THEOLOGICAL DICTIONARY
OF THE
NEW TESTAMENT

EDITED BY

GERHARD KITTEL

Translator and Editor

GEOFFREY W. BROMILEY, D. LITT., D. D.

Volume IV

Λ—Ν

WM. B. EERDMANS PUBLISHING COMPANY
GRAND RAPIDS, MICHIGAN

THEOLOGICAL DICTIONARY OF THE NEW TESTAMENT

Translated from
THEOLOGISCHES WÖRTERBUCH ZUM NEUEN TESTAMENT
Vierter Band: Λ—Ν, herausgegeben von Gerhard Kittel
Published by
W. KOHLHAMMER VERLAG
Stuttgart, Germany

ISBN 0-8028-2246-0

Reprinted, January 1983

PHOTOLITHOPRINTED BY EERDMANS PRINTING COMPANY
GRAND RAPIDS, MICHIGAN, UNITED STATES OF AMERICA

Preface

It fills us with a deep sense of thanksgiving, and augurs well for the future, that, in spite of rumours to the contrary both at home and abroad, we have been able to finish Volume IV of *TWNT* even in the midst of violent international conflict.

I could hardly have carried through my editorial duties had I not had many faithful helpers both young and old, some for longer and some for shorter periods. In both peace and war these have helped me in checking quotations and correcting manuscripts and proofs. Apart from those already mentioned in the Preface to Volume I, I should like to express my thanks to H. Alswede, E. Bammel, R. Burger, A. Debrunner, J. K. Egli, G. Friedrich, H. Fritsch, G. Gross, W. Gutbrod, H. Hanse, A. Hiller, K. Jendreyczyk, H. Kleinknecht, W. Knöpp, H. Kremser, F. Lang, E. Nestle, K. U. Niedlich, G. v. Rad, C. Schiller, K. Schumm, P. Schwen, O. Stumpff, F. Viering, W. Windfuhr, H. Zahrnt.

Tübingen/Vienna, August 1942.

Kittel

Editor's Preface

From the publication of the first volume, and during the years of its long and arduous composition, the *Theologisches Wörterbuch zum Neuen Testament*, familiarly known as Kittel or abbreviated as *TWNT*, has secured for itself a solid place in biblical scholarship, not only as a reference work or a starting-point for further research, but also as a formative contribution to theology.

There has, of course, been some misunderstanding of its role. While it is not a simple lexicon, it obviously cannot replace either the full commentary or the biblical theology. Its task is to mediate between ordinary lexicography and the specific task of exposition, more particularly at the theological level. For this reason attention is concentrated on theologically significant terms, and on the theologically significant usage of these terms.

When this is understood, Kittel is safeguarded against the indiscriminate enthusiasm which would make it a sole and absolute authority in lexical and exegetical matters. It is also safeguarded against the resultant criticism that it involves an illegitimate task for which it uses improper means. Its more limited, yet valid and invaluable role, can be appreciated, and its learning and insights incorporated into the great task of New Testament interpretation.

Hitherto access to the great bulk of *TWNT* has been only in the original language. Some of the more important articles have been translated in the *Key Words* series, and by virtue of the significance of the words selected this series has performed a most useful service. Yet even the chosen articles have undergone some abridgment and editorial redaction, quite apart from the fact that the main part of Kittel has not been translated at all.

By contrast, the present rendering aims to present the whole of *TWNT* in a faithful reproduction of the original. At the cost of less felicity, for German scholarship is no guarantee of stylistic elegance, the rendering is more closely tied to the German. Quotations are fully given in the original Hebrew, Greek and Latin, and the references are left as they are apart from essential changes. For scholars who may wish to consult the original, even the pagination is retained except for a slight fluctuating variation of no more than two or three pages either way. The external size of the volumes has been much reduced, however, and costs have been trimmed so as to provide the student with maximum material at minimum price.

It need hardly be said that the translation and publication of Kittel is no necessary endorsement of everything contained in it. Written by many scholars over a long period, Kittel naturally contains articles of unequal value and varying outlook. Indeed, there are internal disagreements as regards basic presuppositions, historical assumptions and specific interpretations. The ultimate worth of the undertaking lies in its fundamental orientation and its objective findings; for these it is now presented in translation.

In the preparation of the volumes particular thanks are due to Professor F. F. Bruce of the University of Manchester for his many valuable suggestions and corrections in the course of laborious proof-reading. Also deserving of mention in this instance are the publishers for the courage and helpfulness which they have displayed in so monumental an enterprise, and the printers for the skill with which they have handled such difficult material. In spite of every effort, it would be presumptuous to suppose that all errors have been avoided, and the help of readers will be appreciated in detecting and eliminating those that remain.

Pasadena, California, 1967.

G. W. Bromiley

Contents

Contributors

Editor:

G. Kittel

Contributors:

O. Bauernfeind
J. Behm
G. Bertram,
G. Bornkamm
F. Büchsel
R. Bultmann
A. Debrunner
K. Deissner
G. Delling
W. Grundmann
W. Gutbrod
H. Hanse
F. Hauck
H. W. Heidland
V. Herntrich
J. Horst
J. Jeremias
H. Kleinknecht
K. G. Kuhn
R. Meyer
W. Michaelis
O. Michel
A. Oepke
H. Preisker
O. Procksch
G. Quell
K. H. Rengstorf
H. H. Schaeder
C. Schneider
J. Schneider
G. Schrenk
G. Stählin
H. Strathmann
E. Würthwein

Abbreviations

Bau. Ag. = O. Bauernfeind, *Die Apostelgeschichte* (1939).

Bu. J. = R. Bultmann, *Das Johannesevangelium* (1941).

Chr. W. = *Die christliche Welt.*

Chr. Jdt. = *Christentum und Judentum, Studien zur Erforschung ihres gegenseitigen Verhältnisses* (1940).

FGLP = *Forschungen zur Geschichte und Lehre des Protestantismus.*

FJFr = *Forschungen zur Judenfrage* (1937 ff.).

GChrJdt = *Germanentum, Christentum und Judentum, Studien zur Erforschung ihres gegenseitigen Verhältnisses* (1942).

Hirsch Studien = E. Hirsch, *Studien zum Vierten Evangelium* (1936).

Hirsch J. = E. Hirsch, *Das Vierte Evangelium in seiner ursprünglichen Gestalt verdeutscht und erklärt* (1936).

Loh. Mk. = E. Lohmeyer, *Das Markusevangelium* (1937).

Mi. Hb. = O. Michel, *Der Hebräerbrief* (1936).

Oe. Gl. = A. Oepke, *Der Brief des Paulus an die Galater* (1937).

Preisker ZG = H. Preisker, *Neutestamentliche Zeitgeschichte* (1937).

RAC = *Reallexikon für Antike und Christentum,* ed. T. Klauser (1941 f.).

Schl. Past. = A. Schlatter, *Die Kirche der Griechen im Urteil des Paulus, Eine Auslegung seiner Briefe an Timotheus und Titus* (1936).

SDThFr = *Studien zur Deutschen Theologie und Frömmigkeit.*

Stauffer Theol. = E. Stauffer, *Die Theologie des NT* (1941).

VF = *Verkündigung und Forschung, Theologische Jahresberichte.*

† λαγχάνω

"To attain," usually by lot (cf. Hesych.: λαγχάνειν· κληροῦν). With striking frequency it is thus combined with the word group κλῆρος, κληροῦν etc. Even where there is no casting of lots, the attainment is not by one's own effort or as a result of one's own exertions, but is like ripe fruit falling into one's lap. This is always to be kept in mind. For the rest, all that is to be said may be grouped under the four NT passages.

1. In Jn. 19:24 the word has the meaning "to cast lots," the action, not the result. This is not one of the usual Gk. senses.[1]

There are three instances, two interchangeably with the group κληρ-. Isoc., 7, 23 speaks of free choice as distinct from casting lots; λαγχάνειν is absorbed by κλήρωσις. Diod. S., IV, 63, 3 refers to the winning of Helen as wife. Lots are to be cast (διακληρώσασθαι), and one will attain by lot (λαχεῖν) the right to marry her. When they had sworn, "they cast lots (ἔλαχον) and it happened that the lot fell on Theseus," strictly "Theseus attained" (λαχεῖν). There are striking shifts of sense in this passage. Cf. also Demosth. Argumentum, 2, 3 on Or., 21: λαχεῖν περὶ (!) τῶν αὐλητῶν. § 4, λαχόντος αὐτοῦ περὶ τῶν αὐλητῶν ... ἔλαχεν αὐτῷ ὁ κάλλιστος τῶν αὐλητῶν.[2]

Jn. 19:24 tells how the soldiers agreed to cast lots for the coat of Jesus (λάχωμεν περὶ αὐτοῦ). In so doing they fulfilled the prophecy in ψ 21:18, though this reads: ἔβαλον κλῆρον.

2. Lk. 1:9 says of the priest Zacharias: ἔλαχε τοῦ θυμιᾶσαι, "he had attained," or better, "it was his lot (on this day) to make the offering of incense."

This reminds us both linguistically and materially of some Gk. expressions in which λαγχάνειν is used with the inf. for the attainment of an office or public function (Aristoph. Nu., 623; Hdt., VI, 109). More common is the construction which has the title of the bearer of the office in the nominative.[3] The closest to Lk. 1:9 is 1 Βασ. 14:47: ἔλαχε τοῦ βασιλεύειν.[4]

The expression is illuminated by the relevant description of cultic actions in the temple in Rabb. lit., esp. the tractate Tamid.[5] To bring the offering of incense is a special honour with privilege, and it has special redemptive significance for the one concerned. Each priest can be on the list only once. The sequence is decided by lot. This day when he offered incense was of great personal significance for Zacharias.

3. Ac. 1:17 is to some extent similar: ἔλαχεν (sc. Judas) τὸν κλῆρον τῆς διακονίας ταύτης, "he had attained to a share in this ministry," i.e., "he was called with others to the office of an apostle." Here, too, there is a link with

---

λαγχάνω. [1] Pape, *s.v.* omits this sense, and Pass., *s.v.* has only a brief ref. to the verse in Jn.

[2] These three passages are in Liddell-Scott.

[3] One may refer particularly to the attainment of priestly dignity for a year in many of the cults in Gk. cities, since λαγχάνειν is here a tt.: Ditt. Syll.^{3}, 486, 9; 762, 12; 756, 9; 723, 16; 1018, 1. Λαγχάνειν c. nomin. is construed like αἱρεῖσθαι [Debrunner].

[4] The textual tradition is uncertain here: κατακληροῦται ἔργον and ἔλαχε occur together. A Σ reading seems to have found its way into the LXX.

[5] Cf. Str.-B., II, 57 under e. and II, 71 ff.

κλῆρος. The two words together express the fact that Judas, like the others, had not grasped the office for himself, but that it has been allotted to him by God through Christ. We are reminded of the calling of the disciples. When there is reference to λαγχάνειν, man is *mere passivus.* [6]

4. Of particular theological significance is 2 Pt. 1:1: τοῖς ἰσότιμον[7] ἡμῖν λαχοῦσιν πίστιν, "to those who have attained to a faith equal to ours."

The question who is meant has received various answers, laity as distinct from apostles, Pauline Christians as distinct from Petrine, believers *citra visum* as distinct from eye-witnesses (Bengel, *ad loc.*), the congregation which received the letter as distinct from that which sent it, Gentile Christians as distinct from Jewish. Though this is not our primary concern here, the last of these seems to be the most helpful. [8] The "righteousness of our God and Saviour Jesus Christ," to which reference is made, is revealed in the fact that the Gentile world is not worse off, but is summoned to the same salvation and is called to the faith which according to Paul is alone decisive for salvation and is thus "of equal value" for all.

In this sentence the point of λαγχάνειν is that faith has come to them from God with no co-operation on their part. [9] That faith is the work, not of man, but of God or Christ, is not stated with equal clarity in all parts of the NT, but it must be constantly borne in mind. It can be seen plainly in Ac. 13:48, and Ac. 17:31 is particularly relevant in expounding the present passage, for here God proffers faith to all. Again, in R. 12:3 God apportions the measure of faith. The same thought occurs in the chain of R. 8:28-30, and cf. also Hb. 12:2; [10] Jd. 3 (πίστις παραδοθεῖσα). God does not merely give to both Jews and Gentiles the possibility of faith; He effects faith in them. Eph. 2:8 makes it especially plain that all is of grace and that human merit is completely ruled out. To understand the Pauline and then the Lutheran doctrine of jusification it is essential to make it clear that faith is not a new human merit which replaces the merit of works, that it is not a second achievement which takes the place of the first, that it is not something which man has to show, but that justification by faith is an act of divine grace. Faith is not the presupposition of the grace of God. As a divine gift, it is the epitome and demonstration of the grace of God. "Those who have attained to faith" points finally, then, to predestination as a free act of divine grace. Here one is at the very frontiers of theological utterance. All is of grace, and yet God is righteous. The connection in thought between λαγχάνειν and δικαιοσύνη in 2 Pt. 1:1 is to be noted. Wbg. (→ n. 9) rightly says: "With men λαγχάνειν cannot be combined with strictly impartial justice. With the God of Christians, however, free choice, which seems to exclude all justice because it takes place contingently, fuses with real righteousness in a unity which is indissoluble, though beyond the capacity of man to grasp."

Hanse

---

[6] Cf. also H. H. Wendt, *Die Ag.*[9] (1913), *ad loc.*

[7] On the linking of ἰσότιμος and λαγχάνειν cf. Philo Sobr., 54.

[8] Cf. Ac. 10:47; 11:17; also R. 3:29 f., which is particularly plain.

[9] Wbg. Pt., 168, *ad loc.*: "Through an approach which rests on free choice"; E. Kühl, *Die Briefe Petri u. Judae*[6] (1897), 379: "As a gift of grace with no co-operation on their part"; Bengel, *ad loc.*: *non ipsi sibi pararunt;* C. Bigg, ICC, *ad loc.*: "The verb λαγχάνειν implies a gift of favour"; J. B. Mayor, *The Epistle of St. Jude* ... (1907): "Faith itself is the gift of God." The ref. here is to the λαγχάνειν of a spiritual good as in Plat. Phileb., 55b, Polit., 269d, Philo Vit. Mos., I, 157, Decal., 64, also Wis. 8:19, cf. 3 Macc. 6:1 of old age.

[10] Cf. on this A. Schlatter, *Der Glaube im NT*[4] (1927), 531.

† λακτίζω

Found from the time of Hom., this word means "to strike with the foot." It belongs to a root λακ-, also found in the adv. λάξ (from the time of Hom.), "kicking with the foot," λάξας (Lycophron) = λακτίσας and other constr. [1] To judge from Aesch. Eum., 541 it was regarded as a contraction of λὰξ ἀτίζειν. It is used of men and animals, also of flames (Pindar) and the heart (Aristoph.). [2]

The LXX has the compound ἀπολακτίζειν: [3] Dt. 32:15 for בָּעַט, which is rendered "kick" at 1 S. 2:29 (Luther: *löcken*). The LXX does not have it in the verse in 1 S., but Cod Paris B N gr 133 has the Hexap. note ἀπολακτίζετε τὴν θυσίαν μου. Luther's *löcken*, also *lecken* or *läken*, used 6 times for various Heb. and Gr. words ("leap" etc.) and replaced in modern versions, is perhaps related to the Gk. word.

The word occurs in the NT only in the proverbial saying in Ac. 26:14: πρὸς κέντρα λακτίζειν (→ III, 666).

Hanse

(λαλέω → λέγω), † καταλαλέω, † καταλαλιά, † κατάλαλος

καταλαλέω, "to importune someone with speeches," "to prattle something [1] to someone" (Ps.-Luc. Asin., 12), "to blurt out" (Aristoph. Ra., 752), esp. "to speak against, to accuse, someone," with a suggestion of the false and exaggerated: [2] "to calumniate," Polyb., 3, 90, 6: τὸν Φάβιον κατελάλει πρὸς πάντας, 18, 45 (28), 1: κατελάλουν τὸ δόγμα, Diogenes Babylonius Fr., 99 (v. Arnim, III, p. 237, 6): καταλαληθέντες πολλάκις ὑπ' ἰδιωτῶν, Ditt. Syll.³, 593, 6 f. (2nd cent. B.C.): ἵνα μηδ' ἐν τούτοις ἔχωσιν ἡμᾶς καταλαλεῖν. P. Hib., I, 151 (*c.* 250 B.C.): εἰ οὖν τιν' ἐπιχώρησιν ποιεῖ ἔντυχε ἐκείνωι καταλάλησον, συντετάχαμεν γὰρ ... On the whole the word is not very common in secular usage. Like the whole group, it does not occur at all in Joseph., and in Philo it is found only in two passages influenced by biblical usage: Leg. All., II, 66 f.: Miriam κατελάλει Μωυσῆ, based on LXX Nu. 12:8; *ibid.*, 78 (twice); a quotation from LXX Nu. 21:7. [3]

In the LXX καταλαλέω is mostly (9 times) a rendering of דבר ni and pi in the sense of "hostile speaking," and in isolated instances of גדף pi, "to scorn," "to mock at" (ψ 43:16 AS²), כלם hi, "to revile" (Job 19:3), or לשן po, "to calumniate" (ψ 100:5) etc. [4] The main emphasis is on the hostility denoted by κατα-, whether against God (Nu. 21:5, 7; ψ 77:19; Hos. 7:13; Mal. 3:13), his servant Moses (Nu. 12:8), or frequently one's neighbour (ψ 49:20: κατὰ τοῦ ἀδελφοῦ σου, 100:5: τοῦ πλησίον αὐτοῦ,

---

λακτίζω. [1] Boisacq, *s.v.* λάξ; Walde-Pok., II, 420 [Debrunner].

[2] Liddell-Scott, *s.v.*

[3] From the time of Theogn. [Debrunner].

καταλαλέω κτλ. [1] In the NT only with the gen., cf. LXX (Helbing Kasussyntax, 183) and Diod. S., XI, 4, 6; with the acc. cf. the examples given and καταδικάζω (→ III, 621).

[2] As compared with λέγω, λαλέω carries a suggestion of the ill-considered, superficial and irresponsible. This is important in relation to καταλαλέω [Debrunner].

[3] Since our concern is only with the group καταλαλ-, this is not the place to consider the way in which "slander" was viewed in Rabb. Judaism (Str.-B., I, 226-231).

[4] At Prv. 20:13 the Mas. "Love not sleep ..." is freely rendered by the LXX: μὴ ἀγάπα καταλαλεῖν.

Prv. 20:13; cf. 30:10 Θ).[5] In the first instances the essential element in the hostility is contradiction and rejection, whereas in καταλαλεῖν κατὰ τοῦ ἀδελφοῦ it is malice, slander and calumniation.

This sense of speaking evil against one's neighbour is also found in Test. XII: Test. G. 5:4: οὐ καταλαλεῖ ἀνδρὸς ὁσίου, Test. Iss. 3:4: οὐ κατελάλησά τινος πώποτε. It is the only one reflected in the derived noun and adj. καταλαλιά, "evil report," "calumny," is not found in the non-biblical world but only in the biblically influenced admonition in Wis. 1:11: καὶ ἀπὸ καταλαλιᾶς φείσασθε γλώσσης, and, along with καταλαλέω (→ *supra*), in Test. G. 3:3: καταλαλιὰν ἀσπάζεται. κατάλαλος, "spreading evil reports," "slanderous," "slanderer," is found in P. Oxy., XV, 1828 r 3 (3rd cent. A.D.). It does not occur in the LXX or related lit.

The word group is characterised by the fact that it obviously plays no vital role in the ethical exhortation of the non-biblical world. Even the lists of vices in the Stoics and Philo do not contain it, though it might have proved useful. As a warning against malicious or unthinking gossip it occurs first in the Psalms, Proverbs and the Wisdom literature, though even here it occurs only infrequently in admonitions.

In the usage of the NT and the early Church the only emphasis and content of the group is that of speaking evil against one's neighbour. Other words are now used for opposing and blaspheming God (→ βλασφημέω etc.). Whether the main stress, as in a word like "slander," is on the act of spreading a false report is not apparent in the NT passages, though this is naturally included in καταλαλεῖν. The essence of the matter is probably to be sought in the κατα-, i.e., in the hostility and malice of speech directed against one's neighbour.[6] It violates the early Christian commandment because of its uncharitableness rather than its falsity. The importance of resisting evil-speaking for Christianity (cf. also ψ 100:5, where it is the first individual sin) is shown by the fact that the command to do this is often the first in a general list or occurs individually as a special exhortation.[7] This is particularly so in 1 Pt. 2:1 (along with the more general κακία, δόλος, ὑποκρίσεις, φθόνοι, καταλαλιαί constitute the most concrete evil which the regenerate must avoid), but also in Jm. 4:11 (a special admonition alongside the more general admonitions in vv. 7-10), 2 C. 12:20 (the first special admonition after the general words ἔρις, ζῆλος, θυμοί, ἐριθεῖαι), also 1 Cl., 30, 1-3 (beginning of the exhortation), and Herm. m., 2, 1 ff. (the first specific demand). When we have regard to the history of the term, it is obvious that the occurrence of κατάλαλος and καταλαλιά in the lists of vices in R. 1:30 and 2 C. 12:20 is not to be explained in terms of literary style[8] but reflects part of the ethical life

---

[5] In the LXX καταλαλεῖν seems in the first instance to be a literal and not very Greek rendering of דבר with בְּ or with עַל (Mal. 3:13): "to speak against"; Hos. 7:13 also has an object "lies." In these passages דבר has the secondary sense of rejection, while καταλαλεῖν has that of calumniation. In Mal. 3:16 καταλαλεῖν is simply an intensive form of λαλεῖν (so A) in the good sense. In Σ ψ 40:7 καταλαλεῖν is used for the abs. דבר. Here, then, the sin of the tongue indicated by καταλαλεῖν is for the first time clearly characterised as such by the LXX [Bertram].

[6] Cf. Dib. Jk., 210.

[7] Suidas, *s.v.*: ἡ εἴς τινας ὑπό τινων βλασφημία. The definition of Basilius quoted by Hck. Jk., 205, n. 98 reads something in, esp. with its unsubstantiated τὸ κατὰ ἀπόντος ἀδελφοῦ λαλεῖν.

[8] A stylistic form, which is Christian and dependent on Paul, is obviously to be seen in the use of the terms in the lists of vices in the apostolic fathers, e.g., Pol., 2, 2; 4, 3 etc.

of early Christianity. καταλαλεῖν is taken for granted in the pagan world (1 Pt. 2:12; 3:16), but it must be put off by the regenerate (1 Pt. 2:1 f.), not just on moral grounds, but for the sake of the new life in God (1 Pt. 2:3 : εἰ ἐγεύσασθε ὅτι χρηστὸς ὁ κύριος). καταλαλεῖν is not just an offence against one's neighbour. It is also a violation of the Law of God and hence a sin against God (Jm. 4:11).

The unusual frequency of usage in the post-apost. fathers shows plainly that once the first love was past human weaknesses began to emerge in the early churches. But it also shows how seriously the command against evil-speaking was still taken in these churches. Cf. 1 Cl., 30, 1 and 3; 35, 5 and 8; 2 Cl., 4, 3; Barn., 20, 2; Pol., 2, 2; 4, 3; Herm. m., 2, 3 f. (several times); 8, 3; s., 6, 5, 5; 8, 7, 2; 9, 15, 3; 9, 23, 2 f.; 9, 26, 7.

Kittel

λαμβάνω, ἀναλαμβάνω, ἀνάλημψις, ἐπιλαμβάνω, ἀνεπίλημπτος, κατα-, μεταλαμβάνω, μετάλημψις, παρα-, προ-, προσλαμβάνω, πρόσλημψις, ὑπολαμβάνω

λαμβάνω.

The original etymological meaning [1] is "to grasp," "to seize." It develops in two directions.

1. The first is active, "to take," "to bring under one's control on one's own initiative." a. (i) commonly (also in the LXX) with a personal subj. and material or personal obj. "to take to oneself," "to take captive" (e.g. in Jos. 11), also with a double acc. (esp. γυναῖκα, the predicative acc. being either given or left out, both also in the LXX, e.g., Ex. 6:7; (ii) with abstr. obj. "to take," e.g., πεῖραν λαμβάνειν, Plat. Euthyd., 275b (cf. Dt. 28:56), ἀρχήν = "lordship"; αἴσθησιν λαμβάνειν, "to perceive" (Plat. Phaed., 73c → also I, 692); in the language of jurisprudence δίκην λαμβάνειν, "to receive a judgment"; [2] (iii) of things to which one has a claim, "to collect," e.g., the revenue from possessions (in the LXX esp. of regular duties and taxes, Ex. 25:2 f.; Nu. 3:47; 18:28; 1 Macc. 3:31; 10:30, 42; 11:34). b. With material obj. of fate or conditions of body or soul which "seize" a man [3] (in the LXX φόβος, Is. 10:29; Ep. Jer. 4; τρόμος, *passim*; ζῆλος etc.). c. More generally in pleonastic usage, though often with emphasis on the actuality; class. esp. the part. aor., LXX also in other forms.

2. The second direction gives us already in class. Gk. the sense "to receive," "to acquire" (passively), both literally (e.g., μισθούς, Plat. Resp., VIII, 568c; without obj. *concipere*, of the mother, also in the LXX), and also fig. (e.g., δόξαν, Plat. Polit., 290d etc.; τιμήν, Aristoph. Thes., 823; Da. Θ 2:6, cf. Zech. 6:13; ἀρχήν = "beginning"). In religious statements the negative denotes the divine autarchy: God can receive nothing (Corp. Herm., II, 16) because He possesses all things (V, 10b) and wills to be Himself (X, 3).

λαμβάνω. J. H. H. Schmidt, *Synonymik der griech. Sprache*, III (1879), 203 ff.

[1] Acc. to Schmidt, 210 f. this is still predominant in class. usage.

[2] This presupposes a "relationship in which there is right on both sides" (R. Hirzel. *Themis* ... [1907], 127).

[3] Pass. Wört., *s.v.* Cf. Heinr. on 1 C. 10:13.

The mid. is used act. "to hold something or someone to oneself," "to grasp someone or something"; in the LXX Tob. 11:11 S; 2 Macc. 12:35.

In the LXX [4] sense 2. is comparatively rare; it is commonest in the sense "to take" (gifts, bribes); purely pass. "to receive" (λαμβάνειν μισθόν from God, Prv. 11:21). Sense 1. predominates because λαμβάνειν is mostly used for לקח "to grasp," and much less frequently for נשׂא = "to receive." Certain striking phrases are also to be explained in terms of the Heb.: ψυχὴν λαμβάνειν = "to kill" (often; πνεῦμα λαμβάνειν only at Bar. 2:17); ἀριθμὸν λαμβάνειν, "to take a census" (e.g., Nu. 3:40); "to strike up" (a song) (e.g., ψ 80:2: ψαλμόν; commonly θρῆνον λαμβάνειν); λαμβάνειν ἁμαρτίαν "to take guilt to oneself and to bear it" (for others, Lv. 16:22; on the problem of retribution in Ez. cf. Ez. 14:10; 18:19 f.); πρόσωπον λαμβάνειν, "to take a superficial view" (materially → III, 30). With a personal obj. "to fetch" or "to cause to be fetched."

In the NT λαμβάνω is fairly common in narrative in sense 1. c. [5]: "to take" (also with an abstr. obj.: ἀρχήν, ἀφορμήν [point of entry, R. 7:8], πεῖραν Hb. 11:29, 36 etc.). In sense 1. b. it occurs only in Lk.: φόβος (cf. LXX), ἔκστασις, 5:26, and Paul: πειρασμός, 1 C. 10:13, though here there is transition to 1. a. (temptation as a hostile power).

Under 1. a. we find (i) "to take away," "to take to oneself" (with force, or to unburden) (Jn. τινά); (ii) "to take on oneself" (Mt. 10:38: τὸν σταυρόν, i.e., "to be ready for death"), "to take up," "to accept" into the fashioning of one's own spiritual personality or in acceptance of the claim to one's own existence: the witness of Jesus (Jn. 3:11, 32 f.; 12:48; 17:8) and His messengers (13:20), or Jesus Himself as the Logos (1:12; 5:43), and therewith God (13:20). This sense is not opposed to that which is to be established later, but expresses the character of decision in NT religion. The πνεῦμα of the recipient corresponds to the offer of faith. (iii) "To collect" what is due, e.g., in ecclesiastical or political taxes (Hb. 7:8 f.; Mt. 17:24 f.), or in rent, Mk. 12:2 and par. Cf. Ac. 17:9. [6]

Sense 2. is predominant, esp. in theologically significant verses. From this it is apparent how strongly the NT — to some extent in marked contrast to Gk. religion and to Judaism — views the relation of man to God as that of recipient and Giver (→ I, 587). Jesus takes from men ἀσθένειαι (Mt. 8:17). If it is said that God receives worship and praise (Rev. 5:12, εὐλογίαν κτλ.), the emphasis is not on the fact that this is given by men. τιμή and δόξα are objectively immanent to the being of God. Hence they may be ascribed by men only if God makes them pneumatic and thus lifts them out of themselves (though there is perhaps a different emphasis in 4:11).

The basic principle: τί δὲ ἔχεις, ὃ οὐκ ἔλαβες; (1 C. 4:7) applies even to Christ, as Jn. especially emphasises. Commissioning for His earthly work (Jn. 10:18c), His power as eschatological Ruler and Judge (Rev. 2:28), in short, all the power and fulness of all true being (Rev. 5:12), He has received from God (not in separate acts, but in a single reception of power acc. to 2 Pt. 1:17). Because there is no limit to this endowment, Jesus does not describe Himself as one who has received the πνεῦμα. On the contrary, He says that the πνεῦμα promised to Christians receives His gifts from His own fulness of being (Jn. 16:14 f.).

---

4 Cf. Helbing Kasussyntax, 53 (לְ לקח = λαμβάνειν τινὰ εἰς ... e.g., γυναῖκα frequently, εἰς προφήτας, εἰς ἁγιασμόν, Am. 2:11 etc., not in the NT). [Bertram.]

5 On the pleonastic use cf. Pr.-Bauer³, 770; on Mk. 14:65, *ibid.*, 771.

6 On other passages, Pr.-Bauer³.

What man receives from God (or Christ) is in the first instance this πνεῦμα (Jn. 7:39; 20:22; Ac. 1:8; 2:38; R. 8:15; 1 C. 2:12), along with His specific charismatic operations (1 Pt. 4:10). Reception of the πνεῦμα distinguishes Christians from the world (Jn. 14:17) and so unequivocally constitutes them Christians that (in Ac.) the answer to the question whether there has been reception of the Spirit determines absolutely whether a man is a Christian or not (Ac. 10:47; 19:2).[7] Paul lays particular emphasis on the fact that man cannot even prepare the ground for this reception (Gl. 3:2, 14). Materially to the same effect are the statements that the Christian receives as a gift[8] χάρις, καταλλαγή, δικαιοσύνη (R. 1:5; 5:11, 17; cf. also Hb. 9:15; 10:26; ἄφεσιν ἁμαρτιῶν, Ac. 10:43; 26:18; full unity of life with Christ, Phil. 3:12, though → *infra*).

On the other hand the Christian also realises — and here the distinction made elsewhere between πνεῦμα and κόσμος cannot be upheld[9] — that his whole cosmic existence, being willed by God, is something which has been received (1 Tm. 4:4), so that he believes that he should even seek from God an enhancement of this earthly life (Jm. 1:7; 4:3; 1 Jn. 3:22). For this he can appeal to the promise of Jesus: πᾶς ... ὁ αἰτῶν λαμβάνει (Mt. 7:8; Lk. 11:10), αἰτεῖτε, καὶ λήμψεσθε (Jn. 16:24), though it is emphasised that this promise does not refer to his own autonomy (Jn. 16:24: ἐν τῷ ὀνόματί μου).

Thus the Christian knows that at every moment and in his whole cosmic and pneumatic being he stands under the saying: τί ἔχεις, ὃ οὐκ ἔλαβες; He sees that this is true in relation to the incorruptible crown of life which he is to receive (1 C. 9:25; Jm. 1:12; perhaps Phil. 3:12; cf. Mt. 10:41; Jn. 4:36; 1 C. 3:8, 14 μισθόν; also its serious counterpart κρίμα, Mk. 12:40 and par.; R. 13:2; Jm. 3:1). The force of these statements is apparent when we set them against the background of Jewish and Rabbinic tendencies towards legalism and synergism, in which the believer makes a decisive contribution to his own salvation.

The saying twice quoted in 1 C. 4:7 naturally emphasises the ceaseless dependence of the individual on the gift of the Christian community (the Church as the body of Christ). If Paul concedes this less in relation to himself (though → παραλαμβάνω), he still considers his ἀποστολή and διακονία as wholly and utterly received, not as self-elected (R. 1:5; cf. Ac. 20:24). The Giver is Christ (Gl. 1:12).

† ἀναλαμβάνω, † ἀνάλημψις (→ ἀναβαίνω).

ἀναλαμβάνω (already class.), strictly "to take up," "to lift up," then "to take to oneself" with a personal or material (concrete or abstract) object.

It is used thus in the LXX (mostly for נשׂא then for לקח): "to load" (on carts or animals), but also "to bring along on foot" (βόας, Ex. 12:32; στράτευμα, 2 Macc. 12:38), more strictly "to raise" (in the air), "to set on the feet" (Ez. 2:2), fig. "to raise" (a cry, a speech, a song), "to lift up" (the heart in prayer to God), Lam. 3:41, "to take to" (Job 17:9), "to receive" (instruction, Job 22:22; reason, 4 Macc. 5:11), διὰ μνήμης ἀναλαμβάνειν, "to learn by rote," 2 Macc. 2:25. Of God, in figures of speech, Ex. 19:4; Dt. 32:11; abs. "to help," "to keep upright," Is. 46:4; 63:9; ψ 145:9; 146:6. With ref. to the worship of idols, Am. 5:26.

---

[7] On the specific ideas of Ac. in this regard, cf. 8:15 ff.; also H. v. Baer, *Der Heilige Geist in den Lukasschriften* (1926).

[8] δωρεὰν ἐλάβετε, Mt. 10:8, here related to the apostolic endowment of the twelve.

[9] There is here no inconsistency for faith, since in the antithesis κόσμος does not mean the created world but the fallen world. In so far as God still maintains His order in this, it is God-given.

As a tt. (elsewhere μετατιθέναι, Gn. 5:24; Sir. 44:16; Hb. 11:5; Wis. 4:10) ἀναλαμβάνω can be used for temporary rapture, Apc. Zeph. in Cl. Al. Strom., V, 11, 77, 2 (into the fifth heaven); for the definitive rapture of Enoch, Sir. 49:14 (μετετέθη in A), and Elijah, 4 Βασ. 2:9-11; Sir. 48:9; 1 Macc. 2:58; 4 Βασ. 2:11, with great restraint ἀνελήμφθη ... ὡς εἰς τὸν οὐρανόν. In the raptures of Gk. mythology the technical terms are ἁρπάζειν (→ I, 472), ἀφανῆ γενέσθαι, ἀφανίζειν (cf. ἄφαντος, Lk. 24:31).[1] Rapture is here narrated esp. of divinely honoured rulers (e.g., Alexander).[1]

In the NT "to receive up" (Ac. 10:16), "to take with" (2 Tm. 4:11; Ac. 23:31), "on board" (Ac. 20:13 f.); in a quotation from the OT, Ac. 7:43 (Am. 5:26).

Fig. Eph. 6:13, 16, where the technical use of ἀναλαμβάνω for the putting on of weapons is adopted from military speech (also LXX, Dt. 1:41; Jdt. 6:12 etc.).

For the ascension of the Risen Lord[2] after His (single) appearance to the eleven (Mk. 16:19),[3] or at the end of the forty days with them (Lk., cf. Ac. 1:3), the word occurs only in the inauthentic Marcan ending, in Ac. 1 and in 1 Tm. 3:16. In the last of these we have only a very brief and almost formal allusion,[4] and the account in Mk. 16:19 is very concise. In spite of the slight reminiscence of 4 Βασ. 2:11 there is nothing to indicate that the disciples actually saw the event.[5] A fuller description is given in Ac. 1:2, 11 (22), cf. also ἐπήρθη, v. 9. Here Jesus is not taken up in a chariot of fire like Elijah. He is raised up from the surface of the earth by His own power. But the disciples see only the first stage, for a cloud hides Him from their view (this Palestinian tradition is obviously known to Paul, for he depicts the rapture of those still alive at the *parousia* in similar terms in 1 Th. 4:17). The interesting thing for Lk. is plainly the event itself, but in Mk. 16:19 and 1 Tm. 3:16[6] the important thing is the endowment of Christ with divine majesty. That Jesus no longer dwells on the earth, or in the earth, is taken for granted by all NT writers. But with the exception of the Lucan source of Ac. 1 they believe it to be neither their duty nor their right to give a description of the transition to His present existence.[7] On the whole complex of ideas → I, 520, cf. also → I, 472.

ἀνάλημψις a. "taking up," "receiving" (Philo, e.g., of spiritual processes, Rer. Div. Her., 298). b. "Restoration" (in Philo, e.g., taking back of money, Virt., 100; restoration of health, *ibid.*, 176). Both in various connections, but the word does not occur in the NT.

In later Jewish literature it is used for death generally (Ps. Sol. 4:18). Hence the (original) translator of Ass. Mos. 10:12 unthinkingly uses *mors* for it,[8] and we cannot be sure that in Test. L. 18:3 (where it is not found in all MSS) it refers

---

ἀναλαμβάνω κτλ. [1] Cf. Rohde [9] and [10], *s.v. Entrückung.*

[2] In Greek and Jewish stories the ref. is always to those who have not yet died.

[3] But the μετὰ τὸ λαλῆσαι αὐτοῖς of Mk. 16:19 need not stand in any contradiction to Lk. or Ac. 1:3 when regard is had to narrative style under Semitic influence, cf. Mt. 3:1, where a leap of decades is covered by ἐν δὲ ταῖς ἡμέραις ἐκείναις.

[4] A. Seeberg, *Der Katechismus der Urchristenheit* (1903), 122 f.: "Was received by men"; for a correct rendering cf. Dib. Past., *ad loc.*

[5] Any more than that they saw the ἐκάθισεν ἐκ δεξιῶν τοῦ θεοῦ.

[6] Also 1 Pt. 3:22 (πορευθείς).

[7] In its theological, i.e., Christological or soteriological significance the taking up (rapture or enthronement) of Christ is independent of the resurrection or ascension, cf. G. Bertram, "Die Himmelfahrt Jesu vom Kreuz aus u. der Glaube an seine Auferstehung," *Festgabe f. A. Deissmann* (1927), 187 ff., esp. 203 ff.; U. Holzmeister, *Zschr. f. Kathol. Theologie,* 55 (1931), 44-82; T. Steinmann, ZThK, NF, 8 (1927), 304 f. [Bertram.]

[8] Cf. Kautzsch Pseudepigr., 312.

to the rapture of the Messianic priest. In Lk. 9:51 ἀνάλημψις thus refers to the death of Jesus, the time of which has a firm place in the plan of salvation (→ συνπληροῦσθαι). Possibly it also refers to the taking up, or taking back (→ *supra*), to God which begins with death and which is completed with the Lucan ascension.

ἐπιλαμβάνω, † ἀνεπίλημπτος.

ἐπιλαμβάνω means lit. a. "to grasp" (the basic meaning of the simple form emerges clearly in the compound → 5), act. "to seize," also "to stand by,"[1] "to blame"; mid. strictly "to grasp for oneself," "to lay firm hold of," "to bring into one's sphere" etc.; b. "to add to." In the LXX only the mid. is found, and it has obviously taken the sense of the act., with the gen. "to lay firm hold of," "to seize" (something or someone), perhaps by force; also with abstr. subj., e.g., τρόμος ἐπελάβετο αὐτῶν, ψ 47:6; "to cleave to something" (e.g., discipline, Prv. 4:13, wisdom, Bar. 4:2). Of God, who violently seizes those who suffer (Job 16:8), but who also grasps the hand of His people to help (Ιερ. 38:32, cf. Hb. 8:9); of wisdom, which draws protectively to itself those who seek it, and thus gives them an absolutely reliable stay (ἐπιλαμβάνεται τῶν ζητούντων αὐτήν), Sir. 4:11, "to take up someone" in the sense of → ἀντιλαμβάνομαι.[2]

Only the mid. occurs in the NT (→ *supra*, LXX), mostly with the gen., also with the acc. in the Lucan writings:[3] Luc. 20:20 (26) with a second gen. of that on which one lays hands (fig.). The meaning corresponds to that in the LXX (→ *supra*). Lk. 14:4 of the powerful touch of the healing hand of Jesus; Hb. 2:16, "to draw someone to oneself to help," and thus to take him up into the fellowship of one's own destiny, cf. v. 17 f.; 1 Tm. 6:12, 19: ἐπιλαβοῦ (ἐπιλάβωνται) τῆς ... ζωῆς, "to seek the possession of supraterrestrial life with all one's force" (in the fight of faith which finds expression in moral action).

ἀνεπίλημπτος means "inviolable," "unassailable," "blameless" (of the mind, e.g., Philo Spec. Leg., III, 135) etc. It does not occur in the LXX.

In the NT it occurs only in 1 Tm. 3:2; 5:7: one who cannot be attacked (even by non-Christians)[4] because of his moral conduct (→ I, 356); in the context of 3:2 the ἀνεπίλημπτος is further developed in what follows. In 6:14 Timothy, "unassailed" or free from arbitrary interference, is to keep to the ethical proclamation which lays claim to him as ἐντολή.

† καταλαμβάνω.

κατα- orig. "from above to below," hence completely, so that καταλαμβάνω is a strengthening of the simple form.[1] Act. "to seize," "to grasp" (esp. in a hostile manner), also with impersonal subj.; of God, Plot. Enn., V, 8, 11: εἰ δέ τις ... ὑπ' ἐκείνου τοῦ θεοῦ ... καταληφθείς; so also abs. καταληφθῆναι in the sense of ecstasy = ἐνθουσιάσαι, Poll. Onom., I, 16. b. "To light upon," "to overtake." c. "To grasp," "truly to understand" (e.g., Philo Praem. Poen., 40: "God can be perfectly grasped only by Himself," cf. also Mut. Nom., 6 f.). d. "To hold fast." Mid. a. "To requisition for oneself," b. "to grasp," "to understand" (Sext. Emp. Math., VII, 288 ἑαυτόν).

In the LXX act. a. of God, Is. 10:14; Job 5:13: ὁ καταλαμβάνων σοφούς; of man who would force God to himself: ἐν τίνι καταλάβω τὸν κύριον; Mi. 6:6, or who

ἐπιλαμβάνω κτλ. [1] Pass., *s.v.*
[2] Helbing Kasussyntax, 127 f.
[3] The attempt of Pr.-Bauer³ to explain this away is refuted by Lk. 23:26.
[4] Hence the very general moral demands in 3:2.
καταλαμβάνω. [1] [Debrunner.]

makes wisdom his secure inner possession, Sir. 15:1, cf. 27:8 : τὸ δίκαιον. b. Esp. also "to surprise," "to alight upon suddenly," "to overtake" (also with an abstract subj.). On c. cf. Da. LXX 1:20 "to perceive"; Jdt. 8:14 S "to fathom"; Job 34:24 : God is the One who comprehends the incomprehensible. Mid. a. esp. of captured cities (*passim*); b. "to overtake" only at Ju. 18:22.

In the NT a point which has emerged already from this review comes out with particular clarity, namely, that κατά gives to the simple form the character either of intensity (to grasp with force, Mt. 9:18) or of suddenness (to surprise, 1 Th. 5:4 [Jn. 8:3 f. 𝔎 D etc.; 6:17 ℵ D]; Jn. 12:35 of the time after the death of Jesus). The epistemological nature of the term (→ c. and I, 692) is not to be seen except in Lk. (Ac.).

The act is used a. in the positive sense of "to attain definitively," in R. 9:30 in respect of the righteousness of faith, and paradoxically, without any effort (the element of lighting upon or overtaking is still discernible, as in the next passage), or in Phil. 3:12b, 13 in respect of close fellowship with Christ provisionally demonstrated in dying with Him and consummated by the resurrection (with the pneumatic body). The Christian must constantly seek this. He must strive to overtake it. He will finally possess it in the ἐξανάστασις. It must be affirmed afresh each day in the life of faith until it is finally consummated in the resurrection. Cf. also Phil. 3:12c, of the Christian whom Christ draws fully into this fellowship of death and resurrection, and 1 C. 9:24 of the Christian's crown of victory, i.e., the consummation of this fellowship = ζωὴ αἰώνιος. It is also used in the negative sense "to overpower," Jn. 1:5 : The darkness of separation from God has not succeeded in overcoming the light, the new religious life, which is present in the Logos, in the divine Christ. It has not been able to vanquish the power of His light.[2] By the very existence of this light the whole sphere of night is overcome and deprived of its power.

Corresponding is the use of the mid. (only in the intellectual sphere): "to establish" (Ac. 4:13; 25:25), "to grasp fundamentally," "to appropriate to oneself inwardly" (Ac. 10:34; Eph. 3:18 : the all-permeating greatness of the ἀγάπη τοῦ Χριστοῦ).

† μεταλαμβάνω, † μετάλημψις.

μεταλαμβάνω. In accordance with the twofold sense of μετα- this compound means chiefly a. with the gen. "to take part," "to acquire a share" (though also with the acc. of the part whose whole is in the gen.), b. with the acc. "to take later," hence also "to alter," "to change."

In the NT we find a. "to receive the portion accruing to one" in 2 Tm. 2:6 of fruits which one has grown, or more generally "to take nourishment" (from available or common supplies) in Ac. 2:46; 27:33 f. (v. 33 with → προσλαμβάνομαι). Of invisible goods, or fig., in Hb. 6:7: As a land has (with others) its share of the blessing of God in rain, but is later rejected if it does not bring forth fruit, so apostate Christians received with others the blessing of God in salvation in Christ, and thus have no possibility of a second repentance. Hb. is here developing the metaphor used by Jesus in Mt. 13:3 ff. The Christian is ordained to receive a

---

[2] There is a fairly close par. in Act. Thom., 130 (II, 2, p. 238, 10 f.), *v.* H. Ljungvik, *Studien z. Sprache d. apkr. Apostelgeschichten* (Diss. Uppsala, 1928), 88 f.: φῶς τὸ μὴ καταλαμβανόμενον. Cf. also Schl. Jn., *ad loc.*

share in the holiness of God. This sets him his supreme goal. But he cannot also strive against the necessary work of discipline which God does on him.

b. In Ac. 24:25 καιρὸν δὲ μεταλαβών, the commonly accepted sense "if I take an interest" is possible but colourless. Much more likely is "when I later have time," i.e., when I have changed the present unfavourable time for a favourable.

μετάλημψις: 1 Tm. 4:3 forbids the acceptance of certain non-Christian rules about foods. The context shows that these are foods which are supposed to bring under the power of forces which are hostile to God or dangerous to man. In opposition to this view the author stresses the fact that all food is given by the creative will of God and is thus ordained for the confident and thankful participation of those who believe in Christ and who are thus freed from the power of hostile forces.

παραλαμβάνω.

A. παραλαμβάνειν in the Greek and Hellenistic World.

The compound is very closely related to the simple form. It means "to take to oneself," "to take over"; with a personal obj. it means esp. "to take into a fellowship"; with a material obj., e.g., "to take over an office" (as priest, Ditt. Syll.[3], 663, 12), or a position as ruler (βασιλείαν), more specifically "to inherit," esp. of intellectual things, also historical and scientific materials. The term is an established one in this context, e.g., in Plat. and Aristot.

Plat. Theaet., 198b defines the relation of pupil to teacher as that of παραλαμβάνων to → παραδιδούς (cf. La., 197d, Euthyd., 304c; Philo Cher., 68). In respect of intellectual questions he knows that he is necessarily linked to earlier generations (Theaet., 180c: παρειλήφαμεν), also in terminology (Crat., 425e: ὀνόματα ... παρὰ βαρβάρων τινῶν αὐτὰ παρειλήφαμεν). Aristot. is obviously very conscious of material dependence on these in their shaping of destiny (Meteor., I, 13, p. 349a, 15; Poet., 14, p. 1453b, 22). The formula παρειλήφαμεν παρὰ τῶν ... seems to have become a firmly established one in the two writers (cf. also Aristot. Gen. Corr., I, 7, p. 323b, 1 f.; An., I, 2, p. 403b, 27).

This evaluation of παραλαμβάνειν is perhaps linked with the fact that in the time before Plato there was comparatively little literary production and oral instruction was of great importance in the pursuit of knowledge. Even in the great period of Hellenism pedagogy was based on direct tradition from teacher to pupil, and what was mediated was not in the first instance historical (or scientific) material or highly general and impersonal knowledge, but a legacy of thought which raised a strongly authoritarian claim anchored primarily in the personality of the teacher. This demanded a definite relation of confidence on the part of the παραλαμβάνων. Greek φιλοσοφία or learning was eminently practical. Its final goal was moral impulse awakened by knowledge. This was still true even when abstract investigations were pursued. The philosopher was a personal leader (cf. Plat. Resp., VI, 501; VII, 520) who had charge of all Greek education and who exercised a decisive influence in all spheres of life. For this reason the παραλαμβάνων finds in him absolute authority. He may come into material contradiction with him because he outgrows him (though this is rare enough when there is such a strictly personal relation), but he still recognises the claim to personal

---

παραλαμβάνω. A. Seeberg, *Der Katechismus d. Urchristenheit* (1903), 46. On the Qabbala, cf. C. Taylor, *Sayings of the Jewish Fathers* ...[2] (1897), 106-108 (Excursus 1).

confidence. With the decay of this true form of Greek pedagogy, which set teacher and pupil in more than an abstract intellectual fellowship, which united them in an ἔρως, this understanding of παραλαμβάνειν disappeared in the period of middle Hellenism. It still lived on in Neo-Platonism, but took a rather different direction.[1]

It is obvious that Socrates does not fit smoothly into this scheme, yet he stands consciously outside, and even in opposition to, the normative method of instruction in his day. In any case, the relation of Socrates to his pupils certainly leaves the impression that their fellowship rests on personal trust between teacher and pupil and that the primary goal is not the mediation of knowledge but the formation of character. This orientation of the pedagogical method means that even outside the Socratic circle, each in his generation, at least when he himself becomes a teacher, can reach new results of his own which may even be opposed to those of his teacher. For the content of the tradition is not in the first instance the dead stuff of learning — this would rule out all advance — but the basic direction of character and conduct, and even in the sphere of pure scholarship it consists in the formulations of questions rather than in established findings. Even of these it may sometimes be said quite unequivocally that they were preserved with great tenacity for centuries and that they thus blocked the possibility of advance by new formulations (e.g., in the understanding of time).

The theme of παραλαμβάνειν, however, is not just the ἠθικὸς καὶ πολιτικὸς λόγος, which refers to the nature, meaning and goal of the personal and social shaping of life in the great contexts of all being, but also αἱ ἀπόρρητοι καὶ βαθύτεραι διδασκαλίαι (Plut. Alex., 7, 3 [I, 668a] from Aristot.), doctrines mainly of religious content which in virtue of their character as ἀπόρρητα demand the blind confidence of the παραλαμβάνων[2] and thus force him into strongly authoritarian dependence in respect of philosophical instruction.

παραλαμβάνειν is also a tt. for the reception of the rites and secrets of the Mysteries, the Mithraic, Porphyr. Abst., IV, 16; the Eleusinian, Plut. Demetr., 26 (I, 900e), also Suidas, *s.v.*, Schol. Aristoph. Ra., 757 (ed. G. Dindorf, IV, 2 [1838]); Hermetic gnosis, Corp. Herm., I, 26b. The last passage (cf. also Theo. Smyrnaeus, De Rebus Mathematicis, I, p. 15 [ed. E. Hiller, 1878]) emphasises the ability of the παραλαβών to be for the worthy a leader to redemption by God. But this is the only analogy to the NT concept. In the Mysteries the ref. is to a strict secret, whereas the Christian μυστήριον is the Gospel (Eph. 6:19) which is to be declared to the whole world. Again, the legacy which the Mysteries hand on is a fixed esoteric doctrine, whereas in Christianity it is above all things a living faith. How little Paul himself associated παραλαμβάνειν with the Mysteries may be seen from the fact that he never uses παραλαμβάνειν and παραδιδόναι in connection with μυστήριον, even where it would have been natural enough to do so (1 C. 15:51; Eph. 1:9; 3:3; 6:19; Col. 4:3). παραλαμβάνειν does not denote the direct supernatural revelation which is what Paul has in view, but personal or oral impartation.[3]

B. The Question of Tradition in Judaism.

In the Greek world the relation between teacher and pupil is largely controlled by personal confidence. In the Jewish schools, however, it is the material which

[1] Cf. the indexes to the editions of Iamblichus, esp. Vit. Pyth.

[2] Cf. also Iambl. Vit. Pyth., 28, 148 : ἐπίστευον καὶ παρειλήφεσαν. From the standpoint of later ideas an interesting passage is Pliny the Elder, Hist. Nat., XXX, 1, 9 : *certe Pythagoras, Empedocles, Democritus, Plato ... hanc* (*sc. magicen*) *in arcanis habuere.*

[3] So rightly R. Eisler, ZNW, 24 (1925), 161, n. 5.

is the binding link. This is basically restricted to the religious tradition, though this contains legal and other matters as well, and it claims unconditional validity. παραλαμβάνειν is achieved in a fellowship which has its sustaining basis, not in the person of the teacher, but in his office. Personal friendship is not essential. When we read of an attachment of the תלמיד this may be based on a gratitude corresponding to the greatness of what is received (cf. esp. Chag., 15b, where the orthodox pupil pays his heterodox teacher the thanks of an act of deliverance).[4] In view of the fact that the objective tradition claims infallibility, the relation between teacher and pupil is strongly authoritarian. The confidence of the pupil is not in the man, but in the bearer of the tradition. In the last analysis the content of the tradition includes both the Torah and its exegesis (the prophets, too, are regarded as handers on of the Torah),[5] and hence the exegesis acquires a derivative and increasing authority. The tt. for the transmission of the doctrinal content is קִבֵּל (Ab., 1, 1, where the chain is traced back to Moses or God; cf. Pea, 2, 6), though mostly in the phrase מְקֻבָּל אֲנִי = "it was handed down to me."[6]

The Rabbis, too, speak of a secret tradition (→ I, 741), though in the first instance the concealment is for reasons other than those of the Gk. Mysteries. If there is here a certain esoteric element, the main point is fear lest premature impartation of secret doctrines will do religious harm to the immature (Chag., 14b). For this reason the Merkaba, the exegesis of the vision of the chariot in Ez. and the exposition of the creation story (Chag., 2, 1) was handed on only with the greatest exclusiveness,[7] and so, too, were some purely legal materials (Chag., 2, 1).[8]

In the LXX παραλαμβάνω means "to take to (and with) oneself," mostly (in the historical books always except at Nu. 23:20) with a personal obj., occasionally a material; "to take over," "to inherit" (power, rule).

C. παραλαμβάνω in the NT.

1. With a personal obj. (only Gospels and Ac.), "to take to (or with) oneself" (e.g., in close fellowship). In theologically significant statements this is used of the reception of Christ by the world, Jn. 1:11, of acceptance into the kingdom of Christ, 14:3; Mt. 24:40 f., cf. also Lk. 17:34 f. (these statements typify the different conceptions of eschatology in Jn. and the Synoptists). On Col. 2:6 → *infra*.

2. With material obj. act. "to take over" an office, Col. 4:17; "to inherit" (βασιλείαν), Hb. 12:28. As a tt. a. "to take over the legacy of Rabbinic exegesis of the Torah as a prescription of religious law," Mt. 7:4 (with specific ref. to the rules of purification); b. (only in Paul) with closer correspondence to קִבֵּל on the one side, "to receive in fixed form, in the chain of Christian tradition," the account of the institution of the Lord's Supper and of the passion, death and resurrection of Jesus (1 C. 11:23;[9] 15:1, 3; → I, 437) or "to inherit the formulated laws of Christian morality," the Christian *Halakha*[10] (1 Th. 4:1), and with closer ap-

[4] Cf. Kittel Probleme, 69, esp. n. 4: "Pupils ... knew their teacher only as a teacher who was accidentally theirs."
[5] Cf. Bacher Term., I, 165.
[6] W. Bacher, *Tradition u. Tradenten in d. Schulen Palästinas u. Babyloniens* (1914), 2.
[7] Cf. Str.-B., Index, *s.v.* "Merkaba."
[8] Examples in Str.-B., I, 579 and 977.
[9] Cf. on this pt. Kittel Probleme, 64.
[10] C. v. Weizsäcker, *Das Apostolische Zeitalter*[3] (1902), 594 on 1 C. 4:17.

proximation to the original Greek παραλαμβάνω (→ 11) on the other side,[11] "to receive the intellectual and ethical content of religious life," "to inherit it in acceptance of its claim by attachment" to the personal religious life of Paul as the bearer of revelation (or to the author of this life, Gl. 1:12). Paul emphasises very strongly that the life which he passes on is not in any sense inherited by him from human bearers of revelation, that it has not been awakened in him in this way, but that he has received it directly from the Author of this revelation on the Damascus road. Naturally the content of this παραλαμβάνειν cannot be the legacy of the tradition of historical facts concerning Jesus (corresponding to a.). It must be an inward and living faith which gives religious certainty to a historical narrative which is not wholly immune from questioning. For this reason παραλαμβάνειν cannot be (like a.) the reception of purely intellectual materials. It is acceptance into the essential core of personality, which is more than the intellect alone.

This meaning of the term underlies also its use elsewhere. Only in this light can one explain the tremendous claim to validity, to the exclusion of any possible mistake, which is raised on behalf of what those addressed have received from Paul (Gl. 1:9; cf. 1 Th. 2:13). Only thus can one understand the conviction that congregations not evangelised by him have had imparted to them the same Christ (Col. 2:6) in the faith which is kindled in the non-Christian through that of the Christian. This παραλαμβάνειν is obviously effected by God Himself. The λόγος ἀκοῆς is λόγος θεοῦ (1 Th. 2:13). Related to this is finally the fact that the πῶς δεῖ περιπατεῖν also belongs to the content of παραλαμβάνειν, not as the purely formal acceptance of the traditional ethical teaching (cf. 1 Th. 4:1, → 13), since παραλαμβάνειν denotes the reception of an inner understanding of the nature and spirit of the moral life of the Christian which grows out of the contagious power of example (2 Th. 3:6 and Phil. 4:9). For this understanding derives from πίστις, from living union with Christ, so that its attaining can be described as παραλαμβάνειν τὸν Χριστόν (Col. 2:6).

† προλαμβάνω.

The basic meanings correspond to the nuances imparted by the preposition, "to take before," "to anticipate." In the NT the use is along the second of these two lines.

1. "To anticipate," 1 C. 11:21; also Mk. 14:8: Jesus interprets the anointing, which the woman intended as an act of grateful reverence, as an intimation of His imminent death. Since He sees ahead His death as a malefactor, and realises that His disciples will abandon Him, it is not to be expected that any should anoint Him as an act of piety. The saying could hardly have been invented, and this is an argument in favour of the authenticity of sayings which express His expectation of death (→ II, 24, 949).

2. "To surprise," Gl. 6:1: The point of the προλημφθῇ is that Paul has in view a fault into which the brother is betrayed "unawares," so that it is not intentionally wrong. In this case brotherly help is demanded rather than unloving judgment

[11] Paul can hardly have been aware of this connection. If the use of the term in the Mysteries was present to his mind, he completely transformed it. More likely is the suggestion that he developed the קִבֵּל of Rabbinic terminology.

(→ I, 476). There must be readiness to share the burden of offences before God (vv. 1-5 are closely interrelated, so that in v. 4 Paul emphasises that the readiness to find an excuse, indicated by προλημφθῇ, is to extend only to the fault of the brother, not to one's own).

† προσλαμβάνω, † πρόσλημψις.

προσλαμβάνω act. lit. "to take beside," into free or forced fellowship (possession) etc. Mid. "to draw to oneself," "to lend a hand." [1]

In the LXX (all occurrences are noted) the act. occurs only at Wis. 17:10; elsewhere the mid. has assumed the sense of the act., e.g., 2 Macc. 8:1; 10:15. Of God: As He has done with the whole people (1 Βασ. 12:22), He draws the elect to Himself (ψ 64:4), takes him into the closest fellowship with Himself and rescues him from affliction (ψ 17:16) and loneliness (26:10). This fellowship includes a unique feeling of blessedness (64:4) and protection (72:24).

In the NT the word is found only in the mid. (as in the LXX): "to take to oneself" (men, Ac. 17:5; 18:26; nourishment, Ac. 27:33, 36 [v. 36 part. gen.]) or "with oneself" (Mk. 8:32 and par.), "to receive hospitably" (Phlm. 17; Ac. 28:2). R. 14:1, 3; 15:7: As God (or Christ) has taken every member of the Church into fellowship with Himself, so incorporate each other into your Christian circle with no inner reservations (such as might spring from differences in religious custom).

πρόσλημψις means "taking to," "assumption." [2] Not found in the LXX, it occurs in the NT at R. 11:15 (corresponding to the verb) in the sense of the future "drawing to oneself," i.e., of the Jewish world, which is now far off and dead, by God. [3]

† ὑπολαμβάνω.

All the meanings, which are listed only in so far as they are significant in the NT, are ancient. The basic sense is "to take from below," "to catch up."

Hence 1. "to take up someone (protectively)," 3 Jn. 8; this does not mean only hospitable reception, but carries the thought of protecting those who are persecuted.

2. "To receive the words of someone," Lk. 10:30; what follows is therewith denoted as answer.

3. "To assume," "to suppose"; in Lk. 7:43 the speaker plainly selects this cautious word in order to blunt the seriousness of the judgment which Jesus has pronounced in the preceding parable. It is here a probably right assumption, whereas in Ac. 2:15 it is definitely false (in the refutation).

4. "To take up secretly," Ac. 1:9, unless this is an example of the basic meaning. Either way, the word expresses concealment or removal from the field of vision (→ ἀναλαμβάνω).

Delling

προσλαμβάνω κτλ. [1] Pass.

[2] Examples in lexicons.

[3] αὐτῶν (Jews) comes more naturally after πρόσλημψις than ὑμῶν (Gentiles); the antithesis is ἀποβολή — πρόσλημψις.

† λάμπω, † ἐκλάμπω, † περιλάμπω, † λαμπάς † λαμπρός → φῶς.

Contents: A. Meaning. B. The Moral and Religious Sense of the Words outside the NT: 1. The Greek and Hellenistic World; 2. "To shine" in the OT; 3. Judaism. C. λάμπειν κτλ. in the NT: 1. General Presuppositions; 2. The Theological Use of the Words. D. The Church.

A. Meaning.

The simple λάμπειν, which is found in all Gk., is predominantly, though not exclusively, poetic. It normally means intrans. "to shine," "to be bright," though rarely also trans. "to light up," "to cause to shine." So of a fire which leads astray: δόλιον ἀκταῖς ἀστέρα λάμψας (Eur. Hel., 1131). For the NT → 25. In the intrans. λάμπειν is used a. lit. of the sun, Solon (ed. T. Bergk, *Poetae Lyrici Graeci,* II[5] [1915], 13, 23); of lightning, Lk. 17:24; of a comet which brings disaster ἀστὴρ λάμψει, Sib., 3, 334; of resinous fire-brands, Hom. Il., 18, 492 etc.; of a house light, Mt. 5:15. b. fig. of angrily flashing eyes: ἀπ' ὀφθαλμῶν δὲ κακὸν πῦρ ... λάμπεσκε, Theocr. Idyll., 24, 18 f.; cf. Hom. Il., 15, 608; of the joyfully radiant face φαιδρὸς λάμποντι μετώπῳ, Aristoph. Eq., 550; of radiant beauty, Plat. Phaedr., 250d; of renown, Pind. Olymp., 1, 23; personally construed, "to win fame": οὐδ' εἰ Κλέων γ' ἔλαμψε, Aristoph. Vesp., 62; rarely acoustic: παιὰν δὲ λάμπει, Soph. Oed. Tyr., 186.

The compounds are used correspondingly as a stronger form, ἐκλάμπειν mostly intrans., trans. with acc. of the light shone forth, Aesch. Fr., 300, 4, of the darkness lit up, 2 Βασ. 22:29, or of the person illuminated, Iambl. Myst., VIII, 2; περιλάμπειν predominantly trans. with acc. of the thing lit up, Jos. Bell., 6, 290: φῶς περιέλαμψε τὸν βωμὸν καὶ τὸν ναόν, or of the person, apparently only Lk. 2:9; Ac. 26:13. The word is not found in the LXX.

λαμπάς, "torch," of resinous pine or dry twigs covered with pitch.[1] The word is not found in Homer. He knows only fire bowls filled with resin, λαμπτήρ. The torch occurs infrequently too as a means of illumination (Il., 11 554; 17, 663; Od., 1, 428, 434 etc.), especially as a bridal torch (Il., 18, 492). But this is denoted by δᾴς, and only a simple resinous brand is in view. The word λαμπάς is first found in Aesch. Ag., 8: λαμπάδος τὸ σύμβολον. It is then common in the lit. sense. It is used for enterprises by night. Thuc., III, 24, 1: μετὰ λαμπάδων, Ju. 7:16, 20; 15:4 f.; Ac. 20:8; Jn. 18:3:

λάμπω κτλ. RGG[2], III, 1630 ff., 1597 ff. (Bibl.); RE[3], XI, 464 f.; ERE, VIII, 47 ff., *s.v.* "Light and Darkness"; Pauly-W., VI (1909), 1945 ff.; M. Vassits, *Die Fackel in Kultus u. Kunst d. Griechen* (Diss. München, 1900); E. Samter, *Geburt, Hochzeit u. Tod* (1911), 67-82; T. Wächter, "Reinheitsvorschriften im griech. Kult," RVV, 9, 1 (1910), 27, n. 2; 44; 45, n. 1; 51; G. P. Wetter, *Phos* (1915); Reitzenstein Poim., *passim*; Ir. Erl., *passim*; M. Dibelius, "Die Vorstellung vom göttlichen Licht," DLZ, 36 (1915), 1469 ff.; F. J. Dölger, *Ichthys,* II (1922), 14, 386, 430, 434, 438; V. Thalhofer-L. Eisenhofer, *Hndbch. d. katholischen Liturgik*[2] (1912), Index *s.v. Fackeln, Kerze* etc.; K. Holl, "Der Ursprung d. Epiphanienfestes," SAB (1917), 402 ff.; E. Norden, *Die Geburt des Kindes* (1924), 24 ff.; R. Kittel, *Die hell. Mysterienreligion u. das AT* (1924), esp. 22 ff.; A. v. Harnack, SAB (1922), 62 ff.; E. Lohmeyer, "Die Verklärung Jesu nach dem Mk.-Ev.," ZNW, 21 (1922), 185 ff., esp. 208; J. Höller, *Die Verklärung Jesu* (1937); Hck. Mk. on 9:2 ff.; J. Sickenberger, *Die Briefe des hl. Pls. an die K. und R.* (1932); Wnd., Bchm. 2 K. on 4:6; Bau. J. on 1:4; Bss., Charles (ICC), Zn., Loh., Had. Rev. on the passages mentioned in the text. On the Mandaeans and Manichees → n. 23.

[1] On the nature and use of torches, I. v. Müller, *Die griech. Privataltertümer* = Hndbch. KlAW, IV, 1, 2[2] (1893), 65.

μετὰ φανῶν (lanterns) καὶ λαμπάδων (both together also in Dion. Hal. Ant. Rom., XI, 40, 2; P. Lond., 1159, 59). In the pap. λαμπάς is used always for the lamp with oil and wick, which was used from ancient times in Egypt, e.g., P. Oxy., XII, 1449, 19 from a temple inventory (213-217 A.D.): λαμπάδες ἀργυραῖ. The same combination with the same meaning is found in Jdt. 10:22; lamps at the fetching of the bridegroom, Mt. 25:1, 3, 4, 7, 8.[2] The word is a loan word in the Rabbis (לַמְפָּד). Fig. it is used for heavenly phenomena: ἀελίου λαμπάδες, rays of the sun (Eur. Ion, 1467), λαμπάδες κεραύνιαι, lightning (Eur. Ba., 244, 594), esp. when striking: ἄλλαι φαντασμάτων ἰδέαι θεωροῦνται λαμπάδες καὶ δοκίδες, rods, in a purely physical context, Ps.-Aristot. Mund., 4, p. 395b, 11. The word then acquires theological significance, → 18. In a strictly fig. sense it occurs as a name for hetaerae (Athen., XIII, 46 [p. 583e]), dogs (Ael. Nat. An., XI, 13) and ships (A. Böckh, *Urkunden über das Seewesen des Attischen Staats* [1840], *Urkunde* IVb, 5, h, 32, Xb, 158).

λαμπρός, means "shining," "radiant," "bright," and is used 1. of objects, a. lit. stars (Ep. Jer., 59), the sun (Hom. Od., 19, 234; Herm. s., 9, 17, 4), the moon (Thuc., VII, 44, 2; Test. N. 5:4), the morning star (Rev. 22:16), portions of metal (λαμπροῖσι φάλοισι, shining helmets, Hom. Il., 16, 216), water (Aesch. Eum., 695; Xenoph. Hist. Graec., V, 3, 19), stones (Herm. v., 3, 2, 4b; s., 9, 3, 3 etc.), clothes (the coat of Odysseus λαμπρὸς δ' ἦν ἠέλιος ὥς, Hom. Od., 19, 234). Those who seek the oracle are to sit in the temple ἐν ἐσθῆσιν λαμπραῖς, in white clothes (Ditt. Syll.^{3}, 1157, 39 f.). Pythagoras orders: προσιέναι τοὺς θύοντας μὴ πολυτελεῖς, ἀλλὰ λαμπρὰς καὶ καθαρὰς ἔχοντας ἐσθῆτας (Diod. S., X, 9, 6). λαμπρὰ ἐσθής is esp. a tt. for the *toga candida* of the candidate for office (Polyb., 10, 4, 8; Lk. 23:11?).[3] But also the garment of a popular rich man (Jm. 2:2 f., in the sense of "resplendent"). b. Fig.: λαμπρὰ ἔπη, very promising reputation (Soph. Oed. Col., 721), λαμπρὰ μαρτύρια, clear witnesses (Aesch. Eum., 797), ἐδέσματα λαμπρά, attractive dainties (Sir. 29:22), noun πάντα τὰ λιπαρὰ καὶ τὰ λαμπρά (Rev. 18:14), cf. εὐφραινόμενος λαμπρῶς (Lk. 16:19). In the good sense λαμπρὰ καρδία καὶ ἀγαθή (Sir. 30:25), λαμπρὰ καὶ ἀμάραντός ἐστιν ἡ σοφία (Wis. 6:12). 2. Of persons, "smart," "stately," "beautiful" (νυμφίος, Aristoph. Pax, 859), "generous" (at λειτουργεῖν, Demosth. Or., 21, 153, λαμπρὸν ἐπ' ἄρτοις, in respect of the table, Sir. 31:23), "distinguished" (ἐν τοῖς κινδύνοις, Demosth. Or., 19, 269).

B. The Moral and Religious Sense of the Words outside the New Testament.

1. The Greek and Hellenistic World.

a. Used of man and human things, λάμπειν denotes fighting power which awakens fear, e.g., Hom. Il., 6, 319 f.: λάμπετο δουρὸς αἰχμή. Terror seizes the Trojans when they see Pelides τεύχεσι λαμπόμενον, Il., 20, 46. *Ibid.*, 12, 463 of Hector: λάμπε δὲ χαλκῷ, 15, 623: λαμπόμενος πυρί. Elsewhere, too, the word is used of an ideal which is naturally oriented but not on that account low. Manliness brings repute: λάμπει ... ἀρετά, Pind. Isthm., 1, 22. Young wives acquire honour with their children: τέκνων οἷς ἂν λάμπωσιν ... νεάνιδες ἧβαι, Eur. Ion, 475 ff. The words take on a deeper

---

[2] A par. to the *faces nuptiales* (Cic.) of western peoples (→ 19). Cf. F. Zorell, *Verbum Domini*, 10 (1930), 176 ff. But the only meaning which fits the context is "lamp," or at most "torch" in the broader sense. Cf. Raschi on Kelim, 2, 8: In the land of Ishmael it is a custom that the bride should be taken from the house of her father to the house of her husband the night before her entry into the bridal chamber. Before her are carried ten poles, and at the head of each a kind of copper bowl filled with rags and oil and resin. These are lit to light the way before her (Str.-B., I, 969). Such practices do not seem to be known to the Rabbis. Only when Jochebed is brought home for the second time are torches mentioned (Pesikt. r., 43 [180b], Str.-B., I, 510).

[3] P. Joüon, Lk. 23:11: ἐσθῆτα λαμπράν in *Recherches de Science Religieuse*, 26 (1936), 80 ff.

moral sense in the tragic dramatists. Right shines in smoke-blackened huts, Aesch. Ag., 774: δίκα δὲ λάμπει μὲν ἐν δυσκάπνοις δώμασιν. Cf. also an unknown poet: δίκας δ' ἐξέλαμψε θεῖον φάος (TGF, p. 937, No. 500).

b. When we ask concerning the theological meaning, two radically different aspects are to be distinguished, first the connection of deity with light, and second the cathartic and apotropaic use of fire. The first is not predominant in the Greek world.

The Olympian gods are true gods of the day, Zeus who gathers the clouds and hurls the thunder, Apollo who guides the chariot of the sun. But for the Greeks this furthers the human nearness of the conception of deity. The sinister powers of the depths are also honoured as divine. Yet in view of the geological structure of Hellas the fire of Vulcan is not particularly prominent. The result is that the Greek does not specifically associate that which shines with the divine. There is, of course, a numinous sense of light. Homer compares his shining heroes with Ares, Il., 20, 46. Hesiod depicts the appearance of Apollo at the altar in the sacred grove: the grove was radiant with the weapons of the terrible god and with the god himself, Scutum Herculis, 71. Fiery phenomena, esp. in the night sky, may be evil omens (→ 16), but they may also be signs of divine favour and good success. Diod. S., XVI, 66, 3 narrates the journey of Timoleon to Syracuse: δι' ὅλης γὰρ τῆς νυκτὸς προηγεῖτο λαμπὰς καιομένη κατὰ τὸν οὐρανὸν μέχρι οὗ συνέβη τὸν στόλον εἰς τὴν Ἰταλίαν καταπλεῦσαι. A similar account, with Thrasybulos as the hero, is associated with the fiery pillar of the OT narrative in Cl. Al. Strom., I, 24, 163, 1 ff. On Gk. statues only the infrequently depicted Helios bears a halo.[4] The use of torches in the cultus is not to be explained along these lines.

That this is a special circumstance may be seen from the fact that the torch was originally the attribute only of chthonic deities and was used predominantly in their worship. Foremost here are the deities of Eleusis: Demeter, Kore, Iakchos, also Aphrodite and Eros, then, related esp. to Iakchos and particularly venerated in Orphism, Dionysus and his circle, the maenads and satyrs. The nocturnal torch dance of the thyads on wintry Parnassus is a gift of Dionysus to the Delphic god, whether the connection between the gods is ancient or comparatively late (→ II, 451). Hecate, often close to Artemis and surrounded by a swarm of furies, is also a lover of torches. Luc. Pergr. Mort., 28 mockingly holds out for the gifted Peregrinus the prospect of a nocturnal hero cult with the glow of torches on his funeral pyre. Yet many gods are represented without torches, including not only the Olympian deities but also Zeus Meilichios, Zeus Chthonios, Hermes Chthonios and even Hades,[5] though there are usually torches around him. This is best explained if we assume that the Mysteries had their origin in funeral rites. Hence torches originally had cathartic and apotropaic significance. Fire is a means of cleansing. In this respect it is similar to water, though not above it, cf. Plut. Quaest. Rom., 1 (II, 263e): τὸ πῦρ καθαίρει, καὶ τὸ ὕδωρ ἁγνίζει, Servius Comm. in Vergilii Aeneidem, 6, 741 (ed. G. Thilo [1884]): *aut taeda purgant et sulphure, aut aqua abluunt, aut aëre ventilant.*

Like the bath (→ λούω), the torch is found at most human events associated with miasma or threatened by demons. This is true of birth. It protects the newly born child of Iakchos and Zeus, and is essential at ἐγείρειν τὸν Λικνίτην (→ II, 333, n. 1, new

[4] Haas, 13/14 (1928), 38. On the other hand, the halo is found on demons of the underworld depicted on Etruscan graves under Orphic influence, F. Poulsen, *Etruscan Tomb Paintings* (1922), Fig. 35; F. Weege, *Etruskische Malerei* (1921), Plate 60. But oriental influence is likely on both Orphism and the Etruscans.

[5] From the 4th century on there is a change. On the altar relief at Pergamos Helios and Selene fight with a torch against the giants. Eros uses the torch to kindle love, and the Romans depict death with the torch.

birth from the dead).[6] As the wedding torch it is found already in Hom. (→ 16). That this did not shine on those who died young is bewailed on grave stones. The torch burns at the death bed.[7] "To the torch and the coping stone of life" (ἐπὶ τὴν δᾷδα καὶ κορωνίδα τοῦ βίου) is a proverbial saying in Plut. (An Seni Respublica gerenda sit, 9 [II, 789a]). The funeral pyre is lit by a torch. Luc. Pergr. Mort., 36 gives an express description of associated ceremonies and prayers, and these not merely at self-burning. Perhaps the acceptance of cremation is linked with cathartic and apotropaic origins. Attempts were also made to cure sickness by fire. Perhaps the cauterising of wounds was linked with this. The carrying of a torch perhaps preceded the purifying of whole cities or wards by fire, e.g., in time of pestilence. The basic idea is not the transferring of pure fire from one altar to another, nor that of displaying the random nature of fate. It is rather apotropaic. In Athens the course led from the altar of Prometheus in the Academy to the city (Paus., I, 30, 2).

There are some interesting interrelations. Mystic initiation replaces the wedding torch for the one who dies young. "Initiation and marriage complete." This is perhaps the significance of torches on many sarcophagi.[8] There can be no sharp differentiation between protection against danger and the furtherance of life. Fertility rites are also involved. Stumps of torches are laid between the branches of young fruit-trees to stimulate their growth.[9] The chthonic deities are well-known to be to a special degree the gods of fertility. It is thought that one is particularly near to them in caves. This is where they are preferably worshipped. Even technically this implies the need of lighting. Kora, the young corn, associated with Pluto, resides in the corn chamber beneath the ground. The mystery of the seed gives the initiate the hope of eternal life. The shining of the torch in the dark adyton is the bearer of this hope. It is the symbol of life as such. Plato views the sequence of generations as in some sense a torch procession: καθάπερ λαμπάδα τὸν βίον παραδιδόντας ἄλλοις ἐξ ἄλλων, θεραπεύοντας ἀεὶ θεοὺς κατὰ νόμους Leg., VI, 776b.

This helps us to understand the significance of the torch-bearer in the Mysteries. The δᾳδοῦχος (male or female) is particularly close to the deity, which in many cases also bears the torch.[10] He is often mentioned in the inscr. along with the hierophant, Ditt. Syll.³, 83, 25; *ibid.*, 796 B, 28 ff. (honouring of a dead youth, *c.* 40 A.D.): εὐγενείαι τε τῆι 'Αθήνησιν ἀπὸ τῶν ἀρχαίων καὶ πρώτων ἀνδρῶν, ἱερέων καὶ ἱερειῶν τῆς προσωνύμου τῆς πόλεως θεοῦ καὶ ἱεροφαντικῶν καὶ δᾳδουχικῶν οἴκων γνήσιον ὑπάρχοντα. In the temple precincts of Demeter at Pergamos a δᾳδοῦχος endows an altar to the unknown or most holy gods.[11] Among the dignitaries of a Bacchic fellowship in Italy there stands in the second place, even before the ἱερεῖς and ἱέρειαι a ... ηγίλλα δᾳδοῦχος.[12] One may perhaps see at this pt. in the Mysteries, at least where there is oriental influence, the first traces of a religion of light. But Greek religion never became this in the narrower sense.

The home of the Hellenistic religion of light is in Egypt and the Orient. As shown by the discovery of many lamps in graves, the apotropaic significance is known here too. But the worship of light goes much deeper. From ancient times in Alexandria there rang out in the nocturnal mysteries on December 24/25th and January 5/6th the cry:

---

6 There are examples with interesting par. from modern Greece in Vassits, *op. cit.*, 74 ff.

7 Even to-day a burning candle is put in the hands of the dying.

8 Sarcophagus of a girl from Torre Nova, Haas, 9/11, Leipoldt (1926), 186. There are bizarre explanations of the number five for wedding torches in Plut. Quaest. Rom., 2 (II, 263 f.).

9 Vassits, 9.

10 One need only refer to the well-known Niinnionpinax, Photo Alinari, 24, 335, also Haas, 193.

11 2nd cent. A.D. A. Deissmann, *Paulus*² (1925), 226 ff.

12 1st half of the 2nd cent. A.D. *Amer. Journal of Archaeology*, 37 (1933), Plate XXVII, also 239 ff.

ἡ παρθένος τέτοκεν, αὔξει φῶς, or something similar.[13] In the Isis cult *illustrari* plays an important part (Apul. Met., XI, 27-29 *passim*, cf. what is said about the shining of the sun at midnight, 23). The torch is again a symbol, this time in the hand of the initiate dressed and worshipped as the sun-god, 24. As a dogma of Egyptian theology concerning the deities who overcome death (and the mortals united with them ?), Plut. tells us : τὰ μὲν σώματα ... κεῖσθαι, ... τὰς δὲ ψυχὰς ἐν οὐρανῷ λάμπειν ἄστρα (Is. et Os., 21 [II, 359c d]).

The significance of light and to illumine in Hermes mysticism are linked with this worship of light. But oriental influence is also perceptible here (Corp. Herm., 1, 17: ὁ δὲ ἄνθρωπος ἐκ ζωῆς (physical) καὶ φωτὸς ἐγένετο εἰς ψυχὴν καὶ νοῦν, ἐκ μὲν ζωῆς ψυχήν, ἐκ δὲ φωτὸς νοῦν. *Ibid.*, X, 6 (subj. the beauty of the good): περιλάμψαν δὲ [πάντα] τὸν νοῦν [καὶ] τὴν ὅλην ψυχὴν ἀναλαμβάνει[14] καὶ ἀνέλκει διὰ τοῦ σώματος (away from the body) καὶ ὅλον αὐτὸν εἰς οὐσίαν μεταβάλλει (synon. ἀποθεωθῆναι). Light is regarded as the physical substance of God and salvation.[15]

On the whole, the influence of the Orient is more significant than that of Egypt. It is almost impossible to differentiate the effects of the Indian doctrine of totality, Persian dualism, and the astral religion of Babylon,[16] let alone the derived forms of religion.[17] Here, too, elemental conceptions, which are gradually spiritualised, are the starting-point. Light is the matter of the other world which flows on him who is willing to receive it and imparts divine powers. Light and life, and later knowledge, are interchangeable concepts.

Acc. to the ancient Indian view, fire, as it appears at the dawn, and in other forms in wind and water, or as it arises in the fire-box, is the substance of the deities. It has been conjectured that *bráhma* is etym. related to φλέγμα, *flamma, fulmen.* From this it is only a step to the Persian cult of fire and the doctrine of fire as it might still be found among Parsees in India in the second half of the 18th century.[18] Mithra is originally the starry heaven.[19] The two companions of Mithra represent the rising and falling light of the daily and yearly cycle, Kautes with uplifted torch and Kautopates with fallen torch, cf. countless Mithraic monuments. In Mithra shrines hundreds of lamps are found.[20] In an unknown mystery the deity is greeted : χαῖρε νύμφιε χαῖρε νέον φῶς (Firm. Mat. Err. Prof. Rel., 19, 1). In the Attis cult, or a closely related religion, the transition from sadness to joy is marked by the bringing in of a light, *ibid.*, 22, 1: *deinde cum se ficta lamentatione satiaverint, lumen infertur* ; this is followed by anointing with the well-known θαρρεῖτε μύσται κτλ. The torch also appear on altars of the *taurobolium.*[21] The cultic practices,[22] first meant literally, later became symbols of the

[13] The main witness is Epiphanius. Examples in Holl, Kittel, Norden. That the Gk. ritual is not the original may be assumed. The Jan. festival can be traced back to 1996 B.C. It was then at approximately the winter solstice. The doubling is explicable in terms of a gradual shift of the calendar.

[14] A conjecture of Scott. The codices read ἀναλάμπει.

[15] Wetter's Index has about 40 relevant passages from Corp. Herm. alone.

[16] Cf. e.g., the starred horoscope lion of Antiochus of Commagene (60 B.C.), Haas, 115.

[17] Wetter lays one-sided emphasis on the Babylonian influence.

[18] So J. Hertel, "Der Planet Venus im Avesta," *Berichte über d. Verhandlungen der Sächsischen Akademie d. Wissenschaften zu Leipzig, phil.-hist. Kl.*, 87 (1935), I (1936), 3 ff. Hertel finds agreement as well as disagreement with this derivation, e.g., in authorities like W. Streitberg. He emphasises very strongly that it is a mistake to interpret the spiritualised biblical concepts in terms of the Vendidad and Avesta, or even to derive them from these.

[19] J. Hertel, "D. Sonne u. Mithra im Avesta," *Indoiranische Quellen u. Forschungen,* 9 (1927), esp. 179 ff.

[20] A. Minto, *Notizie degli scavi di antichità* (1924), 353 ff.

[21] Haas, 152 and 153 : Attic *taurobolium* altar, 387 A.D.

[22] Cf. Dio Chrys. Or., 12, 33 : σκότους τε καὶ φωτὸς ἐναλλὰξ αὐτῷ φαινομένων.

lofty reality in which it was hoped to participate in religion. Julian says of divinely filled souls that during the mysteries ἐλλάμπει αὐταῖς τὸ θεῖον φῶς, Or., 5, 178b. Iamblichus speaks of the power of the gods shining like the sun (ἐπιλαμπούσης, Myst., 3, 13 [p. 130, 13]). This religiosity develops riotously in the magic pap. A rite for compelling love describes tne shining of a star as a good omen that the beloved will be affected. If it throws out sparks, she is on the way. But if it is drawn out long like a torch, she has already come, Preis. Zaub., IV, 2939 ff. But such trivial secularisation is not common. In the so-called Mithras liturgy God is encircled by fire and is addressed: λαμπροφεγγῆ, Preis. Zaub., IV, 714 f., cf. the many similar predicates, 590 ff. Cf. the prayer: ἐπικαλοῦμαί σε τὸν θεὸν τὸν ζῶντα, πυριφεγγῆ, ἀόρατον φωτὸς γεννήτορα ... εἴσελθε ἐν τῷ πυρὶ τούτῳ ... καὶ διαλαμψάτω ὁ ἔσωθεν, ὁ κύριος (Reitzenstein Poim., 25). In the so-called 8th Book of Moses in the Leiden magic pap. it is said of God that for Him the sun and moon are unwearying eyes shining in (or into?) the pupils of men (οὗ ὁ ἥλιος καὶ ἡ σελήνη ὀφθαλμοί εἰσιν ἀκάματοι λάμποντες ἐν ταῖς κόραις τῶν ἀνθρώπων, Preis. Zaub., XIII, 766 ff.). Another magic prayer (Reitzenstein Poim., 20) names the name of God ἐν οὐρανῷ λαμφθέν. The ruler cult stands under the sign of this religion of light. Ditt. Syll.^{3}, 798, 3 f. of Caligula as the new Helios: συναναλάμψαι ταῖς ἰδίαις αὐγαῖς ... ἠθέλησεν βασιλήας. *Ibid.*, 814, 34 of Nero: νέος Ἥλιος ἐπιλάμψας τοῖς Ἕλλησιν, cf. also 900, 25 f.; Ditt. Or., 194, 20. Cf. also the prayer to the supreme God in Reitzenstein Poim., 28, VII, 2: ὀρθρινὸν ἐπιλάμποντα.

Among the Manichees and Mandaeans[23] the oriental religion of light, conserving what is old or developing new features, continues on its way and constitutes a serious threat to Christianity. There is here special emphasis on the friendly and redemptive aspect of religion. But the dividing line is not between Creator and creature, or good and evil. It is between two basic principles understood predominantly in natural terms. Light mysticism is from the very first a religion of ontological rather than moral redemption. But this does not rule out the possibility of a powerful ethics developing out of it.

Manichaeism repudiates magic religion in the same way as Christianity does Judaism, Hom., 11, 1 ff. But it takes over the basic Zoroastrian principle of the dualism of light and darkness. *In exordio fuerunt duae substantiae a sese divisae: luminis quidem imperium tenebat Deus pater* (Aug. Contra Epistolam Manichaei, 13 [16], MPL, 42, 182). Mani prays to "the perfect man, the virgin of light" (Hom., 53, 8 f.). He calls himself an apostle of light along with Zarathrustra and Christ, *ibid.*, 11, 26; 29, 9. In the consummation the portions of light now dispersed in darkness will be redeemed and will return to their origin. "He will give grace to his fighters whom he has sent to fight against darkness ... and he will reveal to them his image. All light will plunge into him. They will go into the ταμιεῖον and will come out of it again in glory ... King in the two kingdoms: the King of the aeons of light, that is the Father, the King of light ... but the king of the new aeon is the first man," *ibid.*, 41, 13 ff. An attempt is made to distinguish between intelligible light and its material reflection, the light which may be apprehended by the senses. Titus of Bostra Contra Manichaeos, I, 23 (ed. P. de Lagarde [1859]), p. 14, 4 ff.: θεοῦ μέν ἐστι φῶς αἰσθητὸν δημιούργημα, αὐτὸς δὲ φῶς ἂν εἴη νοητόν, οὐκ αἰσθητὸν ... αὐτὸν τὸν θεόν, ὅσπερ ἐστὶ νοερὸν φῶς, ... But Aug. rightly accuses the Manichaeans of having only a sensual concept of light: *lumen cogitare non potestis, nisi quale videre consuestis,* Faust, XX, 7. Light was thought of as a body extended throughout all nature (→ III, 966). This body had twelve members corresponding to the signs of the zodiac. Among the Mandaeans the mythology

[23] On Manichaeism, RGG^2, III, 1959 ff., with bibl. F. C. Baur, *Das Manichäische Religionssystem* (1831, new impress. 1928) is still unsurpassed. Particularly important sources are the Fr. of Turfân, ed. F. W. K. Müller, AAB (1904), Suppl. and *Manichäische Hdschren. d. Sammlung A. Chester Beatty,* I: *Manichäische Homilien,* ed. H. J. Polotsky (1934), quoted as Hom. with page and line.

of light takes a wholly sensual form. The term radiance is particularly favoured, so that one can even read of the smell of radiance (Lidz. Ginza R., III, 69 [p. 66, 9]). The first radiance admonishes his son (*ibid.*, R., XI, 250 [p. 252, 11 ff.]): "Clothe them with radiance, cover them with light, and let them linger in the garment of living fire, the three Uthras who go there from without to cause the call of life to be received." Here the wildest fantasy is given free rein.

2. "To shine" in the Old Testament.

In OT religion light occurs in many connections ranging from natural light to the most refined details of religious and moral experience. It is not possible tc explore these riches here (→ φῶς). In spite of the high significance of the word in the OT world of thought, it would be very misleading to describe OT religion simply as a religion of light. From the historical and material standpoint there are no serious relations between it and the light religions of the East up to the remotest period, → n. 18. For in those religions light is deified, whereas in the OT the living God is always in the strictest sense the Subject.

The distance between God and all created light is even given linguistic expression. None of the Heb. equivalents of λάμπειν (נָגַהּ, זָהַר, צָחַח) is used intrans. of Yahweh, and the last only trans. in hi (Ps. 18:28; 2 S. 22:29). In the second of these God Himself is certainly the lamp of the singer, but even here, quite apart from the strong spiritualisation, an active element is expressed. If there is a close connection between God and light, it is that of Creator and creature. When He made the world, Yahweh first created light (Gn. 1:3). He wraps Himself in light as in a cloak (Ps. 104:2). The starry heaven is the reflection of His glory (Is. 40:12, 26; Am. 5:8; Ps. 8:3; 19:1; 147:4; Job 9:7 ff.). The stars shine for Him (Bar. 3:34 f.: ἔλαμψαν ... τῷ ποιήσαντι αὐτούς). He shines even in the murk of earth. Even the fearsome crocodile is a proof of the hidden greatness of Him who has made it. This numinous element is described in Job 41:10 ff. in phrases from light theology: φέγγος, λαμπάδες καιόμεναι, ἐσχάραι πυρός, πῦρ ἀνθράκων, φλόξ. In Na. 2:5 the conquerors of Nineveh appear in their terribleness ὡς λαμπάδες πυρὸς καὶ ὡς ἀστραπαὶ διατρέχουσαι. Yahweh sends them. But He also effects a more kindly brightness. It is said of the princes of Jerusalem in good times: ἔλαμψαν ὑπὲρ γάλα (Lam. 4:7, wrongly ascribed to the Nazirites in the LXX). But human radiance has true and lasting significance only as a reflection of that of Yahweh. Otherwise it quickly vanishes. In the coming age of salvation Yahweh will make the head men of Judah like a firebrand among the wood καὶ ὡς λαμπάδα πυρὸς ἐν καλάμῃ (Zech. 12:6). God's warrior Elijah possessed valour and the joy of conflict in the higher sense. He was like a fire, and his word burned like a torch (Sir. 48:1). The heavenly messenger of Yahweh appears in a flame of fire (Ex. 3:2). Later ages sometimes represent the face of an angel as lightning and his eyes as flaming torches (ὡσεὶ λαμπάδες πυρός, Da. 10:6, cf. the description of the Easter angel in Mt. 28:3). The covenant God manifests Himself under similar majestic phenomena of light, though His being is neither exhausted nor fully revealed in them. When the covenant is made with Abraham (Gn. 15:17) there appear λαμπάδες πυρός which pass through the parts of the covenant sacrifice. In the pillar of cloud by night (Ex. 13:21) which frightens away enemies (14:24) He leads His people through the desert (→ 18).

At Sinai the people itself perceives with terror not only smoke but also, at the sound of the trumpet, τὰς λαμπάδας (Ex. 20:18; cf. Dt. 4:24). The majesty of the King of heaven (כְּבוֹד יהוה, δόξα κυρίου, → δόξα) is repeatedly depicted as a flaming fire (Ex. 24:17; Lv. 9:23 f.; Nu. 16:35). It appears thus to the prophets (Ez. 1:13: ὄψις λαμπάδων, 27). Idols, on the other hand, have no brightness, Ep. Jer., 66. Nowhere is there any ref. to a passing of the divine substance of light into man. The cleft between the glory of Yahweh and the mortal and sinful child of man is too great for this. Even to see the glory of Yahweh normally brings death and destruction. The very seraphs hide their faces before Him. Only a few chosen ones may see the radiant and gracious presence of Yahweh without dying (Is. 6:1, 2, 5; Ex. 24:10 f.). He gives Himself to be known by whom He will. The radiance of His glory shines on the mediator of the covenant, whether graciously or to destruction (→ III, 559), Ex. 34:33 ff. He causes His face to shine on the congregation on whom His blessing is laid, Nu. 6:25. As in ecstatic vision, the prophet already experiences the day when the light of the day of salvation shines for the people which walks in darkness (Is. 9:1 LXX: φῶς λάμψει ἐφ' ὑμᾶς, 4:2: ἐπιλάμψει ὁ θεὸς ἐν βουλῇ μετὰ δόξης — the LXX has here read its own theology of light into the original; cf. Is. 60:1 ff.; 62:1). Yahweh is the source of life; in His light His people see light, Ps. 36:9; the combination of life and light is to be noted. The ungodly perish, but αἱ ὁδοὶ τῶν δικαίων ὁμοίως φωτὶ λάμπουσιν (Prv. 4:18). Solemn songs of praise see the day coming when the light of Yahweh will shine on all the world and on all nations, Tob. 13:13 א: φῶς λαμπρὸν λάμψει. At the resurrection — the later piety of the OT finally reaches its goal here — the righteous shall shine in the glory of Yahweh: καὶ οἱ συνιέντες λάμψουσιν ὡς ἡ λαμπρότης τοῦ στερεώματος (Da. 12:3 Θ).

3. Judaism.

The traditional ideas of the luminous glory of Yahweh are further developed in Judaism, and, partly under syncretistic influences, they are worked out with some degree of fantasy both on the cosmic [24] and on the transcendent side. [25] Judaism was much concerned with the spiritualised outshining of the divine light on the world.

The Shekinah is represented as radiant light. It illumines the blessed of the first rank, though, as many suppose, behind a curtain. The glow from it (זִיו) is the food of angels. Through a whole series of media God's light shines into the world. Adam was the lamp (נֵר) of the world, jShab., 5b, line 46, Str.-B., I, 237. The Messiah is comparatively little mentioned in this connection. Cf. Test. L. 18:4: "He will shine as the sun on the earth, and take away all darkness from the earth, and there will be peace on the whole earth." The emphasis is mostly on Israel and its privileges. These are, as it were, embodied in the candlestick of the temple. God has no need of lights, Nu. r., 15 on 8:2, Str.-B., III, 717. He gives Israel the opportunity to attain merit by carefully keeping the lamp, and by the flames of the seven-branched candelabra, which is prefigured already in the creation of light and the planets, He seeks to remind Israel to shine for Him. As the oil (or Noah's dove, Cant. r. on 1:15) brings light to the world, so Israel is the light of the world (*ibid.*, on 1:3). [26] Jerusalem is the light of the world, esp. the temple, whose windows are narrow inside and broad outside so that light may stream out but not come in, Pesikt., 21. The Torah and its knowledge is the light of the world. Baba ben Buta said to Herod when Herod had killed the rabbis: "Thou hast put out the light of the world" (bBB, 4a). R. Jochanan b. Zakkai (c. 80) in the hour of his death was addressed by his pupils as the lamp of the world (נֵר עוֹלָם, Ab. R. Nat., 25; cf. bBer., 28b: נר ישׂראל). The ref. is to more than usual knowledge of the Torah, and also to its fulfilment. Test. B. 5:3: "Where the light of good works is present in the mind, darkness yields

[24] Esp. in the Books of Enoch; for details cf. Bousset-Gressm., 497 ff.

[25] For details on the heavenly world of light, *v.* Weber, 162 ff.

[26] The idea would be stronger if we could be sure that the depiction of the seven-branched candelabra had only symbolical significance in Judaism. Cf. K. H. Rengstorf, "Zu den Fresken in d. jüd. Katakombe der Villa Torlonia in Rom," ZNW, 31 (1932), 33 ff. Two seven-branched candlesticks are mentioned as articles of synagogue furniture, at least in the Byzantine period ("Inschrift von Side," JHS, 28, 1 [1908], 195; Schürer, III[4], 22). Lamps were often endowed, Str.-B., IV, 140.

before it."[27] On Rabbinic visions of light, → II, 455 f. Some day the light of God will be visible to His people. In the future world the faces of the righteous, esp. those who have allowed their faces to become black for the sake of the Torah, will shine like the sun. 4 Esr. 7:97: "The sixth (joy of the righteous in the hour of death) is that they will be shown how their faces will one day shine as the sun." Cf. Eth. En. 51:5: "All will become angels in heaven. Their faces will shine for joy."[28]

The simple λάμπειν does not occur in Philo. Several compounds are used. Above all, the matter is there. The natural man cannot grasp the light of God (Deus Imm., 78). Philo compares the creation of the Nous, the shining of divine knowledge in the human spirit, to the creation of light and the sun and sunrise (Som., I, 72 ff.; Praem. Poen., 25; Migr. Abr., 39; Plant., 40). The onset of ecstasy is particularly compared to the sunrise, Rer. Div. Her., 264: ὅταν μὲν γὰρ φῶς τὸ θεῖον ἐπιλάμψῃ, δύεται τὸ ἀνθρώπινον. Ebr., 44: ἐπιλάμψασα γὰρ ἡ τοῦ ὄντος ἐπιστήμη πάντα περιαυγάζει. Cf. Wis. 5:6 (confession of the ungodly): τὸ τῆς δικαιοσύνης φῶς οὐκ ἐπέλαμψεν ἡμῖν καὶ ὁ ἥλιος οὐκ ἀνέτειλεν ἡμῖν. This close connection between light and knowledge is Hellenistic.

C. λάμπειν κτλ. in the New Testament.

1. General Presuppositions.

These correspond first to those of the OT and Judaism. Later the influence of the Hellenistic religion of light may be discerned, though not specifically in relation to these words (→ φῶς, (ἐπι)φαίνω, ἐπιφάνεια). The traditional ideas are given their specific sense by the particular content of the NT. In the NT the world beyond is thought of as a radiant world of light. Especially impressive in this respect are the series of images in Rev. → λυχνία, λύχνος, λευκός, πῦρ, ἥλιος. Similar concrete conceptions may be assumed in the case of the other NT authors, least of all, perhaps, Paul. The light of God is unchangeable (Jm. 1:17) and intrinsically unapproachable (1 Tm. 6:16). But it sets itself in relation to man. Full of light and dispensing light, the upper world comes into the lower both as the manifestation of light and also as a power which gives knowledge, life and moral renewal. Opposed to it is darkness (→ φῶς, σκότος). The new thing is the linking of light to the historical person of Jesus. This is seen especially in John.

2. The Theological Use of the Words.

λάμπειν and compounds are used a. of the appearance of messengers from the other world. Ac. 12:7, when Peter is freed from prison: φῶς ἔλαμψεν ἐν τῷ οἰκήματι.[29] So also the Christmas narrative in Lk. 2:9: δόξα κυρίου περιέλαμψεν αὐτούς. From the awe-inspiring radiance rings out the voice: "Fear not, for lo, I proclaim to you great joy." This is as far from Hellenistic mysticism as from Jewish transcendence or false familiarity. Here the Father speaks of Jesus Christ.

---

[27] Str.-B., I, 237 on Mt. 5:14. Cf. also the examples of particular worthiness, 239 f. on Mt. 5:16.

[28] For further examples cf. Str.-B., I, 673 f. on Mt. 13:43; 752 on Mt. 17:2. Cf. H. Gunkel in Kautzsch Pseudepigr. on 4 Esr. 7:97. On the light which shines on man during his embryonic development (the Rabb. form of the idea that the soul is a body of light), cf. R. Meyer, "Hellenistisches in der Rabb. Anthropologie," BWANT, IV, 22 (1937), Index *s.v. Lichtmotiv*.

[29] D: ἐπέλαμψεν τῷ οἰκήματι.

They are used b. of the Messiah. His coming in glory and power will take place in a majesty which will be seen by all men at once like lightning, Lk. 17:24: ὥσπερ γὰρ ἡ ἀστραπὴ ἀστράπτουσα ἐκ τῆς ὑπὸ τὸν οὐρανὸν εἰς τὴν ὑπ' οὐρανὸν λάμπει, οὕτως ἔσται ὁ υἱὸς τοῦ ἀνθρώπου ἐν τῇ ἡμέρᾳ αὐτοῦ. The transfiguration is a temporary anticipation of Messianic glory in the earthly life of Jesus. Mt. 17:2: καὶ ἔλαμψεν τὸ πρόσωπον αὐτοῦ ὡς ὁ ἥλιος (peculiar to Mt.).[30] The Risen Lord appears to Saul in a light which outshines the brightness of the midday sun and which throws all who see it to the earth, Ac. 26:13: ἡμέρας μέσης κατὰ τὴν ὁδὸν εἶδον, βασιλεῦ, οὐρανόθεν ὑπὲρ τὴν λαμπρότητα τοῦ ἡλίου περιλάμψαν με φῶς.[31]

They are used c. of the dawn of the Christian experience of salvation: 2 C. 4:6: ὅτι ὁ θεὸς ὁ εἰπών· ἐκ σκότους φῶς λάμψει,[32] ὃς[33] ἔλαμψεν ἐν ταῖς καρδίαις ἡμῶν πρὸς φωτισμὸν τῆς γνώσεως τῆς δόξης τοῦ θεοῦ[34] ἐν προσώπῳ Χριστοῦ, "for God, who said, Let light shine out of darkness, has shined in our hearts to (intended result) the shining of the knowledge of the glory of God in the face of Jesus Christ."

Since neither ὁ θεός (unlike θεός without art. in 2 C. 5:5 and perhaps 1:21) nor ὁ εἰπών can be the predicate noun, the predicate follows, lightly connected with ὅς in the form of anacoluthon, in ἔλαμψεν. The creation *fiat* from Gn. 1:3 (cf. Philo Som., I, 75) is altered on the basis of Is. 9:1 or 2 S. 22:29. Like λάμψει, ἔλαμψεν is intrans., the more so as this use is the more common (→ 16), and there is no obj. Acc. to the rule that the first and last times correspond, the first creation of light is followed by a second. What is meant is not a merely inward act, but a second act of cosmic creation.[35] From this it also follows that ἐν is used, as often, for → εἰς (→ II, 433 f.) and denotes, not the place where light has its source, but the goal of its shining.

---

30 Harnack, *op. cit.*, 62 ff. suggests a historical experience of the ecstatically inclined Pt., in terms of which 1 C. 15:5 is also to be understood. So also, though without the last point, Hck. Mk., *ad loc.* E. Lohmeyer, ZNW, 21 (1922), thinks that the multiplicity of visions indicates a legend. But as against this Mk. 9:3 is hardly dispensable, since Jesus in His earthly body is less than the men of God of the OT (in their supraterrestrial form ?), and it is the tendency of legend to glorify Jesus as the Messiah. There is little substance in the view that Hellenistic practices are the source of the shining heavenly garments. The Greek λαμπρὰ ἐσθής is white as a sign of purity. But the Mysteries go on to give to the new god (in distinction from older practice, Apul. Met., XI, 9) a coloured and artistically painted garment, Apul. Met., XI, 24: *floride depicta veste ... colore vario circumnotatis ... animalibus.* The radiant garment of light is more oriental. The god of the Mithras liturgy has a flowing white garment of light, Preis. Zaub., IV, 696 ff. The white clothing of the Mandaeans is supposed to be a reflection of the heavenly clothing of the angels and manas, Lidz. Ginza R., I, 25 (p. 26, 30 ff.); II, 1, 47 (p. 44, 30 ff.); L., II, 15, 58 (p. 481, 24); *ibid.* (p. 482, 6 f.). In the hymn in Act. Thom., 108 and 111 f. the gay colours belong only to the symbolic investiture (II, 2, p. 223, 7: λαμπρότης; 2: φῶς; p. 224, 12: φέγγος). The μετεμορφώθη of Mk. is rightly referred by Mt. and Lk. to the physical transfiguration. This feature, which is accompanied by the change in the clothing, is thus present in Mk. too. The heavenly confirmation of the Messianic confession "is a knowledge which flames up in symbolic rather than conceptual form." Hck. Mk., *ad loc.*

31 Acc. to E. Hirsch, ZNW, 28 (1929), 305 ff. the account in Ac. 26 goes back to Paul's own description, though this need not apply to every detail. On the relation to Hell. par. cf. F. Smend, *Angelos,* I (1925), 35 f.; H. Windisch, ZNW, 31 (1932), 1 ff.

32 λάμψαι C𝔎 G pl. lat Mcion Or; txt: B ℵ* AD* Cl Al sy copt.

33 Not found in D*G 81 it Mcion Chrys.

34 C*D*G it Mcion αὐτοῦ.

35 This counts against the theory that Paul is thinking of his experience on the Damascus road. The ref. is rather to the experience of all believers and preachers. On the Damascus road this drew Paul into its circle.

φωτισμός, as in v. 4, is not the trans. "enlightening" but the intrans. "shining." τῆς γνώσεως is a subj. gen., τῆς δόξης an obj. The knowledge of the glory of God is first to shine into the heart and then by preaching to shine out into the world. This follows from v. 5.

Paul impinges on Hellenistic mysticism when he links God, light, and saving knowledge. But he diverges from it in that he does not think in terms of a mystical union and inner light, but primarily in terms of a historical act of salvation and of the knowledge bound up with salvation history, which is then used by God for missionary transmission.

d. The words are used of the walk of the disciples of Jesus in Mt. 5:15 f.: ... καὶ λάμπει πᾶσιν τοῖς ἐν τῇ οἰκίᾳ· οὕτως λαμψάτω τὸ φῶς ὑμῶν ἔμπροσθεν τῶν ἀνθρώπων. The phrase is perhaps suggested by the parable in v. 15, and the meaning is in this case purely ethical and immanent. But if the saying is set against its Jewish background (→ 23) and brought into relation with the NT context (v. 13, 14a, 16b, cf. also Jn. 8:12), it is clear that the relation to the world of God is here the basic factor. The disciples of Jesus are to cause the light which they have received from the heavenly Father to shine in the world in order to glorify God.

e. They are used of believers in an eschatological context, Mt. 13:43: οἱ δίκαιοι ἐκλάμψουσιν ὡς ὁ ἥλιος ἐν τῇ βασιλείᾳ τοῦ πατρὸς αὐτῶν. The saying is a quotation from Da. 12:3 in a form closer to Θ than LXX. The NT, too, speaks of a similarity of perfected believers to the stars and to angels. For Jewish parallels → 24.

The theological use of λαμπάς is peculiar to Rev. In 4:5, in a depiction of the throne of God, mention is made of lightning and thunder, and then we read: καὶ ἑπτὰ λαμπάδες πυρὸς καιόμεναι ἐνώπιον τοῦ θρόνου, ἅ εἰσιν τὰ ἑπτὰ πνεύματα τοῦ θεοῦ.

The mode of expression is OT (for λαμπάδες πυρός cf. Gn. 15:17; Na. 2:5; Da. 10:6; 1 Macc. 6:39; for λαμπάδες καιόμεναι, Job 41:11). In visions (Zech. 4:2) and in relation to God's throne (Ez. 1:13), lights are traditional. The original features are the number seven and the use in relation to spirits.[36] There is approximation to the latter in sayings like ψ 103:4: ὁ ποιῶν τοὺς ἀγγέλους αὐτοῦ πνεύματα καὶ τοὺς λειτουργοὺς αὐτοῦ πῦρ φλέγον,[37] and S. Bar. 21:6: "The innumerable holy beings which thou hast created from eternity, the flaming and fiery beings which stand about thy throne." The number seven (→ II, 632, cf. Rev. 1:4) suggests a connection with the spirits of the planets.[38] But this is so softened here that the number is more a symbolical representation of the divine totality. There is no ref. to the Holy Spirit in the NT sense. The statement is more in natural terms.

Rev. 8:10: On the blast of the trumpet by the third angel ἔπεσεν ἐκ τοῦ οὐρανοῦ ἀστὴρ μέγας καιόμενος ὡς λαμπάς.

The ref. is to a real star, not a meteor. For the comparison of a star with the torch → 21. Blazing up in its fall and scattering sparks, the star plunges down and makes

---

[36] There is no justification for cutting this out as a gloss (F. Spitta, J. Weiss, J. Wellhausen).

[37] The Heb. is to be construed as by the Rabbis, namely, that God makes the winds His messengers and flaming fire His servant.

[38] On Mithra altars the planets are represented by seven flaming altars, F. Cumont, *Textes et Monuments figurés relatifs aux Mystères de Mithra* (1896 ff.), I, 115, II, 232 etc. Philo and Joseph. explain the seven-branched candelabra in terms of the planets (→ I, 504). The polar rulers of heaven are personal spirits, e.g., Preis. Zaub., IV, 694 ff.

unserviceable a third part of the water which is essential to life. The interest is not in the fall of the star as such, but in this resultant phenomenon as an eschatological disaster. Is. 14:12 is no true par., and Is. 34:4; Rev. 6:13 and Bundahesh (SBE, V), XXX, 18 and 31 (fall of the star Gôkîhar to initiate the final catastrophe) are only distant par.

In its theological usage λαμπρός bears an eschatological character and is found almost exclusively in Rev. The most difficult passage is Rev. 22:16: ἐγώ εἰμι ἡ ῥίζα καὶ τὸ γένος Δαυίδ, ὁ ἀστὴρ ὁ λαμπρὸς ὁ πρωϊνός.

On the various interpretations, esp. in relation to 2:28, → I, 504. Sir. 50:6; Test. L. 18:3; Test. Jud. 24:1; 2 Pt. 1:19 may be adduced as par. The use of the image, which is common in prophetic speech, is not uniform. The ref. here is to the Messiah as the One who comes in glory to usher in a new cosmic day. The adj., which is most appropriate for a star, emphasises the heavenly glory of Him who comes.

Rev. 22:1 of the interpreting angel: καὶ ἔδειξέν μοι ποταμὸν ὕδατος ζωῆς λαμπρὸν ὡς κρύσταλλον, ἐκπορευόμενον ἐκ τοῦ θρόνου τοῦ θεοῦ καὶ τοῦ ἀρνίου.

On λαμπρός as an epithet of water → 17. The superterrestrial clarity of the water is emphasised here because the ref. is to the heavenly river of Paradise.[39]

The other passages speak of heavenly raiment. In Ac. 10:30 Cornelius describes the angel who appeared to him as a man ἐν ἐσθῆτι λαμπρᾷ. In Rev. 15:6 the angels who bear the seven last plagues come out of the temple, ἐνδεδυμένοι λίνον[40] καθαρὸν λαμπρὸν καὶ περιεζωσμένοι περὶ τὰ στήθη ζώνας χρυσᾶς. In 19:8 it is said of the bride of the Lamb, i.e., the community of the *parousia*: καὶ ἐδόθη αὐτῇ ἵνα περιβάληται βύσσινον λαμπρὸν καθαρόν· τὸ γὰρ βύσσινον τὰ δικαιώματα τῶν ἁγίων ἐστίν.

The usual term for heavenly garments is → λευκός, Mt. 17:2 and par.; 28:3; Mk. 16:5; Jn. 20:12; Ac. 1:10; Rev. 3:4 f., 18; 4:4; 6:11; 7:9, 13; white is also the heavenly colour in Rev. 1:14; 2:17; 6:2; 14:14; 19:11, 14a, b; 20:11; Herm. v., 4, 3, 5. λαμπρός in this sense does not mean magnificent, as in Jm. 2:2 f., but white, as in Lk. 23:11 (→ 17). It is radiant in accordance with its heavenly character (cf. Rev. 12:1). This colour is effectively contrasted in Rev. 19:8 with the obtrusive and bloody finery of the great harlot of 17:4; 18:16. It is hardly possible to take the whole verse as an explanatory note of the divine.[41] It belongs to the song of praise. But the concluding words: "For the fine linen is the righteousness of saints," sound like a pedestrian gloss.[42] In favour of this one might also argue that white garments elsewhere denote heavenly transfiguration (→ *supra*) and that the regular Attic sing. of the verb after a plur. neut. subj. is very rare in Rev., though it does occur in 8:3; 13:14; 14:13; 19:14; 20:3, 5; 21:12. 7:14 points in the direction of the half-verse, and works are emphasised elsewhere (14:13; 13:10), though not in the sense of a righteousness of works. On the original of the white heavenly garment → n. 30.

---

[39] Gn. 2:10 ff. On the location of the rivers of Paradise in ecclesiastical tradition cf. J. Zellinger, *Bad u. Bäder in d. altchristl. Kirche* (1928), 114 f.

[40] In spite of its attestation in AC and many Vulgate codices, λίθον is an ancient scribal error to which Ez. 28:13 may have contributed. λίνον (א 𝔎 P sy) instead of the usual βύσσος is odd in Rev. Linen garments were prescribed in Andania, Lebadeia etc., Wächter, 19, but also for the priests of Israel, Ex. 28:42 etc.; Schürer, II⁴, 338.

[41] Had. Apk., *ad loc.*

[42] Bss., Charles (ICC), Loh. Apk., *ad loc.*, though cf. Had.

D. The Church.

1. The words are rare in patristic lit. Herm. v., 4, 1, 6 (literally, but in a vision): ἐξέλαμψεν ὁ ἥλιος. Ign. Eph., 19, 2 of the appearing of the Messiah, based on Mt. 2:2, 9 f., but in a broader depiction: ἀστὴρ ἐν οὐρανῷ ἔλαμψεν ὑπὲρ πάντας. λαμπρός is more common in Herm. (→ 17, also v., 1, 2, 2 of the clothing of the heavenly messenger, 3, 2, 4 of her glittering staff). The early Church has a general sense of being in possession of unique light. At the end of the 1st cent. the Roman church prays to the God who through Christ ἐκάλεσεν ἡμᾶς ἀπὸ σκότους εἰς φῶς, ἀπὸ ἀγνωσίας εἰς ἐπίγνωσιν δόξης ὀνόματος αὐτοῦ (1 Cl., 59, 2). Cf. also Ign. Phld., 2, 1; Just. Apol., 16, 2 and 12; Dial., 113, 5; 121, 3; 131, 3. λαμπρός is later used almost technically in the terminology of baptism. Thus we read of the martyr Chione: τούτων τοίνυν ἡ μὲν καθαρὸν καὶ λαμπρὸν τοῦ βαπτίσματος φυλάττουσα.[43] *candor* is an interchangeable term for *fides* (Altercatio Simonis Judaei et Theophili Christiani, VI, 22, ed. A. Harnack, TU, 1 [1883], 30, 19).

The Hellenistic religion of light continues within Christianity esp. in Christian Gnosticism. In the apocr. Gospels phenomena of light occur at the birth of Jesus (Prot. Ev. Jc., 19) and at His baptism (Ev. Eb. Fr., 6a).[44] In Act. Thom., 153 (cf. 27) the apostle prays in a very dark prison: "It is time for Thee, Jesus, to hurry. For lo, the children of darkness put us in their darkness." σὺ οὖν ἐν φωτὶ τῆς φύσεως ὢν κατάλαμψον ἡμᾶς. The answer comes at once in visible form. καὶ ἐξαίφνης, τὸ δεσμωτήριον ὅλον ἔλαμψεν ὡς ἡ ἡμέρα. Cf. Act. Pt. Verc., 21; Asc. Is. 8:20 ff.; 9:6; Od. Sol. 10:1, 6; 41:6 etc. The motif of light occurs with all the magic of oriental narrative art in the famous hymn in Act. Thom., 108-113.[45] The Gnostic Cl. Al. made such a strong use of similar thoughts that he is an important source for the Hellenistic religion of light.[46] In Gnosticism there is an admixture of more or less natural and pantheistic elements. But the simple piety of the Church never forgot the thought of light. It is powerfully expressed on an inscr. in the church of St. George in Zorava, which was built on the site of a pagan altar: φῶς σωτήριον ἔλαμψεν, ὅπου σκότος ἐκάλυπτεν (Ditt. Or., 610, 2).

2. The use of lamps in Christian worship is attested already in Ac. 20:8, though it does not have here any profound significance. It is impossible to say when the custom arose of going beyond the technical need and distinguishing certain services, or certain high points in the liturgy, by lamps. It was already widespread in the 4th century, and must have arisen earlier. Various causes contributed to its formation, including sheer necessity in vigils and in the catacombs, the example of other religions, esp. Judaism and Mithraism, the traditional symbolism of light, and apotropaic reasons. To put the latter exclusively in the foreground is probably to misread the historical facts. The altar was distinguished by the presence around it of a large number of standing and hanging lamps. Only from the 12th century are lights placed on the altar itself. The eternal lamp is first mentioned by Paulinus of Nola. But there is a model for it in the cult of Ammon. Plut. Def. Orac., 2 (II, 410b) tells of a man who claimed to have heard from the priests of Ammon the remarkable declaration περὶ τοῦ λύχνου τοῦ ἀσβέστου that this lamp uses less oil from year to year and that it thus proves that the years are getting shorter. The Reformed churches rejected the liturgical use of lamps as papistical, but the Lutheran churches maintained the traditional practice in a modified form with their altar lights.

Oepke

---

43 R. Knopf, *Ausgewählte Märtyrerakten*³ (1929), 95, 26.

44 Acc. to Epiph. Haer., 30, 13, Hennecke, 45. Among the Mandaeans the baptismal stream was invested with heavenly fire by incantations.

45 Cf. Reitzenstein Ir. Erl., 70 ff. Mandaean sources are not very critically evaluated there.

46 → Wetter, Index, 183.

λαός

Contents: A. λαός in Non-Biblical Greek: 1. The Form of the Word; 2. The Etymology; 3. The Use in Homer; 4. The Use in the Post-Homeric Period. B. λαός in the LXX: 1. Hebrew Equivalents; 2. The Main and Popular Meaning of λαός in the LXX; 3. The Specific Usage in the LXX: λαός = Ἰσραήλ: a. Israel as λαὸς θεοῦ; b. The Nature of this Relation; c. The Basis of this Relation; d. The Two-sided Nature of this Relation; e. The Battle of the Prophets for its Actualisation; f. Prophecy as the Climax of the History of the Word λαός in the Old Testament. C. λαός in Hellenistic Judaism outside the Bible: 1. Josephus; 2. Philo; 3. Inscriptions. D. People and Peoples in Rabbinic Literature: I. The People: 1. Yahweh's Possession: a. Israel under the Direct Lordship of Yahweh; b. The Father-Son Relation between Yahweh and Israel; c. The People as the Bride of Yahweh; d. The Jews as Friends and Brothers of their God; 2. The Holy People; 3. The People as the Centre of the World; 4. The Meaning and Duration of Suffering: a. Suffering as the Result of Sin; b. Suffering as a Means of Testing; c. Suffering with a View to Purification for the Coming Aeon; 5. The Eternal Character of the People. II. The Peoples: 1. The Remoteness of the Peoples from God; 2. The Sinful Character of the Peoples: a. The Transgression of the Adamic Commands; b. The Violation of the Noachic Commands; c. The Rejection of the Torah by the Peoples; 3. The Success of the Gentiles; 4. The *massa perditionis*. III. The Election and Privilege of the People: 1. Universalism; 2. The Triumph of National Particularism. E. λαός in the New Testament: 1. Occurrence in the New Testament; 2. The Popular Meaning; 3. The National Meaning; 4. The Specific Meaning λαός = Ἰσραήλ; 5. The Figurative Meaning λαός = the Christian Community; 6. The Significance of this Metaphorical Use; 7. Related Transfers. F. λαός in the Usage of the Early Church.

λαός is one of those words in whose history the LXX is of decisive importance. It is very common in Homer and occurs a number of times in Herodotus, the tragic dramatists and Aristophanes. But it hardly occurs at all in Attic prose.[1] In later literature it is found from time to time.[2] Its literary existence, however, is most precarious. The term belongs to an archaic and poetic mode of speech,

---

λαός. Cf. Thes. Steph., Pass., Pape, Liddell-Scott, Cr.-Kö., Pr.-Bauer, Moult.-Mill., Preisigke Wört., Prellwitz Etym. Wört., Boisacq, *s.v.*; H. v. Herwerden, *Lexicon Graecum Suppletorium et Dialecticum*² (1910); special lexicons on individual writers like Aristot. (H. Bonitz [1870]), Dio C. (U. P. Boissevain [1931]), Hdt. (J. Schweighaeuser [1824]), Homer (H. Ebeling, I [1885], ed. R. J. Cunliffe [1924]), Plat. (F. Ast [1835 f.]), Plut. (D. Wyttenbach [1843]), Polyb. (J. Schweighaeuser² [1822]), Soph. (F. T. Ellendt [1870 ff.]), Thuc. (E. A. Bétant [1843/47]), the tragic dramatists (A. Nauck [1892]). λαός does not occur in J. H. H. Schmidt, *Synonymik d. griech. Sprache* (1876 ff.), nor do ἔθνος, δῆμος, ὄχλος. Cf. also Mayser, I, 24; on this A. Thumb, APF, 4 (1908), 489 f.; Harnack Miss., II, c. 7; *Die Apostelgeschichte* (1908), 54 f.; J. Juster, *Les Juifs dans l'Empire Romain*, I (1914), 414, 416; N. Müller-N. Bees, *Die Inschr. d. jüdischen Katakombe am Monte Verde zu Rom* (1919), on No. 145; Comm. on 1 Pt. 2:9; L. Rost, "Die Bezeichnungen f. Land u. Volk in AT," *Festschr. O. Procksch* (1934), 141 ff.; G. v. Rad, "Das Gottesvolk im Dt," BWANT, 3, F H 11 (1929); G. Bertram, *Volkstum u. Menschheit im Lichte d. hl. Schrift* (1937); "Volk u. Völker in d. hl. Schrift," *Kirche im Angriff*, 11 (1935, 19-30.

[1] In Plat. (except in quotations from Hom.) only twice in the form λεώς (Resp., V, 458d and Leg., IV, 707e); not at all in Aristot., nor Thuc., Xenoph., Demosth.; only once in Diels' *Vorsokratiker* (Xenophanes Fr. 2 [I, 129, 5, Diels⁵]).

[2] Once in Polyb. (4, 52, 7), twice in Plut. (Romulus, 26 [I, 34b] and Suav. Viv. Epic., 13 [II, 1096b]); not in Epict. or Dio C.; a few times in Diod. S. (I, 57, 2; III, 45, 6; V, 7, 6; V, 59, 5); only in two inscr. in Ditt. Or. 90, 12; 225, 8; 22; 34); in Ditt. Syll.³ on a hopelessly corrupt Magnesian inscr. and apart from this only on a small group of Jewish burial inscr. from Thessaly (1247; cf. IG, IX, 2, 985-990). The occurrence here is as striking as the non-occurrence elsewhere.

and plays almost no role at all outside the sphere and influence of this mode. [3] In the LXX, on the other hand, it occurs over 2000 times, and it is thus given a new lease of life and a specific sense which became normative in the usage of the early Church. To clarify this, it is first necessary to sketch the usage outside the Bible.

A. λαός in Non-Biblical Greek.

1. The Form of the Word. The form is Doric-Aeolic; the Ionic form is ληός, the Attic λεώς. The tragedians prefer λεώς, also found in Plato. Ἀκούετε λεῴ, "Hear ye people," is the traditional cry of the herald in Athens to introduce his announcements. Herodotus vacillates between λαός and λεώς. This form had for later writers a note of archaic solemnity. Hence Joseph. causes Balaam to begin his oracle concerning Israel: ὁ λεὼς οὗτος εὐδαίμων ..., though elsewhere he always has λαός (Ant., 4, 114).

2. The Etymology. This is uncertain. [4] The ancients linked it with λᾶας, "stone," cf. already Hom. and Pindar, who in Olymp., 9, 43 ff. refers to the legend of Deucalion and Pyrrha. Men rose up from the stones which they threw behind them, and hence they are called λαοί. Hom. Il., 24, 611 alludes to this. The word is not related to λεία "booty," ληίζομαι, "to take as booty" (Prellwitz Etym. Wört.), and it is doubtful whether there is any connection with ἐλεύθερος and the Old High German *liut* (*Leute*), though this corresponds to the predominant original meaning of λαός. Perhaps the word is of Aegean origin, borrowed, that is, by the Indo-Germanic Greeks from a non-Indo-Germanic language spoken by the earlier inhabitants of Greece. [5]

3. The Use in Homer. In Hom. it denotes in the first instance the people as a factual plurality of men with no recollection of what constitutes the plurality a unity (descent, language, religion, custom, culture, the state). It is the "people" as "crowd," "population," "group of inhabitants," and especially the population as distinct from the rulers or in some relationship of subordination to their lord. The plural λαοί denotes the "number of individuals of whom the crowd is composed." The λαός consists of λαοί. Hence it often makes little difference whether λαός or λαοί is used (cf. both Il. and Od.).

Il., 24, 665: The λαός is to be fed at Hector's burial, i.e., the crowd; Od., 3, 304: The λαός is subjected to Aigisthos, i.e., the population; Il., 24, 611: No one buried the sons of Niobe, λαοὺς δὲ λίθους ποίησε Κρονίων, i.e., the people; Od., 3, 214: ἦ σέ γε λαοὶ ἐχθαίρουσ' ἀνὰ δῆμον, "or the multitude of the people will hate thee"; Il., 18, 497 ff. (in the description of the shield of Thetis): Creditors and debtors struggle on the market place, the λαοί adding their lively contribution, but the heralds λαὸν ἐρήτυον (quietened the people). λαοί as the inhabitants of a city, Il., 22, 408 f.: The λαοὶ κατὰ ἄστυ wept with the parents for Hector; Od., 6, 194: ἄστυ δέ τοι δείξω, ἐρέω δέ τοι οὔνομα λαῶν, Od., 13, 155 f.: πάντες ... λαοὶ ἀπὸ πτόλιος. The population of a country, Il., 11, 676: λαοὶ ... ἀγροιῶται, Il., 24, 28: Πρίαμος καὶ λαός, 21, 458: The Trojans are λαοί of Laomedon. In Od., 4, 177 the πάντες λαοί are the total subject population. Il., 17, 390: λαοί of the associates or workers of a tanner; they are his people.

In the Il. λαός and λαοί are then used specifically for the army, the soldiers, especially in distinction from their leaders. Cf. Il., 1, 226: The son of Atreus never arms

---

[3] Cf. Mayser, I, 24.

[4] On the various conjectures cf. Ebeling, *s.v.;* there is nothing about λαός in Walde-Pok.

[5] Cf. A. Debrunner in *Reallexikon d. Vorgeschichte,* ed. M. Ebert, IV (1926), 527; P. Kretschmer, *Einleitung in d. Geschichte d. gr. Sprache* (1896), 235 f., 239.

himself ἅμα λαῷ, 2, 577 f.: πλεῖστοι καὶ ἄριστοι λαοί follow Agamemnon, 5, 473: Hector boasts that he can hold the city ἄτερ λαῶν ... ἠδ' ἐπικούρων, without warriors and (barbarian) auxiliaries, 18, 509: δύω στρατοὶ ... λαῶν, two hosts of warriors, 13, 475: λαῶν ἔθνος, a swarm, a host of men, 13, 492: λαοὶ ἕποντο, 13, 834: ἐπὶ δ' ἴαχε λαὸς ὄπισθεν, after the men rejoiced, 13, 710: λαοὶ ἕταροι (squires) followed Ajax, the son of Telamon, 7, 342: ἵπποι καὶ λαός, the cavalry as distinct from the infantry, 9, 424 and 10, 14: The army as distinct from the navy. From Od. cf. 9, 263: Odysseus and his companions are λαοὶ 'Ατρεΐδεω 'Αγαμέμνονος.

The fairly common expression λαὸς 'Αχαιῶν (e.g., Il., 6, 223) denotes the soldiers by nationality, but it does not mean "people" in the sense of "nation," nor is λαοί ever used by Hom. for the "nations" or "peoples."

4. The Use in the Post-Homeric Period. A development beyond the consistent usage of Homer is to employ λαός for the totality of a population.

Pind. is the first witness, cf. Olymp., 8, 30: Δωριεὺς λαός, Nem., 1, 16b: λαὸς ἵππαιχμος, a people which fights on horseback, Pyth., 9, 54 f.: λαὸς νασιώτας, an island people. Herodotus, too, speaks of the λεώς of the Athenians, VIII, 136, and the tragedians speak of the λαός of the Persians, the Lydians, the Phrygians, the Athenians, the Achaians, and the Thracians (cf. Aesch. Pers., 92; 593; 789; 770; Soph. Phil., 1243; Eur. Fr., 360, 48 [TGF]).

Yet the word is still used for the crowd (Plut. Romulus, 26 [I, 34b]: ἔτι νῦν Ἕλληνες καὶ λαὸν τὸ πλῆθος ὀνομάζουσιν) [6] and we still find λαός and especially λαοί in the sense of population, inhabitants, people, whether generally or specifically.

Cf. Plat. Resp., V, 458d: ὁ πολὺς λεώς, Aristoph. Ra., 676: τὸν πολὺν ὀψομένη λαῶν ὄχλον (in the theatre), Eq., 163: αἱ στίχες τῶν λαῶν (in the popular assembly), Plut. Suav. Viv. Epic., 13 (II, 1096b): ὁ λαὸς τυφλοῦται (of the crowd of spectators). Soph. Oed. Col., 42 f.: ὅ γ' ἐνθαδ' ἂν εἴποι λεώς (the population there). Xenophanes Fr., 2 (I, 129, 5, Diels[5]): εἰ πύκτης ἀγαθὸς λαοῖσι μετείη (among the people of a city). Diod. S., I, 57, 2: King Sesoosis of Egypt built canals ταῖς πρὸς ἀλλήλους τῶν λαῶν ἐπιμιξίαις, to make trade easier among the people. *Ibid.*, III, 45, 6: The land does not receive the usual care διὰ τὴν τῶν λαῶν ἀπειρίαν. Polyb., 4, 52, 7: Prusias of Bithynia must hand over to the Byzantines lands and strongholds καὶ τοὺς λαοὺς καὶ τὰ πολεμικὰ σώματα, the civil population and prisoners of war. λαός means the people as distinct from the rulers in Hdt., II, 124 and 129; of lesser people, Ditt. Or., 90, 12 f.: Ptolemy V remitted some taxes ὅπως ὅ τε λαὸς καὶ οἱ ἄλλοι πάντες (such as priests, officials, soldiers) ἐν εὐθηνίαι ὦσιν, cf. 225, 4 f.: τοὺς ὑπάρχοντας αὐτο[ῖς λαοὺς πα]νοικίους (the subjects with their whole families). In cultic matters the meaning sometimes approximates to that of laity, cf. the inscr. of the priest Apollonius from the shrine of Serapis at Delos, 3rd cent. B.C. (IG, XI, 4, 1299, 90): ἅπας δ' ἄρα λαὸς ἐκείνωι σὴν ἀρετὴν (of Serapis) θάμβησεν ἐν ἤματι. [7] In the pap.

---

6 Hence λαός is not to be expounded in the light of Cic. Rep., I, 25: *populus autem non omnis hominum coetus quoquo modo congregatus, sed coetus multitudinis iuris consensu sociatus.* To this *populus* corresponds the Gr. δῆμος, not λαός, which is more fluid and indefinite (in spite of E. Peterson ΕΙΣ ΘΕΟΣ [1926], 179).

7 A. Dieterich drew attention to this use in his inaugural dissertation De Hymnis Orphicis (Marburg, 1891), 13 with ref. to a passage in the Orphic hymn to Apollo (34, 10 Orph. [Abel]): κλῦθί μευ εὐχομένου λαῶν ὕπερ εὔφρονι θυμῷ. The same usage appears in the mocking epigram, 47 of Callimachus, ed. U. v. Wilamowitz-Moellendorff[4] (1925): Eudemos turns with the address ὦ λαοί to those not initiated into the Samothracian Mysteries and shows them the worthless salt-cellar brought as an offering, to which he owes salvation from the attacks of his creditors. Cf. on this O. Kern, ARW, 30 (1933), 205-207.

λαός, λαοί is consistently used for people, inhabitants, esp. the lower orders as distinct from the rulers. [8] λαοί is used very generally for ἄνθρωποι in Poimandres, I, 27: [9] ἦργμαι κηρύσσειν τοῖς ἀνθρώποις τὸ τῆς εὐσεβείας καὶ γνώσεως κάλλος. ῏Ω λαοί, ἄνδρες γηγενεῖς ... νήψατε. But cf. also ναυτικὸς λεώς, Aesch. Pers., 383; γεωργικὸς λεώς, Aristoph. Pax, 920; λαοὶ ἐγχώριοι, Aesch. Suppl., 517. The predominant use in Hom., at least in the Il., for the men-at-arms has completely disappeared.

B. λαός in the LXX. [10]

When we turn to the LXX, we feel that we have been set in a different world. For one thing, the term is now so common. For another, the singular is so overwhelmingly predominant, for in 2000 instances the plural occurs only some 140 times. Above all, however, there has been a shift of meaning, so that the word is now a specific term for a specific people, namely, Israel, and it serves to emphasise the special and privileged religious position of this people as the people of God.

1. The Hebrew Equivalents.

Apart from some 40 instances, the Heb. is always עַם. Of the 40, 12 have גּוֹי [11] which is usually rendered ἔθνος; 11 have לְאֹם, which is rendered ἔθνος in a similar number of passages; the rest have various terms. [12] The use of λαός for these is usually determined either by special senses which λαός can have (e.g., Jos. 10:5: מַחֲנֶה = λαός = host; Job 31:34 [AVLa]: הָמוֹן = λαός = crowd; Ju. 18:22 [A]: אֲנָשִׁים and 1 S. 24:10: אָדָם = λαός = inhabitants, people), or more often by the fact that the Heb. words are alternatives for Israel. We then have free renderings which are not concerned with the specific content of the Heb. term and which represent a broadening of the dominant reference of λαός to Israel, e.g., when λαός is used for בן, עבד, צאן, קהל in the passages mentioned in the note. Special regard should be had to the 7 passages in which the Heb. גּוֹי, contrary to the usual rule, is rendered λαός. In all these גּוֹי refers to Israel, or is taken by the LXX to do so, cf. Jos. 3:17; 4:1; Is. 9:2; 26:2; 58:2; Jer. 9:8; 40:9 LXX (33:9 HT). [13, 14] The use of λαός here is a further proof of the inclination of the LXX always to choose this word when the ref. is to Israel. There is

---

[8] Examples in Preisigke Wört. and Moult.-Mill. on λαός; cf. also Mayser, I, 27 and 29.

[9] Reitzenstein Poim., 337.

[10] Cf. Bertram, *Volk u. Völker*; also → ἔθνος, II, 364 ff.

[11] We omit ψ 66:2, for, although Sinaiticus has λαοί for גּוֹיִם, ἔθνη is better attested. The λαοί has come in from v. 3, where it occurs twice for עַמִּים.

[12] As אָדָם, 1 S. 24:10. אֻמָּה, ψ 116:1; Da. 3:4. אֲנָשִׁים, Ju. 18:22 (A). בֵּן, Ex. 4:23; 1 Ch. 17:13 (S); Jer. 23:7 (S). הָמוֹן, Job 31:34 (AVLa) מַחֲנֶה, Jos. 10:5. מָקוֹם, Ruth 4:10. מִשְׁפָּחָה, Na. 3:4 (BS). עֶבֶד, ψ 135:22 (S); Is. 48:20 (A). צֹאן, Jer. 23:3. קָהָל, 2 Ch. 30:24.

[13] Here the HT runs: "(The city of Jerusalem) shall be to my praise ... לְכֹל גּוֹיֵי הָאָרֶץ among all the nations of earth." The LXX has παντὶ τῷ λαῷ τῆς γῆς. It read a sing. and took this to apply to Israel in the sense in which עַם הָאָרֶץ is often used: the people of the land, the people dwelling in the land, as distinct from the priests, prophets and rulers, cf. Lv. 4:3, 22, 27; Zech. 7:5; Ιερ. 44:2; Ez. 7:27; 22:29; 46:2, 9; it thus selected λαός for גּוֹי.

[14] There are also 5 instances of the plur. λαοί for the Heb. גּוֹיִם. Here the ref. is to non-Israelite peoples. In three cases it occurs along with ἔθνη and is obviously used for stylistic variety (Is. 55:5; 60:5; Ez. 28:25). Why it is used in the two other cases is not clear.

a corresponding inclination to use ἔθνος instead when עַם does not refer to Israel.[15]

But one can speak only of an inclination. The principle is not applied consistently. λαός does not always occur when גּוֹי refers to Israel. In some cases we find ἔθνος, cf. Ex. 19:6 גּוֹי קָדוֹשׁ = ἔθνος ἅγιον LXX; also Ex. 23:22; Wis. 17:2. Conversely ἔθνος is not always used when the ref. is not to Israel. The Egyptians (Gn. 41:40, 55; Ex. 1:22; 9:27 etc.), the Philistines (Gn. 26:11), the Moabites (Nu. 21:29; 24:14), the Sodomites (Gn. 19:4), the Hittites (Gn. 23:7), the Ethiopians (Is. 18:2; ψ 86:4) and the Scythians (Ιερ. 6:22; 26:24; 27:41) can all be called λαός. But these are exceptions, and the seven גּוֹי passages are a proof how strong the inclination was. The true equivalent of λαός is thus עַם, and the meaning and application of this word are in essentials normative for the use of λαός in the LXX.

2. The Main and Popular Meaning of λαός in the LXX.

The first decisive point is that in its main use λαός = עַם does not now mean people in the sense of crowd or population but people in the sense of a people as a union.[16] Gn. 34:22 is most illuminating. The Shechemites and the family of Jacob are to intermarry ὥστε εἶναι λαὸν ἕνα. A society, a union, is to be established between them. Could a Greek express himself in this way? This union of people could be thought of with varying degrees of comprehensiveness.

The population of a city can be called λαός, e.g., that of Sodom in Gn. 19:4; also the members of a tribe (Δὰν κρινεῖ τὸν ἑαυτοῦ λαόν, Gn. 49:16), or the higher union of a whole people. The dead can be included. The dying Jacob declares in Gn. 49:29: I shall be gathered πρὸς τὸν ἐμὸν λαόν, אֶל־עַמִּי, cf. τὸν λαὸν αὐτοῦ, עַמָּיו Gn. 49:33; 25:8, though the rendering is τὸ γένος αὐτοῦ in 25:17; 35:29. In the LXX λαοί are never the people; they are nations.[17] One cannot say any longer that the λαός consists of λαοί. Nor can one speak of the λαοὶ κατὰ ἄστυ. Every city has one λαός, for λαός is the union of the people. Thus a usage which in Gk. poetry does not go

---

[15] E.g., Ex. 1:9: Pharaoh speaks to his ἔθνος (Heb. עַם). Ex. 15:14: ἤκουσαν ἔθνη (שָׁמְעוּ עַמִּים). Ex. 19:5: ἀπὸ πάντων τῶν ἐθνῶν (מִכָּל־הָעַמִּים). Ex. 21:8: ἔθνει ἀλλοτρίῳ (לְעַם נָכְרִי). Almost always when ἔθνος, ἔθνη is used for עַם, עַמִּים it is because the ref. is to non-Israelites. In Dt. 7:6 and Is. 51:4 עם = Israel is rendered λαός and עַמִּים = other nations ἔθνη. It is highly remarkable that in Solomon's prayer at the dedication of the temple in 1 K. (3 Βασ.) 8:34, 36b and in the saying of Yahweh to Jehu in 1 K. 16:2 — passages which occur only in one part of the textual transmission of the LXX — עם with ref. to Israel is rendered δοῦλος. Did the translators have a text which read עַבְדְּךָ or (in 16:2) עַבְדִּי? In 1 K. 8:59 the text is so altered that Israel, not Solomon, is called the servant of Yahweh and its designation as His people is thus left out: לַעֲשׂוֹת מִשְׁפַּט עַבְדּוֹ וּמִשְׁפַּט עַמּוֹ יִשְׂרָאֵל, τοῦ ποιεῖν τὸ δικαίωμα τοῦ δούλου σου Ἰσραήλ. G. v. Rad, who has written me on the subject, suggests that this alteration may be connected with a collective understanding of the Ebed Yahweh songs.

[16] This corresponds to the Heb. עם to the degree that עם was originally a term of relationship. It first denoted the individual male relative of the father, then collectively the male family in the broader sense. It then came to include the people in the sense of men who were qualified to serve in the army, to take part in the administration of justice and to share in the cultus. Cf. on this Rost, 141 ff. The word λαός as such does not, of course, contain any such connection with relationship. But it does have a male ref., e.g., as applied to the army.

[17] The only exception is Sir. 44:15, where λαοί stands in parallelism with ἐκκλησία and can only mean "the people."

back to Hom. but occurs a few times later, has become predominant in the LXX. Every people can be called a λαός (→ 33). Hence the plur. λαοί is synon. with ἔθνη and either with or without it serves to denote the plurality of nations outside Israel, esp. in the Psalter. The sing. has the same sense with πᾶς, Sir. 24:6: ἐν παντὶ λαῷ καὶ ἔθνει. One can speak of an ὄχλος λαῶν (Ez. 23:24), which is not a host of men or warriors, but of nations. In the striking expression πάντες οἱ λαοὶ τῶν ἐθνῶν (כָּל־עַמֵּי הָאָרֶץ), Ez. 31:12, cf. 2 Εσδρ. 9:11: λαοὶ τῶν ἐθνῶν — which differs pointedly from Homer's ἔθνος λαῶν, a swarm of warriors, Il., 13, 495 — τὰ ἔθνη are the Gentile world and οἱ λαοί the individual members. οἱ λαοὶ τῆς γῆς (עַמְמֵי הָאָרֶץ), 2 Εσδρ. 19:24 = Neh. 9:24, are not the inhabitants but the peoples of the land, i.e., of Palestine, while the λαοὶ τῆς γῆς = עַמֵּי הָאֲרָצוֹת, Neh. 9:30, are the nations of the earth. When Gn. 23:7 refers to the Hittites as the λαὸς τῆς γῆς = עַם הָאָרֶץ, they are designated not merely as the inhabitants but as the people dwelling in the land.

In many cases λαός means the people as distinct from the rulers or upper classes, and there is a fluid boundary between this and the popular use for population.

Thus the Egyptians are the λαός of Pharaoh (Gn. 41:40; Ex. 1:22; Ex. 7-9), or the λαὸς τῆς γῆς αὐτοῦ (2 Εσδρ. 19:10). In Gn. 47:21 λαός denotes the population as distinct from the ground and territory of Egypt; this is sold into Pharaoh's possession as a result of Joseph's speculation in corn. With ref. to Israel ὁ προφήτης καὶ ὁ ἱερεὺς καὶ ὁ λαός, Jer. 23:34, and more often οἱ μεγιστᾶνες καὶ πᾶς ὁ λαός, Ιερ. 41:10; the king and his servants (παῖδες) καὶ ὁ λαὸς τῆς γῆς, Ιερ. 44:2; the ἄρχων as distinct from the λαὸς τῆς γῆς = עַם הָאָרֶץ, Ez. 7:27, cf. Lv. 4:3, 27 — here the term λαὸς τῆς γῆς does not mean country people (as distinct from townsfolk) but the whole population dwelling in the land. On this usage the national identity of those referred to is always self-evidently presupposed.

A looser usage is for the people.

So Nu. 2:6: The serpents bite τὸν λαόν. ἀπέθανε λαὸς πολύς, "many people died"; Jos. 17:14: ἐγὼ δὲ λαὸς πολύς εἰμι, "we are many people"; 2 Ch. 7:10: ἀπέστειλε τὸν λαόν, "he sent away the people who had appeared at the feast"; ψ 17:27: σὺ λαὸν ταπεινὸν σώσεις, "thou wilt help the oppressed people"; Gn. 50:20: God has guided Joseph's destiny ἵνα διατραφῇ λαὸς πολύς, "that much people might be saved"; cf. also Is. 42:5; Sir. 16:17; 42:11. It is worth noting that the Homeric use of λαός (though never λαοί) for men of war is found in the LXX: Pharaoh led πάντα τὸν λαὸν αὐτοῦ after Israel, Ex. 14:6; Joshua ἐτρέψατο τὸν Ἀμαλὴκ καὶ πάντα τὸν λαὸν αὐτοῦ ἐν φόνῳ μαχαίρας, Ex. 17:13; with an explanatory addition, Jos. 8:3: ὁ λαὸς ὁ πολεμιστής; cf. also Nu. 21:23, 33-35; Dt. 20:1; Jos. 10:7, 15, 33; 1 Ch. 11:13; 19:7, 11; Ez. 30:11, and esp. Judith (5:22; 7:1, 7, 11, 13, 26; 14:17). The men who accompany Esau when he meets Jacob (Gn. 33:15) and Jacob's company (32:8; 35:6) are called λαός = עַם. But the basic LXX meaning is hardly affected by these popular or archaic senses found in certain passages.

3. The Specific Usage in the LXX: λαός = Ἰσραήλ.

a. Israel as λαὸς θεοῦ. According to the predominant usage of the LXX λαός means a people or national union. It can be and is sometimes used of any such union. But the truly distinctive feature of LXX usage is the careful restriction of the use of the term to Israel. All else is subsidiary — the exception which proves the rule. This is the decisive point, the point which is important both from the standpoint of the history of religion and also from that of theology. The Heb. OT reveals already a corresponding inclination to use עַם for Israel and גּוֹי for other nations. The distinction is not carried through with absolute consistency in the

LXX, but it is certainly carried much further with a view to laying constant emphasis on the special religious position of Israel.[18] This is grounded in the fact that Israel is the people of God. What counts is not the word λαός as such, but the continual recurrence of the phrase λαὸς θεοῦ. This is what gives colour to the special use of the simple λαός for Israel. λαός in this sense is the national society of Israel according to its religious basis and distinction.[19] It would be intrinsically possible to lend a similar nuance to ἔθνος, cf. 1 Ch. 17:21: οὐκ ἔστιν ὡς ὁ λαός σου Ἰσραήλ (עַם) ἔθνος (גּוֹי) ἔτι ἐπὶ τῆς γῆς. This is obviously not done. λαός is chosen instead. The only reason for this is that this word was so much at home in the poetic sphere, and that as a term of lofty speech it was much better suited to the sanctity and dignity of the relationship to be expressed than a term like ἔθνος, which might easily carry a suggestion of disparagement in virtue of its original sense of "swarm" or "heap." The selection of an archaically poetical and solemn word like λαός thus expresses a sense of distinction from all other peoples on the basis of religion, an awareness that Israel stands in a special relation to Yahweh, who is incomparably superior to all the gods of the nations.

b. The Nature of this Relation. The nature and significance of this relation are brought out in passages like Ex. 19:4-7; Dt. 7:6-12; 32:8 ff.; ψ 134, and especially Dt. 4.

The whole earth belongs to Yahweh (Ex. 19:5). But He divided the nations acc. to the number of the angels, to which He allotted them (Δτ. 32:8; Sir. 17:17; Da. 10:13; 12:1). The sun, moon and stars He allotted πᾶσιν τοῖς ἔθνεσιν τοῖς ὑποκάτω τοῦ οὐρανοῦ (Dt. 4:19). They may worship them. But Israel Yahweh kept for Himself as עַם סְגֻלָּה מִכֹּל־הָעַמִּים, which the LXX renders as λαὸς περιούσιος ἀπὸ πάντων τῶν ἐθνῶν or παρὰ πάντα τὰ ἔθνη (Ex. 19:5; Dt. 14:2; 7:6, or simply λαὸς περιούσιος Dt. 26:18; cf. περιουσιασμός, ψ 134:4; עַם נַחֲלָה = λαὸς ἔγκληρος, Dt. 4:20). This distinctive relation of possession is constantly in mind even when λαός is applied to Israel without the gen. θεοῦ.

Because Yahweh has separated Israel to Himself as a peculiar possession, they are a holy people. They do not have to become a holy people by cultic or moral sanctification; they are this in virtue of the divine distinction: "Thou art a holy people to the Lord thy God," λαὸς ἅγιος εἶ κυρίῳ τῷ θεῷ σου, Dt. 7:6; cf. 14:2, 21; 26:18 f.[20] Korah, Dathan and Abiram revolt against Moses' leadership (Nu. 16:3) on the ground that πᾶσα ἡ συναγωγὴ πάντες ἅγιοι. Hence Israel is the λαὸς ἐγγίζων αὐτῷ (τῷ κυρίῳ), Ps. 148:14, and Yahweh is near to them whenever they call upon Him.

c. The Basis of this Relation. This relation of possession is by the free act of Yahweh. He chose Israel, Dt. 4:37; 7:6; 14:2; ψ 134:4. This took place in full freedom. It was not caused by any outward or inward advantages enjoyed by Israel. Israel is quite insignificant παρὰ πάντα τὰ ἔθνη, Dt. 7:7. It is a λαὸς σκληροτράχηλος without righteousness, Dt. 9:5, 6. The basis of election was God's love for them (Dt. 7:8) or more accurately for the fathers (4:37), and His

---

18 In Jdt., e.g., the non-Israelite nations are regularly called ἔθνη. But Holofernes and those around him almost always use λαός for Israel (5:3, 23; 11:2, 22; the exception is 5:21). Where λαός does not refer to Israel it always means the host in Jdt.

19 Cf. on this v. Rad, and M. Noth, "Das System der zwölf Stämme Israels," BWANT, IV (1930), 120 f. Here it is pointed out that this concept had its final historical roots in the cultic tribal union of the ancient Israelite amphictyony before Israel became a state.

20 Cf. 1 Εσδρ. 8:57; 2 Εσδρ. 8:28; Da. 7:27; 8:24 Θ; 2 Macc. 15:24; 3 Macc. 2:6; Wis. 10:15; 17:2.

faithfulness to the promise which He had sworn to them (7:8). On this basis they were the people to which He laid claim that it should serve Him in the wilderness. He thus demanded its liberation from Pharaoh (Ex. 7:16, 26; 8:16; 9:1, 13, 17; 10:3). In the course of the Egyptian plagues He treats it very differently from Pharaoh and His people (Ex. 8:17, 19; 9:4; 11:7). "My people" (Yahweh's) and "thy people" (Pharaoh's) are deliberately set in antithesis in Ex. 8.

The great historical demonstration of this relation was for Israel the liberation by mighty acts from the iron furnace (Dt. 4:20) and the house of bondage (Ex. 20:2) in Egypt. What no other god had ever attempted, namely, to take to himself one people out of the midst of another (גּוֹי מִקֶּרֶב גּוֹי, ἔθνος ἐκ μέσου ἔθνους), God accomplished with a strong hand and outstretched arm (Dt. 4:34; Ex. 7:5). At the very beginning of the national history of Israel there thus stands the liberation from alien dominion which is unequivocally regarded as the act of God and which alone makes it possible for Israel to become a nation. God freed Israel and bore it on eagle's wings (Ex. 19:4; Dt. 32:11). But it became a nation only with its reception of revelation. It became a nation when it became Yahweh's people with the conclusion of the covenant at Sinai. There Yahweh spoke to the Israelites, gave them distinctive statutes, and declared to them His covenant and promises (Dt. 4:7 ff.).

d. The Two-sided Nature of this Relation. The relation thus established is two-sided. It is a relation of reciprocal obligation, faithfulness and love. Israel is Yahweh's people.

He has rescued it from Egypt and revealed Himself to it. Hence He and He alone is Israel's God: οὐκ ἔσονταί σοι θεοὶ ἕτεροι πλὴν ἐμοῦ (Ex. 20:3). Yahweh has separated Israel to Himself (Lv. 20:26). He now expects that Israel will separate itself for Him. Yahweh has shown Israel His love. He now expects that Israel will love Him and keep His commandments (Dt. 7:9). Israel is holy; it has been taken from the sphere of the secular world of nations for Yahweh. But this indicative carries with it the imperative: Ye shall be holy! Ἅγιοι ἔσεσθε, ὅτι ἐγὼ ἅγιος κύριος ὁ θεὸς ὑμῶν (Lv. 19:2; 11:44; 20:7, 26; Nu. 15:40; Dt. 28:9). Israel is Yahweh's people only if it conducts itself accordingly.

e. The Battle of the Prophets for its Actualisation. Because Israel does not conduct itself accordingly, the prophets wage their great battle. "For ye are not my people, and I am not your [God]," Hos. 1:9. The people of God has become λαὸς Γομόρρας, Is. 1:10. The conduct of Israel does not correspond to the elective act of the divine love. The consequence is the judgment of dispersion and of disappearance among the nations, Dt. 4:27. But the last word is not yet. Israel is still Yahweh's people. Yahweh will not yet wholly reject it. Only when the eternal laws by which the stars move come to an end, i.e., never, καὶ τὸ γένος (זֶרַע) Ἰσραὴλ παύσεται γενέσθαι ἔθνος (גּוֹי) κατὰ πρόσωπόν μου πάσας τὰς ἡμέρας, Ιερ. 38:37 = 31:36 HT. For He will "not forget the covenant of thy fathers which he swore unto them" (Dt. 4:31). He only waits for repentance to treat them again as His people. Even though Israel provokes His judgment so severely, as in the time of Elijah when only 7000 were left who did not bow the knee to Baal (1 K. 19:18), Isaiah is certain that at the last a remnant of Israel (→ λεῖμμα) will return to Yahweh, the Holy One of Israel. This will only be a small remnant, the "poor" of His people. But it will be a remnant that can represent the true Israel and have its refuge on Zion (cf. Is. 10:20-25; 14:32; 10:2). They will return to Yahweh, or rather, according to the wonderful saying of Jer., God Himself will so turn them inwardly that they will do from the heart what is according to His will (Jer. 38:33 LXX = 31:33 HT). The present of possession, however, has now become the future of promise, which as at the first is linked with the condition of obedience to the commandments of Yahweh: Hear my voice, καὶ ἔσομαι ὑμῖν εἰς θεόν, καὶ ὑμεῖς ἔσεσθέ μοι εἰς λαόν (Jer. 7:23, cf. 24:7; 31:33; 32:36 ff.; Ez. 11:20; 14:11; 36:28; 37:23; Is. 41:8-10). Even the predicate ἅγιος will become valid only in the sanctification of the future: καὶ καλέσει αὐτὸν λαὸν ἅγιον λελυτρωμένον ὑπὸ κυρίου (Is. 62:12; cf. Ισ. 30:19 and Is. 60:21: ὁ λαός σου πᾶς δίκαιος). Yet at the same time prophetic proclamation transcends the limits of purely national expectation. This may be seen already in Is. 11:10, where it is said of the Messianic King of salvation: ἐπ' αὐτῷ ἔθνη ἐλπιοῦσιν (cf. Is. 62:10). But this thought is expressed most clearly in Zech. 2:10 f.: "Sing and rejoice, O daughter of Zion: for, lo, I come, and I will dwell in the midst of thee καὶ καταφεύξονται ἔθνη πολλὰ ἐπὶ τὸν κύριον ἐν τῇ ἡμέρᾳ ἐκείνῃ καὶ ἔσονται αὐτῷ εἰς λαὸν καὶ κατασκηνώσουσιν ἐν μέσῳ σου. This is the most pregnant expression of eschatological prophetic universalism, though it is echoed in countless other passages (cf. 1 K. 8:41-43; Is. 25:6, 7; 26:2; 45:18-25; 55:4-7; Jer. 12:16; 16:19; Ez. 47:22; Zeph. 3:9; Zech. 9:7; Ps. 67:5; 117:1; 148:11-13).

f. Prophecy as the Climax of the History of the Word λαός in the OT. Prophetic preaching with all its profundity and force brought to full expression the unique relation between God and Israel which is implied in Israel's designation as the λαὸς θεοῦ and in the resultant and increasing exclusiveness with which עַם = λαός is applied to Israel alone. This relation, which was first the sustaining and normative basis of the constitution of Israel as a people, had now ceased to be a present possession granted by the freely electing love of God and had become instead claim and judgment, longing and promise. Its certainty could now be maintained only by faith, which looked beyond all the contradictions of the national present, both external and internal, and clung simply to the faithfulness of God to His promise. But this necessarily created in Israel itself the preconditions of its actualisation, which was in fact to extend far beyond the frontiers of Israel. One may thus say that the prophetic statements are the climax of the development which the word λαός underwent in the OT.

As compared with this prophetic attitude, the tendency of later writings to speak self-evidently of Israel as the ἅγιοι (1 Εσδρ. 8:57; 2 Εσδρ. 8:28), or as the λαὸς ὅσιος and σπέρμα ἄμεμπτον (Wis. 10:15), or as the ἔθνος ἅγιον (Wis. 17:2), or as the λαὸς ἅγιος (Da. 7:27; 8:24 Θ; 2 Macc. 15:24; 3 Macc. 2:6) represents a certain regression which forms a transition to Pharisaic Judaism with its stubborn insistence on a position of privilege granted once and for all to the people. This is a transition to the spiritual outlook and conduct against which the protest of John the Baptist was directed.

C. λαός in Hellenistic Judaism outside the Bible.[21]

1. Josephus. That Flavius Josephus is a very inconsistent writer[22] is an observation which is confirmed in the present case. In the Bellum Judaicum there is no trace of the ordinary LXX use of the word λαός. ἔθνος is commonly used of the Jewish people: Herod orders mourning in ὅλῳ τῷ ἔθνει, 1, 581; τὸ ἔθνος ἐπαναστήσειν Ῥωμαίοις ἤλπισεν, 1, 232; Florus πόλεμον ... τῷ ἔθνει σκοπούμενος, "wished to drive the people into war," 2, 282. He also uses δῆμος, though without thinking of the people

21 On עַם and עַם הארץ in Rabb. Judaism → ὄχλος.

22 Cf. H. St. J. Thackeray-R. Marcus, *A Lexicon to Josephus,* I (1930), Preface.

as a political entity: Τίτος ... τὸν μὲν δῆμον ἐλεήσας, "had sympathy with the people," 1, 10. δῆμος is the people as a whole (τοῦ δήμου τὸ καθαρώτατον, 2, 345), the ordinary folk compared with the upper classes (2, 338), the public as distinct from the council (2, 641) or the rebellious sicarii (2, 449). For the people as a nation he uses οἱ ὁμόφυλοι or τὸ ὁμόφυλον ἡμῶν, e.g., 1, 150. On the other hand, λαός is used in the popular sense for people, population, crowd. In the context the word often corresponds to πλῆθος: τοῦ λαοῦ περιεστῶτος, "while the people stood around," 1, 122, cf. 457 and 466; Herod incites the crowd (τὸν λαόν), 1, 550; the crowd (ὁ λαός) receives Archelaus in the temple with good wishes, 2, 1; ὁ ἀσθενὴς λαός, the "unarmed population" as distinct from the sicarii, 2, 425; ἀπὸ τῆς ἄκρας τὸν λεὼ συνωθοῦντες ἐφόνευον, 3, 329.

The position is very different in the Antiquities. Here λαός is generally used with ref. to Israel.[23] To be sure, it can sometimes be used for other nations, e.g., the Egyptians (Ant., 2, 301). But the non-Israelite peoples are usually ἔθνη. In the writing against Apion, however, ἔθνος is again predominant for Israel.[24] The change in usage leaps to the eye. One is tempted to ascribe it to the different linguistic aids that Joseph. is known to have used in the edition of his Greek works, and to the very different use of these aids in the individual works.[25] The Attic λεώς in his rendering of the oracle of Balaam (Ant., 4, 114 and Bell., 3, 329)[26] points in this direction. But not much can be made of the Atticist customs of the Graeculi since they vary so much in their use of words. The fluctuation in Joseph. is to be explained rather in terms of the influence which the LXX unavoidably exerted on the presentation of the earlier history of Israel. For if Joseph. boasts in the preface to Ant. (1, 5) that he has drawn his whole account from Hebrew sources, this is a very summary mode of expression. He certainly consulted the LXX quite frequently as well.[27] But he allowed himself to be controlled by its use in respect of λαός only in so far as the material in hand suggested.

2. Philo.[28] Philo uses the Attic form λεώς equally with λαός. He naturally uses the occurrence of the term in the Pentateuch as a basis for his own monotonous, moralising, psychologising and etymologising speculations and considerations thereupon. On Gn. 35:29 (Isaac died καὶ προσετέθη πρὸς τὸ γένος αὐτοῦ) it is said, e.g., that Isaac leaves the corporeal as a type of self-attained insight, and that he is not gathered to the λαός, like those who preceded (e.g., Abraham, Gn. 25:8), but to the γένος (Sacr. AC, 6). The supreme γένος is only one. λαός, however, denotes a plurality. To this belong those who are made perfect only by instruction on the part of others. Only those who have attained to unceasing ἐπιστήμη will be set in the ἄφθαρτον καὶ τελειότατον γένος (Sacr. AC, 7). The λαὸς ἐξαίρετος in Dt. 7:7 is the σοφός, the σπουδαῖος, who, whether ἀνήρ or λαός, is represented as the true head of humanity (Praem. Poen., 123; 125). Balaam is called μάταιος λαός (בַּל־עָם) because he does not understand the battle of the soul for genuine ἐπιστήμη (Cher., 32). Amalek signifies λαὸς ἐκλείχων (לקק lick) because πάθος so licks up the soul as to leave no spark

---

[23] Though the Jews in Alexandria have an ἐθνάρχης, ὃς διοικεῖ τε τὸ ἔθνος καὶ διαιτᾷ κρίσεις κτλ. (Ant., 14, 117).

[24] E.g., τὸ ἔθνος ἡμῶν, 1, 5; 161; 168; 194; 213; 2, 43; 220. So also Vit., 24. Cf. τὸ γένος ἡμῶν, Ap., 1, 1; 2; 219; 278; λαὸς τῶν Ἰουδαίων, 1, 305; 313.

[25] Cf. Ap., 1, 50. Joseph. mentioned the Gr. συνεργοί only with ref. to the Gr. edition of Bell. But close stylistic examination of Joseph. shows that various hands worked differently in different parts of the other works, esp. Ant. Cf. Thackeray-Marcus, *op. cit.* [Debrunner and Kittel].

[26] I owe the ref. Bell., 3, 329 to Kittel.

[27] Cf. O. Stählin, "Die hell.-jüd. Lit.," *Geschichte d. griech. Lit.* = *Hndbch. KlAW*, VII, 2, 1[6] (1920), 594, n. 4 and bibl.

[28] The learned work of I. Heinemann, *Philons griechische u. jüdische Bildung* (1932), which investigates Philo's ethics from the standpoint of the title, pays no attention to the term "people" in Philo. On Leisegang's Index cf. O. Stählin's critical observations in Philol. Wochenschr., 47 (1927), 8-13.

of virtue (Leg. All., III,, 186 f.). The λαὸς πλείων σου (the superior numbers of warriors) are the ζηλωταὶ παθῶν (Migr. Abr., 62).

The specific flavour of the term in the Gk. OT is here completely lost under the sway of speculation which obliterates all historical distinctions.

3. Inscriptions. Among the many names which the congregations had for themselves [29] the inscr. of the Hellenistic *diaspora* include not a few instances of τὸ ἔθνος τῶν Ἰουδαίων [30] but also on occasion λαὸς τῶν Ἰουδαίων [31] or the simple λαός. [32] There is thus applied to the individual congregation what is primarily true of the whole. The whole λαός is present in the spatially limited λαός. That the word is taken to apply only to Jews and not to other peoples is shown by 1st century Jewish burial inscr. from Thessaly in which the departed take leave with a τῷ λαῷ χαίρειν. [33] This greeting is to the people as a whole, not to the local congregation. [34] On two Roman inscr. the deceased is lauded for being a φιλόλαος. [35] The same is undoubtedly meant by the expression *amor generis* on the inscr. of Regina from the Jewish catacomb at Monteverde in Rome. [36] This shows that the usage of Hellenistic Jews of the dispersion was affected by that of the LXX.

Strathmann

D. People and Peoples in Rabbinic Literature.

I. The People.

1. Yahweh's Possession.

One of the basic motifs of the OT is that of the people of God. This recurs in many forms in Jewish literature of late antiquity. In part there is a fresh incursion of ideas from the classical period and in part concepts occur which are attested only in later works.

a. Israel as λαὸς θεοῦ. Thus in Jewish lit. we find a myth with whose help an attempt is made to fix the relation of Yahweh to Israel and to other peoples. This myth builds on the idea that each people has its archon, genius or guardian angel. The oldest literary instance of the idea of a national angel in Palestine is the verse in Sir. 17:17 which will be treated later. That each nation has a genius is the opinion of Da. 10:13, 20 f.; 12:1. Here Michael is the genius of the Jewish people (cf. Eth. En. 20:5), and elsewhere there is ref. to the guardian angels of Persia and of Greece. [37] It may

---

29 Cf. the statistics in J. Oehler, "Epigraphische Beiträge z. Geschichte des Judt.," MGWJ, 53 (1909), 528 ff.; Juster, 414; Schürer, III⁴, 71 ff.

30 Smyrna, Oehler, 529, No. 51; Schürer, III, 14 f.

31 Hierapolis, Oehler, 529, No. 71; Schürer, III, 17.

32 Nysa: Schürer, III, 16; Mantinea: IG, V, 2, 295 = J. B. Frey, Corpus Inscriptionum Judaicarum, I (1936), No. 720; Smyrna: γραμματεὺς τοῦ ἐν Ζμύρνῃ λαοῦ, acc. to Leemann's Griek. Opschr., XII (Ditt. Syll.^{3}, 1247, n.).

33 Cf. IG, IX, 2, 985-990.

34 Cf. Juster, 416. The conjecture that τῷ λαῷ χαίρειν corresponds to the Heb. formula שלום על ישראל is helpful. It makes the Gk. expression all the more distinctive.

35 Frey No. 203, 509; cf. H. Vogelstein-P. Rieger, *Geschichte d. Juden in Rom,* I (1895), 469.

36 Cf. Müller-Bees, 133 ff., No. 145; Frey No. 476; Deissmann LO, 387 ff., who points out that *genus* is often used for the Jewish people in the Lat. Bible, e.g., Phil. 3:5: *ego ex genere Israel.*

37 In Da. Θ 10:13, 20 f.; 12:1; in LXX Da. 10:13 ἄρχων is used for the national genius (→ n. 40).

be said with certainty that this belief in national angels,[38] which derived from the belief in individual guardian angels, did not originate on the soil of Israel.[39] Its probable home was the astral religion of Chaldaea and Persia, since it is unlikely that Platonic conceptions had any influence on belief in the genius or archon.[40]

The idea that each people has its genius was used relatively early as a means of expressing the privileges of Israel over other nations. Thus Δτ. 32:8 f. reads: "When the Most High divided the peoples ... he established the borders of the peoples according to the number of the angels of God, and the portion of the Lord was his people Jacob."[41] The LXX translator thus utilises the intrinsically neutral genius concept to express his opinion concerning the distance of the peoples from God. Alien nations are under the guidance of angels; Yahweh Himself directs the Jewish people. One is tempted to assume that acc. to Δτ. 32:8 f. the original national gods are identified with the national angels. This cannot be proved,[42] but it is strongly supported by the fact that the archons contend ruthlessly for their nations and are thus felt by the Jews to be mythical enemies and representatives of an anti-God principle.

In Palestine the first sure witness to the myth of people and peoples is Sir. 17:17: "He has appointed an archon for each people, and the portion of the Lord is Israel."[43] As already noted, this passage is also the oldest Palestinian instance of the idea of national angels in general. As in Sir. 17:17 so in Jub. 15:30 ff. the genius concept is

---

[38] On the concept of national angels, cf. Str.-B., II, 360; III, 48 and 194; Moore, I, 227, 403 f., 406 f.; Bousset-Gressm., 324 f.

[39] The final origin of the idea of guardian angels is perhaps to be sought in the belief in ghosts, which as the shades of the dead dwell in tombs. This belief is international, cf. the genii in Roman religion and the daemon in later Platonism (cf. K. G. Kuhn, S. Nu. [1935], 515), the *fravashis* in Persian belief (N. Söderblom, *Les Fravashis* [1899]) and the Egyptian idea of *ka* (A. Erman, *Die Religion d. Ägypter* [1934], 210). Judaism, too, was familiar with such ancient ideas. Even in late antiquity there are many stories of ghosts and their life in the cemetery (cf. R. Meyer, "Hellenistisches in d. rabb. Anthropologie," BWANT, IV, 22 [1937], 2 ff.). That the shade, the imperishable part of man, became a heavenly alter ego, the guardian angel, may be ascribed with Bousset-Gressm., 324 to the astral beliefs of Chaldea and Persia. Belief in the guardian angels of all nations is a logical collectivising of the belief in the individual guardian angel, perhaps stimulated by the ancient belief in rulers.

[40] Cf. on this K. G. Kuhn, *op. cit.*, 514 f. and → I, 488 f.

[41] ὅτε διεμέριζεν ὁ ὕψιστος ἔθνη, ὡς διέσπειρεν υἱοὺς Αδαμ, ἔστησεν ὅρια ἐθνῶν κατὰ ἀριθμὸν ἀγγέλων θεοῦ, καὶ ἐγενήθη μερὶς κυρίου λαὸς αὐτοῦ Ιακωβ ... The HT runs: בְּהַנְחֵל עֶלְיוֹן גּוֹיִם בְּהַפְרִידוֹ בְּנֵי אָדָם יַצֵּב גְּבֻלֹת עַמִּים לְמִסְפַּר בְּנֵי יִשְׂרָאֵל׃ כִּי חֵלֶק יְהוָה עַמּוֹ. Jewish tradition is familiar with both readings. For the Mas. cf. Tg. J. I on Dt. 32:8 (ed. M. Ginsburger [1903], 358): ובי היא זימנא אקים תחומי אומיא בסכום שובעין נפשתא דישראל דנחתו למצרים, "And in that time he established the borders of the peoples according to the number of the 70 souls of Israel which went down to Egypt." Tg. O., *ad loc.* also presupposes the HT. K. Marti (in Kautzsch) decides for the Δτ. reading (→ II, 367), but the evidence is hardly adequate. Among early testimonies Str.-B., III, 48 f. lists an account of the scattering of the peoples, and of the appointment of Israel as the people of Yahweh by the election of Abraham, which he finds in Heb. Test. N. 8 ff. But this Heb. version of Test. N., published by M. Gaster, *Studies and Texts,* I (1925), 69 ff., is probably a later Heb. rendering of the Gk., not the original; cf. on this O. Eissfeldt, *Einl. in d. AT* (1934), 690.

[42] This is not sufficiently taken into account by either Bousset-Gressm., 324 or Str.-B., III, 48. Serious note should be taken of K. G. Kuhn's observation that belief in genii has basically nothing to do with heathen deities. Yet it cannot be assumed that conceptions of the genius were always preserved intact in Judaism, cf. the example from Jub. 15:30 ff. quoted → 41.

[43] Ἑκάστῳ ἔθνει κατέστησεν ἡγούμενον, καὶ μερὶς κυρίου Ισραηλ ἐστίν.

used to emphasise the direct relation between Yahweh and His people:[44] "But he has chosen Israel to be his people. And he has sanctified it and assembled it from all the children of men; for many are the nations and numerous the people, and they all belong to him, and he has given the spirits power over them, that they might lead them astray from him. But he has given no angel or spirit power over Israel; but he alone is its ruler, and he watches over it."[45] Here the genii, as angels or spirits, embody the principle which is against Yahweh, and the use of "lead them astray" points clearly to heathen idolatry. If our interpretation is correct, there is here support (→ 40) for the assumption that the gods stands behond the national genii. Acc. to Jub. 15:30 ff. non-Jews were seduced into apostasy from Yahweh by their genii, while the Jewish people was directly ruled by God and kept against all evil.

In many statements the Rabbis of the Tannaitic and Amorean period express the same idea of the close relation between Yahweh and His people on the one side and the remoteness of the nations on the other. An example may be given from Tg. J. I on Dt. 32:8 f. (ed. M. Ginsburger [1903], 358): "When the Most High made over the world to the nations which proceeded from the sons of Noah, and when in the time of the dispersal he established separate writings and languages for men, in that time he threw lots with the 70 angels, the archons of the peoples, with whom he had come to see[46] the city (Babel).[47] And when the holy people[48] fell to the lot of the Lord of the world, Michael arose and said: This is a good portion ... Then Gabriel opened his mouth in praise and said: The house of Jacob is his portion."

b. The Father-Son Relation between Yahweh and Israel. Along with this myth other images from human life are used to express the inner relation of the Jewish people to Yahweh.[49] One might mention first the OT motif of the sonship of Israel.[50, 51] Thus in 4 Esr. 6:58 the people is the firstborn and only son of Yahweh: *Nos autem, populus tuus, quem vocasti primogenitum, unigenitum, aemulatorem, carissimum, traditi sumus in manibus eorum* (sc. non-Jews).[52] The concept of the firstborn carries with it that of the privilege which the people has in relation to Yahweh. This idea is sometimes linked with that of the superfluous merits of the fathers, which are of advantage to their successors. We may quote as an example the exposition of the Amorean Chija b. Abba (c. 280 A.D.) in Ex. r., 15, 27 on 12:2: "What is meant by 'my firstborn is Israel' (Ex. 4:22)? R. Chija (b. Abba) has said: These are the sons whom their fathers have blessed by their deeds, e.g., Abraham, for it is written: Blessed be Abraham by the most high God (Gn. 14:19)."

The thought of sonship is sometimes worked out ethically, but more often in purely natural terms. Both concepts are present in S. Dt., 96 on 14:1: "R. Jehuda (c. 150 A.D.) has said: If you (Israelites) conduct yourselves like sons, you are sons, but if not you are no sons. But R. Meïr (c. 150 A.D.) has said: You are sons of Yahweh, your

---

44 In Eth. En. 89:59 f., however, the genii of heathen nations rule Israel at Yahweh's behest so long as the Jews are under the dominion of non-Jews.

45 Kautzsch Pseudepigr., 67 f.

46 Cf. Gn. 11:7.

47 Here follows an intrusion which disrupts the context. This presupposes Dt. 32:8 f. in the present HT (→ n. 41), whereas the Tg. account treated here represents an extension of the text given in Δτ.

48 עמא קדישא; on this term for the Jewish people → 43.

49 Cf. on what follows S. Schechter, *Some Aspects of Rabbinic Theology* (1909), 46 ff.

50 Cf. Ex. 4:22; Dt. 14:1; Is. 1:2, 4; 30:1, 9; 43:6; 45:11; 63:8; Jer. 3:14; 31:9, 20; Hos. 2:1; 11:1; Ps. 73:15; 80:15.

51 Cf. Str.-B., I, 428 No. 2; II, 12, 530 on Jn. 9:6b; III, 263 f., 257; IV, 852.

52 Cf. B. Violet, 4 Esra I (1910), 124.

God."[53] How widespread in Rabb. Judaism was the idea of the natural sonship of Israel may be seen also from R. Simon b. Jochai (*c.* 150 A.D.) in Shab., 14, 4, where he calls all Israelites royal children. In general, then, it is held that the father-son relation is not destroyed by sinful conduct in the present. R. Akiba (d. 135 A.D.), who in Ab., 3, 14 regards it as a special token of love for the Israelites that they are called the sons of Yahweh in Dt. 14:1, says in Yoma, 8, 9 with ref. to the day of atonement when sins against God will be forgiven: "Hail to you, Israel! Before whom do you purify yourself, and who purifies you? Your father in heaven."[54] Yahweh even bears with His people the suffering of galuth which it has brought on itself by its sinfulness. Thus in bBer., 3a a heavenly voice says three times daily in the ruins of Jerusalem: "Woe to the sons for the sake of whose sins I have destroyed my house and burned my sanctuary and whom I have banished among the Gentiles." In the same passage it is said of Yahweh's grief: "When Israelites go into the synagogues and houses of instruction and say: Blessed be his great name! then the Holy One, blessed be he, shakes his head (for sorrow) and says: Blessed is the king whose household praises him so, but what shall the father do who has banished his sons? and woe to the sons who are banished from the father's table."

c. The People as the Bride of Yahweh. Another image used by the Rabbis to express the close relation between Yahweh and His people is that of love. Whether it be the love of spouse, relative or friend, love is another theme taken from the OT and worked out by the Rabbis.[55] Thus in Ex. r., 15, 31 on 12:2 Yahweh is compared to a king who was betrothed to a wife. At first he gave her only small gifts, but after marriage he gave many gifts. Referred to Yahweh and Israel, this means that the Jewish people is as yet only betrothed to Yahweh, and that correspondingly it has only a small share in His gifts. But the days of the Messiah will bring the marriage and the fulness of Yahweh's gifts to His people.[56] In this connection Akiba's exposition of Cant. deserves mention, esp. as his interpretation had some influence on Christian exposition, → III, 985. Acc. to this view, the Jewish people is the beloved of Yahweh and the chorus of women represents the Gentile nations.[57]

d. The Jews as Friends and Brothers of their God. Along with marital love we also find that of the love of friends and relatives. The idea of brotherhood[58] between Yahweh and the Jewish people is expressed in a saying of the Tannaitic Chanania b. Chakinai (*c.* 120 A.D.) in M. Ex. on 14:15. Here Yahweh said concerning His relation to Israel: "Have I not already caused to be written long ago: 'A brother is born for adversity' (Prv. 17:17)? I am a brother to Israel in its adversity." In the same context the Israelites are accordingly called the brothers of Yahweh. The idea of friendship between Yahweh and the Jewish people is found, e.g., in Tanch. נשא 20. In an exposition of Cant. 5:1: "Eat, O friends; drink, and drink abundantly, O beloved," it is said that those addressed are the Israelites, since they are called friends. Both the concept of friendship and that of relationship are used by the Amorean Simon b. Laqish (*c.* 250 A.D.) when he says

[53] Cf. on this Moore, II, 203. How strong was the thought of the natural link between Yahweh and His people may also be seen from an eschatological picture such as that sketched by Eleazar of Modeïm (d. *c.* 135 A.D.). In Cant. r. on 2:1 the Tannaite, alluding to Mi. 4:5, shows how the genii of the nations — שרי אומות העולם — will then point out to Yahweh that the Jews as well as the Gentiles have been guilty of idolatry, bloodshed and licentiousness. But the accusation does not succeed; the Gentile nations and their genii will have to go to perdition, while Yahweh will keep His people from the torments of hell.

[54] אֲבִיכֶם שֶׁבַּשָּׁמַיִם; For further details on the father-son relationship between Yahweh and Israel → πατήρ.

[55] On love in the OT cf. Eichr., *Theol. d. AT*, I, 127 ff.

[56] Cf. on this Str.-B., IV, 827, 863, 926.

[57] Cf. M. Ex. on 15:2 and par.

[58] Str.-B., III, 682.

in jBer., 13b, lines 38 ff.: "When a man has a relative, he acknowledges him if he is rich and denies him if he is poor. But not so the Holy One, blessed be he; even when Israel comes into the deepest humiliation, he still calls them 'my brethren and my friends' ..." Finally, it may be pointed out that in Rabb. writings the Jews are often called the beloved[59] (חֲבִיבִין = ἀγαπητοί) of Yahweh,[60] e.g., in bMeg., 29a, where the Tannaite Simon b. Jochai (c. 150 A.D.), seeking to emphasise the connection between Yahweh and His people even in times of adversity, says: "Come and see how beloved the Israelites are before the Holy One, blessed be he; for at all places to which they were banished the Shekinah was with them."

2. The Holy People.

The idea that the quality of holiness attaches to the people which Yahweh has chosen as His possession is also taken by the Rabbis from the OT[61] and worked out further. For the Rabb. the basis of the holiness of the people is that the Jews, as believers in Yahweh, have no fellowship with idolaters. Another point is that they are sanctified by the gift of the Torah. Both lines of thought are found together in S. Lv. קדושים Perek, 10 on 20:7. Israel, then, is called the holy people: עם קדוש, a name which belongs to it alone acc. to S. Dt., 97 on 14:2. Holy nation might also be used: אומה קדושה[62] or אומתא קדישתא.[63]

3. The People as the Centre of the World.

A sense of centrality was proper to every ancient religious community once its adherents began to think beyond the limits of tribal or national religion.[64] But in no religion did it receive so distinctive an impress as in later Judaism.[65] Thus the author of 4 Esr. represents as follows the popular view of his Jewish contemporaries on the central significance of their people (6:55 ff.): *Haec autem omnia dixi coram te, domine, quoniam dixisti, quia propter nos creasti primogenitum saeculum; residuas autem gentes ab Adam natas dixisti eas nihil esse, et quoniam salivae adsimilatae sunt et sicut stillicidium de vaso similasti habundantiam eorum ... Et si propter nos creatum est saeculum, quare non hereditatem possidemus nostrum saeculum?*[66] The hope of world dominion even in this aeon as thus expressed in 4 Esr. corresponds to the national hope for the future cherished by the people from the Persian period.[67] After Hadrian the hope of dominion in the present aeon, which is not shared by the author of 4 Esr.,[68] becomes increasingly weaker with political failures and a darkening situation. National hope for the future focuses more and more on the coming aeon. Hence even Rabb. sayings which speak of the significance of Israel for this world are free from any true idea of world dominion.[69] Thus the Amorean Jehuda b. Shalom (c. 370 A.D.) says in discussion of Gn. 1:1 that the world was created for the sake of the Jewish people but he does not say that it will be subject to the dominion of the Jews, cf. Tanch. B בראשית 3 (p. 1b).

---

59 *Ibid.*, 24, 89; IV, 6; cf. also the term *populus carissimus* in 4 Esr. 6:58, → 41.
60 Cf. Moore, I, 398.
61 E.g., Dt. 7:6; 14:2, 21; 26:19; 28:9; → I, 91.
62 Est. r., 4 on 1:15.
63 jShab., 8d, line 16.
64 Thus one may think of the Omphalos conceptions of certain peoples acc. to which the central sanctuary is also the centre of the earth and of growth, cf. W. H. Roscher, *Omphalos* (1913), *passim*; for Judaism cf. Joma, 5, 2; jJoma, 42c, lines 35 ff. and Tanch. פקודי, 3. For the Jewish material cf. J. Jeremias, *Golgotha* (1926), 51 ff.
65 Moore, I, 383, 449 f.
66 Violet (→ n. 52), 122 ff.
67 Cf. on this G. Hölscher, *Geschichte d. israel. u. jüd. Religion* (1922), 153 f.
68 Cf. the passage 4 Esr. 7:10 ff. discussed → 44.
69 Cf. on this Str.-B., III, 248; IV, 847, 852.

In the tractate Gerim, 1, 5 the proselyte, after baptism, is greeted with the words: "Blessed be thou! To whom hast thou joined thyself? To him at whose behest the world was; for the world was created for the sake of Israel alone, and only Israelites are called the children of God." Another Amorean, Jehuda b. Simon (c. 320 A.D.), in Lv. r., 23, 3 on Lv. 18:3 and par. says in a parable that the world has long merited destruction and that only Yahweh's pleasure in His people has thus far preserved the whole race from perishing.[70] In the parable Israel is the rose (?) and the other peoples are thorns and thistles, and this helps to illuminate the other passages, for it shows that the concept of the central position of Israel is taken ethically. The Jewish people is the righteous people to whose being the rest of the world owes its existence. The same idea that the Jews are necessary to the existence of the world is also expressed by a Tannaite in bAZ, 10b before the emperor Hadrian (?), who agrees with his advisers that the Jews are to be regarded as cancerous sores on the Roman people.[71]

4. The Meaning and Duration of Suffering.

The disastrous political situation of the Jews after the downfall of the independent Hasmonean kingdom, and esp. after the destruction of the second temple, was in blatant contradiction to their statements about themselves. This dichotomy between the present and the ideal was adjusted by various theological considerations.

a. Suffering as the Result of Sin. Present suffering[72] is the result of the sinful conduct of the people in relation to Yahweh. This historical interpretation, which has its OT model in the historical work of the Deuteronomist, finds acute expression in a story from the end of the revolt against Hadrian. In jTaan., 68d, lines 60 ff., it is narrated that Eleazar of Modeïm, when the city of Beth Ter was besieged by the Romans, prayed daily: "Lord of the world, let not thy judgment fall to-day." The city was preserved by the effectual prayer of Eleazar, until bKosiba, who had once been greeted by Akiba as a Messianic king, on the ground of a calumny killed the old man with a kick. There then came to bKosiba a heavenly voice announcing imminent destruction. Shortly afterwards the city was taken by the Romans.[73] The significance of suffering for the whole course of history finds expression in the saying in Tanch. אמור, 32 (p. 52a) and par.: "The Holy One, blessed be He, has said: In this world you are delivered up to the peoples of the world because of your sins, but in the coming world 'kings will become your guardians and princesses your nurses'."

Significant from the standpoint of religious history is 4 Esr. 7:10 ff. To the question why things go so ill for the Jews in this world which was created for their sake (→ 43), the seer receives the answer: *Sic est et Israel pars; propter eos enim feci saeculum. Et quando transgressus est Adam constitutiones meas, iudicatum est, quod factum est; et facti sunt introitus huius saeculi angusti et dolentes et laboriosi, paucae autem et malae et periculorum plenae et laborum magnorum fultae ... Si ergo non ingredientes ingressi fuerint, qui vivunt, angusta et vana, non poterunt recipere, quae sunt reposita.*[74] Here the present situation of the people is regarded as a result of the fall. This idea was not developed further in later Rabb. statements. For the Rabb. take the fall into account in their interpretation of the present only in so far as they relate the ebb and flow of history, the presence within it of good and evil, of joy and sorrow, in short, the imperfection of the world, to the fall of Adam. They certainly do not explain their own miserable situation in terms of the fall.

---

70 *Ibid.*, I, 873.
71 *Ibid.*, I, 832 f.
72 On what follows cf. Str.-B., Index *s.v.* "Leiden."
73 Cf. Bacher Tannaiten, I², 187 f.
74 Violet, 130 ff.

b. Suffering as a Means of Testing. In 4 Esr. 7:10 ff. the thought of judgment is accompanied by that of the testing of man. The living must go through the present world to enter the future aeon. This idea of testing enjoyed a considerable vogue among the Rabb. Thus Simon b. Jochai (c. 150 A.D.) says in S. Dt., 32 on 6:5 (p. 57, Kittel) that Yahweh has given the Jewish people three gifts which the nations of the world sought in vain, the Torah, the land of Israel and the coming world. But the Israelites had to suffer for them.

c. Suffering with a View to Purification for the Coming Aeon. Another thought which helped to make the present understandable was that of the atoning power of suffering. The people which is chosen for the future aeon does not have enough power to resist all the temptations of the present world. Hence Yahweh punishes it in order that its slate may be clean when the future aeon comes.[75] This idea is found in Lv. r., 29, 2 on 23:24 and par.: "I (Yahweh) will chastise you with suffering in this world to purify you from your sins for the world to come."

5. The Eternal Character of the People.

The peoples of the world enjoy their apogee in the present. But acc. to Rabb. eschatological expectation the great day of Israel has still to come.[76] In the days of the Messiah the peoples will be gathered against Israel to battle and will be destroyed. Then Jewish world dominion will be set up, and the peoples, in so far as they are not destroyed, will be subject to the Messiah and His people. Yet not the Messianic period alone will be an age of glory for the Jewish people. For the future world, the final aeon of the story of man, will be as a whole a period of glory for the Jewish people. At the beginning of the coming aeon is the great world judgment. This does not have an exclusively collective character, like the judgment of the nations at the beginning of the Messianic age. Acc. to many statements, it applies to individuals, like the judgment immediately after death. But in effect, whatever the individual presentation may be, the Jewish nation as a whole will come through this judgment unscathed, whereas it will be the end for the nations of the world. This is how we are to understand the basic principle, which probably goes back to Akiba, that all Israel will have a part in the future world, Sanh., 11, 1: כָּל־יִשְׂרָאֵל יֵשׁ לָהֶם חֵלֶק לָעוֹלָם הַבָּא.[77] This principle, which enjoyed almost universal recognition in the Tannaitic and Amorean period, may be regarded as proof of a fundamentally collective and national expectation which was linked with belief in the great world judgment.[78] Naturally this hope of collective salvation is not to be taken to mean that mere descent from the patriarchs was enough for the attainment of eternal life. Mortal sinners, generations as well as individuals, upon whom the Bible had already passed sentence of condemnation acc. to the Rabb. view, would be shut out of the coming aeon. Opinions as to the number of those excluded vary with individual Rabb. but in no case is it so large as to disturb the collective expectation, just as the number of pious individuals from the nations[79] which will enter into the future world with Israel is too small to have any effect. All other Jews who are guilty

---

[75] Cf. already 2 Macc. 6:12-16: Παρακαλῶ οὖν τοὺς ἐντυγχάνοντας τῇδε τῇ βίβλῳ μὴ συστέλλεσθαι διὰ τὰς συμφοράς, λογίζεσθαι δὲ τὰς τιμωρίας μὴ πρὸς ὄλεθρον, ἀλλὰ πρὸς παιδείαν τοῦ γένους ἡμῶν εἶναι· καὶ γὰρ τὸ μὴ πολὺν χρόνον ἐᾶσθαι τοὺς δυσσεβοῦντας, ἀλλ' εὐθέως περιπίπτειν ἐπιτίμοις, μεγάλης εὐεργεσίας σημεῖόν ἐστιν. οὐ γὰρ καθάπερ καὶ ἐπὶ τῶν ἄλλων ἐθνῶν ἀναμένει μακροθυμῶν ὁ δεσπότης μέχρι τοῦ καταντήσαντας αὐτοὺς πρὸς ἐκπλήρωσιν ἁμαρτιῶν κολάσαι, οὕτως καὶ ἐφ' ἡμῶν ἔκρινεν εἶναι, ἵνα μὴ πρὸς τέλος ἀφικομένων ἡμῶν τῶν ἁμαρτιῶν ὕστερον ἡμᾶς ἐκδικᾷ. διόπερ οὐδέποτε μὲν τὸν ἔλεον ἀφ' ἡμῶν ἀφίστησιν, παιδεύων δὲ μετὰ συμφορᾶς οὐκ ἐγκαταλείπει τὸν ἑαυτοῦ λαόν.

[76] Cf. on what follows Str.-B., IV, 858 ff., 880 ff., 968 ff.

[77] Cf. on this Str.-B., IV, 1053 f., where Zech. 11:1 ff. is to be emended.

[78] Cf. on the other hand the view of the last judgment in Mt. 25:31 ff.

[79] Cf. Moore, I, 279; II, 386.

of lesser sins will after death have to undergo a process of purification in purgatory [80] before they have a claim to the future aeon. The opinion which Justin represents as the Rabb. doctrine of the eternal character of the Jewish people in Dial., 140: ὅτι πάντως τοῖς ἀπὸ τῆς σπορᾶς τῆς κατὰ σάρκα τοῦ 'Αβραὰμ οὖσι, κἂν ἁμαρτωλοὶ ὦσι καὶ ἄπιστοι καὶ ἀπειθεῖς πρὸς τὸν θεόν, ἡ βασιλεία ἡ αἰώνιος δοθήσεται, is thus polemically crude and materially inaccurate, even when full account is taken of the Rabb. fondness for the idea of a natural union between Yahweh and His people (→ 41).

II. The Peoples.

With the Exile the question of the relation between Israel and the nations became acute. Two attempts were made to solve it in Judaism, the first in terms of universalism, the second in terms of particularism. The national and religious view of the world triumphed (→ 49). In Rabb. literature, which belongs in the main to the period after the destruction of the national power of Israel, we find the final stages of the development to national and religious particularism. With few exceptions the nations of the world are accordingly viewed extremely pessimistically.

1. The Remoteness of the Peoples from God.

It has been pointed out already (→ 39 ff.) that the concept of the people of possession was often linked with that of the genii of the peoples to show that the peoples of the world do not stand under the direct guidance of Yahweh but are led by their archons. In this way the nations are mythically degraded in relation to Israel, for the genii which are bound to them for good or evil [81] belong to the court of Yahweh and are thus only His servants. [82] The result is that the archons do not have temporally unlimited power. They perish with their peoples, just as the genius of a man perishes at his death. [83] The oldest attestation of this idea in M. Ex. on 15:1 runs: "So soon as the Israelites saw the archon of the Egyptian nation fall, they raised a song of praise ... And so it is seen that the Holy One, blessed be He, will punish the kingdoms in the future aeon only when He has first visited their genii." Finally, attention was drawn to a further fact which may be seen particularly clearly in the same passage. Belief in genii explains the second part of this Rabb. statement, but it does not suffice to explain the first part of the Haggada. The fall of the guardian angel is here parallel to a defeat of the Egyptians, not to the definitive destruction of this nation. This can be understood only on the assumption that acc. to the Rabb. an event in heaven corresponded to the battle at the Red Sea. Now it is impossible that the Rabb. should envisage a contest between equal forces in heaven, since there are no gods equal to Yahweh. One is thus tempted to suspect that behind the first part of M. Ex. on 15:1 stand the myth of a battle of the gods, and that even in the softened Rabb. vision the guardian angel is more than a genius, that he is a national god opposed to Yahweh, and that he is accordingly cast

[80] Acc. to Akiba the stay in purgatory is 12 months.

[81] Cf. Tg. J. I on Gn. 11:7 (ed. M. Ginsburger [1903], 18 f.).

[82] How strongly the Rabb. felt this mythical degradation is plain when one realises that it affected even the relation between Yahweh and Israel. Thus Pinchas b. Chama (c. 320) says in Ex. r., 32, 1 on 23:20: "The Holy One, blessed be He, said to the Israelites. You have brought about your own fall. Once you enjoyed direction by the Holy Spirit; now you must make do with direction by an angel." The Rabbi thus feels that the idea of a guardian angel for Israel implies an increase in the distance between Yahweh and His people.

[83] [I owe this ref. to K. G. Kuhn.]

out of heaven by Him.[84] It thus follows also that the archons are not just servants of Yahweh but His enemies, the representatives of an anti-God principle like the heathen gods.

Because of their remoteness from God the peoples of the world do not have the predicates of honour which accrue to Israel as the possession of Yahweh. There are not too many Rabb. sayings which do not ascribe to Yahweh the hostile feelings which Judaism felt for the nations in consequence of its political situation.[85] Thus in a Haggada of Jochanan b. Nappacha, a younger contemporary of Origen (d. 279 A.D.), bSanh., 98b: "What does it mean: 'And all faces have turned pale' (Jer. 30:6)? R. Jochanan has said: By those who have turned pale are to be understood the upper servants and the lower servants in the hour when the Holy One, blessed be He, says: These (the Israelites) are the work of My hands, and those (the peoples) are the work of My hands; why should I destroy the one for the sake of the other?" In this depiction of the last judgment there is the same mixture of universalism and national particularism as in a consideration of the fall of Egypt in bSanh., 39b; here, in an exposition of Ex. 14:20 which goes back to Jonathan b. Eleazar (*c.* 230 A.D.), we read: "In that hour the ministering angels wished to raise a song of praise before the Holy One, blessed be He. Then said the Holy One, blessed be He: The work of My hands is drowned in the sea, and will you raise a song before Me?"

2. The Sinful Character of the Peoples.

Between Yahweh and the peoples the gulf is not just mythical; it is ethical. The peoples have brought down Yahweh's wrath upon them because they have set themselves outside His order. Among the charges which Judaism raised against the nations from the religious standpoint the following are the chief.

a. The Transgression of the Adamic Commands. In the first man the peoples transgressed the so-called Adamic commands.[86] Jehuda b. Simon (*c.* 320 A.D.) says in Gn. r., 24, 5 on 5:1: "The first man was ordained to receive the Torah. The Holy One, blessed be He, said: He is a creation of My hands, and shall I not give it him? But the Holy One, blessed be He, changed (His mind) and said: If I have already given him six commandments and he cannot keep them, how shall I give him 613 commandments? ... I will give them, not to Adam, but to his descendants."

b. The Violation of the Noachic Commands. More common is the thought that the peoples have not kept the seven Noachic commandments. Nechemia (*c.* 150 A.D.) says in S. Dt., 322 on 32:28: "... (Yahweh said): The nations have lost the seven commandments which I gave them." And in relation to proselytes Chanania b. Gamliel (*c.* 120 A.D.) says in bJeb., 48b: "Why are proselytes humbled in this time, and why do sorrows come upon them? Because (before their conversion) they did not keep the seven commandments of the children of Noah."

c. The Rejection of the Torah by the Peoples. The main charge against the peoples was that they knowingly rejected the Torah. It was presupposed that they once had knowledge of it.[87] Pre-Rabbinic literature does not tell us how they had this knowledge.

---

[84] That there is substance behind this conjecture may be seen from Lk. 10:18. The battle of Jesus and His disciples against the kingdom of darkness on earth is accompanied by a battle of God against Satan; thus, when the 70 return triumphantly from their conflict against demons, Jesus can say: ἐθεώρουν τὸν σατανᾶν ὡς ἀστραπὴν ἐκ τοῦ οὐρανοῦ πεσόντα. While it is Satan and his demons who suffer defeat acc. to Lk., in M. Ex. on 15:1 it is the archon of Egypt and his nation. But both represent the same anti-God principle, and in both cases the monotheism is so strong that there is no longer any thought of a real struggle.

[85] Cf. Str.-B., III, 289; C. G. Montefiore, *Rabbinic Literature and Gospel Teachings* (1930), 214.

[86] Adam here is regarded as a non-Jew, cf. Str.-B., III, 41.

[87] Str.-B., III, 38 ff., 596 f.

Rabbinic literature does. Acc. to the tradition in Sota, 7, 5 the Israelites, on entering the land west of Jordan, built an altar on Mt. Ebal. On it were inscribed all the words of the Torah in seventy languages so that the peoples of the world could copy them and make them their own. Thus Jehuda (c. 150 A.D.) says in T. Sota, 8, 6: "The Holy One, blessed be He, put it into their hearts (the 'nations'), and they sent scribes, and these made a copy from the stones in seventy languages." To be sure, the moment the peoples came to know the Torah of Yahweh they rejected the divine Law and were thus irrevocably shut out of the world to come. Hence the Tannaite continues: "In that hour the judgment on the nations in respect of eternal death was sealed." The myth of the apostasy of the nations is also linked with the law-giving at Sinai in M. Ex. on 20:2. Acc. to Jochanan b. Nappacha (d. 279 A.D.) Yahweh spread abroad the Torah among all the nations, but only Israel accepted it, bAZ, 2b. Hence the destiny of the peoples is eschatological destruction, for they received the sentence of death at Horeb in consequence of their rejection of the Law, Tanch. B במדבר, 7 (4b).

Culpable ignorance of the Law is the basis of all the moral and religious charges which the Jews bring against the nations. Since our concern here is only with the main outline, we need not pursue the details of the ungodliness of the nations in Jewish eyes.

3. The Success of the Gentiles.

In obvious contradiction to the thesis that the peoples are remote from God and sinful is their political success, which weighed particularly heavily after the suppression of the revolts. As attempts were made to integrate the suffering of Israel into the world picture (→ 44), so the good fortune of the Gentiles had to be explained. The success of the peoples was viewed as the temporally limited rewarding of the transgressor in this world, just as Israel's suffering was equated with the penal and purgatorial suffering of the righteous in the present age. On the temporal limitation S. Bar. 82:2 ff. says: "But you should know that our Creator assuredly avenges us on all our foes ... and that the end of His judgment is not distant. For now we see the fulness of the prosperity of the peoples, while they commit ungodly acts, but they are like wind." [88] Rabb. writings do not share the eschatological tension of apocalyptic literature — the suppression of the revolt against Hadrian had a sobering effect — but the thought remains that the nations are spared for the great judgment. Their present success is viewed by the Rabbis as the reward which they receive because, although sinful by nature, they have done some good works. So that Yahweh may later punish them justly, He requites their good deeds on the spot. Hence an anonymous tradition in Tanch. משפטים, 5 reads: "The Holy One, blessed be He, has said: I am called the Lord of justice, and should I (already) stretch out My hand against Esau (= Rome)? I can do this only when I have paid him a reward for the little commandment [89] which he has observed in this world." Yahweh deals with the other nations in the same way as with Rome. So R. Alexandrai (c. 270 A.D.) expounds Zech. 12:9 as follows in bAZ, 4a: "I (Yahweh) will (in that day) examine their lists (of works). If they merit a reward I will redeem them, if not, I will destroy them." It is tacitly assumed that the nations will have no more claim to reward. So R. Aibo (c. 320 A.D.) can say in Est. r., 1 on 1:1 (p. 3c, Vilna) that Yahweh will pour out His wrath on the nations only when, after an examination of the heavenly accounts, all claims to reward have been fully met.

---

[88] Kautzsch Pseudepigr., 443.

[89] The ref. is to Esau's love for Isaac; by this he acquired merit on which his descendants, the Romans, draw.

4. The *massa perditionis*.

From what has been said, it is evident that Rabb. Judaism did not ascribe an eternal character to the nations. [90] It is thus superflous to adduce further examples to show that the peoples were only transitory. We need only conclude that because of their sinful remoteness from God the peoples have a right of domicile only in this world and that they are in the main excluded from the world to come by Yahweh's sentence of condemnation. A single example may be adduced to show the sense of superiority which was felt from the standpoint of salvation history towards the Gentile nations as a *massa perditionis*. In bBer., 10a we have an account of the debate between Beruria, the wife of R. Meïr (c. 150 A.D.) and a heretic, who draws attention to the present affliction of Israel. Beruria then expounds Is. 54:1 as follows: "But what is meant by: 'Unfruitful, who has not borne'? Rejoice, O congregation of Israel, that has not borne sons for Gehinnom like them (the Gentiles)."

III. The Election and Privilege of the People.

In respect of the relation of Israel to the world around one may distinguish already in the OT two basic religious attitudes, that of universalism and that of particularism. The view of history in Dt. Is. is the high watermark of the former. [91] This universalism goes so far that it can regard a heathen ruler, Cyrus, as the one commissioned by Yahweh to bring salvation. [92] But along with it, and esp. in the Persian period, particularism begins to permeate the religious writings. Both attitudes are concerned with the nations. But whereas universalism builds on the assumption that the nations will have a share in the salvation which Yahweh brings, particularism views the nations as the enemies of Israel which Yahweh will either destroy or cause to serve His people. Universalism is full of missionary zeal. Particularism is indifferent or even hostile to missions. The goal of its religious yearning is the day of vengeance which Yahweh will cause to come.

1. Universalism.

So far as can be judged from the sources, at the time of transition from B.C. to A.D. universalism is most at home in Hellenistic Judaism. Thus we read in Sib., 3, 753 ff.: "Not war nor drought will there be any more on earth, not hunger nor hail which devastates the fruits, but great peace on the whole earth. And one king will be a friend to the other to the end of times, and the Immortal in the starry heaven will consummate for men one common law on the whole earth ... For He Himself alone is God and there is no longer any other." [93] Cf. also 194 f.: "And then will the people of the great God be strong again, which will be to all mortals guides to the way of life." [94] Since the people has been given by Yahweh the task of instructing other nations, Wis. 18:4 says: "Those (the Egyptians) deserved to be deprived of light and to be kept captive in darkness, since they had tried to hold as prisoners the sons through whom the imperishable light of the Law was to be given to the world," ἄξιοι μὲν γὰρ ἐκεῖνοι στερηθῆναι φωτὸς καὶ φυλακισθῆναι σκότει οἱ κατακλείστους φυλάξαντες τοὺς υἱούς σου, δι' ὧν ἤμελλεν τὸ ἄφθαρτον νόμου φῶς τῷ αἰῶνι δίδοσθαι. Acc. to Philo the people Israel is by God's plan the priestly and prophetic nation for the rest of the world, Abr., 98: Abraham "was not to bear a small number of sons and daughters, but a whole people, the people most loved by God among all peoples. This has, it seems to me, received the priestly and prophetic office for the whole human race," ὃς οὐκ ἔμελλεν ὀλίγων ἀριθμὸν υἱῶν ἢ θυγατέρων γεννᾶν, ἀλλ' ὅλον ἔθνος καὶ

---

[90] → 45.
[91] Moore, I, 228.
[92] → II, 368, n. 15.
[93] Kautzsch Pseudepigr., 199; on what follows cf. Str.-B., III, 98 ff.
[94] Kautzsch Pseudepigr., 188.

ἐθνῶν τὸ θεοφιλέστατον, ὃ μοι δοκεῖ τὴν ὑπὲρ παντὸς ἀνθρώπων γένους ἱερωσύνην καὶ προφητείαν λαχεῖν. Similarly, in Vit. Mos., I, 149 Israel is described as a people "which, (selected) from all others, was to discharge a priestly ministry by always offering prayers on behalf of the human race for turning from evil and participation in the good," ὅπερ ἔμελλεν ἐξ ἁπάντων τῶν ἄλλων ἱερᾶσθαι τὰς ὑπὲρ τοῦ γένους τῶν ἀνθρώπων ἀεὶ ποιησόμενον εὐχὰς ὑπέρ τε κακῶν ἀποτροπῆς καὶ μετουσίας ἀγαθῶν.

Universalism had its limits, of course, even in Hellenistic Judaism. Many references in the relevant lit. emphasise the deep cleavage between Israel and the nations. One has only to think of the LXX additions to Est. Thus it is not uncommon for writers to speak of Gk. culture as a poor copy of the Mosaic, and the idea of the election of Israel, which demands its ministry to the peoples, is turned into that of the privilege of Israel over the nations. Indeed, some passages are found which express national hatred and the desire for vengeance.

Palestinian literature offers fewer express examples of universalism. Yet one may conclude from Mt. 23:15 that active missionary work was being done. Perhaps one may even take the well-known story of the Gentile who wanted to learn from Hillel and Shammai [95] what was the basic rule for the worship of God, as evidence that in Palestine in the days of Jesus a more universalistic stream ran side by side with a particularistic.

2. The Triumph of National Particularism.

Events between 66 and 135 A.D. had a decisive impact on the position of the Jewish people *vis-à-vis* the world around. Universalism, and with it the ancient prophetic heritage, was set aside. Israel was now no longer regarded as the selected people which has a missionary vocation towards the nations, but as the privileged nation which waits to be given its rights by Yahweh, as the world power of the days of the Messiah, as the only nation in the future aeon after the great judgment of the world. [96] The words of Sib. and Philo are no longer heard. The peoples of the world appear only as the enemies of Yahweh and Israel, embodying the principle of evil.

R. Meyer

E. λαός in the New Testament.

1. Occurrence in the New Testament. The word occurs in the NT (apart from Jn. 8:2) 140 times, of which only 8 are in the plur. (Lk. 2:31; Ac. 4:25, 27; R. 15:11; Rev. 7:9; 10:11; 11:9; 17:15; on 21:3 → n. 104). The distribution in individual writings and groups is worth noting. Mk. has three examples (7:6; 11:32 Ꞩ; 14:2), of which 7:6 and 14:2 occur in Mt. and 11:32 and 14:2 in Lk. Mt. has the word 14 times, Lk. 36 times in the Gospel and 48 in Ac. Jn. has 2 instances in the Gospel and 8 or 9 (13:7) in Rev. (5 in the plur.; on 21:3 → n. 104). Paul has 11 instances, Hb. 13, 1 Pt. 2 and 2 Pt. and Jd. one each. More than half the occurrences are thus in Lk. It is surprising that it does not occur at all in the "journey" in Lk. 9:51-18:14 or in the "we-passages" in Ac. Also noteworthy is the fact that apart from Mk. 14:2 = Mt. 26:5 = Lk. 22:2 there is no λαός passage common to Mk., Mt. and Lk. The word is found in the special Lucan material, e.g., 1:10, 21; 7:1, 29, but it is usually introduced by Lk. into passages taken from his two main sources, e.g., 6:17; 8:47; 9:13; 18:43; 19:47; 20:9, 19, 26; 21:38; 23:35. One may thus conclude that it is a favourite word of Luke's. Also worth noting is the paucity of the term in the Fourth Gospel. Often, where Lk. would say λαός, Jn. has

---

[95] bShab., 31a.

[96] Cf. on this G. Kittel, "Die Entstehung des Judentums u. die Entstehung der Judenfrage," FJFr, I (1937), 56 ff. [To be used with caution.]

οἱ → Ἰουδαῖοι (used some 70 times in the Gospel) or ὁ → ὄχλος (20 times in the Gospel).

2. The Popular Meaning. In the LXX λαός mostly signifies people in the sense of "nation." In the NT, however, the statistically predominant sense is the popular one of "crowd," "population," "people," with no implication of membership of one national union in distinction from other peoples. In this sense λαός is always in the singular. Yet this impression is given only by the Lucan writings, for outside Luke this general meaning, with no special significance, is found only twice in Mk. (11:32 vl.; 14:2) and four times in Mt. (4:23; 26:5; 27:25, 64).

In Mt. 27:25 : πᾶς ὁ λαὸς εἶπεν· τὸ αἷμα αὐτοῦ ἐφ' ἡμᾶς κτλ., λαός is to be equated with the ὄχλος of v. 24 (Pilate washes his hands κατέναντι τοῦ ὄχλου). The λαός is thus the mob. The word is used in the same sense in Mk. 11:32 (𝔎 Dpm; T); the members of the Sanhedrin, who deliberate on their answer to the question about John's baptism, ἐφοβοῦντο τὸν λαόν. Mt. 21:26, replacing the objective account by a subjective consideration, has φοβούμεθα τὸν ὄχλον, while in Lk. 20:6 there is a concrete formulation of the fear : ὁ λαὸς ἅπας καταλιθάσει ἡμᾶς. λαός has this sense in the related Mk. 14:2 (cf. Mt. 26:5): ἔλεγον γάρ· μὴ ἐν τῇ ἑορτῇ, μήποτε ἔσται θόρυβος τοῦ λαοῦ. If λαός here means the people as an assembled crowd, in Mt. 4:23 it has the weaker sense of population (Jesus on His journeys healed πᾶσαν μαλακίαν ἐν τῷ λαῷ) [97] and Mt. 27:64 (the members of the Sanhedrin ordered a watch on the tomb, μήποτε ἐλθόντες οἱ μαθηταὶ κλέψωσιν αὐτὸν καὶ εἴπωσιν τῷ λαῷ ...).

If, however, λαός means the "crowd" or the "population" or "people" only in these passages in Mt. and Mk., this is the customary sense in Lk. and Ac.

Cf., e.g., Lk. 1:21 ἦν ὁ λαὸς προσδοκῶν τὸν Ζαχαρίαν, of the crowd before the temple ; also 3:15, 18; 7:1; 8:47; 20:1, 9, 45; 23:35; Ac. 2:47; 3:9, 11, 12; 4:1, 2, 17, 21; 5:13, 20, 25 f., 37; 10:41; 12:4; 19:4; 21:30 etc. In some cases λαός is here, too, another word for a preceding ὄχλος (Lk. 7:29, cf. 7:24; 8:47, cf. 8:42, 45; 9:13, cf. 9:12), or it corresponds to an ὄχλος in Mk. or ὄχλοι in Mt. (Lk. 19:48, cf. Mk. 11:18; Lk. 20:45, cf. Mt. 23:1; Lk. 20:19, cf. Mk. 12:12; Mt. 21:46). Sometimes a πᾶς gives the narrative a popular sound (πᾶς ὁ λαός saw the healing of the blind man at Jericho, Lk. 18:43; πᾶς ὁ λαός, "everybody" was baptised, Lk. 3:21; πᾶς ὁ λαὸς ὤρθριζεν πρὸς αὐτόν, Lk. 21:38; cf. 7:29; 8:47; 9:13; Ac. 3:9; 5:34; 10:41 etc.), or there is ref. to the πλῆθος or πλῆθος πολὺ τοῦ λαοῦ or even πᾶν τὸ πλῆθος τοῦ λαοῦ (Ac. 21:36; Lk. 6:17; 1:10) to suggest the great number present and their full participation in what occurred. λαός is also used for the people at large as distinct from or in opposition to the ruling classes. The members of the Sanhedrin feared the λαός (Lk. 22:2). They complained that Jesus ἀνασείει τὸν λαόν (Lk. 23:5). Pilate summoned them καὶ τὸν λαόν (Lk. 23:13); just before (v. 4) we read that he spoke πρὸς τοὺς ἀρχιερεῖς καὶ τοὺς ὄχλους. There is a similar distinction between the λαός and members of the Sanhedrin in Ac. 6:12, and in Ac. 10:41 πᾶς ὁ λαός is used in antithesis to those called to be witnesses of the Risen Lord, while in 13:15 the λαός assembled in the synagogue is distinguished from the leaders.

This distinction does not occur outside the Synoptic Gospels and Acts. For there is a different reason for the distinction between the high-priest and the people in Hb.

3. The National Meaning. In the popular use discussed thus far the idea of a national union as distinct from other unions plays no part. But this concept is

[97] In the par. Mt. 9:35 the ἐν τῷ λαῷ of the *Koine* text is a secondary intrusion from Mt. 4:23.

decisive in a second group of passages. Only here can one discern the influence of the LXX on NT usage, for this use of the term is the distinctive feature of the LXX (→ B.).

This meaning is first found in the NT in the few passages in which the word occurs in the plur. It is then a regular par. to ἔθνη, e.g., in the quotation which freely conflates three passages from Is. in Lk. 2:30 f.: τὸ σωτήριόν σου (Is. 40:5), ὃ ἡτοίμασας κατὰ πρόσωπον πάντων τῶν λαῶν (52:10) φῶς εἰς ἀποκάλυψιν ἐθνῶν (42:6) (the LXX has ἐθνῶν for λαῶν at 52:10), or in R.15:11 (quoting Ps. 117:1), or in Rev. 7:9; 10:11; 11:9; 17:15, where in dependence on Da. 3:4 λαοί, ἔθνη, γλῶσσαι, φυλαί occur together to denote the whole human race in its national and linguistic distinctions. The listing of these terms in Rev. 5:9; 13:7; 14:6 may be mentioned in this connection, though here we have the sing. with πᾶς instead of the plur. Finally, there is Ac. 4:25, 27. The distinctive point here is that Ps. 2:1 is quoted, where ἔθνη and λαοί stand in parallelism with the same meaning. Acc. to v. 27, however, the point of the word is that Pilate and Herod allied themselves against Jesus σὺν ἔθνεσιν καὶ λαοῖς Ἰσραήλ. This λαοῖς is highly remarkable.[98] The author certainly does not mean that Israel consists of many λαοί. He uses the plur. only in the light of Ps. 2, but this was possible only because the word reminded the author of Israel. He might just as well have been thinking of Israel when using ἔθνη, but under LXX influence this was hardly possible, since in the LXX Israel is the λαὸς κατ' ἐξοχήν as compared with the world outside Israel, which is ἔθνη. The verse thus marks the transition to a specific use in which it acquires a special religious sense. On Rev. 21:3 → n. 104.

4. The Specific Meaning λαός = Ἰσραήλ. The use is first present when there is an antithesis between λαός and ἔθνη, e.g., in Lk. 2:32 (φῶς εἰς ἀποκάλυψιν ἐθνῶν καὶ δόξαν λαοῦ σου Ἰσραήλ, a free conflation of Is. 42:6 and 46:13); Ac. 26:17, 23; 28:27, 28; Rom. 15:10 (quoting Dt. 32:43). It occurs also when various additions, either direct or in the context, indicate that the reference of λαός is to Israel, e.g., ὁ λαὸς Ἰσραήλ, Ac. 4:10; 13:24; ὁ λαὸς οὗτος, Mt. 13:15 (from Is. 6:9 f.); 15:8 (from Ισ. 29:13); Lk. 21:23; Ac. 28:26, 27 (from Is. 6:9 f.); 1 C. 14:21 (from Is. 28:11 f.); ὁ λαὸς οὗτος Ἰσραήλ, Ac. 13:17; ὁ λαὸς τῶν Ἰουδαίων, Ac. 12:11. These passages give evidence of a specific or technical use to the degree that this word and not ἔθνος is always used for Israel.

This is not always true, of course, in the NT. In Jn. 11:48-52 and the related 18:14 λαός is used twice but ἔθνος 4 times for Israel, partly by the high-priests and Pharisees, partly by the Evangelist, and also by Pilate (18:35). The Jews also use it in Lk. 7:5 (ἀγαπᾷ ... τὸ ἔθνος ἡμῶν) with reference to the centurion of Capernaum, the members of the Sanhedrin to Pilate in Lk. 23:2 (τοῦτον εὕραμεν διαστρέφοντα τὸ ἔθνος ἡμῶν), the messengers to Cornelius in Ac. 10:22 (τὸ ἔθνος τῶν Ἰουδαίων), Tertullus in 24:2 (τὸ ἔθνος τοῦτο), Paul in 24:10, 17; 26:4; 28:19 (τὸ ἔθνος τοῦτο or τὸ ἔθνος μου). In Jn. this usage betrays a certain concern to ignore the distinction which Jews would sense between λαός and ἔθνος.

---

[98] Zn. Ac., 176, n. 5 thinks the true reading is λαός, since the λαοῖς of the best MSS is meaningless and must have arisen either by grammatical assimilation to ἔθνεσιν or by confusion with the ΙΣ(ραήλ) which follows. But this contradicts all the basic principles of textual criticism. *Lectio ardua praestat.* The sparsely attested λαός proves only that those who sponsored it found the plur. difficult. In his *Forschungen z. Geschichte des nt.lichen Kanons,* IX (1916), 257 Zahn, having adduced the ancient versions which seem to presuppose the sing., declares rather more cautiously that if λαός is not the earliest tradition it is a *conjectura palmaris* of the early translators. But this conjecture robs the verse of what makes it distinctive.

For it is hardly conceivable that Jn. was unaware of it. This outlook does not arise in relation to Lk. It is to be noted, however, that in the Lucan passages ἔθνος is used of Israel either by non-Jews or with reference to the attitude of a non-Jew or in speeches before non-Jews. The only exception is Ac. 28:19. But here the choice of term is influenced by the preceding addresses of Paul before non-Jews. For the τὸ ἔθνος μου to Jews in Ac. 28:19 can be explained only in terms of Ac. 24:17; 26:4. Seen in this light, all the ἔθνος-Israel passages seem to be a confirmation of the specific or technical use of λαός which is present in the passages adduced previously and from which there is deviation only for special reasons.

This technical usage may be fully seen when λαός means Israel with no elucidatory additions, so that the writer does not even consider the possibility of there being any other λαός.

This is particularly plain in Ac. 21:28: The Jews of Asia protest against Paul that he is the man who is everywhere teaching all men κατὰ τοῦ λαοῦ καὶ τοῦ νόμου καὶ τοῦ τόπου τούτου. Here the people is something just as singular and unique as the Law and the temple; cf. Ac. 28:17: Paul has done nothing contrary τῷ λαῷ ἢ τοῖς ἔθεσι τοῖς πατρῴοις. λαός is also meant thus in Ac. 10:2 (cf. Lk. 7:5): Cornelius rendered ἐλεημοσύνας πολλὰς τῷ λαῷ. Cf. also Lk. 2:10;[99] Ac. 3:23 (from Lv. 23:29); Ac. 10:41, 42 (as compared with 45); 13:17, 31 (as compared with 46); 19:4; 1 C. 10:7 (from Ex. 32:6); 2 Pt. 2:1; Jd. 5; Hb. 2:17; 5:3; 7:5, 11, 27; 9:7, 19; 11:25. The thought of the uniqueness of this people is also present in formulae like οἱ ἀρχιερεῖς καὶ γραμματεῖς τοῦ λαοῦ, οἱ πρεσβύτεροι τοῦ λαοῦ, τὸ πρεσβυτέριον τοῦ λαοῦ (e.g., Mt. 2:4; 21:23; 26:3; Lk. 19:47; 22:66; Ac. 4:8; 23:5). Probably this is true even in the popular use. For the reference here is always to the Jewish population. When it is to a non-Jewish crowd, e.g., of Christians, Lk. never has λαός but always ὄχλος or ὄχλοι; cf. Ac. 13:45 (in Pisidian Antioch); 14:11-19 (Lystra); 16:22 (Philippi); 17:8 (Thessalonica); 17:13 (Berea); 19:26, 35 (Ephesus). Even Hellenes who join the Christian movement in Syrian Antioch are called ὄχλος (11:24, 26). Similarly, the Samaritans in Ac. 8:6 are ὄχλος, not λαός. ὄχλος takes the place of λαός in Ac. when non-Jewish crowds are in question. This is why ὄχλος occurs hardly at all in the first chapters (only 1:15 and 6:7, not in the sense of a crowd but in that of a great number, accompanied by ἀριθμός in 6:7, and not replaceable by λαός). This is also why it is the more common in the later chapters. At first, when the crowds are Jewish, λαός is regularly used.[100] This can be explained only if we assume that the national use, in its specific sense,[101] is implied in the popular.[102]

Naturally the NT also shows that this technical use of λαός has a religious basis. Israel is ὁ λαὸς αὐτοῦ, sc. θεοῦ, Mt. 1:21; Lk. 1:68, 77; 7:16; R. 11:1 f. (from

---

[99] The angel says that great joy will be παντὶ τῷ λαῷ. Because this is unusual, the Syr. in part substituted עלמא (world) for עמא and introduced universalism; cf. Zn. Lk., *ad loc.*

[100] Cf. Ac. 7:17: ηὔξησεν ὁ λαός, but 11:24: προσετέθη ὄχλος ἱκανός. — 4:2: διδάσκειν αὐτοὺς τὸν λαόν, but 11:26: διδάξαι ὄχλον ἱκανόν. — 5:26: ἐφοβοῦντο γὰρ τὸν λαόν, but 13:45: ἰδόντες δὲ οἱ Ἰουδαῖοι τοὺς ὄχλους. — 6:12: συνεκίνησάν τε τὸν λαόν, but 19:26: μετέστησεν ἱκανὸν ὄχλον.

[101] Jn., however, always calls the crowd → ὄχλος (5:13; 6:2, 5, 22, 24; 7:12, 20, 31 etc.). This confirms our observations concerning the use of ἔθνος and λαός in Jn. → 51-53.

[102] The word δῆμος, which denotes the people esp. as a political body, occurs in the NT only in 4 places in Ac. in scenes at Caesarea, Thessalonica and Ephesus (Ac. 12:22; 17:5; 19:30, 33). It is never used of the Jewish people or the Christian community in the NT. It must have been felt to be unsuitable for this.

Ps. 94:14); 15:10 (from Dt. 32:43); Hb. 10:30 (from Ps. 135:14); 11:25 (τῷ λαῷ τοῦ θεοῦ); cf. ὁ λαός μου, Ac. 7:34 (from Ex. 3:7); ὁ λαός μου ὁ Ἰσραήλ, Mt. 2:6 (from 2 S. 5:2); λαός σου Ἰσραήλ, Lk. 2:32. This exclusive relationship finds particularly forceful expression in Lk. 24:19: Jesus was a prophet mighty in word and deed ἐναντίον τοῦ θεοῦ καὶ παντὸς τοῦ λαοῦ.

5. The Figurative Meaning. λαός = the Christian Community. Thus far the NT has built wholly on LXX usage. It goes beyond it by using λαός in the specific national sense for the Christian community, e.g., in Ac. 15:14; 18:10; R. 9:25 f.; 2 C. 6:16; Tt. 2:14; 1 Pt. 2:9 f.; Hb. 4:9; 8:10; 10:30; 13:12; Rev. 18:4; 21:3. It will be noted that this usage occurs especially in Paul and the writings influenced by him. This figurative use is not found at all in the Gospels. At the most, one might see in the formulation of the task of the Baptist in Lk. 1:17: ἑτοιμάσαι κυρίῳ λαὸν κατεσκευασμένον, an indication of the freeing of the term λαός from its national basis in nature and history, especially if the saying in Lk. 3:8 about the stones of which God can raise up children to Abraham is adduced in exposition, since according to this Israel as such is no λαὸς κατεσκευασμένος. It is λαὸς κυρίου only with reservations. The more significant is the observation of James at the Apostolic Council in Ac. 15:14. Simon has told how God for the first time was minded λαβεῖν ἐξ ἐθνῶν λαὸν τῷ ὀνόματι αὐτοῦ (with the conversion of Cornelius, Ac. 10). This was for Jewish ears an astounding and even a revolutionary saying, though the way had been prepared for it in OT prophecy. Thus far λαός and ἔθνη had been mutually exclusive terms. Now there rises up to God's name from the ἔθνη a λαός independent of all national preconditions. The circle of the word λαός is given a new centre. Only faith in the Gospel decides. The title is not herewith taken from Israel. But another λαός now takes its place along with Israel on a different basis. This means, of course, that within Israel only those who meet the decisive conditions belong to this λαός. Thus a new and figurative Christian concept arises along with the old biological and historical view and crowds it out. This transposition of the term is found in Ac. 18:10. The direction to Paul to continue work in Corinth is grounded on the words: διότι λαός ἐστί μοι πολὺς ἐν τῇ πόλει ταύτῃ. This means that there are here many future Christians. These come from the ἔθνη to which Paul here as always must turn, since the Jews reject him. But if the λαός in the old sense rejects him, there arises from the ἔθνη a λαός in the new sense (cf. v. 6; 13:46; 28:26, 27). The passage in R. 9:23 ff. is particularly instructive in this regard, for the two quotations adduced from Hosea both refer in the original to Israel. Israel, which in its present condition can no longer be acknowledged as God's people, will again become this in the time of salvation. Paul, however, sees in the saying καλέσω τὸν οὐ λαόν μου λαόν μου a prophecy of the conversion of the Gentiles which he promotes and experiences in his missionary work. Hence the Gentile Christians are for him "my people." The passage in 2 C. 6:14 ff. is seeking to impress on believers in Corinth the impossibility of compromising with the denial of faith. The temple of God has no room for idols. This is Paul's argument. For "we are the temple of the living God." A mixed quotation from Lv. 26:12 and Ex. 37:27 is adduced in proof. The original speaks of God's relation to Israel. To Israel is given the promise that God will dwell among it and that it will be His people. Paul finds no difficulty in ascribing the quotation to the Christian community, so that here, too, the community is the people of God. Tt. 2:14 goes further along this line when it claims the phrase λαὸς περιούσιος (cf. Ex. 19:5 f.; 23:22; Dt. 7:6;

14:2) for the Christian community. 1 Pt. 2:9 f. goes even further when it transfers to the Christian community not only the title λαὸς περιούσιος but also the other titles of honour ascribed to Israel in these passages, and the full assurance of Christian conviction and its justification in this respect may be seen from the fact that no need is felt to vindicate this bold transposition. Hb. moves wholly in the sphere of the OT cultus. When it uses λαός, the primary reference is to Israel. But all things in the OT are only a likeness of the Christian present, whether the tabernacle, the priesthood or the cultus. Hence the Christian community continually takes the place of Israel as the λαός. This is the reference when it is said of the Son that He became man to expiate "the sins of the people" (2:17). The community is the λαός for which the Sabbath is present (4:9). It is the λαός to which the warning of Ps. 135:14 applies (10:30) and which Jesus sanctified by His blood (13:12). The author of Hb., too, does not feel that this transfer of the title of Israel to the Christian community needs vindication any more than does the referring of suitable OT quotations to Christ and His work or to the Christian community. These are the concealed and true theme of the OT. Hence, when there is reference to the λαός, Israel may be meant in the first instance but the ultimate application is to the Christian community. Finally, in Rev. 18:4 another OT verse (Jer. 51:45 = Ιερ. 28:44) [103] in which ὁ λαός μου refers to Israel is transferred to the Christian community, and in Rev. 21:3 the perfected Christian community of salvation is the λαὸς [104] θεοῦ as foretold in Zech. 2:14 and Ez. 37:27.

6. The Significance of this Metaphorical Use. What is the significance of this transfer? It makes over to the Christian community a concept which is national and religious according to its OT origin, and in which from the very commencement of the history of Israel the national and religious elements are in conflict. The two elements were meant to be united: ἐὰν ἀκοῇ ἀκούσητε τῆς ἐμῆς φωνῆς καὶ φυλάξητε τὴν διαθήκην μου, ἔσεσθέ μοι λαὸς περιούσιος ἀπὸ πάντων τῶν ἐθνῶν, Ex. 19:5. But the harmony was never achieved. Tension between them mounts until we read in Hos. 1:9: "Ye are not my people." The uniting of the two elements becomes the theme of the eschatological hope and proclamation of salvation in prophecy. This salvation will be achieved only by way of severe and almost annihilating judgments on Israel. On the other hand, new members will be added to the λαός from the λαοί = ἔθνη. What OT prophecy foresees the NT community sees to be fulfilled in itself. From the national and religious λαός and from the λαοί = ἔθνη arises a new λαός in the purely religious sense. For the existence of this λαός the biologico-historical or national element is of no significance. It is a third race, as was said later. [105] From the biologico-historical or national standpoint this λαός consists of two or even many λαοί. But these λαοί fuse in the unity of a new λαός, for whose constitution only the fashioning of the religious relationship by God's creative act of redemption in the sending of Christ, and by faith in Christ, is normative. You are all the children of God by faith in Christ Jesus ... there is neither Jew nor Greek, slave nor free, male nor

---

[103] Acc. to the apparatus of Swete the verse is found only in secondary MSS tradition. But the use in Rev. 18:4 shows that the insertion must be of great antiquity. This is one of the many riddles of the LXX text of Jer.

[104] λαός with the *koine*, not λαοί. The plur. is to be regarded as a secondary assimilation to the preceding αὐτοί, cf. Bss. Apk., *ad loc.*

[105] Cf. Harnack Miss.[4] (1924), 259 ff.

female. For you are all one in Christ Jesus. If you are Christ's, then you are the seed of Abraham (Gl. 3:26 ff.; cf. 1 C. 12:13; Col. 3:11). If it is not actually said that you are all the one new λαὸς θεοῦ, this is the thought implied.

It is thus an important concern of the apostle to emphasise the unity of the new λαός which is present in the Christian community and which transcends all the frontiers of the λαοί and ἔθνη. But this has nothing whatever to do with the inclination of the popular philosophy of the time, and of unhistorical and inorganic "Enlightenment" thinking, to disregard and dissolve the natural and historical distinctions between the peoples and their inner biological and social groupings. The saying in Gl. does not ignore the difference between the sexes. It cannot be used as the slogan of a feminist movement. 1 Cor. shows plainly how remote such deductions are from the thinking of the apostle. Similarly, it has nothing to do with a rationalistic obliteration of the given national groupings of the race. It would certainly be false to say that the NT is unfamiliar with the thought of the race as a unity. The term → κόσμος often means humanity. On the other hand, it is equally false to make this the starting-point for a view which would set aside as unimportant the given distinctions between the nations. Ἕκαστος ἐν τῇ κλήσει ᾗ ἐκλήθη, ἐν ταύτῃ μενέτω (1 Cor. 7:20) — this saying applies to national as well as social differences. One cannot deduce from the great truth of Gl. 3:26 ff. that the Jew must become a Greek or the Greek a Jew. To be sure, Paul was a Greek to the Greeks. But he had no thought of surrendering his national consciousness as a Jew. Nor did he require a similar surrender of Greeks. The distinctions remain and are acknowledged in their own national and historical sphere. But they lose their emphasis in the sphere of the Christian community. The all-transcending unity of the λαός neither can nor should be disrupted by them. For it rests on faith in the one κύριος Χριστός.

This caused serious difficulties even in the apostolic period. For in Judaism a religiously coloured and grounded national consciousness struggled against this de-emphasising of national distinctiveness in the Christian community and thus brought about the first serious crisis. The main struggle of Paul is against this nationalism. He repudiates a levelling of all distinctions, but with the same definiteness he stresses that the unity of the community must not be shattered by any national distinctiveness. For this reason he insists that there must be fellowship at table, and at the Lord's Table, between the two parties at Antioch. For the serious Jew, even though he was a Christian, it must have been a hard decision to set aside the regulations which in the time of his national religion had come down to him with his flesh and blood and which forbade him to have table fellowship with non-Jews. But Paul insisted, and saw to it, that the unity of the new λαός on the basis of faith in the one κύριος should be demonstrated in this way. The national and historical distinctions between men and human groups have no place in the Christian community. They have lost their religious significance, and therewith their power to separate. Nationality is no longer a condition of belonging to God.

7. Related Transfers. The transfer of the title λαός (sc. θεοῦ), the nation of God, from Israel to the Christian community is only one of the forms which express the certainty of early Christianity that it possesses and is the fulfilment of OT prophecy, the realisation of the goal of the religion of Israel, the essential reality corresponding to the figurative intimation. If Christ is the fulfilment toward which the Law and prophets move, His community is the true λαός (sc. θεοῦ),

the true Israel of God (Gl. 6:16; 1 C. 10:18; R. 9:6), the true seed of Abraham (Gl. 3:29; cf. R. 9:7 f.), the true circumcision (Phil. 3:3), the true temple (1 C. 3:16), the true קְהַל יהוה (→ ἐκκλησία). It is the true λαός within which God dwells and which has access to Him because, sanctified by Christ, it is holy. In all these phrases there is expressed with unsurpassable succinctness a certainty which historically binds the Christian community and its religious heritage just as firmly to the OT community as it divides it from this preliminary and superseded stage on the basis of the redemptive act of God in Christ.

F. λαός in the Usage of the Early Church.

In the literature of the early Church we find again the primitive Christian uses, first, the popular ("crowd," "population," "people"),[106] then the national for "nations" in general (along with ἔθνη), then the specific for Israel (as distinct from the ἔθνη),[107] then the figurative for Christians and the Christian community, which is often called the λαὸς καινός in contrast to the λαὸς πρεσβύτερος or παλαιός or πρῶτος Israel.[108] How strong was the awareness that the Christian community was a new people of salvation from a twofold historical root may be well seen in an observation of Cl. Al. (Strom., VI, 5, 42, 2): ἐκ γοῦν τῆς Ἑλληνικῆς παιδείας, ἀλλὰ καὶ ἐκ τῆς νομικῆς εἰς τὸ ἓν γένος τοῦ σῳζομένου συνάγονται λαοῦ οἱ τὴν πίστιν προσιέμενοι.

The expression λαός is often used for the congregation assembled in worship (as distinct from the leaders). Cf. Just. Ap., I, 67, 5: When the prayer is ended ὁ λαὸς ἐπευφημεῖ λέγων· τὸ Ἀμήν, and Cl. Al. Strom., I, 1, 5, 1: ᾗ καὶ τὴν εὐχαριστίαν τινὲς διανείμαντες, ὡς ἔθος, αὐτὸν δὴ ἕκαστον τοῦ λαοῦ λαβεῖν τὴν μοῖραν ἐπιτρέπουσιν. This is the Christian continuation of a usage which is found already in Ac. 13:15 with ref. to synagogue worship and also in the pre-Christian period. It is an adaptation of popular use to the specific relationships of the congregation, and the idea of the "laity" developed from it later.

Strathmann

† λάρυγξ

"Larynx," also "gullet," though the proper word for the latter is φάρυγξ.[1] The two were not precisely distinguished, however, and it may be noted that the English "throat" is not a very exact term. Etym. M. says: Λάλυγξ μὲν δι' οὗ λαλοῦμεν καὶ ἀναπνέομεν· φάρυγξ δὲ δι' οὗ ἐσθίομεν καὶ πίνομεν (to which a third πόρος also belongs). Did the Greek catch an echo of the verbal stems λεγ- and φαγ-?

Both λάρυγξ and φάρυγξ are used in the LXX both for the gullet (חֵךְ and מַלְקוֹחַ: Job 6:30 and Cant. 7:9 [10] also suggest in some way the palate) and for the larynx

[106] E.g., Herm. s., 8, 1, 2-5; Cl. Al. Paed., II, 1, 18, 2: David gave a feast παντὶ τῷ ὑπηκόῳ ... λαῷ.

[107] E.g., Sib., 8, 13: The Roman Empire θεσμοὺς θήσει λαοῖς; 8, 12: Rome will drag βασιλεῖς ἐθνῶν to the west; 8, 278: At the feeding twelve baskets are filled εἰς ἐλπίδα λαῶν; 2, 42: πᾶς λαός, i.e., every people = all peoples; 2, 160: The earth is μήτηρ λαῶν; 8, 252: Moses overcame Amalek by faith ἵνα λαὸς (Israel) ἐπιγνῷ; 3, 249: λαὸς ὁ δωδεκάφυλος; 1 Cl., 55, 6; Barn., 8, 1; 12, 6; Herm. v., 2, 3, 4; Dg., 11, 3: God sent the λόγος who ὑπὸ λαοῦ (Israel) ἀτιμασθείς ... ὑπὸ ἐθνῶν ἐπιστεύθη.

[108] E.g., Barn., 5, 7; 7, 5; 13, 1; Cl. Al. Paed., I, 5, 19, 4; 20, 3; 7, 57, 1; 59, 1; III, 11, 75, 3.

λάρυγξ. [1] On λάρυγξ and φάρυγξ *v.* Wettstein on R. 3:13; H. Güntert, *Über Reimwortbildungen im Arischen u. Altgriech.* (1914), 119 [Kleinknecht]. Güntert takes the view that the later λάρυγξ is another form of the Homeric φάρυγξ by association with λάπτω "to lick" or λαφύσσω "to swallow." He discusses other derivations.

(גָּרוֹן). λάρυγξ occurs 17 times (limited to 4 OT books) and φάρυγξ 9 times. There is a par. tradition only at Cant. 2:3 (LXX λάρυγξ, Σ φάρυγξ). λάρυγξ is used 3 times for the palate to which the tongue cleaves, 5 times for the gullet and 9 for the larynx.

An important verse is ψ 5:9 [2] since this is the only verse with λάρυγξ quoted in the NT. The comparison with an open grave seems to suggest the gullet (swallowing), [3] but the commentaries have rightly taken גָּרוֹן here, too, as an instrument of speech. H. Hupfeld [4] thinks the image is suggested by the view of the throat. H. Herkenne [5] finds in the verse a chiastic structure according to which the throat, as the hidden instrument of speech, is parallel to the inner parts. He gives an excellent rendering: "Their opened throat, for all its friendly words, spews out death and destruction."

The use of the verse in R. 3:13 leaves the sense unaltered, for the other quotations from the Ps. are all concerned with sins of speech. Words reveal inward depravity, just as the breath of corruption comes from the entrance to a tomb. [6]

It is worth noting that Luther in his lectures on Romans treats this verse very fully and even indulges in detailed allegorisation. For him the throat is that which kills and swallows.

If in the Scripture proofs in R. 3:10-18 the mouth plays so important a role as the revealer of inward wickedness, this reminds us of the teaching of Jesus in Mk. 7:15, 18-23. What defiles a man is not what goes into him, but what comes out of him; there then follows a list of individual evils which it is rewarding to compare with R. 3.

Hanse

† λατρεύω, † λατρεία

Contents. A. λατρεύω and λατρεία in Non-Biblical Greek: 1. λατρεύω: a. Etymology, Basic Meaning and Occurrence; b. Use; 2. λατρεία. B. λατρεύω and λατρεία in the LXX: 1. λατρεύω: a. Occurrence, Hebrew Equivalents and Basic Character; b. Use; 2. λατρεία; 3. Comparison of Non-Biblical and LXX Usage; 4. Philo's Usage. C. λατρεύω and λατρεία in the New Testament: 1. λατρεύω: a. Occurrence; b. The Purely Religious Character of the Word as Determined by the LXX; c. λατρεύω of the Sacrificial Ministry, Obliteration of the Distinction between λατρεύω and λειτουργέω in Hb.; d. λατρεύω of the Ministry of Prayer; e. λατρεύω in a Generalised Figurative Sense; 2. λατρεία.

A. λατρεύω and λατρεία in Non-Biblical Greek.

1. λατρεύω.

a. Etymology, Basic Meaning and Occurrence. λατρεύειν comes from λάτρον, "reward," "wages"; cf. λάτρις, "hireling," more generally "servant"; cf. also the Lat.

---

[2] In ψ 13:3 ℵ[1] and B (not A) have introduced the text of R. 3:13-18 and the quotation from ψ 5:9.

[3] Cf. Ign. R., 4, 2 and Wettstein, *ad loc.*

[4] *Die Psalmen übersetzt u. ausgelegt*[3] (1888).

[5] *Das Buch d. Ps. übersetzt u. erklärt* (1936) (Bonner Bibel).

[6] Note should be taken of the γέμει of v. 14 (cf. Mt. 23:27). Cf. B. Weiss, *Der Brief an die Römer* (1899), 153, *ad loc.*

λατρεύω κτλ. On lexical aids → under λαός. W. Sanday and A. C. Headlam in ICC on R. 1:9; W. Brandt, "Die Wortgruppe λειτουργεῖν im Hb. u. bei Cl. Romanus," *Jbcher. d. Theolog. Schule Bethel* (1930), 145 ff.; H. Wenschkewitz, "Die Spiritualisierung der Kultusbegriffe," *Angelos Beih.*, 4 (1932).

latro, "robber."[1] Hence the first meaning of λατρεύειν is "to work or serve for reward," then "to render services," "to serve," with no thought of reward and irrespective of whether the one who serves is a slave or free. The oldest instance seems to be an Eleusinian inscr. from the 6th cent.; cf. CIG, I, 11 = Ditt. Syll.[3], 9. The word was not very common. It is not found in Homer nor in Plato and Aristotle. It does not occur in the indexes on Thuc., Polyb., Dio C. by E. A. Bétant (1843/47), J. Schweighäuser (1822) and U. P. Boissevain (1931). Its use in Sophocles, Xenophon, Isocrates, Epictetus, Lucian and Plutarch is only occasional. It occurs only once in the whole of CIG (CIG, IV) acc. to the index of H. Roehl, and in Ditt. Or. and Ditt. Syll.[3] only in the inscr. mentioned above. Acc. to Preisigke's lexicon it is not found at all in the pap.

b. Use. It is used of bodily services (Soph. Trach., 35 of Heracles: τὸν ἄνδρ᾽ ἔπεμπε λατρεύοντα), of workers on the land (Solon, 13, 48, ed. T. Bergk, Poetae Lyrici Graeci, II[5] [1915]), of slavery (Xenoph. Cyrop., III, 1, 36). It is also used figuratively in many different connections, cf. λατρεύειν νόμοις (Xenoph. Ag., 7, 2), λατρεύειν τῷ κάλλει ("to cherish," Isoc. 10, 57), λατρεύειν μόχθοις ("to have to suffer," Soph. Oed. Col., 105), λατρεύειν καιρῷ ("to fit the time," Ps.-Phocylides, 121 [ed. Bergk, p. 98]), λατρεύειν ἡδονῇ (Luc. Nigrinus, 15). In some cases it is used of the service of the gods, e.g., in Eur. Ion, 152 and Plut. Pyth. Or., 26 (II, 407e), where the ὑπηρέται καὶ προφῆται who stand in the service of the Pyth. Apollo are called θεῷ λατρεύοντες. Cf. also Epict. Diss., III, 22, 56: κυνικῷ δὲ Καῖσαρ τί ἐστιν ἢ ἀνθύπατος ἢ ἄλλος ἢ ὁ καταπεπομφὼς αὐτὸν καὶ ᾧ λατρεύει, ὁ Ζεύς; But θεραπεύειν is much more common here. Though the word is rare, its potentialities are thus very large. There are no impulses towards the development of a usage which is even remotely technical.

2. λατρεία.

The noun λατρεία is rather more common. It first means service for reward. Suidas defines it as δουλεία ἐπὶ μισθῷ. It then means service, work, labour generally. Cf. Soph. Trach., 830: ἐπίπονον ἔχειν λατρείαν (of Heracles); Eur. Tro., 823 f. (of the service of the cupbearer): Ζηνὸς ἔχεις κυλίκων πλήρωμα, καλλίσταν λατρείαν), Plut. Romulus, 19 (I, 30a): γυναῖκες ... παντὸς ἔργου καὶ πάσης λατρείας, πλὴν ταλασίας (spinning wool) ἀφειμέναι, Plut. Bruta Animalia Ratione Uti, 7 (II, 990c): Men are ὠνούμενοι μισθοῦ καὶ πόνου καὶ λατρείας τὸ τῆς γενέσεως ἔργον, Plut. Cons. ad Apoll., 11 (II, 107c) of the travail of human life: πῶς οὐκ εὐδαιμονίζειν μᾶλλον προσήκει τοὺς ἀπολυθέντας τῆς ἐν αὐτῷ (τῷ βίῳ) λατρείας, ἢ κατοικτείρειν; Plut. Cons. ad Apoll., 25 (II, 114d) of the laborious care of the body: The dead man is ἀπαλλαγεὶς τῆς τοῦ σώματος λατρείας, Plut. Quaest. Conv., V, 1 prooem (II, 673a): The soul of the dead is πραγμάτων ἀπαλλαγεῖσα καὶ λατρείας, Plut. Def. Orac., 15 (II, 417)e: πλάναι θεῶν, κρύψεις τε καὶ φυγαὶ καὶ λατρεῖαι (in the sagas of the gods — which Plut. would rather ascribe to demons). Special note should be taken of the fact that λατρεία can be used for the worship of the gods. Cf. Plat. Ap., 23c (διὰ τὴν τοῦ θεοῦ λατρείαν); Phaedr., 244e (καταφυγοῦσα πρὸς θεῶν εὐχάς τε καὶ λατρείας); Plut. Adulat., 12 (II, 56e) (εὐσέβεια καὶ θεῶν λατρεία); Is. et Os., 2 (II, 352a) (ἄθρυπτοι [without any luxury] ... ἐν ἱεροῖς λατρεῖαι, of the cultic and ritual preparations for the reception of initiates in the worship of Isis). λατρεία also has a cultic ref. in its one occurrence in the pap, cf. Preisigke Sammelbuch, 1934, 3. The picture is thus exactly the same as in the case of λατρεύειν.

B. λατρεύω and λατρεία in the LXX.

1. λατρεύω.

a. Occurrence, Hebrew Equivalents and Basic Character. The word occurs a round 90 times in the LXX. The distribution is remarkably uneven. For 70 of these instances

---

[1] Acc. to Prellwitz Etym. Wört. and Boisacq from the root *lē:la*, but the etym. is uncertain, Walde-Pok., II, 394.

are in Ex. (17), Dt. (25), Jos. (19) and Ju. (9). The word does not occur at all in the prophets (apart from Ez. 20:32), Ps., S. (apart from 2 S. 15:8) or Παρ. (apart from 2 Παρ. 7:19). This is connected with the method of translation. With a few unimportant exceptions λατρεύω is always used for the Heb. עָבַד.[2] But this word is also very frequently rendered δουλεύειν. It is to be noted that the books which frequently have λατρεύειν use it mostly when עבד has a religious reference, cf. Ex. 3:12; 4:23; 7:16, 26; 8:16; 9:1, 13; 10:3, 7, 8, 24, 26; 20:5; 23:24, 25; Dt. 4:19, 28; 5:9; 6:13; 7:4, 16; Jos. 22:27; 24:14-24, 31. When the ref. is to human relations, the rendering is always δουλεύειν, cf. Ex. 14:5, 12; 21:2, 6; Dt. 15:12, 18; Ju. 3:8, 14; 9:28, 38; and consistently in Gn. In these writings δουλεύειν is used in the religious sense only at Ex. 23:33 (τοῖς θεοῖς); Dt. 13:5 (αὐτῷ, namely, Yahweh, but only in A); 28:64 (θεοῖς ἑτέροις); Ju. 2:7 (τῷ κυρίῳ); 10:6a, 6b, 10, 13, 16 (τοῖς Βααλίμ, θεοῖς ἑτέροις, τῷ κυρίῳ, in B; A always has λατρεύειν except at 10:6b). Conversely, λατρεύειν is always used in these writings in the religious sense. The translators of these books thus attempted to show even by their choice of words that the relation of service in religion is something apart from other relations of service. In the other writings, where the term λατρεύειν hardly occurs at all, there is no such concern. Here δουλεύειν is used almost uniformly for עבד no matter whether the relation is religious or secular. Nevertheless, λατρεύειν is distinctively religious not only in the books where it is chiefly found but wherever it appears in the LXX. The only exception is Dt. 28:48: λατρεύσεις τοῖς ἐχθροῖς σου. But this proves the rule. For here there is a play on words. Because Israel was not willing to "serve" the Lord, who sought only its good, it must "serve" its enemies, who destroy it.[3]

b. Use. The religious connotation of λατρεύειν is not to be taken, however, merely in a general, abstract, spiritual or ethical sense. It is not enough to say that λατρεύειν has religious significance. One must say that it has sacral significance. λατρεύειν means more precisely to serve or worship cultically, especially by sacrifice. Moses is told that the purpose of the Exodus from Egypt is (Ex. 3:12): λατρεύσετε τῷ θεῷ ἐν τῷ ὄρει τούτῳ, namely, in cultic acts, and especially in sacrifices. The whole conflict between Moses and Pharaoh in Ex. 4-10 hinges on the demand of 7:16: Let my people go ἵνα μοι λατρεύσῃ ἐν τῇ ἐρήμῳ (4:23; 7:26; 8:16; 9:1, 13; 10:3, 7, 8, 24, 26). That sacrifices are meant is amply shown by the parallel θύειν κυρίῳ in 8:4 and by the reason for the requirement that the cattle should be taken in 10:26: ἀπ' αὐτῶν γὰρ λημψόμεθα λατρεῦσαι κυρίῳ τῷ θεῷ ἡμῶν. Similarly, definite cultic acts are in view in 2 Βασ. 15:8 when Absalom declares that he will τῷ κυρίῳ λατρεύειν in Hebron in fulfilment of a vow.

The term can be used indifferently of the cultic worship of the God of Israel (e.g., Ex. 23:25; Dt. 6:13; 10:12, 20; 28:47; Jos. 22:27; 24:14, 15; 2 S. 15:8 etc.) or of the worship of εἴδωλα or θεοὶ ἕτεροι or ἀλλότριοι or τῶν ἐθνῶν or τῶν πατέρων ὑμῶν (e.g., Ex. 20:5; 23:24; Dt. 4:28; 5:9; 7:4, 16; 8:19; 11:16, 28; 12:2; 29:17; Jos. 24:14 f.; Ju. 2:19; 4 Βασ. 17:12; 21:21; 2 Ch. 7:19), or concretely of

---

[2] It is twice used for שֵׁרֵת (Nu. 16:9, the Levites serve the Israelites in the cultus; Ez. 20:32, λατρεύειν ξύλοις καὶ λίθοις; cf. → λειτουργεῖν, B. 1. b.); once for הָיָה עֹבֵד, (2 K. 17:33, with no distinction from עבד); once for הָלַךְ אַחַר (Dt. 11:28). In the 6 or 7 passages in Daniel the equivalent is פְּלַח or אִיתַי פָּלַח.

[3] A second exception is Da. 7:14: πᾶσα δόξα αὐτῷ (the Son of Man) λατρεύουσα. He has the βασιλεία. Θ here correctly reads γλῶσσαι for δόξα and translates δουλεύσουσιν.

Melech, Baal or Baalim (e.g., Lv. 18:21;[4] Ju. 2:11, 13; 3:7; 4 Βασ. 7:16). It can also be used of the worship of the ruler, i.e., Nebuchadnezzar (Jdt. 3:8).

The demand continually made upon Israel is that it should not offer worship to these gods but to Yahweh alone, thereby recognising His position as Lord. But if the primary reference of the term is to cultic worship, this is only an expression of the inner attitude, of confident committal to Yahweh, of conduct. This is particularly evident in the way in which the word is quite naturally expounded in this sense in Dt. 10:12 ff. The passage speaks of a λατρεύειν κυρίῳ τῷ θεῷ σου ἐξ ὅλης τῆς καρδίας σου καὶ ἐξ ὅλης τῆς ψυχῆς σου. But this is to demonstrate itself in fear (10:12), in love (11:1) and in keeping the commandments and statutes of Yahweh, also in swearing only in His name. Hence circumcision of σκληροκαρδία is demanded. Also required, of course, is the exclusive cultic worship of Yahweh alone. But the term λατρεύειν is not exhausted by this. It goes much deeper and involves the demand for right disposition of the heart and the demonstration of this in the whole of religious and moral conduct. Here is indeed the true uniqueness of the religion of Israel. The term has the same implications in Jos. 24:19, since here very generally τὰ ἁμαρτήματα καὶ τὰ ἀνομήματα ὑμῶν form the antithesis to the λατρεύειν demanded by Joshua. Much later λατρεύειν seems to be freed from any idea of cultic worship and wholly spiritualised in Sir. 4:14, where there is reference to the ministry of wisdom (οἱ λατρεύοντες αὐτῇ).[5]

If λατρεύειν is thus used more or less exclusively for cultic worship, though naturally with the profounder understanding of Israelite prophecy, it is apparently very closely related to the term → λειτουργεῖν. But only apparently! The two words are very clearly distinguished, for λατρεύειν always denotes the religious conduct of the people generally, including, of course, that of the priesthood, whereas λειτουργεῖν is wholly restricted to priestly functions and is even a tt. for them. There is only one exception. According to 1 Εσδρ. 4:54 Darius orders delivery to the priests in Jerusalem καὶ τὴν ἱερατικὴν στολήν, ἐν τίνι λατρεύουσιν ἐν αὐτῇ. Here one would have expected λειτουργεῖν according to the normal rules of the LXX.

2. λατρεία.

λατρεία occurs only 9 times in the LXX (including the Apocrypha), and so far as the Heb. is available always corresponds to עֲבֹדָה. With one exception the meaning is always cultic. It denotes very generally cultic worship (Jos. 22:27) or else specifically a single practice, namely, the Passover (Ex. 12:25, 26; 13:5). In 1 Macc. it is always used for religion, cf. 2:19: ἀποστῆναι ἀπὸ λατρείας πατέρων, 2:22: ἡ λατρεία ἡμῶν, 1:43, of the unity of religion forced on the nations by Antiochus Epiphanes. Once λατρεία means the priestly ministry, cf. 1 Παρ. 28:13: τὰ λειτουργήσιμα σκεύη τῆς λατρείας οἴκου κυρίου, though just before λειτουργία is used for the same word עֲבֹדָה. Perhaps λατρεία is here introduced merely for the sake of variety. It is also used once in a non-cultic sense at 3 Macc. 4:14: ἡ τῶν ἔργων κατάπονος λατρεία, of the compulsory service of the Jews.

---

[4] Here the LXX reads: ἀπὸ τοῦ σπέρματός σου οὐ δώσεις λατρεύειν ἄρχοντι. It has rightly read לְמֶלֶךְ, but does not make plain what is meant.

[5] Cf. Σ Is. 32:17: λατρεία τῆς δικαιοσύνης.

In the LXX, then, the use of λατρεία is fully parallel to that of λατρεύειν. In the two passages adduced by Trench[6] Augustine finely sums up the matter: λατρεία ... *secundum consuetudinem, qua locuti sunt qui nobis divina eloquia condiderunt, aut semper aut tam frequenter ut paene semper ea dicitur servitus quae pertinet ad colendum deum* (Civ. D., X, 1, 2). *At illo cultu, quae graece λατρεία dicitur, latine uno verbo dici non potest, cum sit quaedam proprie divinitati debita servitus nec colimus nec colendum docemus nisi unum deum* (Faust., 20, 21; CSEL, 25 [1891], 562, 24/7).

3. Comparison of Non-Biblical and LXX Usage. Comparison with non-biblical usage shows that the LXX more or less completely rejects other possible meanings and concentrates on the cultic use, but in such a way that the terms λατρεύειν, λατρεία are hardly at all used for the priestly ministry, but for cultic worship in general. For this non-biblical Greek prefers θεραπεύειν, θεραπεία. But the LXX uses these in a religious sense only at Is. 54:17 and Da. 7:10; elsewhere they have the sense of healing or cherishing. Nor is δουλεύειν considered as a term for general cultic worship. If it was desired to isolate a word for this use (and the LXX constantly shows this tendency), then λατρεύειν had to be the choice.[7]

4. Philo's Usage. In Philo, acc. to Leisegang's index, λατρεύειν occurs only once at Spec. Leg., I, 300 in a paraphrase of Dt. 10:12 f. It means cultic worship, and thus follows LXX usage. In the first instance the same is true of the noun, which occurs six times. Philo uses it in Spec. Leg., II, 167 in the plur. for individual cultic duties and in Decal., 158 in the sing. as a comprehensive term. He also uses it (cf. λατρεύειν in Sir. 4:14) metaphorically of the ministry of virtue (Sacr. AC, 84) and of the spiritual service of God (Ebr., 144: νοῦς λατρείᾳ καὶ θεραπείᾳ θεοῦ μόνῃ χαίρων, where the combination of λατρεία and θεραπεία, obviously felt to be similar words, is to be noted). Finally, it occurs in a secular sense, equivalent to ὑπηρεσία, in Spec. Leg., III, 201 and II, 67: αἱ ἀπὸ τῶν οἰκετῶν λατρεῖαι καὶ ὑπηρεσίαι. Here Philo leaves the LXX world and accommodates himself to non-biblical usage.

C. λατρεύω and λατρεία in the New Testament.

1. λατρεύω.

a. Occurrence. λατρεύειν occurs in the NT 21 times, of which 8 are in Luke (Lk. 1:74; 2:37; 4:8; Ac. 7:7, 42; 24:14; 26:7; 27:23), 6 in Hb. (8:5; 9:9, 14; 10:2; 12:28; 13:10), 4 in Paul (R. 1:9, 25; Phil. 3:3; 2 Tm. 1:3), 2 in Rev. (7:15; 22:3) and 1 in Mt. (4:10). Three of these verses derive from the OT (Mt. 4:10; Lk. 4:8; Ac. 7:7). The particularly strong usage in Hb. corresponds to the significance of cultic ideas in this epistle.

b. The Purely Religious Character of the Word as Determined by the LXX. The influence of the LXX may be seen in the fact that the word never refers to human relations, let alone to secular services. The ministry denoted by λατρεύειν is always offered to God (or to heathen gods: ἐλάτρευσαν τῇ κτίσει παρὰ τὸν κτίσαντα, R. 1:25; τῇ στρατιᾷ τοῦ οὐρανοῦ, Ac. 7:42). Both in the OT and the NT (in spite of the dominant use of the word as a tt.) λειτουργεῖν, λειτουργία always enable us to detect the broader potentialities of usage found in non-biblical Greek, but in neither OT nor NT is this true of λατρεύειν.

---

[6] Trench, *s.v.*

[7] Cf. the note on this in Cr.-Kö.

c. λατρεύω of the Sacrificial Ministry. Obliteration of the Distinction between λατρεύω and λειτουργέω in Hb. According to LXX usage the primary reference of λατρεύειν is to the sacrificial ministry which is to be offered to Yahweh in contrast to other gods. This usage recurs in Ac. 7:7 (cf. Ex. 3:12); 7:42 (cf. Jer. 7:18 LXX); also R. 1:25. A similar reference is to be seen in Hb. at 8:5; 9:9; 10:2; 13:10. But the distinction between λειτουργεῖν (priestly sacrificial ministry) and λατρεύειν (cultic worship generally), which is so strict in the LXX except at 1 Εσδρ. 4:54, is now obliterated. For in Hb. 8:5 and 13:10 λατρεύειν refers primarily to the sacrificial ministry of the priests. According to 8:5 the earthly sacrificial ministry in the tabernacle is a ὑποδείγματι καὶ σκιᾷ τῶν ἐπουρανίων λατρεύειν, since the true tabernacle is in heaven. Similarly, the priests are described as οἱ τῇ σκηνῇ λατρεύοντες in 13:10. The more precise meaning of the verse is contested.[8] It need not concern us here. For there is in any case no doubt that the phrase has the priests in view and not the Jewish community in general, no matter what deductions are made from what is said about the priests. Again, the λατρεύειν of Hb. 9:9 refers, not just to participants in the cultus, but to the priests who offer sacrifice. This is clear from the fact that in the λατρεύων of this verse there is further reference only to the ἱερεῖς τὰς λατρείας ἐπιτελοῦντες of 9:6. The λατρεύοντες in Hb. 10:2 are also the priests. The LXX translators would certainly have chosen λειτουργεῖν in all these cases, cf. the way in which the λατρεύειν of 8:5 is taken up in the λειτουργία of 8:8, cf. also 10:11.

d. λατρεύω of the Ministry of Prayer. In the other NT verses the reference of λατρεύειν is to the cultic worship of praise and prayer which all may offer, or else the word is used in an extended, loose and almost figurative or spiritualised sense to include every form of divine worship.

In the sense of adoration λατρεύειν occurs in the temptation story (Mt. 4:10; Lk. 4:8; cf. Dt. 6:13), where it stands in antithesis to the προσκυνεῖν demanded by the tempter; cf. also Rev. 7:15 (of the blessed martyrs who serve God day and night in His temple) and Rev. 22:3. But the unwearying prayer of Anna in the temple (Lk. 2:37) and the incessant supplication of Israel for the fulfilment of the promise (Ac. 26:7) are also called λατρεύειν, and indeed in the second of these two verses the word simply means "to pray." The verses are worth noting because the dative to denote the recipient is absent. The word is thus used here as a tt. for the ministry of prayer.

e. λατρεύω in a Generalised Figurative Sense. The comprehensive use of λατρεύειν for the whole conduct of the righteous towards God is found first in Lk. 1:74. Zacharias confidently awaits the time when God will grant that, undisturbed by the oppression of enemies, we may λατρεύειν αὐτῷ ἐν ὁσιότητι καὶ δικαιοσύνῃ ἐνώπιον αὐτοῦ. The worship of God to which he here looks forward with yearning is impossible without a true holiness and a keeping of the commandments which is valid in God's eyes too. λατρεύειν then has the same comprehensive sense in Ac. 24:14, where Paul gives the assurance that he serves the God of the fathers. Though this λατρεύειν now takes place κατὰ τὴν ὁδὸν ἣν λέγουσιν αἵρεσιν, i.e., according to the standard of the Gospel, this does not imply any loss of fidelity to the Law and the prophets. Part of the service is that he strenuously exerts himself (ἀσκῶ), ἀπρόσκοπον συνείδησιν ἔχειν πρὸς τὸν

---

8 Cf. *NT Deutsch,* III (1935), *ad loc.*

θεὸν καὶ τοὺς ἀνθρώπους διὰ παντός. Cf. also Ac. 27:23 (τοῦ θεοῦ οὗ εἰμι, ᾧ καὶ λατρεύω, ἄγγελος) and 2 Tm. 1:3 (χάριν ἔχω τῷ θεῷ, ᾧ λατρεύω ἀπὸ προγόνων ἐν καθαρᾷ συνειδήσει). Hb. 12:28 may be cited in this connection. We receive, says the author, an incorruptible kingdom. This pledges us to gratitude (ἔχωμεν χάριν), δι' ἧς λατρεύωμεν (vl. λατρεύομεν) εὐαρέστως τῷ θεῷ, μετὰ εὐλαβείας καὶ δέους. A manner of life which is pleasing to God, and which is sustained both by gratitude and by a serious sense of responsibility — this is Christian τῷ θεῷ λατρεύειν. The word thus serves as a transition to the admonitory section which follows (c. 13). Perhaps the λατρεύειν of Hb. 9:14 also belongs here. The blood of Christ will purge our conscience from dead works εἰς τὸ λατρεύειν θεῷ ζῶντι. Purging of the conscience implies remission of sins (cf. v. 22). One possible rendering is that the Christian now has the ability to come to God, to approach Him, like the priest in sacrificial ministry. In this case there is a figurative reference to priestly λατρεύειν. But another possible meaning is that the goal and result of this purging of conscience is a new manner of life which is true λατρεύειν θεῷ ζῶντι (cf. 12:28). In this case the term is used as in Lk. 1:74.

R. 1:9 has in view the same active religious service except that here the reference is specifically to Paul's missionary work. In R. 1:9 Paul, asserting his unceasing remembrance of the Roman Christians in prayer, calls God to witness, ᾧ λατρεύω ἐν τῷ πνεύματί μου ἐν τῷ εὐαγγελίῳ τοῦ υἱοῦ αὐτοῦ. The conclusion of this observation can only mean that the apostle's service is rendered in the sphere of preaching the Gospel of the Son of God (ἐν τῷ εὐαγγελίῳ as in 2 C. 8:18; 10:14). Hence Paul refers to his missionary work. He calls this a λατρεύειν, an act of religious service, of the worship which he offers to God. Worth noting is the addition ἐν τῷ πνεύματί μου. Paul obviously does not mean that his missionary service is rendered inwardly. Does he mean, then, that his service is rendered "through his spirit," and by "his spirit" does he mean the Holy Spirit imparted to him, i.e., the Spirit of God? But why does he not say this? And what is the point of describing his apostolic office as a charisma in this context? Another suggestion is that he is emphasising that he does this work with his whole heart. But would he express this in the phrase in question? Perhaps two thoughts are present, first, that Paul's λατρεύειν, or service, is rendered outwardly in his missionary work, and second, that it is also rendered in his prayer life, the chief concern of which is, of course, the progress of his missionary work. In this case there is a measure of oscillation in the term λατρεύειν. Paul serves and worships God, he renders divine service, actively in the proclamation of the message and inwardly in intercession for the churches and for the progress of the Gospel.[9] This thought would supply the reason for Paul's appealing to God as witness of his intercession. As an inner process, this is concealed from the congregation but well known to God.

Finally, in Phil. 3:3 we again find λατρεύειν in a broad metaphorical sense in which it comprises the whole of Christian existence. Paul contrasts himself and Christians with the Judaisers, for whom he has very sharp words. We are the true circumcision οἱ πνεύματι θεοῦ (vl. θεῷ) λατρεύοντες. They put confidence in the flesh. Their whole worship of God is in the flesh. Christians worship God through the Spirit of God.[10] This is not to be restricted to prayer. It includes all

[9] Cf. Khl. R. and Zn. R., *ad loc.*
[10] The variation in readings does not affect the sense.

that to which we are impelled by the Spirit. The Christian life fashioned by the Spirit is true λατρεία.

λατρεύειν means to worship cultically. In the OT its primary reference is to the sacrificial cultus. In the NT, however, this is almost completely secondary, except in Hb. It gives place to the ministry of prayer, and then more broadly to the total view according to which the whole life of the Christian is fundamentally brought under the concept λατρεύειν, so that he alone seems to be capable of a λατρεύειν, a worship of God, which is worthy of the name. The cultic concept is now spiritualised.[11]

2. λατρεία.

Of the five occurrences of this word in the NT, three refer to the sacrificial ministry. In R. 9:4, with the giving of the Law and the promise, λατρεία, the sacrificial cultus, is one of the religious advantages which accrue to Israel. The δικαιώματα λατρείας of Hb. 9:1 are cultic ordinances. In Hb. 9:6: οἱ ἱερεῖς τὰς λατρείας ἐπιτελοῦντες, the ordinances are again those of the sacrificial ministry. In Jn. 16:2: ἔρχεται ὥρα ἵνα πᾶς ὁ ἀποκτείνας ὑμᾶς δόξῃ λατρείαν προσφέρειν τῷ θεῷ, the word λατρεία virtually means sacrifice, as shown by the verb προσφέρειν. The concrete idea of sacrifice seems always to cling to the noun no less than to the verb. This is also true in the last verse (R. 12:1), though the use here is metaphorical. The service which Christians are to offer consists in the fashioning of their inner lives and their outward physical conduct in a way which plainly distinguishes them from the world and which corresponds to the will of God. This is the living sacrifice which they have to offer. Using a term which was current in the philosophy of his day,[12] Paul describes this sacrifice as a λογικὴ λατρεία, a service of God which corresponds to human reason, in which, however, divine reason is also at work. If man listens to the voice of reason, he must acknowledge that this is the true service of God. The biblical history of the cultic term λατρεία reaches its climax in this interiorisation, which is also the most comprehensive exteriorisation, and which takes up again the initial prophetic statement in Dt. 10:12 ff. The saying of Paul in R. 12:1 ff. is the crown of this whole development.

Strathmann

† λάχανον[1]

Mostly in the plur., "edible plants," "vegetables," which are grown in the field or garden (λαχαίνειν, "to grub up"),[2] sold on the market (τὰ λάχανα for the vegetable market: Aristoph. Lys., 557; Alexis Fr., 46, 8 [CAF, II, p. 314] etc.) and prepared in the kitchen: from Cratinus Fr., 313 (CAF, I, p. 104); Plat. Resp., II, 372c: βολβοὺς καὶ λάχανά γε, οἷα δὴ ἐν ἀγροῖς ἑψήματα, Athen., II, 81 (69 f.): ἑψητά; also λάχανα ἄγρια, Aristoph. Thes., 456, Pl., 298; Jos. Bell., 5, 437; ἄγρια λάχανα: "Αλλοι (except for 'ΑΣ) at 4 Βασ. 4:39 (for אֹרֹת plants, LXX ἀριώθ). They are characterised botanically in Aristot. De Plantis, I, 4, p. 819b, 8 ff.; Theophr. Hist. Plant., I, 3, 1.

---

[11] Cf. the leading ideas in Wenschkewitz, *op. cit.*
[12] Cf. Ltzm. R., *ad loc.*

λάχανον. [1] Liddell-Scott, Pass., Preisigke Wört., *s.v.*
[2] Walde-Pok., II, 381.

For vegetarian diet, Philostr. Vit. Ap., I, 8; Diog. L., VIII, 20 (38); Preis. Zaub., I, 104 (as distinct from fish and swine's flesh); in medical lit. there are many works with the title περὶ λαχάνων, Diocles in Galen (ed. Kühn, XVIII, 1, p. 712), Chrysippus (fragments in Pliny the Elder), [3] Euthydemus (Athen., II, 53 [58 f.] etc.). In the LXX for יֶרֶק (or יָרָק), Gn. 9:3 : λάχανα χόρτου, ψ 36:2 : λάχανα χλόης (cf. also 'A Gn. 1:30), 3 Βασ. 20:2 : κῆπος λαχάνων (cf. also Dt. 11:10 : κῆπος λαχανείας). The simplicity of vegetable fare, Prv. 15:17.

In the NT we read in Mk. 4:32 par. Mt. 13:32 that the mustard seed, the smallest seed of all, [4] becomes greater than all herbs (hyperbolically a tree in Mt. and Lk.). [5] So the rule of God, after a hidden and insignificant start, will miraculously embrace all the nations of the world. [6]

Lk. 11:42: ἀποδεκατοῦτε τὸ ἡδύοσμον καὶ τὸ πήγανον καὶ πᾶν λάχανον. [7] To pay tithes on garden plants goes beyond the provisions of the Torah (Dt. 14:22 f.). It derives from Rabbinic tradition, which appeals to Lv. 27:30. [8] Strict observance of tithing requirements distinguishes the Chaberim from the Amhaarez. [9] The saying does not attack the practices of the Pharisees but the Pharisees themselves, since under the cloak of rigorous legal observance they really evade the true demand of God (παρέρχεσθε τὴν κρίσιν καὶ τὴν ἀγάπην τοῦ θεοῦ).

In R. 14:2 [10] Paul, who is probably taking up slogans of the Roman church, describes a group of the "weak" (→ I, 491) as vegetarians (ὁ δὲ ἀσθενῶν λάχανα ἐσθίει). For them the eating of flesh — and the drinking of wine (v. 21) — were unclean (v. 14). For this reason they were offended by the free manner of life of the "strong," and condemned them. That this group was Jewish in origin may be concluded from the fact that according to 14:5 their practices included the observance of days (of which the chief was surely the Sabbath), and also from the fact that when Paul takes up again the requirement of 14:1 in 15:7 he sets it in the context of the relation of περιτομή and ἔθνη (vv. 8 ff.). Consistent vegetarianism, as distinct from occasional fasting, was alien to official Judaism in the form represented in the Roman church, [11] but it may be found in some movements within syncretistic Judaism. [12]

---

3 Cf. Pauly-W., III, 2 (1899), 2509 f.

4 The smallness of the mustard seed is proverbial (examples in Str.-B., I, 669).

5 Whether the version in Mt. and Lk. is to be taken hyperbolically depends on the identification of the species as *sinapis nigra* or *salvadora persica*. Only in the former case (which is to be preferred) is it to be reckoned with the γένος λαχανῶδες (Theophr. Hist. Plant., VII, 1, 1 f.). Cf. Kl. Mk., *ad loc.*

6 The figure of a tree which provides shelter and habitation for a world kingdom is common in the OT, Ez. 17:22 f.; 31:6; Da. 4:9, 18.

7 Mt. 23:23 has instead ἡδύοσμον, ἄνηθον and κύμινον. This must correspond to Q, since שְׁבָרָא (πήγανον) can be read for שְׁבֵתָא (ἄνηθον) (E. Nestle, ZNW, 7 [1906], 261) and πήγανον is expressly excluded from the tithe (Shebi., 9, 1). On the tithing of kitchen vegetables cf. b AZ, 7b; Maas., 1, 1; 4, 5.

8 S. Lv. on 27:30; Str.-B., IV, 653.

9 Str.-B., II, 498, 500.

10 Cf. E. Riggenbach, "Die Starken u. Schwachen in d. römischen Gemeinde," ThStKr, 66 (1893), 649 ff. M. Rauer, "Die 'Schwachen' in Korinth und Rom . . .," BSt, 21, 2/3 (1923), 76 ff.

11 Isolated instances (as an expression of sorrow) and also criticism, are to be found in passages like T. Sota, 15, 11-15; bBB, 60b Bar.; Str.-B., III, 307 f.; II, 523.

12 E. v. Dobschütz, *Die urchr. Gemeinden* (1902), 93 ff., 274 ff.; H. Strathmann, *Geschichte d. frühchristl. Askese . . .*, I (1914), *passim* ; Ltzm. R., Exc. on R. 14:1; P. R. Arbesmann, "Das Fasten bei d. Griechen u. Römern," RVV, 21, 1 (1929), 29 ff.; J. Haussleiter, "Der Vegetarismus in d. Antike," RVV, 24 (1935).

In the early history of religion and philosophy there are many instances of the practice and promotion of vegetarianism.[12] It is one of the basic principles of the Orphics, though in the Orphic mysteries the sacramental eating of raw flesh, taken from the Thracian Dionysus cult, also has a place (Porphyr. Abst., IV, 19; Orph. Fr. [Kern] Testimonia, 90, 212, 213, 215). It is also a principle of the Pythagoreans (Iambl. Vit. Pyth., 24, 107 f.),[13] who in this respect are influenced by the Orphics (cf. Empedocles), of some later Academics like Xenocrates (Cl. Al. Strom., VII, 32, 9) and Plutarch (cf. his tractate on the eating of meat [II, 993-999]). Among the Stoics it was espoused by Seneca (esp. Epistulae Morales, XVIII, 5 [108], 17 ff.) and Musonius (p. 57 ff., 94 ff. [Hense]), both under Neo-Pythagorean influence (Diog. L., VIII, 20 [38]), the school of Sextius (Sen., *loc. cit.*), Apollonius of Tyana (Philostr. Vit. Ap., I, 8) and the Neo-Platonists (cf. Porphyr., 4 books περὶ ἀποχῆς ἐμψύχων). Vegetarianism is also found in the circles of Hermetic mysticism,[14] the Therapeutae (Philo Vit. Cont., 37), probably the Essenes[15] and Gnostic sects (Ebionites, Ps.-Clem. Hom., 8, 15; 12, 6; Epiph. Haer., 30, 15, 3), the Encratites (Iren. Haer., I, 28, 1), the followers of Saturninus (Hipp. Ref., VII, 28), the Marcionites (Tertullian Marc., I, 14), the Manicheans (Aug. Faust., XX, 23; De Moribus Ecclesiae Catholicae et de Moribus Manichaeorum, II, 16 [MPL, 32]). Finally, a vegetarian regime is part of the normal asceticism in apocryphal stories of the apostles and monks. The reasons advanced for the practice are many, an early belief in the transmigration of souls, Orphic ideas of purification, mantic asceticism, and later predominantly the motives of humanitarianism, hygiene and dualistic asceticism.

Of the reasons for the vegetarianism and abstinence of the Roman Christians we know nothing beyond what is told us in 14:14. The parallel discussions in 1 C. 8 and 10 seem to suggest that in Rome, too, there was fear of contact with pagan sacrifices. Yet in R. 14 we do not find the decisive terms εἴδωλον, εἰδωλεῖον, εἰδωλόθυτον which would justify this assumption. Hence we must be content to say that this is a religious vegetarianism on general grounds. Certainly in both R. 14 f. and 1 C. 8 ff. Paul quickly disposes of the general question of the "intrinsic" (R. 14:14) rights or wrongs of freedom or abstinence (cf. R. 14:6, 17 and 1 C. 8:8; 10:19, 25 f.), replacing it by responsible concern for that which is "another's" (1 C. 10:24; cf. R. 14:19 ff.; 15:1 ff.). In both epistles, then, the criteria by which the question is to be decided are love, edification and regard for the conscience of the other (as opposed to giving offence). The toleration with which Paul treats the weak in Rome and Corinth shows that we are not to think in terms of the proponents of an error (as in Gl. 4:10; Col. 2:16, 21; 1 Tm. 4:3). If he forbids them to judge others by their own practice, he also recognises their allegiance to conscience and the danger of arbitrarily breaking this allegiance. Hence he enjoins the strong to take this allegiance of the weak into account.

Bornkamm

13 Further instances, including some which disprove the unconditional vegetarianism of Pythagoras and his disciples, are to be found in Haussleiter, 97 ff.

14 Cf. J. Kroll, *Die Lehren des Hermes Trismegistos* (1914), 343.

15 Haussleiter, 37 ff.

† λεγιών

λεγιών, borrowed from the Lat. *legio* from the time of Diod. S., XXVI, 5 (ed. L. Dindorf, IV [1867]); λεγεών is also found,[1] and once (CIG, III, 6627) λεγειών. It is explained in Plut. Romulus, 13 (I, 24d): ἐκλήθη δὲ λεγεὼν τῷ λογάδας εἶναι τοὺς μαχίμους ἐκ πάντων, Otho, 12 (I, 1072a): ... λεγεῶνες (οὕτω γὰρ τὰ τάγματα Ῥωμαῖοι καλοῦσιν), Nicolaus of Damascus, Vita Caesaris, 31 (F. Jacoby, *Die Fr. d. griech. Historiker,* II A [1926], p. 419, 6). On inscr. from the time of the Triumvirate, e.g., the Ephes. inscr. of a tribune λεγεῶνος ἕκτης Μακεδονικῆς,[2] cf. Ditt. Syll.[3], 805 etc.; CIG, I, 1327, 9 f.; III, 4011, 5; III, 4029, 10. It is very common in the pap., e.g., P. Oxy., II, 276, 9 (λεγεὼν δευτέρα); BGU, I, 140, 6 (λεγιὼν τρίτη). It does not occur in the LXX, or Joseph., who uses τάγμα, or Philo. But *legio* was adopted in Palestine: לְגִיוֹן, e.g., מְלָכִים וְלִגְיוֹנוֹתֵיהֶם = οἱ βασιλεῖς καὶ οἱ λεγιῶνες αὐτῶν, Tanch. לך לך 17 (p. 37b, Buber), and also of individual soldiers: The Levites הֵם לִגְיוֹנוֹתַי = αὐτοί εἰσιν οἱ λεγιῶνές μου, Tanch. במדבר 17 (p. 8a, Buber).[3] In the imperial period a Roman legion consisted of about 6000 men on foot and 120 on horse, to which the *auxilia* should be added, i.e., technical branches and special troops.[4]

In the NT the word occurs only in the story of the demoniac in Mk. 5:9 = Lk. 8:30; Mk. 5:15, and in the story of the arrest of Jesus, Mt. 26:53.

In the MSS there is alternation between λεγιών and λεγεών, e.g., at Mk. 5:9 λεγιών S* B* C D L it vg syr[utr] cop, λεγεών AB[2]. In Mk. 5:15 the words τὸν ἐσχηκότα τὸν λεγιῶνα (A C λεγεῶνα) do not occur in D 17, 27 it vg, but they should be retained in view of their ample attestation in other MSS (cf. Tisch. NT, I, *ad loc.*).

It is to be noted that λεγιών as a military unit is used in the NT only of non-human beings, whether demons (Mk. 5:9, 15 = Lk. 8:30), or angels (Mt. 26:53). That is to say, it is used only of beings which represent something powerful, unparalleled and extraordinary which can force man. These beings may be angels which belong to the world of God and which point to God's goodness. But they may also be demons which come from the world of darkness and which remind us of the dark oppression and confusion of the world.[5]

Like the Syncretism of the time, Judaism also believed that the angelic armies were made up of hosts beyond computation.[6] Equally common to the world of Syncretism and Jewish conviction was the idea that the multitude of evil spirits could not be counted.[7] This popular belief underlies the legion sayings in the NT. The name legion

---

λεγιών. [1] Mostly abbreviated λεγ, so that it is hard to say whether ι or ε is earlier. Transition from ι to ε would result from the Lat. pronunciation of i, which is close to the Gk. ε; this probably gave rise to a good deal of confusion between the letters. Cf. W. Dittenberger, Herm., 6 (1872), 129 ff.; T. Eckinger, *Die Orthographie lat. Wörter in griech. Inschr.* (Diss. Zürich, 1892), 29 f.; C. Wessely, "Die lat. Elemente in d. Gräzität d. ägypt. Papyrusurkunden," *Wiener Studien,* 24 (1902), 99 ff.; Ditt. Or. Index; A. P. M. Meuwese, *De rerum gestarum Divi Augusti versione Graeca* (Diss. Amsterdam, 1920), 15.

[2] Cf. A. v. Domaszewski in *Jahreshefte des Österreichischen archäologischen Instituts in Wien,* II (1899), *Beiblatt,* col. 81-86.

[3] Schl. Mt., *ad loc.*

[4] Pauly-W., XII (1924), 1196 (Art. *Legio*).

[5] → II, 1 ff.; Str.-B., IV, 501 ff.

[6] Bousset-Gressm., 325 f.; Str.-B., I, 997, 682.

[7] Bousset-Gressm., 338.

for a demon is not found in any passage independent of Mk. [8] It is certainly a striking name, nor can we explain it in terms of the Rabbinic use of לגיון for the individual legionary, [9] for the point is surely that the sick man is possessed by many demonic spirits, cf. Mk. 16:9; Mt. 12:45 = Lk. 11:26; Lk. 8:2, but that these constitute a single power, Mt. 12:45 = Lk. 11:26, so that the name λεγιών is given in answer to the question of Jesus. [10] The power of demonic forces is thereby intimated. In Mt. 26:53 the 12 legions which God, if He willed, might send to liberate Jesus bear witness both to the omnipotence of God which far transcends all human power and also to the saving love of God. The hosts of men, whether they be the temple guard or the Roman legions which were so much feared by the Jews, are confronted by the heavenly legions with the unique power of God Himself.

An important point in both stories is that λεγιών is used only in relation to Jesus as the embodiment of the δύναμις θεοῦ, as the Son of Man. Because He is the υἱὸς τοῦ θεοῦ, the heavenly legions are at His side, and He shows Himself to be Lord over demonic forces even when they are present as legions. Thus in the NT the word λεγιών is not used for the military world, as elsewhere. It is used to denote transcendent forces. It thus shows us where the Church militant has to fight its war, namely, where the struggle is between the kingdom of God and demonic powers (cf. Eph. 6:12).

Preisker

λέγω, λόγος, ῥῆμα, λαλέω, λόγιος, λόγιον, ἄλογος, λογικός, λογομαχέω, λογομαχία, ἐκλέγομαι, ἐκλογή, ἐκλεκτός

λέγω, λόγος, ῥῆμα, λαλέω.

Contents: A. The Words λέγω, λόγος, ῥῆμα, λαλέω in the Greek World: 1. λέγω: a. The Basic Meaning of the Root; b. "To gather," c. "To count," d. "To enumerate," e. "To narrate," "to say"; 2. λόγος: a. "Collection"; b. "Counting," "reckoning." i. "Calculation," ii. "Account," iii. "Consideration," "evaluation," iv. "Reflection," "ground,"

---

8 O. Bauernfeind, *Die Worte d. Dämonen im Mk.-Ev.* (1927), 26.

9 With Kl. and Schl. Mk., *ad loc.* as opposed to Str.-B., II, 9.

10 Hence the alternation between the sing. (Mk. 5:8: τὸ πνεῦμα, v. 9: αὐτόν, σοι, μοι, v. 10: παρεκάλει) and the plur. (v. 9: ἐσμεν, v. 10: αὐτά, v. 12: παρεκάλεσαν, ἡμᾶς, v. 13: αὐτοῖς, πνεύματα).

λέγω κτλ. On the whole field: R. H. Grützmacher, *Wort u. Geist, eine historische u. dogmatische Untersuchung* (1902); M. Kähler, *Dogmatische Zeitfragen,* I: *Zur Bibelfrage*[2] (1907); K. Barth, *Das Wort Gottes u. die Theologie* = *Gesammelte Vorträge,* I[2] (1925); W. Vollrath, *Das Problem des Wortes* (1925); H. W. Schmidt, *Zeit u. Ewigkeit* (1927); E. Schaeder, *Das Wort Gottes* (1930); *Deutsche Theologie,* III (*Bericht über den Breslauer Theologentag* [1931]); K. Heim, *Jesus der Herr* (1935), 167-201. On A: Pass., Liddell-Scott, Cr.-Kö., Pr.-Bauer[3], *s.v.*; J. H. H. Schmidt, *Synonymik d. griech. Sprache,* I (1876), 1 ff.; E. Hofmann, *Qua ratione* ΕΠΟΣ, ΜΥΘΟΣ, ΑΙΝΟΣ, ΛΟΓΟΣ ... *in antiquo Graecorum Sermone ... adhibita sint* (Diss. Göttingen, 1922). On B: M. Heinze, *D. Lehre vom Logos in d. griech. Philosophie* 1872); G. Teichmüller, *Neue Studien zur Geschichte der Begriffe,* I (1876), 167 ff. and *pass.*; A. Aall, *Geschichte d. Logosidee: in d. griech. Philosophie* (1896), *in d. christ. Lit.* (1899); H. J. Flipse, *De Vocis quae est* ΛΟΓΟΣ *Significatione atque Usu* (Diss. Vrije Univ. Amsterdam, 1902); F. E. Walton, *Development of the Logos-doctrine in Greek and Hebrew Thought* (1911); E. Hoffmann, "Die Sprache u. d. archaische Logik," *Heidelberger Abh. z. Philosophie u. ihrer Geschichte,* III (1925); H. Leisegang, Art. "Logos" in Pauly-W., XIII (1927), 1035-1081; "Der Logos als Symbol,"

"condition"; c. κατάλογος: "enumeration," "catalogue"; d. λόγος: "narrative," "word," "speech," etc. 3. ῥῆμα; 4. λαλέω, λαλιά. B. The Logos in the Greek and Hellenistic World: 1. The Meaning of the Word λόγος in its Multiplicity; 2. The Development of the λόγος Concept in the Greek World: a. The Two Sides of the Concept; b. Heraclitus; c. The Sophists; d. Socrates and Plato; e. Aristotle; 3. The λόγος in Hellenism: a. Stoicism; b. Neo-Platonism; c. The Mysteries; d. The Hermes-Logos-Theology, Hermeticism; 4. The λόγοι of Philo of Alexandria; 5. Hellenistic Logos Speculation and the New Testament. C. The Word of God in the OT; 1. The Hebrew Equivalents of the Greek Terms for Word; 2. The General Use of דָּבָר as a Rendering of λόγος and ῥῆμα; 3. The דָּבָר of Prophetic Revelation: a. Revelation in Sign; b. Revelation in Sign and Word; c. Dissolution of the Sign; d. The Writing Prophets; 4. The דָּבָר as Revelation of Law; 5. The Divine Word of Creation; 6. The Word in Poetry. D. Word and Speech in the New Testament: 1. Basic and General Aspects of the Use of λέγω/λόγος; 2. More Specific and Technical Meanings; 3. The Sayings of Jesus: a. The Quotation of the

---

Blätter f. Deutsche Philosophie, 1 (1927/28), 292 ff.; J. Stenzel, "Zur Theorie des Logos bei Aristoteles," *Quellen u. Studien zur Geschichte d. Mathematik,* B. I (1931), 34 ff.; G. Bornkamm, "Ὁμολογία, Zur Geschichte eines politischen Begriffes," Herm., 71 (1936), 377 ff. On C: OT Theol. by E. König[3, 4] (1923), 75 ff.; E. Sellin[2] (1936), 50 ff.; W. Eichrodt, II (1935), 32 ff.; L. Köhler (1936), 82 ff.; cf. also E. König, *Der Offenbarungsbegriff des AT* (1882); F. Giesebrecht, *Die Berufsbegabung d. at.lichen Propheten* (1897), 38 ff.; F. Buhl, "Über d. Ausdrücke f. Ding, Sache uä. im Semitischen," *Festschr. f. Vilhelm Thomsen* (1912); J. Szeruda, *Das Wort Jahwes* (1921); J. Hänel, *Das Erkennen Gottes bei den Schriftpropheten* (1923), 19 ff.; F. Haeussermann, *Wortempfang u. Symbol* (1932); K. Beyer, *Spruch u. Predigt bei d. vorexilischen Schriftpropheten* (Diss. Erlangen, 1933); O. Grether, *Name u. Wort Gottes im AT* (1934), 59 ff.; L. Dürr, "Die Wertung d. göttlichen Wortes im AT u. im antiken Orient, zugleich ein Beitrag zur Vorgeschichte des nt.lichen Logosbegriffes," *Mitt. d. Vorderasiatisch-Ägyptischen Ges.* 42, 1 (1938, after the conclusion of this art.). On D: E. Krebs, *Der Logos als Heiland* ... (1910); J. Schniewind, *Die Begriffe Wort u. Evangelium bei Pls.* (1910); H. Leisegang, *Der Heilige Geist,* I, 1 (1919), 67 ff.; R. Bultmann, "Der Begriff d. Wortes Gottes im NT," *Glauben u. Verstehen* (1933), 268-293; R. Asting, *Die Verkündigung des Wortes im Urchr.* (1938, after the conclusion of this art.). NT Theol. by H. J. Holtzmann, II[2] (1911), 437 ff.; J. Kaftan (1927), 201 f.; H. Weinel[4] (1928), 437 ff.; P. Feine[6] (1934), 338 ff.; F. Büchsel (1935), 153 f. On D. 13:-15.: Comm. on Jn. 1:1-14 by Bau., Zn., Schl., F. Büchsel in *NT Deutsch,* R. Bultmann (1937/8, after the conclusion of this art.); A. N. Jannaris, "St. John's Gospel and the Logos," ZNW, 2 (1901), 13-25; E. Schwartz, *Aporien im Vierten Ev.,* IV (NGG, 1908), 497-560; J. Lebreton, *Les Origines du Dogme de la Trinité*[2], *Bibliothèque de Théologie Historique,* VIII, 1 (1910), 41-73, 110-120, 143-152, 183-205, 495-506, 515-523; G. Vos, "The Range of the Logos-Title in the Prologue to the Fourth Gospel," *Princeton Theol. Review,* 11 (1913), 365 ff., 557 ff.; W. Bousset, *Kyrios Christos*[2] (1921), 304 ff., 316 ff.; C. F. Burney, *The Aram. Origin of the Fourth Gospel* (1922), 37 ff.; M. J. Lagrange, "Vers le Logos de St. Jean," Rev. Bibl., 32 (1923), 161 ff., 321 ff.; A. B. D. Alexander, "The Johannine Doctrine of the Logos," ExpT, 36 (1924/5), 394 ff., 467 ff.; C. F. Nolloth, *The Fourth Evangelist* (1925), 172 ff.; C. H. Dodd, *The Bible and the Greeks* (1935), Index *s.v.* λόγος; E. Hirsch, *Das Vierte Ev.* (1936), 101 ff.; *Studien z. Vierten Ev.* (1936), 44 f. On the Historical Problem (On D. 14.-15.): R. Reitzenstein, *Zwei religionsgesch. Fragen* (1901), 47-132: *Schöpfungsmythen u. Logoslehre*; J. Kroll, *D. Lehren d. Hermes Trismegistos* (1914), Index *s.v.* λόγος; G. P. Wetter, *Der Sohn Gottes* (1916); R. Reitzenstein, "D. mandäische Buch des Herrn der Grösse u. d. Evangelienüberlieferung," SAH (1919); Hell. Myst., Index *s.v.* λόγος; W. F. Albright, "The Supposed Babylonian Derivation of the Logos," JBL, 39 (1920), 143-151; R. Bultmann, "Die Bedeutung der neuerschlossenen mandäischen u. manichäischen Quellen f. das Verständnis des Joh.-Ev.," ZNW, 24 (1925), 100 ff.; H. H. Schaeder, "Der 'Mensch' im Prolog d. vierten Ev.," *Studien zum antiken Synkretismus aus Iran u. Griechenland = Studien der Bibliothek Warburg,* VII (1926), 306-341; F. Büchsel, *Joh. u. der hell. Synkretismus* (1928), 21 ff., 30 ff., 38 ff.; L. Schmid, *Joh.-Ev. u. Religionsgeschichte* (Diss. Tübingen, 1933), esp. 38 ff. Wisdom: F. Klasen, *Die at.liche Weisheit u. d. Logos d. jüdisch-alexandrinischen Philosophie* ... (1878); Hillen, *Die at.liche Chokma, der platonisch-philonische Logos u. d. chinesische Tao* (Programm Coesfeld, 1882); W. Schenke, "Die Chokma (Sophia) in d. jüdischen Hypostasenspekulation" (*Skrifter utgit av Videns-*

Sayings; b. The Authority of the Sayings; c. The Appeal to the Word of Jesus outside the Gospels; 4. The Old Testament Word in the New Testament; 5. The Special Word of God to Individuals in the New Testament: a. Simeon; The Baptist; b. The Apostolic Period; c. Jesus; 6. The Early Christian Message as the Word of God (outside the Johannine Writings): a. Statistics; b. Content; 7. The Character and Efficacy of the Early Christian Word (outside the Johannine Writings): a. The Word as God's Word; b. The Relation of Man to the Word; c. The Word as Spoken Word; 8. The Word in the Synoptic Account of Jesus; 9. The Word in the Synoptic Sayings of Jesus; 10. λόγος/λόγοι (τοῦ θεοῦ) in Revelation; 11. Jesus Christ the λόγος τοῦ θεοῦ; 12. 1 Jn. 1:1 ff.; 13. The Distinctiveness of the λόγος Saying in Jn. 1:1 ff.; 14. The Concern and Derivation of the λόγος Sayings in the Prologue to John, I: a. The Lack of Speculative Concern; b. The Allusion to Gn. 1:1; c. Other Connections; d. Relation to "Word" Speculations in the Contemporary World; 15. The Concern and Derivation of the λόγος Sayings in the Prologue to John, II: Logos and Torah.

A. The Words λέγω, λόγος, ῥῆμα, λαλέω in the Greek World.

It is hardly possible in this context to give a full history of the Greek words for "to say," "to speak," "to tell," "word," "speech" etc. such as that attempted by J. H. H. Schmidt, I, 1-112, or more briefly E. Hofmann, 120 ff. It must suffice to lay the foundation for the philosophical use of λόγος (→ B.) and for the use of the terms λέγω, λόγος, ῥῆμα and λαλέω in the OT and NT (→ C.D. → ῥῆμα, → λαλέω).

1. λέγω.[1]

a. The Basic Meaning of the Root. The basic meaning of *leg-* is "to gather." This may be seen from the Lat. as well as the Greek (→ b.),[2] for both the simple *legere* (e.g., *oleam, nuces,* also *vestigia, oram*) and the compounds *colligere, deligere* and

---

skapsselskapet i Kristiania, Historisk-Filosofisk Kl., 1912 No. 6 [1913]); H. Windisch, "Die göttliche Weisheit d. Juden u. d. paulinische Christologie," *Nt.liche Studien f. G. Heinrici* (1914), 220-234; J. R. Harris, *The Origin of the Prologue to St. John's Gospel* (1917); "Athena, Sophia and the Logos," *Bulletin of the J. Rylands Library,* 7 (1922), 56-72; R. Bultmann, "Der religionsgeschichtliche Hintergrund des Prologs zum Joh.-Ev.," *Eucharisterion, H. Gunkel-Festschr.,* II (1923), 1-26. Memra: Dalman WJ, I (1898), 187 f.; G. F. Moore, "Intermediaries in Jewish Theology: Memra, Shekinah, Metatron," HThR, 15 (1922), 41-55; F. C. Burkitt, JThSt, 24 (1923), 158 f.; Str.-B., II, 302-333; F. Aber, "Memra und Schechinah," *Festschr. z. 75 jähr. Bestehen des Jüd.-Theologischen Seminars Fraenckelscher Stiftung* (1929), II, 1-10; V. Hamp, *Der Begriff "Wort" in den aram. Bibelübersetzungen, Ein exegetischer Beitrag zum Hypostasen-Problem u. zur Gesch. der Logos-Spekulationen* (1938, after the conclusion of this art.). Torah: A. Schlatter, "Die Sprache u. Heimat d. vierten Evangelisten," BFTh, 6, 4 (1902), 14 ff.; Schl. J., 1 ff.; Str.-B., II, 353-362; K. Bornhäuser, *Das Joh.-Ev., eine Missionsschrift f. Israel* (1928), 5-13. Philo: H. Soulier, *La Doctrine du Logos chez Philon d'Alexandrie* (Diss. Leipzig, 1876); J. Reville, *La Doctrine du Logos dans le quatrième Évangile et dans les Oeuvres de Philon* (1881); P. Wendland, *Philo u. d. kynisch-stoische Diatribe = Beiträge zur Gesch. d. griech. Philosophie u. Religion* (1895), 1-75; E. Sachsse, "Die Logoslehre bei Philo u. bei Johannes," NkZ, 15 (1904), 747-767; J. d'Alma, *Philon d'Alexandrie et le quatrième Évangile* (1910); L. Cohn, "Zur Lehre vom Logos bei Philo," *Iudaica, H. Cohen-Festschr.* (1912), 303-331; E. Bréhier, *Les Idées philosophiques et religieuses de Philon d'Alexandrie*[2] (1925), 83-111; B. Kellermann, "Licht u. Logos bei Philo," *Lewi ben Gerson, Die Kämpfe Gottes,* II (1916), 307-336; E. Turowski, *Die Widerspiegelung des stoischen Systems bei Philo von Alex.* (Diss. Königsberg, 1927), 6 ff.; cf. also F. Überweg-K. Praechter, *Grundriss d. Geschichte d. Philosophie,* I: *Die Philosophie des Altertums*[11] (1920), 209 ff.

[1] E. Hoffmann, 77 ff.

[2] Cf. A. Ernout-A. Meillet, *Dictionnaire Étymologique de la Langue Latine* (1932), 507 ff.

eligere have kept this meaning,[3] which may also be seen in the Albanian *mb-l'eθ*, "gather," "reap."[4] To gather is to pick out things which from some standpoint are alike.[5] It implies on the one side "succession," "repetition," and on the other "judgment," "logical separation." Both ideas are broadly developed in λέγω and λόγος.

b. λέγω is very common in the sense "to gather," e.g., in Hom. ὀστέα (Il., 23, 239), or αἱμασιάς (material for a wall, Od., 18, 359), also mid. "to assemble" (λέξασθαι, Il., 2, 125) and "to collect for oneself" (ὀστέα, Il., 24, 793; ξύλα, 8, 507 and 547; ἄνδρας ἀρίστους, Od., 24, 108 [κρινάμενος, by sifting]); so also the compounds, from the time of Hom. ἀνα-, "to glean" and συλ-, "to gather," and from the class. period ἀπο- and ἐκ-, "to select."

c. "To count." The material or mental gathering one after the other of similar things can often be linked with counting. Thus λέγω can sometimes mean "to count": Hom. Od., 4, 450 ff.: Proteus followed all the seals and counted them (λέκτο δ' ἀριθμόν), among them the Greeks (disguised as seals) (ἡμέας πρώτους λέγε).

d. "To enumerate," i.e., to recall from memory things of the same kind with a view to impartation. So in Hom. and his imitators (ἔργα, κήδεα, "sufferings," ὀνείδεα, "deeds of shame," πάντα, ταῦτα), also with κατα- (from Hom. Od., 16, 235; 22, 417), "to draw up," "to enter on a list," "to enlist" (soldiers). The enumeration usually aims at completeness, hence in Hom. (πᾶσαν) ἀληθείην καταλέξαι acc. to the basic sense of ἀλήθεια: "not concealing or forgetting anything" (→ I, 238), and without obj. with ἀτρεκέως (?), and in Hes. Theog., 627 with ἅπαντα διηνεκέως, "everything thoroughly."

e. "To narrate," "to say." Soon after Hom. a further step was taken, and the complete enumeration of things or events of the same kind became the narration, depiction or recounting of various matters, and then speaking in general.[6] Already in Hes. Theog., 27: ἴδμεν ψεύδεα πολλὰ λέγειν ἐτύμοισιν ὁμοῖα, it is better to translate "narrate" than "enumerate." Then we quickly find many passages in which λέγειν περί τινος means "to speak about something," Sappho Fr., 149 (Diehl, I, 387) and Xenophanes Fr., 8, 4 (I, 131, 10, Diels[5]), cf. λέγειν τι κατά τινος, Theogn., 1239 f. (Diehl, I, 180), λέγειν as the opp. of ᾄδειν from Anacr. Fr., 32 (Diehl, I, 456), ἅσσα λέγω, Xenophanes Fr., 34, 2 (I, 137, 3, Diels[5]). From the time of Pindar and the tragedians the word λέγειν is then common in many shades of meaning, with the acc. and infin. from Pind. Pyth., 2, 60: τῶν πάροιθε γενέσθαι ὑπέρτερον, with the acc. of person and object, esp. κακὰ (ἀγαθὰ) λέγειν τινά(ς), "to speak evil (good) of (to) someone," e.g., Hdt., VIII, 61; Aristoph. Eccl., 435 (also εὖ, κακῶς λέγειν τινά(ς), e.g., Aesch. Ag., 445; Soph. El., 524), with acc. of person and pred., "to name," e.g., Aesch. Ag., 896: λέγοιμ' ἂν ἄνδρα τόνδε with many predicates. With more precise content, "to mean or mention someone or something," e.g., Aristoph. Eq., 1021: ταυτὶ ... ἐγὼ οὐκ οἶδ' ὅ τι λέγει, Aesch. Prom., 946: τὸν πυρὸς κλέπτην λέγω ("I mean"); so also τι, οὐδὲν λέγειν, "to say something, nothing important": Soph. Oed. Tyr., 1475: λέγω τι; "am I right?", Aristoph. Thes., 625: οὐδὲν λέγεις, "nonsense!", Hdt., I, 124: τὰ γράμματα (writing) ἔλεγε τάδε, Plat. Ap., 24e, also πῶς λέγεις, "how do you think that?" Also very commonly λέγουσι, λέγεται, λέγονται, "it is said," Pind. Pyth., 5, 108: λεγόμενον ἐρέω, "I will say something which is commonly said." Of the orator, Isoc., 3, 8: ῥητορικοὺς καλοῦμεν τοὺς ἐν τῷ πλήθει λέγειν δυναμένους. δεινὸς λέγειν, "a skilled orator," e.g., Soph. Oed. Tyr., 545. Several

---

3 *Legere* = "to read" (something written) comes from "to take from the list by letters" (or names from a list etc.).

4 Walde-Pok., II, 422. The root has not been identified for certain in other Indo-European languages.

5 Hoffmann, 77.

6 Cf. "to tell" in relation to the German *zählen, erzählen, sagen,* also "tale" *Zahl* etc.

compounds are linked with this meaning, e.g., ἀντι-, "to contradict" (from the time of the tragic dramatists), ἀμφι(λ)- "to speak pro and con," "to debate about something," "to contest" (esp. in Doric inscr.), προ- "to foretell" (from Hdt. and Soph.), "to proclaim," "to make known" (from Pindar and the tragedians), διαλέγομαι "to talk together" (from Hdt.). With the transition to the sense "to speak," "to say," λέγειν approximates to εἰπεῖν and the root ῥη (→ 3.).[7] Cf. εἰπεῖν aor. "to make an utterance in speech," "to express" and λέγειν pres. ("to enumerate") "to narrate," "to depict," "to draw," e.g., εἶπε, "he made a proposition," ἔλεγε, "he made a speech," λέγε, λεγ', ὦ 'γαθέ, "speak on," Aristoph. Eccl., 213, λέγε δή, "speak about it," Plat. Phaedr., 271c, εἰπέ, "say it," "speak," "mention it" (e.g., εἶπ' ἄγε μοι καὶ τόνδε, φίλον τέκος, ὅστις ὅδ' ἐστίν, Hom. Il., 3, 192); cf. also Zeno Eleates Fr., 1 (I, 255, 19, Diels[5]): ἅπαξ τε εἰπεῖν καὶ ἀεὶ λέγειν. Because of its durative significance λέγειν is better adapted than the instantaneous εἰπεῖν to be the opp. of "to do," "to listen," or "to be silent," cf. Theogn., 1180 (Diehl, I, 177): Fear of the gods hinders man μήθ' ἔρδειν μήτε λέγειν ἀσεβῆ, Democr. Fr., 86 (II, 161, 5, Diels[5]): πλεονεξίη (presumption) τὸ πάντα λέγειν, μηδὲν δὲ ἐθέλειν ἀκούειν, Aesch. Sept. c. Theb., 619: φιλεῖ δὲ σιγᾶν ἢ λέγειν τὰ καίρια.

2. λόγος.[8]

Both in general and in detail the development of λόγος is exactly parallel to that of λέγω.

a. The sense "collection" (cf. 1. b.) is attested only of a number of compounds and derivatives,[9] e.g., σύλλογος, "gathering" (from Hdt. and the tragedians), παλίλλογος, "assembled again," Hom. Il., 1, 126, and in class. times often with -λόγος "assembling" (also → σπερμο-λόγος), and -λογεῖν, and cf. the Hell. → λογεία, λογεύειν.

b. "Counting," "reckoning." This sense, which one would expect from 1. c,, is very rare, cf. Aristoph. Nu., 619: τῆς ἑορτῆς μὴ τυχόντες (the gods) κατὰ λόγον τῶν ἡμερῶν (cf. Hdt., I, 47: ἡμερολογεῖν τὸν λοιπὸν χρόνον, "to count by days"), and the class. γενεαλογεῖν, "to count the generations" (→ I, 663; 665). Related, but also rare, is λόγος in the sense of "number," e.g., Hdt., III, 120: ἐν ἀνδρῶν λόγῳ, Thuc., VII, 56, 4: ὁ ξύμπας λόγος (?), "the totality," Aesch. Pers., 343: ὧδ' ἔχει λόγος (the number previously mentioned). Much more important is the sense of reckoning numbers (though there is nothing corresponding in the case of λέγειν). This is found from the beginning of the class. time, is common throughout the Greek world, and occurs frequently in the inscr. and pap.

i. "Calculation." It is used for accounts: Hdt., III, 142: λόγον δώσεις τῶν μετεχείρισας χρημάτων, 143: ὡς δὴ λόγον τῶν χρημάτων δώσων, IG, I² several times (from c. 434 B.C.; *v.* Index), IG, IV, 1485 (Epidauros, 4th cent. B.C.), 145, 151, 154, 155: λόγος λάμματος, "total income," 161, 173, 178, and 1487, 12 and 18: λόγος δαπάνας, "total expenditure." In Hellenistic Roman Egypt the written calculation becomes the account or balance or financial statement (Preisigke Wört., II, 33 f.).

ii. "Account." More generally the word can be used for an account of other than financial matters, e.g., Hdt., VIII, 100: The Greeks will inevitably become thy slaves δόντας λόγον (as they are punished) τῶν ἐποίησαν νῦν τε καὶ πρότερον, Plat. Polit., 285e: λόγον αἰτεῖν, Demosth. Or., 30, 15: λόγον ἀπαιτεῖν, Plat. Prot., 336c: λόγον δοῦναι καὶ δέξασθαι. → λογίζομαι and derivatives belong under i. and ii.

---

7 Hence the class. suppletive paradigm λέγω ἐρῶ εἶπον εἴρηκα εἴρημαι ἐρρήθην.
8 Cf. Hoffmann, 77 ff.
9 The simple λόγος seems to have been formed, then, only when the simple λέγω had come to have the predominant sense "to reckon," "to speak." Cf. E. Schwyzer, *Griech. Grammatik* = *Handbch. AW*, II, 1, 1 (1934), 31.

iii. From expressions like "to take account of" there arises the sense of "consideration," "review," "evaluation," "value," e.g., Heracl. Fr., 39 (I, 160, 2, Diels[5]): οὗ πλείων λόγος ἢ τῶν ἄλλων, Aesch. Prom., 231 f.: βροτῶν ... λόγον οὐκ ἔσχεν οὐδέν(α), so esp. the class. phrases ἐν (οὐδενὶ) λόγῳ ποιεῖν τινα or τι, (ἐλαχίστου, πλείστου, οὐδενὸς) λόγου γίγνεσθαι or εἶναι etc., ἄξιος λόγου, "worth noting," (also ἀξιόλογος), cf. also → λόγιος. Weaker, "respect," e.g., Thuc., III, 46, 4, ἐς χρημάτων λόγον.

iv. From i. and iii. it is an easy step to the meanings "reflection," "ground," "condition,"[10] which became important in everyday use and in philosophy, e.g., Aesch. Choeph., 515 : ἐκ τίνος λόγου, "on what ground," lit. from what calculation, Leucippus Fr., 2 (II, 81, 5 f., Diels[5]): Everything takes place ἐκ λόγου τε καὶ ὑπ' ἀνάγκης, "for a specific reason and under the pressure of necessity," Gorg. Fr., 11a, 37 (II, 303, 18 f., Diels[5]): ἔχει λόγον, "there is a reason," Hdt., III, 36 : ἐπὶ τῷδε τῷ λόγῳ ὥστε ..., "on the ground of deliberation," i.e., with a purpose, Plat. Gorg., 512c : τίνι δικαίῳ λόγῳ, "on what cogent ground," Hdt., VII, 158 : ἐπὶ λόγῳ τοιῷδε ("on the condition") τάδε ὑπίσχομαι, ἐπ' ᾧ ... ἐπ' ἄλλῳ δὲ λόγῳ οὔτ' ἂν αὐτὸς ἔλθοιμι οὔτ' ἂν ἄλλους πέμψαιμι, Democr. Fr., 76 (II, 159, 17, Diels[5]): νηπίοισιν οὐ λόγος ("rational consideration, understanding or persuasion," "good counsel" ?), ἀλλὰ ξυμφορὴ γίγνεται διδάσκαλος, Hdt., I, 132 and elsewhere: λόγος αἱρέει, "reason counsels." On the further development in philosophy → B.; cf. also → ἄλογος, → ὁμολογεῖν, → ἀναλογία.

c. καταλέγειν, "to count (up)," gives us κατάλογος, "list," "catalogue" (from the time of Aristoph. and Thuc.).

d. "Narrative," "word," "speech," etc. The starting-point, as in the case of λέγειν (→ 1. e.), is "narrative." Hom. has only this sense, and only in the plur.: Il., 15, 393 : τὸν ἔτερπε λόγοις, Od., 1, 56 f.: αἰεὶ δὲ μαλακοῖσι καὶ αἱμυλίοισι λόγοισιν θέλγει, then Hom. Hymn. Merc., 317 and Hes. Theog., 890, more freely Hes. Op., 78 and 789 : αἱμυλίους λόγους. Less clearly Hes. Op., 106 : εἰ δ' ἐθέλεις, ἕτερόν τοι ἐγὼ λόγον ("narrative" or "rational explanation" ?) ἐκκορυθώσω (will propound the main heads; there follows a description of the 4 ages of the world).[11] Yet immediately after the age of the ancient epic λόγος is used for "what is spoken" in the widest and most varied sense. In so doing it replaces ἔπος, which was taken from the Indo-European[12] to denote a "spoken utterance," the "word" (esp. the "idle" or "mere word" as distinct from the act),[13] and → μῦθος, the earlier word for "meaningful statement,"[14] "fable," "dictum."[15] ἔπος came to be almost completely limited to the sense of "verse" and μῦθος to be used only for (invented or not very well established) "history" in contrast to λόγος, (rationally established and constructed) "speech." The victory of λόγος is the result of the permeation of philosophical thinking in the transition from the heroic to the class. period.[16] Of the many nuances we may emphasise various kinds of utterance like "fable" (Plat. Phaed., 60d : οἱ τοῦ Αἰσώπου λόγοι), "legend" (Hdt., II, 62 : ἱρὸς λόγος), "ancient proverb" (Pind. Pyth., 3, 80 : εἰ δὲ λόγων συνέμεν κορυφὰν [the

---

[10] Cf. the Lat. *ratio*, "calculation," "consideration," then "ground," "cause."

[11] These are all the λόγος passages in ancient epic. Hom. Il., 4, 339 (καὶ σὺ κακοῖσι) λόγοισι (κεκασμένε), is an unconvincing variant for δόλοισι.

[12] Identical with the Sanscrit *vacas-* and the *vačah* ("speech," "word") of the Avesta; on the Indo-European root *u̯eku̯* "to speak," which is also present in εἶπον, ὄψ, Lat. *vox* = Sanscrit *vāc*, Lat. *vocare*, cf. Walde-Pok., I, 245.

[13] Hoffmann, 2 ff.

[14] Orig. "thought," cf. Slavic *mysli̇̆*, "thought," "opinion," Hoffmann, 47 f.

[15] Hoffmann, 28.

[16] The derivation from "narrative" is to be seen in the fact that grammatically λόγος (unlike ἔπος, λέξις, ῥῆμα, ὄνομα) is never used for a single word but only for an expression or sentence, Liddell-Scott, *s.v.* λόγος VI.

last sense] ... ὀρθὰν ἐπίστᾳ), "stories" (Hdt., I, 184: ἐν τοῖσι 'Ασσυρίοισι λόγοισι, Xenophanes, 7, 1 [I, 130, 19, Diels[5]]: ἄλλον ἔπειμι λόγον, a story in a dream, Hdt., I, 141), "command" (Aesch. Pers., 363: πᾶσιν προφωνεῖ τόνδε ναυάρχοις λόγον), "promise" (Soph. Oed. Col., 651: simple promise as distinct from formal oath), "good or evil reputation" (Pind. Isthm., 5, 13: λόγος ἐσθλός, Eur. Heracl., 165: λόγος κακός), "tradition" (Hdt., III, 32: διξὸς λέγεται λόγος, Soph. Trach., 1: λόγος μὲν ἔστ' ἀρχαῖος ἀνθρώπων φανείς, ὡς ..., often λόγος ἐστί, "the story is"); "written account," hence "writing" or part of such (Hdt., VI, 19: μνήμην ἑτέρωθι τοῦ λόγου ἐποιησάμην, v. 22: ἐν τοῖσι ὄπισθε λόγοισι ἀποδέξω, Plat. Parm., 127d: ὁ πρῶτος λόγος), "speech" as a work of art," e.g., ἐπιτάφιος λόγος, "funeral oration," Plat. Menex., 236b; "speech" as distinct from action (Democr. Fr., 145 [II, 171, 4, Diels[5]]: λόγος ἔργου σκιή; often λόγῳ μὲν ... ἔργῳ δέ), or from truth (Lyc., 23: ἵνα μὴ λόγον οἴησθε εἶναι, ἀλλ' εἰδῆτε τὴν ἀλήθειαν), or from silence (Pind. Fr., 180: σιγά is often better than λόγος); λόγοι, "conversation" (εἰς λόγους ἐλθεῖν, λόγους ποιεῖν etc.). Formally λόγος is the "utterance of thought in speech" (Plat. Soph., 263e: λόγος—διάνοια) "sentence" (Aristot. De Sophisticis Elenchis, I, p. 165a, 13: the opp. of ὄνομα "word"; among grammarians the μέρη τοῦ λόγου are the parts of a sentence or parts of speech), "prose" (Pind. Nem., 6, 30: opp. of ἀοιδαί, Plat. Resp., III, 390a: of ποίησις, poetry). Sometimes the account of a thing and the thing itself merge, so that λόγος can be translated "thing": [17] Theogn., 1055 (Diehl, I, 169): λόγον τοῦτον ἐάσομεν, Hdt., I, 21: σαφέως προπεπυσμένος πάντα λόγον, VIII, 65: μηδενὶ ἄλλῳ τὸν λόγον τοῦτον εἴπῃς, Soph. Oed. Tyr., 684: τίς ἦν λόγος (682: δόκησις ἀγνὼς λόγων), cf. 699 πρᾶγμα, Isoc., 4, 146: μηδένα λόγον ("material to be recounted") ὑπολιπεῖν.

Cf. the compounds and derivatives → ἄλογος, ἀντιλογία, ἀπολογεῖσθαι, → εὐλογεῖν.

3. ῥῆμα.

The root (ϝ)ερ- (ϝ)ρη [18] only exceptionally in Gk. forms a present, though the other tenses are common: fut. ἐρέω ἐρῶ, aor. pass. ἐρρήθην, Ion. εἰρέθην, Hell. ἐρρέθην, perf. εἴρηκα εἴρημαι. Thus the sense is clearly non-durative, "to state specifically." Of the derivatives [19] the same is true esp. of ῥήτρα (Aeolic ϝράτρα), "saying," "treaty," and the verbal adj. → ῥητός, "definitely stated," "expressly laid down." In related languages the verb is practically never found but the extension is ancient, e.g., Lat. *verbum.* Old Prussian *wirds,* Lithuanian *vardas* ("name"), German *Wort,* Eng. "word." ῥῆμα, [20] then, is what is definitely stated (at first usually in the plur.). Thus in solemn announcement, Archiloch. Fr., 52 (Diehl, I, 226): [ὦ] Λιπερνῆτες πολῖται, τἀμὰ δὴ ξυνίετε ῥήματ(α) (cf. Aristoph. Pax, 603: ὦ σοφώτατοι γεωργοί...), of military orders in the epigram of Simonides (Fr., 92 [Diehl, II, 94]) on the Spartans who fell at Thermopylae: τοῖς κείνων ῥήμασι πειθόμενοι, [21] but with the weaker sense of "statements," "words" already in Theog., 1152 = 1238b (Diehl, I, 174, 180): Do not change the friend δειλῶν ἀνθρώπων ῥήμασι πειθόμενος, Hdt., VIII, 83: τοῖσι δὲ Ἕλλησι ὡς πιστὰ δὴ τὰ λεγόμενα ἦν τῶν Τηνίων ῥήματα, Pind. Nem., 4, 94: ῥήματα πλέκων. So also in the sing., Pind. Pyth., 4, 277 f.: Of a statement of Hom., Hdt., VII, 162: ὁ νόος τοῦ ῥήματος, τὸ ἐθέλει λέγειν, Plat. Prot., 343b: τοῦ Πιττακοῦ, 342e: ῥῆμα ἄξιον λόγου βραχύ (pithy saying in contrast to long speeches, λόγοι). Words as distinct from deeds, Pind. Nem., 4, 6: ῥῆμα δ' ἐργμάτων χρονιώ-

---

17 Hoffmann, 111 f.; Liddell-Scott, *s.v.* λόγος VIII.
18 Walde-Pok., I, 283; Hofmann, 121.
19 Cf. ῥήτωρ, (public) "speaker"; ῥῆσις, "speech."
20 In poetry from Archilochus, in prose from Hdt.
21 Simonides Fr., 13, 16 f. (Diehl, II, 71): καί κεν ἐμῶν ῥημάτων λεπτὸν ὑπεῖχες οὖας, is obscure.

τερον βιοτεύει, Thuc., V, 111, 3: Men fall into misfortune because they submit to the ῥῆμα (previously ὄνομα ἐπαγωγόν, magically enticing word) of expected misfortune. Words as opposed to truth, Plat. Phaed., 102b: οὐχ, ὡς τοῖς ῥήμασι λέγεται, οὕτω καὶ τὸ ἀληθὲς ἔχειν; In Plato's time grammatical and philosophical thought[22] took over the word, at first with a fluid line of demarcation: Plat. Crat., 399b: ῥῆμα, syntactical connection as distinct from ὄνομα, material or personal connection (cf. Aeschin. Or., 3, 72: ῥῆμα, the wording of the whole saying, ὄνομα the offensive word in it), 431b: ὄνομα and ῥῆμα together form the sentence (λόγος), cf. 425a; Theaet., 206d: λόγος is the intimation of the thought μετὰ ῥημάτων τε καὶ ὀνομάτων, Soph., 262a: τὸ μὲν ἐπὶ ταῖς πράξεσιν ὂν δήλωμα (the rendering of acts in speech) ῥῆμά που λέγομεν ... τὸ δέ γ' ἐπ' αὐτοῖς τοῖς ἐκείνας πράττουσι σημεῖον τῆς φωνῆς ἐπιτεθὲν (the phonetic sign for the doers of the acts) ὄνομα,[23] and this distinction between ῥῆμα (active word) and ὄνομα (personal and material designation) led to the grammatical use of ῥῆμα for verb and ὄνομα for noun (from Aristot. Poët., 20, p. 1457a, 11 ff.). Except in this special sense the word does not seem to have lived on in the post-class. period, Ditt. Syll.³, 1175, 5 f., 18 f., 36 f. (cursing tablet from c. 300 B.C.): ῥῆμα μοχθηρὸν ἢ πονηρὸν φθέγγεσθαι, pap. only from the 3rd cent. A.D.[24]

4. λαλέω, λαλιά.

a. λαλέω and related words[25] like the Lat. *lallus* (the "nurse's crooning"), *lallare* ("to lull to sleep"), the Germ. *lallen* and the Eng. "lull" imitate the babbling of small children. Hence to use the word of the speech of adults is a sign of either intimacy or scorn: "to prattle," Aristoph. Eq., 348 (σεαυτῷ), Alexis Fr., 9, 10 (CAF, II, p. 300): λαλεῖν τι καὶ ληρεῖν πρὸς αὑτοὺς ἡδέως in a light whisper, Pherecrates Fr., 131, 2 (CAF, I, p. 183): μελιλώτινον (sweet as Melilotus) λαλῶν (cf. Fr., 2, 3 [CAF, I, p. 145]);[26] "to babble," Aristoph. Lys., 627: καὶ λαλεῖν γυναῖκας οὔσας ἀσπίδος χαλκῆς πέρι, Eccl., 1058: ἕπου ... δεῦρ' ἀνύσας καὶ μὴ λάλει. It is found as the opp. of rational normal speech (λέγειν):[27] Eupolis Fr., 95 (CAF, I, p. 281): λαλεῖν ἄριστος, ἀδυνατώτατος λέγειν, and to correct answering: Plat. Euthyd., 287d: λαλεῖς ... ἀμελήσας ἀποκρίνασθαι. So also of animal sounds as compared with human speech, Philemo Fr., 208 (CAF, II, p. 532): ἡ μὲν χελιδὼν τὸ θέρος, ὦ γύναι, λαλεῖ, Plut. De Placitis Philosophorum, V, 20, 4 (II, 909a): λαλοῦσι μὲν γὰρ οὗτοι (apes), οὐ φράζουσι, Theocr. Idyll., 5, 34: of the locust, Aristophon. Fr., 10, 6 (CAF, II, p. 280): of the grasshopper; also the sounds of musical instruments: Anaxandrides Fr., 35 (CAF, II, p. 149): μάγαδιν λαλήσω μικρὸν ἅμα σοι καὶ μέγαν, Aristot. De Audibilibus, p. 801a, 29: διὰ τούτων (flute etc.).

But λαλεῖν can also be used quite objectively of speech when there is reference to sound rather than meaning, Aristoph. Thes., 267: ἣν λαλῇς, of a man dressed as a woman,[28] Ra., 750 f.: παρακούων δεσποτῶν, ἅττ' ἂν λαλῶσι, Antiphanes Fr., 171, 2 (CAF, II, p. 80): ἀποπνίξεις δέ με καινὴν πρός με διάλεκτον (speech) λαλῶν, Alexis Fr. (CAF, II, p. 369): μετ' Ἀττικιστὶ δυναμένου λαλεῖν. It can even be used of understandable speech, Strato Fr., 1, 45 f. (CAF, III, p. 362): πλὴν ἱκέτευον αὐτὸν (the cook who used many unintelligible words) ἤδη μεταβαλεῖν ἀνθρωπίνως λαλεῖν

---

[22] H. Steinthal, *Geschichte d. Sprachwissenschaft bei d. Griechen u. Römern*, I² (1890), 137 ff.

[23] But in Tim., 49e τόδε is a ῥῆμα; cf. Aeschin. Or., 2, 122: κατὰ ῥῆμα (word for word) ἀκριβέστατα.

[24] Preisigke Wört., *s.v.*

[25] Walde-Pok., II, 376; cf. λαλαγέω, "to babble" (Pind.), "twitter," etc.

[26] Doubtful vl. Demosth. Or., 21, 118 λαλῶν, "gossiping," opp. λέγων καὶ καταιτιώμενος ταῦτα.

[27] Phryn. Anecd. Graec., I, p. 51, 3 (= Phryn. ed. J. de Borries [1911], p. 87, 15) defines λαλεῖν as φλυαρεῖν, λέγειν as ἱκανῶς λέγειν. Cf. → λαλιά.

[28] Herond., VI, 61: "ἐπὴν λαλῇ, one will know that it is Kerdo, not Prexinus."

τε, Ps.-Plat. Ax., 366d : of a crying infant which cannot yet express in words (λαλῆσαι) what it wants. "Speak of something" (acc.): Aristoph. Thes., 577 f.: πρᾶγμα λαλούμενον[29] ("of which one speaks"). "Ability to speak" as a characteristic of man. Aristot. Probl., XI, 1, p. 899a, 1: Only man λαλεῖ, Herond., IV, 32 f.: If it were not a stone statue, one would say : τοὔργον λαλήσει.[30] "To speak" as the opp. of "to be silent" : Simonides in Plut. Athen., 3 (II, 346 f.) calls poetry a ζωγραφία λαλοῦσα, and painting a ποίησις σιωπῶσα, Luc. Vit. Auct., 3 : ἡσυχίη μακρὴ καὶ ἀφωνίη καὶ πέντε ὅλων ἐτέων λαλέειν μηδέν.

In the compounds the meaning in the class. period is always "to prattle" or "babble" : δια-, Eur. Cyc., 175, ἐκ-, Eur. Fr., 219, 2 (TGF), Demosth. Or., 1, 26, Hippocr. Jusiurandum (IV, p. 630, Littré), κατα-, Aristoph. Ra., 752, περι-, Aristoph. Eccl., 230, Fr. 376 (CAF, I, p. 490), προσ-, Antiphanes Fr., 218, 3 (CAF, II, p. 107), Heniochus Fr., 4, 3 (CAF, II, p. 432).

b. λαλιά[31] is defined by Theophr. Char., 7, 1 as ἀκρασία τοῦ λόγου, "excess of speech," cf. also Ps.-Plat. Def., 416 (with the addition of ἄλογος), i.e., "talk," "chatter," Aristoph. Nu., 930 f.: εἴπερ γ' αὐτὸν σωθῆναι χρὴ καὶ μὴ λαλιὰν μόνον ἀσκῆσαι, Aeschin. Or., 2, 49 : ἀποδιατρίβωσι (waste time) τὴν ὑπερόριον (about what is foreign) λαλιὰν ἀγαπῶντες ἐν τοῖς οἰκείοις πράγμασιν, "garrulity" : Aristoph. Ra., 1069 : λαλιὰν ἐπιτηδεῦσαι καὶ στωμυλίαν.

Debrunner

B. The Logos in the Greek and Hellenistic World.

1. The Meaning of the Word λόγος in Its Multiplicity.

Although little used in epic,[32] λόγος achieved a comprehensive and varied significance with the process of rationalisation which characterised the Greek spirit. Indeed, in its manifold historical application one might almost call it symbolic of the Greek understanding of the world and existence.

The etym. enables us to perceive the decisive and, in their συμπλοκή,[33] basically significant features of the concept. The noun of λέγειν, λόγος means fundamentally "gathering" or "gleaning" in the selective and critical sense. Cf. Hom. Od., 24, 107 f.: οὐδέ κεν ἄλλως κρινάμενος λέξαιτο κατὰ πτόλιν ἄνδρας ἀρίστους.

Figuratively, but even as mental activity directed to something present, λόγος has the original sense of "counting," "reckoning," "explaining." Emphasising the critical as well as the counting side of λέγειν (cf. συλλέγειν), the use[34] of λόγος embraces the following senses.

---

29 Post-class. also the act., Theocr. Idyll., 27, 58 : ἀλλήλαις λαλέουσι τεὸν γάμον αἱ κυπάρισσοι, Alciphr. Fr., 5, 2 (p. 156, 9 f., Schepers): πανταχῇ· πάντες αὐτὴν λαλοῦσιν.

30 Cf. Luc. Vit. Auct., 3 : ἐγὼ γὰρ λάλος ("having the gift of speech"), οὐκ ἀνδριὰς εἶναι βούλομαι.

31 From λάλος, "garrulous" (from Aristoph. and Eur.) with the infrequent suffix-ιά, like, e.g., στρατιά from στρατός, νεοσσιά ("nest") from νεοσσός ("young"). In sense the closest is παιδιά ("game") from παιδ-, P. Chantraine, *La Formation des Noms en Grec Ancien* (1933), 81 f.

32 Only twice in Hom., Il. 15, 393 and Od., 1, 56 : αἰεὶ δὲ μαλακοῖσι καὶ αἱμυλίοισι (→ 74) λόγοισι θέλγει, and almost as rare in Hes., e.g., Op., 106, always in the sense of connected speech ; elsewhere ἔπος and μῦθος. Cf. Hoffmann.

33 The transcendent meaning of λόγος is particularly clear when it is a grammatical tt. as compared with ὀνόματα and ῥήματα, Ps.-Plat. Def., 414d : λόγος φωνὴ ἐγγράμματος, φραστικὴ ἑκάστου τῶν ὄντων· διάλεκτος συνθετὴ ἐξ ὀνομάτων καὶ ῥημάτων ἄνευ μέλους. Cf. Plat. Crat., 424e ff.; Soph., 218c; Aristot. Phys., I, 1, p. 184b, 10 (ὄνομα/λόγος).

34 Examples in Flipse, *op. cit.,* 87 ff. and the lexicons. Cf. J. H. H. Schmidt, I, 1 ff. (λέγειν); 113 ff. (ὄνομα).

a. "Counting up," "recounting" (Hdt., II, 123, where λόγος refers to the whole narrative), "account" (→ b.), the sum of individual words (ἔπη) to form the comprehensive construct "speech" or "language" (esp. prose as distinct from ποίησις,[35] Plat. Resp., III, 390a), "sentence" or "saying." Because λόγος, as distinct from → μῦθος,[36] which is a developing or invented narrative or tradition in the poetic or religious sphere, always refers to something material, it is either that which is at issue (Hdt., I, 21; Soph. Trach., 484), or that which is recounted of someone, i.e., good or bad repute (Aesch. Prom., 732; Eur. Phoen., 1251; Heracl., 165), renown (Pind. Nem., 4, 71; Hdt., IX, 78; Heracl. Fr., 39 [I, 160, 2, Diels[5]]), saga (Pind. Nem., 1, 34b), history (Hdt., VI, 137).

b. "Account," "reckoning," "result of reckoning" (a) in a more metaphysical sense as the principle or law which can be calculated or discovered in calculation (Heracl. Fr., 1 [I, 150, 1 ff., Diels[5]]) or often the reason which is the product of thought and calculation (Aesch. Choeph., 515; Leucipp. Fr., 2 [II, 81, 5, Diels[5]]), the argument or explanation (cf. λόγον διδόναι, "to give an account," "to account for"; (b) as an economic or commercial term: "reckoning" (συναίρω λόγον, Mt. 18:23; cf. P. Oxy., I, 113, 28; BGU, 775, 19); "cash account" (δημόσιος λόγος), "account" etc. (very frequently in the pap.).[37]

c. As a technical term in mathematics:[38] "proportion," "relation," "element" in the sense of Euclid (ed. I. L. Heiberg, II [1884]), V Definitio 3: λόγος ἐστὶ δύο μεγέθων ὁμογενῶν ἡ κατὰ πηλικότητά ποια σχέσις, Plat. Tim., 32b; common in Democr.; Plot. Enn., III, 3, 6. Here the orderly and rational character implicit in the term is quite clear. With the interrelation of mathematics and philosophy, λόγος, as the rational relation of things to one another, then acquires the more general sense of "order" or "measure" (Hdt., III, 119; Heracl. Fr., 31 [I, 158, 13, Diels[5]]; Fr., 45 [I, 161, 2, Diels[5]]).

d. From the second half of the 5th century it is used subjectively for man's *ratio*, his ability to think (synon. with → νοῦς), "reason" (Democr. Fr., 53 [II, 157, 1 ff., Diels[5]]), the human "mind" or "spirit," "thought" (Democr. Fr., 146 [II, 171, 6 ff., Diels[5]]).

Since λόγος has so many meanings,[39] for a right understanding it is important that they all converge into one concept and all-embracing content which is more or less systematically dissected again by later grammarians and rhetoricians,[40] esp. in the Scholia Marciana in Artis Dionysianae, 11 (Grammatici Graeci, ed. A. Hilgard, I, 3 [1901], 353, 29-355, 15). Socrates refers back to the material connections present in the concept itself when in Plat. Theaet. he tries to give a progressive explanation of the untranslatable term λόγος, because he wishes to show that it is a significant preliminary stage in the rise of supreme ἐπιστήμη, of which the capacity for λόγον δοῦναι καὶ δέξασθαι is an important aspect, Plat. Theaet., 206d ff.: τὸ μὲν πρῶτον εἴη ἂν (sc. ὁ λόγος) τὸ τὴν αὑτοῦ διάνοιαν ἐμφανῆ ποιεῖν διὰ φωνῆς μετὰ ῥημάτων τε καὶ ὀνομάτων. The λόγος is first, then, the expression of διάνοια in words. It is secondly (206e-208b) the enumeration in correct order of the elements in a subject: τὴν διὰ στοιχείου διέξοδον περὶ ἑκάστου λόγον εἶναι (207c). Finally, it is the establishment of

[35] "For the language of prose is by nature the language of *ratio*; it is *ratio* itself in the form of words," W. Schadewaldt, *Antike*, 10 (1934), 154 f.; in this art. there are some excellent remarks on the origin of the λόγος concept.

[36] On the relation μῦθος/λόγος, cf. Plat. Leg., I, 645b; Xenophanes Fr., 1, 14 (I, 127, 9, Diels[5]).

[37] There are several examples in Preisigke Wört., *s.v.*

[38] Cf. J. Stenzel, *Zahl u. Gestalt bei Plat. u. Aristot.*[2] (1933), 147 ff.; cf. also sense a.: "word" or "speech" as the representation of one thing in another, acc. to Stenzel's formulation, 151.

[39] Cf. also Plat. Resp., VII, 525e; Aristot. Phys., II, 3, p. 194b, 27 etc.

[40] On λόγος in grammar and rhetoric cf. Leisegang, Pauly-W., 1036 ff.

the particular, ᾧ ἁπάντων διαφέρει τὸ ἐρωτηθέν, within the κοινόν (208c), i.e., the definition [41] and sometimes even the nature or essence. [42]

By reason of its structure λόγος in the course of its development necessarily entered into relations and parallels and connections and equations with a whole series of basic philosophical terms [43] such as → ἀλήθεια (Plat. Phaed., 99e ff.; cf. Heracl. Fr., 1 [I, 150, 1 ff., Diels⁵]), though it can also stand in confrontation λόγος/ἔργον (Thuc., II, 65, 9; Anaxag. Fr., 7 [II, 36, 4, Diels⁵]) and even antithesis; ἐπιστήμη (Plat. Symp., 211a; Soph., 265c); → ἀρετή (Aristot. Eth. Nic., I, 6, p. 1098a, 7-16; Plut. De Virt. Morali, 3 [II, 441c]: ἀρετή is λόγος and *vice versa*); → ἀνάγκη (Leucipp. Fr., 2 [II, 81, 5 f., Diels⁵]); → κόσμος (→ III, 873; 878); → νόμος (II, p. 169, 28 f.; III, p. 4, 2 ff., v. Arnim; M. Ant., IV, 4; Plot. Enn., III, 2, 4; Heracl. Fr., 114 together with Fr., 2 [I, 176, 5 ff. and 151, 1 ff., Diels⁵]); → ζωή (Plot. Enn., VI, 7, 11); → εἶδος and → μορφή (*ibid.*, I, 6, 2 f.; VI, 7, 10 f.); → φύσις; → πνεῦμα, esp. in the Stoa (λόγος τοῦ θεοῦ = πνεῦμα σωματικόν, II, p. 310, 24 f., v. Arnim); → θεός (Max. Tyr., 27, 8; God is ὁ πάντων τῶν ὄντων λόγος, Orig. Cels., V, 14). λόγος and ἀριθμός are also related (Ps.-Epicharm. Fr., 56 [I, 208, 5 f., Diels⁵]). Acc. to Pythagorean teaching, the nature of things is expressed in numerical relations, and this gives us a close approximation to λόγος (cf. Plut. Comm. Not., 35 [II, 1077b]); Simpl. in Aristot. = Schol. in Aristot. (ed. C. A. Brandis [1836]), p. 67a, 38 ff.: ἀριθμοὺς μὲν οἱ Πυθαγόρειοι καὶ λόγους ἐν τῇ ὕλῃ ὠνόμαζον τὰ αἴτια ταῦτα τῶν ὄντων ᾗ ὄντα (cf. Plot. Enn., V, 1, 5).

If one may put it thus, the imaginary basic meaning, the ambiguity or wealth of relations (→ 84) sustained by an ultimate unity of sense intrinsic to λόγος, makes the word a philosophical term κατ' ἐξοχήν, and displays the philosophical content which from the very first underlies the very nature of the Greek language.

It should not be overlooked, however, that for the Greeks λόγος is very different from an address or a word of creative power. [44] No matter how we construe it as used by the Greeks, [45] it stands in contrast to the "Word" of the OT and NT. Naturally, concrete utterance is part of its content, especially when it is employed in an emphatic sense, as in human words of command (Hdt., IX, 4; Soph. Oed. Col., 66), divine or oracular sayings (Pind. Pyth., 4, 59), λόγοι μαντικοί (Plat. Phaedr., 275b), or philosophical dialogue. But there is implied the connected rational element in speech, which seeks to discover the issue itself in the demonstration, [46] as distinct from the harmony and beauty of sound, for which the Greek uses ἔπος or ῥῆμα, and especially in contrast to ῥῆμα as the individual and more emotional expression or saying, though this does, of course, fall into a pattern, so that the fact of speech is the essential thing, [47] and ῥῆμα thus denotes

---

41 Cf. Plat. Ep., VII, 342b; Resp., I, 343a: ὁ τοῦ δικαίου λόγος.

42 Plat. Phaedr., 245e: ψυχῆς οὐσία τε καὶ λόγος.

43 Stob. Ecl., I, 79, 8 ff. tells of Chrysipp. (II, 264, 21 ff., v. Arnim): μεταλαμβάνει δ' ἀντὶ τοῦ λόγου τὴν ἀλήθειαν, τὴν αἰτίαν, τὴν φύσιν, τὴν ἀνάγκην, προστιθεὶς καὶ ἑτέρας ὀνομασίας. Cf. Epict. Diss., II, 8, 2: οὐσία θεοῦ ... νοῦς, ἐπιστήμη, λόγος ὀρθός.

44 Only in the later cosmogony of Κόρη κόσμου (Stob. Ecl., I, 388, 13 ff.) does God create Φύσις by His word: ἐμειδίασεν ὁ θεὸς καὶ εἶπε Φύσιν εἶναι ... εἶπεν ὁ θεὸς καὶ ἦν, and in a fragment of Orphic Ὅρκοι (Orph. Fr., 299, Kern) there is distinctive ref. to the αὐδὴ πατρὸς which He φθέγξατο πρῶτον when He ἑαῖς στηρίξατο βουλαῖς the whole world (→ I, 634), expounded and rendered by Justin as ὁ τοῦ θεοῦ λόγος. Cf. Philo Sacr. AC, 65: ὁ γὰρ θεὸς λέγων ἅμα ἐποίει.

45 Cf. the basic expositions of Bultmann, *Glauben u. Verstehen*, 274 ff.; M. Heidegger, *Sein u. Zeit*, I⁴ (1935), 32 ff.; J. H. H. Schmidt, I, 1 ff.

46 Cf. Bornkamm, 379.

47 Cf. Pind. Nem., 4, 6: ῥῆμα δ' ἐργμάτων χρονιώτερον βιοτεύει, Demosth. Or., 24, 191: τῶν ἐκ τοῦ νόμου ῥημάτων ἐκλέξας.

the word as expressed will,[48] as distinct from the explicatory element in λόγος. According to the acute definition of Aristot. (De Interpretatione, p. 16b, 26), λόγος is a φωνὴ σημαντική, a "significant utterance." Expressions like τί λέγεις; ("what is the meaning of what you say?") point to the fact that the essential thing is, not the saying, but the meaning. λέγειν cannot be used for "to command," or "to address," or "to utter a word of creative power." λόγος is a statement (ἀπόφανσις, *ibid.*, p. 17a, 22) whether something ὑπάρχει or μὴ ὑπάρχει (p. 17a, 23). Hence the explanatory words are ἀποφαίνεσθαι (to cause something to be seen, p. 17a, 27); δηλοῦν (p. 17a, 16; cf. Pol., I, 2, p. 1253a, 14: ὁ δὲ λόγος ἐπὶ τῷ δηλοῦν ἐστιν); (λέγειν) τι κατά τινος (p. 17a, 21). "This causing of something to be seen for what it is, and the possibility of being orientated thereby, are what Aristotle defines as 'word' (λόγος)."[49]

It simply illustrates this specific use if in the Gk. magic pap. λόγος (cf. → πρᾶξις) is an important tt. for the magical song or prayer or incantation of powerful demons, Preis. Zaub., I, 156; III, 3 and 17.[50] In this connection we may cite some wholly non-Greek meanings of which there are no examples whatever in secular Gk. Thus Philo speaks of the ζηλωτικὸς λόγος, Leg. All., III, 242, the "spirit of zeal," and Jesus in Mt. 8:16 ἐξέβαλεν τὰ πνεύματα λόγῳ. The Jew Aristobulus is also using a singular turn of phrase when he has the word λόγος in the Jewish sense for that which is spoken essentially and primarily: Eus. Praep. Ev., XIII, 12, 3: δεῖ γὰρ λαμβάνειν τὴν θείαν φωνὴν οὐ ῥητὸν λόγον ἀλλ' ἔργων κατασκευάς.

For the creative Word of God in the OT sense cf. Sir. 42:15: ἐν λόγοις κυρίου τὰ ἔργα αὐτοῦ; in contrast, the classical Gk. λόγος concept is set in characteristic antithesis to ἔργον, cf. Thuc., II, 65, 9; Anaxag. Fr., 7 (II, 36, 4 f., Diels[5]). It is interesting that Wis. and the LXX do not use ῥῆμα for the Word of creation and revelation; it is obviously too narrow. Instead, they have the more profound and comprehensive λόγος, though in the OT, as later in the NT (→ n. 144), λόγος and ῥῆμα are closer to one another (cf. the non-Gk. combinations of the two in Philo Poster. C., 102; Leg. All., III, 173; Cl. Al. Strom., VI, 3, 34, 3: ἡ κυριακὴ φωνὴ λόγος ἀσχημάτιστος· ἡ <γὰρ> τοῦ λόγου δύναμις, ῥῆμα κυρίου φωτεινόν).

2. The Development of the λόγος Concept in the Greek World.

a. The Two Sides of the Concept. We shall pursue the distinctive Gk. use according to two aspects which are still significantly undivided at the starting-point in Heraclitus (→ b.).

First, we have in view the use of λόγος for word, speech, utterance, revelation, not in the sense of something proclaimed and heard, but rather in that of something displayed, clarified, recognised, and understood; λόγος as the rational power of calculation in virtue of which man can see himself and his place in the cosmos; λόγος as the indication of an existing and significant content which is assumed to be intelligible; λόγος as the content itself in terms of its meaning and law, its basis and structure. Secondly, we have in view λόγος as a metaphysical reality and an

---

48 Cr.-Kö., 450.

49 W. Bröcker, *Aristoteles* = *Philosophische Abhandlungen*, 1 (1935), 28; cf. 176 ff.; cf. also the Stoic theory of meaning in Diog. L., VII, 38 (57): ... λόγος ἀεὶ σημαντικός ἐστιν ... διαφέρει δὲ καὶ τὸ λέγειν τοῦ προφέρεσθαι· προφέρονται μὲν γὰρ αἱ φωναί, λέγεται δὲ τὰ πράγματα.

50 On the other hand cf. Plot. Enn., II, 9, 14: ὅταν γὰρ ἐπαοιδὰς γράφωσιν (the Gnostics) ὡς πρὸς ἐκεῖνα λέγοντες, οὐ μόνον τὴν ψυχήν, ἀλλὰ καὶ τὰ ἐπάνω, τί ποιοῦσιν ἢ γοητείας καὶ θέλξεις (enchantments) καὶ πείσεις λέγουσι ὡς λόγῳ ὑπακούειν καὶ ἄγεσθαι.

established term in philosophy and theology, from which there finally develops in later antiquity, under alien influences, a cosmological entity and hypostasis of the deity, a δεύτερος θεός.

It is presupposed as self-evident by the Greek that there is in things, in the world and its course, a primary λόγος, an intelligible and recognisable law, which then makes possible knowledge and understanding in the human λόγος. But this λόγος is not taken to be something which is merely grasped theoretically. It claims a man. It determines his true life and conduct. The λόγος is thus the norm (→ νόμος). For the Greek, knowledge is always recognition of a law. Therewith it is also fulfilment of this law.

b. Heraclitus. Because the same λόγος constitutes the being of both the cosmos and man, it is the connecting principle which forms the bridge and possibility of understanding[51] 1. between man and the world, and also between men (in their political order, → 82), 2. between man and God, and finally in later antiquity 3. between this world and the world above. It is in Heraclitus[52] (Fr., 1 [I, 150, 1 ff., Diels[5]]) that the λόγος is first stated to be that which establishes man in his true being in virtue of this interconnection (sense c. → 78): τοῦ δὲ λόγου τοῦδ' ἐόντος ἀεὶ ἀξύνετοι γίνονται ἄνθρωποι καὶ πρόσθεν ἢ ἀκοῦσαι καὶ ἀκούσαντες τὸ πρῶτον· γινομένων γὰρ πάντων κατὰ τὸν λόγον τόνδε ἀπείροισιν ἐοίκασι, πειρώμενοι καὶ ἐπέων καὶ ἔργων τοιούτων, ὁκοίων ἐγὼ διηγεῦμαι κατὰ φύσιν διαιρέων ἕκαστον καὶ φράζων ὅκως ἔχει. Cf. also Fr., 2 (I, 151, 1 ff., Diels[5]): διὸ δεῖ ἕπεσθαι τῶι κοινῶι· ξυνὸς γὰρ ὁ κοινός. τοῦ λόγου δ' ἐόντος ξυνοῦ ζώουσιν οἱ πολλοὶ ὡς ἰδίαν ἔχοντες φρόνησιν. The λόγος is here the word, speech, or content of speech or book, but also what is meant by the word or in the work, the truth ; for only of it can one say that it is eternally valid (ἀεὶ ἐόντος), and that everything takes place in its sense. Philosophical knowledge, the λόγος or → νοῦς, → σύνεσις, is thus for Heraclitus the means to evoke the words and works of men. Both speech and action follow from it. This λόγος of Heraclitus is to be understood and interpreted as an oracular word. For men are bound by the λόγος and yet they do not see it. They live as though there were an ἰδία φρόνησις (Fr., 2). Heraclitus connects this λόγος with the ξυνόν (→ κοινὸς λόγος), Fr., 2. It is the transcendent and lasting order in which eternal flux occurs, binding the individual to the whole. It is the cosmic law[53] which is comprehended by the λόγος which grows in the soul (Fr., 115 [I, 176, 10, Diels[5]]: ψυχῆς ἐστι λόγος ἑαυτὸν αὔξων, cf. Fr., 45 [I, 161, 1 ff., Diels[5]]); as such it is the opposite of every individual or private δόξα. The deepest ground of the → ψυχή, which none can wholly plumb, is the λόγος. "He who hears the λόγος does not merely accept a claim which springs out of the situation and encounters him. He is aware of a claim, but in such a way that he truly understands it only if he realises that basically it is he himself who must raise the claim to transcend the ἰδία φρόνησις,[54] Fr., 50 (I, 161, 16 f., Diels[5]): οὐκ ἐμοῦ, ἀλλὰ τοῦ λόγου ἀκούσαντας[55] ὁμολογεῖν σοφόν ἐστιν ἓν πάντα εἶναι.

---

[51] Cf. Pos. in Philo Fug., 112 : ὅ τε γὰρ τοῦ ὄντος λόγος δεσμὸς ὢν τῶν ἁπάντων, ὡς εἴρηται, καὶ συνέχει τὰ μέρη πάντα καὶ σφίγγει κωλύων αὐτὰ διαλύεσθαι καὶ διαρτᾶσθαι.

[52] Cf. A. Busse, "Der Wortsinn von ΛΟΓΟΣ bei Heracl.," *Rheinisches Museum*, 75 (1926), 203 ff.; the definitive interpretation of the λόγος concept in Heracl. is to be found in O. Gigon, *Untersuchungen zu Heracl.* (Diss. Basel, 1935), 3 ff.; for the range of the concept cf. J. Stenzel, *Platon der Erzieher* (1928), 43 ff.

[53] On the connection and parallelism of λόγος as speech and as cosmic law cf. E. Hofmann, 3 ff.

[54] Bultmann (n. 45), 275.

[55] Nevertheless, in Heraclitus the λόγος is received more by the eyes than the ears, Fr., 101 (I, 173, 15 f., Diels[5]); the eyes are more reliable witnesses. In Christianity the λόγος is essentially the spoken word ; hence the emphasis on ἀκούειν (→ I, 219).

c. The Sophists. After Heraclitus the word develops in Gk. thought, and the unity of meaning which distinguishes Heraclitus is disrupted. By way of the sense of reckoning and gradual synonymity with → νοῦς, the λόγος now becomes predominantly the rational power set in man, the power of speech and thought. In political life it plays a decisive part as the means of persuasion and direction. Only in Stoicism does it re-emerge as a universal, cosmic, and religious principle.

The great representatives of this development are the Sophists, who not only treated the λόγος apart from any norm or connection with given interests or situations even to the τὸν ἥττω λόγον κρείσσω ποιεῖν (Plat. Ap., 18b), [56] but who were also the first to work out a theory [57] of the λόγος.

In the political life of 4th and 5th century democracy, which was strongly marked by *ratio*, the λόγος naturally took on great significance. In Helenae Encomium, 8 (Fr., 11 [II, 290, 17 ff., Diels[5]]), Gorg. extols the psychagogic power of the λόγος, which is here almost personified: [58] λόγος δυνάστης μέγας ἐστίν, ὃς σμικροτάτωι σώματι καὶ ἀφανεστάτωι θειότατα ἔργα ἀποτελεῖ· δύναται γὰρ καὶ φόβον παῦσαι καὶ λύπην ἀφελεῖν καὶ χαρὰν ἐνεργάσασθαι καὶ ἔλεον ἐπαυξῆσαι, and the one mastered by it is a δοῦλος of the λόγος (cf. Plat. Phileb., 58b). The λόγος may take the most varied turns in detail, e.g., a pedagogic in Isoc. Or., 3, 7: τούτῳ (sc. τῷ λόγῳ) καὶ τοὺς κακοὺς ἐξελέγχομεν καὶ τοὺς ἀγαθοὺς ἐγκωμιάζομεν, and even a creatively cultural, *ibid.*, 3, 6 ff.; Or., 15, 254: καὶ σχεδὸν ἅπαντα τὰ δι' ἡμῶν μεμηχανημένα λόγος ἡμῖν ἐστιν ὁ συγκατασκευάσας. Only the λόγος makes possible the political life which raises us above the level of the beasts. All cultural achievements are owed to it: οὐ μόνον τοῦ θηριωδῶς ζῆν ἀπηλλάγημεν ἀλλὰ καὶ συνελθόντες πόλεις ᾠκίσαμεν καὶ νόμους ἐθέμεθα καὶ τέχνας εὕρομεν (*loc. cit.*). [59] *Ratio, oratio*, and normative force are comprised in the term: οὗτος γὰρ περὶ τῶν δικαίων καὶ τῶν ἀδίκων καὶ τῶν καλῶν καὶ τῶν αἰσχρῶν ἐνομοθέτησεν. Thus the λόγος

---

[56] Cf. the Καταβάλλοντες (λόγοι) of Protagoras Fr., 1 (II, 263, 2 f., Diels[5]), the Δισσοὶ Λόγοι (II, 405 ff.), and the speech-contest of δίκαιος and ἄδικος λόγος in the parody in Aristoph. Nu. 889 ff.

[57] On λόγος as an established term in rhetoric cf. Leisegang, Pauly-W., 1043 ff.

[58] Like many other terms (cf. → αἰών, → δίκη, → νόμος), λόγος is personified quite early in the poets (Hes. Theog., 229; Eur. Iph. Aul., 1013; Phoen., 471; cf. Rev. 19:13). This is not surprising among the Gks. There are movements in this direction in Plato's usage, Phaedr., 264c: δεῖ πάντα λόγον ὥσπερ ζῷον (organism) συνεστάναι σῶμά τι ἔχοντα αὐτὸν αὑτοῦ ... etc. E. Hoffmann, 29 f. points esp. to the role of sophistic and dialectically polemic λόγος in Theaet. Thus it can be said of the λόγος (cf. the NT, examples in Bultmann, *op. cit.*, 280, n. 2) that it fights, conquers, succumbs, dies and rises again (cf. Plat. Phaed., 89b: ἐάνπερ γε ἡμῖν ὁ λόγος τελευτήσῃ καὶ μὴ δυνώμεθα αὐτὸν ἀναβιώσασθαι. On this cf. H. Diels, SAB (1883), I, 488 f. We are to distinguish this from the equation of λόγος with a god or its hypostatisation to an independent divine essence in later antiquity.

[59] The verse from the Politeia of Chrysogonus (end of the 5th cent. B.C.), Ps.-Epicharm. Fr., 57 (I, 208, 8 ff., Diels[5]) seems to me to belong to the context of theories of the rise of culture rather than Hermes theology, as Leisegang suggests in Pauly-W., 1062: ὁ λόγος ἀνθρώπους κυβερνᾶι κατὰ τρόπον σώιζει τ' ἀεί· | ἔστιν ἀνθρώπωι λογισμός, ἔστι καὶ θεῖος λόγος· | ὁ δὲ γε τἀνθρώπου πέφυκεν ἀπό γε τοῦ θείου λόγου | <καὶ> φέρει <πόρους ἑκάστωι> περὶ βίου καὶ τᾶς τροφᾶς. | ὁ δέ γε ταῖς τέχναις ἁπάσαις συνέπεται θεῖος λόγος, | ἐκδιδάσκων αὐτὸς αὐτούς, ὅ τι ποιεῖν δεῖ συμφέρον. | οὐ γὰρ ἄνθρωπος τέχναν τιν' εὗρεν, ὁ δὲ θεὸς τοπάν. On the θεῖος λόγος cf. Plat. Phaed., 85d. Apart from Plut. we also find θεῖος λόγος in Orph. Fr., 245, 5, Kern: εἰς δὲ λόγον θεῖον βλέψας τούτωι προσέδρευε | ἰθύνων κραδίης νοερὸν κύτος, and the Hermetic writings, cf. Cl. Al. Strom., V, 14, 94, 5; Sext. Emp. Math., VII, 129 speaks of the θεῖος λόγος of Heracl.: τοῦτον οὖν τὸν θεῖον λόγον καθ' Ἡράκλειτον δι' ἀναπνοῆς σπάσαντες νοεροὶ γινόμεθα. For the common use in Philo cf. **Leisegang's Index**, *s.v.* θεῖος.

ἀληθὴς καὶ νόμιμος καὶ δίκαιος is finally ψυχῆς ἀγαθῆς καὶ πιστῆς εἴδωλον (*ibid.*, 255).

d. Socrates and Plato. As Socrates and Plato transcend the more individualistic λόγος of the Sophists by pursuing this way to its logical end, a new and deeper conception of the λόγος arises. This is the thought, widespread in the Gk. world, of the power of the λόγος, if only it is linked to the κοινὸς λόγος, to establish fellowship by making possible agreement on the basis of the matter, ὁμολογία.[60] The constantly recurring τί λέγεις; in the Socratic dialogues expresses the fact that here common speech with its words and concepts is recognised, or presupposed, as the common basis. The λόγος as the basic fact in all life in society is the decisive point in the politics of Socrates and Plato, just as there is a kind of pre-existent harmony between the λόγος of the thinking soul and the λόγος of things. Hence man must be on guard lest he become an enemy of the word as another might become the enemy of men. No greater misfortune can befall a man, and both hatred of the word and enmity against men proceed from the same disposition (Plat. Phaed., 89d; 90d e: Hence μὴ παρίωμεν εἰς τὴν ψυχὴν ὡς τῶν λόγων κινδυνεύει οὐδὲν ὑγιὲς εἶναι, ἀλλὰ πολὺ μᾶλλον ὅτι ἡμεῖς οὔπω ὑγιῶς ἔχομεν ..., 99e: ἔδοξε δή μοι χρῆναι εἰς τοὺς λόγους καταφυγόντα ἐν ἐκείνοις σκοπεῖν τῶν ὄντων τὴν ἀλήθειαν). The truth is attained when the λόγος interprets phenomena; but the λόγος must proceed from them. The Socratic-Platonic understanding and use of λόγος rests on this duality. λόγος is thinking as the διά-λογος of the soul with itself (Plat. Soph., 263e: διάνοια μὲν καὶ λόγος ταὐτόν· πλὴν ὁ μὲν ἐντὸς τῆς ψυχῆς πρὸς αὑτὴν διάλογος ἄνευ φωνῆς γιγνόμενος, cf. Theaet., 189e). Here Plato simply expresses philosophically the twofold content found in the word itself. By contrast with the eristic and destructive λόγος of the Sophists, which merely represents what is always the possible failure of the λόγος, the τῶν λόγων αὐτῶν ἀθάνατόν τι καὶ ἀγήρων πάθος (Plat. Phileb., 15d), since it is not oriented ἀφθόνως to the matter, the λόγος is here (Plat. Soph., 259c-264) developed as τῶν ὄντων ἕν τι γενῶν (Soph., 260a), and as such it makes philosophy possible because it is linked to being as to a great κοινωνία. λόγος and κοινωνία belong closely together, Soph. 262c (cf. 259e): τότε δ' ἥρμοσέν τε καὶ λόγος ἐγένετο εὐθὺς ἡ πρώτη συμπλοκή. The συμπλοκή of ὀνόματα and ῥήματα, however small, at once produces a λόγος which has its essence in the fact that it does not merely speak (ὀνομάζει) words but τι περαίνει — 262d — that it says (λέγει) something, a matter, a being (and therewith a sense). As ἀληθής or πιστὸς λόγος (Dio Chrys. Or., 45, 3), it expresses what is as it is.[61] Once again, then, δηλοῦν and σημαίνειν are correlative to λόγος (Soph., 261d/e).

Thought, word, matter,[62] nature, being and norm (cf. the identity of being and thought in Parm.) are all brought into a comprehensive interrelation in the λόγος concept. Thus Plato in Crito, 46b/d can say of the λόγοι of Socrates that they were not just λόγοι ἕνεκα λόγου, a mere speaking, nor were they παιδιά and

[60] Cf. Eur. Suppl., 201 ff. In terms of the λόγος J. Stenzel has suggested a whole new understanding of Socrates and Plato in the art. "Sokrates" in Pauly-W., 2, III, 1 (1927), 811 ff.; cf. Bornkamm, 377 ff.

[61] Plat. Crat., 385b: λόγος, ὃς ἂν τὰ ὄντα λέγῃ ὡς ἔστιν, ἀληθής· ὃς δ' ἂν ὡς οὐκ ἔστιν, ψευδής.

[62] Cf. Pind. Olymp., 1, 28 f.: καὶ πού τι καὶ βροτῶν φάτις ὑπὲρ τὸν ἀληθῆ λόγον (the true, and conceptually possible, content so far as it is expressed in the ode).

φλυαρία (46d), but they were essence and deed, since they stood up even in face of death.[63]

e. Aristotle. Aristotle sums up once again the classical understanding of human existence in his statement: λόγον δὲ μόνον ἄνθρωπος ἔχει τῶν ζῴων, Polit., I, 2, p. 1253a, 9 f. Man has the word in the twofold sense that what he does and does not do are determined by the word or understanding, and that he himself speaks the word, achieving understanding and speech[64] (Aristot. Eth. Nic., I, 6, p. 1098a, 4 f.: τούτου δὲ τὸ μὲν ὡς ἐπιπειθὲς λόγῳ, τὸ δ' ὡς ἔχον καὶ διανοούμενον). The specific ἔργον ἀνθρώπου is the ψυχῆς ἐνέργεια κατὰ λόγον (*ibid.*, a 7).[65] The λόγος is the source of the unique ἀρετή (Eth. Nic., II, 6, p. 1106b, 36 ff.) of man,[66] and consequently of his εὐδαιμονία.

3. The λόγος in Hellenism.

a. Stoicism. In Stoicism[67] λόγος is a term for the ordered and teleologically orientated nature of the world (Diog. L., VII, 74 [149] λόγος, καθ' ὃν ὁ κόσμος διεξάγεται). It is thus equated with the concept of God (→ θεός, III, 75; cf. Zeno in Diog. L., VII, 68 [134] [= I, p. 24, 7 f., v. Arnim] τὸ δὲ ποιοῦν τὸν ἐν αὐτῇ [sc. τῇ ὕλῃ] λόγον τὸν θεόν), with πρόνοια, εἱμαρμένη, with → κόσμος, → νόμος, → φύσις — acc. to Chrysipp. εἱμαρμένη is the Διὸς λόγος (Plut. Stoic. Rep., 47 [II, 1056c]) or ὁ τοῦ κόσμου λόγος or λόγος τῶν ἐν κόσμῳ προνοίᾳ διοικουμένων (II, 264, 18 ff., v. Arnim).[68] As such it can no longer be rendered actively as concrete speech which is uttered on a meaningful basis, as in Socratic-Platonic philosophy. It can be identified only passively with the (cosmic) law of reason. God is ὁ πάντων τῶν ὄντων λόγος, Orig. Cels., V, 14, and the basis of the unity of this world (εἷς λόγος ὁ ταῦτα κοσμῶν καὶ μία πρόνοια ἐπιτροπεύουσα, Plut. Is. et Os., 67 [II, 377 f.]; ὁ τὴν οὐσίαν τῶν ὅλων διοικῶν λόγος, M. Ant., VI, 1). By assimilation to popular religion this world logos is equated with Zeus, as in the well-known hymn of Cleanthes, Fr., 537 (I, p. 122, 7, v. Arnim): ὥσθ' ἕνα γίγνεσθαι πάντων λόγον αἰὲν ἐόντα. It is the principle which creates the world, i.e., which orders and constitutes it

---

[63] Cf. Crito, 46b/c (Socrates says): μηδενὶ ἄλλῳ πείθεσθαι ἢ τῷ λόγῳ ὃς ἄν μοι λογιζομένῳ βέλτιστος φαίνηται. τοὺς δὴ λόγους ... οὐ δύναμαι νῦν (in face of death) ἐκβαλεῖν ... ἀλλὰ σχεδόν τι ὅμοιοι φαίνονταί μοι, καὶ τοὺς αὐτοὺς πρεσβεύω καὶ τιμῶ οὕσπερ καὶ πρότερον ... Here, then, the λόγος is set over against the ἀλήθεια, as, e.g., in Demosth. Or., 30, 34. 26: οὐκ ἔχει ταῦτ' ἀλήθειαν, ... ἀλλὰ λόγοι ταῦτ' ἐστιν ... Plato says of himself in Ep., VII, 328c: μὴ δόξαιμί ποτε ἐμαυτῷ παντάπασι λόγος μόνον ἀτεχνῶς εἶναί τις, ἔργου δὲ οὐδενὸς ἄν ποτε ἑκὼν ἀνθάψασθαι.

[64] Bröcker, 27 and 176 ff., who develops the understanding of human existence in terms of the λόγος. The λόγος as that which underlies man's being and gives him the possibility of freedom (M. Ant., VI, 58) is also found later in the Stoics, cf. Zeno in Stob. Ecl., II, 75, 11 ff.; Epict. Diss., III, 1, 25; Plot. Enn., III, 1, 9; M. Ant., VI, 23.

[65] The λόγος is here quite closely linked to the ψυχή concept: Eth. Nic., I, 13, p. 1102a, 27 ff., esp. 1102b, 13 ff.: ἔοικεν δὲ καὶ ἄλλη τις φύσις τῆς ψυχῆς ἄλογος εἶναι, μετέχουσα μέντοι πῃ λόγου. τοῦ γὰρ ἐγκρατοῦς καὶ ἀκρατοῦς τὸν λόγον καὶ τῆς ψυχῆς τὸ λόγον ἔχον ἐπαινοῦμεν. ὀρθῶς γὰρ καὶ ἐπὶ τὰ βέλτιστα παρακαλεῖ· φαίνεται δ' ἐν αὐτοῖς καὶ ἄλλο τι παρὰ τὸν λόγον πεφυκός, ὃ μάχεταί τε καὶ ἀντιτείνει τῷ λόγῳ. Here Aristot. speaks on the one side of a πειθαρχεῖν and ὁμοφωνεῖν τῷ λόγῳ — this is the ὀρθὸς λόγος, p. 1103b, 32 — but on the other the ψυχή can resist it and strive with it.

[66] Cf. Plut. De Virt. Morali, 3 (II, 441c): κοινῶς δὲ ἅπαντες οὗτοι (Menedemus, Zeno, Ariston, Chrysipp.) τὴν ἀρετὴν τοῦ ἡγεμονικοῦ τῆς ψυχῆς διάθεσίν τινα καὶ δύναμιν γεγενημένην ὑπὸ λόγου, μᾶλλον δὲ λόγον οὖσαν αὐτὴν ὁμολογούμενον καὶ βέβαιον καὶ ἀμετάπτωτον ὑποτίθενται.

[67] Cf. the collection of examples in E. Schwartz, NGG (1908), 555, n. 1. 2, and v. Arnim, Index, *s.v.*

[68] → 79.

(ὁ τοῦ κόσμου λόγος, Chrysipp. [II, p. 264, 18 f., v. Arnim]; M. Ant., IV, 29, 3), which makes it a ζῷον λογικόν (II, p. 191, 34 f., v. Arnim). It is the power which extends throughout matter (ὁ δι' ὅλης τῆς οὐσίας διήκων λόγος, M. Ant., V, 32) and works immanently in all things. The world is a grand unfolding of the λόγος, which is, of course, represented materially (Diog. L., VII, 35 [56]: πᾶν γὰρ τὸ ποιοῦν σῶμά ἐστιν) as → πῦρ, → πνεῦμα (II, p. 310, 24 f., v. Arnim), or αἰθήρ. But as the organic power which fashions unformed and inorganic matter, which gives growth to plants and movement to animals, it is the λόγος σπερματικός (Zeno [I, p. 28, 26, v. Arnim]). That is, it is a seed which unfolds itself, and this seed is by nature reason. As λόγος ὀρθός, the cosmic law, the → νόμος of the world as well as the individual, it gives men the power of knowledge (Pos. in Sext. Emp. Math., VII, 93: ἡ τῶν ὅλων φύσις ὑπὸ συγγενοῦς ὀφείλει καταλαμβάνεσθαι τοῦ λόγου, cf. Diog. L., VII, 52) and of moral action (M. Ant., IV, 4, 1: ὁ προστακτικὸς τῶν ποιητέων ἢ μὴ λόγος κοινός). As all powers proceed from the λόγος, they all return to it again, M. Ant., IV, 21, 2: ψυχαὶ ... μεταβάλλουσι καὶ χέονται καὶ ἐξάπτονται εἰς τὸν τῶν ὅλων σπερματικὸν λόγον ἀναλαμβανόμεναι. The particular logos of man is only part of the great general logos, V, 27; Epict. Diss., III, 3; M. Ant., VII, 53: κατὰ τὸν κοινὸν θεοῖς καὶ ἀνθρώποις λόγον, which achieves awareness in man, so that through it God and man, or the sage or philosopher as the true man who alone has the ὀρθὸς λόγος and who thus lives ἀκολουθῶν τῇ φύσει (Philo Ebr., 34) are combined into a great κόσμος (II, p. 169, 28 f., v. Arnim: κοινωνίαν ὑπάρχειν πρὸς ἀλλήλους [sc. ἀνθρώποις καὶ θεοῖς] διὰ τὸ λόγου μετέχειν, ὅς ἐστι φύσει νόμος. The duality of λόγος as reason and speech (opp. πάθος) develops in Stoic doctrine inwardly into the λόγος ἐνδιάθετος and outwardly into the λόγος προφορικός (Sext. Emp. Pyrrh. Hyp., I, 65). An extension of content signficant for later development is to be found in the equation of λόγος with φύσις (ὁ κοινὸς τῆς φύσεως λόγος, II, p. 269, 13, v. Arnim; M. Ant., IV, 29, 3) as a creative power. In the period which followed this aspect was increasingly emphasised, e.g., in Plut. Is. et Os., 45 (II, 369a): δημιουργὸν ὕλης ἕνα λόγον καὶ μίαν πρόνοιαν. In the Stoic λόγος the rational power of order and the vital power of conception are merged in one (Diog. L., VII, 68 [135 f.] = II, 180, 2 ff., v. Arnim).

b. Neo-Platonism. In debate with Stoicism Neo-platonism [69] championed a developed logos doctrine. Here, too, the λόγος is a shaping power which lends form and life to things and is thus closely related to εἶδος and → μορφή (Plot. Enn., I, 6, 2. 3. 6; III, 3, 6; IV, 3, 10), → φῶς (*ibid.*, II, 4, 5) and → ζωή (*ibid.*, VI, 7, 11: εἰ δὴ κατὰ λόγον δεῖ τὸ ποιοῦν εἶναι ὡς μορφοῦν, τί ἂν εἴη; ἢ ψυχὴ ποιεῖν πῦρ δυναμένη· τοῦτό δ' ἐστι ζωὴ καὶ λόγος, ἓν καὶ ταὐτὸν ἄμφω). Life is artistically fashioning power. τίς ὁ λόγος; it is οἷον ἔκλαμψις (irradiation) ἐξ ἀμφοῖν, νοῦ καὶ ψυχῆς (*ibid.*, III, 2, 16). Where it works, everything is permeated (λελόγωται), i.e., shaped (μεμόρφωται) by the λόγος, III, 2, 16. Nature is life and λόγος and the working power of form, III, 8, 2: ... τὴν φύσιν εἶναι λόγον, ὃς ποιεῖ λόγον ἄλλον γέννημα αὐτοῦ. Indeed, the whole world is λόγος, and all that is in it is λόγος, III, 2, 2, the former as the pure power of form in the intelligible world, the latter in admixture with matter to the final λόγος ὁ κατὰ τὴν μορφὴν τὴν ὁρωμένην ἔσχατος ἤδη καὶ νεκρός, which οὐκέτι ποιεῖν δύναται ἄλλον, and which was unknown to Stoicism in contrast to Neo-platonism, III, 8, 2. Thus Plot., like John's Gospel, can say in III, 2, 15: ἀρχὴ οὖν λόγος καὶ πάντα λόγος. Sometimes this is regarded as a unity, an emanation from → Νοῦς, III, 2, 2: τοῦτο δὲ λόγος ἐκ νοῦ ῥυείς. τὸ γὰρ ἀπορρέον ἐκ νοῦ λόγος, καὶ ἀεὶ — not in singular historicity — ἀπορρεῖ ἕως ἂν ᾖ παρὼν ἐν τοῖς οὖσι λόγος ... οὕτω δὴ καὶ ἐξ ἑνὸς νοῦ καὶ τοῦ ἀπ' αὐτοῦ λόγου ἀνέστη τόδε

[69] H. F. Müller, "Die Lehre vom Logos bei Plot.," *Archiv f. Geschichte der Philosophie*, 30 (1916), 38 ff. Esp. instructive is the Logos chapter in Plot. Enn., III, 2, 16, where basic mathematical meaning as tonal relation is important for the achievement of cosmic harmony.

τὸ πᾶν καὶ διέστη ... τοῦ δὲ λόγου ἐπ' αὐτοῖς τὴν ἁρμονίαν καὶ μίαν τὴν σύνταξιν εἰς τὰ ὅλα ποιουμένου, sometimes as a plurality by which it brings into effect the multiplicity of phenomena; for it is πολὺς καὶ πᾶς, V, 3, 16, εἷς and πολύς, VI, 7, 14. Indeed, the one λόγος divides into warring opposites, III, 2, 16: ἀνάγκη καὶ τὸν ἕνα τοῦτον λόγον ἐξ ἐναντίων λόγων εἶναι ἕνα τὴν σύστασιν αὐτῷ καὶ οἷον οὐσίαν τῆς τοιαύτης ἐναντιώσεως, the antithesis securing its consistence and essentiality. But the formative principle is not, as in Stoicism, τὸ ὑγρὸν ἐν σπέρμασιν; it is τὸ μὴ ὁρώμενον· τοῦτο δὲ ἀριθμὸς (ideal measure) καὶ λόγος, V, 1, 5, the μέτρον, II, 4, 8. By his λόγος man can break free from the φύσεως γοητεία, IV, 4, 43 f., and attain to the λόγος ἀληθής, the truth of being, IV, 4, 12; VI, 7, 4 ff. But the human λόγος does not lead to an ἀκούειν. It is the ἐκ τῶν λόγων ἐπὶ τὴν θέαν ... παιδαγωγῶν λόγος, VI, 9, 4. As such it is not supreme or final. For what one sees in mystic vision is οὐκέτι λόγος, ἀλλὰ μεῖζον λόγου καὶ πρὸ λόγου, VI, 9, 10.

c. The Mysteries. In connection with deities of revelation the λόγος takes on esp. in the Hellen. mysteries an enhanced religious significance as → ἱερὸς λόγος "sacred history," "holy and mysterious doctrine," "revelation," in a sense not found elsewhere in secular Gk. The ἱερός here belongs essentially to the content and is not just traditional. Hdt., II, 51 already appeals to a ἱρόν τινα λόγον of the Cabiri mysteries in Samothrace (Syr. Dea, 15, 4); and we hear of sacred history in the Dionysus cult, among the Pythagoreans (Iambl. Vit. Pyth., 28, 146: Πυθαγόραν συντάξαι τὸν περὶ θεῶν λόγον, ὃν καὶ ἱερὸν διὰ τοῦτο ἐπέγραψεν), cf. the ἱερὸς λόγος of the Orphics[70] (Suid., *s.v.* Ὀρφεύς, No. 654 [Adler]). In the Isis hymn of Andros, v. 12 (ed. W. Peek [1930]) there is ref. to the sacred doctrine of the mysteries of Isis which induces pious awe in the initiate, and in Plut. Is. et Os., 2 (II, 351 f.) in connection with theological logos speculation, we read of the ἱερὸς λόγος, ὃν ἡ θεὸς [sc. Isis] συνάγει καὶ συντίθησι, καὶ παραδίδωσι (!) τοῖς τελουμένοις <διὰ> θειώσεως, and for which δεισιδαιμονία and περιεργία are not enough, 3 (II, 352b). Osiris is the half personified λόγος created by Isis, a spiritual reflection of the world (Is. et Os., 54). In the Ἑρμοῦ τοῦ τρισμεγίστου ἱερὸς λόγος (Corp. Herm., III heading [acc. to Reitzenstein Poim.]) Hermes tells how by God's mercy he became λόγος and hence υἱὸς θεοῦ. As a special gift of God (XII, 12. 13) and as λόγος τέλειος this ἱερὸς λόγος[71] leads to the mystery of union with the deity (IX, 1; XII, 12). Indeed, the λόγος can even be equivalent to → μυστήριον or τελετή (XIII, 13b: the λόγος is the παράδοσις of παλιγγενεσία), and the initiate himself is the personified λόγος θεοῦ, cf. I, 6 (Reitzenstein Poim.): τὸ ἐν σοὶ βλέπον (!) καὶ ἀκοῦον λόγος κυρίου ἐστίν, which extols God in the regenerate and in the λόγος offers Him all things as λογικὴ → θυσία, XIII, 18. 21.

λόγος as prayer, Aesch. Choeph., 509; in connection with → εὐχή it plays a certain role in mystical speculation inasmuch as it is the only worthy way to enter into relation with God, cf. Sallust, 16 (ed. A. D. Nock, [1926]): αἱ μὲν χωρὶς θυσιῶν εὐχαὶ λόγοι μόνον εἰσίν, αἱ δὲ μετὰ θυσιῶν ἔμψυχοι λόγοι· τοῦ μὲν λόγου τὴν ζωὴν δυναμοῦντος, τῆς δὲ ζωῆς τὸν λόγον ψυχούσης). Apollonius of Tyana (in Eus. Dem. Ev., III, 3, 11) teaches that all genuine prayer must be offered through the λόγος; true honouring of God takes place μόνῳ ... τῷ κρείττονι λόγῳ (λέγω δὲ τῷ μὴ διὰ στόματος ἰόντι), and can be known only λόγῳ (Schol. on Epic. Sententia, 1 in Diog. L., X, 31 [139]: τοὺς θεοὺς λόγῳ θεωρητούς). The λόγος shows man the upward way, Max. Tyr., XI, 10: ἐκλαθόμενος μὲν τῶν κάτω οἰμωγῶν ... καὶ δοξῶν ..., ἐπιτρέψας δὲ τὴν ἡγεμονίαν αὐτοῦ λόγῳ ἀληθεῖ καὶ ἔρωτι ἐρρωμένῳ· τῷ μὲν λόγῳ φράζοντι ᾗ χρὴ ἰέναι ..., Plot. Enn., VI, 9, 4: παιδαγωγῶν λόγος. On this way the λόγος ends in mystical σιωπή, Philostr. Vit. Ap., I, 1: καὶ ἡ σιωπὴ δὲ ὑπὲρ

[70] On the much debated Orphic Pythagorean ἱερὸς λόγος (passages in Orph. Fr. [Kern], p. 140 ff.) cf. A. Krüger, Quaestiones Orphicae, Diss. Halle (1934), 13 ff.
[71] Common in the magic pap., Preis. Zaub., I, 62; IV, 2245.

τοῦ θείου σφίσιν ἐπήσκετο· πολλὰ γὰρ θεῖά τε καὶ ἀπόρρητα ἤκουον, ὧν κρατεῖν χαλεπὸν ἦν μὴ πρῶτον μαθοῦσι, ὅτι καὶ τὸ σιωπᾶν λόγος. Cf. VI, 11 (245): διδάσκαλον εὑρὼν σιωπῆς λόγον, Plot. Enn., III, 8, 6: ὃ γὰρ ἐν ψυχῇ λαμβάνει λόγῳ οὔσῃ, τί ἂν ἄλλο ἢ λόγος σιωπῶν εἴη; In Plot. God is λόγου κρείττων, and in Plut. Is. et Os., 75 (II, 381b) φωνῆς γὰρ ὁ θεῖος λόγος ἀπροσδεής ἐστι.[72]

d. The Hermes-Logos-Theology; Hermeticism. Almost all aspects of the philosophical logos concept occur in Gk. theology, personified and comprehended in the figure of the god Hermes[73] and others. If in Gk. theology Helios, Pan, Isis etc.[74] are the λόγος as well as Hermes, there is no implied incarnation of the λόγος but the equation of a revealing and cosmogonic principle with one of the deities of popular religion. This is the kind of identification which is often found in, e.g., the theological system of Stoicism (Zeus-Λόγος, Isis-Φῶς, Isis-Δικαιοσύνη, Isis-Γένεσις, etc.). In other words, a concept is hypostatised as a god, or identified with a god. There is no question of the divine word of power and creation becoming man, incarnate. This kind of Hermes-Logos-theology is to be found in Cornut. Theol. Graec., 16 (cf. Diog. L., VII, 1, 36 [49]: τυγχάνει δὲ ὁ Ἑρμῆς ὁ λόγος ὤν, ὃν ἀπέστειλαν πρὸς ἡμᾶς ἐξ οὐρανοῦ οἱ θεοί, μόνον τὸν ἄνθρωπον τῶν ἐπὶ γῆς ζῴων λογικὸν ποιήσαντες ... ἀλλὰ πρὸς τὸ σῴζειν μᾶλλον γέγονεν ὁ λόγος,[75] ὅθεν καὶ τὴν Ὑγίειαν αὐτῷ συνῴκισαν ... παραδέδοται δὲ καὶ κῆρυξ θεῶν καὶ διαγγέλλειν αὐτὸν ἔφασαν τὰ παρ' ἐκείνων τοῖς ἀνθρώποις, κῆρυξ μέν, ἐπειδὴ διὰ φωνῆς γεγωνοῦ παριστᾷ τὰ κατὰ τὸν λόγον σημαινόμενα ταῖς ἀκοαῖς, ἄγγελος δέ, ἐπεὶ τὸ βούλημα τῶν θεῶν γιγνώσκομεν ἐκ τῶν ἐνδεδομένων ἡμῖν κατὰ τὸν λόγον ἐννοιῶν. New and significant here is the role of Hermes as a mediator and revealer who as κῆρυξ and ἄγγελος declares and makes known to us the will of the gods. He thus has a soteriological role in so far as the λόγος is present for σῴζειν.[76] Indeed, Hermes is the great power of conception and creation, the λόγος σπερματικός of the Stoa, honoured under the image of the Phallos:[77] γόνιμος ὁ λόγος καὶ τέλειός ἐστιν, and he finally rises to the level of the comprehensive κοινὸς λόγος: διὰ δὲ τὸ κοινὸν αὐτὸν εἶναι καὶ τὸν αὐτὸν ἔν τε τοῖς ἀνθρώποις πᾶσι καὶ ἐν τοῖς θεοῖς. It is interesting to see how in later antiquity the λόγος concept, which derives originally from the cultural and intellectual sphere, sinks back increasingly into the sphere of the natural which it was once fashioned to oppose. Thus in Hellenistic mysticism λόγος is essentially a cosmic and creative potency, the guide and agent of knowledge, increasingly represented as a religious doctrine of salvation, the revealer of what is hidden.[78]

---

[72] Cf. O. Casel, De philosophorum Graecorum silentio mystico, RVV, 16, 2 (1919), 66 ff.

[73] Cf. Hermes as god of *ratio, ordo, numerus* and *scientia*, Sen. Ben., IV, 8.

[74] For a full list of the gods identified with the λόγος or its many aspects cf. Leisegang, Pauly-W., 1061 ff. The λόγος is an independent personification and τοῦ Διὸς ἀδελφός in Menand. Epidict., ed. L. Spengel, Rhetores Graeci, III (1856), p. 341, 16.

[75] This has often been compared with Jn. 3:17.

[76] On this idea, of which there are hints already in Plat. Crat., 407e ff. and Stoicism, cf. Ac. 14:12: ἐκάλουν δὲ τὸν Βαρναβᾶν Δία, τὸν δὲ Παῦλον Ἑρμῆν, ἐπειδὴ αὐτὸς ἦν ὁ ἡγούμενος τοῦ λόγου. Leisegang, Pauly-W., 1063 refers to Iambl. Myst., 1: θεὸς ὁ τῶν λόγων ἡγεμών, and Etym. M., *s.v.* Ἑρμῆς: παρὰ τὸ ἐρῶ, τὸ λέγω, Ἑρμῆς, ὁ τοῦ λόγου ἔφορος, cf. also Orph. (Abel), 28, 4 (to Hermes).

[77] Cf. the λόγος as αἰδοῖον in Reitzenstein, *Zwei religionsgeschichtliche Fragen*, 96, or the λόγος with strong sexual connections in Philo Som., I, 200. Plot. (Enn., III, 6, 19), giving a philosophical interpretation of historically developed popular religion, thought the Gks. rightly represented the god Hermes ithyphallically, i.e., as an image of the procreative intelligible λόγος. Porphyr. in Eus. Praep. Ev., III, 11, 42: ὁ δὲ ἐντεταμένος Ἑρμῆς δηλοῖ τὴν εὐτονίαν, δείκνυσι δὲ καὶ τὸν σπερματικὸν λόγον τὸν διήκοντα διὰ πάντων. For the creation of the world through the divine Λόγος, cf. Sib., 8, 446.

[78] Cf. Plut. Is. et Os., 53 (II, 373b): τοῦ Ἑρμοῦ, τουτέστι τοῦ λόγου, μαρτυροῦντος καὶ δεικνύοντος ὅτι πρὸς τὸ νοητὸν ἡ φύσις μετασχηματιζομένη τὸν κόσμον ἀποδίδωσιν. 373d: τὸ πᾶν ὁ λόγος διαρμοσάμενος σύμφωνον ἐξ ἀσυμφώνων μερῶν ἐποίησε.

Under the influence of ancient Egyptian theology this philosophical and noetic concept ends, therefore, in the mystico-religious speculations of Hermeticism [79] concerning creation and revelation. The λόγος comes forth from → Νοῦς (Corp. Herm., I, 5a: the ἐκ τοῦ φωτὸς προελθὼν λόγος ἅγιος ἐπέβη τῇ ὑγρᾷ φύσει). It is the son of God (I, 6: ὁ ἐκ νοὸς φωτεινὸς λόγος is the υἱὸς θεοῦ). It brings order and form into the world as its δημιουργός: Suid., *s.v.* Ἑρμῆς, ὁ Τρισμέγιστος, No. 3038 (Adler): ὁ γὰρ λόγος αὐτοῦ παντέλειος ὢν καὶ γόνιμος καὶ δημιουργικός, ἐν γονίμῳ φύσει πεσὼν καὶ γονίμῳ ὕδατι, ἔγκυον τὸ ὕδωρ ἐποίησε. Almost all the divine attributes are ascribed to it as such. But as the sum of all the δυνάμεις of the supreme deity it is still an intermediary making contact between God and matter, and also between God, the father of the λόγος, and created being, man. The idea of an intermediate λόγος is further developed in the concept of the father-son relation, cf. Schol. on Ael. Arist., III, p. 564, 19 ff., Dindorf. Thus the λόγος is also the son of Hermes, related to Hermes as Hermes is to the supreme deity, Zeus. In accordance with this intermediate position in creation Horus/Osiris in Plut. Is. et Os., 53 (II, 373a/b) is not καθαρός and εἰλικρινής, οἷος ὁ πατὴρ λόγος αὐτὸς καθ' ἑαυτὸν ἀμιγὴς καὶ ἀπαθής, ἀλλὰ νενοθευμένος τῇ ὕλῃ διὰ τὸ σωματικόν. There is a graded connection which in the Hermetic conception of a world organism is elucidated in the thought of the image (→ εἰκών): The λόγος is an εἰκών of God, and man is an image of the λόγος, Cl. Al. Strom., V, 14, 94, 5: εἰκὼν μὲν γὰρ θεοῦ λόγος θεῖος καὶ βασιλικός, ἄνθρωπος ἀπαθής, εἰκὼν δ' εἰκόνος ἀνθρώπινος νοῦς.

The λόγος is not only God's son. It is also λόγος θεοῦ, Orig. Cels., VI, 60: λέγοντες τὸν μὲν προσεχῶς δημιουργὸν εἶναι τὸν υἱὸν τοῦ θεοῦ λόγον καὶ ὡσπερεὶ αὐτουργὸν τοῦ κόσμου, τὸν δὲ πατέρα τοῦ λόγου τῷ προστεταχέναι τῷ υἱῷ ἑαυτοῦ λόγῳ ποιῆσαι τὸν κόσμον εἶναι πρώτως δημιουργόν.

Together with the → βουλὴ θεοῦ and the κόσμος, the λόγος forms a divine trinity inasmuch as it is the divine seed which the βουλὴ θεοῦ fashions into the visible world (→ I, 634).

4. The λόγοι of Philo of Alexandria.

The Logos concept plays a considerable role in Philo. [80] This is shown at once by the fact that he uses it over 1300 times. [81] To the common use there corresponds a confusing vacillation of meanings [82] which raises such a distinctive problem in relation to Philo. E. Schwartz [83] can deny his derivation of the term from Gk. philosophy; he regards λόγος as at heart and in essence a Jewish term ("Word of God"). [84] L. Cohn, [85] on the other hand, declares that the Stoic λόγος τῆς φύσεως is the root of Philo's λόγος θεοῦ (or θεῖος λόγος) in the sense of the "divine reason," the "epitome of divine wisdom."

The vacillation is naturally due to the synthesising tendency in Philo's attempted uniting of Jewish religion and Gk. philosophical speculation. One can do justice to it only if one first considers the various aspects and understandings of the Philonic concept apart, not trying to harmonise them, but separating the incompatible Gk. and non-Gk. elements. In the main it is only the divine logos which is here at issue. The essential

---

[79] Cf. J. Kroll, *Die Lehren des Hermes Trismegistos* (1914), 57 ff.

[80] For the most important lit. cf. Leisegang, Pauly-W., 1077 f.; O. Willmann, *Geschichte d. Idealismus*, I (1894), 617 ff. Cf. also → Bibl.

[81] Acc. to Leisegang, *op. cit.*, 1072; cf. also the Philo Index, *s.v.*

[82] Cf. L. Grossmann, Quaestionum Philonearum altera de Λόγῳ Philonis (1829); Leisegang, *op. cit.*, 1072 ff.

[83] NGG (→ n. 67), 537 ff.

[84] Esp. because of the connection of the λόγος with the → ῥῆμα θεοῦ (Leg. All., III, 173; Poster. C., 102 of the Law).

[85] *Op. cit.*, 303 ff.

features of this cannot be explained in terms of the development of the Gk. logos concept. Even if we cannot be sure of the detailed roots of this new usage, they are manifestly non-Gk. The term is taken from the academic vocabulary of Hellenistic philosophy. [86] But it is decisively refashioned in a new, very different, and primarily mythologising direction.

This λόγος θεοῦ or θεῖος λόγος, as the new use with the gen. shows, is no longer God Himself as in the Stoa (I, p. 24, 7; II, p. 111, 10, v. Arnim; cf. also Orig. Cels., V, 24: ὁ τῶν πάντων λόγος ἐστὶ κατὰ μὲν Κέλσον αὐτὸς ὁ θεός, κατὰ δὲ ἡμᾶς ὁ υἱὸς αὐτοῦ). It is an ἔργον of God (Sacr. AC, 65). It is a god, but of the second rank (Leg. All., II, 86: τὸ δὲ γενικώτατόν ἐστιν ὁ θεός, καὶ δεύτερος ὁ θεοῦ λόγος, τὰ δ' ἄλλα λόγῳ μόνον ὑπάρχει). As such it is called the → εἰκών (Spec. Leg., I, 81: λόγος δ' ἐστὶν εἰκὼν θεοῦ, δι' οὗ σύμπας ὁ κόσμος ἐδημιουργεῖτο) of the supreme God, and in Philo's doctrine of creation it takes on basic significance not only as ἀρχέτυπον παράδειγμα [87] but also as ὄργανον θεοῦ (Migr. Abr., 6; Cher., 127). With Σοφία [88] God has begotten the κόσμος νοητός as His first-born son [89] (Agric., 51: τὸν ὀρθὸν αὐτοῦ λόγον καὶ πρωτόγονον → υἱόν). This is equated with the λόγος (Op. Mund., 24: οὐδὲν ἂν ἕτερον εἴποι [τις] τὸν νοητὸν κόσμον εἶναι ἢ θεοῦ λόγον ἤδη κοσμοποιοῦντος). Thus the λόγος is a mediating figure which comes forth from God and establishes a link between the remotely transcendent God and the world or man, and yet which also represents man to God as a high-priest (Gig., 52) and advocate (Vit. Mos., II, 133), i.e., as a personal Mediator, and not just in terms of the genuinely Gk. ἀνα-λογία (Plat. Tim., 31c; Plot. Enn., III, 3, 6).

As the κόσμος νοητός it is the sum and locus (Op. Mund., 20) of the creative powers of God, His → δυνάμεις (Fug., 101), the ideas, the individual logoi [90] whereby this visible world is fashioned in detail and also maintained in its ordered life (Rer. Div. Her., 188). As δίοπος καὶ κυβερνήτης τοῦ παντός (Cher., 36) it guides the world in exactly the same way as the Stoic νόμος or λόγος φύσεως.

Now W. Theiler [91] has shown that the λόγος as the sphere of divine ideas, the νόησις θεοῦ, and also as the ὄργανον θεοῦ, belongs to the pre-neo-platonic tradition. Yet two things are non-Gk. in this whole concept. The first is the linguistic form with a gen. or adj.: θεοῦ or θεῖος. This gives the term its distinctive reality, and, as Schwartz has rightly pointed out, marks it off from Gk. usage, even if one cannot always render it "Word of God." The second is the fact that a universal concept is conceived of personally [92] (cf. → Σοφία, → Πνεῦμα, → Νοῦς [93]). Closely linked with this is the

---

[86] It is not surprising in his day that Philo should use the term in all the various senses of Platonism and esp. Stoicism, as λόγος σπερματικός (Leg. All., III, 150), προφορικός and ἐνδιάθετος (Vit. Mos., II, 129), ἑρμηνευτικός (Leg. All., I, 74), esp. as ὀρθὸς λόγος (*ibid.*, III, 1 etc.) — along with the sense of Holy Scripture (Poster. C., 142), even as the Stoic moral and cosmic law (Op. Mund., 143; Deus Imm., 71) and destiny (Deus Imm., 176), and including the material qualities of the ἔνθερμος καὶ πυρώδης λόγος (Cher., 30). Cf. the many examples in Grossmann and Leisegang. For distinctions from Stoicism cf. Aall, I, 195 ff.; on Philo's general method in the development of concepts, cf. Schürer, III^4, 698 ff.

[87] Op. Mund., 25: δῆλον ὅτι καὶ ἡ ἀρχέτυπος σφραγίς, ὅν φαμεν νοητὸν εἶναι κόσμον, αὐτὸς ἂν εἴη [τὸ παράδειγμα, ἀρχέτυπος ἰδέα τῶν ἰδεῶν] ὁ θεοῦ λόγος.

[88] Sometimes the λόγος is also equated with this (Leg. All., I, 65 ἡ δὲ [σοφία] ἐστὶν ὁ θεοῦ λόγος).

[89] The younger son is the κόσμος αἰσθητός, also called the λόγος (Deus Imm., 31).

[90] Also called ἄγγελοι (Som. I, 148) or ψυχαὶ ἀθάνατοι (*ibid.*, I, 127).

[91] "Die Vorbereitung des Neoplatonismus," *Problemata*, 1 (1930), 30 ff.

[92] Acc. to E. Hoffmann, "Platonismus u. Mystik im Altertum" (SAH, 1934/5, 2), 58, who even speaks of an oriental style of thought. This personifying type of thought perhaps explains also the very non-Gk., figurative and allegorical identification of the λόγος with OT characters like Melchizedek, the high-priest, and finally a βασιλεύς, διδάσκαλος, σύμβουλος etc. (for the passages cf. Leisegang, Pauly-W., 1077).

[93] Cf. Kroll, 55 ff.

idea of relationship or sonship, which is expressed in metaphors taken from the sphere of procreation (Agric., 51; Det. Pot. Ins., 54), and which applies both to the manner of the origin of the λόγος and to the mode of its operation, i.e., its wedding of the soul (Spec. Leg., II, 29 ff.) and the fact that it is the father of the daughters ἐπιστῆμαι and ἀρεταί (Gig., 17).

The anthropomorphic view of the world expressed in the image of putting on the cosmos like a garment (Fug., 110) is certainly non-Gk., though it is also non-Jewish too, and seems to point rather in the direction of oriental and Egyptian theology. [94]

5. Hellenistic Logos Speculation and the NT.

There is a great difference between Hellenistic Logos speculation and the NT λόγος.

This is shown first by the pronouncedly rational and intellectual character of the λόγος, and by the fact that it occurs in very different connections and more precise senses in profane Gk. To the Christian, "word," "speech," "reason," and "law" in the absolute, being in some way expressions of man's self-understanding, are not important in themselves. The only important thing is what God has to say to man, the λόγος θεοῦ, the fact which cannot be combined with the Greek view of God, namely, that God addresses man in his life here and now. [95] In the Gk. λόγος concept one may see an attempt to adjust to life and in some way to master the world in terms of the spirit, which is more than calculable causality. Thus the logos concept of Stoicism is too much controlled by human *ratio*, which is, of course, rediscovered in nature, world, and God (M. Ant., IV, 4; XII, 26), to offer any parallels to the NT concept, which in the first instance came in the opposite direction from God to man καὶ ἐσκήνωσεν ἐν ἡμῖν (Jn. 1:14). Of course, man has to decide consciously for this λόγος and the life which corresponds to it. But in life κατὰ λόγον (Diog. L., VII, 52 [86]) he does not accept the claim of a will deriving from another world. He comes to himself, to his true being, and attains his → ἐλευθερία, [96] by following the most inward law, and consequently God. [97] Thus the Gk. λόγος is revelation only in the sense that one perceives the inner law of the matter, or of self, and orientates oneself thereby.

A further demonstration is to be found in the fact that secular Gk. (e.g., in Stoicism and Neo-platonism) can split up the λόγος into many creative individual or partial logoi in all the phenomena which invest the world with being and reality. To be sure, the λόγος is an expression of harmony. [98] It is itself the

---

[94] Cf. the interpretation of the Osiris myth in Plut. Is. et Os., 53 (II, 373b), where it is said of Horus, the elder of the two sons, ὃν ἡ Ἶσις εἰκόνα τοῦ νοητοῦ κόσμου αἰσθητὸν ὄντα γεννᾷ. From the Herm. writings cf. passages like Herm., I, 8; VIII, 2; XI, 9; cf. Orig. Cels., VI, 60. On this cf. Reitzenstein Hell. Myst., 49 and 329; Poim., 41 ff.; also Kroll, 55 ff.; Turowski, 9, n. 22.

[95] On the different usage cf. Schwartz, 555; Bultmann (→ n. 45), 275.

[96] Cf. Max. Tyr., 33, 5: ἐγὼ δὲ ἐλευθερίαν ποθῶν νόμου δέομαι, λόγου δέομαι. M. Ant., VI, 58.

[97] Cf. Plut. Aud., 1 (II, 37d): ταὐτόν ἐστι τὸ ἕπεσθαι θεῷ καὶ τὸ πείθεσθαι λόγῳ. Thus in Plut. Ad Principem Ineruditum, 3 (II, 780 f.) the true ruler is called a μίμημα καὶ φέγγος θεοῦ when he has θεοῦ λόγον as διάνοια, cf. *loc. cit.*: ὁ νόμος ... ἔμψυχος ὢν ἐν αὐτῷ λόγος, Stoic. Rep., 1 (II, 1033b): ὁ ... λόγος τοῦ φιλοσόφου νόμος αὐθαίρετος.

[98] On the λόγος as harmony, cf. Plut. Is. et Os., 55 (II, 373d); cf. E. Hoffmann, 42; → n. 69.

spiritual bond which holds the world together at its heart (Pos. in Philo Fug., 112: ὅ τε γὰρ τοῦ ὄντος λόγος δεσμὸς ὢν τῶν ἁπάντων ... καὶ συνέχει τὰ μέρη πάντα καὶ σφίγγει κωλύων αὐτὰ διαλύεσθαι καὶ διαρτᾶσθαι ... ἁρμονίαν καὶ ἕνωσιν ἀδιάλυτον ἄγει τὴν πρὸς ἄλληλα). But it is not a mediating figure which stands independently between God and the world. Only in so far as the constructive principle is also that which reveals the knowability of things can one speak of the Gk. λόγος having a mediatorial role.

Thirdly, the distinction appears in the fact that the Gk. λόγος in its manifestation is not historically unique. It cannot be dated in time. On the contrary, it is an unbroken working and creating. In the eternal cycle of things (according to the Gk. view of the world) it releases creative and constructive forces, and then takes them back into itself in an eternal process which does not begin with the resolve of a personal God but takes place metaphysically, continually, and eternally in a gradual unfolding of being.

A fourth point is that the Gk. λόγος became, or, in Stoicism and Neo-platonism, is the world. As such it is called a υἱός [99] τοῦ θεοῦ, but is no → μονογενής. In the NT, however, the λόγος became this one historically unique man, σάρξ.

From the very first the NT λόγος concept is alien to Gk. thought. But it later became the point of contact between Christian doctrine and Gk. philosophy. [100]

Kleinknecht

C. The Word of God in the Old Testament.

1. The Hebrew Equivalents of the Greek Terms for Word.

The roots אמר and דבר are the main Hebrew equivalents of the Gk. λόγος, also λόγιον, ῥῆμα, ῥῆσις. Rarer is מִלָּה, which in Hebrew, where it is not an Aramaic loan word (cf. 2 S. 23:2), is mostly restricted to Job, though it is frequent in the Aram. sections of Daniel. Other Heb. words are inaccurately rendered λόγος and ῥῆμα (e.g., תּוֹרָה, תְּבוּנָה, שֵׁבֶט, שָׂפָה, קוֹל, פִּתְגָּם, פֶּה, סֵפֶר, מַשָּׂא, מִצְוָה, טַעַם) and hardly call for consideration in relation to the philology of the word.

Our main concern is with the roots אמר and דבר. Here אֹמֶר, "saying" (Ps. 19:2 f.; 68:11; 77:8; Job 22:28) — perhaps [101] the basic form of אֲמָרִים with the relevant suffix constructions — is used only poetically, as is also אִמְרָה. The nouns אֹמֶר and אִמְרָה are found before the exile (Gn. 4:23; Dt. 33:9; Is. 5:24; 28:23; 29:4), but are mostly post-exilic. They are usually rendered λόγος (some 20 times), ῥῆμα (some 29 times), λόγιον, or ῥῆσις. This poetic meaning is plainly distinguished from the verbal concept אָמַר, "to speak," "to say," which is one of the most common words in the language.

[99] On the equation of λόγος and υἱός cf. Plut. Is. et Os., *loc. cit.*; M. Ant., IV, 29, 3.

[100] For the radical conflict between the ancient and the Christian concept of the Logos cf. already Orig. Cels., II, 31: μετὰ ταῦτα Χριστιανοῖς ἐγκαλεῖ (sc. Κέλσος) ὡς σοφιζομένοις ἐν τῷ λέγειν τὸν υἱὸν τοῦ θεοῦ εἶναι αὐτολόγον, καὶ οἴεταί γε κρατύνειν τὸ ἔγκλημα, ἐπεὶ λόγον ἐπαγγελλόμενοι υἱὸν εἶναι τοῦ θεοῦ ἀποδείκνυμεν οὐ λόγον καθαρὸν καὶ ἅγιον ἀλλὰ ἄνθρωπον ἀτιμότατα ἀπαχθέντα καὶ ἀποτυμπανισθέντα ... οὐδενὸς ἀκήκοα ἐπαινοῦντος τὸ λόγον εἶναι τὸν υἱὸν τοῦ θεοῦ, ὡς ὁ Κέλσος εἴρηκε, ... ὡς εἴ γε ὁ λόγος ἐστὶν ὑμῖν υἱὸς τοῦ θεοῦ, καὶ ἡμεῖς (we Greeks) ἐπαινοῦμεν.

[101] So C. Brockelmann, *Grundriss der vergleichenden Grammatik der semitischen Sprachen*, I (1908), 255.

The basic classical word for λόγος in history and law, prophecy and poetry, is, however, דָּבָר, "word." Etymology must start with the noun, not the verb דִּבֶּר, which seems to be denominated from דָּבָר, as shown by the absence of the qal. דָּבָר would appear to be inseparable from דְּבִיר, the "holiest of all," the "back of the temple," which gives us the basic sense of "back." To this corresponds the Arab. *dubr* "back," which brings us to the heart of the matter.[102] The Arab. *dăbăra* means "to have at one's back," the Ethiop. *tadabbara* "to put on one's back," the Aram. *d'bar* "to be behind" (cf. the German *treiben*[103] and also *führen*).

In דָּבָר one is thus to seek the "back" or "background" of a matter. Whereas אֹמֶר and אִמְרָה denote a saying or expression in the indefinite sense, דָּבָר is to be regarded as the definite content or meaning of a word in which it has its conceptual background. No thing is דָּבָר in itself, but all things have a דָּבָר, a "background" or "meaning." It is easy to see that in speech the meaning or concept stands for the thing, so that a thing, as an event, has in its דָּבָר its historical element, and history is thus enclosed in the דְּבָרִים as the background of things.

Analysis of the term דָּבָר shows two main elements which are both of the highest theological significance. We must distinguish between the dianoetic and the dynamic element. Dianoetically, דָּבָר always contains a νοῦς, a thought. In it is displayed the meaning of a thing, so that דָּבָר always belongs to the field of knowledge. By its דָּבָר a thing is known and becomes subject to thought. To grasp the דָּבָר of a thing is to grasp the thing itself. It becomes clear and transparent; its nature is brought to light. In this connection the word is also distinguished theologically from the spirit, since the OT concept of spirit (רוּחַ) does not originally have this dianoetic element. But along with the dianoetic element is the dynamic, even if this is not always so evident. Every דָּבָר is filled with power which can be manifested in the most diverse energies. This power is felt by the one who receives the word and takes it to himself. But it is present independently of this reception in the objective effects which the word has in history. The two elements, the dianoetic and the dynamic, may be seen most forcefully in the Word of God, and the prophets had a profound grasp of this from both sides, so that in this respect they are the teachers of all theology.

2. The General Use of דָּבָר as a Rendering of λόγος and ῥῆμα.

The main Gk. terms for דָּבָר are λόγος and ῥῆμα.

The LXX uses them as full synonyms, so that we may treat the two together. In the usage of the Pentateuch the proportion between λόγος and ῥῆμα is 56 to 147, so that ῥῆμα easily predominates. In Jos., Ju. and Ruth the figures are 26 to 30, almost equal. In the other historical books (S., K., Ch., Ezr.-Neh., Est.) the proportion is 365 to 200, and in the poetical books (Job, Ps., Prv., Qoh., Cant.) 159 to 72, though ῥῆμα is predominant in Job (50 times as compared with λόγος 19). In the prophets (including Da.) we find λόγος 320 times and ῥῆμα only 40, so that λόγος occurs eight times more than ῥῆμα. In the apocr. too (Wis., Jdt., Sir., Tob., Bar., 1-4 Macc.), λόγος is much more common (221 times to 40). Except in the Octateuch λόγος is thus the predominant rendering.

---

102 Cf. Grether, *op. cit.*, 59 ff.

103 Thus the Aram. *dabrā* ("field") and the Heb. *dober* ("pasture") are related. In the case of מִדְבָּר one might ask whether it does not mean "pasture," or, better, "hinterland."

It has to be kept in view that in the LXX the meaning of λόγος and ῥῆμα is much influenced by the basic Heb. דָּבָר. The great significance of λόγος in Stoic philosophy, like that of πνεῦμα, possibly derives from a Semitic root, since Zeno was certainly a Semite.[104] By nature the Gk. word has a mainly dianoetic value; it receives the dynamic element only from the Heb. דָּבָר.

In Gk. attributes like ἀγαθός (ψ 44:1), καλός (Prv. 23:8), ὀρθός (Prv. 16:13), ἄδικος (Prv. 13:5), πονηρός (2 Εσδρ. 23:17; ψ 63:5), σκληρός (Tob. 13:14 א), ψευδής (Jer. 7:4, 8; Ez. 13:8; Sir. 36:19[24]), ἀληθινός (2 Ch. 9:5), σοφός (1 Εσδρ. 3:9) are immediately understandable; and φιλόσοφος (4 Macc. 5:35) and φιλοσοφώτατος (4 Macc. 1:1) are to be explained in terms of Gk., not Heb. But other combinations can be understood only against a Heb. background, e.g., 2 Βασ. 19:44: ἐσκληρύνθη ὁ λόγος; 24:4: ὑπερίσχυσεν ὁ λόγος; ψ 118:74: εἰς τοὺς λόγους σου ἐπήλπισα (cf. v. 81); v. 89: ὁ λόγος σου διαμένει; v. 154: διὰ τὸν λόγον σου ζῆσόν με; ψ 147:4: ἕως τάχους δραμεῖται ὁ λόγος αὐτοῦ; Dt. 30:14: ἔστιν σου ἐγγὺς τὸ ῥῆμα σφόδρα; Jos. 21:45: οὐ διέπεσεν ἀπὸ πάντων τῶν ῥημάτων; 2 Βασ. 14:20: ἕνεκεν τοῦ περιελθεῖν τὸ πρόσωπον τοῦ ῥήματος τούτου; 3 Βασ. 13:21, 26: παρεπίκρανας τὸ ῥῆμα; Tob. 14:4 א: οὐ μὴ διαπέσῃ ῥῆμα ἐκ τῶν λόγων.

Only in the Heb. דָּבָר is the material concept with its energy felt so vitally in the verbal concept that the word appears as a material force which is always present and at work, which runs and has the power to make alive. In connection with ῥῆμα we might mention here דְּבָרִים = ῥήματα, "history," as used in 3 Βασ. 11:41: ἐν βιβλίῳ ῥημάτων Σαλωμών, or Gn. 15:1; 22:1: μετὰ τὰ ῥήματα ταῦτα, etc., whereas the rendering by λόγοι (3 Βασ. 14:29 etc.) in such cases is in keeping with the linguistic sense of the Greeks. History is the event established and narrated in the word, so that the thing and its meaning may both be seen, as expressed by the Heb. דְּבָרִים in the plural. From these examples it may be seen that the LXX concept cannot be wholly explained in terms of the Gk. λόγος or ῥῆμα, but can be fully understood only against the background of the Hebrew דָּבָר.

To the degree that the meaning of a thing is implied in דָּבָר, the whole point is that the word and the thing are co-extensive. Hence the most important attribute of דָּבָר, and of λόγος and ῥῆμα as translations, is truth.

In keeping is the common reference of the word אֱמֶת ("truth") to the word. As Yahweh's words are אֱמֶת (2 S. 7:28), so human words must be (Gn. 42:16, 20; 1 K. 10:6; 17:24; Ps. 45:4; 119:43; 2 Ch. 9:5). If a word is to be valid, the one concerned ratifies it with an Amen (Dt. 27:15 ff. אָמֵן) or Amen, Amen (Nu. 5:22). Similarly, the verb אמן in the ni is used as the sign of attestation of דָּבָר (Gn. 42:20; 3 Βασ. 8:26; 1 Ch. 17:23; 2 Ch. 1:9; 6:17) in so far as words are found to be true; and to this there corresponds the fact that one believes a word (Dt. 1:32; 1 K. 10:7; Ps. 106:12, 24; 2 Ch. 9:6). "The sum of the divine word is truth" (Ps. 119:160: רֹאשׁ דְּבָרְךָ אֱמֶת).

In every spoken word there should be a relation of truth between word and thing, and a relation of fidelity between the one who speaks and the one who hears. Hence the word belongs to the moral sphere, in which it must be a witness to something for the two persons concerned.

---

[104] M. Pohlenz, "Stoa und Semitismus," *Ilbergs Neue Jahrbücher f. Wiss. u. Jugendbildung*, 2 (1926), 258.

3. The דָּבָר of Prophetic Revelation.

a. Revelation in Sign. The history of the theological development of the concept has its roots in prophecy. In what seems to be the oldest Messianic prophecy which we have (2 S. [= 2 Βασ.] 23:1 ff.), where David confesses that he is a prophet (v. 1: נְאֻם דָּוִד), it is said: πνεῦμα κυρίου ἐλάλησεν ἐν ἐμοί, καὶ ὁ λόγος αὐτοῦ (מִלָּתוֹ) ἐπὶ γλώσσης μου. The rare נְאֻם דָּוִד, in contrast to the later נְאֻם יהוה — so that the prophet is the speaker as compared with the later view of Yahweh as the speaker — is very ancient, almost the only other instance being in the Balaam oracles in J (Nu. 24:4, 16, cf. Prv. 30:1). The prophet is seized by God, by His Spirit (רוּחַ) and Word (מִלָּה = λόγος). The power of God finds recognisable expression in the λόγος. The image of the Messianic king, which appears in the λόγος, is evoked by the Spirit. In pneumatic rapture, the prophet receives an ear and eye for this suprasensual picture, and the mystery is thus revealed and imparted.

Equally old is the depiction of the ecstatic Balaam (Nu. 24:4, 16), in whose mouth God sets His Word (Nu. 22:38; 23:5, 16). He speaks as שֹׁמֵעַ אִמְרֵי־אֵל = ἀκούων λόγια θεοῦ, as יֹדֵעַ דַּעַת עֶלְיוֹן = ἐπιστάμενος ἐπιστήμην παρὰ Ὑψίστου (24:16), as one who מַחֲזֵה שַׁדַּי יֶחֱזֶה = ὅρασιν θεοῦ ἰδών in the state of a נֹפֵל וּגְלוּי עֵינָיִם = ἐν ὕπνῳ, ἀποκεκαλυμμένοι οἱ ὀφθαλμοὶ αὐτοῦ. With opened eye he sees the face of God, with opened ear [105] he hears God's sayings (λόγια). In vision and audition revelation is contained as the knowledge of God (דַּעַת עֶלְיוֹן) which comes forth from God and has God's plan as its content. Here again one may see the connection between image and word in earliest prophecy. The Messianic picture contains the word of prophecy. Pictorial language is to be translated into words.

The writing prophets of the classical age are also familiar with pictorial revelation which contains the revelation of word. The visions at the call of Isaiah (6) and Ezekiel (1) present images from which the word can be taken.

One might also refer to the visions which God causes Amos to see (7:1 ff.; 8:1 f.; 9:1 ff.) and with which God's voice is linked. The image as such already contains a complete revelation. In Ez. the transcendent glory of God is pictorially expressed in the vision at his call (2:1 ff.). This finds an echo in the awe of the prophet, which causes him to fall down (2:1 ff.). Amos as גְּלוּי עֵינָיִם at once perceives in the five visions the sign of judgment. The sequence of the visions indicates a heightening of the tension from anxiety at approaching judgment to certainty that it is present, so that the last vision depicts utter destruction (9:1 ff.). But here a divine word of interpretation is always sought in the picture. In Zechariah we again find instantaneous images whose meaning is at once apparent to the watchful prophet without a word (4:1-6, 10 ff.; 5:1-4, 5 ff.). Nevertheless, along with these we also find moving images whose sense cannot be apprehended in a moment but is disclosed only in a temporal process (1:7 ff.; 6:1-8), so that even the prophet himself (1:9; 2:4; 4:4; 6:4) needs an interpretative word, let alone his hearers. This is why the angel of interpretation comes to translate the image into a word.

b. Revelation in Sign and Word. In the great writing prophets, however, the significance of the pictorial revelation is much less than that of the verbal revelation. The original voice which they perceive in themselves is no longer revealed as their own voice (2 S. 23:1: נְאֻם דָּוִד) but as the voice of Yahweh (נְאֻם יְהוָה).

---

105 On the state of the גְּלוּי אֹזֶן cf. Is. 22:14.

In the infinitive נאם, the whispering which is not originally to be regarded as articulated speech, the דְּבַר־יְהוָֹה develops constantly increasing clarity and energy.

The interconnection of image and word, in which דָּבָר is the background and meaning of the sign, may again be seen in the puns of, e.g., Amos 8:2, where קַיִץ ("summer fruit") is linked with קֵץ ("end"), or Jeremiah 1:11 f., where שָׁקֵד ("almond tree") reminds us of the watchful Yahweh (שֹׁקֵד), so that the sign passes into the sound.

The word does not have to be combined with an image. It can be received as a voice. In the prophets the original sound develops into harmonies and rhythms whose divine sense finds expression in the human word. The word of revelation in saying and sermon may be very short or it may be a most powerful oration.[106] In every saying or sermon the original word received from God is the vital nerve so that the finished prophetic address may be described as the Word of God. Reception of God's Word by the prophets can be called a spiritual process, though the close connection between Word and Spirit which we find in the NT is comparatively rarely seen in the OT.

The Spirit is expressly mentioned, however, in the last words of David (2 S. 23:2) and the oracles of Balaam (Nu. 24:2), and Hosea does not avoid the description אִישׁ הָרוּחַ (9:7). Moreover, that which we call spiritual is implicitly contained in every verbal revelation, though according to OT usage spiritual operations are discerned chiefly in the נָבִיא, the ecstatic, who is not identical with the seer (רֹאֶה, חֹזֶה), and who is distinguished, not so much by the sign and word of revelation, but rather by ecstatic gestures and violent actions.[107] It is only as the concept of the seer is gradually merged with that of the ecstatic (cf. 1 S. 9:9) that דָּבָר becomes a mark of the נָבִיא as תּוֹרָה is of the priest (Jer. 18:18).

c. Dissolution of the Sign. In the history of prophecy the דָּבָר increasingly freed itself from the sign and became a pure expression of revelation. The prophet realised that God Himself was addressing him therein. The E formula: Abraham, Abraham (Gn. 22:1 vl.); Jacob, Jacob (46:2); Moses, Moses (Ex. 3:4), suggests the urgency with which the divine voice smites the heart of the hearer and enables him to receive the revelation. The process is very beautifully described in the case of Samuel (1 S. 3:1 ff.). Yahweh reveals Himself (3:21: נִגְלָה יהוה) to him in Shiloh[108] by a summons which implies a call, for previously the Word and revelation of Yahweh were not known to him (3:7: טֶרֶם יִגָּלֶה אֵלָיו דְּבַר־יְהוָֹה). He believes that he is hearing the voice of Eli, i.e., a human voice (3:4 f.), until Eli sets him on the right track and he declares to God his readiness to hear: דַּבֵּר יְהוָֹה כִּי שֹׁמֵעַ עַבְדֶּךָ (3:9, 10). He then receives the prophecy in clear terms, for Yahweh Himself comes and stands before him (v. 10, cf. Gn. 28:13). This reminds us of the traditional revelation of the דָּבָר to Eliphaz in Job 4:12-16, except that here a figure appeared. Later, it is by the דְּבַר אֱלֹהִים that Samuel promises Saul the royal dignity (1 S. 9:27), which is thus a divine charisma; and later still he challenges Saul on the performance of the divine word (1 S. 15:13: הֲקִימֹ) concerning the Amalekite king, and announces judgment because of Saul's scorning (v. 23, 26: מָאַסְתָּ אֶת דְּבַר־יְהוָֹה)

[106] Cf. K. Beyer, *Spruch u. Predigt bei den vorexilischen Schriftpropheten* (Diss. Erlangen, 1933).
[107] A. Jepsen, *Nabi* (1934), 43 ff. seems to me to efface the distinctions.
[108] בדבר יהוה is rightly left out in the LXX.

of the Word of God. The explosive and destructive power of the דְּבַר־יְהוָֹה is here impressively depicted. The דְּבַר־יְהוָֹה which the prophet receives by revelation (1 S. 3:7) embraces both promise and demand. It is despised at the cost of life itself.

From the days of Samuel the דְּבַר־יהוה is the decisive force in the history of Israel. It is given to David through Nathan (2 S. 7:4) and to Elijah (1 K. 17:2, 8). It plays a constructive historical part in the march of events. In K., Jer. and Ez. the formula וַיְהִי דְּבַר־יְהוָֹה is common in connection with the prophet addressed (1 K. 6:11; 13:20; Jer. 1:4, 11; 2:1; 13:8; 16:1; 24:4; 28:12; 29:30; Ez. 3:16; 6:1; 7:1; 12:1). Though it may often be ascribed to the redactor, it shows that the prophetic view of history, with which is linked the Deuteronomic, regards the prophet as an agent of revelation who perceives the secret plan and will of God at work in history. The Word of God is fulfilled (1 K. 2:27: לְמַלֵּא אֶת־דְּבַר יְהוָֹה = πληρωθῆναι τὸ ῥῆμα κυρίου); it comes to pass (Ju. 13:12, 17; 2 K. 22:16: בא), it stands for ever (Is. 40:8: יָקוּם לְעוֹלָם) without any co-operation on man's part. The mystery of God (Ju. 3:19: דְּבַר־ סֵתֶר, v. 20: דְּבַר־אֱלֹהִים) is to be seen herein, and its content is irresistible (2 K. 1:17; 9:36; Is. 9:7; 55:10 f.). Everywhere that the true prophet speaks בִּדְבַר יְהוָֹה = ἐν λόγῳ κυρίου (1 K. 13:1, 2, 5, 9, 17, 32 — ἐν ῥήματι κυρίου only in 3 Βασ. 13:18), things take place כִּדְבַר יְהוָֹה = κατὰ τὸ ῥῆμα κυρίου (1 K. 12:24; 15:29; 16:12, 34).

d. The Writing Prophets. The books of the writing prophets are often opened by the formula דְּבַר־יְהוָֹה אֲשֶׁר הָיָה אֶל־[הוֹשֵׁעַ] (Hos. 1:1; Mi. 1:1; Zeph. 1:1; cf. Mal. 1:1). Perhaps this is added by the collector of a pre-exilic series, since the date as well as the name is regularly given. It is probably later than the titles חֲזוֹן יְשַׁעְיָהוּ (Is. 1:1), דִּבְרֵי עָמוֹס (Am. 1:1; cf. Jer. 1:1), סֵפֶר חֲזוֹן נַחוּם (Na. 1:1), which mention the prophet as author. It is also found in the LXX in Jer. 1:1, where the Mas. is דִּבְרֵי יִרְמְיָהוּ. It certainly implies that the whole book is regarded as דְּבַר־יְהוָֹה. In the written form no distinction is made between the divine voice in the prophet and its expression in poetry, saying, and address. We have here a transition to the final view that not merely the prophetic book, but in the last resort the whole of the OT, is the Word of God. The element of revelation is plainly present in the concept of word. For it is as revelation that the books are collected. But this element is present from the very first in the prophetic concept of the word, cf. the partial title (Is. 2:1) to Isaiah's oldest writing (Is. 2-6), which runs הַדָּבָר אֲשֶׁר חָזָה יְשַׁעְיָהוּ. The bold image of the word which is seen, found also in Jer. 2:31 but not translated by the LXX, suggests in prophetic speech the close connection between sign and word. The book probably opened with the call (Is. 6). Both in time and substance this comes first, whereas the prophecy of international peace (2:2-5) is not so appropriate an opening. The seen word is the divine word of revelation which is embodied in vision and audition. Is. also refers to דְּבַר־יְהוָֹה as the word of revelation within his addresses, e.g., when he introduces a new train of thought (1:10; 9:7; 28:14; 37:22; cf. 38:7), and even within the structure of an address (2:3; 16:13; 28:13; 30:12). It is characteristic that he equates the Word of God with God's teaching (תּוֹרָה), 1:10; 2:3; 30:9, 12, for תּוֹרָה is originally the doctrine of God mediated by the priest (cf. Jer. 18:18).[109] As compared with תּוֹרָה, however, דָּבָר

[109] Cf. J. Begrich, "Die priesterliche Thora," in P. Volz-F. Stummer-J. Hempel, *Werden u. Wesen des AT* = ZAW Beih., 66 (1936), 63-88.

has a dynamic, creative and destructive element; Is. 9:7 is a classical example. Yahweh does not retract the words which He has spoken by the prophet, Is. 31:2. In itself revelation in word is a great blessing, 2:3. This is true even when judgment falls because it is despised, 28:13. The relation here is the same as in Amos, for whom the Word of God is a revelation (3:7) which, when received, forces the prophet willy-nilly to prophesy (3:8; cf. 3:1; 4:1; 5:1). Revelation is a blessing whose absence is felt as a judgment, for they will thirst for the Word of Yahweh and they will not find it (8:11 f.).[110] The Word of Yahweh is a vital force whose withdrawal means that grace ceases.

The most profound theological understanding of the word is to be found in Jer. In accordance with the common usage, Jer. sees the Torah committed to the priest, while the prophet is the specific agent of the דָּבָר (18:18), though, like Is., he closely relates תּוֹרָה and דָּבָר as forms of revelation. His main concern, however, is not with the תּוֹרָה, which, like Hosea (8:12), he knows as a written book (8:8). It is with the דָּבָר whose innermost being he has discovered. Dedicated a prophet from his mother's womb (1:5), he receives at his call the certainty that Yahweh has put His words on his lips (1:9) as He once did with Balaam (Nu. 22:38; 23:5, 16). From the very first revelation, then, he embodies the Word of Yahweh in his addresses (1:11, 12), and the roll of the book which he has Baruch write for him contains nothing but the words of God (36:2). When he speaks of God's Word, he does not have primarily in view the dianoetic sense, though he lays great stress on knowledge. He thinks first of the dynamic content, which he has felt strongly in his constant wrestling with God. In the midst of his sufferings he confesses that God's Word is the joy and delight of his heart (15:16), that he has swallowed it (if we may trust the doubtful Heb. text of 15:16). This he has in fact done. The supreme grace which can come to him through submission of his own will to God in prayer is his renewed appointment as the mouth of God whose witness has the power of conversion for others too (15:19). But the Word also puts him under a divine constraint which his nature resists (20:7 ff.). It is thus sharply differentiated from his human thoughts. The prophet's preaching brings him only mockery and shame, so that he would rather not declare the Word of God. But it is a burning fire in his soul shut up in his bones, so that he cannot contain it.[111] The meaning seems to be that he is inwardly aflame with the Word of Yahweh and will perish if he does not speak. This Word does not well up from his own soul. It is tossed into it like a burning brand. It demands to be passed on in his preaching. The torch which has been kindled must shine out; otherwise it will consume the one who bears it. Never has the constraint of preaching the Word found more poignant utterance. Never has the martyrdom of the prophet been more keenly felt. He has to preach the Word for his own soul's salvation. The specific distinction of this Word from the word of man is thus made plain. The divine constraint as the very opposite of even the most pure and tender human nature is fully perceived. But these conflicts in the soul of Jer. also bring to light the moral nature of the knowledge and power in which his character is purified in wrestling with the Word. It is his supreme burden and joy to be a prophet of the Word, an example of the operation of the Word in the great men of Church

---

110 8:11, reading דְּבַר יְהוָה with LXX Syr Vg.

111 The subj. of Jer. 20:9b α (וְהָיָה) is hardly God, but the דָּבָר, since לֹא אֶזְכְּרֶנּוּ in v. 9a does not refer to God but to the דָּבָר received.

history. The dynamic side of the דָּבָר = λόγος is also forcefully portrayed in Jeremiah's self-differentiation from ordinary prophecy (23:28 f.). The prophet who has dreams tells his dreams; the one in whom is God's Word tells God's Word. The relation of the Word of God to the dream of the prophet is like that of the wheat to the straw. It may be clothed in a vision, but it is independent of it. It is an irresistible force, like the fire in which the chaff is consumed or like a hammer which breaks the rock, 23:29. Thus the דְּבַר־יְהוָה can be depicted only by one who has been seized and broken by it. Here, too, Jer. displays an astonishing ability to analyse the prophetic consciousness into which the Word of Yahweh has come. Since God's Word is power, it is infallibly accomplished. Its authenticity may be known by the fact that it comes to pass, 28:9: בְּבֹא, cf. Ju. 13:12, 17; 2 K. 22:16; Ps. 105:19; 107:20. It may be contained in an event which is apparently indifferent in itself, as when Jer. is asked by his uncle to buy a field for him, and he perceives in this the Word of Yahweh, 32:1 ff. But it can be found only in prayer, 42:1 ff. Only prayer, whether as self-subjection to God (15:10 ff.) or as intercession (42:7 ff.), can give clarity concerning the Word of revelation.

Whereas in Jer. wrestling with the Word of God is a matter of personal destiny, in Dt. Is. the דְּבַר־יְהוָה is a historical force. This theoretician among the prophets seems to see the דָּבָר embodied in the history of prophecy. As living divine revelation it is worked out in terms of the development of things. Nature passes away, but the Word of Yahweh lasts for ever, Is. 40:8. God's prophecy carries its fulfilment within itself. Dt. Is. finds proof of God in this fulfilled Word. Since the prophetic word proclaims a new creation which is being prepared in the old, this new creation will come. The דְּבַר־יְהוָה is presented as absolute by nature in the well-known comparison with rain and snow in Is. 55:10 f. As rain and snow cannot be unfruitful but soak into the earth and cause seeds to sprout, so the Word of Yahweh cannot return to heaven without accomplishing its mission. It executes God's will and does what it is sent to do. The Word is bound to prophecy, yet this does not produce it in its own strength, but receives it from heaven. Every prophetic word is an effectual force, and the epitome of all prophecy is the living and eternal Word of God. As in Jer., the dynamic aspect of the דְּבַר־יְהוָה is here more prominent than the dianoetic. The Word is seen to be a heavenly force which creatively accomplishes its work on earth.

4. The דָּבָר as Revelation of the Law.

The דְּבַר־יְהוָה always contains revelation, and the revelation of the Word is the main form of all divine revelation. The prophetic word establishes a personal and moral relation between God and the prophet. Here is something total, so that the entire work of the prophet can be called דְּבַר־יהוה, Is. 2:1; Hos. 1:1; Mi. 1:1; Zeph. 1:1. He who is smitten by the Word, so that he receives it into himself and is orientated thereto, has become a new man. But along with this is the revelation of the Law, which can also be expressed by דָּבָר, though usually in the plural rather than the singular. Whereas the prophetic word always has topical significance, though the *hic et nunc* can determine the whole life of the prophet, as may be seen from the example of Jer., the legal דָּבָר is valid for the whole people in every age quite independently of the prophetic recipient.

The best example is the Decalogue, whose ten sayings can be called עֲשֶׂרֶת הַדְּבָרִים by J in Ex. 34:28, cf. Dt. 4:13; 10:4, though the ancient Decalogue has here been replaced by a law of a very different kind, Ex. 34:10-26. The ten sayings are the basic law of Israel which underlies the divine covenant (Ex. 34:27 f.), which is inviolably valid in every age, and the transgression of which spells ruin for the people (cf. Hos. 4:2 f.; Jer. 7:9). The same is true of the דְּבָרִים of the book of the covenant (Ex. 24:4, 8 E), which is read by Moses on the making of the covenant (24:7), and to which the people pledges itself. The contents of this book are not imparted. What we now call the book of the covenant (Ex. 20:23 — chapter 23) seems more likely to have arisen, not at Sinai, but at the end of the Book of Joshua (24:25).[112]

Later, Deuteronomy was identified with the Sinaitic book of the covenant. For it bears the name סֵפֶר הַבְּרִית (2 K. 23:2 f., 21; cf. Ex. 24:7), and it purports to proclaim as Moses' testament the divine words which he received on the mount of God (1:1: אֵלֶּה הַדְּבָרִים). In the choice of דְּבָרִים as the title for Dt. one may see the prophetic character of the work, for the words which Moses has to proclaim are words of revelation. The title in 4:44: זֹאת הַתּוֹרָה, which selects the priestly תּוֹרָה (cf. esp. 4:45), is thus to be regarded as secondary. But in the basic singular of Dt. there may be found also the singular הַדָּבָר as the epitome of promise (9:5) and Law (13:1). This is best brought out at the end in 30:11 ff., where הַמִּצְוָה (v. 11) and הַדָּבָר (v. 14) are identified as the sum of Dt. The divine Word which is presented to Israel as מִצְוָה is not beyond the power of Israel to grasp and to do (לֹא נִפְלֵאת הִוא מִמְּךָ, v. 11), as though no inner relation were possible. It is not hidden in heaven or beyond the sea, so that no one can fetch and proclaim it. But קָרוֹב אֵלֶיךָ הַדָּבָר מְאֹד (v. 14). The Word is present revelation. It carries within it the power of performance. The mouth and heart are organs to proclaim and fulfil it. To take effect, it seeks to be proclaimed on the lips and received into the heart. The revelation of God's will becomes preaching. As such, it permeates the length and breadth of the people. It mediates itself through historical agents in the historical world. The thought is analogous to that of Is. 55:10 f., except that Dt. lays greater stress on the commandment than the message. Divine revelation, however, is both. For in Dt. Moses is also a prophet (18:15 ff.). In the original Dt. the priestly תּוֹרָה plays no part, just as דָּבָר plays no real role in priestly legislation, which in P is only rarely called the Law of God (Lv. 4:13; 8:5, 36; 9:6; 17:2). The דָּבָר = λόγος belongs to the prophet, the תּוֹרָה = νόμος to the priest (Jer. 18:18).

5. The Divine Word of Creation.

In the post-exilic period, when the Law was assembled in the Pentateuch and the prophets in the נְבִיאִים רִאשֹׁנִים and אַחֲרֹנִים, so that the Word of God took fixed written form, the prophetic concept of the דְּבַר־יְהוָֹה merges with the legal to form a single whole, even though the written form as such is not given the name דְּבַר־יְהוָֹה. As noted, דְּבַר־יְהוָֹה is chosen as the title for many prophetic books (Hos. 1:1; Mi. 1:1; Zeph. 1:1), and the sing. דָּבָר is also used for Dt. (30:14). Since the Word of Yahweh always contained revelation, whether in the Law or the prophets, it could always be used to denote the revealed will of God. Indeed, there is a third sphere of revelation, namely, in the creation of nature, which is everywhere attributed to the Word of God. This thought, though without the term, is present already in the P creation story (Gn. 1), where the world has its origin in

---

112 Cf. H. Holzinger, *Einleitung in den Hexateuch* (1893), 179 and 250.

the divine Word. It is usually thought that this story is the refashioning of an older account, the work which God does (Gn. 2:2: הַמְּלָאכָה אֲשֶׁר עָשָׂה), being replaced by the word which He speaks (וַיְהִי כֵן). This spiritualising of the work of creation may be traced back to a spiritualising of priestly thinking, though it is not impossible that some influence was exerted by Accadian ideas of the creative power of the word,[113] which are well attested. There can certainly be no doubt that the concept of creation by the Word was pre-exilic, for Ez. is independent of P and he is acquainted with the creative power of the דָּבָר (37:4: דְּבַר־יְהוָה), and is followed in this regard by Dt. Is. (40:26; 44:24 ff.; 48:13; cf. 55:10 f.). The Psalter, whose theology is also an influence on Dt. Is., frequently emphasises this creative power (147:15-18), and in the depiction of the creation of heaven by the דָּבָר in Ps. 33 we find the succinct formulation: כִּי הוּא אָמַר וַיֶּהִי הוּא־צִוָּה וַיַּעֲמֹד.

6. The Word in Poetry.

As the creative power of דָּבָר = λόγος came forth out of nothing (Ps. 33), so in poetry revelation is effected by the Word (Job 4:12). In keeping with its prophetic or legal character, the דָּבָר is here regarded as one of promise or of demand. But everywhere it contains revelation, and everywhere it has both a dianoetic and a dynamic element.

The much misunderstood 119th psalm is a veritable treasury of the various nuances of דָּבָר, and it sheds light on דְּבַר־יְהוָה from every side. Here דְּבַר־יְהוָה is normally in the sing.; דְּבָרֶיךָ with plur. suffix may often be regarded as an original sing. The poetic אִמְרָה can sometimes be substituted for it (v. 38, 41, 103, 123, 154, 162, 170) with no essential alteration of sense. תּוֹרָה in particular is used interchangeably with דָּבָר (v. 1, 18, 34, 44, 51, 61, 72, 97, 126, 136, 163), and from this it is clear that the author is thinking esp. of the Pentateuch as the written Word of God. But תּוֹרָה comprehends both promise and demand, so that the prophetic sense is emphasised as well as the legal. The Word stands in heaven (v. 89). Its sum is truth (v. 160). It is a light on the path (v. 105). It has the content of life, for according to its measure God quickens the righteous (v. 25, 107, 154) and gives him understanding (v. 169). It has within it power, for the poet trusts in it (v. 42 בטח) and hopes in it (v. 74, 81, 114, 147; cf. Ps. 130:5). It demands obedience and observance (v. 57, 101). It thus has moral significance for man. It is both promise and hope, demand and power. As one may say that both the motivation and the rest of faith and of the moral life are to be found in the תּוֹרָה, so one may find these in the Word because it contains God's revelation. Since its quintessence is truth, one can rely on God's Word absolutely.

The Jewish community lived on this treasure of the Word on the basis of the confession stated in the Pentateuch and believed in by the righteous. But with the canonisation of the prophets as well as the Law, the written word of the prophetic collection was also accepted as canonical, and finally the Writings were added too. The διάνοια and δύναμις of Scripture are to be found in the Word.

Procksch

D. Word and Speech in the New Testament.

1. Basic and General Aspects of the Use of λέγω/λόγος.

The emphasis which the whole of the NT places on hearing (→ ἀκούω, I, 219) presupposes a preceding speaking. An essential part of the religious relation im-

---

113 Cf. Grether, *op. cit.*, 139 ff.

plied in the NT is thus expressed both quantitatively and qualitatively by the many words for speech — → ἀγγέλλω and derivatives, → κηρύσσω/κήρυγμα, → μαρτυρέω etc. It is thus no accident, nor is it the result of arbitrary extraneous influences, that the fundamental Gk. word for speech, both as verb and esp. as noun (λέγω/λόγος), should be the vehicle of important NT statements. Even in matters where the whole emphasis seems to be on action, e.g., the baptism and transfiguration, the → φωνὴ λέγουσα (Mt. 3:17; 17:5) is not just an accompanying phenomenon. It is that which gives the event its theme and content.

It is to be noted, of course, that in the use of the term this special content does not claim or attain any exclusiveness. In the NT both as a whole and in detail both the verb and the noun run the whole gamut of usage from the most everyday to the most pregnant.

That the usage remained basically free from necessary implication is shown by the ingenuous way in which many statements can be made that enshrine a negative estimate of the "word." Thus in the NT, as elsewhere in the Gk. world,[114] it can be said of something which is present only as λόγος that it is nothing (Col. 2:23). λόγος is also the term for a bad word. The NT speaks of the σαπρὸς λόγος (Eph. 4:29), κενοὶ[115] λόγοι (Eph. 5:6),[116] λόγοι πονηροί (3 Jn. 10), the λόγος κολακείας (1 Th. 2:5), the λόγος which is comparable with a canker (2 Tm. 2:17), πλαστοὶ λόγοι (2 Pt. 2:3). It describes how the human λόγος works itself out in sin, and exceptions to this rule, though not impossible, are rare:[117] πολλὰ γὰρ πταίομεν ἅπαντες· εἴ τις ἐν λόγῳ οὐ πταίει, οὗτος τέλειος ἀνήρ (Jm. 3:2; → γλῶσσα, I, 721). Above all, 1 C. 1-4 lashes this word of human wisdom (1:17; 2:1, 4, 13) which pretends to be καθ' ὑπεροχήν (2:1) and yet which is mere vaunting (4:19 f.). This speech is called human, not because it is spoken by men, but because its content is human. The same human lips can be instruments of the Word of God (1 Th. 2:13).

Along with this negative estimation we should mention the many occurrences in which there is no judgment. The account of something, whether spoken by Jesus, the disciples, or another, refers to "these words" (Mt. 7:28; Ac. 2:22; 16:36). or collectively[118] "this word" (Mk. 7:29; 10:22),[119] or "many words" (Lk. 23:9). Paul distinguishes between a letter and the spoken word (λόγος, 2 Th. 2:2, 15; 2 C. 10:10; cf. Ac. 15:27), though even in the same sentence (2 C. 10:11) he can call a letter the bearer and reproduction of the λόγος (2 Th. 3:14; cf. Hb. 5:11; 13:22). An address (Ac. 2:41; 20:7), an account (Ac. 11:22), a rumour (Lk. 5:15; 7:17), can all be called λόγος, and also the partial record embodied in a book (Ac. 1:1).[120] Whether in the νοῦς or the γλῶσσα, what is spoken is always a λόγος (1 C. 14:19). In the second case it may be inarticulate. It may not be in

---

114 For examples cf. Pass., *s.v.*; comm. on Col. 2:23.

115 Cf. κενοφωνία in 2 Tm. 2:16.

116 The examples show that with the negative estimation too the plur. and sing. are interchanged at will, even in the same epistle.

117 Schl. Jk., 213: "Regulation of the word is the most difficult thing of all and the last to be attained."

118 How meaningless the distinction often is between the plur. and the collective sing. may be seen from Ac. 2:40 f.: ἑτέροις δὲ λόγοις πλείοσιν διεμαρτύρατο ... οἱ μὲν οὖν ἀποδεξάμενοι τὸν λόγον αὐτοῦ ...

119 On Mk. 9:10 → n. 140.

120 On the πρῶτος λόγος (= Lk.) cf. Philo Omn. Prob. Lib., 1; Gal. De Usu Partium Corporis Humani, II, 1 (III, p. 88, Kühn); Hdt., V, 36. Cf. Zn. Ag., *ad loc.*

the form of connected words and sayings (ῥήματα, → 75; 79). But, as something which involves a λέγειν, it is a λόγος.

Ac. 20:24 :[121] ἀλλ' οὐδενὸς λόγου ποιοῦμαι τὴν ψυχὴν τιμίαν ἐμαυτῷ,[122] "but I do not regard my life as worth a word (worth speaking of) for myself." Cf. Hdt., IV, 28 : λόγου ἄξιον, also the similar form λόγον ποιεῖν or ποιεῖσθαι, "to have regard for something," Hdt., I, 4; III, 25 etc.; Theocr. Idyll., 2, 61; Jos. Ant., 1, 72; 7, 88; 11, 82; Job 22:4. It seems that the text was soon assimilated to this common expression, and at the same time extended, because it was felt to be difficult and unusual. Thus the form arose : ἀλλ' οὐδενὸς λόγον ποιοῦμαι οὐδὲ ἔχω τὴν ψυχήν μου τιμίαν ἐμαυτῷ,[123] "but I have regard for nothing, I count not my life as dear to myself." The reverse possibility that the first form was garbled is less likely.[124]

It is obvious that the main emphasis of the term is always on saying something. This is why there is such a range of possibilities and such a notable vacillation in sense. The word can contain γνῶσις or true σοφία (1 C. 12:8). It can also be opposed to them (2 C. 11:6). Or it can be set alongside them (1 C. 1:5; 2 C. 8:7). In the same way word and act, or word and power, can be mutually exclusive (1 Th. 1:5; 1 C. 4:19 f.), or complementary (Lk. 24:19; R. 15:18; 2 Th. 2:17; Col. 3:17). The emphasis of the sentence will decide whether the word intended is empty sound or whether it carries within it a content which impels towards and necessitates action. This multiplicity of possibilities can express anything said or spoken ; it can embrace any content put in words.

It becomes fully evident when one compares with it the specific theological concept, yet to be discussed, of the word which proffers the Gospel and its message. Even this part of the usage, which is so pregnant, can be accompanied in the same sentence by looser and less pregnant forms. 1 Th. 1:5 f.: ὅτι τὸ εὐαγγέλιον ἡμῶν οὐκ ἐγενήθη εἰς ὑμᾶς ἐν λόγῳ μόνον, ἀλλὰ καὶ ἐν δυνάμει ... καὶ ὑμεῖς ... δεξάμενοι τὸν λόγον ..., 1 C. 2:4 : καὶ ὁ λόγος μου καὶ τὸ κήρυγμά μου[125] οὐκ ἐν πειθοῖς σοφίας λόγοις ..., 1 Pt. 3:1: ἵνα καὶ εἴ τινες ἀπειθοῦσιν τῷ λόγῳ ... ἄνευ λόγου κερδηθήσονται.[126] The material distance between such logos-statements is as great as it could be. Nevertheless, there is no need to change the words even in this close spatial proximity. This shows that the chief and proper emphasis of the word remains the same no matter how strong the impress of a given content. The reference is always to a spoken word. Even in the Prologue to John, the term never becomes a purely formal one. It always contains the living concept of a spoken word, in this case the word spoken by God to the world. When it is the word of revelation, in some way the decisive thing is recollection of the One who in living reality speaks this word. The word is never an independent entity. As a genuine word, it always finds its essence and meaning in the fact that it points to Him who spoke it. The essence of the distinctive NT logos-statement is thus to be found, not in the term or form as such, but in the actual relation to Him.

---

[121] Cf. H. A. W. Meyer[4] (1870), Zn. Ag., *ad loc.*; Schl. Lk., 624.

[122] So ℵ*BC etc.

[123] So text. rec. acc. to EHLP etc.

[124] So Zn. Ag., 716, n. 67.

[125] Note the parallelism of λόγος and κήρυγμα, which gives a highly individual content to λόγος.

[126] Cf. Ac. 6:4 f.; 11:19, 22.

The same is true of the formula which on the lips of Jesus seems particularly to indicate the verbal character of revelation by using the verb. The highly emphatic λέγω of the ἐγὼ[127] λέγω ὑμῖν (and similar formulae), because it is so very common, undoubtedly characterises the authoritative sayings of Jesus. It is also possible that the link with ἀμήν,[127] found only on the lips of Jesus, represents a conscious peculiarity of the word of Jesus. This is not true of the λέγω as such. Even early Christianity did not regard it as a specific Christ formula.[128] In the tradition it was used also of the Baptist (Mt. 3:9 : λέγω γὰρ ὑμῖν). Paul felt no constraint in using it of himself (Gl. 5:2 : ἐγὼ Παῦλος λέγω ὑμῖν).[129] It is even put on the lips of Gamaliel (Ac. 5:38 : καὶ τὰ νῦν λέγω ὑμῖν). It is not authoritarian speech as such which constitutes a Christ saying, but the content which sets aside traditional authorities (Mt. 5:21 ff.) and the fact that this content is offered through Christ (Mt. 13:17).

2. More Specific and Technical Meanings.

In the NT, too, the term λόγος as an expression for something which is really said can be used in a more specific sense. But this is not because the first emphasis is overborne or reduced to silence by a strong accent or content. No λόγος statement is so affected or enhanced by new factors that the original "word" character is transcended by this new and more significant use. This could happen in Philo because for him the categories of speaking and hearing were secondary (→ I, 217). There is no such development in the NT, since all the theocentric and christocentric contents which the word can have find in the idea of speaking and the spoken word a perfectly adequate revelational form beyond which they need not seek a higher. If the basic character is in any way weakened in the NT, it is rather by a loss of emphasis, by a tonelessness due to the influence of current usage.

This development may be noted in 4 respects in the NT.

a. λόγος, "reckoning," "account."[130]

λόγον αἰτεῖν, συναίρειν, διδόναι, ἀποδιδόναι, "to demand or give an account," is a common tt. in business.[131] In the first instance it suggests an oral report, but in everyday speech this emphasis drops away, and we have the commercial sense of "account," with no implication that it has to be rendered orally. When suitable, the NT uses the term thus in a purely secular context, e.g., on the occasion of the Ephesian riot and responsibility for it (Ac. 19:40), cf. also in the same passage the related expression λόγον ἔχειν πρός τινα, "to have a complaint against someone, a matter on which reckoning is demanded" (19:38).

In the NT, however, this expression is predominantly used of the responsibility of the Christian to give an account to men (1 Pt. 3:15), and to God, both for himself (Mt. 12:36) and for the neighbour committed to him (Hb. 13:17). It thus implies the whole of the early Christian concept of eschatological judgment and responsibility (R. 14:12; 1 Pt. 4:5). Already in the parables of Jesus this rendering of an account is an important feature, not only in the parables, but also in the interpretation, cf. the parables of the wicked servant (Mt. 18:23), the talents

---

127 On ἐγώ → II, 343 ff., esp. 345 ff.; on ἀμήν → I, 337 f.

128 This is not altered by the approximation of the formula to the OT ἐγὼ κύριος λελάληκα, Ez. 5:15, 17 etc.

129 Cf. also Gl. 3:17; 4:1; 5:16; 1 C. 7:8, 12 etc.

130 Division into several subsidiary meanings in NT usage is misleading, since this is a single group to the Gk. ear.

131 For examples cf. Pass., Pape, Pr.-Bauer, *s.v.*; Deissmann LO, 94; Schl. Lk., 372; Kl. Mt. on 18:23; → 73; 78.

(Mt. 25:19), and the unjust steward (Lk. 16:2). It is particularly plain in Phil. 4:15, 17 to what degree the term has in this sense the tendency to move out of the commercial sphere as a figure of spiritual things. The λόγος ("account") [132] δόσεως καὶ λήμψεως (v. 15) which first applies to earthly things, i.e., support of the apostle, unexpectedly becomes an image of the καρπὸν τὸν πλεονάζοντα εἰς λόγον ὑμῶν (v. 17), i.e., fruit in a very different eternal sense, since the earthly goods are reckoned as equivalent to the spiritual gift received.

Hb. 4:13 may be cited in the same connection. πρὸς ὃν ἡμῖν ὁ λόγος may well contain only a concluding "with whom we have to do." [133] But even then the basic sense of relation or proportion (i.e., "to whom we stand in relation") is only a variant of the same meaning "reckoning," i.e., a "relation to be reckoned, or reckoned." And if the Peshitta and above all the Gk. fathers [134] are right in detecting here the thought of reckoning, their judgment should be accepted, not merely because they are closer to the living speech, but also because it corresponds best to the context. For "having to do with God" is not an innocuous thing for early Christians. It is not a meaningless rhetorical flourish at the end. It contains a reminder of the responsibility and account which we owe to God as Judge. When the context deals with the laying bare of the thoughts before Him from whom no secrets are hid, [135] it is not impossible that this sense of rendering an account, which is proper to the term and which was known to the author (cf. 13:17), should fix the emphasis. [136]

b. Ac. 10:29: τίνι λόγῳ; "on what ground?" Ac. 18:14: κατὰ λόγον "with reason." In both cases we have a very weak and everyday form of the Gk. sense which uses λόγος with ref. to thought (→ 73 f.) as "reason," "rational consideration," "the result of deliberation," "the reason or rational ground" which results therefrom. [137]

c. λόγος, "the matter (discussed)," "the subject of speech." This is a common meaning in classical and Hellenistic Gk. [138] It occurs several times in the NT. Ac. 8:21: οὐκ ἔστιν σοι μερὶς οὐδὲ κλῆρος ἐν τῷ λόγῳ τούτῳ, namely, the Spirit sought by Simon in v. 19. [139] Ac. 15:6: συνήχθησαν ... ἰδεῖν περὶ τοῦ λόγου τούτου (namely, the demand of v. 5). [140]

---

[132] Mich. Ph., *ad loc.*

[133] So most modern exegetes, G. Lünemann (H. A. W. Meyer[4] [1878]), Rgg., *ad loc.*; F. W. Grosheide, *De Brief aan de Hebreen = Kommentaar op het Nieuwe Testament*, XII (1927), 139; though cf. Lucifer of Calaris (d. 370): *ad quem nobis ratio est* (Rgg. Hb. [2, 3], 117, n. 8), also Calvin Comm., *ad loc.*: *cum quo nobis est ratio* (Vg: *ad quem nobis sermo*). For examples cf. Wettstein, II, 399; F. Bleek, *Der Brief an d. Hb.*, II, 1 (1936), 591; Rgg. Hb. [2, 3], 117, n. 8; Exp. 6th Ser., Vol. VIII (1903), 437; 8th Ser., I (1911), 286 f. Colourless in Wnd. Hb., [1] *ad loc.*: "of whom we speak," Hb. [2]: "... have to speak."

[134] Chrys. Hom. in Hb., VII, 1, *ad loc.* (MPG, 63, p. 62): αὐτῷ μέλλομεν δοῦναι εὐθύνας τῶν πεπραγμένων. Cf. also E. Preuschen, "Altkirchliche antimarcionitische Schrift unter dem Namen Ephräms," ZNW, 12 (1911), 260: λόγον αὐτῷ ἀποδιδόναι.

[135] Cf. also Ign. Mg., 3, 2: τὸ δὲ τοιοῦτον οὐ πρὸς σάρκα ὁ λόγος, ἀλλὰ πρὸς θεόν, τὸν τὰ κρύφια εἰδότα.

[136] So also *ad loc.*, J. C. K. v. Hofmann, *Die Hl. Schrift NT's*, V (1873); Schl. Erl.; G. Hollmann, *Schr. NT.*

[137] Examples in Pape, Pass., Liddell-Scott, *s.v.*; e.g., Aesch. Choeph., 515: ἐκ τίνος λόγου; → 74.

[138] E.g., Hdt., I, 95: τὸν ἐόντα λέγειν λόγον, "to represent the matter as it is"; Demosth. Or., 18, 44: ἕτερος λόγος οὗτος, "this is another matter"; Plut. Them., 11 (I, 117e): ἀνῆγεν αὐτὸν ἐπὶ τὸν λόγον, "he won him for the matter (referred to)." → 78.

[139] τούτῳ shows that there is no ref. back to v. 4 (τὸν λόγον) and v. 14 (τὸν λόγον τοῦ θεοῦ).

[140] Pr.-Bauer includes Mk. 9:10 in this connection, but incorrectly. τὸν λόγον ἐκράτησαν does not refer to the "matter" of the transfiguration of Jesus, but, acc. to v. 10b, to the saying about the resurrection in v. 9. Cf. Kl. Mk., *ad loc.* Pr.-Bauer also mentions the

d. This form of meaning from the Gk. world links up with another which arose as a Semitism from the Heb. דָּבָר, as in Mt. 5:32 and Lk. 4:36. Lk. 4:36: τίς ὁ λόγος οὗτος ...; is incorrectly rendered: "What manner of word (or speech) is this?"[141] The continuation: ὅτι ἐν ἐξουσίᾳ καὶ δυνάμει ἐπιτάσσει τοῖς ἀκαθάρτοις πνεύμασιν καὶ ἐξέρχονται, does not refer only to the word but to its result, namely, the ἐξέρχεσθαι of demons. There is an exact equivalent in the narrative style of the OT in 2 Βασ. 1:4: καὶ εἶπεν αὐτῷ Δαυίδ· τίς ὁ λόγος οὗτος; (Mas. מֶה־הָיָה הַדָּבָר). Here the context shows us the real meaning: "What is this matter?"

In Mt. 5:32 Jesus rejects divorce παρεκτὸς λόγου πορνείας. This obviously does not mean "saving only for an unchaste word." It corresponds to the OT formula in such matters often found in the Rabbis: Dt. 24:1: כִּי־מָצָא בָהּ עֶרְוַת דָּבָר (LXX: ὅτι εὗρεν ἐν αὐτῇ ἄσχημον πρᾶγμα), "because he has found in her some scandal of a matter, or scandalous matter."[142] The question what this might be was much debated by the schools, and there was a good deal of frivolous exegesis. In conscious opposition to this, and in exposition of the formula, the Sermon on the Mount limits the ground of divorce to the λόγος πορνείας, "some form of licentiousness."[143]

3. The Sayings of Jesus.

a. The Quotation of the Sayings. Since the work of Jesus consisted to a large extent in the proclamation of the message, i.e., the spoken word, it is natural that there should be countless references to His λέγειν or λόγοι or ῥήματα. In this respect there seems to be no distinction between λόγος and ῥῆμα.[144]

The ref. may be to an individual saying. In Mk. 10:22 the rich young ruler is displeased ἐπὶ τῷ λόγῳ (the command to sell all); 14:72: Peter remembers the ῥῆμα ὡς εἶπεν ... Ἰησοῦς about the cock crowing. Similarly the plural, a number of sayings, may refer to a definite section of His preaching: Mt. 26:1: πάντες οἱ λόγοι οὗτοι are ended (i.e., the preceding address); also Lk. 7:1: πάντα τὰ ῥήματα αὐτοῦ. But the plural may also indicate the sum of sayings, His total message, Mt. 24:35 and par.: οἱ δὲ λόγοι μου οὐ μὴ παρέλθωσιν, Mk. 8:38: ὃς γὰρ ἐὰν ἐπαισχυνθῇ με καὶ τοὺς ἐμοὺς λόγους, Jn. 15:7: ἐὰν ... τὰ ῥήματά μου ἐν ὑμῖν μείνῃ. Finally, a collective sing. can be used for the word which comprehends His whole proclamation: Lk. 10:39: Mary, sitting at His feet, hears τὸν λόγον αὐτοῦ.

The following formulae are used in quoting the sayings.

τὸ ῥῆμα Ἰησοῦ (Mt. 26:75), τὸ ῥῆμα ὡς εἶπεν ... ὁ Ἰησοῦς (Mk.14:72), τὸ ῥῆμα τοῦ κυρίου (Ac. 11:16), ὁ λόγος ὃν εἶπεν (Jn. 18:9), ὁ λόγος οὗτος ὃν εἶπεν

---

form λόγον ἔχειν πρός τινα in Ac. 19:38 → 103. This is not to be taken in the same way as Ac. 8:21; 15:6, since there is no reference back.

141 Zn., Kl., Hck., *ad loc.*

142 Cf. Str.-B., I, 313 ff.; Kittel Probleme, 100.

143 Cf. S. Dt., 26 on 3:23 (p. 36, Kittel): "It seems that a matter of adultery was found in her (דבר ניאוף = λόγος μοιχείας); T. Shebu., 3, 6: "A matter of violation" (דבר עבירה = λόγος παραβάσεως), cf. Schl. Mt., *ad loc.* There is to be seen in the formula exactly the same reversal of the OT *status constructus* formula as in the NT saying.

144 E.g., Lk. 9:44 f. (v. 44a: τοὺς λόγους τούτους, v. 45 [twice]; τὸ ῥῆμα τοῦτο both related to the intervening statement of Jesus, v. 44b). Cf. also Mt. 26:75; Mk. 14:72 (ῥήματος); par. Lk. 22:61 (λόγου). There is perhaps a certain distinction of emphasis in Lk. 20: v. 20: ἵνα ἐπιλάβωνται αὐτοῦ λόγου, "that they might lay hold of his words" (seen as a whole, in terms of content), and v. 26: οὐκ ἴσχυσαν ἐπιλαβέσθαι αὐτοῦ ῥήματος, "they could not fasten on a single saying." But it may be that this is to read too much into the statements. For ῥῆμα in Pl. cf. Haupt Gefbr. (Eph.), 213, 240; on the original relation between λόγος and ῥῆμα → 79 f.

(7:36), ὁ λόγος τοῦ Ἰησοῦ ὃν εἶπεν (18:32), ὁ λόγος τοῦ κυρίου ὡς εἶπεν (Lk. 22:61), λόγος κυρίου [145] (1 Th. 4:15), οἱ λόγοι τοῦ κυρίου Ἰησοῦ ὅτι αὐτὸς εἶπεν (Ac. 20:35), ἐπιταγὴ κυρίου (1 C. 7:25; 7:10, 12: with παραγγέλλω and λέγω).

The variety shows that there is no fixed formula like the later λέγει ὁ κύριος (2 Cl., 5, 2; 6, 1; 8, 5). But this does not mean that the Lord's sayings do not already have exclusive authority for Paul (1 C. 7:10). The most comprehensive and strongest historical proof of the authoritative character of Jesus' sayings in the apostolic age is the fact of the Gospels with their accounts of what Jesus said. These are preceded by the apostolic witness, which is expressly accredited by the fact that the apostles were present as eye-witnesses (Ac. 1:21 f.). Yet it is also worth pondering that early Christianity could quite freely accept different forms of the same sayings as preserved in the tradition. This is linked with the fact that the Church could use the various Synoptic Gospels alongside one another. It is true, of course, that the Evangelist examines and sifts the tradition. He tries to find the sources and the accounts of eye-witnesses (Lk. 1:1-4). This displays an interest in the historical aspect of the sayings of Jesus. Nevertheless, he and the community do not give way to the resignation which might arise from inability to fix the precise wording of the Beatitudes or the account of the Lord's Supper. Neither a book with literally inspired wording nor the mythically or dogmatically fixed statement of a supernaturally docetic Christ constitutes the authority by which early Christianity lives and dies. This authority is the genuine word which Jesus spoke, which men heard, and which is recounted by men. It is no accident that again and again, both on the lips of Jesus and in narration, the self-evident ὃν (οὓς) ἐλάλησα (Lk. 24:44; Jn. 12:48) or ὃν εἶπεν (→ *supra*) is expressly used of the λόγος of Jesus. This word which is really spoken, and no other, is for early Christianity the Word of Christ. Here, too, the σὰρξ ἐγένετο is taken seriously, and in spite of it, or in it, they see the δόξα.

b. The Authority of the Sayings of Jesus. The Gospel tradition tells us how the sayings of Jesus of Nazareth were received by the hearers. Some are displeased (Mk. 10:22), take offence (Mt. 15:12), and call Him possessed (Jn. 10:20). This is not just because His Word is paradoxical, a hard saying (σκληρός ἐστιν ὁ λόγος οὗτος, Jn. 6:60). It is because the implied claim is unheard of, and is felt to be blasphemous (Mk. 2:7). Opponents can try to catch Him (ἐν) λόγῳ (Mt. 22:15; Mk. 12:13; Lk. 20:20, cf. v. 26: ῥήματος). For His claim, and therewith the threat which He poses, may be seen in His λόγος. Yet on the other side there is astonishment at the same Word. [146] This is not so much evoked by an external impression [147] nor by the psychological operation of a particular depth of ethical or religious insight. It is the devastating effect of the → ἐξουσία displayed in the Word (Mt. 7:28; Lk. 4:32). Because of this the Word of Jesus is different from that of the γραμματεῖς. It testifies to the authority, not of the rabbi, but the Son. Like His acts and His whole appearance, His Word demands faith in the One whom God has sent. This is the heart of the Word according to the Synoptic tradition (Mt. 8:9 f.; Lk. 5:5). The destiny of man is decided by

145 There is no reason to refer this to a saying of the exalted Lord.

146 → θαμβέω, III, 5 f.; → θαυμάζω, III, 36 ff.; ἐκπλήσσομαι.

147 So perhaps λόγοι τῆς χάριτος in Lk. 4:22 ("gracious address"), cf. Zn., *ad loc.*; Schl. and Hck., *ad loc.* take a different view: "sweet words of grace."

the attitude to this Word as the Word of Christ, by the attitude to Him. Because it is His Word, to be ashamed of His words is to be ashamed of Him (Mk. 8:38). Because they are His words, they do not pass away even though heaven and earth pass away (Mk. 13:31).

It is in no sense true that the word and work of Jesus are distinct as two separate functions of His manifestation. This basic insight will call for fuller discussion (→ 108 f.), but already at this point is is evident that His Word is a working and active Word. It is an integral part of His action. This is expressed in the request which has healing action in view but speaks only of εἰπὲ λόγῳ (Mt. 8:8; Lk. 7:7), in the ἐπὶ δὲ τῷ ῥήματί σου χαλάσω τὰ δίκτυα (Lk. 5:5), in the account of His driving out spirits λόγῳ (Mt. 8:16), in the many accounts, characteristic of almost all the miracle stories, of the way in which His spoken Word brings into operation His power of healing (Mk. 2:10 ff.), raising the dead (Lk. 7:14 f.), controlling demons (Mk. 1:25 f.), and ruling the elements (Mk. 4:39). The Word of Jesus, and the power of this Word, do not operate only on a spiritual level beyond the physical and natural. They raise a claim to lordship over the undiminished whole of spirit-corporeality as this characterises all creation as described in the Bible.

How strongly the tradition is controlled by recollection that the saying of Jesus in a specific situation has the definite effectual ἐξουσία of operation may be seen from the fact that in the Gk. account many such sayings are preserved in Aramaic: ταλιθὰ κοῦμ (Mk. 5:41); ἐφφαθά (Mk. 7:34) etc. This fixing of the saying might seem to suggest that it is regarded as a magic formula. But in reality there is no such idea, as all our knowledge of primitive Christianity shows beyond doubt. Sayings of the Lord are quoted to give unconditional authority to a demand (1 C. 7:10). Healings are performed in the name of Jesus Christ (Ac. 3:6). It is never suggested, however, that the miracle is magically performed merely by the utterance of the name. Even though this might seem to be implied when the wording was thought to be so important that the original was preserved, primitive Christianity observed with sure and unerring instinct the boundary between the superstition of magic formulae on the one side, and the account of the ἐξουσία of Jesus, and awareness of its present efficacy in His name, on the other.

The facts firmly and definitely described in the Synoptic tradition are taken up by John and expressed in many compendious statements.[148] The dual effect of faith or rejection is caused, for Jn., both by the work of Jesus (11:45 ff.) and by His Word (6:60 ff.; 10:19 ff.: σχίσμα ἐγένετο ... διὰ τοὺς λόγους τούτους). Men believe in Jesus διὰ τὸν λόγον αὐτοῦ (4:41; cf. 4:50 ff.). They accept His words or not (λαμβάνειν, 12:48). They either keep them or not (τηρεῖν, 8:51; 14:24; 15:20; Rev. 3:8). They abide in His Word (Jn. 8:31; cf. 15:7). His Word enters into them (χωρεῖ ἐν ὑμῖν, 8:37). Rejection of His Word means divine judgment (12:47 f.). But the man who receives and keeps it is καθαρός ... διὰ τὸν λόγον ὃν λελάληκα ὑμῖν (15:3). Of him it is said: ἔχει ζωὴν αἰώνιον καὶ εἰς κρίσιν οὐκ ἔρχεται (5:24), οὐ μὴ γεύσηται θανάτου εἰς τὸν αἰῶνα (8:51 f.).

In Jn. as in the Synoptic tradition the basis of this evaluation of the Word is the fact that Jesus is the Christ and the Son. ὁ λόγος ὃν ἀκούετε οὐκ ἔστιν ἐμὸς ἀλλὰ τοῦ πέμψαντός με πατρός (14:24; cf. 14:10; 17:8). Because these are the words of the Son, they are ῥήματα ζωῆς αἰωνίου (6:68), πνεῦμα καὶ ζωή

---

[148] Jn. usually has λόγος in the sing., often in a collective sense. As a plur. he normally uses τὰ ῥήματα (λόγοι only in Jn. 10:19; 14:24, cf. also vl. 7:40; 19:13); → 13. a.

(6:63). This justifies John's equating of the Word of Jesus with the γραφή: ἐπίστευσαν τῇ γραφῇ καὶ τῷ λόγῳ ὃν εἶπεν ὁ Ἰησοῦς (2:22; 5:47).

This also means, however, that the relation of men to the Word of Jesus is integrated into the relation of active and passive which is integral to the statements of primitive Christianity. To grasp is always to be grasped, and to be grasped is always to grasp. Jn. expresses this in terms of δύνασθαι and esp. in the category of being given: διὰ τοῦτο εἴρηκα ὑμῖν ὅτι οὐδεὶς δύναται ἐλθεῖν πρός με ἐὰν μὴ ᾖ δεδομένον αὐτῷ ἐκ τοῦ πατρός (6:65); οὐ δύνασθε ἀκούειν τὸν λόγον τὸν ἐμόν (8:43). The context of the latter saying makes it clear how remote is the idea that οὐ δύνασθε absolves from responsibility or guilt. The Synoptic statements make exactly the same point. Of Jesus Himself it is said: οὐ πάντες χωροῦσιν τὸν λόγον τοῦτον, ἀλλ' οἷς δέδοται (Mt. 19:11). To this corresponds the statement concerning the aim of speaking in parables: ὑμῖν τὸ μυστήριον δέδοται τῆς βασιλείας τοῦ θεοῦ (Mk. 4:11 and par.).[149] Cf. also Lk. 18:34: καὶ ἦν τὸ ῥῆμα τοῦτο κεκρυμμένον ἀπ' αὐτῶν, and Lk. 9:45: οἱ δὲ ἠγνόουν τὸ ῥῆμα τοῦτο, καὶ ἦν παρακεκαλυμμένον ἀπ' αὐτῶν ἵνα μὴ αἴσθωνται αὐτό.

c. The Appeal to the Word of Jesus outside the Gospels. It may strike us that the Word of Jesus seems to play a lesser role outside the Gospels than one would expect. To be sure, its application is not restricted to the small number of express quotations. Part of the self-evident freedom of the primitive Church in respect of the spoken Word of the Lord is that, in addition to using many different quotation formulae (→ 105 f.), it can freely quote dominical sayings without express reference. Paul refers to the faith which can move mountains in 1 C. 13:2,[150] and James has a wealth of instances,[151] as does also the Didache.[152] Hence it is incorrect to suppose that the application of the Word of Jesus plays a completely negligible role in the apostolic writings, and that His Word was not held in any high regard, especially by Paul. Quite apart from other factors, the existence of the Gospels, and the interest displayed in them (Lk. 1:1-4), rules out this possibility. It should also be remembered that our knowledge of apostolic proclamation is limited to specific extracts, so that to draw conclusions e.g., from epistles to missionary preaching or catechetical instruction is quite impermissible, or should be done only with great and deliberate caution.

In addition, there is the most important and pregnant fact that for the apostolic age there is no autonomous Word of Jesus separate from christological reality as a whole (→ 107). This shows how improbable is the theory of a distinct source of logia or addresses, or at least how uncertain are all the conclusions drawn from the actual or supposed existence of such a source. The words of Jesus are never more than part of a whole. This means, first, that they are viewed together with His ἔργα, secondly, that, like the whole of the earthly life and work of Jesus, they are seen and estimated in the light of the crucifixion and resurrection,

---

[149] Mt. 13:11 continues: ἐκείνοις δὲ οὐ δέδοται; these words are not found in Mk. But Mk. 4:11 makes it clear that the opinion of the ἐκεῖνοι presupposed in him is the same as that recorded in Mt. (→ ἵνα).

[150] = Mk. 11:23; Mt. 17:20; 21:21. Many other examples from Paul are given in H. J. Holtzmann, *Lehrbuch der nt.lichen Theologie*, II² (1911), 232 f.

[151] Cf. Hck. Jk., 13, n. 46; Zahn Einl., I, 87. Dib. Jk. underestimates the real connection in favour of formal analogies (27).

[152] Esp. 1:1 ff.

and, thirdly, that once again like the whole of His accomplished work they are related to the contemporaneity of the work of the ascended and heavenly Lord and His πνεῦμα.

These aspects, esp. the third, are to be borne in mind in respect of most of the not very numerous passages[153] in which there is ref. to Christ's Word, though no express quotation (→ 108), within the primitive Christian literature that has come down to us. Only 1 Tm. 6:3 with its ὑγιαίνοντες λόγοι τοῦ κυρίου ἡμῶν Ἰησοῦ Χριστοῦ refers to the recorded words of Jesus as a basis of διδασκαλία. Hb. 1:3: (ὁ υἱὸς) φέρων τὰ πάντα τῷ ῥήματι τῆς δυνάμεως αὐτοῦ, speaks of the creative Word of Christ. R. 10:17: ἡ πίστις ἐξ ἀκοῆς, ἡ δὲ ἀκοὴ διὰ ῥήματος Χριστοῦ, certainly has in view the recorded ῥήματα; nevertheless, as the Χριστοῦ shows, it refers also to the Word of the present Lord as this is at work in ἀκοή. This aspect is dominant in Col. 3:16: ὁ λόγος τοῦ Χριστοῦ ἐνοικείτω ἐν ὑμῖν πλουσίως, though the other need not be ruled out completely.

The most significant and pregnant result of this fact is an extension in content of the λόγος concept to the whole range of the early Christian message. Whether in the form of λόγος τοῦ θεοῦ, λόγος τοῦ κυρίου, or λόγος in the absolute, this becomes a characteristic feature of early Christian terminology.

4. The Old Testament Word in the New Testament.

a. The NT quotes the OT either[154] as Scripture[155] or as Word.[156] Our present concern is with the latter formulae. They are very varied both in the use of verbal forms and in respect of the speaking subject. This variety is largely due to the adoption of Rabbinic formulae.

As among the Rabbis,[157] both active and passive forms are found: λέγει, φησίν, εἶπεν, λέγων, ἐρρέθη, εἰρημένον, ῥηθέν. In traditional formulae, the passive forms often have no subject; the subject is left indefinite. On the basis of the Heb. perfect אוֹמֵר/אָמַר we find the Gk. aorist εἶπεν or present λέγει,[158] the latter quite irrespective of its setting sometimes in a narrative in the preterite.[159] It is hard to discern any conscious distinction in usage.[160] Both forms became fixed, but their use alongside one another without distinction perhaps contains a recollection that these quotations are both the account of something which took place in the past and also a statement of that which is just as directly alive and active in the present.

---

[153] In Hb. 6:1: ἀφέντες τὸν τῆς ἀρχῆς τοῦ Χριστοῦ λόγον, the τοῦ Χριστοῦ is perhaps an obj. gen. Cf. Rgg. Hb.[2, 3], 146, *ad loc.* The attempt of A. Seeberg in *Der Katechismus der Urchristenheit* (1903), 248 f. to find here a "catechism whose individual parts may be traced back to Christ" is pure imagination.

[154] Naturally there are also mixed forms, e.g., Ac. 15:15: οἱ λόγοι τῶν προφητῶν, καθὼς γέγραπται.

[155] Cf. γέγραπται and γεγραμμένον, → I, 746 ff.; γραφή, → I, 749 ff.; ἀναγινώσκω, → I, 343 f.; βίβλος, βιβλίον, → I, 615 ff.

[156] Apart from the verbs mentioned here cf. προευαγγελίζομαι, → II, 737 f.; κράζω, → III, 900; 902, n. 15 (R. 9:27).

[157] Esp. אמר, אוֹמֵר and נֶאֱמַר. Cf. Bacher Term., I, 5 f.; II, 9 ff., 94; Str.-B., I, 74 f.; II, 1; III, 314, 365 f.

[158] O. Michel, *Pls. u. seine Bibel* (1929), 70 points out the Gk. par., e.g., ὡς (καθάπερ) λέγει Πλάτων, Epict. Diss., I, 28, 4; III, 24, 99; IV, 1, 41 and 73.

[159] Cf. Jn. 19:36 f.

[160] For arbitrary interchange cf. Hb. 1:5 ff.: v. 5: εἶπεν, v. 6: λέγει, v. 7: λέγει, v. 13: εἴρηκεν. Gl. 3:16: ἐρρέθησαν ... λέγει, Ac. 13:34 f.: εἴρηκεν ... λέγει.

The variety of subjects may be seen from a review.

Human subject: Moses:[161] Mt. 22:24; Mk. 7:10; Ac. 3:22; R. 10:19; David:[162] Ac. 2:25, 34; R. 4:6; 11:9; Mt. 22:43 and par.; Mk. 12:36 (ἐν [τῷ] πνεύματι [τῷ ἁγίῳ]); Lk. 20:42: ἐν βίβλῳ ψαλμῶν; the prophet:[163] Ac. 7:48; Isaiah:[164] Jn. 1:23; 12:38 f.; R. 9:27 (κράζει), 29 (προείρηκεν); 10:16, 20 f.; 15:12; Mt. 13:14 (ἡ προφητεία Ἠσαΐου ἡ λέγουσα); 15:7 (ἐπροφήτευσεν ... Ἠσαΐας λέγων); someone: Hb. 2:6 (διεμαρτύρατο δέ πού τις[165] λέγων). In what follows there is often direct ref. to a human subject as well (e.g., with διά).

Superhuman subject: The (pre-existent) Christ:[166] Hb. 2:12 f. (λέγων); 10:5, 8, 9 (λέγει, λέγων, εἴρηκεν); ἡ → σοφία τοῦ θεοῦ: Lk. 11:49; ὁ χρηματισμός: R. 11:4; ὁ νόμος:[167] 1 C. 14:34; τὸ πνεῦμα τὸ ἅγιον (→ n. 175): Hb. 3:7; Ac. 28:25 (ἐλάλησεν διὰ Ἠσαΐου τοῦ προφήτου ... λέγων),[168] ἡ γραφή:[169] Jn. 7:38, 42; 19:37 (ἑτέρα γραφή[170]); R. 4:3; 10:11; Gl. 4:30; 1 Tm. 5:18; Jm. 2:23; 4:5 f.; R. 9:17 (τῷ Φαραώ); 11:2 (ἐν Ἠλίᾳ).

Indefinite subject: with λέγει:[171] R. 15:10; 2 C. 6:2; Eph. 4:8; 5:14; R. 9:15 (τῷ Μωϋσεῖ); 9:25 (ἐν τῷ Ὡσηέ); Gl. 3:16 (interchange with the pass. → *infra*), with φησίν: 1 C. 6:16; Hb. 8:5, ἐρρέθη:[172] Mt. 5:27, 31, 38, 43; Mt. 5:21, 33 (τοῖς ἀρχαίοις);[173] R. 9:12 (αὐτῇ); Gl. 3:16 (τῷ δὲ Ἀβραὰμ ἐρρέθησαν αἱ ἐπαγγελίαι, → *supra*), εἴρηται: Lk. 4:12; τὸ εἰρημένον: R. 4:18; Lk. 2:24 (ἐν τῷ νόμῳ κυρίου); Ac. 2:16 (διὰ τοῦ προφήτου Ἰωήλ); 13:40 (ἐν τοῖς προφήταις), ὁ ῥηθείς Mt. 3:3 (διὰ Ἠσαΐου τοῦ προφήτου λέγοντος), τὸ ῥηθέν: Mt. 2:23 (διὰ τῶν προφητῶν); 13:35; 21:4 (διὰ τοῦ προφήτου λέγοντος); 2:17; 27:9 (διὰ Ἰερεμίου τοῦ προφήτου λέγοντος);[174] 4:14; 8:17; 12:17 (διὰ Ἠσαΐου τοῦ προφήτου λέγοντος); 24:15 (διὰ Δανιὴλ τοῦ προφήτου).

God as subject. The transition from the previous group to this one is naturally fluid, for often we do not have θεὸς εἶπεν, but the context shows that God is the subject, esp. in Hb. Mt. 1:22; 2:15 (τὸ ῥηθὲν ὑπὸ κυρίου [22:31: θεοῦ] διὰ τοῦ προφήτου λέγοντος); 15:4 (ὁ θεὸς εἶπεν); Mk. 12:26 (ἐν τῇ βίβλῳ Μωϋσέως ... πῶς εἶπεν αὐτῷ ὁ θεὸς λέγων); Lk. 1:70 (καθὼς ἐλάλησεν διὰ στόματος τῶν ἁγίων ἀπ' αἰῶνος προφητῶν αὐτοῦ); Ac. 3:25 (λέγων πρὸς Ἀβραάμ); 4:25 (ὁ τοῦ πατρὸς

---

161 Lv. r., 13, 5 on 11:1 (p. 19b Vilna): משה אמר; cf. Bacher, II, 9. On Hb. 9:20 → n. 177.

162 jPea, 16b, 60: וכן דוד הוא אומר.

163 Tanch. שמות, 7 and תצוה, 10 (Buber): אמר הנביא.

164 Tanch. יתרו, 13 (Buber): אמר ישעיה.

165 For par. from Philo → n. 178. The author of Hb. never quotes the author of a book of the Bible by name.

166 Cf. Rgg. Hb.[2, 3], 51 f., 299.

167 M. Ex. on 23:7; S. Nu., 115 on 15:38: אמרה תורה.

168 Pesikt. r., 6, p. 23a: זה הוא שאמרה רוח הקדש על ידי ... ("this is what the Holy Spirit has said through ..."). For further instances cf. Str.-B., I, 74 f.

169 M. Ex. on 12:29: הכתוב אומר; TBQ, 7, 5: אמר הכתוב.

170 M. Ex. on 14:3; Tanch. נשא, 18 (Buber): וכתוב אחר אומר.

171 Cf. the Rabb. אוֹמֵר or הוּא אוֹמֵר, in most cases to be filled out to הַכָּתוּב אוֹמֵר ("Scripture says"), though we also find הַקָּדוֹשׁ בָּרוּךְ הוּא אוֹמֵר ("the Holy One, blessed be He, says"), bShab., 152b. Cf. Str.-B., III, 314, 365 f.

172 Cf. שנאמר, the formula most commonly used by the Rabb. to introduce biblical quotations.

173 The par. R. 9:12; Gl. 3:16, and all other usage, show how impossible it is to regard τοῖς ἀρχαίοις (= ὑπὸ τῶν ἀρχαίων) as an ablative. Cf. also Zn. Mt.[4], 223 f., n. 90.

174 Pesikt. r., 28 (p. 134b): זו היא שנאמרה על ידי ירמיה הנביא ("this is what was said through the prophet Jeremiah"), Str.-B., II, 1.

ἡμῶν διὰ πνεύματος ἁγίου στόματος Δαυὶδ παιδός σου εἰπών); 7:3 (εἶπεν πρὸς αὐτόν); 7:6 (ἐλάλησεν δὲ οὕτως ὁ θεός); 7:7 (ὁ θεὸς εἶπεν); 7:31 (ἐγένετο φωνὴ κυρίου); 7:33 (εἶπεν δὲ αὐτῷ ὁ κύριος); Jm. 2:11 (ὁ γὰρ εἰπών ... εἶπεν καί); Hb. 1:5, 6, 7, 13 (εἶπεν, λέγει, λέγει, εἴρηκεν); 3:15 (ἐν τῷ λέγεσθαι); 4:3, 4 (καθὼς εἴρηκεν); 4:7 (ἐν Δαυὶδ λέγων ... καθὼς προείρηται); 5:5 (ὁ λαλήσας πρὸς αὐτόν); 5:6 (καθὼς καὶ ἐν ἑτέρῳ λέγει); 6:14 (λέγων); 8:8 (μεμφόμενος λέγει); 10:15 (μετὰ τὸ εἰρηκέναι);[175] 10:30 (τὸν εἰπόντα).

In many cases mention of the divine subject is facilitated by the fact that the OT passage quoted is itself an I-saying (Mt. 22:31 f. and par.: "I am the God of Abraham ...") or a statement which the OT narrative sets on the lips of God, e.g., the promise to Abraham (Ac. 3:25). But the examples go further by quoting sayings from the prophets and Psalms as spoken by God (Mt. 1:22; Ac. 4:25; Hb. 1:5 ff. etc.). They show that God Himself is firmly regarded as the One who speaks in Scripture. The only point is that this insight is not a theory which denies or excludes the human authors. These men are not introduced merely indirectly as intermediaries, but directly as the true subjects of what is said. Such dramatic terms can be used of them as → κράζει (R. 9:27 [Is.]) and ἀποτολμᾷ (R. 10:20 [Is.]) (→ 110). For the most part the quotation formulae which refer to the human authors are freely interchangeable with those which refer to the divine subject.[176] These facts are cogent proof that the co-existence of the two groups of formulae does not imply any cross-cutting or antithesis for the NT writers. At most there seems to be something of this in Hb., since this does not have any human subjects apart from the τις of 2:6.[177] In this respect it is influenced by the Alexandrian view of inspiration, which eliminates as far as possible the human subject of the Word of God.[178] But for Paul it implies no diminution whatever of the divine nature of Scripture, or the authority of demonstration from Scripture, to speak very concretely of the κράζει or the ἀποτολμᾷ καὶ λέγει of Is. (R. 9:27; 10:20), and therewith to emphasise as strongly as possible the fact that the adduced verse of Scripture is spoken by a man. Similarly, adoption of traditional forms with λέγει (without subject) or the passive cannot possibly mean evasion of the divine nature of the saying quoted.

For this reason, it is incorrect exegesis to suggest that failure to mention the subject in Mt. 5:21 ff. with its ἐρρέθη is an attempt to avoid a polemical reference to God or to Moses as His prophet.[179] Both the commandment quoted and the formula forbid us to think of anything but a divine saying.[180] If human authors were intended, they

---

[175] The subject is κύριος, not τὸ πνεῦμα τὸ ἅγιον. Cf. Rgg. Hb.[2, 3], 311.

[176] E.g., Mt. 15:4 (ὁ θεὸς εἶπεν) and 15:7 (καλῶς ἐπροφήτευσεν περὶ ὑμῶν Ἠσαΐας). Mt. 15:4: ὁ γὰρ θεὸς εἶπεν, par. Mk. 7:10: Μωϋσῆς γὰρ εἶπεν (both formulae introducing the 5th commandment).

[177] In Hb. 9:20 Moses is the subj. of λέγων (cf. v. 19), but this is an unusual verse, since Ex. 24:8 is not quoted in isolation, but as part of the story in Ex. 24:6-8 (Hb. 9:19-20), in which it is said of Moses that he addressed the people.

[178] Cf. Michel, 69, who refers to Philo Spec. Leg., 49. It is worth noting that the πού τις also corresponds to a Philonic form of citation, though this is used of refs. to Gk. philosophers and poets (Rer. Div. Her., 181 [Plato]; Fug., 61 [Heraclitus]; Som., I, 150 [Homer] etc.) as well as Scripture (Ebr., 61). Cf. Rgg. Hb.[2, 3], 36 f., n. 98.

[179] For older examples cf. H. A. W. Meyer[6] (1876), *ad loc.*; Zn. Mt., *ad loc.* ("not with ref. to that which is written or is to be read in the Law and the prophets"); Wellh. Mt., 19 ("Moses is obviously not intended"); also, as it seems, Kl. Mt., *ad loc.*

[180] Schl. Mt., 165: "The pass. draws attention to the one of whom we all think even though he is not named."

would have to be mentioned. ἐρρέθη here and ὁ θεὸς εἶπεν in Mt. 15:4 are both introductory formulae to commandments (the 6th and the 5th).[181]

b. The use of λόγος and ῥῆμα, in so far as they refer to the OT, is in accord with our findings thus far. Here, too, both the human and the divine aspects may be emphasised.

Human word: Lk. 3:4: ὡς γέγραπται ἐν βίβλῳ λόγων Ἠσαΐου τοῦ προφήτου, Jn. 12:38: ἵνα ὁ λόγος Ἠσαΐου τοῦ προφήτου πληρωθῇ ὃν εἶπεν, Ac. 15:15: καὶ τούτῳ συμφωνοῦσιν οἱ λόγοι τῶν προφητῶν, καθὼς γέγραπται. The relation between the sing. and plur. shows that λόγος means the individual saying, whereas the plur. refers to many sayings, e.g., the βίβλος of a prophet, which can also be called the λόγος of the prophet in a collective sing.

In the sense of the individual passage λόγος can be used without the gen. of the speaker: R. 9:9; 13:9: ὁ λόγος οὗτος, 1 C. 15:54: ὁ λόγος ὁ γεγραμμένος, Gl. 5:14: ἐν ἑνὶ λόγῳ. There is a new development in 2 Pt. 1:19: καὶ ἔχομεν βεβαιότερον τὸν προφητικὸν λόγον (cf. v. 20: πᾶσα προφητεία γραφῆς).

Apart from 2 Pt. 1:19, λόγος and ῥῆμα statements which refer to God as the speaker can mean individual verses or passages in the OT. Mk. 7:13: ἀκυροῦντες τὸν λόγον τοῦ θεοῦ τῇ παραδόσει ὑμῶν (the 5th commandment); Jn. 10:35: πρὸς οὓς ὁ λόγος τοῦ θεοῦ ἐγένετο (Ps. 82:6); R. 9:6: οὐχ οἷον δὲ ὅτι ἐκπέπτωκεν ὁ λόγος τοῦ θεοῦ (the promise concerning Israel); Hb. 2:2: ὁ δι' ἀγγέλων λαληθεὶς λόγος (the Law); 7:28: ὁ λόγος τῆς ὁρκωμοσίας (God); 11:3: κατηρτίσθαι τοὺς αἰῶνας ῥήματι θεοῦ (the word of creation); 12:19: φωνὴ ῥημάτων ... μὴ προστεθῆναι αὐτοῖς λόγον (the giving of the Law); 2 Pt. 3:5-7: ὁ τοῦ θεοῦ λόγος (the word of creation).

In all these cases the specialised use of דְּבַר־יְהוָֹה developed in the OT is not merely the basis of NT usage but maintains its original reference to the OT word of revelation. The fact that it refers to individual passages simply shows that what is in view is not a theory of the Word of God but the concreteness of the divine speaking as a historical event. The way is, of course, left open for a view on which the totality of this work of God in salvation history becomes the Word of God. Thus the old covenant and the new are combined as God's Word in Col. 1:25 (→ 116; 125) and Hb. 4:12 (→ 113). This implies their unity, so that fundamentally the OT Word is on the same level as the NT Word. Both are the Word of God.

The phrase λόγος τοῦ κυρίου is not used in this group of statements in which the NT is referring to the OT Word. This is surprising, since it would be the most direct rendering of the OT דְּבַר־יְהוָֹה. Whatever the reason may be, it is not Marcionite depreciation of the OT; otherwise λόγος τοῦ θεοῦ would also have had to be avoided. λέγει, too, is never used with κύριος to introduce a quotation, but only within a quotation: R. 12:19; 14:11; 1 C. 14:21; 2 C. 6:17 f.; Hb. 8:8 ff.; 10:16; Rev. 1:8. The fact that in part the λέγει (ὁ) κύριος[182] goes beyond the actual OT text makes no difference, since the NT author always quotes it as part of the OT saying. How strongly it is felt to belong to the saying may be seen from the fact that it does not make an introductory formula redundant. Hence λέγει ὁ κύριος is curiously combined with γέγραπται in R. 12:19; 14:11; 1 C. 14:21, with εἶπεν ὁ θεός in 2 C. 6:16 ff., and with λέγει or εἰρηκέναι (with ref. to God) in Hb. 8:8; 10:15 f.[183] κύριος (= θεός) occurs only twice in

[181] *Loc. cit.*
[182] Ac. 2:17: λέγει ὁ θεός, in a quotation.
[183] Cf. Michel, 72; F. Bleek, *Der Brief an d. Hb.* (1828 ff.), 32²

introducing quotations, namely, Mt. 1:22; 2:15: τὸ ῥηθὲν ὑπὸ κυρίου διὰ τοῦ προφήτου λέγοντος.

c. It need cause no surprise that in some cases it is exegetically hard to decide whether the Word of God is the OT or the early Christian message. Cf. Hb. 4:12 (→ 112): ζῶν γὰρ ὁ λόγος τοῦ θεοῦ καὶ ἐνεργὴς καὶ τομώτερος ὑπὲρ πᾶσαν μάχαιραν δίστομον ..., Eph. 6:17: καὶ τὴν μάχαιραν τοῦ πνεύματος, ὅ ἐστιν ῥῆμα θεοῦ.[184] In these and similar cases the idea of an alternative would probably be contrary to the concern of the NT author, since for him — this may be seen most plainly in the λαλεῖν of Hb. 1:1 f. — there are not two Words of God but only one, which is given as such in the continuity and unity of salvation history (from the προφῆται to the υἱός, Hb. 1:1 f.). The first part of this in time is meant to point to the second, the second to fulfil the first. In Hb. 13:7 it is hard to say whether those who have the rule have spoken and taught the OT Word, the NT Word, or both in one.

5. The Special Word of God to Individuals in the New Testament.

a. Simeon; the Baptist. The OT formula that the Word of the Lord came to a man specifically called by God (1 Βασ. 15:10: ῥῆμα κυρίου; 2 Βασ. 24:11: λόγος κυρίου etc.) is also found in a few obviously limited instances in the NT. God's ῥῆμα came to Simeon with the Messianic promise in Lk. 2:29. This is equivalent to the καὶ ἦν αὐτῷ κεχρηματισμένον ὑπὸ τοῦ πνεύματος τοῦ ἁγίου (v. 26). Of the Baptist it is said that ἐγένετο ῥῆμα θεοῦ to him (Lk. 3:2). Both men were placed by Lk. in the category of OT prophets prior to the Christian age.

b. The Apostolic Period. The phrases λόγος τοῦ θεοῦ, λόγος τοῦ κυρίου and ῥῆμα κυρίου are very common in the NT, but, except in the case of these introductory figures, they are never used of special divine directions. It is not that these do not occur in the NT. On the contrary, the apostolic age is full of them. But they are described in many other different ways, e.g., as → ἀποκάλυψις (Gl. 2:2), as direction of the πνεῦμα (Ac. 16:6), as the manifestation of the angel of God (Ac. 27:23), or of the Lord Himself (18:9), or some other divinely caused phenomenon (10:10 ff.). In Rev. (→ 122 f.) it is said that the seer hears the divine φωνή (1:10; 4:1 etc.) but what is said by this voice is at best called the λόγοι τῆς προφητείας (1:3; 22:7; 18) or οὗτοι οἱ λόγοι (21:5; 22:6), never the Word of God imparted to the divine.

The reason for this obvious and remarkable fact is that after the coming of Jesus the Word of God or the Word of the Lord has for the whole of primitive Christianity a new and absolutely exclusive sense. It has become the undisputed term for the one Word of God which God has spoken, and speaks, in what has taken place in Jesus and in the message concerning it. From this time on, the term cannot be used of any other revealing event, no matter how authentic and estimable in the religious sense. Later statistical evidence gives direct expression to the primitive Christian conviction that the revelation which has taken place in Jesus Christ is definitive and unique,[185] and that a new age has been inaugurated therewith (→ καινός; also → 125 f.).

---

[184] It may be left open whether ῥῆμα θεοῦ means the specific saying "which is adapted to this (particular) case"; cf. Haupt Gefbr. (Eph.), 240. Certainly it is not a specific OT or NT saying, but rather the Word which the Spirit "brings to the community and teaches it to use," Schl. Erl., *ad loc.*

[185] This is not expressed in the NT term ἀποκάλυψις — a point to be noted in the doctrinal use of the term "revelation," → III, 585.

c. Jesus. In view of this fact it is doubly surprising that in the account of Jesus Himself there is no reference to the Word of God, to a Word of God, or to words of God, being given to Him, the supreme agent of revelation. For surely the restriction observed in the case of others, including the apostles, did not have to apply to Him too. Yet it is a fact that at no point do we read of a specific declaration of God's will being imparted to Him as the Word of God. The reason for this must be a very profound one, for there are many situations in which this kind of reference would be quite natural, e.g., in the story of Gethsemane (Mt. 26:36-46 and par.) or in other contexts where particular prominence is given to prayer (Lk. 6:12; 9:18).

At two points it is particularly striking that there is no ἐγένετο ὁ λόγος (τὸ ῥῆμα) τοῦ θεοῦ with ref. to Jesus, namely, when there comes a voice from heaven at the baptism and the transfiguration. The descriptions and the forms of expression make it quite plain that according to the intention of the authors the heavenly saying introduced by → φωνὴ ἐκ τῶν οὐρανῶν (Mt. 3:17; Mk. 1:11; Lk. 3:22 [ἐξ οὐρανοῦ]) or ἐκ τῆς νεφέλης (Mt. 17:5; Mk. 9:7; Lk. 9:35) is analogous, not to the דְּבַר יְהוָה, the word of divine direction which comes to the prophets, but to the בַּת קוֹל.[186] It has a very different purpose, namely, that of an impartation, confirmation, or decision granted to the hearers esp. in order that uncertainty may be dispelled where there is doubt. In the case of the voice at the transfiguration the agreed οὗτός ἐστιν ..., the link with Peter's confession, and the intimation of the passion make it plain that it is the disciples who are addressed. But the same is true at the baptism, for, in the form σὺ εἶ ... (Mk. 1:11),[187] the voice is an accreditation of the Son, not a commission laid upon Him.

There can be only one reason why the idea of a detailed Word of God imparted to Jesus Himself has not found its way into the record. This is that such an idea was felt to be inappropriate and inadequate to describe the relationship of Jesus with God. Hence it was consciously or unconsciously avoided. Such phrases as πάντα μοι παρεδόθη ὑπὸ τοῦ πατρός μου and τὸν πατέρα ἐπιγινώσκει (Mt. 11:27) set the unity of Jesus with the Father, and also with the Word of God, on a completely different basis which goes far beyond isolated impartation.[188]

6. The Early Christian Message as the Word of God (outside the Johannine Writings).

a. Statistics. When applied to the complex of NT events and the message which bears witness to this complex, the terms ὁ λόγος τοῦ θεοῦ, ὁ λόγος τοῦ κυρίου, and ὁ λόγος are used alongside one another without any discernible difference (apart from numerical incidence).

---

[186] → φωνή. For material cf. Str.-B., I, 125-134; Schl. Gesch. d. Chr., 89; Schl. Mt., 93.

[187] The 2nd person sing. does not exclude the Bath Qol from being an address to those around, cf. the voice immediately after the martyrdom of Aqiba: "Hail to thee, R. Aqiba ..." (bBer., 61b). This does not answer a question of Aqiba but of the ministering angels. Cf. Str.-B., I, 133.

[188] Jn. 17:8: τὰ ῥήματα ἃ ἔδωκάς μοι, does not refer to specific directions given to Jesus but to all that is given to Him and passed on by Him. There is an exact par. in Mt. 11:27 (or even R. 8:17).

The statistics are as follows.[189]

λόγος τοῦ θεοῦ : Lk.: 4 times ; Ac.: 12; Th.: 2; C.: 3; Phil.: 1 (vl.); Col.: 1; Past.: 4; Hb.: 2; 1 Pt.: 1: a total of 30.

λόγος τοῦ κυρίου : Ac.: 6 times ; Th.: 2 : a total of 8.

λόγος : Mt. 13 : 4 times (the only instances in Mt.); Mk.: 9 times in c. 4 and 1 elsewhere ; Marcan ending : 1; Lk.: 3 in c. 8 and 1 elsewhere ; Ac.: 9 times ; Th.: 1; Gl.: 1; Phil.: 1 (vl.); Col.: 1; Past.: 5; 1 Pt.: 2; Jm.: 1: a total of 40 times.

There is no material distinction in usage either in Paul, in Ac., or elsewhere. Cf. 1 Th. 1:6 (λόγος), 1:8 (λόγος τοῦ κυρίου), and 2:13 (λόγος τοῦ θεοῦ); or Ac. 6:2 (ἡμᾶς καταλείψαντας τὸν λόγον τοῦ θεοῦ), and 6:4 (τῇ διακονίᾳ τοῦ λόγου προσκαρτερήσομεν). If λόγος τοῦ κυρίου is less common, this may be due to the fact that it can also be used to introduce the sayings of Jesus (→ 105 f.). It need cause no surprise that the MSS readings have become interchanged and assimilated to one another, cf. Phil. 1:14; Ac. 13:44, 48 etc. It is no accident that the Johannine writings do not figure in the statistics ; → 13. a. b.

b. Content. The content of the primitive Christian use of "word" can be more precisely established from a comparison of Ac. 6:1 ff. and 1:21 ff. According to 6:2, 4 the διακονία τοῦ λόγου is the essential content of the office of the Twelve which they cannot surrender. When a twelfth apostle is chosen to replace Judas, it is said that this apostle must be an eye-witness of the story of Jesus who can testify to His resurrection (1:21 f.). Here, then, ministry of the Word is equivalent to the witness and message about Jesus. A similar definition may be gleaned from the prologue to Lk. The ἀπ' ἀρχῆς αὐτόπται have become ὑπηρέται τοῦ λόγου (1:2). Obviously these are not two different functions. They are inwardly related. Because these men were eye-witnesses they had an essential qualification for the ministry of the Word, namely, acquaintance with the πράγματα, with the facts concerning Jesus Christ, about whom the Word is the witness and message.

Other passages in Ac. confirm this. 18:5 describes the fulfilment of the λόγος[190] by Paul : διαμαρτυρόμενος τοῖς Ἰουδαίοις εἶναι τὸν χριστὸν Ἰησοῦν. In 17:11 we read first that they accepted the Word and then that they daily examined whether these things were so according to the OT. This obviously means, not that the Word is simply the OT word, but that it is the one fact of salvation to which the OT word points. When in 11:1 those in Jerusalem hear of the conversion of Cornelius, ὅτι καὶ τὰ ἔθνη ἐδέξαντο τὸν λόγον τοῦ θεοῦ, the context makes it quite obvious that the Gentiles had not just received the OT and become Jews, but that they had heard and believed the message concerning Jesus. This is how we are to understand the equation of early missionary preaching and the Word in Ac. 4-19 : λόγον (τοῦ θεοῦ or κυρίου) λαλεῖν, 4:29, 31; 11:19; 13:46; 14:25; 16:32, καταγγέλλειν, 13:5; 15:36; 17:13, διδάσκειν, 18:11, εὐαγγελί-

---

[189] We do not count the many instances where there is fuller definition, e.g., the "sound word," the "word of truth," etc. Also to be distinguished are the many cases in which ὁ λόγος refers to a specific saying or incident, e.g., Mk. 1:45; 9:10; 14:39; also 8:32 : ἐλάλει τὸν λόγον, namely, that mentioned in v. 31 (as opposed to E. Lohmeyer, *Das Mk.-Ev.* [1936], 50, n. 6).

[190] συνείχετο τῷ λόγῳ : "He was wholly given up to, he spent his time in proclamation"; cf. Pr.-Bauer³, 1313. The rendering "he was held fast, constrained, i.e., by a (special) Word of God to him (cf. 16:7)," is intrinsically possible ; it is ruled out, however, by the consistent use of λόγος in Ac. (this is what led to the 𝔎 reading πνεύματι).

ζεσθαι, 8:4; 15:35, ἀκούειν, 4:4; 13:7, 44; 19:10, δέχεσθαι, 8:14; 17:11, δοξάζειν, 13:48, cf. ηὔξανεν ὁ λόγος (τοῦ κυρίου), 6:7; 12:24; 19:20. The missionary preaching of Peter, Paul, and the other apostles, whose content is simply Jesus Christ, was always this Word of God to Israel and the Gentiles. The Word of God is the Word about Jesus.

The same is true in Paul. For him the λόγος (τοῦ θεοῦ or κυρίου) is the message proclaimed by him and accepted by his churches. That is to say, it is simply the message about Christ. The usage is already fixed in Th. The Thessalonians are δεξάμενοι τὸν λόγον (1 Th. 1:6; cf. 2:13). The λόγος τοῦ κυρίου is to τρέχειν and δοξάζεσθαι (2 Th. 3:1). The news (ἐξηχεῖσθαι) of this δέχεσθαι is itself the λόγος τοῦ κυρίου (1 Th. 1:8).

Later epistles tell the same story. What came to the Corinthians is the λόγος τοῦ θεοῦ (1 C. 14:36). The κατηχεῖσθαι of the Galatians is κατηχεῖσθαι τὸν λόγον (6:6). The λαλεῖν of the brethren is λαλεῖν τὸν λόγον τοῦ θεοῦ (Phil. 1:14). The proclamation laid on Paul, with which he pursues no → καπηλεύειν or δολοῦν, is the λόγος τοῦ θεοῦ (2 C. 2:17; 4:2), which is not bound even when the apostle is in bonds (2 Tm. 2:9). Similarly, κήρυξον τὸν λόγον is the task laid on Timothy (2 Tm. 4:2). Particularly clear in content are the two sayings in Col. The λόγος for which a door is to be opened is λαλῆσαι τὸ μυστήριον τοῦ Χριστοῦ, and this λαλῆσαι is the δεῖ, i.e., the task, of Paul, Col. 4:3 f. The οἰκονομία given to Paul is πληρῶσαι τὸν λόγον τοῦ θεοῦ, i.e., the mystery which was once hidden and which is now disclosed, — ὅς ἐστιν Χριστὸς ἐν ὑμῖν, Col. 1:25 ff. (→ 112; 125). Cf. Col. 1:5 and Eph. 1:13, where the λόγος, as λόγος τῆς ἀληθείας, is identical with the εὐαγγέλιον τὸ παρὸν εἰς ὑμᾶς or τῆς σωτηρίας ὑμῶν, i.e., with the message of Christ which has come, and comes, to all men. What God promised πρὸ χρόνων αἰωνίων He has now (καιροῖς ἰδίοις) declared (ἐφανέρωσεν), namely, τὸν λόγον αὐτοῦ. This λόγος of His is to be found in the κήρυγμα entrusted to Paul, Tt. 1:2 f. The content of the λόγος is given in 1 Tm. 1:15 :[191] ὅτι Χριστὸς Ἰησοῦς ἦλθεν εἰς τὸν κόσμον ἁμαρτωλοὺς σῶσαι.

Though there is no definition, 1 Pt. 1:23 is to be understood in the same way: At the beginning of the Christian life, where ἀναγεννᾶσθαι takes place, there stands a λόγος ζῶντος θεοῦ καὶ μένοντος. According to v. 25 this λόγος is no other than τὸ ῥῆμα τὸ εὐαγγελισθὲν εἰς ὑμᾶς.[192] Similarly, the ἔμφυτος λόγος in Jm. 1:21 is the message which saves souls and which has been implanted in proclamation (cf. 1:18 : ἀπεκύησεν ἡμᾶς λόγῳ ἀληθείας).

So far as can be seen, there is no similar fixity of usage in the case of ῥῆμα. To be sure, similar expressions occur, so that one cannot say that ῥῆμα is avoided in this connection. But these expressions are both less frequent than those with λόγος and also much looser, so that we never have the impression of a fixed term. If we ignore Lk. 2:29; 3:2 (→ 113), which describe the pre-Christian situation, and Eph. 6:17 (τὴν μάχαιραν τοῦς πνεύματος ὅ ἐστιν ῥῆμα θεοῦ, → 113), which also refers either wholly or in part to the OT word, we simply have Jn. 3:34; 8:47 (τὰ ῥήματα τοῦ

---

[191] Luther's fine rendering (cf. A.V.: "This is a faithful saying, and worthy ...") is unfortunately not tenable, since it ignores the definite ὁ and also conflicts with the fixed use of πιστὸς ὁ λόγος in the Past. (→ 118).

[192] We need not pursue the question whether behind the ἀναγεννᾶσθαι of 1 Pt. 1:23 there is a recollection of baptism accompanied by the Word (→ I, 674, n. 6); cf. Eph. 5:26.

θεοῦ); Hb. 6:5 (θεοῦ ῥῆμα); 1 Pt. 1:25 (ῥῆμα κυρίου = τὸ ῥῆμα τὸ εὐαγγελισθὲν εἰς ὑμᾶς); Eph. 5:26 (the ῥῆμα which purifies man in baptism).[193]

7. The Character and Efficacy of the Early Christian Word (outside the Johannine Writings).[194]

a. The Word as God's Word. If the Word is identical with the message about Jesus, with the εὐαγγέλιον (Ac. 15:7; Eph. 1:13; Col. 1:5), it is natural that almost anything said about the Gospel can also be said about the Word. It is[195] the λόγος τοῦ σταυροῦ (1 C. 1:18), τῆς καταλλαγῆς (2 C. 5:19), τῆς σωτηρίας (Ac. 13:26), τῆς χάριτος (Ac. 14:3; 20:32), ζωῆς or ζῶν (Phil. 2:16 [cf. Ac. 5:20]; Hb. 4:12; 1 Pt. 1:23[196]),[197] τῆς ἀληθείας (2 C. 6:7; Eph. 1:13; Col. 1:5; 2 Tm. 2:15; Jm. 1:18). The last phrase can simply mean the true and reliable word (e.g., Ac. 26:25: ἀληθείας ῥήματα), but a statement like 2 C. 4:2, in which ἀλήθεια is interchangeable with λόγος τοῦ θεοῦ, shows clearly that the Gospel itself is here described, first as λόγος τοῦ θεοῦ, then as ἀλήθεια (→ I, 244), and that the reference is to the λόγος whose nature as Gospel is denoted by the τῆς ἀληθείας. The Word is the message which corresponds to a reality (ἀλήθεια).

It is this because the One who speaks the Word is God. Whether explicit or not, the τοῦ θεοῦ always controls λόγος statements. 1 Th. 2:13: They have received the Word spoken by Paul: οὐ λόγον ἀνθρώπων ἀλλὰ — καθὼς ἀληθῶς ἐστιν — λόγον θεοῦ. Paul simply has a διακονία (2 C. 5:18) or οἰκονομία (Col. 1:25) in relation to this Word which is given. He has to serve its πληρῶσαι, i.e., to spread across the earth the Word spoken by God (cf. R. 15:19). Because it is given, he guards it cautiously against the alteration or falsification which would make it something of his own; 2 C. 2:17: οὐ γάρ ἐσμεν ... → καπηλεύοντες τὸν λόγον τοῦ θεοῦ, 4:2: μηδὲ δολοῦντες τὸν λόγον τοῦ θεοῦ. As an → ὀρθοτομῶν τὸν λόγον τῆς ἀληθείας one is an ἐργάτης ἀνεπαίσχυντος (2 Tm. 2:15). God Himself is the θέμενος τὸν λόγον τῆς καταλλαγῆς. The apostle is simply a πρεσβεύων, and one through whom (δι' ἡμῶν) God admonishes (2 C. 5:19 f.). ἡμῖν ὁ λόγος ἐξαπεστάλη (Ac. 13:26), says Paul in Antioch; the Word has its origin in the One who sends it. God is the subject of ἐφανέρωσεν ... τὸν λόγον αὐτοῦ, and the ἐν κηρύγματι ὃ ἐπιστεύθην ἐγώ is simply an execution of something given (Tt. 1:3). With this is linked the historical ἀναγκαῖον of the sequence of proclamation of the Word, to the Jew first and then to the ἔθνη (Ac. 13:46).

The efficacy of the Word is dependent on its Author, but is also assured by His will. βουληθεὶς ἀπεκύησεν ἡμᾶς λόγῳ ἀληθείας (Jm. 1:18). It increases

[193] The ref. of the ἐν ῥήματι can hardly be established with certainty. It seems to be the word which accompanies the act of baptism and which is spoken by the baptiser, cf. Haupt Gefbr. (Eph.), 213 f.; Dib. Eph., *ad loc.*

[194] Once the usage is firmly established, there is nothing to prevent all kinds of looser definitions such as "word of truth" and the like. But the general picture is uniform, so that it makes little difference if in some of the expressions there is doubt whether the ref. is simply to the early Christian Word or there is perhaps some reminiscence of the OT word (→ 113).

[195] λόγος δικαιοσύνης in Hb. 5:13 is not the "word of righteousness," but the "right word," though with a suggestion of the other sense too. Cf. O. Michel, *Meyerscher Komm. z. Hb.* (1936), 65.

[196] διὰ λόγου ζῶντος θεοῦ καὶ μένοντος. It is hardly possible to say whether the two participles refer to λόγου or to θεοῦ.

[197] Though cf. → 118.

through His power (Ac. 19:20;[198] 2 C. 6:7). It is itself the δύναμις θεοῦ (1 C. 1:18). It cannot be bound (2 Tm. 2:9). Only God Himself can open the θύρα τοῦ λόγου (Col. 4:3). For this reason we must pray that it may have free course (2 Th. 3:1), or that He may grant λαλεῖν τὸν λόγον (αὐτοῦ) (Ac. 4:29). By the very nature of things prayer and the Word go together (Ac. 6:4; 1 Tm. 4:5), for all prayer derives its promise and power from the Word spoken by God. Hence Paul at Miletus: παρατίθεμαι ὑμᾶς τῷ κυρίῳ καὶ τῷ λόγῳ τῆς χάριτος αὐτοῦ (Ac. 20:32). The Word has within it the effective χάρις of the One who has spoken it. Thus the events described in Ac. 14:3 are simply a manifestation of this intrinsic relation: ἐπὶ τῷ κυρίῳ τῷ μαρτυροῦντι ἐπὶ τῷ λόγῳ τῆς χάριτος αὐτοῦ, διδόντι σημεῖα καὶ τέρατα γίνεσθαι διὰ τῶν χειρῶν αὐτῶν. The non-authentic ending to Mk. gives exactly the same description of the apostolic age in Mk. 16:20: τοῦ κυρίου συνεργοῦντος καὶ τὸν λόγον βεβαιοῦντος διὰ τῶν ἐπακολουθούντων σημείων.

Not in itself as a magical entity, but as the Word of God, i.e., the Word spoken and used by God, the Word is efficacious (ἐνεργής, Hb. 4:12; ἐνεργεῖται, 1 Th. 2:13). This is also implied in the common image of the weapon: Hb. 4:12, sharper than a twoedged sword; Eph. 6:17: τὴν μάχαιραν τοῦ πνεύματος, ὅ ἐστιν ῥῆμα θεοῦ (cf. 2 C. 6:7). The efficacy is supremely concrete. As noted already, the course of the Word cannot be hampered by human and earthly measures, cf. the δεσμοί of 2 Tm. 2:9, or by natural human judgments, cf. the μωρία and σκάνδαλον of 1 C. 1:18, 23. When it takes effect in the one who is smitten by it, ἁγιάζεται (1 Tm. 4:5). If ὁ λόγος τοῦ θεοῦ βλασφημεῖται by the unholy walk of a Christian (Tt. 2:5), this is simply another way of saying that, if it is not resisted, its normal and authentic working is a sanctifying which may be recognised in the concrete traits enumerated in Tt. 2:2 ff. This fact that the Word is efficacious in individual lives is the content of the recurrent πιστὸς ὁ λόγος of the Pastorals.[199] Its reliability is demonstrated in the πίστις and ἀγάπη of the apostle (1 Tm. 1:14), or in the woman who bears her children and is concerned for true ἁγιασμὸς μετὰ σωφροσύνης (1 Tm. 2:15; 3:1). To εὐσέβεια it guarantees the ἐπαγγελία ... ζωῆς τῆς νῦν καὶ τῆς μελλούσης (1 Tm. 4:8 f.), to the ἐκλεκτοί σωτηρία ... μετὰ δόξης αἰωνίου (2 Tm. 2:10 f.). Thus expressions like λόγος τῆς χάριτος (Ac. 14:3; 20:32), τῆς σωτηρίας (Ac. 13:26), ζωῆς (Phil. 2:16), do not simply tell us what the Word speaks and imparts. The genitives are also more precise definitions of the Word which is efficacious because it is God's Word. This Word does not simply point to grace, salvation, and life. It effects grace, salvation and life, for it is grace, salvation and life. Jm. 1:21: τὸν ... λόγον τὸν δυνάμενον σῶσαι τὰς ψυχὰς ὑμῶν.

b. The Relation of Man to the Word. This corresponds in every respect to the genuine and all-pervasive NT dialectic of grasping and being grasped. At the beginning of every relation of man to the Word stands the passive. It cannot be

---

[198] κατὰ κράτος τοῦ κυρίου ὁ λόγος ηὔξανεν. The inverted 𝔎 reading is a natural simplification to ὁ λόγος τοῦ κυρίου.

[199] That this is the right interpretation, and that we do not simply have the introduction to a quotation ("True is the saying ..."), is shown by the fact that this rendering is impossible at Tt. 1:9, → n. 191. In most cases πιστὸς ὁ λόγος does not refer (cf. 1 Tm. 3:1), or does not refer only, to the sentence which follows. It is a confirmation of that which precedes.

expressed more strongly, or in a way which more fully excludes human action, than in the image of birth as this is found in 1 Pt. 1:23: ἀναγεγεννημένοι ... διὰ λόγου ... θεοῦ, and Jm. 1:18: βουληθεὶς ἀπεκύησεν ἡμᾶς λόγῳ ἀληθείας, where the emphasis is uniquely strengthened by the preceding βουληθείς (→ 117). When we are told in 1 Th. 1:6 that the Word has been received μετὰ χαρᾶς πνεύματος ἁγίου, this presupposes the fact that there could have been no reception apart from the gift and work of the πνεῦμα. God's ἐξελέξατο precedes the whole proclamation and hearing of the Word (Ac. 15:7; cf. 13:48). Even of the coming of the Word in detail it is said that God must open the door (Col. 4:3) and let it have free course (2 Th. 3:1).

If this emphasis is strong and ineffaceable, the other side of the picture is equally self-evident. The Word must be received and maintained. This means that it can be accepted or rejected: ἐπειδὴ ἀπωθεῖσθε αὐτόν (= τὸν λόγον τοῦ θεοῦ), Ac. 13:46. The verb δέχεσθαι is linked particularly frequently with the λόγος: Ac. 8:14; 11:1; 17:11; 1 Th. 1:6; 2:13; Jm. 1:21. Cf. πάσης ἀποδοχῆς ἄξιος, 1 Tm. 1:15; 4:9, ἐπέχειν, Phil. 2:16, ἀντέχεσθαι, Tt. 1:9, ἀκατάγνωστος λόγος, Tt. 2:8. The decisive point for understanding this reception of the Word, however, is that the relevant act is not one of mere intellectual agreement but of appropriation by faith. Here again, as always, ἀκούειν reaches its goal only by πιστεύειν, Ac. 4:4; 15:7. These two lines do not contradict or cancel out one another in primitive Christian thinking. This is shown by the fact that in some statements they stand alongside and merge into one another. Paul thanks God that they have received the Word; it works in those who believe (1 Th. 2:13). Those who believe the Word are sealed by the Holy Ghost (Eph. 1:13). Those who magnify and believe the Word are ὅσοι ἦσαν τεταγμένοι εἰς ζωὴν αἰώνιον (Ac. 13:48).

It should be added that δέχεσθαι and πιστεύειν are truly present only where the Word is done, where one is a ποιητὴς λόγου (Jm. 1:22). δέχεσθαι τὸν λόγον means "to lay aside filthiness" (1:21). The Word demands decision between obedience and disobedience (1 Pt. 2:8; 3:1). Where it is not combined with faith in those who hear,[200] it is of no profit (Hb. 4:2). A life which does not concretely observe moral norms consistent with the Word blasphemes the Word (Tt. 2:5). Conversely, it can be said of those who genuinely receive the Word: ἐδόξαζον τὸν λόγον τοῦ κυρίου (Ac. 13:48).

c. The Word as Spoken Word. In all this the λόγος is always genuine λέγειν, or spoken word in all concreteness. One of the most serious errors of which one could be guilty would be to make this λόγος τοῦ θεοῦ a concept or abstraction. Proclamation of the Christ event speaks the Word of God to the world. It is in the last resort a very sober fact, always taken into account by the men of the NT, that the Word is present to be transmitted. No one knows this Word without proclamation. There can be no ἀκοή and no πίστις without this λέγειν and ῥῆμα (R. 10:17). There can be no δέχεσθαι, no Christianity, without this λαλεῖν and καταγγέλλειν of the λόγος τοῦ θεοῦ. All Christian theology, speculation, and instruction have their norm — τὴν ἀσφάλειαν — in the faithfulness with which they repeat and pass on the event which has happened, the Word of God which has been established by God and spoken in the event (Lk. 1:1-4; cf. Tt. 1:9: κατὰ τὴν διδαχήν).

---

200 On the textual problem cf. Michel, 49.

8. The Word in the Synoptic Account of Jesus.

a. Our investigation thus far has produced an essentially uniform picture of usage and content in all essential parts of the primitive Christian writings apart from the Johannine writings on the one side and the Synoptic tradition on the other. Both of these merit special consideration.

In both — and this is natural in the Gospels — we are concerned with the special link between the term "word" and the person of Jesus. The question does not arise only here. We have seen that in apostolic usage διακονία τοῦ λόγου is the witness and message concerning Jesus (→ 115). The Word is the word about Jesus (→ 116).

The prologue to Luke, with its αὐτόπται καὶ ὑπηρέται τοῦ λόγου (1:2; → 115), fully corresponds, as we have seen, to the usage in Ac. and Pl. Quite apart from the common authorship of Lk. and Ac., this is not surprising. For the prologue is related to the situation of Luke and Theophilus, namely, the apostolic age, the very same age as that described in Ac. What the Evangelist does in his work as a collector of the tradition about Jesus and the author of a gospel is proclamation of the Gospel, the fulfilment of a commissioned κήρυξον τὸν λόγον (cf. 2 Tm. 4:2). The special use of the term "word" which we find in the Gospels is twofold. The Gospel narrative applies the word in a specific sense to the work of Jesus. And Jesus Himself, according to the account of the Evangelists, uses the term.

b. Twice in Mk., once in Lk. and once in Ac. it is said of Jesus that He is a preacher of the Word. Mk. 2:2: καὶ συνήχθησαν πολλοὶ ... καὶ ἐλάλει αὐτοῖς τὸν λόγον, Mk. 4:33: καὶ τοιαύταις παραβολαῖς πολλαῖς ἐλάλει αὐτοῖς τὸν λόγον, Lk. 5:1: ἐγένετο δὲ ἐν τῷ τὸν ὄχλον ἐπικεῖσθαι αὐτῷ καὶ ἀκούειν τὸν λόγον τοῦ θεοῦ ..., Ac. 10:36 (Peter's address to Cornelius): τὸν λόγον ὃν ἀπέστειλεν τοῖς υἱοῖς Ἰσραὴλ εὐαγγελιζόμενος εἰρήνην διὰ Ἰησοῦ Χριστοῦ. In these verses[201] the term "word" is used of the preaching of Jesus in exactly the same way as it is of the message of the apostles. Jesus speaks the Word; by Him it is spoken. The usage is so extraordinarily natural that one is astonished at its infrequency. If one compares the very free way in which Ac. and Pl. speak of apostolic preaching as the speaking of the Word, a clear statistical distinction is to be seen. While it is possible to apply the word occasionally to Jesus, the Evangelists are plainly aware that it does not describe the totality of the mission and manifestation of Jesus in the same unmistakable way as it does the mission and task of the apostles. When used and understood in the light of apostolic usage — and in view of the link between Lk. and Ac. a reader like Theophilus would obviously do this — the term carries with it the danger of suggesting that the mission of Jesus is to be regarded as that of passing on in words the preaching laid upon Him by God. Misunderstanding of the word might make of Jesus a teacher or prophet. Perhaps it is no accident that Mt. in particular avoids the word in this connection. In the case of Jewish Christians it is especially necessary to rule out the misconception that Jesus is just a preacher or rabbi.

The task of the messenger is λαλεῖν, namely, telling what he has seen and heard. He passes on the "word" with his λαλεῖν. But the Word which Jesus

201 Verses like Mk. 1:45 (as against Kl. Mk., *ad loc.*); 8:32 (→ n. 189) are not relevant here.

brings is not the object of mere λαλεῖν. It is also presented in the works of Jesus. The λεπροὶ καθαρίζονται is Word as these Evangelists understand it. As the message of the Baptist shows, it is accepted by the sensual act of βλέπειν as well as ἀκούειν (Mt. 11:4). This is perhaps the reason why the formula λαλεῖν τὸν λόγον, which is so common in Ac., is used only occasionally in the account of Jesus. The distinctive Johannine view that Jesus is the Word is not expressly present in the Synoptists. Yet their very reserve in respect of the term ὁ λόγος shows that the first three Evangelists are well aware of the facts to which the distinctive Johannine usage bears witness.

9. The Word in the Synoptic Sayings of Jesus.

a. The occurrence of ὁ λόγος in the sayings of Jesus preserved in the tradition is statistically small. Apart from the interpretation of the parable of the Sower, which is found in all three Gospels, there are only two passages in Lk. Lk. 8:21 gives us the saying about the true relatives of Jesus: μήτηρ μου καὶ ἀδελφοί μου οὗτοί εἰσιν οἱ τὸν λόγον τοῦ θεοῦ ἀκούοντες καὶ ποιοῦντες. Mk. 3:35 and Mt. 12:50 have the statement in the form: ... ὅς (ὅστις γὰρ) ἂν ποιήσῃ τὸ θέλημα τοῦ θεοῦ (τοῦ πατρός μου τοῦ ἐν οὐρανοῖς). Lk. 11:28, which is peculiar to Lk., is the answer of Jesus to the woman who lauds His mother: μενοῦν μακάριοι οἱ ἀκούοντες τὸν λόγον τοῦ θεοῦ καὶ φυλάσσοντες. There is no Synoptic par. to this. The fact that the par. to the first Lucan saying has "do the will of God" rather than "hear and do the Word of God" is a warning against drawing far-reaching conclusions from the Lucan passages. There is no serious reason to doubt the historical authenticity of the sayings, but it must also be said that the tradition gives us no certainty that in both cases Jesus really used the Aram. term for the Word of God and not one which might imply the will of God. The possibility, and even probability, that the expression "Word of God" was introduced here by Lk. is all the greater in view of the fact (1) that the phrase ἀκούειν τὸν λόγον was well-known to the Evangelist and his readers, as Ac. shows, and (2) that this formula quite rightly seemed to him to be a wholly suitable and correct rendering of what Jesus supposedly said and meant in His Aram. saying. It is hardly possible, then, to draw from the Lucan passages the historical conclusion that Jesus Himself actually used the word and applied it to His own preaching.

b. Matters seem to be rather different in the interpretation of the parable of the Sower, where all three Evangelists use the term, Mt. 13:18-23; Mk. 4:13-20; Lk. 8:11-15. It is obvious, of course, that the repetition of the term in this group does not denote more than a single occurrence.[202] Hence this is the only occurrence outside the special Lucan material. In this case, however, the question of authenticity is complicated by the well-known problem of the interpretation and its allegorising. We are thus faced by two facts. The first is that this is the only instance of ὁ λόγος on the lips of Jesus in Mt. and Mk. The second is that it

---

[202] At the beginning of the exposition Mk. has τὸν λόγον (v. 14), but Mt. has τὸν λόγον τῆς βασιλείας (v. 19) and Lk. ὁ λόγος τοῦ θεοῦ (v. 11). The more extended form in Lk. denotes no basic alteration, as may be seen from the presence of both forms in Ac. (→ 115). On the other hand, it cannot be ruled out that the phrase in Mt., which stands at the head of the exposition, and thus forms a commentary on the use of τὸν λόγον without attributes in the succeeding verses, is introduced for the same reason as the avoidance of ὁ λόγος in Mt.'s narrative (→ 120).

occurs in the context of a type of express allegorical interpretation for which there are no par. elsewhere in Jesus' teaching. We may thus conclude that it is at least doubtful whether these are the actual words of Jesus Himself. The current usage of the apostolic community has perhaps exerted some influence here. This is the more likely in view of the fact that all the details of the interpretation find parallels in apostolic depictions of the experiences of primitive Christianity.

> "Satan hinders the course of the Word in 1 Th. 2:18; 3:5; 2 C. 11:3; the Word is received, i.e., taken into the heart, in 1 Th. 1:6; 2:13; 2 C. 11:4; this means joy in 1 Th. 1:6; Ac. 8:8; 16:34; persecution arises for the sake of the Word in 1 Th. 1:6; Phil. 1:7; Phlm. 13; 2 Tm. 1:8; 2:9."[203]

Hence this passage gives us no certainty, or even probability, that Jesus Himself used the term "word" in a special sense. This is not to say, of course, that the statements are right or wrong, correct or incorrect. The true and important factor in this interpretation of the parable is not whether it is the only possible understanding in its explanation of the details,[204] but that it shows Jesus to be the sower who scatters the Word, the Word of the βασιλεία, the λόγος τοῦ θεοῦ, and who demands decision, i.e., fruit. There can be no doubt that the exposition does not have in view any word of God, or a general concept of the Word, but very concretely the Word brought by Jesus. And it has in view this Word, not in the sense of sayings which are adopted but in the sense of the Word of Christ which is received.

c. As in the case of εὐαγγέλιον and its occurrence, "the question whether we have an authentic saying of Jesus or a construct of the community is of secondary importance" (→ II, 728). For, if the interpretation derives from the community, the question is whether the community was faithful to what Jesus had in view or altered it, and whether it gave to the term "word," here ascribed to Jesus, a content which corresponds or not to the real claim which Jesus made. Thus the ultimate question is the question of His Messianic consciousness and His sense of authority. What the interpretation of the parable, and its ascription of the term "word" to Jesus, seeks to attest to is identical with the ultimate background of the whole tradition concerning Jesus as this is reflected in His ἐγὼ δὲ λέγω ὑμῖν, Mt. 5:22 ff., in His judgment on the cities, Mt. 11:20 ff., in the message to the Baptist, Mt. 11:4 ff., in the authority of His word and act *vis-à-vis* the man sick of the palsy, Mt. 9:5 ff.

This total picture must decide, not the detailed authenticity of the use of the specific term "the Word" on the lips of Jesus, but the legitimacy of the way in which Lk., and the three Synoptists in the exposition of the parable of the Sower, laid this term on His lips.

10. λόγος/λόγοι (τοῦ θεοῦ) in Revelation.

a. The character of Rev. as an authentic and not just a literary revelation is reflected in the dominant and recurrent description of its contents, especially at

---

[203] J. Schniewind in *NT Deutsch*, I³ (1937), 75 f. on Mk. 4:15 ff.

[204] Cf. e.g., J. Weiss, *Schr. NT*, I³ 113 f.: "Why should not the birds of the air be equated, not with Satan, but with the cares and sorrows of life, or the thorns with sloth and self-righteousness? This would be just as apposite."

the beginning and the end, as οἱ λόγοι: τῆς προφητείας (1:3), τοῦ βιβλίου τούτου (22:9), τῆς προφητείας τοῦ βιβλίου τούτου (22:7, 10, 18), τοῦ βιβλίου τῆς προφητείας ταύτης (22:19), οὗτοι οἱ λόγοι πιστοὶ καὶ ἀληθινοί (εἰσιν)[205] (21:5; 22:6). In this group of sayings, which refers to the contents of Rev., the phrase "Word of God" is not used.[206]

The plural οἱ λόγοι τοῦ θεοῦ occurs twice. In the first instance (19:9) it refers to a single promise which is given just before, the μακάριοι on those who are called to the marriage feast of the Lamb (v. 9a): οὗτοι οἱ λόγοι ἀληθινοὶ τοῦ θεοῦ εἰσιν.[207] In the second instance it is to be understood by comparison with parallel sayings. 17:17: the βασιλεία is given to the beast, ἄχρι τελεσθήσονται οἱ λόγοι τοῦ θεοῦ, cf. 10:7: καὶ ἐτελέσθη τὸ μυστήριον τοῦ θεοῦ, ὡς εὐηγγέλισεν τοὺς ἑαυτοῦ δούλους τοὺς προφήτας. Here, then, the words of God are the promises spoken by the prophets.

b. Apart from 19:13, the sing. ὁ λόγος τοῦ θεοῦ is restricted to a group of sayings in which it is combined with → μαρτυρία. First of all, these are sayings about the divine himself: ὃς ἐμαρτύρησεν τὸν λόγον τοῦ θεοῦ καὶ τὴν μαρτυρίαν Ἰησοῦ Χριστοῦ, 1:2, and: "Who ... was in the isle that is called Patmos, διὰ τὸν λόγον τοῦ θεοῦ καὶ τὴν μαρτυρίαν Ἰησοῦ", 1:9. Secondly, they are sayings about the martyrs who are slain διὰ τὸν λόγον τοῦ θεοῦ καὶ διὰ τὴν μαρτυρίαν ἣν εἶχον, 6:9, or beheaded διὰ τὴν μαρτυρίαν καὶ διὰ τὸν λόγον τοῦ θεοῦ, 20:4. Martyrs (οὐκ ἠγάπησαν τὴν ψυχὴν αὐτῶν ἄχρι θανάτου) are also in view in 12:11: Those who have overcome the κατήγωρ διὰ τὸ αἷμα τοῦ ἀρνίου καὶ διὰ τὸν λόγον τῆς μαρτυρίας αὐτῶν.

Comparison of the passages answers many exegetical questions. 6:9 and 20:4 show that διὰ τὸν λόγον τοῦ θεοῦ καὶ τὴν μαρτυρίαν (Ἰησοῦ) points to the fact that persecution and wrong are suffered for these things. This rules out any "innocuous" reasons for the stay on Patmos, e.g., the pursuit of solitude for visions, missionary activity, or accident.[208] By reason of the common διά, the gen. μαρτυρία Ἰησοῦ is to be construed as a subj. gen. (cf. the αἷμα τοῦ ἀρνίου in 12:11): the witness of Jesus, not the witness concerning Jesus.[209] Parallelism with λόγος τοῦ θεοῦ supports this: "The Word spoken by God and the witness given by Jesus." So, too, does the description of Jesus as ὁ μάρτυς ὁ πιστός in 1:5. This witness of Jesus is the witness which they hold (6:9), or their witness (12:11).[210]

What is the meaning of ὁ λόγος τοῦ θεοῦ in these statements, which are plainly distinguished from the others by the use of the singular? Obviously the reference is not to the contents of Rev. with its individual λόγοι τῆς προφητείας. The martyrs are not beheaded for these. It is true that 1:2, as the ὅσα εἶδεν shows, establishes a connection with the contents of the book. Yet it does not do so in such a way that in what is seen the λόγος τοῦ θεοῦ and μαρτυρία Ἰησοῦ

---

205 It is self-evident that the addition of τοῦ θεοῦ (Q etc.) is secondary.

206 On the fact that the λόγοι is without subject cf. Loh. Apk., 174.

207 The ref. back to the whole of Rev. (Had. Apk., 186: "in all these visions"), or to the section 17:1-19:8 (Loh. Apk., 153) is as ill supported as the deletion of τοῦ θεοῦ (Bss. Apk., 428).

208 Bss. Apk., 192.

209 Luther suggests the witness about Jesus (1:2).

210 Rev. 19:10: ἔχειν the μαρτυρία Ἰησοῦ is present where the πνεῦμα τῆς προφητείας effects the sealing and confirmation of the μαρτυρία, cf. Had. Apk., 186.

Χριστοῦ are present as something new and singular and only just disclosed. They are both independent of what now happens to John, and, as they appear elsewhere in other forms, so they appear here in that of ἰδεῖν. Both ὁ λόγος τοῦ θεοῦ and ἡ μαρτυρία Ἰησοῦ are given magnitudes. They can be present in the form of apostolic preaching, in that of martyrs who are persecuted and slain, or in that of vision, as with John. The λόγος τοῦ θεοῦ and μαρτυρία Ἰησοῦ always lie behind the form of representation. They are that which is represented. They are the given factors to which the form bears witness. Hence nothing in the impartation of the heavenly Lord depicted in Rev. 1 ff. is to be considered or evaluated alone, i.e., in abstraction from these underlying factors. When this is done, even the finest passages in Rev. become apocalyptic fantasy and frenzy. The impartation of the Lord given in John's visions is simply a presentation, propagation, elucidation, and illustration of the λόγος which is spoken by God and the μαρτυρία which is given by Jesus, i.e., of the given factors which underlie Christianity.

Among statements about what is given to the community we are naturally to number 3:8 : ἐτήρησάς μου τὸν λόγον, and 3:10 : ὅτι ἐτήρησας τὸν λόγον τῆς ὑπομονῆς, the Word of the risen Lord which is given to the community and which is to be kept by it.

When we speak of the given factors described in these phrases, do we refer to two different things, or to one? Are the λόγος τοῦ θεοῦ and the μαρτυρία Ἰησοῦ Χριστοῦ distinct, or are they one and the same thing? If we are to give the opinion of the writer, we cannot answer this question without referring to a verse which is highly singular and yet an integral part of the whole, namely, 19:13. The description of the Christ who appears eschatologically culminates in the saying: καὶ κέκληται τὸ ὄνομα αὐτοῦ ὁ λόγος τοῦ θεοῦ.[211] But this statement is completely distorted if it is seen apart from the total NT picture. It belongs on the one side to the series of primitive Christian λόγος τοῦ θεοῦ sayings, and on the other it is characterised as part of the primitive Christian view of Christ.

11. Jesus Christ the λόγος τοῦ θεοῦ.

a. In primitive Christianity as we have thus far considered it there is an awareness, reflected in the use of the term λόγος, that preaching of what has taken place in the person of Jesus is preaching of the Word, and that reception of the Word implies faith in Jesus. Ministers of the Word does not mean those who repeat sayings — Tannaites[212] — but eye-witnesses who recount what has taken place (Lk. 1:2; Ac. 6:2, 4; cf. 1:21 → 115). In the Synoptic record is reflected a sense that, while it is not incorrect to use the word ὁ λόγος of the λαλεῖν of Jesus, this does not fully express what is to be said (→ 120). The interpretation of the parable of the Sower, whether it derives from Jesus or not, has its true

[211] To delete the verse as an interpolation (Bss. Apk., 431: "It is possible that we have here the idle conceit of a copyist who was anxious to explain the unknown name") is quite arbitrary, since there is no hint of this in the textual tradition; it also robs the context of its crown and climax, as rightly perceived in Loh. Apk., 155 and Had. Apk., 190.

[212] Heb. שנה = Aram. תנא: "to repeat, learn, teach, pass on," hence מִשְׁנָה = "the traditional material (to be repeated)" = the Mishnah; תַּנָּא. תַּנָּאִים = "transmitter(s) of this traditional material" = Tannaite(s). The sayings of the fathers (Pirqe Aboth) are a collection of such sayings memorised and passed on by repetition. Here we have the very thing which early Christian ministers of the Word, for all the formal similarity, were not.

point in the conviction that the seed expounded as the Word is the Christ event which has taken place in Jesus (→ 122). In Colossians (→ 112; 116) the λόγος τοῦ θεοῦ is the μυστήριον which was once hidden but which is now manifest τοῖς ἁγίοις αὐτοῦ. This formulation alone makes it clear that the content of the λόγος and μυστήριον cannot be anything other than the fact of Christ; this is expressly stated in the relative apposition: ὅς ἐστιν Χριστός (Col. 1:25-27).[213] This fact of Christ is the Word of God, the Word which God has spoken to His saints.

It is to be noted however — and this is of absolutely decisive importance — that these statements do not rest on a concept of the "Word." If they are understood conceptually, they are wholly and hopelessly distorted. They arise, and derive their life, only from the event which is given in the person of Jesus. At the head of the train of thought sketched by the term λόγος there stands, not a concept, but the event which has taken place, and in which God declares Himself, causing His Word to be enacted. That apostolic thinking starts originally and dynamically at this point, that a concept is not the starting-point, may be seen particularly clearly in the fact that statements of this kind are in no way bound to the term λόγος. The most obvious example is 2 C. 1:19: God's Son, Jesus Christ, the One whom the apostles — and specifically the three mentioned, Paul, Silvanus, and Timotheus — proclaim, "was not yes and no, but in him was enacted yes" (ναὶ ἐν αὐτῷ γέγονεν). The Word "yes" has taken place in Jesus Christ, which means that He is this Word "yes" in His historical person. Rev. 3:14 is to the same effect: τάδε λέγει ὁ ἀμήν, Christ is the Word "amen." Both passages leave us in no doubt that the speaker of the Word cannot be any other than God Himself, and certainly not a fate or chance alongside God. In Rev. 3:14 the τοῦ θεοῦ of the third member belongs purely grammatically to τῆς κτίσεως and not to ἡ ἀρχή, but this in no way alters the fact that according to the structure of the verse all the members, including especially the three nouns ἀμήν, μάρτυς and ἀρχή, stand in logical apposition, as is clear when the verse is read aloud. In any case, no other speaker is available for the ἀμήν apart from the θεός. In 2 C. 1:19 f. the correspondence between the ἐπαγγελίαι θεοῦ and the ναί is so plain that one can speak of the ναί as a ναὶ θεοῦ, the more so as the continuation (linked by διό) summons to ἀμὴν τῷ θεῷ πρὸς δόξαν in virtue of this "yes" of God enacted in Christ. All these statements show that the saying in Rev. 19:13: "Whose name is the Word of God," gives succinct expression to something present in the whole outlook and utterance of the primitive Church.

b. If this fact is to be rightly evaluated, however, it must be set in a broader context.

In relation to the terms "Word" and "Word of God," and their application to the events of the NT there is repeated the common process whereby a value already present in religious language is filled with a new content and becomes a new value when it passes into the vocabulary of the NT, though the old value is subordinated to the new rather than abolished or negated. Thus the κτίσις, ἐντολή and διαθήκη of the OT are not deprived of their force; they are set in contrast with the καινὴ κτίσις, ἐντολή and διαθήκη (2 C. 5:17; Jn. 13:34; Lk. 22:20) which

---

[213] That the ἐν ὑμῖν added to ὅς ἐστιν Χριστός does not indicate a spiritualising break of the connection with the enacted process "Jesus" is proved beyond doubt by the continuation: ὃν ἡμεῖς καταγγέλλομεν (v. 28). Pauline καταγγέλλειν includes the παράδοσις; cf. Schniewind (→ I, 72).

are constituted by the fact of Christ and in which the old values are fulfilled. Now it is true that we never read of a καινὸς λόγος. But the thing itself is present. When the Christian message speaks of the Word of God, this means no more and no less — as in the case of the other values — than that the value indicated by "word" in the OT, namely, the "Word of God," is shown to be taken up into and fulfilled in the expression which denotes the event of the NT.

Here as elsewhere, however, a second point must be made. This is that according to the common understanding of primitive Christianity this is not a process which stands alongside the person of Jesus Christ. It is not a doctrine proclaimed by Him and passed on by His apostles. It is present only in His person, in the historical occurrence which is given with Him, which He Himself is. Nor is this a theology of the community which the apostolic age introduced. According to the ample witness of the whole tradition it is Jesus' own awareness of His mission. Both the ἦλθον ... πληρῶσαι of Mt. 5:17 and the Ἐγὼ δὲ λέγω ὑμῖν of Mt. 5:22 ff. mean that the καινὴ ἐντολή is present in Him, in His person. The ὅτι τοῦ ἱεροῦ μεῖζόν ἐστιν ὧδε of Mt. 12:6 also points to His person, in which the old value of the temple, which Jesus Himself affirms (cf. Mt. 21:12 ff.), is present in a new form. Again, the καινή [214] διαθήκη is present, not in words, or doctrines, or a theology, but in His blood, i.e., in what takes place in His person, in the life lived by Him, Mt. 26:28 and par. His authoritative Word is the Word of One who knows that the full authority of God is present in His person (Mt. 9:1 ff.). Apostolic proclamation simply continues this line of thought which derives from Jesus' own sense of His mission when it says of Him that He did not merely proclaim, but is, the τέλος of the Law (R. 10:4), that He ἐγενήθη σοφία, δικαιοσύνη, ἁγιασμός, ἀπολύτρωσις (1 C. 1:30), that He does not merely bring a message of peace but ἐστὶν ἡ εἰρήνη (Eph. 2:14). There is not the slightest difference, but full and unremitting correspondence with the fundamental NT fact constantly described herewith, if we say that Jesus is not just the One who brings the Word but the One who incorporates it in His person, in the historical process of His speech and action, of His life and being.

c. This is the point of Rev. 19:13. The phenomenon described in vv. 11-16 characterises the two sides of all Christology, i.e., of all statements about Christ: the recognition and affirmation of the mystery which no one can express, of the name which no one knows (v. 12); and yet at the same time the assertion of what is manifest, of the name which can be known, which is ὁ λόγος τοῦ θεοῦ. The fact that a sword proceeds out of His mouth is to the same effect (v. 15).[215] What He does to His enemies is the work of this Word which exercises effective and irresistible dominion in His person. For this reason it is the same ὄνομα as that of v. 16: βασιλεὺς βασιλέων καὶ κύριος κυρίων. This Word of God is King of kings and Lord of lords.

Here, as always, there is for the divine no bifurcation into an earthly Jesus and an eschatological Christ. In 1:7 He who comes on the clouds is also described

---

[214] Whether the word "new" was part of the original saying is of little importance, since the word simply brings out what is obviously intended, cf. G. Kittel, "Jesu Worte über sein Sterben," *Deutsche Theologie*, 3 (1936), 185 f.

[215] Cf. Eph. 6:17; Hb. 4:12; also Ps. 57:4; 64:3; Is. 49:2. The repetition of the image in Rev. 1:16; 2:16 shows that 19:11-16, and the statement of v. 13, do not stand alone in Rev.

as the One whom they pierced. In 5:12 the Lamb which was worthy to receive power, and to sit on the throne, and to feed the nations, is τὸ ἐσφαγμένον. Similarly, in 19:11 the depiction of the rider on the white horse as the One who is the Word of God establishes the identity of this eschatological figure with Jesus of Nazareth.

This is confirmed by what we said earlier (→ 124) about the content of the twofold statement: ὁ λόγος τοῦ θεοῦ καὶ ἡ μαρτυρία Ἰησοῦ Χριστοῦ (1:2, 9; 6:9; 20:4; cf. 12:11). If the λόγος τοῦ θεοῦ statement of Rev. belongs, as described, to the totality of early christological utterance, it is directly connected with the μαρτυρία Ἰησοῦ Χριστοῦ statement. One and the same basic function of Jesus Christ is described: ὁ μάρτυς ὁ πιστός (1:5; 3:14), who represents as well as bears the μαρτυρία, cf. Jn. 1:7: ἦλθεν εἰς μαρτυρίαν; and: τὸ ὄνομα αὐτοῦ ὁ λόγος τοῦ θεοῦ (19:13). As the Word of God, He is Witness and He bears witness, cf. Jn. 1:18: ἐκεῖνος ἐξηγήσατο. The apostle and the martyr, however, bear witness to τὸν λόγον τοῦ θεοῦ καὶ τὴν μαρτυρίαν Ἰησοῦ Χριστοῦ (1:2), and they are persecuted and put to death on account of this witness (6:9). They do exactly the same thing as described in Ac.; they tell (4:31 etc.) and proclaim (13:5 etc.) τὸν λόγον τοῦ θεοῦ, i.e., the message about Jesus, who is this Word spoken by God.

12. 1 Jn. 1:1 ff.[216]

a. What has been said thus far has given us in large measure, if not completely, a historical point from which to view the term λόγος in 1 Jn. 1:1. The λόγος τῆς ζωῆς is what has been heard, seen, considered, and handled by the apostle. He goes out of his way to emphasise, in threefold repetition (v. 1, 2, 3), the historical, spatio-temporal concreteness of what has been manifested (ἐφανερώθη). It is beyond question that the λόγος is meant to be the historical figure of Jesus Christ.

The question whether the seeing and handling refer to the historical or the risen Jesus is an idle one from the standpoint of the NT author. For the risen Lord is identical with the One whom they saw and heard as Jesus of Nazareth, and the historical Jesus is believed in against the background of Easter. Hence the interrelation of the two testimonies in Ac. 1:21 f.

The apostle has seen and heard the Word in his encounter with this historical manifestation. He has not just heard the Word with his ear. The Word is not just the revelation mediated through the speaking and teaching Jesus. It is the fact of Christ as such. The writer's mission, as he heaps up words to tell us, is simply to pass on what he has heard: μαρτυροῦμεν καὶ ἀπαγγέλλομεν (v. 2 f.), ἀναγγέλλομεν (v. 5). Here the λόγος, in both substance and usage, simply denotes what was described as the apostolic task in the earliest apostolic writings: διακονία τοῦ λόγου (Ac. 6:4), namely, witness (μάρτυς, Ac. 1:22) to the history

---

[216] In this context, which is concerned with the primitive data, we need not discuss the so-called *comma Johanneum* which has come into the text at 1 Jn. 5:7: (τρεῖς εἰσιν οἱ μαρτυροῦντες) ἐν τῷ οὐρανῷ, ὁ πατήρ, ὁ λόγος καὶ τὸ ἅγιον πνεῦμα. καὶ οὗτοι οἱ τρεῖς ἕν εἰσι. This came into the biblical text prior to 400 A.D. "In face of the findings of textual criticism the authenticity of the *comma Johanneum* cannot be upheld, and the context of 1 Jn. 5 supports the external evidence. This is now agreed" (M. Meinertz, *Einl. in das NT*⁴ [1933], 311). Cf. E. Künstle, *Das* Comma Johanneum (1905); E. Riggenbach, "Das *Comma Johanneum*" = BFTh, 31, 4 (1928).

of Jesus in which the apostle was present, cf. ὃ ἑωράκαμεν (1 Jn. 1:3; cf. Ac. 1:21 f.; → 115). The combination with τῆς ζωῆς, which denotes an equation, as the parallel statements of 1 and 2 show, is also to be found earlier, i.e., in Phil. 2:16 (λόγος ζωῆς) and Ac. 5:20 (τὰ ῥήματα τῆς ζωῆς ταύτης).

The saying in 1 Jn. 1:1 shows very plainly that the equation of λόγος with Jesus Christ is still dynamic. It has not yet become a true personification either conceptually or mythically. The statement still reflects the direct idea of the true and actual "Word." This may be seen from the structure (anacoluthon) and especially from the neuter form of the relative pronoun: ὃ ἑωράκαμεν etc. The author is very conscious of the paradox that one cannot see and view and handle a "word." For this reason he deliberately avoids the ὅς corresponding to the masculine λόγος. He thus avoids personification, even if in so doing he gives the sentence a broken form. One detects here the genuine sensibility which causes the NT author consciously to safeguard against any possible mythological misunderstanding of the statement.

b. The whole passage 1 Jn. 1:1 ff., as a statement about the λόγος, is in line with other NT statements concerning the Word. Yet there are no previous analogies for some of the details: ὃ ἦν ἀπ' ἀρχῆς in v. 1, and ἥτις ἦν πρὸς τὸν πατέρα in v. 2. With regard to the former, exposition has been much affected by the tendency to deal with it as an appendix to the exposition of Jn. 1:1 ff. This has overshadowed, and even to a large degree effaced, the profound material connection between 1 Jn. 1:1 and the whole of what the primitive Church has to say about the λόγος. On the other hand, it has to be admitted that within the total witness of early Christianity 1 Jn. 1:1 introduces a new element which finds direct correspondence and development in the prologue to the Gospel.

13. The Distinctiveness of the λόγος Saying in Jn. 1:1.

a. The Johannine use of λόγος is controlled by the use of the term in the prologue. A negative fact makes this clear. This is the fact that the absolute, specific, unrelated ὁ λόγος is never found outside the prologue.[217] This is most surprising, since the Gospel uses λόγος in many different combinations.

ὁ λόγος τοῦ θεοῦ (= OT), 10:35; Ἠσαΐου, 12:38; ὁ ἐν τῷ νόμῳ αὐτῶν γεγραμμένος, 15:25; αὐτοῦ (= God), 5:38; 8:55; σου (= God), 17:6, 14; ὁ σός (= God), 17:17; τοῦ Ἰησοῦ, 18:32; αὐτοῦ (= Jesus), 4:41; ὃν εἶπεν ὁ Ἰησοῦς, 2:22; 4:50; ὁ λόγος οὗτος ὃν εἶπεν, 7:36; ὁ λόγος μου, 5:24; 8:52; 14:23; 15:20; ὁ ἐμός, 8:31, 37, 43, 51; 14:24: ὃν ἐλάλησα, 12:48; ὃν λελάληκα, 15:3; οὗ ἐγὼ εἶπον, 15:20; ὃν ἀκούετε, 14:24; ὁ λόγος οὗτος (with ref. to Jesus), 6:60; 7:40 (vl.); 21:23; οἱ λόγοι οὗτοι (with ref. to Jesus), 7:40 (vl.); 10:19; οἱ λόγοι μου, 14:24. Cf. ῥῆμα (no sing. in Jn.): τὰ ῥήματα τοῦ θεοῦ, 3:34; 8:47; τὰ ἐμὰ ῥήματα, 5:47; τὰ ῥήματα μου, 12:47 f.; 15:7; ταῦτα τὰ ῥήματα, 8:20; 10:21; τὰ ῥήματα ἃ ἐγὼ λελάληκα (λέγω), 6:63; 14:10; τὰ ῥήματα ἃ ἔδωκάς μοι, 17:8 (→ n. 188); ῥήματα ζωῆς αἰωνίου ἔχεις, 6:68.

b. When we consider the usage elsewhere, these findings are remarkable. The situation can hardly be the same as in the Synoptic Gospels, where it seemed to be felt that the innocuous use (e.g., Ac.) should not be applied to Jesus because

---

[217] In view of the poor attestation there can be little doubt that in 7:40 τὸν λόγον (for τῶν λόγων τούτων) is a secondary reading.

there was hesitation to make the Lord a mere speaker, a mere transmitter of the message, which would be to put Him on the same level as the apostles (→ 120). The way in which the Fourth Gospel refers to Jesus' speaking, i.e., the way in which, esp. in the Parting Discourses, it causes Him to speak of His "I have said unto you" and of His mission (→ I, 443), shows that this is no longer a problem. At essential points the whole composition of the Gospel rests on the unity of action and speech. The action is the theme of the speech, the speech exposition of the action.

The situation in the Fourth Gospel is thus quite different. At the time of the Synoptists, as Ac. and Pl. show, the λόγος is the message about Jesus. There is an unmistakable material tendency to regard Jesus Himself as the One who gives and is this Word, not only in His addresses, but in His whole earthly manifestation. This created in the Synoptists, and most strongly on Jewish Christian [218] soil, a hesitation to apply the term λόγος in its developing specific sense to Jesus Himself, since at this stage of development, i.e., before the development was complete, it might give rise to misunderstanding. Now, however, the restraining factor is the definitiveness of the specific use, which may be seen in the prologue to Jn. as nowhere else in the NT. Once the λόγος saying of the prologue was possible, there could hardly be any further place for the kind of use still found in Mk. 2:2; 4:33: "He (= the λόγος) spoke the λόγος to them."

c. A second point also calls for notice, and this explains why Jesus is never again called the λόγος in the Gospel. The emphasis of the λόγος saying in the prologue lies at the point to which we are referred in part by 1 Jn. 1:1, namely, pre-existence. The ἐγένετο of Jn. 1:14 is the point of transition. The historical manifestation is Jesus. He is the Word. The Word is now Jesus. The term λόγος is not used for the very reverse of docetic reasons, namely, because this Jesus is the λόγος wholly and not just partially, because the unconditional identity of the σάρξ or historical manifestation of Jesus with the eternal Word is the first and most radical presupposition of the Fourth Gospel. The Gospel is wholly at one with the beginning of the Epistle. The ἐσκήνωσεν ἐν ἡμῖν and the ἐθεασάμεθα τὴν δόξαν αὐτοῦ of Jn. 1:14 is just as identical in content with the ὃ ἐθεασάμεθα καὶ αἱ χεῖρες ἡμῶν ἐψηλάφησαν of 1 Jn. 1:1 as are the ἐν ἀρχῇ and the πρὸς τὸν θεόν of Jn. 1:1 with the ἀπ' ἀρχῆς and the πρὸς τὸν πατέρα of 1 Jn. 1:1 f. The only difference is that the transition from the one to the other is presupposed in 1 Jn. 1:1 f., whereas in Jn. 1:1-18 it is the true theme of the passage. [219]

d. This, then, is the essential point at which the λόγος saying of the prologue goes beyond the previous λόγος statements of the NT. The essential point is not the equation of the Word with Jesus. This is increasingly revealed to be the kernel of all the NT λόγος sayings which use the word in a specific sense. The new thing (as in 1 Jn. 1:1 f.) is that the λόγος is the pre-existent Christ, and that (as

---

[218] Cf. what was said about Mt. → 120.

[219] An important conclusion regarding the relation of the prologue to the Gospel follows from these observations. On quite other grounds it is unlikely that the prologue, or an early draft of it, was in existence prior to the Gospel itself, e.g., in Aram. form (→ 133). But this does not imply a complete distinction between the two. The facts stated above force us to assume that the Gospel did not receive its form wihout some ref. to the prologue, or at least to the use of the term "word" which is found in the prologue.

distinct from 1 Jn. 1:1) the transition from pre-existence to history is the true theme.

This question dominates the prologue, but is not confined to it. By the very nature of the case it comes out with particularly strong and thematic emphasis at the beginning of the Gospel. But it is also present throughout the Gospel, as may be seen from sayings like 1:30; 6:62; 8:38, 58; 17:5, and also from those which refer to being sent or to coming from heaven: 3:13, 31; 6:33 ff., 46, 50 ff.; 8:23, 42; 16:28, 30 etc. If the name Logos is not again used, for the reasons mentioned, awareness of the pre-temporal existence of the Son is one of the most essential bases of the Fourth Gospel.

The theme itself does not receive its first treatment from this Evangelist. Christological pre-existence sayings are a constituent part of the whole of Paulinism: R. 1:4; 8:3; 1 C. 10:3 f.; 2 C. 8:9; Phil. 2:6 ff.; Gl. 4:4. So, too, are statements concerning Christ's part in creation: 1 C. 8:6; Col. 1:16. Such statements are not informed by speculative concern to disclose a Gnostic secret. They simply try to describe a fact which underlies the manifest reality of Ἰησοῦς Χριστός. If there is reference to this underlying fact, it is not for its own sake, but to illumine that which within it is of immediate concern to believers, e.g., the ethical demand of Phil. 2:1 ff. or the soteriological statement of Col. 1:12 ff. It is thus plain that for Paul awareness of the pre-existence of Jesus Christ is a much deeper thing than the statements alone might suggest.

The same is true, however, of other passages in the NT, and especially of the Word of Jesus Himself. This is not just a question of whether, or how often, Jesus spoke of His pre-existence either by open reference or by hint.[220] It is a question of whether awareness of His sonship, and adoption of the title Son of Man, are possible without the explicit or implicit basis of an awareness of His pre-temporal being with the Father.[221]

In no sense can the statements of the prologue to Jn. be isolated. They stand in the context both of the Fourth Gospel and of all NT Christology. The distinctive thing about them is not their mere existence but 1. the fact that they stand thematically at the head of a Gospel, a description of the earthly life of Jesus, and 2. that they are grouped under the catchword ὁ λόγος.

14. The Concern and Derivation of the λόγος Sayings in the Prologue to John, I.

a. The Lack of Speculative Concern. When enquiry is made into the concern of the statement in the Johannine Prologue, the first point to be made is the negative one that this pre-existence statement is in no sense speculative.

It might seem to be speculative. It might have a speculative ring. Yet it is not speculative for the Evangelist (as distinct from many of his expositors), since his emphasis is on the fact that the statement does not derive from reflection or from a mythical or theological idea of pre-existence, but from the θεᾶσθαι of the

---

220 Cf. esp. on Lk. 10:18: Orig. Princ., I, 5, 5; Orat., 26, 5; Cels., IV, 92. Cf. also J. C. K. v. Hofmann, *Die Hl. Schrift NT's*[5], VIII, 1 (1878), 269 f. The very general modern rejection of reference to a pre-historical event (cf. esp. Zn. Lk., *ad loc.*) demands serious investigation.

221 Cf. G. Kittel, *Jesus Christus, Gottes Sohn u. unser Herr* (1937), 19.

historical figure of Jesus (1:14; cf. 1:51; 2:11 etc.). This, and nothing else, absolutely nothing, has provided him with the witness and message of eternal sonship, of the πρὸς τὸν πατέρα εἶναι of the λόγος. The development of the theological statement in Jn. 1:1 ff. is not to be explained, then, in terms of a rise of faith in Jesus out of awareness of the fact of pre-existence. On the contrary, this apparently speculative statement arises out of, and gains its only light from, the historical process of seeing and hearing Jesus in faith.

For the same reason, it is wrong to speak of a personification of the Logos in Jn. 1:1, 14. This idea arises exclusively under the influence of non-biblical rather than biblical thought. It is possible only where there is something to be personified, i.e., something which may be abstracted from the person and envisaged as an idea outside it. NT thinking, including Johannine, has no primary interest, however, in a world of reason or a semi-divine intermediate being, the Logos, which it is essential to describe, and which, among other things, entered one day into the person of an earthly man. It has no interest in Messianic or toralogical ideas which may be transferred to a specific person. It has no interest in ideas, not even in theological ideas. Its sole concern is with what has taken place in the person of Jesus. This event is set in its eternal framework. It is investigated in terms of its primal and fundamental basis, the light of which is displayed in it. But this basis, without the enacted and experienced event, is never the subject of investigation. This is the point where speculation on the process of personification and incarnation begins. The Evangelist's acquaintance with the ὁ λόγος σάρξ ἐγένετο is not the result of reflection on the λόγος and its personification. Nor does it rest on theological invention. It derives from the fulfilment of ἐθεασάμεθα in this σάρξ, i.e., the historical figure of Jesus. It derives from beholding τὴν δόξαν, from the shining forth of a background of eternal being.

b. The Allusion to Genesis 1:1.

The concern of the prologue is to pursue the origin of this outshining. In this it is helped by the λόγος statement which is developed and present in all primitive Christianity. This refers to the Word of God which is spoken in the event of Jesus of Nazareth. This insight is linked with the question of the being of Jesus Christ rooted before and beyond time, so that allusion is naturally made to the fact that the first statement of the Bible about God is that about His creative activity, and that this activity is depicted as one which is fulfilled only through His Word — "God spake." The result is that the combining of the primitive Christian λόγος statement with the christological pre-existence statement leads necessarily to an assertion of the identity of the historical figure of Jesus with the Word of the divine Creator.

The prologue makes this combination in a way which is obviously intentional. This may be seen from the words ἐν ἀρχῇ. The way in which these are put at the head of the whole Gospel can surely be construed only as a conscious adoption [222] of the very first words of the first book of the Bible, Gn. 1:1: בְּרֵאשִׁית, LXX ἐν ἀρχῇ.

Once this combination is made, the statements of the first verse of the prologue are not complete, but an essential part has been added. It may in fact be said of

222 → I, 482, n. 21. It does not matter whether ἐν ἀρχῇ is a Semitism or not; hence there is no point in pursuing the question.

this Word of creation: πάντα δι' αὐτοῦ ἐγένετο, v. 3. It is ζωή (v. 4), which is simply another way of saying that there could be no creaturely life without the "God spake" of Gn. 1.

In meaning, the statements of Jn. 1:1 simply express the fact that this Word always goes forth as the divine Word, that it cannot be detached from God, that it is always the Word of God. But the formulation of this, both in the phrase καὶ ὁ λόγος ἦν πρὸς τὸν θεόν and also in the phrase καὶ θεὸς ἦν ὁ λόγος, undoubtedly goes further in the direction of apparent personification. The λόγος resembles a magnitude which confronts God, even though it cannot be detached from Him and yet cannot be represented as a mere function of God. The Word is personal, and this aspect finds no basis in the OT creation story. Its basis is the fact that the thinking of the NT author does not start with speculation, not even with speculation on the process of creation, but with a person, namely, the person of Jesus Christ, in whom the σὰρξ ἐγένετο of the Word took place. The pre-existence of the λόγος is in fact the pre-existence of Christ.

c. Other Connections. Perhaps what has been said would suffice if we did not know that in the time and environment of the prologue there were other personified entities accompanied by statements very similar to those of the prologue. This makes it possible to seek other connections.

There can be no question of Jewish Messianic dogma contributing to the prologue. In the Messianology of Judaism there are no pre-existence statements whatever in the sense of Jn. 1:1.[223] Similarly, all attempts to explain the λόγος statements of Jn. 1 in terms of the Targumic מֵימְרָא have failed, since this is never a personal hypostasis, but only a substitute for the tetragrammaton.[224]

On the other hand, at least four concepts may be cited which bear analogy to the λόγος statements of the prologue: the Hellenistic Gnostic λόγος; the oriental Gnostic man; the Hellenistic Jewish σοφία/חָכְמָה; the Palestinian Jewish Torah.

There is no need to adduce detailed examples, since this would merely involve repetition of what has been well said by others. It must be enough to say that attempts have been made to work out a close parallelism for all four:[225] in the case of the λόγος in Philo[226] and the mystics by W. Bauer[227] and many others; in the case of Gnosticism esp. by R. Bultmann;[228] in the case of the primal man Enos by R. Reitzenstein[229] and

[223] Cf. the exhaustive investigation of Billerbeck (Str.-B., II, 333-352), who has definitively shattered all views to the contrary.

[224] Cf. once again Billerbeck, *loc. cit.*; though cf. also Dalman WJ, I, 187 f.; Moore, 41 ff.; Burkitt, 158 f.; Hamp. There is no way of judging how far the *memra* arose under the influence of Alexandrian thought (Bau. J.³, 7), though it may well be that Philo knew it (so Hamp).

[225] In criticism cf. esp. Büchsel, *Joh. u. der Hell. Synkretismus,* 21 ff.

[226] For older writers cf. esp. Holtzmann, II, 437 ff.

[227] Bau. J.³, 8 ff., with bibl.

[228] R. Bultmann, ZNW, 24 (1925), 100 ff., and esp. the comm. *Das Johannesevangelium* (1937/8), 6-15.

[229] Reitzenstein, *Zwei religionsgeschichtliche Fragen* (1901); *Das mandäische Buch* ... (1919); Hell. Myst.; also Reitzenstein's disciple G. P. Wetter.

H. H. Schaeder;[230] in the case of wisdom by R. Harris[231] and R. Bultmann;[232] in that of the Torah by A. Schlatter,[233] P. Billerbeck,[234] and K. Bornhäuser.[235]

The Enos and *chokma* parallels have no direct significance, since there is no material connection with these concepts at least in the existing form of the prologue. One would have to assume that where we now read λόγος one of these other entities originally stood, so that we really have at root a hymn to wisdom[236] or primal man.[237] But this path is methodologically permissible only if all others are barred. It is also forced to presuppose that a first form or original of the prologue precedes in time the Fourth Gospel. The problem where and how a prologue on the λόγος then came to be attached to the Gospel still arises quite apart from these attempted solutions.

On the other hand, there can be little doubt that wisdom did indirectly, i.e., by way of the Torah, have some influence on the prologue (→ 136).

This does not mean that the Gk. term λόγος has always necessarily been the predominant one in the prologue. The question whether the Fourth Gospel is not a translation from Aram. has been impressively raised in many circles in our day.[238] In relation to the Gospel as a whole the details tend to suggest "virtual translation" rather than "real translation."[239] In the prologue itself things may be different. The two most important "mistranslations" which are alleged in discussion of an original Aram. draft are both in the prologue (1:4;[240] 1:18[241]). They both solve otherwise insoluble linguistic and material problems by means of conjectures to which there can be no linguistic objection. Hence the hypothesis of an Aram. original of the prologue has to be taken seriously. The only pt. is that we have absolutely no grounds on which to assume either 1. that this original prologue was not Johannine in the sense of being composed by the author of the rest of the Gospel,[242] or 2. that it had a different — pre-Christian — theme from that of the present prologue, which refers unequivocally to Jesus, or, finally,

---

230 Schaeder, "Der 'Mensch' ..." (1926).

231 Cf. → Bibl., where other works are listed.

232 Bultmann in *Gunkel-Festschr.*, II, 1 ff.

233 Schl. J., 1 ff.; also *Sprache u. Heimat,* 14 ff.

234 Str.-B., II, 353-362.

235 Bornhäuser, 5 ff.

236 Bultmann thinks there was an original in which Hellenistic Jewish circles had already substituted λόγος for σοφία.

237 So Schaeder, 325-341.

238 Cf. Burney, *The Aram. Origin*; C. C. Torrey, "The Aram. Origin of the Gospel of Jn.," HThR, 16 (1923), 305 ff.; M. Goguel, *Revue d'Hist. et Philosophie religieuse,* 3 (1923), 373-382; Kittel Probleme, 45 ff.; M. Burrows, "The Original Language of the Gospel of Jn.," JBL, 49 (1930), 95 ff.; E. C. Colwell, *The Gk. of the Fourth Gospel* (1931).

239 Cf. Burney's distinction and careful analysis, *op. cit.,* 7 and 126 f.

240 The brilliant conjecture of Burney, which solves the ancient problem of the concluding words of v. 3, is that ὃ γέγονεν ἐν αὐτῷ ζωὴ ἦν = דַּהֲוָא בֵיהּ חַיִּין = "for in it was life," cf. *op. cit.,* 29, and Schaeder, *op. cit.,* 312.

241 For the equally elegant solution of the hitherto unexplained μονογενὴς θεός (יחיד אלהא: 1. יְחִיד אֱלָהָא = μονογενὴς θεοῦ, 2. יְחִיד אֱלָהָא = μονογενὴς θεός), cf. Burney, *op. cit.,* 39 f.

242 This is based on two considerations which we cannot pursue here, first, that behind the Fourth Gospel there stands in some way the authoritative authorship of the Lord's disciple, who spoke Aram. but lived on Hellenistic soil, and secondly that from 21:1 ff. (esp. 24 f.) we may deduce some kind of editorship of that which was transmitted under the name of the disciple.

3. that it did not express this ref. to Jesus in the term "word," not in Gk., of course, but in the Aram. equivalent.

d. Relations to "Word" Speculations in the Contemporary World. It is quite conceivable that "word" speculations in the surrounding world were not without influence on the prologue. The situation is that four different streams come together: first, the early Christian view of Jesus as the Word; secondly, early Christian awareness of the divine pre-temporality of Christ; thirdly, recollection of the biblical account of the Word of creation which was uttered in the beginning; and fourthly, the λόγος myths and theories of the time. This situation causes the author of the Fourth Gospel to adopt the slogan of the fourth group and to make it the catchword of his statements. It is a slogan which comes to him from the vocabulary of the Bible and primitive Christianity. But it now finds a new place and emphasis. One might write as a variation on 1 C. 8:5: ὥσπερ εἰσὶν θεοὶ πολλοὶ καὶ κύριοι πολλοὶ — καὶ λόγοι πολλοί ... The author presents *his* λόγος. This is the one and only λόγος which was in the beginning, which is neither speculation on an indefinite intermediary nor the metaphysical personification of a mythical concept, but the person manifested in Jesus, and in Him the Word.

A point to be noted is that there is no polemical or apologetic thrust in this respect. None of the statements is formulated in debate with other λόγοι. All the questions of pre-existence speculation and metaphysics to which they might seem to give rise are completely ignored by the author. If we did not know of their existence from other sources, we could hardly deduce it from the prologue. These things do not interest the author. They are not the theme of his discussion. Their rejection is not the content of his statements. For those acquainted with Philo or other λόγος speculations, they are simply "a restrained opening to the Gospel." [243] Only the formal fact of the putting of the name λόγος on the plane of pre-temporal and personal being betrays any contact. For the rest, there is parallelism, but no connection. The content and concern of the prologue derive from a very different source.

Cf. the comparison of Hellenistic logos speculations and the NT Logos → 90.

15. The Interest and Derivation of the λόγος Sayings in the Prologue to John, II: Logos and Torah.

Things are very different in respect of Rabbinic questions concerning the Torah, for the contrast between λόγος and νόμος is expressly shown to be one of the essential themes of the prologue. This may be seen in the interrelation of v. 14 and v. 17. V. 17 lays down the antithesis: ὁ νόμος (i.e., the Torah) διὰ Μωϋσέως ἐδόθη, ἡ χάρις καὶ ἡ ἀλήθεια διὰ Ἰησοῦ Χριστοῦ ἐγένετο. This is plain enough in itself, since Ἰησοῦς Χριστός is the incarnate form of the λόγος. But the author is so concerned to clarify the reference of this antithesis to the λόγος that he uses the same phrase as that which he used to describe the λόγος in v. 14: πλήρης [244] χάριτος καὶ ἀληθείας. χάρις καὶ ἀλήθεια are the nature

[243] So Hirsch, *Das Vierte Evangelium,* 106; cf. his fine exposition, 101 ff.

[244] If πλήρης is indeclinable, it is to be referred, as Bau. J.^{3}, 26 rightly perceives, to αὐτοῦ rather than δόξαν. But in its case it may also refer quite correctly to λόγος, so Schl. J., 27. Either way, the nature of the λόγος is set forth by apposition.

of the λόγος (v. 14). They are thus the content of the revelation given in Jesus (v. 17b), which replaces the Mosaic νόμος, the Torah (v. 17a).

To the four elements which coalesce (→ 132), we may thus add a fifth. The fourth, the connection with λόγος myths of the age, was of no significance from the standpoint of content. The fifth is of much higher significance. For this reason, parallels from the Torah speculations of the Rabbis are of incomparably greater importance than parallels from Philonic and other logos speculations. These are no problem for the author. They do not even have to be refuted. But the relation between Christ and Law is a basic question throughout the Gospel.[245] The incarnation of the Word has taken place in order that the antithesis to the Jewish Torah may be manifested therein. Nor is the word λόγος accidental, for the Torah, too, is a Word. Throughout Ps. 119 דָּבָר, דְּבָרִים, דְּבָרְךָ (LXX λόγος, λόγοι, λόγος σου) are interchangeable with תּוֹרָה (LXX νόμος, νόμος σου): v. 9, 16, 17, 25, 28, 42, 43, 49, 65, 74, 89 etc. — v. 1, 18, 29, 34, 44, 51, 53, 55, 57, 61, 70, 72, 77, 85 etc. The terms are fully interchangeable (→ 100). In Rabbinic discussion דִּיבּוּר, "utterance," is a tt. for the giving of the Law and for the commandments.[246] But the statements concerning the pre-existence and majesty of the Torah are now intentionally heaped upon the λόγος. It was in the beginning. It was with God. It was God, or divine. All things were made by it. In it was life. It was the light of men. In the Rabbis these are all sayings about the Torah.[247] But they are now statements about Christ. In Him the eternal Word of God, the Word of creation, the Word of the Law, is not just passed on (ἐδόθη) but enacted (ἐγένετο). Christ is not just a teacher and transmitter of the Torah. He is Himself the Torah, the new Torah. Mosaism, which is provisional and intermediary, has passed. In Jesus Christ the Word of God has taken place in truth. What they behold (ἐθεασάμεθα) is the content of this true, final, and only Torah: χάρις καὶ ἀλήθεια.

ἐν ἀρχῇ, the pre-existence of the Torah. bPes., 54a, Bar.: "Seven things were created before the world was created, namely, the Torah, repentance, the Garden of Eden, Gehenna, the throne of glory, the sanctuary, the name of the Messiah." πρὸς τὸν θέον, the eternal being of the Torah with God. Midr. Ps. on 90:3 § 12 (Buber, 196a): "It lay on God's bosom, while God sat on the throne of glory." θεὸς ἦν ὁ λόγος, the divine nature of the Torah. Lv. r., 20, 10 on 16:1: "God spake ... My daughter, that is the Torah." πάντα δι' αὐτοῦ ἐγένετο, the Torah as the mediator and means of creation. Gn. r., 1, 1 on 1:1: "Through the first-born God created the heaven and the earth, and the first-born is none other than the Torah." ζωή, the Torah is life. S. Dt., 306 on 32:2: "... the words of the Torah are life for the world." φῶς, the Torah is light.[248] 4 Esr. 14:20 f.: "The world lies in darkness, its inhabitants are without light; for thy Law is burned." πλήρης ... ἀληθείας, the Torah is truth. Midr. Ps. on 25:10 § 11 (Buber, 107a): "Truth, the Torah is meant."

---

[245] For all the serious criticisms brought against him, it is the lasting merit of E. Hirsch's two works on Jn. to bring out as impressively as hardly anyone before him this theme of the Gospel. Perhaps he exaggerates, and makes Jn. too Pauline, but this in no way affects the service which he has rendered by reminding us of a truth which is often overlooked.

[246] Levy Wört., I, 374a.

[247] Cf. the comprehensive examples in Str.-B., II, 353-358; III, 129-131, and → νόμος. Bornhäuser, *op. cit.*, 6 has shown particularly impressively the significance of these connections by means of the term toralogy, which he coined. In the next paragraph we simply give a few examples from Str.-B. to illustrate our thesis.

[248] Cf. also Jn. 8:12, and on this Str.-B., II, 521 f.

Ref. to the Torah, and the transferring of the Torah statements to Jesus, is not limited to the prologue. It may often be seen in the body of the Gospel, cf. the water of 4:10 [249] and the bread of 6:35. [250]

The prologue to Jn. (1:1-18) is another witness — and a most emphatic witness — to the basic insight of primitive Christianity already mentioned (→ 125), namely, that in the person and event of Jesus Christ traditional religious values are present in a new and personal way. One might take up the saying in Mt. 12:6: "Lo, here is greater than the temple," and say: "Lo, here is greater than the Torah." Or, as a parallel to the ἡ καινὴ διαθήκη of the Lord's Supper, one might speak of ὁ καινὸς νόμος, always with ref. to the Word of God which has gone forth and become an event, flesh, history, in His person.

The σοφία and חָכְמָה speculations of Jewish wisdom literature are of no direct significance in relation to the λόγος of the prologue to Jn. (→ 133). Nevertheless, it is no accident that they offer a striking parallel to the λόγος sayings. [251] The Rabbis increasingly, and from an early period, identified wisdom with the Torah. OT and later statements concerning *chokma* were transferred directly to the Torah. Cf. already Sir. 24:1-22 with 24:23 ff.; Bar. 3:15 ff. with 4:1. [252] Prv. 8:22: "Yahweh has created me (wisdom) as the beginning of his way, as the earliest of his works, from of old," is used as a proof text for the pre-existence of the Torah, bPes., 54a, Bar.; cf. Prv. 8:30: Ex. r., 30, 9 on 22:1.

† λόγιος.

This word is found from the time of Pind. (Pyth., 1, 183) in the twofold sense of a. "eloquent," "skilled in speech," Plut. Pomp., 51 (I, 646e), opp. ἄφωνος; of Hermes, Luc. De Gallo, 2 (λογιώτατος θεῶν ἁπάντων), Apologia, 2 (ὁ λόγιος); and b. "skilled in knowledge," "educated," "cultured" (for the Gks. to have the λόγος was equivalent to the development of learning), Pind. Nem., 6, 51 (opp. ἀοιδός); Hdt., I, 1 etc. (with a good knowledge of history); Heliodor. Aeth., 4, 7: λόγιος ἰατρός (a well-trained physician).

Sense b. is more common in Philo and Joseph. Only in one passage in Philo can we be sure of a.: Cher., 116: μικρὰ νόσου πρόφασις οὐ τὴν γλῶτταν ἐπήρωσεν, οὐ τὸ στόμα καὶ τῶν πάνυ λογίων ἀπέρραψεν (close the mouth even of the very eloquent). On the other hand, in at least eight passages sense b. is sure or probable, Vit. Mos., I, 2: τῶν παρ' Ἕλλησι (Leg. Gaj., 237: τῶν κατὰ τὴν Ἑλλάδα) λογίων, *ibid.*, I, 23: Αἰγυπτίων οἱ λόγιοι παρεδίδοσαν, etc., and with φρόνιμος, σώφρων, δίκαιος, δόκιμος, Leg. Gaj., 142; Virt., 174; Poster. C., 162. Sense a. does not seem to occur in Joseph., but sense b. is common: Bell., 1, 13: ἐπιτιμήσαιμ' ἂν αὐτὸς δικαίως τοῖς Ἑλλήνων λογίοις, 6, 295: ἰδιῶται — λόγιοι (par., 291: ἄπειροι — ἱερογραμματεῖς), Ant., 1, 175 and 2, 75: Αἰγυπτίων οἱ λογιώτατοι (the most wise or cultured), 17, 149: Ἰουδαίων λογιώτατοι καὶ παρ' οὕστινας ἐξηγηταὶ τῶν πατρίων νόμων, Ap., 1, 235: τῶν λογίων ἱερέων ("learned" priests). Cf. Eus. De Martyribus Palaestinae, 11, 1 (GCS, Schwartz, 933, 5): λόγιοί τε καὶ ἰδιῶται, cf. Eus. Hist. Eccl., VI, 15.

---

249 Cf. Str.-B., II, 433, 435 f. For water as a symbol of the Torah cf. the mural at Dura with its depiction of the water miracle of Ex. 15:27; → II, 386 f.

250 Cf. Str.-B., II, 483.

251 Cf. Bultmann, *loc. cit.* (→ n. 232).

252 Str.-B., II, 353, where there are further examples.

λόγιος. Liddell-Scott, Pass., Moult.-Mill., Pr.-Bauer³, *s.v.*; Wettstein, II, 578; Schl. Lk., 616; Zn. Ag., 471, n. 80, 669, n. 82; E. Orth, *Logios* (1926).

In the NT the word is used only once at Ac. 18:24 of Apollos, who is called an ἀνὴρ λόγιος. It is not possible to decide with certainty between the two senses. Some of the older translations have *eloquens* etc. (lat, cf. syr, arm), but the accompanying clause:[1] δυνατὸς ὢν ἐν ταῖς γραφαῖς, corresponds so closely to the use attested in Joseph. that the sense of "learned" is at least very probable. If most expositors prefer "eloquent" this is due to v. 25 (ζέων τῷ πνεύματι ἐλάλει) and the picture of Apollos derived from 1 C. 1:12; 3:5 f.

† λόγιον.[1]

A. The Pre-Christian Use of λόγιον.

1. "Saying," "pronouncement," esp. "saying which may be traced back to the deity," then almost the equivalent[2] of χρησμός, "oracular saying." Hdt., VIII, 60, 3: ἐν τῇ ἡμῖν καὶ λόγιον ἐστι τῶν ἐχθρῶν καθύπερθε γενέσθαι, Eur. Heracl., 406: βέβηλα καὶ κεκρυμμένα λόγια παλαιά, Aristoph. Vesp., 800: ὅρα τὸ χρῆμα, τὰ λόγι' ὡς περαίνεται, Eustath. Thessal. Comm. in Il., 2, 233: τὰ λόγια, ἤγουν οἱ χρησμοί, Philo Spec. Leg., I, 315; Leg. Gaj., 110: τὰ Γαΐου λόγια (but in conscious analogy [ἄξιον τούτοις ἀντιθεῖναι] to the above-mentioned χρησμοί of Apollo), Gig., 49: λόγιόν ἐστι τοῦτο χρησθὲν τῷ προφήτῃ, Jos. Bell., 6, 311-313: alternation between ἐν τοῖς λογίοις and ἐν τοῖς ἱεροῖς γράμμασιν (Daniel), and between χρησμός and λόγιον (Daniel), Test. B., 9, 1 (c): ἀπὸ λογίων 'Ενὼχ τοῦ δικαίου (prophetic word).

2. In the LXX λόγιον is used for the Word of God, e.g., when Balaam receives the oracular saying (Nu. 24:4, 16), or in relation to individual sayings (Is. 28:13), e.g., the commandments (Dt. 33:9), but usually as a general statement about the word or words of God. Is. 5:24: τὸ λόγιον τοῦ ἁγίου 'Ισραὴλ παρώξυναν, ψ 18:14: ἔσονται εἰς εὐδοκίαν τὰ λόγια τοῦ στόματός μου, 106:11: παρεπίκραναν τὰ λόγια τοῦ θεοῦ. Thus λόγιον τοῦ θεοῦ is more or less equivalent to λόγος τοῦ θεοῦ, though λόγιον is mostly used for the Heb. אֵמֶר, אִמְרָה, λόγος for דָּבָר. Yet this is not a fixed rule. Cf. ψ 147:4 (15): ὁ ἀποστέλλων τὸ λόγιον (אִמְרָתוֹ) αὐτοῦ τῇ γῇ, ἕως τάχους δραμεῖται ὁ λόγος (דְּבָרוֹ) αὐτοῦ, but also 118:154/169: διὰ τὸν λόγον σου (לְאִמְרָתְךָ) ζῆσόν με ... κατὰ τὸ λόγιόν σου (כִּדְבָרְךָ) συνέτισόν με. ψ 118 is most instructive, for it very often equates the two terms. λόγος occurs 24 times, λόγιον 22 times (textual uncertainty as between them 4 times), and there is no palpable difference in sense. While τὰ λόγια predominates elsewhere, the sing. τὸ λόγιον θεοῦ (or σου) is found in this psalm, though not exclusively.

---

[1] There is nothing to suggest that "learnedness in the Scriptures is specifically emphasised along with λογιότης," H. A. W. Meyer, Ag.[4] (1870), 412.

λόγιον. F. D. Schleiermacher, "Über das Zeugnis des Papias von unseren beiden ersten Evangelien," ThStKr (1832), 735-768; Zahn Kan., I, 857 ff., II, 790 ff.; P. Feine-J. Behm, *Einl. ins NT*[8] (1936), 46; R. Harris, *Testimonies*, I (1916), II (1920); B. W. Bacon, *Studies in Matthew* (1930), 443-451.

[1] Purely formally there are three possible derivations: 1. λόγιον neut. of the adj. λόγιος; 2. with -ιον from λόγος, not diminutive; 3. the same, diminutive (so Bengel, *ad loc.*). 3. is more recent than 2., and in terms of the sense is not very likely. 1. would have to imply derivation from λόγιος "(good) story-teller" (Liddell-Scott, "versed in tales or stories"), Pind., Hdt., but this hardly gives us "oracle." -ιον in 2. seems to imply a more individual ref., cf. οἶκος, "dwelling" — οἰκία (Hom.) "individual rooms," also μηρία, "thigh bones," cf. P. Chantraine, *La formation des noms en Grec ancien* (1933), 59. λόγιον seems to fit in here best: λόγος "(longer) narrative" — λόγιον "(shorter) individual utterance." It is hardly possible to be more definite [Debrunner].

[2] Thuc., II, 8, 2: πολλὰ μὲν λόγια ἐλέγετο, πολλὰ δὲ χρησομολόγοι ᾖδον; Schol.: λόγιον is an oracular saying in prose, χρησμός in verse. But it may be doubted whether this distinction has any material significance. Cf. Wettstein, II, 36.

The sense of oracular saying disappears from the developed usage of the LXX. The term has become a vehicle for the biblical conception of revelation by Word.

B. λόγιον in the New Testament.

1. At Ac. 7:38: ἐδέξατο (Moses) λόγια ζῶντα, plainly refers to the OT revelation at Sinai, especially the Torah (or the Decalogue), which was received by Moses. It does not mean that Moses himself uttered the λόγια, but that he received them to pass on. With this emphasis [3] the phrase λόγια ζῶντα might well be characteristic of the pre-Pauline Stephen.

Cf. jPea, 15b: [4] "It is not a vain word — for you" (Dt. 32:47): if it is vain, it is for you, since you are not concerned about it. "But it is your life" (Dt. 32:47). When is it your life? When you are concerned about it.

2. R. 3:2 deals with the λόγια τοῦ θεοῦ imparted to the Jews. [5] It is obvious that the reference is to the OT promises, though there is no apparent reason [6] why it should be restricted to these. Literally, τὰ λόγια τοῦ θεοῦ is simply a reference to God's speaking, which for Paul takes place just as much in OT as NT salvation history. Paul can say that the "yes" of God has taken place in Jesus. This occurrence is for him no less λόγια τοῦ θεοῦ than what takes place in the OT. But the salvation history of both OT and NT did not take place just anywhere. It was entrusted to Israel (ἐπιστεύθησαν). R. 15:8: [7] λέγω γὰρ Χριστὸν διάκονον γεγενῆσθαι περιτομῆς ... εἰς τὸ βεβαιῶσαι τὰς ἐπαγγελίας τῶν πατέρων.

3. Hb. 5:12 reproves believers who might be teachers but who, because of their dullness, again need a teacher to teach them the στοιχεῖα τῆς ἀρχῆς τῶν λογίων τοῦ θεοῦ, "the rudiments of the words of God." It is obvious that this must include more than the OT revelation. For the context makes it plain that there would be no sense in making out that this needs to be taught afresh. Possibly it is included, and the expression, as in R. 3:2, unites the divine revelation in OT and NT. [8] But the chief, if not the only, emphasis is, in the context of Hb., undoubtedly laid on the Christ revelation which God ἐλάλησεν ἡμῖν ἐν υἱῷ (1:2). It is these λόγια τοῦ θεοῦ which must be taught to them afresh. [9]

4. 1 Pt. 4:10 f.: the καλὸς οἰκονόμος ... χάριτος θεοῦ, when he speaks, declares ὡς λόγια θεοῦ in exactly the same sense as later he exercises his διακονεῖν in the power of God, and also in the sense of v. 14: ὅτι τὸ τῆς δόξης καὶ τὸ τοῦ θεοῦ πνεῦμα ἐφ' ὑμᾶς ἀναπαύεται. Thus, as the seer who proclaimed the oracle was the agent and mouthpiece of a λόγιον according to the ancient sense, the

---

[3] It is worth noting that the reading λόγια θεοῦ ζῶντος is early (Iren. Haer., IV, 15, 1: *praecepta Dei vivi*). Cf. Pr. Ag., 42; W. Sanday-C. H. Turner, *NT Sancti Irenaei* (1923), 101.

[4] Str.-B., II, 681.

[5] Cf. on what follows J. C. K. v. Hofmann, *Die Hl. Schrift NT's*, III (1868), *ad loc.*: Zn. R.³, *ad loc.*

[6] Zn. R.³, 149 rightly calls this "pure arbitrariness."

[7] Cf. Zn. R.³, 149.

[8] O. Michel, *Der Hebräerbrief* (1936), 64, n. 5.

[9] So Rgg. Hb. ²,³, 142.

utterance of him who bears the Spirit is a Spirit-inspired utterance which bears in itself the nature of the λόγια θεοῦ. In this passage, in close relation to the terminology of 1 Pt., the NT usage comes nearest to the non-biblical usage. But the intentional ὡς makes it clear that in primitive Christian consciousness the term was reserved exclusively for the divine Subject. There is hesitation to say that the believer utters λόγια θεοῦ. He declares ὡς λόγια θεοῦ.

In sum, there are two lines of NT usage. The first is a continuation of the ancient use for an individual divine saying, Ac. 7:38: the oracles delivered to Moses at Sinai; 1 Pt. 4:11: the words and statements spoken by the charismatic. The second refers, not to a saying, but to the divine action fulfilled as the salvation history of the old and new covenant, to the oracle of God, or to what God says to the world. R. 3:2: Individual oracles, biblical sayings and promises are undoubtedly given to the Jew, but there is also given to him the whole event of salvation history in which God spoke πολυμερῶς καὶ πολυτρόπως (Hb. 1:1) up to what took place in Jesus Christ. Cf. esp. Hb. 5:12: The admonition certainly does not mean that they are to learn or memorise afresh individual sayings or texts or sayings of Jesus, but that they are again to immerse themselves, and to be instructed, in the event of revelation which has taken place in Jesus, the λόγια τοῦ θεοῦ which have taken place in Him, and which do, of course, include His words and sayings. Recognition of the two lines of usage is of great importance later.

C. λόγιον in the Usage of the Early Church.

1. The sense of "individual saying" still continues.

It may be used of an OT verse, 2 Cl., 13, 3 f.;[10] Just. Apol., 32, 14; Eus. Hist. Eccl., IX, 9,7; X, 1, 4. 7. 28, but also in relation to NT and esp. dominical sayings, Just. Dial., 18, 1: ἐκείνου (τοῦ σωτῆρος) ... λόγια (Mt. 23), Eus. Hist. Eccl., IX, 7, 15: τὸ θεῖον ἐκεῖνο λόγιον (Mt. 24:24). There is an obvious ref. to dominical sayings in Iren. Haer., I, 8, 1. Here the κυριακὰ λόγια are par. to the παραβολαὶ κυριακαί, and in the account these are grouped with the ῥήσεις προφητικαί and the λόγοι ἀποστολικοί, and are clearly distinguished from τὰ ἐκτὸς τοῦ Πληρώματος mentioned in I, 8, 2. It is interesting that τὰ λόγια τοῦ θεοῦ are here the general concept which embraces the three subordinate groups of prophetic, apostolic and dominical sayings.

2. But λόγιον and λόγια can also be used, not merely for a number of such sayings, but also for the sum of them, and for the divine revelation of the old and new covenant comprehended in them.

Even in 1 Cl., 13, 4: τρέμοντά μου τὰ λόγια,[11] it may be asked whether the ref. is to individual threats or to the total word embraced by them. Similarly in 19, 1 the humble men of the old covenant were καταδεξάμενοι τὰ λόγια αὐτοῦ ἐν φόβῳ καὶ ἀληθείᾳ. 62, 3 is particularly plain: the missive is to those who have immersed themselves εἰς τὰ λόγια τῆς παιδείας τοῦ θεοῦ, and even more so 53:1: You know τὰς ἱερὰς γραφάς, and have immersed yourselves εἰς τὰ λόγια τοῦ θεοῦ. Here the accompanying "holy scriptures" shows that the ref. is not just to individual texts. This

---

[10] λόγια τοῦ θεοῦ obviously refers to the preceding OT sayings (v. 2) rather than the succeeding NT sayings (v. 2), though cf. Pr.-Bauer[3], *s.v.*

[11] Quoting Is. 66:2; LXX: λόγους.

is confirmed in Cl. Al. Strom., I, 31, 124, 2: The restoration of the OT Scriptures by Ezra: ὁ τῶν θεοπνεύστων ἀναγνωρισμὸς καὶ ἀνακαινισμὸς λογίων. Cf. also Cl. Al. Prot., 10, 107, 1: A beautiful song of praise to God is the immortal man who is built up in righteousness and in whom τὰ λόγια τῆς ἀληθείας ἐγκεχάρακται (are engraved). Eus. Hist. Eccl., V, 17, 5: ἡ περὶ τὰ θεῖα λόγια σπουδή ("the Word of God" = "theology," cf. De Martyribus Palaestinae, 11, 2); Hist. Eccl., VI, 23, 2: Work on the θεῖα λόγια ("Holy Scripture"), of the comm. of Origen.[12] Particularly clear is Hist. Eccl., X, 4, 43: (the cedars of Lebanon,) ὧν οὐδὲ τὸ θεῖον λόγιον τὴν μνήμην ἀπεσιώπησεν ... φάσκον (ψ 103:16 is then quoted). Here τὸ θεῖον λόγιον is not the individual text; it declares and contains the individual text; the individual text is a constituent part of the divine Word. Instructive, too, is the usage in Ps.-Ign.[13] Magn., 9 (Gebhardt-Harnack-Zahn, II [1876], p. 202, 13): Quotations from 2 Th. 3:10 and Gn. 3:19 are linked and rounded off[14] with φασὶ τὰ λόγια. Smyrn., 3 (*ibid.*, p. 244, 28 f.): φασὶ γὰρ τὰ λόγια (there follows the saying of the angel in Ac. 1:11b). τὰ λόγια is not the collection of sayings but the Word of Scripture, i.e., the Word spoken by God in the Scriptures of the OT and the NT.

3. These observations show that the widespread usage found in LXX ψ 118 and Hb. 5:12 continued to exert an influence in the early Church. They are a warning that we should examine carefully some of the relevant λόγια τοῦ Κυρίου passages.

Pol., 7, 1: ὃς ἂν μεθοδεύῃ τὰ λόγια τοῦ Κυρίου πρὸς τὰς ἰδίας ἐπιθυμίας καὶ λέγῃ, μήτε ἀνάστασιν μήτε κρίσιν εἶναι, Iren. Haer., I, praef. 1: ῥᾳδιουργοῦντες τὰ λόγια Κυρίου, ἐξηγηταὶ κακοὶ τῶν καλῶς εἰρημένων γινόμενοι, cf. Ps.-Just., ep. ad Zenam et Serenum, 2 (ed. J. C. T. v. Otto, III, 1³ [1880], p. 70). Here already we have to ask whether the emphasis is on the falsification and misrepresentation of individual sayings of the Lord or on the falsification of His whole Gospel. Thus the conflict of Iren. in the praef. is not just against the ἐφαρμόζοντες τὰ ἐντός but also τὰ ἐκτὸς τοῦ Πληρώματος, cf. I, 8, 1/2 (→ 139). As may be seen, either the narrower or the broader meaning of λόγια Κυρίου or κυριακά is suitable in his case. Similarly, the broader meaning is at least implied also in Cl. Al., Quis Div. Salv., 3, 1: He who would help the rich man must show him by the necessary exposition (μετὰ τῆς δεούσης ἐξηγήσεως) τῶν λογίων that there is still hope. This is exposition not merely of individual sayings but also of the whole message revealed in them. Cl. Al. Paed., II, X, 113, 3: In exposition of the long and colourful garment of Jesus he refers to the blossoms of wisdom, the manifold and never-withering γραφάς, τὰ λόγια τοῦ Κυρίου which are illumined by the beams of truth. Here, too, emphatic restriction to sayings of the Lord can hardly be intended.

4. The use of the term in Papias is of particular interest (Eus. Hist. Eccl., III, 39, 15 f.). It fits in with our findings thus far. The title of Papias' work: λογίων κυριακῶν ἐξηγήσεις (III, 39, 1), is obviously not meant to limit the work to a collection of sayings, for in the light of our investigation it includes many other things.[15] Of the composition of Mk. Papias says that Mk., οὐ μέντοι τάξει, wrote down accurately what had been said and done by the Lord (τὰ

---

[12] II, 13, 7: κατά τι παρ' αὐτοῖς λόγιον ἔγγραφον, "a writing preserved by them."
[13] The question of authorship need not be discussed here; the letters belong to the 4th or 5th cent.
[14] It is possible that the concluding formula refers only to the second quotation from Gn. 3:19; cf. Zahn Kan., II, 792, n. 4.
[15] Cf. Zahn Kan., I, 860 f.

ὑπὸ τοῦ Κυρίου ἢ λεχθέντα ἢ πραχθέντα). The additional sentence: ἀλλ᾽ οὐχ ὥσπερ σύνταξιν τῶν κυριακῶν ποιούμενος λογίων, obviously does not mean that he has omitted individual sayings — he has written down λεχθέντα, and that he did so οὐ τάξει has been stated already in the first clause — but that he has not aimed to give a full collection of the tradition as a whole. The fuller phrase "what the Lord said or did" and the shorter expression τὰ κυριακὰ λόγια clearly mean one and the same thing.[16]

This shows us what is meant by Papias' reference to the composition of Mt.: τὰ λόγια συνετάξατο. Though there is no express τοῦ Κυρίου or κυριακά, it is self-evident from the context that the λόγια of the Κύριος are meant. That theoretically this might mean "sayings," i.e., a collection of dominical sayings after the manner of the "sayings of the fathers" or the collections in the Wisdom literature, is quite incontestable. But it is just as clear and indisputable that in the light of the usage of the LXX, NT and early Church the more comprehensive meaning is also possible. In terms of this τὰ ὑπὸ τοῦ Κυρίου ἢ λεχθέντα ἢ πραχθέντα, as in Hb. 5:12, are simply called τὰ λόγια.[17] Whatever merit there may be in modern theories which postulate a λόγια source (Q), i.e., a collection of dominical sayings, these theories cannot appeal to what the Papias fragment tells us about Mt.

† ἄλογος.

ἄ-λογος, i.e., without λόγος. a. Without λέγειν in the strict sense, "without speech," "speechless," "dumb," Soph. Oed. Col., 131; Plat. Leg., III, 696d. Phil. Rer. Div. Her., 16: ἰσχνόφωνος (endowed with a weak voice) καὶ βραδύγλωσσος καὶ ἄλογος, Jos. Bell., 4, 170: ἐξ ἀγέλης ζῴων ἀλόγων ἑλκομένου ... οὐδὲ φωνήν τις ἀφῆκεν ..., LXX Ex. 6:12: ἐγὼ δὲ (Moses) ἄλογός εἰμι (Mas. עֲרַל שְׂפָתַיִם) b. Without λόγος, i.e., "without reason, basis, meaning, calculation": Thuc., VI, 46; BGU, 74, 8: καὶ γὰρ ἂν ἄλογον εἴη.[1] Corp. Herm., I, 11; X, 19b, Philo: very common[2] (like λόγος), Jos. Ant.,[3] 10, 262; 17, 61 and 307; 19, 201; Bell., 1, 335; 4, 211; Ap., 1, 15. 224. 271 (ἀλόγως, Ant., 15, 17; Bell., 6, 176; Ap., 1, 92. 109), LXX: Nu. 6:12; Job 11:12 (vl.); Wis. 11:15 (par. ἀσύνετος); 3 Macc. 5:40; 4 Macc. 14:14, 18; Σ Job 13:4.

In the NT we find sense b. at Ac. 25:27: ἄλογόν μοι δοκεῖ, "it seems to me to be contrary to reason." At 2 Pt. 2:12; Jd. 10 it is hard to decide whether the beasts are called dumb, irrational, or both. ὡς (τὰ) ἄλογα ζῷα.

We often find ζῷα ἄλογα. Both senses are suggested by the Gk. phrase. Jos. Bell., 4, 170 (→ *supra*) lays emphasis on the fact of being without speech, but in most cases the term refers equally well to the irrationality of the beast[4] (Wis. 11:15; 4 Macc. 4:14, 18; Philo Virt., 117; Vit. Cont., 8; Jos. Ant., 10, 262; Ap., 1, 224).

---

[16] *Ibid.*, 859.

[17] The Syr. transl. of Eus. Hist. Eccl., III, 39, 16 bears witness to this understanding by rendering τὰ λόγια "Gospel."

ἄλογος. [1] For further examples from pap. and inscr. cf. Moult.-Mill., 24.

[2] Leisegang, 82 ff.

[3] Cf. Schl. Lk., 645.

[4] Modern Gk.: τὸ ἄλογο = "horse" [Debrunner].

† **λογικός.**

a. With ref. to λέγειν, "belonging to speech" (Plut. Gaius Marcius, 38 [I, 232b]: μέρεσι λογικοῖς = "instruments of speech"). b. With ref. to λόγος, "belonging to reason," "rational." In this sense it is a favourite term in Gk. philosophy, esp. among the Stoics.[1] Man is a ζῷον λογικόν, Epict. Diss., II, 9, 2; M. Ant., II, 16, 6 etc.; Philo Abr., 32. "Belonging to the sphere of the λόγος or reason," "spiritual," M. Ant., VII, 55, 4: λογικὴ καὶ νοερὰ κίνησις, opp. αἰσθητικὴ κίνησις. The term does not occur in the LXX or Joseph., but is found in Gk. synagogue prayers, Const. Ap., VII, 34, 6.[2]

Sense a. does not occur in the NT. The meaning "spiritual" or "suprasensual" is plain in 1 Pt. 2:2: the λογικὸν ἄδολον → γάλα which the regenerate seeks, nourishment from the sphere, not of the αἰσθητικόν (→ *supra*), but the νοερόν, that which belongs to the level of the νοῦς rather than the senses, or, to use other NT terms, the πνευματικόν rather than the ψυχικόν. That this paraphrase is not against the context may be seen from v. 5: οἰκοδομεῖσθε οἶκος πνευματικός ... ἀνενέγκαι πνευματικὰς θυσίας. The sacrifice and house on the level of the πνεῦμα correspond to milk on the level of the λόγος.

Yet the question arises why in v. 2 λογικόν is used in respect of γάλα rather than πνευματικόν, even though the meaning may be the same. This can hardly be accidental, since the image of milk as sacramental food is part of the terminology of the mysteries (→ I, 646), and λογικός, like λόγος, is found not only in the vocabulary of philosophy but also in that of mysticism.

Philo, in his use of λογικός, forges links with both mysticism and Stoicism,[3] cf., e.g., Cher., 39; Migr. Abr., 185. The mystical use is predominant in Corp. Herm., cf. I, 31 (Scott, I, p. 130, 22 f.): δέξαι λογικὰς θυσίας ἁγνὰς ἀπὸ ψυχῆς καὶ καρδίας πρὸς σὲ ἀνατεταμένης, ἀνεκλάλητε,[4] ἄρρητε,[4] σιωπῇ φωνούμενε, XIII, 18 (I, p. 252, 7): ὁ σὸς λόγος δι' ἐμοῦ ὑμνεῖ σέ· δι' ἐμοῦ δέξαι τὸ πᾶν λόγῳ λογικὴν θυσίαν.

The quotations adduced show that λογικός can be a term to express the spiritualising of the cultic. This is its characteristic function in R. 12:1, where the παραστῆσαι τὰ σώματα ὑμῶν is called a θυσία ζῶσα ἁγία, and this in turn is equivalent to λογικὴ λατρεία. Materially, the thought is quite clear. As in pre-Christian θυσία and λατρεία the σώματα of beasts are brought to the hecatombs, so the bodies of Christians are now that which is sacrificed to God, i.e., given to Him to be His possession. This is the form of λατρεία befitting the λόγος. The πνευματικαὶ θυσίαι of 1 Pt. 2:5 bear exactly the same meaning.[5]

λογικός. Zn. R.³, 536 f. (cf. n. 12); Schl. R., 333; Ltzm. R., Exc. on 12:1; Reitzenstein Hell. Myst.³, 328 f.; O. Casel in *Jbch. f. Liturgiewissenschaft*, 4 (1924), 37 ff.; B. Schmidt, *Das geistige Gebet* (Diss. Breslau, 1916); R. Perdelwitz, *Die Mysterienreligion u. d. Problem des 1 Pt.* = RVV, 11, 3 (1911), 56 ff.; H. Wenschkewitz, "Die Spiritualisierung der Kultusbegriffe Tempel, Priester u. Opfer im NT," *Angelos*, 4 (1932), 70-230, esp. 180 ff.; T. Arvedson, *Das Mysterium Christi* = *Arbeiten u. Mitteilungen aus dem Nt.lichen Seminar zu Uppsala*, VII (1937), 231 f.

1 Pr.-Bauer³, *s.v.*

2 Cf. Ltzm., *op. cit.*; W. Bousset, NGG (1915), 467 f.

3 Cf. Wenschkewitz, 149 and 180.

4 Mystical predicates of the Godhead, cf. *op. cit.*, 121.

5 So also Zn. R.³, 537, n. 12.

Paul was not the only one to accomplish a moral spiritualising of the cultus. This occurs in Judaism in echo of the prophetic demand of Ps. 51:16 ff.; Hos. 6:6. Test. L. 3:6: προσφέροντες τῷ Κυρίῳ ὀσμὴν εὐωδίας λογικὴν (vl. λογικῆς) καὶ ἀναίμακτον θυσίαν, Philo Spec. Leg., I, 277: παρὰ θεῷ μὴ τὸ πλῆθος τῶν καταθυομένων εἶναι τίμιον, ἀλλὰ τὸ καθαρώτατον τοῦ θύοντος πνεῦμα λογικόν. S. Dt., 41 on 11:13 (p. 95, Kittel): "Hast thou then a עֲבוֹדָה (= sacrifice) in the heart? ... This is prayer ... As the worship of the altar was called a עֲבוֹדָה, so prayer is called a עֲבוֹדָה." Similar ideas are found in technical and popular philosophy:[6] Sen. Ben., I, 6, 3; Apollonius of Tyana De Sacrificiis (Eus. Praep. Ev., IV, 13).

The essential characteristic of Pl. is not just that he ethicises and spiritualises the concept of sacrifice and the cultus. Nor it is merely that this inward sacrifice must correspond to the nature of the λόγος or πνεῦμα. The real point is that the reconstruction takes place διὰ τῶν οἰκτιρμῶν τοῦ θεοῦ (R. 12:1), i.e., on the basis of the merciful action of God in Jesus Christ which he has described in the preceding chapters. It is unlikely that the terminology of Pl., as distinct from that of 1 Pt. 2:2, is dependent on that of the mysteries. He is simply using λογικός in a refined sense, cf. Test. L. 3:6 (→ *supra*).[7] The question is not of supreme importance, since in any case the norm of conformity to the λόγος is to be found in the πνεῦμα Ἰησοῦ Χριστοῦ.

† λογομαχέω, † λογομαχία.

The verb and noun occur once each in the Past. 2 Tm. 2:14: Warning μὴ λογομαχεῖν, for this profits nothing and subverts the hearers. 1 Tm. 6:4: He who does not keep to the λόγοι of Christ and sound (κατ' εὐσέβειαν) doctrine becomes νοσῶν περὶ → ζητήσεις καὶ λογομαχίας. The terms need no explanation. The warning implied in them corresponds to the warning against sins of the tongue which is often found in primitive Christianity.

In profane use few examples of λογομαχία have been found: Porphyrius in Eus. Praep. Ev., XIV, 10, 2; the title of a Menippean satire of Varro in which he calls the debate between the Stoics and Epicureans a λογομαχία, Porphyrius on Hor. Sat., II, 4 (ed. A. Holder [1894], 308; cf. F. Buecheler, Petronii Saturae[5] [1912], 209).[1] The paucity of examples is naturally no argument against the presence of the words elsewhere.

Kittel

[6] Cf. Ltzm., *op. cit.*
[7] Wenschkewitz, 190.
λογομαχέω κτλ. [1] I owe this ref. to Debrunner.

† ἐκλέγομαι.

Contents: A. On the Common Greek Meaning of ἐκλέγομαι. B. Election in the Old Testament: 1. The LXX Rendering of the Hebrew; 2. בחר and Related Expressions; 3. בחר in Common Parlance; 4. בחר as an Act of Religious Confession; 5. The Election of Individuals by Yahweh; 6. The Choice of the King; 7. The Election of the People. C. ἐκλέγομαι in the LXX and Jewish Hellenistic Writings: 1. General; 2. The Nature of the Selection; 3. Religious Election in ἐκλέγομαι: a. The Election of Specific Classes; b. The Nature of the Selection; c. The Election of the People; d. Reprobation or Non-Election; e. The Purpose in Election; f. Other Meanings of ἐκλέγομαι. D. The Idea of Election in ἐκλέγεσθαι in 1. Apocalyptic; 2. The Damascus Document. E. ἐκλέγομαι in the New Testament; 1. The Synoptists; 2. The ἐκλέγεσθαι of the Disciples in John; 3. Acts; 4. Paul and James: The Election of the Community; 5. The Idea of Reprobation.

A. On the Common Greek Meaning of ἐκλέγομαι.

Since the NT, and almost without exception the LXX (though cf. 1 Macc. 9:25; 11:23 S †), does not have the act. ἐκλέγω, our investigation of the general Gk. background can be restricted at once to the mid. and pass. The mid. "to choose something for oneself," "to make one's choice," with the acc. is already found in the absolute in Hdt., I, 199. There is ref. to the object of selection in Plat. Tim., 24c, cf. P. Magd., 29, 4 (3rd cent. B.C.): τὸν τόπον. Of men, Xenoph. An., II, 3, 11: τὸν ἐπιτήδειον. The choice of slaves, imposts, payments etc. is common in the pap. and inscr.: P. M. Meyer, *Gr. Texte aus Ägypten* (1916), 8, 12 (2nd cent. A.D.); P. Oxy., II, 237, IV, 8. The choice of abstract things may be seen in Plat. Symp., 198d: the most beautiful of what is to be praised; Xenoph. Mem., I, 6, 14: something good from literary treasures. We continually find ἐκ, Hdt., III, 38; Polyb., 3, 93, 4, or instead the gen., Polyb., 39, 4, 1. The pass. with ἐκ, Xenoph. Mem., III, 5, 2. The Attic perf. pass. is ἐξειλεγμένος, "choice," "chosen": Ps.-Plat. Alc., 121e. This is used instead of or interchangeably with ἐκλεκτός in Philo Cher., 7: ὁ νοῦς ἐξειλεγμένος (to be read instead of ἐπειλημμένος), and Gig., 64; Jos. Ant., 7, 12. On the other hand, in Zeph. 3:9 ᾿ΑΘ χεῖλος ἐξειλεγμένον (ברר) means "pure lip." ἐκλελεγμένος [1] is late Gk.: Polyb., 5, 79, 4; Cant. 5:10 ᾿Α (Σ ἐπίλεκτος); 1 Macc. 6:35; Ign. Eph. appendix of the church at Ephesus; 1 Cl., 50, 7; Pol., 1, 1; Herm. v., 4, 3, 5 of believers. On Lk. 9:35 א B → ἐκλεκτός E. 2 and n. 17.

Schrenk

ἐκλέγεσθαι. H. St. J. Thackeray, *A Grammar of the Old Testament in Greek*, I (1909), 274; Bl.-Debr.[6] § 316, 1; § 101 (λέγειν); Nägeli, 82. On Lk. 14:7: A. T. Robertson, *A Grammar of the Gk. NT* ... (1914), 811; J. H. Moulton, *A Grammar of NT Gk.*, I, Prolegomena (1906), 157. On Ac. 15:22: Robertson, *op. cit.*, 808. On Jm. 2:5, *ibid.*, 480. On Eph. 1:4 ff.: E. Lohmeyer, "Das Proömium des Epheserbriefes," ThBl, 5 (1926), 120-125; E. Gaugler, "Heilsplan u. Heilsverwirklichung nach Eph. 1:3-2:10," *Internat. kirchl. Zschr.*, 20 (1930), 201-216. On B: → διαθήκη. Cf. A. Bertholet, *Die Stellung d. Israeliten u. d. Juden zu d. Fremden* (1896); K. Galling, *Die Erwählungstraditionen Israels* (1928); G. v. Rad, *Das Gottesvolk im Dt.* (1929); *Das Geschichtsbild des chronist. Werkes* (1930); A. Weiser, *Glaube u. Gesch. im AT* (1931); W. Caspari, "Beweggründe d. Erwählung nach d. AT," NkZ, 32 (1921), 202 ff.; J. M. P. Smith, "The Chosen People," *American Journal of Semitic Languages and Literatures*, 45 (1928/29), 73 ff.; P. Volz, "Der Glaube an d. Erwählung Israels im AT," *Deutsches Pfarrerblatt*, 41 (1937), 213 ff.; W. Staerk, "Zum at.lichen Erwählungsglauben," ZAW, NF, 14 (1937), 1 ff.

[1] Cf. Bl.-Debr.[6] § 101 (λέγειν).

B. Election in the Old Testament.

1. The LXX Rendering of the Hebrew.

The verb ἐκλέγεσθαι (mid.), rarely ἐκλέγειν (act.) corresponds for the most part in the LXX (108 times) to the Heb. בחר. In the few cases it which it translates other Heb. roots this is partly due to the desire for stylistic variation (e.g., Jl. 2:16 by reason of the heaping up of synonyms for קבץ "to gather"), partly due to the opposite desire to bring together differing expressions (1 Ch. 21:11: ἔκλεξαι σεαυτῷ for קַבֶּל־לָךְ in assimilation to 2 Βασ. 24:12), partly due to a liking for choice expressions (Prv. 24:32: ἐκλέξασθαι παιδείαν for לקח מוּסָר), and not least, since ἐκλέγεσθαι has great theological significance as the chief rendering of בחר, due to a desire to speak theologically (Dt. 1:33: Yahweh went before you לָתוּר לָכֶם מָקוֹם = ἐκλέγεσθαι ὑμῖν τόπον). It may well be that the use four times for ברר "to sift," "to separate," is linked with theological associations: Ez. 20:38: ἐκλέξω (so rightly AQ instead of ἐλέγξω B) ἐξ ὑμῶν τοὺς ἀσεβεῖς, Da. 11:35; Da. Θ 12:10 of the purifying of the wise prior to the dawn of the age of salvation; 1 Ch. 16:41 of the temple singers.[2]

The caprice of the translator is more apparent in the use of the verbal adj. ἐκλεκτός. It is finely used for pass. constructions of בחר[3]: בָּחוּר (8 times), נִבְחָר (Prv. 8:19), and בָּחִיר (13 times), also for the nouns מִבְחָר (7 times, elsewhere rendered τὸ κάλλος) and מִבְחוֹר (2 K. 3:19 vl.; 19:23), "that which is choice or excellent" (cf. the gloss טוב in Ez. 31:16). It is used rather more freely for phrases with חֶמְדָּה, "what is desired, or costly" (4 times, e.g., Jer. 3:19 γῆ ἐκλεκτή), חֵפֶץ (Is. 54:12) and יָקָר (Ez. 27:22 A). The summary use of בָּרוּר in Heb. is repeated in the case of ἐκλεκτός: Is. 49:2 of the arrow as an image of the Ebed; 1 Ch. 7:40 of the heads of tribes; 9:22 of the keepers of the gates; 2 Εσδρ. 15:18 of sheep. What is costly in the concept of the pure (בָּרָה adj. fem.) is brought out by ἐκλεκτός in Cant. 6:9 (synon. with אַחַת "unique"), 6:10 (ἐκλεκτὴ ὡς ὁ ἥλιος). Less clear, perhaps because defective in the Mas., is Ps. 18(17):26: עִם־נָבָר תִּתְבָּרָר = μετὰ ἐκλεκτοῦ ἐκλεκτὸς ἔσῃ. ἐκλεκτός also emphasises the choice or excellent element when used for בֹּחַן "test" (Is. 28:16: אֶבֶן בֹּחַן = ἐκλεκτὸς λίθος; cf. the plur. in Ezr. (2 Εσδρ.) 5:8 for the Aram. אֶבֶן גְּלָל) and צְבִי "adornment" (Ez. 7:20; 25:9). In Prv. 17:3 it is more or less inaccurately substituted for בחן (though → n. 5), or in Gn. 41:2, 4, 5, 7, 18, 20 for בָּרִיא "fat" (of cattle and ears), Am. 5:11 for בַּר "wheat," 1 K. 5:3 (3 Βασ.) for בַּרְבֻּרִים (meaning obscure), and 6 times for בָּחוּר "young man."[4] Not good are the renderings in Ez. 27:24 (for בְּרֹמִים, "material"), 17:3, 22 vl. (for צַמֶּרֶת "top"), Ps. 141(140):4 (for מַנְעַמִּים "dainties"), Job 37:11 (for בְּרִי) and Ex. 30:23 (מָר־דְּרוֹר); it may be that Ez. 19:14 (for בַּד "twig") is a scribal error. The noun ἐκλογή is found only in 'A (Is. 22:7), ΣΘ (Is. 37:24) for מִבְחָר, and Ps. Sol. 9:4 perhaps for רָצוֹן or חֵפֶץ.

The idea of choice suggested by the Heb. root בחר is often expressed, or changed, in the Gk. Bible by other words apart from those mentioned. ἐκλέγεσθαι, on which ἐπιλέγειν or ἐπίλεκτος is 7 times a variation (3 times for מִבְחָר), is the chief term for

---

[2] The reading בֹּרוּ (from ברר) for M בְּרוּ in 1 S. 17:8 is doubtful, though the latter may be a scribal error for בַּחֲרוּ = ἐκλέξασθε.

[3] ἐκλεκτός occurs 44 times in LXX and Hexapla as a rendering of בחר and derivatives.

[4] The reverse error בָּחוּר "to select" = νεανίσκος is found in 2 S. (2 Βασ.) 10:9, cf. 2 Ch. 13:3, 17 δυνατός. On the etym. → n. 5.

בחר. In addition we find αἱρεῖν (4 times, including Jos. 24:15 A), αἱρετίζειν (13 times, 5 in Ch.), ἐξαιρεῖν (doubtful in Is. 48:10 → n. 5; Job 36:21), αἱρετός (Prv. 16:16; 22, 1 for נִבְחָר). Less suitable are ἀρεστός (Prv. 21:3 for נִבְחָר) διακρίνειν (Job 9:14; 15:5), εὐδοκεῖν (Sir. 37:28), εὐδοκιμεῖν (Sir. 41:16), δοκιμάζειν (Prv. 8:10), and more sharply ἐπιθυμεῖν (Is. 1:29, correct in sense), and ζηλοῦν (Prv. 3:31; → III, 478, n. 32). Select terms are κάλλος (Is. 37:24) and ἐκσεσαρκισμένος (Ez. 24:4) for מִבְחָר. At Prv. 10:20 πεπυρωμένος seems to derive from the Aram. נִבְחָר (→ n. 5), and μέτοχος at 1 S. (Βασ.) 20:30 goes back to חבר rather than the Mas. בחר. ἐκδέξασθαι is a common variant in the MSS (2 Βασ. 19:39 A; Job 34:33 S; Is. 66:4 B); it is probably a scribal error for ἐκλέξασθαι.

2. בחר and Related Expressions.

The verb בחר "to elect" [5] occurs 164 times [6] in the Heb. Bible, predominantly as qal, only 7 times as niph'al and once (Qoh. 9:4 in doubtful ketib) as pu'al. Its theological significance may be seen from the fact that in 92 instances the subject is God, and in 13 instances of the pass. בָּחִיר the election is by God. When used of God's electing the verb is always act.; the niph'al constructions, the pass. part. qal בָּחוּר and the nouns מִבְחָר (12 times) and מִבְחוֹר (2 K. 3:19; 19:23) for election in the sense of selection, belong to secular usage, as do many instances of the qal. Among the instances in which בחר denotes a human decision a particular place is occupied in which the object of choice is God, His Law, or similar normative definitions of the divine will. These are few in number, but they deserve special attention on account of Jos. 24:15, 22 (→ 150 ff.).

The use of בחר may be arranged in three groups of functions. The first, which has no theological importance, is the common use of the term. The second belongs to the sphere of sacral concepts; God and His norms are elected by man. In the third בחר is a statement of religious ideology; God decides on means and ways by choosing from what is possible.

The third group is not the only theologically significant one, but it is the most fruitful from this angle. In the later strata of the Canon from Dt. on it is the favourite term in formulation of the fact of the divine revelation within the concept of the covenant. Nowhere, not even in the pre-Dt. literature, are there any full synonyms, and our LXX findings simply indicate Heb. roots which might be regarded as partially synon. with בחר. The true content of the term is not congruent with any other Heb. word to the same degree as, e.g., ἐκλέγεσθαι is with ἐξαιρεῖσθαι in Gk. For 1. the element of willed decision which distinguishes בחר is not quite so unequivocal elsewhere, and 2. the words for calling, selecting, desiring, claiming etc. are not religious expressions in the same strong and precise sense as בחר, so that this verb, when the subject is God, seems almost always to be a technical doctrinal term which does not need to be explained and for which there is no equivalent.

---

5 Whether an Aramaism בחר "to test" for Heb. בחן is to be distinguished from the pure Heb. בחר "to choose" (so Ges.-Buhl) is important only in respect of the gloss Is. 48:10 (par. צרף "to melt") and Prv. 10:20 (כֶּסֶף נִבְחָר ἄργυρος πεπυρωμένος), and possibly also Job 29:25; 34:4, → n. 20. No etym. connection has been demonstrated between בָּחוּר "young man," בְּחוּרִים "youth," and בחר "to choose." It is likely that there is an independent root which possibly, with dialect changes, underlies the more modern Heb. בחל pi, "to ripen."

6 Constr. of the object with בְּ (Kautzsch § 119k) has a popular ring, → n. 27. 1 S. 20:30 (constr. with לְ); 2 S. 21:6 (cf. BHK³); 2 Ch. 34:6; Qoh. 9:4 seem to be errors.

As a verb of willing, הוֹאִיל (hi), "to insist on" (Hos. 5:11), has a particular interest when used of God. The word has many gradations, but basically it always denotes a resolve of the will. This is emphatically called unbreakable, or tenaciously held, in 1 S. 12:22, which is an instructive comment on statements about election: "God has insisted on making you his people." There is even an added element here, for its express appeal to His great name is meant to exclude all doubt. But other verbs of willing are also used religiously, esp. חפץ if it is to be reckoned as such, e.g., Nu. 14:8; Is. 62:4; 2 Ch. 9:8, with ref. to the king who is motivated by Yahweh's love for Israel, which has לְהַעֲמִידוֹ לְעוֹלָם as its goal. Among the words already mentioned under 1. the closest is ברר, "to separate," though the sparing use of this contrasts with the rich usage of בחר, and adds nothing essential to its understanding.[7] The alternation of קַבֶּל־לָךְ, "take," and בְּחַר־לְךָ, "choose," in 1 Ch. 21:11 and 2 S. 24:12 denotes a certain degree of synonymity, into which לקח may also be drawn. Perhaps it had this sense in current speech, but it is rare in religious terminology, cf. Ex. 6:7: "I take (וְלָקַחְתִּי) you to me for a people." On the other hand, in contexts such as this לקח may be interpreted simply as a verb of movement, "to fetch," e.g., Gn. 24:7; Jos. 24:3 (of Abraham). Very incomplete, too, is the congruence of words like חזה in connection with מִן or ראה, "to choose one from among others," Ex. 18:21 of the appointment of officials; 1 S. 16:1 of the appointment of David; Gn. 22:8 of the selection of an animal for sacrifice.

There is a certain relation to these expressions, since they occur in contexts which are bound up with an understanding of revelation which may be called belief in election in the broader sense. On the other hand, they are only loosely connected with the basic thought of God's choice suggested by בחר, since they avoid laying any stress on the free decision of the divine will. Of unique significance is ידע, "to know."[8] In Am. 3:2 רַק אֶתְכֶם יָדַעְתִּי מִכֹּל מִשְׁפְּחוֹת הָאֲדָמָה, "you only have I known[9] of all the families of the earth," this may be regarded as the earliest attempt at a formulated conception of the popular belief in election. The only thing lacking is the catchword "election" itself. That the content is present is shown by the fact that knowledge is here used in the sense of essential appropriation,[10] as with men who know one another as יוֹדְעִים, "friends" (Job 19:13).[11] This is expressed by the combination with רַק and מִן partitive: Yahweh knew only Israel in distinction from (all) other peoples. In this way ידע is given an emphasis which enables it to be regarded as a free and efficacious act of will. This volitional element is not present, however, without the partitive particles. When it is simply said that God knew Israel, this means that He for His part did the same as He demands from the man who is to know God (cf. the parallelism of דַּעַת אֱלֹהִים and חֶסֶד) in Hos. 6:6); He enters into him and creates the state of *shalom*. The meaning is the

---

[7] In Ez. 20:38 it represents an act of judgment in necessary correction of the act of revelation denoted by בחר in v. 5.

[8] → γινώσκω I, 696 ff.; cf. also → n. 91.

[9] Suppression of the preterite (so already J. Wellhausen, *Die kleinen Propheten* [1892], 74; cf. also L. Köhler, *Theol. d. AT* [1936], 64: "You only will I know") involves paraphrase rather than translation. The statement may be "flatly thematic" (Galling, 9, cf. Wellhausen), but the theme derives from history. This is pointed out in v. 1b, though it is almost self-evident.

[10] Cf. on this J. Pedersen, *Israel*, 109.

[11] The sexual sense of ידע is quite impossible here (Galling, 3; K. Cramer, *Amos* [1930], 32: "My covenant of marriage is with you"); this is simply a special euphemistic use. At a pinch it might be conceivable in Hosea, but one cannot seriously maintain that Amos has before him the picture of a paterfamilias (Cramer, 57). If so, one might say, on the basis of Gn. 18:19, that God made a covenant of marriage with Abraham.

same in a few related expressions[12] such as that in Dt. 9:24: "Since the time that he[13] knew you." In Jer. 1:5 יְדַעְתִּיךָ is made more specific as calling by the addition: "I appointed you a prophet," and in cases where the expression is related to historical figures like Moses (Ex. 33:12: יְדַעְתִּיךָ בְשֵׁם, cf. v. 17), or Abraham (Gn. 18:19), and perhaps David (2 S. 7:20), it is possible to detect an analogy to Am. 3:2. "To know," however, is just an alternative for providential care when the expression lies outside the narrow sphere of salvation history or prophetic calling, cf. Na. 1:7: "Yahweh knows those who take refuge in him"; Ps. 1:6: He "knows" the way of the righteous; Ps. 144:3: "What is man, that thou takest knowledge of him? or the son of man that thou takest account of him?" (חשב pi; cf. Ps. 8:4).[14]

Other variations of the concept of election may be found in general expressions which refer to the Lord of the world separating His possession out from the course of events. Thus Yahweh "calls" (קרא) in Ex. 31:2; 35:30, and He entrusts with a particular task. Dt. Is. in particular is fond of this expression, 49:1; 51:2, with שֵׁם 43:1; 45:3 (Cyrus).[15] Or Yahweh "separates" (הִבְדִּיל, Dt. 10:8), "takes" (הֶחֱזִיק, Is. 41:9), "desires" (אִוָּה, Ps. 132:13 par. בחר, with Zion as obj.) etc. Fruitful also in the development of the concept in legal terminology, from which we have certain expressions which are formally instructive. Yahweh "redeems" (פדה, Dt. 9:26 etc.), "releases" (גאל, Ex. 15:13), "acquires by purchase" (קנה,[16] cf. esp. Ex. 15:16: עַם־זוּ קָנִיתָ; Ps. 74:2: עֲדָתְךָ קָנִיתָ קֶּדֶם; Is. 11:11). But these phrases are historically rather than theologically orientated. The concept of election is not necessarily implicit in them. The same is true of verbs like "to lead out" or "to deliver" used to describe the basic act of Yahweh in relation to Israel. Again, nouns like "people" and "inheritance" refer in the first instance to the covenant and can be used as witnesses to belief in election only with great caution. Is. 45:3 (the call of Cyrus) might even be regarded as polemical.

In sum, it is only occasionally that these close expressions, even ידע, are drawn into theological or religious service, whereas בחר is in this field an obvious key to the interpretation of faith's insight into the divine work, and it thus takes on a significance extending far beyond the OT Canon. Thus the content of the belief in election in the strict sense is almost exclusively tied to this word which, because of its secular rootage, is excellently adapted to provide an interpretation of historical revelation.

3. בחר in Current Usage.

בחר, like the word "to choose," denotes the complicated rather than the simple act of will, for which the Heb. is אבה. The one who chooses decides in favour of one of many

---

[12] The יְדַעְתִּיךָ בַּמִּדְבָּר of Hos. 13:5 is uncertain, cf. מַרְעִית in v. 6 and the context, which deals with the monarchy.

[13] דַּעְתּוֹ (Samaritanus) is the original and is materially correct, cf. C. Steuernagel (1900), *ad loc.* The banal thought of the Heb. that Moses knew Israel from a certain point in time is impossible in the framework of the tradition. It simply derives from the concern of scribes lest God's knowledge should seem to be limited, cf. A. Geiger, *Urschrift u. Übersetzungen d. Bibel*[2] (1928), 336. V. 7 shows that the מִיּוֹם refers to the day of Yahweh's intervention in Israel's history.

[14] In Hos. 5:3 יָדַעְתִּי is purely informative in view of the parallelism with לֹא נִכְחַד מִמֶּנִּי.

[15] Is. 41:9 (Israel as obj.), compared with v. 4 (the generations of humanity as obj.), shows, however, that in Dt. Is. קרא is the broader term as compared with בחר.

[16] This verb can also mean to create, Ps. 139:13; with ref. to the people, Dt. 32:6. Perhaps we really have two different roots, and the strained attempts at combination are superfluous.

possibilities and rejects the others (מאס). The motive is not indicated by the word. בחר can sometimes mean "to value highly" and מאס "to value lightly" or even "to detest,"[17] but these are emphases which derive from the logic of the context when the simple "to choose" or "to reject" seems to be too restrained. The verbs themselves are never strengthened by intensive construction.[18] This fact, and the many examples of current usage, prove the restrained character of the words. When the objects are things, an element of purpose is indicated. One chooses a piece of land (Gn. 13:11), stones for slinging (1 S. 17:40), suitable wood (Is. 40:20), a fitting animal (1 K. 18:23, 25) etc. The stone not used in building is rejected (Ps. 118:22).[19] This element is well brought out when בחר and מאס are purposefully contrasted in Is. 7:15 f. ("to refuse the evil, i.e., that which is ill-adapted, and to choose the good, i.e., that which is well-adapted") in order to show the ability of the growing youth to use his own intelligence.[20] The element of purpose is also present in the choice of persons. Thus the sons of the gods choose the daughters of men because they are beautiful (Gn. 6:2). Again, Moses chooses men for office (Ex. 18:25). The expression אִישׁ בָּחוּר is common for those selected on mobilisation (Ju. 20:15 etc.). Thus the term carries with it an implication of approval and recognition.[21] A "chosen" countenance is both imposing and attractive (Cant. 5:15). Even in a bad sense the word can explain impulsive desire (Is. 1:29[22] of adherence to alien cults) or indicate evil kinship, cf. Job 15:5, where the crafty man chooses crafty speech, or Is. 41:24, where he who is an abomination chooses an abomination. "My soul chooses strangling" in Job 7:15 means that this would be the best for it. The emphases, then, can vary greatly. One chooses on the basis of intelligence. Yet one does not have to do so, for sometimes a choice may be grounded in emotion or even compulsion. Basically, however, the rational element predominates. To choose is a matter of intelligence[23] quite apart from the part played by the emotions, which usually find their own linguistic expression.

4. בחר as an Act of Religious Confession.

בחר still retains an unmistakable rational element even in the few cases in which it has as object God (Jos. 24:22; false gods, 24:15; Ju. 5:8 (?);[24] 10:14), God's

[17] Cf. Lv. 26:44 with געל, Am. 5:21 with שׂנא, Is. 33:8 with the gloss לֹא חָשַׁב.

[18] An emotional emphasis is imparted in Heb. by the piel. The pual in Qoh. 9:4 is incorrect, cf. BHK.

[19] Cf. Jer. 6:30: Israel is rejected as unserviceable metal.

[20] A process in criminal law, whereby several punishments are laid before the guilty for choice, seems to be suggested in 2 S. 24:12. Something similar seems to underlie Dt. 30:19 (heaven and earth as witnesses of the choice between life and death) and Jer. 8:3 (death preferred to life). In Job 34:4 מִשְׁפָּט נִבְחֲרָה לָּנוּ seems to be a technical expression for finding the right (Aramaism for בחן in v. 3? → n. 5). Jos. 24:22 has a legal ring in view of the appeal to attestation, → n. 30.

[21] Cf. Is. 58:5 f.: Yahweh recognises the fast. Is. 66:4 is ironical: "I will make their devices my own."

[22] חמד is par. Cf. Ju. 10:14 → 151.

[23] Though on the question of objectivity in the biblical expression cf. J. Köberle, *Natur u. Geist nach der Auffassung des AT* (1901), 212 ff.

[24] The obscure statement in the Song of Deborah at Ju. 5:8: יִבְחַר אֱלֹהִים חֲדָשִׁים leaves too much play for interpretation and is not controlled by any obvious ref. The LXX (B) with its ἐξελέξαντο θεοὺς καινούς seems to be better than attempts to take אֱלֹהִים as subj. (cf. Luther: "God has chosen a new thing"), since the song uses the name Yahweh but not the appellative. On the other hand, the thought of choosing new gods is so isolated in the context that no confidence can be put in the accuracy of this view or of the text generally. The suggestion that אֱלֹהִים refers here to some kind of officials is merely an attempt to avoid the difficulty.

Law or way (Ps. 119:173; 25:12; 119:30; negatively, Prv. 3:31), the fear of God (Prv. 1:29), or the sanctuary (Ps. 84:10 ?). It is no accident that these often occur in the stylistic forms of Wisdom poetry. Yahweh shows the righteous the way he is to choose (Ps. 25:12). Instruction in the way brings conviction that it is the right one, and this conviction underlies the decision of the pupil to take it. In this sense one can speak of a knowledge which those who do not choose the fear of Yahweh hate (Prv. 1:29). Less evident is the rational pedagogic climax at which choosing what is pleasing to Yahweh is identical with keeping the covenant (Is. 56:4) and thus denotes an act of confession.[25] It is possible, though not very likely, that such modes of expression are influenced by the significantly older statement in Jos. 24:22. Because of its setting, this demands special attention.

It is part of the E account of the council at Shechem which is the climax and conclusion of the Joshua stories and of the early history of the people of Yahweh. V. 15 speaks of a choice which Israel must make between other gods if "it seems unprofitable" (רַע) to them to serve Yahweh. The word בחר is then used in v. 22 to denote the act of confession by which the tribes acknowledge Yahweh as their God at Shechem. "Ye are witnesses against yourselves," says Joshua, "that ye have chosen you the Lord, to serve him." They have done this because they have been convinced by Joshua's demonstration that Yahweh has always shown Himself to be a Guide and Helper since the days of Abraham.

It seems that one could hardly say more precisely than by using the concept of choice that Israel's confession of its covenant God, which took place at the beginning of its common history as a people and a divine community, consisted in a rationally grounded act of will. But for those who have just read Dt. it is surprising that the word בחר, which is there used for God's sovereign action, for the normative divine initiative which is accountable to none, should now be used to describe human responsibility for the coming into existence of an inviolable commitment to God. The question arises whether this unmistakably impressive choice of the same word is to be construed as a pedagogic device to kindle a sense of responsibility in the reader (just as the covenant is sometimes shown to be two-sided, Dt. 26:17; → II, 122 f.), or whether it is more correct to assume that this anthropocentric idea of election is quite independent of the theocentric presentation in Dt. It seems hard to find any serious arguments in favour of the first alternative, since the texts quoted, whose related usage may well be modelled on that of Jos. 24:22, hardly suffice to prove that the polar relation of this verse to the Deuteronomic view of election is grounded in literary intent. Thus interpretation must seek elsewhere than in Dt.[26] in any attempt to find the elements of psychological and historical truth in this almost completely isolated statement concerning an election of Yahweh by the people.

A critical difficulty is posed at once by the fact that the combination of the statements containing בחר in v. 15 and v. 22 does not seem to be too secure. It is only ironically that Joshua in v. 15 calls for a choice among the gods, Yahweh being expressly excluded. These words presuppose a readiness to leave Yahweh, and the answer of the people in

---

[25] Negatively Is. 65:12; 66:3. Proselytes are in view in the נִלְוִים of 56:6.

[26] The suggestion of O. Procksch (*Das nordhebräische Sagenbuch* ... [1906], 167) that vv. 14b-23 are a Deuteronomic addition is not adequately supported by the mere fact of its polemic against the gods. V. 24 obviously presupposes a similar polemic.

v. 16 mentions the attitude which Joshua has in mind with his words "if it seems unprofitable to you." Only those who have forsaken Yahweh — v. 27 uses the stronger כחש — can choose which of the gods they will serve. This is the same sarcastic depreciation of the choice of gods as is found in Ju. 10:14:[27] "Go and cry unto the gods which ye have chosen; let them deliver you in the time of your tribulation." Here, too, one finds the bitter and resigned assumption that Yahweh has been forsaken, v. 13. Here, too, the choice of gods is tacitly but clearly referred to as something which must seem to be absurd to the people, as a heathen error into which only the unfaithful can fall back.[28] The more strange it seems, then, that in v. 22 Israel's confession of fidelity to its God can be called a choice, since this statement completely disregards the satirical element in the choice of v. 15 and can hardly be regarded as a direct continuation. One is tempted to conclude that the term בחר is a crude gloss on v. 15, on a sarcastic application of heathen practice to the relation of Israel to Yahweh, whose sarcastic intent was not recognised. In other words, the statement is an addition to the original narrative, whose unity is in any case suspect.[29]

Whether one draws this conclusion or not, v. 22 does take up the thought of the conditional clause of v. 15: "If it seems unprofitable to you to serve Yahweh." Adopting the בחר of v. 15 positively, without regard to its sarcastic emphasis, it coins a bold formula. Possibly the בחר of v. 22 rests on a very different usage from that of v. 15, deriving from treaty law and esp. from the law of kingship,[30] and excluding from the very outset the element of irrational caprice predominant in v. 15. In fact, the solemn declaration: "Ye are witnesses against yourselves that ye have chosen you the Lord," is indicative of a formal, attested, and binding act integral to the use of בחר. In the form of a compact it asserts the legal obligation implicit in the spontaneous homage paid to the superior God.[31]

Even if one ignores v. 22 and finds the centre of the story in the "if it seems unprofitable to you" of v. 15, the idea of a choice of Yahweh by the tribes of Israel is still present, though less obtrusively. The only point is that there is now quite clearly no place either for the rivalry of other gods or for man's complete freedom to choose among the gods. The verse unmistakably expresses the passionate conviction that loyalty must and shall be upheld.[32] To be sure, the reason for cleaving to Yahweh is that it is not unprofitable. But to emphasise the opposite term טוב ("profitable," "meaningful") would be to incur the guilt of exaggeration, since the story is obviously designed to rule out any synergistic ideas about the establishment of covenant fellowship with Yahweh. From the time that Yahweh brought (לקח, v. 3) Abraham out of a race given up to the service of other gods, He has led, saved and blessed Israel. To show Him sincere and perfect service (עִבְדוּ אֹתוֹ בְּתָמִים וּבֶאֱמֶת v. 14), and to put away all other gods, is now an obvious duty, no matter how impossible its attainment might seem to be, v. 19. Those who realise this have no choice. The role of human choice in fellowship with God is thus presented strictly in terms of spontaneous gratitude and loyalty, as in the E passage at Ex. 32:26, where at a moment of dangerous crisis the cry: "Who is on the Lord's side?" is quite unambiguously a resolute appeal to loyalty: "Let him come unto me." If the service of Yahweh seems to be profitable, if a man tries to choose

---

[27] The construction with בְּ is designed to sharpen the sarcasm, → n. 6.

[28] → III, 88 f. Rejection of Yahweh corresponds (1 S. 10:19). There is point to this, since Yahweh is in fact a national God.

[29] Cf. the literary analysis of Jos. 24 by M. Noth, *Das System d. zwölf Stämme Israels* (1930), 133 ff. The elimination of v. 22 is here suggested on other grounds.

[30] 1 S. 8:18; 12:13. Cf. → 156.

[31] → n. 20. On Mi. 4:5 → 160.

[32] Cf. M. Buber, *Königtum Gottes*[2] (1936), 115.

Yahweh or believes that he can do so, he has obviously not understood this God. Mention of the bitter possibility of rejection by the hearers, and the sharp contrast of the unchanging loyalty of Joshua and his house, impart a strong note of urgency to the speech.

In the setting, then, the psychological cogency of the "ye have chosen you the Lord" is very limited, and this is perhaps one of the main reasons why the strong formulation played only a minor role, or exerted no influence at all, within the Canon. It cannot be said with equal certainty whether the same restriction may be asserted in respect of the element of historical truth in the story. It seems that in this form of expression, as at other points in these saga-like stories, one has to assume historical reminiscence, even if, with some modern scholars,[33] we replace the view that Jos. 24 is a historically valueless doublet of the story of the Mosaic covenant in Ex. 19; 24; 34 by the suggestion that the chapter is an aetiologically oriented account of entry into the Yahweh cultus at Shechem, after the conquest, by tribes, presumably the Leah tribes, which had hitherto stood outside the worship of Yahweh. Those whom Joshua addresses, and whom he differentiates from his house, probably the house of Joseph, have been moved to enter into the covenant by the impression which the great acts of Yahweh have made on them. Such a confession by tribes and tribal groups may well have contained some prudential elements in the age of political and military conflict with Canaan and in the sphere of unbroken polytheism; these are the elements implied in what is said about rejection of Yahweh.[34] For the coalescence of tribal groups under a cultic obligation was always in fact an act of political resolve. The decision was taken to recognise a sacral organisation as binding and to claim it as a centre of forces. An account of this nature could be the historical kernel of the story of the council at Shechem insofar as this finds expression in what is said about a choice of Yahweh.

It may be that Dt. 33:5: "And he was king in Jeshurun, when the heads of the people and the tribes of Israel were gathered together," alludes to a similar or even to the same historical process,[35] so long as one assumes a point which the obscure style of the poem unfortunately does not allow to be proved, namely, that the king who "came to be" (וַיְהִי) in Jeshurun was Yahweh. Reasons may also be advanced for believing that the ref. is to a human king, e.g., Saul.[36] In this case the gathering would be a military concentration such as that described in 1 S. 11:7.

5. The Election of Individuals by Yahweh.

Among statements in which God is the subject of electing there are only a few in which the divine choice refers specifically to individuals. Disregarding those which speak of the king (→ 6.), we find the following.

a. Because of its early attestation, the proper name יִבְחָר (2 S. 5:15), which is borne by one of the sons of David, must be treated first.

---

[33] Cf. E. Sellin, "Seit welcher Zeit verehrten die nordisraelitischen Stämme Jahwe?" *Oriental Studies* (*Festschr. f. P. Haupt,* 1926), 124 ff.; M. J. Bin Gorion, *Sinai und Garizim* (1926), 311 ff.; M. Noth, *op. cit.* (→ n. 29), 65 ff.; A. Alt, "Josua" (ZAW, Beih. 66 [1936], 124 ff.).

[34] Cf. Nu. 11:20; 1 S. 10:19 etc.

[35] So E. Sellin, *Geschichte d. israelitisch-jüdischen Volkes,* I (1924), 99 f. notwithstanding the uncertainties of translation.

[36] So K. Budde, *Der Segen Moses* (1922), 13 f., though cf. M. Buber, *op. cit.,* 126 f.

It is short for יבחר־אל [37] or יבחריה: "El, or Yahweh, elects," or, as a wish: [38] "May He elect." It cannot be taken for certain, of course, that the obj. of election is a person, namely, the bearer of the name. The wish, or whatever it is, might refer to his family as in יוסף, יבניה etc., or even to his people, as in אלישיב. [39] Nevertheless, the latter suggestion is as little likely as the view that the name is influenced by the fact that a king is in view. In particular, however, the meaning of the desired or actual election is uncertain. Perhaps the point is simply to indicate the motive which might have governed God, or did govern Him, in the election of this man, i.e., to assure the bearer of the name of God's recognition and favour, as in אלידע. It can hardly be to mark him off from the non-elect. The value of this incidental witness is thus essentially restricted to the fact that it attests to a religious use of the term in the age of David for what seems in all probability to be a personal and willed relation of Yahweh to an individual.

b. It is perhaps surprising that the closely related concept of prophetic calling, the distinctive self-awareness of the prophet, which is rooted in personal encounter with God, is nowhere with complete certainty construed as election in the OT. [40] Only one prophet, Dt. Is., uses election and calling interchangeably to describe a sense of mission, and this is in no sense typical of prophetic thinking, since there are special reasons for it.

In the address to the "servant of rulers" [41] in Is. 49:7 we read that the Holy One of Israel has "chosen thee," while v. 1 speaks of calling from the mother's womb. Similarly in 42:1 God speaks of the servant as "mine elect," while he is "called" in v. 6. Quite apart from the question whether this favours an interpretation of the *Ebed* as a collective symbol for Israel, [42] and quite apart from the question whether the elect is supposed to be a prophet or something else, it may be stated that the word "to elect" implies the introduction into prophecy of a new term designed to indicate a mission which is to be equated, not with that of the priest or king, but with that of the people generally. It is worth noting that this takes place in an author whose style is distinctively characterised by a very definite tendency towards the kind of plerophory which easily reduces language to a common level. [43] The election and calling of the servant are one and the same, and, if this is meant seriously, the equation seems to be undertaken for the sake of election. Election is established calling to be a light to the nations (42:6).

Nevertheless, it is no accident, but rests on a sense of the distinctive dimensions of election and calling, that in the terminology of prophetic self-awareness the concept of election is nowhere found outside Dt. Is. Calling and election are, of course, related as modes of experiencing the sovereign will of God, but they are probably regarded as different in compass, though the difference is never so palpable as in Mt. 22:14: πολλοὶ γάρ εἰσιν κλητοί, ὀλίγοι δὲ ἐκλεκτοί. [44] It may be that in the concept of election the

[37] For this form, though with no examples, cf. M. Lidzbarski, *Handbuch der nordsemitischen Epigraphik* (1898), Index.
[38] So M. Noth, *Die israel. Personennamen* ... (1928), 209.
[39] Though in this case the post-exilic origin gives rise to the interpretation, cf. Noth, *op. cit.*, 213.
[40] → καλέω, III, 487 ff.
[41] If we may read it thus, cf. BHK, *ad loc.*
[42] Is. 41:8 f.; 43:10, 20; 44:1 f.; 45:4; 48:12 plainly refer to the national history, → 167. In Jl. 2:32 those whom God calls are Gentiles if the "all flesh" of v. 28 still applies.
[43] L. Köhler says of the rhetorical style of Dt. Is. (*Dtjs* [1923], 79): "He expresses himself well, but he does not express himself exactly"; 81: "Fulness must pass for precision." This must be remembered in all theological conclusions drawn from this work.
[44] Though cf. → n. 15 and → III, 495.

psychical process in the one who elects, which finds expression in specific action, is more strongly felt than in the concept of calling, which envisages only the action. Yet in election there is always a judgment which distinguishes the recognised from the rejected, while this element of recognition is completely absent from calling.

Of a piece with this is the fact that, apart from one very doubtful case, the prophets never have the sense of being elected. The process in the divine psyche which led to their being addressed did not concern them. Their concern was exclusively with the command which they received to "go, prophesy" (Am. 7:15). He who hears the call must obey (Am. 3:8).

What is said about the call of Jer. in 1:4-8 betrays close affinity to the song of Is. 49:1-6. Yet Jer. does not use the obvious term election for his appointment as a prophet. He uses the word "to know," which only in its specific sense is a possible synonym (ידע, 1:5).[45] This term, which pregnantly describes God's impartation of spiritual power to man,[46] is hardly comparable with choice, which corresponds, and is designed to correspond, to rejection, and which expresses primarily an order and only by extension a personal relation. With good reason one might certainly say of Jer. that he was elected, since others who even in his own opinion were more mature and eloquent and fitted for the prophetic office than he[47] were not called, just as one might say the same of Is. when he accepted the challenge of the One who commissioned him: "Who will go for us?" (6:8), or of Amos, who knew that he was called even though he was not a prophet by vocation (7:14). But this idea of other possibilities open to God is meaningless for the prophets. Their intolerance has other roots, and no cogent reasons can be found for introducing the concept of election in interpretation of prophetic calling.[48] So far as Dt. Is. is concerned, his desire for magniloquence leads him to adopt a terminology which was by no means so fixed in the days of pre-exilic prophecy that it could influence the expression of a sense of prophetic mission, quite apart from the fact that it was not particularly adapted for such a function.

c. In the light of these findings it is perhaps as well to bring other statements about the election of individuals who were not prophets into connection with the circle of prophetic thinking. It is occasionally said of the national heroes, e.g., Abraham (Neh. 9:7), or Moses (Ps. 106:23; cf. also Ps. 105:26), or David (Ps. 78:70;[49] 89:4), or Zerubbabel (Hag. 2:23), that they were elected.

The attestation is sparse and strikingly late. It reminds us of the personification of the people in Dt. Is. Apart from the ref. to David, who was a king, it follows a usage which is alien to the tradition about these men, though in other respects the tradition is plain enough in these passages. Thus the ref. to Abraham may even be regarded as an interpretation of the Gn. tradition. It sees the sequence election,[50] testing, covenant. Election is not the only presupposition of the covenant, for stress is also laid on the proving of the elect ("and foundest his heart faithful before thee," Neh. 9:8).

---

45 → 147 f.; Is. 49:1 has "called" instead of this difficult word.

46 The par. is "I sanctified thee"; cf. Dt. 34:10: יָדַע פָּנִים אֶל־פָּנִים.

47 The similar words of Moses, which are motivated by the same doubts, are even blunter. What they amount to is: "Send whom thou wilt" (Ex. 4:13).

48 The idea of conversion is closer (Jer. 3:7 etc.); cf. J. Hempel, "Berufung und Bekehrung" (*Festschr. G. Beer* [1935], 41 ff.).

49 Par. "took him from the sheepfolds."

50 Is. 51:2 speaks of calling.

d. Apart from what is said about the election of the people, these occasional references to that of national heroes have no independent theological significance. Nor have scattered references to election to the priestly office.

The oldest and most independent of these concerns the election of the house of Eli (1 S. 2:28), though there is not sufficient evidence to support the implied ideology. Only in Chronicles (1 Ch. 15:2; 2 Ch. 29:11) is there express ref. to the election of the Levites by Yahweh. There are glosses on the Levites in Dt. (18:5; 21:5).[51] The note about Aaron in Ps. 105:26 might equally well be applied to Moses, and does not necessarily imply specific election to the priesthood.

e. It is thus fairly evident that the spiritual context which has fashioned these occasional turns of phrase is to be found in the belief in the election of the community of Yahweh. This is certainly expressed plainly and strongly where the elect are the community, Is. 65:9, 15, 22; Ps. 105:6, 43; 106:5; 1 Ch. 16:13. In particular, those who pray in the forecourt are conscious of their election (Ps. 65:4; Nu. 16:7). This shows that belief in election is the power which sustains the inner life of the community. Those who may come to the sanctuary gain joy from the fact that they are preferred to others who cannot and may not do so. For them election is experience of God's grace as this is renewed in the cultus. If, in speaking about this, they mark themselves off from other members of the nation whom God abhors (Ps. 5:5 ff.), they do this as Israel κατὰ πνεῦμα, as responsible bearers of the grace of election. Thus under the title of elect we find both the nameless righteous and the holders of great names. All are personal symbols of the people which has experienced election, and all the statements about individuals exemplify the one concept which derives from the community's heritage of faith and which stands or falls with the living sense of fellowship.

6. The Choice of the King.

With certain reservations imposed by historical development the same applies to the use of the concept of election, and the relation of this circle of thought, to the monarchy and its representatives. In this connection the ideology of kingship takes on real significance, since the monarchy in Israel and Judah strongly fosters the typical spiritual attitude which appears in many forms in the religious and political thought of Israel, and which may be called a belief in national election. Personally elected by God, the ruler of the people of Yahweh guarantees the divine direction of its destiny in virtue of the religious basis of his position.[52] Faith in the election of the king was more vital and popular in Israel and Judah than the belief of foreign myth in the divinity of the ruler.[53] It is a special form of expression, and the earliest attempt at fixing conceptually the belief in the election of the people. It was for the sake of His people Israel that Yahweh established the disputed kingship of David. This was what David learned from his first successes (2 S. 5:12). The king's people is God's people (Ps. 28:8; 72:2).

---

[51] The use of בחר for Yahweh's decision in the ordeal (Nu. 16:5-7) seems to belong to this complex. He hereby proclaims who is His and who is holy. Yet the motif of choice in this account may also be linked with the oracle by lot (1 S. 10:20 f.).

[52] Cf. the combination of king and people in many motifs in the royal psalms, H. Gunkel, *Einleitung in d. Psalmen* (1933), § 5.

[53] → I, 565 f.

In the establishment and description of the legal position of the kings the thought of the divine election does not play any explicit role, and the use of בחר in connection with the monarchy is only within comparatively narrow limits.[54] Ref. to the anointing is more common; it is self-evident that when this is done by an ecstatic nabi[55] the divine designation of the person is implied. This may be the reason why emphatic and explicit references to the election of the king are limited to the sources dealing with the rise of the monarchy.

These sources show us, of course, that the theopolitical use of the concept cannot be regarded as *ipso facto* the only valid one. The choice of a king was hardly linked so firmly with obedience to the divine will that it could be forgotten that it represented a process of political construction grounded in a conflict of political forces.[56] On two occasions in these accounts (1 S. 8:18; 12:13) בחר is used with a human subject for the voice of the people (1 S. 8:7) in the sense of the city elders or the national levy.

It is worth noting, however, that there is here the same sceptical undertone as in the choice of God in Jos. 24 (→ 150 f.): "Ye shall cry out in that day because of the king which ye shall have chosen you; and the Lord will not hear you in that day," 1 S. 8:18; 12:13; cf. 12:25: "both ye and your king."[57] This is even clearer in passages which make it as plain as possible that to make a man king is to reject Yahweh as King (1 S. 8:7; 12:12). The political views and forces which work in this direction are unequivocally disapproved, and hence they are not stated. Yet it is easy enough to see what they were. The account of Saul's victory over the Ammonites in 1 S. 11 leaves us in no doubt that the power of the first king was based on a deployment of national force which, by setting up an agreed executive authority, created an institution which would ensure the continued life of the nation. Later David is acclaimed as king by the leading classes, first in Judah (2 S. 2:4, 7), then in Israel (2 S. 5:3).[58] Abimelech had been similarly acclaimed in Shechem (Ju. 9:6), and the monarchy was not entirely separated from this democratic foundation when in Judah it came to be confined to the house of David (2 S. 23:5). The "people of the land" were still a force which maintained this connection in times of crisis and prevented it from developing into tyranny.[59] In Dt., too, the sombre law of monarchy refers explicitly to the popular will and its demand for a king, and to that degree it is strongly limited (17:14-20).

---

[54] Objects of the divine choice are Saul, 1 S. 10:24 (2 S. 21:6? → n. 62); David, 1 S. 16:8, 9, 10; 2 S. 6:21 (in his own words to Michal); 1 Ch. 28:4; 1 K. 8:16 (Deuteronomic); 2 Ch. 6:6; Ps. 78:70 (par. "he took him"); Absalom, 2 S. 16:18; Solomon, 1 Ch. 28:5 f.; 29:1 (in the words of David); Zerubbabel, Hag. 2:23; generally נָגִיד, 2 Ch. 6:5 (1 Ch. 28:4, the stem of Jesse as נָגִיד). Statistically the main use is in Ch.

[55] In other cases it is more a confirmation than a transfer of divine dignity, → n. 76.

[56] Cf. A. Alt, *Reallexikon d. Vorgeschichte*, 7 (1926), 27 ff.; RGG², III, 1134 ff.; *Die Staatenbildung der Israeliten in Palästina* (1930); A. Wendel, *Säkularisierung in Israels Kultur* (1934), 133 ff.; K. Galling, *Die israelitische Staatsverfassung in ihrer vorderorientalischen Umwelt* (1929).

[57] Cf. the mocking speech of Jehu in 2 K. 10:3: "Look even out the best" (i.e., as rival king).

[58] The arrangement between king and leaders is a בְּרִית.

[59] People of the land means "fully authorised members of a common political or cultic body, of a city state ... These people live in the city concerned, and have their main possessions within the city — in this case הָאָרֶץ": E. Gillischewski, ZAW, 40 (1922), 141. Cf. also E. Würthwein, "Der *'amm ha'arez* im AT," BWANT, IV, 17 (1936).

Criticism of this political development,[60] and opposition to it, could never cease to be concerned lest it should imply a reduction of the theocratic principle.[61] On the other hand, those who championed monarchy argued that the easier solution of national crises which it offered was a proof of its divine authority and mission. This also seemed to meet the objection that in acting according to political insights or desires those responsible for the institution of the monarchy or the anointing of a usurper were guilty of a serious mistake. For the decisive matter was God's decision in favour of this man, not the preceding deliberations. There thus arose a view which is everywhere recognised in the OT, even if it is only seldom formulated,[62] namely, that the bearer of the kingly office is the elect of Yahweh. This sacral conception so outweighs interpretations in terms of realistic politics that the latter hardly count at all.

In fact, a secular monarchy without sacral sanction would have been impossible, and all attempts in this direction failed. The tyranny of Abimelech (Ju. 9:1-6) could not establish its authority in spite of the election in Shechem.[63] Eshbaal, who was made king as a successful soldier (2 S. 2:8 f.), remained an unfortunate minor figure; we never hear of his anointing. Adonijah's failure was decided the moment Solomon was anointed before him (1 K. 1:38 ff.).

The narrative of 1 S. 10:17 ff. tries to depict the irrational process of the choice of a king by God. The tribes were summoned to Mizpah and there they "asked" (v. 22: וַיִּשְׁאֲלוּ־עוֹד) for His decision. The lot was cast (נִלְכַּד) and in this way it was learned which was the tribe, family and individual whom Yahweh had elected (v. 24). There is no question of any act of will on the part of the assembly. Its role is purely passive. God elects in its place and from within it.[64]

The historical value of this account is hard to estimate, since it seems to be more or less superfluous in view of the accompanying story (c. 10) of the victory over the Ammonites and the consequent elevation of Saul to be king. Yet if one notes the role of Samuel in the events described, one will probably conclude that there is a historical basis in the fact that nabiism, in this case represented by

---

60 Hosea's sharp words (7:3; 8:4; 10:3; 13:10 f.) refer more to actual abuses than to the monarchy as such. More radical is the lesson of the fable of Jotham (Ju. 9:8-15): Only a bramble becomes king.

61 There is a polemical formulation in the words of Gideon in Ju. 8:23: "The Lord shall rule over you," and a dogmatic formulation in the leading motif of the so-called enthronement psalms: "The Lord has become king" (Ps. 93:1 etc.).

62 The use of בְּחִיר יְהוָה with ref. to Saul in 2 S. 21:6 is of value only as testimony to the view of the writer, cf. BHK, *ad loc.*; in Ps. 89:4 the LXX reads בְּחִירַי as a plur.

64 The form of rule corresponds to the αἱρετὴ τυραννίς which the Gks. call αἰσυμνητεία, cf. Aristot. Pol., III, 15, p. 1285b, 25 f.

64 In fact it might be argued that the divine choice is a ratification of the political decision of men. An instructive example is that of Thotmes III, who supported his claim to the throne by a declaration of the god Amun, cf. J. H. Breasted, *History of Egypt* (Germ. 1936, p. 175). Comparable is the case of a Nubian king who, at the demand of the army, was elected by Amun as described on a royal election stele from Napata (6th cent., cf. H. Gressmann, AOT, 100 f.). As in 1 S. 16:1 ff., brothers are put forward for election, and God designates one of them. Cf. G. Hoffmann-H. Gressmann, "Teraphim," ZAW, 40 (1922), 110 ff. On the other hand, the casting of lots on the installation of the yearly archon in Assyria (B. Meissner, *Bab. u. Ass.* II [1925], 275; H. Zimmern, KAT, 518) is no true analogy, since it does not relate to the finding of the official.

Samuel,[65] gave dominant and emphatic support to the view that the king is instituted by God,[66] with the apparent result that the popular choice came to be regularly confirmed by the word of a nabi accompanying the anointing.[67]

The initiative of nabiism also offers a certain guarantee that the ideology of election had its root in the power of the experience of an act of Yahweh which leaves little or no opportunity for the development of mythical ideas. One might, of course, adduce the frequently denounced copying of foreign models (1 S. 8:5) and say that this also applied to expression of the thought of election. But the decorative rigidity with which this appears in, e.g., the political ideology of Egypt[68] is hardly comparable with the great emotional power with which the religion of Yahweh gripped the nation. When the principles of government of greater states had been introduced into the united kingdoms of Israel and Judah this analogy, and the idea of divine sonship, perhaps received some stress in courtly address, though there is no direct attestation of this (1 Ch. 28:6 ?). But the relation of בחר to mythical thinking is only free and formal.[69] Furthermore, belief in a divine ordination demonstrated in *charismata* of leadership had already been a live one in the days of the Judges,[70] and it is certainly older than the use of the concept of election for it. The traditional term for the divine appointment of a ruler, and perhaps one of the oldest of all the words which gives formal shape to the thought of the divine direction of the people's destiny, seems to be נָגִיד, which is used both pass. and act., and for which "prince" or "leader" is not a wholly adequate translation.[71] The נָגִיד possesses a gift which men can only acknowledge, not impart. Hence the point of the account of Saul's anointing as נָגִיד (1 S. 10:1) in the complex of stories about the rise of the monarchy, which is built up from very different traditions, is to make it clear to the reader that Saul is already selected by Yahweh even when he takes up the struggle against the Amalekites,[72] though doubts may arise as to the exact historicity of the secret anointing. Saul was victor in the conflict because he was נָגִיד, and the army's approval of the one shown to be נָגִיד by this act of deliverance is his nomination as king.[73]

---

[65] Whether Samuel was a nabi is another question, cf. A. Jepsen, *Nabi* (1934), 99 ff.

[66] Cf. also the divine sayings in 2 S. 3:18; 5:2.

[67] Cf. esp. Neh. 6:7, and on this Jepsen, 176 f.; also O. Procksch, *König u. Prophet in Israel* (1924), 6 f.

[68] In full style Egyptian kings are more often called "son of Re" than "elect of Re" (*śtp n r'*, Akkad. *šatip na ria*, Gk. ὃν ἐδοκίμασεν or προέκρινεν), cf. the first name of Ramses II (F. Bilabel, *Gesch. Vorderasiens u. Ägyptens* [1927], 107) and A. Erman-H. Grapow, *Wörterbuch d. ägypt. Sprache*, 4 (1930), 337 f. under *śtp*.

[69] The expression takes mythological form in the Canon in the expressions which Is. uses of the call of Cyrus by Yahweh (Is. 44:28 ff.): Yahweh takes his right hand, opens doors before him, precedes him. The premisses of this type of expression are not to be found in belief in Yahweh, but in the so-called courtly style adopted by Dt. Is., cf. H. Gressmann, *Der Messias* (1929), 59 ff.

[70] They are divinely sent helpers (מוֹשִׁיעַ), 2 K. 13:5; Is. 19:20, → σωτήρ.

[71] A. Alt, *Staatenbildung*, 29, n. 1 regards the *nagīd* as the one "declared" by God ("raised up" acc. to Wendel, *op. cit.*, 152). On the linguistic form cf. J. Barth, *Die Nominalbildung in den semit. Sprachen*, I (1889), 161 f. The secular counterpart seems to be *nasi'* (Ezr. 1:8 etc.), which is used in Gn. 34:2 for a city prince. Wendel, 184 ff. believes that the word is originally sacral.

[72] Cf. the view of 1 S. 16:1 ff. that David is chosen by God before all the mighty deeds which distinguish him, while his brothers are set aside (מאס, v. 7). The Egyptian text mentioned in → n. 64 should be compared with this scene.

[73] 1 S. 11:15 : וַיַּמְלִכוּ. The LXX is materially correct when it adds καὶ ἔχρισεν Σαμουήλ. The editorial verses 12-14 dubiously call this a renewal of the monarchy in an attempt to forge an inner link with 1 S. 10:19 ff.

In this development one may see the element of truth which underlies the consideration that choice of a king cannot be a purely human affair. The law of the monarchy in Dt. 17:14-20 distinguishes between institution (שׂים, v. 15) and election; the one is done by men, the other by God. [74] Only sarcastically are the roles interchanged, as in 1 S. 12:13: "Behold the king whom ye have chosen." [75] If it may thus be said in Ps. 89:19 that one chosen out of the people is exalted by God, this may be historically correct and politically unobjectionable, but it is not a view which is inspired by undivided sympathy for the monarchy as an instrument of God. This should be concerned to lay the whole emphasis, as regards the institution of the ruler and the monarchical form of government, quite unequivocally on the divine decision. A stronger expression, though not quite precise enough, is to be found in the statement which is no doubt flattery in relation to the usurper Absalom, but which for this very reason keeps to the proper form: The king "whom Yahweh, and this people, and all the men of Israel, choose" (2 S. 16:18). According to theocratic theory, the people does not choose; it simply ratifies. This custom established itself in Judah with the establishment of the Davidic dynasty; [76] it is also seen in Israel in the case of Jehu (2 K. 10:5). Yahweh alone appoints; the anointing is sacral ratification of the divine choice. This is the view of Chronicles, [77] though here the rather different concept of divine sonship (→ πατήρ) is intermingled with that of election in a way which stylistically is open to criticism (1 Ch. 28:6: "For I have chosen him to be my son").

7. The Election of the People.

a. From the ideology of kingship the term בחר seems to have passed over to that of nationhood. Dt. here seems to have been the first work to give a strict and precise meaning to the nation and its history, and to express this in the succinct form of an article of faith: "The Lord hath chosen thee for himself as a possession out of all the nations that are upon the earth" (Dt. 14:2).

Nevertheless, the idea behind this precise formulation of the concept of election was a vital one from the very beginning of the nation's existence as the "people of Yahweh" (Ju. 5:11). Only the term election was needed to give the idea its significance from the standpoint of salvation history. On the basis of the Gn. tradition it seems to be likely enough that the idea had already given a distinctive impress to the forms of patriarchal religion. [78] It certainly bears testimony to the spiritual outlook which characterises all the impulses in the national life of Israel from an early period, and which is usually described as the belief in election in the broader sense. Without any essential restriction of content one might describe this in secular terms as a sense of nationality [79] originating in, and

---

[74] It may be asked, however, whether the words in v. 15: אֲשֶׁר יִבְחַר יְהוָה אֱלֹהֶיךָ בּוֹ are not an expansion. No gap arises if they are omitted; indeed, the permissive "thou shalt set a king over thee" becomes a stronger authorisation.

[75] Worth noting is the softening "and whom ye have desired."

[76] 2 K. 11:12; 14:21; 21:24; 23:30; cf. also → n. 55.

[77] 1 Ch. 11:1-3 gives stronger emphasis than 2 S. 2:1-4 to the role of the prophet in the appointment of David.

[78] Cf. A. Alt, *Der Gott der Väter* (1929), 68 ff.; also → 171.

[79] Cf. on this concept E. Meyer, *Gesch. d. Altertums,* I, 1^5 (1925), 79: "Only very gradually, in the course of historical development, does there arise, at first half-consciously,

strengthened by, a legacy of common experience.[80] The obvious and exemplary significance of the national history of Israel is to be found in the fact that it offers us adequate source material from which to observe the operation of national forces in close concentration.[81] If one asks concerning the spiritual presuppositions of this operation, it is evident that a rare and happy blend of religion and nationality made the concentration possible. From the days of Moses belief in God was the impulse behind the deployment of national powers and the constructive principle in their development. This was the foundation and guarantee of national unity even when it did not exist politically (Jer. 31:10). Later ages confess it with the same bitter pride as the fathers: "For all people will walk every one in the name of his god, and we will walk in the name of the Lord our God for ever and ever" (Mi. 4:5).[82] In the days of the wars of Yahweh the interrelations of gods were regulated by the solution of political conflicts,[83] and when Yahweh gave the peoples of Canaan into the hands of His people He acted in undisputed sovereignty, even though the same might be said of Chemosh, the god of the Moabites, when he caused them to see a triumph over all who hated them.[84] This sense of the supremacy of God was closely linked with the power of the nation, and this in turn with the loyalty to God which gave it a readiness to venture. Those who love God are like the rising sun in strength (Ju. 5:31). With this pride in the wars of Yahweh poets also fashioned the imperishable symbol of national power, the lion which rises up certain of its prey.[85] A saying of such prophetic richness as that of Balaam: "The people shall dwell alone, and shall not be reckoned among the nations" (Nu. 23:9), also expresses with innocent purity the guiding motif of the national history, and in the depth of its vision it enables us to discern the original basis of election, namely, recognition of the unique and imperishable meaning of the history of the people of Yahweh among the nations. A confession like this, which is not hampered by reflection but vitally sustained by a powerful experience, leaves an impression of the strength of the feelings which underlie the concept of national election and which thereby exercise a fruitful influence on thinking in terms of salvation history.

For the idea of the people of God obviously cannot have great theological value apart from an adequate concept of God. In essence, what we see in the early period is still a form of religion which according to prophetic insight is not able to bear the weight of an omnipotent divine will or to measure up to the responsibility implicit in the national history. The shaping of this vigorous and proud idea into the religious dogma of the election of the people under the leader chosen by Yahweh had to come with almost logical necessity as the faith of the

---

a sense of close relationship, an idea of national unity. The supreme climax, the idea of nationality itself, is the most delicate and complicated structure which historical development can fashion; it translates actual unity into a conscious, active and constructive will to present a specific unity distinct from all other groups and to put this into effect."

[80] J. Burckhardt, *Weltgeschichtliche Betrachtungen* (Kröner-Ausgabe [1935]), 25.

[81] Cf. G. van der Leeuw, *Phänomenologie d. Religion* (1933), 250: "The Jewish people is the first historical example of a nation. The other peoples of antiquity are either tribes or empires."

[82] It is sometimes thought that this statement is an addition of the redactor.

[83] Ju. 11:23; Nu. 21:29.

[84] Mesha-stele, line 4: הראני בכל שנאי; cf. also the word רית = רְאִיַת on line 12, and the expression in Ps. 118:7. 2 K. 18:25 is ironical.

[85] Nu. 23:24; with ref. to Judah Gn. 49:9.

people of Yahweh faced with increasing urgency the task of maintaining itself among alien cultures and their resources, and as in the course of the prophetic movement it began to accept the insight of the omnipotence of its God.

b. The historically necessary encounter between nationality and the belief in a universal God produced the statement on election which we find, e.g., in Dt., by posing afresh the meaning of this nation living under the saving promise of Yahweh within the experience of the world which it gained in political life and which far surpassed the measure of its earlier insights. The fact that Yahweh spoke with Israel and entered into covenant with it was regarded as the decision of His will. From all the nations He chose Israel to lead it through history as His own possession. Why did He do this? To what end? How can such a stupendous statement be proved? What value will a proof have, no matter what it may be?

The multiplicity and breadth of the statement of election led in Israel's spiritual history to conflicts which are unique in reality and severity, which lay bare the polar forces in human existence, and to which virtually the whole of prophetic literature owes its existence. In the struggle to shape historical destiny there is a clash between self-awareness in its most vital form as the living will of the people and faith in God as unconditional commitment to the ethical. With material urgency the course of the conflict poses for every observer the question of the truth or falsity of the divine message.

c. In the four centuries of political life between the rise of Saul and the reforms of Josiah and beyond, the harmonious unity of religion and nationality underwent severe crises and was finally broken. If faith in God had begun to learn from the prophetic message to escape the dominant influence of national forces and to perceive its absolute obligation, nationality for its part proved to be not yet sufficiently advanced to accept the reduction of its value as a norm and to make this serve the development of the nation. In Israel even more than Judah a religiously impregnated nationalism was fostered which thought it could evade the unconditional authority of the norms of the divine will and safeguard itself by a strongly cultic understanding of the divine presence, supported by popular prophecies of salvation: "Is not Yahweh among us? No evil can come upon us" (Mi. 3:11). This belief, which finds powerful expression in hymns about Zion (cf. Ps. 46), is too exclusively orientated to political self-preservation not to fall into the danger of being blind to inner crises and moral problems. "God is with us," [86] "we are secure" (Jer. 5:12; 7:4, 10) — these are the weighty slogans with which every prophet of disaster is successfully combatted. The cry is "peace, peace" when there is no peace (Mi. 3:5, 11; Jer. 6:14; 8:11; Ez. 13:10, 16), but only disaster except in the balance of the great powers. [87] Already in the 8th cen-

---

[86] Immanuel is found in Is. 8:10, and a similar form in Am. 5:14, as a theopolitical watchword, and it seems to have been taken up in Is. 7:14 as a symbolical name for the Messiah. The words seem to have penetrated into Is. 8:8 only by dittography from v. 10; possibly the scribe or redactor, but not the author, regarded them as a conclusion to the threat of vv. 6-8 ("Yes, this is Immanuel," Galling, *op. cit.*, p. 80).

[87] In Amos (6:1) the "proud in Zion" are mentioned as well as the "secure on the hill of Samaria." Amos is thus speaking of Greater Israel, as Galling (p. 68) calls the ideal denominator of the national sense of election. Yet the difficulties in this view suggest that

tury unassailable pride had arrogated to itself the proud title of "first of the nations"[88] which had once been the challenging expression of a sovereign nomadic group (Nu. 24:20), and which summed up the sense of strength in an age of political power. "From the road of Hamath to the Araba"[89] was the watchword of national assertion, reflecting the pride of victory.

d. This sense represented a spiritual power, the inner force of the nation. It had found the most noble form. But at this very point there then came the prophetic message with the reproving question of God to the "first of the nations": "Are you better than Calneh, Hamath or Gath?" and with the warning: "I will raise up against you a nation that shall cause you to go from the road of Hamath to the Araba."[90] This makes it plain that in spite of political success there has been a denial of nationality that makes all pride illusory.

This is the situation in which for the first time Amos introduced the concept of election into the prophetic message. In negative rather than positive terms, he brings out its meaning with classical pregnancy: "You only have I known of all the families of the earth: therefore I will punish you for all your iniquities" (Am. 3:2).[91] Divine election does not mean dominion or primacy. Though he does not formulate the concept, Amos sees in the fact of the revelation of Yahweh a very different meaning. The exodus, deliverance from a hopeless situation, is not for him an experience from which to derive a claim to precedence over the nations. As he says in reproof (9:7), the Philistines or Aramaeans could draw similar conclusions in their own favour, since their history, too, stands under the direction of the Almighty. "Have not I brought up ... the Philistines from Crete and the Aramaeans from Kir? Are not the Ethiopians as dear to me as the children of Israel?" More important than the exodus is the fact that in this people God has raised up men to proclaim His will and to summon to right and righteousness, to life in obedience to God. It is thus that He has known Israel more than all nations. Because He has done this, or, in Deuteronomic terms, chosen it out of the nations, He sees its every fault. "I scrutinise you more closely than any nation on earth," is the sense. God's work in relation to Israel is to examine its life. The task of those whom He knows is to stand up under His searching gaze, to keep the faith which is demanded, to live before the nations as one ought to live in righteousness and truth. "Prepare to meet thy God" (Am. 4:12). What interest has God in

we should also consider the rendering of A. Weiser, *Die Prophetie des Amos* (1929), 229 f.: "Woe to those who are proud on Zion and trust in the hill of Samaria." This gives us a more concrete picture of the situation.

[88] Am. 6:1. That the term refers to rank or quality rather than age is evident from analogies like ר׳ שְׁמָנִים (6:6) "best ointment" or ר׳ הָאָרֶץ "best land" (Ez. 48:14; Dt. 33:21). Jer. 2:3 ("Israel is holy to Yahweh, the best of his harvest") seems to be a similar slogan; the introduction of the cultic sense of the term is a variation.

[89] Am. 6:14; cf. 2 K. 14:25; Ez. 6:14. Another catchword to express the idea of Greater Israel is perhaps to be seen in "from Dan to Beersheba" (Ju. 20:1; 1 S. 3:20; 2 S. 17:11). Possibly the same stylistic form occurs in Am. 8:14.

[90] Acc. to Weiser (*loc. cit.*) the order should be Am. 6:1, 13, 2, 3, 14.

[91] On the construction → n. 9. In secular use פקד is the activity of the official who demands an account, the פָּקִיד (Gn. 41:34; Ju. 9:28), or the military commander at a review (1 S. 11:8; 2 S. 18:1 etc.). Amos uses it as an intensive form of ידע, which thus includes פקד and like it presupposes obligation. For the language of prayer, cf. Ps. 17:3.

Israel's greatness? one might ask. His whole concern is with righteousness and fidelity. The only point of His fellowship with Israel is that of all fellowship: Faithfulness for faithfulness' sake.

e. Dt. established the concept of election in the sense of the designation of Israel as the people of God.[92] It is here distinctively accompanied by an interpretation from which one may perhaps conclude that the term was already current and stood in danger of a restriction of meaning. In Dt. 7:6, in a context which makes a duty of strict exclusiveness in relation to the seven nations of the land, which are "greater and mighter than thou," a statement is made which is the basis of this duty: "For thou art a people, holy for Yahweh, thy God: Yahweh, thy God, hath chosen thee to be a people for him as a possession out of all peoples." This is the fundamental saying which is plainly (כִּי) meant to bring out sharply the duty of drawing the practical consequences of the confession of faith. It is followed at once by an explanatory analysis: "Not because ye were more in number than any people did Yahweh take you in his arms (חשק) and elect you, for ye were the fewest of all people. But because Yahweh loveth you, and keepeth the oath which he hath sworn to your fathers, he hath led you out with a mighty hand, and redeemed you out of the house of slaves, out of the power of Pharaoh king of Egypt. Thou shalt know, therefore, that thy God Yahweh is God, the true God, who keepeth the covenant of faithfulness with those who love him and live according to his commandments ..." The patriarchal history was itself a proof (Dt. 4:37; 10:15) of the love of God working itself out in the election of the children.

The strength, theological value, and didactic fruitfulness of the concept derive from the unique blending of rational and demonstrable thought with the suprarational certainty of faith, from the taking up of concrete history into the sphere of experience of God. It is hereby shown to be of universal and not just national and restricted validity. In the basic statement the rational colouring of the content is surprisingly strong. The statement rests on theological reflection, on meditation on the suprarational. Conceptual analysis is thus easy and illuminating, so that one may well say that next to the legally rooted idea of the covenant no statement of faith in the OT is logically clearer or theologically more fruitful than that of election. It offers a plastic, yet also a sure and bold characterisation of the divine action in revelation, an objective statement concerning a process in the divine psyche which certainly cannot be fathomed by man's understanding but which can be fully grasped in its actual outworking in the inner and outer life of the divine community. There are, of course, no evident reasons why Israel should be the people of God or why a power which bursts all human restrictions should develop in those who proclaim and fulfil the divine will. But the statement of faith declares how this came to pass with its assertion of God's election. "I have chosen thee, and not rejected thee" (Is. 41:9). Love and faithfulness, it is added, determine the divine choice.

f. But this objective character also determines the double nature of the concept, which in its use both inside and outside the OT is worked out now on the one side

[92] If the place in which Yahweh causes His name to dwell (Dt. 12:14 etc.; 14:23; 15:20 etc.) is also called elect, the idea is an adaptation to traditional cultic ideology and its expression is more rigid and less open to development in cultic phraseology. On these expressions → Staerk, 15 ff.

and now on the other. From one standpoint, it is a useful instrument to show the particular status of the elect, and Dt. is obviously concerned to define this correctly as a task, and thus to exclude from the concept the element of placid security. Election establishes an authority which must be regarded by the people of God and which will bring its moral powers into play: "Thou art a people, holy for Yahweh, thy God." To be apprehended by God, to be drawn into His sphere, can only mean to be at the service of His purposes. From the second standpoint, the problem of the history of God with man is disclosed with unrestricted totality, and the question as to the meaning of the decision taken in God's election is tacitly abandoned. The nations, all the nations according to the express emphasis, stand in the circle of the speaker's view. No longer do we have a narrow national religion which only eclectically takes note of one or another nation. Something of Amos and Isaiah may be seen in this breadth of outlook. We find a view of man similar also to that taught in the pre-history of Gn. The Lord of the earth makes His will known in a historical process and an immanent development which is clear enough at specific points. The concept of election thus underlies and sustains the idea of universal salvation history, i.e., history as the place of God's revelation. An action such as man usually performs, the free resolve of the will in a concrete case, is ascribed to God, and thereby God's being in its living, concrete relation to the world is outlined with a precision which rules out all chance of misunderstanding who God is, and which emphatically refers religion to history: there are the signs of God's activity and the norm of His will. God lays hold of a "possession" in the world (Ex. 19:5).

g. But the problem of the Gentiles also arises the moment the divine revelation ceases to be a purely internal concern of the Israelite groups and the God who chooses out of and rules over all the nations is known. Negatively, electing means rejecting (מאס). The nations did not experience what Israel experienced. In the days of Israel's consolidation as the people of Yahweh they were enmeshed in cultic religions to varying degrees. "Thou shalt destroy their altars, break down their images, cut down their sacred trees, and burn their graven images with fire" (Dt. 7:5, 25). In the form of a demand for action a judgment on Gentile religions is thus pronounced. This is inevitable in the light of the thought of election and the movement to total faith in God. The gulf is obvious. There can be no fellowship between the God of gods and idolatry. If this seems fanatical, [93] the exhortation of Dt. 4:19 is also concerned with the problem of the Gentiles even though it has a superior conception of the legacy of faith. Israel is forbidden to worship the stars, for Yahweh has allotted them to the Gentiles, but "Yahweh hath taken you ... out of the iron furnace ... to be unto him a people" (v. 20). With respectful tenderness, and no blustering polemic, the view of the divine which characterises the nature religions is woven into the universal concept of God. Whether the stars be gods or not, they are not the Lord of the world. All nations

[93] Animosity against the Gentile world more often led to outbreaks of national hate after the downfall of the state and in the age of humble suffering, Ps. 137:7 ff.; Is. 19:17. The insight that unrestricted nationalism can awaken hatred just as much as love is more keenly and demonically attested in passages dominated by the glow of faith and the motifs of ancient military poetry (Ju. 5:31) than in the sources of secular history. This is a factor which often clouds the theological clarity of the biblical concept of election, so that it is often regarded as a historically conditioned idea rather than a constructive force in interpretation of a national history which ended in sombre tragedy.

are responsible to Him. It would be unworthy to try to press this thought theoretically. It is wholly emotional. Be concerned for what you have experienced. Wherever it leads, militantly maintain the covenant faithfulness which you have sworn. The history of revelation is always present history. "The Lord made not this covenant with our fathers, but with us, even us, who are all of us here alive this day" (Dt. 5:2 f.).

Anger at heathenism is caused by recognition that the life of heathen does not correspond to the norm of God, since it gives evidence of cults and customs which are unworthy of man. Thus Dt. 9:5 refers frankly to the wickedness on account of which Israel must avoid pagan nations.[94] In the very same breath, however, there is a warning against arrogance: "Think not, when thy God doth chase them out before thee, that it is for the uprightness of thine heart. Remember, and forget not, that thou hast provoked thy God to wrath." Hence one cannot argue that chauvinism is the real substance of this view. The point of this explicit presentation is indeed to keep this out of the belief in election, to lift the belief above the emotionalism of national feeling, to make it serve the fruitful observance of the demands of the covenant.[95]

h. Also of far-reaching significance, however, is the attempt, consonant with the pedagogic tendencies, to protect the total thought of the book against rigidity, and to make it vital and fruitful, by incorporating an element of emotion in the form of the love of God. It is because the God of the world loved you that He elected you. The sober thought of mystery is linked with this. It would be obviously arbitrary to draw out the opposite implication that He did not love the nations. For the reference is not to the nations. It is to the fact that He spoke with Israel. The basis of love is not a logical basis. It is the admission, proceeding from the strongest possible feeling, that the election is an inexplicable fact. In so far as it can be explained and interpreted, this can be only in terms of its factuality, not of the motives, as a comprehensive explanation would demand. Instructive at this point is the attempt of the author to show formally that there could be no question of God being controlled by a motive for taking Israel out of the nations which could be justified on logical grounds or reached by logical examination. Neither imposing greatness or power (7:7), nor uprightness and purity (9:5), can have impressed Him, since this tiny and wayward people does not possess either of these two characteristics (9:6). The people has to be formally urged to accept the gift of love,[96] and the nations are astonished at the gift (4:6 ff.).

---

94 The main ref., of course, is to unbridled sexuality in worship and life, Gn. 9:20 ff.; 19:30 ff.; Nu. 25:1 ff. But Is. (7:10 ff.) already has in view as well the destructive imperialistic illusions of the large states, and the prophecies in Jer. 46-51 are to be set against the background of terrible experience.

95 That the belief in election establishes a claim which is prejudicial to the nations is an idea found even in so sober an author as R. Smend, *Lehrbuch d. at.lichen Relgesch.*[2] (1893), 294; 364. But those who begin to think along these lines will soon begin to see themselves threatened everywhere, and there will be continual charges of misanthropy where exclusive tendencies appear, even in the secular field. → II, 371 f. (ἔθνος), I, 546 ff. (βάρβαρος); Gn. 43:32; Ex. 8:22. The term תּוֹעֵבָה "abomination" is derogatory only where its ritual basis is misunderstood and where it is forgotten that religious feelings are not subject to human codes of honour.

96 Hos. 2:18. → I, 31 f. (ἀγάπη).

i. Closely connected with this is the thought of education. "Know in thy heart that thy God will bring thee up as a man brings up his son (יסר pi)," Dt. 8:5. Hence God's action in election is seen to be meaningful and purposeful. Israel is to become something which it is to be according to God's will.[97] This thought, which is understood quite esoterically, is so predominant in Dt. that it crowds out the different and wholly irrational thought of love beyond measure. Education is introduced and claims all our attention. Nevertheless, the reader perceives the primitive force behind the whole work of education. Because the process of election is wholly concentrated in the person, indeed, the emotion of God, it has a full share in the riddle of all personal feeling. Wherever it occurs, it thus dispays an irrational distinctiveness which cannot be mastered theologically. Interpretation cannot be guided by purely rational lines of thought. This process is not just a product of theological meditation. It rests in mystery. The unique intertwining of theology and faith, interpretation and mystery, invests all the statements which express belief in election with a distinctive charm and great didactic value.

k. The idyllically presented traditions concerning the God of the fathers in the Genesis sagas bring the early period, too, within the compass of the belief in election. God caused the people to come into being out of one family. The sons of Abraham are to be as numerous as the stars of heaven, as is said with figurative hyperbole and in terms of a specific view of blessing. In this fulness they are to bring blessing, i.e., the fulfilment of life, salvation, and fortune to all the nations of earth (Gn. 22:18; 26:4). This will come to pass because Abraham, the servant of God (26:24), in obedience and trust and against every consideration and custom, followed God's call to the unknown. With all the means at his command the author tries to make the reader aware of the irrationality of this promise given to an alien with no status in a foreign land. The wife of the alien can be taken from him just because she is beautiful. Serious crises arise. Finally, his wife is barren, both are old, and they have no son. The saying about blessing to all nations seems to be a subject for laughter (צחק), 18:11 f. But for all the dubious and all too human elements,[98] we suddenly come on the statement that Abraham believed (15:6). Crisis then follows crisis up to the journey to Egypt. In the whole account there are rational elements as well as numinous. The simple believer cannot help enquiring into the divine motives. For him the obedience of Abraham explains the miraculous direction of the destinies of the patriarchs. God acknowledges the faith of Abraham: "He imputed it to him" (15:6). Even where this motivation is not present (18:19), and the numinous mystery of the "knowing" of Abraham is not prejudiced by subsidiary ideas, there may be seen an aetiological purpose. Why is the way of Yahweh traditionally the way of salvation for the people? (Jer. 5:4). Because already by Abram God willed to lead, and did lead, to righteousness and judgment (Is. 51:2; Neh. 9:7).

---

[97] G. E. Lessing, *Die Erziehung des Menschengeschlechts* (1780), § 8 displays a keen and accurate awareness of the normative significance of Dt. 8:5 for the orientation which was given to the whole OT Canon by those who collected and edited it.

[98] In the acute crisis of existence ethical norms yield to necessity; cleverness is what counts, stupidity is a crime. The authenticity of the presentation may refresh one reader, but it can also disturb another. The redactors knew very well what they were doing, and tried to purify the realism, cf. the climax in the stories of the threat to Sarah, Gn. 12;20; 26. Their concern, however, was to set man and God in contrast.

l. The idea of election is thus illustrated in the material of colourful popular saga, as the construction and harmony of the individual stories shows. This being so, the national element is very strong in the concept of election, and for this reason it is the more difficult to achieve a productive understanding both of the sagas and the concept. This difficulty is an expression of the fact that insight into the meaning of the national history, which the concept was at hand to mediate, was attained only by a long process. The idea of prerogative was present in national religion before this came into collision with prophetic preaching, and was vanquished by the prophetic interpretation. The differences between the older popular and the newer prophetic belief in election are so great that one may say with truth that the OT reader can watch a battle of the belief in election against the belief in election.[99] Dramatic examples are the encounter between the prophet Amos and the priest Amaziah in the state sanctuary at Bethel (Am. 7:10 ff.), the temple sermon of Jeremiah (Jer. 7:26), Jeremiah's conflict with Hananiah, the prophet of salvation (Jer. 28), and especially the tumultuous trial for treason which Jeremiah had to suffer in the last days of Judah's political independence (Jer. 37 f.). In all these cases it is only too easy to condemn the antagonists of the prophets, as though it were a simple matter to subjugate national pride to obedience to God, as was demanded even in the most critical situation. With their politically orientated belief in election these men could not understand that Yahweh would deliver back to shameful slavery the people which He had brought out of the house of bondage and established as a nation. How could He allow His safe stronghold to fall? They thus defended Zion and freedom to the last ditch against the superior power which threatened them. Yahweh was for them a πολιοῦχος, as He was for many after them right up to John of Gischala, the last defender of the sanctuary against the Roman legions. They represented the withering shoot of a powerful spiritual history filled by the battle for the truth of election, which lasts well beyond the OT. In many cases, and as a whole, their action presents a tragic picture of human greatness though one may also discern features of a demonism in which in no salvation.

m. The other shoot, weak and sparse in its human representation, though strong and fruitful in its fulness of spiritual content, has remained alive in the history of the Bible right up to our own day. The unique combination of particularism and universalism in the belief in election, the insight that the God who chose a small national community because He loved it is God in the true sense as the Holy One and the Lord, is developed with increasing clarity in exilic prophecy to the point where the nations who do not yet know Him will learn to do so. If election had for Amos a particular purpose (→ 162), this is now the purpose. The elect people and its heralds are witnesses. "Ye are my witnesses, saith Yahweh, and my servant whom I have chosen, that they may know and believe in me and understand that I am he" (Is. 43:10). To what are they to bear witness? We simply have the brief and clear-cut statement אֲנִי הוּא "I am he." This is the whole truth which the servant of 42:1 is to take to the Gentiles, the teaching for which the isles are waiting. Now there are also national features in this prophecy. Israel is to be restored.[100] But this takes place in order that all nations may take note

---

[99] P. Volz, *Deutsches Pfarrerblatt*, 37 (1936), 213 ff.

[100] A note of lordship may also be heard, e.g., in Is. 49:22 f.; 60:10 ff. The poem in Joel 2:28 ff., a variation on Is. 44:1-5 (→ n. 42), is also, with its attempted transformation into

and not be blind and deaf as this people has been in its variable history. A light to the Gentiles (49:6) is to shine forth from this history. This development of the belief in election into the concept of witness to the truth of God is to be regarded as the consummation of the OT message of salvation. It is the surest and boldest interpretation of the historical experience of God to be found in the whole history of religion, and it grows with almost logical necessity out of the story of almost a thousand years of spiritual conflict. If divine providence now seems to be an almost self-evident rational truth, there can be no doubt that it has become so under the influence of biblical proclamation. For all the prophets became, like Jeremiah (1:5), prophets to the nations, and the chosen witness carried the truth to the nations even in perishing. The question arises: Was he also elected to do this? The one thing which remains vital in the OT concept of election is the element of the mysterious and the inexplicable which Dt. expresses in the words: "He has loved you." The universal power of God was seen in this mystery. Experience of the absolute derived from it. "The nations shall walk in thy light" (Is. 60:3).

Quell

C. ἐκλέγομαι in the LXX and the Jewish Hellenistic Writings.

1. General. In the LXX ἐκλέγεσθαι in the sense of "to select," "to elect," is used with the gen., 2 Ch. 6:38: τῆς πόλεως ἧς ἐξελέξω, cf. Gn. 6:2, more rarely the dat., ψ 24(25):12 'A: ἐν ὁδῷ ᾗ ἐκλέξεται, but usually the acc., e.g., Nu. 16:7; Job 15:5 Σ; Is. 7:16: ἐκλέξασθαι τὸ ἀγαθόν. Often we find ἐν, sometimes with the acc., 'Ιερ. 40:24 Θ; 2 Ch. 6:34, though also without it, 1 Βασ. 16:9; 3 Βασ. 8:16. This corresponds to the Heb. בחר ב.[101] Cf. Test. R. 6:11.[102] The mid. use often has an emphatic ἑαυτῷ, ἑαυτοῖς, Gn. 13:11; 1 Βασ. 17:8; ψ 134:4; Test. L. 19:1. Cf. Damasc. 7:16. To emphasise the element of preferring one above others ὑπέρ with acc. is used, 2 Βασ. 6:21; cf. Test. Jud. 21:5. Relation to the available mass from which selection is made can also be denoted by ἐκ, 1 Βασ. 13:2 B; 1 Ch. 19:10, or ἀπό, Dt. 14:2; 1 Ch. 28:5; Sir. 45:16; Tob. 1:4. The gen. is very occasionally used alone, 1 Macc. 11:23 S † (here as in 1 Macc. 9:25 the rare ἐκλέγω act.). In Joseph. we find ἐκλέγω only 4 times, ἐκλέγομαι 9 times, but ἐπιλέγω 16 times and ἐπιλέγομαι 12 times, both in the same sense as the combination with ἐκ (→ 182).

2. The Nature of the Selection. It may be a selection from many things, e.g., stone: 1 Βασ. 17:40; wood: Is. 40:20; animals: Ep. Ar., 93, cf. Damasc. 1:14; Jos. Ant., 8, 339; gifts: Ant., 8, 175; a field: Ant., 8, 355, or persons, e.g., in selecting men, 1 Βασ. 13:2 B; 1 Macc. 10:32; Jos. Bell., 2, 588, or, abstractly, from what has been learned: Ep. Ar., 239. Or the selection may be between two or three things: 3 Βασ. 18:23, 25: one of two bullocks, or abstractly life or death (Dt. 30:19), light or darkness, the Law of the Lord or the works of Beliar (Test. L. 19:1). With verb and μᾶλλον ἤ, ψ 83:10. David has a choice of three things in 2 Βασ. 24:12; Jos. Ant., 7, 321, and he selects pestilence rather than famine or war.

---

the great motif of "all flesh," a characteristic illustration of the two souls of the people of God. The living strength of the national will often prevents these later messengers from seeing clearly, as Jeremiah and the author of the Ebed songs saw, that their calling is to be prophets for all peoples. Cf. Is. 55:4, where the combination of witness and leader plainly shows how paradoxical the message of a universal God was felt to be. On Da. 7 → σωτήρ.

[101] Cf. the Rabb. par. in Schl. J., 184.

[102] Thus ἐν αὐτῷ does not here mean "in him," in spite of Kautzsch Pseudepigr., *ad loc.*

3. Religious Election in ἐκλέγεσθαι. The most common use in the NT, i.e., for God's ἐκλέγεσθαι, is found in respect of places, individuals or a people consecrated to Him. It presupposes selection from among many, → 168, though this is not always explicitly stated, yet cf. 3 Βασ. 11:32 of Jerusalem: ἣν ἐξελεξάμην ἐν αὐτῇ (→ 168) ἐκ πασῶν φυλῶν Ἰσραήλ, Sir. 45:4, 16 of Moses and Aaron: ἐξελέξατο αὐτὸν ἐκ πάσης σαρκός or ἀπὸ παντὸς ζῶντος, Dt. 7:6 f.; 10:15 of the people: παρὰ πάντα ἔθνη, cf. 14:2: ἀπὸ πάντων τῶν ἐθνῶν.

a. It many cases it may be the choice of places, esp. Jerusalem → *infra*; 4 Βασ. 21:7; 2 Ch. 35:19d; Zech. 2:16 Αλλ etc., cf. 3 Macc. 2:9 in the prayer of the high-priest Simon; Test. L. 10:5; Zeb. 9:8; also the temple as the place of worship, Jos. 9:27; Dt. 12:5-26:2; Neh. 1:9 etc.; cf. 1 Macc. 7:37; 2 Macc. 5:19; Test. L. 15:1.

b. Men are also elected in the sacred history, e.g., Abraham, Neh. 9:7 (= 2 Εσδρ. 19:7), cf. 4 Esr. 3:13; Apc. Abr., 14 (ed. N. Bonwetsch [1897], 25), though Test. N. 8:3 Heb. (p. 242, Charles) says that Abraham chose God, and Gn. r., 44 (27a) in Str.-B., III, 579 that Israel is elected in Abraham; for Moses cf. Sir. 45:4 → *supra*. More often ἐκλέγεσθαι is used of the king whom God or the people has elected, Dt. 17:15; 1 Βασ. 8:18; cf. Saul, 1 Βασ. 10:24; 12:13; David, ψ 77:70; Solomon, Jos. Ant., 7, 372 and Eupolemos in Eus. Praep. Ev., IX, 26. It can also be used of Levi and Aaron, Nu. 17:20 (Mas. 17:5); 1 Βασ. 2:28; ψ 104:26; Sir. 45:16 → *supra*; Test. L. 51, older Gr. Fr. (p. 251, Charles): ἐξελέχθης εἰς ἱεροσύνην ἁγίαν. Of great influence as regards the Messianic application is what is said about the servant in Is. 43:10: ὁ παῖς, ὃν ἐξελεξάμην, which, partly under the influence of Daniel, is worked out apocalyptically in the election of the Son of Man in Eth. En. 46:3; 49:4; 48:6: "The Lord of spirits has chosen him," or: "He is elected by the Lord of spirits according to his good-pleasure," which also means: "He was hidden with him before the world was made, and will be in eternity." Cf. ἐκλεκτός, → 184.

c. The election of the people (→ *supra*) in terms of ἐκλέγεσθαι is given greater attention by the translators, cf. → 183 f. Thus we find ἐξελεξάμην for ᾑρέτισα in ʼΑΣΘ Ez. 20:5, and ἐκλέξεται for the LXX ᾑρετίσατο in ψ 24:12 ʼΑ. Cf. also Prv. 8:9 Σ. Jos. does not use either ἐκλέγω or ἐπιλέγω for the election of the people.

d. Only a minor part is played by rejection or non-election as the opp. of ἐκλέγεσθαι. In Is. 41:9 ἐκλέγεσθαι is the opp. of being despised, and the latter does not apply to Israel. Cf. the interpretation in Gn. r., 44 (27a), Str.-B., III, 579. ψ 77:67 says that God did not choose the tribe of Ephraim, but this simply means that the king is not chosen from this tribe. Cf. Bar. 3:27 of the γίγαντες (Gn. 6:4) whom God has not chosen — οὐδὲ ὁδὸν ἐπιστήμης ἔδωκεν αὐτοῖς. We strike off in a very different direction in a saying like Damasc. 2:6, which reads that God has not elected sinners, → 171.

e. Important in clarification of the concept is the definition of purpose often added with εἴς τι and a ἵνα or inf. This occurs very generally in 1 Esr. 5:1, and more specifically in relation to places and national or cultic officials. Thus Jerusalem and the temple are chosen in order that God's name may dwell there, 3 Βασ. 8:16 (inf.); 1 Macc. 7:37 (inf.); Jub. 32:10; opp. in Apc. Abr. 13, to choose as the habitation of impurity. Again, Jerusalem is chosen in order that the tribes may sacrifice there, Tob. 1:4 (εἰς τό with inf.). God chose David to rule over Israel (τοῦ εἶναι βασιλέα ἐπί), Solomon to sit on the throne of the kingdom (inf.), 1 Ch. 28:4 f. In the case of priests and Levites the purpose is defined in terms of παρεστάναι ἔναντι κυρίου, λειτουργεῖν, εὐλογεῖν, Dt. 18:5 (inf.); 1 Ch. 15:2 (inf.). Cf. 1 Cl., 43, 4 with ἱερατεύειν (εἰς τό with inf.). There is here a link with Jn. (→ 173), and cf. Herm. v., 4, 3, 5: οἱ ἐκλελεγμένοι ὑπὸ τοῦ θεοῦ εἰς ζωὴν αἰώνιον.

f. In addition to the idea of choosing or selecting from a big number, the LXX also uses ἐκλέγεσθαι for the related idea of picking out a few, cf. "to pick out," "to sift," for ברר, Ez. 20:38; Da. 11:35 LXX Θ; Da. 12:10 Θ, along with "to purge," "to purify," → 144. Cf. the trying of the heart by God in Prv. 17:3 א* (Swete), καρδία ἐκλέγεται. In psychological terms we also find the senses: "to be pleased," 2 Βασ. 19:39; Is. 58:5 f., "to decide for something," ψ 118:173 ᾿ΑΘ; Is. 7:15; 56:4. Cf. also the verses which refer to decision between God and idols, Jos. 24:22; Ju. 5:8 B; Is. 41:24. Finally, we find the sense of "determine" in Job 29:25 LXX Θ; cf. 34:33. Cf. ἐκλέξασθαι παιδείαν in Prv. 24:32 (לקח); Sir. 32:14 B², where a decision of will is again in view.

D. The Idea of Election in 1. Apocalyptic and 2. the Damascus Document.

1. Jewish writings, esp. of the Maccabean period, give evidence of an understandable development of the sense of election, which is established in oppression and conflict, in spite of all appearances to the contrary, Jub. 2:20; 15:30; 19:18; 22:9 f. → ἐκλεκτός, 183. Eschatology promotes this sense. For one thing, pressure is adapted to strengthen this comfort as a final core of resistance. But it also fosters the dangerous aspects of the idea, esp. when the better motivation of election in the OT, the concept of mission (→ 167), is submerged in a spirit of revenge and exultation at victory over enemies. In Jub. the focus is the name of Jacob, and here the sense of election as compared with Ishmael or Esau (cf. esp. 15:30; 19:18 f.) rallies opposition in face of the inscrutability of the ways of God and the struggle against all the forces which seek to destroy the Jews. Based on Dt. 7:6 f.; 10:15 the παρὰ πάντα τὰ ἔθνη of Ps. Sol. 9:9 (here used with αἱρετίζω) sets the tone. It is impressive that at the very time when early Christianity uses election in a new universal sense, and even after the disaster of 70 A.D., this Jewish pride in election remains unbroken, S. Bar. 48:20, and this even in terms of merit, namely, that the people is chosen because none is more worthy. The mark of preference and the basis of its highly renowned name is the Law which still dwells in Israel, S. Bar. 48:22, 24. This sense mounts even higher in the battle against gloomy pessimism, 4 Esr. 6:59: "If, however, the world was created for our sake, why do we not hold this world in possession?" In place of the elect temple and city there now comes even more definitely the consolation of hope, 4 Esr. 8:52: "For you paradise is opened, the tree of life is planted, the future world is prepared, blessedness is made ready, the city is built, the home chosen, good works completed, wisdom prepared." This is the selfish view of election projected into the hereafter. The fig. passage 4 Esr. 5:23-27 contrasts the one vine, the one plant, the one lily, the one stream, the one Zion, the one dove, the one sheep, the one people, as sharply as possible with all other peoples. The forms of election are developed by heaping up synonyms. To be elected is to be sought out, selected, called, foreknown, won. There is here a Jewish model or parallel for Paul's use in R. 8 (→ 175). Cf. also 4 Esr. 6:54. How dangerous is this national pride in election, even in the Synagogue, may be seen in Tanch. נשא § 13 (16a, Buber):[103] "The Holy One, blessed be He, has said: In this world I have abhorred all peoples (תיעבתי אותם) because they come from unclean seed (מזרע הטומאה), but I have chosen you because you come from genuine seed" (מזרע אמת). Cf. Tanch. נשא § 7 (252b, Horeb). While Tanch. B speaks of the nations — אומות — Tanch. speaks of non-Jews — נכרים. The contrast is less sharp in Midr. Ps., 2 § 13 (15b): "All nations are subsidiary (טפילין, 'of less account') compared with Israel." This may be seen from the fact that the commandments of circumcision, tassels, phylacteries and boxes on the doorposts are given only to the Jews.[104]

---

[103] Str.-B., III, 141.
[104] Cf. Str.-B., IV, 35 and the par. given there.

2. Also worth noting is the fact that the document of the new covenant in Damascus,[105] which is perhaps to be dated in the Maccabean period, uses election in an even narrower sense. Like ἐκλεκτός (→ 183) in apocalyptic, it expresses the sense of election of the Jewish sect which feels itself to be the remnant or the elite. Cf. also the Mandaean writings, → 185. Acc. to Damasc. 6:2 the sons of Zadok are the elect and are called by names which will last to the end of the days. Acc. to 9:11 B (Charles, II, 817) they are the designated ones for whom (9:43 B) a book of remembrance is written and salvation and righteousness arise. Acc. to 5:6 (cf. v. 7: the priests, Levites and sons of Zadok), as those who cleave fast to Him, they are ordained to eternal life and all the glory of men will be their portion. Here, too, the opposite judgment of reprobation is more strongly individual. Acc. to 2:6 God did not elect sinners from the foundation of the world, but He knew their works even before they were created.[106] This is a new phase in the development of the doctrine among isolated Jewish groups. The one who is faithful to the covenant in the sense of the new, special group is elect; the sinner is non-elect. Already we find traces of specialisation in the sense of selection

[105] On the contested problem of dating cf. the bibl. in RGG, I, 1776.

[106] כי לא בחר אל בהם מקדם עולם ובטרם נוסדן (נוצרו ?) ידע את מעשיהם. The idea represented in the Damascus document that Yahweh created the world for the sake of the righteous but allowed evil and foresaw the deeds of the wicked is one which is often found among the Rabb. Thus creation is described as follows in Pesikt. r., 40 (166, 67a): "When the Holy One, blessed be He, willed the creation of the world, He considered the works of the wicked ..., and willed not to create the world. And again the Holy One, blessed be He, considered the works of the righteous ... and He said, Because of the wicked I do not create the world, but, lo, I do create it (for the sake of the righteous)." Related to this is a haggada of the Amorean Berekiah (*c.* 350), 8 § 4: "When the Holy One, blessed be He, set about to create the first man, He saw that righteous and sinners would both spring from him. He said, If I create him, righteous and wicked will spring from him; if I do not create him, how will the righteous spring from him? What did the Holy One do, blessed be He? He did not consider the way of the wicked (הפליג דרכן שלרשעים מכנגד פניו)... and He created him (the first man)." We should also compare a third haggada attributed to Chaninah (*c.* 225): "When (Yahweh) willed to create the first man, he consulted the ministering angels. He said to them, We will to make a man. They said to Him, What will his nature be? He said to them, Righteous ones will spring from him ... He revealed to them that the righteous would spring from him, but not that the wicked should also spring from him, for if He had revealed to them that the wicked would also spring from him, the measure of righteousness would not have permitted that the first man be created." In Yahweh's plan, however, only the righteous (הצדיקים) have a place. Though the verb בחר is not used, they are the elect. The concept of uprightness has here a very specific sense; the צדיק belongs pre-eminently to the Jewish people (though cf. T. Sanh., 13, 2), and even within the people צדיק is used only of those who have a special inner relation (which the Gentile may also have, bBQ, 38a, par.) to the Law given by Yahweh and interpreted by the Rabbis. The sinner, on the other hand, is the one who stands outside the people (Esau is a prototype), or who, even within the people, does not belong to the fellowship of faith and the Law established by the Rabb., i.e., the *'Am-ha-Arez,* the Sadducee, the Samaritan, the Jewish Christian. The existence of this mass of perdition cannot be denied. On the other hand, Yahweh did not will sin or sinners. It is thus tempting to divide the work of creation as in Plat. Tim., 41d (cf. Philo Conf. Ling., 178 f.). But Rabb. Judaism does not follow this path. It is content with a formal separation between evil and Yahweh, Gn. r., 3 on 1:5: "Never does the Holy One, blessed be He, connect His name with evil, but only with good" (cf. Tanch. תזריע § 12 [40b, Buber]). To save Yahweh's omnipotence, however, this formal separation is not enough, and we thus find the concept of foreknowledge, as in Damasc., 2, 6 and the passages adduced above, cf. also Gn. r., 53 on 21:17 par. There thus arises the paradox that Yahweh foreknows the deeds of the righteous and the wicked, but they are not foreordained to election or perdition. On this whole question cf. R. Meyer, *Hellenistisches in d. rabb. Anthropologie* (1937), 41, n. 3; 75, n. 3 [R. Meyer].

from the whole people or community. Already we find a sectarian restriction which is to play a significant role in the later history of religion.

E. ἐκλέγομαι in the New Testament.

1. The Synoptists.

General. Two passages which along the lines of → 168 bear the meaning "to select from among many possibilities" or "to decide between two possibilities" are Lk. 14:7: τὰς πρωτοκλισίας ἐξελέγοντο, and Lk. 10:42 (on the basis of the reading B L 1. 33 bo aeth Orig): ὀλίγων δέ ἐστιν χρεία ἢ ἑνός — Μαρία γὰρ τὴν ἀγαθὴν μερίδα ἐξελέξατο.

The only other Synoptic ref. is in Mk. 13:20, where the word ἐκλεκτός, used of the community of the last time → 188, is supported by a verb: διὰ τοὺς ἐκλεκτούς, οὓς ἐξελέξατο.[107] Elsewhere ἐκλέγεσθαι is used only of the election of the apostles. According to Lk. 6:13: ἐκλεξάμενος ἀπ' αὐτῶν δώδεκα, this is selection from a larger number. On ἀπ' αὐτῶν instead of ἐκ → 168. This election of the disciples is mentioned also in Ev. Eb., 2, lines 18 and 21, and Barn., 5, 9, where the purpose is also added: τοὺς μέλλοντας κηρύσσειν τὸ εὐαγγέλιον αὐτοῦ.

2. The ἐκλέγεσθαι of the Disciples in John.

ἐκλέγεσθαι in Jn. is strikingly different from the use in the Mandaean writings (→ ἐκλεκτός, 185), whereas these and Eth. En. represent a related type. If Jn. has connections with this sphere, he certainly differs at this decisive point from the Jewish sectarian tradition, and this may be traced to conscious demarcation from the Jewish sense of election. The reading ἐκλεκτός at Jn. 1:34 (→ 189, n. 18), if original, is the only link with the usage of Jewish apocalyptic. On the other hand, the usual expressions found in Jn. are along the lines of those of the Synoptists, → *supra*. It will be seen that a true doctrine of election cannot be connected with this concept, but only with that which goes beyond it.

In Jn. ἐκλέγεσθαι is especially related to the problem how Judas can belong to the twelve and yet be a traitor. Three stages may be discerned in the treatment of the word. The problem is posed in Jn. 6:70: οὐκ ἐγὼ ὑμᾶς τοὺς δώδεκα ἐξελεξάμην; καὶ ἐξ ὑμῶν εἷς διάβολός ἐστιν.[108] The final answer is given in Jn. 13:18 f. just before the unmasking of the traitor. The true and full development of the thought of election then follows in 15:16 ff. after the sifting out of Judas. Characteristic of all the statements is that Jesus is the One who elects, always in solemn ἐγώ statements, 6:70; 13:18; 15:16, 19. Election, then, takes place in the life of the disciples, and God's only instrument is election through Jesus. Hence election is not a secret counsel of God. It is enacted through the electing Son. Nevertheless, the Father always stands behind this election by Jesus. The condition of coming to Him goes before in 6:65: δεδομένον ἐκ τοῦ πατρός. In 13:18 the ἐξελεξάμην is amplified by the necessity of the betrayal as prophesied in Scripture. In c. 15 the basic and determinative Father-Son relation underlies the

---

[107] This combination is found in Ginza, 272, 32; 297, 3 f.; 381, 26 f.; Liturg., 193, 10.
[108] Schl. J., 184: "For Jn. the case of Judas was a greater puzzle than the fall of Jerusalem and the rabbinate."

whole. Equally uniform, however, is the supplementing of this approach by the reference to human responsibility. The electing will is worked out in the sphere of faith and unbelief, obedience and disobedience. The mark of those whom the Father has given Him is faith in His words. Thus the division among the disciples is set under this alternative. Judas is not given, and he does not believe, 6:63-65. The reverse is illustrated in the faith and confession of Peter in 6:68 f. What is said about obedience is parallel. The οὐ περὶ πάντων ὑμῶν λέγω of 13:18 is preceded by the blessing of ποιεῖν which is necessarily bound up with knowledge. Judas shows that he is not given by the fact that he is no ποιῶν. The great development of the goal of election is first found in 15:16 f. It is the bringing forth of fruit in obedience, in love, and in dependence on the Father and the Son. Here is the decisive reference to the living activity of discipleship.

Of these two approaches, the second is the one which throws light on the riddle in the existence of Judas, namely, the fact that he is elected and yet a διάβολος. Jesus Himself, not confessing Peter, is the One who, without any attempt at excuse, unfolds the riddle, cf. 6:68 f. and 6:70 f. 6:70 does not refer to an election *ad malam partem,* to foreordination as διάβολος. No support is to be found here for the dogmatic formulation of double election, nor in the Synoptic "called, but not chosen" (→ 186). The problem in Jn. is that of being a chosen apostle and yet, as it is shown, not given by the Father, not a believer, but rather an antagonist, a διάβολος. This painful conclusion is not a deduction of metaphysical or speculative enquiry. The problem is posed by the reality of Christ on the one side and the existence of Judas on the other. The riddle is thus restricted to the question whether Christ acts rightly here. Is not his office as Christ challenged by the existence of the traitor? Did Jesus make a mistake? Was He deceived? The answer is that the Father's counsel and guiding power is over all these things. They have to take place thus. Cf. 6:70 with 6:64 f. and the reference to Ps. 41:9 in 13:18. Here the ἐκλέγεσθαι is not used in a different sense from that of 6:70, as though the οὐ περὶ πάντων were contrasted with the τίνας, to give the meaning: I say this only of those whom I have elected in truth, which is not true of Judas. On this interpretation, the dogmatic formulation of election to salvation is an underlying postulate. Always in Jn., however, ἐκλέγεσθαι is restricted to the apostles, and throughout the Gospel it is emphasised that Jesus knows of the treachery of Judas, 6:64 (ᾔδει ἐξ ἀρχῆς), 70, 71; 13:11; 18:4. Hence 13:18 is a succinct account of the following train of thought: I do not disclose my tasks and promises to all of you; they do not apply to Judas. I know those whom I chose. Even the election of the traitor was not a mistake. It took place with full foreknowledge. It had to take place in order that Ps. 41:9 should be fulfilled according to the Father's will. The key to these statements is to be found in 6:64 and 13:18. The only difference between 13:18 and 6:70 is that Scripture is now adduced to show that the betrayal is divinely determined. Thus Christ's action stands unshaken even in face of the existence of Judas.

That the purpose of the ἐκλέγεσθαι should only be fully developed after the departure of the traitor, since the fruit can now be mentioned without restriction in 15:16 ff., is quite understandable in the light of 15:19. Election is ἐκ τοῦ κόσμου (→ 186, Mand.). This means that the κόσμος will fight and hate the disciple. For the one who is not ἐκ τοῦ κόσμου is not τὸ ἴδιον for the world. There is no comfortable distinction between the rejected and those who bear fruit. The decision made in the existence of Judas applies to the whole apostolic band, 15:6. In relation to the purpose of election it is emphasised that the ἐκλέγεσθαι does not proceed from the disciples but from the sovereign electing Christ. Only thus is the bearing of lasting fruit possible, cf. 15:16 f. Thus election makes sense only as the basis and source of fruitful service.

As Calvin sees it, [109] Jn. 6:70 refers only to the *delecti ad munus apostolicum*, not to the *aeternum Dei consilium*. He thus tries to avoid false deductions in terms of the doctrine of election: *neque enim fieri potest, ut quisquam eorum excidat, qui praeordinati sunt ad vitam*. On the other hand, at 15:16 ff. [110] he moves on from the *electio particularis* of the apostles to the election of the community, of which he says: *his verbis complectitur*. The main objection to this view (→ 172) is that all the ἐκλέγεσθαι passages in Jn. refer to the *munus apostolicum*. Only in the light of the total conception of Jn. can one say how these passages relate to the idea of the community. It is certainly true that 15:16, 17 has the whole Church in view (cf. 17:20). The Evangelist uses the case of the disciples to illustrate something which applies to the whole community. The meaning of election for all is best seen at its source, the apostolic band. The whole community learns from the riddle of Judas that even the severest conflicts in the Church find their solution in the decision of the Lord. The question of the beloved disciple at the suggestion of the leading disciple in 13:24 expresses this confidence. Thus the right way is established, namely, the way of subjection to divine necessity, of a right attitude to the fallen brother, and above all of confidence that even the worst that can happen among disciples is infallibly and perfectly apprehended by Jesus in judgment and in grace.

3. ἐκλέγεσθαι in Acts.

Ac. uses ἐκλέγεσθαι in many senses, but never for the election of the community of Christ. Thus the word occurs for 1. the selection of officers: a. the apostles by Jesus, → 172. In accordance with the leading motif of Ac., the guidance of the community by the risen Lord, prayer is directed to the κύριος in 1:24 that He will show which of two He has chosen, cf. → 168; b. the deacons by the community, 6:5; c. delegates to Antioch by the apostles, the elders and the whole community, 15:22, 25 (ἐξ αὐτῶν). It is also used 2. of the election of the fathers (cf. 2 Macc. 1:25 and → πατήρ) in Paul's sketch of the history of revelation at Pisidian Antioch (13:17), where he takes seriously the election of Israel. It is finally used 3. specifically and in the absolute, with ensuing inf., by Peter in his speech to the apostolic council (15:7), cf. Jos. LXX 24:15, 22 (and inf.). The ref. is to God's resolve to have regard to the Gentiles, as worked out in the story of Cornelius. [111]

4. ἐκλέγεσθαι in Paul and James: The Election of the Community.

In 1 C. 1:27-29 Paul's threefold ἐξελέξατο expresses the fact that the community in its humanly feeble manifestation corresponds to the judicial will of God, who hereby puts to shame wisdom, power, and carnal fame. The threefold ἵνα and the ὅπως μή emphasise the purpose of God's electing will in fashioning the community thus, and they show that the goal of election is that God alone should be supreme. In this sense the term involves a radical break with selfish concerns about election, → 170; 184.

---

[109] *J. Calvini in NT Comm.*, III (1833), ed. A. Tholuck, p. 135.

[110] *Op. cit.*, p. 288.

[111] Finely put by Calvin, *ad loc.*: *Verbum eligendi statuere et discernere significat*. The ἀφ' ἡμερῶν ἀρχαίων refers to the story of Cornelius in view of the διὰ τοῦ στόματός μου (Peter). The frequently suggested relating of ἐξελέξατο and ἔθνη, or the supplying of an ἐμέ (Zn. Ag.), overlooks the sense in the LXX, which likewise has a dependent inf. clause.

The hymn of praise concerning εὐλογία πνευματική in Eph. 1:4 deals comprehensively with the basis, mediator and goal of election.

Three elements are essential. 1. ἐκλέγεσθαι is here primary. The consideration is from above, in contrast to R. 8, where the predestinarian formulae (πρόθεσις, προγιγνώσκειν, προορίζειν, ἐκλεκτός) in the great presentation of salvation serve retrospectively to bring out the eternal basis of justification after starting with its declaration in human history. The πρὸ καταβολῆς κόσμου in 1:4 corresponds to the starting-point. This is the one place in the NT where we find ἐκλέγεσθαι with an express accent on eternity.[112] But cf. κατὰ πρόγνωσιν with ἐκλεκτός in 1 Pt. 1:2, → 190. 2. On the ἐν αὐτῷ, cf. the development of the train of thought in v. 5 f. Election and predestination are for the state of adoption, and this takes place through the ἠγαπημένος, the elect. The connection here is obviously that the Elect (Christ) bears the elect, → Eth. En., 184. On the other hand, 1 Cl., 59, 3 simply deduces from the word the equation οἱ ἀγαπῶντες = ὁ ἠγαπημένος. 3. The purpose of election is described as responsible calling to a consecrated walk in the presence of God, in love.[113] If love, the end of self-seeking, characterises the walk, the fact is here taken seriously, as in 1 C. 1:27-29, that election is the negation of selfishness (cf. χάρις, χαριτόω, v. 6). The opposite is the perversion of the idea of election, namely, the idea that the community of God is more important than the whole world, S. Bar. 48:20; 4 Esr. 6:59; 5:23-27; → 170.

Jm. 2:5 is a par. to 1 C. 1:26-28, except that the standpoint is social; there is here a polemic against discrimination between the rich and the poor. Here, too, emphasis is laid on the experience of the community that God receives the needy. They become rich only by election. The two accusatives express the gift bound up with election. As in Eph. 1:5 f., the free gift of grace given with ἐκλέγεσθαι is emphasised, for the poor man who is lifted up can allege no merit before either God or man. Hence the triumph of divine grace is clearly expressed by ἐκλέγεσθαι both in Pl. and in Jm.

5. The Idea of Reprobation.

Nowhere in the NT is ἐκλέγεσθαι explicitly contrasted with reprobation. The same is in part true in relation to similar trains of thought, for in R. 9:13 the opposites ἀγαπᾶν/μισεῖν strictly belong to the quotation (Mal. 1:2 f.) and are equivalent to the ἐλεεῖν/σκληρύνειν of R. 9:18. The reference is not to the foreordination of two classes, the one to blessedness, the other to perdition, but in the case of the OT model to the preference of Jacob over Esau in leadership, and in the actual situation of the community to the temporary supersession and hardening of Israel as compared with the blossoming of the Gentile Church. Rather different is the grim formulation in 4 Esr. 2:17 (Riessler, 128): "Thou savest whom thou wilt, and thou destroyest whom thou wilt." In particular ἐκλέγεσθαι is not adapted to serve as the basis of a dogma of election and reprobation. It is unfortunate that the concept of election has been linked with the predestinarian controversy. This controversy is more concerned with προγιγνώσκειν, προετοι-

---

112 Cf. on this the Rabb. idea of the ideal pre-existence of Israel: It was created before the world was created, or: The thought of Israel, the contemplation of God preceded all else, Gn. r., 1 (2b) in Str.-B., I, 974; II, 335; III, 579 f.

113 For reasons of style, and in view of the structure, ἐν ἀγάπῃ is to be related to the first clause and not to προορίσας.

μάζειν, προορίζειν, προτίθεσθαι, πρόγνωσις, πρόθεσις. Even καλεῖν, κλῆσις and κλητός are much more closely involved in the NT.

† ἐκλογή.

Contents: A. ἐκλογή in General Greek Usage. B. ἐκλογή in Aquila, Symmachus and Theodotion. C. ἐκλογή in other Jewish Hellenistic Writings. D. ἐκλογή in the New Testament: 1. In Acts; 2. In Paul; 3. In 2 Peter. E. ἐκλογή in the Early Church: 1. In the Apostolic Fathers and Early Apologists; 2. In Origen and Gnosticism.

A. ἐκλογή in General Greek Usage.

The act. "selection" is predominant, and this from qualitative angles.[1] Thus in Plato it is used for the selection of rulers and guardians, i.e., officials with specific tasks, Resp., III, 414a; VII, 535a; 536c. In Plat. Leg., VII, 802b τὴν ἐκλογὴν ποιεῖσθαι is the selecting of officials, of a commission of experts for the poetry and dancing to be introduced into the state. Aristot. Eth. Nic., X, 10, p. 1181a, 18 uses ἐκλογή for the selection of laws, which presupposes insight.

There are 15 instances in Polyb., 7 with κατ' ἐκλογήν, → Pl. in R., 179 f. The ref., however, is not to what is selected as the result of the action, as in R. 11:7, but to the act itself. What is meant is always careful sifting on the basis of aptness and serviceability for a specific end. a. In the military sphere it is used of special levies in 5, 63, 11 — cf. the whole section 6, 19-21 — and esp. of the selection of legions by the tribunes, 6, 20, 4; 7; 9, and the cities, 6, 21, 5. For the selection of core troops, cf. 1, 47, 9; 1, 61, 3; 10, 12, 8. For appointment for special tasks, 6, 34, 8: the soldier to give the nightly password; 9, 13, 9, a troop for dangerous missions. Only once is it not used of persons, 31, 20, 12 (vessels). b. Of rulers in the aristocracy, 6, 4, 3. Of the elders of Lycurgus, 6, 10, 9. c. When the common κατ' ἐκλογήν is used, the principle of selection is usually added. In 6, 10, 9 the elders are selected ἀριστίνδην, by merit or birth, cf. 6, 20, 9, the cavalry levy is πλουτίνδην, according to income (in this case not with κατά). But cf. 1, 61, 3; 6, 4, 3; 10, 12, 8, where there is always more precise elucidation of the κατ' ἐκλογήν. Cf. also the negatively ironical use in 38, 2, 8: οὗτοι δὲ ἦσαν ὥσπερ ἐπίτηδες ἐξ ἑκάστης πόλεως κατ' ἐκλογὴν οἱ χείριστοι, definitely the worst people. Sometimes, when the connection is self-evident, the principle of selection can be left out, 6, 34, 8; 31, 20, 12. d. In combination with verbs (→ *supra*) we find λαμβάνειν τὴν ἐκλογήν (6, 20, 4) and ποιεῖσθαι τὴν ἐκλογήν (6, 21, 5), both with ref. to levies. Elsewhere it occurs simply with γίγνεσθαι, 6, 20, 7 and 9. Thus Polyb. confirms the usage in Plat.; the emphasis is always on commissioning for service. In relation to Pl. it may be asked whether the military use had some influence: the community is the elite corps or shock troop, cf. R. 8:23. It is possible that the concept of election was somehow influenced by metaphorical understanding along these lines. This is at least a possibility worth further exploration.

ἐκλογή. P. Riessler, *Altjüdisches Schrifttum ausserhalb d. Bibel* (1928), *Erläuterungen* 1268, 1269, 1271, 1273, 1282, 1283, 1284, 1294, 1301 f., 1322. A. v. Harnack, TU, 42, 3 (1918), *Die Terminologie d. Wiedergeburt u. verwandter Erlebnisse in d. ältesten Kirche*, 103; E. Jacquier, *Les Actes des Apôtres* (1926), 290; J. Lagrange, *Épitre aux Romains*[4] (1931) on 11:7.

[1] Eus. has τὴν τοῦ κρείττονος ἐκλογήν in Laus Constantini, Prologue, line 14 (ed. J. A. Heikel [GCS], p. 195, 13 f.). Plur. Dem. Ev., VI, 18, 29: ἐν ἐκλογαῖς γε μὴν [μὴ] διατριβόντων, as the monks, whose concern is for the selection of the best. In Hist. Eccl., IV, 26, 13 and 14 the extracts taken by Melito from the OT are ἐκλογαί. On this cf. Liddell-Scott, *s.v.*

In the pap. and inscr. ἐκλογή is the function of "seeking out" or "selecting." The ref. may be to a field, P. Tebt., I, 5, 166 (118 B.C.) or to the bride acc. to the formula of the marriage contract, P. Oxy., III, 496, 15.[2] The element of free choice is always emphasised here, cf. BGU, III, 717, 21 (2nd cent. A.D.): [ἐκλογῆς] σοι οὔσης ἤ τ(ι)να ἱμάτια ἢ τὴν συντίμησιν (instead of συν εἴμησιν): "you must have a free choice of receiving clothes or their equivalent value."[3] When it is a matter of a supplementary payment to balance an exchange, the concept of exchange defines the ἐκλογή, BGU, IV, 1158, 13 (9 B.C.); IV, 1013, 16 (Claudius or Nero); P. Ryl., II, 157, 6 (135 A.D.); P. Flor., I, 47, 14 (213-217 A.D.) in Mitteis-Wilcken, II, 2 (1912), 146, 14 (p. 158). Directly influenced by R. 11:7 (→ 180) is the burial inscr. of M. Julius Eugenius, Bishop of Laodicea (340-342 A.D.) in W. M. Ramsay, Exp. 7th Ser., Vol. IX (1910), 53. ἐκλογή is also found as a proper name, Preisigke Sammelbuch, I, 4315, 3.

The terms ἐκλέγομαι, ἐκλογή take on a distinctive anthropological and philosophical sense in Stoicism. The ref. here is to free choice between two things in practical decisions of personal life. The term always signifies preferring one to the other, Epict. Diss., I, 1, 27. This does not take place when circumstances are accepted as given, I, 12, 28; II, 5, 10; IV, 10, 30. But in adiaphora there is a task of ἡγεμονικόν, of testing, choosing, and rejecting, IV, 7, 40; II, 6, 9 (acc. to Chrysipp.). Acc. to the practice of middle Stoicism Epict. sets up the telos formula: ἡ ἐκλογὴ τῶν κατὰ φύσιν (II, 10, 6), esp. in relation to means of livelihood and of securing external goods. Also in the use of these things a rational choice has to be made as to what is in keeping with nature. Even if προηγμένον is to be regarded as an ἀδιάφορον, this is by no means an indifferent matter. As ἐκλογή it is a secondary work of virtue.[4]

B. ἐκλογή in Aquila, Symmachus and Theodotion.

In the LXX ἐκλογή is not found in canonical writings, and only sparsely in 'ΑΣΘ. Since the latter show some sense of Synagogue usage, it is likely that the few cases stand under the influence of the Synagogue בְּחִירָה.[5] 'A renders the מִבְחָר of Is. 22:7 lit. as ἐκλογαὶ κοιλάδων, while the LXX has ἐκλεκταὶ φάραγγες. Again, ΣΘ have ἐκλογή for מִבְחָר at Is. 37:24: τὴν ἐκλογὴν τῶν ἀρκεύθων or τῶν βραθέων. The LXX has the better Gk. translation τὸ κάλλος τῆς κυπαρίσσου. Elsewhere מִבְחָר, "choice," "best," is rendered ἐκλεκτός in the LXX, Gn. 23:6; Is. 22:7; 'Ιερ. 22:7; Da. 11:15 Θ → 145. Unless בחירה is the basis of 'ΑΣΘ, these simply have a more lit. rendering, since ἐκλογή was well-known in Gk. (→ 176).

C. ἐκλογή in other Jewish Hellenistic Writings.

Here the element of free choice (→ *supra*) is predominant. In the prayer in Ps. Sol. 18:6 the petition is that God may purify the people in view of the ἡμέρα ἐκλογῆς. Here ἐκλογή is the decisive, sifting choice which the Anointed will make within Israel when He comes to rule. Elsewhere the term is used of men. In Ep. Ar., 33 ἐκλογή is that which artists choose when they freely select precious stones. The explanatory ὧν ἂν προαιρῶνται shows that the choice is one which derives from προαίρεσις or free

---

[2] For further examples cf. Preisigke Wört., *s.v.*

[3] Cf. Wilcken, *ad loc.*, also Preisigke Wört., I, 449. Materially related is the sense of the debtor's right to choose between alternatives, Preisigke Fachwörter, *s.v.*; A. Berger, *Die Strafklauseln in den Pap.* (1911), 113.

[4] On ἐκλογή, ἐκλέγεσθαι in Epict. and his predecessors cf. A. Bonhöffer, *Die Ethik des Stoikers Epiktet* (1894), Index.

[5] בֵּית הַבְּחִירָה is the old Synagogue name for the temple, the house of election, cf. Pesikt., 100a; Str.-B., I, 853; S. Nu., 6, 23 § 39 (12a); Str.-B., II, 311 Ba α.

resolve. Cf. Jos. Ant., 12, 41. The ref. in Ps. Sol. 9:4 is to a free decision of the human will: τὰ ἔργα ἡμῶν ἐν ἐκλογῇ καὶ ἐξουσίᾳ τῆς ψυχῆς ἡμῶν, τοῦ ποιῆσαι δικαιοσύνην καὶ ἀδικίαν ἐν ἔργοις χειρῶν ἡμῶν. Here, in a Pharisaic writing, the anthropological doctrine of free will (→ n. 8, 9) is applied in such a way that all our action takes place acc. to the will and decision of the heart. ἐκλογή here corresponds to, e.g., רָצוֹן or חֵפֶץ. Joseph., too, uses the term in this sense. In Ant., 1, 169 Abraham gives Lot the ἐκλογή in the dividing of the land, i.e., a free choice (with αἵρεσις). In Ant., 7, 322 ἐκλογή is used for the choice which David must make between famine, pestilence and war, and in Ant., 8, 24 for the selective desire of Solomon. [6] But in Bell., 2, 165 we find the same anthropological and philosophical use as in Ps. Sol. 9:4. Here it is said of the Sadducees: φασὶν δ' ἐπ' ἀνθρώπων ἐκλογῇ τό τε καλὸν καὶ τὸ κακὸν προκεῖσθαι καὶ κατὰ γνώμην ἕκαστον [7] τούτων ἑκατέρῳ προσιέναι. Good and evil are for man to choose freely, and each comes to one or the other acc. to his resolve. This implies that God's purpose and work do not affect human action, Bell., 2, 164. [8] It is a mere accident that this sense of free decision is used in relation to the Sadducees, for all good Jews, Pharisees and Rabbis alike, championed free will in this way. [9]

---

[6] Jos. Ant., 8, 24: παρὰ τὴν ἐκλογήν God promises Solomon also what he has not chosen. On παρά τι in Jos. cf. Schl. Theol. d. Judt., 189, n. 1.

[7] ἕκαστον instead of ἑκάστου, cf. Schl. Theol. d. Judt., 188, n. 1.

[8] Jos. Bell., 2, 164: The Sadducees completely deny εἱμαρμένη — καὶ τὸν θεὸν ἔξω τοῦ δρᾶν τι κακὸν ἢ ἐφορᾶν τίθενται. On the vl. κακόν after τι, cf. Schl. Theol. d. Judt., 188, n. 1. In Jos. Ant., 13, 173 the rejection of εἱμαρμένη by the Sadducees is identical with the statement: ἅπαντα δὲ ἐφ' ἡμῖν αὐτοῖς κεῖσθαι, "everything is up to us." The continuation shows that the ref. is to the human happiness or unhappiness which we bring on ourselves. To the Pharisees Jos. ascribes a synergistic attitude, Bell., 2, 162 f.; Ant., 13, 172; 18, 13. Much, but not all, is the work of destiny. The Sadducean statement of Bell., 2, 165 becomes for them (2, 163): καὶ τὸ μὲν πράττειν τὰ δίκαια καὶ μὴ κατὰ τὸ πλεῖστον ἐπὶ τοῖς ἀνθρώποις κεῖσθαι, βοηθεῖν δὲ εἰς ἕκαστον καὶ τὴν εἱμαρμένην. On the textually difficult passage Ant., 18, 13 cf. Schl. Theol. d. Judt., 209, n. 1. Here it is clear that the human function in question is described as an impulse of the will (ὁρμή) complementing the divine βουλευτήριον. Finally the Essenes, acc. to Jos., assume complete dependence on εἱμαρμένη, Ant., 13, 172. On εἱμαρμένη in Jos., cf. Schl., 32-35. Jos. also uses τύχη, Ant., 16, 397 f., or τὸ χρεών, 8, 409 and 419. But the ref. is not always to the foreordained necessity of human actions.

[9] Cf. on this R. Meyer, "Hellenistisches in d. rabb. Anthropologie," BWANT, IV, 22 (1937), 63 ff. The emphasis on human freedom and responsibility may be seen already in Sir. 15:11-20, where in v. 14 we have διαβούλιον for ἐκλογή, and θέλειν and εὐδοκεῖν are also used for what man can do, vv. 15-17. Acc. to Eth. En. 98:4 men sin of themselves. They are able to fulfil the divine commandments. Cf. the examples in Str.-B., I, 814 f. By controlling the evil impulse they make observance easier (Ab., 4, 2, Ben Azzai, c. 110; cf. Str.-B., IV, 8) and can achieve sinlessness (Str.-B., I, 814), so that God's power strengthens them in the good. With this emphasis on freedom of choice Pharisaism combines the ref. to predestination in world history. Cf. Ab., 3, 15 f. (R. Akiba): Everything is foreseen by God, but freedom of decision (רְשׁוּת) is given to man, so that he cannot escape an account. Everything is in the hand of heaven except the decision either for fear of God or ungodliness, Ber., 33b par., cf. BM, 107b, par. (R. Chanina, c. 225); Tanch. פקודי § 13, 127a in Str.-B., II, 343, lines 27 ff., cf. Nidda, 16b, Str.-B., III, 266. The combination of εἱμαρμένη and διαβούλιον is expressed thus. God predetermines the constitution, disposition, endowment, social position etc., but not whether a man will be ungodly or righteous. Cf. also Str.-B., I, 982 f. On Tanch., *op. cit.* and non-Jewish influences cf. Meyer, *op. cit.*, c. VII, 88 f. The combination of freedom and foreordination in personal destiny finds an obvious model in Platonic thought, cf. Plat. Resp., X, 617 d. e. Cf. also human will and the immutable decree of God in Apc. Abr., 26, 5. To say with Riessler, *op. cit.* that the predestinarian element in apocalyptic is Essene is advisable only when other Essene traits are discernible. Thus 4 Esr. 6:6 is not Essene when it says that creation and the end are foreknown and foreordained (cf. also 7:42). The same is true of the foreordination of the times in all apocal.

D. ἐκλογή in the New Testament.

1. ἐκλογή in Acts.

In Ac. 9:15 the κύριος says to Ananias concerning Paul: ὅτι σκεῦος ἐκλογῆς ἐστίν μοι οὗτος. The Hebraic gen. qual. ἐκλογῆς is here used for the adjective ἐκλεκτόν. In what follows appointment to serve (→ Jn. 15 ἐκλέγεσθαι, 173 f.) comes emphatically to the fore. Paul has an ἐκλογή to apostolic tasks before nations, kings and the children of Israel.

2. ἐκλογή in Paul.

Paul has a fivefold use of the word in 1 Th. and R.

a. He uses it for the divine selection in the history of the patriarchs, R. 9:11. The electing divine will (on κατ' ἐκλογήν → Polyb., 176) ordains the destiny of the sons of Jacob prior to their birth or to their works (whether "good" or "evil," so that there can be no question of a moral process). The reference here is not to salvation, but to position and historical task, cf. the quotation from Gn. 25:23 in v. 12: "The elder shall serve the younger." If in the story of the patriarchs the ἐκλογή of the one implies the setting aside of the other, the application is to the present precedence of the Gentile Church and the setting aside of Israel. What God does is intentional and purposeful: ἵνα ἡ κατ' ἐκλογὴν πρόθεσις τοῦ θεοῦ μένῃ, οὐκ ἐξ ἔργων ἀλλ' ἐκ τοῦ καλοῦντος. καλεῖν takes the place of merit. Thus ἐκλογή lays emphasis on the free decision of God, and it does so in such a way that the prototype of d. (→ 180) is found is the history of revelation. Mal. 1:2 f. in v. 13 refers even more strongly to the seriousness of divine judgment on the majority in Israel, for in the figurative language of Mal. 1 hatred denotes the act of judgment manifested in the destruction of Edom. There can be no doubt that ἀγαπᾶν and μισεῖν are here understood in terms of πρόθεσις, but not outside the sphere of human responsibility and conduct.

b. Paul also uses the term for the election of all Israel in the fathers, R. 11:28. If the Israelites are κατὰ τὸ εὐαγγέλιον ἐχθροὶ δι' ὑμᾶς, they are κατὰ τὴν ἐκλογὴν ἀγαπητοὶ διὰ τοὺς πατέρας, cf. Ac. 13:17 ἐκλέγεσθαι, → 174. Here the reference is not to a part (cf. R. 9:11; 11:5, 7; → 180) but to the whole people.

c. The word is used again for the election of the whole Christian community to faith, with no special regard to its dual origin, 1 Th. 1:4. As the ὅτι clause shows, this ἐκλογή is manifested in the powerful operation of the Spirit in the community. Hence ἐκλογή is not just a dogmatic thesis. It denotes the manifestation of election, → II, 730. The ἠγαπημένοι ὑπὸ τοῦ θεοῦ is an interpretation of election, cf. Col. 3:12 under ἐκλεκτός → 189 f.; 2 Th. 2:13, 16; R. 8:37 with Eph. 1:6; → 175.

All that is ordained for being God has sketched and set before Him, Apc. Abr. 22:3. For each man God's decree, and what is written, is immutable, Test. Isaac 3:10 (Riessler, 1138). The Lord of spirits has decreed all things for His saints, their habitation and inheritance, Eth. En. 39:8. Moses is selected, predesignated and prepared as mediator from the beginning of the world, Ass. Mos. 1:14. Cf. the selecting scales set up in Lidz. Joh., 226, 5 ff. (Liturg., 154, 8). This predestinarianism seems to be strengthened by apocal. belief in εἱμαρμένη, though it is found also in the Synagogue and was transmitted to Paul as the heir of Judaism.

d. Another use is for God's selecting of a part of Israel out of the whole, R. 11:5: λεῖμμα κατ' ἐκλογὴν χάριτος. This remnant of Christian believers in Israel is chosen according to the principle of grace (Polyb. → 176). Here ἐκλογή act. is the selection of a part from the whole — Israel as a national community — to a place of privilege. Cf. → λεῖμμα. In the NT, however, we never read of an elite in the Christian community itself, as in the case of the Jewish sects → 171; 184. Applied to Israel, the thought of selection is closely controlled by the OT use of λεῖμμα.

e. This ἐκλογή in sense d. is found in the pass. in R. 11:7: the elected portion in distinction from the λοιποί of Israel as a whole. The chosen number of believing Israelites has attained to that which Israel strove after, whereas the rest (the majority) were hardened.

3. ἐκλογή in 2 Peter.

2 Pt. 1:10: σπουδάσατε βεβαίαν ὑμῶν τὴν κλῆσιν καὶ ἐκλογὴν ποιεῖσθαι, has in view the election and calling of the community of believers in Christ. On the parallelism of κλῆσις and ἐκλογή cf. the κλητοί καὶ ἐκλεκτοί of Rev. 17:14; → ἐκλεκτός, n. 10. In the Synoptists to be called (invited) but not chosen (→ 186) has a different sense. Only in appearance is election here a more dogmatic term (cf. Origen, → 181), for the passage shows that there is no static rigidity. The word is used in the movement of responsibility and with an eschatological reference in which regard is had to teleological ordination. This finds expression in the fact that the purely divine aspect is made sure only by men. This means that man has to be taken with full seriousness in relation to the divine rule. In the Synoptic Gospels, too, the ἐκλεκτός is established by obedience, → 187. This involves resolute purification, zeal in availing oneself of power, and experience of God and His promises, 1:3 ff. [10]

E. ἐκλογή in the Early Church.

1. In the Apostolic Fathers and Early Apologists. Dg., 4, 4 speaks of the circumcision of the Jews, on which they plume themselves as on the μαρτύριον ἐκλογῆς. 1 Cl., 29, 1 refers to the Christian sense of election. The Father has made us ἐκλογῆς μέρος ἑαυτῷ, His elect portion, i.e., the true Israel (cf. Just. Dial., 11, 5). This use is related to the pass. of R. 11:7. Mart. Pol., 20, 1, with ref. to the martyrs, speaks of the κύριος: τὸν ἐκλογὰς (plur.) ποιοῦντα ἀπὸ τῶν ἰδίων δούλων. This is close to the sectarian sense, since the martyrs are a selection from the whole community. In Just. Dial. the Jew twice uses ἐκλογή of the elect Christ in the sense of the adoption of man: 48, 3: ἐκλογὴ γενόμενος εἰς τὸν Χριστόν, 49, 1: οἱ λέγοντες ἄνθρωπον γεγονέναι αὐτὸν καὶ κατ' ἐκλογὴν (→ 176) κεχρῖσθαι.

2. In Origen and Gnosticism. Origen is strongly influenced by the usage of Pl. in R.: Princ., IV, 1, 4: τῶν ἀσυνέτων ἐθνῶν ἐκλογή, IV, 1, 6: τῆς ἀπὸ τῶν ἐθνῶν ἐκλογῆς. He also adopts the pass. use of R. 11:7, Comm. in Joh., II, 3, 24: God is τῶν ὅλων τῆς ἐκλογῆς θεὸς καὶ πολὺ μᾶλλον τοῦ τῆς ἐκλογῆς σωτῆρος. He also likes to use ἐκλογή where the NT has ἐκλέγεσθαι, ἐκλεκτός or καλεῖν. Cf. the Jewish sense of election in Comm. in Joh., VI, 9, 54: κατ' ἐκλογὴν θεοῦ. In the case of the κεκλημένοι in Lk. 14:16 f., *ibid.*, XIII, 34, 221: μυστήριον τῆς κλήσεως καὶ

---

[10] Cf. Kn. Pt. and Schl. Erl., *ad loc.*

ἐκλογῆς. Concerning the election of Judas (Jn. 13) he says (*ibid.*, XXXII, 18, 235): εἷς τῶν ἐν ἐκλογῇ μοι τετιμημένων ἀποστόλων. On Eph. 1 (Orat., 5, 5) he ventures to say of the elect Christian: ἀμήχανον αὐτὸν τῆς ἐκλογῆς ἐκπεσεῖν. Here ἐκλογή is a key word and it almost becomes a dogmatic term, taking on a fixed sense which is not found in the NT (→ 192). Distinctive is the use of the term for the purely future goal in Hom. in Jer., IV, 3: "to attain" ἐπὶ τὴν ἐκλογὴν τοῦ θεοῦ καὶ τὴν μακαριότητα, which will apply only to few. Origen also knows ἐκλογή in the sense of shock troops, Comm. in Joh., XIII, 59, 411.

The sectarian use of ἐκλογή in the spirit of Valentinian Gnosticism in found in Heracleon, Orig. Comm. in J., XIII, 51, 341. In Jn. 4:39 he contrasts the many Samaritans ὡς πολλῶν ὄντων ψυχικῶν with the one woman: τὴν δὲ μίαν λέγει τὴν ἄφθαρτον τῆς ἐκλογῆς φύσιν καὶ μονειδῆ καὶ ἑνικήν. When ἐκλογή is allegorised we have the πνευματικοί as distinct from the ψυχικοί. On Euseb. → 176, n. 1.

† ἐκλεκτός.

Contents: A. Ordinary Greek Use. B. Use in the Greek Bible and Hellenistic Jewish Writings: 1. General; 2. The Religious Meaning of ἐκλεκτός. C. ἐκλεκτός and the Thought of Election in Apocalyptic: 1. Israel or its Elite as the Elect; 2. The Messiah as the Elect among the Elect; 3. The Angels as the Elect. D. "Elect" in the Mandaean Writings. E. ἐκλεκτός in the New Testament: 1. The ἐκλεκτοί in the Synoptics; 2. Christ as the Elect in Luke; 3. ἐκλεκτός in Paul; 4. ἐκλεκτός and συνεκλεκτός in 1 Peter and the Johannine Epistles; 5. Summary. F. ἐκλεκτός in the Apostolic Fathers.

A. Ordinary Greek Use.

In class. Gk. the predominant meaning of the adj. is "choice," "selected." Of soldiers, Thuc., VI, 100 for selected lightly armed troops. The tt. *judices selecti* for Rome, Ditt. Or., 499, 3 (2nd cent. A.D.), cf. 567, 10: ἐπίλεκτον κριτήν, finds a par. already in Plat. Leg., XII, 946d: εἰς τοὺς ἐκλεκτοὺς δικαστάς. Plat. Leg., XI, 938b has instead ἐν τῷ τῶν ἐκλεκτῶν δικαστηρίῳ, though δικαστῶν should be supplied. In the pap. and inscr. the word has the sense of "choice" for things of the best quality, P. Rein., 43, 9

ἐκλεκτός. On Lk. 18:1-8: J. A. Robertson, "The Parable of the Unjust Judge," Exp. T., 38 (1926/1927), 389-392; D. Buzy, "Le juge inique," *Rev. Bibl.*, 39 (1930), 377-391. On 1 Pt.: T. Spörri, *Der Gemeindegedanke in 1 Pt.* (1925), 24-26, 163-167. On the doctrine of election (→ 175 f.) in Pl.: B. Weiss, "Die Prädestinationslehre des Ap. Pls." in *Jahrbücher f. deutsche Theologie* (1857), 54-115; E. Ménégoz, *La prédestination dans la théologie paulinienne* (1885); V. Weber, *Krit. Geschichte d. Exegese des 9. Kp. ... des Römerbriefs bis auf Chrys. u. Aug. ...* (1889); K. Müller, *Die göttliche Zuvorersehung u. Erwählung ... nach dem Ev. des Pls.* (1892); E. Grafe, *Das Verhältnis der paul. Schriften zur Sap. Sal.* (1892); J. Dalmer, *Die Erwählung Israels nach d. Heilsverkündigung des Ap. Pls.* (1894); "Zur paul. Erwählungslehre," *Greifswalder Studien f. H. Cremer* (1895), 183-206; W. Beyschlag, *D. paul. Theodizee R. 9-11*^{2} (1896); E. Kühl, "Zur paul. Theodizee," *Theol. Studien f. B. Weiss* (1897); H. E. Weber, *Das Problem d. Heilsgeschichte nach R. 9-11* (1911); R. Liechtenhan, *Die göttliche Vorherbestimmung bei Pls. und in d. Posidonianischen Philosophie* (1922); E. v. Dobschütz, "Zeit u. Raum im Denken d. Urchristentums," JBL, 41 (1922); T. Hoppe, "Die Idee d. Heilsgeschichte bei Pls. ...," BFTh, 30, 2 (1926); F. W. Maier, *Israel in d. Heilsgeschichte nach R. 9-11* (1929); E. v. Dobschütz, "Die Paradoxie im NT," ZSTh, 8 (1930/31), 181-200; "Prädestination," ThStKr, 106 (1934/5), 9-19; E. Stauffer, "ἵνα u. d. Problem des teleologischen Denkens bei Pls.," ThStKr, 102 (1930), 232-257; R. Hoffmann, "D. göttliche Vorherbestimmung nach d. Lehre d. Pls.," *Wartburg*, 29 (1930), 444-452; Damascus Document, cf. W. Stärk in BFTh, 27 (1922) and P. Riessler, *Altjüd. Schrifttum ausserhalb d. Bibel* (1928), 920 ff.

(102 A.D.): ἐκλεκτὸν ἀνδρῶνα, chamber, or ἐκλεκτοί of baskets, P. Fay., 102, 3, or oil, BGU, II, 603, 18 and 38 (*c.* 167 A.D.). Cf. CIA, 1122, 23 and 24. [1]

B. Use in the Greek Bible and Hellenistic Jewish Writings.

1. On the Heb. words which underlie ἐκλεκτός in the LXX → 145. Worth noting is that as ἐκλέγεσθαι becomes more prominent in 'ΑΣΘ, so does ἐκλεκτός in the LXX of Ez., where there are 10 renderings for words never translated thus elsewhere. If it is only in the fig. language of 19:12, 14 that these passages show a ref. to the election of Israel, this motivation is the natural explanation of the love for ἐκλεκτός. The adj. (LXX and Hexapla 56 times) and the noun (47) are fairly equally balanced. Verbal constructions like ἐκλεκτόν (ἐστι) ἤ are rare. As at Prv. 22:1 'ΑΘ, they are usually based on the ni of בחר, cf. 2 Macc. 1:25 : ὁ ποιήσας τοὺς πατέρας ἐκλεκτούς. The general, secular use of ἐκλεκτός is a. for natural products, esp. plants, animals, minerals, and the meaning is choice, select, costly, sterling, purified, profitable, best of its kind, of top quality, → 145. When used b. of persons, as noted → 148, it often occurs for בָּחוּר, which can denote young men or chosen fighters. The meaning may vacillate. Ju. 20:15; 2 Βασ. 10:9 'ΑΣ. Cf. Jdt. 2:15; 1 Macc. 4:1; 15:26; Ep. Ar., 13; Sib. 3:521. Jos. Ant., 7, 59 has ἐκλεκτός only once in this sense (based on the LXX), whereas he uses ἐπίλεκτος 33 times, always in the military sense for shock troops, bodyguards etc. (→ 168).

2. The Religious Meaning of ἐκλεκτός. a. The word is closely related to קדשׁ and is sometimes used for it, Sir. 49:6 of Jerusalem as ἐκλεκτὴ πόλις, 1 Βασ. 10:3 Ἄλλος (Field): ἐκλεκτή of the sacred oak of Tabor, Ιερ. 26:15 (46:15): ὁ μόσχος ὁ ἐκλεκτός σου, of the sacred Apis bull of Memphis. It can also be used for "pure," e.g., Cant. 6:10 → 144; 169 f. Here the thought of election perhaps combines with the exegesis of the Synagogue (the bride = Israel). This is also the sense in ψ 17:26 = 2 Βασ. 22:27: μετὰ ἐκλεκτοῦ ἐκλεκτὸς ἔσῃ, → 145. This passage is important, since it is the only one in which ἐκλεκτός is used of God Himself (cf. its special use for light in the Mandaean writings, → 185). The idea of "holy or elect for" carries a religious and especially a cultic ref. From the time of Isaiah (740) קדשׁ in the abs. is applied to God, though the first sense remains. This is a new development, and it logically raises the question : For whom is God holy ? There is among the Mandaeans a similar transfer of "elect" to God as in the case of קדשׁ in the OT.

b. In keeping with the relation to קדשׁ is the common cultic use of ἐκλεκτός. This may be seen in σμύρνη ἐκλεκτή with ref. to the holy oil of anointing, Ex. 30:23 (דרור), and also to sacrifices dedicated to God, Dt. 12:11 (מִבְחַר). Cf. the sacrilege of stealing ἐκλεκτά, Test. L. 14:5; Test. Job 15:9 (Riessler, 1112). The rare dat. also emphasises the cultic ref., 1 Ch. 9:22 : οἱ ἐκλεκτοὶ ταῖς πύλαις, → 145. Related is 2 Βασ. 21:6, where those who have fallen to Yahweh, and who are impaled in judicial expiation, are called ἐκλεκτοὶ κυρίου. This sense is almost always present in the case of λίθοι ἐκλεκτοί, i.e., stones for the temple and the new Jerusalem, Is. 54:12; → 190 f.; Ιερ. 38:39. Cf. Test. Sol. 21:2 vl. (p. 64* n. ed. McCown) χαλκὸν ἐκλεκτόν in the temple. The most influential saying in this connection is Is. 28:16 : ἰδοὺ ἐγὼ ἐμβαλῶ εἰς τὰ θεμέλια Σιὼν λίθον πολυτελῆ ἐκλεκτὸν ἀκρογωνιαῖον ἔντιμον (בֹּחַן): the sacred stone as the head of the corner and the final stone in the temple. [2]

c. The express religious concept of election. This occurs in relation to ἐκλεκτός in four forms, men of God in salvation history, the land, the city and the people. i. Of

---

[1] In K. Meisterhans-E. Schwyzer, *Grammatik d. attischen Inschr.*[8] (1900), 109.

[2] Cf. J. Jeremias, "Golgotha," *Angelos, Beih.* 1 (1926), Index on Is. 28:16.

the patriarchs neither Abraham nor Isaac is called ἐκλεκτός in the LXX. But we find the term in Philo's allegorical exegesis of the name of Abraham, Abr., 82; 83; Cher., 7; Gig., 64; Mut. Nom., 66; 69; 71. Ἀβράμ is אב רם μετέωρος πατήρ, who is occupied with astrology. The nature philosopher then becomes Ἀβραάμ, אב בר הם, πατὴρ ἐκλεκτὸς ἠχοῦς, explained in terms of ὁ τοῦ σπουδαίου λογισμός, the νοῦς τοῦ σοφοῦ. Hence Abraham the sage becomes the friend of God. Synon. to ἐκλεκτός (ἐπίλεκτος) is ἀστεῖος, ἀγαθός, opp. φαῦλος. For the interchangeability of ἐκλεκτός and ἐπίλεκτος cf. Joseph. → 168; 182. Abraham is "thine elect" in Apc. Abr. (→ 169) 20:6, and Michael says to Isaac: "Elect son," in Test. Is. (→ Riessler, 1134) 1:2. In the OT writings Jacob (Israel) is ἐκλεκτός: Is. 42:1 LXX. Here the servant is understood with ref. to the people, whereas Θ follows the Mas.: ὁ ἐκλεκτός μου ὃν ηὐδόκησεν ἡ ψυχή μου (בְּחִירִי). Sir. 47:22 also refers to Jacob. Then Moses in ψ 105:23 is the chosen one who, as a mediator, stands in the breach, cf. the elect as the mediator in the Mandaean writings, → 185. For Joshua cf. Nu. 11:28, for David Sir. 47:22, where the Gk. has for the chosen race a masc. that refers both to Jacob (→ *supra*) and David. Cf. Test. Sol. D., I, 2 (p. 88* McCown) of David: ὁ ἐκλεκτὸς τοῦ θεοῦ. In apocal. there is an increase in the use of the term for biblical figures, cf. Jeremiah in Paral. Jerem., 1, 1 and 4; 3, 4 and 5; 7, 15; Ezra in the Gk. Ezr. Apc. (ed. C. Tischendorf, Apocalypses Apocryphae [1866], 24 ff.; cf Riessler, 126 ff.); here the prophet in 1, 8 is "Thou elect of God" and in 3, 3 God's chosen son. For Job cf. Test. Job 4:11 (Riessler, 1106). ii. Palestine is the chosen land in Ιερ. 3:19, where the LXX again strengthens the thought of election, and Zech. 7:14; cf. S. Bar. 40:2. iii. Jerusalem is ἡ ἐκλεκτή (κατ' ἐξοχήν) in Tob. 13:13 S. This is the model for Rev. 21, cf. esp. 13:17, which deals with the future of the city. Later, Paral. Jerem., 1, 5. iv. God's people as the elect is found already in Dt. Is. in the sense of the faithful in Israel, the servants of God, as distinct from sinners, Is. 65:9, 15. The eschatological view of God's people in the new age, which is the sense in Eth. En. → 185, is already implied in Is. 65:23. The τὸ γένος τὸ ἐκλεκτόν of 1 Pt. (→ 191) may be seen in Is. 43:20, cf. Est. 8:12 t. God's people is also elect in ψ 104:43, synon. λαός; ψ 105:5, synon. ἔθνος; 1 Ch. 16:13; Sir. 46:1. This concept is further developed in apocal. (→ *infra*) and undergoes sectarian narrowing (→ 184).

3. One may say in sum that though there is a marked growth in the use of "elect" by the translators as compared with the Mas., this is not always explicitly due to a liking for the religious motif of election. The motif is plain, however, in an addition like that at Hag. 2:22 A. In ψ 88:3; Hab. 3:13 Αλλ the ref. to the people is imported; the Mas. simply speaks of David, Jacob, or the anointed prince. Predilection for the concept may also be seen in passages where the exegesis of the Synagogue establishes the ref. to the chosen people, e.g., the vineyard in Is. 5:2 Σ; Ez. 19:12, 14, the shepherd and the flock in Zech. 11:16; cf. the bride in Cant. 6:9 f. (→ 182). Many mistakes, e.g., at Nu. 11:28; 2 Βασ. 21:6; Is. 1:25 Ἀ; Ιερ. 10:17; Am. 5:11; Job 37:11 LXX Θ; Prv. 12:24; Cant. 5:13 Ἀ certainly show a growing liking for ἐκλεκτός. The increasing inclination to emphasise the election of Israel is to be seen particularly in the fact that the Gk. translators make ἐκλεκτός a single catchword for a whole series of terms in the OT.

C. ἐκλεκτός and the Thought of Election in Apocalyptic.

The role of the elect in this group of writings may be seen in Eth. En. The work is specifically destined for them, 1:1, 3, 8. The term is so overworked as to be debased as compared with Dt. Is. or the Ps., though it is strikingly absent from Slav. En. When we consider related writings, a common feature is the eschatological emphasis. Synon. to the elect are the righteous or the saints, Eth. En. 38:2-5; 41:2; 48:1; 61:13; 70:3. The opp. are sinners and the wicked, 5:7; 41:2; 50:1 f. In the use of the predicate three aspects are to be distinguished.

1. Israel or its Elite as the Elect. In the Ten Weeks Apocalypse in Eth. En. 93; 91:12-17, the oldest part of the book (prior to 167 B.C.), where the cosmic drama is unfolded in ten acts from the birth of Enoch to the Messianic judgment, we still find the original equation of the elect with all Israel, cf. 93:1 f., 10: The elect of the world, the children of righteousness, the plant of righteousness and uprightness.[3] To this corresponds the *plebs excepta* of Ass. Mos. 4:2 (after Herod the Gt.), cf. Jub. 22:9; S. Bar. 21:21, where Israel is always called the chosen people, the inheritance out of all peoples, the favourite people. For a developed form of the sense of election cf. 4 Esr. 5:23-27 (→ ἐκλέγεσθαι, 170). An infallible mark of all these works is the instinct of revenge, Eth. En. 48:9; 56:8; 62:11-15; cf. 5 Esr. 15:53, 56 (O. F. Fritzsche, Libri Apocryphi Veteris Testamenti [1871], 648 f.), which delights in the thought that sinners are punished as an enjoyable spectacle for the elect. An isolated expression occurs in Test. B. 10:10: He chastises Israel ἐν τοῖς ἐκλεκτοῖς ἔθνεσι. In face of Eth. En. 46:8; 53:6; 56; 60:6, it can hardly be maintained that there is no thought of any national boundary[4] in 37-71 (before 64 B.C.). Here, too, the elect are those who acknowledge the righteous law, 60:6. The war of the Gentiles (Medes and Persians?) is against Jerusalem and the land of the elect, 56, esp. v. 6 f. The Synagogue in 46:8 and the hope set on the house of the community in 53:6 betray a Jewish concern. Cf. the elect of Israel in Jub. 1:29, and believers and the elect of the Hebrews in Sib. 3:69. In the symbolism, however, there is a restriction of the concept of election to an elite in Israel. This motif, based on the biblical idea of the remnant (→ λεῖμμα), makes great strides in apocal. It occurs esp. where there is emphasis on the tension between the righteous and the ungodly in Israel, and it is pointed out that the true result is what matters fundamentally in the divine covenant and election. Thus in Wis. 3:9 the elect are the πεποιθότες ἐπ' αὐτῷ, οἱ πιστοὶ ἐν ἀγάπῃ, and in 5 Esr. 16:74 f. (Fritzsche, 653) it is the tested who will be delivered from the days of tribulation (cf. Lk. 18, → 187). Thus from the time of Da. there is hope that the righteous will be raised again. Eth. En. 51:1 f. speaks of a selection of righteous and the saints from among the dead in Hades. Cf. Gk. Esr. Apc. 7:2. This community of the elect and the saints will be "sown," Eth. En. 62:8. The idea of a definite number arises in S. Bar. 30:2; 75:5 f. Acc. to Apc. Abr. 29:17 this is predetermined and kept secret with God (cf. v. 13). Cf. 5 Esr. 2:38.[5] Here, then, is a process of development. The thought of election is transferred from all Israel to a narrower group. It applies only to the righteous, to those who keep the Law strictly, among the people.[6] This seems to be a result of the great struggle against alien Hellenistic influence and everything that threatens to destroy the national and religious uniqueness of Israel. The sectarian view of election is easily combined with this. The narrowing of the concept may be seen clearly in Damasc. 6:2, where the sons of Zadok are the elect of Israel. Of these it is said expressly that as the bearers of this name they will do service at the end of the days.[7]

2. The Messiah as the Elect among the Elect. In the OT one can say that the Messiah is called elect only if the servant passages in Dt. Is are taken messianically. In apocal., however, there is a typical development in this respect. A favourite theme of Eth. En. is that of the connection and correspondence between the one elect and the elect. This is worked out systematically. The Messiah is righteous and elect, 53:6; 62:1. He is the elect of righteousness and fidelity, 39:6 f. The elect and the righteous cor-

---

[3] Cf. Str.-B., III, 293; Volz Esch., 352.

[4] Volz Esch., 352.

[5] In keeping is the idea of the righteous written in the book of life, Da. 12:1. For further examples cf. Volz Esch., 292 and → I, 619, n. 21 (βιβλίον). The concept of separation is also promoted by the dividing of the righteous into sages, martyrs, ascetics, cf. Volz, 352. Liking for a fixed number may still be seen in Rev. In the apost. fathers, 1 Cl., 2, 4; 59, 2.

[6] Volz, *loc. cit.*

[7] For the increase in the use of the word for biblical characters in apocal. → 183.

respond to him, 39:6 f. etc. The power of the Lord of spirits brings Him out of obscurity and declares Him the elect, 62:7; cf. 62:1, also Apc. Abr. (→ 169) 31:1: God sends Him at the end of the days. Here, too, there is a strict analogy. As the Son of Man (the Elect) was hidden from the beginning, kept by the Most High in the presence of His power (62:7), so the elect are kept with the Lord of spirits, and will be magnified with Him, 40:5. When he appears and is set on the throne of His glory, 49:2; 51:3; 52:9; 55:4; 61:8, He will make from His throne the final choice of the elect, 45:3 f. He selects in the resurrection the righteous and the saints, 51:1 f. As His glory endures from eternity to eternity, 49:2, cf. Test. B. 11:4 β S[1] (p. 231, Charles): καὶ ἔσται ἐκλεκτὸς θεοῦ ἕως τοῦ αἰῶνος, so He dwells among the elect on the transfigured earth, 45:3-5; 51:5 (61:4 ?). Cf. Eph. 1 and 1 Cl., 64 : Jesus as the Elect (verb), and we elected by Him (→ 175).

3. The Angels as the Elect. In the song of Raguel in Tob. 8:15 BA οἱ ἐκλεκτοί is synon. to ἄγγελοι. [8] In Eth. En. 39:1, cf. 6:2 the angels are chosen and holy children of heaven who acc. to Gn. 6:1 ff. come down to earth. Cf. 61:10 for the elect along with angels of power, dominion etc. It may be that the elect and beloved in 56:3 f. are the sons of fallen angels (or possibly those seduced by them). Cf. Joseph and Asenath, 16, 14. In Lidz. Ginza, too, the angels are described as elect (p. 96, 15; 74, 16).

D. "Elect" in the Mandaean Writings.

The Gnostic baptist sect uses the term (בהיריא or בהירא) almost more lavishly even than the writings already mentioned. The incidence in Ginza and Liturg., also Joh., is very high. The verb (ביהרה, "he elected") is comparatively rare, Lidz. Liturg., 88, 5; 89, 7 and 12; 95, 8; → 172 on Mk. 13:20. A threefold use is to be distinguished, though this shows that basically the one conception of the divine character of light is at work in this whole world of thought.

1. "Elect" is a term for fundamental religious concepts such as life and divine light, Ginza R, XV, 17, 353 (p. 371): Elect life, which has elected itself, cf. XV, 16, 351 (p. 368, 32 f.): the great life as the elected ; also XV, 14, 340 (p. 353). The same is said of the radiance of the kingdom of light, Liturg., 83, 10, → 186. Cf. the use for angels, → *supra*.

2. This life sends the messenger, the apostle, the helper, the son of life as the elect, Ginza R, XVI, 6, 367/68 (p. 391, 20 ff.), *ibid.*, p. 392, cf. Joh., 69, 10 etc. The mediating powers in the mission are given various names. Thus Jawar is the elect, the pure one, Liturg., 252-262, cf. Ginza R, XV, 15, 342 (p. 355); XV, 16, 345 (p. 360, 23). In Liturg., 204, 1 the Word appears as the Helper, also the Creator, the beloved first creation, the Architect, the great radiance of life, cf. Ginza R, V, 1, 172 (p. 176); XIV, 292 (p. 289), etc. Similarly, Ptahil-Uthra, the demiurge, is the elect. He, too, is sent, and life has set up for him a throne in the place of light, Joh., 210, 16; 211, 8. Anos bears the same name ; the song of the elect in the I style refers to him, Ginza R, XII, 3, 275 (p. 273). Hibil (Abel) is the great elect in XV, 2, 306 (p. 305, 12 f.). Cf. also Sum bar Nu (Shem), Joh., 62, 19. The call of Manda dHaije, personified γνῶσις ζωῆς, goes out to his elect, though the word is not used of gnosis itself. But Kusta (כושטא, truth) is called the good one, the elect of life, in Joh., 176, 6 f.; cf. Ginza R, XII, 2, 274 (p. 271). It has taken a place in the hearts of the elect, *ibid.*, p. 272, 27 f. Here too, then, though in varied mythological form, one finds the relation which is so important in apocalyptic. The elect mediator joins himself to the elect.

---

[8] In Tob. 8:15 we have the parallel members οἱ ἅγιοί σου καὶ πᾶσαι αἱ κτίσεις σου on the one side, and καὶ πάντες οἱ ἄγγελοί σου καὶ οἱ ἐκλεκτοί σου on the other.

3. It is only logical that this great process of redemption should produce elect. The ref. is to the Nasoraeans or Mandaeans, Ginza R, I, 170 (p. 26), 177 (p. 27). Cf. Hegemonius, Acta Archelai, 10, 5 (GCS, XVI, p. 16.11 and 13), ἐκλεκτοί of the Manichees. Pist. Soph., 27 (p. 28, 10 and 14, Schmidt) describes the elect as those who have received the mysteries. In Ginza R, XV, 1 (p. 296), *ibid.*, 297, 4, they are chosen from the world, cf. XV, 11, 328 (p. 337, 4), → 173. Synonyms are the perfect, I, 142 (p. 22) etc.; the good, Ginza L, III, 13, 91 (p. 529); R, XII, 3, 276 (p. 274). The elect are startled and aroused from sleep by the word of exhortation, R, XV, 1, 299 (p. 296); 14, 341 (p. 354, 34 f.). Hence the countless times when it is a leading term in admonition: "My elect," Ginza R, I, 104 (p. 17); Joh., 180, 6; 18; 22; Liturg., 165, 2; 5; 6. The awakening entails the illumining of the sons of Adam, their liberation from the earthly body, and their ascent to light. Thus Adam becomes the elect, the sinless, the pure, Ginza R, XVI, 6 (p. 391); *ibid.*, p. 392; cf. Joh., 69, 10; Ginza L, I, 2, 16 (p. 435). Thus redemption reaches its goal, the souls of the elect go to the house of life, the kingdom of light, R, XII, 7, 284 (p. 282); XV, 13, 337 (p. 349); Joh., 221, 21 ff.; Liturg., 207, 5 ff. The individual soul, too, is addressed as elect and pure, Ginza L, III, 4, 79 (p. 512) etc.; Liturg., 102, 12. Cf. the related view of the process of redemption in Eth. En. 5:7 f.

4. Finally, it is important in the battle of the sects for the title of elect that Ginza R, IX, 1 (p. 226 f.) speaks antagonistically of the elect of Ruha and of Christ in terms of rejection, if the conjecture of Lidzbarski is correct that the גיביא used here is a distortion of the Syr. גְּבַיָּא, "the elect." [9]

E. ἐκλεκτός in the New Testament.

1. The ἐκλεκτοί in the Synoptics.

In the Synoptic Gospels ἐκλεκτός is always used in an eschatological connection.

a. The meaning of the final sentence in the parable of the marriage feast in Mt. 22:14: πολλοὶ γάρ εἰσιν κλητοί, ὀλίγοι δὲ ἐκλεκτοί, is lit up by the whole trilogy in Mt. 21-22. Under the figures of sons, labourers and guests the relation of Israel to God's invitation is presented. In the first parable we simply find the righteous and sinners (21:31). In the second we have Israel and the Gentiles (ἄλλοι γεωργοί, v. 41 cf. with v. 43). The third refers to the same groups. The κεκλημένοι of 22:3, 4, 8 are those invited from Israel who set their own earthly interests above the Messianic wedding (cf. 22:6 with 21:35). Judgment executed on the Jewish state by the hosts of the king (v. 7) is the divine answer. The city is destroyed by fire, but there is a significant development outside, for the invitation now goes out to those on the street-corners (v. 9), the Gentiles, cf. in the parable of the vineyard, 21:41. They, too, are now κλητοί. But are they all ἐκλεκτοί? It undoubtedly belongs to the idea of the ἐκλεκτός that the reference should be to God's final choice in the light of the universal principle of the calling of the Gentiles. But the very word ἐκλεκτός shows that the invitation implies an obedience corresponding to grace. The condition of the wedding-garment is given a solid interpretation by the trilogy as a whole, 21:31: ποιεῖν τὸ θέλημα; 21:43: ποιεῖν τοὺς καρπούς. Total obedience is always at issue. Even the man without the garment is κλητός, but because he brings his disobedience to the wedding, and does not have the conduct which corresponds to blessing, he cannot

---

[9] Cf. Lidz. Ginza, p. 226, n. 2; on Ruha, the Holy Spirit, *ibid.*, *Einl.*, p. XI.

be a real participant. Election is fulfilled only in obedience. Hence we do not have here a static doctrine of election but a dynamic theology which is oriented to the right attitude of the elect. To receive gifts is of no avail if there is no readiness to obey. Thus the concept of election is set in living history. It demands responsibility and decision. To be sure, it is an eternal pronouncement, like everything which has to do with God's work. But it is not one which enslaves historical movement and decision fatalistically. On the contrary, it establishes decision. Nowhere do we read that those invited are forced to refuse. The whole point of the parable is that one does not have to decline or to appear in an unsuitable garment.[10]

The vl. at Lk. 14:24 GHXΓΛ eth, which introduces the same saying in connection with the parable of the wedding feast, is taken from Mt. 22:14. This was a natural interposition, since Lk. 14:7-24 uses the words καλεῖν and καλεῖσθαι 8 times. The vl. shows that the glossator understood the ἐκλεκτοί of the addition as those who obeyed the invitation, though the sifting out of those who come is not dealt with.

The predominantly western reading at Mt. 20:16 CDN lat sy arm eth, which has the same addition, is not authentic, since the parable of the labourers in the vineyard (Mt. 20:1-6) already culminates in the saying about the first and the last. But here, too, the gloss has value, for it shows that the ἐκλεκτοί are those who give evidence of a right attitude of faith in response to unmerited grace.

The different forms of the parable in Mt. and Lk. do not affect the meaning of ἐκλεκτός in Mt. The three groups invited in Lk. probably comprise the three classes present in the great trilogy of Mt., the righteous in Israel, the *'am-ha-'ares,* and the Gentiles.[11] In both cases there is a comprehensive historical view. If the twofold division of Mt. is simpler, the political aspect (the armies burn the city) and the condition of the garment are both stylistically and figuratively more complicated. One can hardly think that either version was dependent on the other. Lk. draws from his independent source. Both make application in terms of their own standpoint and composition.

b. The saying at the end of the parable of the unjust judge in Lk. 18:7 is introduced for no less practical reasons: ὁ δὲ θεὸς οὐ μὴ ποιήσῃ τὴν ἐκδίκησιν τῶν ἐκλεκτῶν αὐτοῦ τῶν βοώντων αὐτῷ ἡμέρας καὶ νυκτός, καὶ μακροθυμεῖ ἐπ' αὐτοῖς;[12] Here, too, ἐκλεκτοί is used eschatologically of the community of the end time. Like Mt. 22:14, the parable leads to unconditional trust on the one side and to fear and obedience on the other. The elect can influence God by their believing prayer. They can have an effect on history. They are heard and receive justice (→ II, 446). They are delivered. This is their consolation. Without it, the parable would be meaningless and dead. Nevertheless, it is instructive that what is said does not offer any basis for election. It simply shows what is the right standing and attitude of the elect. The controlling question is whether the Son of Man will find faith on the earth. No less than Mt. 22:14 and Mk. 13 and par. (→ 188), this implies the shattering of self-confidence, of human assurance of

[10] There is a similar grouping in Rev. 17:14. The victors who accompany the coming king, the whole company of martyrs of the end time, are κλητοί, ἐκλεκτοί, πιστοί. Here calling, election and perseverance are combined. The truth of Mt. 22:14 f., namely, that those who believe and obey are elected, has been stated as follows by J. Brenz in his comm. on Eph. (ed. W. Köhler, 1935, p. 11, 31 f.): *Occupat te formido, ne sis predestinatus, age, cape verbum, vive iuxta verbum, et predestinaberis.*

[11] Though cf. Schl. Lk., *ad loc.*

[12] On οἱ ἐκλεκτοὶ αὐτοῦ cf. Herm. v., 1, 3, 4; 2, 2, 5; 1 Cl., 2, 4; 59, 2; 2 Cl., 14, 5, always of those who believe in Christ.

election. The possibility of falling away is not suppressed; otherwise the final question would be pointless. This does not conflict with faith's looking to the God who conducts to the goal. Election is not a logical point of rest. It is the serious responsibility which confronts the community with the question of final decision. To close in this way after the word of unconditional consolation is to appeal to the centre of the conscience of the community. It is highly significant that the concept is always found in this context of exhortation.

c. The word ἐκλεκτοί occurs again in the Synoptic apocalypse, Mk. 13:19-27; Mt. 24:21-31. We have here Jewish ideas which have been worked over, reshaped, and given a universal scope: the antichrist, the elect, the flight, the shortening of the last time, expectation of the Son of Man coming out of concealment, the gathering of the dispersed community.[13] The close connection between the Son of Man and the elect is also found in Mt. 13:26 f. and par., though the phrase "the Elect and the elect" does not occur (Eth. En. → 184 f.). If ἐκλεκτός has an eschatological content, as in Jewish apocalyptic, there is no particularist or sectarian element. As in vv. 20, 22, the elect gathered from the four winds in Mk. 13:27[14] are believers in Christ throughout the world. They are the universal community of the end time which replaces Israel and which puts all its hope on the *parousia* of Christ.[15] The verbal οὓς ἐξελέξατο (13:20) which makes the term more explicit shows that it is used advisedly (→ 172).

The true theme of the discussion is the threat to the ἐκλεκτοί at the end, their preservation, and their conducting to the goal. Thus Mk. 13:20-23, Mt. 24:22 ff. and Lk. 18:7 f. all bear the same message. The only point is that it is now clearer (though cf. the ἐν τάχει of Lk. 18:8) that the divine mercy of preservation will be by the shortening of the days. Without this there would be no salvation, not only for πᾶσα σάρξ, but even for the ἐκλεκτοί (v. 20).

Already in apocal. there are two lines in relation to the end. The first is that a fixed time is appointed, 4 Esr. 4:37: it has been measured and reckoned, cf. 11:44. The second is what Schl. Mt., 707 f. calls the "flexibility of the divine government," cf. Apc. Abr. (→ 169) 29:13 on the shortening, or breaking off, of the aeon of the ungodly; S. Bar. 20:1. For the sense of the time of the world hastening to its end cf. 4 Esr. 4:26; 1 C. 7:29. There is a kind of synthesis of the two views in S. Bar. 83:1: The Most High most certainly causes His time to hasten by, and brings in His times. There is a different thought in Eth. En. 80:2, where the curse which acts on nature shortens the years as an act of judgment.

The shortening of Mk. 13:20 is characterised by the fact that it is wholly in the interests of the ἐκλεκτοί, cf. the εἰ μή, οὐκ ἄν of v. 20 with the εἰ δυνατόν of v. 22, all expressing the unshakable counsel of grace. The threat to the ἐκλεκτοί lies in the unprecedented θλῖψις (Mk. 13:19) and in false messianism and prophecy (13:21 ff.). Here too, as in Mt. 22:14; Lk. 18:7 f., warning is given to the elect,

---

[13] On this cf. Str.-B., I, 959; III, 153 and 854; IV, 891 and 902-910.

[14] Not without reason Schl. Mk., 247 raises the question whether at Mk. 13:27 (ἕως ἄκρου οὐρανοῦ) a scribe was also thinking of the resurrection. In view of Da. and Eth. En. this is a justifiable question. On this whole mode of expression cf. Eth. En. 57:2.

[15] Calvin on Mt. 24:22 interpreted the passage in the light of R. 11 and referred it to the remnant of Israel. But in Mt. 24, cf. v. 9, 14, 31, the ref. is always to the universal community from all nations. Calvin also intruded the categories of the elect and the reprobate into the text.

and yet everything is fixed on the keeping grace which leads to fear and trust. In particular the εἰ δυνατόν (cf. Jn. 10:28) points to the power of the divine preservation. Cf. the αὐτοῦ, which is well attested in Mt. 24:31, and added at Mk. 13:27: they are His elect. As such they are not only kept; they are also gathered and finally brought to the goal. But if the elect are only those who are kept, this means that election gives no logically satisfying certainty. It gives the assurance which is combined with holy fear. This is the assurance of standing in grace and of being made responsible thereby in a life of trust.

2. Christ as the Elect in Luke.

Common to the sayings in Lk. 9:35 and 23:35 is the fact that Christ in connection with His passion is called ὁ υἱός μου ὁ ἐκλελεγμένος (→ 144) at His transfiguration, just before entering the way of suffering, [16] and then ὁ χριστὸς τοῦ θεοῦ ὁ ἐκλεκτός as He hangs on the cross. [17] The first saying is a declaration of the heavenly voice, the second a contemptuous doubting of His claim by His enemies. It is in Lk., who in 24:26, 46 shows the passion to be a necessary point of transition to the glory, that this designation as the Elect is brought into connection with the suffering. He is the Elect, not merely in or in spite of His passion, but in His appointment thereto. The scorn of His adversaries proves that this Elect refuses to help Himself. Herewith His claim to be ἐκλεκτός is shown to imply a complete break with human ideas of success. The electing divine will does not depend on appearances. The combination ἐκλεκτός/ἐκλεκτοί is not found here, though it is striking that Lk. is the only Evangelist who has both in his gospel (cf. 18:7). Nevertheless, he does not say expressly that the ἐκλεκτός produces the ἐκλεκτοί, as does Paul in the case of the υἱός, Gl. 3:26; cf. 4:3, 5, 6, 7; R. 8:3, 9, 11, 14, 15, 19; also Hb. 2:10: The Son produces sons (cf. Eph. 1:4 ff. → 175). [18]

3. ἐκλεκτός in Paul.

It is surprising how little use Pl. makes of ἐκλεκτός. Is the former Pharisee afraid of using a word which was so often misapplied in later Judaism? He does have it, of course, in R. 8:33 at the climax of the letter. Here its sums up emphatically all that has been said in 8:14 f. about the bearers of the Spirit, the υἱοὶ θεοῦ, the ἀγαπῶντες τὸν θεόν. In conclusion, then, the whole of the divine work, salvation, and new creation, from its pre-temporal origin (8:28-30) [19] to the final

[16] Cf. Lk. 9:31: Moses and Elijah speak with Him about His ἔξοδος.

[17] In both cases abs., as apposition, not adj., cf. the usage of apocal. → 184. On ἐκλελεγμένος → II, 740. The reading ἐκλελεγμένος is authentic, ℵ BLΞa ff^{2} (*electus*) sy^{c} sy^{hlmg} eth bo sa arm. — ἀγαπητός as Mt. 17:5; Mk. 9:7: ACDNΨ vg sy^{c} sy^{pesh} sy^{hl} Marc. For textual criticism cf. A. Merx, *Die Ev. d. Mk. u. Lk.* (1905), 266. A. v. Harnack, *Studien,* I (1931), 129.

[18] It is not wholly impossible that the reading ὁ ἐκλεκτός for ὁ υἱὸς τοῦ θεοῦ at Jn. 1:34 represents an older text which was gradually replaced on Christological grounds. It is found in P. Oxy., II, 208, fol. 1$^{r\,7}$ (3rd. cent.), ℵ* 77. 218. sy^{sc}e ff^{2} Ambros, and cf. the mixed text (ἐκλεκτός with υἱός), sy^{hc} a b ff^{2} Corr. This view is accepted by F. Blass, *Euangelion secundum Joh.* (1902); Zn. J.; A. Merx, *Das Ev. des Joh.* (1911), *ad loc.*; A. Harnack, SAB (1915), 552-556 = *Studien,* I (1931), 127-132. On the other hand, an isolated ἐκλεκτός as compared with the common υἱός sounds non-Johannine, and Jn. does not hesitate elsewhere to put his own terms on the lips of the Baptist (as against Harnack, 131).

[19] In R. 8, as in Rev. 17:14, κλητός is used alongside ἐκλεκτός, cf. v. 28 with v. 33.

glorification, is summed up in the one term. Because the community consists of the ἐκλεκτοὶ θεοῦ, there is no more accusation or condemnation, since, grounded thus, it cannot be separated from the love of God (8:37-39). This view of R. 8:33 is confirmed by the fact that in Col. 3:12 the ἐκλεκτοὶ τοῦ θεοῦ [20] are the ἅγιοι καὶ ἠγαπημένοι. [21] Here, too, the whole community is addressed. As the elect, Christians must love one another. The aim of election is love. He who is loved by God can now love in truth. R. 16:13, where Rufus is called ὁ ἐκλεκτὸς ἐν κυρίῳ, shows that the individual member as well as the whole community can be described in this way. [22]

The use in the Past. is more formal, cf. Tt. 1:1. Yet cf. also 2 Tm. 2:10, where the reference to the final goal should be noted. 1 Tm. 5:21 is an example of the designation of angels as ἐκλεκτοί (→ 185).

4. ἐκλεκτός and συνεκλεκτός in 1 Peter and the Johannine Epistles.

1 Pt. is the only NT work in which ἐκλεκτός has from the very outset thematic significance. Here everything is worked out in terms of this controlling concept. In 1:1 the readers are characterised at once as ἐκλεκτοὶ παρεπίδημοι διασπορᾶς, and there then follow the names of provinces or districts in Asia Minor. The ref. is to Gentile Christians, who are figuratively aliens, living in dispersion here on earth. In this age their position is that of foreigners, but they belong to the community of the elect. They are ἐκλεκτοὶ παρεπίδημοι, v. 2: κατὰ πρόγνωσιν θεοῦ πατρός, ἐν ἁγιασμῷ πνεύματος, εἰς ὑπακοὴν καὶ ῥαντισμὸν αἵματος Ἰησοῦ Χριστοῦ. Here already one may see a kind of doctrine of election, or at least a view of the Christian state, its basis, means and goal in trinitarian order, which rests on the eternal election. There can be no doubt (cf. 1:20 : προεγνωσμένου πρὸ καταβολῆς κόσμου in a Christological sense) that the πρόγνωσις implies the eternal pronouncement which is the pre-temporal basis of election. The ἐν denotes the means whereby election is enacted : the ἁγιασμός of the Spirit, dedication to God. The εἰς tells us that the goal of election is obedience and the actualistion of the central sacrificial act of Christ in the life of believers.

As may be see from 2:11 : ὡς παροίκους καὶ παρεπιδήμους, this opening theme is further developed in 2:4-10. The supremely important point here is that basic OT promises and predicates, which originally applied to the people of Israel, are now transferred to the universal Christian community. Christianity knows that it is the elect Israel. Christ is the chosen corner-stone of the temple (λίθον ἐκλεκτόν, v. 4, 6 → 182). Through Him the community becomes a temple, a priesthood offering sacrifices (→ III, 250). It is a γένος ἐκλεκτόν (→ 183), a holy people, a people of possession. The transfer is wholly grounded upon, and executed by, Christ. There can be little room for doubt that emphasis is here laid upon the link between the λίθος ἐκλεκτός (Christ) and the γένος ἐκλεκτόν,

[20] ἐκλεκτοὶ τοῦ θεοῦ is common in the post-apost. fathers, 1 Cl., 1, 1; 46, 4; 49, 5; Herm. v., 2, 1, 3; 3, 8, 3.

[21] On ἅγιος with ἐκλεκτός cf. Eth. En. → 185; Wis. 4:15 (3:9 S); ὅσιος, Ign. Tr. inscr. → 191, n. 27; Mart. Pol., 22, 1.

[22] Why this singling out of an individual ? Pr.-Bauer[3], *s.v.* considers the sense of "outstanding Christian," as is said of Rheus Agathopus in Ign. Phil., 11, 1: ἀνδρὶ ἐκλεκτῷ. This is linguistically possible but unlikely in Pl., who is surely more concerned to show that any excellence of Rufus has its spiritual norm ἐν κυρίῳ.

along the lines of Eph. 1:6 (→ 175). The similarity of designations is intentional. In content a total view of the images suggests that the λίθος ἐκλεκτός creates and upholds the γένος ἐκλεκτόν (→ 184).

In 2:7, 8 (note the antithetical ὑμεῖς δέ which introduces the further statement about election), the unbelieving and disobedient are contrasted with this elect generation.[23] It is certainly not said that from all eternity the world has been divided into the predestined and the reprobate. What is said is that everything depends upon whether one is willing or not to believe in Christ and to obey Him. The community (1:1 f.) knows that its own status is eternally grounded. Hence in relation to the unbelieving and disobedient it is not dealing with human contingencies but with God's judicial action. Nevertheless, it is illegitimate to extend the εἰς ὃ καὶ ἐτέθησαν of 2:8 to mean that they cannot do otherwise because hereto foreordained from all eternity. Again with reference to responsible decision, the saying is again stating that even when it is confronted by the hardened unbelief and disobedience of others, the community has to do with God. In assessing the situation, it must look beyond men and be still in the presence of the divine overruling and the divine judgment. Here is both the meaning and the limit of the statement.[24]

Vital here is the emphasis laid on the ministry bound up with the ἐκλεκτός — cf. the εἰς of 1:2 esp. with the ὅπως τὰς ἀρετὰς ἐξαγγείλητε of 2:9. The universal calling of the elect people of God is to proclaim the powerful mercy revealed in this election and calling, v. 10. It is thus that the divine goal is fulfilled. The whole exhortation of the epistle is anchored in this basic ordination. It makes quite impossible both a false sense of election and a proud isolation from unbelievers.

In 1 Pt., however, the thought of election does not just apply to the community as a whole (γένος ἐκλεκτόν may be compared with the body of Christ in Pl.) or to its manifestation in the individual ἐκλεκτοί. Quite logically in 5:13 it is also used for the local congregation from which the author is writing, the συνεκλεκτὴ ἐν Βαβυλῶνι which as a single ἐκλεκτή realises that it is combined with the other ἐκλεκταί to constitute the whole.[25] At 2 Jn. 1, 13 (ἐκλεκτὴ κυρία and τὰ τέκνα τῆς ἀδελφῆς σου τῆς ἐκλεκτῆς) we are also to think in terms of the personified congregation.[26] Belief in election does not stop short of the individual form of the community. It consistently applies the ἐκλεκτός to every concrete manifestation.[27]

---

[23] For the contrast ἄπιστοι/ἐκλεκτοί cf. Mart. Pol., 16, 1.

[24] Cf. *ad loc.*: Schl. Erl.; Schl., *Petrus u. Paulus nach dem 1 Pt.* (1937), 98; Wnd., Gunkel (*Schr. NT*³), Kn., Wbg. Pt. Cf. also Spörri, 165. Here, too, one should remember the dependence of 1 Pt. on R. Paul's treatment of the hardening of the Jews in R. 9-11 is similar.

[25] On the view that the ref. is to Peter's wife, Zn. Einl., II, 16, n. 11. ἐκκλησία is to be supplied with συνεκλεκτή; א pesh vulg Hier put this before συνεκλεκτή. On a probable allusion to Rome (→ I, 516) in secret apocal. speech, cf. Papias, Jer., Hilary (Zn. Einl., II, 20 ff.). Schl. Gesch. d. erst. Chr., 303 favours Babylon on the Euphrates, cf. also his *Petrus u. Paulus* ..., 176-179.

[26] On 2 Jn. 1, 13 cf. B. Weiss, *Br. des Ap. Joh.*⁶ (1899), 168 f. The κυρία is to be construed as *domina familiae*, hardly as the wife of the κύριος (Zn. Einl., II, 593, n. 8). Such a play on words would hardly be in keeping with the seriousness of the Joh. writings. Cl. Alex. Adumbrationes in 2 Jn. 1 in Zahn Forsch., III, 92 is not at all clear.

[27] Cf. Ign. Tr. inscr.: ἐκκλησίᾳ ἁγίᾳ τῇ οὔσῃ ἐν Τράλλεσιν τῆς Ἀσίας, ἐκλεκτῇ καὶ ἀξιοθέῳ.

5. Summary.

a. Against the historical background of later Judaism, with its nationalistic pride in election and its sectarian restriction, primitive Christianity gives a wholly new turn to the concept on the basis of Christ Himself. It has in view the election of a universal community in which there is no place for the developments mentioned.

b. For it, too, election denotes the eternal basis of salvation. But in the NT we never find the danger against which the history of dogma has continually to fight, namely, that of bringing the concept of election into too close proximity to a view which is to be described as enslavement to εἱμαρμένη or fate. It is never separated from responsibility and decision. It is never remote from living history. If anchored in eternity, it is also functional in history.

c. The truth that election does not aim at the preferential treatment of one part of the race involves the further positive truth that the community as a whole is elected for the whole of the human race. It is commissioned to fulfil eschatological and teleological tasks in the service of the divine overruling.

F. ἐκλεκτός in the Apostolic Fathers.

These writings manifest an extraordinary increase in the use of ἐκλεκτός. 1 Cl. and Herm. are particularly fond of it. In connection with the growing use it is instructive that in phrases like 1 Cl., 46, 8 : ἕνα τῶν ἐκλεκτῶν μου σκανδαλίσαι (millstone), or 2 Cl., 14, 5 : ἃ ἡτοίμασεν ὁ κύριος τοῖς ἐκλεκτοῖς αὐτοῦ, there is an alteration of NT sayings. 1 Cl. shows a great interest in the idea of the number of the elect (→ 184). But we can still find πολὺ πλῆθος ἐκλεκτῶν in 1 Cl., 6, 1. This usage in the post-apost. fathers shows how sparse is the NT use. Of course, even the post-apost. fathers fall far short of the unrestricted use in Eth. En. (→ 183). On Christ as ἐκλεκτός → ἐκλέγεσθαι, 175 and → ἐκλογή, 180.[28]

Schrenk

---

[28] On this cf. A. v. Harnack, *Studien*, I (1931), 131, n. 1; Epiph. Haer., 55, 8, 3.

† λεῖος

Common in class. and later Gk. from the time of Hom. [1] in the sense of "smooth," "level," "offering no resistance," esp. of plants, animals, stones, objects (fig. in the sense of "fine," "tender," "sweet," but also "smooth," "hard to grasp." In connection with the one use in the NT we may refer to the sense of level ground (squares or streets), Il., 12, 30; 23, 330, 359; Od., 5, 443; 10, 103; Hes. Op., 288; Hdt., VII, 9; IX, 69; Aristot. Hist. An., IX, 37 ff., p. 622a, 33; V, 17, p. 549b, 14. Opp. τραχύς, Xenoph. Mem., III, 10, 1; Aristot. Cat., 8, p. 10a, 17, 22 f.; Gen. An., V, 8, p. 788a, 23, 25. Ditt. Syll.³, 972, 119; BGU, I, 162, 5; III, 781, Col. II, 15. In the LXX for חָלָק (חָלוּק), Gn. 27:11 (of smooth skin without hair); 1 Βασ. 17:40 (of pebbles); fig. Prv. 2:20: ... εὕροσαν ἂν τρίβους δικαιοσύνης λείους; also Prv. 12:13; 26:23. [2] Is. 40:4 (AQS^cC, cf. Lk. 3:5): ὁδοὺς λείας (Mas. בִּקְעָה).

In the NT the adj. occurs only at Lk. 3:5 in introducing the story of the Baptist. Lk. quotes Is. 40:3 (cf. Mt., Mk.) and also v. 4 f. with some slight deviation from the Mas. and LXX: καὶ ἔσται τὰ σκολιὰ εἰς εὐθείας καὶ αἱ τραχεῖαι εἰς ὁδοὺς λείας (for ... εἰς εὐθεῖαν καὶ ἡ τραχεῖα εἰς πεδία), "and the crooked shall be made straight, and the rough ways shall be made smooth."

Lk. differs from Mk., as does Mt., by omitting the quotation from Mal. and also by putting the quotation from Is. after the main sentence. He also differs from both Mk. and Mt. in respect of the quotation formula, the directness of the quotation, and the omission of a description of the Baptist and his success. In many ways the express quotation as a whole reveals a theological concern. It identifies the Baptist from the very first as a messenger of joy (cf. 3:18 and → II, 719). The dawn of the Messianic age will reverse human standards of what is exalted and base. Witness is also borne to the universal scope of salvation (3:6). In addition, the prophecy, and the preceding synchronism (3:1 f.), give the appearance of the Baptist its place both in history and also in salvation history, and the section 3:1-6 serves as a special prologue to the account of the Baptist which follows (3:7-20).

Bornkamm

λεῖος. [1] Pass., Liddell-Scott, Preisigke Wört., *s.v.* Root *lei* (Lat. *lēvis*) Prellwitz Etym. Wört., *s.v.*; Walde-Pok., II, 389 f.

[2] In 2 passages in Prv. there is no Heb. original. λεῖος is used for חלק at 26:23; the LXX probably read חלק. S seems to confirm this with its δόλιος, which is found for חלק at ψ 11:2; in fact, the Hexapla translators often use λεῖος for חלק [Bertram].

† λεῖμμα, † ὑπόλειμμα, † καταλείπω (κατά-, περί-, διάλειμμα)

Contents: A. Greek Usage: 1. λεῖμμα; 2. Compounds. B. The "Remnant" in the Old Testament: 1. Usage; 2. The Rise of the Concept of the Remnant; 3. The Remnant established by God; 4. The Conversion of the Remnant; 5. The Remnant and the Nations; 6. The Remnant Community and the Messiah. C. The Thought of the Remnant in Paul as compared with its Occurrence in Apocalyptic and the Rabbis: 1. The Remnant in R. 9-11; 2. Comparison and Summary.

A. Greek Usage.

1. λεῖμμα (from λείπω) means τὸ λείψανον, μέρος ὑπολειφθέν, ὑπόλοιπον, ὑπολειπόμενον, κατάλοιπον, [1] "what is left over," "what remains," "surplus." Since ει is pronounced as ῑ, we also find the incorrect λίμμα. [2]

a. In general usage the term finds many applications. Hdt., I, 119 has τοῦ παιδὸς τὰ λείμματα for the remains of the slaughtered son of Harpagus, cf. also τὰ λοιπὰ τῶν κρεῶν. Plut. Quomodo Quis Suos in Virtute Sentiat Profectus, 5 (II, 78a) has τὰ σὰ λείμματα for the fragments which Diogenes uses at mealtime. Plut. Nicias, 17 (I, 534d) has it for the rest of the as yet uncompleted wall of Syracuse. It is found in

---

λεῖμμα κτλ. F. Baumgärtel, *Die Eigenart d. at.lichen Frömmigkeit* (1932); W. Baumgartner, "Kennen Amos u. Hosea eine Heilseschatologie?" *Schweizerische Theol. Zeitschrift,* XXX (1913), 30-42, 95-124, 152-170; J. Boehmer, "Die Eigenart d. prophetischen Heilspredigt des Amos," ThStKr, 76 (1903), 35 ff.; W. Cossmann, "Die Entwicklung des Gerichtsgedankens bei den at.lichen Propheten," *Beih.* ZAW, 29 (1915); K. Cramer, "Amos, Versuch einer theol. Interpretation," BWANT, 15 (1930), 130 ff.; E. K. Dietrich, *Die Umkehr (Bekehrung u. Busse) im AT u. im Judentum* ... (1936); H. Dittmann, "Der heilige Rest im AT," ThStKr, 87 (1914), 603 ff.; G. Gloege, "Reich Gottes u. Kirche im NT," *Nt.liche Forschungen, 2. Reihe,* 4 (1929), 212 ff.; H. Gressmann, "Der Ursprung d. israelitisch-jüdischen Eschatologie," *Forschungen z. Religion u. Literatur des A. u. NT,* 6 (1905), esp. 229 ff. (2nd ed.: *Der Messias,* NF, 26 [1929]); J. Hempel, "Vom irrenden Glauben," ZSTh, 7 (1929/30), 631-660; "Gott u. Mensch im AT," BWANT, *3. Folge* 2^2 (1936); G. Hölscher, "D. Ursprünge d. jüdischen Eschatologie," *Vorträge d. theol. Konferenz zu Giessen, 41. Folge* (1925); J. Köberle, *Sünde u. Gnade im religiösen Leben des Volkes Israel bis auf Christum* (1905); L. Köhler, *Theol. d. AT* (1936); E. König, *Geschichte der At.lichen Religion*^{2} (1915); *Theol. d. AT*^{3,4} (1923); H. H. Krause, "Der Gerichtsprophet Amos, ein Vorläufer des Deuteronomisten," ZAW, NF, 9 (1932), 221 ff.; J. Meinhold, *Studien z. israelitischen Religionsgeschichte,* I: *Der heilige Rest* (1903); S. Mowinckel, *Psalmenstudien,* II: *Das Thronbesteigungsfest Jahwäs u. d. Ursprung d. Eschatologie* (1922), esp. 276 ff.; E. Sellin, *D. at.liche Prophetismus* (1912), 105 ff.; M. Weber, *Ges. Aufsätze z. Religionssoziologie,* III: *Das antike Judt.* (1923); A. Weiser, "Die Profetie d. Amos," *Beih.* ZAW, 53 (1929); H. W. Wolff, "Die Begründungen der prophetischen Heils- und Unheilssprüche," ZAW, NF, 11 (1934), 1 ff.

[1] Joseph., who does not use λεῖμμα, normally (18 times) has τὸ λείψανον and plur.: of the people, Ant., 11, 213; Bell., 4, 410; 5, 522; of the land, Bell., 2, 90; 4, 556; of the city, 6, 365; 7, 376; also abstr., 1, 29; 3, 465; 4, 657. Occasionally (4 times) we also find τὰ λειπόμενα, ὑπολελειμμένα, 4, 413 (of Jerusalem); Ant., 10, 165 (of Israel). But the theological and prophetic idea of the remnant does not occur. On τὸ λείψανον cf. Stob. Hermetica Excerpt 23, 19 and 30 (Corp. Herm., I, p. 468, 474).

[2] Westcott and Hort have this in the NT, though the weight of evidence in the MSS does not support λίμμα.

the sense of a deficit in accounts in, e.g., P. Tebt., 115, 23 (2nd cent. B.C.), IG, V (1), 1432, 9 (Messene, 1st cent. B.C. to 1st cent. A.D.). b. In early Gk. musical theory [3] the "canonics" (c. 300 B.C.), who tried to fix intervals with mathematical exactness on a Pythagorean basis, used it for an interval. λεῖμμα is here the diatonic half-tone step which is left as the rest of the pure fourth after the deduction of the two whole tone steps. [4] c. The Gk. translators of the OT use it of things, Ιερ. 27:19 Θ: τὸ λεῖμμα τῶν σκευῶν (יֶתֶר), of persons and groups, rarely for descendants, 2 Βασ. 14:7 AL+, O—AM (instead of κατάλειμμα B). This promotes in Lv. 18:6, 12, 17; 20:19 "Αλλ the false rendering λίμμα ("Αλλ reads שְׁאָר, for שְׁאֵר flesh, blood-relative). One who remains or survives, Dt. 2:34 and 3:3 'Α (שָׂרִיד). The remnant of the people, Ιερ. 52:15 'Α (יֶתֶר), with no special religious sense. On the prophetic view → 200 ff.; 4 Βασ. 19:4 A (שְׁאֵרִית); [5] Is. 37:4 ΣΘ (שְׁאֵרִית), where the LXX has οἱ καταλελειμμένοι.

2 The compounds ὑπόλειμμα, κατάλειμμα, περίλειμμα have the same sense.

ὑπόλειμμα displays a. even outside the Bible the same variety in use. It is especially common in a scientific context, Aristot. Gen. An., II, 6, p. 744b, 15 synon. to περίττωμα. Cf. Hist. An., VI, 2, p. 559b, 21; Theophr. De Causis Plantarum, 5, 15, 6: τὰ ὑπολείμματα τῶν ῥιζῶν, cf., 5, 1, 5; 1, 11, 3. Of what is left on the sale of wine, P. Greci e Latini, VII, 860, 8 (3rd cent. B.C.). Of remnants of rebellion, Plut. Pomp., 16 (I, 626e) ὑπολείμματα τῶν στάσεων. b. In the Gk. transl. of the Bible [6] it is used for the remains of food, supplies etc.: 1 Βασ. 9:24 (שְׁאָר ni); Job 20:21 (שָׂרִיד) LXX Θ; 1 Macc. 6:53; Wis. 13:12 A plur. of the remains of burned wood (BS: ἀποβλήματα), though also the prophetic remnant, for שְׁאֵרִית, שְׁאָר 4 Βασ. 21:14; Mi. 4:7; 5:6 (7); 5:7 (8); Is. 11:11 'ΑΣΘ, cf. Eus. Dem. Ev., II, 3, 119. [7]

τὸ κατάλειμμα, in secular Gk. Gal., XIV, p. 456, 13 (Kühn): of what remains of sickness. In OT translations, a. of plants, Is. 37:30, the rest of what has grown (Mas. שָׁחִים, what has grown of itself); Ιερ. 30:3 BS (Mas. 49:9), cf. Swete, gleanings of grapes (עֹלֵלוֹת). b. Descendants for שְׁאֵרִית, Gn. 45:7; 2 Βασ. 14:7 B → λεῖμμα, *supra;* Is. 14:30 of the Philistines; Is. 14:22 of Babylon (שְׁאָר); Tob. 13:17 א: τὸ κατάλειμμα τοῦ σπέρματός μου. c. The remnant of the people, with no specific religious sense: 1 Βασ. 13:15 B (not in the Heb.); 3 Βασ. 12:24y B (not in the Heb.); Ιερ. 8:3 'ΑΣ (שְׁאֵרִית); 47 (Mas. 40):11 (A+ plur.); 1 Macc. 3:35; what is left of Jerusalem; the remnant of the house of Ahab, 4 Βασ. 10:11 (שָׂרִיד), synon. οἱ καταλειφθέντες. The

---

[3] Already Plato in Plut. De Animae Procreatione, in Timaeo Platonis, 12 (II, 1017 F) speaks of the musical λεῖμμα. Cf. then Nicomachus Enchiridion (excerpta), c. 2, p. 269 in Musici Scriptores Graeci (1895); Aristides Quintilianus, De Musica (ed. A. Jahn [1882], p. 27), 1, 18 has the definition: λεῖμμα δὲ ἐν ῥυθμῷ χρόνος κενὸς ἐλάχιστος; cf. also Gaudentius, c. 13, p. 342 f. (ed. A. Jahn). For recent presentations cf. T. Reinach, *La musique grecque* (1926), 23 f.; C. Sachs, "Die Musik d. Antike," *Hndbch. der Musikwissenschaft,* IVc, 19 (1928), 22; M. Emmanuel, "Grèce" in *Encyclopédie de la Musique,* I (1928), 464.

[4] To be distinguished from the ἀποτομή, the chromatic half-tone step, which arises with the deduction of the λεῖμμα from the whole tone step. Cf. H. Riemann-A. Einstein, *Musiklexikon* (1929), Art. *Apotome u. Tonbestimmung.*

[5] The λήμματος of B (cf. Thackeray, 84) has nothing to do with λῆμμα (gain, advantage) but like κατάλημμα in Ju. 5:13 B (שָׂרִיד deserter, one who runs away; the text is defective, Moore having ישראל) it has the incorrect η for ει.

[6] Cf. the use of ὑπολείπειν in the LXX, which is also a transl. of שְׁאָר ni and hi.

[7] Difficult texts, Mal. 2:15 for שְׁאָר, where in the Mas. the ref. is to God's seed in the sense of pure Jewish descent; Ιερ. 15:11 'Α (שְׁאֵרִית); Job 4:21 "Αλλ wrongly has ὑπόλειμμα for יֶתֶר, "tent-rope."

remnant of other peoples, Ιερ. 27 (Mas. 50):26, the Chaldeans; 29:5 (Mas. 47:5) 'Α κοιλάδων, strictly Anakites, both times שְׁאֵרִית. Rest of opponents, Job 22:20 LXX Θ (יֶתֶר). d. The prophetic concept of the remnant, 4 Βασ. 19:31 (שְׁאֵרִית); Is. 10:22 (שְׁאָר); cf. R. 9:27 → 210; Sir. 44:17 ABS[2] of Noah: διὰ τοῦτον ἐγενήθη κατάλειμμα τῇ γῇ (שְׁאֵרִית) a reading of Gn. in the light of prophecy, cf. Eth. En. 83:8 → 212. In Sir. 47:22 God will leave Jacob a remnant. [8]

περίλειμμα, too, means "remnant." Plat. Menex., 236b of fragments of a funeral oration. [9]

διάλειμμα is used in Plut. Quomodo Quis Suos in Virtute Sentiat Profectus, 3 (II, 76d): διάλειμμα προκοπῆς, the arrest in growth, denied for philosophy. It plays a special part in medicine. Hippocr. acc. to Gal., VII, p. 414, 11 (Kühn, 1824) uses it for the intermission of fever. Cf. also VII, p. 420, 17 f.; 425, 17; 427, 3; IX, p. 552, 16. Gal. also has the verb διαλείπειν for this. Joseph. in Ant., 1, 330; Bell., 6, 17 has ἐκ διαλειμμάτων for the spaces between sections.

Schrenk

B. The "Remnant" in the Old Testament.

1. Usage.

a. In the OT there are four roots to express the idea of the remnant, of "being left" or "delivered," of "having escaped": שאר, פלט, שרד, יתר. Of these שאר with its derivatives occurs in the OT 220 times (the noun שְׁאָר 25 times and שְׁאֵרִית 66 times), פלט with derivatives 80 times, שרד with derivatives 29 times, יתר with derivatives 103 times (the noun יֶתֶר 91 times). Often individual expressions are combined or occur in parallelism, e.g., השאיר־להם שריד ופליט, Jos. 8:22; פליט ושריד לשארית, Jer. 44:14; שריד and פליט Jer. 42:17; Lam. 2:22; השא ר שריד, Nu. 21:35; Dt. 2:34; 3:3; Jos. 8:22; 10:28, 30, 33, 37, 39, 40; Jos. 11:8; 2 K. 10:11. שאר ישראל ופליטת בית־יעקב, Is. 10:20; שארית ופליטה, 2 K. 19:31 (Is. 37:32); Ezr. 9:14; cf. Gn. 45:7; את שארית הפליטה, 1 Ch. 4:43; פליטת בית־יהודה הנשארה, 2 K. 19:30 (Is. 37:31); נשארנו פליטה, Ezr. 9:15; להשאיר פליטה, Ezr. 9:8; הנשאר והנותר, Is. 4:3; את יתר הפלטה, Ex. 10:5; נותרה־בה פלטה, Ez. 14:22; הותיר שריד Is. 1:9, cf. also Gn. 32:9; Neh. 1:2; 2 Ch. 30:6. Along with the sense of rest or remnant פלט carries the sense of escape or deliverance, שרד contains the element of fear and flight, שאר and יתר are largely synon. (though the sense "to have the advantage" is found for יתר in the hi [?] at Gn. 49:4; cf. יֶתֶר for "advantage" in Gn. 49:3; the basic sense of יתר is "to span," intr. "to be stretched out," "to surpass," and it may be that שְׁאָר too, has this sense of "advantage" at Mal. 2:15, cf. Tg. שְׁארוּתָא)

b. For the nouns שְׁאָר and שְׁאֵרִית, which are most important theologically, the LXX usually has verbal forms of καταλείπειν or ὑπολείπειν. שְׁאָר is rendered τὸ καταλειφθέν, Is. 10:19 ff.; 11:11, 16; 28:5; or τὸ κατάλοιπον, Is. 21:17; 2 Ch. 24:14: οἱ κατάλοιποι; Ezr. 4:3; Neh. 11:1; 2 Ch. 9:29. Nouns used are κατάλειμμα, Is. 10:22; 14:22, and ὑπόλειμμα, Mal. 2:15. As derivatives of the simple form τὸ λοιπόν, Is. 17:3; Neh. 11:20, and οἱ λοιποί, Esth. 9:16; Ezr. 4:7; 1 Ch. 16:41. שְׁאֵרִית is translated τὸ κατάλοιπον, Is. 15:9; 46:3; Jer. 24:8; 2 Ch. 34:9; οἱ κατάλοιποι, Jer. 8:3; 15:9; 23:3; 39(46):3; 40(47):15; 41(48):16; 42(49):2, 19; 43(50):5; 44(51):12, 28; 47(29):4 f.; Ez. 5:10; 9:8; 11:13; 25:16; 36:3; Am. 1:8; 9:12; Mi. 2:12; 7:18; Zeph. 2:9; 3:13; Hag. 1:12, 14;

---

[8] The influence of the remnant idea may be seen in the mistranslation of נִיר, at 3 Βασ. 15:4 LXX Θ. Ιερ. 32:38 (Mas. 25:38) Q (Heb. סֻכּוֹ) is a misreading for κατάλυμα ABS.

[9] Cf. περιλείπομαι in Pr.-Bauer, *s.v.* and the use of περιλείπειν (שְׁאָר ni) in the LXX.

2:2; Zech. 8:6, 12; 1 Ch. 4:43; 2 Ch. 36:20; οἱ καταλελειμμένοι, Is. 37:31 f.; τὰ κατάλοιπα, Jer. 6:9; κατάλειμμα, Gn. 45:7; 2 S. 14:7; 2 K. 19:31; Is. 14:30; Jer. 40(47):11; 50(27):26; τὸ ἐπίλοιπον, Jer. 25(32):20.

c. When one reviews the usage, a first impression is that the predominant use of שׁאר, פלט, שׂרד, יתר and derivatives is secular. The ref. might be to the wood left over in making an idol (Is. 44:17, 19), the remainder of trees of the forest (Is. 10:19), or the land still left to be taken (Jos. 13:1), the nations remaining (Jos. 23:4, 7), or the rest of a series of years (Lv. 25:52), of food (1 S. 9:24), of the coal (fig. 2 S. 14:7), of strength (Da. 10:8), of breath (Da. 10:17), of blood (Lv. 5:9). Occasionally שְׁאֵרִית can take on the sense of descendants, Gn. 45:7; 2 S. 14:7; Is. 14:22; Jer. 11:23.[10] In enumerations "all the rest" can mean all those remaining, Hag. 1:12, 14 (?); 2:2; Zech. 12:14; Esth. 9:12; 9:16; Ezr. 3:8; 4:3, 7; Neh. 7:71; 10:29; 11:1, 20; 1 Ch. 12:39; 16:41; 2 Ch. 9:29; 34:9; cf. also a similar use in Arabic. We also find the expression "not one remained" in the sense of "all," Jos. 8:17; 2 K. 10:21. As a term for complete destruction one also reads that the remnant (i.e., those remaining, all) was destroyed, Dt. 7:20; 2 K. 10:11, 17; Is. 14:30; Jer. 15:9; 21:7; 44:12; 47:4, 5; 50:26, 29; Ez. 5:10; 17:21; 25:16; Am. 1:8; 1 Ch. 4:43; cf. Ezr. 9:14. For terrible destruction one finds the phrase "nothing remained but ...," 2 K. 13:7; 17:18; 24:14; 2 Ch. 21:17. If here the remnant denotes the greatness of the judgment, it can also be used positively, Gn. 14:10; 42:38; Dt. 3:11; Jos. 13:12; 1 S. 5:4; 11:11; 2 K. 3:25; 25:12, 22; Jer. 34:7; 37:10; 38:22; 39:10; 52:16.

Often the remnant is a definite historical entity, e.g., the remnant of a people which survives a disaster. Thus the people is called a remnant under Hezekiah, 2 K. 19:4; Is. 37:4, and those who remained under Josiah are the remnant, 2 Ch. 34:21, as are also those who remain in Jerusalem after the deportation of 597 under Zedekiah, 2 K. 25:11; Jer. 24:8; 52:15; Ez. 9:8; 11:13; 2 Ch. 36:20. This remnant is taken to Babylon in 586, but some vine-dressers still remain. Those left behind under Gedaliah are called the remnant, 2 K. 25:22; Jer. 40:6, 11, 15; 41:10, 16; 42:2, 15, 19; 43:5; 44:12, 28. Of these remaining there is no remnant when they go to Egypt, Jer. 42:17; 44:7, 14. Finally, the Jews who come back from exile are the remnant, e.g., Hag. 1:12, 14; 2:2; Zech. 8:6, 11, 12; Ezr. 9:8, 13, 14, 15; Neh. 1:2, 3.

d. If the ref. here seems to be to those who survive historical catastrophes, there is a whole series of verses in which it is hard to say whether the remnant consists of those who are delivered from historical catastrophes or from eschatological judgment, Am. 5:15; Mi. 2:12; Jer. 6:9; 8:3; 11:23; Ez. 6:12; 9:8; 11:13. The reason for this lies in the distinctive nature of OT eschatology, which views historical and eschatological events together. Eschatology is concerned not only with the end of the time of this world, but also with the invasion of this time by God's reality.[11] Thus the prophets proclaim the coming of God into the here and now, but they also understand all history as eschatological occurrence which takes its meaning from the "to-day" of prophetic preaching. The history of the past, too, speaks of the coming of God which the prophet now proclaims. If along these lines we consider that in the course of the history of God's people the thought of the remnant was constantly applied to those who survived the great catastrophes of judgment, it is obvious that the boundary between the secular and the theological use of the concept will be a fluid one, e.g., Ezr. 9:8.

e. It may also be seen — very clearly from the time of Is. — that the thought of the remnant as a theological concept belongs to the context of expectation of salvation and judgment, e.g., Is. 1:8, 9; 4:2 ff.; 7:3; 10:20 ff.; 11:11 ff.; 37:32 (2 K. 19:31); 46:3; Jer. 23:3; 31:7; Jl. 2:32; Mi. 4:7; 5:6, 7; Zeph. 2:9; 3:12, 13; Ob. 17; Zech. 14:16. That this is a fixed theological term may be seen especially from the fact that the word can be

---

[10] Though → 202, n. 31.
[11] On OT eschatology → Baumgärtel, 66 ff.

used without more precise definition, e.g., Mi. 4:7, and also from the fact that it can be kept even where its content is transcended, e.g., Is. 46:3. Also significant in this connection is the fact that שׁאר, פלט, שׂרד, יתר and derivatives are to a large extent formally interrelated.[12]

In content, the idea of the remnant is under double control. It contains a ref. to preceding judgment or sifting. But it also denotes the limitation of this judgment. The remnant has escaped it. Hence the term implies both judgment and salvation.

The question thus arises whether judgment or salvation is the more determinative. In answering this question it is as well to consider chiefly the passages in which it does not have the fixed theological sense, since this brought with it a shift in the original meaning. These passages show that it has in the main a comforting character. This may be seen first from verses which express the totality of a judgment by saying that no remnant survived, Nu. 21:35; Dt. 3:3; Jos. 8:22; 10:28; 1 K. 16:11; Jer. 11:23; 44:7, 14; 50:26. Note should also be taken of sayings in which the thought of the remnant, because of its comforting character, is drawn into a context of judgment only by additions, or more precise definitions, or the associated image, e.g., Is. 16:14; 30:17. The positive significance of the term is clear from the combination of שֵׁם and שְׁאֵרִית, 2 S. 14:7; Is. 14:22. The ref. to salvation is quite plain in the theological use of the idea of the remnant, e.g., Is. 10:21; 37:32 (2 K. 19:31); Jl. 2:32; Mi. 4:7; Ob. 17.

Yet the ref. to judgment remains. Thus the greatness of the judgment is brought out in Am. 5:3. Is. 10:22 is directly linked with a verse which clearly brings out the comforting character of what is said about the remnant, but the other aspect of the concept is now emphasised: "Only a remnant shall return." Nevertheless, this is simply a development of the ref. to judgment which is also implicit in the term. It cannot affect the essential orientation of the concept to salvation.

2. The Rise of the Concept of the Remnant.

The question of the rise of the fixed theological concept of the remnant is very closely connected with the question of the origin of OT eschatology. Both questions can be answered only in the light of the nature of prophetic preaching, or the OT revelation of God. For it is within prophetic proclamation that what is said about the remnant has decisive significance. In the concept three lines seem to meet which define prophetic proclamation in a distinctive way.

This threefold structure of prophetic preaching may first be seen in a developed form in Amos. The prophet preaches 1. the complete destruction of the people of God (e.g., 8:1 ff.; 9:1 ff.); 2. the salvation which God will grant to the people (9:11 ff.); and 3. the opportunity of the people to save its existence by undertaking to seek God, or the good (5:6, 14). Within this threefold preaching, which does not give evidence of any clear bond or interrelation, may be found the message of the remnant (5:15: "Hate the evil, and love the good, and establish judgment in the gate; it may be that Yahweh, the God of hosts, will have mercy on the remnant of Joseph"). The same threefold structure is to be seen in the prophets after Amos. The question of an understanding of prophetic preaching is that of the relation of the three lines to one another. This is why the question of the place of the remnant idea is so important in prophetic proclamation.

Gressmann[13] was the first to feel in all its sharpness the largely unadjusted juxtaposition of the message of salvation and judgment. He thought the facts could be ex-

[12] On the question of the significance of the concept within the totality of OT eschatology it should be noted that in fact expectation of the deliverance of the "remnant" often occurs in verses in which the words for remnant or remaining are not found. But these verses can be used to fix the theological meaning only if there is a clear explication of the concept of the "remnant," of "remaining," or of "being delivered."

[13] Cf. Gressmann, *Der Ursprung,* 229 ff.

plained only by supposing that the prophets adopted both the eschatology of salvation and that of disaster from popular views, and that they left them in the disjointed state which they had perhaps had in Israel from the very first.[14] Both are originally mythical in nature, and acc. to Gressmann's conviction, which he shares with Winckler and Gunkel, they go back to the ancient Babylonian reckoning of the times, which has its basis in observation of the procession of the sun. In the eschatology of Israel the two expectations are non-organically and defectively linked by the idea of the remnant.[15] On Gressmann's view this belongs originally to the eschatology of disaster. All perish apart from a remnant.[16] There is nothing comforting about the thought. But with a change of the original sense it became a technical dogmatic term in the eschatology of salvation, though remnant and the preaching of salvation are mutually exclusive, since the object of salvation ought not to be a remnant, but the new people.[17] Acc. to Gressmann this adoption of the idea in the eschatology of salvation, as a bridge between salvation and disaster, is earlier than Amos. It occurs in the pre-canonical prophetic schools which give the concept its technical sense. For the people the remnant may be identical with Israel, but the prophets understand the word in the original sense. The canonical prophets then adopt it. But in their proclamation the word is no true bridge between the word of salvation and that of judgment. In spite of the remnant idea, these are in unadjusted juxtaposition. It may well be that emphasis on repentance for the remnant is a new prophetic concept, but the fact remains that the prophets are not greatly concerned to achieve a true interrelating of the preaching of salvation and disaster by means of the remnant concept. Since on Gressmann's view the whole eschatology of salvation is in radical contradiction with the character of prophetic eschatology,[18] adoption of the remnant concept is merely an incidental accommodation to the popular belief which they either affirm or reject according to time and mood. Thus, quite apart from the remnant concept, the logical contradiction between the message of salvation and that of judgment may often be resolved chronologically by assuming that the prophets changed the content of their message at different times.[19] Hence Gressmann finally accepts the customary understanding of prophetic preaching whereby the juxtaposition of salvation and disaster is for the most part explained psychologically.[20]

Acc. to → Mowinckel the idea of the remnant originates in the enthronement myth. Like the older eschatology, this myth expected an almost universal period of distress, oppression and destruction which threatened to swallow up Israel and Jerusalem and which was caused by the enemies of Yahweh and Israel. Against this danger Yahweh intervenes in the form of a no less comprehensive catastrophe which destroys the enemies but rescues Israel and Jerusalem at the last moment. The remnant which thus escapes is originally Israel itself, which alone is delivered from the hostile threat and the catas-

---

14 *Ibid.*, 233.

15 Gressmann finds an organic connection between salvation and judgment in the concept of the resurrection in later apocal. eschatology, though he leaves open the question whether the people from whom Israel took the eschatology had this concept. He certainly does not think it occurs in ancient Israel, *ibid.*, p. 238.

16 *Ibid.*, p. 233.

17 *Loc. cit.*

18 *Ibid.*, 236.

19 Gressmann, *Der Messias*, 71.

20 Along with the critical solution of the interrelation of the two messages, which we need not discuss here, the psychological is the customary one. It explains the double message of salvation and disaster in the preaching of the same prophet in terms of the moods of the prophet, which may vary from time to time. Ref. is thus made to the happy inconsistency of the prophets, who do not play only on the one string, and who change their views acc. to the situation and the conduct of the people. Cf. Meinhold, 108.

trophe of judgment.[21] The thesis that the remnant is not strictly a remnant of Israel, but the whole people, is grounded on the usage, in which the remnant is never שְׁאָר מִיִּשְׂרָאֵל or the like, but always שְׁאָר יִשְׂרָאֵל. Mowinckel also points to Mi. 4:7; Zeph. 2:7, 9; Jl. 2:32, which, as he sees it, show that the remnant is the people. Is. adopted the term in this sense. But he then proclaimed that the remnant is a remnant of the people, and to belong to it depends on conversion. The term is not originally linked with an eschatology of judgment, as Gressmann supposes, but with an eschatology of salvation. It does not have to mediate between the two, since salvation and judgment, like the remnant, find their origin and unity in the enthronement myth.

Gressmann's interpretation is untenable in view of the actual data. Quite apart from the fact that in the mythical explanation of the eschatology of salvation and disaster he confuses the content with the imagery, his interpretation is destroyed by the fact that the remnant concept belongs originally to the eschatology of salvation as well as judgment. Hence the conclusions which Gressmann draws from the supposed reorientation of an originally different concept also fall to the ground. Moreover, he fails to see the true nature of the concept, which is not a bridge between the two eschatologies in the sense of preserving the continuity of history beyond total judgment by means of men and their conversion. This is the basic error in all attempts to explain the remnant idea psychologically. In the message of the remnant disaster and salvation are in fact united in such a way that the continuity of history is grounded solely in the work of God, who establishes a remnant.[22]

This objection may also be brought against Mowinckel's interpretation. Furthermore, Mowinckel overlooks the fact that the very concept makes his interpretation impossible. The linguistic considerations (שְׁאר ישׂראל etc.) do not justify the conclusions which Mowinckel draws from them. This is shown by the expression שארית הגוים, פליטי הגוים, from which one would then be forced to conclude that the nations are originally the remnant. The verses which Mowinckel quotes (Mi. 4:7; Zeph. 2:7, 9; Jl. 2:32) rule out the equation of Israel with the remnant. When there is ref. to the remnant, judgment on the people is always presupposed, and a remnant survives. The idea of sifting and separating is inherent in that of the remnant. The same is true of passages in which, in a distinctive development of the concept, there is reference to the whole remnant.

The question of the rise of the remnant concept is not the question of the origin of an idea but the question of witness to the reality of God, who establishes a remnant in His own action. Hence the question can be finally answered only with a consideration of the structure of the testimony to the three acts of divine revelation which stand distinctively at the heart of the history of God's people: first, the election of the people; secondly, the calling of the prophets; and thirdly, the promise of the Messiah.

The question of the origin of the witness to the remnant is difficult because, although the remnant idea is common in the canonical OT, it is never comprehensively explained. Even in Is., where it has a central place, there is no unfolding of the concept itself. Yet in Is. we find the answer to the question of the remnant in the testimony to the calling of the prophet (c. 6). Even externally there is here

---

[21] Mowinckel, 281 f.

[22] Another pt. is that the remnant idea and the belief in the resurrection are not antithetical, as Gressmann believes. This would be so only if hope of the remnant were hope of the conversion and amendment of men. But hope of the remnant, like hope of the resurrection, is hope for God's action. Hence the remnant concept is not a non-organic and defective link between salvation and disaster. The concept expresses both the continuity of history and also the nature of the age of salvation as the new beginning of God.

an evident connection between the call and the message of the remnant, both at the end of the chapter (6:13) and also in the direct link between c. 6 and c. 7, in which the term שְׁאָר appears for the first time in the name of the son.[23] Even plainer, however, is the close inner connection between the call and the remnant in Is. 8:16-18, where the prophet proclaims that the remnant is already symbolically present in God's people in the form of the prophet himself and the disciples whom God has given him. Here, then, the remnant has its origin in the calling of the prophet. This means, however, that the message of the remnant has its origin at the same point as eschatology generally, namely, in the coming of God into this world-time in which He reveals Himself to men as the Holy One.

According to the witness of Is. 6 this coming of God means for the man to whom He comes destruction and death (6:5: "Woe is me, for I am undone"). Even the sense of election gives no security or salvation in face of this coming. But God Himself gives life (6:6, 7). Destroying sin, He calls the prophet. In the story of the call of Is., then, judgment is shown to be only the other side of salvation. The remnant is grounded solely in the fact that God establishes it. To the remnant belong those whom God calls (cf. Is. 8:18: "the disciples whom Yahweh has given me"; also Jer. 1:5; Jl. 2:32); this is one side of the matter. To the remnant belong those who believe (cf. Is. 6:8; 7:9); this is the other side of the matter.

If the content of the remnant message is fully developed in Is. 6-8,[24] one can say retrospectively that the essential core of the idea is presented when there is reference to the election of Israel. For the election has its basis in the coming of God to His people. In so far as Israel is elected, it is established as the remnant of Israel.[25]

Thus we read in Is. 46:3: "Hearken unto me, O house of Jacob, and all the remnant of the house of Israel, which are borne by me from the belly, which are carried from the womb." From the very beginning, from the first entry into history, God has carried the house of Jacob, the remnant of Israel. He carries it through time. In eternity He will set up on Mount Zion His royal dominion over the remnant (Mi. 4:7). In view of Is. 53 and Da. 7, and the relation of the Ebed or Son of Man to the community as it is found in these chapters, it is significant that along the lines indicated the sayings concerning the remnant and those concerning the Messiah very largely correspond (cf. Mi. 5:1 ff.; Is. 9:6).

This does not tell us where the remnant idea first occurs in the literature which has come down to us. It simply brings out the essential structure of the concept. In view of the present state of the OT documents one can hardly answer the

---

23 This connection remains even though the direct link between c. 6 and c. 7 is not regarded as original from the literary standpoint.

24 The element of sifting or separation is present in Is. 6:6, 7.

25 This is to say implicitly that the core of OT eschatology is also to be found here. To be sure, eschatology does not derive spontaneously in the hearts of God's people from a living hope, grounded in the Sinai revelation, that Yahweh will come again to set up a lasting kingdom (Sellin, 148). It has its basis in the coming of God Himself, which is continually thought to be present and active in the actual event of revelation (Baumgärtel, 67). Nevertheless, I cannot agree with Baumgärtel that eschatology is possible only when the question of theodicy arises (*op. cit.*, 76, n. 92). Thus the witness of Is. 6 is undoubtedly controlled by eschatology, and here the question of theodicy is not expressly posed or answered. On the question of the relation between election and the remnant we should also consider the passages in which the eschatological deliverance of the remnant is connected with the deliverance out of Egypt (cf. Is. 4:2 ff.; Mi. 2:12, 13; Jer. 23:5 ff.; 31:31 ff.; Is. 11:16).

question of temporal origin.[26] The concept is first to be found quite incontestably in Is.[27] Even in Amos, however, the presence of the concept can be contested only if the prophetic office is not properly understood. For questioning of the passages in which the message of the remnant is either linguistically or materially present depends less on the actual facts than on the assumption that Amos could prophesy only disaster. But this assumption is in conflict with the claim of the text itself. The remnant concept is not present only in Am. 5:6, 14, 15. Regard should also be had to the passages in which the prophet in his own distinctive dialectic combats a false understanding of the remnant message, and dialectically overthrows the idea (Am. 3:12; 9:1; cf. 6:9). The "perhaps" of Am. 5:15 safeguards the remnant message against false objectification, and thus affirms the concept as well as denying it.[28]

The exegetical question how far it is meaningful that Amos should summon all Israel to repent in the hope that Yahweh will then be gracious has always led either to the ascribing of the term "remnant of Joseph" to the Israel of the time and the rejection of an eschatological interpretation, or to the elimination of the whole verse because of its contradictory content. Now in view of the totality of the prophetic judgment, and passages like Am. 7:2, 5, it cannot be contested that even in the days of Jeroboam II Amos might have called the northern kingdom the remnant of Joseph. On the other hand, within the context of the total message 5:15 has to be taken eschatologically. But because eschatology means God's coming here and now, the remnant of Joseph is the people to which He comes in the to-day of the prophetic word. The prophetic word always means quite definitely that the time sequence is broken. Thus the question of time sequence does not arise in relation to 5:15.

Already, then, Amos presupposes that the remnant concept is eschatologically oriented.[29] Before him we find the concept in 1 K. 19:18: "Yet I have left me seven thousand in Israel, all the knees which have not bowed unto Baal." Here the number esp. suggests that we have a fixed phrase even though the remnant message is not developed in this verse. The remnant is established by God. It means sifting in Israel. Those who are loyal to Yahweh belong to the remnant.

E in Gn. 45:7 distinctively links שְׁאֵרִית with פְּלֵיטָה.[30] Here, too, the text, and esp. this combination, shows that a definite expression is being used.[31] In J the essential core of the remnant concept is to be found at Gn. 7:23b (cf. 6:8; 7:1, 5). The fact that Noah survives when all else is destroyed is grounded in the grace of Yahweh.

---

[26] Thus some exegetes ascribe decisive significance to the remnant concept in the preaching of Amos (e.g., Weber, 345), whereas others deny that it is there at all (Mowinckel, 280).

[27] Here, too, the authenticity of all the passages which speak of the remnant (apart from 7:3) is disputed.

[28] The remnant message is just as much exposed to the danger of objectification and consequent perversion as is the testimony to election. In this case belief in the deliverance of the people becomes the basis of self-security.

[29] Hos., on the other hand, makes no mention of the remnant. In his preaching the people of God as a whole (northern Israel) receives salvation after the judgment.

[30] l c sam G al פליטה, cf. BHK.

[31] Cf. F. Delitzsch, *Komm.* (1887), *ad loc.*: "The terms שארית and פליטה, which later became highly significant in prophecy, are here set on the lips of Joseph, the deliverer of his family, and in it of the future people, the type of Christ." It is true that in the light of 2 S. 14:7 שארית is usually rendered "posterity" or "race" (cf. H. Gunkel, *Komm.*[5] [1922], *ad loc.*), but even in 2 S. 14:7 we cannot be sure that this is the correct transl. (cf. W. Caspari, *Komm.* [1926], *ad loc.*). Gunkel suggests splitting Gn. 45:7 and assigning 7a to J, but this is most unlikely, since שארית and פליטה are combined as a formula elsewhere.

3. The Remnant established by God.

a. The remnant has its origin, not in the quality of those saved, but in the saving action of God. This is apparent in the texts quoted (Gn. 7:23b; 45:7; 1 K. 19:18; Am. 5:15). It is even plainer in passages in which the concept is unequivocally a fixed theological term in prophetic eschatology. Thus in Mi. 4:7 the prophet uses שְׁאֵרִית in the absolute: "I will make her that halted a remnant, and her that was worn out a strong people." God Himself will gather the remnant of Israel (2:12). The remnant of Jacob will be as dew from Yahweh (5:7) which independently of men, and outwith their control, comes directly from God. Distinctive in these passages is the eschatological orientation of the prophetic discourse. The remnant is an entity in the world (Mi. 5:6, 7). But it is also a company established by God at His final coming in that day (cf. the connection between Mi. 4:1-4 and 5:1 ff.). We are told nothing concerning the faith or holiness of the remnant. God establishes it. This is enough. For even though the term שׁארית ישׂראל, שׁארית יעקב denotes a relation to the people of God, the absolute use of the concept indicates the direction in which this relation is developed.

In Is. the remnant is established already in the story of the call of the prophet. In Is. 8:16-18 it is emphasised that the community of disciples is God's gift (אשׁר נתן־לי יהוה). The prophet does not have the task of creating or gathering the remnant. God creates it. This is expressly stated in the prologue to Is. (1:8, 9). Here we read that only the daughter of Zion survives God's judgment. Nor does this pitiful remnant derive its existence from itself. "Except Yahweh of hosts had left unto us a remnant, we should have been as Sodom and like unto Gomorrah." [32] The remnant has its existence in Yahweh alone. The same is true in 7:3. The name of the prophet's son does not imply that a remnant is left on the condition that Ahaz or the people of God repents. שְׁאָר יָשׁוּב is an unconditional promise: "A remnant will come to a right condition." The question is not whether there will be a remnant; the real question is who will belong to it. Hence the promise of a remnant is a summons to faith. For judgment is also implied in the promise: "If you will not believe, you will not be established" (7:2, 9; cf. 10:20 ff.). The remnant is also promised in Is. 6:13. The image of the seed shows that it will be a new creation. God will redeem the remnant of His people (11:11) and gather the scattered of Israel (11:12). He will make a highway for the remnant of His people (11:16). God Himself will be the crown and ornament of the remnant (28:5). This is also the message of Is. 4:2 ff., where there is an individual application: He will belong to the remnant, who is written in the book of life. The man who does belong to the remnant will be called holy. Here, too, it is clear that the deliverance of the remnant does not depend on the holiness of its members (4:4). It is not a remnant which goes forth out of Zion (not מירושׁלם, מציון), [33] but a remnant established in Zion. Elsewhere (37:32, cf. 2 K. 19:31) we also read, however, that Yahweh's zeal will cause the remnant to go out from Jerusalem and a host of those who have escaped from Zion. These many statements in Is. are summed up in 28:16, where, even though the term is not used, we read, as in 8:16-18, of the establishment of the remnant: "Therefore thus saith the Lord Yahweh: Behold, I lay on Zion for a foundation a stone, a corner stone of pre-

[32] In v. 9 we should omit כמעט with GLSV, cf. BHK.
[33] Cf. O. Procksch, *Komm.* (1930), *ad loc.*

cious foundation: 'He that believeth shall not be put to shame.'" God Himself creates a foundation for the remnant. The saying about faith is the other side of the statement. Faith is the guarantee of existence in the to-day (7:9), in the new community (28:16). But faith is not a work of man. God lays the corner stone on which the saying about faith is written.[34]

Zeph. 3:12, 13 is in harmony with the statements of Is. about the remnant. God is He who leaves a humble and lowly people as the remnant of Israel. Among those who have escaped judgment is he whom Yahweh calls (Jl. 2:32, cf. 3:16). There is a distinctive development of the remnant concept in Ez. When Jerusalem is destroyed, Yahweh will leave a remnant in order that it may be perceived thereby how just is the judgment (14:21 ff.).[35] God can even establish a remnant of the Philistines and incorporate this remnant into the Messianic kingdom (Zech. 9:7). But the remnant of Israel will be the wonderful new creation of God. "Thus saith Yahweh of hosts; If it seems impossible to the people in that day, should it seem impossible to me?" (8:6). In Ezr. 9:13, too, the escaped remnant is presented as the gift of God (ונתתה לנו פליטה).

The establishment and preservation of the remnant are based upon the zeal of God (2 K. 19:31; Is. 37:32), the righteousness of God (Is. 10:20 ff.; Ezr. 9:13, 14), the grace of God (Gn. 6:8; Jer. 31:2), the mercy of God (Am. 5:15; Is. 46:3), the help of God (Jer. 31:7), and the forgiveness of God (Jer. 50:20; Mi. 7:18).

b. The fact that the remnant is grounded in God's action is emphasised in two ways. First, there are passages in the prophets which speak of total judgment (e.g., Ez. 7:7, 16, 24, 25; Jl. 2:3; Am. 3:12; 5:1, 2; 6:9, 10; 8:1 ff.; 9:1 ff.; Lam. 2:22). If, in spite of total judgment, there is reference to the deliverance of a remnant, the existence of this remnant is necessarily grounded in the divine action. The relation between total judgment and the deliverance of the remnant is worked out in Is. 1:8, 9. Then there are passages in which the deliverance of the remnant is related to the redemption of the people out of Egypt. This lays particular stress on the fact that the existence of the remnant rests on the divine act of deliverance. The relation may be seen in Is. 4:2 ff. and Mi. 2:12, 13. Again, in Jer. 23:5 ff. and 31:31 ff. the new creation of the community is contrasted with the redemption out of Egypt and the making of the first covenant. In Is. 11:16 we read: "And there shall be a highway for the remnant of his people, which shall be left, from Assyria; as there was for Israel when Israel came up out of Egypt."

c. If the remnant is preserved only by God's action, the remnant concept cannot be a quantitative one in the sense that the remnant has to be small. The concept certainly contains a reference to the greatness of the judgment, but not to the small number of those who are delivered (though cf. Dt. 4:27; 28:62; Is. 10:22). Thus in Mi. 4:7 remnant is in parallelism with "strong people." The figure of the dew in Mi. 5:6, 7 contains implicitly a reference to the great number of the remnant, and it is said in Jer. 23:3 that the remnant will increase and be fruitful in

---

[34] As against Meinhold, 134: "For an Isaiah faith is hardly established by Yahweh; it is an act of men (Is. 7:1 ff.). Controlling his own will, man has either to proffer faith or to withhold it. That this will, too, is under divine influence is not an idea which is present in Isaiah."

[35] On the relation of this passage to the doctrine of individual responsibility proclaimed by Ez. cf. J. Herrmann, *Komm.* (1924), *ad loc.*

the land. This idea is often found in passages where the remnant concept is materially, if not linguistically, present.

d. The uniqueness of eschatological proclamation in the OT includes the fact that the remnant is referred to as both a present and a future entity. It is present in the time before Amos (cf. Gn. 7:23; 45:7; 1 K. 19:18), and in Amos the remnant of Joseph is the people of God to whom the prophet proclaims God's coming (5:15). In Is. 1:8, 9 Zion is the remnant which God has left. The prophet and his disciples are the remnant in Israel (8:16-18). The distinctive interrelation of historical and eschatological events is particularly to be seen in Is. in Messianic passages in which the coming of the Messiah is directly imminent (7:10 ff.), and indeed in process of enactment (9:5). The prophet also says that the Messiah will be given "us" (7:10 ff., "Immanuel"; 9:5 twice לָנוּ). The לָנוּ can only be the remnant whose presence is referred to in 8:16-18.

Ez. speaks of the remnant in the same way. It consists of those who in the present of prophetic vision undergo the final judgment of God (9:8; 11:13), or of the servants of Yahweh who have the mark and who are delivered from this judgment (9:4). Temporal distinction is completely set aside in Is. 46:3. The remnant is the house of Jacob which the prophet addresses in the present, but which from the very beginning God has borne and will bear.

If the remnant is a present entity, this carries with it the basic possibility of identifying it with a present historical entity. This is particularly apparent in the post-exilic texts in which the remnant is widely identified with the Jews who returned from exile (e.g., Zech. 8:6; Ezr. 9:8, 13, 15; Neh. 1:2, 3).[36]

e. The question of the identity of the remnant with a historical entity is also posed by the common linking of the remnant with Jerusalem or Zion. Zion is the remnant in Is. 1:8. God establishes the remnant in Zion in Is. 28:16, 17. This is the home of those who remain in Is. 4:2 ff. Is. and his disciples are a sign for the God who dwells on Zion (8:16-18). A remnant will go out from Jerusalem, and a host of those who have escaped from Zion (37:32; cf. 2 K. 19:31). In Micah, too, the remnant is connected with Zion (4:1 ff.) or Bethlehem (5:1 ff.). Yahweh will leave a humble and lowly people on His holy hill, Zeph. 3:11-13; cf. Is. 11:4; 14:32. In Jer. 23:3 ff. the gathered remnant is brought into relation with the holy land, and in Jer. 31:6, 7 the remnant is summoned to come to Zion. Salvation will be on Zion in the day of Yahweh (Ob. 17). There each of the survivors whom Yahweh calls will find salvation (Jl. 2:32). The new creation of the remnant by Yahweh will take place in Jerusalem (Zech. 8:1-6). In the day of Yahweh part of the population of Jerusalem will remain as the remnant (Zech. 14:2). The delivered remnant and Jerusalem are also closely connected in Ezra and Nehemiah (Ezr. 9:8, 13, 15; Neh. 1:2, 3).

If this connection between the remnant and Jerusalem or Zion is to be found especially in post-exilic texts, one should not overlook the fact that even in Is. the remnant is spoken of in a way which seems to link it with Zion. One can hardly refer to this as an "antique" trait in the prophecy of Is. On the contrary,

---

[36] Though cf. also 2 K. 25:11, 22; Is. 37:4 (2 K. 19:4); Jer. 24:8; 40:6, 11, 15; 41:10, 16; 42:2, 15, 17, 19; 43:5; 44:7, 12, 14, 28; 52:15; Ez. 9:8; 11:13; Hag. 1:12, 14; 2:2; Zech. 8:6, 11, 12; 2 Ch. 34:21; 36:20.

the message of the remnant is shown thereby to be one of the statements of faith which are made in the sphere of the history of the people of God as this is controlled by election and the covenant.

In this relation to Zion one finds expressed the same explicit reference as may be seen in phrases like שארית ישראל, שארית יוסף, פליטת ישראל, שארית יעקב which link the remnant concept with the name of God's people. These expressions, too, raise the question who belongs to the remnant and where it is established. If there may be seen here on the one side an intention to identify the remnant with a historical entity (and in particular sections of the history of God's people the entity which is called the remnant may vary), if there is a special tendency to link the remnant with Israel or Zion, it should not be overlooked that the very idea of the remnant fundamentally resists this identification, so that even in the OT itself one may see how the concept is developed in such a way as to transcend every restriction or relation. This development is found especially when the term is used in the absolute (e.g., Is. 7:3; Mi. 4:7). Above all, it should be noted that in most cases the question of the limit of the remnant cannot be answered merely from the text itself. This is particularly plain in passages in which faith is the other side of the establishment of the remnant by God (cf. Is. 7:2-9; 28:16, 17; 8:16-18). Obviously Is. in his encounter with Ahaz does not mean Judah when he speaks of the remnant. He means believers to whom the promise applies. Judah as a political entity, and even the office of the king who sits on David's throne, is called in question by this promise. If it is asked what is the limit of the circle of believers, no more answer is given to this than to the question of the לָנוּ to whom the Messiah is given (Is. 7:10 ff.; 9:5).[37] Individualising of the concept also implies its radical extension (cf. Is. 1:9; 4:2 ff.; 7:2-9; 7:10 ff.; 8:16-18; 9:1 ff.; Ez. 9:4). If one can say that the prophet represents the remnant at his call (cf. Is. 6:1 ff. with 8:16-18), the Ebed and his relation to the people of God is spoken of in a way (Is. 40 ff.) which seems to entail an inclusive relation between the deliverer and the remnant community. That is to say, the Ebed is the representative of the people of God. But this restriction involves extension (cf. Is. 42:1, 3, 4, 6). For the question of the limit of the רַבִּים is not answered by the text, and in principle it cannot be answered (cf. Is. 52:13 ff.).

4. The Conversion of the Remnant.

If the establishment of the remnant has its basis in the gracious action of God, the conversion of men cannot be the essential presupposition for the existence of a remnant. It is true that in 2 Ch. 30:6 the conversion of the Israelites is a condition for God's gracious turning to the remnant, but even here it is presupposed that survivors have been left as a remnant in the judgment.

In fact the primary reference is always to the deliverance of the remnant with no condition as a basis, and only then do we read of its conversion or faith. If one might conclude from the prophetic imperatives in Am. 5:6, 14 that human conduct is the norm of deliverance, this misunderstanding is ruled out by the "perhaps" of 5:15. In Is. 10:20, 21 it is said that the remnant from Jacob shall build on Yahweh, the Holy One of Israel, and shall return to the אל גבור. But here, too, judgment and the deliverance of the remnant are already presupposed, not

[37] Cf. also Is. 11:4; 14:32.

made dependent on the conversion of the remnant. It is true that v. 22 might seem to suggest otherwise. But here it is best to render שְׁאָר יָשׁוּב, "A remnant comes to a right condition," since there is no mention of turning to God.[38] The attitude of the remnant is one of patient waiting (8:16-18; cf. also 30:15-18). He who believes belongs to the remnant (7:9). But the statement can be reversed: He who belongs to the remnant believes (28:16, 17). Hence faith is not the condition for belonging to the remnant. It is simply the other side of the establishment of the remnant. Again, in Is. 4:2 ff. the holiness of the remnant is not the basis of its existence. Those who have been left are called holy. Only in this sense can one speak of a holy remnant. Even in Zeph. 3:12, 13 the faith and sanctification of the remnant are simply the other side of the establishment of the remnant by Yahweh. The two aspects come together in statements concerning what constitutes the essence of the remnant, cf. Jl. 2:32: "Whosever shall call on the name of Yahweh shall be delivered: for in mount Zion and in Jerusalem shall be deliverance, as Yahweh has said, and among those who have escaped is he whom Yahweh calls" (cf. 2:12; Ez. 9:4).[39]

That the remnant does not have its existence in the holiness of its members may be seen finally in passages in which there is reference to the sins of the remnant. God himself must wash away the filth of the daughter of Zion and the blood-guiltiness of Jerusalem with the spirit of judgment and of fire (Is. 4:4). He must forgive the sin of the remnant of His inheritance (Mi. 7:18). "In those days, and in that time, the saying of Yahweh is that one will search for the iniquity of Jerusalem, and it shall not be there, and for the sins of Judah, and they shall not be found; for I will forgive those whom I leave" (Jer. 50:20). Those who escape must be forgiven because all the remnant remains of "this evil family" (Jer. 8:3). Similarly, the context of Ez. 9:8; 11:13 shows plainly that the remnant spoken of here is not sinless. Nor is the remnant of Lv. 26:36 defined in moral or religious terms. The sinfulness of the remnant is emphasised in Ez. 14:22, for this remnant is saved only in order that the righteousness of the divine judgment may be set in relief by its sin. This emphasis on the sin of the remnant certainly finds its basis in the fact that the reference is always to a definite historical entity, and the actual state of the remnant necessarily implies a reference to sin. Nor should the point be missed that the reference to sin is finally grounded in the structure of the concept. For this reference brings out the more clearly the fact that it is God who newly creates the remnant. God Himself in that day roots out the names of idols and the unclean spirit out of the land (Zech. 13:2). He brings the saved third part into the fire and smelts it as one smelts silver, and purifies it as gold (Zech. 13:8, 9).[40] That the members of the remnant commit no more wrong and speak no more lies is the response to their deliverance (Zeph. 3:12, 13).

---

[38] Cf. F. Delitzsch, *Komm.*[4] (1889), *ad loc.* The arguments of B. Duhm, *Komm.*[4] (1922), *ad loc.* for putting vv. 20-23 in the 2nd cent. are not convincing. O. Procksch, too, thinks that vv. 22-23 are a later addition, since pessimism prevails in contrast to the optimism of vv. 20-21. In fact v. 22 looks like later exegesis as compared with v. 21. Yet one should remember that the remnant concept itself contains the two different elements emphasised in v. 21 and v. 22. Hence it is by no means impossible that Is. himself also developed the thought along the lines of v. 22.

[39] The way in which expositors speak of the conversion, uprightness, piety or holiness of the remnant is hardly justifiable in the light of this witness of the OT itself.

[40] At the same time it should be noted that within the proclamation of the remnant the idea of a purifying judgment does not have quite the meaning usually ascribed to it.

God will then destroy the weapons of war and the cultic objects taken over from the Canaanites (Mi. 5:9 ff.), and as the purging of the remnant must take place through the spirit of judgment (Is. 4:4), so the renewal of the remnant will be effected through the gift of the Spirit of God bringing about new obedience (Ez. 36:24-27; 37:23, 24; 39:29; Jl. 2:28 ff.).

5. The Remnant and the Nations.

If the remnant is constituted by the act of God, it is still an entity within the world. Thus the question of its relation to the nations arises. At this point the nature of the remnant is depicted in very realistic colours. The remnant will exist among many nations (Mi. 5:6). But it will not be dependent on men (*loc. cit.*). It will rule over the nations "as a lion among the beasts of the forest, as a young lion among the flocks of sheep, who, if he go through, both treadeth down, and teareth in pieces, and none can deliver" (5:8). In particular — and here one may see the historical relation of the remnant to the people of God — it will lay waste and inherit the neighbours of Israel (the Moabites and the Ammonites) (Zeph. 2:9). It will possess the coast and dwell in the houses of Ashkelon (2:7). But these statements are in sharp tension with 3:12, where the remnant is a humble and lowly people. In the main, the relation of the nations to the saved community in the last time is depicted in more positive terms. The nations will go up to Zion to receive instruction (Is. 2:2-4; Mi. 4:1-5).

In the OT we read not only of a remnant of the people of God but also of a remnant of the Gentiles. Judgment on the nations is an established part of eschatological expectation. But the nations are not extirpated. A remnant of them will remain. Thus in Dt. Is. those who remain of the Gentiles are called upon to gather together to find salvation and deliverance in Yahweh, the only Helper (Is. 45:20 ff.). Those who survive the last judgment on the nations will be set in the service of God. They will not only be sent to the Gentiles to proclaim to them God's glory as revealed in the judgment. They also receive the commission to bring "your brothers" from all the nations to be incorporated into the service of Yahweh (Is. 66:19 ff.). Neither here nor in Jl. 2:28 ff. can one say for certain whether "your brethren" (cf. "all flesh" in Jl. 2:28) are the Jews of the dispersion, or whether there is to be an incorporation of Gentiles into the community.[41] In any case it is said in Zech. 9:7 that the remnant of the Philistines remains for Yahweh, and in 14:16 that the remnant of the nations which attacked Jerusalem will go up year by year to worship Yahweh and to keep the feast of tabernacles. Formally, Ez. 36:3, 5 also refers to the remnant of the nations, and in 36:36 it is said that the remnant of the nations will see God's act in the bringing back of the people of God.[42]

6. The Remnant Community and the Messiah.

As a connection may be seen between the remnant and Zion, there is a similar relation between the remnant and the Messiah. It is not worked out in detail how the Messiah is related to the "us" to which there is reference in the name Immanuel

---

[41] On the other hand יֶתֶר אֶחָיו (Mi. 5:2) can hardly be taken to refer to the remnant of the Gentiles.

[42] In Ez. and post-exilic prophetic writings may be seen the beginnings of a more detailed systematisation of eschatological expectation.

and in Is. 9:5, but it is obvious that the Messiah is given specifically to the "us," who figuratively embody the remnant within God's people, cf. Is. 8:16-18; 1:9; 7:10 ff.; 9:5; 11:1 ff. This remnant will turn to the אֵל גִּבּוֹר (Is. 10:21), which on the basis of 9:5 must be construed as a designation of the Messiah. There also seems to be a relation between the remnant and the Messiah in Is. 4:2 ff. According to Jer. 23:3 ff. God will raise up David to the remnant as a righteous branch, and in him God Himself will be the righteousness of His people (v. 6). Similarly, in Mi. 5:1 ff. the promise of the Messiah is closely linked with the remnant message. The birth of the Messiah is the dawn of the age of salvation for the remnant (cf. Ez. 34:12, 13, 23 ff.; 37:23 f.).

In these verses it is not expressly stated that the remnant community has its existence in the Messiah alone. The time of salvation which dawns for the remnant with the coming of the Messiah, or among whose gifts the raising up of the righteous branch is to be reckoned, will be brought in by God. Yet the connection between the remnant and the Messiah is already so close that we can see plainly the lines leading up to the sayings of Dt. Is. about the relation between the Ebed and the people of God. For already in Is. 28:16 f. it is hard to say whether the corner stone of precious foundation is simply the remnant or in the first instance the Messiah, in which case the link with the remnant is established by the saying: "He who believes will not be put to shame." For the Messiah is the foundation on which the new building is built. [43] Even less is it possible to separate the Ebed and the people of God in Dt. Is. Here the Ebed who has borne the sins of many is the representative of God's people, and only in Him does the new community have its life.

Herntrich

C. The Thought of the Remnant in Paul as compared with its Occurrence in Apocalyptic and the Rabbis.

1. The Remnant in Romans 9-11.

a. The prophetic concept of the remnant is growing and adaptable. Its application changes with changing situations, though one may always discern the intention to link the remnant to Israel and Zion, → 205. Paul makes use of only a small part of the great prophetic heritage. He simply wants to show the fulfilment in his own time. The passages used by him undoubtedly bring out the theological aspect of the concept and its firm reference to Israel.

The contents of R. 9-11, into which the theme is interwoven, are all related to the actual missionary situation of Paul's day. [44] On the one side this involves Israel's rejection of the righteousness of God, and on the other the coming of the Gentiles to Christ. Is the obvious fate of Israel a testimony against God's righteousness? Paul's answer is that the hardening of Israel does not hopelessly confuse everything but simply confirms God's ancient word. A distinction has always had to be made between the physical Israel and the true Israel. Already in the story of the patriarchs the calling of God — and not a purely natural factor — creates the true Israel. Thus Jacob, in his commission and life's task in the national history,

[43] Cf. O. Procksch, *Komm.* (1930), *ad loc.*

[44] Cf. G. Schrenk, "Der Römerbrief als Missionsdokument," in *Aus Theologie u. Geschichte d. reformierten Kirche, Festgabe f. E. F. K. Müller* (1933), 39 ff.

is given precedence over Esau. The history as a whole reveals this differentiation, which is not injustice but the working out of a selection. The same is confirmed in Moses; mercy is shown to the one whom God freely exalts. Quite apart from any righteousness of merit, this act of divine mercy underlies the destiny of Israel. The reverse side may be seen in Pharaoh, for in his hardening is manifested the judicial severity of the divine majesty, which here, too, maintains its sovereign sway. Silent submission to the incomprehensible overruling of sovereign calling and choice is the only possible attitude (vv. 19-21).

How this truth, which is exemplified in salvation history, applies to-day, may be seen clearly when it is referred to the existence of the new community, which is made up of Jews and Gentiles. In this the two continuing aspects of God's action may be seen, namely, wrath and mercy. Concerning hardened Israel on the one side it is said: "God willed to show his wrath and display his power by patiently bearing vessels of wrath prepared for destruction." On the other hand, the vessels of mercy which are ordained for glory are the Gentile Church. The distinction is not, of course, absolute, since Israelites are also incorporated into the new community. Hence the words are intentionally added: "As he has called us as such, not only of the Jews, but also of the Gentiles."

b. Here the idea of the remnant is introduced. In terms of the proof from the history of the patriarchs and Moses, this is the sum of the prophetic message. Prophecy's contribution to the understanding of God's work of sifting and differentiation in relation to Israel is all comprehended for Paul in the concept of the remnant. This is the climax and conclusion of the exposition thus far, and the free and uninfluenced sovereignty of the God of grace and judgment is then supported from the nebiim. Three quotations from the prophets are related to the constitution of the community. The first and main point is that the Gentiles, who are not a people, have been called. This is foretold by Hosea. There then follow two verses from Is. 10:22 f. and 1:9, both introduced by Ἠσαΐας δὲ κράζει ὑπὲρ τοῦ Ἰσραήλ. These expressly proclaim the idea of the remnant to be a prophecy concerning Israel (v. 29). Hence they are just as relevant as the saying of Hosea about the Gentiles. "Though the number of the children of Israel were as the sand of the sea (i.e., it is not numbers that count), (only) τὸ ὑπόλειμμα [45] will be delivered." By means of the συντέμνων of the quotation in 9:28 — which denotes stern and pitiless cutting off — Paul effectively emphasises the thought of judgment. But the fact that the σπέρμα remains to which the σωθήσεται refers is a vindication of God's faithfulness and mercy.

Paul does not need to expound the remnant concept, since it throws vivid light on the actual state of the new community. It is the ὑπόλειμμα of Israel among the hosts of the ἔθνη. Quite obviously a qualitative principle is involved. The remnant concept helps to deal with the misunderstanding in the community which troubles those who seek to win all Israel. It is not transferred by extension to the ἔθνη. On the other hand, the connection with faith in Christ is close and firm. The ὑπόλειμμα consists of believers in Christ. The whole train of thought which leads to this conclusion stands under the sign of God's sovereign appointment and election. Wrath and mercy, perdition and salvation, sifting and comforting, are

[45] R. 9:27: ὑπόλειμμα: ℵ AB Euseb; κατάλειμμα: DEFGKLP. LXX: κατάλειμμα.

bound up with one another. This may be seen in R. 11. We are dealing only with a remnant. In Paul the thought of dividing and sifting (→ 204 ff.) is still inherent in the concept. The question of the human responsibility of Israel, the other side of the same truth, is first found only in 9:30-10:21. Deliberately, attention is first focused on God's free action. In this way, if the argumentative theologian thinks he can be absolutely sure of God, his sense of freedom is crushed. The present situation is to be assessed as follows. God has a right to be gracious to the Gentile hosts and to save only a remnant of Israel. The promise to Israel is not broken thereby. The universalism of salvation is not truncated. But the fact that the Gentiles believe, and Israel does not, is in the first instance an offence, and needs elucidation.

c. This is why Paul deals with the responsibility of Israel before developing the remnant concept as a basis of hope in R. 11. The fundamental reason for Israel's fall is that it has stumbled on the stone of offence. Fanatical disputing of God's righteousness in favour of self-righteousness, failure to see that faith is the only way to God, persistence in unbelief in spite of all God's concern through His messengers in open ἀκοή, ἀκούειν which does not become ὑπακούειν, this is the answer to the question of Israel's guilt which must be seen side by side with the other truth that God ordains all things on the basis of His own free decision. Conversely, the remnant must consist of those who are ἐκ πίστεως, οὐκ ἐξ ἔργων, who, when they come up against the λίθος ἐν Σιών experience, not God's judgment, but His gracious promise, which is emphatically added in 9:33. Cf. later 11:7. Only the ἐκλογή (= λεῖμμα) has reached the goal (the righteousness of God). According to this purifying message of repentance the whole consoling power of hope in the λεῖμμα can be indicated without danger of misconception. The first word of comfort to Israel is clothed in the concept of the remnant. In Paul himself it is shown that God has not cast off the people which He foreknew. In the OT the calling of the prophet was closely related to the idea of the remnant (along with the election of the people and the promise of the Messiah), → 200. Now the calling of the apostle from fanatically opposed Jewish circles is a confirmation of the divinely ordained remnant. The Scripture proof which Paul adduces in 11:2 ff. is from 3 Βασ. 19:10, 18, a much older part of the OT than the sayings from Is. in c. 9. This verse brings out the connection between the process in the OT community and that in the NT community. Now, as then, the same principle is to be seen. In serious situations what counts is the sovereign ἐκλογή. In the days of Elijah the majority were hardened and God caused only a λεῖμμα of 7000 to remain. So it is to-day. There is a λεῖμμα κατ' ἐκλογὴν χάριτος.[46] The comparatively few Israelites in the Christian community are the λεῖμμα. The quantitative aspect of the concept is again indispensable. As in c. 9 the reference is present, not future. According to 11:7-10 the other Israelites are judicially hardened by God.[47]

d. The surprising development which the prophetic saying about the salvation of all Israel brings in 11:25-32 is prepared for in 11:11-24. The λεῖμμα is not the final goal. The goal is the re-adoption, the salvation of all Israel, 11:15 f. In the

---

[46] For an analogous construction to R. 9:11: ἡ κατ' ἐκλογὴν πρόθεσις → ἐκλογή, 179.

[47] The expression in 11:17: "Some of the branches," is deliberately milder.

words πώρωσις ἀπὸ μέρους τῷ Ἰσραὴλ γέγονεν in 11:25 there is further reference to the λεῖμμα; the hardening is shown to be partial. It is also temporary, and will last only until the πλήρωμα [48] of the Gentiles has come in. It is here plain that the remnant concept is provisional for Paul. [49] The remnant will become the totality. [50] It is thus a productive number, not an unchangeable minority.

2. Comparison and Summary.

a. The remnant and Israel. In apocal. as well as the OT the remnant is closely linked to Israel. It is what is left of the whole people. There are passages which are orientated to final cosmic catastrophes and which seem to leave Israel out of account, cf. Eth. En. 83:8 (date uncertain). Nevertheless, the definition in relation to Israel may be seen again in S. Bar. 40:2, where the Messiah protects the remnant of the people, which is located in the Holy Land. This ref. to the Holy Land along with the remnant is common in 4 Esr. 9:7 f.; 13:48; 12:31-34: The Messiah destroys the Roman Empire, but will "graciously redeem the remnant of my people which have remained in my land." Messianic salvation appears in Palestine, for those who remain, and there is also ref. to the redemption of all creation, 13:26. In Eth. En. 90:30 (*c.* 135-105 B.C.) the remaining sheep, who with all other animals (the nations) do homage to the shepherd (the martyred leader), are the righteous remnant of Israel. The ref. to the remaining wise people of Israel in Sib., 5, 384, however, seems to bear witness to the significance of Israel as a whole.

In Rabb. theology the remnant concept is secondary to the expectation that the people as a whole will partake of salvation. The few Jews who are eternally rejected, and the small number of righteous from among the nations, hardly count in comparison → λαός, 45 ff. But the exegesis of the Synagogue always finds it necessary to give some account of the term. [51]

For Paul, as we have shown, the remnant is not Israel. It is only a part of Israel, but a new seed which points forward to all Israel, and has this as its goal. Paul in his day makes use of a concept which was variable, and variously applied, in the OT. He explains it in terms of Jews who believe in Christ. The concept stands at a decisive point in his eschatological view of history, but is also filled with a sense of the present. In the OT the word is always linked with the prospect of coming disaster. In 4 Esr. references to the *derelicti, relicti, residuus populus meus,* or *relinqui* → *supra,* cf. ἐλείφθη, Sib., 5, 384, always imply that these remnants of the people escape the coming woes of the last time. But in Paul's use of the concept the apocalyptic idea of the woes of the last time is very secondary. He no longer speaks of a remnant which is awaited. The remnant is present and set up already in the λεῖμμα κατ' ἐκλογὴν χάριτος. To be sure, this present entity is eschatological, for everything which has occurred since the coming of Christ is ἔσχατον. Nevertheless, though the prophecy of the remnant is fulfilled, it is so only in the form of a first beginning.

b. Election and the remnant concept. In the apocal. sense of the election shared by believers in the last time the basic point is a sectarian restriction of the remnant concept. The special characteristic of this literature is that the saved remnant, which is marked

---

[48] Here πλήρωμα means the full number, in 11:12 full entry, opp. of ἥττημα.

[49] In 11:16 ἀπαρχὴ ἁγία, ῥίζα ἁγία refers, not to the λεῖμμα, but to the beginnings in the history of the patriarchs.

[50] Cf. later Eus. Dem. Ev., II, 3, 47: ὑπόλειμμα τοῦ παντός.

[51] This paragraph is by R. Meyer.

off from Israel as a whole, is a term to denote those who hope to be among the elect (→ ἐκλογή, 184) in the last time. In Damasc. 2:9; 9:10 B, cf. → 171, the Zadokite community is regarded as the remnant which is spared for the land. Here the concept is applied to a specific group, and this group stands behind it with its consciousness of election. This represents a significant change in relation to earlier prophecy.

It might be argued that Paul makes a corresponding transfer to the new group of Jewish believers in Christ. But to say this is to overlook the fact that through faith in the definitive salvation manifested in Christ this transfer leaps all previously existing boundaries. Also to be noted is the fact that for Paul, as for OT prophecy, the essential core of the concept of the remnant is the inviolable election of Israel. The remnant is a proof of election in the deepest need, a creation of wondrous mercy, a result of the grace of God in calling and salvation — of the God who according to R. 9:3-5 has entered into a unique relation to His covenant people. Aiming at the incorporation of Israel into the new community, He brings His covenant will to its goal.

c. The remnant and the Messiah. The Messianic ref. of the concept is emphasised in apocal. Acc. to 4 Esr. those who remain of the people of God experience the preliminary Messianic age, 6:25; 7:27 f.; 9:7; 12:34; 13:24, 26, 48 f. Acc. to 7:28 this lasts for 400 years. The gift of salvation is also heavily stressed in 4 Esr. They are delivered from the pains of oppression, and experience the salvation and joy of the Messianic time, but also *finis saeculi mei* and the end of the day of judgment, 6:25; 12:34.

The new turn in Paul is that the remnant is now related only to the Christ who has appeared. The remnant has its existence only in Him. It consists, not only of those who are faithful to Yahweh, but rather of those who believe in God's righteousness in Christ. The λίθος ἐν Σιών of Is. 28:16 f. is Christ alone, and those who believe in Him are the remnant.

d. The remnant and faith. The opp. of the κατ' ἐκλογὴν χάριτος is the righteousness of works, R. 11:6. This is not overcome in apocal., though there foreordination is also linked with the remnant concept, cf. Apc. Abr. 29:17; those remaining are a number kept secret, → 184 f. On this cf. also R. 11:4 : κατέλιπον ἐμαυτῷ.

In the Rabb. the righteousness of works is very strong. In Tg. Is. 1:9, Str.-B., III, 275 and Tg. Is. 53:10, Str.-B., I, 482 the idea of gracious appointment is relatively pure, but elsewhere it is human action (keeping the Torah, letting go sin and pride) which constitutes the remnant, Tg. Is. 4:3, Str.-B., II, 125; Tg. Is. 10:22 f., Str.-B., III, 275; bSanh., 98a, Str.-B., II, 104 n. Along the same lines it is said in Lv. r., 35 on 26:3, Str.-B., II, 170 (referred here to the resurrection) that the one who is left is he who is occupied with the Torah, or, more scholastically, the pupil of the scribes, bChul., 133a; bSanh., 92a; bMeg., 6a, Str.-B., IV, 1074; II, 617; 469. There is a unique exposition of Is. 1:9 in Cant. r., on 8:9 f., Str.-B., II, 562 : The Bath-Qol is the remnant of prophecy.

Paul's concern is with conversion to the present Christ. Hence in a full use of prophecy he can do justice to two elements which are truncated in apocalyptic, namely, that of the conversion of the remnant (Is. 7:3; 10:21 f.; Am. 5:15) and that of the condition of faith (Is. 7:9; 10:20 ff.; 11:4; 28:16). The *sine qua non* of belonging to the remnant is faith in righteousness through Christ, R. 10:4. But to be saved is to be raised from the dead, R. 10:4, 9. On the presupposition that conversion and faith are the other side of God's appointment (→ 206 f.) one must maintain that the remnant exists on the condition of faith. God's appointment is thus correlated with man's decision in such a way that the one entails the other.

Faith is the operation of the God who so activates man to the work of faith that faith is man's own act under grace. It is not a self-produced ἔργον which guarantees the continuity of grace. But the fact that it is man's act must not be minimised. Paul, too, speaks first of the salvation of the remnant and only then of its conversion or faith. Cf. R. 9 with R. 11. But in view of R. 11:23: κἀκεῖνοι δέ, ἐὰν μὴ ἐπιμένωσιν τῇ ἀπιστίᾳ, ἐγκεντρισθήσονται (cf. also 11:20), one has to say *sub conditione fidei.* If Paul immediately goes on to say: "For God is able to graft them in again," this is the other side of the same fact.

e. The remnant and the nations. Paul is aware of the universal triumph to which his line of thought leads. Here again prophecy is taken into account, Mi. 5:6 f.: the remnant of Israel among the nations. The position in apocalyptic writings is very different. In 4 Esr. 13:49 the destruction of the nations runs parallel to the preservation of the remnant of Israel. In R. 11:11 f., however, we have the new and characteristic view that salvation comes to the nations through the hardening of all Israel (apart from the remnant). Again, in apocalyptic there is a harsh dissonance between Israel and the Gentiles. Paul, however, ventures a comprehensive prophecy in respect of all the nations and all Israel together, R. 11:25 f., 31 f. Thus, in his use of the remnant concept Paul avoids all particularism and sectarianism. He sets the concept to work in the service of comprehensive missionary activity which summons all men under the dominion of grace. Though he does not expressly refer to Is. 6:13; Jer. 31:7; Mi. 2:12, in the spirit of this message he views the remnant as a holy seed, as the root of a perfected community. But this is closely related to his hope for the whole Gentile world. Hence Israel loses its special position, and everything is swallowed up in mercy on all.

Schrenk

λειτουργέω, λειτουργία, λειτουργός, λειτουργικός

† λειτουργέω, † λειτουργία.

Contents: A. λειτουργέω, λειτουργία in non-biblical Greek: 1. The Form of the Word; 2. The Etymology and Basic Meaning; 3. The Usage: a. Technical Political Usage; b. This Usage Extended; c. Weaker Popular Use; d. Specialised Cultic Use. B. λειτουργέω, λειτουργία in the LXX and Hellenistic Judaism: 1. λειτουργέω: a. Occurrence and Hebrew Equivalents; b. λειτουργέω as a Technical Cultic Term; 2. λειτουργία; 3. The Relation of LXX to non-biblical Usage; 4. The Usage of Greek Speaking Judaism; C. Cultic Ministry in the Usage of Rabbinic Judaism: 1. Lexical Review; 2. The Idea of Cultic Ministry: a. The Use of Verbal Forms; b. The Use of Nouns; 3. The Spiritualisation of the Concept. D. λειτουργέω, λειτουργία in the New Testament: 1. Occurrence and Use; 2. The Findings and Their Significance. E. Transition to Later Ecclesiastical Usage.

The modern ecclesiastical use of the word liturgy is quite different from the original meaning of λειτουργέω, λειτουργία, which were wholly secular terms. On the other hand, it bears some relation to non-biblical usage. Nevertheless, the only way to understand the change in meaning is by way of the LXX and its almost uniform cultic and priestly use of the words. The ecclesiastical use is the result of a transfer to the Christian cultus of OT concepts in Greek garb. This may be seen very clearly in the literature of the 4th century. The role played by the NT in this history of signification will have to be determined in what follows.

A. λειτουργέω, λειτουργία in non-biblical Greek.

1. The Form of the Word. In the OT and NT we find only λειτουργεῖν, λειτουργία.[1] The older form is ληιτουργεῖν, ληιτουργία. But from about 300 B.C., as with

---

λειτουργέω κτλ. Lexical aids → λαός. Cf. also K. F. Hermann-V. Thumser, *Lehrbuch d. gr. Staatsaltertümer,* I, 2[6] (1892), § 121; A. Boeckh, *Die Staatshaushaltung d. Athener,* I[3] (1886), 368 f., 534 f.; G. Busolt, *Gr. Staatskunde,* II (1926), Index *s.v.* "Leiturgien"; W. Liebenam, *Städteverwaltung im Römischen Kaiserreich* (1900), 418, 489; W. Otto, *Priester u. Tempel im hell. Ägypten,* I (1905), II (1908), Index; F. Oertel, "Die Liturgie," *Studien z. ptolemäischen u. kaiserlichen Verwaltung Ägyptens* (1917), 2 ff.; Wilcken Ptol., I (1927), Index; Ostraka, I (1899), I, 1, c. 8; I. Elbogen, *Der jüdische Gottesdienst in seiner geschichtlichen Entwicklung*[3] (1931); L. Eisenhofer, Art. "Liturgie," Lex. Th. K.[2], VI; G. Rietschel, *Lehrbuch d. Liturgik,* I (1900), 3 f.; E. Achelis, *Praktische Theol.,* II (1891), 1 f.; Deissmann B, 137 ff.; W. Brandt, "Die Wortgruppe λειτουργεῖν im Hb. u. bei Cl. Romanus" (*Jbchr. d. Theol. Schule Bethel* [1930], 145-176); O. Casel, "λειτουργία — *munus*" (*Oriens Christianus,* III, 7 [1932], 289-302); H. Wenschkewitz, "Die Spiritualisierung der Kultusbegriffe ...," *Angelos, Beih.* 4 (1932).

[1] Along with λειτουργία we also find λειτούργημα, cf. Plut. Sept. Sap. Conv., 18 (II, 161e) of the dolphins who alternately bore Arion διαδεχόμενοι ὡς ἀναγκαῖον ἐν μέρει λειτούργημα καὶ προσῆκον πᾶσιν, Plut. Ages., 36 (I, 616d) λειτούργημα δημόσιον. P. Lond., III, No. 1247, 13 (345 A.D.): certain persons are εὔποροι καὶ ἐπιτήδιοι πρὸς τὸ λιτούργημα (of ὑδροφυλακία).

many other words, the ηι was replaced by ει in Attic inscr. and the *koine.* [2] There is reflected here a shift in pronunciation from ē̃i to long e. [3] In the Roman period, though not yet in the NT texts, this came to be pronounced, and sometimes written, ι. [4]

2. The Etymology and Basic Meaning. λειτουργεῖν is formed from λήϊτος, "concerning the people or national community," and the root ἐργ-, which occurs both as noun (ἔργον) and verb (Homeric ἔρδω, ἔρξα). (The compound ληιτουργός is the equivalent of λήιτα ἐργαζόμενος, cf. δημιουργός and δήμια ἐργαζόμενος; and hence ληιτουργεῖν, -γία, as κακοῦργος, -γέω, -γία [Debrunner].) Thus Suid. (ed. Adler) notes on λειτουργία: κυρίως ἡ δημοσία ὑπηρεσία (public discharge of office), παρὰ τὸ λήϊτον καὶ τὸ ἔργον. The expression is thus linked with the national use of → λαός for the national community, as found in Pind. though not in Hom. The word is not possible in Hom. λειτουργεῖν is to do things which are related, not to private concerns, but to the national community as a political unity, or more briefly to the body politic. More precisely, it is "to render service to the people (as a common political entity)" by discharging a true task for society. λειτουργεῖν is the discharge of the task, or "service to the nation" (Pape). Hence Plut. An Seni Respublica Gerenda Sit, 19 (II, 794a): διακονικαὶ λειτουργίαι.

3. The Usage.

a. Technical Political Usage. Though the etymology yields a general basic sense, the dominant usage on the first appearance of the term is technical. In distinction from the fulfilment of financial tasks, especially in respect of taxation (εἰσφορά), [5] λειτουργέω is the direct discharge of specific services to the body politic. Citizens with an income above a fixed level had by law to accept these at their own expense, or else they could do so voluntarily, whether for motives of patriotism or vainglory or both.

The system was not just Athenian but was widespread in the Gk. democracies. A feature of these acc. to Aristot. was the fleecing of the wealthy by liturgies. He advances the principle that in democracies one should spare the well-to-do and even prevent them λειτουργεῖν τὰς δαπανηρὰς μὲν μὴ χρησίμους δὲ λειτουργίας (discharging costly liturgies which serve no useful function) (Pol., V, 8 [p. 1309a, 18]). The opp. is the perverted practice which he commonly sees in democracies known to him. [6] This practice is particularly highly developed in Athens. There are the regular (ἐγκύκλιοι, Dio C., 44, 40, 3) solemn liturgies in relation to the phyla (χορηγία, γυμνασιαρχία, λαμπαδαρχία, ἑστίασις, i.e., feeding the members, ἀρχιθεωρία, i.e., leading a sacred embassy), and also extraordinary liturgies on the occasion of extraordinary needs (esp. the τριηραρχία and προεισφορά, i.e., the payment of military taxes in advance for those weak in performance), and finally special liturgies involving

---

[2] Hence the lexicographer Moeris (ed. I. Bekker, Harpocration [1833], 202, 36 f.): λητουργεῖν διὰ τοῦ η Ἀττικοί, διὰ δὲ τῆς ει διφθόγγου Ἕλληνες· λήϊτον γὰρ τὸ δημόσιον. Cf. on this Mayser, I[2] (1925), 126 and K. Meisterhans-E. Schwyzer, *Grammatik d. attischen Inschr.*[3] (1900), 38, 6.

[3] Cf. E. Schwyzer, *Gr. Grammatik* (1934), 201.

[4] For an example of λιτουργεῖν cf. P. Lond., II, No. 331 (p. 154), 165 A.D. (λιτουργῆσαι ἐν τῇ προκιμένῃ κώμῃ ἐφ᾿ ἡμέρας ἕξ), and in an agreement for private service, P. Oxy., IV, No. 731, 8/9 A.D. (ἐφ᾿ ᾧ λιτουργήσω ὑμεῖν κατὰ μῆνα ἐνάτῃ καὶ δεκάτῃ ...).

[5] Hence, e.g., in Aristot. Pol., V, 11, p. 1314b, 14 εἰσφοραὶ καὶ λειτουργίαι.

[6] Cf., *ibid.*, 5, p. 1305a, 3; 8, p. 1309a, 17; VI, 5, p. 1320b, 4. There were liturgies in Aegina, Byzantium, Keos, Mytilene, Orchomenos, Siphnos, Thebes and the Gk. cities of Asia Minor.

μέτοικοι (αἱ τῶν μετοίκων λειτουργίαι as distinct from πολιτικαί, i.e., those to be discharged by πολῖται, Demosth. Or., 20, 18). From Attic orators like Isaios, Demosth. etc. it may be seen that some performed allotted liturgies under compulsion and grudgingly, but others willing and freely with no regard to obligation, e.g., Isaeus, IV, 27 and 29; V, 36 and 45; VI, 60 f. Often the inscr. emphasise that the one honoured by them discharged the imposed liturgies in the best way, e.g., Ditt. Syll.[3], 385 (282/1 B.C.); 409 (275/4 B.C.); 547 (211/10 B.C.); Ditt. Or., 339, 50 (2nd cent. B.C.); 529; 537, 10; 542, 10. The verb is either used in the abs., technically, or with the acc. of performance (λειτουργεῖν λειτουργίαν, λειτουργίας, also τὰς ἀρχάς, cf. GDI, II, 1539, 35, or with περὶ τὰς ἀρχάς, cf. Aristot. Pol., IV, 4, p. 1291a, 35) and the dat. of the recipient (τῇ πόλει, cf. Isaeus, V, 45; Xenoph. Mem., II, 7, 6; τῇ πατρίδι, cf. Dio C., 69, 3, 6; ὑμῖν, cf. Isaeus, IV, 29).

b. This Usage Extended. With the system, the technical political usage extended to cover all kinds of services to the body politic.

This is esp. true in the pap., since the imperial government in Egypt used the system of compulsory state and communal services to the greatest possible degree. λειτουργεῖν, λειτουργία serve to denote here public and constitutionally regulated services in the discharge of all kinds of compulsory tasks and the execution of all possible offices. Questions as to the obligation, limitation and apportionment of these services (ἀνάδοσις τῶν λειτουργιῶν), complaints about the burden they imposed, the question of exemption from them (ἀλειτουργησία, ἀτέλεια), e.g., on the basis of a money payment (λειτουργικὸν τέλος), play a prominent part.[7]

c. Weaker Popular Use. From the technical and wider technical use there then develops a general and non-technical use in which the words simply denote rendering a service and the significance of the λήϊτος is lost.

Aristot. uses λειτουργεῖν, e.g., for the private services of slaves to their masters or of workers to their taskmasters, Pol., III, 5, p. 1278a, 12, or of the functions of the body, De Iuventute et Senectute, 3, p. 469a, 2 ff.: φανερὸν τοίνυν ὅτι μίαν μέν τινα ἐργασίαν ἡ τοῦ στόματος λειτουργεῖ δύναμις, ἑτέραν δ' ἡ τῆς κοιλίας περὶ τὴν τροφήν. He speaks of a λειτουργεῖν πρὸς τεκνοποιίαν, Pol., VII, 16, p. 1335b, 28 f. He calls the suckling of young by mother animals a λειτουργία, De Animalium Incessu, 12, p. 711b, 30, and speaks of λειτουργία to nature, Oec., 3, p. 1343b, 20: ἡ τῶν τέκνων κτῆσις οὐ λειτουργίας ἕνεκεν τῇ φύσει μόνον ... Thus, apart from the use for public services of all kinds, the terms can be applied in every conceivable way. They are used for the services friends render one another, Plut. De Amicorum Multitudine, 6 (II, 95e); An Seni Respublica Gerenda Sit, 6 (II, 787a); Luc. Salt., 6: ἕτοιμος φιλικὴν ταύτην λειτουργίαν ὑποστῆναι, or the services rendered by a father to his son, Plut. An Seni Respublica Gerenda Sit, 17 (II, 792e), or those of the organs of the body, Plut. Marcius Coriolanus, 6 (I, 216c), or co-operation in theatrical performances, Epict. Diss., I, 2, 12: Ἀγριππῖνος Φλώρῳ σκεπτομένῳ, εἰ καταβατέον αὐτῷ ἐστιν εἰς Νέρωνος θεωρίας, ὥστε καὶ αὐτόν τι λειτουργῆσαι, ἔφη· κατάβηθι, or the services of a courtesan, Anth. Pal. (ed. F. Duebner, I [1864], V, 49, 1 [Aelius Gallus]). There are also many examples of the general sense of rendering service in the pap., cf. B. Grenfell-A. Hunt, *Greek Pap. Ser.* II (*New Classical Frag-*

---

[7] Cf. Wilcken Ptol., I, 173 (156 B.C.); P. Lond., II, p. 154, No. 33 (165 A.D.). P. Oxy., IV, 705, 71 f. (200-202 A.D.): Complaints by villages of Oxyrhynchos district that they σφόδρα ἐξησθένησαν ἐνοχλούμενοι ὑπὸ τῶν κατ' ἔτος λειτουργιῶν. III, 487, 10 f. (156 A.D.): Request to the ruler (κράτιστος) to be freed from a function ἐμοῦ ... καταβαρηθέντος ἐν ταῖς λιτουργίαις καὶ χραιώστου γενομένου (the petitioner is encumbered by liturgies). Cf. also Preisigke Wört., *s.v.* λειτουργεῖν and λειτουργία.

ments) (1897), No. 14c, lines 1 ff. (3rd cent. B.C.): Asclepiades asks Polycrates for the sending of Timoxenos: χρείαν ἔχομεν ... Τιμοξένου, ... καλῶς ... ποιήσεις γράψας αὐτῶι λεοτουργῆσαι ἡμῖν, Mitteis-Wilcken, I, 2, No. 198, 11 (3rd cent. B.C.): ὑποζυγίοις ... τοῖς λειτουργοῦσιν, P. Oxy., III, 475, 18 (2nd cent. A.D.): κροταλιστρίδων (dancing girls with castanets) λειτουργουσῶν κατὰ τὸ ἔθος, P. Tebt., I, 5, 181 (2nd cent. B.C.): ἕλκειν εἰς ἰδίας λειτουργίας (to enforce private services), P. Oxy., IV, 731, 4 ff. (8/9 A.D.): ἐφ' ᾧ (against the agreed payment) λιτουργήσω ὑμεῖν κατὰ μῆνα ἐνάτῃ καὶ δεκάτῃ καὶ Εἰσίοις ἡμέρας δύο. P. Masp. (67), 151, 192 (6th cent. A.D.): ἡ τῶν ἀῤῥώστων φροντὶς καὶ λειτουργία (care of the sick), also Preisigke Wört. It is only a special instance of this general usage that in Polybius λειτουργεῖν and λειτουργία are used of certain military services and commands, e.g., 6, 33, 6: τῶν ... τριῶν σημαιῶν ἀνὰ μέρος ἑκάστη τῷ χιλιάρχῳ λειτουργεῖ λειτουργίαν τοιαύτην, 10, 16, 5: τοῖς ἐπί τινα λειτουργίαν ἀπεσταλμένοις.

d. Specialised Cultic Use. Particular note should be taken of another specialised use, i.e., for cultic functions.

An example of λειτουργεῖν in the cultic sense is to be found on an inscr. from Messene concerning the mysteries of Andania (92 B.C.): οἱ ἱεροὶ προγραφόντω κατ' ἐνιαυτὸν τοὺς λειτουργήσαντας ἔν τε ταῖς θυσίαις καὶ μυστηρίοις αὐλητὰς καὶ κιθαριστάς, ὅσους κα εὑρίσκοντι εὐθέτους ὑπάρχοντας, καὶ οἱ προγραφέντες λειτουργούντω τοῖς θεοῖς.[8] Cf. also Inscr. Magn. (196 B.C.): τοῦ λητουργοῦντος θύτου (sacrifices) τῆι πόλει.[9] An inscr. of Eleusis (177/80 A.D.): λιτουργεῖν τοῖν θεοῖν.[10] An Athenian inscr. (100 B.C.): ἐλειτούργησαν ἐν τῶι ἱερῶι εὐτάκτως.[11] Dion. Hal. Ant. Rom., II, 22, 2: ὅσα μὲν γὰρ αἱ κανηφόροι καὶ ἀρρηφόροι (the so-called basket-bearers and the bearers of secret cultic objects on certain sacral occasions) λεγόμεναι λειτουργοῦσιν ἐπὶ τῶν Ἑλληνικῶν ἱερῶν ... In the same passage λειτουργεῖν is used as an equivalent of ἱερὰ ἐπιτελεῖν. Plut. (An Seni Respublica Gerenda Sit, 17 [II, 792 f.]) serves the Pythian Apollo many pythiades (οἶσθά με ... λειτουργοῦντα, including θύειν, πομπεύειν, χορεύειν acc. to the context). Jul. Ep., 89 (303b): πρέπει ... τοῖς ἱερεῦσιν ἔνδον μέν, ὅτε λειτουργοῦσιν, ἐσθῆτι χρῆσθαι μεγαλοπρεπεστάτῃ, *ibid.* (299b): οὕτω ... ἡμᾶς πρέπει τοῖς θεοῖς λειτουργεῖν. The cultic sense also occurs on a Delphic inscr. of the 2nd cent. B.C.: αἱ τῶν θεῶν λειτουργίαι;[12] on a 1st cent. inscr. of Antiochus of Commagene on the Nemrud Dagh: The temple employees τὰς λειτουργίας ... ποιείσθωσαν;[13] on an Athenian inscr. from 178 A.D.: ὁ ἱερεὺς ... ἐπιτελείτω τὰς ἐθίμους λιτουργίας (the traditional cultic functions) ... εὐπρεπῶς;[14] in Diod. S., I, 21, 7: τὰς τῶν θεῶν θεραπείας τε καὶ λειτουργίας; Dion. Hal. Ant. Rom., X, 53, 6: τῆς περὶ τὰ θεῖα λειτουργίας ἀπέστησαν (they ceased therewith); Jul. Ep., 89 (297b): εἰς ἣν εἰσι κατεσκευασμένοι λειτουργίαν; *ibid.* (298c): ὅτι τὴν λειτουργίαν ταύτην διαθήσῃ καλῶς (of the priestly ministry of Theodorus); *ibid.* (302c): ἡ ἐν τοῖς ἱεροῖς λειτουργία. In the pap. the texts about the twins Thaues and Taus in the Serapeum at Memphis give us many examples of the cultic use. It is constantly said that they are λειτουργοῦσαι ἐν τῷ πρὸς Μέμφει μεγάλῳ Σαραπιείῳ or ποιούμεναι μεγάλας λειτουργίας τῷ θεῷ, or there is ref. to their παρέχεσθαι λειτουργίαν. They had to bring offerings to the god Serapis and the accompanying Isis, and to perform certain cultic actions.[15]

---

[8] Ditt. Syll.³, 736, 73 f.
[9] *Ibid.*, 589, 17 f.
[10] *Ibid.*, 872, 17.
[11] *Ibid.*, 717, 28 f.
[12] *Fouilles de Delphes*, III, 2, ed. M. G. Colin (1909/13), No. 68, line 76.
[13] Ditt. Or., 383, 170; cf. also line 185.
[14] Ditt. Syll.³, 1109, 111 ff.
[15] Wilcken Ptol., I, No. 17 ff.

Similarly, the cultic acts of the Choachytes, who had to make regular offerings to the dead, and the embalming of sacred animals by those called thereto, were described as λειτουργίαι.[16]

In these examples one may see the movement towards a new technical use in the cultic sphere. One might be tempted to connect this with the original political use, since the cultus is also a matter of common concern. Ἔτι ... τὰ πρὸς τοὺς θεοὺς δαπανήματα κοινὰ πάσης τῆς πόλεώς ἐστιν, says Aristot. (Pol., VII, 10, p. 1330a, 8 f.). Thus one part of the common property should serve εἰς τὰς πρὸς τοὺς θεοὺς λειτουργίας, the other εἰς τὴν τῶν συσσιτίων δαπάνην (*ibid.*, lines 12 f.). But if there are contacts between the political and the cultic concept of liturgy, there is no recollection of the political relation in most of the instances of cultic use. The idea is not that one can render service to the nation through the cultus. The very general idea of service is applied to the cultic relation to the gods, and it is applied in such a way that there is approximation to a new technical usage. This is, of course, only one strand in the history of the meaning of the terms. But the future belongs to this strand, by way of the LXX.

B. λειτουργέω and λειτουργία in the LXX and Hellenistic Judaism.

1. λειτουργέω.

a. Occurrence and Hebrew Equivalents. The term occurs some 100 times, and first in Ex. 28:35, i.e., in the context of cultic legislation. This is no accident. Most of the instances are found in Ex. 28-39 (13); Nu. (25); Ch. (20); and Ez. 40-46 (16), i.e., in writings in which the cultus plays a prominent part.

As a rule, but only as a rule, λειτουργεῖν is used for שֵׁרֵת. With few exceptions, however, שֵׁרֵת is rendered λειτουργεῖν only when the reference is cultic. When other services or relations are at issue, other words are chosen, e.g., παριστάναι τινί (Gn. 40:4 of Joseph and the chief butler and chief baker in prison, παρέστη αὐτοῖς; Is. 60:10 of the queens of strangers and Jerusalem; Ex. 24:13 of Joshua and Moses), or λατρεύειν (Ez. 20:32; Nu. 16:9; Sir. 4:14), or δουλεύειν (Is. 56:6), or διάκονος, διακονία (Est. 1:10; 2:2; 6:3, 5, of royal eunuchs), or θεράπων (Ex. 33:11 of Joshua and Moses), or ὑπουργός (Jos. 1:1, Α λιτουργῷ), or διάδοχος (Sir. 46:1), or very free renderings (1 Ch. 28:1; Is. 60:7; Gn. 39:4). Particular note should be taken of Is. 56:6; Nu. 16:9; Sir. 4:14. In the former the reference is to aliens who attach themselves to Yahweh to serve Him. But the service is only general worship, not the priestly cultus. Hence the Heb. שֵׁרֵת is rendered δουλεύειν, not λειτουργεῖν. In Nu. 16:9 it is said of the sons of Korah that Yahweh has brought them near to Himself לַעֲבֹד אֶת־עֲבֹדַת מִשְׁכַּן יהוה and to stand before the congregation לְשָׁרְתָם. Though the LXX usually has λατρεύειν for עָבַד and λειτουργεῖν for שֵׁרֵת, it here takes the opposite course, since λειτουργεῖν must not be used of service to men. In Sir. 4:14 we read that to serve wisdom is to do service to the Holy One (God). The Heb. uses שֵׁרֵת in both cases. But in Greek we have οἱ λατρεύοντες αὐτῇ λειτουργήσουσιν ἁγίῳ. The selection seems to be designed to express the fact that this is the true cultus. It is striking that in Dt. 21:5 שֵׁרֵת is rendered παριστάναι: God has chosen the priests, the Levites, to serve Him (παρεστηκέναι αὐτῷ). But the reference here is to expiation of murder

[16] Cf. Otto, I, 99 ff., 109 f.

by someone not known, not to service of the temple. Perhaps this explains the choice of the term.

Though λειτουργεῖν is not used for non-cultic service, the LXX does not scruple to use it of pagan cults. To be sure, in Ez. 20:32 we find λατρεύειν (not λειτουργεῖν) ξύλοις καὶ λίθοις, in spite of the Heb. שֵׁרֵת. But in Ez. 44:12 and 2 Ch. 15:16 λειτουργεῖν is used of the cult of idols and of Astarte.

There are only a few exceptions to the rule that only the cultic שֵׁרֵת is to be rendered λειτουργεῖν, namely, 1 K. 1:4, 15, of Abishag the Shunammite and David; 1 K. 19:21, of Elisha and Elijah; 2 K. 6:15 A (!), of the personal servants of Elisha; 1 Ch. 27:1, γραμματεῖς ... λειτουργοῦντες τῷ λαῷ, for which R, probably correctly, reads τῷ βασιλεῖ; 2 Ch. 17:19, λειτουργεῖν τῷ βασιλεῖ; 2 Ch. 22:8 B, λειτουργεῖν τῷ Ὀχοζίᾳ; ψ 100:6, οὗτός μοι ἐλειτούργει, i.e., David; and finally Nu. 3:6, of the Levites and Aaron, where the word seems to be chosen because the service rendered Aaron has a cultic connection, so that this is only an apparent exception.[17]

On the other hand, λειτουργεῖν can be used not only for the cultic שֵׁרֵת but also for the cultic עָבַד or עֲבֹדָה (14 times), and also for the cultic צָבָא (7 times), both almost exclusively in Nu.; it is also used once each for כִּהֵן (2 Ch. 11:14) and שְׁמַשׁ (Da. 7:10), but only in Θ; the LXX has θεραπεύειν.

If λειτουργεῖν stands aloof from the non-cultic use of שֵׁרֵת, it also tends to attract to itself other words for cultic service. Apart from the two pagan instances in Ez. 44:12 and 2 Ch. 15:16 the reference is always to the worship of Yahweh performed by the priests and Levites either in the tabernacle or the temple.

b. λειτουργέω as a Technical Cultic Term. Thus the word becomes a definite tt. for this cult.

Hence we find λειτουργεῖν τὴν λειτουργίαν or τὰς λειτουργίας τῆς σκηνῆς (e.g., Nu. 8:22; 16:9; 18:21, 23); λειτουργεῖν (τῷ) κυρίῳ (e.g., Jdt. 4:14; 2 Ch. 11:14; 1 Βασ. 3:1; Jl. 2:17; Ez. 45:4) or θεῷ (Jl. 1:13), or τῷ προσώπῳ κυρίου (1 Βασ. 2:11), or τῷ ὀνόματι κυρίου (Dt. 18:7), or θυσιαστηρίῳ (Jl. 1:9, 13), or τῷ οἴκῳ (Ex. 44:11; 45:5; 46:24).

Once we find λειτουργεῖν τῷ κυρίῳ θεῷ ὑμῶν καὶ τῷ λαῷ αὐτοῦ Ἰσραήλ (2 Ch. 35:3). But this does not imply that κύριος and λαός are equally the recipients of ministry. The explanation is to be found in Ez. 44:11, where λειτουργεῖν αὐτοῖς consists in λειτουργεῖν τῷ οἴκῳ by fulfilment of the sacrificial cultus. The people cannot bring its offerings directly to God, but only by way of the priests, who help the people in its worship of Yahweh.

The distinctive feature, however, is the common absolute use (Ex. 28:35; 35:19; 36:33; Nu. 3:31; 4:3, 23 ff.; Dt. 10:8; 2 K. 25:14; Jer. 52:18; Ez. 42:14; 44:17; 2 Ch. 31:2), and the use where the function is more closely defined only by an indication of place like ἐν τοῖς ἁγίοις (Ex. 29:30), ἐν τῷ ἁγίῳ (Ex. 39:1 = 39:12 LXX Rahlfs = 39:13 Swete; Ez. 44:27), ἐν τῇ σκηνῇ (Nu. 1:50), ἐναντίον τῆς κιβωτοῦ (1 Ch. 16:37),

---

[17] There is also a non-cultic use in 2 Βασ. 19:19, where Ziba and his men ἐλειτούργησαν τὴν λειτουργίαν τοῦ διαβιβάσαι τὸν βασιλέα. This is not found in the Mas. Cf. also Sir. 8:8: λειτουργῆσαι μεγιστᾶσιν, and 10:25: οἰκέτῃ σοφῷ ἐλεύθεροι λειτουργήσουσιν. It should also be mentioned that Ἀ, Σ and Θ at Is. 56:6; 60:7, and Ἀ at Gn. 40:4, render the non-cultic שרת by λειτουργεῖν [Bertram]. It may be suspected that Ἀ, whose method of translation is pedantically stereotyped, ignores any nuances of meaning in שרת. This is obviously retrogressive as compared with the selectivity of the LXX.

ἐν οἴκῳ κυρίου (1 Ch. 23:28), πρὸς τὸ θυσιαστήριον (Ex. 28:43 etc.), or by an expression like ἐπὶ τῷ ὀνόματι κυρίου (Dt. 17:12; 18:5; 1 Ch. 23:13), or ἐνώπιον κυρίου (1 Βασ. 2:18). The phrase which Sir. 45:15 uses for the work of Aaron (λειτουργεῖν καὶ ἱερατεύειν) is a double expression for the same thing.

Though the same is meant, and the author wishes to say that the high-priest Simon correctly discharges the ministry of the altar (συντέλειαν λειτουργῶν ἐπὶ βωμῶν, Sir. 50:14), there is unquestionably in Jesus Sirach a trend towards the spiritualising of the cultus, e.g., when in 4:14 we read of the servants of wisdom that they λειτουργήσουσιν ἁγίῳ, or in 24:10 wisdom confesses of itself that it does service (ἐλειτούργησα) in the σκηνὴ ἁγία. A figurative use is found in Da. 7:10 Θ, where the heavenly hosts of angels serve the Ancient of Days, i.e., worship Him (ἐλειτούργουν αὐτῷ). The term is also used figur. at Wis. 18:21, where it is said of Moses that he interceded for the people τὸ τῆς ἰδίας λειτουργίας ὅπλον, προσευχὴν καὶ θυμιάματος ἐξιλασμὸν κομίσας. Like the offering of expiatory sacrifices, prayer is here subsumed under the concept of liturgy.

2. λειτουργία. The noun, too, became a tt. for the priestly cultus. It occurs some 40 times, almost always for the Heb. עֲבֹדָה.[18] But the relation of the two words is like that of λειτουργεῖν and שֵׁרֵת. Usually only a cultic עֲבֹדָה is rendered λειτουργία.[19] In other cases we find a variety of words such as ἀποσκευή, κατασκευή, παρασκευή for the erection of the tabernacle, and ἔργον, ἐργασία, ἐργάζεσθαι, δουλεία, σύνταξις for the forced service of Israel in Egypt, or Jacob's service with Laban, or work on the land (1 Ch. 27:26). On the other hand, other words for the cultus are rendered λειτουργία (צָבָא in Nu. 8:24, 25; מְלָאכָה in 1 Ch. 26:30; פָּלְחָן in Ezr. 7:19 → 223, and n. 23; פְּעֻלָּה in Ez. 29:20, though there is a special ref. here → *infra*). With the solitary exception of 2 Βασ. 19:19, where there is λειτουργία to the king (→ n. 17), λειτουργία is always used of the ministry of the priests and Levites in and at the sanctuary, especially the ministry of the priests at the altar.

These functions are called λειτουργία or λειτουργίαι τῆς σκηνῆς (κυρίου, τοῦ μαρτυρίου) (e.g., Nu. 16:9; 18:4, 6), or λειτουργία οἴκου τοῦ θεοῦ (κυρίου) (1 Ch. 9:13; 2 Ch. 31:4), or λειτουργία κυρίου (2 Ch. 35:16), or ἔργα τῆς λειτουργίας (1 Ch. 9:19). The vessels used are τὰ σκεύη τῆς λειτουργίας (1 Ch. 9:28); the actions are λειτουργίαι τῶν θυσιῶν (2 Macc. 3:3). λειτουργία is always used literally in these passages. The only figur. use is at Ez. 29:20, where the siege of Tyre is a λειτουργία which Nebuchadnezzar has rendered (ἐδούλευσεν) to Yahweh (as the Heb. adds).

3. The Relation of LXX to non-biblical Usage.

How are we to assess the relation of LXX usage to that of non-biblical Greek? There is no trace of the older technical political use. Such liturgies are not found in the OT. Of the more general or popular use there are only scanty relics. Apart from a few exceptions the object of the ministry is neither the city, state, people, citizens, nor specific individuals. It is the tent, the house, the altar, God Himself, or the name of God. The LXX translators obviously felt a need to try to fix a regular and exclusive term for priestly ministry, and thereby to show that the cultic relation to God is something special as compared with all the other relations of service in which men might stand. They selected λειτουργεῖν, λειτουρ-

[18] On two occasions (Nu. 4:32; 7:9) we find λειτούργημα for עֲבֹדָה. It is used for the service which the Levites render as porters in the sanctuary.

[19] For exceptions cf. Nu. 4:19 (ἀναφορά); 8:24 (ἐνεργεῖν); Ex. 30:16 (κάτεργον τῆς σκηνῆς). In all these cases λειτουργία might have been used.

γία for this purpose. It could well be that the uniformity of LXX use is to be explained in terms of existing use in the Hellenistic Synagogue to which the translators belonged. But why were these words chosen? It has been noted above that on the basis of popular usage a specialised cultic use had already developed in non-biblical Greek. Are we to conclude that this sacral use of the terms was adopted and expanded? Are we to conclude that the Alexandrian translators were particularly influenced by the Egypto-Greek usage as found in the "twin-texts" in Memphis? At a first glance it might seem so. Nevertheless, this is hardly tenable. If the words were known to the translators as technical terms in the pagan cultus, and if they had this fact in view, they would surely have avoided them.[20] It is more likely that they were thinking of the older official or technical political use in which the words denoted a ministry on behalf of the whole which was legally ordered and which was invested with great solemnity in its chief forms. For them, of course, the recipient of the service is God, not the people, though the service promotes the national welfare, which depends on the gracious disposition of God. The people receives the service merely to the degree that it can offer its sacrifices only through the mediation of the priests (cf. 2 Ch. 35:3; Ez. 44:11). Nevertheless, the priestly cultus is official, legally prescribed and solemn service. If the LXX translators desired a term which would express this characteristic element, they could hardly use λατρεύειν, θεραπεύειν, or even διακονεῖν and the corresponding nouns. They had to choose λειτουργεῖν, λειτουργία.

4. The Usage of Greek Speaking Judaism. Joseph. uses the words only of the priestly cultus, cf. Ant., 20, 218: λειτουργεῖν κατὰ τὸ ἱερόν, 3, 107: λειτουργία ἕνεκα τοῦ θεοῦ, Bell., 1, 39: τὰ πρὸς τὰς λειτουργίας σκεύη, 6, 299: The priests went into the temple πρὸς τὰς λειτουργίας. We also find other terms like → λατρεία, Bell., 2, 409: οἱ κατὰ τὴν λατρείαν λειτουργοῦντες, or ἱερατεύειν, or θεραπεία τοῦ θεοῦ (Ant., 3, 212). The most common term for the cultus is ἱερουργία, which is not found in the LXX; cf. Ant., 3, 150; 152; 158; 180; 224. Philo uses λειτουργεῖν of the priestly ministry, e.g., λειτουργεῖν τὰς ἱερὰς λειτουργίας, Spec. Leg., I, 82; ἔνδον λειτουργεῖν (in the holiest of all), Vit. Mos., II, 152. But he also uses it figur., e.g., Rer. Div. Her., 84 of the νοῦς, ὅτε μὲν καθαρῶς λειτουργεῖ θεῷ, and generally for service, e.g., Det. Pot. Ins., 66: ὁ ... λόγος λειτουργήσει τοῖς παιδείαν μετιοῦσι διεξιὼν τὰ σοφίας δόγματα. The word λειτουργία is often used in Philo, as in the LXX, as a tt. for the priestly cultus, though also figur. for the spiritual worship of God, e.g., Poster. C., 185: The human race will enjoy peace ὑπὸ νόμου φύσεως διδασκόμενον, ἀρετῆς, θεὸν τιμᾶν καὶ τῆς λειτουργίας αὐτοῦ περιέχεσθαι. This is πηγὴ εὐδαιμονίας. It is not surprising that the Egyptian Philo should also know the term in the sense of official public functions, cf. Omn. Prob. Lib., 6, where there is ref. to ἄλλαι λειτουργίαι along with ἀγορανομία and γυμνασιαρχία.

Strathmann

C. Cultic Ministry in the Usage of Rabbinic Judaism.

1. Lexical Review. Rabb. Judaism uses the following stems for cultic ministry: a. עבד with the nominal construction עֲבוֹדָה, already found in OT usage (→ 220); b. deriving from OT usage, שרת (in the pi) with the class. nominal construction שֵׁרֵת. From שרת

---

[20] What Trench, 75 says in this respect about the development of Christian terminology applies also to the LXX. Debrunner (in a letter) considers the rather different possibility that the words were chosen in order to contrast their own cult, the true one, with pagan cults.

(pi) we also find in the Mishnah stage the qittul constr. שֵׁירוּת, not found in the OT. The corresponding Jud.-Aram. constr. is שֵׁירוּתָא; c. In Rabb. lit. we find the stem שׁמשׁ (in the pi), which does not occur in the Heb. OT and probably came into later Heb. by way of Aram.[21] The modern nominal form corresponding to the stem שׁמשׁ (pi) is a qittul constr. שִׁמּוּשׁ. In the same way the noun שַׁמּוּשָׁא is formed from the Aram. root שׁמשׁ (pa'el).[22] d. The root פלח and nominal constr. פּוּלְחָן are also used in Rabb. lit. for cultic ministry. Since the Heb. parts of the OT do not have the stem פלח for this, we may assume that it is another Aram. enrichment.[23] The Jud.-Aram. nominal constr. from the stem פלח is correspondingly פּוּלְחָנָא[24]

2. The Idea of Cultic Ministry.

Rabb. Judaism uses the stems mentioned, and their nominal constr., both with ref. to the worship of Yahweh and also with ref. to pagan cults.

a. The Use of Verbal Forms. bChul., 24b speaks of the temple ministry of the priests of Israel: "A minor is not qualified for the ministry of the temple (פסול לעבודה) even though he is without blemish. From what point is he qualified for the ministry of the temple (כשר לעבודה)? From the moment when he attains puberty. Yet his colleagues will not let him officiate (עבד) until he has reached the age of twenty-one." Here the root עבד is used, but in, e.g., Men., 13, 10 we have the stem שמש: "Priests who have discharged their office (שמשו) in the temple of Onias[25] may not do service (לא ישמשו) in the temple at Jerusalem." עבד refers to the single cultic act (e.g., bMen., 109a b) in expressions like עבד עבודה and עבד שירות, and שמש is used in Yom., 7, 5 for the ministry of the temple on the Day of Atonement: "The high-priest celebrated (on the Day of Atonement) in eight vestments, the ordinary priest in four."

The same stems are used for the cultic action of the layman, whether in bringing offerings or attending divine service in the temple. Thus we read in Sanh., 7, 6 that a Jew who worships idols (עובד עבודה זרה) must be stoned, no matter whether he takes part in (עובד) the customary cultic act of paganism or confesses the alien deity in some other way. The following definition of an *ashera* is found in AZ, 3, 7: "What is an *ashera*? Any (tree) under which is an idol.[26] R. Simon[27] has said: Any (tree) under which one worships (שעובדין אותה) i.e., performs a cultic act." Acc. to Tem., 6, 1 no animal should be brought to the Jerusalem altar which has also received cultic adoration, for which the Mishnah uses the part. ni of עבד.[28] The performing of a cultic act by a layman is also mentioned in bGit., 57b in the legend of the mother and her seven mar-

---

[21] The oldest example is Da. 7:10.

[22] The same root is found in the NT syr for λατρεύειν and λειτουργεῖν, cf. Lk. 1:23, where λειτουργία, and R. 12:1, where λατρεία, is rendered תשמשתא.

[23] פלח is first found in a cultic sense at Da. 3:12, 14, 17, 18, 28; 6:17, 21; 7:14, 27; Ezr. 7:24; פָּלְחָן = worship of God in Ezr. 7:19. The stem פלח is also used for worship in OT syr, e.g., Ex. 9:1, 13.

[24] It does not need to be proved that the stems and derivatives also have secular meanings.

[25] בית חוניו, cf. on this Schürer, III[4], 144 f.; S. Krauss, *Synagogale Altertümer* (1922). 82 ff.; Schl. Gesch. Isr., 33; 123; 127; 344; Moore, I, 43; 230; II, 11.

[26] עבודה זרה = abstr. pro concreto; on this use → 224.

[27] The ref. is to Simon b. Jochai (*c.* 150 A.D.).

[28] In the same context we have the definition: איזהו הנעבד? כל שעובדין אותו.

tyred sons. Here we find a summons to pay cultic honour to the idol by bending the knee: פלח.פלח[29] לעבודת אלילים is used in bAZ, 11a, where there is ref. to cultic action at the burying of a non-Jew. פלח is used not only for a single cultic action but also for the cultic observance of a festival, cf. TAZ, 1, 4: "Although all (Gentiles) keep (עושין) the Kalends as a festival, one may not have dealings only with those who cultically celebrate (the day) (פולחין)."

b. The Use of Nouns. The worship of the temple, or of God, whether in its totality or its individual parts, is usually called עֲבוֹדָה in later Heb. There is ref. to the temple worship at Jerusalem in, e.g., Ab., 1, 2, where Simon the Just reckons עֲבוֹדָה among the three things on which the world rests. Ref. is made to the order of temple worship (סדר עבודה) in, e.g., bMen., 109b. The Rabb. also refer to the ministry of the temple in their forms of protestation; thus העבודה means "by the ministry of the temple," e.g., bJeb., 32b.[30] עבודה also occurs in the sense of a single priestly function in bYoma, 32a: "Hence it may be seen that every priest who goes from one cultic action to another (מעבודה לעבודה) should take a bath."

If pagan worship is to be denoted, this is mostly through the expressions עבודה זרה, עבודת אלילים and עבודת כוכבים ומזלות.[31] Thus in Sanh., 7, 4 a Jew who takes part in a pagan cultus is called עובד עבודה זרה, a servant of idols, and the Babylonian Rab (d. 247) in bShab., 56b speaks of the idolatry of Israel when he uses the figure עבד עבודת כוכבים ומזלות (perhaps originally עבד עבודה זרה).[31] Since a Jew hesitates to mention a god by name, he uses terms for idolatry to describe idols and the other symbols of non-Jewish religion. Thus עבודה זרה is used for a pagan cultic symbol which stands under a tree (AZ, 3, 7 → 223). The expression עבודת אלילים to denote an idol is also found in bGit., 57b (→ *supra*) and bShab., 82a b, where along with עבודה זרה and עבודת כוכבים ומזלות one also finds the vl. עבודת אלילים in the sense of idols. Also used for this is the abstr. טעות Aram. טעותא, e.g., jSanh., 28d, 47. The servant of idols is thus עובד עבודה זרה (shortened to עע״ז), עובד עבודת אלילים (shortened to עע״א), or עובד כוכבים ומזלות (shortened to עכו״ם or עכומ״ז; → n. 31). This is used from the very first for the servant of idols, i.e., the Jew who worships another god instead of Yahweh, cf. Sanh., 7, 4 (→ 223) and Sanh., 5, 1. Since the main difference between Jews and Gentiles is in respect of worship, the use of servant of idols for non-Jew became firmly embedded in Judaism.

Apart from עבודה, ministry in the temple is expressed by שָׁרֵת, e.g., in כְּלֵי שָׁרֵת, Sota, 2, 1 etc., which finds a model in Nu. 4:12 and 2 Ch. 24:14. More common is the later שֵׁירוּת; thus we read in bSota, 38a that the priestly blessing (ברכה) is like the ministry of the temple (שירות) in so far as both are performed standing. שירות is also used for the individual cultic act, e.g., in bMen., 109a: "Slaying (a sacrifice) is not a priestly function (שירות)." The ministry of the temple is also called שִׁמּוּשׁ e.g., Nu. r., 3 on 3:6, where it is said that Yahweh alone chose the Levites to stand in His service (לעמוד בשימושו). The Jud.-Aram. form שִׁמּוּשָׁא is found, e.g., in Tg. O. on Ex. 31:10:

---

29 → n. 26.

30 Cf. further Str.-B., I, 335; Moore, I, 377. The 17th benediction of the Sh. E. is also called עבודה; "Bring back the priestly ministry (העבודה) into the holiest of all in thy temple ... and may the ministry of thy people Israel (עבודת ישראל עמך) be to lasting good-pleasure." The shorter Pal. recension does not have עבודה, like the longer Bab.

31 Worship of stars and signs of the zodiac, though it is possible that this is a later invention, cf. Strack Einl.[5], 54, n. 1.

בִּגְדֵי הַשְּׂרָד = לְבוּשֵׁי שִׁמּוּשָׁא and Tg. O. on Nu. 4:12: כְּלֵי הַשָּׁרֵת = מָנֵי שִׁמּוּשָׁא. Finally ref. may be made to פּוּלְחָן or פּוּלְחָנָא for temple ministry or cultic worship.[32] Thus in Tg. O. on Gn. 22:2 Palestine is the land of the cultic worship of Yahweh: ארע פולחנא (acc. to Levy Chald. Wört.; vl. ארעא פולחנא). In Tg. J. I on Gn. 23:2 Mount Moriah is the mount of divine worship: טור פולחנא. The question whether a temple ministry (פולחן Heb.) arose in Babylon is raised in S. Dt., 41 on 11:13 with ref. to Da. 6:11, 21, and a negative answer is given. In Tg. lit. heathen worship is called פולחנא נוכראה (Tg. J. I on Nu. 23:1), or פולחנא נכריתא, (Tg. J. II on Dt. 14:1); these forms correspond exactly to the Heb. עבודה זרה.

3. The Spiritualisation of the Concept.

Along with the cultic concept of service Rabb. Judaism is also acquainted with the ethical. This ethical service is in view in Tg. O. on Gn. 17:1 when Yahweh says to Abraham: "Serve me" (פלח קדמי), or Tg. on Qoh. 5:11 with its ref. to the man who serves the Lord of the world (די פלח למרי עלמא). If here already there is a spiritualisation, the development of Jewish religion made it inevitable that there should be a spiritualisation of the concept in the sphere of cultic worship as well. Long before the destruction of the second temple synagogue worship became most important in both Palestine and the dispersion. When this is perceived, it is obvious that the spiritualising of the cultic concept was by inner compulsion. The ministry of the Word and of prayer became the chief features in the cultic life of the synagogue, as may be seen already in the days of Jesus. The synagogue could serve the mass of the people as the temple could not do. Even in the case of the Palestinian Jew sacrificial worship was largely replaced by that of the synagogue. Hence even the terrible blow of the destruction of the temple did not involve any inner religious crisis. In the spiritualised form of the cultus[33] prayer took the form of material sacrifice as an offering and a means of expiation. Thus prayer is mentioned as a means of expiation along with incense in Wis. 18:21: σπεύσας γὰρ ἀνὴρ (sc. Moses) ἄμεμπτος προεμάχησεν τὸ τῆς ἰδίας λειτουργίας ὅπλον προσευχὴν καὶ θυμιάματος ἐξιλασμὸν κομίσας. Again, Test. L. 3:6 refers to the rational savour and unbloody sacrifice which the angels offer in the heavenly service of God: προσφέροντες τῷ κυρίῳ ὀσμὴν εὐωδίας λογικὴν καὶ ἀναίμακτον θυσίαν.[34] There are similar spiritualisations in the Rabb. writings.[35] Thus with ref. to Da. 6:11, 21 in S. Dt., 41 on Dt. 11:13 (→ *supra*) par. we read: "As the ministry of the altar (עבודת מזבח) is called ministry (עבודה), so prayer is also called ministry (עבודה)." bTaan., 2a, Bar. is dependent on S. Dt., 41. Here, in allusion to Dt. 11:13, prayer is called the ministry of the heart (עבודה שבלב). Cf. also Raba (d. 352) in bBQ, 92b, where the demand to "serve the Lord your God" (Ex. 23:25) is taken to refer to the recitation of the "Hear, O Israel" and the prayer of 18 petitions. Study of the Torah as well as prayer is divine service on the Rabb. view; thus Tg. on 1 Ch. 4:23 refers to service of God through the study of the Torah (פולחן אורייתא).

R. Meyer

---

[32] → n. 23.

[33] On the spiritualisation of λειτουργία in Sir. and the figur. use of λειτουργεῖν in Da. 7:10 (Θ) → 221.

[34] vl. προσφέρουσι δὲ κυρίῳ ὀσμὴν εὐωδίας λογικὴν καὶ ἀναίμακτον προσφοράν, cf. Charles in Test. XII, p. 34.

[35] Cf. Str.-B., II, 437; III, 26, 296; Moore, II, 84 f., 217 f., 240.

D. λειτουργέω and λειτουργία in the New Testament.

1. Occurrence and Use.

What has been said gives us the presuppositions of the significance of λειτουργεῖν and λειτουργία in the NT, both as regards the paucity of use and the way in which the terms are applied. The word λειτουργεῖν occurs only 3 times, once each in Lk. (Ac. 13:2), Pl. (R. 15:27) and Hb. (10:11). λειτουργία is found 6 times (Lk. 1:23; 2 C. 9:12; Phil. 2:17, 30; Hb. 8:6; 9:21). The use is thus restricted to a small circle of writings. Hb. figures three times. If we add → λειτουργός and → λειτουργικός, we have another six instances, and three of these are in Hb. This is naturally no accident. The author of Hb. is deeply rooted in the outlook and vocabulary of the OT cultus, by means of which he elucidates the meaning of Christ's person and work. In this world the terms λειτουργεῖν and λειτουργία are of supreme significance. Thus the author could hardly avoid using them. In so doing he remains wholly in the sphere of LXX usage. This is esp. true in Hb. 10:11, where it is said of the priest of the OT cultus: ἕστηκεν καθ' ἡμέραν λειτουργῶν καὶ τὰς αὐτὰς πολλάκις προσφέρων θυσίας. The λειτουργεῖν of the priests consists in the offering of sacrifices. Hence in Hb. 9:21, as in the LXX, the OT cultic vessels are called σκεύη τῆς λειτουργίας. These sacrifices which have to be repeated continually, because they can never attain the goal of purifying the conscience, are contrasted by the author with the superior, once-for-all, definitive and effectual sacrificial act of Christ, of whom it is said in 8:6 that He διαφορωτέρας τέτυχεν λειτουργίας. His ministry is better because it is more effective, or, strictly, it alone is effective. The λειτουργία of the OT priesthood is only a shadowy prefiguring. Lk. 1:23 (ἐπλήσθησαν αἱ ἡμέραι τῆς λειτουργίας αὐτοῦ, sc. of the priest Zacharias) is also within the framework of OT usage.

This is not true, however, of Ac. 13:2. Five prophets and teachers of the Christian church at Antioch are listed in v. 1. Then we read: λειτουργούντων δὲ αὐτῶν τῷ κυρίῳ καὶ νηστευόντων εἶπεν τὸ πνεῦμα τὸ ἅγιον· ἀφορίσατε δή μοι τὸν Βαρναβᾶν καὶ Σαῦλον κτλ. The reference is obviously to a fellowship of prayer on the part of the five. The effectiveness of prayer is supported by fasting.[36] The prayer is heard. The Spirit issues a missionary order. The term λειτουργεῖν is used of this common prayer. This is new as compared with LXX usage, though the passage seems not to be aware of this. Movements towards a general figurative use (cf. λειτουργία for righteous conduct) may be found, however, in Sir. as well as Philo. λειτουργία is also used of the prayer of Moses (along with the offering of atoning incense) in Wis. 18:21, and it is used for the worship of God by angels in Da. 7:10 (Θ). Cf. also Test. L. 3:6 (→ 225), though λειτουργία itself is not used there.

If these are isolated verses, they are confirmed and given enhanced significance by the fact that the same spiritualising tendency may be seen in the Rabb. use of עֲבוֹדָה (→ C.). Hence, though Lk.'s use of the term in Ac. 13:2 stands in contrast with the LXX, Jewish Christian circles of the time would not regard it as unprecedented or strange. Nevertheless, the verse demands special attention. For it is the first to attest a transfer of the important OT cultic term to the purely

---

[36] Cf. on this Mk. 9:29 vl. and H. Strathmann, *Geschichte d. frühchristl. Askese* ..., I (1914), 63-69.

spiritual Christian service of God, even though the reference be only to a small prayer fellowship of leading men. It thus opens up the way for broader development.

In Paul, R. 15:27 and 2 C. 9:12 belong together. The verb in the former and the noun in the latter both refer to the collection for the congregation in Jerusalem.

Commentators are often inclined either to catch here the basic secular sense — the choice of term implies that the contribution is a ministry to the public welfare of the Christian community [37] — or to interpret the words in terms of the technical cultic significance in the LXX. The collection is thus brought into a sacral and cultic relation. It is a sacred ministry, and is called an act of divine service of a high order. [38] Probably neither explanation is the right one. Both are refuted by the fact that in Phil. 2:30 Paul uses λειτουργία for the monetary gift which the Philippians had made to Paul, and which Epaphroditus had brought at the risk of his life, thus doing what they could not do (ἵνα ἀναπληρώσῃ τὸ ὑμῶν ὑστέρημα τῆς πρός με λειτουργίας). Here there is no sense either of a ministry to the public welfare of the Christian community or of the priestly cultus of the OT. If Paul had either in view, he would not have spoken of a λειτουργία to himself.

It is thus best to see in these three verses the popular sense of rendering a service, of which we gave sufficient examples under → A. 3. c., and to refrain from reading deeper implications into the text [39] and speaking of sacred ministry and the like. On the other hand, in the fourth and last Pauline verse (Phil. 2:17) proximity to θυσία suggests an OT and cultic nuance for λειτουργία.

The meaning varies as one links the ἐπὶ τῇ θυσίᾳ καὶ λειτουργίᾳ τῆς πίστεως ὑμῶν either with the preceding ἀλλὰ εἰ καὶ σπένδομαι or the succeeding χαίρω καὶ συγχαίρω πᾶσιν ὑμῖν. In the former case, either the faith of the Philippians seems to be a sacrificial gift which is offered (by Paul ?) to God, and to which Paul will soon add the drink offering of his martyrdom (though can there be an obj. gen. of this kind with λειτουργία ?), or we have the imprecisely expressed thought that the apostle's missionary work is a service which aims at the establishment of their faith, to which he has thus far given himself in suffering, and in which he may very well suffer martyrdom. In the latter case it is the faith of the Philippians which offers θυσία and λειτουργία. This would consist in their total walk in faith. In virtue of their faith they are both a sacrifice offered to God and priests who offer God sacrifices.

Either way, the close connection with θυσία shows that λειτουργία is here meant in the sense of cultic and priestly ministry. This is a figure to characterise either the missionary work of Paul or the Christian walk of the Philippians.

2. The Findings and Their Significance.

The use of λειτουργεῖν, λειτουργία in the NT is connected partly with the general popular use (R. 15:27; 2 C. 9:12; Phil. 2:30), partly with the preceding OT cultus (Lk. 1:23; Hb. 9:21; 10:11), and partly with an isolated figurative use of LXX terminology to bring out the significance of Christ's death (Hb.) or to characterise either Paul's missionary work with its readiness for martyrdom, or

---

[37] E.g., B. Weiss, *NT*, II² (1902); Heinr. 2 K., *ad loc.*
[38] So, e.g., Bchm. K., *ad loc.*
[39] Cf. Ltzm. K. on 2 C. 9:12.

the Christian walk of the community (Phil. 2:17). Movement towards a new Christian terminology is to be found only in the one verse Ac. 13:2, where λειτουργεῖν is used for a fellowship of prayer, which hereby is indirectly described as a spiritualised priestly ministry.

On the other hand, the terms are never used for the services or offices of leading personalities in the new community such as apostles, teachers, prophets, presbyters, bishops etc. Such a use could not develop on the soil of primitive Christian thought. For the tasks of Christian office-bearers were not comparable with those of the priestly sacrificial cultus. The cultus had reached its end with the self-offering of Christ, as Hb. impressively shows. The messengers of Christ and leaders of individual congregations do not have to fulfil a λειτουργία for the community. Their task is to proclaim in the word of the crucifixion of Christ the λειτουργία which has been fulfilled once and for all. In this circle of ideas it was certainly possible to explain with the help of figures taken from the OT priestly ministry the significance of self-sacrifice in the service of Christ, or of the faithful life of Christians, or of the gathering of the congregation for prayer. But the cultic terms could not be applied specifically to Christian offices as such. The new community had no priests, for it consisted of priests. "We can be bold to enter into the holiest through the blood of Jesus" (Hb. 10:19). We may thus conclude, both from the paucity of use and especially from the complete lack of any parallels in the Christian application, that the Christian message is something new and revolutionary.

E. Transition to Later Ecclesiastical Usage.

The position seems to be much the same in the post-apostolic fathers.

The words are used for the cultic functions of the OT priests; cf. 1 Cl., 32, 2 (λειτουργεῖν τῷ θυσιαστηρίῳ); 40, 2 (προσφοραὶ καὶ λειτουργίαι); 43, 4 (εἰς τὸ ἱερατεύειν καὶ λειτουργεῖν αὐτῷ); also 40, 5 (the λειτουργίαι of the high-priest along with the διακονίαι of the Levites). The cultic terms are then transferred to righteous conduct; cf. 1 Cl., 9, 2 and 4 (the conduct of Enoch etc. is a λειτουργεῖν τῇ μεγαλοπρεπεῖ δόξῃ αὐτοῦ); Herm. s., 7, 6; m., 5, 1, 2 and 3 (of the Holy Spirit dwelling in man who λειτουργεῖ τῷ θεῷ); s., 5, 3 and 8 (true fasting is a θυσία δεκτή and a λειτουργία καλὴ καὶ ... εὐπρόσδεκτος τῷ θεῷ). They are then used of the angels and the winds which serve God's will, 1 Cl., 34, 5; 20, 10. But they are used esp. with ref. to relations in the Christian community. Particular note should be taken here of 1 Cl., 40 ff. The authority of orderly office in the community is to be protected. The author takes the cultic hierarchy of the OT as an example. The tasks of the high-priest, priests, Levites and the λαϊκὸς ἄνθρωπος are all prescribed by specific regulations (40, 5). Hence each member of the Christian community must please God in his own place and not transgress τὸν ὡρισμένον τῆς λειτουργίας αὐτοῦ κανόνα (41, 1). If here λειτουργία refers to the task of every member of the community, in 44, 2-6 it applies specifically to that of the bishops and presbyters.

This becomes an established usage, cf. Eus. Hist. Eccl., III, 13, where it is said of the Roman bishop Linus that for 12 years he discharged τὴν λειτουργίαν and then handed it to Anencletus, or III, 34: Κλήμης Εὐαρέστῳ παραδοὺς τὴν λειτουργίαν ἀναλύει τὸν βίον. In the Const. Ap., λειτουργεῖν, λειτουργία are used of the offices of bishops, presbyters and deacons (VIII, 4, 5; 18, 3; 47, 28 and 36).

It should never be forgotten that in the first instance λειτουργεῖν, λειτουργία simply denotes service, the pious service which is rendered to God (Herm. s., 9,

27, 3) and also to the community (1 Cl., 44, 3: λειτουργεῖν τῷ ποιμνίῳ, and Did., 15, 1). But comparison with the relations of the OT, and the contrast between the priesthood and the λαϊκὸς ἄνθρωπος in 1 Cl., suggest the beginnings of an approximation of the terms for Christian office to those for the OT priesthood, and this was bound to exert an influence on the history of the meaning of λειτουργεῖν, λειτουργία. In this context we cannot pursue the further development. The final result, however, was a thoroughgoing transfer of the OT concept of the priest to the Christian clergy.

Cf. Const. Ap., II, 25, 5: The clergy have a right to support like the Levites, οἱ λειτουργοῦντες τῇ σκηνῇ τοῦ μαρτυρίου, ἥτις ἦν τύπος τῆς ἐκκλησίας κατὰ πάντα. II, 25, 27: ὑμεῖς οὖν σήμερον, ὦ ἐπίσκοποι, ἐστὲ τῷ λαῷ ὑμῶν ἱερεῖς Λευῖται, οἱ λειτουργοῦντες τῇ ἱερᾷ σκηνῇ. The tasks and rights of the clergy are a fulfilment of the λειτουργίαι of the priestly office. Cf. Const. Ap., VIII, 47, 15: If a presbyter or deacon or anyone else from the κατάλογος τῶν κληρικῶν leaves his own παροικία, and against the will of the bishop enters upon another, τοῦτον κελεύομεν μηκέτι λειτουργεῖν ... ὡς λαϊκὸς μέντοι ἐκεῖσε κοινωνείτω. Cf. also the εὐχὴ ὑπὲρ ἐπισκόπου καὶ τῆς ἐκκλησίας in the Sacramentarium Serapionis, 11, 3:[40] Holy also are the deacons ἵνα ὦσιν "καθαροὶ καρδίᾳ" καὶ σώματι καὶ δυνηθῶσιν "καθαρᾷ συνειδήσει" λειτουργεῖν καὶ παραστῆναι τῷ ἁγίῳ σώματι καὶ τῷ ἁγίῳ αἵματι, Thdrt. Hist. Eccl., II, 24, 8: Leontius τῆς μὲν λειτουργίας ἔπαυσεν τὸν 'Αέτιον, τῆς δέ γε ἄλλης αὐτὸν θεραπείας ἠξίου. Cf. also *ibid.*, I, 23, 5: τὰς θείας ἐπιτελεῖν λειτουργίας. II, 27, 2: τὴν τοῦ θείου βαπτίσματος ἐπιτελεῖν λειτουργίαν. IV, 14, 2: τὴν ἑσπερινὴν λειτουργίαν ἐπιτελεῖν.

λειτουργεῖν, λειτουργία are thus used to denote the cultus, and important cultic actions, especially the eucharist. OT cultic concepts celebrate their resurrection. Along with the spiritualisation there is a new materialisation.

† λειτουργός.

One might expect that the Gk. would use λειτουργός for the man who undertook a "liturgy" on behalf of the whole body, but the term is rare, and expectation is disappointed, at least so far as Attic lit. is concerned. It simply occurs a few times in the inscr.[1] In the pap. λειτουργός is often used for liturgical officials.[2] Plut. recalls the connection with the original meaning when he notes in Romulus, 26, 4 (I, 34b) that the *lictores* had previously been called λιτῶρεις, which corresponded to the Gk. λειτουργοί; λήϊτον γὰρ τὸ δημόσιον. But there is no sense of this connection in the use elsewhere in non-biblical Gk. Occasionally it is used as an adj. for "ministering," more often as a noun for one who ministers, usually in the form of manual work, hence a worker. For the adj. cf. Iambl. Myst., 9, 2: One calls the demons ἀπό τε τῶν δεκανῶν καὶ τῶν λειτουργῶν ζῳδίων τε καὶ ἄστρων κτλ. For the noun cf. CIG, I, 181, 21; 182, 11; 200, 33; also Dio C., 38, 41, 7: κριταὶ ἅμα καὶ λειτουργοὶ τοῦ πολέμου γιγνόμενοι. In the sense of military labourers, esp. those who work on intrenchments (pioneers), we find it in Polyb., 3, 93, 5 and 7; 5, 2, 5; 10, 29, 4. In the pap. it is simply

---

[40] Const. Ap. (Funk), II, p. 168.

λειτουργός. [1] Cf. CIG, II, 2774, 2 ff.: ἄνδρα τῶν ἐν τέλει, πατρὸς καὶ προγόνων ἀρχικῶν καὶ λιτουργῶν. 2881, 13: λειτουργὸς τῶν ἐν παισὶ λειτουργιῶν πασῶν. 2882, 6/7: τέλιος λειτουργός. 2884, 6: ἄνδρα ... τῶν πρὶν λειτουργῶν οὐδενὶ λειπόμενον. 2886, 1: προγόνων λειτουργῶν τῆς πόλεως. 2928, 5: ... λειτουργόν ...
[2] Examples in Preisigke Wört., *s.v.*, all from 3rd-6th cent. A.D.

used for workers.[3] It is very rarely used in the sacral sense.[4] In an inscr. in the Delphinium at Miletus the sons of Marcus Aurelius Granianus Posidonius, προφήτης καὶ τέλειος λειτουργός, and Marcus Aurelius Granianus Diodorus, στεφανηφόρος καὶ προφήτης καὶ τέλειος λειτουργός, honour their mother, who is herself described as στεφανηφόρος and coming from a family of προφῆται and στεφανηφόροι.[5] In the context λειτουργός can only be a cultic title. Another example is the inscr. Waddington, II, 3, No. 57, in which two daughters honour their father Alexander τὸν ἐκ προγόνων καὶ ἀπὸ παιδὸς ἡλικίας λιτουργὸν τὸν μιμαντοβάτην καὶ ἱερέα θεοῦ Ἀλεξάνδρου κτλ. Cf. also Dion. Hal. Ant. Rom., II, 2, 3: ἅπαντας ... τοὺς ἱερεῖς τε καὶ λειτουργοὺς τῶν θεῶν ἐνομοθέτησεν ἀποδείκνυσθαι μὲν ὑπὸ τῶν φρατριῶν, ἐπικυροῦσθαι δὲ ὑπὸ τῶν ἐξηγουμένων τὰ θεῖα διὰ μαντικῆς, *ibid.*, II, 73, 2: λειτουργοὶ θεῶν with ἰδιῶται and ἄρχοντες; also ἱερεῖς ἅπαντες with ὑπηρέται αὐτῶν and λειτουργοὶ οἷς χρῶνται πρὸς τὰ ἱερά. But this use is isolated. Preisigke cannot give a single instance from the pap.

Nor is the word common in the LXX. Including the apocr. it occurs 14 times, almost always for מְשָׁרֵת, cf. → 220. But while λειτουργεῖν = שֵׁרֵת usually refers to the priestly ministry, λειτουργός has a cultic sense only in Is. 61:6 (ὑμεῖς δὲ ἱερεῖς κυρίου κληθήσεσθε, λειτουργοὶ θεοῦ), 2 Εσδρ. 20:40 (= Neh. 10:40) (οἱ ἱερεῖς οἱ λειτουργοί) and Sir. 7:30,[6] where the λειτουργοί correspond to the ἱερεῖς of v. 29. Elsewhere the priests are λειτουργοί in Ep. Ar., 95. Normally the word is used for the servant (not slave) of another, a superior, e.g., of Moses (Jos. 1:1 A of Joshua), Amnon (2 Βασ. 13:18), Solomon (3 Βασ. 10:5; 2 Ch. 9:4), Elisha (4 Βασ. 4:43; 6:15), the κριτὴς τοῦ λαοῦ (Sir. 10:2), Ptolemy (3 Macc. 5:5). In ψ 102:21 and 103:4 the λειτουργοί of God are the angels. For the Gk. reader even the λειτουργοὶ οἴκου θεοῦ in 2 Εσδρ. 7:24 would be simply servants, though the original פלח may refer to cultic worship, cf. Da. 3:12. Priests and Levites are mentioned earlier; these λειτουργοί do not have cultic functions.

Of the five NT references 3 are in Paul (R. 13:6; 15:16; Phil. 2:25) and 2 in Hb. (1:7; 8:2). In Hb. 8:2 Christ is called τῶν ἁγίων λειτουργὸς καὶ τῆς σκηνῆς τῆς ἀληθινῆς. The reference is to the high-priestly ministry which He performs in the true and heavenly tabernacle. Here, then, the word has a cultic sense. One might translate "priest of the sanctuary." R. 15:16 also moves in the realm of priestly and cultic ideas. Paul describes himself as λειτουργὸν Χριστοῦ Ἰησοῦ εἰς τὰ ἔθνη. This does not have to include the idea of a sacral function. But if not, he might just as well have used διάκονος. What follows shows that he is using λειτουργός cultically almost in the sense of priest. For he construes it in terms of ἱερουργεῖν τὸ εὐαγγέλιον. He discharges a priestly ministry in relation to the Gospel. The final clause which follows shows how. He wins the Gentiles to the Christian faith and leads them to God. They are thus an acceptable sacrifice. The context thus shows us that λειτουργός had for Paul a sacral ring. This alone explains the phrases that follow. But we do not have to interpret the other verses in the light of these two. In none of the others do we find the priestly and cultic

---

[3] E.g., P. Petr., II, No. 4, 9, line 11 (ἀπόστειλον δὲ λειτουργούς [cf. Preisigke Wört., II, 13]); λειτουργοί with οἰκοδόμοι, *ibid.*, II, No. 14, 3, line 4; III, No. 46, 4, line 8.

[4] We do not include the erroneously adduced passage Plut. Def. Orac., 13 (II, 417a): οἷς δίκαιόν ἐστι ταῦτα λειτουργοῖς θεῶν ἀνατιθέντες, ὥσπερ ὑπηρέταις καὶ γραμματεῦσι (cf. W. Otto, *Priester u. Tempel im hell. Ägypten*, I [1905], 234 f.; II [1908], 33, n. 2). For here the ref. is to demons, not priests. These are the λειτουργοί of the gods.

[5] Cf. G. Kawerau-A. Rehm, *Das Delphinion in Milet.* (1914), 396.

[6] Unless the part. of the Sinaiticus is original.

sense. This is true of Hb. 1:7. The angels are λειτουργοὶ θεοῦ as the agents of His will.[7] In Phil. 2:25 Paul calls Epaphroditus λειτουργὸν τῆς χρείας μου because he has ministered to him in his need by bringing the gift of the Philippians. In R. 13:6 rulers (ἄρχοντες, v. 3) are λειτουργοὶ θεοῦ because they minister to God's will by suppressing evil and promoting good. The term does not imply they discharge a priestly function. Their task is comparable with that of angels in Hb. 1:7. The διάκονος of v. 4 is simply another term for the same thing.[8] It may be that Paul, who does not use the term often, is conscious of an aura of solemnity deriving from the LXX, but one can hardly say that he intends it sacrally. Even in the LXX the term λειτουργός (as distinct from λειτουργεῖν and λειτουργία) does not contain as such the thought of the priestly cultus. Where it is linked with this, it is in virtue of the context. The same is true in the NT. In R. 13:6 and Hb. 1:7 it is not the word λειτουργός which gives the expression its strong religious colouring, but the fact that God or Christ is the recipient of the service.

In 1 Cl. λειτουργοί is used of the priests who fulfil the sacrificial cultus in the temple (41, 2), of the prophets who are λειτουργοὶ τῆς χάριτος τοῦ θεοῦ (8, 1), and of angels (36, 3) on the model of Hb. 1:3 ff. There are other examples of the use for angels,[9] but in its ecclesiastical development the word very largely took on a clerical and sacral nuance.[10]

† λειτουργικός.

This word is found a few times in the pap. λειτουργικόν denotes a tax for the performance of λειτουργίαι, e.g., P. Petr., II, No. 39e, 3rd cent. B.C. Ἡμέραι λειτουργικαί are the days when individual priests did their service and drew the income from it.[1] The word λειτουργικός occurs 6 times in the LXX (and λειτουργήσιμος, which has the same meaning, once in 1 Ch. 28:13). It always bears a sacral sense, "belonging to the cultus," with ref. to cultic vessels and vestments (Ex. 31:10; 39:12; Nu. 4:12, 26; 7:5; 2 Ch. 24:14).

The only NT use is at Hb. 1:14: the angels are λειτουργικὰ πνεύματα εἰς διακονίαν ἀποστελλόμενα διὰ τοὺς μέλλοντας κληρονομεῖν σωτηρίαν. They are ordained to ministry, i.e., the διακονία of believers. Hence the use is not cultic, and is independent of the LXX.

Strathmann

---

7 Hence they are λειτουργικὰ πνεύματα in Hb. 1:14.

8 Thus in Est. 1:10; 2:2; 6:3 מְשָׁרֵת is not rendered λειτουργός as in other OT passages → 230, but διάκονος.

9 E.g., Cl. Al. Exc. Theod., 27, 2; Strom., VI, 17, 157, 4; Method. Resurrect., I, 49, 1-4.

10 Cf. the burial inscr. of a 4th cent. deacon from Iconium, which was published by W. M. Ramsay (*Byzantinisch-Neugriech. Jbchr.* [1923], 344 f.) and on which the deceased is called λιτουργὸς καθολικῆς ἐκκλησίας καταστάθις (= κατασταθείς).

λειτουργικός. 1 W. Otto, *Priester u. Tempel im hell. Ägypten*, II (1908), 33, n. 2. Mitteis-Wilcken, I, 2, p. 146.

† λεπίς

a. "Shell": egg-shell, Schol. Aristoph. Pax, 198 (ed. G. Dindorf [1838]), shell of a nut, Anth. Pal., I, 622, 102, skin of an onion, Schol. in Luc. De Historia Quomodo Conscribenda Sit, 26, ed. H. Rabe (1906), p. 228. b. "Scale" of fishes, Hdt., VII, 61; Aristot. Hist. An., 1, 1, p. 486b, 21; I, 6, p. 490b, 23; III, 10, p. 517b, 5; LXX: Lv. 11:9, 10, 12; Dt. 14:9, 10 (Heb. קַשְׂקֶשֶׂת), of snakes, Nicand. Theriaca, 154. Figur. of metal plates, Hdt., VII, 61; Polyb., 10, 27, 10; BGU, II, 544, 8 (the making of scale-armour); LXX: Nu. 17:3 (Heb. פַּח); Preis. Zaub., IV, 258 etc.; snow-flakes, Theophr. Hist. Plant., IV, 14, 13. At Lv. 13:2, 7 an unknown translator has λεπίς for rash, leprosy.

In the NT the only use is at Ac. 9:18 in the story of the conversion, blinding, and healing of Saul: καὶ εὐθέως ἀπέπεσαν αὐτοῦ ἀπὸ τῶν ὀφθαλμῶν ὡς λεπίδες, "and forthwith there fell as it were scales from his eyes."

This proverbial expression is to be explained in terms of the healing of the eyes in antiquity. [1] λεπίς is not found as a tt. in medical lit. dealing with the eyes, but a passage from Pliny (the Elder) suggests that it was. In Hist. Nat., XXIX, 1, 21 Pliny censures the conduct of doctors who in greed give a palliative to those suffering from a white scar on the horny coat of the eye instead of effecting a radical cure (*arcana praecepti, squamam* (= λεπίς) *in oculis emovendam potius quam extrahendam*), cf. also XXXII, 7, 71. [2] The term de-scaling derives from the removal of the πτερύγιον, a growth of skin covering the eye and causing blindness. Both ailments are related in terms of therapy, [3] so that there can easily be confusion in popular description of the trouble and its cure. Thus the comm. rightly adduce Tob. 11:12 in explanation of Ac. 9:18: διέτριψε τοὺς ὀφθαλμοὺς αὐτοῦ, καὶ ἐλεπίσθη ἀπὸ τῶν κανθῶν τῶν ὀφθαλμῶν αὐτοῦ τὰ λευκώματα. [4]

Thus the expression in Ac. 9:18 is not a freely constructed metaphor. It draws on medical terminology: there happens to Paul what takes place in desquamation. As Tob. 11:12 shows, the expression does not involve any technical medical knowledge. Hence it cannot be used to show that Luke was a physician. [5] It is also a mistake to combine the passage with verses in the epistles (2 C. 12:7; Gl. 4:15)

λεπίς. [1] In what follows I am indebted to Prof. Regenbogen of Heidelberg.

[2] J. Hirschberg, *Gesch. d. Augenheilkunde* (Graefe-Saemisch, *Hndbch. d. gesamten Augenheilkunde*, XII) [2] (1899), 307 f.

[3] *Ibid.*, No. 27-29, pp. 384 ff.

[4] In S the blindness of Tob. is due to faulty medical treatment; in AB it is a natural accompaniment. Talmudic medicine has for this affliction which leads to blindness the etym. suitable term בַּרְקָא = παράλαμψις = λεύκωμα. Cf. J. Preuss, *Biblisch-talmudische Medizin* (1911), 301 and 307 ff.; Hirschberg, 29, 86.

[5] W. K. Hobart, *The Medical Language of St. Luke* (1882), 39 f.; A. Harnack, *Lk. der Arzt* (1906). In any case, Hobart gives examples only of the more general use of λεπίς (scales of bone and skin). In pharmacology λεπίδες are a copper preparation which serves as medication (Diosc. Mat. Med., V, 78).

and to conclude that Paul was suffering from an affliction of the eyes.[6] If the phrase is chosen to emphasise the fact that the healing is just as effective[7] as with medical treatment, the metaphorical significance of the healing should not be overlooked. Paul loses the light of his eyes because the risen Lord has overcome him as an enemy (Ac. 22:6 ff.), and he receives it back as His witness, commissioned to go to the Gentiles "to open their eyes, and to turn them from darkness to light" (Ac. 26:18).

Bornkamm

† λέπρα, † λεπρός

The adj. λεπρός (from λέπω, "to scale or peel off") has the sense of "scaly," "scabby," "not smooth on the surface." It can be used of uneven and stony ground, but also of leprosy, in which the skin becomes rough and scabby. The related noun λέπρα and the derivatives λεπράω, λεπρόω etc. are used only of leprosy.[1] The LXX uses λέπρα for צָרַעַת, which is found esp. in Lv. 13 f., or נֶגַע־צָרַעַת, Lv. 13:20; λεπρός, λεπράω, λεπρόομαι are also found in the LXX.

In the NT λέπρα and λεπρός refer to the same ailment, or group of ailments, as the words denote in the OT or LXX. This is proved by the reference to the OT in Lk. 4:27; Mt. 11:5 and par., and to the OT ritual of purification in Mk. 1:44 and par.; Lk. 17:14.[2] Whether this sickness is what we now call leprosy may be questioned.[3] But the precise medical identification of the disease does not affect our estimation of the accounts of healing.[4] If the tradition emphasises particularly that Jesus healed lepers, this is linked with the fact that Judaism expected the removal of this affliction in the time of Messianic salvation,[5] cf. the reply of Jesus

---

[6] On Paul's sickness cf. Ltzm. K., Exc. on 2 C. 12:10; Wnd. 2 K., Exc. on 12:7; Bchm. K., II[4] (1922), 399 ff.; F. Fenner, "Die Krankheit im NT," UNT, 18 (1930), 30 ff. → III, 204; 819 f.

[7] The use of medical terms in accounts of healing is common elsewhere, cf. in relation to blindness the votive tablets of Epidauros assembled by Hirschberg, 57 ff.

λέπρα κτλ. [1] Cf. the non-biblical instances in Liddell-Scott, *s.v.*

[2] J. Jadassohn, *Die Lepra* (1930) = *Hndbch. d. Haut- u. Geschlechtskrankheiten*, Vol. X.

[3] Doubts are raised by, e.g., G. N. Münch, *Die Zaraath (Lepra) d. hbr. Bibel* (1893) = *Dermatologische Studien*, XVI; W. Ebstein, *D. Medizin im NT u. im Talmud* (1903), 38 f., 90 f., 272 ff. Cf. also Loh. Mk. (1937), 45; R. Otto, *Reich Gottes u. Menschensohn* (1934), 299; F. Fenner, *D. Krankheit im NT* (1930), 67 f. = UNT, 18; A. Sandler, Art. "Lepra" in EJ, X (1934), 798 ff. But C. v. Orelli, Art. "Aussatz" in RE[3], II (1897), 296-9 (older bibl.); XXIII (1913), 149 thinks it was modern leprosy. Cf. also J. Preuss, *Biblisch-talmudische Medizin* (1911), 369. Philo, who often deals with OT rules about leprosy, groups it in Spec. Leg., I, 80 with scabs and similar sores, and in Poster. C., 47; Som., I, 202 calls it πολύμορφος καὶ πολύτροπος. Cf. also Str.-B., IV, 745-763, Exc. 27: "Aussatz u. Aussätzige."

[4] → III, 207.

[5] Str.-B., I, 593 ff.

to the Baptist in Mt. 11:5 and par.,[6] and the power given to the disciples in Mt. 10:8. Accounts of such healings are to be found in Mk. 1:40 ff. and par.;[7] Lk. 17:12 ff. (cf. also Mt. 10:8 and par.).[8] → III, 424.

Michaelis

† Λευ(ε)ί, Λευ(ε)ίς

Gk. rendering of the name לֵוִי, either unchanged and indeclinable,[1] or made declinable by the addition of ς (gen. and dat. Λευ(ε)ί, acc. Λευ(ε)ίν).[2]

1. The name occurs in the NT in the Lucan genealogy of Jesus for the great-grandfather of Joseph,[3] and then again for a link about halfway between David and Zerubbabel (Lk. 3:24, 29). Nothing else is known of these two.

In evaluation of Lk. 3:29 it should be noted that the use of patriarchal names as personal names seems to begin only in the Hellenistic period.[4] The earliest example of Levi is in Ep. Ar. (48), where in the group of translators we read of a Λευίς along with Isaac, Jacob, Joshua, Sabbataios and Simon. The four who bear the name in Joseph. belong to the 1st cent. A.D. לֵוִי בַּר סִיסִי appears as a Tannaite of the 5th generation.[5]

2. In Lk. 5:27, 29 we read of a tax-collector called Levi whom Jesus called from his post to be a disciple, and who then made a great supper for publicans and sinners to which he invited Jesus. In Mk. this man is more accurately called the son of Alphaeus (2:14).

In Luke's list of the apostles we do not find this Levi at either Lk. 6:13 ff. or Ac. 1:13. Nor does he occur in Mk., where we have instead James the son of Alphaeus.[6] Hence many texts thought they should put James for Levi at Mk. 2:14.[7] The father seems to be the same, and a disciple whose calling is recounted in this way should surely belong to the apostolic band. It is worth considering whether the τὸν τοῦ Ἁλφαίου of Mk. 2:14 does not owe its origin to the same feeling. In the First Gospel there is no

[6] On the relation to Mandaean texts, cf. Kl. Mt., *ad loc.*

[7] On the version of this pericope in *Unknown Gospel*, lines 32 ff., cf. K. F. Schmidt and J. Jeremias, "Ein bisher unbekanntes Evangelienfragment," in ThBl, 15 (1936), 34 ff.

[8] Zn. Mt., *ad loc.*

Λευ(ε)ί κτλ. [1] Bl.-Debr. § 53, 1.

[2] *Ibid.*, § 55, 1e.

[3] On the omission of Matthat and Levi in the text of Lk. 3:24 in Julius Africanus as the result of a deliberate correction of the genealogy, cf. Zn. Lk. [3, 4] (1920), *ad loc.*, 213 ff.

[4] For instances cf. art "Levi" by G. Hölscher in Pauly-W., XII (1925), 2207.

[5] Strack Einl., c. 13 § 7.

[6] Cf. also Lk. D.

[7] D Θ φ it Tat; Origen, too, knew this variant. Cf. Zn. Forsch., I, 130.

tax-collector Levi, but only Matthew, who is said to have been called in the same way, and also to have made the supper, and who appears in the list in Mt. 10:3 as Matthew the publican, though he is not called this in the other three lists. Here the linking of the call with a well-known apostle is fully accomplished.[8]

The relation of the three accounts can hardly be explained by supposing that the same event took place twice with different persons.[9] Either Levi and Matthew are one and the same, or the story of the one has been transferred to the other.[10]

According to the spirit in which the Gospels were written, the important thing is to lay simple emphasis on the fact that the one called, and made worthy of table-fellowship with Jesus, belonged to the despised and hated company of tax-collectors. Bearing an honoured name from the patriarchal period, he had grown rich on his fellow-countrymen. In the Christian community there was no need to excuse or to hide the past of even worthy members. For in this community there is repentance, forgiveness, and καινὴ κτίσις. The Christian community can speak quite truthfully of the past of its members. For it does not believe in the significant personalities within it. It believes in the One to whom it owes everything. That Levi was a publican simply shows the greatness of Christ. Levi had been a publican. But ἀναστὰς ἠκολούθησεν αὐτῷ.

3. In the three remaining NT passages (Hb. 7:5, 9; Rev. 7:7) Levi is the third son of Jacob by Leah.

a. The OT tradition derives the priestly tribe of Levi from him. We cannot go into the difficult questions relating to the meaning of the name or the origin and history of the tribe. May it be that there was once a secular tribe which perished because of an act of shameful subterfuge (Gn. 34), and its scattered members then devoted themselves to the priesthood? May it be that, irrespective of the secular tribe, the priestly order of Levi was an independent group, a kind of religious order, a society, which was linked with the priesthood of the sanctuary in Kadesh (Nu. 18:19; Mal. 2:4-9)? What was the relation of the Levitical priesthood to the Aaronic, and then, after the settlement in Canaan, to the existing pre-Israelitish priesthoods in existing shrines, and then to the Zadokite priesthood in Jerusalem? How did the legal position and ministerial functions of the Levites develop in relation to the temple priests in consequence of the Deuteronomic centralisation of the cultus?[11] Setting aside such questions, we can only point out that acc. to the dominant OT view the tribe of Levi was charged with the priesthood. Cf. Ex. 2:1 ff.; 6:20; 32:25-29; Dt. 10:8; 17:9; 33:9-11; Ju. 17:13.

---

[8] The disciple Levi also occurs in Ev. Pt., 14, 60 on the occasion of the appearance of the risen Lord at the Sea of Galilee; also in Didasc., where on Easter Sunday the Lord shows Himself to him in his dwelling (ed. H. Achelis-J. Flemming, TU, 25, 2 [1904]), 107; in an unpublished Coptic Gnostic work, where Levi intervenes for Mary in a dispute between Peter and Mary about revelations of the risen Lord (cf. on this Hennecke, 69 f.); acc. to Cl. Al. Strom., IV, 9, 71, 3, the Valentinian Heracleon in his Comm. on Lk. 12:11 f. tells us that Levi was one of the first fathers who did not suffer martyrdom (οὐ γὰρ πάντες οἱ σῳζόμενοι ὡμολόγησαν τὴν διὰ τῆς φωνῆς ὁμολογίαν καὶ ἐξῆλθον, ἐξ ὧν Ματθαῖος, Φίλιππος, Θωμᾶς, Λευὶς καὶ ἄλλοι πολλοί).

[9] One might also mention the view of Photius, Catena Possini (1645), 50 that there were two publicans in the apostolic band.

[10] In this context we cannot take up this complicated question.

[11] Cf. on these questions the careful discussion in Eichr. Theol. AT, I, 209 ff.; R. Kittel, *Gesch. d. Volkes Israel*, I² (1912), 217-326, 407 f., 540; II² (1909), 74 f., 270 ff.; G. A. Cooke in Hastings DB, III (1900), *s.v.*; S. Mowinckel in RGG², III, *s.v.*; E. Auerbach in EJ, X (1934), *s.v.*; P. Heinisch in Lex. Th. K.², VI (1934), *s.v.*; Hölscher, *op. cit.*, 2155-2208.

b. In later Judaism the Book of Jub. and the Jewish basis of the Test. XII display a striking interest in Levi and his tribe. Along with Judah Levi is given a privileged position among the sons of Jacob, and even over Judah he has the precedence. When Jacob visits the dying Isaac, only these two go with him. Isaac is filled with the spirit of prophecy, and takes Levi by his right hand, Judah by his left, and blesses Levi and his descendants. First, they are promised priestly ministry in the sanctuary. Then we read: "Princes and judges and rulers will they be to all the seed of the children of Jacob; they will proclaim the Word of God in truth, and set up His judgment in righteousness, and proclaim my ways to Jacob and my paths to Israel" (Jub. 31:14 f.). Levi is thus to be priest, prince and prophet in one. Acc. to Dt. 33:8-11 he is to serve as priest, to deliver oracles, and to give instruction. But his position as prince and ruler is new as compared with the OT, as is also his exalting above Judah. Also divergent from the OT is the assessment of the massacre of Shechem by Simeon and Levi (Gn. 34). The OT condemns this cruel and crafty act (Gn. 49:5), but it is lauded in Jub. 30:23, and heavenly blessing is ascribed to its perpetrators, for they have "exercised judgment, justice and revenge on sinners." [12] Closely related to this assessment of Levi is that of the Jewish basis of the Test. XII. Naturally Levi has the priesthood, with which he is most solemnly invested. He has visions and receives revelations like an OT prophet. He exhorts to study and faithful observance of the Law of God. [13] But his tasks and position are in no way limited to this alone. The striking thing is that God has given him dominion along with and even above Judah. [14] Others can do nothing against him. [15] Hence the demand in Test. Jud.: "Love Levi that you may abide, and do not rise up against him, that you be not destroyed. To me (Judah) the Lord gave the monarchy and to him the priesthood, and he placed the monarchy under the priesthood. To me he gave what is on earth, to him what is in heaven. As heaven is above the earth, so is God's priesthood above the monarchy on earth." [16] It can even be said: "I and my brethren become rulers of our sceptres (tribes), Levi first, I the second ..." [17] In a race on the Mount of Olives Levi grasps the sun and Judah the moon, and a youth gives Levi 12 palm branches as a sign of the blessing of all the tribes. [18]

The evaluation of Levi in these writings can be understood only against the background of the Maccabean wars and the development which accompanied them. Mattathias, the father of Judas Maccabeus and his brothers Jonathan and Simon, who successively held the office of high-priest, was of legitimate priestly descent. So too, then, was the whole Hasmonean dynasty. They belonged to the sons of Jojarib. [19] They united in themselves the dignities and tasks of priesthood and secular monarchy, completely so after Jannaeus Alexander (103-77) took the crown. Even to Joseph. this seemed to be an ideal arrangement. For he notes with ref. to Hyrcanus I (135-105) that God had honoured him with the greatest gifts, namely, rule over his people, high-priestly dignity, and the prophetic gift. [20] Jub. and Test. XII are an echo of this. [21] This seems to apply even to the changed view of Gn. 34. For Hyrcanus, too, exercised judgment on Shechem and Samaria. This seems to be indirectly approved in Jub. 30.

---

[12] Cf. on this pt. Bousset-Gressm., 13 f.
[13] Test. L. 8:2, 13.
[14] Test. R. 6.
[15] Test. S. 5.
[16] Test. Jud. 21:1-4.
[17] *Ibid.*, 25:1.
[18] Test. N. 5.
[19] 1 Macc. 2:1; 14:29; cf. 1 Ch. 24:1-7.
[20] Hyrcanus I died τριῶν τῶν μεγίστων ἄξιος ὑπὸ τοῦ θεοῦ κριθείς, ἀρχῆς τοῦ ἔθνους καὶ τῆς ἀρχιερατικῆς τιμῆς καὶ προφητείας (Ant., 13, 299; Bell., 1, 68). On the prophetic gift of the high-priest, cf. Jn. 11:51.
[21] Cf. Schürer, III[4], 339 ff. Bousset-Gressm., 109 f.

Levi enjoys the gift of prophecy in Damasc. 4:15, where there is ref. to the three nets of Belial "of which Levi, the son of Jacob, spoke, and with which he will take the house of Israel."[22] The basis of this prophetic gift is found in the OT ref. to the oracle of the Urim and Thummim (Ex. 28:30; Nu. 27:21; Dt. 33:8).

In Philo Levi, like everything else, is made to serve the end of moralistic allegorising. He is a type of the φιλόθεος who, as esp. developed in Dt. 10:9; 33:9, leaves or mortifies the body to cleave to God alone.[23]

c. The NT verses display as little influence of the Hasmonean period as they do contact with Philonic trains of thought. They simply rely on the Pentateuchal record. Thus Rev. 7:7 shows no interest in the special position of Levi. It is simply one of the twelve tribes, and 12,000 of its members belong to the 144,000 who are marked by God's seal. In Hb. 7:5, 9 Levi is the ancestor of the legitimate OT priesthood. This is compared with the priesthood according to the order of Melchisedec in order to show the superiority of Jesus as the NT high-priest. The basis is ψ 109:4; a Messianic reference to Jesus is regarded as self-evidently justified, as elsewhere in the NT.[24] The superiority is based on the fact that in Gn. 14:18-20 Melchisedec exercises the priestly right of receiving tithes from (Nu. 18:21), and imparting blessing to (Dt. 10:8), both Abraham and his descendant Levi. In two respects this was paradoxical. Only he who can show descent from the sons of Levi may discharge priestly functions, but there can be no question of this in the case of Melchisedec. It is not just that he comes much earlier than Levi — Hb. does not stress this. The point is that he has no genealogy. How grotesque! A priest without genealogy![25] Moreover Abraham is lit up by the great promise of Gn. 12:2. Nevertheless, he is blessed by Melchisedec. Hereby one may see how exalted this mysterious and unknown personage is. But if, according to ψ 109, Jesus is a priest after the order of this Melchisedec, it may be concluded that His priesthood is superior to the Levitical, and that the Levitical is thus superseded as inadequate. In fact, as Hb. 7:11-19 goes on to show, this conclusion is vindicated by the religious inadequacy of the Levitical priesthood, which cannot achieve perfection (7:11), or access to God (7:19), or purification and perfecting of the conscience (9:14, 9), or remission of sins (9:22; 10:4). The thinking of the learned author of Hb. is characterised, however, by the fact that the formal deduction from ψ 109 is for him more important than the material justification of the change which has taken place. That in which the priesthood of Israel took the greatest pride, its correct descent, was the cliff on which it foundered. The descent of Christ from the tribe of Judah is by no means an argument

---

[22] Cf. S. Schechter's and L. Rost's ed., also W. Staerk, *Die jüd. Gemeinde des neuen Bundes in Damaskus* (1922), 57, *ad loc.*, which deals, too, with the literary relation of Damasc. to Test. XII.

[23] πατέρα καὶ μητέρα ..., τὸν νοῦν καὶ τὴν τοῦ σώματος ὕλην, καταλείπει ὑπὲρ τοῦ κλῆρον ἔχειν τὸν ἕνα θεόν (Leg. All., II, 51; cf. Plant., 63 f.). Ex. 32:27 f. is construed in terms of the mortification of the body, not the killing of national brethren who worshipped the golden calf: διὰ τοῦτο καὶ "ἀδελφόν," οὐκ ἄνθρωπον, ἀλλὰ τὸ ψυχῆς ἀδελφὸν σῶμα ἀποκτενοῦμεν, τουτέστι τοῦ φιλαρέτου καὶ θείου τὸ φιλοπαθὲς καὶ θνητὸν διαζεύξομεν. ἀποκτενοῦμεν καὶ τὸν "πλησίον," πάλιν οὐκ ἄνθρωπον ἀλλὰ τὸν <αἰσθήσεων> χορὸν καὶ θίασον (Ebr., 70). The name Levi is σύμβολον ... ἐνεργειῶν .. .καὶ πράξεων σπουδαίων καὶ λειτουργιῶν ἁγίων (Som., II, 34).

[24] Cf. Mt. 22:44; 26:64; Ac. 2:34; 7:56; 1 C. 15:25; Col. 3:1; Eph. 1:20; Hb. 1:3, 13; 10:12 f.; 1 Pt. 3:22; Rev. 3:21.

[25] Cf. Jos. Vit., 1.

against His high-priestly dignity. On the contrary, His high-priestly dignity is an argument in favour of the view that the Levitical priesthood is superseded and ended. This implies a radical liberation of the Christian community from the OT cultus. Τοίνυν ἐξερχώμεθα πρὸς αὐτὸν ἔξω τῆς παρεμβολῆς (Hb. 13:13). To expound this is the function allotted to Hb. in the circle of NT writings. Levi must yield his place to Christ.[26]

4. Early Christian attempts to trace the descent of Jesus from the tribe of Levi. Hb. emphasises that the descent of Jesus is from the tribe of Judah, and knows nothing of any genealogical connection with that of Levi. This would in fact disturb the argument of c. 7; he could not justify the high-priestly dignity of Jesus along these lines. Nevertheless, there were those in early Christianity who tried to maintain such a connection through Mary, and thought it important. It is true that the Church accepted the view that Mary was of Davidic descent, as Justin was the first to maintain in his Dialogue with Trypho.[27] The concern of this thesis, as Augustine noted,[28] is that only thus can Jesus, who is not conceived by Joseph, be literally of the blood of David. There is no support for the opinion in the NT.[29] Indeed, Lk. 1:36 (Elisabeth is Mary's συγγενίς) seems to hint that Mary was of Levitical descent, since Elisabeth (1:5) was of the daughters of Aaron, and συγγενίς may well denote belonging to the same family and not just the same people.[30] On the other hand, this genealogical connection with Levi through Mary is shadowy and isolated in the NT, and no importance attaches to it. The situation is very different in the Christian part of Test. XII,[31] for here it is constantly emphasised that Christ descends from Levi as well as Judah, from the one as priest and the other as king, the two offices being united in Him. Particularly clear is Test. Jos. 19: "Keep the commandments of the Lord, and honour Judah and Levi, for from their seed[32] will come forth for you the Lamb of God, which through grace saves the Gentiles and Israel."[33] On the basis of Test. S. 7 it is also maintained in a fr. attributed to Iren. that Christ ἐκ τοῦ Λευὶ καὶ τοῦ Ἰούδα τὸ κατὰ σάρκα, ὡς βασιλεὺς καὶ ἱερεὺς ἐγεννήθη.[34] The Manichee Faustus also claimed that Mary

[26] Cf. the exposition of Hb. 7 in *NT Deutsch.*

[27] C. 43; 45; 100; 120. Along with this Prot. Ev. Jc. 10 is the earliest instance. This view is predominant in Roman Catholic theology, cf. the art. "Maria" by L. Kösters in Lex. Th. K., VI² (1934), 888. On the other hand cf. Zahn Forsch., VI, 328 ff.; Zn. Lk. ³, ⁴ (1920), 76, n. 80.

[28] Cf. Aug. Faust., 23, 4.

[29] At least not in the traditional text of the only relevant verse (Lk. 1:27). For to link ἐξ οἴκου Δαυίδ with the more distant παρθένον instead of the preceding Ἰωσήφ is somewhat arbitrary. Things would be different if we had to cut out ἐμνηστευμένην ἀνδρὶ ᾧ ὄνομα Ἰωσήφ as a secondary intrusion (so M. Dibelius, *Jungfrauensohn u. Krippenkind* [1932], 12 f.) (SAH, 22, 4 [1931/2]). But there still remains the συγγενίς of Lk. 1:36.

[30] Cf. Zn. Lk. ³, ⁴ (1920), 89 f.; W. Bauer, *Das Leben Jesu im Zeitalter d. nt.lichen Apkr.* (1909), 9 ff.; Kl. Lk., *ad loc.* Zn. rightly emphasises that the stress on the Levitical descent of the Baptist (Lk. 1:5) is connected with this.

[31] A double relation to Levi and Judah seems to be suggested also in 1 Cl., 32, 2: ἐξ αὐτοῦ (sc. Jacob) γὰρ ἱερεῖς τε καὶ Λευῖται πάντες οἱ λειτουργοῦντες τῷ θυσιαστηρίῳ τοῦ θεοῦ· ἐξ αὐτοῦ ὁ κύριος Ἰησοῦς τὸ κατὰ σάρκα· ἐξ αὐτοῦ βασιλεῖς καὶ ἄρχοντες καὶ ἡγούμενοι κατὰ τὸν Ἰούδαν. It is worth noting that Jesus is not said to descend from Judah but from Jacob, and that He is set between the two tribes of Levi and Judah as though descending from both κατὰ σάρκα. He unites in Himself the dignities of both. For He is our High-Priest and Defender (ἀρχιερεὺς καὶ προστάτης).

[32] ἐκ τοῦ σπέρματος αὐτῶν, vl. ἐξ αὐτῶν, obviously meaning the same, so that there can hardly be any question of purely spiritual descent.

[33] Cf. also Test. S. 7 ff.; L. 2; D. 5; G. 8; also Schürer, III⁴, 345.

[34] Iren., ed. W. Harvey, II (1857), 487. Yet elsewhere Iren. takes the view that Mary was of Davidic descent.

was of Levitical descent, and that her father Joachim was a priest (Aug. Faust., 23, 4 and 9).[35] He seems to have built on an older form of the Prot. Ev. Jc. which took this view as distinct from the form which has come down to us.

Strathmann

† Λευ(ε)ίτης

This word occurs in LXX, Philo,[1] Joseph.,[2] and Plut.[3] It denotes a member of the tribe of Levi.[4] But since the Levite takes part in the cultus, it comes to denote a cultic officer of the second rank who renders subordinate services in the sanctuary. The division of the priesthood into the two classes of priests and Levites, who, in spite of their interconnection, are separate castes, seems to derive in principle from the reform under Josiah. Then the sanctuaries were all removed and the Zadokite priesthood in Jerusalem experienced a consequent enhancement of power, while the rural priests lost their sphere of operation. It is true that Dt. ascribes equality to all members of the tribe of Levi,[5] but the Jerusalem priests successfully circumvented these demands.[6] The first actual ref. to a division of the cultic personnel into two groups is to be found in the sketch of a temple order in Ez. 44:6 ff. Here the true service of the temple and the altar is assigned to the Levitical priests, the sons of Zadok, i.e., the earlier Jerusalem priesthood, while the Levites must be content with inferior tasks such as keeping the temple gates, cleansing the temple, slaughtering the animals, and serving the people. They are thus given cultic duties which had been discharged by those of other stock prior to the destruction of the temple.[7]

In the time immediately following, that part of Ezekiel's sketch which exerted an influence was the idea of separating the priests and Levites. Acc. to P the Levites serve the Aaronic priesthood.[8] In the early post-exilic period we find, along with the Levites,[9] singers,[10] door-keepers,[11] and temple servants.[12] The subordinate position

---

[35] Some further traces of this view are mentioned in Zn. Lk.[3,4] (1920), 76, n. 80 and 90, n. 11.

Λ ε υ (ε) ί τ η ς. Pass.-Cr., Pr.-Bauer[3], Thes. Steph., *s.v.* For bibl. Schürer, II[4], 291 ff. (older bibl.), 328 ff.; G. A. Barton, Jew. Enc., VIII, *s.v.*; G. Hölscher, Pauly-W., XII (1925), 2155 ff.; Bousset-Gressm., 102, 105; V. Aptowitzer, *Die Parteipolitik d. Hasmonäerzeit* ... (1927), *passim*; S. Mowinckel, RGG[2], III, 1603 ff.; I. Heinemann, *Philons gr. u. jüd. Bildung* (1932), Index *s.v.*; G. v. Rad, *Das Geschichtsbild d. chronistischen Werkes* (1930), 80 ff.; 88 ff.; K. Moehlenbrink, ZAW, NF, 11 (1934), 184 ff.; J. Gutmann and D. J. Bornstein, EJ, X (1934), *s.v.*; also bibl. → 235, n. 11.

[1] → Heinemann, Index *s.v.*

[2] Jos., ed. Niese, Index *s.v.*

[3] Quaest. Conv., IV, 6, 2 (II, 671e).

[4] On the question whether Levi is a tribe or order → 235.

[5] Dt. 18:1, 6 f.

[6] 2 K. 23:9.

[7] Cf. A. Bertholet-K. Galling, *Ez.* (1936), 157.

[8] Nu. 3:11 f.; 3:6 ff.; 8:19; 18:2 ff. → v. Rad, 90.

[9] Ezr. 2:40.

[10] Ezr. 2:41.

[11] Ezr. 2:42.

[12] Ezr. 2:43 ff.

of the Levites makes their position less enviable. This is expressed in the records in the small number of Levites who return from Babylon.[13] Yet in the time after P there are signs of a struggle for emancipation on the part of the Levites. This can be followed very well in the work of the Chronicler, whose central concern is "the position of the Levites in the organism of post-exilic Israel."[14] In this period the singers and door-keepers come to be numbered with the Levites for reasons not known to us. The aim of the Levites was equality with the priesthood. But this could be attained only by participation in the sacrifices. Since sacrifice was in the hands of the priests, the Levites could find an opening only in respect of the liturgical accompaniment. Here, however, the Levitical singers secured for themselves already in the time of the Chronicler a secure place at the centre of cultic life.[15]

The movement of emancipation led to rivalry between the two classes which lasted up to the destruction of the second temple. A high point in the story of the Levites was when the Hasmoneans were appointed hereditary priest-princes,[16] for they belonged to the tribe of Levi. We find many ref. to this time when the tribe of Levi played a leading part in the common life of Judaism.[17] The final goal of all attempts at emancipation, equality with the priests, was reached shortly before the destruction of the temple. As we are told in Jos. Ant., 20, 216 ff., Agrippa II called a synod at the instigation of the Levites,[18] and it was here resolved that the Levitical singers should wear the same linen garments as the priests. At the same time those who discharged lesser functions were allowed to train for the higher rank of singers. The anger which this victory of the Levites provoked among the priests may be seen clearly enough from Josephus, who himself belonger to the higher priestly aristocracy.

But the priests did not remain inactive in face of the emancipation movement. As one may gather from Talmudic accounts, a few yrs. before the destruction of the temple they wrested from the Levites their source of income, the Levitical tithes.[19] When after the war things began to settle again in Palestine, this law was found, though its origin was obscure. Since it contradicted the rest of the tradition, there was considerable debate about the point.[20]

The Levites takes second place after the Aaronites as compared with other Jews.[21] A 2nd cent. ref. speaks of their privileges.[22] In regard to their duties in the sanctuary,[23] from the time of the Chronicler they are in charge of 1. the liturgy,[24] the singers being

13 v. Rad, 81 f.

14 *Ibid.*, 119.

15 *Ibid.*, 98 ff.

16 On Levi's righteousness and piety, *v.* Damasc. 6:10; S. Dt., 350 on Dt. 33:9; bJoma, 66b; jJoma, 38b. Hence the dignity of his priestly office, Jub. 30:18 ff.; Philo Vit. Mos., II, 170 ff. The institution of the Hasmoneans as priest-princes is expressed in Jub. 32:1: "Levi dreamed that they had instituted him and made him the priest of the Most High God." More explicitly, Test. L. 8:1 ff.

17 Cf. Jub. 31:11 ff.; Test. N. 5:1 ff.; Test. Jud. 25:1; 21:1 ff.; R. 6:5 ff.; Ex. r., 5 on 5:4; Nu. r., 13 on 7:13.

18 Under the procuratorship of Gessius Florus in 62 A.D.; cf. Gutmann, 840; Str.-B., IV, 653-9.

19 Cf. bJeb., 86a b; bKet., 26a; jMS, 56d.

20 Cf. H. Graetz, "Eine Strafmassregel gegen die Leviten," MGWJ, 35 (1886), 97 ff.

21 Cf. Qid., 4, 1.

22 Jos. Ant., 12, 142; here the Levites are called ἱεροψάλται after the normative class of temple singers ; on the privileges of the Levites cf. also Bek., 1, 1; 2, 1; 8, 1; bBek., 47a. Cf. also theoretical discussions of their cities and houses ; cf. Bornstein, 842 f.

23 There are also priests and Levites in the temple of Onias, Jos. Ant., 13, 63.

24 Jos. Ant., 7, 305; 8, 176; 9, 269; Tamid, 7, 3 f.; bRH, 31a, Bar.; Sukka, 5, 1 ff.; cf. Str.-B., II, 76 f., 806. Priests are also temple singers, though in smaller numbers, Tamid, 7, 3; Sukka, 5, 4. But the singers are mostly Levites, cf. Plut. → n. 3; 22. Philo does not allude to this.

divided into 24 classes like the priests,[25] and 2. policing the temple. In this respect they see to law and order. Here again we find the figure 24, for there are 24 police posts. Of these 21 are manned by Levites, and 3 in the inner court by priests.[26] The captain of the temple (στρατηγὸς τοῦ ἱεροῦ, Ac. 4:1; 5:24, 26) is also a priest. Their offices also include 3. keeping the doors[27] and 4. helping in the sacrifices. Apart from the cultic duties we read of their participation in governing the community.[28] The teaching office which they had from the time of Ezra[29] is reflected in the prominence which they enjoyed, along with the priests, in the ritual of the synagogue. In reading the Torah, the priest is called on first, then the Levite, then the ordinary Jew. If no Levite is present in divine service, he can be replaced only by the priest who is called on first, not by an ordinary Jew.[30]

In the NT a Levite is mentioned in the parable of the Good Samaritan, Lk. 10:32: ὁμοίως δὲ καὶ Λευίτης κατὰ τὸν τόπον ἐλθὼν καὶ ἰδὼν ἀντιπαρῆλθεν. He takes the same attitude as the priest who comes first. Both are representatives of the privileged classes in Israel. In sharp contrast stands the despised Samaritan who unselfishly helps the man who had fallen among thieves. In Jn. 1:19 the embassy sent by the Jews to John the Baptist consists of priests and Levites. According to Ac. 4:36 Joseph surnamed Barnabas, a Jewish Christian from Cyprus, belongs to the tribe of Levi.

R. Meyer

† λευκός, † λευκαίνω

1. λευκός comes from the root *leuk,* Lat. *lux,* Germ. *licht,* Eng. *light,* also in → λύχνος, λυχνία. In acc. with its etymology it often means "radiant," "bright," "light" (a particularly apposite rendering in eschatological and apocalyptic contexts because it kindles the right associations). Mostly the word denotes the colour "white" in its various shades to "gray white," "light gray" and "gray." The word thus has a relatively large sphere of meaning in the range of colours, though it shares this peculiarity with all other such terms, esp. its antithesis → μέλας. (This phenomenon is not restricted to the Gk. world or to antiquity, nor is it due to weakness in observation and differentiation; it reflects the fact that colours are for man relative rather than absolute values whose precise definition depends on choice, shifting possibilities of comparison, the inner constitution of the one who beholds them etc.) λευκός occurs from the time of Hom. in all branches of Gk. poetry and prose,[1] e.g., of milk, snow (cf. the

25 Jos. Ant., 7, 367; Taan., 4, 2; TTaan., 4, 2 f.
26 Jos. Ant., 18, 29 f.; Philo Spec. Leg., I, 156; Mid., 1, 1 ff.; Tamid, 1, 1.
27 Jos. Ap., 2, 119; Bell., 6, 293. The inner gates are also kept by the priests; cf. Mid., 1, 9.
28 Jos. Ant., 4, 214; Test. R. 6:8. Cf. v. Rad, 94 f.
29 v. Rad, 95 f.; also Test. R. 6:8; here it is said of Levi: ὅτι αὐτὸς γνώσεται νόμον θεοῦ. Test. L. 13:2 ff.
30 Git., 5, 8; bGit., 59b.

λευκός κτλ. 1 Cf. Liddell-Scott and Pass., *s.v.*

common comparison "as white as milk, or snow"; these two phenomena obviously fix the original range of the colour), flowers, fruits, animals, esp. the faded or white hair of old age (hence also λευκὸν γῆρας). On the metaphorical use → *infra*; 243. The noun τὸ λευκόν is used for a white garment, e.g., λευκὸν ἀμπέχει, Aristoph. Ach., 1024 (also the colour "white," the "white of an egg" etc.). On inscr. it is the colour of sacrificial animals (cock, lamb, ram etc.), also of the garments of priests and initiates, Ditt. Syll.³, 1018, 1 f. (3rd cent. B.C.); 736, 13; 15 f.; 24 f. (92 B.C.), also of the clothing of the dead and mourners, *ibid.*, 1218, 2 f. (5th cent. B.C.); 1219, 9 (3rd cent. B.C.): λευκὸς λίθος (also λευκόλιθος) in temples, e.g., Ditt. Or., 268, 16 f. (3rd cent. B.C.): τὰ δεδογμένα ἀναγράψαι εἰς στήλην λευκοῦ λίθου (cf. also Moult.-Mill., 374). λευκός is common in the pap. for various animals (camels, asses, goats, pigs) and for clothes and linen, along with ἱμάτιον, ἐσθής, στολή (cf. Preisigke Wört., II, 16 *s.v.*).

λευκαίνω, the verb from λευκός, "I make white," though rarer, is found from Hom. on: λεύκαινον ὕδωρ ἐλάτῃσι, "they beat the water white with the oars," Od., 12, 172; λευκαίνων ὁ χρόνος, the time which makes hair white, Theocr., 14, 70; also mid. and intr. It does not occur on inscr. and pap., though we find the related λευκόω (cf. Ditt. Syll.³, Index, *s.v.*).[2]

The significance of white in the life and thinking of Gk. and Roman antiquity, which finds expression in the great no. of constructions with λευκός, has thus far been adequately developed in monograph form only for the sphere of the cultus.[3] Here it played a prominent part, being a colour esp. pleasing and suitable to the gods, cf. Plat. Leg., XII, 956a: χρώματα δὲ λευκὰ πρέποντ' ἂν θεοῖς εἴη. Often sacrificial animals had to be white. In Hom. Il., 3, 103 f. a white sheep is offered to Helios and a black sheep to the earth; this brings out the relation of the colour white to light. In other cases the rarity of this colour is the reason why it is preferred. But white can also count as a cathartic or apotropaic colour.[4] Helpful deities are called white, e.g., Hermes Λευκός of Tanagra, the white goddess of the sea Λευκοθέα, Hom. Od., 5, 333 ff. In contrast to black, it is also the colour of joy, fortune, and victory, cf. λευκὴ ἡμέρα. It is not possible to advance a single explanation why this colour was so significant in ancient religion, and even in detail the motivation is often obscure, e.g., why white as well as the common black should be the colour of mourning and should be related to the cult of the dead.[5] White was also important in superstition and magic, as may be seen in the magic pap., e.g., Preis. Zaub., II, 73; III, 303, 305, 693; IV, 35 f., 165 ff., 698, 2190.

2. In the sphere of Heb. and Jewish culture, too, white always had a particular significance, as a natural colour (of milk, teeth etc.), or as an artistic colour richly used in ceramics, murals, and frescoes.[6] Gay and varied colours were highly valued on clothes; linens and woollens were dyed, though they were also worn white, and bleached

---

[2] *Loc. cit.* On the derivation of λευκαίνω, cf. E. Fraenkel, *Gr. Denominativa* (1906), 14; A. Debrunner, *Indogerm. Forschungen*, 21 (1907), 29 f., and *Gr. Wortb.* § 220. For instances of λευκόω, Fraenkel, 139. The relation between adj. and verbs of colour in Gr. is dealt with in a larger context in L. Weisgerber, "Adjektivische u. verbale Auffassung d. Gesichtsempfindungen," *Wörter u. Sachen*, XII, 2 (1929), 197 ff. [Debrunner].

[3] G. Radke, *Die Bdtg. d. weissen u. schwarzen Farbe in Kult u. Brauch d. Gr. u. Römer*, Diss. Berlin (1936); older bibl., 5 ff.

[4] Cf. S. Eitrem, "Opferritus u. Voropfer d. Gr. u. Römer" (*Skrifter utgit av Videnskapsselskapet i Kristiania*, 1914, II *Hist.-Fil. Kl.*, No. 1 [1915]), 492; Index, *s.v.* "Weiss"; esp. 196, 225, 268, n. 3. Radke gives many examples of the magical use of white: bringing blessing (35 ff.), apotropaic (38 ff.), lustral (47 ff.), sympathetic (50 ff.).

[5] Cf. the ref. of A. Bertholet, Art. "Farben" (1. Religionsgeschichtlich), RGG², II, 514 ff., and Radke, 44.

[6] K. Galling, Art. "Farbe" and "Färberei" in *Biblisches Reallexikon* (1937), 150 ff. Later white, with red, was regarded as a basic substance in the human body; cf. R. Meyer, "Hellenistisches in d. rabb. Anthropologie," BWANT, 4 F. 22 (1937), 15 ff.; 33 ff. etc.

linen (*byssus*) was dear and fashionable.[7] White was predominant for priestly vestments. and was the basic cultic colour in general. Though this was also true in the surrounding world,[8] it is to be explained less in terms of general views and more in terms of the fact that the seriousness and clarity of the OT concept of God helped other basic conceptions to emerge even in the field of the symbolism of colour, including the complete exclusion of black and the predominance of white.[9] What influenced the choice of white was not so much the character of the divine world as light in a more natural sense, but rather the prominence of the concept of holiness. It is also true that "vitality, life, light, holiness, and joy on the one side, and inertia, darkness, evil and sorrow on the other, are interchangeable concepts in the Bible, and white and black are a phenomenal expression of the two series of antitheses."[10]

In Heb., too, the words for colour are imprecise. White includes half-yellow, so that *byssus* is called white even when it has a yellow shimmer.[11] The main adj. used is לָבָן; the verb לָבַן is found only in the hi ("to make white," "to become white") and the hitp (neither word is common, but there are several derivatives which attest and extend the use of white).[12] In Cant. 5:10 we find the adj. צַח ("blinding white") from צחח, "to shine" (Lam. 4:7: "like milk"). In Is. 32:4 this is used of clear speech, just as λευκός can mean a clear voice, or expression, or speech. In Ju. 5:10 we find צְחֹר (of white she-asses).[13] In transl. A is vague here (ἐπιβεβηκότες ἐπὶ ὑποζυγίων), while B has: ἐπιβεβηκότες ἐπὶ ὄνου θηλείας μεσημβρίας (צְחֹר is obviously connected with the noun צַח [mid-day] heat, cf. Is. 18:4: ὡς φῶς καύματος μεσημβρίας = כְּחֹם צַח עֲלֵי־אוֹר). צַח in Cant. 5:10 is rendered λευκός, and לָבָן is usually translated λευκός (Lv. 13:24 ἔκλευκος, once χλωρός, also the verbal λευκαίνω etc.). λευκός corresponds esp. to לָבָן. In Gn. 31:8 עָקֹד is λευκός, though in 30:35, 39 f.; 31:10, 12 we have διάλευκος (not found elsewhere). At Gn. 30:32 A has διάραντον καὶ λευκόν (others διάλευκον καὶ ῥαντόν). At Da. 7:9 LXX and Θ use λευκός for נְקֵא though the order of words differs. At 2 Macc. 11:8 we find ἐν λευκῇ ἐσθῆτι (no Heb.). About half the λευκός refs. occur in Lv. 13; λευκός is used 16 times of the whitening of the skin or hair in leprosy (cf. Hdt., I, 138: λέπρην ἢ λεύκην ἔχειν). λευκαίνω also occurs in the LXX 5 times (mostly for לָבַן hi). Da. Θ 12:10 B ἐκλευκαίνω, with λευκανθίζω or λευκαθίζω; also λεύκωμα several times in Tob. and λευκότης in Sir. 43:18: κάλλος λευκότητος αὐτῆς ἐκθαυμάσει ὀφθαλμός (of snow in the hymn to the glory of God's works).

3. Philo has τὸ λευκόν and esp. the opp. τὸ λευκόν and τὸ μέλαν when he wishes to illustrate from outward appearance: πῶς ἡμῶν ὁ νοῦς καταλαμβάνει, ὅτι τουτὶ

---

[7] Galling, *loc. cit.*, also Art. "Byssus" and "Kleidung." The shirt in particular seems to have been mostly white, though cf. P. Thomsen, Art. "Kleidung" (D. Palästina-Syrien) in *Reallexikon d. Vorgeschichte*, VI (1926), 389 ff.

[8] Galling, Art. "Priesterkleidung," *op. cit.*, 429 ff.

[9] For details cf. Delitzsch (Lotz), Art. "Farben in d. Bibel," RE[3], V (1898), 755 ff.

[10] *Ibid.*, 760.

[11] *Ibid.*, 756.

[12] Debatable is how far we are to reckon לְבֵנָה ("tile"), and לָבֵן, found only in q (cf. Ges.-Buhl, *s.v.*). The Gks. counted dust and stucco as white (cf. Schol. on Aristoph. Vesp., 921: λέγεται καὶ γῆ σκιρράς, λευκή τις ὡς γύψος). Cf. also the phrase in Iren., III, 17, 4 which presupposes that milk and gypsum look the same: *In Dei lacte gypsum male miscetur.*

[13] To be derived from צחר, "to be buff or yellow" (connected with Sahara, cf. Ges.-Buhl, *s.v.*). In Ju. 5:10 Σ has στίλβω and in ψ 103:15 it uses this for צהל: στίλβειν πρόσωπον τῷ ἐλαίῳ (cf. Field). The LXX has στίλβω some 9 times with no Heb. original. It is used for צהב at 2 Εσδρ. 8:27 = 1 Ezr. 8:56. In the NT στίλβω is found only at Mk. 9:3: τὰ ἱμάτια αὐτοῦ ἐγένετο στίλβοντα λευκὰ λίαν [Bertram].

λευκὸν ἢ μέλαν ἐστίν, εἰ μὴ βοηθῷ χρησάμενος ὁράσει; Leg. All., II, 7, cf. II, 39; III, 57 f. (λευκαίνω is also used once in this connection : ὀφθαλμὸς λευκαίνεται νῦν ὑπὸ τοῦ παρόντος λευκοῦ, when white is present the eye receives the impression of white, Leg. All., II, 43). For Philo white and black are typical antitheses, and always come in lists of such, Leg. All., III, 61; Ebr., 186; esp. Rer. Div. Her., 209 : life and death, sickness and health, white and black, right and left, righteousness and unrighteousness etc. Cf. the allegorical interpretation of the white colour of manna, Fug., 138 f., and even more clearly Plant., 110 f., where the white on the staves (Gn. 30:37) shows that we should free the good from all the evil that surrounds it. The statements about leprosy in Lv. 13:12 f. (also allegorised in Deus Imm., 130) teach us to put off gaudy, evil and unstable passion and to put on the one simple colour of truth ἀνενδοίαστον ἀληθείας ἁπλοῦν χρῶμα δεξώμεθα. In Leg. All., III, 171 it is emphasised that divine reason is called λευκόν : τί γὰρ ἂν εἴη λαμπρότερον ἢ τηλαυγέστερον θείου λόγου; (Cf. Test. Sol. C Prologue, 1 [McCown]: ἰδοὺ ἔση βλέπων πᾶσαν τὴν σοφίαν λελευκασμένην ὡς χιόνα ἐνώπιόν σου καὶ τῶν ὀφθαλμῶν σου). In the description and interpretation of the priestly vestments and liturgical colours Philo uses λευκός as rarely as Joseph. Both speak in this connection of the *byssus* ; the prominence of white is thus evident. In Ant., 20, 216 f. Joseph. mentions that Agrippa II gave the Levitical singers the right to wear (white) linen clothes like the priests. In Bell., 7, 29 we are told how Simon ben Giora, after the capture of Jerusalem, suddenly rose up from the ground at the place where the temple had stood and startled the Romans ; he λευκοὺς ἐνδιδύσκει χιτωνίσκους. Since he had also fastened on a purple over-garment πορφυρᾶν ἐμπερονησάμενος χλανίδα, he obviously wished to pretend to be a priest, or a ghost in priestly clothing. [14] In Ant., 11, 327, 331 we are told that, while the priests went to meet the besieger in their *byssus* vestments, the whole people joined the procession (ἐν ταῖς) λευκαῖς ἐσθῆσιν. They had been told to put these on, so they represented, not their usual dress, but clothes chosen for effect. Acc. to Ant., 8, 186 Solomon on his daily ride was λευκὴν ἠμφιεσμένος ἐσθῆτα. After the prior description of the magnificence of his horses and riders, this is obviously meant to indicate his royal glory. Esp. worth noting is the fact that in Jos. Bell., 2, 123 we are told that the Essenes always went clothed in white λευχειμονεῖν διαπαντός [15] (cf., 137 λευκὴν ἐσθῆτα δόντες). This can hardly mean festive garments, but clothes of white fabric, which acc. to 2, 126 were worn until they grew ragged. [16]

4. The picture might be filled out with details which in some cases are important for the NT. Rabb. sources [17] display a great fondness for white clothes. They are worn on joyous occasions or feast days, but they are also regarded as a mark of distinction, so that men of eminence, or those who wish to make a parade of their position, wear white and leave gay colours to the common people. [18] White also denotes purity, and so even white linen clothes are specially washed. [19] In Judaism from the first cent. A.D.

---

[14] Hence this passage is not a sure example of the custom (attested elsewhere → n. 20) of burying the dead in white. Cf. S. Krauss, *Talmudische Archäologie*, I (1910), 550, n. 212.

[15] Krauss, *loc. cit.* sees in this a literal following of Qoh. 9:8a : ἐν παντὶ καιρῷ ἔστωσαν ἱμάτιά σου λευκά. But this is unlikely, for Qoh. 9:8b goes on : καὶ ἔλαιον ἐπὶ κεφαλήν σου μὴ ὑστερησάτω, and Jos. tells us that the Essenes avoided oil because it stained, and if any of them were involuntarily anointed, they carefully cleansed themselves (→ II, 472).

[16] The Therapeutae, on the other hand, used white clothes only rarely for feasts. Acc. to Philo Vit. Cont., 66 they were clothed in white for their feast of the 50th day (λευχειμονοῦντες φαιδροί).

[17] The neut. λευκόν passed as a loan word (לבקן, לווקן etc.) into Rabb. speech, cf. S. Krauss, *Gr. u. lat. Lehnwörter in Talmud, Midrasch u. Targum*, II (1899), 304, 309; *Archäologie*, I, 245; II (1911), 409.

[18] For details *v.* Krauss, *Archäologie*, I, 144 f., 547 ff. The scribes and their pupils wore white linen clothes (cf. *ibid.*, 162, 592, n. 459).

[19] Krauss, I, 133 (for the Sabbath).

onwards the dead were buried in white linen clothes[20] (→ 242; cf. also Mt. 27:59: σινδόνι καθαρᾷ and par.). If Qoh. 9:8 is expounded in terms of cleansing from sin (→ n. 15),[21] other passages show that those who are found upright at the last judgment will be robed in white, e.g., bShab., 114a: "R. Jannai said to his sons: My children, do not bury me in white robes or in black: (not) in white, for perchance I shall not be found upright, and will be as a bridegroom among mourners; (not) in black, for perchance I shall be found upright, and shall be as a mourner at a wedding."[22] The comparison is not necessarily based on the idea of the Messianic wedding, but more likely on the general thought of marriage and burial. Similarly, we do not have to deduce from it a primary reference to joy or sadness. The guiding thought is that the righteous and the guilty will then have to wear white or black, just as the accused had to appear in court in black clothing.[23] This idea of the just being robed in white was undoubtedly influenced by the burial of the dead in white clothes, but it is hard to say how much it may also owe to the idea that white is the colour appropriate only to God and the heavenly world.[24] Like the concept of guilt and innocence, this idea plays a role in the development of OT colour symbolism, and there is hardly any need to turn to non-Jewish parallels for its better understanding. It may be that the origin is to be sought in the idea of heavenly clothing which is one of the gifts of the future life, or which represents this life. This idea is found in later Jewish writings (esp. Eth. En. 62:14; Slav. En. 22:8),[25] and we find it in the Rabbis,[26] though it is to be distinguished from the reference already made. For here there is no thought of the recognition of guilt or innocence. Strong emphasis is laid on the fact that this clothing is a divine gift. Nor is there any idea of the expression of festive joy. The main thought is that of transfiguration to heavenly glory such as is proper to God and heavenly beings. As the heavenly colour white has become the eschatological colour. In the background one may detect the definite concept of the supraterrestrial substance of light as divine — an idea which is never so clearly evident in the OT. In this respect, then, we do best to assume foreign influences. Nevertheless, the concept of כָּבוֹד or → δόξα contains all the elements from which the thought of the white clothing of heavenly or transfigured beings might have developed. Indeed, Da. 7:9, following up OT statements about the significance of white, refers to the white clothing of God Himself. Hence it is not really necessary to assume that alien influences came into later Judaism.[27] It should be borne in mind that the varied and originally distinct uses of white mutually influenced one another, and also that in the concept of heavenly robes an originally stronger realism gave way to more symbolical usage.[28]

---

[20] I. Scheftelowitz, *D. altpersische Religion u. d. Judentum* (1920), 170, n. 2: as a "symbolical sign that the dead man moves forward in festal array to the heavenly banquet," though white is rather the colour of purity (→ *infra*). Black was still the colour of mourning, cf. Krauss, I, 145; II, 57 and 71.

[21] Cf. Qoh. r. on 9:8 and other examples in Str.-B., III, 795; I, 878.

[22] Str.-B., I, 506; cf. also the variants, I, 878; III, 795.

[23] E.g., Jos. Bell., I, 506: μελαίνῃ ἐσθῆτι; Ant., 14, 172: A sign of a bad conscience and guilt rather than sorrow.

[24] R. Jirmeja, without considering the decision of the last judgment, orders that at his burial he be clothed in a white robe "that I may be ready when Messiah comes" (jKil., 32b, 7, Str.-B., II, 192). This expresses the idea that one can go to the Messiah only as a heavenly being clothed in white. It carries with it, then, the assurance of being one of the righteous who will meet the Messiah.

[25] For details cf. Bousset-Gressm., 277 f. and Loh. Apk. on 3:4 f. (Mandaean examples).

[26] Str.-B., I, 752 f.

[27] Clemen, 242 f.; G. Kittel, Art. → δόξα, esp. II, 247, 252.

[28] Difficulty is caused by the fact that one can rarely date the various ideas with precision. Thus it is not much to the point for R. Eisler, *Weltenmantel u. Himmelszelt* (1910), 296, n. 1 to adduce a series of interesting but obviously, in meaning and origin, later Jewish statements, e.g.: "When the righteous man appears in Paradise, the angels will go to meet him, take off his burial clothes, and put on robes of purest ether."

5. In the NT this eschatological use, which forms the conclusion of our deliberations thus far, occupies the field almost exclusively. That is to say, in the NT white is mentioned almost always in eschatological and apocalyptic contexts or as the heavenly colour.

a. The other rich possibilities of use found in the non-biblical and OT sphere no longer come into account. This is connected with the fact that the whole world of colour is hardly mentioned in the NT.[29] The setting of narratives or parables can be referred to with hardly a ref. to colour.[30] Mt. 6:29 mentions the lilies of the field which can be compared with the δόξα of Solomon, but gives no description of their gay beauty. The cultus can be described with no mention of the gorgeous colours, and the only point about the temple which is emphasised is its monumental size.[31] Details of clothing are mentioned only when there is a particular reason, e.g., in relation to John the Baptist in Mk. 1:6 and par., or the rich man in Lk. 16:19 : ἐνεδιδύσκετο πορφύραν καὶ βύσσον.[32]

There are few references to the clothes of Jesus. The mocking in Mk. 15:16 ff. and par. tells us that His own clothes were in no way royal since He had to be forcibly clothed with a purple robe in order to be given the appearance of a king.[33] From the transfiguration scene in Mk. 9:1 ff. and par. (→ 247) one may deduce that His clothing only once, and only for a brief period, displayed the heavenly colour in keeping with His dignity, and that normally He wore ordinary clothes, He did not wear white like the priests and Levites, or the Pythagoreans, and He could not be recognised as a saint by His clothes.[34] Jesus must have worn coloured garments like common folk. Hence the soldiers in Mk. 15:24 and par. could dice for His clothes. "No one would be outstanding who wore them after Jesus."[35]

Only in two places (apart from the comparison in Mk. 9:3c; cf. → 248) is white not an eschatological or heavenly colour. The first is Jn. 4:35 : "Lift up your eyes καὶ θεάσασθε τὰς χώρας, ὅτι λευκαί εἰσιν πρὸς θερισμόν," the ripe ears are white or

[29] The use of colours, when it occurs, must be evaluated in terms of this mode of looking at things which has little regard for colour. It may be asked whether this general lack of joy in colour (Rev. is the NT book which revels most in colour) is a weakness or an advantage. It did not prevent an open and thoughtful regard for the beauty of nature (esp. in Jesus), though the criterion is obviously not aesthetic. Cf. J. Leipoldt, *Jesus und Paulus — Jesus oder Paulus?* (1936), 31 f.

[30] The green grass is not mentioned in Mk. 6:39 because it is pleasing to the eye. Cf. E. Lohmeyer Mk. (1937), 127: "The groups of men are spread over the green field like beds of flowers (πρασιαί)."

[31] Mk. 13:1; in this respect there is no great difference in the par. Lk. 21:5 (cf. Hck. Lk., *ad loc.*).

[32] Only here is there ref. to *byssus* in the NT (apart from τὸ βύσσινον in Rev. 18:12, 16; 19:8, 14). Cf. Pr.-Bauer, *s.v.*

[33] H. Windisch, "Die Notiz über Tracht u. Speise des Täufers Johannes u. ihre Entsprechung in d. Jesusüberlieferung," ZNW, 32 (1933), 83.

[34] So rightly Windisch, *loc. cit.*; for another view cf. R. Eisler, ΙΗΣΟΥΣ ΒΑΣΙΛΕΥΣ ΟΥ ΒΑΣΙΛΕΥΣΑΣ, II (1930), 281, n. 4. Jesus did not dress like the scribes (→ n. 18). Of James the Just, the Lord's brother, it is reported by Hegesipp. (Eus. Hist. Eccl., II, 23, 5 f.) that he wore σινδόνας, white linen robes like the priests. Cf. also P. Oxy., V, 840, 27 f. (Kl. T., 31).

[35] Windisch, *op. cit.*, 84.

golden.[36] Then in the Sermon on the Mount, Mt. 5:36, we read: μήτε ἐν τῇ κεφαλῇ σου ὀμόσῃς, ὅτι οὐ δύνασαι μίαν τρίχα λευκὴν ποιῆσαι ἢ μέλαιναν. To swear by one's own head, as though one were master of it, is to forget that God's power and man's weakness are displayed here in the fact that God alone can make one's hair black or white, i.e., dark in youth and white in old age. This enables man to see his nothingness, for it is not in his own power to fix his age, or to alter it at wish. This thought (cf. the related saying in Mt. 6:27; → II, 942) is brought out by the illustration of the colour of the hair.[37]

b. The situation is very different in Rev. 1:14, where in the description of the heavenly figure of Christ (based on Da. 7:9) we read: ἡ δὲ κεφαλὴ αὐτοῦ καὶ αἱ τρίχες λευκαὶ ὡς ἔριον λευκὸν ὡς χιών. In Da., even though there is reference to the Ancient of Days, the white hairs do not signify old age, for just before the περιβολή (LXX; ἔνδυμα Θ) is also called white.[38] Similarly, in Rev. 1:14 the reference is not to age or length of days, for the head is also white. White denotes "the radiance of the heavenly being which makes perceptible the majesty of the upper world." The adoption of this trait from Da. 7:9 also shows that for the author "Christ is equal to God in essence and appearance."[39] The phrase "white as snow-white wool"[40] combines the comparisons with snow and wool used in Da. 7:9. The favourite comparison of antiquity, "white as snow" (→ 242; 243 f.; Is. 1:18; Ps. 51:7; Eth. En. 106:2, 10) is also found in Mt. 28:3 and is inserted into Mk. 9:3 in ℜ D sy^{s} etc.[41] (cf. also Mt. 17:2 D).

In Rev. 1:14 only the κεφαλή and τρίχες are radiant with heavenly glory. The raiment of Christ is not expressly called white in v. 13.[42] At the transfiguration, however, there is reference not merely — at least in Mt. 17:2; Lk. 9:29 — to the πρόσωπον or εἶδος τοῦ προσώπου but also, in all three Gospels, Mk. 9:3 and par., to the ἱμάτια (Lk. ἱματισμός). Of them it is said that they became white: Mt.: λευκὰ ὡς τὸ φῶς, Lk.: λευκὸς ἐξαστράπτων, Mk.: στίλβοντα λευκὰ λίαν. There is no doubt that this is not meant to be a negative statement

---

[36] Cf. → 241 and esp. 242 f. Wettstein, I, 865, *ad loc.* refers to Ovid Fast., V, 357: *An quia maturis albescit messis aristis?* and Vergil Ecl., IV, 28: *molli paullatim flavescet campus arista.* R. Bultmann J. (1938), 145, n. 2 thinks that Jn. 4:35 stands in an eschatological context, though this is true only if eschatology is conceived more broadly.

[37] In antiquity white and black hair are often used for age and youth, cf. → 242, and the Rabb. examples in Schl. Mt., 182. The art of dyeing the hair black was known to the ancients (cf. Wettstein, I, 306, *ad loc.*, and esp. Jos. Ant., 16, 233: Herod the Gt. had his hair dyed, and thus sought to remove the treacherous signs of age μελαίνοντα τὰς τρίχας καὶ κλέπτοντα τὸν ἔλεγχον τῆς ἡλικίας). That the saying of Jesus does not consider this possibility is perhaps linked with the fact that the opp. possibility (making black hair white) was not known so widely, but the main explanation is that the simple country people to whom Jesus was speaking found such practices alien.

[38] We need not discuss the meaning of light and fire in Da. 7:9, or the explanation of these traits in terms of the history of religion. Cf. M. Haller, *Das Judentum* (*Die Schriften d. AT*, II, 3)[2] (1925), *ad loc.*

[39] J. Behm Apk. (*NT Deutsch*), *ad loc.*

[40] Had. Apk. wrongly translates "white like white wool, like snow."

[41] The secondary character, proved by the attestation, cannot be contested in terms of the fanciful ref. of R. Eisler, 281, n. 5: "This trait may well be part of the original account, since the setting of the story is the snowy peak of Hermon, and comparison between the radiance of the heavenly garment and the snowy background is quite appropriate." Cf. also Loh. Mk., 174, n. 5.

[42] If the ref. in 1:13 is to a priestly or high-priestly garment, it will be white. Cf. Zn. Apk., 201, n. 44.

to the effect that the clothes have lost their (gay; → n. 34) colour and become unearthly pale, [43] or even evaporated. The statement is a positive one; the clothes, too, have a part in the μεταμορφοῦσθαι; they take on another colour, namely, supraterrestrial white, which is proper to heavenly beings, and is ascribed also to Moses and Elijah in Lk. 9:31: ὀφθέντες ἐν δόξῃ, cf. also the νεφέλη φωτεινή of Mt. 17:5. Is this a temporary disclosure of the true nature of Jesus, a revelation of His δόξα (in this sense)? Would not this be too Johannine (though there is in Jn. no revelation of the δόξα of Jesus, not even in 12:27 f., comparable to the Synoptic transfiguration)? In view of the fact that Mk. 9:1 and par. speak of the *parousia* of Jesus, and Mk. 9:9 and par. of His resurrection, are we not better advised to say that "Jesus appears to His disciples in the form which He will have as the Messiah-Son of Man," i.e., "in the form of the resurrection from the dead"? [44] "His transfiguration is an anticipation of His eschatology." [45]

White is here a specifically eschatological colour: εἶδαν τὴν δόξαν αὐτοῦ, Lk. 9:32, a "representation of δόξα," Mk. 9:1 and par. [46] Mt. emphasises the supraterrestrial character of this white by his comparison ὡς τὸ → φῶς, Lk. by the use of δόξα in 9:31 f., and Mk. by the addition, found only in his Gospel, of the phrase: οἷα γναφεὺς ἐπὶ τῆς γῆς οὐ δύναται οὕτως λευκᾶναι. [47] It is self-evident that this heavenly colour does not apply only externally to the clothes, but implies the transfiguring of the whole nature. [48] Indeed, we do well to consider whether there has not been some influence here of the common eschatological equation of clothes and mode of existence, so that the reference is to the whole nature even though there is fig. mention only of the clothes. This procedure, which may be found poetically in ψ 103:2 (ἀναβαλλόμενος φῶς ὡς ἱμάτιον), is controlled by the thought of heavenly clothes (→ 245), esp. when the clothes are mentioned so exclusively, or with such emphasis, that they can hardly mean the external vesture alone. Something of this may be seen in the NT, cf. → 249 and the image of clothing in 2 C. 5:2 ff. [49] (clothing as εἰκών in 1 C. 15:49, as σῶμα in 1 C. 15:44, and ἱμάτια λευκά as σῶμα τῆς δόξης in Phil. 3:21). [50]

---

[43] In antiquity air was not without colour, but, in distinction from ether, was black (→ μέλας).

[44] J. Schniewind Mk. (*NT Deutsch*), *ad loc.*

[45] → II, 248 f. On the transfiguration, and esp. that of the clothing, cf. E. Lohmeyer, "Die Verklärung Jesu nach dem Markus-Evangelium," ZNW, 21 (1922), 185 ff., 203 ff.; J. Höller, *Die Verklärung Jesu. Eine Auslegung d. nt.lichen Berichte* (1937), esp. 52 ff. (with bibl.); → 25, n. 30.

[46] B. Weiss Mk. Lk.[9] (1901), on Lk. 9:29.

[47] The statement in Kl. Mk., *ad loc.*: "Mk. is not thinking of the white robes of the priests, but this white is supraterrestrial," might easily and quite wrongly suggest that Mt. and Lk. are thinking of priestly or other garments. Loh. Mk., *ad loc.* brings out very well the way in which Mk.'s comparison refers to a small village economy (cf. → n. 37).

[48] The statement of Hck. (Mk., *ad loc.*) that the radiance streaming from Jesus causes His clothes to be radiantly white is open to question, since the clothes themselves are radiant.

[49] This use of clothing (related to the Χριστὸν ἐνδύεσθαι of Gl. 3:27 etc.) needs no addition to emphasise its heavenly character. It is also worth recalling that the same thought can be expressed in terms of light as well as the white garment, cf. οἱ δίκαιοι ἐκλάμψουσιν ὡς ὁ ἥλιος in Mt. 13:43 and similar passages, also the terms → δόξα and → φῶς, and → 26.

[50] No Hell. models are needed to explain either the transfiguration itself, or that of the clothes. Cf. → 245; II, 249, n. 64, and the significant explanation in Loh. Mk., 174, n. 7. The idea of heavenly clothes is not to be regarded merely as a special feature of the depiction of epiphanies (cf. F. Pfister, Art. "Epiphanie," Sctn. 39; "Glanz," Pauly-W. Suppl.-Bd., IV [1924], 315 f.), nor does it have much to do with the clothing mysticism of the mystery religions (cf. C. Schneider, *Einführung in d. nt.liche Zeitgeschichte* [1934], 108 ff.,

c. The closest par. to Mk. 9:3 is Mt. 28:3, where the description of the angel at the tomb says that his face and clothes shone with heavenly radiance: ἦν δὲ ἡ εἰδέα αὐτοῦ ὡς ἀστραπή, καὶ τὸ ἔνδυμα αὐτοῦ λευκὸν ὡς χιών.[51] The par. Mk. 16:5 refers only to the clothes: περιβεβλημένον στολὴν λευκήν (cf. Rev. 6:11; 7:9, 13). So, too, does the par. Lk. 24:4: ἐν ἐσθῆτι ἀστραπτούσῃ (cf. 9:29). In Jn. 20:12 we read of the two angels at the empty tomb: ἐν λευκοῖς καθεζομένους,[52] and in Ac. 1:10 of the two ἄνδρες (hereby characterised as angels):[53] ἐν ἐσθήσεσι λευκαῖς. In the last two passages the reference to white clothes is such that they alone are enough to indicate heavenly nature, → 248. This type of reference, not yet found in the OT, is to angels: "The white clothes are not a description, but an indication of the transcendental character of their δόξα."[54]

Nevertheless, though the white clothes of Jesus are emphasised in Mk. 9:3 and par., one cannot conclude that He is meant to be described as an angel.[55] For in Rev. white clothes do not point to angels but to membership of the heavenly world. To be sure, the 24 elders in Rev. 4:4, who are robed ἐν ἱματίοις λευκοῖς, are probably angels.[56] But the investing of those who overcome with white garments (3:4 f.; 6:11; 7:9, 13)[57] does not mean their elevation to the rank of angels (and certainly not their deification). It signifies the gift of eternal life in fellowship with the exalted Lord before the throne of God (cf. 3:4; 7:15 ff.). There is thus a change by which those who are changed are made like Him (cf. 1 C. 15:51, 49; Phil. 3:21; 1 Jn. 3:2). But the exalted Lord in no way forfeits His position as the Kurios,[58] nor, acc. to Rev., is the special position of angels violated, for elsewhere in Rev. these are clearly differentiated from the transfigured conquerors.[59] That the white clothes are a gift is so strongly emphasised in

117 ff.). On the Gnostic view of clothing, and the identification of the body and clothing, cf. E. Käsemann, "Leib u. Leib Christi," *Beiträge z. hist. Theologie*, 9 (1933), esp. 87 ff.; J. Dey, ΠΑΛΙΓΓΕΝΕΣΙΑ, *Nt.liche Abh.*, XVII, 5 (1937), 88 f., 96 f. Material from the fathers may be found in E. Peterson, "Theologie des Kleides," *Benediktinische Monatsschrift*, 16 (1934), 347 ff.

51 εἰδέα (→ II, 373, n. 2), along with raiment, denotes appearance rather than the figure as a whole. Cf. τὸ εἶδος (D ἰδέα) τοῦ προσώπου, Lk. 9:29 (= ὄψις Rev. 1:16). In v. 3b we see some influence of the Θ version of Da. 7:9, → 247.

52 λευκά is an ellipse (or neuter subst. → 242); so also Rev. 3:4; cf. ἐν μαλακοῖς, Mt. 11:8, the use of βύσσινον (→ n. 32), ἐν πενθικοῖς, Ex. 33:4. Cf. Wettstein, I, 958 and Bl.-Debr. § 241, 7.

53 I.e., in this context; no one would relate the ἐν ἐσθῆτι λαμπρᾷ of Jm. 2:2 to an angel, but cf. Ac. 10:30; cf. also the description of the angel at the tomb in Ev. Pt. 13:55: περιβεβλημένον στολὴν λαμπροτάτην.

54 → I, 84, n. 67.

55 → I, 85.

56 Cf. the comm. Since they sit on thrones, these elders may be regarded as kings, and, in view of 5:8, as priests (Loh. Apk., *ad loc.*; though cf. Zn. Apk., *ad loc.*). But their white garments are not priestly vestments or royal robes, as against H. Gunkel, *Zum religionsgeschichtlichen Verständnis des NT* (FRL, 1)² (1910), 42. Indeed, white is not the colour of royal robes (cf. R. Delbrück, "Der spätantike Kaiserornat," *Die Antike*, VIII [1932], 1 ff.). The white clothes show that the elders belong to the heavenly world. In Rev. 19:14 the στρατεύματα τὰ ἐν τῷ οὐρανῷ are also clad in white (for wide-ranging speculation cf. Had. Apk., *ad loc.*).

57 Cf. also 3:18. The exposition in Had. Apk., *ad loc.*: "white clothes instead of luxurious black," overlooks the fact that white clothes, like pure gold and eye ointment, must be costly. It is best to see here an approximation to the usage elsewhere.

58 Cf. Mich. Ph., 64.

59 The question arises whether the literary peculiarity of Rev. permits us to emphasise it as a precise point of teaching that the martyrs wear white clothes "even before their resurrection" (Zn. Apk., 300, n. 40).

3:5 that the ref. cannot be to personal clothes when we read in 3:4: ἃ οὐκ ἐμόλυναν τὰ ἱμάτια αὐτῶν. It is also clear that 7:14: ἔπλυναν τὰς στολὰς αὐτῶν καὶ ἐλεύκαναν αὐτὰς ἐν τῷ αἵματι τοῦ ἀρνίου must be in harmony with 6:11.[60] 7:14, with its ref. to cleansing (→ I, 174 f.), prevents us from relating 6:11 to the recognition of an existing innocence.[61] Indeed, it is as well not to regard the white clothes as a symbol of purity of heart;[62] they express heavenly δόξα.[63]

White as a heavenly colour also occurs in Rev. 14:14: νεφέλη λευκή,[64] 6:2 and 19:11: ἵππος λευκός, also 19:14: ἐφ' ἵπποις λευκοῖς,[65] and 20:11: εἶδον θρόνον μέγαν λευκόν.[66] The white stone in 2:17, whatever its meaning or basis, also has eschatological significance in the context of Rev. In this connection it is important that Rev. is the book in whose realistic descriptions white is so prominent (most of the λευκός passages in the NT are found in Rev.). In less concrete terms, there are, of course, many other NT refs. to the significance of δόξα, esp. in Pl. and John's Gospel.[67]

Michaelis

---

[60] Cf. Behm Apk. (*NT Deutsch*), *ad loc.* For all the differences the verse is the only NT par. to the promise of Is. 1:18.

[61] Had. Apk. on 6:11: "The symbol of innocence, a pledge that God will declare innocent those who were put to death as guilty and infamous." Had. is inclined to regard white as the colour of innocence. Cf. → 244 f.

[62] This truncation of the biblical view is common, e.g., G. Leroux, Art. "Stola" in Darembg.-Saglio, IV, 2, p. 1522: "Enfin, dans la littérature chrétienne, la *stola candida* est le vêtement sacré que doivent revêtir les élus et qui symbolise la pureté du coeur."

[63] The thought of white as the colour of the victor (perhaps in keeping in 6:2) is not predominant. Tertullian Scorpiace, 12 thinks of a triumphal garment in connection with the white robes of the heavenly hosts in Rev.; Radke, 63, n. 526 thinks Roman ideas have played some part here.

[64] Cf. νεφέλη φωτεινή in Mt. 17:5 and Loh. Apk., *ad loc.*

[65] → n. 63; III, 338 f.; Wettstein, II, 770 f.; Loh. Apk. and Behm Apk. on 6:2. Cf. also ἅρμα λευκόν in the description of the procession of the great king in Xenoph. Cyrop., VIII, 3, 12, also ἅρματι λευκοπώλῳ at the beginning of P. Giess., 3 (the heavenly journey of the dead emperor Trajan). The Messiah sits on a white horse in Rev. 19:11 and so, too, does the first rider in 6:2 (not identical with the Messiah, cf. Bss. Apk., *ad loc.*; → III, 338, n. 11). This shows, as does 19:14, that there is in 19:11 no special idea of the Messiah as a rider on a white horse.

[66] → III, 165. Delitzsch, 760: "The throne of God, which Ez. (1:26; 10:1) sees like a sapphire above the crystal base, and which is thus deep blue, is white when the visions of the NT seer come to the transition of temporal history into the eternal form of the hereafter."

[67] It is worth noting that in the post-apost. fathers λευκός occurs only in Herm. (20 times, cf. Pr.-Bauer, *s.v.*) as an eschatological colour (cf. esp. v., 4, 3, 5: τὸ δὲ λευκὸν μέρος ὁ αἰὼν ὁ ἐπερχόμενός ἐστιν, and as a colour of virgin purity. Cf. Dib. Herm. on v., 1, 2, 2; 4, 2, 1; s., 8, 2, 3; 9, 8, 5, and exc. on s., 9, 2, 1-4. Is. 1:18 is quoted in 1 Cl., 8, 4; cf. 1 Cl., 18, 7: ὑπὲρ χιόνα λευκανθήσομαι. In the Apologists the word group occurs only in OT quotations (Is. 1:18 in Just. Apol., 44, 3 and 61, 7; Da. 7:9 in Just. Dial., 31, 2 and Gn. 49:12 in Dial., 52, 2), and in a secular sense in Athenag., 17, 2.

† λέων

λέων, "lion,"[1] is found from the time of Hom. (the fem. λέαινα is later), both in general and in many fig. senses,[2] e.g., as the constellation, or the sign of the zodiac,[3] or a brave or violent man. No beast of prey is mentioned so often in Hom., nor does any animal play so big a role in fables (usually as a symbol of power and courage).[4] Many depictions of lions have come down from antiquity, esp. from Egypt and Babylon, where the lion (cf. the Heracles saga or the Cybele cult) had an important place in mythological and religious thought.[5] The Babylonian Nergal as the god of the glowing sun is given the bodily shape of a lion; this god is mentioned in 2 K. 17:30 because its worship spread to Samaria.[6] Babylonian or Syrian art influenced the excellent depiction of a roaring lion on the seal of שמע found at Megiddo.[7] In the OT lions are depicted on the throne of Solomon, 1 K. 10:19 f.; 2 Ch. 9:18 f., and on the bases in the temple, 1 K. 7:29, 36. The cherubim in Ez. 1:10 ff., 41:19 have the heads of lions; this reflects ancient mythological notions.[8] The lion is often mentioned in the OT,[9] usually

λέων. [1] The etym. is uncertain, cf. Steier, Art. "Löwe," Pauly-W., XIII (1927), 968 ff.; A. Walde-J. B. Hofmann, *Lat. etymol. Wört.*[3] (1930), 785; Boisacq[3], 575. Though it has not been explained in detail, there is a connection with the Heb. לָבִיא, Assyr. *labbu*.

[2] Cf. Pass. and Liddell-Scott, *s.v.* λέων is rare on inscr.; in Ditt. Or., only on the inscr. of King Silko of Nubia, 201, 15 (A.D.): ἐγὼ γὰρ εἰς κάτω μέρη λέων εἰμί, καὶ εἰς ἄνω μέρη ἄρξ (= ἄρκτος) εἰμι, cf. 1 S. 17:34 ff., Am. 5:19. On the other hand the word is common in the pap. in various senses, as a military title first in the Byzant. period (λέων is attested as a degree in the Mithra cult in Pophyr. Abst., IV, 16). Cf. Preisigke Wört., II, 17 and Moult-Mill., 374 *s.v.*

[3] Cf. W. Gundel, Art. "Leo," 9 (sign of the zodiac). Pauly-W., XII (1925), 1973 ff. (with further details on mythological connections). In the magic pap. observation of the constellation τῇ συνόδῳ τῇ γενομένῃ λέοντι is important, Preis. Zaub., IV, 780 (cf. VII, 299 and 814).

[4] Cf. Steier, 984 ff. for many instances of refs. to the lion in proverbs, fables and poetry.

[5] Selected examples in K. Galling, Art. "Götterbild (männliches)," *Biblisches Reallexikon* (1937), 200 ff. (206 ill.). Egyptian influence (Osiris) may be seen in the mention in Preis. Zaub., IV, 2112 f. of a human figure with a lion's head ἀνδριὰς λεοντοπρόσωπος (cf. also Test. Sol. 2:3: εἰς τρεῖς μορφὰς μεταβαλλόμενος ... πότε δὲ ὄψιν λέοντος ἐμφαίνω).

[6] The conjecture נרגלים in Cant. 6:4, 10 is uncertain; cf. A. Jeremias, Art. "Nergal" in RE[3], XIII, 711 f. (he rejects decisively the suggestion "that there is a connection between certain christological ideas and the Babyl. cult of Nergal"; his conclusion is worth quoting: "The Christian view of the world is not refined mythology").

[7] AOB, Ill. 578; for another lion seal cf. Galling, Art. "Siegel," 487 (486 ill. 11). For lions on Jewish glasses, cf. G. Kittel, *Religionsgesch. u. Urchr.* (1932), 57 and n. 113; E. L. Sukenik, *The Ancient Synagogue of Beth Alpha* (1932), Plate VIII, depictions of Daniel in the lion's den, → II, 384 f., n. 14 and 22; the lion in the zodiac, Plate X, and on this 31-34 (→ II, 383).

[8] The home of these fabulous beings is probably among the partially non-Semitic hill-people of Asia Minor, cf. Galling, Art. "Mischwesen" (→ n. 5), 384 f.

[9] Sometimes there were so many lions in Palestine as to constitute a plague, cf. I. Benzinger, Art. "Jagd bei den Hebräern," RE[3], VIII, 520.

in comparisons (cf. the verses mentioned in n. 2, 11 f., 14 ff.).[10] In the LXX λέων occurs some 150 times, 32 times for אֲרִי (always λέων), 58 for אַרְיֵה (always λέων, except once λέαινα), 17 for כְּפִיר (also σκύμνος, "young," esp. young lion, and δράκων), 5 for לָבִיא (also λέαινα).[11] Philo mentions lions, sometimes in renderings of the OT, cf. Deus Imm., 117; Vit. Mos., I, 109, 284, 291; Decal., 113; Praem. Poen., 89; Omn. Prob. Lib., 40; Egyptian worship of animals, Leg. Gaj., 139; Decal., 78; Vit. Cont., 8.

In all the verses in the NT in which λέων occurs we have OT allusions of greater or lesser force. Hb. 11:33: ἔφραξαν στόματα λεόντων "they (the OT heroes of faith) stopped the mouths of lions," is based on Da. 6:17 ff., esp. 6:23 Θ: (ὁ θεὸς) ἐνέφραξεν τὰ στόματα τῶν λεόντων (cf. 1 Macc. 2:60).[12] In Rev. we find ancient (astral) mythological ideas, mediated through the OT, when in 4:7 the first of the four ζῷα (→ II, 873) is depicted ὅμοιον λέοντι (cf. Ez. 1:10; 10:14; 41:19)[13] and when in 9:8 the ὀδόντες,[14] in 9:17 the κεφαλαί,[15] and in 13:2 the στόμα of lions[16] are used to describe the apocalyptic beasts. In 5:5 it is said of the lamb: ἐνίκησεν ὁ λέων ὁ ἐκ τῆς φυλῆς Ἰούδα; the basis here is Gn. 49:9, a passage which later Judaism interpreted in terms of the Messiah.[17] In 10:3 it is said of the angel with the opened book: καὶ ἔκραξεν φωνῇ μεγάλῃ ὥσπερ λέων μυκᾶται; here an image is adopted which in Hos. 11:10; Am. 3:8 (cf. also Is. 31:4) is applied to God Himself.[18] Related is the warning against apostasy in 1 Pt. 5:8: ὁ ἀντίδικος ὑμῶν διάβολος ὡς λέων ὠρυόμενος περιπατεῖ ζητῶν τινα καταπιεῖν (→ I, 374; II, 80), cf. ψ 21:13 (22:13).[19] When Paul

---

[10] P. Thomsen, Art. "Löwe, E. Palästina-Syrien," *Reallexikon d. Vorgeschichte*, VII (1926), 318 f. Cf. also A. Wünsche, *Die Bildersprache des AT* (1906), 57 ff.

[11] Poetically also לַיִשׁ (the strong?), Is. 30:6; Prv. 30:30 (LXX σκύμνος λέοντος); Job 4:11 (LXX μυρμηκολέων), also several times שַׁחַל (the roarer?) (LXX πανθήρ at Hos. 5:14; 13:7; λέαινα or λέων at Job 4:10; 10:16; 28:8; not understood at ψ 90:13; Prv. 26:13).

[12] We are not to think of Samson or David in Ju. 14:5 f.; 1 S. 17:34 ff., as Wettstein, II, 430, *ad loc.*, cf. Rgg. Hb.[2, 3], 377, n. 87. ἐμφράσσειν στόμα (of men) occurs often in the LXX.

[13] The depiction of Rev. is simpler than that of Ez. The use of ὅμοιον brings the remnant of a mythological view into the sphere of symbol (Loh. Apk., *ad loc.*). When the attributes of the 4 Evangelists are later seen in the ζῷα, Mk. is usually the lion, though also Jn. and Mt. (cf. Bss. Apk., *ad loc.* and *ibid.*, 50).

[14] Following Jl. 1:6 (also Sir. 21:2). Loh. Apk., *ad loc.*: "An ὡς is added here which brings the depiction into another sphere" (cf. Rev. 9:17; 13:2).

[15] The LXX often πρόσωπον λέοντος (פָּנִים).

[16] Cf. Da. 7:4 (LXX Θ: λέαινα); Bss. Apk., *ad loc.*

[17] Cf. Str.-B., III, 801 (on the other hand Test. Jud. 24:5 [cf. Loh. Apk., *ad loc.*] follows Is. 11:1, 10), though some Rabb. apply this only to the tribe of Judah (Had. Apk., *ad loc.*, following Schlatter; Had. also mentions a Zionistic interpretation). Rev. 5:5 is not influenced here by a nationalistically orientated Jewish Christianity (as against Bss. Apk., *ad loc.*). It rests on a confession of the OT Messianic promise which is orientated to the death and resurrection of Jesus. The picture of the lion is not intended politically, so that there is no opposition to the political world (so — more with ref. to ἐνίκησεν — E. Peterson, *Zeuge d. Wahrheit* [1937], 79).

[18] LXX has ἐρεύγεσθαι at Hos. 11:10 and Am. 3:8, ἀνακράζειν at Jl. 3:16, βοᾶν (with κράζειν) at Is. 31:4. μυκᾶσθαι is elsewhere used of the bull (the lion in Theocr. Idyll., 26, 20 f.; cf. → n. 19). The image of the roaring lion is used of the Messiah in 4 Esr. 11:37; 12:31.

[19] There is also ref. to the ὠρύεσθαι of the lion in Ju. 14:5; Jer. 2:15; Ez. 22:25; Zech. 11:3; Zeph. 3:3 (cf. βρυγμός, Prv. 19:12, also Sir. 51:3; → n. 7, 11 [שַׁחַל], 18). The ancient

in 2 Tm. 4:17 writes: (through the κύριος) ἐρρύσθην ἐκ στόματος λέοντος, he has in view 1 Macc. 2:60: (Daniel) ἐρρύσθη ἐκ στόματος λεόντων (א λέοντος), also ψ 21:21: σῶσόν με ἐκ στόματος λέοντος, and similar passages. It may be assumed that he was influenced by OT usage.[20, 21] There is no means of deciding how far these NT passages may rest on personal observation of the different qualities of the lion. The promise that lions will be peaceful in the last time (Is. 11:6 f.; 65:25) finds no echo in the eschatological statements of the NT.[22]

Michaelis

---

lexicographers are divided whether one should say ὠρύεσθαι or βρυχᾶσθαι of the lion (cf. Wettstein, II, 697 *ad loc.*). The lion's unceasing search for prey, Nu. 23:24: οὐ κοιμηθήσεται, ἕως φάγῃ θήραν, καὶ αἷμα τραυματιῶν πίεται. Cf. also Job 10:16; ψ 16:12; Sir. 27:10, 28. On καταπίνειν: μάχαιρα κατέφαγεν τοὺς προφήτας ὑμῶν ὡς λέων ὀλεθρεύων, Jer. 2:30 and esp. ψ 7:2: μήποτε ἁρπάσῃ ὡς λέων τὴν ψυχήν μου (cf. Na. 2:13; Ez. 22:25). Against misleading historical par. cf. Clemen, 357.

20 As against Dib. Past., who looks elsewhere than to OT models. In 4:18 ῥύσεται and σώσει correspond, so that the LXX verses which use σῴζειν (ψ 21:21; Da. 6:21, 23) are a direct par.; cf. also 1 Βασ. 17:37; Δα. 6:16 f.; Da. Θ 6:21, 28, also Am. 3:12). There can be no question of condemnation *ad bestias*, or of deliverance from Satan (1 Pt. 5:8). It is doubtful whether we are to think of Nero (cf. the ref. to the death of Tiberius in Jos. Ant., 18, 228: τέθνηκεν ὁ λέων). Perhaps the situation is that of the hearing at which Paul had to champion the Gospel before the lion. Cf. Εσθ. 4:17 s: δὸς λόγον εὔρυθμον εἰς τὸ στόμα μου ἐνώπιον τοῦ λέοντος (in the prayer of Esther ῥύεσθαι is also used several times).

21 In ψ 21:21, then in 2 Tm. 4:17, λέων is used for death or its kingdom, which in the OT is often depicted as the power which swallows up life, Prv. 1:12; Is. 25:8; Job 18:13 LXX, cf. also Hab. 2:5 and Is. 5:14. In pagan and Christian antiquity we find sarcophagi with the heads of lions, which are to be taken as symbols of death in the sense of the σαρκοφάγος. Cf. e.g., the Christian shepherd sarcophagus in C. M. Kaufmann, *Handbuch d. christl. Archäologie*[3] (1922), 491 and the pagan lion sarcophogus of Tarragona in H. Laag, "Die Coemeterialbasilika v. Tarragona," *Festgabe f. V. Schultze* (1931), 145. A representation of death on the lion is also to be found as the mechanical figure on a clock on the minster in Heilsbronn, Bayrisches Nationalmuseum, No. 3450. Here the influence of antiquity may be seen. The lion is the beast on which death rides in a Ruthenian tableau of the 14th cent., W. Molsdorf, *Christl. Symbolik d. mittelalterlichen Kunst* (1926), 244, No. 1136. The lion can also symbolise the power of hell, cf. the passages mentioned, and others, esp. as used in the Christian liturgy. This idea is found in Aug. Serm., 263 (MPL, 38 [1845], p. 210) with ref. to ψ 21:21 and Gn. 49:9: *Quis non incurreret in dentes leonis huius, nisi vicisset Leo de tribu Juda?* Depictions are first found only in medieval Christian art, e.g., on monuments where the deceased stands on the lion (cf. Ps. 91:13). These refer to the victory of the righteous over the power of hell in their lives. The true victor is Christ, also represented as a lion. Cf. K. Künstle, *Ikonographie d. christl. Kunst*, I (1928), 126-128 (with further examples). For material on the symbolical reference of the lion to Christ cf. F. X. Kraus, *Gesch. d. christl. Kunst*, I (1896), 106; 110; II, 2 (1908), Index, *s.v.* Cf. also Molsdorf and Kaufmann, *et al.* [Bertram].

22 Cf. Vergil Ecl., IV, 22; E. Norden, *Die Geburt des Kindes* (1924), 52. Post-apost. fathers, Mart. Pol., 12, 2 of the condemnation to fight with lions; 1 Cl., 35, 11 (= ψ 49:22 ὡς λέων from ψ 7:2; cf. A. Rahlfs, *Psalmi cum Odis* [1931] on ψ 49:22); 1 Cl., 45, 6, ref. to Da. 6:16 f.

† ληνός, † ὑπολήνιον

1. ἡ (also ὁ) ληνός denotes a vat or tub shaped vessel, mostly the "press," Anecd. Graec., I, p. 277, 17: γεωργικὸν σκεῦος· ἔστι δὲ ἀγγεῖον δεκτικὸν οἴνου, ξύλινον, ὃ ἀποδέχεται τὸ ῥέον ἐκ τῶν ὀργάνων τῶν πιεζομένων. Theocr. Idyll., 25, 28; Diod. S., III, 63, 4; Anth. Pal., XI, 63, 3; P. Amh., 48, 7; P. Oxy., IV, 729, 19 etc. Of **other uses** [1] **the only one to arise in OT and NT writings is in** Gn. 30:38, 41 for רַהַט, the pitcher for watering cattle (cf. also Hom. Hymn. Merc., 104 etc.). In the OT the "press" is often specifically the "winepress" or "oilpress" as found in the olive grove or vineyard, hewn out in the cliff (Is. 5:2; cf. Mk. 12:1; Mt. 21:33; cf. P. Oxy., III, 502, 36 f.). It would consist of two containers, an upper one (Heb. גַּת [Gethsemane = oil-press, Dalman Gr.^{2}, 191], Gr. ληνός) in which the fruits were pressed (cf. Mi. 6:15), usually by trampling (πατεῖν [דָּרַךְ], Is. 16:10; Jer. 48:33 = Ιερ. 31:33; Lam. 1:15; Neh. 13:15 = 2 Εσδρ. 23:15), and a lower one (Heb. יֶקֶב = Gr. ὑπολήνιον, or προλήνιον [Is. 5:2], Jl. 3:13; Hag. 2:16; Zech. 14:10; Is. 16:10) into which the juice flows. [2]

Grapes were pressed to cries of jubilation and songs [3] (Is. 16:9 f.; Jer. 48:33). The wine harvest is a joyous feast, and the filling and overflowing of the vats (Jl. 2:24; Σιρ. 33:17) is the epitome of rich blessing. [4] The sharper the contrast, then, when the same figure is used to depict the terror of judgment. In Jer. 25:30 the roaring of Yahweh as He comes to judgment is compared with the wild cries of those who tread the press.

ληνός κτλ. Thes. Steph., Passow, Liddell-Scott, Preisigke Wört., Pr.-Bauer^3, *s.v.* E. C. A. Riehm, *Handwörterbuch d. Bibl. Altertums,* I (1884), 821; H. Guthe, *Kurzes Bibelwörterbuch* (1903), 360; S. Krauss, *Talmud. Archäologie,* II (1911), 233 ff.; G. Dalman, *Arbeit u. Sitte in Palästina,* IV (1935), 354 ff. On the motif of the wine-treader, which is common in patristic and medieval exegesis, also in sermons, hymns, and depictions of the passion in the Middle Ages, which arose out of the allegorical interpretation and combination of OT sayings (esp. Gn. 49:11 and Is. 63:1 ff.), and which is centred on Christ, along with the idea that He is the fruit which is pressed, cf. W. Molsdorf, *Christl. Symbolik d. mittelalterlichen Kunst* (1926), 206 f.; K. Künstle, *Ikonographie d. christl. Kunst,* I (1928), 489 f.; A. Thomas, "Die Darstellung Christi in der Kelter," (*Forschungen u. Volkskunde,* Heft 20/21 [1935]).

1 For other uses *v.* the dict. The press is important in the Dionysus cult; Dionysus is the god of the press (Diod. S., IV, 5, 1 Ληναῖον δὲ ἀπὸ τοῦ πατῆσαι τὰς σταφυλὰς ἐν ληνῷ [sc. ὀνομάσαι]). On the Lenaia as a Dionysus festival, Lenaion as the name of the month and Lenaios a name for Dionysus, cf. Pauly-W., XII (1925), 1935 ff. On the isolated ληνός = coffin (Poll. Onom., V, 150; Anecd. Graec., I, p. 51, 14), cf. R. Eisler, *Orpheus — The Fisher* (1921), XXXIV; ληνοί for initiates of Dionysus, cf. O. Kern, *Die Religion d. Griechen,* III (1938), 204.

2 On ὑπολήνιον cf. Poll. Onom., X, 130; P. Oxy., XIV, 1735, 5; A. Wikenhauser, BZ, 8 (1910), 273.

3 LXX calls Ps. 8, ψ 80 and 83 winepress songs: ὑπὲρ τῶν ληνῶν, by incorrect derivation of the title עַל־הַגִּתִּית from גַּת. On such songs cf. R. Eisler, "Orphisch-dionysische Mysteriengedanken in d. christl. Antike," *Vorträge d. Bibliothek Warburg,* II, 2 (1925), 269 ff.

4 For rules regarding offerings from the wine harvest cf. Ex. 22:29: ἀπαρχαὶ ἅλωνος καὶ ληνοῦ, Nu. 18:27: ἀφαίρεμα ἀπὸ ληνοῦ, Nu. 18:30: γένημα ἀπὸ ληνοῦ, cf. Did., 13, 3: ἀπαρχὴν γεννημάτων ληνοῦ, and Pr.-Bauer^3, 258.

In Lam. 1:15 He Himself is the treader who declares a festival of destruction in Judah and destroys the young men. Similarly, in Is. 63:1-6 judgment falls on Edom, and Yahweh returns, His garments covered with blood, sprinkled red like those of one who treads the winepress: "I have trodden the winepress alone; and of the people there was none with me: for I trod them in mine anger, and trampled them in my fury; and their juice sprinkled on my garments, and I stained all my raiment" (v. 3). In Jl. 3:13 the call goes out to the helpers of Yahweh: "Put ye in the sickle, for the harvest is ripe; come to tread, for the press is full, the vats overflow; for their wickedness is great."

2. The 4 NT passages which refer to the press are all under OT influence. In Mk. 12:1 par. Mt. 21:33 the parable of the wicked husbandmen opens with a reference to Is. 5:2.[5] If it is wrong to apply every individual detail (the fence, the press, the tower), it is also wrong to overlook the allegorical character of the parable, which is suggested in Mk. and more explicit in Mt. and Lk. (cf. esp. Mt. 21:39; Lk. 20:15 with Hb. 13:12 as distinct from Mk. 12:8). The express use in Mk. and Mt. of the traditional image, whose features no longer serve the original point, shows that the Jewish people was always seen in the vineyard.

3. The other verses are Rev. 14:19 f. and 19:15 in the depiction of judgment. Both use prophetic images. The double figure of the grain and wine harvest for judgment in Jl. 3:13 is found again in Rev. 14:14-20. To the double call ἐξαποστείλατε δρέπανα ... εἰσπορεύεσθε πατεῖτε ... there correspond two separate acts: a first angel summons the sickle of the Son of Man to reap the harvest, and a second angel summons the sickle of an ἄλλος ἄγγελος to cut clusters from the vine of the earth. The wine harvest is followed by an enigmatic depiction of wine-treading: καὶ ἔβαλεν εἰς τὴν ληνὸν τοῦ θυμοῦ τοῦ θεοῦ τὸν μέγαν. καὶ ἐπατήθη ἡ ληνὸς ἔξωθεν τῆς πόλεως, καὶ ἐξῆλθεν αἷμα ἐκ τῆς ληνοῦ ἄχρι τῶν χαλινῶν τῶν ἵππων, ἀπὸ σταδίων χιλίων ἑξακοσίων (v. 19 f.). In 19:15 the Messiah Judge is the one who treads the press, and the figure of the Judge bears the features of the God who in Is. 63:1 ff. returns after destroying His enemies.

The first vision raises many problems both because of its position and also because of the details. It obviously describes a final judgment which no further events will follow. Various attempts have been made to show that 14:14-20 is the end of an underlying source or writing, or at least to see in it an originally independent and detached fragment.[6] No less puzzling than the position of the vision in the general context of Rev. are some of the details: 1. the unexpected appearance of an angel of judgment along with the Son of Man (v. 14 and v. 17); 2. the note on the place, καὶ ἐπατήθη ἡ ληνὸς ἔξωθεν τῆς πόλεως (v. 20a); 3. the mixing of the motifs of the winepress and battle (v. 20b); 4. the note on the extreme bloodiness of the event, ἀπὸ σταδίων χιλίων ἑξακοσίων.[7]

Both the question of an independent source and the problem of the details in 14:19 f. are solved if it is noted that the vision, at least from v. 17 on, is conceived with a view to c. 19. Hence it is an intentionally mysterious first sketch of events which will be more plainly and broadly described later. The connection between the winepress and

---

[5] Lk. 20:9 is content with ἐφύτευσεν ἀμπελῶνα, which is adequate in the context, since the ref. in the parable is to the wickedness of the workers, not to the disproportion of the concern and the futility of the work, as in Is. (where a winepress is set up, προλήνιον in Is., ὑπολήνιον in Mk., ληνόν in Mt.).

[6] Cf. Bss. Apk., Exc. on 14:14-20.

[7] ℵ* syp^h: 1200; 2036; 1606.

the battle is clear enough in the light of c. 19 (or Is. 63:1 ff.). The description of the winepress (which does not derive from Jl.) as that of the wrath of God in 14:19 points forward to 19:15: καὶ αὐτὸς πατεῖ τὴν ληνὸν τοῦ οἴνου τοῦ θυμοῦ τῆς ὀργῆς τοῦ θεοῦ, [8] and the indefiniteness of the pass. in 14:20 is resolved by the more precise statement in 19:15. The dependence of the vision on 19:11 ff. also explains the mention of the angel of judgment in 14:17, which seems to compete with the appearance of the Son of Man in 14:14. Even in the second act of the harvest the seer can think only of the Messiah, as the same attribute in 14:14 and 14:17, and the solution in 19:15, indicate. He is introduced as ἄλλος ἄγγελος for concealment, since the final Messianic judgment will be the theme of later depiction. [9] The location of the press outside the city is in keeping with the Jewish tradition that the final destruction of enemies will take place at the gates of Jerusalem (Jl. 3:2, 12; Zech. 14:4; 4 Esr. 13:35; S. Bar. 40:1). Since Rev. 14:18 f. is based on Jl. 3:13, there is allusion to the (unspecified) vale of Jehoshaphat (or judgment) of Jl. 3:2, 12, 14. Here again one may see a connection between the winepress and the place of destruction mentioned in 19:20, which for its part is equated with → γέεννα (ἔβαλεν εἰς τὴν ληνόν, 14:19, ἐβλήθησαν ... εἰς τὴν λίμνην τοῦ πυρὸς τῆς καιομένης ἐν θείῳ, 19:20). The topographical note in v. 20 may be explained by the fact that acc. to Jewish tradition the entrance to Gehinnom is at Jerusalem, [10] and the ref. gains its point from the mention of the angel of fire directly before in 14:18. [11] But the note on the stream of blood stretching 1600 furlongs is still puzzling. If the referring of the winepress to Gehenna is correct, the number is perhaps a schematic observation on the great size of the place of judgment. [12] Neither in

---

[8] Is. 63:5 f.: καὶ ὁ θυμός μου ἐπέστη καὶ κατεπάτησα αὐτοὺς τῇ ὀργῇ μου καὶ κατήγαγον τὸ αἷμα αὐτῶν εἰς γῆν. The description of the massacre in 14:20 is formal: En. 100:3: "A horse will wade up to its breast in the blood of sinners, and a chariot will sink to its full height." jTaan., 69a, 7 f.: "The people of Beth-ter was slaughtered until a horse sank up to its nostrils in blood" (Str.-B., III, 817). Eka r. on 2:1 :"So many of the inhabitants were smitten that the horse sank up to its nose in blood." Lidz. Ginza R., XVIII, 390 f. (p. 417, 15 ff.): "Then comes that king, lets loose his horse, and this strides over them up to its saddle in blood, and the stream of blood reaches to the sides of its nose."

[9] The common idea that God exercises judgment on hostile nations by the angel of judgment makes possible the variation in 14:17 ff. as compared with 19:11 ff. Cf. En. 100:4; 10:11, 16, 20; 53:3 ff.; 56:1 ff. etc.; Str.-B., IV, 868 ff. Nevertheless, these are not different events, for in 19:14 (as distinct from Is. 63:3) the Messiah is accompanied by a heavenly host. There is ref. to this host in 14:20, though He Himself is not mentioned in 14:17. The objection that the Son of Man is openly introduced in 14:14 is met by the fact that the θερισμός of vv. 14-16 is the gathering of believers (Loh. Had. etc., *ad loc.*), and the divine needs to speak openly here because he has not previously stated the precise relation of the Messiah to the redeemed. On the other hand, it is only later that the Messiah will emerge as the final victor (cf. the proclamation of his name in 19:16).

[10] In En. 90:26 all will be judged, found guilty, cast into the bowl of fire and burned; this abyss was to the right of the house. Cf. also En. 26:1-27:4; Str.-B., IV, 1029 f., also 1115; P. Volz, *Die Eschatologie d. jüdischen Gemeinde*[2] (1934), 329 f. On the identity of the valley of Jehoshaphat or decision in Jl. 3:12 ff. and Gehinnom, cf. Midr. Ps. 62 § 2 on 62:3; Str.-B., IV, 1106 f. also → n. 13.

[11] It may be asked whether the striking change of article in 14:19: εἰς τὴν ληνόν ... τὸν μέγαν, does not also carry an allusion to Gehinnom, which is expressly called "the great" (Midr. Ps. 62 § 2 on 62:3). It is, of course, more obvious to relate the change to the double gender of ληνός (hardly as *constructio ad sensum*, related to θυμός, Had., *ad loc.*). Cf. Radermacher[2], 110, and for further examples of the predilection for the masc. in Rev., which often leads to incongruence, cf. Bl.-Debr.[6] § 136, 3.

[12] It is thus idle to seek geographical identification. The extent of Palestine (from Tyre to the Egyptian border) is 1664 stadia in the itinerary of Antonius, but the divine can hardly have known this, and it has no bearing here. Victorinus takes it to apply schematically to the whole earth (*per omnes mundi quattuor partes*), cf. Bss. and Loh., *ad loc.*, and for other figures on the extent of Gehinnom, Volz, 328.

14:17 ff. not 19:11-16 are we told who the enemies are, but in 19:17-21, which is based on Ez. 39:17-20, we learn that they are the βασιλεῖς, χιλίαρχοι and ἰσχυροί and their troops who, representing the beast and his pseudo-prophet, made war on the Messiah and His host. There is in 19:17 ff. a distinction of judgment; [13] only the beast and the false prophet come into the λίμνη τοῦ πυρός (as later Satan in 20:10 and θάνατος and ᾅδης in 20:14), while the rest fall to the sword of the Messiah. But in 14:17 ff. only a single image is used. Yet the allusions of c. 19 are plain. 19:15 combines the motifs of the winepress and the wine of wrath in 14:8, 10, 19 f., and the mention of the beast in 19:20 corresponds to 14:9, 11, which for their part refer back to c. 13. In 14:9 ff. and 20:15 [14] those who worship the beast are also consigned to the λίμνη τοῦ πυρός.

Bornkamm

† ληστής

A. ληστής outside the NT.

1. From the root *lāu,* "to win," "to take," "to seize," "to enjoy," come the nouns λεία (ληΐη) or ληΐς, "prey" by way of the verb ληΐζομαι, "to gain as booty" [Debrunner], and from these again ληστής, originally "the one who takes booty." The word does not unconditionally imply lack of honesty; hence it can be used for the regular soldier or mercenary, who in antiquity had a right to plunder. It is still found in this sense in the Gk. Bible, though, quite understandably from the standpoint of those affected, the use is for enemy soldiers (Jer. 18:22; Σιρ. 36:26). [1] But the bad sense has always been predominant. Already in Soph. Oed. Tyr., 534 f. ληστής is used with φονεύς, and on the lips of Oedipus it describes Creon as a man who seeks both his life and his power. [2] In the period which follows it becomes a word for any kind of

[13] The same distinction is to be seen in En. 53 and 54. Acc. to 53:1 the place where kings and great men of the earth are destroyed is a deep valley with an open abyss (cf. Jl. 3:2, 12), but this is not the same as the deep valley with burning fire, or Gehenna (54:1), which is for the hosts of Azazel (54:5). Yet the distinction is not topographical in Rev., nor indeed in En., since we find the kings and mighty men in the second valley in 54:2.

[14] It need hardly be said that the above analysis cuts the ground from under the feet of those who would detach 14:14-20 on critical grounds. In essence, the only independent feature in this passage is the quotation from Jl. For the rest, it fits both retrospectively and prospectively into the total plan of Rev. On the motifs of form and composition which apply both to c. 14 and c. 19 and also to the book as a whole, cf. G. Bornkamm, "Die Komposition d. apokalyptischen Visionen d. Offenbarung Johannis," ZNW, 37 (1938), 132 ff., esp. 141 f.

ληστής. For bibl. → ζηλωτής, II, 884, n. 7. Cf. also J. Pickl, *Messiaskönig Jesus in d. Auffassung seiner Zeitgenossen* (1935); Schl. Gesch. Isr., 264, 322 ff.

[1] The εὔζωνος ληστής, who because of his restlessness is not worthy of confidence, is a rendering of גְּדוּד צָבָא (cf. 1 Ch. 7:4) in the Heb. of Sir. 36:31, which denotes the regular squadron.

[2] Vv. 532-535:

οὗτος σύ, πῶς δεῦρ' ἦλθες; ἢ τοσόνδ' ἔχεις
τόλμης πρόσωπον, ὥστε τὰς ἐμὰς στέγας
ἵκου, φονεὺς ὢν τοῦδε τἀνδρὸς ἐμφανῶς
ληστής τ' ἐναργὴς τῆς ἐμῆς τυραννίδος;

robber (plunderer, highwayman, pirate [3] etc.), and also for undisciplined soldiers (Philo Flacc., 5: ληστεία), yet always with the implication of a ruthless use of force in seeking the goods of others. Thus there is a distinction from κλέπτης, but the two words are on the same level (cf. already Plato Resp., I, 351c). In Plato Gorg., 507e Socrates calls a βίος which is controlled by unbridled impulses, which is thus thoroughly a-social, a ληστοῦ βίος. The implication of force guides the use in many passages in the LXX. At Jer. 7:11 (σπήλαιον ληστῶν, cf. 12:9 A) it is used for פָּרִיץ, and at Ob. 5 (with κλέπτης) for שׁוֹדֵד, two words which denote men who do violent acts (cf. Ep. Jer. 13, 17, 57, here with κλέπτης). This emphasis on violence [4] enables it to be listed in M. Ant., VI, 34 along with other violent men such as κίναιδοι, πατραλοῖαι and τύραννοι.

2. In Joseph. it is constantly used for the Zealots [5] who, along with those who help, accept or merely tolerate them, make armed conflict against Roman rule the content of their life, and are prepared to risk everything, even life itself, to achieve national liberty (→ ζηλωτής, esp. II, 884 ff.). The movement as such was called into being at the time of the tax evaluation under Quirinius. Under a certain Judas of Galilee it was a protest against the dominion of Rome thereby manifested, Ant., 18, 4 ff.; Bell., 2, 117 f. But it had a prior history, as Joseph. himself tells us. For the Hezekiah whom Herod, soon after the beginning of his reign, arrested and executed along with his companions through Phasael (cf. Ant., 14, 158 ff., Bell., 1, 204 f.), [6] is called ἀρχιληστής by Joseph. (Ant., 14, 159; 17, 271; Bell., 1, 204), while his companions are λησταί and their company is a ληστήριον or robber band (Ant., 14, 159 f.). Since no record is given of him, there is at least the possibility that Hezekiah was not a bandit but a political revolutionary, perhaps with Messianic aims. The later Zealots rejected Roman rule, not because it was Roman, but because it was alien, and it is well known that Jews who inclined to Pharisaism never recognised the family of the Idumean Herod as a legitimate dynasty. Thus immediately after the death of Herod the son of Hezekiah called for a revolt against his successors, and at first achieved some notable success (e.g., the capture of Sepphoris, Ant., 17, 271). When Joseph. tells us that he even sought royal dignity (βασίλειος τιμή, Ant., 17, 272), the Messianic character of the revolutionary movement is surely plain. [7] But the Jewish narrator calls his following a πλῆθος ἀνδρῶν ἀπονενοημένων (Ant., 17, 271), and this betrays his later [8] aversion to all such movements. But this is hardly a true account of those concerned. [9] In addition to Judas, whose father Hezekiah he describes as μέγα δυνηθείς in Ant., 17, 271, Joseph. mentions many other Messianic pretenders of the same period (Ant., 17, 273 ff., Bell., 2, 57 ff.), some for Peraea and Samaria. Their actions, aimed at the removal of Ῥωμαῖοι and βασιλικοί (Bell., 2, 62), are indeed comparable to those of λησταί, esp. as they showed no regard even for their own compatriots. Constantly on the run from superior forces, they often had to take what they needed without asking too many questions. Nor did things change in later decades. It is thus the more noteworthy that the sympathies of the people were always on the side of the Zealots (→ 260). They shared

[3] The sense of pirate occurs already in Hom. Od., 3, 73.

[4] Something of the same sense underlies the German *Raub* and Eng. "robbery."

[5] For abundant material cf. Pickl, esp. 14 ff.

[6] When Joseph. says that Herod received much thanks and praise for this, we see his tendency to set Herod in a good light.

[7] The revolt collapsed when the Romans intervened under Varus (Ant., 17, 289; Bell., 2, 68). This intervention showed the Jews once again the fact that the rule of the house of Herod meant Roman rule. Joseph. does not tell us that Judas himself perished in the struggle, but we learn this from Lk. in Ac. 5:37.

[8] In the great war which led to the destruction of Jerusalem he had held a high-ranking military post on the side of the revolt.

[9] In Bell. 2, 56 he simply calls them οἱ περὶ αὐτόν.

with the Zealots the view that the concern for liberation from foreign rule was a wholly religious concern. God alone is the Lord of the Jewish world (→ II, 45). Hence the only tolerable βασιλεία is the βασιλεία τοῦ θεοῦ. In relation even to definitely Messianic groups Joseph. still speaks of λῃστήρια (Ant., 17, 285). Those who belong to them are λῃσταί. His usage in this respect is uniform.

Two things are to be noted about the usage of Joseph. The first is that he uses the term for the Zealot movement as seen through the eyes of the Roman rulers. The word stamps it as an illegal, armed political movement composed of malcontents, rebels, bandits and highwaymen. The outlook of Joseph. is that of an outsider. It should be noted, however, that the Romans themselves did not in fact treat as λῃσταί the Zealots whom they captured. Their punishment was crucifixion, and this alone was enough to show that they were regarded and treated as political offenders. If they were called λῃσταί, this expresses a sense of political security and complete superiority on the part of the Romans. Joseph. thus adopts the Roman standpoint. Secondly, the use of λῃσταί for the Zealots indicates the scattered nature of the movement, its lack of inner and outer cohesion. Thus, when he speaks of the revolt of the whole people in the years 66 ff., Joseph. calls the rebels οἱ Ἰουδαῖοι, [10] and only later, when in addition to the conflict with Rome there were bloody inner struggles between individual Zealot leaders and their factions, does he begin to speak of λῃσταί (Bell., 4, 135), [11] and to use λῃστεία comprehensively for their actions (4, 134). The word thus carries with it some criticism of the Zealot movement in its traditional form. It indicates the degree to which personal aims damaged the common cause of the people, and besmirched and misused the religious basis.

3. Rabb. Judaism borrowed λῃστής and λῃστεία from the Gk. in the form of the loan words לִיסְטִים [12] and לִיסְטְיָא, לִיסְטִיּוּת. The usage is not so clear as in the case of Joseph. Yet the texts make it evident that there is an inner connection. To be sure, לִיסְטִים is often found in a context which shows that the ref. is to ordinary robbers (e.g., Shab., 2, 5), and לִיסְטִים was used in this way when the Zealot movement had been destroyed and recollection of the insecurity of the country under its dominion had faded. But even in Shab., 2, 5 לִיסְטִים occurs along with גּוֹיִם, and the ref. is thus to Jews as distinct from non-Jews. Their place is isolation (cf. Ber., 1, 3). An anecdote tells of לִסְטַיָּא in Judaea (דָּרוֹמִית) (Gn. r., 92, 6 on 44:1 ff.) who acted like bandits but could have been members of the Zealot movement. [13] The Mishnah uses גָּנַב for stealing and גָּזַל for robbery, but not every robber is a לִיסְטִים, and some לִיסְטִים act like thieves, e.g., when they reap the fields of others (like Samaritans) by night (Pea, 2, 7 f.). [14] In BQ, 6, 1 we even find rules as to the obligation of לִיסְטִים to make good the damage done by them. These are perhaps recollections of a day when it was taken for granted that the לִיסְטִים would come under the Law as traditionally expounded. [15] It should also be noted that in these texts the usual punishment for the לִיסְטִים is crucifixion (Qoh. r., 7, 26; Est. r., 3, 14 on 1:12 etc.), and this is a Roman punishment (→ σταυρός).

---

[10] They are νεωτερίζοντες (Bell., 4, 120) and their spiritual leaders ταράσσοντες (4, 117). They are also στασιώδεις (4, 86 etc.) or even (ἄνδρες) ἐκ τοῦ διεφθαρμένου τάγματος (4, 93), but not λῃσταί.

[11] Here we have ἀρχιλῃστής for leaders of individual groups of λῃσταί (→ 258).

[12] Plur. לִיסְטִים (לִיסְטִים).

[13] The hero of the story is R. Meïr (c. 150 A.D.). In his time the movement had been long since broken, but was not yet rooted out. There were still pockets in South and East Judaea. Naturally the border between rebels and robbers tended to become more and more tenuous, since the לִיסְטִים had to take steps to secure their lives and freedom.

[14] The Mishnah seems to presuppose that they come under the Pea obligation.

[15] Zelotism is a branch of Pharisaism, cf. Schl. Gesch. Isr., 261 ff.

We also find the principle אֵשֶׁת לִיסְטִים כְּלִיסְטִים (jKet., 26d, 38), [16] and this points to martial law, since it was not usual to make women responsible for the faults of their husbands. Perhaps, then, one can say that in spite of the later change in use the Rabb. לִיסְטִים originally denoted the Zealot. But the word could be adopted in this sense only if the Zealots themselves regarded as a title of honour the term of reproach used by their enemies [17] — something for which history affords many parallels. [18] At the same time, the use of the term in Rabb. texts expresses the partial Rabb. repudiation of Zelotism as the proclamation of individual war against the pagan state in the name of God. [19] The Rabbis were waiting for God Himself to act and to set up His rule, for they were certain that He would not abandon His people (cf. Gamaliel in Ac. 5:35 ff.). The impreciseness of their use of לִיסְטִים, which arises from the fact that it may denote both a bandit and a Zealot, is perhaps rooted in their inner and outer rejection of the methods of the Zealots. At this point there is a connection between their usage and that of Joseph. (→ 258).

B. ληστής in the NT.

1. In 2 C. 11:26 Paul mentions κίνδυνοι λῃστῶν among the many perils to which he was exposed in the discharge of his apostolic office. Here ληστής bears the ordinary sense attaching to it in antiquity (→ 257 f.). Paul is thinking of the bandits who in their thirst for the goods of others lie in wait for the traveller in lonely places.

2. In Mt. 21:13 and par. Jesus, when He cleanses the temple, raises against the priestly aristocracy responsible for its holiness [20] the charge that they have made that which God appointed an οἶκος προσευχῆς (Is. 56:7) [21] into a σπήλαιον λῃστῶν, a den to which robbers can return as needed and in which they have an indispensable retreat. The meaning may best be seen from the corresponding statement in Jn. 2:16: οἶκος ἐμπορίου. His anger is directed against the linking of divine worship and trade, which, in connection with the priestly aristocracy, He saw before Him in the buying and selling of sacrificial animals in the forecourt of the temple, and in such a form that the temple and its cult were made to serve the ends of personal enrichment and the satisfaction of cupidity. In terms of its basic meaning (→ 257) ληστής is here the right word for those who are censured. With the use of the phrase σπήλαιον λῃστῶν Jesus also quotes from Jer. 7:11 [22] and thus sets the temple and the priests under the declaration of judgment pronounced therein. Where the worship of God amounts to no more than ceremonial it not only will not prevent God's judgment but will bring it on (Jer. 7:8 ff.).

---

[16] We also find the principle שׁוּתַּף לִיסְטִים כְּלִיסְטִים (jSanh., 19b, 19: Jochanan ben Zakkai, c. 70 A.D.) which ranks the friend and associate of the Zealot with him. These far-reaching principles cast a serious light on the way in which Jesus made the fate of His disciples dependent on His own (cf. esp. Mt. 10:16 ff. and par.). Cf. also Tat. Or. Graec., 18, 1: ὁ τῷ ληστεύοντι συνδειπνήσας, κἂν μὴ ληστὴς αὐτὸς ᾖ, ... τιμωρίας μεταλαμβάνει [G. Bertram].

[17] Cf. terms like Protestants, Pietists etc.

[18] A. Schlatter also seems to assume this (Gesch. Isr., 264).

[19] *Ibid.*, 261 f.

[20] I.e., for respecting the fact that the temple as God's house is His property and stands under His will.

[21] In Mk. the quotation agrees with the LXX. Mt. leaves out the final phrase. There are slight variations in Lk.

[22] The phrase is also found in Jer. 12:9 A for σπήλαιον ὑαίνης LXX; cf. also the ἄλλος of Origen. Mas. 7:11: מְעָרַת פָּרִיצִים, → 257. For par. in Joseph. cf. Schl. Mt., 613.

3. In Lk. 10:30, 36 the λησταί could well be bandits (→ 257 f.), but they do not have to be. Since the Zealots had to sustain themselves as well as seeking to overthrow their enemies, it is quite possible that they are the λησταί of the story. Perhaps it is significant that the man who fell among thieves suffered injury to property and person, but did not lose his life. The parable makes it apparent that he was a Jew. We know that the Zealots took no more from their own countrymen than was necessary, unless there were other reasons (treachery etc.) for more extreme measures.[23] If the man in the story suffered physical hurt, it would be because he resisted. Since the Pharisees continually tried to get Jesus to adopt a clear practical attitude to the Zealot movement, cf. Mt. 22:15 ff. and par., it could well be that in His answer to the scribe's question about one's neighbour Jesus intentionally tells this story of the man who fell among λησταί, and of his experiences, in order to express the fact that He does not sanction the way in which the Zealots think they serve God.[24]

4. Similarly, ληστής in the parable of the Good Shepherd in Jn. 10:1 ff. may bear this meaning, though it is accompanied by a κλέπτης and could very well be taken literally in the context of the imagery, v. 1, 8. The λησταί here are all those, including the Zealots, who try to bring in God's kingdom without regard to the person of Jesus and His divine approval, and who thus bring the community into danger of error and destruction. The material par. in the Synoptic Gospels is to be found in Mt. 24:4 ff. and par.[25]

This interpretation is suggested by the Palestinian usage (Joseph., the Rabb.), which is repeated in the Gospels (with the exception of the quotation in Mt. 21:13 and par.). Yet there are also signs that the figure behind the Johannine writings had connections with Zelotism.[26] If so, it is understandable that he should preserve, in this form, a saying in which Jesus repudiates the movement.

5. There is an unmistakable reference of ληστής to Messianism in Mt. 26:55 and par. in the saying of Jesus to His captors: ὡς ἐπὶ ληστὴν ἐξήλθατε μετὰ μαχαιρῶν καὶ ξύλων συλλαβεῖν με. "He who rejects the royal claim of Jesus ranks Him with the leaders of Zealot bands."[27] While this action takes place at the instigation of Jewish leaders,[28] it is done through the Roman procurator. The setting is the Passover, the day for remembering the constitution of the people and the attainment of national freedom by the exodus from Egypt. The procurator actually allows the people to choose between the freedom fighter Barabbas and Jesus (Mt. 27:15 ff. and par.; Jn. 18:39 f.). The implied attempt to include Jesus in the Zealot movement and to stamp Him as a Zealot leader is given emphasis in

---

[23] BQ, 10, 2 reckons with the possibility, very rare in ordinary robbery, that the לִיסְטִים might take the victim's coat but give him another instead. Pious tradition forbade the seizure of an upper garment on the ground that it was indispensable at night, cf. Schl. Mt. on 5:40.

[24] That the λησταί of Lk. 10:30 ff. were Zealots is the view of K. Bornhäuser, *Studien zum Sondergut des Lk.* (1934), 69.

[25] Obviously, if this is the meaning of ληστής it explains only one aspect of the allegory, not the allegory as a whole.

[26] Cf. Schl. Gesch. d. erst. Chr., 65 f.

[27] Schl. Mt., 756, *ad loc.*

[28] The part of the Roman soldiers in the arrest in Jn. 18:3, 12, cf. the later attitude of Pilate in 18:28 ff., is at the instigation of Jewish leaders.

the texts by the description of Barabbas as a λῃστής in Jn. 18:40, a στασιαστής (→ n. 10) in Mk. 15:7 (cf. Lk. 23:19), and a δέσμιος ἐπίσημος in Mt. 27:16.

The text gives us some reason to suppose [29] that the first name of Barabbas [30] was also Jesus, and that this was intentionally suppressed. It was a sorry jest on the part of Pilate that he allowed the people to choose between Jesus Barabbas and Jesus, the son of Joseph, of Nazareth, both being presented as men of the same stamp, i.e., Zealot leaders. It is true that in the present form of the texts Barabbas is not expressly called a Zealot leader. Yet some versions of Jn. 19:40 call him ἀρχιλῃστής, i.e., *princeps latronum,* instead of λῃστής. [31] If the ἐπίσημος of Mt. 27:16 means leader on the model of Joseph.Bell., 2, 585, [32] we have a clear description of Barabbas as a leading Zealot, but this is not an assured interpretation.

When Jesus was crucified, and was thus punished as a political rebel against Rome, two others condemned as λῃσταί suffered with Him (Mt. 27:38 ff. and par.). The title on the cross marked Him as one of them, and indeed as one who aimed at the crown, as more or less all Zealot leaders had done from the time of the first Judas (→ 258, Mt. 27:37 and par.). His crucifixion as a λῃστής was at the request of His own people (Mt. 27:21 ff.), which decided against His Messianism and in favour of that of the Zealots, and which thus elected war against Rome and its own crucifixion [33] instead of the peace which the Messiah of God brings (cf. Lk. 19:42 with 19:38 and 2:14; → Χριστός). How far this decision affected the judgment of Judaism on Him is nowhere more clearly seen than when Celsus calls Jesus a λῃστής and thus seeks to dismiss Him as a false Messiah. [34]

Rengstorf

[29] Cf. Mt. 27:16 Θ λ sys. Cf. A. Deissmann, "Der Name Jesu," in *Mysterium Christi* (1931), 35 ff.

[30] This is how he is known, cf. Mk. 15:7: ὁ λεγόμενος Βαραββᾶς, and Deissmann, 35 f.

[31] Cf. Tischendorf's apparatus in his Editio octava critica maior of the NT (1869).

[32] With Pickl, 247.

[33] During the siege Titus set around Jerusalem a ring of crosses on which untold numbers met a painful end.

[34] Orig. Cels., III, 59 (I, 253, 24 ff., ed. Koetschau).

† λίβανος, † λιβανωτός

The use of incense was very widespread in the ancient world, both generally and cultically (in the latter case usually along with offerings, sometimes with sacrifices, and rarely as an independent offering).[1] The incense most commonly favoured came from the resin of various trees and bushes of the species boswellia in Arabia and on the Somali coast (also the East Indies).[2] This was a much sought after commodity.[3] λίβανος is occasionally used for the tree, but mostly for incense (also λιβανωτός),[4] and it is a Semitic loan word.[5] The LXX always has λίβανος for לְבוֹנָה (לְבֹנָה) (only at 1 Ch. 9:29 do we find λιβανωτός). It often uses it when there is no Mas. equivalent, cf. also λιβανωτός in 3 Macc. 5:2.[6] Philo has this in Spec. Leg., I, 175 and 275; Rer. Div. Her., 197 and 226, though λίβανος occurs in the quotation from Ex. 30:34 f. in Rer. Div. Her., 196 and 198. Joseph. uses λίβανος in, e.g., Ant., 3, 143 and λιβανωτός in 3, 256. Cf. also 1 Cl., 25, 2 λίβανος, Mart. Pol., 15, 2 λιβανωτός.

λίβανος κτλ. C. v. Orelli, Art. "Räuchern" in RE³, XVI (1905), 404-409; R. Zehnpfund, Art. "Weihrauch in d. Bibel," *ibid.*, XXI (1908), 54 f. (older bibl.); F. Pfister, Art. "Rauchopfer" in Pauly-W., 2nd. Ser., I (1920), 267-286; M. Löhr, *Das Räucheropfer im AT* (1927) = *Schriften d. Königsberger Gelehrten Gesellschaft, Geisteswissenschaftliche Klasse*, 4. Jahr, Heft 4; S. Eitrem, *Opferritus u. Voropfer d. Griechen u. Römer* (*Skrifter utgit av Videnskapsselskapet* ... II, *Hist.-Fil. Kl.* [1914], No. 1) (1915), Index, *s.v.* "Weihrauch."

1 Cf. the discussion in Pfister and the review in Löhr, 1-9. It may be doubted whether the cultic use grew out of the secular. Löhr points out that the Egyptian word for incense (*śntr*) denotes that which qualifies for dealings with deity.

2 I. Löw, *Die Flora d. Juden*, I, 1 (1926), 312 ff., IV (1934), Index, *s.v.* It is arguable whether it was cultivated in Palestine, cf. A. Bertholet, Art. "Weihrauch" in RGG², V, 1795; K. Galling, Art. "Harze" 4 in *Bibl. Reallexikon* (1937), 266.

3 Cf. Rev. 18:13; T. Reil, *Beiträge z. Kenntnis d. Gewerbes im hell. Ägypten*, Diss. Leipzig (1913), 146 f.; U. Wilcken, "Alexander d. Grosse u. d. hell. Wirtschaft" in Schmoller's *Jbch. f. Gesetzgebung, Verwaltung u. Volkswirtschaft im Deutschen Reiche*, 45 (1921), 408 f.; A. Schmidt, *Drogen u. Drogenhandel im Altertum* (1924).

4 Liddell-Scott, *s.v.* The pap. have both forms, cf. Preisigke Wört., II, 20; Moult.-Mill., *s.v.*; Mayser, II, 1 (1926), 32. λιβανωτός is more common in the inscr., cf. Ditt. Or. and Syll.³, *s.v.* The magic pap. have λίβανος, e.g., Preis. Zaub., I, 10 and 62; II, 13, 19 f.; IV, 1909 f.; XIII, 18; cf. Test. Sol. 6:10. Phryn., p. 187 (Lobeck) schematises the usage. The gender of λίβανος cannot be determined from the NT; elsewhere it is masc. or fem. Worth noting are the very many comp. with λίβανος, cf. Liddell-Scott. Bss. Apk., 195 f. rightly emphasises that χαλκολίβανος(ν) in Rev. 1:15; 2:18 has nothing to do with λίβανος = "incense"; cf. also Zn. Apk., 199, n. 41.

5 Cf. Heb. לְבוֹנָה; H. Lewy, *Die semitischen Fremdwörter im Gr.* (1895), 44 f.; Löhr, 2, n. 1.

6 On the offering of incense in the OT, cf. Löhr, 10 ff. and v. Orelli; on incense cf. also Zehnpfund.

In the NT λίβανος is used for incense not only in Rev. 18:13 (→ n. 3) but also in Mt. 2:11, where, with gold [7] and myrrh [8] it is one of the costly gifts [9] brought by the wise men [10] to the child in the manger to honour and recognise Him as the King of the Jews. [11]

λιβανωτός occurs in the NT at Rev. 8:3, 5 in a sense not attested elsewhere, namely, "censer." In 8:3 the divine sees an angel with a golden λιβανωτός in his hands coming to the heavenly altar (θυσιαστήριον, → III, 182 f.), where much incense (θυμιάματα πολλά) is given him ἵνα δώσει ταῖς προσευχαῖς τῶν ἁγίων κτλ. [12] Then in 8:5 the angel fills the λιβανωτός with fire from the altar and casts it on the earth as a sign of the divine wrath.

Usually the censer for glowing coals, on which the incense was laid for burning, is called θυμιατήριον. [13] The LXX uses this for מִקְטֶרֶת, which occurs only at 2 Ch. 26:19; Ez. 8:11 and which denotes a vessel or pan for incense. [14] θυμιατήριον is also used in this sense in 4 Macc. 7:11. The true word for the censer is מַחְתָּה which the LXX renders θυΐσκη and πυρεῖον. In the NT θυμιατήριον occurs only at Hb. 9:4, where it may very suitably be translated altar of incense. [15]

Michaelis

---

[7] Is. 60:6 must have had some influence (cf. also ψ 71:15).

[8] ψ 44:8 (so Clemen, 195) is less normative than esp. Cant. 3:6 (cf. Kl. Mt., *ad loc.*) and Σιρ. 24:15, where frankincense and myrrh are combined (also, e.g., Diod. S., II, 49, 2; Athen., III, 59 [101c]; Ditt. Or., 214, 58). Cf. A. Deissmann, "Weihrauch u. Myrrhen," ThBl, 1 (1922), 13.

[9] The frankincense must have been particularly expensive, since oriental spices were attainable by the poor, and incense was "the luxury of the common man," cf. Pfister, 280.

[10] The gifts tell us nothing very specific about the native country of the magi, → n. 2 and Zn. Mt.[4], 91, n. 70.

[11] On the fulfilment of the Jewish expectation that the Gentiles would bring gifts to the Messiah, cf. ψ 71:10 f. and Str.-B., *ad loc.* The character of the gifts is thus the impressive thing, not the possible use, e.g., of incense. On the later symbolical interpretation, cf. Kl. Mt., *ad loc.*; Zn. Mt.[4], 103, n. 93; Bengel, *ad loc.*

[12] On the dat. commodi ταῖς προσευχαῖς in 8:4 cf. Bl.-Debr.[6] § 188, 1. Incense is a sweet-smelling accompaniment and purification of the prayers, acc. to the paraphrase of Had. Apk. The idea is rather different from that of 5:8 (Bss. Apk., 293, n. 3). On the relation between incense and prayer cf. also E. Lohmeyer, "Vom göttlichen Wohlgeruch" in SAH (1919), 9. Abh. and → II, 793. To say that the Mandaeans regarded incense as a kind of divine being ascending to heaven — so Bertholet with ref. to R. Reitzenstein, ARW, 27 (1929), 274 — is to say too much.

[13] On other expressions, inc. λιβανωτίς and λιβανωτρίς, cf. A. Hug, Art. "Thymiaterion" in Pauly-W., 2nd Ser., VI (1936), 707 and Liddell-Scott, *s.v.*

[14] Cf. v. Orelli, 409.

[15] Cf. Rgg. Hb.[2, 3], 241 ff., n. 73 and O. Michel, *Hb.* (1936), 105, who definitely takes the view that the ref. is to the censer, though his examples from Jos. demand further investigation (as distinct from S. Bar. 6:7, which refers to a censer). In Lk. 1:11 the altar of incense is the θυσιαστήριον τοῦ θυμιάματος, as usually in the LXX. It may be added that in the NT θυμίαμα also occurs in Lk. 1:10 f.; Rev. 5:8; 8:3 f.; 18:13, and θυμιάω in Lk. 1:9.

† Λιβερτῖνοι

In Ac. 6:9, in a general characterisation of the work of Stephen, we read: ἀνέστησαν δέ τινες τῶν ἐκ τῆς συναγωγῆς τῆς λεγομένης Λιβερτίνων[1] καὶ Κυρηναίων καὶ Ἀλεξανδρέων καὶ τῶν ἀπὸ Κιλικίας καὶ Ἀσίας συζητοῦντες τῷ Στεφάνῳ.

The opponents of Stephen are from different groups, though exegetes are not agreed how many.[2] Yet there is no real reason for dissension. The different names are plainly divided into two groups by the twofold τῶν. The second group consists of men, obviously Jews, from Cilicia and Asia. In what way they constitute a separate group we are not told, but one can guess on the analogy of the first group. This is a synagogal union to which belong the Libertines, Cyrenians and Alexandrians. That this union possessed a building is possible and even probable. Indeed, there is much to support the view that a Gk. inscr. of a certain Theodotus, son of Vettenos, which was found in Jerusalem in 1913/4 by R. Weill, refers to this synagogue.[3] But here, as again in Ac. 9:2, the primary thought is that of a religious union to which the opponents of Stephen belong.[4] The point to be emphasised is not that they came from the building but that this union was the true seat of the attack which was later supported by those from Cilicia and Asia. To this union belong the Cyrenians and Alexandrians, i.e., Hellenistic Jews from these places now settled in Jerusalem, and along with them the

Λιβερτῖνοι. [1] Already T. Beza (in the Lat. NT[4] of R. Stephanus in 1556), and later Wettstein, *ad loc.*, then more recently F. Blass (*Philology of the Gospels* [1898], 69 f.), argue that Λιβυστίνων is the original, and they refer this to Libyans, as in the Armenian Vulgate. But these probably come from 2:10, and are usually Λιβυστικοί. Cf. Jackson-Lake, III, 58 (1926), *ad loc.* The reading τῶν λεγομένων for τῆς λεγομένης is found in Tisch. NT on the basis of ℵ, A and other witnesses, but the attestation is poor and it is to be rejected also on material grounds. The name of the συναγωγή had to be given but the freedmen were so in fact and were not "so-called" freedmen.

[2] Pr. Ag., 37 thinks there was a single synagogue which included all those mentioned, as does also Holtzmann NT, I, 357 f. H. Lietzmann seems to assume 5 different synagogues, cf. ZNW, 20 (1921), 172, so too B. Weiss, *Das NT*, III[2] (1902), 64. H. H. Wendt, *Ag.*[9] (1913), 135 and esp. Zn. Ag., 238 f. decide for two. Schürer, II[4], 87 vacillates between 1 and 5, but inclines to 5 (502 f., n. 7). For older exegesis cf. J. Patrick, Art. "Libertines" in Hastings DB, III. On the synagogues in Jerusalem cf. also Str.-B., II, 266.

[3] Cf. on this L. H. Vincent, *Rev. Bibl.*, 30 (1921), 247-277; also H. Lietzmann, ZNW, 20 (1921), 171 ff.; Deissmann LO, 378-380, with good bibl. The French scholars who first found and published the inscr. believe that the synagogue mentioned by Theodotus is that of Ac. 6:9 (R. Weill, T. Reinach, Clermont-Ganneau and L. H. Vincent). Deissmann is sceptical. But it is highly probable that Vettenos, the father of Theodotus, was a Roman freedman, and it is fairly certain that the inscr. is prior to 70 A.D. We cannot be sure that the synagogue of Alexandrians dwelling in Jerusalem, which is incidentally mentioned in TMeg., 3, 6 (p. 224, 26, Zuckermandel), has anything to do with that of Theodotus and finally with that of Ac. 6:9. Cf. Schürer, II[4], 87.

[4] Cf. Zn. Ag., *ad loc.*; Schürer, II[4], 504; III[4], 81 f. The transfer of the term to the place of assembly does, of course, govern NT usage.

Libertines.[5] This word loaned from Roman law[6] denotes one-time slaves who had gained their freedom, and their children.[7] There were freedmen everywhere. But since the word is mentioned along with the Cyrenians and Alexandrians, it must have a precise geographical reference. One can only think of descendants of the great numbers of prisoners of war whom Pompey had taken to Rome and who formed a great part of the Jewish population in Rome.[8] The text gives no support for thinking of one-time imperial slaves on the ground that membership of Καίσαρος οἰκία (Phil. 4:22) might foster a community sense which would not be present in the freedmen of private individuals.[9] This theory also disregards the point that the Libertines did not form their own congregation, but united with Egyptian Hellenists.

The account in Ac. which tells us that the first Christian persecution started with militant opposition to the new movement on the part of Hellenistic groups settled in Jerusalem (Ac. 8:1 ff.) is most instructive and wholly credible. For it agrees with other evidence of the divisive attitude of Hellenistic Judaism, and also with what we know of its ideal of piety.[10]

Strathmann

---

[5] Though the grouping is unusual, this does not justify conjectures which deviate from the text; → n. 1.

[6] Like κῆνσος, κολωνία, σπεκουλάτωρ etc., cf. Bl.-Debr. § 5, 1. For λιβερτῖνος the only example from the inscr. in Liddell-Scott is IG, XIV, 1781.

[7] For the legal position and development of the *libertini*, cf. the art. "Libertini" by A. Steinwenter in Pauly-W., XIII (1927), 104 ff.

[8] Cf. Philo Leg. Gai., 155: Ῥωμαῖοι (the Roman Jews) δὲ ἦσαν οἱ πλείους ἀπελευθερωθέντες· αἰχμάλωτοι γὰρ ἀχθέντες εἰς Ἰταλίαν ὑπὸ τῶν κτησαμένων ἠλευθερώθησαν, οὐδὲν τῶν πατρίων παραχαράξαι βιασθέντες. On this cf. Schürer, III⁴, 127 f. On the strength of the Roman Jews, cf. Jos. Ant., 17, 300; 18, 84; Bell., 2, 80; Tac. Ann., II, 85. It is possible that the Roman synagogues of the Augustesians, Agrippesians and Volumnesians, attested on the inscr., were recruited from these freedmen; cf. Schürer, III⁴, 82 [Kittel].

[9] Deissmann LO, 380, following E. Bormann, *Wiener Studien*, 34 (1912), 363 ff. Cf. also N. Müller-N. Bees, *Die Inschriften d. jüd. Katakombe am Monte Verde zu Rom* (1919), 98 f.

[10] Cf. H. Strathmann, *Geschichte der früh-christl. Askese*, I (1914), 107 ff.

† λιθάζω, † καταλιθάζω, † λιθοβολέω

As regards the origin, history, and legal and religious evaluation of stoning, many questions arise.[1] There is ref. to it in the earliest attestation of class. antiquity, esp. among the Gks. Nor is it merely a violent expression of aroused passion, but an ordered legal instrument. It is significant that in the related decision and execution there is almost always total action. Stoning is one of the punishments carried out by the group as a whole (cf. par. acts in ancient German law).[2] The malefactor, in a dramatic form of outlawing, is chased out of the community. It is open to question whether death was necessarily intended.[3] "Throwing stones ... expresses in a tangible way, almost as a primitive reflex action, the breaking of all fellowship."[4] In the OT stoning is one of the capital sentences laid down by the Law.[5]

Except when phrases like λίθους βάλλειν are preferred, λιθάζειν, λιθοβολεῖν, λεύειν, καταλεύειν are the usual tt. in non-biblical Gk.[6] The LXX has λιθάζειν only at 2 Βασ. 16:6, 13 (contempt by throwing stones). Elsewhere it uses λιθοβολεῖν (καταλιθοβολεῖν, Ex. 17:4; Nu. 14:10). Philo has καταλεύειν,[7] Joseph. λεύειν, Ant., 17, 216; Ap., 2, 206; often καταλεύειν, e.g., Ant., 3, 307; 4, 12; καταλιθοῦν, 4, 282, also paraphrases.[8]

In the Synoptic Gospels λιθοβολεῖν is found as *species atrox* of killing in Mt. 21:35,[9] cf. also 23:37 and par., and καταλιθάζειν (the only instance) at Lk. 20:6.[10] In Jn. 10:31-33; 11:8 λιθάζειν is used for attempts on the part of the

---

λιθάζω κτλ. [1] For basic material cf. R. Hirzel, "D. Strafe d. Steinigung" in ASG 27, 7 (1909), 222-266; K. Latte, Art. "Steinigung" in Pauly-W., 2nd Ser. III (1929), 2294 f.; J. Pfaff, Art. "Lapidatio" in Pauly-W., XII, 1 (1924), 775 f.

[2] Hirzel, 238 (with instances).

[3] The thesis of Hirzel that the basic aim was to chase out rather than to kill the offender is accepted by Latte, but doubt is briefly expressed by R. Wünsch, ARW, 14 (1911), 560 and E. König, RE³, XXIV (1913), 529. If death is in view, this is not so much against the demonistic background of locally banishing the souls or spirits of malefactors by thickly covering their corpses (A. Bertholet, Art. "Steinigung" in RGG², V, 781) but rather as a typical instance of remote killing so as not to come in direct touch with the victim. In S. Nu., 7 on 5:12 it is mentioned that if a rabbi was excommunicated and died in excommunication, the court should stone his coffin, which could be done by placing a stone on it (bMQ, 15a) [Kuhn]. Cf. Str.-B., I, 696, 793; IV, 309 f., 320.

[4] Latte, 2295.

[5] Cf. E. König, Art. "Steinigung bei d. Hebräern" in RE³, XVIII (1906), 792-794. Sanh., 6, 1 ff. is important. Hirzel also deals with Judaism, but his treatment suffers from his dependence on older works (esp. J. D. Michaelis, *Mosaisches Recht,* V [1774], who himself followed his father C. B. Michaelis, *De iudiciis poenisque capitalibus in Sacra Scriptura commemoratis* [1749]).

[6] Cf. Liddell-Scott, *s.v.*

[7] Cf. Leisegang, *s.v.,* and esp. Vit. Mos., II, 202.

[8] On the avoiding of λιθοβολεῖν cf. Schl. Mt., 628; also Schl. J., 242 on 10:31.

[9] Kl. Mt., *ad loc.*; B. Weiss, Mt.[10] (1910), 368.

[10] Kl. Lk. and Hck. Lk., *ad loc.*

Jews to stone Jesus as a blasphemer, cf. also 8:59.[11] In 8:5, in the story of the woman taken in adultery, λιθοβολεῖσθαι 𝔎 would be Synoptic (D etc. have λιθάζειν).[12] In Ac. 5:26 the ref. may be simply to throwing stones (λιθάζειν),[13] but stoning is meant in 14:5 (λιθοβολεῖν).[14] The stoning of Paul in 14:9 (λιθάζειν, cf. 2 C. 11:25 : ἅπαξ ἐλιθάσθην) was without a trial,[15] but this is doubtful in the case of Stephen in 7:58 f. (λιθοβολεῖν).[16] Cf. also Hb. 11:37 (λιθάζειν), 12:20 (λιθοβολεῖν, quotation from Ex. 19:13). Cf. 1 Cl., 5, 6; 45, 4; Ev. Pt., 11, 48 (λιθάζειν).

Michaelis

λίθος, † λίθινος

(→ γωνία [ἀκρογωνιαῖος, κεφαλὴ γωνίας], πέτρα).

Contents : A. λίθος in the Literal Sense. B. Living Stones. C. Christ as λίθος : 1. The Verses ; 2. The Reference of OT λίθος-statements to the Messiah in Later Judaism ; 3. Christ the Stone : a. Jesus as the Key Stone and Foundation Stone of the True Temple of God ; b. The Stone which Crushes and the Stone of Offence ; c. The Significance of Christ the Stone for Salvation and Perdition ; d. The Dispenser of Living Water ; e. Christ the Stone in Post-NT Writings. D. Christians as Living Stones.

In the NT (and LXX), as in the *koine*, λίθος is always masc.[1]

The Aram. equivalent is either אַבְנָא (stone, weight) or כֵּיפָא (stone, rock).[2] The saying of the Baptist in Mt. 3:9 supports אַבְנָא if there is a play on the words בְּנַיָּא — אַבְנַיָּא, though this is not very likely (→ 270). כֵּיפָא rests on 1. Mt. 3:9 and Mk. 15:46 etc., where the meaning of λίθος is rock (→ 271), and 2. on the fact that sy^s c (also sy^pal for the Gospels) always[3] have כיפא (כאפא) for λίθος (even at Mt. 3:9).

---

[11] Schl. J., 221; Zn. J.[5, 6], 468; Str.-B., II, 527, 541 f.; Moulton, 210. Cf. Unknown Gospel, lines 23 f.

[12] Bau. J., *ad loc.*; Str.-B., II, 520; Zn. J., *ad loc.* Cf. also Jn. 8:7.

[13] Zn. Ag., *ad loc.*

[14] Though cf. Zn. Ag., *ad loc.*

[15] Pr. Ag., *ad loc.* is too sceptical.

[16] Str.-B., II, 685; Zn. Ag., *ad loc.*; K. Bornhäuser, *Studien z. Ag.* (1934), and on this ThLBl, 55 (1934), 291 ff. On cries at stoning, cf. Hirzel, 231.

λίθος. A. Jeremias, *Babylonisches im NT* (1905), 79 f.; A. Schlatter, "Das AT in d. johann. Apk.," BFTh, 16, 6 (1912), 32 f., 49; R. Harris, *Testimonies* (1916), I, 18 f., 26 ff.; II, 59 ff., 137, 139; Joh. Jeremias, *Der Gottesberg* (1919), 146; Joach. Jeremias, *Golgotha* (1926), 51 ff., 77 ff.; Κεφαλὴ γωνίας — 'Ακρογωνιαῖος, ZNW, 29 (1930), 264-280; "Jesus als Weltvollender," BFTh, 33, 4 (1930), 48-52; H. Schlier, "Christus u. d. Kirche im Eph.," *Beiträge z. historischen Theol.*, 6 (1930), 47, 49, n. 1; H. J. Cadbury in Jackson-Lake, I, 5 (1933), 373 ff.; H. Schmidt, *Der heilige Fels in Jerusalem* (1933); "Das vierte Nachtgesicht des Propheten Sach.," ZAW, NF, 13 (1936), 48 ff.

[1] Moult.-Mill., 375b. The fem. occurs 5 times in Philo.

[2] On כֵּיפָא = rock cf. Mt. 16:18.

[3] Only as a vl. do we find אבנא. The MSS B C of the Pal. Syr. lectionary have for λίθος at Mt. 21:42 (= ψ 117:22) אבנא (A. S. Lewis-M. D. Gibson, *The Pal. Syriac Lectionary of the Gospels* [1899], 154) and כיפא (*ibid.*, 89), while MS A has כיפא (154) or כאפא (89) twice. For the sake of completeness it might be mentioned that sy^s c have *raḥja daḥmara* (grind-stone) for λίθος μυλικός at Lk. 17:2. Cf. A. Dell, ZNW (1914), 19.

A. λίθος in the Literal Sense.

ὁ λίθος in the NT means a. "stone," whether hewn or not, more precisely defined as "millstone" (Lk. 17:2; Rev. 18:21),[4] or precious stone (Rev. 4:3; 15:6 vl.; 17:4; 18:12, 16; 21:11, 19);[5] b. at Mt. 3:9 (par. Lk. 3:8) very probably "rock" (→ 271), cf. Mk. 15:46; 16:3 f.; Mt. 27:60, 66; 28:2; Lk. 24:2; Jn. 20:1; Ev. Pt., 32 for the unhewn block of stone which was rolled before the tomb of Jesus;[6] also c. "stone image" at Ac. 17:29 and Dg., 2, 2.

Stone was regarded as the most enduring writing material, hence the stone tables of the Mosaic Law (2 C. 3:3, 7; Barn., 4, 7; cf. Ex. 24:12; 31:18; 34:1, 4). Because of their weight rolling stones and blocks were used for security at the low entrance to sepulchres (Jn. 11:38 f., 41 and the verses mentioned → *supra*).[7] Because stone vessels (as distinct from earthen) were not susceptible to Levitical impurity,[8] they were used for water employed for ritual purposes (Jn. 2:6).

The stone is an image of what is dead and of what cannot be enjoyed, so that it is often brought into contrast with God (Ac. 17:29),[9] man (Mt. 3:9, par. Lk. 3:8; Lk. 19:40), flesh (2 C. 3:3),[10] or bread (Mt. 4:3, par. Lk. 4:3; Mt. 7:9, par. Lk. 11:11 vl.). The precious stone is a symbol of luxury and wealth, and the triad gold,[11] precious stones and pearls (Rev. 17:4; 18:12, 16, cf. 21:11-21) are a superlative expression of what is costly on earth. The walls of the future Jerusalem will be built of precious stones (Rev. 21:18-20, on the basis of Is. 54:11 f., Tob. 13:17). The brightness of precious stones is an image of the brilliant radiance and the purity of God (Rev. 4:3), of the sacred city of God (21:11), and of angels (15:6 vl.).

The meaning of the important agraphon in P. Oxy., I, 1 is debated: ἔγει[ρ]ον τὸν λίθο[ν], κἀκεῖ εὑρήσεις με· | σχίσον τὸ ξύλον, κἀγὼ ἐκεῖ εἰμι. Either the proverb is to be taken pantheistically: Christ may be found in wood and stone, so that the doctrine of His ubiquity is pushed to the extreme point of pan-Christism,[12] or, in antithetical allusion to Qoh. 10:9, we have a saying about the blessing of the work before us, all work — even the heavy toil of those who work with wood and stone — being sanctified by the presence of Christ, so that it is service of God.[13] If the second inter-

[4] λίθος μυλικός (Lk. 17:2) or μύλινος (Rev. 18:21) is the upper stone of the mill worked by an animal.

[5] On the other hand the λίθοι τίμιοι of 1 C. 3:12 can hardly be precious stones but are probably marble blocks like the λίθοι καλοί of Lk. 21:5 (cf. also 3 Βασ. 6:1a; 7:46 ff.) (Bl.-Debr.[6], IV, A. Deissmann, *Paulus*[2] [1925], 244-247, as against E. Schwartz, GGA, 173 [1911], 663 f.).

[6] It can hardly be a round stone, since Mk. 15:46 and Mt. 27:60 have no art., and in Mt. 28:2 the angel sits on the stone, which would not be possible if it were round, cf. G. Dalman, *Orte u. Wege Jesu*[3] (1924), 395 f., also 391 f.

[7] Cf. Str.-B., I, 1051; Dalman, *loc. cit.*

[8] Str.-B., II, 405 ff.

[9] This antithesis has a solid place in the Jewish battle against pagan worship, Dt. 4:28; 28:36, 64; 29:16; LXX 4 Βασ. 19:18, par. Is. 37:19; Jer. 2:27; 3:9; Ez. 20:32; Da. 5:23; Wis. 13:10; Philo Vit. Cont., 7; Sib. Fr., 3; also early Christian writings, Rev. 9:20; Dg., 2, 2 f.; 7, 9; 2 Cl., 1, 6.

[10] Cf. the stony heart of Job 41:16; Ez. 11:19; 36:26; Barn., 6, 14.

[11] Plus silver, Rev. 18:12.

[12] T. Zahn, ThLBl, 18 (1897), 428. This view is taken by Reitzenstein, Poim. (1904), 239 f.; ZNW, 6 (1905), 203; GGA, 183 (1921), 165-170. Also A. Resch, *Agrapha*[2] = TU, NF, 15, 3-4 (1906), 69; Hennecke[2], 37; A. Oepke, → II, 334, n. 3.

[13] A. Harnack, *Über d. jüngst entdeckten Sprüche Jesu* (1897); J. Leipoldt, *Die ersten heidenchristlichen Gemeinden* (1916), 17; H. G. E. White, *The Sayings of Jesus from Oxyrhynchus* (1920), LXIII; J. Leipoldt, *Der Gottesdienst d. ältesten Kirche* (1937), 19 f.

pretation is correct, and Mt. 18:20 seems to support it, the saying is worth noting, since the Gospels do not contain any sayings of Jesus about everyday work.

B. Living Stones.

1. Lk. 19:40 refers to stones crying out: λέγω ὑμῖν, ἐὰν οὗτοι σιωπήσουσιν, οἱ λίθοι κράξουσιν. The passage is usually taken to imply songs of praise raised by the stones. If men deny adoration to Jesus, inorganic nature will render it (→ III, 901). This interpretation is possible. But biblical usage points in a different direction. For the Bible often speaks of the accusing cry of lifeless objects invoking divine retribution. Thus the blood of the murdered Abel cries out (Gn. 4:10; Hb. 12:24). So does the plundered field (Job 31:38). So does the withheld reward of workers (Jm. 5:4).[14] So does the stone as an involuntary witness of wrong and violence, Hab. 2:11: λίθος ἐκ τοίχου βοήσεται. Rabb. lit. often has references in this sense to the accusing cry of the stone (on the basis of Hab. 2:11).[15] Construed along these lines Lk. 19:40 says that if my disciples were to withhold their acclamation, the stones by the wayside would cry out and accuse them.[16]

2. A singular saying is that of the Baptist in Mt. 3:9 = Lk. 3:8: λέγω γὰρ ὑμῖν ὅτι δύναται ὁ θεὸς ἐκ τῶν λίθων τούτων ἐγεῖραι τέκνα τῷ Ἀβραάμ. In interpretation it is not enough to suggest a play on words in the original Aram. (→ 268), or to recall that proverbially the stone is the most worthless of all things in Palestine.[17] For these and similar explanations evade the main difficulty, namely, that while in LXX and NT (not secular) Gk. the trans. ἐγείρειν with personal obj. can often mean "to cause to appear, to arise in history" (→ II, 334), the Semitism ἐγείρειν ἔκ τινος means "to cause to be born,"[18] "to cause to come forth as progeny."[19] Thus a striking figure is intentionally used: God can give

[14] Related, though different, is Jos. Bell., 1, 197: Antipater tears his garment and points to his scars in proof of his loyalty: κεκραγέναι γὰρ τὸ σῶμα σιωπῶντος. The motif here is that of dumb witness, not of a cry for vengeance.

[15] Str.-B., II, 253. Apocal. found in the cry of stones a sign of the end: *de ligno sanguis stillabit et lapis dabit vocem suam* (4 Esr. 5:5); καὶ ἔδωκε (Jonas) τέρας ἐπὶ Ἰερουσαλὴμ καὶ ὅλην τὴν γῆν· ὅτε ἴδωσι λίθον βοῶντα οἰκτρῶς ἐγγίζει τὸ τέλος (Prophetarum Vitae Fabulosae, 31, 13 ff. par. 84, 12 ff., 101, 1 f., ed. T. Schermann [1907]). Here we have the motif of the prodigy which kindles terror, cf. 4 Esr. 5:7: "The sea of Sodom will cry at night with a voice which many will not understand but all will hear."

[16] Schl. Lk., 409 f. also takes this to be an accusation, though on the basis of the fut. in Lk. 19:40 and the context of 19:43 f. he thinks it is a prophecy. If Jewish resistance makes confession of Jesus impossible, instead the stones of overthrown Jerusalem will bear witness that Christ was rejected. But does not this interpretation of ἐὰν οὗτοι σιωπήσουσιν go too far afield from the concrete situation of the entry into Jerusalem?

[17] L. Haefeli, *Sprichwörter u. Redensarten aus d. Zeit Christi* (1934), 12. Cf. 1 K. 10:27: "And the king made silver as plentiful as stones in Jerusalem."

[18] P. Joüon, *L'Évangile de Notre-Seigneur Jésus-Christ* = *Verbum Salutis*, V (1930), 12.

[19] Tanch. לך לך 5, p. 32a, Buber: Eka r. on 5:3. Schl. Mt., 74 refers to these passages. In both we find העמיד מן (= ἐγείρειν ἐκ τινος) = "to cause to go forth from someone (as descendant)." Cf. also Dt. 18:15 נָבִיא מִקִּרְבְּךָ מֵאַחֶיךָ כָּמֹנִי יָקִים לְךָ (LXX προφήτην ἐκ τῶν ἀδελφῶν σου ὡς ἐμὲ ἀναστήσει σοι); 18:18; Ac. 3:22; 7:37; 2 Βασ. 7:12 ἀναστήσω τὸ σπέρμα σου μετὰ σέ, ὃς ἔσται ἐκ τῆς κοιλίας σου. Esp. cf. Ac. 13:23 vl. τούτου (David) ὁ θεὸς ἀπὸ τοῦ σπέρματος κατ' ἐπαγγελίαν ἤγαγεν (C D pm ἤγειρε) τῷ Ἰσραὴλ σωτῆρα Ἰησοῦν. In all these verses the ἐκ (or ἀπό) shows that the ref. is to physical descent.

stones the power to bring forth men.[20] The strange image of stones which bring forth men is based on Is. 51:1-2, where Abraham is compared with a rock, and his descendants with stones hewn out of the rock.

Is. 51:1-2 runs as follows: "Look unto the rock whence ye are hewn, and to the hole of the well whence ye are digged. Look unto Abraham your father, and unto Sarah that bare you." Contemporary exegesis found in the comparison of Abraham's children with stones hewn from the rock and material dug from the pit[21] a ref. to the wonderful birth of Isaac. This understanding of Is. 51:1 f. underlies the saying of the Baptist in Mt. 3:9. As God then caused the children of Abraham to spring up miraculously out of the rock Abraham, so He can now in the same way call children of Abraham to life. If this is correct, then it is evident 1. that the Gk. λίθος corresponds to an Aram. כֵּיפָא (→ 268)[22] in the sense of rock; 2. that the stones are mentioned, not because they are worthless, but because they are lifeless (they cannot pass on life); and 3. that the image in Mt. 3:9 (par. Lk. 3:8) has nothing whatever to do with mythical motifs (belief in mother earth,[23] Deucalion and Pyrrha), but derives directly from a scriptural saying (Is. 51:1 f.).

The figure of the rock which brings forth children rejects with cutting severity the Jewish dogma that salvation depends on pure lineage.[24] If those who are children of Abraham by racial descent refuse to repent, then God can again cause children of Abraham to come forth from the rock. That is to say, He can arouse spiritual life in the spiritually dead, with perhaps a hint of the transfer of the promise to the Gentiles.

3. On the λίθοι ζῶντες of 1 Pt. 2:5 → 279.

C. Christ as λίθος

1. The Verses.

In a series of verses in the NT Christ is compared with a stone (λίθος): Mk. 12:10 par. Mt. 21:42 and Lk. 20:17 (= ψ 117:22); Lk. 20:18 par. Mt. 21:44 vl. (cf. Da. 2:34 f., 44 f.); Ac. 4:11 (ψ 117:22); R. 9:32 f. (Is. 8:14 combined with 28:16); 1 Pt. 2:4-8 (ψ 117:22; Is. 28:16; 8:14). Also materially relevant are 1 C. 10:4c (ἡ πέτρα δὲ ἦν ὁ Χριστός), Eph. 2:20 (ὄντος ἀκρογωνιαίου αὐτοῦ Χριστοῦ Ἰησοῦ) and the call of the Saviour in Jn. 7:37 ff. when He makes use of the idea of the holy rock which dispenses the water of life — an idea firmly associated with the feast of the tabernacles. Perhaps the concept of the rock is also present in Lk. 2:34 (οὗτος κεῖται εἰς πτῶσιν καὶ ἀνάστασιν πολλῶν ἐν τῷ Ἰσραήλ) with its suggestion of either stumbling or being established. Certainly the twofold effect which is ascribed to Christ as the stone bringing salvation or destruction in R. 9:33 and 1 Pt. 2:4-8 strongly suggests an allusion to Is. 8:14 in

---

20 Schl. Mt., 74.

21 Tg. Is. 51:1 (Vilna, 1893): "Note that you are hewn like a stone out of the rock and dug like rubbish out of an empty well."

22 צוּר would be possible (Tg. Is. 51:1 = Is. 51:1), but if so we should expect πέτρα (not λίθος) in Mt. 3:9.

23 L. Köhler, ZNW, 9 (1908), 77-80; W. Dittmar, *ibid.*, 341-344.

24 On this dogma cf. Joach. Jeremias, *Jerusalem zur Zeit Jesu*, II B (1937), 172 ff.

Lk. 2:34. Finally, we should mention two references to a verse already mentioned, namely, Is. 28:16. Thus Is. 28:16b is quoted in R. 10:11 (πᾶς ὁ πιστεύων ἐπ' αὐτῷ οὐ καταισχυνθήσεται), though there is no sign of any use of the image in 28:16a. The second reference is in 1 Tm. 1:16 (πρὸς ὑποτύπωσιν τῶν μελλόντων πιστεύειν ἐπ' αὐτῷ εἰς ζωὴν αἰώνιον); the construction πιστεύειν with ἐπί and the dative to denote the one in whom faith is fixed is unusual, and occurs only three other times in the NT (R. 9:33; 10:11; 1 Pt. 2:6). In each of these three cases it occurs in quotation of Is. 28:16b, [25] so that we may assume that 1 Tm. 1:16 is also influenced by this verse. But in both R. 10:11 and 1 Tm. 1:16 the concrete image of the stone has faded from view.

This is even more true of Rev. 5:6, where it is said of the → ἀρνίον that it had "seven eyes, which are the seven spirits of God sent forth into all the earth." This is a plain allusion to Zech. 4:10 (3:9). If the image of the stone is set aside in Rev., it is worth noting that the passage presupposes a Messianic interpretation of Zech. 4:10 [26] such as is found in later Judaism, → 273.

2. The Reference of the OT λίθος-statements to the Messiah in Later Judaism.

The christological rock (or stone) passages of the NT mentioned under 1. rest almost entirely on OT verses: Ps. 118:22; Is. 28:16; Da. 2:34 f., 44 f.; Ex. 17:6 and Nu. 20:7 ff. (Zech. 4:10). How these verses came to be referred to Christ is obvious when we see that many of them were already associated with the Messiah in later Judaism.

The oldest example of Messianic interpretation of an OT stone statement is to be found in the LXX addition ἐπ' αὐτῷ to Is. 28:16 (B: ὁ πιστεύων οὐ μὴ καταισχυνθῇ; A min: ὁ πιστεύων ἐπ' αὐτῷ οὐ μὴ καταισχυνθῇ). That this addition is prior to the NT may be presumed from the fact that it is quoted in R. 9:33; 10:11 and 1 Pt. 2:6. [27] It essentially alters the sense of Is. 28:16 to the degree that the stone now becomes a ground of assurance or the object of faith, and this at least suggests a personal understanding. The stone is Messianically interpreted in the Tg. with its paraphrase: "Behold, I set in Sion a king, a mighty king, mighty and terrible, whom I will uphold and strengthen; the prophet says: And the righteous in whom is confidence shall not tremble when affliction comes." [28]

In Rabb. lit. there are many instances of the reference of the stone of Da. 2:34 ff. to the Messiah. [29] Nu. r., 13, 14 on 7:13: "Whence (comes it that the Messiah will reign)

---

[25] We might finally refer to a late attested variant of Mt. 27:42 (ℵ). Lk. 24:25 (πιστεύειν ἐπὶ πᾶσιν οἷς ἐλάλησαν οἱ προφῆται) is hardly relevant here. The fact that ἐπί with the dat. refers to a thing, not a person, shows that ἐπί denotes here the motive rather than the object of faith. The object of faith is God who fulfils His promises, cf. A. Schlatter, *Der Glaube im NT*[4] (1927), 591 f.

[26] Schlatter, 49.

[27] *Ibid.*, 591; Wnd. Pt. on 1 Pt. 2:7 f. Cf. also 3 Macc. 2:7 τοὺς δὲ ἐμπιστεύσαντας ἐπὶ σοί (God). But cf. H. Strathmann, *Theologie der Gegenwart*, 29 (1935), 171, n. 3: "The ἐπ' αὐτῷ may have penetrated (into the LXX) from R. 9:33; 1 Pt. 2:6." If so, one must assume (with P. Feine-J. Behm, *Einl. in das NT*[8] [1936], 239 f. etc.) the direct literary dependence of 1 Pt. on R. (as against Harris, I, 29; Wnd. Pt. on 1 Pt. 2:7 f. and Exc. before 1 Pt. 2:13).

[28] Ed. Vilna (1893).

[29] Dalman WJ, I, 197, n. 1; Schlatter, 33; Schl. Mt., 633; Str.-B., I, 877; III, 506; IV, 879.

on the earth? (Answer:) for it is written: Ps. 72:11 ...; Da. 7:13 f. ...; Da. 2:35: The stone ... filled the whole earth." [30] Tanch. תרומה, 6 on Da. 2:34: (You were looking until a stone was loosed): "Resh Laqish (c. 250) has said: This is the king Messiah"; [31] Tanch. תולדות, 20 [32] par. Aggadat Bereshit, 33a, 7; [33] Tanch. עקב, 10 [34] (where, with Str.-B., III, 506g, we are to read משיח for משה). Esp. important is the fact that we learn from Jos. that the Messianic interpretation of the stone of Da. 2:34 ff. was accepted in the 1st cent. Jos. concludes his exposition of the vision of Da. 2 with the striking words: "Daniel also expounded the stone to the king. But I have resolved not to speak of this, since I have to indicate what is past and what has taken place, not what is future," Ant., 10, 210. [35] Jos. does not regard it as opportune to mention Messianic expectation in his work, but he can hardly refrain from alluding to it. [36]

Finally, Rabb. lit. refers to the Messiah the stone of Gn. 28:18 (Tanch. תולדות, 20 [37] par. Aggadat Bereshit, 33a, 6 [38]), Is. 8:14 (bSanh., 38a), Zech. 4:7 (Tg. Zech. 4:7 paraphrases וְהוֹצִיא אֶת־הָאֶבֶן הָרֹאשָׁה: "And he will reveal his Messiah whose name is known from of old"; [39] Tanch. תולדות, 20 [40] par. Aggadat Bereshit, 33a, 5 [41]), and Zech. 4:10 (Tanch. תולדות, 20 [42] par. Aggadat Bereshit, 33a, 3 [43]). On the other hand, in spite of assertions to the contrary, the rock of Horeb was not interpreted Messianically in Judaism. [44] The Messianic understanding of Ps. 118:22 does not arise here, since its attestation is very late. [45]

The fact that Rock is often a name for Yahweh in the OT prepared the ground and made the way smoother for the Messianic understanding of many OT stone passages. [46] How common this name was may be seen from the LXX, which often has θεός for צוּר, and also from Gn. r., 70, 9 on 29:2: "And the stone (הָאֶבֶן) was great. This is the Shekinah." [47]

---

[30] p. 53d, 25 ff., Vilna.

[31] p. 46b, 7 f. Buber; ed. Stettin (1864) תרומה 7, p. 140b, 26.

[32] p. 70b, 17 f., Buber; ed. Stettin (1864) תולדות, 14, p. 48b, 17 f.

[33] Ed. Warsaw (1876).

[34] Ed. Stettin (1864), p. 317b, 7.

[35] Cf. Schlatter, 33; Theol. d. Judt., 257 and 259.

[36] It should be noted that 4 Esr. bases its strange idea of the hill which the man himself hews out on Da. 2:34 ff.: 13:6 f., 12, 36 (Dalman WJ, I, 197, n. 1). Here the stone which has become a mountain is not the Messiah Himself, but an attribute of the Messiah.

[37] p. 70b, 16, Buber.

[38] Ed. Warsaw (1876).

[39] Ed. Vilna (1893).

[40] p. 70b, 16, Buber; ed. Stettin (1864) תולדות, 14, p. 48b, 16.

[41] Ed. Warsaw (1876).

[42] p. 70b, 12 ff.; Buber; ed. Stettin (1864) תולדות, 14, p. 48b, 12 and 14.

[43] Ed. Warsaw (1876).

[44] Str.-B., III, 408 has shown decisively that the assertion of older scholars (C. Schöttgen, J. J. Wettstein, L. Bertholdt, H. St. J. Thackeray, *The Relation of St. Paul to Contemporary Jewish Thought* [1900], 211) that Tg. Is., 16, 1 referred the rock which followed to the Messiah, rests on a wrong translation of the Tg. Yet this view is still cautiously advanced by E. Stauffer in his supplementary notes on Bchm. 1 K.^{4}, 501.

[45] The Mess. interpretation of Ps. 118:22 is first found in Rashi (d. 1105) on Mi. 5:1: C. Schöttgen, *Horae Hebraicae et Talmudicae* (1733), I, 174; Str.-B., I, 876.

[46] A. Wiegand, "Der Gottesname צור ...," ZAW, 10 (1890), 85 ff.; H. Schmidt, *Der heilige Fels in Jerusalem* (1933), 87.

[47] p. 137d, 23, Vilna.

3. Christ the Stone.

Several OT conceptions underlie the Christ-λίθος-statements mentioned above (→ 271). In the foreground is the thought of the temple of the age of salvation, whose corner stone and foundation stone is Christ. A second group of passages speaks of Christ as the stone which crushes. Finally, Christ as the one who dispenses living water is compared with the rock of Horeb and the sacred stone of the Jerusalem temple.

a. Jesus as the Key Stone and Foundation Stone of the True Temple of God. According to Mk. 12:10 and par. and Lk. 20:18 Jesus Himself was the first to apply the metaphor of the stone to Himself.[48] At the end of the parable of the wicked husbandmen[49] He quotes ψ 117:22: λίθον ὃν ἀπεδοκίμασαν οἱ οἰκοδομοῦντες, οὗτος ἐγενήθη εἰς κεφαλὴν γωνίας. For an understanding of the quotation it is important that, according to the agreed testimony of the Syr. translation of Ps. 118:22,[50] Symmachus,[51] Test. Sol.,[52] Hipp.,[53] Tertullian,[54] Aphraates,[55] Prudentius,[56] and Synagogue poetry,[57] the κεφαλὴ γωνίας is the stone which crowns the building, or, more precisely, the key stone[58] of the structure probably set above the porch.[59, 60] Only in this light can one understand the imagery of Mk. 12:10. Jesus reads His fate in the psalm. He will be rejected as an unsuitable stone by men. But God will exalt Him to be the key stone, or, in plain words, the King and Ruler (Tg. Ps. 118:22). The building of which Jesus speaks is the

---

[48] In favour of authenticity note 1. that Ps. 118 belongs to the Hallel which Jesus prays with His disciples after the passover (Mk. 14:26); 2. the Messianic interpretation of the passage in Mk. 8:31; Lk. 9:22; 17:25 (ἀποδοκιμάζειν); and 3. the Messianic interpretation of Ps. 118:26 in Mt. 11:3; Lk. 7:19 f. (ὁ ἐρχόμενος); Mt. 23:39 par. Lk. 13:35; Mk. 11:9 f. par. Mt. 21:9; Lk. 19:38; Jn. 12:13.

[49] On the question whether Mk. 12:10 originally belongs to the parable (often denied since Jülicher GlJ, II, 405) note should be taken of 1. the Rabb. custom of concluding parables with a text, and 2. the common application of the image of builders to scribes or the Sanhedrin (Str.-B., I, 876).

[50] "Head of the building."

[51] Σ ψ 117:22 ἀκρογωνιαῖος (cf. Σ 4 Βασ. 25:17).

[52] 22:7-23:4 (ed. McCown) → I, 792.

[53] Ref., V, 7, 35: κεφαλὴ γωνίας is the original man as absolute head, who is called ἡ κορυφή in what follows (V, 8, 13).

[54] Marc., III, 7: *lapis summus angularis post reprobationem adsumptus et sublimatus in consummationem templi* (CSEL, 47, p. 386, 23).

[55] Homily, 1, 6 f. (ed. W. Wright [1869], I, 10 f.; J. Parisot [1894], I, 15 ff.): "head of the building."

[56] Dittochaeum, Stichos 31 (MPL, 60, p. 104): *caput templi.*

[57] 13th *ḳeroba* (*ḥuppa*) on the 9th of Ab. concerning 24 priestly orders (P. Kahle, "Masoreten des Westens," BWANT, NF, Heft 8 [1927], 20*), VI, 17: "The precious corner stone is firm, and not loose, at its portals" [Bertram]. Cf. also VI, 1 f. (Kahle, 18*): "The stone which you have chosen to be the head of each tabernacle (cf. Ps. 118:22) was beautified with *boḥan* stones (cf. Is. 28:16) and *ekdaḥ* stones (cf. Is. 54:12)."

[58] Test. Sol. 22:7; Tertullian → n. 54; Aphraates, Homily, 1, 6 f. → n. 55; 13th *ḳeroba* on the 24 priestly orders, VI, 17 → n. 57.

[59] Test. Sol. 23:3 f.

[60] For details → J. Jeremias, Κεφαλὴ γωνίας, 264-280. On Test. Sol. 22:7 ff. cf. also Jeremias, "Die 'Zinne' des Tempels (Mt. 4:5; Lk. 4:9)," ZDPV, 59 (1936), 195-208; "Eckstein-Schlussstein," ZNW, 36 (1937), 154-157.

future temple, i.e., the holy community of the last time.[61] Hence the insertion of the key stone can belong only to the *parousia*. Mk. 12:10 is thus a Messianic pronouncement in the form of the mashal. Jesus directs it against His opponents[62] as a word of eschatological threat and a summons to repentance. At His coming God will show them that they have laid hands on the Lord and Consummator of the holy community.

Jesus' referring of Ps. 118:22 to Himself was followed up in early Christian writings, and first in Ac. 4:11. The rejection of the stone is here again the death of Jesus, but the raising up of the key stone, as the context (4:10) and the aor. part. γενόμενος show, is now the resurrection rather than the *parousia*. Thus Ps. 118:22 becomes an early Christian proof text for the death and resurrection.[63]

Eph. 2:20-22 also speaks of Jesus as the key stone. Here the one community of Jews and Gentiles is compared to a temple whose foundation is formed of the apostles and prophets (cf. Rev. 21:14; Mt. 16:18) and whose key stone (ἀκρογωνιαῖος)[64] is Christ, v. 20. If the building is said to grow in v. 21, the image of a building is here fused with that of the ἀνὴρ τέλειος whose head is Christ (4:11-16). Conversely, in 4:11 ff. the figure of the ἀνὴρ τέλειος is fused with that of building (v. 12, 16). The interrelating of the two metaphors expresses the fact that the spiritual temple is not static but is in process of growth and aiming at completion. There is a twofold shift in application as compared with Mk. 12:10. The temple is no longer the future, but the present community of salvation. The final stone is Christ, not just as the One who comes again, but as the exalted Lord.

If Christ is the foundation stone as well as the key stone, this is to be explained in the light of the OT. The verse in Is. which speaks of the foundation of the new temple that God Himself has laid (28:16: ἰδοὺ ἐγὼ ἐμβαλῶ εἰς τὰ θεμέλια Σιων λίθον πολυτελῆ ἐκλεκτὸν ἀκρογωνιαῖον ἔντιμον εἰς τὰ θεμέλια αὐτῆς, καὶ ὁ πιστεύων ἐπ' αὐτῷ οὐ μὴ καταισχυνθῇ) is referred to Christ (1 Pt. 2:4-6; cf. R. 9:33; 10:11 [1 Tm. 1:16 → 272]). The christological interpretation is suggested by the LXX text (→ 272). The saying was important for early Christianity because of the promise therewith given to the believer that he would not be put to shame (Is. 28:16b). The saving significance of Christ as the stone was nowhere in the OT so plainly stated as here.

b. The Stone which crushes and the Stone of Offence. According to Lk. 20:18 (Mt. 21:44 vl.) Jesus added to the quotation of Ps. 118:22 a further eschatological threat which develops in parallelism the image of the stone: πᾶς ὁ πεσὼν ἐπ' ἐκεῖνον τὸν λίθον συνθλασθήσεται· ἐφ' ὃν δ' ἂν πέσῃ, λικμήσει αὐτόν. This, too, rests on the OT. The second part refers to the vision of Nebuchadnezzar (Da. 2:31-45) in which he saw a stone which smashed the image and became a mountain[65] — a passage which soon came to be understood Messianically in Judaism (→ 272 f.; → λικμάω, 280).

[61] J. Jeremias, *Jesus* ..., 39 f., 43 f., 79-81.
[62] So at least in the present context, → n. 49.
[63] Ps. 118:22 is also referred to Christ in 1 Pt. 2:4, 7 → 277; Barn., 6, 4 → 279.
[64] Apart from LXX Is. 28:16 (and quotations of this verse) ἀκρογωνιαῖος everywhere means the stone which crowns the building (Σ ψ 117:22, cf. Σ 4 Βασ. 25:17; Test. Sol. 22:7; 23:2-4; Hipp. Ref., V, 7, 35; Tert. Marc., V, 17; Aphraates, Hom., I, 7 → I, 792) or the final stone (Test. Sol. 22:7; 23:2-4).
[65] Da. 2:34 f., 44 f., cf. esp. 2:44 Θ: καὶ → λικμήσει πάσας τὰς βασιλείας.

Whether there is in the first line an allusion to Is. 8:14 ("and he [Yahweh] shall be ... a stone of stumbling and a rock of offence") is not certain, since Lk. 20:18a does not say that men stumble over the stone but that it falls on them. It is thus more likely [66] that the Da. saying is combined with a proverb like the saying of R. Shim'on ben Jose ben Laqonja (c. 200) which was handed down in Midr. Est., 7, 10 on 3:6 and combined with Da. 2:45: "If the stone (כֵּיפָה) falls on the pot, woe to the pot! If the pot falls on the stone, woe to the pot! Either way, woe to the pot!" [67]

Both lines depict the crushing effect of the stone (Christ) smashing and pulverising its opponents. The first line tells us that running up against it leads to destruction, [68] the second (in the metaphor of the falling stone) that Christ as Judge will destroy His enemies at the last judgment. [69]

Lk. 20:18 contains implicitly a broader christological statement. The stone of Da. which becomes a great mountain filling the whole earth (2:35) represents the final rule of Israel which will overthrow all kingdoms (2:44 f.). Referred to Christ, this means that the returning Lord will be Ruler of the whole world. It is worth noting, however, that the OT text is altered at a decisive point. There is no ref. in Lk. 20:18 to the predominance of Israel. The point is that in relation to Christ as the stone Israel has to make a decision, and that destruction will come upon all those in Israel who resist Him.

Another OT verse which speaks of the destructive operation of the stone is also referred to Christ. This is Is. 8:14. In the metaphor of the stone of stumbling there are seen the consequences of taking offence at Christ, namely, falling, or the missing of eternal salvation (R. 9:32 f.; 1 Pt. 2:8; cf. Lk. 2:34).

c. The Significance of Christ the Stone for Salvation and Perdition. From what has been said it may be seen that the metaphor of the stone can be used in different ways. The content is sometimes promise and sometimes threat. In Christ God's goodness and wrath are both revealed. Christ the stone is at one and the same time a symbol of salvation and perdition. The difference in orientation may best be seen in passages which present both operations.

R. 9:32 f. is a mixed quotation from Is. 8:14 and 28:16. Paul is dealing with the question why Israel does not attain to righteousness in spite of all its concern for the Law. He finds the answer in Is. Confronted by Christ with His demand for faith, the Jews have stumbled as at a stone (λίθος προσκόμματος καὶ πέτρα σκανδάλου). Thus it is their own fault that Christ means perdition for them. They have denied Him faith. To believers, however, applies the saying about the stone in Sion in 28:16: ὁ πιστεύων ἐπ᾿ αὐτῷ οὐ καταισχυνθήσεται. Whether Christ as the stone is for salvation or perdition is decided by faith.

1 Pt. 2:4 f. admonishes the newly baptised to come to the living stone [70] and to let themselves, as living stones, be built up into a spiritual house. The descrip-

---

[66] Hck. Lk., *ad loc.*

[67] Cf. already Sir. 13:2b: "What kind of fellowship can the pot have with the kettle? For this will dash against it and it will be broken"; Aesop Fabula, 422 (ed. C. Halm [1868], p. 204).

[68] Heb. נָפַל, Aram. and Syr. נְפַל, often has the aggressive sense, e.g., sy$^{p\,ph}$ Mk. 4:37, of the waves coming into the ship.

[69] Schl. Mt., 633.

[70] The description of Christ as λίθος ζῶν has nothing to do with mythological ideas. It is also doubtful, in spite of the spiritual rock of 1 C. 10:4, whether the stone is called

tion of Christ as the stone in vv. 6-8 rests on three quotations of which the first (Is. 28:16) refers to the saving significance of the stone (Christ) for the community, while the other two (ψ 117:22; Is. 8:14) refer to the fact that it entails perdition for unbelievers. The believer will not be put to shame (1 Pt. 2:6); unbelievers προσκόπτουσιν (2:8), i.e., they stumble, and fall (this addition is demanded by the ensuing εἰς ὃ καὶ ἐτέθησαν, which only makes sense when construed thus). [71] Again it is faith which decides. Lk. 2:34 (οὗτος κεῖται εἰς πτῶσιν καὶ ἀνάστασιν πολλῶν ἐν τῷ Ἰσραήλ) may also be understood in this way. The falling and rising are decided by faith.

The working of Christ the stone to salvation or perdition is also present in Barn. 6, 2 f. This refers Is. 28:16a to the operation to perdition; Christ is set up as a powerful stone to grind down, 6, 2. Is. 28:16b is then referred to the saving operation. Here the LXX text is altered to express the life-giving power of Christ: "He who believes in him will live for ever" (Barn., 6, 3).

d. The Dispenser of Living Water. In 1 C. 10:4 the rock of Horeb which gave forth water, and which according to legend accompanied Israel through the desert, is referred to the pre-existent Christ (→ πέτρα). There is a close material connection between 1 C. 10:4 and the call of the Saviour in Jn, 7:37 f.:

ἐάν τις διψᾷ, ἐρχέσθω [72]
καὶ πινέτω ὁ πιστεύων εἰς ἐμέ. [73]

In interpretation of this saying, it should be noted that it comes on the last day of the Feast of Tabernacles (Jn. 7:37). [74] One may recall that at the heart of the accompanying rites stood the pouring out of water. Water drawn from the pool of Siloam was led in solemn procession to the temple, and along with the wine of the daily morning drink offering poured into a vessel on the altar of burnt offering, Str.-B., II, 799 ff. Like the other rites, the shaking of the festal tuft [75] and the procession around the altar of

---

living by allusion to the rock which dispenses the water of life (i.e., the Spirit). On the other hand, the adj. ζῶν is not just a reference to the allegorical significance of the description of Christ as a stone (Wnd. Pt. on 1 Pt. 2:4-5; Holtzmann NT, *ad loc.*). Probably the adj. is meant to express the living connection between Christ, the living Lord who dispenses life, and His community.

[71] The sentence οἳ προσκόπτουσιν τῷ λόγῳ ἀπειθοῦντες, εἰς ὃ καὶ ἐτέθησαν (1 Pt. 2:8) seems at a first glance to suggest that some men were predestined to stumble at the stone Christ. But this can hardly be the meaning. If one remembers that the προσκόπτειν contains the idea of falling as a result of stumbling, the εἰς ὃ καὶ ἐτέθησαν can hardly imply that it was God's will that unbelievers should fall. The reference is to the results of unbelief, not to reprobation.

[72] + πρός με BLT.

[73] It is debated whether the sentence ends with πινέτω (Luther, and modern exegetes like J. Behm → III, 789) or includes εἰς ἐμέ. The second view (→ III, 902, n. 14) is supported by 1. the resultant parallelism; 2. the parallelism in the materially related verses Rev. 22:17 and Jn. 6:35; 3. the unity thereby given to the passage: vv. 37-38a speak of Jesus as the One who dispenses the water of life, v. 38b gives scriptural proof for the fact that the Redeemer dispenses living water, v. 39 is an exegetical note of the Evangelist to the effect that the water of life is the Spirit, and v. 40 is the echo of the crowd describing Jesus as the second Moses who repeats the miracle of Horeb.

[74] Joh. Jeremias, *Der Gottesberg,* 146; Joach. Jeremias, *Golgotha,* 54 ff., 60 ff., 80-85; *Jesus,* 46-50.

[75] Str.-B., II, 791; Jeremias, *Golgotha,* 61.

burnt offering,[76] this is a rain rite. "Why has the Torah commanded: Pour out water on the Feast of Tabernacles? The Holy One, blessed be He, has commanded: Pour out water before me on the Feast of Tabernacles, in order that the rain (of the coming year) may bless you."[77] It was assumed that the channels from the altar of burnt offering reached down to the abyss.[78] "Thus said R. El'azar: So soon as the water is poured out on the Feast of Tabernacles, one flood says to another: Let your waters gush forth."[79] It was thought that the blessing of water poured forth from the אֶבֶן שְׁתִיָּה, the sacred rock of the Most Holy, over the whole world. "R. Jose[80] (*c.* 150) said: Why is it called אֶבֶן שְׁתִיָּה? Because from it the world was founded (הושתה). R. Hijja (*c.* 200) taught: Why is it called אֶבֶן שְׁתִיָּה? Because from it the world was given to drink (הושתה, he derives שְׁתִיָּה from שָׁתָה, "to drink from")."[81] But it was not just water that was drawn on the Feast of Tabernacles. The pouring out of water was also a symbol of the pouring out of the Holy Spirit.[82] "Why was the place called the 'place of drawing'? Because there the Holy Spirit was drawn in virtue of the saying (Is. 12:3): With joy shall ye draw water out of the wells of salvation."[83] In this light one can easily see how from an early time the pouring out of water at the Feast of Tabernacles was regarded as a ref. to the last Messianic age in which the stream of blessing from the Most Holy,[84] the sacred rock,[85] would be poured over the whole earth[86] acc. to the prophecy of Ez. 47:1 ff. Then would be fulfilled the expectation: "As the first redeemer (Moses) caused the spring to arise (when he divided the rock in Horeb, Ex. 17:6), so the last redeemer will cause water to rise up, as it is written: A fountain shall come forth of the house of Yahweh (Jl. 3:18)."[87]

There can be little doubt that when Jesus calls on men to draw water from Him He is using the ideas associated with the Feast of Tabernacles. As the One who can give the water of life to the thirsty, i.e., to believers (Jn. 7:38a), He compares Himself with the sacred rock which provides the world with water.

e. Christ the Stone in Post-NT Writings.[88] Already in the NT stone-sayings from the OT are combined, cf. Lk. 20:17 f. (ψ 117:22; Da. 2:34); R. 9:32 f. (Is. 28:16; 8:14); 1 Pt. 2:4-8 (ψ 117:22; Is. 28:16; 8:14). These combinations become increasingly popular in the post-NT period, for OT stone-sayings become a constituent part of the christological proof from Scripture.[89]

---

76 D. Feuchtwang, MGWJ, 55 (1911), 56 f. rightly recalls ancient Arab processions around the sacred stone to ask for and to bring down rain.

77 bRH, 16a. Par. in Str.-B., II, 804. The saying goes back to R. 'Aqiba (d. 134 A.D.). Cf. also Jeremias, *Golgotha,* 60 ff. The idea is old, Zech. 14:16 f.

78 bSukka, 49a, and on this Jeremias, *op. cit.,* 63.

79 bTaan, 25b, and on this Jeremias, 62-64.

80 So with T. Joma, 3, 6 instead of R. Johanan.

81 jJoma, 42c, 35 ff., also Jeremias, 56 f.; Str.-B., III, 182 f.

82 Str.-B., II, 434.

83 jSukka, 55a, 48 f., cf. also Jeremias, 63 f. (Gn. r., 70 on 29:2-3).

84 jSheq, 50a, 4 Bar. (par. in Str.-B., III, 855).

85 Jeremias, 54 and 57.

86 T. Sukka, 3, 3 and Str.-B., II, 805 and 800; Mid., 2, 6.

87 Qoh. r. on 1:9 (p. 4d, Vilna).

88 Harris, II, 60 f., 137, 139; Cadbury, 373 f.

89 Barn., 6, 2-4; Just. Dial., 34, 2; 36, 1; 70, 1; 76, 1; 86, 2 f.; 90, 5; 100, 4; 113, 6; 114, 2 and 4; 126, 1. Tertullian Marc., 3, 7; Cyprian Testimonia, 2, 16 f. (CSEL, 3, 1, p. 82-84); Orig. Comm. in Joh. I, 36 and 265 on Jn. 1:1; Aphraates, Hom., 1, 6-8. For further examples cf. Harris.

Thus Barn., 6, 2-4 combines the following sayings: Is. 28:16a, 16b; 50:7; ψ 117:22, and Barn. seems to be answering possible objections to this kind of proof when he himself asks: "Do we set our hope only on a stone?", and he bases his negative answer on Is. 50:7 (καὶ ἔθηκέν με ὡς στερεὰν πέτραν): The steadfastness of Jesus in suffering is brought out by the metaphor, 6, 3. The stone recurs in Just. in three long lists of the OT epithets of Christ (Dial., 34, 2; 100, 4; 126, 1; cf. also 36, 1). This shows that the stone statements had become part of the proof from Scripture. In detail Just., in various passages, applies the following verses to Christ: Da. 2:34, the stone which broke loose without human aid (Dial., 70, 1; 76, 1; 114, 4); Gn. 28:18, the stone of Bethel (Dial., 86, 2-3); Ex. 17:12, the stone on which Moses sat when he prayed for victory over the Amalekites (Dial., 90, 5); Jos. 5:2 f., the stone knives used in circumcision (Dial., 113, 6 = the words of Christ, the stone); Is. 28:16, the λίθος ἀκρογωνιαῖος (Dial., 114, 4). The first of these is related to the miraculous birth of Christ (Dial., 76, 1, cf. Ac. Pt. Verc., 24). The myth of Mithra born of the rock is for Just. a pagan imitation of Da. 2:34 (Dial., 70, 1). In Just. the prophets proclaimed Jesus as stone ἐν παραβολῇ (114, 2; cf. 113, 6; 36, 1). In Cyprian the stone is an OT name for Jesus, as the title of his collection of OT stone passages shows: *Quod idem et lapis dictus sit* (Testimonia, 2, 16).[90] In 2, 16 f. he has Is. 28:16; Ps. 118:22; Zech. 3:8 f.; Dt. 27:8; Jos. 24:26 f.; Gn. 28:18; Ex. 17:12; 1 S. 6:14 f.; 17:49 f.; 7:12; Da. 2:31 ff. Finally, the Syrian bishop Aphraates in his first homily on the demonstration of faith (c. 337) has the following verses: Ps. 118:22; Is. 28:16; Da. 2:34; Zech. 4:7; 3:9 (Homily, 1, 6-8).[91]

The Preaching of the Naassenes shows that Gnostic circles linked Ps. 118:22; Is. 28:16; Da. 2:45 with speculations about the first man. The upper Adamas is the κεφαλὴ γωνίας (ψ 117:22) and the ἀκρογωνιαῖος (cf. Is. 28:16), while Da. 2:45 and Is. 28:16 are referred to the ἔσω ἄνθρωπος who falls from the upper Adamas and is enclosed in the human body.[92]

D. Christians as Living Stones.

As Christ is the λίθος ζῶν (1 Pt. 2:4), so Christians are λίθοι ζῶντες (2:5). They form the spiritual house, namely, in a change of image, a "holy priesthood which offers up spiritual sacrifices, acceptable to God" (2:5). The description of Christians as stones is first found in Eph. 2:20, and the context here shows that this image is a development of the idea that the apostles and prophets are the foundation of God's building. The attribute "living" (1 Pt. 2:5) is certainly intended to bring out the allegorical character of the image, but it is also meant to express the fact that the community owes the spiritual life which it possesses solely to Christ, the living stone.[93]

The metaphor is further developed by Ign. in Eph., 9, 1 when he says that the stones are lifted into place by the lifting beam of Christ, i.e., the cross, while the Holy Spirit serves as the rope. This is a variation on the Gnostic idea of the zodiac as a well-wheel with which the one who is sent draws up souls entangled in matter, i.e., in the body.[94]

---

[90] CSEL, 3, 1, pp. 82 ff.

[91] Ed. W. Wright, *The Homilies of Aphraates* (1869), I, 10, 5 ff. Cf. Joach. Jeremias, ZNW, 29 (1930), 273-276.

[92] Hipp. Ref., V, 7, 35 f.; cf. also R. Reitzenstein-H. H. Schaeder, *Studien z. antiken Synkretismus* = *Stud. d. Bibliothek Warburg,* VII (1926), 165 f. Cf. Schlier, 47; 49, n. 1; J. Jeremias, ZNW, 29 (1930), 268 ff. That ἀκρογωνιαῖος is a pre-Christian title of Adamas, as Schlier conjectures, 49, n. 1, cannot be proved.

[93] → n. 70.

[94] Cf. H. Schlier, *Religionsgeschichtliche Untersuchungen zu den Ignatiusbriefen* = ZNW *Beih.,* 8 (1929), 110 ff.

Twice in Herm. the comparison of Christians with stones is worked out in exhaustive detail, namely, in the visions of the tower in v., 3 (the building of the tower above the flood) and s., 9 (the building of the tower on the rock). In both cases the Church is the tower which Christ causes to be erected, and in both cases the main point is the distinction between stones which are serviceable, those which are temporarily unserviceable, and those which are unserviceable. The author's main concern is with the second group, whose members can be saved if they repent. The seriousness of sin and the urgency of the call to repent are brought home to them in constant applications and depictions of the image.[95]

J. Jeremias

† λικμάω

λικμᾶν (also λικμίζειν): a. "to winnow," "to separate the wheat from the chaff," Hom. Il., 5, 500; Xenoph. Oec., 18, 6; Anth. Pal., VI, 53, 4; Plut. Quaest. Conv., VII, 2 (II, 701c); Philo Jos., 112; P. Greci e Latini, V, 522, 2; P. Ryl., 442, 3; BGU, III, 698, 15; 18; 19; IV, 1040, 11 etc. LXX Ju. 3:2; Sir. 5:9. The process may be portrayed as man's act as he tosses the wheat with the shovel or uses the fan, Am. 9:9 : λικμιῶ ... ὃν τρόπον λικμᾶται ἐν τῷ λικμῷ (Heb. נוּעַ, "to shake," hi and ni), so that the chaff is scattered (Heb. usually זָרָה q ni pi). But it can also be the work of the wind, which really accomplishes the job. From this derives the sense b. "to blow apart," "to scatter," Job 27:21: ἀναλήμψεται αὐτὸν καύσων καὶ ἀπελεύσεται καὶ λικμήσει αὐτὸν ἐκ τοῦ τόπου αὐτοῦ (Heb. שָׂעַר pi, "to whirl up," "to snatch away in a storm"); Wis. 5:23 : ὡς λαῖλαψ ἐκλικμήσει αὐτούς, hence fig. 11:20 : λικμηθέντες ὑπὸ πνεύματος δυνάμεώς σου,[1] and with other obj. Is. 30:22 : λικμήσεις ὡς ὕδωρ (זרה), Ez. 26:4 : λικμήσω τὸν χοῦν (Heb. סָחָה pi, "to sweep away"). This leads to a further development in which the idea of destroying what is worthless, already present in winnowing, becomes predominant : c. "to pulverise," "to destroy." There are not many instances of this use in secular Gk., cf. BGU, I, 146, 8 f. (2nd/3rd cent. A.D.): ἐλίκμησάν μου τὸ λάχανον (a complaint against those who have destroyed fruits of the field or garden on the threshing-floor [?]).[2] Joh. Lyd. De Ostentis, 20 (p. 297, 23, Bekker): λικμητὸν ἀνθρώποις ἀπειλεῖ (λικμητός = ἀπώλεια).[3] That this became an established sense

[95] Dib. Herm., 465 f.

λικμάω. Liddell-Scott, Pr.-Bauer[3], Moult.-Mill., Preisigke Wört., *s.v.*, Boisacq, 581; Walde-Pok., II, 321. H. A. A. Kennedy, *Sources of NT Greek* (1895), 126 f.; Deissmann NB, 52 f.; E. Nestle, ZNW, 8 (1907), 321; F. Boll, *Aus d. Offenbarung Joh.* (1914), 130, n. 1.

[1] How strong this sense could be may be seen in Wis. 11:18c : (θῆρας) βρόμον λικμωμένους καπνοῦ, where the par. part. φυσῶντας in 18b proves that the unusual act. med. has the meaning "to blow out." This is so unusual that it has led to emendation in some MSS, cf. W. J. Deane, *The Book of Wisdom* (1881), 172.

[2] That λικμᾶν here means more than simply "to scatter" is shown by the "no mean punishment" (line 10) which overtakes the offenders. Obviously they aimed to inflict serious damage on the owner. We cannot say how they destroyed the fruits (plucking or trampling ?).

[3] Boll, *op. cit.*

is shown not merely by these examples adduced by Deissmann and Boll but also by Theophylacti Simocattae Historia, IV, 11, 3:[4] ταύταις γὰρ ταῖς μεγίσταις ἀρχαῖς τὰ ἀπειθῆ καὶ φιλοπόλεμα ἔθνη λικμίζονται. Cf. also Jdt. 2:27: τὰ πεδία αὐτῶν ἐξελίκμησεν, and Da. 2:44 Θ: λεπτυνεῖ καὶ λικμήσει πάσας τὰς βασιλείας (LXX: πατάξει καὶ ἀφανίσει).[5]

In the OT this is a common metaphor for judgment (under the twofold image of winnowing and threshing, Is. 41:15 f.) a. temporary, Ιερ. 38:10: ὁ λικμήσας τὸν Ἰσραὴλ συνάξει αὐτόν, Ez. 36:19 ff., and b. final, Jer. 15:7 Mas. (LXX: διασπερῶ ... ἐν διασπορᾷ);[6] Ez. 26:4; 30:23, 26.

In the NT the word occurs only at Lk. 20:18 par. Mt. 21:44:[7] πᾶς ὁ πεσὼν ἐπ' ἐκεῖνον τὸν λίθον συνθλασθήσεται· ἐφ' ὃν δ' ἂν πέσῃ λικμήσει αὐτόν (Vulg. *comminuet illum*), "whosoever shall fall on that stone shall be broken; but on whomsoever it shall fall, it will grind him to powder." The saying is here appended to the quotation of ψ 117:22 in v. 17, and in this context it means that the stone which the builders rejected, but which God has made the corner stone (→ I, 793; → 274), will bring ineluctable judgment on its opponents. Da. 2:34 f., 44 f. undoubtedly underlies the saying. To 18a there are material parallels in Is. 8:14 and 28:16, though one can hardly say that the whole of v. 18 is a deliberate combination of prophetic sayings. The Messianic reference of the Da. text is attested elsewhere,[8] and it is obvious that this is behind the linking of the saying with ψ 117:22 (v. 17). Nevertheless, it is best not to attempt too elaborate an exposition[9] and simply to take from the proverbial[10] and pithy saying the thought of the ineluctability of judgment.[11]

Bornkamm

---

[4] Ed. C. de Boor (1887).

[5] Nestle, *op. cit.*, on the basis of the relation between Lk. 20:18 and Da. 2:44 Θ, considers a possible dependence of Theodotion on the NT. But this is unlikely, as there are parallels to the deviation of Theod. from the LXX at Is. (LXX) 30:22: ... λεπτὰ ποιήσεις καὶ λικμήσεις, and 41:15 f.: καὶ λεπτυνεῖς βουνοὺς καὶ ὡς χνοῦν θήσεις καὶ λικμήσεις.

[6] The Hexap. translators also use λικμάω here: Ἀ: καὶ λικμήσω αὐτοὺς ἐν τῷ λικμῷ ἐν πύλαις γῆς, Σ: καὶ λικμήσω αὐτοὺς ἐν λικμητηρίῳ ἐν πόλεσιν τῆς γῆς. The fig. of winnowing is present here, but often we have the weaker sense "to scatter," so 3 Βασ. 14:15 LXX (A) Ἀ; Lv. 26:33 Ἄλλος; ψ 43:11 Σ; Jer. 51 (LXX: 28): 2 ἈΣ; Mal. 2:3 Ἀ. LXX has διασπείρω or σκορπίζω, Mas. usually זרה [Bertram].

[7] The saying came into Mt. from Lk. It is not found in D it syr[s] Or, and does not fit the context, since it is separated by v. 42c (= ψ 117:23 = Mk. 12:11) and v. 43 from the basic saying (λίθον ... εἰς κεφαλὴν γωνίας), whereas it follows on at once in Lk.

[8] Str.-B., I, 877; → 272 f.

[9] J. Jeremias, *Golgotha* (ΑΓΓΕΛΟΣ, *Beih.* 1 [1926]), 79 f.: "In these words, based on the verse in Da., Jesus is thinking ... of the plunging down of the sacred rock, i.e., of the great judgment at the *parousia*." To harmonise the ideas in v. 17 and v. 18 — for the falling of the stone makes no sense if referred to the corner stone over the porch — Jeremias suggests a play on words, and takes the first πίπτειν ἐπί to imply an attack on the stone acc. to the Aram. נפל (cf. Lk. 11:17). The exact correspondence of the two halves of the verse, which demands the same sense for the twofold πίπτειν, is thus broken.

[10] Cf. already Sir. 13:2: "Why dost thou lift up what is too heavy for thee, and for what cause dost thou have dealings with one who is richer than thou? What fellowship can the pot have with the metal vessel? For this will dash against it, and it will be broken" (cf. Aesop Fab., 422, ed. Halm, 1929, 204), also Midr. Esth., 7 on 3:6 → 276 (λίθος), Lidz. Liturg., 23: "Each *dew* who hurls himself on me will be broken, and each on whom I fall I will smash to pieces."

[11] The OT basis of the saying has given rise to the idea of an apocr. from which Lk. perhaps took a collection of sayings. Cf. Jülicher Gl. J., II, 401 f.; A. Loisy, *L'Evangile selon Luc* (1924), *ad loc.*; R. Harris, *Testimonies*, II (1920), 96.

† λογεία

λογεία and the related verb λογεύω [1] are not found in literary speech. [2] Thus prior to acquaintance with the pap. a natural attempt was made to derive the word λογεία direct from λέγω. [3] In reality both words go back to λόγος in the sense (for which there is no direct evidence) of "collection" and "to engage (officially) in collection." [4] In pap. and inscr. from Egypt and Asia Minor from the 3rd cent. B.C. on there are many instances of both words. λογεύω, "I collect," P. Rev., 4, 1; 39, 14; 52, 20 (258 B.C.); CIG, III, 4956 (49 A.D.) etc. [5] λογεία, "collection," "collection of money," "tax," the oldest example P. Hibeh, I, 51, 2 (245 B.C.), esp., as it seems, in the sense of an extraordinary tax, cf. P. Oxy., II, 239, 8: ὀμνύω ... μηδεμίαν λογείαν γεγονέναι ὑπ' ἐμοῦ ἐν τῇ αὐτῇ κώμῃ. [6] BGU, II, 515, 7: τὰ ὑπὲρ λογίας [ἐπ]ιβληθέντα, as distinct from σιτικὰ δημόσια. Often a "sacral collection of money," "collection," [7] e.g., Ostraka, II, 413 (August 4th, 63 A.D.): ἀπέχω παρὰ σοῦ (δραχμὰς) δ ὀβολ(ὸν) τὴν λογίαν Ἴσιδος περὶ τῶν δημοσίων (collection of Isis, contribution for official services), [8] cf. also No. 402, 412, 415-418, 420; Ditt. Syll.³, 996, 26 (Smyrna, 1st cent. A.D.): κλεῖν κεχρυσωμένην καὶ ἐμπεφιασμένην [9] πρὸς τὴν λογήαν καὶ πομπὴν τῶν θεῶν, "a vessel which is gilded ..., for the collection and procession of the gods." [10]

In the NT it occurs only at 1 C. 16:1 f. In Corinth, as in Galatia, the λογεία εἰς [11] τοὺς ἁγίους arranged by Paul is now to be gathered in orderly fashion so that λογεῖαι will not be necessary when he comes. In evaluating the procedure, it is essential to bear in mind that in the use of λογεία, especially the sacral use, the primary emphasis obviously does not fall on the element of regular taxation.

λογεία. Liddell-Scott, Moult.-Mill., Pr.-Bauer³, *s.v.*; Deissmann B., 139 ff. NB, 46 f.; LO, 83 ff.; Mayser, I, 67 and 417.

[1] Hence the correct form λογεία, not, like NT MSS apart from B 1 C. 16:2, λογία. Cf. Bl.-Debr.⁶ § 23; Heinr. 1 K., 510 f. But the pap. occasionally have λογία, cf. Deissmann LO, 83, n. 2.

[2] For this reason many exegetes erroneously thought the word had been coined by Paul, so T. C. Edwards, *A Comm. on the First Epistle to the Corinthians* [1885], 462 (quoted in Deissmann B, 139, n. 5). H. Grotius and others even suggested emending to εὐλογίας on the basis of 2 C. 9:5, cf. Wettstein, II, 174.

[3] So Wilke-Grimm³ (1888), *s.v.*

[4] Debrunner, cf. → 73.

[5] For further examples cf. Deissmann B, 140 f.; Mayser, I, 463; Preisigke Wört., *s.v.*

[6] Cf. the editor's note: "λογεία is used for irregular local contributions as opposed to regular taxes"; cf. Moult.-Mill., 377.

[7] There are many examples in Ostraka, I, 253 ff.; Preisigke Wört., *s.v.*; W. Spiegelberg, *Zschr. f. ägypt. Sprache*, 54 (1918), 116.

[8] Cf. Deissmann LO⁴, 84; also W. Otto, *Priester u. Tempel im hell. Ägypten*, I (1905), 359 ff.

[9] = ἠμφιασμένην, "clothed." The vessel was thus borne in the procession like the ἀγάλματα ... ἐμπεφιεσμένα (lines 20 ff.) [Debrunner].

[10] Deissmann LO, 83, n. 10: "The ref. is to a procession at which the spectators were expected to contribute money."

[11] On the εἰς cf. LXX Bel et Draco 6: ὅσα εἰς αὐτὸν δαπανᾶται.

The choice of the word does not imply any reference to an assessment, evaluation or "levy which the mother congregation lays on Gentile Christians." [12] It makes it clear that this is not an imposed tax but a gift gathered, even if in orderly fashion, as a collection. In keeping is the fact that the synonyms which Paul uses for this λογεία are not taken from the area of taxation [13] but from that of edification. In other words, they depict acts of love: χάρις, v. 3; 2 C. 8:4 ff.; κοινωνία, R. 15:26; διακονία, R. 15:31; 2 C. 8:4; 9:1; εὐλογία, [14] 2 C. 9:5.

This does not rule out the possibility that Paul regarded this collection made by his congregations for the original church as an action parallel to certain Jewish collections. The point is, however, that the real analogy is not the temple tax [15] to which there is ref. in Mt. 17:24, which does not fall only on the *diaspora* but is an impost on all adult male Israelites both in Palestine and abroad, and which is an established religious tax on the basis of Ex. 30:11 ff. and Neh. 10:33 f. [16] We are rather to think of the additional voluntary love offerings made to Jerusalem; these are mentioned from the Maccabean period and came mostly from the *diaspora*. Cf. 2 Macc. 3:2; Jos. Ant., 18, 82 (the Roman lady Fulvia sends πορφύραν καὶ χρυσὸν εἰς τὸ ἐν Ἱεροσολύμοις ἱερόν). After the destruction of Jerusalem the scribes became very poor; this led to the מְגְּבַת חֲכָמִים (collection for the scribes) which seems to be very similar to Paul's λογεία. [17] From this there later developed the so-called "patriarchal tax," a kind of continuation of the temple tax, though originally voluntary. [18] In connection with the sending of these voluntary gifts we often find the terms ἀποστέλλω, ἀποστολή, *apostoli*, שְׁלִיחוּת) שלח (שְׁלוּחִים: [19] Neh. 8:10, 12 = 1 Εσδρ. 9:51, 54; 1 Macc. 2:18; 2 Macc. 3:2; Cod. Theodosianus (ed. T. Mommsen-P. M. Meyer, I, 2, p. 890), 16, 8, 14 (Apr. 11, 399); Jul. Ep., p. 281, 4. This corresponds to the NT use of ἀπόστολοι and ἀποστείλαντες for those who bring collections, 2 C. 8:23; Phil. 2:25; Ac. 11:30.

Kittel

[12] So — as an essential part of his argument as to the relationship between the Pauline churches and the original congregation — K. Holl, *Der Kirchenbegriff des Pls. in seinem Verhältnis zur Urgemeinde* (1921) = *Ges. Aufsätze zur Kirchengeschichte*, II: *Der Osten* (1928), 60 f.

[13] The nearest is λειτουργία in 2 C. 9:12.

[14] The changing of εὐλογίαν to λογείαν, which Deissmann B, 141 considers, is unnecessary, cf. Wnd. 2 K., 274; → II, 763.

[15] Cf. Holl, *op. cit.*, 58, n. 1, who refers back to the conjectures of O. Pfleiderer and H. J. Holtzmann.

[16] For examples and details cf. Str.-B., I, 760-770.

[17] *Ibid.*, III, 317 f.

[18] Cf. Rengstorf → I, 417 and esp. n. 64.

[19] Cf. Str.-B., III, 316.

λογίζομαι, † λογισμός

A. The Word Group outside the New Testament.

1. λογίζομαι.[1]

In profane Gk. there are two distinctive uses. Common to both is the idea of an act of thought acc. to strict logical rules. a. In commercial dealings λογίζεσθαι is a tt. for "reckoning," and is found as such in the legal language of Demosthenes and Lys., then esp. in the pap. and inscr., e.g., for "evaluating" (Demosth. Or., 27, 39; P. Oxy., XII, 1434, 8 (107-108 A.D.), for charging up a debt (Demosth. Or., 27, 46), ἐν ἐλασσώματι "to losses," P. Lond., 259, 94 (1st cent. A.D.). When εἰς is added, it indicates the scale (or currency) used for estimating the value of an object (χρήματα ... εἰς ἀργύριον λογισθέντα, Xenoph. Cyrop., III, 1, 33; P. Lips., 34, 15 [375 A.D.], or, in charging up, the object or debt to be paid (εἰς ὄψον μὲν δυοῖν παιδίοιν ... πέντε ὀβολοὺς ... ἐλογίζετο, Lys., 32, 20; P. Lond., 1323, 1 [7th cent. A.D.], or occasionally in the sense of ἐν the person who is to meet the account (P. Fay., 21, 9 [134 A.D.]). b. In class. literature λογίζεσθαι means to "deliberate, to conclude." Esp. in Plato it is the typical term for the non-emotional thinking of the philosopher seeking suprapersonal knowledge, in this case, the receptive apprehension of something objectively present: ἆρ' οὖν οὐκ ἐν τῷ λογίζεσθαι εἴπερ που ἄλλοθι κατάδηλον αὐτῇ (sc. τῇ ψυχῇ) γίγνεταί τι τῶν ὄντων; Plat. Phaed., 65 c, cf. also a and b. The term then takes on political significance in Demosth., whose speeches are an appeal to λογίζεσθαι as the only way to express the facts as they are (Or., 5, 12). But in later historical writing this whole sense becomes less important. Philo occasionally leans on Plato with his emphasis on the rational course of thought, Sacr. AC, 2; Spec. Leg., III, 194. The sense "to regard as" is rare, Aristoph. Vesp., 74:5; it is found with ὡς and part. in Plat. Phileb., 18c; Ditt. Or., 665, 28.

In the LXX λογίζεσθαι has two additional nuances. a. As the act of thought it takes on a subjective, emotional and even volitional character. This is because λογίζεσθαι with only 5 exceptions is used for חָשַׁב.[2] But in 123 instances the Heb. is used only 7 times (of these 6 times pi) for reckoning in the commercial sense. On the other hand, in 56 cases it has a sense alien to λογίζεσθαι, namely, that of emotional devising, mechanical invention, or volitional planning, and in 43 cases it has a sense rare for λογίζεσθαι, namely, that of "to regard as," "to be reckoned with something," "to count something to someone as," with a personal and emotional overtone alien to the Gk. Thus in 53 instances the LXX uses other verbs, e.g., ἡγεῖσθαι (6 times), even ἀρχιτεκτονεῖν (Ex. 35:32) and ποιεῖν (Est. 8:3), and in 16 cases out of the 53 it has more precise compounds of λογίζεσθαι, esp. for commercial reckoning, e.g., with σύν,

---

λογίζομαι κτλ. H. W. Heidland, "Die Anrechnung des Glaubens zur Gerechtigkeit" = BWANT, IV, 18 (1936); also Liddell-Scott, Moult.-Mill., Preisigke Wört., Pr.-Bauer³, Wilke-Grimm, Cr.-Kö., *s.v.* λογίζεσθαι from → λόγος ("reckoning," "account," "deliberation").

[1] Cf. Heidland, 24 ff.

[2] For הָיָה 2 Βασ. 19:44 in a free rendering as "to be regarded"; for קָרָא ni Dt. 3:13, "to count as"; for מָנָה ni 2 Ch. 5:6, "to be counted"; Is. 53:12, "to be reckoned among"; for שׁוּב Is. 44:19, "to consider." Each of these senses is also class.

Lv. 25:27, 50, 52; ἐξ, 4 Βασ. 12:16; 22:7; πρός, Lv. 27:18 (cf. ψ 87:4). The simple form occurs in this sense only in Lv. 27:23; elsewhere it is most common with διά (→ II, 95). The predominant use of λογίζεσθαι is perhaps to be explained in terms of a close approximation between these two in the first translation of the Pent. (cf. in this connection the few instances of commercial reckoning, also the sense "to count as" in Gn. 31:15; Lv. 25:31; Dt. 2:11, 20), the possibility that various theological reasons led to the use of λογίζεσθαι (Gn. 15:6; Lv. 7:18; 17:4; Nu. 18:27, 30; → b.), [3] and the later schematic adoption of the same equation in later translation in which it was not really justified. In such cases the context is usually strong enough to impart the Heb. sense to the Gk. term, esp. when the Heb. syntax is alien to the Gk. There thus arises the meaning "to devise evil" (ψ 51:2; 139:2; Qoh. 10:3; Mi. 2:1; Zech. 8:17; Ez. 11:2; 38:10); ἐπί τινα, "against someone," 2 Βασ. 14:13; Mi. 2:3; Nah. 1:9; Ἰερ. 31:2; 1 Macc. 3:52; εἴς τινα, Hos. 7:15 (neither prep. is usual with λογίζεσθαι in this sense); also with the inner obj. λογισμός for מַחֲשָׁבָה, Jer. 11:19; 18:11, 18; Ἰερ. 27:45; 30:14, 25; 36:11; Da. 11:24 f. (Θ). That this sense took on its own life may be seen in Qoh. 10:3, where it is meaningfully present without the Heb. חָשַׁב. In "to count something as" and similar constructions it is alien to the Gks. that the judgment should have no objective basis but often be a purely subjective and emotional evaluation, Gn. 31:15; 1 Βασ. 1:13; 2 Ch. 9:20; Job 41:21, 24; Hos. 8:12; Is. 5:28; 29:17; 40:15, 17; 53:4; Lam. 4:2. Syntactically worth noting in the sense "to be reckoned (regarded) as something" is the ὡς before the predicative (Heb. כְּ), which is rare with λογίζεσθαι in secular Gk. and found only before the part., which tends to be weaker in meaning and which can be omitted in transl., e.g., Hos. 2:5 (B); Is. 14:17. The same is true of the form λογίζεσθαί τι εἴς τι ("to regard something as," 1 Βασ. 1:13; Job 41:24; pass. 2 Ch. 9:20; Hos. 8:12; Is. 29:17; 40:17; Lam. 4:2), also τινί τι εἴς τι ("to reckon something to someone as," Gn. 15:6; ψ 105:31; 1 Macc. 2:52; cf. → 289). The εἰς is usually construed prepositionally like ἐν ("to reckon in a sphere, to an account"), [4] but it is better to take it predicatively. [5] This is supported by 1. the intr. use, Wis. 2:16; Orig. Orat., 26, 6 ("to reckon to somebody as," which would be impossible with λογίζεσθαι ἐν); 2. Job 41:19, where ἡγεῖσθαι is used for חָשַׁב with לְ; 3. the interchangeability of εἰς and ὡς (Hos. 8:12 Heb. כְּ, LXX εἰς); 4. the use of εἰς for the simple Heb. predicate in Gn. 15:6. This predicative εἰς is found in the *koine* with other verbs, [6] though not with λογίζεσθαι. Originally it denotes the change which the obj. undergoes as a result of the evaluation, but like ὡς it loses its emphasis. Hence one may see a subjective act of judgment here too, though naturally this does not exclude the possible presence of a commercial sense in some cases. Here again the LXX use becomes both formally and materially independent, cf. ὡς with the predicative in Wis. 7:9, and εἰς in Wis. 2:16; 3:17; 9:6.

b. λογίζεσθαι is found also in the religious sphere. It is used 19 times of God, 5 of men (Nah. 1:9, 11: "to devise mischief against the Lord"; Is. 53:3 f., 12; → 287). In Jer. it is plainly influenced by the Heb. and denotes God's counsel to bring evil on a disobedient people (18:8, 11; Ἰερ. 27:45; 30:14; 33:3; 43:3; cf. Mi. 2:3), though He has thoughts of peace if it repents (Ἰερ. 36:11). Heb., too, is the evaluation of the nations in the light of God's greatness (Is. 40:15, 17: ὡς σίελος; εἰς οὐθέν). Plainly different is the righteous judgment on faith (Gn. 15:6; ψ 105:31; 1 Macc. 2:52; → 289)

[3] The translators must have been aware of the difference, for they have δοκεῖν in Gn. 38:15, βουλεύεσθαι in Gn. 50:20, and various terms for manual skills in the 12 instances in Ex. 26:31 etc.

[4] Helbing Kasussyntax, 66 f.; Bl.-Debr.[6], 298. Also εἴς τινα in Hos. 7:15 is only a formal par. to P. Fay., 21, 9, since in deliberation εἰς rather than ἐπί (cf. Bl.-Debr.[6] § 207, 1) denotes the direction of the mind (Winer[7], 381), cf. Paul in 2 C. 12:6.

[5] Wilke-Grimm (= εἰς τὸ [ὥστε] εἶναί τι).

[6] Bl.-Debr.[6] § 145 (with bibl.).

and sin (ψ 31:2; → 292), cf. also imputing in the sphere of cultic regulations (Lv. 7:18), also with the predicative "as something" (Lv. 17:4). Acc. to the strict sense of חָשַׁב the judgment of Lv. 17:4, where blood is imputed to the one who does not make his offering before the door of the tabernacle, has its *locus* in the will of God, who punishes this disobedience — an idea which is in conformity with the prophetic spirit. In the context as thus understood λογίζεσθαι can take on some of the elements of חָשַׁב as in other places. Acc. to the genuine Gk. sense, however, the judgment 1. stands on the ground of general reason and its law, and 2. can be understood as charging to one's account in the financial sense. Both these ideas are common in post-exilic Judaism. Hence a community which shared such notions would naturally and intentionally use the Gk. term in such a verse. The spirit of Gk. and later Judaism thus work hand in hand.

2. λογισμός. [7]

The noun denotes the actual fulfilment of λογίζεσθαι, and it thus has the par. meaning "reckoning," "charging to" (esp. pap.), "thought," "consideration." But the specific content of the term lies elsewhere. a. In secular Gk. the idea of counting causes it to be used even in class. Gk. as a specialised term for arithmetic (Plat. Prot., 318e). The general logical sense is important in the diatribe. In Aristot. (Metaph., I, 1, p. 980b, 28) λογισμός is the supreme activity which constitutes man as such, and in Stoicism there is an ethical orientation. As the supreme function it controls all others, including impulses. Cf. in 4 Macc. the sermon περὶ αὐτοκράτορος λογισμοῦ: ὁ γὰρ λογισμὸς τῶν μὲν ἀρετῶν ἐστιν ἡγεμών, τῶν δὲ παθῶν αὐτοκράτωρ (1:30). More precisely: λογισμὸς μὲν δὴ τοίνυν ἐστὶν νοῦς μετὰ ὀρθοῦ λόγου προτιμῶν τὸν σοφίας βίον (1:15). λογισμός, then, is not just reason in general (the νοῦς). It is reason in its concrete form in the consciousness and worked out in life as action. The norm of λογισμός — here the preacher seems to differ from Stoicism — is the Mosaic Law (2:6, 14). But for him this is identical with the principle of reason, the νοῦς. b. In the LXX λογισμός, like λογίζεσθαι, takes from חָשַׁב, and its derivatives מַחֲשֶׁבֶת, חֶשְׁבּוֹן, חִשָּׁבוֹן, an emotional and volitional emphasis, and it denotes "plan" in the neutral sense (ψ 32:10), good when used of God's plan to save (Ἰερ. 36:11), but usually bad (Ez. 38:10). In the same sense we also find διαλογισμός in ψ 39:5, βουλή in Job 5:12, and ἐνθύμημα in 1 Ch. 28:9. The formula λογίζεσθαι λογισμόν, which is modelled on the Heb., is not good Gk. (though cf. the purely logical use in Plat. Tim., 34a b). In Wis. λογισμός is the concept of self-glorious reason apart from God: σκολιοὶ γὰρ λογισμοὶ χωρίζουσιν ἀπὸ θεοῦ (1:3, cf. v. 5; 9:14 etc.).

B. The Word Group in the New Testament.

Paul — and this is indicative of his literary position — uses λογίζεσθαι in all its nuances, though he bends it to his own purpose. On the other hand λογισμός occurs only twice, and then in Hell. garb. The rest of the NT follows current usage. λογίζεσθαι is rare (6 times, including two quotations) and weak (1 Pt. 5:12). The commercial sense does not occur, nor does λογισμός.

1. Thought taken captive to Christ. [8]

Paul was not merely acquainted with the popular philosophical idea of thought. He expressed it exactly in his use of λογισμός. The apostle even uses it in a

[7] Cf. the lexicons.

[8] What follows is to be regarded only as an exposition of the terms λογίζεσθαι and λογισμός. On NT thought cf. H. Leisegang, *Der Ap. Pl. als Denker* (1923); E. Stauffer, *Grundbegriffe einer Morphologie des nt.lichen Denkens* (1929).

positive sense in R. 2:15. This is because he stands on the same ground as the diatribe when in his conflict with paganism he mentions the general moral law and conscience. He gives force to the existence of this common law with his reference to the thoughts which either accuse or excuse us. [9] This reference is meaningful, however, only because it belongs to the nature of these thoughts to judge according to the law, to be dependent on it. [10] Since this is not stated directly, the idea must have been a common one which could be presupposed. That this was so may be seen from 4 Macc., whose view is in striking agreement with what is here presupposed. If, then, λογισμός is in R. 2:15 a pregnant concept like νόμος and συνείδησις, one should not overlook the fact that the reference is only to the judicial activity of λογισμός, and no room is left for the high estimation which might also be linked with it.

In 2 C. 10:4, on the other hand, there is no longer any common ground. Both materially and metaphorically (v. 3, 5) there is open conflict against the λογισμοί, which are again to be taken in the very special sense, i.e., in the first instance the unfavourable judgments of Paul's opponents mentioned in v. 2. Since this λογίζεσθαι is not only hostile to Paul (an echo of the LXX) but also presupposes an overestimation of the rational mind (cf. the particular situation in Corinth), the philosophical term is in view. [11] When the metaphor of the fortress and ὕψωμα is also taken into account, we have a view of λογισμοί similar to that found in Wis. They are the thoughts of a reason which in its self-vaunting shuts itself off from God.

These thoughts are not destroyed by carnal weapons. The ground of reason has to be abandoned. The apostle's weapons are δυνατὰ τῷ θεῷ. To reason he opposes the reality of God as this is manifested at the cross. That λογίζεσθαι grounded in reason will fall when confronted by this reality is stated in Lk. 22:37 in a quotation from Is. 53:12: καὶ μετὰ ἀνόμων ἐλογίσθη. [12] The purely conceptual transcending of the Gk. sense of λογίζεσθαι as an apprehension of truth is here a picture of the collapse of heaven-storming reason before the revelation of this heaven.

It is possible that the translator of Is. 53:12 used λογίζεσθαι to bring into the passage the emotional overtone which it had gained as an equivalent of חָשַׁב, for ἀριθμεῖσθαι (so 'ΑΣ) is a stricter rendering of the original. At any rate, λογίζεσθαι takes on here, and keeps (cf. v. 3 f.), the character of an unbelieving and blinded judgment. Indeed, this became the *locus classicus* for this type of thinking: Mk. 15:28 (interpolation from Lk.); 1 Cl., 16, 3 f. and 13; Just. Dial., 13, 4; 89, 3; Apol., I, 50, 2; 51, 5; Eus. Dem. Ev., III, 2, 68 ff.

---

[9] A special question is whether the μεταξὺ ἀλλήλων refers to the Gentiles or the thoughts. In the former case (Khl. R., *ad loc.*) the thoughts as a judgment on others are a special witness along with self-judgment; in the latter (Zn. R., *ad loc.*) they are simply an expression of this συνείδησις, cf. → n. 10.

[10] In the context both the accusations and the excuses refer back to the law, not the latter to the person (Ltzm. R., *ad loc.*). If we link the μεταξὺ ἀλλήλων with the thoughts, and thus assume a conflict, this is against the unequivocal nature of the νοῦς, and might here give rise to doubts as to the existence of the law. For this reason it is best to construe μεταξὺ ἀλλήλων as the mutual judgment of the Gentiles "among themselves."

[11] For a judgment arising from superiority, cf. R. 2:3, also Ac. 19:27, with a clear echo of the LXX (Is. 40:17; 2 Ch. 9:20).

[12] LXX: ἐν τοῖς ἀνόμοις. Lk. does not go back to the Heb. but uses another edition, cf. Just. Apol., I, 50, 2.

But if λογισμοί are hurled from their high keep, Paul takes them prisoner εἰς τὴν ὑπακοὴν τοῦ Χριστοῦ, 2 C. 10:5. Far from repudiating λογίζεσθαι altogether, he demands its renewal, 1 C. 4:1; 2 C. 10:7, 11; 12:6. [13] But now it must be oriented to the facts established by the reality of God. [14] Thus λογίζεσθαι becomes the term for the "judgment of faith" (R. 3:28; [15] 6:11; 8:18; 14:14; Phil. 3:13). All questions are framed in terms of such a conclusion: What are the consequences of the crucifixion for the righteousness of man (R. 3:28)? or: How are we to think of present sufferings in the light of the glory of the τέλειον (R. 8:18)? The norm of λογίζεσθαι is outside and above it. As saving event, it can be grasped only by faith. It is a fact, not a principle, and the act of thought must be orientated to this fact. Then λογίζεσθαι is obedient.

A mark of the judgment of faith is its unconditional validity. When Paul judges concerning the state of his perfection (Phil. 3:13) or his position as an apostle (2 C. 11:5), no objections can be raised by the community. According to R. 14:14 the faith of the weak is overthrown if he takes meat sacrificed to idols. His judgment that this meat is unclean is for him a binding reality whose violation means that he himself is shaken. Thus the obedient apprehension of the reality of faith in λογίζεσθαι poses the demand that life should be subordinated to this reality. The imperative of R. 6:11: λογίζεσθε yourselves to be dead to sin and alive to God, implies, then, that conduct should be in conformity with this judgment.

2. λογίζεσθαι in the Ministry of the Apostle.

οὐχ ὅτι ἀφ' ἑαυτῶν ἱκανοί ἐσμεν λογίσασθαί τι ὡς ἐξ ἑαυτῶν, ἀλλ' ἡ ἱκανότης ἡμῶν ἐκ τοῦ θεοῦ, 2 C. 3:5. Paul is here referring in general terms to his work. [16] If it is called a λογίζεσθαι, this does not mean that the apostle is a thinker. It is explained by the broad understanding of the term. He has in view the whole work of thought within the framework of apostolic activity, i.e., thinking, judging, planning and resolving. This extension of meaning may be found already in the LXX when it uses the word for חָשַׁב. It is also to be seen in 1 C. 13:11 and 2 C. 10:2. Here Paul intends to meet his opponents resolutely. But this intention is not a purely logical act as distinct from deeds. It is the beginning of a deed. Again, only God enables the apostle to come to this judgment. As obedience must follow the judgment in its narrower sense, so his plans and conclusions must be accompanied in his missionary work by a continual openness to the Spirit. [17] Even though the conferring of the λογίζεσθαι makes the office διακονία τοῦ πνεύματος ... ἐν δόξῃ (2 C. 3:8), the ἱκανότης does not imply essential relationship, but ministry, or, in view of the broader significance of λογίζεσθαι, commitment to action.

---

[13] 2 C. 12:6: εἴς τινα, is closer to the LXX Hos. 7:15: "to imagine something against someone," than to the secular "to put to an account," → n. 4.

[14] Cf. Hb. 11:19.

[15] Acc. to the reading here preferred (λογιζόμεθα γάρ, cf. Zn. R., *ad loc.*), the judgment is the basis of v. 27: "For we are of the opinion that ..." whereas the reading οὖν makes it appear that the judgment is a sum of the ideas developed in vv. 21-27: "We thus conclude ..." But surely the conclusion ought to come after v. 26.

[16] So in most modern comm. Acc. to Wnd. 2 K., *ad loc.* the τί refers to the evaluation of the calling (λογίζεσθαι = "to ascribe to oneself a title"); acc. to Thdrt., de Wette, Neander it refers to the doctrine or preaching (λογίζεσθαι = "to excogitate, invent").

[17] Earlier commentators took the passage to be a general ref. to human insufficiency (Augustine, Calvin, Bengel).

3. λογίζεσθαι in the Life of the Community.

ὅσα ... ἀληθῆ, ὅσα σεμνά, ... ταῦτα λογίζεσθε, Phil. 4:8. It is not the custom of Paul to summon his congregations to reflection, at least at the end of his epistles. The community is to consider how it is to do good. On the basis of the LXX there is here a clear emotional ring.[18] If the passage offers us a list of virtues, i.e., something borrowed from the Gk. world, it is simply another example of the independent way in which Paul handles what he borrows from the world around: οὐ λογίζεται τὸ κακόν, 1 C. 13:5. The usual translation (cf. 2 Tm. 4:16) tends to create a divergence between Paul and the LXX, and even assumes, if there is allusion to Zech. 8:17,[19] that he misunderstands the LXX in favour of the Gk. sense. But quite apart from Zech. the Heb. meaning "not to imagine evil" is quite possible in view of the common use of this expression in the LXX.

The practical side is strongly to the fore, so much so, indeed, that for Greeks this activity would no longer come in the sphere of λογίζεσθαι. A statement like the ἀγάπη λογίζεται of 1 C. 13:5 is just as unthinkable to the Greeks as it is natural to the Hebrews. This type of reflection is not following a principle. It is living in accordance with the event of salvation (Phil. 2:5 ff.) or after the example of the apostle, who is the instrument of Christ (Phil. 4:9). If Christ is the normative factor, this means for λογίζεσθαι the power to live. Nor is it arbitrarily or aimlessly that λογίζεσθαι is impelled to action. Having its source in the saving event, it unfolds in the community established by this event, and it finds its fulfilment in the edification of this community (1 C. 12; 14).

4. λογίζεσθαι as the Saving Act of God.

a. The imputing of faith, Jm. 2:23; R. 4:3 ff., 9 ff., 22 ff.; Gl. 3:6; Gn. 15:6 is quoted.

LXX: καὶ ἐπίστευσεν Αβραμ τῷ θεῷ, καὶ ἐλογίσθη αὐτῷ εἰς δικαιοσύνην. Cf. also v. 6b, ψ 105:31 and 1 Macc. 2:52 (B א; the simple pred. nom. of A is to be preferred as the more difficult reading), also Philo Rer. Div. Her., 94: λογισθῆναι τὴν πίστιν εἰς δικαιοσύνην αὐτῷ; and more freely Leg. All., III, 228: δίκαιος ἐνομίσθη, cf. Barn., 13, 7: πιστεύσας ἐτέθη εἰς δικαιοσύνην, or simply ἐδικαιώθη, Just. Dial., 23, 4. For v. 6a alone cf. Philo Abr., 262; Migr. Abr., 44. The whole verse occurs in Jub. 14:6; Jm. 2:23; R. 4:3; Gl. 3:6; 1 Cl., 10, 6, though (apart from Gl. 3:6) in a form with δέ more suitable for quotation.

The peculiarity of the mode of expression is that it links salvation with faith, and thus poses acutely the problem of merit.

This may be perceived already in the redaction which embraces both J and E: וְהֶאֱמִן בַּיהוָה וַיַּחְשְׁבֶהָ לּוֹ צְדָקָה.[20] In relation to the basic theme of the Abraham stories as the prophetic narrator seems to have understood them, namely, that of free election, the believing Abraham can only be a recipient, just as Yahweh condescends as the Lord in the ensuing making of the covenant (Gn. 15:9 ff.). This is implicit in the meaning of חָשַׁב. Faith is reckoned for righteousness because this is pleasing to the will of Yahweh, not because faith has this value intrinsically. If in the final redaction Yahweh also makes a demand on Abraham when the covenant is concluded (v. 8), it

[18] Cf. ψ 139:3; Jer. 11:19.
[19] Heinrici, J. Weiss, *ad loc.*; Pr.-Bauer,[3] *s.v.*
[20] Whether Gn. 15:6 is J (Gunkel) or E (Procksch) it is not possible to decide.

may be suspected that along with the judgment of righteousness a concession is made to the demand for recognition contained in the faith of Abraham. In this sense faith is also a merit. If the meaning of חָשַׁב is in tension with this view, in Ps. 106:31, where the judgment on Abraham is transferred to the act of Phinehas, an attempt is made, by changing the kal into ni, to adapt the quotation to the less personal way of speaking about God in post-exilic times, and thereby to take the judgment out of the sphere of personal will and to turn it into a general recognition. The Rabb. tends to weaken the sense even more by putting זְכוּת for צְדָקָה.[21] In this respect it is worth noting that in the Rabb. writings חָשַׁב is seldom used for the recording of human achievements in the religious sphere. Among other terms, the most common is הֶעֱלָה כְּאִלּוּ.[22] This commercial expression gives the value of an achievement by comparing it with another act whose value is known: "When a man honours his father and mother, says the Holy One ...: I reckon it to them as though I dwelt among them and they honoured me" מעלה אני עליהם כאילו דרתי ביניהם וכבדוני, bQid, 30b. The word חָשַׁב, on the other hand, does not carry any direct ref. to the idea of book-value. The act is assessed in terms of its quality (whether a merit or a fault), so that the implication is: "The honouring of parents I reckon to them as righteousness." But if חָשַׁב (and with it Gn. 15:6) is not fully adequate either in form or content from the standpoint of Rabb. terminology, the real adaptation of the content of the quotation to post-exilic theology takes place in the Gk. sphere. For when the LXX used λογίζεσθαι for חָשַׁב, it found a term which embraces both the idea of imputation (the noting of human achievements in heaven) and also merit (God's recognition of the value of faith). Thus understood — and in the first instance λογίζεσθαι could, of course, be understood only in its Gk. sense — the quotation tells us that it is by merit, i.e., because it actually has this value, that faith is reckoned for righteousness. Gn. 15:6 thus becomes a solid proof of the merit of father Abraham and of faith in general, 1 Macc. 2:52; Jub. 14:6; Philo Abr., 262; Leg. All., III, 228; Migr. Abr., 44; Rer. Div. Her., 90 and 94.

In the NT a reaction may be seen already in Jm. 2:23 (→ II, 201). No matter how we take this whole passage, the use of the word is plainly distinguished from its use in later Judaism by the fact that the emphasis falls, not on the meritoriousness of faith, but on its commitment to action. It is not possible to say anything very definite about the precise meaning of λογίζεσθαι here, since Gn. 15:6 is to be taken in its totality as a saying.

Things are otherwise in Paul. Here we have a radical break with Judaism at the very point of the understanding of λογίζεσθαι. Having introduced the quotation in R. 4:3, Pl. goes on to expound it as follows: τῷ δὲ ἐργαζομένῳ ὁ μισθὸς οὐ λογίζεται κατὰ χάριν ἀλλὰ κατὰ ὀφείλημα· τῷ δὲ μὴ ἐργαζομένῳ, πιστεύοντι δὲ ἐπὶ τὸν δικαιοῦντα τὸν ἀσεβῆ, λογίζεται ἡ πίστις αὐτοῦ εἰς δικαιοσύνην (4:4 f.). With reference to this λογίζεσθαι there are three possibilities. 1. One may take faith itself as the only point of comparison with Gn. 15:6, ignoring as inadequate the nature of the judgment in view of its use in later

---

21 Cf. Moore, II, 237; A. Meyer, *Das Rätsel des Jk.* (1930), 137; Str.-B., III, 199 ff.

22 Weber, 280 ff.; Str.-B., III, 121 ff. In this respect the "just as if" should be noted. The achievement is always smaller than what Yahweh imputes. But the same is true of transgressions. More common is the subst. חֶשְׁבּוֹן, cf. Ab., 3, 1: דִּין וְחֶשְׁבּוֹן in the commercial sense. It can be used fig. of God's accounting. On bQid, 30b cf. the account of the religious background in R. Meyer, "Hellenistisches in d. rabb. Anthropologie," BWANT, IV, 21 (1937), 20 ff.

Judaism.[23] 2. One may begin with the Greek sense[24] and refer the imputing to the content of faith to which there is here legal and objective correspondence.[25] 3. One may follow Paul's own explanation, negative and general in v. 4, positive and with closer reference to the actual formulation in v. 5, with a distinction between λογίζεσθαι κατὰ χάριν and κατὰ ὀφείλημα. The latter is in contrast to the λογίζεσθαι meant in Gn. 15:6, and denotes the statutory reckoning of a reward for those who can produce achievements. But the former, which describes the judgment of the quotation, denotes a gracious gift given to those who abandon all the claims that works might have and trust in the God who justifies sinners who have no claims.[26] We are surely right to see in the λογίζεσθαι κατὰ ὀφείλημα a description of the Jewish recording of merits (i.e., the Greek sense), while κατὰ χάριν corresponds exactly to the חָשַׁב of the original (in R. [J E]). There is no need to look for a zeugma in λογίζεσθαι κατὰ χάριν.[27] On the contrary, one may assume that when Paul uses this term, even though he may not be quoting the original directly, he intentionally has in view the Hebraic λογίζεσθαι of the LXX (which he also uses elsewhere), and is playing this off against the Gk. use.[28]

This interpretation, with its strict evaluation of κατὰ χάριν in R. 4, offers a clear solution to the problem of Gn. 15:6. For it excludes all thought of merit by emphasising that there is no idea of recording in the Heb. term. One might equally well say that faith is acknowledged to him for righteousness, or even better that righteousness is allotted to the believer.[29] Moreover, the seat of the judgment is in the gracious will of God, and this makes it quite impossible for human insight to anticipate the judgment in terms of merit. What faith is intrinsically is of no relevance.[30] This is the one answer to the question why faith is declared to be righteous. The very question is rejected as false. Attention is directed away from human weakness or supposed human strength to the grace of God. Everything depends on this. Once the idea of merit is banished, a positive answer can then be given, though without ascribing any particular worth or deserving to faith as a human attitude. In the light of the typical faith of Abraham this runs as follows. Faith confidently subjects itself to the judgment and grace of the cross. It is thus the only human attitude in face of which God's λογίζεσθαι takes place (v. 16a). Only the believer is ready to live by God's grace. Hence this grace is allotted to him as righteousness (v. 20 ff.). The meaning of λογίζεσθαι never allows us to forget that this is possible only as a repetition of the justification effected at the cross, i.e., in faith (v. 23 f.). What was said earlier about the realistic aspect of the judgment

---

23 Cf. A. Deissmann, *Paulus*² (1925), 132; A. Schweitzer, *Die Mystik d. Ap. Pls.* (1930), 202; W. Michaelis, "Rechtfertigung aus Glauben bei Pls." in *Festgabe f. A. Deissmann* (1927), 122.

24 In this case the term would correspond to its use, e.g., in R. 2:26; 9:8.

25 So G. Schrenk, → II, 207; H. D. Wendland, *Die Mitte d. paul. Botschaft* (1935), 43.

26 Cf. Khl. R., Ltzm. R., Schl. R., *ad loc.* They miss the pt., however, that λογίζεσθαι has a different sense in secular Gk. and later Judaism.

27 I.e., in relation to the usual Gk. sense.

28 Cr.-Kö., *s.v.* and Zn. R., *ad loc.* suggest a special meaning for λογίζομαι in the LXX though without emphasising its distinction from the secular meaning. The Heb. meaning may also be present with a simple dat. constr. (as against Zn.). The first translator of Gn. 15:6 may have had the Gk. sense in view, but this would not prevent the later penetration of the Heb. sense in view of its presence elsewhere.

29 This would be the logical development of the train of thought from v. 4, but we do not find it because Paul returns to Gn. 15:6 (Ltzm. R., *ad loc.*).

30 Cf. (also for what follows) G. Schrenk, → II, 207; Schl. R., *ad loc.*

is now important. Justification is not a fiction alongside the reality.[31] If God counts faith as righteous, man is wholly righteous in God's eyes. And the reality of God's judgment is normative for man. He becomes a new creature through God's λογίζεσθαι. Hence Gl. 3:2-6 can equate justification with the receiving of the Spirit and quote Gn. 15:6 in support of justification.

The demarcation from Judaism is thus complete. It is to be taken the more seriously because Paul in using Gn. 15:6 wrests the main argument from his opponents, thereby correcting the LXX and reviving the prophetic view. On the other hand, λογίζεσθαι may rightly be used along with δικαιοῦν in spite of the polemical situation. If δικαιοῦν presents God as Judge, λογίζεσθαι presents Him as Father. Hence the two words necessarily complement one another, and only from this twofold standpoint is the cross fully presented as both judgment and grace.

After Paul this understanding was quickly lost, and Gn. 15:6 became a pious phrase. The fact of Abraham's faith was valued only for the purposes of exhortation (1 Cl., 10, 6), and if it was desired to avoid the Gk. sense ἐλογίσθη was replaced by ἐτέθη (Barn., 13, 7) or ἐδικαιώθη (Just. Dial., 23, 4).

b. Non-imputation of sin, R. 4:7 f.; 2 C. 5:19; based on ψ 31:2.

LXX: μακάριος ἀνήρ, οὗ οὐ μὴ λογίσηται κύριος ἁμαρτίαν (A). א ac has ᾧ corresponding to the Heb. לוֹ. There are also differences in quotation: R. 4:8 οὗ BאDG, ᾧ AC𝔎 pl; 1 Cl., 50, 6 οὗ A, ᾧ 𝔎; Just. Dial., 141, 2 ᾧ. In spite of the vacillation the distinction between οὗ and ᾧ might well be significant. Thus, if the LXX has οὗ for the Heb. לוֹ, the intention might be to avoid the commercial sense, which in routine transl. would be suggested by λογίζεσθαί τινι. Hence λογίζεσθαι has perhaps the sense of "regard" as in Is. 13:17; 33:8; 53:3. In any case the LXX deviates from the Gk. sense, since the non-imputation is grounded in the subj. rather than the obj. (that is, there is no connection of guilt between the act and the one who performs it).

The intrusion of grace into the divine righteousness offended the Greek linguistically and the Jew materially. Only at the cross are these two things united as they never are in the OT. If in 2 C. 5:19 God does not impute sins, this is because Christ has become sin for us.[32] In this full sense ψ 31:2 is used along with Gn. 15:6 in R. 4:8, and it provides the negative basis of the antithesis δικαιοσύνη χωρὶς ἔργων (v. 6) as Gn. 15:6 had previously provided the positive basis.

There is in this passage no equation of Gn. 15:6 and ψ 31:2, as though the imputation of faith were the same as the non-imputation of sin. This would in fact restrict considerably the range of Gn. 15:6. The connecting link in the chain is the word λογίζεσθαι. This word, in its unmistakable Hebrew character (ψ 31:2) as a judgment of grace, is the point of comparison. By contrast, Just. Dial., 141, 2 f. (ᾧ) is still thinking in Gk. terms, and he cancels out the element of grace by suggesting that man's expiation by repentance is the ground of non-imputation.

Heidland

λογικός → 142.
λόγιος → 136.
λογομαχέω, -ία → 143.
λόγιον → 137.
λογισμός → 286.
λόγος → 69 ff.

---

[31] Cr.-Kö. and Zn. come close to this in their exposition of λογίζεσθαι.
[32] As an example of substitutionary reckoning in business cf. Ditt. Or., 595, 13 ff.: τὰ γὰρ ἕτερα ἀναλώματα ... ἑαυτοῖς ἐλογισάμεθα, ἵνα μὴ τὴν πόλιν βαρῶμεν.

† λοιδορέω, † λοιδορία,
† λοίδορος, † ἀντιλοιδορέω

→ βλασφημέω, → ὀνειδίζω.

A common Gk. word group, not attested only in the pap., with the unanimous sense "to reproach," "insult," "revile," even "blaspheme," though it is not a religious term. In public life in Greece insult and calumny played a considerable part, whether among the heroes in Hom., in political life in the democracies, in comedy, or in the great orators. Not to be susceptible was part of the art of living, though in fact a great deal of objective harm was done by this love of denigration. [1]

In the LXX [2] we usually find λοιδορεῖν and λοιδορία for ריב (λοιδόρησις in Ex. 17:7 for the place-name מְרִיבָה). The sense, then, is that of "to wrangle," "quarrel," "remonstrate angrily." The word is close to the Gk. in Ιερ. 36:27, where it is used for "to chide" (simple form in א and later transl., συλλοιδορεῖν in AB), in Prv. 10:18, where it occurs for דִבָּה in the sense of "calumny," "evil report" (other words are used elsewhere), in 2 Macc. 12:14 (the verb), and λοιδορία 3 times in Sir. The adj. λοίδορος is found 3 times in Prv. and once in Sir. in the sense of "contentious." The compound διαλοιδόρησις is found in Sir. 27:15. Materially Sir. 22:24 deserves special mention. The idea that abuse which injures the reputation is a preliminary form of murder reminds us of the exposition of the 6th commandment in the Sermon on the Mount, except that for Jesus anger (cf. Did., 3, 2) and calumniation are an actual transgression of the commandment. [3] The context of the term in Sir. 29:6 is to be noted; it is used along with κατάρα and ἀτιμία. In Test. XII B. 5:4 the adj. λοίδορος takes up again the thought in the verb ὑβρίζειν. In Phil. Decal., 75 λοιδορία is used in the sense of "mockery" in logical connection with κατάρα; in Som., II, 168 it occurs in a kind of list of vices; in Agric., 110 there is ref. to competition in invective (λοιδορίας ἅμιλλα).

In the NT we find the verb 4 times, the noun twice, and the adjective twice, in the usual Greek sense. One may group the passages under the following heads.

1. λοιδορεῖν is an unchristian trait in those guilty of it. Thus λοίδορος is twice found in lists of vices (1 C. 5:11; 6:10). On the OT view it is especially forbidden in relation to superiors. Thus Paul is asked in Ac. 23:4: τὸν ἀρχιερέα τοῦ θεοῦ λοιδορεῖς; In his reply (v. 5) he says that he would have abstained from this intentional calumniation (v. 3: τοῖχε κεκονιαμένε) had he recognised the high-priest. [4] For it is written ἄρχοντα τοῦ λαοῦ σου οὐκ ἐρεῖς κακῶς. This verse has a religious aspect. The high-priest stands before God. To abuse him, especially

λοιδορέω κτλ. [1] Cf. on this J. Burckhardt, *Griechische Kulturgeschichte* (ed. J. Oeri), II[3] (1930/31), 353-363 [Kleinknecht].

[2] Cf. Helbing Kasussyntax, 20 ff.

[3] Cf. G. Bertram, "Bergpredigt u. Kultur," *Ztschr. f. d. evang. Religions-Unterricht*, 43 (1932), 338 f.

[4] Perhaps there is biting irony here; from his conduct one could not see that this man was the high-priest.

in the discharge of his office, is blasphemy. The situation is the same in Mart. Pol., 9, 3. The aged Polycarp cannot revile Christ (λοιδόρησον τὸν Χριστόν), for He is his King and Saviour, whom he cannot βλασφημῆσαι.

2. Several passages deal with the way in which the Christian is to comport himself when he is the object of λοιδορεῖν or stands under λοιδορία. 1 Tm. 5:14 stands alone in suggesting that the Christian must avoid all occasion for calumny (λοιδορία). That Christians are particularly exposed to calumniation for the Lord's sake is the tacit presupposition, cf. Mt. 5:11; 10:25. The man born blind (Jn. 9:28) has to learn this when the words of abuse which fall on him (ἐλοιδόρησαν αὐτόν) are really directed against Jesus (ἐκείνου, cf. v. 29: "We know not whence he is").

Christians are thus to take Jesus as their example, for He did not revile again [5] when He was reviled, 1 Pt. 2:23. This reminds us especially of the passion narrative, cf. Mt. 26:63; 27:29, 44; Jn. 18:23. The final verse deserves special notice, particularly in comparison with Ac. 23. Jesus is not completely silent when reviled, but He stresses the fact that His words were not spoken κακῶς.

The Christian, too, does not revile again when reviled. He does not answer railing with railing (μὴ ἀποδιδόντες λοιδορίαν ἀντὶ λοιδορίας, 1 Pt. 3:9). [6]

But he does not remain wholly silent when he suffers abuse, like the holy man praised in Test. B. 5:4, who is silent out of sympathy for the reviler, and who humbles him thereby. On the contrary, the Christian overcomes railing by repaying it with blessing: 1 Pt. 3:9: τοὐναντίον δὲ εὐλογοῦντες. [7]

This leads to the pregnant formula of 1 C. 4:12: λοιδορούμενοι εὐλογοῦμεν, "being reviled, we bless" (i.e., for Christ's sake, v. 10). This is echoed in Dg., 5, 15.

The world-conquering power of genuine Christianity is thus displayed even in respect of sins of the tongue. At this point human laws are transcended as in the Sermon on the Mount. When blessing is the answer to reviling the kingdom of God has broken in and the new creation is a reality.

Hanse

[5] ἀντιλοιδορεῖν, for which א* vg have the simple form, is very rare, though not without literary attestation.

[6] He is thus like one of those of old of whom Philo tells us in Agric., 110 that when challenged to a competition in reviling he said that he would never enter into such a competition, in which the victor would be worse than the vanquished.

[7] The verse is also taken up in Pol., 2, 2, where other members are added (including κατάρα) and it is combined with Mt. 7.

† λούω, † ἀπολούω, † λουτρόν [1] → βαπτίζω, καθαρίζω.

Contents: A. The Terms in Hellenism: 1. The General Usage. Bathing in Antiquity and the Attitude of the Church to it; 2. Sacral Baths and Purifications. B. λούειν κτλ. in the Old Testament and Judaism: 1. The Old Testament; 2. Judaism. C. λούειν κτλ. in the New Testament: 1. The Secular Sense; 2. Theological Reflection; 3. Examination of Pertinent Passages. D. λούειν κτλ. in the Church.

A. The Terms in Hellenism.

1. The General Usage. Bathing in Antiquity and the Attitude of the Church to it.

As distinct from πλύνειν for the washing of clothes and νίζειν or νίπτειν for washing the face, hands, or feet, λούειν is normally used for the complete cleansing of the body (rarely with a material obj. → P. Flor., 384, 30) in the sense "to wash," "to bathe," trans. τὸν δ' Ἥβη λοῦσεν, Hom. Il., 5, 905, usually med. "to wash oneself," "to take a bath," abs. P. Flor., III, 332, 11, with gen. (ποταμοῖο, Hom. Il., 6, 508), with ἀπό (κρήνης, Hdt., III, 23), also with dat. and acc. (ὕδατι τὸ σῶμα, Hdt., IV, 75). ἀπολούειν is used in the same sense, though often with a material obj. (λούειν ἄπο βρότον, "to wash away blood," Hom. Il., 14, 7) or a double acc. (Πάτροκλον λούειν

λούω κτλ. RE[3], XVI, 564 ff.; RGG[2], IV, 1847 ff.; Pauly-W., 2 (1896), 2743 ff.; I. v. Müller, *Die griech. Privataltertümer* = Hndbch. Kl. AW, IV, 1, 2[2] (1893), 132 ff.; H. Blümner, *Die römischen Privataltertümer, ibid.*, IV, 2, 2[3] (1911), 420 ff.; P. Stengel, *Die griech. Kultusaltertümer, ibid.*, V, 3[3] (1920), 155 ff.; Rohde [9, 10], esp. II, 71 ff., 405 ff.; L. Deubner, *Attische Feste* (1932), Index, *s.v.* "Bad," "λουτρίδες," "Reinigungen"; T. Wächter, "Reinheitsvorschriften im griech. Kult," RVV, 9, 1 (1910); J. Heckenbach, "De Nuditate Sacra," RVV, 9, 3 (1911), 3; E. Fehrle, "Die kultische Keuschheit im Altertum," RVV, 6 (1910), Index, *s.v.* "Baden, kultisches," "Weihwasser, über das Waschen von Götterbildern," 171 ff.; J. Zellinger, *Bad u. Bäder in d. altchristl. Kirche* (1928); F. J. Dölger, *Ichthys*, II (1922), Index, *s.v.* "Bad," "λούεσθαι," "λουτρόν" etc.; *Antike u. Christentum*, I (1929), 143 ff., 156 ff.; *Sol Salutis*[2] (1925), 20 f., 343 f.; Steinleitner, esp. 85 ff.; Schürer, Index, *s.v.* "Rein u. unrein," "Reinigungen," "Händewaschen," "Waschungen," "Essener"; Bousset-Gressm., Index, *s.v.*, "Reinheitsvorschriften"; Str.-B., esp. I, 108 ff.; W. Brandt, *Die jüd. Baptismen* (1910); Deissmann NB, 53 f.; LO, 86; W. Ramsay, Exp. 7th Ser., Vol. VIII (1909), 280; Bchm., Joh. W. 1 C. on 6:11; Dib. Past. on Tt. 3:5; Wnd. Kath. Br. on 2 Pt. 2:22; Bau., Zn., Tillm. J. on 13:10; H. Windisch, *Joh. u. d. Synpt.* (1926), 70 ff.; G. A. F. Knight, ERE, V, 814 ff. *s.v.* "Feetwashing"; E. Schwartz, NGG *phil.-hist. Kl.* (1907), 344 ff.; J. Kreyenbühl, *Das Ev. der Wahrheit* (1905), II, 102 ff. (he finds in Jn. 13:10 a heretical attack on Christian baptism, cf. R. Reitzenstein, *Die Vorgeschichte d. christl. Taufe* [1929], 160, n. 1); R. Eisler, "Zur Fusswaschung am Tage vor dem Passah," ZNW, 14 (1913), 268 ff. (he regards the footwashing as a mystical symbol of the marriage between Christ and the community); P. Fiebig, "Die Fusswaschung," *Angelos*, III (1930), 121 ff.; B. W. Bacon, Exp. T., 43 (1931/32), 218 ff. (points to sacramental footwashing in Ephesus on the eve of the Passover, along the same lines as Eisler); H. v. Campenhausen, "Zur Auslegung von Jn. 13:6-10," ZNW, 33 (1934), 259 ff.; F. M. Braun, *Rev. Bibl.*, NS, 44 (1935), 22 ff. (rightly links Jesus' action as Saviour with His example). → βαπτίζω, Bibl.

[1] Lat. *lavare*, New High German *Lauge*.

ἄπο βρότον, Il., 18, 345), also med. with acc. (σῶμα, Longus, I, 13, βρότον, Hom. Il., 23, 41). λουτρόν is the place for bathing, the bath-house, usually in the plur. from Hom. to the pap. (τὰ δημόσια λουτρά, P. Oxy., X, 1252, Verso 22 [3rd cent. A.D.]), though also in the sing. from the time of Hes.; also the water for bathing, the bath (λουτρόν ἐστιν, οὐ πότος, Alexis Fr., 9, 11, CAF, II, 300).

From an early time the Greeks were accustomed to bathe in rivers or the sea. There is also early evidence of swimming pools. Swimming was almost one of the rudiments in Athens (μήτε γράμματα μήτε νεῖν ἐπίστωνται, Plat. Leg., III, 689d). Warm baths are known from the pre-Homeric period. Bathrooms are an established feature in Cretan and mainland Mycenaean palaces. A cold bath often preceded the bath proper. The bath was not so much for cleansing as for strengthening and nursing, esp. after severe exertion. In the 3rd cent. B.C. the Gk. bath was adopted by the Romans under the existing name *balneum* (= βαλανεῖον). The Romans, with their heating system, made bathing into a new luxury. A list mentions 856, 927 or even 956 baths in imperial Rome. Bathing took an important place in the life of antiquity. Successive warm and cold baths were taken, accompanied by curative perspirings and anointings. If by reason of its situation a village could offer its inhabitants θερμῶν ὑδάτων λουτρά for the health and nurture of the body, this was regarded as a special amenity (Ditt. Syll.^{3}, 888, 124 f. [238 A.D.]). A man confesses that he avoids baths and ointments since his wife has gone from him (P. Oxy., III, 528, 10). The Church was not resolutely opposed to the bathing customs of the time, but it fought against excesses.

2. Sacral Baths and Purifications.

According to primitive ideas there is a higher degree of impurity. In certain conditions and processes of human life, e.g., birth, menstruation, and sickness, demons are at work. These homeless souls are also about human corpses, especially the souls of murdered men as vengeful spirits. They also hover around the carcases of animals. Behind such animistic views lies an even more primitive conception which thinks only in terms of impersonal powers or material μίασμα. The man affected by this is not only in supreme danger himself. He is also a danger to those around him, and he is thus in need of purification. Holy and unholy taboos are very close to one another, and in much the same way they make purification necessary (→ III, 414 f.). These notions are in the first instance physical and natural. Only gradually do moral judgments arise, though they may well be present before being brought to expression. Throughout antiquity these are the presuppositions which underlie sacral baths.

On Egypt → I, 530 f., 533, 534, n. 30. With a glance at corresponding Persian customs, Strabo says of the Babylonians: ὁσάκις δ' ἂν μειχθῶσιν ἀλλήλοις, ἐπιθυμιάσοντες ἐξανίστανται ἑκάτερος χωρίς· ὄρθρου δὲ λούονται, πρὶν ἀγγείου τινὸς ἅψασθαι· παραπλησίως γάρ, ὥσπερ ἀπὸ νεκροῦ τὸ λουτρὸν ἐν ἔθει ἐστίν, οὕτω καὶ ἀπὸ συνουσίας, XVI, 20, p. 745, ed. A. Meineke (1877). Cl. Al. knows similar customs in his own area, → I, 531, and he is already aware of religious and cultic parallels: τῶν μυστηρίων τῶν παρ' Ἕλλησιν ἄρχει μὲν τὰ καθάρσια, καθάπερ καὶ τοῖς βαρβάροις τὸ λουτρόν, Strom., V, 11, 70, 7.

Primitive rites of purification are not yet solidly attested in the sphere of Cretan and Mycenaean culture. Perhaps the Greeks brought them with them from Asia. Though the Greeks were not particularly scrupulous in the religious field, purifications affected their lives at every point. It was supposed that the very presence, and esp. the contact, of a menstruous woman would destroy seeds and make fruit bitter. Hes. is perhaps alluding to the bath which she had to take in Op., 753 ff.: μηδὲ γυναικείῳ λουτρῷ χρόα φαιδρύνεσθαι ἀνέρα, "for on it stands heavy penance." There is a firm ref. to it in the cultic order of Sunion (→ 298). Before marriage both bride and bridegroom took baths in their houses, and the water was to be brought from a sacred spring.[2] Sexual intercourse demanded a full bath (→ I, 531 f.). After a birth, both mother and child and all who touched the woman in child-bed were unclean. A miscarriage caused particularly serious impurity, since death was also involved (→ 298). Acc. to the cultic order of Eresos a full bath was adequate for the cleansing of a woman after labour (→ 298; lines 25 ff., to be filled out from the context). The purification of the child took place in the so-called amphidromia, originally on the 5th day when the newborn child was taken around the hearth. There is here a possible hint of lustration by fire, cf. also the use of torches (→ 18). There is no sure attestation of the bathing of the child as a sacral custom (Ditt. Syll.³, 1168, 6 is secular), but by analogy it seems likely. Callim. Hymn., I, 15 f. could be taken in this sense. In sickness baths were used to set aside the miasma and demons. Aesculapius often prescribes baths to heal and to reduce pain: αὐτὸν δι' αὐτοῦ λοῦσθαι ... λουόμενος δὲ οὐκ ἤλγησα (Ditt. Syll.³, 1170, 8 and 22, on accompanying rational cures, → III, 208 f.). In Epidauros a senator endows Ἀσκληπιοῦ λουτρόν (Paus., II, 27, 6). Madness in particular is regarded as the operation of hostile powers necessitating lustrations. Ajax, who murdered the flocks in his madness, cries out in a tragic allusion to his death (Soph. Ai., 654 ff.): ἀλλ' εἶμι πρός τε λουτρὰ καὶ παρακτίους | λειμῶνας, ὡς ἂν λύμαθ' ἁγνίσας ἐμὰ | μῆνιν βαρεῖαν ἐξαλύξωμαι θεᾶς.[3] In particular, anything linked with death is regarded as unclean and makes purification necessary. Death itself is unclean,[4] and makes everything that comes in contact with it unclean, e.g., clothes, the house of death, and especially relatives. The required lustrations are with water. τοὺς μιαινομένους λουσαμένους ... ὕδατος χύσι καθαροὺς ἶναι (burial ordinance of Keos, 5th cent. B.C.), Ditt. Syll.³, 1218, 30. Cf. also the cultic orders → 298. On leaving the house of death one must cleanse oneself by sprinkling water from the vessel before the door. The water must be fetched from another house, because the well is rendered unclean. Participation in, or even encounter with, a funeral makes a bath necessary, so that Julian orders funerals to be held at night (Jul. Ep., 76 [77], p. 601, 20 f., Hertlein): τοῖς δὲ εἰς τὰ ἱερὰ βαδίζουσιν οὐ θέμις προσελθεῖν ἐστι πρὶν ἀπολούσασθαι. Murder evokes particular horror. At this point there is an increasing intermingling of moral considerations, as when it is said that those who judge or bear witness contrary to the right, and who thus share in the offence, carry serious impurity into their houses, Antiphon Or., IV, 1, 3, ed. F. Blass [1871]. Nevertheless, the basis is still physical. Even accidental death, e.g., in a competition, or the blood revenge which is felt to be a duty, still carries with it an uncleanness which extends to everything the murderer touches or everyone he looks on.[5] He affects the city in which he stays and brings destruction on the ship in which he sails, with everyone in it, *ibid.*, V, 82. In distinction from other purifications, that of the murderer must be accomplished by others, not himself, → 299. Baths again play a leading role. The water must come from running springs or rivers or the sea (θάλασσα κλύζει πάντα τἀνθρώπων κακά, Eur. Iph. Taur., 1193) because

---

2 Cf. I. v. Müller, 148.

3 It is worth noting that quacks and hedge priests whom a disciple of Hippocr. tried to drive away, forbade baths to epileptics (Hippocr. Morb. Sacr., 1 [VI, p. 354, Littré]). This was perhaps for supposed hygienic or ascetic reasons. Purifications were carried out with blood.

4 With this is linked bathing before interment, a custom which led Antigone to give her life for her brother (τὸν μὲν λούσαντες ἁγνὸν λουτρόν, Soph. Ant., 1201, cf. 901; Eur. Tro., 1152; Phoen., 1667; on the other hand χθόνια λουτρά· τὰ τοῖς νεκροῖς ἐπιφερόμενα, Hesych. *s.v.*, gifts poured out like water). The dying Oedipus commands his children: ῥυτῶν | ὑδάτων ἐνεγκεῖν λουτρὰ καὶ χοάς ποθεν, Soph. Oed. Col., 1599. Related is the apotropaic use of torches at the death-bed, → 19.

5 It is remarkable that we never hear of purification of returning warriors. Perhaps originally only the killing of those of one's own kith and kin made unclean, though it is possible that the purification of the army at regular intervals was based on lustrations after campaigns.

in them the power of cleansing is particularly strong. In severe cases only three (Menand. Fr., 530, 22 [CAF, III, 152]), five (Emped. Fr., 143 [I, p. 369, 14 Diels[5]]), seven (Varro Human., 11, Probus in Vergil, ed. H. Keil [1848], p. 4, 1 ff.) or even twice times seven springs can bring full purity (Suid., *s.v.* ἀπὸ δὶς ἑπτὰ κυμάτων [A 3298, Adler]), if it can be had at all. Thus Oedipus cries out in Soph. Oed. Tyr., 1227 ff.: οἶμαι γὰρ οὔτ' ἂν Ἴστρον οὔτε Φᾶσιν ἂν νίψαι καθαρμῷ τήνδε τὴν στέγην, ὅσα κεύθει.

Purity is indispensable for cultic participation. On the cultus in Syrian Hierapolis Ps.-Luc. Syr. Dea, 53 (ed. G. Dindorf) says: ἢν μέν τις αὐτῶν νέκυν ἴδηται, ἐκείνην τὴν ἡμέραν ἐς τὸ ἱρὸν οὐκ ἀπικνέεται, τῇ ἑτέρῃ δὲ καθήρας ἑωυτὸν ἐσέρχεται. αὐτέων δὲ τῶν οἰκηίων τοῦ νέκυος ἕκαστοι φυλάξαντες ἀριθμὸν ἡμερέων τριήκοντα καὶ τὰς κεφαλὰς ξυράμενοι ἐσέρχονται· πρὶν δὲ τάδε ποιῆσαι, οὐ σφίσιν ἐσιέναι ὅσιον. The cultic order of Lycian Xanthos for the sanctuary of Men Tyrannos which he established in Sunion ordains μηθένα ἀκάθαρτον προσάγειν (Ditt. Syll.[3], 1042, 2 f. 2nd/3rd cent. A.D.). Individual directions are then given as to the required lustrations. καθαριζέσθω δὲ ἀπὸ σκόρδων καὶ χοιρέων (the eating of garlic and swine's flesh) καὶ γυναικός (sexual intercourse)· λουσαμένους δὲ κατακέφαλα (a complete bath from head to foot) αὐθημερὸν εἰσπορεύεσθαι· καὶ ἐκ τῶν γυναικέων (menstruation) διὰ ἑπτὰ ἡμερῶν λουσαμένην κατακέφαλα εἰσπορεύεσθαι αὐθημερόν, καὶ ἀπὸ νεκροῦ διὰ ἡμερῶν δέκα καὶ ἀπὸ φθορᾶς (miscarriage rather than abortion) ἡμερῶν τετταράκοντα (lines 3 ff.). A bath is ordered in all cases, but the periods of quarantine vary. Mourning in one's own house requires twenty days, sharing the mourning of another only three (ἀπὸ μὲν κάδεος ἰδίω περιμένναντας ἀμέραις εἴκοσι· ἀπὸ δὲ ἀλλοτρίω ἀμέραις τρεῖς λοεσσάμενον, cultic statute of Eresos, 2nd/1st cent. B.C., Dialectorum Graecarum exempla epigraphica, ed. E. Schwyzer [1923], No. 633, 4 ff.). There is no mention of murder. But this is not because it is viewed more lightly. The par. to Ditt. Syll.[3], 1042 in IG, III, 1, 73, which is to be regarded as a first draft,[6] has at the relevant pt. the strict requirement ἀνδροφόνον μηδὲ περὶ τὸν τόπον, "a murderer is not to come near the sanctuary." If this was later omitted, it was because severity against murder was self-evident, and the main aim of the cultic rule is to set the required times. Here, then, it is apparent that murder could not be expiated in the usual cultic ways. Elsewhere, too, we find moral distinctions. In the temple to Athene at Pergamos marital intercourse is differentiated from extra-marital, though this is pardoned easily enough (οἱ ... ἀπὸ μὲν τῆς ἰδίας γυναικὸς καὶ τοῦ ἰδίου ἀνδρὸς αὐθημερόν, ἀπὸ δὲ ἀλλοτρίας καὶ ἀλλοτρίου δευτεραῖοι λουσάμενοι, Ditt. Syll.[3], 982, 4 ff. = Inscr. Perg., 255, 4 ff., after 133 B.C.).[7]

Because there might always be impurity without a specific cause, lustration was customary before all cultic acts. Bathing (Hom. Od., 4, 750) or at least washing the hands (*ibid.*, 2, 261) preceded private prayer or the sacrifice to Hecate (ἀκαμάτοιο ῥοῇσι λοεσσάμενος ποταμοῖο, Apoll. Rhod. Argonautica, III, 1030) or entering the Eleusinion (εἰσῆλθεν εἰς τὸ Ἐλευσίνιον, ἐχερνίψατο ἐκ τῆς ἱερᾶς χέρνιβος, Lys., 6, 52) etc. Bowls specially provided with many spouts[8] were set up everywhere in the forecourts of the temple. Bathing and sprinkling before entering the sanctuary is mentioned as a pagan custom by Justin (Apol., I, 62, 1). On the Isis mysteries in Corinth → I, 530 n. 4; 534. The man who approaches deity is called λουσάμενος, Ditt. Syll.[3], 1159, 6; Orac. Trozeum, 5th cent. B.C.; cf. also the Egyptian books of the dead: a man whose feet are cleansed.[9] The priest esp. must be clean. During his period

---

[6] Cf. on this Leges Graecorum sacrae, ed. L. Ziehen (1906), 148 ff.

[7] More serious and yet more free is the outlook of the Pythagorean Theano, who, in answer to the question when to go into the temple after intercourse, replied: ἀπὸ μὲν τοῦ ἰδίου παραχρῆμα, ἀπὸ δὲ τοῦ ἀλλοτρίου οὐδέποτε.

[8] W. Dörpfeld, Ath. Mitt., 14 (1889), 124.

[9] Quoted from Dölger, *Ichthys*, II, 50, n. 1.

of duty the priest of Athena Cranaia in Elateia had to take special baths in traditional tubs, Paus., X, 34, 8. Because the transition from the sacred to the profane, or from a holy sphere to another, is always dangerous, a bath is necessary after a sacrifice or expiatory offering (Porphyr. Abst., II, 44 : No-one goes after into the city μὴ πρότερον ἐσθῆτα καὶ σῶμα ποταμοῖς ἢ πηγῇ ἀποκαθήρας) or a sacrifice to Zeus or Aesculapius, Paus., V, 13, 3. Formal bathing took place before the popular festivals of the mysteries, esp. in connection with the Eleusinian Mysteries. On the 16th of Boedromion there was general bathing in the sea which included the young pigs to be sacrificed.[10] In Eleusis itself one of the two salty watercourses called Ῥειτοί was used for the purification of the initiates, cf. Hesych., *s.v.* Ῥειτοί : ἐν τῇ Ἀττικῇ δύο εἰσὶν οἱ πρὸς τῇ Ἐλευσῖνι Ῥειτοὶ ῥωγμοί. καὶ ὁ μὲν πρὸς τῇ θαλάττῃ τῆς πρεσβυτέρας θεοῦ (Demeter) νομίζεται, ὁ δὲ πρὸς τὸ ἄστυ τῆς νεωτέρας (Kora), ὅθεν τοῖς λουτροῖς[11] ἁγνίζεσθαι τοὺς θιάσους. On similar festivals → I, 531 n. 6.

Private devotion pushed lustrations to extremes. In the religio-philosophical division of time by the Pythagoreans there was a regular place for the daily bath, Iambl. Vit. Pyth, 21, 98. There is a delightful sketch of the δεισιδαίμων[12] in Theophr. Char., 16. He is a man ἀπονιψάμενος τὰς χεῖρας καὶ περιρρανάμενος ἀπὸ ἱεροῦ. He is certainly one of those who sprinkle themselves liberally with sea-water. Each month he goes with his wife and children, or, if his wife has no time, with the nurse and children (to bathe out of religious devotion).[13] If he sees any wreathed with garlic at the cross-roads, on returning home he washes himself from head to foot (κατὰ κεφαλῆς λούσασθαι), calls the priest, and commissions him to purify him with a squill or young dog. Severe penitential exercises, which are linked with a threefold dip in the frozen Tiber early in the morning, are described in Juv. Sat., VI, 520 ff., cf. also Plut. → I, 532. We find a last wild off-shoot of these views in the magic rituals, which prescribed a bath at the commencement, Preis. Zaub., III, 381 λουσάμενος, → I, 531.

In lower purifications, the one who acts is the one in need. But in more serious cases, e.g., blood guilt, the purification must be done by others. In the early mythical period one hero purifies another. Thus Odysseus purifies Achilles after the murder of Thersites. In the historical period the priest comes on the scene (θύει ἱαρεὺς καὶ ἀπορραίνεται θαλάσσᾳ, *Inscr. of Cos,* ed. W. R. Paton and E. L. Hicks [1891], 38, 23). In Athens those of the Phytalidae and Eupatridae had this privilege (Plut. Thes., 12, 1 [I, 5c]; Paus., I, 37, 4; Athen., IX, 78 [p. 410a]). Gods, too, take a more or less direct part, e.g., Zeus Catharsios, Athene, Hermes, Apollo. An Eleusinian relief from the middle of the 5th cent. B.C. depicts a goddess pouring a vessel over a man, who is represented as small, → I, 530, n. 1. One might see here a sense that purification is not finally in human power. On the other hand, the gods themselves need cleansing on the Gk. view. When Apollo and Artemis kill Python, they are purified in Crete by Carmanor and Chrysothemis.[14] There are many ref. to washing statues of the gods. In Athens the old wooden image of Athene Polias was washed in sea-water by two maidens called πλυντρίδες or λουτρίδες on the festival of the Plynteria.[15] The silver statue of Cybele in Rome was washed in the Almo (*lavatio*)[16] at the end of the Attis festival early in the year. In both cases we have a purification of the ἱερὸς γάμος. The Egyptian religion of the sun regarded the daily progress of the sun through the ocean as a purifying and vivifying bath. This idea, originally referring to Osiris, was syncretisti-

---

[10] Cf. Deubner, 75.

[11] So with A. Mommsen, *Feste d. Stadt Athen* (1899), 228, n. 5 as opposed to the traditional but meaningless τοὺς λουτρούς.

[12] Untranslatable, midway between the bigot and the superstitious person.

[13] This is important in view of infant baptism in the early Church.

[14] Cf. Wächter, 66.

[15] Cf. Deubner, 18.

[16] F. Cumont, *Die orientalischen Religionen im römischen Heidentum*[3] (1931), 53.

cally transferred to other Hellenistic deities, as may be well seen on the inscr. in Preisigke Sammelbuch, I, 4127.[17] The address is to Mandulis Titan Macareus Apollon Aion Helios. The text is corrupt and hard to understand. But line 14 is plain: ἐν ᾧ καὶ ἁγίῳ τῷ τῆς ἀθανασίας ὕδατι λουσάμενος. A widespread mythical interpretation relates the "bath of the sun"[18] to believers who journey "in the ship of Osiris." The Gk. also says of his dead: τὸν ἀθάνατοι φιλέεσκον· | τοὔνεκα καὶ πηγαῖς λοῦσαν ἐν ἀθανάτοις (Epigr. Graec., No. 366, 4 f.). Melito of Sardis sees in the bath of the sun a hint of baptism (Περὶ λουτροῦ, 3, ed. E. Goodspeed [1914], 311).

A progressive feature in the Gk. world is the constantly recurrent recognition of the distinctiveness and special significance of the moral element. χεῖρας καὶ γνώμην καθαροὺς καὶ ὑγιεῖς ὑπάρχοντας καὶ μηδὲν αὑτοῖς δεινὸν συνειδότας, is how an inscr. from Rhodes describes members of the cult and the conduct required of them (Ziehen, No. 148, 4 ff., 2nd cent. A.D.). Moral purity is also required in Eleusis. Lampridius Alexander Severus, 18, 2 (Script. Hist. Aug., XVIII): *Quem ad modum in Eleusiniis sacris dicitur, ut nemo ingrediatur, nisi qui se innocentem novit.* Even in antiquity it was said often enough that the purifications had a blunting moral effect[19] because they were so many and frequent, → I, 534. To this context belongs a quotation of unknown provenance in Cl. Al. Strom., IV, 22, 142, 3: ἴσθι μὴ λουτρῷ, ἀλλὰ νόῳ καθαρός. But these voices are few and late, and since they make moral blamelessness a condition of approaching deity, they fall into the opposite error of moralisation. Hellenism has no understanding of the purification which is once-for-all, which comes into a life with revolutionary force, which is given unconditionally, and yet which carries with it an absolute moral commitment. It does not have any of the presuppositions of such an understanding.

B. λούειν κτλ. in the Old Testament and Judaism.

1. In the OT λούειν (ἀπολούειν only at Job 9:30; 2 Βασ. 11:4 ['A]; Prv. 30:12 [Θ]) is the regular transl. of רָחַץ (only Ps. 6:7 of שָׂחָה hi). In the q trans. this means "to wash" and intr. "to wash oneself," "to bathe," the latter also in the hitp, in the pu "to be washed." Both words are used in the first instance of care of the body, the newly born (Ez. 16:4 [9 ?]), women (Ex. 2:5; 2 Βασ. 11:2; Sus. [Θ] 15, 17), to enhance beauty (Ru. 3:3), for unlawful ends (Ez. 23:40). In men bathing is a sign of the end of self-mortification, 2 Βασ. 12:20. In 3 Βασ. 22:38 (cf. 3 Βασ. 20:19) there seems to be a hint of the superstitious use of the royal blood. 4 Βασ. 5:10, 12, 13 illustrate the use of the bath for purposes of healing. Semi-sacral ideas linked with the Jordan show the transition from λούεσθαι to later synonyms which became technical, → βαπτίζεσθαι, v. 14 (→ I, 535). In most cases the present words indicate bathing for ritual purity. It applies to those made unclean, e.g., by eating carcases (Lv. 11:40), leprosy (14:8 f. — after healing), sick discharges (15:5 ff.; Dt. 23:12), menstruation (Lv. 15:21 f.; 2 Βασ. 11:4 ['A, LXX ἁγιάζεσθαι]),[20] hemorrhage (Lv. 15:25 ff.), touching the dead (Tob. 2:5 [Σ 9]).[21] The priest in particular had to bathe before consecration and official actions (Ex. 29:4; 40:12; Lv. 8:6; 16:4) or after these (Nu. 19:7 f.).

---

[17] From Tamis (Kalabsha), 2nd/3rd cent. A.D. To the bibl. should be added A. D. Nock "A Vision of Mandulis Aion," *Harvard Theological Review,* XXVII (1934), 53-104.

[18] This idea is touched on also in Ovid Metamorphoses, IV, 214 ff.

[19] In another religious context this is also true of the many sacral baths of the Mandaeans, though the ethical plane is in many respects higher, → I, 536 f.

[20] Nowhere in the OT is there any sure ref. to normal sexual intercourse necessitating purification. Lv. 15:18, if it is not a later addition, refers to a special case. Cf. RE^3, XVI, 566 f.

[21] For the purifying water cf. Nu. 19.

In all these matters Israel is like other peoples of antiquity. The manistic and animistic background is the same. But under the influence of the unique knowledge of God there dawns at an early period and with incomparable passion and certainty a recognition of the distinctiveness of the moral element. Nowhere in the OT do we read of the purification of a murderer by a bath or similar means. The murderer falls victim to revenge or execution. The avenger of blood is not unclean. Cities of refuge are open only for those who slay unintentionally. These rules are expressly based on the fact that the land of Yahweh must not be polluted by blood, Nu. 35:9 ff., 27, 30 ff.; Dt. 4:41 ff.; 19:1 ff. If popular religion in every age was inclined to wash away guilt by ritual, among the classical representatives of the religion of Yahweh, especially the prophets, there is never any doubt that this is too easy a way of dealing with sin. Nevertheless, purifications occur, whether as fossil remains (if viewed historically), or as duties by which Yahweh tests the obedience of His people (if viewed within the total context of OT religion).

The idea of cleansing is certainly applied to liberation from moral defects, but only figuratively. Nowhere do the classical proponents of OT religion think that disobedience to the moral will of Yahweh can be expiated by external washing. The call is always for repentance and effective amendment. Cf. Is. 1:16: λούσασθε, καθαροὶ γένεσθε, ἀφέλετε τὰς πονηρίας ἀπὸ τῶν ψυχῶν ὑμῶν, ἀπέναντι τῶν ὀφθαλμῶν μου, also Prv. 30:12 and Jer. 4:14. This cleansing is also prayed for as the saving act of Yahweh (Ps. 51:7), and it is promised, especially for the last time of salvation (Is. 4:4; Zech. 13:1; Ez. 36:25). This does not exclude the thought of amendment and repentance. It supplements and transcends it by the idea of the divine grace exceeding and preceding all human achievement (Is. 43:25; 44:22). Without falling into superficial moralising, the prophets thus keep constantly alive the sense that external washing cannot undo the wrong (Jer. 2:22).

λουτρόν is found in the LXX only at Cant. 4:2; 6:6 of the washing-place for animals (cf. 5:12, λούεσθαι of doves), and at Sir. 34:25 of purification after contact with the dead, here fig. of cleansing from sin by fasting, which is useless if the offence is repeated. In Aquila it is used in ψ 59:8; 107:9 for washpot (LXX: λέβης τῆς ἐλπίδος).

2. In Judaism the emphasis falls on the ritual character of the washings, but instead of the present words טָבַל and → βαπτίζειν become tt. (also → νίπτειν for hands and feet, Mk. 7:3 f.; Mt. 15:2; cf. Lk. 11:38). On these purifications → III, 421. If there might seem to be a danger that Judaism would confuse the moral and the ritual, there remains a keen awareness that mere washing with water does not give remission (→ I, 536, n. 34). It is worth noting that Judaism did not find here, where it really lay, its superiority over pagans. It based this on the assumption that it was in advance in respect of its ritual washings.

In Judaism as among the Gentiles (→ 297), though perhaps not yet in Israel (→ 300, n. 20), a bath was customary after intercourse.[22] Joseph. uses ἀπολούσασθαι for this (Ap., 2, 203; → I, 531 f.). Cf. also bBer., 21a ff. The significance of washings in Judaism is finely illustrated, though possibly with tendentious and legendary features, in a fragment which may belong to the Ev. Naz., P. Oxy., V, 840.[23] A Pharisee forbids Jesus to enter the temple μήτε λουσα[μ]έν[ῳ] ... (line 14). No one must enter the holy place εἰ μὴ λουσάμενος (18 f.). When Jesus asks him if he is clean, he replies:

---

[22] Even if the original point was different, this might be a means of protection against non-moral defilement, bBer., 22a. For additional refs. cf. Brandt, 143.

[23] Cf. Hennecke, 31.

καθαρεύω, ἐλουσάμην γὰρ ἐν τῇ λίμνῃ τοῦ Δαυείδ (24 f.). Scrupulous washing of the hands in the morning is a protection against demons, Str.-B., IV, 533. Even Yahweh bathes after burying Moses. This is not because He needs cleansing, but to keep the Law, as when He also puts on phylacteries. When a heretic took Rab Abbahu up on this on the ground that all the waters on earth would not be enough for Yahweh, he gave the ready answer: "He bathed in fire" (bSanh., 39a, Str.-B., II, 21). Fire was a valid means of cleansing, → *infra*.

A few individuals or groups like Bannus or the Essenes (→ I, 537) pushed scrupulosity to the limit in their search for Levitical purity. Joseph. uses the present terms for their daily baths before meals (Bell., 2, 129: ἀπολούονται, 2, 161: λουτρὰ δὲ ταῖς γυναιξὶν ἀμπεχομέναις ἐνδύματα, καθάπερ τοῖς ἀνδράσιν ἐν περιζώματι).[24]

Philo is acquainted with the everyday use (λούεσθαι, Leg. All., II, 16, λουτρόν, Vit. Mos., II, 148, Det. Pot. Ins., 19), but more often he uses the words for the OT washings (λούειν, Vit. Mos., II, 143, λούεσθαι and ἀπολούεσθαι, Spec. Leg., I, 261, III, 89, 205 f., λουτρόν, Spec. Leg., 258, 261, of the purification of the fruit of the vineyard, Plant., 116). He also knows their ritual sense among the Gentiles (Deus Imm., 8: None may enter a sanctuary, ὃς ἂν μὴ πρότερον λουσάμενος φαιδρύνηται τὸ σῶμα, Leg. Gaj., 235: λουσάμενοι τῷ συγγενικῷ αἵματι — τοιαῦτα γὰρ τὰ λουτρὰ τοῖς εἰς ᾅδου φαιδρυνομένοις). He emphasises that external washing does not cleanse man (Mut. Nom., 49: ἄπειρα μέν ἐστι τὰ καταρρυπαίνοντα τὴν ψυχήν, ἅπερ ἐκνίψασθαι καὶ ἀπολούσασθαι παντελῶς οὐκ ἔνεστιν). To work out his philosophical outlook in terms of the OT, he distinguishes between washing the body and washing the soul (Cher., 95: τὰ μὲν σώματα λουτροῖς καὶ καθαρσίοις ἀπορρύπτονται, τὰ δὲ ψυχῆς ἐκνίψασθαι πάθη, οἷς καταρρυπαίνεται ὁ βίος, οὔτε βούλονται οὔτε ἐπιτηδεύουσι, Plant., 162: σώματα καὶ ψυχὰς καθηράμενοι, τὰ μὲν λουτροῖς, τὰ δὲ νόμων καὶ παιδείας ὀρθῆς ῥεύμασι), or he understands the external washings symbolically and allegorically as inner cleansing (Som., I, 82: τὰς τῶν κενῶν δοξῶν ἐκνίπτεσθαι καὶ ἀπολούεσθαι κηλῖδας, cf. Spec. Leg., I, 207: τὸ τοὺς πόδας ἀπολούεσθαι is to be understood symbolically, Rer. Div. Her., 113: ἀπολουσάμενοι τὰ καταρρυπαίνοντα ἡμῶν τὸν ἄθλιον ... βίον, Mut. Nom., 124: τὰ φρονήσεως λουτρά). This inner cleansing is his favourite theme. Thus in Som., I, 148 he distinguishes between those being purified (οἱ ἔτι ἀπολουόμενοι) and those who are fully purified (οἱ ἄκρως κεκαθαρμένοι).

λούεσθαι is used for an ethical proselyte baptism in Sib., 4, 165 → I, 535 f.

C. λούειν κτλ. in the New Testament.

1. The Secular Sense. Only λούειν occurs in a purely secular sense. It is used of the living in Ac. 16:33, of washing a corpse (with a weak sacral background?) in Ac. 9:37, of an animal in the bath, but fig., in 2 Pt. 2:22. Like the last ref., all others are related to freeing from sin, and esp. to baptism. λουτρόν is used only for this (Eph. 5:26; Tt. 3:5). The terms do not occur at all in the Synpt.

2. Theological Reflection. This must start with the fact that Christianity begins with a sharp protest against the interchanging and confusing of ritual and moral purity, and against confidence in external works. Because of this Jesus breaks dramatically and provocatively with Jewish custom (Mk. 7). Paul follows the same line[25] (→ I, 540).

---

[24] The girdle was also good manners among the Gks. and Romans, at least for both sexes in the *balnea mixta*. The Essenes demand more for women. This is perhaps the first ref. to a bathing costume.

[25] The primitive community felt a little differently. It was more Jewish than Jesus Himself. This is particularly true of James, the Lord's brother, Gl. 2:12. The popular idealisation

Cf. the continuation of the Gospel Fr. already mentioned, P. Oxy., V, 840, 32 ff.: (Jesus is speaking to the Pharisee) σὺ ἐλούσω τούτοις τοῖς χεομένοις ὕ[δ]ασιν ἐν οἷς κύνες καὶ χοῖροι βέβλην[ται] νυκτὸς καὶ ἡμέρας, καὶ νιψάμε[ν]ος τὸ ἐκτὸς δέρμα ἐσμήξω, ὅπερ [κα]ὶ αἱ πόρναι καὶ α[ἱ] αὐλητρίδες μυρί[ζ]ου[σιν κ]αὶ λούουσιν (there follows a description of inward uncleanness). ἐγὼ δὲ καὶ οἱ [μαθηταί μου] οὓς λέγεις μὴ βεβα[πτίσθαι βεβά]μμεθα ἐν ὕδασι ζω[ῆς αἰωνίου]. A sound NT concept may be seen here through the strange apocryphal garb.

As the NT sees it, there is no possibility of comparing the λούεσθαι of believers, which stands at the very heart of NT religion, with the external washings of paganism or Judaism. Any sacral and magical or ritualistic and legalistic over-evaluation of external cleansing would be a relapse from the basic NT position. Even the moralising view that baptism is a symbol of the sinner's resolve to break with the past and to begin a new life, on which basis he is cleansed before God, misses the true point and content of the NT message. The proper starting-point is the understanding of the remission of sins in the OT (→ 301; → I, 510). This is orientated to the holy and gracious person of God. In this light it is self-evident that fellowship with God is moral in character. God can and will have fellowship only with those who break with sin. But it is no less evident that the conversion of the sinner is not an adequate ground for fellowship with God. This ground is to be found only in God's mercy. Full cleansing from sin will come only in the consummation. The eschatological fulfilment which is nevertheless a present reality in Christ is the true theme of the NT witness. It is compressed in the crucifixion (and resurrection) of Christ. Believers are "elect ... to sprinkling with the blood of Christ" (1 Pt. 1:2). This is their cleansing (1 Jn. 1:7). Baptism, which constitutes the community, is for individuals the actualisation of this relation to salvation history. Hence, even though it resembles outwardly the cultic baths of pagans and Jews, it is not λουτρόν and λούσασθαι in the same sense, but in a new and unique sense,[26] → I, 540. Thus it is distinctive from the very first. The use of the words in the NT is to be interpreted against this background.

3. Examination of Pertinent Passages. All the relevant passages show that, so far as theological usage is concerned, λούειν and λουτρόν are baptismal terms.

a. In the text rec used by A.V., Rev. 1:5b runs as follows: τῷ ἀγαπήσαντι ἡμᾶς, καὶ λούσαντι ἡμᾶς ἀπὸ τῶν ἁμαρτιῶν ἡμῶν ἐν τῷ αἵματι αὐτοῦ. This would be a NT thought, indirectly related to baptism. But a better reading is: τῷ ἀγαπῶντι ἡμᾶς καὶ λύσαντι[27] ἡμᾶς ἐκ τῶν ἁμαρτιῶν ἡμῶν ἐν τῷ αἵματι αὐτοῦ.

b. In most of the other verses the connection with baptism in the sense indicated is quite obvious. Ac. 22:16 (Ananias to Saul): ἀναστὰς βάπτισαι καὶ ἀπόλουσαι τὰς ἁμαρτίας σου. The demand is rooted in the appearance of the

of Hegesipp. in Eus. Hist. Eccl., II, 23, 4 ff. is, of course, valueless as a source for the apostolic period, cf. G. Kittel, ZNW, 30 (1931), 145. The words βαλανείῳ οὐκ ἐχρήσατο are enough to show how little the author knew about the historical relations of the time of James.

[26] The development is to some degree par. to that of the concept of sacrifice. Repeated sacrifices are rendered superfluous by the perfect sacrifice of Christ, and in the same way ritual cleansings are no longer necessary in view of the one cleansing in the crucifixion and baptism.

[27] With ℌ 1 pm h sy Prim against ℜ P al gig vg.

risen Lord to Paul. 1 Cor. 6:11 is exhortatory, after a glance back at the heathen past of the readers: ἀλλὰ ἀπελούσασθε, ἀλλὰ ἡγιάσθητε, ἀλλὰ ἐδικαιώθητε ἐν τῷ ὀνόματι τοῦ κυρίου Ἰησοῦ Χριστοῦ καὶ ἐν τῷ πνεύματι τοῦ θεοῦ ἡμῶν. By washing, divine appropriation and pardon,[28] the connection with the sinful past is broken. Hence the need to guard against fresh defilement (→ I, 540 f.).

On the analogy of the two other verbs one might expect the pass. of λούειν. But this is very rare.[29] Furthermore, there is a clear allusion to pagan and Jewish lustrations, and these suggest the med. The Christian use of βαπτίζειν is different, → I, 540.

In Eph. 5:26 Christ gave Himself for the community, ἵνα αὐτὴν ἁγιάσῃ καθαρίσας τῷ λουτρῷ τοῦ ὕδατος ἐν ῥήματι. He did this with a view to bridal unity with it in unspotted sanctity (v. 27).

The part. does not supply something preceding the main verb but the means of its fulfilment. ἐν ῥήματι is a closer definition of καθαρίσας. The cleansing takes place through the specified bath (double art.) by means of the word. The word is that spoken at baptism. This word brings the preceding word of proclamation to its goal. It is neither to be perverted into magic nor dissolved into mere symbolism. It goes back to God and Christ, and thence derives its efficacy.[30]

In Hb. 10:22: προσερχώμεθα μετὰ ἀληθινῆς καρδίας ἐν πληροφορίᾳ πίστεως, ῥεραντισμένοι τὰς καρδίας ἀπὸ συνειδήσεως πονηρᾶς καὶ λελουσμένοι τὸ σῶμα ὕδατι καθαρῷ, the reference is not to an ultimately unrelated juxtaposition of outer and inner cleansing (so Philo → 302; I, 534, and Joseph., → I, 535), but to an inseparable relationship between the outer process and the sacramental operation, → I, 540. Tt. 3:5: Not on the basis of our works, but according to His mercy God saved us διὰ λουτροῦ παλιγγενεσίας καὶ ἀνακαινώσεως πνεύματος ἁγίου.

Since reception of the Spirit is constantly connected with baptism in the NT, there is no reason to combine ἀνακαινώσεως κτλ. directly with διά. λουτρόν is the master concept for both the gen. which follow. The more individualistic view of regeneration and renovation is probably Hellenistic rather than genuinely Pauline.[31] The more significant, then, is the close link with forgiveness indicated by λουτρόν. This is undoubtedly Pauline, → I, 540.

2 Pt. 2:22 of Gnostic Libertines: συμβέβηκεν αὐτοῖς τὸ τῆς ἀληθοῦς παροιμίας· κύων ἐπιστρέψας ἐπὶ τὸ ἴδιον ἐξέραμα, καί· ὗς λουσαμένη εἰς κυλισμὸν βορβόρου. The first half of the verse is a quotation from Prv. 26:11, and the second half is a proverb. What is meant is that after baptism the false teachers return to sin, and incur unforgivable guilt according to Hb. 6:4 ff.; 10:26 ff.; 12:17; 1 Jn. 5:16.

---

[28] We are not to stress the order of the verbs. These are not carefully defined and systematically arranged terms. They are three distinctive Christian words which are virtually synonymous. To try to take them in the direct ethical sense is to cut the nerve of the exhortation.

[29] Liddell-Scott, *s.v.* λούω.

[30] Cf. Haupt Gefbr., *ad loc.*

[31] In R. 6 a similar thought is formulated very differently in connection with eschatology. Cf. A. Schweitzer, *Die Mystik des Ap. Pls.* (1930), 13 ff. and on the other side Dib. Past. Excursus *ad loc.*, and → I, 688.

Even in the second half there must be two acts. εἰς κυλισμὸν βορβόρου does not depend on λουσαμένη, certainly not in the simple spatial sense, and hardly as an εἰς final. It independently represents a finite verb. Thus we do not have the general sense that the sow bathes in the mire (cf. λούεσθαι ἐν πηλῷ, Aristot. Hist. An., VIII, 6, p. 595a, 31), but that after being washed it returns to the mud.[32]

c. The reference to baptism is not so clear in Jn. 13:10: λέγει αὐτῷ (Peter) Ἰησοῦς· ὁ λελουμένος οὐκ ἔχει χρείαν [εἰ μὴ τοὺς πόδας][33] νίψασθαι, ἀλλ' ἔστιν καθαρὸς ὅλος. Here the meaning of λελουμένος, and the significance of the whole action, is much debated.

The main difficulty is that the story has two points, the example of ministering love in v. 14 f. and cleansing by Jesus in vv. 8 ff. This can be avoided if we either restrict the service to helping to attain forgiveness[34] or base forgiveness on following the example of Jesus and His ministering love, in which case baptism is ruled out.[35] The first view is too narrow, and does not yield an adequate interpretation of vv. 12 ff., cf. esp. v. 16. But the second is also faced by the problem that if λελουμένος, as also νίψασθαι, refers to the feetwashing, there are no solid grounds for the change of term[36] or the perf.[37] The heavily stressed ὅλος emphasises the difference between total cleansing and partial cleansing, i.e., feetwashing. The idea that there can be total cleansing by ethical means is quite alien to the NT and esp. Jn. Nor is the inner unity of the story saved by finding in it a reference to objections raised against the practice of baptism by sprinkling, and an express equation of the foot-bath of the latter with the full bath of tradition.[38] This is to lead right away from the ethical purpose which is quite indisputable in view of vv. 12 ff. Nor is it the custom of the Evangelist to emphasise details. The most serious obstacle to this view, however, is the λελουμένος, which is taken to refer, not to baptism, but to a preceding cleansing. The ref. to Jn. 15:3 is not enough to explain this divergence from the symbolism. Even the conjecture that the author is thinking of the institution of a sacramental action for "ideal agape" which would be par. to the Eucharist, or that he does not have in view any ecclesiastical rite at all,[39] is not convincing. The term λελουμένος is very suggestive of baptism. Nor can it refer to the baptism of John, which is not regarded too highly in the Fourth Gospel;[40] it must refer to Christian baptism.[41] The question whether the

---

[32] Of the par. adduced by Wnd. 2 Pt., *ad loc.* the only one that is strictly appropriate is that from the Achikar Story, 8, 18 Syr., ed. R. H. Charles (*Oxford Ed. of the Apocrypha and Pseudepigr.* [1913], 772): "Thou wert to me, my son, as a pig which went into a bath, and when it saw a miry hole, it went in and bathed in it." This passage might have been known to the author. On the date cf. R. Smend, Beih. z. ZAW, 13 (1908); EJ, I (1927), 720 ff.; Schürer, III, 247 ff.

[33] The words in parentheses are not found in ℵ vg codd Orig Tert, but are convincingly attested by 𝔇 𝔎 pl lat, and are demanded by the sense (in spite of E. Schwartz and M. J. Lagrange, St. Jean² [1925], *ad loc.*). So also Tillm. J., *ad loc.*

[34] Zn. J., *ad loc.*

[35] P. Fiebig, 125 paraphrases as follows: "He who is now washed by me in respect of his feet, does not need further washing, but is already completely clean by the foot-bath ... Similarly, he is clean who does what I have done with the feetwashing."

[36] If λούεσθαι and abs. νίπτεσθαι are synon. in P. Oxy., V, 840, 32 and 34 f. (→ 303), this proves nothing regarding Jn. generally, let alone the present passage.

[37] The ref. to the so-called *casus pendens* in Heb. (T Pea, 2, 6) is no true analogy for a present, and overestimates the Hebraic element in the Fourth Gospel (so rightly v. Campenhausen, 270).

[38] So v. Campenhausen on the basis of archaeological material, though this is mostly later.

[39] H. Windisch, *Joh. u. d. Synpt.* (1926), 77. On additional and even less probable views → Bibl.

[40] Zn. J., *ad loc.* including the Word of Jesus received in faith.

[41] Bau. J. Excursus on 13:20.

twelve received it is answered by the fact that the relation of discipleship is a substitute.[42] But baptism is brought up. As so often, the Evangelist speaks to his age. Yet if the feetwashing is interpreted as baptism, is not the latter repeated? To try to see in this washing which follows the general cleansing a ref. to the Lord's Supper is not advisable,[43] since there is nothing to indicate it, and it is hard to see how a washing can symbolise a meal.[44] Indeed, Jn. 6 shows us that the Evangelist links the idea of life-giving rather than cleansing with the Lord's Supper. Thus it seems best to refer the τοὺς πόδας νίψασθαι to the partial forgiveness which follows and as it were continues baptism. This leaves us with two main thoughts, cleansing by Jesus, and the example of His ministering love. But there is no more reason to suspect a story than a parable because it has two points.[45] Indeed, the Evangelist uses multiplicity of meaning as a mode of exposition. The two basic thoughts are closely linked in this story. The one cleansing which is renewed daily is a supreme proof of the ministering love of Jesus, and in connection with the example of Jesus it will be for the true disciple the source of power f : his own ministry in love. Exactly the same combination of ideas, though in the reverse order, is to be found in Mk. 10:42-45. The story of the feetwashing is the best illustration of this saying, and finds in it its authentic commentary. Thus there is an inner unity to the story. This can be better felt than stated.

In the light of this discussion, we conclude that here, too, there is a reference to (Christian) baptism. The basic cleansing (λελουμένος) needs no repetition. It makes the one who has received it wholly (ὅλος) clean. For the individual sins which remain in the life of the baptised, however, there is cleansing with Jesus (τοὺς πόδας νίψασθαι). The man who refuses this has no part in Him (v. 8). Hence we have here one of the many NT sayings about the daily forgiveness of sins.[46] This is to be differentiated from the grace of baptism, but is closely related to it. The passage thus leads in the direction of Luther's view that the Christian has to return continually to his baptism.[47]

D. λούειν κτλ. in the Church.

In the post-apost. fathers we find only λούεσθαι in the sense "to bathe," Herm. v., 1, 1, 2 and also 1 Cl., 8, 4 quoting Is. 1:16. The word group is not found in most of the Apologists, but is much favoured by Justin. He uses λούειν and λούεσθαι (quoting Is. 1:16) once without ref. to baptism (Apol., I, 44, 3), once with indirect ref. to it as a term for pagan washings (I, 62, 1), elsewhere as a direct ref. to it (I, 61, 7. 10. 13 etc.; Dial., 12, 3; 18, 2; 44:4); ἀπολούεσθαι only Dial., 13, 1 of the external washing away of bloodguiltiness, which Is. does not have in view, but baptism; λουτρόν always of baptism, Apol., I, 61, 3. 10. 12 etc.; Dial., 13, 1; 14, 1; 18, 2; 44, 4. Sometimes Justin expressly links baptism and remission (Apol., I, 66, 1; Dial., 44, 4: λούσασθαι τὸ ὑπὲρ ἀφέσεως ἁμαρτιῶν ... λουτρόν). But he feels a need to give greater force to the idea with a ref. to the illumination given in baptism (φωτίζεσθαι, φωτισμός, Apol., I, 61, 12 f.), or the regeneration (ἀναγέννησις, I, 66, 1), or gnosis (λουτρὸν τῆς μετανοίας καὶ τῆς γνώσεως τοῦ θεοῦ, Dial., 14, 1).

---

[42] Cf. Tillm. J., *ad loc.*

[43] Bau. J. Exc. on 13:20, cf. O. Holtzmann etc.

[44] Windisch, *op. cit.*, 76 f.; v. Campenhausen, 262.

[45] On the many points of Jewish parables cf. P. Fiebig, *Die Gleichnisreden Jesu* (1912), 27.

[46] On the position of this in the NT cf. L. Ihmels, *D. tägliche Vergebung d. Sünden* (1916).

[47] So also E. Hirsch, *Das 4. Ev. in seiner urspr. Gestalt* (1936), 331 ff. Perhaps correctly, he sees an ultimate slender connection between the feetwashing and the Lord's Supper.

On the whole the use remains true to that of the NT. But later the Church became increasingly syncretistic, and there was a consequent increase in the danger of the heathen view of the sacral bath gaining a foothold. Baptism became a syncretistic mystery (→ I, 543). But this meant that the Church's action was surrounded by many illegitimate offshoots of the wild stock of paganism, e.g., cleansing of sins, healing of sickness, protection and assistance. The Church resolutely opposed the superstition that baths can wash away sin. It had to do this in order to ensure the uniqueness of baptism. But on inner grounds, too, it maintained with fidelity and some measure of success the biblical doctrine of the seriousness of sin. "What is the significance of washing the body?" exclaims Chrysostom (Hom. in 2 Tm., VI, 4, MPG, 62, 634 f.). "An expiatory ritual which is meaningless and valueless unless it affects the soul ... There are those who all the day cover themselves with guilt and sin,[48] and in the evening they take a bath (λουόμενοι) and then come confidently to church and lift up their hands in prayer as though they had washed away every fault in their basin of water (διὰ τῆς τῶν ὑδάτων κολυμβήθρας)." On the other hand, the Church could protect itself against insurgent paganism only by eliminating the worst excesses and then validating and if possible christianising the rest.

To bathe at the traditional place of Jesus' baptism in the Jordan held promise of healing for lepers and the blessing of children for the barren.[49] Church canons demand the washing of the hands before prayer as a reminiscence of baptism. In Tertullian this gains a place in the liturgy. Soon every church has bowls of water for at least a symbolical purification. It is true that the inscr. of one Cantharus in Constantinople urges a washing away of sin and not just external cleansing — whether read forwards or backwards it bears the same sense: νίψον ἀνομήματα μὴ μόναν ὄψιν (Inscr. Antiquae, ed. J. Gruter *et. al.*, II² [1707], 1047, 9). But all these interpretations of consecrated water — and there are plenty of them to-day — do not alter the fact that in bowls of holy water a cultic practice of antiquity lives on in Christianity.

Oepke

---

[48] The ref. is esp. to sins of licentiousness, including those of an unnatural character. We have here a direct continuation of the traditional bath after sexual intercourse, → 297.
[49] For examples from the sources, and other rich materials, cf. Zellinger, 93 ff.

† λύκος

A. The Wolf outside the New Testament.

As a terrible beast of prey, spread over almost all the ancient world,[1] the wolf is mentioned from earliest times in many places in the writings of antiquity. It is common in depictions of war, e.g., as a symbol of fierce bravery, Pind. Pyth., 2, 84 : ποτὶ δ' ἐχθρὸν ἅτ' ἐχθρὸς ἐὼν λύκοιο δίκαν ὑποθεύσομαι, Solon, 24, 26 f. (Diehl, I, 37): τῶν οὕνεκ' ἀλκὴν πάντοθεν ποιεύμενος ὡς ἐν κυσὶν πολλῇσιν ἐστράφην λύκος. Homer constantly compares those who fling themselves wildly on the enemy with wolves, Il., 4, 471; 11, 72; 16, 156 ff.;[2] Vergil Aen., 2, 355 ff. The very name suggests that the wolf is a ravening beast.[3] A common epithet is ἅρπαξ, Lycophron Alexandra, 1309 (vl. Ἄτρακας) (ed. E. Scheer, I [1881]); Ps.-Oppian Cynegetica, III, 302 ff.; Horat. Carmina, 4, 4, 50; Epodi, 16, 20; Velleius Paterculus (ed. C. Stegmann v. Pritzwald [1933]), II, 27 (the Carthaginians as *raptores Italicae libertatis lupi*); Macrob. Sat., I, 20, 14; Seneca Oed. (ed. F. Leo [1878/9]), 150; cf. also Cl. Al. Strom., IV, 9, 12, 4; Protr., I, 4, 1. With other beasts it was particularly to be feared by flocks of sheep, Hom. Il., 16, 352; Ps.-Oppian Cynegetica, I, 432; II, 409; III, 287; Ovid Fast., 2, 85 f.; Metamorphoses, XI, 370 ff.; commonly in fables, Aesop, 268 ff. (ed. C. Halm [1868], p. 131 ff.) etc. The insatiable appetite of the hungry wolf is proverbial, λύκος ἔχανεν, Diogenianus, 6, 20 (CPG, I, 273); Aristoph. Lys., 629 etc.[4] So, too, is the implacable hostility between wolf and sheep, Hom. Il., 22, 263 : οὐδὲ λύκοι τε καὶ ἄρνες ὁμόφρονα θυμὸν ἔχουσιν; Aristoph. Pax, 1076 : πρίν κεν λύκος οἶν ὑμεναιοῖ (*ibid.*, 1112).[5] Whether the sheep became a prey depended on the conduct of the shepherd, Hom. Il., 16, 352 ff.;[6] Statius Thebais, 8, 691 f. (ed. R. Jahnke [1898]); Themist. Oratio, I, 9d : καὶ ποιμνίον ἐκεῖνο εὔκολον τοῖς λύκοις ὅτῳ ὁ ποιμὴν ἀπεχθάνοιτο. Cf. the proverbial saying λύκος ποιμήν, Diogenianus, 5, 96 (CPG, I, 269); Cic. In Antonium, III, 11, 27; also "to entrust the sheep to the wolf," Plaut. Pseudolus, 140; Terentius Eunuchus (ed. Kauer-Lindsay [1926]), 832. But λύκος ποιμήν can also describe the dangerous pretences of a noxious person, Apostolius, 10, 96b (CPG, II, 513): expounded ἐπὶ τῶν μετὰ σχήματος φιλικοῦ ἐπιβουλευόντων τισί. M. Ant., XI, 15, 5 : οὐδέν ἐστιν αἴσχιον λυκοφιλίας (cf. also Jul. Or., p. 591, 14, Hertlein); Cl. Al. Strom., II, 4, 16, 1: ὑποκρίνεται δὲ τὴν πίστιν ἡ εἰκασία ... καθάπερ ὁ κόλαξ τὸν φίλον καὶ ὁ λύκος τὸν κύνα. The wiles of the wolf, who stalks his prey with cunning, are described in Xenoph. Eq. Mag., 4, 18-20.[7] In fable we find the crafty wolf (Aesop, 266, 268, 269 etc.) as well as the clumsy (Babrius, Fabulae Aesopeae, ed. O. Crusius [1897],

---

λύκος. [1] O. Keller, *Thiere d. classischen Alterthums* ... (1887), 158 ff.

[2] H. Fränkel, *Die homerischen Gleichnisse* (1921), 62, 73 ff.

[3] Indogermanic *u̯lquos*, perhaps from the root *u̯el*, "to rend, ravish, wound," Walde-Pok., I, 304 f., 316 f.

[4] Also in Lat., Plaut. Stichus, 605; Trinummus, 169 etc. For further Gk. and Lat. instances cf. A. Otto, *Sprichwörter ... d. Römer* (1890), 198; also Keller, *op. cit.*, 401, n. 78.

[5] Similar hyperboles to describe an ἀδύνατον, Aristoph. Av., 967 f. ὅταν οἰκήσωσι λύκοι πολιαί τε κορῶναι ἐν ταὐτῷ, Horat. Carmina, 1, 33, 7 f.: *sed prius Apulis iungentur capreae lupis.*

[6] Cf. Fränkel, *op. cit.*, 59 f., 75 f.

[7] For details cf. Keller, 162.

122, Aesop, 274). The mortal terror which the wolf induces when it suddenly appears, and the greatness of the danger, are again expressed in proverbs: λύκον ἰδεῖν is to lose one's speech for fright, Theocr., XIV, 22.[8] To the same context belongs the phrase *lupus in fabula* (Terentius Adelphi, 537; Cic. Att., XIII, 33) (*lupum in sermone*: Plaut. Stichus, 577): If one speaks of the wolf, he is not far away (originally in the sense of magic: one should not talk of the devil).[9] To be in unavoidable danger is expressed in the Gk. and Lat. proverb: to have the wolf by the ears (οὔτε γὰρ κατέχειν οἷόν τε οὔτε ἀφεῖναι ἀκίνδυνον, Macarius, 8, 44 [CPG, II, 220]).[10]

The wolf has a considerable role in ancient mythology[11] and superstition. This may be seen in the Lycaon saga and the cult of the Lycaean Zeus and Lycian Apollo in which the wolf is sometimes a symbol of the fugitive who seeks protection (both deities are also called Φύξιος) and sometimes the epitome of demonic powers which the deity proves mighty to avert (Apollo as λυκοκτόνος, Soph. El., 6; Plut. De Sollertia Animalium, 9 [II, 966a] etc.). To indicate the part of the wolf in superstition it is enough to recall the ancient and widespread idea of the werewolf (the sudden change of a man into a wolf).[12]

In the OT there is ref. to the wolf (זְאֵב) in Jer. 5:6 in description of a terrible judgment: καὶ λύκος ἕως τῶν οἰκιῶν ὠλέθρευσεν αὐτούς. The word occurs mostly in metaphors and similes, Gn. 49:27: Βενιαμιν λύκος ἅρπαξ to describe valour in war, but mostly in a bad sense, Hab. 1:8 (of snappish horses): ὀξύτεροι ὑπὲρ τοὺς λύκους τῆς Ἀραβίας, Ez. 22:27: οἱ ἄρχοντες αὐτῆς ἐν μέσῳ αὐτῆς ὡς λύκοι ἁρπάζοντες ἁρπάγματα τοῦ ἐκχέαι αἷμα, Zeph. 3:3: οἱ κριταὶ αὐτῆς ὡς λύκοι τῆς Ἀραβίας, as a picture of selfish cruelty.[13] The hostility between wolf and sheep is found in the simile in Sir. 13:17: τί κοινωνήσει λύκος ἀμνῷ; οὕτως ἁμαρτωλὸς πρὸς εὐσεβῆ. It provides the background for the state of peace in the Messianic kingdom when the wolf will lie down with the sheep (Is. 11:6; 65:25) and peace reigns over the new creation.

There is a distinctive use of λύκος in Rabb. lit. As the basis of a judicial degrading of the priestly order Bilga there is in TSukka, 4, 28 an account of the fearful crime of Miriam when she went out from this order and relapsed into paganism: "When the Greeks burst into the temple Miriam went in and beat on the altar and said to it לוּקִיס לוּקִיס, thou destroyest the resources of the Israelites, but thou dost not stand by them in the hour of need." K. Rengstorf has expounded this remarkable anecdote and esp. the insult to the altar (= God).[14] The blasphemy obviously consists in a frivolous play on words: לוקיס = לוקוס = *locus* = τόπος = מָקוֹם (substitute for the name of God), but here also = λύκος, i.e., God, the מָקוֹם/*locus* shows Himself to be a λύκος in His attitude to His oppressed people.[15] In the Talmudic par. with their slight deviations the original play on words seems to have been lost in favour of the meaning λύκος (par. bSukka, 56b, Bar.; jSukka, 55d, 40 ff.: Str.-B., I, 466).

---

[8] Lat. examples, Otto, 200 f.

[9] Cf. Otto, 200.

[10] Cf. Otto, 199.

[11] Keller, 170 ff.; M. P. Nilsson, *Griech. Feste v. religiöser Bdtg.* (1906), 8 ff.; F. Schwenn, "Die Menschenopfer bei d. Griech. u. Römern," RVV, 15, 3 (1915), 20 ff.; Roscher, *s.v.* "Lykaios u. Lykaon"; P. Kretschmer in *Kleinasiatische Forschungen,* I (1930), 14 f.; F. Altheim, "Griech. Götter im alten Rom," RVV, 22, 1 (1930), 148 f.; *Röm. Religionsgeschichte,* II (1932), 52 f.

[12] Petronius Saturae (ed. F. Buecheler-W. Heräus[6] [1922], 61, 5 ff. Cf. Keller, 164 ff., 403, n. 122; esp. M. Schuster, *D. Werwolf u. die Hexen* (*Wiener Studien,* 48 [1930]), 149 ff.

[13] Παροιμ. 28:15: λέων πεινῶν καὶ λύκος διψῶν ὃς τυραννεῖ πτωχὸς ὢν ἔθνους πενιχροῦ. The Mas. has דֹּב ("bear"), but wolf seems to fit better in the LXX.

[14] *Orientalistische Studien* (*E. Littmann zu seinem 60. Geburtstag* [1935]), 59 ff.

[15] *Ibid.,* 61.

B. The Usage in the New Testament.

In the NT λύκος is found in the warning of our Lord against false prophets in Mt. 7:15: "Beware of false prophets, which come to you in sheep's clothing, but inwardly they are ravening wolves (λύκοι ἅρπαγες)." Since these false prophets seem to belong to the community, and turn this appearance to destructive ends (wolves in sheep's clothing), the reference is to false teachers. The criterion by which to distinguish between appearance and reality is offered in the accompanying saying about the tree and its fruits.

If we are to understand this correctly, we must set aside the popular view that outward success and activity are a proof of divine mission, and concentrate on the following points. 1. The question to be decided is a problem within the community and is not concerned with the vague general distinction between words and acts. 2. Proclamation is one of the fruits, as may be seen from the par. Lk. 6:43 ff. and Mt. 12:33 ff. 3. The activity is not viewed in and for itself, but in the light of its source (the goodness or badness of the tree). 4. The ambiguity of purely external appearance is emphasised in Mt. by the fact that wolves cannot be distinguished externally from sheep acc. to 7:15, and also by the fact that acc. to vv. 21 ff. false disciples can produce outstanding achievements before the heavenly Judge, and yet they will be rejected by Him because they have not done the one thing that matters, i.e., the will of the Father. We may thus conclude that the acts of those who come as prophets do enable the community to distinguish between truth and appearance to the degree that they are an evident fulfilment or non-fulfilment of the divine will. In other words, the acts themselves stand under an ultimate criterion, and only thus can they serve as a standard of judgment.[16]

In Ac. 20:29, when taking leave of the Ephesian elders, Paul assumes that destroyers will come into the congregation: "After my departing shall grievous wolves (λύκοι βαρεῖς) enter in among you, not sparing the flock." In view of v. 30 it is apparent that these are false teachers. They come from without in v. 29, and rise up from within in v. 30.

No account is given of these false teachers. The image of v. 29 and the description of the presbyters as overseers and shepherds (v. 28) shows that the error is not a minor evil but represents a mortal threat to the community which has to be averted.

The defenceless vulnerability of the disciples when Jesus sends them out is the theme of the metaphor used in the charge in Mt. 10:16a; Lk. 10:3: "Behold, I send you forth as sheep in the midst of wolves." The disciples are herewith warned of the danger which threatens them (cf. Mt. 10:16b ff.) but they are also comforted, for this is no unforeseen disaster, but exposure to danger is involved in the very fact that they are sent out by Jesus.[17] In a series of sayings from v. 11 on

---

[16] This verse in the Sermon on the Mount finds a par. in the Mandaean Ginza, Lidz. Ginza R. XIII, 287 (p. 285, 11 ff.): "Mandaeans who acknowledge the name of Mandā dHaijē only with their lips, but are without faith in the heart, are like bad trees which drink the water of life but bear no fruits, like the ravening wolf and springing lion ... we invoke the powerful first life as a witness against them ..." There can be no doubt that the sayings in Mt. 7:15 ff. underlie this passage; though the order is different, we have echoes of verses 7:21, 16 f., 15. Fig. Ginza R. V, 2, 179 (p. 183, 1 ff.) also speaks of wolves, i.e., those who lead believers astray; cf. also R. XV, 11, 333 (p. 343, 31).

[17] The parable of the sheep among wolves is also found in the Rabb., Tanch. תולדות § 5: Hadrian said to R. J^ehoshua (c. 90): Great is the sheep (i.e., Israel) which has remained alive among 70 wolves (the 70 nations of the world). He replied: Greater is the shepherd who delivers and keeps it, and who breaks the wolves before them (Israel), Str.-B., I, 574.

Mt. brings out the eschatological significance of the relation of the disciples to the world by clearly contrasting their authority and the persecution which awaits them.[18]

Finally, Jn. 10:12 reads: "He that is an hireling, and not the shepherd, whose own the sheep are not, seeth the wolf coming, and leaveth the sheep, and fleeth: and the wolf catcheth them, and scattereth the sheep." Who the wolf is, is not stated. The serious nature of the threat, the faithfulness of the shepherd, and the unfaithfulness of the hireling, are best grasped if one does not try to say what is precisely the peril to the community depicted under the image of the wolf. That the reference is simply to false teachers is nowhere indicated, and is in fact excluded by the link with v. 11 (the good shepherd gives his life for the sheep). We are thus to think of the unforeseeable threat posed to the community by the enemy of God, and from the fact that the content shatters the image we may draw the following deductions in respect of the relation between the wolf, the flock, the hireling and the shepherd: 1. the good shepherd sees the onset of the danger, and gives his life to protect the flock; his death plainly shows that the flock belongs to him alone, and genuinely remains his possession; 2. the hireling sees the approach of danger, and in saving his own life loses the flock, thus making it clear that the flock was never his; 3. when confronted by the danger, the flock sees to whom it truly belongs and does not belong; 4. the dreadful possibility that the flock might succumb to the fatal rapacity of the wolf which suddenly bursts in upon it, and that it might lose both its protection and its life, is shown by these words of Jesus to be a danger which is already averted, since the community lives even now in virtue of the self-sacrifice of the Good Shepherd, and by this sacrifice its unity is established and sealed as a promise (10:11-17).

In later literature λύκος is often used for the false teacher or the one who corrupts the community (Mt. 7:15 is often quoted): Did., 16, 3; Ign. Phld., 2, 2; 2 Cl., 5, 2-4; Just. Apol., I, 16, 13; Dial., 35, 3; 81, 2. Rhodon in Eus. Hist. Eccl., V, 13, 4 speaks of Marcion as the Ποντικὸς λύκος.[19]

Bornkamm

[18] Cf. the apocryphon quoted in 2 Cl., 5, 2-4, which combines Mt. 10:16 par. with 10:28 par.: "For the Lord says: You shall be as lambs among wolves. But Peter answered him and said: What if the wolves rend the lambs? Jesus said to Peter: The lambs shall not fear the wolves after their death; do not fear those who kill you and can then do no more to you, but fear him who after your death has power over your soul and body, to cast them into the lake of fire."

[19] A. v. Harnack, *Marcion*[2] (1924), 321 finds here an allusion to Marcion's Cynic mode of life (he refers to Luc. Pergr. Mort., 30), but the fig. is a common one. Cf. Just. Apol., I, 58, 2, Eus. Hist. Eccl., IV, 24 and W. Bauer, *Rechtgläubigkeit und Ketzerei* (1934), 134 f.

† λυμαίνομαι

* λυμαίνομαι. Mid. dep., from the time of Aesch. in the sense "to treat disgracefully," then more generally "to do an injury," "to hurt," "to imperil" (e.g., the health of the body, the constitution of the state), "to destroy" (physically or morally), "to devastate" (places in war), seldom abs., usually with acc. or dat.[1] Inscr., e.g., IG, V, 2, 6, line 16 f. (4th cent. B.C.); Ditt. Syll.[3], 997, 3, par. with ἀδικέω; 1238, 11 (2nd. cent. A.D.), par. with λωβάομαι, "to treat infamously," "to injure"; also pap.[2] In the LXX λυμαίνομαι occurs 16 times, 7 times for שחת pi, hi and ho, 2 for סלף pi (cf. also Da. Θ 6:23). Abs. 2 Ch. 16:10; Is. 65:25; otherwise always with acc.[3] The meaning is "to destroy" (γῆν, Ιερ. 28:2; ὀχύρωμα, Ιερ. 31:18; ὕδατος ἔξοδον, Prv. 25:26), "to corrupt" or "to disfigure" (gifts pervert ῥήματα δίκαια, Ex. 23:8; λόγους καλούς, Prv. 23:8), "to shame" (τὸ κάλλος σου, Ez. 16:25; τὰ ἁγνὰ τῆς παρθενίας, 4 Macc. 18:8), "to annihilate", often, as outside the Bible, with a suggestion of the arbitrary, irrational and wanton (e.g., ἀφροσύνη ἀνδρὸς λυμαίνεται τὰς ὁδοὺς αὐτοῦ, Prv. 19:3; ὑβριστὴς ὅστις τὰ ἀλλότρια λυμαίνεται, 27:13). Philo uses λυμαίνομαι 13 times:[4] Spec. Leg., IV, 62 quoting Ex. 23:8; Spec. Leg., IV, 226, a command not to harm πόλεως ἐχθρᾶς τὴν ἀρετῶσαν γῆν; Vit. Mos., I, 108 of injury by gnat-stings; Migr. Abr., 164 of the inconsiderate egoism of the drone; Deus Imm., 136 and 142 with φθείρω; often of the devastation of the soul by ἡδονή, πάθη and ἐπιθυμία, cf. Sacr. AC, 29; Cher., 9; Mut. Nom., 203. In Joseph. cf. Ant., 12, 256 pass. of martyrdom: μαστιγούμενοι καὶ τὰ σώματα λυμαινόμενοι ζῶντες ἔτι καὶ ἐμπνέοντες ἀνεσταυροῦντο. Cf. also Ep. Ar., 164.

The only occurrence in the NT is at Ac. 8:3: Σαῦλος δὲ ἐλυμαίνετο τὴν ἐκκλησίαν. This is a more forceful term than ἐδίωξα in 1 C. 15:9 or even ἐπόρθουν in Gl. 1:13, cf. 23. The fierce and relentless nature of the persecution depicted in Ac. 8:3; 9:1; 22:4 is reflected in the choice of this word.[5]

Michaelis

λυμαίνομαι. Deriv. from the noun λύμη (from the time of Eur. and Hdt.) in the sense of "shameful treatment" (also "uncleanness") is argued by E. Fraenkel, *Griech. Denominativa* (1906), 9 and 49. Deriv. from the noun λῦμα (from Aesch. and Eur. on) in the sense "corruption" (also "filth") is favoured by A. Debrunner, *Indogerm. Forschungen,* 21 (1907), 22, who considers the possibility that "to dirty" may be the original sense [Debrunner].

[1] Cf. Pass. and Liddell-Scott, *s.v.*; Wettstein, II, 504 on Ac. 8:3.

[2] Preisigke Wört., II, 41 *s.v.*: "to treat shamefully," P. Petr., III, 27, 3 (3rd cent. B.C.), mostly "to destroy." The rare pass. use of the dep. is found in the pap., cf. Mayser, II, 1 (1926), 121 and Pr.-Bauer[3], *s.v.* Cf. also Preis. Zaub., 13, 302 (2nd/3rd cent. A.D.): πῦρ, οὐ μή μου λυμάνῃς σάρκα, for the act. λυμαίνω (otherwise the earliest non-Christian use is in Lib.; cf. Pass. and → n. 5). Mostly with acc., though the Atticists prefer the dat.; cf. Mayser, II, 2 (1934), 302 and R. Helbing Kasussyntax (1928), 14. On λοιμαίνομαι cf. Mayser, I (1906), 111.

[3] The aor. 2 Ch. 16:10; ψ 79:13; Am. 1:11; Is. 65:8; Ez. 16:25; Da. Θ 6:23; 4 Macc. 18:8 always ἐλυμηνάμην; cf. Helbing Gramm., 94. Cod. B. writes λοιμαίνομαι 6 times (→ n. 2); cf. Moult.-Mill., 382, s.v.

[4] Acc. to Leisegang, *s.v.* Moreover, λύμη, which does not occur in the LXX, is found 7 times in Philo, cf. Spec. Leg., III, 51; IV, 184 with ζημία (→ II, 889).

[5] Wdt. Ag., *ad loc.* suggests *drangsalieren,* "to harass." There may be allusion to ψ 79:13: ἐλυμήνατο αὐτὴν σῦς ἐκ δρυμοῦ, which refers to the devastation of the national community of Israel under the fig. of the vine (Zn. Ag., *ad loc.*). On the acc. cf. Bl.-Debr.[6] § 152, 1. Post-apost. fathers, Herm. v., 3, 9, 3: λυμαίνομαι (cf. 3b pass.) of the harming of the body by gluttony; cf. also v., 4, 1, 8 (πόλιν); 4, 2, 4; the act. λυμαίνω "to destroy" (earliest example; → n. 2).

λύπη, λυπέω, ἄλυπος, περίλυπος, συλλυπέομαι

λύπη, λυπέω.

A. The Greek Understanding of λύπη.

1. λύπη, "pain," "sorrow" (λυπεῖν, "to cause pain," λυπεῖσθαι, "to experience sorrow," "to be sad"), is in the broadest sense the experience of the natural impulse of both man and animals in the pursuit of ἡδονή.[1] Since the natural impulse is the ψυχή, λύπη is a matter of the ψυχή,[2] and since this is for the Gks. the sphere of bodily vitality as well as the intellectual life, λύπη can mean physical pain as well as sorrow of spirit.[3] πόνος can be used as a par.,[4] and ἀλγηδών is a common alternative.[5] The opp. is ἡδονή, though χαρά, εὐφροσύνη, εὐπάθεια etc. also occur. The Sophists and Stoics undertook a fundamental differentiation between the various terms for joy, but it is typical that there is no similar attempt in respect of those for sorrow (→ εὐφροσύνη, II, 772; → χαρά).

Physically λύπη can denote any pain, though esp. that caused by hunger or thirst, by heat or cold (Plat. Phileb., 31e f; Phaed., 85a), or by sickness (Soph. Ai., 338). This leads fig. to the common use of πικρά along with it (Soph. El., 654; Eur. Or., 1105), and it is often characterised as δάκνειν, δῆγμα (Hdt., VII, 16 [α]); Aesch. Ag., 791 f.; Stoics, v. Arnim, III, 93, 5 f.; 107, 26; Plut. Tranq. An., 19 (II, 476 f.). Spiritually λύπη is sorrow, pain or anxiety at misfortune or death, or anger at annoyances or hurts, esp. insults and outrages. As in Plat. Phileb., 47e (cf. 48b; 50b) ὀργή, φόβος, πόθος, θρῆνος, ἔρως, ζῆλος, φθόνος are λῦπαι, so, e.g., Thuc., VI, 59, 1 speaks of ἐρωτικὴ λύπη. It is singular, but significant, that Orestes in Eur. Or., 396 ff. describes the σύνεσις, ὅτι σύνοιδα δείν' εἰργασμένος as λύπη μάλιστά γ' ἡ διαφθείρουσά με.[6]

2. Joy and sorrow in their alternation are part of human life: δεῖ δέ σε χαίρειν καὶ λυπεῖσθαι· θνητὸς γὰρ ἔφυς (Eur. Iph. Aul., 31 f.; cf. Soph. Ai., 554 f.;[7] Trach., 126 ff.; Menand. Fr., 281, 8 ff.). λῦπαι and ἡδοναί are intermingled not merely in the dramas of poets but in the whole tragedy and comedy of life (Plat. Phileb., 50b). To live μήτε χαίροντα ἔτι μήτε λυπούμενον is ὥσπερ λίθον ζῆν (Plat. Gorg., 494a). But it is understandable that there should be a desire to live without λύπη (Aesch. Fr., 177; Eur. Ion, 632; Menand. Fr., 410; Soph. Ant., 1165 ff.: the man who lives without ἡδονή and χαίρειν is an ἔμψυχος νεκρός); everyone

---

λύπη κτλ. Trench, 150 ff.; H. G. Gadamer, *Platos dialektische Ethik* (1931).

[1] E.g., Aristot. Eth. Nic., VII, 13, p. 1153a, 14 f.; 14, p. 1153b, 10 f.: ἡδονή is present where there is the ἐνέργεια of a ζῷον ἀνεμπόδιστος. Ἡδονή occurs when the state of a ζῷον corresponds to its nature, when it is in harmony etc., while λύπη is the disturbing of this condition. Cf. Plat. Phileb., 31c ff.; Aristot. Eth. Nic., X, 2, p. 1173b, 7 ff.; Rhet., I, 11, p. 1369b, 33 ff.

[2] For definitions of ἡδονή (hence indirectly of λύπη) as κίνησις of the ψυχή, Plat. Resp., IX, 583e; Aristot. Eth. Nic., X, 2, p. 1173a, 29 ff.; Rhet., I, 11, p. 1369b, 33 f.

[3] Physical and spiritual ἡδοναί and λῦπαι are expressly distinguished in Plat. Phileb., 31b ff.; cf. 36a.

[4] Cf. Antiphon Fr., 49 (II, 358, 4 f., Diels[5]); Aristot. Eth. Nic., VII, 15, p. 1154b, 7 f.

[5] In Epic. ἀλγηδών is used instead of λύπη as the opp. of ἡδονή, e.g., Diog. L., X, 34 (23).

[6] And this can all be a ἡδύ, cf. Aristot. Rhet., I, 11, p. 1369b, 33-1372a, 3. Antiph. Fr., 107: ἅπαν τὸ λυποῦν ἐστιν ἀνθρώπῳ νόσος ὀνόματ' ἔχουσα πολλά.

[7] For the dead there is no more χαίρειν or λυπεῖσθαι, Aesch. Fr., 266 (TGF).

seeks ἡδύ and flees λυπηρόν (Aristot. Eth. Nic., X, 1, p. 1172a, 25 f.; 2, p. 1172b, 9-23), and Cyclops extols as his Zeus eating and drinking and λυπεῖν μηδὲν αὑτόν (Eur. Cyc., 338). But according to Plat. Phileb., 21c a life in mere self-forgetful ἡδονή would be the vegetating of an oyster. In fact there is no ἡδονή without λύπη. The two are strangely linked (Plat. Phaed., 60b c); λῦπαι καὶ πόνοι follow ἡδοναί, indeed, πᾶσαι ἡδοναὶ ἐκ μεγάλων λυπημάτων ἐθέλουσι παραγίνεσθαι; in life everything is ἀναμεμειγμένα λύπαις μεγάλαις (Antiphon Fr., 49 [II, 358, 13 f., Diels[5]]; Fr., 51 [II, 360, 11 f., Diels[5]]). Things which seem to be joyous, like marriage and the blessing of children, bring λύπη (Eur. Alc., 238 f.; Democr. Fr., 276 [II, 202, 2 f., Diels[5]]). We bring sorrow on ourselves (Democr. Fr., 88 [II, 161, 9, Diels[5]]), or attract it to us by our deeds (Soph. Ai., 1085 f.). The worst pain is that which we cause ourselves (Soph. Ai., 260 ff.; Oed. Tyr., 1230 f.). In carousing especially ἡδοναί are brief and λῦπαι are πολλαὶ <καὶ μακραί> (Democr. Fr., 235 [II, 192, 8 f., Diels[5]]; cf. Critias Fr., 6 [II, 379, 16 f., Diels[5]]). Hence the advice of Solon (I, 63, 14 f., Diels[5] [II, 215, 11, Diels[4]]: ἡδονὴν φεῦγε, ἥτις λύπην τίκτει, or the counsel: εὐγνώμων ὁ μὴ λυπεόμενος ἐφ' οἷσιν οὐκ ἔχει, ἀλλὰ χαίρων ἐφ' οἷσιν ἔχει (Democr. Fr., 231 [II, 191, 13, Diels[5]]; cf. Isoc., 1, 42). He who goes beyond the mean is a fool, for he does not think of the days of λύπη which are still ahead (Soph. Oed. Col., 1211 ff.). And Thuc. realises ὡς οἵτινες πρὸς τὰς ξυμφορὰς γνώμῃ μὲν ἥκιστα λυποῦνται, ἔργῳ δὲ μάλιστα ἀντέχουσιν, οὗτοι καὶ πόλεων καὶ ἰδιωτῶν κράτιστοί εἰσιν (Thuc., II, 64, 6).

3. Philosophy dealt with the problem of λύπη only indirectly in treating of ἡδονή. If according to Plat. Phileb., 31b there can be no ἡδονή without λύπη, the understanding of λύπη is not regarded as an independent task. Direct interest is always focused on ἡδονή. Indeed, ἡδονή itself (along with λύπη) is part of the question of the ἀγαθόν. According to Aristot. Pol., I, 2, p. 1253a, 9 ff. man is distinguished from the beast only by the fact that, in addition to the αἴσθησις of λυπηρόν and ἡδύ, he has the λόγος to differentiate between good and evil, right and wrong. According to Plat. Leg., III, 689b λύπη and ἡδονή belong to the lower part of the soul: τὸ γὰρ λυπούμενον καὶ ἡδόμενον αὐτῆς (τῆς ψυχῆς) is like the broad mass of the people. The κατὰ λόγον δόξα must rule over it. According to Phileb., 21d, to be sure, a βίος without ἡδονή and λύπη is as little a αἱρετὸς βίος as life in mere self-forgetful ἡδονή, for in Plato "Hedone and Lupe are the basic modes of awareness of existence, since they are the ways in which existence understands itself in terms of the world." [8] But the question then arises what are true ἡδοναί, Phileb., 36c ff. For Plato it is clear that they can be only spiritual ἡδοναί; yet even here there are also true and false. For joy is a way of discovering the world. It thus involves an evaluation. Hence there is the possibility of error. What is unpleasant and even unreal can be regarded as delightful. Or joy may be alloyed because it conceals and forgets present pain. Pure joy and pure delight is joy in the pure forms of the beautiful and in the knowledge of the true. It is the joy of the pure perception which recognises the δύναμις of the good in the φύσις of the beautiful, Phileb., 64e. [9] If the meaning of true joy

---

[8] Gadamer, *op. cit.*, 132.
[9] *Ibid.*, 119 ff.

is thus traced back to discovery and contemplation of the ἀγαθόν, a characteristic limitation is set from the very first for the opposite emotion of λύπη. It is seen that in every sorrow there is raised the question of its *raison d'être,* so that pain, too, unveils the world for being. On the other hand, it is not considered that pain, as an interruption of the self-forgetfulness of being, summons this out of the world and back to itself and to isolation. [10]

Aristotle gives a critical account of the discussion whether ἡδονή is an ἀγαθόν (and therewith, indirectly, λύπη is a κακόν), Eth. Nic., VII, 12-15; X, 1-5. [11] It seems to him to be incontrovertible that ἡδονή is an ἀγαθόν, but he does not agree that it is the absolute ἄριστον (VII, 13, p. 1152b, 25 f.). Indeed, he rejects the whole question of an absolute ἀγαθόν and raises instead that of the relative good, the οἰκεῖον ἀγαθόν of each ζῷον. As each ζῷον has its οἰκεῖον ἔργον, so it has its οἰκεία ἡδονή, X, 5, p. 1176a, 3 f. ἡδονή is found with the ἐνέργεια which attains unhampered to its goal, though ἡδονή itself cannot be made the goal, X, 4, p. 1174b, 14 ff. For this reason, ἀρετή is the standard by which to judge whether any given ἡδονή is right or wrong, X, 5, p. 1176a, 17 ff.

Acc. to Epicurus ἡδονή is an οἰκεῖον πάθος for each ζῷον, and ἀλγηδών an ἀλλότριον, Diog. L., X, 34; 128 ff.; 139 f. Of course, not every ἡδονή is to be chosen, and there are some ἀλγηδόνες which are better than ἡδοναί because they lead to greater ἡδονή, 129. [12]

Stoicism groups λύπη with φόβος, ἐπιθυμία and ἡδονή among the πάθη, from which the wise man is free. [13] λυπεῖσθαι is a ἁμάρτημα, v. Arnim, III, 119, 25 f.; 136, 22 f.; 137, 10. It is no easy thing to free oneself from it, I, 85, 18 f.; III, 94, 39 ff. If λύπη is defined as δόξα πρόσφατος κακοῦ παρουσίας, I, 52, 9 f.; III, 94, 17 f.; 115, 29 etc., there is a characteristic modification of this δόξα aspect as compared with Plato. Acc. to Stoic rationalism a false opinion is responsible for the existence of the πάθος, I, 51, 15 ff.; III, 92, 32 ff.; 95, 42 f.; 116, 3 ff. It seems that for Stoicism, too, there is no recognition of the positive meaning of pain. [14] Even in later Stoics we still find the same view that λύπη is a πάθος and hence a ἁμάρτημα from which the sage must be free. [15] It is typical that for Epict. and M. Ant. λύπη is a sign of ungodliness which opposes the divine διοίκησις of the κόσμος, Epict. Diss., III, 11, 2; 24, 43; IV, 4, 32; Fr., 3, 13 f.; M. Ant., X, 25, 2; XI, 20, 5, while the man who trusts in God as ποιητής, πατήρ and κηδεμών can be free from λῦπαι and φόβοι, Epict. Diss., I, 9, 7. The presupposition of this view is always that λύπη comes to man from within as an emotion based on error. It derives from the world only to the degree that man does not understand his inner independence of the world and thus delivers himself up to its assaults. The wise man avoids encounter with the world. The basic assumption, then, is that man is a non-historical and rational being, so that there can be no positive understanding of λύπη as an occurrence by which the true being of man is disclosed in

---

10 *Ibid.*, 145.

11 Cf. H. Karpp, *Untersuchungen zur Philosophie des Eudoxos von Knidos* (Diss. Marburg, 1933).

12 On the difference between the Epicurean and Cyrenaic views of ἡδονή and ἀλγηδών cf. Diog. L., X, 136 f.

13 v. Arnim, I, 51, 32 ff.; III, 92, 15 f.; 95, 14 ff.; 261, 17 etc.; the different εἴδη of λύπη, III, 99, 36 f.; 100, 3 ff. etc.

14 The justification of sorrow at the death of relatives in Sen. Epistulae, 99, 19 is not really a positive estimation : *inest quiddam dulce tristitiae.* Again, the statement : *est aliquis et dolendi* (*flendi?*) *decor* (99, 21), is simply to the effect that the wise man can be dignified even in sorrow.

15 Cf. the story of Poseidonios in Cic. Tusc., II, 61, who, beset by sorrows, cries out : *nihil agis, dolor! quamvis sis molestus, nunquam te esse confitebor malum.*

hostile encounter with the world. Stoicism distinguished from the πάθος of ἡδονή the true joy of the sage (→ εὐφροσύνη, II, 772; → χαρά), but it did not consider the question of meaningful λύπη.

4. In Greek antiquity there are at least the beginnings of a positive estimation of suffering. The view that it can be meaningful in the form of sympathy is to be found in the words of Tecmessa (Soph. Ai., 265 ff.):

πότερα δ' ἄν, εἰ νέμοι τις αἵρεσιν, λάβοις
φίλους ἀνιῶν αὐτὸς ἡδονὰς ἔχειν
ἢ κοινὸς ἐν κοινοῖσι λυπεῖσθαι ξυνών;

though the chorus answers:

τό τοι διπλάζον, ὦ γύναι, μεῖζον κακόν.

The Greek world certainly recognises that suffering leads to knowledge (παθήματα — μαθήματα, Hdt., I, 207). This is true not only in the sense that the πάθημα of the one who suffers can be instructive to others (Aesch. Prom., 553; Soph. Ai., 121 ff.; Oed. Tyr., 1524 ff.), but also in the sense that it can be instructive to himself. According to Aesch. Ag., 176 ff. Zeus brings it about that man learns from his suffering (πάθει μάθος) by means of μνησιπήμων πόνος, the torment of sorrowful remembrance.[16] Euripides knows the self-accusing pain of remorse (→ 313),[17] of which it is said: δεινὴ γὰρ ἡ θεός, ἀλλ' ὅμως ἰάσιμος (Eur. Or., 399). The δική which inflicts pain but also leads to salvation is compared by Plato to ἰατρική when he shows in Gorg., 476a ff. that, contrary to naive ideas, δίκην διδόναι and κολάζεσθαι is better for the ἀδικῶν than to remain unpunished, since by chastisement he becomes βελτίων τὴν ψυχήν. Mythologically it is then said: εἰσὶ δὲ οἱ μὲν ὠφελούμενοί τε καὶ δίκην διδόντες ὑπὸ θεῶν τε καὶ ἀνθρώπων οὗτοι οἳ ἂν ἰάσιμα ἁμαρτήματα ἁμάρτωσιν· ὅμως δὲ δι' ἀλγηδόνων καὶ ὀδυνῶν γίγνεται αὐτοῖς ἡ ὠφελία καὶ ἐνθάδε καὶ ἐν Ἅιδου· οὐ γὰρ οἷόν τε ἄλλως ἀδικίας ἀπαλλάττεσθαι (Gorg., 525b). One might suspect that in Orphic and Pythagorean circles, and in Empedocles, where this world is the scene of the curse, there would be the possibility of finding the meaning of suffering in the fact that it kindles an awareness of the alienation of the soul from the world, and thus contributes positively to redemption. Perhaps this kind of tradition lies behind Gorg., 525b. At any rate, there arises later a disquiet and a sense of sin which under oriental influence leads to an interpretation of misfortune as a divine punishment, to the practice of penance, and to sorrow at sin.[18] Plut. describes how the δεισιδαίμων views misfortune and sickness as a ὑπὸ τῶν θεῶν κολάζεσθαι, as πληγαὶ θεοῦ, and how he in deep sorrow ἐξαγορεύει τινὰς ἁμαρτίας αὐτοῦ καὶ πλημμελείας, Superst., 7 (II, 168a-d). Here, of course, there is no sorrow of genuine self-accusation, since the man afflicted by misfortune, although he confesses that he is ἀσεβής and hated by God, also makes divine destiny responsible for his sin, 168b.[19] On the other hand, the significance

---

[16] Cf. Aesch. Ag., 249 f.: δίκα δὲ τοῖς μὲν παθοῦσιν μαθεῖν ἐπιρρέπει. Soph. Oed. Col., 7 f.

[17] Cf. also Democr. Fr., 174 (II, 179, 15 — 180, 3, Diels[5]). On the other hand, cf. the counsel to let bygones be bygones in Soph. Ai., 377 f.; Oed. Col., 509 f.

[18] Cf. K. Latte, ARW, 20 (1920/21), 293 ff.

[19] Cf. also in this connection Corp. Herm., X, 20, which deals with the κόλασις of the ἀσεβὴς ψυχή: the soul is more grievously tormented by ἀσέβεια than by a δακετὸν θηρίον, and it cries out: καίομαι, φλέγομαι.

of λύπη is seen to be that of remorse in Plut. Tranq. An., 19 (II, 476 f): τὰς μὲν γὰρ ἄλλας ἀναιρεῖ λύπας ὁ λόγος, τὴν δὲ μετάνοιαν αὐτὸς ἐργάζεται δακνομένης σὺν αἰσχύνῃ τῆς ψυχῆς καὶ κολαζομένης ὑφ' αὑτῆς.[20] Some statements of Philo (→ 319) make it likely that others thought along these lines. In Gnostic dualism there is, of course, no reference to this type of pain, yet here, too, there is the possibility of a positive interpretation of λύπη to the degree that λύπη is one of the τιμωρίαι under which earthly life in the body is set, Corp. Herm., XIII, 7. The ὑλικὸν σῶμα is πάντοθεν ἐσφιγμένον κακίᾳ, καὶ πόνοις καὶ ἀλγηδόσι, καὶ ἐπιθυμίαις καὶ ὀργαῖς, καὶ ἀπάταις καὶ δόξαις ἀνοήτοις, Corp. Herm., VI, 3.[21] Similarly, souls imprisoned in bodies in the κόρη κόσμου (Corp. Herm., Vol. I, 474, 20 ff.) complain that this κόλασις, this λυπεῖσθαι, is suspended over them. This does not mean that λύπη takes on the positive significance of a break with the world, but it is explained (*ibid.*, 482, 4 ff.) that the man who in his τόλμα would search out the mysteries of φύσις and his own origin cannot live ἀμέριμνος and ἄλυπος but will be disciplined by λύπη.[22] The possibility of learning through λύπη the alienation of the soul and its relationship to deity is at least intimated in Plotinus when he speaks of the gains which the soul that has plunged into the depths brings back with it on its re-ascent. It "has learned what it really means to live in the upper world, and perceived more clearly what the higher means by comparison with its opposite. For experience of the bad gives a clear knowledge of the good to those whose strength is too weak to know the bad by pure knowledge prior to all experience."[23] But Plotinus does not follow up this possibility of attaining to a positive understanding of λύπη, and in his discussion of κάθαρσις, e.g., λύπη, along with θυμός, ἐπιθυμία etc., is a πάθος from which the soul must purify itself (Enn., I, 2, 5, p. 54, 25 ff.).

B. The Understanding of Sorrow in the Old Testament and Judaism.

1. λύπη (λυπεῖν) in the LXX is not the accepted or even the preferred rendering of any one Heb. word. It is used for many words indicating pain, sorrow, annoyance etc. λύπη is used for 7 and λυπεῖν for 13 different words, relatively the most frequently for the stem עצב. Other Gk. words are also used for these terms. Thus we find λύπη 4 times for יָגוֹן which is 8 times rendered ὀδύνη. λύπη and λυπεῖν occur twice each for רָעָה, which is normally translated κακός and derivatives (also πονηρός and derivatives). λυπεῖν is also used once for אָבֵל, mostly πενθεῖν; 5 times for חָרָה, usually θυμοῦν and ὀργίζειν; 5 times for קָצַף, for which ὀργίζειν is used 10 times; and 2 for רָגַז, which is 6 times rendered ὀργίζειν and 8 times ταράσσειν. When there is an antonym, it is usually → εὐφροσύνη.

---

20 This passage is quoted in Wnd. 2 K., 232, with a ref. also to Ceb. Tab., 11, which deals with the μετάνοια that leads to παιδεία. But there is here no ref. to λύπη, though Plut. Ser. Num. Pun., 3 (II, 549c) shows a connection between παιδεία and λύπη. μετάνοια as λύπη is also found in Plut. Terrestriane An Aquatilia Animalia Sint Callidiora, 3 (II, 961d); cf. Gen. Socr., 22 (II, 592b), where μεταμέλεια and αἰσχύνη stand alongside one another as ἀλγηδών.

21 Corp. Herm., VI, 1b reads: λύπη γὰρ κακίας μέρος, but in connection with statements from the Stoic tradition that God is not ἐνδεής and hence knows no ἐπιθυμία and λύπη.

22 Cf. how acc. to Valentinian teaching σωματικὰ τοῦ κόσμου στοιχεῖα arise from the λύπη and ἔκπληξις of σοφία, Iren., I, 4, 2; cf. 4, 5; 5, 4. Cf. the lamenting ψυχή in Hipp. Ref., V, 10, 2, p. 103, 5 f.

23 Enn., IV, 8, 7, p. 151, 14 ff. (Harder).

The meaning of λύπη (λυπεῖν) varies accordingly. It can denote physical exertion and trouble (Gn. 3:17; Prv. 10:22), also pains (Gn. 3:16; Da. 3:50); but esp. suffering, e.g., sorrow at the death of relatives (Gn. 42:38; 44:29, 31 'A; Sir. 38:17 ff.), at foolish children (Prv. 10:1; Sir. 22:4 ff.), lamentation at the overthrow of Jerusalem or the people (Lam. 1:22; Tob. 2:5 vl. πένθος; 14:4 א), also anxiety (Is. 32:11; ψ 54:2), annoyance and wrath (1 Βασ. 29:4; 4 Βασ. 13:19; Jon. 4:1, 4, 9).

2. The phenomenon of pain and sorrow is plainly seen in the OT and Judaism, both in the prophets and the Psalms, in Lamentations and Job. But except in Hellenistic Judaism the emotion is never the theme of theoretical reflection. Indeed, it is only in the secular prudence of the Wisdom literature that pain and trouble are considered as such. This literature perceives that in Israel, too, joy and sorrow are inseparably intermingled in human life (Prv. 14:13). There is an hour both for weeping and for laughter, and human effort cannot alter this (Qoh. 3:4). If Qoh. regards sorrow as better because it is a *memento mori* (7:3 f.), the normal advice of the Wisdom literature is rather different. It warns against surrender to grief (Sir. 30:21 ff.; 38:18 ff.), for good things are not wanting to those of good cheer (Sir. 30:16), and the end of care is death (Sir. 38:18).[24] As Noah, the first to cultivate the vine, brought consolation to man (Gn. 5:29), so Prv. 31:6 admonishes those who are in trouble to drink and forget their grief (cf. Qoh. 9:7; 10:19).

For the rest, the emotions are considered only indirectly, attention being focused — not from the standpoint of theoretical knowledge, but from that of faith — on the objects or causes of joy and sorrow. When there is reference to joy or sorrow, there is no discussion of the constitution or attitude of the soul as these might stand under the question of the ἀγαθόν. Joy and sorrow are understood from the standpoint of the reasons for them. Interest centres, not in joy as such, but in good fortune, not in sorrow as such, but in suffering, trouble and need. For this reason pain stands under the question of theodicy. For it is obvious that suffering and pain are things which ought not to be. God has imposed physical pain and the toil of work on the human race as a punishment for the sin of Adam and Eve (Gn. 3:16 f.). From the time of the fall the world stands under God's judgment, and this aeon is full of trouble and sorrow (4 Esr. 7:11 f.). But in the time of salvation sorrow and sighing will vanish (Is. 35:10; 51:11; cf. 25:8). In so far as suffering is a divine punishment, it brings with it grief and lamentation. Yet one can hardly say that this is the positive meaning of sorrow. This occurs only when suffering is regarded not merely as a punishment by which guilt is expiated but as a divine means of instruction. This occurs first in respect of the people as a whole, so that suffering or affliction is understood as an eschatological phenomenon (→ θλῖψις, → παιδεία; λύπη did not become a characteristic term for this). But individual suffering, too, is regarded as a divine means of instruction.[25]

---

[24] Cf. Test. XII D. 4:6: καὶ ἐὰν ζημιωθῆτε ἑκουσίως [ἢ ἀκουσίως ?] μὴ λυπεῖσθε· ἀπὸ γὰρ λύπης ἐγείρεται καὶ θυμὸς μετὰ ψεύδους. M. Dibelius quotes this verse on Herm. m., 10, 1, 1 (*Handbuch zum NT*, Suppl.), and tries to trace back both passages to Persian tradition.

[25] Cf. the Rabb., e.g., Ex. r., 15 on 12:11 in Str.-B., III, 253 on R. 8:20 f.; MQ, 3, 9, *ibid.*, 805 on Rev. 7:17; also Str.-B., IV, 965 f.

Hence faith in God sees a firm connection between suffering and salvation, between grief and joy.[26] Those who sow in tears reap in joy, Ps. 126:5, cf. Tob. 13:16: μακάριοι ὅσοι ἐλυπήθησαν ἐπὶ πάσαις ταῖς μάστιξίν σου, ὅτι ἐπὶ σοὶ χαρήσονται θεασάμενοι πᾶσαν τὴν δόξαν σου; Test. XII Jud. 25:4: οἱ ἐν λύπῃ τελευτήσαντες ἀναστήσονται ἐν χαρᾷ. Nevertheless, so long as this connection is seen only from the standpoint of divine punishment or instruction, the inner unity between pain and the genuine joy which is given by God is not perceived, nor is the truly positive meaning of suffering. So long as sorrow is simply the opposite of joy, it is not seen that the possibility of joy is given with pain itself.

3. In Hell. Judaism we find some common, secular, moralistic or general religious reflections on λύπη. If in Wis. 8:9 σοφία is the παραίνεσις φροντίδων καὶ λύπης, in Ep. Ar., 232 f. he will escape λύπη who follows after δικαιοσύνη, never harms anyone, and always does good. In face of unavoidable θάνατοι, νόσοι and λῦπαι one must pray to God. One ought to be concerned about the misfortune of friends, but one should not bewail the dead. All men complain only about that which is τὸ πρὸς ἑαυτοὺς συμφέρον, Ep. Ar., 268. In 4 Macc. 1:23 λύπη is listed with the πάθη in Stoic fashion.

Philo's account of λύπη stands particularly under Stoic influence. Philo often presents the Stoic doctrine of λύπη, e.g., Leg. All., III, 200; Rer. Div. Her., 268 ff.; Jos., 79; Decal., 144; Spec. Leg., II, 30.[27] If on this view λύπη is a πάθος like ἡδονή (also ἐπιθυμία and φόβος), it is also contrasted with → χαρά and → εὐφροσύνη, II, 773 f. (and cf. also → ἐλπίς, II, 529 f.), e.g., in Leg. All., III, 216-219; Det. Pot. Ins., 119 ff., 124, 140; Mut. Nom., 163 and 167 ff.; Som., II, 165 and 191. All λυπηρόν is banned from the soul of the righteous, Det. Pot. Ins., 121. χαρά and εὐπάθεια without λύπη and φόβος are signs of εὐδαιμονία, Spec. Leg., II, 48. To be sure, full χαίρειν belongs to God alone, whose φύσις is ἄλυπος and ἄφοβος, Abr., 202. As Abraham offered his son, so the wise man must offer to God his κατὰ διάνοιαν εὐπάθεια and χαρά (*loc. cit.*). But God gives it back to him (*ibid.*, 203 f.). There is for man no ἄκρατος καὶ ἀμιγὴς λύπης χαρά (205). But God does not will that the human race should be just tormented by λῦπαι, ὀδύναι and ἄχθη. He gives merriness to the soul, and the life of the σοφός in particular should be full of joy (207; Spec. Leg., II, 55). Only the fratricide will have unmixed λύπη and φόβος (Praem. Poen., 71; Virt., 200).

This does not yield a positive understanding of λύπη, but we find something along these lines when Philo speaks of the pain of remorse, Spec. Leg., I, 314; Exsecr., 170 and esp. Leg. All., III, 211, where a twofold στεναγμός (defined as σφοδρὰ καὶ ἐπιτεταμένη λύπη) is distinguished: 1. that of the φαῦλος, whose longing is vain, and 2. that of the μετανοῶν καὶ ἀχθόμενος ἐπὶ τῇ πάλαι τροπῇ.

C. λύπη in Primitive Christian Writings.

1. The Greek contrast between ἡδονή and λύπη is not found in the first Christian writings, for ἡδονή is here used, not as the emotion of joy, but as an

---

[26] W. Wichmann, *Die Leidenstheologie* (1930). Naturally, the Gk. idea of the development of the soul is very different from the OT and Jewish concept of instruction. Instruction is the correction which causes the one thus corrected not to do any further wrong.

[27] Acc. to the theory of Middle Stoicism the πάθη are sometimes called βοηθοί of the νοῦς, and as such they are necessary to life, Philo Leg. All., II, 8; cf. Abr., 236-244; Congr., 81; W. Bousset, *Jüdisch-christlicher Schulbetrieb in Alexandria u. Rom* (1915), 74 ff. On the other hand, Stoic theory is sometimes modified along the lines of Cynicism; ἡδονή here appears as the ἀρχή and θεμέλιος of ἐπιθυμία, λύπη and φόβος, Leg. All., III, 113; cf. Op. Mund., 167; Bousset, 82.

ethical term for the desire of the world. On the other hand, we find λύπη-χαρά in Jn. 16:20 ff.; 2 C. 2:3; 6:10; 7:8 f.; Phil. 2:27; Hb. 12:11; Herm. v., 3, 13, 2; s., 1, 10, and also λυπεῖν-εὐφραίνειν in 2 C. 2:2; 2 Cl., 19, 4.

λύπη is used generally for sorrow, pain (2 C. 7:10; Hb. 12:11; 1 Pt. 2:19), esp. sorrow of soul, e.g., the sorrow of the disciples in Gethsemane in Lk. 22:45, their sorrow at the parting of Jesus in Jn. 16:6, 20, 22,[28] Paul's sadness at the unbelief of the Jews in R. 9:2 (combined with ὀδύνη τῇ καρδίᾳ), the grief which Paul is spared when Epaphroditus does not die in Phil. 2:27, and sorrow at the στάσις in Corinth in 1 Cl., 46, 9.

2. The question of the ἀγαθόν or κακόν of λύπη is not raised. As in the OT, sorrow is obviously something which ought not to be. The desire to be spared it, or relieved from it, is justifiable. Paul naturally does not want to suffer λύπη because of the unbelief of the Jews or the revolt at Corinth (R. 9:2; 2 C. 2:1 ff.). He is glad when God spares him a λύπη, and he would like to be ἀλυπότερος (Phil. 2:27 f.). As in the OT and Judaism, there is obviously hope that in the coming age of salvation sorrow and pain will have disappeared (Rev. 7:17; 21:4 etc.), and that those who mourn will be comforted (Mt. 5:4; cf. Lk. 6:21). The time of salvation will be the ἀλύπητος αἰών in view of which there need be no λυπεῖσθαι for the εὐσεβής in the sufferings of the present time (2 Cl., 19, 4).

If λύπη poses an ethical question, it does so only in the sense that we should not cause sorrow to our brethren (R. 14:15). If Paul is going to cause the Corinthians λύπη, this is not for the sake of λύπη. It is in order that their λύπη should be a means whereby they see his love and are led to repentance (2 C. 2:4; 7:9; → 321).

Nor is the question of theodicy raised in the first Christian writings. It is, of course, noted that to be afflicted by sorrows is a problem for the one afflicted, and Hb. 12:11 admonishes those who are being put off by suffering: πᾶσα μὲν παιδεία πρὸς μὲν τὸ παρὸν οὐ δοκεῖ χαρᾶς εἶναι ἀλλὰ λύπης, ὕστερον δὲ καρπὸν εἰρηνικὸν τοῖς δι' αὐτῆς γεγυμνασμένοις ἀποδίδωσιν δικαιοσύνης (cf. the whole passage 12:4-13). As in the OT and Judaism, the idea of divine correction is the answer to the question of suffering. The same thought is to be found in 1 Pt. 1:6 f.; Herm. v., 4, 3, 4; also Jm. 1:2 f. (though λύπη is not used here).

3. Yet this is not the specifically Christian approach to λύπη. This is to be found in the thought that λύπη is essentially bound up with the Christian life. For the Christian life begins with a turning from the world, a break with it, and it involves a constant maintaining of this attitude to the world.

This concept finds its first expression in a Christian modification of the ancient Hellenistic idea of the salutary pangs of remorse. Paul alludes to this, though he does not expressly develop the theme, when he speaks of λυπεῖσθαι εἰς μετάνοιαν or κατὰ θεὸν λύπη in 2 C. 7:9-11, and contrasts this λύπη with the λύπη τοῦ κόσμου. If the λύπη τοῦ κόσμου is the concern of the man who sees his worldly well-being and desires shattered, the κατὰ θεὸν λύπη is the sorrow of the man who has become aware of his lostness in the world, and who cries again to God

[28] The bodily pain of a woman in childbirth involves λύπη (Jn. 16:21), but it is here linked with anguish.

in μετάνοια from the world. As worldly λύπη works death, because the man who has become a slave of the world perishes with the world, so λύπη κατὰ θεόν works σωτηρία. And it manifests itself in conduct according to the divine requirement (v. 11). Paul speaks here of this λύπη as something within the Christian life, for the Corinthians are already Christians. But it is self-evident that the same holds good of the μετάνοια of conversion to Christianity. 2 C. 7:9-11 simply shows that the basis of the Christian life in μετάνοια is not secured once and for all by conversion. It must be maintained by constant renewal.

Apart from this λύπη of self-judgment, there also belongs essentially to the Christian life the kind of λύπη known by the world. The Christian life is especially affected by this because the Christian realises that he has broken with the world and is in opposition to it. As a Christian he is thus a particular target of its hostility. He has thus to accept what the world calls λύπη and what he himself continually experiences as such inasmuch as he constantly detects, and must overcome, the world in himself. But just because he also experiences a new freedom from the world in this acceptance of λύπη, he has attained to a new understanding of λύπη, which does not mean the same for him as for the worldly. For the latter, λύπη is the constant hampering of life and its ultimate extinction. But for Christians it is the constant liberation and growth of the power of life. For Christians the break with the world and liberation for life is grounded in the death and resurrection of Christ. Hence this acceptance of λύπη is no other than acceptance of the cross of Christ, through which the world is crucified for them and they to the world, Gl. 6:14; cf. R. 6:6. It is no other than fellowship with the resurrection of Christ, Phil. 3:10 f.; 2 C. 4:7 ff. It is true that Paul does not develop this thought specifically in terms of λύπη. But what he says about suffering in 2 C. 4:8 f.; 11:23 ff. falls under the worldly concept of λῦπαι, and in the antitheses in 2 C. 6:7 ff., which depict the Christian life in its acceptance and paradoxical transvaluation of sufferings, we find the antithesis: ὡς λυπούμενοι, ἀεὶ δὲ χαίροντες. In the same way the sickness mentioned in 2 C. 12:7 f. would be a λύπη from the worldly standpoint, and the statement: ἡ γὰρ δύναμις ἐν ἀσθενείᾳ τελεῖται, shows plainly the Christian understanding of λύπη.

The same thought is developed in Jn. 16:6 f., 20-22. For the λύπη in which the disciples are plunged by the departure of Jesus is not to be misunderstood along the lines of psychology or fiction. On the contrary, it characterises the situation of loneliness which is the lot of those whom Jesus has called out of the world (15:19; 17:16) and who are yet in the world (17:11) and against whom the hatred of the world is directed (15:18 ff.). To this λύπη corresponds the χαρά of the κόσμος (16:20). The κόσμος rejoices at the going of Jesus, because His presence challenges its security, and it hates His own, because their existence constantly calls it in question. Belonging to Jesus, His own must accept this loneliness in the world and the world's hatred. For they now belong to Jesus and not to the world (15:19). In the first instance this means for them ταραχή (14:1),[29] θλῖψις (16:33) and λύπη. For their situation is not an obvious one. They must find their way into it. λύπη must be experienced if the meaning of belonging to Jesus is to be grasped. Jesus must go away from them. He does not have for them the significance of an

---

[29] λύπη is also linked with ταραχή in, e.g., ψ 54:2. The combination is given currency by Stoicism, cf. Epict. Diss., II, 1, 24; 22, 6; III, 11, 2; 22, 61; Ench., 5; Plot. Enn., IV, 8, 8 (Volkmann, II, p. 152, 27).

enhancement and ensuring of their being in the world, for He Himself does not belong to the world. If they are to remain bound to Him, they must be alone. But for this very reason their λύπη is the origin of their χαρά (16:21 f.). In turning from the world they experience fellowship with Him, and they thus stand in a joy which is eternal (16:22) because it does not derive from the world. The world is overcome for them by Him (16:33). In Jn., as distinct from Pl., one side of λύπη is particularly emphasised, namely, that in Christian λύπη apparent isolation from Jesus must be suffered as well as isolation in the world. The paradox of fellowship with Him is thereby made clearer.

4. The specifically Christian understanding of λύπη is also found in 1 Pt. when in 2:19, in a special exhortation to slaves, we read: τοῦτο γὰρ χάρις, εἰ διὰ συνείδησιν θεοῦ ὑποφέρει τις λύπας πάσχων ἀδίκως; for in the διὰ συνείδησιν θεοῦ, as in the ἀδίκως, we find the thought that commitment to God and separation from the world includes a readiness for λύπη. Thus the admonition in vv. 21 ff. (εἰς τοῦτο γὰρ ἐκλήθητε) is grounded in a reference to relationship with Christ, who gave an ὑπογραμμός by His suffering. The same idea is found in 1 Pt. 3:13 ff.; 4:12 ff., though λύπη is not used.

Rather apart is the admonition in Eph. 4:30: μὴ λυπεῖτε τὸ πνεῦμα τὸ ἅγιον τοῦ θεοῦ, ἐν ᾧ ἐσφραγίσθητε εἰς ἡμέραν ἀπολυτρώσεως, where λυπεῖν is used in the current sense of "to wound," "to insult." This warning is obviously a strengthening of the admonition in v. 29 to guard against corrupt words.[30] Perhaps the phrase is influenced by the tradition which is also found in Herm. (→ C. 5.).[31]

5. λύπη is used for sorrow over sins in Herm. v., 1, 2, 1 f., and more emphatically in connection with saving μετάνοια, m., 10, 1-3. Yet these are Christian additions to the basic tradition.[32] This tradition presents λύπη as the worst of all πνεύματα. It corrupts man, and drives out the Holy Spirit. The ἱλαρὸς ἀνήρ despises λύπη, while the λυπηρὸς ἀνήρ wounds (λυπεῖ) the Holy Spirit and is unable to pray. Hence we must purify ourselves of λύπη and put on ἱλαρότης (→ III, 299). Similarly, in s., 9, 15, 3 λύπη is one of the 12 vices. The warning, μηδὲ λύπην ἐπάγειν τῷ πνεύματι τῷ σεμνῷ καὶ ἀληθεῖ, is also found in m., 3, 4, where it is plain that the πνεῦμα, in distinction from Eph. 4:30, is thought of as παρακαταθήκη, m., 3, 2. The tradition here, which can hardly be Stoic, comes from a Persian source, as par. in the Test. XII and Corp. Herm. show.[32] On the other hand, we have in v., 4, 3, 4 a Christian discussion of the testing sorrows by which believers are freed from λύπη and στενοχωρία.

In Tat. Or. Graec., 11, 1, in the context of Stoicising ideas, we find the phrase λύπη μου τὴν ψυχὴν οὐκ ἀναλίσκει. There is little else worthy of note in the Apologists. In the Gnostic sphere we might refer to the prayer for the soul preparing for the heavenly journey in Act. Thom., 142, p. 249, 5 ff.: ἰδοὺ ἀπαλλάττομαι λύπης καὶ χαρὰν ἐνδύομαι μόνον. ἰδοὺ γίνομαι ἄφροντις καὶ ἄλυπος ἐν ἀνέσει διατρίβων.

---

30 λυπεῖν through wounding words, e.g., Eur. Med., 474; Plat. Ap., 41e; Luc. Nigrinus, 9; IG, XIV, 1857, 3.

31 The admonition of Eph. 4:30 is quoted as a saying of the Lord in Ps.-Cyprian De Aleat., 3 (p. 95, 1, ed. G. Hartel, 1868/71): *nolite contristare spiritum sanctum qui in vobis est, et nolite exstinguere lumen quod in vobis effulsit.*

32 M. Dibelius on Herm. m., 10, 1, 1 in *Handbuch,* Suppl.

† ἄλυπος.

ἄλυπος, "without sorrow or care," a word found from the time of Soph.,[1] fairly common also in the pap.[2] It has a particular role in Stoicism, where it is a characteristic of the σοφός (v. Arnim, III, p. 110, 23) and therewith of the εὐτυχής (M. Ant., 4, 49). It occurs frequently, then, in Epict., e.g., along with ἀτάραχος (Diss., IV, 6, 8 → 321, n. 29) and ἄφοβος (III, 22, 48; IV, 1, 5; 6, 16; Ench., 12, 1). Though it does not occur in the LXX, Philo uses it as an attribute of God (Cher., 86 with ἄφοβος) or of the φύσις of God (Abr., 202), also of the high-priest (Spec. Leg., I, 115) and the ζωή of Isaac (with ἄφοβος) as a type of χαρά (Praem. Poen., 35).

In the NT it occurs only in Phil. 2:28 (→ 320).

In Just. Dial., 117, 3 it serves with ἄφθαρτος and ἀθάνατος to characterise the blessed, as does ἀλύπητος in 69, 7. This word, found from the time of Soph., does not occur in the pap., but is used in 2 Cl., 19, 4 (→ 320). ἀλυπία is also a feature of blessedness in Just. Dial., 45, 4; cf. Act. Thom., 142, p. 249, 7, → *supra*.

† περίλυπος.

περίλυπος, "afflicted beyond measure," "deeply sorrowful," attested from the time of Hippocr., not found in the pap. Its antonym in Isoc., 1, 42 is περιχαρής. It occurs 8 times in the LXX: with γίγνεσθαι in Gn. 4:6 (for חָרָה); Da. 2:12 (for קְצַף); with εἶναι in ψ 41:5, 11; 42:5 (for שׁוּחַ or שִׂיחַ hitpal); also 1 Esr. 8:68 f.; Tob. 3:1 א. It is not found in Philo or Joseph.

The use in the NT gives evidence of LXX influence: Lk. 18:23 of the rich young ruler περίλυπος ἐγενήθη (Mk. 10:22; Mt. 19:22: λυπούμενος); Mk. 6:26 of Herod περίλυπος γενόμενος (Mt. 14:9 λυπηθείς); Mk. 14:34; Mt. 26:38 of Jesus in Gethsemane περίλυπός ἐστιν ἡ ψυχή μου ἕως θανάτου.[1]

1 Cl. has the word in a quotation from Gn. 4:6; it is strengthened by λίαν in Herm. v., 3, 10, 6.

† συλλυπέομαι.

συλλυπεῖν "to make sorrowful with" (Aristot. Eth. Nic., IX, p. 1171b, 7), συλλυπεῖσθαι, "to sorrow with," "to feel sympathy," common from the time of Hdt., also in the LXX at Is. 51:19; ψ 68:20 for נוּד.

In the NT it occurs only at Mk. 3:5: καὶ περιβλεψάμενος αὐτοὺς μετ᾽ ὀργῆς, συλλυπούμενος ἐπὶ τῇ πωρώσει τῆς καρδίας αὐτῶν, λέγει ... Since the op-

ἄλυπος. [1] Of Ionic derivation? *v.* Nägeli, 25.
[2] Cf. Preisigke Wört., *s.v.*

περίλυπος. [1] Of the ψυχή also in Plut. Suav. Viv. Epic., 21 (II, 1101e). λυπεῖσθαι is found with ἕως θανάτου in Jon. 4:9, λύπη in Sir. 37:2; cf. also Ju. 16:16 B: ὠλιγοψύχησεν ἕως τοῦ ἀποθανεῖν, *v.* Schl. Mt., 751. The meaning is obvious: "to be so full of sorrow that I would rather be dead," not "of sorrow which leads to death," or "which lasts until death," or even "as if death were approaching."

ponents have no λύπη, συλλυπούμενος seems to be simply a stronger form of λυπούμενος.

Bultmann

λύτρον, λυτρόω, λύτρωσις, λυτρωτής → λύω, 328.

† λύχνος, † λυχνία

λύχνος comes from the well-known root *leuk,* which is seen in → λευκός, Lat. *lux,* Germ. *Licht,* Eng. light.[1] It is common from the time of Hom. (with λύχνοι we also find, though less frequently, λύχνα as a plur.).[2] If in the earliest instance (Hom. Od., 19, 34) we are perhaps to think more of a candlestick,[3] elsewhere λύχνος always means "lamp."[4] From the original open bowl with an inset for the better disposition of the wick there developed from the 5th cent. B.C. the closed lamp which has an opening in the middle for filling up with oil and which usually has only one hole for the wick, though in other respects it may be made in the most varied forms.[5] To give the light a greater range the lamp is usually elevated by being put on a stand, though the lamp and stand could also be made in one piece. For the stand the usual word is λυχνία,[6] though we also find λυχνεῖον[7] and λυχνοῦχος.[8] In Israel and Judah lamps and lampstands had great significance as elsewhere in antiquity.[9] In the LXX λύχνος occurs some 50 times (plur. always λύχνοι). The Heb. is almost always נֵר, and this in turn is almost always λύχνος (only twice each λαμπτήρ and φῶς). λυχνία occurs 37 times, 7 in Ex. 25:31-35, 8 in Ex. 26-40, and 6 in Nu. The Heb. is always מְנוֹרָה, and this is always λυχνία except in Ex. 37:19 (LXX 38:16).[10] The seven-branched candelabra in

---

λύχνος. [1] Walde-Pok., II, 409.

[2] Cf. Liddell-Scott and Pass., *s.v.* Also inscr., cf. Ditt. Syll.³, 57, 34 (450/49 B.C.) and pap. (Preisigke Wört., II, 43; Moult.-Mill., IV, 383); → n. 14.

[3] Cf. Hug, Art. "*Lucerna* (λύχνος), die Lampe" in Pauly-W., XIII (1927), 1567.

[4] In this sense the word passed into Lat. as the loan word *lychnus* (along with the more common *lucerna*). Cf. Hug, *op. cit.*

[5] The extraordinary number of lamps found in burial places has given us an exact knowledge of the various types, their dates and distribution. Cf. Hug, 1566-1613, and works with particular ref. to Palestine and Syria, K. Galling, "Die Beleuchtungsgeräte im israelitisch-jüdischen Kulturgebiet," ZDPV, 46 (1923), 1-50 (with Plates I-IV); P. Thomsen, Art. "Beleuchtung, C: Palästina-Syrien" in *Reallexikon der Vorgeschichte,* 1 (1924), 384-390, also the review in K. Galling, Art. "Lampe (und Leuchter)" in *Biblisches Reallexikon* (1937), 347-350.

[6] λυχνία (from the beginning of the 3rd cent. B.C.) is related to λύχνος as οἰκία to οἶκος or κοπρία to κόπρος. Derivates in -ία from substantive o stems are rare in this or a related sense. On λυχνία cf. Mayser, I, 3² (1936), 28, 4 ff., on derivates in -ία, P. Chantraine, *La formation des noms en Grec Ancien* (1933), 81 [Debrunner]. Cf. Liddell-Scott and Pass., *s.v.* Inscr. late and rare, but more common in pap., cf. Preisigke Wört., II, 43, the earliest P. Eleph., 5, 7 (284/3 B.C.).

[7] Also λυχνίον (or λύχνιον); diminutive of λύχνος, "little lamp." Cf. Phryn., ed. Lobeck, 313 f.

[8] In Lat. as the loan word *lychnuchus.* Mau, Art. "Candelabrum" in Pauly-W., III (1899), 1461-1464, considers only the Roman aspect.

[9] Cf. the special bibl. in → n. 5, also S. Krauss, *Talmudische Arch.,* I (1910), 68 ff.

[10] Neither λυχνοῦχος not other derivates of λύχνος occur in the LXX. But for other vessels we find → λαμπάς (some 20 times, almost always for לַפִּיד), λαμπάδιον (-εῖον, 5 refs.), λαμπτήρ (4 times in Prv.), φωστήρ (6 times). We do not find φανός, "lantern" (cf. Galling, ZDPV, *op. cit.,* 5 [n. 1], 32); cf. also → n. 24. Nor is there any mention of candles, though these were known in Judaism (cf. Krauss, I, 73).

the tabernacle and the temple deserves special mention (it is called λυχνία, and its seven lamps are λύχνοι).[11] So, too, does the candlestick described in Zech. 4:2.[12] Both in connection with the OT and also independently, both Philo[13] and Joseph.[14] often use λύχνος and λυχνία. Lamps are part of the furnishings of the synagogue.[15] It must be emphasised that, while a fig. use of λύχνος is rare elsewhere,[16] the lamp (though not the stand) is often used as a metaphor in the OT and LXX. It denotes length of days, vitality, the possibility of action: 2 Βασ. 21:17: οὐ μὴ σβέσῃς τὸν λύχνον Ἰσραήλ, ψ 17:28: σὺ φωτιεῖς λύχνον μου, κύριε, ψ 131:17: ἡτοίμασα λύχνον τῷ χριστῷ μου. There are many refs. to the lamp of the ungodly which will be put out (Job 18:6; 21:17; other passages with λαμπτήρ). It also denotes the source of strength, helping power and the grace of preservation: Job 29:3: ὡς ὅτε ηὔγει ὁ λύχνος αὐτοῦ (God) ὑπὲρ κεφαλῆς μου, 2 Βασ. 22:29: σὺ ὁ λύχνος μου, κύριε, of the Law: Prv. 6:23: λύχνος ἐντολὴ νόμου καὶ φῶς, ψ 118:105: λύχνος τοῖς ποσίν μου ὁ νόμος σου (also rendered ὁ λόγος acc. to the Mas.); cf. also Prv. 20:27. The connection with similar sayings in which → φῶς is used (also λάμπω κτλ. → 22) is obvious.[17]

---

[11] For an express description cf. LXX Ex. 25:31 ff. Cf. R. Kittel, Art. "Stiftshütte" in RE³, XIX (1907), 38 f. and Art. "Tempelgeräte," *ibid.*, 501 ff.; also K. Galling, *Biblisches Reallexikon*, 349. → 23, n. 26.

[12] Cf. → n. 11, also K. Möhlenbrink, "Der Leuchter im 5. Nachtgesicht des Proph. Sach.," ZDPV, 52 (1929), 257 ff., and the reconstruction in Galling, *Biblisches Reallexikon*, 348.

[13] Leisegang, *s.v.*

[14] Cf. the collection in G. Schmidt, "De Flavii Josephi elocutione observationes criticae," *Jbch. f. Phil.*, Suppl. Vol. NF, 20 (1894), 529. In Ant., 18, 93 Jos. also uses τὸ λύχνον, of which there are a few instances in the pap. in the Christian era, Preisigke Wört., II, 43; BGU, I, 338, 1 [2nd/3rd cent.]) and Ant., 18, 74 the plur. τὰ λύχνα.

[15] Str.-B., IV, 140 → 23, n. 26. Cf. Galling, Art. "Schrein" in *Biblisches Reallexikon*, 471 (seven-branched candelabra in the synagogue).

[16] Cf. Pass., *s.v.*

[17] Often the use of the image in the LXX is uncertain. Thus in 4 Βασ. 8:19 and 2 Παρ. 21:7 we find δοῦναι αὐτῷ λύχνον, and in 2 Βασ. 14:7 σβέσουσιν τὸν ἄνθρακά μου. But sometimes the image is dropped, cf. 3 Βασ. 11:36 (θέσις) and 15:4 (κατάλειμμα, with Θ; 'ΑΣ keep λύχνος). In the difficult verse Nu. 21:30 the LXX finds the image of the נֵר and uses σπέρμα (as κατάλειμμα in 3 Βασ. 15:4); this does not presuppose a different text (unlike BHK ²˒ ³, which assumes that the Heb. original is נִין "posterity"). But it may be that instead of נֵר the LXX reads in these verses נִיר ("newly cleared land") in the sense of a Jewish exegesis which is still current (*v.* Mandelkern, *s.v.* ניר and נזר), and which might also explain 2 K. 8:19 and 2 Ch. 21:7. This word is known for certain in the LXX, and distinguished from נֵר only in Jer. 4:3, where νεοῦν and νέωμα are used for the verb and the noun ניר. In Prv. 13:23 the LXX uses a different text from the Mas. In Prv. 21:4 it has λαμπτήρ, which is also found in 20:20 (LXX 9a); 24:20 for נֵר, also in another rendering 20:27 (LXX φῶς, in many MSS ἢ λύχνος). In 16:28, too, the LXX obviously read ונרגן from נֵר and used λαμπτήρ. These passages show the liking of the LXX for the lamp-light topology. David is a light for his people, and his race remains this for him and for Israel. Thus the term takes on a Messianic character. How far a cosmic symbolism is recognised and felt in the seven-branched candelabra (in terms of the seven planets) is open to question. Cf. also A. Jeremias, *Das AT im Lichte des Alten Orients*³ (1916), *s.v.* "Leuchte, Leuchter," esp. 475. On the ἐπιλύχνιος εὐχαριστία (ἐπιλύχνιος ψαλμός, Const. Ap., VIII, 35, 2 [I, 544, Funk]) in the early Church cf. F. J. Dölger, "Lumen Christi. Untersuchungen zum abendländischen Lichtsegen in Antike u. Christentum. Die Deo-Gratias-Lampen von Selinunt in Sizilien und Cuicul in Numidien," *Antike u. Christentum*, 5 (1936), 1-43 [Bertram].

The widespread acquaintance with lamps and stands is the basis of Jesus' allusion to the obvious rule that if a lamp is to give its full illumination it must be set on a stand and not irrationally placed under a bed or covered with a bushel. [18] This is used to give point to a law in the spiritual life, Mk. 4:21; Mt. 5:15; Lk. 8:16; 11:33. For all the interrelation of these passages there are differences in detailed form which may not only reflect different stages of the tradition, and show the influence of the contexts in which they are put and the independent interpretations of the Evangelists, but which may also be linked with the fact that Jesus used the comparison on different occasions and in different senses. [19] This makes exposition more difficult, especially as no interpretation is ever appended. One might think of the duty of the disciples to pursue their ministry publicly and not to withhold the glad tidings from any (this interpretation is particularly suggested in Mt. 5:15; cf. 5:14, where the disciples are called τὸ → φῶς τοῦ κόσμου). [20] But one might also think of the tendency towards full outworking and the universal extension of help which is immanent in the Gospel itself. [21] Nor is it impossible that the reference is to Jesus and His significance or the course of His life (cf. Jn. 1:5; 8:12). [22] Lk. adds to 11:33 the parable which is found in another context and a shorter version in Mt. 6:22. In 11:34 He calls the eye the λύχνος τοῦ σώματος. On its health depends whether the blessings of light come to man. We must be fully open to the light of Jesus, or of the Gospel. [23] The admonition in Lk. 12:35 : ἔστωσαν ὑμῶν ... οἱ λύχνοι καιόμενοι, an obvious figure for constant readiness, reminds us of the situation in the parable in Mt. 25:1 ff. [24] The woman in the parable of the lost coin lights a lamp (ἅπτει λύχνον,

[18] Exceptions, e.g., the dazzling of a sick person by the lamp (Shab., 2, 5), or the covering of the lamp with a bushel on the Sabbath so that the flame will not catch the beams (16, 7), do not affect the rule. The ref. is obviously to a house with one room (Kl. Mt., *ad loc.*; Galling, ZDPV, *op. cit.*, 34), to simple conditions, and to a stand which is not too big or heavy (as against Zn. Mt.[4], 205, n. 60 and Lk.[3, 4], 344, n. 18).

[19] Cf. Wbg. Mk., 136. Zn. Lk.[3, 4], 344, n. 18 and 469; J. Schniewind, Mk. (*NT Deutsch,* 1), 76: "Fine examples of the many meanings of an unexplained parable."

[20] In spite of Mt. 5:16, we are not to think of the conduct of the disciples. The admonition that they should not obscure the Gospel, nor get in the way of its operation, is certainly implied, but the main emphasis is on the positive demand. Cf. also → 26.

[21] That the saying is taken eschatologically by Mk., and refers to the manifestation of the kingdom, cannot be deduced from the ἔρχεται (as against E. Lohmeyer, *Kommentar z. Mk.* [1937], *ad loc.*). Perhaps we should not seek too close a connection with the temporarily concealing character of the parables in Mk. Is more than Israel in view? Cf. Kl. Lk. on 8:16; Schl. Mk., 101 f.

[22] Though not in such a way that κρύπτῃ in Lk. 11:33 refers to the death of Jesus in the sense of sepulchre, and the whole saying to His resurrection, by which He, and with Him His Gospel, come to light again (so Zn. Lk.[3, 4], 470). → III, 975.

[23] In Lk. there is certainly "an association in terms of λύχνος" (Kl. Lk., *ad loc.*), but Lk. sees a material connection with 11:33: it is man's fault that, even though the light shines forth, he does not let it affect him. Is this an explanation of Jewish rejection? The parable presents many detailed problems, esp. τὸ → φῶς τὸ ἐν σοί, Lk. 11:35; Mt. 6:23, and the exclusively Lucan conclusion in 11:36, in which λύχνος occurs again.

[24] Cf. W. Michaelis, *Es ging ein Sämann aus, zu säen* (1938), 151 f., 174. The ten virgins carry λαμπάδες rather than λύχνοι (Galling, ZDPV, *op. cit.*, 32, "lamps on poles"). λαμπάς is also found in Jn. 18:3; Ac. 20:8 (to illuminate an obviously large upper room); Rev. 4:5; 8:10; → 17 and 26. In Jn. 18:3 we find φανός, "lantern." In Phil. 2:15 (cf. Da. 12:3) φωστήρ is used for "lampstand," though it means "light" in Rev. 21:11. On these partial synonyms cf. Trench, 96 ff. (§ 28 : φῶς, φέγγος, φωστήρ, λύχνος, λαμπάς), also → n. 10. The plur. (λύχνοι) is found only in Lk. 12:35.

Lk. 15:8) in order to see into all corners of the house. This, too, is a feature which everyone can understand. [25]

According to Jn. 5:35 Jesus says of John the Baptist: ἐκεῖνος ἦν ὁ λύχνος ὁ καιόμενος καὶ φαίνων. Here we have an intentional (cf. 1:8) limitation; John is a lamp, but not the light itself. [26] Yet the saying also bears witness, to John's honour, that he fulfilled the task which he was given, ἵνα μαρτυρήσῃ περὶ τοῦ φωτός (1:8). [27] The description of the two witnesses in Rev. 11:4 as αἱ δύο λυχνίαι is based on Zech. 4:2, 11, though the comparison is independently changed. [28] The depicting of the seven churches of the letters of Rev. under the metaphor of 7 golden λυχνίαι (1:12 f., 20; 2:1, 5) is also influenced by Zech. 4 (rather than Ex. 25), though the image of Mt. 5:14 (Phil. 2:15) probably had some influence. [29] In Rev. 21:23 the Lamb Himself is ὁ λύχνος αὐτῆς (the heavenly Jerusalem). [30]

The (seven-branched) λυχνία of the ancient cultus is mentioned in Hb. 9:2. [31] The phrase ὡς λύχνῳ φαίνοντι ἐν αὐχμηρῷ τόπῳ in 2 Pt. 1:19 is designed to characterise the task of the προφητικὸς λόγος. [32]

Michaelis

---

25 This passage, with Mt. 5:15, is rightly claimed as evidence that the custom that private houses should have an everlasting lamp was not followed in Judaism at this time. Cf. Galling, ZDPV, *op. cit.*, 34; Krauss, I, 404, n. 224.

26 On related Rabb. predications (usually with no distinction between light and lamp), cf. Str.-B., I, 236 f., II, 466; → 23. The description of Elijah in Sir. 48:1: καὶ ἀνέστη Ηλιας προφήτης ὡς πῦρ, καὶ ὁ λόγος αὐτοῦ ὡς λαμπὰς ἐκαίετο, is so similar that one might think this verse had some influence (Zn. J.[5, 6], 309 f.). Can one deduce from the art. (ὁ λύχνος) a corresponding expectation of Elijah (so also Bl.-Debr.[6] § 273, 1)? Cf. also → II, 937, n. 75.

27 The order shows that καιόμενος is the presupposition of φαίνων and does not mean burning itself out in the sense of the decrease of Jn. 3:30. Hence the Mandean passages cited in Bau. J.[2], 85 ("extinguished like a lamp") are no true par.

28 Cf. D. Haug, *Die zwei Zeugen. Eine exegetische Studie über Apk. 11:1-13* (*NT.liche Abh.*, 17, 1) (1936), 16 f., 137. Here, too, we are to think of Elijah (and Moses), cf. → n. 26; II, 939. The conjecture in Loh. Apk., 89 that Moses and Elijah represent the Law and the prophets cannot be pressed in spite of passages like those quoted on → 325.

29 Cf. also → 325, and n. 26. On the historical background cf. Clemen, 368 ff. On Rev. 2:5 cf. → III, 718. On the equation of the 7 candlesticks with 7 stars → I, 504.

30 Cf. Is. 60:19 f. and → 325. The relation to → φῶς (e.g., Jn. 8:12) and φωστήρ is plain in Rev. 21:11; cf. J. Behm, *Apk.* (*NT Deutsch,* 11), *ad loc.* φῶς λύχνου in Rev. 18:23; 22:5 is based on Jer. 25:10.

31 Str.-B., III, 705 ff.; O. Michel, *Der Brief an d. Hebräer* (1936), *ad loc.*

32 It is striking how strong is the influence of the OT in these passages as compared with the sayings of Jesus in the Synpt. Post-apost. fathers: In 1 Cl., 21, 2 we have a very independent use of Prv. 20:27 (with λύχνος from Cod A); there is a paraphrase of Lk. 12:35 in Did., 16, 1.

λύω, ἀναλύω, ἀνάλυσις, ἐπιλύω, ἐπίλυσις, καταλύω, κατάλυμα, ἀκατάλυτος, λύτρον, ἀντίλυτρον, λυτρόω, λύτρωσις, λυτρωτής, ἀπολύτρωσις

The Word Group in the Old Testament.

Contents: 1. λύω and Compounds; 2. λύτρον: a. כֹּפֶר, b. גאל, c. פִּדְיֹן; 3. λυτροῦσθαι and Derivatives: a. λυτρόομαι, b. λύτρωσις, c. λυτρωτής, d. ἀπολύτρωσις.

1. λύω and Compounds. [1]

The Gk. word λύω "to loose" is rich in compounds which give nuances to the basic meaning. In the LXX we find ἀναλύω (only in the Apocr.), also ἀπολύω, διαλύω, ἐκλύω, ἐπιλύω (Ἀ Gn. 40:8; 41:8, 12 and Θ Jer. 46:3), καταλύω, παραλύω, περιλύω, συλλύω, ὑπολύω, of which all but the last three also occur in the NT. Of the many Heb. equivalents for λύω the most important are פָּתַח "to open" (Gn. 42:27; Job 39:5; Ps. 102:20; Is. 5:27; 14:17; 58:6; Jer. 40:4) and הִתִּיר (Ps. 105:20; 146:7). The Aram. is שְׁרָא (Da. 3:25; 5:12).

The simple λύω is used for the freeing of those in prison (Tob. 3:17 א; Jdt. 6:14; Job 5:20; Ps. 102:20; 105:20; 146:7; Is. 14:17; Jer. 40:4; Da. 3:25; 3 Macc. 6:29; 4 Macc. 12:8 f.), but also for the opening of things that are closed (Gn. 42:27: τὸν μάρσιππον; 1 Εσδρ. 9:46: τὸν νόμον), and also for the destruction of foundations and walls (2 Εσδρ. 5:12 B [סתר]; 1 Εσδρ. 1:52), also of fetters (Ex. 3:5; Jos. 5:15; Job 39:2, 5; Is. 5:27; 58:6; Da. 5:12; 3 Macc. 6:27) which are put off. This idea is present when sin (ἁμαρτία) is the obj. of λύω (Job 42:9; cf. Sir. 28:2: δεηθέντος σου αἱ ἁμαρτίαι σου λυθήσονται, Is. 40:2). Here God is the subj.; He breaks sin like a fetter. [2] Of the compounds ἀναλύω means "to leave" and is used of sin in Sir. 3:15. ἀπολύω means "to release," [3] once in the pass. of liberation from sin (2 Macc. 12:45: τῆς ἁμαρτίας ἀπολυθῆναι). διαλύω means "to loosen," "resolve," and is used for 8 Heb. words in the 8 instances. ἐκλύω means "to loosen" (Job 19:25 גאל), mostly pass. in the sense "to relax," "to grow weary," for a total of 19 Heb. words. The opp. of ἀναλύω is καταλύω, "to break off," used of a journey, so that it is common in the historical books (15 times) as a rendering of the Heb. root לין "to pass the night," though

---

λύω κτλ. The Word Group in the OT. J. Herrmann, *Die Idee der Sühne im AT* (1905).

[1] Walde-Pok., II, 406.

[2] In Lat. authors man himself pays the debt which he has incurred (Liv., 30, 15: *luo temeritatem*; Horat. Carmina, III, 6, 1: *delicta*) or the equivalent (Curtius, ed. T. Vogel [3, 4] [1903 ff.], X, 2, 25: *aes alienum*; Cic. Att., III, 9, 1: *poenas*).

[3] In the LXX and NT ἀπολύω is mostly used in the sense of "release" or "free," and med. in the sense of "break out." It is often a figure or euphemism for "to die" (Gn. 15:2; Nu. 20:29; Tob. 3:6, 13; Lk. 2:29).

sometimes it can also mean "to destroy" (4 Βασ. 25:10 vl.), a common sense in the NT. In the LXX παραλύω, which in 15 canonical passages is used for 13 Heb. words, is the compound for "to destroy." In 3 instances it is used for the Heb. רפה "to become slack," with special ref. to the failure of the hands (in the NT the παραλυτικός is the lame person, i.e., failure of the knees and hips, cf. Sir. 25:23). Other words which have no relevance from the standpoint of the NT are περιλύω, "to release round about" (apart from 'A, only once in א at 4 Macc. 10:7), συλλύω, "to part," i.e., those who are fighting with a view to reconciliation (1 Macc. 13:47; 2 Macc. 11:14; 13:23), and ὑπολύω, "to untie," of sandals.

2. λύτρον.

Theologically the derived noun λύτρον, "ransom," is much more important than λύω and its compounds. In contrast to Mk. 10:45; Mt. 20:28, λύτρον is always used in the plur. in the LXX (except for Prv. 6:35; 13:8). Except for Is. 45:13 (מְחִיר = λύτρα), where a different rendering is found elsewhere in the Gk., λύτρον has three Heb. equivalents, namely, כֹּפֶר, גאל and פדה, which are all theologically significant, and which must be dealt with separately.[4]

a. כֹּפֶר. The subst. singulare tantum כֹּפֶר, which is 6 times the original of λύτρον (Ex. 21:30; 30:12; Nu. 35:31, 32; Prv. 6:35; 13:8), means "cover." In the Heb. verb כִּפֶּר "to atone," which does not occur in the q, the basic meaning "to cover" has been lost.[5] But it is still to be seen in the ritual of expiation.

A derivation from the Assyr. *kuppuru* "to wash away" is not to be recommended for כִּפֶּר in view of its connection with כֹּפֶר, since "to cover" is still the meaning in the Arab. *kafara*. Yet it is to be noted that כֹּפֶר, as distinct from כִּפֶּר, has a wholly civil, not a sacral, meaning. As a "cover" כֹּפֶר always denotes an equivalent, just as one speaks of covering a fault, so that the term is always one of value. With this is linked the thought of substitution, which is always present in כֹּפֶר. The idea is not that of simple freeing from a fault, but of its recognition and expiation in the substitutionary offering.

Thus when λύτρον (-α) is used for כֹּפֶר it always denotes a vicarious gift whose value covers a fault, so that the debt is not just cancelled. Indeed, in the equation כֹּפֶר = λύτρον the offering is always for a human life (ψυχή). This is even true of Prv. 6:35 in the light of the preceding יוֹם נָקָם; we are to read: לֹא יִשָּׂא פָנֶיךָ לְכֹפֶר (G. Beer in BHK³ S 1162). In itself life is forfeit, whether to a man (Ex. 21:30) or to God, and sacrally this amounts to the same thing. The λύτρον — only τὰ λύτρα in the Pentateuch — seems to be money in all the examples given (cf. Prv. 13:8: λύτρον ἀνδρὸς ψυχῆς ὁ ἴδιος πλοῦτος). The creditor may freely choose whether he will accept the כֹּפֶר = λύτρον (Ex. 21:30); he cannot be forced. But there are cases in which he is not allowed to accept. Thus there can be no λύτρα for the murderer (רֹצֵחַ) in sacral law, Nu. 35:31 f. His life is unconditionally forfeit.

It is to be noted that כֹּפֶר is not an absolute equivalent of λύτρον, but only where the ref. is to a substitute for human life. In other cases, where other matters are at

[4] Cf. *Deutsche Theologie,* II (Theologentag, 1929), 130 ff.: *Der Erlösungsgedanke im AT*; G. Dalman, *Jesus-Jeschua* (1922), 109 f.

[5] In Gn. 6:14, however, כָּפַר is related to כֹּפֶר ("pitch").

issue, כֹּפֶר is rendered differently in the LXX, e.g., ἐξίλασμα in 1 Βασ. 12:3 (used for a human life in ψ 48:7), ἄλλαγμα in Is. 43:3, also Am. 5:12 (B ἀντάλλαγμα), περικάθαρμα in Prv. 21:18. But this makes it all the clearer that in Mk. 10:45; Mt. 20:28, where λύτρον is the ransom for a human life, the Heb. equivalent is to be sought in כֹּפֶר. The Aram. *purqânâ* ("ransom money") is not exactly the same as the Heb. כֹּפֶר.

b. גאל. λύτρον is also used for גאל; this is particularly true in respect of the verb → λυτροῦσθαι.

If כֹּפֶר belongs to the sphere of private law, גאל is a term from family law. The גֹּאֵל, rendered ἀγχιστεύς in the legal terminology of the Pentateuch, also in Joshua (20:3, 5, 9) and Ruth (2:20; 3:13; 4:1 ff.), is strictly the responsible closest relative in family affairs. He must redeem for the family lives or goods which have fallen into bondage, so that גאל can be translated "to redeem." In particular the גֹּאֵל is the blood avenger (גֹּאֵל הַדָּם = ἀγχιστεύων, Nu. 35:12, 19, 21, 24 ff.; Dt. 19:6, 12; Jos. 20:3, 5, 9; 2 S. 14:11). As the nearest kinsman the blood avenger "releases" the blood of the victim. In Heb., as in Arab., we are to think primarily of the father, brother, or son acc. to the basic principle: נֶפֶשׁ תַּחַת נָפֶשׁ.[6] But the גֹּאֵל is also responsible for redeeming from slavery (Lv. 25:48) or recovering possessions (Lv. 25:25, 48 ff.). Jeremiah redeems by purchase the field of his cousin Hanameel (Jer. 32:7) acc. to the מִשְׁפַּט הַגְּאֻלָּה. Even though he himself is in prison, he does this in order that the family possessions may be maintained. In Ruth, too, the גֹּאֵל is the nearest relative who is under obligation to buy back the lands of Elimelech, and also in this case to marry the widowed daughter-in-law (2:20; 3:9; 4:3 ff.), though here the גֹּאֵל can transfer his right and duty to the next close relative, Boaz. In P גְּאֻלָּה can be used similarly in the sense of λύτρον on the occasion of the year of jubilee (Lv. 25:24, 26, 51 f., cf. 27:31), when fields go back to their original owners.

Applied to God, the גֹּאֵל thus denotes in family law the dignity of the nearest relative whose duty it is to redeem His elect, whether it be the forefather Jacob (Gn. 48:16) or the people Israel. Understood thus, the term leads us to the very heart of the relation between God and man. This is here a bond of kinship which commits God to the duty of redemption, not, of course, by the law of blood, but by that of election. Dt. Is. in particular applied the term גֹּאֵל to God in order to bring out for Israel the whole comfort of the thought of election (Is. 41:14; 43:14; 44:24; 47:4; 48:17; 49:7, 26; 54:5, 8; 60:16). God is the Holy One of Israel. He will be its Redeemer (41:14; 54:5) as He was its Creator (יוֹצֵר). Hence Israel's redemption is fully assured. For by His very nature the Holy One of Israel is in antithesis to the sinfulness of the people, whom He Himself has sold into bondage. God is most penetratingly presented as גֹּאֵל in Job (19:25). Here גֹּאֵל = ὁ ἐκλύειν μέλλων has the ancient sense of the blood avenger who treads on the dust of the victim (אַחֲרוֹן עַל עָפָר יָקוּם). But it is God Himself who smites Job. Hence, as his blood avenger, He enters the lists against Himself when He enables Job to see Him after death. The slain and risen Job is in the hands of the same God even though this be the *Deus absconditus*. It is thus necessary to examine the Heb. term if we are wholly to understand its Gk. rendering by λυτρούμενος and ῥυόμενος.

c. פִּדְיֹן. If כפר and גאל are specific terms in Heb. law, פִּדְיֹן, from the root *pdj*, belongs to an ancient Semitic circle of concepts.

---

[6] E. Merz, *Die Blutrache bei den Israeliten* (1916), 93 ff.

This is found esp. in the Arab. *fidan, fadan, fida'un, fidjatun* ("ransom money"), also in the Accad. *padû* ("to set free"). The noun פִּדְיֹן (= λύτρα, Ex. 21:30; = λύτρωσις, Ps. 49:8) is rare, but very old, since it occurs in the pre-monarchy book of the covenant. The subsidiary form פִּדְיֹם = plur. λύτρα (Nu. 3:49, 51) is perhaps to be read פְּדוּיִם,[7] and thus to be taken as an abstract like גְּאוּלִים (Is. 63:4). Almost everywhere the Heb. root פדה is rendered λύτρον, λυτροῦν; only at Is. 50:2; Job 5:20; 6:23 do we find ῥύεσθαι, and at Job 33:28 σῴζειν. In Arab. *fidan* is the ransom for a prisoner, usually 100 camels, and thus as high as the price of blood (*dijatun*).[8] This basic meaning is perhaps present in the Heb., though Ex. 21:30 refers to the redemption of a life which has fallen victim to death (פִּדְיֹן נַפְשׁוֹ).

In distinction from גאל, פדה does not refer to the relationships of family law. The פֹּדֶה can be the one responsible (Ex. 21:30), but also another who is not a relative. It does not matter who puts down the פִּדְיֹן so long as it is put down. The emphasis is on the payment. The object of פִּדְיֹן is never inanimate. It is always an animal (Ex. 34:20) or a human life which in sacral law has fallen forfeit to God, e.g., the first-born, who must be redeemed (Ex. 13:13, 15; 34:20; Nu. 18:15), or which in civil law, or by force, has come under alien control. To sacral law belongs the idea of the Levites being a payment for the first-born (Nu. 3:12, 46 ff.) that should be dedicated to God. Here, then, men are the equivalent payment for men, except in so far as silver must be paid to make up for any deficiency in numbers. Even in sacral law the פִּדְיֹן for a human life can consist in another human life, as probably in the redemption of Jonathan (1 S. 14:45). God Himself is the redeemer (פֹּדֶה) in the story of David (2 S. 4:9; 1 K. 1:29), but this idea is found mainly in the Deuteronomic age, since the redemption is not carried through in Hos. 7:13; 13:14. In Dt. God is regularly called the redeemer of Israel from the house of bondage in Egypt (7:8; 13:6; cf. 9:26; 15:15; 21:8; 24:18). The same thought occurs in 7th century prophecy, e.g., Micah (6:4) and Jeremiah (15:21; cf. 31:11), but Jeremiah applies it to his personal life, since God's voice is heard in him as the voice of the Redeemer. There is transferred to him, the man of God, that which God has done for, and ascribed to, His people. As Yahweh's name is uttered over him (15:16) rather than Israel (14:9), and he is thus claimed as Yahweh's possession, God's work of redemption is done in him in a new and deeper way than in the redemption of Israel out of the house of bondage. It is worth noting, however, that פֹּדֶה, unlike גֹּאֵל, never became a nominal term with any special role in law. In family law much depends on the גֹּאֵל as the responsible redeemer. But in the case of פדה, as already mentioned, the emphasis is on the action, not the subject. Thus the thought of grace is contained in פָּדָה

3. λυτροῦσθαι and Derivatives.

a. From λύτρον comes the verb λυτροῦν, "to free for ransom," which is used in the act. in class. Gk., e.g., Plat. Theaet., 165e (cf. also Diod. S., V, 17, 3) (cf. Ex. 21:8: ἀπολυτροῦν = הֶפְדָּה), but in the LXX occurs only in the med. "to redeem" and the pass.[9] Of the three Heb. words for λύτρον, namely, גאל, כפר

[7] Ges.-Buhl, 634.

[8] G. Jacob, *Altarabisches Beduinenleben*² (1897), 137 and 145; O. Procksch, *Über die Blutrache bei den vorislamischen Arabern* (1899), 52 ff.

[9] Cf. Cr.-Kö., 704 f.

and פדה, כפר drops out in respect of λυτροῦσθαι, since the Heb. verb כִּפֶּר "to atone" belongs to the sacral sphere, and there is a clear distinction between "atonement" and "redemption." Atonement is a sacral act in which sacrifice is the means of expiation. Almost always, except in a few secondary instances, it is accomplished by the bloody sacrifice. But the cultic element does not belong originally to the idea of redemption. Hence λυτροῦσθαι is mostly used for גאל (45 times) and פדה (42 times), for both of which ῥύεσθαι occurs only infrequently. On 4 occasions λυτροῦσθαι is used for פרק in the Aram. sense "to loose" (Ps. 7:2; 136:24; Lam. 5:8; Da. 4:24), and once each it is used for פִּלֵּט (Ps. 32:7), פָּצָה (Ps. 144:10), קנה (Ex. 15:16 A), שִׂגֵּב (Ps. 59:1), שֵׁיזִב (Da. 6:28).

In the Pentateuch, where the subst. גֹּאֵל "redeemer" as the גֹּאֵל הַדָּם "avenger of blood" is not rendered λυτρούμενος but ἀρχιστεύων in the LXX (Nu. 35:19, 21, 24; Dt. 19:6, 12; cf. Rt. 2:20; 3:9; 4:3 ff.), גאל = λυτροῦσθαι is used of the ransoming of the lost freedom of the debtor (Lv. 25:48 f.) or of the family property (Lv. 25:25, 29, 30, 33), and the part played by brothers, uncles, and cousins (25:48 f.) plainly reflects the basic meaning in family law. The point is to maintain the family in terms of men and possessions. It is as well to remember this original relation to property which lies behind the term. There is a special, if secondary, use of גאל = λυτροῦσθαι in connection with the law of holiness (Lv. 27), where the ref. is to the redemption of gifts dedicated to the sanctuary (vv. 13 ff.).

In prophecy גָּאַל is almost wholly restricted to Dt. Is. (Is. 41:14; 43:1, 14; 44:22 ff.; 52:3; 62:12; 63:[4,]9 = λυτροῦσθαι, and 44:6; 47:4; 48:17, 20; 49:7, 26; 51:10; 52:9; 54:5, 8; 59:20 = ῥύεσθαι).[10] If קְדוֹשׁ יִשְׂרָאֵל bears the stamp of Is., גֹּאֵל יִשְׂרָאֵל is peculiar to Dt. Is. One must assume that the prophet is depicting God as the responsible relative of Israel, though by adoption. If the Creator of the world, the Maker of Israel, the Holy One of Israel, reveals Himself as the Redeemer, this yields the infallible certainty of Israel's redemption from the Babylonian captivity. As He is the גֹּאֵל יִשְׂרָאֵל, they are the גְּאוּלֵי יהוה (62:12; cf. 35:9). In this connection the thought of ransom (כֹּפֶר = ἄλλαγμα) is used in an extraordinary way. Silver is not the price by which Israel is redeemed (52:3). God as the Lord of the nations frees His people in accordance with His will. He gives Egypt, Cush and Seba as a ransom (כֹּפֶר) for it (43:3). But then the prophet moves on to the even bolder thought that God does not pay any price to Cyrus for Israel's redemption (45:13: οὐ μετὰ λύτρων οὐδὲ μετὰ δώρων). Egypt, Cush and Seba are given to Israel as a voluntary acquisition, for they come to Jerusalem and recognise that the God of Israel dwells there as the Saviour (v. 14).[11] Hence alien peoples become, not the slaves of Cyrus, but the possession of Jerusalem, and as such they are included in God's world-embracing plan of redemption (vv. 18 ff.). In Dt. Is., then, the idea of redemption is split off from that of ransom. Israel's redemption is a free act of God's grace which embraces the Gentiles too.

---

[10] Elsewhere only in Hos. 13:14; Jer. 31:11; 50:34; Mi. 4:10, and Is. 35:9 under the influence of Dt. Is. In Zeph. 3:1 we find גאל=געל "to pollute."

[11] In Is. 45:14 a α there is no address, e.g., לְבַת יְרוּשָׁלַם, after כה אמר יהוה, since a fem. is presupposed. בזקים יעברו is an addition acc. to Duhm, Marti and Buhl.

While a family relation is presupposed in גאל, and this is echoed in the thought of redemption,[12] there is in פדה no necessary relation drawn from family law. פדה is originally a loosing or releasing by money payment. Thus the verb פדה is regularly the original of λυτροῦσθαι when the reference is to the redemption of the first-born (πρωτότοκα) of man and beast (Ex. 13:13, 15; 34:20; Nu. 18:15-17) by a substitutionary offering (cf. 1 S. 14:45). It is used especially of freeing from bondage or imprisonment under an alien power. Dt., where גאל is restricted to the concept of a blood avenger (19:6, 12 גֹּאֵל הַדָּם), uses פדה = λυτροῦσθαι exclusively of the redemption of Israel out of bondage in Egypt. Decisive here is the state from which the people is brought out into freedom, not the means by which it happens. God does not pay a ransom. He acts in His own power (Dt. 7:8; 9:26; 13:6; 15:15; 21:8; 24:18). Whereas in Dt. Is. God as גֹּאֵל accomplishes freedom in voluntary commitment to Israel, in Dt. this takes place in complete freedom. But in both cases there is liberation from bondage, and in neither is there a ransom, since Yahweh, as God of the world (cf. Dt. 4:32 ff.), owns both Israel and the nations. Thus the terms גאל and פדה approximate closely in post-exilic theology, which is very largely controlled by Dt. Is. and Dt. These words are used as synonyms for the redemption of Israel out of bondage, and they are both rendered λυτροῦσθαι (Ex. 6:6; 2 S. 7:23; 1 Ch. 17:21; Neh. 1:10). This is particularly true in the Psalter, where the thought of redemption is a very important theologoumenon (Ps. 25:22; 44:26; 74:2; 77:15; 78:42; 106:10; 107:2; 130:8; 136:24), פדה being used exclusively in the first book and predominantly in the second.[13] It is especially noteworthy that the idea is practically never connected with sin; only in ψ 129:8: λυτρώσεται τὸν Ἰσραὴλ ἐκ πασῶν τῶν ἀνομιῶν αὐτοῦ, do we find this connection. But with the individualising of the life of faith, redemption comes to be referred increasingly not merely to Israel but to the individual believer as well (Ps. 144:10; cf. 2 S. 4:9; 1 K. 1:29 David; Jer. 15:21 Jeremiah). This comes out clearly when there is reference to the redemption of the soul (ψυχή), for this can hardly be construed as the soul of the people (Ps. 34:22; 49:15; 55:18; 71:23). Again, when it is the I who prays for redemption one has to think of the righteous individual (Ps. 26:11; 31:5; 32:7; 59:1; 119:134, 154). The need for redemption grows on the personal side as well as the national. The trouble from which redemption is sought is often called צַר, צָרָה ("affliction"), which is found in early passages such as 2 S. 4:9; 1 K. 1:29. This may be any national or personal distress into which the soul falls. The final emergency is that of death (Hos. 13:14; Ps. 103:4; Sir. 51:2), and the prayer is to be kept from it. But the question of redemption out of death is also raised in Ps. 49:7 ff. No man can pay a ransom for his life (פָּדֹה יִפְדֶּה אִישׁ) or make to God a substitutionary offering (כֹּפֶר = ἐξίλασμα).[14] But the poet knows that it is God who redeems the soul (v. 16: יִפְדֶּה נַפְשִׁי = [ὁ θεὸς] λυτρώσεται τὴν ψυχήν μου [ψ 48:15]) when He snatches it from the power of the underworld. Probably לקח refers to

[12] Cr.-Kö. rightly emphasises this, though wrongly extends it to פדה as well.

[13] Cr.-Kö., 705.

[14] The text of Ps. 49:7 f. is doubtful. Since one expects a contrast to v. 6, אַךְ, attested by 8 MSS, is preferable to the Mas. אָח, so that the brother drops out of the relation between God and man. In v. 8a we should read וְיֵקַר פִּדְיוֹן נַפְשׁוֹ, unless this is a variation of v. 7. Cf. P. Volz, ZAW NF, 14 (1937), 235 ff.

snatching from the state of death through which man must pass. Self-redemption is impossible here, but God's redemption is valid in face of death. Thus Job believes in the גֹּאֵל = ἐκλύων who will awaken to new life the life which has fallen victim to death (19:25). As regards the individual as well as the nation there are few references to redemption from sin. This is connected with the fact that the concept of atonement applies in this sphere. Though it derives from כָּפַר ("cover"), the term for atonement כִּפֵּר = ἱλάσκεσθαι, ἐξιλάσκεσθαι) adopts a sacral element which is almost indispensable in expiation, and this gives it a new content which theologically goes beyond that of redemption (λυτροῦσθαι).

Only in comparatively few passages does the word group λύτρον κτλ. enable us to follow the development of the concept of redemption in the Gk. OT. Sir. uses λυτροῦν not only for פדה (51:2: καὶ ἐλυτρώσω τὸ σῶμά μου ἐξ ἀπωλείας = כי פדית ממות נפשי), but also for ישע (48:20: καὶ ἐλυτρώσατο [God] αὐτοὺς ἐν χειρὶ Ησαιου = ויושיעם ביד ישעיהו; 49:10: καὶ ἐλυτρώσαντο [the twelve minor prophets] αὐτοὺς ἐν πίστει ἐλπίδος = וישעוהו בתקות אמת), and for עזר (51:3: ἐλυτρώσω με κατὰ τὸ πλῆθος ἐλέους καὶ ὀνόματός σου = עזרתני כרוב חסדך; 50:24: καὶ ἐν ταῖς ἡμέραις ἡμῶν λυτρωσάσθω ἡμᾶς = ולזרעו כימי שמים [for זרע the LXX obviously read עזר, and it thus construed the sentence differently]). In all these passages we have the religious view of redemption. The legal idea of buying back from an alien power is missing. Even in 49:10, where He acts through the prophets, God is the One who redeems from the hostile forces that would ruin His people. Thus redemption is an act of salvation and grace which presupposes that all hostile powers are subject to God. λύτρωσις is to be taken in the same sense when it came into Lv. for אשם acc. to the witness of the marginal note of Cod. X on 5:18, 25; 6:10; 7:37; 14:12. In all these verses the LXX has πλημμέλεια or the like. At Lv. 27:24, along with the LXX ἀποδοθήσεται, we have in marg. Cod. 85 λυτρώσεται [15] or λυτρωθήσεται [16] for יָשׁוּב. In Ex. 15:16 B etc. have the literal ἐκτήσω for Heb. קנה, but A has a formula which gives confessional expression to the belief in Israel's redemption out of Egypt by God: ὁ λαός ... ὃν ἐλυτρώσω ... There seems to be a misunderstanding of the Heb. in Zeph. 3:1: ὢ ἡ ἐπιφανὴς καὶ (ἀπο)λελυτρωμένη, ἡ πόλις ἡ περιστερά. [17] The Mas. has גאל II in the sense "to pollute," while the LXX takes it as גאל I "to redeem." On the other hand, the idea of redemption is intentionally imported into Zeph. 3:15. In place of the colourless "take away" (פִּנָּה אֹיְבֵךְ) we find λελύτρωταί σε ἐκ χειρὸς ἐχθρῶν σου. It is doubtful, of course, whether פנה should be taken in the sense of "take away," since elsewhere it always means to restore to an earlier condition. [18] At Is. 29:22 Σ with its ὁ λυτρωσάμενος τὸν Αβρααμ gives a literal rendering of the Mas., while the LXX introduces a different sense. In the martyr piety of Hell. Judaism the thought of redemption acquires again its original relation to expiatory sacrifice, though in a new sense and in new terms. Thus we read in 4 Macc. 6:29: ἀντίψυχον αὐτῶν λαβὲ τὴν ἐμὴν ψυχήν, and in 17:21: ὥσπερ ἀντίψυχον γεγονότας τῆς τοῦ ἔθνους ἁμαρτίας. Acc. to Da. 4:34 the sufferings and humiliations which the king has suffered have counterbalanced his sins: αἱ ἁμαρτίαι μου καὶ αἱ ἄγνοιαί μου ἐπληρώθησαν ἐναντίον τοῦ θεοῦ τοῦ οὐρανοῦ. [19]

---

[15] Acc. to R. Holmes, *Vetus Test. Gr. cum var. Lectionibus* (1798), on Lv. 27:24.
[16] Cf. Field, *ad loc.*
[17] There is frequent confusion of גאל II with I. Thus in 2 Εσδρ. 2:62; 17:64 (= Neh. 7:64) it is rendered ἀγχιστεύειν, and in 23:29 (= Neh. 13:29) ἀγχιστεία. Again, ἐκλαμβάνειν in Job 3:5 is based on I.
[18] Cf. F. Schwally, ZAW, 10 (1890), 205 f.
[19] **This paragraph is by Bertram.**

b. λύτρωσις. From λυτρόω there developed many nouns and adjectives in which the Hebrew roots גאל and פדה recur. The rare λύτρωσις ("loosing") has an act. sense outside the Bible, corresponding to the act. λυτροῦν (→ 331). But in the Bible, both LXX and NT, it is passive ("redemption," "release").

Is. 63:4 : שְׁנַת גְּאוּלַי בָּאָה = ἐνιαυτὸς λυτρώσεως πάρεστιν, with an allusion to the year of jubilee when possessions reverted to their original owners. Lv. 25:29, 48 : גְּאֻלָּה = λύτρωσις, right to redeem a possession which has been sold. In פדה = λύτρωσις we see again the element of releasing by a substitutionary gift, cf. the first-born in Nu. 18:16 and esp. Ps. 49:8 : וְיֵקַר פִּדְיוֹן נַפְשׁוֹ = καὶ τὴν τιμὴν [וִיקָר] τῆς λυτρώσεως τῆς ψυχῆς αὐτοῦ, so that there is no means of redeeming the human soul. In Ps. 111:9; 130:7 פְּדוּת = λύτρωσις is the redemption of the people regardless of the means. ʼA Qoh. 12:6 and Θ Prv. 6:35 (λύτρωσις = כֹּפֶר), and other translators, also use the word. [20]

c. λυτρωτής "Redeemer" (= גֹּאֵל) is twice used of God in the Psalter (Ps. 19:14; 78:35), cf. גֹּאֵל in Dt. Is. λυτρωτής is also found in Lv. 25:25 Samarit. and Αλλ. for גאל LXX ἀγχιστεύων. [21]

The pass. λυτρωτός, "capable of being redeemed," is used in Lv. 25:31, 32 for גְּאֻלָּה, the "right of redemption." In the year of jubilee there is for the houses concerned, in so far as they are λυτρωταί, the right of redemption.

d. ἀπολύτρωσις, "redemption." In non-biblical Gk. this means the gift offered as ransom money (cf. LXX Ex. 21:8) when derived from the act. ἀπολυτροῦν, and "ransom" when derived from the med. ἀπολυτροῦσθαι. The biblical sense of "redemption," which became highly significant in the NT, followed the second meaning in LXX Da. 4:34 : ὁ χρόνος μου τῆς ἀπολυτρώσεως ἦλθε, but this is the only example, and it is set on the lips of Nebuchadnezzar. The Aram. equivalent is missing here ; in the Peshitta *purqânâ* corresponds to ἀπολύτρωσις at Lk. 21:28.

Sometimes the Heb. גאולים would better correspond to the NT ἀπολύτρωσις (Is. 63:4; cf. Lk. 21:28 ; R. 8:21, 23; Eph. 4:30 [ἡμέρα ἀπολυτρώσεως]), but when the ref. is to ransom פְּדוּיִם is better (R. 3:24; Eph. 1:7; Col. 1:14).

Procksch

† λύω → δέω.

This is commonly attested, in various senses, in Gk. lit. from the time of Homer. Of religious importance is the use of λύω (λύσις) in the Gk. hymn to denote the redemption which deity grants to man from πόνοι, μόχθοι, ἄλγη, φόβοι. [1] In the NT the word means a. "to loose," "release," with the obj. of that which binds : τὸν ἱμάντα ("latchet") in Mk. 1:7; Lk. 3:16; Jn. 1:27; σφραγῖδας ("seals") in Rev. 5:2 (→ σφρα-

[20] Lv. 5:18, 25; 6:10; 7:1, 37; 14:12; 25:26, 29.
[21] Cf. Field, *ad loc.* I owe the ref. Lv. 25:25 to Bertram.
λ ύ ω. Pr.-Bauer³, Cr.-Kö., Liddell-Scott, Pape, *s.v.*
[1] Cf. K. Keyssner, *Gottesvorstellung u. Lebensauffassung im griech. Hymnus* (*Würzburger Studien*, 2 [1932], 110 ff.).

γίς), fig. ἐλύθη ὁ δεσμὸς τῆς γλώσσης αὐτοῦ ("the cords of his tongue were unloosed," Mk. 7:35), or with the obj. of what is bound: the foal of the ass, Mk. 11:2, 4 f.; Mt. 21:2; Lk. 19:30 f., 33; τὸν βοῦν, Lk. 13:15; sandals, Ac. 7:33; 13:25; prisoners, 22:30 (24:26); Rev. 9:14 f.; 20:3, 7; one who is wrapped up, Jn. 11:44; fig. λυθῆναι ἀπὸ τοῦ δεσμοῦ τούτου, Lk. 13:16; λέλυσαι ἀπὸ γυναικός, 1 C. 7:27. With a personal obj. it takes on the sense "to free," esp. when used fig. On Mt. 16:19; 18:18 → II, 60 f. b. λύω also means "to dissolve something into its parts," "to destroy," e.g., to break down a wall.[2] Jn. 2:19, the temple; Eph. 2:14, the Law as a wall of partition; Ac. 27:41: ἡ πρύμνα ἐλύετο, the hinder part broke in pieces; 2 Pt. 3:10-12 in the prophecy of the end of the world; to break up an assembly,[3] Ac. 13:43.

The sense "to break up," "to destroy," "to dismiss" is often theologically important. In the struggle for the validity of the OT Law we find the phrases λύσῃ μίαν τῶν ἐντολῶν τούτων τῶν ἐλαχίστων (Mt. 5:19); ἔλυεν τὸ σάββατον (Jn. 5:18); ἵνα μὴ λυθῇ ὁ νόμος Μωϋσέως (7:23); and the weighty οὐ δύναται λυθῆναι ἡ γραφή (10:35). The best rendering here is "to set aside," "to invalidate."[4] In the battle for the validity of Jesus as the Christ we read in 1 Jn. 4:3: ὃ λύει[5] τὸν Ἰησοῦν. λύειν here is to be construed as the opp. of ὁμολογεῖν Ἰησοῦν Χριστὸν ἐν σαρκὶ ἐληλυθότα. It does not mean "to dissolve the unity of the person of Jesus," e.g., by separating the man Jesus from the supraterrestrial λόγος. This question does not arise in 1 Jn. or Jn. Nor to it mean "to reject the true doctrine concerning Jesus." In 1 Jn. we do not have doctrine about Jesus, but confession of Jesus as the Christ, the Son of God, and faith in Him (2:23; 4:15; 5:1, 5). The meaning is to dismiss Jesus as an object of Christian confession, so that He is just one among many figures of the past, and there can be no question of faith in Him.[6] In the conflict against moral laxity 1 Jn. 3:8 says that the Son of God manifested Himself ἵνα λύσῃ τὰ ἔργα τοῦ διαβόλου. According to the exact par. in 3:5: And you know that he was manifested ἵνα τὰς ἁμαρτίας ἄρῃ, destroying the works of the devil is the same as taking away sins, so that they are not committed any more (v. 9).[7] Rev. 1:5 calls Jesus the One who has redeemed, i.e., ransomed (λύσαντι)[8] us from our sins by His blood.[9] In Ac. 2:24,

---

[2] Cf. Hom. Il., 16, 100; Xenoph. An., II, 4, 17 and 19; Herodian Hist., VII, 1, 7; Joseph. Bell., 6, 32; 1 Εσδρ. 1:52.

[3] Hom. Il., 1, 305; Od., 2, 257; Apoll. Rhod. Argonautica, I, 708; Xenoph. Cyrop., VI, 1, 2; Diod. S., XIX, 25, 7; Joseph. Ant., 14, 388.

[4] Isis texts of Nyssa in Diod. S., I, 27: ὅσα ἐγὼ ἐνομοθέτησα, οὐδεὶς αὐτὰ δύναται λῦσαι; Str.-B., I, 241 gives בִּטֵּל as the Heb. equivalent and בַּטֵּל as the Aram.

[5] The usual reading μὴ ὁμολογεῖ is wrong, cf. Zahn Einl., II[3], 585; Bü. Jn., 63.

[6] Cf. Büchsel, *op. cit.*, 64 ff.

[7] Cf. Büchsel, 49-53.

[8] Along with λύσαντι we also find λούσαντι. The idea of washing is more vivid and fits the context of Rev. 7:14, but λύσαντι is better attested, cf. also → 303, n. 27. λύειν ἐκ τῶν ἁμαρτιῶν does not occur elsewhere in the NT, but we find λύειν ἐκ and ἀπό in the sense "to free" at Rev. 20:7; Lk. 13:16. There is no citation from the OT in spite of the printing and the allusions to ψ 129:8 and Is. 40:2 in Nestle. The LXX uses λύειν with ἁμαρτία, but only ἁμαρτία as the obj. of λύειν act. in Job 42:9 and the subj. of the pass. in Sir. 28:2; Is. 40:2 in the sense "to atone" or "to forgive." We do not find expressions like λύειν ἐκ τῆς ἁμαρτίας.

[9] The ἐν τῷ αἵματι αὐτοῦ shows that λύσαντι is here used in the sense of redemption → λύτρον, → ἀπολύτρωσις, → ἐξαγοράζειν. This meaning is not found elsewhere in the NT, but cf. Hom. Il., 1, 13 and 20; Plat. Resp., IX, 574d: αἱ νεωστὶ ἐκ δουλείας λελυμέναι etc. Cf. Pape under λύω 3. One cannot be more precise about Rev. 1:5.

in Peter's sermon at Pentecost, the resurrection of Jesus (in its significance for the sorrowing disciples) is described as follows: λύσας (ὁ θεὸς) τὰς ὠδῖνας τοῦ θανάτου.[10]

There can be little doubt that the LXX took this ὠδῖνες τοῦ θανάτου fig. rather than lit., in the sense, not of the pangs of birth, but of grievous sorrows. The idea of a birth at which death suffers or causes sorrows is quite alien to ψ 17:4, 5; 114(116):3; 2 Βασ. 22:6, even though we have the phrase ὠδῖνες τοῦ θανάτου. This is shown by the verbs περιέσχον, ἐκύκλωσαν. Moreover the LXX, like the OT, often used ὠδῖνες for grievous sufferings (cf. Ex. 15:14; Hos. 13:13; Na. 2:11; Is. 13:8; 21:3 etc.). Thus Ac. 2:24 cannot be understood along the lines of Job 39:3, where λύειν ὠδῖνας means "to end the pangs (by birth)."

† ἀναλύω, † ἀνάλυσις.

This means lit. "to undo again," Hom. Od., 2, 105, and it has a richly developed usage. In the NT its predominant meaning is "to leave" (→ καταλύω).[1] It is used euphemistically for death in kindly concealment of its terror, i.e., "to depart" (Phil. 1:23: ἐπιθυμίαν ἔχων εἰς τὸ ἀναλῦσαι).[2] ἀνάλυσις accordingly means "leaving,"[3] "departing":[4] 2 Tm. 4:6: ὁ καιρὸς τῆς ἀναλύσεώς μου.

The special sense of "to return"[5] occurs at Lk. 12:36: πότε ἀναλύσῃ ἐκ τῶν γάμων, though here, too, ἀναλύσῃ might mean leaving, with the thought of return only in the ensuing ἵνα ἐλθόντος καὶ κρούσαντος.

† ἐπιλύω, † ἐπίλυσις.

ἐπιλύω, lit. "to release"; Ac. 19:39 "to resolve" (a disputed question); Mk. 4:34: κατ' ἰδίαν δὲ τοῖς ἰδίοις μαθηταῖς ἐπέλυεν πάντα, "to explain," "to interpret," which is not attested elsewhere.[1] Hence ἐπίλυσις is "exposition."[2] Thus in 2 Pt. 1:20: πᾶσα προφητεία ... ἰδίας ἐπιλύσεως οὐ γίνεται, "no prophecy should be expounded[3] according to private opinion."[4]

---

[10] On ὠδῖνες τοῦ θανάτου → ὠδῖνες.

ἀναλύω κτλ. [1] P. Tor., I, 2, 16; P. Par., 15, 30; 22, 29; P. Lond., 44, 17 f.

[2] Luc. Philopseudes, 14: ὀκτωκαιδεκαέτης ὢν ἀνέλυε, Epigr. Graec., 340, 7: ἐς θεοὺς ἀνέλυσα, IG, XIV, 1794, 2.

[3] Philo Flacc., 115; Jos. Ant., 19, 239.

[4] Philo Flacc., 187: τὴν ἐκ τοῦ βίου τελευταίαν ἀνάλυσιν.

[5] Wis. 2:1: οὐκ ἐγνώσθη ὁ ἀναλύσας ἐξ ᾅδου, Tob., 2, 9: ἀνέλυσα θάψας καὶ ἐκοιμήθην, 2 Macc. 8:25; 12:7; Polyb., Pap. in APF, 1 (1901), 59 ff. It is not clear how ἀναλύω could come to mean "to return"; perhaps it has something to do with the unyoking of draught animals.

ἐπιλύω κτλ. [1] Sext. Emp. Pyrrh. Hyp., 2, 246; Vett. Val., IV, 11 (p. 173, 6); Athen., 10 (p. 249e); Philo Agric., 16; Gn. 40:8 'A; 41:8, 12 'A; Herm. s., 5, 3, 1 f.; 5, 4, 2 f.; 5, 5, 1; 9, 11, 9.

[2] Sext. Emp. Pyrrh. Hyp., 2, 246; Vett. Val., V, 9 (p. 221, 9); IX, 1 (p. 330, 10); Heliodor., I, 18; Cl. Al. Paed., II, 1, 14, 2; Gn. 40:8 'A.

[3] There can be no question of the sense "destruction" here, cf. Kn. Pt., *ad loc.*

[4] ἰδίας refers to the expositor, not the προφητεία. Cf. Philo Vit. Mos., I, 281: λέγω (Balaam) γὰρ ἴδιον οὐδέν, ἀλλ' ἅττ' ἂν ὑπηχήσῃ τὸ θεῖον, cf. also 286.

† καταλύω, † κατάλυμα.

The meaning of κατά ("downward") is still present in καταλύω, which is a strengthened form of λύω in the sense "to put down." It is used in various connections, but in the NT usually has the same meaning as the simple form.

a. It is used of the destroying of a building, [1] e.g., the temple. Mk. 14:58; 15:29 (Mt. 26:61; 27:40); Ac. 6:14 (καταλύσει τὸν τόπον τοῦτον. ὁ τόπος οὗτος is the temple); or the stones of a building, Mk. 13:2 (Mt. 24:2; Lk. 21:6). When the body is thought of as an οἰκία in 2 C. 5:1 καταλυθῇ can be used of it. As with the metaphorical use of → οἰκοδομεῖν, καταλύειν, too, can be used of the work of God in man, R. 14:20 (cf. v. 19). The same antithesis is found in reverse order in Gl. 2:18 : εἰ γὰρ ἃ κατέλυσα ταῦτα πάλιν οἰκοδομῶ. καταλύειν is also used more freely of the frustration of a plan or work, or of men as its agents, Ac. 5:38, 39 : ὅτι ἐὰν ᾖ ἐξ ἀνθρώπων ἡ βουλὴ αὕτη ἢ τὸ ἔργον τοῦτο, καταλυθήσεται· εἰ δὲ ἐκ θεοῦ ἐστιν, οὐ δυνήσεσθε καταλῦσαι αὐτούς ...

b. "To invalidate," of the Law in Mt. 5:17 → 336. [2]

c. "To unyoke" (lit. of draught animals or beasts of burden), [3] "to rest" on a journey, "to put up," [4] Lk. 9:12 : ἵνα πορευθέντες (the people at the feeding) εἰς τὰς κύκλῳ κώμας καὶ ἀγροὺς καταλύσωσιν [5] καὶ εὕρωσιν ἐπισιτισμόν, 19:7: ὅτι παρὰ ἁμαρτωλῷ ἀνδρὶ (Zacchaeus) εἰσῆλθεν καταλῦσαι. From this sense comes κατάλυμα, the "place of lodging," "inn," [6] Lk. 2:7, also freely of a chamber or dining-room, Mk. 14:14; Lk. 22:11 (though it does not mean dining-room). [7]

† ἀκατάλυτος.

The verbal adj. of καταλύω, "to dissolve," "to cause to cease," with α- privative, hence "indissoluble," "indestructible," "endless." Its literary attestation is late, 4 Macc. 10:11: διὰ τὴν ἀσέβειαν καὶ μιαιφονίαν ἀκαταλύτους καρτερήσεις βασάνους (a Jewish martyr to Antiochus Epiphanes) and Dion. Hal. Ant. Rom., X, 31, 5 : οἰόμενοι μάλιστα τὸ τῆς δημαρχίας ἀκατάλυτον ἔσεσθαι κράτος, ἐὰν τὸ στασιάζον ἐξ αὐτῆς ἀναιρεθῇ. The only instance in the Bible is at Hb. 7:16 : ὃς οὐ κατὰ νόμον ἐντολῆς σαρκίνης γέγονεν ἀλλὰ κατὰ δύναμιν ζωῆς ἀκαταλύτου. In Dion. Hal., in a secular context, the word means historical duration. In 4 Macc. and Hb., in a religious context, it denotes the eternity of the divine.

καταλύω κτλ. [1] 2 Εσδρ. 5:12; Jos. Ant., 9, 161.

[2] Xenoph. Mem., IV, 4, 14; Isoc., 4, 55; Philostr. Vit. Ap., 4, 40; Philo Som., II, 123; 2 Macc. 2:22.

[3] Hom. Od., 4, 28.

[4] Thuc., I, 136; Demosth. Or., 18, 82; Ditt.-Syll.³, 978, 8; Gn. 19:2; 24:23, 25; Sir. 14:25, 27; 36:27; Jos. Vit., 248.

[5] Not "to disperse."

[6] Polyb., 2, 36, 1; Diod. S., XIV, 93, 5; Ditt. Syll.³, 609, 1.

[7] In the other instances given in Pr.-Bauer³, *s.v.* (1 Βασ. 1:18; 9:22; Sir. 14:25) it does not have this sense.

ἀκατάλυτος. Cr.-Kö., *s.v.*; the comm., Rgg. Hb., Wnd. Hb. and O. Michel (1936), *ad loc.*

In effect there is a contrast here between the Law and power, between that which has its basis in the flesh and indestructible life. Herein is expressed the whole superiority of Jesus, a high-priest after the order of Melchisedek, over the Levitical high-priests. That Jesus has this life is proved in v. 17 by a reference to Ps. 110:4: "Thou art a priest for ever after the order of Melchisedek." Scripture is the proof, not the facts of the story of Jesus. In this context the primary reference is to the risen Lord. This may be seen from vv. 25-28: He is made higher than the heavens (v. 26), and is perfected (perf. part. pass.) in eternity (v. 28). Unceasing life belongs particularly to Jesus after His resurrection,[1] though it does not begin then, for in Hb. the historical as well as the risen Jesus is High-priest. If it is by His resurrection, on the basis of His death, that He is fully what He is, He begins to be it already in His historical life.[2] This applies also to the power of indestructible life, which in some sense belongs already to the historical man, Jesus. Wnd. is right when he observes, *ad loc.*, that "it is not explained how this Son can still be 'dead' for a space." Nevertheless, 9:14 offers some explanation when it says that by the eternal Spirit He offered Himself spotless to God.[3] The eternal Spirit of God who is at work in Him is the power of indestructible life in the man Jesus. One has to understand 9:14 in the context of the strong religious concept of the Spirit in primitive Christianity. Spirit is God's presence in man, not the eternal part of man, as on a metaphysical view. Hence He does not have the power of an indestructible life in Himself, e.g., because He has a divine nature.[4] He has it in fellowship with God. God calls Him an eternal High-priest by His Word in Ps. 110:4. In the power of this saying He is thus full of the power of indestructible life even as mortal man.[5] This is not a paradox any more than the possession of the Spirit by believers is a paradox. It is certainly a miracle. His death is not the decease of a man like other men. It is upheld by the power of an indestructible life. This may be seen unmistakeably in the fact that it is the sacrifice of the High-priest who has received the promise of eternity from God's Word. He offers Himself to God as a spotless sacrifice, and the eternal Spirit enables Him to do so. In His death He is above death. He is not under external compulsion. Even as He dies, He does not have to die. If this is true of all martyrs, it is supremely true of Him and only partially true of them. For they fall victim to death by reason of their sinfulness, whereas He is sinless and offers up Himself freely. The secret of the Christology of Hb. is to be found in 7:16.[6]

---

[1] The exaltation of Jesus is His resurrection from the dead, 13:20.

[2] This relation between the historical life and the resurrection gives us the rule that we should begin with what is said about the risen Lord, since this is less equivocal.

[3] Cf. F. Büchsel, "Die Christologie des Hb.," BFTh, 27, 2 (1922), 50 ff. and Michel, 85.

[4] Wnd. Hb. on 9:14 does not get beyond this mistaken view.

[5] It is only as a believer, i.e., in the personal attitude and decision of divine ministry and fellowship, that the Christ of Hb. is the Son of God and Saviour of men, 12:2, cf. 2:13. He is the reflection of God's glory and image of His nature (1:3) only in personal fellowship with God. This is not stated in 1:3, but it can hardly be contested, since in 1:5 He is the Son of God in virtue of the Word of God addressed to Him. If His divine Sonship were a natural or substantial relation to God, it would hardly be possible to refer a saying like Ps. 2:7 to Him.

[6] For this reason the verse must be protected against superficial interpretations which empty it of its true meaning.

† λύτρον.

A. λύτρον and Ideas of Ransom outside the NT.

1. λύτρον is formed from λύω with the ending -τρον. In the oldest stratum nouns formed thus denote a means, ἄρο-τρον, "plough," φέρ-τρον, "bier." In post-Homeric constructs the means usually has the sense of payment for something, θρέπ-τρα, "reward for instruction," μήνυ-τρον, "for information," δίδακ-τρον "for teaching," and similarly λύτρον "money paid as a ransom." [1] The word is not found in Hom., but it occurs in Herodot. and the tragedians, [2] also inscr. and pap. [3] It is commonly used in the plur., since a sum of money is needed for ransom. Related are → ἀντάλλαγμα, ἀντίψυχον, and → ἀντίλυτρον.

λύτρον is esp. the money paid to ransom prisoners of war, [4] but it is then used for slaves, [5] or for release from a bond. [6] The word is infrequently used cultically for the payment made to a deity to which man has incurred indebtedness. [7] It is also found, however, in the sense of "expiation" or "compensation." [8] The usage of the LXX is much the same as secular usage except that there is a more common and specific cultic use, → 329 ff. Philo's usage follows that of the LXX. [9] In Joseph. λύτρον is often used in the sense of ransom for prisoners of war or booty seized in war, Ant., 12, 28. 33. 46; 14, 107. 371; 15, 156; Bell., 1, 274 and 384; Vit., 419. [10] It will be seen that this was a current practice in the time of Joseph.

2. It is common to all antiquity that when a ransom is demanded, paid, or fixed by law, the amount is in some sense a matter of agreement, like all other prices. It may be fixed for all time, like the shekel which Yahweh demanded from all Israelites as a ransom (Ex. 30:12). It may be fixed according to everyday things like the market price of slaves. It can also be a matter of arrangement be-

---

λύτρον. Pape, Liddell-Scott, Pr.-Bauer³, *s.v.* Zn., Schl. on Mt. 20:28; Kl., Hck., J. Schniewind (*NT Deutsch*) on Mk. 10:45; G. Hollmann, *Die Bedeutung d. Todes Jesu* (1901), 101-108. NT theologies by P. Feine⁶ (1934), 115-117 (with notes on earlier works) and H. Weinel⁴ (1928), 158 f.; Schl. Gesch. d. Chr. (1921), 428 ff.; O. Schmitz, *Die Opferanschauung des späteren Judt.* (1910), 199 f.; J. Herrmann, *Die Idee d. Sühne im AT* (1905); B. B. Warfield, "The NT Terminology of Redemption," *Princeton Theological Review,* 15 (1917), 201-249; G. Dalman, *Jesus-Jeschua* (1922), 109-111; G. Kittel, "Jesu Worte über sein Sterben," *Deutsche Theologie,* 3 (1936), 166 ff.

[1] Debr. Griech. Wortb., 177; cf. E. Fränkel, *Gesch. d. gr. Nomina agentis,* I (1910), 203 f.; P. Chantraine, *La formation des noms en Grec Ancien* (1933), 330 ff.

[2] Cf. the dictionaries.

[3] Cf. Pr.-Bauer³ and Preisigke Wört., *s.v.*

[4] For the ransoming of prisoners of war among the Gks. cf. the art. in Pauly-W., XIV, 1 (1928), 72 ff.

[5] P. Oxy., I, 48 and 49; IV, 722. Cf. also L. Mitteis, *Reichsrecht u. Volksrecht* (1891), 388.

[6] Liddell-Scott, *s.v.* under 1.

[7] Steinleitner, 36 f., cf. 59 finds it on two inscr. from Asia Minor (2nd and 3rd cent. A.D., cf. 9). Luc. Dialogi Deorum, 4, 2: ὑπισχνοῦμαί σοι καὶ ἄλλον παρ' αὐτοῦ κριὸν τυθήσεσθαι λύτρα ὑπὲρ ἐμοῦ. Aesch. Choeph., 48: λύτρον αἵματος.

[8] Liddell-Scott, *s.v.* λύτρον plays no part in Gk. philosophical usage. Philo in Sacr. AC, 121 says: πᾶς σοφὸς λύτρον ἐστὶ τοῦ φαύλου, and v. Arnim, III, p. 162, 4 f. claims that this is Stoic. It certainly corresponds to statements in which the Stoics extol the sage, but it may be that Philo is simply imitating such statements. Epict. does not use λύτρον.

[9] Cf. Leisegang. On the Stoic or stoicising formula that every wise man is a ransom for the bad → n. 8. In λύτρα καὶ σῶστρα, a phrase often used by Philo, σῶστρον is not the sacrifice of salvation or thanksgiving, but the means of deliverance.

[10] Cf. Schl. Mt., 602.

tween the parties, and the price will often be inflated by the one who holds to ransom.[11] Legislation in fixing the price is usually inclined, out of a sense of equity, to protect or even to represent the claims of the purchaser, and so far as possible to restrict the arbitrary attempts of the owner to raise the price, e.g., Lv. 25:24, 26, 51, 52. But assessment of a ransom cannot be objective. For the equation between the money and the object of ransom is not intrinsic. It is a matter for the one who fixes or acknowledges the price, whether this be the legislator or the parties in the transaction. The ransom must be in due legal form in order to make sure that the person ransomed is really freed. But the legality does not depend on whether the price is equivalent to the object of ransom. In many cases there is no means of calculating this. Whether or not there is a ransom depends basically on seigniorial law, whether it be that of the legislator or that of the one who must accept the ransom.

Where ransom takes place in the cultus, its assessment is more positive, since it is fixed by the deity, or the tradition of the sanctuary. What is for the deity equivalent to forfeited human life is not invariable, but changes according to the circumstances of forfeiture. Acceptance of a ransom shows, however, that the deity is gracious, not implacable. Yet for this reason, as with men, so with gods, there may be cases in which a payment is no longer accepted.[12] The ransom is one of the points where law and grace meet.[13]

3. The Jewish view is the same as the general view of antiquity. "Ransom money (*purkan*) ... is ... an equivalent for forfeited life. In Rabb. law the ref. is to death decreed by God, from which there is release by ransom ... It is significant that the acceptance and amount of the ransom are dependent on the good will of the one to whom it is offered. The ransom does not belong to the sphere of strict law with its fixed sanctions, and it cannot be applied in the case of murder (Nu. 35:31 f.). It arises only when the law is not applied in its stringency."[14] Since the Rabb. accept the principle that a ransom is an expiation,[15] it is easy for them, though not obligatory, to make the transition from the idea of ransom to that of expiation (→ III, 312 ff.; I, 254 ff.). For the Jew, then, the ref. to a ransom can easily carry with it the thought of expiation by the vicarious sufferings of the righteous, so that finally the ransom idea can become a form of the belief in the atoning power of righteous suffering.

B. The λύτρον-Saying in the New Testament.

1. λύτρον occurs in the NT only at Mk. 10:45 and Mt. 20:28 in the saying in which Jesus explains the meaning of His death. In Lk. 22:24-27 there is a par. to what is said about ministry, which in Mk. 10:42-45 and Mt. 20:25-28 precedes the saying about the ransom, but there is no par. to the ransom saying itself. The Lucan form is obviously late in style, later than the form in Mk. and Mt. (cf. νεώτερος and ἡγούμενος

---

[11] Cf. the art. mentioned in → n. 4.

[12] Nu. 35:31, 32, cf. also Ps. 49:7; Mk. 8:37 and par.

[13] With the end of slavery the practice of ransoming gradually disappeared, and to demand it is now usually an offence. Nevertheless, fines are in some respects similar, since they free man from guilt (in place of imprisonment etc.). But there is the basic difference that the ransom is primarily based on loss of freedom, not guilt. If the victor in war or the master of a slave believes the prisoner or slave is guilty in relation to him, he does not accept a ransom but gives free rein to his anger.

[14] Dalman, 110.

[15] bBQ, 40a, 41b, bMak., 2b; cf. also Str.-B., III, 644.

in v. 26, and διακονῶν in v. 27). That Lk. reported the saying about ministry in its original form can thus be ruled out. Hence one cannot prove from Lk. 22:24-27 that the ransom saying was a later addition to an original saying which dealt only with ministry.[16] If Lk. had had it too this would be a support for authenticity, but this support is not indispensable.[17]

Since the saying about the ransom which the Son of Man in His self-offering will give on behalf of many derives from Mk., and since the only difference between Mk. and Mt. — Mt. uses ὥσπερ and Mk. καὶ γάρ to connect with what precedes — is of no significance, the exegetical task is simple. We have simply to establish the meaning in the context of Mark's Gospel or the Markan depiction of Jesus. Only then do other questions arise.

2. In Mk. 10:45 Jesus is the Son of Man. The significance of this title is Messianic.[18] Mk.10:45 is thus expounding the Messianic work of Jesus. Its meaning is service, i.e., service in the full sense as opposed not merely to rule but also to the conduct of worldly rulers described in v. 42. The service in which the royal will of Jesus is manifested is fulfilled in His giving of Himself. ψυχή is the life, not as a state of the self, but as the self itself. Hence δοῦναι τὴν ψυχὴν αὐτοῦ is to be taken as the equivalent of δοῦναι ἑαυτόν.[19] δοῦναι τὴν ψυχήν is the same as τίθημι τὴν ψυχήν in Jn. 10:11, 15, 17; in this context it can apply only to the death of Jesus,[20] and it expresses the element of voluntariness or self-sacrifice in the death of Jesus as Mk. describes it, i.e., as an act of willing obedience to God, not as a mere succumbing to the hostility of the Pharisees and the Sanhedrin. ἀντί means "for" in the sense of "in place of" rather than "to the advantage of" (→ I, 372 [ἀντί]). πολλοί can denote an indefinite multitude; οἱ πολλοί, following Semitic usage, can mean the totality in question, so that it is equivalent to πάντες. The closest parallel is in Mk. 14:24; Mt. 26:28: "This is my blood of the covenant which is shed for many." Since πολλοί has no art. here, the first meaning is more likely than the second, though an emphasis on the universal significance of the death of Jesus fits the context in both passages.[21] The position

---

[16] It certainly cannot be said that the ransom saying is Pauline in character or origin, since Paul does not use the word λύτρον, and it is open to grave doubt whether the ἀντίλυτρον of 1 Tm. 2:6 is Pauline. Bultmann (Trad., 154, *Jesus* [1926], 196) believes that the saying in Lk. is older, and that the form in Mk. and Mt. derives from the Hell.-Christ. doctrine of redemption. He fails to note 1. that Lk. 22:24-27 is the form which gives evidence of Hell.-Christ. influence, and 2. that the material link with 1 C. 15:3 ("he died for our sins acc. to the Scriptures") shows Mk. to be older in content. For 1 C. 15:3 ff. belongs in content (cf. the witnesses of the resurrection in vv. 5-7), and probably also in expression (Aram.), to the primitive community.

[17] It is hard to say whether the text of Mk. used by Lk. contained the ransom saying or not. Perhaps Lk. intentionally left out the story of the sons of Zebedee, which the ransom saying concludes, because it censures the sons of Zebedee (cf. 9:22 f., where he omits the censure of Pt. found in Mk. 8:33 and Mt. 16:23). If the omission involves the loss of a saying of Jesus about His death, he could not have thought this more significant than the omission of the similar important insight in Mk. 8:33 ("thou dost not think what is of God, but what is of man"). In view of this par. one certainly cannot argue that Mk. 10:35-45 was not in the original Mk.

[18] Cf. F. Büchsel, *Theol. des NT*[2] (1937), 52 f.

[19] Cf. Bl.-Debr.[6] § 283, 4, and the bibl. there.

[20] Cf. v. 39. Attempts, like that of F. Spitta, *Streitfragen der Gesch. Jesu* (1907), 219 ff.; "Die Hirtengleichnisse des 4. Ev. I," ZNW, 10 (1909), 73 ff., to explain the saying apart from the death of Jesus, are rightly ignored.

[21] Zn. Mt., 616, n. 94 on 20:28 points to R. 5:12-19 in favour of πολλοί = πάντες; there is a detailed exposition in J. Jeremias, *Die Abendmahlsworte Jesu* (1935), 69 and 84.

shows that ἀντὶ πολλῶν depends on the noun λύτρον, not the verb δοῦναι, → I, 373 (ἀντί). It must surely strike all readers that there is no mention of any recipient of the ransom. Nor are we told from what the many are set free. For Jesus the true misery of man is his separation from God, his subjection to death, his sin. Hence the liberation is obviously liberation from sin. It cannot be merely liberation from death, since this never has in itself the same significance for Jesus. That many are freed from sin, so that they are truly and definitively set free, is the result of the death of Jesus. It has this result because it is a Messianic act.

3. The ransom saying undoubtedly implies substitution. For, even if the ἀντί be translated "to the advantage of," the death of Jesus means that there happens to Him what would have had to happen to the many. Hence He takes their place. The saying plainly looks back to Mk. 8:37; Mt. 16:26 (→ ἀντάλλαγμα). What no man can do, He, the unique Son of God, achieves. Attempts have often been made to expound this concept of substitution in terms of the OT idea of ransom, or sacrifice, or the Servant of God who dies vicariously for many (Is. 53:6, 12), but methodologically these attempts are open to the objection that it is not possible to refer Mk. 10:45 with the necessary certainty to anything specific in the OT.[22] The method breaks down at the decisive point. "How far the many have lost this life (with God), and how Jesus represents them with the offering up of His life, cannot be deduced from any theory of sacrifice, but only from the reality of the life, death and resurrection of Jesus."[23] By intention, the saying of Jesus is only allusive. It gives an insight into the mystery of God which is to be humbly venerated and yet also protected against over-subtle curiosity; hence its figurative form. It is to be understood in terms of the history narrated in the Gospels. It is not a fragment of a dogmatic doctrine of the atonement in relation to which the presuppositions and conclusions implied within it can or should be reconstructed. It is part of the history of the death of Jesus, and it manifests to us the will which gave rise to this history and which determined its form, the transcendently lofty and sacred will of God which is clasped by the will of Jesus. Only those who see it from this standpoint can fully understand it. The ransom saying and the death of Jesus plainly correspond to one another in Mk. and Mt. In these Gospels Jesus experiences death, not as one who is at least inwardly sustained by God's miraculous protection, but as one who is abandoned by God to the derision of His enemies, so that out of the darkness which engulfs Him He can only cry to God: "My God, my God, why hast thou forsaken me?" Inconceivable though it may appear, He experiences death as one of the many who have fallen victim to corruption. He has taken their place. He, the beloved Son of God, is the divinely smitten shepherd of the flock, Zech. 13:7; Mk. 14:27; Mt. 26:31. God has laid on Him the necessity of dying. Because He thinks what is of God, He must die, Mk. 8:31, 33; Mt. 16:23. In spite of His humble request, the Father does not let the cup pass from Him, Mk. 14:36; Mt. 26:39. His blood is shed on behalf of

---

[22] It cannot be denied that there is a similarity between the ransom saying and Is. 53. It may also be conceded that Is. 53 played an important role in its formation. But there is no express or even clear allusion to Is. 53; hence it is methodologically incorrect to make Is. 53 the starting-point of exposition. This is overlooked in P. Feine, 115 ff. Feine gives us a penetrating examination, and his main point is of value, but he has not proved that it is methodologically correct to start from Is. 53.

[23] J. Schniewind, *NT Deutsch*, I, 137.

many, for the new covenant of God with men is established with His blood, Mk. 14:24; Mt. 26:28. All this is finally based on the fact that His life is a ransom for men, that He offers Himself as a substitute.

4. What has been said leaves us in no doubt but that God is the recipient of the ransom. Jesus serves God when He dies, and God inexorably demands suffering from His Son. God smites Him. All possibility that Satan might receive the ransom is thus ruled out. Satan does not figure at all in the passion story in Mk. and Mt. Satan desires the death of Jesus so little that He tries to divert Him from this path, Mk. 8:33; Mt. 16:23. It is by no means commensurate with Jesus' powerful concept of God that the many should have to be rescued from bondage to Satan. This concept demands that they be liberated from indebtedness to God. If Jesus does not mention God's name here, this is not merely in accordance with the Jewish practice, which Jesus follows elsewhere, of using paraphrases for this name (Mk. 14:62; Mt. 26:64), but it is also in keeping with hesitance to mention the name of the judge into whose hands man has fallen; cf. Mt. 10:28, where there is dispute whether God or the devil is meant, and yet the reference can only be to God. If we do not understand the deep and self-abasing respect with which the ransom saying tacitly alludes to God, we do not understand the saying at all. The God of this saying is the God of Ps. 90 who reduces man to the dust, whose wrath is shown by our death to be the reality of our being, and with whom and of whom one can speak only as out of the depths, Ps. 130.

5. If we approach the ransom saying in a probing spirit, the question arises why God demands the death of Jesus for the freedom of the many. Could He not free them without this ransom? In the reported words of Jesus, however, this question is neither raised nor answered. The saying nowhere unveils the ultimate reasons for God's treating His Son like this. It simply shows that the Son is ready to bow to God's will, to respect this will, to offer up Himself, even though we are not shown what are the reasons for the divine will, cf. Mt. 11:25, 26; Mk. 13:32; 14:35, 36; 15:34. This complete subjection to God's will is an integral part of the service which Jesus renders to God. For Jesus, God does not owe anyone, not even the Son, a manifestation of His reasons, let alone a justification of His acts and demands. What God wills and does, He does for reasons which are holy, just and wise. But this does not mean that He will disclose the reasons. There is a purpose behind God's will; it is not caprice. But man can know this purpose only if and in so far as God reveals it to him. What is here revealed to man is that the death of Jesus is service to God, and that it is a vicarious death for many in virtue of which they find freedom from sin. More than this is not revealed.

6. But the question raised above then changes into the further question why Jesus, who had long since forgiven sins (Mk. 2:5), should now see in His death the condition of the remission of the sins of the many. This question can be answered only on the basis of a profound consideration of the nature of the forgiveness which Jesus conferred. Mk. undoubtedly implies that Jesus is the first who as man grants to men a freedom from guilt which is true and valid in the eternal judgment of God. According to Mk. such remission can be given only in the name of Jesus. He is the first and only man among men with whom there is full and eternally valid forgiveness. He does not grant a mere soothing of the sense of guilt or a mere hope of the release which God will later confer. Nor does He impart a forgiveness which moralistically understands itself in terms of itself. On the contrary, He forgives as one who accepts the holy judgment of

God on every sin, even on that which might appear to be the most trivial. He forgives as one for whom the eternal condemnation of sinners is an indisputable reality, Mk. 9:42-48. He forgives as one who knows that a divine miracle is needed if man is to be saved, since this is impossible with man, Mk. 10:27. His forgiveness is God's miracle towards man in present reality. It is thus so bold that it provokes the charge of blasphemy, Mk. 2:7-12. For this reason, there arises in consequence of His forgiveness the danger of a flabby or even an insolent confidence which regards guilt as empty and obedience toward God as outdated, one of the most dreadful forms of all sin, and at the same time the climax of the dishonouring of God by sin.[24] Only the death of Jesus, only death in the service of God, offers cogent proof and a convincing revelation of the fact that in spite of, or along with, His forgiveness, He also presents the divine will and requirement in all its holy seriousness and without the slightest subtraction from its validity. Up to His death there might still be doubt whether for Him, as for others, there was a limit to obedience toward God. Would the disobedience of weakness or self-glory set in on the far side of this limit? In other words, would His forgiveness be at odds with holiness? Jesus could, of course, pronounce the word of forgiveness and impart true forgiveness before His death. But what His forgiveness meant, its range and force, could be revealed only when He died and was raised again for the sake of it. Only those who have not yet realised how truly monstrous it was that Jesus as man should forgive sins in the full sense of the word, eternally, as God forgives, can fail to see that His death was needed to safeguard this forgiveness against the dangers inherent in such an act. To impart true remission of sins to true sinners, i.e., to men who are chained by their sin in disobedience to God, to declare that now these men are eternally free from their guilt, is something which He alone could do who lifted up these sinners out of the world of their disobedience to God, out of the sphere of wanton self-glory, into the field of His own perfect obedience to God which does not flinch from any self-sacrifice, and who did this by creating in the world a place where the full holiness of God would be manifested by the offering up of His own life to God. To give His life a ransom for many was the ineluctable inner condition of His forgiveness. On this basis His forgiveness could bring with it a renewal of life to self-sacrificial obedience.[25] It could thus be prevented from sinking to the level of what man's offer of God's forgiveness so easily becomes, namely, a lulling of the sense of guilt which is already weak enough in itself. To object that this is the mission of the Word of Jesus is to forget that words without deeds are the worst form of religious weakness, if not hypocrisy. They are the worst form of the very sin from which Jesus had to redeem men, and only by His death did

---

[24] This is in fact a sin which is so widespread in Christianity that one cannot possibly doubt that it is real and not just imaginary, cf. R. 6:1.

[25] In this light it is clear how the forgiveness of Jesus differs from that which He had before Him in the old covenant. The temple sacrifices ordained by the Law did not bring about the renewal of the life for sacrificial obedience to God. As Hb. 9:14 puts it, they could not purge the conscience from dead works to serve the living God. The free prayer to God depicted in the Ps. certainly sought a pure heart and an established spirit (Ps. 51:10), but attainment of these could not be guaranteed, nor did the prophecy of inner renewal in Jer. 31:33; Ez. 36:26 give any assurance of the same. If there had already been this renewal by forgiveness, Jesus would not have been rejected as a blasphemer on the ground of His forgiveness. Forgiveness prior to Jesus is provisional. It is an exercise of patience with a view to Him who is to come (R. 3:25 f.). It is simply a tacit intimation of the one full forgiveness in the crucifixion and resurrection of the Son of God.

redeem them. That His words were acts could be established and revealed only as He Himself demonstrated the obedience which they demanded by His own acts, even to the offering up of His life. Obviously His death would have had no power to overcome sin if it had not been accompanied by His words. But the reverse is also true. His words had to be accompanied by His death to guarantee their power to overcome sin. [26]

If we recognise that the willing suffering of death by Jesus was the inner condition of His right to impart forgiveness of sins, we have already answered the question why God demanded this ransom. We also understand why Jesus did not specify this reason for the demand. The disciples were to discover this power of His death in themselves. There was no point in speaking of it more explicitly before His death was a reality and could exercise in them its power to overcome sin and to renew to perfect obedience. Jesus counted on it that God would complete His work in the disciples and bring home to them the deepest meaning of His death. [27] It has been shown already (→ 341) that the estimation of the death of Jesus as a ransom does not have to imply that the death and what the many owe to God are objectively equivalent. If they are equivalent for God, it is because the self-offering of Jesus is a demonstration of His obedience, and as such it overcomes sin as a power in men. [28]

7. Yet the previous question returns at this point in a new form. Did Jesus not know a forgiveness of God which was imparted also to those who did not stand under the operation of His Messianic work or within the circle of His ransom?

---

[26] Bultmannn in his discussion of Jesus' forgiveness (*Jesus* [1926], 179-200) has laid his whole emphasis on the fact that God's forgiveness becomes an event, and he believes that it does so only by the Word, alongside which we cannot place either the saving facts (the death and resurrection of Jesus, 195) or guarantees like His miracles or personal qualities, 197. Now we can agree that forgiveness becomes an event, but everything depends on how it does so, i.e., on both the safeguarding and the demonstration of the holiness of forgiveness. For the Jews around Jesus forgiveness was undoubtedly an event. The annual day of atonement had this significance for the people at large, and John with his baptism and preaching had it for individuals. The special feature of Jesus' forgiveness lies in the way in which it takes place, not in the fact that it does so. It does not rest on the cultus, or on a publicly acknowledged office, but on Jesus Himself, on His fellowship with God, on His obedience to God, i.e., on His personal qualities. (It is worth noting that when Bultmann develops more fully the concept of personal qualities, he does not speak of fellowship with God or obedience to Him, 198.) These personal qualities of Jesus are no less than the basis of His forgiveness. But this means that the death of Jesus, which is the crown of His obedience, has the value and meaning of a saving fact. (So, too, does the resurrection, without which the death would be defeat.) Bultmann rightly emphasises that we are to estimate Christ's person in terms of His divine mission as "the bearer of the Word" (198). But to be sent by God and to be the bearer of His Word is the basis of the qualities mentioned and would be impossible without them. For the Word does not stand alongside His person and qualities; it is in them.

[27] What is said in Jn. 14:26; 16:12-15 is indispensable for anyone who would ascribe to the historical and mortal man the revelatory significance which He claims for Himself.

[28] If it is not strictly maintained that Jesus' forgiveness in general, and His dying for the right to forgive in particular, have the significance of overcoming sin in man and introducing a complete renewal of man, we remain on the surface. It is very dangerous to say that Jesus' forgiveness removes guilt without also destroying the power of sin. If so, it sinks back to the OT level. The danger that this might happen is by no means negligible. If Christ is found on every page of the OT, there is a very real peril not only that the OT will be unhistorically overestimated but also that the significance of Jesus will be unhistorically depreciated.

There can be no doubt that each day Jesus saw His Father exercise His grace towards enemies, Mt. 5:45.[29] There can be no doubt that He expected to find many Gentiles in the kingdom of heaven, Mt. 8:11; Lk. 13:28. But the God who shows grace each day to His enemies was for Him also the God who condemns man to hell, Mt. 5:29; 10:28, and according to Jesus the grace which God granted each day never saved anyone from hell. The Gentiles who come into the kingdom come only through the personal grace of Jesus Himself, Mt. 25:31-40. For Him there was absolutely no other eternally valid forgiveness than that which He Himself dispensed. For with the utmost seriousness He maintained that He was the Christ, the divinely appointed Judge of all men, so that there could be no deliverance from perdition apart from Him and His Messianic work.[30] Men who came into the kingdom behind His back He did not know. If in Lk. 15:11-32 He describes God as the father who with infinite kindness pardons, the point of the story is undoubtedly to justify the grace which Jesus Himself shows to sinners, Lk. 15:1-2.[31] This story establishes the right of Jesus to grant to sinners fellowship with Himself and therewith a share in the kingdom of heaven. It does not teach timelessly (and unhistorically) valid truths concerning the relation of man to God, or the right of man to ignore his guilt in cheerful confidence that it is without significance before God. When in Mt. 18:23-35 Jesus describes God as a king who in pity forgives an enormous debt, the point of the story is to remind Peter and all the disciples of the greatness of the forgiveness which has been granted them through Jesus, so that they will be merciful to their brethren (vv. 21-22). The parable also says that God executes strict justice, and that this threatens the disciples of Jesus, and the appended saying of Jesus in v. 35 brings this out with full clarity. Jesus never prevented any man from hoping for God's forgiveness or from seeking it, so long as he would seriously turn and do God's will. He knew that there would be joy in heaven over a single sinner repenting, Lk. 15:7, 10. No one should despise the publican who asks for pardon. Nevertheless, if he returns to his house justified, it is not the publican himself, nor the Pharisee, who says it, but only Jesus. In the story of Jesus the publican is not sure of the forgiveness shown him,[32] and the Pharisee regards him as a child of hell, Lk. 18:9-14. If the publicans and harlots really go into the kingdom of heaven, Jesus can say this in Mt. 21:31 f. only because He is the Judge of the world, and He knows who may hope for pardon at the last judgment, because He Himself will pronounce it. All who enter into the kingdom of heaven, including those who have not known Him (Mt. 25:37-39), will do so only in virtue of His forgiveness. But His right to forgive, as we have seen, rests finally on the divine service which He renders in His death. Without this it would not be possible. Hence this service rendered in His death is in fact the ransom for many. Since full remission cannot be separated from the person of Jesus, it cannot be separated from His death.

---

[29] Since v. 45 underlies the requirement of love in v. 44, God's benevolence to His enemies is to be understood as a demonstration of personal love and not merely as a material gift more or less impersonally dispensed. It also includes pardon.

[30] Cf. the quotation from M. Kähler in → III, 936, n. 63.

[31] To ignore this and similar sayings on the ground that they are editorial additions to the original parables of Jesus is childish. For the parables are undoubtedly uttered in a concrete situation. If He had not imparted forgiveness, He did not need to speak of it thus, nor could He have done so. It was from His forgiveness and the related problems for His disciples and enemies that there arose the situation in which alone the stories could be meaningful.

[32] He is simply praying, not giving thanks.

8. To find the answer to the question raised under 5. in speculations concerning God's nature, the relation of His grace and righteousness, the meaning of His honour and its re-establishment etc. (cf. Anselm), does not correspond to the service which Jesus renders to God or to the fellowship which He has with Him. For Him God is to be known only by His revelation. The speculations of Scholasticism and later Protestantism may be vast and profound, but they do not provide an adequate basis for understanding the saying of Jesus. Nor is such a basis to be found in rational discussion of man's need of salvation and the satisfaction of this need in the death of Jesus — a discussion which sets the anthropocentric theology of the Enlightenment in place of the above speculations. Jesus' saying about His death is to be interpreted neither in terms of an example of punishment which serves as a deterrent,[33] nor in terms of man's need of a demonstration of the infinite love of God.[34] Neither approach leads us to the decisive point in the saying, for in neither is the true theme of the doctrine of the atonement either God as He is or man as he is, with the result that the relation between God and man does not take on the decisive significance which properly belongs to it. Jesus, on the other hand, lives in the strength of God's action towards man. He serves this action. He thinks in terms of the relationship of fellowship between God and man. For Him this relationship between God and man is created by God, and it is grounded in the living unity of God's judgment and blessing.[35] Both are equally holy for Him, and man stands equally in need of both. For Him the living unity of the two is to be found in God. He did not think it His task to reconstruct them in terms of human thought. His task was so to reveal the living unity of the two to men that real fellowship would be established between God and man. He made His own life, Himself, the revelation of the living unity of God's grace and judgment by making it the basis of His teaching, of His action towards men, of His suffering at their hands, and finally of His dying for this cause. One thing He achieved thereby. In His community there can be no faith in God's pardoning grace which does not take seriously the holy demand of the divine will and the holy justice of the divine punishment, which does not unceasingly accept commitment to obedience, even to the final extreme of self-sacrifice. To accept the forgiveness of Jesus is to accept the gift of Him who in willing obedience made of His whole existence, of His life and death, an offering to God, so that those who accept this forgiveness are not left at rest until they render the same obedience to God. This completed sacrifice of the life and death of Jesus was necessary for us if we were to have fellowship with God. The depth of our fall into sin and our dishonouring of God made it necessary. The saying of Jesus brings this out when it calls His life a ransom for many. Those who know the gravity of sin (Anselm) know that man cannot create for himself a faith which is sure of forgiveness and which overcomes evil. They can only receive this from what Jesus has done to and for humanity. They also know that finally everything depends on whether we are brought by the divine forgiveness, imparted by Jesus, to the invincible obedience of genuine love for God and man. When we are, we confess that Jesus is right and we appropriate His

---

[33] Cf. H. Grotius.

[34] Cf. Abelard, A. Ritschl.

[35] Marcionitism, which differentiates the God of grace from the God of justice, is not a renewal of the Gospel when measured by the word and work of Jesus. It is paganism, the self-made religion of those who do not know God.

death as our ransom. For this reason the understanding of Jesus' death as a ransom for us is a basic element in the Church's confession which it cannot surrender. This confession is possible only as a personal confession of Him who was crucified for us. But this confession is also a duty for all who believe.

† ἀντίλυτρον.

This is a rare word and its attestation is late. It does not occur in the LXX. [1] The two instances, [2] Orph. Lithica, 593 (p. 129, Abel) and P. Lond., 1343, 31 (8th cent. A.D.), are both later than the NT. But the verb ἀντιλυτρόω is found already in Aristot. Eth. Nic., IX, 2, p. 1164b, 35. Materially ἀντίλυτρον is the same as λύτρον. The compound is an example of the liking of Hell. Gk. for compounds.

In the NT ἀντίλυτρον occurs only at 1 Tm. 2:6: Χριστὸς Ἰησοῦς ὁ δοὺς ἑαυτὸν ἀντίλυτρον ὑπὲρ πάντων. The statement is plainly based on Mk. 10:45 (Mt. 20:28): δοῦναι τὴν ψυχὴν αὐτοῦ λύτρον ἀντὶ πολλῶν. [3] The deviations are typical of the Past. Instead of the Semitic τὴν ψυχὴν αὐτοῦ we have the good Gk. ἑαυτόν; [4] instead of the indefinite πολλῶν the expressly universal (cf. 2:4) πάντων; instead of the simple form the elegant compound. The same thought recurs in Tt. 2:14: Χριστοῦ Ἰησοῦ, ὃς ἔδωκεν ἑαυτὸν ὑπὲρ ἡμῶν, ἵνα λυτρώσηται ἡμᾶς ἀπὸ πάσης ἀνομίας. With its forceful content and breadth of meaning in a didactic context it is typical of the Past.

† λυτρόω. [1]

"To free by ransom." The act. denotes the action of one who has to free prisoners of war etc., hence "to let free for a ransom." [2] But it can also be used of the one who gives the ransom, hence "to buy back by a ransom." [3] The med. means "to purchase for a ransom," [4] the pass. "bought by ransom," or "set free." [5] The usage of Philo is the same as that of the LXX. He can use λυτροῦσθαι like ἐλευθεροῦν, Sacr. AC, 114 (quoting Ex. 13:13).

ἀντίλυτρον. Pr.-Bauer³, *s.v.*; comm. on 1 Tm. 2:6.

[1] Field, II, 170 has on ψ 48:8 וְיֵקַר פִּדְיוֹן... LXX: καὶ τὴν τιμὴν τῆς λυτρώσεως. ["Αλλος· καὶ ἀντίλυτρον], with the note *lectio suspecta*. Cod. 281 *ad vocem* ἐξίλασμα v. 8 *in margine affert* ἀντίλυτρον. It is thus open to doubt whether the Hexapla has ἀντίλυτρον.

[2] Pr.-Bauer³, *s.v.*

[3] Moult.-Mill., 171 suggests an actual quotation of Mk. 10:45, but this is going too far.

[4] → λύτρον 342.

λυτρόω. Liddell-Scott, Pr.-Bauer³, Cr.-Kö., *s.v.*; Zn.R., 179-185; Rgg. Hb., 262 f.

[1] On the linguistic formation cf. Debr. Gr. Wortb. § 198-207; E. Fränkel, *Gr. Denominativa* (1906), 75.

[2] Plat. Theaet., 165e: ἐλύτρου χρημάτων ὅσων σοί τε κἀκείνῳ ἐδόκει, Diod. S., XIX, 73, 10: τῶν στρατιωτῶν οὓς μὲν ἐλύτρωσεν.

[3] P. Oxy., III, 530, 14 (2nd cent. A.D.): λυτρώσασά μου τὰ ἱμάτια (redeeming my [pledged] clothes). The common view (cf. Zn. R., 179) that λυτρόω in the act. means only "to release," not "to buy back," is now exploded by the pap., cf. Liddell-Scott, *s.v.*

[4] Polyb., 18, 16, 1: τὴν ἱερὰν χώραν ... ἐλυτρώσατο χρημάτων αὐτοῖς οὐκ ὀλίγων, IG, XII (5), 36, 12. Diod. S., V, 17, 3: ἀντὶ μιᾶς γυναικὸς τρεῖς ... ἄνδρας διδόντες λυτροῦνται.

[5] Demosth. Or., 19, 170: λελυτρῶσθαι ἐκ τῶν ἰδίων. Aristot. Eth. Nic., IX, 2, p. 1164b, 34; P. Eleph., 19, 8.

In later Jewish Rabb. usage גָּאַל and פָּדָה correspond to λυτρόω. Both are used indifferently for "to redeem." Redemption in later Jewish usage is always the redemption of Israel from the dominion of Gentile peoples, often the exodus from Egypt,[6] but also the many other redemptions in Jewish history, e.g., from oppression by Antiochus Epiphanes IV.[7] Very commonly redemption is the final redemption for which the people longs and which will be achieved for it in the last age by God Himself or His Messiah. The Jew makes repeated daily petition for it.[8] In all the frequent refs., redemption is always from bondage to the nations. The decisive NT concept of redemption from sins is not found. The final redemption is also related to the present, for its coming is hastened by the presence of the righteous and their correct and pious conduct, but delayed by sinners and their ungodly manner of life.[9] The idea of ransom plays no part in all this, but it occurs in Rabb. Judaism. The use of גאל for the freeing of Jewish slaves from Gentile masters,[10] which is a religious duty on the basis of Lv. 25:48 f., introduces the thought of ransom into the religious use of גאל. But it is found with full clarity in S. Nu., 115 on 15:41:[11] "A comparison with a king whose friend's son was taken prisoner. When the king purchased him (פדה), he purchased him not as a free man (i.e., to freedom) but as a slave, so that if he commanded something and the other would not do it, he could say: Thou art my slave! ... So also when God purchased (פדה) the seed of Abraham his friend (out of bondage in Egypt), he purchased them, not as his children, but as his slaves, so that when he commanded something which they would not do he might be able to say to them: You are my slaves!"[12]

In the NT we find only the med. λυτροῦσθαι, and it is used exclusively for the redeeming act of God or of Jesus. The usage seems to be the same as that of the LXX. The only point is how far it carries with it the idea of a ransom. This can hardly be so in Lk. 24:21: ὁ μέλλων λυτροῦσθαι τὸν Ἰσραήλ, since it had no part in Jewish expectation, and Lk. does not have the ransom saying of Jesus. On the other hand, it is present in Tt. 2:14: ὃς ἔδωκεν ἑαυτὸν ὑπὲρ ἡμῶν ἵνα λυτρώσηται ἡμᾶς ἀπὸ πάσης ἀνομίας καὶ καθαρίσῃ ... and 1 Pt. 1:18 f.:

---

[6] Cf. the prayer אֱמֶת וְיַצִּיב which acc. to the *sch'ma* is to be said at morning: "Out of Egypt hast thou redeemed us (גאל), and out of the house of bondage hast thou freed us (פדה)."

[7] For examples cf. Str.-B., I, 70 under b and IV, 861 under k.

[8] At the end of the prayer in → n. 6: "Rock of Israel, ... free (פדה) Judah and Israel acc. to thy word, redeem (גאל) us ... Blessed be thou Lord, thou redeemer (גוֹאֵל) of Israel," and in the 7th benediction of the *Sch'mone Esrē*; for many other examples cf. Str.-B., IV, 860-862 under g-l; I, 67 ff.; III, 741 (on Hb. 9:12); also Ps. Sol. 8:11, 30: λυτρούμενος, 9:1: κύριος ὁ λυτρωσάμενος αὐτούς (of God or His Messiah), here fully synon. with the usual κύριος (θεός) σωτὴρ αὐτῶν (ἡμῶν) in 3:6; 8:33; 17:3. Generally λυτροῦσθαι and σῴζειν are par. for the Jewish גאל and פדה, cf. αἰωνία λύτρωσις at Hb. 9:12 with σωτηρία αἰώνιος at Hb. 5:9.

[9] Cf. Cant. r. on 2:2 (R. Meyer): "As the lily is only for the scent, so the righteous are created only for the redemption of Israel." "As the lily is prepared for the sabbaths and feasts, so Israel is prepared from the morning for redemption." bMeg., 15a: "He who passes on something (a Rabb. saying) in the name of the one who first pronounced it (not in his own name or without a name) brings redemption for the world (מֵבִיא גְאֻלָּה לָעוֹלָם)."

[10] So, e.g., in bQid., 15b, where it is disputed whether the גְּאֻלָּה of a Jewish slave by relatives or other compatriots is a purchase to freedom or to slavery (under a master of his own race).

[11] Cf. K. G. Kuhn, S. Nu. (1932 ff.), 350 f. and notes.

[12] The last half of this paragraph is by K. G. Kuhn.

οὐ φθαρτοῖς, ἀργυρίῳ ἢ χρυσίῳ, ἐλυτρώθητε ἐκ τῆς ματαίας ὑμῶν ἀναστροφῆς πατροπαραδότου, ἀλλὰ τιμίῳ αἵματι ὡς ἀμνοῦ ἀμώμου καὶ ἀσπίλου Χριστοῦ. The reference to the self-offering of Jesus and to His ransom saying in Mk. 10:45 is here so plain that λυτροῦσθαι must be translated "to buy back." The facts are interesting in the sense that they show that the weaker use of λυτροῦσθαι, which is to be noted in the LXX when the reference is to God's redeeming acts, has now become more specific. "The thought of a ransom, a payment, is now restored." [13] Probably the fact of the death of Jesus, and its understanding as a ransom, had some influence here, even if only to a restricted degree. Certainly it would be quite wrong to say of Tt. 2:14 and 1 Pt. 1:18 that because in LXX usage λυτροῦσθαι as God's act does not contain the idea of ransom, it is not contained in these passages either. [14]

† λύτρωσις.

Similar to λυτρόω, "liberation by ransom." It usually means "redemption," [1] but we also find "release from an obligation." [2] λύτρωσις does not occur in Philo.

In the NT it is the redemption which is awaited for Israel or Jerusalem, Lk. 1:68; 2:38, i.e., from the yoke of enemies, Lk. 1:71. The reference is not to a ransom but to a redeemer, cf. Lk. 24:21. At root we have here the same ideas of the redemption of Israel by God's pardoning grace as in ψ 110:9; 129:7, so that λύτρωσις is virtually the same as σωτηρία, cf. Lk. 1:69, 77. Hb. 9:12: αἰωνίαν λύτρωσιν εὑράμενος, does not show so close a connection with the OT. Here λύτρωσις has the general sense of redemption, naturally from sin (v. 14). There is no thought of a price, though reference is made to the blood of Jesus. The idea is more cultic than legal in Hb.

† λυτρωτής.

Nomen agentis of λυτρόω, "the liberator," "redeemer," not thus far attested outside the Bible. It occurs in the NT only at Ac. 7:35 as a title for Moses par. with ἄρχων. Moses is λυτρωτής as the divinely sent liberator of Israel from Egypt. There is no more thought of a ransom in Ac. 7:35 than in ψ 18:14; 77:35.

† ἀπολύτρωσις.

The verb ἀπολυτρόω, derived from → λυτρόω and then from → λύτρον, "to set free for a ransom," does not occur in the NT, [1] but the related noun ἀπολύτρωσις

---

[13] Cr.-Kö., 706. It is to be noted that in common use λυτρόω always means "to free by money payment."

[14] There is no doubt that Tt. 2:14 is based on ψ 129:8: καὶ αὐτὸς λυτρώσεται τὸν Ἰσραὴλ ἐκ πασῶν τῶν ἀνομιῶν αὐτοῦ, and 1 Pt. 1:18 on Is. 52:3, but this does not mean that the sense of λυτροῦσθαι is the same in the NT and OT verses.

λύτρωσις. → Bibl. on λυτρόω.

[1] Plut. Aratus, 11 (I, 1032a): λύτρωσις αἰχμαλώτων, ransom of prisoners; P. Tebt., 120, 41 (1st cent. A.D.) redemption of a pledge.

[2] P. Oxy., VIII, 1130, 20 (5th cent. A.D.).

ἀπολύτρωσις. [1] ἀπολυτρόω is found already in Plat. Leg., XI, 919a; Demosth. Or., 12, 3; Polyb., 2, 6, 6; 21, 38, 3; Ep. Ar., 20; in the LXX only Ex. 21:8; Zeph. 3:1.

is used quite often, Lk. 21:28, in Paul at R. 3:24; 8:23; 1 C. 1:30; Eph. 1:7, 14; 4:30; Col. 1:14, also Hb. 9:15; 11:35. If λύτρωσις is also found in Lk. and Hb., Paul uses only ἀπολύτρωσις. Elsewhere the word is sparsely attested, and only from the 2nd or 1st cent. B.C. [2] It means "setting free for a ransom," and is used of prisoners of war, [3] slaves, [4] and criminals condemned to death (Hb. 11:35 → 354). The LXX uses it only at Da. 4:34 of the release of Nebuchadnezzar from his madness, and this verse shows that there does not have to be a ransom. It is used in this way, however, by Jews who write in Gk., Ep. Ar., Philo, Joseph. (→ n. 4). Acc. to Chrysostom on R. 3:24 (MPG, 60, p. 444b) the difference between ἀπολύτρωσις and λύτρωσις is that between definitive liberation and liberation at will (ὡς μηκέτι ἡμᾶς ἐπανελθεῖν πάλιν ἐπὶ τὴν αὐτὴν δουλείαν). In the NT ἀπολύτρωσις is always definitive redemption or manumission, but the same is true of λύτρωσις, cf. Hb. 9:12. Hence there are no grounds for the distinction. The prominence of ἀπολύτρωσις in the NT is due to the Hell. liking for compounds, cf. ἀντίλυτρον and λύτρον, ἀποκαταλλάσσειν and καταλλάσσειν, etc.

In Lk. 21:28 ἀπολύτρωσις is the redemption which the disciples longingly and painfully await and which will mean release from afflictions and persecutions at the return of the Son of Man. This liberation is unique, because definitive, and for this reason it is hoped for with unparalleled desire. The whole glow of eschatological expectation is in the word. The reference is not just to liberation from sin or to a ransom. The religious attitude from which it takes its distinctive content is rooted in the Jewish hope of the kingdom of heaven, but it is given new depth by the word and destiny of Jesus. ἀπολύτρωσις here corresponds to λύτρωσις in Lk. 1:68; 2:38. Probably a traditional Jewish phrase stands behind Lk. 21:28. [5]

ἀπολύτρωσις also occurs in this eschatological sense in R. 8:23; Eph. 1:14; 4:30. The ἀπολύτρωσις τοῦ σώματος in R. 8:23 is not redemption from the body, but the redemption of the body. Comparison with v. 21 proves this beyond cavil. As creatures attain to the freedom of the glory of the children of God when they are freed from bondage to corruption, so we shall attain to the υἱοθεσία, i.e., institution to sonship and its glory, when our body, which is dead because of sin (v. 10), is freed from this curse of death and puts on incorruption or immortality (1 C. 15:53 f.). For Paul, to be without the body is not redemption. It is a state from which he shrinks (2 C. 5:2-4). He hopes for a new body (1 C. 15:35-57). Our lowly body will be transformed in accordance with the model of the glorious body of the risen Lord (Phil. 3:21), so that incorruption, glory and power will replace corruption, humiliation and weakness (1 C. 15:42 f.). Here eschatological expectation is no less fervent than in Lk. 21:28. Indeed, it is greater, or at least more profound, since human misery, which is to be overcome, is pursued to its form of existence as physical being. To be forced to yearn in this way, and to be able to do so, is for Paul the work of God's Spirit in man. All present spiritual possessions are simply an instalment [6] on the inheritance, which will consist in

---

[2] The oldest instance is on the Kos inscr. (→ n. 4) from the 2nd or 1st cent. B.C. Since the verb occurs in Plato, the noun may well be older than this inscr.

[3] Diod. S., Fr., 37, 5, 3 (ed. L. Dindorf [1866/68], V, 149, 6); Plut. Pomp., 24 (I, 631b).

[4] Ep. Ar., 12; 33; Jos. Ant., 12, 27, Kos inscr. (Paton-Hicks, *The Inscr. of Kos* [1891], p. 52, No. 29,7 = R. Herzog, *Koische Forschungen u. Funde* [1899], 39, 7). Philo Omn. Prob.Lib., 114.

[5] Cf. En. 51:2: "For the day of their redemption is nigh"; Cant. r. on 2:13: "The time for Israel to be redeemed has come" (Str.-B., II, 256, *ad loc.*).

[6] → ἀρραβών, ἀπαρχή.

the whole existence of man being given up and made conformable to the Spirit, σῶμα πνευματικόν (1 C. 15:44). ἀπολύτρωσις is also used eschatologically in Eph. 1:14 and 4:30. In both verses the relation between possession of the Spirit and future redemption is strongly to the fore. In Eph. 4:30 we are to look forward with longing and joyous hope to the day [7] which in R. 2:5 is the day of wrath and of the revelation of the righteous judgment of God, for this is now the day of redemption on which we shall receive our portion of the inheritance, Eph. 1:14. This complete reversal of what seems to be self-evident to man is spiritual (pneumatic) piety. [8]

For believers, however, ἀπολύτρωσις is not just the object of hope. It is also a present possession, an existing reality, Col. 1:14; Eph. 1:7 and 1 C. 1:30; R. 3:24. In these verses redemption is either explicitly (Col. 1:14; Eph. 1:7) or implicitly (R. 3:24; 1 C. 1:30) equated with the forgiveness of sins. But this is no contradiction of the use in R. 8:23; Eph. 1:14; 4:30. For here, too, the reference is to redemption on the day of judgment, and whatever else this may mean or bring, it certainly implies remission of sins. The corruption from which the body is redeemed in R. 8:23 is for Paul the consequence of sin, R. 5:12. The present nature of ἀπολύτρωσις, which is particularly clear in the ἔχομεν of Col. 1:14 and Eph. 1:7, is the same as that of σωτηρία in R. 8:24: τῇ γὰρ ἐλπίδι ἐσώθημεν, i.e., it does not stand in mutually exclusive antithesis to futurity. The forgiveness of sins is not palpably a present reality. It is the act and attitude of the transcendent God, revealed and imparted to us by His Word. We have it only as a given promise, which does indeed have present effects on our lives, but which will in the full sense be a palpable reality which renews our being externally only in the final judgment. In the Word of God remission of sins is already present, and this Word is a Word of power, R. 1:16. But it is quite unpauline to limit God's gifts to His Word and to what this Word contains. Believers are redeemed, but only in such a way that they wait for (the consummation of) redemption. [9]

One can speak of a historical actuality of ἀπολύτρωσις on the basis of 1 C. 1:30 and R. 3:24 only if one keeps strictly to the idea of a history of God with man as distinct from history in the more usual sense. [10] Jesus Christ, in whom is redemption according to R. 3:24, and who is made unto us redemption in 1 C. 1:30, is the crucified and risen Lord who is proclaimed in the Gospel. He is not just historical in the modern, secular sense of the term. [11] He constitutes the middle point of God's history with man, for He is the Son of God in power (R. 1:4), who is also the last Adam, the second man (1 C. 15:45, 47), our first-born brother

---

7 → ἡμέρα.

8 The gen. περιποιήσεως in Eph. 1:14 is best taken epexegetically: the redemption which consists in taking possession of the inheritance previously mentioned. This combination is perhaps obscure, but it is in keeping with the style of Eph. (cf. Hpt. and Dib. Gefbr., *ad loc.*), and it is better than the idea of a redemption which makes into a possession, since there is no ref. in the context to becoming a possession (of God).

9 There is here a strict parallelism between redemption and justification, which is also both present and future, or better, both future and present, cf. F. Büchsel, *Theologie des NT*² (1937), 123-132.

10 Cf. F. Büchsel, *Die Offenbarung Gottes* (1938), 3-7.

11 For Schleiermacher, e.g., redemption comes from the historical Jesus. By virtue of His historical influence, He takes us up into the power and blessedness of His consciousness of God, which is also a being of God in Him. Paul has in view a different basis, not man's consciousness of God, but the work of God towards man.

(R. 8:29).[12] If redemption is to be found in Him who by the way of the cross comes to the right hand of God (Phil. 2:8 f.), in Him who is hid in God (Col. 3:3) and is yet to be manifested in His glory, this means that redemption will come to its consummation and full manifestation only at that day when we attain to union with Him (1 Th. 4:17), to glorification in His image (1 C. 15:49). Only then will it be truly present.

ἀπολύτρωσις is bound up strictly with the person of Jesus. We have it in Him, Col. 1:14; Eph. 1:7; R. 3:24. By God He is made unto us ἀπολύτρωσις, 1 C. 1:30. Redemption cannot be regarded, then, as a fact which He has indeed established, but which then has its own intrinsic life and power apart from His person, so that one can have it without being in personal fellowship with Him. To give to redemption this objective autonomy is to part company with Paul. For him there is redemption only within the circumference of faith in Jesus. It is an outworking of His love and self-offering for us, Gl. 2:20. It can be had only by those who are set in the sphere of His lordship, Col. 1:13. Thus ἀπολύτρωσις is truly and finally effected by God. One cannot speak of Jesus winning redemption from God or even of His bringing it to God. God has made Him redemption, 1 C. 1:30. As the dear Son (Col. 1:13; Eph. 1:6), He is the One in whom we have redemption. Redemption is brought about by the grace of God, R. 3:24. Here the concept of redemption is fully parallel to that of atonement.[13]

In Hb. 11:35: οὐ προσδεξάμενοι (the martyrs and heroes of faith) τὴν ἀπολύτρωσιν, ἀπολύτρωσις is (proffered) liberation. The words are to be explained by 2 Macc. 6 and 7. Release from death was offered to Eleazar in 6:22, 30: ἀπολυθῆναι τοῦ θανάτου, on condition that he renounced Judaism, and so also to the youngest of the seven brothers, 7:24-29. But they would not accept it. Here ἀπολύτρωσις is used in the common Gk. sense.[14] In Hb. 9:15: ὅπως θανάτου γενομένου εἰς ἀπολύτρωσιν τῶν ἐπὶ τῇ πρώτῃ διαθήκῃ παραβάσεων ..., the sense is, however, rather different. Sins cannot be liberated. The meaning is "cancellation" or "remission," which is also the material sense in Col. 1:14 and Eph. 1:7. Strictly, we ought to have ἀπολύτρωσις ἀπὸ τῶν ... παραβάσεων. But a shift took place, as with καθαρισμός, which strictly is the purifying of man from sin, but which then came to be related directly to sin, Hb. 1:3: καθαρισμὸν τῶν ἁμαρτιῶν ποιησάμενος.[15] A similar shift in meaning may also be seen in the case of ἱλασμός.[16]

A final question must now be put. How far is the idea of a λύτρον, a ransom or the like, still implied in ἀπολύτρωσις? Are we to assume that whenever ἀπολύτρωσις is used there is also a suggestion of λύτρον? In none of the ἀπολύτρωσις passages is there any express reference to a ransom. In the eschatological verses (Lk. 21:28; R. 8:23; Eph. 1:14; 4:30) it is indeed impossible to append the idea; it lies completely beyond the horizon of these passages.[17] Even the other

---

[12] Luther's rendering of R. 3:24: "Which took place through Jesus Christ," presupposes this view of history. In terms of the secular view of history it would be incorrect.

[13] → καταλλάσσω.

[14] → n. 3 and 4.

[15] Cf. Rgg. Hb.[2, 3], 271, esp. the passage which he adduces from Philo Spec. Leg., I, 215: δι' οὗ (the altar) πάντων ἁμαρτημάτων καὶ παρανομημάτων ἀπολύσεις γίνονται καὶ παντελεῖς ἀφέσεις.

[16] → III, 317.

[17] This is esp. true of Da. 4:34, the only OT ref. → 352.

Pauline verses (R. 3:24; 1 C. 1:30; Col. 1:14; Eph. 1:7) do not have in view an act in virtue of which liberation comes. They think only of the act of emancipation itself, and of what it implies. The only verse where there is perhaps a hint of the λύτρον is R. 3:24. Yet in 3:25 Paul is thinking in cultic, not commercial, terms.[18] He has in view a payment in Gl. 3:13; 4:5, but this does not mean that this is also implied in R. 3:24. For he uses ἀπολύτρωσις in R. 8:23; Eph. 1:14; 4:30 with no thought at all of a ransom. Hence one cannot argue that, because the context of justification in R. 3:21-31 is legal, this demands the implication of a ransom in ἀπολύτρωσις. For the payment of a ransom is a commercial transaction in legal form, not strictly a legal action such as, e.g., punishment, → 334 f. Law recognises and recognised acts of grace without any payment at all. Legal release from a penalty is not linked with the payment of a ransom. To show how redemption is brought to pass, Paul uses the concept of ἱλαστήριον, but this would be superfluous if there were any thought of a ransom in ἀπολύτρωσις. The more concretely we take the idea of ransom, the less it is in place alongside that of ἱλαστήριον. Hence there is no real implication of ransom in R. 3:24. Of the two Hb. passages, 11:35 has no suggestion of a λύτρον,[19] though it may be present in 9:15, where the death of Jesus is described as the cause of ἀπολύτρωσις. Nevertheless, the use of ἀπολύτρωσις is so weak in this verse that it is most unlikely that there is any thought of a ransom.[20] The original, etymologically grounded sense is thus watered down in biblical usage,[21] and only a very general sense remains.[22] The true rendering, then, is "redemption" or "liberation," not "ransom."[23] "Release" is also possible in Hb. 11:35 and "remission" in Hb. 9:15. In primitive Christianity the word was used to express a religious content, and it thus took on a special sense which is not found elsewhere. To this use as a tt. there corresponds the fact that primitive Christianity does not have a verb ἀπολυτρόω or the like alongside the noun ἀπολύτρωσις,[24] and also the fact that Paul uses only ἀπολύτρωσις and not λύτρον or any of its other derivates.

---

18 → ἱλαστήριον, III, 320 ff.

19 Cf. 2 Macc. 6:22, 30, where the ref. is only to death, not to that by which the martyr may be released.

20 Cf. what is said about Hb. 9:12 under → λύτρωσις.

21 Zahn R., 179 and 181. If the reverse is said of λυτρόω (→ *supra*), this applies only to the usage of the Past. and 1 Pt., not Lk. and Pl.

22 The same is true of the Lat. *redemptio*, which originally meant ransom, but then in Church usage took on the more general sense, so that the first and narrower sense virtually disappeared.

23 Deissmann, *Licht vom Osten* (1909), 246 f., claims that ἀπολύτρωσις means "ransoming" in Pl., and he takes it that Pl. "extends the master concept of ransom and adjusts it to the Gk. world." But he bases this view, not on an exegetical examination of the Pauline verses, which he does not provide, but on ancient records of the manumission of slaves. Yet surely, if we are to find out what Paul means by the word, we must first consult his epistles. Contemporary non-pauline records may be important, but they can never take the first place in this kind of enquiry. The method of Deissmann inevitably results in an obscuring of what is distinctively Pauline, cf. Zn. R., 180 f. The eschatological element in Paul's view of ἀπολύτρωσις is completely ignored by Deissmann. Pr.-B., *s.v.*; P. Feine, *Nt.liche Theologie* (1922), 240; Althaus in *NT Deutsch, ad loc.*; and rather more cautiously Lietzmann, *ad loc.*, also regard it as more or less self-evident that ἀπολύτρωσις means ransom in R. 3:24, yet incorrectly, since they adduce no adequate arguments.

24 It should be noted in contrast how often we use "to redeem" and "redeemer" as well as "redemption."

ἀπολύτρωσις is not one of the chief concepts in early Christian proclamation and teaching. It is not found at all in Mk.-Mt., Jn., the Catholic Ep., or Rev. Its use in Lk. is sparse. In Paul it cannot compare in importance with δικαιοσύνη or καταλλαγή. As distinct from these words, ἀπολύτρωσις is not a point of crystallisation in Paul's world of thought. The reason is that it is not so concrete or so full of content. To a much higher degree the word ἀπολύτρωσις has to be given its content. It is worth noting that Pl. does not use it when he speaks of emancipation from the Law or from the necessity of sin. The word group ἐλεύθερος, ἐλευθερία, ἐλευθεροῦν plays generally a bigger role in Pl. than ἀπολύτρωσις. The meaning of redemption in the NT is distinguished from that which the word acquired in later doctrine by the strong emphasis which the NT lays on the eschatological element implicit within it. In Paul's concept of ἀπολύτρωσις there is no place whatever for any physical redemption in the sense of redemption brought about by natural means.

Büchsel

† μάγος, † μαγεία, † μαγεύω (→ γόης).

† μάγος.[1]

1. μάγος in the Greek World.

Four meanings are found together in almost every age. a. The specific meaning of a "member of the Persian priestly caste" (which acc. to Hdt., I, 101 was one of the 6 tribes of the Medes), about which the Gks. had various opinions. Strabo, XV, 3, 15 tells of a fire cult; acc. to Hdt., I, 132 they had to be present to speak the sacred words at sacrifices; in VII, 37 they are the interpreters of special signs.[2] Heracl. Fr., 14, (I, 154, 13 ff., Diels[5]) ascribes to them mysteries which put them on the same plane as followers of Dionysus; he also realises plainly that they are the rulers of a distinctive religion. Their religious ideas are thought to be strongly influenced by philosophy; for this reason the Gk. philosophers are often portrayed as their pupils. This idea occurs again and again in Democr. esp.[3] If later this is linked up with a Romantic veneration for the exotic, this assertion, though it cannot be checked in detail, may contain a grain of truth and may point to a historical cultural and intellectual link. Something of the

---

μάγος. T. Hopfner, Art. "Mageia," Pauly-W., XIV (1928), 302 f., 373 ff.; F. Pfister, Art. "Epode" (19), PaulyW., Suppl. IV (1924), 342; C. Clemen, Art. "Magoi," Pauly-W., XIV, 509 ff.; Str.-B., I, 76; A. Abt, *Die Apologie d. Apul. v. Madaura* (1908), *passim*, esp. 32 ff. (= RVV, 4); A. D. Nock, "Paul and the Magus," Excurs. 14 in Jackson-Lake, V (1932), 164 ff. → I, 693, n. 14. A. Christensen, *Die Iranier* (*Kulturgesch. d. Alten Orients*, III, 1 [1933] = *Hndbch. AW*, III, 3, 1, 233 and 289 f.); S. Nyberg, *D. Religion d. alten Iran* (1938), 335 ff., 374 ff., 388 ff., 395 ff.; G. Messina, *I Magi a Betlemme e una Predizione di Zoroastro* = *Sacra Scriptura Antiquitatibus Orientalibus Illustrata*, III (1933).

[1] μάγος is not found in Hom., and rather strangely it is not listed in Preisigke Wört. (though cf. perhaps μαγιανός); v. Arnim, Ditt. Syll.[3]

[2] For further accounts cf. Plut. Quaest. Conv., IV, 5, 2 (II, 670d); Diog. L. prooem, 1 (1); 6-9 (5-6).

[3] Diels[5], I, 284, 26 ff.; II, 81, 11 f.; 84, 30 ff.; 86, 38 f.; 94, 30 f.; 209, 1 f.

same may be seen in the more likely account of the education of Protagoras by the magi at the time of the campaign of Xerxes (c. 480 B.C.; Protagoras Fr., 2 [II, 255, 17 ff., Diels[5]]). Even if this account is to be rejected on chronological grounds, the total presentation does at least show the possibility of such a contact. Ps.-Plat. Alc., I, 122a (written in the 4th cent.) refers to the activity of the Persian μάγοι as teachers; μαγεία is here quite correctly defined as θεῶν θεραπεία. Nor does the Platonic school see anything incongruous in causing Socrates to speak of a λόγος, ὅν ἐμοὶ ἤγγειλε Γωβρύης, ἀνὴρ μάγος (Ps.-Plat. Ax., 371a). Aristot. has more exact information about the philosophical labours of the magi: τὸ γεννῆσαν πρῶτον ἄριστον τιθέασιν καὶ οἱ Μάγοι (Metaph., XIII, 4, p. 1091b, 10). Cf. Philo Spec. Leg., III, 100 → 358.

The content of the Gk. philosophies had also a strong religious impulse (→ παραλαμβάνω). Obviously, along the traditional lines of the magi, there was a close, inward and indissoluble connection between philosophy and religion, as may be seen in the strongly religious form of the doctrine of the two principles, which is also known in the Gk. tradition concerning the magi (Aristot. Fr., 8, p. 1475a, 35 f.). This explains how, with a strong restriction of understanding, a second meaning could develop out of the original sense, with no national limitation. It is no longer possible to discern the deeper reasons for the development.[4]

b. More generally "the possessor and user of supernatural knowledge and ability." Thus by his initiations he protects the soul of the dying against Hades (ἄξουσι τὴν ψυχὴν ἄνω, Python Fr., 1, 5 ff. [TGF, p. 811]); cf. on this Heracl. Fr., 14. He foretells the future (the way Socrates will die, Aristot. Fr., 27, p. 1479a, 13 ff.; this one is from Syria; cf. Herm. m., 11, 2). Comparing Joseph. Ant., 10, 195 with 216 we find that μάγος is a comprehensive term (used here for the interpreter of dreams). The boundary line with the next meaning is fluid; it should be recalled how in the popular mind those who place no value on superstitious devices and ideas are thought to believe in nothing.

c. "Magician" (cf. Phot. Lex., 240, 13:[5] μάγους = τοὺς μαγγανεύοντας = exercising magic). His arts are connected with the name of a Persian magus Ost(h)anes (II, 216, 28 ff.; 217, 1 ff., Diels[5]); but Orpheus and Pythagoras had to put up with the same (*ibid.*, 216, 35 ff.), so that this religious bridge is an artificial construction. The μάγος as a magician is in general higher than the → γόης,[6] but he, too, works with compulsion, accomplishing, e.g., purification and expiation by magical means, Philo Spec. Leg., III, 100. The meaning is sometimes the same as that of γόης, cf. Act. Thom., 152. In a derogatory sense it may also be used for the missionary of a new religion whose success can then be explained in terms of the use of magical compulsion, Act. Thom., 101, cf. 20. The religious antithesis may be seen clearly in the question put to the missionary: μάγος or θεός, Mart. Mt., 22. The pagan thus distinguishes sharply between a divine gift which is given, and forced (demonic) magic.

d. Figuratively, "deceiver," "seducer." This sense may be found on the lips of those who know of genuine magic but do not uncritically accept all that claims to be such, and also on the lips of those who rationalistically refuse to accept magic as real power. It has not been explained how μάγος could come to take on this general sense so

---

[4] There is only a remote possibility that the word μάγγανον = "magical means," which is older than the borrowing of μάγος from the Persian [Debrunner: a word inherited by Gk. from the Indo-Germanic], influenced the meaning of μάγος. Nock § 2 seeks to explain the meaning along these lines; The Gks., who knew little of Persian and were poor observers of alien religions, confused the rites of the magi with magic. But this is hardly an adequate explanation, and in a private communication Nock himself says that the development was more or less accidental.

[5] Quoted in TGF Adespota, 592, p. 956.

[6] Cf. Pauly-W., XIV (1928), 378: Magic turns to higher classes of demons and already uses the higher magical prayer.

early, cf. Plat. Resp., IX, 572e in a purely ethical sense of corrupters of youth; Soph. Oed. Tyr., 387, probably deceiver. Later it is, of course, very common.

2. μάγος in Judaism.

For Philo the work of the μάγος is sub-religious; he is grouped with the σοφιστής (Vit. Mos., I, 92) or the φαρμακευτής (Spec. Leg., III, 93), and his technique is contrasted with the πνεῦμα προφητικόν (Vit. Mos., I, 277). Philo accepts μαγεία only as (scientific) research (Spec. Leg., III, 100: τὰ φύσεως ἔργα διερευνώμενοι πρὸς ἐπίγνωσιν τῆς ἀληθείας, Omn. Prob. Lib., 74). This forces him to give partial acknowledgment to the Persian μάγοι (*loc. cit.*).

In the Rabb. μάγος is a loan word which is found under various forms, usually in the sense of magician.[7] Nevertheless, we still find the original sense of Persian priest (or adherent of the religion of Ormuzd-Ahriman), bSanh., 39a. It is obviously forbidden to Jews to have anything to do with them: "He who learns from a magus is worthy of death," bShab., 75a.

In the LXX it is used for אַשָּׁף only at Da. 2:2 (cf. v. 10): μάγοι ... τῶν Χαλδαίων along with ἐπαοιδός, φαρμακός (cf. Barn., 20, 1; Did., 2, 2), σοφός, Χαλδαῖος, and it thus means the possessor of the religious and magical arts of Babylonian mediators between the higher powers and men. If is often found in the same sense in Da. Θ.

3. μάγος in the New Testament.

There is no means of determining whether the μάγοι ἀπ' ἀνατολῶν of Mt. 2:1 (7, 16) are specifically Babylonian astrologers[8] or astrologers in general.[9] The former is more likely, since it is only in Babylon, by contact with the exiles, that the μάγοι would acquire an interest in the Jewish king (Messiah).[10] μάγος here means the "possessor of special (secret) wisdom," especially concerning the meaning of the course of the stars and its interconnection with world events[11] (→ I, 505).

In Ac. 13:6, 8 μάγος is used of a Jew along with → ψευδοπροφήτης in sense b.[12] The word μάγος does not primarily emphasise a distinction between magic and true religion (as in Philo). The reference is rather to the conflict between two religions, in which Christianity emerges victorious.

We cannot accept the impossible equation of the μάγος of Ac. 13:8 with the Ἄτομος mentioned in Jos. Ant., 20, 142, for Jos. says expressly that under the mask of a μάγος (μάγον εἶναι σκηπτόμενον) this man sought (and gained) entry to Drusilla. The passage does not say that Jews appeared as μάγοι. On the relation of the names → *infra*.

Nock gives a more vivid picture of the μάγος in Ac. 13:8. He reminds us of the Jewish exorcists of Ac. 19:13. The mysterious and impressive name of their God con-

---

7 Str.-B., I, 76, though cf. bShab., 75a, where the meaning might be "blasphemer."

8 Kl. Mt. on 2:1; for the most convincing reasons cf. Zn. Mt.[2] on 2:1 (90 f.).

9 Schl. Mt. on 2:1.

10 A. Jeremias, *Babylonisches im NT* (1905), 52 wrongly appeals to Test. L. 18 in favour of the view that the Jewish Messianic hope spoke of a star of the Messiah, for here ἄστρον is meant fig., as may be seen from the masc. φωτίζων associated with it (though → I, 505).

11 Those who take the story as a legend can naturally find here symbolical favouring of the Persian cult of Mithras above Christ (A. Dieterich, ZNW, 3 [1902], 1 ff.; *v.* H. Usener, ZNW, 4 [1903], 19 ff.); there is a convincing reply in Jeremias, 51 ff., esp. 55 f.

12 Against sense d. is the fact that μάγος ψευδοπροφήτης would then be tautological. The conjunction of the two words in Herm. m., 11, 2 is only a formal par.

stituted for the Jews a temptation to use this name magically. Hence the man mentioned in Ac. 13:8 is a man of religious power. His position is similar to that of the house philosopher of the time.[13] Along with other aims mentioned, the story is also designed to show the sharp contrast between Christianity and magic.[14]

† μαγεία, † μαγεύω.

μαγεία is the "activity of the → μάγος."[1]

μαγεύω is a. "to belong to the order of μάγοι"; b. "to do the work of the μάγος."

These words are found in the NT only in Ac. 8:9, 11 in relation to Simon Magus[2] (the introduction of this name in place of Ἄτομος in Jos. Ant., 20, 142 may well be due to confusion with Ac. 13:8 on the part of Christian copyists of the Josephus codex). In Ac. 8:9, 11 it is stressed that by his work in Samaria he had started a deep religious movement. This shows at least that he knew how to relate his activity to the religious ideas of the Samaritans. He may even have regarded himself as the forerunner of the Messiah. Certain visible signs of mission could be expected in the case of the forerunner of the Messiah as well as the Messiah Himself. More strongly than in Ac. 13:8 (→ μάγος) it is emphasised in Ac. 8:9, 11 by the use of μαγεύων and μαγείαις that the influence of Simon could not be traced to the possession of the genuine πνεῦμα θεοῦ but only to the use of extradivine powers. The efficacy of these powers is not denied. In fact, Ac. 8 admits the dangerous and influential force of the work of Simon. That he probably regarded himself as the Taëb is supported by his swift conversion to faith in the Messiah Jesus — a conversion which would tear down the barrier existing between Samaritans and Jews. On the other hand, it may simply denote an impulsive nature.

Delling

---

[13] § 5. Cf. also H. Gressmann, "Die Aufgaben d. Wissenschaft des nachibiblischen Judt.," ZAW, NF, 2 (1925), 9 ff.: "Jao u. d. Zauberreligion" [Bertram].

[14] § 7. It may be mentioned that for Ign. in Eph., 19, 3 the real power of μαγεία is only overthrown with the appearing of Christ.

μαγεία κτλ. [1] What is said under → μάγος n. 1 applies also to μαγεία.

[2] Bibl. on Simon Magus in H. Waitz, RE³, XVIII, 351. Waitz' source criticism of Ac. 8 in ZNW, 7 (1906), 341 ff. tears the living text into dead fragments on account of the difficult contents. His summary "Simon Magus in der altchristl. Lit.," ZNW, 5 (1904), 121 ff. is of value.

Μαγώγ → I, 789 ff.

μαθητεύω, μαθητής → μανθάνω.

† μαίνομαι

μαίνομαι, "to rage," "to be furious" (the Indo-Germanic root *men-* always means "to think" except in Gk.; in Gk. it means "to be in transports," "to rage"). It is used in Hom. for the terror-evoking manner of fighting of the god or hero, Il., 5, 717 of Ares the god of war (εἰ οὕτω μαίνεσθαι ἐάσομεν οὖλον Ἄρηα), also of Ares in Aesch. Sept. c. Theb., 343; Hom. Il., 21, 5 of Hector (ὅτε μαίνετο φαίδιμος Ἕκτωρ); of the rage of battle also in Soph. Ant., 135 f. (ὃς τότε μαινομένᾳ ξὺν ὁρμᾷ βακχεύων ἐπέπνει). It also describes the effect of intoxicating drink, e.g., wine in Hom. Od., 21, 297 f.; Luc. Dialogi Deorum, 18, 2. Then it is used of great anger in Hom. Il., 8, 360 (cf. also 2 Macc. 4:4 vl.), or sorrow (Aesch. Sept. c. Theb., 967: μαίνεται γόοισι φρήν). It can be used, too, of the wild raging of desire, Eur. Phoen., 535 (with ἐπί and dat.), cf. 4 Macc. 7:5; also of passionate love, μαίνεσθαι ὑπὸ ἐπιθυμιῶν καὶ ἐρώτων, Plat. Resp., IX, 578a, δι᾽ ἔρωτα μανείς, Phaedr., 253c; or the raging of the mind, or frenzy, Soph. Ant., 765; Oed. Col., 1537; Plat. Symp., 173e (with παραπαίω); P. Oxy., I, 33, Col. IV, 9 ff. (ἰώθαμεν καὶ ἡμεῖς μαινομένους ... σωφρονίζειν); P. Herm., 7, 18; madness, Aesch. Prom., 977 (κλύω σ᾽ ἐγὼ μεμηνότ᾽ οὐ σμικρὰν νόσον); Plat. Lys., 205a; Epict. Diss., I, 21, 4; 22, 18; II, 11, 12; III, 9, 5; M. Ant., 11, 33 (σῦκον χειμῶνος ζητεῖν μαινομένου, "mad is he who seeks a fig in winter"). Hence the antonym σωφρονεῖν in Plat. Phaedr., 244a. Here (244 ff.) Plato describes the blessing of divinely sent madness (μανία, μαίνεσθαι), which gives different insights from the knowledge acquired by the more sober. He points to the Pythia, the priestesses of Dodona, and divinely inspired poets. μαίνεσθαι can also be used for Bacchic possession and inspiration : Hdt., IV, 79 (ὑπὸ τοῦ θεοῦ μαίνεται), for being filled with the spirit of divine rapture, Eur. Ba., 298 ff.: μάντις δ᾽ ὁ δαίμων ὅδε· τὸ γὰρ βακχεύσιμον καὶ τὸ μανιῶδες μαντικὴν πολλὴν ἔχει· ὅταν γὰρ ὁ θεὸς εἰς τὸ σῶμ᾽ ἔλθῃ πολύς, λέγειν τὸ μέλλον τοὺς μεμηνότας ποιεῖ ("the god is also a seer, for he plunges us into an ecstasy of self-forgetfulness. This gives us clear vision, and when the soul has wholly taken the god into itself, it can prophesy in rapture"). [1] Rarely we find the act. μαίνω, "to make mad," e.g., Eur. Ion, 520 : σ᾽ ἔμηνε θεοῦ τις ... βλάβη. For the Gks., then, μαίνεσθαι (μανία) is not just a pathological expression. It is not just a malady or the result of wrong instruction (so Plat. Leg., XI, 934d). To be in ecstasy to the point of frenzy is a divine transposition from customary states (Plat. Phaedr., 265a). [2] It is a strongly affirmed religious phenomenon. Even a god, Dionysus, is a μαινόμενος in Hom. Il., 6, 132, and the supreme blessing of this frenzied god is to draw his followers into the same μαίνεσθαι, because the "stirring up of the death-encompassed foundations of life" constitutes his mien and aspect. [3]

In the LXX μαίνεσθαι is used once for the raging waves of human passion, Ιερ. 32:16, of the raging of the nations under the terror of war which Yahweh suspends over them as a punishment. [4] In 4 Macc. 8:5; 10:13 the faithfulness even to death of

---

μαίνομαι. [1] Cf. U. v. Wilamowitz-Moellendorff's transl. (1923).

[2] E. Rohde, *Psyche,* II [9, 10] (1925), 4.

[3] W. F. Otto, *Dionysos* (1933), 132.

[4] The LXX finds in μανία a direct punishment for sin, Hos. 9:7; cf. Zech. 12:4; Dt. 28:28, 34. Even prophetic μανία is estimated negatively, though in Ιερ. 36:26 a distinction is, of course, made between true prophecy and false.

Eleazar and his sons has the appearance of madness to Antiochus Epiphanes. The obedience and fidelity of pious Jews to the Law also seems to be μαίνεσθαι to those who oppose the Law. The term thus belongs to the sphere where religious decisions are made and the ways of men part. It admits that the worlds of belief and unbelief do not understand one another. Similarly, Teiresias in Eur. Ba., 359 says that Pentheus rages in madness (μέμηνας ἤδη· καὶ πρὶν ἐξέστης φρενῶν), not because he falls into Bacchic frenzy, but because he will have nothing whatever to do with Bacchic madness and Dionysiac rapture. The only point here is that it is the believer who regards the unbeliever as mad, whereas in the LXX it is the non-Jew who declares that the Jew who joyfully embraces martyrdom is mad. In both cases, however, there is decision, and the opposing party does not understand, but rejects or persecutes. Philo uses μαίνεσθαι only in the sense of delusion, Vit. Mos., I, 161; Leg. Gaj., 233; Flacc., 162; Cher., 32; Spec. Leg., III, 126; Agric., 84 (περὶ ἡδονὰς καὶ ἐπιθυμίας καὶ ἔρωτας ἀκαθέκτους μεμηνώς), hence with παραπαίω, Som., II, 83; Flacc., 6, with μεθύω, Leg. All., III, 210 (ὁ μεθύων μέντοι καὶ μεμηνὼς ἔστιν), and as the opp. of σωφρονεῖν, Cher., 69. Joseph. has μαίνεσθαι in the sense "to be mad" in Ap., 1, 204. In Ant., 1, 116 the building of the tower of Babel is madness to God (οὕτως δὲ μεμηνότας αὐτοὺς ὁρῶν ὁ θεός). In Bell., 1, 352 (= Ant., 14, 480) it is used of the raging of the victors (ὥσπερ μεμηνότες).

In the NT μαίνομαι is used only to characterise the messengers of God with their unheard of proclamation. Thus we read in Jn. 10:19 ff. that a division arose among the Jews because of the message of Jesus. Those who did not understand His claim or preaching, who had no ear for the uniqueness of His Word, rejected Him, and their reason was that He had an evil spirit and was out of His mind (10:20). The unheard of seems to be madness to unbelief. In Ac. 12:15 the girl Rhoda is told that she is mad when she comes to tell the disciples that the imprisoned Peter is standing outside the door. μαίνεσθαι is here used of one who carries the news of an incredible divine miracle. In Ac. 26:1-23 Paul makes his defence before King Herod Agrippa II at the court of the Roman governor Festus. Even the Roman governor cannot remain indifferent to this learned and passionate speech with its message of the victory of the risen Christ over death (v. 23). But since he will not let himself be convinced by the message, there is only one other possibility. He breaks the tension and resists Paul with the only remaining gesture (v. 24): "Thou art mad." Enquiry into the final mysteries, thought and knowledge concerning them, higher learning and the unheard of message, have robbed Paul of his understanding. What are ἀληθείας καὶ σωφροσύνης ῥήματα to the believer (v. 25) are μαίνεσθαι to the unbeliever. In 1 C. 14:23 divinely inspired speaking with tongues must seem mad to non-Christian visitors to gatherings of the congregation. The unbeliever has no understanding of this spiritual gift, and he rejects this type of charismatic proclamation as frenzy. In the NT, then, μαίνεσθαι expresses the judgment of unbelief on divinely filled witness, on the inconceivable act of divine salvation.

Preisker

† μακάριος, † μακαρίζω, † μακαρισμός

Contents: A. The Greek Usage. B. The Stylistic Form of the Beatitude. C. μακάριος in the LXX and Judaism. D. The Word Group in the New Testament.

A. The Greek Usage.

First found in Pindar, μακάριος is a poetic word, also found later in common speech. It is a subsidiary form of μάκαρ. The latter is referred predominantly, at first, to the gods (οἱ μάκαρες = the gods; Hom. uses μάκαρ only 8 times of men). It denotes the transcendent happiness of a life beyond care, labour and death, Hom. Od., 5, 7.[1] μάκαρ is then used of men to denote the state of godlike blessedness hereafter in the isles of the blessed.[2] The synon. poetic ὄλβιος extols human happiness; possession and happiness are inseparably connected here. εὐδαίμων, another synon. not known to Homer, strictly denotes one who has a good daemon; it thus looks to the origin of happiness.[3] But it then means simply "rich." It becomes a leading philosophical term for inner happiness.[4] It seems not to have come into common use. εὐτυχής, "the one who is provided or favoured with a happy destiny," is also a more lofty term.

In keeping with its relation to μάκαρ, μακάριος describes first the happy state of the gods above earthly sufferings and labours; it thus goes beyond mere εὐδαίμων.[5] Like μάκαρ, it is then used for the dead who have attained to the supraterrestrial life of the gods.[6] From the time of Aristot. it becomes a very common and much weaker everyday term, and it is thus avoided by poets (Aesch., Soph.) and orators. It is used to describe the social stratum of the wealthy who in virtue of their riches are above the normal cares and worries of lesser folk (Plat. Men., 71a: κινδυνεύω σοι δοκεῖν μακάριός τις εἶναι).[7] It is often used synon. with εὐδαίμων (Plat. Resp., I, 354a: ὅ γε εὖ ζῶν μακάριός τε καὶ εὐδαίμων). Aristot. (→ n. 4) differentiates between the two. He ascribes full blessedness only to the gods who live in θεωρία, conceding only relatively lesser εὐδαιμονία to men, who in accordance with their earthly nature necessarily live in earthly activity, Eth. Nic., XI, 8, p. 1178b, 20 ff. More rarely μακά-

---

μακάριος κτλ. G. L. Dirichlet, *De Veterum Macarismis,* RVV, 14, 4 (1914); J. H. H. Schmidt, *Synonymik d. gr. Sprache,* IV (1886), 402 ff.; L. Schmidt, *Ethik d. Griechen,* II (1882), 133 ff.; E. Norden, *Agnostos Theos* (1913), 100, n. 1.

[1] μάκαρες θεοὶ αἰὲν ἐόντες.

[2] Hes. Op., 141 ff.: μάκαρες θνητοί; μακάρων νῆσοι, so from Hes. on; cf. Op., 170 f.; Theogn., 1013; Rohde[9, 10], I, 308, n. 1.

[3] Hes. Op., 826: εὐδαίμων τε καὶ ὄλβιος; Plat. Tim., 90c.

[4] Aristot. Eth. Nic., I, 2 ff., p. 1095a, 16-1099b, 8; VII, 14, p. 1153b, 9-21; M. Heinze, *Der Eudämonismus in d. gr. Philosophie, Abh. d. Sächs. Gesellschaft d. Wissenschaften zu Leipzig* (1883), 645 ff.

[5] Epicur. in Diog. L., X, 123 (27): πρῶτον μὲν τὸν θεὸν ζῶον ἄφθαρτον καὶ μακάριον νομίζων, ὡς ἡ κοινὴ τοῦ θεοῦ νόησις ὑπεγράφη, μηθὲν μήτε τῆς ἀφθαρσίας ἀλλότριον μήτε τῆς μακαριότητος ἀνοίκειον αὐτῷ πρόσαπτε· πᾶν δὲ τὸ φυλάττειν αὐτοῦ δυνάμενον τὴν μετὰ ἀφθαρσίας μακαριότητα περὶ αὐτὸν δόξαζε.

[6] Plat. Leg., XII, 947d; cf. the later Christian use in P. Giess., I, 55, 6.

[7] Cf. Plat. Resp., I, 335e.

ριος is used of material things or states, e.g., μακάριαι τύχαι, Eur. Tro., 327; βίος μακάριος, Cratinus Fr., 238 (CAF, I, 85); Ditt. Or., 519, 9 (c. 245 A.D.): ἐν τοῖς μακαριωτάτοις ὑμῶν χρόνοις.

The verb μακαρίζω, "to extol as blessed," "to declare to be blessed," *gratulari*, corresponds in content to the various Gk. ideas of happiness (→ *infra*), cf. Od., 15, 538; Hdt., I, 31; Aristoph. Vesp., 1275; Epict. Diss., III, 17, 5; Vett. Val., II, 22 (p. 88, 25), of one born under lucky stars: ὑπὸ πολλῶν μακαρισθήσεται.[8]

The noun μακαρισμός, "extolling as happy," is first found in Plat. Resp., IX, 591d: οὐκ ἐκπληττόμενος ὑπὸ τοῦ τῶν πολλῶν μακαρισμοῦ, of the admiring praises with which the people exalt honoured men, cf. Stob. Ecl., III, 57, 13 f. of blessing on the basis of experienced fortune: γίνεται δὲ ὁ μὲν ἔπαινος ἐπ' ἀρετᾷ, ὁ δὲ μακαρισμὸς ἐπ' εὐτυχίᾳ. Aristot. is the first to use the word as a tt., Rhet., I, 9, p. 1367b, 33, in the sense of macarism (beatitude).[9]

B. The Stylistic Form of the Beatitude.

From mere statements there obviously developed in Gk. a specific genre of beatitude to extol the fortune accruing to someone and to exalt this person on the basis or condition of the good fortune.[10] There are many forms of beatitude.[11] The most common is the formula μακάριος, ὅς(τις) or ὄλβιος ὅς(τις).[12] But the stronger τρισμακάριος is also favoured.[13] Since the saying often lays value on developing the thought as a general truth, it has a tendency to become gnomic.[14] Breaking forth at decisive points, it is often found in epitaphs[15] or epinicia.[16] It is frequently evoked by the contrast of painful reality, and hence it can have a strongly emotional quality. In content beatitudes, which are common in both poetry and prose throughout the centuries, reflect the sorrows and afflictions, the aspirations and ideals, of the Greeks.[17] Practical Greek philosophy breathes in them. Orientated to earth, the Gk. mind first draws its happiness from earthly goods and values. Thus parents are extolled for fine children, mothers for admirable sons[18] (cf. Lk. 11:27), the bridegroom for winning an excellent

---

[8] For further examples → Dirichlet, 52, 57 f. etc.

[9] μακαρισμὸς δὲ καὶ εὐδαιμονισμὸς αὐτοῖς μὲν ταὐτά. Cf. Plut. Tranq. An., 11 (II, 471c): "ὦ μάκαρ Ἀτρείδη, μοιρηγενές, ὀλβιόδαιμον" ἔξωθεν οὗτος ὁ μακαρισμὸς ὅπλων καὶ ἵππων καὶ στρατιᾶς περικεχυμένης. Philo Som., II, 35; L. Schmidt, 133 ff.

[10] → Dirichlet, 24.

[11] E.g., Hom. Od., 24, 192: ὄλβιε Λαέρταο πάϊ ...; Menand. Adelphi Fr., 1: ὦ μακάριόν με ...; Theogn., 1013: ἆ μάκαρ εὐδαίμων τε καὶ ὄλβιος, ὅστις ...; Bion (in Bucolici Graeci, ed. U. v. Wilamowitz-Moellendorff [1910]), IX, 1: ὄλβιοι οἱ φιλέοντες, ἐπὴν ἴσον ἀντεράωνται; for further instances, Dirichlet, 28 ff.; Norden, 100, n. 1.

[12] Hes. Theog., 954 f.: ὄλβιος ὃς μέγα ἔργον ἐν ἀθανάτοισιν ἀνύσσας ναίει ἀπήμαντος καὶ ἀγήραος ἤματα πάντα, *ibid.*, 933; Hom. Hymn. Cer., 480; Theocr., 12, 34; ὄλβιος ὅστις παισὶ φιλήματα κεῖνα διαιτᾷ, Menand. Fr., 114 (CAF, III, 34): μακάριος ὅστις οὐσίαν καὶ νοῦν ἔχει ...; Pind. Pyth., 5, 46: μακάριος, ὃς ἔχεις κτλ.

[13] Aristoph. Ach., 400: ὦ τρισμακάρι' Εὐριπίδη κτλ., cf. τρὶς ὄλβιοι, Soph. Fr., 753 (TGF, 308); τρισμάκαρες Δαναοί, Hom. Od., 5, 306; τρισευδαίμων ἀνήρ, Bacchyl., 3, 10 etc.

[14] Bion, IX, 1 → n. 11; Menand. Fr., 114, → n. 12. Hes. Theog., 95: ὁ δ' ὄλβιος ὅντινα Μοῦσαι φιλῶνται.

[15] Dirichlet, 45; 46, n. 2.

[16] *Ibid.*, 47.

[17] L. Schmidt, II, 133 ff.

[18] Hdt., I, 31; Aristoph. Vesp., 1512: ὦ Καρκίν', ὦ μακάριε τῆς εὐπαιδίας, cf. Petronius Sat. (ed. F. Bücheler-W. Heräus [1922]), 94, 1: *O felicem, inquit, matrem tuam, quae te talem peperit.* Dirichlet, 29-32.

bride.[19] But the bachelor can also be lauded for remaining unmarried.[20] Praise is naturally accorded to those who have found the great happiness of love.[21] It is accorded also to the wealthy whose possessions give them a good position in life,[22] but even more so to those who also have a good understanding or who are free from tribulations. If regard is had for inner values, he is extolled who has attained to fame, honour and manly virtue.[23] In view of the vanity of earthly things even the dead can be called blessed,[24] or in comparison with man the beast, which is not encumbered with human cares.[25] The righteous man is extolled for the outer and inner advantage conferred by piety,[26] also the wise man for the blessing of the knowledge which accrues to him.[27] The beatitude seems to have played an important role in the mystery rites, for initiates were called particularly blessed because of their distinctive and direct experience of God.[28]

Hauck

C. μακάριος in the LXX and Judaism.

μακάριος or μακαρίζειν is often used in the LXX for other words than אֶשֶׁר with the same or similar radicals, so Is. 31:9 the relative, Prv. 4:14 'ΑΘ (LXX : ζηλοῦν), ψ 16:11 Σ, perhaps also at Sir. 25:23 the verb אשר ("to stride") and Nu. 24:17 the verb שׁוּר ("to behold"). Once in Σ at Qoh. 4:2 שׁבח is rendered μακαρίζειν; the LXX has ἐπαινεῖν. Here, as also elsewhere in the OT, μακαρίζειν has the weaker sense "to bless," cf. Cant. 6:9; 4 Macc. 1:10. On the other side, it can also mean "to make happy," Sir. 25:23; 45:7; ψ 40:2; cf. Σ: μακαριστὸς ἔσται ἐν τῇ γῇ; 2 Macc. 7:24: μακαριστὸν ποιεῖν. Only once, at Prv. 31:28, does the LXX not use μακαρίζειν (so 'ΑΣΘ) for אשר. It has there πλουτεῖν.

The number of beatitudes is thus greater in the Gk. than the original, though on the whole the form and content remain the same. The beatitude begins with the predicative μακάριος (-οι), and the basis or content comes in a relative clause, a participle, or a ὅτι clause. It is only comparatively rarely that μακαρίζειν is a finite verb, but we do occasionally find it in direct speech to introduce or support the macarism. Cf. Gn. 30:13; ψ 40:2; 143:15; Sir. 25:7; 31:9. Only very rarely do we have divergent formulations such as Prv. 20:7; Sir. 26:1; 34:15 (31:17). Here μακάριος, like εὐτυχής (cf. Hdt.,

---

19 Hom. Od., 24, 192; Eur. Alc., 915.

20 Menand. Fr. 1 (CAF, III, 3): ὦ μακάριόν με· γυναῖκα οὐ λαμβάνω.

21 Bion, IX, 1, → n. 11.

22 Bacchyl., 5, 50: ὄλβιος ᾧτινι θεὸς μοῖράν τε καλῶν ἔπορεν σύν τ' ἐπιζήλῳ τύχᾳ ἀφνεὸν βιοτὰν διάγειν.

23 Pind. Olymp., VII, 11: ὁ δ' ὄλβιος ὃν φᾶμαι κατέχοντ' ἀγαθαί, cf. also Dirichlet, 43 f.

24 Chilon: τὸν τετελευτηκότα μακάριζε (I, 63, 23, Diels[5]); Aesch. Pers., 712: ... νῦν τέ σε ζηλῶ θανόντα, πρὶν κακῶν ἰδεῖν βάθος. Eur. Tro., 1170. Cf. Vergil Aen., 11, 158; Ovid Metamorphoses, 13, 521 of Priam: *felix morte sua est.*

25 Menand. Fr., 534 (CAF, III, 159): ἅπαντα τὰ ζῷ' ἐστὶ μακαριώτατα καὶ νοῦν ἔχοντα μᾶλλον ἀνθρώπου πολύ. Philemon Fr., 93 (CAF, II, 507): ὦ τρισμακάρια πάντα καὶ τρισόλβια τὰ θηρί', οἷς οὐκ ἔστι περὶ τούτων λόγος. Cf. Dirichlet, 55 f.

26 Eur. Fr., 256 (TGF, 434): μακάριος ὅστις νοῦν ἔχων τιμᾷ θεὸν καὶ κέρδος αὑτῷ τοῦτο ποιεῖται μέγα. Aristot. Eth. Eud., I, 4, p. 1215b, 11 f.: αὐτὸς (Anaxagoras) δ' ἴσως ᾤετο τὸν ζῶντα ἀλύπως καὶ καθαρῶς πρὸς τὸ δίκαιον ἤ τινος θεωρίας κοινωνοῦντα θείας, τοῦτον ὡς ἄνθρωπον εἰπεῖν μακάριον εἶναι. Cf. Dirichlet, 61 f.

27 Plat. Leg., II, 660e: ὁ μὲν ἀγαθὸς ἀνὴρ σώφρων ὢν καὶ δίκαιος εὐδαίμων ἐστὶ καὶ μακάριος. Cf. Rohde, II[2], 279, 1.

28 Cf. the formula of the Eleusinian mysteries in Hom. Hymn. Cer., 480: ὄλβιος ὃς τάδ' ὄπωπεν, cf. Dirichlet, 62 ff.; Norden, 100, n. 1.

I, 31 f. → 363; 366) and εὐδαίμων, denotes the state of blessedness in which a man finds himself, while formal beatitudes express the acknowledgment of this state before God and man. μακαριστός is used like μακάριος in Prv. 14:21; 16:20; 29:18. It always stands behind the participial phrase to which it is related as a predicate noun.

In content the OT beatitudes are controlled by prevailing desires and ideals. They are part of the practical wisdom of the OT, and are thus common in the Wisdom lit.; [29] only a few are found elsewhere. In keeping with the distinctive nature of OT piety, the different secular and religious ideals existed alongside one another. It is impossible to date them with certainty. So far no direct formal par. have been found in the wisdom of the Near East. [30] That there were collections of beatitudes may be seen from Sir. 25:7-10, where we have 9 or 10, some of them found also elsewhere.

In the OT the beatitude always refers to a person, never a thing or state. Even the blessing of the land whose king is born free (Qoh. 10:17) is no true exception, since the ref. is obviously to the inhabitants of the land who are his subjects. Only in 4 Macc. do we find ref. to the μακαριότης τοῦ ἱεροῦ τόπου (4:12), the μακάριος αἰών (17:18), and the μακαριότης (א μακρότης) τῶν ἡμερῶν (18:19). γῆρας (7:15), θάνατος (10:15), ἀποθνῄσκειν (12:1), and ὑπομένειν (7:22) are also called μακάριος. In marked distinction from Hell. usage God is not called μακάριος in the Bible. The only exceptions are in 1 Tm. 1:11; 6:15. God is the Giver of all blessedness. Blessedness is fulness of life; it relates first to earthly blessings, a wife (Sir. 25:8; 26:1), children (Gn. 30:13; 4 Macc. 16:9; 18:9; ψ 126:5; Sir. 25:7), [31] beauty (Cant. 6:9 [8]), earthly well-being, riches, honour, wisdom (Job 29:10, 11, cf. also Is. 32:20). In keeping with the whole tenor of Scripture wisdom is often the theme, Prv. 3:13; Sir. 14:20; 25:9; 37:24; 50:28; ψ 1:1 f.; [32] 3 Βασ. 10:8 = 2 Ch. 9:7. God's will is known to His people Israel; this is its privilege and the basis of its blessedness, Mal. 3:12; Bar. 4:4. Wisdom and piety are God's gift and the presupposition of all blessedness. So one may not introduce the eudaemonistic idea of recompense even where the keeping of legal demands seems to be the basis of macarisms, cf. ψ 1:1; 40:1, 2; 105:3; 118:1, 2; 127:1; Prv. 8:32 (BS), 34; 14:21; 20:7; 29:18; Sir. 31 (34):8, 9; Is. 56:2. Men can easily go astray in their judgment, Is. 3:12; 9:15. They go too much by outward success, Mal. 3:15. Thus the blessing of the Israelites by the Egyptians when they went into the desert is to be explained subjectively by the fact that they had been spared the terrible experience of the plagues (Wis. 18:1), and the blessing of ψ 136:8, 9 flows from the human heart in its desire for revenge. The OT warns us against rash judgment acc. to appearance, Sir. 11:28: πρὸ τελευτῆς μὴ μακάριζε μηδένα, καὶ ἐν τέκνοις αὐτοῦ γνωσθήσεται ἀνήρ. The Heb. word אַחֲרִית ("end") is taken by the LXX in the sense of posterity. [33]

---

[29] Cf. F. Maas, *Formgeschichte d. Mischna* (1937), 64.

[30] W. Baumgartner, *Isr. u. altorientalische Weisheit* (1933); "D. isr. Weisheitsliteratur," ThR, NF, 5 (1933), 259-288. A broad religious and liturgical context is found for the macarism by T. Arvedson, *Das Mysterium Christi, Eine Studie zu Mt. 11:25-30* (1937), 95 ff. Here Norden's critical method is rejected, and the beatitude is associated with the blessing, so that its cultic character (esp. in the Psalms) is protected against its one-sided understanding as a wisdom saying. B. Gemser, *Sprüche Salomos* (1937), on 3:13 takes the macarism as a hymnic form midway between a statement and an admonition, cf. also W. Zimmerli, ZAW, NF, 10 (1933), 185, n. 1.

[31] In Wis. 3:13, 14 the beatitude is for the unfruitful wife or unmarried woman, who, if she avoids defilement or wrong, is more highly praised than sinful parents. We see here a trend towards rigorous asceticism, though cf. J. Fichtner, *ad loc.*

[32] In many of these passages (Sir. 14:20; 50:28; ψ 1:2) concern for wisdom is expressed in the Heb. verb הגה. As well as the lit. translation μελετήσει (S^2) at Sir. 14:20, the LXX uses for this τελευτήσει (BS^1 A) and at 50:28 ἀναστραφήσεται. Thus the ref. is sometimes clearer in the original than in the Gk. translation.

[33] The LXX uses the same or corresponding words for אַחֲרִית at the following places: Prv. 23:18; 24:20 (ἔκγονος); Nu. 23:10; 24:20 (σπέρμα); ψ 108:13; Ιερ. 38 (31):17; Sir. 32 (35):22 (τέκνον).

The main thought, which is emphasised in the Heb. parallelism by the negative and positive form,[34] corresponds materially to the well-known dictum of Solon from the story of Croesus: πρὶν δ' ἂν τελευτήσῃ, ἐπισχεῖν μηδὲ καλέειν κω ὄλβιον, ἀλλ' εὐτυχέα (Hdt., I, 32). Here the word εὐτυχής stands for fleeting earthly happiness. ὄλβιος, or μακαρίζειν in the story of Cleobis and Biton in I, 31,[35] denotes the true happiness which endures through the changes of Tyche. But the biblical understanding of the warning may be seen clearly in the positive turn which the thought it given in Wis. 2:16: μακαρίζει ἔσχατα δικαίων. The end itself is decisive. It reveals that the righteous is near God. Thus characteristic biblical beatitudes refer simply to the one who trusts in God,[36] who hopes and waits for Him, who fears and loves Him, ψ 2:12; 33:8; 39:4; 83:12; 111:1; Prv. 16:20; 28:14; Sir. 34:15 (31:17); Is. 30:18; Tob. 13:15. God's people, the righteous elected by Him, are to be blessed as such, Dt. 33:29; ψ 32:12; 64:4; 83:4, 5; 88:15; 143:15; 145:5. Happy are those whose sins are forgiven, ψ 31:1, 2, and also those who are protected against specific sins, or particularly dangerous sins, Sir. 14:1, 2; 25:8; 28:19. Blessed is the righteous even in suffering, Da. 12:12 LXX, Θ; 4 Macc. 7:22, which is regarded as divine chastisement, Job 5:17; ψ 93:12; Tob. 13:16. Martyrdom is ultimate blessedness, 4 Macc. 7:15; 10:15; 12:1; also 18:13. εὐτυχία occurs as a synon. for the only time in the Bible at 4 Macc. 6:11:[37] it denotes the inner attitude of the martyr as this is determined by the eternal blessedness which is before him. μακάριος also in fact takes on this eschatological significance in 4 Macc. 17:18; 18:19 (A). In many OT texts the beatitude is used in an eschatological connection. ψ 71:17 and Is. 31:9 (not the Heb., → 364) also have Messianic significance. Nu. 24:17 is also to be taken in this way (not the Mas. → 364), and Sir. 48:11 refers to the coming again of Elijah.

In Philo the formal beatitude is not common, cf. Som., I, 50; Spec. Leg., IV, 115. The word almost always applies to a transcendental reality which impinges on the earthly sphere for the righteous. It is often used of God. Indeed, in the true sense blessedness belongs to Him alone. Thus we read in Abr., 202: ἄλυπος δὲ καὶ ἄφοβος καὶ παντὸς πάθους ἀμέτοχος ἡ τοῦ θεοῦ φύσις εὐδαιμονίας καὶ μακαριότητος παντελοῦς μόνη μετέχουσα. Cf. also Deus Imm., 55; 161; Sacr. AC, 101: μόνος μακάριος; 40; 95; Spec. Leg., I, 329; II, 53 etc. Blessedness is proper to the divine nature, Deus Imm., 108; Som., I, 94; Spec. Leg., III, 178; IV, 48 and 123. Only as this nature invades creation do heavenly and earthly beings, including man, have a part in it, and therewith in the divine blessedness. Man can attain to it in bearing the troubles of earthly existence — here Philo is near to Gk. ways of thought — and in philosophical endeavour. Thus we read in Vit. Mos., II, 184: ὁ δὲ τλητικῶς καὶ ἀνδρείως ὑπομένων τὰ δυσκαρτέρητα σπεύδει πρὸς μακαριότητα. Cf. also Vit. Cont., 6; 13; Op. Mund., 135; 172; Leg. All., I, 4; Omn. Prob. Lib., 96 (quotation); Cher., 86; Det. Pot. Ins., 86; Sacr. AC, 27; Rer. Div. Her., 111; 285; Som., I, 50; Praem. Poen., 63; 122; Spec. Leg., II, 141; 230; III, 1; IV, 115; Decal., 104. Thus the word group has for Philo a specific transcendental sense. Men as such, however eminent, are bound to earth; hence Philo can call them happy only in the subjective and relative sense of popular estimation, Conf. Ling., 164; Decal., 4.

---

[34] לפני מות אל תאשר גבר ובאחריתו ינכר איש "Do not call a man blessed before his death, for a man is known at his end."

[35] Here we read: Ἀργεῖοι μὲν γὰρ περιστάντες ἐμακάριζον τῶν νεηνιέων τὴν ῥώμην, αἱ δὲ Ἀργεῖαι τὴν μητέρα αὐτῶν, οἵων τέκνων ἐκύρησε.

[36] In the same sense as μακάριος we have at Ιερ. 17:7: εὐλογημένος (בָּרוּךְ) ὁ ἄνθρωπος, ὃς πέποιθεν ἐπὶ τῷ κυρίῳ. Cf. also Lk. 1:28, 42; Mt. 25:34, also ψ 117:26; Mt. 21:9. These are salutations, as also esp. Ps. 1:1; 112:1; 128:1; Dt. 33:29; Is. 56:2. Cf. H. Schmidt (1934) on Ps. 1:1 and F. Baethgen, *Die Ps.*[3] (1904) on 1:1.

[37] Unless, with Deissmann in Kautzsch Apkr. and Pseudepigr., we are to read εὐψυχία (א). So also A. Rahlfs LXX.

In Philo, as in 4 Macc., one may discern Hellenistic influences. The effects of this shift from biblical usage on Hell. soil may be seen in the later Christian period on burial inscr. of the 5th-8th cent., which plainly presuppose and apply the equation of μακάριος and eternal blessedness without any direct relation to the NT. [38]

In contrast to this development or reorientation Rabb. Judaism maintained the OT beatitude. Thus Rabban Jochanan ben Zakkai (d. c. 80) cried to two of his pupils (bChag., 14b): [39] "Hail to you, and hail to the mothers that bare you! Hail to mine eyes, that they have seen this!" Here we have familiar motifs. The content of this group of beatitudes is obviously controlled by the theological and legal ideals of the Rabbis.

Bertram

D. The Word Group in the New Testament.

1. The special feature of the group μακάριος, μακαρίζειν, μακαρισμός in the NT is that it refers overwhelmingly to the distinctive religious joy which accrues to man from his share in the salvation of the kingdom of God. Thus the verb μακαρίζειν, which occurs only twice in the NT, is used in Lk. 1:48 of the blessing of the mother of the Messiah by all generations (Lk. 11:27), and in Jm. 5:11 of the righteous who endure (ὑπομείναντας). The noun μακαρισμός is found only 3 times, at Gl. 4:15 for the blessedness of receiving the message of salvation, and at R. 4:6, 9 with reference to the remission of sins. In both passages it is used almost technically by Paul. μακάριος is very common in the NT, and it is used almost always in direct beatitudes. [40] As in the Gk. world and the OT the reference is to persons. Only occasionally is it to things, e.g., individual members of the body (Mt. 13:16: ὀφθαλμοί, ὦτα; Lk. 11:27: κοιλία, μαστοί). One may see here the influence of Jewish modes of thought in which members of the body are in some sense regarded as independent bearers of life. [41] The formula often found in the Gk. world and also in the LXX, on the basis of the Heb. אַשְׁרֵי הָאִישׁ אֲשֶׁר, namely, μακάριος ὅς(τις), is seldom found in the NT (only Mt. 11:6 and par.; Lk. 14:15). This is a sign of the independence of the NT beatitudes as compared with the surrounding world. [42] The NT, like the LXX in many cases, prefers a predicative μακάριος first, then the person with art. (cf. Mt. 5:3 ff.; Rev. 1:3; 14:13 etc.), and finally the reason for the blessedness, or a description of it, in a subsidiary clause (ὅτι Mt. 5:3 ff.; Lk. 1:45 etc.). In general the NT macarisms are in the 3rd person (cf. the Heb. אַשְׁרֵי). [43] As distinct from those of the OT, they are not part of practical wisdom but come in the context of eschatological proclamation. [44] For this reason they occur for the most

---

[38] Examples may be found in Preisigke Wört., II, 46 f.

[39] So Str.-B., I, 189, where further material may be found. On the understanding of the OT passages by the Rabbis → ἔργον, II, 649.

[40] The NT uses only μακάριος; other Gk. terms like ὄλβιος, εὐδαίμων etc. are not found at all.

[41] Cf. Str.-B., II, 187 f.

[42] Cf. Norden, 100, n. 1: "Where the question is that of causal relation," differences of style "are more decisive than similarities of thought, which might have arisen independently."

[43] Hence the Lucan form (2nd person) is probably secondary, by way of approximation to the Woes. Attempts are made at a rendering back to Aram. in C. F. Burney, *The Poetry of our Lord* (1925), 166; K. Köhler, "Die urspr. Form d. Seligpreisungen," ThStKr, 91 (1918), 157-192.

[44] Cf. Bultmann Trad., 113 f.

part in the Synpt. and Rev. In keeping with the tension into which the dawn of the age of salvation sets the soul, the NT beatitudes have great emotional force (Mt. 13:16; Rev. 19:9). As in Gk. macarisms, there is often contrast with a false estimation as to who is truly blessed (Mt. 5:3-6, 10 f.; Lk. 11:28; Jn. 20:29; 1 Pt. 3:14; 4:14). A clear difference from the Gk. beatitudes is that all secular goods and values are now completely subsidiary to the one supreme good, the kingdom of God, whether it be that the righteous man may hope for this, is certain of it, has a title to it, or already has a part in it. The predominating estimation of the kingdom of God carries with it a reversal of all customary evaluations.

Thus the NT beatitudes often contain sacred paradoxes (Mt. 5:3 ff.; Lk. 6:20-22; 1 Pt. 3:14; 4:14; Rev. 14:13). This is particularly true of the striking beatitudes which obviously formed the introduction to the Sermon on the Mount in the very earliest tradition.[45] In the impressive form of beatitudes basic statements are here made about those who may regard themselves as citizens of the kingdom of God. The power of the statements lies in their reversal of all human values. In Lk. the beatitudes consist more of eschatological consolation. Men in certain circumstances, the poor, the hungry, the weeping, the hated, are promised the blessings of the kingdom of God. In Mt. the factor of their own moral and religious conduct is more prominent, and the connection between right conduct and heavenly recompense is emphasised.[46] There is in fact no material distinction between the two forms, for even the partially earlier form in Lk. includes righteousness on the part of those who are called blessed. The blessing of Jesus is for pious *aniyim*,[47] who are depicted partly as humble and oppressed (→ πτωχοί, Lk. 6:20; Mt. 5:3 + τῷ πνεύματι; cf. Lk. 1:52 f.; Ps. 10:2; 14:6; 18:27), partly as those who are filled with longing (πεινῶντες, Lk. 6:21; Mt. 5:6 + καὶ διψῶντες τὴν δικαιοσύνην, cf. Is. 55:1), partly as those who are much disturbed, whether at the poor state of the world or at their own imperfection (Lk. 6:21 κλαίοντες, Mt. 5:4 πενθοῦντες, cf. Is. 61:2 f.). The self-conscious and impenitent rich, and the proud and self-righteous models of piety, are their antithesis, Lk. 18:9. The beatitudes in Mt. which are additional to those of Lk. mention also men whose mind corresponds in content to the higher law of the kingdom of God: ἐλεήμονες, v. 7; καθαροὶ τῇ καρδίᾳ, v. 8; εἰρηνοποιοί, v. 9. Here, too, there is to some degree a contrast with the attitude of the righteous among the Jews. What counts before God is simple pity (Mt. 25:31 ff.) rather than cold knowledge of the Law, purity of heart (Ps. 24:4) rather than self-righteous external purity (Mt. 23:26), unselfish readiness to assist the cause of peace (→ II, 419). The final beatitude in the 2nd person[48] refers the disciples paradoxically to the blessing of being listed among the most honoured of the prophets as a result of persecution. As they remain steadfast in martyrdom they can be sure of the divine reward. The blessing extends also to those who, in distinction from the unsatisfied longing of the upright in days past, may now experience the coming of the kingdom of God (Mt. 13:16 f. and par.).[49] It applies also to those who meet the decisive revelation of God with

---

[45] The simpler Lucan tradition (3 short beatitudes with one longer one in the 2nd person) has become 7 plus 1 in Mt. Mt. 5:5 is open to textual objection.

[46] H. Windisch, *Der Sinn d. Bergpredigt* (1929), 61; Hck. Lk., 83.

[47] Cf. Kittel Probleme, 53 f.; Kl. Mt., 34; W. Sattler, *Die Anawim im Zeitalter Jesu* (1927).

[48] In Mt. the (secondary) penultimate and ultimate, Bultmann Trad., 115.

[49] Cf. Ps. Sol. 17:44.

genuine faith (Lk. 1:45; Mt. 16:17); hence also to those who accept the revelation of God without cavil (Mt. 11:6 and par.) and make no false demands upon it (Jn. 20:29); and to those, too, who bring the true presupposition of faith in readiness to hear the Word of God (Lk. 11:28). As Jesus sets before men the terrible twofold destiny of judgment or salvation, He blesses those who will find a divine reward by steadfast watchfulness (Lk. 12:37 f.; Rev. 16:15), fidelity (Mt. 24:46; Lk. 12:43), or the general fulfilling of Christian requirements (Lk. 14:14; Jn. 13:17). Similarly, those who stand fast are called blessed in Jm. 1:12, for their earthly endurance brings them eternal salvation. The thought of a sure reward is also present when the righteous doer is called blessed in Jm. 1:25. In all these verses the light of future glory shines over the sorry present position of the righteous. Thus the NT beatitudes are not just intimations of the future or consolations in relation to it. They see the present in the light of the future. As the Gk. world often blesses the one who escapes serious misfortune, so women who are unfortunate enough to be childless are called blessed under the threat of impending judgment on Jerusalem (Lk. 23:29). The honour of a woman is most enhanced by great sons, and for this reason the mother of the Messiah is called blessed (Lk. 11:27). In a non-personal use in Ac. 20:35 Christian giving is blessed as compared with selfish receiving.

While there are many beatitudes in the Synoptists, there are hardly any in Paul, nor do Pauline beatitudes have a specific gnomic form. Yet the few Paul has are theologically important. The twofold macarism which he takes from the OT (Ps. 32:1 f.) in R. 4:7 f. calls the man blessed who enjoys remission of sins. This is the blessing of salvation in special measure. In R. 14:22 Paul calls blessed the man who in his decisions on disputed ethical matters has no reason for self-reproach. In a comparison he calls the unmarried blessed because they are spared worldly θλῖψις and can give themselves more wholeheartedly to the Lord, 1 C. 7:40.

Finally, beatitudes figure strongly in Rev. There are 7 as compared with 14 οὐαί,[50] and they have a pronounced gnomic form, and are full of the whole tension which the time just before the end implies for the community. Five of them — and this enhances their force — are from heavenly lips. They thus speak with supreme and indisputable authority (14:13; 16:15; 19:9; 22:7, 14). The whole book stands in the framework of the blessing of those who attain to and keep the blessed revelation of the mysteries of God (1:3 confirmed in 22:7). In 14:13 the witnesses of Christ who will find martyrdom ἀπ' ἄρτι, i.e., from the beginning of the final struggle against the community, are called blessed. Their work, which accompanies the soul to judgment (4 Esr. 7:35), and which in this case is endurance even to death, will receive from God an everlasting reward.[51] Also blessed is the faithful Christian who perseveres in watching and in keeping himself during his time on earth (16:15), esteeming the heavenly promise more highly than all the attractions and apparent treasures of the world. Blessed, too, are those whom God invites to the consummation (19:9). Blessed are those who take part in the first resurrection, and who thus escape final death (20:6). The final macarism is a judicial sentence. In contrast to the wicked who are excluded, it blesses those who in full holiness (forgiveness) and sanctification are counted worthy to enter into the eternal city.

---

[50] Loh. Apk., 181 f.

[51] *Ibid.*, 186 f.; Bousset-Gressm., 285.

2. The purely secular concept of counting someone blessed is found in Ac. 26:2.

3. In the Past. μακάριος is used in a more Gk. and Hellenistic sense (→ 362) to describe the blessed transcendence of God above earthly suffering and corruptibility, 1 Tm. 1:11; 6:15.[52] There is a non-personal use of μακάριος in Tt. 2:13 with reference to Christian hope, which belongs to the sphere of the incorruptible and blessed God.[53]

Hauck

† μάκελλον

"Enclosure," "railing," "fenced place." (The Sicilian place name Μάκελλα denotes a settlement as a protected place.) "Food market." Acc. to Varro, De Lingua Lat., V, 146 (ed. Goetz and Schoell) the word is of Doric-Ionic origin. But modern etymologists suspect that it is Semitic. They trace it back to the Heb. מִכְלָה, "fold," "enclosure," "enclosed place."[1] This seems to be supported by the explanation of Hesych., III, 65: μακέλα· φράγματα δρύφακτοι, μάκελος· δρύφακτος. In the Hell. period the μάκελλον was regarded as essentially Roman. Hahn[2] conjectures that the word passed from Gk. into Lat. and then passed back into Gk. as apparently a Lat. term. However that may be, μάκελλον is of Gk. origin. Borrowing from Lat.[3] can be ruled out, for the word occurs *c.* 400 in Epidauros (on a building inscr. in the temple of Aesculapius of Argolis), GDI, III, 1, 3325, 107; 296; 298; 301.[4] Nevertheless, the Lat. *macellum* appears on Roman inscr. in Italy and Lat. speaking colonies more frequently than the Gk. μάκελλον on Gk. inscr.[5] The Aram. מקולין is to be regarded as a Lat. loan word[6] or a word taken from the *koine*.[7]

In Gk. we find the masc. μάκελλος as well as the neut. μάκελλον, though it is rare as a clear masc., BCH, 20 [1896], 126, line 45 (= Ditt. Syll.³, 783, 45); Schol.[8]

---

[52] Cf. Epicur. in Diog. L., X, 123 (27) → n. 5; for further examples cf. Dib. Past., 15 f. on 1 Tm. 1:11 and 19 on 1 Tm. 1:17.

[53] Cf. μακαριστὰς ἐλπίδας, Ditt. Or., 383, 108.

μάκελλον. [1] So A. Walde, *Lat. Etym. Wörterb.*² (1910), 450 and *Indogermanische Forschungen*, 39 (1921), 82; Moult.-Mill., *s.v.*; H. Lewy, *Die semitischen Fremdworte im Griech.* (1895), 111 f.

[2] L. Hahn, *Rom u. Romanismus im griech.-römischen Osten* (1906), 249, n. 6.

[3] So Bl.-Debr.⁶, 6, n. 2. Debr. now rejects this thesis (in a letter).

[4] Cf. on this A. Cameron, *Amer. Journal of Philology*, 52 (1931), 249 f.

[5] For a good collection of inscr. with the Lat. *macellum* cf. H. Dessau, Inscriptiones Latinae Selectae, II, 1 (1902), No. 5578-5592. Even fuller is the list in K. Schneider, Pauly-W., XIV, 1 (1928), 129 ff.

[6] So S. Krauss, *Gr. u. lat. Lehnwörter im Talmud*, II (1899), 349; *Talmudische Archäol.*, II (1911), 365 f.; Str.-B., III, 420. On the orthography cf. Dalman Wört.², *s.v.*

[7] So Bl.-Debr.⁶, 6, n. 2.

[8] The passage reads: ὁ δὲ κύκλος Ἀθήνησίν ἐστι καθάπερ μάκελλος ἐκ τῆς κατασκευῆς τὴν προσηγορίαν λαβών· ἔνθα δὴ πιπράσκεται χωρὶς κρεῶν τὰ ἄλλα ὤνια, καὶ ἐξαιρέτως δὲ οἱ ἰχθύες.

Aristoph. Eq., 137 (ed. G. Dindorf, IV, 2 [1838], 184); IG, V, 2, 268, 45.[9] The word occurs on Gk. inscr. in Phrygia,[10] Pisidia,[11] Mantinea,[12] and several other cities of Asia Minor[13] and the Gk. mainland.[14]

It is worth noting — and this supports Hahn's thesis (→ n. 2) — that the word is found in only two Gk. authors, Plut. Quaest. Rom., 54 (II, 277d)[15] and Dio C., 61, 18. Dio C. explains it by ἀγορὰ τῶν ὄψων.[16] In Christian Gk. lit. it is first found again only a long time after Paul, Pall. Hist. Laus, 22 (MPG, 34, 1066 D); Socrates, Historia eccl., I, 38 (MPG, 67, 177 A); Asterius of Amasea Homilia XXI in psalm VII (MPG, 40, 473 B). Cf. also a Gk. pap. from Egypt, P. Herm., I, 127, verso 5 (263/4 A.D.) (building account from Hermopolis): Ἁδριανείου καὶ τῆς ἐκ λιβὸς στοᾶς καὶ μακέλλου καὶ στοᾶς ἐκτὸς μακέλλου.[17] In the 6th cent. we find τὸ μακελλάριον (food market), P. Oxy., VI, 1000: τοῦ γεουχικ(οῦ) μακελλαρ(ίου). On an inscr. from the island of Delos, 2nd cent. B.C.: θύρας μακελλωτάς ("grated"), Inscr. Delos (ed. F. Durrbach [1929]), 442 B 238.

The word means not only a meat market but a food market in general. The meat market is part of the μάκελλον. The arrangement of such markets is known to us from excavations.[18] It seems to have been everywhere the same: a rectangular court of pillars with a fountain in the middle and over it, supported by the pillars, a dome-shaped roof (Tholus); the booths on the sides; before them porticos. In Pompeii there was found on the narrow east side a chapel of the imperial cult adorned with statues; to the south-east there was probably a room for sacrificial repasts.[19]

It is most significant that the account of Paul in 1 C. 10:25 is confirmed by a Lat. inscr. found in Corinth which contains the word *macellum*.[20] Acc. to the researches of H. J. Cadbury[21] this *macellum* existed in the days of Paul.[22]

---

[9] Acc. to Liddell-Scott, *s.v.* the masc. also occurs in P. Lond. ined., 2487, 43 (cf. also ὁ μακελλάριος, Aesop, ed. C. Halm [1868], 134). In modern Gk. the word is used in the masc. Cf. G. Meyer, *Neugriech. Studien,* III. *Die lat. Lehnworte im Neugriech. Sitzungsberichte d. Wiener Akademie, phil.-hist. Kl.,* 132 (1895), 41: μάκελλος, "slaughter-house." In Lat. the masc. *macellus* is found in Mart., X, 96, 9; also L. Pomponius Fr., 38 (O. Ribbeck, Comicorum Romanorum Fragmenta, II³ [1898], 276).

[10] BCH, 17 (1893), 261, line 45: ἡ γερουσία τὰ ζυγοστάσια πρὸς τῷ μακέλλῳ ἐκ τῶν ἰδίων ποιήσαντα (Phrygia).

[11] *V.* on this K. Lanckoronski, *D. Städte Pamphyliens u. Pisidiens,* II (1892), No. 250, line 4 (inscr. from Selge: μα]κέλου).

[12] BCH, 20 (1896), 126, line 45 (μάκελλος ἐκ θεμελίων ὑψοῦτο πολυτελής) = Ditt. Syll.³, 783, 45; IG, V, 2, 268, 45.

[13] Inscr. Magn., 179, 21.

[14] IG, IV, 2, 102 and 107 (Epidaurus); IG, V, 1, 149, 7 (Sparta).

[15] Διὰ τί τὰ κρεοπώλια 'μάκελλα' καὶ 'μακέλλας' καλοῦσι;

[16] Τότε μὲν δὴ τοσαῦτα σωτήρια, ὡς δὴ ἔλεγεν, ἑώρτασε, καὶ τὴν ἀγορὰν τῶν ὄψων, τὸ μάκελλον ὠνομασμένον καθιέρωσε.

[17] Cf. on this C. Wessely, *Die lat. Elemente in d. Gräzität d. ägyptischen Pap.-Urkunden, Wiener Studien,* 24 (1902), 138.

[18] Cf. on this Pauly-W., XIV, 1 (1928), 129 ff. (K. Schneider): *macellum.* On the *macellum* in Pompeii, A. Mau, *Pompeji in Leben u. Kunst* (1900), 85 ff.

[19] The plan of the *macellum* in Pompeii is also sketched by Lietzmann 1 K., 52.

[20] *Corinth. Results of Excavations conducted by the American School of Classical Studies at Athens,* VIII, 2: Lat. Inscr. (1896-1926), ed. A. B. West, Cambridge (Mass.) (1931), 100 ff., No. 124 and 125. The Lat. word shows that Corinth, a Roman colony, bore a strong Roman impress.

[21] "The Macellum of Corinth," JBL, 53 (1934), 134 ff. Cadbury gives an express account of the results of the excavations.

[22] *Ibid.,* 140 f. The Q. Maecius mentioned on inscr. 124 belongs to the early imperial period, so J. Geffcken, Pauly-W., XIV, 1 (1928). Acc. to Cadbury, *op. cit.,* 138, n. 14 the date is in any case prior to 40 A.D.

In 1 C. 10:25 Paul gives directions how Christians are to act in relation to the meat which was sold on the market and which might well have come from pagan temples. In a city like Corinth it is likely that very little other meat was available.[23] Paul forbids enquiry into the origin of the meat lest the consciences of Christians be unnecessarily burdened.[24]

J. Schneider

† μακράν, † μακρόθεν

μακράν is an adv. acc. construction used both of space and time; ὁδόν should be supplied. μακρόθεν is an adv. of location in -θεν; it is not used of time. The prep. ἀπό is prefixed for this old form of the question "whence" to strengthen analytically what the suffix -θεν suggests synthetically.[1] a. As an adv. of place: μακράν, "far off," Aesch. Prom., 312: μακρὰν ἀνωτέρω θακῶν, Soph. Oed. Tyr., 16; Phil., 42: προσβαίη μακράν, Plat. Leg., VI, 753a: μακρὰν ἀποικοῦσιν; Xenoph. An., III, 4, 17; P. Zen. (Preisigke Wört.), 59605, 3: οὐ μακράν σου ἀπέχομεν ("to be a long way off"), 59647, 13: ὅπως μὴ μακρὰν ὦμεν ἀπεσπασμένοι ἀπὸ σοῦ. μακρόθεν, "from afar," Chrysipp. Athen. IV (p. 137 f.); Strabo, III, 3, 4: μακρόθεν τε ῥέων παρὰ Νομαντίαν, Epict. Diss., I, 16, 11: μακρόθεν κέκραγεν ἡμῶν ἑκάστου ἡ φύσις, Ael. Nat. An., 15, 12; P. Tebt., 230. μακράν with gen., Eur. Iph. Taur., 629; Polyb., 3, 50, 8. b. Adv. of time: μακράν, Soph. El., 323: ἐπεὶ τἄν οὐ μακρὰν ἔζων ἐγώ, Eur. Med., 1158: μακρὰν ἀπεῖναι, Xenoph. Cyrop., V, 4, 21: οὐκ εἰς μακράν. With ref. to speeches it then comes to mean "verbose": μακρὰν λέγειν, τείνειν, Aesch. Ag., 1296. Finally, μακράν is used as a prep.: μακράν τινος, P. Oxy., I, 113, 18. c. οὐ μακράν as a term for the nearness of God, Dio Chrys. Or., 12, 28 (I, 162, 10 ff., ed. J. v. Arnim [1893]): ἅτε γὰρ οὐ μακρὰν οὐδ' ἔξω τοῦ θείου διῳκισμένοι καθ' ἑαυτούς, ἀλλὰ ἐν αὐτῷ μέσῳ πεφυκότες, μᾶλλον δὲ συμπεφυκότες ἐκείνῳ καὶ προσεχόμενοι πάντα τρόπον, οὐκ ἐδύναντο μέχρι πλείονος ἀξύνετοι μένειν.

In the LXX both words are used first a. in the spatial sense: μακράν, Gn. 44:4; Nu. 9:10; Is. 27:9; Prv. 2:16; 13:19; Sir. 13:10 etc.; μακρὰν ἀπό is very common, Dt. 13:8; 14:24; 20:15 (ἀπὸ σοῦ); Ju. 18:7; ψ 118:155 (μακρὰν ἀπὸ ἁμαρτωλῶν); μακρὰν ἀπέχειν, Jl. 3:8; Ez. 22:5 (ταῖς μακρὰν ἀπεχούσαις ἀπὸ σοῦ); 1 Macc. 8:4. μακρόθεν, Gn. 21:16; 22:4; 1 Βασ. 26:13; ψ 137:6; Is. 60:4 etc. As we read ἕως εἰς γῆν μακράν in Mi. 4:3, so ἐκ γῆς μακρόθεν in 2 Ch. 6:32; Jer. 4:16; 8:19; ἀπὸ μακρόθεν ἔστησαν, ψ 37:11, also ἀφέστηκας μακρόθεν ψ 9:21. There is then a special use of μακρόθεν for standing clear of holy places where God appears, Ex. 20:18: φοβηθέντες δὲ πᾶς ὁ λαὸς ἔστησαν μακρόθεν, 20:21; 24:1: προσκυνήσουσιν μακρόθεν τῷ κυρίῳ.

Fig. both terms are used for the remoteness of God, ψ 9:21: ἵνα τί, κύριε, ἀφέστηκας μακρόθεν, or the fact that salvation (Is. 59:11) or righteousness (Is. 59:14) is far off; or they may refer to man's distance from God, Jer. 2:5: ἀπέστησαν μακρὰν ἀπ'

---

[23] So Joh. W. 1 K., 263.
[24] Cf. on this Schl. 1 K., 303; Ltzm. K., 51 f.

μακράν. [1] K. Dieterich, "Untersuchungen zur Geschichte d. griech. Sprache," *Byzantinisches Archiv*, 1 (1898), 183 f.

ἐμοῦ,[2] or from righteousness, Is. 46:12: οἱ μακρὰν ἀπὸ τῆς δικαιοσύνης. In Dt. 30:11 μακράν has the sense of "unattainable": ἡ ἐντολὴ ... οὐδὲ μακρὰν ἀπὸ σοῦ. The opp. is ἐγγύς, Is. 57:19; Ez. 6:12; Est. 9:20. μακράν is often used in an ethical and religious sense in the Wisdom lit. in admonition to remain aloof from sin, Prv. 4:24; 5:8; Sir. 15:8. The sinner feels that he is far from God, ψ 21:1; salvation is far from sinners, ψ 118:155; God holds aloof from sinners, Prv. 15:29. b. For time μακράν is almost always used, 2 Βασ. 7:19 (εἰς μακράν); Sir. 16:22; Ἱερ. 36:28: μακράν ἐστιν ("it lasts a long time yet"); Ez. 12:22: μακρὰν αἱ ἡμέραι ("the days are prolonged"). μακρόθεν is found for time ("from of old") only once at 4 Βασ. 19:25 in the reading of Orig. c. μακράν is used as a prep. with the gen. in Sir. 15:8. Joseph., too, has μακράν both of space (Ant., 8, 108, God is present in the temple [πάρει καὶ μακρὰν οὐκ ἀφέστηκας]) and of time (Ant., 6, 278, οὐκ εἰς μακράν, "in brief"; 20, 153).

In the NT μακράν and μακρόθεν are used 1. in the original sense adverbially to denote place, Mt. 8:30: ἦν δὲ μακρὰν ἀπ' αὐτῶν ἀγέλη χοίρων πολλῶν βοσκομένη. In Jn. 21:8 it is said of the disciples on the lake: οὐ γὰρ ἦσαν μακρὰν ἀπὸ τῆς γῆς. In Ac. 22:21, in the account of Paul's conversion, the apostle's mission is εἰς ἔθνη μακράν. Similarly μακρόθεν is an indication of place in Mk. 11:13: ἰδὼν συκῆν ἀπὸ μακρόθεν. It is also recounted of the Gadarene demoniac in Mk. 5:6: καὶ ἰδὼν τὸν Ἰησοῦν ἀπὸ μακρόθεν. In Mk. 8:3 we read of the 4000 gathered around Jesus: καί τινες αὐτῶν ἀπὸ μακρόθεν εἰσίν. Of Peter it is said in Mk. 14:54 that he followed Jesus ἀπὸ μακρόθεν into the court of the high-priest; Lk. has μακρόθεν at 22:54, and Mt., too, uses [ἀπὸ] μακρόθεν in this scene (26:58). It will be noted that Mk. normally has ἀπό.[3]

2. In a figurative sense ἀπὸ μακρόθεν occurs in Mk. 15:40 = Mt. 27:55 = Lk. 23:49. While some around the cross express scorn and hatred, the women stand afar off. This is not out of fear. According to the picture given in the Synoptics, they stand afar off because they cannot join the mockers, and can be witnesses of the crucifixion only at a distance and silently. Thus ἀπὸ μακρόθεν does not so much fix their location as express the pious awe and sense of distance which grips the women when they are confronted by what God does at the cross. Reverence and pious adoration demand distance and quiet. Lk. 16:23 points in the same direction. It is said of the rich man: καὶ ἐν τῷ ᾅδῃ ἐπάρας τοὺς ὀφθαλμοὺς αὐτοῦ, ... ὁρᾷ Ἀβραὰμ ἀπὸ μακρόθεν. Here the phrase ἀπὸ μακρόθεν depicts in a spatial image the great cleft between heaven and hell. Similarly, the ἀπὸ μακρόθεν of Rev. 18:10, 15, 17 expresses the numinous horror felt by the kings of the earth, the merchants, the shipmasters, the sailors and the fishermen when they see the judgment of God on Babylon. Only from afar dare they watch the burning of the great city, for God's judgment on their own conduct is herein declared. The sense of distance is very strongly present in the μακρόθεν of Lk. 18:13, as the continuation proves. The publican in the sanctuary stands afar off from the altar and the worshippers, and dare not lift up his eyes to heaven. Even in this metaphorical sense Lk. can leave out the ἀπό, whereas Mt. and Mk. always use it with μακρόθεν.

μακράν, too, can be used figuratively. In the LXX it expresses the remoteness of God and His salvation from sinful man. In the NT, however, οὐ μακράν (cf.

---

[2] Ez. 11:15: μακρὰν ἀπέχετε ἀπὸ τοῦ κυρίου, has in view distance from the holy land as the dwelling-place of Yahweh.

[3] If at Lk. 7:6 we are to read αὐτοῦ οὐ μακρὰν ἀπέχοντος τῆς οἰκίας with ℵ D λ φ, μακράν is here used as a prep.

Dio C. → 372) is often used to denote the overcoming of the separation between God and man. In Mk. 12:34 Jesus says to the scribe that he is not far from the kingdom of God. In Lk. 15:20 the spatial distance of the son from the father is emphasised merely for the sake of showing how anxious the father is to overcome the spiritual as well as the spatial distance. In Ac. 17:27 the national orders of creation are established in order that men should seek after God, and this presupposes that God is οὐ μακρὰν ἀπὸ ἑνὸς ἑκάστου ἡμῶν. In Eph. 2:13 Gentile Christians are reminded of God's gift that those who were once far from God, οἵ ποτε ὄντες μακράν, have been brought near to Him by Christ and become His children. In Eph. 2:17, which sets Is. 57:19 in the context of salvation history (→ 373), the Gentiles are told that to them, who are far from God (τοῖς μακράν), Christ brought peace and salvation no less than to the Jews, so that the distant and the near, Gentile and Jewish Christians, experience as the great mystery of God through Christ their union into the new people of God. Cf. the allusion to Is. 57:19 in Ac. 2:39. Thus μακρόθεν and μακράν, when used metaphorically, are terms which express the *numinosum* and *fascinosum* of faith.

Preisker

† μακροθυμία, † μακροθυμέω, † μακρόθυμος, † μακροθύμως

Contents: A. Occurrence and Meaning in non-biblical Greek. B. The Theological Significance of the Terms in the OT (LXX) and Later Judaism. C. The Rabbis. D. μακροθυμ- in the New Testament: 1. Synoptic Gospels; 2. Paul: a. The Longsuffering of God; b. The Longsuffering of the Christian; c. The Pastorals; 3. The Catholic Epistles: a. James; b. Hebrews; c. 1 Peter; d. 2 Peter.

A. Occurrence and Meaning in non-biblical Greek.

Other words formed with → θυμός are found fairly early, e.g., μεγάθυμος from the time of Homer,[1] and ὀξύθυμος, which forms something of an antonym

---

μακροθυμία κτλ. Cr.-Kö., *s.v.*; also Thes. Steph., Pass., Pape, Liddell-Scott, Moult.-Mill., G. Abbott-Smith, *A Manual Greek Lexicon of the NT*[2] (1923); Pr.-Bauer[3], Wilke-Grimm; F. Zorell, Lexicon Graecum Novi Testamenti[2] (1931); A. Konstantinides, Μέγα Λεξικὸν τῆς Ἑλληνικῆς Γλώσσης, III (1904); Sophocles Lex.; Schleusner. The word is not found in Phryn. or Suid. Cf. also the art. "Langmut" in D. Schenkel's *Bibel-lexikon*, IV (1872), "Geduld" in RE[3] and RGG[2], "Langmut Gottes" in *Bibl. Reallexikon* (E. Kalt, 1931), "Geduld" in Jüd. Lex. W. Meikle, "The Vocabulary of Patience in the OT," Exp. 8th Ser., Vol. XIX (1920), 219 ff.; "The Vocabulary of Patience in the NT," *ibid.*, 304 ff. ERE, *s.v.* "Longsuffering." On the etym. of → μακρός, which is a suffix construction in *-ro, -rā*, and which gives us the Old High German *magar, mager*, cf. K. Brugmann-A. Thumb, *Griech. Grammatik* = Handbuch KlAW, II, 1[4] (1913), 227; H. Hirt, *Handbuch d. gr. Laut- u. Formenlehre* (1902), 252. On the etym. of θυμός → III, 167.

[1] Cf. H. Ebeling, *Lexicon Homericum*, I (1885), 1025 *s.v.* μεγάθυμος, "high-minded."

for μακρόθυμος, from the tragic poets.[2] But μακρόθυμος and its derivates are comparatively late in the non-biblical Gk. world, and they are also rare.

When μακροθυμία occurs first in Menand., it is not without a certain element of "resignation" or forced "acceptance." For men, as distinct from the blessedness of the gods who know no suffering, the only option is μακροθυμία, the patience which must be resigned: ἄνθρωπος ὢν μηδέποτε τὴν ἀλυπίαν | αἰτοῦ παρὰ θεῶν, ἀλλὰ τὴν μακροθυμίαν. | ὅταν γὰρ ἄλυπος διὰ τέλους εἶναι θέλῃς, | ἢ δεῖ θεόν σ' εἶναί τιν' ἢ τάχα δὴ νεκρόν. | παρηγόρει δὲ τὰ κακὰ δι' ἑτέρων κακῶν.[3]

In Strabo μακροθυμία has the sense of desperate patience which in the supreme emergency of siege leaves no stone unturned to try to stave off the inevitable end: ἐθαύμαζεν, ὡς ἔοικεν, ὁ Ἀννίβας τῆς μακροθυμίας.[4]

In Artemid. μακροθυμία and μακροθυμεῖν are used in a context which suggests delay or procrastination, the putting off of an action, μακροθυμεῖν καὶ μὴ κενοσπουδεῖν,[5] μακροθυμίας καὶ παρολκῆς.[6]

μακροθυμίη (Ionic) is found in Aret.[7] in a good sense for the patience and endurance of the physician in treating severe chronic illnesses with only doubtful hopes of a cure.

Similarly in Plut. it is used of the steadfastness of the general or soldier in putting up with hardships, i.e., "endurance" until a goal is reached.[8]

The verb μακροθυμεῖν is found in the same sense when those engaged in the battle of life are compared to swimmers in the sea who seek safety on the shore: αὐτοὺς ἐξαμιλλᾶσθαι καὶ μακροθυμεῖν, δι' οἰκείας πειρωμένους ἀρετῆς σῴζεσθαι καὶ τυγχάνειν λιμένος.[9]

It is worth noting that μακροθυμία is not found in the Stoics.[10] Yet it does occur once in Marc. Aurel., where part of the ideal of him who is ὀλίγοις ἀρκούμενος is to be φιλόπονος καὶ μακρόθυμος, i.e., "persevering in his work."[11]

---

[2] E.g., Aesch. Eum., 705. Also Eur., Aristoph., cf. Thes. Steph., *s.v.* ὀξύθυμος, ὀξυθυμία, ὀξυθυμέω "to be irritable." Πραΰθυμος is first found in Christian authors. Thes. Steph., *s.v.*, also ὀλιγοθυμέω, which is used by Eustath. Thessal. to explain a Homeric ὀλιγηπελέω thereby: ἀγείρει δὲ θυμὸν ὁ ὀλιγοθυμήσας, Comm. in Il., 15, 240 (III, p. 264, 28, Stallbaum).

[3] Fr., 549, CAF, III, 167.

[4] Geographica (ed. C. Müller-F. Dübner [1853]), V, 4, 10, p. 249. But here μακροθυμία attains its goal. A rather derogatory sense is still found in an epigram of Palladas (4th cent. A.D.) where a stubborn donkey is called μακρόθυμος υἱὸς τῆς βραδυτῆτος, Anth. Pal., XI, 317.

[5] Oneirocr., IV, 11.

[6] *Ibid.*, II, 25.

[7] Aret., III, 1 in CMG, II, p. 36, 12.

[8] Lucull., 32 (I, 514a): ἀξιῶν αὐτοὺς μακροθυμίαν ἐμβαλέσθαι ταῖς ψυχαῖς. *Ibid.*, 33 (I, 514c): ἀρετὴν μὲν ἀπεδείκνυτο καὶ μακροθυμίαν ἡγεμόνος ἀγαθοῦ. Joseph. uses the word in exactly the same way when he puts it on the lips of Titus in an address to his soldiers to kindle them to steadfastness by the example of the Jews: ἡ Ἰουδαίων μακροθυμία καὶ τὸ καρτερικὸν ἐν οἷς κακοπαθοῦσιν, Bell., 6, 37.

[9] Gen. Socr., 24 (II, 593 f.).

[10] Cf. the index to v. Arnim. Concepts like καρτερία and ὑπομονή may be found, and μεγαλοψυχία, if not μακροθυμία, figures in their lists of virtues. This sheds a significant light on the estimation of μακροθυμία in the total Stoic view.

[11] M. Ant., VI, 30, 10, cf. *ibid.*, 7: ὡς ἐπ' οὐδὲν ἔσπευδεν. An addition: ... καὶ οἷος εἶ μακροθυμεῖν in Epict. Ench., 12, 2 is rejected by Schenkl as a Christian paraphrase. Hence the word is not in Epict.

B. The Theological Significance of the Terms in the Old Testament (LXX) and Later Judaism.

The word takes on a distinctive depth in biblical usage. Quite literally the Gk. Bible translates the Heb. הֶאֱרִיךְ אַף and אֶרֶךְ אַפַּיִם, "to delay his wrath, i.e., its outbreak," "to be longsuffering," [12] by μακροθυμέω, μακρόθυμος and μακροθυμία. [13] Already in the Torah, in statements concerning God's dealings with His people, including His אֶרֶךְ אַפַּיִם, [14] the self-revelation of the glory of God gives basic significance to the biblical usage: κύριος ὁ θεὸς οἰκτίρμων καὶ ἐλεήμων, μακρόθυμος καὶ πολυέλεος καὶ ἀληθινὸς καὶ δικαιοσύνην διατηρῶν κτλ., Ex. 34:6 f. μακροθυμία can no longer be used in detachment to denote a human attitude. The divine attitude, God's dealings with men, have become the content indissolubly linked with μακροθυμία, so that even the human attitude of μακροθυμεῖν is set in a new light. [15] The majestic God, whose wrath Israel must recognise as soon as it experiences the revelation of God, [16] surprisingly attests Himself to the people as the God who will restrain this wrath and cause His grace and lovingkindness to rule. The wrath and the grace of God are the two poles which constitute the span of His longsuffering. [17]

The set formula of Ex. 34:6 echoes again and again through the biblical writings and into later Judaism. [18]

The μακροθυμία of God is displayed in His saving work for Israel and thus finds soteriological confirmation, cf. Wis. 15:1 ff., [19] where the predicate of longsuffering is linked with the confession: "We are thine even though we have sinned; for σὺ δέ, ὁ θεὸς ἡμῶν ... μακρόθυμος καὶ ἐλέει διοικῶν τὰ πάντα. καὶ γὰρ ἐὰν ἁμάρτωμεν, σοί ἐσμεν, and where this confirmation clearly demarcates from the fate of idolaters who perish. In post-exilic Judaism, however, the μακροθυμία of God is also based on more general considerations as to the shortness of human life and the weakness of the race, whose few years are a mere drop in the bucket compared with the eternity of God. For this reason the mercy of God ἐπὶ πᾶσαν σάρκα is affirmed: διὰ τοῦτο ἐμακροθύμησεν κύριος ἐπ' αὐτοῖς. [20] His μακροθυμία consists in His forgiveness (ἐξιλασμός), for He sees the misery of man's final end. [21]

---

[12] Ges.-Buhl, *s.v.* from ארך, "to be long," hi "to make long," "to draw out at length." Cf. also the dict, of J. Fürst, I (1857) and E. König [2, 3] (1922), *s.v.* Also *s.v.* ארך (adj.), אֶרֶךְ אַפַּיִם also אֶרֶךְ רוּחַ (e.g., Qoh. 7:8). For further examples, *loc. cit.* Also אֹרֶךְ (subst.).

[13] Hatch-Redp., *s.v.*, with Suppl., *s.v.* ארך and derivates. At Job 6:11 (אאריך נפשי), where the LXX has ἀνέχεταί μου ἡ ψυχή, 'A finely renders μακροθυμήσω. At Is. 57:15 the LXX understands שפל רוח as the gift of salvation along the lines of ταπεινοφροσύνη, and translates ὀλιγοψύχοις διδοὺς μακροθυμίαν.

[14] Acc. relationis, cf. B. Baentsch, *Ex.-Lv.-Nu.* (1903), on Ex. 34:6. Cf. also the opp. in Mi. 2:7, where the possibility of divine impatience is rejected: הֲקָצַר רוּחַ יהוה, "Is Yahweh impatient?" But the people can be said to become impatient: καὶ ὠλιγοψύχησεν ὁ λαὸς ἐν τῇ ὁδῷ, Nu. 21:4.

[15] Thus a word which is not very significant in secular Gk. takes on a new and unexpectedly profound significance. Cf. Deissmann LO, 61 on the linguistic creativity of early Christianity; the same is true of the LXX.

[16] Ex. 19:12; cf. Hb. 12:18 ff.

[17] ἔλεος γὰρ καὶ ὀργὴ παρ' αὐτῷ, Sir. 5:6, cf. 4; Nah. 1:2 ff.; Prayer of Man. 7 and 10 etc.

[18] Nu. 14:18; ψ 85:15; 102:8; Jl. 2:13; Jon. 4:2; 2 Εσδρ. 19:17; Σιρ. 2:11 S; Prayer of Man. 7; 4 Esr. 7:33 (*longanimus*). Cf. also Bousset-Gressm., 383 and n. 4.

[19] Esp. 16:1 ff.-19:12.

[20] Sir. 18:8 ff., 11, 13.

[21] *Ibid.* 12 (cf. A. Eberharter, *Das Buch Jesus Sir.* ... [1925], *ad loc.*).

This is perhaps the bridge which, esp. in the Wisdom lit., leads to the requirement of μακροθυμία from man too. Man should pity his neighbour (πλησίον), though naturally the mercy of God is infinitely more extensive (ἐπὶ πᾶσαν σάρκα).[22] Man should not allow his anger to break forth. He should restrain it,[23] considering the work of God. To be sure, it often seems that a purely rational basis is given for longsuffering. It is extolled as a quality of the prudent, esp. in the proverbs of Solomon[24] and in Sirach.[25] Nevertheless, it is commanded by Yahweh, and what is demanded of the wise man is already done to him,[26] even though the idea of the saving power of a good work seems to obtrude.[27]

Occasionally μακροθυμία still has a secular sense in allusion to the warlike virtue of Roman endurance, 1 Macc. 8:4.[28]

Yet there is no relaxing of the immanent tension between wrath and mercy. In Ex. 34:6 f. already the declaration of μακρόθυμος does not mean the complete end of wrath. There is no overlooking or renouncing.[29] As in the Heb. original, the καὶ ποιῶν ἔλεος is accompanied by a καὶ οὐ καθαριεῖ τὸν ἔνοχον ἐπάγων ἀνομίας πατέρων ἐπὶ τέκνα κτλ.[30] In biblical usage μακροθυμεῖν does not imply renunciation of the grounds for wrath. What it does mean is that alongside this wrath there is a divine restraint which postpones its operation[31] until something takes place in man which justifies the postponement. If this new attitude does not eventuate, then wrath is fully visited: κύριός ἐστιν μακρόθυμος ... ἔλεος γὰρ καὶ ὀργὴ παρ' αὐτῷ.[32]

We find these two aspects close together in Nah. 1:2 ff. as well: God is μετὰ θυμοῦ[33] (→ θυμός) and μακρόθυμος. θεὸς ζηλωτὴς καὶ ἐκδικῶν κύριος, ἐκδικῶν κύριος μετὰ θυμοῦ ... κύριος μακρόθυμος, καὶ μεγάλη ἡ ἰσχὺς αὐτοῦ. For the one to whom it is revealed this means that he is required to repent ἐπιστρά-

---

[22] *Ibid.* 13. Cf. the model in Egyptian ethics, where special stress is laid on meeting the angry with silence: "God will know how to answer him," or: "Put yourself in the arms of God, and your silence will overthrow your opponents" etc. A. Erman, *Die Religion d. Ägypter* (1934), 162 f.

[23] Qoh. 7:8 ff.

[24] Prv. 14:29 f. (corresponding to πραΰθυμος → n. 2); 15:18, where the ἀνὴρ θυμώδης is the opp. of the μακρόθυμος; 16:32: κρείσσων ... μακρόθυμος ἰσχυροῦ, and 17:27: μακρόθυμος ἀνὴρ φρόνιμος. Here the LXX prefers the religious μακρόθυμος to "cold-blooded" (קַר רוּחַ). Cf. also 25:15.

[25] Sir. 1:23; 5:11: ἐν μακροθυμίᾳ φθέγγου ἀπόκρισιν (cf. the conjectures of Kautzsch Apkr., *ad loc.* on the original Heb.).

[26] Prv. 19:11: ἐλεήμων ἀνὴρ μακροθυμεῖ, cf. v. 17: δανίζει θεῷ ὁ ἐλεῶν πτωχόν. Sir. 29:8 f.: ἐπὶ ταπεινῷ μακροθύμησον ... χάριν ἐντολῆς ἀντιλαβοῦ πένητος.

[27] Sir. 29:12 f.

[28] κατεκράτησαν [οἱ 'Ρωμαῖοι] τοῦ τόπου παντὸς τῇ βουλῇ αὐτῶν καὶ τῇ μακροθυμίᾳ. Cf. Joseph.'s use in the same sense, Bell., 6, 37 (→ n. 8).

[29] This is true in spite of the strange statement in Wis. 11:23: παρορᾷς ἁμαρτήματα ἀνθρώπων εἰς μετάνοιαν; for against this should be set μετ' ὀργῆς κρινόμενοι ἀσεβεῖς in v. 9.

[30] וְנַקֵּה לֹא יְנַקֶּה, cf. also Nu. 14:18.

[31] ψ 7:11: ὁ θεὸς κριτὴς δίκαιος καὶ ἰσχυρὸς καὶ μακρόθυμος μὴ ὀργὴν ἐπάγων καθ' ἑκάστην ἡμέραν. Here the LXX reverses the sense of the original by taking אל as a negation and adding μακρόθυμος. The Mas. reads: "God is a just judge, and a God who chides every day."

[32] Sir. 5:4 ff. Thus there can be no presuming on God's patience for continuing in sin: μὴ εἴπῃς· ἥμαρτον, καὶ τί μοι ἐγένετο;

[33] The deliberate echoing of θυμός ("wrath") in μακρόθυμος is to be noted, cf. also Test. D. 2:1.

φητε πρὸς κύριον τὸν θεὸν ὑμῶν ὅτι ... μακρόθυμος ..., Jl. 2:13.[34] And the new attitude to which man is brought by the μακροθυμία of God will show itself on the one hand in the fact that he himself exercises μακροθυμία towards his neighbour,[35] and on the other hand in the fact that he will learn to understand the affliction and suffering in which he stands as a πειρασμός which instructs him in μακροθυμία and brings him to faith.[36]

Thus μακροθυμεῖν is a gift of God, not an arbitrary cultivation of the virtue of self-control.[37]

Now it may be that the breadth of God's μακροθυμία, which is subject only to His own sovereignty, awakens opposition in those who want God to intervene, as in Jer. 15:15, where the prophet, at the end of his resources, beseeches God to take vengeance in wrath on his persecutors μὴ εἰς μακροθυμίαν,[38] for otherwise he fears that he will succumb to them. The Book of Jonah is a unique reply to the opposition of particularist Judaism to the universal sweep of the μακροθυμία which God exercises even in respect of the Gentiles.[39] In 2 Macc. 6:14 ff. it is shown that God's μακροθυμία is displayed for a time to the nations (ἀναμένει μακροθυμῶν) until His punishment falls when they have filled up the measure of their sins, whereas in the case of Israel He already sends corrective punishments in order that His vengeance may not fall when sin has run its length, ἵνα μὴ ... ὕστερον ἡμᾶς ἐκδικᾷ.

This passage shows how the post-exilic concept of retribution is in danger of preventing the sovereignty of God's μακροθυμία, exercised in ἔλεος and ὀργή, from being taken with full seriousness.[40] This is clear in Sir.[41] 35(32):19 f.: καὶ ὁ κύριος οὐ μὴ βραδύνῃ οὐδὲ μὴ μακροθυμήσῃ ἐπ' αὐτοῖς, ἕως ἂν συντρίψῃ ὀσφὺν ἀνελεημόνων καὶ τοῖς ἔθνεσιν ἀνταποδώσει ἐκδίκησιν.[42] In Da. Θ 4:27 ff. the longsuffering of God is a reward for corresponding good works on the part of man: καὶ τὰς ἁμαρτίας σου ἐν ἐλεημοσύναις λύτρωσαι καὶ τὰς ἀδικίας σου ἐν οἰκτιρμοῖς πενήτων· ἴσως ἔσται μακρόθυμος τοῖς παραπτώμασίν σου ὁ θεός.[43]

Thus the data in the OT and LXX show that in the struggle to understand God's μακροθυμία there is always an unresolved uncertainty[44] whether it will finally serve to deliver the man who in prayer tries to seek refuge in it. Wrath

---

[34] Cf. also ψ 7:12 f.

[35] Cf. Sir. 18:13; Qoh. 7:8 f.

[36] Sir. 2:1, 4, 6: ἑτοίμασον τὴν ψυχήν σου εἰς πειρασμόν ... ἐν ἀλλάγμασιν ταπεινώσεώς σου μακροθύμησον ... πίστευσον αὐτῷ, καὶ ἀντιλήμψεταί σου. Cf. Ιωβ 7:16 (*v.* B. Duhm, *Das Buch Hi.* [1897], *ad loc.*): Job will not be patient any longer. Test. Jos. 2:7: ἐν δέκα πειρασμοῖς δόκιμον ἀπέδειξέ με, καὶ ἐν πᾶσιν αὐτοῖς ἐμακροθύμησα· ὅτι μέγα φάρμακόν ἐστι ἡ μακροθυμία καὶ πολλὰ ἀγαθὰ δίδωσιν ἡ ὑπομονή.

[37] Is. 57:15. The opp. here is ὀλιγόψυχος. Cf. Cr.-Kö., *s.v.* μακροθυμία.

[38] Cf. the comm. of B. Duhm (1901) and P. Volz[2] (1928), *ad loc.*

[39] Jon. 4:2. Cf. B. Stade-A. Bertholet, *Bibl. Theol. d. AT,* II[1,2] (1911), 154 f.

[40] Thus it can even be said in Bar. 4:25: τέκνα, μακροθυμήσατε τὴν παρὰ τοῦ θεοῦ ἐπελθοῦσαν ὑμῖν ὀργήν. In view of the retribution which will shortly fall (ἀπώλειαν ἐν τάχει) on the enemies of Sion, the righteous can endure God's wrath with patience.

[41] Cf. Stade-Bertholet, II, 189.

[42] Cf. 2:11.

[43] Cf. also Test. D. 2:1: ἐὰν μὴ φυλάξητε ἑαυτοὺς ἀπὸ τοῦ πνεύματος τοῦ ψεύδους καὶ τοῦ θυμοῦ, καὶ ἀγαπήσητε τὴν ἀλήθειαν καὶ τὴν μακροθυμίαν, ἀπολεῖσθε. (Here it should be noted how θυμός re-echoes in μακροθυμία in the juxtaposition of the two.)

[44] This is not a subjective "disharmony of moods" (Bousset-Gressm., 384); it is objectively grounded.

and grace? Wrath or grace? Will God really show the righteous a σημεῖον εἰς ἀγαθόν?[45]

It is almost inevitable that in the use of μακροθυμεῖν in later Judaism there should come in from secular thought an element which weakens it. There are perhaps traces of this in Prv. In Ep. Ar. the king is advised to strengthen his reign by clever complaisance and mild punishments μιμούμενος τὸ τοῦ θεοῦ διὰ παντὸς ἐπιεικές· μακροθυμίᾳ γὰρ χρώμενος ... But the μακροθυμία of God is not an ἐπιεικέστερον.[46] While this has a pious ring, it comes from a very different world.

C. The Rabbis.

Among the Rabb. individual aspects of μακροθύμια are distinctively expounded. In an exposition based on Jl. 2:13, where the plur. אֶרֶךְ אַפַּיִם suggests one longsuffering towards the righteous and another towards the ungodly, R. Chanina attacks the view that longsuffering is indulgence. "He who says that the Almighty is indulgent, may he perish; the Almighty is longsuffering, but he exacts his due" (jTaan., 65b, 49 f.).[47] Acc. to bJoma, 69b (Str.-B., III, 77 f.) it is a particular merit of the men of the great synagogue that they re-established the predicates of God as great, strong and terrible (Dt. 10:17). "His greatness is seen in the fact that he suppresses his impulse (to destroy) and makes longsuffering a portion of the ungodly, and these are the proofs of his terribleness," cf. Wis. 11:23; 12:16. Also worth noting is the discussion of the question why God exercises patience towards the ungodly in this world, and the answer of R. Joshiyya: 1. They might repent; 2. they might keep the commandments, so that God will give them their reward in this world; 3. they might produce righteous sons (Qoh. r. on 7:15, Str.-B., III, 78). There are signs of a casuistical reduction of the unrestricted sovereignty of God by calculation of the measure of God's grace in terms of the weighing of merit and guilt (cf. Str.-B., III, 78 on R. 2:6). Indeed, an attempt can even be made casuistically to set a limit to God's patience, Gn. r., 26 on 6:2 (cf. Schl. Mt. on 18:26) עַל הַכֹּל ה׳ מַאֲרִיךְ אַפּוֹ חוּץ מִן הַזְּנוּת. Also important are the concepts which make of God's patience an obligation: "So should you display longsuffering to one another for good," Seder Eliyyahu r., 24 (135), Str.-B., III, 595. The mildness of Hillel is highly praised as compared with the attitude of Shammai: "The mildness of Hillel has brought us under the wings of the shekinah, the raging of Shammai would drive us out of the world" (bShab, 30b and 31a, Str.-B., I, 198 f.).

μακροθυμεῖν does not occur in Philo, and μακροθυμία has only a secular sense in Joseph.[48]

D. μακροθυμέω and μακροθυμία in the New Testament.

1. Synoptic Gospels.

In the parable of the wicked servant in Mt. 18:23-35 there is an appeal to the μακροθυμεῖν of the king and then of the servant in the emphatic twofold μακροθύμησον ἐπ' ἐμοί, καὶ (πάντα) ἀποδώσω σοι (26, 29). The parable makes it clear how Jesus both adopts and yet also transcends the Jewish understanding of μακροθυμία.

---

[45] ψ 85:15-17.
[46] Ep. Ar., 188.
[47] Str.-B., III, 77; cf. Stade-Bertholet, II, 355 f.
[48] → n. 8; cf. Schl. Mt. on 18:26. The note of Schl. is to be augmented accordingly.

The thought of judgment is maintained in the idea of a reckoning, and judgment is linked with the emotion of anger (v. 34: ὀργισθείς). Similarly, there is an insistence on the full obligation of the debtor with life and limb, though the debts which by human judgment ought to bring down immediate judgment are so inconceivably great (10,000 talents) [49] that they seem to be completely impossible in the situation depicted. The πάντα ἀποδώσω σοι is no doubt understandable as an anxious cry on the lips of the defaulting servant, [50] but hearers recognise at once that it cannot be implemented when the κύριος is God. On the other hand, when the σύνδουλος makes the same pledge to a man, the wicked servant, there is every hope of fulfilment in view of the smallness of the sum (100 denarii).

When appeal is made to his patience, the κύριος does not have the servant at once imprisoned for debt, but cancels the enormous sum. This transcends Jewish casuistry and the "Pharisaic theory of compensation," [51] which always deal in measurable and comparable amounts. Here the mercy of God (σπλαγχνισθείς, v. 27) is unlimited and the debt of man is so incalculably great that he cannot possibly pay it. In this parable, materially if not in express words, the man to whom ἀπέλυσεν and ἀφῆκεν (v. 27) are shown by God is in the same position as Paul with regard to justification. The μακροθυμία of God to which the debtor appeals consists essentially, not in indulgence or postponement, but in the full and unsurpassable readiness of generous and forgiving grace. Nevertheless, this is so highly estimated that it must be expected that the man who has really taken it seriously will be basically altered in his own attitude to his fellows. Thus the relating of God's μακροθυμία to an obligation of human μακροθυμία towards one's neighbour, which is perceived already in Judaism (→ 376; 379), is carried by Jesus to the final point where a failure of readiness for μακροθυμία on man's part will necessarily call in question again the divine forbearance. The possibility of judgment by the God of sovereign decision is not ruled out by a display of μακροθυμία. The one who benefits by it must not make of it a law which he may then turn against God to escape the obligation of reciprocal μακροθυμία towards his σύνδουλος. If he does, wrath falls upon him (ὀργισθείς, v. 34), he is put in prison, and the claim upon him will be pressed with the utmost rigour ἕως οὗ ἀποδῷ πᾶν τὸ ὀφειλόμενον αὐτῷ (v. 34). This indissoluble relating of the known love of God with neighbourly love is something which we find again and again in Jesus (→ I, 44 ff.). The new relation between men in love must spring forth from the new relation to God in which the believer has known and understood the μακροθυμία of God (→ I, 47).

Cf. the application in v. 35; also Lk. 6:36; Mt. 5:7 par.; 5:25 par.; 6:12 par.; 14 f. par.; cf. 1 Cl., 13, 1 f.; Pol., 6, 2. The ἕως οὗ ἀποδῷ at the end of the parable indicates the decidedly eschatological reference of the μακροθυμία of God in the NT.

In the Synoptic Gospels there is an echo of this in Lk. 18:7. If the καὶ μακροθυμεῖ ἐπ᾽ αὐτοῖς [52] of the explanation gives rise to great difficulties, and if the original connection of the parable (vv. 2-5) with the explanation (6-8) is not un-

---

[49] This is 600,000 times the 100 denarii (cf. Kl. Mt., *ad loc.*). The amount has not been exaggerated later; an exorbitant sum was chosen because the debt is infinite (*loc. cit.*).
[50] Kl. Mt., *ad loc.*
[51] Schl. Mt., 559 f.
[52] The well attested μακροθυμεῖ, ℵ A B D L Q 1. 157. 209. e .... is to be preferred to μακροθυμῶν Γ Δ Λ R ..., cf. Zn. Lk., *ad loc.*, n. 61.

disputed,[53] the parable of the unjust judge and the widow is clear enough in itself, and it throws light on the interpretation. The persecuted community[54] in its longing expectation that justice will be done to it by its enemies (this is how ἐκδίκησις is to be construed acc. to → II, 444; 446) is to realise that this ἐκδίκησις cannot possibly fail. It rests in God's hands. Hence, in the question introduced by οὐ μή, which demands an absolutely certain answer, it may believe that ἐκδίκησις will come: ποιήσει τὴν ἐκδίκησιν ἐν τάχει, i.e., suddenly, unexpectedly.[55] But this leaves the tormenting question why ἐκδίκησις is not yet manifest, since the community suffers like the oppressed widow. The tension in which the community stands between the promise ἐν τάχει and the need to pray for the coming of God's kingdom finds its solution and answer in the saying: καὶ μακροθυμεῖ ἐπ' αὐτοῖς. The harassed elect need God's μακροθυμεῖν. This μακροθυμεῖν is not immediately suggested by the parable, since the unjust judge cannot be compared with God. An objectionable figure who offers no true comparison is deliberately chosen because of the difference between this aeon and the coming aeon. Hence the term μακροθυμεῖν is expressly introduced as the key to understanding. In this context it indicates that ἐκδίκησις means not only final judgment for adversaries but also serious self-examination for the elect. When the Son of Man comes, will He find faith on the earth? (v. 8b). Only in faith can they go into the ἐκδίκησις of the last judgment and pray for its coming. Thus God's μακροθυμεῖν ἐπ' αὐτοῖς is for them a necessary interval of grace which should kindle the faith and prayer that moves mountains (17:6 par.). In the μακροθυμεῖν of God there now lies the possibility of the existence of believers before God, in full realisation that they are dependent on God's decision, and yet in confidence that they may beseech His righteousness and grace.[56]

---

[53] Bultmann Trad., 189: "The application ... is undoubtedly secondary"; "the added application is undoubtedly right, for the specific point of the parable is prayer for the coming of God's rule," 209. Jülicher Gl. J., II, 288 ff. But cf. Wellh. (Kl. Lk., *ad loc.*), Zn., Hck., *ad loc.*

[54] Schl. Lk., Zn. Lk., *ad loc.*, n. 69.

[55] Cf. Zn. Lk., *ad loc.*, n. 67.

[56] Because of the difficulties it raises, Lk. 18:7 has been much discussed, cf. J. C. K. v. Hofmann, *Die hl. Schrift neuen Testaments* ..., VIII, 1 (1878), 437 ff.; Jülicher Gl. J., II, 285 ff.; B. B. Warfield, Exp. T., 25 (1913/14), 69 ff.; the comm., esp. Zn. and Kl. It seems to be generally accepted that οὐ μὴ ποιήσῃ τὴν ἐκδίκησιν is to be taken as a question. If this ends with ἡμέρας καὶ νυκτός, v. 8a: λέγω ὑμῖν, ὅτι ποιήσει κτλ., seems to be a smooth answer. But how, then, are we to take the clause μακροθυμεῖ ἐπ' αὐτοῖς? Does it belong to the question or to the answer? To take it with the question introduced by οὐ μή is hardly possible linguistically, since it would go only with the μή and not the οὐ (Zn., Kl. Lk., *ad loc.*). Even to bring it into the question in connection with βοώντων, "who cry to him and concerning whom he is longsuffering," is linguistically impossible. The rendering: "And shall he not show patience with them (the adversaries)?" — which relates the ἐπ' αὐτοῖς to the enemies — is without linguistic support in the text. On the other hand, to translate: "Does he not tarry long with them?" or: "Does he not keep them waiting?" (K. v. Weizsäcker, *Das NT übers.*[10] [1922]; B. Weiss, *Die Ev. d. Mk. u. Lk.*[9] [1901]; Pr.-Bauer[3], *s.v.*; Hck. Lk., etc.), which sees a ref. to the elect (ἐκλεκτοί), is not in keeping with the NT use of μακροθυμεῖν ἐπί τινι (Hofmann, Zn. Kl.), for the NT no longer employs the secular sense "to delay." In any case, the fact that the ἐκδίκησις has not yet come makes this plain enough. Thus it is best to follow Hofmann and others in taking the clause as an answer in the form of a simple statement. This is linguistically possible in Gk. (Hofmann, Zn., Kühner-Blass-Gerth, II, 540, n. 2). Hence: "And he shows patience (even) with them." If this is correct, the punctuation of the Gk. in Tisch. NT, H. v. Soden, *D. Schriften d. NT* ..., II (1913), Nestle, is incorrect. The clause is syntactically parenthetical, but it is necessary to the understanding of the whole and cannot

2. Paul.

a. The longsuffering of God. In Paul,[57] too, God's longsuffering is related to His wrath, R. 2:4; 9:22. There is a clear influence of the Semitic אֶרֶךְ אַפַּיִם. The wrath of God, though manifested already, R. 2:5; cf. 1:18; 9:22 f., will reach its climax only on the day of wrath, 2:5. By virtue of the eschatological reference to this climax of its manifestation in the δικαιοκρισία[58] (cf. ἐκδίκησις in Lk. 18:7), the righteous judgment of God,[59] μακροθυμία can never imply irresolution on the part of God, as though He could decide only after a period of waiting.[60] Nor does it imply compliance[61] or indulgence. God's patience does not overlook anything. It simply sees further than man. It has the end in view. It has the true insight which knows best. It is not swayed by human emotions. The fact that divine μακροθυμία stands alongside God's ὀργή means that this ὀργή is freed from anthropomorphic misunderstanding. The words χρηστότης and → ἀνοχή, with which μακροθυμία is associated in R. 2:4, must not be misunderstood psychologically. They refer to a historical action on the part of God[62] (cf. R. 9:22; cf. v. 17, Pharaoh).[63] χρηστότης gives to μακροθυμία the nuance of kindness, ἀνοχή that of the restraint of wrath,[64] though this is not hereby removed or softened (θησαυρίζεις). While τὸ χρηστὸν τοῦ θεοῦ in R. 2:4 leads to μετάνοια, to the question of conversion, it has also to be recalled that the capital of wrath (θησαυρίζεις) increases with the μακροθυμία shown, and this side is emphasised even more clearly in R. 9:22. Here the reason for μακροθυμία is not so much to allow time for repentance.[65] The delay is simply to bring out more clearly what God already wills (θέλων)[66] and knows, but what He allows to

---

be eliminated. Jülicher and others believe it is a kind of gloss from Sir. 35:19. One may accept the influence of Sir., esp. in view of the χήρα in Sir. 35:14 ff., but the idea of a gloss runs into the difficulty of the change of μακροθυμήσῃ (vl. μακροθυμήσει) into μακροθυμεῖ, for which there is no satisfactory explanation. Even if elsewhere in Lk. there is a tendency to introduce short parenthetical comments into the tradition (cf., e.g., the πλὴν τὰ ἐνόντα δότε ἐλεημοσύνην in 11:41a, and on this J. Horst, ThStKr, 87 [1914], 441), it has to be considered that the real problem is posed by the parable itself, and that this is not solved by the introductory δεῖν πάντοτε προσεύχεσθαι καὶ μὴ ἐγκακεῖν in v. 1, nor by the promise ἐν τάχει, but only by the statement concerning the μακροθυμεῖν of God with its positive ref. to the elect. Hence the writer himself must have formulated the saying, possibly under the influence of Sir. or of the fragment of a dominical saying (Zn. sees it again in 2 Pt. 3:9, Zn. Lk., *ad loc.*) which he took from another logion or which in the tradition was already part of this whole pericope, in which case we have to assume either "bad Greek or bad translation" (Well. Lk., *ad loc.*). On this whole question cf. Warfield, *op. cit.*, 70 ff.

[57] μακροθυμία is found 14 times in the NT, 10 times in Pl.; μακροθυμέω 10 times in the NT, twice in Paul.

[58] Cf. Deissmann LO, 72.

[59] Here μακροθυμία comes to be related to the righteousness of God (justification).

[60] This is ruled out by R. 9:22.

[61] As against Khl. R. on 2:4.

[62] πλοῦτος is to be related only to χρηστότης; ἀνοχῆς and μακροθυμίας are not dependent gen., cf. Zn. R., *ad loc.*

[63] Hofmann, *ad loc.*

[64] Cf. on ἀνοχή Zn. R., *ad loc.*, n. 27. Cf. also Ign. Eph., 11, 1: φοβηθῶμεν τὴν μακροθυμίαν τοῦ θεοῦ, ἵνα μὴ ἡμῖν εἰς κρίμα γένηται ἢ γὰρ τὴν μέλλουσαν ὀργὴν φοβηθῶμεν.

[65] Ltzm. R., *ad loc.*

[66] Cf. the comm.

come to plain fulfilment in man.[67] In no case, then, does μακροθυμία give the sinner a possibility of securing a claim on God's goodness.[68] This would be "to think of it as is not befitting" (ἀγνοῶν),[69] "to despise it."[70] It can indeed be an aggravation, namely, for vessels of wrath. Thus μακροθυμία does not carry with it any true pedagogical purpose of amendment.[71] It is simply a making clear of God's dealings with men in respect of their eschatological orientation. Nevertheless, the goal of God's πολλὴ μακροθυμία is never the purely passive one of restraining ὀργή. It is finally lit up by the revelation of God's glory.[72] Even where He has prepared σκεύη ὀργῆς (κατηρτισμένα εἰς ἀπώλειαν), these, too, are under His will, which only in this antithesis makes the community called by Him (v. 24) vessels of mercy.[73] The vessels of wrath and their preparation for destruction serve to display God's δόξα in all the richness with which it is spread over the community. This, then, is the aim of God's μακροθυμία.[74]

b. The longsuffering of the Christian. This understanding of μακροθυμία as a demonstration of God's δόξα to the community points again to the indissoluble relationship in virtue of which true perception of the μακροθυμία of God pledges believing Christians to μακροθυμία in the community. This is why exhortation must include the admonition μακροθυμεῖτε πρὸς πάντας, 1 Th. 5:14. It is not just that all members of the community stand in need of forbearance and patience,[75] for what is based on human need is no virtue.[76] The truth is that God's dealings with the community manifested in Christ, which set the members and their faults in the light of the *parousia* (v. 23, cf. 1 ff.), must also find expression in mutual correction controlled by μακροθυμία. But this cannot be a virtue attained among other virtues. It is a fruit of the Spirit, Gl. 5:22. Far from being one among other forms of ethical conduct, it grows from the common root and bears fruit only along with all others.[77] Love (→ ἀγάπη) takes precedence in this list of manifestations of the Spirit. By this supremely μακροθυμία is controlled, though also by χρηστότης (friendliness),[78] which Paul likes to relate to

---

[67] Cf. Hofmann, *ad loc.*
[68] Cf. Schl. R., *ad loc.*
[69] Ltzm. R., *ad loc.*
[70] Schl., *ad loc.*
[71] Hofmann, *ad loc.* A weakening of the μακρόθυμον βούλημα of God is found only later πῶς ἀόργητος, 1 Cl., 19, 3, cf. Dg., 8, 7 f. θεὸς οὐ μόνον φιλάνθρωπος ἐγένετο ἀλλὰ καὶ μακρόθυμος ... χρηστὸς καὶ ἀγαθὸς καὶ ἀόργητος.
[72] This should not lead, as with Hofmann and the Erlangen school, to a kind of softening of the θέλων ὁ θεὸς ἐνδείξασθαι τὴν ὀργήν and the σκεύη ὀργῆς κατηρτισμένα εἰς ἀπώλειαν.
[73] Bengel on v. 22: *observandus est sermo eius de vasis irae, parcior, de vasis misericordiae uberior.*
[74] Cf. on πλοῦτον τῆς δόξης (v. 23) πλούτου τῆς χρηστότητος ... καὶ τῆς μακροθυμίας, 2:4.
[75] Dob. Th., *ad loc.* Cf. the notes on ὀλιγόψυχοι. μακροθυμία is not indulgence; it is restraint from hasty and angry judgments. Dob. relates the πάντας to all members of the community, Wbg. Th. to all men. At least the admonition μακροθυμεῖτε is given to members of the community, and consequently it is not a general virtue.
[76] The Semitic form of the exhortation (Dib. Th., *ad loc.*; E. Norden, *Agnostos Theos* [1913], 365 f.) and the word μακροθυμέω are arguments against the influence of popular Stoicism, → 375.
[77] Zn. Gl., *ad loc.* Only later are there attempts to bring the virtues, including μακροθυμία, into a system. Wnd. Barn. on 2, 2; cf. 2 Pt. 1:5 ff.; Herm. s., 9, 15, 2.
[78] A. Oepke, *Der Brief d. Pls. an die Gl.* (1937), *ad loc.* on the individual items in the list. In Herm. s., 9, 15, 2 Μακροθυμία is among the first 4 maidens, Ἀγάπη is the last.

μακροθυμία.[79] Indeed, it receives different nuances from all the others in the list. Thus μακροθυμεῖ can even be a predicate of ἀγάπη: μακροθυμεῖ ἡ ἀγάπη. This is, in fact, the first thing said about ἀγάπη in the whole hymn (1 C. 13:4).[80] In the statement that the power behind it is love the NT understanding of μακροθυμεῖν finds succinct and essential expression. In 2 C. 6:6 Paul includes μακροθυμία in the list of missionary qualifications which he displays in model fashion as a διάκονος θεοῦ. It comes here between γνῶσις and χρηστότης. To make μακροθυμία possible there is needed not only friendliness and love, but also true insight, the better knowledge of man's situation before God as this is granted through the revelation of Christ.[81] Again in Col. 1:11 longsuffering is related to the special knowledge of God (ἐπίγνωσις τοῦ θεοῦ) and is a necessary part of περιπατῆσαι ἀξίως τοῦ κυρίου, connected here with ὑπομονή.[82] The dynamic content of NT longsuffering is plainly revealed in this passage. It is no mere endurance,[83] much less feeble indulgence, but a specifically spiritual force which has its source in the δόξα θεοῦ[84] and which works itself out in longsuffering ἐν πάσῃ δυνάμει δυναμούμενοι κατὰ τὸ κράτος τῆς δόξης αὐτοῦ εἰς πᾶσαν ὑπομονὴν καὶ μακροθυμίαν. If the list of virtues in 3:12 seems to be systematised,[85] it is plain that this ἐνδύσασθε, this slipping into[86] μακροθυμία and the other virtues (cf. πραΰτης and ἀνεχόμενοι ἀλλήλων) as into a garment, is a reality for the ἐκλεκτοὶ τοῦ θεοῦ only through the ἐν πᾶσιν Χριστός. The example of Jesus Himself is not without influence in these combinations with ταπεινοφροσύνη and πραΰτης.[87]

In Eph. 4:2 ἀξίως περιπατῆσαι ... μετὰ μακροθυμίας is again combined with ταπεινοφροσύνη and πραΰτης and ἀνεχόμενοι ἐν ἀγάπῃ (cf. Col. 3:12).[88] The demand for longsuffering is here based particularly on the reference to → κλῆσις.[89] The fact of calling to the ἓν σῶμα and ἓν πνεῦμα and εἷς κύριος etc., and the

---

[79] R. 2:4; 2 C. 6:6; Col. 3:12; 1 C. 13:4. Paul relates μακροθυμία and χρηστότης both in respect of God's action (R. 2:4) and also in respect of the Christian's. On this combination, which is peculiar to Paul in the NT, cf. Heinr. 2 C. on 6:6; Hofmann on 1 C. 13:4. The Rabb. tradition, which goes back to the OT root of μακροθυμία, could have influenced Paul's formulation. Cf. Ab., 6, 5 (*Giessener Mischna, ad loc.*, p. 172) among the 48 demands on those occupied with the Torah בְּאֶרֶךְ אַפַּיִם and בְּלֵב טוֹב; this corresponds to the combination in Paul.

[80] Note again the association with χρηστεύεται and with οὐ ζηλοῖ (cf. ὀργή). Cf. also Bchm. 1 K.[4], *ad loc.* (397 n.); cf. also 1 Cl., 13, 1.

[81] Cf. also Barn., 3, 6: ὁ μακρόθυμος προβλέψας.

[82] Much has been said about the distinction between ὑπομονή and μακροθυμία. The latter refers more to persons, the former to things. But this distinction is not absolute. Trench, 119 ff. § 33; Abbott-Smith, *s.v.* ἀνοχή; Hastings DB, *s.v.* "forbearance," "longsuffering"; J. A. H. Tittmann, *De Synonymis in NT*, I (1829), 194, *s.v.* ὑπομονή and ἀνοχή. Cf. also Ew. Gefbr., *ad loc.*, n. 2; Ign. Eph., 3, 1; 1 Cl., 64.

[83] As against Ew., *loc.cit.* Nor is this true of ὑπομονή. Cf. also Herm. m., 5, 2, 3.

[84] On the eschatological ref. of this passage cf. Loh. Kol., *ad loc.*

[85] Cf. Dib. Gefbr., *ad loc.* But Paul is closer to the scribal tradition of Judaism than to the list of virtues in Epictet., cf. Ab., 6, 5 f. → n. 79.

[86] Ew. Gefbr., *ad loc.* For the distinction between the 5 nouns cf. Loh. Kol., *ad loc.* For the consistent understanding of μακροθυμία cf. also v. 8: ἀπόθεσθε ... ὀργήν, θυμόν, v. 6: ὀργὴ τοῦ θεοῦ, v. 13: μομφήν.

[87] Cf. Phil. 2:3 ff.; Mt. 11:29; Loh. Kol., *ad loc.*

[88] Cf. J. T. Beck, *Erklärung d. Briefes Pauli an d. Eph.* (1891), *ad loc.* On the combination cf. also Ew. Gefbr. and W. M. L. de Wette, *Kurze Erklärung d. Briefe an d. Kol., Phlm., Eph. u. Phil.*[2] (1847), *ad loc.*

[89] Cf. also Herm. s., 8, 11, 1.

uniform direction of hope which this gives, make μακροθυμία one of the marks of the wrestling ἐκκλησία.

c. The Pastorals. In the Past. Christ Himself is the acting subject of the divine longsuffering at 1 Tm. 1:16: ἵνα ἐν ἐμοὶ πρώτῳ ἐνδείξηται Ἰησοῦς Χριστὸς τὴν ἅπασαν μακροθυμίαν.[90] Paul's experience of this waiting patience, which bore with the persecutor until it overcame him, should strengthen the faith of the community in relation to adversaries and offenders, whom this μακροθυμία fashions πρὸς ὑποτύπωσιν[91] if it has destined them for faith. Thus no one is to be given up. This μακροθυμία leads to praise (the doxology in v. 17). On the other hand, under the command of love, it is also an obligation in missionary service according to Paul's example: σὺ δὲ παρηκολούθησάς μου τῇ διδασκαλίᾳ ... τῇ πίστει, τῇ μακροθυμίᾳ, τῇ ἀγάπῃ, 2 Tm. 3:10. The main reference here is to missionary teaching, and especially to the fight against false teachers, cf. 4:2: ἐν πάσῃ μακροθυμίᾳ καὶ διδαχῇ.[92] What is wanted in face of opposition is the longsuffering which surrenders no doctrine and refuses to retreat (ἐπίστηθι). This is an expression of the belief that normative decision rests, not with angry human judgment, but with the Judge of the quick and the dead — Χριστοῦ Ἰησοῦ τοῦ μέλλοντος κρίνειν ζῶντας καὶ νεκρούς.[93]

3. The Catholic Epistles.

a. James. In a section in which μακροθυμία is the main theme (5:7-11),[94] and in the admonition μακροθυμήσατε (v. 7, 8),[95] James brings out an aspect of μακροθυμία which is very close to that found in the Synoptists.[96] Under the constraint of having to suffer unjustly, μακροθυμία comes to be orientated to perseverance, to expectation of the *parousia*, μακροθυμήσατε ἕως τῆς παρουσίας, v. 7, cf. v. 8. In connection with κακοπάθεια, (endurance of) affliction and ὑπομονή, persistence, it comes to suggest a triumphant steadfastness which does not come from the heroic depths of one's own heart but from certainty of the proximity of the *parousia*,[97] i.e., of the Lord who is Judge (v. 10). Awareness of His nearness — ὁ κριτὴς πρὸ τῶν θυρῶν ἕστηκεν — quenches all angry feelings against opponents and all overhasty sighings and murmurings against brothers, μὴ στενάζετε, ἵνα μὴ κριθῆτε,[98] since both parties will stand before this Judge.

---

[90] Cf. also Dg., 9, 2, where the καιρός of the self-sacrifice of the Son is seen as the climax of the μακροθυμία of God: ἐμακροθύμησεν ... τὸν ἴδιον υἱὸν ἀπέδοτο λύτρον ὑπὲρ ἡμῶν.

[91] A. Schlatter, *Die Kirche d. Griechen im Urteil des Pls.* (1936), *ad loc.* Cf. also P. Leo, "Das anvertraute Gut" in O. Schmitz, *Die urchr. Botschaft,* 15 (1935), *ad loc.* (p. 23). Longsuffering is the "utter indissolubility of His relation to men."

[92] Cf. Hofmann, *ad loc.*

[93] Cf. J. Jeremias, *NT Deutsch, ad loc.*

[94] Wnd. Kath. Br., *ad loc.*

[95] On this imp. aor. Bl.-Debr.[6] § 337, 2.

[96] Cf. the βοαὶ τῶν θερισάντων of v. 4 with the βοώντων of Lk. 18:7 and v. 9 with Mt. 18:23 ff. Cf. also Schl. Jk., *ad loc.*

[97] The στηρίξατε τὰς καρδίας ὑμῶν is controlled by the ὅτι ἡ παρουσία τοῦ κυρίου ἤγγικεν of v. 8. Cf. Hck. Jk., *ad loc.*

[98] Verbal link with Mt. 7:1; Schl. Jk., *ad loc.*

Furthermore, what the circle of brothers may expect in persistent longsuffering is the certainty of a precious fruit, v. 7.[99]

b. Hebrews.[100] Here the element of refraining from overhasty wrath is less prominent than the positive connection with πίστις:[101] ἐνδείκνυσθαι σπουδὴν πρὸς τὴν πληροφορίαν τῆς ἐλπίδος ἄχρι τέλους ... μιμηταὶ ... τῶν διὰ πίστεως καὶ μακροθυμίας κληρονομούντων τὰς ἐπαγγελίας, 6:11 f. μακροθυμία denotes here the steadfast endurance of faith which is not vexed by waiting.[102] If in Paul μακροθυμία is an essential mark of ἀγάπη,[103] in Hb. it is an essential mark of πίστις.[104] ἐλπίς, too, is involved in μακροθυμία.[105] The active nature of this μακροθυμία is denoted by σπουδήν (v. 11). Its basis is the promise of the righteous God:[106] οὕτως μακροθυμήσας ἐπέτυχεν τῆς ἐπαγγελίας, 6:15.[107]

c. In 1 Pt. 3:20 ἀπεξεδέχετο ἡ τοῦ θεοῦ μακροθυμία[108] has a closer relation to a period of time,[109] i.e., that of the generation of Noah.[110] This μακροθυμία of God allows the development of the obedience and disobedience (ἀπειθήσασιν) which in judgment are manifested in deliverance (διεσώθησαν) and destruction. In the age of the community it is characterised by the spiritual operations of Christ through the word of proclamation (ἐκήρυξεν) and the sacrament of baptism (v. 21).[111]

d. μακροθυμία and μακροθυμεῖν are used only occasionally in the NT, even though they are related to central themes like the *parousia*, justification and the Christian walk. In 2 Peter, however, the patience of God is the key concern. In the μακροθυμία τοῦ κυρίου the epistle finds the solution to the difficult problem which the community then had to face,[112] namely, that the promise of the *parousia* had not yet been fulfilled (3:4). If the strong antithesis of the sharp formula in R. 9:22 has here yielded to a statement in which only one side, i.e., the saving forbearance of God, is pedagogically emphasised: οὐ βραδύνει κύριος τῆς

---

[99] On the constr. μακροθυμῶν ἐπ' αὐτῷ cf. Lk. 18:7 and Hck. Jk. *ad loc.*

[100] It is striking that μακροθυμία and μακροθυμεῖν occur only in the section 6:9-15, whereas the word group ὑπομονή is confined to the last part of the epistle, O. Michel Hb.[7] (1936), *ad loc.*, n. 1.

[101] Luther: *pulchre coniungit utrumque fidem et patientiam*, J. Ficker, *Luthers Vorlesung über den Hb. 1517/18* (1929); Schol. 71.

[102] Rgg. Hb., *ad loc.*

[103] 1 C. 13:4.

[104] Wnd. Hb., *ad loc.* and exc. on 11:40.

[105] Michel, *ad loc.*

[106] v. 10: οὐ γὰρ ἄδικος ὁ θεός.

[107] μακροθυμήσας ἐπέτυχεν belong close together, Rgg. Hb., *ad loc.*

[108] Here μακροθυμία is the subj. of God's action.

[109] The ref. is to the 120 yrs. of Gn. 6:3, Wbg. Pt., *ad loc.*

[110] Cf. Mt. 24:37 ff.

[111] With Hofmann and Wbg. we may take the τοῖς ἐν φυλακῇ πνεύμασιν πορευθεὶς → ἐκήρυξεν (v. 19) to refer to the preaching of the pre-existent Christ to the generation of Noah, or with expositors like Wnd., Hck. (*NT Deutsch*) we may take it to refer to the preaching of Christ in the underworld between His death and resurrection, but in terms of the emerging creed of vv. 18-22 the emphasis is not on the incidental illustration of the generation of Noah but on the present spiritual activity of the risen Lord (πνεύματι, v. 18), who fills the interval up to the *parousia* with longsuffering, and through the κήρυγμα and βάπτισμα, word and sacrament, delivers members in the ark of the Church. The ὀλίγοι makes us aware again of the serious background of this μακροθυμία of God.

[112] Cf. already Mt. 24:48 χρονίζει.

ἐπαγγελίας[113] ... ἀλλὰ μακροθυμεῖ εἰς ὑμᾶς,[114] μὴ βουλόμενός τινας ἀπολέσθαι ἀλλὰ πάντας[115] εἰς μετάνοιαν χωρῆσαι (3:9), the essential features of the early Christian insight into the patience of God are here brought to mind in an attempt to cut the ground from under a superficial disappointment that the *parousia* has not yet taken place.[116] The misconception that God's μακροθυμεῖν is a βραδύνειν, a negligent delay, is met by an elimination of the human concept of time. The idea of judgment is maintained on two sides, for the ungodly (v. 7), but also for believers who ought seriously to use the interval for a blameless walk (v. 14 f.).[117] The meaning of God's μακροθυμία, and of time generally, for the community, is its σωτηρία: τὴν τοῦ κυρίου ἡμῶν μακροθυμίαν σωτηρίαν ἡγεῖσθε (3:15).

† μακροθύμως.[1]

This adv. from μακρόθυμος is found only in Ac. 26:3 in the secular sense of "patiently." In his address to Agrippa Paul does not wish to be disturbed by angry or impatient interruptions such as came from Festus in v. 24.[2]

Horst

---

[113] This is a gen. not found elsewhere (Is. 46:13 acc., Grotius conjectures τάς), cf. Bl.-Debr.[6] § 180, 5; Cr.-Kö., 28 ff., though cf. also Hofmann and Wbg. Pt., *ad loc.* Textually cf. Sir. 35:19.

[114] On the more striking εἰς with μακροθυμεῖν in BCKLP min, arm, bo as against the smoother but less well attested δι' ℵ, A m vg sa sy aeth T, cf. Knopf Pt., *ad loc.* Usually μακροθυμέω is found with the prep. ἐπί, Mt. 18:26; Lk. 18:7; Jm. 5:7; or πρός, 1 Th. 5:14; only here with εἰς, E. Kühl, *D. Briefe Petri u. Judae*[6] (1897), *ad loc.*; Bl.-Debr.[6] § 196.

[115] It cannot be decided exegetically whether the πάντας (or τινας) refers universally to all men or to the members of the community, cf. the comm. In view are all who will come into the community up to the *parousia.*

[116] Wnd. Kath. Br., *ad loc.*

[117] ὑπομονή is used for human patience in 1:6.

μακροθύμως. [1] The adj. μακρόθυμος occurs in the LXX (e.g., Ex. 34:6 etc., Hatch-Redp.), also in the post-apost. fathers, 1 Cl., 19, 3; Did., 3, 8; Barn., 3, 6; Dg., 8, 7; Herm. v., 1, 2, 3; m., 5, 1, 1; 2; 8, 10; s., 8, 11, 1. It is not found in the NT.

[2] Cf. also 22:22 and 23:7; Pr. Ag., *ad loc.*

† μαμωνᾶς

1. The Gr. μαμωνᾶς is a rendering of the *status emphaticus* מָמוֹנָא of the current Aram. noun מָמוֹן.[1] The derivation is uncertain, though it most likely comes from אמן = "that in which one trusts" (J. Buxtorf).[2] The orig. Aram. of the saying in Lk. 16:10 f. would thus contain a pun, for πιστός, πιστεύσει, τὸ ἀληθινόν also belong to the stem אמן. That the community did not render מָמוֹן by a Gk. word (e.g., οὐσία) is perhaps due to the untranslatable ethical and religious nuance, or possibly because it had come into the Gk. of Syria as a loan word.[3]

2. מָמוֹן does not occur in the OT,[4] though cf. Heb. Sir. 42:9, Damasc. (14, 20) in a corrupt passage, often in the Targum, → 389, the Mishnah, e.g., Ab., 2, 12; Sanh., 1, 1, and the Talmud, probably also the basic text of En. 63:10, here, as often in the Targum, in the phrase "unrighteous mammon," cf. Lk. 16:9, 11. The meaning and usage are made clearer by a comparison of several Tg. passages with the corresponding Heb. originals.

a. מָמוֹן is used obj. for resources, not merely in money, but also in property and anything of value (e.g., slaves). In the legal language of the Mishnah מָמוֹן as possessions is contrasted with the life (נֶפֶשׁ) or body as man's living possession. Thus דִּינֵי מָמוֹנוֹת are property cases as distinct from דִּינֵי נְפָשׁוֹת, those which decide life and death, Sanh.,

---

μαμωνᾶς. Art. "Mammon" in RE³, XII, 153 f. (G. Dalman); BW, 411 (G. Beer); Hastings DB, III, 224 (W. H. Bennett); EB, III, 2912 ff. (E. Nestle); ERE, VIII, 374 f.; Levy Wört., III, 138; Levy Chald. Wört., *s.v.*; Zahn Einl., I, 12; E. Riggenbach, *Theol. Abhandlungen f. A. Schlatter* (1922), 21 ff.; S. Krauss, *Talmud. Archäologie*, II (1911), 320 and 404; J. Lightfoot, *Horae Hebraicae* ..., I² (1684), 843 ff.; A. Merx, *Die 4 kanon Ev.*, II, 2 (1905), 327 ff.; S. Ejger, *Das Geld im Talmud* (Vilna, 1930); S. Helfer, *Geld u. Kredit bei d. Juden in talmud. Zeit* (Diss. Berlin, 1922).

1 The Gk. and Syr. MSS prefer to spell with one μ, and this is important in relation to the origin. Only the Lat. (and later Gk.) have the double μ, cf. Bl.-Debr.⁶ § 40 (assimilation to *mamma, annona* etc. ?).

2 Dalman, 153 "deposited," "put in safety"; Dalman Gr., 170, n. 1: the Syr. grammarians derive from אמן, Nestle, 2914. Other suggestions (Str.-B., I, 434) are: 1. from מון or מנה, "to apportion," F. Delitzsch, *Zschr. f. lutherische Theologie* ... (1876), 600; Levy Wört., III, 138b; 2. from טמן, "lay up," מַטְמוֹן, מַמּוֹן. P. de Lagarde, *Übersicht* ... (1889), 185. The single μ is against this, also the fact that Sir. uses both מטמון (42:9) and מָמוֹן (34:8); 3. from the Arab. root *ḍamina-maḍmun*, which would give the Aram. מעמון; מאמון or ממון would be a weaker form, P. de Lagarde, *Mitteilungen* ... (1884), 229, though in this case we should expect the double μ; 4. from the Babyl. *man man*, a name of Margal, hence μαμωνᾶς = gold = filth of hell, H. Winckler, *Babyl. Kultur* (1902), 47 f.; A. Jeremias, *Das AT im Licht des Alten Orients*³ (1916), 671; 5. acc. to Aug. De Sermone Domini in Monte ..., II, 14, 47 (MPL, 34, 1290) μαμωνᾶς was a Punic word meaning *lucrum*, cf. בצע. On this cf. Z. S. Harris, *A Grammar of the Phoenician Language* = *American Oriental Series*, VIII (1936), 120. There is no basis for the idea that μαμωνᾶς was a Syrian deity = Πλοῦτος, cf. Zn. Mt. on 6:24.

3 Schl. Lk., 368.

4 The LXX has πλούτῳ for אֱמוּנָה at Ps. 37:3 and perhaps θησαυροῖς at Is. 33:6. It might have read מָמוֹנָא.

1, 1. The Rabb. contrast מָמוֹן שֶׁל שֶׁקֶר and מָמוֹן שֶׁל אֱמֶת[5] and thereby recognise expressly that there is a mammon which is free from ethical objection. Thus it is used neutrally in the Targum for רְכוּשׁ, "property" (Gn. 14:12), for הוֹן, "goods" (Ps. 44:12 and Prv. 3:9, where the command to honour God with one's substance shows that there is no ethical incompatibility between מָמוֹן and God), also for מְחִיר "purchase price," "means of payment" (Is. 55:1).

b. The Tg. often uses מָמוֹן for בֶּצַע, "gain" (Ju. 5:19), esp. "dishonest gain," "damage," "spoiling one's neighbour's property" (בצע, "to cut off," Ps. 10:3, "to cheat," Ex. 22:12). It denotes the dishonest profit which a man makes in a matter or transaction by selfishly exploiting the situation of another, Tg. O. on Gn. 37:26; Tg. Ju. 5:19. Unselfish integrity which comes from fear of God is a mark of the honest man, who is well adapted to be a judge, Tg. O. on Ex. 18:21.[6] The man who hates dishonest gain (bribes) will live, Tg. Prv. 15:27. The wickedness of the sons of Eli (priest-judges) in 1 S. 8:3 and of the bad princes in Ez. 22:27 is shown by their readiness for dishonest gain (bribes, personal advantage). In the last three passages the emphatic מָמוֹן דִּשְׁקַר gives the desired sense.[7]

c. מָמוֹן is also used for כֹּפֶר, which is partly the ransom or compensation imposed by the judge (Tg. O. on Ex. 21:30) but also the bribe which is silently brought to the judge (Tg. O. on Nu. 35:31; Tg. Am. 5:12). Samuel advances it as a proof of his blamelessness in office that he has been absolutely impervious to such payments, Tg. 1 S. 12:3. Thus מָמוֹן can be used directly for שֹׁחַד, "bribe," Tg. Is. 33:15. (In the last two passages we again find מָמוֹן דִּשְׁקַר.) Cf. Tg. Is. 45:13.

Thus already in Judaism מָמוֹן has an ignoble sense and is used in censure. To make this clear דִּשְׁקַר is often added. In some circles at least (cf. the piety of the *Anawim*)[8] the idea of the impure, dishonest and worldly is intrinsically bound up with the word. In Eth. En., esp. in the admonitions (94-105), one may see the same hostility to love of mammon (→ πλούσιος, πτωχός) as is later found in Jesus. The righteous who love God rather than earthly possessions (108:7) stand opposed to the rich and powerful who trust in dishonestly won money and property (94:6, 8; 97:8) and who exploit their position with injustice and violence (94:6 ff.; 96:5 ff.). In the hereafter, when the position will be reversed (94:10; 96:8; cf. Lk. 16:19 ff.), the rich will lament: Our souls are sated with unrighteous mammon, but this does not prevent us from plunging into the flames of hell (63:10).

3. In the NT μαμωνᾶς occurs only on the lips of Jesus. In the first instance it means "property," "earthly goods," but always with a derogatory sense of the materialistic, anti-godly and sinful. In the earthly property which man gathers (Mt. 6:19 ff.), in which he erroneously seeks security (Lk. 12:15 ff.), to which he gives his heart (Mt. 6:21), and because of which he ceases to love, Jesus finds the very opposite of God (Mt. 6:24 par.). Because of the demonic power immanent in possessions, surrender to them brings practical enslavement (Mt. 6:19 ff.). The righteous must resolutely break free from this entanglement and stand in exclusive religious dependence on God, Mt. 6:24 par. This realistic view of the actual facts makes it impossible for Jesus to think of earthly possessions

---

[5] Ex. r., 31 on 22:26; Str.-B., II, 220.

[6] Heb. אַנְשֵׁי אֱמֶת שֹׂנְאֵי בָצַע.

[7] Here we might also mention Hos. 5:11, where the Tg. seems to have read Heb. בֶּצַע for צַו.

[8] Ps. 34:11; Lk. 1:53; Jm. 1:10 f.; 2:5 f.; 5:1; Dib. Jk., 37 ff.: Rich and poor.

with religious optimism or to regard them as a mark of special divine blessing (Job 1:10). The phrase μαμωνᾶς τῆς ἀδικίας in Lk. 16:9 (= ἀδίκῳ μαμωνᾷ, 16:11) corresponds exactly to the Aram. מָמוֹן דִּשְׁקַר, = possessions acquired dishonestly.[9] The saying of Jesus need not have been originally directed against publicans, for in practice no property can be acquired except with some element of injustice (cf. Σειρ. 26:29). The estimation of God as the supreme good, and the high ethical emphasis placed on brotherly love, especially in expectation of the imminent end, rule out all ideas of using mammon in the world to serve cultural aims and concerns. The only possibility for Jesus is the renunciation of earthly wealth as this is expressed in giving it to the poor. This ethically unobjectionable and religiously prudent use of earthly riches in the service of love for others is something which the righteous may learn from the ethically unjustifiable but clever use of money for corrupt purposes as this may be seen in the world (Lk. 16:1-7, 9). Even in respect of modest earthly wealth, the righteous is under the obligation of faithfulness, Lk. 16:11. Faithfulness in small things is the presupposition of participation in the eternal (great) things which are the true wealth of the disciples (τὸ ἀληθινόν, play on words → 388).

Hauck

μανθάνω, καταμανθάνω, μαθητής, συμμαθητής, μαθήτρια, μαθητεύω

† μανθάνω.

Contents: A. μανθάνω among the Greeks: 1. Ordinary Use; 2. Philosophical Use: a. Beginnings; b. The Metaphysics of Learning in Socrates/Plato; c. The Intellectualising of the Learning Process in the Philosophy of the Schools; 3. μανθάνω as a Special Cultic Term in Hellenism. B. μανθάνω in the Old Testament and Judaism: 1. לָמַד/μανθάνω in the Old Testament (LXX); 2. לָמַד in the Usage of the Rabbis; 3. Josephus; 4. Philo. C. μανθάνω in the New Testament: 1. The General Situation; 2. Ordinary Use; 3. Learning from Scripture; 4. The New Learning; 5. The Threat Posed to Piety by μανθάνειν in the Pastorals; 6. Hb. 5:8. D. The Usage of the Early Church.

---

[9] Cf. Tg. Prv. 15:27: "He destroys his house who gathers the mammon of dishonesty." Cf. also Str.-B., II, 220; Merx, 327 f.

μανθάνω. Pr.-Bauer³, Pass., Liddell-Scott, *s.v.* On A.: B. Snell, *Die Ausdrücke f. den Begriff des Wissens in der vorplatonischen Philosophie* = *Philologische Untersuchungen*, 29 (1924), 72 ff.; J. Stenzel, *Platon der Erzieher* (1928); W. Freymann, *Platons Suchen nach einer Grundlegung aller Philosophie* (1930), 79 ff.; C. Ritter, *Die Kerngedanken d. platonischen Philosophie* (1931); J. Stenzel, *Metaphysik des Altertums* (1931); W. Nestle, *Menschliche Existenz u. politische Erziehung in d. Tragödie des Aischylos* = *Tübinger Beiträge z. Altertumswissenschaft*, 23 (1934), 82 ff. On B.: S. Krauss, *Talmud. Archäologie*, III (1912), 199 ff.; Bacher Term., I, 94, 199 ff.; II, 96 f., 234 f.; Schl. Theol. d. Judt., 101 f.; I. Heinemann, *Philons gr. u. jüd. Bildung* (1932). On C.: Cr.-Kö., *s.v.*

A. μανθάνω among the Greeks.

1. Ordinary Use.

a. μανθάνω is formed from the aor. ἔ-μαθ-ο-ν, which comes from the root *mn̥dh-, *men-dh- (*men-dhē) and which has the basic meaning "to direct one's mind to something." [1] From this come the individual meanings of the term. In some sense one can still see how the original sense is developed in them. [2]

(a) In the three passages in which the word occurs (in the aor.) in Hom. [3] it cannot be rendered "have learned." [4] It has more the sense of "to have accustomed oneself to something." There is an element of compulsion in so far as something essential to the man concerned is denoted. [5] Thus Hector is ἐσθλός (Il., 6, 444); the ragged beggar behind whom Odysseus conceals himself is of use only for ἔργα κακά (Od., 17, 226 f.; 18, 362 f.). This use has continued and is still found in modern Gk. [6] But the emphasis is more on that to which one becomes accustomed than on that which is essential, and this controls the use. From Empedocles comes the statement: ἓν ἐκ πλεόνων μεμάθηκε φύεσθαι, Fr., 26 (I, 323, 6, Diels⁵). Here there is no personal subj. The situation is even plainer when we read in Hippocr. Acut., II, 8 (II, p. 430, Littré): μεμαθήκασι δὲ μακροὶ οἱ πυρετοὶ οἵδε γίνεσθαι, and Erotian (c. 60 A.D.) has the gloss: μεμαθήκασι· εἰώθασι (p. 60, Nachmanson). [7] The meaning here is "to be used." [8]

(b) The basic meaning then gives us "to experience." Here again intellectual concern is implied, so that the word in the present stem can mean "to seek to experience." Both senses are found together in Hdt., VII, 208: ἔτυχον δὲ τοῦτον τὸν χρόνον Λακεδαιμόνιοι ἔξω τεταγμένοι ... ταῦτα δὴ θεώμενος ἐθωύμαζε καὶ τὸ πλῆθος ἐμάνθανε. μαθὼν δὲ πάντα ἀτρεκέως ἀπήλαυνε ὀπίσω κατ' ἡσυχίην. In this sense, too, the word loses its distinctive flavour with time. [9]

(c) With the acc. of person the word means "to learn to know," so Xen. Hist. Graec., II, 1, 1: οἷς δὲ ταῦτα ἀρέσκοι κάλαμον φέρειν ἐδόκει, ἵνα ἀλλήλους μάθοιεν· ὁπόσοι εἴησαν, or a later (5th/6th cent. A.D.) non-literary text (P. Greci e Latini, V, 480, 6 f.): οὐ θέλει ὁ εὐδοκιμ[ώτατος] Φοιβάμμων σε μαθεῖν. In direct proximity to this use is that for "to note" (from some standpoint), e.g., Soph. Phil., 12 ff.: ἀκμὴ γὰρ οὐ μακρῶν ἡμῖν λόγων, | μὴ καὶ μάθῃ μ' ἥκοντα κἀκχέω τὸ πᾶν | σόφισμα, τῷ νιν αὐτίχ' αἱρήσειν δοκῶ, Hdt., I, 5: ἐπεὶ δὲ ἔμαθε ἔγκυος ἐοῦσα ...

---

[1] Walde-Pok., II, 270 f.; Boisacq, 607: *"appliquer son esprit à qc."* Snell, 73 postulates a basic meaning "to makes intellectually one's own something which has a specific effect."

[2] Snell, 72, though the ref. is rather to μάθημα.

[3] Il. 6, 444 f.: οὐδέ με θυμὸς ἄνωγεν, ἐπεὶ μάθον ἔμμεναι ἐσθλὸς | αἰεὶ καὶ πρώτοισι μετὰ Τρώεσσι μάχεσθαι ...; Od., 17, 226 f.: ἀλλ' ἐπεὶ οὖν δὴ ἔργα κάκ' ἔμμαθεν, οὐκ ἐθελήσει | ἔργον ἐποίχεσθαι ...; Od., 18, 362 f.

[4] In Hom. true learning is διδάσκεσθαι, Il., 11, 830 ff.: ἐπὶ δ' ἤπια φάρμακα πάσσεν | ἐσθλά, τά σε προτί φασιν 'Αχιλλῆος δεδιδάχθαι, | ὃν Χείρων ἐδίδαξε ..., cf. Il., 16, 811: διδασκόμενος πολέμοιο; cf. Snell, 72, n. 1 and → II, 135, also A. Debrunner, *Annuaire de l'Inst. de Philol. et d'Hist. Orient.*, 5 (1937, *Mélanges E. Boisacq*), 251 ff.

[5] Here is the starting-point for the later philosophical use, → 393.

[6] For examples cf. Snell, 72, n. 3.

[7] These and other early examples may be found in Snell, 72, n. 2.

[8] There is a par. use of the Lat. *didici* in poetic usage, cf. Thes. Ling. Lat., V, 1 (1934), 1333 f.

[9] Cf., e.g., BGU, II, 602, 10: ἵνα μάθω, τί πράξω (2nd cent. A.D.); P. Greci e Latini, IX, 1033, 9 ff.: ἀξιῶ δέ σε μαθεῖν παρὰ τοῦ ὑπηρέτου [Διοφάντο]υ ὅπως ἐξῆλθεν ἡ παῖς (166 A.D.); III, 226, 12 f.: ἵνα μάθω εἰ ἐκῖ ἐστιν εἴτε ἐξῆλθεν (4th cent. A.D.); Achill. Tat., VI, 3, 3 (Erotici Scriptores Graeci, I, 157, 24 ff., Hercher): ὁ γὰρ Σωσθένης ὁ τὴν Λευκίππην ὠνησάμενος, ὃν ἡ Μελίτη τῆς τῶν ἀγρῶν ἐκέλευσεν ἀποστῆναι διοικήσεως, μαθὼν παρεῖναι τὸν δεσπότην τούς τε ἀγροὺς οὐκέτι ἀφῆκε τήν τε Μελίτην ἤθελεν ἀμύνασθαι.

(d) In dialogue μανθάνω is used to show understanding or non-understanding (cf. Aristoph. Ra., 195 [Dionysus]: μανθάνεις; [Xanthias]: πάνυ μανθάνω, Plat. Theaet., 174b: μανθάνεις γάρ που, ὦ Θεόδωρε· ἢ οὔ; [Theodorus:] ἔγωγε· καὶ ἀληθῆ λέγεις. Cf. also Epict. Diss., II, 6, 4). The choice of the word in the answer expresses the willingness of the person questioned to follow the thoughts of the questioner.[10]

(e) μανθάνω is also used for "learning skills under instruction" (cf. Xenoph. Mem., II, 1, 28: εἴτε διὰ πολέμου ὁρμᾷς αὔξεσθαι ..., τὰς πολεμικὰς τέχνας αὐτάς τε παρὰ τῶν ἐπισταμένων μαθητέον καὶ ὅπως δεῖ αὐταῖς χρῆσθαι ἀσκητέον).[11] Since man's capacity for this is not unlimited, we sometimes read of an age of learning (Plut. Cicero, 2, 1 [I, 861d]: ἐν ἡλικίᾳ τοῦ μανθάνειν γενόμενος.[12] In this sense μανθάνειν is part of the constitution of man.[13]

(f) Plut. uses the word once for "receiving direction from deity in an oracle" (Parallela, 41 [II, 316a]).[14] Here, too, one may match an echo of the philosophical use, → 393.

(g) The word becomes stereotyped in the phrase τί μαθών, "why?" Yet a connection with the original sense may still be discerned here, for the question seeks the rational basis and inner motive of an action,[15] while the par. τί παθών is concerned with emotion and the external motive. It often has an ironical note,[16] and there is always something of reproach. Hence τί μαθών can finally be used in statements which suggest the incomprehensibility of an attitude.[17]

b. Though broad, the ordinary use is consistent to the degree that, if not always with equal clarity, an intellectual process is always implied and this always has external effects. The process is related to the individuality of the man concerned, if there is a personal reference; and things are much the same with material subjects (→ 391). The word also points to an intellectual initiative, whether conscious or unconscious.

This means that μανθάνω can be elucidated but not replaced by other words. εἴωθα is not the same as μεμάθηκα,[18] even though Erotian explains the latter by it, → 391. διδάσκεσθαι has in view the influence to which one is exposed, cf. Soph. Phil.,

---

[10] *audire* is often used in this way in Lat.

[11] Cf. also Ael. Var. Hist., III, 32 ('Αλέξανδρος ... ἐμάνθανε κιθαρίζειν) and the sentence in M. Ant., IV, 31: τὸ τεχνίον (diminutive of τέχνη), ὃ ἔμαθες, φίλει. There are also many non-literary examples, P. Greci e Latini, VIII, 871, 11 ff. (66 A.D.): ὥστε μαθεῖν τὴν χαλκοτυπικὴν τέχνην, P. Tebt., II, 385, 9 f. (117 A.D.): ὥστε μαθῖν αὐτὸν [τὴν δηλο]υμ[ένη]ν γε[ρ]διακὴν τέχνην. Cf. also BGU, IV, 1124, 21; 1125, 10 (both 1st cent. B.C.).

[12] The same thought, elliptically expressed, may be found in Plut. Cato Minor, 1, 3 (I, 759 f.): ὡς οὖν εἰς τὸ μανθάνειν ἧκε, νωθρὸς ἦν ἀναλαβεῖν καὶ βραδύς ...

[13] Cf. Cic. Fin., III, 66 (v. Arnim, III, p. 84, 3): *ita non solum ad discendum propensi sumus verum etiam ad docendum.*

[14] Τηλέγονος, 'Οδυσσέως καὶ Κίρκης, ἐπὶ ἀναζήτησιν τοῦ πατρὸς πεμφθεὶς ἔμαθε πόλιν κτίσαι, ἔνθα ἂν ἴδῃ γεωργοὺς ἐστεφανωμένους καὶ χορεύοντας.

[15] Cf. Eupolis Fr., 357, 3 (CAF, I, 353): ὅ τι μαθόντες τοὺς ξένους μὲν λέγετε ποιητὰς σοφούς, Philostr. Vit. Ap., V, 25 (I, 183, 30 f.): ἐρομένου δ' αὐτὸν τοῦ ἱερέως, τί μαθὼν οὐχ οὕτω θύοι ...

[16] Cf. Aristoph. Ach., 826: τί δὴ μαθὼν φαίνεις ἄνευ θρυαλλίδος (wick), cf. Vesp., 251.

[17] Cf., e.g., Plat. Euthyd., 283e: εἰ μὴ ἀγροικότερον ... ἦν εἰπεῖν, εἶπον ἄν· "Σοὶ εἰς κεφαλήν," ὅτι μαθών μου καὶ τῶν ἄλλων καταψεύδῃ τοιοῦτον πρᾶγμα.

[18] ἔθω, εἴωθα is "acc. to character to be wont" (Snell, 73, n. 1). The πυρετός naturally has no ἔθος.

1012 ff.[19] and esp. Aesch. Prom., 8 ff.[20] and Soph. Phil., 538.[21, 22] There is no more synonymity here than with συνίημι (the basic meaning of the fig. use: "to declare oneself," "to express one's solidarity with a word from the other side")[23] or γιγνώσκω (basic meaning: "to accept," "to take something for what it really is").[24, 25] Nor is τί μαθών equivalent to τί βουλόμενος, which is sometimes mentioned in elucidation of the strange expression.[26] All this is of fundamental importance in relation to the specific use of μανθάνω as a philosophical term.[27]

2. Philosophical Use.

a. Beginnings.

In Homer there is no co-existence of the practical and the theoretical in the sense that the two spheres are consciously differentiated.[28] His use of μανθάνω confirms this (→ 391). Later the intellectual aspect of the Greek world became increasingly stronger with the desire for pure knowledge. Since μανθάνω denotes from the very outset an intellectual process which serves to develop the personality, the word meets the indispensable prerequisites for adoption into the vocabulary of theories of knowledge. The transition is made already in pre-Socratic philosophy, and to some extent in tragedy. Here μανθάνω is a constituent part of the process in the course of which knowledge arises. This is true even when there is intellectual guidance from the other side, so long as the process is fruitful.

Heracl. of Ephesus makes γινώσκειν dependent on μανθάνειν, at least in those — and this is the common rule — who do not have the ability of φρονεῖν, of sober deliberation.[29] For them the philosopher is, in a saying of Parmenides Fr., 8, 52 (I, 239, Diels[5]), the guide: μάνθανε κόσμον ἐμῶν ἐπέων ἀπατηλὸν ἀκούων. The normal situation, then, is that a man learns,[30] no matter whether he be mastering a craft

---

19 Philoctetus to Odysseus: ἡ κακὴ σὴ ... ψυχή ... | εὖ προυδίδαξεν ἐν κακοῖς εἶναι σοφόν.

20 Cratos to Hephaestus about Prometheus: τοιᾶσδέ τοι | ἁμαρτίας σφε δεῖ θεοῖς δοῦναι δίκην, | ὡς ἂν διδαχθῇ τὴν Διὸς τυραννίδα | στέργειν, φιλανθρώπου δὲ παύεσθαι τρόπου.

21 Philoctetus: ἐγὼ δ' ἀνάγκῃ προὔμαθον στέργειν κακά.

22 Cf. Snell, 73, n. 2, though Snell is inclined to stress the inner relation of the various words, → II, 135.

23 Snell, 40 ff.; συνιέναι is by way of the ear.

24 Snell, 20 ff. and → I, 689 ff.

25 Cf. a Schol. on Pind. Olymp., 9, 75 (μαθεῖν Πατρόκλου βιατὰν νόον): γνῶναι ὅτι γενναῖος ἦν ὁ Πάτροκλος (Snell, 73, n. 3).

26 Snell, 72, n. 4 mentions Hesych. and Photius on Aristoph. Vesp., 251. On βούλομαι → I, 629.

27 Pr.-Bauer[3], *s.v.* mentions the sense "to be the disciple of someone" and refers to Mart. Pol. Epilogus (e Codice Mosquensi descriptus), 1 (ἐν οἷς μέμνηται Πολυκάρπου, ὅτι παρ' αὐτοῦ ἔμαθεν). But this can be taken in the usual sense.

28 Snell, *passim*, also 73 on μανθάνω.

29 Heracl. Fr., 17 (H. Diels, *Herakleitos von Ephesus*[2] [1909], 20): οὐ γὰρ φρονέουσι τοιαῦτα <οἱ> πολλοί, ὁκοίοις ἐγκυρεῦσιν, οὐδὲ μαθόντες γινώσκουσιν, ἑωυτοῖσι δὲ δοκέουσι. What is meant is that most men cannot press on from the cleavage of the sensual world to the unity of the logos in which all nature is related in its multiplicity, Diels, n. 17, *ad loc.*

30 Protagoras of Abdera (born c. 485 B.C.) Fr., 3 (II, 264, Diels[5]): ἀπὸ νεότητος δὲ ἀρξαμένους δεῖ μανθάνειν.

(τέχνη) or attaining intellectual capacity (σοφίη).[31] Yet μανθάνειν is not the only possible way. Along with it is that of ἐξευρίσκειν which takes place δι' αὔταυτον καὶ ἰδίᾳ. The only trouble is that this is reserved simply for the ἐπιστάμενοι ζητεῖν.[32] Naturally ἐξευρίσκειν is better than μανθάνειν, for it denotes fruitful independent research, whereas the latter can easily become mechanical reception. Even when a man absorbs much knowledge, he is usually still far from true learning.[33] Thus we should set the saying of Democr. (Fr., 65 [II, 158, Diels[5]]): πολυνοΐην, οὐ πολυμαθίην ἀσκέειν χρή, alongside his other saying (Fr., 85 [II, 161, Diels[5]]): ἀφυὴς ἐς μάθησιν[34] ὢν χρή. The ideal is the ability and the will to exercise one's own νοῦς, not just to amass information, necessary though this may be. Formally Plato is pursuing the same line of thought when he can distinguish between μάθησις and ζήτησις as different processes in this sequence.[35]

Tragedy must also be mentioned.[36] μανθάνειν is a common and favourite term here.[37] It describes the actual "attitude of the one who seeks to live in harmony with the whole."[38] Acc. to Aesch. Ag., 176 f. it is a law of life ordained by Zeus: πάθει μάθος. The πάθη are there in order that man may learn, i.e., attain to σωφρονεῖν, *ibid.*, 179 ff., 249 f. One might almost say that with many variations πάθει μάθος determines the aim of tragedy,[39] thus giving it its consciously educational character.[40] An experience or word leads to an insight which should determine an attitude or act.[41] If it does, the man or even the god (Zeus in Aesch. Prom., 926) learns, grows up into the task imposed on him to comprehend himself in his limitations as a part of reality. μανθάνειν is thus an intensification of the being of man by way of an intensification of the νοῦς. The use of the word in Plato is thus in essence more strongly prepared for in tragedy than it is in older philosophy.

b. The Metaphysics of Learning in Socrates/Plato.

(a) The movement to a consciously speculative use of the word and concept took place in Socrates. It did so in connection with his central interest in the objective solution of the problem of education. In Socrates learning is for the first time an indispensable prerequisite for the development of moral judgment, which is the basis of moral action.

The need to abandon the traditional form of education, which was aesthetic, philological and gymnastic, arose out of the great economic, social and political tasks which young men from the best circles in Athens had to face in the time of Socrates. Socrates himself saw to it that the question was kept alive, in deliberate opposition to the

---

[31] Democritus of Abdera Fr., 59 (II, 157, Diels[5]): οὔτε τέχνη οὔτε σοφίη ἐφικτόν, ἢν μὴ μάθηι τις. On the relation between τέχνη and σοφίη cf. Snell, 15 f. (also bibl., 16, n. 1).

[32] Archytas of Tarent. Fr., 3, 1 ff. (I, 437, Diels[5]): δεῖ γὰρ ἢ μαθόντα παρ' ἄλλω ἢ αὐτὸν ἐξευρόντα, ὧν ἀνεπιστάμων ἦσθα, ἐπιστάμονα γενέσθαι. τὸ μὲν ὦν μαθὲν παρ' ἄλλω καὶ ἀλλοτρίαι, τὸ δὲ ἐξευρὲν δι' αὔταυτον καὶ ἰδίαι· ἐξευρεῖν δὲ μὴ ζατοῦντα ἄπορον καὶ σπάνιον, ζατοῦντα δὲ εὔπορον καὶ ῥάιδιον, μὴ ἐπιστάμενον δὲ ζητεῖν ἀδύνατον.

[33] Cf. Democr. Fr., 64 (II, 158, Diels[5]): πολλοὶ πολυμαθέες νοῦν οὐκ ἔχουσιν.

[34] Up to Plato we find μάθησις as the noun of μανθάνειν.

[35] Plat. Tim., 88a: (ἡ ψυχὴ) ὅταν εἴς τινας μαθήσεις καὶ ζητήσεις συντόνως ἴῃ, κατατήκει, Theaet., 144b: ὁ δὲ οὕτω λείως τε καὶ ἀπταίστως καὶ ἀνυσίμως ἔρχεται ἐπὶ τὰς μαθήσεις τε καὶ ζητήσεις μετὰ πολλῆς τῆς πρᾳότητος ...

[36] H. Kleinknecht drew attention to this.

[37] Cf. the quotations → *infra*.

[38] Nestle, 82, and numerous examples, 82 ff.

[39] For Soph. cf. H. Weinstock, *Sophokles* (1931), 244 ff.; for Aesch. Nestle 84-87.

[40] Cf. the short observations in K. H. Rengstorf, "Griechentum und Christentum," *Die Volkskirche*, 7 (1934), 74a.

[41] Cf. Nestle, 83.

Sophists, who thought that the emergency could be met by formal education.[42] He refused to follow the example of the Sophists by gathering around him a fixed circle of pupils (μαθηταί), nor would he be paid as the Sophists were.[43] Acc. to Plat. La., 200a-e he did not wish to be a teacher of youth.[44] His goal was simply to kindle a moral sense in his hearers as one part of self-awareness, and thereby to open the way for moral action in the existing situation. The dialectical method which he used was for this purpose. In the course of discussion his companion, under his guidance, would come to insights which would fit together and produce the attitude sought. Socrates himself describes his method as τέχνη τῆς μαιεύσεως (maieutics).[45] In Plato[46] and Xenophon[47] he himself describes as μανθάνειν the intellectual movement which he initiates thereby in the συγγιγνόμενοι αὐτῷ. This is in keeping with the basic sense of the word, → 391. Yet a passage like Theaet., 150d (→ n. 46) shows that μανθάνειν has for Socrates a suprapersonal accent when used for the process of perception. Here is the new element in him as compared with the older philosophy. The metaphysics of learning developed by Plato is already present *in nuce* in Socrates,[48] most plainly so in his own person. If he did not refuse to be called σοφός (→ n. 45), it was because he always had the sense that he was in all things learning,[49] that he was thus becoming, and that in so doing he was fulfilling the destiny divinely ordained for him (Plat. Theaet., 150c; → n. 45).

Plato is a genuine pupil of Socrates in his radical rejection of the teaching and learning practised in the Sophist schools. This did not mean, however, that he any more than his master[50] regarded a good formal education as secondary. He thought that learning rudimentary knowledge and skills was indispensable for all members of the state, and this was part of his programme in both the *Republic* and the *Laws*. Here, too, the goal is ἀρετή, the awakening of a sense of the ἀγαθόν.

He thought there should be compulsory education for both sexes between the years 10 and 18. The subjects should be reading and writing, song and music, and elementary arithmetic, geometry and astronomy. Physical education was naturally included as well.

---

[42] Cf. H. Maier, *Sokrates* (1913), 189 ff.

[43] Notwithstanding Xenoph. Mem., IV, 7, 1: ὧν δὲ προσήκει ἀνδρὶ καλῷ κἀγαθῷ εἰδέναι, ὅ τι μὲν αὐτὸς εἰδείη, πάντων προθυμότατα ἐδίδασκεν· ὅτου δὲ αὐτὸς ἀπειρότερος εἴη, πρὸς τοὺς ἐπισταμένους ἦγεν αὐτούς, Plat. Ap., 33a-b is quite plain: οὓς δὴ διαβάλλοντες ἐμέ φασιν ἐμοὺς μαθητὰς εἶναι. ἐγὼ δὲ διδάσκαλος μὲν οὐδενὸς πώποτ' ἐγενόμην· εἰ δέ τίς μου λέγοντος ... ἐπιθυμοῖ ἀκούειν, ... οὐδὲ χρήματα μὲν λαμβάνων διαλέγομαι ... On the contradiction between the two passages cf. Maier, *op. cit.*, 107 f., 170 ff., 193 f.

[44] Cf. Maier, 194, n. 3.

[45] Plat. Theaet., 150b, cf. c: μαιεύεσθαί με ὁ θεὸς ἀναγκάζει, γεννᾶν δὲ ἀπεκώλυσεν. εἰμὶ δὴ οὖν αὐτὸς μὲν οὐ πάνυ τι σοφός ...

[46] Plat. Theaet., 150d: οἱ δ' ἐμοὶ συγγιγνόμενοι τὸ μὲν πρῶτον φαίνονται ἔνιοι μὲν καὶ πάνυ ἀμαθεῖς, πάντες δὲ προϊούσης τῆς συνουσίας, οἷσπερ ἂν ὁ θεὸς παρείκῃ, θαυμαστὸν ὅσον ἐπιδιδόντες, ὡς αὐτοῖς τε καὶ τοῖς ἄλλοις δοκοῦσι· καὶ τοῦτο ἐναργὲς ὅτι παρ' ἐμοῦ οὐδὲν πώποτε μαθόντες, ἀλλ' αὐτοὶ παρ' αὐτῶν πολλὰ καὶ καλὰ εὑρόντες τε καὶ τεκόντες. τῆς μέντοι μαιείας ὁ θεός τε καὶ ἐγὼ αἴτιος.

[47] So Xenoph. Mem., I, 4, 17: ἔφη, κατάμαθε ὅτι καὶ ὁ σὸς νοῦς ἐνὼν τὸ σὸν σῶμα ὅπως βούλεται μεταχειρίζεται.

[48] Stenzel, 62 ff. recalls that at the time of Socrates reading as well as hearing was identical with learning, at least in the result; he hereby draws attention to an important prerequisite for the success of the mode of instruction developed by Socrates.

[49] To this aspect of Socrates, which was not sufficiently appreciated for a long time, Stenzel, 54 has again drawn attention. He agrees that Socrates did not wish to be a teacher (→ n. 43), cf. also O. Dittrich, *Geschichte der Ethik*, I (1926), 173.

[50] There may be a grain of truth in Xenoph. Mem., IV, 7, 1, but only in this respect.

(b) The new element is Plato's discussion of the learning process. He relates this to his doctrine of the pre-existence of the ψυχή, which he shared with the Pythagoreans.[51] μανθάνειν is more precisely defined as ἀνάμνησις, i.e., the recollection of what was known before time: ἡμῖν ἡ μάθησις οὐκ ἄλλο τι ἢ ἀνάμνησις τυγχάνει οὖσα (Phaed., 72e).[52] In this saying he goes beyond a theory of knowledge and raises the learning process to the level of metaphysics.[53] So far as the method of the teacher is concerned, this means that the maieutic procedure of Socrates alone corresponds to reality. It may be said: ἀεὶ ἡ ἀλήθεια ἡμῖν τῶν ὄντων ἐστὶν ἐν τῇ ψυχῇ (Plat. Men., 86b). But if so, the teacher's only task is to bring a man from unconscious to conscious knowledge, and thus to lead him to ἀρετή, and to make him capable of independent moral action.

Plato explicitly expounds the metaphysics of the learning process in the dialogue Meno.[54] He begins with the question of Meno to Socrates (70a): ἔχεις μοι εἰπεῖν, ὦ Σώκρατες, ἆρα διδακτὸν ἡ ἀρετή; ἢ οὐ διδακτὸν ἀλλ' ἀσκητόν; ἢ οὔτε ἀσκητὸν οὔτε μαθητόν, ἀλλὰ φύσει παραγίγνεται τοῖς ἀνθρώποις ἢ ἄλλῳ τινὶ τρόπῳ; With the help of his peculiar method Socrates points the questioner beyond the mere concept of ἀρετή to the insight that the perception and definition of ἀρετή in its manifoldness is possible only if a basic and comprehensive attitude of the soul, which is always present in individual things, produces virtue or ἀρετή in each case.[55] The attempt of Meno to define ἀρετή as such for Socrates (77a ff.) is a failure. He must admit that though he thought he knew it he no longer knows what ἀρετή is.[56] Socrates himself does not know it and never did (80c). But he will now join with Meno in investigating what it is (80d). Since he has also to bring out for Meno the paradox of the co-existence of practical knowledge and theoretical ignorance, this enquiry will be an analysis of the learning process by which a man passes from ignorance to knowledge. Since it has not proved possible (→ *supra*) to proceed by way of concepts to general and necessary truths, the only remaining possibility is that these are latent in the ψυχή and simply need to be brought to light (81a ff.). Socrates takes this path. Adopting the doctrine of the immortality of the soul, he argues: ἅτε οὖν ἡ ψυχὴ ἀθάνατός τε οὖσα καὶ πολλάκις γεγονυῖα, καὶ ἑωρακυῖα καὶ τὰ ἐνθάδε καὶ τὰ ἐν Ἅιδου καὶ πάντα χρήματα, οὐκ ἔστιν, ὅτι οὐ μεμάθηκεν (81c). He proves the truth of his view in the famous scene in which, with the help of leading questions, he brings an uneducated slave to see that the diagonal of a square is the side of the square with the doubled surface (82a-85b). Finally, this result is evaluated both in respect of the learning process and in respect of the initial question (85c ff.): ἀρετή is not ἐπιστήμη (knowledge) in the usual sense, and hence it cannot be taught; it can

---

[51] Cf. Empedocles Fr., 115 (I, 358, Diels^5) and on the historical connections, W. Jaeger, *Paideia*^{2}, I (1936), 225 ff. Probably the starting-point of the whole speculation is to be found among the Orphics.

[52] Cf. also Aristot. Topica, IV, p. 124a, 21 ff.: ... καὶ εἰ τὸ μανθάνειν ἀναμιμνήσκεσθαι, καὶ τὸ μεμαθηκέναι ἀναμεμνῆσθαι ...

[53] W. Freymann, *Platons Suchen nach einer Grundlegung aller Philosophie* (1930), 79 ff.; E. Grassi, *Il problema della metafisica platonica* (1932); K. Hildebrandt, *Platon* (1933), 163. F. Schleiermacher was the first to see his way clearly in these matters; cf. *Platons Werke*, II, 3^2 (1826), 16.

[54] For an analysis cf. Stenzel, 147-163. This underlies the present sketch. Cf. also Klara Buchmann, "Die Stellung des Menon in d. platonischen Philosophie," *Philologus Suppl.*, 29, 3 (1936); E. Grassi.

[55] Stenzel, 149; cf. Men., 77a ff.: The point is to comprehend ἀρετή as a totality: ἀλλ' ἴθι δὴ πειρῶ καὶ σὺ ἐμοὶ τὴν ὑπόσχεσιν ἀποδοῦναι, κατὰ ὅλου εἰπὼν ἀρετῆς πέρι ὅτι ἐστίν (77a).

[56] Men., 80b: καὶ πάνυ εὖ, ὥς γε ἐμαυτῷ ἐδόκουν· νῦν δὲ οὐδ' ὅτι ἐστὶν τὸ παράπαν ἔχω εἰπεῖν.

be achieved only by way of μανθάνειν through ἀνάμνησις, for it τῶν ἐν τῇ ψυχῇ τί ἐστιν (88c). Through ἀνάμνησις, which takes place in discussion of the basis (αἰτίας λογισμῷ) of the ὀρθὴ δόξα, in which ἀρετή is enclosed, there arises this ἐπιστήμη in the higher sense (98a).

In this light one can appreciate the inner consistency of the many statements of Plato about the nature of μανθάνειν in various contexts. Learning and forgetting are for him intermediate states between εἰδέναι and μὴ εἰδέναι.[57] In learning man is never passive; he is always active, even when receiving.[58] Hence μανθάνω and εὑρίσκω can be used almost synonymously.[59] μανθάνειν is more demanding than gymnastics (Resp., VII, 535b). The latter applies only to the σῶμα, the former to the whole man. The less, then, should it be forced.[60] One ought to learn by play, for thus one may better establish for what μάθημα there is aptitude.[61] Part of true μανθάνειν is the desire (χάρις) rooted in ἀλήθεια.[62] The Platonic view of learning also enables us to see why mathematics (τὰ μαθήματα)[63] is so important for Plato in the learning process.[64]

c. The Intellectualising of the Learning Process in the Philosophy of the Schools.

Of Socrates' pupils Plato was the only one to understand him and to develop his teaching. This is illustrated by the treatment of μανθάνω by the philosophers of the period which followed. The word was increasingly intellectualised and rationalised.

In Mem., IV, 7, 2 ff. Xenophon causes Socrates to advise the ὁμιλοῦντας αὐτῷ to learn (μανθάνειν) only so much geometry, astronomy, arithmetic and medicine as an ὀρθῶς πεπαιδευμένος should know. Though put on the lips of Socrates, this restriction of μανθάνειν has nothing to do with him. What is presented is the ideal of Xenophon himself, who knows not only the blessings of knowledge but also the dangers which threaten the traditional view of knowledge, and its progress, which it is his own concern to preserve.[65] In Xenophon μανθάνω is completely rationalised again (cf. Mem., I, 1, 9; 2, 17; III, 9, 3 etc.).[66] For him μανθάνοντες are μαθηταί ("pupils," → μαθητής), which they are not for Plato.[67]

---

[57] Cf. Theaet., 188a, 191c ff.

[58] *Ibid.*, 197e: ἣν δ' ἂν ἐπιστήμην (partial knowledge) κτησάμενος καθείρξῃ (καθείργνυμι, to include) εἰς τὸν περίβολον (supply τῆς ψυχῆς), φάναι αὐτὸν μεμαθηκέναι ἢ ηὑρηκέναι τὸ πρᾶγμα οὗ ἦν αὕτη ἡ ἐπιστήμη (i.e., to which ἐπιστήμη related itself), καὶ τὸ ἐπίστασθαι τοῦτ' εἶναι, cf. Hildebrandt, *op. cit.*, 158; P. Friedländer, *Platon*, I (1928), 193.

[59] → n. 58 and → 394.

[60] Resp., VII, 536e f.: οὐδὲν μάθημα μετὰ δουλείας τὸν ἐλεύθερον χρὴ μανθάνειν. οἱ μὲν γὰρ τοῦ σώματος πόνοι βίᾳ πονούμενοι χεῖρον οὐδὲν τὸ σῶμα ἀπεργάζονται, ψυχῇ δὲ βίαιον οὐδὲν ἔμμονον μάθημα.

[61] *Ibid.*, 537a: παίζοντας τρέφε, ἵνα καὶ μᾶλλον οἷός τ' ἦς καθορᾶν ἐφ' ὃ ἕκαστος πέφυκεν. Cf. also Leg., VII, 819a ff.

[62] Leg., II, 667c.

[63] On the history of μάθημα cf. Snell, 76 ff. In his evaluation of μαθήματα Philo follows earlier philosophy, esp. Pythagoras, for whom mathematics was *the* science.

[64] Cf. Freymann, 105 ff. It is a matter of the structural control of being.

[65] Maier, 171 f.

[66] Xenoph. Sym., 3, 5 uses μανθάνω for learning by heart: ὁ πατὴρ ..., ὅπως ἀνὴρ ἀγαθὸς γενοίμην (→ n. 60) ἠνάγκασέ με πάντα τὰ Ὁμήρου ἔπη μαθεῖν· καὶ νῦν δυναίμην ἂν ... ἀπὸ στόματος εἰπεῖν.

[67] It should be noted that acc. to the Socrates of Xenophon one could learn all that is needed as a member of the *polis* from Homer (Sym., 4, 6), who is *the* σοφός; cf. also

In Aristot. it is hard to see the intellectual link with Socrates/Plato when we consider his use of μανθάνω. There are express refs. to Plato,[68] but the total attitude is very different. Aristotle is a pure theoretician. This attitude controls his view of the learning process. He rejects the Platonic doctrine of ἀνάμνησις. For Aristotle the νοῦς is immortal rather than the ψυχή, though only in so far as it is the active principle in the process of knowledge (cf. An., III, 5, p. 430). ἐπιστήμη is called the ὄργανον of the νοῦς (Probl., 30, 5, p. 955b, 36 ff.). Hence it may be said: ὥσπερ τὸ μανθάνειν λέγεται ξυνιέναι, ὅταν χρῆται τῇ ἐπιστήμῃ ... (Eth. Nic., VI, 11, p. 1143a, 12 f.). Knowledge proceeds in such a way that the receptive part of the νοῦς is, in Aristotle's own image, an empty tablet (An., III, 5, p. 430). In practice this means that learning (μανθάνειν) loses any irrational features and remains wholly in the sphere of the rational: ἃ γὰρ δεῖ μαθόντας ποιεῖν, ταῦτα ποιοῦντες μανθάνομεν, οἷον οἰκοδομοῦντες οἰκοδόμοι γίνονται καὶ κιθαρίζοντες κιθαρισταί (Eth. Nic., II, 1, p. 1103a, 32 ff.).[69] Hence Aristotle can explain the fact that with increasing age men have μᾶλλον νοῦν, but in youth they learn faster (θᾶττον μανθάνομεν), by saying that the νοῦς needs first to be endowed with natural dispositions, and that this is so with the young διὰ τὸ μηδέν πω ἐπίστασθαι. ὅταν δὲ ἐπιστώμεθα, οὐκέτι ὁμοίως δυνάμεθα (Probl., 30, 5, p. 955b, 23 ff.). How far he is from Plato may be seen from the fact that for him ἀρετή ... διανοητικὴ τὸ πλεῖον ἐκ διδασκαλίας[70] ἔχει καὶ τὴν γένεσιν καὶ τὴν αὔξησιν, ... ἡ δ' ἠθικὴ ἐξ ἔθους περιγίνεται (Eth. Nic., II, 1, p. 1103a, 15 ff.). Perhaps Probl., 30, 6, p. 956a, 11 ff. is even more instructive in this connection: διὰ τί ἀνθρώπῳ πειστέον μᾶλλον ἢ ἄλλῳ ζῴῳ; ... ἢ ὅτι μιμητικώτατον; μανθάνειν γὰρ δύναται διὰ τοῦτο.

The later philosophy of the schools simply concludes the process.

Neither in the Peripatetics nor the Stoics is there anything special about μανθάνω. Epict. uses the word for the mastering of technical skills (Diss., I, 26, 7) and the technique of thought (I, 22, 19: σὺ παρὰ τῶν φιλοσόφων μανθάνεις συλλογισμόν), but also for the adoption of philosophical and theological insights.[71] In these matters the point is to fall in with the man who knows what one does not know.[72] Practice is thus important, esp. in the ethical sphere.[73] So is the appeal to the example (Socrates!).

Mem., I, 6, 14 and Maier, 172 ff. Stoicism treads a similar path, cf. I. Heinemann, *Poseidonios' metaphysische Schriften* II (1928), 54 ff., and the significance of Homer for Stoicism, e.g., Epict.

[68] An. Post., I, 1, p. 71a, 29 f.: ... τὸ ἐν τῷ Μένωνι ἀπόρημα συμβήσεται· ἢ γὰρ οὐδὲν μαθήσεται ἢ ἃ οἶδεν, cf. lines 1 f.: πᾶσα διδασκαλία καὶ πᾶσα μάθησις διανοητικὴ ἐκ προϋπαρχούσης γίνεται γνώσεως. → also n. 46.

[69] Cf. Metaph., VIII, 8, p. 1049b, 27 ff.: εἴρηται δ' ἐν τοῖς περὶ τῆς οὐσίας λόγοις ὅτι ἅπαν τὸ γιγνόμενον γίγνεται ἔκ τινός τι καὶ ὑπό τινος, καὶ τοῦτο τῷ εἴδει τὸ αὐτό. διὸ καὶ δοκεῖ ἀδύνατον εἶναι οἰκοδόμον εἶναι μὴ οἰκοδομήσαντα μηδὲν ἢ κιθαριστὴν μηδὲν κιθαρίσαντα· ὁ γὰρ μανθάνων κιθαρίζειν κιθαρίζων μανθάνει κιθαρίζειν, ὁμοίως δὲ καὶ οἱ ἄλλοι. ὅθεν ὁ σοφιστικὸς ἔλεγχος ἐγίγνετο ὅτι οὐκ ἔχων τις τὴν ἐπιστήμην ποιήσει οὗ ἡ ἐπιστήμη· ὁ γὰρ μανθάνων οὐκ ἔχει, ἀλλὰ διὰ τὸ τοῦ γιγνομένου γεγενῆσθαί τι καὶ τοῦ ὅλως κινουμένου κεκινῆσθαί τι (δῆλον δ' ἐν τοῖς περὶ κινήσεως τοῦτο) καὶ τὸν μανθάνοντα ἀνάγκη ἔχειν τι τῆς ἐπιστήμης ἴσως. Cf. also An. Post., I, 18; 81a, 38 ff. ... μανθάνομεν ἢ ἐπαγωγῇ (induction) ἢ ἀποδείξει (deduction).

[70] It should be noted that μανθάνειν is part of διδασκαλία.

[71] Cf. e.g., Diss., II, 14, 11: λέγουσιν οἱ φιλόσοφοι, ὅτι μαθεῖν δεῖ πρῶτον τοῦτο, ὅτι ἔστι θεός, καὶ προνοεῖ τῶν ὅλων ...

[72] Diss., II, 17, 3: τίνος δ' ἕνεκα προσερχόμεθα τοῖς φιλοσόφοις; μαθησόμενοι παρ' αὐτοῖς ἃ οὐκ οἰόμεθα εἰδέναι. τίνα δ' ἐστὶ ταῦτα; τὰ θεωρήματα. ἃ γὰρ λαλοῦσιν οἱ φιλόσοφοι μαθεῖν θέλομεν ὡς κομψὰ καὶ δριμέα, οἱ δ', ἵν' ἀπ' αὐτῶν περιποιήσωνται.

[73] Diss., II, 14, 10: ὁρῶμεν οὖν ὅτι ὁ τέκτων μαθών τινα γίνεται τέκτων, ὁ κυβερνήτης μαθών τινα γίνεται κυβερνήτης. Cf. Aristot. Metaph., VIII, 8, p. 1049b, 27 ff. → n. 69 and also Diss., II, 9, 10 f., also M. Ant., XII, 6 (ἐθίζειν).

The finest example is in the 1st book of M. Ant., Τὰ εἰς ἑαυτόν.[74] Here appeal is made to Socrates, but there is no trace of what Plato had in mind as the follower of Socrates.[75]

3. μανθάνω as a Special Cultic Term in Hellenism.

The Corp. Herm. suggests that in the circle of cultic mysticism μανθάνειν was used to denote reception of the ἱερὸς λόγος by initiates, this acceptance being an essential part of rites of initiation. It is in keeping with the situation that the word is found in close proximity to γινώσκειν.

The dialogue with which the Corp. Herm. begins gives some particulars. The recipient of revelation tells how, when he is in an exalted mood, the question is put to him by Poimandres (I, 1): τί βούλει ἀκοῦσαι καὶ θεάσασθαι, καὶ νοήσας μαθεῖν καὶ γνῶναι; and he answers (I, 3): μαθεῖν θέλω τὰ ὄντα καὶ νοῆσαι τὴν τούτων φύσιν, καὶ γνῶναι τὸν θεόν ... Then it is said to him: ἔχε νῷ σῷ ὅσα θέλεις μαθεῖν, κἀγώ σε διδάξω. μανθάνειν, and on the other side διδάσκειν (I, 24, 27, 29; XIII, 2, 16 etc.; cf. also XVI, 1b: Hermes as διδάσκαλος), as expressions for central religious processes, show plainly the trend towards intellectualisation in the piety of Corp. Herm. τὴν τῶν ὄντων φύσιν μαθεῖν (cf. XIV, 1) "is almost a formula for seeing God."[76] True piety and knowledge of the world are much the same.[77] Both are rooted in the νοῦς.

Perhaps Apul. Met. should be mentioned here. Luc. tells how to him, as an Isis initiate, the priest of the goddess revealed the ceremonial which related to initiation (τελετή) (*indidem mihi praedicat, quae forent ad usum teletae necessario praeparanda*). This instruction takes place in the form of reading from books with strange signs and animal figures, i.e., in hieroglyphics, and it has a definite didactic character.[78] We have some depictions which suggest that such instruction was common in the mysteries. Thus a bas relief in the Louvre shows behind an altar with fruits a reading-desk on which is the roll of a book,[79] and in the Villa Item in Rome we have in the so-called chamber of the mysteries a mural depicting the instruction of a young girl who is to be initiated into the Dionysus mysteries. This is almost an illustration of the scene in Apul.[80] The only thing lacking in Apul. is a word corresponding to μανθάνειν for the reception by the initiate of the instruction given by the priest. When *praedicare* is used for the work of the priest, this suggests authoritative pronouncement as well as the impartation of things not previously known. Much later, in Firmicus Maternus Err. Prof. Rel., 18, 1 we find the Attis symbol in a form which even in the choice of words attests a close connection between the rites of initiation and objective instruction: *de tympano manducavi, de cymbalo bibi, et religionis secreta perdidici.* It may be that this is a later stage of the mysteries in which the didactic element is strongly to the fore as compared with

---

[74] Cf. esp. I, 8: Παρὰ Ἀπολλωνίου ... καὶ τὸ ἐπὶ παραδείγματος ζῶντος ἰδεῖν ἐναργῶς ...

[75] To be sure, acc. to Xenoph. Mem., III, 5, 8 ff. Socrates regarded ἀναμιμνήσκεσθαι of the πρόγονοι as an important factor in the education of the people in civic virtues. But both he and Plato have in view something very different from the mere setting up of moral examples, as in the Stoa, cf. J. Bannes, *Platon. Die Philosophie des heroischen Vorbildes* (1935), esp. 21 ff.

[76] Reitzenstein Hell. Myst.[2] (1920), 141.

[77] G. Heinrici, *Die Hermes-Mystik und das NT* (1918), 18.

[78] Cf. also Liv. XXXIX, 11, 1.

[79] Phot. A. Giraudon, 1840 (J. Leipoldt, *Der Gottesdienst d. ältesten Kirche* [1937], 6, n. 2). In this case the book possibly contained prayers (cf. Apul. Met., XI, 17), but its mere presence is important enough to call for notice.

[80] Phot. Andersen, 26,380 and 26,553, cf. J. Leipoldt, *Dionysos* (ΑΓΓΕΛΟΣ *Beih.*, 3) (1931), 29 and n. 217.

the mystic rite.[81] But the development presupposes that the didactic element was already present earlier.[82] If the older texts found little place for it, this may be linked with the *disciplina arcana* to which initiates were subject.[83] There can be no doubt that symbolic formulae were found in the various mysteries,[84] and even their understanding, let alone their meaningful use, would not have been possible without searching instruction.[85] Thus διδάσκειν and μανθάνειν must have had a place in the mysteries as soon as the mystery cults led to the formation of religious societies which proselytised for their god. A σύμβολον/*signum* was needed both for the sake of the society and also for that of new recruits if they were to recognise one another as members of the same group. Here may be seen some of the decisive presuppositions for the rise of the Christian creed, → 412.[86]

B. μανθάνω in the Old Testament and Judaism.

1. לָמַד/μανθάνω in the Old Testament (LXX).

a. μανθάνω occurs in the LXX and other Gk. transl. of the OT some 55 times. Of the 40 instances in which there is a Heb. original, it is used almost 30 times for a form of the root למד: למד is thus the true original for μανθάνω. Alongside it, other terms play only a minor part. It is twice used for forms of ידע, and quite appropriately, for in both cases the ref. is to personal information (לְדֵעָה, Ex. 2:4; לָדַעַת, Est. 4:5; → 391). In Prv. 22:25 we find μανθάνω for אָלַף, "to accustom oneself to," in a good, if not literal, translation (→ 401). It also occurs in Is. 47:12 for יָגַע, "to exercise oneself," in Sir. 8:9a for שָׁמַע, and in Sir. 8:9b; 16:24 for לָקַח, "to receive." לָמַד (qal) is fairly regularly rendered μανθάνω by the LXX. At 1 Ch. 5:18 we find לְמוּדֵי מִלְחָמָה translated δεδιδαγμένοι πόλεμον, but this, too, is apposite, for → διδάσκειν is customarily used for לִמֵּד and passive forms of לָמַד → διδάσκειν.[87]

---

[81] Cf. M. Dibelius, "Die Isisweihe bei Apul. and verwandte Initiationsriten," SAH, 1917, 4, 7 ff., esp. 10 f., and for analogies in Ps.-Apul. cf. Reitzenstein. On Aesculapius in Ps.-Apul., ARW, 7 (1904), 393 ff., esp. 410.

[82] The judgment of Aristot. on the demands on initiates in Synesius of Cyrene (c. 370-415 A.D.), De Dione (ed. G. Krabinger [1850], p. 171 f.): Ἀριστοτέλης ἀξιοῖ τοὺς τελουμένους οὐ μαθεῖν τι δεῖν, ἀλλὰ παθεῖν καὶ διατεθῆναι, γινομένους δηλονότι ἐπιτηδείους, may simply indicate that the mysteries imparted knowledge in a way quite different from that of the philosophy of the schools (→ 397). One might refer to Pythagoreanism from an older period. Novices were given comprehensive esoteric instruction before reception into the society. Some data were known to Aristot. (Ael. Var. Hist., II, 26), but we have no precise picture of the earlier Pythagorean rite.

[83] Cf. on this Dibelius, 15 f.

[84] *Ibid.*, 11 ff.

[85] *Ibid.*, 15 for a summary on the nature of such symbols.

[86] So far there has not been found in the mysteries any term for the symbol derived from μανθάνω, like the μάθημα of the early Church.

[87] At 1 Βασ. 1:9 we find in A ἐμάθετο for יָשַׁב, where we should read ἐκάθητο as in 4:13 (ἐκάθητο is not found in either verse in B). Θ has μανθάνειν for לקח in Ez. 16:61, relating לֶקַח to "teaching." Sometimes the LXX, too, equates the words in arbitrary interpretation of the Heb. Thus at Job 34:36 the Mas. has בחן, and the LXX the more intellectual μανθάνειν. The same tendency appears when in Prv. 17:16a the LXX improves on the Mas. by transferring to the σκολιάζων τοῦ μαθεῖν what 17:20 Mas. says about the evil that will befall those who sin with the tongue. In Is. 32:4 we have a free rendering of the difficult Heb. Yet here, too, μαθεῖν is suggested by בין in the first half of the verse. The same may well apply in Is. 28:19 [Bertram].

b. If the picture is fairly uniform, one cannot say this of the usage. This is partly linked with the particular character of למד and partly with the penetration of the ordinary use of μανθάνω into the Gk. translation or the Gk. parts of the OT. Nor does a consistent usage gradually develop. Ordinary use occurs throughout the OT.[88] Nevertheless, the word also comes plainly within the circle of divine revelation, and this gives to it, as to → διδάσκω, a special nuance, the more so as revelation of God is in the OT the declaration of His will. Thus the word is in some sense used for the process wherein man subjects himself to fulfilment of the will of God as this is intimated especially in the Law.

The objects of μανθάνω are instructive. In Dt. the obj. is always the fear of God (4:10: ὅπως μάθωσιν φοβεῖσθαί με, cf. 14:23; 17:19; 31:12 f.) as the goal which God Himself set when He gave δικαιώματα καὶ κρίσεις (חֻקִּים וּמִשְׁפָּטִים, 4:14) in order that the people should be instructed in them by Moses. The attitude sought in μανθάνοντες is that of the obedience of the whole man to God in the doing of His will (ποιεῖν αὐτά), and not just a more or less clear insight into the divine will. Hence everything depends on obedience even when elsewhere we read only of μανθάνειν τὰ δικαιώματά σου (אֶלְמַד חֻקֶּיךָ) (ψ 118:71, 73) and not explicitly of φυλάσσειν (as, e.g., in ψ 118:7 f.; Dt. 5:1 לַעֲשֹׂתָם). It is in keeping with the practical attitude at issue that we also find as objects δικαιοσύνη (Is. 26:9), καλὸν ποιεῖν (Is. 1:17), ὑπακούειν and λαλεῖν εἰρήνην (Is. 29:24). All this, living and walking acc. to God's will, is summed up in biblical language as the דֶּרֶךְ (→ ὁδός) (hence μανθάνειν τὴν ὁδὸν τοῦ λαοῦ μου, Jer. 12:16; cf. also ψ 24:9, though here with διδάσκω). Only he can walk thus who has learned → φρόνησις (Bar. 3:14), → σύνεσις (Sir. 8:9), ἐπιστήμη (Sir. 16:24) and → σοφία (Wis. 6:9; 7:13), and who thus knows what he has to do.[89] All this knowledge, in whose evaluation in the apocr. there may be noted the influence of Gk. rationalism on Judaism in the form of a certain intellectualising of its piety, is enclosed in the Law. For this reason the ultimate requirement is to learn the Law, i.e., consciously and totally to set oneself under the will of God laid down in the νόμος (תּוֹרָה). Where there is no access to the Law, the possibility of μανθάνειν in the strictest sense[90] no longer exists.[91] When the word is used in this connection, an

---

[88] Cf., e.g., Mi. 4:3 (cf. Is. 2:4): καὶ οὐκέτι μὴ μάθωσιν πολεμεῖν (וְלֹא יִלְמְדוּן עוֹד מִלְחָמָה; here the basic meaning of למד, "to exercise," "to grow accustomed to" may well have had some influence); Ez. 19:3, 6: ἔμαθεν τοῦ ἁρπάζειν ἁρπάγματα (image of the young lion: וַיִּלְמַד); Sus. 38: μάθωμεν τίνες εἰσὶν οὗτοι (cf. 1 Macc. 10:72); Da. 7:16 Θ in AB^c: ἐζήτουν παρ' αὐτοῦ μαθεῖν περὶ πάντων τούτων (cf. Ex. 2:4; Est. 4:5 → 400; 2 Macc. 7:2; 3 Macc. 1:1); Παροιμ. 6:8a: μάθε ὡς ἐργάτις ἐστίν (of the bee). For this side of μανθάνω, too, there is a corresponding use of διδάσκω (→ II, 128).

[89] In the LXX σοφία has in general nothing to do with the speculative σοφία of the Gks. Like חָכְמָה, it means knowledge of right conduct (→ σοφία); experience is a source as well as the Torah. *Mutatis mutandis* the same is true of the par. words mentioned above, cf. the partly corresponding verbs in Wis. 6:1. Nevertheless, one may perceive some Gk. influence, esp. in the part played by σοφία in Sir. (cf. R. Sander, *Furcht u. Liebe im palästinischen Judentum* [1935], 40, with bibl.).

[90] Cf. on this 4 Macc. 1:17; 9:5; 10:16, where μανθάνω is used always with a view to personal championing of God's will and work to which others are exposed. Also instructive is Ιωβ 34:36: οὐ μὴν δὲ ἀλλὰ μάθε, Ἰώβ, μὴ δῷς ἔτι ἀνταπόκρισιν ὥσπερ οἱ ἄφρονες. Acc. to the context of this badly preserved text μανθάνω refers to reflection on the will and purpose of God. Job (cf. vv. 29-31) has not previously spoken as συνετὸς καρδίας, σοφός (v. 34), ἐν συνέσει, ἐν ἐπιστήμῃ (v. 35), as he should have done. Now he must learn to do so.

[91] Cf. Is. 8:16: οἱ σφραγιζόμενοι τὸν νόμον τοῦ μὴ μαθεῖν ...

act of will is always in view. Hence, as in similar instances of διδάσκω (→ II, 137), the word can be used even when, under ungodly influences, there is a decision for another will than that of God (cf. Παροιμ. 17:16a; Prv. 22:25; Jer. 10:2; 13:23).

The distinctiveness of the biblical usage as compared with the secular is plain to see. In contrast to the later philosophy and ethics of antiquity, the reference is here to the whole man. With μανθάνω, as with διδάσκω, the object and goal are the same. Thus, even though it be by way of definite information, we learn only what is ultimately to be practised or fulfilled.[92] What this is, God Himself decides. To this degree God Himself in His will is the One around whom all learning in the true sense revolves.

2. לָמַד in the Usage of the Rabbis.

a. Here, too, we find a secular use of לָמַד. Thus it is found for learning a trade (Qid., 4, 14) or for getting information about something (Jeb., 15, 3b; Ed., 1, 12) or for drawing knowledge from a book (BM, 2, 8a).[93] As a past part. it is normally used for an existing custom (cf. Ter., 11, 10; Nid., 9, 9 f.; Lv. r., 25, 1 on 19:23 etc.). Ab., 4, 1 describes the חָכָם thus: הַלּוֹמֵד מִכָּל אָדָם. In the first instance this is to be taken very generally.

b. Yet for the most part Rabbinic usage develops and concludes the movement found in the OT. לָמַד in the abs. usually means occupation with the Torah with the aim of knowing and doing the will of God. In view of the position of the Law in the thought and life of later Judaism, it is inevitable that all learning, including that of the rudiments of knowledge, serves the purpose of making all members of the people or community into men who are versed in the Law.[94] Occupation with Holy Scripture is thus only the first stage for learners. From this, if they want real knowledge, they must move on to the traditional exposition of Scripture in the Mishnah, the Talmud and the Midrash,[95] which control the whole life of the scholar (→ μαθητής B. 4 ff.). These, too, are learned not least with a view to maintaining the known will of God and making it profitable for others also.[96]

Things are much the same here as with לִמֵּד (→ διδάσκω, II, 137 f.) except that the standpoint is now that of the recipient. Learning and learning the Torah are equated. This may be seen from the fact that sometimes in the same passages some verses, usually the older, regard לָמַד as enough, while others add an explanatory תּוֹרָה.[97] Thus learning

---

92 The same is true of a saying like Sir. 18:19: πρὶν ἢ λαλῆσαι μάνθανε, though it is possible that the Gk. version here rests on a mistranslation, cf. V. Ryssel in Kautzsch Apokr., 321, n. d *ad loc.*, and R. Smend, *Die Weisheit des Jesus Sirach erklärt* (1906), 167.

93 This and other passages do at least touch on the sphere of the authority of the Torah.

94 It is worth noting that the teacher's chair is called קָתֶדְרָא דְמשֶׁה (Krauss, III, 208, 340, n. 54).

95 Cf. Ab., 5, 21: "With five years for Scripture, ten for the Mishnah, fifteen for the Talmud." The Mishnah and Talmud here are not the works we now know, but the process of learning and teaching — the Mishnah as exposition of Scripture and the Talmud as exposition of the Mishnah — which finally produced them. We should also remember that acc. to the Rabb. the prophets and writings contained nothing not already in the Torah (cf. Str.-B., IV, 446 ff.).

96 Cf. Ab., 4, 5: הַלּוֹמֵד עַל מְנָת לְלַמֵּד מַסְפִּיקִין בְּיָדוֹ לִלְמוֹד וּלְלַמֵּד: "He who learns in order to teach is given (by God) enough room to learn and to teach."

97 Cf., e.g., Ab., 2, 14 in K. Marti-G. Beer, 'Abôṯ (1927), 189.

is a mark of the righteous,[98] and the prudent will begin to learn in good time while the memory is still receptive (Ab., 4, 20).[99] In the Tann. Midrash formulae like אֶלְמַד לָמַדְתִּי are constant elements in the presentation.[100] But לָמַד is also used when one part of Scripture serves to elucidate another. In this case the second is that which learns, and we thus read: הֲרֵי זֶה בָּא לְלַמֵּד וְנִמְצָא לָמֵד.[101] From this the 12th of the 32 exegetical rules of R. Eliezer[102] took its name (דָּבָר שֶׁבָּא לְלַמֵּד וְנִמְצָא לָמֵד). לָמַד comes to be used increasingly not merely for appropriation of the contents of Scripture but also for familiarity with the methods with whose help alone the true, final and deepest sense of Scripture can be attained. He who reads and follows Scripture without having learned, and continuing to learn, may be full of good intentions but for the Rabbis he has no access to it, and he must be prepared to be contemptuously reckoned by them among the ὄχλος ὁ μὴ γινώσκων τὸν νόμον (Jn. 7:49) and regarded as a severe burden on the chosen people.[103] The Holy God desires a holy people (Lv. 19:2). But for the Rabbis only he can be holy who knows God's holy will from the legal tradition and exact knowledge of it. This is why R. Eleazar ben Shammua (c. 150) could call those who were gathered in the house of instruction to learn the holy people (עַם קוֹדֶשׁ) = Israel, bSota, 39a. Acc. to Rabb. teaching Israel was created, or elected by God as His people, only to occupy itself with the pre-existent Torah.[104] Hence members of the people are ordained to learn the Torah. The ideal is that all should do so.[105] Thus in the age of the Messiah, the age of the consummation of salvation history and the history of the people, it is expected that there will be study of the Torah by all the people, and that the Messiah will take the lead in this.[106] The glory of the Messiah will rest not least in the fact that he is a student as well as a teacher of the Torah (Midr. Ps., 21, 4 on 21:6).

c. The use of לָמַד in Rabb. Judaism gives evidence of a further intellectualising of Jewish piety as compared with the OT.[107] The process may be seen already in the Apocrypha with its evaluation of σοφία as a knowledge which one has (→ n. 89). The Greek influences which come to light here continue their work. The development comes to a head in some sense in the decision which the Rabbis took under the leadership of Akiba at the time of the persecution under Hadrian, namely, that study of the Law is of higher rank than practising it (S. Dt., 41 on 11:13; bQid., 40b). The decision was in part fostered by the outward situation of the Jews (the prohibition of the cultus by the Romans). But it was also in line with earlier development, as is shown by the fact that its validity was not questioned even when keeping the Law was no longer attended by such serious

---

98 Ab., 5, 10-19 and → I, 323.

99 bShab., 119b, alluding to Jer. 6:11, has the statement of an Amor. that Jerusalem will be destroyed because school-children are kept from learning.

100 W. Bacher, *Die exegetische Terminologie d. jüd. Traditionsliteratur,* I (1899), 94; II (1905), 96 f.

101 Examples in Bacher, I, 95.

102 Cf. the list in Strack Einl., 100 ff.

103 Cf. the Rabb. material on this in Str.-B., II, 494 ff.

104 *Ibid.*, IV, 488-490.

105 In bAZ, 3b Rab. Jehuda (d. 299) hands down a saying of his teacher Rab (d. 247 A.D.) to the effect that God Himself spends 3 hours each day with the Torah (עוֹסֵק) and is thus the great example for His people.

106 Cf. the examples in Str.-B., IV, 918.

107 → on this and on what follows διδάσκω, II, 142 and n. 42.

difficulties.[108] In this connection one might also mention the fact that the later period, which had to come to some terms with the loss of the temple, gave precedence to study of the Torah over penitence, fasting, benevolence and even prayer, when considering things which God would count as the equivalent of sacrifices on the part of His people.[109] Among the factors which ensure the preservation of the race it is reported that Shim'on the Just had already reckoned the Torah above the temple cultus and works of love (Ab., 1, 2). But Shim'on, the son of the elder Gamaliel, could still say that observance rather than study is the chief thing, although in so doing he had now to oppose a different view. The time when the change came is to be put about the time of destruction of the temple. This gave the Rabb. tendency towards religious theory and intellectualistic piety the seeming external justification which it needed to establish itself. In pursuing it the Rabbis avoided outwardly the temptation to hellenise Judaism. But inwardly they still tended to fall victim to the very danger which they sought to escape. Thus the history of לָמַד on the soil of later Judaism is in some ways an instructive part of the history of the Hellenisation of the very Judaism which sought to be wholly faithful to the Law.[110]

If the Rabb. view of לָמַד approximates to Hellenism, there are still characteristic differences. The Greek uses two different words for "to learn" and "to teach," nor is "to learn" the same as "to be taught."[111] But the Hebrew uses the same root for both words. Historical research shows the significance of this. For the Greeks learning and being taught have their own content and goal, and there can also be different ways of approaching the matter. But in the biblical and later Jewish world they are united by the fact that the content and goal of all learning and teaching are established once and for all in the will of God in the Torah. To this degree the more intellectualised לָמַד of later Judaism is still within the circle of the historical revelation of God in His Word to His people. Thus the same word is used, but there may be discerned in it an anthropocentric view of things on the one side and a theocentric on the other.

3. Josephus.

In the use of μανθάνω in Joseph. the formal aspect is predominant. There are many points of contact with the philosophy of the schools, → 397. Yet OT influences are to be seen as well.

---

[108] The textual variants are instructive. Thus a well-known statement of Jochanan ben Zakkai (Ab., 2, 8) originally reads: אִם עָשִׂיתָ תּוֹרָה הַרְבֵּה אַל תַּחֲזִיק טוֹבָה לְעַצְמְךָ כִּי לְכָךְ נוֹצָרְתָּ: "When you have done much of the Torah, do not reckon it a merit, for thereto you were created." Under the influence of the decision at Lydda later tradition substitutes לָמַדְתָּ for עָשִׂיתָ, and thus gives the saying a very different point. Cf. the apparatus in the editions, *ad loc.*

[109] Cf. H. Wenschkewitz, "Die Spiritualisierung der Kultusbegriffe Tempel, Priester und Opfer im NT," ΑΓΓΕΛΟΣ, 4 (1932), 93 f. In bShab., 10a Raba (d. 352 A.D.) censures a colleague for praying too long on the ground that "they leave eternal life and concern themselves with temporal life." Another Amoraean in a similar situation cites Prv. 28:9.

[110] This development calls for more research. Thus far we have solid information only at individual points. But we now have enough to show that the absolute antithesis been Hellenism and the Rabbis is no longer tenable. On this question cf. esp. the hints in P. Feine, *Der Apostel Paulus* (1927), 511 ff. Cf. also R. Meyer, "Hellenistisches in der rabb. Anthropologie," BWANT, IV, 22 (1937), esp. 133 ff.

[111] → n. 4 and 393.

In many instances μανθάνω simply means "to experience." Yet even in this sense it has something distinctive which differentiates it from synonyms. As distinct from πυνθάνομαι and γιγνώσκω, it aims at intellectual assimilation of the object. Thus it can be said of the Greeks with reference to the learning of alphabetic writing, on the one side: ὀψὲ καὶ μόλις ἔγνωσαν φύσιν γραμμάτων, and on the other παρὰ Φοινίκων καὶ Κάδμου σεμνύνονται μαθεῖν (Ap., 1, 10). γινώσκω means here "to penetrate something in terms of knowledge," μανθάνω "to appropriate it intellectually."[112] Hence Joseph. can also say of the Gk. historians: ἢ τίς οὐ παρ' αὐτῶν ἂν τῶν συγγραφέων μάθοι ῥᾳδίως, ὅτι μηδὲν βεβαίως εἰδότες συνέγραφον; (Ap., 1, 15), or of the Philistines that they had bribed the wife of Samson μαθεῖν παρὰ τοῦ Σαμψῶνος τὴν αἰτίαν τῆς ἰσχύος, ὑφ' ἧς ἄληπτός ἐστι τοῖς ἐχθροῖς (Ant., 5, 307).[113] The influence of the OT לָמַד may be seen in Ap., 2, 176: καὶ τοσοῦτον οἱ πλεῖστοι τῶν ἀνθρώπων ἀνέχουσι τοῦ κατὰ τοὺς οἰκείους νόμους ζῆν, ὥστε ... παρ' ἄλλων μανθάνουσιν, ὅτι τὸν νόμον παραβεβήκασιν. In opposition to the divine will μανθάνω is found as in the OT (→ 402), Ant., 8, 317:[114] (But Ahab) ἔγημε ... γυναῖκα ... 'Ιεζαβέλην δὲ ὄνομα, ἀφ' ἧς τοὺς ἰδίους αὐτῆς θεοὺς προσκυνεῖν ἔμαθεν. Yet it is in connection with the νόμος (תּוֹרָה) that we see how formal the word is in Joseph. Acc. to Ant., 16, 43 the Sabbath serves τῇ μαθήσει τῶν ἡμετέρων ἐθῶν καὶ νόμου with the aim of avoiding offences against them. Here Joseph. shows acquaintance with scribal custom.[115] In the whole process of education[116] the νόμος is κάλλιστον καὶ ἀναγκαιότατον παίδευμα (the means of education), Ap., 2, 175. It is to be carefully learned by heart (ἀκριβῶς ἐμμανθάνειν), 2, 175, and indeed ἀπὸ τῆς πρώτης εὐθὺς αἰσθήσεως, 178; cf. Bell., 7, 343. In παιδεία there is both τρόπος λόγῳ διδασκαλικός and τρόπος διὰ τῆς ἀσκήσεως τῶν ἐθῶν, Ap., 2, 171. The inner relation to Stoicism disclosed here is underlined by the definition of the goal τὰ περὶ τοὺς νόμους καὶ τῶν προγόνων τὰς πράξεις ἐπίστασθαι, τὰς μὲν ἵνα μιμῶνται, τοῖς δ' ἵνα ... μήτε παραβαίνωσι μήτε σκῆψιν ἀγνοίας ἔχωσι, 2, 204. There is no further trace in Joseph. of the fact that the point of learning the Law is the full orientation of man by the will of God. His νόμος is distinguished from human νόμοι merely by its ultimate derivation from God and not from a human νομοθέτης, Ant., 3, 86 ff.[117]

4. Philo.

μανθάνω is rare in Philo.[118] His usage shows no special features. Plato's doctrine that ἀνάμνησις is the essence of the learning process is known: ὄντως γὰρ ἡ μὲν τοῦ μεμνημένου ψυχὴ καρποφορεῖ ἃ ἔμαθεν οὐδὲν ἀποβάλλουσα αὐτῶν, ἡ δὲ τοῦ ἀναμνήσει χρωμένου ἔξω λήθης γίνεται, ᾗ πρὶν ὑπομνησθῆναι κατέσχητο, Congr., 41; cf. 39 ff. But it is freed from its mythological elements, personalised,[119] and set in the framework of a speculative philosophy of revelation. The basis is Scripture, and Moses is the great pioneer who will not lead the μανθάνων astray.[120] The point of μανθάνειν in Philo is always the perception of ultimate reality in God. Moses him-

---

112 On the relation of πυνθάνομαι, "to learn (by investigation)" and μανθάνω, cf. Bell., 1, 649: οἱ τότε τὸν βασιλέα πυνθανόμενοι ταῖς ἀθυμίαις ὑπορρέοντα καὶ τῇ νόσῳ, also Vita, 62: ἐπεὶ δ' ... ταῦτα παρὰ τῶν ἀπαγγειλάντων ἔμαθον ...

113 μανθάνω also (→ 392) of the learning of a trade, Ant., 18, 314.

114 Acc. to Schl. Mt., 386.

115 Cf. also Ac. 15:21 and Str.-B., IV, 183 ff.: "Der altjüdische Synagogengottesdienst."

116 The quotations which follow are partly from Schl. Theol. d. Judt., 101 f.

117 Cf. the many other examples in Schl. Jos., 69 f. Joseph. shares the Rabb. view that Moses is simply the mediator of the divine will.

118 Leisegang mentions some 120 instances.

119 Cf. also Det. Pot. Ins., 65: τὸν μνήμονα ὧν ἔμαθεν ...

120 Deus Imm., 108: μαθὼν παρὰ Μωϋσέως ἀποκρινοῦμαι ..., Leg. All., III, 194: μαθὼν παρὰ Μωϋσέως δίδαγμα καὶ δόγμα ἀναγκαῖον.

self owes his absolute knowledge, e.g., about the origin of man's knowledge of God, to God Himself, who has revealed it to him, Det. Pot. Ins., 86 : τὴν γὰρ αἰτίαν χρησμῷ μαθὼν αὐτὸς ἡμῖν ὑφηγήσατο. Here as always μανθάνειν is guided. This may be through a person, but also through things or words, Poster. C., 179 : προσέσχη τε τῷ λεχθέντι καὶ μαθοῦσα παλινῳδίαν ἱερωτάτην ἐποίησε, cf. Gn. 30:24, also through events, Vit. Mos., 1, 122 : ἢ οὔπω μανθάνεις ἐκ τῶν γινομένων, ὅτι ἀπόλωλεν Αἴγυπτος; [121] Through μάθησις, which presupposes readiness to hear, [122] the way leads to γνῶσις, Vit. Mos., II, 280. [123] In Philo, too, we find ἄσκησις alongside learning, Abr., 53, and the example also plays a role, Sacr. AC, 43 etc. To a large extent μανθάνω is the same as allegorical work on Scripture, Det. Pot. Ins., 12 etc. How strongly piety is intellectualised may be seen also from the fact that it is possible to teach πίστις, which is understood gnostically, Ebr., 40, [124] and is indeed a product of thought, Leg. All., II, 89 : πῶς ἄν τις πιστεύσαι θεῷ; ἐὰν μάθῃ, [125] ὅτι πάντα τὰ ἄλλα τρέπεται, μόνος δὲ αὐτὸς ἄτρεπτός ἐστι. One is forced to say that in thus linking faith and individual knowledge Philo leaves the OT sphere, nor is he at one here with the Palestinian Rabbis, [126] though Holy Scripture is for him too the normative source of knowledge. [127]

C. μανθάνω in the New Testament.

1. The General Situation.

When we come from the usage outside the NT to the NT itself, it is with some astonishment that we find only 25 occurrences of μανθάνω in the whole of the NT. [128] The word plays a comparatively minor role. διδάσκω is four times as frequent, and this is the more surprising in view of the close material connection between the two terms. But the most instructive aspect of the statistics is that Mt. uses the word only 3 times, Mk. once (but cf. → n. 128), and Jn. twice, while it is not found at all in Lk. and only once in Ac. (23:27). In other words, whereas more than half the instances of διδάσκω are in the Gospels, we find here only one fifth of the occurrences of μανθάνω. Obviously the term is only weakly related to the true concern of the Gospels; otherwise it would be more common. This needs the more emphasis in view of the fact that μαθητής is the most common word to denote the men whom Jesus associated with Himself. The linguistic findings, and investigation of the various passages, show that ἀκολουθεῖν rather than μανθάνειν is the true mark of the μαθητής (→ I, 213). This is what corresponds to the preaching of Jesus. His concern is not to impart information, nor to deepen an existing attitude, but to awaken unconditional commitment to Himself. That the μαθητής, as ἀκολουθῶν, is also μανθάνων, is self-evident (cf. simply

---

[121] Cf. Leg. All., II, 39 : μαθεῖν δὲ ἐκ τῆς ἐναργείας (what is before one) ῥᾴδιον.

[122] Cf. Sacr. AC, 7: μανθάνειν ἐξ ἀκοῆς καὶ ὑφηγήσεως, Praem. Poen., 49 : τὸν μανθάνοντα πιστεῦσαι δεῖ τῷ διδάσκοντι περὶ ὧν ὑφηγεῖται (here Philo, even if only indirectly, is a pupil of Aristot., cf. A. Schlatter, *Der Glaube im NT*⁴ [1927], 67, n. 1).

[123] Cf. also Gig., 37; Deus Imm., 64 etc.

[124] Cf. Schl. Theol. d. Judt., 103, n. 2 and 106, n. 1.

[125] That μανθάνω can mean "to think" as well as "to engage in allegorical exposition of Scripture" is linked with the fact that Philo basically finds the material for his speculative thought in Scripture. This is also the reason why πίστις and γνῶσις come at the end, not the beginning, of the way of the righteous, Rer. Div. Her., 98 f.; cf. H. Windisch, *Die Frömmigkeit Philos* (1909), 26 f.

[126] Cf. on this Schlatter, *Glaube*³ (1905), 13.

[127] Cf. the details in Windisch, 90 ff.

[128] Basically Mt. 24:32 and Mk. 13:28 are only one instance.

Mt. 11:29). But μανθάνειν, as distinct from the תַּלְמִיד of the Rabbis (→ μαθητής, B. 4-5), is not what makes him a μαθητής. In Jn. Jesus Himself makes the situation very clear when in 8:31 He says to the Jews who come to faith in Him: ἐὰν ὑμεῖς μείνητε ἐν τῷ λόγῳ τῷ ἐμῷ, ἀληθῶς μαθηταί μού ἐστε. The distinction between the NT use of μανθάνω and the use outside the NT, and especially the Rabbinic use of לָמַד, is caused by the Word of Jesus as His Word. This means finally that it is caused by His person.

2. Ordinary Use.

The only sure instance where there is no overtone is Ac. 23:27. Perhaps we might add Rev. 14:3, though here the word may well be used with fixed intention.

a. In the letter which the tribune Claudius Lysias sent to the governor Felix in Caesarea along with the prisoner Paul (Ac. 23:26 ff.), the writer explains why he rescued Paul from mortal danger — contrary to the earlier account in Ac. 21:31 ff.[129] — by saying: μαθὼν ὅτι Ῥωμαῖός ἐστιν (23:27). This is the only instance of μανθάνω in Lk. The use is wholly in line with what we find in Gk. writers (→ 391) and there are par. in Joseph. (→ 405). It means here "to discover."

b. Rev. 14:3:[130] καὶ ᾄδουσιν ᾠδὴν καινὴν ἐνώπιον τοῦ θρόνου καὶ ἐνώπιον τῶν τεσσάρων ζῴων καὶ τῶν πρεσβυτέρων· καὶ οὐδεὶς ἐδύνατο μαθεῖν τὴν ᾠδὴν εἰ μὴ αἱ ἑκατὸν τεσσεράκοντα τέσσαρες χιλιάδες, οἱ ἠγορασμένοι ἀπὸ τῆς γῆς. The question is whether μαθεῖν simply means "to learn" in the ordinary sense[131] or whether it is to be taken in a more technical sense for hearing of a higher kind.[132] A clear-cut decision is hardly possible, but there are certain passages which seem to favour the second view. Thus we might refer to 2 C. 12:4, where Paul says with reference to his rapture into Paradise: ἤκουσεν ἄρρητα ῥήματα, ἃ οὐκ ἐξὸν ἀνθρώπῳ λαλῆσαι. Now it is true that the 144,000 of Rev. 14:3 are not ἄνθρωποι after the manner of the ἄνθρωπος of 2 C. 12:3 f. Yet one must allow that there is a connection, especially as it is not certain that the song sung by those who have overcome in Rev. 15:3 is identical with that mentioned in 14:3. Perhaps Corp. Herm., XIII, 15 is not without a bearing on this verse.[133] From the discussion between Hermes and his son Tat it emerges that only the κεκαθαρμένος is in a position to learn (μανθάνειν) the ὕμνος to the heavenly δυνάμεις which the prophet has heard (ἀκοῦσαι) in his rapture: What has already been communicated to the expert in his way, the adept may learn in the same way. μανθάνω can be used here because the reference is to finding out for oneself under the necessary guidance (→ 392) and with the result of intellectual appropriation. In this light the μαθεῖν of Rev. 14:3 might be understood

[129] "This is either a gross error on Luke's part or it is intentional: the tribune gives a false but favourable account of what transpired" (A. Harnack, *Die Apostelgeschichte* [1908], 163).

[130] Cf. the comm., *ad loc.*; F. Boll, *Aus d. Offenbarung Johannis* (1914), 19 f.

[131] So Bss. Apk., *ad loc.*; Zn. Apk., *ad loc.*; Schl. Erl., *ad loc.*

[132] So, following Boll, Loh., *ad loc.*; J. Weiss, *Schr. NT* "to understand."

[133] Quoted by Boll, 20, cf. R. Reitzenstein Poimandres (1904), 345: ἐβουλόμην, ὦ πάτερ, τὴν διὰ τοῦ ὕμνου εὐλογίαν <μανθάνειν>, ἣν ἔφης ἐπὶ τὴν Ὀγδοάδα γενομένου σου ἀκοῦσαι τῶν δυνάμεων (addition by Reitzenstein, described as excellent in Boll, 20, n. 1). Καθὼς <ἀνιόντι μοι εἰς τὴν> Ὀγδοάδα ὁ Ποιμάνδρης ἐθέσπισε, τέκνον, καλῶς σπεύδεις λῦσαι τὸ σκῆνος· κεκαθαρμένος γάρ.

as a deepened hearing.[134] In this sense μανθάνω is sometimes expressly differentiated from ἀκούω.[135]

3. Learning from Scripture.

The native soil of the NT may be seen from the degree to which the NT μανθάνω is controlled by the OT and later Jewish use of לָמַד. The general primitive Christian character of this use is evident from the fact that it is found both in the Gospels and in Paul.

a. The word occurs twice in disputations between Jesus and His opponents, and in both cases He uses it to point them to the Scriptures, thus binding them and also subjecting them to His claim, for the γραφαί bear witness to Him (Jn. 5:39). In Mt. 9:13 He refers the Pharisees, the champions of legal practice, to Hos. 6:6. This saying vindicates Him when He holds fellowship with the publicans and sinners, and it puts his questioners in the wrong with their concern only for ritual tradition and form (θυσία). The material par. in Mt. 12:7: εἰ δὲ ἐγνώκειτε τί ἐστιν· ἔλεος θέλω καὶ οὐ θυσίαν, οὐκ ἂν κατεδικάσατε τοὺς ἀναιτίους, shows how His demand: πορευθέντες δὲ μάθετε τί ἐστιν· ἔλεος θέλω καὶ οὐ θυσίαν, is to be construed. μανθάνειν takes place when God's will is learned from Scripture and taken up into one's own will. In the μάθετε we see that the concern of Jesus is in fact for God's will, not His own. But the revelation of God's will is one great reference to Jesus as the Christ. The Fourth Evangelist in his own way expresses the same thought as Mt. in Jn. 6:45: ἔστιν γεγραμμένον ἐν τοῖς προφήταις· καὶ ἔσονται πάντες διδακτοὶ θεοῦ· πᾶς ὁ ἀκούσας παρὰ τοῦ πατρὸς καὶ μαθὼν ἔρχεται πρὸς ἐμέ. Since hearing reaches its goal in learning, and since the πατήρ in everything He says points to the υἱός, learning necessarily includes acceptance of Jesus (cf. Jn. 6:44).[136] It is worth noting that even externally μανθάνειν corresponds here, not to a διδάσκειν of Jesus, but to that of God Himself.

b. μανθάνω is also used as a technical term for academic study of Scripture in Jn. 7:15. Here Jesus must accept the fact that His right to proclaim God's will on the basis of Scripture (διδάσκειν, v. 14) is doubted by the Jews because He has not gone through the normal course of instruction (μὴ μεμαθηκώς).[137] He answers by pointing out that God's will is done in His own person and teaching. Thus he who does God's will will see the nature of Jesus' teaching, namely, that He speaks with divine authority.

Paul uses μανθάνω in a similar way in Gl. 3:2: τοῦτο μόνον θέλω μαθεῖν ἀφ' ὑμῶν, ἐξ ἔργων νόμου τὸ πνεῦμα ἐλάβετε ἢ ἐξ ἀκοῆς πίστεως; The choice of μαθεῖν, which Paul never uses for mere information, shows that he is making an important point[138] against the Galatians, who in their legalism know nothing

---

[134] So Had. Apk., *ad loc.*: "But no one can learn (i.e., hear and appropriate) this song except the man who has experience of what is extolled.

[135] Polyb., III, 32, 9: ὅσῳ διαφέρει τὸ μαθεῖν τοῦ μόνον ἀκοῦσαι, τοσούτῳ καὶ κτλ. (Bau. J. on 6:45).

[136] Cf. on this what was said about Rev. 14:3 (→ 407).

[137] μανθάνω does not need an explanatory obj. since it is clear in the light of לָמַד (→ 400, and cf. Schl. J., *ad loc.*).

[138] The comm. do not take up the word. Pr.-Bau.[3], *s.v.* groups Gl. 3:2 with Ac. 23:27, and expositors tacitly take the same course.

higher than study of the Law (cf. 4:21: λέγετέ μοι ... τὸν νόμον οὐκ ἀκούετε;).[139] This gives to the ἀφ' ὑμῶν, too, its point and weight.[140] Paul does not wish to learn from the Galatians. He wishes to learn by them, i.e., as they become for him a means of knowing the divine will, which in this case is the saving will of God disclosed in Scripture, i.e., in the νόμος. Paul thus keeps to the line indicated by μαθεῖν when, after a few intervening verses from v. 6 ff., he adds to the verse quoted a scriptural proof for his own thesis and against that of the false legalistic teachers in Galatia. He takes this from the νόμος which the false teachers thought they could successfully advance against Paul. Though he does not say it, Paul thus assumes that only through the life and death of Jesus does μαθεῖν find the standpoint without which it is a human affair and can remain only provisional and uncertain in its effect. The ground slips from beneath one's feet, however, if one thinks one need not stand by what is written to know the will of God. Paul states emphatically in 1 C. 4:6 (cf. 1:31) that Scripture alone gives man a basis on which he can stand before God. He himself is the best example of this.

4. The New Learning.

a. The most important verse is Mt. 11:29, the saying of Jesus to the κοπιῶντες καὶ πεφορτισμένοι: ἄρατε τὸν ζυγόν μου ἐφ' ὑμᾶς καὶ μάθετε ἀπ' ἐμοῦ. Here He sets His own person and authority against the scribes with their claim that they alone can rightly expound Scripture. Though the Hebraic Gk. of Mt. forces us to consider that the ἀπό simply corresponds to a מִן which might also be rendered παρά,[141] note should be taken of the ἀπό. In the light of the total attitude of Jesus it suggests that He is not a διδάσκαλος like the Rabbis, but views Himself as the σημεῖον wherein is manifested the coming of the βασιλεία τοῦ θεοῦ[142] in which God's holy and righteous will is done. Hence He can promise ἀνάπαυσις (→ I, 350) to those who come to Him. From Him one can learn that the will of God and its fulfilment are not a burden and torment but bring rest and joy to all those who subject themselves to this will in fellowship with Jesus.

b. Mt. 24:32 par. gives us a variation on this usage. The demand of Jesus on His disciples: ἀπὸ δὲ τῆς συκῆς μάθετε τὴν παραβολήν, is based on the truth that for the disciples everyday things become an expression of the eternal laws of God continually declared and proclaimed in the words of the prophets. This prophetic view of things becomes a possession of the community under the guidance of the Spirit, in whom Jesus Himself is active as the living Lord after His resurrection and exaltation. The disciplinary nature of early Christian prophecy is displayed when Paul defines its goal as follows in 1 C. 14:31: ἵνα πάντες μανθάνωσιν καὶ πάντες παρακαλῶνται. Prophecy serves the clear proclamation of the will of God, not the satisfaction of curiosity. The community needs it when it, or one of its members, needs guidance in a particular situation and does not find it in Scripture (cf. e.g., 1 Tm. 4:14).[143]

---

139 It should be noted that we again find ἀκούειν here (*v. supra*).

140 The usual prep. with μανθάνω is παρά when it is stated from whom, i.e., under whose instruction, one learns (so 2 Tm. 3:14).

141 Cf. the passages in Schl. Mt., 307 on 9:13. Schl. always translates מִן by ἀπό when it is used with לָמַד.

142 Cf. Origen's term αὐτοβασιλεία and → I, 589.

143 By reason of its relationship 1 C. 14:35 also belongs to this context. But we have also to consider a specific moral use in the narrower sense (→ 410).

c. In Eph. 4:20 we find the phrase ἐμάθετε τὸν Χριστόν. According to the context μανθάνειν has here more of the sense of ἀκούειν than διδάσκεσθαι. It implies full acceptance of Christ and His work, even in respect of the direction of life. Its ethical character, in the broadest sense, is thus clear. Explicitly or implicitly there stands behind the expression opposition to the thesis that the way to an ordered life is only by μανθάνειν νόμον. The new man is nourished by the Gospel, in which Christ does His work according to the plan and purpose of God. μανθάνω seems to be used in the same sense in 2 Tm. 3:14 and R. 16:17, here with reference to the apostolic διδαχή (→ II, 164).[144] And when Paul confesses in Phil. 4:11: ἐγὼ γὰρ ἔμαθον ἐν οἷς εἰμι αὐτάρκης εἶναι, this can only be because he has learned Christ (cf. the context).

5. The Threat Posed to Piety by μανθάνειν in the Pastorals.

In the Pastorals μανθάνω is more common than διδάσκω. Learning here seems to be a threat to the faith of the community. Officiousness and an intellectualistic piety are widespread, especially among the women (2 Tm. 3:6 f.; 1 Tm. 5:13),[145] and they give false teachers the opportunity of insinuating themselves into the congregations. The piety propagated by them is legalistic. The old connection between νόμος and μανθάνω persists, but in a form which should have been long since superseded. Gk. influences have also to be taken into account. In face of this, Paul reminds the women of the fact that they must exercise restraint even when they seek instruction (1 Tm. 2:11) and he also admonishes the children and grandchildren first (πρῶτον) to learn (μανθανέτωσαν) to achieve piety at home, repaying parents and grandparents for the things they owe to them; possibly the fifth commandment is in the background here (1 Tm. 5:4). But there is also, as in Phil. 4:9, a corresponding and comprehensive word for the whole community, Tt. 3:14. Paul speaks with the certainty that members of his churches will always be fruitful in piety if they will accept and learn from the Gospel as the new Law (Tt. 3:14).

6. Hebrews 5:8.

Hb. 5:7 ff.: [ὁ Χριστὸς ...] ὃς ἐν ταῖς ἡμέραις τῆς σαρκὸς αὐτοῦ δεήσεις τε καὶ ἱκετηρίας πρὸς τὸν δυνάμενον σῴζειν αὐτὸν ἐκ θανάτου μετὰ κραυγῆς ἰσχυρᾶς καὶ δακρύων προσενέγκας καὶ εἰσακουσθεὶς[146] ἀπὸ τῆς εὐλαβείας, καίπερ ὢν υἱός, ἔμαθεν ἀφ' ὧν ἔπαθεν τὴν ὑπακοήν, καὶ τελειωθεὶς ἐγένετο πᾶσιν τοῖς ὑπακούουσιν αὐτῷ αἴτιος σωτηρίας αἰωνίου ...

We can deal with the many difficulties in this verse only in so far as they are connected with the words ἔμαθεν ἀφ' ὧν ἔπαθεν τὴν ὑπακοήν. There seems to be here a play on words which is not infrequent in Greek literature[147] and which

---

[144] Cf. also Col. 1:7:

[145] On the text *v.* Dib., *ad loc.*; P. W. Schmiedel, ThBl, 1 (1922), 222; *Zürcher Bibelübersetzung* (1931), *Anhang zum NT*, 5 reads with older authors λανθάνουσιν.

[146] On the text, whether we are to read εἰσακουσθείς or a conjectured οὐκ εἰσακουσθείς, cf. A. v. Harnack, "Zwei alte dogmatische Korrekturen im Hebräerbrief," SAB (1929), 69 ff. = *Studien zur Geschichte des NT u. d. alten Kirche,* I (1931), 245 ff.; Wnd. Hb., 43 f.; O. Michel, *Der Brief an die Hb.* (Meyer, XIII[7]) (1936), 61 f.; → II, 753 (Bultmann); → 412.

[147] Many instances are given in Wettstein, and most of the par. in the comm. are based on his list. The oldest is Aesch. Ag., 177: πάθει μάθος, → 394.

is found also in Jewish Hellenists.[148] Yet the parallels do not help us to understand the verse. To do this, we must consider the different ideas suggested by πάσχειν on the one side and the other. In other works πάσχειν is used of outside influences which sway human emotion (→ 394). In Hb., however, it is used of the unique and once-for-all suffering laid by the Father on the Son in the discharge of His office (2:10; 9:26; 13:12).[149] The πάσχειν of Jesus is not a destiny which causes the one afflicted by it to grow and mature in the sense of idealism. When the Son suffers, this is only because God wills it, because it thus seems right to Him (2:10). Thus these few words embrace the whole path of the Son. They state that Jesus, by suffering in undeviating acceptance of the divine will as His own will, honours God as His Father, and entrusts Himself to Him, confident that He will give Him His office and dignity (5:5 etc.). If the author introduces the word μανθάνειν, the only possible reason is that for him, and for the passion tradition which he used, the attitude of Jesus when He went to the cross was controlled by Scripture. From Scripture He learned that even to the smallest details (ἀφ' ὧν) His passion was grounded in the saving will of God and could not be separated from His calling.[150] Thus the saying is a witness to the conscious demonstration of obedience which is a mark of the Son and which Jesus renders without restriction. In full clarity and freedom, and with no resistance, He went to suffering and death because Scripture, and in it God, pointed Him in this direction for the sake of His office.

The history of the word rules out any other solution. This is particularly true of expositions which find evidence of a development of Jesus in these words, no matter whether this be moral growth in the sense of an increasing capacity for obedience[151] or a developing maturity of Jesus for the fulfilment of His task.[152] All such explanations fall into the error of idealism. They overlook the fact that for biblical Gk. μανθάνειν takes place in the handling of Scripture as the revealed will of God. They fail to see that throughout the Gospel tradition Jesus' awareness of Himself and His mission is shaped by Scripture. We have here the same thought as in Phil. 2:8: γενόμενος ὑπήκοος μέχρι θανάτου, θανάτου δὲ σταυροῦ. The difference between Hb. 5:8 and Phil. 2:8 is simply that Paul regards the crucifixion as grounded in the obedience of Jesus without saying anything about its origin, while Hb. measures the depth of the obedience of Jesus by the passion to which He is appointed by God acc. to the testimony of Scripture. Nevertheless, it is true that for Hb. "the new thing is not in the last analysis the learning of obedience, but its nature and manner as denoted by ἀφ' ὧν ἔπαθεν."[153] The accent in the saying is on ἔπαθεν.[154] This is what binds the saving power of Jesus to His going to the cross (12:2).[155]

---

148 Often in Philo, e.g., Fug., 138: ἔμαθον μὲν ὃ ἔπαθον, cf. also Wnd. Hb., *ad loc.*

149 πάσχειν is used in Hb. only of the passion of Jesus, while πάθημα is used in 10:32 for the suffering of Christians too.

150 Here the author of Hb. is close to the man to whom Lk. owes his special material on the passion and the resurrection. The connecting pt. is that both believe that Jesus in His exodus consciously fulfilled Scripture (cf. simply Lk. 22:37 and 24:25 ff., 44 ff.).

151 So E. K. A. Riehm, *Der Lehrbegriff des Hb.*² (1867), 328 f.

152 Cf. the over-subtle presentation of F. W. Grosheide, *De brief aan de Hb. en de brief van Jakobus* (1927), 152, where appeal is made to 2:17 f.

153 J. C. K. v. Hofmann, *D. hl. Schrift neuen Testaments zusammenhängend untersucht*, V (1873), 222.

154 Cf. v. Hofmann, also F. Delitzsch, *Comm. z. Briefe an die Hb.* (1857), 185 (with criticism of v. Hofmann).

155 Only here (though cf. 6:6) does Hb. speaks expressly of the cross of Jesus; cf. on this Schl. Theol. d. Ap., 470.

The immediate context supports this reading. The καίπερ ὢν υἱός is to be understood in the light of the paradox that the Son is ordained to suffer. He does not "have" the position linked with sonship. He receives it from the Father's hand only when He has suffered death in the most shameful form (12:2; 2:1 ff.).[156] This paradox is not expressed for the first time by ἔπαθεν. It occurs already in v. 7 in the description of the attitude of the Son in παθήματα, and then in v. 8 it is simply brought to full expression by means of a pun which the author thinks is particularly apposite here because of its pregnancy. Hence the thesis of A. v. Harnack that on grammatical grounds καίπερ ὢν υἱός can be related only to what precedes[157] is only formally and not materially correct. The paradox is expressed afresh in what follows even if only to emphasise it in terms of the uniqueness of this Son. Thus the words καίπερ ὢν υἱός conclude what precedes in the form of an unavoidable question, and in some sense they prepare the way for what follows as Jesus' own answer to this question.[158]

The answer is completed only with the τελειωθείς (5:9) in so far as God validates the filial attitude of Jesus by His action, and in God's own Word the answer of Jesus is given relevance (ἀρχιερεύς). We must again distinguish between the formal and the material aspects of the thought presented. Formally μανθάνειν and τελειοῦσθαι go together, for "only he who learns becomes perfect."[159] But materially it is suffering, not learning, which brings the Son to the goal appointed for Him by God (2:10). Thus the idea is pressed to the end in terms of the total view of Hb. Its sharp form finally makes it unnecessary to add an οὐκ before εἰσακουσθείς in v. 7 (→ n. 146), for the contrast is not between the sonship and the fact that he is not heard, but between the sonship and the act which it brought with it. The traditional form of the text is in keeping with this, especially in view of the emphasis which is placed on the fellowship between Jesus and God in the words which follow. If it is God's Word which causes Him to accept suffering, it is in keeping that God's ear should be open to Him in His suffering.

D. The Usage of the Early Church.

The use of μανθάνω in the early Church reflects the intellectualising of faith which is one of the marks of the commencement and continuation of the Hellenisation of Christianity.

The usage of the post-apost. fathers is already instructive in this regard. There is no ordinary use of the word in the true sense. This may well be accidental. Yet it is worth noting that wherever one might at first have assumed the ordinary use a specific moral attitude is the obj. of μανθάνειν (1 Cl., 57, 2: ὑποτάσσεσθαι; Ign. R., 4, 3: μηδὲν ἐπιθυμεῖν; Ign. Magn., 10:1: κατὰ Χριστιανισμὸν ζῆν).[160] In Barnabas esp. μανθάνειν is the way in which one gets special knowledge with the help of one who knows,[161] e.g., the kind of knowledge which comes through the use of allegorical exegesis or through special revelation. Hence the author continually demands of his

---

[156] Finely stated by M. Kähler, *Der Hebräerbrief in genauer Wiedergabe seines Gedankenganges*[2] (1889), 11: "... and in spite of his described position as the Son, he learned and rendered his confessed obedience in suffering even to death."

[157] *Op. cit.*, 247 ff.; cf. also A. v. Harnack in Michel, 61, n. 2.

[158] Hence most comm. are materially right when they see a connection both with what precedes and what follows.

[159] So O. Michel, "Die Lehre v. d. christlichen Vollkommenheit nach der Anschauung des Hebräerbriefes," ThStKr, 106, NF, 1 (1934/35, 333-355), 349, cf. 338 f. with a ref. to 1 Παρ. 25:8. Cf. already F. Büchsel, "D. Christologie des Hb.," BFTh, 27, 2 (1922), 33.

[160] Cf. also Barn., 21, 1: καλὸν οὖν ἐστιν μαθόντα τὰ δικαιώματα (→ 401) τοῦ κυρίου, ὅσα γέγραπται, ἐν τούτοις περιπατεῖν.

[161] Cf. also Dg., 4, 1 and 6.

readers: μάθετε (6, 9; 9, 7 ff.; 14, 4; 16, 2, 7 f.). Hermas, too, emphasises the need of μανθάνειν (s., 9, 1, 3). It is simply another step on the same path when Christianity itself becomes the obj. of μανθάνειν, whether in its distinctive λόγος [162] or its distinctive θεοσέβεια. [163] In the Apol., e.g., Justin, [164] μανθάνειν is used specifically for the appropriation of individual saving truths, e.g., the divine sonship of Jesus, through instruction (Apol., I, 13, 3). At the head of the chain of tradition composed of those who give and those who receive, διδάσκοντες and μανθάνοντες, stands Jesus Himself as the absolute διδάσκαλος (πάντων διδάσκαλος), who as such can be compared with Hermes (I, 22, 2; → II, 157 f., esp. n. 58), who in Hermes mysticism (cf. Corp. Herm., XVI, 1b) stands at the beginning of all religious knowledge in this sense. Hence one may say that in this use of the word there may be noted the influence of the linguistic usage of the mysteries (→ 398). The presupposition for the adoption of this usage is that Christianity relatively soon took on the same characteristics of an esoteric religion. [165]

The hints in Justin are fully developed in Hippolyt., for whom μανθάνειν is clearly and unequivocally a tt. for the impartation of the central truths of Christianity to catechumens. Acc. to his account (Contra Noetum, 1 [p. 43, 30, ed. P. de Lagarde, 1858]) the presbyters of Smyrna (c. 180-190) affirmed their faith against the heretical views of their colleague Noetus, with express emphasis on its traditional intactness: ταῦτα λέγομεν ἃ ἐμάθομεν. The context shows that μανθάνειν carries an allusion to the creed, the form in which they had received the faith. [166] In the same way Marcellus of Ancyra tried to prove his orthodoxy in a letter [167] to bishop Julius of Rome some 150 years later, and in this he said that he had "learned" his faith (τὴν ἐμαυτοῦ πίστιν μετὰ πάσης ἀληθείας ... γράψας ἐπιδοῦναι, ἣν ἔμαθον ἔκ τε τῶν θείων γραφῶν ἐδιδάχθην). [168] It is not surprising, then, that along with ἡ πίστις and τὸ σύμβολον we find τὸ μάθημα as a common term for the baptismal symbol as the confession of faith, esp. in the East. [169] In this term the Church itself bears witness through its theological teachers that the πίστις, in permeating the Church, has been intellectualised by the Gk. spirit, and has thus become the διδαχή to which only the initiate has true access. [170]

---

[162] Mart. Pol., 10, 1: εἰ δὲ θέλεις τὸν τοῦ Χριστιανισμοῦ μαθεῖν λόγον ...

[163] Dg., 1, 1: ὁρῶ ... ὑπερεσπουδακότα σε τὴν θεοσέβειαν τῶν Χριστιανῶν μαθεῖν.

[164] The use of μαθεῖν δύνασθε ἐκ, which is common in Justin with ref. to the basis of Christian knowledge in official documents and private writings (Apol., I, 28, 1; 34, 2; 48, 3), seems to go back to the current use of μαθεῖν ἐκ for "to learn by examination" (cf. Phlegon of Tralles, De longaevis, I, and on this S. Lösch, *Diatagma Kaisaros* [1936], 67 ff., 70).

[165] On the *disciplina arcana* of early Christianity, even in the NT, cf. J. Jeremias, *Die Abendmahlsworte Jesu* (1935), 45 ff. The question urgently needs investigation. Thus I do not think it likely that Lk.'s account of the Last Supper gives evidence of *disciplina arcana.*

[166] Cf. T. Zahn, *Das apostolische Symbolum* (1893), 23 and 24, n. 1.

[167] Preserved in Epiphanius Haer., 72, 2 f., p. 257, 6, Holl. The letter has other instances of the usage here in question (cf. 72, 3, 1 and 3; p. 258, 14 f., 20 f., Holl); cf. also Caspari, 32 (→ n. 168).

[168] Cf. C. P. Caspari, *Ungedruckte, unbeachtete u. wenig beachtete Quellen zur Geschichte des Taufsymbols u. der Glaubensregel,* III (1875), 28 ff., 161, esp. 30 f.

[169] Since we cannot appeal to Eus. (F. Kattenbusch, *Das apost. Symbol,* I [1894], 228, n. 4), the Constantinopolitan in Socrates Hist. Eccl., III, 25 is the oldest example. It is particularly interesting because the context plainly shows the connections of the word with the *disciplina arcana* (cf. Kattenbusch, II [1900], 235). For further examples cf. Kattenbusch, 235 and 467, also Caspari, "Aus historisch-kritischen Studien über das kirchliche Taufbekenntnis, I," *Zeitschrift f. d. gesammte lutherische Theologie u. Kirche,* 18 (1857), 634 ff.

[170] μάθημα is found for an object of learning from the time of Aristoph. It is later a special term for knowledge, esp. the mathematical sciences. The emphasis is on the obj., which guarantees correct knowledge if the right method is followed. Cf. Snell, 76 ff., esp. 79. It would be a rewarding enterprise to study the development of usage in the early Church (Clement of Alexandria).

† καταμανθάνω.

καταμανθάνω is in some sense the intensive of μανθάνω in the sense "to examine closely," "to learn," "to grasp," "to note," as in Plut. Quomodo Adulator ab Amico Internoscatur, 34 (11, 65a) of the probing of a wound, or in a pap. APF, 3 (1906), 370 [1] of the examination of a pregnant woman; P. Fay., 114, 8 ff. (c. 100 A.D.) of getting to know an oliveyard; Hdt., 7, 146 of the watching of spies, also without obj. for "to come to see" etc., as in P. Fay., 20, 19 (late 3rd or 4th cent.). For the special nature of the word as compared with the simple form, Plat. Theaet., 198d is instructive: οὐκοῦν ἡμεῖς ἀπεικάζοντες τῇ τῶν περιστερῶν κτήσει τε καὶ θήρᾳ ἐροῦμεν ὅτι διττὴ ἦν ἡ θήρα, ἡ μὲν πρὶν ἐκτῆσθαι τοῦ κεκτῆσθαι ἕνεκα, ἡ δὲ κεκτημένῳ τοῦ λαβεῖν καὶ ἔχειν ἐν ταῖς χερσὶν ἃ πάλαι ἐκέκτητο. οὕτως δὲ καὶ ὧν πάλαι ἐπιστῆμαι ἦσαν αὐτῷ, μαθόντι καὶ ἠπίστατο αὐτά, πάλιν ἔστι καταμανθάνειν ταὐτὰ ταῦτα ἀναλαμβάνοντα τὴν ἐπιστήμην ἑκάστου καὶ ἴσχοντα, ἣν ἐκέκτητο μὲν πάλαι, πρόχειρον δ' οὐκ εἶχε τῇ διανοίᾳ. The intellectual character which it plainly has here is to be seen also in Philo [2] (Leg. All., 1, 61; II, 17 [with ἰδεῖν]; Post. C., 168 [of the activity of the λογισμός] and Joseph. [3] (Ant., 6, 230 f.; Vit., 10 of getting to know the Jewish sects).

The surprising thing in the Gk. Bible is that the compound, unlike μανθάνω, bears no relation to the root למד. The original Heb. words all [4] have to do with the process of seeing, usually with emphasis on the closeness of scrutiny. The most prominent is רָאָה (Gn. 34:1; Lv. 14:36; Eccl. 4:7 Σ; 8:17 Σ; Ασμα 6:11 Σ), [5] which has more of the sense of testing or scrutinising than mere seeing, [6] usually in respect of moral conduct. With the same nuance καταμανθάνω is used in Ιωβ 35:5 for שׁוּר, in Gn. 24:21 for מִשְׁתָּאֵה, and also in 1 Εσδρ. 8:41. Sometimes the result of the καταμανθάνειν is an attitude which the author rejects; it is obvious that his judgment is directed against the aim of the καταμανθάνειν (cf. Σιρ. 9:5 for הִתְבּוֹנֵן; 9:8 for הִבִּיט). Only once is the word used for learning a technical skill (Σιρ. 38:28: the χαλκεύς is καταμανθάνων ἔργα σιδήρου). Even here it is possible that the orientation of καταμανθάνειν is to the action. On the whole, then, one may say that biblical καταμανθάνω, though it is obviously rather colourless, is distinguished from non-biblical καταμανθάνω to the degree that its relation to μανθάνω brings it under the influence of למד.

The only occurrence in the NT is at Mt. 6:28: καταμάθετε τὰ κρίνα τοῦ ἀγροῦ, πῶς αὐξάνουσιν ... Here pre-NT biblical usage does not allow us to see in καταμανθάνειν merely "viewing" or "pleasing contemplation of the beautiful." [7] On the other hand, the context does not permit us to take the word in the sense that regarding the κρίνα τοῦ ἀγροῦ will impart to us a specific knowledge of God. The invitation of Jesus to those who are anxious (→ μεριμνάω) is designed to overcome their inner insecurity, which is based on a lack. Jesus points

---

καταμανθάνω. [1] Placed by Preisigke Wört., *s.v.* in the 2nd cent., by U. Wilcken, APF, 3 (1906), 374, n. in the 3rd.

[2] Leisegang has 10 instances.

[3] Cf. Schl. Mt., 231.

[4] The only exception is Ju. 5:28 A, where κατεμάνθανεν is used for יַבֵּב (וַתְּיַבֵּב, "to call loudly"). But perhaps we should read וַתַּבֵּט (from נבט); the Talmud has מְדִיקָא. Cf. the comm., *ad loc.*, with other possibilities. Altogether καταμανθάνω occurs only 12 times in the Gk. Bible.

[5] In the last three passages the LXX has εἶδον or ἰδεῖν.

[6] So, e.g., Schl. Mt., 231.

[7] Zn. Mt., *ad loc.*

to the order of nature, which bears witness to the plenitude of possibilities and means at the disposal of the Creator. To the one who is able to see and perceive (cf. Lk. 12:27: κατανοήσατε) this can bring awareness that it befits him to put unbounded confidence in the Creator who has also made him.

μαθητής.

Contents: A. The Term in the Greek World: 1. The General Use; 2. Pupil or Disciple? 3. Master and Disciple: a. Socrates, Plato and the Academy; b. The Mystery Religions; c. The Master-Disciple Relation with a Religious Aspect; 4. The Fellowship of Disciples and the Principle of Tradition: a. The Fellowship of Disciples; b. The Principle of Tradition. B. The Term in the Old Testament and Judaism: 1. The Use of μαθητής/תַּלְמִיד in the OT (LXX): a. μαθητής in the LXX; b. תַּלְמִיד in the OT; 2. The Material Problem in the Old Testament: a. The Reason for the almost complete Absence of תַּלְמִיד/μαθητής from the OT (LXX); b. The Absence also of the Master-Disciple Relation from the OT; c. The Absence of the Principle of Tradition from the OT; 3. The Reason for the Absence of the Master-Disciple Relation and the Principle of Tradition from the OT; 4. The Rabbinic Use of תַּלְמִיד: a. The Meaning of the Word; b. The Different Groups of תַּלְמִידִים; c. Only Men as תַּלְמִידִים; d. תַּלְמִיד as a Title of Honour; e. The Targumic Usage; 5. The תַּלְמִיד as the Member of a School and Tradition: a. The תַּלְמִיד as a Pupil; b. The תַּלְמִיד as a Listener; c. The School; d. The תַּלְמִיד and Tradition; e. The Rabbinate as the School of Moses; 6. The Origin of Rabbinic Views of the תַּלְמִיד as the Member of a School and Tradition: a. The Impossibility of Development from the OT; b. Hellenistic Influences; c. The Adoption of the תַּלְמִיד from Hellenistic Teaching (cf. Josephus); 7. The Theology Implied in the Later Jewish תַּלְמִיד; 8. Philo. C. The Term in the New Testament: 1. The Usage: a. Statistical Data; b. The Uniformity of Usage; c. The Relation of μαθητής to תַּלְמִיד, d. Peculiarities of the Usage; 2. Jewish μαθηταί in the NT: a. The μαθηταὶ τῶν Φαρισαίων; b. τοῦ Μωϋσέως μαθηταί; 3. The Disciples of Jesus: a. The Call of the Disciples of Jesus; (a) The Initiative of Jesus; (b) Some Disciples not Personally Called? b. The Disciples of Jesus in their Relation to Him: (a) The Commitment of the Disciples of Jesus to His Person; (b) The Obedience of the Disciples to Jesus; (c) The Obligation of the Disciples to Suffer with Jesus; c. οἱ μαθηταί, οἱ δώδεκα, οἱ ἀπόστολοι; d. The Band of the (Twelve) Disciples of Jesus as an Intimation of His Way of Suffering: (a) The Failure of the Disciples to Understand; (b) The Composition of the Band; e. The Share of the Disciples in the Work of Jesus; f. The Principle of Tradition in Jesus' Band of Disciples: (a) The Lack of a Principle of Tradition; (b) The Reasons for this Lack; g. Summary; 4. The μαθηταί of John the Baptist: a. The Disciples in the Lifetime of John; b. The Disciples after the Death of John (Ac.); 5. μαθητής as a Term for Christians in Ac.: a. The Linguistic Problem; b. The Material Problem; 6. μαθηταί of Paul in Ac. 9:25? D. The Usage of the Early Church.

μαθητής. J. Wach, *Meister u. Jünger* (1925); R. Schütz, *Apostel u. Jünger* (1921); A. Harnack, *Entstehung u. Entwicklung der Kirchenverfassung u. des Kirchenrechts in den zwei ersten Jahrhunderten* (1910), 5 ff.; J. Wellhausen, *Einleitung in die drei ersten Ev.*[2] (1911), 138-147: "Die Zwölf, Die Jünger und die Apostel"; Harnack Miss.[4], I, 410 ff.; J. Ranft, *Der Ursprung des katholischen Traditionsprinzips* (1931); Talmid Ḥakam: Jew. Enc., XI, 678 f. Cf. Wach, 35: "There has been far too little work done on the disciples of Jesus."

A. The Term in the Greek World.

1. The General Use.

a. As a *nomen actoris* [1] from μαθ-, μαθητής denotes the man who directs his mind to something. In its earliest literary use it takes on the sense of pupil in analogy to μανθάνω (→ 391 f.). The oldest instance is in Hdt., 4, 77, where the Scythian Anacharsis is called τῆς Ἑλλάδος μαθητής in this sense. He has adopted Gk. wisdom and culture, and become their champion. The context is instructive, for it shows us that there is no derogatory sense such as might cling to "tyro." The emphasis is not so much on the incompleteness or even deficiency of education as on the fact that the one thus designated is engaged in learning, that his education consists in the appropriation or adoption of specific knowledge or conduct, and that it proceeds deliberately and according to a set plan. There is thus no μαθητής without a διδάσκαλος. The process involves a corresponding personal relation.

b. The almost technical sense of the word, which implies a direct dependence of the one under instruction upon an authority superior in knowledge, and which emphasises the fact that this relation cannot be dissolved, controls the whole usage, no matter whether the reference is to the winning of technical or academic information and skill.

μαθητής is the usual word for "apprentice." The pap. esp. yield many examples, e.g., P. Oxy., IV, 725, 15, the apprentice of a weaver, who is called διδάσκαλος in line 14. [2] We find this use in Plat. when in Men., 90e he calls the man learning to play a flute a μαθητής (cf. also 89d, where διδάσκαλος, too, is used). The doctor in training is a μαθητὴς ἰατρικῆς (sc. τέχνης) (Plat. Resp., X, 599c), with a trained physician in the background (cf. Men., 90c). But any student is a μαθητής if he has a teacher, cf. the students of a rhetorician in Plut. Cons. ad Apoll., 36 (II, 120e); Apophth., 13 (II, 182d), or the disciples of the Sophists in Plat. Prot., 315a: τῶν Πρωταγόρου μαθητῶν, etc. μαθητής could also be used to show the allegiance of a philosopher to a given school. Thus the associates of Socrates can also be called his μαθηταί, though he himself bitterly opposed this, Plat. Ap., 33a; [3] → 2. Later the word is regularly used to show to what school one belongs in the history of philosophy, e.g., Athen., [4] Diog. L., [5] Plut., [6] and Cicero. [7] We find this usage in Joseph. too, for in Ap., 1, 14 he says of Pherecydes, [8] Pythagoras and Thales that according to common consent they were Αἰγυπτίων καὶ Χαλδαίων μαθηταί. We find the same use when he speaks of Clearchos in Ap., 1, 176 as ὁ Ἀριστοτέλους ὢν μαθητής. [9]

c. Finally, μαθητής is used in a broader sense when the reference is to an intellectual link between those who are considerably removed in time. In this con-

---

[1] Bl.-Debr.[6] § 109, 8.

[2] Cf. also P. Oxy., VII, 1029, 25; BGU, I, 328 Col. I, 34; IV, 1125, 9.

[3] Cf. also the mocking words to Socrates in Aristoph. Nu., 501 f.: ἢν ἐπιμελὴς ὦ καὶ προθύμως μανθάνω, | τῷ τῶν μαθητῶν ἐμφερὴς γενήσομαι;

[4] So VII, 281c (p. 212): Ἐρατοσθένης γοῦν ὁ Κυρηναῖος μαθητὴς γενόμενος Ἀρίστωνος τοῦ Χίου, ὃς ἦν εἷς τῶν ἀπὸ τῆς Στοᾶς (v. Arnim, 1, 341) etc.

[5] Cf. also VI, 84 (3): Μένανδρος Διογένους μαθητής. VI, 85 (1): οἱ ἐλλόγιμοι τοῦ Κυνός μαθηταί. In VI, 94 (1 vl.) Metrocles is called the μαθητής of Crates; then in 95 (2 ff.) his own μαθηταί and their μαθηταί are listed.

[6] E.g., Laud. s. Inv., 17 (II, 545 f.): τὸ πλῆθος τῶν Θεοφράστου μαθητῶν.

[7] E.g., Acad., II, 42: *Euclides, Socratis discipulus.* Strabo has the same thing in view when he calls Euclid Σωκρατικός in IX, 1, 8.

[8] Pherecydes (from the island of Syros) is the first Gk. prose writer (the middle of the 6th cent.) as the author of Ἑπτάμυχος, a cosmogonic work (Diels[5], I, 43 ff.).

[9] Then Aristot. is even more definitely called his διδάσκαλος.

nection we should mention especially the widespread view that Socrates is the true μαθητής of Homer because he is his ζηλωτής and imitates him.

Already in Xenophanes Fr. 10 (I, 131, Diels[5]) Homer is the teacher of all Greece.[10] In Plat. Resp., X, 606e Socrates himself quotes this idea, recalling the admirers of Hom. acc. to whom τὴν Ἑλλάδα πεπαίδευκεν οὗτος ὁ ποιητὴς καὶ πρὸς διοίκησίν τε καὶ παιδείαν τῶν ἀνθρωπίνων πραγμάτων ἄξιος ἀναλαβόντι μανθάνειν τε καὶ κατὰ τοῦτον τὸν ποιητὴν πάντα τὸν αὑτοῦ βίον κατασκευασάμενον ζῆν. The same point is made in Xenoph. Sym., 4, 6 (→ μανθάνω, n. 67): Ὅμηρος ὁ σοφώτατος πεποίηκε σχεδὸν περὶ πάντων τῶν ἀνθρωπίνων. But while the Socrates of Plat. Resp., X, 606e accepts the view only with reservations (607a),[11] a later age connected the greatest philosopher of Greece indissolubly with its greatest poet, through whom Greece "achieved a unity of national consciousness."[12] Dio Chrys. in his 55th address (De Homero et Socrate) advanced the thesis (3) ὅτι Σωκράτης τό γε ἀληθὲς Ὁμήρου μαθητὴς γέγονεν. The long span of time between the two cannot shake the thesis, since Socrates is the ζηλωτής of Homer. This is proved as follows: (4) εἴπερ οὖν ζηλωτής, καὶ μαθητὴς εἴη ἄν. ὁ γὰρ ζηλῶν τινα ὀρθῶς ἐπίσταται δήπου ἐκεῖνον ὁποῖος ἦν καὶ μιμούμενος τὰ ἔργα καὶ τοὺς λόγους ὡς οἷόν τε ἐπιχειρεῖ ὅμοιον αὑτὸν ἀποφαίνειν. (5) ταὐτὸ δὲ τοῦτο καὶ ὁ μαθητὴς ποιεῖν ἔοικε· μιμούμενος τὸν διδάσκαλον καὶ προσέχων ἀναλαμβάνει τὴν τέχνην. τὸ δὲ ὁρᾶν καὶ ξυνεῖναι οὐδέν ἐστι πρὸς τὸ μανθάνειν.[13] It is then shown in detail how Socrates as a philosopher can be the μαθητής of the poet Homer. Among the arguments the most important is that the theme of both is ἀρετὴ ἀνθρώπων καὶ κακία, i.e., the sphere of moral and religious life, the only difference being that the one handles it διὰ τῆς ποιήσεως, the other καταλογάδην (v. 9).

The significant thing here is the way in which μαθητής is expounded in terms of μιμεῖσθαι. The centre of gravity of μαθητὴν εἶναι is thus removed from the formal side of the relation between μαθητής and διδάσκαλος to the inner fellowship between the two and its practical effects, and this to such a degree that the latter is basic to the whole relationship. This is not without considerable significance in relation to the development of the Christian use of μαθητής (→ D.).

2. Pupil or Disciple?

a. The character of μαθητής in which, as in διδάσκαλος (→ II, 149), the technical and rational element takes precedence of the inner fellowship, very definitely restricts the possible range of usage. It is not in place when the reference is not merely to an external connection with the goal of picking up certain information or aptitudes under expert direction, but to a materially grounded fellowship which arises under a goal which is certainly directed by an individual, but towards which all who participate are equally striving. This explains the aversion of Socrates and his circle to this word, an aversion whose effects may

---

10 Cf. W. Jaeger, *Paideia* (1934), 63-88: "Homer als Erzieher." It should be noted that Homer was much read even in Rabb. circles (jSanh., 28a, 18; Jad., 4, 6 and cf. B. Heller, MGWJ, 76 [1932], 330 ff.).

11 The reason is that for Plato restriction of the content of truth in the poems of Homer carries with it a diminished regard for them (Jaeger, *op. cit.*, 63 f.).

12 Jaeger, *op. cit.*, 88.

13 In proof it is pointed out that many watch flute-players exercising their skill without in any way learning to play the flute themselves.

be seen throughout the history of its use on Greek soil. The desire is to have disciples, not pupils.[14]

Socrates refused to be called a διδάσκαλος, or to let his teaching be called διδάσκειν (→ II, 150). Similarly, μαθητής was not for him the word to describe the relation of his companions to him. He would have called the use of this word a calumny,[15] just as he expressly rejected the phrase μαθητὴν εἶναι in personal application.[16] The Sophists have μαθηταί,[17] but not he. If his followers were called μαθηταί, this would have made him a teacher after the manner of the Sophists.[18] He uses the word[19] ironically in Plato for a disciple, so Euthyphr., 5a: Ἆρ' οὖν μοι, ὦ θαυμάσιε Εὐθύφρων, κράτιστόν ἐστι μαθητῇ σῷ γενέσθαι ...[20] As in Plato, so in Xenophon μαθητής is not used for a follower of Socrates (but → 419). Aristotle, too, stands under the influence of the Socratic-Platonic judgment on the relation between master and disciple, for he generally avoids μαθητής when compelled to mention these relations. In the one passage in which he uses it (Metaph., I, 5, p. 986b, 21 ff.)[21] it serves to denote, not the relation between teacher and pupil, but the incontestable dependence of the pupil on the teacher, here within the school or trend of the Eleatics. The word came strongly back into favour in the philosophy of the schools (→ 416), and rightly so in view of its character, since here the μίμησις of the master is cultivated.[22] But it is also used in cases where it is modified by co-ordination with another term, e.g., ἑταῖρος (Plut. Cons. ad Apoll., 36 [II, 120e]) etc. In Epict., who emphatically calls himself a διδάσκαλος (→ II, 150), μαθητής plays only a minor role.[23]

b. Though the disciple is so closely bound with and to his master, there are not a few words to express his independence and a certain personal dignity. Along with γνώριμος we find designations like οἱ συγγιγνόμενοι, οἱ συνόντες, οἱ ὁμιλοῦντες, ἀκόλουθος, ζηλωτής, ἑταῖρος (→ II, 699 f.) etc.

---

[14] On this distinction cf. Wach, 7 ff., who differentiates between disciple and pupil. But μαθητής becomes more specific, for it is not just a sociological term, as in Wach, but a pedagogical.

[15] Plat. Ap., 33a: ... οὐδενὶ πώποτε συγχωρήσας οὐδὲν παρὰ τὸ δίκαιον οὔτε ἄλλῳ οὔτε τούτων οὐδενὶ οὓς οἱ διαβάλλοντες ἐμέ φασιν ἐμοὺς μαθητὰς εἶναι. ἐγὼ δὲ διδάσκαλος μὲν οὐδενὸς πώποτ' ἐγενόμην ... Only the διδάσκαλος can have μαθηταί, cf. 33b.

[16] Plat. La., 186e: οὔτε γὰρ εὑρετὴς οὔτε μαθητὴς οὐδενὸς περὶ τῶν τοιούτων γεγονέναι. Cf. on this H. Maier, *Sokrates* (1913), 168.

[17] The usage is fixed, cf. → 416, and Aristoph. Nu., *passim* as well as Plato.

[18] This is the aim of Aristoph. Nu. Cf. the saying of a μαθητής of Socrates, which is typically Sophist in its exclusivism, 140: οὐ θέμις πλὴν τοῖς μαθηταῖσιν λέγειν, with the witness of Socrates himself in Plat. Ap., 33b: εἰ δέ τίς φησι παρ' ἐμοῦ πώποτέ τι μαθεῖν ἢ ἀκοῦσαι ἰδίᾳ ὅτι μὴ καὶ οἱ ἄλλοι πάντες, εὖ ἴστε ὅτι οὐκ ἀληθῆ λέγει.

[19] On the ordinary use in Plato → 416.

[20] Cf. what follows (esp. → 5. a, and cf. Gorg., 455c [Socrates to Gorgias]: καὶ ἐμὲ νῦν νόμισον καὶ τὸ σὸν σπεύδειν· ἴσως γὰρ καὶ τυγχάνει τις τῶν ἔνδον ὄντων μαθητής σου βουλόμενος γενέσθαι, ὡς ἐγώ τινας σχεδὸν καὶ συχνοὺς αἰσθάνομαι, οἳ ἴσως αἰσχύνοιντ' ἄν σε ἀνερέσθαι. Euthyd. 272e f. [Socrates]: καὶ ὀλίγῳ ὕστερον εἰσέρχεσθον τούτω — ὅ τ' Εὐθύδημος καὶ ὁ Διονυσόδωρος — καὶ ἄλλοι μαθηταὶ ἅμα αὖ πολλοὶ ἐμοὶ δοκεῖν.

[21] Ξενοφάνης δὲ πρῶτος τούτων ἑνίσας [ἑνίζω: "to declare as one," here used of ὄν] (ὁ γὰρ Παρμενίδης τούτου λέγεται μαθητής) οὐδὲν διεσαφήνισεν [διασαφηνίζω: "to explain clearly"].

[22] Cf. Democr. Fr., 154 (II, 173, Diels[5]): γελοῖοι δ' ἴσως ἐσμὲν ἐπὶ τῶι μανθάνειν τὰ ζῶια σεμνύνοντες, ὧν ὁ Δημόκριτος ἀποφαίνει μαθητὰς ἐν τοῖς μεγίστοις γεγονότας ἡμᾶς ... κατὰ μίμησιν.

[23] There is nothing special about the only two occurrences (IV, 6, 11; 8, 24).

γνώριμος is perhaps the most widespread, though only later writers use it in this special sense, Athen., II, 55 f. (p. 130) etc.; Stob. Floril., 57, 12 (cf. v. Arnim, I, p. 69, No. 312) etc.; Diog. L., VII, 36 (31) etc.; Strabo I, 2, 2 etc., and they do so in contrast to μαθητής when it is desired to emphasise fellowship with the master rather than dependence on him.[24] In γνώριμος there is also a suggestion of some intimacy, cf. Philostratus when in his Vit. Ap. he calls the companions of Apollonius γνώριμοι (IV, 47 etc.) as well as the common ὁμιληταί (I, 16 etc.) and θεράποντες (I, 18). The same is true with Epictet. or Arrian (Diss., I, 29, 66 : τοῖς γνωρίμοις, τοῖς δυναμένοις, αὐτὰ ἀκοῦσαι ... cf. III, 22, 1). The common συνήθης points in the same direction.

Avoiding all specialised terms, Socrates himself simply speaks of οἱ δ' ἐμοὶ συγγιγνόμενοι (Plat. Theaet., 150d), while various words to the same effect alternate in Xenophon : οἱ συνόντες, Mem., I, 4, 19; I, 7, 5 etc.; οἱ ὁμιλοῦντες (αὐτῷ), Mem., IV, 7, 1 etc.[25] These terms later give place to γνώριμος, but they do not wholly disappear, and οἱ συνόντες is strikingly found in Epictet. Diss., III, 16, 5 for those gathered around Socrates,[26] so that the old ideal still has its echoes. One cannot say that it is renewed in the circle around Epictet.; the rational element is now too strong, → II, 150.

c. Xenophon uses a special word.

Avoiding μαθητής, he shows that he has taken up, or tried to take up, the concern of Socrates (→ 418). But by occasionally using οἱ μανθάνοντες, even in connection with the work of Socrates (Mem., I, 2, 17), he also gives evidence that he has not succeeded in grasping, or in expressing beyond possibility of misunderstanding, the distinctiveness of Socrates. Though he did not put Socrates on the same level as the Sophists, he failed on the other hand to get beyond the commitment of hearers to the teacher, or to understand their mutual relation in common commitment to the object. For Xenophon, as distinct from Plato, Socrates is finally the great personality who draws into his circle and thus has pupils even though one can still see the powerful influence of Socrates' own concern, → 420 and 394. Cf. esp. the Oec. and the portrait of Socrates there.

3. Master and Disciple.[27]

Antiquity knows the master-disciple relation in two forms. The first is in the sphere of philosophical culture, the second in that of cultic and religious activity. The two forms come together where philosophical and religious elements intersect in the person of the master. This may be seen at the time of early Christianity.

a. Socrates, Plato and the Academy. The first time that master and disciple meet on the soil of Greek culture is when Socrates associates with his circle in deliberate avoidance of the teacher-pupil relation which was taken for granted among the Sophists. This is by its very nature rational and professional, and those concerned were in part aware of this. It was now replaced by a purely ideal fellowship between the one who gave out intellectually and those who received intellectually. In the academy founded by Plato this relation was given its classic form which continued to exert an influence for centuries and which was still in some sense the model for the great schools of a later age.

---

[24] Cf. Athen., VII, 281c (p. 212) with VI, 251b (p. 61). *V.* also H. Diels, *Philosophische Aufsätze, Eduard Zeller gewidmet* (1887), 245. The oldest instance acc. to H. Usener, *Pr. Jahrb.*, 53 (1884), 10 is in Lycon, who led the Peripatetic school from 270-236 B.C. γνώριμος in this sense is also common in Joseph., cf. Schl. Theol. d. Judt., 206, n. 2.

[25] On Plato and Xenoph. cf. also O. Dittrich, *Geschichte d. Ethik,* I (1926), 173.

[26] Elsewhere in Epictet. οἱ συνόντες means much the same as "entourage," cf. Diss., IV, 11, 32; Ench., 33, 3 etc.

[27] In what follows we are again indebted to Wach, though → n. 14.

Protagoras [28] was the first Sophist and also the first to take μαθηταί for a fee. In return for this he imparted to them knowledge of practical value. [29] Later writers say that he demanded a high sum. [30] Perhaps this was exaggerated, though there can be little doubt that he asked a good deal. It is a mark of his self-esteem that if pupils thought it exorbitant he left it to them, after serious examination in the temple, to give him what they thought that which they had learned was worth. [31] His success was such that wherever he went great crowds of students gathered around him and followed him enthusiastically. [32] What is true of him is more or less true of the other Sophists. Fundamentally the image which they present with their μαθηταί is the same, for everywhere the intellectual direction of the διδάσκαλος must be compensated by financial contributions of the μαθηταί. [33]

It is in keeping that Socrates, when he refused to allow the relation between himself and his listeners to be described in terms of διδάσκαλος/μαθητής (→ 395), should also reject any compensation or payment: ἐγὼ δὲ διδάσκαλος μὲν οὐδενὸς πώποτ' ἐγενόμην· εἰ δέ τίς μου λέγοντος καὶ τὰ ἐμαυτοῦ πράττοντος ἐπιθυμεῖ ἀκούειν, εἴτε νεώτερος εἴτε πρεσβύτερος, [34] οὐδενὶ πώποτε ἐφθόνησα, οὐδὲ χρήματα μὲν λαμβάνων διαλέγομαι μὴ λαμβάνων δὲ οὔ, ἀλλ' ὁμοίως καὶ πλουσίῳ καὶ πένητι παρέχω ἐμαυτὸν ἐρωτᾶν, καὶ ἐάν τις βούληται ἀποκρινόμενος ἀκούειν ὧν ἂν λέγω (Plat. Ap., 33, a-b). The basis of the relation is Socrates himself rather than the knowledge at his disposal. He is the master around whom disciples gather. Young and old become his disciples because he grants to them his fellowship, allowing them a share in his intellectual life. The avoidance of μαθητής in the circle around Socrates is thus justified not only on formal grounds (→ 395, n. 43) but also on material. Plato, [35] and, with some reservations (→ 419), Xenophon, [36] rightly understood him [37] at this point, and Aristotle also followed him in this respect. [38] An external expression of the relation, which was marked both by personal freedom in relation to Socrates [39] and also by the material attachment of the listeners to him, is to be found in the meals which he often shared with a familiar circle. [40] He did not in fact found a school. The same is true of Plato, his greatest disciple, and the academy founded by him. In this there was a fellowship of life as well as intellect, so that the picture resembles that of the Pythagorean circle. [41] It is worth noting in this connection that → ἑταῖρος was often used to describe those who belonged to the academy. [42] The director is the first among equals. This was true even in the way that his office, with common consent, was freely

---

[28] What follows is based on the material in E. Zeller, *Die Philosophie d. Griechen*[6], I, 2 (1920), 1340-49.

[29] Plat. Prot., 348e/349a.

[30] Diog. L., IX, 50 (1) and 52 (3) tells us that the fee for a whole course was a hundred minas.

[31] Plat. Prot., 328b-c; cf. also Aristot. Eth. Nic., IX, 1, p. 1164a, 24 ff.

[32] For details cf. Plat. Prot., 310b ff.

[33] For the more important Sophists cf. on Gorgias, Diod. S., 12, 53; on Prodicus, Plat. Crat., 384b; on Hippias, Plat. Ap., 19e; Hi., I, 282d-e; on the Sophists generally, Xenoph. Mem., I, 6, 13; *v.* also Zeller, I, 2, 1345.

[34] Since the Sophists turned to the young, there is here too a distinction between them and Socrates.

[35] Cf. Gorg., 450c ff.

[36] Mem., I, 6, 14 etc.

[37] Plato demands that the state should guarantee the freedom of philosophers by undertaking their support.

[38] Eth. Nic., IX, 1, p. 1164a, 24 ff.

[39] Xenoph. Mem., III, 14, 1 ff.

[40] Cf. on this Plat. Theaet., 151b; Xenoph. Mem., III, 1, 1 ff.

[41] Cf. already in the circle around Socrates the ἑταῖρος in Plat. Prot., also Xenoph. Mem., II, 8, 1, and later Plut. Timoleon, 6 (I, 238d) etc.; → II, 700, n. 1.

[42] Zeller[5], II, 1, 982 ff., esp. 985, and n.

transferred by the incumbent to his successor before death. [43] Both the Platonic and Aristotelian circles adopted the common meal from Socrates. Epictet., too, can sometimes call his disciples ἑταῖροι, [44] thereby expressing the fact that he does not seek to rule over them, but wishes to be of profit to them. [45]

b. The Mystery Religions. The mystery religions are another area where one finds the specific master-disciple relation. The initiate needs the master to introduce him to the mysteries of the god and the cultus in order that he may become a member of the society gathered around the god. Thus the mystagogue is the master for the adept. By the very nature of the case this is true here only in so far and so long as the initiate stands under the direction of the expert. The latter has significance for him only in the discharge of his function. For this reason he remains in the sphere of anonymity and never becomes personal.

The need briefly to mention this aspect is based on the fact that "teaching" and "learning" very probably had no little significance in the mysteries (→ μανθάνω, 398 f.). If those who took part in the processes described by these words were not actually called διδάσκαλος and μαθητής, the reason is obvious. Learning in the mysteries is a necessary process, but not an end in itself. For the goal of the rites is not knowledge of the god ; it is fellowship with him. Hence it is more natural to think of the mysteries in terms of a family rather than a school when they wish to describe relations not only with the god but also with the religious leaders and among members. For this reason the head of the priestly hierarchy in the Mithras mysteries is called father, [46] and it seems likely that the same term was used for the leading priests of individual cultic societies in the Attis mysteries, [47] → πατήρ. Here then, and quite logically in terms of the basic ideas behind the mystery religions, the master-disciple relation was construed naturally, though only in symbol.

c. The Master-Disciple Relation with a Religious Aspect. There is a definite religious side to the relation in men like Pythagoras, Epicurus and Apollonius of Tyana. Legend and myth have clustered around all these figures, so that the attempt to give a clear and historically objective picture is extraordinarily difficult. Nevertheless, the original sources in their various layers enable us fix on the basic element at issue here, namely, the religious veneration of the master by his disciples.

The followers (μαθηταί, Diog. L., VIII, 3 [3] etc.; Iambl. Vit. Pyth., 254 etc.; γνώριμοι, Diog. L., VIII, 14-15 [12-15]; συνήθεις, VIII, 39 [31]; ἑταῖροι, *loc. cit.*) of Pythagoras seem to have constituted a religious and moral community from the very first. [48] The heart of this was the word [49] and person of the philosopher, and entry into it was by examination, in which proof of worthiness had to be given. [50] His person,

---

[43] Epict. Diss., II, 15, 4.

[44] This is not finally religious, so that there is no essential distinction from the academy of Plato. Tradition finds different degrees among the disciples of Pythagoras ; the esoteric core of his teaching is not accessible to all of them, cf. Zeller[6], I, 1, 400.

[45] He also seeks to make "men" of his listeners.

[46] Cf. F. Cumont, *Die Mysterien des Mithra*[3] (1923), 142 ff.

[47] For details cf. H. Hepding, *Attis, seine Mythen u. sein Kult* (1903), 187 f.

[48] Herodot., II, 81 already draws attention to certain cultic peculiarities of the Pythagoreans. Plato speaks expressly of a Πυθαγόρειος τρόπος τοῦ βίου, Resp., X, 600b.

[49] Cf. the phrase αὐτὸς ἔφα (Diog. L., VIII, 46 [25] and 44 [23]), which makes absolutely binding on adherents the teachings which have come down by tradition from the master.

[50] Details were supplied later (cf. esp. Iambl. Vit. Pyth., 71 ff.), though it is likely that there was a good deal of accretion, even if one cannot always distinguish with certainty.

which pious saga soon took in hand, became increasingly more important for his later followers, so that he has a divine aspect for the succeeding world, and is equated with Apollo.[51] This development is understandable, however, if impulses towards it are already present in the direct relation between him and his μαθηταί, and in the general picture which his contemporaries had of him. The rapid spread of Pythagoreanism in his own lifetime and the 5th century points in the same direction.

What has come down to us concerning the relation of Epicureans to their master seems related in many ways. Epicurus seems from the very first to have bound his disciples primarily to his own person. Acc. to tradition he certainly made them learn by heart sayings of his own (Diog. L., X, 12 [6] and 7 [3]) which were called κύριαι δόξαι (*ibid.*, X, 29 [18] etc. → 425 and n. 69); and also acc. to tradition he disparaged other philosophers in the eyes of his γνώριμοι or μαθηταί (so Diog. L., X, 22 [11] etc.), cf. Diog. L., X, 7 f. (4) etc. Acc. to the accounts we have, his estimation of himself must have been high, and there are traits which present him more as the founder of a religion than a philosopher.[52] Even in his lifetime he was honoured by his disciples as a god,[53] and in the 1st cent. B.C. his follower and enthusiastic propagandist in Latin, Lucretius, lauds him in the exalted terms : ... *Epicurus ..., qui genus humanum ingenio superavit et omnis restinxit, stellas exortus ut aetherius Sol* (De rerum natura, III, 1042-1044). In none of the schools of antiquity is the memory of the master so cultivated or his legacy so carefully preserved as in Epicureanism. The almost religious veneration of the person of Epicurus and the careful transmission of his thoughts and most important sayings in literal form[54] go hand in hand.[55]

In the days of early Christianity we find the Neo-Pythagorean Apollonius of Tyana. Here again the tradition has many strata, but already the sources used by Philostr.[56] make it apparent that the personality of Apollonius was calculated to make an unusual impression on his contemporaries, and actually did so.[57] It is fairly certain that Apollonius did not regard himself as divine.[58] The more resolutely, then, did his followers see in him more than a man. This is shown by the fact that the tradition is rich in miracles, and certain historical traits (visions, healings etc.) seem to form a starting-point.[59] There is no doubt that his relation to his disciples is definitely religious in

---

[51] Ael. Var. Hist., II, 26 : 'Αριστοτέλης λέγει ὑπὸ τῶν Κροτωνιατῶν τὸν Πυθαγόραν 'Απόλλωνα 'Υπερβόρεον προσαγορεύεσθαι. Cf. also Diog. L., VIII, 11 (9): καὶ αὐτοῦ οἱ μαθηταὶ δόξαν εἶχον περὶ αὐτοῦ ὡς εἴη 'Απόλλων ἐξ 'Υπερβορέων ἀφιγμένος. *Ibid.*, VIII, 14 (15): οὕτω δὲ ἐθαυμάσθη ὥστε ἔλεγον τοὺς γνωρίμους αὐτοῦ παντοίας θεοῦ φωνάς (vl. ed. Cobet [Paris, 1862]: τοὺς γνωρίμους αὐτοῦ μάντιας θεοῦ φωνάς, *ut appellarent eius discipulos "Vates divinae vocis"*).

[52] Cf. E. Schwartz, *Characterköpfe aus der antiken Lit., 2. Reihe*³ (1919), 27 f. and 37 ff. For an ed. of the Κύριαι Δόξαι cf. C. Bailey, *Epicurus* (1926), 94-104. On the basis of the Hercul. Fragments (ed. A. Vogliano [1928]), R. Philippson defends Epicurus against the charge of calumniation in NGG [1929], 148.

[53] This may be seen best in the writings of his immediate disciple Metrodorus of Lampsacos; cf. the remains in the ed. of A. Koerte, *Jbch. f. Phil. Suppl.*, 17 (1890), 529 ff. Cf. also Schwartz, 42 f. and Diog. L., X, 18 (10) with Epicurus' own institution by will of a monthly veneration of his person after the manner of a hero.

[54] Cf. Diog. L., X, 139-154 (list of the κύριαι δόξαι) and also the "Epicurean book in stone" in Oenoanda in Pisidia (cf. the ed. of J. William, *Diogenis Oenoandensis Fragmenta* [1907]).

[55] Cf. on this Schwartz, 29.

[56] Cf. R. Reitzenstein, *Hellenistische Wundererzählungen* (1906), 41 ff.; J. Hempel, *Untersuchungen z. Überlieferung von Apollonius von Tyana = Beiträge z. Religionswissenschaft*, 4 [1920], 37 ff.

[57] Hempel, 62 f.

[58] *Ibid.*, 64 ff.

[59] *Ibid.*, 68 ff.; cf. M. Wundt, "Apollonius v. Tyana," ZwTh, 49 (1906), 309 ff. Cf. also Philostr. Vit. Ap., VIII, 13 : τότε πρῶτον κατενόησα (subj. Damis) τοῦ ἀνδρὸς θεσπέσιόν τε εἶναι αὐτὸν καὶ κρείσσω τῆς ἡμεδαπῆς σοφίας.

character. Indeed, some aspects seem astonishingly close to the NT, though it is unlikely that there are any literary connections.[60] Hence there is no reason for surprise if we occasionally read of enthusiastic groups of disciples who spread abroad the fame of their master when he went on his great journeys: ἠκολούθησαν δὲ αὐτῷ οἱ γνώριμοι πάντες ἐπαινοῦντες καὶ τὴν ἀποδημίαν καὶ τὸν ἄνδρα, Philostr. Vit. Ap., IV, 47.

It may be mentioned by way of supplement that the picture which Lucian gives of the position of the μαθηταί of Peregrinus Proteus (Pergr. Mort., 28; ὁμιληταί in 30, and ἑταῖροι in 29 and 41) is not dissimilar, e.g., when he mentions the possibility that they erected a sanctuary to him at the site of his self-immolation by fire (*ibid.*, 28).

4. The Fellowship of Disciples and the Principle of Tradition.

a. The Fellowship of Disciples. The groups which assembled around the great philosophical teachers of antiquity were much too solidly established to disintegrate when the teachers died. This was not just because of the personal regard which the masters enjoyed and which gave them influence even after death. The true presupposition for the continuation of groups of disciples is to be found, not merely at the personal level, but in the cause advocated and presented by the teachers. In the last resort these groups were formed by common acknowledgement of insights peculiar to the masters concerned. The groups regarded these as truth which they could not give up but had to propagate with all their power. The death of the teachers could not alter this. On the contrary, it increased responsibility for the work and strengthened commitment to it. This sense of responsibility in the groups of disciples went hand in hand with the natural desire of the teachers to know that their cause would be represented with true dedication after their death. The suprapersonal interest on both sides led to the formation of communities of disciples out of the original groups of students. It is worth noting that this principle embraces not only fellowships of a religious character, like the Pythagoreans and Epicureans,[61] but also groups like the Peripatetics and Stoics, not to speak of the Platonic academy. Alongside the resolute will to continue the master's work in fellowship, it is fundamentally a secondary question whether there was always success in remaining faithful to the master's intentions.[62] We cannot go into this question here.

By public position as well as organisation the oldest philosophical schools were θίασοι, i.e., religious unions. Even the Platonic academy is no exception to this general rule. This fact throws light on the dominant position of the master even at the level of organisation. He usually has at least the opportunity to influence the continuation of the fellowship along his own lines by appointing his nearest follower as his successor. It is reported of no less a figure than Aristotle that shortly before his death he chose Theophrastus as his successor in directing the Peripatetic school founded by him, though only after *omnis eius sectatorum cohors* had urgently requested him to settle the question of his successor in the teaching office himself.[63] This procedure bears testimony to the

---

[60] Cf. Philostr. Vit. Ap., I, 19, which is typical even though Damis is speaking: ὁ μὲν δὴ Ἀσσύριος προσηύξατο αὐτόν, ... καὶ ὥσπερ δαίμονα ἔβλεπε, συνῆν τε αὐτῷ ἐπιδιδοὺς τὴν σοφίαν καὶ ὅ τι μάθοι μνημονεύων ... τοιοῦδε μὲν ἑταίρου καὶ ἐραστοῦ ἔτυχεν, ᾧ τὸ πολὺ τοῦ βίου συνεπορεύθη. Cf. also VII, 38 (*v.* Hempel, 64, n. 1) or even VIII, 11 ff.

[61] → 421 f.

[62] For details cf. the histories of philosophy.

[63] A. Gellius (c. 160 A.D.), Noctes Atticae, XIII, 5.

situation of the fellowship of disciples as outlined above. Its distinctive nature is the result of an interplay of various factors. More frequently the future leaders are in fact chosen by the schools themselves.[64] Nevertheless, one may say that increasingly in all schools the centre shifts from the official leaders to the schools as such, since the members consciously seek to propagate the cause of the school as the cause of its founder. This may be seen particularly well in the Epicurean Lucretius in the 1st century B.C. (→ 422). The Stoics might be mentioned along with the Epicureans in this connection, the more so as they very largely determined the intellectual image of the world into which early Christianity came.

b. The Principle of Tradition. In keeping with the origin of the fellowships in the work of the master is the fact they remained inwardly committed to him, and were aware of this. Outward expression of it is to be found in a principle which controlled the whole life and work of the fellowships. This can best be called the principle of tradition. At issue here is that the intentions of the master should be cultivated, and his sayings carefully preserved and transmitted. The principle is to be found everywhere up to and beyond the time of the NT. But it does not appear to have been equally comprehensive in every case. Another essential point is that the tradition does not seem to have operated mechanically, but in a process of constant movement which enables us to see that we have here the opposite of schematism and rigidity, namely, a living appropriation in both freedom and commitment.

It has long since been recognised that the Gk. philosophical schools both at the time of their formation and in the manner of their operation were working fellowships under the decisive leadership of the master who formed their centre.[65] There are also important reasons for assuming that this was true from the very first, and not just from the time of Plato and Aristotle.[66]

This sheds a significant light on the fact of the development of this principle of tradition in the philosophical schools, on the natural way in which it was everywhere handled, and also on the fact that it was never felt to impose a restriction on personal freedom. On the one side the school lives by its tradition, on the other the tradition has in the school which cultivates it the soil by which it is continually renewed. It can thus happen that when Aristotle takes issue with Pythagoreanism he never speaks of the teaching of Pythagoras, nor does he deal with individual representatives of the movement known to him, but he concerns himself always with the Πυθαγόρειοι, i.e., the whole school.[67] It is also true that among the Pythagoreans themselves, in the phrase αὐτὸς ἔφα, constant appeal is made to the authority and word of the master.[68]

It is among the Epicureans that there is strongest orientation to the person of the master. Strikingly, a number of sayings stands here at the heart of the tradition. These were supposedly formulated by Epicurus himself, and they were handed down from generation to generation as the most succinct and pertinent sum of his teaching. These

---

[64] It may thus be pointed out that acc. to Gellius Aristotle recognised his successor in a symbolical gesture, thereby simply indicating that he personally desired this man, but not intending to force him on the school.

[65] Cf. H. Usener, "Organisation der wissenschaftl. Arbeit, Bilder aus d. Geschichte der Wissenschaft," *Pr. Jahrb.*, 53 (1884), 1 ff., esp. 9 ff.

[66] H. Diels, "Über d. ältesten Philosophenschulen der Griechen," *Philosophische Aufsätze, Eduard Zeller gewidmet* (1887), 239 ff.

[67] Diels, *op. cit.*, 247. He rightly sees in this fact "the most eloquent proof of the importance of the school."

[68] → n. 49. Cf. also the formula Πυθαγόρου δόξαι, Philostr. Vit. Ap., I, 7.

κύριαι δόξαι [69] are authentic in content, and this is the important point in this connection, not whether they were really collected by Epicurus, which is not very likely. [70] Though there is not always complete agreement in wording, [71] many of the sayings collected in Diog. L. are found through the centuries both in literary and non-literary sources, [72] including Christian. Finally, the school of Epicurus has also a very definite discipline. [73]

Things are much the same among the Stoics. [74] What we know of the origins of Stoicism enables us to see how the specific Stoic tradition was established. After the death of Zeno, *a quo coepit Stoicorum rigida ac virilis sapientia* (Seneca ad Helviam, 12, 4), the school founded by him threatened to break up, not least because he intentionally allowed his disciples the freedom to think independently. Then Chrysippus [75] restored the threatened cohesion of the school. Though he was a creative thinker and came to not a few new insights, for the sake of the school he did not present these as his own teaching, but as a development of the doctrine of Zeno, even when in fact he was going his own way. [76] Serving to maintain and increase the authority of Zeno, he was thus the one to whom the Stoa owed, not its existence, but its preservation and high repute in the ancient world. [77] Anti-Stoic polemic was largely directed against him for this reason, esp. from the beginning of the 2nd cent. A.D. [78] "But in many cases, when accounts were given of the orthodox dogma of the school, reference was made, not to the Stoics, but to τοὺς ἀπὸ Ζήνωνος, or simply to the name of the founder of the school, with no careful enquiry whether he was in fact personally responsible for the individual doctrine." [79] Perhaps nothing shows more clearly how strong and vital and dominant in Stoicism too was the principle of tradition (in the above sense) together with the sense of being a school.

The principle of tradition is thus an inherent feature of the philosophical fellowship of disciples in the Greek or Hellenistic world. Since it is often taken for granted that on Greek soil a principle of tradition obtained only in the mystery religions, and that it there served the esoteric transmission of religious and cultic secrets, [80] this finding represents a notable widening of our horizon which is bound to have important consequences (→ B. 6). The traditional view certainly has in its favour the fact that the word group παραδιδόναι, παράδοσις etc., which is used to describe the process of tradition in the mystery religions, [81] is very rare [82]

---

[69] → 422. Ancient witnesses to the use of this phrase to describe the core sayings of the Epicureans may be found in Usener, *Epicurea* (1887), 68 ff.

[70] *Ibid.*, XLIII ff.; F. Überweg, *Grundriss d. Geschichte der Philosophie des Altertums*[12], I (1926), 443 f.

[71] Usener, XLIV. Cf. the different versions of the δόξαι in Diog. L. and Oenoanda (→ n. 54).

[72] Cf. the *Sententiarum selectarum testimonia* in Usener, 394 ff. and → n. 54.

[73] Cf. R. Philippson, Herm., 60 (1925), 478 ff.; NGG (1930), 6 ff.

[74] Cf. v. Arnim, who gives rich materials, though only of Stoics up to the middle of the 2nd cent. B.C.

[75] Diog. L., VII, 179 (1): Χρύσιππος ... μαθητὴς Κλεάνθους; Luc. Macrob., 19: Κλεάνθης δὲ ὁ Ζήνωνος μαθητής ...

[76] Cf. M. Pohlenz, "Zenon u. Chrysipp," NGG *phil.-hist. Klasse, Fachgruppe*, I, NF II, 9 (1938).

[77] Cf. Diog. L., VII, 183 (5): εἰ μὴ γὰρ ἦν Χρύσιππος, οὐκ ἂν ἦν στοά.

[78] Cf. v. Arnim, I, 1 ff. (*praefatio*) *passim.*

[79] Pohlenz, *op. cit.*, 174.

[80] Cf. the comprehensive discussion in Ranft, esp. 179 ff.

[81] → II, 171, n. 19; 173, n. 7.

[82] So M. Valerius Probus (2nd half of the 1st cent. A.D.) in Verg., p. 10, 33, ed. Keil (cf. v. Arnim, I, 102, p. 29): *ex his (quattuor elementis) omnia esse postea effigiata Stoici tradunt, Zenon ... et Chrysippus ... et Cleanthes.* Cf. v. Arnim, I, 496, p. 111 (*tradunt*);

in relation to the principle of tradition in the philosophical schools. [83] Nevertheless, it may be shown that the group was not so apt in this field. In any case, this is not our present concern. All that we are pointing out is that the principle of tradition is generally accepted, and that it is so in the framework of the self-awareness of the school as a fellowship of disciples.

B. The Term in the Old Testament and Judaism.

1. The Use of μαθητής/תַּלְמִיד in the OT (LXX).

a. μαθητής in the LXX. The term μαθητής does not occur in the established LXX tradition. It is simply found in three passages in A. [84] These verses add nothing to the history of the word.

Ιερ. 13:21 [85] (to Jerusalem: καὶ σὺ ἐδίδαξας αὐτοὺς ἐπὶ σὲ μαθητὰς (A) εἰς ἀρχήν, Mas. וְאַתְּ לִמַּדְתְּ אֹתָם עָלַיִךְ אַלֻּפִים לְרֹאשׁ). The usual reading here is μαθήματα (as hapaxlegomenon). In similar cases (Prv. 16:28) the underlying Mas. אַלּוּפִים is rendered φίλος. It is perhaps in view of αὐτούς that A substitutes the personal μαθητής for the impersonal μαθήματα. But this does not clarify the Gk. The very fact that a word formed from μαθ- is used can be explained only by assuming an attempt to carry over into Gk. the juxtaposition of לִמֵּד ("to teach") and the rare אָלַף ("to learn") seen in the original. [86]

On the other hand it is hard to see what A had in view at Ιερ. 20:11 (καὶ κύριος μετ' ἐμοῦ καθὼς μαθητὴς ἰσχυρός for Mas. וַיהוָה אוֹתִי [87] (כְּגִבּוֹר עָרִיץ, where the usual reading is μαχητὴς ἰσχύων. Even more puzzling is Ιερ. 26:9 = Jer. 46:9: ἐξέλθατε, οἱ μαθηταὶ Αἰθιόπων ... instead of οἱ μαχηταὶ Αἰθιόπων for Mas. הַגִּבּוֹרִים כּוּשׁ. [88]

b. תַּלְמִיד in the OT. The Heb. תַּלְמִיד, which is later (→ B. 4) the usual equivalent for μαθητής, is found in the OT only at 1 Ch. 25:8 along with מֵבִין. Both words are general, and in translation the part. μανθάνοντες is used rather than μαθηταί. If the term is rather specialised, the refusal to use μαθητής (→ μανθάνω, 401) is justified, but the almost complete absence of תַּלְמִיד even from the later parts of

---

II, 586, p. 181 (*tradit*); I, 558, p. 127 (Cicero Off., III, 3 (§ 11): *itaque accepimus Socratem exsecrari solitum eos, qui* ...); II, 411, p. 135 (Gal. Methodi medicinae, I, 2: ἕτοιμα δ' ἤδη παραλαβόντες οὐκ ἐφιλονίκησαν οἱ περὶ τὸν Χρύσιππον ...).

[83] On the terminology of the philosophical school tradition cf. Aristot. Metaph., IV, 5, p. 1009b, 25 ff.: Ἀναξαγόρου δὲ καὶ ἀπόφθεγμα μνημονεύεται πρὸς τῶν ἑταίρων τινάς ... The enclitic φασιν is common, also phrases like οἱ ἀπὸ τῆς Στοᾶς λέγουσιν etc. Cic. Divin., I, 27 (§ 56): *somnia, quae creberrume commemorantur a Stoicis* ...

[84] The readings are not well attested in Ιερ. 13:21; 20:11. At Ιερ. 26:9, since μαθηταί is only in A^1 (Hatch-Redp.), it does not even occur in A. Rahlfs' apparatus to the LXX; he simply regards it as a scribal error (cf. I, p. XV of his ed.).

[85] For the textual material cf. P. Volz, "Studien zum Text des Jeremia," BWANT, 25 (1920), 119.

[86] Cf. Volz, *op. cit.* B. Duhm, *Das Buch Jeremia* (1901), *ad loc.* finds in this misunderstanding of אלפים the reason for the present disorder of the verse in the Mas. The Tg. (רברבין) is not guilty of the misunderstanding, so that one may ask whether it does not arise only with Christianity.

[87] Read אִתִּי.

[88] → n. 84.

the OT is striking. When we take into account the parallel absence of μαθητής a special problem arises, since the significance of teaching (→ II, 136) and learning (→ 400) in the OT would at a first glance suggest the development of a special term for learners.

2. The Material Problem in the OT.

a. The Reason for the almost complete Absence of תַּלְמִיד/μαθητής from the OT (LXX). In the way in which the LXX uses μανθάνω one may see the influence of לָמַד, of which it is the normal rendering (→ 401). לָמַד stands always in conscious relation to the revealed will of God. It denotes the process in course of which man makes this will his own. Hence other words and concepts occur when there is no question of the formation and filling of one's own will in the light of God's will, especially as this is summed up in the Torah. For the direction of man, the usual word is יָסַר and derivates, for which the LXX uses παιδεύειν, παιδεία etc. [89] More particularly, however, the whole people is always the subject of learning. God has chosen His people in order that as a whole it may serve Him as the Lord by fulfilling His will. [90] If the same demand is made on the individual, this is because, as a member of the chosen people of God, he has a special task, e.g., as king, [91] and he shares the responsibility of the whole people in this specific way. The self-awareness of the OT community is thus controlled by the fact of its divine election, and on this basis it is quite impossible for it to use a noun formed from לָמַד to denote the individual who gives himself specially to לָמַד, and thereby to differentiate him from the other members of the chosen people. [92] *Mutatis mutandis* the same applies to the use of μαθητής. It is thus no accident, but wholly in keeping with the facts of the situation, that תַּלְמִיד and μαθητής play only a very minor role in the OT, and that תַּלְמִיד occurs only once in one of the later writings. [93]

b. The Absence also of the Master-Disciple Relation from the OT. If the term is missing, so, too, is that which it serves to denote. Apart from the formal relation of teacher and pupil, the OT, unlike the classical Greek world and Hellenism, has no master-disciple relation. Whether among the prophets or the scribes we seek in vain for anything corresponding to it.

(a) The relation between Moses and Joshua, as this is portrayed in the OT, is on a very different level.

Joshua is always the servant (מְשָׁרֵת) [94] of Moses, who stands at his side. He does not gradually grow into Moses's office as his disciple and heir, so that he has simply to assume this office on the death of Moses. He is publicly appointed Moses' successor by

---

[89] Cf. on this G. Bertram, *Der Begriff d. Erziehung in d. griech. Bibel* (1932).

[90] Cf. esp. Dt. 4:10; 5:1 etc.

[91] Cf. Dt. 17:19.

[92] Nothing bears stronger witness to the truth of this statement than the expectation that the whole community of the new covenant will be a community of men who know God and who thus need no mutual instruction (Jer. 31:34). Thus at Ησ. 54:13 (Heb. לִמּוּדֵי יְהוָה) the LXX appropriately calls them διδακτοὶ θεοῦ (→ II, 165, cf. 1 Th. 4:9).

[93] There is thus repeated what had to be said about διδάσκαλος (→ II, 151). Where this word occurs in the LXX, it is either secondary or in a later text.

[94] Ex. 24:13; Nu. 11:28: παρεστηκώς; Ex. 33:11: θεράπων.

express command of God (Nu. 27:15 ff.). It is worth noting that the account of this does not touch on the personal relation between the two. Moses does not ask God for this successor, nor does the narrator explain the succession along these lines.[95] The decision is with God alone, who directs Moses already to impart to Joshua some of his הוד/δόξα (→ II, 242). In keeping with this, Joshua does not discharge his office in the shadow of his predecessor but in terms of the full authority with which he is vested by God (Jos. 1:2 ff., esp. v. 5a;[96] 4:14; cf. Dt. 34:9).

(b) The OT prophets had no disciples. This is true both of the popular prophets and of men like Elijah, Elisha and Jeremiah, who had assistants who looked after them and who to some extent were more than servants.

The *nebi'im* are organised in guilds (2 K. 6:1 ff.). Sometimes we see that these guilds had a head (1 S. 19:20).[97] But there is nothing else to suggest hierarchical organisation. Above all, membership of the guild does not rest on a personal relation to the leader. What binds the members is the guidance and filling of the Spirit of God who takes possession of them (cf. 1 S. 10:10 ff.; 19:20 ff.). Thus there is only one comprehensive name for them : בְּנֵי־הַנְּבִיאִים/υἱοὶ τῶν προφητῶν, and this, in keeping with the established use of בֵּן/υἱός,[98] simply suggests that they belong to the נְבִיאִים/προφῆται.[99]

The assistant of Elijah is not a disciple, but a servant. First he is a נַעַר (1 K. 18:43; LXX : παιδάριον, → παῖς) whose name is not known. Then it is Elisha (19:19 ff.). Of the latter it is stated emphatically in 19:21 that he served Elijah (וַיְשָׁרְתֵהוּ), and 2 K. 3:11 leaves us in no doubt that he performed the kind of services rendered by slaves. Later Gehazi is regularly called the נַעַר of Elisha (2 K. 4:12, 25, 38; 5:20; 6:17; 8:4), though his activity is also described as that of a מְשָׁרֵת (→ *supra*). The circumstances in which Elisha became the companion of Elijah point in the same direction. When Elijah casts his mantle over the young husbandman as he is ploughing (1 K. 19:19), this tacit but immediately understood gesture does not imply "the dedication of Elisha as a nabi and the successor of Elijah."[100] It is a distraint on Elisha ; he is now to be at the disposal of Elijah.[101] It is thus correct to take the וַיֵּלֶךְ אַחֲרֵי אֵלִיָּהוּ of 1 K. 19:21 simply as a ref. to the entry of Elisha into the service of Elijah, and not, acc. to later usage,[102] as the beginning of the discipleship of Elisha. The presupposition and background of the whole scene is the authority of Elijah. The context gives us no reason to suppose that binding power goes forth from the mantle of Elijah.[103] For the rest,

---

[95] The description of Joshua as ὁ ἐκλεκτός (Αριθμ. 11:28) rests, like Luther's "the one whom he (Moses) had chosen," on a misunderstanding of the Mas. מִבְּחֻרָיו (Nu. 11:28) as בְּחָרוֹ.

[96] M. Noth, *Das Buch Josua, Hndbch. z. AT,* I, 7 (1938), 7, thinks that vv. 7-9, which bind Joshua to the book of law given by Moses, are secondary. But even if not, the picture given above would not be fundamentally affected.

[97] Cf. the brief collection of material in H. Gressmann, "Die älteste Geschichtsschreibung u. Prophetie Israels," *Die Schriften des AT,* II, 1 (1910), 31 f. → προφήτης.

[98] Cf. Dalman WJ, I, 94 f.; for details → υἱός.

[99] Neither here, nor in passages like 2 K. 4:38 ff.; 6:1 ff. etc., nor with ref. to בְּנֵי־הַנְּבִיאִים, can one speak of pupils or disciples of the prophets, though this is customary.

[100] Cf. also I. Benzinger, *Die Bücher der Könige* (1899), 113, *ad loc.*

[101] Cf. Rt. 3:9 and on this J. Wellhausen, ARW, 7 (1904), 40 f.; H. Gunkel, *Reden u. Aufsätze* (1913), 76 f.

[102] Perhaps it is of significance, however, that the piel is used in the Rabb., whereas here we have the kal.

[103] So esp. H. Gunkel, *Elias, Jahwe u. Baal* (1906), 26 and 71 f.; also Gressm., 268, *ad loc.*; though O. Eissfeldt in Kautzsch, *ad loc.* leaves the matter open.

1 K. 19:16, which comes from the same source as 19:19 ff., shows that Elisha is to be the successor of Elijah in his prophetic office. But for all his fellowship with Elijah (cf. 2 K. 2:1 ff.), he no more grows into this office than does Joshua (→ 427 f.). He receives it the moment Elijah leaves the scene (2 K. 2:9 ff.), and he exercises it, not in Elijah's name, but, like Elijah (2:15), solely in the name of God (3:11 ff.).

The decisive aspects may be seen again in the relation between Baruch and Jeremiah. How this came into being we do not know. But the records we have seem to show that Baruch served Jeremiah as Gehazi served Elisha (cf. Jer. 32:12 ff. with 2 K. 4:27 ff.; 5:19 ff.), except that Baruch is more of a scribe and sees to the publishing of what is written (Jer. 36:4 ff.; 45:1 ff.). Jer. 43:3 presupposes that Baruch spoke when the prophet himself was prevented.[104] This brings out the closeness of the working partnership between them (cf. also 36:26). Baruch undoubtedly had a hand in giving literary form to the original parts of the Book of Jeremiah.[105] But there is no hint of any independent work of Baruch alongside or after Jeremiah. He is the assistant and interpreter of Jeremiah, no more. Hence it is fitting that the assistant should disappear from the scene along with the prophet. This would not happen on Gk. soil, where the master lives on in his disciples and their teachings.

On Is. 8:16 → 430.

(c) To the degree that there are scribes in the OT, the presence of early impulses towards the formation of schools will always be an open question.

1 Ch. 2:55 speaks of מִשְׁפְּחוֹת סוֹפְרִים (LXX πατριαὶ γραμματέων). The phrase suggests that we have here a first attestation of the fact that after the return the סֹפְרִים consolidated themselves, in distinction from the חֲכָמִים, as a group especially concerned with the Torah (cf. 1 Macc. 7:12 : συναγωγὴ γραμματέων).[106] But the text is hardly reliable, so that it is inadvisable to draw far-reaching conclusions from it.[107] At best one can only deduce[108] that the scribes were organised in guilds like the *nebiim* (→ 428).

c. The Absence of the Principle of Tradition from the OT. Finally, we search the OT in vain for a principle of tradition of the kind found in Greek and Hellenistic philosophy and its off shoots in the religious sphere. This is the more remarkable in that the OT is consciously "Mosaic."

The religion of Israel stands or falls with Moses and his work.[109] Alongside the great figures of the age that follows, whose names are known and among whom we are to mention esp. the prophets, the great anonymous men of the OT also stand on the shoulders of Moses and continue his work.[110] Even a great religious leader like Samuel is simply preserving the legacy left by Moses.[111] Hence the religion of Israel may rightly be called Mosaism, the more so as the very existence of the people is rooted in the lifework of Moses.

It is thus remarkable that in the OT administration of the legacy of Moses is not bound up with veneration of his person. Though the prophets steadfastly follow his intentions, Moses is mentioned by them only a few times along with others (Mi. 6:4;

---

[104] Cf. P. Volz, *Der Prophet Jeremia* (*Komm. z. AT*, X[2] [1928]), *ad loc.*

[105] Cf. on this the comm. on Jer.

[106] Cf. Sir. 38:24-39:11.

[107] Cf. E. Sellin, *Geschichte d. israelitisch-jüdischen Volkes*, II (1932), 183. J. W. Rothstein-J. Hänel, *Komm. z. ersten Buch d. Chronik* (1927), 35, thinks it purposeless to try to make even general deductions in view of the state of the text.

[108] Cf. R. Kittel, *Geschichte d. Volkes Israel*, III, 2 (1929), 661.

[109] Cf. on this P. Volz, *Mose u. sein Werk*[2] (1932).

[110] Cf. on this P. Volz, *Prophetengestalten des AT* (1938), on J, 86 ff.

[111] *Ibid.*, 75 ff., and cf. Moses and Samuel in Jer. 15:1.

Jer. 15:1; Is. 63:11 f.; Mal. 3:22). Nowhere is he presented as a hero, even in the background, though he accomplished the redemption of his people out of Egypt.[112] Nor is he honoured even as the founder of a religion. The prophets look back to the time of Moses, not to Moses himself (cf. Am. 5:25; Hos. 2:16 ff.; Jer. 2:1 ff.).[113] The thing is what counts, not the man.

From the very outset, then, the principle of tradition is alien to the OT in the sense of orientation to the person of the master, i.e., in the form which it takes on Gk. and Hellen. soil, where a significant personality initiates intellectual movements (→ 424).[114] It will be seen later that this is rooted in the very nature of religion in Israel, and is thus a necessary feature (→ 3.).

In these circumstances, it is hardly surprising that in the prophetic movement there are no moves towards the formation of a religious or moral tradition linked with individual prophets. Even Is. 8:16 is no exception. Here a few exegetes see evidence of the founding by the prophet of a fellowship of disciples whose members will save his witness and teaching for a better time.[115] But the state of the text is such[116] that no certain results can be attained from it. Even if this view is right, the preservation of תּוֹרָה/νόμος is the task of the community, and these point beyond the prophet and his word to God Himself, on whom they rest (→ 427 and *supra*). Hence it is better to speak, not of a fellowship of disciples, but of the new community gathered around the prophet. In this the community of faith will be fashioned out of the national community for the first time in the history of Israel.[117]

3. The Reason for the Absence of the Master-Disciple Relation and the Principle of Tradition from the OT.

The religion of Israel is a religion of revelation. Here, then, the religious speech of man is simply the means which God uses to make known Himself and His will. Testimony is borne to the authenticity of the sense of calling and purpose of the agents and representatives of OT revelation by the fact that they never even try to interpose themselves as a factor of independent worth in the dialogue between God and His people. They never speak on their own account, and, when they have to defend their cause, they never fight for their own persons.[118] Their whole work is based on the divine commission which they have received. God has given them knowledge of His will, and put His Word on their lips.[119] This commits them[120] to pass on what they have received, for it comes to them for the sake of their people, which is God's people. It also makes them stewards who pass on what they have received as that which has been received, i.e., God's Word. If the word of the commissioned witness of God implies commitment, this

---

[112] *Ibid.*, 48.

[113] *Ibid.*, 124.

[114] We are not asking whether there is a tradition in the OT, what kind it is, or what are its laws. This is a matter of introduction which does not affect the present question. Hence we can rightly ignore it here (as against Ranft, 118 ff., who links the two issues).

[115] Cf., e.g., O. Procksch, *Jesaja*, I (1930), 138 ff., *ad loc.*; H. Guthe in Kautzsch, *ad loc.*

[116] Cf. the LXX, which deviates from the Mas., also the comm. with their various conjectures.

[117] Cf. Procksch, 140, also Volz, *op. cit.*, 211 f., who, referring to Is. 50:4, finds in the לִמֻּדָי of 8:16 God's disciples among the people; cf. also the phrase לִמּוּדֵי יְהוָֹה in Is. 54:13 and → n. 92.

[118] Ex. 32; Dt. 5:1 ff.; Jer. 11:18 ff. By the very nature of the case we know just as little about the lives of the prophets. Interest is directed, not to them, but to what they have to say, and to the fact that they say it, cf. Volz, *op. cit.*, 41.

[119] Cf. Ex. 4:12 (Moses) and Jer. 1:6 ff.; cf. also Is. 40:6 f.

[120] Cf. Nu. 11:10 ff.; Jer. 20:14 ff.

is commitment to God, not to men, no matter how profound a vision these men may have of the mysteries of God. In the sphere of revelation there is no place for the establishment of a master-disciple relation, nor is there the possibility of setting up a human word alongside the Word of God which is proclaimed, nor of trying to ensure the force of the divine address by basing it on the authority of a great personality (→ n. 118). For here God's Word alone is justified, no matter whether we be dealing with Moses or the prophets. Moses is indeed the first of the great line of divine witnesses. But the whole revelation of God is not present in him. If prophecy would have been impossible without Moses, new insight is still given to the prophets as compared with Moses. If in the OT there is no place whatever for the veneration of the religious leader as master, or for the cultivation of his memory as an almost religious duty, the final reason for this is that in the OT the disclosure of God is regarded as continuous and dynamic.[121]

So far as Moses is concerned, it is impossible to give a firm historical picture of him. We know him simply through the impression which he made and the influence which he exerted. Both affected the OT portrait. But the feature with which we are here concerned is definite enough. He is simply a minister in the cause of God (cf. Ex. 4:10 ff.). The declaration of the divine will constantly controls his acts, Ex. 5 ff. It is worth noting that the legislation, in which he seems to play the part of a mediator (Ex. 19:20 ff.),[122] comes only after the liberation, which throughout the OT is presented as God's own act. Having prepared a people for Himself, God sets this people under His will. The decisive point is that materially the two things belong together, and, as God's election of Israel to be His own people, they are uniformly understood as God's own action.[123]

Since it is this act of God which binds Israel to God, the prophets hold up before runagate Israel, not the person of Moses, but the time when it became God's people under his guidance (→ 430). They do not appeal to Moses or invoke his aid to get a hearing. Their word goes forth in the name of Yahweh, and it is He who, through their constant fellowship with Him, gives them a true understanding and the right word in a given moment,[124] and leads them from insight to insight, but always in such a way that each renders his service in exclusive dependence on God. Thus God Himself is their Master and Teacher. This means that there is for them no other master, not even Moses. Nor do they themselves have either the desire or the ability to be masters for others, even though they are the great and highly blessed religious guides of their people.[125]

4. The Rabbinic Use of תַּלְמִיד.

a. The Meaning of the Word. Since לָמַד is used for learning a trade (→ 402), one might expect that the common noun תַּלְמִיד would also denote an apprentice. But this is not so.[126] It is used exclusively for the one who gives himself (as a

---

[121] It would be instructive to compare these things with the background of the religious environment of the OT, but this would take us too far afield.

[122] Cf. also Gal. 3:19 : ἐν χειρὶ μεσίτου.

[123] Cf. simply Ex. 20:2 f.; Dt. 5:6 f.

[124] Cf. Jer. 18:2 ff.

[125] Cf. Volz, *op. cit.*, 26 f.

[126] S. Krauss, *Talmudische Archäologie*, II (1911), 256 f. gives the sense of apprentice, but there is no instance of this supposed meaning in the passages adduced by him, 624, n. 54. Usually the father teaches the son his own trade (Krauss, 254 f. and n. on p. 623), so that there is no need for a special word for apprentice. The Aram. uses שׁוּלְיָא for this, cf. Levy Wört., IV, 519b, *s.v.* for examples.

learner) to Scripture and to the religious tradition of Judaism. The word stands wholly under the influence of the specific sense of לָמַד (→ μανθάνω, 403). לָמַד in the specific sense constitutes the תַּלְמִיד.

It is hardly necessary to give examples of the many instances in Rabb. texts, → 434, and on the תַּלְמִידִים of Jesus → 442.

b. The Different Groups of תַּלְמִידִים. Rabbinic usage distinguishes two groups of תַּלְמִידִים. The first are the so-called תַּלְמִידֵי־חֲכָמִים, the second the ordinary תַּלְמִידִים. The latter are in some sense beginners in the study of scribal materials. In distinction from them the תַּלְמִידֵי־חֲכָמִים [127] have reached the stage which enables them to make independent decisions in religious law even though they have not yet been formally ordained rabbis or given public recognition as authorities.

The תַּלְמִיד is the first step towards the rabbi, who in later Judaism is the religious authority for those who are bound by traditional piety. He who would follow the Law in all things cannot do without the constant instruction and guidance of the rabbi. Only the rabbi, on the basis of his familiarity with the materials of religious law, can say for certain what is right in individual cases. Hence the pious ideal is that all Jews should be occupied in the Torah and its exposition and application, so that they can and will do what is right in a given situation. [128] The fulfilment of this ideal is expected in the Messianic age. This will be a time when all Israelites will zealously study the Torah, and the Messiah will be the great example. [129] Indeed, the opinion is ventured (R. Chanin, c. 300 A.D.) that God Himself will teach His people the Torah. [130] Until then the rabbi is indispensable, and תַּלְמִידִים are needed who are preparing for the office. In respect of the goal of making all Jewry a people of the casuistically expanded Torah, two complementary rules are to be noted. The one is for the pious Jew who wants to learn: עֲשֵׂה לְךָ רַב (Ab., 1, 16; Rabban Gamaliel the Elder at the time of Jesus), the other is for rabbis: הַעֲמִידוּ תַּלְמִידִים הַרְבֵּה (Ab., 1, 1, ascribed to the men of the Great Synagogue). [131] Teachers and pupils belong together (→ 434), and indeed teachers are continually augmented from the תַּלְמִידִים. This is the ref. of the statement ascribed to Hillel: "He who does not learn is worthy of death." [132] Israel is the people of God because it is the people of the Torah. [133] Not to study the Torah is to despise God and disrupt His work of election, and this makes worthy of death. For this reason contempt [134] and even hatred of those who learn [135] is ascribed to members of the people who are not constantly engaged in investigating the Torah and the divine intentions which are contained in it, but which are disclosed only with considerable effort, i.e., to the עַמֵּי־הָאָרֶץ or the ὄχλος ὁ μὴ γινώσκων τὸν νόμον (Jn. 7:49).

Generally reckoned as תַּלְמִידֵי־חֲכָמִים are the תַּלְמִידִים who have carried their studies so far that they equipped for the work of the rabbi: A תַּלְמִיד־חָכָם is one who is asked

---

[127] Cf. Str.-B., I, 496-498; A. Marmorstein, *Religionsgeschichtliche Studien,* II: "Die Schriftgelehrten" (1912), 17 ff.; Jew. Enc., XI, 678 f.

[128] Cf. simply the expectation that Messiah will come when Israel has kept just one Sabbath as prescribed, Str.-B., I, 600.

[129] Str.-B., IV, 882 f.

[130] Cf. Str.-B., III, 704; IV, 919.

[131] Cf. K. Marti-G. Beer, Abôṯ (1927), 3 ff.

[132] Ab., 1, 13: דְּלָא יַלֵּף קְטָלָא חַיָּב.

[133] Str.-B., III, 126 ff.

[134] Hillel in Ab., 2, 5: "No *'amm hā-āreṣ* is pious" (לֹא עַם־הָאָרֶץ חָסִיד).

[135] Cf. the material in Str.-B., II, 504 ff., esp. 515 f., also Jn. 7:49 and → I, 451.

and who answers (כָּל שֶׁשּׁוֹאֲלִין אוֹתוֹ וְהוּא מֵשִׁיב: jMQ, 83b, 18 f. Bar.).[136] The term tells us on the one side that he is no longer among the תַּלְמִידִים and on the other that he is not yet numbered with the חֲכָמִים, ordained scholars or rabbis (→ σοφός). These form a kind of guild (→ ῥαββί) which can be entered only when certain material conditions are met (comprehensive knowledge of Scripture and tradition, and dealings with תַּלְמִידֵי־חֲכָמִים: Lv. r., 3, 7 on 2:3) and the candidate is 40 years of age. He is then ordained by laying on of hands (→ χείρ).[137] From Sanh., 4, 4 (cf. T. Sanh., 8, 2) it may be seen that ordination does not automatically come at this stage, but is according to need, so that there is always a great number of תַּלְמִידֵי־חֲכָמִים available. These either execute the measures taken by a court[138] or, later at least, they have their own tasks, so long as those whom they have to serve are ready to accept their judgment.[139] jMakk., 31d, 74 ff. suggests that sometimes a school (בֵּית וַעַד) was built for a תַּלְמִיד־חָכָם.[140] In any case this shows that a תַּלְמִיד־חָכָם could be highly esteemed. Tradition reports many men of rank who were not ordained; this may be linked with the fact that in times of persecution a rite like ordination might carry with it the danger of execution.[141] Nor does the term תַּלְמִיד have a derogatory ring, as may be seen from a statement, based on Ps. 21:6, which ascribes הוֹד שֶׁל רַב as well as הָדָר שֶׁל תַּלְמִיד to the Messiah (Midr. Ps. 21:4, ed. S. Buber [1890], p. 179), so that he is both the perfect teacher and also the perfect student of the Torah.[142]

c. Only Men as תַּלְמִידִים. The word is used only of men. This is connected with the general position of women in later Judaism. Religiously women are on a lower level and cannot give themselves to the work of teaching and learning. → I, 781 and → μαθήτρια.

d. תַּלְמִיד as a Title of Honour. The תַּלְמִיד is highly esteemed by pious Jews. He shares the glory of the Torah, which he studies so diligently.

The sources offer many instructive illustrations. They naturally give prominence to the תַּלְמִיד־חָכָם. Best known, perhaps, is the statement which sets a bastard[143] who is a תַּלְמִיד־חָכָם above the high-priest as a עַם־הָאָרֶץ (T. Hor., 2, 10[144]).[145] bSanh., 52b con-

---

[136] In Rabb. lit. the question who is a "ת"ח is put and answered 6 times (cf. Marmorstein, 22 f.). The passage quoted here is the only Tannaitic one.

[137] → II, 700 and n. 6.

[138] This is presupposed in Makk., 2, 5, where two "ת"ח are given the murderer on his way to the city of refuge to intercede for him, if need be, with the avenger of blood.

[139] Cf. Str.-B., I, 496 f.

[140] *Ibid.*, 497b gives us the instructive anecdote concerning the precise circumstances under which a תַּלְמִיד־חָכָם can have an office.

[141] Cf. the tradition about the death of R. Jehuda bBaba because of ordination under Hadrian, bAZ, 8b.

[142] Different definitions of the "ת"ח are given by Marmorstein and S. Krauss, *Sanhedrin-Makkot* (1933), 344 on Makk., 2, 5. Krauss takes him to be a teacher, Marmorstein (20, n. 6 with bibl.) identifies תלמידי־חכמים with חכמים and understands by a חכם simply a scribe who has special knowledge of Scripture. Neither writer does justice to the terminological differentiation.

[143] The bastard (מַמְזֵר) is the child of a union forbidden by law (Jeb., 4, 13; Dt. 23:3: מַמְזֵר = ἐκ πόρνης; Philo Spec. Leg., I, 324 ff.; cf. V. Aptowitzer, *Hebrew Union College Annual*, 5 [1928], 262 ff.).

[144] This is based on Prv. 3:15.

[145] Perhaps we catch here an echo of anti-Sadducean polemic. Pursuing this thought, R. Meir (c. 150) puts even the non-Jew who studies the Torah on a level with the high-priest.

tains a Tannaitic saying, perhaps from the 1st cent., to the effect that the dignity of a תַּלְמִיד־חָכָם demands that he not even speak with a עַם־הָאָרֶץ, let alone engage in friendly intercourse with him. The conduct of the תַּלְמִיד־חָכָם is also regulated elsewhere (cf. bBer., 43b, Bar.). Thus a father takes precedence of the teacher of his son only when he himself is a תַּלְמִיד־חָכָם [146] (BM, 2, 11). bPes., 113a, Bar., warns not to stir even a תַּלְמִיד קָטָן to anger. Finally, the passages in Ab., 6, 1 ff. impressively describe how he who gives himself to study is inwardly and outwardly changed by the subject-matter, the Torah. Thus even תַּלְמִיד is always a title of honour which exalts the one who bears it above his fellow-countrymen and fellow-believers. Even proselytes can profit by it, of whom we find some among the תַּלְמִידֵי־חֲכָמִים and later חֲכָמִים. [147]

e. The Targumic Usage. The usage of the Targum deserves special mention. Here the Aram. equivalent תַּלְמִידָא can be used for terms which have no linguistic or material connection with למד to denote the one who receives, or who is influenced, in a personal relation.

The בְּנֵי־הַנְּבִיאִים are often תַּלְמִידֵי נְבִיַּיָּא (2 K. 2:15 etc.), and the מִשְׁפְּחוֹת of 1 Ch. 2:53, 55 תַּלְמִידַיָּיא. Tg. O. translates Nu. 32:14 תַּרְבּוּת אֲנָשִׁים חַטָּאִים ("brood of sinners") by תַּלְמִידֵי גַּבְרַיָּא חַיָּיבַיָּא (cf. also Tg. J., I). In each of these instances the word, which is almost completely alien to the OT (→ 426), is imported into the text, so that the idea in the transl. is quite different from that of the Mas. On the reason for this change → 438; 440.

5. The תַּלְמִיד as the Member of a School and Tradition.

a. The תַּלְמִיד as a Pupil. There is no תַּלְמִיד without a teacher (רַב). He who has no teacher is no תַּלְמִיד, no matter how diligently he studies. [148] This is most plainly expressed in bBer., 47b Bar.: "Even though a man has read Scripture and learned the Mishnah, but not served (שִׁמֵּשׁ) תַּלְמִידֵי־חֲכָמִים he is a עַם־הָאָרֶץ." Only entry into the fellowship gathered around a teacher, and subjection to the authority of the teacher, constitutes the תַּלְמִיד. Hence a pre-Christian writer (Joshua b. Perachiah) counsels: "Take to yourself a teacher and acquire a companion (חָבֵר)" Ab., 1, 6. Gamaliel I adopted this principle and based it on the fact that in cases of doubt only adherence to a teacher can give certainty, Ab., 1, 16.

The term שִׁמֵּשׁ expresses external submission to the teacher. It is the first mark of the תַּלְמִיד, for it makes his purpose plain to all. The תַּלְמִיד owes his רַב the same services as does the slave his master apart from certain particularly menial tasks like untying shoes (bKet., 96a; R. Joshua b. Levi, c. 250; cf. Mk. 1:7 par.). [149] The texts show that the

[146] Acc. to the reading of the Budapest and Cambridge MSS, also jTalm., as against the חכם of bTalm.

[147] Shemaia and Abtalion, the first of the "pairs" (Ab., 1, 10; cf. bJoma, 71b, Bar.; bGit., 57b, Bar.), were said to be proselytes. Another proselyte was Aquila, whose transl. of the OT was designed to replace the LXX, now claimed by Christians, in Gk. Judaism.

[148] It is worth noting that the non-Jew who studied the Torah (עוסק) was rated as highly as the high-priest (→ n. 145) but was not declared to be a תלמיד־חכם or even a תלמיד.

[149] Cf. the material in Str.-B., I, 527 ff. Akiba has a תלמיד to attend him in prison (bErub., 21b, Bar.; cf. Eka r., 3, 43). He also reached halachic decisions there, which presupposes the presence of תלמידים (T. Sanh., 2, 8; T. Ahilut, 4, 2). Cf. A. Schlatter, *Die Tage Trajans und Hadrians* (1897), 16 ff. In praise of Jochanan b. Zakkai it is said that he served scholars for 40 years (S. Dt. § 357 on 34:7).

honour paid the teacher is finally for the Torah to whose investigation the teacher has dedicated his life, cf. bBer., 7b; Str.-B., I, 527. Service of the teacher also provides a valuable opportunity of practical growth in the halacha according to his example.[150] If the תַּלְמִיד follows the teacher on the way (→ I, 212 f.), this simply corresponds to the fact that he serves him, as may be seen already in the OT (→ 428). No specific meaning attaches to the "following" (→ I, 213).

b. The תַּלְמִיד as a Listener. Learning takes place by listening to what the rabbi says, and appropriating what is heard. Thus שָׁמַע describes the true function of the תַּלְמִיד.

In Rabb. teaching both teacher and pupil sat,[151] and the teacher lectured, with an opportunity for questions.[152] The questioning תַּלְמִיד is a recurrent figure in anecdotes from the house of instruction. The question put by the listener would open up a discussion in which the others took part. This older method of teaching was perfected by a man like Akiba, who demanded that questions should be put.[153] Yet Akiba is also the best example to prove that questioning was not an obligation on the listeners. According to tradition he was silent for thirteen years in the house of instruction, and then became at a stroke one of the acknowledged authorities of his day.[154] Rabb. rulings make it plain that the only task of the תַּלְמִיד was to acquire knowledge from his teacher,[155] though not without critical reflection.[156] The latter is not ruled out by the common use of שָׁמַע. All Rabb. listening stands in an ultimate relation to Scripture (→ I, 218). But the rabbi is the instrument to make possible for the תַּלְמִיד the right hearing which is his concern. Thus his word, too, is to be heard and appropriated.[157] Nevertheless if it is dangerous on the one side to form one's own understanding of Scripture (→ 434), testing of what is presented by the rabbi is also a duty of his hearers on the other.[158]

c. The School. The predominant position of the rabbi in the work of teaching means that schools come into existence. The circle of תַּלְמִידִים around a teacher becomes a fellowship under his influence, and this is controlled both outwardly and inwardly by his message and conduct.

The two great schools of Hillel (בֵּית הִלֵּל) and Shammai (בֵּית שַׁמַּי) are well known.[159] Their debates dominate many parts of the older tradition (e.g., Ed., 4-5). On the whole

---

150 Cf. esp. Akiba's own confession, jNaz., 56a, 69 ff., and on this P. Billerbeck, "Rabbi Aqiba. Leben und Wirken eines Meisters in Israel," *Nathanael,* 32 (1916), 119.

151 Cf. Str.-B., II, 763 f.; Ac. 22:3.

152 Cf. Str.-B., II, 150 f.; Lk. 2:46.

153 Cf. Billerbeck, *op. cit.*, 118 f.

154 Pes., 6, 2 f.; jPes., 33b, 66 ff.

155 Jochanan b. Zakkai praises Eliezer b. Hyrcanos when he calls him a sealed cistern which does not allow a single drop to escape, Ab., 2, 8.

156 This is in view when Ab., 5, 15 uses the image of the winnowing fan for the model תלמיד, who separates the wheat from the chaff (cf. Dalman, *Arbeit u. Sitte in Palästina,* III [1933], 290 ff.).

157 R. Eliezer (c. 90 A.D.) is lauded for keeping the Rabb. principle : אָדָם חַיָּב לוֹמַר בִּלְשׁוֹן רַבּוֹ (Ed., 1, 3) with particular fidelity : He would not say a word which he had not heard in his own lifetime (or : from his teacher) (T. Jeb., 3, 4). One of the marks of the חָכָם is : עַל־מַה שֶּׁלֹּא שָׁמַע אוֹמֵר לֹא שָׁמַעְתִּי Ab., 5, 7. Cf. also Jochanan b. Zakkai (c. 70 A.D.). Jad., 4, 3; Ed., 8, 7: ...שֶׁשָּׁמַע מֵרַבּוֹ וְרַבּוֹ מֵרַבּוֹ.

158 Cf. R. Meir's (c. 150) relation to his teacher Elisha b. Abuya, who became an apostate, bChag., 15b.

159 Cf. the short account in Schl. Gesch. Isr., 250 ff.

the former prevailed, largely on the basis of the methodological rules enunciated by Hillel and adopted and further developed by his pupils.[160] But his successors also played a notable role here, for they took over from him the intellectual leadership from which the patriarchal office later developed.[161] Yet within the great schools the individual rabbi can also have his special school. We see this most clearly in Akiba. He developed to perfection the method by which each letter of Scripture has its distinctive sense, and thus made possible both an extension of the halachic tradition and also an exegetical establishment of oral tradition (תּוֹרָה שֶׁבְּעַל פֶּה, הֲלָכָה לְמֹשֶׁה מִסִּינַי) so far as this was feasible (though cf. S. Lv. צו, 11, 6 on 7:12).[162] At the same time Akiba was also the first to arrange systematically the materials of religious law, and thus to lay the basis for its coherent transmission.

The degree to which a fellowship of pupils is also externally controlled by the teacher (materially → 435) may finally be seen from the school of Akiba.[163] His attachment to the Zealot movement, for which he found self-evident justification in his method, was followed by the allegiance of his school, and since he had so many pupils this had a big influence on the course taken at that time by the Rabbinate,[164] disastrously so for those who believed they should follow him, since he dragged them down to destruction with him.

d. The תַּלְמִיד and Tradition. In the school the individual תַּלְמִיד is necessarily the representative of the tradition established by the rabbi and the member of a chain composed of the various generations of the school.

The Rabb. method of teaching, in which everything depends on listening (→ 435), is designed to make the תַּלְמִיד a bearer of tradition. In keeping is the fact that the material of religious law is in fact passed down from lip to lip,[165] with express mention of names in so far as teachers helped to form it or in so far as there were at certain points differences between different teachers. Almost every chapter of the Mishnah gives examples of the current formula "R. NN has said" or variations of it. This does not express, of course, biographical interest in the rabbi concerned. For the Rabbinate the real centre of concern is the matter advocated by the teacher, not the teacher himself.[166]

Nevertheless, one cannot go so far as to ascribe a purely incidental significance to the persons of the teachers for the תַּלְמִיד.[167] The great teachers are regarded with respect, cf. Ab., 1, 1 ff. When Joshua b. Chananiah publicly calls Akiba a תַּלְמִיד of Jochanan b. Zakkai (Sota, 5, 5) even though he never served him, this is not just to mention the association, but to honour Akiba because of this direct connection.[168] The bearer of the tradition and the man cannot be separated in the image of the teacher or in the eyes of the pupils, as may be seen from the fact that in serving the תַּלְמִידִים

---

160 Cf. Strack Einl., 96 ff.

161 Gamaliel I, Paul's teacher, with whom the dynasty began, was either Hillel's son (d. c. 20 A.D.) or, less likely, his grandson, *ibid.*, 120.

162 Cf. Billerbeck, *op. cit.*, 97 ff., which brings out plainly Akiba's significance both in relation to the Rabb. struggle with Sadduceanism for the validity of tradition and also in relation to the broad victory of the specific tradition of Hillel as compared with that of Shammai. Cf. also W. Bacher, *Tradition u. Tradenten Palästinas u. Babyloniens* (1914), 22-4, 33 ff., though 34 f. gives rise to some questions.

163 Cf. A. Rahlfs, *Septuaginta* I: Genesis (1926), 9 f.

164 Schlatter, *Tage Trajans*, 51 f.; Billerbeck, *Nathanael*, 34 (1918), 46 ff.

165 Cf. the self-witness of Rabbinism at the beginning of Abot, → 435.

166 Kittel Probleme, 68 f.

167 *Ibid.*, 69, n. 4.

168 This is how Maimonides took the story, cf. R. Sander, *Furcht u. Liebe im palästinischen Judt.* (1935), 71 f.

were seeking to learn from the example as well as the word of the teacher, → 434. All this is ultimately based on the fact that Rabb. Judaism is a religion of attainment. On this soil the righteous man has his part, even though his true task is to pass on the tradition. Thus the numerous statements made by Akiba do not merely exalt the Torah ; they also increase his own fame.[169] The individual link in the chain is responsible both as scholar and teacher for the loyal transmission of the tradition. The many lists preserved for us[170] express the seriousness with which this responsibility was felt.[171]

e. The Rabbinate as the School of Moses. In Rabbinic teaching, though the individual teacher has an important place, the dominating element is the Torah. In the form controlled by the prominence of tradition this means that Moses is the starting-point and absolute teacher. Rabbinic Judaism is a conscious Mosaism.

The authority of the Torah and the tradition contained in it may be seen in the fact that it limits the authority of individual rabbis. Since the Torah was given to Israel through the mediation of Moses, and he was the first to make Israel acquainted with it, the decisive pt. for individual rabbis is to be in agreement with Moses.[172] For the Rabbinate Moses is the greatest teacher of the Torah who sets the direction for all who follow. Joshua and the wilderness generation are related to Moses as the תַּלְמִיד to the rabbi.[173] The same is true of the prophets, to whom on this view תַּלְמִידִים are subject in the בְּנֵי־הַנְּבִיאִים.[174] In T. Sot., 4, 7 Elisha is called a תַּלְמִיד of Elijah, who for his part is תַּלְמִיד of Moses. In S. Dt. § 26 on 3:23 Moses and David are the pillars of doctrine. It is also possible that תַּלְמִידָיו שֶׁל־מֹשֶׁה is used by the Pharisaic Rabbinate as an emphatic anti-Sadducean self-designation (oral and written Torah deriving from Moses), cf. bJoma, 4a, Bar.; 53a, Bar. In any case, this would again fit in with the thought developed in the introduction to Abot. Finally, the description of the teaching chair in the house of instruction as קַתֶּדְרָא דְמֹשֶׁה (→ μανθάνω, n. 94) tells us that he who sits in it does his work in the name of Moses.[175] This is an important feature if we are to understand the Rabbinate's view of itself.

6. The Origin of Rabbinic Views of the תַּלְמִיד as the Member of a School and Tradition.

a. The Impossibility of Development from the OT. The links between these Rabbinic views and the OT are comparatively slight. The only real connection is the superiority of the divine material in the Torah (the revelation of God's will) to those who represent it, though this supremacy is affected by the emphasis on Moses and other teachers of the Torah. Detailed derivation from the OT is hardly possible.

---

[169] Cf. a legend like that of bMen., 29b, or the claim of his teacher Joshua b. Chananiah to be a pupil of Akiba (תַּלְמִיד תַּלְמִידְךָ, Sota, 5, 5; → *supra*).

[170] Cf. Bacher (→ n. 162).

[171] Sometimes the contradictory sayings of two rabbis are handed down for centuries without any attempt to remove the difficulty by compromise, cf. the case in bSanh., 59a, and on this M. Guttmann, *Entwicklungsstufen jüdischer Religion* (1927), 55 f.

[172] Cf. Ex. r., 2, 6 on 3:5.

[173] Joshua (Ab., 1, 1) seeks his teacher after the death of Moses (בקש יהושע רבו) and does not find him : Dt. r., 11, 10 on 31:14; Moses is רבינו ("our teacher") for the wilderness generation : M. Ex. ויסע בשלח 4 on 16:22, 25, p. 168, 9; 169, 1, Horowitz etc.

[174] Cf. Ab., 1, 1 and also the instructive passage S. Dt. § 34 on 6:7 *s.v.* לבניך: "thy sons" — these are thy תלמידים!.. (2 K. 2:3). Were they sons of the prophets ? Were they not rather תלמידים?

[175] Cf. also Marmorstein, 44 f.

Thus we do not find in the OT even the first beginnings of a school or a principle of tradition (→ 429) such as may be seen in Rabbinism. Nor is there conscious Mosaism in the sense of reposing everything on the person of Moses (→ 430).

b. Hellenistic Influences. In developing these views later Judaism was under influences which could come only from Hellenism, where they were firmly established.[176] For here were schools in the sense of fellowships of disciples (→ 423), and here, too, the principle of tradition was accepted (→ 424). Greek influences may certainly be seen, or are very probable, at least at certain points.

(a) There is an unbroken chain of Rabb. tradition only up to the Maccabean period.[177] This corresponds to the facts.[178] A special class of סוֹפְרִים/γραμματεῖς is found for the first time in Sir. 38:25-39:11, though not in the special sense of the later Rabbinate. It is thus formed at the time of the decisive conflict between Palestinian Judaism and Hellenism.[179] This imposes on the Rabbinate the unavoidable task of ensuring the survival of Judaism in its traditional form. In fact, apologetic debate with Hellenism and its philosophy continues throughout the work of the Rabbis.[180]

(b) If the outward cause of the formation of a teaching office which would guard the pious tradition of Judaism was the attack of Hellenism upon it, we have also to consider that the form of this work was strongly affected by Hellenism. Thus the way in which Akiba conducts a disputation gives unmistakable evidence of the influence of the methods of the Gk. schools. For example, the opposition of the hearer is provoked in order to lead him to independent apprehension of the truth.[181] Indeed, discussion as such is fundamentally alien to Judaism, and is of Gk. origin.[182]

(c) The way in which older authorities, and esp. one's own teacher or the head of one's school, are cited, is par. to the form customary in Stoicism; cf. the formula which occurs times without number: ...אָמַר רַבִּי or רַבִּי...אוֹמֵר with Gk. formulae like φησὶν ... ὁ Ἀρίστων (v. Arnim, I, 88, 11 ff. [Plut.]; φησὶ ... Χρύσιππος (I, 90, 13 [Diog. L.]); Ἀντίγονος ... φησί (I, 94, 24 ff. [Athen.]); *Aristo Chius dicere solebat* (I, 78, 23 f. [Cic.]); *Ariston ait* (I, 85, 28 [Sen.]); *Ariston aiebat* (I, 88, 21 [Sen.]) etc. In the same connection it is worth noting that Joseph. — for whatever motives — describes the Φαρισαίων αἵρεσις as παραπλήσιος τῇ παρ' Ἕλλησιν Στωϊκῇ λεγομένῃ (Vit., 12).

(d) Another Gk. feature is the lionising of Moses, which distinguishes Judaism from the OT.[183] The oldest instance is Sir. 45:1 ff. An extract from the passage extolling

---

[176] Cf. on this and the next sentences Schl. Gesch. Isr., 93 ff.; A. Schlatter, "Jochanan Ben Zakkai, der Zeitgenosse der Apostel," BFTh, 3, 4 (1899), 11 ff.

[177] Between the first of the "pairs" (Ab., 1, 4) and the next to the oldest authority Antigonos of Sokho (1, 3) there is perhaps no direct link, cf. Marti-Beer, 11 f., *ad loc.* Since the third "pair" (1, 8) belongs to the beginning of the 1st cent. B.C., the first may perhaps be put around 170 B.C.

[178] Schlatter, "Jochanan," 14.

[179] The saying of Jose b. Joezer, who is in the oldest of the five "pairs": "Thy house be a house of instruction for the wise (חכמים)" (Ab., 1, 4) seems to presuppose that in his time (→ n. 177) there was still no official education with special schools (F. Maas, *Formgeschichte der Mischna mit bes. Berücksichtigung des Traktats Abot* [1937], 43). It should also be noted that in the lists the title rabbi is only used after Hillel and Shammai (Ab., 1, 1 ff.). Later it could sometimes be accorded to the "fathers" (cf. for Jehuda b. Tabbai, T. Sanh., 6, 6).

[180] Bibl. in Strack Einl., 178 f.

[181] → 434; 437.

[182] More precise research into the detailed links is needed.

[183] On the significance of the Gk. concept of ἀρετή for Hell. Judaism → I, 458, and in relation to the development of the Pharisaic doctrine of righteousness, Schl. Theol. d. Judt., 198.

the fathers (44:1-50:24) enables us to see already the direction in which we are led by the Rabbinate: מֹשֶׁה רַבֵּינוּ (cf. 45:5 and → 437). For Joseph. Moses is a θεῖος ἀνήρ (Ant., 3, 180), and both in Joseph. and the Rabb. he is encircled by magnifying legends which culminate in the account of his assumption (cf. also Ass. Mos.).[184] That in this lionising everything revolves around the fact that he mediates the divine will is inevitable in view of his position in the religion of Israel as a religion of revelaton. Even Moses the hero is still the Moses who is and does all things for God's sake.[185]

(e) Greek teachers take fees (→ 420). The Rabbinate allowed this only for elementary teachers;[186] scribal instruction had to be given free.[187] But perhaps this is a rule first introduced by Hillel (Ab., 1, 13) and not always scrupulously observed.[188] At any rate, it is said of Hillel himself that so long as he was תַּלְמִיד he could not always pay the modest fee for entering the school of Shemaiah and Abtalion (bJoma, 35b). It is possible that genuine reminiscence underlies the anecdote.[189] This would show that at least in earlier times the Rabbis were like Gk. teachers at an important point.

c. The Adoption of the תַּלְמִיד from Hellenistic Teaching (cf. Josephus). We may finally venture to say that the תַּלְמִיד as such came into Judaism from the educative process of the Greek and Hellenistic philosophical schools.

(a) Linguistically the use of תַּלְמִיד corresponds closely to the use of μαθητής to denote intellectual fellowship where there is no direct link. The phrase תַּלְמִידָיו שֶׁל־מֹשֶׁה (→ 437) is in every way par. to the Gk. μαθητὴς Ὁμήρου (→ 417). Cf. also formulae like תַּלְמִידוֹ שֶׁל־אַבְרָהָם אָבִינוּ, תַּלְמִידוֹ שֶׁל־בִּלְעָם הָרָשָׁע (Ab., 5, 19), תַּלְמִידָיו שֶׁל אַהֲרֹן (1, 12), תַּלְמִידוֹ שֶׁל־הִלֵּל, תַּלְמִידוֹ שֶׁל־עֶזְרָא (bSanh., 11a). In these it should be noted esp. that תַּלְמִיד sometimes has no further connection at all with the specific sense of לָמַד, from which it was formed (→ 431). This seems to support the view that תַּלְמִיד is analogous to μαθητής.

Excellent examples may also be found in the usage of Joseph. in so far as he remains in the Jewish sphere.[190] Thus Joshua is the μαθητής of Moses (Ant., 6, 84). Elijah has a θεράπων (8, 344, cf. 348), but then in Elisha he finds a μαθητὴς καὶ διάκονος (8, 354; cf. 9, 28 and 33). In its twofold sense this term describes exactly what the Rabbinate understands by a תַּלְמִיד but it follows Gk. usage by reserving μαθητής for the one who enters into intellectual rapport with his master and makes his cause his own.[191] The description of Elisha as μαθητής presupposes that Elijah for his part

---

[184] Cf. Str.-B., IV, 1249, Index *s.v.* "Mose"; S. Rappaport, *Agada u. Exegese bei Flavius Josephus* (1930), 26 ff. (R. believes that the account of Moses the warrior in Jos. Ant., 2, 238 ff., also known to the later Midrash, is of Palestinian origin, 28 f.); Schl. Gesch. Isr., 190 ff. For details → Μωϋσῆς.

[185] This may be seen most clearly in the figure of the מורה צדק expected by the community of the new covenant in Damascus (Damasc. 9, 53 [B], p. 32, 32, Rost). For this predecessor of the Messiah Moses is obviously the model.

[186] Str.-B., I, 563 f.

[187] *Ibid.*, 561 f.

[188] Cf. *ibid.*, 564 h.

[189] Cf. Schürer, II, 379 f.

[190] On μαθητής for "apprentice" → n. 1. Gk. usage (→ 416) may also be seen in Κλέαρχος γὰρ ὁ Ἀριστοτέλους ὢν μαθητής ... (Ap., 1, 176).

[191] In Bell., 4, 460 Elisha, in Gk. fashion, is called Elijah's γνώριμος (→ 419) καὶ διάδοχος (cf. on this Luc. Macrob., 19: Κλεάνθης δὲ ὁ Ζήνωνος μαθητὴς καὶ διάδοχος, and cf. Schl. Theol. d. Judt., 206, n. 2). Examples of γνώριμος for Rabb. disciple in Joseph. may be found in Schl. Mt., 130. In Vit., 11 Joseph. calls himself a ζηλωτής of an Essene Bannus, with whom he spent three years, but only to learn his way of life, not to be his μαθητής. On the use of μαθητής by Joseph. cf. also Schl. Lk., 63 on 5:30.

officially represents the Torah. In fact, for Joseph. this man who is zealous for God (as in the OT) is also zealous for God's ἐντολαί (8, 337) and the πάτριοι νόμοι (8, 361). This view of Elijah was common in the Judaism of the day, as may be seen from 1 Macc. 2:58, where ζῆλος νόμου is ascribed to him. Elisha, too, has a διάκονος (9, 54 ff.), but along with him (9, 68 f.) we also find his μαθηταί (the πρεσβύτεροι (זְקֵנִים) of 4 Βασ. 6:32), and these are hearers as well as ministers, so that the picture is repeated again; cf. also Ant., 9, 106 with 4 Βασ. 9:1. In Jos. Baruch is the μαθητής of Jeremiah (10, 178). In 15, 3 μαθητής is used in the sense of the Rabb. תַּלְמִיד.[192] The total picture is rounded off when in Ant., 18, 11 f.; Bell., 2, 119 ff. Joseph. takes the further step of calling the three trends in current Judaism φιλοσοφίαι, i.e., schools. Sometimes he sets the Pharisees alongside the Stoics (→ 438) and the Essenes alongside the Pythagoreans (Ant., 15, 371). On Philo → 441.

(b) Materially we find two Gk. names amongst the oldest names in the official lists, Antigonos of Sokho (Ab., 1, 3) and Abtalion[193] (1, 10). The latter, who was one of the teachers of Hillel (→ 439), was not necessarily a proselyte (→ n. 147), but he certainly came from a Gk. background and knew the situation there, so that he provided the necessary presuppositions for adopting Gk. elements into the Jewish system of instruction.

7. The Theology Implied in the Later Jewish תַּלְמִיד.

a. The formal dependence of the Rabbinate on Hellenism in respect of the תַּלְמִיד may be taken as certain.[194] Unlike the rabbi, the תַּלְמִיד is of Greek origin.

b. The Greek form, however, is not simply taken over as it stands. It is integrated into the central concern of Judaism, i.e., concern for the Torah. Hence the Rabbinic תַּלְמִיד is never an individualist. If so, he would place himself outside the fellowship. He stands always within the Jewish community, seeking to help it to a right orientation of the service which it renders to God.

c. In the existence and continued gathering of תַּלְמִידִים, quite apart from their origin etc. (→ 434), there may thus be seen the claim to absolutism which characterises the classical Torahism of the Rabbinate and its theology. This confronts the philosophical schools of the age, and their attempts to understand the world, with the certainty that the answer to all questions, and the sum of all necessary ordinances, is to be found in the will of the God of heaven and earth as this is laid down in the Torah.

d. Torahism's confession of its own absoluteness finds its echo in the assertion that the chain of tradition begins with Moses and in the projection of the תַּלְמִיד institution back into the lives of the great figures in the national history. At the same time Torahism seeks a historical basis along these lines; it claims to be an integral part of the history of revelation from the very first (cf. on this 1 Macc. 2:49 ff., esp. 2:58 [Elijah], and → 437). To this extent the Rabbinic use of תַּלְמִיד

---

192 Cf. also Ant., 13, 289 and on this Schl. Theol. d. Judt., 206.

193 There is agreement that this is based on a Gk. name, but not on what the name is: Εὐθαλίων (Schl. Jos., 121 f.), Πτολλίων (Marti-Beer, *ad loc.*), or Πολλίων (Jos. Ant., 15, 3); cf. Schl. Theol. d. Judt., 199, n. 1.

194 Cf. Schlatter, "Jochanan," 11, though Schlatter derives the rabbi from contact with Gk. philosophy, and does not specifically mention the תַּלְמִיד.

also makes a contribution to the Rabbinic understanding of the history of Israel, and therewith of history in general.[195]

8. Philo.

The use of μαθητής in Philo is essentially the same as the general Gk. usage (→ 416): "apprentice" (Spec. Leg., 2, 227); "pupil," esp. one who seeks divine wisdom (Poster. C., 146). The word has no derogatory nuance (Poster. C., 136: σπουδαῖος μαθητής), but in Philo it is distinctively associated with γνώριμος (*ibid.*, 151). The occasional combination of ὁ μανθάνων and ὁ μαθητής (Sacr. AC, 64) suggests that the μαθητής is a student who has already reached a certain ripeness, as distinct from a beginner. This explains phrases like τοῦ μόνου σοφοῦ μαθηταί (Sacr. AC, 64) and ὁ θεοῦ φοιτητὴς ἢ γνώριμος ἢ μαθητής (*ibid.*, 79), which materially lead us to Philo's mysticism. Perhaps the most important point, however, is that even Philo is in the stream of one Jewish scholastic tradition. Its presence has always to be inferred, and it is to some extent very different from that cultivated in Palestinian Judaism,[196] though there is, of course, kinship between them.[197]

C. The Term in the New Testament.

1. The Usage.

a. Statistical Data. In the NT μαθητής occurs only in the Gospels and Acts. As distinct from the comparatively rare μανθάνω (→ 406) it is a common word, attested for certain some 250 times.[198] The usage is from the very first characterised by the fact that, apart from a few exceptions, μαθητής denotes the men who have attached themselves to Jesus as their Master. In the Gospels association with Him is in these cases either expressly mentioned or to be assumed from the context. Acts has an absolute use of μαθητής in the sense of a disciple of Jesus. As will be shown, this developed within the community, and it thus represents a distinctively Christian use (→ 457). In all the Gospels the word is also used a few times for the "disciples of John the Baptist"; this phrase is always expressly used. In Ac. 9:25 we find disciples of Paul, and in Mk. 2:18 par.; Mt. 22:16 μαθηταὶ τῶν Φαρισαίων. Finally, in the Fourth Gospel there is preserved a saying in debate in which the opponents of Jesus are described as τοῦ Μωϋσέως μαθηταί, Jn. 9:28.

b. The Uniformity of Usage. The first thing to emerge from this review is the uniformity of usage.

μαθητής always implies the existence of a personal attachment which shapes the whole life of the one described as μαθητής, and which in its particularity leaves no doubt as to who is deploying the formative power.

There is a good example in Mk. 2:18. The μαθηταί of John the Baptist and those of the Pharisees on the one side, and the μαθηταί of Jesus on the other, are distinguished

---

[195] Cf. on the problem of history in the thinking of the Rabbinate, N. N. Glatzer, *Untersuchungen zur Geschichtslehre d. Tannaiten* (1933), and on this K. H. Rengstorf in *D.-Lit.-Zeitung*, 3rd Ser., 6 (1935), 931 ff.

[196] Cf. W. Bousset, *Jüdisch-Christlicher Schulbetrieb in Alexandria und Rom* (1915), 8 ff.; Schl. Gesch. Isr., 300 ff.

[197] Schl. Gesch. Isr., 302 f.

[198] In a few other cases the text vacillates between μαθητής and other words, Mt. 20:17; Lk. 9:1; Ac. 1:15; 20:7 etc. Elsewhere μαθητής is obviously added in some texts for clarification (cf. Bruder, *s.v.*).

by the fact that the former exercise the pious discipline of fasting [199] while the latter do not. It is in full keeping with the situation if, in seeking the reasons for the conduct of the disciples of Jesus, ref. is made, not to them, but to Jesus, who is thus regarded as the head of the school. There is a par. in Mk. 2:23 f. par. It is expected that Jesus will direct His disciples not only to do what is right but also not to do what is regarded as wrong.

The control of the μαθηταί by the man to whom they have committed themselves extends in the NT to the inner life. This may be seen from the fact that the circle around the Baptist had a prayer which it had received from John and which united the individual members of this circle. Hence the disciples of Jesus also asked for a similar prayer as a sign of their fellowship with Him and with one another (Lk. 11:1). [200] In the NT we do not find any instances where μαθητής is used without this implication of supremely personal union. The common non-NT Greek use for purely formal dependence never occurs in the NT.

Some scholars [201] find the general sense of "pupil" or "scholar" (as distinct from teacher) in Mt. 10:24 f.; Lk. 6:40. But in view of the fact that NT usage is so unequivocal this could be justified only if the verses mentioned were proverbial sayings. Thus far, however, Rabb. par. have been found only for Mt. 10:25b. [202] This leads us to suppose that 10:24a, 25a are formulated in relation to the context. But the point at issue is not the relation of scholars to their teacher; it is the destiny of the disciples of Jesus in so far as this is bound up with the person of Jesus. In Lk. 6:40 the ref. is not to the imperfection of the pupil compared with the master, but to the responsibility which the disciples of Jesus bear because they are disciples.

c. The Relation of μαθητής to תַּלְמִיד. In its fixity of usage the NT μαθητής is closely related to the Rabbinic תַּלְמִיד. Explicitly or implicitly the μαθητής is always accompanied by the διδάσκαλος around whom the μαθηταί gather. In this is repeated [203] what was said under → B. 5 (434) about the Rabbinic תַּלְמִידִים. We refer essentially to terminological kinship, no more; a more precise comparison of the μαθηταί of Jesus with the תַּלְמִידִים of the Rabbis will make this clear (→ 444). The linguistic kinship is confirmed by the fact that the Rabbinate itself spoke of the תַּלְמִידִים of Jesus, bSanh., 43a, Bar.: Jesus had five תַּלְמִידִים, Mattai, Naqqai, Nezer, Buni and Toda ... [204]

d. Peculiarities of the Usage. Lk. especially proves that in early Christian usage μαθητής was the common term for the disciples of Jesus. He found the word as a fixed term in all the sources which he used, including the special material worked over by him (Lk. 11:1; 14:26 ff. etc.). It is thus the more remarkable that in his Gospel (as distinct from Mt. and Mk., also Jn.) the description of the disciples of Jesus as μαθηταί breaks off at 22:45 (Gethsemane), and is never resumed. This can be explained only if we assume that it was due to theological

[199] On fasting as a pious exercise cf. Str.-B., II, 241 ff.; I. Abrahams, "Fasting," in *Studies in Pharisaism and the Gospels*, I (1917), 121 ff.
[200] Cf. Schl. Lk., *ad loc.*
[201] So Pr.-Bauer³, *s.v.*
[202] Cf. Str.-B., I, 577 f.; Schl. Mt., *ad loc.*
[203] Apart from what is said under → b.
[204] On this cf. Str.-B., II, 417 (with the notes of Billerbeck, esp. on the names, 417 ff.); cf. also H. L. Strack, *Jesus, die Häretiker u. die Christen nach den ältesten jüdischen Angaben* (1910), 19, 43* f.

considerations (→ 446). The term appears again only from Ac. 6:1 onwards, and here it refers, not specifically to the personal disciples of Jesus, but to all Christians. It is regularly used in this sense in Ac.; indeed, its occurrence may even be regarded as a special feature of the source which Lk. uses here.[205]

2. Jewish μαθηταί in the NT.

a. The μαθηταὶ τῶν Φαρισαίων. The phrase μαθηταὶ τῶν Φαρισαίων (Mk. 2:18 = Lk. 5:33; Mt. 22:16) causes some difficulty, since the Pharisees were the practical exponents of nomism as distinct from the γραμματεῖς, who as the Rabbinate championed it theoretically, and in later Judaism the μαθητής (תַּלְמִיד) is always close to a rabbi (→ 435). This fact has led to the conclusion that Mk. 2:18 has been worked over, and that the μαθηταὶ τῶν Φαρισαίων, and the Pharisees, have been brought in later.[206] But the par. in Mt. 9:14 certainly speaks of Φαρισαῖοι, and the formula also occurs in Mt. 22:16, and is thus found in the Evangelist whose acquaintance with the Judaism of the time of Jesus is generally recognised. Nor should it be overlooked that in Mt. 12:27 (Lk. 11:19) there is ref. to οἱ υἱοὶ ὑμῶν (i.e., τῶν Φαρισαίων), which presupposes the currency of a formula οἱ υἱοὶ τῶν Φαρισαίων. Since בַּר/בֵּן /υἱός is often used to describe a fellowship which implies kinship of species,[207] and since Jos. can use μαθηταί for the בְּנֵי־הַנְּבִיאִים of the OT (→ 439), this amounts to the same as οἱ μαθηταὶ τῶν Φαρισαίων. Thus there is no reason to suspect the difficult οἱ μαθηταὶ τῶν Φαρισαίων in terms of contemporary usage.

Material explanation is more difficult. But this, too, is possible when two points are remembered. First, it is to be noted that, while the NT has the distinction between theoretical and practical exponents of the Law with its γραμματεῖς and Φαρισαῖοι, the boundaries between the two are fluid, for often the γραμματεῖς are Φαρισαῖοι, and are even in many cases leaders of the Pharisaical societies.[208] Secondly, for Rabbinic תַּלְמִידִים teachers are not just purveyors of nomistic knowledge but also examples of a life acc. to the precepts of the Law (→ 434 f.). Nor should it be overlooked that the concern in both Mk. 2:18 ff. and Mt. 22:16 is with important matters of Pharisaic practice. Thus the ref. to μαθηταὶ τῶν Φαρισαίων is quite possible in terms of the material relation, even though the phrase involves some measure of obscurity. Perhaps it also carries with it a recollection that opposition to Jesus began with the Pharisees, since His rejection of formalism wounded them at a sensitive point in their religious self-awareness.[209]

b. τοῦ Μωϋσέως μαθηταί. In Jn. 9:28 the Ἰουδαῖοι of the Fourth Gospel call themselves τοῦ Μωϋσέως μαθηταί in emphatic antithesis to one whom they call a μαθητής of Jesus. Here Moses is regarded as "our teacher," as he was often called by the Rabbinate (→ 437). Those who call themselves his disciples consciously regard themselves as links in the chain which stretches back to Moses and at the beginning of which is the clear and unequivocal revelation of the will of God for the people through him (cf. v. 29a). As compared with Moses, Jesus is unknown and unproved (v. 29b). Thus the self-designation as τοῦ Μωϋσέως

---

[205] Cf. on this J. Jeremias, "Die antiochenische Quelle d. Apostelgeschichte u. die Datierung der ersten Missionsreise," ZNW, 36 (1937), 213 ff., esp. 215 and 220, with bibl. On Ac. 19:1 ff. → 456.

[206] Cf. E. Lohmeyer, *Das Evangelium des Markus* (Meyer, I, 2^{10} [1937], *ad loc.*).

[207] Cf. on this the material in Dalman WJ, I, 94 f.

[208] Cf. Str.-B., IV, 334; J. Jeremias, *Jerusalem zur Zeit Jesu,* II B (1938), 125 ff. The community of the new covenant in Damascus is a good example of a Pharisaic society under scribal leadership, cf. Jeremias 130 ff.

[209] In view of the nature of the sources it is hard to be more specific at this point.

μαθηταί denotes a deliberate contesting of the authority of Jesus by the Ἰουδαῖοι on the ground that His authority is personal authority. At this point Jn. is close to the Synoptists, for he bases the decision for or against commitment to Jesus (μαθητής) on a personal relation to Him and not on material considerations. This is underlined in Jn. 9:35 ff., where the point at issue is the faith of the man born blind, → II, 156.

3. The Disciples of Jesus.

a. The Call of the Disciples of Jesus.

(a) The Initiative of Jesus. A fundamental mark of the μαθηταί of Jesus in the tradition is that they are called by Him to discipleship. This aspect dominates all the Gospel accounts of the way in which they began to follow Jesus. It is not always so linguistically clear as in Mk. 1:17; Mt. 4:19 (where Jesus addresses to Peter and Andrew a δεῦτε ὀπίσω μου), or in Mk. 2:14 par. (the call of Levi), or in Mk. 10:21 (the rich young ruler), or in Lk. 9:59; Jn. 1:43 (Philip), where the challenge is ἀκολούθει μοι. But materially every such incident is exclusively marked by the initiative of Jesus. This is attested not only by Lk. 9:57 f.; 9:60 ff., but also by a passage like Mk. 5:18 ff. (Lk. 8:37 ff.), and esp. by the Lukan account of the calling of the first disciples (Lk. 5:1 ff.), where there is no formal call, but where the main point is that Peter and Andrew simply obeyed Jesus when they left all and followed Him. In this matter the tradition is quite unambiguous. If there are differences in detail regarding the call of the first disciples (cf. Mk. 1:16 ff. [Mt. 4:18 ff.] with Lk. 5:1 ff.), there is complete agreement at this point.[210] Nor does the Johannine tradition (Jn. 1:35 ff.; cf. also 15:16 etc.) differ in this regard.[211]

The way in which disciples commit themselves to Jesus is thus fundamentally different from what we usually find in the Rabbinate.[212] There the prospective תַּלְמִיד must see to it that he links up with a teacher, and a rule from the early days of the Rabbinate (Ab., 1, 6; cf. 1, 16) expressly makes this a duty for the righteous. But here the initiative is with Jesus Himself, both in respect of forming a circle of disciples, and also with respect to its composition. Decisive here is the fact that He calls to Himself disciples who do not seem to enjoy the necessary qualifications for fellowship with Him, e.g., the tax-gatherer Levi (Mk. 2:13 ff.), for by their calling tax-gatherers were regarded as sinners and were thus shunned by the pious (Lk. 15:1 f.).[213]

(b) Some Disciples not Personally Called? On the other hand, the question arises whether there were also among the μαθηταί of Jesus those who attached themselves to Him without express calling. The usage of the Evangelists is not absolutely clear on this matter. This may be due to deeper causes than lack of linguistic precision. It may well be that the ambiguity of μαθητής in respect of whether every μαθητής of Jesus had to be personally called by Him reflects the

---

[210] Since our concern is simply with the fact, we need not go into the critical questions. On these cf. the comm., also the attempt at an analysis of this complex by L. Brun, "Die Berufung der ersten Jünger Jesu," *Symbolae Osloenses,* 11 (1932), 35 ff.

[211] On Jn. 1:45 ff., cf. J. Jeremias, "Die Berufung des Nathanael," ΑΓΓΕΛΟΣ, 3 (1930), 2 ff.

[212] → also 447.

[213] → I, 327 and J. Jeremias, "Zöllner u. Sünder," ZNW, 30 (1931), 293 ff. But cf. also the significant self-witness of Peter in Lk. 5:8.

actual circumstances of the early days of His activity when the people flocked to Him from all sides. Above all, the fact that He gave the impression of being a רַבִּי/διδάσκαλος may have had some influence. The more significant it is, then, that the whole tradition is agreed that finally it was Jesus Himself who decided the matter of belonging to Him. From this standpoint a passage like Jn. 6:60 ff. has great significance in this context.

Expressions like ἠκολούθησαν αὐτῷ πολλοί (Mt. 12:15), ὄχλος πολὺς μαθητῶν αὐτοῦ (Lk. 6:17), ἅπαν τὸ πλῆθος τῶν μαθητῶν (Lk. 19:37), πολλοὶ ... ἐκ τῶν μαθητῶν αὐτοῦ (Jn. 6:60; cf. 66), make it clear that the circle of μαθηταί gathered around Jesus was not small, and a passage like Lk. 10:1 (ἑτέρους ἑβδομήκοντα) confirms this with a number. The tradition even gives us some names, e.g., Cleopas in Lk. 24:18, Joseph of Arimathea in Jn. 19:38, perhaps Ananias in Ac. 9:10 and Mnason in Ac. 21:16 (ἀρχαῖος μαθητής, → 458, n. 283). There are not so many accounts of express callings as these figures would cause us to expect, though it should be noted that the tradition also does not give accounts of those who were later members of the circle of the twelve (cf. Lk. 9:59). Here and there we find instances of the readiness of Jesus to accept into fellowship, i.e., to allow to become a μαθητής, without issuing any summons thereto (Lk. 9:57, 61; Mk. 5:18 par.). Thus the impression might easily arise that there are two groups of μαθηταί, a wider circle of those who believe in Him, and a narrower circle which always accompanies Him.[214] On the other hand, in, e.g., Jn. 6:66, μετ' αὐτοῦ περιπατεῖν seems to be a definite feature of the μαθηταί. The impression given by Jn. is that there was at first a large group of disciples, but at a distinct point in time this broke up because offence was taken at the self-testimony of Jesus. Thus what Jn. tells us confirms in its own way the fact that the composition of the circle of disciple depends, not on the disciples, but on Jesus.

In the development of this initiative by Jesus we are perhaps tempted to detect a Greek trait in Jesus.[215] But it will be seen that the roots of this wholly non-Jewish relation of Jesus to His disciples are to be found, not in the affinity of Jesus to Hellenism, but in Himself.

b. The Disciples of Jesus in Their Relation to Him.

The relation between Jesus and His disciples is always presented in the tradition as unique. It is wholly personal, whether as the relation of Jesus to the disciples or as that of the disciples to Jesus. The factor on which the whole emphasis lies is exclusively the person of Jesus. As it is He who finally decides whether a man enters into discipleship, so it is He who gives form and content to the relationship of His disciples.

(a) The Commitment of the Disciples of Jesus to His Person. The detailed circumstances under which calling takes place are most instructive. In recollection it is never the isolated Word of Jesus which either attracts to allegiance or repels. The Word develops its true and binding force only when there is already commitment to Him.[216] Thus Lk., e.g., seems to presuppose that Jesus was not unknown to Peter, and perhaps also the sons of Zebedee, when He came to their

---

[214] Zn. Lk., 405 on 9:60.

[215] E. Wechssler, *Hellas im Evangelium* (1936), 242 ff., esp. 253 ff., tries to group Jesus with the wandering Cynic-Stoic preachers, and thus to relate Him to Hellenism. While he mentions Jesus' relation to His followers, he does not take up the question of their call.

[216] Cf. Jn. 6:68; also Ac. 4:20, where the εἴδαμεν καὶ ἠκούσαμεν (in this order) is worth noting.

boats by the lake (5:1 ff.), for the sermon in the synagogue at Capernaum and the healing of Peter's wife's mother come just before this scene and are closely related to it (4:31 ff.). Nevertheless, it is only the powerful direct impression of the person of Jesus on Peter and the others which, along with His personal Word, impels them to follow Him and causes them to becomes His μαθηταί. The emphasis is on the inner effect on Peter of what Jesus does. His self-awareness crumbles before the One who confronts him. He repents and believes, and it is thus, as a believer, that he is made a disciple by Jesus. The calling of Nathanael is in every way parallel (Jn. 1:45 ff.). Only the impression which Jesus makes on this man makes it natural that he should leave all and follow Him. The accounts of calling in Mk. 1:16 ff.; Mt. 4:18 ff. presuppose a similar train of events.[217]

The personal allegiance of the disciples to Jesus is confirmed by their conduct in the days between the crucifixion and the resurrection.[218] The reason for the deep depression which marks these days is to be found in the fate which has befallen the person of Jesus. No matter what view we take of the story of the walk to Emmaus, the fact that "He" is the theme of their conversation on the way (Lk. 24:19 ff.) corresponds in every sense to the relation of the disciples to Jesus before His arrest and execution. On the other hand, it is nowhere stated or even hinted that after the death of Jesus His teaching was a source of strength to His followers, or that they had the impression of having a valuable legacy in the Word of Jesus. This is a point of considerable importance for a true understanding of the μαθητής of Jesus.

Finally, note should be taken of the detailed circumstances of the reconstitution of the circle of disciples.[219] The tradition is unanimous in seeing in it the personal work of the risen Jesus, and it makes it apparent (Lk. 24:36 ff.; Jn. 20:24 ff. with Jn. 20:8; also Mt. 28:17b) that considerable resistance had to be overcome. It is striking that we meet again the two points which are found in the accounts of calling, i.e., acceptance into personal fellowship, and calling to be disciples. The first is to be seen in the fact that Jesus restores the fellowship with Himself which had been broken by the unfaithfulness of the disciples (forgiveness of sins).[220] From the standpoint of the Easter experience of the disciples it is quite natural that His μαθηταί could not be content merely to transmit His διδασκαλία but had to be His witnesses, i.e., witnesses to the revelation disclosed in His person, whether or not Jesus Himself ordained them as such (Lk. 24:48; Ac. 1:8).

Some linguistic observations may be made on the personal nature of the relation of the μαθηταί of Jesus to Jesus. They apply especially to Lk.[221] and Jn.

Lk. ceases to use μαθητής for the disciples of Jesus at the end of the Gethsemane story (22:45). From then on he has οἱ περὶ αὐτόν (22:49; cf. also 22:56, 58, 59), οἱ γνωστοὶ αὐτῷ (23:49, based on Ps. 38:11; 88:8, 18), οἱ ἕνδεκα καὶ πάντες οἱ λοιποί (24:9), αὐτοί (24:13), οἱ ἕνδεκα καὶ οἱ σὺν αὐτοῖς (24:33). The avoidance of μαθητής, which seems to be peculiar to the special source used by Lk.,[222] may be seen also early in Ac. The only possible explanation is that the behaviour of the disciples

217 Cf. K. H. Rengstorf, *Das Evangelium nach Lukas* (1937), 60.
218 Cf. K. H. Rengstorf, *Ich glaube an den Herrn Jesus Christus*² (1939), 7 f.
219 Since our concern is simply with the material understanding of μαθητής, we cannot go into questions of historical criticism here.
220 Cf. on this E. Hirsch, *Jesus Christus der Herr*² (1929), 36 ff.
221 Cf. Rengstorf, *Das Ev. nach Lk.*, 258 on Lk. 22:49.
222 In Mt.-Mk. μαθητής is used right to the end.

of Jesus during the passion is equivalent to a breach of the relationship by them, and that it is the task of Jesus to gather disciples afresh after His resurrection. In this connection it may be significant that after the denial (22:62) Peter is no longer called by this name which is his as a disciple, but is always Simon. But the position is not so clear in this respect.[223]

Jn.[224] refers very generally to οἱ μαθηταί in 6:66. But with the disintegration of the wider circle through offence at the self-testimony of Jesus, he begins to speak of the δώδεκα (μαθηταί). He thus underlines the fact that the mark of the disciple of Jesus is faith in Him (cf. 6:64). He also emphasises this esp. by having Jesus confront the disciples in full freedom with the decision whether they will remain with Him in faith or cease to be His μαθηταί.

Here, then, the fundamental difference between Jesus and representatives of the Rabbinate is to be seen in the disciples on both sides. What leads תַּלְמִידִים in swarms to a man like Akiba is his knowledge and method. Moreover, the תַּלְמִיד is welcomed by the rabbi so long as he is ready to accept what the rabbi has to offer with all the concern and faithfulness at his command (→ 435). In the case of Jesus, however, everything depends on His person. If on the one side respect for the knowledge and ability of the teacher determines the relation of the תַּלְמִיד to him, faith is the controlling factor in the relation of the disciples of Jesus to their Master.

But one can go a step further and say that Jesus represents something new as compared not merely with the Rabbinate but also with the Greek master after the manner of Socrates. If allegiance to the rabbi has its ultimate source in the תּוֹרָה which he expounds, the basis of allegiance to Socrates is to be found in the idea which he personally represents. In contrast to both, Jesus binds exclusively to Himself. The rabbi and the Greek philosopher are at one in representing a specific cause. Jesus offers Himself. This obviously gives a completely different turn to the whole relation of the disciples to Him. The difference which may be seen at this point becomes even clearer when the external relation of the disciples of Jesus to Jesus is considered (→ 453 on the principle of tradition).

(b) The Obedience of the Disciples to Jesus. A man like Akiba left all that he had to become a תַּלְמִיד,[225] and it is recounted of another תַּלְמִיד־חָכָם that he renounced marriage and posterity for the sake of study of the Torah.[226] Thus there are parallels in Rabbinism for the radicalness with which Jesus breaks all other ties and binds His disciples to Himself alone. Nevertheless, the situation is not really the same. Sometimes the Rabbinic תַּלְמִיד may give up a great deal, but he knows that more will accrue to him. For the Torah, to whose investigation and fulfilment he devotes his powers, is incontestably God's Word for His people, which lives by it as it has also to live for it. The personal authority which a teacher of the

[223] Simon seems to be the name used by the special source of Lk. We find Πέτρος at 24:12 in a passage which many expositors regard as apocryphal, though there is something to be said for its authenticity (J. Schniewind, *Die Parallelperikopen bei Lukas u. Johannes* [1914], 88 f.). If it is an original part of the Gospel, its relation to the special source is a matter of debate.

[224] Cf. Schl. J., 183 on 6:67.

[225] Cf. bNed., 50a; Ket., 62b-63a. Cf. generally the anecdotes assembled in bKet., 62b.

[226] T. Jeb., 8, 4. The man concerned, Ben 'Azzai, was not ordained, perhaps because he was not married.

Torah enjoys he owes, for all the recognition of his own personal gifts, to the Torah which he sacrificially studies. The great teachers of later Judaism are not sought out by throngs of students because they are men of intellectual endowment and practical wisdom like the popular Greek philosophers, but because they are teachers of the Torah. It is surely significant that Jesus does not seek any material foundation for His authority, but expects His μαθηταί to renounce for His sake alone all that has hitherto seemed indispensable to them (Mt. 10:37 ff. par.).

Even more significant is the fact that the disciples unconditionally accepted His authority, not just inwardly by believing in Him, but also outwardly by obeying Him. It has long since been noted that here the relation of the μαθηταί of Jesus to Him is quite different from that of the Rabbinic תַּלְמִידִים to their teacher even though the terminology of the NT integrates Jesus and His disciples into the world of the νομοδιδάσκαλοι of His day.[227] The fact that μαθηταί can be parallel to δοῦλοι (Mt. 10:24 f.; Jn. 13:16; 15:20) is quite alien to later Judaism (→ 442). In this connection we may cite the parables relating to the second coming, in which Jesus is the κύριος and the disciples are δοῦλοι (Mt. 24:45 ff.; 25:14 ff.; Lk. 12:35 ff., 42 ff.)[228] in a way not current among the Rabbis. The picture outlined here finds historical confirmation in two scenes from the last days of Jesus. On the occasion of the entry He sends His disciples to find a donkey (Mk. 11:1 ff. par.), and later the disciples at His command make ready the last supper (Mk. 14:12 ff. par.).[229] These are services which go far beyond what a תַּלְמִיד־חָכָם was obliged to render to his teacher,[230] especially when one considers the detailed conditions under which the disciples fulfilled it. It has also to be remembered that in the parables mentioned as well as the accounts the service of the disciples is regarded as quite natural, and that it is with this understanding that they render it.[231] What is to be seen here is more than respect. Jesus is obeyed because it is believed that He is the Messiah. It is no accident that scenes like those portrayed in Mk. 11:1 ff. par. and Mk. 14:12 ff. par. are connected with the public manifestation of the Messianic consciousness of Jesus.

The traditions associated here enable us for the first time clearly to differentiate the μαθηταί of Jesus from the תַּלְמִידֵי־חֲכָמִים of the Rabbinate in terms of the self-understanding of the two groups of disciples. For the תַּלְמִיד־חָכָם discipleship is only a transitory stage. The goal at which he aims is obviously to belong in due course to those whom it is now a supreme honour for the תַּלְמִיד־חָכָם to serve (→ 434). For him his rabbi is certainly indispensable (→ 434), but for this very reason his concern is to be like the rabbi, and thus independent of or even superior to him. For the disciple of Jesus, however, discipleship is not a first step with the promise of greater things to come. It is the fulfilment of his destiny. This is so only because he is the disciple of Jesus. He is called by Him and believes in Him.

---

227 Cf., e.g., W. Foerster, *Herr ist Jesus* (1924), 228 ff.

228 *Ibid.*, 231 f.

229 Bultmann regards this as a legendary accretion to the story of the entry (Trad., 281). But he is notably more restrained in relation to Mk. 14:12 ff. (Trad., 283 f.). In any case, even if legendary elements are assumed in both cases, the passages are highly instructive regarding the very non-Jewish picture which the tradition presents of the disciples of Jesus and their relation to their Master, especially if one agrees with Bultmann that a passage like Mk. 14:12 ff. could have arisen only in the Palestinian community (Trad., 284).

230 Cf. Str.-B., I, 527 (services to be rendered by a non-Jewish born slave), also → 434.

231 What Foerster, 232 has to say about this stands in need of modification.

Whereas the תַּלְמִיד־חָכָם hopes in some sense to master the Torah, it is the business of the μαθητής of Jesus to be stamped and fashioned by Him.

The Synoptic Gospels confirm this picture at every point, and what they say is the more impressive the more clearly Jesus and His disciples are seen against the Jewish background. Jesus does not differentiate Himself externally from contemporary teachers of the Torah. He expounds Scripture and gathers around Him a group of disciples. This is taken into account by the terms used (διδάσκαλος, μαθητής etc.; → II, 153). Mt. rightly emphasises that the ἐξουσία which marked His teaching gave Him a special position from the very first (7:28 f.). But this uniqueness is to be seen with full clarity only when note is also taken of His μαθηταί. Thus it should be fully considered that the μαθηταί are never presented as engaged in discussion with Jesus. Discussions are started only by the opponents of Jesus (Mt. 21:23 ff. par.; 22:15 ff. par. etc.) except when Jesus forces them into debate (Mt. 22:41 ff. par.). Jesus' own disciples are always listeners[232] who simply put questions when they do not understand what Jesus says (Mk. 4:10 ff. par.). The decisive thing, however, is not intellectual appropriation but acceptance of the Word of Jesus by the will, and its implementation (Mt. 7:24 ff. par.).[233]

The Syn. statements are supplemented by Jn. In a series of sayings which in form and content are typically Johannine, the only proper attitude of the disciples is described, in analogy to the Syn. picture, as one of obedience.[234] It is expressly affirmed that the basis of this is to be found in the call by Jesus (15:16). Where the believer abides in the Word of Jesus (8:31) and keeps His ἐντολαί (13:34 f.; 14:15 ff.; 15:10 ff.), he is ἀληθῶς His μαθητής (8:31), and from a δοῦλος is raised to be His φίλος (15:14 ff.). This last statement is important. The Fourth Gospel avoids γνώριμος when describing the disciples of Jesus in terms of fellowship, though this word, along with ἑταῖρος, was the acknowledged term in contemporary usage (→ 419). A theological insight finally lies behind the avoidance of these two terms. The μαθηταί of Gk. and Hell. philosophers are γνώριμοι in so far as they are united with their masters in the fellowship of pursuit after knowledge. ἑταῖροι groups them as *pares* under a *primus inter pares* (→ 420). For John's Gospel, however, Jesus is always the One who gives and with whom there can be no equal partnership. Even the fellowship of the disciples with Him is His gift. Since He is before them as the steward of the divine will, He can and will give only to those who take Him seriously in His office, and who allow themselves to be moulded by Him.[235]

(c) The Obligation of the Disciples to Suffer with Jesus. The nature of the calling of the disciples of Jesus, and their resultant dependence on Him, means that there is nothing in the life of disciples which is apart from Jesus and His life. With all they have and are they are drawn into fellowship with Him. But the way of Jesus leads to the cross. Hence entry into His fellowship as His μαθητής carries with it the obligation to suffer. The tradition is unanimous that in fact Jesus left His disciples in no doubt that they were committing themselves to suffering if they followed Him.

Most of the sayings of Jesus which hold out suffering before the disciples are not, in the Gospel tradition, addressed to disciples in general, but are part of the information and instruction given to the (twelve) apostles (Mt. 10:17 ff.; Jn.

---

232 It is to be noted that they are ἀκούοντες, not ἀκροαταί.

233 The Sermon on the Mount is relevant here, esp. if it is regarded as instruction of the disciples.

234 Cf. the catena of such sayings in Jn. 8:31 ff.; 15:1 ff.

235 Religious par. (Mandaean in Bau. J., *ad loc.*; there are no Rabb.) are of little help

15:18 ff.; 16:1 ff.).[236] Here they are indispensable, for in all things the apostle is as his master. If the Lord has to suffer, suffering will naturally fall on the apostle too.[237] But some sayings of this kind apply to disciples in general (Mk. 8:34 ff. par.[238] and esp. Lk. 14:26 f.),[239] and leave us in no doubt that extreme affliction is involved in following Jesus, though there is always comfort too for those who die with and for Jesus. The band of disciples broke up when its members ran away from the danger into which they were set by the arrest of Jesus (→ *infra*). The change took place in the Easter days. There then took root a joyous readiness for the suffering which Christians, as disciples of Jesus, have had to endure and have constantly endured for centuries.

c. οἱ μαθηταί — οἱ δώδεκα — οἱ ἀπόστολοι.

The differences between the three groups are complicated, and cannot always be indicated with the clarity one would desire. It can be shown, however, that on the one side it is part of the image of the ἀπόστολος that he should be a μαθητής, whereas not by a long way are all the μαθηταί also ἀπόστολοι, and that on the other side οἱ δώδεκα and ἀπόστολοι are not at all equivalent. οἱ δώδεκα (μαθηταί, ἀπόστολοι) denotes the narrower circle around Jesus as compared with the wider circle either of μαθηταί or ἀπόστολοι.

In all essentials ref. may here be made to earlier arts. On the use of οἱ μαθηταί — οἱ δώδεκα — οἱ ἀπόστολοι in the Gospels → I, 424, 425, 427; on the origin and significance of the group of the δώδεκα (μαθηταί, ἀπόστολοι) → II, 325.

d. The Band of the (Twelve) Disciples of Jesus as an Intimation of His Way of Suffering.

The self-awareness of Jesus is revealed in His calling of the disciples (→ 447). When out of the circle of disciples He chooses twelve men to be His companions (Mk. 3:13 f.), He thereby manifests His claim to be sent by God to the whole people for its salvation (→ II, 326). Only against this background can one see clearly what is the significance of the twelve as the core of the fellowship of disciples, both in respect of its understanding of Jesus, and also in respect of its composition with a view to His way.

(a) The Failure of the Disciples to Understand. According to the Synoptists lack of understanding not merely of the goal of Jesus but also of His proclamation accompanies the relation of the disciples to Him to the very end. In this context we might mention their failure to see clearly what following Him demands (Mt. 8:19 ff.; Lk. 9:57 ff.), their fear and anxiety even when with Him (Mt. 8:23 ff. par.; 14:13 ff. par.; 15:32 ff. par.), scenes like that in Mk. 9:33 ff. par.; Lk. 22:24 ff.

---

towards an understanding of Jn. 15:14 f. It seems to me that Is. 41:8 stands in the background, and regard should be had to the understanding of this passage in James (2:21 ff.). If the link with Is. 41:8 is correct, Jn. 15:14 f. reveals the self-awareness which everywhere characterises the Johannine Christ.

[236] Sayings like Mk. 13:9 ff. par., which the Evangelists bring into close proximity to the passion, are also addressed to the inner circle.

[237] Cf. K. H. Rengstorf, *Apostolat u. Predigtamt* (1934), 22 ff.

[238] In this light Mt. 10:38 f. appears to some to be of secondary composition (Bultmann Trad., 86).

[239] Jn. 12:25 f. may also be cited here; cf. Schl. Erl., *ad loc.*

(their quarrels about rank, cf. Mt. 20:20 ff. par.); Mk. 10:13 ff. par. (the disciples try to prevent the mothers and children from coming to Jesus), defective understanding of His preaching (Mk. 4:10 f. par.; Mt. 13:36), inner and outer protests against His passion (Mt. 16:22 ff. par.; Mt. 26:51 ff. par.;[240] Lk. 22:38).[241] The flight of the disciples on the arrest of Jesus (Mt. 26:55 f. par.) is the logical result of this attitude, as is also their doubting of His resurrection when God had not prevented His execution and had thus, according to the impression of the disciples as well as the opponents of Jesus, withheld confirmation of the testimony which He had borne to Himself (cf. Lk. 24:19 ff.). A note of the third Evangelist on the occasion of the third prophecy of the passion shows as clearly as possible how little understanding the disciples of Jesus had for His way to the cross (Lk. 18:34). Only the risen Lord brought about a change in this respect.[242]

The same picture is presented in John's Gospel except that here the reflection of the Evangelist plays a stronger role than in the Synoptic Gospels. While Jn. says that the disciples of Jesus believed on Him (2:11), he also says from the very first that they had no real knowledge of His nature or understanding of His words (2:21 f.; 12:16; cf. 16:19 ff.). Jn. agrees especially with Lk. in testifying that it was only the resurrection which brought about a great change in the understanding of the disciples (2:22; 12:16; → also 446).

The Evangelists do not fail to point out on occasion that the disciples' lack of understanding was a severe burden to Jesus (cf. on the one side Mk. 9:19 par.; Mt. 16:22 f., and on the other Jn. 14:9). Perhaps Gethsemane, with its intermingling of the great desire of Jesus for fellowship with His disciples and the actual loneliness of Jesus, is to be understood from this standpoint. It is hard to see why these aspects of the tradition should not be regarded as original, since they serve to glorify neither Jesus nor the disciples. There can certainly be no doubt that Jesus was finally left in the lurch by the disciples, and that this was a logical development. His patience with them, the tirelessness with which He made their salvation His concern, shines out in sayings like Lk. 22:31 f.; Jn. 16:12; 17:1 ff., and also in acts like those in Lk. 22:51; Jn. 13:1 ff.; Jn. 18:8, even though the presentation may owe some of its details to the later piety of the community of Jesus.

(b) The Composition of the Band. From the emphasis which the whole tradition places on the fact that the disciples of Jesus were called by Him to discipleship, the composition of the band takes on significance in any attempt to evaluate the role of the disciples as participants in His history. This is particularly true with respect to Judas, who betrayed Him. In this connection[243] it is less important that Judas finally delivered Jesus into the hands of His enemies than that Jesus brought Judas into the band of disciples when He realised long before what Judas pur-

---

240 Cf. also Jn. 18:10: Peter. If Peter finally denies Jesus, then he, the rock man, and spokesman for the band of disciples (Lk. 22:33 f. etc.), represents here the whole group, and shows how fragile was their faith in Jesus prior to Easter (cf. also Mt. 8:26: ὀλιγόπιστοι; Mt. 14:31 to Peter: ὀλιγόπιστε).

241 → III, 295.

242 Cf. the opening up of the Scriptures to the disciples by the risen Lord (Lk. 24:26 f., 44 ff.).

243 Obviously we cannot deal here with the problem of Judas as such, whether in detail or more generally. We must certainly not try to explain what he did. Luke (22:3; cf. 4, 13) and John (13:2, 27) can understand his betrayal only on the assumption that he was a tool of Satan.

posed to do (Lk. 22:21 ff.; Mt. 26:20 ff.; Jn. 13:21 ff.; cf. 6:64, 70 f.). If one also considers that the second Simon in the circle was undoubtedly a Zealot (→ II, 886 f.), that both the Gospel and the Apocalypse of John give indications that the author had connections with the Zealots,[244] that there was also a publican among the disciples (→ 444), and we find Greek as well as Semitic names, and that, if ὁ Ἰσκαριώτης or Ἰσκαριώθ (Mk. 3:19 par.) really describes Judas as the man from Karioth,[245] the band included a Judaean as well as Galilaeans, then the circle of the disciples is in fact a microcosm of the Judaism of the time. In it we find all the powers and thoughts of the people, even in their divergence. In its own way it thus bears witness to the fact that Jesus sought to do it service with a full realisation of the relationships around Him, and that this was a service to the people as it was, not as He imagined it to be. The calling of the disciples thus shows Jesus to be a sober realist. But it also shows Him as the One who is ready obediently to bear all that may result when He comes to a people which, while it is conscious of its election, no longer perceives why it is called, and undertakes to tell this people afresh what is its obligation to God.[246]

e. The Share of the Disciples in the Work of Jesus.

The call of Peter to discipleship (Lk. 5:1 ff.) is also a call to work with Jesus (5:10). This is no accident, nor is it exceptional. It perhaps corresponds to the fact that the disciples called by Jesus are *His* disciples. As He Himself does not turn inwards into Himself, but girds Himself for service, so He directs the gaze and powers of His disciples to His task, which by their association with Him is also theirs. Sayings from the instruction of the disciples in Mt. 5:13 ff., parables such as Mt. 25:14 ff. par., and directions like those given by Mt. in the charge in Mt. 10:5 ff. correspond to sayings of the Johannine Jesus such as we find in 17:13 ff., esp. 15.

The participation of the disciples of Jesus in His work finds classic expression in the twofold establishment of the apostolate by Jesus (→ I, 424, 430). To understand this it should be recalled that, while not all μαθηταί became apostles, the apostle was normally a μαθητής of Jesus (→ 450). To this degree Luke's account of the sending out of the seventy after the twelve (Lk. 10:1 ff.) represents a broadening of the picture which we have of the drawing of the disciples by Jesus into co-operation with Him.[247] In the first instance this co-operation is worked out externally in the customary Jewish forms. Jesus sends out the disciples two by two (Mk. 6:7; Lk. 10:1) according to the direction of the Torah which demands two witnesses for authentic testimony (Dt. 17:6; 19:15).[248] This gave rise to a Christian custom which is also found in the life of Paul when the church at Antioch sends him out with Barnabas on missionary work (Ac. 13:2 ff.; cf. 15:36 ff.). Inwardly the work of the disciples is stamped by Jesus' own work and arises from His ἐξουσία (Lk. 10:1 ff., 17; Mk. 6:7, 12 f.; Mt. 10:7 f.). The decisive

[244] Cf. Schl. Gesch. d. erst. Chr., 65 f.

[245] Jn. 6:71 ℵ Θ φ; 12:4 𝔎 D; 13:2 De; 14:22 D. For bibl. on this cf. Pr.-Bauer[3], *s.v.* Ἰσκαριώθ.

[246] The disciples, then, are not at all companions whom Jesus needs (as against Wach, 33).

[247] On the detailed problems of Lk. 10:1 ff. → II, 634.

[248] Rabb. material in Str.-B., I, 790 on Mt. 18:16. Schl. Mt., 325 f. appositely points out that the list of apostles in Mt. 10:2 ff. shows signs of arrangement in pairs, and recalls that pre-Christian Rabb. tradition was represented by pairs (cf. Ab., 1, 4 ff.; also in Schl. examples from Jos.).

thing is that over their work stands: δωρεὰν ἐλάβετε, δωρεὰν δότε (Mt. 10:8). In keeping this rule[249] (cf. Ac. 3:6 and 20:33 ff.) the disciples of Jesus showed that in fact they did not seek to be more than fellow-workers (cf. also 1 C. 3:9; 1 Th. 3:2 D*), and they also showed that they realised it was grace both to be called to the status of disciple and also to be called to share in the work of Jesus.[250]

A difficult special question is raised by Jn. 3:22, 26; 4:1 f. If Jesus Himself really baptised and His disciples helped Him, this would be another form of working with Him. But the relevant statements are not wholly clear; → I, 538.

f. The Principle of Tradition in Jesus' Band of Disciples.

(a) The Lack of a Principle of Tradition. Both on Greek-Hellenistic soil and also in Rabbinism disciples (μαθηταί, תַּלְמִידִים) are as such the representatives of a principle of tradition. Every μαθητής/ תַּלְמִיד is also the member of a chain of tradition at whose beginning is the head of the school to whom it owes its existence and to whose knowledge it owes its *raison d'être* (→ 423; 434). It is thus natural to ask what is the situation of Jesus' disciples in this respect. This is the more natural in view of the unique personal relation of the disciples to Jesus.

Now there is no doubt that we find tradition, and the material of tradition, in the NT. We also see a clear dependence here on later Jewish forms.[251] Apart from the few passages which are expressly stated to be based on tradition (1 C. 11:23 ff.; 15:3 ff.), the whole of the material used by the Synoptists, and a good deal of that in the Fourth Gospel, derives from oral tradition. It is even possible to some degree to reconstruct the history of the formation and composition of this material. We thus seem to be forced to the conclusion that the Gospels give clear evidence of a definite principle of tradition in the circle from which they took their origin, and that certain statements of Paul (→ *supra*) give excellent corroboration. This conclusion has in fact been drawn. It makes of the early community the representative of a principle of tradition in which Greek elements from the mysteries combine with the law of oral tradition on the soil of later Judaism to produce a new entity which distinctively corresponds to the Gospel as the theme of early Christian tradition.[252]

Though we cannot go into this whole subject here, attention may be drawn to certain facts which show, however, that, in spite of certain formal analogies, the first Christian generation and the New Testament are far removed from any principle of tradition, whether Greek or Rabbinic.

The most significant point is that recollection of Jesus as a teacher seems to have been quite secondary. This may be seen not only in the epistles of Paul, the oldest Christian sources which have come down to us,[253] but also in the oldest and surest part of the Gospel tradition, which contains, not the sayings of Jesus, but the story of His death and passion (→ II, 157).[254] The freedom in the form

[249] Its observance by the Rabbis is not certain, though many Rabb. voices speak in its favour, → 439.

[250] Cf. the linking of χάρις and ἀποστολή in R. 1:5.

[251] Cf. Kittel Probl., 63 ff.; → Ranft, 248 ff.

[252] Ranft, esp. 304 ff.

[253] Only occasionally does Paul quote a saying of Jesus, and then quite freely (1 C. 7:10). On the other hand, there are many reminiscences of dominical sayings (e.g., 1 Th. 5:1 ff.).

[254] It is worth noting that Rabb. tradition concerning Jesus confirms this. It accepts Him as having תלמידים, but regards Him as a false prophet rather than a teacher. Cf. Strack, *op. cit., passim.*

in which the sayings of Jesus are transmitted may be seen from the different versions in which we now have them. Since it is combined with a strong interest in material precision, this freedom is most instructive. It tells us no more and no less than that the early Christian emphasis lay on the history of Jesus as the history of the divine confirmation of His claim to faith, and that the words of Jesus were significant because God had in fact acknowledged Him. For the disciples Jesus is nowhere the head of a school; He is the living Lord of His people.

In keeping is the fact that the first Christian generation placed high value on the fact that its leading men were eye-witnesses. When addition was made to the circle after Easter, this was the main concern, Ac. 1:21 f.; → I, 436. Possibly the difficulties with which Paul had to contend when he sought the recognition of primitive Christianity for his own apostleship were due to the fact that he was not an eye-witness in the accepted sense, and that, while he was an apostle, he was not a μαθητής (→ I, 437). The fact that after emphasising his apostleship in 1 C. 9:1 he goes on to say: οὐχὶ Ἰησοῦν τὸν κύριον ἡμῶν ἑόρακα; [255] possibly points in this direction. If he has seen the Lord, he is also in direct fellowship with Him.

At this point ref. might be made to the fact that in Ac. 9:26 Paul is also called μαθητής. Is there an attempt here to take the stigma from him?

It must also be remembered that Jesus deliberately kept His disciples aloof from the Rabbinic system of His time. Part of the chain of tradition was that the μαθητής would become one who himself had μαθηταί and who would be honoured by them as a master. Jesus drew a clear line of separation between His disciples and this whole world (cf. Mt. 23:6 ff.). Nor did He find His disciples among the σοφοί but among the νήπιοι, and the wisdom of God's guidance is seen herein (Mt. 11:25). [256] In all its details this saying is rooted in the situation of Jesus. [257] It also finds a close parallel in the Beatitudes (Mt. 5:3 ff.; Lk. 6:20 ff.). Along the same lines, the exercise of love is made a sign of the μαθητής to the world in John's Gospel, Jn. 13:34 f.

(b) The Reasons for this Lack. In the Gospel, then, the disciples are witnesses, not bearers of a tradition. This is no accident. It necessarily results not merely (positively) from the significance which attaches to His person in fellowship with Him (→ 445) but also (negatively) from the attitude which Jesus Himself adopted towards religious tradition and the principle of tradition.

So far as we can see, He never expounded His position comprehensively. But there is no doubt that He constantly opposed traditionalism, as may be seen especially from the accounts of healings on the Sabbath (Mk. 3:1 ff. par.; Lk. 13:10 ff.; 14:1 ff.). His repudiation of not inconsiderable portions of pious Jewish tradition, and therewith of the principle of tradition as the foundation of service to God, [258] does not spring from a critical spirit or from a liberal attitude to what is

---

[255] Cf. also 1 C. 15:8, where Paul concludes the chain of eye-witnesses (ὤφθη κἀμοί).

[256] On Mt. 11:25-30 cf. T. Arvedson, *Das Mysterium Christi. Eine Studie zu Mt. 11:25-30* (1937). For Arvedson Jesus is a teacher, but a teacher of wisdom, not a rabbi after the manner of Rabbinic authorities. Yet he also emphasises the uniqueness of Jesus even as a teacher of wisdom.

[257] Cf. J. Schniewind in *NT Deutsch*, 2 (1937), *ad loc.*, esp. 146.

[258] Cf. on this W. G. Kümmel, "Jesus u. der jüd. Traditionsgedanke," ZNW, 33 (1934), 105 ff.

traditional. It is grounded in His self-awareness, which also shaped the relation of His disciples to Him. He is the One in whom prophetic Scripture and the hope of His people have been fulfilled (Lk. 4:16 ff.). As the fulfilment, He ends the pious tradition of His people. This is a definitive end, not a new beginning in a new form. If the members of the chain of tradition are at their own points fellow-workers in the perception and stewardship of the truth, He is Himself the truth (Jn. 14:6). This means that His μαθηταί, unlike the μαθηταί/תַּלְמִידִים of the Rabbinate, are not the faithful mediators of insights. They are His obedient witnesses (cf. Lk. 24:48; Ac. 1:8; Jn. 19:35; 21:24).[259]

g. Summary.

Investigation of the statements of the Gospels about the disciples of Jesus thus leads us to two conclusions.

(a) Notwithstanding the formal kinship between the תַּלְמִיד of later Rabbinic Judaism and the μαθητής of Jesus, there is between the two no inner relation. The reason is that both in origin and nature the disciples of Jesus are moulded by the self-awareness of Jesus. He is for them, not the rabbi/διδάσκαλος, but their Lord. The fact that they are μαθηταί does not affect this.

(b) The relation in which the disciples are set by Jesus to Himself implies already that witness to Him is the task to which they are called as His disciples. Since early Christian proclamation, so far as we can see, was from the very first witness to Jesus and not the reception and transmission of His own proclamation, this is a finding of great significance. It bases this fact, whose authenticity has often been disputed, on the personal relation of the disciples of Jesus to Him.[260] It also helps us to understand why primitive Christianity knows nothing of discipleship of Jesus in the sense of an *imitatio Christi*.[261]

4. The μαθηταί of John the Baptist.

a. The Disciples in the Lifetime of John. In the Gospels John as well as Jesus is surrounded by μαθηταί.[262]

We are not told how they came to attach themselves to him. It may be that they entered into fellowship with him without any special summons, as the young Joseph. associated for three years with the hermit Bannus and shared his life (Vit., 11).[263]

---

259 In this respect the picture needs to be broadened out and filled in, but this must be done in some other context. It may at least be noted, however, that the Palestinian church had a kind of Christian Rabbinate (cf. Schl. Gesch. d. erst. Chr., 362 ff., esp. 368 ff.). Whether the Evangelist Mt. belonged to this (*v.* E. v. Dobschütz, "Matthäus als Rabbi u. Katechet," ZNW, 27 [1928], 338 ff.) is, of course, more than doubtful. The common features adduced are only only formal, and even v. Dobschütz cannot produce any more solid examples. The situation is naturally quite different when we come to the teaching system of the early Catholic Church.

260 Cf. also K. Bornhäuser, *Das Joh.-Ev. eine Missionsschrift für Israel* (1928), 156 (of the eleven): "But these are not further scribes ; they are witnesses."

261 Cf. on this R. Seeberg, "Die Nachfolge Christi," *Aus Religion u. Geschichte* (1906), 1-41, esp. 9 ff.

262 Cf. on this E. Lohmeyer, *Das Urchristentum, 1. Buch :* "Johannes der Täufer" (1932), 114 ff.

263 Jos., however, uses ζηλωτής, not μαθητής (→ 439, n. 191).

The picture is significant because the μαθηταί of the Baptist are not presented as a loose throng constantly coming and going. They are a solid group, closed both inwardly and outwardly, and closely related to the Baptist.

In the light of Jn. 4:1 their number cannot have been small. They also seem to have had a rule, for we hear that they fasted (Mt. 9:14 par.) and that they had a prayer which John had given them and the use of which characterised them (Lk. 11:1).[264] In Jn. 3:25 the disciples of the Baptist champion him in disputation with the Jews about καθαρισμός, which is here presumably the baptism of John (→ III, 429 f.).[265] Later they come to John in prison and can pass on from him a question to Jesus (Mt. 11:2 par.).[266] After his execution he is buried by disciples (Mt. 14:12 par.).[267] Hence the fellowship goes on even after his death.

The disciples of John have direct significance in the NT because according to Jn. the first disciples of Jesus came from this circle, and they did so on the basis of a saying of the Baptist which pointed them in this direction (Jn. 1:35 ff.). In the light of the preaching of the Baptist in Jn. this step was logical.[268] The more surprising it is, then, that John himself did not take it, and that many of his disciples obviously did not do so (→ *infra*). Perhaps the reason is that John's doctrine of baptism consolidated the circle of his μαθηταί more than he intended (cf. on this Jn. 3:26 and passages like Ac. 18:25; 19:1 ff.).[269] In view of the lack of more precise information about the μαθηταί of the Baptist, it is hard to be more definite.

Attempts have been made to show that Jesus Himself was originally a disciple of John, esp. in view of His designation as Ναζωραῖος (Mt. 2:23), which characterises Him as an observant. But in spite of the many linguistic and material arguments advanced, this is a very dubious thesis.

b. The Disciples after the Death of John (Ac.). There is certainly no doubt that the disciples assembled by John continued to be a firm circle long after his death. This is attested by the mere fact that Josephus *c.* 90 A.D. had at his disposal living testimonies to the Baptist.[270] Quite apart from any possible religious implications, these reports are interesting because twice in Ac. we read of believers in Christ who are not baptised in the name of Jesus, but know only the baptism of John. The first reference is to Apollos, an Alexandrian[271] Jew and later a fellow-worker with Paul (1 C. 1:12; 3:6; Ac. 18:24). The second reference is to a group of 12 (Ac. 19:7; → II, 322) Ephesian μαθηταί. It is best to take the accounts as

---

[264] Schl. Lk., 296 rightly concludes from 11:1 that the source used by Lk. knew of a definite circle of disciples of the Baptist. In this it agrees with Jn., who distinguishes the disciples of the Baptist from the Ἰουδαῖοι.

[265] Cf. also Schl. J., 105 f. *ad loc.*, who also quotes Jos. Ant., 18, 117 to elucidate the point at issue.

[266] Akiba, too, had a תַּלְמִיד to serve him in prison, cf. P. Billerbeck, *Nathanael*, 34 (1918), 55 ff.

[267] Cf. the par. in Jn. 19:38.

[268] There are many reasons for thinking that the author of the Fourth Gospel came from the circle of John's disciples, *v.* Lohmeyer, *op. cit.*, 119, n. 1.

[269] Cf. Lohmeyer, 117 ff.

[270] Cf. Schl. Gesch. d. Chr., 74.

[271] This account shows that the preaching of the Baptist had spread to the Egyptian *diaspora*, and it thus gives us a clear indication of the extent of the influence of the Baptist on the Jewish world as a whole (cf. Mt. 3:5 with Lk. 3:15; Jn. 1:19 ff.).

they stand[272] and to see here μαθηταί of the Baptist. They then give us an instructive glimpse of religio-sociological relations at the middle of the 1st century. The boundaries between the movements initiated by John and Jesus have neither disappeared nor hardened. This corresponds to the personal relation of the Baptist to Jesus, which was never clarified rationally and remained to the very end a question of faith (cf. Mt. 11:2 ff. par.). If is was possible to lead Apollos and the men of Ephesus quite easily to Jesus (Ac. 18:26; 19:3 ff.), this is finally because the community of John turned so seriously to Jesus in accordance with Jn. 1:29 ff.

A problem bound up with the existence of disciples of John long after his death is that of the ultimate fate of these supporters. The only certain point is that research leads us at once away from the NT and partly into the history of Jewish sects, partly beyond the confines of Judaism into syncretistic Gnosticism.[273] For many years there was an inclination to find a direct link between the baptismal sect of the Mandaeans and the movement of the Baptist; indeed, it was even suggested that John and his group belonged to the wider circle of the Mandaeans. But this line of enquiry is now closed, for it has been shown that the Mandaean rites presuppose the baptismal ritual of Christian Syrians, and in particular that the figure of John belongs to the latest stratum of the Mandaean tradition.[274] This also undermines the conjecture that Jesus as a disciple of the Baptist was related through him to the Mandaeans.[275] It also makes it unnecessary to pursue the question further in this context.

5. μαθητής as a Term for Christians in Acts.

Except for 19:1 and 9:25 (→ 459) μαθητής is regularly used in Ac. for a Christian as such. We have still to ask how this usage arose and what makes it so distinctive. The problem has both a linguistic and also a material aspect.

a. The Linguistic Problem. Linguistically, it is to be noted first that μαθητής is used for Christians only in specific sections of Acts.

It occurs first in 6:1 and stretches, with breaks, to 21:16. Before 6:1 Christians are οἱ πιστεύσαντες (2:44; 4:32), οἱ ἀδελφοί (1:15, also frequently between 6:1 and 21:16, e.g., 11:1, 29; 12:17; 14:2 etc., and after 21:16, 21:17; 28:14 ff.), οἱ φίλοι, οἱ ἅγιοι etc.[276] The use of μαθητής is so unsystematic that it has even been treated as a principle for differentiating the sources of Ac.[277] Another feature of the linguistic picture is that there is a certain tendency in the textual tradition to increase the use of μαθητής at the expense of other words: 1:15 (for ἀδελφός) ℵ D pm sy; 20:7 (for ἡμῶν) HLP,[278] or to introduce it by way of clarification: 6:5 D h. Finally, it is worth

[272] W. Michaelis, "Die sog. Johannes-Jünger in Ephesus," NKZ, 38 (1927), 717 ff. (cf. also Jackson-Lake, I, 4 [1933], 231 ff.) tries to show that those called μαθηταί in Ac. 19:1 (also Apollos, Ac. 18:24) were Christians who had simply been baptised by John and who esp. knew nothing about Pentecost. If this were so, the use of μαθητής in Ac. would be more fixed than is the case if 18:24; 19:1 ff. refer to disciples of John. But the question is still an open one.
[273] Cf. the brief observations in Lohmeyer, 184 ff.
[274] H. Lietzmann, "Ein Beitrag zur Mandäerfrage," SAB (1930), 27, with bibl.; for additional bibl. cf. Bau. J.[3]
[275] Cf. Lidz. Joh., 30; R. Bultmann, ZNW, 24 (1925), 100 ff., esp. 143 ff.
[276] Cf. the list in Jackson-Lake, I, 5 (1933), 375 ff. (Note XXX: "Names for Christians and Christianity in Acts").
[277] R. Schütz, "Das Quellenproblem der Ag.," *Harnack-Ehrung* (1921), 44 ff. Cf. also Joachim Jeremias (→ n. 205).
[278] Jackson-Lake, I, 3 (1926), 192, *ad loc.*

noting that μαθητής does not occur in the so-called "We" passages except at 21:4, 16, where the first ref. is to Christians in general, but the second to Mnason, an ἀρχαῖος μαθητής (cf. 9:10 of Ananias). → n. 283.

Normally μαθητής is used without explanatory addition. Only occasionally is there more precise designation (9:1: οἱ μαθηταὶ τοῦ κυρίου). This supports the view that when Ac. has the word for Christians it is following a special usage which for its part derives from the way Palestinian Christians described themselves.

A review of the passages quickly shows that the term means Christians in general and not just personal disciples, i.e., that it includes those who did not know Jesus personally. Timothy is called a μαθητής in 16:1, and it can hardly be assumed that he had any contact with Jesus. In fact, this is ruled out by 1 Tm. 1:2; 2 Tm. 1:2 (τέκνον); 1:5. On the first missionary journey μαθηταί appear in the course of the narrative as the fruit of the work of Barnabas and Paul (13:52; 14:20 ff.; cf. also 18:23). The phrase πληθυνόντων τῶν μαθητῶν (6:1) has in view the missionary success of the primitive community.

That we have in Ac. a special usage is supported by the fact that μαθητής without addition is not found for Christians generally outside Acts.[279] The full significance of this is realised only when one considers that Paul never has μαθητής in this sense (or at all), that the source of the "We" passages also does not have it in this sense (→ 443),[280] and that the post-NT writings are increasingly hellenised linguistically.[281] All these factors enable us to conclude that the use in Acts goes back to the common name by which Palestinian Christians called themselves.[282] If so, we may take it that the simple תַּלְמִידִים was the original.[283]

b. The Material Problem. As regards the material aspect of the use of μαθητής for Christians in Acts, the primary point to notice is that the relevant sections of Acts use it in the sense of those who have come to believe in Christ. In this respect the usage is analogous to that of John's Gospel.

The mark of μαθηταί in Ac. 6:7 is ὑπήκουον τῇ πίστει. In 9:26 the Jerusalem Christians doubt concerning Paul ὅτι ἐστὶν μαθητής, i.e., whether he has come to faith. Acc. to 14:22 Barnabas and Paul confirmed the souls of the μαθηταί by the admonition ἐμμένειν τῇ πίστει (cf. also 18:23). The link between μαθητής and πιστεύω may be seen also in 18:27.

The classic passage for this link in Jn. is 8:31. Here we even find the same formulae as in Ac. Jesus tells the Ἰουδαῖοι who have come to faith that they are ἀληθῶς His μαθηταί (πεπιστευκότες) if they abide in His Word (ἐὰν ὑμεῖς μείνητε ἐν τῷ

---

279 Harnack Miss., I, 411, n. 4.

280 In the case of the ἀρχαῖος μαθητής Mnason in 21:16 this would mean, in spite of Harnack Miss., I, 411, n. 2, that he was a personal disciple of Jesus (so also Jackson-Lake, I, 5, 377). Neither the Gk. name (→ 452) nor the fact that he came from Cyprus (cf. Barnabas, who was probably an apostle as well as a μαθητής, → I, 422 f.) is a decisive argument to the contrary. On 21:4 (16) → n. 283.

281 Cf. the instances in Harnack Miss., I, 411 f., n. 4.

282 If this is correct, the source used by Luke in which we find this usage must be of Palestinian origin. Perhaps it is not wholly adequate to call it Antiochene.

283 Ac. 21:4, 16 raises no difficulties, since the background is Palestinian (Tyre). There is also a certain par. in the Johannine writings. Only the Gospel speaks of the μαθηταί of Jesus, whereas the epistles and Rev. do not use the term. Since the Johannine concept is so clear and basic (→ b.), this can only mean that the word was not apposite in the epistles and Rev. → also n. 280.

λόγῳ τῷ ἐμῷ, cf. Ac. 14:22). For further links between μαθητής and πίστις cf. Jn. 2:11; 20:24 ff., and esp. 6:60 ff., where leaving Jesus is an expression of unbelief and thus signifies the end of discipleship (→ 449).

John's Gospel thus gives us real help towards an understanding of μαθητής in this sense. As it is the mark of a תַּלְמִיד/μαθητής that he should keep to what he has heard from his teacher (→ 435), so it is a mark of the μαθηταί of Jesus that they should abide in His Word (8:31). Here תַּלְמִיד can establish spiritual fellowship, even across the generations, quite apart from personal fellowship (→ 439). This usage was taken over by the primitive community. This was the more readily possible in view of the fact that the presence and activity of the Holy Spirit ensured constant direct fellowship with Jesus. At this point too — the link between discipleship and possession of the Spirit — Ac. agrees with Jn. (cf. Jn. 14:15 ff.; 15:26 f. with Ac. 9:17[27]; 13:52; 19:1 ff. [μαθηταί without the Spirit are no true μαθηταί]; 21:4). On the other hand, it was not so easy for the Greek communities to take over μαθητής in this sense because this might give rise to the idea that Christianity was simply a philosophical movement.[284] It may thus be seen why the usage did not make its way in the Greek world,[285] and why μαθητής for disciple of Jesus or Christian declined in primitive Christianity.

6. μαθηταί of Paul in Acts 9:25?

In Ac. 9:25 we read with reference to Paul: λαβόντες δὲ οἱ μαθηταὶ αὐτοῦ νυκτὸς διὰ τοῦ τείχους καθῆκαν αὐτὸν χαλάσαντες ἐν σπυρίδι. This text speaks unambiguously of disciples of Paul. It thus states something which is quite possible, since Paul as a recognised rabbi might well have μαθηταί. Yet the question arises whether what is meant are not Christians whom he assembled in Damascus, for the μαθηταί save his life, and Ac. never uses μαθητής elsewhere in the sense of Rabbinic disciples. If we cannot be more precise, the usage of the NT as a whole does at least suggest the possibility that μαθηταὶ αὐτοῦ were those who went with Paul to Damascus, who through his leadership and witness themselves came to faith, and who then rescued him from mortal peril.

There is no doubt that αὐτοῦ is in the original.[286] The reading αὐτὸν οἱ μαθηταί in EHLP S gig e syp^h sa bo is a smoothing of the difficulty.[287] It is also unlikely that αὐτοῦ could be an obj. for λαβόντες. On the other hand, there is no doubt that it is materially difficult.

In a less acute form the critical problem arises again at Ac. 14:20, where D d Ee (but not h) read: κυκλωσάντων δὲ τῶν μαθητῶν αὐτοῦ or *eius* (rather than αὐτόν).[288] If the αὐτοῦ is undoubtedly secondary here, it is more easily explained if we accept αὐτοῦ at 9:25.

---

[284] The Apologists took this intellectualistic way for apologetic reasons. Tert. even speaks occasionally of a *Christi schola* (Scorpiace, 12). Cf. Harnack Miss., I, 411, n. 4.

[285] As against this Harnack recalls (411, n. 2) that in a source used by Epiphanius (Haer., 29, 7) the Christians who moved from Jerusalem to Pella were still called μαθηταί.

[286] Zn. Ag.³, 328, n. 16, *ad loc.* rejects this on the ground that we never read of μαθηταί of Paul in the NT. J. H. Ropes shares this view in his critical ed. of Ac. (Jackson-Lake, I, 3, 89, n. *ad loc.*).

[287] There is also some support for οἱ μαθηταὶ αὐτόν or simply οἱ μαθηταί (Ropes, *ad loc.*). Zn. explains the widely attested reading αὐτοῦ as an attempt to avoid a double αὐτόν (after λαβόντες δέ and καθῆκαν). But the material objections considered by Zn. and Ropes make it very unlikely that αὐτοῦ would establish itself later.

[288] E even reads κ. δ. αὐτὸν τῶν μαθητῶν αὐτοῦ.

D. The Usage of the Early Church.

This is marked by the incursion of the Greek and Hellenistic use of μαθητής for intellectual adherence without direct commitment, and in close relation to this by the inevitable emergence of the idea of imitating Christ.[289] This is already so strong in Ignatius that only the martyr is the μαθητὴς ἀληθὴς τοῦ Χριστοῦ (R., 4, 2; 5, 3).[290] Hence the conclusion of the NT story of μαθητής is a contribution to the question of the Hellenisation of Christianity.

† συμμαθητής.

This word is rare outside the NT. The oldest instance is in Plato (Euthyd., 272c: ἐγὼ δ', ὦ Κρίτων, ἐκεῖσε μὲν ἄλλους πέπεικα συμμαθητάς μοι φοιτᾶν πρεσβύτας) in the sense of "fellow-pupil" or "fellow-apprentice." The same meaning may be seen in Ps.-Callisthenes, I, 13, 5 (p. 14, 11, ed. G. Kroll [1926]): μετὰ γὰρ τὴν διδαχὴν πᾶσαν διέσχιζε κατὰ μέρος τοὺς συμμαθητάς. It is also found in pre-Christian times in Anaxipp. Fr., 1, 2 (CAF, III, 296). Galen (p. 12, 835, ed. C. G. Kühn [1826]) quotes a remedy Διονυσίου συμμαθητοῦ for the healing of ἕλκωσις (cf. NT ἕλκος) and thus takes it to mean "fellow-student" (cf. also Diog. L., VI, 2 (2). It is not found in Preisigke Wört., nor is it used by Joseph.[1] or the LXX.

In the NT it occurs only at Jn. 11:16 for "fellow-disciple" (of Jesus), in dependence on the NT use of μαθητής, and in a context which emphasises the fellowship of the μαθηταί with Jesus, and on this basis their fellowship with one another.

In Mart. Pol., 17, 3 συμμαθητής is used already under the influence of the old Catholic use of μαθητής. The μαθηταί of Jesus embody the ideal of discipleship which one must strive to attain.

† μαθήτρια.

This is a rare word.[1] There are material reasons for this, for women are essentially outside organised education. The term is used only by later writers. Thus Diog. L., VIII, 42 (22) tells us that Pythagoras had a μαθήτρια called Theano. The same author in IV, 2 (5) mentions two women who are supposed to have belonged to the Platonic academy. In these cases the meaning is the same as that of μαθητής, "pupil." Philo has μαθητρίς in a phrase analogous to the Gk. μαθητὴς καὶ διάδοχος (Luc. Macrob., 19), i.e., μαθητρὶς καὶ διάδοχος (Deus Imm., 5). The word does not occur in Joseph.[2] or the LXX. Nor does the Rabbinate have a corresponding תַּלְמִידָה. The Rabb. view of women would preclude their studying the Law.[3] We read of certain women learned in

---

[289] → 458, and cf. Harnack Miss., I, 411 f., n. 4. Naturally μαθητής can still be used for the historical μαθηταί of Jesus, but they embody the ideal of discipleship.
[290] Cf. on this F. Kattenbusch, ZNW, 4 (1903), 124 f.; H. Schlier, *Religionsgeschichtliche Untersuchungen zu den Ignatiusbriefen* (1929), 56 f.

συμμαθητής. Liddell-Scott, Pr.-Bauer[3], *s.v.*; Bau. J.[2] on 11:16.
[1] Schl. J., 393.

μαθήτρια. Pr.-Bauer[3], *s.v.*; Leisegang, *s.v.*
[1] The same is true of the form μαθητρίς.
[2] Schl. Lk., 589 on Ac. 9:36.
[3] Cf. Str.-B., III, 561 and → I, 781 f.

Scripture, like Beruria (Valeria),[4] the wife of R. Meïr, but these are exceptions, and they raise no claim to be called תַּלְמִיד or תַּלְמִידָה.

The only NT use is at Ac. 9:36. Here Tabitha is called μαθήτρια, and the obvious meaning is that she is either "a disciple of Jesus" or "a Christian." The use of μαθητής makes the first possible, for in the Gospels we read of women followers (Mk. 15:40 f. par.; cf. Lk. 8:2 f.), and Ev. Pt., p. 21, 9 f. (Swete) calls Mary Magdalene a μαθήτρια τοῦ κυρίου. But in view of the general usage of Ac. the second sense is more likely.

† μαθητεύω.

Constructed from μαθητής, this means intrans. "to be (a.) or to become (b.) a pupil," e.g., Plut. De Vitis Decem Oratorum, IV (II, 837c): ἐμαθήτευσε δ' αὐτῷ (Isocrates) καὶ Θεόπομπός ὁ Χῖος καὶ Ἔφορος ὁ Κυμαῖος ... (sense b.) or *ibid.*, VI (II, 840 f): οἱ δὲ εἶπον μηδὲ μαθητεῦσαί τισι τὸν Αἰσχίνην (sense a.). The word does not occur in the LXX, Philo,[1] or Joseph.[2]

In the sense current in non-NT Greek the word occurs only in a vl. (B𝔎 pm) at Mt. 27:57: (Joseph of Arimathea) ἐμαθήτευσεν τῷ Ἰησοῦ. Here the inner and outer kinship with the use of μαθητής in the Gospels is palpable. Elsewhere in the NT we find a trans. use of μαθητεύω different from non-NT usage (Mt. 13:52; 28:19; Ac. 14:21), i.e., "to make disciples." Behind this peculiar NT use there possibly stands the insight that one can become a disciple of Jesus — this also stands behind Mt. 13:52 — only on the basis of a call which leads to discipleship.[3]

Rengstorf

---

[4] Cf. Jew. Enc., III, 109 f. and e.g., bEr., 53b ff.; T. Kelim BQ, 4, 17 etc.

μαθητεύω. [1] Acc. to Leisegang.

[2] Schl. Lk., 603 on Ac. 14:21.

[3] Cr.-Kö., *s.v.* notes a par. trans. use of βασιλεύω. Cf. also Bl.-Debr.[6] § 148, 3; 309, 1; suppl. p. 309 on p. 178, 11.

† Μάννα

1. Linguistic Data.

מָן — manna — is used in the OT for the miraculous food by which the Israelites were fed during the wilderness journey, Ex. 16:31, 33, 35; Nu. 11:6 f., 9; Dt. 8:3, 16; Jos. 5:12; Neh. 9:20; Ps. 78:24a. "Heavenly bread" is also used in Ps. 105:40b, "bread from heaven" in Ex. 16:4a, "bread" in Ex. 16:8, 12, 15, 22, 32, "heavenly grain" in Ps. 78:24b, and "angels' food" in Ps. 78:25a. [1]

Related in sound is the Gk. ἡ μάννα, "morsel," "crumb," "grain," esp. used for grains of incense. This is found in Gk. lit. from the time of Hippocr.; cf. also a remedy against nose-bleeding in P. Oxy., VIII, 1088, Col. I, 21 ff. (1st cent. B.C.): μάνναν φύρασον χυλῶι πράσωι καὶ ἐνάλιψον τὸν χυλὸν ἔνδοθεν, "mix incense with the juice of onions and apply inwardly to the flux." Because of the similarity of sound it may be that the Heb. μάν — so Ex. 16:31, 32 f., 35 — became the indeclinable neut. μάννα.

The LXX uses μάννα [2] for מָן at Nu. 11:6 f., 9; Dt. 8:3, 16; Jos. 5:12; 2 Εσδρ. 19:20; ψ 77:24. Philo then adopted it, e.g., Decal., 16; Congr., 173; Sacr. AC, 86; Leg. All., III, 166. Cf. Joseph. Ant., 3, 32, where we also have μάν for the sake of the popular etymology of Ex. 16:15.

The NT uses τὸ μάννα in Jn. 6:31, 49; Hb. 9:4; Rev. 2:17. It is then found in Christian usage, e.g., Ev. Eb. 4 (Epiph. Haer., 30, 13), Preisigke Sammelbuch, I, 5977.

2. Manna in the Old Testament.

Manna is found in the oldest narrative stratum of the Pentateuch. [3] It occurs along with the miraculous provision of water and quails. The ideas about manna

---

Μάννα. Thes. Steph., Pape, Pass. (-Cr.), Liddell-Scott, Moult.-Mill., Pr.-Bauer^{3}, *s.v.* On 2: Ges.-Buhl^{17}, 432; H. Gressmann, *Mose und seine Zeit* (1913), 124 ff., 136, 386, 462; H. Guthe, RE^{3}, 21, 537 ff.; P. Haupt, "Manna, Nectar and Ambrosia," *Proceedings of the American Philos. Society*, 61 (1922), 227 ff.; *American Journal of Philology*, 43 (1922), 247 ff.; A. Kaiser, "Der heutige Stand der Mannafrage," *Mitteilungen d. Thurgauischen Naturforschenden Gesellschaft*, 25 (1924), 99 ff.; L. Köhler, RGG^{2}, III, 1975 f.; A. Macalister, Art. "Manna" in Hastings DB, III, 236; M. Seligsohn, Art. "Manna" in Jew. Enc., 8, 292 ff.; cf. also bibl. in Pr.-Bauer^{3}, Ges.-Buhl, A Kaiser etc. On 3: Jew. Enc., *loc. cit.*; Moore, I, 445 ff.; Str.-B., I, 86 f.; II, 481 f.; III, 411, 737, 739, 793; IV, 506, 509, 890, 954; Volz Esch., 388 f., 404. On 4: Comm. on Jn. 6:31, 49; Hb. 9:4; Rev. 2:17.

[1] לֶחֶם אַבִּירִים; ψ 77:25: ἄρτος ἀγγέλων, cf. Wis. 16:20: ἀγγέλων τροφή.

[2] μάννα can also be used as a transcription of מִנְחָה, "tribute," "meal offering," though the correct Gk. form is μαναα.

[3] J. Hempel, *Altheb. Lit. u. ihr hellen.-jüd. Nachleben* (1930), 92 takes a different view, but he can hardly be right.

are not uniform, and the sources give evidence of redaction.[4] Two main views may be discerned, that in J[5] and that in P.[6]

Acc. to J the manna falls with the dew from heaven (Ex. 16:4a, 13b). It is a granular deposit like frost (v. 14), and when the people see it they ask with astonishment: מָן הוּא, "What is this?" Hence the name מָן, "manna"[7] (v. 15a, 31a). It is like coriander seed and tastes like honey (v. 31b). It is gathered daily as required (v. 21a), early in the morning before the sun melts it (v. 21b). Yahweh sent this miraculous food to His people during the 40 years of wandering (v. 35a). The view in the different strata of P, and in the editorial Nu. 11:7-9,[8] is rather different. Here it is baked and cooked (Ex. 16:23; Nu. 11:8), after having been ground in handmills and beaten in a mortar (Nu. 11:8; cf. Ps. 78:24b). It also becomes uneatable through corruption (Ex. 16:20, 24), tastes like fresh oil, and is compared with coriander seed and bdellium (Nu. 11:7, 8b).[9]

Obviously different natural phenomena sponsored the two accounts.[10] Behind J is tamarisk manna, a honey-like fluid, and behind P the manna lichen.[11] Both are magnified and idealised in the accounts, and various features are developed independently and then imported into the original.

3. Manna in Later Literature.

In the ideal picture of the wandering projected later, manna plays an essential part. Acc. to the Rabb. view manna, with the well, i.e., the rock from which Moses smote water,[12] was created on the evening of the sixth day just before Yahweh began to keep the Sabbath.[13] It was also considered why Yahweh created it. R. Jehuda b. Jose (c. 180) says: "Three good providers (פרנסים) rose up for Israel, Moses, Aaron and Miriam, and for their sakes three good gifts were given, the well, the pillar of cloud and the manna. The people owed the well to Miriam, the pillar of cloud to Aaron, and the manna to Moses."[14] In Ex. r., 25 on 16:4, however, the people receives miraculous food and drink as a reward for accepting the Torah.

---

[4] How widely students differ here may be seen from a comparison between Gressmann, 124, n. 2; Holzinger on Ex. 16:11 ff. in Kautzsch, I, 119 ff.; also on Nu. 11:4 ff., *ibid.*, 217 f.; and O. Eissfeldt, *Hexateuch-Synopse* (1922), 37 ff., 139* ff., 161*; cf. also the comm. on Ex. 16.

[5] Following Gressmann, 124, n. 2 we attribute Ex. 16:4a, 13b-15a, 31, 21, 35a to J. Acc. to Gressmann, 126 this is the oldest part of J and does not yet contain the Sabbath commandment, though Gressmann sees two variants into which the Sabbath motif is interwoven (16:4b, 5, 27, 29-30). On this cf. Gressmann, 128, n. 3 with 124, n. 2. It is perhaps better to ascribe Ex. 16:27-30, with 22-26, to P, with Holzinger; v. 5 is an editorial anticipation of v. 22. To J also belongs Nu. 11:4-6; cf. Gressm., 124, n. 2 and Holzinger, *ad loc.*

[6] Acc. to Gressm. P includes Ex. 16:1-3, 6 f. (with editorial additions), 9-13a, 15b-17, 19 f., 22-26, 32, 34a, 35b. Vv. 22-26 are late (Holzinger, Ps), cf. also 32a, 34a. It is perhaps better to take 32-34 as a unity, cf. Holzinger (Ps) and Eissfeldt, 141* f. Nu. 11:7-9 is editorial.

[7] On the popular etym. cf. Gressmann, 126, n. 3, and for another (mistaken) view, Haupt, *Amer. Journ.*, 248: "The popular etymology ... must be a late gloss."

[8] Since the ideas of P and the redactor are the same, the relevant materials can be treated together.

[9] P is marked by a strong theological spiritualising of the story, cf. v. Rad, "Die Priesterschrift im Hexateuch," BWANT, IV, 13 (1934), 56 f. Dt. 8:3 takes a further step [G. v. Rad].

[10] For a different view, which can hardly be correct, cf. Gressm., 135 ff.

[11] Kaiser, 103 ff., 115 ff.

[12] Ex. 17:6.

[13] S. Dt. § 355 on 33:21; Ab., 5, 6; M. Ex. on 16:32; bPes., 54a; Tg. J. I on Nu. 22:28; cf. Str.-B., IV, 506.

[14] T. Sota, 11, 10; also bTaan., 9a; cf. M. Ex. on 16:35; Seder Olam r., 10; Nu. r., 1 on 1:1; Tanch. B במדבר § 2 (1b); Lv. r., 27 on 22:27 etc. Cf. also jSota, 17c, 11 ff. Cf. Str.-B., II, 482.

It is to be noted that the manna and water are here mentioned together, and that acc. to the Rabb. both accompanied the Israelites through the wilderness.[15] This combination may have been suggested by the idea of the food and drink of the gods, nectar and ambrosia.[16] That something of the kind was in the mind of the Rabb. is suggested by the description of the food. Acc. to Ps. 78:25a (late) it is angels' food[17] of which one can never tire, since it satisfies all tastes (Wis. 16:20). The Rabb. worked out this thought further, cf. S. Nu., 89 on 11:8.[18] That manna was divine food may be seen also in a later addition to P, Ex. 16:32-34 (→ n. 6). Here manna is obviously laid out for Yahweh, like the showbread.[19] It is true that the original meaning of the cultic act is no longer clear to the author; he simply sees in it a recollection of Yahweh's miracle of feeding.

Acc. to the Rabbis the ark contained a phial[20] or little basket[21] with manna. When the ark was hidden under Josiah, the manna disappeared. Only Elijah will bring it back.[22] Since Ex. 16:32-34 indicates the presence of manna in the later temple, the Rabb. statements are to be viewed as constructions designed to idealise the past.[23]

In contrast to Joseph. Ant., 3, 31 the Rabb. and apocr. writings say that there is no manna for the present inhabitants of earth. As divine food it is reserved for those who dwell in heaven. Acc. to R. Meïr (*c.* 150) the mills which grind the manna for the righteous deceased are in the third heaven.[24] That the righteous eat manna in the hereafter is also the view of Zabdai b. Levi (*c.* 240) in Tanch. בשלח 21 (33b, Buber). Along somewhat the same lines the legendary phoenix takes to itself "the manna of heaven and the dew of earth"[25] in Gr. Bar. 7.

The manna motif also occurs in teaching about the Messianic kingdom. It is true that manna is no longer needed here, since unheard of fruitfulness is part of this kingdom. If it still has a place, this is probably because of the belief that the coming age of salvation must correspond to the ideal past. Divine food given to men is part of this past, and hence it must be present in the Messianic kingdom. Thus we are told in Sib. Fr., 3, 84 ff. that those who worship the true God will dwell for ever in the green garden of Paradise and eat the sweet bread which comes from the starry heaven. Acc. to S. Bar. 29:8 manna again falls from heaven in the age of salvation, and Eleazar Chasama (*c.* 110) in M. Ex. 16, 25 even expects manna on the Sabbath.[26] Worth noting is the saying of R. Jizchaq (*c.* 300) in Qoh. r. on 1:9: "Corresponding to the first redeemer (is also) the last redeemer ... As the first redeemer caused manna to fall (from heaven), so the last redeemer will cause manna to fall ... As the first redeemer caused the well to gush forth, so the last redeemer will cause the well to gush forth."[27] In

[15] The same idea is presupposed in 1 C. 10:3 f. → n. 31.

[16] Cf. on this K. Wernicke, Pauly-W., I (1894), 1809 ff.

[17] Aqiba (d. *c.* 135) calls manna the food of ministering angels in bYoma, 75b, Bar.; cf. M. Ex. on 16:15; S. Nu., 88 on 11:6; Midr. Ps. 78 § 3 (173a).

[18] The Gentiles, on the other hand, could not eat manna, cf. Tanch. B בשלח § 22 (34a). For further examples of its many possibilities of use cf. M. Ex., 18, 9; 16, 21; bYoma, 75a; Nu. r., 7 on 5:1; Ex. r., 25 on 16:4. Cf. Str.-B., II, 481.

[19] Cf. Gressmann, 136, n. 1.

[20] Tg. O. on Ex. 16:33 f.; cf. Tg. J. I, *ad loc.*

[21] T. Yoma, 3, 7; Ab R. Nath, 41 (67a).

[22] M. Ex. 16:33 par.; cf. Str.-B., III, 739 f.

[23] Though cf. W. Oesterley-T. Robinson, *Hebrew Religion* (1930), 144.

[24] Cf. bChag., 12b; on this R. Meyer, "Hellenistisches in d. rabb. Anthropologie," BWANT, IV, 22 (1937), 52 f.

[25] V. Ryssel, Kautzsch Pseudepigr., 453.

[26] For further material cf. Volz Esch., 388 f.

[27] Cf. Rt. r. on 2:14; Pesikt. r., 15 (72b); Pesikt., 49b; Cant. r. on 2:9 f.; Nu. r., 11 on 6:22; Str.-B., II, 481.

the age of salvation men will enjoy the same miraculous food and drink as did the wilderness generation.

4. New Testament Views of Manna.

a. In the NT the manna motif occurs first in Jn. 6:31, 49. The word is used twice in alternation with "bread from heaven" [28] (ψ 77:24). The phrases "bread of life" and "living bread" (→ I, 477, 25 ff.) have no parallels in the OT or Jewish writings. Jn. 6:1-13 is an account of the miraculous feeding by the Sea of Tiberias. Jesus has here shown Himself to be a prophet, and the Galileans want to crown him king (v. 14 f.). The story of crossing the lake follows (vv. 16-21), and then Jn. 6:22-31 describes a disputation with the Jews which culminates in the demand for a sign (v. 30 f.): τί οὖν ποιεῖς σὺ σημεῖον, ἵνα ἴδωμεν καὶ πιστεύσωμέν σοι; τί ἐργάζῃ: οἱ πατέρες ἡμῶν τὸ μάννα ἔφαγον ἐν τῇ ἐρήμῳ, καθώς ἐστιν γεγραμμένον· ἄρτον ἐκ τοῦ οὐρανοῦ ἔδωκεν αὐτοῖς φαγεῖν (ψ 77:24).

As Moses showed the wilderness generation that he was the redeemer by providing it with manna, so Jesus should work a corresponding miracle, and then they would believe that He was the Messiah. The demand for a sign is rather strange immediately after the miraculous feeding, which is obviously an attestation in Jn. The explanation of this difficulty in composition is perhaps that Jn. needs a transition to the sermon on the bread of life. Thus 6:32 ff. is an answer to the demand for a sign and also a transcending of the Messianic hope of the people with its orientation to the ideal past. To the statement of opponents (v. 31): "Our fathers ate manna in the wilderness," the Johannine Jesus replies: "Moses did not give you bread from heaven" (v. 32). Heavenly bread, or manna, as divine food, would necessarily confer immortality. But the wilderness manna did not have this lifegiving power. Hence Jesus says in v. 49: "Your fathers ate manna in the wilderness and are dead." [29] Thus Moses — to fill out Jn. — is not a perfect image of the redeemer. The age of salvation which dawns with Jesus is quite different from the Messianic future expected by the Jews and prefigured in the wilderness period. In contrast to the manna of the past, the food of the age of salvation which has come with Jesus confers immortality. This food is the true bread from heaven which God Himself gives (v. 32b). It gives life both to the cosmos (v. 33, 51) and to the individual (v. 50, 51). Jesus Himself is this living bread (v. 35, 48). [30] Jn. thus rejects the idea that manna is an expression both of the ideal past and also of the Messianic future. He cannot accept the Jewish model as adequate. He also offers us some early Christian reflection on the Lord's Supper. [31]

b. Hb. 9:4 also refers to manna. Here the manna is laid up in the ark in a golden vessel along with the tables of the Law and Aaron's rod: στάμνος χρυσῆ

---

[28] Jn. 6:32 f., 41, 50 f., 58.

[29] Cf. v. 58.

[30] Cf. the important par. in Philo; for him manna is the prototype of the *logos* and the heavenly food of the soul, → I, 477. The idea is materially stronger in Jn., since the Lord's Supper is the presupposition of the whole address.

[31] It is to be noted that Pl. in 1 C. 10:3 ff. commences his discussion of the Lord's Supper and its proper use with a ref. to the miraculous wilderness feeding. The supernatural food and drink of the wilderness period (v. 3 f.) find par. in the bread and cup of the Lord's Supper (v. 16). Instructive here is the predominance of the ethical aspect over the sacramental. The idea that the Lord's Supper is manna, the food of the inaugurated age of salvation, is to be found on an ancient communion vessel with the inscr. φάγε μάνα (→ 462).

ἔχουσα τὸ μάννα. It is no accident that Hb. 9:4 concurs closely at this point with Rabbinic tradition, e.g., in T. Yoma, 3, 7 par. (→ n. 21). For in both cases we have a scribal deduction concerning the ark on the basis of Nu. 17:4, 16 ff. and Ex. 16:33. Hb. 9:4 has no more historical value than the Rabbinic tradition. According to 1 K. 8:9 [32] only the tables were laid in the ark. [33]

c. Rev. 2:17 is also related to later Jewish belief: τῷ νικῶντι δώσω αὐτῷ τοῦ μάννα τοῦ κεκρυμμένου. If manna is in time taken from men and given only to those who finally persevere and triumph, this corresponds exactly to the later idea that manna is the food of the blessed in the last time. As in contemporary Jewish literature, the manna of Rev. 7:17 has a counterpart in water: τὸ ἀρνίον ... ὁδηγήσει αὐτοὺς ἐπὶ ζωῆς πηγὰς ὑδάτων; cf. also Rev. 21:6; 22:1, 17.

R. Meyer

† μαραναθά

1. This occurs in the NT only at 1 C. 16:22 in the greeting in the apostle's own hand: εἴ τις οὐ φιλεῖ τὸν κύριον, ἤτω ἀνάθεμα. μαραναθά. [1] ἡ χάρις τοῦ κυρίου Ἰησοῦ (Χριστοῦ) μεθ' ὑμῶν. It is found also in Did., 10, 6 at the end of a series of eucharistic prayers: Ἐλθέτω χάρις καὶ παρελθέτω ὁ κόσμος

---

[32] Cf. 2 Ch. 5:10; Damasc., 5, 3 (= Charles, 7, 5).
[33] Cf. K. Galling, *Bibl. Reallexikon* (1937), 343 f.

μαραναθά. Comm. on 1 C. 16:22 by J. C. K. v. Hofmann² (1874); F. Godet; P. W. Schmiedel² (1892); Heinr. 1 K.; J. Weiss⁹ (1910); Holtzmann NT, II; Ltzm. K.; J. Sickenberger⁴ (1932); Schl. K.; Bchm. K.⁴ (1936). Comm. on Did., 10, 6, Zahn Forsch., III (1884), 294; A. Harnack, TU, II, 1-2 (1886), 34; C. Taylor, *The Teaching of the Twelve Apostles* (1886), 77 ff.; P. Drews, *Hndbch. zu den nt. lichen Apokryphen* (1904), 269 ff.; R. Knopf, Lietzmann's Hndbch., Suppl. I (1920), 29 f.; H. Lietzmann in RGG², I, 32. Art. "Maranatha," EB, III, 2935 f. (H. W. Hogg); Hastings DB, III, 241 ff. (J. H. Thayer); DAC, I, 56, *s.v.* "Anathema" (R. W. Moss); F. Vigouroux, *Dictionnaire de la bible*, IV (1908), 712 ff. (F. Vigouroux); J. Orr, *International Standard Bible Encyclopaedia*, III (1925), 1984; G. Kittel, RGG², III, 1983; H. Leclerq, *Dictionnaire d'Archéologie chrétienne*, X, 2 (1932), 1729 f.; Lex. Th. K., VI, 862 (O. Pretzl); Pr.-Bauer³, 813. Also A. Klostermann, *Probleme im Aposteltexte* (1883), 220-246; E. Nestle, *Theol. Studien aus Württemberg*, 5 (1884), 186-188; E. Kautzsch, *Grammatik des Bibl. Aramäischen* (1884), 12 and 174; W. Riedel, "A u. Ω," ThStKr, 74 (1901), 295 f.; T. Nöldeke, GGA (1884), 1023; N. Schmidt, JBL, 13 (1894), 50-60; JBL, 15 (1896), 44, n. 14; Dalman WJ, I, 147 ff., 268 ff.; Dalman Gr., 152, n. 3; 357; n. 1; Dalman, *Jesus-Jeschua* (1922), 12; E. v. d. Goltz, *Das Gebet in d. ältesten Christenheit* (1901), 82, 132, 212 f., 218; Zahn Einl., I³ (1906), 216 f.; A. Deissmann, *Die Urgesch. d. Christentums im Lichte d. Sprachforschung* (1910), 26-28; R. Seeberg, *Aus Religion u. Geschichte*, I (1906), 121; II (1909), 311-313; *Der Ursprung des Christusglaubens* (1914), 15; *Lehrbuch d. Dogmengesch.*, I³ (1920), 166 f.; E. Hommel, ZNW, 15 (1914), 317-322; J. Weiss, *Das Urchristentum* (1917), 28 f., 47, 131, 255, 351; F. J. Dölger, *Sol Salutis*² (1925) (*Liturgiegesch. Forschungen* 4/5), 198-210; E. Peterson, Εἷς θεός (1926), 130 f.; *Byzantinisch-Neugriechische Jbchr.*, 3 (1922), 185; C. Fabricius in *R. Seeberg-Festschr.*, I (1929), 26-32.

[1] As regards textual criticism cf. the collection of various spellings in the MSS in N. Schmidt, JBL, 13 (1894), 50 f.

οὗτος· Ὡσαννὰ τῷ θεῷ Δαβίδ. εἴ τις ἅγιός ἐστιν, ἐρχέσθω· εἴ τις οὐκ ἔστι, μετανοείτω· μαραναθά· ἀμήν.

It is found more frequently in later ecclesiastical use, often with ἀνάθεμα, to give weight to a solemn curse. There is always quotation from, or allusion to, 1 C. 16:22.[2] Thus in a Christian burial inscr. from Salamis (either 4th or 5th cent., CIG, IV, 9303) we read: (Whoever lays another corpse in this grave between the two who rest here) ... ἀνάθεμα ἤτω· μαραναθάν. Cf. also the canon of the Fourth Council of Toledo (633 A.D.): *qui contra hanc nostram definitionem praesumpserit, anathema maranatha hoc est, perditio in adventu domini sit* (can. 75).[3]

2. The term is undoubtedly Aram. But it is hard to explain it linguistically. It may represent מָרַנָא תָא or מָרַן אֱתָא, "Our Lord, come!" or מָרַן אֲתָא, "Our Lord has come."

There are considerable linguistic and material difficulties in the way of any other explanation, and derivations other than from the verb אתא are out of the question.[4] So A. Klostermann's view[5] that μαραναθά = מָרַן אָתָא = "Our Lord is the sign," a phrase used when giving the brotherly kiss (as supposedly intimated in the φιλεῖν of 1 C. 16:22a). Independently of Klostermann, E. Hommel[6] gives the same linguistic explanation (Aram. אָתָא, Heb. אוֹת, "sign"), but applies it differently, pointing out that the Aram. and Heb. words are made up etymologically of the first and last words of the alphabet (א and ת), so that the meaning is: "Our Lord is the sign" = the א and ת = τὸ ἄλφα καὶ τὸ ὦ (Rev. 22:13).[7] Hofmann's explanation[8] (מַר אַנְתָּה, "Thou art Lord") is to be rejected on the same grounds.[9]

In interpretation one should begin with the first of the two words, the Aram. מָרֵא (st. determ.: מָרָא from *mār'ā*) "lord" with the suffix of the first person plur. In older Aram. this suffix is *-ánā*, cf. bibl. Aram.,[10] the Nabatean inscr.[11] and to some degree Jewish-Palestinian Aram.[12] In later Aram. the unstressed *ā* disappears. Hence we find the suffix *-an* in Jewish-Palestinian Aram.[13] (with *-ánā*), Christian Palestinian,[14]

---

[2] So also Zahn Einl., I³, 217.

[3] Leclerq, 1729 f.; for a further list of instances of later ecclesiastical use cf. Vigouroux, 713 f.

[4] Against these explanations cf. Zahn Einl., I³, 216.

[5] *Probleme* ... (1883), 220-246.

[6] ZNW, 15 (1914), 317-322.

[7] And earlier Riedel, 296. Acc. to Peterson, *Jahrbücher*, 3, 185 the view of Klostermann and Hommel was also presented by Bruston in *Revue de théol. et des questions relig.*, XXII, 402-8.

[8] v. Hofmann, 401 f.

[9] On Luther's *maharam motha* (Heb. מַחֲרָם מוֹתָה, "devoted to death") cf. P. W. Schmiedel, *Thess.-Kor.*² (1892), 208 f., *ad loc.*; Klostermann, 227 ff.; N. Schmidt, JBL, 13 (1894), 51.

[10] H. Bauer-P. Leander, *Gramm. d. Bibl.-Aram.* (1927) § 20 q. But in the P. Eleph. we always find מראן *mār'an* "our lord" (common as a title); cf. A. Cowley, *Aram. Papyri of the Fifth Century B.C.* (1922), Index, *s.v.* מרא.

[11] Always מראנא *mar'ánā* (once מרנא) "our lord" (title of the Nabatean kings); *v.* J. Cantineau, *Le Nabatéen*, II (1932), 117 with many examples.

[12] So in Tg. O.: Dalman Gr., 109; 202 f.

[13] Dalman Gr., *loc. cit.*

[14] F. Schulthess, *Gramm. d. christl.-pal. Aram.* (1924) § 57.

Syriac,[15] Mandaean,[16] and the language of bTalmud.[17] It is hard to say for certain whether "our lord" would be מָרַנָא[18] or מָרַן in popular Aram. in Palestine (and Syria) in NT times; either is possible.[19]

But this distinction does not affect the interpretation of μαραναθά. This depends more on the second word, either the imp. or perf. of אתא "to come." a. The imp. is either אֱתָא (so mostly in Jewish Pal. Aram., with the less common תָא[20] though we also find the initial א in the imp. in Christian Pal. Aram.[21]), or תָא (rare in Jewish Pal. Aram.;[22] always in Syriac and the language of bTalmud).[23] In this light μαραναθά is מָרַנָא תָא[24] or מָרַן אֱתָא,[25] "our Lord, come." Both are linguistically possible. b. The perf. is also free from objections: מָרַן אֲתָא, "our Lord has come." The early Church

---

[15] T. Nöldeke, *Syr. Gramm.*[2] (1898) § 65.

[16] T. Nöldeke, *Mand. Gramm.* (1875), 88.

[17] In bTalmud we occasionally find the older *-ānā* as well as *-an,* but this is due to the secondary influence of Targumic on the authors [G. Dalman in a letter]. In solemn titles (e.g., מרנא ורבנא) this *-ānā* even persists into medieval Jewish Aram.

[18] Thus מָרַנָא is the grammatically correct vocalisation, not the commonly found מָרָנָא (cf. Pr.-Bauer[3], *s.v.*). It is true that in Bibl. Aram. we find the Masoretic form of the suffix *-ānā* (e.g., Da. 3:17 אֱלָהַנָא), but MSS with supralinear pointing have the correct *-ănā* with the short *a*.

[19] G. Dalman expresses in a letter the view that *maran* did not become the popular form of "our lord," cf. Schl. K., 460: The full suffix *ana* was no longer common. On the other hand, one may refer to the name of the god Μάρνας of Gaza (first found on the coins of Hadrian, more common in the 3rd cent. A.D.). This can only be מרנא ("our lord") in Gk., cf. W. Baudissin, *Kyrios* (1929), II, 38-41; IV, 186 f.; for further bibl. on Μάρνας cf. Dölger, *op. cit.*, 201, n. 4. On the other hand, one might cite in favour of מָרַן the Μάριν in Philo Flacc., 39, the cry with which the Alexandrians mockingly greeted Agrippa I as king in 38 A.D. But whether this Μάριν = מָרַן "our lord" is doubtful. Dalman Gr., 152, n. 3 sees מָרִי "my lord."

[20] Dalman, 356 f.

[21] אתא or אתי = *ethē*: F. Schulthess, 73. In P. Eleph., too, we once find the imp. אתי (Achiqar narrative, line 118). Bibl. Aram, too, has the initial א in the imp.: Da. 3:26 אֱתוֹ (imp. plur.).

[22] Acc. to Dalman, 97 the form תָא is esp. Galilean, where omission of the initial א and vocalisation is common in other cases. C. Brockelmann, *Syrische Gramm.*[5] (1938) § 32, n. 2 suggests that the אֱ dropped away because in the common imperatives תָא ("come") and זיל ("go," from אזל) the emphatic command gave rise to a quick form without vocalisation.

[23] In Mandaean we find the form אתא (Nöldeke, *Mand. Gramm.*, 259). The final *a* of אֱתָא and תָא (as distinct from the paradigm of the verba tertiae י,ו) is to be explained as the relic of an original inflection tertiae א (thus root אתא, not אתי); Nöldeke, *Gramm. d. neusyrischen Sprache* (1868), 244, n. 1.

[24] So first G. Bickell, *Zschr. f. Katholische Theol.,* 8 (1884), 403, n. 3 and J. Halévy, *Revue des études juives,* 9 (1884), 9, with the assent of T. Nöldeke and J. Wellhausen (GGA, 1884, p. 1023); also E. Kautzsch, ZwTh, 28 (1885), 128 and ThStKr, 74 (1901), 296, n. 1, after initial rejection (*Gramm. d. Bibl.-Aram.* [1884], 174); Dalman Gr., 152, n. 3; Zahn Einl., I[3], 216, and most scholars to-day.

[25] So esp. G. Dalman, *Jesus-Jeschua* (1922), 12. αθα is just as possible as εθα as a transcription of אֱתָא; cf. Dalman Gr., 84 f. and esp. the examples in N. Schmidt, JBL, 13 (1894), 52.

always takes it this way.[26] Yet this interpretation does not really fit the sense and context too well (→ 472). Thus modern expositors usually modify it by seeing here a prophetic perf.: "Our Lord will (soon) come" (at the *parousia,* cf. Phil. 4:5 : ὁ κύριος ἐγγύς).[27] But, though we find the prophetic perf. in bibl. Heb., to the best of my knowledge there is not a single instance in all Aram.[28] Hence to construe the perf. אָתָא as "our Lord comes" in the fut. tense is hardly possible.[29] On the other hand, to take it as a present perf.: "Our Lord has come, is present," is free from linguistic difficulties.[30]

For the linguistic form of μαραναθά we may refer to a historical par.[31] with an analogous Aram. formula in a Gk. text. Stephanus Byzantinus quotes from Philo Byblius, *s.v.* Λαοδίκεια a passage[32] in which the earlier name of the city (Ῥάμιθα) is explained : κεραυνωθεὶς γάρ τις ποιμὴν ἔλεγε Ῥαμάνθας, τουτέστιν ἀφ' ὕψους ὁ θεός· Ῥάμαν γὰρ τὸ ὕψος, Ἄθας δὲ ὁ θεός. Here the shepherd's cry ῥαμάνθας when struck by lightning is undoubtedly interpreted incorrectly.[33] ῥάμαν is the name of the Syrian god (of thunder) Hadad-Rammān (OT Rimmon).[34] W. Baudissin[34] (adopting the conjecture of Salmasius :[35] ῥαμανάθας) thus explains ῥαμάνθας as רמן את, "Ramman (the thunderer) art thou," while R. Dussaud[36] rightly refers to אתא, "to come." Adopting the same conjecture, he interprets it as רַמָּן אֲתָא, "Ramman has come, is present" (in the annihilating flash of lightning). But one might just as well keep to the traditional text and take ῥαμάνθας as רַמָּן תָּא: "Ramman, come." It is true that on this view the cry does not stand in direct logical connection with the situation of the smitten shepherd. But this is a cultic legend in which the stereotyped cry : "Ramman, come," which was constantly used in the worship of this god, is placed on the lips of the shepherd as his last cry when struck by lightning (visited by the god). In the case of this ῥαμάνθας, too, both the perf. and the imp. are possible.[37]

Linguistic research thus offers three equally possible meanings of μαραναθά : 1. The prayer "Lord, come" as a petition for the *parousia* ; 2. the confession "our Lord has come" (into the world in lowliness); 3. the statement "our Lord is now

[26] Chrys., Thdrt., etc.; cf. also Dölger, *op. cit.,* 200, n. 2; Zahn Einl., I[3], 216; the fullest patristic examples are in F. Vigouroux, *Dict. de la bible,* IV (1908), 713. The Copt. Did. Fr. in the Brit. Museum also has μαραναθά at 10, 6 with ὁ κύριος ἦλθεν, C. Schmidt, ZNW, 24 (1925), 98.

[27] Cf. Schl. K., 460 : "With the Syr. perfect the one who cries sets himself at the moment when the Lord comes ... His new coming in glory is proclaimed."

[28] Cf. C. Brockelmann, *Grundriss d. vgl. Gramm. d. semitischen Sprachen,* II (1913), 151 ff. J. C. K. v. Hofmann, 1 K.[2] (1874), 401 f. already notes this against a prophetic perf., cf. also F. Field, *Otium Norvicense,* III (1881), 110 f.; Nestle, *Theol. Studien,* 5, 187; Zahn Einl., I[3], 216; stressed esp. by N. Schmidt, JBL, 13 (1894), 54.

[29] G. Dalman assures me in a letter that the prophetic perf. may be ruled out.

[30] So Zahn Forsch., III, 294 on Did., 10, 6.

[31] D. Heinsius, *Sacrarum Exercitationum ad NT libri XX*[2] (1640), 392 on 1 Cor. 16:22 draws attention to this, through it is not adduced in modern theological lit.

[32] K. Müller, *Fragm. historic. graec.,* III (1840), 575.

[33] Quite wrong is the interpretation of A. Berkelius in Stephanus Byzantinus, III (1825), 974 : *"Rham attha vel Rham anth = celsus es tu,"* cf. T. de Pinedo, *ibid.,* IV (1825), 737: "ῥαμάνθας = רם (Heb.): *excelsus* + אנתה (Aram.): *tu."*

[34] W. Baudissin in RE[3], XVII, 5, R. Dussaud in Pauly-W., VII (1912), 2158.

[35] Cf. Stephanus Byzantinus, II (1924), 397.

[36] → n. 34, and more fully *Journal asiatique,* 1910, II, 646 f.

[37] Taylor, 77 ff. believed he had found another par. to μαραναθά in the sense "Lord, come" in later Jewish literature, namely, the אמן בא, "Amen, come," in the acrostic of an ancient synagogue prayer. But this is a misconception on Taylor's part, for what we have here is not אמן בא, but אמן ב״א = אמן ברוך אתה; Dalman, *Jesus-Jeschua* (1922), 28.

present" (i.e., in worship, and especially the Lord's Supper). Decision between these possibilities can be made only on the basis of the origin of the word and the context of 1 C. 16:22 and Did., 10, 6.

3. The question of origin is closely linked with the problem of an Aram. term in the Greek text. Why does Paul, when writing to Corinth, where Aram. was not current, conclude with an untranslated Aramaic statement?[38] It is hardly adequate to reply that Paul wished to give a special hint or warning in their own secret language to the Judaisers against whom he had just pronounced the ἀνάθεμα.[39] For one thing, it is not certain that in 1 C. 16:22a he has in view specific opponents in Corinth. Perhaps, in this short final greeting, he is speaking more generally.[40] Again, such a special hint would not really demand a sudden transition into Aramaic.[41] The untranslated Aram. term is meaningful only if it is a fixed formula well-known in the churches. Such a formula might well have arisen in a congregation which spoke only Aramaic, and attained there such special significance and so fixed a form that it remained in the original Aramaic when adopted in Greek speaking congregations. This means that the origin of μαραναθά can be sought only in the first Palestinian community, that it had an important place already in the worship of this community, and that as a fixed term, like the Hebrew ἀμήν or ὡσαννά, it was then adopted untranslated into the worship of the Greek speaking Christian world.

Thus μαραναθά is an important and authentic witness to the faith of the primitive Palestinian community.[42] This confessed Jesus, the exalted Christ, as its Lord. It spoke of Him and prayed to Him[43] as "our Lord." Here, then, is the origin of the ascription of the name "Lord," the title κύριος, to Jesus — a title which in Paul especially takes on profound and comprehensive significance in opposition to the κύριοι of the Hellenistic world.[44]

The derivation of μαραναθά from the first Palestinian community has been contested by Heitmüller and Bousset in the interests of their thesis that the title κύριος ("Lord") is first ascribed to Jesus in Hellenistic Christianity. μαραναθά did not have to arise in Palestine. It could have come into use in bilingual Antioch or Damascus, and become familiar to Paul there.[45] Decisive against this view is the fact that it is impossible to

---

[38] It is to be noted in contrast that the Aram. ἀββᾶ is always translated, Mk. 14:36; R. 8:15; Gl. 4:6.

[39] So the comm. of Hofmann, Schmiedel etc., *ad loc.*; Zahn Einl., I³, 217; Weiss, *Urchristentum,* 131, 255; P. Althaus, NkZ, 26 (1915), 517; also Schl. K., 460: "To those who come from the Orient Paul presents in the form in which they know it the cry which resounds through the whole Church and which proclaims to them the Judge ..."

[40] This is emphasised by Bchm. 1 K., *ad loc.*

[41] This is rightly emphasised by Klostermann, *Probleme,* 222 f.

[42] Origin in the first Pal. community is emphasised by Deissmann, 27 f.; v. d. Goltz, *Das Gebet,* 132; R. Seeberg, *Aus Religion,* II, 313; *Der Ursprung,* 15; Weiss, *Urchristentum,* 28 f.; P. Feine, *Nt.liche Theol.*⁴ (1922), 140; C. Fabricius, 26 ff. ("a primitive confession of Christianity"); Ltzm. 1 K., *ad loc.*; G. Kittel in RGG², III, 1983; "Jesus Christus, Gottes Sohn u. unser Herr" (*Wittenberger Reihe, Heft* 7) (1937), 12; cf. also → n. 46.

[43] v. d. Goltz, 82: "The oldest prayer to Jesus Himself."

[44] J. Weiss, *Urchristentum,* 351; Ltzm. R., Excurs. on 10:9; Deissmann LO, 298; W. Foerster, → III, 1094.

[45] W. Heitmüller, ZNW, 13 (1912), 333 f.; in a weaker form ZThK, 25 (1915), 176 f.; W. Bousset, *Kyrios Christos*¹ (1913), 103, n. 3; ² (1921), 84; cf. H. Böhlig, ZNW, 14 (1913), 28 f. The suggestion of W. Bousset, *Jesus der Herr* (1916), 22 f. that μαραναθά was a Jewish oath or conjuration, and that the title *māran* ("Lord") thus refers to God rather than Jesus, was soon abandoned by him (*Kyrios Christos*² [1921], 84, n. 3); cf. on

explain why an Aram. formula should spread into the Greek speaking world from bilingual Antioch. Such an occurrence is conceivable only if the term originates with the primitive Aramaic speaking Palestinian community.[46] Even the Syrian ῥαμάνθας (→ 469), which Bousset did not know, does not contradict this. It simply proves something which need cause no surprise, namely, that there were divine cults which had similar "come" formulae .

4. In Did., 10, 6 μαραναθά is closely linked with the Lord's Supper. It does not come directly in the eucharistic prayer, however, but in the context: "Whoso is unholy (may not come to the Lord's Supper, but first) μετανοείτω, μαραναθά. It is obvious that μαραναθά is here to be construed as a confirmation or basis of the warning to repent.[47] This would fit in well with the interpretation: "Our Lord is present." As a threat it is then a reference to the presence of the risen Lord at the Lord's Supper.[48] This presence will not tolerate the unholy (cf. the same thought in 1 C. 11:27-30). It is easy enough to see in the term a similar threat in 1 C. 16:22, for the context is much the same: "He who does not love the Lord, let him be cursed. μαραναθά." Thus, if we take it to mean "the Lord is present," Paul is saying: "You know that in the congregation we confess the presence of the risen Lord with the cry μαραναθά, and His presence, expressed in this cry, excludes from membership those who do not love Him."

If we adopt the other linguistic interpretation and see in μαραναθά the prayer "Lord, come," we cannot link it so directly with the context of 1 C. 16:22 or Did., 10, 6.[49] Nevertheless, this view finds strong support in Rev. 22:20, where the promise of Jesus: "I come quickly," evokes the response of the community: "Amen, yes, come, Lord Jesus." Here again the basis is probably ancient liturgical usage in the worship of the primitive community.[50] The ἔρχου κύριε Ἰησοῦ seems to be a translation of μαραναθά, "Lord, come."[51] In Did., 10, 6 this "Lord, come" would then be a cry at the Lord's Supper, and by quoting it in 1 C. 16:22 Paul would be impressing on the Corinthian congregation once again in short and pregnant form the decisive content of the Christian expectation of faith.

Either way it seems that μαραναθά is connected with celebration of the Lord's Supper.[52] This is the original setting of the cry of the community. For on the one side an essential element in the Lord's Supper is the certainty of the personal

---

this the note of G. Kittel, RGG², III, 1983. As regards the fact that *māran* can refer only to Jesus cf. the note on Syriac usage in P. Schwen, "Afrahat," *Neue Studien zur Geschichte d. Theologie u. d. Kirche,* II (1907), 74.

[46] Cf., with ref. to μαραναθά, the criticism of W. Bousset by Althaus, 517 f.; P. Wernle, ZThK, 25 (1915), 19 f.; W. Foerster, *Herr ist Jesus* (1924), 28 etc.; → III, 1094.

[47] This is rightly seen by Peterson, Εἷς θεός, 130 f. But he goes too far when he deduces that μαραναθά is to be taken simply as a form of exorcism in an apotropaic sense. The inscr. of Salamis, CIG, IV, 9303 lends no support to this (→ 467).

[48] Zahn, *Forschungen,* III, 294.

[49] This is emphasised, e.g., in DAC, I, 56; Nestle, *Theol. Studien,* 188; O. Holtzmann and Bchm. 1 K., *ad loc.*

[50] Loh. Apk., *ad loc.*

[51] In Semitic the personal pronoun is needed in the address ("my lord," "our lord"), but in Gk. the absolute κύριε is all that is needed (as in German, English etc.). Thus κύριε is a correct rendering of מָרַנָא or מָרַן Dalman WJ, I, 147 ff., 268 ff.; Althaus, 518 f. Cf. the relevant essay of E. Littmann, "Anredeformen in erweiterter Bdtg.," NGG, *phil.-hist. Kl.* (1916), 94 ff.

[52] So v. d. Goltz, 212 f., 218; R. Seeberg, *Aus Religion,* 121; II, 311-313; *Der Ursprung,* 15; *Lehrb.,* I³ (1922), 166 f.; T. Schmidt, *Der Leib Christi* (1919), 38 f.; J. Behm → III, 737.

presence of the Lord of the community.[53] On the other, yearning expectation of the *parousia* is linked with the Lord's Supper.[54]

The third possibility (→ 469), namely, "our Lord has come," stands in no meaningful relation either to the context of 1 C. 16:22 and Did., 10, 6 or to original liturgical usage, and it is thus to be discarded.

μαραναθά, then, is either the confession of the exalted Christ present in the community, especially at the Lord's Supper ("our Lord is present"), or it is the cry of the waiting and longing community for His coming again in glory — a cry which is made to the Lord of the community with particular force and fervour at the Lord's Supper ("Lord, come").

K. G. Kuhn

† μαργαρίτης

Pearls were usually regarded as precious stones in antiquity.[1] They were taken esp. from the Red Sea, the Persian Gulf and the Indian Ocean.[2] In the Gk. West they first came to be better known after the conquest of the Orient by Alexander, and in Rome only after the annexation of Greece by Sulla (69).[3] In Egypt the cult of pearls reached its height under the Ptolemies,[4] in Rome during the imperial period.[5] Pearls, used for necklaces and other ornaments, were regarded as very costly,[6] so that the word came to be a figure of speech for something of supreme worth.[7]

---

[53] Behm → III, 737; 739.

[54] 1 C. 11:26: ἄχρι οὗ ἔλθῃ; Did., 10, 6: ἐλθέτω χάρις καὶ παρελθέτω ὁ κόσμος οὗτος; Weiss, *Urchristentum*, 47; Behm → III, 739.

μαργαρίτης. RW, II, 265; HW, II, 1158 f.; BW, 508; RE[3], X, 523, 16 ff.; K. Möbius, *Die echten Perlen* (1858); S. Krauss, *Talmudische Archäologie*, I (1910), 200 f.; O. Keller, *Die antike Tierwelt* (1913), II, 552 ff.; H. Usener, "Die Perle" (*Theol. Abh. C. v. Weizsäcker gewidmet* [1892]), 203-13; C. Daremberg-E. Saglio, *Dictionnaire des Antiquités*, III, 2 (1904), 1595 f. Art. "Margarita"; Pauly-W., XIV, 2 (1930), 1682-1702, Art. μαργαρῖται; ZNW, 9 (1908), 174.

[1] μαργαρίτης is first an adj. and λίθος should be supplied; on other Gk. terms for pearl cf. Pauly-W., 1683 f. -ιτης is a common suffix for stones (even to-day; cf. anhydrite, diorite etc.) [Debrunner].

[2] Pliny the Elder, Hist. Nat., 112 f.; Strabo, 15, 69.

[3] The oldest Gk. ref. is in Theophr. (pupil of Aristot.) De Lapidibus, 36 (p. 345, 37, Wimmer).

[4] Cf. the hypogeion of Cleopatra, which was adorned with pearls, and the costly pearls of Cleopatra, valued at 100 million sesterces, Pliny the Elder, Hist. Nat., IX, 119 ff.; Keller, 555 f.

[5] Lollia Paulina, wife of Caligula, had ornaments of pearls and emeralds to the value of 40 million sesterces, Pliny Hist. Nat., IX, 117; Caesar gave the mother of his later assassin Brutus a pearl valued at 6 million sesterces, Suet. Caes., 50.

[6] On Roman Hell. life cf. Pliny Hist. Nat., IX, 105 ff., esp. 106: *principium columenque omnium rerum pretii margaritae tenent;* on Jewish life, Krauss, I, 200.

[7] E.g., a much loved child, inscr. in Daremberg-Saglio, 1596 and n. 12; CIL, VI, 13637: *margarition* of a much loved boy.

μαργαρίτης does not occur in the LXX.[8] Test. Jud. 13:5 mentions pearls (μαργαρίτης) along with gold as something of great price. In Judaism the pearl (מרגניתא, מרג'ין) because of its high value, is used metaphorically for a valuable saying.[9] The older Jewish form of preaching, with its catenae of biblical verses, was compared to strings of pearls.[10] Eschatological fantasy speaks of pearls of great size which, as pearls were pierced for adornment, will serve as gates for the holy city.[11] A city wall with its gates is like a chain or band adorned at intervals with pearls.

The NT refers to the pearl a. generally as something of great worth, Rev. 18:12, hence a simile for the saving benefits of the kingdom of God, Mt. 13:45 f.; 7:6;[12] b. as a costly ornament, 1 Tm. 2:9; Rev. 17:4; 18:16;[13] c. as an eschatological motif to depict the glory of the future Jerusalem (→ *supra*): The twelve gates of the new Jerusalem, which correspond to the heavenly gates of the twelve signs of the Zodiac, are formed each of a miraculous giant pearl, Rev. 21:21 (→ n. 11).

Hauck

---

8 Heb. פְּנִינִים Prv. 8:11 and 31:10 (λίθων πολυτελῶν), Job 28:18 (ὑπὲρ τὰ ἐσώτατα), in spite of the resemblance to πίννα (mussel), is coral rather than pearl in view of Lam. 4:7 (ἐπυρρώθησαν ὑπὲρ λίθους). רָאמוֹת (Job 28:18; Ez. 27:16; Prv. 24:7) used to be translated pearl, but the LXX does not take it in this way. Etym. μαργαρίτης comes from Sanskrit (so Arrian Indica, 8, 9 [ed. A. Ross, 1928]) *mañjarī*, "pearl," "little knot of flowers" (Keller, 553; Boisacq, *s.v.*), to be preferred to derivation from the Babylonian *margalittu*, "child of the sea" (F. E. Peiser, *Mitteilungen der vorderasiatischen Gesellschaft*, 5, 2 [1900], 29-32). The Arabic Persian word *gauhar* — and this is not without importance for the understanding and meanings of μαργαρίτης — means "pearl," "jewel," "innermost part," "soul," "spiritual force," R. Reitzenstein, *Festschrift f. Andreas* (1916), 46; cf. also H. Gressmann, ZDMG, 60 (1906), 671 f.

9 bQid, 39b: "The mouth which produced pearls ...," Str.-B., I, 447 f.; III, 325, with other examples.

10 *Ibid.*, IV, 176.

11 bBB, 75a (cf. Bss. Apk. on 21:21): "J. Jochanan once sat and said: The Holy One, blessed be He, will one day make precious stones and pearls 30 (ells) big. The same will be hollowed out to a height of 20 and a breadth of 10 to serve as gates for Jerusalem" (expounding Is. 54:12).

12 Often in the Rabb. the pearl is a figure for an excellent thought or fine saying, cf. Qid., 39b: "The mouth which produced pearls must now lick the dust," cf. also Str.-B., I, 447 f., 450.

13 Gnosticism referred the pearl to Christ Himself, cf. Act. Pt., 20 (I, p. 68, 12). It had in view a story about the origin of the pearl acc. to which it was conceived in the sea in the flesh of the mussel through a stroke of lightning (a spark, God, Zeus) (Athen., III, p. 93e), Pliny Hist. Nat., IX, 107 f.; Orig. in Mt. 13:45 (46) (GCS, X, p. 8). In the myth this referred to the birth of the sea-goddess Aphrodite, who was venerated as the pearl goddess (Usener, 207; the flash of lightning = Zeus). Applied to Christ this is a picture of the virgin birth which even ecclesiastical authors use (Cl. Al. Paed., II, 12, 118, 4; Ephraem [ed. Assemani], II, p. 263c; cf. Usener, 204, 3). In Mandaean writings the pearl is a common figure of the soul which comes from the divine world and perfumes (gives life to) the stinking body. Lidz. Ginza L, III, 6, 81 (p. 515, 20 ff.); III, 5, 80 f. (p. 514, 16 ff.) etc., *v.* Index, *s.v.* "Perle," also Index to Act. (Lipsius-Bonnet), *s.v.* μαργαρίτης, e.g., Act. Joh. 109; 113 (II, 1, p. 213, 12 vl.); Act. Thom. 108 (II, 2, p. 220); 148 (II, 2, p. 256, 8 vl.); W. Bousset, "Manichäisches in d. Thomasakten," ZNW, 18 (1917/18), 23 ff.; W. Weyh, ZNW, 9 (1908), 174.

μάρτυς, μαρτυρέω, μαρτυρία, μαρτύριον, ἐπιμαρτυρέω, συμμαρτυρέω, συνεπιμαρτυρέω, καταμαρτυρέω, μαρτύρομαι, διαμαρτύρομαι, προμαρτύρομαι, ψευδόμαρτυς, ψευδομαρτυρέω, ψευδομαρτυρία

† μάρτυς, † μαρτυρέω, † μαρτυρία, † μαρτύριον.

Contents: A. Form of the Word, Etymology and Formation. B. Use of μάρτυς, μαρτυρέω, μαρτυρία, μαρτύριον in non-biblical Greek: 1. Witness to Facts in the Legal Sphere; 2. Witness to Facts generally, and also to Truths or Views; 4. Applications of the Use in the Sense of Witness to Truths or Views; the Special Use in Epictetus. C. μάρτυς, μαρτυρέω, μαρτυρία, μαρτύριον in the LXX: 1. The Heb. Words: a. for μαρτυρέω, μαρτυρία; b. for μαρτύριον; 2. The Use of μάρτυς, μαρτυρέω, μαρτυρία: a. In the Legal Sphere; b. In the Religious Sense in Dt. Is.; 3. The Use of μαρτύριον. D. The Idea of the Martyr in Later Judaism; the Usage in Josephus and Philo. E. μάρτυς, μαρτυρέω, μαρτυρία, μαρτύριον in the New Testament: 1. Occurrence; 2. The Use of μάρτυς: a. General Use (Witness to Facts); b. The Special Lukan Use (Combination of Witness to Facts and Witness in the Sense of Evangelistic Confession); c. The In-

μάρτυς κτλ. For lexical and other general philological aids → λαός. μάρτυς in Gk. law, E. Leisi, *Der Zeuge im attischen Recht,* Diss. Zürich (1907); K. Latter, *Heiliges Recht. Untersuchungen z. Geschichte der sakralen Rechtsformen in Griechenland* (1920), 28-39. On the development of the Christian concept of the martyr, F. Kattenbusch, "Der Märtyrertitel," ZNW, 4 (1903), 111-127; J. Geffcken, "Die christl. Martyrien," Herm., 45 (1910), 481-505; K. Holl, "Die Vorstellung vom Märtyrer u. d. Märtyrerakte in ihrer geschichtlichen Entwicklung," *N. Jbch. Kl. Alt.,* 33 (1914), 521-56 (also in *Ges. Aufsätze z. Kirchengeschichte,* II [1928], 68 ff.); "Der ursprüngliche Sinn des Namens Märtyrer," *ibid.,* 37 (1916), 253-259; ψευδόμαρτυς, Herm., 52, 2 (1917), 301-7; R. Reitzenstein, *Historia Monachorum u. Historia Lausiaca* (1916), 79-90; "Bemerkungen z. Martyrienlit.," NGG, *Phil.-hist. Kl.* (1916), 417-467; "Der Titel Märtyrer," Herm., 52, 2 (1917), 442-452. A. Schlatter, "Der Märtyrer in den Anfängen d. Kirche," BFTh, 19, 3 (1915); R. Corssen, "Begriff u. Wesen des Märtyrers in d. alten Kirche," *N. Jbch. Kl. Alt.,* 35 (1915), 481-501; "μάρτυς u. ψευδόμαρτυς," *ibid.,* 37 (1916), 424-427; H. Strathmann, "Der Märtyrer. Ein Bericht über neue Untersuchungen z. Gesch. des Wortes u. der Anschauung," ThLBl, 37 (1916), 337 ff., 353 ff.; G. Krüger, "Zur Frage nach d. Entstehung des Märtyrertitels," ZNW, 17 (1916), 264-69; G. Fitzer, *Der Begriff des μάρτυς im Judt. u. Urchr.,* Diss. Breslau (1928, unpublished); O. Michel, "Prophet u. Märtyrer," BFTh, 37, 2 (1932); "Biblisches Bekennen u. Bezeugen," *Evangelische Theologie,* 2 (1935), 231-45; H. W. Surkau, "Martyrien in jüd. u. frühchristlicher Zeit," FRL, 54 (1938). N. Bonwetsch, Art. "Märtyrer u. Bekenner," RE³, 12, 48-52; H. Lietzmann, Art. "Martys," Pauly-W., XIV, 2 (1930), 2044 ff.; K. Latter, Art. "Martyria," *ibid.,* 2032 ff.; H. Leclercq, Art. "Martyr," "Martyrium," F. Cabrol-H. Leclercq, *Dictionnaire d'Archéologie Chrétienne,* X, 2 (1932), 2359 ff.; H. Delehaye, *Sanctus, Essai sur le culte des saints dans l'antiquité* (1927), 74-121; *Les origines du culte des martyrs*² (1933); M. Viller-K. Rahner, *Aszese u. Mystik in der Väterzeit* (1939), 29-40; J. B. Lightfoot, *St. Clement of Rome. The Two Epistles to the Corinthians* (1869), on 1 Cl., 5, 4; R. P. Casey, Μάρτυς (Jackson-Lake, I, 5 [1933], Note V, 30-37); H. v. Campenhausen, *Die Idee des Martyriums in d. alten Kirche* (1936); E. Peterson, *Zeuge d. Wahrheit* (1937); F. J. Dölger, "Der Kampf mit dem Ägypter in d. Perpetua-Vision; Das Martyrium als Kampf mit d. Teufel," *Antike u. Christentum,* III (1932), 177-188. On the main points in martyr theology and its historical development in the early Church cf. the introd. notes (545-9) in E. Stauffer, "Märtyrertheologie u. Täuferbewegung," ZKG, 52 (1933), 545-98. Older bibl. on the subject of martyr acts may be found in Mitteis-Wilcken, cf. → n. 23. Cf. also H. Niedermayer, *Über antike Protokoll-Lit.,* Diss. Göttingen (1918). Bibl. in G. Krüger, *Ausgewählte Märtyrerakten*³ (1929), X f. and O. Stählin in W. v. Christ, *Gesch. d. griech. Lit.* = *Handbuch Kl. AW,* VII, 2, 2⁶ (1924), 1246 ff.

cipient Separation of the Two Elements in Luke ; d. μάρτυς τῶν τοῦ Χριστοῦ παθημάτων in 1 Pt. 5:1; e. μάρτυς in the Johannine Writtings ; 3. The Use of μαρτυρέω : a. Of the Human Declaration of Facts ; b. Of the Good Report ; c. Of the Witness of God, the Spirit, or Scripture ; d. Of Religious Witness ; e. The Special Use in the Johannine Writings ; f. 1 Tm. 6:13; 4. The Use of μαρτυρία : a. Outside the Johannine Writings ; b. In the Johannine Writings ; 5. The Use of μαρτύριον : a. Occurrence ; b. The Use in the Sense of Witness for the Prosecution ; c. Witness to Something ; d. Witness in the Active Sense. F. The Development and Establishment of the Specific Martyrological Use in the Early Church : 1. Review ; 2. Usage ; 3. Understanding.

A. Form of the Word, Etymology and Formation.

1. Form of the Word. [1] ὁ, ἡ μάρτυς, gen. μάρτυρος, acc. μάρτυρα and occasionally μάρτυν, dat. plur. μάρτυσι. The ancient epic form is ὁ μάρτυρος, nom. plur. μάρτυροι, dat. plur. μαρτύροις in Hom., also some inscr., esp. Delphic (CIG, I, 1699, 1702-1707), once in P. Gen., 54, 6 (4th cent. A.D.): μάρτυρός ἐστιν ὁ θεός, ὅτι κτλ. [2] The form repeatedly called Aeolian by Herodianus Technicus, i.e., μάρτυρ, [3] is also found in the inscr. of Cnidos, GDI, 3591, 23 = Ditt. Syll.³, 953, 22. It becomes quite common later in ecclesiastical usage. [4]

2. Etymology and Formation. [5] μάρτυς would seem to come from the root *smer*, "to bear in mind," "to remember," "to be careful," cf. the Gk. μέρμερος, "that which demands much care or deliberation ; he who considers or deliberates much," then μερμαίρω, μερμηρίζω, "consider, deliberate, hesitate," μεριμνάω, μέριμνα, the Lat. *memor, memoria,* Gothic *maúrnan,* Anglo-Saxon *murnan,* Old High German *mornēn,* "to be anxiously concerned." Hence μάρτυς was probably "one who remembers, who has knowledge of something by recollection, and who can thus tell about it," i.e., the witness. To the verb μαρτυρεῖν applies something which is true of verbs in -έω formed from nouns and adj. of all declensions, namely, that they denote a state or habitual activity, but can often take on trans. significance. [6] μαρτυρεῖν thus means "to be a witness," "to come forward as a witness," "to bear witness to something." The secondary noun μαρτυρία, whether referred to μάρτυς or μαρτυρεῖν, [7] has in the first instance, like most such nouns, an abstract significance : the bearing of witness. But it can then mean the witness thus borne. On the other hand, μαρτύριον, like other nouns in -ιον, is more concrete and denotes witness from the more objective standpoint as the proof of something. Any μαρτυρία can become a μαρτύριον, but not conversely. μαρτυρία and μαρτύριον are related like ναυαγία ("shipwreck") and τὰ ναυάγια ("the remains of the ship") or γυμνασία ("bodily exercise") and γυμνάσιον ("the place of exercise"). [8]

---

[1] Cf. Kühner-Blass-Gerth, I, 1 §§ 139, 140; E. Schwyzer, *Griech. Gramm.,* I (1934), 260.

[2] Cf. H. v. Herwerden, *Lexicon Graecum suppletorium et dialecticum,* II (1910). Thes. Steph. also has *s.v.* μάρτυρος Bas. Ep. ad Chilonem (ἅπερ τοῖς μαρτύροις τοῦ Χριστοῦ ἐπήγγελται), though MPG, 32, p. 357c has here μάρτυσι.

[3] Herodiani Technici Reliquiae, ed. A. Lentz, I (1867), p. 47, 4 : (μάρτυρ) γίνεται ... ἐκ τοῦ μάρτυς κατὰ τὴν Αἰολέων διάλεκτον· ἐκεῖνοι γὰρ τὸ σ̄ εἰς ρ̄ μεταβάλλουσι, II (1868), p. 548, 22 : τὴν μάρτυς εὐθεῖαν ἡ Αἰολέων διάλεκτος διὰ τοῦ ρ̄ προφέρει. The Aeolians said, e.g., οὗτορ instead of οὗτος, ἵππορ instead of ἵππος, cf. 615, 35 f. and 747, 28. Cf. also Kühner-Blass³, I, 1 (1890), 510.

[4] Cf. Pass. (-Cr.) and Liddell-Scott, *s.v.* ("became general").

[5] Cf. Walde-Pok., II, 689 under *smer-;* also Boisacq, *s.v.*

[6] Kühner-Blass³, I, 2 (1892), 260; cf. Debr. Griech. Wortb. § 191-3.

[7] Kühner-Blass³, I, 2, 276.

[8] Cf. P. Chantraine, *La Formation des Noms en Grec Ancien* (1933), 59 [Debrunner]; legal terms in -ιον, cf. Debr. Griech. Wortb. § 289; Blass-Debr.⁶ § 111, 4. On what follows cf. Kühner-Blass³, I, 2, 274 f.

B. Use of μάρτυς, μαρτυρέω, μαρτυρία, μαρτύριον in non-biblical Greek.

1. Witness to Facts in the Legal Sphere. The proper sphere of μάρτυς is the legal, where it denotes one who can and does speak from personal experience about actions in which he took part and which happened to him, or about persons and relations known to him. He may be a witness at a trial, or, in legal transactions of different kinds, a solemn witness in the most varied connections.[9] The witness at a trial and his μαρτυρίαι are dealt with fully by Aristot. in his Rhet. and also by Anaximenes of Lampsacos in his Ars Rhetorica ad Alexandrum, which is found among the works of Aristot.[10] The inscr. and esp. the pap. offer an almost inexhaustible number of examples of the solemn witness in every possible kind of written agreement and record, including official records.[11]

The function of the witness is normally denoted by the verb μαρτυρεῖν. This can be used in the abs., "to come forward as a witness," but also commonly with the dat.

---

[9] On this distinction cf. Latte and Leisi.

[10] Anaxim. links μαρτυρία, βάσανος (statement induced by torture) and ὅρκος as means of legal proof. In Rhet. ad Alexandrum, 18, p. 1432a, 33 ὅρκος is defined as μετὰ θείας παραλήψεως φάσις ἀναπόδεικτος (an unprovable statement with invocation of the gods). Βάσανος δ' ἐστὶ μὲν ὁμολογία περὶ συνειδότος, ἄκοντος δέ, c. 17. On the other hand μαρτυρία is ὁμολογία συνειδότος ἑκοντί, c. 16. What is attested can be πιθανόν, ἀπίθανον or ἀμφίβολον πρὸς πίστιν, and accordingly the witness can be πιστός, ἄπιστος or ἀμφίδοξος. If what is attested is credible and the witness ἀληθινός, οὐδὲν δέονται αἱ μαρτυρίαι ἐπιλόγων. If there is suspicion, it is to be demonstrated in support that he neither χάριτος ἕνεκεν οὔτε τιμωρίας ἢ κέρδους τὰ ψευδῆ μαρτυρεῖ (that he lies neither out of partiality nor the desire for revenge or gain). Δεῖ δὲ καὶ διδάσκειν ὅτι οὐ συμφέρει τὸ ψεῦδος μαρτυρεῖν· αἱ μὲν γὰρ ὠφέλειαι μικραί, τὸ δ' ἐξελεγχθῆναι χαλεπόν ... Τοὺς μὲν οὖν μάρτυρας οὕτω πιστοὺς ποιήσομεν. On the other side, the methods for attacking the statement of a witness are considered: Ἀντιλέγοντας δὲ μαρτυρίᾳ δεῖ τὸν τρόπον τοῦ μάρτυρος διαβάλλειν, ἂν ᾖ πονηρός (he is brought under moral suspicion), ἢ τὸ μαρτυρούμενον ἐξετάζειν, ἂν ᾖ πιθανὸν κτλ. Σκεπτέον δὲ καὶ εἰ φίλος ἐστὶν ὁ μάρτυς ᾧ μαρτυρεῖ ... ἢ ἐχθρός ἐστιν οὗ καταμαρτυρεῖ, ἢ πένης. For all such are suspect, τὰ ψευδῆ μαρτυρεῖν. Καὶ τὸν τῶν ψευδομαρτυριῶν νόμον ἐπὶ τούτοις τεθεικέναι φήσομεν τὸν νομοθέτην· ἄτοπον οὖν εἶναι τοῦ νομοθέτου τοῖς μάρτυσι μὴ πιστεύσαντος τοὺς κρίνοντας πιστεύειν αὐτοῖς, κατὰ τοὺς νόμους κρίνειν ὀμωμοκότας. τοὺς μὲν οὖν μάρτυρας οὕτως ἀπιθάνους ποιήσομεν. At the end of the chapter there is then ref. to the surreptitious gaining of oral witness (κλέπτειν τὴν μαρτυρίαν). The section closes with the expression that now one knows μάρτυσι ... καὶ μαρτυρίαις ... ὡς δεῖ χρήσασθαι. Information on the handling of witnesses and witness may be gained from the inscr. of Kalymna (Ditt. Syll^3, 953) which deals with a dispute between some Koans and the Kalymna community.

[11] In agreements the text comes first. Often the concluding formula is ἡ συγγραφὴ κυρία. A Μάρτυρες then leads to the signatures of the individual witnesses. Cf. Preisigke Sammelbuch, III, 6709, 6 (purchase of slaves); 6742a, 18 (a loan); 6759, 18 (lease); IV, 7450, 25 (all 3rd cent. B.C.); V, 7532, 24 (1st cent. B.C.). Cf. also wills, Mitteis-Wilcken, II, 2, 301, 30; P. Petr., I, 11, 13; 13, 2, 4; 13, 3, 6; 14, 21; 19, 30; III, 1, 1, 18; 4(2), 23; 6a, 37; 7, 20; 10, 11; 11,25; 12, 13 (all 3rd cent. B.C.). Often an exact personal description of the witnesses is given with any special marks, scars, birth-marks, etc., as in a warrant, e.g., P. Petr., I, 19, 30 (= Mitteis-Wilcken, II, 2, 301, 20 ff.): μάρτυρες: Πάρις Θεοφίλου Θεσσαλὸς τῆς ἐπιγονῆς ὡς ἐτῶν [τριάκ]οντα μέσος μεγέθει μελίχρως μακροπρόσωπος τετανόθριξ [οὐλὴ με]τώπωι μέσωι καὶ φακὸς παρ' ὀφθαλμὸν δεξιόν ... Often each witness, unless illiterate, must write in his own hand: μαρτυρῶ τῇ τοῦ δεῖνα διαθήκῃ; Mitteis-Wilcken, II, 2, 303, 14 ff. (2nd cent. A.D.). We often find witnesses on public records; thus the Delphic records of the liberation of slaves usually close with μάρτυρες οἱ ἱερεῖς καὶ οἱ ἰδιῶται or the like, cf. CIG, I, 1702-1707 etc. The inscr. concerning Phokian tributes to Delphi have the μάρτυρες by name on both sides. Acc. to Plato Leg., XII, 953e conditions for going bail are listed in a συγγραφή "καὶ ἐναντίον μαρτύρων μὴ ἔλαττον τριῶν." Cf. also P. Ryl., II, 160a, 6 (1st cent. A.D.): ἐπιτε[τάχα]μεν τοῖς μάρτυσι γράφειν.

to denote the one for whom one testifies or the agreement to which one is a witness,[12] then the acc., or περί and the gen., or an ὅτι clause, for the content of the statement in so far as the witness is testifying to anything specific. Similarly, the noun μαρτυρία, in acc. with its basic meaning as a *nomen actionis,* is used for the coming forward of a witness, or the giving of the witness. But it can then denote the witness itself.[13] Often it is hard to differentiate. A fine example of the legal use of μαρτυρεῖν, μαρτυρία is to be found in P. Hal., 1, lines 222-233 (3rd cent. B.C.), a passage which concerns the summoning and examining of witnesses:[14] line 222: εἰς μαρτυρίαν κλῆσις. Ε[ἰς] μαρτυρίαν καλείσθω ἐναντίον (223) δύο κλ[η]τόρων παρόντα ἀγορεύοντα καθ' ἓν ἕκαστον ὅτι ἄ[ν] (224) δέηι μ[αρ]τυρεῖν. ὁ δὲ καλεσάμενος γραφέτω τὴν μαρ(225)τυρίαν εἰς π[ι]ν[ά]κι[ον], ὁ δὲ κληθεὶς μαρτυρείτω ἐ[π]ὶ [τῆ]ι (226) ἀρχῆι καὶ ἐπὶ τ[ῶι] δικαστηρίωι ἐφ' οἷς παρῆν ἢ εἶδε[ν ὀ]μόσας (227) τὸν ν[ό]μιμον ὅρκ[ο]ν ἀληθῆ μαρτυρεῖν τὰ ἐν τῶι π[ινα]κίωι (228) γεγρα[μμέν]α, ἄλλην δὲ μὴ μαρτυρείτ[ω. 'Ε]ὰν <δὲ> μὴ φῆι [⟦παρα⟧] (229) παρεῖναι μηδὲ ἰδεῖν περὶ ὧν ἂν κελεύηι μαρτυρεῖν (230), ἐξομοσάσθω τὸν νόμιμον ὅρκον παραχρῆμα μήτε εἰδέ[ν]αι μήτε (231) παρεῖναι περὶ ὧν ἂν κληθῆι εἰς μαρτυρίαν. ἐὰν δ[ὲ] (232) τῆς μαρτυρίας τὰ μὲν φῆι εἰδέναι, τὰ δὲ μή, ἃ μὲν ἂν φῆ[ι] (233) συνειδέναι, μαρτυρείτω, ἃ δ' ἂν φῆι μὴ συνειδέναι, ἐξομο[σ]άσθ[ω].

In the case of μαρτύριον, on the other hand, there is no special affinity to the sphere of the courts or the law generally. This denotes the objective, witness, the proof, which can be adduced to confirm a statement or fact, whether this be the saying of a third person (e.g., a poet — a very common use), or a series of facts, or something which serves as proof. In the latter case one sees clearly the objective character of the term: The olive wreath with which bravery is crowned is laid up in the temple of the gods of war — μαρτύριον εἰς τὴν τῶν ἀριστείων κρίσιν παντὸς τοῦ βίου κτλ., Plat. Leg., XII, 943c. Every man becomes a poet when *eros* lays hold of him: ᾧ δὴ πρέπει ἡμᾶς μαρτυρίῳ χρῆσθαι, ὅτι ποιητὴς ὁ Ἔρως ἀγαθός, Plat. Symp., 196e. The saying of Plato confirms this fact of experience. A writing may be handed to the authorities πρὸς μαρτύριον (Preisigke Sammelbuch, IV, 7363, 15 [168 A.D.]). For the assertion that many foods cause bad dreams, μαρτυρίοις ἐχρῶντο τοῖς τε κυάμοις καὶ τῇ κεφαλῇ τοῦ πολύποδος, Plut. Quaest. Conv., 8, 10 (II, 734 f.). μαρτύρια δὲ τούτων τρόπαια ἐστήσαντο τῶν πολεμίων, Gorg. Fr., 6 (II, 286, 8 f., Diels[5]). μαρτύριον δὲ τῶν εἰρημένων καὶ τὸ πᾶσι ὑπάρχειν ... αὐτήν, Aristot. Part. An., III, 4, p. 666a, 22. μαρτύρια τὰ ἡμερινὰ ἔργα τῶν νυκτερινῶν ποιούμενος, Dio C., 38, 22, 3. In support of the view that Caesar often showed clemency out of sheer generosity of soul, μέγιστον μὲν καὶ ἐκεῖνο μαρτύριόν ἐστιν ..., Dio C., 44, 47, 1. The Carian graves on Delos are μαρτύριον to the settlements which the Carian pirates once established there, Thuc., I, 8, 1. Any recollection that the stem word originally belonged to the legal sphere, esp. trials, has now completely faded. The ref. is always to the proving of facts.

2. Witness to Facts generally, and also to Truths or Views. But the stem words μάρτυς, μαρτυρεῖν and μαρτυρία also find a very general use outside the legal sphere. In so doing they undergo a broadening of meaning and thus

---

[12] The expression μαρτυρῶ τῇ ... διαθήκῃ is common in P. Oxy. μαρτυρεῖ Σωταίρωι Διογένης, P. Petr., II, 21d, 2; μαρτυρεῖ μοι ὁ θεός, P. Oxy., VIII, 1164, 11.

[13] εἰς μαρτυρίαν καλείσθω, P. Hal., I, 222; εἰς μαρτυρίαν κληθείς, Plat. Leg., XI, 937a. IG, V, 2, 357, 10 ff. The witness who refuses to testify must swear that he has no knowledge. This is then an ἐξωμοσία (P. Eleph., 34, 1). Acc. to this ἐξωμοσία "ἀφεώσθω τὰς μαρτυρίας." Dio C., 55, 19, 2: Livia in a statement to Augustus: Many regarded the administration of justice as wholly corrupt; οὔτε γὰρ τὰς μαρτυρίας οὔτε τὰς βασάνους οὔτ' ἄλλο τι τῶν τοιούτων ὡς καὶ ἀληθὲς ὂν κατ' αὐτῶν προσίενται.

[14] Cf. *Dikaiomata, Auszüge aus alexandrinischen Gesetzen und Verordnungen in einem Papyrus des philologischen Seminars der Universität Halle* (1913), 125.

come to be used in two senses. The group now refers not merely to the establishment of events or actual relations or facts of experience on the basis of direct personal knowledge. It signifies also the proclamation of views or truths of which the speaker is convinced. It thus relates to things which by their very nature cannot be submitted to empirical investigation. This distinction is plainly developed by Aristot. in Rhet., I, 15. Aristot. first compares πίστεις ἄτεχνοι and ἔντεχνοι, i.e., natural means of proof and those fashioned by methodical art (I, 2, p. 1355b, 35 f.). He cites five πίστεις ἄτεχνοι: νόμοι, μάρτυρες, συνθῆκαι, βάσανοι (statements under torture), ὅρκοι, which he discusses in detail (I, 15, p. 1375a, 24 f.). Among witnesses he distinguishes between those who belong to the past and those who belong to the present (παλαιοί and πρόσφατοι). Among the past witnesses are those who testify to past events and those who testify to the future. To the latter group belong χρησμολόγοι (those who expound oracles), but also αἱ παροιμίαι μαρτύριά ἐστιν. In relation to πρόσφατοι μάρτυρες we have the judgments of worthy persons which are made without respect to the immediate point at issue, but on the other hand we may also have μάρτυρες μετέχοντες τοῦ κινδύνου. Of these it is then said (p. 1376a, 12 ff.): οἱ μὲν οὖν τοιοῦτοι τῶν τοιούτων μόνον μάρτυρές εἰσιν, εἰ γέγονεν ἢ μή, εἰ ἔστιν ἢ μή, περὶ δὲ τοῦ ποῖον οὐ μάρτυρες οἷον εἰ δίκαιον ἢ ἄδικον, εἰ συμφέρον ἢ ἀσύμφορον. Hence a distinction is made between μαρτυρίαι περὶ τοῦ πράγματος and those περὶ τοῦ ἤθους. Only in the former case do we have legal witnesses in the sense of Anaximenes (→ n. 10). Though the terms μάρτυς, μαρτυρεῖν, μαρτυρία are used on both sides, the sense is obviously quite different. In the former case the reference is to the examination of facts observable from without, whether these be events or states. In the latter case the reference is to ethical judgments, to expressions of moral convictions, or more generally to views. On the one hand, statements are made about objective events, on the other personal convictions are made known. On the one hand the point at issue is whether a thing is or was really so, on the other whether it is true and valid from the standpoint of the one who states it.

Yet the distinction does not arise merely at this point. It is to be noted already when μάρτυρες is used with reference to the future. For in this case witness can be borne only by the faith that this or that will happen, no matter what may be the basis of this faith. The fact that the terms μάρτυς, μαρτυρεῖν, μαρτυρία can embrace both meanings is of decisive importance for their further history.

3. Applications of the General Use in the Sense of Witness to Facts. In this sense there was from very early times a use with ref. to the gods. Appeal was made to the gods as witnesses in treaties, solemn agreements or declarations, assurances and oaths. Even if no other witness was present, they, the omniscient, could confirm the truth of a statement or the fact of an agreement. Those who appealed to them as witnesses did so in the belief that should they be lying, or should they break the agreement, they would fall victim to divine punishment.[15] The word is also used for men as witnesses

[15] Hom. Il., 3, 280: At the offering before the duel between Alexander and Menelaus, Zeus, Helios etc. are invoked as witnesses to the solemn agreement which they are to observe: ὑμεῖς μάρτυροι ἔστε, φυλάσσετε δ' ὅρκια πιστά, Il., 22, 254 f.: Hector's challenge to Achilles: We will look up to the gods τοὶ γὰρ ἄριστοι μάρτυροι ἔσσονται καὶ ἐπίσκοποι ἁρμονιάων; with ref. to the gods of the underworld as those who are invoked to punish perjury, Il., 14, 274: μάρτυροι ὦσ' οἱ ἔνερθε θεοὶ Κρόνον ἀμφὶς ἐόντες, cf. Il., 7, 76; Od., 14, 394; ἄμμιν μάρτυς ἔστω Ζεύς, Pind. Pyth., 4, 297: μάρτυρας καλῶ θεούς, Soph. Trach., 1248; P. Gen., 54, 6: μαρτυρός ἐστιν ὁ [θ]εὸς ὅτι οὐ διὰ

by eye or ear to all kinds of things. It would be superfluous to give examples of this everyday use.[16] Finally, there is a figur. use for impersonal witnesses.[17] In the same way μαρτυρεῖν is used in the sense of to confirm or prove, and similarly μαρτυρία. These words even have the weaker sense of "making a statement about someone or something," or a "statement thus made," esp. in a favourable sense, i.e., a good witness, or the confirmation of, e.g., a fact of experience.[18]

4. Applications of the Use in the Sense of Witness to Truths or Views; the Special Use in Epictetus. The sense of testifying to a view held, or a truth of which one is convinced, may first be illustrated by some examples from Plato. The χορός of young men up to 30 yrs. of age is first devoted to the task of convincing youth that the best life is also the happiest — τὸν ... Παιᾶνα ἐπικαλούμενος μάρτυρα τῶν λεγομένων ἀληθείας πέρι, Leg., II, 664c. The Athenian rejects the homosexuality of the Spartans — μάρτυρα παραγόμενος τὴν τῶν θηρίων φύσιν, Leg., VIII, 836c. For the view that the brave conduct of citizens in revolution is to be more highly estimated than bravery in battle against external foes, the Athenian appeals to the poet Theognis of Megara — ποιητὴν δὲ καὶ ἡμεῖς μάρτυρ' ἔχομεν, Θέογνιν κτλ., Leg., I, 630a.

λῆμ[μ]α μάχομε, ἀλλὰ μάχομε διὰ σέ. The Elkesaites were later advised in their repeated baptisms and their conjurations against the bite of mad dogs to invoke ἑπτὰ μάρτυρας, τὸν οὐρανὸν καὶ τὸ ὕδωρ καὶ τὰ πνεύματα τὰ ἅγια καὶ τοὺς ἀγγέλους τῆς προσευχῆς καὶ τὸ ἔλαιον καὶ τὸ ἅλας καὶ τὴν γῆν, cf. Hipp. Philos., IX, 15, 2 and 5.

[16] Yet we may mention two examples from Hom., Il., 1, 338 f.: Achilles hands over Briseis to the heralds of Agamemnon, but also appeals to her as a witness to the injustice done him: τὼ δ' αὐτὼ μάρτυροι ἔστων πρός τε θεῶν μακάρων πρός τε θνητῶν ἀνθρώπων. Again, in Il., 2, 301 f. Odysseus reminds the Achaeans of the sign of the great length of the campaign which they received on departing from Aulis (the snake under the altar which swallowed 8 young sparrows and their mother): ἐστὲ δὲ πάντες μάρτυροι, οὓς μὴ Κῆρες ἔβαν θανάτοιο φέρουσαι. Cf. also the idea of the eye- and ear-witness in Hom. Hymn. Merc., 372: οὐδὲ θεῶν μακάρων ἄγε μάρτυρας οὐδὲ κατόπτας. Dio C., 41, 33, 1: Caesar in an address in Placentia to the legions before punishing mutineers: ἐγὼ συνεκάλεσα ὑμᾶς, ἵνα καὶ μάρτυρας καὶ ἐπόπτας τῶν τε λεγομένων καὶ <τῶν> πραττομένων ποιήσωμαι. Dio C., 46, 56, 2: ὅπως καὶ ἐπήκοοι ... καὶ μάρτυρες τῶν ὡμολογημένων σφίσι γένωνται. Cf. also 53, 24, 3. Plut. Adulat., 32 (II, 71a): The admonition which a friend gives a friend must be discreet, μὴ ... μηδὲ μάρτυρας καὶ θεατὰς συνάγουσαν.

[17] E.g., ἁμέραι δ' ἐπίλοιποι μάρτυρες σοφώτατοι, Pind. Olymp., 1, 54; ἔθηκε ναυτιλίας ἐσχάτας μάρτυρας, of the pillars of Hercules, Pind. Nem., 3, 22. In Plat. Ap., 31c Socrates appeals to his poverty in witness against the suspicion he made a business out of philosophy: ἐγὼ παρέχομαι τὸν μάρτυρα ... τὴν πενίαν. Plut. de Amicorum Multitudine, 2 (II, 93e): τὸν μακρὸν καὶ παλαιὸν αἰῶνα μάρτυρα τοῦ λόγου καὶ σύμβουλον λάβωμεν: The course of the world should give witness and advice as to the conduct of true friends.

[18] E.g., P. Oxy., VIII, 1164, 11: μαρτυρεῖ μοι γὰρ ὁ θεός. Dio C., 50, 3, 5: Antonius in his will τῷ Καισαρίωνι (the son of Cleopatra) ὡς καὶ ἐκ τοῦ Καίσαρος ὄντως γεγονότι ἐμεμαρτυρήκει. *Ibid.*, 57, 15, 3: Tiberius ἑκατοντάρχου ἑλληνιστὶ ἐν τῷ συνεδρίῳ μαρτυρῆσαί τι ἐθελήσαντος οὐκ ἠνέσχετο. Inscr. from Olbia on the Black Sea (2nd cent. B.C.) in Deissmann LO, 69, n. 2: ἀλλὰ καὶ (μέχρι) περάτων γῆς ἐμαρτυρήθη τοὺς ὑπὲρ φιλίας κινδύνους μέχρι Σεβαστῶν συμμαχίᾳ παραβολευσάμενος: "Witness was given him that in the interests of friendship he exposed himself to dangers by lending support in the dispute even to the imperial courts." Μαρτυρίη occurs only once in Hom. at Od., 11, 325. On the basis of μαρτυρίαι of Dionysus concerning an event observed by him, Artemis prevents Theseus from bringing Ariadne to Athens. Dio C., 56, 25, 6: Augustus orders that no τιμή be shown any of the ἄρχοντες by subjects during their period in office and 60 days after ὅτι τινὲς μαρτυρίας παρ' αὐτῶν καὶ ἐπαίνους προπαρασκευαζόμενοι πολλὰ διὰ τούτου ἐκακούργουν: to do this was very wrong. Μαρτυρία for declaration or demonstration (in a council meeting) is found in P. Oxy., I, 41, 18 (3rd cent. A.D.).

τὸν ἀδικοῦντα οὐκ εὐδαίμονα εἶναι is a basic conception of Socrates. Polos can easily adduce a swarm of witnesses to contest the truth of this teaching: ἐὰν βούλῃ κατ' ἐμοῦ μάρτυρας παρασχέσθαι ὡς οὐκ ἀληθῆ λέγω· μαρτυρήσουσί σοι, ἐὰν μὲν βούλῃ, Νικίας κτλ., Gorg., 472a. In the opposite evaluations of ecstasy μάρτυσι καὶ ἐπαινέταις χρώμενοι ἐπαινοῦμεν ἑκάτεροι — both parties support their views by witnesses and panegyrists, Leg., I, 638d. Here it is particularly worth noting that μάρτυρες and ἐπαινέται are obviously felt to be synonymous.

In all these examples the ref. is not to facts which are to be established by the witness but to views or convictions which he approves, expresses and emphatically champions as right, to truths which he accepts and espouses. This takes place in the form of the judgments which he makes. But the trial of Socrates, and the way it is handled in Plato's Apol., show that men are more effectively convinced by conduct than by word. If the terms μάρτυς, μαρτυρεῖν, μαρτυρία are not used in this sense here, materially the whole Apol. is one long glorification of Socrates from the standpoint that he invincibly demonstrated the truth of what he taught by his conduct both in life and esp. in death.[19] Socrates is a model of loyalty to conviction irrespective of the consequences, and he is extolled as such, as a moral hero.

When centuries later Epictet. magnifies the πεπαιδευμένος as the divinely called witness to practical philosophical wisdom, apart from the Stoic garb he simply reduces to a formula a view which is already present in Plato's Apol. and which had considerable influence. In fact the theme of the philosopher as a witness plays a considerable role in Epictet., and he gives us the most important examples of the use of the terms μάρτυς, μαρτυρεῖν, μαρτυρία in this sense.[20, 21] The philosopher, the true Cynic, is or ought to be a witness to the truth of Stoic-Cynic wisdom with its doctrine of the unimportance of everything external, of everything which one cannot control. The πεπαιδευμένος shows himself to be a witness when he maintains a cheerful equanimity of soul in face of disgrace, exile, or whatever else may befall him. He comes forward as a divinely summoned witness to testify to God in face of accusers who question the divine government of the world: ὡς μάρτυς ὑπὸ τοῦ θεοῦ κεκλημένος. "ἔρχου σὺ καὶ μαρτύρησόν μοι· σὺ γὰρ ἄξιος εἶ προαχθῆναι μάρτυς ὑπ' ἐμοῦ. μή τι τῶν ἐκτὸς τῆς προαιρέσεως ἀγαθόν ἐστιν ἢ κακόν; μή τινα βλάπτω; ..." (God does not ordain ill to any man when the external blows of fate smite him?) God has

---

[19] Cf. Ap., 28d: Where someone has chosen his place to the best of his knowledge, or is appointed by an ἄρχων, ἐνταῦθα δεῖ, ὡς ἐμοὶ δοκεῖ, μένοντα κινδυνεύειν, μηδὲν ὑπολογιζόμενον μήτε θάνατον μήτε ἄλλο μηδὲν πρὸ τοῦ αἰσχροῦ. This is the situation of Socrates. For (Ap., 28e) he is convinced τοῦ θεοῦ ... τάττοντος ... φιλοσοφοῦντά με δεῖν ζῆν, and nothing will shake this. Ap., 29d: When he is promised a pardon if he will keep silence — ἐγὼ ὑμᾶς ... ἀσπάζομαι μὲν καὶ φιλῶ, πείσομαι δὲ μᾶλλον τῷ θεῷ ἢ ὑμῖν, καὶ ἕωσπερ ἂν ἐμπνέω ... οὐ μὴ παύσωμαι φιλοσοφῶν. Ap., 32c d: Socrates has shown οὐ λόγῳ ἀλλ' ἔργῳ that he does not fear death and has only one concern, μηδὲν ἄδικον μηδὲ ἀνόσιον ἐργάζεσθαι. Hence he must remain true to his task (τὰ ἐμαυτοῦ πράττειν, Ap., 33a). For ἐμοὶ ... τοῦτο προστέτακται ὑπὸ τοῦ θεοῦ (33c). He goes to death with the conviction which he proves by his conduct: Οὐκ ἔστιν ἀνδρὶ ἀγαθῷ κακὸν οὐδὲν οὔτε ζῶντι οὔτε τελευτήσαντι οὐδὲ ἀμελεῖται ὑπὸ θεῶν τὰ τούτου πράγματα, 41d. The trial ends as a complete moral victory for the accused over his accusers and judges.

[20] It may be viewed as a transition when Aristot. (Metaph., I, 10, p. 995a, 7 f.) speaks of custom determining our judgment of the way men speak to us. Some demand mathematically strict deduction, others that we speak παραδειγματικῶς; οἱ δὲ μάρτυρα ἀξιοῦσιν ἐπάγεσθαι ποιητήν: They demand a saying from the poets in witness, not to facts, but to the truth of a judgment. Cf. also Dio C., 52, 16, 1: Maecenas gives Caesar certain political advice; ὅτι ταῦτα ἀληθῆ λέγω, μαρτυρεῖ τὰ γεγονότα: History proves the truth of certain political judgments.

[21] Cf. on this Geffcken, Hermes, 45, 481 ff.; Reitzenstein, *Historia,* 85 ff.; *Bemerkungen,* 445 ff.; Delehaye, *Sanctus,* 95 ff.

based the true profit of each on his own decision. τίνα μαρτυρίαν δίδως τῷ θεῷ; The man struck by misfortune begins to complain. Epictet. writes: ταῦτα μέλλεις "μαρτυρεῖν" καὶ καταισχύνειν τὴν κλῆσιν ἣν κέκληκεν, ὅτι σε ἐτίμησεν ταύτην τὴν τιμὴν καὶ ἄξιον ἡγήσατο προσαγαγεῖν εἰς μαρτυρίαν τηλικαύτην; Diss:, I, 29, 44-49. On the philosopher's view of temporal evils, Zeus willed τοῖς ἄλλοις ἀνθρώποις προάγειν με μάρτυρα τῶν ἀπροαιρέτων, namely, as witnesses to the unimportance of ἀπροαίρετα. Zeus sends evils, not out of ill-will or indifference, ἀλλὰ γυμνάζων καὶ μάρτυρι πρὸς τοὺς ἄλλους χρώμενος (III, 24, 110-114). The philosophically educated are μάρτυρες, οἷς μόνοις χρῆται [ὁ θεὸς] παραδείγμασιν πρὸς τοὺς ἀπαιδεύτους, ὅτι καὶ ἔστι καὶ καλῶς διοικεῖ τὰ ὅλα ... καὶ ὅτι ἀνδρὶ ἀγαθῷ οὐδέν ἐστι κακὸν οὔτε ζῶντι οὔτε ἀποθανόντι ... (III, 26, 28). Practical Stoic-Cynic wisdom is thus the truth which the true philosopher in the sense of Epictet. attests by the steadfast equanimity with which he accepts all the blows of fate. Thereby he is also a witness for God against those who accuse Him. Thereby he proves himself a μάρτυς, with the sense of being called and brought to this position by Zeus. In this consists his μαρτυρία.[22] In some cases this may involve suffering death. But this is not essential to the concept of the witness in Epictet. Naturally, he attests the truth of this view of life by words too. But Epictet. applies the terms μάρτυς, μαρτυρεῖν, μαρτυρία, not to this, but to practical demonstration in a crisis, to the οὐ λόγῳ, ἀλλ' ἔργῳ τὰ τοῦ καλοῦ καὶ ἀγαθοῦ ἐκτελεῖν, III, 24, 110. Nor is it the point to prove the factuality of external events. The point is to express conviction as to the truth of a doctrine by one's conduct in adverse circumstances.[23]

Yet there can be no question of a technical use of the words. How little this is so may be seen from Diss., III, 22, 87 f., where Epictet. uses μάρτυς of the body of the philosopher: The health of the body is a proof, a witness to the correctness of the Cynic ideal of a simple and natural mode of life which despises luxury. The term is sometimes used in Epictet. for an act which confesses a truth. In the last resort this would be death, though it does not have to be. Neither Socrates, nor Musonius, nor any other of the lauded models of a genuine philosophical attitude are described as μάρτυρες. The relation between Christian usage and that of Epictet. (if one may speak of such) is only external.

---

[22] Cf. also Porphyr. Marc., 8: δεῖ οὕτως βιοῦν ὅστις ἐπίστευσεν, ἵνα καὶ αὐτὸς πιστὸς ᾖ μάρτυς περὶ ὧν λέγει τοῖς ἀκροωμένοις.

[23] On the basis of a note of U. v. Wilamowitz in GGA (1890), 690, and an essay of A. Bauer in APF, 1 (1901), 29 ff., it is customary to cite as pagan martyrologies a series of pap. texts of the 1st and 2nd centuries which extol upright citizens ready to suffer death in the courts of imperial Rome. (Cf. on this Schürer, I^3, 65-71; U. Wilcken, "Zum antiken Antisemitismus." *Abh. d. kgl. sächs. Ges. d. Wissenschaft,* 57 [1909], 783-839; Mitteis-Wilcken, I, 1, 44 f.; I, 2, 14 and 20; W. Weber, "Eine Gerichtsverhandlung vor Kaiser Trajan," Hermes, 50 [1915], 47-92; H. I. Bell, *Jews and Christians in Egypt* [1924], 25 ff.; "Juden u. Griechen im röm. Alexandrien," *Beih. z. AO,* 9 [1926], with bibl.). The ref. is to the champions of the Gk. opposition to Roman rule who, condemned by the emperor, suffered death as moral victors. (This view that the "acts" are fragments of a group of political pamphlets was first advocated by M. Rostovtzeff in "Die Märtyrer der griechischen Kultur" [1901, Russian]; cf. Rostovtzeff, *Gesellschaft und Wirtschaft im römischen Kaiserreich* [1930], I, 99 f. and esp. 284.) Like the later Christian martyrologies, the depictions make use of the form of trial records. It is debated whether they are based on authentic records, but everywhere conceded that there has been progressive literary development. The accounts are part of the literature which honours heroes of conviction, like the work of Timotheus of Pergamon Περὶ τῆς τῶν φιλοσόφων ἀνδρείας, which is mentioned in Cl. Al. Strom., IV, 8, 56, 2. There is thus some relation to Plato's Apol., though the conviction and attitude are now purely political. The similarity of literary form, and some similarities of treatment, suggest inevitably a comparison with Christian accounts. (The genealogical relation is handled by A. Bauer, *op. cit.,* 45 with exemplary restraint.) But the terms μάρτυς etc. are not applied to the champions of the opposition in Alexandria. In so far as these men die for fearlessly proclaimed convictions, one can speak of a formal similarity to the Christian idea of the martyr, but the texts tell us nothing about the history of the concept.

C. μάρτυς, μαρτυρέω, μαρτυρία, μαρτύριον in the LXX.

1. The Hebrew Words.

When we consider μάρτυς κτλ. in the LXX attention is directed primarily to μαρτύριον. In respect of μάρτυς, μαρτυρεῖν, μαρτυρία the LXX remains by and large within the confines of popular usage and its various possibilities. The only exception is 4 Macc. 12:16 (A): οὐκ ἀπαυτομολῶ τῆς τῶν ἀδελφῶν μου μαρτυρίας, if we are to follow A with Swete and not to read ἀριστείας (א) with Rahlfs.[24] But a few passages in Dt. Is. also have a bearing. The main interest, however, centres on μαρτύριον.

a. μάρτυς occurs some 60 times, always for Heb. עֵד with the single exception of Gn. 31:47, unless we are to follow Rahlfs there in reading τῆς μαρτυρίας (D). In this verse the original is שָׂהֲדוּתָא, used by the Aramean Laban. The cairn erected on the occasion of his covenant with Jacob is called by him יְגַר שָׂהֲדוּתָא and by Jacob גַּלְעֵד. On the other side, עֵד is some 8 or 9 times rendered μαρτύριον, some 6 times μαρτυρεῖν, and a few times, inexactly, by other terms, though without any particular significance.[25] μαρτυρεῖν (some 15 times), when there is a Heb. original, is used once each for ענה and עוּד q. and twice for עוּד hi. which is usually translated → διαμαρτύρεσθαι. μαρτυρία (some 10 times, 6 times with Heb. equivalent) is found in Gn. 31:47 for שָׂהֲדוּתָא, in the verses mentioned in → n. 25 for עֵד, in ψ 18:7 for עֵדוּת (usually μαρτύριον), and in 1 Βασ. 9:24 for מוֹעֵד, unless (with Rahlfs) we read μαρτύριον here, as usually in the LXX.

b. In the case of μαρτύριον things are rather complicated. Used some 250 times, it is first the rendering of מוֹעֵד, almost always (over 100 times) in the expression אֹהֶל מוֹעֵד (ἡ) σκηνὴ (τοῦ) μαρτυρίου. Some 40 times it is used for עֵדָה and עֵדוּת, 8 or 9 times for עֵד, once for תְּעוּדָה. In many cases the use of μαρτύριον is very mechanical, and is to be explained by the view of the translator that the Heb. term to be translated was in some way connected with עוּד, עֵד, which is not always true, and which can make it hard to make sense of the rendering. This is very generally true of the rendering of מוֹעֵד by μαρτύριον. מוֹעֵד means the agreement or appointment (Ju. 20:38), or the content of the agreement, or the place or time agreed upon or appointed. The expression אֹהֶל מוֹעֵד means the appointed place where Yahweh will meet with Moses by agreement to impart His demands for Israel (Ex. 25:22). When the expression is rendered ἡ σκηνὴ τοῦ μαρτυρίου, it is obviously because the translator in some way perceived עוּד, עֵד as a constituent part in מוֹעֵד. The rendering is linguistically incorrect, but materially not unsuitable, and certainly not without point (→ 485). But when μαρτύριον is used in translation of הַמּוֹעֵד אֲשֶׁר (שָׂם) שְׁמוּאֵל (1 S. 13:8), of מוֹעֵד הַיָּמִים (1 S. 13:11), or of מוֹעֵד דָּוִד (1 S. 20:35), the Greek makes no sense. For מוֹעֵד here means the appointed time, and is elsewhere properly rendered καιρός (e.g., 2 Βασ. 20:5) or ὅρος (e.g., Ex. 9:5). Equally mechanical and meaningless is the use of μαρτύριον in Mi. 7:18 (God does not hold His wrath לָעַד) and Prv. 29:14 (the throne of the king who deals justly with the lowly will stand לָעַד), where the rendering εἰς μαρτύριον can be explained only in terms of a false reading of לָעַד, cf. also Am. 1:11 and Hos. 2:14:

---

[24] The μαρτυρία in 4 Macc. 12:16 A is a variant which we are to explain in terms of the later views of the Church. Orig. extolled Eleazar and the seven brothers as παράδειγμα κάλλιστον ... ῥωμαλέου μαρτυρίου, Exhort., 23.

[25] ἄνθρωπος, Is. 8:2; ἐγγυᾶν, Prv. 19:28; ἔτασις, Job 10:17; μαρτυρία, Ex. 20:16; Dt. 5:20; Prv. 25:18.

καὶ θήσομαι αὐτὰ εἰς μαρτύριον, HT : וְשַׂמְתִּים לְיַעַר. On the other hand, in Zeph. 3:8 the LXX is right in reading לְעֵד = εἰς μαρτύριον instead of the Mas. לְעַד. In Ιερ. 37:20 (30:20 HT): τὰ μαρτύρια αὐτῶν = עֵדָתוֹ or עֵדֹתָם, and in Job 15:34 : עֲדַת חָנֵף = μαρτύριον ἀσεβοῦς, עֵדָה ("congregation") is confused by LXX with עֵדָה*, עֵדוֹת ("commandments"). Literally, but by reason of the corruption of the text quite obscurely, μαρτύριον is put for עֵדוּת in 4 Βασ. 11:12. Nor can the Gk. reader make much of μαρτύριον τῷ 'Ασάφ = עֵדוּת לְאָסָף in the title of ψ 79.

2. The Use of μάρτυς, μαρτυρέω, μαρτυρία.

a. In the Legal Sphere. In the LXX, too, μάρτυς belongs to the legal world and denotes the witness before the judgment, in the first instance the witness for the prosecution, cf. Nu. 5:13; 35:30; Dt. 17:6, 7; 19:15. False witness stands under the severe threat of the *lex talionis,* Dt. 19:16 ff. The μάρτυς ἄδικος, δόλιος or ψευδής, also the overhasty witness (μάρτυς ταχύς) is particularly worthy of contempt, Ex. 23:1; ψ 26:12; 34:11; Prv. 6:19; 12:17, 19; 19:5, 9; 21:28, whereas the μάρτυς πιστός is praised, Prv. 14:25, 5. μαρτυρεῖν is used for judicial witness in Nu. 35:30; Dt. 19:15, 18; Sus. 41; μαρτυρία in Prv. 25:18. The witness to an agreement is found in Ιερ. 39(32):10, 25, 44 and Rt. 4:9, 10, the eye- or ear-witness to an event in Lv. 5:1; Nu. 23:18; Is. 8:2. For an appeal to Yahweh as witness cf. the agreement between Laban and Jacob in Gn. 31:44, and the pact between David and Jonathan in 1 S. 20:23, 42; also the agreement of the Jews who wish to go down to Egypt and Jeremiah in Ιερ. 49(42):5. Yahweh can also be a witness in judgment in Mal. 3:5; Ιερ. 36(29):23. He is a witness to the integrity of Samuel in 1 S. 12:5 f. (along with the king), to the innocence of Job (16:19): ἰδοὺ ἐν οὐρανοῖς ὁ μάρτυς μου; to the innocence of those who die rather than fight on the Sabbath in 1 Macc. 2:37, to what goes on in the inner part of man in Wis. 1:6; ψ 88:37 (ὁ μάρτυς ἐν οὐρανῷ πιστός). In the judgment of Yahweh the people are witnesses against themselves (Jos. 24:22), the song of Moses bears witness (μαρτυρεῖν) against Israel (Dt. 31:19, 21), and illegitimately begotten children are μάρτυρες πονηρίας κατὰ γονέων (Wis. 4:6). μαρτυρία is used generally and weakly for the proof or confirmation of something in Sir. 31:23 f. and 4 Macc. 6:32 (the death of Eleazar is a proof that λογισμός rules over the πάθη; otherwise I would have given them τὴν τῆς ἐπικρατείας μαρτυρίαν, and confirmed their superiority).[26] Similarly in Lam. 2:13 μαρτυρεῖν simply means to declare. In a few verses not mentioned here the bearing is obscure (cf. Ex. 21:36; 1 S. 9:24; 1 K. 17:20; 2 Ch. 28:10; Wis. 17:10).

b. In the Religious Sense. Along with all these passages in which there is nothing distinctive as compared with non-biblical popular use, a few verses from Dt. Is. deserve special attention.[27] We refer to the sections Is. 43:9-13 and 44:7-11.[28] Here Yahweh arranges before the nations a kind of trial in which it will be

[26] At Sir. 45:17 the μαρτύρια of B is more probably the original than the μαρτυρία of A, for this alone, as a par. to ἐντολαί, κρίματα, νόμος, corresponds to the usage of the LXX.

[27] Though he does not adduce the witness passages, K. Holl already in his essay of 1914 points out that acc. to Dt. Is. the prophet must die for his witness (p. 79). F. Dornseiff, ARW, 22 (1923/4), 133 ff. saw in these passages a decisive point for the development of the meaning of the term. E. Lohmeyer ("Die Idee des Martyriums im Judt. u. Urchr.," ZSTh, 5 [1927], 232 ff.), G. Fitzer in his unpublished diss., and esp. O. Michel, who even speaks of a prophetic martyr theology, all take up and develop this thought. The terms prophet and witness are even equated. But cf. Delehaye, *op. cit.,* 76, n. 1, who refuses to appeal either to the OT in general or even to Dt. Is. in particular: "Il n'y a rien là qui, de près ou de loin, donne l'idée d'un témoignage qui va jusqu'au sacrifice de la vie."

[28] The Gk. is inexact in both passages. In 43:10 (cf. also 12) it has after γένεσθέ μοι μάρτυρες or ὑμεῖς ἐμοὶ μάρτυρες a κἀγὼ (God) μάρτυς. In 44:8 the suffix of עֵדַי is not translated. In 44:9 the distinctive expression וְעֵדֵיהֶם הֵמָּה בַּל־יִרְאוּ וּבַל־יֵדְעוּ is left out. The meaning, however, is not affected by these deviations.

shown who is truly God, Yahweh or the gods of the Gentiles. The nations seem to be here both spectators and also judges who will decide (v. Rad). But they are also interested parties as advocates and witnesses on behalf of their gods. They are interested witnesses who must come forward to demonstrate the deity of their gods from their experiences (43:9; 44:9). To this extent they are also accusers of Yahweh, though vanquished by Him, 44:11. For these witnesses or deities have nothing whereof to testify. They see nothing and hear nothing. The makers of idols are impotent. Their favoured gods are of no use to them. In this trial they will be put to shame (44:9-11). In contrast, Israel is told three times: "You are my witnesses," 43:10, 12; 44:8. "Ye are my witnesses, saith the Lord, and my servant whom I have chosen, that ye may know, and believe me, and understand that I am he: before me there was no god formed, neither shall there be after me. I, even I, am the Lord; and beside me there is no saviour. I have declared, and have saved, and I have shewed, and there was no strange god among you: therefore ye are my witnesses, saith the Lord. I am God. Yea, from eternity I am he; and there is none that can deliver out of my hand," 43:10-13. "Who is like unto me? Let him come forth, and call, and declare it to me, and set in order for me ... and the things that are coming, and shall come, let them shew unto them. Fear not, neither be afraid. Have not I told thee long before, and declared it? Yea, ye are my witnesses. Is there a God beside me? Yea, there is no rock; I know not any," 44:7-9. In this trial between God and the nations and their gods, Israel, on the basis of the guidance, deliverance and revelation which is grounded in its election and which it has experienced, will declare to the nations of the world the uniqueness, reality, and deity of God. Hence they are His witnesses. For the prophets the deity of God is a fact, His particular saving action in the history of Israel is a fact. But it is not the kind of fact which can be observed and attested like any other externally demonstrable fact. It is a fact which is certain only to faith, which only the man who is not blind and deaf can see and attest, 43:8. The content of the witness is thus a religious truth of which the witness is convinced on the basis of his experience. It is a religious certainty whose content he emphatically represents, for whose acknowledgment he strives, but for the correctness of which he cannot give any rational proof or present any empirical demonstration. It is grounded, then, on the prophetic experience of revelation which is original, and which by nature is not subject to rational control. This is certainty to the prophet. It is also certainty to Israel in so far as it follows the spiritual leadership of prophecy. The witness to this reality of God which is believed and experienced in faith bears the character of a religious confession advanced with the claim to recognition.

If one compares the statements of Dt. Is. with those of Epictet., too much stress should not be laid on the fact that in Epictet. we have the witness of conduct whereas in Dt. Is. we have witness of mouth. The decisive point is the difference in content. The view of the witness in Dt. Is. is superior to that in Epictet. to the same degree that the prophetic historical view of God in the OT is superior to the rational Enlightenment philosophy of Epictet. The witness of Epictet. retreats into the capsule of apathy. The witness of Dt. Is. proclaims with holy passion the living God, whether by his conduct or by his existence (v. Rad). On the one hand we have philosophy or religion, on the other revelation. The word draws its life from its content.

Significant though this is, however, it is to be noted that one cannot speak of a witness concept in Dt. Is., though the great goal of evangelising the nations shines before him, 42:4; 49:6; 62:10; → λαός, 37. In him the term is a figurative one which he uses from time to time without in any way developing a technical use. In particular, there is no more precise connection between the function of witness discharged by the servant of Yahweh, Israel, and the suffering of the *'ebed Yahweh,* especially if we are to see in this *'ebed* a figure like the suffering king.[29] It is thus straining things exegetically to press the metaphor, to pour all that the book says about the servant of the Lord into the figure of the witness of Yahweh, to speak of the prophetic martyr theology of Dt. Is., or even to work this up into a formal theological system. There is certainly no direct connection with the early Christian concept of the witness, let alone with the concept of the martyr in the 2nd century Church.

3. The Use of μαρτύριον.

In respect of μαρτύριον one may first see traces of the popular use, though this quickly takes on a religious flavour. The total picture is thus controlled by a distinctively religious use.

In the sense of an objective witness or means of demonstration or the confirmation of the factuality of events or the correctness of an assertion, we find μαρτύριον in connection with the drawing off of the shoe in Rt. 4:7 in testimony of the renunciation of the right of redemption to Boaz. The 7 lambs which Abimelech receives from Abraham serve as a μαρτύριον that Abraham has dug the well of Beersheba, or as an acknowledgment of this fact by Abimelech, Gn. 21:30. The cairn in Gn. 31:44 serves as a μαρτύριον to the fact of the agreement between Jacob and Laban. In the same sense the altar erected by the Jordan in Jos. 22 is a μαρτύριον to the compact made there. In Is. 55:4 we read with ref. to David: μαρτύριον ἐν ἔθνεσιν ἔδωκα αὐτόν, which means that David, in virtue of all that Yahweh has granted him, is a factual proof of Yahweh's grace and power — in Sir. 36:14 there seems to be prayer for a similar proof of the authenticity of faith in Yahweh. But the witness to facts can also be accusation. The stone of Shechem serves as a μαρτύριον to the fact of the covenant made with Yahweh, and this is a threat when Israel breaks the covenant, Jos. 24:27. Thus the Law laid up in the ark can be ἐν ὑμῖν εἰς μαρτύριον in the sense of accusing witness, like the song of Moses extolling the acts of Yahweh towards Israel, Dt. 31:19, 26. On the other side Yahweh Himself can become εἰς μαρτύριον, not in leveling accusations, but in executing judgment, Mi. 1:2; Zeph. 3:8. Through the judgment which He executes He establishes beyond cavil the fact of the guilt of those on whom it falls. This is how Hos. 2:14 LXX is to be understood. God will make the devastated plantings of Israel εἰς μαρτύριον, namely, a proof of the reality of their sin and also of His judgments on them; cf. the expression μαρτύριον τῆς πονηρίας (Wis. 10:7) with ref. to the wasted and smoking fields of Sodom etc. Thus the witness against men becomes an attestation of God Himself. It is this thought which controls the expressions σκηνὴ τοῦ μαρτυρίου, κιβωτὸς τοῦ μαρτυρίου. This does not really correspond to Gk. usage, according to which there is something objective about the word μαρτύριον. For the tent or ark cannot be described as μαρτύριον. Nor can it be said that there is in them an objective μαρτύριον or demonstration. One can think only in terms of the tables of the Law which acc. to Ex. 25:15(16), 20(21) are laid up in the ark. But these are τὰ μαρτύρια. Hence the phrase σκηνὴ τοῦ μαρτυρίου neither could nor did suggest these to the Gk. reader — the phrase is σκηνὴ τοῦ μαρτυρίου, never σκηνὴ τῶν μαρτυρίων — but it pointed him to the fact that here the attestation of God takes place through the directions there imparted to Moses for Israel (Ex. 25:22). μαρτύριον always takes on here the sense of revelation, the revelation of divine commandments.

---

29 Cf. on this W. Eichrodt, *Theologie des AT* (1933), 262, n. 6 and the bibl. given there. But v. Rad points out that the *Ebed* is usually thought to refer to the prophet himself.

If the rendering of אֹהֶל מוֹעֵד by σκηνὴ τοῦ μαρτυρίου is linguistically inexact, it is materially appropriate. But the term μαρτύριον is also materially appropriate in the admittedly not very many cases where the phrases אֹהֶל הָעֵדוּת (Nu. 9:15; 17:22, 23; 18:2; 2 Ch. 24:6) or מִשְׁכַּן הָעֵדוּת (Nu. 1:50, 53; 10:11) or אֲרוֹן הָעֵדוּת (= κιβωτὸς τοῦ μαρτυρίου, e.g., Ex. 25:10, 22; 26:33 f.; 40:5 A, 21; Nu. 4:5; 7:89) were being translated.

In all these combinations μαρτύριον is always in the sing. The only exception is ἡ κιβωτὸς τῶν μαρτυρίων in Ex. 30:6. This reminds us that acc. to Ex. 25:15 ff. τὰ μαρτύρια, the Mosaic Law (עֵדוּת), lay in the ark ; cf. τὸ ἱλαστήριον τὸ ἐπὶ τῶν μαρτυρίων, Lv. 16:13; ἀπέναντι τῶν μαρτυρίων, Ex. 30:36; 40:20.[30] To be sure, in Ex. 31:18; 32:15 we find πλάκες τοῦ μαρτυρίου. But elsewhere the plur. τὰ μαρτύρια is used for the concrete statutes of the divine attestation from which the Mosaic Law proceeded. This corresponds in some instances to עֵדוּת, but usually to the plur. of עֵדָה. This plur. is formally a par. for δικαιώματα, κρίματα, προστάγματα, ἐντολαί, διαθήκη, νόμος (cf. Dt. 4:45; 6:17; 3 Βασ. 2:3; 4 Βασ. 17:13-15; 1 Ch. 29:19; Ιερ. 51:23; ψ 77:5; 80:5 f.; 98:7; 118 *passim;* 131:12).[31]

Hence a distinctive point in the LXX use in so far as it goes beyond the popular is the fact that Yahweh Himself is the subject of the μαρτυρεῖν contained in μαρτύριον. But this μαρτυρεῖν is worked out in the revelation imparted to Moses. The commandments are its content. The full appropriation of the word μαρτύριον and its plural μαρτύρια for the self-witness of God in the Mosaic legislation is a highly significant process for the development of OT nomism.

D. The Idea of the Martyr in Later Judaism ; the Usage in Josephus and Philo.

"The Jewish religion is a religion of martyrdom. It is born out of martyrdom and the sufferings of the righteous in the Maccabean age. At the end of our epoch stands the figure of the martyr Akiba, who rejoices because in his martyrdom he first fulfils in truth the saying : Thou shalt love God with thy whole soul."[32] Already in the early Church, cf. Orig. Exhort. → n. 24, it became the custom to bring the events to which we refer into close connection with the development of the early Christian μάρτυς concept.[33] Now it may well be that one can discern this kind of influence in the further history of the idea, so that in the Church's tradition the Maccabean martyrs could even be enrolled among the Christian martyrs.[34] Nevertheless, this approach is not correct so far as the origin of the early Christian concept is concerned, and it hampers a clear understanding of the uniqueness of this concept.

The figure of the prophet who for the sake of his mission, or the righteous man who for the sake of his piety, suffers calumny, persecution and even death, was known to Israel prior to the time of the Maccabees. One has only to remember Elijah, or the prophets put to death by Jezebel, or the martyrdom of the prophet Uriah (1 K. 19:10; Jer. 26:20 ff.). The true prophet says nothing to tickle

---

[30] Cf. also Dt. 9:15, where μαρτύρια (πλάκες τῶν μαρτυρίων) is used in A for בְּרִית. Similarly μαρτύρια is used for חֹק at Sir. 45:17 [Bertram].

[31] In their usage Σ etc. offer nothing of material significance as compared with the LXX.

[32] Bousset-Gressm., 374.

[33] Bousset-Gressm., 190; Holl, *Ges. Aufsätze,* II, 79 f.; A. Schlatter; O. Michel. On this v. Campenhausen, *op. cit.,* 1-3. Cf. also E. Bickermann, *Der Gott der Makkabäer* (1936) [G. Kittel].

[34] Cf. on this Schürer, III⁴, 486 f.

the fancy of people. He is irrevocably committed to preach repentance. The echo which he finds is in all ages הַאַתָּה זֶה עֹכֵר יִשְׂרָאֵל (1 K. 18:17), and sometimes he must suffer the consequences. Alongside the prophet with his special mission is the righteous man (cf. Ps. 69:8-10), and indeed the whole people, which is forced to complain: "For thy sake are we killed" (Ps. 44:22).[35] This experience did, of course, reach its climax in the atrocities of the Syrian persecution, and it is only natural that now and later, when the newly kindled zeal found itself exposed to new pressures, attention should be directed to the figures who had defied the demand for apostasy, and crowned their faithfulness and obedience to the Law with steadfast endurance even to death. 1 Macc. tells their story with simple objectivity (chapters 1 and 2). 2 Macc. glories in the παρρησία with which the victims went to their execution, and in the obedience to the Law which triumphed over every pain. To 4 Macc., which in a Hellenistic spirit causes the depiction of the Maccabean martyrdoms to serve the message of the triumph of reason over sufferings, the whole of the OT from the murder of Abel onwards is a collection of illustrations of the true martyr spirit (18:11 ff.). Josephus describes with quiet admiration the Essenes, who defy all threats, ἵν' ἢ βλασφημήσωσιν τὸν νομοθέτην ἢ φάγωσίν τι τῶν ἀσυνήθων, and who without any sign of pain, and even smiling (μειδιῶντες ἐν ταῖς ἀλγηδόσιν), suffer the most exquisite tortures even to death (Bell., 2, 151-153; cf. also 1, 648-655 on the σοφισταί, i.e., the rabbis Judas and Matthias and their 40 pupils, who died ὑπὲρ τοῦ πατρίου νόμου). We may also recall the martyrdom of Isaiah (who did not cry out when he was sawn asunder, for his mouth conversed with the Holy Ghost, Mart. Is. 5:14), En. 47:2; Hb. 11:35-38, and the adornment of the graves of the prophets (Mt. 23:29), whose violent death seems to have come to be taken for granted in the days of Jesus (Mt. 23:37; Lk. 13:33; Mt. 5:11 f.; Ac. 7:52).[36] All this gives us some idea how vital for the people was the ideal of the righteous man who proves his loyalty to the faith and the Law by suffering persecution and death. That this ideal lived on may be seen in the Rabbinic tradition concerning the end of various pious teachers of the Law in older and more recent times, especially R. Akiba in the Barcochba revolt.[37]

But though this much is clear, and though the general regard for heroes of faith and obedience may be seen in the adornment of the stories and the legendary poetry (cf. Da. 3), nevertheless it is surprising that nowhere are the terms μάρτυς,

---

[35] How strong this idea was throughout the OT has been finely shown by K. F. Euler, "Die Verkündigung vom leidenden Gottesknecht aus Js. 53 in der griech. Bibel," BWANT, 4. F., 14 (1934), 114-119, to which G. Bertram refers. But the concept of martyrdom and its history are to be distinguished from the idea of martyrdom and its history. The concept itself does not occur. The same must be said in relation to Job, whom, as v. Rad points out, R. Hempel brings into relation to the idea of martyrdom in his essay "Das theologisches Problem des Hiob," ZSTh, 6 (1928/9), 645. Yahweh had stated that Job would not curse Him even in misfortune. Thus Job is a witness to God by his attitude. Nevertheless, he does not suffer persecutions etc. because of His faith. And, as Hempel himself observes, the term "witness" is not applied to him. In → Surkau, too, there is no clear distinction between the concept of martyrdom and ideas and motifs linked with it.

[36] Cf. on this Schlatter, *op. cit.*, 18 f.

[37] There is rich material in Str.-B., I, 221-226 on Mt. 5:10 and I, 581 on Mt. 10:28, where the most celebrated martyrs of the Rabb. tradition are listed. Cf. also F. Weber, *Jüdische Theologie*[2] (1897), 26 f.; Schürer, I[3], 200 f., 696 f.; also the bibl. in v. Campenhausen, 2, n. 4.

μαρτυρεῖν, μαρτυρία used in this context.[38] This is no accident. In the case of the Christian martyr it is always recalled that witness is borne to someone (as in Is. 43 and 44), that he turns with a message to others. This is not so with the martyrs of Judaism. The high estimation of martyrs is wholly within the framework of the Pharisaic ideal of piety. Suffering and death for the Law is a work of piety *par excellence.*[39] Nowhere is this more apparent than in the statement of R. Akiba already mentioned. Only if we take the word martyr in the very general sense to denote one who suffers for his convictions can it be used of the Maccabean heroes of faith and obedience. But this does not contribute to an understanding of the early Christian concept.

In keeping with this is the fact that there is nothing distinctive about the use of the terms μάρτυς κτλ. in the writings here in question.[40] In Joseph.[41] it is worth noting that in spite of the fixed usage of the LXX he simply says σκηνή or κιβωτός rather than σκηνὴ (or κιβωτὸς) τοῦ μαρτυρίου. He also avoids the plural μαρτύρια = ἐντολαί = νόμος (Ant., 3, 6). Perhaps his *graeculi* had a hand in this. It is understandable that they should not take kindly to this use of the word μαρτύριον.

Nor does Philo's usage offer any deviation from the normal use. μάρτυς, μαρτυρεῖν, μαρτυρία belong to the legal sphere (witness at trials or to agreements),[42] to the attestation of individual facts or events, or to facts of general experience,[43] or to the

[38] The only passage which is supposed to prove the Jewish use of μάρτυς for the suffering prophet, i.e., Rev. 11:3 ff., which "assuredly derives from Jewish sources" (Holl, *Ges. Aufsätze,* II, 80), is hardly adequate to support an assertion or conjecture to the contrary. For even if there is or might be a Jewish basis, it does not follow that μάρτυς was here related to the suffering prophets. This is in fact most unlikely. For details on the passage → 495. Nor are the terms applied to the Jewish righteous of Da., who, defying the threats of Nebuchadnezzar, refuse to worship the image which he had set up, remaining true to their God and to His worship alone (Da. 3:17 f.; cf. also c. 6). Moreover the king is brought to understanding, not by their defiance (3:18), but by their miraculous deliverance.

[39] This has been rightly emphasised by v. Campenhausen, 3 f.

[40] There are passages from Jub. and Apc. Bar. in Str.-B., I, 475 on Mt. 8:4.

[41] Ant., 4, 219: εἷς ... μὴ πιστευέσθω μάρτυς, but at least two, ὧν τὴν μαρτυρίαν ἀληθῆ ποιήσει τὰ προβεβιωμένα. γυναικῶν δὲ μὴ ἔστω μαρτυρία διὰ κουφότητα καὶ θράσος τοῦ γένους αὐτῶν. μαρτυρείτωσαν δὲ μηδὲ δοῦλοι διὰ τὴν τῆς ψυχῆς ἀγένειαν. Vita, 360: παρ' εἰδότων ἔμελλες τῆς ἀκριβείας τὴν μαρτυρίαν ἀποφέρεσθαι. Ap., 1, 93: τῆς ἀρχαιότητος ταύτης παρατίθεμαι τοὺς Αἰγυπτίους μάρτυρας.

[42] Philo Spec. Leg., I, 55: Those who are zealous for ἀρετή are, e.g., βουλευταί, δικασταί, στρατηγοί, ἐκκλησιασταί, κατήγοροι, μάρτυρες, νόμοι, δῆμος in one person; Spec. Leg., IV, 54. Decal., 140: Those engaged in proceedings, if other proofs are lacking, ἐπὶ μάρτυρας καταφεύγουσιν; Plant., 173: the Aristotelian distinction between ἔντεχνοι and ἄτεχνοι ἀποδείξεις, witnesses belonging to the latter; Spec. Leg., IV, 30 (witness to an agreement).

[43] Poster. C., 59; Conf. Ling., 57 (ὄψει πρὸ ἀκοῆς σαφεστέρῳ χρησάμενος μάρτυρι); Abr., 190; Jos., 208; Spec. Leg., I, 341; Conf. Ling., 157; Cher., 40; Leg. All., II, 54 f.; often of God, Spec. Leg., II, 10 and 252; IV, 32; Plant., 82; Migr. Abr., 115; Jos., 265; Decal., 86: The oath is μαρτυρία θεοῦ περὶ πραγμάτων ἀμφισβητουμένων (a common definition in Philo e.g., Spec. Leg., II, 10; Leg. All., III, 205), but in the sense that one θεὸν μάρτυρα καλεῖ, Decal., 90 — μαρτυρία can then mean almost emphatic statement (Rer. Div. Her., 4 ἡ τοῦ προφήτου μαρτυρία) or proof of something (Migr. Abr., 43: εἰς μαρτυρίαν πίστεως ἣν ἐπίστευσεν ἡ ψυχὴ θεῷ that Abraham by his conduct may prove that he believes in God); Jos., 234 f. (Joseph had already secured two μαρτυρίαι for the conduct of his brothers towards Benjamin; but τρίτην ἐπενόησε).

confirmation of certain views expressed or truths maintained,[44] etc. Here, too, μαρτύριον usually has an objective nuance, e.g., as applied to quotations which show this or that statement to be correct, or to facts which serve as proof.[45] There is in Philo not even the first impulse towards a specific use along the lines of that found in primitive Christianity.

E. μάρτυς, μαρτυρέω, μαρτυρία, μαρτύριον in the New Testament.

1. Occurrence.

The distribution in the various writings is worth noting: μάρτυς 34 times (with Lk. 11:48 35 times), 4 (5) times in the Synoptics, 0 in Jn., 13 in Ac., 9 in Paul (incl. Past.); 2 in Hb., 1 in 1 Pt., 5 in Rev.; μαρτυρεῖν 76 times (with Lk. 11:48 77), 2 (3) in the Synoptics, 33 in Jn., 11 in Ac., 8 in Pl., 8 in Hb., 10 in 1 and 3 Jn., 4 in Rev.; μαρτυρία 37 times, 4 in the Synoptics, 14 in Jn., 1 in Ac., 2 in Pl. (Past.), 7 in 1 and 3 Jn., 9 in Rev.; μαρτύριον 20 times, 9 in the Synoptics, 0 in Jn., 2 in Ac., 6 in Pl., 1 in Hb., 1 in Jm., 1 in Rev. A striking feature is that we find μαρτυρεῖν 47 times in the Johannine writings, μαρτυρία 30 times, and μάρτυς and μαρτύριον not at all in the Gospel. A strong proportion of the instances of μάρτυς and μαρτυρεῖν is in Ac. This statistical finding seems to be external, but it is not, since it is connected with the development of the distinctively Christian use of the terms.

2. The Use of μάρτυς.

To understand the NT use it is basic to remember that non-biblical Gk. already uses the concept of witness both in the sense of witness to ascertainable facts and also in that of witness to truths, i.e., the making known and confessing of convictions (→ B.). Both uses are also found in the NT, and the development of the distinctive Christian use is the result of their application to the content of Gospel proclamation and to the circumstances in which this took place.

a. General Use; Witness to Facts.

The original sense of witness to facts, i.e., the man who can speak about them from his own direct knowledge, especially in legal proceedings, is to be found in Mk. 14:63 = Mt. 26:65. When Jesus, in answer to the high-priest's question whether he was the Christ, confessed that He was the Son of Man of Daniel, the high-priest cried out in relief, for this blasphemy in the very ears of his fellow-members on the council made it unnecessary to proceed by the method of proof by witness, hitherto attempted in vain: τὶ ἔτι χρείαν ἔχομεν μαρτύρων.[46] A trial witness, again in proceedings against blasphemy, is also meant in Ac. 6:13; 7:58. False witnesses (μάρτυρες ψευδεῖς) are set up to bring about the condemnation of Stephen, and though there seems to be no orderly sentence he is

---

[44] Philo, Jos., 134: μάρτυρες τῶν ἐνυπνίων οὐκ ἄνδρες μόνον, ἀλλὰ καὶ πόλεις κτλ. (for the truth of the dreams of Joseph); Abr., 29: our senses with the tongue and the νοῦς as the seventh are μάρτυρες to the previously intimated significance of the number seven; Det. Pot. Ins., 99 (of poets); Som., II, 297 (μάρτυς δὲ καὶ χρησμός); Migr. Abr., 3 (μάρτυς Μωυσῆς); Poster. C., 121 (μάρτυς ὁ νόμος); Spec. Leg., I, 37; Vit. Mos., II, 120 and 284; Aet. Mund., 102 (πρὸς μαρτυρίαν in confirmation); Cher., 124; Leg. All., III, 129 (μαρτυρεῖ ... ὁ ἱερώτατος χρησμός); Det. Pot. Ins., 52 (μαρτυρεῖ δέ μου τῷ λόγῳ ἡ φύσις).

[45] Cher. 88 (αἱ ἐτήσιοι ὧραι — the times of the year — are μαρτύριον ἐναργέστατον for the κακοπάθεια, the torment of the cosmos which is in ongoing movement); Aet. Mund., 25 (μαρτύρια καὶ τὰ ἐν Τιμαίῳ); Spec. Leg., IV, 136 (of eye-witnesses).

[46] On the witnesses in the trial of Jesus cf. Str.-B. on Mt. 26:60.

then stoned according to the statute in Dt. 17:7.[47] In this connection we might also mention Hb. 10:28, where in the second warning against irremediable apostasy there is a reminder of the decree of Dt. 17:6 that if a man is guilty of an impious breach of the OT covenant by worshipping other gods, then he must be put to death by stoning if his act is proved by at least two or three witnesses.[48] The legal principle that one witness is not enough for condemnation is stated very generally in Dt. 19:15, and the regulation of Mt. 18:16 borrows from this verse. If in the brotherhood of the Christian community a disciple has offended against another, and the wounded party cannot turn him from his wrongdoing between themselves, then he must repeat the attempt before one or two others, ἵνα ἐπὶ στόματος δύο μαρτύρων ἢ τριῶν σταθῇ πᾶν ῥῆμα. If this attempt also fails, the statements of these witnesses about what has occurred will serve as a basis for the decision which must then be made by the community. According to 1 Tm. 5:19 the Deuteronomic principle that there must be more than one witness also applies when accusation is made against one of the elders of the Christian congregation. Again, in 2 C. 13:1 Paul appeals to the same principle to establish the seriousness of his intention of purifying the congregation on his approaching third visit: Τρίτον τοῦτο ἔρχομαι πρὸς ὑμᾶς· ἐπὶ στόματος δύο μαρτύρων καὶ τριῶν σταθήσεται πᾶν ῥῆμα.[49]

Paul seems to compare his different visits to Corinth to two different but agreed witnesses in a trial who dispose of all doubts concerning the facts. The point at issue is his firm resolve to purify the congregation. On the very first visit his goal was a congregation which would separate itself from sin (cf. 1 C. 6:9). The second aimed to deal with flagrant abuses. It failed. The firmer, then, is Paul's resolve to create pure relations on his imminent new visit. In this case, the relation between the original saying in Dt. 19:15 and Paul's use of it is, of course, very loose. For there is no judicial process, nor are there two or three distinct witnesses, only the repeated assertion of the same witness. The point of comparison is merely that in virtue of repetition on the one side, different witnesses on the other, there can be no doubt as to specific facts in the one case, and a fixed purpose in the other. The seriousness of the statement is in both instances beyond all question.[50] The passage is thus an example of the freedom with which the apostle makes use of OT sayings without concern as to their exact meaning. It is also an example of the freedom which he permits himself in the formal movement of thought.

---

[47] *Ibid.* on Ac. 7:58.

[48] *Ibid.* on Mt. 18:16.

[49] The passage is often taken to mean that Paul is describing the way in which he will exercise discipline, i.e., the way which acc. to Dt. 19:15 "is adapted to lead to the orderly ascertaining of that which needs to be punished," so Heinr., *ad loc.;* B. Weiss, *Das NT, Handausgabe,* II[2] (1902), *ad loc.;* Schl. K., 675: "On every offence Paul will establish what has happened by two or three witnesses." Pl. is thus thought to be applying the Jewish legal rule (Dt. 19:15) to Church discipline. But Pl. in no way believes there is about the misdeed any doubt which needs to be cleared up by formal depositions. His judgment is just as firm as is his conviction of the need for punishment (c. 7; 12:21). The only point is whether those who are at first opposed will finally yield. Moreover, on this interpretation one cannot do justice to the apparently intentional connection between the τρίτον at the beginning of the verse and the three witnesses at the end.

[50] Thus it is not tacitly implied that the decision is confirmed through this twofold or threefold witness before God (cf. D. Wendland, *NT Deutsch, ad loc.*). This would be to dislocate the whole of Paul's chain of thought. Nor does God need the statements of human witnesses to establish facts.

The idea of a witness to facts takes on a more general sense beyond the judicial when Paul frequently calls upon God as a witness to processes and motives in his inner life, no other factual witnesses being available to prove the veracity and authenticity of what he affirms (R. 1:9; 2 C. 1:23; Phil. 1:8; 1 Th. 2:5), or when he invokes the Thessalonians, and with them God, who in the last resort is alone able to judge as He who knows the heart, as witnesses "how holily and justly and unblameably we behaved ourselves among you that believe" (1 Th. 2:10). The observation in 2 C. 1:23 is rather different from these verses in the sense that here Paul appeals directly to God as witness (whereas elsewhere he is simply content to assert that God is his witness), and by adding μάρτυρα τὸν θεὸν ἐπικαλοῦμαι "ἐπὶ τὴν ἐμὴν ψυχήν" he invokes a formal curse against his own soul if his statement does not correspond to the truth. The saying thus takes on the formal character of an oath, though in this capacity it expresses an element which lends particular weight to the appeal to God as witness only where there is faith in Him, or at least no decided lack of faith.

μάρτυς is used for the human witness to facts in Lk. 11:48, where to the Jews who build the graves of the prophets whom their fathers killed Jesus proclaims: ἄρα μάρτυρές ἐστε καὶ συνευδοκεῖτε τοῖς ἔργοις τῶν πατέρων ὑμῶν. If the meaning of συνευδοκεῖτε is not very clear, it is obvious enough that the present generation with its cult of the graves bears witness to the fact that the fathers murdered the prophets. μάρτυς is used in the same sense, not only in 1 Th. 2:10, but also in 1 Tm. 6:12: Timothy has made the good confession (his baptismal confession) ἐνώπιον πολλῶν μαρτύρων (cf. Did., 7, 4; Just. Apol., I, 61). In the phrase ἃ ἤκουσας ... διὰ πολλῶν μαρτύρων, ταῦτα παράθου in 2 Tm. 2:2 there is again a reference to the fact that Timothy has received baptism (or possibly ordination) in the presence of many witnesses, and that the tradition, the παραθήκη, has been committed to him thereby. The μάρτυς is also a witness to an externally perceptible event in Hb. 12:1. After the long list of examples of faith in c. 11, the author proceeds in 12:1: τοιγαροῦν καὶ ἡμεῖς, τοσοῦτον ἔχοντες περικείμενον ἡμῖν νέφος μαρτύρων, ὄγκον ἀποθέμενοι πάντα καὶ τὴν εὐπερίστατον ἁμαρτίαν, δι' ὑπομονῆς τρέχωμεν τὸν προκείμενον ἡμῖν ἀγῶνα κτλ. The readers are represented as runners who have entered the arena. They make ready to run by laying aside everything that would impede them. Around them on the stands are the packed ranks of spectators, the νέφος μαρτύρων, who with avid interest follow the course of the runners as eye-witnesses.[51] The distinctive thing here is, of course, that this νέφος μαρτύρων consists of those who according to c. 11 have received witness (acknowledgment) from God because of their faith (ἐμαρτυρήθησαν, 11:2; cf. 11:4, 5, 39). As such, they bear witness by the very fact of their existence to the authenticity of faith. It thus seems that the factual witness is also implicitly a confessing witness. But the witness which a man receives is different from that which he gives. The movement from a passive "attested by reason of faith" to an active "witness to the validity of faith" is not intimated by the text itself. Without exact analysis one might easily presuppose here a technical use of μάρτυς which is certainly not present in Hb. One is forced to concede, however, that in 12:1 the term has a certain ambivalence in the light of c. 11.

---

51 Expositors often resist this most obvious meaning. But B. F. Westcott, *The Epistle to the Hebrews* (1889) is forced to admit: "It is impossible to exclude the thought of the spectators in the amphitheatre"; cf. Class. Rev., 5 (1891), 21b.

b. The Special Lukan Use (Combination of Witness to Facts and Witness in the Sense of Evangelistic Confession).

In all the instances thus far adduced the use of μάρτυς remains within the framework of popular usage.

It is Luke's usage in Lk. 24:48 and Ac. which takes us beyond this, but in such a way that here, too, the term first denotes one who declares facts directly known to himself. The facts in question, however, are the facts of the history of Jesus, especially His resurrection, which is treated by Luke as no less an objective fact than the passion. But witness cannot be borne to these facts unless their significance is also indicated and an emphatic appeal is made for their recognition in faith. This, too, is from God's standpoint a fact. But it is a fact on a different level from that of the facts in the story of Jesus. It cannot be confirmed by witnesses; it can only be believed and then attested by proclamation. The distinctiveness of the object referred to in this witness implies also that the declaration of specific facts and the believing, confessing, evangelising confession of their significance are indissolubly united in the concept of the witness. The witness to facts and the witness to truth are one and the same — the unavoidable result of the fact that the Gospel presents a historical revelation. But the fact that Luke applies the concept of the witness to the content of the Gospel is grounded in his marked concern to expound clearly the historical foundations of the evangelical message.[52] At issue are, not doctrines, myths, or speculations, but facts which took place in the clear light of history at a specific time and place, facts which can be established and on which one can rely.[53] Hence one must speak of witnesses. Nor are these witnesses in general. They are those who are qualified to be witnesses because they themselves lived through the events. They were indeed specifically called to be such (Lk. 24:47; Ac. 1:8, 22-26). They were given the necessary equipment for their task (Lk. 24:48; Ac. 5:32). Herein may be seen Luke's concept of, and interest in, the witness. This concept coincides with that of the apostle in the narrower sense, and, unless it undergoes reconstruction, it is equally bound to disappear as historical development proceeds.

All the essential elements are present already in the first and only instance in Lk., i.e., in the missionary command of the risen Lord to the eleven[54] in Jerusalem (24:48). Jesus first shows that according to the statements of Scripture Christ had thus (i.e., as He did) to suffer and on the third day to rise again. He then says that on the basis of His name repentance for the remission of sins is to be proclaimed to all nations beginning at Jerusalem. In the last phrase the reference to scriptural statements becomes the missionary charge to the disciples. The addition ὑμεῖς μάρτυρες τούτων shows why the disciples are fitted for this task, and how they will discharge it. They are fitted because from experience they can bear witness to the factuality of the suffering and resurrection of Jesus, and also because they have grasped in faith the significance of Jesus, and can thus attest it. They discharge the task by proclaiming both the facts and their significance

[52] Cf. on this v. Campenhausen, 30 f.

[53] Hence the short prologue to the Gospel and the chronological data in Lk. 2:1 f.; 3:2. It would be superficial to see here only the pleasure which the historian takes in exact dating. The motive at work is the same as that which brought Pontius Pilate into the Apostles' Creed.

[54] Lk. 24:33 mentions τοὺς σὺν αὐτοῖς as well as the eleven, but does not shed any further light on this.

as they have grasped this in faith. Only thus does the *kerygma* become the *kerygma*. As special equipment they have the prospect of the Spirit whom the Father has promised and whom Jesus will send (v. 49).

What is intimated in Lk. is developed in Ac. The missionary charge to the apostolic band is repeated with the phrase ἔσεσθέ μου μάρτυρες (1:8). The primary thought is that they can and will proclaim from first-hand knowledge the story of Jesus (1:22; 10:39) and especially the fact of His resurrection (2:32; 3:15; 5:31 f.; 10:41). But in so doing they will always emphasise its saving significance (cf. esp. 10:42). It is at once apparent that this condition can be met only by a select circle whose members had the honour of personal encounter with the risen Lord (10:41; 1:22). These are μάρτυρες αὐτοῦ πρὸς τὸν λαόν (13:31).

The latter quotation from Paul's address in the synagogue at Pisidian Antioch is worth noting because here only the older apostles "who came up with him from Galilee to Jerusalem," and by whom "he was seen many days," are called μάρτυρες αὐτοῦ, whereas Paul uses of himself and Barnabas the word εὐαγγελίζεσθαι. The emphasis is, of course, that these are μάρτυρες αὐτοῦ πρὸς τὸν λαόν (i.e., Israel in Palestine), whereas ἡμεῖς ὑμᾶς εὐαγγελιζόμεθα (in the Hellenistic world outside Palestine, though first in the Synagogue). Nevertheless, the choice of terms is no accident. It is controlled by the fact that μάρτυς could not be used of Paul (or Barnabas) in the sense in which it had thus far been used in Ac.

c. The Incipient Separation of the Two Elements in Luke.

The more surprising it is, then, that the term is used of Paul in Ac. 22:15 and 26:16, and that Stephen, too, is called μάρτυς σου (of Jesus) in 22:20.

When Paul receives his sight back, Ananias tells him in 22:14 that God has foreordained him to know His will καὶ ἰδεῖν τὸν δίκαιον καὶ ἀκοῦσαι φωνὴν ἐκ τοῦ στόματος αὐτοῦ, ὅτι ἔσῃ μάρτυς αὐτῷ πρὸς πάντας ἀνθρώπους ὧν ἑώρακας καὶ ἤκουσας. In 26:16 Jesus Himself says to Paul on the Damascus road: εἰς τοῦτο γὰρ ὤφθην σοι, προχειρίσασθαί σε ὑπηρέτην καὶ μάρτυρα ὧν τε εἶδές [με] ὧν τε ὀφθήσομαί σοι κτλ. In both passages the concept of the witness is applied to Paul's missionary work in the sense of the witness to facts, as in the case of the older apostles in the passages previously mentioned. But in this sense, in the sense of Ac. 1:22, he is not really a witness to facts. At best, he is this only with reference to the Damascus vision, and in both instances the concept is limited to this and to the visions which followed. But limited, or totally reorientated in this way, the concept is not very well adapted to characterise the content of Paul's missionary work. For the heart of this is the crucifixion, not the Damascus vision. Hence both passages must be regarded as an artificial and not wholly successful attempt to make applicable to Paul the concept of the factual witness which was so decisive for Luke in respect of the older apostles. Apart from the Damascus appearance, Paul could be described as a witness only in respect of the implied element of witness to the significance of the person and story of Jesus, i.e., in the sense of the confessing witness. That this is so may be seen in Ac. 22:15, for here (and here alone) we read ἔσῃ μάρτυς αὐτῷ (for Christ) where one might have expected the genitive. Paul will bear witness for Him by expounding His significance and summoning to faith in Him. Naturally, an assertion of the factuality of the story of Jesus is contained in this witness. But the witness can no longer be called such because he can tell the story from his own experience. Paul is not a factual witness in the same sense as the older apostles. For he cannot guarantee the story of Christ from first-hand knowledge.

He is, however, a witness to truth who seeks to propagate the Christian faith by confession. The result is that, when the term μάρτυς is applied to Paul, the second aspect begins to predominate over the first, whereas the reverse is true when the term is used of the older apostles. The two elements begin to separate, and this enables the term to survive when by the very nature of the case there are no more apostolic witnesses to the facts in the original sense.

A further step is taken when Stephen is called "thy witness" in Ac. 22:20. It is true that the phrase ἐξεχύννετο τὸ αἷμα Στεφάνου τοῦ μάρτυρός σου does not mean that here already we have the later ecclesiastical martyr concept. The genitive σου shows that we are still wholly in the sphere of the original sense. Stephen is not called a witness because he dies; he dies because he is a witness of Christ and because of his evangelistic activity. Nevertheless, there is no sense any more of the man who from first-hand knowledge can bear witness to the facts of Jesus' history. He is simply the confessional witness. All the apostles were, of course, confessional witnesses. But Stephen is called this in an emphatic and distinctive way because by suffering death he gave final proof of the seriousness of his confessional witness. His martyrdom underlies the fact, not that he is called μάρτυς, but that he is so in this emphatic way. To this degree the usage here prepares the ground for the later technical use in the Church.[55] The fact of persecution rather than special ecstatic experiences of the martyrs led to the development of this specialised usage.

d. 1 Pt. 5:1.

A distinctive and equivocal use is to be found in the phrase μάρτυς τῶν τοῦ Χριστοῦ παθημάτων with which Peter in 1 Pt. 5:1 establishes the authority of his admonition to the elders of the community concerning the way in which they should discharge their office: πρεσβυτέρους ... παρακαλῶ ὁ συμπρεσβύτερος καὶ μάρτυς τῶν τοῦ Χριστοῦ παθημάτων. He can give the admonitions of 2 f. because he has the same task as the presbyters, though in a wider circle, and yet at the same time[56] he is μάρτυς τῶν τοῦ Χριστοῦ παθημάτων. At a first glance it might seem that Peter is here calling himself an eye-witness of the passion of Jesus[57] in order to remind the presbyters of His exemplary attitude to suffering. But the continuation ὁ καὶ τῆς μελλούσης ἀποκαλύπτεσθαι δόξης κοινωνός shows that the reference is to personal participation, including participation in Christ's sufferings, and not just to being there as an eye-witness[58] (cf. the description of the sufferings of Christians in persecution as κοινωνεῖν τοῖς τοῦ Χριστοῦ παθήμασιν in 4:13). That the sufferings endured in persecution or in fulfilment of the missionary call should be thought of in this way is a common notion in the NT.[59] The expression also implies that Peter knew persecution, to whose

[55] K. Holl has tried to base the application of the term to Stephen on the fact that just before his death he saw the glory of God and the exalted Son of Man at God's right hand. He is thus a witness of the resurrection of Christ. Hence his confession is based on direct vision. He is a factual witness to supraterrestrial reality. For this reason he is called μάρτυς (*Ges. Aufsätze*, II, 70 f.). But there is no support for this view in Ac. Even less is it possible to see here the later use. On this cf. v. Campenhausen, 32 f. and Delehaye, *Sanctus*, 101 ff.

[56] It is to be noted that μάρτυς τῶν τοῦ Χριστοῦ παθημάτων is linked to the preceding συμπρεσβύτερος by the one art.

[57] So, e.g., Zahn, *Einl.*, II³ (1907), 15, n. 9; R. Reitzenstein, NGG (1916), 436, n. 4.

[58] Cf. the corresponding contrast in R. 8:17; 2 C. 1:7; 2 Tm. 2:11 f.

[59] Cf. also 2 C. 1:5; Col. 1:24; 1 Pt. 2:21; Mt. 10:38; 16:24.

patient and even joyful endurance he repeatedly summoned (1:6 f.; 2:20; 3:14; 4:1, 12 f.), from his own experience, so that he was well able to speak of it and of its meaning and blessing. He does not speak as a blind man speaks of colour when he gives directions as to the right attitude under pressure. He speaks as one who from his own life can say what is meant by the παθήματα τοῦ Χριστοῦ.[60] There can here be no question of a technical martyrological sense, for Peter is still alive.

e. μάρτυς in the Johannine Writings.

Of the Johannine writings, only Rev. uses μάρτυς. In 2 of the 5 references Jesus Christ Himself is thus designated (1:5; 3:14). Of the others 11:3 refers to the two prophets who bear witness for 1260 days in Jerusalem, now doomed to be destroyed by the Gentiles, and who are then put to death by the beast. They are not witnesses because they are put to death, but by reason of their prophetic activity. Similarly Antipas in 2:13 is not a witness because he is put to death; he is put to death because he is a witness, i.e., in the sense of proclamation of the Gospel. Yet he is a faithful witness (emphatic) because he cannot be deflected from his witness by death. This gives us the clue to 17:6 where it is said that the woman is drunk ἐκ τοῦ αἵματος τῶν ἁγίων καὶ ἐκ τοῦ αἵματος τῶν μαρτύρων Ἰησοῦ. The term μάρτυρες cannot be taken here in the later martyrological sense because there is reference also to "martyred" saints.[61] To note this is decisive for a true grasp of the concept of witness in Rev. Those who suffer death for their evangelistic witness are mentioned as well as those who are killed simply because of their faith. Not every committed Christian who dies for his faith is called μάρτυς. The name is reserved for those who are at work as evangelistic witnesses. There is no further place here for the idea of the witness to historical facts. The witness is now the one who persuasively declares the truth of the Gospel. But again not every one who does this is μάρτυς. The term is reserved for those who prove the final seriousness of their witness by suffering death. These are faithful witnesses, and only faithful witnesses are witnesses in the full sense, true witnesses. The concept of the witness in Rev. is the same as that of Ac. 22:20.

In this light one can truly see why Jesus Christ Himself is called ὁ μάρτυς ὁ πιστός in Rev. 1:5 and ὁ μάρτυς ὁ πιστὸς καὶ ἀληθινός in 3:14. The phrase is taken from ψ 88:37: ὁ μάρτυς ἐν οὐρανῷ πιστός. In the psalm it applies to God; here it has a Messianic reference. The sense may be seen from 1:1, 2. The revelation is the revelation of Jesus Christ, who simply passes on what He has received from God. Hence it is called μαρτυρία Ἰησοῦ Χριστοῦ (1:2). This task

[60] Cf. H. v. Soden in *Theol. Handkomm. z. NT*³ (1899), *ad loc.;* H. v. Campenhausen, 63 f. Acc. to Wbg. Pt. the author is rather saying that he accepted it as his task to bear witness to the sufferings of Christ by word and work. This is what marks him as an apostle and missionary. But on this view proper justice is not done either to the contrast with ὁ καὶ τῆς ... δόξης κοινωνός or to the κοινωνεῖν τοῖς τοῦ Χριστοῦ παθήμασι in 4:13.

[61] It is a misconception to say that "all the blood of the saints which great Babylon on the scarlet beast drinks is the blood of the witnesses of Jesus," cf. also Had. Apk. on 1:5. If Rev. is called the book of martyrs, this cannot mean that it believes all Christians must suffer martyrdom, cf. L. Brun, "Übriggebliebene und Märtyrer in d. Apk.," ThStKr, 102 (1930), 215-231, who attacks the one-sidedness of the view of R. H. Charles, *The Revelation of St. John* (1920); A. Loisy, *L'Apocalypse de Jean* (1923); Loh. Apk.; also H. Windisch, RGG², III, 330 ff. *s.v.* "Johannesapokalypse" [Bertram].

He reliably fulfils. This is emphasised in the salutation (1:5) and at the beginning of the last letter (3:15), where it brings out the seriousness of the warning therein contained. But this does not exhaust the meaning of the term. Jesus Christ bears the title, not merely with reference to the revelation, but also more generally: I am born and have come into the world ἵνα μαρτυρήσω τῇ ἀληθείᾳ (Jn. 18:37). He showed Himself faithful to this calling by dying. In evaluating His designation as μάρτυς πιστός one cannot overlook the fact that the martyr Antipas bears the same title. The crucified Lord is the model of the Christian witness.

3. The Use of μαρτυρέω.

a. Of the Human Declaration of Facts.

μαρτυρεῖν denotes the activity of a μάρτυς. It is first used in the NT for the declaration or confirmation, on the basis of first-hand knowledge, of individual acts or general facts of experience, though it so happens that there is no special use for testifying in court. Cf. Mt. 23:31 (of the Pharisees, with reference to the cult of the graves of the prophets): μαρτυρεῖτε ἑαυτοῖς ὅτι υἱοί ἐστε τῶν φονευσάντων τοὺς προφήτας. R. 10:2 (with reference to the Jews): μαρτυρῶ ... αὐτοῖς ὅτι ζῆλον θεοῦ ἔχουσιν. Gl. 4:15: μαρτυρῶ ... ὑμῖν, ὅτι εἰ δυνατὸν τοὺς ὀφθαλμοὺς ὑμῶν ἐξορύξαντες ἐδώκατέ μοι. Cf. Col. 4:13 (of Epaphras): μαρτυρῶ ... αὐτῷ ὅτι ἔχει πολὺν πόνον ὑπὲρ ὑμῶν. 2 C. 8:3 (of the contributions of the Macedonian churches to the collection): γνωρίζομεν ... ὅτι κατὰ δύναμιν, μαρτυρῶ, καὶ παρὰ δύναμιν ... ἔδωκαν. 1 C. 15:15: ἐμαρτυρήσαμεν κατὰ τοῦ θεοῦ ὅτι ἤγειρεν τὸν Χριστόν (i.e., if there is no resurrection of the dead, as some maintain in Corinth, and hence if Christ is not raised). Ac. 22:5: ὡς καὶ ὁ ἀρχιερεὺς μαρτυρεῖ μοι καὶ πᾶν τὸ πρεσβυτέριον (that Paul has persecuted the Christian movement). Ac. 26:5: The Jews are προγινώσκοντές με ἄνωθεν, ἐὰν θέλωσι μαρτυρεῖν, ὅτι κατὰ τὴν ἀκριβεστάτην αἵρεσιν τῆς ἡμετέρας θρησκείας ἔζησα Φαρισαῖος. Jn. 2:25: Jesus did not need ἵνα τις μαρτυρήσῃ περὶ τοῦ ἀνθρώπου· αὐτὸς γὰρ ἐγίνωσκεν τί ἦν ἐν τῷ ἀνθρώπῳ. Jn. 3:28 (the Baptist): αὐτοὶ ὑμεῖς μοι μαρτυρεῖτε ὅτι εἶπον· οὐκ εἰμὶ ἐγὼ ὁ χριστός. Jn. 18:23: The servant of the high-priest should say what is the κακόν in what Jesus said. Jn. 19:35: ὁ ἑωρακὼς μεμαρτύρηκεν (concerning the spear wound in the side of Jesus). Cf. also Jn. 4:39; 12:17. With reference to the future Jn. 13:21 (intimation of the treachery of Judas) and Rev. 22:18 (with reference to the threat which protects the book). As concerns a general fact of experience Jn. 4:44: Ἰησοῦς ἐμαρτύρησεν ὅτι προφήτης ἐν τῇ ἰδίᾳ πατρίδι τιμὴν οὐκ ἔχει.

b. Of the Good Report.

To this section belong all the verses in which μαρτυρεῖν is used in the abs. for "to give a good report," whether actively with the dat. of the person to whom it applies (so Lk. 4:22; cf. also Ac. 13:22 [62] and Hb. 11:4) or passively in the sense of receiving a good report (the seven in Ac. 6:3; Cornelius, 10:22; Timotheus, 16:2; Ananias, 22:12; with special grounds, the widow, who must be ἐν ἔργοις καλοῖς μαρτυρουμένη, 1 Tm. 5:10; cf. also 3 Jn. 3, 6, 12). For the meaning is always that on the basis of direct observation the nature or conduct of those

[62] With ref. to God and David: ᾧ καὶ εἶπεν μαρτυρήσας. The ᾧ is to be taken with μαρτυρήσας; cf. Wdt. Ag., *ad loc.*

concerned is said to be satisfactory and the one who judges is ready in some sense to vouch for it.

c. Of the Witness of God, the Spirit, or Scripture.

A special group is formed by passages in which God, the Spirit, or Scripture is the subject of such judgments (Ac. 13:22; 15:8; Hb. 11:2, 4, 5, 39) or guarantees the correctness of specific statements. Thus the term can often mean "to declare emphatically, on the guarantee of an existing authority"; cf. Hb. 7:8: μαρτυρούμενος ὅτι ζῇ (of Melchisedec); Hb. 7:17: μαρτυρεῖται ... ὅτι σὺ ἱερεὺς εἰς τὸν αἰῶνα κατὰ τὴν τάξιν Μελχισέδεκ (of Christ in ψ 109:4); Hb. 10:15: μαρτυρεῖ δὲ ἡμῖν καὶ τὸ πνεῦμα τὸ ἅγιον (with reference to Jer. 31:33); R. 3:21: μαρτυρουμένη ὑπὸ τοῦ νόμου καὶ τῶν προφητῶν (of the righteousness of God which is revealed without Law); Ac. 10:43 (τούτῳ πάντες οἱ προφῆται μαρτυροῦσιν, ἄφεσιν ἁμαρτιῶν λαβεῖν διὰ τοῦ ὀνόματος αὐτοῦ πάντα τὸν πιστεύοντα εἰς αὐτόν). On the other hand, in Ac. 14:3 (παρρησιαζόμενοι ἐπὶ τῷ κυρίῳ τῷ μαρτυροῦντι τῷ λόγῳ τῆς χάριτος αὐτοῦ, διδόντι σημεῖα καὶ τέρατα γίνεσθαι ...) the thought is that the apostolic proclamation is supported by the factual divine witness of miracles, which confirm the truth of the Gospel (cf. Hb. 2:4).

d. Of Religious Witness.

The three last passages are distinguished from those which precede by the fact that here μαρτυρεῖν refers to the central content of the Gospel as such. Seen from the standpoint of faith this content is a fact. God has established it. But it is a fact of higher order which cannot be observed and attested like other facts of earthly occurrence. If the witness refers to this, it becomes the witness to revealed and believed truth. The factual witness in the popular sense becomes evangelistic confession. [63] But where the whole life revolves around this centre, and the proclamation of this truth is the task which takes precedence of all else, the word becomes — almost, one might say, unavoidably — a technical term for this activity. It has this character in Ac. 23:11, where Paul in a night vision is given the direction: ὡς ... διεμαρτύρω τὰ περὶ ἐμοῦ εἰς Ἰερουσαλήμ, οὕτω σε δεῖ καὶ εἰς Ῥώμην μαρτυρῆσαι. Here we see how language is shaped by the actual forces of historical development.

e. The Special Use in the Johannine Writings.

The final sense leads us close to the Johannine use in the Gospel and the First Epistle, except that here the reference is solely to the figure of Jesus as such, to His person and significance. [64] To be sure, the verb sometime occurs with no specific reference (cf. 2:25; 3:28; 4:39, 44; 12:17; 13:21; 18:23). The Johannine

---

[63] This orientation to evangelisation is what distinguishes the term from ὁμολογεῖν. All μαρτυρεῖν is a ὁμολογεῖν, but not *vice versa*. The point of μαρτυρεῖν is that believers should be won. In ὁμολογεῖν there is a firm declaration of what is in a man, but with no necessary effect on those around. The opp. of ὁμολογεῖν is ἀρνεῖσθαι, that of μαρτυρεῖν διώκειν. The Pharisees confess angels and the resurrection (Ac. 23:8), but they do not bear witness to them. Sins are confessed, but one does not testify to them. One can, of course, "witness" a confession (1 Tm. 6:13). The task of the witness in the early Christian sense is to make known a specific fact or truth. In ὁμολογεῖν one stands personally behind something which one thinks, or believes, or has done, before a judge (Ac. 24:14), or men (R. 10:9 f.), or persecutors (Mt. 10:32), or the congregation (1 Tm. 6:12).

[64] On what follows cf. the discussion in v. Campenhausen, 33 ff., with bibl.

usage is given its distinctive colouring by the numerous passages which speak of witness to Jesus. This is not witness to the factuality of His history, though this is presupposed and even emphasised (1 Jn. 1:2; 4:14; Jn. 15:27; 21:24; also 3:11, in so far as the address of Jesus here actually becomes the preaching of the Evangelist). Nor is it witness to certain significant events in the story, whether His birth, death or resurrection, with the sole exception of 19:35. The witness is simply to the nature and significance of His person. Hence μαρτυρεῖν περὶ αὐτοῦ, 1:15; in the addresses of Jesus περὶ ἐμοῦ or περὶ ἐμαυτοῦ, 5:31-39; 8:13-18; 10:25; 15:26; but 3:26 ᾧ σὺ μεμαρτύρηκας (of the Baptist). The content of this witness is ὅτι οὗτός ἐστιν ὁ υἱὸς τοῦ θεοῦ, 1:34; hence His eternity, 1:15, or ὅτι ὁ πατήρ με ἀπέσταλκεν, 5:36 f.; or ὅτι ὁ πατὴρ ἀπέσταλκεν τὸν υἱὸν σωτῆρα τοῦ κόσμου, 1 Jn. 4:14; or ὅτι ζωὴν αἰώνιον ἔδωκεν ὁ θεὸς ἡμῖν καὶ αὕτη ἡ ζωὴ ἐν τῷ υἱῷ αὐτοῦ ἐστιν, 1 Jn. 5:10 f. If it is emphatically said of the Baptist that he himself is not the light, but has simply come ἵνα μαρτυρήσῃ περὶ τοῦ φωτός, the content of the witness is that Jesus, the incarnate Logos, is this light, the light of the world which Jesus attests Himself to be in 8:12, the light which is the light of life for those who believe in Him (1:7) or who follow Him (8:12). Because He is the incarnate Word, because He has come from heaven, when He speaks of God He bears witness to what He has seen and heard (cf. 3:32; cf. also 3:11). He is the truth (14:6) and thus to bear witness to it (5:33; 18:37) is to bear witness to Him (3:26) or about Him (5:32). For this is always to declare Him as the σωτὴρ τοῦ κόσμου sent by God (4:42). This took place, and does take place, through the Scriptures (5:39), through the Baptist (1:7 f., 15, 32, 34; 3:26; 5:33), through God (5:32, 37; 8:18), through the works which the Father causes Him to do (5:36; 10:25), through Jesus Himself, since in His divine mission He is in the Fourth Gospel the only theme of His addresses (5:31; 8:13 f., 18). It is only the reverse side of His self-witness that He testifies to the world which hates Him that its works are evil (7:7). When Jesus Himself no longer stays on earth, there follows the witness of the Spirit who is the Spirit of truth or simply the truth (15:26; 1 Jn. 5:6), and who especially in baptism and the Lord's Supper bears His witness to the Son of God as the One who gives eternal life (1 Jn. 5:5-11). For believers constantly have fresh experience of Him as such in the sacraments. Finally, the witness is given by the disciples themselves (15:27; 1 Jn. 4:14). Their witness is confession. μαρτυρεῖν and ὁμολογεῖν merge into one another (1 Jn. 4:14 f.).

The ref. in 1 Jn. 5:7 is to three who bear witness now (μαρτυροῦντες). Hence the water and blood of v. 8 can hardly be the baptism and death of Jesus (the latter is given a specific anti-gnostic emphasis). They must surely refer to the sacraments observed by the community. Basically there is only one witness of the Spirit who gives inward assurance to believers. Only recollection of the legal rule (Dt. 17:6; 19:15; cf. Mt. 18:16; also Jn. 8:17) leads to the mention of three witnesses in v. 8. If the concepts of water and blood here undergo a change without any specific note to this effect, this corresponds to the Johannine love of an interrelated wealth of elastic terms. It is not impossible that there is even a ref. to the happening in Jn. 19:34 f., and that here, too, the two sacraments are in view. For the emphasis here on the witness to the truth of what took place shows how decisively important the event was for the Evangelist. Nor is there any wholly satisfying explanation of it apart from the relation suggested.

The author of Jn. and 1 Jn. certainly claims to have been a witness in the historical sense, i.e., an eye-witness to the historical Jesus. But in his view of the witness this is not so important as it is for Lk., namely, to prove the historicity of certain events. It is important in the much deeper sense of endowment with the possibility of receiving a direct impression of the δόξα of Jesus ὡς μονογενοῦς παρὰ πατρὸς πλήρης χάριτος καὶ ἀληθείας, to which he is inescapably bound to testify. The man who is simply an eye-witness in the historical sense sees nothing of this δόξα. It is disclosed only to the believer (1 Jn. 5:9 f.). Nor is it disclosed merely to believers who were eye-witnesses in the historical sense, but to all believers. For ὁ πιστεύων εἰς τὸν υἱὸν τοῦ θεοῦ ἔχει τὴν μαρτυρίαν ἐν αὐτῷ, 1 Jn. 5:10. Hence new witnesses can arise, i.e., those who confess evangelistically who Jesus was and what He signified. With this clear and decisive development of the concept of the religious witness, and its separation from that of the historical witness, we are on the same line as that noted in respect of μάρτυς in Ac. 22:20 (Stephen) and Rev. 2:13; 11:3; 17:6. The only difference is that with the verb there is no discernible movement towards reserving the term for those witnesses who have suffered martyrdom as such.

Nor is there any such movement in Rev. Here μαρτυρεῖν occurs only 4 times, and it refers always to the contents of the book in so far as these are attested to the recipients by Jesus Christ (22:20) or by the divine (1:2; 22:16), apart from 22:18, where the divine, addressing "every man that heareth the words of the prophecy of this book," bears witness to the threat by which it is protected.

f. 1 Tm. 6:13.

There is perhaps an intimation of the later use in the one verse not yet discussed, namely, 1 Tm. 6:13, where Timothy is admonished ἐνώπιον ... Χριστοῦ Ἰησοῦ τοῦ μαρτυρήσαντος ἐπὶ Ποντίου Πιλάτου τὴν καλὴν ὁμολογίαν. The good confession, an expression which seems to be chosen as a parallel to the preceding (baptismal ?) profession of Timothy, is Jesus' acknowledgment of His Messianic mission which He made expressly, or by patiently suffering death as the Messiah, or by both. The fact that the verb μαρτυρεῖν is used for this confession of the passion (rather than the ὁμολογεῖν used for Timothy's profession in v. 12), is worth noting, and reminds us of what was said at the end of a. [65]

4. The Use of μαρτυρία.

a. μαρτυρία outside the Johannine Writings.

μαρτυρία occurs in the NT only 7 times outside the Johannine writings, where it is found 30 times. Of the 7, 6 are religiously neutral. In 4 instances the term is court witness to facts, i.e., the witness for the prosecution in the trial of Jesus (Mk. 14:55, 56, 59; Lk. 22:71), cf. → 489. Once it is a good report; in 1 Tm. 3:7 it is said of the bishop that he must μαρτυρίαν καλὴν ἔχειν ἀπὸ τῶν ἔξωθεν; cf. → 496. Once it refers to a quotation from the poets: Tt. 1:13: ἡ μαρτυρία αὕτη ἐστὶν ἀληθής, with ref. to a verse of Epimenides concerning the moral worthlessness of the Cretans, cf. → 479. The term has a specific religious and Christian reference only at Ac. 22:18. Praying in the temple, Paul sees in an ἔκστασις the heavenly Christ who commands him to leave Jerusalem quickly διότι οὐ παραδέξονταί σου μαρτυρίαν περὶ ἐμοῦ, cf. → 493. μαρτυρία here is evangelistic witness for the faith, and Christ is its content.

b. μαρτυρία in the Johannine Writings.

It is the more surprising, then, that the specific religious and Christian ref. completely dominates the usage in the Johannine writings. It is true that in

---

65 Cf. v. Campenhausen, 50 f. and bibl., esp. Dib. Past., 55.

Jn. 8:17 μαρτυρία means human witness on the basis of Dt. 17:6; 19:15. In 3 Jn. 12 it means the witness of a good Christian report in the case of Demetrius. The first μαρτυρία in 1 Jn. 5:9: εἰ τὴν μαρτυρίαν τῶν ἀνθρώπων λαμβάνομεν, possibly carries with it a reminiscence of the Dt. passages, which is certainly present in v. 8. This would forge a link with the second μαρτυρία, the witness which men give one another.

The other passages (27) are dominated by the specific sense of the evangelistic witness to Christ's nature and significance which aims at faith. This is in keeping with the Johannine use of → μαρτυρεῖν. Corresponding to the fundamental meaning in accordance with the formation of the word (→ A.), μαρτυρία is twice used in the active sense of bearing witness (Jn. 1:7: John ἦλθεν εἰς μαρτυρίαν, ἵνα μαρτυρήσῃ, and Rev. 11:7 of the two prophetic witnesses: ὅταν τελέσωσιν τὴν μαρτυρίαν αὐτῶν). Elsewhere it has the passive sense of the witness given. It is given by the Baptist (1:19), by Jesus Himself (3:11, 32, 33; 8:13 f., which is not in contradiction to 5:31, since here only autonomous self-witness is repudiated), by God through the works which He causes Jesus to do (5:32, 36), by the Evangelist, whose whole book is called a μαρτυρία (21:24), not merely or primarily in the sense of external historical attestation but in the sense of witness to what faith has come to know of Jesus. In 19:35, with its reference to the thrust of the spear in Jesus' side and, the blood and water which flow from it, it is stated with solemn emphasis: ὁ ἑωρακὼς μεμαρτύρηκεν, καὶ ἀληθινὴ αὐτοῦ ἐστιν ἡ μαρτυρία. The obvious point at issue here is not the historical attestation of a remarkable event but the witness to an event which intimates the saving efficacy of the death of Jesus and which is attested by a believer "that ye might believe."

In 1 Jn. 5:9-11, too, the reference is to God's witness to His Son. The content of this witness is ὅτι ζωὴν αἰώνιον ἔδωκεν ὁ θεὸς ἡμῖν καὶ αὕτη ἡ ζωὴ ἐν τῷ υἱῷ αὐτοῦ ἐστιν. According to the context this witness of God is identical with the witness of the Spirit referred to just before in v. 6 f. The distinctive phrase in v. 10a (ὁ πιστεύων εἰς τὸν υἱὸν τοῦ θεοῦ ἔχει τὴν μαρτυρίαν ἐν αὐτῷ) shows that this witness of the Spirit is the *testimonium spiritus sancti internum* in virtue of which man may be sure of the content of the divine μαρτυρία.

The expression "to have the witness" leads to Rev., where it occurs more than once (6:9; 12:17; 19:10). But the most striking feature in Rev. is the phrase ἡ μαρτυρία Ἰησοῦ or Ἰησοῦ Χριστοῦ, which is found in 6 of the 9 occurrences (1:2, 9; 12:17; 19:10 twice; 20:4), cf. also 6:9.[66] The gen. is a subj. gen.[67] Only twice is there reference to human witness (11:7; 12:11). In many cases the λόγος τοῦ θεοῦ (1:2, 9; 6:9; 20:4) or ἐντολαὶ τοῦ θεοῦ (12:17) are closely related to the μαρτυρία Ἰησοῦ, so that we have a twofold expression. The combination is not to be construed as referring to the OT on the one hand and the Christian message on the other. We have rather a "plerophoric expression for the Christian revelation in general."[68] The Word of God and the witness of Jesus Christ are inseparably interwoven.

In 1:2 there is a special reference to the contents of the book. God has given these to Jesus Christ, who has then showed them as His witness to John. The

[66] On Rev. 6:9 cf. Loh., Bss. Apk.; J. Behm, *NT Deutsch*, III (1935), *ad loc.*
[67] Cf. Zn. Apk. 19:10, n. 13.
[68] Bss. Apk., 183 on 1:2.

difficult 19:10c is perhaps to be taken in the same way.[69] Here the angel of revelation forbids the self-prostration of the seer because he is only a fellow-servant with him and with his brothers who have the μαρτυρία Ἰησοῦ. The angel or the author — we need not go into this question here — then adds: ἡ γὰρ μαρτυρία Ἰησοῦ ἐστιν τὸ πνεῦμα τῆς προφητείας (v. 10c). According to the parallel 22:9 the brothers referred to are not believers in general but the prophets. Here, too, they are characterised as such. This is the point of v. 10c.[69] If they have the μαρτυρία Ἰησοῦ, they have the spirit of prophecy, i.e., they are prophets, and as such they stand alongside the divine, who is himself a prophet, like the angel, who simply stands in the service of the μαρτυρία Ἰησοῦ (cf. 1:1). This is why the angel is their σύνδουλος. For as the mediators of what God seeks to impart the prophets are His δοῦλοι in a special sense, cf. 1:1; 10:7; 11:18; 22:3; also 19:2 and perhaps 2:20. The μαρτυρία Ἰησοῦ is the witness which they have, not as Christians, but as Christian prophets. They have it, not as a secure possession, but as a task, i.e., in order that they may pass it on, as John himself attests the witness of Jesus. This is why they are prophets. This is also what is indicated by the phrase ἔχειν τὴν μαρτυρίαν. The reference is to a special obligation resting on them. The idea of martyrdom does not arise.

In the other verses, however, μαρτυρία Ἰησοῦ refers to the Christian revelation in general. This is particularly true of 1:9. For the reference can be only to the banishment of John to Patmos, which took place "for the word of God and the witness of Jesus," i.e., to prevent their further proclamation.[70] This is also the meaning in 12:17 and 20:4, also in 6:9, where we do not have the genitive Ἰησοῦ (Χριστοῦ). Because of this witness the martyrs are slain (6:9) or beheaded (20:4), and according to 12:17 the dragon fights against them because they have this witness. One might think that this phrase, which occurs in 6:9, would simply denote Christians. But this does not seem to be so. In 6:9 the cry for vengeance is uttered by the souls of those who are slain διὰ τὸν λόγον τοῦ θεοῦ καὶ διὰ τὴν μαρτυρίαν (sc. Ἰησοῦ). They are comforted "until their fellow-servants also and their brethren, that should be killed as they were, should be fulfilled." There is a distinction between the fellow-servants and the brethren. The latter are Christians in general. The former are servants in the same special sense as those who cry. They thus have a special task, which is naturally to proclaim the μαρτυρία Ἰησοῦ. The phrase ἔχειν τὴν μαρτυρίαν again seems to be designed to express this. Things are much the same in 20:4, where those who are beheaded for the witness of Jesus and the Word of God are accompanied by those who have not worshipped the beast or his image nor accepted his mark on their foreheads and hands. Only in 12:17 does ἔχειν τὴν μαρτυρίαν Ἰησοῦ seem to refer to Christians in general. For the formula οἱ τηροῦντες τὰς ἐντολὰς τοῦ θεοῦ καὶ ἔχοντες τὴν μαρτυρίαν Ἰησοῦ is comprised under one article and relates to the total remnant of the seed of the woman.

In view of the statements of John's Gospel about the self-witness of Jesus, it is not surprising that occasionally in Rev. the Christian message of salvation should be called μαρτυρία Ἰησοῦ, perhaps in combination with λόγος or ἐντολαί

---

[69] Cf. esp. Zn. Apk., *ad loc.* The difficulty may be seen from the fact that older commentators usually set aside v. 10c as a secondary gloss: "The whole saying leaves the impression of an unskilfully interpolated gloss" (Bss. Apk., 429).

[70] So E. Lohmeyer, W. Hadorn (1928), J. Behm in their comm.; also v. Campenhausen, 42 f.

τοῦ θεοῦ. Nevertheless the phrase is a remarkable one. For it involves the isolation of one expression which in the Gospel occurs with others (witness of the Baptist, of God). This expression alone is made a formula for the Gospel. This is possibly linked with the fact that the divine reserves the term → μάρτυς for those who have confirmed their witness by their death. It is also linked with the fact that Jesus, like Antipas, is from this standpoint given the title "faithful witness." In the expression μαρτυρία 'Ιησοῦ there is a reminiscence of the passion of Jesus, cf. 1 Tm. 6:13. Under the impress of the current experience of the Church, μαρτυρία, like μάρτυς, takes on an affinity to the instances where death proved the final seriousness of the witness and his witness. The term begins to acquire a martyrological nuance. This may be seen in the phrase ἔχειν τὴν μαρτυρίαν 'Ιησοῦ. For this is used always of those who have suffered death or are in the total situation of martyrdom. Even in 11:7, which speaks of the μαρτυρία of the two prophets in Jerusalem, the term naturally means oral witness. But it is used of those who seal their witness with their death. In 12:11 the martyrological orientation of the word seems to be even plainer. After the victory of Michael and his angelic hosts over the dragon there is heavenly jubilation that "the accuser of our brethren is cast down." "And they overcame him διὰ τὸ αἷμα τοῦ ἀρνίου καὶ διὰ τὸν λόγον τῆς μαρτυρίας αὐτῶν, by[71] the blood of the Lamb, and by the word of their testimony,"[72] i.e., the word which they attest, or rather, since they have given their lives, attested. Now here, too, the term means evangelistic confession of Jesus rather than the testimony of blood. Nevertheless, it is used of a confession which culminates in the sacrifice of life.

The results of this investigation of the terms μάρτυς, μαρτυρεῖν, μαρτυρία overlap and support one another. What we find in the Johannine writings, especially Rev., but also in some verses in Ac., forms a preliminary step towards the martyrological concept of the witness (μάρτυς = martyr) which emerged at once in the early Church.[73]

5. The Use of μαρτύριον.

a. Occurrence.

This word (used 20 times) is less common than μάρτυς, μαρτυρεῖν and μαρτυρία. It is not found at all in the Johannine writings except at Rev. 15:5, where the OT ἡ σκηνὴ τοῦ μαρτυρίου is adopted with ref. to the heavenly temple, cf. Ac. 7:44. Of the other 18 instances half are in the Synoptists (Mk. 1:44 par. Mt. 8:4; Lk. 5:14; Mk. 6:11 par. Lk. 9:5; Mt. 10:18 and 24:14 par. Mk. 13:9; Lk. 21:13; in fact there are thus only three references).

b. Use in the Sense of Witness for the Prosecution.

In respect of the use and meaning, our starting-point must be the fact that, unlike μαρτυρία, μαρτύριον does not mean the process of giving testimony. Even in witness we are to think less of the content than of the fact that the objective testimony, whether it be an object, act or utterance, is primarily a means of proof. This is everywhere apparent in the NT, where the phrase εἰς μαρτύριον is used

---

71 On διά with the acc. cf. Bl.-Debr.⁶ § 222.

72 This is the right translation, not "by their word of witness"; λόγος is the objective word of revelation. The ref. is to that which objectively makes the triumph possible.

73 Cf. Delehaye, 79: "Le NT ne nous fournit ... aucun exemple certain du mot μάρτυς ou de ses dérivés employés dans le sens restreint et précis de martyr qu'il a fini par prendre dans le langage chrétien."

with the dat. of the person for whom the witness is significant, usually as witness against him. This sense is apparent already in the OT use, cf. Gn. 31:44; Dt. 31:26; Jos. 24:27. In the NT it is plainly the meaning in Jm. 5:3: the rust on the gold and silver of the rich εἰς μαρτύριον ὑμῖν ἔσται καὶ φάγεται τὰς σάρκας ὑμῶν ὡς πῦρ. They would rather let their possessions rot than use them in works of mercy. Thus the rust on their gold will be a witness for the prosecution against them on the day of judgment.[74] Mk. 6:11 is to be construed in the same way. Where the disciples are not accepted with their message, they are to leave the place and to shake off the dust from their feet εἰς μαρτύριον αὐτοῖς (correctly expounded in Lk. 9:5 as εἰς μαρτύριον ἐπ' αὐτούς). The fact that they leave their hearers with this gesture will be a witness against their resistance and unbelief on the day of judgment. The direction which Jesus gives the cleansed leper that he should show himself to the priest and bring the prescribed offerings εἰς μαρτύριον αὐτοῖς (Mk. 1:44 par.) could be taken in the same way.[75] If the cleansing is confirmed by the priest, this will be a severe indictment of the unbelief in which the people (αὐτοῖς) lingers still. The passage is to be expounded in terms of Mt. 11:20-24. Also to be taken in this sense are Mk. 13:9 and the par. Mt. 10:18, also 24:14, though Lk. 21:13 stands apart. In Mk. 13:9; Mt. 10:18 it is envisaged that for Jesus' sake the disciples will be brought before the local Jewish courts, whipped in the synagogues, and arraigned before rulers and kings εἰς μαρτύριον αὐτοῖς (Mk.) or αὐτοῖς καὶ τοῖς ἔθνεσιν (Mt.). The αὐτοί here seem to be the Jews in contrast to the Gentiles represented by the rulers and kings. According to the context the μαρτύριον cannot be the evangelistic witness of missionary preaching, which offers the chance of conversion. The goal of this witness is to make opponents guilty.[76] In Mt. 24:14: "This gospel of the kingdom must be preached in all the world εἰς μαρτύριον πᾶσιν τοῖς ἔθνεσιν, it is apparent from v. 9 (ἔσεσθε μισούμενοι ὑπὸ πάντων τῶν ἐθνῶν διὰ τὸ ὄνομά μου) that the reference is to the witness which makes the Gentiles guilty. Hence we cannot translate: "That they may be given a chance to believe."[77] Only Lk. gives a different turn to the saying with his ἀποβήσεται ὑμῖν εἰς μαρτύριον (21:13).

---

[74] Cf. Hck., Dib. Jk., *ad loc.*

[75] Exposition varies to an extraordinary degree at this pt. Most widespread is the view that the ref. is to a testimony to those around that the leper is really cleansed, so that intercourse with him may be resumed. Others take it that Jesus is proving to opponents His fidelity to the Law, or that His Messiahship is to be accredited by the miracle. Yet others combine the various possibilities. Cf. the comm. of, e.g., J. Holtzmann, E. Klostermann, F. Hauck, T. Zahn, *ad loc.* The first interpretation would be possible only if the εἰς μαρτύριον αὐτοῖς could be linked with a direction of Moses, which is ruled out by Lev. 13 f. The second has no support in the context. To turn to Mt. 5:17 for light on Mk. 1:44 is arbitrary. These explanations also overlook the OT background. Only in so far as this is taken into account is the third explanation correct.

[76] So also E. Meyer, *Ursprung u. Anfänge des Christentums,* I (1921), 128; also v. Campenhausen, *op. cit.,* 24 ff.; Schlatter on Mt. 10:18 and 24:14. The observation of Zn. on Mt. 10:18 that the witness affects Jews and Gentiles in different ways is quite contrary to the context.

[77] On the above exposition of the εἰς μαρτύριον αὐτοῖς κτλ. cf. Ign. Tr., 12, 3: "I beseech you to hear me in love ἵνα μὴ εἰς μαρτύριον ὦ ἐν ὑμῖν γράψας ("that through my epistle I do not become a witness to, i.e., against you"). Ign. Phld., 6, 3: ἵνα μὴ εἰς μαρτύριον αὐτὸ κτήσωνται, i.e., Ignatius' desire for all is that his words should not become an accusing witness against them. The translation of Krüger: "That (in my words) they may find no witness (against themselves)" (Hennecke, 530) completely misses the point of the saying by subjectivising it.

This means, not martyrdom in the later sense, but the opportunity which the disciples are given of making their witness. As always in Lk., the alteration is a thoughtful one, and is designed to form a transition to the ensuing promise that Jesus will help them at the trials. Their witness will thus be of irresistible power (v. 15), so that they will emerge unscathed from the most dangerous situations (v. 18 f.).

c. Witness to Something.

The small alteration here made by Lk. is important because it introduces us to another circle in which μαρτύριον is not witness as a means of proof but witness to something, occasionally in an active sense. The genitive used with it denotes either the subject (τὸ μαρτύριον τῆς συνειδήσεως ἡμῶν, 2 C. 1:12; τὸ μαρτύριον ἡμῶν, 2 Th. 1:10) or the object to which the statement relates (τὸ μαρτύριον ... τῆς ἀναστάσεως, Ac. 4:33; τὸ μαρτύριον τοῦ Χριστοῦ, 1 C. 1:6; τὸ μαρτύριον τοῦ θεοῦ, 1 C. 2:1, unless we are to read τὸ μυστήριον here;[78] τὸ μαρτύριον τοῦ κυρίου, 2 Tm. 1:8). μαρτύριον is here synonymous with εὐαγγέλιον, κήρυγμα or διδασκαλία.[79] The same is true of the designation of the Christian message as τὸ μαρτύριον καιροῖς ἰδίοις in 1 Tm. 2:6.[80]

d. Witness in the Active Sense.

μαρτύριον takes on the active sense of attestation in Hb. 3:5. Moses was faithful in all his house as a servant εἰς μαρτύριον τῶν λαληθησομένων, i.e., the directions, especially the legal statutes, which he receives from God in the tabernacle and is then to attest to the people.[81] This active use is contrary to Greek sensibility and is to be explained by the σκηνὴ τοῦ μαρτυρίου of the LXX, → 485.

In clear distinction from μάρτυς, μαρτυρεῖν, μαρτυρία, there is in the NT no trace of any inclination to develop the use of μαρτύριον in the direction of the Church's martyrological usage in the 2nd century (cf. Mart. Pol., 1, 1; 2, 1; 18, 2; 19, 1).

F. The Development and Establishment of the Specific Martyrological Use in the Early Church.

1. Review.

In the 2nd century the impulses found in the NT, especially in the Johannine writings, are carried a stage further. Like the beginnings, the development was due to the persecutions which fell on the Christian community. As is only natural, the popular use with its various meanings lived on.[82] So, too, did the older

[78] The great Egyptian witnesses read μυστήριον, but the western have μαρτύριον, which has also come into B. One might say that μαρτύριον is secondary in the light of 1:6, or that μυστήριον is secondary in the light of 2:7; 4:1. If one chooses τὸ μαρτύριον τοῦ θεοῦ, the gen. must be taken as an obj. gen., i.e., witness of God's saving acts in Christ. But τὸ μαρτύριον τοῦ θεοῦ is not a very clear phrase for this. In the whole discussion of σοφία μυστήριον fits better than the neutral μαρτύριον. Cf. Ltzm. K., who reads μυστήριον, and esp. Joh. W. 1 K., *ad loc.*

[79] Cf. v. Dobschütz on 2 Th. 1:10; 1 Th. 2:2.

[80] Cf. also Pol., 7, 1: πᾶς γάρ ὃς ἂν μὴ ὁμολογῇ Ἰησοῦν Χριστὸν ἐν σαρκὶ ἐληλυθέναι, ἀντίχριστός ἐστιν· καὶ ὃς ἂν μὴ ὁμολογῇ τὸ μαρτύριον τοῦ σταυροῦ, ἐκ τοῦ διαβόλου ἐστίν.

[81] Cf. Rgg. Hb., *ad loc.*

[82] There are many instances in Cl. Al. (cf. Stählin's index), Origen and Eusebius.

specifically Christian use for verbal evangelistic witness to the truth of the Gospel. The only thing to fade was recollection that the reference was originally to those who were specifically charged to give this witness, or who did in fact give it. The terms are now applied to those who, even if only on occasion, bear witness under threat, for only this is regarded as full witness. Hence the distinction between ὁμολογεῖν and μαρτυρεῖν disappears, as may be seen especially in the accounts of the South Gaul martyrdoms in Eus. Hist. Eccl., V, 1, where the two terms are fully interchangeable. But they also draw apart, for the term witness is reserved for those who seal the seriousness of their witness or confession by death, and it becomes a tt. in this sense.

2. The Usage.

Whether μαρτυρεῖν is used in this martyrological sense in 1 Cl., 5, 4 and 7 is open to debate.[83] As an example of a ἕως θανάτου ἀθλεῖν (5, 2) Peter is first mentioned, ὃς ... οὐχ ἕνα οὐδὲ δύο ἀλλὰ πλείονας ὑπήνεγκε πόνους καὶ οὕτω μαρτυρήσας ἐπορεύθη εἰς τὸν ὀφειλόμενον τόπον τῆς δόξης (5, 4). It is said of Paul that he δικαιοσύνην διδάξας ὅλον τὸν κόσμον, καὶ ἐπὶ τὸ τέρμα τῆς δύσεως ἐλθὼν καὶ μαρτυρήσας ἐπὶ τῶν ἡγουμένων, οὕτως ἀπηλλάγη τοῦ κόσμου (5, 7). In the first verse there has been no mention of Peter's preaching, only of his sufferings. Hence it seems to be said that he suffered a martyr's death. But in what is said about Paul the μαρτυρεῖν seems to refer to his preaching, though this is, of course, the preaching of one who died for the sake of his ministry. The usage is thus fluid.[84] To reserve judgment on this epistle, which comes from the Roman church, is particularly appropriate when one recalls that the Shepherd of Hermas, which also comes from Rome, obviously does not show acquaintance with the technical use of μάρτυς etc. Hermas mentions martyrs, and is vitally concerned about their ecclesiastical rank and heavenly reward, cf. esp. s., 9, 28; v., 3, 1, 9; 2, 1; 5, 2. But his regular term for them is οἱ παθόντες διὰ τὸ ὄνομα or εἵνεκα τοῦ ὀνόματος. No less surprising is the complete lack of any martyrological use of the word group in Ignatius. Ignatius is full of the idea of martyrdom. The content associated with the idea is richly developed by him. He is an imitator, a bearer of Christ. As one who goes to martyrdom, he is on the point of becoming a true disciple of Christ. But nowhere do we find μάρτυς, μαρτυρεῖν etc. He shows no acquaintance whatever with the later use. The same is also true of Justin, who does not use the terms either.

The first work to have all four words μάρτυς κτλ. in the fixed martyrological sense is the Martyrdom of Polycarp written just after Polycarp's death (Feb. 23, 155) by the church of Smyrna to tell the church of Philomelium about it, cf. Mart. Pol., 19, 1: ... Πολύκαρπον, ὃς σὺν τοῖς ἀπὸ Φιλαδελφίας δωδέκατος ἐν Σμύρνῃ μαρτυρήσας ... οὐ μόνον διδάσκαλος γενόμενος ἐπίσημος, ἀλλὰ καὶ μάρτυς ἔξοχος, οὗ τὸ μαρτύριον πάντες ἐπιθυμοῦσιν μιμεῖσθαι κατὰ τὸ εὐαγγέλιον Χριστοῦ γενόμενον, and 13, 2: παντὶ ... καλῷ πρὸ τῆς μαρτυρίας ἐκεκόσμητο. Cf. also μάρτυς in 2, 2; 14, 2; 15, 2; 16, 2; 17, 3; μαρτυρεῖν in 1, 1; 21, 1; 22, 1; epil. 3; μαρτυρία in 1, 1; μαρτύριον in 1, 1; 2, 1; 18, 3. It may also be noted that a little later Melito of Sardis in his work Περὶ τοῦ πάσχα uses the simple ἐμαρτύρησεν when telling of the martyrdom of Bishop Sagaris (Eus. Hist. Eccl., IV, 26, 3), and that a little later still Polycrates of Ephesus, in his letter to Victor of Rome about the paschal

[83] Cf. the notes of J. B. Lightfoot on 1 Cl., 5, 4 in his edition (1869), 46 f. Cf. also Delehaye, 79: μαρτυρεῖν here undoubtedly means "souffrir le martyre"; also v. Campenhausen, 54; Leclercq in Cabrol-Leclercq, X, 2 (1932), 2360 f.; H. Lietzmann, "Petrus röm. Märtyrer," SBA (1936), 29; E. Molland, ThLZ (1937), 439-444 [Bertram]. For a different view K. Heussi, "War Petrus in Rom?" (1936), 24 f.; "War Petrus wirklich römischer Märtyrer?" (1937), 3 ff.

[84] In 1 Cl., 38, 2 μαρτυρεῖν is used in the ordinary sense, as is μάρτυς in 63, 3.

question, uses what is almost the fixed double formula ἐπίσκοπος καὶ μάρτυς for the bishops Polycarp of Smyrna, Thraseas of Eumenia and the above Sagaris.

Thus in the church at Smyrna, and, one might say, in the church throughout Asia Minor, we find a fixed and technical martyrological use of the terms by the middle of the second century. We find this use, then, in the area which was the home of Rev., in which the first clear steps are taken towards such a development. Elsewhere at this time no traces of the later concept are to be found. One may conclude that the sphere in which the martyr concept developed was the church in Asia Minor.[85]

We also find the beginnings of a use of the term witness for those who confess at the risk of their lives but without suffering death. Thus acc. to Hegesippus the descendants of Jude, the brother of Jesus, who were haled before Domitian but escaped free and later played a leading role in the Palestinian church, are called μάρτυρες (Eus. Hist. Eccl., III, 20, 6; 32, 6). Hippolytus also uses the word for those who had to do forced labour in the Sardinian mines and who were later liberated (Philos., IX, 12, 10 and 11). He also speaks of the μαρτυρεῖν and μαρτυρία of that dubious Christian the later Pope Calixtus, who had temporarily done forced labour in Sardinia (§ 4). In a letter of Serapion of Antioch there is ref. to a bishop who signed himself Αὐρήλιος Κυρίνιος μάρτυς (Eus. Hist. Eccl., V, 19, 3). In Eus. Hist. Eccl., V, 18, 5 f. there is a Montanist leader Themison, ὁ μὴ βαστάσας τῆς ὁμολογίας τὸ σημεῖον, who purchased his freedom by a big money payment, and also an Alexander, both of whom called themselves witnesses and were honoured as such by their followers.

The usage is only occasional. But it spread rapidly. It is found in the Acts of Justin (c. 6: οἱ ἅγιοι μάρτυρες ... ἐτελείωσαν τὸ μαρτύριον ἐν τῇ τοῦ σωτῆρος ἡμῶν ὁμολογίᾳ). Dionysius of Corinth in his letter to Rome wrote that Peter and Paul εἰς τὴν Ἰταλίαν ὁμόσε διδάξαντες ἐμαρτύρησαν κατὰ τὸν αὐτὸν καιρόν (Eus. Hist. Eccl., II, 25, 8). He obviously took the μαρτυρεῖν of 1 Cl., 5, 4 and 7 in the sense of martyrdom. Hegesippus uses μαρτυρεῖν in this sense of the martyrdom of Simon, son of Cleopas, in the time of Trajan (Eus. Hist. Eccl., III, 32, 3), and esp. of the death of the Lord's brother, James. After being thrown from the top of the temple and stoned, James received a blow on the head from a fuller: καὶ οὕτως ἐμαρτύρησεν, Eus. Hist. Eccl., II, 23, 18; cf. also μετὰ τὸ μαρτυρῆσαι Ἰάκωβον τὸν δίκαιον, ὡς καὶ ὁ κύριος, IV, 22, 4. But μαρτυρεῖν is also used by Hegesippus in the ordinary sense (μαρτυροῦμέν σοι καὶ πᾶς ὁ λαὸς ὅτι δίκαιος εἶ, II, 23, 10), and μαρτυρία can mean oral witness to the faith, II, 23, 14, cf. 23, 2. Both ideas are combined at the end of the account: μάρτυς οὗτος ἀληθὴς Ἰουδαίοις τε καὶ Ἕλλησιν γεγένηται ὅτι Ἰησοῦς ὁ Χριστός ἐστιν (23, 18). His oral witness is consummated in his death. Both are one act. He is thus a μάρτυς in the full sense. But the ὅτι clause shows that μάρτυς needed to be filled out in content.[86]

Particularly instructive is the account of the persecution in S. Gaul at the time of Marcus Aurelius (Eus. Hist. Eccl., V, 1 f.), esp. because here for the first time we find the distinction between ὁμόλογοι and μάρτυρες which later carried the field, and the title μάρτυς or ἡ τῆς μαρτυρίας προσηγορία is reserved for Christ Himself and for those οὓς ἐν τῇ ὁμολογίᾳ Χριστὸς ἠξίωσεν ἀναληφθῆναι, ἐπισφραγισάμενος αὐτῶν διὰ τῆς ἐξόδου τὴν μαρτυρίαν (V, 2, 3). The Christians there, for all the terrible tortures they have already had to suffer — οὐχ ἅπαξ οὐδὲ δὶς ἀλλὰ πολλάκις μαρτυρήσαντες, says the account (V, 2, 2) — refused to be called martyrs by their

---

[85] Lightfoot, 47: "Doubtless the Neronian persecution had done much to promote this sense." More important were the heavy blows which smote the young church in Asia Minor.

[86] The technical use of μαρτύριον for martyrdom in § 19 (the siege of Jerusalem by Vespasian began at once μετὰ τὸ μαρτύριον αὐτοῦ) is not part of the account, but comes from Eus.

fellow-believers until they were perfected; they were only ὁμόλογοι μέτριοι καὶ ταπεινοί. The account itself, of course, is not so strict in its usage. If it says of those condemned to death προσετίθεντο τῷ τῶν μαρτύρων κλήρῳ etc. (V, 1, 26 and 48), it can already call the living μάρτυρες in so far as they have had to suffer torments for their confession. What is usually ὁμολογία can also be called τὴν καλὴν μαρτυρίαν (V, 1, 30). It speaks of the repeated μαρτυρεῖν of the same persons (V, 2, 2). It even says of Attalos that he ἀεὶ μάρτυς ἐγεγόνει παρ' ἡμῖν ἀληθείας (V, 1, 43), using the term in the older sense of evangelistic witness. But these are echoes of a less developed and earlier use. Such echoes never die away altogether. We also find spiritualisations, esp. in Cl. Al., cf. Strom., IV. But in the strict sense martyrs are now only those put to death for their faith: κυρίως μόνους μάρτυρας ὠνόμασαν τοὺς τῇ ἐκχύσει τοῦ ἑαυτῶν αἵματος μαρτυρήσαντας τῷ τῆς θεοσεβείας μυστηρίῳ (Orig. Comm. in Joh., 2, 210). For as the prophets are perfect (τέλειοι) in prophecy, so οἱ μάρτυρες ἐν ὁμολογίᾳ (Cl. Al. Strom., IV, 21, 133, 1). The content and the current relation of μαρτυρεῖν and ὁμολογεῖν are correctly stated in this observation. Those not yet condemned are, in Tertullian's phrase (Mart., 1), *martyres designati*. The strict sense of witness is only a distant echo in this technical Christian use. The word has acquired a new sense. This is why the Latin speaking church took over the Greek term instead of translating it (by *testis*).

It remains only to note that μαρτύριον, in accordance with its objective trend, was often used later for the place where a martyr was buried or his remains were to be found, cf. P. Oxy., VI, 941, 4 (6th cent. A.D.): ἀντὶς τοῦ μαρτυρίου, over against the altar of the martyr. [87]

3. Understanding.

The new concept which arose in this way naturally associated itself at once with ideas which had been long in preparation. The Christian who goes forward to martyrdom does not wrestle with flesh and blood. Those who torture him or try to make him recant are agents of the devil. He stands in an ἀγών with this great foe. The conflict with the Egyptian (Egypt is the land of devilish magic) finds particularly graphic description in a vision in the Martyrdom of Perpetua and her companions, c. 10. [88] In this struggle Christians imitate Christ. They also continue His sufferings. Indeed, He Himself fights in them and stands at their side. They are supported by Him and by the Spirit. They are thus enabled to endure without a murmur, and even with a smile, the most terrible torments. In not a few cases they have the privilege of seeing the δόξα κυρίου. They are prepared, encouraged and strengthened by visions and heavenly voices. As they suffer, they are in transition to the heavenly state, μηκέτι ἄνθρωποι, ἀλλ' ἤδη ἄγγελοι (Mart. Pol., 2, 3). It is little wonder that when their bodies are consumed by the flames there comes from them a divine savour. If they are perfected, they go directly to heavenly glory.

These ideas are found very clearly in the older martyrdoms, e.g., of Polycarp, Justin, Perpetua, and the S. Gaul martyrs, though not every trait is present in all of them. [89] The basic elements, namely, the conflict with Satan, the imitation and extension of the sufferings of Christ, His mysterious support, the infilling of power and joy, are fully developed in the epistles of Ignatius. All the decisive

[87] In Eus. Vit. Const. the sepulchre of Jesus, and the Church of the Sepulchre, are thus designated, cf. the index in Heikel's edition; cf. also F. J. Dölger, *Sol salutis* (1925), 269, n. 3 and 324, n. 3 [Bertram].

[88] Cf. Dölger.

[89] We refrain from adducing examples, which are readily accessible in the sources. For good material cf. H. Achelis, *Das Christentum in den ersten drei Jahrhunderten*, II (1912), c. 7 and Excursus 87.

points go back to ideas found in the NT itself.[90] Thus disciples who are persecuted for the sake of Christ are called blessed in Mt. 5:11 f. The support of the Spirit is promised to those brought before courts in Mt. 10:17 ff. The promise of life is given to those who offer up their lives in Mt. 16:24 ff. Here and in the eschatological discourses the Gospel tradition offers a wealth of motifs which come together at this point. The note in Ac. 5:41 (they rejoiced because they κατηξιώθησαν ὑπὲρ τοῦ ὀνόματος ἀτιμασθῆναι) breathes the whole mood of martyrdom, not to mention the death of Stephen. To Paul the sufferings which he endures in his missionary work seem to be an ἀνταναπληροῦν of the ὑστερήματα τῶν θλίψεων τοῦ Χριστοῦ (Col. 1:24). This thought determines his whole view of his missionary sufferings. As such, they are sufferings in the service of Christ. The joyous mood of martyrdom is also expressed in Rom. 5:3 and 8:17. In 1 Pt. those who are persecuted are summoned to joy at κοινωνεῖν τοῖς τοῦ Χριστοῦ παθήμασιν (4:13) and exhorted to ἐπακολουθεῖν τοῖς ἴχνεσιν αὐτοῦ, namely, those of the Christ who suffered for others (2:21 ff.). Before the eyes of the seer in Rev. stands Christ, the Lamb slain, the original martyr, the faithful witness κατ' ἐξοχήν. In the NT, however, these elements are not yet firmly associated with the concept of the martyr. They cannot be, for the development of the martyrological sense is only a consequence of the martyrdom experienced by the Church. When it arose, this sense necessarily assimilated all the other ideas, and it thus had new implications (e.g., in respect of merits) which it is beyond the scope of this dictionary to pursue.

† ἐπιμαρτυρέω, † συμμαρτυρέω, † συνεπιμαρτυρέω, † καταμαρτυρέω.

The meaning of these compounds is closely related to the popular sense of μαρτυρεῖν (→ μάρτυς B. 2 and 3).

ἐπιμαρτυρεῖν[1] (Plat., Plut., Lucian, Joseph., very occasionally pap.) is not found in the LXX at all.

ἐπιμαρτυρεῖν occurs in the NT only at 1 Pt. 5:12. It means "to attest (a preceding assertion)," not just "to attest emphatically" (cf. P. Lond., 1692a, 19 [6th cent. A.D.]: τῶν δεῖνα ἐπιμαρτυρούντων). The ἐπι- simply strengthens an element in the μαρτυρεῖν. But ἐπιμαρτυρεῖν can also mean "to affirm," "to agree," and it can be used of the protestation, not of a fact, but of a view or opinion, so that the basic sense of μαρτυρεῖν is lost, cf. Ep. Ar., 197: ἐπιμαρτυρήσας δὲ τούτοις, where ἐπιμαρτυρεῖν means the same as the preceding ἐπιφωνεῖν, ἐπαινεῖν, ἀποδέχεσθαι. There can be no question here of a witness or proof in the strict sense. This may be explained in terms of what was said in → μάρτυς B. 2. In 1 Pt. 5:12 what is attested is stated in the ensuing acc. c. inf.

συμμαρτυρεῖν is a common compound (Soph., Eur., Isocr., Xenoph., Plut., pap.) which does not occur in the LXX and is used in the NT only at R. 2:15; 8:16; 9:1. It first means "to bear witness with," "to attest or confirm something as one witness along with another or several others." It has this sense in, e.g., BGU, I, 86, 40 ff. (2nd cent. A.D.), where a list of witnesses is linked with the first witness by a συμμαρτιρῶ (or συμμαρτυρῶ) καὶ συνσφραγιῶ (*sic*); cf. also Plut. Comparatio Thesei c. Romulo,

---

[90] Cf. the fine collection of material in v. Campenhausen and the works he mentions.

ἐπιμαρτυρέω κτλ. [1] ἐπι- must have signified originally "to what has gone before," i.e., "to add to the assertion the witness, the proof, or simply agreement" [Debrunner]. Cf. also → 510, n. 1 on ἐπιμαρτύρεσθαι, "to aver as a warning."

6, 5 and 7 (I, 39b) ὁ χρόνος ἐστὶ μάρτυς ... τῷ δὲ τοσούτῳ χρόνῳ συμμαρτυρεῖ καὶ τὰ ἔργα. But then recollection of the basic meaning fades, and συμμαρτυρεῖν simply means "to confirm" (i.e., the statement of another of any kind, whether about a fact or an opinion), or, with the dat., "to agree." Cf. Plat. Hi., I, 282b: συμμαρτυρῆσαι δέ σοι ἔχω ὅτι ἀληθῆ λέγεις, "I must agree with you that you are right" (i.e., with the view expressed). Xenoph. Hist. Graec., VII, 1, 35: ἔλεγε δὲ ὁ Πελοπίδας ὅτι ... συνεμαρτύρει δ' αὐτῷ ταῦτα πάντα ὡς ἀληθῆ λέγοι ὁ 'Αθηναῖος Τιμαγόρας, Timagoras confirms the account of Pelopidas. With ref. only to a belief, without mentioning who held it, Plut. Quaest. Conv., VIII, 4, 4 (II, 724c/d): σκύλων δὲ Πυθοῖ καὶ ἀκροθινίων καὶ τροπαίων ἀναθέσεις ἆρα οὐ συμμαρτυροῦσιν ὅτι τῆς εἰς τὸ νικᾶν καὶ κρατεῖν δυνάμεως τῷ θεῷ τούτῳ πλεῖστον μέτεστιν, the votive offerings confirm the opinion of faith that God will help to victory. "Distinction between the two meanings to testify with and to confirm alone does justice to the usage; συμμαρτυρεῖν never denotes, like μαρτυρεῖν, purely authoritative assertion, but always confirmation." [2]

Our starting-point now must be the three passages in Romans. 2:15: οἵτινες ἐνδεικνυνται τὸ ἔργον τοῦ νόμου γραπτὸν ἐν ταῖς καρδίαις αὐτῶν (by their actual conduct, v. 14), συμμαρτυρούσης αὐτῶν τῆς συνειδήσεως. Conscience confirms the ἔνδειξις of the actual conduct of the Gentiles (that they ἑαυτοῖς εἰσιν νόμος, or that the works demanded by the Law are written on their hearts). The constant impulses of the living moral consciousness have independent significance along with the individual acts performed. Similarly, R. 9:1: ἀλήθειαν λέγω ἐν Χριστῷ, οὐ ψεύδομαι, συμμαρτυρούσης μοι τῆς συνειδήσεώς μου ἐν πνεύματι ἁγίῳ. The judgment of Paul's conscience as directed by the Holy Spirit accompanies and confirms the statement which he has made or begun to make. It is really true that the unbelief of Israel is a great burden to the apostle. In R. 8:16: αὐτὸ τὸ πνεῦμα συμμαρτυρεῖ τῷ πνεύματι ἡμῶν ὅτι ἐσμὲν τέκνα θεοῦ, the divine → πνεῦμα confirms what τὸ πνεῦμα ἡμῶν already says, namely, that we Christians are the children of God. The first πνεῦμα is the πνεῦμα υἱοθεσίας by which the sons of God are impelled and which enables them to call upon God as Father (v. 14 f.). The πνεῦμα ἡμῶν can only be the spiritual ego of man, the νοῦς, or, as we would say, the soul. πνεῦμα is also used for soul in R. 1:9; 8:10; 1 C. 5:3-5; 7:34; 16:18; 2 C. 2:13; 7:1, 13; Gl. 6:18; Phil. 4:23; Col. 2:5; Phlm. 25. [3] If we take συμμαρτυρεῖν strictly, it is implicitly said that the spiritual ego of the man in Christ already declares him to be a child of God. But it is hard to think that Paul could say this. Hence we are forced to give to συμμαρτυρεῖν here the simple sense of "bear witness." [4] If, on the other hand, we think that when Paul relates the πνεῦμα to man he always, or here at least, means the personal life of the Christian as this is shaped by the Spirit of God, then we can take συμμαρτυρεῖν strictly. The statement of faith made by this Christian ego which is aware of being a child of God is confirmed by the Spirit. "Here Paul sets alongside the act of faith the inspirative process. He assigns this to the second place; the first is occupied by the faith based on the message of Jesus." [5] But could the Roman Christians read this from τῷ πνεύματι ἡμῶν? Does it not finally amount to the fact that the Spirit of God confirms Himself?

---

2 Acc. to Cr.-Kö.
3 Cf., e.g., Ltzm. on R. 8:16, 11.
4 E.g., Ltzm. R., also P. Althaus in *NT Deutsch*, II (1933), *ad loc.*
5 So Schl. R., 266.

συνεπιμαρτυρεῖν, which is common in non-biblical Gk. (Aristot., Polyb., Plut.), does not occur in the LXX and is found in the NT only at Hb. 2:4. The salvation first preached by the Lord Himself is confirmed in us by the hearers, συνεπιμαρτυροῦντος τοῦ θεοῦ σημείοις κτλ. On the meaning cf. Ep. Ar., 191: συνεπιμαρτυρήσας δὲ τούτῳ τὸν ἐχόμενον ἠρώτα, "(the king) agreed with this one and asked the next." Cf. also 1 Cl., 23, 5: συνεπιμαρτυρούσης καὶ τῆς γραφῆς. The saying does not imply the presence of another witness who confirms what has been said and with whom there is then a second. It simply means that something seen by another, whether a fact, opinion, or conviction, is accepted by a second as true.

Thus Hb. 2:4 does not carry a reference to yet other μάρτυρες, so that the preachers (ὑπὸ τῶν ἀκουσάντων ... ἐβεβαιώθη) are indirectly described as such. They have given assurance and made an impression thereby. But God Himself has confirmed the truth of the preaching by the witness of the σημεῖα. In the case of συνεπιμαρτυρεῖν the situation is much the same as in that of συμμαρτυρεῖν.

καταμαρτυρεῖν (Lys., Demosth., Isaeus, Epict., Dio C., occasionally the pap.) is used with the gen. of person for "making a statement in witness against someone." It occurs a few times in the LXX (for עוד hi, עָנָה or אֲכַל קַרְצֵי דִי פ׳), mostly of false witnesses for the prosecution. It does not have to mean false witnesses; this either emerges from the context (3 Βασ. 20:10 [not B], 13; Sus. 21 Θ) or is expressly indicated by the addition (μαρτυρίαν) ψευδῆ (Prv. 25:18; Sus. 43;49 Θ). The term does not have this implication in Job 15:6: τὰ δὲ χείλη σου καταμαρτυρήσουσίν σου, or Da. 6:25: οἱ καταμαρτυρήσαντες τοῦ Δανιήλ. Cf. also Epict. Diss., IV, 8, 32, of the witness of the genuine Cynic who by his conduct τῇ ἀρετῇ μαρτυρεῖ καὶ τῶν ἐκτὸς καταμαρτυρεῖ (bears witness against the value of everything external).

In the NT the word occurs only at Mk. 14:60 = Mt. 26:62, where the high-priest asks Jesus: οὐκ ἀποκρίνῃ οὐδὲν τί οὗτοί σου καταμαρτυροῦσιν; and Mt. 27:13, where Pilate puts to Him the question: οὐκ ἀκούεις πόσα σου καταμαρτυροῦσιν; (Mk.: ἴδε πόσα σου κατηγοροῦσιν). The context shows that there is no basis for the statements.

† μαρτύρομαι, † διαμαρτύρομαι, † προμαρτύρομαι.[1]

μαρτύρεσθαι originally, "to invoke someone as a witness about something," esp. the gods (Plat. Phileb., 12b: μαρτύρομαι νῦν αὐτὴν τὴν θεόν, Eur. Med., 1410: δαίμονας, Eur. Phoen., 626: γαῖαν καὶ θεούς), but also men, Aesch. Eum., 643: ὑμᾶς δ' ἀκούειν ταῦτ' ἐγὼ μαρτύρομαι, Plat. Resp., II, 364d: οἱ δὲ τῆς τῶν θεῶν ὑπ' ἀνθρώπων παραγωγῆς τὸν Ὅμηρον μαρτύρονται, Aristoph. Pl., 932: ὁρᾷς ἃ ποιεῖ; ταῦτ' ἐγὼ μαρτύρομαι, namely, the witness who is addressed (σε to be supplied), cf. Ra., 528; Vesp., 1436; Nu., 1222 and 1297; Plut. Alcibiades, 12 (I, 196d): τὸν Διομήδη ... μαρτυρόμενον θεοὺς καὶ ἀνθρώπους, Plut. Aristid., 18 (I, 330a): Ἀριστείδης ... μαρτυρόμενος Ἑλληνίους θεοὺς ἀπέχεσθαι μάχης, Marcellus, 7 (I, 301d): Ζεῦ, μαρτύρομαί σε ... σοὶ καθιεροῦν, P. Oxy., VIII, 1114, 23 ff. (3rd cent. A.D.): ἐμαρτύρατο τοὺς τόδε τὸ μαρτυροποίημα σφραγίζειν μέλλοντας ... Αὐρηλίαν Ἀπολλωνίαν ... ἀδιάθετον τελευτῆσαι. It thus passes into general use. Strictly, we should be told what the occasion is.[2] If we are told only to what the

μαρτύρομαι κτλ. [1] ἐπιμαρτύρεσθαι occurs a few times in the LXX (for עוד on the verbal constr. cf. Helbing Kasussyntax, 226 f.), usually in the sense "to aver as a warning"; cf. 3 Βασ. 2:42; Am. 3:13; 2 Εσδρ. 19:29 f.; 23:15, 21 (*vl.*).

[2] On the meaning of the med. cf., e.g., δικάζειν, "to judge," δικάζεσθαι, "to seek judgment"; μισθοῦν, "to hire out," med. "to hire" [Debrunner]. Cf. also Helbing, 225 [Bertram].

witness refers, μαρτύρεσθαι comes to mean "to make a solemn declaration about." This can then have the sense of an emphatic affirmation that something is so, cf. Plat. Phileb., 47d: ταῦτα δὲ τότε μὲν οὐκ ἐμαρτυράμεθα, νῦν δὲ λέγομεν; Dio C., 41, 3, 2: εἶπόν τε πολλὰ καὶ ἐμαρτύραντο, or simply "to attest": P. Oxy., VIII, 1121, 8 (3rd cent. A.D.): μαρτυρομένη τὰ εἴς με ἐπιχειρηθέντα, cf. line 23 f.: ἐπιδίδωμι τάδε τὰ βιβλία μαρτυρομένη μὲν τὸ ἐπιχείρημα ἀξιοῦσα δὲ ..., also 1120, 11; 1114, 23 (→ *supra*), or an emphatic demand, requirement or admonition, cf. P. Lips., 37, 25 (4th cent. A.D.): διὰ τοῦτο ἐπιδίδωμι τούσδε τοὺς λιβέλλους μαρτυρόμενος καὶ ἀξιῶν τούτους ἐν ἀσφαλεῖ εἶναι μέχρις τῆς ἐπιδημίας τοῦ ἄρχοντος.

In the LXX it occurs (along with the rather more common ἐπιμαρτύρεσθαι, 9 times) only twice, at Jdt. 7:28: μαρτυρόμεθα ὑμῖν τὸν οὐρανὸν καὶ τὴν γῆν καὶ τὸν θεὸν ἡμῶν, to support a demand previously expressed; and 1 Macc. 2:56, where Caleb receives an inheritance ἐν τῷ μαρτύρασθαι τῇ ἐκκλησίᾳ, because he bore witness to the community in the sense of a summons not to be discouraged by the report of the spies, but to begin the conquest of Canaan trusting in God. Σ has it in ψ 49:7 (for עוד hi) in the sense "to declare solemnly."

In the NT μαρτύρεσθαι is found twice in Ac. and three times in Pl. It has the meaning of emphatic demand in 1 Th. 2:11 f.: παρακαλοῦντες ὑμᾶς ... καὶ μαρτυρόμενοι εἰς τὸ περιπατεῖν ὑμᾶς ἀξίως τοῦ θεοῦ κτλ., and Eph. 4:17: τοῦτο οὖν λέγω καὶ μαρτύρομαι ἐν κυρίῳ, μηκέτι ὑμᾶς περιπατεῖν καθὼς καὶ τὰ ἔθνη περιπατεῖ. The translation "I adjure you" strikes a false note, since there is no thought of calling on God to give force to the admonition. In the other three passages it has the sense of emphatic affirmation, each time with the dat. of person. It may be a factual assertion, as in Ac. 20:26: διότι μαρτύρομαι ὑμῖν ... ὅτι καθαρός εἰμι ἀπὸ τοῦ αἵματος πάντων. Paul assures the Ephesian elders that he bears no responsibility if anyone perishes. It may refer to a truth to be observed, as in Gl. 5:3: μαρτύρομαι δὲ πάλιν παντὶ ἀνθρώπῳ περιτεμνομένῳ ὅτι ὀφειλέτης ἐστὶν ὅλον τὸν νόμον ποιῆσαι. In particular, it refers to the message of the Gospel which Paul attests both to small and great (Ac. 26:22).[3]

There is hardly any difference in meaning between διαμαρτύρεσθαι and μαρτύρεσθαι. The first meaning is "to invoke someone (gods or men) as witness with reference to something," "to declare with an appeal to witnesses," and then secondly "to declare emphatically," whether with ref. to facts or truths (so esp. Demosth.) or in the sense of a summons, admonition, or warning.[4]

It occurs a few times in the LXX, almost always for עוד hi, but once each for זהר hi, עוד hoph, and twice for ידע hi. It has its basic sense at Dt. 4:26: διαμαρτύρομαι ὑμῖν (against you) σήμερον τόν τε οὐρανὸν καὶ τὴν γῆν, ὅτι ἀπωλείᾳ ἀπολεῖσθε

[3] The dat. with μαρτύρεσθαι should be noted; it proves that in the case of μαρτύρομαι there is transition from "to invoke as witness" to "to attest" or "affirm," and hence fusion with μαρτυρεῖν; → *supra* [Debrunner]. The dat. also occurs in the LXX (with the acc. of the one invoked as witness) at Jdt. 7:28. Here, then, the term has both senses.

[4] This expression is esp. common, cf. Plut. Cim., 16 (I, 489b): Ἐφιάλτου δὲ κωλύοντος καὶ διαμαρτυρομένου μὴ βοηθεῖν κτλ.; Plut. Crass., 16 (I, 553a): ὁ δ' Ἀτήϊος ... ἐκώλυε καὶ διεμαρτύρετο μὴ βαδίζειν ..., Demosth. Or., 33, 20: διαμαρτυρομένου τοῦ ἀνθρώπου ἐναντίον μαρτύρων μὴ ἀποφαίνεσθαι ..., Xenoph. Cyrop., VII, 1, 17: καὶ σὺ μὴ πρότερον ἔμβαλλε τοῖς ἐναντίοις, διαμαρτύρομαι, πρὶν ἂν φεύγοντας ... θεάσῃ, Polyb., I, 33, 5: Ξανθίππου διαμαρτυρομένου μὴ παριέναι τὸν καιρόν, III, 15, 5: διεμαρτύροντο ... ἀπέχεσθαι ... καὶ ... μὴ διαβαίνειν, III, 110, 4: πολλὰ διαμαρτυρομένου καὶ κωλύοντος τοῦ Λευκίου. For the pap. cf. Preisigke Wört. and Moult.-Mill., *s.v.*

κτλ., cf. 30:19; 31:28; in Ιερ. 39:10, 44 (διαμαρτύρεσθαι μάρτυρας) the ref. is to the part of witnesses at the signing of agreements. Elsewhere it means "to declare emphatically," whether with ref. to statutes to be followed (Ex. 18:20; 19:10, 21; 1 Βασ. 8:9), to representations made to someone (Ex. 21:29; 2 Εσδρ. 23:21), occasionally to a promise given (Zech. 3:6), or commonly to prophetic warnings to repent (4 Βασ. 17:13; 2 Παρ. 24:19; 2 Εσδρ. 19:26, 34; ψ 49:7; [5] 80:8; Ιερ. 6:10; Ez. 16:2; 20:4 in these two passages with the obj. τὰς ἀνομίας). With these meanings we often find the dat of person, e.g., Dt. 32:46; Ex. 19:21. [6] There is a special use in Mal. 2:14: ὅτι Κύριος διεμαρτύρατο ἀνὰ μέσον σοῦ καὶ ἀνὰ μέσον γυναικὸς νεότητός σου, "He was present as a witness."

Of the 15 NT occurrences, 10 are in the Lucan writings (9 in Ac.), 3 in the Past., one each in 1 Th. and Hb. The meaning is never "to invoke as witness." "To declare emphatically" in the sense of a warning is the meaning in Lk. 16:28: ὅπως διαμαρτύρηται αὐτοῖς, ἵνα μὴ καὶ αὐτοὶ ἔλθωσιν εἰς τὸν τόπον τοῦτον τῆς βασάνου, and 2 Tm. 2:14: διαμαρτυρόμενος ἐνώπιον τοῦ θεοῦ μὴ λογομαχεῖν. Here the ἐνώπιον τοῦ θεοῦ reminds us of the original sphere of the term. This is also true in 1 Tm. 5:21 and esp. 2 Tm. 4:1, where the meaning is "to declare emphatically" by way of admonition. In the latter passage: Διαμαρτύρομαι ἐνώπιον τοῦ θεοῦ καὶ Χριστοῦ Ἰησοῦ ... καὶ τὴν ἐπιφάνειαν αὐτοῦ καὶ τὴν βασιλείαν αὐτοῦ· κήρυξον τὸν λόγον, διαμαρτύρεσθαι is similar to ὁρκίζω τινά τι in Mk. 5:7; Ac. 19:13; cf. 1 Th. 5:27, and it obviously has the sense "to adjure." To avoid this we should have to take τὴν ἐπιφάνειαν κτλ. as the object of διαμαρτύρομαι, which is against the context. In all other instances the meaning is (emphatic) "affirmation" that a thing is or will be so, cf. the intimation of Paul's imprisonment in Ac. 20:23, the adducing of a truth attested in the OT in Hb. 2:6, Paul's preaching of future judgment in 1 Th. 4:6, and in Ac. (up to 20:23) the apostolic preaching of the Gospel with the object τὸ εὐαγγέλιον τῆς χάριτος τοῦ θεοῦ (20:24), τὴν βασιλείαν τοῦ θεοῦ (28:23), τὸν λόγον τοῦ κυρίου (8:25), τὰ περὶ ἐμοῦ (Christ, 23:11), τὴν εἰς θεὸν μετάνοιαν καὶ πίστιν εἰς τὸν κύριον ἡμῶν Ἰησοῦν (20:21). In 18:5 the content is given by the phrase εἶναι τὸν χριστὸν Ἰησοῦν and in 10:42 by a ὅτι clause. In 2:40 it is made clear by the context.

προμαρτύρεσθαι occurs for the first time outside the Bible in an 8th cent. pap. in the sense "to summon to something in advance" (P. Lond., IV, 1356, 32: προμαρτυρόμενος [αὐτοὺς εἰ]ς τὸ σχεῖν τὸν φόβον τοῦ θεοῦ πρὸ ὀφθαλμῶν).

It does not occur in the LXX and the only NT instance is at 1 Pt. 1:11 in the sense "to attest or declare in advance as a fact (which will come to pass)." The πνεῦμα (of Christ) dwelling in the prophets was προμαρτυρόμενον τὰ εἰς Χριστὸν παθήματα (the sufferings ordained for Christ) καὶ τὰς μετὰ ταῦτα δόξας. [7]

[5] The fact that Σ uses the simple form shows that the two are equivalent in meaning [Bertram].

[6] Cf. Helbing, 225 f.

[7] Moult.-Mill. translate: "Called to witness, summon to witness." But this sense, deduced from the basic sense of μαρτύρεσθαι, cannot apply to the two passages in question.

† ψευδόμαρτυς, † ψευδομαρτυρέω, † ψευδομαρτυρία.

ψευδόμαρτυς, "the false witness." Like ψευδομαρτυρεῖν and ψευδομαρτυρία it occurs already in class Gk., cf. esp. Anaxim. in Ps.-Aristot. Rhet. Al., 16, p. 1431b, 20 ff., esp. 41 f., where there is an express discussion *de testimoniis et testibus*, and all three words are found. On the other hand, they do not occur at all in the pap., though we find ψευδομαρτύριον (→ 514). The construction is not to be explained in the same way as ψευδοφίλιππος (Luc.), ψευδηρακλῆς (Menand.), ψευδόχριστος (Mt. 24:24), ψευδοπάρθενος (Hdt.), ψευδόχρυσος (Plut.), ψευδόδειπνον (Aesch.) etc., where the ψευδο- implies that what the main word denotes is claimed only ψευδῶς or falsely. On the contrary, the main word is taken verbally as in ψευδάγγελος (declaring lies, false messenger, Hom., Aristot.), ψευδοκῆρυξ (Soph.), ψευδόμαντις (Aesch., Soph.).[1] The word thus means one who attests something which is false. It is not contested that the person concerned is a witness, as though he had no direct knowledge of the persons, relations or events at issue. What is disputed is the correctness of what he says; τὰ ψευδῆ μαρτυρεῖν, ψευδομαρτυρία, ψευδόμαρτυς correspond (cf. Anaxim. Rhet. Al., 16). When in Plat. Gorg. (472b), in the discussion of the thesis of Socrates τὸν ἀδικοῦντα οὐκ εὐδαίμονα εἶναι, Polos brings against Socrates the whole host of the Athenians as witnesses, and Socrates calls all these ψευδομάρτυρας with whose help ἐπιχειρεῖς ἐκβάλλειν με ἐκ τῆς οὐσίας καὶ τοῦ ἀληθοῦς, he is not saying that they cannot be regarded as witnesses, but simply that οὗτος ὁ ἔλεγχος οὐδενὸς ἄξιός ἐστι πρὸς τὴν ἀλήθειαν (471e) because they testify to what is false. Whether a man is μάρτυς or ψευδόμαρτυς depends on whether or not he tells the truth.

The biblical usage is similar. In the LXX ψευδόμαρτυς occurs only in Sus. 60 (cf. Θ v. 61), where it is said of Daniel and the two elders who laid traps for Susannah: αὐτοὺς κατέστησεν ἀμφοτέρους ψευδομάρτυρας, "he convicted them both as false witnesses."

In the NT the word is used at Mt. 26:60 for those who bore witness against Jesus at His trial. The high-priest and the whole council sought ψευδομαρτυρίαν κατὰ τοῦ Ἰησοῦ, ὅπως αὐτὸν θανατώσωσιν, καὶ οὐχ εὗρον πολλῶν προσελθόντων ψευδομαρτύρων. Here the standpoint of the narrator merges into that of the assembly inasmuch as his judgment of the quality of the witnesses becomes a description of the purpose of the Sanhedrin.

The only other instance of ψευδόμαρτυς is at 1 C. 15:15. If Christ is not risen, our preaching is in vain and so is your faith. εὑρισκόμεθα δὲ καὶ ψευδομάρτυρες τοῦ θεοῦ, ὅτι ἐμαρτυρήσαμεν κατὰ τοῦ θεοῦ ὅτι ἤγειρεν τὸν Χριστόν, ὃν οὐκ ἤγειρεν εἴπερ ἄρα νεκροὶ οὐκ ἐγείρονται. Here, too, the starting-point is that ψευδόμαρτυς denotes the one who as a witness, i.e., claiming to be a witness, says something untrue. Paul has done this if, as he says in v. 8, he proclaims from his own experience that Christ is risen and yet all the time it is established *a priori* that resurrection from the dead is not possible. The reference of the observation is to the content of the witness, not to the fact that the character of Paul is set in a bad light because he falsely claims the title of μάρτυς.[2] Quite apart from contradicting the sense of ψευδόμαρτυς, this would also, in defiance of the context, entail a diverting of attention from the material question to a personal consideration. The genitive ψευδομάρτυρες τοῦ θεοῦ makes no difference in this

ψευδόμαρτυς κτλ. Bibl. on → μάρτυς; Holl, Reitzenstein, Corssen, also P. Corssen, *Über Bildung u. Bedeutung der Komposita* ψευδοπροφήτης, ψευδόμαντις, ψευδόμαρτυς, Sokrates, 72 (1918), 106-114; *Indogerm. Jbch.*, 5 (1918), 123 f. (bibl.); v. Campenhausen, *op. cit.*, 28 f.

[1] Cf. Debr. Griech. Wortb. § 114 and Bl.-Debr.[6] § 119.

[2] Cf. Heinr. Sendschr., I, 487.

respect. If this is taken as a subj. gen. (witnesses whom God has appointed and who obey Him),[3] this would mean that the incidental note echoes a title (μάρτυς τοῦ θεοῦ) not found elsewhere in Paul. This compels a wresting of the sense of ψευδόμαρτυς and a deflection from material considerations to personal. The point is also missed that the ὅτι clause which follows is a comment on the phrase. This is the correct explanation.[4] Though it is linguistically difficult to take the gen. as an obj. gen., the usual exegesis is right here. Paul would be a ψευδόμαρτυς τοῦ θεοῦ because, to use Plato's words, καταψευδομαρτυρηθείη ἄν ὁ θεὸς ὑπ' αὐτοῦ, that He has done something which in reality He has not done, i.e., raise up Christ (cf. Plat. Gorg., 472a).

Apart from a vl. in Sus. 61 Θ, ψευδομαρτυρεῖν occurs in the LXX only at Ex. 20:16 = Dt. 5:20 (17): לֹא תַעֲנֶה בְרֵעֲךָ עֵד שָׁקֶר, of false witness in court.

There is reference to this statute of the Law in Mt. 9:18 = Mk. 10:19 = Lk. 18:20. At R. 13:9 it has made its way — from this source — into א and some other MSS as a secondary reading. The only other instance is in Mk. 14:56 f. of the witnesses at the trial of Jesus.

ψευδομαρτυρία does not occur in the LXX.

It is found in the NT at Mt. 26:59 with reference to the trial of Jesus (→ ψευδόμαρτυς) and in the plural in the list of vices, based on the second table of the Decalogue, in Mt. 15:19: ἐκ γὰρ τῆς καρδίας ἐξέρχονται διαλογισμοὶ πονηροί, φόνοι, μοιχεῖαι, πορνεῖαι, κλοπαί, ψευδομαρτυρίαι. In P. Hal., 1 (→ μάρτυς n. 14) we have express accounts of the proceedings at trials for false witness (ἡ τοῦ ψευδομαρτυρίου δίκη). The normal expression here is ψευδομαρτύριον.

Strathmann

† μασάομαι

From the root μάω = "to touch," Hom. μάσταξ = "mouth," Lat. *mando*. Attic-Ionic,[1] first in comedy; the tragedians and older prose writers avoid it because of its harsh ring: "to bite," "to chew," "to eat."[2] Without obj. Aristoph. Eq., 717; Vesp., 780; Theophr. Char., 20, 5; P. Lond., I, 46, 280 f.; with obj. ἀμυγδάλας (almonds), Eupolis Fr., 253 (CAF, I, 327); κρέας, Aristoph. Pl., 320 f.; σηπίας (cuttle-fish), Aristoph. Eccl., 554; τοὺς ἄρτους, Artemid. Oneirocr., IV, 33; τὸν πάπυρον, Theophr. Hist. Plant., IV, 8, 4; Cassius Felix, 32 (ed. V. Rose [1879]) uses τὸ μασώμενον of a medicament for the teeth; Philostr. Vit. Ap., VII, 21 μασάομαι [τὰ χείλη] with συγγελάω in the sense of making a wry mouth in mockery.

There is only one instance in the LXX in a free rendering of Job 30:4: οἳ καὶ ῥίζας

---

[3] So K. Holl, "Ψευδόμαρτυς" (*Ges. Aufs. z. Kirchengesch.*, II [1928], 113).

[4] So v. Campenhausen, 29, n. 4, though in the main he is inclined to follow Holl's interpretation of the gen.

μασάομαι. Liddell-Scott, 1082; Wilke-Grimm., 273; Pr.-Bauer, 777, [3] 819; Walde-Pok., II, 270.

[1] Hence the occasional spelling μασσάομαι is wrong.

[2] In the NT only impf. ἐμασῶντο.

ξύλων ἐμασῶντο ὑπὸ λιμοῦ μεγάλου, with no Heb. equivalent.[3] Joseph. Bell., 6, 197: μασάομαι τὰ δέρματα τῶν θυρεῶν.

It occurs in the NT only at Rev. 16:10: "And they gnawed their tongues for pain" as a result of the fifth vial which the angel poured on the throne of the beast, and the darkness connected with this.[4]

It can hardly be assumed that the darkness and pain are results of stinging scorpions which darken the sun (9:1 ff.), or that the darkness alone is πόνος, or that there is textual confusion.[5] It seems rather that there is reflected here the genuine experience of the divine. In hallucinations men bite their own tongues in circumstances of great excitement; the confusion of images shows that the sense of pain on experiencing the vision was so strong that it could not find adequate plastic expression.[6]

The same experience is to be seen in Apc. Pt. Akhmim text, 28 f., though here it is worked into the retribution schema of the Apc. and rationalised.[7] Men and women who blaspheme God or the way of righteousness are forced in punishment to bite their lips, and false witnesses their tongues.[8]

Carl Schneider

† μαστιγόω, † μαστίζω, † μάστιξ

→ μώλωψ, πληγή, ῥαβδίζω.

† μαστιγόω, † μαστίζω.

Etym. related to μαίομαι, "to go over something," cf. Hom. Il., 5, 748; 8, 392: μάστιγι ... ἐπεμαίετ' ἄρ' ἵππους. μαστίζω from Hom. Il., 5, 366 and 768; Od., 6, 82; μαστιγόω from Epicharm. (CGF) Fr., 35, 12; Hdt., I, 114; III, 16; VII, 54; "to whip," "to beat with a lash or whip": Anth. Pal., 9, 348; Nonnus Dionys., 2, 645; Xenoph. Cyrop., I, 4, 13; Plat. Resp., II, 361e; Leg., VIII, 845a; XI, 914b; fig. a. "to lash with words," Epigr. Graec., 303, 5; b. "to torment," "to plague," Max. Tyr. (ed. Hobein), 19, 5e (of torments of the soul).

LXX in the lit. sense for נָכָה, Ex. 5:14, 16; Dt. 25:2 f.; 2 Ch. 25:16; Nu. 22:25; also 3 Βασ. 12:24r; Tob. 3:9 (of slaves); 2 Macc. 3:26; 6:30 (scourging of a martyr); Prv. 27:22 (of a fool). Fig. a. "to beat the air with birds' wings," Wis. 5:11; b. "to plague," "to torment," "to punish" (usually by God) for נָכָה Ιερ. 5:3; for נָגַע ψ 72:5; for שָׂטַם Job 30:21; also Tob. 11:14; 13:2, 5, 10; Jdt. 8:27; Job 15:11; Prv. 3:12; Wis. 12:22; 16:16

---

[3] Sir. 19:9 can only be μισήσει (against Codex A with BS).
[4] On ἐκ τοῦ πόνου Bl.-Debr.[6] § 212, p. 125.
[5] Bss., Loh., Zn. Apk., *ad loc.*
[6] C. Schneider, *Die Erlebnisechtheit der Apk. d. Joh.* (1930), 103.
[7] In the Eth. text c. 9 has the biting of the tongue for blasphemy and of the lips for false witness, also c. 11 the biting of the tongue for disobedient slaves.
[8] In Rev. 16:11 the blasphemy is a result of the pain, in Apc. Pt. the other way round. Here, too, Rev. is true to life, Apc. Pt. artificial.

μαστιγόω κτλ. Pr.-Bauer[3], 819 f.; Liddell-Scott, 1083; Walde-Pok., II, 219 f.; Tractate Sanh.-Makkot; T. Mommsen, *Römisches Strafrecht* (1899); H. Fulda, *Das Kreuz u. die Kreuzigung* (1878); H. Diels, "Zwei Fr. Heraklits," SAB (1901), 199 f.; Weinreich, AH, 60 f.; E. Feder, *Die Prügelstrafe* (1911); Str.-B., III, 527 ff.

(with the Egyptian plagues); Sir. 30:14 (with sickness); 2 Macc. 3:34, 38; 5:18; 3 Macc. 2:21. Θ has it at Is. 53:4 for נָגוּעַ.[1]

1. In Mt. 10:17 and 23:34 the disciples are told that with other persecutions they will have to face whippings in the synagogues. The sayings do not have to have been shaped by later experience in times of persecution.[2] The fact that the tt. is used only in Mt. points to a Palestinian origin.

There is a thorough treatment of punishment by scourging in Sanh.-Makkot.[3] Three, and sometimes as many as 23, judges were needed to secure condemnation to whipping in the local synagogues (Sanh., 1, 2; bSanh., 10a f.). These had specific tasks during execution of the sentence. One recited Dt. 28:58 f.; 29:8; Ps. 73:28, the second counted the blows, the third gave the command before each blow.[4] Offences were calumniation of a woman (Dt. 22:13-19), wounding the body (cf. Dt. 25:1-3), false witness if not punished more severely, the cursing of a master by a slave, certain forms of incest, keeping Hellenistic customs, breaking Nazarite vows, performing holy functions in a state of cultic uncleanness, sacrificing outside the temple, transgressing certain laws of diet, esp. Lv. 3:17, breaking the bones of the paschal lamb, imitating incense or anointing oil, flagrant offences against the Ten Commandments.[5] In the case of ordained scholars the punishment could be a substitute for expulsion. Dt. 25:3 limits the number of strokes to 40 as compared with 60 in the Code of Hammurabi[6] and as many as 80 or even 100 in the Koran.[7] But acc. to 2 C. 11:24; Mak., 3, 10; Joseph. Ant., 4, 238 and 248 the synagogue reduced this to thirty-nine; the fortieth might be omitted. There were thirteen strokes on the breast and 26 on the back. Before the whipping it had to be considered whether the person could stand the punishment. If not, it was reduced to a lesser number divisible by three. If it turned out that the estimate was too low, he was released all the same. The punishment was administered by the servant of the synagogue, who usually stood on a stone behind the sentenced person.[8] The mode varied, for sometimes the victim would stand by a pillar with his hands tied,[9] sometimes he would bend, sometimes he would be beaten lying down,[10] sometimes he would cower on the seats.[11] The instrument was the lash → μάστιξ. If it tore, a new one was not supplied; the victim was released. If there seemed to be danger of death, the whipping was to stop, though deaths were recorded.[12] Since the number of strokes had not to be exceeded, there might be more than one whipping for some offences.[13] Women were whipped as well as men.[14] Theoretically the punishment might sometimes be a substitute for a capital sentence when there was repentance.[15]

---

1 Cf. K. F. Euler, *Die Verkündigung vom leidenden Gottesknecht aus Js. 53 in der griechischen Bibel* (1934), 62 f., 139 f.

2 Bultmann Trad., 119 f.

3 Cf. also Schl. Mt. on 10:17; Str.-B., III, 527 ff.; S. Krauss, *Synagogale Altertümer* (1922), 186 f.

4 bMak., 23a, Bar.; for a rather different practice, Yoma, 5, 3.

5 Mak., 3, 1 ff. Scourging for transgressing Rabb. laws (מַכַּת מַרְדּוּת) is to be distinguished from that ordained by the Bible, Nas., 4, 3; bKet., 45b; bShab., 40b; bJeb., 52a [R. Meyer].

6 § 202 (ed. H. Winkler [1904], 104).

7 Bertholet-Leh., I, 717.

8 Mak., 3, 12; he had to strike with all his might, 3, 13.

9 Mak., 3, 12 ff.; bRH, 22b.

10 Tg. J., I on Dt. 25:2 f. S. Krauss, Sanhedrin-Makkot (1933), 372, n. 3. suggests that all three come to the same thing, i.e., binding to the pillar in a bending position.

11 jBik., 64a, 29.

12 Mak., 3, 11 and 14.

13 bMak., 16b ff.

14 Mak., 3, 14.

15 Mak., 3, 15. Cf. Epiph. Haer., 30, 11, where the Jews whip a convert to Christianity and then drown him; cf. also Eus. Hist. Eccl., V, 16, 12.

2. The scourging of Jesus in Jn. 19:1 and in the prophecies of the passion in Mt. 20:19 = Mk. 10:34 = Lk. 18:33 is not the synagogue punishment but the Roman *verberatio.*

Mt. 27:26 = Mk. 15:15 have the Lat. loan word φραγελλόω instead of μαστιγόω. Lk. 23:16 has the weaker παιδεύσας and says nothing about its execution. Here is one of the many instances of Luke's softening of the passion story. Jn. seems to think in terms of a compromise between true *verberatio* and a separate whipping. The aim of Pilate is to awaken pity by the scourging. It seems as though he wants to impose only a scourging without crucifixion. [16]

Acc. to Roman law the *verberatio* always accompanied a capital sentence, *condemnatio ad metalla,* and other degrading punishments with the loss of freedom or civil rights. [17] In many cases it was itself fatal. It usually preceded crucifixion. [18] It was so terrible that even Domitian was horrified by it. [19] Women were exempted. [20] We know little about the details. The number of strokes was not prescribed. It continued until the flesh hung down in bloody shreds. Slaves administered it, and the condemned person was tied to a pillar. [21] On the *flagellum* → μάστιξ.

3. The whipping with which Paul was threatened in Ac. 22:24 f. was an examination, [22] cf. also that of Ac. 16:22 ff. On 2 C. 11:25 → ῥαβδίζω. Since Paul's offence was not clear to those who questioned him, he was to be examined under torture. He was thus either tied to the scourging pillar or strapped to a bench. But the scourging in Ac. 16:22 ff. might also be a primary punishment. This was sometimes administered to provincials and often to slaves.

Torture, which is based on the legal principle that there can be no condemnation without confession, is found in the imperial period esp. in relation to traitors, but also citizens and freemen. [23] Only from the time of Marcus Aurelius are all upper classes and soldiers exempt in principle. [24] A *quaesitor* is in charge, [25] and *tortores,* mostly slaves, administer it. [26] Blows are the mildest form. [27] Only much later in Roman law is whipping a primary punishment; originally it is simply a means of coercion. [28] Sometimes we hear of unfair contestants being beaten, but hardly by the courts. Only slaves were frequently beaten by their own masters with the permission of the judicial authorities. [29] But at the time of the Second Punic War the *pontifex maximus* could even whip a vestal virgin. [30] From the time of the Lex Porcia of the older Cato, however, no citizen could be punished by beating: *Porcia lex virgas ab omnium civium Roma-*

---

16 This would be a kind of examination, cf. 3. and Schl. J. on 19:1.

17 Cic. Rep., II, 37, 62; Digesta (ed. T. Mommsen [1868], 9, 9; Liv., 10, 9, 4 f.; Jos. Bell., 2, 306; 5, 449; Sallust Catilina, 51, 39. → n. 31.

18 Jos. Bell., 2, 306 ff.: Florus has prominent Jews of Jerusalem whipped and crucified by his courts. In Bell., 5, 449 there is also rough handling by the executioners, as in the case of Jesus. Cf. also Liv., 34, 27; Cic. Verr., V, 62 and 162; Luc. Piscator, 2.

19 Suet. Domitian, 11.

20 T. Mommsen, 928, n. 3.

21 Plaut. Bacchides, 823; Suet. Claudius, 34.

22 Jackson-Lake, I, 5, 318 f. is wrongly critical here. There are many examples of similar situations, → n. 23.

23 Suet. Augustus, 27; Tiberius, 58; Domitian, 8; Dio C., 57, 19; Tac. Ann., 11, 22; 15, 56.

24 T. Mommsen, 406 f.

25 Cic. Pro Sulla, 28 and 78.

26 Cic. Pro Milone, 21 and 57.

27 Aug. Ep., 133, 2.

28 T. Mommsen, 984 f. Only much later could fines be redeemed by beatings.

29 Valerius Maximus (ed. Kempf [1888]), 8, 4, 1; Digesta, 47, 10, 15. 34. 42; Plaut. Mostellaria, 1087 f.; Terentius (ed. Fleckeisen [1898]), Hecyra, 773; Jos. Bell., 6, 302 ff.

30 Liv., 28, 11; Valerius Maximus, 1, 6. Cf. also Apul. Met., VI, 9.

norum corpore amovit, is the classical formulation of Cicero.[31] Nevertheless, there were exceptions, though increasingly illegal.[32]

4. The word is used figuratively in Hb. 12:6 (quoting Prv. 3:12) for "to impart corrective punishment." As the education of a beloved child may sometimes demand blows, so God may sometimes smite His childen. Suffering will be regarded by the Christian as a proof of God's educative love.[33]

Similar ideas occur in Ps. Sol., cf. 10:2; 13:6-10; 14:1, but they are also part of the common Hellenistic and Jewish heritage.[34]

There is in the NT none of the religious flagellation found in the surrounding world.[35]

† μάστιξ.

Fem. from the time of Hom., strictly "horsewhip," then any "lash" or "whip." Plur. sometimes "lashes," Hom. Il., 5, 748; 8, 392; 11, 532; Hdt., IV, 3; VII, 56 and 103; Soph. Ai., 242; Aristoph. Thes., 933; Xenoph. An., III, 4, 25 etc. Fig. "trouble," "suffering," esp. older divinely sent suffering, Διὸς μάστιξ, Hom. Il., 12, 37; 13, 812; μάστιξ θεία, Aesch. Prom., 682; Sept. c. Theb., 608; Ag., 642; inscr. μάστειγα αἰώνιον, W. M. Ramsay, *Phrygia,* I, 2 (1897), 520, No. 361. After Aesch. the term loses its religious significance and is used generally for "suffering" or even "want."

In the LXX it is used lit. for שֵׁבֶט Job 21:8 (God's scourge) or שׁוֹט, 1 K. 12:11, 14; 2 Ch. 10:11, 14 (any lash); Prv. 26:3; Na. 3:2 (horsewhip), also Sir. 28:17; 30:1; 2 Macc. 7:1, 37; 4 Macc. 6:3, 6; 9:12. Fig. for שׁוֹט, Job 5:21; cf. Sir. 26:6 (lash of the tongue); for נֶגַע, Ps. 39:10 (ψ 38:10); 89:32 (ψ 88:32, punishment sent by God, cf. 2 Macc. 9:11); 91:10 (ψ 90:10, plague generally); cf. ψ 72:3; Sir. 23:11; 40:9; for מַכָּה, Is. 50:6 (blow); Jer. 6:7 (blows); for שְׁפָט, Prv. 19:29 (blow); for מַכְאוֹב, Ps. 32:10 (ψ 31:10, the sorrows of the sinful); for צֶלַע, ψ 37:17 (suffering); also Sir. 22:6 (chastisement); 23:2 (scourge of conscience).

1. Literally μάστιξ occurs only in Ac. 22:24 and Hb. 11:36. The ref. in the first verse is to Roman torture (→ 517). In the second passage, which enumerates the sufferings of the martyrs, the reference is to stripes received in the synagogue.

The synagogue scourge consisted of a strap of calf leather which was divided into four thongs and through which smaller thongs were plaited to make it stronger. In the handle there was a device to make the strap longer or shorter.[1] Basically the form is

[31] Cic. Pro Rabirio Perduellionis Reo, 4, 12; also Verr., V, 54, 140; 63; Dion. Hal. Ant. Rom., V, 19, 4; Pliny the Elder Hist. Nat., VII, 43, 136; Sallust Catilina, 51, 22; Valerius Maximus, 4, 1, 1.

[32] Cic. Verr., *loc. cit.* Cf. also Wnd. 2 K., 356.

[33] On Prv. 3:12 cf. G. Bertram, "Der Begriff d. Erziehung in d. griech. Bibel," *Imago Dei, Festschr. f. G. Krüger* (1932), 38 f.

[34] Sen. De Providentia, 1, 6; Philo Congr., 177; cf. also Str.-B., III, 747 and Wnd. Hb. on 12:6.

[35] This may be a religious test of bravery like the annual διαμαστίγωσις of boys at the altar of Artemis Ὀρθία in Sparta, cf. Pauly-W., II (1896), 1395 [Kleinknecht]. There is also the whipping at the Mithras initiation, cf. the pictures of Capua (Haas, 15, J. Leipoldt, *Mithra* [1930], 45), also at the Dionysus initiation, if the well-known depiction at the Villa Item (Haas, 9/11, J. Leipoldt [1926], XX and 169 f.) is to be understood thus. There is also the ascetic practice, as in the cults of Syria and Asia Minor, esp. Attis and Ma Bellona, cf. F. Cumont, *Die orientalischen Religionen im römischen Heidentum*[3] (1931), 37, 47, 50, and the depiction on the relief of Civita Lavinia → μάστιξ, n. 3.

μάστιξ. [1] אַבְקָתָא bMak., 23a; it could also be made from the leather of the ass.

Egyptian or Asiatic. On the stele of Esarhaddon in the Berlin Museum there is a whip with two thongs and on the relief of Kuyunjik in the British Museum there is a horsewhip with three thongs. In the Codex Hammurabi it is made of ox leather. The Roman scourge, the *horribile flagellum*,[2] also *flagrum*, was a leather strap with interwoven bones and bits of metal.[3] This is the most terrible instrument for beating; milder forms are *scutica* (from σκῦτος), a leather whip, *virga*, the rod, and the *ferula*, a stick.[4]

2. Fig. μάστιξ is used in Mk. 3:10; Lk. 7:21 as a comprehensive term for the ills cured by Jesus, and at Mk. 5:29, 34 for a feminine ailment which He healed.[5]

Carl Schneider

μάταιος, ματαιότης, ματαιόω, μάτην, ματαιολογία, ματαιολόγος

† μάταιος.

A. μάταιος outside the NT.

1. The word μάταιος[1] — and the related word group — corresponds to the older sense of "vain." It denotes the world of appearance as distinct from that of being. The emphasis may be on the fact that what is called μάταιος, e.g., a word, does not rest on the causes which it alleges, "deceptive," Hdt., VII, 10 η. The absence of an effect may also be stressed, "in vain," "to no purpose": τὰ μάταια ἀναλώματα, P. Oxy., I, 58, 20. If the ref. is to the human will, μάταιος may castigate an offence, "wicked": αὐτουργίαι μάταιαι, of the act of Orestes, Aesch. Eum., 337; but often it simply means "pointless," χαρὰ ματαία, Aesch. Sept. c. Theb., 442. Both the basic meaning and the more detailed senses may be applied to persons too.[2]

→ κενός is sometimes used fig. along with μάταιος. But the words are not wholly synon., for in μάταιος there is always the implication of what is against the norm, unexpected, offending what ought to be. κενός means worthless, because without content, μάταιος worthless because deceptive or ineffectual. κεναῖς χερσίν, Plat. Leg.,

---

2 Horat. Sat., I, 3, 119.

3 Cf. the relief of Civita Lavinia, now Museo Capitolino (W. Helbig, *Führer durch die Sammlungen klass. Altertümer in Rom.*[3] [1912], No. 987). Here we have a whip with three thongs with pieces of bone interwoven at regular intervals. For lead, cf. Lib. pro Aristoph. Or., 14, 15, 429.

4 J. Marquardt, *Das Privatleben d. Römer*[2] (1886), I, 182 ff.

5 In the OT leprosy is often called נֶגַע, Lv. 13:2 f., 9, 20, 25, 27; 14:3, 32, 54; Dt. 24:8. In post-NT writings μάστιξ is used for the troubles of the sinner, 1 Cl., 22, 8; Herm. v., 4, 2, 6; for the Egyptian plagues, 1 Cl., 17, 5; for the mischief caused by the tongue, 1 Cl., 56, 10.

μάταιος. 1 To the same group belong μάτη (→ μάτην, n. 1), ματάω, "to waver," and ματεύω, "to seek"; the basic sense always seems to be "to fumble," "to grope uncertainly." Cf. Prellwitz Etym. Wört., *s.v.*; also Trench, 111 f.

2 μάταιος can thus often mean "foolish," or, as a noun, "fool." It is a mark of Gk. intellectualism that foolish and ineffectual mean much the same. Folly cannot achieve anything. This idea is present in the weaker use of μάταιος in Plat. Resp., V, 452d: μάταιος ὃς γελοῖον ἄλλο τι ἡγεῖται ἢ τὸ κακόν [Kleinknecht].

VII, 796b (with empty hands) has quite a different ring from ματαίαις χερσίν, Soph. Trach., 565 (with unclean hands). Cf. also κοὐδ' ἐν χρόνῳ μακρῷ διδαχθῆναι θέλεις θυμῷ ματαίῳ μὴ χαρίζεσθαι κενά, Soph. El., 330 f. That a χαρίζεσθαι turns out to be empty is a pity, but no more than a mishap; that the θυμός is said to be μάταιος is more than a mishap.

There may be many different norms whose transgression is described in terms of μάταιος. It is not that the ethical or intellectual norm predominantly controls the word and gives it its distinctiveness. The peculiarity of the term is that it retains its comprehensive metaphysical undertone. The result is that, in accordance with the more optimistic or sceptical view of the life of the one who uses it, its range may be narrow or very broad. This is important, since it does not become a weak and quickly fading formula. When it is used and when it convinces, or begins to convince, a value is assailed and a part of supposed being begins to sink into the world of mere appearance. Acc. to the nature of the value affected, this has either a liberating or a harmful effect. When the clique of those who despise their homeland is called Φῦλον ματαιότατον in Pindar Pyth., 3, 21, this is liberating. But when the shadow of the μάταιον falls on joy (Aesch. Sept., 442), or prayer (Eur. Iph. Taur., 628), or the τύχαι of a royal house (Aesch. Choeph., 83 f.), the effect is harmful. In the last act of Antigone (1339 f.) Creon, king of Thebes, is according to his own judgment a μάταιος ἀνήρ. Why? Because of the fate which hangs over him and from which no ἀπαλλαγή brings release. So says the chorus, the same chorus which at the climax of the play (332 ff.) had sung: πολλὰ τὰ δεινά, κοὐδὲν ἀνθρώπου δεινότερον πέλει ("nothing is more powerful than man"). In face of this we are forced to conclude that the tragedians — who often use the word — put to their readers the question whether there is finally any sphere which escapes the verdict of μάταιος, whether deep reflection does not lead to the view that all values are subject to it. Where the answer to this question is to be sought is perhaps indicated by Aesch. when in Suppl., 197 f. he uses the phrase μὴ μάταιον: τὸ μὴ μάταιον δ' ἐκ μετωποσωφρόνων ἴτω προσώπων (countenances with serious brow). The human face is the place where μὴ μάταιον is, or ought to be, seen. It is there that σωφροσύνη rules. Thus the question of the limitation of the μάταιον, even though μάταιος is not in itself an ethical or religious term, is an ethical and ultimately a religious[3] question. If we try to get beyond this individual hint, and seek a comprehensive answer from all the tragic poets and the Greek world as a whole, the answer will still be religious. Only words of faith can hold in check a tormented or weary μάταιος. "All earthly being is as smoke; ... only the gods abide." The portion of man in μὴ μάταιον is to be measured by his portion in the divine. But, to stay for a moment with the tragic poets, the plurality of the gods makes it doubtful whether Schiller's reply on behalf of the Greek world can really arrest the dangerous expansion of the μάταιος concept. An Aesch. realises that the troubles of Cassandra are μάταιοι (Ag., 1150) even though a god, Apollo, has ordained them. What Aesch. knows of Apollo or the gods can hardly restrain the μάταιον; only his firm and honest faith in Zeus can do this. But this faith in its very honesty leaves open many questions, at least for later readers. What Zeus now is, he was not always (Prom.). Will he always be it in the future? It is natural to suppose that among the many presuppositions of the later Greek world the term μάταιος would be a favourite instrument for struggling with these problems, and that the question of the μὴ μάταιον would constantly be put in this concrete form. In fact, this did not happen in the true Gk. sphere. So far as we can see, the word group played only a subordinate role later in spite of its force, or perhaps just because of its dangerous and in some sense defeatist force. This is, of course, an area where we can argue only from silence. Hence caution is demanded. But we may at least say that a relativism or nihilism which gives up everything to the

[3] Cf. Xenoph. Mem., I, 3, 1: Socrates regards as περίεργοι and μάταιοι all those who in cultic things act otherwise than prescribed by the Delphic Apollo through the lips of the Pythia.

verdict μάταιος is always exposed to grotesque self-contradictions so long as those who espouse it do not take their own lives. The men of antiquity had too much native σωφροσύνη for such a view. On the other hand, an optimism which can wholly exclude the spirit of negation in the word μάταιος demands a higher measure of certainty than the Gk. gods could give. Hence there must be deeper reasons for the restraint in the use of μάταιος. The later observer will have regard to these reasons. In this area, too, he will find the "magic of antiquity" in the fact that it understood how to "pass by quietly."

2. With the OT, however, μάταιος statements of a ruthlessly radical kind — indeed, an extended catena of such statements — came into Greek literature. Here there is no question whatever of quietly passing by. It is as though a considerable number[4] of Hebrew words had been waiting to pour their negative content into the Greek μάταιος (cf. esp. also → ματαιότης). No-one can here escape the question whether this luxuriant growth is to be understood from the standpoint of such human presuppositions as the abandonment of healthy restraint or the impulsive love of negation, or whether a very different outlook prevails. If we are to form an independent judgment, we shall be well advised to compare closely the texts of the tragic poets with those of Ps. and Qoh. This will show that the distinctiveness of the term in the LXX is not to be seen in the fact that, e.g., beauty (Prv. 31:30) and understanding (ψ 93:11) also fall under the judgment of μάταιος. The ugly Socrates had already shown that "man is of more value than beautiful man," and his "I know that I know nothing" had not been forgotten. Indeed, even the sweeping judgments μάταιοι οἱ υἱοὶ τῶν ἀνθρώπων (ψ 61:9) and ματαία σωτηρία ἀνθρώπου (ψ 59:11) differ from the statements already quoted from the end of Antigone only formally in virtue of their didactic character, not materially in virtue of their radicalness. The distinctiveness of μάταιος in the LXX is — purely lexically — that it is constantly used for the other world. The gods of the ἔθνη are primarily μάταια, i.e., the very gods who in the Greek world are supposed in some way to be the guarantors of that which escapes the

[4] Cf. Hatch-Redp. Mostly commonly the word group is used for the root הבל, which denotes a breath of wind, and which becomes a figure for mortality. Apart from this, it is used esp. for the concept of futility in so far as this is bound up with falsehood or deception, i.e., for שָׁוְא, also כזב (in Mi. 1:14 אַכְזִיב, which in the Heb. is a pun on אַכְזָב = "deceitful," is derived from this root), and שקר. The idea of what is empty, vain or futile is present in the rendering of רֵיק, חִנָּם and תֹּהוּ. The use of μάταιος for חַטָּאת in 3 Βασ. 16:2 expresses the fact that sin is by nature man's desire for nothingness, and the context shows that the primary ref. is to idolatry (→ ἁμαρτία, I, 288). Again, μάταιος can be used not merely for Heb. terms for idols which denote their unreality, e.g., הֶבֶל (→ n. 4) and אֱלִיל (Zech. 11:17), but also for contemptuous words like שָׂעִיר (Lv. 17:7; 2 Ch. 11:15). אָוֶן is 4 times rendered μάταιος, and הַוָּה 3 times. Finally, it is worth noting that the word group is often related to the fool (רֵיק); → n. 2; → ἄφρων; → μωρός. Cf. on this W. Caspari, "Über den biblischen Begriff der Torheit," NkZ, 39 [1928], 681, n. 3). In many places the LXX introduces μάταιος independently, whether with ref. to the gods and their worship (Hos. 5:11; Is. 2:20; 30:15; Ez. 8:10) or with ref. to the vanity of human effort (Is. 28:29; 33:11; in Is. 30:7, 28 [*vl.*] the word occurs twice in the LXX, only once in the Mas.).

μάταιον. Only the one God is the living God. Who beside Him can raise the claim not to be μάταιον, vain, relative? Again, it is supremely ignorance of God which makes men φύσει μάταιοι (Wis. 13:1). But God is known only to those to whom He has made Himself known. There can be no possibility of being kept from nothingness unless it is given by this one God. And His possibilities are under no πεπρωμένη. That which distinguishes the LXX from the Greek tragedians, the certainty, the instructive calm, with which the sphere of μάταιος is extended to all the lower and higher and highest values attainable by man, derives, not from a historically conditioned joy in negation, but primarily and exclusively from faith in the one God. Whether this God for His part is a product of the human will for negation, or whether He is as He says in the OT, is itself not a matter for investigation, but for faith.

The sayings of false prophets are also μάταια (Ez. 13:6 ff.). λαμβάνειν ἐπὶ ματαίῳ is a phrase for misuse of the name of God (Ex. 20:7). The term can also be used for "empty rumours" (Ex. 23:1). From Philo we need only quote Som., I, 244: μάταιος δ' ὅστις μὴ θεῷ στήλην ἀνατίθησιν, ἀλλ' ἑαυτῷ.

B. μάταιος in the NT.

In the NT there is no mitigation of the ruthless comprehensiveness of the LXX. It is a biblical truth that even in the most favourable circumstances human reflection does not escape μάταιον: 1 C. 3:20: κύριος γινώσκει τοὺς διαλογισμοὺς τῶν σοφῶν, ὅτι εἰσὶν μάταιοι (ψ 93:11); cf. R. 1:21 → ματαιόω. Speculation is still speculation even though it be pious speculation: Tt. 3:9: μωρὰς δὲ ζητήσεις καὶ γενεαλογίας ... περιΐστατο· εἰσὶν γὰρ ἀνωφελεῖς καὶ μάταιοι. This would apply even to the resurrection of Jesus if it were only the product of man's religious notions and not a credibly attested historical event; this purely unreal and hypothetical conclusion is drily stated in 1 C. 15:17: εἰ δὲ Χριστὸς οὐκ ἐγήγερται, ματαία ἡ πίστις ὑμῶν. A faith orientated to a resurrection which did not take place in the field of history could not be regarded as a noteworthy or even a supreme religion. It would be just as relative and empty as the other thoughts of men.

If the main objects of the LXX statements are the pseudo-divine powers to which man cleaves and by which he seeks to avoid the μάταιον, this is also the main NT usage. μάταιος has always its basic sense of unreal or vain. Everything which resists the first commandment comes under the judgment of μάταιος, whether it be vaunting human thought (as in the passages already quoted), or the concrete gods of paganism, or the conduct controlled by them: Ac. 14:15: ἀπὸ τούτων τῶν ματαίων ἐπιστρέφειν ἐπὶ θεὸν ζῶντα (from these vain idols); 1 Pt. 1:18: ἐλυτρώθητε ἐκ τῆς ματαίας ὑμῶν ἀναστροφῆς πατροπαραδότου.

In the latter verse, the fact that, with no special emphasis, μάταιος is quite naturally set alongside a word like πατροπαράδοτος, is quite shattering for the man who for his part thinks that he may use this word with thankfulness. It should not be forgotten that even the community comes under the judgment of μάταιος the moment it ceases to cleave solely to God's revelation. It must receive this warning with full seriousness. Its πίστις becomes ματαία once it ascribes to God an act which He has not done (→ *supra* on 1 C. 15:17). Its θρησκεία becomes vain once it sets aside the divine command in arrogant self-deception: Jm. 1:26: εἴ τις δοκεῖ θρησκὸς εἶναι, μὴ χαλιναγωγῶν γλῶσσαν ἑαυτοῦ ἀλλὰ ἀπατῶν καρδίαν ἑαυτοῦ, τούτου μάταιος ἡ θρησκεία.

† ματαιότης.

In secular lit. this is a rare word. Philodem. Philos. Rhet., 2, p. 26 (ed. S. Sudhaus 1892) speaks of the ματαιότης ἀνθρώπων, "the nothingness of man." The LXX makes frequent use of it:[1] πλὴν τὰ σύμπαντα ματαιότης, πᾶς ἄνθρωπος ζῶν, ψ 38:6; ἄνθρωπος ματαιότητι ὡμοιώθη, 143:4. The word was given an unexpected turn by Qoh.[2]: ματαιότης ματαιοτήτων, εἶπεν ὁ Ἐκκλησιαστής, ματαιότης ματαιοτήτων, τὰ πάντα ματαιότης, 1:2; 2:1 etc. The stern and irrefutable *vanitas vanitatum* ends the futile struggle which living man, in his desire for life, wages against his own insight into vanity. Since it is a biblical saying, it also points him to God, with whom is no ματαιότης.

R. 8:20 is a valid commentary on Qoh. The passage does not solve the metaphysical and logical problems raised by *vanitas*. In detail it allows of different possibilities of understanding (→ κτίσις, → ὑποτάσσω). But it tells us plainly that the state of ματαιότης ("vanity") exists, and also that this has a beginning and end. Before its beginning and beyond its end is God, and a κτίσις without ματαιότης. τῇ γὰρ ματαιότητι ἡ κτίσις ὑπετάγη, οὐχ ἑκοῦσα, ἀλλὰ διὰ τὸν ὑποτάξαντα, ἐφ' ἐλπίδι. διότι καὶ αὐτὴ ἡ κτίσις ἐλευθερωθήσεται ἀπὸ τῆς δουλείας τῆς φθορᾶς εἰς τὴν ἐλευθερίαν τῆς δόξης τῶν τέκνων τοῦ θεοῦ. Paul could speak of ἐλπίς and δόξα with an authority not found in Qoh.

Of the effect of vanity in human society, of worthlessness, we read in Eph. 4:17: ... περιπατεῖ ἐν ματαιότητι τοῦ νοὸς αὐτῶν, and also, in bold hyperbole, in 2 Pt. 2:18: ὑπέρογκα ματαιότητος.

† ματαιόω.

This is a biblical word. It occurs in the act. only once in the sense "to present what is vain," "to deceive": ματαιοῦσιν ἑαυτοῖς ὅρασιν, Ιερ. 23:16. Otherwise it is always passive, "to be delivered up to vanity" (not to nothing, but to → ματαιότης). With ref. to the first commandment: ἐπορεύθησαν ὀπίσω τῶν ματαίων καὶ ἐματαιώθησαν, Ιερ. 2:5. Μεματαίωταί σοι, 1 Βασ. 13:13: it has become for you a vain enterprise.

R. 1:21: ἐματαιώθησαν ἐν τοῖς διαλογισμοῖς αὐτῶν, "they have become vain." The διαλογισμοί are the antithesis to the δοξάζειν and εὐχαριστεῖν of v. 21, which should have been the answer to God's φανεροῦν in v. 19; cf. 1 C. 3:20 → μάταιος. The state of ματαιότης begins in this world; it exists already.

† μάτην.

Adv.[1] (a) "in vain," Pind. Olymp., 1, 83; βλέποντες ἔβλεπον μάτην, Aesch. Prom., 447; ἢ ... λόγοι πεδάρσιοι θρώισκουσι θνήισκοντες μάτην ("or ... go there forth only high-sounding words, dying in vain?"), Aesch. Choeph., 845 f.;[2] μάτην ἐπάταξα τὰ τέκνα ὑμῶν, παιδείαν οὐκ ἐδέξασθε, Ιερ. 2:30. (b) "Groundlessly," "pointlessly," οὐ γὰρ δίκαιον οὔτε τοὺς κακοὺς μάτην χρηστοὺς νομίζειν, Soph. Oed. Tyr., 609 f. (c) "Deceitfully," of a dream, Aesch. Ag., 423. Εἰς μάτην ἐγενήθη σχοῖνος ψευδὴς γραμματεῦσιν, Ιερ. 8:8. The particular ring of the word group → μάταιος may be detected in all the passages mentioned.

ματαιότης. [1] Cf. Hatch-Redp.
[2] Here הֶבֶל is the only original (36 times).

μάτην. [1] Strictly acc. εἰς μάτην, cf. Ιερ. 8:8 (μάτη = mistake, nonsense).
[2] Cf. also → ματαιολόγος.

Mt. 15:9; Mk. 7:7, on the basis of Is. 29:13: μάτην δὲ σέβονταί με (a) "in vain"; cf. → μάταιος ..., 522.

† ματαιολογία.

"Empty prattle," Plut. Lib. Educ., 9 (II, 6 f.). Cf. μαντεύεσθαι μάταια, Ez. 13:6 ff.

It is used in 1 Tm. 1:6 of those who have turned their backs on the πίστις ἀνυπόκριτος: ἐξετράπησαν εἰς ματαιολογίαν.

There seems to be a sense of the distinction between μάταιος and κενός in the expression κενὴ ματαιολογία in Pol., 2, 1.

† ματαιολόγος.

"Empty prattler." μάταν ἀχόρευτος ἅδε ματαιολόγων φάμα προσέπταθ' Ἑλλάδα μουσοπόλων ("meaninglessly and joylessly these whisperings of prattlers flew in the service of the Muses through Hellas"), Telestes Lyricus (Poetae Lyrici Graeci, III, 628).

Tt. 1:10: εἰσὶν γὰρ πολλοὶ ἀνυπότακτοι, ματαιολόγοι.

Bauernfeind

† μάχαιρα

μάχαιρα, which seems to be related to → μάχομαι, is very common from the time of Hom., first in the sense of "knife," at sacrifice, slaughter, the chase, cooking (though not at meals, since knives and forks were not used), for clipping, shaving, and as a tool in various occupations, tanners, gardeners etc. As a weapon from the time of Hdt.: "small sword," to be distinguished from the sword proper (→ ῥομφαία) "dagger," "sabre" (in Xenoph. Eq., 12, 11 a curved weapon as distinct from the ξίφος, the pointed weapon or sword).[1]

Things are much the same in the world of Israel and Judah.[2] μάχαιρα is found some 180 times, a third of these in Jer. The usual Heb. equivalent is חֶרֶב, which is more

---

μάχαιρα. [1] Cf. Liddell-Scott, Pass., *s.v.*; also pap. (Preisigke Wört., II, 55), but rare in inscr. For archaeological material cf. A. Mau, Art. "Culter, μάχαιρα" in Pauly-W., IV (1901), 1752 f.; S. Reinach, Art. "Culter" in Daremberg-Saglio, I, 2, 1582-1587. On the cultic use of the knife cf. S. Eitrem, *Opferritus u. Voropfer der Griechen u. Römer* (*Videnskaps-Akademi-Skrifter, Kristiania,* II. *Hist.-Filos. Klasse* [1914], No. 1) (1915), 488, Index, *s.v.* "Messer."

[2] For archaeological material cf. P. Thomsen, Art. "Messer C: Palästina-Syrien," in *Reallexikon d. Vorgeschichte,* VIII (1927), 172-174; also art. "Dolch C: Palästina-Syrien," *ibid.,* II (1925), 436-438, and art. "Schwert C: Palästina-Syrien," *ibid.* XI (1927/8), 439-442; K. Galling, Art. "Messer" in *Biblisches Reallexikon* (1937), 378 f., also art. "Dolch," 129-135, and "Schwert," 472-475. Cf. S. Krauss, *Talmudische Archäologie,* I (1910), 266; II (1911), 262, 310 f., 313 ff.; III (1912), 53. The diminutive μαχαίριον (e.g., Jos. Ant., 17, 183 for a fruit-knife) was used by the Rabb. as a loan word מכירין, cf. S. Krauss, *Gr. u. Lat. Lehnwörter im Talmud, Midr. u. Tg.,* I (1898), 203 f., 235. On the other hand, the connection between מְכֵרָה (unknown weapon, only Gn. 49:5) and μάχαιρα is not certain.

commonly rendered ῥομφαία, much less frequently ξίφος (the Gk. terms vary a little in the MSS). Only rarely does μάχαιρα mean a knife, e.g., the stone knife of circumcision in Jos. 5:2 f. (Mas. חֶרֶב): 21:42d; 24:31a, the knife of Abraham at the offering of Isaac, Gn. 22:6, 10 (Mas. מַאֲכֶלֶת).[3] It is mostly a weapon, "dagger" or "(small) sword."[4] It is seldom used fig., cf. ψ 56:4; Prv. 24:22c; Is. 49:2.[5] The warlike and rather terrible nature of the μάχαιρα passages in the OT is also reflected in later Jewish apocalyptic.[6]

In the NT μάχαιρα is used for 1. a weapon in the accounts of the arrest of Jesus. It is carried by His opponents, who come out μετὰ μαχαιρῶν καὶ ξύλων (Mt. 26:47 par. Mk. 14:43;[7] cf. later the question of Jesus, Mt. 26:55 par. Mk. 14:48; Lk. 22:52). In defence of Jesus it is also carried by a disciple (Mt. 26:51 par. Mk. 14:47; Jn. 18:10; cf. Lk. 22:49). Jesus rebukes the disciple and bids him put the μάχαιρα back in its sheath (Mt. 26:52a par. Jn. 18:11).[8] In Mt. 26:52b, in a saying which finds an echo in Rev. 13:10,[9] Jesus warns all who take to the μάχαιρα that they will perish ἐν μαχαίρῃ.[10, 11] Violent death (in war, persecution etc.) is also ascribed elsewhere to the μάχαιρα, cf. the OT events recalled in Hb. 11:34 (cf. 1 K. 19:1 ff.), 37 (cf. 1 K. 19:10; Jer. 26:23),[12] the fate of Judaea in the last time (Lk. 21:24),[13] the execution of James the son of Zebedee (Ac. 12:2).[14] μάχαιρα

---

[3] For שַׂכִּין, which occurs only in Prv. 23:2 and which is not translated in the LXX, ʼΑΘ have μάχαιρα in the sense of knife (cf. סכין "knife" which is common in the Rabb.).

[4] E.g., Ju. 3:16, where the meaning is "small sword" or "dagger" (Jos. Ant., 5, 193 has ξιφίδιον). But in the light of the Heb. חֶרֶב there is no set distinction between μάχαιρα and ῥομφαία.

[5] Other verses in Prv. also have a fig. or metaphorical use of μάχαιρα. Thus in 5:4 the effect of the harlot folly on those who consort with her is like the cut of a sharp knife. Words are compared to a sword or knife in 12:18. So, too, are the teeth of the wicked who rend the poor and humble in 30:14. In 25:18 the sword, with the club and bow, is used of the false witness. There is also a fig. use of μάχαιρα for knife in 23:2 ʼΑΘ [Bertram].

[6] Cf. H. Windisch, *Der messianische Krieg u. das Urchr.* (1909). In 4 Εσδρ. 13:9 the Messiah has no sword but He destroys His enemies with a stream of fire from His mouth.

[7] The mention of μάχαιρα does not have to imply the participation of Roman legionaries (as against Zn. Mt.[4], 703). Cf. F. Lundgren, "Das palästinische Heerwesen in d. nt.lichen Zeit," PJB, 17 (1921), 61.

[8] Knives and daggers were also carried in sheaths, Krauss Archäologie, II, 313; Schl. J., 329.

[9] But the version in Cod. A is more independent and perhaps original, cf. Loh. Apk., 110.

[10] On the endings -ρης and -ρῃ cf. Bl.-Debr.[6] § 43, 1; Thackeray, 141 f.; Helbing, 31 ff.; Mayser, I, 12.

[11] Mt. 26:53 f., peculiar to Mt., gives the context of 26:52b, but not its meaning. Perhaps the ref. is to acts of violence. R. 13:4 (the sword as a symbol of the penal power of the state) and military service hardly seem to be meant, nor perhaps self-defence in case of need. On the other hand, the Matthean material does not allow us to suppose that the cutting off of the ear was not meant as defence or attack, but simply to make the man concerned ridiculous (cf. M. Rostovtzeff, Οὖς δεξιὸν ἀποτέμνειν, ZNW, 33 [1934], 196 ff.).

[12] ἐν φόνῳ μαχαίρας is common in the LXX: Ex. 17:13; Nu. 21:24; Dt. 13:16; 20:13.

[13] On στόματι μαχαίρας (also Hb. 11:34 στόματα μαχαίρης) cf. LXX Gn. 34:26 etc.

[14] Here and sometimes elsewhere the μάχαιρα is the long sword (also Ign. Sm., 4, 2, where μάχαιρα, elsewhere in the post-apost. fathers only 1 Cl., 8, 4 = Is. 1:20, is used twice for the sword of execution). The distinction between μάχαιρα and ῥομφαία may be seen at Lk. 2:35 and in 6 verses in Rev., cf. Cod. D Lk. 21:24, → ῥομφαία, n. 12, but under LXX influence it is rarely felt in the NT. Sanh., 7, 3; 9, 3; 10, 4 uses for beheading with the sword סַיִף (= ξίφος; cf. Krauss Archäol., II, 313 and Syr. סיפא). The attempt at suicide on the part of the Philippian gaoler may also be mentioned in this connection (Ac. 16:27), also the mortal wound of the beast (Rev. 13:14).

is also a pregnant term (perhaps for execution) in R. 8:35; hence its use for the dreadful bloodshed of Rev. 6:4. [15]

2. On the other hand, the saying of Jesus in Mt. 10:34: οὐκ ἦλθον βαλεῖν εἰρήνην ἀλλὰ μάχαιραν, is also related to Rev. 6:4 in its antithesis of μάχαιρα and → εἰρήνη, but it can hardly refer to military conflict. [16] It tells us figuratively that he who decides for Jesus must be prepared for the enmity even of those who are most closely related to him (cf. 10:35 and the Lukan version in 12:51; → II, 414). Hence the saying has no connection with later Jewish conceptions of the days of the Messiah as a period of the sword. [17] It also involves no contradiction with sayings which depict Jesus as One who brings peace (→ II, 413). No less figurative, though in a different sense, is the direction of Jesus in Lk. 22:35 ff., which is peculiar to Lk. and which has been so much debated. Here the disciples are to have a μάχαιρα for the future. "Jesus was not speaking of increasing their weapons. But just because He was not thinking of their weapons, the disciples needed the courage which regards a sword as more necessary than a cloak, and which will surrender its last possession but cannot give up the fight." [18] Jesus' attitude to the aggressive use of weapons is consistently one of disapproval. [19] But it is plain that He demands from His disciples an equal readiness for self-sacrifice.

3. In the depiction of the spiritual armour of the Christian we read in Eph. 6:17: (δέξασθε) καὶ τὴν μάχαιραν τοῦ πνεύματος, ὅ ἐστιν ῥῆμα θεοῦ. [20] So far as concerns the fight against πνευματικὰ τῆς πονηρίας ἐν τοῖς ἐπουρανίοις (6:12) the Christian needs only spiritual weapons. The spiritual sword [21] with which he can defend himself is the Word of God. [22]

4. Hb. 4:12 uses μάχαιρα in much the same way, though the orientation is different. The λόγος τοῦ θεοῦ is not called a μάχαιρα directly, but we read that it is τομώτερος ὑπὲρ πᾶσαν μάχαιραν δίστομον. The choice of μάχαιρα

---

[15] This is referred by J. Behm Apk. (*NT Deutsch*, 11), *ad loc.* particularly to the horrors of civil war.

[16] Though cf. Schl. Mt., 349 f.: The success of Jesus causes the opponents of Christianity to take to the sword and to try to root it out. Cf. also J. Schniewind Mt. (*NT Deutsch*, 2), *ad loc.*

[17] Str.-B., I, 585 f.; IV, 865, 979, 981, 988. Cf. Windisch, 45 ff.

[18] Schl. Lk., 429; A. Schlatter, "Die beiden Schwerter Lk. 22:35-38," BFTh, 20, 6 (1916); → III, 295. Here, as always, the Vg has *gladius*. Would the doctrine of the two swords (→ III, 296) have appealed to Lk. 22:38 if it had been clear that the ref. was not to swords but much less impressively to knives or daggers? Yet we can hardly think in terms of the knives which the disciples must have had with them for killing the paschal lamb (so Zn. Lk. [3, 4], 685, n. 71).

[19] Windisch, 48 f. suggests that Jesus underwent a change between Lk. 22:35 ff. and Mt. 26:51 f.

[20] Is. 11:4 (cf. 2 Th. 2:8) is perhaps the basis (cf. Eph. 6:14 and Is. 11:5). But Is. is referring to the Messiah who with the λόγος τοῦ στόματος αὐτοῦ will smite the earth and ἐν πνεύματι διὰ χειλέων ἀνελεῖ ἀσεβῆ. Hence there is no material par.

[21] The sword is not the → πνεῦμα but the Word of God; τοῦ πνεύματος characterises the sword as that which proceeds from the Spirit and is given by Him (Ew. Gefbr., *ad loc.*). Eph. 6:17 led Christian art to depict the apostle Paul with a sword. Cf. W. Straub, *Die Bildersprache des Apostels Paulus* (1937), 112.

[22] If (instead of following the λόγος of Is. 11:4) → ῥῆμα is chosen, it is perhaps because, as in the temptation of Christ in the wilderness, a divine saying is the sword in each individual case (Haupt Gefbr., *ad loc.*).

(cf. Is. 49:2 [23]) distinguishes this verse from Rev. 1:16; 2:12, 16; 19:15, 21, where → ῥομφαία (δίστομος or ὀξεῖα) is used. But the image is also different. The sword is not used to punish and destroy, but pitilessly to disclose the secret thoughts of the heart of man. [24] Hence μάχαιρα is not a sword. To cut the joints and marrow one does not use a sword. The picture is that of the knife used by the priest or butcher, [25] or even perhaps the surgeon. [26]

Michaelis

μάχομαι, μάχη, ἄμαχος, θεομάχος, θεομαχέω

† μάχομαι, † μάχη, † ἄμαχος.

The word group is frequently used for physical combat in the military sense (the adj. act. and pass.) or for sporting contests (with → ἀγών). In the general sense of conflict, for battles of words (Hom. Il., 1, 304 : μαχησαμένω ἐπέεσσιν, Plat. Resp., 1, 342d : μάχεσθαι = "to dispute"; Plat. Tim., 88a : μάχας ἐν λόγοις ποιουμένη ... δι' ἐρίδων καὶ φιλονικίας γενομένων), the noun is usually in the plur. Sometimes logical contradictions are set in confrontation by μάχεσθαι or μάχη (Plat. Theaet., 155b : ὁμολογήματα τρία μάχεται αὐτὰ αὑτοῖς ἐν τῇ ἡμετέρᾳ ψυχῇ; Epict. Ench., 52, 1: τί γάρ ἐστιν ἀπόδειξις, τί ἀκολουθία, τί μάχη, τί ἀληθές, τί ψεῦδος). In the LXX the military use predominates, but in 2 Εσδρ. 15:7; 23:11, 17, 25 μάχεσθαι means (justifiable) opposition and censure, and in Cant. 1:6 unjustifiable grumbling. Philo often speaks of the necessary μάχεσθαι against ἐπιθυμίαι, ἡδοναί and πάθη (Leg. All., I, 86; III, 21 and 116), also of the battle of opinions (Det. Pot. Ins., 32). Acc. to Leg. All., I, 106 there is between physical death which liberates the body and the death of the soul through desires a μάχεσθαι (σχεδὸν οὗτος ὁ θάνατος μάχεται ἐκείνῳ). Rer. Div. Her., 100 f., which follows Gn. 15:8, refers to an apparent μάχεσθαι between knowledge and faith.

In the NT the group can be related for certain to physical conflict only in Ac. 7:26 : ὤφθη αὐτοῖς μαχομένοις. In Jn. 6:52 ἐμάχοντο ... πρὸς ἀλλήλους οἱ Ἰουδαῖοι we have a strife of words on the basis of spiritual division. It is not

---

[23] In the 2nd OT comparison of the Word with a sword in Wis. 18:15 we find ξίφος ὀξύ.

[24] Hence it is not advisable to link Hb. 4:12 with a doctrine of the eschatological sword of God as we find it in Is. 27:1; 34:5; 66:16; Ez. 21:33, as against E. Käsemann, "Das wandernde Gottesvolk," FRL, NF, 37 (1939), 1, n. 4.

[25] It may be that sacrifice stands behind the τετραχηλισμένον of 4:13, though the image does not have to be uniform.

[26] Ordinary knives are not usually two-edged (cf. C. A. Seyffert, "Das Messer," in *Archiv f. Anthropologie*, NF 10 [1911] 148; Galling, 379). The LXX has δίστομος at Ju. 3:16; Prv. 5:4 with μάχαιρα; ψ 149:6; Sir. 21:3 with ῥομφαία. Surgeons' knives might be two-edged, cf. K. Sudhoff, Art. "Chirurgische Instrumente" in *Reallexikon d. Vorgeschichte*, II (1925), 310. Cf. also T. Meyer-Steineg and K. Sudhoff, *Gesch. d. Medizin im Überblick mit Abbildungen*[2] (1922); T. Meyer-Steineg, "Chirurgische Instrumente des Altertums," *Jenaer medizinisch-historische Beiträge*, Heft 1 (1912); Krauss Archäol., I (1910), 266 and 719; J. Preuss, *Biblisch-talmudische Medizin. Beiträge zur Gesch. d. Heilkunde u. d. Kultur überhaupt* (1911), 219 and 282. In the Epidauros inscr. Ditt. Syll.[3], 1168, 98 f. the person healed tells how during incubation he had the experience of the god cutting his breast open with a μάχαιρα. μαχαίριον is often used for the surgeon's knife (μαχαίριον ἰατρικόν in Aristot. and Plut., cf. Liddell-Scott, *s.v.*).

clear whether the μάχαι to which Paul was exposed in 2 C. 7:5 embraced physical threats. Also debatable is Jm. 4:1 f.: πόθεν πόλεμοι καὶ πόθεν μάχαι ἐν ὑμῖν; ... μάχεσθε καὶ πολεμεῖτε, "whence come wars and fightings among you? ... You fight and war." If Jm. is referring to the Jews (Schl. Jk.) he might mean bloody events, but otherwise it is more likely that he means spiritual wars and fightings. More important than the question of the frontier between physical and spiritual battles is the fact that never in the NT is the word group used positively for the warfare of the Christian life. All μάχεσθαι is rejected as inconsistent for the Christian. 2 Tm. 2:23 f.: τὰς δὲ μωρὰς καὶ ἀπαιδεύτους ζητήσεις παραιτοῦ, εἰδὼς ὅτι γεννῶσιν μάχας· δοῦλον δὲ κυρίου οὐ δεῖ μάχεσθαι, ἀλλὰ ἤπιον εἶναι πρὸς πάντας, "in awareness that they produce (only) strife. But a servant of the Lord should not strive." Tt. 3:9 : καὶ ἔριν καὶ μάχας νομικὰς περιΐστασο, "... you must avoid legal disputes." The bishop in 1 Tm. 3:3, and the Christian in Tt. 3:2, must be ἄμαχος, "peaceful." The word group thus has a negative ring in the NT which it does not have by nature [1] or in the LXX. [2] What is true of Jm. 4:1 f. is true of the NT as a whole. Where there is μάχεσθαι, human lust is finally, if secretly, at work. [3] The fact that the Christian lives by the divine mercy and loves his enemies does not relieve him of → ἀγωνίζεσθαι or → ἐλέγχειν. He takes the field and captures strongholds (2 C. 10:3 f.). To those around, who measure him by their own standards, he might often seem to be a very contentious disturber of the peace (Ac. 17:6). In reality, however, he cannot serve the μάχεσθαι which fills the world and which is directed especially against him. He offers the world no μάχαι.

† θεομάχος, † θεομαχέω.

Both the verb ("to strive against God") and the adj. ("striving against God") are rare. [1] In Eur. Ba., 45 and 325 (cf. 635), also 1255 the verb or concept denotes fatal opposition to the triumphant march of the god Dionysus. [2] The adj. does not occur in the LXX, and the verb only at 2 Macc. 7:19 with ref. to Antiochus Epiphanes. Σ translates רְפָאִים by θεομάχοι at Job 26:5; Prv. 9:18; 21:16.

Ac. 5:39 : μήποτε καὶ θεομάχοι εὑρεθῆτε, "that you may not be found even to be strivers against God." Materially this is a good description of the attitude which some in Pharisaic circles had taken up. [3] That Lk. in his rendering chooses this word is not due to LXX influence but to the direct or indirect influence of Eur. There is, of course, nothing comparable to the Gospel and its triumph, and he makes this clear. But he obviously does not fail to see the formal similarity to many religious battles in the pagan past. [4]

Bauernfeind

μάχομαι κτλ. [1] Cf. Plat. Tim., 88a.
[2] Cf. Sir. 28:8 : ἀπόσχου ἀπὸ μάχης, also Prv. 24:67 (30:32); but more likely Sir. 8:16 : μετὰ θυμώδους μὴ ποιήσῃς μάχην, or Prv. 25:8.
[3] Cf. Schl. Jk., 241.

θεομάχος κτλ. [1] Pr.-Bauer³, *s.v.*
[2] Cf. W. Nestle, *Philol.*, 59 (1900), 46 ff.; ARW, 33 (1936), 246 ff.; O. Weinreich, *Tübinger Beiträge zur Altertumswissenschaft*, 5 (1929), 334 f.
[3] Cf. Schl. Gesch. d. erst. Chr., 100 f.; O. Bauernfeind, *Die Apostelgeschichte* (1939), 94 ff.
[4] Ag., 23, 9 𝔎 μὴ θεομαχῶμεν is not original, but an addition and paraphrase based on 5:39.

μέγας, μεγαλεῖον, μεγαλειότης, μεγαλοπρεπής, μεγαλύνω, μεγαλωσύνη, μέγεθος

μέγας.

Contents: A. μέγας outside the New Testament. B. μέγας in the New Testament: 1. General Use; 2. Great and Small in the Kingdom of Heaven; 3. The Greatest Commandment; 4. The Johannine Use; 5. τοῦ μεγάλου θεοῦ, Tt. 2:13; 6. ἡ μεγάλη δύναμις, Ac. 8:10.

A. μέγας outside the New Testament.

1. The basic meaning of μέγας is "great," first with reference to visible phenomena, people, animals, inanimate objects. It is said of Achilles: ἐν κονίῃσι μέγας μεγαλωστὶ τανυσθεὶς κεῖτο, Hom. Il., 18, 26 f.; cf. εἶδος δὲ μάλα μέγας ἦν ὁράασθαι, Hom. Od., 18, 4; μέγας δὲ πλευρὰ βοῦς, Soph. Ai., 1253. In Xenoph. grown men as distinct from children, being recognised as such by their size, are οἱ μεγάλοι ἄνδρες, Cyrop., I, 3, 14; cf. also Hom. Od., 18, 217: νῦν δ' ὅτε δὴ μέγας ἐσσὶ καὶ ἥβης μέτρον ἱκάνεις· Ex. 2:11: μέγας γενόμενος Μωυσῆς. Also inanimate objects: μεγάλαι πόλεις, Pind. Pyth., 4, 19; μεγάλα πεδία, Aesch. Sept. c. Theb., 733; Gn. 1:16: ἐποίησεν ὁ θεὸς τοὺς δύο φωστῆρας τοὺς μεγάλους. Since there can be greatness in various directions, the term can mean "high" (μέγαν οὐρανὸν Οὔλυμπόν τε, Hom. Il., 1, 497); "long" (δόρυ μέγα νήϊον, *ibid.*, 17, 744); "wide" (μέγα λαῖτμα θαλάσσης, Hom. Od., 4, 504; ἡ θάλασσα ἡ μεγάλη, Nu. 34:6 f.; ... τὴν ἔρημον τὴν μεγάλην καὶ τὴν φοβερὰν ἐκείνην, Dt. 2:7); "broad" (μεγάλην αὐλήν, Hom. Il., 24, 452).

In addition to the basic meanings there are also the fig. In connection with persons and objects which have force or power we have the sense of "powerful," "mighty," of gods and deities (→ 538 on μέγας θεός) — a common name for Zeus: μέγας ὠδύσατο Ζεύς, Hom. Il., 18, 292; Διὸς κούρῃ μεγάλοιο, *ibid.*, 6, 304; cf. also μεγάλη Μοῖρα, Soph. Phil., 1466, see also Aesch. Choeph., 306. Also of men — τὸ ὄνομα τῶν μεγάλων τῶν ἐπὶ τῆς γῆς, 1 Παρ. 17:8: ... ποιήσω σε εἰς ἔθνος μέγα, Gn. 12:2; the Persian king is μέγας βασιλεύς, Aesch. Pers., 24; cf. ὁ μέγας βασιλεὺς Ἀσσυρίων, 4 Βασ. 18:19; ὁ μέγας ἀνὴρ ἐν πόλει, Plat. Leg., V, 730d; μεγάλαι ψυχαί, Soph. Ai., 154.[1] Also of natural forces and dangers: μέγας χειμών, Soph. Ai., 1148 f.; μεγάλου ὑπὸ κύματος, Hom. Od., 5, 320; μέγας κίνδυνος, Pind. Olymp., 1, 81; θάνατος μέγας σφόδρα, Ex. 9:3. Also abstr. μέγας χρόνος for "mighty time," Soph. Ai., 714, or for man's emotional states (πένθος μέγα, Gn. 50:11; ὀργὴ μεγάλη, Sir. 26:8; also Zech. 1:2, 15; ἐλυπήθη Ιωνας λύπην μεγάλην, Jon. 4:1; καὶ ἐχάρη

μέγας. Pass., Thes. Steph., Liddell-Scott, *s.v.*; B. Müller, Μέγας θεός (Diss. Hal. [1913]); Pauly-W., XV (1932), 221 ff.

1 In titles we find ὁ ἱερεὺς ὁ μέγας in Lv. 21:10 etc. (NT Hb. 10:21 in an OT quotation, otherwise → ἀρχιερεύς). In Hb. Jesus Christ is μέγας ἀρχιερεύς (μέγας powerful, accomplishing what His counterpart, the earthly high-priest, cannot do), 4:14. Cf. also 13:20: τὸν ποιμένα τῶν προβάτων τὸν μέγαν ..., where μέγας expresses the might and efficacy ascribed to Christ as in the OT to Yahweh.

Ιωνας ... χαρὰν μεγάλην, Jon. 4:6), or impressions on human hearing (ἀνεβόησεν φωνὴν μεγάλην, Gn. 27:34), i.e., great, strong, loud or powerful. μέγα ἔργον is an important or significant work (Hom. Od., 3, 261); μέγας λόγος an important speech (Plat. Phaed., 62b); ἐγίγνωσκον ὅτι ταῦτα μέγιστα ("highly significant") εἴη, Xenoph. Cyrop., VII, 5, 52.

μέγας and derivates are also used in connection with epiphanies of deities and heroes, e.g., Hdt., VIII, 38; Dior. Hal. Ant. Rom., VI, 13; Xenoph. Cyrop., VIII, 3, 14; Plot. Enn., V, 5, 3 etc.,[2] also — μέγας in the superlative μέγιστος — in court ceremonial as titles of honour.[3]

Finally, there can be a censorious ring: μηδὲν μέγ' εἴπῃς, Soph. Ai., 386 etc. μεγάλα φρονεῖν, "arrogant thinking" (Aristoph. Ach., 988); μὴ μέγα λέγων μεῖζον πάθῃς, Eur. Herc. Fur., 1244.

2. In the LXX the meanings of μέγας generally correspond to the Heb. root גדל, esp. the adj. גָּדוֹל, for which μέγας usually occurs. With ref. to extension and intensity גָּדוֹל can express the same nuances of the concept of greatness as μέγας, so that the two words are co-extensive. This does not mean that, in view of the range of the concept, other Gk. words cannot be used with comparative frequency for גדל, or that μέγας cannot be used for many other Heb. roots. In Gk. there are, apart from μέγας and derivates, 17 other terms for גָּדוֹל, though they are used only occasionally. Except in cases of free translation, which adapt the term to the context (e.g., ἅγιος in Ez. 36:23 A; ἔσχατος in Jos. 1:4; εὐγενής in Job 1:3), these words express specific aspects of greatness (e.g., ἁδρός in 4 Βασ. 10:6, 11; Jer. 5:5; δυνάστης, Lv. 19:15; Prv. 18:16; 25:6; ἰσχυρός, Da. 10:1, 7; 11:44; πολύς in Gn. 15:14 etc.; πρεσβύτερος in Gn. 27:1 etc.; ὑπέρογκος, Ex. 18:22). There are synon. neither for μέγας nor גָּדוֹל. When other Heb. words are translated μέγας, they are usually generalised. Thus μέγας is often used for רב, רבה ("many") and מְאֹד ("very"), Ex. 19:16; also כָּבֵד ("heavy"); Is. 33:21, 22; Ez. 17:8 for אַדִּיר and Is. 60:22 for עָצוּם ("powerful," "strong"); for גָּבַהּ "to become high," Ez. 31:10; for titles, גְּבִירָה "lady" (3 Βασ. 11:19), ראשׁ "high-(priest)" (2 Ch. 24:11); for loudness: Dt. 27:14 רָם, with raised, Jer. 4:5 מָלֵא, with full, עֲצִיב with strained voice, Da. 6:21; Job 36:24 for שׂגא hi, "to lift up with praise"; for the "extraordinary," פלא in Job 42:3; Is. 9:5 or the "terrible," ירא Job 37:22; finally very freely הָמוֹן in Is. 5:14 for the noisy multitude (with a suggestion of *hubris*),[4] Is. 26:4 for צור "rock" (a name for God) and for לִוְיָתָן μέγα κῆτος (Job 3:8). In Is. particularly many Heb. words are weakly rendered μέγας. μέγας occurs here 32 times, and only 13 times for גדל. In other passages we either have a free translation or an independent understanding of the text.[5]

B. μέγας in the New Testament.

1. General Use.

In the NT the term is used within the framework of general Greek and Hellenistic usage. Some special instances may be mentioned out of the many examples.[6] We read of τὸ δεῖπνον τὸ μέγα τοῦ θεοῦ (Rev. 19:17) to which the birds are invited and which will be supplied by the flesh of kings and mighty men (→ δεῖπ-

---

[2] Cf. Pauly-W., Suppl., IV (1924), 314.

[3] Preisigke Wört., *s.v.*

[4] G. Bertram, "Das Problem der Umschrift und die religionsgeschichtliche Erforschung der LXX," ZAW *Beiheft*, 66 (1936), 107.

[5] This paragraph is by Bertram.

[6] Cf. Pr.-Bauer[3], *s.v.* μέγας.

νον, II, 34); of the μεγάλη πίστις (Mt. 15:28) which the woman of Canaan had (→ πίστις); of God as μέγας βασιλεύς (Mt. 5:35; cf. ψ 46:2), the mighty King; of the severer judgment awaiting the teacher (μεῖζον κρίμα λημψόμεθα, Jm. 3:1); of the μικροί and μεγάλοι (Rev. 11:18; 13:16; 19:5, 18; 20:12, in connection with other antonyms: great and small in the various senses of the terms).[7] It is said of John the Baptist: ἔσται ... μέγας ἐνώπιον κυρίου ... (Lk. 1:15); also of Jesus:[8] οὗτος ἔσται μέγας ... (Lk. 1:32) = significant, great; cf.: προφήτης μέγας ἠγέρθη ἐν ἡμῖν (Lk. 7:16). The basis of this greatness according to Hb. 11:24 is faith: πίστει Μωϋσῆς μέγας γενόμενος ...[9] In the Magnificat Mary confesses: ... ἐποίησέν μοι μεγάλα ὁ δυνατός, "he that is mighty has done great things for me" (Lk. 1:49). The term ὁ δυνατός invests μεγάλα with its meaning as that which is astonishing, which is beyond understanding.[10]

Paul speaks impressively of love as the greatest of the χαρίσματα: ζηλοῦτε δὲ τὰ χαρίσματα τὰ μείζονα ... νυνὶ δὲ μένει πίστις, ἐλπίς, ἀγάπη, τὰ τρία ταῦτα· μείζων δὲ τούτων ἡ ἀγάπη, 1 C. 12:31; 13:13. Love is the eternal thing in the world, its meaning and value. As may be seen from 14:4, 5 (μείζων δὲ ὁ προφητεύων ἢ ὁ λαλῶν γλώσσαις, for ὁ ... προφητεύων ἐκκλησίαν οἰκοδομεῖ, v. 4), greatness and its evaluation are according to the value of the gift for the moulding and edifying of the congregation. According to the judgment of John's Gospel love reaches its climax in the loving sacrifice which Jesus makes, but which is here related to loving self-sacrifice in general: μείζονα ταύτης ἀγάπην οὐδεὶς ἔχει, ἵνα τις τὴν ψυχὴν αὐτοῦ θῇ ὑπὲρ τῶν φίλων αὐτοῦ, Jn. 15:13.

The relation between husband and wife, with its promise that they will be one flesh, is understood by Paul in the light of the relation between Christ and the community, which he calls a great mystery: τὸ μυστήριον τοῦτο μέγα ἐστίν ..., Eph. 5:32. The whole Christ event confessed in the hymn in 1 Tm. 3:16 is ὁμολογουμένως μέγα, namely, as τὸ τῆς εὐσεβείας μυστήριον. Piety itself, linked with αὐτάρκεια, is for man a πορισμὸς μέγας, great gain (1 Tm. 6:6). In the same sense παρρησία as confident freedom toward God has μεγάλην μισθαποδοσίαν (Hb. 10:35).

The eschatological day of divine judgment to which expectation is orientated is μεγάλη ἡμέρα. In allusion to Zeph. 1:14 (ἐγγὺς ἡ ἡμέρα κυρίου ἡ μεγάλη), it is called this in Jd. 6: εἰς κρίσιν μεγάλης ἡμέρας, and Rev. 6:17: ἡ ἡμέρα ἡ μεγάλη τῆς ὀργῆς, cf. also Ac. 2:20 quoting Jl. 2:31.

2. Great and Small in the Kingdom of Heaven.

Special attention must be paid to the use of the term in certain theologically important contexts. In His proclamation of the kingdom of God Jesus raises the question of great and small in the kingdom. The basis of the question is the struggle

[7] The expression ἀπὸ μικροῦ ἕως μεγάλου ... (Ac. 8:10; Hb. 8:11), as may be seen from the second passage, has its origin in LXX usage; cf. Gn. 19:11; 1 Βασ. 30:2 etc. It is designed to characterise an embracing totality. 1 K. 9:11: μέγα = "is it then something strange or surprising ...?"; cf. also 2 C. 11:15.

[8] If the appearance of the angel to Mary was originally an appearance to Elisabeth, as argued by D. Völter, *Die ev. Erzählungen von der Geburt und Kindheit Jesu* (1911); E. Norden, *Die Geburt des Kindes* (1924), this saying, too, is a promise to the Baptist.

[9] We have here a spiritualised exposition of Ex. 2:11 (→ 529), which simply says: "When Moses was grown ..."

[10] On the usage cf. Dt. 10:21: ὅστις ἐποίησεν ἐν σοὶ τὰ μεγάλα καὶ τὰ ἔνδοξα ταῦτα, Dt. 34:11 f.: ποιῆσαι ... τὰ θαυμάσια τὰ μεγάλα.

of the apostles for rank, which in Mt. takes the form: τίς ἄρα μείζων ἐστὶν ἐν τῇ βασιλείᾳ τῶν οὐρανῶν (18:1), and in Lk.: τὸ τίς ἂν εἴη μείζων αὐτῶν (9:46).[11] If in Lk. (and Mk.) the point of the dispute is who should have the greater prominence and worth, in Mt. it is a matter of their relations in the kingdom of God. This presents a view of the heavenly kingdom which understands it as a state and reality within which there are distinctions as in earthly forms of society.[12] Schlatter notes that the question of greatness permeated the whole of Palestinian piety. "At all points, in worship, in the administration of justice, at meals, in all dealings, there constantly arose the question who was the greater, and estimating the honour due to each was a task which had to be constantly fulfilled and which was felt to be very important."[13]

It is an established fact in Palestinian religion that there are small and great in the world to come. "We read in Job 3:19: 'Small and great are there.' Does not everyone know then that small and great are there? It teaches thee that one does not know in this world who is small and who is great ...," Pesikt. r., App. 3 (198b).[14] As distinct from shifting relations in this world, those in the world to come are fixed: "In this world he who is small can become great, and he who is great small; but in the future he who is small cannot become great, nor he who is great small," Rt. r., 1, 17. The saying in Job 3:19 is expounded as follows in bBM, 85b: "He who makes himself small in this world on account of the words of the Torah will be great in the future world; and he who makes himself a slave in this world on account of the words of the Torah will be free in the future world." The future world, symbolised in Gan Eden,[15] had seven classes or divisions into which the blessed were divided. The debate was which was the best and first.[16] It was allotted to martyrs, or to the upright, or to faithful students of Scripture and the Mishnah.

Jesus decides the question in a way which is in keeping with His proclamation of God and His understanding of the kingdom of God. R. Otto says in relation to this pericope: Here "there blows the new spirit which threatened and overcame the emerging Judaism of the Rabbis."[17] Taking an illustration from life, He set a child in the midst — all three Evangelists record this enacted parable. In relation to the action He utters a saying which is most pertinently reported in Mt.: ἐὰν μὴ στραφῆτε καὶ γένησθε ὡς τὰ παιδία, οὐ μὴ εἰσέλθητε εἰς τὴν βασιλείαν τῶν οὐρανῶν (18:3).[18] He then adds a saying peculiar to his Gospel: ὅστις οὖν ταπεινώσει ἑαυτὸν ὡς τὸ παιδίον τοῦτο, οὗτός ἐστιν ὁ μείζων ἐν τῇ βασιλείᾳ τῶν οὐρανῶν (18:4), which stands in antithetical relation to the Rabbinic saying

[11] Mk. has the account, but raises the question indirectly through the materially identical saying: εἴ τις θέλει πρῶτος εἶναι, ἔσται πάντων ἔσχατος καὶ πάντων διάκονος, Mk. 9:33-35.

[12] The usage may be traced back to this, cf. ὁ μέγας ἀνὴρ ἐν πόλει, Plat. Leg., V, 730d; τὸ ὄνομα τῶν μεγάλων τῶν ἐπὶ τῆς γῆς, 1 Ch. 17:8; μέγας ἦν ἐν τῇ βασιλείᾳ, Est. 10:3.

[13] Schl. Mt., 543.

[14] Str.-B., I, 249.

[15] *Ibid.*, IV, 1016 ff.: "Sch^e^ol, Gehinnom und Gan Eden."

[16] Cf. esp. *ibid.*, IV, 1139; also I, 773.

[17] R. Otto, *Reich Gottes und Menschensohn* (1934), 96.

[18] There corresponds to this in Mk. the general saying in the story of the blessing of the children: ἀμὴν λέγω ὑμῖν, ὃς ἂν μὴ δέξηται τὴν βασιλείαν τοῦ θεοῦ ὡς παιδίον, οὐ μὴ εἰσέλθῃ εἰς αὐτήν (Mk. 10:15); cf. Lk. 18:17. Acc. to Lohmeyer (*Das Evangelium d. Markus* [1937], 206) the saying formulates the point of the story as a general community rule. Where Mt. has the saying we find in Mk. and Lk.: ὃς ἂν ἓν τῶν τοιούτων

about making oneself small for the sake of the words of the Torah.[19] It may be said of the parable and the attached saying that it "makes the child an example of those who belong to the kingdom of God."[20] The striving for greatness which marks Rabbinic Jewish piety is ruled out. The nature of the child is to take openly and confidently what is given. This positive attitude is commended. The distinction is incisive. While the Rabbis discuss which children will belong to the kingdom of heaven, Jesus includes the child in the absolute. While they say: "Prattling with children puts a man out of the world" (Ab., 3, 14), Jesus enacts His parable with the child. The unchildlike piety of achievement is overcome by childlike reception and trust.[21] When man adopts this childlike attitude (ταπεινώσει ἑαυτόν ..., "the ταπεινός is not impelled by the will for power, but in the small sphere assigned to him fulfils his allotted task with perfect love"),[22] he is a μείζων ἐν τῇ βασιλείᾳ τῶν οὐρανῶν. Thus the question of greatness is answered in the new piety which receives from God and which consists in being a child of God.

The saying in the incident of the sons of Zebedee illustrates the thought expressed in the special logion in Mt.: ... ὃς ἐὰν θέλῃ ἐν ὑμῖν μέγας γενέσθαι, ἔσται ὑμῶν διάκονος (Mt. 20:26, also in a different order of words Mk. 10:43).[23] This saying is directed against the order of earthly rule. The order of life for the common dealings of the disciples is to be the ministry of love. Hence the question of greatness is transformed into the task of service. This does not rule it out as invalid, but the way on which the disciple is set overcomes the resultant strife and opposition towards one another and towards God. Lk. 22:26 f. puts the saying in a different context and gives it the form: ὁ μείζων ἐν ὑμῖν γινέσθω ὡς ὁ νεώτερος, καὶ ὁ ἡγούμενος ὡς ὁ διακονῶν. A. Schlatter excellently describes the difference in situation: "In Mk. the sayings answer the question how one may be great; only by being small, only by service, does one become great. The new series of sayings asks to what end the disciple will use the greatness given to him ... The meaning of the greatness to which Jesus has exalted the disciples is

---

παιδίων δέξηται ἐπὶ τῷ ὀνόματί μου, ἐμὲ δέχεται ..., Mk. 9:37; cf. Lk. 9:48. Jesus answers the question who is the greater by saying that he who does works of love like receiving children is great in the kingdom of heaven. There can be no doubt that Jesus gave rules and directions of this kind, but did He do so in answer to this question? One might consider the suggestion of E. Winkel, *Das Ev. nach Markus* (1937), 54 that we should read ἐκ for ἕν, as in WΘφ it vg: "Whoso takes from such children to himself ..." The only difficulty is that in view of the continuation this would lead to the idea of receiving Christ and God along the lines of inward and mystical reception, and there are hardly any instances of such usage in Jesus. The different forms of the saying in Mk. 9:37, Mt. 18:5 (ἓν παιδίον τοιοῦτο) and Lk. 9:48 (τοῦτο τὸ παιδίον), also the ἕν or ἐκ τῶν τοιούτων παιδίων or τῶν παιδίων τούτων, show that the tradition is uncertain.

[19] There can be no doubt that the setting and the special saying are related in Mt.

[20] E. Lohmeyer, 205. Cf. also W. Grundmann, *Die Gotteskindschaft in der Geschichte Jesu u. ihre religionsgeschichtlichen Voraussetzungen* (1938), 78 ff.

[21] Cf. R. Otto, 94: "'Accepting' and 'receiving as children' — this is the new way of salvation to which Jesus points. It is the way which corresponds least to the Pharisaic attitude. Indeed, it is its direct opposite. It is opposed to it not merely in details or principles but as a total inner attitude of a very different kind. The specific Pharisaic attitude could not be described in better or more striking words than by saying that it is 'unchildlike,' 'contrary to the manner of a child.'"

[22] Schl. Mt., 545.

[23] In both Evangelists there is attached the saying which is also quoted by Mk. in the different context of the strife about rank: καὶ ὃς ἂν θέλῃ ἐν ὑμῖν εἶναι πρῶτος, ἔσται ὑμῶν δοῦλος (Mk. πάντων δοῦλος).

service."[24] The form νεώτερος introduces into μείζων the thought of the elder. The reference in Mk. is to contention at the Last Supper about the question: τὸ τίς αὐτῶν δοκεῖ εἶναι μείζων, and in His answer Jesus alludes to His own manner: τίς γὰρ μείζων, ὁ ἀνακείμενος ἢ ὁ διακονῶν; οὐχὶ ὁ ἀνακείμενος; ἐγὼ δὲ ἐν μέσῳ ὑμῶν εἰμι ὡς ὁ διακονῶν.[25] He, the greater, is their servant. They must study and imitate His manner.

But this leaves one question open. It is clear how Jesus answers the question of greatness. But it is not clear whether it was put to Him or whether He Himself spoke of great and small in the kingdom of heaven. In the Sermon on the Mount in Mt., in the context of the sayings about the Law and righteousness, we find a saying which is with reason much debated and which is in fact limited by the sovereign attitude of Jesus to the Law: ὃς ἐὰν οὖν λύσῃ μίαν τῶν ἐντολῶν τούτων τῶν ἐλαχίστων καὶ διδάξῃ οὕτως τοὺς ἀνθρώπους, ἐλάχιστος κληθήσεται ἐν τῇ βασιλείᾳ τῶν οὐρανῶν· ὃς δ' ἂν ποιήσῃ καὶ διδάξῃ, οὗτος μέγας κληθήσεται ἐν τῇ βασιλείᾳ τῶν οὐρανῶν (Mt. 5:19). The saying which follows demands a better righteousness than that of the scribes and Pharisees as a condition for entry into the kingdom of God. The illustrations (5:21 ff.) contrast the commandment of Jesus with the halacha of the scribes (ἠκούσατε ὅτι ... ἐρρέθη — not ἐγράφη)[26] and assert the validity of the Law, understood as an expression of God's will for the whole man, in opposition to the halacha, which seeks to be a "hedge about the Torah" (Ab., 1, 1), but which in fact erodes it. The scribes, not Jesus, erode the Law. Hence the new righteousness must be better than theirs. 5:19 is to be understood in the light of this. Since they erode the Law and so teach, even though it be only in respect of the smallest commandment, they can be only the least in the kingdom of heaven. Indeed, according to v. 20 they will not even enter into it. As the saying puts it, in opposition to the Pharisees, one's position in the kingdom of heaven is bound up with unremitting fulfilment of the will of God. The Sermon on the Mount shows that this will embraces the whole man and aims at truth and love, at openness to God and trust in Him.

Finally, there is reference to great and small in the kingdom of heaven in the saying of Jesus in connection with the discussion initiated by the question of the Baptist: ἀμὴν λέγω ὑμῖν, οὐκ ἐγήγερται ἐν γεννητοῖς γυναικῶν μείζων Ἰωάννου τοῦ βαπτιστοῦ· ὁ δὲ μικρότερος ἐν τῇ βασιλείᾳ τῶν οὐρανῶν μείζων αὐτοῦ ἐστιν, Mt. 11:11; Lk. 7:28. As is shown by what follows, the point at issue is the gulf which separates the time of Jesus from that of the prophets and John as the time of fulfilment, of entry into the kingdom of God, of the proclamation and expectation of this kingdom. In the time just ended, John is, according to the

---

[24] Schl. Lk., 424.

[25] Str.-B., II, 257 draws attention to the Palestinian colouring of the question: "Who is greater, he who guards or he who is guarded? ... Who is greater, he who bears or he who is borne ...?" Gn. r., 78, 1 on 32:27; with other examples. Cf. also the instance from M. Ex. on 18:12, where there is ref. to the extraordinary situation of a greater serving someone less at table, and in defence Abraham is cited, who served the three men even though he took them for bedouins who worshipped idols, and also God, who hourly gives food to all.

[26] It may be seen clearly from vv. 33-37, and also from other expressions, that we do not have in the Sermon on the Mount an exposition of the Decalogue but opposition to the scribal halacha. Cf. K. Bornhäuser, *Die Bergpredigt* (1923); W. Grundmann, *Die Frage d. ältesten Gestalt u. des ursprünglichen Sinnes der Bergrede Jesu* (1939), 6 f.

judgment of Jesus, the greatest born of woman. But the delimitation is at once added: ὁ δὲ μικρότερος ἐν τῇ βασιλείᾳ τῶν οὐρανῶν μείζων αὐτοῦ ἐστιν. Does this mean that John is excluded from the kingdom of God? This is hardly likely. It is open to Abraham, Isaac and Jacob (Mt. 8:11). Could Jesus have wished to exclude the one whom He called the greatest born of woman? It is obviously open to the prophets. Shall he who is the περισσότερον προφήτου (v. 9) be left out? Who is then the μικρότερος ἐν τῇ βασιλείᾳ τῶν οὐρανῶν who is the μείζων αὐτοῦ? It may be the disciple who experiences the coming of the kingdom (Mt. 13:16 f.). But it is more probably Jesus Himself, who in the concealment which provokes the question of the Baptist, in the servant form which disappoints all expectations, seems to be the μικρότερος αὐτοῦ, and yet, as He who brings the kingdom of God, is really the μείζων.[27] This exposition brings the saying into line with that which, characterising the mission of Jesus: τοῦ ἱεροῦ μεῖζόν ἐστιν ὧδε (Mt. 12:6), sets Him above the temple and establishes His freedom in respect of the Rabbinic exposition of the Law (cf. 12:41, 42).[28]

3. The Greatest Commandment.

In the disputes which introduce the passion narrative, Mt. and Mk. raise the question of the greatest commandment.[29] In both cases it is a νομικός, a scribe, who puts the question: ποία ἐντολὴ μεγάλη ἐν τῷ νόμῳ; Mt. 22:36; ποία ἐστὶν ἐντολὴ πρώτη πάντων; Mk. 12:28. In both cases Jesus answers by giving a summary from Dt. 6:5 and Lv. 19:18: "Thou shalt love the Lord thy God with all thy heart and with all thy soul and with all thy mind (strength, Mk.)," and: "Thou shalt love thy neighbour as thyself." The two commandments are brought together in Mt.: αὕτη ἐστὶν ἡ μεγάλη καὶ πρώτη ἐντολή. δευτέρα ὁμοία αὐτῇ ... ἐν ταύταις ταῖς δυσὶν ἐντολαῖς ὅλος ὁ νόμος κρέμαται καὶ οἱ προφῆται (22:38-40),[30] and in Mk.: μείζων τούτων ἄλλη ἐντολὴ οὐκ ἔστιν (12:31). And the νομικός himself says: ... περισσότερόν ἐστιν πάντων τῶν ὁλοκαυτωμάτων καὶ θυσιῶν (v. 33). It is evident that Jesus sees the will of God and its fulfilment in combined and inseparable love for God and love for man. Besides this, everything else is unimportant. This is the position from which Jesus Himself acts and because of which He gives offence, e.g., in the question of the Sabbath. It is possible that the question itself was evoked by the conduct of Jesus in respect of the Law.

What is the relation of the question, and of the answer which Jesus gives, to Palestinian piety? This piety recognises that there is a distinction between lighter and weightier, smaller and greater commandments. Since by ancient tradition[31] the Law consists of 613 individual statutes, 248 commands and 365 prohibitions,

---

[27] This exposition is already found in the fathers. Cf. F. Dibelius, ZNW, 11 (1910), 190 f. and the comm.

[28] But cf. W. Bousset, *Kyrios Christos*[3] (1926), 45, who regards the saying as a product of the community.

[29] Lk. has the dialogue in another form at 10:25 ff. He puts the answer on the lips of the νομικός and then has him ask who is one's neighbour, and in answer gives the parable of the Good Samaritan.

[30] As in Mt. 7:12 etc., the relation to the Law is emphasised.

[31] Rabbi Shim'on ben Azzai, c. 110 A.D. refers first to the 365 prohibitions, and Rabbi Shim'on ben Eleazar (c. 190 A.D.) to the whole 613, but both assume that they are already known; cf. Str.-B., I, 900.

the question is quite understandable. Evaluation as light or weighty, small or great, is according to the nature of the demand for human achievement or the nature of possible expiation for infringement of prohibitions. In no case can there be dispensation from even the smallest commands. To all 613 statutes the principle applies: ἐπικατάρατος πᾶς ὃς οὐκ ἐμμένει πᾶσιν τοῖς γεγραμμένοις ἐν τῷ βιβλίῳ τοῦ νόμου τοῦ ποιῆσαι αὐτά (Gl. 3:10). The answer of Jesus shows that He goes much deeper than distinction between less and weighty in terms of demand or the possibility of atonement. His concern is for the will of God, not for individual commands or prohibitions. His answer takes the question to be a question concerning the principle of the Law. Now this question of principle was both raised and answered in Rabbinic Judaism.[32] Thus, when a proselyte asked for the whole Law in a nutshell, Shammai indignantly rejected the question, while Hillel answered it in a negative form of the Golden Rule.[33] The division between the two shows, however, that Rabbinic Judaism did not favour such attempts, and insisted on fulfilment of the whole Law, as Paul emphasises in Gl. 3:10. To show the principle of the Law is to enter on a way which leads out of the nomism so current in Judaism. The story of Jesus shows that He took this way, and His answer shows that He did so deliberately. Moreover, when attempts to state the principle are considered, it is plain that Jesus is also distinctive in respect of the principle which He espouses. For Him the will of God aims at the love which is one as love for God and for one's neighbour. The general position of Judaism is well stated in Ab., 1, 2: "The world rests on three things: the Torah, sacrificial worship, and expressions of love." Jesus does not merely set love above the Torah and sacrifice; He ignores the last two altogether. Again, for Him love is not just benevolence expressed in works of love and sometimes set above sacrifice even in Judaism on account of its atoning significance (Ab. R. Nat., 4).[34] Love is for Him the inner commitment of man to God. It is committal to God in divine sonship. It is the commitment and committal which works itself out in a similar commitment to men. Here man reflects and works out the love which he has received from God (cf., e.g., Mt. 5:44, 45, 48). This is the only essential thing — μείζων τούτων ἄλλη ἐντολὴ οὐκ ἔστιν — beside which all else is non-essential — "infuriating audacity to the Rabbinic understanding."[35] It carries with it the radical overthrow of Jewish nomism, and in some sense of Judaism itself as a religion.[36] The cross is a natural outcome.

4. The Johannine Use.

Jesus tells Nathanael, who saw that he was known by Him: μείζω τούτων ὄψῃ (Jn. 1:50). This promise is elucidated by the general promise: ὄψεσθε τὸν

[32] Cf. Str.-B., I, 907.

[33] bShab., 31a; cf. also Tob. 4:15; on this Grundmann, 87 f.

[34] Str.-B., I, 500. → καλὰ ἔργα, III, 545 f.

[35] E. Lohmeyer, 261; cf. the complete exposition of the pericope.

[36] Jesus thus took up in relation to Jewish nomism a position which may be pertinently called freedom from the Law in commitment to God. It should be continually pointed out that the best and most relevant exposition of His proclamation is His history. This confirms our judgment. Paul did not at first enjoy this freedom. His estimation of the Law was Rabbinic. Because he had to find his way to the position of Jesus, the Law, and questions related to it, play in his theology a role which they do not have in Jesus. Here is an essential point in the relation between Paul and Jesus to which adequate attention has not been paid.

οὐρανὸν ἀνεῳγότα ...[37] The reference is to seeing the δόξα of Jesus, in which they will share when they are drawn into it.[38] This takes place because through and in Jesus they see God and are set in fellowship with Him. Jesus expects for Himself: ὁ ... πατὴρ φιλεῖ τὸν υἱὸν καὶ πάντα δείκνυσιν αὐτῷ ἃ αὐτὸς ποιεῖ, καὶ μείζονα τούτων δείξει αὐτῷ ἔργα, ἵνα ὑμεῖς θαυμάζητε, 5:20. He does not do His miracles of Himself. He fulfils what the Father, with whom He is one in love, manifests to Him. He will show Him greater works than the miracle wrought at the pool of Bethesda on the man who had been lame for 38 years. What this greater thing is may be seen in the following verse. It is a matter of ζωοποιεῖν. This is the greater thing compared with the miracles which He performs.[39] To the disciple who abides in faith in Christ the promise is made: μείζονα τούτων ποιήσει, and the basis of this is His going to the Father (14:12). This going to the Father gives Him the possibility of greater efficacy exercised through the disciples.

The promise of the greater thing, and the power to do it, make Jesus greater than the fathers. The Samaritan woman senses this from His saying: μὴ σὺ μείζων εἶ τοῦ πατρὸς ἡμῶν Ἰακώβ; (4:12). The Jews ask the same question: μὴ σὺ μείζων εἶ τοῦ πατρὸς ἡμῶν Ἀβραάμ; (8:53). He Himself confesses: ἐγὼ δὲ ἔχω τὴν μαρτυρίαν μείζω τοῦ Ἰωάννου (5:36). The question is whether this is a witness greater than John had or than John gave.[40] In view of v. 33 the latter is more probable. Jesus lays before those who would judge Him two witnesses: the works which the Father gives Him, and Scripture, in which the Father has testified to Him. The witness of John is mentioned only for the sake of His hearers. He does not emphasise it, for He will not accept the witness of men. It is said of the witness of God as compared with the witness of men: ἡ μαρτυρία τοῦ θεοῦ μείζων ἐστίν (1 Jn. 5:9).

A special question is raised by the textually uncertain saying in 10:29: either ὁ πατήρ μου ὃς δέδωκέν μοι πάντων μείζων ἐστίν (ℵ LD syr^sin pesh Basil Chrysost Cyril Alex), or: ὁ πατήρ μου ὅ δέδωκέν μοι πάντων μεῖζόν ἐστιν (AB Tert Aug latt).[41] In the first case Jesus grounds His authority to grant eternal and inalienable life in the greatness of the Father, which is above all things, so that nothing can pluck those who belong to Jesus out of the hand of the Father.[42] In the second case the power of Jesus as a shepherd is described as the highest and supreme thing.[43] Whereas in the first case the greatness of Jesus is grounded in the Father, in the second it is said of this greatness which the Father has given Him that it cannot be challenged by anything. Though Jesus speaks of His unity with the Father, and this is the foundation of Johannine Christology,

---

[37] Cf. on this H. Windisch, ZNW, 30 (1931), 215 ff.; J. Jeremias, *Angelos*, 3 (1930), 2-5.

[38] On the question of different strata in the pericope cf. R. Bultmann, *Das Johannesevangelium* (1937), 74 f.

[39] → II, 869; 875; E. Hirsch, *Das vierte Evangelium* (1936): "The greatest thing which He shows and gives Him is the power to create life out of death ... Jesus' works should not be confused with His signs. The works go beyond the signs. They embrace them, but are His total action towards us," 161.

[40] For the one view cf. Bau., *ad loc.* and Zn. J., 305; for the other Schl. J., 156 f.

[41] There are also variations within the main groups. Cf. the critical apparatus in H. v. Soden and E. Nestle.

[42] In this reading there is no αὐτά after δέδωκέν μοι.

[43] In this reading v. 29b limps badly and seems to be an editorial addition.

He does not equate Himself with the Father. This is plain in the saying: ὁ πατὴρ μείζων μού ἐστιν (14:28). The First Epistle declares: μείζων ἐστὶν ὁ θεὸς τῆς καρδίας ἡμῶν, namely, as He who pardons, who overcomes the accusing heart (3:20). For this reason it can say: ὑμεῖς ἐκ τοῦ θεοῦ ἐστε, τεκνία, καὶ νενικήκατε αὐτούς (namely, the ψευδοπροφῆται), ὅτι μείζων ἐστὶν ὁ ἐν ὑμῖν ἢ ὁ ἐν τῷ κόσμῳ (4:4). God, who is in the community, is greater than Satan, who is in the world.

The Johannine Christ forbids the disciples to exalt themselves above Him. He also commands them to love and serve as He does: οὐκ ἔστιν δοῦλος μείζων τοῦ κυρίου αὐτοῦ, οὐδὲ ἀπόστολος μείζων τοῦ πέμψαντος αὐτόν (Jn. 13:16). In so doing they will experience the hatred of the world like Himself: μνημονεύετε τοῦ λόγου οὗ ἐγὼ εἶπον ὑμῖν· οὐκ ἔστιν δοῦλος μείζων τοῦ κυρίου αὐτοῦ· εἰ ἐμὲ ἐδίωξαν, καὶ ὑμᾶς διώξουσιν. But also: εἰ τὸν λόγον μου ἐτήρησαν, καὶ τὸν ὑμέτερον τηρήσουσιν (Jn. 15:20).

In 1 Jn. 3:19 f. we have the saying: "Herein — namely, in love in deed and in truth — we shall know that we are of the truth, and shall assure our heart before him. For if our heart condemns us, God is greater than our heart, and knoweth all things." The greatness of God, which is above both accusation and Satan, to whom all accusations go back (cf. 1 Jn. 4:4), consists in the forgiveness which remits guilt and in the power which gives fulfilment of the commandments.[44]

5. τοῦ μεγάλου θεοῦ, Tt. 2:13.

προσδεχόμενοι τὴν μακαρίαν ἐλπίδα καὶ ἐπιφάνειαν τῆς δόξης τοῦ μεγάλου θεοῦ καὶ σωτῆρος ἡμῶν Χριστοῦ Ἰησοῦ, Tt. 2:13. The exegetical question posed by this verse is as follows: How are the words τοῦ μεγάλου θεοῦ καὶ σωτῆρος ἡμῶν Ἰησοῦ Χριστοῦ related? There are three possibilities: 1. Jesus Christ is the great God and Saviour; 2. The great God and our Saviour Jesus Christ are distinguished; 3. Jesus Christ is in apposition to δόξα, and τοῦ μεγάλου θεοῦ καὶ σωτῆρος ἡμῶν refers to God. It is possible to decide only when one has reviewed the problem bound up with the phrase ὁ μέγας θεός,[45] which is found elsewhere in the NT, e.g., when Diana is called μεγάλη θεά in Ac. 19:27 f., and the cry goes up: μεγάλη ἡ Ἄρτεμις Ἐφεσίων (cf. also v. 34 f.).

The question of the greatness of God is raised in the OT and is there closely linked with the development of monotheism. Ex. 18:11 reads: μέγας κύριος παρὰ πάντας τοὺς θεούς. Other refs. say the same: ὁ γὰρ κύριος ὁ θεὸς ὑμῶν, οὗτος θεὸς τῶν θεῶν καὶ κύριος τῶν κυρίων, ὁ θεὸς ὁ μέγας καὶ ἰσχυρὸς καὶ ὁ φοβερός, Dt. 10:17; μέγας ὁ θεὸς ἡμῶν παρὰ πάντας τοὺς θεούς ..., 2 Ch. 2:4; κύριος ... βασιλεὺς μέγας ἐπὶ πᾶσαν τὴν γῆν, ψ 46:2; τίς θεὸς μέγας ὡς ὁ θεὸς ἡμῶν, ψ 76:13.[46] ... σὺ εἶ ὁ θεὸς μόνος ὁ μέγας, ψ 85:10; θεὸς μέγας κύριος καὶ βασιλεὺς μέγας ἐπὶ πάντας τοὺς θεούς, ψ 94:3. The basic monotheistic thrust in conflict

---

[44] Cf. the basic discussion of this passage in F. Büchsel, *Die Johannesbriefe* (1933), 58-61. On the question whether an earlier work is used, which seems to be suggested by the strange antithesis of v. 21, cf. R. Bultmann, "Analyse des ersten Johannesbriefes," *Festschrift f. Adolf Jülicher* (1927), 150 f.

[45] Cf. Müller; Pauly-W., 15, 221 ff.; E. Peterson, εἷς θεός (1926), 196 ff.; Deissmann LO⁴, 229, n. 3.

[46] The following verses describe the greatness: σὺ εἶ ὁ θεὸς ὁ ποιῶν θαυμάσια, ἐγνώρισας ἐν τοῖς λαοῖς σου τὴν δύναμίν σου· ἐλυτρώσω ἐν τῷ βραχίονί σου τὸν λαόν σου ...

with other gods is clear and unmistakable. The greatness of God's individual attributes is also extolled: His ἰσχύς (Ex. 32:11; Dt. 4:37); His δύναμις (Dt. 8:17; οὐχ ᾧ μεγίστη δύναμις, Job 26:3); His ἔλεος (ψ 85:13; 107:5; Is. 54:7); His δόξα (ψ 137:5). The → ὄνομα of God, which contains and expresses His nature and being, is great (ψ 75:1; 98:3; Mal. 1:11; Tob. 11:14). God's works are great (Ju. 2:7; Tob. 12:22). Statements concerning the greatness of God and His being are increasingly multiplied in the later parts of the OT and in the so-called Apocrypha.[47] God is the ὕψιστος μέγιστος ζῶν θεός (Est. 8:12q). This fact is related to the debate with paganism, where the μέγας θεός has an established place (cf. Sib., 3, 702: "the sons of the great God").

In class. Gk. μέγας is an epithet applied to almost all the gods.[48] But, as in the OT examples, μέγας can also be a common part of cultic epiclesis. This is relatively rare in relation to Gk. deities. It comes from the Orient. An ancient example is the inscr. of Darius I (522-486) in Persepolis: "A great god is Ahura Mazda, who is the greatest of all gods ..."[49] "Great" is also used for almost all Egyptian deities from the very earliest times. In Hellenism, with its fusion of the oriental and Greek worlds, the phrase μέγας θεός is found everywhere. A few examples may be given: Διὶ μεγίστῳ Κεραυνίῳ ὑπὲρ σωτηρίας ... τὴν καμάραν ᾠκοδόμησεν ..., CIG, III, 4501; μέγας Ἀπόλλων Λειμηνός, JHS (1887), p. 386 and 15; ... ἱερέως διὰ βίου τοῦ μεγίστου καὶ ἐνφανεστάτου θεοῦ Ἡλίου ..., CIG, II, 2653; ... τῆς μεγάλης θεᾶς Ἀρτέμιδος πρὸ πόλεως ἱερεῖς (Ephesus), CIG, II, 2963c;[50] cf. ὁ κράτιστος ... μέγιστος θεῶν Ζεύς, CIG, II, 2170; Διὶ ὑψίστῳ μεγίστῳ καὶ ἐπηκόῳ ..., CIG, III, 4502. Such formulae are common in the magic pap. and in writings associated with magic; cf. κύριε, χαῖρε, μεγαλοδύναμε, μεγαλοκράτωρ, βασιλεῦ, μέγιστε θεῶν, Ἥλιε, ὁ κύριος τοῦ οὐρανοῦ καὶ τῆς γῆς, θεὲ θεῶν, Preis. Zaub., IV, 640; ἐπικαλοῦμαί σε, τὸν μέγιστον θεόν, δυνάστην Ὧρον Ἁρποκράτην ..., *ibid.*, 987; ἐπικαλοῦμαι ὑμᾶς ... παρέδρους τοῦ μεγάλου θεοῦ, τοὺς κραταιοὺς ἀρχιδαίμονας *ibid.*, 1345; ... ὁρκίζω ... τὸν πάντα κτίσαντα θεὸν μέγαν Σαρουσιν, *ibid.*, 1710.[51] Peterson refers to the inscr. assembled by Steinleitner,[52] in which we find various forms of *megas* acclamation, e.g., μεγάλη μήτηρ ..., followed by confession of sins;[53] μεγάλη Ἀναεῖτις ...[54] He characterises them as exhomologesis, "which is both confession of sin and acclamation of the god, and which presupposes the epiphany of the god."[55] In all these context μέγας has a strong suggestion of "mighty one," for the greatness of the deity is seen in his power. It is thus exalted above the world of men. The phrase is not motivated by a monotheistic tendency in Hellenism, e.g., καὶ τῶν συννάων θεῶν μεγίστων, or: καὶ οἱ σὺν αὐτοῖς θεῶν μεγίστων, or: καὶ τοῖς συννάοις θεοῖς μεγίστοις.[56] Several gods may be mentioned and invoked together. The phrase passed

---

[47] Cf. Βηλ καὶ Δράκων v. 18 Θ: μέγας εἶ, Βήλ ...; v. 41: καὶ ἀναβοήσας φωνῇ μεγάλῃ εἶπεν Μέγας εἶ, Κύριε ὁ θεὸς τοῦ Δανιήλ, καὶ οὐκ ἔστιν πλὴν σοῦ ἄλλος.

[48] Cf. the many examples in Müller.

[49] F. H. Weissbach, *Die Keilinschriften d. Achämeniden* (1911), 85 § 1.

[50] Cf. *Forschungen in Ephesus, veröffentlicht vom österreichischen archäol. Institut,* I (1906), II (1912); II, 128, No. 27: ... τὴν μεγίστην θεὸν Ἄρτεμιν τειμᾶν (v. 12) ... τῇ μεγίστῃ θεᾷ Ἐφεσίᾳ Ἀρτέμιδι (v. 143) etc.

[51] Cf. μεγάλη μήτηρ for Cybele (B. Müller, 300-307) and the μέγας Δαίμων.

[52] F. Steinleitner, *Die Beicht im Zusammenhange mit der sakralen Rechtspflege in der Antike* (Diss. Munich, 1913).

[53] *Ibid.*, 10.

[54] *Ibid.*, 26 ff.

[55] E. Peterson, 202. In this connection Peterson draws attention to the beginning of Augustine's Confessions: *Magnus es domine et laudabilis valde; magna virtus tua et sapientiae tuae non est numerus.*

[56] Cf. Müller, 379 f. with many examples. Cf. also the inscr. on the Andania mysteries, Müller, 294 f.; also μέγας εἶ ὦ Ἀπόλλων καὶ πάντες οἱ λοιποὶ θεοί, Anal. Boll., 29 (1910), 273, 12.

from the cult of deities into that of rulers, e.g., τὸν αἰώνιον τοῦ μεγίστου θεῶν Τιβερίου Σεβαστοῦ Καίσαρος οἶκον, BCH, 6 (1882), p. 613.[57] With the μέγας formula we also find the μέγα ὄνομα formula, e.g., εἷς θεός, τὸ μέγιστον, τὸ ἐνδοξότατον ὄνομα βοήθη . . . ;[58] μέγα τὸ ὄνομα τοῦ θεοῦ, μέγα τὸ ὅσιον, μέγα τὸ ἀγαθόν.[59]

The Ephesian formula μεγάλη ἡ Ἄρτεμις Ἐφεσίων is explained by these examples and is just another instance of such acclamations. But the statement in Tt. 2:13 also belongs to the same context. The God of Christians, on whom their faith and hope is set, is for them the μέγας θεός. The saying is not to be explained in terms of the OT alone, for the OT itself is part of the world of cultic forms and speech which has its origin in the East and which in Hellenism spreads to the West. The later use of the phrase in stories of martyrdom and other Christian writings[60] demands this broader context. But who is the μέγας θεός? We may dismiss the idea that the Χριστοῦ Ἰησοῦ is in apposition to τῆς δόξης, for σωτήρ refers to Christ in Tt. Hence we have to take Jesus Christ as the μέγας θεός. This is demanded by the position of the article, by the term ἐπιφάνεια (the return of Jesus Christ will be an epiphany), and by the stereotyped nature of the expression. With its cultic and polytheistic background the phrase is better adapted to refer to Jesus Christ as God than to God the Father in the narrower monotheistic sense. Hence the best rendering is: "We wait for the blessed hope and manifestation of the glory of our great God and Saviour Jesus Christ."

6. ἡ μεγάλη δύναμις, Ac. 8:10.

In Ac. 8:10 Simon Magus is called ἡ δύναμις τοῦ θεοῦ ἡ καλουμένη μεγάλη. He ranks as μέγας.

The phrase μεγάλη δύναμις belongs to the context of the μέγας θεός. Cf. εἷς θεὸς ἐν οὐρανοῖς, μέγας Μὴν οὐράνιος, μεγάλη δύναμις τοῦ ἀθανάτου θεοῦ.[61] Peterson[62] finds in this inscr. a threefold acclamation. He compares: μεγάλη ἡ δύναμις τοῦ ξένου θεοῦ, μέγας ὁ θεὸς ὁ κηρυττόμενος παρὰ τοῦ ξένου Ἀνδρεά . . . μέγας ὁ θεὸς Ἀνδρέου, Martyr. Andreae prius, 6. Cf. also: μέγας ὁ κύριος ἡμῶν καὶ μεγάλη ἡ ἰσχὺς αὐτοῦ, Descensus Christi ad inferos, 10; μεγάλη ἡ δύναμις τῆς ἁγίας τριάδος, Inscr. Prentice, No. 203. The phrase μεγάλη δύναμις is linked with these acclamations. On Palestinian soil it is also found for the divine name (cf. Mt. 26:64; Mk. 14:62 [not Lk. 22:69], though without μεγάλη. → II, 297); e.g., Eus. Hist. Eccl., II, 23, 13: . . . ἐκ δεξιῶν τῆς μεγάλης δυνάμεως . . . (in the witness of James to Christ); Ev. Pt.: "My power, my power, why hast thou forsaken me?"[63] → μεγαλοπρεπής.

---

[57] Müller, 394 f. for further instances.

[58] Peterson, 281 f.

[59] J. Keil, *Österreichische Jahreshefte,* XI (1908), *Beibl.,* 154-156; Peterson, 205; cf. 208-210.

[60] Cf. Peterson, 196-199 for examples.

[61] J. Keil and A. v. Premerstein, "Bericht über eine zweite Reise in Lydien," *Denkschr. d. Wiener Akademie, Phil.-Hist. Klasse,* 54 (1911), 109 f., No. 211.

[62] Peterson, 268 f.

[63] Cf. E. Lohmeyer, *Galiläa u. Jerusalem* (1936), 69 f., n. 1. Lohmeyer rightly sees in the phrase "great power" the name for God of a particular Jewish eschatological trend, but his judgment that "it is natural enough to seek the origin of this peculiar development in Galilee" needs modification. For Galilee itself was open to influences which suggest the religious world of Syria and Asia Minor. This is the ultimate place of origin.

When Simon Magus is called ἡ δύναμις τοῦ θεοῦ ἡ καλουμένη μεγάλη, this form of expression is part of the world of Hellenistic magic piety which had made its way into Palestine and combined with popular Jewish ideas. The phrase characterises Simon as a θεῖος ἄνθρωπος, a mediator of revelation, an incarnation of the μεγάλη δύναμις τοῦ θεοῦ. The λέγων εἶναί τινα ἑαυτὸν μέγαν (v. 9) has the same meaning in the context.[64]

† μεγαλεῖον.

The noun τὰ μεγαλεῖα is formed from the adj. μεγαλεῖος, α, ον, "great," "powerful," e.g., Xenoph. Mem., IV, 1, 4: μεγαλείους καὶ σφοδροὺς ὄντας, *ibid.*, IV, 5, 1: μεγαλεῖον κτῆμα. Also in connection with a divine epiphany in the case of the emperor god Caligula: ... τὸ μεγαλεῖον τῆς ἀθανασίας, Ditt. Syll.³, 798, 5.

τὸ μεγαλεῖον, "greatness," "pomp": τὸ μεγαλεῖον τῶν πράξεων, Polyb., 3, 87, 5; τὸ μεγαλεῖον τῶν ἔργων, Sir. 17:8 f.; τὰ μεγαλεῖα, the mighty acts, Dt. 11:2; ὁ θεός, ἕως ὑψίστων ἃ ἐποίησας μεγαλεῖα ..., ψ 70:19; ἀπήγγειλεν ... τὰ μεγαλεῖα τὰ γενόμενα αὐτῷ, Tob. 11:15; τὰ μεγαλεῖα τοῦ μεγίστου θεοῦ ποιήσαντος, 3 Macc. 7:22.

μεγαλεῖον, which is used in the LXX for גֹּדֶל, גָּדוֹל or עֲלִילָה, and in Sir. also for גְּבוּרָה, almost always refers in the Gk. Bible to the mighty acts or works of God. Only in Tob. 11:15 does it stand for the strange adventures of Tobit in Media and in Sir. 45:24 for the high-priesthood (כהונה גדולה) ἱερωσύνης μεγαλεῖον. Σ also has the word, found in the LXX in Sir. and ψ, as an adj. in Jer. 39(32):21. → ἔργον, II, 638 ff.[1]

In the NT: ἀκούομεν λαλούντων αὐτῶν ταῖς ἡμετέραις γλώσσαις τὰ μεγαλεῖα τοῦ θεοῦ, Ac. 2:11. τὰ μεγαλεῖα are the mighty acts of God which relate to, and consist in, the story of Christ, and which form the content of NT proclamation. The context is Hellenistic, and the reference is probably to the mighty acts of God which are contained in His epiphany in Christ.

† μεγαλειότης.

μεγαλειότης, "greatness," "pomp," "majesty," e.g., προσκυνήσας τὸν Ἥλιον Ἅρμαχιν ἐπόπτην καὶ σωτῆρα τῇ τε τῶν πυραμίδων μεγαλειότητι καὶ ὑπερφυείᾳ τερφθείς, Ditt. Or., 666, 24 f.; ... τῆς τοῦ αὐτοκράτορος δυνάμεως καὶ μεγαλειότητος, 669, 9.

In the LXX: ... κατὰ τὴν μεγαλειότητα Σαλωμων τοῦ υἱοῦ αὐτοῦ (sc. David), 1 Εσδρ. 1:4 (the glory of king Solomon); ... αὐτῇ (namely, τῇ ἀληθείᾳ) ἡ ἰσχὺς καὶ τὸ βασίλειον καὶ ἡ ἐξουσία καὶ ἡ μεγαλειότης τῶν πάντων αἰώνων, 1 Εσδρ. 4:40; καὶ ἔσται (namely, not remembering sins) εἰς εὐφροσύνην καὶ εἰς αἴνεσιν καὶ εἰς μεγαλειότητα παντὶ τῷ λαῷ τῆς γῆς ..., Ιερ. 40:9.

There is no Heb. term which strictly corresponds to μεγαλειότης. In Jer. 33:9 the Mas. has תִּפְאֶרֶת, and the meaning is: "The good which God shows Jerusalem redounds (לִי, says God) to his praise among all peoples." LXX (Ιερ. 40:9) leaves out לִי and has

---

[64] On the whole idea cf. esp. G. P. Wetter, *Der Sohn Gottes* (1916).
μεγαλεῖον. [1] This paragraph is by Bertram.
μεγαλειότης. Deissmann LO, 311, n. 4 and Deissmann B, 277 ff.

the sing. "people" for "peoples." This gives the new sense that the good which God does redounds to the glory of the Jewish people. Hence the universalist missionary revelation of Jer. is nationalistically distorted by the translators. In Da. 7:27 the nationalistic thrust is already present in the Mas. Here we have the Aram. רְבוּ ("greatness"), so that the ref. is to power in the political sense. In 1 Εσδρ. 1:4 μεγαλειότης is arbitrarily added by the translator. Neither the Mas. nor the LXX has an original in the corresponding verse in 2 Ch. 35:4 on which 1 Εσδρ. 1:4 is based. In 1 Εσδρ. 4:40 it comes in the story of the three youths, for which there is no Heb. original. Here, too, μεγαλειότης is formal. The term is found in a secondary tradition at Lv. 7:35. There is no Heb. original. LXX here has χρῖσις. The translator took מִשְׁחָה to mean, not a share in the sacrifice, but anointing. μεγαλειότης probably suggests a prerogative of the priest. Θ has μεγαλειότης at Ez. 31:18 of the majesty of a tree (for גֹּדֶל). In ψ 130:1 ʼΑΘ have it, and in ψ 70:21 ʼΑΣΘ, for derivates of גדל. The ref. in ψ 130:1 is to ungodly power and pomp, while in ψ 70:21 we have a prayer to God for increase of the greatness of the righteous. LXX goes its own way here, and speaks of the μεγαλωσύνη (vl. δικαιοσύνη) of God.

The term is used with ref. to God in Joseph.[1] It has the character of a title and occurs in liturgical contexts. Thus we read in Ant., 8, 111: τὴν σὴν εὐλογεῖν μεγαλειότητα. It is also found liturgically in the cultic vocabulary of Christianity. Cf., e.g., Cl. Al. Quis Div. Salv., 42, 20 in the concluding doxology: ὁ πατὴρ ὁ ἀγαθὸς ὁ ἐν τοῖς οὐρανοῖς, ᾧ ... εἴη δόξα, τιμή, κράτος, αἰώνιος μεγαλειότης.[2]

In the NT it occurs at Lk. 9:43. After Jesus has expelled the devil which the disciples could not control, ἐξεπλήσσοντο δὲ πάντες ἐπὶ τῇ μεγαλειότητι τοῦ θεοῦ (the majesty or power of God). It also occurs in 2 Pt. 1:16: ἐπόπται γενηθέντες τῆς ἐκείνου μεγαλειότητος (the reference is to the majesty of Christ which was manifested at the transfiguration and of which the disciples were initiated eye-witnesses; ἐπόπτης is a term from the mysteries). A third use is in Ac. 19:27: ... μέλλειν τε καὶ καθαιρεῖσθαι τῆς μεγαλειότητος αὐτῆς (namely, Diana of Ephesus) → μέγας θεός (538 f.).

† μεγαλοπρεπής.

This word, composed of μέγας and πρέπειν, means a "great man," i.e., "of great and noble disposition," hence "magnanimous or noble." E.g., νεανικοί τε καὶ μεγαλοπρεπεῖς τὰς διανοίας, Plat. Resp., VI, 503c; "splendid," "magnificent," ἔδωκέ σφι [= αὐταῖς] δωρεὴν μεγαλοπρεπεστάτην, Hdt., VI, 122, 2; καλοὶ λόγοι καὶ μεγαλοπρεπεῖς, Plat. Symp., 210d; "generous," μεγαλοπρεπέως ξεινίζειν, Hdt., VI, 128. The word is used of God in Dt. 33:26: ὁ μεγαλοπρεπὴς (Mas. גַּאֲוָה) τοῦ στερεώματος (the great, majestic, exalted One). 2 Macc. 8:15: ... (ἐπίκλησις) τοῦ σεμνοῦ καὶ μεγαλοπρεποῦς ὀνόματος αὐτοῦ.

μεγαλοπρεπής, the adv. μεγαλοπρεπῶς, and the noun μεγαλοπρέπεια, which in the Ps. is used for such Heb. words as גַּאֲוָה, "majesty," הָדָר, "splendour," הוֹד, "excellence," תִּפְאֶרֶת, "honour," are constantly used in the LXX for God, His works, and His Messiah (ψ 8:1; 20:6; 28:4; 67:34; 70:8; 95:6; 103:1 [A]; 110:3; 144:5, 12). μεγαλοπρεπής is once used in 2 Macc. 15:13 of a vision of Jeremiah alongside θαυμαστός. In 2 Macc. 4:22 and probably 4:49 we should read μεγαλομερῶς instead of μεγαλοπρεπῶς. Outside the Ps. Θ has the noun once at Is. 35:2 with ref. to God for הָדָר.[1]

---

[1] Cf. Schl. Theol. d. Judt., 4.
[2] The last two paragraphs are by Bertram.
μεγαλοπρεπής. [1] This paragraph is by Bertram.

In the NT we have only the one occurrence at 2 Pt. 1:17: ... ὑπὸ τῆς μεγαλοπρεποῦς δόξης ..., for God: "He received from God the Father honour and glory, when there came such a voice to him from the excellent glory." There is a similar use for God in Test. L. 3:4: ... ἡ μεγάλη δόξα ὑπεράνω πάσης ἁγιότητος; Eth. En. 14:20: the great majesty. The term is closely parallel to μεγάλη δύναμις.

† μεγαλύνω.

This is a verb derived from μέγας, [1] and it means "to make great," "to magnify," e.g., τοὺς πολεμίους, Thuc., V, 98; τὴν δύναμιν, Diod. S., I, 20, 6; τὰ κράσπεδα (τῶν ἱματίων), Mt. 23:5; μεγαλυνῶ τὸ ὄνομά σου, Gn. 12:2; τί γάρ ἐστιν ἄνθρωπος, ὅτι ἐμεγάλυνας αὐτόν, Job 7:17; cf. ψ 19:6; 103:24; also in a spiritual and moral sense ἀπῄει μεγαλυνόμενος ὑπὸ τῶν ἐπαίνων, Plut. Lycurgus, 14 (I, 48a): ... καθὼς ἐμεγαλύνθη ἡ ψυχή τοῦ σήμερον ..., οὕτως μεγαλυνθείη ἡ ψυχή μου ἐνώπιον κυρίου, 1 Βασ. 26:24: ἐμεγάλυνας τὴν δικαιοσύνην σου, Gn. 19:19; also "to magnify with words," "to extol," τὸ Πενθέως ὄνομα, Eur. Ba., 320; τὸ δίκαιον ... μεγαλύνων, Plut. Lysander, 7 (I, 437a); μεγαλυνθείη τὸ ὄνομά σου ἕως αἰῶνος, 2 Βασ. 7:26; ... μεγαλυνθήτω ὁ κύριος, ψ 34:27.

The Heb. original is normally the root גדל; only occasionally do we find another verb. Thus גבר hi. "to show strength (with the tongue)" = "to speak arrogantly," Ps. 12:5; פלא pi. "to fulfil a vow" (?), Nu. 15:3, 8; רבב, "to be manifold," Ps. 104:24; רבה "to become much," Gn. 43:34; Aram. pe. "to become great," pa "to make great," Da. 2:48 etc. in Θ, also שׂרר, "to rule," Prv. 8:16 of the μεγιστᾶνες. The LXX goes its own way in Ju. 5:13. In Mi. 1:10 גדל seems to be presupposed; μεγαλύνειν has here the sense "to boast of." [2]

In the NT Mt. 23:5 ("to make great," "to enlarge"); Lk. 1:58 (ἐμεγάλυνεν κύριος τὸ ἔλεος αὐτοῦ μετ' αὐτῆς); Ac. 5:13 ("to extol," namely, the apostles). It can also mean "to extol," "to praise" in Lk. 1:46: μεγαλύνει ἡ ψυχή μου τὸν κύριον (in the Magnificat); ... μεγαλυνόντων τὸν θεόν, Ac. 10:46; ἐμεγαλύνετο τὸ ὄνομα τοῦ κυρίου Ἰησοῦ, Ac. 19:17. In the last two cases the context suggests μέγας acclamations on the proclamation or experience of mighty divine acts. Phil. 1:20: ὡς πάντοτε καὶ νῦν μεγαλυνθήσεται Χριστὸς ἐν τῷ σώματί μου, εἴτε διὰ ζωῆς εἴτε διὰ θανάτου. The whole life of Paul is a magnifying of Christ, and his death as well. Herein he sees the meaning of life. This praise is accomplished through his life — the ἐν is instrumental — which he has placed in the service of Christ and which he can also sacrifice for Him. In such a life the κύριος Ἰησοῦς is efficacious action.

In 2 C. 10:15 Paul hopes that he will be magnified in the Corinthians (ἐν ὑμῖν μεγαλυνθῆναι ...) with the growth of their faith. "He will become great in them by the fact that he can unite the congregation and confirm it in the knowledge of God." [3]

μεγαλύνω. [1] Cf. E. Fraenkel, *Griech. Denominativa* (1906), 36, 63 f.; A. Debrunner, *Indogermanische Forschungen*, 21 (1907), 73 ff.; Gr. Wortb. (1917), 113.
[2] This paragraph is by Bertram.
[3] Schl. K., 625.

† μεγαλωσύνη.

μεγαλωσύνη,[1] biblical Gk. meaning "loftiness," "majesty," e.g., δότε μεγαλωσύνην τῷ θεῷ ἡμῶν, Dt. 32:3; Sir. 39:15; cf. also: ... κατὰ τὴν μεγαλωσύνην τοῦ βραχίονός σου ... ψ 78:11; cf. Prv. 18:10; Ep. Ar., 192.

The word is used in the NT for the divine name: ἐκάθισεν ἐν δεξιᾷ τῆς μεγαλωσύνης ἐν ὑψηλοῖς, Hb. 1:3; also 8:1; it occurs, too, in the great doxology in Jd. 24 f.: ... δόξα μεγαλωσύνη κράτος ...

† μέγεθος.[1]

μέγεθος is the noun of μέγας and means "greatness," whether physical or spiritual: μέγεθος λαμβάνειν, "to become great," "to grow," Xenoph. Cyrop., I, 4, 3. It can also, like μέγας, take on the sense of "power": ἔρωτος μεγέθει πάντα ἐπέχοντος, Xenoph. Sym., 8, 1. In Plut. Alex., 14 (I, 671e) it means Diogenes' "greatness of soul."[1] τὸ μέγεθος τοῦ θεοῦ ("the greatness of God") on an inscr.[2] In the LXX: μεγέθει βραχίονός σου ἀπολιθωθήτωσαν, Ex. 15:16; δέκα πήχεων μέγεθος, 3 Βασ. 6:23.

In the LXX μέγεθος usually means "height" or "growth," and is used almost exclusively for קוֹמָה, once for גֹּבַהּ. Only at Ex. 15:16 is גָּדֹל the original. Here and in 2 Macc. 15:24 the greatness of God's arm is a symbol of His power. In Wis. 6:7 the ref. is to the greatness of the earthly ruler, and in 13:5 the greatness and beauty of creation are adduced in proof of God. The difficult verse Bar. 2:18 possibly refers to the fallen greatness of Israel.

At Prv. 18:10 an unknown translator renders מִגְדַּל־עֹז שֵׁם יְהוָה, not like the LXX: ἐκ μεγαλωσύνης ἰσχύος ὄνομα κυρίου, but by the materially better: ἐκ μεγέθους ἔργων (ʼΑΘ: πύργος κράτους, "a safe tower"). At Qoh. 2:9 Σ has μεγέθει ὑπερέβαλον for גדל instead of the LXX ἐμεγαλύνθην. At Is. 37:24 ΣΘ have μέγεθος for קוֹמָה. The ref. is to the height of the cedars.[3]

The word occurs in the NT at Eph. 1:19: καὶ τί τὸ ὑπερβάλλον μέγεθος τῆς δυνάμεως αὐτοῦ εἰς ἡμᾶς ...,[4] to describe the content of Paul's petition, which is that the community may know the outstanding greatness of the power of God.

Grundmann

μεγαλωσύνη. [1] Abstract nouns in -σύνη are common in Hell. Gk., cf. Bl.-Debr. § 110, 2; Debr. Gr. Wortb., 162; P. Chantraine, *La formation des noms* (1933), 212 f.; in the NT cf. ἁγιωσύνη, ἀγαθωσύνη, ταπεινοφροσύνη etc. The last of these is also found in Joseph. and Epict., and there are instances of ἁγιωσύνη outside the Bible. Cf. Nägeli, 43; Moult.-Mill., *s.v.* [Bertram].

μέγεθος. [1] On the mathematical sense cf. the dict.

[2] W. M. Ramsay, *Cities and Bishoprics of Phrygia*, I, 2 (1897), 700, No. 635, 4.

[3] The last two paragraphs are by Bertram.

[4] The third in the clauses introduced by τίς, τί (τίς ... ἡ ἐλπίς ... τίς ὁ πλοῦτος τῆς δόξης ... τί τὸ ... μέγεθος τῆς δυνάμεως), dependent on ... εἰς τὸ εἰδέναι.

† μέθη, † μεθύω, † μέθυσος † μεθύσκομαι

A. The Word Group outside the New Testament.

All these words are mostly used a. in the lit. sense. μεθύω, "to be drunk," Hom. Od., 18, 240; Pind. Fr., 128 (90): ὄφρα σὺν Χειμάρῳ μεθύων, Eur. Cyc., 535; Epict. Diss., III, 1, 16; P. Hal., I, 193 f.; the opp. is νήφω, Plat. Resp., III, 395e (μεθύοντας ἢ καὶ νήφοντας); Aristot. Pol., II, 12, p. 1274b, 19 f.: τὸ τοὺς μεθύοντας, ἂν τυπτήσωσι, πλείω ζημίαν ἀποτίνειν τῶν νηφόντων, Epict. Gnom. Stob., 25 (35). Hence μεθύσκω means "to intoxicate," "to make drunk," mostly pass. "to get drunk," Hdt., I, 133; Xenoph. Cyrop., I, 3, 11: πίνων οὐ μεθύσκεται, Plat. Symp., 176c; 203b: μεθυσθεὶς τοῦ νέκταρος.

μέθυσος, "drunk" (with wine). In early lit. use is restricted to the feminine sex, Aristoph. Nu., 555: γραῦν μεθύσην, but from Menand. it is used of both, Menand. in Athen., X (p. 442d): πάντας μεθύσους τοὺς ἐμπόρους ποιεῖ τὸ Βυζάντιον, Plut. Brutus, 5, 2 (I, 986b): κράτει, μέθυσε, Luc. Tim., 55: μέθυσος καὶ πάροινος, P. Oxy., XV, 1828, 3, where μέθυσος occurs with κατάλαλος, ψεύστης, πλεονέκτης, ἀποστερητής in a kind of list of vices.

μέθη, "drink," P. Giess., 3, 8, mostly "over-rich drinking," Plat. Resp., IX, 571c: ἢ σίτων ἢ μέθης πλησθέν, often "intoxication," "drunkenness": Hdt., V, 20: καλῶς ἔχοντας ὑμέας ὁρέω μέθης, Xenoph. Cyrop., IV, 2, 40; Soph. Oed. Tyr., 779: ἀνὴρ γὰρ ἐν δείπνοις μ' ὑπερπλησθεὶς μέθῃ, Democr. Fr., 159 (II, 175, 23, Diels[5]); Plat. Symp., 176e: μὴ διὰ μέθης ποιήσασθαι τὴν ... συνουσίαν, ἀλλ' οὕτω ... πρὸς ἡδονήν, Plat. Phaedr., 256c: ἐν μέθαις, Aristot. Pol., II, 12, p. 1274b, 11: ἔτι δ' ὁ περὶ τὴν μέθην νόμος, Epict. Diss., III, 26, 5: διαρραγέντας ὑπὸ ἀπεψιῶν καὶ μέθης (bursting with undigested delicacies and drunkenness); cf., IV, 2, 7.[1] In Plat. Leg., I, 637-650 "drinking" is a means of education to test and develop σωφροσύνη.[2] For Plotin. intoxication with nectar (μεθυσθεὶς τοῦ νέκταρος), on the basis of Plat. Phaedr. and Symp., is used to describe the state of mystical enthusiasm and union with the deity, Enn., VI, 7, 30 and 35; cf. V, 8, 10; III, 5, 9.

In oriental-Hellenistic Gnosticism we often hear of dreams and intoxication in connection with ἀγνωσία (just as watchfulness and sobriety belong to γνῶσις): ὦ λαοί, ἄνδρες γηγενεῖς, οἱ μέθῃ καὶ ὕπνῳ ἑαυτοὺς ἐκδεδωκότες [καὶ] τῇ ἀγνωσίᾳ τοῦ θεοῦ, νήψατε, παύσασθε δὲ κραιπαλῶντες [καὶ] θελγόμενοι ὕπνῳ ἀλόγῳ Corp. Herm., I, 27 (= Reitzenstein Poim., 337, 7 ff.).[3] Men should be roused from the stupor of ignorance.[4] In the Od. Sol. 11:8 the drunkenness brought about by the water

μέθη κτλ. [1] A common theme in Stoic ethics.

[2] Wine kindles the emotions and gives self-reliance, though drunkenness reduces to childish helplessness, Plat. Resp., IX, 573b c; Leg., I, 645e, 646a. A reasonable use of wine makes a man mellow and receptive to good influences, Leg., II, 666b c.

[3] Cf. J. Kroll, *Die Lehren des Hermes Trismegistos* (= *Beiträge zur Gesch. d. Philos. d. Mittelalters*) (1914), 376 ff.; Dib. Th. on 1 Th. 5:6.

[4] In Corp. Herm., VII, 2 μεθύειν denotes the walk of the carnal man, while νήφειν is used for ecstatic vision.

of the logos is contrasted with the μέθη τῆς ἀγνωσίας. The fig. sense b. (except for μέθυσος, which is never employed thus) occurs as follows: μεθύω, Xenoph. Sym., 8, 21; μεθύοντα ὑπὸ τῆς Ἀφροδίτης, Plat. Lys., 222c: μεθύομεν ὑπὸ τοῦ λόγοι (discussion, enquiry); Oppian Cyn., 2, 576: δέμας ὕπνοισιν μεθύοντες (drunk with sleep).

Cf. also μεθύσκω, Plat. Resp., VIII, 562d: ἀκράτου αὐτῆς (= τῆς ἐλευθερίας), Plut. Quaest. Conv., VII, 5 (II, 704d): τὴν μουσικὴν παντὸς οἴνου μᾶλλον μεθύσκουσαν, also μέθη, Plat. Leg., I, 639b: κἂν δειλὸς ὢν ἐν τοῖς δεινοῖς ὑπὸ μέθης τοῦ φόβου ναυτιᾷ (frenzy of fear).

In the LXX all the words occur a. in the lit. sense. Thus μεθύω, Gn. 9:21; 1 Βασ. 1:13 f.; 2 Βασ. 11:13; Is. 19:14; 28:1; Jl. 1:5; 1 Macc. 16:16 etc. μεθύω can also be used for what is dry being blessedly saturated with moisture (rain), Is. 55:10; ψ 64:10; Sir. 39:22. μεθύσκω occurs with οἴνῳ in Prv. 23:31: μὴ μεθύσκεσθε οἴνῳ, Test. Jud. 14:1. μέθυσος is used for the drunkard in Prv. 23:21; 26:9; Sir. 19:1; 26:8; 4 Macc. 2:7 (here with γαστρίμαργος, the "glutton"). μέθη means drunkenness in Is. 28:7; Ez. 23:33; Jdt. 13:15 (ἐν ταῖς μέθαις); Tob. 4:15 (οἶνον εἰς μέθην μὴ πίῃς); Prv. 20:1; Sir. 31:30. Joseph. has μεθύσκομαι in the lit. sense in Bell., 2, 29; Vit., 225, and μεθύω in Bell., 6, 196; Ant., 8, 376. b. In the fig. sense we do not find μέθυσος or μέθη, but for μεθύσκω cf. Is. 34:5: ἐμεθύσθη ἡ μάχαιρά μου ἐν τῷ οὐρανῷ, Ιερ. 28:39, 57; αἷμα is often the intoxicating drink, Is. 34:7; 49:26; Ιερ. 26:10; ψ 35:8: μεθυσθήσονται ἀπὸ ποιότητος τοῦ οἴκου σου, Cant. 5:1 (ἔπιον οἶνόν μου for bridal love); Na. 3:11 (καὶ σὺ μεθυσθήσῃ of the cup of divine wrath), also Is. 51:21. Fig. μεθύσκω can often be used for a refreshing drink, e.g., Ιερ. 38:14: μεθύσω τὴν ψυχὴν τῶν ἱερέων υἱῶν Λευι, "I will refresh the souls of the priests"; 38:25: ἐμέθυσα πᾶσαν ψυχὴν διψῶσαν, in the sense of Hellen. mysticism.[5] Fig. wine can denote an antinomian impulse when παράνομος is added, Prv. 4:17: οἴνῳ δὲ παρανόμῳ (of the wine of life contrary to the Law, par. to the preceding σῖτα ἀσεβείας) μεθύσκονται.[6]

In Philo[7] we find only μεθύω and μέθη, a. in the lit. sense. Plant., 163 speaks of μεθύειν as follows: ἀπὸ τούτου γέ τοί φασιν τὸ μεθύειν ὠνομάσθαι, ὅτι μετὰ τὸ θύειν ἔθος ἦν τοῖς πρότερον οἰνοῦσθαι. It thus follows, ὅτι τὸ μεθύειν ἦν τὸ οἰνοῦσθαι, Plant., 174, that μεθύειν means to get drunk with wine; cf. Plant., 139 ff.; 154; 174; Jos., 45; Fug., 166; Ebr., 27 and 206. Hence the opp. is νήφειν, Plant., 172; Poster. C., 175. Similarly μέθη means "intoxication" (μεθύων ... μέθην, Fug., 166). Philo wrote a whole work under the title περὶ μέθης (de ebrietate). Wine and drunkenness belong together (ἐν οἴνῳ καὶ μέθῃ), Vit. Mos., I, 270, and μέθη is for him δημιουργὸς κακῶν, Sobr., 2, the cause of ἔκστασις and παραφροσύνη, Ebr., 15. Like sleep (ὕπνος), this μεθύειν is the mark and symbol of the blind and ignorant man who is sunk in the material world, while the man of vision is sober (νήφων), Som., II, 101 f., cf. 162; Plant., 177; Ebr., 154 f. μέθη means ἀναισθησία in the body and ἄγνοια in the soul, 154. Yet Philo commends μέθη and μεθύειν for the wise man as the drinking of wine, not to excess (ἄδην) nor unmixed (ἄκρατον), Plant., 162 f., but with moderation and joy, since this leads to peace and the coming of the soul to itself (μεθέσεως ψυχῆς αἰτία γίγνεται), 165, and enables one to enjoy relaxation, rest and cheerfulness, 166. This "intoxication" does not harm virtue, but the effect of μεθύειν depends on the one who drinks, whether he is of the ἀγαθοί or the φαῦλοι, 172.[8] Philo also uses μεθύειν and μέθη b. in the fig. sense. He not only distinguishes διττὴν μεθύοντας μέθην, τὴν μὲν ἀσεβείᾳ, τὴν δὲ οἴνῳ, Spec. Leg., III, 126, or Vit. Mos., II, 162: μέθη ... ἐξ οἴνου ... καὶ ἀφροσύνης, but he also knows another divine

---

[5] → II, 227 f.

[6] J. Hempel, *Mystik u. Alkoholekstase* (1926); H. Schmidt, *Die Alkoholfrage im AT* (1926).

[7] H. Lewy, "Sobria ebrietas," ZNW *Beih.*, 9 (1929).

[8] Cf. Ebr., 27, 125 f., 128 ff., 138, 151 f.; Som., II, 160, 192, 200; Plant., 147 ff.

intoxication which is independent of wine. In Vit. Mos., I, 187, in the account of the changing of the bitter spring into a sweet spring by Moses, he speaks of the grateful joy of the people: μεθύοντες οὐ τὴν ἐν οἴνῳ μέθην ἀλλὰ τὴν νηφάλιον, ἣν ... λαβόντες παρὰ τῆς εὐσεβείας, and he thus differentiates this sober intoxication from drunkenness with wine. In Leg. All., I, 84 he again speaks of gratitude: μεθύει τὴν νήφουσαν μέθην. Acc. to Leg. All., III, 82 Melchizedek helps to θείᾳ μέθη νηφαλεωτέρᾳ νήφεως αὐτῆς. He compares the drunkenness of the toper with the sober ecstasy of the ascetic in Omn. Prob. Lib., 12 f.; Op. Mund., 71 (μέθῃ νηφαλίῳ κατασχεθείς), making use here of Platonic images and concepts; in Vit. Cont., 89 ff. he describes the beautiful intoxication (μεθυσθέντες ... τὴν καλὴν ταύτην μέθην) of the ascetic therapeutae when they worship the sun with hands outstetched to heaven. He uses a favourite expression νηφάλιος μέθη ("sober intoxication") to extol the union of the soul with deity, alluding to ecstatic forms cultivated in the Dionysus cult by the drinking of wine.

B. The Word Group in the New Testament.

1. In the NT we find μέθυσος ("drunkard") only in the lists of vices in 1 C. 5:11 and 6:10, and μέθη ("drunkenness") only in similar lists (along with κῶμοι, "excessive feastings") in R. 13:13; Gl. 5:21.

2. μεθύω and μεθύσκομαι are mostly used lit. in the NT for "to be drunk" and "to get drunk." μεθύσκομαι is used with no ethical or religious judgment in Jn. 2:10 in connection with the rule [9] that the poorer wine is served only when the guests have drunk well. In 1 Th. 5:6 Paul admonishes the community not to live indifferently in all kinds of vices (the stupor of sins), but, with a sense of the imminence of the *parousia*, to be awake in a sanctified life. To fill out the picture he demands sobriety, and issues a special warning against the tension which might easily be caused by eschatological expectation. [10] This twofold demand [11] is based on the fact that Christians live in the dawn of the new aeon which has arrived with the resurrection of Jesus. They live in the day of Christ, so that what belongs to the night must be alien to them. In this connection he interposes in v. 7 an appeal to the common fact of experience that those who are drunk are drunk in the night. [12] In the parable in Mt. 24:45-51 = Lk. 12:42-46 the Christian attitude, alertness on the basis of inward reconstitution, is depicted in terms of a wise and faithful steward, with whom is contrasted the bad servant who does not live in eschatological tension or in integration into the divine rule, and who thus on the one side loses himself in a life of violent egoism, and on the other side, in corruption of natural needs, falls victim to hedonistic license in μεθύειν (Mt. 24:49), μεθύσκεσθαι (Lk. 12:45). Here μεθύειν is radically condemned. μεθύσκεσθαι is ruled out by eschatological possession and eschatological certainty. But it is also ruled out because the early Christian is filled with the Spirit. Paul censures the Corinthians in 1 C. 11:21. They destroy the fellowship of the Lord's Supper. The rich separate themselves from the poor, and some are hungry while others are swollen with excess and drunk with wine. The important point here — in opposition to the Dionysus cult which was well established at Corinth — is that

[9] ZNW, 14 (1913), 248 ff.
[10] Dob. Th., *ad loc.*
[11] → 546.
[12] There is no reason here to take μεθύσκεσθαι and μεθύειν in a spiritual sense, as suggested by A. Schaefer, *Die Bücher d. NT*, I (1890), *ad loc.*

intoxication and the Lord's Supper are incompatible. In contrast to the Dionysus cult, μεθύειν is not only no part of the celebration; it makes a Christian celebration impossible. Dionysiac intoxication and πνευματικὸν πόμα (1 C. 10:4) are irreconcilably opposed. Hence Peter in his Pentecost sermon must resist as strongly as possible any suspicion of μεθύειν (Ac. 2:15). If the spiritually controlled speech of the disciples is unintelligible to unbelievers, and gives the impression of intoxication, the power of the Spirit of God has nothing whatever to do with drunkenness with wine. The fundamental difference between early Christian fulness of the Spirit and the orgiastic enthusiasm of Hellenism is indicated in Eph. 5:18. The life and liturgy of Christians are not marked by sensual ecstasy or Bacchantic frenzy (μεθύσκεσθαι οἴνῳ) [13] but by infilling with the Spirit (πληροῦσθε ἐν πνεύματι). The distinction could hardly be more succinctly expressed: orgiastic enthusiasm on the one side, and on the other the fulness of the Spirit which finds liturgical expression in praise and thanksgiving (5:18-20) and practical expression in ἀγάπη (5:21-6:9). In this respect Paul emphasises explicitly the fact that μεθύσκεσθαι is not the result of ἀγνωσία, as the Hermetic writings and Philo suppose, but of ἀσωτία, i.e., a corrupt and profligate nature.

3. The two terms are used figuratively in Rev. In 17:2 the inhabitants of earth are accused of being drunk with the wine of their whoredom, i.e., idolatry. There can be no doubt that μεθύσκεσθαι is used symbolically here, though the vividness of the image is fully grasped only if we also catch an allusion to the orgiastic nature of Hellenistic cults. μεθύω is unequivocally metaphorical in 17:6. Here in the familiar LXX figure (→ 546) the woman (the epitome of the demonic and ungodly world) is drunk with the blood of the saints and the blood of the witnesses of Jesus.

Preisker

μεθοδία → ὁδός.

[13] The very fact that the admonition is set in the context of the cultus (5:19) means that we have to think, not simply of the exalted feelings of the natural man (Haupt Gefbr.), but of the Hellenistic cults and their enthusiasm.

† μέλας

μέλας, a commonly used adj. from Homer, "black," "dark," the opp. of → λευκός, like all terms for colour fairly elastic in meaning, so that it might indicate "dark red," "dark blue," "dark grey" etc. (e.g., μέλας οἶνος; μέλας πόντος, μέλαν αἷμα), the colour of hair (in youth), of sun-burned skin, the hides of animals etc.[1] It is common in a fig. sense. For the men of antiquity black (cf. the Lat. *niger, ater*) means sinister, dreadful, terrible, sad, unlucky, hence μέλας θάνατος (already Hom. Il., 2, 834; Od., 12, 92), μέλας φόνος, μέλαν ὄναρ, μέλαινα ἀνάγκη, also of the disposition etc.[2] Black has a cultic role,[3] and is widespread as the colour of mourning (already Eur. Alc., 427: μελαμπέπλῳ στολῇ).[4] The neut. subst. τὸ μέλαν, "black colour," "blackness," is found from Plato for the ink made up of sepia or soot; it would be more like Indian ink.[5]

Black had the same meaning in the Israelite and Judaean world of culture.[6] It should be specially noted, however, that it had no part in the cultus.[7] The Heb. words for "black," "dark," are חוּם, only at Gn. 30:32 f., 35, 40, rendered φαιός ("blackish" or "grey") in the LXX (Gn. 30:40 ποικίλος), also שָׁחֹר: Lv. 13:31, 37 of dark hair, also

---

μέλας. G. Radke, *Die Bedeutung der weissen u. schwarzen Farbe in Kult u. Brauch d. Griechen u. Römer*, Diss. Berlin (1936); older bibl., 5 ff.

1 Cf. Pass. and Liddell-Scott, *s.v.* Rare in inscr. (cf. Ditt. Syll.³, Index, *s.v.*), though common in pap.: Preisigke Wört., II, 64 and Moult.-Mill., 395, *s.v.* On Μέλας as a name for persons and rivers, cf. Pauly-W., XV, 1 (1931), 437 ff., on Μέλαινα as a name, *ibid.*, 384 ff. Cf. also → n. 21.

2 Cf. the dict. and the review in F. J. Dölger, "Die Sonne der Gerechtigkeit u. der Schwarze. Eine religionsgesch. Studie zum Taufgelöbnis" (*Liturgiegesch. Forschungen, Heft* 2) (1918), 58 ff., esp. the note "that the equation μέλας = κακός, πονηρός seems to have been very common and virtually self-evident in the language of ancient culture," 61.

3 Radke discusses "black as the colour of the night and the chthonic deities, also as the colour of harmful demons" (14 ff.). He also discusses "the use of black in sacrifice" (27 ff.), "black as an unfavourable omen" (33 ff.), and "the apotropaic significance of the colour black" (51 ff.). Cf. S. Eitrem, "Opferritus u. Voropfer d. Griech. u. Röm." (*Videnskaps-Akademi-Skrifter, Kristiania,* II. *Hist.-Filos. Klasse* [1914], No. 1) (1915), 490, Index, *s.v.* "Schwartz," esp. 401. In superstition and magic the observation of black was of supreme significance (milk from a black cow, the horn of a black ram etc.), e.g., Preis. Zaub, I, 5 and 58 f.; II, 46; IV, 165 ff., 403, 673 ff., 909, 2052, 2551, 3117 f., 3149; VII, 327, 433, 539; XII, 108; XIII, 129 and 687.

4 Cf. Radke, 69 ff.; G. Wilke, Art. "Totenkultus: B. Europa § 9" in *Reallexikon d. Vorgeschichte,* XIII (1929), 411; G. Herzog-Hauser, Art. "Trauerkleidung" in Pauly-W., 2. *Reihe,* VI, 2 (1937), 2225 ff.

5 Cf. Pass. and Liddell-Scott, *s.v.* The use is also well attested in the pap.: Preisigke Wört. and Moult.-Mill.; Mayser, II, 1 (1926), 3 f. The expression μέλαν γραφικόν is later. For a full discussion of all questions relating to the composition and use of inks in antiquity cf. O. Roller, "Das Formular der paul. Briefe" (BWANT, 4. *Folge, Heft,* 6 [1933], 6 f. and 268 ff., n. 32 ff. In the magic pap. we have recipes for magical colours mixed with the blood of animals, Preis. Zaub., IV, 2109 ff., 2207, 2393 f.; XXXVI, 72; the addition of myrrh was very common, II, 34 f.; XII, 399; XIII, 322 (hence commonly σμυρνόμελαν, "ink of myrrh": I, 233; II, 30; IV, 3212; VII, 468 and 521; XIII, 409; XXXVI, 103 etc.; cf. also I, 8; V, 309 f.).

6 K. Galling, Art. "Farbe" and "Färberei" in *Biblisches Reallexikon* (1937), 150 ff.

7 F. Delitzsch (Lotz), Art. "Farben in der Bibel" in RE³, V (1898), 755 ff., esp. 759 f.

Cant. 5:11 of raven dark (ὡς κόραξ) hair, 1:5 of sun-burnt skin, Zech. 6:2, 6 of (apocalyptic) black horses; in all these verses the LXX has μέλας, only in Lv. 13:31 is there another rendering under the influence of 13:32 (cf. also Prv. 23:29 vl. for μέλας). μελανοῦσθαι is also found in the LXX at Job 30:30 (vl. for ἐσκότωται); Cant. 1:6; Ep. Jer. 20 (cf. also the other renderings at Job 30:30; Ez. 9:2, 11). At Jer. 36:18 we have the Heb. דְיוֹ for ink or Indian ink; the LXX does not translate this at Ιερ. 43:18.[8]

Philo often uses μέλας in the antithesis black and white (for examples → 243 f.). In a series of other passages we find the view that ὁ ἀήρ, which acc. to the Stoic distinction between the sub-lunar and the heavenly region (shared by Philo) is the air between the earth and the moon (as distinct from the αἰθήρ), is black (μέλας), which has here the sense of dark or dark red, since the use of hyacinth colour in the cultus is explained in this way in the description of the temple curtains in Vit. Mos., II (III), 88 and the vesture of the high-priest in Spec. Leg., I, 85 and 94; cf. also Congr., 117. Hence it is said also of light in Abr., 205: τὸ φῶς ἐν οὐρανῷ μὲν ἄκρατον καὶ ἀμιγὲς σκότους ἐστίν, ἐν δὲ τοῖς ὑπὸ σελήνην ἀέρι ζοφερῷ κεκραμένον φαίνεται. The spots on the moon are also explained in this way in Som., I, 145: τό γε ἐμφαινόμενον αὐτῇ (sc. τῇ σελήνῃ) μέλαν, ὃ καλοῦσί τινες πρόσωπον, οὐδὲν ἄλλο εἶναι ἢ τὸν ἀναμεμιγμένον ἀέρα, ὃς κατὰ φύσιν μέλας ὢν ἄχρις οὐρανοῦ τείνεται. Philo (cf. already Abr., 205) thus comes to equate ἀήρ and → σκότος: God called ἀέρος ἰδέαν σκότος, ἐπειδὴ μέλας ὁ ἀὴρ τῇ φύσει, Op. Mund., 29.[9] Distinctive is the attempt in Leg. All., II, 67, in exposition of Nu. 12, to find in the Ethiopian whom Moses married τὴν ἀμετάβλητον καὶ κατακορῆ γνώμην, the immutable and pure mind (as the seer is black of eye, so the spiritual seer is called an Ethiopian).[10] Joseph. mentions, e.g., in Ant., 16, 233, the art of dyeing the hair black (→ 247, n. 37), and also the black clothes of an accused person, Ant., 14, 172; Bell., 1, 506 (→ 245 and n. 23), or of one burdened with debt, or of a person asking for grace, Ant., 16, 267; Vit., 138; cf. also the black of mourning in Ant., 16, 287 and Bell., 4, 260. The preference for mourning clothes of black is also attested in Rabb. sources.[11] For the rest, the use of black is much the same as elsewhere. Hair is dark in youth,[12] worn coins, esp. of silver, are called black,[13] dark wine is black wine,[14] etc. The loan word מילן (= μέλαν) is sometimes used as well as the OT דְיוֹ (דיותא) for "ink" or "Indian ink."[15]

---

[8] Only a few minusc. add ἐν μέλανι, cf. E. Nestle, *Das Buch Jer. gr. u. hbr.* (1925), *ad loc.*

[9] Cf. Dölger, 50 f. Though the full seriousness of the biblical concept σκότος is not perhaps expressed in Philo, the equation of ἀήρ and σκότος is to be noted in expounding e.g., Eph. 2:2; 6:12. Cf. Apc. Pt. 21: οἱ κολάζοντες ἄγγελοι σκοτεινὸν εἶχον τὸ ἔνδυμα κατὰ τὸν ἀέρα τοῦ τόπου.

[10] Is the explanation to be sought in the fact that κατακορής is used in the sense of pure or unmixed as well as thick or dark (of colour), so that Philo was here able to make the desired equation of black and pure? Elsewhere Ethiopians are mentioned only in a derogatory sense in respect of their colour (Dölger, 52 ff.). Xenophanes Fr., 16 (I, 133, 6 f., Diels[5]) says: "The Ethiopians have gods with blunt noses and black, the Thracians with blue eyes and red hair."

[11] S. Krauss, *Talmudische Archäologie*, I (1910), 145, 550, n. 211; II (1911), 71; Str.-B., I, 506. On black clothes at the last day cf. → 245. We also find black as the colour of mourning in the readings of Test. Sol. 20:19 which change τεθλιμμένον καὶ πενθοῦντα into κατὰ πένθος καὶ μελανῷ (or μεμελασμένῳ) προσώπῳ.

[12] Krauss, I, 191 and 641, n. 815 f.

[13] *Ibid.*, II, 410.

[14] I. Löw, *Die Flora der Juden*, I, 1 (1926), 97.

[15] Krauss, III (1912), 148 f., 309 f.; *Griech. u. lat. Lehnwörter im Talmud, Midrasch u. Targum*, II (1899), 336 (here, and I [1898], 79 and 132 also on μέλαινα and μελάνη as loan words in Rabb. writings); Str.-B., III, 499 ff.

In the NT μέλας is comparatively rare. We see here something of the influence of OT restraint in the use of the colour (→ 549).

In Mt. 5:36, in a saying of Jesus, we have a reference to black or white hair as a mark of youth or age (→ 247). Black hardly ever occurs as an apocalyptic colour. Rev. 6:5 : ἵππος μέλας, is influenced by Zech. 6:2, 6 (→ III, 337 ff.; IV, 250, n. 65). In Rev. 6:12 we read : ὁ ἥλιος ἐγένετο μέλας ὡς σάκκος τρίχινος; this image for the darkening of the sun (cf. also Mt. 24:29 : ὁ ἥλιος σκοτισθήσεται) finds no exact equivalent in the OT (cf. Am. 8:9; Jl. 2:10; 2:31; Is. 13:10; Ez. 32:7 f.), though σάκκος is used in the same way at Is. 50:3 : καὶ ἐνδύσω τὸν οὐρανὸν σκότος καὶ θήσω ὡς σάκκον τὸ περιβόλαιον αὐτοῦ, and the use of σάκκος in Rev. 6:12 (cf. 11:3 and Mt. 11:21 par. Lk. 10:13) is controlled by the fact that σάκκος (loan word from the Semitic : Heb. שַׂק) was a Jewish mourning garment.[16] μέλαν is used for "ink" in 2 C. 3:3,[17] also 2 Jn. 12 and 3 Jn. 13.[18]

In the post-apost. fathers 1 Cl., 8, 3, in a paraphrase of OT passages, says of ἁμαρτίαι : ἐὰν ὦσιν ... μελανώτεραι σάκκου (→ n. 16). In relation to Rev. (→ *supra*), it is interesting that only in Herm. does black become a more definitely apocalyptic colour. In v., 4, 1, 10 (which continues the old four colour tradition of Zech. 1:8; 6:1 ff.; Rev. 6:1 ff.[19]) we read of the black colour of an apocalyptic beast ; in explanation of the colour it is said in v., 4, 3, 2 : τὸ μὲν μέλαν οὗτος ὁ κόσμος ἐστίν, ἐν ᾧ κατοικεῖτε. In s., 9, 1, 5 there is mention of the black hill ; of those who come from it, it is said in s., 9, 19, 1: τούτοις δὲ μετάνοια οὐκ ἔστι, θάνατος δὲ ἔστι, καὶ διὰ τοῦτο καὶ μέλανές εἰσιν· καὶ γὰρ τὸ γένος αὐτῶν ἄνομόν ἐστιν. In s., 9, 6, 4; 9, 8, 1 f. and 4 f. we find black = poor, unserviceable stones (= the unworthy) in the building of the tower. In s., 9, 9, 5; 9, 13, 8; 9, 15, 1 and 3 we read of twelve beautiful women in black garments (μέλανα or μέλανα ἱμάτια); these are equated with the twelve vices of the previous passage.[20] In s., 9, 1, 5 and 9, 6, 4 we have ὡς (or ὡσεὶ) ἀσβόλη, "black as pitch." It is in line with this usage that the devil is ὁ μέλας in Barn., 4, 9; cf. also 20, 1: ἡ δὲ τοῦ μέλανος ὁδός (notwithstanding 18:1: ἡ τοῦ σκότους sc. ὁδός we are not to assume the neut. τὸ μέλαν = τὸ σκότος but the masc. ὁ μέλας; cf. ἄγγελοι τοῦ σατανᾶ, 18, 1, and ὁ δὲ ἄρχων καιροῦ τοῦ νῦν τῆς ἀνομίας, 18, 2).[21]

Michaelis

---

16 The שַׂק, which left the upper body free (Galling, Art. "Kleidung," *op. cit.*, 337), more an apron (P. Thomsen, Art. "Kleidung : D. Palästina-Syrien," in *Reallexikon der Vorgeschichte*, VI [1926], 391), was made of coarse cloth and was mostly dark (cf. 1 Cl., 8, 3 : μελανώτεραι σάκκου). Wilke, *op. cit.*, 411 refers to the fact that there is other evidence that outmoded styles persisted in mourning clothes. On τρίχινος cf. Wbg. Mk., 42, n. 15. Cf. the (non-apocalyptic) Rabb. par. in Str.-B., I, 955 : "When the sun is like a sack, then arrows of hunger come into the world." On the astronomical explanation cf. Clemen, 142 ff., 385, 391.

17 Cf. Wnd. 2 K., *ad loc.*

18 Cf. Wnd. Kath. Br., *ad loc.*

19 Cf. Dib. Herm., *ad loc.* and Excurs.: "Die Tiervision."

20 Dib. Herm., *ad loc.* Here, too, an older tradition is worked over. On μέλανα, s., 9, 9, 5 cf. → 249, n. 52.

21 That in the comparison ὁ μέλας = ὁ → πονηρός (Barn., 4, 10; 2, 10) general ancient views of the colour black, and the idea of the black gods of death (esp. the black Dis), have had some influence, has been shown by Dölger, 49 ff., and has met with the approval of L. Ziehen, "Der Mysterienkult von Andania," ARW, 24 (1926), 29 ff., who on 48 ff. has investigated the question of the deities honoured under the names Μέλας, Μέλαινα.

† μέλι

μέλι, "honey," bee honey (cf. μέλισσα, "bee") from the time of Hom. [1] The possible ways of using honey — for the beginnings of beekeeping cf. Hom. Od., 13, 103 ff. — were extraordinarily rich in antiquity. Honey was the sugar of the ancients. [2] It was used in medicine and also in cosmetics, as a means of preservation. [3] Beekeeping was an important occupation, [4] and the trade in honey reached significant proportions. [5] Comparisons with honey, esp. on account of its sweetness, were common in proverb and poetry from the time of Hom. Il., 1, 249: τοῦ ἀπὸ γλώσσης μέλιτος γλυκίων ῥέεν αὐδή. [6] In the cultus, often with milk, honey played a great role as a gift to the dead with an apotropaic and cathartic character, then as an offering to the deities of death, then as a sacrifice to other gods, until finally it came to be regarded as the food of the gods and of the heavenly world. [7] What ideas were bound up with honey in popular use, and later in the piety of the mysteries, it is hard to say. [8] The fact that it was important in superstition and magic is in keeping with its general significance. [9]

In the OT honey is mentioned some 60 times. More than a third of the refs. are in the promise of the אֶרֶץ זָבַת חָלָב וּדְבָשׁ (LXX: γῆ ῥέουσα γάλα καὶ μέλι), Ex. 3:8, 17, many verses in the Pentateuch, Jos. 5:6; Sir. 46:8; Ιερ. 11:5; 39:22; Bar. 1:20; Ez. 20:6, 15. Many alien mythological ideas may underlie the expression, but, though Palestine was

μέλι. [1] Cf. Pass. and Liddell-Scott, *s.v.* In the pap. from the 3rd cent. B.C.: Preisigke Wört., II, 65, *s.v.* On the etym. (the root may be found in many languages) cf. Boisacq, 624; Walde-Pok., II, 296; M. Schuster, Art. "Mel" in Pauly-W., XV, 1 (1931), 364.

[2] Schuster, *op. cit.*, 372; 367, where there are further details on the kinds of honey, its gathering and preservation. Cf. also Olck, Art. "Biene" in Pauly-W., III (1899), 431 ff. and "Bienenzucht," 450 ff.

[3] Schuster, 372 ff. and G. Lafaye, Art. "Mel" in Daremberg-Saglio, III, 2, 1701 ff. For the medical use cf. also healing inscr., Ditt. Syll.[3], III, 1170, 15 ff. (Epidaurus); 1171, 15 (Aesculapius inscr. from Crete); 1173, 13 ff. (Aesculapius inscr. from Rome; cf. Deissmann LO, 108).

[4] Thus in Egypt beekeeping, while not a monopoly, was strongly under the influence of royal finance. Cf. Mitteis-Wilcken (I, 1), 252.

[5] Schuster, 378.

[6] Schuster, 382 f., with bibl. 383 f.

[7] On this development of the sacral use cf. S. Eitrem, "Opferritus u. Voropfer d. Griechen u. Römer," *Videnskaps-Akademie-Skrifter, Kristiania,* II. *Hist.-Filos. Kl.* (1914), No. 1 (1915), 102 ff. But cf. also H. Usener, "Milch u. Honig," *Rhein. Museum NF,* 57 (1902), 177 ff. (= *Kleine Schriften,* IV [1913], 398 ff.), who believes that the idea of honey as divine food was original, and who regards the giving of honey to the dead as their consecration to Elysium.

[8] Schuster, 381, takes too simple a view when he says that "honey represents symbolically the threshold of another world," nor can we merely take over the materials which Usener has made use of in his construction (→ n. 7). It would seem that to honey, as to milk (cf. Schlier in → I, 646), sacramental force was ascribed (cf. its use in Mithraism). In so far as it was used in Christian baptism (→ Schlier, I, 647) there is also obvious influence of the OT. It is no convincing explanation to say, as Schuster does (382), that in comparisons the poet and the seer were closely connected with the bee and honey "because they could enrapture men for a short time."

[9] For examples from lit. cf. Schuster, 383; cf. also F. J. Dölger, *Ichthys,* II (1922), 610, Index, *s.v.* Also Preis. Zaub., I, 5 and 20 (καὶ λαβὼν τὸ γάλα σὺν τῷ μέλιτι ἀπόπιε ... καὶ ἔσται τι ἔνθεον ἐν τῇ σῇ καρδίᾳ), 287; III, 325 and 426; IV, 755, 781, 908, 2192; VII, 192; XII, 215.

not a particularly fertile land, there was in fact a good deal of honey there (cf. Ep. Ar., 112 and Jos. Bell., 4, 469; Ez. 27:17, and Gn. 43:11, where it is an export).[10] In the OT verses in which it is used fig., we are to think of wild bees, for beekeeping came into Palestine only in the Hell. period. It is possible, however, that in some passages דְּבַשׁ[11] means the honey of grapes or fruit (cf. Arab. *dibs*).[12] In Fug., 138 Philo calls manna (divine wisdom) γλυκύτερον μέλιτος (cf. Ex. 16:31), and in what follows he expounds this allegorically. Again, in Det. Pot. Ins., 117 (in an exposition of Dt. 32:13) he compares the θεοῦ σοφία to sweet honey, and combines manna with it in 118. The rule in Lv. 2:11 that there is to be no leaven or honey in offerings he explains in Spec. Leg., I, 291 f. by saying that either the bee is ζῷον οὐ καθαρόν or that all superfluous joy is unholy.[13]

In the NT, Rev. 10:9 f. — where we have an intimation and description of what follows when the divine consumes the βιβλαρίδιον (→ I, 619; II, 695) — uses the comparison: γλυκὺ ὡς μέλι or ὡς μέλι γλυκύ. Though reconstructed independently, this draws on Ez. 3:1 ff., which in 3:3 contains the comparison: ὡς μέλι γλυκάζον (cf. Ju. 14:18; ψ 18:10; 118:103; Sir. 24:20; 49:1).[14]

Honey is also a means of nourishment. Thus in Mk. 1:6 par. Mt. 3:4 it is said of John the Baptist that he ate ἀκρίδας καὶ μέλι ἄγριον.[15] ἄγριον[16] rules out

---

[10] H. Guthe, Art. "Palästina," RE³, XIV (1904), 592; P. Thomsen, Art. "Biene: B Palästina-Syrien," *Reallexikon d. Vorgeschichte,* II (1925), 20. Honey plays only a slight role in the cultus (as an independent firstfruits only 2 Ch. 31:5). On "the land flowing with milk and honey" cf. the essays in *Mitteilungen u. Nachrichten d. Deutschen Palästina-Vereins* 1902 ff. (also → n. 12). E. Hahn, Art. "Honig" A. in *Reallexikon d. Vorgeschichte,* V (1926), 380 tries, not very cogently, to link the phrase with a Cretan Zeus cult. Cf. also K. Galling, Art. "Ackerwirtschaft" in *Bibl. Reallexikon* (1937), 2.

[11] The LXX always has μέλι for דְּבַשׁ apart from μελισσών at 1 Βασ. 14:25 f. (the only instance of μελισσών). Again, μέλι is always דְּבַשׁ, except for נֹפֶת (elsewhere κηρίον "honey-comb") at Prv. 5:3.

[12] It would be quite wrong to think that the ref. in the "land flowing with milk and honey" is to fruit honey rather than bee honey. S. Krauss, "Honig in Palästina," ZDPV, 32 (1909), 151 f. takes this view with appeal to Rabb. exposition; cf. also his *Talmudische Archäologie,* II (1911), 137, 147 ff.; I. Löw, *Die Flora d. Juden,* I, 1 (1926), 93. The Rabb. quotations in Krauss' essay have been examined by H. Hänsler, "Noch einmal 'Honig im hl. Lande'" in ZDPV, 35 (1912), 186 ff. It is not contested that much fruit honey (from dates, figs, carobs, grapes) was used in the Rabb. period. The compound οἰνόμελι ("honey wine") passed into the vocabulary of the Rabb. as the loan word אנומלין or יינומלין.

[13] That the Essenes esp. were beekeepers acc. to Philo (Krauss, *Talm. Arch.,* 523, n. 966) is an exaggeration of Eus. Praep., Ev., VIII, 11, 8: ἔνιοι δὲ σμήνη μελιττῶν ἐπιτροπεύουσιν (there is nothing corresponding in the depiction of the Essenes in Omn. Prob. Lib., 75 ff.).

[14] In exposition cf. esp. Loh. Apk., *ad loc.*

[15] We cannot discuss here what is meant by ἀκρίδες, but cf. E. Lohmeyer, *Das Urchristentum,* I, "Johannes d. Täufer" (1932), 50, n. 4. When we read of the Baptist in Ev. Eb. (Epiph. Haer., 30, 13): καὶ τὸ βρῶμα αὐτοῦ μέλι ἄγριον, οὗ ἡ γεῦσις ἡ τοῦ μάννα ὡς ἐγκρὶς ἐν ἐλαίῳ, this is obviously based on the description of manna in Ex. 16:31: τὸ δὲ γεῦμα αὐτοῦ ὡς ἐγκρὶς ἐν μέλιτι (cf. also Dt. 32:13, and Philo's exposition → *supra*; also the combination of μέλι and ἔλαιον or ἐλαία, Dt. 8:8; 4 Βασ. 18:32; 2 Παρ. 31:5; Ιερ. 48[41]:8; Ez. 16:13, 19). It is possible that behind the use of ἐγκρίς ("cakes") in Ev. Eb. there is not just confusion with the ἀκρίδες of Mk. 1:6 par. but another tradition, or even intentional alteration in the interests of vegetarianism, cf. Kl. Mk., *ad loc.* It is going too far to conjecture that the ἀκρίδες of Mk. 1:6 par. was finally based on the ἐγκρίς of Ex. 16:31.

[16] The suggestion of A. Pallis in *Notes on St. Mark and St. Matthew*² (1932), 1 ff. that the original reading was καρπὸν ἄγριον (καρπόν miscopied as κηρίον, and this later replaced by the synon. μέλι) is rightly rejected by H. Windisch, "Die Notiz über Tracht

both the honey from beekeeping and fruit honey which comes from human labour (→ n. 12). On the other hand, it is debatable whether the reference is to honey from wild bees or to the sweet exudations from certain trees. Since the use of μέλι ἄγριον for the latter is poorly attested in antiquity,[17] and this type of honey was unlikely in the Jordan valley,[18] there can be little doubt that the honey of wild bees is meant.[19] Such honey was accepted as clean food.[20] It was the modest food of those who lived on the steppes, and would be in keeping with the fact that John appeared in the wilderness (→ II, 659).[21]

In Lk. 24:42, in the account of an appearance of the risen Lord in Jerusalem, we read: οἱ δὲ ἐπέδωκαν αὐτῷ ἰχθύος ὀπτοῦ μέρος. The *koine* MSS and the older versions almost all have an addition which is found also in the fathers: καὶ ἀπὸ μελισσίου κηρίου, "and of a honeycomb."[22] This can hardly be an original reading which was later dropped because of the use of honey in Gnostic rites.[23] On the other hand, it can hardly be explained as a fairly early addition which the early Church put in because of the cultic[24] or symbolical[25] significance of honey. Nor can there be any connection with rites for the dead,[26] and the partaking of honey is certainly not accompanied by resuscitation.[27] It seems much more likely that in accordance with current custom a sweet dessert of honey was added to the main fish course.[28, 29]

Michaelis

u. Speise d. Täufers u. ihre Entsprechungen in d. Jesusüberlieferung," ZNW, 32 (1933), 66, n. 1.

17 Only Diod. S., XIX, 94, 10 and Suid., *s.v.* Cf. B. Weiss, Mt.-Ev.[10] (1910), *ad loc.* The etym. connection with μέλισσα is rightly left out of account. In Strabo, 12, 3, 18 μαινόμενον μέλι is used for wild honey.

18 Cf. Schl. Mt., *ad loc.* But cf. G. Dalman, *Orte u. Wege Jesu*[2] (1921), 78 f. (with ref. to the later attested plant name μελιάγριον).

19 The later attested designation of the carob (Ceratonia Siliqua) as the tree of St. John's bread (cf. Löw, II [1924], 399) was based on the idea that John ate the juice of the carob (modern Gk. *ikratomeli*), which was much fancied in the Orient.

20 Str.-B., I, 100 on Mt. 3:4. Philo Spec. Leg., I, 291 f. (→ 553) is no proof to the contrary, since we have here only a conjecture.

21 It is correct that the prophetic stature of the Baptist is expressed in his way of life. Does this mean that he should be called a "desert saint" (Windisch, 80)? It is certainly questionable whether one can speak in his case of sacred food or of a material concept of holiness (as against Lohmeyer, 51 f.). The wild honey certainly does not support Essene influence (→ n. 13). On the account of John's food in Slav. Jos. cf. W. Bienert, *Der älteste nichtchristliche Jesusbericht. Josephus über Jesus* (1936), 118 ff.

22 Cf. Tisch. NT, *ad loc.* (also on vl. within the addition). The adj. μελίσσειος is not found elsewhere (cf. Liddell-Scott, *s.v.*; on Μελισσαῖος as a name for Zeus cf. Pauly-W., XV, 1 [1931], 528 f.). Moult.-Mill., 395 has a ref. to μελικηρίς ("honey wafers or cakes") in P. Oxy., VI, 936, 10 (3rd cent. A.D.).

23 So A. Merx, *Die 4 kanonischen Evv.*, II, 2 (1905), 541 ff.

24 So Hck. Lk., *ad loc.*

25 So Kl. Lk., *ad loc.*

26 As against Schuster, 381. There is no question of a gift to the dead or a meal for the dead.

27 So Krauss, "Honig in Palästina," 163 (he alludes to the Glaucos saga: Γλαῦκος πιὼν μέλι ἀνέστη, in E. Maass, *Griechen u. Semiten auf dem Isthmus von Korinth* [1903], 30).

28 Cf. E. Nestle, "Gebratener Fisch u. Honigseim," ZDPV, 30 (1907), 208 f.; E. Graf v. Mülinen, 35 (1912), 105 ff. (fresh bee honey was eaten with the comb); L. Köhler, *ibid.*, 54 (1931), 289 ff. (it was regarded as healthy to eat honey after fish; examples from Pliny the Elder on); G. Dalman, *ibid.*, 55 (1932), 80 f. = PJB, 9 (1913), 51 (his own inquiries in Palestine). Cf. Windisch, 80.

29 Post-apost. fathers, Barn., 6, 8, cf. v. 10 and 13 (Ex. 33:3); in 6, 17 milk and honey are regarded as children's nourishment (cf. Wnd. Barn., *ad loc.*). In Herm. m., 5, 1, 5 f. there is an exhortation on the incompatibility of honey and gall (cf. Dib. Herm., *ad loc.*).

† μέλος

Contents: A. The Usage of Secular Greek: 1. General Use; 2. The Mysteries and Gnosticism. B. The Use on Jewish Soil: 1. LXX; 2. Philo and Josephus; 3. Rabbinic Writings. C. μέλος in the New Testament: 1. Synoptists; 2. Pauline Epistles; 3. Epistle of James. D. Post-apostolic Use.

A. The Usage of Secular Greek.

1. μέλος, a. "member of the body," b. "song." In Hom. the word is found in the plur. only for members of the body (men and animals) μέλε' ἤλδανε ποιμένι λαῶν (sc. 'Αθήνη), Od., 18, 70; 24, 368; then also the body itself as opp. to → θυμός: θυμὸν ἀπὸ μελέων δῦναι δόμον "Αϊδος εἴσω, Il., 7, 131; cf. also 13, 672; 16, 607.[1] Also Hesiod. It is only in the plur. in Pind. too (opp. of → ψυχή, Nem., 1, 47) μαχαίρᾳ τάμον κατὰ μέλη, member by member, Olymp., 1, 49. So, too, the tragedians and Herodot.

In the sense of "organ" Parmenides sets μέλη in a relation to thought, Fr., 16, 3 (I, 244, Diels[5]), and Empedocles has in view the harmony of the members (in the sphairos) οὐ στάσις οὐδέ τε δῆρις ἀναίσιμος (unseemly strife) ἐν μελέεσσιν, Fr. 27, a (I, 324, Diels[5]) which comes into contrary motion through the conflict between νεῖκος and φιλία (Fr., 30, 1 [I, 325, Diels[5]]; 35, 11 [I, 327, Diels[5]]). This conflict moves not only the universe but human members as well βροτέων μελέων, Fr., 20, 1 (I, 318, Diels[5]). In him μέλη takes on a sense which points in the direction of "elements," and it thus acquires an abstract character.

In Plato we find the later very common link with μέρη:[2] τῶν τοῦ σώματος αὐτοῦ μελῶν καὶ μερῶν, Leg., VII, 795e, 794d, cf. Tim., 76e etc. In him we also find μέλος in the sing. (cf. already Pindar) in the sense of "melody," "song,"[3] ὅτι τὸ μέλος

μέλος. Thes. Steph., Pass., Liddell-Scott, Pr.-Bauer[3], Moult.-Mill., *s.v.* On this whole question → σῶμα. Cf. also H. Lüdemann, *Die Anthropologie des Ap. Pls. u. ihre Stellung innerhalb seiner Heilslehre* (1872); R. Bultmann, ThR, NF, 1 (1929), 26 ff.; "Kirche u. Lehre im NT," ZdZ, 7 (1929), 22; T. Schmidt, *Der Leib Christi* (1919); W. Gutbrod, *Die Paulinische Anthropologie* (1934); E. Käsemann, *Leib u. Leib Christi* (1933); H. Schlier, *Religionsgeschichtliche Untersuchungen zu den Ignatiusbriefen* (1929); *Christus u. d. Kirche im Epheserbrief* (1930); E. Schlink, *D. Mensch in d. Verkündigung d. Kirche* (1936); O. Koch, "Was ist 'theologische Anthropologie'?" *Berliner Börsenzeitung*, No. 37 (1937); P. Althaus, *Die letzten Dinge*[4] (1933), 123 ff.

1 Cf. J. Böhme, *Die Seele u. das Ich im homerischen Epos* (1929), 32. On this cf. B. Snell, *Gnomon*, 7 (1931), 75. The body in Homer is only the sum of individual organs as μέλη, not a single organism.

2 Etym. M., 385, 43 calls μέρη καὶ μέλη synon. (→ μέρος). Cf. also later δύναται δὲ καὶ μέρος τὸ αὐτὸ λέγεσθαι καὶ μέλος, Anecd. Graec., III (ed. J. A. Cramer [1836]), 50, 30; 51, 2 f.

3 Attention is often drawn to the German "Lied" and "Glied," but etym. these are quite unrelated (*Lied* early German *leuþ-*, *G-lied* Gothic *liþus*) [Debrunner]. On the etym. of μέλος, Walde-Pok., II, 293; Prellwitz Etym. Wört., 196. F. A. Wright seeks the connection between member and song (*The Class. Review*, 30 (1916), 9b) in the dance as the most ancient art. μέλος is the member, esp. the lower member (leg), and from the movement of this in dancing comes the musical sense when the movement of the voice is expressed by the same term as that which denotes the movement of the body in the dance.

ἐκ τριῶν ἐστι συγκείμενον, λόγου τε καὶ ἁρμονίας καὶ ῥυθμοῦ, Resp., III, 398d. τὸ πάτριον μέλος ἐφυμνεῖν, Leg. XII, 947c. It also has this sense in Herodot., 5, 95: ἐν μέλεϊ ποιεῖν τι, "to sing in a lyrical poem." [4]

Aristot. gives definitions of the μέλη acc. to the parts (μέρη): ἔνια οὐ μόνον μέρη ἀλλὰ καὶ μέλη καλεῖται. [5] He can also speak of the μέλος αἰσθανόμενον which we do not see in plants. [6] Thus we find in him first the sing. for a bodily member. So also in Strabo ἡ κατὰ μέλος τομή (II, 1, 30), Galen etc.

In Epictet. μέλος is used both in the sing. and plur. only in the musical sense of song or melody (Diss., I, 1, 2 and 3). It is characteristic, however, that in him, as a thinking Gk. who knows that he is part of a πόλις, into the organism of which he is integrated, we should find the statement: τί γάρ ἐστιν ἄνθρωπος; μέρος πόλεως, πρώτης μὲν τῆς ἐκ θεῶν καὶ ἀνθρώπων, II, 5, 26. [7]

This idea of the organism is particularly clearly expressed in the famous fable of Menenius Agrippa, [8] which often recurs in Stoic literature. [9] The members of the body make together a στάσις against the belly, and they have to realise that if the stomach no longer nourishes them they themselves will decay, until, better instructed, they enter again into the organism of the body.

The human body and its members are expressly compared to the πόλις in Dion. Hal.: ἔοικέ πως ἀνθρωπείῳ σώματι πόλις. σύνθετον γὰρ καὶ ἐκ πολλῶν μερῶν ἐστιν ἑκάτερον (VI, 86, 1). Marc. Aurelius, too, calls the sage a μέλος logically integrated into a harmonious and organic whole. He contrasts this sense of integration with the view that one is just a μέρος, a single member of the whole: μᾶλλον ... ἐὰν πρὸς ἑαυτὸν πολλάκις λέγῃς, ὅτι μέλος εἰμὶ τοῦ ἐκ τῶν λογικῶν συστήματος. Ἐὰν δὲ ... μέρος εἶναι ἑαυτὸν λέγῃς, οὔπω ἀπὸ καρδίας φιλεῖς τοὺς ἀνθρώπους ... οὔπω ὡς ἑαυτὸν εὖ ποιῶν; VII, 13 (Schenkl).

In the pap. μέλος has the fixed sense of a member of the body: ἐ]πήνεγκά[ν μο]ι πληγὰς εἰς πᾶν μέλ[ο]ς το[ῦ σ]ώματος, P. Tebt., II, 331, 10 f. (131 A.D.). [10] Burial inscr. from the 1st and 2nd cent. set the μέλη (body) in contrast with the life which departs from it: πνεῦμα μελῶν ἀπέλυε and ψυχῆς ἐκ μελέων ἀποπταθείσης, Epigr. Graec., 547, 7 and 261, 22.

2. The Mysteries and Gnosticism. Under the influence of oriental ideas the distinctively Greek philosophical application of the image of the σῶμα and the μέλη as organ and organism of the intellectual life is accompanied by religious speculation concerning the term. In the Orphic myth the consuming of the members of Dionysus plays a part. [11]

---

[4] The plur. in the musical sense is found earlier, e.g., Hom. Hymn., 19, 16; Theogn. Tragg.

[5] Hist. An., I, 1, p. 486a, 5 ff., cf. also Part. An., I, 5, p. 645b, 36 f.; Περὶ φυτῶν, I, 3, p. 818a, 17.

[6] Περὶ φυτῶν, I, 1, p. 815b, 23. The note in Pass. that even in Aristot. μέλη is found only in the plur. for members of the body has thus to be corrected.

[7] Cf. also II, 10, 3 f.: πολίτης εἶ τοῦ κόσμου καὶ μέρος αὐτοῦ. Cf. also Sen. Epistulae Morales, XV, 95, 52: *omne ... quo divina et humana conclusa sunt, unum est: membra sumus corporis magni.*

[8] Liv., II, 32; Dio Chrys. Or., 33, 16. W. Nestle, "Die Fabel d. Menenius Agrippa," *Klio*, 21 (1927), 350-360.

[9] Acc. to Joh. W. on 1 C. 12:12 ff. the passages adduced in the imposing lists in Wettstein and Ltzm. on R. 12:4 and 1 C. 12:12 go back to this fable and the similar one in Aesop. W. Jaeger, "Tyrtaios über die wahre ἀρετή," SAB, 1932 (*23. Sonderausgabe*, 32) says that "the story finally goes back to an old λόγος προτρεπτικὸς πρὸς ὁμόνοιαν which has its origin in the Sophist doctrine of the state ... Livius ... or the author takes it from a Greek source. It hardly matters where Paul took it from, since the Greek origin is clear enough."

[10] For members of the human body cf. also an ostrakon of the Roman period: μέλη ἀνθρώπ[ινα], U. Wilcken, *Griech. Ostraka* (1899), II, 1218.

[11] RGG², IV, 791.

These are found again in men as the most noble legacy at creation. In the myth of the world god the members of this god are seen in the κόσμος.[12]

In Gnostic speculation this world god is equated with the man god, the primal man (→ III, 676). This takes place in the myth of the primal man and redeemer. But the Gnostic idea of συγγένεια is also produced in this way. The individual can be thought of as a member of the primal man. This may be seen in the Gnosticism which has a Christian tinge. The redeemer gathers the members from dispersion; the redeemed receive a new form and imitate him.[13] In the O. Sol. we read: "They received my blessing and came to life; they gathered around me and were redeemed. For they became my members and I their head. Praise be to thee, our head, Lord Christ" (17:14 ff.).[14] In Pistis Sophia the members take on the significance of forces, forces of the Father of all, whose members constitute myriads upon myriads of forces.[15] In the fragments of a Gnostic prayer we read: "Deliver all my members, who from the beginning of the world are dispersed in all the archontes ... of the ... aeon, and gather them and receive them into the light."[16] In comparison with the Pauline Epistles, esp. Ephesians, it should not be overlooked that the passages adduced in support of this speculative development of the μέλος concept are post-Pauline.[17]

B. The Use on Jewish Soil.

1. LXX. In the LXX the word is used for the bodily members of men (e.g., Ju. 19:29 B; Job 9:28) and animals (e.g., Ex. 29:17). It is also used for song and melody.[18] This may be a song of pleasure: μέλος μουσικῶν ἐφ' ἡδεῖ οἴνῳ, Sir. 32:6[19] or a lament: ἐγέγραπτο ... θρῆνος καὶ μέλος καὶ οὐαί, Ez. 2:10.[20] It is esp. used to denote the parts into which the animal is cut up when sacrificed.[21] Here we also have the verb μελίζω, which does not occur in the NT: μελιοῦσιν αὐτὸ κατὰ μέλη, Lv. 1:6. There is more frequent refs. to the members of the body in Macc., where the bodies of confessors must endure the pains of martyrdom, or be wounded or maimed

---

12 Zeus, the world god, whose head, body and feet, reaching through heaven, the air, and the earth to the underworld, embrace all things. The world is thus depicted in human form, Kern Orph. Fr., 168 (→ III, 676). Cf. also the Sarapis oracle to King Nicocreon of Cyprus, Macrob. Sat., I, 20, 17, quoted → III, 676. On this whole question Käsemann, 59 ff., → III, 676 ff.; W. Kranz, "Kosmos u. Mensch in d. Vorstellung frühen Griechentums," NGG, *phil.-hist. Kl., Fachgruppe* 1, *Altertumswissenschaft* NF, Vol. II, 7 (1938) [Kleinknecht].

13 In Act. Joh., 100 the Gnostics do not yet have a single form. This means that not every member of the descended Lord has yet been brought in: οὐδέπω τὸ πᾶν τοῦ κατελθόντος συνελήφθη μέλος, cf. Schlier Eph., 44; also cf. Epiph. Haer., 26, 13, 2; Act. Thom., 121.

14 Acc. to Gressmann in Hennecke, 453. Cf. O. Sol. 17:4; 6:15.

15 For examples cf. Käsemann, 78.

16 C. Schmidt, *Koptisch-gnostische Schriften*, I (1905), 330, 7 ff.

17 Cf. the review of Käsemann's *Leib und Leib Christi* by W. Michaelis, ThLBl, 54 (1933), 387 ff.

18 μέλος is not used in this sense in the NT.

19 Cf. Sir. 40:21; 47:9; 50:18.

20 Cf. Mi. 2:4; 3 Macc. 5:25; 6:32.

21 Ex. 29:17; Lv. 1:6, 12; 8:19 f.; 9:13; Sir. 50:12; Ez. 24:6. In the sense of member μέλος is used only for נֵתַח, though this means piece, or piece of flesh, rather than member. This word is usually rendered μέλος, though just after at Ex. 29:17; Lv. 1:8; Ez. 24:4 the LXX has the more exact διχοτόμημα. The concept of member does not seem to occur at all in Heb. But cf. Ges.-Buhl, *s.v.* בַּד II on Job 18:13 and יצרים, Job 17:7. The Heb. words occasionally rendered μέλος by Σ (ψ 67:13; Lam. 4:7; Ez. 17:3) do not have this sense [Bertram].

22 1 Βασ. 11:7; 3 Βασ. 18:23, 33. For human members Ju. 19:29; 20:6; Mi. 3:3.

in battle, or where corpses are quartered. Man's activity in the use of his members displays that which characterises the person. The more serious, then, is their destruction. But believers gladly let their members be mutilated for God (ἡδέως ὑπὲρ τοῦ θεοῦ τὰ τοῦ σώματος μέλη ἀκρωτηριαζόμεθα, 4 Macc. 10:20).[23] On the other side we have the dismembering (μέλη ποιήσαντες, 2 Macc. 1:16) of the corpse of the ungodly king.[24]

In LXX usage, then, we have ref. to the concrete member of the body. The body is never used as a figure for the harmonious whole to which the members are subject. The body is created by God and dependent on Him. It is subject to death, "flesh." OT anthropology cannot think of it apart from its dependence on God. In the main attention is directed to the function of each individual member, not to its harmonious integration in the whole. This is shown, e.g., by the use of the head (→ κεφαλή) to denote lordship, the feet to denote standing, the eyes seeing, the ears hearing. The member is regarded as an effective instrument of the human will.

2. Philo and Josephus. Philo, too, begins with the concrete functions of the members δυσκινητότερα τὰ μέλη ποιεῖ (unmixed wine),[25] but he then assimilates this basic Jewish understanding to Gk. thought by giving ontological significance to the activity of the member, as in the allegorical exposition of the parts in sacrifice. The dismemberment of the sacrificial beast teaches unity: ἡ δὲ εἰς μέλη τοῦ ζῴου διανομὴ δηλοῖ, ἤτοι ὡς ἓν τὰ πάντα ἢ ὅτι ἐξ ἑνός τε καὶ εἰς ἕν ..., Spec. Leg., I, 208.[26] He is thus distinct from the pre-Socratic thinkers, in whom the image primarily illustrates a philosophical principle (→ 555, Emped.) which, as the primary thought, seeks the help of the metaphor. Instead, Philo exerts himself to show that the philosophical thought is already there in the fact concretely present in the Bible. Here too, then, the Greek formulations wrestle with the Jewish understanding.[27] Like the OT, Philo thinks that the head denotes the head or ruler of a society, → III, 674 f. It is the chief member, under which the others are simply parts of a body, receiving life only through the forces in the head which is over them: κεφαλὴ μὲν πρῶτον καὶ ἄριστον ... τῶν μελῶν ... κεφαλὴν μὲν τοῦ ἀνθρωπείου γένους ἔσεσθαι ... τὸν σπουδαῖον ..., τοὺς δὲ ἄλλους ἅπαντας οἷον μέρη σώματος ψυχούμενα ταῖς ἐν κεφαλῇ καὶ ὑπεράνω δυνάμεσιν, Praem. Poen., 125.

Under the influence of the OT concept of God he rejects the idea that God can have bodily parts,[28] but adds that being itself cannot be subject to any passion: θεῷ δὲ οὔτε ψυχῆς ἄλογα πάθη οὔτε τὰ σώματος μέρη καὶ μέλη συνόλως ἐστὶν οἰκεῖα, Deus Imm., 52. As the combination μέλη καὶ μέρη, which he often uses for members of the body,[29] is distinctive in Philo, so he often uses the combination μέτρα καὶ μέλη, verse and melody, in places where he has μέλος in the musical sense.[30]

---

[23] Cf. 2 Macc. 7:7; 4 Macc. 9:14, 17; 2 Macc. 8:24.
[24] Cf. 9:7.
[25] Spec. Leg., I, 99. Cf. Virt., 32: The general examines the members of each individual soldier: σῶμα μὲν ἐξετάζων ... εἰ τοῖς μέρεσι καὶ μέλεσι πᾶσιν εὖ ἡρμοσμένον πρὸς τὰς ἐπιβαλλούσας ἑκάστῳ σχέσεις τε καὶ κινήσεις, Exsecr., 143: αἱ σωματικαὶ νόσοι μέλος ἕκαστον καὶ μέρος ἰδίᾳ κατεργαζόμεναι (here once in the sing. as in Vit. Mos., I, 128). So also ἔτι τῶν ὀργανικῶν μελῶν συνεστηκότων (Op. Mund., 103): Death comes even though the active members are still together. As in other expressions of man's physical and spiritual capacities, so in bodily members the number 7 is important: μέλη δὲ σώματος ὁμοίως ἰσάριθμα· κεφαλή, τράχηλος, στέρνον, χεῖρες, κοιλία, ἦτρον, πόδες, Leg. All., I, 12.
[26] Cf. Spec. Leg., I, 199.
[27] Cf. Rer. Div. Her., 133: καθάπερ γὰρ ἡμῶν τὴν ψυχὴν καὶ τὰ μέλη μέσα διεῖλεν ὁ τεχνίτης, οὕτως καὶ τὴν τοῦ παντὸς οὐσίαν, ἡνίκα τὸν κόσμον ἐδημιούρει.
[28] Cf. J. Geffcken, *Zwei griechische Apologeten* (1907), 177 f.
[29] Cf. in addition to the passages cited the Index, *s.v.*
[30] Vit. Cont., 84 etc.; *v.* Index, *s.v.*

Josephus uses the metaphor of the inflammation of an important member, which affects all the others, only in order that he may illustrate from concrete observation the way in which, in the Jewish revolt, all parts of the land were forced by circumstances to share in the suffering of the chief city (πάντα τὰ μέλη συνενόσει, Bell., 4, 406). The idea of an organism is not present here. Similarly, there is a ref. only to the functions of the members in Bell., 1, 656 : σπασμοὶ πάντων τῶν μελῶν = spasms in all his members (in the description of Herod's sickness), and Ant., 9, 240 : πάρεσις τῶν μελῶν = weakness of the limbs.

3. Rabbinic Writings. Rabb. theology considered how many members a man has, and related the number to the Torah. Thus, acc. to jBer., 8b, 60 ff., Hezekiah prays : "Lord of the world, I have gone through the 248 members which thou hast given me, and I have not found that I have kindled thee to wrath with any one of them." [31] There are in the Torah 248 commandments corresponding to the members and 365 prohibitions according to the number of the days of a year. [32] The Rabb. also asked which member is the most important and should rule the others. The head esp. is found to be the one by which the others should direct themselves הכל הולך אחר הראש, [33] but also the heart and the reins. The tongue, too, is regarded as mistress of all others members in Ps. 39:1. In the Midrash a physician dreams that his members are in conflict. Feet, hands, eyes, heart and tongue all claim to be the most important for the body. But the tongue, which the others despise because it is in a place of darkness and has no bone in it, saves the others and is thus acknowledged as mistress. [34] Much more seriously supernatural powers strive for mastery over members of the human body. The evil impulse gains dominion over all 248 members when the voice of the good impulse is impotent. [35] Indeed, the human body can be compared to a little town with only a few men, its members, within it. The great king who makes war on it is the evil impulse. The good impulse is a poor man who saves the city by wisdom. [36] But we do not find the Greek idea of the πόλις as an organism. There is also a distinction between the 3 members which God created, the hands, feet and mouth (or tongue), and the 3 which are not in His power, the eyes, ears and nose (or smell). [37]

C. μέλος in the New Testament.

1. Synoptists.

In the saying in Mt. 5:29-30 Jesus contrasts a single member (ἓν τῶν μελῶν) with the whole body (ὅλον τὸ σῶμα). [38] He calls the eye and hand members which have to fulfil the most important functions, [39] which characterise man con-

---

[31] Str.-B., I, 815.

[32] bMak., 23b : Str.-B., I, 901.

[33] PRE, 42 (24a), cf. also T. Taan., 2, 5 : Str.-B., III, 446 f. A parable of R. Joshua b. Levi (c. 220 A.D.), Dt. r., 1, 13 on 1:10 is obviously influenced by a corresponding fable of Aesop, 344 (ed. C. Halm, 169 f.): The tail of a snake, tired of the precedence of the head, seized the leadership, but was soon taught better by the misfortunes which followed [R. Meyer].

[34] Midr. Ps., 39 § 2 (128a): Str.-B., III, 447.

[35] Str.-B., IV, 470 ff. with examples.

[36] bNed., 32b and Qoh. r., 4, 13 (24a): Str.-B., IV, 472.

[37] Tanch. תולדות, 34a : Str.-B., III, 757.

[38] In D sys the 2nd clause has dropped out (on account of the homoioteleuton, cf. Zn. Mt., *ad loc.*). The variants, e.g., βληθῇ in v. 30 instead of ἀπέλθῃ, are insignificant.

[39] In Mk. 9:43 ff. = Mt. 18:8 f. the foot too. Bultmann Trad., 90 thinks that this is a secondary addition by way of analogy. In the preceding verse in Mt. 5:28 Jesus also mentions the heart as the instrument of sinning related to the eye. Cf. Rashi on Nu. 15:39 : The eye sees, the heart desires, the body accomplishes the sin. The evil impulse gains power over the one whose eyes see, cf. Str.-B., I, 302.

cretely as one who knows and acts.[40] Palestinians do not refer to the abstract activity but to the specific member which is responsible for it. Hence the members are the acting subject: εἰ δὲ ὁ ὀφθαλμός σου δεξιὸς (ἡ δεξιά σου χεὶρ) σκανδαλίζει σε.[41] The more radical, then, is the command of Jesus that the right member,[42] which is privileged and which gives promise of success, should be sacrificed, that the eye should be plucked out, the hand hacked off, that both should be cast away (ἔξελε αὐτὸν καὶ βάλε ἀπὸ σοῦ), if they are a means of offence which would cause the hearers to perish. But what is the offence, the σκανδαλίζειν? Mt. includes the saying in his antitheses to legal piety, and in the context of vv. 27 ff. he has in view the adulterous glance of the eye.[43] Nevertheless, the similar Mt. 18:8 f. = Mk. 9:43 ff.,[44] which is not so closely related to the 7th commandment, must be our point of departure. Here the σκάνδαλον is obviously in the question of decision for the βασιλεία τοῦ θεοῦ,[45] namely, for Jesus Himself, for faith (τῶν πιστευόντων, Mk. 9:42; τῶν πιστευόντων εἰς ἐμέ, Mt. 18:6).[46] The danger of σκάνδαλον may obviously arise also out of persistence in adulterous glances or acts. Just as Jesus unconditionally demands that we renounce possessions,[47] family, the natural orders,[48] and even life itself,[49] if these things keep us from discipleship, so He also demands that we unconditionally give up the sinful activity of the members.[50]

The question whether He demands a literal fulfilment of the ἔξελε (ἔκκοψον) καὶ βάλε ἀπὸ σοῦ is falsely put. When He requires the surrender of life He is not demanding physical suicide. Similarly, He is not demanding physical self-mutilation. Every member of the body which God has created, indeed, every hair, is in God's hand, Mt. 10:30. But for the sake of the unconditional rule of God these members must not be put in the service of sinful desire. The sinful member must be renounced in respect of this function in order that ὅλον τὸ σῶμα be not cast into → γέεννα. According to both Mt. 5:29 f. and 18:8 f. the saying implies κρίσις on every man and pronounces him guilty of γέεννα,[51] but Jesus can

---

40 J. Schniewind Mt., *ad loc.* refers to everyday words in which the act is described in terms of the member (cf. the English "to handle" [hand], "to eye" [eye]).

41 Schl. Mt., 177. Acc. to Jewish thought the evil impulse is localised in the members, Hck. Mk., 116 (on v. 43 ff.).

42 Schl. Mt., *ad loc.* ἡ δεξιά is not found in the par. Mk. 9:43 ff., cf. Bultmann Trad., 340.

43 Cf. also K. Wolfram, *Kazanie na górze,* I [the Sermon on the Mount], Warsaw (1934), 116 f. As may be seen from the saying of R. Tarphon about the licentious hand, such an understanding of the 7th commandment was possible with ref. to the activity of the hand too, Str.-B., I, 302 B.

44 Though in a different respect, this is a broadening as compared with Mt. 5:29 f., cf. J. Schniewind on Mt. 18:8, 9.

45 All these sayings of Jesus relate to the βασιλεία τοῦ θεοῦ. Hence they cannot be divorced from His own person. Cf. Schniewind on the verses in Mt. and Mk. Cf. Mt. 11:6 (ἐν ἐμοί).

46 J. Schniewind, 192 on Mt. 18:6 calls this a phrase of the Church. This is the only instance of faith "in" Jesus in the Synpt.

47 Mk. 10:21 ff. par.

48 Mt. 10:37 ff.; Lk. 14:26 f.

49 Mk. 8:34 ff. par.

50 Cf. the way in which the Maccabean martyrs gladly let their members be mangled for God's sake, 4 Macc. 10:20, → 557 f.

51 Cf. Luther's exposition, Schniewind, *ad loc.*

pronounce this radical judgment because determined μετάνοια carries with it σῴζεσθαι.[52]

As concerns the relation between μέλη and σῶμα it is to be noted that the radical ἔξελε καὶ βάλε ἀπὸ σοῦ is in contradiction with the view of the body as a harmonious whole whose malfunctioning can be corrected by a mere integration into the organic autonomy. On the other hand, it is obvious that, though members can be renounced in respect of their sinful functions, the σῶμα as human existence is more than the perfection of the members. The members can perish as parts, but ὅλον τὸ σῶμα has a destiny in the next aeon.

Why, then, does Jesus heal sick members?[53] The healings are σημεῖα that in the coming aeon man will have a renewed existence like the angels of God in a resurrection body which does not bear certain members but which need not renounce a σῶμα.[54]

2. Pauline Epistles.

a. In Paul a man's members are not something autonomous whose πρᾶξις or activity (R. 12:4)[55] he may arbitrarily control. Man with his physical body stands responsible to God the Creator who has set the members in the body (ὁ θεὸς ἔθετο τὰ μέλη, ἓν ἕκαστον αὐτῶν ἐν τῷ σώματι καθὼς ἠθέλησεν, 1 C. 12:18). He is thus involved in the conflict of superhuman forces which poses radical division into two fronts for percipient believers (οὐκ οἴδατε, R. 6:16).[56] This conflict is not just a spiritual conflict of ideas. It embraces active man in his actuality. This is shown by the mounting concreteness from ὑμεῖς, by way of σῶμα, to μέλη in R. 6:11 f. These members are weapons either of ἀδικία or of δικαιοσύνη. By speaking of ἁμαρτία (ἀδικία) and δικαιοσύνη Paul refers to positions rather than leaders.[57] The μηδὲ παριστάνετε τὰ μέλη ὑμῶν ὅπλα ..., ἀλλὰ παραστήσατε κτλ. rings out like a command.[58] The sinister power of sin needs the members of the mortal body in order to accomplish the actual doing of wrong by subjecting man to desires (ὑπακούειν ταῖς ἐπιθυμίαις).[59] Sin in its position of strength is here a military leader, but the metaphor is quickly changed into that of a slaveowner (6:19).[60] The members of the slave (→ δοῦλος II, 274) are the property of the owner. They are not at the disposal of the slave himself. This bondage has been broken by Christ, so that members which have been enslaved to ἀκαθαρσία and ἀνομία are liberated and are to stand in the service of δικαιοσύνη: οὕτως νῦν παραστήσατε τὰ μέλη ὑμῶν δοῦλα τῇ δικαιοσύνῃ.[61] This can only mean that they have received a wholly new meaning

---

52 The beatitudes also stand over Mt. 5:29 f.; Schniewind, *ad loc.* and Mk. 9:43 ff.

53 E.g., Mk. 3:1, 5 χείρ, Mt. 9:29 ὀφθαλμοί, Mk. 7:33 ὦτα and → γλῶσσα.

54 Mt. 22:30 par.; cf. 15:17; 1 C. 6:13. μέλος does not occur in John's Gospel. Cf. the note in Schl. J. on 2:21.

55 Cf. 8:13.

56 1 C. 6:15.

57 When God Himself is mentioned (13), the comprehensive ἑαυτούς corresponds to τῷ θεῷ, and only then do we read τὰ μέλη ὑμῶν ὅπλα δικαιοσύνης τῷ θεῷ.

58 Cf. οὕτως ἑαυτοὺς παραστήσεσθε πρὸς τὴν μάχην, Polyb., 3, 109, 9. This is the point of the image rather than the comparison with sacrifice to which Ltzm., *ad loc.* points.

59 Cf. Gutbrod, 159.

60 Cf. Zn. R., *ad loc.*

61 Paul is quite clear that in view of the ἐλευθερωθέντες he cannot properly describe as bondage the surrender of the members to the new master δικαιοσύνη. Hence the preceding ἀνθρώπινον λέγω, which restricts the metaphor. Cf. Zn. R., *ad loc.*

(ὡς ζῶντας) and goal which renders service in ἀκαθαρσία impossible. If the μέλη receive this high significance, so does the actual bodily life of the Christian. There is no trace here of an asceticism which degrades the function of any member or regards it as of lower moral value. It is true that the members are not held in unbroken esteem in and for themselves. The new and positive affirmation of the function of the members is illumined by the sharp antithesis of the dark τότε of v. 21: ὅτε ἦμεν ἐν τῇ σαρκί, τὰ παθήματα τῶν ἁμαρτιῶν τὰ διὰ τοῦ νόμου ἐνηργεῖτο ἐν τοῖς μέλεσιν ἡμῶν εἰς τὸ καρποφορῆσαι τῷ θανάτῳ, R. 7:5. In the light of what precedes this cannot mean that "sinful passions [62] had as it were their seat in the members," but that "the states of passion brought about by sins were given expression by means of our members." [63] With the help of the Law, the sinister power of sin uses the members as an instrument to express itself in actions (ἐνηργεῖτο) which come to maturity in the terrible fruit of death, and to which the instrument itself falls victim.

It is this reference to θάνατος which finally imposes a heavy destiny on being ἐν σαρκί. This being ἐν σαρκί, which is defined by θάνατος, finds expression in concrete actions of the μέλη which cannot but bring forth this fruit of death in so far as this being ἐν σαρκί remains the only sphere of man's somatic existence. [64] With logical and pitiless force this power of sin works itself out in the members even against man's better knowledge (νοῦς), [65] which is directed with equal strictness to the willing of the good: ἕτερον νόμον ἐν τοῖς μέλεσίν μου ἀντιστρατευόμενον τῷ νόμῳ τοῦ νοός καὶ αἰχμαλωτίζοντά με ἐν τῷ νόμῳ τῆς ἁμαρτίας τῷ ὄντι ἐν τοῖς μέλεσίν μου, R. 7:23. Here, then, the μέλη are always mentioned rather than ἐγώ, ἡμεῖς, σῶμα, σάρξ, παλαιὸς ἄνθρωπος etc. to denote the real man whose sinning is a concrete sinful action. Similarly, the ἁγιασμός for which the members of the believer who has risen to new life ἐν Χριστῷ are destined is no mere mental experience but a true demonstration of the justifying faith which has given to the members a new master (6:19). This mention of the μέλη rules out any psychological or speculative misunderstanding of the realistic view of the σῶμα and σάρξ in Paul.

Only on the basis of an understanding of these passages can one proceed to what is said about the σῶμα and the many μέλη in the well-known passages R. 12:4 f. and 1 C. 12:12 ff. Normally the image of the body and members presupposes the idea of the community as an organism. There is thus presupposed an appeal to the fable of Menenius Agrippa about the στάσις of the members against the stomach, which was commonly used in contemporary, especially Stoic, writings. [66] Underlying the fable is the Greek idea of the πόλις. Hence the fable itself reflects an unreal situation, namely, the time when the members did not

---

[62] Ltzm. R., *ad loc.*

[63] Schl. R., 228, *ad loc.* Cf. Pass., *s.v.* πάθημα. Since Paul does not elsewhere use παθήματα for passions, he can hardly do so here.

[64] The relation between σάρξ and μέλη is different in 7:25 inasmuch as we there simply have σάρξ instead of the μέλη ruled by sin, Gutbrod, 157.

[65] R. 7:23 τῷ νόμῳ τοῦ νοός μου.

[66] So also Jaeger, *op. cit.*, n. 9: "The apostle ... writes to the Christian congregation in Corinth, a state within the state, which must also be edified in order that its members may learn to integrate themselves into the cosmos," cf. also → n. 9, the list of similar refs. in Wettstein on R. 12:5 and 1 C. 12:14 ff., also Ltzm. and Joh. W. on 1 C. 12:12 ff. etc.

see that the organism of the body was a necessary law, and could thus conspire against the stomach, until, on the edge of self-destruction, they saw their error and integrated themselves into the law of organism immanent within them. But this idea is alien to the biblical view, which starts with the realistic observation of the functions of the members which God has created. The unity of a body with many members to which Paul points (ἐν ἑνὶ σώματι πολλὰ μέλη, R. 12:4, τὸ σῶμα ἕν ἐστιν καὶ μέλη πολλὰ ἔχει, 1 C. 12:12) does not derive from the law of organism which holds the members together. It is the ongoing act of the creative will of God: ὁ θεὸς ἔθετο τὰ μέλη, ἓν ἕκαστον αὐτῶν ἐν τῷ σώματι καθὼς ἠθέλησεν, v. 18.[67] Since God has brought the members into this unity, none of them can argue that it does not belong thereto, v. 15 ff.[68] Each member has its distinctive function. Hence very different functions are at the command of the body. If it had only one, it would not be the σῶμα which is rich in members.[69] In the same way, it is the miracle of the new creation that Christ has integrated the most diverse members into one body. Paul does not speak in general of a σῶμα, and then go on to speak of the σῶμα Χριστοῦ. From the very first he has in view the σῶμα of the community which belongs to Christ, and he illustrates this by the metaphor of the σῶμα and μέλη. To the different backgrounds of religion and nationality (εἴτε Ἰουδαῖοι εἴτε Ἕλληνες), to the differences in social standing (εἴτε δοῦλοι εἴτε ἐλεύθεροι, v. 13), must be added the differences in congregational function according to the various χαρίσματα, 12:4 ff., 28 ff. This miracle of creation has been accomplished by the πνεῦμα, who permeates believers as does life the members, and who in the sacraments of baptism and the Lord's Supper demonstrates His reality as the One who binds together in unity: ἐν ἑνὶ πνεύματι ἡμεῖς πάντες εἰς ἓν σῶμα ἐβαπτίσθημεν κτλ., v. 13. The

[67] Cf. v. 24 συνεκέρασεν. Though assuming that Paul took the metaphor from popular Stoic philosophy, Joh. W. perceived many distinctive Pauline alterations, and since then theological interpretation has increasingly abandoned the idea of an organism. Schlier, Ign., 90 f., Eph., 40, finds a basis in popular Greek philosophy, but for him sacramental nourishment constitutes the unity of the body. The figure of the body and members is applied to the community, but with no emphasis here (as distinct from Eph.) on the fact that the community as the body is related to Christ. In Pauline works, unlike deutero-Pauline, he sees no Gnostic influence. Käsemann does not find any thought of an organism in Paul. He thinks that the metaphor is simply an aid. The real thrust of the passage lies in the οὕτως καὶ ὁ Χριστός in 1 C. 12:12. But he does discern Gnostic influence here, as in other genuine Pauline writings, 171, 160 ff., 98. Cf. also K. L. Schmidt, → III, 512: "If we follow Paul, we must not speak too loudly ... of the organism." Barth R.², *ad loc.* rejects an understanding in terms of natural philosophy, i.e., the idea of an organic bodily nexus built up of cells. The body is neither the sum of individual members nor their mutual interrelation, but the one confronting the other in the invisible unity which transcends all the members and each one in particular. Cf. also K.D., I, 2 (1938), 235 ff. (E.T. C.D., I, 2 [1956], 210 ff.); R. Bultmann, "Kirche u. Lehre," *op. cit.*, 22.

[68] Schl. K.: In comparison with the others and the establishment of what it lacks; Wendland K.: Because it does not have the gift of glossolalia, which is regarded as essential.

[69] Paul mentions as the most important active members the foot and the hand, then the instruments of the senses, the οὖς (echoing the earlier πούς, the ὀφθαλμός, ἀκοή, ὄσφρησις (sense of smell, for nose), κεφαλή, and finally other members whose use is merely indicated by comparison with the rest, "the breast and the lower parts of the body, which we modestly cover," Schl., *ad loc.* The members are compared and evaluated in terms of their power (ἀσθενέστερα), the honour paid them (ἀτιμότερα), and their decorousness (εὐσχήμονα — ἀσχήμονα). God, who has put the body together (συνεκέρασεν), has given the greater honour to the member which has to stay in the background τῷ ὑστερουμένῳ περισσοτέραν δοὺς τιμήν.

miracle brings it about that elements which are so different (v. 13) come to be related like members: τὸ αὐτὸ ὑπὲρ ἀλλήλων μεριμνῶσιν τὰ μέλη, v. 25. This pneumatic interrelation finds expression in suffering and rejoicing with one another: εἴτε πάσχει ἓν μέλος, συμπάσχει πάντα τὰ μέλη· εἴτε δοξάζεται μέλος, συγχαίρει πάντα τὰ μέλη, v. 26. In view of the common life of the members in the πνεῦμα they can now be addressed as the σῶμα Χριστοῦ: ὑμεῖς δέ ἐστε σῶμα Χριστοῦ. Nevertheless, this does not imply a mystical obliteration of the boundaries of individuality. The whole is the σῶμα which belongs to Christ. Seen in part, they are members, and each is a specific member: καὶ μέλη ἐκ μέρους, v. 27.

The conclusion is not that they should integrate themselves.[70] They are already integrated. What is needed is that they should avoid ὑπερφρονεῖν, arrogance, R. 12:3. In a congregation threatened by faction and the playing off of specific gifts, they must keep in view what is given to them in their unity: οἱ πολλοὶ ἓν σῶμά ἐσμεν ἐν Χριστῷ, R. 12:5. We are all one body, and we are this in Christ, and in Him alone. We belong to one another only as we are related in faith to Christ. Membership does not consist in belonging to a social body. The οὕτως καὶ ὁ Χριστός of 1 C. 12:12 is often rendered: So it is with Christ.[71] But when Paul uses the metaphor of the body he speaks of the πρᾶξις of the μέλη (R. 12:4). So, here, he speaks of this and of the ἐνεργεῖ of the πνεῦμα.[72] Hence οὕτως καὶ ὁ Χριστός is not just an ontological statement. It can be paraphrased as follows: So Christ does this. This is justified by the fact that what Christ does by the πνεῦμα is again expressed by an active term in the verse which follows: εἰς ἓν σῶμα ἐβαπτίσθημεν. Similarly, R. 12:5 does not mean that Christ is one body and we are the members, but that we are one body, and that we are this in Christ: τὸ δὲ καθ' εἷς ἀλλήλων μέλη. It is worth noting that here, too, there precedes a statement emphasising the underlying creative act of God: ὡς ὁ θεὸς ἐμέρισεν μέτρον πίστεως.

As Paul can say that we are members in one σῶμα which Christ controls, so, remembering that the members of the community are persons, he can say conversely in another context: τὰ σώματα ὑμῶν μέλη Χριστοῦ ἐστιν, 1 C. 6:15. It does not say here that your members are members of Christ, but your bodies. Now σῶμα and μέλη are not interchangeable terms. Hence the apostle shows that Christ does not make a mechanical use of the members when He accomplishes His will through them in the community. He does this through the σῶμα of Christians, through the whole of their personal, physical and spiritual life as this is determined by baptism. The σωμα is here more than the sum of its members. For, as concerns the κοιλία, Paul grants the Corinthians that this will fall victim to destruction by God like the corruptible food which ὁ θεὸς καταργήσει (v. 13); he also concedes that the members "which make the man a man and the woman a woman"[73] will share the same fate. But the σώματα which stand in the mutual relation τὸ σῶμα τῷ κυρίῳ and ὁ κύριος τῷ σώματι (v. 13) are not appointed by God to destruction, but, as in the case of Christ's σῶμα, to resurrection. In

---

[70] So P. Althaus R., *ad loc.*
[71] Cf. the comm.
[72] 1 C. 12:11.
[73] Schl. 1 K., *ad loc.*

relation to the libertinistic deduction of the Corinthian extremists, who regard intercourse with a harlot as a function of the members no less indifferent than the eating of meats, Paul points out that what is at issue is not perishable members but the σῶμα. In personal conduct the man who yields his members to a harlot, so that she has control of them, surrenders the σῶμα. The believer who gives to a harlot members which belong to Christ takes them away from Christ (ἄρας, v. 15), and in so doing he makes them the members of a harlot. For according to Scripture this union is more than an incidental function of the members. It is a coming together as one σῶμα, [74] and it is thus of far-reaching significance for the whole physico-spiritual personal life. With this somatic and carnal union with a harlot, which denies Christ, is contrasted the pneumatic union with Christ: τῇ πόρνῃ — ἓν σῶμα; τῷ κυρίῳ — ἓν πνεῦμα (16 f.), which self-evidently includes the full control of the Lord over the σῶμα and μέλη of the Christian, but which also shows that the σῶμα-μέλη statements burst through the limitations of the comparison even though they present a relevant image which cannot be capriciously replaced by a different one. In other words, the comparison cannot do full justice to the true reality of the relation to Christ, as the choice of the word μέλη particularly emphasises. There can be no question in Paul of any essential influence of the Greek concept of organism or of any mystical and speculative broadening of the metaphor into Gnosticism.

b. In Col. and Eph., too, one must start with the basic understanding of the relation of the μέλη to the σῶμα in the older Pauline letters. [75] In this light we are to construe the νεκρώσατε τὰ μέλη [76] τὰ ἐπὶ τῆς γῆς, πορνείαν, ἀκαθαρσίαν κτλ. in Col. 3:5 in such a way that here again the reference is to the members which constitute active and concrete corporeality [77] under sin, cf. R. 8:13: πνεύματι τὰς πράξεις τοῦ σώματος θανατοῦτε. [78] As in the latter verse we have τὰς πράξεις τοῦ σώματος rather than τὸ σῶμα, so here we have τὰ μέλη. How this νεκρώσατε τὰ μέλη is to be understood in face of the existence of man in earthly corporeality is shown fundamentally by what precedes: συνηγέρθητε τῷ Χριστῷ κτλ. (1 f.), and by what follows: ἀπεκδυσάμενοι τὸν παλαιὸν ἄνθρωπον σὺν ταῖς πράξεσιν αὐτοῦ καὶ ἐνδυσάμενοι τὸν νέον κτλ. (9 f.). [79] The example of a specific member clarifies this: ἀπόθεσθε ... ὀργὴν κτλ. ἐκ τοῦ στόματος ὑμῶν (8). This means that the sinful use of the tongue, being radically condemned to death, can have no more place. Only secondarily may we consider whether the five vices and five virtues are reminiscent of a schema of five spiritual members in the Persian redemption mystery. [80]

---

[74] σῶμα can here be used instead of the σάρξ of the original saying.

[75] For a fuller discussion → σῶμα.

[76] There is fairly good attestation for the addition ὑμῶν (A ℜ D G pl lat), but it is not tenable in face of the contrary witness.

[77] Cf. K. v. Hofmann, *Die Hl. Schrift NT* (1870), *ad loc.*

[78] Cf. also 1 C. 6:15 ff. on μέλη-πορνείαν for what is meant (also Mt. 5:29 f.).

[79] Here, too, the proper starting-point is the παλαιὸς ἄνθρωπος (→ I, 365 f.) of R. 6:6 and the ἔσω ἄνθρωπος (→ II, 698 f.) of R. 7:22, not the redeemer myth of oriental and Hellenistic Gnosticism.

[80] Cf. Dib. Gefbr., *ad loc.*, who starts at R. 6:4 and concludes that this is "in fact only a schema." But this means that the word μέλη must not be dropped in translation. "The term μέλη does not ignore the distinction between the physical and the spiritual," but over against a possible Hellenistic abstraction of the vices mentioned ... πάθος, ἐπιθυμίαν κακήν ... (5) it sets from the very outset the unmistakable seriousness of the fact that concrete human members are the instruments of sinning (as against Käsemann, 150).

As in R. 12:5 and 1 C. 12:25 there is emphasis on the thought of the reciprocal ministry of the members in their interrelationship (ὑπὲρ ἀλλήλων) and for the sake of their belonging to Christ, so the same idea occurs in the crisp formulation of Eph. 4:25 : ὅτι ἐσμὲν ἀλλήλων μέλη.

Similarly, the ὅτι μέλη ἐσμὲν τοῦ σώματος αὐτοῦ of Eph. 5:30 is a stereotyped formula after a comparison between the ἐκκλησία and the γυνή. Here again, however, the older epistles supply the starting-point for the comparison, which gives a distinctive nuance to the formula. Thus in 1 C. 6:15, which has the community in view, the members must not belong to the πόρνη. Hence it involves no very difficult transition in the use of the image to see the members of Christ, the σῶμα of the ἐκκλησία, as united in legitimate marriage to the Lord (→ III, 511 f.). In Eph. 4:16, however, there seems to be a new use which goes beyond the figurative employment of σῶμα and μέλη in the earlier letters: ἡ κεφαλή, Χριστός, ἐξ οὗ πᾶν τὸ σῶμα συναρμολογούμενον καὶ συμβιβαζόμενον διὰ πάσης ἁφῆς τῆς ἐπιχορηγίας κατ' ἐνέργειαν ἐν μέτρῳ ἑνὸς ἑκάστου μέρους [81] τὴν αὔξησιν τοῦ σώματος ποιεῖται εἰς οἰκοδομὴν ἑαυτοῦ ἐν ἀγάπῃ (→ ἐκκλησία, III, 509 ff.). One might suppose that the Greek concept of organism has exerted a stronger influence here. In the διὰ πάσης ἁφῆς [82] (ligaments) regard is had to that which binds the individual members together in their common action. Nevertheless, there is no autonomous law in this growth of the body. [83] Christ creatively permeates and dominates the whole, although in what has now become a very complicated metaphor κεφαλή and σῶμα can be mentioned alongside Χριστός. The significance which is given to Christ transcends the strict metaphor of the σῶμα, for it goes beyond what can be assigned to the κεφαλή as a member. Christ is both κεφαλή and σῶμα. [84]

Is this complicated image to be interpreted only in terms of Gnostic teaching? Col. like Eph. shows [85] that in the struggle against incipient Gnostic tendencies in the Church the older Pauline metaphor of σῶμα and μέλη necessarily took on a specific colour and wider significance. This is because the chief member, the κεφαλή, becomes a christological term and is used against Gnosticism. The metaphorical character of the σῶμα changes accordingly. [86] Christ is increasingly brought into the picture: αὐτός ἐστιν ἡ κεφαλὴ τοῦ σώματος, τῆς ἐκκλησίας, Col. 1:18, and His revelation is seen against the broadest possible background of cosmological significance. This does not mean, however, that we are to take the post-Pauline Gnostic content of the terms as our starting-point and then to ex-

---

[81] AC 14. 66 mg vg syp Bas Chr Cyr Thphyl Hier have μέλους. But the better attested μέρους (ℵBDEFGKLO defg Bas Euthal Thdrt etc.) undoubtedly has here the sense of "member." Cf. μέλη καὶ μέρη from the time of Plato (→ 555) and Philo.

[82] Cf. Dib. Gefbr. on Col. 2:19; Ew. Gefbr., *ad loc.*, 202, n. 3; Pr.-Bauer³, *s.v.*

[83] Cf. Käsemann, 158.

[84] If He is both a member and also the whole σῶμα, the meaning of κεφαλή cannot be expounded simply in competition with the other μέλη, for even in OT and Rabb. thought the κεφαλή is self-evidently the member which rules over the others, → n. 33 (as against H. J. Holtzmann, *Lehrb. d. Nt. lichen Theologie*² (1911), II, 255 f.

[85] On the differences between the epistles in respect of the image cf. Dib. Gefbr. on Eph. 4:16 Exc.

[86] How easily Paul comes to allegorise his images and comparisons may be seen from 1 C. 3:10 ff.; R. 11:17 ff.; Gl. 4:22 ff.; 1 Th. 5:2 ff. The idea of Christ as the head is already intimated in 1 C. 11:3 (Christ the head of the man).

plain the μέλη of Eph. in the light of a Χριστός-εἰκών-μέλη schema.[87] To do this would be to rob the terms of their true meaning. We are rather to begin with the older Pauline epistles[88] and their realistic biblical view of the members. We can then appreciate the distinctive nuance which the term μέλη acquires in debate with the newer Gnostically orientated opponents, from whose ideas the Christology of the NT is plainly enough differentiated. In spite of statements which may seem to have a speculative bent, in the last resort being a member of the body of Jesus Christ simply means being redeemed by His death and resurrection (1:7, 20), and being integrated into His community, to which He gives comprehensive significance, but which, obedient in faith, stands actively at His disposal in pure service to others, as explicitly stated in the exhortations and household tables.

3. Epistle of James. This epistle displays a meaning of μέλος which is essentially the same as that of later Judaism. The tongue is astonishingly small as compared with other members, ἡ γλῶσσα μικρὸν μέλος, 3:5.[89] Nevertheless, it has a firm place among our members,[90] καθίσταται ἐν τοῖς μέλεσιν ἡμῶν, v. 6, which enables it to affect ὅλον τὸ σῶμα.[91] Here reference is made only to the harmful working of this most powerful member,[92] which is almost personified as an effective instrument in place of the activity of speech for which it is used.[93] The members are not regarded as an independent part of man. Here, too, they are controlled by forces which, impelled by desires, initiate conflict by means of the active members,[94] ἐκ τῶν ἡδονῶν ὑμῶν τῶν στρατευομένων ἐν τοῖς μέλεσιν ὑμῶν (4:1). The reference, then, is to conflict, though there is no explanation in terms of "the law of sin," as in Paul.[95]

D. Post-Apostolic Use.

1 Cl., 37, 5 : τὰ ἐλάχιστα μέλη τοῦ σώματος ἡμῶν ἀναγκαῖα κτλ., shows clear dependence on 1 C. 12:12 ff.,[96] and in 46, 7 the comparison of Menenius Agrippa echoes only formally in the στασιάζομεν πρὸς τὸ σῶμα ... ὥστε ἐπιλαθέσθαι ἡμᾶς ὅτι μέλη ἐσμὲν ἀλλήλων.[97] In the Ep. to Diognetus, however, the Gk. concept may be seen in the dualistic relation between the soul and the body with the members into which it is split up : ἔσπαρται κατὰ πάντων τῶν τοῦ σώματος μελῶν ἡ ψυχή. With this ψυχή are compared Χριστιανοί, scattered κατὰ τὰς τοῦ κόσμου πόλεις (Dg., 6, 2). We then read : ἡ ψυχὴ τὴν μισοῦσαν ἀγαπᾷ σάρκα καὶ τὰ μέλη (6, 6).

In the Ep. of Ignatius it is no longer just the creative overruling of the electing grace of God which brings about the pneumatic miracle of the σῶμα of the community

---

[87] Käsemann, 150.

[88] In these, too, Käsemann sees Gnostic influence, cf. → n. 67.

[89] Cf. the parable in Midr. Ps. 39:1; Str.-B., III, 447, → n. 34.

[90] Schl., *ad loc.*; Hck., *ad loc.*: "stands among them."

[91] Cf. Mt. 5:29 f.

[92] B. Stade-A. Bertholet, *Bibl. Theol. d. AT,* II (1911), 93 f., 168 f., 183 f.

[93] Schl., *ad loc.* The use for which God claims this member ἐν αὐτῇ εὐλογοῦμεν τὸν κύριον καὶ πατέρα is streaked through by the fact that the member which praises God brings itself to curse (v. 9).

[94] Since on the Rabb. view the evil impulse is thought to dwell and grow in man, the ἐν could also be taken locally, Str.-B., IV, 468; III, 95 h.

[95] On this passage and R. 7:23, Schl. Jk., 46.

[96] Not on the Stoic diatribe, cf. Knopf, *ad loc.* (Ltzm.); cf. also Just. Dial., 42, 3.

[97] The view of the σῶμα πολυμερές in πάντα τὰ μέλη on the basis of ἕνωσις and συμφωνία may be seen more clearly in the apology of Aristides, 13, 5.

consisting of many members, for here the divine acknowledgment that one is a member of His Son is based on good works: ἵνα ... ἐπιγινώσκῃ, δι' ὧν εὖ πράσσετε, μέλη ὄντας τοῦ υἱοῦ αὐτοῦ,[98] and this in the context of blameless agreement with the bishop.[99] Gnostic influence may be seen here.[100] In R., 5, 3 μέλος is used of the physical members, συγκοπὴ μελῶν at martyrdom.

Horst

† Μελχισεδέκ

1. Μελχισεδέκ (Heb. מַלְכִּי־צֶדֶק) is in Gn. 14:18 the King of Salem and priest of the Most High God (אֵל עֶלְיוֹן), a contemporary of Abraham with whom the latter has dealings in an independent anecdote.[1] In Ps. 110:4 there is ref. to this anecdote in a saying of God to the king: "Yahweh has sworn, he will not repent: Thou art a priest for ever after the manner of Melchizedek." Kingship and priesthood originally went together, and they will do so in the present and future. Similar ideas were at work in the Maccabean period (Jonathan in 1 Macc. 9:30 f.; 10:20 f.; Simon in 1 Macc. 14:41: ἡγούμενος καὶ ἀρχιερεὺς εἰς τὸν αἰῶνα). Traces may be found esp. in Test. XII (cf. Test. L. 5:1-7; 8:1-19; 17:1-11; 18:1-14; Test. Jud. 24:1-6). Apocalyptic expected the renewal of the priesthood and a future priestly monarchy, the overcoming of sin and

---

[98] Ign. Eph., 4, 2.

[99] 4, 1 and 3: οὕτως συνήρμοσται τῷ ἐπισκόπῳ, ὡς χορδαὶ κιθάρᾳ.

[100] On the relation to Gnosticism and Eph. cf. Schl. Ign., 88 ff.

Μελχισεδέκ. [1] On the name cf. F. C. Burkitt, *The Syriac Forms of NT Proper Names* (1912), 28; on his historicity and the story, G. Wuttke, "Melchisedech, der Priesterkönig von Salem," *Beih. zu* ZNW, 5 (1927); M. Friedländer, "La Secte de Melchisédec et l'épître aux Hébreux" (*Revue des études Juives*, V [1882], 1 ff., 188 ff.; VI, 187 ff.). M. Simon, "Melchisédech dans la polémique entre Juifs et Chrétiens et dans la légende," *Revue d'Histoire et de Philosophie Religieuse*, 17 (1937), 1. W. Hertzberg, "Die Melchisedektraditionen," JPOS, 8 (1928), 169-179. H. Storck, *Die sogenannten Melchisedekianer mit Untersuchung ihrer Quellen auf Gedankengehalt u. dogmengesch. Entwicklung* (1928). J. Gamble, "Symbol and Reality in the Epistle to the Hebrews," JBL, 45 (1926), 162-170. Cf. also the comm. on Gn., Ps., Hb. The name seems to be an ancient Canaanitish name constructed like Adonizedek: "My king is Zedek." W. Hertzberg conjectures that the story is "the ἱερὸς λόγος of an ancient Canaanitish sanctuary later taken over by Israel" (178) and he links it with the Palestinian sites: "The tradition of the Canaanitish priest king, which originally came from Tabor, moved to Jerusalem and the temple for Jews, to Gerizim for Samaritans, and to Golgotha for Christians. It is very probable that Melchizedek belonged to North Canaan, and that the little we know of him is one of the relics which still remain to us of the traditions appertaining to the northern territories of Palestine" (179). A. Jirku, *Geschichte d. Volkes Israel* (1931), 63, n. 25 says "that in Hb. (7:3) it is said of this Melchizedek that he was ἀπάτωρ ἀμήτωρ ἀγενεαλόγητος. As P. Haupt (JAOS [1918], 332) points out, these terms remind us of the words which Abdihipa of Jerusalem writes to the King of Egypt in one of the El Amarna letters (ed. J. A. Knudtzon [1915], I, 286, 9 ff.): 'Neither my father nor my mother has set me in this place; the mighty hand of the king has brought me into the house of my father.' Has Hb. preserved the ancient courtly style of Jerusalem?" H. Gressmann, *Der Messias* (1929) also argues that Israel took over from the Canaanites the Messianic hope and courtly style, and that the royal priesthood of Melchizedek was important in this sense in the development of Israel's religious history. One is certainly inclined to see in Gn. 14 an element of ancient Palestinian tradition.

the opening of Paradise. In Rabb. exegesis it was often conjectured that Melchizedek was another name for Shem, the son of Noah (Tg. J. I on Gn. 14:18), and interest was shifted to Abraham (PRE, 27; Seder Eliahu r., 25).[2] If Abraham paid tithes of all, his descendants receive blessing in all (Gn. r., 43 on 14:20). Doubt is sometimes cast on whether the progenitor paid tithes, and it is maintained that Yahweh Himself gave tithes to Abraham.[3] Acc. to R. Ishmael Melchizedek forfeits his priesthood by putting Abraham's name before God's in Gn. 14:19. God transfers this priestly dignity to Abraham in terms of Ps. 110:4 (Lv. r., 25 on 19:23; bNed., 32b). Sometimes we find Kohen Zedek as an eschatological entity alongside the Messiah, and it seems that there is here a link with Melchizedek (Cant. r., 2, 13; bSukka, 52b; Ab. R. Nat., 34 [Rec. A]; ed. S. Schechter [1882], 100 on Zech. 4:14). It is noteworthy that there is this eschatological Malki-Zedek or Kohen Zedek alongside the Messiah, for it implies that the personal union of priestly monarchy was not attained. For the Rabb. Melchizedek is a link in the chain of tradition: Noah-Shem-Abraham-Aaron. The fact that this stranger received tithes from Abraham is concealed in many ways, usually by focusing interest on Abraham and telling the story to his special honour. One may suppose that the Rabbinate opposed from an early period the Christian understanding of Ps. 110 and the person of Melchizedek, cf. R. Ishmael c. 135 A.D.[4]

Joseph. mentions Melchizedek in Bell., 6, 438 and Ant., 1, 180 ff. He depicts him as the founder and first priest of the city of Jerusalem, which owes its name to him (Ἱεροσόλυμα = ἱερόν and Σαλήμ).[5] Like Philo and the Rabb., he tries to work back from the name to the one who bears it, an obvious thing to do in this case. It is significant that he accepts the historicity of the story and the person, including the offence that it relates to a Χαναναίων δυνάστης. But his rationalising and moralising exegesis expunges the ancient features from Gn. 14, and, like that of the Rabbis, puts Abraham and his virtues in the forefront. The historical concern of Joseph. is not found in Philo, who mentions Melchizedek only occasionally, though with lively interest. The OT text furnishes him with the slogans βασιλεύς and ἱερεύς, so that the philosopher finds in Melchizedek the βασιλεὺς νοῦς and λόγος, Leg. All., III, 79-82. He is also the friend of Abraham, who perceives in Abraham's act the help of God, Abr., 235 f. Finally, he is an "autodidact" of the knowledge of God, whose priestly dignity is understood in this sense, Congr., 99.[6] Speculative philosophical thinking strains the concrete historical person to the very limit of the possible.

2. Starting with a christological understanding of Ps. 110, primitive Christianity comes up against the mystery of the person of Melchizedek. As the Messiah, Christ was also priest, or high-priest (ἀρχιερεύς, → III, 274 ff.). He fulfilled ancient apocalyptic expectation (already in Mk. 12:36 ?).[7] Hb., expounding homiletically the terms "Son" and "High-priest," takes up the ancient questions and themes of apocalyptic (Test. XII), and in connection with Ps. 110:4 comes to speak of

[2] Cf. also the tradition of the Samaritans in Epiph. Haer., 55, 6.

[3] Jer., too, adduces as the opinion of the Hebrews: *ambiguum habetur,* it is not known who gave and who received tithes (Ep. ad Evangelum, 73, 6): Wuttke, 20 f., n. 5; Rgg. Hb., 190, n. 25.

[4] Cf. the important exc. in Str.-B., IV, 452-465: "Der 110. Ps. in d. altrabb. Lit.," and on this J. Jeremias, ThBl (1937), 308-310.

[5] Jerome is acquainted with a Saloumias south of Scythopolis and a Salem in the same area; the ruins of the palace of Melchizedek were to be seen there. This area was described and linked with Melchizedek in the Peregrinatio Silviae. But the main interest of tradition centred on Jn. 3:23 (Aenon near to Salim). Cf. Hertzberg, 177.

[6] ὁ τὴν αὐτομαθῆ καὶ αὐτοδίδακτον λαχὼν ἱερωσύνην, Congr., 99 — a feature later taken up in the exposition of the Church.

[7] Acc. to the OT Melchizedek is a priest, but he is never called ἀρχιερεύς in the LXX, Philo, or Joseph.; he is ὁ μέγας ἱερεύς in Philo Abr., 235.

Melchizedek (5:6, 10; 6:20; 7:1 ff., 10 ff.). It then advances the mysterious understanding of Gn. 14:17-20, an example of more profound and perfect teaching (6:1). The name and dignity point to the Messianic gifts of righteousness and peace (7:2). The lack of a father's name or genealogy points to miraculous origin: he is without father, mother, or descent (7:3).[8] Silent concerning his birth and death, Scripture indicates his eternity and imperishable priesthood (7:3). In spite of these lofty statements Melchizedek is only a shadow and reflection of the Son of God (ἀφωμοιωμένος, 7:3). He has no independent significance to salvation; he is simply a divine intimation of the Son. Gn. 14:17-20 shows that he is greater than Abraham and Levi (→ 237 f.), and Ps. 110:4 proves that with him there begins a new order (τάξις) which cannot be combined with the Aaronic priesthood. Melchizedek implies the dissolving of the Jewish Law and cultus. He is at one and the same time person, intimation and order, primal history and eschatological history, the divine plan of salvation and human fulfilment (τελείωσις). Peculiar to this account are the wonderful colours of 7:2-3 (are they original to Hb.?), the christological understanding (ἀφωμοιωμένος, 7:3), and acceptance of the historical offence (non-integration into the tradition of Abraham, Levi and Aaron).[9]

3. The mysterious exposition of Hb. had a constant attraction for the later speculation of the Church and Gnosticism. Pist. Soph. and the Books of Jeû list Melchizedek among the Gnostic redeemers as a mysterious force of the kingdom of light.[10] Jewish Michael

---

[8] Acc. to Wuttke, 6 ff. Hb. uses a model in 7:2-3: "The author has taken over an original because of its highsounding form and finely polished predicates, with no profound interest in the content." We thus have the ancient courtly style, with perhaps traces of pre-Christian Melchizedek gnosis. It is certainly worth noting that the great statements of 7:2-3 are not expounded, and definitely not exploited, in Hb. E. Käsemann, *Das wandernde Gottesvolk* (1939), 134: "Neither in the case of Philo nor Hb. can one dispute acquaintance with secret traditions concerning the heavenly high-priest or insist on a pure Scripture gnosis derived from Ps. 110." Acc. to Käsemann the remarkable attributes of 7:2-3 coincide with those which Gnosticism applies to an aeon. "Is this accidental? One may deny this in respect of the very exact acquaintance of Hb. with Gnosticism, and herein corroborate the fact that Philo's Melchizedek speculation is that of a specific Jewish Gnostic tradition." F. J. Jerôme, *Das geschichtliche Melchisedek-Bild u. seine Bedeutung im Hb.* (Diss.-MS Freiburg, 1920); B. Murmelstein, "Adam, ein Beitrag zur Messiaslehre," *Wiener Zeitschrift f. die Kunde des Morgenlandes*, 35 (1928), 242-275; 36 (1929), 51-86, and Käsemann, 130 show that Gnosticism had a distinctive blend of belief in the primal man with the high-priesthood. Melchizedek can be regarded as an incarnation of the primal man and to that degree as a bearer of the Messianic high-priesthood, as elsewhere Moses, Elijah-Phinehas, Metatron, Shem or Michael. The figures change, but the schema remains. Melchizedek, who is a great high-priest in the Adam writings, discharges his office at the middle point on earth, and is also buried there (Melchizedek fragment in Slav. En.); the same is true of Adam in ancient speculations. In the Christian Book of Adam in the East this is presented in such a way that Melchizedek ministers at the tomb of Adam, carries the body of Adam to the hill of Calvary, as the bearer of his body receives his high-priestly functions, and is thus the link between the high-priest Adam and the third high-priest Christ. In the Armenian Adam writings Shem buries the corpse of Adam on Golgotha (Jerôme, 10-15; Käsemann, 130).

[9] We obviously have here an example of early Christian typology, not an allegory. Typology and allegory have a different relation to history (cf. the different approaches of Philo and Hb. to the historical past). Yet we should not miss the fact that Hb. presupposes the very specific methods and principles of later Jewish Rabb. exegesis, without which it could not reach its results.

[10] C. Schmidt, *Koptisch-gnostische Schriften* (1905); Pist. Soph. (1925).

speculation was also bound up with him at a later date (Lueken).[11] The Melchizedekians seem to have paid him cultic homage and to have imperilled the saving work of Christ by their Gnostic series of redeemers (acc. to Hipp. Ref., VII, 36; X, 24; Epiph. Haer., 55). Melchizedek, as they see it, is above Christ, and Christ is only a reflection of this divine power.[12] In this Gnostic speculation the relation between the two is often reversed and the text of Hb. misunderstood. But in Church circles, too, the mysterious hints of Hb. gave rise to many opinions and speculations (Epiph. Haer., 55),[13] though we do not find here the cultic setting which made heretical Gnosticism so dangerous.

Michel

† μέμφομαι, † μεμψίμοιρος † ἄμεμπτος, † μομφή

μέμφομαι means "to blame," "to scold," "to upbraid," common from Hesiod, also Hellen. τοὺς ἀγαθοὺς ἄλλος μάλα μέμφεται, ἄλλος ἐπαινεῖ, Theogn., 797; μέμφομ' αἶσαν τυραννίδων, Pind. Pyth., 11, 53; μηδὲ πρὸς ἄτης θηραθεῖσαι μέμψησθε τύχην, Aesch. Prom., 1072; "to chide," "to reproach," e.g., τῷ δὲ Λοξίᾳ ... μέμψιν δικαίαν μέμφομαι ταύτην, Aristoph. Pl., 10; "to declare oneself dissatisfied with something," οἵ σε ποιήσαντα ἀνόσια, νόμῳ δικαίῳ χρεώμενοι, ὑπήγαγον ἐς χεῖρας τὰς ἐμάς, ὥστε σε μὴ μέμψεσθαι τὴν ... δίκην, Hdt., VIII, 106, 8 ff.; τῶν γεωργούντων τὴν χώραν μεμφομένων, Ditt. Or., 669, 6. In the LXX Sir. 11:7: πρὶν ἐξετάσῃς, μὴ μέμψῃ ("to blame," "to scold"); πατρὶ ἀσεβεῖ μέμψεται ("to bring reproaches") τέκνα, ὅτι δι' αὐτὸν ὀνειδισθήσονται, Sir. 41:7; μεμψάμενος αὐτοῖς 2 Macc. 2:7.

In the LXX there is no established Heb. original. At Sir. 11:7 it is used for סלף, which is found only here in Sir. and which occurs 7 times in the Mas. (4 times in Prv.), being variously translated in Gk. In Sir. 41:7 and 2 Macc. 2:7 the personal obj. is in the dat. Cf. also Job 1:22 Heb.: οὐκ ἐμέμψατο τῷ θεῷ for לֹא־נָתַן תִּפְלָה לֵאלֹהִים (LXX: οὐκ ἔδωκεν ἀφροσύνην τῷ θεῷ). In Job 33:27 ἀπομέμψεται ἑαυτῷ has no original in the Mas.[1]

μεμψίμοιρος is based on the combination μέμφεσθαι μοῖραν (which is not attested, but is to be assumed on the model of μέμφεσθαι τύχην, δίκην): "one who bemoans his fate or destiny," "who is dissatisfied with it," "who complains or grumbles." Isoc., 12, 8: οὕτω τὸ γῆρας ἐστι δυσάρεστον καὶ μικρολόγον καὶ μεμψίμοιρον, Luc. Jup. Trag., 40: ἐκείνη (Diana) μεμψίμοιρος οὖσα ἠγανάκτησεν, Aristot. Hist. An., IX, 1, p. 608b, 8 ff.: γυνὴ ἀνδρὸς ... φθονερώτερον καὶ μεμψιμοιρότερον.[2]

---

[11] Rgg. Hb., 179; Wuttke, 24.

[12] Hipp. Ref., VII, 36, 16 f.: τοῦτον εἶναι μείζονα τοῦ Χριστοῦ, οὗ κατ' εἰκόνα φάσκουσι τὸν Χριστὸν τυγχάνειν; X, 24, 13: φάσκοντες αὐτὸν ὑπὲρ πᾶσαν δύναμιν ὑπάρχειν.

[13] Cf. also Marcus Eremita, MPG, 65, p. 1117 ff. On this J. Kunze, *Marcus Eremita* (1895) and Wuttke, 32 ff. Acc. to the teachers combatted by Epiph. and Marcus Eremita Melchizedek was an appearance of the λόγος θεός prior to the historical incarnation.

μέμφομαι κτλ. [1] This paragraph is by Bertram.

[2] But cf. the definition in Cl. Al. Paed., I, 9, 80, 3: μεμψιμοιρία δέ ἐστι λάθριος ψόγος, τεχνικῇ βοηθείᾳ καὶ αὐτὴ σωτηρίαν οἰκονομουμένη ἐν παρακαλύμματι (... a hidden fault, yet with skilful help she will bring deliverance in disguise).

ἄμεμπτος, [3] a person or object which is "without blame," "blameless," so ἄμεμπτος, Plat. Leg., XI, 924a; ἄμεμπτος ὑπὸ τῶν φίλων, Xenoph. Ag., 6, 8; ἄμεμπτον δεῖπνον, Xenoph. Sym., 2, 2; ἄμεμπτος δίκη, Plat. Leg., XII, 945d, also used act.: ἄμεμπτόν τινα ποιεῖν, Xenoph. Cyrop., IV, 5, 52. In the LXX this word is surprisingly common in Job (elsewhere only Gn. 17:1; Wis. 10:5, 15; 18:21). Job is an ἄνθρωπος ... ἀληθινός, ἄμεμπτος, δίκαιος, θεοσεβής, 1:1, 8; 2:3. One of his friends raises the question: μὴ καθαρὸς ἔσται βροτὸς ἐναντίον κυρίου ἢ ἀπὸ τῶν ἔργων αὐτοῦ ἄμεμπτος ἀνήρ; (4:17), to which he expects a negative reply. Another gives the similar admonition: μὴ ... λέγε ὅτι καθαρός εἰμι τοῖς ἔργοις καὶ ἄμεμπτος ἐναντίον αὐτοῦ (11:4), cf. also 15:14; 22:3; 33:9; though cf. Job himself, 9:20; 12:4. The orientation of ἄμεμπτος in the LXX is thus more specific than in Gk. use, for the final decision concerning it is not in the hands of a human court. What is at issue is an ἄμεμπτος before God.

For ἄμεμπτος, as for most words constructed with an α privativum, there is no direct equivalent in Heb. Several positive terms are used such as pure, perfect, pious, righteous, cf. בַּר, זָכָה, זָכַךְ, חַף (only Job 33:9 in the Mas.), טָהֵר, נָקִי, תָּם, תָּמִים, צַדִּק, יָשָׁר. All these words objectively reflect a state, whereas the LXX ἄμεμπτος expresses a subjective judgment, just as μέμφομαι (as distinct from μωμάομαι) expresses subjective blame. In an anon. Gk. tradition ἄμεμπτος is used at Ps. 1:1 for אֶשֶׁר; it is also used 3 times in the Ps. for תָּמִים. [4]

μέμψις, from Aesch., "censure": μέμψιν μέμφεσθαι, Aristoph. Pl., 10; μέμψις δέ ἐστι ψόγος ὡς ὀλιγωρούντων ἢ ἀμελούντων (namely, τὸν θεόν), Cl. Al. Paed., I, 9, 77, 3. In the LXX at Wis. 13:6 and Job 33:10: μέμψιν ... κατ' ἐμοῦ εὗρεν, cf. 33:23; 39:7.

There is no direct Heb. term for μέμψις either. תְּנוּאָה in Job 33:10 is an occasion for enmity. In the only other passage where it occurs in the Mas. (Nu. 14:34) the LXX has τὸν θυμὸν τῆς ὀργῆς μου. Acc. to Ges.-Buhl it here means God's alienation from man. תְּשֻׁאוֹת, "noise," "tumult," occurs 4 times in the Mas.: in Is. 22:2 βοῶντες perhaps comprises the various synonyms for noise. At Zech. 4:7 and Job 36:29 the LXX has ἰσότης, at Job 39:7 μέμψις. The LXX thus seems not to be properly acquainted with the Heb. term, but to render it arbitrarily. On the other hand, at Qoh. 7:15 it has μέμψις for מאום, which it obviously assumes instead of מְאוּמָה Mas. The root מאום, however, is normally translated by the synon. μωμᾶσθαι in the LXX. [5]

μομφή — constructed like νομή from νέμω [6] — means "blame" or "reproach," μομφὰν ἔχει παίδεσσιν Ἑλλάνων, Pind. Isthm., 4, 61; μομφῆς ἄτερ, Aesch. Sept. c. Theb., 1010; ἓν μὲν πρῶτά σοι μομφὴν ἔχω, Eur. Or., 1069. It does not occur in the LXX.

In the NT Hb. 8:8 reads: μεμφόμενος γὰρ αὐτοὺς λέγει ... (there follows a prophetic word of promise and censure to the covenant-breaking Israelites). God does not reject the ancient covenant. The faithless Israelites are the occasion of new covenant action on the part of God. Their unfaithful conduct is an object of μέμφεσθαι, and they have robbed the old covenant of its significance (εἰ γὰρ ἡ πρώτη ἐκείνη ἦν ἄμεμπτος, οὐκ ἂν δευτέρας ἐζητεῖτο τόπος, 8:7).

R. 9:19: τί ἔτι μέμφεται; Paul raises an objection (ἐρεῖς μοι οὖν) which takes the form of this question. The objection is to the thesis which he espouses, and which he finds confirmed in the history of Israel, namely, that God is free in His

---

[3] Cf. Pass. (-Cr.), *s.v.*
[4] This paragraph is by Bertram.
[5] This paragraph is by Bertram.
[6] P. Chantraine, *La formation des noms en grec ancien* (1933), 20 f.

acts, and that man is subject to the free sovereignty with which God brings all things to pass. History is brought to pass by God, and it serves His purpose, namely, the demonstration of His power and the declaration of His name throughout the world. Both His mercy and His hardening serve this end. His will and purpose embrace both positive and negative action. The question thus arises how in these circumstances God can speak a word of blame,[7] for it is impossible to resist His will. Paul rejects the question with a reference to the fact that man has no right to dispute with God. The problem is that of the omnicausality of God and the fault of man.

In Phil. 3:6 Paul says of himself: κατὰ δικαιοσύνην τὴν ἐν νόμῳ γενόμενος ἄμεμπτος. This judgment agrees with his self-assessment in Gl. 1:14 and is a significant testimony to Pharisaic self-understanding.[8] One should not emphasise in this self-evaluation the fact of blamelessness in respect of righteousness according to the Law. This is simply the presupposition of the other statements: κατὰ ζῆλος — Gl. 1:14: περισσοτέρως ζηλωτὴς ὑπάρχων τῶν πατρικῶν μου παραδόσεων — διώκων τὴν ἐκκλησίαν. The sin of Paul is the persecution of the Church.[9] But this persecution is zeal for the Law of the fathers and the fulfilment of Halachic exposition. Thus zeal for the Law and fulfilment of the Halacha becomes sin, and righteousness by the Law becomes impossible, not because he cannot keep the Law, but because keeping it is itself sin. This is the Damascus experience which gives rise to the question of the righteousness of faith.[10]

For Paul it is the destiny of Christians to be ἄμεμπτοι before God: ... ἵνα γένησθε ἄμεμπτοι καὶ ἀκέραιοι ..., Phil. 2:15; εἰς τὸ στηρίξαι ὑμῶν τὰς καρδίας ἀμέμπτους ἐν ἁγιωσύνῃ ἔμπροσθεν τοῦ θεοῦ καὶ πατρὸς ἡμῶν ἐν τῇ παρουσίᾳ τοῦ κυρίου ἡμῶν Ἰησοῦ ..., 1 Th. 3:13. The verdict ἄμεμπτος is the eschatological judgment of God on His day. To be ἄμεμπτοι ἔμπροσθεν τοῦ θεοῦ is the task of Christians. It is possible because as those who are justified by faith they have received the gift of the Holy Spirit whose fruit and operation is pleasing to God. Thus ἄμεμπτος can be both a motif of admonition and a sum of life's purpose (→ ἔπαινος, II, 587). Paul can now bear this testimony concerning his apostolic office: ὁσίως καὶ δικαίως καὶ ἀμέμπτως ὑμῖν τοῖς πιστεύουσιν ἐγενήθημεν, 1 Th. 2:10. And the blessing which he pronounces is a request for the preservation of the whole man: ἀμέμπτως ἐν τῇ παρουσίᾳ τοῦ κυρίου ἡμῶν Ἰησοῦ Χριστοῦ (1 Th. 5:23).

μέμψις does not occur in the NT, but μομφή is found in Col. 3:13: ἀνεχόμενοι ἀλλήλων καὶ χαριζόμενοι ἑαυτοῖς, ἐάν τις πρός τινα ἔχῃ μομφήν ("reproach").

---

7 So rightly E. Kühl, *Brief d. Pls. an d. R.* (1913), 328 as opposed to Zn. R., 453.

8 → ἁμαρτωλός, I, 327, also Erik Sjöberg, "Gott und die Sünder im palästinischen Judentum," BWANT, IV, 27 (1939), 152, n. 2. Lk. 1:6 of the parents of John the Baptist: πορευόμενοι ἐν πάσαις ταῖς ἐντολαῖς καὶ δικαιώμασιν τοῦ κυρίου ἄμεμπτοι.

9 E.g., 1 C. 15:9 f.; Gl. 1:13 f.; Eph. 3:8; 1 Tm. 1:13 ff.

10 Cf. esp. R. 9:30-10:4. There is here a decisive difference from Luther's experience in the cloister with its non-fulfilment of God's will, and from the outline of his doctrine of justification. R. 7 should not be used to explain the Damascus experience in terms of a moral cleavage. Cf. W. G. Kümmel, *Römer 7 u. die Bekehrung des Pls.* (1929) and R. Bultmann, "Römer 7 und die Anthropologie des Pls.," *Imago Die, Festschr. f. G. Krüger* (1932), 53 ff.

In Jd. 16 the false teachers are called μεμψίμοιροι. If their opposition to the order of the community is expressed by the ἀντιλογία τοῦ Κόρε (v. 11), the γογγυσταὶ μεμψίμοιροι shows that they are in opposition to God [11] and to the destiny (μοῖρα) which He has laid upon them. They are dissatisfied with God and they criticise His guidance.

Grundmann

μένω, ἐμ-, παρα-, περι-, προσμένω, μονή, ὑπομένω, ὑπομονή

μένω.

The concept of remaining or abiding takes different forms according to the different relations and antonyms in view.

μένειν means 1. intrans. a. "to remain in a place," "to tarry," opp. to go away. Polyb., 30, 4, 10; Plat. Euthyphr., 15b; Gn. 24:55; 45:9; Rev. 17:10; "to stay in the house," Aesch. Fr., 300; Lk. 8:27; 19:5, then esp. in the Hell. period "to stay overnight" (cf. *manere, mansio*), Ju. 19:9 ʼΑ (לִין), "to dwell," Jn. 1:38 f.; Preisigke Sammelbuch, 2639 : ποῦ μένι Θερμοῦθις; "to stay alive," Epict. Diss., III, 24, 97; Diog. L., VII, 174(5) (opp. ἀπιέναι); fig. "to remain in a sphere," Plat. Ep., 10, 358c : μένε ἐν τοῖς ἤθεσιν οἷσπερ καὶ νῦν μένεις, Prot., 356e : τὴν ψυχὴν μένουσαν ἐπὶ τῷ ἀληθεῖ, Test. Jos. 1:3 : ἔμεινα ἐν τῇ ἀληθείᾳ Κυρίου. b. "To stand against opposition," "to hold out," "to stand fast," opp. to waver, to flee, Hom. Il., 16, 838; Hdt., VIII, 62; Epict. Diss., II, 16, 42 (opp. φεύγειν); in legal disputation, P. Tebt., II, 391, 24 : ὁ μένων, the party which remains true to the agreement. c. "To remain," "to stay still," opp. to move, to be moved, to be changed, Hom. Od., 17, 570; Aristot. Cael., II, 8, p. 290a, 21: οἱ μένοντες, the fixed stars as compared with the planets ; Philo Som., II, 221 of the eternal God : ἑστὼς ἐν ὁμοίῳ καὶ μένων, ἄτρεπτος ὤν, πρὶν ἢ σὲ ἤ τι τῶν ὄντων εἰς γένεσιν ἐλθεῖν, of the unchanging and perfect Word of God, Fug., 13 : μένει γὰρ ἡ αὐτὴ ποιότης ἅτε ἀπὸ μένοντος ἐκμαγεῖσα καὶ μηδαμῇ τρεπομένου θείου λόγου. d. "To remain," "to last," esp. "to remain in legal force," opp. to perish, Hom. Il., 17, 434; Plat. Crat., 440a (opp. μεταπίπτει); Crito, 48b (ὁ λόγος); Eur. Andr., 1000 : ὅρκοι; Epict. Diss., III, 24, 10 (opp. κινεῖσθαι); so esp. of legal agreements, BGU, I, 2, 17 f. (3rd cent.): πρὸς τὸ μένειν ἐμοὶ τὸν λόγον πρὸς αὐτοὺς περ[ὶ τούτο]υ, CPR, 228, 10 (3rd cent.): μένοντός μοι τοῦ λόγου πρὸς ὑμᾶς, P. Amh., 85, 21 (1st cent.) ὅπως ... μένηι ἡ μίσθωσις βεβαία, BGU, I, 361, col. II, 30 f.: διαθήκη ἄλυ[τος] μένῃ. Religiously μένειν is a mark of God and of what is commensurate with Him, Porphyr. Vit. Pyth., 38 : τὸ μένον, Philo Ebr., 212 : τὰ μένοντα τῆς φύσεως

11 → γογγυστής, I, 737 and → γογγύζω.

λαμπάδια ἄσβεστα; Leg. All., III, 100 of the νοῦς: ὅστις οὐκ ἀπὸ τῶν γεγονότων τὸ αἴτιον γνωρίζει ὡς ἂν ἀπὸ σκιᾶς τὸ μένον. Det. Pot. Ins., 75: Men, artists died, αἱ δὲ τούτων ἰδέαι μένουσι καὶ τρόπον τινὰ βιοῦσιν ἰσοχρόνιοι τῷ κόσμῳ. 2. trans. "to expect someone," Hom. Il., 8, 565; 2 Macc. 7:30; Ac. 20:5.

The LXX uses μένειν mostly for עמד ("to stand," "to last," "to remain," "to endure," "to remain alive"), commonly for קום ("to stand up," "to stand," "to take place," Is. 7:7, "to be lasting," Job 15:29, "to stand on something," Is. 32:8, "to be in force," Nu. 30:5), more rarely for ישב ("to remain sitting," Gn. 24:55, "to dwell," "to remain undisturbed," Zech. 14:10), חכה ("to delay," 2 K. 7:9; Is. 8:17), קוה ("to wait," Is. 5:2, 4, 7) etc.

In the OT the abiding of God and the things and persons relating to God is of religious and theological significance. As distinct from the mutability and transitoriness of everything earthly and human, God is characterised by the fact that He endures. To speak also of eternity simply gives strength to the thought (ψ 9:7; 101:12). Perishing is partly a characteristic of what is earthly or less than divine (Is. 40:8; ψ 101:12), partly a consequence of divine judgment (Job 15:29; Ιερ. 26[33]:15; Da. 11:6). God is θεὸς ζῶν καὶ μένων εἰς τοὺς αἰῶνας. He is thus superior to false gods (Da. 6:27, קים). God's counsel remains (Is. 14:24, קום), while all the plans of His enemies are bound to fail and to be broken by Him (ψ 32:11, עמד; Prv. 19:21; Is. 7:7, קום). His Word, especially His Word of address and promise, abides (Is. 40:8, קום). In eschatological expectation the wealthy among men, who perish, stand contrasted with the dominion of God, which endures (Da. 4:26, קים). The new heaven and the new earth will also remain (Is. 66:22, עמד). The new Jerusalem is the city which will know no destruction (Zech. 14:10, ישב). Divine wisdom remains, and will make all things new (Wis. 7:27). The righteous and their generation will share in God's abiding (Sir. 44:13). Their δικαιοσύνη endures (ψ 111:3, 9). Their counsel stands in face of the ungodly (Is. 32:8, קום).

In the NT, too, μένειν is used 1. of the immutability of God and the things of God, e.g., His counsel, which cannot be changed, R. 9:11, His Word, which remains as compared with what is human and corruptible, 1 Pt. 1:23, 25,[1] the office of the NT as compared with the transitory (καταργούμενον) office of the OT, 2 C. 3:11, πίστις, ἐλπίς, ἀγάπη as things which abide, 1 C. 13:13 (compared with πίπτει, καταργηθήσονται, παύσονται, v. 8, cf. 4 Esr. 9:37).[2] μένειν is particularly common in the Johannine writings.[3] The statement that Jesus Himself abides in Jn. 12:34 is undoubtedly designed to assert apologetically the eternal character of the dignity of Jesus in face of Jewish protests which deny His Messiahship on the basis of His transitory earthly existence.[4] The abiding of the

μένω. [1] V. 23: ζῶντος θεοῦ καὶ μένοντος, seems to echo Da. 6:27, though in view of what follows in v. 24 f. it is to be taken with λόγου, cf. Kn. Pt., 81; Wnd. Kath. Br., 55.

[2] The statement in 1 C. 13:13 is not logically constructed. In the context one would expect to hear only of the abiding of love in contrast to the transitoriness of the *charismata* previously mentioned (v. 8). Joh. W. 1 K., 320 f. suggests that Paul uses a fixed formula, A. Harnack, SAB (1911), 132-163; R. Reitzenstein, GGA, *Phil.-hist. Kl.* (1916), 367-416; (1917), 130-151; (1922), 256; ThStKr, 94 (1922), 94 f. E. Lehmann-A. Fridrichsen on 1 C. 13).

[3] μένειν occurs 112 times in the NT, 66 times in the Johannine writings (40 in the Gospel, 23 in 1 Jn., 3 in 2 Jn.). On the Johannine μένειν cf. H. Hanse, "'Gott haben' in der Antike u. im frühen Chrt.," RVV, 27 (1939), 132.

[4] On the eternal duration of the Messianic age, cf. Ez. 37:25; Ps. 110:4; Ps. Sol. 17:4; En. 49:1; 62:14; Sib. 3:49, 50, 767: Str.-B., II, 552.

Spirit on Christ in Jn. 1:32 lifts Him above the prophets, who are honoured only with temporary inspiration. It also lifts His filling with the Spirit, and the later filling of Christians, above the passing ecstatic states of pagans. The endowment of the Spirit is a continuing state in the Christian religion.

2. Along the lines of the common Greek expression μένειν ἐν (→ 1. a) the NT often refers to the psychological abiding of the righteous in the things which belong to salvation, 1 Tm. 2:15 : ἐν πίστει καὶ ἀγάπῃ, 2 Tm. 3:14 : ἐν οἷς ἔμαθες, cf. Ign. Pol., 5, 2 : ἐν ἁγνείᾳ. In the Johannine writings such phrases are developed into distinctive personal statements concerning the lasting immanence between God and Christ or Christians and Christ (→ II, 542 f.). This is a stronger form of the Pauline ἐν Χριστῷ (→ II, 541 f.).

The Johannine use is built on earlier models and analogies. The idea of a spirit dwelling in man is a formal analogy in Mt. 12:43 ff. Paul speaks analogously of the → οἰκεῖν of the Spirit or of Christ in the believer, and *vice versa,* R. 8:8 ff. Philo speaks in Stoic fashion of the dwelling of the divine λόγος or νοῦς in man, Poster. C., 122; Mut. Nom., 265; Det. Pot. Ins., 4 (ἐνοικεῖν, ἐμπεριπατεῖν). On the basis of Gn. 6:3 LXX he draws a distinction : πνεῦμα θεῖον μένειν μὲν δυνατὸν ἐν ψυχῇ, διαμένειν δὲ ἀδύνατον, ὡς εἴπομεν, Gig., 28 (cf. 19). Judaism speaks of the dwelling of the Shekinah in the people of God or among believers. [5]

By the use of μένειν Jn. seeks to express the immutability and inviolability of the relation of immanence. In so doing he elevates the Christian religion above what is attained in Hellenistic rapture or even in the prophecy of Israel. Thus God abides in Christ, 14:10. Believers abide in Christ (6:56; 15:4-7; 1 Jn. 2:6, 27 f.; 3:6, 24) and Christ in them (Jn. 15:4-7; 1 Jn. 3:24). God abides in believers (1 Jn. 4:16), and believers in God (1 Jn. 2:24; 4:16). The eschatological promise of salvation becomes immediate possession in virtue of this statement in the present tense. Nevertheless, Jn. keeps to an expression (μένειν ἐν) which maintains biblical theism and avoids the assertions of identity found in Hellenistic mysticism. [6] After the analogy of the personal statement Jn. uses μένειν ἐν for the abiding of the expressions of divine life in believers, e.g., God's Word in Jn. 5:38; 15:7; 1 Jn. 2:14; life, 1 Jn. 3:15; love, 1 Jn. 3:17; truth, 2 Jn. 2; anointing, 1 Jn. 2:27. Believers, too, abide in divine things, e.g., in God's house, Jn. 8:35; love, Jn. 15:9, 10; light, 1 Jn. 2:10; doctrine, 2 Jn. 9. Here again the relationship of salvation is both enduring and present. The same is true of perdition. Unbelievers abide in darkness (Jn. 12:46) and death (1 Jn. 3:14).

† ἐμμένω.

a. "To abide in something," Xenoph. An., IV, 7, 17; Herm. v., 3, 6, 3. b. "To keep to something," Hdt., IX, 106, 28 f. (ὁρκίοισι ἐμμενέειν καὶ μὴ ἀποστήσεσθαι); M. Ant., IV, 30 (τῷ λόγῳ); Polyb., 3, 70, 4 (ἐν τῇ πίστει); Plat. Crito, 50c (ἐμμενεῖν ταῖς δίκαις αἷς ἂν ἡ πόλις δικάζῃ); 53a; common in legal documents in connection with penal clauses for not fulfilling an agreement, CPR, 224, 5 f. (5th/6th cent. A.D.):

---

[5] Examples in Str.-B., I, 794. For Mandaean usage cf. Lidz. Ginza, Index, *s.v.* "Wohnung"; R. Reitzenstein-H. H. Schaeder, "Studien z. antiken Synkretismus ...," *Studien d. Bibliothek Warburg,* 7 (1926), 316 ff.

[6] Cf. Corp. Herm., V, 11.

ἐμμένειν ἐν πᾶσι τοῖς γεγε[νημένοις κατὰ τὴ]ν γραφὴν τῆς ὁμολογίας (agreement), ἣν συγγέγραμμαί σοι, BGU, II, 600, 6 (2nd/3rd cent. A.D.): ἐνμένω πᾶσι τοῖς προγεγραμμέν[α]ις [ἐν]τολαῖς. Jos. Ap., 2, 144; Ant., 16, 177 (τοῖς νόμοις).

Once in the LXX for חכה [1] at Is. 30:18 of the righteous waiting on God, also 8 times for קום (→ μένω), esp. in sayings about abiding by one's promised word, e.g., an alliance (φιλία) in 1 Macc. 10:26, the ἐντολαί of God, Sir. 28:6, vows, Ιερ. 51(44):25 (ὁμολογίαις), esp. in threats for unfaithfulness to an agreement (→ *supra*), Dt. 27:26: ἐπικατάρατος πᾶς ἄνθρωπος, ὃς οὐκ ἐμμενεῖ ἐν πᾶσιν τοῖς λόγοις τοῦ νόμου τούτου τοῦ ποιῆσαι αὐτούς. The OT contrasts God's reliable keeping to His Word (Nu. 23:19) with man's inconstancy: Is. 8:10 (man's word); 28:18 (false hope); Ιερ. 38(31):32 (covenant unfaithfulness).

In the NT it has a topographical reference at Ac. 28:30 (ἐν ἰδίῳ μισθώματι). Religiously it is used of persistence in faith in spite of pressing temptations (Ac. 14:22), and of abiding in διαθήκη with God (Hb. 8:9 = Ιερ. 38[31]:32). It also occurs in warnings against not keeping an agreement in Gl. 3:10, where by additions to Dt. 27:26 LXX Paul strengthens the reminiscence of the current legal formula: πᾶς ὃς οὐκ ἐμμένει πᾶσιν τοῖς γεγραμμένοις ἐν τῷ βιβλίῳ τοῦ νόμου. In this way Paul expresses the more clearly that human sin is a failure to keep the covenant and automatically brings down upon itself the threats attached thereto.

† παραμένω.

a. "To remain in place," "to stay," P. Flor., III, 365, 7 (3rd cent.): ἐνθάδε παραμένειν. "To remain in the house," Hdt., I, 64; "to remain in a place or spot," opp. to run away, esp. of a slave, Plat. Men., 97e: ὥσπερ δραπέτην ἄνθρωπον — οὐ γὰρ παραμένει, of a warring army, "to stand firm," Il., 13, 151; Thuc., VII, 15, 1: ἀδύνατός εἰμι διὰ νόσον νεφρῖτιν παραμένειν· ἀξιῶ δ' ὑμῶν ξυγγνώμης τυγχάνειν, abs. "to remain alive," Hdt., I, 30; of things, "to endure," "to remain": of nature, Eur. El., 942: ἀεὶ παραμένουσα, Xenoph. Cyrop., I, 6, 17: ἡ ὑγίεια, Lys. Or., 25, 28. b. With the dat. of person, "to stay with someone," "steadfastly to stand by him," Hom. Il., 11, 402; Aristoph. Pax, 1108: παράμεινον τὸν βίον ἡμῖν, P. Oxy., IV, 725, 43; esp. of a slave, who is to stay in someone's service: Xenoph. Oec., 3, 4; hence commonly Παρμένων as a slave's name. In wills manumission is often granted on the condition ἐφ' ᾧ παραμενεῖ αὐτῇ τὸ[ν] τῆς ζωῆς αὐτῆς χρόνον, Ditt. Syll.³, 1210, 7 ff. παραμένειν is here almost a euphemism for "to serve," P. Petr., III, 2, 21 (236 B.C.): Slaves should be free, ἐάμ μοι παραμείνω[σιν ἕ]ως ἂν ἐγὼ ζῶι, BGU, IV, 1126, 8 (8 B.C.); Ditt. Syll.², 850, 5 (173/172 B.C.); similarly of an apprentice, e.g., in the agreement in P. Tebt., II, 384, 21 f. (10 B.C.): παρεξόμεθα τὸν ἀδελφὸν ὑμῶν (read ἡμῶν) Πασίωνα π[αραμέ]νοντα αὐτῷ ἐνιαυτὸν ἕνα. Of things, "to remain with someone," Jos. Ant., 11, 309: τῆς ἱερατικῆς τιμῆς ... τῷ γένει παραμενούσης, Plat. Leg., VI, 769c: σμικρόν τινα χρόνον αὐτῷ πόνος παραμενεῖ πάμπολυς. c. With dat. of object: "to remain or persist in an occupation or state," Jos. Ant., 9, 273 of the priests: ἵνα ἀεὶ τῇ θρησκείᾳ παραμένωσιν.

In the LXX a. Jdt. 12:7: παρέμεινεν ἐν τῇ παρεμβολῇ, of the unfaithful and untrustworthy friend: Sir. 6:8: οὐ μὴ παραμείνῃ ἐν ἡμέρᾳ θλίψεώς σου, Prv. 12:7:

ἐ μ μ έ ν ω. Deissmann NB, 76 f.: A. Berger, *Die Strafklauseln in den Papyrusurkunden* (1911), 3 f.; O. Eger, "Rechtswörter u. Rechtsbilder in den paul. Briefen," ZNW, 18 (1917/18), 94.

[1] For חכה we elsewhere have ὑπομένω, ψ 32:20; 105:13; Is. 64:3, or μένω, Is. 8:17.

of the house or family of the righteous which endures (עָמַד), unlike the ungodly whom God overthrows and destroys. God, the Eternal and Almighty, makes judicial decision concerning being and perishing. b. In Gn. 44:33 Judah volunteers to remain (יָשַׁב) with Joseph as a slave — serving (→ 577). In Sir. 11:17 (δόσις κυρίου παραμένει εὐσεβέσιν), as in Prv. 12:7 (→ *supra*), God is addressed as the superior power on which abiding depends.

In the NT παραμένειν means 1. "to stay with someone" (→ a.) with a hint of service (→ 577). Since Paul has in view his missionary work, the word has the profoundest possible content. Thus in 1 C. 16:6: πρὸς ὑμᾶς ... παραμενῶ [1] ἢ καὶ παραχειμάσω. The winter, which is no use for travel, is to be devoted to the Corinthian church. In Phil. 1:25 Paul characteristically changes the expected avoidance of martyrdom (μένειν, "to remain alive") into the ethical παραμενῶ πᾶσιν ὑμῖν εἰς τὴν ὑμῶν προκοπὴν καὶ χαρὰν τῆς πίστεως. Instead of attaining by martyrdom to the union with Christ for which he yearns, he will stay to serve them. Selfish desires are subordinated to the service and furtherance of the congregation. [2]

2. "To continue in a matter or occupation" (→ c.). Christ, who remains a high-priest for ever, is contrasted with the OT priests, who cannot remain in their priesthood because of the law of death, Hb. 7:23. [3] In Jm. 1:25 παραμείνας (along with παρακύψας εἰς νόμον τέλειον τὸν τῆς ἐλευθερίας) has in view an abiding in the Law which is ready to receive and to obey it, [4] as contrasted with the superficial man, who goes away from the mirror of God's Word without amendment, 1:23. Only this willing abiding in the Law, which is prepared to be effectively transformed by it, can lead to salvation (cf. Jn. 8:31).

† περιμένω.

a. "To expect," with acc. of person, Hdt., IV, 89; Xenoph. An., II, 4, 1; P. Giess., 73, 3 f. (time of Hadrian): ἐκομισάμην σου τὴν ἐπιστολὴν ἡδέως καὶ περιμένω σε, also with acc. of obj.: Plat. Phaed., 115a: οὕτω περιμένει (sc. the dying sage) τὴν εἰς Ἅιδου πορείαν ὡς πορευσόμενος, ὅταν ἡ εἱμαρμένη καλῇ. M. Ant., V, 10, 9: περιμένειν τὴν φυσικὴν λύσιν (dissolution, death); V, 33, 15. b. Of events: "to await someone," Soph. Ant., 1296: τίς με πότμος (destiny) ἔτι περιμένει, Plat. Resp., X, 614a: ἃ τελευτήσαντα ἑκάτερον περιμένει. c. Abs., like the simple μένω, "to wait," "to stand still," Hdt., VII, 58; Plat. Ap., 38c: ὀλίγον χρόνον, with inf., Plat. Resp., II, 375c: οὐ περιμενοῦσιν ἄλλους σφᾶς διολέσαι, with ἕως, Plat. Phaed., 59d: περιμένειν ... ἕως ἀνοιχθείη τὸ δεσμωτήριον, Polyb., 5, 56, 2: μηδ᾿ ἕως τούτου περιμεῖναι μέχρις ἂν οὗ τοῖς ὁμοίοις τἀδελφῷ παλαίῃ συμπτώμασιν.

It occurs only twice in the LXX. In Gn. 49:18 (for קוה pi) [1] it is the tense waiting

---

παραμένω. [1] So ℌℜ DG as opp. to B 1739: καταμενῶ.

[2] Loh. Phil., 67, also n. 3.

[3] τῇ ἱερωσύνῃ should be supplied from v. 24 (Rgg. Hb., *ad loc.*), since otherwise there would be tautology with τὸ θανάτῳ κωλύεσθαι.

[4] Cf. Ps. 1:2; Dt. 6:6 ff.

περιμένω. [1] קוה, connected with קַו, tense thread, "to be tense," of the expectant spirit, esp. the righteous who, in spite of worldly happenings, set their expectant hope in God, q: Ps. 25:3; 37:9; Is. 40:31; pi: of the hope of the righteous in God, Ps. 25:5; 39:7; 40:1; of the yearning expectation of those in trouble for the end of their distress, Job 7:2 (LXX ἀναμένω); 30:26 (LXX ἐπέχω).

of a dying man for divine aid (יְשׁוּעָה, σωτηρία), and in Wis. 8:12 it denotes the respectful, silent waiting of the lowly for the pronouncement of the wise man.

The only instance in the NT is at Ac. 1:4, where it signifies waiting for the fulfilment of the promise of the end.[2]

† προσμένω.

a. Abs. "to remain," "to stay on," "to wait longer," Hdt., I, 199; Ditt. Syll.[3], 615, 7 (180 B.C.). b. With dat.: "to stay with someone or something," "to be attached, or faithful, to him," πάθεα προσμένει τοκεῦσιν, Aesch. Eum., 497. c. Trans. "to expect someone," "to wait for someone," Soph. Oed. Tyr., 837.

It occurs only twice in the LXX. For a. cf. Ju. 3:25 : προσέμειναν (חיל)[1] αἰσχυνόμενοι καὶ ἰδοὺ οὐκ ἦν ὁ ἀνοίγων τὰς θύρας, for b. Wis. 3:9 : οἱ πιστοὶ ἐν ἀγάπῃ προσμενοῦσιν αὐτῷ, of the righteous who on the basis of the grace which they have received wait hopefully for God. This expression corresponds to the common Heb. יחל, which in the pi (Ps. 31:24; 33:18, 22; 69:3; 130:7 etc.) and in the hi (Ps. 38:15; 42:5, 11; 43:5; 130:5 etc.) depicts the righteous as those who in faith wait upon God and cling fast to Him.[2]

In the NT cf. for a. abs. Ac. 18:18; 1 Tm. 1:3, and for b., "to remain with someone," Mk. 8:2; Mt. 15:32 of the multitude which stayed whole days with Jesus, with an implicit element of believing adherence and confident personal commitment to Him as the divinely sent Helper. Ac. 11:23 refers to faithful going on with the Lord, which is a decisive demand made upon Christians in addition to the initial decision of conversion (cf. Lk. 8:15). Perseverance in face of all the disturbing experiences of suffering is also included (cf. ἐμμένειν, Ac. 14:22). Faithful cleaving to the saving revelation of God is contrasted with the vacillation which for the slightest reason lets go of the salvation found (Ac. 13:43; cf. Mk. 4:17 πρόσκαιροι). The righteous widow of 1 Tm. 5:5 is known by her faithful and confident persistence in prayer as compared with giddy younger widows who are quickly turned from Christ by attractive worldly goals (v. 11).

† μονή.

a. "Stay," "tarrying," Eur. Tro., 1129; Hdt., I, 94 (opp. ἔξοδος ἐκ τῆς χώρας); Plat. Leg., IX, 856e; Crat., 437b (opp. φορά, movement); Aristot. Phys., III, 5, p. 205a, 17 (opp. κίνησις); Philo Abr., 58 : Nothing is higher than God, πρὸς ὃν ... μονὴν εὐχέσθω καὶ στάσιν. μονὴν ποιεῖσθαι, "to take up abode," Jos. Ant., 8, 350; 13, 41; "abiding," Philo Vit. Mos., I, 316 : διὰ τὴν ἔνδον μονήν, I, 64; "persistence," Plat. Crat., 395a (along with καρτερία); tt. for staying in service as opp. to leaving it, BGU, II, 581, 6 ff. (2nd cent.): ἐγγυᾶσθαι ... μονῆς καὶ ἐμφανείας. "Procrastination," Philo Vit. Mos., I, 330; "continuance," Polyb., 4, 41, 4 f. (along with στάσις); Philo Som., II, 237; Aet. Mund., 116 (ἀσαλεύτου μονῆς); Vit. Mos., II (III), 125 : τὴν διαιωνίζουσαν αὐτῶν μονήν, Spec. Leg., I, 58; "permanence," 1 Macc. 7:38 : μὴ δῷς αὐτοῖς μονήν. b. "Abiding place," Apc. Pt. Fr. (acc. to Cl. Al.), 2 : ἵνα γνώσεως

---

[2] vl. Ac. 10:24 D, of the expectant and respectful waiting of the Gentile centurion for the apostle of Christ.

προσμένω. [1] Ges.-Buhl, *s.v.* חיל III.

[2] For יחל the LXX elsewhere has μένω (2 Βασ. 18:14), ὑπομένω (Job 6:11; 14:14; 32:16; Mi. 7:7 etc.) and esp. (cf. the verses mentioned above) ἐλπίζω.

μεταλαβόντα τῆς ἀμείνονος τύχῃ μονῆς, "place of halt" on a journey, "inn," Paus., X, 31, 7 (*mansio*), "watch-house" in a police district: E. J. Goodspeed, *Greek Papyri from the Cairo Museum* (1902), 15, 19, "hut for watching" in a field, P. Masp., 107, 10 (6th cent.). [1]

In the NT μονή occurs only twice in John's Gospel (14:2, 23). Probably intentionally, the two statements correspond. In 14:2 the heavenly dwellings which are the goal of salvation (the movement is from below upwards), and to which believers will go after their earthly separation from God, are called abiding places [2] which are fully prepared for them in the Father's house. [3] The word seems to be deliberately chosen to express the fact that our earthly state is transitory and provisional compared with eternal and blessed being with God. On the other hand, 14:23 (the movement is from above downwards) depicts salvation after the departure of the Saviour as a permanent abiding of Christ and God in believers. [4] God's dwelling among His people is expressed cultically in the OT (Ex. 25:8; 29:45; Lv. 26:11) and is expected by promise in the last time (Ez. 37:26 f.; Zech. 2:14; Rev. 21:3, 22 f.). In spiritual form it has now come into the community's present. Both passages have in view individual rather than universal and eschatological salvation. Salvation consists in union with God and Christ. This takes place through the immanence of God and of Christ in believers and through the taking of believers home to Christ and to God. The permanence, indestructibility and continuation of this union is expressed by μονή (→ μένειν). In Johannine fashion there is no theological adjustment of the two metaphors of faith (cf. 1 Jn. 1:8 and 9 f.).

The idea of the heavenly dwellings of the righteous has its roots in Persian belief, [5] and from here it penetrated into later Judaism, [6] so that the older conception of *sheol* was essentially reconstructed. [7] Along with the belief in a temporary stay in *sheol*, where the righteous may rest in a place of peace, [8] there arises that of immediate entry into the heavenly world after death, cf. Lk. 16:22; 23:43 (→ παράδεισος). En. 39:4 ff.; 15:7, 10; 22:9 ff.; 71:15 f. describe the dwellings of the righteous and the resting places of the saints in heaven. Acc. to the Talmudic view the abodes of the ministering angels and the blessed righteous stand in concentric circles around the throne of God as the innermost section (מְחִיצָה) of heaven. [9] Acc. to Tanch. אמור § 9 (p. 45a, Buber) each of the righteous has his own dwelling place (מָדוֹר) in Paradise. [10] The Mandaean writings are also dependent on Persian ideas. Here the return of the soul to the dwellings of the blessed in light in the great paternal house of God is the centre of the belief in re-

μονή. [1] For details cf. Preisigke Wört., Moult.-Mill., Preisigke Fachwörter, *s.v.*

[2] Orig. Princ., II, 11, 6 construes μονή (*mansio*) as stations or halts in the journey of the soul to God. Only after testing in these can it proceed. Cf. Cl. Al. Strom., IV, 6, 36, 3; VI, 14, 114, 1. For further interpretations of the fathers cf. H. Smith *Antenicene Exegesis of the Gospels*, 5 (1928), 275 ff.; Bernard ICC, *ad loc.*, II, 532 f.

[3] Hardly for this reason μοναί, so J. Grill, *Untersuchungen über d. Entstehung d. 4. Ev.*, II (1923), 214 f.

[4] παρά has much the same meaning as ἐν, as v. 17 shows; Bau. J., 181.

[5] W. Bousset, "Himmelsreise d. Seele," ARW, 4 (1901), 155 ff.; Reitzenstein Ir. Erl., 207 ff.; J. Kroll, *Himmelsreise d. Seele* (1931); H. Jonas, *Gnosis u. spätantiker Geist* (1934), 100 ff.

[6] RGG², I, 626.

[7] Str.-B., II, 264 ff.; IV, 1016 f., 1020 f.

[8] Examples in Str.-B., IV, 1017 f.

[9] *Ibid.*, II, 266.

[10] Schl. J., 292.

demption.[11] Lidz. Ginza R., V, 1, 136 (p. 152, 23 ff.) says: "In that world he created for me 10,000 times 1,000 worlds of light ... in each world he created me 360,000 uthras, in each individual skina (שכינתא) he created for me 360,000 skinas."[12] Plato[13] speaks in Phaed. (53-63) of the heavenly dwellings to which the soul returns home. Cf. also Philo Som., I, 256: οὕτως γὰρ δυνήσῃ (sc. the soul) καὶ εἰς τὸν πατρῷον οἶκον ἐπανελθεῖν. Like Jn., Philo also speaks of the dwelling in man of the λόγος or νοῦς,[14] or even God.[15]

† ὑπομένω, † ὑπομονή.

Contents: A. The Greek World. B. The Old Testament and Later Judaism: 1. ὑπομένειν towards God: to wait on God, to cleave to God; 2. ὑπομένειν towards the World: to endure, stand fast, bear patiently. C. The New Testament: 1. ὑπομένειν towards God: to expect, to wait; 2. ὑπομένειν towards the world: to stand fast, to persevere.

ὑπομένω a. "to stay behind," "to stand still," Hom. Od., 10, 232; Jos. Ant., 18, 328; Lk. 2:43; Ac. 17:14; "to stay alive," Hdt., IV, 149. b. "To expect," "to await," "to wait for," Xenoph. An., 4, 1, 21; Hdt., IV, 3; VII, 121a. c. "To stay," "to wait for hostile attacks," "to stand firm against them," Hom. Il., 16, 814, also abs., "to endure," "to remain firm," Hom. Il., 5, 498; 15, 312; Hdt., VI, 96; Plat. Theaet., 177b: ἀνδρικῶς ... ὑπομεῖναι καὶ μὴ ἀνάνδρως φυγεῖν, with acc. of that which one resists: πολιορκίαν, Polyb., 1, 24, 11; πόλεμον, 4, 84, 9, or with inf.: φόρους ἐνεγκεῖν, Polyb., 2, 43, 6, or with part.: Plat. Gorg., 505c: οὗτος ἀνὴρ οὐχ ὑπομένει ὠφελούμενος καὶ αὐτὸς τοῦτο πάσχων, περὶ οὗ ὁ λόγος ἐστίν, κολαζόμενος. d. "To endure," "to bear," "to suffer": δουλείαν, Hdt., VI, 12; αἰσχρόν τι, Plat. Ap., 28c; οὐχ ὑπέμειναν τὰς παρ' ἐκείνου δωρεάς, Isoc., 4, 94, they did not accept bribes, but rejected them. e. "To stay or persevere with something," τῇ γνώμῃ, Appian De Bellis Civilibus, 5, 54.

ὑπομονή: a. "Holding out," "standing fast," "endurance," "steadfastness": so esp. of enduring evils, e.g., λύπης, Ps.-Plat. Def., 412c; πόνων, Jos. Ant., 2, 7; Democr. Fr., 240 (II, 193, 10, Diels⁵): τὴν τῶν ἀκουσίων (sc. πόνων) ὑπομονήν. Like ὑπομένειν, it covers courageous active resistance to hostile attack, and in this sense is used alongside ἀνδρεία and καρτερία. b. "Expectation," "waiting," Aristot. Rhet., III, 9, p. 1410a, 4 (opp. ἀκολούθησις).

A. The Greek World.

In the first instance ὑπομένειν is ethically neutral. It simply means "to hold out." But as ὑπομονή later came to hold a prominent place in the list of Greek virtues, so there predominates in ὑπομένειν the concept of the courageous endurance which man-

---

[11] Lidz. Liturg., 5, 12, 14 f., 18, 21, 30; Lidz. Ginza R., I, 16 (p. 7, 17), 27 (p. 9, 17), 44 (p. 11, 22), 53 (p. 12, 10).

[12] שכינתא predominantly "residence," sometimes personified for higher beings, Lidz. Ginza, 7, n. 4; uthra is an emanation of deity, 6, n. 3.

[13] Under Orphic-Pythagorean influence, Bousset, 255.

[14] Poster. C., 122: ὥσθ' οἷς μὲν ὁ ψυχῆς βίος τετίμηται, λόγος θεῖος ἐνοικεῖ; Fug., 117: ὁ ἱερώτατος οὗτος λόγος ζῇ καὶ περίεστιν ἐν ψυχῇ.

[15] Som., I, 149: σπούδαζε οὖν, ὦ ψυχή, θεοῦ οἶκος γενέσθαι, Cher., 98, 100 f.; Sobr., 62 ff.

ὑπομένω κτλ. J. H. H. Schmidt, *Synonymik d. griech. Sprache*, I (1876), 424 ff.; ERE, IX, 674 f. ("Patience"); Trench, 121 f.; A. Carr, "The Patience of Job," Exp. Ser., 8, Vol. VI (1913), 511-517; W. Meikle, "The Vocabulary of Patience in the OT," *ibid.*, 8, Vol. XIX (1920), 219-225; in the NT, 304-313; C. Spicq, "Patientia," *Revue des Sciences Philosophiques et Théologiques*, 19 (1930), 95-106; A. M. Festugière, "ὑπομονή dans la Tradition Grecque," *Recherches de Science Religieuse*, 30 (1931), 477-86.

fully defies evil. Unlike patience, it thus has an active content. It includes active and energetic resistance to hostile power, though with no assertion of the success of this resistance. It is plainly distinguished from synonyms like πάσχειν (cf. Mt. 16:21; 1 Pt. 2:21, 23; 4:1), which is a pure antonym to δρᾶν (in the good and bad sense), Plat. Euthyphr. 11a. In the syn. φέρειν (cf. R. 9:22), which depicts the bearing of a burden more from the standpoint of movement and success (Xenoph. Cyrop., VIII, 2, 21; Isoc., 6, 60 f.), the element of standing firm is less prominent. ὑποφέρειν (cf. 1 C. 10:13; 2 Tm. 3:11; 1 Pt. 2:19) depicts one who bears a burden, and is used of physical and spiritual ability (Isoc., 1, 30; Plat. Leg., IX, 879c). ἀνέχεσθαι is close to ὑπομένειν (cf. Mt. 17:17; 2 C. 11:1, 4, 20; Eph. 4:2; 2 Th. 1:4), but suggests standing erect against an external factor without being disturbed or unsettled by it, so primarily in the physical sense, e.g., of the wounded who bear their pains (Od., 11, 375 f.), then in a moral connection of staying calm, without excitement, fear, or passion, in face of the assaults of destiny, Hom. Il., 24, 549; Od., 19, 27; Thuc., I, 122, 3. Thus ἀνέχεσθαι is used for the Stoic attitude, Epict. Fr., 10, 34; M. Ant., V, 33, 6. → καρτερεῖν (κάρτος = κράτος from καρτερός = κρατερός, "strong") again contains the element of strong, courageous and brave resistance and endurance (Plat. La., 194a). The poetic τλῆναι, from the root ταλ "to bear," denotes the endurance of pains and afflictions with a steadfast spirit, without being bowed down by them, Hom. Od., 5, 362; Il., 19, 308; 5, 382. In prose the content of τλῆναι goes beyond that of ὑπομένειν, which means above all perseverance in face of hostile forces. This may be against attacks (πολιορκίαν, Polyb., 1, 24, 11), fate (συμφοράς, Isoc., 6, 86), or bodily torments (βασάνους, Plut. Apophth. Lac. [II, 830c]), or it may be a kind of heroism in face of bodily chastisement (Aristophon Fr., 4, 6 [CAF, II, p. 277], cf. 1 Pt. 2:20), or the power to resist attempts at bribery, which a whole man repels (Demosth. Or., 21, 93 : οὐχ ὑπεμείναμεν).[1]

Ethically ὑπομένειν may be a brave resistance which honours man (cf. Plat. Theaet., 117b) or a cowardly acceptance of what degrades man, e.g., ὑπομένειν δουλείαν, Hdt., VI, 12; τυραννίδα, Aristot. Pol., IV, 10, p. 1295a, 23; δεσποτικὴν ἀρχήν, III, 14, p. 1285a, 22. The Greek is proud of his sense of freedom which will not tolerate humiliating demands. In the system of Greek virtues ὑπομονή is, along with καρτερία, a sub-division of ἀνδρεία.[2] This treats περὶ τὰς ὑπομονάς, δικαιοσύνη περὶ τὰς ἀπονεμήσεις (v. Arnim, III, p. 64, 18). δειλός is the πάντα φεύγων καὶ φοβούμενος καὶ μηδὲν ὑπομένων (Aristot. Eth. Nic., II, 2, p. 1104a, 19 ff.). Aristot. grants that ethically it is often hard to decide τί ἀντὶ τίνος ὑπομενετέον, III, 1, p. 1110a, 30. But the brave man has to summon from within himself the power of resistance. As he must not stand firm just for fear of social ostracism (→ αἰσχύνη, Plat. Ap., 28c; Hb. 12:2), so he must not do so from the hedonistic motive of enticing hope. The brave man must stand fast for love of honour (→ αἰδώς).[3] He must endure hard things καλοῦ ἕνεκα.[4] Aristot. distinguishes ἐγκράτεια and καρτερία by saying that the ἐγκρατής is ὁ κρατῶν τῶν ἡδονῶν, the καρτερῶν ὑπομένων τὰς λύπας. He similarly distinguishes

[1] → Schmidt, 424 ff.

[2] Aristot. Eth. Nic., III, 10, p. 115b, 17-23 : ὁ ἀνδρεῖος ὑπομένει, 1117a, 32-35 : τῷ δὴ τὰ λυπηρὰ ὑπομένειν ἀνδρεῖοι λέγονται. v. Arnim, III, p. 64, 1: ἡ δὲ ἀνδρεία τοῖς ὑπομενετέοις, *ibid.*, 72, 37: (ὁ ἐνάρετος) ὑπομενετικῶς ποιεῖ. Demetrius of Phaleron in Stob. Ecl., III, 345, 13 ff.: ἀνδρεία commands μένειν ... καὶ τὴν τάξιν διαφυλάττειν· "ἀλλὰ βάλλουσιν"· ὑπόμενε· "ἀλλὰ τρωθήσομαι"· καρτέρει.

[3] Aristot. Eth. Eud., III, p. 1229b, 31 ff.: καὶ γὰρ ὁ θυμὸς ἡδονὴν ἔχει τινά· μετ' ἐλπίδος γάρ ἐστι τιμωρίας. ἀλλ' ὅμως οὔτ' εἰ διὰ ταύτην οὔτ' εἰ δι' ἄλλην ἡδονὴν ὑπομένει τις τὸν θάνατον ἢ φυγὴν μειζόνων λυπῶν, οὐδεὶς δικαίως ἀνδρεῖος λέγοιτο τούτων ... p. 1230a, 16 ff. ἀλλὰ πάντων τῶν τοιούτων αἰτίων οἱ διὰ τὴν αἰδῶ ὑπομένοντες μάλιστα φανεῖεν ἀνδρεῖοι. Eth. M., I, 22, p. 1191a, 5 ff. Cic. Tusc., III, 14 ff.

[4] Aristot. Eth. Nic., III, 10, p. 1115b, 23 f.: καλοῦ δὴ ἕνεκα ὁ ἀνδρεῖος ὑπομένει καὶ πράττει τὰ κατὰ τὴν ἀνδρείαν. Ps.-Plat. Def., 412c : καρτερία ὑπομονὴ λύπης ἕνεκα τοῦ καλοῦ.

μαλακία and ἀκρασία: the μαλακός is ὁ μὴ ὑπομένων πόνους, the ἀκρατής is ὁ μὴ δυνάμενος ὑπομένειν ἡδονὰς ἀλλὰ καταμαλακιζόμενος (weak, yielding) καὶ ὑπὸ τούτων ἀγόμενος.[5] In the Stoic system, too, ὑπομονή has a high place as a sub-division of ἀνδρεία.[6] The Stoic strives for strength of soul. This is to be attained by schooling the will, both ἀποχῇ τῶν ἡδέων and ὑπομονῇ τῶν ἐπιπόνων.[7] Under Stoic influence Philo, too, links ὑπομονή with ἀνδρεία and καρτερία.[8]

B. The Old Testament and Later Judaism.

1. ὑπομένειν towards God: to wait on God, to cleave to God.

The distinctive note of the OT is that it gives the word a religious turn, and instead of relating it to the object of hostile power it links it by an acc. or dat. to the person for whom one waits or to whom one holds fast with expectant hope. Thus ὑπομένειν is mostly used in the OT in the phrase "to wait upon God." It is on the one side equivalent to πεποιθέναι (ψ 24:2, בטח') and on the other to ἐλπίζειν (ψ 5:11; 7:1; 15:1; 16:7, חסה).[9] Hence it is normally used in the OT for the 3 verbs קוה, יחל, and חכה.

קוה, related to קַו (tense string), depicts expectation and hope as a tense attitude on man's part.[10] It is rendered some 25 times by ὑπομένειν, e.g., Job 3:9; 17:13; ψ 24:3, 5, 21; Lam. 3:25 (ἀγαθὸς κύριος τοῖς ὑπομένουσιν αὐτόν).

יחל pi, hi, related to חיל III (wait, Ju. 3:25; Gn. 8:10; Ps. 37:7), means "to wait," "to wait for." It is continued and persevering expectation. Thus common translation by ὑπομένειν is natural, e.g., Job 6:11; 14:14; 32:16; Lam. 3:21, 26 (alongside ἡσυχάσει). In relation to God, the Protector and Refuge of His people, this is confident waiting which will not be shown to be false, Mi. 7:7 (ἐπὶ τῷ θεῷ τῷ σωτῆρί μου).

חכה q, pi means "to wait patiently," Job 32:4, "to wait," ψ 105:13, opp. they hastened. As simple and quiet waiting (2 K. 7:9; 9:3) it has a natural affinity to the Gk. ὑπομένειν. In relation to God it is confident waiting which is patient until His intervention, ψ 32:20; Is. 64:3; Hab. 2:3 (when the prophecy tarries); Zeph. 3:8; Da. 12:12 Θ (μακάριος ὁ ὑπομένων).

The noun ὑπομονή is similarly a rendering of מִקְוֶה, "hope," confidence," 1 Ch. 29:15; 2 Εσδρ. 10:2, with religious concentration on God as the hope of Israel, Jer. 14:8; 17:13 and of the individual, ψ 38:7. It is also used for תִּקְוָה, "tense expectation," "hope," ψ 9:18 (ἡ ὑπομονὴ τῶν πενήτων); 61:5; 70:5 (σὺ εἶ ἡ ὑπομονή μου, κύριε· κύριος ἡ ἐλπίς μου ἐκ νεότητός μου); Job 14:19 (ὑπομονὴν ἀνθρώπου ἀπώλεσας); Sir. 16:13; 41:2 (ἀπολωλεκότι ὑπομονήν).

---

5 Eth. M., II, 6, p. 1202b, 29 ff.

6 Sen. Ep. Moral., 67, 10; P. Barth, *Die Stoa* 3, 4 (1922), 119 ff.; v. Arnim, III, p. 65 ff.; Epict. Diss., II, 2, 13; I, 2, 25; cf. A. Bonhöffer, *Die Ethik d. Stoikers Epict.* (1894), 20 ff.: "Die Übel des Lebens."

7 Muson., p. 25, 8 f.; 12 f.: ῥώννυται δὲ ἡ ψυχὴ γυμναζομένη διὰ μὲν τῆς ὑπομονῆς τῶν ἐπιπόνων πρὸς ἀνδρείαν, διὰ δὲ τῆς ἀποχῆς τῶν ἡδέων πρὸς σωφροσύνην. p. 28, 7 f.

8 Deus Imm., 13; Leg. All., I, 65: ἡ μὲν φρόνησις περὶ τὰ ποιητέα ὅρους αὐτοῖς τιθεῖσα, ἡ δὲ ἀνδρεία τοῖς ὑπομενετέοις, ἡ δὲ σωφροσύνη τοῖς αἱρετέοις, ἡ δὲ δικαιοσύνη τοῖς ἀπονεμητέοις, Mut. Nom., 197: ὑπομονῆς ἄξιον ἡ ἀνδρεία, φυγῆς ἡ δειλία, Cher., 78; → also n. 15.

9 Ἀ often has ὑπομονή (Job 4:6; 6:8; 17:15) where the LXX has ἐλπίς.

10 Related to the Arab. קוי "to be tense, strong," and the Syr. קוי "to brace the spirit," "to hope," Ges.-Buhl, *s.v.*

According to the common OT formula the righteous are those who wait upon God (οἱ ὑπομένοντες τὸν κύριον, ψ 36:9, 34; 24:3). God is the Deliverer upon whom the hope of the righteous is directed, ψ 24:5. Surrounded by unrighteousness and in much inward distress, the righteous know that they are protected by God and that they have only to wait for His liberating action which will bring an alleviation of their situation, Mi. 7:7 (τῷ σωτῆρί μου). God is the Almighty, who is above the whole world of man, Is. 51:5. Above all, He is the covenant God, who will substantiate His promise of help and justice, ψ 51:9; 129:4 f. Waiting for God is thus inwardly inspired by the thought of the covenant (Zeph. 3:8), and it is a special expression of the piety of Israel. The subject of waiting is primarily Israel, and God is called the hope of Israel (Jer. 14:8; 17:13). Only secondarily does the individual wait for the personal help of God (ψ 9:18; 38:7; 61:5; 70:5; Lam. 3:25). It is an expression of wicked ungodliness to abandon hope in God (Sir. 2:14). The general concept of pious waiting on God takes on particular force in eschatological thinking. God will fulfil the promise of eschatological salvation. Israel and the righteous wait expectantly for this decisive action of God (Hab. 2:3; Is. 25:9 vl.; 49:23 vl.; 51:5). Those who endure and reach the final fulfilment will be saved (Da. 12:12 Θ; Zech. 6:14).

This OT use of ὑπομονή carries with it a shift of content as compared with the current use in secular Greek. Attention is not directed earthwards to hostile powers which one resists, nor does the one who endures draw the power of resistance from within himself. The point of nerving oneself is to hold fast to God and not to mistake His power and faithfulness. This divinely orientated ὑπομονή is also an active attitude full of the strongest inner tension. It is manly perseverance (so ψ 26:14 along with ἀνδρίζεσθαι). This pious waiting on God prevents us from falling into αἰσχύνη (Is. 49:23). But the righteous man does not endure in the power of his own steadfastness (Job 6:11). His strength to do so has its source in cleaving to God. It is the result of his waiting on God (Is. 40:31). Thus OT religion does not incite the righteous directly to manly and courageous steadfastness. With confidence in the God who protects and finally establishes the right, it grants indirectly a strong inner ability to persevere which can then take on strongly the quietistic character of a patience which waits and endures. While the Greek moralist censured the linking of ὑπομονή with hope as an inadmissible weakening, OT ὑπομονή issues almost wholly in hope. What sustains the righteous is that God will establish justice and reward righteousness (ψ 141:8; Sir. 36:15).

2. ὑπομένειν towards the World: to endure, stand fast, bear patiently.

As compared with ὑπομένειν towards God, ὑπομένειν towards the world in the sense of enduring, standing fast, in face of various evils plays only a secondary role in the OT. The later books offer some examples, cf. without obj. Job 9:4; 22:21; 41:3 (three times for שׁלם, "to remain safe and sound," hence with a significant alteration of sense); Sir. 22:18; with the acc. of what one resists, Mal. 3:2 (ἡμέραν εἰσόδου αὐτοῦ, for כול pilp: "to endure"); Wis. 16:22 (πῦρ); Sus. 57 Θ (τὴν ἀνομίαν) or with the inf., Wis. 17:5 (καταυγάζειν).

Job is an example of pious endurance. The frequent occurrence of ὑπομονή in this book is no accident (verb, 13 times, noun once). Eight different Heb. words are rendered by ὑπομονή, so that the thought of standing firm is obviously stronger than in the Heb. (e.g., in the rendering of שׁלם, → *supra*). Man's own power is not strong enough for perseverance, 6:11. It is not possible for man, especially for the ungodly, to stand against God (9:4; 15:31; 22:21). God Himself shatters purely human hope and expectation, 14:19. Job waits his whole life for God to intervene, 14:14; 17:13. God Himself finally reminds Job that none can stand against Him, 41:3.

Later Judaism, which in many ways makes religion more inward under the pressure of experience, develops the sense of pious steadfastness more strongly than the OT. The Test. Job represents Job as one who endures with steadfastness and piety.[11] The righteous must remain steadfast in face of temptation. Endurance is an inward work which is of great profit to the righteous.[12] Abraham is a special example of the tested saint; he stood fast in 10 temptations (Jub. 17, 18). ὑπομένειν becomes a tt. for the steadfastness of the martyr.[13] This may be seen esp. in 4 Macc., where Jewish piety is expressed in Stoic forms. The book is a great hymn of praise to steadfastness, which faith demands and effects. This is demonstrated in the patriarchs (Isaac, 13:12; Noah, 15:31), in the prophets (Daniel, 16:21), and esp. in the martyrs,[14] above all the seven brothers and their mother. As in Stoicism, ὑπομονή is grouped here with ἀνδρεία (1:11; 6:21 as opp. to ἄνανδροι). It endures triumphantly all πόνοι (5:23) and βασανισμοί (9:6; 15:32). It perseveres steadfastly even to death (16:1; 17:7). It thus evokes religious astonishment even from the tyrant (17:17), and carries loyalty to the faith to triumph against him (1:11: νικήσαντες τὸν τύραννον τῇ ὑπομονῇ). It surpassed Stoicism, however, in the fact that this steadfastness is διὰ τὸν θεόν (16:19), and also that the martyrs of faith prove hereby their fear of God (9:6: διὰ τὴν εὐσέβειαν καὶ βασανισμοὺς ὑπομείναντες εὐσέβησαν, cf. 2 Pt. 1:6). Philo gives an allegorical interpretation of the name of Rebekah in terms of קוה and רב, and he thus extols her as a model of the patience which endures.[15] But in Stoic fashion he also links ὑπομονή with ἀνδρεία and καρτερία.[16]

C. The New Testament.

ὑπομονή as the basic attitude of the righteous, as developed in the OT and later Judaism, finds a natural continuation in the eschatologically orientated thinking of the NT. The endurance which is given with hope for the realisation of the kingdom of God is a basic attitude of the Christian too as he faces the attacks of a hostile and unbelieving world and as he finds himself in the midst of its temptations. It is a decisive precondition if the individual is to attain personally to the final salvation of God. In these circumstances it is the more surprising that the OT description of the righteous as ὑπομένοντες τὸν κύριον or τῷ θεῷ is not continued in the NT. Apparently the centrality of faith and the prominence given to ἐλπίς as primary Christian virtues leave no place for the OT formula. Perhaps, too, ὑπομένειν was not thought to be so appropriate in view of the ἐγγύς ἐστιν (cf. → δέχεσθαι and compounds). In the NT ὑπομένειν

---

[11] Test. Job (ed. M. R. James in *Texts and Studies*, V, 1 [1899]), 1, 4, 5, 26. F. Spitta, *Zur Gesch. u. Lit. d. Urchr.*, III, 2 (1907), 160, 171 ff., 201 ff.; J. H. Korn, Πειρασμός, BWANT, 4. F., 20 (1937), 68 ff. on Job.

[12] Test. Jos. 2:7: ἐν δέκα πειρασμοῖς δόκιμον ἀπέδειξέ με καὶ ἐν πᾶσιν αὐτοῖς ἐμακροθύμησα· Ὅτι μέγα φάρμακόν ἐστιν ἡ μακροθυμία καὶ πολλὰ ἀγαθὰ δίδωσιν ἡ ὑπομονή. 10:1: ὁρᾶτε οὖν, τέκνα μου, πόσα κατεργάζεται ἡ ὑπομονὴ καὶ ἡ προσευχὴ μετὰ νηστείας. 17:1; Korn, 48 ff.

[13] K. F. Euler, "Die Verkündigung vom leidenden Gottesknecht," BWANT, IV, 14 (1934), 114 ff. → μάρτυς, 474 ff.

[14] K. Holl, *Jbch. f. klass. Altertumswissenschaft*, 33 (1914), 521 ff. The martyrdoms, too, are to be regarded as temptation, Korn, 71 ff.

[15] Det. Pot. Ins., 30, 45, 51; Plant., 169 etc.; cf. A. Meyer, *Das Rätsel des Jk.-Briefes*, ZNW, *Beih.* 10 (1930), 273 and 283 f.

[16] → n. 8.

is preponderantly used either in the absolute for "to endure," or in the same sense with the accusative, more rarely the part. or inf. It is used comparatively rarely for "to wait," "to wait for," "to expect."

1. ὑπομένειν towards God: to expect, to wait.

There is an example of the Godward use, corresponding to that of the LXX, in 2 Th. 3:5. The ὑπομονὴ τοῦ Χριστοῦ is here expectation of the Christ who will come again in glory. [17] The Christian must direct his whole heart to this and to ἀγάπη τοῦ θεοῦ (v. 5). Similarly, in Rev. 1:9 [18] the ὑπομονὴ Ἰησοῦ is to be construed as expectation of Jesus, since the saying of the exalted Christ in 3:10 (ἐτήρησας τὸν λόγον τῆς ὑπομονῆς μου) is plainly intended to praise the loyal preservation of faith in the *parousia* in the community. [19] Pious waiting for Jesus is the heart-beat of the faith of the NT community. In some passages, especially in the Past., there is room for doubt whether the orientation of ὑπομένειν is to God or to the world (→ 587).

2. ὑπομένειν towards the World: to stand fast, to persevere.

In most of the NT passages ὑπομένειν refers to the steadfast endurance of the Christian under the difficulties and tests of the present evil age.

a. In the Synoptic Gospels ὑπομένειν and ὑπομονή are found in religious and ethical statements only three times, always on the lips of Jesus. Lk. at 8:15 adds ἐν ὑπομονῇ to καρποφοροῦσιν in the interpretation of the Parable of the Sower. In contrast to vv. 12, 13, 14 the righteous are characterised by the steadfastness and persistence with which they cling to piety of life and work in spite of all opposition and temptation. ὑπομονή is here an active force, demonstrated and proved with a view to the final reward. In Mk. 13:13 (par. Mt. 24:13; 10:22) endurance or perseverance to the end under all the trials (martyrdom etc.) of the terrible last period is a presupposition for attaining salvation. Lk. has an active formulation of the same thought in 21:19 (ἐν τῇ ὑπομονῇ ὑμῶν κτήσεσθε τὰς ψυχὰς ὑμῶν, cf. Ac. 14:22).

b. The main features of ὑπομονή as a basic Christian virtue and attitude are most richly sketched by Paul, especially if we include instances from the Past. and also the references in Pt. As concerns the steadfast and patient endurance of the Christian it is noteworthy that this does not derive from personal bravery (→ 581 f.) or stoical insensitivity (1 Pt. 2:20: κολαφιζόμενοι ὑπομενεῖτε). As in the OT and later Judaism, it draws its power from religious faith, and here especially from Christian hope (R. 8:25: δι' ὑπομονῆς ἀπεκδεχόμεθα). The most Greek is 2 Pt. 1:6, where ὑπομονή develops out of self-control, though here, too, the righteous man demonstrates his εὐσέβεια thereby, as in the thinking of the OT or later Judaism (→ 585). Unbreakable and patient endurance in face of the evil and injustice of the world is the true attitude of the Christian (1 C. 13:7), his inner action in the present evil aeon (R. 12:12: τῇ θλίψει ὑπομένοντες, 15:4).

---

[17] Dob. Th., 309; but cf. Dib. Th., 45: Patience of Christ = the patience which is in believers on the basis of Christ's indwelling; so also O. Schmitz, *Die Christus-Gemeinschaft d. Pls. im Licht seines Gen.-Gebrauchs* (1924), 139 f.

[18] Zn. Apk., I, 182 f.; Loh. Apk., 13; text with Dionys. (*v.* Nestle, *ad loc.*) ἐν ὑπομονῇ Ἰησοῦ, cf. Zn. Apk., 179, n. 2; J. Heikel, ThStKr, 106 (1934/35), 317.

[19] Zn. Apk., I, 306 f.; though cf. Bss. Apk., 228: "The patience exercised by me (Christ)," "the commandment to exercise patience like Jesus." 2 Th. 3:5 is also to be taken in this way.

ὑπομονή is sometimes more active in persevering good works (R. 2:7, καθ' ὑπομονὴν ἔργου ἀγαθοῦ; 2 C. 12:12),[20] sometimes more passive in the steadfast and patient endurance of suffering. Since the Christian should also bear evil passively (1 Pt. 2:20), Christian ὑπομονή takes on a more quietistic aspect (2 Th. 1:4 alongside ἀνέχεσθαι). Greek ethics, which has no understanding of the inner bravery hereby manifested, would regard this as servile and shameful. Christianity ennobled this passive ὑπομένειν. In the NT, too, the endurance of sufferings is wholly active (2 C. 1:6: τῆς ὑμῶν παρακλήσεως τῆς ἐνεργουμένης ἐν ὑπομονῇ τῶν αὐτῶν παθημάτων). This is particularly evident in 1 Pt. 2:20, where it is mentioned along with the inevitable overwhelming (v. 19: πάσχων ἀδίκως) by injustices. As Christians have a call to suffer (Ac. 14:22; 1 Pt. 2:21), so they are summoned to ὑπομονή, in which they must prove their standing in the faith by perseverance to the final redemption (2 C. 6:4). Paul realises that he is under obligation to endure as an example (2 Tm. 2:10). It is of the very essence of NT piety that ὑπομονή is not so much endurance under self-selected burdens (as in the Greek world) but rather endurance under imposed sufferings and religious temptation. Tribulation, piously endured, accomplishes as its result (R. 5:3: κατεργάζεται) in the Christian highly estimable ὑπομονή, and this the even higher δοκιμή (5:4). The battle which has to be fought through in the Christian sphere (Hb. 10:32: ἄθλησιν παθημάτων) is thus more inward as compared with that in the Greek sphere. The reference of ὑπομονή is to endurance in face of unfavourable relationships; in this respect ὑπομονή differs from μακροθυμία, which is — often at least — patience with people (the two occur together in Col. 1:11; 2 C. 6:4 ff.; 2 Tm. 3:10). Hence the ὑπομονὴ Ἰώβ (Jm. 5:11) is contrasted with the μακροθυμία of God (ψ 85:15; 102:8; 1 Pt. 3:20; 2 Pt. 3:15). ὑπομονή is not attributed to God (on R. 15:5 → *infra*) since He is not subject to external pressure. The endurance of the Christian will not be complaining, weary, despondent or grumbling. It is inspired and filled by a pious and heroic will to hold firm (Jm. 1:2 f.). In persevering, the Christian is not referred to his own power. The needed power of resistance is given him by God Himself (Col. 1:11: δυναμούμενοι ... εἰς πᾶσαν ὑπομονήν), who for this reason is called ὁ θεὸς τῆς ὑπομονῆς (R. 15:5), i.e., the God who imparts ὑπομονή. Christ and His example also enable Christians to hold fast under sufferings (1 Pt. 2:21 in continuation of v. 20).

Because of its central significance, ὑπομονή is often in the Past. set alongside the basic and decisive Christian attitudes of πίστις[21] and ἀγάπη (1 Tm. 6:11; 2 Tm. 3:10; Tt. 2:2; cf. Rev. 2:19). It has a particular affinity to them. The model Christian is described in Tt. 2:2 in terms of the triad faith, love, and (hoping, steadfast, patient) endurance (cf. 1 C. 13:7), just as the triad πίστις, ἐλπίς, ἀγάπη gives us the main Christian virtues in 1 C. 13:13. While ἐλπίς directs one's gaze more to the future, ὑπομονή summons to perseverance under the attacks of the world; it is thus indispensable for the attaining of salvation. ὑπομονή here is very close to ἐλπίς. The phrase ὑπομονὴ τῆς ἐλπίδος in 1 Th. 1:3[22] expresses the way in which Christian hope seeks to be steadfast under uncertainty and threat. The causal connection between perseverance in the present age of suffering and the future attainment of salvation is expressly stated in 2 Tm. 2:12 (εἰ ὑπομένομεν,

---

20 Wnd. 2 K., 397.
21 With πίστις alone in 2 Th. 1:4.
22 Subj. gen.: Hope endures, cf. the preceding genitives, Dob. Th., 65 f.; Schmitz, 140 ff.

καὶ συμβασιλεύσομεν).[23] In virtue of mystical fellowship with Christ the suffering of Christians with Him (v. 11) is followed by their reigning with Him (v. 12). The patient endurance of the apostle on behalf of his congregations has a similar effect on his fellow-believers (2 Tm. 2:10).

c. Hb., which is written to a church under persecution, impressively exhorts to ὑπομονή. The readers, who have already resisted steadfastly the hostile attacks of serious persecution (10:32: ἄθλησιν ὑπεμείνατε παθημάτων), must now display the same steadfastness (v. 36) if they are to attain the promise. In the metaphor of the race (12:1) ὑπομονή reminds us of the tense perseverance to victory which is necessary if the prize is to be won. The gaze of the Christian who is thus summoned to endurance should be fixed on Christ Himself, the model martyr, whose passion is depicted as a physical and spiritual endurance of the terrible death of the cross (ὑπέμεινεν σταυρόν) in renunciation of joy, contempt for the external shame and the suffering of hostile repudiation (ὑπομεμενηκότα ... ἀντιλογίαν), 12:2 f.[24] The steadfast endurance of trials and afflictions will have for them the value of a divine παιδεία, 12:7.

d. James is also directed to Christians under affliction, and it has a sharp exhortation to steadfast endurance both at the beginning and at the end. The tests which come upon us (πειρασμοί, 1:2; 1:12) serve to confirm faith and thus to strengthen steadfastness (1:3), while believing steadfastness for its part brings forth a perfect work (1:4; cf. Abraham's works in 2:21 f.; Gn. 22).[25] Job is the great example of this perseverance under affliction (5:11; cf. Job 1:21 f.).[26] As his believing steadfastness received from God a rich reward, so blessing and the crown of victory are for those who persevere (5:11; cf. 1:12; Da. 12:12; Mt. 5:12). The prophets are mentioned as earlier examples of martyrs of faith (5:10).

e. Rev. especially, the book of the martyr church, in sevenfold repetition extols ὑπομονή as the right and necessary attitude of believers in the last hour of the old aeon. The two-sidedness of ὑπομονή, its orientation to God and to the world, is particularly clear in Rev. "ὑπομονή is an endurance which is grounded in waiting, a waiting which expresses itself in endurance."[27] Waiting for Jesus (1:9;[28] 3:10) is on the one side the attitude which fills the whole soul of believers. On the other side salvation depends on their steadfastness to the end. It is particularly necessary as the suffering and enduring patience of martyr believers under persecution (2:2 f.; 19). The final clash between the power of the world and the community will also be the final and supreme test of faith. It will demand of believers supreme steadfastness if everything is not finally to be in vain (13:10; 14:12). It is no accident that in Jn., as distinct from Rev., ὑπομένειν and ὑπομονή do not occur, for here eschatological tension is greatly relaxed with the bringing of salvation very largely into the present in mystical union with the Redeemer.

Hauck

---

[23] W. T. Hahn, *Das Mitsterben u. Mitauferstehen mit Christus bei Pls.* (1937), 156 ff.
[24] Paul, on the other hand, never uses ὑπομένω for the patient suffering of Jesus.
[25] It may be that behind ὑπομονή in Jm. 1:2-4 there is allegorisation of the name of Rebekah, as in Philo (→ n. 15); cf. Meyer, 274 f.; Hck., *ad loc.* (*NT Deutsch*), 4 and 7.
[26] → n. 11.
[27] Loh. Apk., 20 ff.
[28] → 586, also n. 18.

μεριμνάω, προμεριμνάω, μέριμνα, ἀμέριμνος

† μεριμνάω, † προμεριμνάω, † μέριμνα.

1. Greek Usage.

μεριμνάω (μέριμνα) has the same wealth of meaning as the Eng. "to care" ("care"). [1] It means a. "to care for someone or something," e.g., children, Soph. Oed. Tyr., 1460; mostly the "for" can be left unspoken when it is self-evident that the one concerned cares for himself. Then it means b. careful or anxious "concern about something," Soph. Oed. Tyr., 1124: ἔργον μεριμνῶν ποῖον ἢ βίον τίνα; "What work was incumbent on you, what vocation?" [2] Then οὐ μεριμνᾶν can take on the sense of "ignoring (something)," Philodem. Philos. Volumina Rhetorica, ed. S. Sudhaus, II (1896), 143, 9 f. This concern for or about something may have a future orientation, and it can thus mean either c. "to be intent on something," e.g., of a hound in Aesch. Eum., 132: μέριμναν οὔποτ' ἐκλείπων πόνου, "to strive after something," Pind. Olymp., 1, 109; 2, 60, even to the point of "ambition," Pind. Nem., 3, 69; Xenoph. Cyrop., VIII, 7, 12, combination with ἐλπίς often serving to bring out the future ref. (Pind. Isthm., 8, 13 ff.; Pyth., 8, 88 ff.), or d. "anxious expectation of something," "anxiety in face of something, of what may come," Aesch. Sept. c. Theb., 843; Ag., 460; Soph. Oed. Tyr., 728; Eur. Ion, 404, in this sense often linked with φόβος, Aesch. Sept. c. Theb., 287 ff.; Pers., 165 ff. But the future ref. may be secondary and may almost disappear, so that μέριμνα has the sense of e. "solicitude" or "grief" about something, with an approximation to λύπη, Aesch. Sept. c. Theb., 849; Soph. Ant., 857; Eur. Hipp., 1157, [3] or of f. "brooding," "speculating," "enquiring"; hence in the eyes of poets philosophers are οἱ λεπτῶς μεριμνῶντες, Plat. Resp., X, 607c = Poetae Lyrici Graeci, ed. T. Bergk, III (1882), Fr. Adespota, 135. [4]

Often without any specific object there is ref. to cares as the worrying and tormenting cares which belong to human life like λῦπαι and πόνοι. [5] Usually we then have the plur. μέριμναι, and typical attributes are χαλεπαί (Hes. Op., 178), κακαί (Theogn.,

---

μεριμνάω κτλ. [1] In accordance with the reciprocity of such Gk. terms μέριμνα can also mean what causes care, Hom. Hymn. Merc., 160.

[2] In sense b. or a. there can also be ref. to θεῶν μέριμνα, Bacchyl., 3, 57 f.

[3] μέριμνα can mean specifically the troubles of love, Sappho, 1, 25 f. (Diehl, I, 327); Bacchyl., 11 (10), 85 f.; cf. also Hippocr. Vict. (VI, p. 648, 15, É. Littré): ψυχῆς τινα τάραξιν ... ὑπὸ μερίμνης.

[4] So also Aristoph. Nu., 949 ff.; 1404 (here 101 the mocking construction μεριμνοφροντισταί); in a critical sense also Xenoph. Mem., I, 1, 14; IV, 7, 6. In the first sense Emped. Fr., 2, 11 and 110 (I, 309, 1; 313, 18; 353, 1 f., Diels[5]). Philodem. Philos. Volumina Rhetorica, ed. S. Sudhaus, I (1892), 135, 28. Thus the Gk. natural scientists are μεριμνηταί in Hipp. Ref., IV, 12, 1; 15, 3 (p. 44, 24 f.; 49, 8, GCS).

[5] μέριμνα is several times linked with λύπη (Menand. Fr., 1083 [CAF, III, 263]; Diphilos Fr., 88 [CAF, II, 570]; Apollodor. Fr., 3 [CAF, III, 289]), with πόνος (Ps.-Plat. Amat., 134b; Vett. Val., II, 40 [p. 131, 2 ff.]) etc. (cf. Anth. Pal., IX, 359; here, as in Aesch. Pers., 161 ff., e.g., also with φροντίς, with which μέριμνα is related in this sense, cf. Soph. Trach., 147 ff.). The decisive feature in φροντίς (the true Gk. word for "care") is the constant thought which leads to nothing.

343 [Diehl, I, 134]), καματώδεες (Pind. Fr., 124a b, 5 ff.), ἄσπετοι (Bacchyl., 19[18], 34), θαμειαί (Hom. Hymn. Merc., 44). One can hardly live one's life without cares.[6] They even disturb sleep.[7] The frivolous try to drown them in love[8] or drink.[9] But at the last only death can free us from them.[10]

μέριμνα or μεριμνᾶν is found in Gk. from the time of Hesiod or Soph.; it also occurs in the pap. Surprisingly, it is not found in the Stoa, where φροντίς etc. are used instead. Among the Romans one finds *cura, solicitudo* and *metus* as corresponding features of human life.

2. Hellenistic-Jewish Use.

As in the Stoa, so in Philo, Joseph. and the Test. XII we do not find μέριμνα and μεριμνᾶν; φροντίς and φροντίζειν are used instead. μέριμνα occurs in the LXX 5 times for יְהָב (only ψ 54:22) and דְּאָגָה, and 7 times besides. μεριμνᾶν is found 7 times for various Heb. words. μέριμνα denotes intentness on or striving after something in Prv. 17:12; Sir. 38:29 (cf. the whole passage vv. 26-30); Est. 1:1 n. It is linked with φροντίς in Ep. Ar., 271. In vl. with σοφία at Jdt. 8:29. μεριμνᾶν means to be intent on something at Ex. 5:9 both for עָשָׂה[11] and for שָׁעָה (elsewhere rendered ἐπιδεῖν or προσέχειν). In Ep. Ar., 296 it means "to consider well," "to weigh beforehand." Mostly μέριμνα has the sense of "anxious care," Job 11:18 (with φροντίς); Da. 11:26 (plur.); 1 Macc. 6:10 (sleeplessness with worry); ψ 54:22 (for יְהָב, whose meaning is uncertain); Sir. 30(31):24; 34:1 ff.; 42:9 (in all 4 verses for דְּאָגָה, "anxiety," elsewhere rendered θλῖψις, ταραχή etc.; in the last two verses linked with sleeplessness). Thus μεριμνᾶν can mean "to be worried or anxious," 2 Βασ. 7:10; 1 Ch. 17:9 (both times for רָגַז, elsewhere transl. λυπεῖν, ταράσσειν, φοβεῖν etc.); ψ 37:18 (for דָּאַג, elsewhere φοβεῖσθαι, φροντίζειν etc.); Prv. 14:23 (for עֶצֶב, "struggle," rendered λύπη at Prv. 10:22; Gn. 3:16, elsewhere ὀδύνη, πόνος etc.). Finally μεριμνᾶν is used at Ez. 16:42 for כָּעַס, "to chide" (elsewhere transl. θυμοῦν, ὀργίζειν etc.). The usage in LXX and Ep. Ar. is the same as the Gk., and what is said about care in Sir. is what we find in the Gk. world and universally. The only verse of theological significance is ψ 54:22: ἐπίρριψον ἐπὶ κύριον τὴν μέριμνάν σου, καὶ αὐτός σε διαθρέψει.[12]

3. μέριμνα and μεριμνᾶν in Primitive Christian Literature.

a. μέριμνα and μεριμνᾶν occur several times in the NT, but only rarely in other early Christian writings: μέριμνα only 3 times in Herm., μεριμνᾶν once in Dg. and 3 times (2 in NT quotations) in Just.[13] The structure of the term is the old one.

---

[6] Vett. Val., IX, 11 (p. 355, 6); Anth. Pal., IX, 359, 5 f.

[7] Aristoph. Nu., 420; Ps.-Plat. Amat., 134b; Apollodor. Fr., 3 (CAF, III, 289).

[8] Anacreontea, 32, 18 (p. 26, Preisendanz).

[9] Pind. Fr., 124a b, 5 ff.; Eur. Ba., 378 ff.; Anth. Pal., XI, 24.

[10] Diphilos Fr., 88 (CAF, II, 570); Anth. Pal., IX, 359; burial inscr., Eranos, 13 (1913), 87 (Inscr., 9, 6).

[11] Perhaps the LXX, unless translating freely, reads עָשָׂה for שָׁעָה in the first part of the verse.

[12] μέριμνα also several times for דְּאָגָה in 'ΑΘ: Ez. 4:16 (LXX ἔνδεια); 12:19 (the same); Prv. 12:25 (LXX: φοβερὸς λόγος); for יָגוֹן, ψ 12:2 Σ (LXX ὀδύναι); ψ 30:10 'Α (LXX ὀδύνη); for שִׂיחַ, ψ 54:2 Αλλ. (LXX ἀδολεσχία).

[13] φροντίζειν, which is related in meaning to μεριμνᾶν, is found in the NT only at Tt. 3:8 (καλῶν ἔργων προΐστασθαι). It then occurs in Ign. Pol., 1, 2. φροντίς is not found in the NT but occurs in 1 Cl., 7, 2 (διὸ ἀπολίπωμεν τὰς κενὰς καὶ ματαίας φροντίδας, cf. Job 11:18, → *supra*); 63, 4 (anxious care for the community); Dg., 5, 3. Both are more common in the Apol. Cf. also Act. Thom., 42, p. 160, 5.

μέριμνα is "caring for," usually unexpressed if the ref. is to self (cf. in respect of the means of life in Mt. 6:25-34 etc.); it is "care about something" (περὶ πολλά, Lk. 10:41; τὰ τοῦ κόσμου or τὰ τοῦ κυρίου, 1 C. 7:32-34); it is "intentness on something," "striving after something" (τί φάγωμεν ἢ τί πίωμεν, Mt. 6:31; πῶς ἀρέσῃ τῇ γυναικί, or τῷ ἀνδρί, or τῷ κυρίῳ, 1 C. 7:32-34);[14] it is "anxiety in face of something" (1 Pt. 5:7; Herm. v., 4, 2, 5; also Phil. 4:6). There is always a hint of the future, but in relation to the antonym ἡδονή (Lk. 8:14) μέριμνα has the sense of "sorrow," and in Mt. 10:19 par. μεριμνᾶν means "to consider," "to prepare."[15]

b. The NT, too, realises that human life is swayed by care. The exhortations not to worry[16] presuppose that every man naturally cares for himself and his life, that he is concerned about himself, that he is always intent on something and concerned about something. This is by no means ruled out as illegitimate. Indeed, it is accepted that man is concerned about himself and and that he strives after things. But the why and wherefore of his concern and striving are given a new orientation, and so, too, is his understanding of himself and his life.

This would not be so if the admonitions not to care, but to cast one's care on God,[17] were based on the idea that God guarantees the fulfilment of all striving. Phil. 4:6 shows, however, that in petitionary prayer, which is based on anxiety, the man who prays attains a certain aloofness from his wishes when he puts them before God μετὰ εὐχαριστίας, and he thus finds liberation from care. 1 Pt. 5:7 (cf. v. 6) also shows that to cast one's care on God does not mean to think of Him as the One who guarantees one's wishes, but to see in Him the One who knows what we need better than we do ourselves. These exhortations to prayer are thus designed to give absolute freedom from care as anxiety.

To anxiety concerning food and clothing, or the βιωτικά,[18] is opposed concern for the βασιλεία τοῦ θεοῦ, to care for τὰ τοῦ κόσμου, concern for τὰ τοῦ κυρίου. This does not mean, of course, that man is torn out of natural life, which necessarily involves μεριμνᾶν. Men, as distinct from plants and animals, sow and reap, work and spin. This is presupposed in Mt. 6:26, 28 (→ *supra*), and Paul earns his bread by work, and exhorts others to work (1 Th. 2:9; 4:11; cf. 2 Th. 3:10 etc.). The point is, however, that man is given to understand that he must not believe that he can secure his life by his μεριμνᾶν (Mt. 6:27; cf. Lk. 12:15-21). If he is genuinely concerned about himself, he must strive after the βασιλεία τοῦ θεοῦ and care for τὰ τοῦ κυρίου. This means, however, that he must realise not merely that he does not draw his life from this present world but also that if, in self-concern,

---

[14] That μεριμνᾶν means "to strive for" is supported by the fact that it can be an alternative to ζητεῖν. Thus Mt. 6:33; Lk. 12:29 have ζητεῖν for the μεριμνᾶν of Mt. 6:31. The ζητεῖν τὸ ἑαυτοῦ of 1 C. 10:33; 13:5 corresponds to the ὑπὲρ ἀλλήλων μεριμνᾶν of 1 C. 12:25; cf. Phil. 2:20, 21. In Mk. 4:19 μέριμνα is linked with ἐπιθυμία.

[15] Cf. Demosth. Or., 21, 192: ὁ μεριμνήσας τὰ δίκαια λέγειν νῦν. Ep. Ar., 296. In the par. to Mt. 10:19 Mk. 13:11 reads προμεριμνᾶν, while for this word, which is not attested elsewhere, Lk. 21:14 has προμελετᾶν.

[16] Mt. 6:25-34; Phil. 4:6; 1 Pt. 5:7; Herm. v., 4, 2, 4; Dg., 9, 6; Just. Apol., 15, 14-16.

[17] 1 Pt. 5:7 (cf. ψ 54:22; also Herm. v., 3, 11, 3; 4, 2, 5); Phil. 4:6. Cf. Act. Thom., 42, p. 160, 4 f. in the depiction of the life which is not bothered by the evil demon: πανταχόθεν με εἰρήνη περιεῖχεν καὶ οὐδενὸς μέριμναν ἐποιούμην, cf. on this G. Bornkamm, *Mythos u. Legende in den apokr. Thomas-Akten* (1933), 43.

[18] The scope of μέριμναι βιωτικαί is made clear by passages like Mk. 4:19 par.; Lk. 21:34; Mt. 24:38; 1 C. 7:29-34.

he cares for the things of this world, he will fall victim to this world. For his life is in fact controlled by that for which, about which, after which, before which and concerning which he cares. It is the constant tendency of this world to lead him to apostasy to it through the μέριμναι βιωτικαί (Lk. 21:34), the μέριμνα τοῦ αἰῶνος (sc. τούτου, Mk. 4:19 par.). Herein is the ἀπάτη τοῦ πλούτου (Mk. 4:19 par.).

In so far as man must take care for the means of life, he must restrict this care to the bare minimum in order that the ἀγαθὴ μερίς may not be lost (Lk. 10:41 f.). He must confront all worldly ties at the distinctive distance of the ὡς μή (1 C. 7:29-31). For, if he is genuinely a believer, he no longer belongs to this world. He belongs to the world to come. Hence he must strive after this future world (Mt. 6:33 par.). He must be ready for its coming (Lk. 21:34). He must care πῶς ἀρέσῃ τῷ κυρίῳ (1 C. 7:32-34). The believer is thus released from μέριμνα, for his existence is an eschatological existence. This will be shown by whether, in conflict with the hostile world, he can rest, not on the strength of his own calculations, but wholly on the Spirit given him from the world to come (Mt. 10:19 par.).

It is self-evident, however, that this means the requirement rather than the suspension of care for others, which for believers stands under the eschatological orientation and goal (2 C. 11:28; Phil. 2:20). For individuals are members of the body of Christ, and the ὑπὲρ ἀλλήλων μεριμνᾶν of the members is God's command (1 C. 12:25).

c. Only in Mt. 6:25-34 par. is there an explicit discussion of care, and this passage must be expounded separately. μεριμνᾶν is self-concern in respect of the future (εἰς τὴν αὔριον, Mt. 6:34). It is concern for the means of life (Mt. 6:25, 28 par.), for one's own life (for ψυχή and σῶμα, which in synthetic parallelism denote life in Mt. 6:25). That the care is anxious is shown by the questions τί φάγωμεν; τί πίωμεν; τί περιβαλώμεθα; (Mt. 6:31 par.), and especially by the comparison with the birds and plants, which follows the rule of *a maiori ad minus* (Mt. 6:26, 28 par.). For if there is reference to these creatures, which cannot provide for the future by work, it is presupposed that men do this, but that in view of these creatures they ought to do so without μεριμνᾶν. What makes a proper concern foolish is anxiety and the illusion to which it gives rise in its blindness, namely, that life itself can be secured by the means of life for which there is concern. (Hence the paradox of Mt. 6:25 : οὐχὶ ἡ ψυχὴ πλεῖόν ἐστιν τῆς τροφῆς καὶ τὸ σῶμα τοῦ ἐνδύματος; for the hearers might well reply that it is just because their life is so infinitely precious that they are anxious.) Such anxiety is futile ; for the future which they think they can provide for is not in their hands. This is stated expressly if → ἡλικία in Mt. 6:27 par. means length of days; if it is stature the statement refers mockingly to the fact that man can achieve ridiculously little by his worrying, much less procure for himself security. In any case, worry is unnecessary. God has lifted it from man. In spite of the ταῦτα ... προστεθήσεται ὑμῖν (Mt. 6:33 par.), which is the normal case, this can hardly mean, in view of Mt. 10:29-31 par., that man can always be certain that his life is secured by God. What it does mean is that this uncertainty need not cause him anxiety. Whatever happens will be under God's control. The presupposition of being able to defeat μεριμνᾶν in this certainty is to be found, of course, in obedience to the admonition ζητεῖτε κτλ. (Mt. 6:33 par.). The man who is concerned about himself, and who tries to find security in the means of life, is shown that he must make the lordship of God his first concern, and then anxiety about his life will wither away.[19] Mt. 6:34 (no par. in Lk.) adds a bit of worldly wisdom which in itself does not seem to be typical of Jesus.[20] It is absurd to add the worry of tomorrow to that of to-day. If the disciple worries about tomorrow, to his shame he will be reduced *ad absurdum* even by secular wisdom with its resigned humour.

† ἀμέριμνος.

ἀμέριμνος[1] is found in Soph. Ai., 1207 in the sense of "a man who cares for no one"; from the time of later comedy it means "unconcerned," e.g., Menand. Fr., 1083 (CAF, III, 263), ἀμέριμνος βίος, Vett. Val., IX, 11 (p. 355, 6), σπάνιον γάρ τινα ἀμέμπτως τὸν βίον καὶ ἀμερίμνως διευθῦναι, Herodian, IV, 5, 15, ἀμέριμνως βιοῦν, on a burial inscr., Eranos, 13 (1913), 87, Inscr. 9, 5 ff., τὸν ἄπονον, ἄφοβον, ἡδύν <νήδυμον> ἀμέριμνον αἰώνιον ὕπνον εὕδεις. Not infrequent in the pap.

In the LXX the word occurs in Wis. 6:15: ὁ ἀγρυπνήσας δι' αὐτὴν ταχέως ἀμέριμνος ἔσται, i.e., for the sake of wisdom, 7:23: wisdom is a πνεῦμα ... βέβαιον, ἀσφαλές, ἀμέριμνον ..., Test. Jud. 3:9: ἀμέριμνος ἐν τοῖς πολέμοις. The burial inscr. in IG, XIV, 1839, 11 is possibly Jewish: ἔλιπε ψυχὴν ἀμερίμνως. ἀμερίμνως is used for לָבֶטַח in Is. 14:30 'Α,[2] for בטח in ψ 111:7 Σ; Is. 32:11 Σ (in the Hexapla trans. we also find ἀμεριμνᾶν and ἀμεριμνία).

In the NT ἀμέριμνος occurs only at 1 C. 7:32 (θέλω δὲ ὑμᾶς ἀμερίμνους εἶναι, → 592); Mt. 28:14 (the Jews to the guards at the tomb: καὶ ἐὰν ἀκουσθῇ τοῦτο ἐπὶ τοῦ ἡγεμόνος, ἡμεῖς πείσομεν καὶ ὑμᾶς ἀμερίμνους ποιήσομεν). In Herm. m., 5, 2, 3 it is used alongside ἱλαρός, ἀγαλλιώμενος to characterise μακροθυμία. In Sib., II, 316 the righteous are promised that the angels εἰς φῶς ἄξουσιν (them) καὶ εἰς ζωὴν ἀμέριμνον.

In Ign. Pol. we also find the noun ἀμεριμνία (found from Plut.; also ψ 107:10 Σ [LXX ἐλπίς] and Jos. Bell., 1, 627) in 7, 1: κἀγὼ εὐθυμότερος ἐγενόμην ἐν ἀμεριμνίᾳ θεοῦ.

Bultmann

---

19 This thought distinguishes the admonition in Mt. 6:25-33 par. from Stoic par. (Epict. Diss., I, 9, 7 ff.; 16:1 ff.; III, 26, 27 ff.; Sen. De Remediis Fortuitorum, 10 [p. 104, 18 f., Rossbach, *Breslauer Phil. Abh.*, II, 3, 1888]; on Mt. 6:29 par. cf. the saying of Solon in Diog. L., I, 51), in which anxious concern for the means of life is at least shown to be foolish in view of the animals. For in Stoicism freedom from care is grounded in conviction as to the divine πρόνοια which has furnished man, like every other creature, with what is necessary for him, and esp. in the dogma of the freedom of man acc. to which man's true life is his inner spiritual life, which cannot be affected by outward destiny (cf. R. Bultmann, ZNW, 13 [1912], 106 f.). Nor is there any true analogy in the Rabb. par. (Str.-B., I, 436 f.; P. Fiebig, *Jesu Bergpredigt* [1924], 129 f.). These usually argue acc. to the rule *a maiori ad minus*: If the animal need not work, then man, whom the animals serve and who for his part should serve the Creator, ought not to have to care for his life with all the toil and trouble of work. The difference is, however, that man has to do this because of his sins. Hence the sayings do not exhort to freedom from worry because it is bondage to this world. They show that care is a divine punishment on man.

20 Cf. the Jewish and Gentile par. in the comm., Str.-B., Fiebig, 130; G. Heinrici, *Beiträge z. Geschichte u. Erklärung d. NT*, III (1905).

ἀμέριμνος. 1 On ἀμέριμνος and ἀμεριμνία cf. Pr.-Bauer³.

2 ZAW, NF, 11 (1934), 181.

† μέρος

A. μέρος outside the NT.

1. Secular Greek Usage.

From the root (σ)μερ-, "to get as a share," "to have a share in," μείρομαι, ἔμμορε. (σ)μερ- is perhaps identical with the Indo-Eur. root *smer-*, "to have in mind," "to care" (→ μέριμνα).[1] It is found from the Hom. Hymn. and Pind.

a. "Part" as distinct from the whole, esp. "part of the body, of a building, or a city." τὰ μέρη, "the territory, country, district," e.g., Thuc., II, 96. Fig. (esp. common in pap.) "sphere of office," "circle of occupation," "department of administration."[2] Politically, "party."[3] μέρος also plays an important role in the spheres of law (party at law, in a trial or contract), the army (division of an army) and mathematics (parts of numbers).[4] "Allotted portion," "share," often with the verbs μετέχειν, ἔχειν, λαμβάνειν. Eur. Alc., 474: "allotted destiny." Cf. also Aesch. Ag., 507: μεθέξειν φιλτάτου τάφου μέρος, Isoc., 10, 54: κάλλους γὰρ πλεῖστον μέρος μετέσχεν. c. "Fixed time," "series," "place." Aesch. Choeph., 827 f.: ὅταν ἥκῃ μέρος ἔργων, when the time comes for deeds. d. μέρος is very commonly used with prep. (ἀπὸ, ἐκ μέρους; ἐπὶ, ἐν μέρει; κατὰ, πρὸς, ὑπὸ μέρος; μέρος τι), usually in the sense "partially."[5] Esp. characteristic is the common use of ἐκ μέρους ἔχειν in government organisation. This means "to discharge an office by participation," i.e., to share the burden with several persons.[6] So BGU, II, 574, 10: ἐγ μέρους ἀγορ(ανόμος), I, 144, col. II, 7 f. often has ἐγ(μέρους) ἐξηγητ(εύσας) (or ἐγ [μέρους] ἀγορανο[μήσας]).[7]

2. The Use in the LXX and Philo.

In the LXX μέρος is found for many different Heb. words of different meaning. It is esp. used of buildings or objects (the temple tabernacle, appurtenances) for צַד, צֵלָע, מִקְצוֹעַ, יַרְכָּה, יָד etc. It is also used topographically or geographically, whether physically or politically, for צַד, שָׂפָה. פֶּלֶךְ, פֵּאָה, עֵבֶר etc. Sociologically it is used only for קֵץ and cognates, Ju. 18:2 etc. קֵץ and cognates are the most common originals in various senses. Legally μέρος denotes a portion. In Da. the term is often used in the partitive sense for מִן. Finally it denotes fractions for יָד, or it is used with the Gk. ordinal number for the Heb. fraction alone. On the other hand it is not used in the biological sense for the part or side of man or animal.[8]

μέρος. [1] Cf. Boisacq, 621; Walde-Pok., II, 689 f. [Debrunner].

[2] Cf. the many examples in Preisigke Wört., *s.v.* and Fachwörter, 121; *v.* esp. P. Flor., I, 89, 2: πάντα μέρη τῆς διοικήσεως, "(representatively conducting) the business of financial administration."

[3] P. Oxy., X, 1278, 24; P. Flor., I, 47, 17; P. Lond., 1028, 18; also Jos. Bell., 1, 143.

[4] Cf. on this the dict., esp. Liddell-Scott and Preisigke Wört., *s.v.*

[5] Cf. the dict., esp. Preisigke Wört., II, 75 f. and Mayser, II, 2, Index, 610.

[6] Cf. on this F. Preisigke, *Städtisches Beamtenwesen* (1903), 14, n. 4 and 68, n. 5.

[7] Cf. on this *ibid.*, 14, n. 4.

[8] I am indebted to G. Bertram in this paragraph.

In detail it occurs a. for "part," esp. the last part of a land, district or sea, hence side, margin, border, end: south side, Ez. 47:19; east side, Jos. 18:20; west side, Ez. 47:20; sides of the cherubim, Ez. 1:8 ff.; of the forecourt, Ez. 40:47; of the altar of burnt offering, Ez. 43:16 f. The edges of the road, μέρη ὁδοῦ (S^1: λόγου), Job 26:14; on both sides, ἐξ ἑκατέρου μέρους, 2 Macc. 3:26. b. τὰ μέρη, "the district," Is. 9:1 (8:23) AB^2S; 1 Βασ. 30:14: τὰ τῆς Ἰουδαίας μέρη, Tob. 8:3 S; τὰ μέρη Αἰγύπτου (AB: τὰ ἀνώτατα Αἰγύπτου), upper Egypt. Fig. Sir. 23:19: ἀπόκρυφα μέρη (the most secret corners). c. μέρος "place" (2 Macc. 15:20: τῶν θηρίων ἐπὶ μέρος εὔκαιρον ἀποκαταστaθέντων). d. "Division of an army," 1 Macc. 4:19; 9:11; δύο μέρη, the two wings of an army, 1 Macc. 6:38; τὸ δεξιὸν μέρος, the right "wing," 1 Macc. 9:15 S. e. "Share," "possession," Job 31:12: πῦρ ... καιόμενον ἐπὶ πάντων τῶν μερῶν, 2 Εσδρ. 4:20, the share demanded (tribute); Prv. 17:2, the share left (inheritance); 3 Macc. 5:17, taking part in a meal (εἰς εὐφροσύνην καταθέσθαι μέρος). f. With prep., e.g., κατὰ μέρος, "partially," 2 Macc. 15:33 etc.; 11:20: τὰ κατὰ μέρος, "individual parts." ἐν μέρει, Job 30:1 etc. At Da. 11:45 Θ, instead of the LXX καὶ ἥξει ὥρα τῆς συντελείας αὐτοῦ, we find ἥξει ἕως μέρους αὐτοῦ (to his end) (Heb. עַד־קִצּוֹ).

Philo refers to the part of the body, the soul, the world, philosophy etc. He is esp. concerned with the problem of the whole and the parts, cf. Congr., 145: ἡ (φιλοσοφία) τὰ ὅλα καθορῶσα θεᾶται καὶ τὰ μέρη. [9] God is a whole (ὁ δὲ θεὸς ὅλον, Poster. C., 3). With Plato and the Stoics, Philo espouses the unity of the world, while the Epicureans maintain that the universe consists of infinitely many individual worlds, Op. Mund., 171. Since the world is one, Philo accepts the doctrine of the communion of the parts and the sympathy of the whole, Migr. Abr., 180. The totality is everywhere decisive. Only for the sake of the whole do the parts have the right of participation in it, Vit. Mos., I, 323. Ethically, the truly perfect good is a whole. Individual goods, which are only parts of the perfect good, cannot be called perfect goods, Det. Pot. Ins., 7. Man is μέρος τοῦ παντός, Som., II, 116. [10] As μέρος, however, he is not directly an image of God. He is only an image of the divine logos, Op. Mund., 25.

B. μέρος in the NT.

1. The Usage.

In the NT we find the two basic senses of μέρος seen throughout the writings of antiquity, namely, "part" and "share."

1. "Part." μέρος is a part of the body, Lk. 11:36, of a competence, Lk. 15:12, of the proceeds of a sale, Ac. 5:2, of a garment, Jn. 19:23, of a fish, Lk. 24:42, of a city, Rev. 11:13; [11] 16:19. τὰ μέρη means "district" in Mt. 2:22; 15:21; 16:13; Mk. 8:10; Ac. 2:10; 19:1 (τὰ ἀνωτερικὰ μέρη, the high country); 20:2. μέρος is also the side of a ship, Jn. 21:6 τὰ δεξιὰ μέρη τοῦ πλοίου, the right side (as the lucky side). It

[9] On the philosophical problem of the whole and the parts cf. esp. Aristot. Metaph., IV, 25, p. 1023b, 12 ff. and IV, 26, p. 1023b, 26 ff. Aristot. defines μέρος as follows: μέρος λέγεται ἕνα μὲν τρόπον εἰς ὃ διαιρεθείη ἂν τὸ ποσὸν ὁπωσοῦν ... ἄλλον δὲ τρόπον τὰ καταμετροῦντα τῶν τοιούτων μόνον· ... ἔτι εἰς ἃ τὸ εἶδος διαιρεθείη ἂν ἄνευ τοῦ ποσοῦ, καὶ ταῦτα μόρια λέγεται τούτου. "We call a part on the one side that into which what is quantitative can be in some way divided, ... and also that into which form can be divided apart from quantity, e.g., the forms are parts of the species." On the definition of "part" in the history of philosophy cf. R. Eisler, *Wörterbuch d. philosoph. Begriffe,* III (1930^4), 216.

[10] Cf. on this Plat. Leg., X, 903c. Acc. to Plato the individual, understood as part of the whole, is there for the sake of the whole, not the whole for the sake of the part. The aim of everything individual is to be found in the good of the whole.

[11] The expression τὸ δέκατον (sc. μέρος) τῆς πόλεως in Rev. 11:13 is not classical. Cf. Bl.-Debr. § 241, 7; cf. also § 164, 5.

occurs again in this sense only in Herm. s., 9, 2, 3; v., 3, 1, 9 : τὰ δεξιὰ μέρη; 3, 2, 1: τὰ ἀριστερὰ μέρη; s., 9, 9, 3 : τὰ ἐξώτερα μέρη τῆς οἰκοδομῆς, the outside of the building. Religiously τὸ μέρος can be the party which has come into being for theological or political reasons, Ac. 23:6 : τὸ ἓν μέρος ἐστὶν Σαδδουκαίων, τὸ δὲ ἕτερον Φαρισαίων, 23:9 : τὸ μέρος τῶν Φαρισαίων. Ac. 19:27 shows that in the *koine* μέρος can mean a trade, though always against the background that the craft (that of the goldsmiths in Ephesus) is part of the total business life (of the city).

2. "Share." One can have a share in a person (Jesus, Jn. 13:8), a group of persons (hypocrites and ungodly, Mt. 24:51; Lk. 24:46), a thing (the tree of life, Rev. 22:19; the lake of fire, Rev. 21:8), or an event (the resurrection, Rev. 20:6). In the case of persons we have μέρος μετά τινος (Jn. 13:8; Mt. 24:51; Lk. 12:46), in that of things or events μέρος ἔν τινι (Rev. 20:6; 21:8) or ἀπό τινος (Rev. 22:19).

3. Adv. phrases in the NT : ἀνὰ μέρος, "after one another," 1 C. 14:27 (those who speak with tongues must speak after one another for the sake of order); ἀπὸ μέρους, "partially," R. 15:5; 2 C. 2:5; "a little," "to some degree," R. 15:24; 2 C. 1:14; ἐκ μέρους, "in part," 1 C. 13:9, 10, 12 (of expressions of the gifts of the Spirit in this aeon); ἐν τούτῳ τῷ μέρει, "in this connection or instance," 2 C. 3:10.[12] Cf. 2 C. 9:3 : "in this matter or point." Col. 2:16 : ἐν μέρει ἑορτῆς, "in respect of festivals." κατὰ μέρος, "in detail" (Hb. 9:5, of detailed expositions of a head of Christian doctrine). Adv. acc. μέρος τι, "in part," 1 C. 11:18.

2. Theologically Important Statements.

The adverbial ἐκ μέρους, along with the verbs γινώσκειν and προφητεύειν, serves in 1 C. 13:9, 12 to denote the situation of Christians in this age. There is now no perfect knowledge, no full exercise of the prophetic gift. Though controlled by the Spirit, the earthly existence of Christians stands under the sign of the partial. Only in the future aeon will what is partial (τὸ ἐκ μέρους, 1 C. 13:10) be replaced by what is perfect (→ τὸ τέλειον).

Salvation history, in so far as it applies to Israel, is also put by Paul in the category of μέρος. Paul has a secret knowledge of the counsel of God which is concealed from men (→ μυστήριον).[13] On this basis he declares in R. 11:25 that a partial hardness has come on Israel which will last until the divinely ordained number of the Gentiles has been brought to salvation.[14] Then the whole counsel of God, which rests on the promises, will be brought to fulfilment. Israel as a whole will finally be saved. Hence ἀπὸ μέρους refers to what takes place now. God's gracious action applies now to only one part of Israel. The other part, which is obviously the majority for Paul, stands for the time being under the sign of πώρωσις.

In 1 C. 12:27 (→ 564) Paul declares : ὑμεῖς δέ ἐστε σῶμα Χριστοῦ καὶ μέλη ἐκ μέρους, "but you are the body of Christ, and each is a member according to his portion."[15] Paul is affirming two things. The first is that Christians are not unrelated individuals. They belong to an organism which is distinguished from

---

[12] There is a verbal par. in Polyb., 18, 35 (18), 2. J. Weiss, *Die Aufgaben der nt.lichen Wissenschaft* (1908), 32 strikes out ἐν τούτῳ τῷ μέρει as a gloss on ἕνεκεν. But a glance at the passage in Polyb. shows that this is unnecessary. The phrase is wholly justified in the context of 2 C. 3:10.

[13] Cf. on this J. Schneider, " 'Mysterion' im NT," ThStKr, 104 (1932), 267 f.

[14] Cf. on this Schl. R., 327: "The closing of the Jewish world to the work of God is for the period during which those who belong to the nations are called."

[15] D vg Latt, acc. to Nestle also sy^h, have ἐκ μέλους for ἐκ μέρους; this is a scribal error. Cf. also Ltzm. K., 63.

all others by the addition of the gen. Χριστοῦ to σῶμα. In this organism Christians are indissolubly bound together in unity and fellowship. The second point is that the σῶμα Χριστοῦ is an integrated organism in which there are μέλη. Thus the individuality of each Christian is recognised and established. But this individuality is not an autonomous whole. It can be understood only as part of a whole. Hence the fact of the individual Christian always presupposes the fact of the σῶμα Χριστοῦ.

Eph. 4:16 may be mentioned in this connection. This does not simply call the ἐκκλησία the σῶμα Χριστοῦ. It also speaks of the relation of the σῶμα to its κεφαλή, to Christ. The body receives from Christ the strength to grow. But it is held together by bonds (ἁφαί) which have different powers allotted to them. According to the measure of the power which they have received (ἐν μέτρῳ ἑνὸς ἑκάστου μέρους) these must contribute to the building up of the whole body. Paul is saying that the decisive vital forces for the growth of the Church come from Christ, but that the members to whom a special position and power are given (the apostles, prophets, evangelists, pastors and teachers, v. 11), [16] are under obligation to serve the edifying of the Church at their own place and according to the measure of the gifts with which they are endowed.

In Jn. 13:8 Jesus makes it clear when He washes the feet of Peter that only the purified disciple can have any part in Him (ἔχεις μέρος μετ' ἐμοῦ). Purification (from sin) is an unconditional presupposition for fellowship with Christ Jesus.

When this aeon ends and the new one begins, fellowship with Jesus will lead to participation in the first resurrection (Rev. 20:6) [17] which precedes the general resurrection of the dead (→ ἀνίστημι, I, 373). The Christian who has a part in this will then have a share in the tree of life (Rev. 22:19: τὸ μέρος αὐτοῦ ἀπὸ τοῦ ξύλου τῆς ζωῆς), [18] i.e., he will participate in the imperishable benefits of eternal life.

Participation is thus of fateful significance for man. Jesus leaves His disciples in no doubt that unfaithful discipleship can entail loss of all share in the kingdom of God. In Mt. 24:51 (Lk. 12:46) He assigns the unfaithful disciple a place (μέρος) with the hypocrites (Lk. μετὰ τῶν ἀπίστων). [19] In Rev. 21:8 the ungodly are allotted a share in the lake which burns with fire and brimstone. This is the second death i.e., eternal destruction. [20]

Eph. 4:9 (κατέβη εἰς τὰ κατώτερα μέρη τῆς γῆς) may refer to a journey of Christ to the underworld or to His earthly journey. Büchsel (→ κατώτερος, III, 640 f.) has given plausible reasons for the opinion that what is in view is not

---

[16] So also A. Klöpper, *Der Brief an d. Eph.* (1891), 136: The ref. is to "the various individuals who have specific charismata." Cf. also Schl. Erl., *ad loc.* Others, e.g., Haupt Gefbr., 175; Ew. Gefbr., 199, (incorrectly) relate the expression to all members of the community.

[17] On ἔχειν μέρος ἔν τινι (Rev. 20:6: μακάριος καὶ ἅγιος ὁ ἔχων μέρος ἐν τῇ ἀναστάσει τῇ πρώτῃ), cf. Dalman WJ, I, 103 f.

[18] On ξύλον τῆς ζωῆς cf. → ξύλον.

[19] τὸ μέρος μετά τινος is a Semitism. Cf. ψ 49:18 μετὰ μοιχῶν τὴν μερίδα σου ἐτίθεις and the Rabb. examples in Schl. Mt., 718; cf. also Str.-B., I, 969. The reading in Lk. (μετὰ τῶν ἀπίστων) is to be regarded as secondary.

[20] There is a counterpart to this in Ign. Pol., 6, 1: μετ' αὐτῶν μοι τὸ μέρος γένοιτο σχεῖν ἐν (vl. παρὰ) θεῷ, "I would have my place with them in (or with) God"; and Mart. Pol., 14, 2: τοῦ λαβεῖν μέρος (place) ἐν ἀριθμῷ τῶν μαρτύρων.

the earthly journey of the Redeemer but Christ's going into the realm of the dead by death.[21]

In 1 Cl., 29, 1 Christians are called ἐκλογῆς μέρος, the selected portion (of all humanity). Acc. to Herm. v., 3, 6, 4 there is still an evil portion even in Christians: τινὰ δὲ μέρη ἔχουσιν τῆς ἀνομίας, "they still have certain parts of unrighteousness."[22]

J. Schneider

† μεσίτης, † μεσιτεύω

Contents: A. Occurrence and Meaning: I. Hellenistic Usage; II. The Term and Concept in Israelite-Jewish Usage: 1. The Old Testament; 2. Rabbinic Judaism; 3. Hellenistic Judaism: Josephus and Philo. B. The Theology of Mediatorship outside the Bible: 1. The Deity as a Guarantor of Human Agreements; 2. Cosmic Soteriological Intermediaries in

---

[21] The view which I expressed in → I, 522 f. is to be amended accordingly.
[22] Pr.-Bauer[3], 837.

μεσίτης κτλ. RGG[2], IV, 121 f.; Wettstein on Gl. 3:19; Hb. 6:17; J. Behm, *Der Begriff* διαθήκη *im NT* (1912), 77 ff.; Liddell-Scott, Pr.-Bauer[3], Moult.-Mill., Cr.-Kö., *s.v.*; → διαθήκη, ἀποκαλύπτω, ἔγγυος, Bibl. On A: Preisigke Wört. and Fachwörter, *s.v.*; O. Schulthess, Pauly-W., XV (1932), 1097 ff.; L. Mitteis, "Zur Berliner Papyruspublikation, IV. Μεσίτης," Herm., 30 (1895), 616 ff.; *Berichte d. Sächs. Gesellsch.*, 62, 1 (1910), 124 ff.; O. Gradenwitz, *Einführung in die Papyruskunde*, I (1900), 31, n. 3; 94; J. Partsch, *Griechisches Bürgschaftsrecht*, I (1909); O. Eger, *Zum ägyptischen Grundbuchwesen in römischer Zeit* (1909), 43 ff.; E. Weiss, *Pfandrechtliche Untersuchungen*, 1 (1909), 21, n. 1; A. B. Schwarz, *Hypothek u. Hypallagma* (1911), 143 ff.; G. Semeka, *Ptolemäisches Prozessrecht*, I (1913), 217 ff. On B: W. H. Roscher, "Der Omphalosgedanke bei verschiedenen Völkern, bes. den semitischen," *Berichte d. Sächs. Gesellsch.*, 70 (1918), 1 ff.; F. Cumont, *Textes et Monuments figurés relatifs aux Mystères de Mithra*, I (1899), Index, *s.v.* μεσίτης, II (1896), 33 ff.; *Die Mysterien des Mithra*[3], transl. K. Latte (1923); C. Clemen, "D. griech. u. lat. Nachrichten über d. persische Religion," RVV, 17, 1 (1920), 155 ff.; J. Hertel, "Die Sonne u. Mithra im Awesta," *Indo-iranische Quellen u. Forschungen*, IX (1927); H. Lommel, "Die Yäšts des Awesta übersetzt u. eingeleitet," *Quellen d. Religionsgesch.*, 15 (1927), esp. 61 ff.; A. Meillet, "Le Dieu Indo-Iranien Mitra," *Journal Asiatique*, 10, 10 (1907, II), 143 ff.; R. Eisler, *Weltenmantel u. Himmelszelt*, II (1910), 417 ff.; H. Güntert, *Der arische Weltkönig u. Heiland* (1923), 49 ff.; C. Schmidt and H. J. Polotsky, "Ein Mani-Fund in Ägypten," SAB (1933), 4 ff.; "Manichäische Homilien," *Manichäische Handschr. der Sammlung A. Chester Beatty*, I, ed. H. J. Polotsky (1934); "Kephalaia," *Manichäische Handschr. der Staatlichen Museen Berlin*, ed. C. Schmidt, I (1935 ff.); Lidz. Ginza → 607 f.; O. v. Wesendonk, *Urmensch u. Seele in d. iranischen Überlieferung* (1924); W. Staerk, "D. sieben Säulen d. Welt u. des Hauses d. Weisheit," ZNW, 35 (1936), 232 ff. On C: W. Eichrodt, *Theologie d. AT*, I (1933), 150 ff.; P. Volz, *Mose u. sein Werk*[2] (1932); *Js. II übersetzt u. erklärt* (1932), 149 ff.; K. Elliger, *Dtjs. in seinem Verhältnis zu Tritjs.* (1933), esp. 6 ff.; G. v. Rad, "D. Konfessionen Jeremias," *Evangelische Theol.*, 3 (1936), 265 ff. On D: Levy Wört., *s.v.* סרסור; Moore, I, 416 ff., 437 f.; "Intermediaries in Jewish Theology," HThR, 15 (1922), 41-85 (Memra, Shekinah, Metatron = *metator*, not intermediary hypostases); Str.-B., esp. II, 302 ff.; III, 512 ff.; 556; G. Dalman, *Der leidende u. der sterbende Messias d. Synagoge im ersten nachchristlichen Jahrtausend* (1888); J. Jeremias, "Erlöser u. Erlösung im Spätjudt. u. Urchr.," *Deutsche Theol., Bericht über den 2. deutschen Theologentag in Frankfurt a.M.* (1929), 106 ff.; B. Murmelstein, "Adam, ein Beitrag zur Messiaslehre,"

Comparative Religion; 3. Men as Mediators. C. Mediatorship in the Old Testament: 1. Divine Mediatorship; 2. Men as Mediators. D. The Theological Concept of the Mediator in Judaism: 1. Rabbinic Judaism; 2. Hellenistic Judaism. E. The New Testament Concept of the Mediator: 1. The Use of the Terms; 2. The Theology of Mediatorship in the New Testament: a. Jesus; b. The Primitive Community; c. Paul; d. The Gospel and Epistles of John; e. The Other NT Writings. F. The Church.

A. Occurrence and Meaning.

I. Hellenistic Usage.

μεσίτης is non-Attic (Moeridis Atticistae Lexicon Atticum, ed. G. A. Koch [1830], 235: μετέγγυος Ἀττικῶς· μεσίτης, Ἑλληνικῶς). Aristot. Eth. Nic., V, 7, p. 1132a, 22 ff. avoids it, hesitates to introduce μεσίδιος (καλοῦσιν ἔνιοι), and prefers δικαστὴς μέσος. On μέσῳ δικαστῇ in Thuc., IV, 83 the scholiast (ed. C. Hude [1927], p. 268) notes: ἀντὶ τοῦ μεσίτῃ καὶ διαιτητῇ (umpire). The word is found occasionally in Hellen. writers from Polyb. on, and is common in the pap. from the 3rd cent. B.C. It has not been found thus far on inscr. Formed like πολίτης (from πόλις), τεχνίτης (from τέχνη) etc., it denotes the one in the middle who discharges the function of a μέσος. For the most common technical use we should start with the specific meaning of μέσος as "between contestants or parties," "neutral," τὸ μέσον "no man's land." [1] In Hom. Il., 18, 507: κεῖτο (in the council portrayed on Achilles' shield) δ' ἄρ' ἐν μέσσοισι δύω χρυσοῖο τάλαντα (to fall as a prize for the best of the judges), this meaning may be seen. It is clear in Xenoph. An., III, 1, 21: ἐν μέσῳ ... κεῖται ταῦτα τὰ ἀγαθὰ ἆθλα. The expression ἐς μέσον ἀμφοτέροισι δικάζειν (Il., 23, 574) leads directly to μέσος δικαστής and μεσίτης.

1. The "neutral" whom both sides can trust. He may be an umpire (cf. Thuc., IV, 83: ἕτοιμος ὢν Βρασίδᾳ μέσῳ δικαστῇ ἐπιτρέπειν, → *supra*) or a "negotiator of peace" (Polyb., 28, 17, 8: ἐβούλετο τοὺς Ῥοδίους προνύξας μεσίτας ἀποδεῖξαι). But acc. to context he may be one who guarantees agreements (Diod. S., IV, 54, 7: The repudiated Medea flees to Heracles. τοῦτον γὰρ μεσίτην (guarantor) γεγονότα τῶν ὁμολογιῶν ἐν Κόλχοις ἐπηγγέλθαι βοηθήσειν αὐτῇ παρασπονδουμένῃ). Thus μεσίτης can be a syn. of (μετ)έγγυος, "guarantor." It became one of the most varied technical terms in the vocabulary of Hellen. law. Ignoring more delicate nuances, we may see the following senses in the pap.: a. The arbiter in civil legal transactions (μεσίτης· ὁ εἰρηνοποιός, Suid., *s.v.*). The fairly common combination μεσίτης καὶ κριτής or the like (e.g., P. Cattaoui verso col. I, 3, APF, III [1906], 62 and 103) reminds us of the Roman juxtaposition of *iudex* and *arbiter*, and may have been influenced by this in Roman Egypt. Yet there is the material difference that the *arbiter* is part of the legal process, whereas the appointment of one or more μεσῖται (cf. the work of the village mayors under the permanent control of the *strategos*) is designed to avoid

---

WZKM, 35 (1928), 242 ff.; 36 (1929), 51 ff.; P. Seidelin, "Der Ebed Jahwe u. d. Messiasgestalt im Jesajatargum," ZNW, 35 (1936), 194 ff. On E: NT Theol. by Holtzmann and Weinel, Index *s.v.* "Mittler"; E. Käsemann, "Das wandernde Gottesvolk," FRL, 55 (1938), esp. 58-156; Sieffert, Zn., Burton, Lagrange, Loisy, Ltzm., Oepke Gl. on 3:19 f.; B. Weiss, Dib., Schl. Past. on 1 Tm. 2:5; Rgg., Wnd., Michel Hb. on 6:17; 7:22; 8:6; 9:15; 12:24; G. Kittel, "Jesu Worte über sein Sterben," DTh, 3 (1936), 166 ff.; "Jesus oder Pls.?" AELKZ, 69 (1936), 578 ff.; A. Oepke, "Hat Pls. 'die Jesusreligion verdorben'?" *ibid.*, 410 ff.; "Das Christuszeugnis des Joh.-Ev.," *Sächs. Kirchenblatt, NF*, 1 (1937), 252 ff. On F: E. Brunner, *Der Mittler*[2] (1930); E.T. *The Mediator* (1947); W. Künneth, *Theologie der Auferstehung*[2] (1934), esp. 143 ff.

[1] On the constr. cf. Debr. Gr. Wortb., 180; P. Chantraine, *La Formation des Noms en Grec Ancien* (1933), 312; Mayser, I, 3[2] (1936), 76 ff. Derivation from law as the mediator between two extremes in Aristot. Eth. Nic., V, 7, p. 1132a, 22 ff. is a philosophical construction.

or to smooth official procedures, and is thus opposed to the δικαστήριον. P. Lond., I, 113, 1, 26 ff. (6th cent. A.D.): After further negotiations it took place μεσητίαν (= μεσιτείαν) γενέσθαι μέσων εἰρηνικῶν ἀνδρῶν ἀγαθῶν ... μέλλοντος τοῦ πράγματος εἰς δικαστήριον κατάγεσθαι, ὕστερον ἤρεσεν τοῖς μέσοις καὶ τοῖς μέρεσε[ι]ν ἔδοξεν (the agreement follows). The arbiter may be named by the judge (Greek Papyri from the Cairo Museum, ed. E. J. Goodspeed, *The Decennial Publications of the Univ. of Chicago*, I, 5 [1904], 29, col. III, 5 : μεσίτην ἡμῖν δός, P. Lille, I, 28, 11: αὐτοῖς ἐδώκαμεν μεσίτην, Pap. Grecs et Démotiques ... publiés par T. Reinach [1905], 44, 3 [104 A.D.]: ὁ κατασταθεὶς κριτὴς μεσίτης) or selected by the parties (Mitteis-Wilcken, II, 2, 87, 13 : ἕλεσθε τίνα βούλεσθε μεσίτην). b. The "witness" to a legal transaction or "guarantor" of the execution of an agreement. CPR, 19, 10 f. (relating to a sale of land ; the purchaser does not reimburse certain outlays): καὶ πολλάκις ταύτῃ ἠνώχλησα (have reminded) μετὰ τοῦ μεσίτου ἀποδοῦναί μοι ἃ παρέσχον. The clerk who has notified the contract of purchase (line 16 : ὁ μεταξύ, line 23 : ὁ μεταξὺ μεσίτης) sees to its execution. The handing over of an inheritance takes place παρόντων (τῶν) μεσιτῶν (BGU, II, 419, 8 and 18) even when there is no dispute.[2] c. The "sequestrator," a neutral with whom a disputed object or sum is temporarily left.[3] BGU, I, 4, 16 f. (relating to a refused deposit): ἔχοντός μου μεσείτην Συρίωνα Ἰσιδώρου. μεσίτης, perhaps along with d., can here denote an occupation. CPR, 45, 3 (214 A.D.): παρὰ Μάρκου Αὐρηλίου Σερήνου μεσίτου ἀπὸ ἀμφόδου (name of a street).[4] d. "Pawnbroker." This meaning arises because to those untrained in law there is a similarly between sequestration and pawnbroking.[5] It cannot be attested, but is to be postulated. μεσιτεία means pledging or pledge. BGU, III, 907, 4 and cf. 7: ὑποθήκην καὶ μεσειτίαν, I, 68, 13 : ὧν ὀφείλει μυ (= μοι) ἐπεὶ (= ἐπὶ) μεσειτέᾳ (→ also μεσιτεύειν, 601). e. Occasionally "guarantor" in the sense of one who goes bail with his own funds for another (derived from d.), P. Lond., II, 370, 6; 9; 14.[6] f. Later the "warehouse official" who notes down invoices on corn accounts and assigns dues to individual owners. BGU, II, 683-689 (from the Arab period): κυ(ρίῳ) μεσί(τῃ) ὁρρ(ίων) πολιτῶν.

---

[2] The witnesses who acc. to Roman law have to sign a will along with the testator are usually μάρτυρες, the executors ἐπίτροποι, the accountants λογοθέται. But can one say that μεσίτης διαθήκης is an alien term in this sphere (→ Behm, 79, n. 1)? Cl. Al., in an exposition of the meaning of symbols in Strom., V, 8, 55, 4, writes : καὶ τὰ παρὰ Ῥωμαίοις ἐπὶ τῶν διαθηκῶν γινόμενα τάξιν εἴληχε, τὰ διὰ δικαιοσύνην ἐκεῖνα ζυγὰ καὶ ἀσσάρια καρπισμοί τε καὶ αἱ τῶν ὤτων ἐπιψαύσεις, τὰ μὲν γὰρ ἵνα δικαίως γίνηται, τὰ δὲ εἰς τὸν τῆς τιμῆς μερισμόν, τὸ δ᾽ ὅπως ὁ παρατυχών, ὡς βάρους τινὸς αὐτῷ ἐπιτιθεμένου, ἑστὼς ἀκούσῃ καὶ τάξιν μεσίτου λάβῃ. He is here alluding to the symbolical purchase of inheritance connected with the making of a will in Rome. The *familiae emptor,* a legally appointed representative of the heir or heirs, knocked on the scales (ζυγά) with a bronze or gold piece (ἀσσάρια) and gave it to the testator as a sign of taking over the *familia pecuniaque* (slaves and cattle). Slaves to be emancipated were touched (καρπισμοί) with the rod (καρπίς). The ears of the representative also seem to have been touched (τῶν ὤτων ἐπιψαύσεις) to lay on him the burden of responsibility and the duty of listening (e.g., to complaints etc.). The scales (which are for Cl. a symbol of *iustitia*) are to remind him of the task of deciding rightly. He thus receives a kind of investiture (τάξις) as μεσίτης διαθήκης, a guarantor of the orderly execution of the terms of the will. The expression is borrowed from the Egyptian. In explanation of the difficult text cf. Pauly-W., *2. Reihe,* V, 1 (1934), 987; Pass., *s.v.* καρπίς.

[3] Isidor. Hisp. Etymologiae (ed. W. Lindsay [1911]), X, 260; *Sequester dicitur, qui certantibus medius intervenit, qui apud Graecos* ὁ μέσος *dicitur, apud quem pignora deponi solent.* The etymology : *quod eius ... utraque pars fidem sequatur,* is dubious. *Sequester* is rather related to the old Lat. *secus,* along, alongside, hence "one who stands by," "a neutral." In etym. and meaning it thus corresponds exactly to the Gk. μεσίτης.

[4] C. Wessely renders "agent." But this can hardly be a separate sense, though there is perhaps a weakening in this direction.

[5] Mitteis, Herm., 618.

[6] Cf. the introductory remarks of Kenyon on the pap.

In addition to the technical sense the word seems to have had two less precise meanings: 2. the "intermediary" in the general spatial sense; 3. the "mediator" or "negotiator" in the sense of one who establishes a relation which would not otherwise exist. There are as yet no certain examples of these meanings in secular Gk. But they may be deduced from the use of the related verb, → also 602; 617. On the other hand, the sense of "conveyer" or "giver," found in the later fathers, is doubtful (→ n. 84, also *infra*).

μεσιτεύω: 1. technical, "to act as umpire or peacemaker." In the fable the crayfish, which seeks to make peace between the dolphins and whales, is the model of a busy but insignificant politician playing a tragi-comic role: τούτοις παρῆλθε καρκίνος μεσιτεύων (synon. εἰρηνεύων, Babrius, ed. W. G. Rutherford [1883], 39, 2). With inner obj. (μεσιτεύειν τὴν διάλυσιν), Polyb., 11, 34, 3. With simple obj., Eustath. Thessal. Comm. in Il., 1338, 50 (IV, 336, Stallbaum): μεσιτεύειν ἰσότητα τιμῆς τοῖς μὴ ἐπίσης ἀρίστοις, "to adjudge as umpire" (synon. τιθέναι τιμήν τινι). There is no ground for postulating a sense "to give," "to impart," on the basis of this passage. The guaranteeing of agreements and their execution may be included. Ephesus and Sardis make a treaty guaranteed by a third power, probably Pergamos. If through violation a ban is pronounced on one of the signatories by the league to which it belongs, the choice of the power charged to execute it shall be arranged ἀπὸ τῆς μεσιτευούσης τὰς συνθήκας πόλεως [7] (Inscr. Perg., 268 E, 21 = Ditt. Or., II, 437, 76, 1st cent. B.C., cf. C, 23: μεσιτεύειν, E, 24: πρὸς τὸν μεσιτεύοντα δῆμον, E, 28: ἐπὶ τὸν μεσιτεύοντα δῆμον, also BCH, IV [1880], 265, line 7 [Carpathos]: μεσιτεύοντος τοῦ δάμου). Most of the meanings of the noun are repeated here: "to deposit with a sequestrator" (anon. in Suid., *s.v.*: τὰ χρήματα μεσιτεύειν); "to pledge" (μεσιτεύειν καὶ παραχωρεῖν, BGU, III, 709, 18; 906, 7; CPR, 1, 19: to pledge and alienate); Eustath. Thessal. Comm. in Il., 1342, 39 f. (IV, 341, Stallbaum): ὑπὲρ χρεώστου ἀρρώστου μεσιτεύειν, to intercede or pledge oneself for a sick debtor. 2. Spatially, "to occupy the middle place." The four and seven μεσιτεύουσι μονάδος καὶ δεκάδος, Iambl. Theol. Arithm., ed. V. de Falco (1922), 44, i.e., they are equidistant from the outer numbers, perhaps with a subsidiary mystical significance in terms of 1. or 3. Cl. Al. Strom., III, 12, 81, 4: γάμου τοῦ σώφρονος μεσιτεύει συμφωνία. 3. "To establish a relation" between two hitherto unrelated entities, "to mediate" their coming together. This sense grows out of 1. and 2. in such a way that precise distinction is hardly possible. On the border is Diod. S., XIX, 71, 6: μεσιτεύσαντος τὰς συνθήκας Ἀμίλκου τοῦ Καρχηδονίου. The shift is perhaps clearer in Dion. Hal., IX, 59, 5: μετὰ τοῦτο συνθῆκαι γίνονται ταῖς πόλεσι μεσιτεύσαντος αὐτὰς τοῦ ὑπάτου τοιαίδε. The consul is not a neutral, nor an umpire, nor the guarantor of an agreement, but an authorised negotiator for the one party, the Roman Senate, which simply dictates peace. A better though later example is Eustath. Thessal. Comm. in Il., 1166, 25 (IV, 102, Stallbaum): Daidalos τῇ Πασιφάῃ πρὸς ἀλλόκοτον ἔρωτα τὸν τοῦ ταύρου ἐμεσίτευσε, he served as mediator, he it was who by making the wooden cow brought together the woman and the bull, paired off the queen and the bull. Luc. Amores in 27 calls the table and in 54 the desire for pederasty φιλίας μεσῖτις. Here, too, the sense of establishing a relationship may be glimpsed. This permits of inferences in respect of μεσιτεύειν and μεσίτης.

II. The Term and Concept in Israelite-Jewish Usage.

1. The Old Testament. μεσιτεύω does not occur in the LXX and μεσίτης only at Job 9:33: εἴθε ἦν ὁ μεσίτης ἡμῶν καὶ ἐλέγχων καὶ διακούων ἀνὰ μέσον ἀμφοτέρων· לֹא יֵשׁ־בֵּינֵינוּ מוֹכִיחַ יָשֵׁת יָדוֹ עַל־שְׁנֵינוּ, ὁ μεσίτης is thus an incorrect rendering of בֵּינֵינוּ, which shows the associations of the term to the Hellenistic ear. In sense מוֹכִיחַ (rendered ἐλέγχων) is closer. There is no single term for "mediator" in the Heb. or Gk. OT. אִישׁ הַבֵּנַיִם is the warrior who, coming between the hosts, decides the war by

[7] One is reminded of the sarcastic depiction in Aristot. Pol., V, 6, p. 1306a, 26 ff. ἐν τῇ εἰρήνῃ διὰ τὴν ἀπιστίαν τὴν πρὸς ἀλλήλους ἐγχειρίζουσι τὴν φυλακὴν στρατιώταις καὶ ἄρχοντι μεσιδίῳ, ὃς ἐνίοτε γίνεται κύριος ἀμφοτέρων.

single combat, 1 S. 17:4, 23: Goliath; v. 23 Orig. and Lucian: ἀνὴρ ὁ μεσαῖος, no LXX. מֵלִיץ is strictly the "mocker," then the "interpreter," perhaps because he speaks a strange and garbled speech, Gn. 42:23, LXX ἑρμηνευτής. It finally means the "negotiator" or "envoy," 2 Chron. 32:31, LXX πρεσβευτής; Is. 43:27 LXX οἱ ἄρχοντες ὑμῶν; Job 33:23: LXX quite wrong. This concept is closer to the Hebrew and Jewish cultural and linguistic sense than that of a neutral and trusted umpire. The function of the latter did not establish itself here in independence of the regular judicial office.

2. Rabbinic Judaism. Only in post-bibl. Heb. and Aram. do we find the typical and religiously technical term for the concept in question, namely, סַרְסוּר, Aram. סַרְסוּרָא.[8] This comes from the field of commerce rather than law. It means the negotiator who arranges business deals and contracts and who thus brings together those previously unrelated. BB, 5, 8 (purchase of wine): If they have a broker and the vessel breaks, the broker bears (the loss). Gn. r., 8, on 1:26 and Ex. r., 6 on 6:2 have parables of a king using a negotiator for the purchase of wine or the marriage of his daughter. That the thought of setting in relation predominates may be seen from the fig. use for the couch as the mediator of increase (jBer., 6a, 6) or the heart and eyes as the brokers of sin (jBer., 3c, 19). The verb סרסר always means "to negotiate" or "to mediate," never "to be umpire," "to guarantee," "to transmit."

3. Hellenistic Judaism. In Joseph. the terms are used only in a secular sense, and the Hellenistic use predominates in sense 1. When Alexander and Aristobulus, accused by their father Herod before the emperor, propose: διόπερ ἐπὶ τῷ πάντων δεσπότῃ Καίσαρι μεσιτεύοντι τὸν παρόντα καιρὸν συντιθέμεθα ταύτην τὴν συνθήκην (Ant., 16, 118), the emperor is designated as supreme umpire, though perhaps also without sharp distinction as the guarantor of an agreement to be concluded (→ 599). The meaning of guarantor or pledge (→ 600) is present when it is said of the Midianites: ταῦτα ὀμνύντες ἔλεγον καὶ θεὸν μεσίτην ὧν ὑπισχνοῦντο ποιούμενοι (Ant., 4, 133, cf. Luc. Amores, 47 of Pylades and Orestes: θεὸν τῶν πρὸς ἀλλήλους παθῶν μεσίτην λαβόντες ὡς ἐφ' ἑνὸς σκάφους (ship) τοῦ βίου συνέπλευσαν). Similarly, μεσιτεία in Ant., 20, 62 means "surety," ὅρκους καὶ μεσιτείαν. On the border between 1. and 3. is Ant., 7, 193, where it is said of Joab: ἐμεσίτευσε πρὸς τὸν βασιλέα (in favour of Absalom). The ref. is to the conclusion of peace, not by arrangement between two equally justified parties, but by the king's intervention. Joab is the mediator or advocate. Sense 3. is even stronger in Ant., 16, 24: τῶν παρὰ Ἀγρίππα τισὶν ἐπιζητουμένων (neut.) μεσίτης ἦν. Herod saw to it that suppliants could make contact with Agrippa, the legate of Augustus. He was their middle-man, their counsel in the unofficial sense. μεσίτης is here close to סַרְסוּר.

Philo, too, begins with the Hellenistic use in sense 1. Synon. of μεσίτης are διαιτητής (umpire, Som., I, 142, cf. μεσιτεύειν καὶ διαιτᾶν, Plant., 10) and διαλλακτής (peace-maker, Vit. Mos., II, 166). But the further synon. κηδεμών (guardian) and παραιτητής (advocate, Vit. Mos., *loc. cit.*) show that what is at issue is something very different from neutral decision between equal parties. It is appeal to a higher court. This may be explained only partially in terms of 3. Nor does the influence of סַרְסוּר (→ *supra*) wholly explain the usage. The concept "mediator" has here been given a specific depth and fulness by religion. There is a hint of this in the fact that Philo always uses μεσίτης, and almost always μεσιτεύω,[9] in a technical religious sense.

[8] Str.-B., III, 512, 556. Levy Wört., III, 595 f., *s.v.* vocalised סִרְסוּר. Subsidiary forms are סַפְסָר, טַפְסִירָא. The related abstract terms are סַרְסָרוּת and סַפְסִירוּתָא, "negotiation," "mediation."

[9] The only exception is Migr. Abr., 158: Many ... wish that their lives may remain on the middle road, on the border between human and divine virtues, that they may remain in contact with both (μεσιτεύειν τὸν ἑαυτῶν βίον ἀξιοῦντες καὶ μεθόριον ἀνθρωπίνων τε καὶ θείων ἀρετῶν τιθέντες).

B. The Theology of Mediatorship outside the Bible.

1. The Deity as a Guarantor of Human Agreements.

Instances have already been seen of the deity as the guarantor of human relationships in sense 1. (→ 602). This idea underlies the oath, and like the oath it is common to all religions.

Simplicius in Epicteti enchiridion, 33, 5 (ed. J. Schweighäuser, IV [1800], 423) says: ὁ γὰρ ὅρκος μάρτυρα τὸν θεὸν καλεῖ καὶ μεσίτην αὐτὸν καὶ ἐγγυητὴν ἐφ' οἷς λέγει προΐσχεται. One of the gods particularly concerned here is Mithra. From Xenophon on, Greek authors commonly put on the lips of Persians the affirmation μὰ τὸν Μίθρην. Perhaps Mithra derives his title from the function of sanctifying treaties (→ 605). As a highly personal God, Yahweh, too, is to a supreme degree a God of oaths (→ ὀμνύω, ὁρκίζω). In relation to him the verb is used as well as the noun (→ 602). Philo Spec. Leg., IV, 31: ἀοράτῳ δὲ πράγματι πάντως ἀόρατος μεσιτεύει θεός, ὃν εἰκὸς ὑπ' ἀμφοῖν μάρτυρα καλεῖσθαι. The ref. is not to an oath, but to the laying up of a deposit, which in good faith is done under four eyes, simply with divine knowledge. A rabb. par. is interesting here because it contains a definition of μεσίτης. S. Lv. on 5:21 (p. 27d, 6 ff., Weiss): "He who (simply) lends, ... lends on a bill of exchange and before witnesses ...; but he who gives something to his friend to keep for him does not wish a soul to know about it, but only the third who is between them (i.e., God). If he denies it, he does so before the third who is between them." It is hard to say whether there is here a Hellenistic influence or parallel. The true theological problem goes deeper.

2. Cosmic Soteriological Intermediaries in Comparative Religion.

In our consideration of the various lights which play on the idea of the mediator, we do best to begin with the primitive notion that the earth or cosmos is a universal body.[10] Particular respect is paid to the navel of this body and to the middle deities, and here already it may be noted how cosmogonic and cosmological ideas subsequently acquire soteriological force. Most peoples have from the very first the idea that their country occupies a privileged position as the middle kingdom.[11] The geographical or religious centre of the kingdom is the navel of the earth, and if such points are not distinguished already by natural elevation, they are marked off by omphalos stones in the shape of beehives.[12] The local deities are portrayed as sitting either on or by the stones. The omphalos deity grants salvation. From Eleusis Triptolemos at the command of Demeter brings corn and culture to the whole world. In the Kora cult eternal life is sought there.

Herm. Trismeg. speaks more speculatively of the advantage of the middle situation in Stob. Ecl., I, 412, 7 ff.: ἐπειδὴ δὲ ἐν τῷ μέσῳ τῆς γῆς κεῖται ἡ τῶν προγόνων ἡμῶν ἱερωτάτη χώρα, τὸ δὲ μέσον τοῦ ἀνθρωπίνου σώματος τῆς καρδίας ἐστὶ σηκός, τῆς δὲ ψυχῆς ὁρμητήριόν ἐστιν ἡ καρδία, παρὰ ταύτην τὴν αἰτίαν, ὦ τέκνον, οἱ ἐνταῦθα ἄνθρωποι τὰ μὲν ἄλλα ἔχουσιν οὐχ ἧττον ὅσα καὶ πάντες,

---

10 A view still found in Orphism, → III, 964.

11 This idea is not just Chinese. It also found among the pygmies of Central Africa. The Indians regard Aryn, the Assyrians and Babylonians Nineveh and Babylon, the Egyptians Thebes, the Arabians Mecca, the Greeks Athens, Eleusis, Delphi or Epidauros as the navel of the earth.

12 For good material cf. esp. Roscher, "Omphalosgedanke." Depictions of the Eleusis omphalos on the Niinnionpinax (photo. Alinari, 24335), on a vase of Sta. Maria di Capua (Roscher, 68), and on a Cretan vase (72). The original of the Delphi omphalos has been discovered (→ II, 452, n. 14).

ἐξαίρετον δὲ τῶν πάντων νοερώτεροί εἰσι. Here the idea of the navel is replaced by the more spiritual one of the heart as the centre of the body and life. This may be seen elsewhere, esp. in respect of the individual organism. Philo is acquainted with the view that the tree in the midst of Paradise is the heart, ἐπειδὴ αἰτία τε τοῦ ζῆν ἐστι καὶ τὴν μέσην τοῦ σώματος χώραν ἔλαχεν. He himself rejects this, not on anatomical grounds, but because it is more ἰατρική than φυσική, Leg. All., I, 59.[13] If the whole world be regarded as a giant organism, it is natural to regard the deity as its heart, and to locate it at the heart of the world. In this sense Corp. Herm., XVI, 7 says of the sun: μέσος γὰρ ἵδρυται στεφανηφορῶν τὸν κόσμον καὶ καθάπερ ἡνίοχος ἀγαθὸς τὸ τοῦ κόσμου ἅρμα ἀσφαλισάμενος καὶ ἀναδήσας εἰς ἑαυτόν, μή πως ἀτάκτως φέροιτο. εἰσὶ δὲ αἱ ἡνίαι ζωὴ καὶ ψυχὴ καὶ πνεῦμα καὶ ἀθανασία καὶ γένεσις.[14] It does not allow the cosmos to separate itself from it, but holds it in close relation to itself. By nature the cosmos tends to err, but the sun holds it fast by the bridle. In so doing it manifests the supreme God.

The individual parts of the world also strive away from or against one another. If the earth and heaven are pictured as a giant building with a dome-like roof, care must be taken that the dome be supported. Earth and heaven must be kept apart. This is the special task of the middle deities. An Egyptian depiction of the New Kingdom represents the goddess of heaven, Nut, supported by the god of the air. Between the arms of this god may be seen the four pillars of heaven.[15] In Gk. mythology Atlas has the same function of holding up the vault of heaven, Hom. Od., 1, 52 ff.; Hes. Theogn., 517 ff.; Aesch. Prom., 348 ff. Philo uses similar ideas in allegorical exposition of the OT. The ladder of heaven is the symbol of the atmosphere: κλῖμαξ τοίνυν ἐν μὲν τῷ κόσμῳ συμβολικῶς λέγεται ὁ ἀήρ, οὗ βάσις μέν ἐστι γῆ, κορυφὴ δ᾽ οὐρανός (Som., I, 134). The angels ascend and descend on it as μεσῖται (→ 617).

Philo refers similar ideas, some of them very old, to the *logos*. Stretching from the middle of the world to the ends, and back from the extreme edges to the middle (ἀπὸ τῶν μέσων ἐπὶ τὰ πέρατα καὶ ἀπὸ τῶν ἄκρων ἐπὶ τὰ μέσα ταθείς), he holds together all parts of the world, Plant., 9. He it is who prevents the world from sinking back into chaos, who as an arbiter holds in check the mutually hostile elements, who reconciles them to one another. The earth does not suck in the water, fire is not extinguished by the air, nor does it burn up the air.[16] How is this? It takes place τοῦ θείου λόγου μεθόριον τάττοντος αὑτὸν καθάπερ φωνήεντα (the vowels) στοιχείων ἀφώνων (between the consonants) in order that the whole may have the harmony of the word as by the persuasion of the intermediary decision is made in face of the threats of the hostile elements (τὰς τῶν ἐναντίων ἀπειλὰς πειθοῖ τῇ συναγωγῷ μεσιτεύοντος τε καὶ διαιτῶντος, Plant., 10). To understand this it is necessary to note that → στοιχεῖα means both letters and elements, or elemental spirits (on the latter cf. Kore Kosmu, 54 and 62; Stob. Ecl., I, 403, 12; 405, 12). This brings us suddenly to the technical meaning of the word (sense 1.). But we are in the sphere, not of the metaphorical speech inspired by the Hellen. concept of dialysis, but of ancient cosmology. This finds practical outworking as soteriology. For the preservation of cosmic order is salutary to man.

Armed with these preliminary considerations, we may tackle the best known and most difficult of all the examples of mediatorial theology outside the Bible. Plut. Is. et Os., 46 (II, 369e) writes: "Zarathustra called the good god of light Ahuramazda, the evil god of darkness Ahriman, μέσον δ᾽ ἀμφοῖν τὸν Μίθρην εἶναι· διὸ καὶ Μίθρην Πέρσαι τὸν μεσίτην ὀνομάζουσιν. He taught that we should bring vows and thank-

---

[13] The idea that the heart is the centre of the body may be seen still in the heart of Jesus cult.

[14] Quoted from Reitzenstein Poim., 351, 3 ff. Scott, as always, relies heavily on conjectures.

[15] Haas, 2/4, Bonnet (1924), Ill. 2.

[16] Philo seems to have overlooked the fact that water quenches fire.

offerings to the one, but apotropaic and dark sacrifices to the other. For they crush a plant called ὄμωμι[17] (= haoma) in a mortar. They call upon Hades and darkness. They then mix it with the blood of a slaughtered wolf, carry it to a place where there is no sun, and pour it out." There can be no doubt that this account is ancient.[18] Opinions differ strongly as to its significance. The debate is whether Mithra owes his title as μεσίτης in the first instance to his position as a cosmic or as an ethical and religious mediator, i.e., whether sense 2. or sense 1. is basic. Both sides allow that there could be later transition from the one to the other. Apart from the similarity of μεσίτην and μέσον, it is argued for the first view[19] that the Mithra of Persian sources is originally the starry heaven,[20] then the light which streams from it. For the magi Mithra is the god of light. Since light is carried by the air, he is thought of as the ruler of the middle zone of air between heaven and the underworld. He mediates the transition between night and day, and makes it rich in blessing. Yašt, 10, 13: "Who as the first Yazata (= spiritual god worthy of veneration) comes over the harā (= the mountains of the world) in advance of the immortal sun, who with the swift horses reaches the beautiful gold-tinted summits first."[21] After sunset he holds in his hands the club of which pernicious Ahriman is afraid (95 ff.). He also mediates the transition between increasing and decreasing light during the course of the year. Thus he stands in the midst between Kautes and Kautopates. He seems to have been identified with the Babylonian Shamash. But acc. to the Chaldean view the sun occupied a middle place among the planets. As a reminder of Mithra's middle place, the sixteenth or middle day of the month and the seventh or middle month of the year were sacred to him. The second view, however, points out in opposition[22] that Mithra is personified agreement as the Gk. Dike is personified law. The name is thought to derive from a root *m(e)i*, "to bind," and the instrumental suffix *-tra*. Both recur in the Gk. μί-τρη, "girdle," "head-band." In Sanskrit *Mitra* means masc. "friend," neut. "friendship," in Zend *Mithra* masc. "agreement," plur. "leagues." Mithra is the *ṛta*, order in person, the god of truth and fidelity, the god of treaties and decisions (cf. Yašt, 10, 2 and 8 f.). The equation is so clear that sometimes it is hard to decide whether the ref. is to the god or the treaty.[23] Later connections with the sun may easily be explained, since bright light is inimical to all that is secretive.

---

[17] μῶλυ is a conjecture of Bernardakis with no MS support, cf. J. H. Moulton, Class. Rev., 26 (1912), 81 f.

[18] That Plut. follows Theopomp. (b. 376 B.C.) is not apparent from what he says, for he mentions him only in 47 (II, 370b). The links with Poseidonios are very doubtful. Even if we read μῶλυ (with Lagarde etc.), and Diosc. was right to maintain a Cappadocian origin of the saying, this would not imply a late origin. For Zarathustrianism came into Cappadocia very early. If Plut. drew on an Alexandrian compilation (Cumont, *Textes et Monuments,* II, 33), this could have followed earlier sources.

[19] Cf. Cumont, I, 303 ff.; Clemen, *Griech. u. lat. Nachrichten,* 157 f.

[20] J. Hertel, *Die Sonne u. Mithra im Awesta* (1927). The coloured Mithra of Santa Maria Capua vetere (*Notizie degli Scavi di Antichità* [1924], Plate 17) shows Mithra's mantle billowing in the wind in the form of a heavenly vault, lined with blue on the inside and decorated with golden stars.

[21] Transl. acc. to H. Junker, who gave some other valuable refs. F. Wolff, *Avesta, d. heiligen Bücher der Parsen* (1924) and Lommel regard the horses as an attribute of the sun.

[22] M. A. Meillet, "Le Dieu Indo-Iranien Mitra," *Journal Asiatique,* 10, 10 (1907, II), 143 ff. E. Lehmann in Chant. de la Saussaye, II, 226.

[23] E.g., Yašt, 10, 2, the non-man who deceives Mithra, the treaty breaker. Both have a claim to faithfulness (Mithra), the ungodly and the righteous. The refrain is "those who do not deceive Mithra (= break the treaty)." On the equation cf. Lommel, 61 ff.; Güntert, 64. Hertel, *op. cit.,* 229 f. is doubtful as to the etym., but does not dispute the identity of Mithra and treaty, though he regards it as secondary, 219.

Though these two views seem at first glance to be so different, in fact they are not antithetical. One has only to grasp the outlook of antiquity to see this. For the ancient the cosmos was not a place of impersonal natural laws. The order of the cosmos was regarded as the work of personal forces, as order in the strict sense, as the model of all law. The preservation of the world depends on the preservation of this order. Mithra is appointed to watch over it by the supreme god. As the middle force in the cosmos he is also the arbiter between the opposing cosmic forces, the preserver of cosmic balance, the absolute upholder of law. Sacrifice falls within this function. For it is a basic rule that life proceeds from death. The world lives by sacrifice. Mithra is thus the mediator of personal salvation to all who believe in him. Ascended to heaven as victor, he is the spokesman and giver of eternal life to all who serve him faithfully. In the Turfân fr. we find the invocation : "Mithras, great messenger of the gods, mediator of the religion of the elect." [24]

In this light it seems obvious that the title μεσίτης for Mithra is not accidental. It sums up what the name in all its manifoldness of meaning conveys to the Persian ear. Several reasons make it likely that μεσίτης, if not a literal transl., is a meaningful interpretation of the name Mithra. So far no Persian equivalent has been found. The equivalent is the name Mithra itself. Again, Plut. does not say, as one would expect, Μίθρην Πέρσαι μεσίτην καλοῦσιν, but τὸν μεσίτην ὀνομάζουσιν. This seems more like an interpretation of the name than a mere designation of function. Final confirmation is found in what Šahrastani says about the Persian Marcionites : "They assume two fundamental beings, eternal and mutually opposed ... but also the righteous mediator, the uniter ; he is the cause of fusion, for the two contending and hostile beings come together only through the one who unites them. They say the mediator is on the stage below light and above darkness." [25]

If the above interpretation is correct, then sense 1. is normative. "Personified *ṛta* can hardly be better expressed in Gk. than by μεσίτης. In the first instance this designation does not imply that Mithra is the mediator between God and man." [26] It hardly needs to be shown, however, that for the Gk. ear sense 3. and sense 2. (cf. Plut.) could also be present. The idea of intermediaries mediating dealings between gods and men is known, e.g., to Plato. In Symp., 202e Plato defines the daimonion as a being which by nature stands between the divine and the mortal (μεταξὺ θεοῦ τε καὶ θνητοῦ). "It translates and conveys to the gods that which comes forth from men, and to men that which comes forth from the gods, prayers and offerings on the one side, commands and recompenses on the other. Standing between the two, it fills the intervening space, so that the whole is bound together (ἐν μέσῳ δὲ ὂν ἀμφοτέρων συμπληροῖ, ὥστε τὸ πᾶν αὐτὸ αὑτῷ ξυνδεδέσθαι)." To this middle position of the daimonion the whole art of the priest and the seer is traced back. One of the chief daimons is Eros. He has the role of a mediator. In connection with a half jocular threat of punishment we read : "For this reason all should admonish one another to exercise piety towards the gods, in order that we may escape this and attain that whereto Eros leads us ... Let none act against him ; he acts against him who incurs the hatred of the gods. For if we befriend and reconcile the god (φίλοι γὰρ γενόμενοι καὶ διαλλαγέντες τῷ θεῷ), we shall come up against our own lovers and partake of them" (Symp., 193 a/b). These statements occur in a long address of praise to pederasty. In spite of all Plato's exertions to mark

---

[24] F. W. K. Müller, *Handschriftenreste in Estrangelo-Schrift aus Turfân*, II, AAB (1904), 77.

[25] Cf. the transl. of T. Haarbrücker, *Religionsparteien und Philosophenschulen*, I (1850), 295. The above interpretation is supported by Güntert 50 ff., but R. Eisler is rather fanciful in *Weltenmantel u. Himmelszelt*, II (1910), 418 when he says that Mithra is the sign which unites Ahuramazda and Ahriman as the upper and lower halves of the world egg.

[26] The view of Dib. Past. on 1 Tm. 2:5 (cf. also Pr.-Bauer³, *s.v.* μεσίτης) that Mithra is called μεσίτης because he laid down the rules of sacrifice and was thus a direct mediator between God and man, rests on an understanding of the text which can hardly be right. The subj. of ἐδίδαξε is Zarathuštra, not Mithra.

off *eros* from purely sensual love, the question whether we have here a material par. to the NT concept of the mediator needs no discussion.

In Hellenism the view often recurs that the gods of favourite special cults are mediators between the supreme deity and their devotees. How far the designation "lord" has here technical signification is debated. → κύριος.

But there are also impersonal intermediaries. The Vedic Agni is hardly more than a personification of sacral fire. He is called the nearest of the *devá-* to us. He takes our offerings on his war chariot to the *devá-* and is also called the mouth of the *devá-*, because he consumes the offerings for them. He also takes to himself corpses on the funeral pyre and leads them in the fiery body to the heaven of light. [27]

Finally, there are mixed figures, half personal conceptions. The real sphere in which these flourish is Gnosticism, behind which is varied oriental mythology fructified by western philosophy. In view of recent findings at the main point of interest Manicheanism will serve as an example. [28] In particular, this has three mediating hypostases, [29] which by way of the "mother of the living" emanate from the "father of greatness." There is the first one who is sent (primal man, → 608), the living spirit, and the one who is sent. The last, as Jesus, is already sent to Adam to show him his devilish origin and his destiny of light. He then appears in three precursors, the historical Jesus, Zarades (Zoroaster) and Buddha. He finally finds embodiment in Mani, the promised Paraclete. Mani calls himself an apostle of Jesus Christ. He is not inferior, however, but a perfecter. The whole emphasis falls on wisdom, teaching. Real mediatorship is accomplished in the three sent ones as more than historical beings. It is their task, by means of a natural, cosmogonic process, which issues, however, in a comparatively high ethics, to free the particles of light chained to darkness. Manicheanism does not appear to have any real word for mediator. The concept of the sent one is a substitute. The Gk. form ἀπόστολος is also used in the Coptic texts. If Mani equated his second sent one with Mithra, [30] he found the connecting factor in cosmic soteriological mediation.

The Mandaean religion, too, puts the thought of the mediator in the centre. [31] It uses the same term, the sent one. [32] While the emanations, the uthras, from the original being, the great mana of glory, number several thousands, [33] there is ref. only to three, [34] and to only one sent one. [35] He is called Hibil-Ziwa. In the background is the biblical Abel. He is also identified with Ptahil-Gabriel, and represents Mandā d'Haije, the personified gnosis of life, whose son he is. We cannot pursue here the complex details. But here, too, the main task of the mediator of revelation is to bring saving knowledge. Neither here nor in Manicheanism should this be misunderstood intellectualistically. The dualism underlying all Gnostic and mystical systems traces the moral antithesis of good and evil back to the ontic antithesis of spirit and matter or light and darkness (→ λάμπω, 21). Within man the moral antithesis thus corresponds to the two main parts of man,

---

[27] [J. Hertel in a letter]. Cf. also his book "Die arische Feuerlehre," *Indo-Iranische Quellen u. Forschungen*, VI (1925), 147 ff.

[28] On this cf. H. H. Schaeder, RGG², III, 1959 ff. with good bibl. The remains of the original works of Mani since found in Egypt are discussed by Schmidt-Polotsky, *Ein Mani-Fund*, and cf. Polotsky's ed. of the *Manichäische Homilien* (1934) and Schmidt's ed. of *Kephalaia* (1936 ff.).

[29] This threefold schema intersects with a fivefold schema, five fathers with three emanations each, Schmidt-Polotsky, *Ein Mani-Fund*, 62 ff.

[30] Schaeder, RGG², III, 1969.

[31] For bibl. on the Mandaeans → I, 537, n. 37 and 38.

[32] Lidz. Ginza Index, *s.v.* "Gesandter."

[33] Ibid., R. V, 1, 136 (p. 152, 23 ff.): Ten thousand times a thousand worlds of light each with 360,000 uthras.

[34] *Ibid.*, R. II, 1, 47 (p. 44, 23).

[35] The first pure and true sent one of life, light, etc., Lidz. Index. On the higher and lower beings in general cf. Lidz. Ginza, 597 ff.

soul and body. Knowledge implies a strengthening of the good and spiritual in man by attachment to the original reality of the good, the spiritual deity of light. The task of the mediator includes action. He comes down to fight darkness. He takes the "navel of earth" and "binds it to the heart of heaven." [36] He also binds the evil influences of the planets. Here is a mixture of western and eastern wisdom (→ 604). As is increasingly recognised to-day, [37] the palm of priority by no means goes to the East. For, as eastern mythology has often fructified the West, so Greek philosophy has often sparked eastern speculation. The ideas before us are post-Christian, mostly very much so, and are demonstrably influenced by the NT. [38] But they also contain ancient ideas whose origin in respect of country and race can be determined only with reservations. [39]

This is particularly clear in the primal-man-speculation which is often present in the mediator concepts. [40] As distinct from the primitive idea of an original author, [41] this always rests on a pantheistic interfusion of original divine and human life. The primal man, who is not identical with the first historical man, is at first the bearer of the transcendental and purely spiritual life of light. Then he falls victim to matter and darkness, and is finally freed by a very complicated process of redemption. He is the God-man, both redeemer and redeemed, the mediator between the world of light which remained intact and the human world. Thus in Manicheanism the first sent one is the primal man. In narrative form the hymn of the Act. Thom. [42] describes the journey of the royal son after the costly pearl, i.e., the redemption of the individual soul through the primal man. The Pistis Sophia [43] describes the encounter between the redeemer and his heavenly brother. All individual souls are posited in the primal man as *anima generalis*. As bats in a musty cave cling to one another and to the rock, so souls cling to one another and to the primal man Adamas, the ἔσω ἄνθρωπος (cf. the preaching of the Naassenes in Hippolytus). [44] The primal man is now enclosed in the body as a tomb, but as God he cannot remain in death. [45] What happens to him happens also to (elect) individual souls. This oriental teaching moved also into the West. In the cosmogony of Poimandres there is a rather artificial combination of the ὁ τοῦ θεοῦ Λόγος, which is ὁμοούσιος with the supreme God Nous, [46] and Ἄνθρωπος, whom Nous begot αὐτῷ ὅμοιον. [47] This corresponds to the fusion of two different views of the world.

Here again it is impossible to trace back the mediator doctrine simply to the idea of the primal man. Mediators like Hermes-Tat and Aesculapius are not connected with the latter. They come into religio-philosophical speculation from the Egyptian pantheon. Pantheistic ideas do not exclude mediator concepts even in personal form. But the ornate

---

[36] Lidz. Ginza, R. III, 97 (p. 103, 29 ff.); R. III, 98 (p. 104, 13 ff.). The binding is a torture which expresses complete subjection, cf. R. III, 118 (p. 132, 11).

[37] Cf. esp. the researches of F. Cumont and H. H. Schaeder.

[38] On the Mandaean problem → I, 536 f.

[39] Reitzenstein Poim. rather one-sidedly champions an Egyptian provenance, and in the Iranian mystery of redemption even more so a Persian. Pan-Babylonianism and Pan-Arism mix what may be precisely established with loose and rather tendentious presuppositions. More sober is the position of O. v. Wesendonk, *Urmensch u. Seele in der iranischen Überlieferung* (1924), 18 ff. Acc. to more recent research, as Syriasms show, the North Iranian texts are to be reckoned with the "western" tradition, Schmidt-Polotsky, *op. cit.*, 80.

[40] Review (with bibl.) by L. Troje, RGG², V, 1416 f. Käsemann, 61 ff.

[41] On this cf. N. Söderblom, *Das Werden des Gottesglaubens*² (1926), 93 ff.

[42] Act. Thom., 108-113; Hennecke, 277 ff.

[43] 120, cf. the transl. of C. Schmidt (1925). Cf. also H. Leisegang, "Der Bruder des Erlösers," *Angelos,* I (1925), 24 ff. On the sevenfold manifestation of the primal man cf. Staerk, ZNW, 35 (1936), 232 ff.

[44] Cf. Reitzenstein Poim., 89.

[45] *Ibid.*, 93.

[46] Corp. Herm., I, 10.

[47] *Ibid.*, I, 12.

façade of many mediators should not hide from us the fact that in pantheistic mysticism we are dealing fundamentally with a religion in which is no mediation.

3. Men as Mediators.

Along with divine and semi-divine mediators are also human, and in many cases there is no sharp distinction between the two groups. The king, often regarded as god or the son of god, is a mediator of the people before the godhead, receiving divine laws and offering national sacrifices.[48] Alongside him the priest is a mediator both for the whole people and for pious individuals, sacrificing, praying and issuing directions. Ancient connections between the two are indicated by the fact that the king discharges some priestly functions, by the occurrence of the royal designation in priestly terminology,[49] and by the initiation of the king into secret priestly doctrine (→ III, 963). Apart from purely sociological origins, both types of mediator go back to a single type, that of the charismatic, the man endowed with force (θεῖος ἄνθρωπος, → III, 567 f.), who continues to exist independently in the ecstatic, the miracle-worker, the man of God, the prophet. Thus the concept of the mediator develops quite early into the schema of the *munus triplex*. Though with many disruptions, it keeps alive the awareness that between God and man there is an essential distinction which is intensified by man's transgression, though the possibility of fellowship is not hereby excluded. For details cf. → βασιλεύς, I, 564 f.; ἱερεύς, III, 257 ff.; προφήτης.

Supreme fulfilment of the type of human mediator is to be found in the founder of religion. As distinct from lesser mediators, he does a unique work of lasting influence. The emphasis usually falls on the revelation of saving knowledge. In the faith of the community the image of the founder usually takes on superhuman features. Thus Zoroaster is surrounded by a halo of rich legend.[50] The sober moralist Confucius, though later, is by imperial decree adopted into the Chinese pantheon.[51] After the death of Mani the community addressed to him prayers and hymns with his crucifixion as the theme. For the elect and catechumens he is the god before whom they appear annually at the Bema festival to receive the *consolamentum*, the remission of sins, and whom they greet as the bridegroom with the evangelical greeting.[52] Mohammed becomes the embodiment of the pre-existent light of revelation. He comes to the centre of the universe as a cosmic principle. The tomb of the sinless, wonder-working prophet becomes the holiest place of pilgrimage. Altars are erected and sacrifices brought to him.[53] Buddha, particularly in northern Buddhism and in connection with Amida, becomes the pre-existent Buddha, infinite light, the object of faith and worship,[54] having the stature of the supreme personal God rather than a mediator. That these founders of religion were simply revered as pioneers of knowledge would be too sober a rationalisation or statement of the case. Where it is thought that an invocation repeated a thousand or million fold, or even a single invocation in the hour of death, can save, where images are held out before the dying, where a cord from them is bound around the wrist so that they may have a firm hold and enter into Paradise, there we have a real concept of saving mediation. For this form of faith in Japanese sects, the possibility of Christian

---

[48] Cf. Hammurapi before the sun god at the head of the Paris stele with the so-called Codex Hammurapi, cf. RGG², I, 704 f., Plate VI, 4. Antiochus I of Commagene before Mithra on the relief of Nemrud-dagh, Haas, 15, Leipoldt (1930), 6. For sacrificing and praying kings in Egypt, Haas, 2/4 (1924), Bonnet, 76-91.

[49] *Basileus* and *Basilinna* in the Attic, *rex sacrificulus* in the Roman cult. Chant. de la Saussaye, II, 449.

[50] Chant. de la Saussaye, II, 204 f.

[51] *Ibid.*, I, 213 f.

[52] Schmidt-Polotsky, *Mani-Fund*, 32 f.

[53] Chant. de la Saussaye, I, 674.

[54] *Ibid.*, 382-410. Also esp. H. Haas, "'Amida Buddha unsere Zuflucht,' Urkunden zum Verständnis des japanischen Sukhāvatī-Buddhismus," *Quellen d. Religionsgesch.*, 2 (1910).

influence arises, mediated through the Nestorian missions to China in the 7th century.[55] But this influence could hardly have prevailed if it had not been met by a tendency already present in other founded religions.

For the most part this tendency cannot be traced back to the founders themselves. The historical Buddha is remote from all ideas of mediation, for he does not seek by faith to lead to fellowship with God and salvation hereafter, but to lead by knowledge to Nirvana. His teaching is fundamentally atheistic, and hence a-religious. Mohammed, apart from his prophetic task, claims to be no more than fallible man. Acc. to a canonical tradition he is supposed to have hurled a curse at all veneration of men. Even the relatively highly developed self-awareness of Mani does not involve more than a divinely authorised and definitive mediator of wisdom. Comparative religion thus raises the problem whether the development from the restrained sense of mission of founders of religion to the transcendental mediator concept of their followers is a regularly repeated process according to a definite law, and whether Christianity with the formation of its mediatorial Christology does not fall under this law. In such a law there might be discerned again, and paradoxically, a tendency towards a direct relationship to God, a religion without mediation.

C. Mediatorship in the Old Testament.

1. Divine Mediatorship.

From the standpoint of comparative religion it is noteworthy and striking that the idea of a cosmic mediatorship of Yahweh is completely absent from OT religion. The nearest to this is Gn. 1:6-8. Yahweh places between the waters the vault of heaven, a firm, thin mass, and He thereby restricts the forces of chaos to their own allotted space. But there is here a great difference. At the beginning is the Creator, not chaos. Without Him there would be no initial waste and void. Yahweh fashions the world without effort or struggle by His mere Word (→ κτίζω, III, 1010). He sees to it that cosmic balance is preserved, never as an inner cosmic potency or world soul which is only relatively superior to other cosmic powers, but as that which is absolutely exalted above the earth (cf. Am. 5:8; Is. 40:12 ff., 22 ff.; Ps. 104; Job 9:5 ff.). It would be an infringement of His dignity to try to bind Him to the centre of the earth or the world. Omphalos ideas are known in Israel.[56] Jerusalem is the city which Yahweh has set in the midst of the nations (Ez. 5:5). At the end of the days the mountain of the house of Yahweh will be firmly set on high among the mountains and above the hills, and all peoples will go up to it (Is. 2:2 ff.; Mi. 4:1 ff.). Other sites in Palestine, like Shechem (Gn. 12:6 f.; Jn. 4:20) or Bethel, the place of the heavenly ladder (Gn. 28:11 ff.; 35:1 ff.), perhaps contested the honour with the holy city. But the example of Sinai shows that the supposed or, nationally, real centre was never decisive. Yahweh does not receive His honour from places; the places which in His free historical guidance He chooses (Dt. 12:5; 15:20 etc.) receive their honour from Him. As the exalted Ruler of the world He is not the middle point of the world. In complete independence He is the omnipresent and supraterrestrial Sovereign who rules in all things, Jer. 23:23 f.; Ps. 139. Here is a sharp protest against all pagan pantheism and dualism.

Hence Yahweh is not in any sense a cosmic soteriological mediator. But He does occupy a mediatorial position in the battle of Job against the God of the

---

[55] Chant. de la Saussaye, I, 382.
[56] Roscher, "Omphalosgedanke," 12 ff., 48 ff.

dogma of retribution. Job 9:33 expresses for the first time what is in the first instance a spontaneous desire for an arbiter (מוֹכִיחַ, LXX μεσίτης, → 601 f.) between Job and the God who so incomprehensibly tortures him. He reaches a resolve to go to law (הוֹכִחַ, LXX ἐλέγξω, 13:3) with God, and he is finally crowned with the certainty that there is already in heaven a witness and guarantor (עֵד, LXX μάρτυς, שָׂהֵד, LXX συνίστωρ) who will vindicate man against God and his fellow-men (16:18 ff.). Job knows that his redeemer (גֹּאֵל, LXX μέλλων ἐκλύειν) lives, and as the last will raise himself up on the dust, 19:25. He thus appeals to God against God. Distinction is made between God as a party and God as the umpire above or between the parties. Formally then, though with no necessary genealogical connection, the mediator concept corresponds to Hellenistic usage, and materially it is near the height of the NT view. This is quite unique in the OT.[57]

On the other side, Yahweh has His mediators, quite apart from human instruments of revelation (→ 2.). He reveals Himself. OT monotheism gained increasingly in strength, but without becoming abstract, attenuated or poverty-stricken. God's dealings with the world are through intermediary hypostases. There are three of these in particular. First, from the earliest to the latest times, there is the מַלְאַךְ יהוה, the visible and for the most part helpful messenger of Yahweh; then the רוּחַ יהוה, known by its operations, which were at first merely ecstatic and later also moral; and finally the hypostatised divine חָכְמָה, corresponding to the Greek *logos* concept.[58] The relations of these three entities to one another and to Yahweh raises important questions which we cannot discuss here. → ἄγγελος, I, 76 ff., πνεῦμα, σοφία. The original man in the OT is neither demi-god nor mediator. He is created in the image of God, but is sharply differentiated from Him → I, 141 ff. Only in apocalyptic literature do we perhaps see the syncretistic myth of the primal or heavenly man.

2. Men as Mediators.

The OT knows human mediators such as we find in comparative religion (→ 609). Most weakly developed is the religious significance of the king.[59] The king is sometimes called the son of Yahweh (2 S. 7:14; Ps. 2:7), but not in a metaphysical sense. Royal mediation finds central significance only in the future figure of the ideal anointed, the Messiah. The true distinctiveness of OT religion as compared with paganism is to be seen in the mediatorial position of the priest and especially the prophet, → βασιλεύς, I, 564 f.; ἱερεύς, III, 257 ff.; προφήτης. In the course of the development of salvation history the *munus triplex* becomes increasingly the vessel which is fitted to contain the NT concept of the mediator.

But the OT concept reaches its climax at the beginning and end of the creative period in two figures which are only loosely related to the *munus triplex*. At the beginning of the history of Israel's religion is Moses, the absolute mediator to later ages. This figure, who is normative for the religion of Israel in every age, cannot be fitted easily into any of the available forms. He is "an organiser without political power, a leader without military force, an architect of divine worship

[57] [G. v. Rad].

[58] The autonomy of the divine Word in the OT hardly goes beyond personification, → λόγος. R. Bultmann, *Das Joh.-Ev.* (1937 ff.), on 1:1.

[59] In the OT the monarchy is seen predominantly in the light of Deuteronomistic criticism. But this undoubtedly preserves much of the thinking of ancient Israel.

without a priestly character, a founder and mediator of the new knowledge of God without the sanction of prophetic utterances, a worker of miracles who is far above the sphere of the purely magical." [60] In this paradoxical uniqueness he is the specially called and equipped mediator between Yahweh and the people whom Yahweh has chosen. The story of his call in Ex. 3:1 ff. enables us to see that Yahweh had a special work for him. His is a particular commissioning to a particular task. What is at issue is the basic act of liberation which in fulfilment of the promise given to the fathers creates for the people the possibility of its own national and religious existence. The new turn is marked in E by the fact that at this point in the story he introduces the divine name Yahweh (Ex. 3:13 f.). As the commissioned spokesman of Yahweh Moses now comes before the people and the Egyptian king (Ex. 4:29; 5:1). Though the word is not used, the mediator concept is twice given classical formulation in this context. Aaron, who as the more eloquent brother speaks to the people and Pharaoh, is the mouth of Moses, and Moses is God speaking through him (Ex. 4:16; 7:1). The mediator in the OT is thus the commissioned spokesman. Moses is uniquely at work as a mediator in the giving of the Law (Ex. 19:3 ff., 9 ff., 21 ff.; 20:18 ff.; 34:1 ff., 29 ff.; Dt. 5:5, 23 ff.). He alone can stand before Yahweh. Between Yahweh and the people, he receives the directions of Yahweh and passes them on to the people. This may be seen again on other occasions (Ex. 33:5 ff.). The priestly statutes are handed on as commands to Moses (Ex. 35:1, 4; Lv. 1:1; 4:1; 5:14; 6:1 etc.). The mediatorship rests indeed on Yahweh's commission, but it is two-sided in the sense that the people expressly desires that Moses should speak the word of Yahweh to it and intercede with Yahweh on its behalf (Ex. 20:19; Nu. 21:7; Dt. 5:24; 18:16). The people cries to Moses, and he prays to Yahweh (Nu. 17:27 f.). The mediatorship of Moses is perhaps most profoundly expressed in his intercession. Thus, after the sin with the golden calf, he even asks that he may be vicariously stricken out of the book of Yahweh (Ex. 32:11 ff., 30 ff.; 33:12 ff.). He includes himself in the prayer for forgiveness, though he had in fact no personal part in the sin in question (Ex. 34:8 f.). Aaron can sometimes take his side in this respect (Nu. 17:10 ff., 25; Lv. 11:1 etc.). But express emphasis is laid on the unique position of Moses as compared with him or with the later prophets. Yahweh speaks with Moses face to face (in spite of Ex. 33:20; the two views may be attributed to E and J respectively). He speaks to him as a man speaks to his friend (Ex. 33:11; Dt. 34:10, Deuteronomistic addition). Cf. also Nu. 11:25 ff.; 12:2 ff. There is a different slant in Dt. 18:15, 18. Here the meaning is that revelation is always present in Israel. Nevertheless, here too Moses is both the first in the series and also the normative embodiment of mediatorship for every age. The figure of Moses is presented with particular depth in Dt. Moses is here a suffering mediator. He prays and fasts forty days for the apostate people (9:8 f.). He wrestles with God (9:26 ff.). His death outside the promised land is substitutionary suffering (3:23 ff.). It may well be that later ages have helped to produce the Moses of these texts. But the core is historical in the strict sense. For our present purpose it is more important to bring out what is theologically significant than to try to sift out what is original. [61]

The other great OT figure is the Ebed Yahweh of Dt. Is. The songs which

[60] Eichrodt, I, 151.

[61] P. Volz, *Mose u. sein Werk*[2] (1932) [v. Rad].

present him (Is. 42:1-4 [5-9 ?]; 49:1-6 [7-13 ?]; 50:4-9 [10 f. ?]; 52:13-53:12) are deliberately mysterious and will always be puzzling. But it is brought out with mounting clarity that the Ebed is a concrete historical figure, possibly the prophet himself. The first songs are part of a profound autobiography. They speak of a powerful sense of mission which is directed not merely to Israel but to all nations and which aims to bring them right and light by gentle preaching. They speak of strong inner conflicts which amount almost to despair, and of outward assaults which can even take the form of severe maltreatment. But they also speak of steadfast endurance, of success, and of believing confidence. The final song does not fit into this autobiographical understanding. The view has been advanced that it is an addition by Tr. Is., a pupil and admirer of Dt. Is., whose hand is also discerned at points in the other songs.[62] The following picture of the situation results. Dt. Is. hailed Cyrus as the chosen and anointed of Yahweh, the liberator of Israel. He also recognised the historical significance of the leadership of Israel. The whole people, which ought to have been Yahweh's servant, does, of course, refuse, and becomes deaf and blind (42:19). The more forcefully, then, does the prophet, Yahweh's servant in the concrete sense, seek to shake it out of its non-participation. In Dt. Is. a sense of world mission emerges for the first time in full strength. But his word is not just for Israel; it is for all nations. We cannot say for certain if the prophet himself took any practical part in fulfilling this commission, whether by not taking part in the return to Palestine or by voluntarily going into exile again. In any case, he met with mistrust and opposition from the political leaders, and possibly also from his own compatriots. He was put in prison, and badly treated, but remained steadfast. A miserable and shameful death was, from the human standpoint, the end. But Tr. Is. could not believe that all his work and patience had been in vain. He wrestled through to the solution in the final song that the suffering of the Ebed had been a divinely willed and vicarious intercession for the sins of the people, and that God had ways and means of turning the suffering into a blessing for the servant, for Israel, and for the world. Starting with the actual situation, the author of the song perceived something which was not exhausted by it. The concept of the mediator reaches here its final metaphysical and soteriological profundity prior to Christ.

The description of the perfect righteous man in Plat. Resp., II, 361e is often adduced as a par. "If this is so with the righteous man (i.e., if he does nothing unrighteous, but has the appearance of unrighteousness, because otherwise his righteousness would not be truly confirmed), he is whipped and tortured, and put in chains, his eyes are burned out and after all these torments he is finally crucified (ἀνασχινδυλευθήσεται)." The par. is striking, and seems to be almost an unwitting pagan foreshadowing of Christ. But in reality it is quite external and irrelevant. It occurs in a hymn of praise to imperfect righteousness by the sophist Glaucon. Hence it does not represent the true view of Socrates or Plato. It is simply dialectical skirmishing. It reaches the conclusion that the righteous man, in consequence of his experiences, will realise that it is not worth while to be righteous, but only to appear righteous. Suffering is simply postulated as a concept. It is not deduced from the inexorable conflict between good and evil. Hence we have here no glorification of martyrdom. Much less is there any ref. to mediatorial intercession by the righteous for the unrighteous. Nor is this a historical

---

[62] Cf. Elliger, 66 ff. P. Volz, *Komm. z. Js.*, II (1932), 149 ff., takes the same view, but he understands the last song eschatologically, and attributes it to a great figure of a later age, perhaps the 4th or 3rd cent. For the academic discussion and the vast bibl. cf. the books mentioned. → παῖς.

event. It is a fiction of thought deliberately exaggerated to the point where it ceases to be natural.

The profound conception of prophetic mediation in Dt. Is. and Tr. Is. did not arise without preparation. There is constant allusion to the figure of Moses in Dt. (→ 612). Ezekiel and Jeremiah were also significant forerunners. The former uses twice a metaphor taken from a besieged city, "to stand in the breach" (עָמַד בַּפֶּרֶץ, 22:30; 13:5). In the former case the political leaders, and in the latter the false prophets, are accused of failing to stand in the gap in this way. "I sought for a man among them who would make up the wall, and stand in the gap before me for the land, that I should not destroy it, but I found none" (22:30). "Like jackals in the ruins, so are your prophets, O Israel! You have not gone up into the breach nor made up the wall around the house of Israel, to stand fast in the battle on the day of Yahweh" (13:4, 5). Between the lines one can see that Ez. is claiming this mediatorial prophetic ministry for himself. Under severe physical sufferings he has faithfully fulfilled his calling (→ νόσος).

The confessions which Baruch possibly interwove into the prophetic book give a moving picture of the suffering mediatorship of Jeremiah.[63] In 15:16 ff. the prophet complains that because of his almost instinctive concern for God he is lonely and despised among men. But in so doing he is unfaithful to his calling. Yahweh gives him the strict though consoling answer that he can effectually proclaim God's Word only if he is absolutely faithful, but that he may genuinely do so if he is. Hence he must take upon himself the burden of suffering which his commission entails. He suffers even more profoundly when he sees the success of the ungodly and the misery of his people, whom Yahweh does not help (12:1-5; 8:18-23). His distress rises to terrible heights when he threatens to lose confidence in his calling. The Word of Yahweh, which comes on him with irresistible power, exposes him to the contempt and derision of all men. Yet he cannot suppress it. It burns within him like a fire. Under this dreadful pressure the struggling prophet curses the day of his birth and the messenger who told his father about it (20:7-9, 14-18). Yet in such hours there wells up within him the certainty that Yahweh is with him as a strong Hero, and with startling severity there breaks forth from him the prayer that God will let him see himself avenged on his enemies (20:11-13). Jer. does not attain to the solution of Tr. Is. that prophetic suffering is a mediatorial ministry for the community. This is the OT limit of his mediatorship. The mediator himself is involved in guilt.[64]

Though the word is not used, mediatorship is at the heart of OT religion. The theologically significant point is that God cannot be approached at our pleasure, but only when He offers Himself for fellowship. The basis of fellowship with Him is His unconditional moral demand both on the community and on each member individually, and the two in indissoluble combination. Yet fellowship with God does not mean only the demand. It also implies prior election. Thus the mediator, commissioned by God, carries a twofold, though intrinsically united, divine claim. He stands over against God on the side of the community represented by him. If the

---

[63] W. Baumgartner, *Die Klagegedichte des Jeremia* (1917), esp. 68 ff., advances strong reasons against the authenticity of these confessions. As he sees it, Baruch writes a passion story which accords none too well with the one-sided view of the prophet as a bearer of the Word of God. Jeremiah is not just God's commissioned messenger to men. He himself is also a man, and in their profound distress he takes them to himself.

[64] Cf. the exposition of v. Rad.

majority fails to meet God's claim, the mediator stands in the breach, first in intercession, then in substitutionary self-offering (cf. Ex. 32:11 ff., 30 ff.; 33:12 ff.; 34:8 f. with Is. 53:12, 4-10). Whereas the pagan concept of the mediator is based on natural presuppositions (→ 603 f.), the OT concept is orientated to the personality of God and His saving sway in history. There is no tendency whatever to glorify the mediator as a divine or semi-divine being.[65] It is increasingly plain, however, that mediatorship in Israel is ultimately focused on the race as a whole. In its greatness as well as its limitations the OT concept points to the One in whom mediatorship will find its fulfilment.

D. The Theological Concept of the Mediator in Judaism.

1. Rabbinic Judaism.

The term "mediator" is first used in its theological sense in Judaism. Its use in Philo and Paul shows that this had already taken place by the 1st cent. A.D. Since the Rabb. have the loan word מֵיסוֹן for μέσον, but use a Heb. term for μεσίτης, Palestinian usage is the starting-point. Though Rabb. sources are later, it is thus as well to begin with Rabb. Judaism. Here, in correspondence with the meaning of סַרְסוֹר (→ 602), the sense of "broker," "negotiator," "interpreter," is basic, and in essentials the term is used exclusively for Moses as the commissioned agent of God.

As the broker had to replace the wine if a vessel broke, so God says to Moses: Thou art the סַרְסוֹר between me and my children; thou hast broken (the tables), and must replace them (Dt. r., 3, 12 on 10:1; Str.-B., III, 512). In the latter ref. the same thought is clarified by the concept of the deposit. This corresponds to the Hell. use of μεσίτης (→ 603). But the term סַרְסוֹר is not used in this connection; it occurs only with a shift of the image. This brings out plainly the distinction between the Heb. linguistic sense and the Hell. Two parables about kings are worth noting. One king, who wishes to marry his daughter, uses a small citizen as סַרְסוֹר, and this makes him arrogant. So said God to Moses: Who causes thee to speak so proudly? I, even I, who have raised thee up so high (Ex. r., 6 on 6:2). In another parable in which the king himself seeks a wife, the סַרְסוֹר is the match-maker. When the woman marries another, he tears up the marriage bond. So Moses broke the tables of the Law (Ex. r., 43 on 32:11). Moses as mediator is thus the go-between who brings together Yahweh and His people. Ex. r., 3 on 3:13 (Str.-B., III, 556): Moses said: I will be the סַרְסוֹר between thee and them if thou wilt give them the doctrine of the Law. Because the Torah was all fire, so was the face of the סַרְסוֹר (Ex. 34:30; Tanch. יתרו § 16, 97a, Warsaw, 1879). The Israelites could not look on the face of Moses because of their sin with the calf, Pesikt. § 5, p. 45a (Str.-B., III, 515, cf. 31). As the Torah was given by the hand of a mediator (עַל יְדֵי סַרְסוֹר, cf. Gl. 3:19), so it may be passed on only עַל יְדֵי סַרְסוֹר, i.e., by an interpreter distinct from the reader, jMeg., 74d, 12 f.; Str.-B., III, 556). Thus the mediator concept is focused in the main on Moses. Quite unusual is the note in Tanch. יתרו § 10, p. 95b (Warsaw, 1879) that the mediator is threefold, Miriam, Aaron, Moses. Though so emphatically singled out from the rest, Moses is still a fallible man. He falls victim to pride (→ *supra*). He also has to suffer for the sin of the people. While the greatest angels could not look on him prior to the worship of the golden calf, later he could not bear the glance of the camp-followers of the angels (continuation of the quotation → *supra*). Only rarely is it claimed that he kept the whole Torah. This was more readily claimed for others, e.g., his father, than for him (Str.-B., I, 815 f.). Never-

---

[65] The attempt to understand Is. 53 in terms of the oriental myth of the god who dies and rises again (cf. J. Jeremias, 118 f.) is regarded by Volz (II, 187) as inadequately supported.

theless, under the influence of the myth of the primal man, in later Jewish sagas he was exalted to more than human proportions. [66]

Rabb. Judaism at first shows little understanding of the magnificent and profound development of the mediator concept in the figure of the suffering servant. This is surprising, since from Sir. 48:10 ff. it may be deduced, though not conclusively, that the Servant Songs were construed messianically even in the pre-Christian period. Very typical is the lack of emphasis in the Targum on Is. 52:13-53:12. [67] Here the Ebed Yahweh of the songs is taken to be the Messiah. But no place is found for vicarious suffering within the Messianic concept. Instead, the text is consistently reinterpreted in terms of the exaltation of Israel and the overcoming of the nations by force. The vicarious action is reduced to a mere remnant of Messianic intercession. In the Targum paraphrase the decisive verses run as follows: "3. Hence the glory of all kingdoms will be turned to contempt and disappear; they will be weak and poor. Lo, like a man of sorrows appointed for sickness, and as when the face of the shekinah is turned from us, they will be despised and not accounted. 4. Therefore will he pray for our guilt, and for his sake he will forgive our transgression, while we are reckoned as those who are crushed, rooted out before Yahweh and humbled. 5. And he will build the temple which is desecrated because of our iniquity and abandoned because of our transgression, and through his teaching there will be great peace for us, and when we gather around his words, our sins will be forgiven us ... 7. When he prays he is answered, before he opens his mouth he receives. The strong of the nations he will hand over like a lamb to the slaughter, and like a sheep dumb before the shearer, and before him there is none that opens his mouth or speaks a word ... 10. And before Yahweh it was his good-pleasure to purge and cleanse the remnant of his people, to purify their soul from sin; they will see the kingdom of their Messiah. Their sons and daughters will be many, they will have a long life, and if they serve the Torah of Yahweh in his good-pleasure, they will find happiness." This complete misunderstanding is the more surprising because the idea of vicarious suffering was by no means alien to Judaism (cf. 4 Macc. 6:28 f.; 17:22; BM, 85a, R. Eleazar), and traditions about a suffering and dying Messiah may certainly be traced back to the 2nd cent. A.D. [68] For material reasons, however, it was very difficult for Judaism to link this with Is. 53. [69] Only in the Middle Ages, through profounder study of Scripture, heavy external pressure and polemical discussion with Christianity, was Judaism led to the figure of a Messiah who suffers, though he does not die, as mediator. [70]

Apart from the further development in wisdom teaching (Sir. 24:3 ff.; Bar. 3:9 ff.; Eth. En. 42:1 f.; 91:10 etc.), the doctrine of divine intermediaries is carried further in Judaism only in so far as the transcendent apocalyptic Messiah developed out of

---

[66] For full materials cf. Murmelstein, 51 ff.

[67] Dalman, Seidelin. Cf. also the text in Str.-B., I, 482 f. Seidelin's transl. is our basis. Many details are debatable, but there is little doubt as to the main thrust.

[68] Mostly assigned to Messiah ben Joseph and Messiah ben David. 4 Esr. 7:29 should not be adduced, since it refers to Messiah's death after his reign. Messiah ben Joseph (first in bSukka, 52a, Bar.) will at first triumph and reign happily for forty years, but he will then be slain in street-fighting against Gog and Magog, and will be despairingly bewailed by Israel, Leqach Tob. Nu. 24:17; Str.-B., II, 298. It may be that this reflects the tragic fate of the Zealots in the Jewish wars. No atoning or mediatorial significance is ascribed to his death. Cf. on this R. Meyer, *Der Prophet aus Galiläa* (1939), 80 ff. The sufferings of Messiah ben David are before he enters on his office and they serve to confirm him in it (first in bSanh., 98a b). Both examples are Tannaitic. That expectation of a suffering Messiah in the sense of Is. 53 was a secret tradition among the people in NT days (J. Jeremias, 106 ff.) is not very likely in spite of the incontestable allusions to the servant of Yahweh in apoc. writings, cf. older scholars like Schürer, II, 648 ff., also Volz, *Is.*, II, 185, n. 2, G. Kittel, *D. Th.*, 3 (1936), 166 ff., esp. 175 ff., Seidelin, 230 f.

[69] The Targum may even be polemicising against the idea of a suffering Messiah.

[70] For details cf. Dalman, esp. 49 ff. Cf. the fine song from the Polish Machzor, 72 f., which probably goes back to Eleazar ben Qalir.

Da. 7:13 f. and ultimately out of the myth of the primal man, → υἱὸς τοῦ ἀνθρώπου. On the other hand, the Memra Adonai is not a (mediating) hypostasis, Str.-B., II, 302 ff. And Metatron (→ *metator*, land-surveyor, billeting officer, or scribe, → III, 164, n. 30) is simply the preceding angel. Yahweh Himself can be called this inasmuch as he shows Moses the promised land or goes before the people. There is here no thought of the mediator. [71]

2. Hellenistic Judaism.

In Philo the angels are occasionally, though with marked restraint, the mediators between heaven and earth. They go up and down on the heavenly ladder, οὐκ ἐπειδὴ τῶν μηνυσόντων ὁ πάντη ἐφθακὼς θεὸς δεῖται, ἀλλ' ὅτι τοῖς ἐπικήροις ἡμῖν συνέφερε μεσίταις καὶ διαιτηταῖς λόγοις χρῆσθαι, "because we are plunged into astonishment and fear before the Lord of all and the great power of His dominion" (Som., I, 142). Here the use is Hebraic in sense 3. The angels or λόγοι connect heaven and earth. This sense has even rubbed off on διαιτητής. For there is, strictly, no support for the view that the angels are umpires between God and men. διαιτητής has here something of the sense of "reconciler." But the juxtaposition of the two synon. shows that μεσίτης has something of sense 1. The use in Test. XII is just the same. Test. D. 6:2 says of the angel who intercedes for Israel (παραιτουμένῳ ἡμᾶς): ὅτι οὗτός ἐστι μεσίτης θεοῦ καὶ ἀνθρώπων καὶ ἐπὶ τῆς εἰρήνης τοῦ Ἰσραὴλ κατέναντι τῆς βασιλείας τοῦ θεοῦ [72] (cf. Test. L. 5:6). The ideas of negotiator and peace-maker here merge into one another. Moses is the absolute mediator. [73] Philo speaks of him as well as the angels (→ *supra*) in Som., I, 143: οὗ λαβόντες ἔννοιαν ἐδεήθημέν ποτέ τινος τῶν μεσιτῶν λέγοντες· (there follows Ex. 20:19). Another synon. is ὑπηρέται ἄλλοι. Here again we see the Hebraic use. But when applied to Moses the concept broadens, the OT content being poured into the Hellenistic term (sense 1.) as into a prepared form. In connection with the story of the idolatry of the Israelites at Sinai it is said of Moses in Vit. Mos., II (III), 166: καταπλαγεὶς δὲ καὶ ἀναγκασθεὶς πιστεύειν ἀπίστοις πράξεσιν οἷα (as a just) μεσίτης καὶ διαλλακτὴς οὐκ εὐθὺς ἀπεπήδησεν, ἀλλὰ πρότερον τὰς ὑπὲρ τοῦ ἔθνους ἱκεσίας καὶ λιτὰς ἐποιεῖτο συγγνῶναι τῶν ἡμαρτημένων δεόμενος. εἶτ' ἐξευμενισάμενος ὁ κηδεμὼν (provider) καὶ παραιτητὴς (intercessor) τὸν ἡγεμόνα ἐπανῄει χαίρων ἅμα καὶ κατηφῶν. The synon. for μεσίτης are worth noting. Whereas here everything is on the human level, in other passages Philo inclines to apply the cosmological mediator concept (→ 604) to Moses, and thereby to approximate him to the *logos*. Moses lauds the gift received: "κἀγὼ εἱστήκειν ἀνὰ μέσον κυρίου καὶ ὑμῶν" (Dt. 5:5), οὔτε ἀγένητος ὡς ὁ θεὸς ὢν οὔτε γενητὸς ὡς ὑμεῖς, ἀλλὰ μέσος τῶν ἄκρων (in the middle of extremes), ἀμφοτέροις ὁμηρεύων (to enter into contact, to serve as hostage or pledge), παρὰ μὲν τῷ φυτεύσαντι πρὸς πίστιν τοῦ μὴ σύμπαν ἀφηνιάσαι (to slip off the reins) ποτὲ καὶ ἀποστῆναι τὸ γεγονὸς ἀκοσμίαν ἀντὶ κόσμου ἑλόμενον, παρὰ δὲ τῷ φύντι πρὸς εὐελπιστίαν τοῦ μήποτε τὸν ἵλεω θεὸν περιιδεῖν τὸ ἴδιον ἔργον (Rer. Div. Her., 206). The assimilation of cosmological and soteriological motifs is highly individual. μεσιτεύειν, too, is in this sense technical in Philo, → 602.

---

[71] Bousset-Gressm., 353 f. Moore, HThR, 62 ff. The view of Weber, 178 ff. is wrong. The attempt to derive Metatron from *mediator* is quite erroneous.

[72] Most interesting is the weakly attested but original and meaningful variant ἐχθροῦ. Is there again reflected here the umpire between the elements?

[73] So also Ass. Mos. 1:14: *itaque excogitavit et invenit me, qui ab initio orbis terrarum praeparatus sum, ut sim arbiter testamenti illius*, Gr. in Gelasius, Commentarius actorum concilii Nicaeni (Schürer, III^4, 294): καὶ προεθεάσατό με ὁ θεὸς πρὸ καταβολῆς κόσμου εἶναί με τῆς διαθήκης αὐτοῦ μεσίτην. The work was written soon after the death of Herod. We see arising here the concept of the pre-existence of the mediator of the covenant. On μεσίτης τῆς διαθήκης → 600. The transl. *arbiter* has the Hell. sense (1.), but the Palestinian original had in view sense 3.

Only with Judaism is the mediator concept worked out technically. At the same time the wealth and depth of the basic OT understanding is only partially grasped, by Hell. Judaism more than Rabb. Under alien influences there manifests itself a tendency to exalt the mediator of the covenant to semi-divine status.

Thus Philo says of the high-priest: βούλεται γὰρ αὐτὸν ὁ νόμος μείζονος μεμοιρᾶσθαι φύσεως ἢ κατ' ἄνθρωπον, ἐγγυτέρω προσιόντα τῆς θείας, μεθόριον, εἰ δεῖ τἀληθὲς λέγειν, ἀμφοῖν, ἵνα διά μέσου τινὸς ἄνθρωποι μὲν ἱλάσκωνται θεόν, θεὸς δὲ τὰς χάριτας ἀνθρώποις ὑποδιακόνῳ τινὶ χρώμενος ὀρέγῃ καὶ χορηγῇ (Spec. Leg., I, 116).

E. The New Testament Concept of the Mediator.

1. The Use of the Terms.

Both words are rare in the NT. μεσίτης is found only in the Pauline corpus and Hb., μεσιτεύειν only in the latter, and there as a hapaxlegomenon. In interpretation we must begin with the Jewish Greek sense (3.). In Hb. there is an admixture of the specific Hellenistic sense (1.). Sense 2. does not occur.

Gl. 3:19 f.: τί οὖν ὁ νόμος; τῶν παραβάσεων χάριν προσετέθη, ἄχρις οὗ ἔλθῃ τὸ σπέρμα ᾧ ἐπήγγελται, διαταγεὶς δι' ἀγγέλων, ἐν χειρὶ μεσίτου, ὁ δὲ μεσίτης ἑνὸς οὐκ ἔστιν, ὁ δὲ θεὸς εἷς ἐστιν. The preceding verses have shown that the promise to Abraham and his descendants did not rest on the Law and could not be invalidated by the Law. The question thus arises whether the Law had a divine goal. Paul seeks to give a positive answer (vv. 21 ff.). But first his answer might well cause offence. [74] God had a hand in the giving of the Law. But the Law was only a temporarily valid (ἄχρις οὗ κτλ.) and strictly contradictory addition to the testament of promise (προσετέθη, cf. παρεισῆλθεν, R. 5:20; παρεισῆλθον, Gl. 2:4). It had the task of increasing transgressions (τῶν παραβάσεων χάριν, cf. R. 4:15; 5:20; 7:7 ff.; 11:32). The words which follow are strenuously debated, but they are surely designed to depreciate rather than magnify the Law. Only on this view could one with apparent logic reach the antinomian conclusion of v. 21, which is, of course, rejected. The part of the angels in the giving of the Law is not mentioned, then, in laudation, as on the Jewish view (Dt. 33:2 LXX; Jos. Ant., 15, 136; Jub. 1:29 [Str.-B., III, 554 ff.]; cf. Ac. 7:38, 53; Hb. 2:2), but in disparagement, → I, 85. A disputed point is whether the angels are for Paul subordinate agents of the divine Lawgiver or relatively independent authors (→ II, 67). The context might seem to support the latter. The view linked with the mediator concept also fits this explanation best. ἐν χειρὶ μεσίτου in v. 19 is a Hebraism for "בְּיַד, jMeg., 74d, 12 f. (Str.-B., III, 556): The Torah is given עַל יְדֵי סַרְסוֹר. By μεσίτης Paul means concretely Moses. But Moses is not called ὁ μεσίτης; he is subsumed under the concept of μεσίτης. The use is pure Jewish Gk. (sense 3.). [75] V. 20 adds a note which refers rather to the concept of negotiator or spokesman than to the concrete figure of Moses. Hence the generic art. here. V. 20a is thus a general statement. The first δέ links it with 19b, the second δέ looks forward to 20b as a second and antithetical statement. ἑνός thus corresponds to εἷς and is also masc. It is disputed whether the two terms refer to the duality of the contracting parties or to plurality on one of the two sides. The first view leads to the thought that since a mediator usually acts between two, but God is one, the Law is a contract or compromise given through a mediator, not a direct expression of the will of God. [76] But in this case mention of the angels

---

[74] Even Christian copyists took offence, as the variants show. It is wholly objectionable to Jewish thought.

[75] There is no ground in the text for thinking of Moses as the trustee of the Law, the bridge between Abraham and Christ (→ Mitteis, Herm., 617, cf. Halmel).

[76] F. Sieffert[9] (1899); E. W. Burton (1921); Lagrange, *ad loc.*

in v. 19b is superfluous. The second view fits the context better, namely, that since a mediator usually represents a plurality (or two pluralities), the Law does not come directly from God, who is one, but from the plurality, i.e., the angels, mentioned in v. 19b.[77] On this view the objection of v. 21 is quite logical. Here, then, the use of μεσίτης is purely Jewish, unaffected by Christianity. Description of Christ as μεσίτης might have endangered the apostle's argument, since it would suggest a similar conclusion in respect of the promise.

The case is different in 1 Tm. 2:5 f.: εἷς γὰρ θεός, εἷς καὶ μεσίτης θεοῦ καὶ ἀνθρώπων, ἄνθρωπος Χριστὸς Ἰησοῦς, ὁ δοὺς ἑαυτὸν ἀντίλυτρον ὑπὲρ πάντων, τὸ μαρτύριον καιροῖς ἰδίοις. Here the mediator concept is Christianised. The statement confirms the universality of the divine will to save stated in v. 4.[78] This demands the thought of the singularity and uniqueness of God and the Mediator. εἷς is thus a predicate in both cases.[79] The mediator between God and Israel, on which Jewish particularism[80] relies, is replaced by the μεσίτης θεοῦ καὶ ἀνθρώπων, who in correspondence with the singularity of God and total humanity is one. He is expressly called man to emphasise that he belongs to all who bear the face of man.[81] The universal validity of His mediatorial self-offering to death gives all a share in salvation from God's standpoint. This saving act is the central theme of the apostolic witness addressed to all. The μεσίτης is the One who represents God to men and men to God, and brings them together. He is the attorney and negotiator (sense 3. with the meaning of סַרְסוֹר). That He makes peace between God and man is not so strongly emphasised in the text that we can assume a direct ref. to sense 1. This is implied only indirectly to the degree that, along with the OT, it is involved in the dissemination of the religious mediator concept in the Jewish Greek world, so that μεσίτης acquires something of the sense of reconciler (→ 602, 617). The new thing as compared with all previous conceptions is that the function of the μεσίτης is related exclusively to Christ and the uniqueness and universality of the relation is maintained on this basis. The mediator concept thus has a positive significance which it is hard to reconcile with the negative estimation in Gl. 3:19 f. But Pauline dialectic leads not uncommonly to formal logical contradictions.[82] Materially it corresponds to the view of Paul that the boundlessness of God's will to save follows from the unity of God, and that this will to save is actualised, not in human experience, but in Christ, in His self-sacrifice in death (R. 3:30; 5:18; 11:32; 1 C. 15:22; Gl. 1:4; 3:14 etc.). The use of μεσίτης for this function of Christ is as little excluded by Gl. 3:19 as is the phrase νόμος τοῦ Χριστοῦ by the antithesis to the Mosaic Law (Gl. 6:2). Christ is the antitype of Moses (1 C. 10:2, cf. with 1:13; R. 6:3).

The word μεσίτης takes a more Hellenistic turn in Hb. 8:6: νῦν δὲ διαφορωτέρας

---

77 Ltzm., A. Loisy, A. Oepke, Gl., *ad loc.*; A. Schweitzer, *D. Mystik d. Ap. Pls.* (1930), 71; Zn. Gl., *ad loc.* and J. Gründler, NkZ, 39 (1928), 549 ff. think the people which receives is the plurality, though this is hardly the meaning of the apostle.

78 Not just, as B. Weiss, *ad loc.* thinks, the unity of the way of salvation (v. 4b). Reproduction of a religious formula (Dib. Past., *ad loc.*) would not rule out a close material connection.

79 All the analogies (R. 3:30; Gl. 3:20; cf. also 1 C. 8:6; E. Peterson, ΕΙΣ ΘΕΟΣ [1926], 134; 227 ff.; 254 ff.) are against εἷς as subj. (B. Weiss, apparently also Dib. Past.). No decisive weight should be laid on the absence of the art.

80 Only by spiritualising exegesis can one find here a polemic against particularism (Schl. Past., *ad loc.*). There is displayed rather the self-awareness of the "catholic" Church.

81 The correspondence between ἀνθρώπους in v. 4, ἀνθρώπων and ἄνθρωπος in v. 5, is obvious. Christ is obviously not called man to rule out His deity, or in opposition to Docetic inclinations, or as ideal man or member of the one party, but to show that He belongs to all men without distinction.

82 Thus in Gl. 3:16 Paul argues from the sing. σπέρμα even though he realises clearly (R. 4:16) that this can include all the descendants. R. 5:13: ἁμαρτία οὐκ ἐλλογεῖται μὴ ὄντος νόμου, stands in contradiction with R. 2:12 ff., and the *lex paradisiaca* of R. 5:14 is in tension with Gl. 3:17. If, of course, the Past. are non-Pauline, the difference need cause no surprise.

τέτυχεν λειτουργίας, ὅσῳ καὶ κρείττονός ἐστιν διαθήκης μεσίτης, ἥτις ἐπὶ κρείττοσιν ἐπαγγελίαις νενομοθέτηται, 9:15: καὶ διὰ τοῦτο διαθήκης καινῆς μεσίτης ἐστίν, ὅπως θανάτου γενομένου εἰς ἀπολύτρωσιν τῶν ἐπὶ τῇ πρώτῃ διαθήκῃ παραβάσεων τὴν ἐπαγγελίαν λάβωσιν οἱ κεκλημένοι τῆς αἰωνίου κληρονομίας, 12:24 (in an enumeration of the blessings of salvation beginning with προσεληλύθατε in v. 22): καὶ διαθήκης νέας μεσίτῃ Ἰησοῦ, καὶ αἵματι ῥαντισμοῦ κρεῖττον λαλοῦντι παρὰ τὸν Ἄβελ. Characteristic of all these passages is the linking of μεσίτης with διαθήκη. On the basis of the LXX the latter term means God's "covenant" or "saving disposition." But in 9:16 ff., to show that the death of Christ was necessary, the author incidentally gives it the sense of "last will and testament" which became technical in the later secular *koine*.[83] The same holds good for μεσίτης. The primary meaning is everywhere that Jesus transcends and replaces the mediator of the old covenant, Μωϋσῆς 8:5; 9:19; 12:21. The author did not coin the theological concept μεσίτης independently on the basis of Hellenistic presuppositions. He took it from the Jewish or Christian tradition. Hence "mediator" is a pertinent translation (sense 3. = סַרְסוֹר).[84] But there are two reasons why we cannot stop at this. 1. In 7:22 Jesus is called κρείττονος διαθήκης ἔγγυος. The strong agreement makes it probable that → ἔγγυος is for the author a synon. of μεσίτης. This is only possible, however, if as a good Hellenist he also finds sense 1., esp. e. and perhaps b., in the theological concept. This leads to the idea of a contracted obligation whose fulfilment Jesus guarantees, in a sense by sharing the debt. The divine promise of salvation is here in view. In relation to men Jesus has undertaken to see to it that this will not go unfulfilled, that deliverance will be accomplished.[85] 2. In 6:17 we read: ἐν ᾧ περισσότερον βουλόμενος ὁ θεὸς ἐπιδεῖξαι τοῖς κληρονόμοις τῆς ἐπαγγελίας τὸ ἀμετάθετον τῆς βουλῆς αὐτοῦ ἐμεσίτευσεν ὅρκῳ. Here μεσιτεύειν cannot mean "to mediate," "to convey," since there is no obj., nor "to be mediator," since there is no higher court which God might represent in relation to men. The only possible translation is "to guarantee," "to vouch for."[86] In giving the promise. God is as it were one of the parties. But with His oath, and as its Guarantor (→ 603), He puts Himself on neutral ground and pledges the fulfilment of the promise. This means again that μεσίτης bears sense 1. b. This Hellenistic understanding is helped by the fact that μεσίτης διαθήκης is a possible, if rare, phrase in the Hellen. law of inheritance, → 600. But since the basic meaning is still mediator, μεσίτης is in fact more than ἔγγυος. The latter simply stresses the guaranteeing of salvation, the former its accomplishment, which also entails mediatorial death.

2. The Theology of Mediatorship in the New Testament.

The fact that the term does not occur on the lips of Jesus, but arises only in the community, raises the question whether the concept, in accordance with the law of → 610, is not a later contribution of the community. Much depends on this, and it is a basic problem of NT theology. The answer is that the mediator concept is original. It clothes itself increasingly in forms which lie ready to hand. But it maintains its NT individuality.

---

[83] → διαθήκη, II, 131. To translate "testament" in every case (Rgg. Hb.) is just as impossible as always to render "covenant" (Milligan, Carr). For a similar flexibility in Pl. cf. 2 C. 3:6, 14; Gl. 3:15.

[84] Rgg. Hb. on 8:6: Mediator of a blessing. But the explanations of Theophylact.: μεσίτης καὶ δότης (τοῦ εὐαγγελίου), and Euthymius: μεσίτης ἀντὶ τοῦ ὑφηγητὴς καὶ δοτήρ, rest on a sense which is at least very refined and which is perhaps invented for the occasion, → 601. διαθήκης is an obj. gen. in the sense of inner obj., → 601.

[85] → II, 329. That Christ vouches for men before God (O. Michel, *Der Brief an d. Hebräer* [1936], on 7:22) is alien to the distinctive thought of Hb.

[86] So Rgg., Wnd., Michel Hb., *ad loc.*

a. Jesus. The lack of self-testimony in the Synoptics, and esp. passages like Lk. 18:9-14 and Lk. 15:11 ff., have led to the conclusion that the historical Jesus proclaimed a religion without mediation. But even so the fact remains that the parables are simply designed to bring out sharply the point at issue in the context, without offering any full allegorical description of salvation. The publican in the temple prays as a Jew to the God of revelation. In the story of the prodigal son Jesus is justifying His own attitude to sinners. He pronounces remission of sins to the paralytic in a way which seems blasphemous to the leaders of Judaism (Mk. 2:1 ff.; cf. Lk. 7:36-50). The self-testimony, historically convincing in its very reserve, is not entirely absent from the Synoptics even apart from the final open confessions (Mt. 21:1 ff.; 26:64 and par.). Jesus makes total demands (Mt. 10:37 ff. and par.) and grants total peace (Mt. 11:28 ff.). He alone knows and reveals the Father (Mt. 11:27 and par.). He makes man's destiny dependent on confession of His person (Mt. 10:32 f. and par.). He is the Judge of the world (Mt. 25:31 ff.). In the eschatological situation the only psychologically convincing Jesus is the Jesus offered by the sources,[87] not the Jesus of psychological investigation.

Jesus's sense of majesty clothes itself in the historical forms ready to hand. Least emphasis falls on the fact that He is the antitype of Moses. In Mt. 5:20 ff., speaking from the mount, He is not giving a new Torah but showing by examples that He increases rather than softens moral demands as compared with Rabbinic casuistry.[88] The historical Last Supper, especially if it took place at the Passover (→ III, 734), has the redemption out of Egypt and the conclusion of the covenant at Sinai as its background but leaves us in no doubt as to the difference between the old covenant and this new one which was expected according to Jer. 31:31 ff. Comparison of Mt. 11:25 ff. with Sir. 51 makes it plain that Jesus realises His oneness with divine wisdom.[89] The main form of His sense of mediatorship is apocalyptic and messianic divine and human sonship (→ υἱὸς τοῦ ἀνθρώπου). It seems to be His original and most proper act indissolubly to combine this ideal of power with the ideal of humility expressed in the suffering servant of God (→ 612 f.). His sense of mission is predominantly orientated to Dt. Is. (and Tr. Is.),[90] though explicit allusion is rare. As the Servant of God He gives His life λύτρον ἀντὶ πολλῶν (Mk. 10:45 and par.), and knows that God will acknowledge this mediatorship of His. Only as the One who died and rose again is He in the full sense of the word the Mediator.

---

[87] "The chaotic confusion of the narratives ought to have suggested the thought that the events have been thrown into this confusion by the volcanic force of an incalculable personality, not by some kind of carelessness . . . in the tradition," A. Schweitzer, *Geschichte der Leben-Jesu-Forschung*[4] (1926), 391, ET (1954), p. 349. J. Jeremias, "Jesus als Weltvollender," BFTh, 33, 4 (1930), has a correct view of the whole, though there are still many detailed problems. Attempts to dismiss the mediatorial consciousness of the historical Jesus by way of criticism (E. Winkel, *Der Sohn*[2] [1938]; R. Thiel, *Jesus Christus u. d. Wissenschaft* [1938]) do not stand up to scientific investigation. Except in details, E. Hoskyns and N. Davey give a convincing presentation in *The Riddle of the New Testament* (1931).

[88] περισσεύειν in Mt. 5:20 is a quantitative rather than a qualitative term. Only in the light of this basic insight can one understand both the verses which precede and those which follow. Cf. A. Oepke, "Jesus u. d. AT" (*Theologia militans*, No. 21 [1938]).

[89] For details, though with debatable conclusions, cf. E. Norden, *Agnostos Theos* (1913), 280 ff.

[90] Wrongly contested by P. Volz, *Js.*, II, 185.

b. The Primitive Community. The common conjecture that the primitive community, on the basis of its faith, created the image of Jesus portrayed in the Gospels, is shattered already by the simple but masterly portrayal, which could only correspond to the actuality, and also by the shortness of the time available. In Buddhism and Islam centuries were needed to make demi-gods out of the human founders of religion. In the faith of the primitive community as we may see it quite well in Ac. and Pl. there lives on from the very first the Lord who by the resurrection is exalted to heavenly glory and whose coming again to establish the rule of God is awaited with longing.[91] The rise of Christianity would be quite inexplicable if the earthly life of Jesus were not fundamentally different from that of a favourite teacher or prophet, and if the primitive community itself had attributed to Him saving and mediatorial significance.[92]

The faith of the primitive community patently rests on the synthesis which Jesus Himself made between the Son of Man and the Suffering Servant. What is added is simply the fulfilment of Good Friday, Easter and Pentecost. Ideas of pre-existence cannot be proved, but they are already in the air. It is often asserted that syncretistic myth adds its quota to Christianity, but this is most unlikely.

c. Paul. When Paul came to faith in the risen Lord on the Damascus road, he adopted, though with his own independent experience, the faith of the primitive community. That he never preached a religion without mediation, that he never claimed for himself the position of a mediator in the absolute sense, needs no demonstration. Without evaporising or minimising the earthly life of Jesus, he sets the crucifixion and resurrection more exclusively in the centre. In this twofold divine act the change from the old aeon to the new was accomplished. Baptism is into the final act of the old age, and the inaugural act of the new, as these were basically fulfilled in the Mediator (R. 4:25; 6:1 ff.). The final consummation is only a matter of time. But Paul also believes that the pre-existent Christ played a part in the creation of the world (1 C. 8:6; Col. 1:16). The OT idea of wisdom had some influence here. Belief in the Kyrios (→ III, 1088), though adopted by the primitive community (1 C. 16:22), is now emphasised antithetically (1 C. 8:5) and is thus developed more strongly (→ διά, II, 67; ἐν, II, 541). Also new in Paul (→ I, 141) is the parallel between Adam and Christ (R. 5:12 ff.; 1 C. 15:22, 45 ff.). It is unlikely that this was simply a new form of the self-testimony of Jesus concerning the Son of Man. Along with Jewish speculations about Adam the syncretistic myth of the primal man (→ 608) perhaps had an indirect influence here. But Paul's use of it is new and different. In Paul Christ is always the last Adam. This overthrows the mystical equation of the mediators of ruin and salvation, the pantheistic dissolving of the antithesis between the Creator and fallen creation, the whole religion of ontological redemption. Redemption does not consist in man's orientation to the divine in the strict sense, but in his being redeemed. Adam is a mediator only of ruin. As compared with him, Christ is quite different. He is the mediator of salvation in the true sense. The mediator is not the timeless heavenly man. He is the incarnate Son of God who came into history. Where Gnosis knocks at the door, there arise constructs of thought which to some degree find the cosmic mediatorial position of the deity (→ 604) fulfilled in Christ. The all is com-

[91] As against the partially erroneous view of Bousset, cf. P. Wernle, "Jesus u. Pls.," ZThK, 25 (1915), 1 ff.

[92] D. A. Frövig, "Der Kyriosglaube des NT u. das Messiasbewusstsein Jesu," BFTh, 31, 2 (1928).

prehended in Him (ἀνακεφαλαιώσασθαι, Eph. 1:10), and brought to peace (ἀποκαταλλάξαι, εἰρηνοποιήσας, Col. 1:20). He in whom the whole → πλήρωμα dwells (Col. 1:19) holds all things together and fills them with His life (τοῦ τὰ πάντα ἐν πᾶσιν πληρουμένου, Eph. 1:23). But now the thinking takes a highly significant turn. The universal body which He rules as Head, the *pleroma* which He for His part fills, is in the full sense, not the cosmos, but the → ἐκκλησία (Eph. 1:22). Whereas in paganism soteriological mediatorship proceeds from the cosmic, the relation is reversed in Christian Gnosis. To be sure, there stands at the beginning the creation-mediatorship of the πρωτότοκος πάσης κτίσεως (Col. 1:15 f.), and at the end the manifestation or cosmic glorification of Christ and His people is awaited (Col. 3:4). But in between is history with its whole descent, paradox and distance. The tendency is to bind the cosmos to salvation, not salvation to the cosmos.[93]

d. John's Gospel and Epistles. Though the term is not used, Johannine theology is strongly impregnated by the attempt to show that Christ is the fulfilment of all mediatorship. We catch echoes of motifs from all the religious yearning of the world around the Evangelist. But as Pauline Gnosis raises Christ above the series of aeons and gives His mediatorship an absolute character (Col. 2:3), John sets all those who claim to be guides to God (Jn. 10:8; 5:43) in contrast with the One who is the way, the truth and the life (14:6).[94] Here, too, mediatorial representation culminates in intercession (17; 1 Jn. 2:1) and death (10:11; 12:32; 17:19 etc.). The atoning significance of this is particularly emphasised in 1 Jn. (1:7; 2:2). Allusion to Is. 53 is again patent (Jn. 1:29; → I, 339). Between the earthly Jesus and the risen Lord no distinction can be made. The Mediator in Johannine theology is seen from the standpoint of the Easter faith of the community.

e. The Other New Testament Writings. In the rest of the NT Jesus Christ as Mediator is comparatively less prominent only in Jm. This is connected with the distinctive nature of the work. But the epistle, as it stands to-day, is to be interpreted on the assumption that what seems to be missing is tacitly presupposed. In respect of the other writings there is no room for doubt. Hb. uses the mediator concept, even where it does not use the term, to show that the Church is the true people of God in the age of salvation.[95] 1 Pt. begins with sprinkling with the blood of Christ and the renewing of the world by the resurrection of Jesus Christ from the dead (1:2 f.), and from this it moves on to the antitypical election of the holy, royal and priestly generation (2:9). Though in different ways, both works are formally saturated by belief in the Mediator. Jude and 2 Pt. belong to a slightly less primitive time. But their dogmatic and liturgical formulae show how firmly rooted is the mediator concept in the faith of the Church — a development which was not, of course, without its dangers (Jd. 1, 4, 17, 21, 25; 2 Pt. 1:1, 2, 8, 11; 2:20; 3:18). For the Apocalyptist Christ is the Lion of the tribe of Judah and the Lamb which was slain. He is the personal fulfilment of the united ideals of power and

---

[93] H. Schlier, *Christus und die Kirche im Epheserbrief* (1930).

[94] A. Oepke, "Das Christuszeugnis des Johannesevangeliums," *Sächs. Kirchenblatt,* NF, 1 (1937), 252 ff.; R. Bultmann, *Das Joh.-Ev.* (1937 ff.) on 1:1 ff. Par. between Jn. and Eph. are sensitively worked out in B. W. Bacon, *The Gospel of the Hellenists* (1933), 370 ff.

[95] Cf. on this Käsemann, though he starts too one-sidedly with Gnosticism, and, in spite of his sense of the distinctiveness of the Gospel, pays too little regard to the biblical connections.

humility. He alone can open the seven seals of the book and unravel the mysteries of the divine government of the world, 5:5 ff. Hence originally cosmic symbolic relations are systematically applied to Him, the numbers seven and twelve as they originally belonged to the planets and the signs of the zodiac (1:12 ff.; 21:14), the splendour of the sun, the moon and the morning star (12:1 ff.; 22:16). Christ does not merely stand at the centre of the world. He leads His community from the one epoch to the other.

Hence NT religion in its whole range is strictly and exclusively orientated to the mediator concept, not in the sense that outside the Mediator there is no place for witness to or contact with God (→ III, 586), but in the sense that in the Mediator Christ there is accomplished the decisive self-offering of God to the full fellowship to which we are absolutely directed. NT revelation cannot be integrated into a schema derived from comparative religion. It is something new and independent. But it is also the fulfilment of the mediator concept as such.

F. The Church.

If the infrequent occurrence of the term in the NT is surprising, even more so is its almost complete absence from the earliest Christian writings. μεσιτεία is used technically of the mediatorship of Christ in Act. Andr., 2 (Bonnet, 38, 25). μεσίτης does not recur until Cl. Al. Paed., III, 1, 2, 1: τὸ θέλημα τοῦ πατρὸς ὁ μεσίτης ἐκτελεῖ· μεσίτης γὰρ ὁ λόγος ὁ κοινὸς ἀμφοῖν, θεοῦ μὲν υἱός, σωτὴρ δὲ ἀνθρώπων. The thought is elucidated with the help of an inexactly quoted saying of Heraclitus which was meant in a very different pantheistic and rational sense: ἄνθρωποι θεοί, θεοὶ ἄνθρωποι, λόγος (mind, reason) γὰρ αὐτοῖς, cf. Heracl. Fr., 62 [I, 164, 9 f., Diels[5]]).[96] μεσιτεύειν is found in a corresponding theological sense in Cl. Al. Prot., XII, 122, 3: μεσιτεύοντος τοῦ λόγου. Instances remain sporadic. But it would be just as mistaken to conclude that the matter is absent as in the case of the NT. On the other hand, it did not for a while become a central concept in dogmatics. Other designations for Christ, e.g., κύριος, or the θεοῦ υἱός and σωτήρ comprised in the fish symbol, were at first much more influential. Perhaps the mediator concept suffered from its strong secular and Jewish associations. In Roman Catholicism the Church and its agents largely took over the mediatorial function. In contrast, Reformation theology looked to the one Mediator, Christ (cf. Conf. Aug., XX). It is no accident that in the 20th century, when, after a period of liberal and rational thought, theology was finding its way back to the biblical and Reformation message, the word "mediator" became one of the slogans of the new outlook.[97]

Oepke

---

[96] Cf. also Lact. Inst., IV, 25, who keeps the Gk. term. Latins like Tertullian and Prudentius use *mediator*. Cf. A. Forcellini-J. Furlanetto-V. de Vit, Totius Latinitatis Lexicon, IV (1868), 74. Worth noting is the monstrous etym. in Etym. Gud. (ed. Sturz, 388, 17): Μεσίας, ὁ Χριστός, παρὰ τὸ μέσος.

[97] Cf. the works by Brunner and Künneth.

† μεσότοιχον

The neut. μεσότοιχον or masc. μεσότοιχος has so far been found, apart from Eph. 2:14, only in Hesych., *s.v.* κατῆλιψ, two inscr. from Argos[1] and Didyma,[2] and fig. τὸν τῆς ἡδονῆς καὶ ἀρετῆς μεσότοιχον, Eratosthenes of Cyrene in Athen., VII, 14 (p. 281d); the adj. μεσότοιχος in P. Amh., II, 98, 8 ff.: ὁμολογῶ πεπρακέναι σοι ... οἰκίαν καὶ τὴν ἐνοῦσαν αὐλὴν καὶ ἥμισυ μέρος τῶν μεσοτοίχων (μεσοτύχων? there is some doubt as to the reading) οἰκιῶν. The construction is mainly Hellenistic with the sense of "partition" or "dividing wall."[3] It does not occur in the LXX.

The only occurrence in the NT is at Eph. 2:14. The sense here is not wholly clear, but in the total context τὸ μεσότοιχον τοῦ φραγμοῦ seems to be the wall of partition which consists in the fence between God and man. μεσότοιχον is more fully elucidated by ἔχθρα and φραγμός by νόμος τῶν ἐντολῶν. By His incarnation and death Christ did away with the νόμος τῶν ἐντολῶν and removed the enmity between God and man.[4] To refer the passage to the removal of the antithesis between Greek and Jew, with reminiscence of the temple barriers,[5] the walls of the Law as a protection against Gentiles,[6] or the barricades of the ghetto,[7] is hardly convincing or even possible in the light of v. 16 and v. 17.[8]

Carl Schneider

Μεσσίας → Χριστός.
μεταβαίνω → I, 523.
μετάθεσις → τίθημι.
μετακαλέομαι → III, 496.
μετακινέω → III, 720.
μεταλαμβάνω, μετάλημψις → 10.
μεταλλάσσω → I, 259.

μεσότοιχον. Liddell-Scott, 1108; Pr.-Bauer, 798; [3] 841; Wilke-Grimm, 279.
[1] BCH, 33 (1909), p. 452, No. 22, 16.
[2] *Siebenter vorläufiger Bericht über die ... in Milet u. Didyma unternommenen Ausgrabungen.* AAB (1911), 56.
[3] In modern Gk. only μεσότοιχος.
[4] For a review of the arguments cf. Haupt Gefbr., *ad loc.*
[5] Jos. Bell., 5, 193 f.; Ditt. Or., II, 598. Dib. Gefbr., *ad loc.* rightly asks: "Would the readers of Eph. 2:14 have understood such an allusion?"
[6] Ep. Ar., 139: Moses surrounded Israel ἀδιακόποις χάραξι καὶ σιδηροῖς τείχεσιν, cf. also 142.
[7] Ew. Gefbr., *ad loc.*
[8] That the hostility between Greeks and Jews can be done away by abolishing the Law as a way of salvation is by no means obvious. There can be no doubt, however, that the passage is dealing with the new relationship of the Gentiles to God.

† μεταμέλομαι, † ἀμεταμέλητος

1. μετανοεῖν and μεταμέλεσθαι are distinct in class. Gk. → μετανοεῖν means a change of heart either generally or in respect of a specific sin, whereas μεταμέλεσθαι means "to experience remorse." [1] μετανοεῖν implies that one has later arrived at a different view of something (νοῦς), μεταμέλεσθαι that one has a different feeling about it (μέλει). But it is easy for the two ideas to come together and even merge, since a change of view often carries with it an uncomfortable feeling. The pass. deponent is attested from Thuc. To Democr. is attributed the statement: μεταμέλεια ἐπ' αἰσχροῖσιν ἔργμασι βίου σωτηρίη, Fr., 43 (II, 155, 13 f., Diels[5]). [2] μετάνοια and the related μεταμέλεια are common on class. soil, but, as the sentence of Democr. shows, they were not understood merely intellectually. They were differently estimated and could even be rejected. ταραχή and μεταμέλεια are in Plato two related signs of sickness in the human soul: καὶ ἡ τυραννουμένη ἄρα ψυχὴ ἥκιστα ποιήσει ἃ ἂν βουληθῇ, ὡς περὶ ὅλης εἰπεῖν ψυχῆς. ὑπὸ δὲ οἴστρου (prick, strong emotion) ἀεὶ ἑλκομένη βίᾳ ταραχῆς καὶ μεταμελείας μεστὴ ἔσται, Resp., IX, 577e. In keeping is the fact that Aristot. says of the σπουδαῖος ἀνήρ: ἀμεταμέλητος γάρ, Eth. Nic., IX, 4, p. 1166a, 29. μεταμέλεια is for Aristot. a sign of lack of inner consistency in thought and action because it involves a shift of concern (μεταμέλεια acc. to its basic sense). It is thus understandable that the Stoics polemicise against μεταμέλεια and μετάνοια (μεταμέλεια as πάθος), and that our understanding of penitence is strictly alien to the class. Gk. [3] μετάνοια and μεταμέλεια could then awaken a new moral interest through the preaching of the Cynics and Pythagoreans. A new sense of guilt and a summons to conversion affected wide circles of the population. For the word group μεταμέλομαι — μεταμέλεια later cf. Plut. Ser. Num. Pun., 3 (II, 549c); Tranq. An., 19 (II, 476 f.); Apophth., 22 (II, 178 f.); Gen. Socr., 22 (II, 592b); Ceb. Tab., 35, 4; Philo Spec. Leg., I, 242; the decree of the Gk. cities in Ditt. Or., 458, 10 f.: ὅ ἐστιν πέρας καὶ ὅρος τοῦ μεταμέλεσθαι, and BGU, IV, 1040, 20. μετάμελος (noun) is found earlier in Thuc. and then only in the Hell. period (Varro [ed. Buecheler, 1922], Sat., 239: Metamelos Inconstantiae filius). Along with μετανοεῖν and μεταμέλεσθαι note should be taken of μεταβάλλεσθαι, though this is intellectualistic (Isoc., 8, 23; Eur. Ion, 1614).

μεταμέλομαι κτλ. [1] For bibl. cf. E. F. Thompson, *Μετανοέω and μεταμέλει in Greek Lit. until 100 A.D.* (Diss. Chicago, 1908); H. J. Holtzmann, ThLZ, 33 (1908), 459-460; Wnd. 2 K., 229; Pr.-Bauer[3], *s.v.*; Helbing Kasussyntax, 112; Trench, 167 ff.; E. Norden, *Agnostos Theos* (1913), 134 ff.; W. Jaeger, GGA, 175 (1913), 569-610. Weber, 316-321 (תְּשׁוּבָה); E. K. Dietrich, *Die Umkehr* (*Bekehrung und Busse*) *im AT u. im Judt.* (1936); H. Pohlmann, *Die Metanoia als Zentralbegriff der christlichen Frömmigkeit* (1938); J. Schniewind, "Evangelische Metanoia," *Bekennende Kirche, Heft* 25 (1935); O. Michel, "Die Umkehr nach der Verkündigung Jesu," *Ev. Theol.*, 5 (1938), 403-414.

[2] Cf. Norden, 136: "Here there are two possibilities. Either this saying (which is not in Stob.) is not by Democr., or, if it is genuine, it must have anticipated future development of the concept by centuries." Jaeger, 590: "The polemic of the Stoics against μετάνοια, which is found in many authors, seems to me to point to the widespread existence of a type of ethics in which it had high value." Cf. Democr. Fr., 43 (II, 155, 13 f., Diels[5]) and Ceb. Tab., 10, 4; 11, 1; 32, 2; 35, 4.

[3] Cf. v. Arnim, *s.v.* μεταμέλεια; Norden, 134-140. μετάνοια is opposed and condemned as a πάθος in Epict., M. Ant. and Ar. Did.; cf. Jaeger, 589.

2. In the LXX we find μεταμέλει (אשם, נחם and נחם ni), μετάμελος (4 Βασ. 3:27; Prv. 11:3; 3 Macc. 2:24: οὐδαμῶς εἰς μετάμελον ἦλθεν) and once μεταμέλεια (Hos. 11:8).[4] The phrase is hazarded that God repented (1 Βασ. 15:35: καὶ κύριος μετεμελήθη, also 1 Ch. 21:15: εἶδεν κύριος καὶ μετεμελήθη ἐπὶ τῇ κακίᾳ, ψ 105:45: καὶ ἐμνήσθη τῆς διαθήκης αὐτοῦ καὶ μετεμελήθη κατὰ τὸ πλῆθος τοῦ ἐλέους αὐτοῦ, 109:4: ὤμοσεν κύριος καὶ οὐ μεταμεληθήσεται, Jer. 20:16: αἱ πόλεις, ἃς κατέστρεψεν κύριος ἐν θυμῷ καὶ οὐ μετεμελήθη, → III, 109). Amos in his prayer counts on it that God will hear his protestation: μετανόησον, κύριε, ἐπὶ τούτῳ (Am. 7:3, 6). In fact God yields to his request (נִחַם יהוה). The OT thus believes that there are divine words and acts in which God's repentance (μεταμελεῖσθαι, μετανοεῖν = נִחַם) is expressed. On the other hand, it is concerned that the seriousness of the message of judgment should not be weakened by this teaching. God is not a man that He should go back on His word (Nu. 23:19; 1 S. 15:29; Jer. 4:28; 20:16; Zech. 8:14).[5] Hence the repentance of God is not capricious. It does not overthrow the idea of judgment. It is not a false human love. On the contrary, the seriousness of the divine judgment is confirmed and established by the proclamation of divine repentance. OT sayings about the repentance of God speak of a twofold possibility: a. God rejects in spite of His prior grace and election (1 S. 15:35); b. in spite of His prior judgment God renews His grace and mercy (1 Ch. 21:15; Ps. 106:45). Thus God's grace always includes the possibility of His wrath, His election the danger of rejection. On the other hand, His judgment and punishment are not distinct from His kindness and mercy, but surrounded by them. Every divine repentance is thus the fulfilment of a possibility already present. "All love is precisely for the one who stands above the beloved a victory, a waiver, a sacrifice, and this is particularly true of divine grace."[6] This tension in the outworking of God's action in salvation history — the tension between judgment and grace, election and rejection — is still felt by later Judaism. God is both the Judge and the Merciful One. As Judge He is Elohim, as the Merciful One Yahweh.[7] Judaism and primitive Christianity are distinguished by the way in which they understand this tension. If the OT says that God did not and does not repent (Ps. 110:4; Jer. 4:28; 20:16), there is in this negation a ref. to His constancy and faithfulness. No human opposition frustrates His action. His will attains its goal.

When "remorse" is ascribed to man, there is an obvious difference from repentance (μετανοεῖν), though the LXX does pay tribute to the Hell. attempt to assimilate μεταμέλεσθαι and μετανοεῖν (cf. Jer. 4:28: οὐ μετανοήσω, and 20:16: καὶ οὐ μεταμελήθη). Remorse does not have to be pleasing to God. It can be simply a change in mood (Ex. 13:17; 1 Macc. 11:10). It is often the natural result of imprudent and unjust action (Sir. 33:20; cf. μεταμέλεσθαι ἐπ' ἐσχάτων in Prv. 5:11; 25:8). In re-

[4] 2 K. 3:27: Mas. קֶצֶף = wrath. Originally the ref. was to the wrath of the god Chemosh which forced Israel to retreat when the king of Moab sacrificed his son to Chemosh. But Israel thought in terms of the anger of the people at human sacrifice. The LXX, too, sees a ref. to the psychological attitude of the people. It puts μετάμελος for קֶצֶף in the sense of grief, cf. the same meaning in Prv. 11:3. Mas. תֻּמַּת יְשָׁרִים תַּנְחֵם וְסֶלֶף בֹּגְדִים וְשָׁדֵּם, "the integrity of the upright guides them, and the falsity of the unfaithful destroys them." In the first half the LXX thinks of מוּת "to die" and נִחַם "to repent," and it thus has: ἀποθανὼν δίκαιος ἔλιπεν μετάμελον, πρόχειρος δὲ γίνεται καὶ ἐπίχαρτος ἀσεβῶν ἀπώλεια, "When the righteous died, he left grief behind, but the destruction of the ungodly will be taken lightly and awakens pleasure."

[5] Important is 1 Βασ. 15:29: καὶ οὐκ ἀποστρέψει οὐδὲ μετανοήσει, ὅτι οὐχ ὡς ἄνθρωπός ἐστιν τοῦ μετανοῆσαι αὐτός.

[6] W. Lütgert, *Schöpfung u. Offenbarung* (1934), 392.

[7] Lv. r., 29, 9 f. on 23:24; S. Dt., 27 on 3:24; on the problem cf. also Weber, 154. E. Sjöberg, "Gott u. d. Sünder im paläst. Judt.," BWANT, IV, 27 (1938), 6, 11 ff.; R. Sander, "Furcht u. Liebe im paläst. Judt.," BWANT, IV, 16 (1935).

morse (μεταμέλεσθαι) a man sees the bitter end of sin, in repentance (μετανοεῖν) he breaks free from it. Remorse comes of itself at the end of a sinful and foolish way. But a man is called to repentance by the one who brings the divine Word (μετανοεῖτε, Mk. 1:15).

3. In Hellen. lit., too, we often find μετάνοια and μεταμέλεια (or μετάμελος) alongside one another, several times as equivalents in a refined usage, though sometimes distinct.[8] μετάνοια is the word of the Synagogue and the Church (= תְּשׁוּבָה), μεταμέλεια (μετάμελος) that of general literature, philosophy and wisdom teaching. In biblical thought, too, μετάνοια can have a broad sense (cf. Hb. 12:17).[9] In Philo μεταμέλεια is the presupposition and proof of remission of sins (Spec. Leg., I, 242: ὅτι οἷς ἁμαρτημάτων εἰσέρχεται μεταμέλεια ἵλεω τὸν θεὸν ἔχουσιν), but we also find μετάνοια and μετανοεῖν (Leg. All., III, 106: ὁ θεὸς ... δίδωσι χρόνον εἰς μετάνοιαν) and Som., I, 91: τὸ μετανοεῖν ἀδελφὸν νεώτερον ὂν τοῦ μηδ' ὅλως ἁμαρτεῖν ἀποδέχεται). Jos. is perhaps aware that μετάνοια is more than μεταμέλεια: "Alongside μετάνοια, the change of will, is μετάμελος, remorse, through which man suffers the pain of self-accusation."[10] Characteristic, at least, are the expressions: κατήφεια ... καὶ τῶν πραγμάτων μετάμελος (Ant., 2, 108); λύπη τῶν πεπραγμένων ... καὶ μετάμελος (8, 362). There is an interesting alternation in Bell., 1, 81: ἡ περὶ τοῦ μίσους μεταμέλεια and Ant., 13, 314: τῆς ἀδελφοκτονίας μετάνοια. After the OT account of Saul's rejection we also find these words: μετανοεῖν ... ἔλεγε (Ant., 6, 143; δῆλος ἦν μεταμελόμενος 6, 145).

4. The only NT instances are Mt. 21:30, 32; 27:3; 2 C. 7:8 and Hb. 7:21 (quoting ψ 109:4); Pl. also uses the adj. ἀμεταμέλητος at R. 11:29 and 2 C. 7:10. μετανοεῖν and μετάνοια thus take precedence. In the parable of Jesus in Mt. 21:28-32 μεταμέλεσθαι occurs twice. The son who has rejected his father's request rues his answer and goes to work in the vineyard (μεταμεληθεὶς ἀπῆλθεν). The publicans and harlots believed John, but the high-priests and elders, who saw this, did not think better and believe him (οὐδὲ μετεμελήθητε ὕστερον τοῦ πιστεῦσαι αὐτῷ). The formulation of the reproach in 21:32 refers back to the parable (μεταμεληθείς, 21:30). The son changed his mind (not in the religious sense), but the elders of the Jewish people maintained their resistance. The reproach οὐδὲ μετεμελήθητε ὕστερον has in view the concrete rejection of the message and person of the Baptist. In Mt. 21:30, 32, then, μεταμέλεσθαι is not equivalent to μετανοεῖν.[11] When Judas saw that Jesus was condemned, he was filled with remorse (μεταμεληθείς, 27:3) and brought back the thirty pieces of silver. The reference here is to remorse, not repentance. Judas sees that his action was guilty, and he gives way under the burden. The remorse of Judas (Mt. 27:3) and of Esau (Hb. 12:17) does not have the power to overcome the destructive operation of sin. "For a Jewish conscience, however, remorse necessarily entails the duty of restoring what has been wrongfully won"[12] (cf. Lk. 19:8). In 2 C. 7:8-10 there is again a plain distinction between μεταμέλεσθαι and μετανοεῖν. Paul is not sorry that he sent a severe letter (οὐ μεταμέλομαι, 7:8). Even if it caused pain, this was according to God's will. It might be that he vacillated earlier (εἰ καὶ μετεμελόμην, 7:8), but it is now clear to him that the pain was necessary to bring the Corinthians to a change of heart (ἐλυπήθητε εἰς μετάνοιαν, 7:9). Suffering

[8] How μετάνοια and μετανοεῖν change meaning in Hell. is shown by Wnd. in his excursus, 2 K., 233 f.
[9] Cf. on this Rgg. Hb., 407-410.
[10] Schl. Theol. d. Judt., 147.
[11] Though cf. Zn. Mt., *ad loc.*
[12] Schl. Mt., 768.

which corresponds to God's will brings about a change of heart which is to salvation and which will not be rued (hence the oxymoron μετάνοια ἀμεταμέλητος, 7:10). What is of God causes no remorse. Human "repentance" is here natural reconsideration with no content of faith (μεταμέλεσθαι, 7:8), whereas real change of heart (μετάνοια, 7:9) is a divine operation in spite of and precisely in suffering. In this repentance is new salvation (7:10) and new life (7:11). In R. 11:29 Paul says that the gracious gifts (χαρίσματα) and calling (κλῆσις) of God are irrevocable (ἀμεταμέλητα). He has in view the inflexible goal that in spite of the disobedience and hardness of men God will accomplish His will to save. Similarly, the ἀμεταμέλητος of 2 C. 7:10 is sometimes linked with σωτηρία (vg *in salutem stabilem*).[13] But preference should be given to the combination μετάνοια ἀμεταμέλητος.

In Hb. 7:21 Ps. 110:4 is quoted to confirm the divinely sworn superiority of the new priesthood over the old. When God swears, He makes His own person the pledge of the truth of His Word (6:13 ff.). The institution of the eternal priest is immutable and unchangeable; hence in this negation, as in the ἀμεταμέλητος of R. 11:29, there is a reference to God's faithfulness and to the reliability of His promise. When, therefore, the NT separates the meanings of μεταμέλεσθαι and μετανοεῖν, it displays a clear awareness of the unchangeable substance of both concepts. In contrast, Hellenistic usage often effaced the boundary between the two words.

Michel

μεταμορφόομαι → μορφή.
μετανοέω, μετάνοια → νοῦς.
μεταπέμπομαι → I, 403.
μεταστρέφω → στρέφω.
μετασχηματίζω → σχῆμα.
μετατίθημι → τίθημι.
μετέχω → II, 830.

---

[13] ἀμεταμέλητος occurs also in 1 Cl., 2, 7; 54, 4; 58, 2. On its Gk. use elsewhere cf. Wnd. 2 K., 232. On ἀμετανόητος cf. A. Bonhöffer, "Epiktet u. d. NT," RVV, 10 (1911), 106 f.; Norden, 135; Jaeger, 589 f.

† μετεωρίζομαι

Act. μετεωρίζω means "to raise on high," "to exalt," or (P. Oxy., VI, 904, 6; Philo Spec. Leg., III, 152) "to suspend someone"; fig. "to raise up someone by hope," "to encourage," "to stir" (Polyb., 5, 70, 10; 25, 3, 4). In the mid. and pass. μετεωρίζω (also the adj. μετέωρος) is most common in the fig. sense. This embraces two different meanings: a. "to lift up oneself," "to soar" (of the human spirit), "to exalt oneself," "to be arrogant or proud," "to be greedy for"; b. "to be unsettled, anxious, restless, tense, excited by joy, fear or hope," "to hover between fear and hope." μετεωρίζομαι occurs in sense a. in Aristoph. Av., 1447; Polyb., 3, 82, 2 (μετέωρος ... καὶ θυμοῦ πλήρης); 16, 21, 2 (μετέωρος καὶ φιλόδοξος), and is common in Philo; μετεωρίζομαι: Philo Rer. Div. Her., 269; Leg. All., 186 (here and often in a good sense, of the νοῦς: ὁ νοῦς ἐπειδὰν μὲν ἐξάρῃ αὑτὸν ἀπὸ τῶν θνητῶν καὶ μετεωρισθῇ); Ebr., 93; Poster. C., 115; μετεωρίζω: Spec. Leg., I, 44; Rer. Div. Her., 71 (καίτοι μετεωρίζοντος καὶ φυσῶντος ἑαυτόν); Vit. Mos., I, 195; II, 139; μετέωρος: Som., II, 16; Flacc., 142; Ebr., 128.

In the LXX we find only the first fig. meaning (a.), and always in the bad sense, esp. for arrogance. μετεωρίζομαι: ψ 130:1 (οὐδὲ ἐμετεωρίσθησαν οἱ ὀφθαλμοί μου); 2 Macc. 5:17; 7:34; 3 Macc. 6:5; μετέωρος: 2 Βασ. 22:28; Is. 2:12; 5:15; μετεωρισμός: Sir. 23:4 (μετεωρισμὸν ὀφθαλμῶν); 26:9 (ἐν μετεωρισμοῖς ὀφθαλμῶν); 2 Macc. 5:21 (διὰ τὸν μετεωρισμὸν τῆς καρδίας).[1]

μετεωρίζομαι is not so common in sense b. Particularly clear is P. Oxy., XIV, 1679, 16 f.: μὴ μετεωρίζου ("do not be upset"), καλῶς διάγομεν; also Jos. Ant., 16, 135 (acc. to Niese's conjecture);[2] μετέωρος (excited, unsettled, tense): Thuc., II, 8, 1; Jos. Ant., 8, 218 (μετεώρου τοῦ λαοῦ παντὸς ὄντος); Polyb., 3, 107, 6 (τῶν δὲ συμμάχων πάντων μετεώρων ὄντων ταῖς διανοίαις, cf. 5, 70, 10: ᾧ χρησάμενος μεγαλοπρεπῶς πολλοὺς ἐμετεώρισε τῶν παρὰ τοῖς ἐναντίοις ἡγεμόνων).[3]

Because of the double meaning, it is hard to fix the sense of μετεωρίζομαι in its one NT occurrence at Lk. 12:29. The words of Jesus uttered in connection with the warning against anxiety: μὴ μετεωρίζεσθε, have in historical exegesis

---

μετεωρίζομαι. A. Harnack, *Sprüche u. Reden Jesu* (1907), 10; K. Köhler, "Textkritische Bemerkungen zu der Perikope vom Sorgen im Lk. Ev.," ThStKr, 86 (1913), 452 ff.; K. F. Euler, "Die Verkündigung vom leidenden Gottesknecht aus Js. 53 in d. griech. Bibel," BWANT, IV, 14 (1934), 97; Pass., Pr.-Bauer[3], *s.v.*

[1] Even Ez. 3:14 is no exception to the regular use of the LXX. Only if μετέωρος (in 'A etc.) corresponds to the Mas. מַר ("bitter," "sad," "displeased") could it denote the "deep depression" "which might be linked with the situation mentioned at the end of v. 15" (J. Herrmann, *Ez.* [1924], 24); in this case μετέωρος at Ez. 3:14 would have sense b. But מַר can hardly be original. More likely μετέωρος is for "רָם (part q) or מוּרָם (part ho) 'to lift up,' 'lifted up,' or at least a form of רום, for in Ez. 10:19 G has μετεωρίζεσθαι for רום qal and ni, and at 17:23 μετέωρος for מָרוֹם" (*ibid.*, 7). In Ez. 3:15 μετέωρος is put for תֵּלֵא (Mas. תֵּל אָבִיב).

[2] Zn. Lk.[3, 4] (1920), 500, n. 27.

[3] The adj. μετέωρος, common in the pap., has here the sense of "left hanging," "unfinished" (of services); Preisigke Wört., *s.v.*

been taken in both the figurative senses:[4] a. "Do not be arrogant in your claims," "do not fly high" (Luther), "do not set your mind on high things," or b. "Do not be upset," "do not worry," "do not excite yourselves," "do not vacillate between fear and hope." The weight of the LXX passages and the Vulgate rendering (*nolite in sublime tolli*) have usually been regarded as decisive, and certainly merit consideration. On the other hand, the oldest versions take μὴ μετεωρίζεσθε in the other sense, e.g., the Old Latin (*nolite solliciti esse*), also the Peshitto;[5] the Latin text of Cod. D also has *abalienatis vos*. If these are strong supports for the second sense, the context inclines decisively in this direction. The warning against arrogance and the exhortation to moderation are certainly a constituent part of early Christian exhortation. Reference may rightly be made to R. 12:16 or 1 Tm. 6:17 ff. Inner humility and perfect contentment at the gift of God — this is the positive side of the demand — are certainly an attitude which is grounded in Jesus Himself and which characterised the first disciples. Nevertheless, the context points to a different understanding. The words of Jesus from v. 22 on unfold the full greatness of the goodness of God as Creator, the lavishness of His gifts, which ought to deflect us from the anxious concern, the "little faith" (v. 28), in which man constantly tries to secure his own existence. At the same time, attention is directed to the final gift, the "dominion" of God, which is quite sure for the Christian, and which completely drives out all fear (v. 32). In this context, the only admonition which makes sense is that we be not anxious, unsettled or insecure, since God guarantees all gifts, even those of the last time. Hence the passage with its admonition: μὴ μετεωρίζεσθε, is a witness to the fact that the eschatological attitude of the first Christians kept them from torturing anxiety and unsettlement. This view is confirmed in, e.g., Phil. 4:4-7, where the dawn of the age of joy overthrows the restless cares associated with human thought, because with it the peace which passes all understanding is granted to the Christian.

Deissner

μέτοχος, μετοχή → II, 830.

μετριοπαθέω → πάσχω.

---

[4] For an account of the different views *v.* Köhler, 454 ff.

[5] A. Merx, *Die vier kanon. Evv.*, II, 2: *Das Ev. Mk. u. Lk.* (1905), 302; Köhler, 456.

† μέτρον, † ἄμετρος, † μετρέω

1. The Word Group outside the NT.

μέτρον (from Hom.: Il., 7, 471; 12, 422; Od., 2, 355; 9, 209 etc.) means a. "measure" as an instrument of measuring (whether cubic or of length); b. "proportion," "order" (common in the class. poets, also the pap.); [1] c. "measure of verse or syllables"; d. "what is measured as the result of measuring," "the measured part" (place, road, time), both literally and figuratively.

The term μέτρον became particularly significant in Gk. philosophy. The μέτρον πάντων, the abs. measure of all things, esp. of values, was set by Protagoras exclusively in men: πάντων χρημάτων μέτρον ἐστὶν ἄνθρωπος, τῶν μὲν ὄντων ὡς ἔστιν, τῶν δὲ οὐκ ὄντων ὡς οὐκ ἔστιν (Fr., 1 [II, 263, 3 ff., Diels[5]]). In contrast, Plato finds it only in God (Leg., IV, 716c: ὁ δὴ θεὸς ἡμῖν πάντων χρημάτων μέτρον ἂν εἴη μάλιστα, καὶ πολὺ μᾶλλον ἤ πού τις, ὥς φασιν, ἄνθρωπος). This thought is particularly important in Neo-Platonism: Plot. Enn., I, 8, 3; cf. VI, 8, 18: περίληψις πάντων καὶ μέτρον; V, 5, 4: μέτρον γὰρ αὐτὸ καὶ οὐ μετρούμενον.

In the LXX μέτρον is mostly used for מִדָּה, apart from some secular refs.: 1. with ref. to the cultic measurements of the tabernacle and temple, esp. Ez. 40-48; 2. of correct measures and weights which stand under God's protection and are superintended in the temple, Lv. 19:35; Dt. 25:14 f.; Prv. 20:10; Am. 8:5; 1 Ch. 23:29; 3. of the measures of the world as an expression of the belief in creation: Job 11:9; 28:25; 38:5; Wis. 11:20; 4. in threats of destruction and judgment sayings: 4 Βασ. 21:13; Is. 5:10; Ez. 4:11, 16; Lam. 2:8; ψ 79:5; Zech. 5:6 ff.; 5. in the salvation saying in Zech. 1:16.

μετρέω (at least from Hom.: Od., 3, 179) means a. "to measure," "to traverse" (the sea); fig. "to evaluate," "to judge"; b. in the phrase τινί τι, "to measure something to someone" (from Eur. and Aristoph.). In the LXX μετρέω is used for מָדַד, e.g., Ex. 16:18. It is found in the pap. [2]

2. The Word Group in the NT.

In the NT μέτρον is used several times in the Gospels in sense a., e.g., in the prohibition of judging, Mt. 7:2: ἐν ᾧ μέτρῳ μετρεῖτε μετρηθήσεται ὑμῖν (cf. Mk. 4:24 and Lk. 6:38b: ᾧ γὰρ μέτρῳ μετρεῖτε ἀντιμετρηθήσεται ὑμῖν; here in Lk. in a more comprehensive sense than in Mt., → 634); Lk. 6:38a: μέτρον καλὸν πεπιεσμένον σεσαλευμένον ὑπερεκχυννόμενον, "a good (abundant) measure, pressed down, shaken, overflowing"; Jn. 3:34: οὐ γὰρ ἐκ μέτρου δίδωσιν τὸ πνεῦμα (→ 634); Mt. 23:32: πληρώσετε (not πληρώσατε) τὸ μέτρον τῶν πατέρων ὑμῶν, "you will fill up the measure of sin which the fathers have not yet filled up"; also Rev. 21:15, 17, here specifically of length, v. 17: μέτρον ἀνθρώπου, ὅ ἐστιν ἀγγέλου, "measure of a man, which is that of the angel."

μέτρον κτλ. Pass., Pape, Pr.-Bauer[3], Liddell-Scott, Preisigke Wört., *s.v.*; Kl. Mt., 65; Schl. Mt., 241; Str.-B., I, 444-446; Bau. J.[3] (1933), 64 f.; Schl. J., 110 f.; Str.-B., II, 431; Zn. J.[5, 6] (1921), 227 ff.; K. Bornhäuser, *Die Bergpredigt*[2] (1927), 187 ff.

[1] Preisigke Wört., *s.v.*

[2] *Loc. cit.*

Senses b. and c. do not occur in the NT, but d. (fig.) is common, R. 12:3: ἑκάστῳ ὡς ὁ θεὸς ἐμέρισεν μέτρον πίστεως, "each as God has given him the measure of faith"; 2 C. 10:13: ἡμεῖς δὲ οὐκ εἰς τὰ ἄμετρα καυχησόμεθα, ἀλλὰ κατὰ τὸ μέτρον τοῦ κανόνος οὗ ἐμέρισεν ἡμῖν ὁ θεὸς μέτρου, "we would not boast beyond measure, but acc. to the measure of the territory which God has assigned to us as a measure"; Eph. 4:7: ἑνὶ δὲ ἑκάστῳ ἡμῶν ἐδόθη ἡ χάρις κατὰ τὸ μέτρον τῆς δωρεᾶς τοῦ Χριστοῦ, "to each of us was grace given acc. to the measure as Christ granted it to him"; Eph. 4:13: μέχρι καταντήσωμεν οἱ πάντες ... εἰς ἄνδρα τέλειον, εἰς μέτρον ἡλικίας τοῦ πληρώματος τοῦ Χριστοῦ, "until we all come ... to a perfect man, to the measure of the age of maturity of Christ"[3] (cf. the expression ἥβης μέτρον ἱκνέομαι in Hom. Il., 11, 225; Od., 11, 317; 18, 217; 19, 532: "to reach the full measure of youth," i.e., the maturity of youth); Eph. 4:16: κατ' ἐνέργειαν ἐν μέτρῳ ἑνὸς ἑκάστου μέρους, "acc. to the power which corresponds to the measure of each part."

ἄμετρος, "without measure," "immeasurable," "incommensurable," "immoderate," "extravagant," in the latter sense twice in the NT at 2 C. 10:13 (→ *supra*), 15 in rejection of immoderate boasting.

μετρέω occurs in the NT in sense a. in Rev. 11:1, to measure the temple of God; 11:2: not to measure the outer court; 21:15, 16, 17, to measure the city, its gates and walls.

A fig. use of a. is found in 2 C. 10:12: αὐτοὶ ἐν ἑαυτοῖς ἑαυτοὺς μετροῦντες, "they measure themselves by themselves, i.e., by human, self-established measures, I by the measure which God has given me."[4]

Sense b. applies in the verses mentioned already under μέτρον (→ 632), namely, Mt. 7:2 and Mk. 4:24 (Lk. 6:38b has the compound ἀντιμετρηθήσεται instead of μετρηθήσεται).

The passages which characterise the NT use of μέτρον and μετρέω refer a. to the judicial work of God in the Last Judgment and b. to the gift of grace allotted to us.

a. In the proverbial expression ἐν ᾧ μέτρῳ μετρεῖτε μετρηθήσεται ὑμῖν in Mt. 7:2 (cf. Mk. 4:24 and Lk. 6:38b) there comes to full expression the eschatological seriousness with which Jesus establishes the μὴ κρίνετε by reference to the divine judgment corresponding to human judging. The rule finds in Rabbinic writings many parallels in wording or meaning; in Sota, 1, 7 it runs: בְּמִדָּה שֶׁאָדָם מוֹדֵד בָּהּ מוֹדְדִין לוֹ, "with the measure with which a man measures, one (i.e., God) will measure to him."[5] Nevertheless, in the application of the norm there is a fundamental difference between Jesus and the Rabbis. With the help of this rule the latter establish and regulate human judging; Jesus, however, rejects all judging, and His prohibition is absolute: μὴ κρίνετε. "The reason for this contradictory use of the same principle is that Jesus did not see the one and

---

[3] Cf. Pr.-Bauer[3], *s.v.*

[4] Ltzm. K., *ad loc.*

[5] Cf. the material in Str.-B., I, 444 ff. and Schl. Mt., 241. Str.-B. adduces examples of the shorter formula "measure for measure" and an equivalent proverb: "In the pot in which a man cooks he will be cooked." Cf. also the ref. of Str.-B. to Wis. 11:15 f.; 12:24 f.; 18:4 ff. In view of this material the saying from Hes. which sounds like Mt. 7:2 and to which G. Heinrici draws attention (*Beiträge z. Gesch. u. Erklärung des NT,* III [1905], 81), as to other sayings from Sen., Epict. etc., is of little significance. Since we have in the words ἐν ᾧ μέτρῳ κτλ. a common proverbial expression designed to support the μὴ κρίνετε, Bornhäuser's understanding of the verse (187 ff.) in terms of the two measures of God, that of goodness and that of justice, is not very pertinent.

ultimate will of God in the norm which demands retribution."[6] The reverse side of κρίνειν is forgiveness, which Jesus requires of His disciples in view of God's readiness to forgive.

At the end of a series of sayings in which the positive duty of exercising forgiveness is set in juxtaposition with the prohibition of judging, Lk. 6:38b has the words: ᾧ γὰρ μέτρῳ μετρεῖτε ἀντιμετρηθήσεται ὑμῖν. These seem first to be the basis of the divine reward which is certain for those who show mercy. But they should not be related only to v. 38a. They refer to the whole group of sayings, including the μὴ κρίνετε κτλ. of v. 37. This solves the difficulty which seems to be presented by the fact that in the preceding words: μέτρον καλὸν πεπιεσμένον κτλ. (v. 38a), emphasis is laid on the superabundant reward of God, whereas the saying: ᾧ γὰρ μέτρῳ κτλ. stresses "the quantitative equivalence of retribution."[7] The form of the text in Mt. and Mk. is more original than that in Lk.[8]

b. But the figure of the μέτρον is also used to express the diversity and manifoldness of the gifts of grace allotted to each man, Eph. 4:7 (with emphasis on the ἑνότης, as in 1 C. 12);[9] Eph. 4:16; R. 12:3. To show what is the one final goal of the members of the community — the goal which the various gifts must serve — μέτρον is then used in the sense of full measure in Eph. 4:13 (→ 633). In 2 C. 10:13, in contrast to the unmeasured boasting of his opponents in Corinth, the measure by which Paul would be measured is the sphere of missionary activity which God has assigned to him as an apostle. This measure is not human; it is indicated by God.

If it is true of all the gifts of Christians that they have a measure and limit, Christ Himself has received the gift of the Spirit from God without measure or restriction. This is the meaning of Jn. 3:34: οὐ γὰρ ἐκ μέτρου δίδωσιν τὸ πνεῦμα.[10] Although the present δίδωσιν might lead us to take the statement as a general rule, the context shows that it refers only to Christ, and according to the context again God alone can be the subject.[11] This is shown plainly both by what precedes (v. 34a) and what follows (v. 35).

c. μετρέω has a distinctive sense in Rev. 11:1 f. In this vision, which is influenced by Ez. 40:3 ff., μετρέω in v. 1, considered along with v. 2, takes on the sense "to preserve."[12] The temple of God is to be measured, i.e., preserved, but the outer court, which is not to be measured, will not be preserved.

Deissner

---

[6] Schl. Mt., 241.

[7] As against B. Weiss, *Die Ev. des Mk. u. Lk.*[9] (1901), *ad loc.*, who sees incongruity here.

[8] Cf. Schl. Lk., 246: "The minor Hellenising, the dropping of the ἐν and the adding of ἀντί to the verb, are to be ascribed to Lk."

[9] Cf. Dib. Gefbr., *ad loc.*

[10] οὐκ ἐκ μέτρου, not yet attested in Gk. (Pr.-Bauer[3], *s.v.* and Bau. J.[3], 64 f.), means "not on the basis of a (restricting) measure," hence without measure or restriction; cf. also Schl. J., 110 f. The opp. would be ἐν μέτρῳ (Ez. 4:11, 16; Jdt. 7:21), Bau. J.[3], 65.

[11] As against Zahn (J., 227 ff.), who takes the statement to be a general rule which applies "only to the prophets, including the Baptist, not to Jesus," and who thinks τὸ πνεῦμα is the subject. On our view, the distinction between Christ and all other prophets is emphasised, for they have the Spirit only ἐκ μέτρου; cf. on this Str.-B., II, 431, which quotes the saying of R. Acha in Lv. r., 15 on 13:2: "The Holy Ghost himself, who rests on the prophets, rests (on them) only by weight (במשקל, measure); one of them prophesied one book, another (like Jer.) two."

[12] Cf. Loh. and Had. Apk., *ad loc.*

† μέτωπον

From μετά + ὤψ, this means strictly the part of the forehead between the eyes, but mostly the whole forehead. It is commonly used of men in Hom.: Il., 4, 460; 6, 10; 13, 615 (in the original sense); 15, 102; 16, 798; Od., 6, 107; 22, 86. 94. 296; of animals, Il., 23, 454; then generally for the human forehead. We find the expressions ἀνασπᾶν and χαλᾶν τὸ μέτωπον, "to knit and smooth the brow," Aristoph. Eq., 631; Vesp., 655. Of animals, Soph. El., 727; Eur. Hel., 1568; Rhes., 307; Xenoph. Cyrop., I, 4, 8; a mountain as γαίας μέτωπον, Pind. Pyth., 1, 30 f.; fig. "front of a helmet," Hom. Il., 16, 70; front of a building, or front gen., Hdt., I, 178; II, 124 (pyramid); IX, 15; Thuc., III, 21; common on inscr.; front or frontal array of an army: Aesch. Pers., 720; Xenoph. Cyrop., II, 4, 2; Hist. Graec., II, 1, 23; Polyb., 1, 33, 6; 3, 65, 5; 5, 82, 10.

In the LXX it is used for מֵצַח, Ex. 28:38; 1 Βασ. 17:49; 2 Ch. 26:19 f.; Is. 48:4; Ez. 9:4, always of the human brow. In Θ, however, it occurs also at Ex. 28:25 for the front of the ephod (מוּל פָּנִים), and in Σ at Jer. 9:25 for border (פֵּאָה).

In the NT it is found only in Rev. in three different connections.

1. The servants of God bear on their foreheads the seal (→ σφραγίς) of God, the name of Christ and God (→ ὄνομα). This protects them against divine judgment, against the apocalyptic plagues, Rev. 7:3; 9:4; 14:1; 22:4.

2. In contrast the enemies of God allow the → χάραγμα of the beast, the mysterious number which contains his name, to be stamped on their forehead and one hand.[1] This gives them great opportunities of economic and commercial advance, but brings them under the wrath of God and excludes them from the millennial kingdom, Rev. 13:16; 14:9; 20:4.

This metaphor, which brings out sharply the externally recognisable distinction between the saved and the lost, and their adherence to two opposing rulers,[2] has three roots. a. There would obviously seem to be a direct allusion to Ez. 9:4: Those who do not take part in idolatry in Jerusalem have ת marked on their foreheads by an angel. The Old Heb. ת is in the form of a cross; it is thus the form of cruciform σφραγίς

μέτωπον. Pr.-Bauer, 811; ^{3}, 853 f.; Liddell-Scott, 1123; Wilke-Grimm, 283; W. Foerster, "Die Bilder in Offenbarung 12 f. und 17 f.," ThStKr, 104 (1932), 279 ff.; Deissmann LO, 289 f.; J. Behm, *Gott u. d. Geschichte* (1925), 7 ff.; R. Schütz, *Die Offenbarung des Joh. u. Kaiser Domitian* (1933), 53 ff.; B. Stade, "Das Kainszeichen," ZAW, 14 (1894), 250 ff.; Deissmann B., 262 ff.; A. Hug, Art. Στιγματίας in Pauly-W., *2. Reihe,* III (1929), 2520 ff.; C. Lécrivain, Art. "Stigma" in Daremberg-Saglio, IV, 2, 1510; R. Herzog, *Die Wunderheilungen von Epidauros* (1931), 133 f.; C. Schneider, *Die Erlebnisechtheit der Apk. des Joh.* (1930), 62 f.

1 The right hand is mentioned only in 13:16. There are as yet no certain instances of marking on both the forehead and the hand except in the case of the tephillin. This supports the allusion conjectured under a.

2 Schütz, 56 rightly stresses the difference between sealing and stamping. But possibly σφραγίς is chosen for Christians only because it was a tt. in the mysteries and on the basis of expressions like 2 C. 1:22; Eph. 1:13; 4:30. It is not certain, but not impossible, that there is also a hint of baptism as in Herm. s., 8, 6, 3; 9, 16 f.; 2 Cl., 7, 6; 8, 6.

which can be most easily inscribed and which is attested also of Isis (→ n. 10). Whether there is any connection with the mark of Cain is more than doubtful. [3] We do best to think of the passover sign before the Exodus (Ex. 12:13), where those marked are also spared a plague. [4] As regards the sign of the beast, all three passages seem fairly clearly to refer to the tephillin, since both forehead and hand are mentioned. [5] If this is so, it would support a certain anti-Jewish trend in Rev., and the meaning of Rev. 13:16 is that he who does not bear the tephillin will be boycotted by the Jews. It has been suggested that in the days of Rev. one of the forces behind persecution was Jewish influence at the imperial court from the days of Nero. [6] b. In the Hell. religions a mark on the forehead was either a sign of adherence to a god or an amulet. The Egyptian gods have their hieroglyphics on the forehead. [7] This can then be transferred to the priest, who either wears the mask of the god [8] or his head-piece. [9] The cruciform σφραγίς [10] on the forehead of the priests of Isis is to be regarded as a sign of adherence, and acc. to Tert. Praescr. Haer., 40, 4 Mithras marks *in frontibus milites suos*. We find amulets with pictures of the cultic gods on the foreheads of the priests of Attis-Cybele. [11] Both senses have a bearing on the signs of Rev., which were cruciform in the case of believers. Adherence is specifically emphasised in Rev. 22:4, the apotropaic aspect in 7:3 and 9:4. [12] c. It is obvious that both author and readers of Rev. must have seen similar marks on slaves. The branding of letters — rarely more than 1 to 3 — on the foreheads of slaves [13] was usually a punishment for running away or other offences; [14] a delightful inscr. from Epidauros tells how Aesculapius removed a brand by charming it onto a bandage. [15] Constantly in the pap. we hear of people with an οὐλή on the right, left,

---

[3] So Stade. But cf. also Ex. 13:9, 16; Is. 44:5, and esp. the sign of the prophet in 1 K. 20:38, 41. Cf. J. Herrmann, *Ezechiel* (1924) on 9:4.

[4] Yet it is not certain that the original OT ref. is to the form of the sign ת. [Bertram regards this as perhaps a Christian view. He points out that 'Α and Θ are the first to refer Ez. 9:4 to the Gk. T, and refers also to Barn., 9, 8 and A. Jeremias, *Das AT im Lichte d. alten Orients*³ (1916), 624.]

[5] It is by no means certain that in NT times the tephillin were usually on the left arm. The oldest refs. in Ep. Ar., 159; Jos. Ant., 4, 213 do not say so, nor does the OT. It is first assumed only in Tg. J., I, Ex. 13:9, 16; Dt. 6:8; 11:18 (not Tg. O.), but one can see from M. Ex., 13, 9 that even in Tannaitic times it was seen that the left arm was chosen only for practical reasons, the right being needed to tie the thongs. On this whole question cf. Str.-B., IV, Exc. 11, pp. 250 ff.

[6] P. Corssen, "Die Zeugnisse des Tac. u. Ps.-Joseph. über Christus," ZNW, 15 (1914), 138 ff.

[7] There any many examples in Haas, 2/4, Bonnet (1924).

[8] Cf. the Anubis mask in the Pelizäus museum in Hildesheim, Bonnet, 144.

[9] It is thus uncertain whether almost all Hell. statues of Isis and many depictions of Dionysus represent the deity, the priest, or the believer. Only in clear portraits or labelled works can one infer transfer mysticism.

[10] Cf. W. Helbig, *Führer durch die öffentlichen Sammlungen klass. Altertümer in Rom*³, I (1912), 827; Haas, 9/11, Leipoldt (1926), 49.

[11] Leipoldt, 150.

[12] P. L. Couchoud, *L'Apocalypse* (1930), 140. From Ez. 9:4 and this passage arose the apotropaic custom of crossing, perhaps preceded by the scratching of a cross on the forehead, Cyr. Cat., XIII, 3. 36 (MPG, 33, p. 773b f., 816a f.); Jerome on Ez. 9:4; Tert. De corona militis, 3; Marc., 3, 22; Lact. Epitome, 46; Aug. in Joh.-Ev. Tract., 11, 3; Prud. Contra Symmachum, II, 712 f.; cf. also F. J. Dölger, *Sphragis* (1911), *passim*.

[13] Sometimes also soldiers (Hug, 2521), whence the custom in Mithraism, though as a sign of adherence not a punishment, or perhaps a test of bravery.

[14] For marks on the foreheads of slaves, prisoners or criminals cf. Herond. Mim., V, 63-79; Plat. Leg., IX, 854 f.; Petronius (ed. F. Buecheler⁶ [1922]), 102 ff.; Aristoph. Av., 760; P. Lille, 29, II, 36; Aeschin. Or., 2, 79; Ael. Var. Hist., II, 9; Diphilos in Athen., VI, 6 (p. 225); Luc. Tim., 17; Diog. L., IV, 7 (46); Plut. Pericl., 26 (I, 166d); Poll. Onom., III, 78 f.; Quint. Inst. Orat., VI, 4, 14; Apul. Met., IX, 12; Sen. De Ira, III, 3, 6; Mart., III, 21.

[15] Ditt. Syll.³, III, 1168, 48 ff.

or centre of the forehead.[16] Freed slaves tried to hide this mark of shame by every possible means, e.g., the cut of the hair. It may be that there is some sense of this in Rev. Those who are branded by God are an offence in this world.

3. In Rev. 17:5 the harlot, who personifies all worldly abominations, whether concretely as Rome or abstractly as a demonic power, bears on her forehead the mark of her true nature in a mysterious allusion to Babylon.[17]

The basis is the modish custom of Roman harlots, who had their names on bands round their foreheads.[18] The divine must have seen this.[19]

Carl Schneider

† μηλωτή

Though not common,[1] this word is used in Gk. lit. (Apollon. Dyscol. Synt., 191, 9) and is found in Ditt. Or., 629, 32; P. Tebt., 38, 22, also the LXX (3 Βασ. 19:13, 19; 4 Βασ. 2:8, 13 f. = אַדֶּרֶת) in the sense of "sheep's skin."[2] On the basis of the biblical tradition acc. to which Elijah wore a hairy coat, it then occurs in Hb. 11:37 and the account in 1 Cl., 17, 1 based on it, also in patristic lit. (Cl. Al. Strom., III, 6, 53, 5; IV, 17, 105, 4; Paed., II, 10, 112). If Elijah was a hairy man (אִישׁ בַּעַל שֵׂעָר), as described in 2 K. 1:8, and if prophets wore a hairy cloak (אַדֶּרֶת שֵׂעָר) as in Zech. 13:4, one may assume that the μηλωτή was a kind of prophetic garb. Hb. 11:37 distinguishes between the skins of sheep and goats, but we are to think in terms of the raw, undressed skins with their wool and hairs, not of garments manufactured from the hairs.[3]

Hb. obviously sees in this striking dress of the prophets an indication of their antithesis to the world, of their need and affliction, of their lonely life in the desert and mountains. There is a self-evident link with the clothing of the Baptist (Mk. 1:6: ἐνδεδυμένος τρίχας καμήλου), and a later age associates the skins of sheep and goats and clothes of camel's hair as the prophetic garb (e.g., Cl. Al., *loc. cit.*).

---

[16] P. Amh., 111, 8 f.; 112, 26; BGU, I, 183, 26 f.; 196, 9; 197, 8; 232, 5; 251, 2; 252, 12; 290, 7 f.; 297, 23; 339, 6 f.; 350, 3; II, 454, 22; 526, 26; 644, 11; III, 713, 13; 854, 9; 856, 8. 11; 901, 8; 910, 18; 911, 5 ff.; 975, 8 f.; IV, 1013, 6 f. etc.

[17] Cf. also Gl. 6:17 in this connection.

[18] Juv., VI, 122 f.; Sen. Rhet. Contr., I, 2, 7.

[19] Visionaries see "important personal impartations ... in bright phosphorescent writing," cf. W. Mayer-Gross, "Psychopathologie u. Klinik der Trugwahrnehmungen," O. Bumke, *Handbuch der Geisteskrankheiten*, I (1928), 449.

μηλωτή. [1] Liddell-Scott, 1127.

[2] For bibl. cf. F. Bleek, *Der Brief an d. Hebräer*, II, 2 (1840), 839 f.; on the use of the word Bleek writes on 840: "μηλωτή seems to have been little used by the Gks. Acc. to Poll. it was found in the comedian Philemon (in the 3rd cent. B.C.), but neither in Stephanus nor elsewhere have I found any other instance in Gk. authors." Cf. Liddell-Scott, 1127.

[3] Etym. M. defines μηλωτή as προβάτειος δορά, Poll. Onom., X, 176 as ἡ τοῦ προβάτου δορά, Theophylactus in Hb. 11:37 (MPG, 125, p. 365a) says similarly: μηλωτὴ δὲ, τὸ τοῦ μήλου, ἤτοι τοῦ προβάτου δέρμα.

In later ecclesiastical accounts of the life and clothing of monks *melotes* is explained to be *pellis caprina.* [4]

Michel

† μήν, † νεομηνία

1. In non-biblical use μήν originally means the moon as a measure of time (root *mē,* related to *metiri* and "measure"), [1] then the portion of time marked off by the moon, the "month." [2] This begins originally with the new moon (in Greece too); hence the number of months is not the same in all years. Only with the reform of the calendar under Solon (Plut. Solon, 25 [I, 92c]) was this changed. With the other heavenly bodies, the moon was created that "there might be time" (Plat. Tim., 38c). It goes round the earth in the sphere nearest to it (38d). Its course embraces a month (39c). Its progress has helped to give man the concept of number and time (47a).

The new moon (νεομηνία) first denotes the beginning of the month, but it soon takes on religious significance through the powers attributed to the moon. Among the beneficial effects of the moon Philo (Spec. Leg., II, 143 etc.) enumerates the swelling of the waters and the growing and ripening of seeds and trees. The fact that Philo shares these common views shows that they are not just magical ideas. In Preis. Zaub., IV, 2554 f. it is said of the moon (cf. 2441) that it begets everything in the earth and sea. [3] Thus it confers life and happiness, and gives particular force to magic (cf., *ibid.,* III, 338 and 416). The idea of fruitful effects is obviously linked with the dew, which is attributed to it (cf. Apul. Met., XI, 2 : *u[n]dis ignibus nutriens laeta semina,* of Isis, who is equated with the moon).

It is no wonder that the new moon is joyfully hailed as the time when its beneficial operations begin afresh. [4] Those born at the new moon are naturally regarded as lucky, and are given the name Νουμήνιος or Νουμῆνις, child of the new moon (e.g., IG, VII, 559; 1556; 3197, 8; 3220; BGU, IV, 1206, 5; 1207, 8; P. Oxy., IV, 715, 22). [5] For

---

[4] Cassian, De Institutis Coenobiorum, I, 7 (CSEL, 17, 1888): *Ultimum est habitus eorum pellis caprina, quae melotis* (GH; *melotes* Lv) *vel pera appellatur, et baculus, quae gestant ad imitationem eorum, qui professionis huius praefiguravere lineas iam in veteri testamento* (quoting Hb. 11:37, 38 and expounding *pellis caprina*). Isidore of Seville, Etymologiarum, XIX, 24 (MPL, 82, p. 691b): *melotes, quae etiam pera vocatur, pellis est caprina, a collo pendens, praecincta usque ad lumbos. Est autem habitus proprie necessarius ad operis exercitium. Fiebat autem prius, ut quidam aestimant, de pelliculis melonum. Unde et melotae vocatae sunt.* Cf. also the Regula Pachomii (ed. B. Albers, 1923).

μ ή ν κ τ λ. F. Ginzel, *Handbuch d. mathematischen u. technischen Chronologie* (1911), II, 36 ff., 315 ff.; W. Sontheimer, Pauly-W., XVI, 1 (1933), 44 ff.; Lesky, PaulyW., XV, 1 (1931), 689-697; more expressly, W. Drexler, Roscher, II, 2, 2687-2770; W. Baudissin, RE³, XIII, 337 ff.; P. Fiebig, Rosch haschana. Giess. Mischna, II, 8 (1914), esp. 13-31; Henle, "Der Men- und Mithrakult in Phrygien," Theol. Quart., 70 (1888), 590-614.

[1] Cf. Boisacq³ (1938), 633; Walde-Pok., II, 271 f.

[2] On the reckoning or division of the month cf. Sontheimer. The twofold meaning "moon" or "month" is already early Indo-European [Debrunner].

[3] On the moon and life in Babylonian astral religion cf. Chant. de la Saussaye, I, 508 f.

[4] Διὰ μὲν δὴ ταῦτα ... νουμηνία τετίμηται καὶ τάξιν ἔλαχε τὴν ἐν ταῖς ἑορταῖς, Philo Spec. Leg., II, 144. Cf. the Babyl. religion, Chant. de la Saussaye, I, 546 f.

[5] Cf. Benchodeš in the Canaanite or Syro-Phoenician cult, from which Chant. de la Saussaye derives the festal character of the day of the new moon.

these reasons the moon is paid divine honours,[6] under the name Μήν. Votive inscr. to Μήν are found in Attica from at least the 3rd cent. B.C. (IG, II, 3, 1587. 1593; III, 1, 140. 73 f.). The cult came into Asia Minor, where it was often important (cf. Strabo, XII, 3, 31, p. 557) and is much attested, e.g., in Galatia.[7] In the age of religious syncretism it naturally mingled and was equated with other deities, e.g., Attis[8] and Adonis (Orph. Fr. [Kern], 201). The Orphics try to systematise here by speaking of spheres of influence in the cosmos and allotting that of the moon to Attis or Adonis. In this connection Μήν is always the moon. The division of time is deified only in philosophical discussions which are not important here.[9]

In acc. with its religious significance the new moon is celebrated from the time of Hom. (Od., 20, 156 and 276-8), later with special offerings and meals (Porphyr. Abst., II, 16). The sickle of the new moon is usually a symbol of mounting life. We find it almost everywhere in ancient religion outside class. Greece. It is found in Babylon,[10] also in depictions of Mithras.[11] The devotees of Isis carry it,[12] and the horns of the goddess herself later resemble it.[13] Not Selene alone is βαριδοῦχος (Preis. Zaub., IV, 2274).[14]

In the philosophical discussions of the Stoa the popular view is adapted. The moon is a goddess (v. Arnim, II, p. 315, 22 f.)[15] in the sense of an ensouled natural force. Chrysipp. takes this to mean that the universal soul reigns in it, i.e., the world principle as the force of the cosmos (*ibid.,* 25 ff.; cf. also Cic. Nat. Deor., I, 36). The unity of the forces permeating all things is also maintained by the Orphics with express mention of the moon (Ps.-Aristot. Mund., 7, p. 401a, 12 ff.). In the popular belief here transmuted by Stoic or Orphic theology the moon (like other heavenly bodies) is naturally regarded as an independent and personal force with which there may be links by prayer and magic.

Finally, it should be mentioned that the moon is a transitory station for souls on their way to earth and away from it (Sext. Emp. Math., IX, 71-74).[16] The idea is palpably old,[17] but not originally Gk. It can easily be merged with the concept of transmigration found among the Pythagoreans and Orphics.[18]

2. In the LXX μήν and νουμηνία are used predominantly for חֹדֶשׁ. This denotes the month or the beginning of the month, though a more exact designation may be used for the latter (the first or beginning of the month). Cf. רֹאשׁ in Nu. 28:11 with its list of the festal offerings to be brought on this day, and Nu. 10:10, where the festival of the new moon is mentioned among the feasts, and given emphasis by the use of wind instruments. One goes to the prophet on the new moon as a holy day, 4 Βασ. 4:23; here the day is set alongside the sabbath, cf. also 2 Ch. 2:3; 31:3; 1 Ch. 23:31; Neh. 10:34 (33); Hos. 2:13(11); Is. 1:13; 2 Εσδρ. 3:5. The many examples show that (contrary to

---

[6] Only a few examples can be given here, cf. Roscher, *s.v.* "Selene"; C. F. H. Bruchmann, Epitheta Deorum (1893), *s.v.* Σελήνη; also μήν.

[7] Drexler, 2690-2733; by accident there is no instance from Colossae.

[8] On the name Menotyrannus etc. cf. H. Hepding, "Attis," RVV, 1 (1903), 208 f., 86 f. On the new moon in Syria cf. Chant. de la Saussaye, I, 628.

[9] In Proclus. For examples cf. Drexler, 2688 f.

[10] Chant. de la Saussaye, I, 523 and 546.

[11] Hepding, 208 f., n. 8.

[12] Haas, 9/11, Leipoldt (1926), 52.

[13] *Ibid.,* 23 and 37; on the equation of Isis and the moon, Apul. Met., XI, 2.

[14] The term means "holder of the boat," and it is worth noting that the first part is Egyptian, βᾶρις = "skiff." The motif is present in altered form in depictions of Mary.

[15] Cf. on this idea F. Cumont, *Astrology and Religion among the Greeks and Romans* (1912), 39 f.

[16] Cf. K. Reinhardt, *Kosmos u. Sympathie* (1926), 308 ff.

[17] Cumont, 175.

[18] Cf. *ibid.,* 196 f.

many conjectures) the day was always of religious importance. In ψ 80:3 it is emphasised as εὔσημος ἡμέρα ἑορτῆς ἡμῶν. The praying community naturally assembles for the prescribed offerings of the feast (Ez. 46:3, 6 f.). Philo gives an allegorical exposition of the number of offerings on the day of the new moon (Spec. Leg., I, 177 f.), and he offers a philosophical and moral rationale for keeping the day (II, 140-142).

The new moon festival maintained its importance in the Jewish cultus up to NT times.[19] The time was not set by astronomical calculations but by observation (bRH, 20a).[20] A great part of the tractate RH is devoted to the procedures for the establishment of the new year by witnesses. The lengthy discussion is understandable when we consider the decisive significance which the more legalistic Judaism of a later period attached to exact observance of the feasts. Thus the original marking of the beginning of the feast by fire signals was no longer enough (2, 2). It was demanded that (in unfavourable weather) as many witnesses as possible should report the appearance of the sickle to the appropriate authorities (1, 6), and a careful system of questioning was worked out (2, 6). The new moon was then consecrated by the chairman of the commission (2, 7; 3, 1) and made known to the community by the notes of wind instruments (4, 1; cf. bRH, 30a). In a special prayer for the day the moon in its renewal then becomes a symbol of the resurrection (bSanh., 42a).

The OT expressly forbids veneration of the moon (Dt. 4:19). This is punished with death (Dt. 17:3 ff.). The severity is necessary because of the danger of influence by the moon cult in the non-Israelite world around (Ju. 8:21, 26).[21] This could at times make its way into the national religion (2 K. 23:5), and even the righteous who repudiated it could feel its sensual and aesthetic attraction (Job 31:26 f.). For them, however, the moon was only a measure of time (Ps. 104:19), and if there are references to a rule of the moon (Ps. 136:9; Gn. 1:16), it is understood quite plainly that this is given it by the one God.

3. The New Testament.

μήν is found in the NT a. in measurements of time in connection with the birth of Moses (Ac. 7:20), of the Baptist (Lk. 1:24,[22] 26, 36) and of Jesus (Lk. 1:56).[23] There is a corresponding use in the account of Paul's visits and work in Ac. 18:11; 19:8; 20:3; 28:11. It is also used in historical presentation in Lk. 4:25; Jm. 5:17.[24]

A distinctive mark of the reporting in the historical books of the NT is that no months are mentioned in Mt., Mk. or Jn., whether to date an event by its day or month in the year or to fix the time between events. Lk. shows a more lively interest in dating in Ac. (→ *supra*), and he was probably concerned about it in

[19] Cf. Fiebig. Liturgically cf. I. Elbogen, *Der jüd. Gottesdienst*³ (1931), 140 ff. (122 ff. for the service on the days of the new moon) [R. Meyer].

[20] Cf. also Islam, Chant. de la Saussaye, I, 712.

[21] We find there amulets in the form of the moon (LXX μηνίσκος), also as ornaments in Is. 3:18. Cf. Preisigke Wört., *s.v.* μηνίσκιον and μηνίσκος. The border between an ornament and an (astrological) amulet was fluid. On the moon cult in the oriental and Hellen. world in its contact with the religion of Israel and Judah and with Christianity cf. the material in A. Jeremias, *Das AT im Lichte des alten Orients*⁴ (1930), Index and Index of Subjects, also F. J. Dölger, *Ichthys*, II: "Der heilige Fisch in den antiken Religionen u. im Christentum" (1922), Index; *Antike u. Christentum*, I (1929), 136; cf. also K. Galling, Bibl. Reallexikon (1937), *s.v.* "Amulett" [Bertram].

[22] Cf. on this Str.-B., *ad loc.*: "The withdrawal is perhaps connected with the fact that the child is to be a Nazirite, cf. Ju. 13:4 ff."

[23] On these generally cf. F. Spitta, ZNW, 7 (1906), 281 ff.

[24] On the different reckoning of these 3½ years in Rabb. tradition cf. Str.-B., III, 760 f. on Jm. 5:17; also G. Kittel, *Rabbinica* (1920), 31 ff. We have here a round figure in the sense of a few years.

his Gospel too (cf. Lk. 1:3 καθεξῆς), but it seems likely that his researches led to no very solid results except in the infancy stories. For the original narrators of the events of the Gospels the dating of the stories of Jesus was a secondary matter. The decisive point for them was the fact, not the time. What results from an investigation of the understanding of time in the NT (apart from Lk.) is confirmed by these observations. The NT authors, who were not moulded by Greek thought, did not regard history primarily as an ongoing stream of past events but as the sum of forces at work in the present. They view it from the standpoint of energy, not of continuity.

b. This is, however, only a more naive conception of time; it is not a rejection of all calculation of time. In connection with the future such calculation is greatly favoured in Rev. But it is often not meant to be taken literally. It is a veiled reference which only initiates can understand, cf. Rev. 9:5, 10 (→ II, 17). Five here is not to be taken as a round number,[25] for there are many round numbers, nor is it meant to be the life-span of the locust,[26] for the ref. is neither to real locusts nor real months. It represents an apocalyptic tradition. Cf. also Rev. 11:2; 13:5 (→ III, 134 f.), where the 42 months are undoubtedly the 1150 days of Da. 8:14.[27] The dates of these eschatological events are hidden from men, even believers, but they are not arbitrary; the days and months have been fixed (9:15). The wealth of joys awaiting the redeemed in the final kingdom is realistically expressed in the fruit which the trees bear each month (Rev. 22:2); the influence of Jewish apocalyptic may be seen here (cf. already Ez. 47:12).

c. Finally, μήν occurs in Gl. 4:10 in connection with Judaising aberrations in the churches, cf. the νεομηνία of Col. 2:16 (the only occurrence in the NT). The two statements correspond in structure (ἡμέρας — σαββάτων, καιρούς — ἑορτῆς [→ III, 459], μῆνας and ἐνιαυτούς — νεομηνίας); for the observation of months naturally consists in the celebration of the feast of the new moon, as does that of years in the celebration of New Year's Day, cf. the treatment of these feasts together in RH, → 640). If the error of the Galatians is not exactly the same as that of the Colossians, the latter approximating closer to syncretism, it is still possible to treat the two passages together from our standpoint.

We have spoken already of the celebration of the first of the month in Judaism (→ also 639 f.). If people came into the churches who demanded circumcision (Gl. 5:2 f.; 6:12 f., also Col. 2:11), this would also involve keeping the feasts prescribed in the OT. Now it has been pointed out already that the cult of a moon god was widespread in the areas in question.[28] It is thus natural to assume that the day of the return of the moon, from which so much good was expected, would be hailed with festive joy. As the dispenser of life, which it was taken to be in paganism, the moon would be, from the biblical standpoint, one of the στοιχεῖα from whose power and service the believer in Christ is liberated (Gl. 4:3, 9; Col. 2:8, 20). But young Christians could easily see in the Jewish feast of the new moon a relic of the worship which they had previously liked, for in the Jewish prayer at the new moon they could still confess: "Blessed art thou, O Lord, who renewest the new moon" (bSanh., 42a; and cf. also the thought of resurrection, → 640). As concerns

---

[25] Loh. Apk. on 9:5; on five as a common number cf. Kittel, *op. cit.*, 39 f.

[26] Had. Apk. on 9:5.

[27] Cf. in the NT Rev. 12:14 (→ III, 461; 459) on the basis of Da. 12:7. But cf. also Str.-B., IV, 986 ff.: Exc. "Vorzeichen u. Berechnung der Tage des Messias, II;" acc. to Kittel, 31 ff. a round number.

[28] There is a strange confusion of possible connections in Henle, 611 ff.

Colossae, it is even possible that there was for members of the community a connection between earlier adoration of the moon and their present reverence for angels (2:18) or "powers" (1:16), → I, 482 f.

Delling

† μήτηρ

The position which the mother occupied in non-biblical antiquity did not wholly coincide with the general evaluation of woman and marriage. [1] Philo Decal., 120 refers to the very high estimation of mothers (and parents generally), e.g., in Stoicism: πατὴρ καὶ μήτηρ ἐμφανεῖς εἰσι θεοί. Cf. the touching witness in a pap. letter: ὀφίλομεν γὰρ σέβεσθε τὴν τεκοῦσαν ὡς θε[όν] μάλειστα τοιαύτην οὖσαν ἀγαθήν. [2] Early matriarchal relations, whose significance was underrated until J. J. Bachofen drew attention to them and went to the opposite extreme, had little effect. [3] On the other hand, the worship of mother deities (from Asia Minor, with mother earth predominant in Greece) exerted a strong influence. [4] There are traces of matriarchy in the OT too. [5] The OT is rich in important mothers. The LXX adds new features in Tob. and Sir., and esp. through the ἱερὰ καὶ θεοσεβὴς μήτηρ of 4 Macc. The term μήτηρ occurs over 300 times in the LXX, with 4 exceptions for אֵם where the Mas. is to hand. There is a fig. use in Is. 50:1; Jer. 27:12; Tob. 4:13; Hos. 4:5: μήτηρ as the personification of the people. [6] In 2 Βασ. 20:19, however, the LXX has μητρόπολις for אֵם in designation of a city. [7] Philo often uses μήτηρ fig. Particularly important is the idea of wisdom as the mother of the world and the *logos*, as μήτηρ καὶ τιθήνη τῶν ὅλων (Ebr., 31; cf. Det. Pot. Ins., 54 and 116), as the mother of the high-priest (Fug., 109). In Ebr., 31 Philo refers to the view found in Plat. Tim., 50d, 51a that matter is the mother (or nurse, cf. 49a, 52d) of all things. [8]

μήτηρ. [1] In the lit., also on woman and marriage in early Christianity (→ I, 776 Bibl.), sufficient regard is not always had to the position of woman as mother.

[2] Deissmann LO, 160, 28 f.; more generally 426, Index, *s.v.* "Mütter."

[3] R. Thurnwald, Art. "Mutterrecht" A in *Reallex. der Vorgeschichte*, 8 (1927), 360-380; E. Kornemann, Art. "Mutterrecht" in Pauly-W., *Suppl.-Bd.*, VI (1935), 557-571; RGG², Index, *s.v.* "Mutterrecht."

[4] F. Schwenn, Art. "Kybele" in Pauly-W., XI (1922), 2250-2298; Art. "Meter," *ibid.*, XV (1932), 1372 f.; A. Dieterich, *Mutter Erde*³ (1925, new impression 1938); L. Franz, "Die Muttergöttin im vorderen Orient u. in Europa," AO, 35, 3 (1937); C. Schrempf, "Der Mutterglaube in der antiken Welt," *Gelbe Hefte. Historische u. politische Zschr. für das christliche Deutschland*, 13 (1937), 593-610; K. Leese, "D. Mutter als religiöses Symbol," *Sammlung gemeinverständlicher Vorträge*, 174 (1934); RGG², Index, *s.v.* "Muttergottheiten." Cf. also W. Bousset, "Hauptprobleme der Gnosis," FRL, 10 (1907), Index, *s.v.* Μήτηρ, "Mutter" etc.

[5] I. Benzinger in RE³, 5 (1898), 739 f., Art. "Familie u. Ehe bei den Hebräern."

[6] In Hos. 2:4, 7, though the people is meant, μήτηρ is to be understood in the light of the metaphor of marriage. God is compared to a mother in Is. 49:15 (γυνή = mother); 66:13.

[7] ψ 86:5: μήτηρ Σιών is a scribal error (Rahlfs μη τη, Schleusner, III, 557 μητι). Cf. also Jer. 15:8. For non-biblical examples of this use cf. Liddell-Scott, *s.v.* Cf. also Str.-B., III, 574.

[8] Cf. J. Pascher, "Η ΒΑΣΙΛΙΚΗ ΟΔΟΣ. Der Königsweg zur Wiedergeburt u. Vergottung bei Philon von Alexandreia," *Studien z. Geschichte u. Kultur des Altertums*, XVII, 3/4 (1931), 65, 70, 112, 153, 156, 222, 261.

The OT commandment: τίμα τὸν πατέρα σου καὶ τὴν μητέρα (Ex. 20:12, quoted as ἐντολὴ πρώτη ἐν ἐπαγγελίᾳ in Eph. 6:2, → II, 552), is not merely endorsed by Jesus (Mt. 15:4a par. Mk. 7:10a; Mt. 19:19 par. Mk. 10:19; Lk. 18:20). He also endorses the threat against its violation, Ex. 21:16 (Mt. 15:4b par. Mk. 7:10b) and protects it against the sophistical exposition of the Pharisees (Mt. 15:5 f. par. Mk. 7:11 f., cf. → III, 865). Just as the rule of Gn. 2:24, which is repeated in Mt. 19:5 par. Mk. 10:7 f.; Eph. 5:31, does not cancel the 5th commandment, neither does the demand of Jesus that we should love Him more than father and mother (Mt. 10:37) and even hate father and mother if attachment to them is a hindrance to discipleship (so the Hebraic par. in Lk. 14:26; cf. the use of Mi. 7:6 in Mt. 10:35 par. Lk. 12:53). The promise which Jesus gives (Mt. 19:29 par. Mk. 10:29 f.; Lk. 18:29 γονεῖς) to those who leave father and mother ἕνεκεν τοῦ ἐμοῦ ὀνόματος (Mk. τοῦ εὐαγγελίου, Lk. τῆς βασιλείας τοῦ θεοῦ) is parallel to the saying about His true relatives, which He uttered when He Himself was faced by the opposition of His own family (Mt. 12:46 ff. par. Mk. 3:31 ff.; Lk. 8:19 ff.).[9]

Apart from the passages just mentioned and Mt. 13:55 (par. Mk. 6:3 without μήτηρ; cf. Jn. 6:42) the mother of Jesus is mentioned in the Synoptists only in the infancy stories in Mt. and Lk. (μήτηρ Mt. 1:18; 2:11, 13 f., 20 f.; Lk. 1:43; 2:33 f., 48, 51; cf. also the reference to the mother of the Baptist in Lk. 1:60). In Jn. the mother of Jesus is present at the wedding in Cana and the scene at the cross, never with her name Mary, 2:1, 3 as ἡ μήτηρ τοῦ Ἰησοῦ, 2:5, 12; 19:25 as ἡ μήτηρ αὐτοῦ (cf. 19:27), twice — almost as a proper name — as ἡ μήτηρ (19:26). But this use, as shown by the position of Mary elsewhere in Jn.,[10] does not imply any particular veneration of her person. In the infancy stories there is understandably a great interest in the figure of the mother of Jesus, though overestimation is expressly forbidden by the saying of Jesus in Lk. 11:28.[11] In the rest of the NT the only reference to the mother of Jesus is in Ac. 1:14.[12]

Other mothers are the mother of the sons of Zebedee, Mt. 20:20; 27:56, the Mary mentioned in Mt. 27:56 par. Mk. 15:40 (cf. → I, 144 n. 4 f.), Mary the mother of John in Ac. 12:12, the mother at the death-bed in Mk. 5:40 par. Lk. 8:51, the mother at the bier in Lk. 7:12, 15, Herodias the mother of Salome in Mt. 14:8 par. Mk. 6:24; Mt. 14:11 par. Mk. 6:28. The expression ἐκ κοιλίας μητρός, found already in the OT (ψ 21:10; 70:6 etc.), recurs in Mt. 19:12; Lk. 1:15; Ac. 3:2; 14:8; Gl. 1:15 (cf. Jn. 3:4: εἰς τὴν κοιλίαν τῆς μητρὸς αὐτοῦ, → III, 787, n. 7). Paul never mentions his mother (or

---

[9] Cf. → I, 145. Mention of the mother shows that the ref. must also be to brothers after the flesh (→ I, 145, n. 5).

[10] On the possibility of allegorical interpretation of the passages in Jn. cf. the comm. On Jn. 2:1 ff. cf. Clemen, 267 f.

[11] In primitive Christianity the mother of Jesus was far less important than the mother of the founder in other religions. H. Neumann, *Die Mutter des Religionsstifters* (Phil. Diss. Leipzig [*Religion u. Geschichte,* 1] 1935), examines the traditions concerning the mothers of Buddha, Mohammed and Zoroaster. Veneration of Mary, which brought the motifs of ancient mother religion into Christianity (though cf. F. X. Steinmetzer, "Die christliche *Mater Dei* u. d. babylonische Mythe," *Prager Theol. Blätter* [1938], 3 ff.), begins only after the NT. Cf. G. Bertram, Art. "Maria" in RGG², III, 1995 f. and Leese, *op. cit.* On the Church as μήτηρ παρθένος in Iren. and Tertullian cf. H. Koch, "*Virgo Eva — Virgo Maria.* Neue Untersuchungen über die Lehre von der Jungfrauschaft u. d. Ehe Mariens in der ältesten Kirche," *Arbeiten zur Kirchengeschichte,* 25 (1937), 42 f. and Appendix 1 (92 ff.): "Die Kirche als jungfräuliche Mutter und Maria ihr Vorbild."

[12] On Gl. 4:4 cf. A. Oepke, *Der Brief des Pls. an d. Galater* (1937), *ad loc.* In Rev. 12 the queen of heaven as the mother of the Messiah is a mythological figure.

father), but behind 2 Tm. 1:5 there is perhaps grateful recollection that his mother passed on to him his religious heritage. Respect for one's mother is expressed in 1 Tm. 5:2 [13] and R. 16:13. [14] It may also be seen in Gl. 4:26, where Paul, following OT usage (→ 642) which has also influenced Rev. 17:5 (though → I, 515, n. 3), says of the Jerusalem which is above: ἥτις ἐστὶν μήτηρ (+ πάντων A 𝔎) ἡμῶν. [15]

If the position of the mother in the NT is free from emotional exaggeration, mythological excess, or elevation to a religious symbol, there is a sense of the significance of the mother and what she stands for, and of her place in God's creation. [16]

Michaelis

μιαίνω, μίασμα, μιασμός, ἀμίαντος

† μιαίνω.

a. In the neut. sense: "to paint in colour," [1] Hom. Il., 4, 141 (φοίνικι). b. Censoriously, "to spot," "to stain," first materially, then in the religious or cultic sense. μιαίνειν is used esp. for staining by bloodguiltiness. [2] In primitive thought this was understood physically like dirt or infection. [3] But the act does not affect only the doer.

---

[13] Par. from antiquity (esp. Plat. Resp., V, 463c, cf. Dib. Past., *ad loc.*) do not affect this estimation of the saying. Cf. also 1 Tm. 2:15.

[14] Cf. the pap. par. in Moult.-Mill., *s.v.*

[15] The idea of a marriage between Christ as the second Abraham and the Church pre-existing as the Holy Spirit has been read in. Similarly, the theses of S. Hirsch, *Die Vorstellung von einem weiblichen* πνεῦμα ἅγιον *im NT u. in d. ältesten christlichen Lit.* (Theol. Diss. Berlin, 1926) are exaggerated, though the view of Hb.-Ev. that the Holy Spirit is the mother of Jesus (→ πνεῦμα) calls for notice, and shows that popular belief in maternal deities lived on. But there is no trace of this in the NT itself. Neither Mt. 3:9 nor 1 C. 15:47 is related in any way to belief in mother earth; cf. ZNW, 9 ff. (1908 ff.) and Dieterich, 116 ff.

[16] What is said about parents in the house-tables, and passages like Jn. 16:21; 1 Th. 2:7, also deserves mention, also the wider circle of statements about birth, childhood etc. Cf. Gl. 4:19, where Paul seems to apply to himself the metaphor of the mother (→ ὠδίνω). In the post-apost. fathers 1 Cl., 18, 5 (ψ 50:5); 35, 8 (ψ 49:20); Pol., 3, 3 (Gl. 4:26, though referred to faith); Herm. v., 3, 8, 5 (faith as the mother of Christian virtues).

μιαίνω. Trench², 106 f.; E. Williger, "Hagios," RVV, 19, 1 (1922), 64 ff.; P. Stengel, *Die griech. Kultusaltertümer*³ (1920), 155 ff.; T. Wächter, "Reinheitsvorschriften im griech. Kult.," RVV, 9, 1 (1910); RGG², IV, 1839 ff. ("Rein u. unrein"). J. Döller, "Die Reinheits- u. Speisegesetze d. AT in religionsgeschichtlicher Beleuchtung," *At.liche Abh.*, VII, 2/3 (1917), → καθαρός, III, 413 ff.

[1] Acc. to Walde-Pok., II, 243 μιαίνω is etym. related to the Old High German and Middle High German *meil, Mal* ("stain"); esp. of blood; Phot. Lex., I, 423, *s.v.* μίασμα = βαφή, immersion.

[2] Hom. Il., 4, 146; Plat. Leg., VI, 782c: τοὺς τῶν θεῶν βωμοὺς αἵματι μιαίνειν, IX, 868a; 871a; 872e; Luc. Alex., 56.

[3] Stengel, 156.

The doer transfers the stain to his fellow-citizens, the city, the temple of the gods.[4] Cultic cleansing by water or sacrifice is needed to purge away the stain.[5] In primitive thought there is no sense of the pricking of conscience. Spotting is particularly incurred by processes in which there was originally thought to be participation in the demonic, e.g., sexual intercourse or decomposition.[6] Even bad news can make the ear unclean.[7] Only later (in Plato, the tragedians) is staining felt to be a moral and spiritual matter.[8]

The OT reflects these primitive and cultic ideas. In the LXX μιαίνω is predominantly used for טמא (q, ni, pi, pu, hitp). This is a cultic term, and occurs a great deal in P and Ez., who has a strong cultic interest.[9] A developed casuistry works out the rules of cultic defilement and its removal. Judgment concerning what defiles is often linked with primitive and direct feelings (aversion) and experiences, or with earlier religious connections (demonism).[10] In particular all contact with alien cults defiles.[11] The unclean person can disqualify or desecrate holy objects by contact.[12] In all such cases μιαίνω is thought of in cultic and ritual terms. Distinction between the ritual and the moral develops with the OT (prophecy).[13]

Peculiar to the LXX is the declarative use of μιαίνω, "to declare unclean" (Lv. 13, 3). In accordance with his tendency to ethicise the Jewish religion, Philo often uses μιαίνω for spiritual defilement.[14]

In the Mishnah the 6th order (טהרות) deals with the different possibilities of defilement and its removal, e.g., tractate כלים (vessels), אהלות (defilement by corpses), נגעים

---

[4] Plat. Leg., IX, 868a: ὅστις δ' ἂν τῶν ἀποκτεινάντων πάντων μὴ πείθηται τῷ νόμῳ, ἀλλ' ἀκάθαρτος ὢν ἀγοράν τε καὶ ἄθλα καὶ τὰ ἄλλα ἱερὰ μιαίνῃ, Plut. Sulla, 35, 2 (I, 474a): τὴν οἰκίαν.

[5] Stengel, 156 f.; Wächter; Rohde [9, 10], I, 275, n. 2; II, 69 ff.; → ἁγνίζειν; Eur. Herc. Fur., 1324; a tt. for expiation of murder is καθαίρειν.

[6] The pregnant, Phot. Lex., *s.v.* ῥάμνος, Wächter, 31, n. 1; women in childbed, Theophr. Char., XVI, 9; Wächter, 25 ff.; O. Gruppe, *Griech. Mythologie* (1906), 858; 1272, n. 7; in menstruation, Geoponica (ed. H. Beckh [1895]), XII, 25, 2; Wächter, 36 ff.; corpses, Theocr., 23, 55 f. (p. 129); Wächter, 43 ff.; the house of the dead: L. Ziehen, Leges Graeciae et Insularum, Leges Graecorum Sacrae, II, 1 (1906), 93 n., v. 24 ff.; even fire in the house of the dead is defiled, Wächter, 47. The Pythagoreans esp. were careful to avoid defilement, Porphyr. Abst., IV, 16: μεμίανται τό τε λέχους ἅψασθαι (contact with a woman in childbed) καὶ τὸ θνησειδίων (eating of dead animals), J. Haussleiter, "Der Vegetarismus in d. Antike," RVV, 24 (1935), 126, n. 1, 218, 340.

[7] Aesch. Ag., 636 f.; Eur. Hipp., 317 (φρήν); here, too, the thinking is primarily in physical categories.

[8] Plat. Resp., X, 621c: τὴν ψυχὴν οὐ μιανθησόμεθα, Aesch. Sept. c. Theb., 344 (εὐσέβειαν); Ag., 1669 (τὴν δίκην μιαίνειν); Eur. Hel., 999 f. (κλέος πατρὸς μιαίνειν). Williger, 63 ff.

[9] μιαίνω 48 times in P, esp. Lv. and Nu., only twice for חלל in JE (Gn. 49:4; Ex. 20:25), 28 times in Ez., 7 in Jer. (e.g., 3:1, 2 for חנף; 2:7, 23; 7:30 for טמא), elsewhere only 16 times in the OT, 9 in the Apcr., esp. Macc. (1 Macc. 1:46, 63; 4:45; 7:34; 14:36), once in Wis. (7:25).

[10] Defiling are sexual processes (Lv. 12:1-5), leprosy (13:14), death and decomposition (21:1 ff.), B. Stade-A. Bertholet, *Bibl. Theol. des AT*, I (1905), 140 f.; Eichrodt Theol. d. AT, I, 61. Döller, 1 ff.

[11] The declaration of animals as unclean (Lv. 11; Dt. 14:4 ff.) is mostly because of connections with alien cults or magical actions, e.g., swine (Canaanite domestic and sacrificial animals), mice, snakes, hares (magical belief) etc., Stade-Bertholet, 39, 141 f.; Eichr., 61; RGG², IV, 1842 ff.; Döller, 168 ff. Idolatry defiles the land, Nu. 35:34; 4 Βασ. 23:10.

[12] Lv. 5:3; 15:31; 20:3; Nu. 5:3; Hag. 2:13 f. Döller, 5 f.

[13] Is. 1:15 ff.; Hos. 6:6, 10; Ez. 14:11 ἵνα μὴ μιαίνωνται ἔτι ἐν πᾶσι τοῖς παραπτώμασιν αὐτῶν.

[14] Leg. All., III, 148 (τὴν ψυχὴν πάθει μιαίνειν); Vit. Mos., II, 196 (μεμιασμένῃ ψυχῇ τε καὶ γλώττῃ); Deus Imm., 89 (τὸν νοῦν μιαίνουσα); Jos. in the cultic sense, Ant., 11, 300; 18, 271; Bell., 4, 201, 215, 242; 5, 402 etc.

(leprosy), טהרות (lesser defilements which last only to sunset), מקואות (baths), נדה (uncleanness of the wife), ידים (defilement of the hands) etc.[15]

In the NT, which no longer thinks in ritual and cultic terms, μιαίνω is very rare.

1. It is used in the cultic sense in connection with the Jewish religion in Jn. 18:28. The Jews avoid entering the house of Gentiles so as not to defile themselves cultically.

2. It is also used in the religious and moral sense of the defilement of the person by inner apostasy from God. In Hb. 12:15 the apostate, by his turning from God's grace, pollutes the other members of the community (alongside πόρνος and → βέβηλος, v. 16; opp. ἁγιασμός, v. 14). In Tt. 1:15 it is used of the inner defilement (νοῦς, συνείδησις) which results from adopting Gnostic libertinism. The champions of this trend are themselves called μεμιαμμένοι (alongside ἄπιστοι in v. 15, βδελυκτοί, ἀπειθεῖς, v. 16). Jd. 8: σάρκα ... μιαίνουσιν — not of the sexual act itself, but licentious sexual action which treats the commandments of God with contempt.[16]

† μίασμα.

This means "defilement" as the result of an action. The word follows the religious changes in the meaning of → μιαίνω. It denotes esp. ritual and cultic pollution, which along the lines of primitive thought is first held to be corporeal. μίασμα arises esp. from bloodguiltiness. It clings to the doer, but can be transferred from him to the countries, sanctuaries and images of the circle which tolerates him in its midst,[1] also to unjust judges and witnesses who prevent expiation.[2] It must be set aside by καθαρμός or ἱλασμός.[3] Later it is employed for moral defilement.[4]

There is no true original for μίασμα in the Mas., and it is rare in the LXX.[5] Jdt. 9:4 (bloodguiltiness); 9:2 (licentiousness); 1 Macc. 13:50 (Gentile defilement); also Ιερ. 39(32):34 (for שִׁקּוּץ); Ez. 33:31 (for בֶּצַע; the LXX seems to have read עָצָב); Lv. 7:18 (פִּגּוּל, cultically forbidden flesh); in the moral sense, Jdt. 13:16 alongside αἰσχύνη. The word is common in Joseph. in the sense of cultic pollution.[6] Philo uses it for ritual, then for moral, defilement.[7]

---

[15] Cf. Strack Einl., 59 ff.; → καθαρός, III, 418 ff.

[16] Kn. Pt., 226 suggests unnatural licentiousness in view of the allusion (ὁμοίως) to the example of the Sodomites (v. 7).

μίασμα. → μιαίνω Bibl. Stengel, 155 ff., 165; Wächter, 3, 14, 28, 58, 64 f.; E. Fehrle, "D. kultische Keuschheit," RVV, 6 (1910); Williger; B. Brüne, *Flavius Josephus* (1913), esp. 86 ff.

[1] Aesch. Ag., 1645; Clytaemnestra is described as χώρας μίασμα καὶ θεῶν ἐγχωρίων, Eur. Alc., 22 f.: ἐγὼ δέ, μὴ μίασμά μ' ἐν δόμοις κίχῃ, λείπω μελάθρων τῶνδε φιλτάτην στέγην, Plat. Leg., VI, 782c: οὐχ ὅσιον ... τῶν θεῶν βωμοὺς αἵματι μιαίνειν.

[2] Antiphon. Or. Tetralogia, III, 1, 3.

[3] Eur. Herc. Fur., 1324: ἐκεῖ χέρας σὰς ἁγνίσας μιάσματος, Hipp., 317: χεῖρες μὲν ἁγναί, φρὴν δ' ἔχει μίασμά τι, here, too, the pollution being regarded as essentially physical, though with a movement towards the spiritual; similarly Hipp., 655; cf. Rohde [9, 10], I, 275, n. 2; II, 71 ff.; Williger, 64 ff.

[4] Polyb., 36, 16, 6.

[5] 7 times, 4 in the Apcr. (3 in Jdt., 1 in Macc.).

[6] Jos. Bell., 2, 455 (murder of the Roman garrison on the sacred soil of Jerusalem); 2, 473 (to expect God's ποινὴ ἀξία on this account); only God's κάθαρσις (by fire) can cleanse the city, 6, 110; 4, 323.

[7] Philo Spec. Leg., III, 121 (φόνου); Decal., 93 (καθαρεύει ψυχὴν καὶ σῶμα ... τὴν μὲν παρανομίας, τὸ δὲ μιασμάτων); Spec. Leg., I, 281 (παθῶν); I, 102 ([πόρνη] σπουδάσασα μιασμάτων καθαρεῦσαι); III, 127; Det. Pot. Ins., 170.

It occurs in the NT only at 2 Pt. 2:20 for "pollution by partaking in that which is contrary to the holy will of God," ἀποφυγόντες τὰ μιάσματα τοῦ κόσμου ἐν ἐπιγνώσει τοῦ κυρίου. Κόσμος here has the sense of the ungodly world, in practice paganism.

† μιασμός.

"Defilement" as an action or state (→ μιαίνω, μίασμα), first cultic, Plut. Solon, 12 (I, 84c): ἄγη καὶ μιασμοὺς δεομένους καθαρμῶν, then moral, Test. B. 8:2 (alongside πορνεία, opp. διάνοια καθαρά); Test. L. 17:8.

It occurs in the LXX only at 1 Macc. 4:43 (of the pagan βωμός on the θυσιαστήριον of God) and Wis. 14:26: ψυχῶν μιασμός ("moral corruption of the soul,"[1] along with forgetfulness of the grace of the covenant, and sins of licentiousness).

The only NT occurrence is at 2 Pt. 2:10, where the reference is to the licentious affirmation of sexual impulses by the libertines: τοὺς ὀπίσω σαρκὸς ἐν ἐπιθυμίᾳ μιασμοῦ πορευομένους (cf. Jd. 8: σάρκα μιαίνειν).

† ἀμίαντος.

"Undefiled," "clean," physically, Pind. Fr., 108b of light, then esp. cultic purity, Plut. Numa, 9 [I, 66b] of the virginal purity of the Vestals, fig. in the moral sense.[1] ἀμίαντος is often used to strengthen καθαρός and has thus the sense of perfect and inviolate purity, Plut. Is. et Os., 79 (II, 383b); Pyth. Or., 3 (II, 395e). Freedom from pollution is the presupposition of cultic proximity to God.[2]

In the LXX ἀμίαντος, for which there is no Heb. term, occurs only 5 times in the Apcr.: 2 Macc. 14:36; 15:34 of keeping the temple cultically pure; a few times for sexual purity in Wis. 3:13: ἡ ἀμίαντος, ἥτις οὐκ ἔγνω κοίτην ἐν παραπτώματι, 8:19 f.: ψυχῆς ἀγαθῆς ... σῶμα ἀμίαντον, 4:2: ἀμιάντων ἄθλων ἀγῶνα, of the life of the unmarried.

In the NT it is used 1. in the narrower sense of purity from sexual transgression in Hb. 13:4.

2. More generally, it is used of the moral purity of true worship, Jm. 1:27 (along with καθαρός), of the perfect purity of the heavenly inheritance, 1 Pt. 1:4 (along with ἄφθαρτος and ἀμάραντος), of the perfect moral purity of the high-priest, Christ, Hb. 7:27 (along with ὅσιος and ἄκακος, → III, 482).

Hauck

μιασμός. [1] K. Siegfried in Kautzsch Apkr., *ad loc.*

ἀμίαντος. → μιαίνω Bibl.

[1] Plat. Leg., VI, 777e: ἀμίαντος τοῦ τε ἀνοσίου πέρι καὶ ἀδίκου σπείρειν εἰς ἀρετῆς ἔκφυσιν ἱκανώτατος ἂν εἴη, Plut. Pericl., 39 (I, 173c): εὐμενὲς ἦθος καὶ βίον ἐν ἐξουσίᾳ καθαρὸν καὶ ἀμίαντον Ὀλύμπιον προσαγορεύεσθαι, Plut. Nikias, 9 (I, 529a): ἀμίαντον καὶ ἀπόλεμον βίον.

[2] Cf. Wächter; Stengel, 156 ff. On Jewish soil cf. Test. Jos. 4:6: τοῖς ἐν καθαρᾷ καρδίᾳ καὶ στόμασιν ἀμιάντοις αὐτῷ προσερχομένοις. Cf. 1 Cl., 29, 1 (of praying hands); 2 Cl., 6, 9 (along with ἁγνός).

† μικρός († ἐλάττων, † ἐλάχιστος)

1. In Gk. μικρός (and σμικρός, with secondary forms μικκός, μικός) is attested from the time of Hom.: Il., 5, 801; 17, 757; Od., 3, 296; Hes. Op., 361 etc. The word is common both in the class. and the later period (inscr., pap.).[1] It means a. "small in outward or physical size": Il., 5, 801: Τυδεύς τοι μικρὸς μὲν ἔην δέμας, ἀλλὰ μαχητής, 17, 757: ὅ τε σμικρῇσι φόνον φέρει ὀρνίθεσσιν. It is found as a nickname in Κλειγένης (ὁ μικρός), Aristoph. Ra., 709; Ἀμύντας (ὁ μικρός), Aristot. Pol., V, 10, p. 1311b, 3.[2] Cf. on this Plat. Prot., 323d: οἷον τοὺς αἰσχροὺς ἢ σμικροὺς ἢ ἀσθενεῖς τίς οὕτως ἀνόητος ὥστε τι τούτων ἐπιχειρεῖν ποιεῖν; ταῦτα μὲν γάρ οἶμαι ἴσασιν ὅτι φύσει τε καὶ τύχῃ τοῖς ἀνθρώποις γίγνεται, τὰ καλὰ καὶ τἀναντία τούτοις. "One is not so lacking in understanding as to take warning steps (instructive or penal) against ugly, small or weak men, for one knows that these things come upon men by nature or accident, whether defects of this kind or the corresponding advantages." Aristot. Eth. Nic., IV, 7, p. 1123b, 6 ff.: ἐν μεγέθει γὰρ ἡ μεγαλοψυχία, ὥσπερ καὶ τὸ κάλλος ἐν μεγάλῳ σώματι, οἱ μικροὶ δ' ἀστεῖοι καὶ σύμμετροι, καλοὶ δ' οὔ. b. "Small in compass": Hes. Op., 361: εἰ γάρ κεν καὶ σμικρὸν ἐπὶ σμικρῷ καταθεῖο καὶ θαμὰ τοῦτ' ἔρδοις, τάχα κεν μέγα καὶ τὸ γένοιτο. Hes. emphasises the value of what is small. "Little added to little becomes great; if a man adds to what he has and does not think that what he has he may consume, he will never be in want. But it must be laid up carefully; abroad it will soon be lost (vessels, wood, grain in bundles etc.). If one has a stock, one may take from it, but a man should never be put in the position of having to borrow."[3] Aristoph. Vesp., 878: Ἀντικυραίου μέλιτος μικρὸν τῷ θυμιδίῳ (diminutive of θυμός) παραμείξας. c. "Little, insignificant." Thus Theogn., 323 admonishes: Μήποτ' ἐπὶ σμικρῇ προφάσει φίλον ἄνδρ' ἀπολέσσαι, πειθόμενος χαλεπῇ, Κύρνε, διαβολίῃ, similarly Soph. Oed. Col., 443: ἀλλ' ἔπους σμικροῦ χάριν φυγάς σφιν ἔξω πτωχὸς ἠλώμην ἀεί, Trach., 361 f.: ἔγκλημα μικρὸν αἰτίαν θ' ἑτοιμάσας ἐπιστρατεύει ..., Oed. Tyr., 961: σμικρὰ παλαιὰ σώματ' εὐνάζει (bring to rest) ῥοπή (inclination). The word is also used of people (opp. μέγας): Pind. Pyth., 3, 107: σμικρὸς ἐν σμικροῖς, μέγας ἐν μεγάλοις ἔσσομαι, or Soph. Ai., 160 f.: μετὰ γὰρ μεγάλων βαιὸς (little) ἄριστ' ἂν καὶ μέγας ὀρθοῖθ' ὑπὸ μικροτέρων. Soph. seems to have a proverb in mind, cf. also Plat. Leg., X, 902d: οὐδενί, χωρὶς τῶν ὀλίγων καὶ σμικρῶν πολλὰ ἢ μεγάλα· οὐδὲ γὰρ

μικρός. [1] Cf. Liddell-Scott, 1132-1134; many compounds are listed there, e.g., μικραδικητής, μικροβασιλεία, μικρόμματος, μικρόμυρτος; μικρότης and μικρύνω are also from the same stem.

[2] W. L. Newman, *The Politics of Aristot.*, IV (1902), 428: "The addition of ὁ μικρός is not altogether respectful: see Meineke, Fragm. Com. Gr., 3, 497 and note on 1335a, 14 and cp. Plato, Protag. 323 D." A. Meineke, Fragmenta Poetarum Comoediae Mediae = Fragmenta Comicorum Graecorum, III (1840), 497: "ὁ μικρός *haud rarum apud Athenienses sive cognomen sive convicium.* Ita Κλειγένη τὸν μικρόν *habemus apud Aristoph. Ra.*, 720: Ἀριστόδημον τὸν μικρὸν apud Xenoph. Mem., I, 4, 2 et Plat. Symp., 1, 7." Linguistically, μικρός = σμικρός cf. Bl.-Debr.[6] § 34, 4.

[3] U. v. Wilamowitz-Moellendorff, Hesiodos Erga *erklärt* (1928), 4. In gen. the word μικρός = σμικρός has a derogatory sense in Gk., as opp. to μέγας. Hes. Op., 361 does not go beyond popular wisdom and proverbs, cf. "Look after the pennies and the pounds will look after themselves."

ἄνευ σμικρῶν τοὺς μεγάλους φασὶν λιθολόγοι (gathering stones) λίθους εὖ κεῖσθαι. Cic. Nat. Deor., II, 66, 167: "The gods watch over big things but neglect small (*magna di curant, parva neglegunt*). d. Of time (χρόνος) or age, "a short time," "young." Pind. Olymp., 12, 12: ἐν μικρῷ πεδάμειψαν χρόνῳ, Plat. Resp., VI, 498d: εἰς μικρόν γ', ἔφη, χρόνον εἴρηκας. There are many adv., μικρῶς, μικροῦ, μικρόν, ἐπὶ or κατὰ μικρόν, παρὰ and μετὰ μικρόν.[4] Later[5] cf. P. Gen., 28, 11: ὁ δεῖνα ἐπικαλούμενος μικρός, P. Flor., III, 322, 28 and 67: κλῆρος μικροῦ Πολύφωνος, P. Eleph., 27, 5: Ψινταῆς μικρὸς Ἐστφήνιος, 16, 11; 18, 1; BGU, III, 712, 2: Πτολεμαῖος μικρός, P. Flor., III, 322, 10: δι' Ἀπιανοῦ μικροῦ, 372, 4: Ἀπιανὸς μικρός, P. Amh., 155, 9: Πέτρου μικροῦ. The word is common as an addition to various names, always in the sense of "small." But it can also mean "young," P. Lond., III, 897, 30: ἀσπάζου Ἀφροδοῦν τὴν μικράν, P. Oxy., I, 131, 7: ὁ μικρότερός μου ἀδελφός, P. Giess., 78, 7, and reminds us of the various other uses mentioned (short time, small measure, quantity etc.), μικκός (P. Fay., 127, 12 and 13; P. Lond., II, 239, 16; 418, 21) = μικρός. ἀπὸ μικρόθεν, from childhood, P. Oxy., IX, 1216, 5.

2. In the LXX it is used for many Heb. words, (צָעוּר) מִצְעָר, מְעַט, מִיכַל, (מִזְעָר) זְעֵיר, קָטָן, קָלַל ni, שִׁפְלַת קוֹמָה, שֶׁצֶף.[6] The most prominent of these is קָטָן, which like the Gk. μικρός can be used in many ways. Thus it can mean "small in size," e.g., Dt. 25:13: "Thou shalt not have in thy bag divers weights, a great and a small," or Ez. 43:14: "... and from the lesser settle even to the greater settle four cubits." Or it can mean shortness of time, youth, e.g., Gn. 9:24: "... Noah knew what his youngest son had done to him (בְּנוֹ הַקָּטָן = LXX ὁ υἱὸς αὐτοῦ ὁ νεώτερος). It can also express insignificance, Is. 22:24; 36:9; Zech. 4:10: "Who hath despised the day of small things?" LXX: διότι τίς ἐξουδένωσεν εἰς ἡμέρας μικράς;). "Small and great" is often used for "all," e.g., Nu. 22:18; Jer. 6:13; ψ 103:25; 113:21; 1 Macc. 5:45 (ἀπὸ μικροῦ ἕως μεγάλου). Ezr. 8:12 mentions Johanan the son of Hakkatan (LXX 2 Εσδρ. 8:12: Ἰωαναν υἱὸς Ἀκαταν). In the OT the style of modesty and humility calls for special notice. Thus Gideon says to the angel of Yahweh in Ju. 6:15: "Wherewith shall I save Israel? Behold, my family is the weakest in Manasseh, and I am the least in my family" (Mas. וְאָנֹכִי הַצָּעִיר בְּבֵית אָבִי; LXX: καὶ ἐγώ εἰμι μικρὸς ἐν τῷ οἴκῳ τοῦ πατρός μου, B: καὶ ἐγώ εἰμι ὁ μικρότερος ἐν οἴκῳ πατρός μου). This trait of modesty is typical of election and calling. It displays a right attitude on the part of the elect and called. It also manifests the freedom and majesty of the divine action. Similarly, in 1 S. 9:21 Saul says to Samuel: "I am only a Benjamite, one of the smallest of the tribes of Israel, and my family is the least of all the families of the tribe of Benjamin" (LXX: οὐχὶ ἀνδρὸς υἱὸς Ἰεμιναίου ἐγώ εἰμι ... ἐξ ὅλου σκήπτρου Βενιαμείν, καὶ ἵνα ἐλάλησας πρὸς ἐμὲ κατὰ τὸ ῥῆμα τοῦτο). This confession is taken up again in 1 S. 15:17: "Art thou not, though little in thine own eyes, the head of the tribes of Israel?" (LXX: οὐχὶ μικρὸς σὺ εἶ ἐνώπιον αὐτοῦ ἡγούμενος σκήπτρου φυλῆς Ἰσραήλ). Solomon, too, says to Yahweh that he is only a young man who does not know how to go out or to come in (1 K. 3:7, LXX: καὶ ἐγώ εἰμι παιδάριον μικρὸν καὶ οὐκ οἶδα τὴν ἔξοδόν μου καὶ τὴν εἴσοδόν μου). This is obviously a specific mode of expression for modesty and humility in prayer or in conversation with others.[7]

3. Str.-B.[8] comments on Mt. 10:42: "There are no Rabb. examples to show that קָטָן or זְעֵיר, זְעֵירָא, for μικρός, means "pupil" or "disciple" when used abs. All the

[4] *V.* the lexicons.
[5] Preisigke Wört., II, 105 f.
[6] *V.* Hatch-Redpath, II, 926 f.
[7] What λαμπρότης τῆς ψυχῆς and μεγαλοψυχία on the part of a king is may be seen in Ep. Ar., 15-20, where, on the request of Aristeas that more than a hundred thousand prisoners should be freed, the king answers with majesty and grace: μικρόν γε ... Ἀριστέας ἡμᾶς ἀξιοῖ πρᾶγμα.
[8] I, 591 f.

instances known to us seem to have a different bearing. Ab., 4, 20 : R. Jose b. Jehuda from Kephar ha-Babli used to say : "He who learns from the small (הקטנים), to whom is he like ? He is like one who eats sour grapes and drinks wine from the winepress. And he who learns from the old, to whom is he like ? He is like one who eats ripe grapes or drinks old wine." The small here are obviously not pupils but young scholars. The same holds good in jMQ, 82d, 25 : "Great (significant scholars) are before him, and he asks the small (insignificant, זעיריא)." bSota, 22a, Bar.: "A girl who is a devotee, and a widow who goes around idly and a little one (קטן) whose months (in the mother's womb) are not yet fulfilled, lo, these ruin the world. Who is meant by the little one whose months are not yet fulfilled ? It has been explained that this is a pupil who rebels against his teachers. R. Abba (*c.* 290) has said : This is a pupil who is not yet able to make decisions, but makes them (just the same)." Here again the little one is not just a pupil, but an immature pupil.[9] But this common Rabbinic habit of disparagingly calling young scholars small (as compared to the old and great) is connected with the fact that children are also called little ones. Thus Gn. r., 42 on 14:1 says : "If there are no little ones, there are no pupils, if no pupils no scholars, if no scholars no elders, if no elders no prophets, if no prophets, God does not cause his *shechina* to rest upon them (Israel)." Here the little ones are obviously children. It is also the be noted that Ze'era, Ze'ura (cf. Παῦλος) is attested as the name of various Amoraeans (jBer., 5c, 53; jPes., 35d, 4).[10]

4. New Testament Use I.

NT usage corresponds in the main to that found elsewhere.[11] In Lk. 19:3 Zacchaeus is reported to be small in stature (ὅτι τῇ ἡλικίᾳ μικρὸς ἦν). More difficult is the addition to the proper name in Mk. 15:40 : Ἰακώβου τοῦ μικροῦ. Does this mean little of stature like Lk. 19:3 ?[12] This is just as possible as the distinction between a younger (= Lat. *minoris*) and an older James. The brief reference does not enable us to reach any solid conclusions. The phrase μικροὶ καὶ μεγάλοι, which occurs both in the OT and in Hellenism, is also found in the NT ; it occurs several times in OT quotations or in allusion to OT style.[13] μικρὸν χρόνον or μικρόν (neut.) is common, though μικρόν can have many different references, temporal, local and quantitative.[14] More important is the fact

---

[9] *Loc. cit.*

[10] Cf. Levy Wört., I, 547; Str.-B., II, 713.

[11] On this whole matter cf. O. Michel, " 'Diese Kleinen' — eine Jüngerbezeichnung Jesu," ThStKr, 108 (1937/8), 401-415; A. v. Harnack, "Die Terminologie der Wiedergeburt u. verwandter Erlebnisse in d. ältesten Kirche," TU, 42, 3 (1918), 97-143; Schl. Mt., 353 f.; Bultm. Trad.[2], 152 f., 155.

[12] Pr.-Bauer[3], 864 is inclined to understand Mk. 15:40 along the lines of Lk. 19:3. E. Lohmeyer Mk. (1937), 348 takes a different view (= Lat. *minor*): "Here alone do we find the addition 'the small' to the name of James, which distinguishes a younger from an elder." It is possible, but not probable, that ὁ μικρός is connected with Jesus' use of οὗτοι οἱ μικροί for the disciples.

[13] Ac. 8:10 : ἀπὸ μικροῦ ἕως μεγάλου; 26:22 : μαρτυρόμενος μικρῷ τε καὶ μεγάλῳ; Hb. 8:11 (quoting Ιερ. 38[31]:34): ἀπὸ μικροῦ ἕως μεγάλου αὐτῶν; Rev. 11:18 : τοῖς μικροῖς καὶ τοῖς μεγάλοις; cf. 13:16; 19:5, 18; 20:12. The NT use is often enough based on the OT (cf. Hb. 8:11), but it should not be overlooked that the same phrase occurs elsewhere, P. Oxy., X, 1350 : προσαγορεύομαι πάντας ἀπὸ μικρῶν ἕως μεγάλων (cf. also Preisigke Wört., II, 105).

[14] Often μικρὸν χρόνον, Rev. 6:11; 20:3; Jn. 7:33; 12:35; shortened to μικρόν : Jn. 13:33; 14:19; 16:16 ff.; Mk. 14:70; Mt. 26:73. μικρόν can also be used of place (Mk. 14:35; Mt. 26:39) or quantity (2 C. 11:16; cf. 11:11: μικρόν τι ἀφροσύνης): Schl. J., 300 on 14:19 :

that the Jesus of the Synoptic tradition often speaks of "these little ones" (οὗτοι οἱ μικροί). He is referring to people who are present, without disparagement, and without having children in view. Mt. 10:42: "And whosoever shall give to drink unto one of these little ones a cup of cold water only in the name of a disciple, amen I say unto you, he shall in no wise lose his reward"; Mt. 18:6: "But whoso shall offend one of these little ones which believe in me, it were better for him that a millstone were hanged about his neck, and that he were drowned in the depth of the sea" (par. Mk. 9:42; Lk. 17:2); Mt. 18:10: "Take heed that ye despise not one of these little ones; for I say unto you, That in heaven their angels do always behold the face of my Father which is in heaven";[15] Mt. 18:14: "Even so it is not the will of your Father which is in heaven, that one (ἕν; vl. εἷς) of these little ones should perish." Here are individual sayings (promises and warnings) in the proclamation of Jesus whose common link is that Jesus extends special protection to these little ones.

Behind μικρός stands the Heb. קָטָן and the Aram. זְעֵירָא, זְעֵיר. Bultmann lists these *logia* among legal sayings and rules for the community which with certain alterations were integrated into the community tradition.[16] We are faced by the question whether sayings of Jesus which originally dealt with the child became in community usage sayings about the little ones i.e., lowly Christians, whether sayings about the little ones refer to pupils,[17] or whether Jesus is saying something specific with this remarkable

---

"ἔτι μικρὸν καί. Hos. 1:4: "כִּי עוֹד מְעַט וּ" = LXX: διότι ἔτι μικρὸν καί. Is. 10:25; Jer. 51:33 μικρὸν ἔμπροσθεν, shortly before, Jos. Ant., 8, 405; 9, 79. Cf. Mt. 26:39, 73." κατὰ μικρόν, "in brief": Barn., 1, 5; παρὰ μικρόν, ψ 72:2; Ez. 16:47; Herm. s., 8, 1, 14: παρὰ μικρὸν ὅλας χλωράς (almost). μικρὸν ὅσον ὅσον, Hb. 10:37; 1 Cl., 50, 4 (both quoting Is. 26:20). Cf. Bl.-Debr.[6] § 304 and Suppl., p. 308.

[15] Acc. to the Rabb. view the angels cannot behold the face of God (Str.-B., I, 783 f.). A tradition attributed to R. Akiba and often cited maintains that even the holy creatures which uphold the throne of glory cannot see the glory of God. So S. Lv., 1, 1 (p. 4a, 23 ff., Weiss) and par. S. Nu., 103 on 12:8. A special light is shed on Mt. 18:10 by this. The guardian angels of these little ones have the privilege of always (διὰ παντός) beholding the face of the Father of Jesus in heaven. Mt. 18:10 is thus in strong contrast to Rabb. theology. J. Schniewind in *NT Deutsch,* I, 2, 193: "But this world government of God is for the smallest. The NT view thus takes a new turn as compared with Judaism and also Hellenism, which was acquainted with speculations about spiritual heavenly beings. Jewish tradition says expressly that the angels cannot see God. But here the very opposite is promised to the smallest. The Jewish and Greek world stood in great awe of these heavenly beings; they had to be reverenced in order to come to God with their help. Here, however, the mighty heavenly beings serve the very smallest who belong to Christ."

[16] Bultmann Trad., 152: "If one considers Mk. 9:37, 41 and Mt. 10:40, 42 together, it is obvious that the παιδία or μικροί of the first part of Mk. and the second of Mt. belong originally to the saying and originally have a place in both parts, while the ὑμεῖς at the beginning in Mt. and the end in Mk. is a secondary correction to facilitate the application of the saying to the Christian community. For undoubtedly the παιδία or μικροί were originally meant strictly. Receiving and refreshing a child is as important as doing good to the lofty. Later the παιδία or μικροί were understood fig. of (lowly) Christians." On Mt. 18:10 cf. Bultmann Trad., 155: "A saying which originally warns against despising children is Christianised, the μικροί being referred contextually to the Christian community. Here, too, it is impossible to say where the saying comes from." On Mt. 10:40-42 par. cf. *ibid.,* 153, n. 2: "Similar Rabb. sayings about those who show hospitality (which is estimated like veneration of the *shekhina*), esp. to students, may be found in Str.-B., I, 589 f. One may even consider whether 'disciple' was not meant in the original saying. Nevertheless, Str.-B., I, 591 f. shows that the abs. 'little ones' (for children) was not used for pupils. Hence one must refer to the Rabb. par. in Str.-B., I, 774 about the repayment of altruism to orphans."

[17] Str.-B. seems to rule this out → n. 16.

usage. On the whole one is forced to say that in spite of notable differences (cf. Mt. 10:42 with Mk. 9:41) the distinctive phrase οὗτοι οἱ μικροί is firmly anchored in the text and is plainly different from sayings about the child. Indeed, the suggestive links between the sayings and the context are not pursued. We have in Mt. 10:42 and Mk. 9:41 two different forms of the same saying, both of which can claim equal value. Mk. 9:42 could not have affected 9:41. Mt. 10:40 ff. interrelates the address and the promise to these little ones without assimilating them. It seems obvious that the Evangelists could not distinguish in sense between the disciples (Mt. 10:42: εἰς ὄνομα μαθητοῦ, Mk. 9:41: ὅτι Χριστοῦ ἐστέ) and these little ones (οὗτοι οἱ μικροί). [18]

The saying in Mt. 10:42 is interesting from another angle. Unlike Mk., it begins with the words: καὶ ὃς ἐὰν ποτίσῃ ἕνα τῶν μικρῶν τούτων. Luther, relying on cod D, the old Lat and Vg, translates: "And whoso gives one of these little ones to drink only with a cup of cold water ..." [19] But this involves a softening of a difficult reading. The saying of Jesus is not dealing with a comparison of human relations and honours, but with objective smallness, a form of the μετάνοια of ταπεινοῦν (or ταπεινὸν εἶναι), relationship with πτωχός and ταπεινός, with עָנִי and עָנָו. Protection of the least in the community is in keeping with the commandment of Jesus, but is less than Jesus' original radical designation of the disciples.

The saying in Mt. 10:42 is also important in another respect. One must read 10:40-42 in context to do justice to the Evangelist. There is a deliberate interrelating of prophet, righteous man and finally these little ones. Perhaps the saying about the little ones was originally independent, and from another context Mt. added to it the two members about the prophet and the righteous man. [20] It is more likely, however, that two different community traditions grew together, and that these little ones — one might call this paradoxical — claim the same spiritual dignity as a prophet or righteous man. The reviving of pneumatic and charismatic gifts does not contradict the humility referred to in Mt. 10:42.

Whereas the term "the small" is used disparagingly in the Rabbis (the immature, those who are not yet great and old), and whereas μέγας has a particular glory in the Greek and Hellenistic world, and μικρός is usually disdained (at best it is only a means and way for the μέγας), the saying on the lips of Jesus seems to point paradoxically to a secret, a concealed inner or future dignity. In the term "little" (קָטָן, μικρός) there may be implied both insignificance for and in the sight of men and also the sign of conversion (תְּשׁוּבָה, μετάνοια), the battle against the Pharisaic or general striving to be great. Perhaps the sociological and the religious elements are interrelated (cf. the spiritually poor of Mt. 5:3 and the poor of Lk. 6:20). God has called the mean and poor (Mt. 11:25, 29; 1 C. 1:26 f.). He who is called by God is mean and poor. He makes and keeps himself as lowly as a child (Mt. 18:4: ὅστις οὖν ταπεινώσει ἑαυτὸν ὡς τὸ παιδίον τοῦτο). The sayings about the little ones are related to those about children (παιδία) because

[18] If we compare Mt. 10:42 and Mk. 9:41 we find that for all their differences in detail they agree in the decisive point. For both these little ones are really the disciples of Jesus. Mt. says: εἰς ὄνομα μαθητοῦ, Mk. ὅτι Χριστοῦ ἐστε. The promise to these little ones in Mt. becomes an address to the disciples in Mk. and then in Mk. 9:42 turns into a promise to these little ones. One may see how the sayings took an independent turn from the first and have nothing to do with the different παιδία sayings.

[19] Vg: *Et quicumque potum dederit uni ex minimis istis*; Mt. 18:6: *unum de pusillis istis*; cf. Mk. 9:42 and Lk. 17:2; Mt. 18:10, 14.

[20] Jewish tradition? cf. Bultmann Trad., 158.

both groups belong to the context of the preaching of μετάνοια (תְּשׁוּבָה).[21] Yet one can also think of the eschatological reference. He who is small in this aeon will be called great in the future aeon (cf. Mt. 5:19: ἐλάχιστος κληθήσεται ἐν τῇ βασιλείᾳ τῶν οὐρανῶν, 18:1: τίς ἄρα μείζων ἐστὶν ἐν τῇ βασιλείᾳ τῶν οὐρανῶν). It may be seen that the saying calls for some elasticity in interpretation.[22] Perhaps light is hereby shed on Mt. 11:11 = Lk. 7:28 (Q), where Jesus says of the Baptist: "Amen I say unto you, Among them that are born of women there hath not risen a greater than John the Baptist; nothwithstanding he that is least in the kingdom of heaven (?) is greater than he."

Bultmann[23] characterises the tension in the saying as follows: "... while some parts present the Baptist as a Christian comrade, others emphasise his inferiority to Jesus. This is understandable, for both views were demanded by controversy with the Jews and followers of the Baptist. The restrictive addition Mt. 11:11b par. is found already in Q, and probably comes from the primitive community. It is certainly Christian, like the interwoven Mt. 11:10 par."[24] Is this verse a sign of the cleaving of the aeons? Is the least in the kingdom of heaven really greater than the Baptist?[25] Or is the old exegesis, revived by F. Dibelius,[26] closer to the mark, namely, that He who is now small, namely, Jesus, will be greater than the greatest of men when the kingdom is manifested? In this case the Son of Man will be revealed as the greater. The mysterious word "little" with its complement and counterpart "great," the revealing and yet also concealing self-awareness of Jesus, and the high acknowledgment of the Baptist are

[21] In the address in Mt. 18 the term "these little ones" occurs no less than 3 times (18:6, 10, 14). This can hardly be accidental; it was surely intentional. Worth noting is the fact that there are three sayings about the child (παιδίον) as well as three about the little ones (18:1-3, 4, 5). There is here a sequence which brings together the different requirements of conversion. Nor does the δέχεσθαι of 18:5 break the context of the preaching of conversion, as Lk. 9:48 teaches. Both groups are externally related by the same Heb. term הַקְּטַנִּים. Both the parable of the child and the description of the disciples as little ones are part of the preaching of conversion. Yet one should not try to make a closer connection between the groups as in Bultmann's redaction hypothesis. Their external separation is an argument against the view that παιδία or μικροί originally referred to the child and then came to be transferred to (lowly) Christians.

[22] J. Schniewind on Mt. 18:10 in *NT Deutsch*, I, 2, 193 sees the link between the קְטַנִּים (= μικροί) and the עֲנָוִים (= πτωχοὶ τῷ πνεύματι, Mt. 5:3): "The little ones are the lowly in the broadest sense, the poor, uneducated, socially inferior; certainly children too, but it would be wrong to derive the idea of a children's angel from this saying." This would mean that equation with the μαθηταί of Jesus came only with the composition of the address, whereas it is quite possible that the Evangelist is right in making this equation.

[23] Trad., 177.

[24] *Op. cit.*, 178.

[25] Job 3:19 is important for the Rabb. (Str.-B., I, 598). Rt. r., 3 on 1:17 "Small and great are there, and the servant is free of his master" (Job 3:19). R. Simon (c. 280) has said: He who is little in this world can become great, and he who is great can become little; but he who is little in the future world cannot become great, and he who is great cannot become little. In Pesikt. r., App. 3 (198b) R. Jonathan (*c.* 220) says with ref. to Job 3:19: "Does not everyone know that small and great are there? The verse teaches that in this world it is not known who is small and who is great." Cf. bBM, 85b: "R. Yirmeya (c. 320) said to R. Zeïra (c. 300): What is meant by Job 3:19, that small and great are there etc.? Do we not know that small and great are there? The meaning is that he who makes himself small in this world for the sake of the words of the Torah will be great in the future world, and he who makes himself equal to a slave in this world for the sake of the words of the Torah will be a free man in the future world." On the Rabb. view the distinction between small and great is thus not removed in the future aeon.

[26] ZNW, 11 (1910), 190.

factors which set in a new light the hypothesis of F. Dibelius.[27] Schlatter[28] sees in Mt. 11:11 the conflict of Jesus against the Jewish goal of greatness: "The disciple can be even greater than the one who is greater than all. He does so when he is smaller, and since by human judgment it is a contradiction for the smaller to be greater because he is smaller, there is need to add ἐν τῇ βασιλείᾳ τῶν οὐρανῶν. The battle of Jesus against human greatness is seen not only in individual statements and actions like 11:25; 18:1; 19:14, 30; it is a continually active and visible mark of His whole activity.[29] "In his ministry and suffering the disciple is smaller than the Baptist, and he is thereby greater than the greatest of all."[29] When He speaks of the mystery of littleness, Jesus combats the human ideal of greatness.[30]

In Mk. 4:31; Mt. 13:32 the grain of mustard seed is the smallest of all seeds when sown. But when sown it grows and becomes greater than all plants, putting forth great branches.[31] The secret of God is concealed in this growth and in this change from the small to the great. In Lk. 12:32 Jesus addresses His disciples with the promise: Μὴ φοβοῦ, τὸ μικρὸν ποίμνιον. Jesus is aware of the temptation caused by the smallness of the company. But here, too, the divine mystery is concealed in the μικρόν. To it will be given a share in the rule of heaven. Lk. 9:48: ὁ γὰρ μικρότερος ἐν πᾶσιν ὑμῖν ὑπάρχων, οὗτός ἐστιν μέγας, again attacks the human striving to be great at the root, and describes littleness as the way to greatness.[32] Littleness corresponds to the ταπεινοῦν of Mt. 18:4 ("Whosoever therefore shall humble himself as this little child, the same is greatest in the kingdom of heaven"); cf. Mt. 23:12: ὅστις δὲ ὑψώσει ἑαυτὸν ταπεινωθήσεται, καὶ ὅστις ταπεινώσει ἑαυτὸν ὑψωθήσεται (cf. Lk. 14:11; 18:14). This ταπεινοῦν ἑαυτόν, recognising that one is little and insignificant before God, is an expression of the humility of Jesus similar to the μικρὸν εἶναι of the Synoptic tradition. It expresses conversion. Hence it is not an artificial work of legal righteousness, but

---

[27] Note should be taken of the testimony of the fathers, Chrys. Hom. in Mt. XXXVII, 2 (MPG, 57, p. 421): περὶ μὲν γὰρ ἑαυτοῦ λέγων, εἰκότως κρύπτει τὸ πρόσωπον διὰ τὴν ἔτι κρατοῦσαν ὑπόνοιαν, καὶ τὸ μὴ δόξαι περὶ ἑαυτοῦ μέγα τι λέγειν, καὶ γὰρ πολλαχοῦ φαίνεται τοῦτο ποιῶν. *Loc. cit.* (p. 422): μικρότερος κατὰ τὴν ἡλικίαν, καὶ κατὰ τὴν τῶν πολλῶν δόξαν· καὶ γὰρ ἔλεγον αὐτὸν φάγον καὶ οἰνοπότην· καὶ· οὐχ οὗτός ἐστιν ὁ τοῦ τέκτονος υἱός; Hilary of Poictiers, Comm. in Mt. XI, 6 (MPL, 9, p. 980 f., c ff.): *Et quomodo Christum ignorare creditur, qui missus in angeli potestate viam venturo paraverit, et quo ex natis mulierum nullus maior propheta surrexerit; nisi quod qui minor eo est, id est, qui interrogatur, cui non creditur, cui testimonium nec opera sua praestant, hic in regno coelorum maior est?* Tert. Marc., 4, 18: *sive enim de quocumque dicit modico sive de semetipso per humilitatem, quia minor Johanne habebatur.*

[28] Schl. Mt., 366 f.

[29] *Loc. cit.*

[30] J. Schniewind on Mt. 11:11 in *NT Deutsch,* 139: "To God's dominion belongs a new existence, a new birth." "The Baptist himself proclaimed this with his baptism, which signified a dying and being raised again ...; but the Baptist in his own work is still one who waits." "And the least who sees the kingdom of heaven, who experiences it and enters into it, has something which even the Baptist as yet did not have." "Current expectation of the days of the Messiah spoke in the same vein: Well with the least who experiences them as with the least who lived through the liberation from Egypt; he saw more than the greatest prophets."

[31] Cf. F. Jehle, "Senfkorn u. Sauerteig in d. Hl. Schrift," NkZ, 34 (1923), 713 ff. Schl. Mt., 442: "The minimum of action is accompanied by totality of success. He who stoops to what is small achieves the great, the whole. The relation of this parable to the situation of the disciples is easily discerned ... God's whole greatness is at work in these small processes. In them is grounded and begun the totality which will infallibly reach its goal."

[32] Schl. Lk., 108.

the very nature of Jesus (ὅτι πραΰς εἰμι καὶ ταπεινὸς τῇ καρδίᾳ, Mt. 11:29).[33] Rev. 3:8 reminds us of the promise which God gives the μικρὸν εἶναι: ὅτι μικρὰν ἔχεις δύναμιν, καὶ ἐτήρησάς μου τὸν λόγον καὶ οὐκ ἠρνήσω τὸ ὀνομά μου.[34] This is the new thing in the proclamation of Jesus. He overcomes both Pharisaic and general striving for greatness, and He also overcomes the temptation implicit in littleness. He finds in littleness before God, in the birth of this littleness, in self-humiliation and self-abasement, the way to win the kingdom of heaven and to be great in the new aeon. Paul takes up this message in Phil. 2:8 (ἐταπείνωσεν ἑαυτόν) and Phil. 2:3; Col. 3:12 (ταπεινοφροσύνη). He sees Christ in this light, and sets himself under the same word (Phil. 4:12: οἶδα καὶ ταπεινοῦσθαι).

It is as well not to overlook small factors and events, as popular wisdom itself reminds us (little causes, great effects). Paul loves the saying: μικρὰ ζύμη ὅλον φύραμα ζυμοῖ (1 C. 5:6; Gl. 5:9),[35] and Jm. 3:5 warns similarly: οὕτως καὶ ἡ γλῶσσα μικρὸν μέλος ἐστὶν καὶ μεγάλα αὐχεῖ.[36] Even evil can deploy uncanny power. Later the usage becomes weaker and adapts itself to general modes of expression. In 2 Cl., 1, 1 f. we find μικρὰ φρονεῖν περί τινος (μικρὸν φρονεῖν, Soph. Ai., 1120; Plut. Quomodo Adolescens Poetas Audire Debeat, 9 [II, 28c]): "We should not think meanly about our salvation" (καὶ οὐ δεῖ ἡμᾶς μικρὰ φρονεῖν περὶ τῆς σωτηρίας ἡμῶν). "For if we think meanly about Him (Jesus), we hope to receive only small things; and if we listen as though only to little things, we sin, for we do not realise whence we are called, and by whom, and to what place, and what sufferings Jesus Christ bore for our sakes." 2 Cl., 8, 5 quotes as a dominical saying (λέγει γὰρ ὁ κύριος ἐν τῷ εὐαγγελίῳ): Εἰ τὸ μικρὸν οὐκ ἐτηρήσατε, τὸ μέγα τίς ὑμῖν δώσει; λέγω γὰρ ὑμῖν ὅτι ὁ

---

33 Schl. Mt., 543: "The question of greatness took on great significance because the striving to be great permeated all Palestinian piety. On all occasions, at worship, at court, in common meals, in every affair, the question constantly arose who was the greater, and according to each his due honour was an important matter which caused constant concern. By breaking the disciples free from this tradition Jesus gave His community a completely new form." On the pre-Christian view of ταπεινοῦν ἑαυτόν cf. Schl. Mt., 545. In Joseph. ταπεινοῦν is connected with weakness and shame. The Rabb. linked self-humiliation with confession of sin. Str.-B., I, 774: Lv. r., 1, 5 on 1:1: "Hillel (*c.* 20 B.C.) said: My (self-) humiliation is my exaltation, my (self-)exaltation my humiliation." This saying was repeated and expounded in many ways. Ex. r., 45, 5 on 33:12: R. Tanchuma b. Abba (*c.* 380) opened his discourse with Prv. 25:7: For it is better that a man say to thee: Come up hither, than that he humiliate thee. Hillel said: My (self-)humiliation, that is my exaltation, and my (self-)exaltation is my humiliation. It is better for a man that one say to him: Come up higher, than: Go down lower. In Rabb. writings David is an example and model of self-humiliation and exaltation (Ps. 56:1; 113:5 f.; 1 Ch. 14:17).

34 Had. Apk., 60: "The small power relates not only to the small number of members but also, as in 1 C. 1:26, to their social position, their lack of significance, esteem or influence." But this is not a secure interpretation of μικρὰ δύναμις.

35 Joh. W. 1 K., 133: "In the οὐκ οἴδατε the apostle not only reminds them of the familiar saying but also appeals to their own judgment. Is it not as the saying has it, and does it not apply fully to you? The image, which occurs in Gl. 5:9 too, does not have to be a mere echo of the parable of Jesus (Mt. 13:33 = Lk. 13:21); indeed, φύραμα (R. 9:21; 11:16) for ἄλευρον is against this. It may be a proverb used by both Jesus and Paul." Schl. K., 179 f.: "The same principle, illustrated by the leaven, that an apparently small process can have significance for the whole, is found in Gl. 5:9. It had proverbial currency; Jesus used the same comparison. The closest par. is Mt. 16:6, and it occurs also in the Rabbis." For leaven as the impelling force behind a doctrine, jChag., 76c, 42 and Pesikt., 121a; Str.-B., I, 728 f.

36 Jm. 3:4: μετάγεται ὑπὸ ἐλαχίστου πηδαλίου, may also be quoted. The contrast between small and great is present in both 3:4 and 3:5. ἐλάχιστος in 3:4 is not a superlative, but a strengthened μικρός (as commonly in Hellen. Gk.). Bl.-Debr.[6] § 60, 2; Schl. Jk., 215 (with examples from Jos.).

πιστὸς ἐν ἐλαχίστῳ καὶ ἐν πολλῷ πιστός ἐστιν (cf. Lk. 16:10).[37] Herm. s., 8, 10, 1 knows the phrase μικρὰ κατ' ἀλλήλων ἔχειν ("to have little things against one another"), and he ventures to speak of petty desires (μικραὶ ἐπιθυμίαι): ἐλάχιστον δὲ (ἐξή)μαρτον διὰ μικρὰς ἐπιθυμίας καὶ μικρὰ κατ' ἀλλήλων ἔχοντες ("they are always good and believing and in regard before God, but they have committed little sins out of petty evil desire, and have had petty quarrels with one another").

5. The New Testament Use II: Comparative and Superlative.

The comparative ἐλάττων (Jn. 2:10; R. 9:12; Hb. 7:7; 1 Tm. 5:9) and the superlative ἐλάχιστος (Eph. 3:8: ἐλαχιστότερος) correspond to the positive μικρός and confirm what we have said thus far.[38] Mt. 2:6, quoting Mi. 5:1, 3, boasts of Bethlehem: καὶ σὺ Βηθλέεμ, γῆ Ἰούδα, οὐδαμῶς ἐλαχίστη εἶ ἐν τοῖς ἡγεμόσιν Ἰούδα. Bethlehem had thus far been regarded as insignificant (Tg. Mi. 5:1), but it is not so according to the Evangelist.[39] In Mt. 5:19 none is to break even one of the least of these commandments, or to teach men so, or he will be called least in the kingdom of heaven (opp. of ἐλάχιστος κληθήσεται: μέγας κληθήσεται).[40] In Mt. 25:40: ἐφ' ὅσον ἐποιήσατε ἑνὶ τούτων τῶν ἀδελφῶν μου τῶν ἐλαχίστων, ἐμοὶ ἐποιήσατε, 25:45: ἐφ' ὅσον οὐκ ἐποιήσατε ἑνὶ τούτων τῶν

---

[37] On 2 Cl., 8, 5 as an apocr. saying of the Lord, and its attestation, *v.* Kn. Did., 166. Iren., II, 34, 3: *et ideo dominus dicebat ingratis exsistentibus in eum: si in modico fideles non fuistis, quod magnum est quis dabit vobis? significans quoniam qui in modica temporali vita ingrati exstiterunt ei qui eam praestitit, iuste non percipient ab eo in saeculum saeculi longitudinem dierum;* cf. also Hipp. Ref., X, 33, 7; Knopf, *loc. cit.*: "For 2 Cl. τὸ μικρὸν τηρεῖν = τὴν σάρκα ἁγνὴν τηρεῖν and the μέγα is ζωὴ αἰώνιος.

[38] On the comparative ἐλάττων cf. Bl.-Debr.[6] § 34, 1; cf. also ἐλαττοῦν and ἐλαττονεῖν. Also § 61, 1 f. (opp. of κρείσσων Jn. 2:10; Hb. 7:7; of μείζων, R. 9:12); ἔλαττον adv. "less" (1 Tm. 5:9). On the superlative ἐλάχιστος § 60, 2 (*perexiguus*); a new popular construction is ἐλαχιστότερος, Eph. 3:8; *v.* § 60, 2 and 61, 2; on ἐμοὶ εἰς ἐλάχιστόν ἐστιν, 1 C. 4:3, cf. § 145, 2; 393, 6. ἐλάσσων (ἐλάττων) is found in class. Gk. from Homer; it also occurs in inscr., pap. and the LXX; ἐλάχιστος occurs in Hom. Hymn. (Merc., 573) and Hdt., also inscr., pap. and LXX. ἐλάχιστος of insignificant persons: Ditt. Syll.[3], II, 888, 56 ff. καὶ γὰρ ὡς ἀληθῶς ἀπὸ πολλῶν οἰκοδεσποτῶν εἰς ἐλαχίστους κατεληλύθαμεν. Cf. also Pr.-Bauer[3], 411 f. and Liddell-Scott, 529 f.

[39] Tg. Mi. 5:1: Thou Bethlehem Ephratha, how small hast thou been in number compared with the thousands of the house of Judah — but out of thee shall come the Messiah to take dominion over Israel, whose name is named from the beginning, from the days of the world. Str.-B., I, 83; LXX Mi. 5:1: καὶ σύ, Βηθλεεμ οἶκος τοῦ Εφραθα, ὀλιγοστὸς εἶ τοῦ εἶναι ἐν χιλιάσιν Ιουδα· ἐκ σοῦ μοι ἐξελεύσεται τοῦ εἶναι εἰς ἄρχοντα ἐν τῷ Ἰσραηλ, καὶ αἱ ἔξοδοι αὐτοῦ ἀπ' ἀρχῆς ἐξ ἡμερῶν αἰῶνος. On the relation of Mt. to the Heb. cf. Schl. Mt., 35.

[40] Cf. F. Dibelius, "Die kleinsten Gebote," ZNW, 11 (1910), 188-190: "The 'smallest' commandments are the shortest." "One thinks immediately of a group of commandments which are undoubtedly the shortest: Thou shalt not kill, Thou shalt not commit adultery, Thou shalt not steal — sayings of only two words in the Heb." Cf. also Schl. Mt., 157 f.: "These smallest commandments are the familiar core of the written Law, the Decalogue." "Since the Semitic has no comparison of the adj., Mt. uses the comparative and superlative sparingly. Apart from ἐλάχιστος he has only πλεῖστος, and the comp. only in respect of measure and number: πλείων, μείζων, μικρότερος, περισσότερος. Cf. also χείρων, πονηρότερος, εὐκοπώτερον, ἀνεκτότερον. J. Schniewind on Mt. 5:19 in *NT Deutsch,* 53 f. points out that gradations are here presupposed in the kingdom of heaven, and that the passage demands radical obedience to the Law. Mt. 5:19 is connected with later Jewish discussion about the Law, and with questions of primitive Christianity. Perhaps in relation to μέγας we should recall that the teacher is called "the great one" (רַב).

ἐλαχίστων, οὐδὲ ἐμοὶ ἐποιήσατε, Jesus speaks of the least of these His brethren.[41] In this context Jesus ranges Himself with them, and the question is whether He means those who are hungry, sick, or in prison, and is giving a standard by which He will judge all (Mt. 5:3-10), or whether He is identifying Himself with the fate of the disciples, and making their affliction His own (Mt. 10:40-42). Lk., too, is fond of this superlative. It expresses the impotence of man in 12:26: εἰ οὖν οὐδὲ ἐλάχιστον δύνασθε ... In 16:10 it appears in the well-known saying of Jesus: ὁ πιστὸς ἐν ἐλαχίστῳ καὶ ἐν πολλῷ πιστός ἐστιν, καὶ ὁ ἐν ἐλαχίστῳ ἄδικος καὶ ἐν πολλῷ ἄδικός ἐστιν.[42] Lk. 19:17 is similar: εὖ γε, ἀγαθὲ δοῦλε, ὅτι ἐν ἐλαχίστῳ πιστὸς ἐγένου. "Not merely is natural possession small; even what is received from Jesus is an ἐλάχιστον. The situation in which the disciples are put by the death of Jesus confers on them no great power. Something very small is given them when one bears in mind the Messianic goal."[43] It is noteworthy that Paul in 1 C. 15:9 calls himself ὁ ἐλάχιστος τῶν ἀποστόλων, obviously, as the same verse tells us, because he is not worthy to be called an apostle, since he persecuted the community of God.[44] In the same connection Eph. 3:8 has the superlative comparative: ἐμοὶ τῷ ἐλαχιστοτέρῳ πάντων ἁγίων ἐδόθη ἡ χάρις αὕτη, τοῖς ἔθνεσιν εὐαγγελίσασθαι τὸ ἀνεξιχνίαστον πλοῦτος τοῦ Χριστοῦ.[45] It may be seen clearly that ἐλάχιστος can have serious significance in the NT, and must be co-ordinated with μικρός.

Paul also uses ἐμοὶ δὲ εἰς ἐλάχιστόν ἐστιν (1 C. 4:3) in the sense: "It makes no odds to me."[46] εἰς ἐλάχιστόν ἐστιν is made up of ἐλάχιστόν ἐστιν and εἰς

---

[41] Apart from the comm., which try to show the point of the passage, cf. also A. Wikenhauser, "D. Liebeswerke in dem Gerichtsgemälde Mt. 25:31-46," BZ, 20 (1932), 366-377; W. Brandt, "Die geringsten Brüder. Aus dem Gespräch d. Kirche mit Mt. 25:31-46," *Jbch. d. Theol. Schule Bethel,* 8 (1937), 1-28. Cf. also H. Graffmann, "Das Gericht nach den Werken im Mt.-Ev.," *Barth-Festschrift* (1936), 124-135. Acc. to Bultmann Trad., 130 f. it is possible that Mt. 25:31-46 derives from Jewish tradition. "The passage contains a specifically Christian element perhaps in the statements that good works or their omission are seen to be related to the Son of Man" (130). "The king and world judge equates the least of his brethren with himself (v. 40, 45). The risen Lord speaks similarly when He vanquishes persecuting Paul (Ac. 26:4 par.). The incarnate Lord also spoke of good shown to His own" (J. Schniewind on Mt. 25:40, 45, *NT Deutsch,* 248).

[42] Bultmann Trad., 79 regards Lk. 16:10-12 as wisdom sayings, vv. 11-12 being a development of v. 10 (p. 90). Materially cf. Schl. Lk., 370; K. H. Rengstorf, *ad loc.* in *NT Deutsch,* I, 3, 175. It is rightly seen that ἐλάχιστον is here elative rather than superlative. That the saying was not later forgotten, but grew with similar sayings in the tradition, may be seen, e.g., from 2 Cl., 8, 5.

[43] Schl. Lk., 406.

[44] Schl. K., 402: "He who because of his guilt is the least of all has by his labours become the first of all." Joh. W. 1 K. (1910), 352: "ἐλάχιστος is quite natural on the lips of the apostle in comparison with the pointless exaggerations charged to him (Eph. 3:8; 1 Tm. 1:15)." Perhaps 1 Tm. 1:15 with its difficult ὧν πρῶτός εἰμι ἐγώ means that Paul sees that he is a sinner of a special kind.

[45] Eph. 3:8: "ἐμοὶ τῷ ἐλαχιστοτέρῳ πάντων ἁγίων ἐδόθη ἡ χάρις αὕτη," reminds us of 1 C. 15:9 and 1 Tm. 1:15. ἐλαχιστότερος is a new popular construct, Bl.-Debr.[6] § 60, 2 and 61, 2. Paul is thinking primarily of his special guilt as in 1 C. 15:9 and 1 Tm. 1:15. But what G. C. A. Harless says in his *Commentar über den Brief Pauli an d. Eph.* (1834), 291 is also true: "In the inmost depths each of us sees only himself; what he sees in himself he does not see in others. What he sees tells him that sin dwells in him." Paul sees in himself the true παράδειγμα of the sinner, and in this sense, too, he draws a line of separation between himself and others.

[46] Ltzm. K., *ad loc.*

ἐλάχιστον γίγνεται.[47] κριτήρια ἐλάχιστα in 1 C. 6:2 means "the smallest legal matters."[48]

τὰ ἐλάχιστα τῶν ζώων in 1 Cl., 20, 10 means "the smallest animals," τὰ ἐλάχιστα μέλη τοῦ σώματος in 1 Cl., 37, 5 "the smallest parts of our body." But the term is most fancied and used by Herm., e.g., m., 5, 1, 5: ἐὰν γὰρ λαβὼν ἀψινθίου μικρὸν λίαν εἰς κεράμιον μέλιτος ἐπιχέῃς, οὐχὶ ὅλον τὸ μέλι ἀφανίζεται, καὶ τοσοῦτον μέλι ὑπὸ τοῦ ἐλαχίστου ἀψινθίου ἀπόλλυται ...; "For if you take a very little gall and put it in a big pot of honey, will not the whole of the honey be corrupted? And so much honey will be corrupted by so little gall ...?" μικρόν and ὅλον, ἐλάχιστον and τοσοῦτον, are here two corresponding antitheses. One is reminded of the Synoptic saying about leaven (ζύμη).[49] Elsewhere, too, it may be seen that Herm. uses ἐλάχιστον as an elative, like μικρόν. Herm. m., 11, 20 f. is designed to show that "very tiny things which fall from heaven to earth have great force" (ὅτι τὰ ἄνωθεν ἐλάχιστα πίπτοντα ἐπὶ τὴν γῆν μεγάλην δύναμιν ἔχουσιν): "Hail is a very little grain (ἐλάχιστόν ἐστιν κοκκάριον), and yet what damage it does when it falls on the head!" (corresponding antithesis: ἐλάχιστος — μέγας). Herm. s., 6, 4, 2: [ἐλάχιστον, φημί, κύριε, βασανίζονται·] ἔδει γὰρ τοὺς οὕτω τρυφῶντας καὶ ἐπιλανθανομένους τοῦ θεοῦ ἑπταπλασίως βασανίζεσθαι (antithesis ἐλάχιστον — ἑπταπλασίως), s., 6, 4, 4: βλέπεις οὖν, φησίν, ὅτι τῆς τρυφῆς καὶ ἀπάτης ὁ χρόνος ἐλάχιστός ἐστι, τῆς δὲ τιμωρίας καὶ βασάνου πολύς (antithesis ἐλάχιστος — πολύς). Herm. must realise that the time of carousing and deceit is very short, that of punishment and torment long. s., 8, 1, 14: ἐλάχιστον δὲ τῶν ῥάβδων αὐτῶν ξηρὸν ἦν, αὐτὸ τὸ ἄκρον, 8, 1, 15: ἑτέρων δὲ ἦν ἐλάχιστον χλωρόν, 8, 5, 5: ἐλάχιστον δὲ (ξηρὸν) καὶ σχισμὰς ἐχούσας, 8, 5, 6: οἱ ἐλάχιστον ἔχοντες χλωρόν, τὰ δὲ λοιπὰ μέρη ξηρά. The parable has in view certain Christians with whose faith Herm. has fault to find. Cf. s., 8, 10, 1: ἐλάχιστον δὲ [ἐξή]μαρτον διὰ μικρὰς ἐπιθυμίας καὶ μικρὰ κατ' ἀλλήλων ἔχοντες. 8, 10, 1-3: "Those who had handed back their staves green, with only the tips dried up and full of rents ..., have committed little sins out of petty evil desire, and have had petty quarrels with one another ... But those who have handed back their staves withered and with very little green are those who have only believed, but the works they do are works of unrighteousness."[50] s., 9, 8, 7: ἐκ τούτων ἐλάχιστοι ἐμελάνησαν, καὶ ἀπεβλήθησαν πρὸς τοὺς λοιπούς (testing of the stones in the parable of the building of the tower). Herm. sees among believers a special group who are for him the ideal of all piety. They are like innocent children into whose minds no evil comes and who have not learned what sin is, who remain always innocent. They will certainly have a dwelling in the kingdom of God, for they have not in any point defiled the commandments of God, but have maintained the same innocent disposition all the days of their lives (s., 9, 29, 1 f.). "All you ... who remain so, and become as children without any wickedness, you are more glorious than those mentioned before; for all children are glorious before God, and stand at the head beside

[47] Cf. Bl.-Debr.[6] § 145, 2; 393, 6.

[48] Ltzm. K., *ad loc.*

[49] Cf. on this Dib. Herm., 515: "The root of the whole may well be a proverb, *v.* the Muratorian Canon, 67 f.: *fel enim cum melle misceri non congruit.* The saying belongs to a series of metaphors which show that it is foolish to associate incompatibles." Cf. Ign. Tr., 6, 2; Iren., III, 18, 3; Tert. De Anima, 3; Marc., 1, 55 f.; also Herm. m., 10, 3, 3: "For as gall and wine no longer have the same taste when mixed, so sadness, mixed with the Holy Spirit, does not have the same power of prayer."

[50] On this cf. the exc. in Dib. Herm., 587 ff.: "Die Allegorie vom Weidenbaum." 589: "He used the metaphor of the testing of the members of God's people simply to split off from it as it were a second picture, the restoration of the withered members. His main interest, then, is to show, not the authentication of the righteous, but the success of the message of repentance among Christians, and to warn the community by depicting the unreadiness of some sinners to repent."

Him. Blessed are you who have shunned iniquity and devoted yourselves to innocence; before all others you will have life with God" (s., 9, 29, 3).[51]

In intimation of later development in the fathers, original Christian preaching is here combined with the motif of childlike innocence, which is common to antiquity, whether Hellenistic or Rabbinical. The essential point is, however, that this motif of antiquity is not found in primitive Christianity. In the NT what Jesus says about the "little ones" is not the same as what He says about "children."[52]

Michel

† μιμέομαι, † μιμητής † συμμιμητής

Contents: 1. Secular Usage; 2. The Cosmological Concept of Mimesis; 3. The Septuagint and Pseudepigrapha; 4. Philo and Josephus; 5. The Word Group in the New Testament; 6. The Word Group in the Post-Apostolic Fathers.

1. Secular Usage.

The word group μιμέομαι etc., which does not occur at all in Hom. or Hes., arose in the 6th cent., and came into common use in both prose and poetry. μιμέομαι has the sense "to imitate," "to mimic," i.e., to do what is seen to be done by someone else.[1]

---

[51] Cf. Dib. Herm., 636 f.; H. Windisch, *Taufe u. Sünde im ältesten Christentum bis auf Origenes* (1908), 359: "ἁπλότης and νηπιότης are excellent terms for these sinless beings. Sinless childhood is realised in them." "To all who remain and become as children without sin (κακίαν μὴ ἔχοντες) the Shepherd promises outstanding glory." "Thus the metaphor of the innocent child, well-known to us from earlier writings, is used to illustrate the Christian ideal of sinlessness. The author believes there have really been sinless men in the Christian community. The preaching of repentance is simply designed to increase the number of these men who are like sinless children."

[52] On the exposition of the παιδία sayings of Mt. 18 in the fathers cf. Michel, *op. cit.* Windisch wrongly reads the innocent, guileless, sinless character of childhood into 1 Pt. 2:2 (ὡς ἀρτιγέννητα βρέφη τὸ λογικὸν ἄδολον γάλα ἐπιποθήσατε), *op. cit.*, 237. A. Schlatter, *Pt. u. Pls. nach dem 1. Pt.* (1937), 90 rightly says: "Since recipients of the word are called regenerate, their demand for the word is compared with the attitude of the newly born child, which desires milk."

μιμέομαι κτλ. Cf. Cr.-Kö., 730 f., *s.v.*; Joh. W. 1 K. on 4:16; E. Eidem, "Imitatio Pauli" (Swed.) in *Teologiska Studier tillägnade Erik Stave* (1922), 67-85; E. G. Gulin, "Die Nachfolge Gottes," *Stud. Or.*, I (1925), 34-50; "Die Freude im NT," *Annales Academiae Scientiarium Fennicae*, Ser. B, tom. XXVI, 2 (1932), 234 ff.; A. Oepke, "Nachfolge u. Nachahmung Christi im NT," AELKZ, 71 (1938), 850-857, 866-872; J. M. Nielen, "Die Kultsprache der Nachfolge u. Nachahmung Gottes u. verwandter Bezeichnungen im nt.lichen Schrifttum," *Heilige Überlieferung. Ausschnitte aus d. Geschichte des Mönchtums u. des heiligen Kultes ... Ildefons Herwegen dargeboten* (= *Beiträge zur Gesch. des alten Mönchtums u. des Benediktinerordens, Suppl.-Bd.*) (1938), 59-85; → ἀκολουθέω, I, 210, Bibl.

[1] Cf. Pass., Liddell-Scott, *s.v.* The group is rare in inscr. Ditt. Syll.³, 783 (after 27 B.C.) in the *laudatio* of a married couple whose ὁμόνοια is extolled, says of the wife in line 39 f.: ἥ τε σεμνοτάτη καὶ φίλανδρος Ἐπιγόνη μειμησαμένη τὸν γαμήσαντα καὶ αὐτή, "she has not remained behind her husband, but has rivalled him." Cf. also Ditt. Or., 669, 14 f.

τό τε γὰρ μιμεῖσθαι σύμφυτον τοῖς ἀνθρώποις ἐκ παίδων ἐστίν, says Aristot. Poet., 4, p. 1448b, 5 f., and Democr. Fr., 154 (II, 173, 11 ff., Diels[5]) explains that the beginnings of human culture came when men took animals as their examples and learned (μανθάνειν) from them, e.g., weaving and sewing from the spider, building from the swallow, and all this κατὰ μίμησιν, i.e., by imitating them. Hippocr. Vict., 1, 11 ff. (I, 185, 25 ff., Diels[5]) emphasises that different artisans, τέκτονες, οἰκοδόμοι, etc., took the different parts of the human body and their functions as models for their activity: φύσιν ἀνθρώπου μιμέονται is the guiding thought in this discussion, in which is interwoven a cosmological consideration to the degree that man is regarded as ἀπομίμησις τοῦ ὅλου (1, 10 = I, 185, 9 ff., Diels[5]; cf. 1, 22 = I, 188, 6). Art, which deliberately seeks to copy, is often called imitation. This applies not merely to drama [2] but also to painting and sculpture, music and dancing, and esp. poetry: all are μιμητικαὶ τέχναι. Already Heracl. Fr., 10 (I, 153, 1 f., Diels[5]) calls τέχνη (he mentions painting, music and writing) τὴν φύσιν μιμουμένη, here with ref. to a specific feature, the creation of harmony out of opposites, not things like. In this he turns against his teacher Plato, who certainly thought the poet a μιμητής, but in a derogatory sense. God, who created the essence or idea of, e.g., a bed (Plato's example in Resp., X, 597d), is the φυτουργός; the carpenter who fashions a bedstead is the δημιουργός; the painter, who simply paints a bed without being able to make it, comes third and is the μιμητής, and the tragic poet is similar (597e). In the background is Plato's distinctive differentiation between idea and phenomenon. Yet painters and poets are not μιμηταί because they give expression to the idea. They copy reality, which in this connection is not called an imitation of the idea, only in an inadequate and even deceptive way (in 598d the μιμητής is associated with the → γόης), for they fashion only an → εἴδωλον, an image of reality (ὁ τοῦ εἰδώλου ποιητής, ὁ μιμητής, 601b). The μιμητής remains quite remote from the truth (the idea) itself (τοῦ δὲ ἀληθοῦς πόρρω πάνυ ἀφεστῶτα, 605c; cf. 597e). Hence Plato will not have epic or tragic poetry in his state, since they set up a κακὴ πολιτεία in the souls of men (605b; cf. also III, 388c, where he criticises Hom. for daring to present Zeus in a way which is so unlike him, τολμῆσαι οὕτως ἀνομοίως μιμήσασθαι).

Elsewhere, too, the group is used in a bad sense, whether for what is showy and aped, or for weak and unoriginal copying. [3] Yet the terms were also quickly adopted into the ethical sphere and there used seriously. Democr. Fr., 39 (II, 155, 5, Diels[5])

(68 A.D.). μίμημα, not used in the NT, but found in the LXX and post-apost. fathers, means "image" in Ditt. Or., 383, 63 (and the shorter version of the same inscr., 404, 26). The pap. show the popular use of μιμέομαι: οὐκ ἐμιμησάμην σε, "I have not done it as thou," P. Oxy., X, 1295, 3 (2nd cent. A.D.); μιμοῦ τὸν πατέρα τὸν φιλότιμον τὸν γέροντα φῶτα, P. Ryl., II, 77, 34 (192 A.D.). For further instances cf. Preisigke Wört., II, 106, Moult.-Mill., 412, *s.v.* μίμησις occurs only in Byzantine pap. in the weaker meaning "corresponding" (cf. also Test. Sol. D, VIII, 5). We may mention from the magic pap. κύριε, ἀπομιμοῦμαί σε ταῖς ζ' φωναῖς, "Lord, I imitate thee with the 7 vowels," Preis. Zaub., XIII, 700 f. (346 A.D.). ἀπομιμέομαι, ἀπομίμησις, ἀπομίμημα are rare cf. Pass., *s.v.*; they do not occur in the biblical writings.

[2] The noun μῖμος, from Aesch., means above all the actor, the mime. A simple joy in imitation, along with an element of merriness and parody, characterises the particular art of the theatre called Mimos, which was widespread from an early time (Plato valued it greatly acc. to Diog. L., III, 13 [18]), and which in the last pre-Christian centuries reached a climax which was to exercise an influence on into the Middle Ages. Cf. E. Wüst, Art. "Mimos" in Pauly-W., XV, 2 (1932), 1727 ff.; K. Kerenyi, *Apollon* (1937), 142 ff. Mimos "presented everyday life with sharp realism. In content and language it simply met the need of the lower classes for entertainment. Fundamentally it was non-literary. It consisted in improvised solo scenes which emphasised the typical, not the dramatic" (Wüst, 1730).

[3] Thus μίμησις was the first (serious) watchword of classicist literary aesthetics, which, itself uncreative, is impelled by a great love for its object and will accept as art only a faithful imitation of classical models. Cf. W. Schmid, W. v. Christ's *Gesch. d. gr. Lit.*[6], II, 1 (1920), 21 and 462.

emphasises: ἀγαθὸν ἢ εἶναι χρεὼν ἢ μιμεῖσθαι, "one must either be good or imitate a good man," cf. Fr., 79 (II, 160, 5 f.): χαλεπὸν μιμεῖσθαι μὲν τοὺς κακούς, μηδὲ ἐθέλειν δὲ τοὺς ἀγαθούς, "it is bad to imitate the wicked and not even to wish to imitate the good." The relation which there ought to be between parents and children (cf. Eur. Hel., 940 f.: μιμοῦ τρόπους πατρὸς δικαίου) or teachers and pupils in instruction and obedience is also expressed in terms of μιμέομαι, e.g., Xenoph. Mem., I, 6, 3: εἰ οὖν ὥσπερ καὶ τῶν ἄλλων ἔργων οἱ διδάσκαλοι τοὺς μαθητὰς μιμητὰς ἑαυτῶν ἀποδεικνύουσιν, οὕτω καὶ σὺ τοὺς συνόντας διαθήσεις, νόμιζε κακοδαιμονίας διδάσκαλος εἶναι (cf. I, 2, 3).

2. The Cosmological Concept of Mimesis.

The term mimesis took on special significance in cosmology. Basic here are the discussions of Plato, the creator of this terminology, in the Tim. Reality is regarded as an imitation of the idea; time imitates eternity (χρόνου ... αἰῶνα μιμουμένου, Tim., 38a); the visible is a μίμημα of the invisible (48e: μίμημα is here synon. with εἰκών → II, 389). In the creation myth the ὁρατοὶ θεοί, in creating mortal ζῷα, imitate the divine creator of the world (ὁ τόδε τὸ πᾶν γεννήσας, 41a); they ought, he charges them, to go to work as μιμούμενοι τὴν ἐμὴν δύναμιν περὶ τὴν ὑμετέραν γένεσιν (41c; cf. μιμούμενοι τὸν σφέτερον δημιουργόν, 42e). Men must also exercise mimesis; God has found for them, and lent them, the power of vision ἵνα τὰς ἐν οὐρανῷ τοῦ νοῦ κατιδόντες περιόδους χρησαίμεθα ἐπὶ τὰς περιφορὰς τὰς τῆς παρ' ἡμῖν διανοήσεως, συγγενεῖς ἐκείναις οὔσας, ... μιμούμενοι τὰς τοῦ θεοῦ πάντως ἀπλανεῖς οὔσας, τὰς ἐν ἡμῖν πεπλανημένας καταστησαίμεθα (47b/c). It is plain that these deliberations are controlled by the thought form of analogy; the more true this is, the further is the concept of mimesis from genuine imitation as an act of free decision, and the more it is a schematic concept of relation which regards the connection of the lower world of phenomena with the higher world of ideas as (imperfect) correspondence, their original → συγγένεια being presupposed. Thus, when Plato says in the Cronos myth in Leg., IV, 713e: μιμεῖσθαι δεῖν ἡμᾶς οἴεται πάσῃ μηχανῇ τὸν ἐπὶ τοῦ Κρόνου λεγόμενον βίον, καὶ ὅσον ἐν ἡμῖν ἀθανασίας ἔνεστι, τούτῳ πειθομένους κτλ., it seems here that, though there is a requirement to fulfil, obedience is the (more or less compulsory) development of an existing disposition. Thus in Phaedr. it can certainly be said that those who worship a god imitate this god (μιμούμενοι, 253b; cf. 252c/d) and try to lead their παιδικά to ὁμοιότης with the god (ποιοῦσιν ὡς δυνατὸν ὁμοιότατον τῷ σφετέρῳ θεῷ, 253a), but it is also said expressly that this is no more than reflection on the image of the god retained in the memory (μνήμη), than the actualisation of a disposition orientated to the correspondence of idea and phenomenon. In other words, the more strongly the mimesis concept is tied to the cosmological schema of original and copy, the less prominent is the thought, sustained by ethical responsibility, of the obedient following of a model.

The Platonic views sketched above had great influence on the understanding of the world in the age which followed. We can see their effects on the Neo-Pythagoreans, who were, of course, working over older Pythagorean views when they took the earthly world to be a μίμησις of the higher world of ἀριθμοί, cf. Diels[5], I, 454, 15; Aristot. Metaph., I, 6, p. 987b, 11 ff.; Iambl. Vit. Pyth., 69 (p. 39, 21 f., Deubner), 33 (229) (p. 123, 20 f., Deubner). The Stoics may also be mentioned, cf. Muson. Fr., 17 (p. 90, 4 f., 13 f., Hense); Epict. Diss., II, 14, 12 ff. Philo is strongly influenced by the Platonic mimesis concept, → 664. The Hellen. ruler theology shows similar traits, → n. 8. Later one may adduce Plotinus, acc. to whom the sensually perceptible (τὰ αἰσθητῶς ὄντα), by its μετοχή to the intelligible (τὰ νοητῶς ὄντα), acquires the capability of εἶναι εἰς ἀεί by imitating intelligible nature as far as possible μιμούμενα τὴν νοητὴν καθ' ὅσον δύναται φύσιν, Enn., IV, 8, 6. In Procl. in Rem. Publ., I, 138, 18; II, 7, 14. 225, 2 etc. the relation of the lower to the upper gods is described as a μιμεῖσθαι (cf. also Plot. Enn., V, 5, 3).

As these examples show, the cosmological mimesis concept was most influential.

A more thorough investigation than this art. allows would no doubt be of great value.[4] But it would be caused considerable difficulty by statements in which cosmological ideas are not the true theme, but can only be conjectured as the background. Thus even in Plato it may be asked whether a statement like Menex., 238a : οὐ γὰρ γῆ γυναῖκα μεμίμηται κυήσει καὶ γεννήσει, ἀλλὰ γυνὴ γῆν, refers without reservation to cosmological and anthropological connections. In particular, light is needed on the question how far the imitation of God by men, where it is an ethical demand, may be understood as an exponent of the cosmological idea of original and copy, or whether the ethicising of μίμησις (in this respect → ὁμοίωσις is closely related) does not signify a breaking loose from cosmological connections. One may refer to Plut. Alex. Fort. Virt., 10 (II, 332a): Ἡρακλέα μιμοῦμαι καὶ Περσέα ζηλῶ, καὶ τὰ Διονύσου μετιὼν ἴχνη. Worth noting in this verse — cf. also Plut. Aud., 6 (II, 40b) — is the parallelism between μιμέομαι and ζηλόω (cf. → II, 877, 882), also the use of ἴχνος (→ III, 403). There also seems to be ethicising in Plut. Laud. s. Inv., 5 (II, 550e): οὐ γάρ ἔστιν ὅ τι μεῖζον ἄνθρωπος ἀπολαύειν θεοῦ πέφυκεν ἢ τὸ μιμήσει καὶ διώξει τῶν ἐν ἐκείνῳ καλῶν καὶ ἀγαθῶν εἰς ἀρετὴν καθίστασθαι; though the context, in which Plut. refers to Plat., shows that mimesis is not exclusively ethical here. Though the idea of imitating God may be originally only a specific instance of the great over-arching relation between the world and the upper world, which is essentially constituted by the lower world's imitation of the higher, the question still remains how far these connections are still consciously retained in statements with an ethical orientation. This is particularly true of the formulation, classical in its brevity, in Sen. Ep., 95, 50 : *vis deos propitiare? bonus esto. satis illos coluit quisquis imitatus est ;* cf. 95, 47: *deum colit qui novit,* and De ira, II, 16, 2 : Man, instead of taking animals as examples, should think of God, *quem ex omnibus animalibus, ut solus imitetur, solus intelligit.* In the background is Plat. Theaet., 176b : φυγὴ δὲ ὁμοίωσις θεῷ κατὰ τὸ δυνατόν· ὁμοίωσις δὲ δίκαιον καὶ ὅσιον μετὰ φρονήσεως γενέσθαι. It would seem that in such statements the *imitatio dei* is not too closely bound to the cosmological mimesis concept.[5]

---

[4] J. Kroll, *Die Lehren d. Herm. Trismeg.* (1914), who finds the mimesis view in the Corp. Herm. (cf. Index, *s.v.* "Nachahmung"), calls for such an investigation, 114.

[5] On Sen. Ep., 95, 50 cf. W. Theiler, *Die Vorbereitung d. Neuplatonismus* (1930), esp. 106 ff. On the mimesis problem generally cf. also H. Willms, *Eikon. 1. Teil : Philon v. Alex.* (1935); W. Kranz, "Kosmos u. Mensch in der Vorstellung frühen Griechentums," NGG *phil.-hist. Klasse, Fachgruppe I Altertumswissenschaft,* NF, 2, 7 (1938), 122 ff. The Göttingen Diss. of G. Abeken, *De* Μιμήσεως *apud Platonem et Aristotelem notione* (1836), is concerned almost exclusively with poetry or art as μίμησις. For → 2. Kleinknecht placed his collections on the mimesis problem at our disposal, and these have been selectively used, though not always as he interpreted them. Acc. to Kleinknecht the religious history of antiquity was from the very first largely dominated by mimesis of the divine. The starting-point for him was cultic action as mimesis of a corresponding mythical action of the gods. He refers to Plat. Numa, 14 (I, 69 f.): ἡ δὲ περιστροφὴ τῶν προσκυνούντων λέγεται μὲν ἀπομίμησις εἶναι τῆς τοῦ κόσμου περιφορᾶς, and, alluding to Hes. Theog., 535 ff., champions the thesis that even sacrifice was originally no more than imitation of the eating of the gods, mimesis of their meals. Hes. tells us that when gods and men were gathered in Mekone Prometheus so divided a bull that the flesh, concealed under a cover of skin, was allotted to men, but to Zeus only the white bones artfully clothed in fat ; but Zeus at once noted the deception. Since then, as we read in verses 556 f., which may be an interpolation, men may always be seen burning white bones to the gods on their altars. But this passage from Hes. is a slender base for so broad a thesis. For the comprehensive character of the mimesis idea Kleinknecht refers to the statements in Strabo, 10, 9 (467), which are to be ascribed to Pos. There we read : ἥ τε κρύψις ἡ μυστικὴ τῶν ἱερῶν σεμνοποιεῖ τὸ θεῖον, μιμουμένη τὴν φύσιν αὐτοῦ φεύγουσαν ἡμῶν τὴν αἴσθησιν, the mystical secrecy of the sacraments exalts the holiness of the deity, imitating thereby his nature, which escapes our perception. We then read : εὖ μὲν γὰρ εἴρηται καὶ τοῦτο τοὺς ἀνθρώπους τότε μάλιστα μιμεῖσθαι τοὺς θεοὺς ὅταν εὐεργετῶσιν· ἄμεινον δ' ἂν λέγοι τις ὅταν εὐδαιμονῶσι· τοιοῦτον δὲ τὸ χαίρειν καὶ τὸ ἑορτάζειν καὶ τὸ φιλοσοφεῖν καὶ μουσικῆς ἅπτεσθαι, for if it is right that men are closest to the gods when they do good,

This concept bears no relation to the NT statements about imitating God and Christ, for acc. to the context in which they stand these are not integrated into the cosmological and anthropological schema of original and copy, and they also have quite plainly an ethical thrust. [6]

3. The Septuagint and Pseudepigrapha.

μιμέομαι and μίμημα occur in the LXX, but they are very rare and are found only in the Apocr., since we cannot accept the scribal error ἐμίμησας (for ἐμίσησας) in ψ 30:7 B. In Wis. 9:8 μίμημα means copy: the temple as μίμημα σκηνῆς ἁγίας ἣν προητοίμασας (cf. Ἀ Ez. 23:14 ἀνδρῶν μίμημα for LXX ἄνδρας ἐζωγραφημένους, Mas. אַנְשֵׁי מְחֻקֶּה; Ez. 16:61 Ἀ ἐν τῷ μιμήσασθαι for LXX ἐν τῷ ἀναλαβεῖν, obviously reading, instead of בְּקַחְתֵּךְ, בַּחֲקֹתֵךְ from חקה "to engrave," "to draw," "to paint," later Heb. "to imitate"). μιμέομαι occurs in Wis. 4:2: παροῦσάν τε μιμοῦνται (Α τιμῶσιν) αὐτήν (sc. ἀρετήν), and 15:9: χαλκοπλάστας τε μιμεῖται, "he imitates the brass-founders," also in 2 passages in 4 Macc. In 9:23 the eldest cries out to his brothers during the torture: μιμήσασθέ με, ἀδελφοί, "take me as an example," "do as I do," and be martyred rather than transgress the Law. In 13:9 the statement is put on the lips of the seven young men: μιμησώμεθα τοὺς τρεῖς τοὺς ἐπὶ τῆς Ἀσσυρίας νεανίσκους, οἳ τῆς ἰσοπολίτιδος (preparing the same fate) καμίνου κατεφρόνησαν (cf. Da. 3:17 ff.). Though the ref. in 4 Macc. is to martyrdom, μιμέομαι cannot be understood as a tt. for a certain view of martyrdom. On the whole the idea of imitation is foreign to the OT. In particular, there is no thought that we must imitate God. [7]

---

it is even more true that they are this when they are happy. A help here is joy and celebration and philosophising and surrender to music (cf. K. Reinhardt, "Poseidonios über Ursprung u. Entartung," *Orient. u. Antike*, 6 [1928], 47 f.). Here the cultus, philosophy, music etc. are not regarded directly as imitation, but as powers which can link to the divine (πρὸς τὸ θεῖον ἡμᾶς συνάπτει or τρέπει πρὸς τὸ θεῖον) because they derive from "primitive enthusiasm as man's original and native relation to deity" (Reinhardt, 50). For the rest, Kleinknecht regards the use of the mimesis concept in the ancient theory of technics and art (cf. Aristot. Poet.) as a secondary development compared with the philosophical use, and for him the cosmological and anthropological application precedes the ethical. It may be mentioned that Gulin, *op. cit.*, 46 (with ref. to Platonic passages which use ἕπεσθαι τῷ θεῷ) takes the view that the ethically orientated following of God grew out of an original cultic and mimic imitation of God: "In the cultus one imitated God, and in so doing one had the sense of becoming God. At this pt. Plato simply spiritualised and ethicised the concept"; 45: "In Greece imitating the gods seems originally to have implied this mimic cultus." In what the Stoics, esp. Epict., say about following God Gulin (47) sees the influence of an original cultic imitation, "though Epict. understood it in purely ethical terms." At issue is not just ethical interpretation, but the overcoming of the cultic and mimic by the ethical. The dramatic and mimic element kept a place in the mystery religions. Thus it is said of the Attis devotees in Ps.-Luc. Syr. Dea, 15: Ῥέη δὲ τέμνονται καὶ Ἄττεα μιμέονται. For other examples cf. G. P. Wetter, *Altchristl. Liturgien: Das christl. Mysterium* (FRL, NF, 13) (1921), 67.

[6] Cf. also → II, 395 f., 397 on εἰκών. The ancient mimesis idea is first found clearly in the early Church in Cl. Al. (→ n. 43).

[7] In the OT itself God is incomparable and inimitable in being and action, Is. 46:5: לְמִי תְדַמְּיוּנִי וְתַשְׁווּ וְתַמְשִׁלוּנִי וְנִדְמֶה. The verse has 3 verbs which are important in this connection, דמה, שׁוה and משׁל. The LXX, which is influenced by the following section (interpolated?) on those who make idols, has the free rendering: τίνι με ὡμοιώσατε; ἴδετε τεχνάσασθε, οἱ πλανώμενοι. To make oneself equal to God is the result of sinful human arrogance such as is seen in the oriental idea of the divine king, Is. 14:14 [Bertram]. The Rabbis are the first to bring the idea of imitation of God to the OT (→ I, 212). M. Buber, "Nachahmung Gottes," *Kampf um Israel* (1933), 68 ff. (= *Der Morgen*, I [1926], 638 ff.) shows how this imitation of God is meant to be a development of the divine likeness of

The situation is different in the pseudepigr. Here the demand is raised that we should imitate exemplary men (Test. B. 4:1: μιμήσασθε ... τὴν εὐσπλαγχνίαν αὐτοῦ sc. τοῦ ἀγαθοῦ ἀνδρός [Joseph]; esp. 3:1: μιμούμενοι τὸν ἀγαθὸν καὶ ὅσιον ἄνδρα Ἰωσήφ etc., as concerns love for God and keeping His commandments). But we also find the idea of imitating God. In Test. A. 4:3 the ἀγαθὸς ἄνθρωπος is righteous before God even when he sins, for the general judgment that the whole work is good remains: μιμεῖται κύριον, he imitates the Lord who does not approve what seems to be good along with what is actually bad. One should compare 4:5, where it is said definitively of the good man: ἐν ζήλῳ θεοῦ πορεύονται, ἀπεχόμενοι ὧν καὶ ὁ θεὸς διὰ τῶν ἐντολῶν μισῶν ἀπαγορεύει κτλ. To emulate God, i.e., to imitate the Lord, is to keep His commandments. In Ep. Ar. μιμέομαι occurs 4 times in the "mirror of the prince" with ref. to imitating specific qualities of God: μιμούμενος τὸ τοῦ θεοῦ διὰ παντὸς ἐπιεικές, 188, τὴν → ἀγωγὴν αὐτοῦ (sc. τοῦ θεοῦ) μιμούμενοι, 280, also 210, 281 the demand that the king should take God as his model in dealing with his subjects. [8] It is part of the situation of a discussion at table between the Gentile king and his Jewish guests that obligation to the commandments of God is not mentioned, nor is imitation of God orientated to this. Cf. also S. Bar. 18:1 (cf. 17:4).

4. Philo and Josephus.

In Philo the word group is very common. μίμημα, found over 60 times, is largely par. with ἀπεικόνισμα (opp. ἀρχέτυπος and παράδειγμα). Its use shows how strongly Philo was influenced by Plato's view that the heavenly and earthly worlds correspond (→ 661). In the discussions in Op. Mund. about the relation of the κόσμος νοητός and the κόσμος αἰσθητός (→ III, 877) it is emphasised in 16: μίμημα καλὸν οὐκ ἄν ποτε γένοιτο δίχα καλοῦ παραδείγματος οὐδέ τι τῶν αἰσθητῶν ἀνυπαίτιον, ὃ μὴ πρὸς ἀρχέτυπον καὶ νοητὴν ἰδέαν ἀπεικονίσθη, and in 25 we find the principle: σύμπας οὗτος ὁ αἰσθητὸς κόσμος ... μίμημα θείας εἰκόνος.

Though μίμημα is often in Philo a tt. for the cosmological idea of original and copy, this is seldom true of μιμέομαι (and μιμητής). μιμέομαι occurs over 40 times. [9] It is not always conscious imitation of a model. It can also be used where there is only

man, though he sees the OT data in the light of Rabb. exposition, and in his NT quotations evidently fails to distinguish between discipleship and imitation. The Rabb. material is none too plentiful, cf. Str.-B., I, 372 f.; III, 605.

[8] H. G. Meecham, *The Letter of Aristeas. A Linguistic Study with Special Reference to the Greek Bible* (1935), has no notes on this passage. Kleinknecht think that we have here typical ideas from Hellen. ruler theology. In fact the mimesis idea was also applied to the relation of the earthly king to the eternal rule of the gods or the supreme God. Cf. Themist. Or., 2 (p. 41, 13, Dindorf): τὸν μὲν γὰρ τοῦδε τοῦ ξύμπαντος βασιλέα ὁ μὲν ἐπίσταται μόνον, ὁ δὲ καὶ μιμεῖται; Sthenidas of Locroi in Stob. Ecl., IV, 7, 63 (270, 14 ff.): οὗτος γὰρ καὶ φύσει ἐντὶ (the divine king of the world) καὶ πρᾶτος βασιλεύς τε καὶ δυνάστας, ὁ δὲ (the earthly king) γενέσει καὶ μιμάσει; Diotogenes Pyth., *ibid.*, IV, 7, 62 (270, 10 f.): θεόμιμόν ἐντι πρᾶγμα βασιλῆα. The king is thus regarded as the μιμητής of God. But this is to be understood in terms of the original-copy schema. As the bearer of divine revelation the king is God's μίμημα on earth. As μίμημα he is in Plut. Princip. Inerudit., 3 (II, 780 f.) compared to the sun which God placed in heaven as περικαλλὲς εἴδωλον ἑαυτοῦ ... ἐνίδρυσε. Cf. E. R. Goodenough, "The Political Philosophy of Hellenistic Kingship," *Yale Class. Studies*, 1 (1928), 55 ff. (esp. devoted to clarification of the designation of the king as νόμος ἔμψυχος); here it is plain that the imitation of the king by his subjects is not regarded as ethical, but as a consequence of the "dynamic and personal revelation of deity" which is mediated to them through the king in virtue of his "relationship with deity," 90 f. Since the statements in Ep. Ar. are ethical imperatives, there is an obvious distinction from the mimesis idea of Hellen. ruler theology.

[9] In Fug., 74; Mut. Nom., 208 we also find (attested only in Philo) the verb μιμηλάζω or μιμηλίζω (derived from the adj. μιμηλός) in the same sense. μίμησις occurs 9 times, 3 of them κατὰ μίμησιν (in Abr. 38 μίμησις and ἐναντίωσις are contrasted). In Migr. Abr., 167 we find the otherwise rare adj. μιμητικός (μιμητικαὶ τέχναι).

comparison, as when in Spec. Leg., IV, 83 it is said of ἐπιθυμία that it violently seizes possession of the soul of man and leaves no part unaffected, just as fire gains the upper hand when it finds plenty of combustible material, μιμουμένη τὴν ἐν ἀφθόνῳ ὕλῃ πυρὸς δύναμιν (cf. Aet. Mund., 135 : τὸ πυρὸς σχῆμα μιμουμένη). But it is usually imitation of a model, e.g., in Sacr. AC, 123, where in relation to caring for men who perish irremediably under their burdens, it is said that one should follow the example of worthy physicians (μιμουμένους τοὺς ἀγαθοὺς τῶν ἰατρῶν) who do what is humanly possible even in hopeless cases, or in Vit. Mos., I, 158, where it is said of Moses that he set himself and his life in the world as a model for all who would imitate it, παράδειγμα τοῖς ἐθέλουσι μιμεῖσθαι (cf. the use of τύπος in the final sentence, 159; in many other cases μιμέομαι is combined with παράδειγμα, e.g., Spec. Leg., IV, 173 and 182, or with ἀρχέτυπος, Vit. Cont., 29). Worth noting is Sacr. AC, 68 : Obedient children necessarily do good if they imitate their fathers, δεόντως οὖν μιμούμενοι τὴν τοῦ πατρὸς φύσιν οἱ ὑπήκοοι παῖδες ... τὰ καλὰ δρῶσιν. Mention of obedience shows that imitation has the character of keeping the commands of fathers, and this element is also present in Migr. Abr., 149, where Lot refuses to imitate the better (to take Abraham's advice), and thus to become better, οὐχ ἕνεκα τοῦ μιμησάμενον τὸν ἀμείνω βελτιωθῆναι. Esp. important is the fact that when Philo speaks of imitating God this side is prominent in spite of the relation of such statements to the idea of original and copy. The *logos* after his birth imitated the ways of the Father and, considering the models created by Him, fashioned the forms, μιμούμενος τὰς τοῦ πατρὸς ὁδούς, πρὸς παραδείγματα ἀρχέτυπα ἐκείνου βλέπων ἐμόρφου τὰ εἴδη, Conf. Ling., 63 (is there here too, in the use of → ὁδοί, the idea that the *logos* is obedient ?). Philo says several times that men should imitate God, Decal., 111; Leg. All., I, 48 : μιμεῖσθαι θεοῦ τὰ ἔργα; Virt., 168; Spec. Leg., IV, 73 : τί δ' ἂν εἴη κρεῖττον ἀγαθὸν ἢ μιμεῖσθαι θεὸν γενητοῖς τὸν ἀΐδιον. In Op. Mund., 79 it is stated that God created man last in order that he should have the rich treasures of nature ready for his use ; it is then said that if men would imitate the author of the human race, μιμούμενοι τὸν ἀρχηγέτην τοῦ γένους, they would be able even now to live in superfluity without toil or trouble. Here to imitate God is to fit into His plan at creation rather than squandering His gifts by transgressing His commandments. Philo often calls the procreation of children an imitation of God, Decal., 51 and 120; Spec. Leg., II, 225. He does not emphasise so much that this is a gift from God (there is more of a comparison), but in Decal., 120 he attacks the idea that parents should be regarded (as in Stoicism) as visible deities, μιμούμενοι τὸν ἀγένητον ἐν τῷ ζῳοπλαστεῖν, and in Spec. Leg., II, 225 he has the reservation : μιμούμενοι καθ' ὅσον οἷόν τε, so far as is possible, τὴν ἐκείνου δύναμιν (cf. καθ' ὅσον οἷόν τε, Virt., 168). Philo does not overlook the limits within which alone one can speak of imitation of God.[10] μιμητής occurs 4 times. Mostly ungrateful men should take an example from the beasts, some of which are well able to show themselves grateful to their benefactors : μιμηταὶ θηρίων ἐνίων, ἄνθρωποι, γίνεσθε, Decal., 114. In Virt., 66 Joshua is called a pupil φοιτητής of Moses and an imitator of his attractive character μιμητὴς τῶν ἀξιεράστων ἠθῶν.

---

[10] Similar results are reached by W. Völker, "Fortschritt u. Vollendung bei Philo v. Alex.," TU, 49, 1 (1938), who shows that Philo's ethic is centrally controlled by the demands of the OT (199), while Platonic, Stoic etc. formulations are only aids to the elucidation of unalterable biblical ideas "with the means of contemporary culture" (57). Acc. to Völker this is also true of the mimesis idea. To be sure, the biblical data (under Buber's influence → n. 7) are a little distorted by him. But the insight is important that only the terminology really reminds us of Plato (207, 216, 333), while the content is orientated to the OT, with obedience to the divine requirement predominant (cf. the discussions of πείθεσθαι or ἕπεσθαι θεῷ, 220, 327 f.; Leg. All., III, 209 : τὸ γὰρ ἕνεκα θεοῦ μόνου πάντα πράττειν εὐσεβές). The mimesis idea is linked with the motif of gratitude (278): "By μίμησις θεοῦ Philo understands in the broadest sense the consecration of the whole life which is offered to God" (333). Willms, *op. cit.*, 86 f. also emphasises that the mimesis concept has an ethical stamp in Philo.

The ref. can hardly be to conscious imitation. What is meant is resemblance to Moses in this respect. In Congr., 70 Gn. 28:7: εἰσήκουσεν (LXX ἤκουσεν) Ἰακὼβ τοῦ πατρὸς καὶ τῆς μητρὸς αὐτοῦ, is expounded as follows: οὐ τῆς φωνῆς οὐδὲ τῶν λόγων — τοῦ γὰρ βίου μιμητὴν ἔδει τὸν ἀσκητήν, οὐκ ἀκροατὴν λόγων εἶναι κτλ.; the μιμητής is thus compared with the ἀκροατής: an ἀκροατής or μανθάνων models himself on the individual saying, the μιμητής on the whole βίος or conduct of the one whom he obeys (κατὰ τὸν λέγοντα and not κατὰ τὸν ἐκείνου λόγον). Cf. also Migr. Abr., 26.

The employment of the word group in Joseph. remains within current usage. μίμημα (Ant., 12, 75; Bell., 7, 142) and μίμησις (3, 111; 12, 77) are found in descriptions of technical achievements. In 3, 123 the plan of the tabernacle is called a μίμησις τῆς τῶν ὅλων φύσεως. μιμέομαι, e.g., Ant., 12, 241; 18, 291; Bell., 4, 562; Ap., 1, 165; 2, 283; and μιμητής, e.g., Ant., 8, 315; 12, 203; 17, 97 (cf. also μίμησις, 5, 98) are mostly used for the conscious imitation of the qualities or acts of others in either a good or a bad sense. Sometimes there is only a comparison, e.g., 8, 315; 9, 44; 17, 97. Joseph. does not speak of imitating God. In Ant., 1, 19 creation in its order and regularity (not God Himself; cf. Ap., 2, 191) is the model which man should have in his life and work. Towards God, as may be seen from Ant., 1, 20, what is required is ἕπεσθαι (cf. 8, 337; → I, 210). One can, of course, "imitate" theology, Ap., 1, 225.

5. The Word Group in the New Testament.

In the NT the word group is represented by μιμέομαι and μιμητής, also συμμιμητής. It is comparatively rare, being found only in Paul's Epistles (1 and 2 Th.; 1 C.; Eph.; Phil.) apart from Hb. and 3 Jn. The 𝔎 reading (τοῦ ἀγαθοῦ) μιμηταί for ζηλωταί at 1 Pt. 3:13 (→ II, 887 f.) is to be regarded as secondary. For all the relation between the terms (→ 662; 664; 674) it is a softening. It is unlikely that 3 Jn. 11 exerted any influence, e.g., on the ground that 3 Jn. preceded 1 Pt. in the order of the Catholic Epistles.

The admonition of 3 Jn. 11: μὴ μιμοῦ τὸ κακὸν ἀλλὰ τὸ ἀγαθόν, is general, but it stands in close relation to what precedes and follows. Gaius must not be ensnared by the Diotrephes who is denounced in v. 9 f. He should follow the Demetrius who is praised in v. 12.

In Hb., which in 11:4 ff.; 12:1 ff. holds out before the readers so many examples of faith without ever specifically emphasising the duty of imitating them (though cf. 12:2 f.), we read in 13:7: ὧν (sc. τῶν ἡγουμένων ὑμῶν) ἀναθεωροῦντες τὴν ἔκβασιν τῆς ἀναστροφῆς μιμεῖσθε τὴν πίστιν. What makes faith exemplary in this case is that it is maintained even in death. Faith is here not just the content of faith; it is the attitude. For faith is not a human virtue. It is a being gripped by Jesus Christ. Hence μιμεῖσθαι embraces, not just striving to live up to the example, but necessarily and by no means finally a willingness to take the same way of faith. Imitation does not imply surrender of individuality. The example is not a schema. It is a summons to keep the faith in one's own life and death. At Hb. 6:12: ἵνα μὴ νωθροὶ γένησθε, μιμηταὶ δὲ τῶν διὰ πίστεως καὶ μακροθυμίας κληρονομούντων τὰς ἐπαγγελίας, μιμηταί has a strongly activist colouring in comparison with νωθροί (cf. 6:11). But it is conceivable that the statement already has in view the result of overcoming indolence, so that a simple comparison is presented: That you may attain to the promised inheritance like those of whom this is true according to our conviction.

There is also a comparison in 1 Th. 2:14: ὑμεῖς γὰρ μιμηταὶ ἐγενήθητε, ἀδελφοί, τῶν ἐκκλησιῶν τοῦ θεοῦ τῶν οὐσῶν ἐν τῇ Ἰουδαίᾳ ἐν Χριστῷ Ἰησοῦ, ὅτι τὰ αὐτὰ ἐπάθετε καὶ ὑμεῖς ὑπὸ τῶν ἰδίων συμφυλετῶν, καθὼς καὶ αὐτοὶ ὑπὸ τῶν Ἰουδαίων. Even though there is an active element in πάσχειν ("to endure patiently" = ὑπομένειν), this is not to the fore, as shown by the construction with ὑπό.[11] For this reason, even though the Thessalonians might have had details of the persecutions of Christians in Palestine,[12] there can be no question of taking their fate (not their conduct) as an example. What is meant is that (through nothing that you have done) the same fate has overtaken you; you have to suffer the same things as they did before. What Paul is saying is that you are not the first on whom this fate has fallen. It is no exception, but the rule, as the example of the first Christian churches can teach you. It is important that this instance is found in Paul, for it shows very plainly that the term μιμητής is not to be taken too narrowly in the apostle, and that more than one meaning of μιμέομαι etc. has to be taken into account.

In a series of references Paul holds up himself as a model whom his congregations should imitate. The δεῖ gives us reason to suppose that this idea had already had a place in his oral missionary preaching: αὐτοὶ γὰρ οἴδατε πῶς δεῖ μιμεῖσθαι ὑμᾶς 2 Th. 3:7. The πῶς is developed in the ὅτι clause which follows, 3:7 f. The exemplary conduct of the apostle is that he earns his bread with the work of his own hands and does not become a burden on anyone in the community. This might have been learned by the ἄτακτοι, and by the congregation in its handling of the ἄτακτοι. In 3:9 Paul emphasises (he has a different point in view in 1 C. 9:12) that in this he was guided by the desire ἵνα ἑαυτοὺς τύπον δῶμεν ὑμῖν εἰς τὸ μιμεῖσθαι ἡμᾶς. That → τύπος is less the pattern to be copied than the example to be followed, and that μιμεῖσθαι thus implies recognition of authority, may be seen from the parallelism with the παράδοσις which is to be followed according to 3:6.

The term τύπος is also used in Phil. 3:17: συμμιμηταί μου γίνεσθε, ἀδελφοί, καὶ σκοπεῖτε τοὺς οὕτω περιπατοῦντας καθὼς ἔχετε τύπον ἡμᾶς. To be sure, Paul is first a τύπος to the extent that the Philippians are to judge the οὕτω περιπατοῦντες by this τύπος. But the statements are in many ways synonymous. As the Philippians become συμμιμηταί[13] of the apostle, they take him as a τύπος for their own walk, and as they mark the οὕτω περιπατοῦντες, they are also their μιμηταί. It is true that the order and choice of words imply a certain differentiation between the apostle and the οὕτω περιπατοῦντες, so that it is not advisable to assume a full equation between συμμιμηταί γίνεσθε with the genitive and σκοπεῖτε with the accusative. On the other hand, it is also as well not to isolate completely the exemplariness of the apostle, as though it were quite different from that of the οὕτω περιπατοῦντες.[14] The particular position which

---

[11] As against Dob. Th., *ad loc.*; it is a *petitio principii*, with no basis in usage elsewhere, to say: "There has to be moral conduct which one can imitate." On the other hand, Dob. rightly refuses to follow Wbg. Th., *ad loc.*, who relates ἐν Χριστῷ Ἰησοῦ to μιμηταὶ ἐγενήθητε.

[12] Yet it is to be considered that (if 1 Th. was written during the 3rd missionary journey) the apostle may be referring to certain events in the immediate past of which he had knowledge (perhaps as an eye-witness) (cf. Ac. 18:22), which were very much on his mind, and which the Thessalonians now heard about for the first time.

[13] This noun, derived from συμμιμέομαι in Plat. Polit., 274d, occurs only here. In the context συν- cannot mean "with me," but at most "all of you together, one as the other." But it may well be a tautological construction (cf., e.g., συνέπομαι) meaning μιμητής (→ n. 39).

[14] As against Loh. Phil., *ad loc.*, who sees in the οὕτω περιπατοῦντες "the perfect who suffer martyrdom" (and in those mentioned in 3:18 f. the *lapsi*), so that the claim of martyrs to be examples is supposed to be expressed here.

Paul takes up is connected with his apostolic authority (the οὕτω περιπατοῦντες may also be engaged in missionary work, like the Christians attacked in 3:18 f.). But whether or not the demand links up with 3:16 or introduces what follows, the concept of imitation contains here, too, more than the attempt to take as a model, and to imitate, an example already being given. Though the walk of the apostle has this exemplary character (he makes this plain, though without boasting, and in full realisation how uncertain his exemplariness is, cf. 1 C. 9:27), the reference is not to his person or "perfection" (Phil. 3:12 ff.), but to the authority with which he is invested and in the light of which he claims a hearing for his preaching and imitation for his walk. συμμιμηταί μου γίνεσθε certainly means: Walk as I do, but it also means (and primarily): Recognise my authority, follow what I say, be obedient. Imitation here is not repetition of a model. It is an expression of obedience.

The element of obedience is particularly clear in 1 C. 4:16: παρακαλῶ οὖν ὑμᾶς, μιμηταί μου γίνεσθε. For in 4:17 Paul writes that, in order to help them to follow this admonition, which is always in force, he has sent Timothy to them, ὃς ὑμᾶς ἀναμνήσει τὰς ὁδούς μου τὰς ἐν Χριστῷ, καθὼς πανταχοῦ ἐν πάσῃ ἐκκλησίᾳ διδάσκω. Now obviously the → ὁδοί which the Corinthian Christians had almost forgotten, and of which Timothy is to remind them, can hardly be the personal walk of the apostle. [15] For they are part of the solid core of his διδάσκειν, and they are thus directions for the leading of a Christian life. It is obvious here that to be μιμηταί of Paul is to follow his ὁδοί, to accept his διδαχή with its character as command, to obey his directions. [16] Cf. also Phil. 4:9 with the preceding ἃ καὶ ἐμάθετε καὶ παρελάβετε.

When the same expression recurs later in 1 C. at 11:1: μιμηταί μου γίνεσθε, it can hardly be understood apart from 4:16. To be sure, Paul refers just before to himself as an example. To the admonition to the Corinthian Christians in 10:32 he adds in 10:33, with the καθὼς κἀγώ and a short statement which reminds us of 9:19 ff., the reference to himself, in order to show that he has adopted as his own criterion that which he expects of his readers. To this degree the μιμηταί μου γίνεσθε which follows might be no more than a repetition of the same thought, a summons to follow his example. [17] Nevertheless, 4:16 leads us to conclude that this interpretation is not adequate. μιμηταί μου γίνεσθε has to mean: "Be told, take it to heart, keep to it, be obedient." In other words, the phrase relates not merely to 10:33, but also and especially to the admonition in 10:32. The Corinthians will show themselves to be μιμηταί of the apostle by obeying his warning call, which is backed by a reference to his own conduct. The apostle then adds the further statement: καθὼς κἀγὼ Χριστοῦ, i.e., he points to the fact that he himself is, or seeks to be, a μιμητὴς Χριστοῦ. If he previously had a model in view, 11:1 would mean that they are to take him as a model as he takes Christ. But it would then be hard to explain why Paul does not call Christ directly a model for the Corinthians. It would also be surprising that he does not say more precisely in what connection Christ is a model for him. To be sure, one may refer

[15] The difficulties involved in trying to find in 4:16 the exemplary qualities of a father which his children ought to imitate may be seen in Bchm. K., *ad loc.* The metaphor of father and children simply shows that the question of obedience is central.

[16] Cf. Joh. W. 1 K.

[17] In so far as there is admonition in 10:32 the reference in 10:33 acquires the value of an encouraging example. But in the first instance καθὼς καί implies only a comparison, cf. 1 Th. 2:14; R. 15:7; Col. 3:13.

to R. 15:1-3, which is undoubtedly related to 10:33. One may also refer to Phil. 2:4 ff. In this light 10:33 can easily be transferred to Christ, though with the proviso that ἵνα σωθῶσιν, in this transfer understood as the goal of Christ's saving work, points to a distinction between Paul and Christ which rules out all imitation. But there is here nothing corresponding to R. 15:1-3. Even 10:24 does not amount to this, and in the related discussion earlier there is no hint of a reference to Christ as example. If one has really to take into account a reference to Christ as example in 11:1, the space allotted to this consideration stands in no relation to the breadth of the argument from 9:1 and even 8:1. The following point should also be borne in mind. Normally only the fleeting thoughts of an author are conveyed in the form of this kind of addition. But the exemplariness of Christ is hardly a fleeting thought for Paul. In R. 15:1-3 the exemplariness of Christ, or the duty of following His example, is plainly stated by him. Indeed, that which is expected of the community, and that of which it is said that God will give it, is described in 15:5 as τὸ αὐτὸ φρονεῖν ἐν ἀλλήλοις κατὰ Χριστὸν Ἰησοῦν.[18] Again, even in Phil. 2:4 ff. it is not unconditionally certain that the thought of the exemplariness of Christ is central.[19] It is thus advisable to seek another explanation of the καθὼς κἀγὼ Χριστοῦ. This is that to be the μιμητής of someone means to follow his command, to be obedient to him. The apostle means that I have commanded you, and Christ has commanded me. Be my μιμητής by heeding the admonition of 10:32, as I am Christ's μιμητής by understanding my apostolic ministry as He wishes (10:33). The statements in 10:32 f. and 11:1, in which the καθὼς κἀγώ (found only here) is repeated, are of similar construction, and their parts correspond. Hence the commission of Christ, by following which Paul shows himself to be a μιμητής, is directly related to the admonition to the Corinthians in 10:32. This means that the admonition is not simply based on Paul's authority as an apostle. Paul derives it from the superior authority of Christ, whom he obeys when he gives the admonition. Often in 1 C. Paul refers to this superior authority of Christ, as he does here, when he is rounding off the long discussion of a subject. Thus 11:1 reminds us of the position of 7:40b at the end of c. 7. With its mention of a climax, not of examples but of authorities, 11:1 is related to the chain of tradition in 11:23.[20] Does not this mean that 11:2 (reference to the παραδόσεις = ὁδοί, 4:17) is to be brought into closer relation to 11:1 than is usually the case, and that only in 11:3, as shown by the introductory θέλω δὲ ὑμᾶς εἰδέναι (cf. the similar οὐ θέλω ὑμᾶς ἀγνοεῖν in 10:1, which is always at the beginning of a section), does Paul definitely take up a new theme? Certainly 11:1 does not refer to examples to be emulated, let alone to models to whom one is to become similar or equal by imitation, but to authorities whose command and admonition are to be obeyed.[21]

---

[18] κατὰ Χριστὸν Ἰησοῦν (cf. κατὰ Χριστόν, Col. 2:8; κατὰ κύριον, 2 C. 11:17; κατὰ θεόν, Eph. 4:24) means according to the will rather than the example (cf. the transl. of E. Brunner, *Der Römerbrief* [*Bibelhilfe f. d. Gemeinde, nt.liche Reihe, Bd. 6*], *ad loc.*).

[19] Cf. Mich. Ph., *ad loc.*

[20] Here too (→ n. 17) καθὼς κἀγώ first introduces a comparison. There is a climax only because Paul is in both clauses (cf. 11:3 and on the other hand Eph. 5:23). The position of Paul between Christ and the community is not expressly that of a mediator. Even though the ref. of 11:1 be to exemplariness, Paul cannot be regarded as a mediator who must be accepted as an example representing Christ (as against Gulin, *op. cit.*, 254, n. 3; cf. G. Bertram, "Paulus Christophoros," *Stromata* [1930] 32). Cf. also 1 Th. 1:6.

[21] If the ref. is not to exemplariness, there is no further pt. to the question raised by Joh. W. 1 K., *ad loc.* whether Χριστός refers to the earthly Jesus (cf. R. 15:3) or the heavenly Christ. The authority which the apostle accepts is that of the heavenly Lord.

1 Thess. 1:6 reads: καὶ ὑμεῖς μιμηταὶ ἡμῶν ἐγενήθητε καὶ τοῦ κυρίου. The co-ordination of Paul and the Lord here does not prevent us from seeing in καὶ τοῦ κυρίου an intensifying, whether it be by way of self-correction (cf. 1 C. 15:10),[22] or whether it be that the recognition afforded the community is to be deepened and extended. The addition δεξάμενοι τὸν λόγον ἐν θλίψει πολλῇ μετὰ χαρᾶς πνεύματος ἁγίου does not, one may first assume, tell us when the Christians in Thessalonica became μιμηταί. It shows to what degree they then became μιμηταί. The thought may be that of following an example which Paul and the Lord have given. The stress would then fall on ἐν θλίψει πολλῇ κτλ. rather than δεξάμενοι τὸν λόγον, for in Paul's case we are not to think of his conversion as the time when he received the Word, and in Christ's case we cannot speak of any specific time at all when He received the Word. But it may quite easily be said of Paul that in Thessalonica he preached the Gospel ἐν θλίψει πολλῇ (cf. 2:2 ἐν πολλῷ ἀγῶνι) but also μετὰ χαρᾶς πνεύματος ἁγίου (cf. 1:5; 2:2), and it is true of the Lord that in the passion particularly He experienced much θλῖψις, yet χαρά did not desert Him (cf. Hb. 5:7). The difficulty that perhaps only hesitantly *tale quale* may we apply the phrase μετὰ χαρᾶς πνεύματος ἁγίου to Jesus is possibly alleviated by the consideration that the participial construction applies primarily to the Thessalonians, and that καὶ τοῦ κυρίου is an addition to the basic ἡμῶν. If Paul and Christ are thus regarded as examples, it is, of course, open to question whether conscious imitation is at issue. If not, the statement is much more like a comparison (cf. also 2:14). Certainly the term τύπος occurs in 1:7 (cf. 2 Th. 3:9; Phil. 3:17) as Paul continues: ὥστε γενέσθαι ὑμᾶς τύπον πᾶσιν τοῖς πιστεύουσιν ἐν τῇ Μακεδονίᾳ καὶ ἐν τῇ Ἀχαΐᾳ. Thus μιμηταί and τύπος seem to be related. Those who thus far have been only μιμηταί are now a τύπος (there is, of course, no question of the deliberate offering of a τύπος as in 2 Th. 3:9).[23] But the Thessalonian Christians are a τύπος of this kind, as 1:8 f. plainly shows, in the very general sense that they have become believers and have turned to God. Since the relation between μιμηταί and τύπος can hardly be dissolved, does not this mean, however, that the stress in 1:6b falls on δεξάμενοι τὸν λόγον, not on ἐν θλίψει πολλῇ κτλ.? But if the Thessalonians became μιμηταί of Paul and Christ by receiving the Word, this rules out the idea of following an example (→ *supra*).[24] The train of thought can only be as follows. When the Thessalonians received the Word, they did what was expected of them; for this was why Paul preached the Word to them as thereunto commissioned by the Lord. In this sense the verse is related to 1 C. 11:1, the only difference being that the reference here is to the first acceptance of the authority of the apostolic Word, to commitment to Paul and the Lord, to the beginning of following and discipleship.[25]

---

[22] So Dob. Th. and Dib. Th., *ad loc.*, also Gulin, 236, and cf. Eidem, *op. cit.*, 75 on 1 C. 11:1.

[23] The meaning certainly cannot be that the Thessalonian church, as the first, became the τύπος for those that followed, since the Philippian church had already come into being in Macedonia.

[24] It is hardly possible to say with Dob. Th., *ad loc.*: "Thus Paul is here thinking first of reception of the Gospel as that in which similarity is manifested." It is precisely in this respect that one cannot speak of a "similarity of conduct" "between Jesus, Paul and the readers."

[25] Paul himself never speaks of discipleship because, as G. Kittel explains → I, 215, this term is in the NT reserved for the relation to the historical Jesus. The ref. here, however, is not to the historical Jesus, nor even to "the historical picture of the suffering Christ"

There remains Eph. 5:1: γίνεσθε οὖν μιμηταὶ τοῦ θεοῦ, ὡς τέκνα ἀγαπητά. The οὖν points back to 4:32: γίνεσθε δὲ εἰς ἀλλήλους χρηστοί, εὔσπλαγχνοι, χαριζόμενοι ἑαυτοῖς καθὼς καὶ ὁ θεὸς ἐν Χριστῷ ἐχαρίσατο ὑμῖν. 4:32 offers a comparison, though one which involves definite obligation. The question arises, however, whether we are justified in construing the reference to God as though God were set up as a model. Is not the argument rather that he who has received forgiveness from God must not fail to forgive his neighbour?[26] There is a clear parallel to 4:32 in 5:2: καὶ περιπατεῖτε ἐν ἀγάπῃ καθὼς καὶ ὁ Χριστὸς ἠγάπησεν ὑμᾶς καὶ παρέδωκεν ἑαυτὸν ὑπὲρ ἡμῶν προσφορὰν καὶ θυσίαν τῷ θεῷ εἰς ὀσμὴν εὐωδίας. Between 4:32 and 5:2 stands the demand of 5:1: γίνεσθε οὖν μιμηταὶ τοῦ θεοῦ. If this means imitating God as an example, then logically 5:2 must be referred to following the example of Christ. Yet there are several objections to this understanding of 5:2.[27] The reference to Christ is to be evaluated rather as an ethical motive which does not have to include the idea of imitating an example. But this means that 4:32 should be taken in the same way (also Col. 3:13), and 5:1 is to be expounded accordingly. It is no accident that in 5:1 ὡς τέκνα ἀγαπητά is added to strengthen the admonition. The readers are to be μιμηταί of God in their capacity as His dear children. This puts the idea of following the fatherly will of God strongly to the forefront. It is also emphasised that as μιμηταὶ τοῦ θεοῦ the readers do not cease to be His τέκνα. Indeed, they show that they are His τέκνα hereby. In 5:1 the distance between God and man is firmly maintained. There can be no possible reference to an imitation whereby we become similar or equal to the model. To take God as a model means here to bear constantly in mind that as His children we live wholly by His love and forgiveness. Hence the passage does not go beyond what Paul says elsewhere, and it leaves no un-Pauline impression.

Reviewing the passages from Paul, we find it necessary to distinguish three different uses of μιμέομαι and μιμητής. First, there is simple comparison. The older example seems to be imitated, but there is no conscious imitation. This type occurs in 1 Th. 2:14 and possibly 1 Th. 1:6. Then there is the following of an example.[28] This use is found in 2 Th. 3:7, 9; Phil. 3:17, and Paul is always the

---

(against Dib. Th., *ad loc.*). What is meant by discipleship, or its commencement, in the Gospels is here expressed by μιμηταὶ τοῦ κυρίου. Perhaps this is the real reason why it is necessary to add καὶ τοῦ κυρίου.

[26] Cf. Mt. 18:33: οὐκ ἔδει καὶ σὲ ἐλεῆσαι τὸν σύνδουλόν σου, ὡς κἀγὼ σὲ ἠλέησα. Here the meaning is not that the unfaithful servant has failed to take his lord as an example, but that the mercy which he had received ought to have been an incentive to being merciful himself. Cf. W. Michaelis, *Das hochzeitliche Kleid. Eine Einführung in die Gleichnisse Jesu über die rechte Jüngerschaft* (1939), 166, 282, n. 21.

[27] Cf. the discussion in Ew. Gefbr., *ad loc.*

[28] It may be asked how far it is advisable to speak of imitating an example at all. With A. Fischer, "Nachahmung u. Nachfolge," ARPs, I (1914), 68-116, one may distinguish between external imitation, which consists in the adoption of the external conduct of another, and internal imitation, which seeks to produce the inner disposition of soul underlying the conduct (78 ff., 83 ff.). But Fischer then compares (89 ff.) these two types with the discipleship in which one seeks to lead one's own life independently in accordance with the principles displayed in the example, because one hopes in so doing to come to true selfhood. This comparison shows that even inner imitation, though higher than external, still involves copying and dependence. Our own usage is in keeping with this in so far as even serious imitation means a lack of independence, since the imitator does not follow his own bent. If we put the matter in these terms, what is at issue in the Pauline refs. is neither external nor internal imitation, but discipleship (→ n. 25). Hence in translation it is perhaps

example.[29] Recognition of the authority of Paul is plainly implied in these passages, so that following his example carries with it obedience to his commands. In the third group obedience is predominant, so exclusively so in 1 C. 4:16 that the thought of an example is quite overshadowed, and in 1 C. 11:1; 1 Th. 1:6; Eph. 5:1 it is quite obvious that the main stress falls on the element of obedience. In this third group alone are Christ and God associated with Paul as authorities in relation to whom one must be a μιμητής.[30]

The occurrences of μιμέομαι etc. are of particular importance in relation to the question of the significance accorded by the NT to the thought of the example, for here, if one starts with the basic meaning of the word group, i.e., "to imitate," there seems to be emphatic reference to imitating an example. The statements of Paul in particular have been very largely understood in this way.[31] Examination has shown, however, that this line of interpretation must at least be subjected to considerable restriction. If the churches are called μιμηταί of the apostle, the thought is that they are to be obedient, that they must act in accordance with his directions.[32] When Pauls calls himself a μιμητὴς Χριστοῦ, or when he tells the Thessalonians they must show themselves to be μιμηταὶ τοῦ κυρίου, the point is that both he and they are followers of their heavenly Lord. There is thus no thought of an imitation, whether outward or inward, of the earthly life of Jesus in either individual features or total impress.[33] The call for an *imitatio Christi* finds no support in the statements of Paul. But the idea of imitation as a mystical re-

---

best to avoid "imitate." Eidem, 83 f. effaces the distinction between discipleship and imitation by relating discipleship to exemplariness in general, while imitation is following a special example.

[29] It may be noted that Gl. 4:12: γίνεσθε ὡς ἐγώ, often adduced as a further example, is no true par.; Paul here continues: ὅτι κἀγὼ ὡς ὑμεῖς. Eidem, 77 thinks we should supply γέγονα or ἐγενόμην; cf. on this A. Oepke Gl. (1937), *ad loc.*

[30] The use of the word group in Pl. is not unrelated to usage outside the NT (→ 1.-4.). But Cr.-Kö., *s.v.* rightly emphasises that the group here takes on its "most profound significance."

[31] Prominence should be given to the correct definition of Cr.-Kö., *s.v.*: "To follow, to attach oneself to someone, to enter into fellowship with someone who shows himself to be akin in disposition and mode of action." Oepke takes the view that the thought of the model, "the taking shape of the master in his disciples" (853), is not forgotten even in passages which speak of discipleship; the idea of exemplariness is particularly present in Pauline statements which use μιμέομαι etc. But Oepke emphasises that in so far as Christ is called an example the statements have a christological character, for Paul always argues from living fellowship with the risen Lord (868). "Hence to imitate Christ means always to seek to emulate both the earthly and the heavenly Christ, and both in indissoluble relation. Mythologising and historicising of the example are equally un-Pauline, though in different directions" (869). But how can one seek to emulate the heavenly Christ? Oepke does not work out the sense of obedience, which ought to be mentioned here.

[32] There can thus be no question of Paul's being an example, an object of imitation, as an apostle (or martyr).

[33] This applies also to a view like that of M. Dibelius, Art. "Nachfolge Christi I, Im NT," RGG², IV, 395: "Before the apostle is not the man but the Son of God come down from heaven, not the course of history but the myth in which the historical life of Jesus is only a period; the qualities to be imitated are not the virtues of a human person but the properties of a divine person." Cf. R. Bultmann, "Die Bedeutung des geschichtlichen Jesus f. d. Theologie des Paulus," ThBl, 8 (1929), 147: "Christ is not an example. He can, of course, be an example of serving one another, of ταπεινοφροσύνη ... But it is everywhere the pre-existent Lord who is the example. This means, however, that only the One recognised already as Lord can be an example; the exemplariness of the historical Jesus does not make Him the Lord": H. J. Ebeling, "Das Messiasgeheimnis u. d. Botschaft des Marcus-Evangelisten," ZNW, *Beih.* 19 (1939), 166: "... not *imitatio*, but *conformitas*." "Christ is no mere example, but the ground of the possibility and obligation of such a life."

lation to the risen Lord is also to be ruled out.[34] Fellowship with Christ certainly includes being made like him (→ II, 396 f.). But the passages in question make it plain that one can be a μιμητὴς Χριστοῦ only by concrete obedience to the word and will of the Lord. Thus Paul does not speak of true imitation of Christ or God. His reference is simply to obedient following as an expression of fellowship of life and will. The → μαθητής (Paul does not use this word) and the μιμητής are one and the same.[35]

Though these observations are restricted to passages in which μιμέομαι occur, they have a more general bearing and fit into a total picture. Cf. → I, 214, 441, 773; II, 33; III, 403 ff.

6. The Post-Apostolic Fathers. In the post-apostolic fathers, as the number of instances shows, the group takes on greater significance than in the NT or even Paul. In 1 Cl., 17, 1, after a depiction of the exemplariness of Christ (16, 17 ὑπογραμμός, → I, 773) we read: μιμηταὶ γενώμεθα κἀκείνων οἵτινες ... περιεπάτησαν κηρύσσοντες τὴν ἔλευσιν τοῦ Χριστοῦ; the ref. is to the example of a patient and modest nature (τὸ ταπεινόφρον καὶ τὸ ὑποδεές, 19, 1), though it is to be noted that acc. to 19, 1, and in full agreement with Paul, the imitation is διὰ τῆς ὑπακοῆς and runs par. to καταδέχεσθαι of the λόγια of God.[36] In Dg., 10, 4-6 it is stated that man ought to be a μιμητής of the χρηστότης of God; worth noting is 10, 4: μὴ θαυμάσῃς, εἰ δύναται μιμητὴς ἄνθρωπος γενέσθαι θεοῦ· δύναται θέλοντος αὐτοῦ.

In Ignatius μιμητής and μιμέομαι are fairly common. The usage is not fixed but displays a certain fluidity. In Sm., 12, 1 there is added to the mention of the one who brings the letter, Burrhus, the wish: καὶ ὄφελον πάντες αὐτὸν ἐμιμοῦντο, ὄντα ἐξεμπλάριον θεοῦ διακονίας. In Mg., 10, 1 we find the sentence: ἐὰν γὰρ ἡμᾶς μιμήσεται, καθὰ πράσσομεν, οὐκέτι ἐσμέν, "if he (Jesus Christ) were to act as we,"[37] i.e., in the context, if He were not so kind as He is, but as we unfortunately are not. In the introductory statements in Eph., 1, 1 and Tr., 1, 2, in a general sense, Ign. calls these churches μιμηταὶ θεοῦ.[38] There is here some influence of Eph. 5:1, and Phld., 7, 2: μιμηταὶ γίνεσθε Ἰησοῦ Χριστοῦ ὡς καὶ αὐτὸς τοῦ πατρὸς αὐτοῦ, also shows Pauline influence (cf. the climax in 1 C. 11:1), though the idea that Christ is a μιμητὴς θεοῦ as well is new, even if it does indicate that the concept of obedience is present in μιμητής.[39] In Eph., 10, 2 the readers are warned against repaying opponents of the Gospel in kind, μὴ σπουδάζοντες ἀντιμιμήσασθαι αὐτούς: You

---

34 As against J. Schneider, "Die Passionsmystik des Pls.," UNT, 15 (1929), 130; H. Windisch, "Pls. u. Christus," UNT, 24 (1934), 251 ff.

35 The essay of Nielen does not define the terms discipleship and imitation clearly enough, nor is there any exact examination of the NT verses which use μιμέομαι. The adducing of numerous cultically tinged terms is no substitute. (Only at 1 C. 11:1 does the author spread himself, and even then he makes no great contribution.)

36 The passage should not be related to the example of martyrs (as against Loh. Phil., 151, n. 2), for the prophets Elijah and Elisha, who are meant and mentioned, did not die as martyrs, and their humility is shown by the fact that in spite of their high commission they appeared ἐν δέρμασιν αἰγείοις καὶ μηλωταῖς.

37 The rendering of Pr.-Bauer³, *s.v.* is to be preferred here to that of Bau. Ign., *ad loc.*

38 In Eph., 1, 1, unless the phrase is conventional, it must be asked whether Jesus Christ is not meant by the θεός (Bau. Ign., *ad loc.*); cf. the ἀναζωπυρήσαντες ἐν αἵματι θεοῦ which follows (also R., 6, 3).

39 It is thus doubtful whether a predominantly Hellen. view of imitation is normative here (Gulin, "Nachfolge," 47, n. 5; 49, n. 2). On Phld., 7, 2 Gulin observes: "This explains the title of the famous *De imitatione Christi* by Thomas à Kempis, though the Vulgate always has *sequi*." It should be pointed out, however, that in the NT passages the Vulgate always renders μιμεῖσθαι or μιμητής by *imitari* or *imitator* (the simple form also in Phil. 3:17).

should not consider doing the same to them.[40] In 10, 3 we are then told that we should rather strive to be μιμηταὶ τοῦ κυρίου: τίς πλέον ἀδικηθείς, τίς ἀποστερηθείς, τίς ἀθετηθείς; If the ref. of what the Lord had to suffer is definitely and pre-eminently to His passion, then the sufferings which disciples must accept as His μιμηταί include martyrdom, though this aspect is not stressed and the concluding admonition is very general: (ἵνα) ἐν πάσῃ ἁγνείᾳ καὶ σωφροσύνῃ μένητε ἐν Ἰησοῦ Χριστῷ σαρκικῶς καὶ πνευματικῶς. R., 6, 3 is the only place where the term μιμητής is plainly and exclusively related to martyrdom. Here Ign. asks the community: ἐπιτρέψατέ μοι μιμητὴν εἶναι τοῦ πάθους τοῦ θεοῦ μου (i.e., of Christ). The significance for Ign. of the idea of the fellowship and discipleship of suffering can hardly be overestimated, for it is attested at every point in his epistles. Nevertheless, one may ask whether the idea of μιμητής is not overvalued when it is made a key to the interpretation of his terminology elsewhere (e.g., συμπαθεῖν αὐτῷ, Sm., 4, 2; ἀποθανεῖν εἰς τὸ αὐτοῦ πάθος, Mg., 5, 2).[41] The one verse R., 6, 3 is too slender a base for this, nor is it certain that the narrower idea of imitation is present even here.[42]

The picture is very different in the Mart. Pol., for all three refs. which call for consideration refer to martyrdom. There is a definite ref. to martyrs in 17, 3 (obviously in opposition to a tendency to make them an object of προσκυνεῖν like Christ): τοὺς δὲ μάρτυρας ὡς μαθητὰς καὶ μιμητὰς τοῦ κυρίου ἀγαπῶμεν (cf. the terms for martyrs in the account of the churches of Vienne and Lyons in Eus. Hist. Eccl., V, 2, 2: ζηλωταὶ καὶ μιμηταὶ Χριστοῦ). The statement concludes: ὧν γένοιτο καὶ ἡμᾶς κοινωνούς τε καὶ συμμαθητὰς γενέσθαι. If μιμηταί is not repeated here, it is applied to all brethren in 1, 2: ἵνα μιμηταὶ καὶ ἡμεῖς αὐτοῦ γενώμεθα. In 19, 1 it is said that Polycarp has become a μάρτυς ἔξοχος, οὗ τὸ μαρτύριον πάντες ἐπιθυμοῦσιν μιμεῖσθαι κατὰ τὸ εὐαγγέλιον Χριστοῦ γενόμενον. Here, since the depiction is strongly assimilated to the passion of Jesus, external imitation cannot be ruled out. Finally, we find in 8, 2 the demand: μιμηταὶ οὖν γενώμεθα τῆς ὑπομονῆς <αὐτοῦ>, cf. the reason then given: τοῦτον γὰρ ἡμῖν τὸν ὑπογραμμὸν ἔθηκε δι' ἑαυτοῦ, and Ign. Eph., 10, 3. In Pol., 1, 1 imprisoned brothers in faith whose cause the church has espoused are called μιμήματα τῆς ἀληθοῦς ἀγάπης (the phrase is not clear in detail, for, while Christ is called true love, have those concerned portrayed Christ, or have they not rather become copies?).[43]

Michaelis

---

[40] ἀντιμιμέομαι, ἀντιμίμησις and the adj. ἀντίμιμος are very rare, cf. Pass. and Liddell-Scott, *s.v.*

[41] This objection must be raised against H. Schlier, "Religionsgesch. Untersuchungen z. d. Ign.-Briefen" (ZNW, *Beih.*, 8 [1929]), esp. 158 ff. Cf. also the questions put by H. v. Campenhausen, *D. Idee d. Martyriums in der alten Kirche* (1936), 76 ff.

[42] Gulin, "Freude," 241, n. 1; 237, n. 3 feels the Ign. passages are Hellenistic. In "Nachfolge" he distinguishes between the Semitic type of obedient discipleship and the Hellen. type of imitation with its minimal impress, cf. → n. 5. In Ign. there is a certain excitement and exaggeration in the statements about the discipleship of suffering, but this does not have to mean that we have here an imitation which goes beyond that of Paul.

[43] It should be noted that in Cl. Al. the Gnostic is often called μιμούμενος τὸν θεόν. Cf. Strom., II, 97, 1: οὗτός ἐστιν ὁ "κατ' εἰκόνα καὶ ὁμοίωσιν," ὁ γνωστικὸς ὁ μιμούμενος τὸν θεὸν καθ' ὅσον οἷόν τε, μηδὲν παραλιπὼν τῶν εἰς τὴν ἐνδεχομένην ὁμοίωσιν, ἐγκρατευόμενος, ὑπομένων, δικαίως βιούς, βασιλεύων τῶν παθῶν ... οὗτος "μέγιστος ἐν τῇ βασιλείᾳ" ... μιμούμενος τὸν θεόν; IV, 171, 3: θεὸν χρὴ μιμεῖσθαι εἰς ὅσον δύναμις τῷ γνωστικῷ; VII, 16, 3: ὁ γνωστικὸς ... τὴν θείαν προαίρεσιν μιμούμενος εὖ ποιεῖ τοὺς ἐθέλοντας τῶν ἀνθρώπων κατὰ δύναμιν. Here is obviously a development of Stoic ideas, cf. also Prot., 117, 1: οὐ γὰρ μιμεῖσθαί τις δυνήσεται τὸν θεὸν ἢ δι' ὧν ὁσίως θεραπεύει οὐδ' αὖ θεραπεύειν καὶ σέβειν ἢ μιμούμενος, which reminds us strongly of Sen. Ep., 95, 50 (→ 662). Plato, too, has exerted some influence, cf. the quotation from Theaet., 176b in Prot., 122, 4 and Theiler, *op. cit.*, 106. The transition to the ethical, however, is quite evident. Cf. also Wetter, *op. cit.*, 105 on Prot., 111 ff.

μιμνῄσκομαι, μνεία, μνήμη, μνῆμα, μνημεῖον, μνημονεύω

μιμνῄσκομαι.

μιμνῄσκομαι (cf. also the common compounds ἀναμιμνῄσκω and ὑπομιμνῄσκω) is frequently attested in classical and Hellen. Gk. from the time of Hom., [1] and is also found in inscr. and pap. [2] The deponent means "to remember," "to be mindful of."

1. In the LXX this concept became central to the biblical view of God. It corresponds almost exclusively to the Mas. זָכַר. God remembers certain persons and turns to them in grace and mercy (Gn. 8:1; 19:29; 30:22; Ex. 32:13; 1 S. 1:11, 19; 25:31). The fact that He does so means that a new situation is created and effective help is extended to man in his need. God's remembering is thus an efficacious and creative event. Above all, God remembers His covenant which He made with the fathers Noah, Abraham, Isaac and Jacob, and He binds Himself afresh to the grace promised therein (Gn. 9:15-16; Ex. 2:24; 6:5; Lv. 26:42; ψ 104:8; 105:45; 110:5; Ez. 16:60; 2 Macc. 1:2). [3] God remembers the patriarchs and is thus merciful to Israel (Ex. 32:13; Dt. 9:27). Conversely, a basic element in OT piety is that man remembers the past acts of God, His commandments and His unexhausted possibilities (Nu. 15:39-40; Dt. 8:2, 18). Dt. especially develops a theology of remembering (Dt. 5:15; 7:18; 8:2, 18; 9:7; 15:15; 16:3, 12; 24:18, 20, 22; 32:7). The severe visitation in Egypt should especially be remembered by Israel (μνησθήσῃ ὅτι οἰκέτης ἦσθα, Dt. 15:15; 16:12; 24:18, 20, 22) and should lead them to new obedience and trust, and to the avoidance of disobedience and arrogance. All recollection serves to maintain the purity of faith. There is, of course, a carnal remembering which is opposed to the μιμνῄσκομαι which God wills (Nu. 11:5). This does not fulfil the will of God; it resists it. Part of the salutary discipline of faith is to remember one's guilt against God (Dt. 9:7). Because God's remembering, though ineffable, is a concrete and actual event, faith can turn to Him with the request μνήσθητι (Ju. 16:28; 2 K. 20:3; 2 Ch. 6:42; Job 7:7; 10:9; ψ 73:2; 18:22; 88:50; 102:14; 105:4; 118:49; 131:1; 137:7; Is. 38:3). It is a feature of OT prayer that in severe assault and distress the cry μνήσθητι goes up and reliance is placed on God's Word. If God remembers His servant, there comes a new turn in the situation and the prayer is answered (ψ 77:35, 39). God's remembering does not always bring grace and mercy; God can also remember the wicked acts of the enemies of Israel, and take vengeance on them (ψ 24:6, 7; 136:7; 1 Macc. 7:38). The request for retribution is against the enemy of the people because he is also the enemy of God. Thus in the Nehemiah tradition it is possible to find together in the prayer: μνήσθητι, a sense of one's own guilt, hope in God's mercy, ex-

---

μιμνῄσκομαι. [1] Liddell-Scott, 1135; Pr.-Bauer[3], 865 f., cf. 96 f. and 1402 f.

[2] Preisigke Wört., II, 106 f.

[3] Cf. the related use of μεταμέλομαι. ψ 105:45 reads: καὶ ἐμνήσθη τῆς διαθήκης αὐτοῦ καὶ μετεμελήθη κατὰ τὸ πλῆθος τοῦ ἐλέους αὐτοῦ.

pectation of an acknowledgment of one's own righteousness, and also expectation that the adversaries of God will be punished (Neh. 1:8; 5:19; 6:14; 13:14, 22, 29, 31). The limitation of OT μνήσθητι may be seen in this unexplained juxtaposition.[4] It is no violation of God's dignity constantly to summon the people to repentance with the admonition: μνήσθητι (Mi. 6:5; Is. 43:26; 44:21; 46:8-9; Sir. 7:16, 28; 14:12; 18:24-25; 23:14; 28:6-7; 38:22; 41:3).[5] In dealings between men, too, the request: μνήσθητί μου, recurs (Gn. 40:14) when one desires a specific service and seeks to bring someone to remembrance.

2. In the NT tradition the terms (ἀνα)μιμνῄσκεσθαι, μνημονεύειν and μνείαν ἔχειν or ποιεῖσθαι are close to one another. Their meaning: "to remember," "to be mindful of," should not be regarded as an exclusively mental process. A word or act can serve the memory and bring to remembrance (εἰς ἀνάμνησιν, εἰς μνημόσυνον).[6] Recollection can strike someone (Mt. 5:23) or it may constantly accompany him (1 C. 11:2). In the canticles of the Lucan infancy stories, with their strong OT colouring, there is often a connection between the saving action of God and effective remembering: 1:54: ἀντελάβετο Ἰσραὴλ παιδὸς αὐτοῦ μνησθῆναι ἐλέους, 1:72: ποιῆσαι ἔλεος μετὰ τῶν πατέρων ἡμῶν καὶ μνησθῆναι διαθήκης ἁγίας αὐτοῦ — in both cases the μνησθῆναι is added to the proclamation of the Messianic event by way of theological explanation: God's gracious remembering is now manifested.[7] Hb., too, recalls the God who thinks on man but can also withdraw from him (2:5-8 = Ps. 8:4-6), and who in the new covenant will remember the sins of His people no more (8:12; 10:17 = Jer. 31:31-34). In Hb., as in Lk., the usage is governed by quotation from the OT.[8] Archaic phrases are used in the story of Cornelius: αἱ προσευχαί σου καὶ αἱ ἐλεημοσύναι σου ἀνέβησαν εἰς μνημόσυνον ἔμπροσθεν τοῦ θεοῦ (Ac. 10:4), αἱ ἐλεημοσύναι σου ἐμνήσθησαν ἐνώπιον τοῦ θεοῦ (10:31). Prayers and alms come before God and induce His intervention. Perhaps remembrance and mention are here much the same.[9] But remembrance before God can also lead to the judgment of Babylon

---

[4] Neh. is certainly aware that in his just and unjust actions he is under the divine judgment and mercy, but he does not break free from a human reservation (Neh. 13:22).

[5] The close relation between the divine requirement μνήσθητι and the summons to repentance is esp. plain in Is. 46:8: μνήσθητε ταῦτα καὶ στενάξατε, μετανοήσατε, οἱ πεπλανημένοι, ἐπιστρέψατε τῇ καρδίᾳ. The call to remember is also part of the teaching style of the Rabbis.

[6] λαληθήσεται εἰς μνημόσυνον αὐτῆς (זִכָּרוֹן), Mk. 14:9; Mt. 26:13; αἱ προσευχαί σου καὶ αἱ ἐλεημοσύναι σου ἀνέβησαν εἰς μνημόσυνον ἔμπροσθεν τοῦ θεοῦ, Ac. 10:4; τοῦτο ποιεῖτε εἰς τὴν ἐμὴν ἀνάμνησιν, 1 C. 11:24; ἀλλ' ἐν αὐταῖς ἀνάμνησις ἁμαρτιῶν κατ' ἐνιαυτόν, Hb. 10:3. Recollection is achieved in the word and act.

[7] The construction of Lk. 1:54 allows of various possibilities. Should one take μνησθῆναι ἐλέους with τῷ Ἀβραὰμ καὶ τῷ σπέρματι αὐτοῦ εἰς τὸν αἰῶνα? Or (in accordance with the Heb. לִזְכֹּר) should one make it co-ordinate: as He remembers? If God is concerned about His people's present, this is a new proof of grace to Abraham himself. The seed thus includes the patriarch (Lk. 1:54, 72) as the patriarch also includes his posterity (Hb. 7:9-10).

[8] It is quite possible that Hb. 2:6 refers to the dereliction of man and of the Son of Man, Jesus Christ (2:9 reading χωρὶς θεοῦ?). Because God does not remember Him, is not concerned about Him, a special darkness lies on the death of Jesus. But the exegetical connection is not wholly clear, and χάριτι θεοῦ demands consideration as well as χωρὶς θεοῦ. Cf. on this A. v. Harnack, "Zwei alte dogmatische Korrekturen im Hb.," SAB (1929).

[9] Tg. II Est. 6:1: "In this night (from the 14th to the 15th Nisan) came the recollection of Abraham, Isaac and Jacob before their Father in heaven, so that an angel was sent from the heights, namely, Michael, the prince of the hosts of Israel." One is reminded of the ministry of angels depicted in Rev. 8:3-5. The expression ἐνώπιον τοῦ θεοῦ denotes the

(Rev. 16:19: καὶ Βαβυλὼν ἡ μεγάλη ἐμνήσθη ἐνώπιον τοῦ θεοῦ, 18:5: καὶ ἐμνημόνευσεν ὁ θεὸς τὰ ἀδικήματα αὐτῆς). Every event on earth has its "effect" on God. His remembrance is concealed in His acts of grace and judgment. The fact that God remembers is revealed by the word of His messengers. Lk. 16:25 sounds like the OT with its call for remembrance: τέκνον, μνήσθητι ὅτι ἀπέλαβες τὰ ἀγαθά σου ἐν τῇ ζωῇ σου, καὶ Λάζαρος ὁμοίως τὰ κακά. The thief on the cross, sensing the future glory of Christ, lays his fate in the hands of Jesus: Ἰησοῦ, μνήσθητί μου ὅταν ἔλθῃς εἰς τὴν βασιλείαν σου (Lk. 23:42). The prayer style of the old covenant is to be found again in the early Church with its prayer in Did., 10, 5: μνήσθητι, κύριε, τῆς ἐκκλησίας σου τοῦ ῥύσασθαι αὐτὴν ἀπὸ παντὸς πονηροῦ καὶ τελειῶσαι αὐτὴν ἐν τῇ ἀγάπῃ σου. How the Word of God can itself become a kind of remembering may be seen in Barn., 13, 7: εἰ οὖν ἔτι καὶ διὰ τοῦ Ἀβραὰμ ἐμνήσθη, ἀπέχομεν τὸ τέλειον τῆς γνώσεως ἡμῶν.

The Word of Jesus displays its power in the fact that it is alive in the disciples through recollection (Mk. 14:72; Mt. 26:75; Lk. 22:61).[10] In a firm Gospel tradition it is told how after the resurrection the disciples remember, and now for the first time understand, the words of Jesus. Lk. emphasises this explicitly in the Easter story (μνήσθητε, ὡς ἐλάλησεν ὑμῖν, 24:6; καὶ ἐμνήσθησαν τῶν ῥημάτων αὐτοῦ, 24:8). Recollection of the Word of Jesus is part of the Easter message, and the resurrection gives new might to this Word. The Fourth Gospel also perceives that sayings and events were not understood prior to the resurrection — ταῦτα οὐκ ἔγνωσαν αὐτοῦ οἱ μαθηταὶ τὸ πρῶτον (12:16). Only after the resurrection do the disciples remember, perceive and believe the Scripture and the Word which Jesus has spoken (2:22; 12:16). This Johannine remembrance is a new and true knowledge, and it thus belongs to the doctrine of the Spirit of God (14:26: ἐκεῖνος ὑμᾶς διδάξει πάντα καὶ ὑπομνήσει ὑμᾶς πάντα ἃ εἶπον ὑμῖν ἐγώ).[11] The Holy Spirit ratifies, confirms and explains the work of Jesus and thereby brings definitive and conclusive remembrance. The story of the cleansing of the temple (Jn. 2:17 = Ps. 69:9) also shows how dealings with Jesus taught the disciples how to understand the OT. Here, too, remembrance (ἐμνήσθησαν) is a comprehensive term for the new understanding of Scripture, the knowledge of the Messianic fulfilment.

Apostolic preaching is not just recollection; it also demands recollection. Timothy in 1 C. 4:17 is instructed to bring to remembrance the ways of Paul as he himself teaches them in every congregation.[12] The church is to remember the apostle and what he has delivered (1 C. 11:2). A solid tradition is passed on, confirmed, and called to remembrance. A specific vocabulary develops, especially later, cf. 2 Pt.

---

presence of God and the environs of His heavenly throne (Rev. 8:3-4). Cf. ἐπιλελησμένον ἐνώπιον τοῦ θεοῦ (Lk. 12:6). This ἐνώπιον can sometimes be simplified to ὑπό (Pr.-Bauer³, *s.v.* μιμνῄσκομαι).

[10] In the denial scene we read expressly: καὶ ἐμνήσθη ὁ Πέτρος τοῦ ῥήματος Ἰησοῦ εἰρηκότος ... (Mt. 26:75; cf. the compounds in Mk. 14:72: καὶ ἀνεμνήσθη ὁ Πέτρος τὸ ῥῆμα ὡς εἶπεν αὐτῷ ὁ Ἰησοῦς, Lk. 22:61: καὶ ὑπεμνήσθη ὁ Πέτρος τοῦ λόγου τοῦ κυρίου). The saying prepares the ground for μετάνοια.

[11] Cf. Jn. 16:12-15.

[12] ὁδούς does not mean the apostle's manner of life (vv. 11, 12), for this would leave the καθὼς isolated. It means the general principles, a sense which is quite natural, and which might very well develop from the image of the two ways (Did., 1, 1; cf. W. Bousset, *Rel. d. Judts.*² [1906], 317) and on the model of the Heb. הלכות (Bousset), cf. also 12:31 (Ltzm. K.² [1923], 22).

1:12, 13 (διεγείρειν ἐν ὑπομνήσει); 3:2; Jd. 5, 17; 2 Tm. 2:14 (ὑπομίμνῃσκε). There is worked out a firm, anti-heretical understanding of the apostolic tradition, and older kerygmatic material is usually passed on in recollection. As exegesis of 2 Pt. 3:1-3 will show, μιμνῄσκεσθαι is not meant in a historicising or intellectualistic sense in the NT, though it easily misunderstood along these lines. What is at issue is neither the quickening of a past tradition nor the keeping in memory of religious truths, but a specific understanding of the Word of God as this emerges especially at a later time. To remind the congregation is to bear witness to the Gospel, to remind oneself is to place oneself under the Word of Jesus. Here, too, the whole man is embraced.

Recollection of the sayings of Jesus lies behind all genuine decisions of the Church (Ac. 11:16: ἐμνήσθην δὲ τοῦ ῥήματος τοῦ κυρίου) and — since it is a special form of attestation — plays a particular part in the composition of the NT Scriptures (2 Pt. 3:1).[13] In no circumstances should we misinterpret this biblical μιμνῄσκομαι along historicising or intellectualistic lines. It includes total dedication to God, concern for the brethren, and true self-judgment (Hb. 13:3). It carries with it the thinking in terms of salvation history and the community which the whole of Scripture demands.

μνεία.

μνεία is often found in Gk. (Soph. El.) and Hellen. (inscr., pap., LXX) usage in the sense of "recollection," "mention." Common both here and in the NT are combinations like μνείαν ποιεῖσθαι (cf. Paul's mention in prayer, R. 1:9; Eph. 1:16; 1 Th. 1:2; Phlm. 4; Phil. 1:3); μνείαν ἔχειν (1 Th. 3:6; 2 Tm. 1:3). The LXX also has μνείᾳ μιμνῄσκεσθαι (Dt. 7:18; Jer. 38:20); ἐστὶ μνεία (Zech. 13:2); μνεία γίνεται (Is. 23:16; Ez. 21:37; 25:10). μνείαν ποιεῖσθαι means "to think of, to mention, someone" (cf. ψ 110:4: μνείαν ἐποιήσατο τῶν θαυμασίων αὐτοῦ), μνείαν ἔχειν, "to have in remembrance" (τινός). The original OT זָכַר or זֵכֶר may be constantly detected.

As the NT understanding of ἀνάμνησις is bound up with a specific proclamation and action (Lk. 22:19; 1 C. 11:24, 25; Hb. 10:3), so Ps. 111:4 ("he hath instituted a remembrance of his wonderful works") refers to a specific proclamation and celebration of the community, i.e., the Passover. This remembrance (זֵכֶר) is a definite acknowledgment of the saving action of God. When Paul thinks of his congregations or brethren in intercession, making mention of their names before God and making their welfare his concern in prayer, this mention is part of his calling as an apostle, and it sets all human relations under the grace of God. According to 1 Th. 3:6 the church has him in good remembrance (ὅτι ἔχετε μνείαν ἡμῶν ἀγαθὴν πάντοτε); this includes the fact that their mutual relations are unruffled.[1]

1 Cl., 56, 1 prays for the guilty brethren, and hopes that this mention (μνεία) before God and the saints will bear fruit. The purity of Pauline intercession is here maintained

---

[13] Wnd. Kath. Br., 99: The author simply has the task of keeping alive recollections of the ancient traditions (the OT prophecies and the directions of Jesus passed on by the apostles, Mt. 28:19b; Jn. 13:34).

μνεία. [1] Worth noting is the reading ταῖς μνείαις τῶν ἁγίων κοινωνοῦντες (R. 12:13 acc. to D*G it vg cod Chr). Cf. Kl. R., 427: "μνείαις is a noteworthy western reading (cf. its adroit defence by Zn.) for χρείαις. It cannot be explained on the ground of intrusion of veneration for martyrs (Weiss), for the saying about commemorations does not have to be interpreted in terms of martyrs."

intact. Barn., 21, 7 hopes, not that they will bear the author in good remembrance, but that there will be remembrance of the good (εἰ δέ τίς ἐστιν ἀγαθοῦ μνεία, μνημονεύετέ μου μελετῶντες ταῦτα). In Herm. v., 3, 7, 3 we find εἰς μνείαν ἔρχεταί τινι (= *in mentem venit alicui*): "If it occurs to you that the truth demands chastity, you will be of another mind ..."

μνήμη.

In the Gk. world μνήμη, μνεία and μνημοσύνη play a particular anthropological, philosophical and mythological role, but μνήμη occurs only once in the NT (2 Pt. 1:15) in the expression μνήμην ποιεῖσθαι (cf. μνείαν ποιεῖσθαι). Platonic philosophy in particular allots an important place to the human and poetic faculty of μνήμη.[1] μνήμη is the mother of the muses (acc. to Plat. Euthyd., 275d), or the muse itself, to which there were sacrifices in Boeotia (Paus., 9, 29, 2). μνήμη, μνεία and μνημοσύνη were cultically venerated;[2] "as μνήμη in particular maintained the beloved dead in the recollection of the living, so μνημοσύνη in heroic poetry kept the vanished great and their dead from being forgotten."[3] 2 Pt. 1:15 is simply using a general Hellen. phrase (cf. P. Fay., 19, 10: τῶν πραγμάτων μνήμην ποιεῖσθαι). But there is a deeper connection with Gk. thought in Herm. s., 6, 5, 3: ἡ γὰρ τρυφὴ καὶ ἀπάτη μνήμας οὐκ ἔχει διὰ τὴν ἀφροσύνην, ἣν ἐνδέδυται, ... μνήμας γὰρ μεγάλας ἔχει ἡ τιμωρία.[4] Cf. also Mart. Pol., 18, 2: εἴς τε τὴν τῶν προηθληκότων μνήμην καὶ τῶν μελλόντων ἄσκησίν τε καὶ ἑτοιμασίαν.[5]

μνῆμα.

μνῆμα means lit. "memorial," but it is connected esp. with remembrance of the dead (from Hom.) and can even mean the grave (Hdt., Plat., Ditt. Syll.[3] and BGU, common in the LXX = קֶבֶר and קְבוּרָה); μνῆμα and μνημεῖον may be used without distinction, cf. (κατα)τιθέναι ἐν μνήμασι, εἰς μνῆμα, ἐν μνημείῳ, εἰς μνημεῖον. In antiquity the grave is a lonely place to which one may withdraw and which can be in some sense

μνήμη. [1] Cf. Crat., 437b: ἔπειτα δὲ ἡ μνήμη παντί που μηνύει, ὅτι μονή ἐστιν ἐν τῇ ψυχῇ, ἀλλ' οὐ φορά; Phaedr., 253a: καὶ ἐφαπτόμενοι αὐτοῦ (sc. τοῦ θεοῦ) τῇ μνήμῃ; Resp., V, 490c: ὅτι ξυνέβη προσῆκον τούτοις ἀνδρεία, μεγαλοπρέπεια, εὐμάθεια, μνήμη. Cf. Ast, Lexicon Platonicum.

[2] Roscher, 3075-3080; Pauly-W., XV, 2 (1932), 2257 f.; 2265-2269.

[3] Pauly-W., *op. cit.*, 2265.

[4] The author of 2 Pt. 1:12 ff. is concerned to see that the community will keep the memory of the Christ event alive after his death. Here μνήμη is found as ἀπαξλεγόμενον alongside ὑπομιμνήσκειν and ὑπόμνησις (→ ἀνάμνησις) in v. 15. The author is perhaps influenced by the "testament of Moses" in Jos. Ant., 4, 177 ff. (cf. Wnd. Kath. Br., 87 f.).

[5] In the LXX μνήμη is regularly used for the root זָכַר. It refers to remembrance of the acts of God (ψ 29:4; 144:7; 'Α ψ 6:5). It also refers esp. to the remembrance of men after death as preserved for the righteous, Prv. 10:7: μνήμη δικαίων μετ' ἐγκωμίων ('Α: εἰς εὐλογίαν). In the 'Α form this saying was often used on inscr., cf. A. Deissmann in N. Müller-N. Bees, *Die Inschr. d. jüdischen Katakombe am Monteverde zu Rom* (1919), No. 118. Cf. also Wis. 4:1: ἀθανασία γάρ ἐστιν ἐν μνήμῃ αὐτῆς (ἀρετῆς). For this conj. καὶ μνήμη ἐν αὐτῇ, for elsewhere, and acc. to the context, the author does not find immortality only in the remembrance of posterity (cf. K. Siegfried in Kautzsch, *ad loc.*). Wis. 8:13 reads: μνήμην αἰώνιον τοῖς μετ' ἐμὲ ἀπολείψω, and in 2 Macc. 7:20 the mother of the martyr brothers is described as μνήμης ἀγαθῆς ἀξία. Prv. 1:12 speaks of the vain attempt of the ungodly to root out the remembrance of the ungodly (not the Mas.). Qoh. 1:11; 2:16; 9:5 refers to the perishing of the remembrance of all men. This applies esp. to the ungodly in Wis. 4:19; cf. also Σ Is. 26:14. μνήμη means historical recollection in Wis. 10:8: τῆς ἀφροσύνης ἀπέλιπον τῷ βίῳ μνήμην; "they left behind for the living a remembrance of their folly," and 2 Macc. 2:25. Cf. also Σ 2 Βασ. 8:16.

a dwelling (Luc. Vit. Auct., 9). This is particularly true of the Palestinian tombs hewn out of the rock, which can serve as hide-outs. Acc. to popular belief, however, the burial ground is a sinister place, for the souls of the dead wander around there (*vulgus existimat mortuorum animas circa tumulos oberrare,* Lact. Inst., II, 2, 6). Living in graves is definitely forbidden for the first time in Judaism, which teaches that uncleanness and unclean spirits rule over the dead. It can be a sign of madness to lodge among tombs (jTer., 1, 40b, 23; bChag., 3b., Bar.). It is also feared that the one concerned is sacrificing to demons or will draw to him the spirit of uncleanness (bSanh., 65b, Bar.; bNidda, 17a). In this case "a man sins against his own soul and his blood is on his own head" (he is responsible).

According to Mk. 5:3 (Lk. 8:27) the demoniac in the country of the Gerasenes had his dwelling among the tombs and came forth thence to meet Jesus. The Gospels narrate that the tomb of Jesus was hewn out of the rock (Mk. 15:46; cf. Is. 22:16), that a stone was rolled in front of the entrance (Mk. 15:46; Mt. 27:60), and that it had not been used before (Mt. 27:60; Lk. 23:53; Jn. 19:41). According to the Johannine tradition it was in a garden (κῆπος, Jn. 19:41; Ev. Pt. κῆπος Ἰωσήφ).[1] One Easter tradition is linked to this sepulchre (μνῆμα), Mk. 16:2; Lk. 24:1, and the story of the empty tomb was from the very first regarded as an attestation and confirmation of the Easter message (ἠγέρθη). Such traditions are early and persistent. According to Ac. 2:29 the tomb of David could still be shown, and Ac. 7:16 (Gn. 23:16 ff.; 50:13; Jos. 24:32) implies that the tombs of other patriarchs had their definite history. Graves are indeed memorials (μνῆμα) for those who come after. Because there is a desire to hate and dishonour the two great witnesses of God even after death, they are left unburied (Rev. 11:9; Ps. 79:3).[2] The 3½ days correspond to the 3½ years of their work.

μνημεῖον.

μνημεῖον is originally a memorial or monument like μνῆμα (from Pind.), and is often related to the dead (Eur. Iph. Taur., 702 and 821; Thuc., I, 138, 5; Xenoph. Hist. Graec., II, 4, 17; III, 2, 15; Plat. Resp., III, 414a). It then commonly means the grave

---

μνῆμα. [1] Cf. also J. Jeremias, *Golgotha* (1926), 3. This topographical note in Jn. leaves an impress of authenticity.

[2] "Indeed, they carried their malice so far as to leave unburied the bodies from which the souls had fled, whereas the Jews take such concern for the burial of their dead that before sunset they take down and bury even the bodies of those condemned to be crucified," Jos. Bell., 4, 317 (Soph. Ant.).

μνημεῖον. [1] 1 Macc. 13:27 ff. tells of the erection of a great sepulchre with pyramids and pillars (στῦλοι). Herod the Great had a monument (μνῆμα) erected at the entrance to the graves of David and Solomon, which he had first pillaged, Jos. Ant., 16, 182. Jos. also mentions the sepulchre (τὰ μνημεῖα) of the patriarchs in Hebron, which is made of costly marble and may still be seen, Bell., 4, 532. He mentions, too, the grave of Aaron (Ant., 4, 83 f.), of the high-priest Eleazar (5, 119), and of Herod Agrippa (Bell., 5, 108). In form these buildings could be very different (blocks, pillars, pyramids), but materially they always served to commemorate the dead (1 Macc. 13:29 : εἰς ὄνομα αἰώνιον). This branch of architecture seems to have been very popular and is part of later Jewish piety. The more surprising, then, is the rejection of this popular piety in the Rabb. saying in Gn. r., 82 on 35:20 : Rabban Shimon b. Gamliel (c. 140) said : One does not erect monuments (בְּפָשׁוֹת) to the righteous ; their words are their memorial (זִכְרוֹנָם). Cf. Str.-B., I, 938. Schl. Mt., 684 f.: "The building of the graves of the prophets with the associated pilgrimages was a dangerous development, not merely because it gave free rein to legend, but also because it sought to strengthen prayer by the wrong means, and thought it could arbitrarily force God's grace and help."

itself, inscr. and pap. (Ditt. Syll.[3], 1229, 4; 1232; 1234; 1242; P. Flor., 9, 10), cf. also the usage of the LXX (μνημεῖον = קֶבֶר and קְבוּרָה), though the original sense may be glimpsed in e.g., Wis. 10:7: ἀπιστούσης ψυχῆς μνημεῖον ἑστηκυῖα στήλη ἁλός. It is attested in the Synpt. tradition that the graves (μνημεῖα) of the righteous were adorned (Mt. 23:29) and built over (Mt. 23:29; Lk. 11:47).[1] Jesus reproaches the scribes and Pharisees for honouring and recognising the prophets and righteous men in their tombs (Mt. 10:41; 13:17; 23:29) but rejecting, like their fathers, the word which came to them through the messengers of God. As μνῆμα and μημεῖον are used in the same sense in the Gospels, the same tradition stands behind the comparatively rare τάφος (LXX = קֶבֶר and קְבוּרָה, cf. Mt. 23:27 and Lk. 11:44; Mt. 23:29 and Lk. 11:47).[2]

In Lk. 11:44 Jesus, upbraiding His opponents, compares them with unrecognisable (Mt. 23:27 whitewashed) graves. The point of the saying is that they conceal their true nature (i.e., death and uncleanness).[3] According to Jn. 5:28 all who rest in the graves will hear the voice of the Son of Man and rise again to life or judgment. The story of Lazarus in Jn. 11:1-44 is a provisional confirmation and fulfilment of this eschatological promise. It refers in 11:38 to a cave with a stone in front of it.[4] The future event of the resurrection also casts its shadow before in Mt. After the death of Jesus the graves open, and the dead come out of them and go into the holy city and appear to many (Mt. 27:52 f.). These events also serve to bear witness to what has taken place. The opening (ἀνοίγειν) of what is closed, the raising of what is dead, is primarily God's work (cf. the promise in Ez. 37:13 and the idea of God's power of the keys, Tg. J. I, Dt. 28:12; Tg. J. II, Gn. 30:22; Taan., 2a; Sanh., 113a; Rev. 1:18).[5]

While Mk. and Lk. use μνῆμα and μνημεῖον together (Mk. 5:2 and 3; Lk. 23:53 and 55), Mt. and Jn. prefer μνημεῖον. μνημεῖον and τάφος are sometimes interchangeable in Mt., but Jn. restricts himself exclusively to μνημεῖον.

---

[2] The account in Mk. 5:1 ff. alternates between μνημεῖον (v. 2) and μνῆμα (v. 3, 5); the story of the tomb in Mt. 27:60 ff. speaks of μνημεῖον (v. 60) and τάφος (v. 61, 64, 66). Gn. 23 also uses μνημεῖον (v. 6, 9) with τάφος (v. 4, 20). τάφος is primarily the burial ground, μνημεῖον or μνῆμα the actual grave or tomb or monument. Family graves were common outside Jerusalem in caves or clefts of the rock. Then a man could rest with his fathers (Str.-B., I, 1049 f.). The Mishnah gives the normal size and number of niches in a rock tomb (BB, 6, 8), though there were layer graves as well as niche graves. The tomb was closed by the great stone (גּוֹלֵל) and the smaller supporting stone (דּוֹפֵק), Str.-B., I, 1051.

[3] The same basic thought is thus worked out in two different ways in Lk. 11:44 and Mt. 23:27. Lk. 11:44 expresses the risk, Mt. 23:27 the reprehensibility, of religious showmanship (ὑποκριτής). Kl. Mt. on 23:27 f. suggests two different explanations of the same original saying: "One knows your true nature as little as that of graves." Certainly, the metaphor comes from the preaching of Jesus. Here, too, awareness that Jesus is and gives life (ζωή, ζωὴ αἰώνιος, ὕδωρ ζῶν) is the necessary complement and counterpart of the Synoptic metaphor of the tomb (Synpt. and Jn.).

[4] Acc. to Bau. Jn.[2] on 11:38 the tomb is either a grotto in the rock or a hole in the ground. It is possible that a specific tomb tradition lies behind the story of Lazarus.

[5] Mt. 27:52-53 links this resurrection of the saints with the death as well as the resurrection of Jesus (μετὰ τὴν ἔγερσιν αὐτοῦ). Whether these words are to be regarded as a later correction in terms of 1 C. 15:20; Col. 1:18, or whether "after their resurrection" was originally meant is an open question. The opening of graves, like any opening or shutting (cf. the concordances), is God's work. This is a special (Jerusalem?) tradition of the First Gospel, not a legendary addition to the passion narrative. That God opens graves is expressly promised in Ez. 37:13.

μνημονεύω.

μνημονεύω is common from Hdt., attested in inscr., pap. and LXX. It means "to remember," "to mention," and corresponds in the LXX to the Mas. זָכַר (זְכַר). Part of the gratitude of faith is to remember the past acts of divine deliverance, the works and miracles of God. In this sense we constantly find the admonition μνημόνευε (Tob. 4:5, 19) or μνημονεύετε (Ex. 13:3; 1 Ch. 16:12). This remembering is both praise and confession. Hence μνημονεύειν is combined with ἐξομολογεῖσθαι (ψ 6:5; 1 Ch. 16:8). The festivals of Israel, esp. the Passover and Tabernacles, are also appointed for remembrance of the past (μνημονεύετε, Ex. 13:3; μνημόσυνον, Ex. 12:14; 13:9). The term (τὸ) μνημόσυνον, which is central in the LXX (= זֵכֶר, זִכָּרוֹן, אַזְכָּרָה), belongs to this context.[1] God Himself promises, and faith proclaims, that His remembrance will go down from generation to generation (Ex. 3:15; ψ 101:12; 134:13). God's commandments and sacrifices, His feasts and cultic vessels, serve this remembrance. We are also told sometimes how words and narratives take written form to assist the remembrance of the congregation (Ex. 17:14; Est. 9:32). The remembrance (μνημόσυνον) of the righteous stands under God's protection (ψ 111:6), but God blots out the remembrance of sinners (ψ 9:5 f.; 33:16).

On the basis of these OT presuppositions of the word group μνημονεύω/μνημόσυνον one may easily perceive its significance in the Gospels from the standpoint of salvation history. Jesus pronounces the admonition with weighty authority, and He points not merely to the important events of the past (Lk. 17:32) but also to His own Word and miracles (Jn. 15:20; 16:4; Mt. 16:9; Mk. 8:19). What Jesus has said and done has been for remembrance by the community, just as the anointing in Bethany was authoritatively dedicated to the remembrance of the woman (λαληθήσεται εἰς μνημόσυνον αὐτῆς, Mk. 14:9; Mt. 26:13 = זִכָּרוֹן). In this light the saying at the Last Supper: τοῦτο ποιεῖτε εἰς τὴν ἐμὴν ἀνάμνησιν (1 C. 11:24 f.; Lk. 22:19), is a confirmation of the whole tradition, but it also shows that a new cultic action is to serve the remembrance of Jesus (זִכָּרוֹן). Hence the word and action of the community serve His remembrance (ἀνάμνησις, μνημόσυνον). Paul is aware of the duty of recalling the words of Jesus (Ac. 20:35: ὅτι ... δεῖ ... μνημονεύειν τε τῶν λόγων τοῦ κυρίου Ἰησοῦ), and he cites a dominical saying otherwise unattested. 2 Tm. 2:8 lays expressly upon the office-bearer the obligation to keep Jesus in mind as Paul proclaimed Him. But the admonition μνημονεύετε also embraces the word and work, life and suffering, of the apostle himself (1 Th. 2:9; 2 Th. 2:5; Col. 4:18). It is, in fact, the duty of the community to remember its preachers, leaders and teachers (Hb. 13:7). Because Christ remains in the remembrance of the community, so, too, does His apostle and messenger. Elsewhere we find the principle that we are to remember those from whom we have received the Word. Paul in Gl. 2:10 speaks of the need to remember the poor in Jerusalem (ἵνα μνημονεύωμεν). The collection for Jerusalem is for remembrance and recognition. Remembrance carries with it recognition and confession. The admonition μνημόνευε (μνημονεύετε) is also a call for self-re-

---

μνημονεύω. [1] On אַזְכָּרָה it may be noted that this term signifies for the Rabb. mention of the name of God, then the name itself, the tetragrammaton (→ III, 982, 31 ff.).

[2] On intercession and remembrance (μνημονεύειν) in prayer cf. A. Deissmann, *Die LXX Pap.-Veröffentlichungen aus der Heidelberger Pap.-Sammlung*, 1 (1905), 6, 15: παρακαλῶ οὖν, δέσποτα, ἵνα μνημονεύῃς μοι[μου ?] εἰς τὰς ἁγίας σου εὐχάς.

flection. Once we were among the uncircumcised outside Christ (Eph. 2:11 f.). Once the congregation was particularly blessed (Rev. 2:5; 3:3). This remembrance, too, should lead to acknowledgment, confession and repentance. Thus the command μνημόνευε (μνημονεύετε) demands gratitude to God, but it speaks also of the seriousness of the summons to repentance (= μετανόησον). That all remembrance of God's saving acts is recognition, confession and orientation to God Himself may be seen from the usage in Hb. 11:15, 22. Faith itself implies remembrance. Thus the NT Scripture is an attempt to serve the remembrance of Jesus Christ and His apostles.

In the post-apostolic period, too, μνημονεύω embraces the most varied possibilities of remembrance (Ign. Eph., 12, 2; 21, 1; Mg., 14, 1; Sm., 5, 3; Tr., 13, 1; R., 9, 1; Barn., 21, 7; Pol., 2, 3; Mart. Pol., 8, 1; 2 Cl., 17, 3; Herm. v., 1, 3, 3 and 2, 1, 3 = *memoria tenere*; v., 4, 3, 6; s., 1, 7; 6, 5, 4; m., 4, 1, 1). One remembers the commandments of God and the words of Jesus Christ; the writer of an epistle asks to be remembered; important, too, is intercession in prayer (esp. in Ign.).[2] On μνημόσυνον note 1 Cl., 22, 6; 45, 8; the expression πρὸς ἀνάμνησιν γράφομεν (1 Cl., 53, 1) belongs to the same context. Christ and His messengers remember the community; hence the community is to remember them (Ign. Eph., 21, 1).

Michel

† μισέω

Contents: 1. The Use in Secular Greek; 2. The OT and LXX: a. The Aversion and Hostility of Men among Themselves; b. God's Hating; c. Hatred of God and the Righteous; d. Fraternal Hatred; 3. Palestinian Judaism; 4. Philo; 5. Hatred and Hating in the New Testament: a. The Aversion of Men among Themselves; b. Hatred of the Community of God; c. Hatred in Discipleship of Jesus; d. The Rejecting Hate of God; e. Love and Hate in John; f. Rom. 7:15; g. The Many Facets of the Concept; h. The Distinctiveness of the Concept; 6. The Post-Apostolic Age.

1. The Use in Secular Greek.

The term occurs in Gk. from Hom., where it is used only in Il., 17, 272 of Zeus: μίσησεν δ' ἄρα μιν δηΐων κυσὶ κύρμα γενέσθαι Τρῳῇσιν. Zeus disliked the idea (hence no personal obj.) that Patroclus should fall prey to the dogs of his enemies. Pind. Pyth., 4, 284 (Schroeder, p. 125): ἔμαθε δ' ὑβρίζοντα μισεῖν. The group μισεῖν-μῖσος is also found elsewhere in class. authors. Menand. Epit., 216: θεῖον δὲ μισεῖ μῖσος ἄνθρωπ[ό]ς μέ τι stands in antithesis to the preceding ἐρᾶσθαι μὲν ἐδόκουν. The harpist Habrotonon says: "It seemed as though he loved me, but he hates me with a divine hatred."[1] The term μισεῖν occurs occasionally on inscr. (Ditt. Syll.^{3}, 1268, 22) and pap. (Soc., 41, 22; P. Oxy., VI, 902, 17; VIII, 1151, 2). We find μισόθεος in Aesch. Ag., 1090: μισόθεον μὲν οὖν, πολλὰ συνίστορα αὐτόφονα κακὰ καρατόμα (Cassandra on the house of the Atridae); μισόθεος also Luc. Tim., 35: καὶ μὴν εἰκὸς ἦν μισάνθρωπον μὲν εἶναί σε τοσαῦτα ὑπ' αὐτῶν δεινὰ πεπονθότα, μισό-

μισέω. [1] The rendering: "I believed he was in love with me, but he hates me as though it were a divine command" (C. Robert, *Szenen aus Menanders Komödien* [1908], 23) is hardly an accurate translation of θεῖον μῖσος.

θεον δὲ μηδαμῶς, οὕτως ἐπιμελουμένων σου τῶν θεῶν. [2] There are many compounds with the stem μισ-. [3] μισόκαλος is Hellen. (Philo), μισοπόνηρος is found from Demosth. and is commonly attested later. Very old is the idea of being hated by the gods. Aiolos forbids Odysseus his island because he is a man ὅς κε θεοῖσιν ἀπέχθηται μακάρεσσιν. ἔρρ', ἐπεὶ ἀθανάτοισιν ἀπεχθόμενος τόδ' ἱκάνεις (Hom. Od., 10, 74 f.). Similarly ὤ μοι ἐγὼ σέο, τέκνον, ἀμήχανος· ἦ σε περὶ Ζεὺς ἀνθρώπων ἔχθαιρε θεουδέα θυμὸν ἔχοντα (19, 363 f.). If it is a common notion that Zeus allots good to the just and punishment to the unjust (Hesiod), this undergoes particularly serious development by Aesch. He has many expressions for the dislike or hatred of deity (θεοστύγητος, Choeph., 635; θεόπτυστος, Sept. c. Theb., 604; θεῶν στύγος, *ibid.*, 653; μίσημα θεῶν, Eum., 73). The opp. is θεοφιλία, adj. θεοφιλής (Eum., 869; Fr., 350, 3). Prometheus is θεοῖς ἔχθιστος (Prom., 37), Διὸς ἐχθρός (120, opp. of διίφιλος). Clytaemnestra is θεῶν στύγος (Choeph., 1208). The house of Laios is Φοίβωι στυγηθέν (Sept. c. Theb., 691). "In the serious religion of Aesch. *dike* rules, or, as we might say, Zeus, and the dark deeds of the past, as told by sacred history, stand out sharply against this overruling *dike* — they are a στύγος, and those who commit them are God's enemies." [4]

Soph. does not emphasise in the same way as Aesch. the religious background of overruling *dike*, but the idea of being hated by the gods is found in him (Oed. Tyr., 1345 f.: ἔτι δὲ καὶ θεοῖς ἐχθρότατον βροτῶν, 1519: ἀλλὰ θεοῖς γ' ἔχθιστος ἥκω, Phil., 1031: ὦ θεοῖς ἔχθιστε). Eur. borrows from the vocabulary of Aesch., but without religious seriousness (El., 19, 130, 619, 708; Hel., 74, 903, 1678; Heracl., 722; Cyc., 396, 602; Tro., 1213; Med., 468, 1323; Iph. Taur., 948; Suppl., 494). The way is here prepared already for the usage of comedy, in which the penal hostility of the gods is no longer taken seriously. Yet there persists the more ethical view that the gods are averse to disreputable passions, Eur. Or., 708 f.: μισεῖ γὰρ ὁ θεὸς τὰς ἄγαν προθυμίας, μισοῦσι δ' ἀστοί. One also finds in the Gk. world an ethical imperative; hatred as renunciation: ὕβριμ μείσει, is demanded already in the *praecepta Delphica*. [5] θεοισεχθρία occurs in Aristoph. Vesp., 418; Archippus has the fuller πανουργία τε καὶ θεοισεχθρία (Fr., 35 K). In Diphilus, the contemporary of Menander, the stomach is θεοῖς ἐχθρά (Fr., 60, 9 K). In Xenarchos sea-crabs are θεοῖς ἐχθροί (Fr., 8 K). In rhetoric the positive θεοῖς ἐχθρός is often raised to a superlative (common in Demosth.). μισόθεος is usually act. "hating the gods," θεοστυγής pass. "hated by God" (θεοστυγής, R. 1:30). μῖσος does not occur in the NT, nor does the fear of the hatred of deity. On Epict. cf. Diss., I, 18, 9: ἄνθρωπε, εἰ σὲ δεῖ παρὰ φύσιν ἐπὶ τοῖς ἀλλοτρίοις κακοῖς διατίθεσθαι, ἐλέει αὐτὸν μᾶλλον ἢ μίσει. ἄφες τοῦτο τὸ προσκοπτικὸν καὶ μισητικόν, II, 22, 34: καὶ ὑμῶν ὅστις ἐσπούδακεν ἢ αὐτός τινι εἶναι φίλος ἢ ἄλλον κτήσασθαι φίλον, ταῦτα τὰ δόγματα ἐκκοπτέτω, ταῦτα μισησάτω, ταῦτα ἐξελασάτω ἐκ τῆς ψυχῆς τῆς ἑαυτοῦ, III, 4, 6: τί οὖν σε ἐλοιδόρουν; ὅτι πᾶς ἄνθρωπος μισεῖ τὸ ἐμποδίζον, III, 24, 113: οὐ μισῶν· μὴ γένοιτο· τίς δὲ μισεῖ τὸν ἄριστον τῶν ὑπηρετῶν τῶν ἑαυτοῦ, IV, 1, 60: ὅταν ταῦτα φιλῶμεν καὶ μισῶμεν καὶ φοβώμεθα, ἀνάγκη τοὺς ἐξουσίαν αὐτῶν ἔχοντας κυρίους ἡμῶν εἶναι. Hatred is a human impulse which can and should be transcended and vanquished. The ethical imperative (ταῦτα μισησάτω) still remains. In the pap.

---

[2] Acc. to Luc. Tim., 35 Hermes says to Timon: "I realise that you are an enemy of men (μισάνθρωπος), having suffered so much and such monstrous injustice at their hands, but I do not see how you can be an enemy of the gods (μισόθεος), since they care for you so graciously." The antithesis between μισάνθρωπος and μισόθεος is to be noted.

[3] Cf. Pass., *s.v.* μισο — is in contrast to φιλο —; cf. Debr. Griech. Wortb. § 77.

[4] F. Dirlmeier, "θεοφιλία-φιλοθεΐα," Philol., 90, NF, 44 (1935), 57 ff.; 176 ff., esp. 184-5. Related but distinct is the motif of the enemy of God, the θεομάχος, cf. W. Nestle, "Legenden vom Tod d. Gottesverächter," *Archiv f. Religionswissenschaft*, 33 (1936), 246-269; also H. Windisch, ZNW, 31 (1932), 10 ff.

[5] Ditt. Syll.³, III, 1268, I, 22.

cf. Soc., 41, 22; P. Oxy., VI, 902, 17; VIII, 1151, 2 (φεύγε πν[εῦμ]α μεμισιμένον, Χ[ριστό]ς σε διώκει).

μισεῖν is also common in the Hermetic writings, e.g., VI, 6: τοιαῦτα τὰ ἀνθρώπεια ἀγαθὰ καὶ [τὰ] καλά, ὦ Ἀσκληπιέ, ἃ οὔτε φυγεῖν δυνάμεθα οὔτε μισῆσαι, IX, 4b (of those who stand in knowledge [οἱ ἐν γνώσει ὄντες]): μισούμενοί τε καὶ καταφρονούμενοι καὶ τάχα που καὶ φονευόμενοι. Also important is IV, 6b: ἐὰν μὴ πρῶτον τὸ σῶμα μισήσῃς, ὦ τέκνον, σεαυτὸν φιλῆσαι οὐ δύνασαι. Commands to love, prohibitions of hatred, and the golden rule are found in Mandaean writings. These are signs of later syncretism and Christian influence. "O ye believers and perfect! All that is hateful to you, do not do to your neighbour" (Ginza R., 1, 150). "Let there be no hate, envy, or division among you" (*ibid.*, 2, 1, 61).[6]

2. The OT and LXX.

a. The Aversion and Hostility of Men among Themselves. The word group μισέω, μῖσος, μισητός is also found in the LXX, and μισητὸν ποιεῖν is common, mostly for שָׂנֵא (noun שִׂנְאָה).[7] This hatred or dislike may be of different kinds and may show itself in different external relations. The word is first used when men are at enmity, e.g., Gn. 26:27; Ju. 11:7; 2 S. 5:8; 13:22; 18:28 B; 22:18, 41; 1 K. 22:8 = 2 Ch. 18:7. In a trial it is noted whether a man who has killed hated or did it unintentionally, Dt. 4:42; 19:4, 6, 11; Jos. 20:5. Very often a man hates or is tired of the wife he has lived with, Gn. 29:31, 33; Dt. 21:15; 22:13, 16; 24:3; Ju. 14:16; 15:2; 2 S. 13:15; Sir. 42:9; Is. 54:6; 60:15. It is natural that the political enemy should come within this hatred which divides men, Da. 4:16; 1 Macc. 7:26; 11:21; 4 Macc. 9:3.[8] The opp. of "to hate" in the OT is always "to love." Of two wives it may be that a man loves the one and hates the other, Dt. 21:15 and n. 23 f., or that love turns to hate, Ju. 14:16; 2 S. 13:15. To hate is to feel distaste, Dt. 22:13; 24:3; Ju. 14:16; 15:2, or to slight, Dt. 21:15 ff.; Is. 60:15, to be unfriendly or not to love, Ex. 20:5; Dt. 7:10.[9] Typical is 2 Βασ. 13:15: καὶ ἐμίσησεν αὐτὴν Ἀμνων μῖσος μέγα σφόδρα, ὅτι μέγα τὸ μῖσος, ὃ ἐμίσησεν αὐτὴν ὑπὲρ τὴν ἀγάπην ἣν ἠγάπησεν αὐτήν. To love is also the opp. (ἀγαπᾶν/μισεῖν) in 2 Βασ. 19:7; Prv. 13:24; Eccl. 3:8; Mi. 3:2; Mal. 1:2, 3. Into this world of passions which ineluctably overtake men there comes the divine command to overcome hate, Lv. 19:17: οὐ μισήσεις τὸν ἀδελφόν σου τῇ διανοίᾳ σου, ἐλεγμῷ ἐλέγξεις τὸν πλησίον σου καὶ οὐ λήμψῃ δι' αὐτὸν ἁμαρτίαν. The reprimand (ἐλεγμός) is to replace hate by love. The later rule of wisdom in Tob. 4:15a points in the same direction: καὶ ὃ μισεῖς, μηδενὶ ποιήσῃς. Both apply to the personal dealings of men, originally within the limits of the national community (Lv. 19:17).

---

6 On the golden rule cf. Tob. 4:15; Heb. Test. Napht. 1:6 (Charles, p. 239); Tg. J. I, Lv. 19:18; Slav. En. 61:1 etc.; Str.-B., I, 460.

7 In the LXX and, so far as may be known, the Hexapla translators, the root שׂנא is rendered by μισεῖν and derivates. The content of the Heb. and Gk. terms is thus equated. Only in the Wisdom writings, esp. Prv., do we often have ἐχθρός and ἔχθρα for part. and subst. Three times (Prv. 16:3 [15:32]; Is. 33:15; 54:6) μισεῖν is used for מאס. The similarity of consonants may have contributed to this choice, as in many cases. Is. 54:6 (cf. 60:15) refers to the wife who is less loved; hence μισεῖν is used as in Dt. 21:15 ff.; 24:3. Cf. on this J. Ziegler, *Untersuchungen zur Septuaginta des Buches Isaias* (1934), 128 f.

8 2 Βασ. 18:28 B: Εὐλογητὸς κύριος ὁ θεός σου, ὃς ἀπέκλεισεν τοὺς ἄνδρας τοὺς μισοῦντας τὴν χεῖρα αὐτῶν ἐν τῷ κυρίῳ μου τῷ βασιλεῖ (better ἀντάραντας A or ἐπαραμένους Lucian). 2 Βασ. 22:18, 41 (= Ps. 18), thanksgiving for deliverance from enemies who hate the opponent. H. Birkeland, *Die Feinde des Individuums in d. israelitischen Psalmendichtung* (1933), 29-30: "In genre this (Ps. 18 = 2 Βασ. 22:2-51) belongs to the individual psalms of thanksgiving; in specific content it is sung by a king after a victory."

9 Cf. on this E. König, *Hbr.-Aram. Wörterbuch z. AT* ^{4,5} (1931), 467.

The word is most common in the Ps. and the Wisdom literature (esp. Prv. and Sir.). The Ps. often refer to enemies who hate the one who prays. God can save from their power, and the psalmist prays that He will (Ps. 25:19; 69:14) or thanks Him for so doing (Ps. 18:17; 106:10). Yahweh even helps by destroying his enemies (Ps. 18:40; 21:9 f.). It may be that these are royal psalms which are directed against external enemies and which regard national opposition as religious.[10] In another group the distinction is between the wicked and the righteous. The wicked hate the righteous (34:21; 36:2, 3; 86:17; Prv. 29:10), though without a cause (35:19; 69:4), but even here there emerges the assurance (cf. Wisdom teaching): "Evil shall slay the wicked, they that hate the righteous shall suffer for it" (Ps. 34:21). The belief in election links God's action with Israel's destiny, and the conviction that Israel's foes are also God's (Nu. 10:35; Dt. 7:15; 30:7; 33:11; Ps. 89:23; 105:25; 129:5; Tob. 13:14 = LXX: ἐπικατάρατοι πάντες οἱ μισοῦντές σε).

b. God's Hating. The OT concept of God includes the fact that God can and does hate. A basic element in biblical proclamation is that He hates alien worship, Dt. 12:31; 16:22; Jer. 44:4; Ez. 23:38 LXX A. The prophets put the cultus without heart obedience on the same level as idolatry; Yahweh hates it too, Am. 5:21; Hos. 9:15; Is. 1:14; 61:8; Zech. 8:17; Mal. 2:13. Idolatry and false worship are thus specifically hated by God. In Wisdom teaching His hatred falls especially on ἀσέβεια, ἀδικία and ὑπερηφανία. Wis. 14:9 f. says of idolatry: God is hostile both to the sinner and his sin. The deed is punished with the doer. Jdt. 5:17 is a fixed phrase with almost a formal ring: θεὸς μισῶν ἀδικίαν. According to Sir. 10:7 pride (ὑπερηφανία) is hated both by God and men. Wisdom teaching holds firmly to the principle that God hates the sinner and recompenses his sin, Sir. 12:6; 27:24 LXX. God's hate implies aversion and hostility to the sin, judgment and retribution for the sinner. Sometimes the thought of love breaks through. God loves all His creatures and pardons all; He is the Lord of life, Wis. 11:24-26.[11] This thought is Hellenistic in form and basis, cf. 12:1. It thus reminds us of Greek philosophy. But it also stands in clear relation to the biblical preaching of repentance (μετάνοια, 11:23).[12] Prv. 6:16-19 shows how the members of man become an abomination to Yahweh, so that He must hate them. Deviating from the Mas., the LXX says about this ἄφρων and παράνομος: ὅτι χαίρει πᾶσιν οἷς μισεῖ ὁ κύριος, 6:16. There is a similar enumeration of the wicked attributes and actions which Yahweh hates in Prv. 8:13 (φόβος κυρίου μισεῖ ἀδικίαν).[13] Sir.

---

[10] So rightly Birkeland, *loc. cit.* The psalms fall into different groups and are not to be understood in terms of the same presuppositions. Cf. also H. Gunkel, *Ausgewählte Ps.* (1917) and *Ps.-komm.* (1926); S. Mowinckel, *Psalmenstudien,* I (1921). The close link between national and religious thinking may be seen esp. in ψ 44, cf. 22: "For thy sake are we killed all the day long; we are counted as sheep for the slaughter" (Maccabean ?).

[11] ἐν ἴσῳ γὰρ μισητὰ θεῷ καὶ ὁ ἀσεβῶν καὶ ἡ ἀσέβεια αὐτοῦ. καὶ γὰρ τὸ πραχθὲν σὺν τῷ δράσαντι κολασθήσεται (Wis. 14:9 f.). μισητὴ ἔναντι κυρίου καὶ ἀνθρώπων ὑπερηφανία, καὶ ἐξ ἀμφοτέρων πλημμελὴς ἡ ἀδικία (Sir. 10:7). ὅτι καὶ ὁ ὕψιστος ἐμίσησεν ἁμαρτωλοὺς καὶ τοῖς ἀσεβέσιν ἀποδώσει ἐκδίκησιν (Sir. 12:6). ἀγαπᾷς γὰρ τὰ ὄντα πάντα καὶ οὐδὲν βδελύσσῃ ὧν ἐποίησας οὐδὲ γὰρ ἂν μισῶν τι κατεσκεύασας (Wis. 11:24).

[12] Cf. on the religious distinctiveness of Wis. 11:24-26 C. L. W. Grimm, *Ex. Hdbch. zu den Apokr. d. AT,* VI (1860), 217 f.; also E. K. Dietrich, *Die Umkehr* (*Bekehrung u. Busse*) *im AT u. im Judt.* (1936), 242-269; E. Sjöberg, *Gott u. d. Sünder im pal. Judt.* (1938), 204.

[13] Prv. 8:13 LXX runs: φόβος κυρίου μισεῖ ἀδικίαν, ὕβριν τε καὶ ὑπερηφανίαν καὶ ὁδοὺς πονηρῶν. μεμίσηκα δὲ ἐγὼ διεστραμμένας ὁδοὺς κακῶν. Cf. also Ex. 18:21: ἄνδρας δυνατοὺς θεοσεβεῖς ἄνδρας δικαίους μισοῦντας ὑπερηφανίαν, and Sir. 10:7: μισητὴ ἔναντι κυρίου καὶ ἀνθρώπων ὑπερηφανία (→ n. 7).

15:11 warns: "What God hates, thou shalt not do" (the LXX reads ποιήσεις and ποιήσει).

As God hates evil, so do the righteous. This is demanded in Ps. 97:10; Sir. 17:26. Distinctive of biblical thinking is that this hatred is regarded as natural, Ex. 18:21; Job 34:17; Am. 5:15; Is. 33:15; Ps. 97:10; 119:104, 128, 163; Prv. 8:13; 13:5; 28:16; Sir. 17:26; 19:6; 25:2; 27:24 LXX. When the righteous of the old covenant hate evil, this is not primarily an emotion of the human heart. It is a passionate disowning in faith of the evil or the evil person whom God Himself has rejected. In his hatred the wise man is on the side of the divine judgment.[14] In this holy and passionate rejection lies the religious distinctiveness of the biblical ethos, though with OT limitations, for in the OT one's own sinfulness is not seen radically enough, nor is there a sharp enough distinction between evil as a power and the human doer. Disowning separates from the sinner, but cannot overcome him. Hence μισεῖν and ἀγαπᾶν are always antonyms in the Wisdom literature. The righteous love the good and hate the evil, the ungodly love the evil and hate the good, Mi. 3:2. Thus in Wisdom style the objects of μισεῖν are παιδεία (ψ 49:17; Prv. 5:12), αἴσθησις (Prv. 1:22), σοφία (Prv. 1:29), ἔλεγχος (Prv. 12:1), ἐλεγμός (Sir. 21:6), ἀλήθεια (Prv. 26:28). What is meant is not so much an emotion as a rejection in will and deed.[15] Intrinsic to the same style is the balancing of love and hate in a loose and non-psychological sense, an indication of what lies behind them, e.g., Prv. 13:24: ὃς φείδεται τῆς βακτηρίας, μισεῖ τὸν υἱὸν αὐτοῦ, ὁ δὲ ἀγαπῶν ἐπιμελῶς παιδεύει, 14:20: φίλοι μισήσουσιν φίλους πτωχούς, φίλοι δὲ πλουσίων πολλοί, 19:7: πᾶς ὃς ἀδελφὸν πτωχὸν μισεῖ, καὶ φιλίας μακρὰν ἔσται, cf. also 29:24: μισεῖ τὴν ἑαυτοῦ ψυχήν. Hatred has here the sense of rejection, and denotes man's aversion from something which seems to him to be petty or false.

c. Hatred of God and the Righteous. As God hates evil and the righteous hate the ungodly, so on the other side there arises man's hate against God, the hatred of the ungodly for the righteous. God visits the misdeeds of the fathers on the children to the third and fourth generation of them that hate Him (τοῖς μισοῦσίν με, Ex. 20:5; Dt. 5:9; 7:10; 32:41, 43). One can love Yahweh, and one can also hate Him. One hates God by consciously transgressing His commandments, ignoring His will, and mocking and persecuting the righteous. Hatred against God is thus a sign of rejection and obduracy. The prayer of the psalmist is against the enemies of God who hate Him (Ps. 68:1; 74:4, 23; 83:2). The assurance is given in Ps. 139:21: "Do not I hate them, O Lord, that hate thee? and do not I abhor them that rise up against thee?" Prv. 9:8 LXX prays: μὴ ἔλεγχε κακοὺς ἵνα μὴ μισῶσίν σε· ἔλεγχε σοφὸν καὶ ἀγαπήσει σε. Psalter and proverb depict the enemies of the righteous, their power and number, the futility of their misdeeds, their evil disposition which repays evil for good (Ps. 34:21; 35:19; 38:19 f.; 69:4; 86:17; Prv. 29:10).

---

[14] Commonly in the Psalter the hate which separates from the ungodly: ψ 25:5: ἐμίσησα ἐκκλησίαν πονηρευομένων καὶ μετὰ ἀσεβῶν οὐ μὴ καθίσω, 100:3: ποιοῦντας παραβάσεις ἐμίσησα, 118:113: παρανόμους ἐμίσησα καὶ τὸν νόμον σου ἠγάπησα, 138:21f.: οὐχὶ τοὺς μισοῦντάς σε, κύριε, ἐμίσησα καὶ ἐπὶ τοῖς ἐχθροῖς σου ἐξετηκόμην; τέλειον μῖσος ἐμίσουν αὐτούς, εἰς ἐχθροὺς ἐγένοντό μοι.

[15] For similar scorn, which is not so much hate in the modern psychological sense, cf. Prv. 15:10b: οἱ δὲ μισοῦντες ἐλέγχους τελευτῶσιν αἰσχρῶς, 15:27b: ὁ δὲ μισῶν δώρων λήμψεις σῴζεται, 17:9b: ὃς δὲ μισεῖ κρύπτειν, διίστησιν φίλους καὶ οἰκείους. Worth noting, too, is Prv. 29:24: ὃς μερίζεται κλέπτῃ, μισεῖ τὴν ἑαυτοῦ ψυχήν.

d. Fraternal Hatred. This is generally forbidden both in the OT (Lv. 19:17; Dt. 19:11) and in the Rabbinic tradition. S. Lev. 19:17 (352a) says expressly: "Scripture teaches: 'in thine heart'; I speak only of the hate which is seated in the heart." [16] S. Dt., 186 f. on 19:11 fears that transgression of the commandment to love will carry with it violation of the prohibition of hatred, and then will follow revenge, anger, and finally bloodshed. In the style of Wisdom preaching Ab., 2, 16 says: "R. Jehoshua (c. 90) said: An envious eye and the evil impulse and hatred of men remove men from the world (cf. Sir. 20:25)." Ab. R. Nathan, 12 (M) (on Hillel's saying in Ab., 1, 12: "Love men"): "This teaches that one should love men and not hate them; for so we find among the people of the generation of the dispersion; because they loved one another, God would not destroy them from the world, but scattered them to the four winds of the world. But the people of Sodom, because they hated one another, God expunged from this world and the world to come." Derek Erez, 11: "R. Eliezer said: He who hates his neighbour is among the shedders of blood (Dt. 19:11)." [17]

3. Palestinian Judaism.

Like the OT itself, Rabbinic tradition is aware of the hatred which is legitimate and even imperative. [18] Ab. R. Nathan, 16 mentions as those whom one must hate Epicureans (free-thinkers), seducers, misleaders, and informers (traitors). Express appeal is made to the saying of David in Ps. 139:21 f. [19] The command of love in Lv. 19:18 is correspondingly restricted: If he acts according to the way of thy people, thou shalt love him; if not, thou shalt not love him. bYoma, 22b/23a records as a saying of R. Jochanan (d. 279) in the name of R. Shimeon b. Jehozadak (225): A student who does not take revenge and bear hate like a serpent (for an injury suffered) is no (true) student. Lv. 19:18 is expressly weakened (not for a personal injury). S. Lv. 19:18 (352a) also distinguishes between revenge and wrath, which are forbidden towards sons of the people, but allowed towards others.

Acc. to bYoma, 9b the second sanctuary (Herod's temple) was destroyed because there was uncaused hatred within it, and this was just as serious a sin as idolatry, licentiousness and bloodshed (TMen., 13, 22: Reason for the destruction of the second temple: Because men loved Mammon, and one hated the other). It is pointed out [20] that Judaism itself regarded lurking animosity as the worst sin of the people during the decades before the destruction of the temple. Cf. also Ps. Sol. 7:1: μὴ ἀποσκηνώσῃς ἀφ' ἡμῶν, ὁ θεός, ἵνα μὴ ἐπιθῶνται ἡμῖν οἳ ἐμίσησαν ἡμᾶς δωρεάν, or 12:6: φυλάξαι κύριος ψυχὴν ἡσύχιον μισοῦσαν ἀδίκους. The battle against hatred is important in apocalyptic. The Test. Gad has many warnings to the effect: "Be not seduced by the spirit of hatred. In all human sayings it is evil" (3:1). "Guard yourselves against hatred, my children. It is a sin against the Lord. It does not heed the command to love one's neighbour; it sins against God" (4:1). "Wicked is hatred; it constantly sides with falsehood, and fights the truth" (5:1). "Now my children, let each love his brother, and root out hatred from your hearts. Love in deed and word and mind" (6:1). This overcoming of hate and instruction in brotherly love is of particular significance: "So love one another from the heart. And if one sin against thee, tell him so in peace.

16 Str.-B., I, 364.
17 Cf. 1 Jn. 3:15: πᾶς ὁ μισῶν τὸν ἀδελφὸν αὐτοῦ ἀνθρωποκτόνος ἐστίν, καὶ οἴδατε, ὅτι πᾶς ἀνθρωποκτόνος οὐκ ἔχει ζωὴν αἰώνιον ἐν αὐτῷ μένουσαν.
18 Str.-B., I, 364-366.
19 TShab., 13, 5 tells of a discussion whether one should save books of the minim from burning because they contain the name of God. Ps. 139:21 f. is quoted here too. Cf. also bShab., 116a.
20 Str.-B., I, 642.

Thus set aside the poison of hatred. Do not keep cunning in thy soul. If he confesses and repents, forgive him. If he denies it, do not strive with him. Otherwise he will swear and thou art doubly guilty" (6:3-4).[21] The apocalyptic mood of Od. Sol. 7:20 is similar: "And hatred will be taken away from the earth, and overthrown along with envy."

4. Philo.

Philo's usage is close to Gk. thought. He has many compounds with the stem μισ-: μισάδελφος, μισάλληλος, μισανθρωπία, μισάνθρωπος, μισάρετος, μισογύναιος, μισόκαλος, μισόπολις, μισοπονηρία, μισοπονηρός, μισοπονία, μισοτεκνία. Of God in Leg. All., 3, 77: ὥσπερ οὖν ἡδονὴν καὶ σῶμα ἄνευ μεμίσηκεν αἰτιῶν ὁ θεός, for no stated cause God has declared desire and the body to be worthy of hate (cf. Herm., 4, 6b). Rer. Div. Her., 163: οὐκοῦν ὁ φιλοδίκαιος θεὸς ἀδικίαν βδελύττεται καὶ μεμίσηκε στάσεως καὶ κακῶν ἀρχήν. Spec. Leg., I, 256: (of God) μισοῦντος ἀλαζονείαν. Of hate which is wrong, Deus Imm., 143: ταύτην τὴν ἀτραπὸν μισεῖ καὶ προβέβληται καὶ φθείρειν ἐπιχειρεῖ πᾶς ὁ σαρκῶν ἑταῖρος. στέργειν and μισεῖν are contrasted in the story of Joseph and his brethren: Jos., 5: μισοῦντες ὅσον ἐστέργετο· τὸ δὲ μῖσος οὐκ ἐξελάλουν, ἀλλ' ἐν ἑαυτοῖς ἐταμίευον. Spec. Leg., III, 101: (of magic) καὶ στέργοντας μὲν εἰς ἀνήκεστον ἔχθραν μισοῦντας δὲ εἰς ὑπερβάλλουσαν εὔνοιαν ἄξειν ὑπισχνούμενα. Exposition of the OT phrase concerning the loved and hated wife, Rer. Div. Her., 47; Leg. All., II, 47 f.; Sacr. AC, 20; Poster. C., 63; Mut. Nom., 254. In Leg. All., II, 47 f. Gn. 29:31 and Dt. 21:15 f. are taken to mean that virtue (ἀρετή) is naturally hated by the mortal race, but that God honours it and gives the first-born to the hated. "For this first and most perfect conception is that of hated virtue, and that of beloved sensual desire is the last." Hate, fear and shame (μῖσος, φόβος, αἰδώς) are mentioned together as motives for flight in Fug., 3 and 23. Congr., 85 speaks of the hate which is forbidden: παραγγέλλων μισεῖν τὰ ἔθη καὶ τὰ νόμιμα καὶ τὰ ἐπιτηδεύματα αὐτῶν. Man should hate the passions of childhood and the vices of age. Rer. Div. Her., 43: εἰρωνείαν γὰρ μισεῖν ἀκαταλλάκτως ἐπαιδεύθημεν, Spec. Leg., IV, 170: καὶ μισεῖν ὡς ἐχθρὸν καὶ μέγιστον κακὸν ἀλαζονείαν. The change from hate to love is mentioned in Somn., II, 107-108: "When in gradual return to amendment ... he proclaims what he has thoroughly apprehended by suffering, namely, that he belongs to God (Gn. 50:19), and no longer to any creature which may be perceived by the senses, then his brothers enter into reconciling negotiations with him and change their hatred into love and their ill-will into good-will ..." We should also note the related ἔχθρα group, which is to be differentiated from μῖσος as is enmity from hatred: Soph. Ant., 523: οὔτοι συνέχθειν, ἀλλὰ συμφιλεῖν ἔφυν. Ep. Ar., 225 puts the question. πῶς ἂν καταφρονοίη τῶν ἐχθρῶν, and answers: ἠσκηκὼς πρὸς πάντας ἀνθρώπους εὔνοιαν καὶ κατεργασάμενος φιλίας λόγον οὐθενὸς ἂν ἔχοις. τὸ δὲ κεχαριτῶσθαι πρὸς πάντας ἀνθρώπους καὶ καλὸν δῶρον εἰληφέναι παρὰ θεοῦ τοῦτ' ἐστὶ κράτιστον. In the Gk. world, as in later Judaism, there is some awareness of the evil consequences of hatred, enmity and envy; there is a demand that these passions should be overcome by ἀγάπη, φιλία and εὔνοια. Ethical hatred is also known with its distinction between man and evil. Apocalyptic sees the relation between love, peace and forgiveness, also between hatred and falsehood. Hellenism speaks of the virtue which is hated. It is thus aware of the dissonance between the divine command and the nature of man. But by its antithesis to the body (μισεῖν τὸ σῶμα) it destroys the unity of human existence and creatureliness (Hermet., Philo). The new thing which the NT brings is Christ Himself as the concrete reality of divine love and as the true victory over hate. If hate is here overcome, it is by the exclusive gift and requirement of ἀγάπη (εὔνοια, Eph. 6:7).

---

[21] Cf. on this G. F. Moore Judaism, II, 155.

5. Hatred and Hating in the New Testament.

a. The Aversion of Men among Themselves. Only μισέω occurs in the NT (not μῖσος or μισητός, μισητὸν ποιεῖν). Here, as in the LXX, it has different nuances. It first denotes the personal aversion of man for man, with no religious background. When Jesus in Mt. 5:43 quotes the saying: "Thou shalt love thy neighbour and hate thine enemy," the saying reminds us of the command of Lv. 19:18 on which Judaism had put false restrictions, though the second half of the saying is not actually attested. "The saying as a whole is a popular maxim in accordance with which the average Israelite shaped his conduct towards friends and foes in the days of Jesus."[22] Jesus is thus referring to a particular interpretation of the OT, not to the OT itself. He fundamentally forbids His disciples to repay hatred with hatred: "Love your enemies, do good to them which hate you" (Lk. 6:27). Jesus lays on His disciples the obligation of love for all men, even enemies. He knows no holy hatred against men. He thus brings to light an irresolvable discord in the OT and especially in Judaism. The antonyms ἀγαπᾶν/μισεῖν take on a special flavour in Mt. 6:24; Lk. 16:13, where, in dependence on Dt. 21:15-17 and Ex. r., 51 (104) they mean "to prefer" ("to be faithful to") and "to slight" ("to despise").[23] We have here a Hebraism, as in the requirement for discipleship (Mt. 10:37: ὁ φιλῶν ὑπὲρ ἐμέ, Lk. 14:26: καὶ οὐ μισεῖ).[24]

b. Hatred of the Community of God. The Gospels speak of a present (Lk., Jn.) and future (esp. Mt., Mk.) hatred which persecutes the community of God. The righteous in the infancy stories of Lk. are already assailed by hostility and hatred, 1:71. To be hated is also the fate of the disciples in Lk. 6:22, 27. In the prophecy of Jesus μισεῖν takes on theological significance. It is an assault and a sign of the apocalyptic future, Mt. 10:22; 24:9; Mk. 13:13; Lk. 21:17. The coming of Jesus according to the Synoptic tradition means deliverance from hatred (Lk. 1:71), victory over it (6:22, 27), but also its increase (Mt. 10:22; 24:9 f.).[25]

c. Hatred in Discipleship of Jesus. The requirement for discipleship in Lk. 14:26 (Mt. 10:37); Jn. 12:25 is striking: "Hatred of all we are under obligation to love, including our own souls, is the condition of fellowship with Jesus, of working together with Him."[26] The reference is not to hate in the psychological sense, but to disowning, renunciation, rejection (καὶ τὴν ψυχὴν ἑαυτοῦ), as in the

---

[22] Str.-B., I, 353.

[23] The OT already distinguishes between the אֲהוּבָה and the שְׂנוּאָה, the loved and the hated or less loved, Dt. 21:15-17. So, too, tradition, Ex. r., 51, 6 on 38:21: "Why is the mount of the Law called Sinai? Because God disregarded (שׂנא) the lofty and loved (אהב) the lowly." Cf. on this Str.-B., I, 434; J. Lagrange, *Evangile selon Luc* (1921), 408 f.

[24] Bultmann Trad., 172 f.; Kittel Probleme, 54 f.; Kittel, "Das Urteil des NT über den Staat," ZSTh (1937), 671 f.; J. Denney, "The Word 'Hate' in Lk. 14:26," Expos. T. (1909), 41 f.; W. Bleibtreu, "Paradoxe Aussprüche Jesu," *Theol. Arbeiten aus dem wissenschaftl. Predigerverein der Rheinprovinz*, NF, 20 (1926), 15-35; on Lk. 14:26 in comparison with Mt. 10:37 cf. also Zn. Lk., 554, n. 50; A. v. Harnack, *Sprüche u. Reden Jesu* (1907), 62. Kittel Probleme, 54 f. rightly observes: "Again the Jewish Christian of the Matthew tradition renders the original Aram. saying of Jesus more freely but quite accurately: ὁ φιλῶν πατέρα ἢ μητέρα ὑπὲρ ἐμέ, whereas the Lucan form yet again shows the remote non-Palestinian who sticks anxiously and pedantically to the original form of his tradition."

[25] Note the increase of hatred in the future; the disciples will be hated by all (Mt. 10:22: ὑπὸ πάντων, 24:9: ὑπὸ πάντων τῶν ἐθνῶν, 24:10: καὶ μισήσουσιν ἀλλήλους, Mk. 13:13; Lk. 21:17: ὑπὸ πάντων).

[26] Schl. Lk., 243.

Wisdom literature of the OT.[27] Those who become disciples of Jesus must be committed exclusively to Him; they cannot be bound to anyone or anything else. The term "hate" demands the separation of the disciple, and the warning not to love anyone or anything more is the test. This abnegation is to be taken, not psychologically or fanatically, but pneumatically and christocentrically.

d. The Rejecting Hate of God. The idea of divinely willed hate reminds us of the OT. In R. 9:13, Mal. 1:2 f. is quoted in connection with the doctrine of election: "Jacob have I loved, but Esau have I hated." The prophetic saying does not advance, however, a particularistic claim to election. It emphasises the free counsel of God which is independent of man. The love of God is the mystery of His election; His hate is the enigma of His hardening. The μισεῖν of God belongs to the context of His office as Lord and Judge. Rev. 2:6 refers to the hate of Jesus and His church at Ephesus; they both hate the works of the Nicolaitans. Hate here denotes differentiation and disavowal, punishment and judgment. In the Spirit of God the community rejects temptation.[28] It is thus understandable that Hb. 1:9 should apply to the lordship of Jesus Christ the saying in Ps. 45:7: ἠγάπησας δικαιοσύνην καὶ ἐμίσησας ἀνομίαν. Jesus Christ has acknowledged righteousness and repudiated iniquity. His office as Lord and Judge is herewith described.[29]

e. Love and Hate in John. The contrast ἀγαπᾶν/μισεῖν reaches a climax in Johannine thinking. The divine movement of love (ἀγάπη) here too comes into conflict with the cosmic movement of hate (μῖσος). Both are so exclusive and comprehensive that they disclose the nature of God and the world. In this hate of the world for God, for Christ, for the disciples, and for the community, lies true sin and murder. Light is here differentiated from darkness.[30] He who does evil hates the light and does not come to it, lest his works should be reproved (3:20). To hate the light is to be blinded and impelled by the power of darkness. Hence one does not hate of oneself. To hate is to live in hostility to the light, to reject it, to avoid its sphere. If we understand Jn. aright, this profound hate is the counterpart of the fact that God is light and love. Just because Christ is the light of the world and the act of divine love, the hatred and opposition of the world is intensified. The mystery of iniquity is concealed in the word "hate." The world hates Jesus (7:7; 15:18). In so doing it also hates God (15:23 f.), and it hates the disciple too (15:18; 17:14; 1 Jn. 3:13). To live in the sphere of light is necessarily

---

[27] One may thus associate μισεῖν τὴν ψυχὴν ἑαυτοῦ (Lk. 14:26) with [ἀπ]αρνεῖσθαι ἑαυτόν (Lk. 9:23). The No to self becomes a No to one's own life. Cf. A. Plummer, *St. Luke* (ICC[5], 1922), 364; also J. Lagrange, *op. cit.*, 408-409, who points out that to hate is to regard as an enemy of the cause of God.

[28] Hate, as the antithesis of the love to be practised among believers, implies sharp separation from the world; the Nicolaitans are reckoned with the world when the community in hate marks itself off from them, Loh. Apk., 21. J. Behm, *NT Deutsch*, III, 18 speaks in terms of a repudiation in holy intolerance.

[29] Though Hb. 1:9 does not rule out the history of Jesus, the aorists refer to the eternal lordship of the exalted Lord. Cf. O. Michel, *Komm. z. Hb.* (1936), *ad loc.*; H. Windisch[2] (1931), *ad loc.*

[30] It is distinctive of Jn. that in 1 Jn. 2:15 he does not demand hate (μισεῖτε), but in the paraphrase μὴ ἀγαπᾶτε τὸν κόσμον μηδὲ τὰ ἐν τῷ κόσμῳ he makes a new demand on the disciples which is related to the cosmic concept. Comparison of Lk. 14:26 with 1 Jn. 2:15-17 throws light on the relation between the Synoptists and Jn. In spite of the relation between the Gospel and Rev. there are certain differences in usage, as the employment of μισεῖν shows (Rev. 2:6). The Synoptic tradition has clearly influenced the Gospel (cf. Jn. 12:25; 15:25).

to be a target of the hate of darkness. He who does not live in this sphere cannot be hated (7:7). Thus the warning against hating the brethren takes on particular theological significance in 1 Jn. To hate the brethren is to live in the sphere of darkness rather than light (1 Jn. 2:9, 11; 3:15; 4:20). The epistle does not show how this hatred finds expression. What is meant, however, is that a power of darkness determines the relation to the brethren. Hate becomes a demonic metaphysical power.

One should not forget, of course, that along with this deeper concept of μισεῖν in Jn. the older tradition still lives on. Thus we see the influence of the Synoptic requirement for discipleship in Jn. 12:25. A complaint from the Psalter (Ps. 35:19; 69:5 : a psalm of suffering) is echoed in Jn. 15:25. Rev. 2:6 is connected with the holy hatred of the OT.

f. R. 7:15. In the depiction of the plight of man under the Law in R. 7 we find in 7:15 the saying: "For that which I do I know not; for what I would, that do I not; but what I hate, that do I." θέλειν and μισεῖν here correspond. The positive and negative will of the ego does not produce action. It is forced by sin (7:17) and the flesh (7:18) which show themselves to be more powerful. Perhaps it is not accidental that μισεῖν here denotes rejection by the ἐγώ, as distinct from Epict., II, 26, 4: ὃ θέλει οὐ ποιεῖ καὶ ὃ μὴ θέλει ποιεῖ. Through the Law man is led not merely to non-willing but also to hatred and rejection (μισεῖν).[31]

g. The Many Facets of the Concept. The use of μισεῖν is more secular in Lk. 19:14; Rev. 17:16, where it denotes political enmity. In Rev. 18:2 ὄρνεον ἀκάθαρτον καὶ μεμισημένον means "bird hated by God and man."[32] Comparison of Rev. 2:6; 17:16; 18:2 shows that the term has retained its many meanings in the apocalyptic tradition. The fine admonition in Eph. 5:28 ff. lays sharply upon the husband the duty of loving his espoused wife: "He who loves his wife loves himself, for she is as his own body, not another which does not belong to him, but his second ego."[33] "For no one has ever yet hated his own flesh, but he nourishes and cherishes it as does Christ the church (5:29a). Eph. repeats the divinely willed order of life and human experience, though these are limited by discipleship of Jesus (cf. also R. 13:14). It presents an action which it would be παρὰ φύσιν to leave undone."[34] According to Tt. 3:3 it is of the essence of the old aeon, and of the life which Christians used to lead in it, to be hateful and to hate one another (στυγητοί, μισοῦντες ἀλλήλους). This conclusion of the list of vices, which corresponds to the verdict of Judaism concerning itself, reveals the full corruption of human relationships. We are reminded by it of the Johannine concept of μισεῖν, though this has absolute significance and does not form part of a chain. The conclusion of the direction in Jd. 23 has a strange ring: "And have mercy on others in fear, full of loathing for the garment spotted by the flesh." The false teacher who is combatted should experience mercy from the Church, but he is so dangerous that all spiritual or physical contact with him is to be avoided. The pollution is either to be taken literally in the sense of licentious-

---

[31] Cf. the comm. of T. Zahn, E. Kühl, K. Barth, A. Schlatter and P. Althaus, also R. Bultmann, "Röm. 7 und d. Anthropologie des Pls.," *Imago Dei* (1932), 53 ff.; W. G. Kümmel, *Röm. 7 und d. Bekehrung des Pls.* (1929); W. Gutbrod, *Die paul. Anthropologie* (1934); P. Althaus, *Pls. u. Luther über den Menschen* (1938).

[32] A. Carr, "The Meaning of 'Hatred' in the NT," Exp. 6 Ser., 12 (1905), 153-160.

[33] C. v. Harless, *Comm. über den Brief Pauli an d. Ephesier*[2] (1858), *ad loc.*

[34] *Ibid.*, 505.

ness or it is to be understood in terms of the ancient popular belief that a man's spiritual manner and force, whether pneumatic or demonic, imparts itself to his apparel (Mk. 5:27 f.; Ac. 19:11 f.).[35] Behind Jd. 23 there finally stands the OT idea of a divine hatred which has been adopted also in the NT (cf. Rev. 2:6). But the question remains open whether this hatred of wickedness is to be extended also to men and objects (Jd. 23). If so, it should be emphasised that this μισεῖν implies theologically the separation of the cause of Jesus Christ from the wickedness of this aeon and cosmos, and that for the community it means the shunning of the false teacher.

h. The Distinctiveness of the Concept. Jesus forbade His disciples to hate (Lk. 6:27). Apostolic proclamation represented hatred of the brethren (1 Jn. 2:9, 11; 3:14; 4:20), and the hatred of men for one another (Tt. 3:3), as bondage to darkness and the old aeon. Thus all passion in the dealings of men with one another, whether general, national or religious, is attacked at the root. But the idea of a holy hatred, of disavowal and repudiation for God's sake, which affects both cause and person in the OT, is also purified in the NT. The NT, too, teaches a holy rejection and repudiation of iniquity, but this is directed against the thing, not against the person. No challenge is offered to the supremacy of the law of love. It is worth noting that Rev. 2:6 speaks of hatred for the works of the Nicolaitans, not of hatred for the men themselves. When Jesus presents the requirements for discipleship, He certainly says that the disciple must renounce the natural and legal ties which bind him to his relatives (Lk. 14:26; Mt. 10:37), and to his own life (Jn. 12:25). But here, too, the reference is not to a psychologically conditioned shunning of men explicable in human terms. It is to the unconditional and exclusive character of the claim of Jesus, which will not stop at even the most important of earthly bonds, including the Law itself. There is in the NT a holy repudiation and abnegation (μισεῖν), but it is embraced and interpreted by love as the power and content of the new world of God. Because the love of God in Christ sanctifies and cleanses, holy hate is forbidden. A repudiation which does not derive from love, or lead to love, cannot appeal to the NT. The NT overcomes all possible forms of hate between man and man, including religious. It teaches, however, a holy repudiation of wickedness and a commitment to Christ with no human reservations or conditions.

6. The Post-Apostolic Age.

In the post-apostolic age the distinctiveness of the Christian law of love and the prohibition of hatred are for the most part preserved. Did., 1, 3 quotes the commandment of love in Lk. 6:27 ff.: "But love those who hate you, and so you will have no enemy." Similarly 2 Cl., 13, 4 appeals to Lk. 6:32, 35. There is an explicit prohibition in Did., 2, 7: "Thou shalt hate no man ..." Cf. also Ign. Eph., 14, 2 : "No man who confesses the faith sins, and he who has love does not hate." Cf. too the list of vices in Herm. s., 9, 15, 3. The commandment of love and forbidding of hate became a fixed part of the Church's teaching. It sounds sometimes, however, as though the law of love is a particularly clever rule of human wisdom. Thus, in distinction from the NT, which never does this, regard is had to the effect of love on men : Did., 1, 3 : "And so you

[35] Wnd. Kath. Br., 47; Kn. Pt., 243 : "Here too, then, the strictest separation and differentiation is demanded ; if one is to avoid the undergarment, how much more so the man who lurks within it." Related is Did., 2, 7: οὐ μισήσεις πάντα ἄνθρωπον, ἀλλὰ οὓς μὲν ἐλέγξεις, οὓς δὲ ἐλεήσεις, περὶ δὲ ὧν προσεύξῃ, οὓς δὲ ἀγαπήσεις ὑπὲρ τὴν ψυχήν σου. The law of love is not abandoned.

will have no enemy," and 2 Cl., 13, 4: "When they hear that, they will be astonished at the excess of goodness." It is overlooked here that the effect of Christian love is exclusively God's concern. Ign. Eph., 14, 2 is close to the absolute statements of Johannine thinking: "He who has love does not hate." In the post-apostolic age the hatred of the world was suffered without agitation, though with no attempt to conceal the seriousness of the situation. 1 Cl., 60, 3 prays: "Save us from those who hate us unjustly" (cf. Dg., 2, 6; 5, 17; 6, 5-6). Did., 16, 3 f. has a threat which reminds us of the Synoptic apocalypse: "Love will turn into hate" (16, 3). "For with the increase of lawlessness they will hate and persecute and betray one another" (16, 4). We often find the command to hate what is not pleasing to God, esp. hypocrisy (Did., 4, 12; Barn., 19, 2). We see the influence of OT usage and formulations when the community is summoned to hate wickedness, lusts and vices. Barn., 4, 1 admonishes: "And we hate the error of the present time in order that we may experience love in the time to come." Cf. also 2 Cl., 6, 6: "We believe that it is better to hate what is present, since it is petty and transitory and corruptible, and to love the goods which are incorruptible." But this statement shows how great is the distance from the NT and its use of μισεῖν. The NT does not reject any earthly good because it is petty and transitory and corruptible. With this mood of virtual flight from the world we find the resolute call: "Hate evil to the last" (Barn., 19, 11).[36] The imagery of Dg., 6, 5 f. throws a particular light on the position and ministry of post-apostolic Christianity: "The flesh hates the soul, which has done nothing to it, and fights against it because it prevents it from yielding to lusts; so the world hates Christians, who have done nothing to it, because they set themselves against lusts. The soul loves the flesh and blood in spite of its hate; so Christians love those who hate them." A large-scale anthropological comparison of Hellen. origin is used to present the relation of Christians to the world, but it displays the distinctiveness and self-understanding of early Christianity.

Michel

[36] Barn., 19, 11: εἰς τέλος μισήσεις τὸ πονηρόν, cf. ψ 96:10: οἱ ἀγαπῶντες τὸν κύριον, μισεῖτε πονηρόν. The reading μισήσεις τὸν πονηρόν, which Hennecke, 517 prefers in translating Barn., 19, 11, is perhaps thinking of Satan.

μισθός, μισθόω, μίσθιος, μισθωτός, μισθαποδότης, μισθαποδοσία, ἀντιμισθία

A. The Use of the Word Group μισθός κτλ.

1. The Use outside the New Testament.

(1) The Word Group in the Graeco-Roman World.

μισθός: a. "Reward for work" (daily, monthly or yearly recompense), Hom. Il., 21, 445 (μισθὸς ῥητός, agreed reward); Hdt., VIII, 4, 2 (πείθουσι Θεμιστοκλέα ἐπὶ μισθῷ), Eur. Iph. Aul., 1169; Plat. Prot., 328b; Xenoph. Ap., 16; Oec., 1, 4; Demosth. Or., 18, 51; 19, 94; P. Fay., 91, 41 (ἡμερήσιος μισθός); P. Tebt., II, 384, 20 (for weavers in a textile factory); BGU, IV, 1106, 14 (for a nurse); Ditt. Syll.³, 244, I, 58 and 60; 252, 36; 244, 56 (attendants and butchers at sacrifice); hence P. Oxy., IV, 724, 5 (μισθοῦ

μισθός κτλ. Cf. the dict., Liddell-Scott, Pape, Pass., Pr.-Bauer³ and the bibl. under κρίνω →, III, 921 f., also histories of the ethics of antiquity: T. Ziegler, *Die Ethik d. Griechen u. Römer* (1881); F. Jodl, *Gesch. d. Ethik in der neueren Philosophie*, I (1882); I. Schmidt, *Die Ethik d. alten Griechen*, I (1882); K. Köstlin, *Die Ethik d. classischen Altertums* (1887); C. E. Luthardt, *Die antike Ethik in ihrer geschichtl. Entwicklung* (1887); M. Wundt, *Geschichte d. griech. Ethik*, I (1908); L. Ihmels, *Der Lohngedanke in der Ethik Jesu* (1908); V. Kirchner, *Der Lohn in d. alten Philosophie, im bürgerlichen Recht, bes. im NT* (1908); O. Dittrich, *Die Systeme d. Moral*, I (1923); E. Howald, *Ethik d. Altertums* = *Handbuch d. Philosophie*, III (1927); F. Wagner, "Geschichte des Sittlichkeitsbegriffes, I: Der Sittlichkeitsbegriff in der antiken Ethik," *Münsterische Beiträge z. Theol.*, 14 (1928); K. Weiss, "Die Frohbotschaft Jesu über Lohn u. Vollkommenheit," *Nt.liche Abhandlungen*, 12, 4/5 (1927); H. Gomperz, *Die Lebensauffassungen d. griech. Philosophie u. das Ideal der inneren Freiheit* (1927); F. K. Karner, *Die Bedeutung des Vergeltunsgedankens f. d. Ethik Jesu* (Diss. Leipzig, 1927); H. Braun, "Gerichtsgedanke u. Rechtfertigungslehre bei Paulus," UNT, 19 (1930); M. Wagner, "Der Lohngedanke im Ev.," NkZ, 43 (1932), 106-112; 129-139; O. Michel, "Der Lohngedanke in d. Verkündigung Jesu," ZSTh, 9 (1932), 47 ff.; U. v. Wilamowitz-Moellendorff, *Der Glaube der Hellenen*, I, II (1931-1932); F. V. Filson, *St. Paul's Conception of Recompense* (1932); H. W. Heidland, *Die Anrechnung des Glaubens zur Gerechtigkeit* (1936). Cf. the NT Theologies of Feine, Holtzmann, Weinel, Büchsel; also O. Schulthess, Art. μισθός, Pauly-W., XV (1932), 2078 ff.

τοῦ συμπεφωνημένου, agreed recompense); P. Gen., 34, 5 (ἄνευ μισθοῦ, free of charge); BGU, IV, 1067, 15 (ἄνευ μισθῶν, without cost).[1] b. "Fee" or "compensation" in the arts and sciences, for orators, poets, actors, doctors, Xenoph. Mem., I, 2, 6 (τοὺς δὲ λαμβάνοντας τῆς ὁμιλίας μισθὸν ἀνδραποδιστὰς ἑαυτῶν ἀπεκάλει, διὰ τὸ ἀναγκαῖον αὐτοῖς εἶναι διαλέγεσθαι παρ' ὧν λάβοιεν τὸν μισθόν); Plat. Prot., 311b; 349a; Leg., I, 650a; Aristoph. Ra., 367; P. Oxy., VII, 1025, 19 f. (for actors); P. Grenf., II, 67 (for a dancer); Ditt. Syll.³, 672, 10 and 20 (teacher); Aristot. Pol., III, 16, p. 1287a, 36 (doctor). c. Soldiers' "pay," Thuc., 1, 143, 2; IV, 124, 4; VI, 8, 1 (sailors' wages), Xenoph. An., VII, 3, 13; 6, 1; Demosth. Or., 14, 31 (μισθοφορεῖν); Ditt. Syll.³, 192, 10; 193, 9; 502, 11. d. "Rent" for possession of ground or a house,[2] Ditt. Or., 595, 10 and 26; "reimbursement" for temporary use, BGU, I, 21; III, 20 (καμήλου); e. "Priests' honorarium," Eur. Ba., 257; Ditt. Syll.³, 42, 91, 130 (the priests of Eleusis received payment from devotees). f. "Payment for visiting a popular assembly" (μισθὸς ἐκκλησιαστικός).[3] g. "Expenses," P. Fay., 103, 3; Ditt. Syll.³, 245, I, 33 (μισθὸς δραχμαὶ δέκα ἕξ). h. "Payment as a bribe," Soph. Ant., 294 (παρηγμένους μισθοῖσιν εἰργάσθαι τάδε). On the dangers of a golden reward cf. Pind. Pyth., III, 55.

i. "Reward (fig.) by man or God." It should be stated in advance that in general the Greek did not accept the concept of reward outside the sphere of industry and commerce. He viewed things rather from the standpoint of δίκη, δικαιοσύνη (→ II, 178 ff.). Only occasionally do the poets speak metaphorically of reward. Thus in Isoc. Or., 15, 220 (ὅτι σοφιστῇ μισθὸς κάλλιστός ἐστι καὶ μέγιστος, ἢν τῶν μαθητῶν τινες καλοὶ κἀγαθοὶ καὶ φρόνιμοι γένωνται) the Sophist's finest reward is to have good pupils. As thanks (μισθὸν οὐκ αἰσχρόν) for bringing her message home Iphigenia offers Orestes the saving of his life, Iph. Taur., 593. Pindar thinks that renown or praise is the finest reward the great can receive from men, Ne., VII, 63. There is a verbal (though not material) par. to R. 4:4 in Pyth., I, 75 ff. (ἀρέομαι πὰρ μὲν Σαλαμῖνος Ἀθαναίων χάριν μισθόν). In Plut. Cons. ad Apoll., 14 (II, 109a) Apollo sends Trophonius and Agamedes a peaceful and blessed death as a μισθός for building a temple. The idea of a reward from the gods leads to euphemistic use j. for "punishment," Hdt., VIII, 116 f. (what is meant is that the father puts out the children's eyes as a punishment for disobedience); Aesch. Ag., 1261; Callim. Hymn. in Dianam, 263; Dion. Hal. Ant. Rom., X, 51, 2. In Eur. Hipp., 1050 the wrongdoer is given the recompense of having to lead the life of a beggar far from home.

μισθόω (-όομαι) means "to hire or let for payment," or "to hire or rent." Plat. Leg., VII, 800e (hired choirs and mourners); Plat. Resp., IX, 580b (κήρυκα); Plat. Prot., 347d (φωνὴν τῶν αὐλῶν); Demosth. Or., 23, 150 (αὑτόν, to hire oneself for service); 27, 15 (οἶκον μισθοῦν, *locare*); Hdt., II, 180 (τὸν νηὸν τριηκοσίων ταλάντων); I, 24; IX, 34; Lys. Or., 17, 8; Epict. Diss., III, 9, 14 (τὸ πλοῖον μισθούμεθα); BGU, II, 606, 16 (barn); P. Lips., 111, 11 (μισθῶσαι ἐργάτας); P. Oxy., VII, 1035, 1 (tools); P. Lille, 3, 75 (mid. to rent land); BGU, II, 591, 8 (τοὺς ἐκπεπτωκότας φοινικίνους καρπούς, to rent fallen olives); P. Masp., 240, 8 (pasture); hence ὁ μεμισθηκώς, "the lessor," BGU, II, 538, 20; ὁ μεμισθωμένος, "the lessee," BGU, I, 197, 12.

μισθωτός (adj. and noun) means "one who is hired for reward," "day-labourer": Plat. Polit., 290a along with θῆτας; Leg., XI, 918b; P. Soc., 359, 6; Plat. Resp., IV, 419 (ἐπίκουροι μισθωτοί, mercenary auxiliaries); Demosth. Or., 18, 38 (hired traitor).

μίσθιος (from the 3rd cent. B.C.), "hired," noun, "hired man," Anth. Pal., VI, 283, 3 (μίσθια ... πηνίσματα κρούει, to weave for money); Plut. Lyc., 16, 7 (I, 50a) (along with ὠνητός, "bought": τοὺς δὲ Σπαρτιατῶν παῖδας οὐκ ἐπὶ ὠνητοῖς οὐδὲ μισθίοις

[1] Cf. Durrbach, *Inscriptions de Délos*, 1. fasc. (1926) and 2. fasc. (1929); F. Heichelheim, *Wirtschaftliche Schwankungen der Zeit von Alexander bis Augustus* (1930).
[2] For details cf. K. Gerth, *Beiträge zur Wirtschaftskunde von Delos* (Diss. Hamburg, 1922, unpublished).
[3] On this cf. A. Boeckh-M. Fraenkel, *Die Staatshaushaltung der Athener* (1886), 148 ff.

ἐποιήσατο παιδαγωγοῖς ὁ Λυκοῦργος); P. Amh., 92, 19 (οὐχ ἕξω δὲ κοινωνὸν οὐδὲ μίσθιον γενόμενον τῆς ὠνῆς ὑποτελῆ, "I will not take any partner nor any paid helper who has stood in the service of state leasing"); P. Flor., 9B, 10 (μισθίοις ἐργάταις); P. Masp., 95, 7 (γεωργὸς μίσθιος, agricultural labourer); P. Oxy., I, 138, 45.

μισθαποδότης, "one who renders hired service," "who is paid," P. Gen., 14, 27 (Byz. period: ὁ μισθαποδότης θεός). The word is elsewhere found only in ecclesiastical authors.

μισθαποδοσία is not found at all elsewhere, nor ἀντιμισθία (from ἀντίμισθος, Aesch. Suppl., 270: "serving as reward," "rewarding").

(2) In the LXX.

μισθός. a. "Wage" (= שָׂכָר, מַשְׂכֹּרֶת, פְּעֻלָּה), usually for the manual worker: Gn. 29:15; 30:28, 32 f.; 31:7 f.; Ex. 2:9; 22:14; Lv. 19:13; Dt. 15:18; 3 Βασ. 5:20; Tob. 2:12, 14; 4:14; 5:3; 12:1, 2 (S), 3 (S); Job 7:1 (A), 2; Eccl. 4:9; Sir. 34:22; Zech. 8:10; Hag. 1:6 (reward for licentiousness in Is. 23:18). There is esp. criticism when the payment is reduced (ἀπαδικεῖν), Dt. 24:14, or withheld, Jer. 22:13, or beaten down, Mal. 3:5, or paid late, Dt. 24:15; evading (ἀποστερεῖν) payment is equivalent to homicide in Sir. 34:22. Other expressions are μισθὸν διδόναι or ἀποδιδόναι, or the plastic μισθὸν ἱστάναι in Zech. 11:12. We also find μισθοὺς συνάγειν in Hag. 1:6, μισθὸν ἀναμένειν in Job 7:2. b. "Reimbursement," "recompense," "payment," Ez. 27:15 (Mas. הֵשִׁיבוּ אֶשְׁכָּרֵךְ, "they paid thee tribute"). c. "Goods" (עִזְבוֹן), Ez. 27:27. d. "Reward for military services," "soldiers' pay" (שָׂכָר), Ez. 29:18 f. e. "Payment for Levitical services in the sanctuary" (μισθὸς ἀντὶ τῶν λειτουργιῶν, Nu. 18:31). f. "Remuneration of priests," Mi. 3:11 (מְחִיר). g. "Rent for temporary use of a beast of burden," Ex. 22:14.

h. Metaphorically, "reward which God gives" (usually with διδόναι or ἀποδιδόναι), Prv. 11:21 (μισθὸν πιστὸν λαμβάνειν); Gn. 15:1; 30:18; Sir. 51:30; 2 Ch. 15:7; ψ 126:3; Wis. 5:15 (ἐν κυρίῳ); Sir. 2:8; 11:22; 51:22, 30; Is. 40:10; 62:11; Ιερ. 38:16. Wisdom also gives a reward, Wis. 10:17. This is naturally assigned only to the righteous, Wis. 2:22; 5:15. In Prv. 11:18b an earlier translator expressed a different sense: σπέρμα δικαίων μισθὸς ἀληθείας, "the posterity of the righteous is their true reward"; the lit. rendering of the Mas. comes only at 11:21. This reward is not strictly a matter of contract. It is not so much recompense as a sign of God's grace and blessing, Is. 40:10; Sir. 2:7 f.; 11:22. It is given to the righteous in this life, e.g., Gn. 15:1; 30:18; Ιερ. 38:16; ψ 126:3; Sir. 2:8; 11:22; 51:30; Eccl. 9:5, or it consists in eternal life, Wis. 5:15 (δίκαιοι δὲ εἰς τὸν αἰῶνα ζῶσιν, καὶ ἐν κυρίῳ ὁ μισθὸς αὐτῶν). i. "Penal recompense," Ez. 27:33; 2 Macc. 8:33.[4]

μισθόω (-όομαι) (= שָׂכַר). a. "To hire for reward," e.g., troops, Ju. 9:4; 2 Βασ. 10:6; 4 Βασ. 7:6; 1 Ch. 19:6 f.; Is. 7:20 (vl.); 1 Macc. 5:39; labourers, 2 Ch. 24:12; prophets, Dt. 23:5; Neh. 13:2 (both with ref. to Balaam); priests, Ju. 18:4; for a night's intercourse, Gn. 30:16. b. "To bribe" (= סָכַר), 2 Εσδρ. 23:2; 16:12. c. "To buy" (כָּרָה), Hos. 3:2.

μισθωτός. a. Adj. "hired," Ex. 22:14. b. Noun, "hired worker," "day-labourer" (שָׂכִיר), Ex. 12:45; Lv. 19:13; 22:10; 25:6, 40, 53; Dt. 15:18; Jdt. 4:10; 6:2, 5; Job 7:2; 14:6; Mal. 3:5; Is. 16:14; 21:16; 28:3. c. "Mercenary," Ιερ. 26:21; 1 Macc. 6:29.

---

[4] Or else we are told that the wicked are without hope of reward, Wis. 2:22. Sometimes the LXX imports the concept. Thus at Prv. 17:8 the Mas. reads: "A magical stone is a bribe in the eyes of the giver," but the LXX has: μισθὸς χαρίτων ἡ παιδεία τοῖς χρωμένοις, "discipline brings a reward of grace for them that exercise it" [Bertram]. Cf. G. Bertram, "Der Begriff d. Erziehung in d. griech. Bibel," *Imago Dei, Krüger-Festschrift* **(1932), 43 f.**

μίσθιος, "hired worker," Lv. 19:13 (A); 25:50; Tob. 5:12; Job 7:1; Sir. 7:20; 34:22; 37:11.

μισθαποδότης, μισθαποδοσία, ἀντιμισθία are not found in the LXX.

(3) In Philo and Josephus.

Philo uses μισθός for the payment of manual labourers in Agric., 5 or Vit. Mos., I, 24, τοῖς ἐπὶ μισθῷ συναγορεύουσι, for the remuneration of priests in their sacred ministry, Spec. Leg., IV, 98. In Virt., 88, e.g., we find the expressions μισθόν (wages) ἀποδιδόναι, ἀπολαμβάνειν, κομίζεσθαι. Part of the duty of love is to give the poor their payment on the same day, *ibid.*, 88. Philo also uses μισθωτός for "labourer," Spec. Leg., II, 82 f., but the other words do not occur in his writings.

Joseph., too, speaks of μισθός in everyday life, Ant., 4, 206; Vit., 78 (soldiers' pay). For reward from God he usually has other terms, e.g., δωρεά in Ant., 8, 22 or ἐπιτίμιον in Bell., 1, 596. But he can occasionally use μισθός for this, Ant., 1, 183; 18, 309. As he sees it, reward and punishment (Ant., 3, 321; 18, 268 etc.) proceed from God's δίκη.

2. The Word Group in the New Testament.

(1) μισθός.

i. In the sense of the payment which is due the labourer for the work he has done we find in Lk. 10:7 and 1 Tm. 5:18 the general rule [5] that the labourer is worthy of his hire. [6] In Jm. 5:4, as often in the OT, [7] it is a sin on the part of the rich to withhold the workers' wage, which cries out to heaven in accusation, i.e., the workers bring before God their complaint against the rich. In Mt. 20:8 the owner of the vineyard charges his steward: κάλεσον τοὺς ἐργάτας καὶ ἀπόδος τὸν μισθόν. According to Lv. 19:13; Dt. 24:15 and the Mishnah payment of wages can be demanded on the evening of the working day. [8]

ii. A stereotyped expression is μισθὸς (τῆς) → ἀδικίας, Ac. 1:18; 2 Pt. 2:13, 15; cf. Jd. 11 (τῇ πλάνῃ τοῦ Βαλαὰμ μισθοῦ). In Ac. 1:18 μισθὸς τῆς ἀδικίας is obviously the money paid to Judas for his betrayal of Jesus. The tempting and demonic power of money is even more strongly emphasised in the other passages; here, too, μισθὸς ἀδικίας is the payment for unrighteousness. In 2 Pt. 2:15 there is no doubt that μισθὸς ἀδικίας means the greedy and dishonest acquisition of money. [9] Hence μισθὸς ἀδικίας in 2 Pt. 2:13 does not refer to eschatological judgment. [10] It is to be construed along the same lines as 2 Pt. 2:15. The false teachers want to make sure of a reward, i.e., of money and influence, by their gluttonous and licentious conduct. Hence this reward is called the μισθὸς ἀδι-

---

[5] It is hard to say whether this is a secular proverb (Bultmann Trad.) or a sacred apocryphon (Dib. Past. on 1 Tm. 5:18). Also doubtful is whether 1 Tm. 5:18 is thinking of Lk. or whether both independently quote a current saying.

[6] Mt. 10:10 offers τροφή instead of μισθός — an alteration due either to the context or to abuses (Kl. Mt., *ad loc.*). If the version in Mt. is original, it shows what Jesus understood by reward, not opulence, but simply sustenance.

[7] → 697.

[8] Str.-B., I, 832.

[9] F. Spitta, *Der 2. Brief des Pt. u. der Brief des Jd.* (1885), 196; Zn. Jd., *ad loc.* Hence ἀδικίας is obj. gen., not subj. gen. or gen. auct.

[10] So Wnd. Kath. Br., *ad loc.*

κίας.[11] The author does, of course, promise them that imminent judgment will overtake them, so that they will attain to the μισθὸς ἀδικίας for which they look.[12]

iii. μισθός is used metaphorically in Jn. 4:36. The inhabitants of the Samaritan city of Sychar come in great numbers to Jesus, and in this success He sees the reward for His work in which He both sows and reaps. There is a similar fig. use in 1 C. 9:18. Paul wants to make clear to the Corinthians the fact that they should be able to abstain for the sake of the weak, and he gives an illustration from his own conduct. Where is he to find a renunciation in terms of which he can speak of καύχημα, v. 15? It is natural that he should think of his preaching of the Gospel. But, he goes on to say, only those who take this up voluntarily could have praise, or expect a reward (v. 17), therefrom. This is for him, however, an impossible assumption. For he was constrained by God to be an apostle (1 C. 15:5 ff.; Gl. 1:12 ff.). Hence he is a slave without rights before God, and he can expect no particular recompense.[13] Yet Paul will not allow his praise to be taken from him. Hence he must bring special offerings and do extraordinary things. He does this by preaching the Gospel without being supported by the communities, i.e., by bringing the Gospel without charge (v. 18). In this unselfish action is the reward which he has made for himself (v. 18). The μισθός thus lies in the particular nature of the apostle's activity, in his disposition, in his voluntary renunciation of the customary reimbursement. The term μισθός is here assimilated to καύχημα in content. The outstanding and favoured conduct which is worthy of reward, the unselfish renunciation, becomes the reward.[14]

iv. "The reward which God gives in recognition of the doing of His will." The OT and Jewish idea of an earthly reward is now abandoned. μισθός belongs wholly to God's world. It is God's affair, and as such comprehensive (πολύς), Mt. 5:12 = Lk. 6:23. In this is seen the unbridgeable gulf between the attitude of God to His children and the attitude of the world. The disciples of Jesus are persecuted by the world. God's dealings are the direct opposite. He shows to them, not the rejection and hatred of the world, but the acceptance of His love. He has for them a reward in the heavens, so that there can be only joy and gladness (Mt. 5:11 f. = Lk. 6:22 f.). The distinctiveness of the divine reward is so radical, however, that if a man seeks human recognition and earthly gain for his acts he thereby forfeits the acceptance which God wills to grant him in the μισθός. Those

---

[11] Spitta, *op. cit.*, 186; Kn. Pt., *ad loc.*

[12] In the text (note the pun) ἀδικούμενοι is to be accepted as the more difficult reading (Bℵ P syph) rather than κομιούμενοι (ACK 33 vg syh): "to suffer loss from the reward for their unrighteousness."

[13] Ltzm. K., *ad loc.*

[14] Only thus can one rightly grasp the meaning of τίς οὖν μού ἐστιν ὁ μισθός. The explanation of G. P. Wetter, *Der Vergeltungsgedanke bei Paulus* (1912), 131 f. is quite impossible. In his translation he must not only say "hope of reward," but he must also render "basis of my hope of reward." That is, he has to supply the terms "basis" and "hope," which is linguistically unjustifiable. Moreover, the point which Paul is making in the context is that his conduct is an example of voluntary renunciation. He is not trying to prove that his hope of reward is well founded. The ref., then, is to a μισθός which lies in the conduct, not to the basis of a hope of reward, which would be quite different from what Paul has in mind. Wetter's treatment is the more surprising when we consider that he sees the relation to καύχημα.

who seek a human reward will be paid in full (ἀπέχειν), [15] Mt. 6:2, 5, 16. Those who make their right conduct toward men a matter of reckoning place themselves outside the divine sphere: "You have no reward from your Father in heaven" (Mt. 6:1). [16] For God's rewarding generosity is only for pure obedience which is free from all selfish calculation or external display (Mt. 6:2, 5, 16). Only thus does man obey in conformity with the absoluteness of God, and only in such a case does God reward as He alone can. Even then man receives a reward only when his obedience is supreme. Only the man who in love does what is unusual and unheard of may hope for God's reward: ἐὰν γὰρ ἀγαπήσητε τοὺς ἀγαπῶντας ὑμᾶς, τίνα μισθὸν ἔχετε (Mt. 5:46); [17] only where love shows itself to be without limits will there be the great reward of heaven (Lk. 6:35). This reward is not a future depicted in individualistic terms. As ἀγάπη is relationship to the neighbour, so its reward is connected with the final destiny in the kingdom of God of those to whom it refers. Thus he who receives a prophet because he is a prophet, or a righteous man out of regard for the greatness of the obedience which he demonstrates (Mt. 10:41), [18] or he who in the burning heat of the eastern sun simply gives a disciple a cup of cold water because he is a disciple (Mt. 10:42), will have a place with him in the kingdom of God (μισθὸν λαμβάνειν).

Paul speaks no less clearly of the reward which God gives. It is evident to him that each man who busies himself in work for the Christian community [19] will receive a reward which corresponds to his inner commitment [20] and activity and which is allotted to him (as distinct from others), 1 C. 3:8. That this has nothing to do with recognition or success or joy in achievement, [21] but refers to reward in the last judgment, may be seen plainly from what follows. In 3:14 Paul is certain that the builder of a congregation whose work endures, i.e., that he as the apostle and father of the church, will then receive a special reward from God as distinct from the missionary whose work perishes and who is himself saved only by the skin of his teeth, as one who tottered on the edge of perdition.

The distinctiveness of the Pauline concept of reward may be seen fully in R. 4:4, where we find the unique combination — a model of the almost misleading pregnancy of the apostle's polemical slogans — ὁ μισθὸς ... κατὰ χάριν. It would be the very opposite of the apostle's attitude of faith if this were a matter of achievement, if the reward were not of grace but corresponded to merit — a possibility which Paul has to reject out of hand as Judaising aberration. [22] In 2 Jn. 8 also a full reward [23] for one's own works is expected as self-evident. And the classical book of martyrs, the Revelation of John, sees the time coming καὶ δοῦναι τὸν μισθὸν τοῖς δούλοις σου τοῖς προφήταις καὶ τοῖς ἁγίοις ..., 11:18.

God's judgment is in full correspondence with man's conduct. Hence it will

---

[15] ἀπέχειν = "to receipt," cf. Deissmann LO, 88 f.

[16] Cf. also → 716 f.

[17] Lk. 6:32 has χάρις here; Just. Apol., I, 15, 9 has the fine variant τί καινὸν ποιεῖτε;

[18] Meyer Ursprung, I, 143, n. 1; Schl. Mt., *ad loc.*

[19] → III, 829 f.

[20] ἴδιος is to be taken qualitatively rather than quantitatively, J. Weiss 1 K., *ad loc.*; Wetter, 122.

[21] So Zn. 1 K., *ad loc.*

[22] → 719 ff.

[23] Cf. Tg. Rt. 2:12: "Thy reward will be complete (אַגְרִיךְ שְׁלֵימָא) in the future world"; Tg. Qoh. 1:3: "To receive a full reward in the future world."

reward the righteous, and especially martyrs, with the salvation of the kingdom. It will also punish and destroy the wicked and the enemies of God.

v. μισθός can thus have the sense of "punishment": ἰδοὺ ἔρχομαι ταχύ, καὶ ὁ μισθός μου μετ' ἐμοῦ, ἀποδοῦναι ἑκάστῳ, ὡς τὸ ἔργον ἐστὶν αὐτοῦ, Rev. 22:12.

(2) Derivates.

i. In a purely secular sense we find μισθόω(όομαι), which occurs twice in the familiar parable in Mt. 20:1 ff. in the sense "to hire" (as a labourer in the vineyard), 20:1, 7.

μισθωτός is used in the NT only as a noun in the sense of a "day-labourer." It can be used in Mk. 1:20 for the hired sailor, and in Jn. 10:12 it has the more specific sense of "hired shepherd" = נוֹשֵׂא שָׂכָר ("paid keeper").

μίσθιος is also used only as a noun in the sense of "day-labourer," Lk. 15:17, 19.[24]

ii. The following words have ethical and religious content.

μισθαποδότης, like μισθαποδοσία, is used in the NT only in Hb. (11:6). It refers to the God who rewards those that seek Him. In this and the term which follows one may see how the belief in God in Hb. rests on (Alexandrian) Jewish soil, and how strongly normative the idea of reward is for it. But here[25] another aspect is to the fore. Faith is the only presupposition for drawing near to God. This is more precisely characterised as the certainty that God is no mere concept but a reality. Nor is this reality just superior to men. Human action has to prove its integrity before God (v. 4, 6). Hence Hb. in its Judaising way speaks of God as μισθαποδότης. He who would draw near to God must be in awe of His greatness and holy transcendence. Otherwise he cannot have the awareness of approaching none other than God Himself.

μισθαποδοσία, which also occurs only in Hb., means "recompense of reward." (a) In Hb. 10:35 the author warns his readers that in spite of persecution they should not weakly toss aside the good confidence which they have in God by faith, for to them alone is the great recompense of full future salvation (v. 25) promised. The meaning of μισθαποδοσία is thus the reward which comes with the blessing of salvation. The schema of payment by contract is transcended. The reference is not to a legal claim which God admits where there is trust. This παρρησία is the obedience which is demanded by God and which He rewards with His promise. As it is impossible without faith to please God (11:6), because faith is the obedience which God expects of man, so joy in God is the presupposition of His recompensing will to save (11:40). The concept of reward is thus integrated into the plan and promise of God.[26] This eschatologically orientated μισθαποδοσία is a powerful motive in the moral struggle. When the community has to choose between accepting the suffering and shame of Christ and living for worldly enjoyment and undisturbed possession, there shines upon it from

[24] Cf. also v. 21 in BאD.
[25] H. J. Holtzmann, *Lehrbuch d. nt.lichen Theologie*, II[2] (1911), 331.
[26] Cf. K. Bornhäuser, *Die Bergpredigt* (1923), 118; Rgg. Hb., *ad loc.*

heaven, in the full splendour of eschatological glory, God's recompense of reward (11:26). Moses was aware of this. He preferred the shame of Christ[27] to the treasures of Egypt. But this was possible only because he looked forward to the promised recompense, μισθαποδοσία. Here, too, the expression has nothing to do with the hiring of labourers. Nor is the motivation simply eudaemonistic. In the ἀποβλέπειν εἰς τὴν μισθαποδοσίαν may be discerned the attitude of faith which is a passionate yearning, a warm orientation to the world of God's radiant promise and its fulfilment.

(b) Thus far μισθαποδοσία has been used *sensu bono*. But it can also have the opposite meaning and signify "penal reward," "punishment as reward," *sensu malo*. It is found in this sense in Hb. 2:2, where the added ἔνδικον shows that its background is that of law. To warn his readers against despising the NT word of salvation, the author points out that even transgression of the OT commandment met with just and lawful recompense (punishment), ἔνδικον μισθαποδοσίαν.

Thus μισθαποδοσία, which occurs in the NT only in Hb., points clearly to the distinctive background of the author, who comes from Judaism and shares its mode of thought, but who still proclaims a passionate eschatological certainty of faith.

ἀντιμισθία means (a) "recompense" (in the good sense). In 2 C. 6:13 it means that the Corinthians, confronted by the warm and forgiving approach of the apostle (ἡ καρδία ἡμῶν πεπλάτυνται), should give him the answer, the grateful and childlike recompense (ἀντιμισθία), of whole-hearted trust. The emphasis is thus on the answer (ἀντί), which consists here in love responding to the glad and open love which has been received.

It can also mean (b) "penal recompense." In R. 1:27 the unnatural sexual aberration of men is regarded as a punishment for the fact that they do not pay God the honour which is His due. Where men worship idols instead of God the destruction of human society is the evident consequence (1:28 ff.). So, too, is the misuse of the beautiful body which is elsewhere extolled. This is the divinely willed recompense for turning aside from the true knowledge and worship of God.

The term does not occur in Gk. lit., nor in the pap. and inscr. It is found in 2 Cl., where it bears (1, 3 and 5;[28] 9, 7; 15, 2) much the same sense of grateful response as in 2 C. 6:13. But in 2 Cl. this response is to Christ or God for His saving action. It is thus plain that ἀντιμισθία contains the thought of a notable achievement on man's part. The sense is different in 2 Cl., 11, 6. Here it is used of the reward which God gives to balance the good works of the righteous. The term is thus integrated again into the idea of eschatological retribution which towards the end of the 1st century came into early Christianity from Judaism.[29]

---

[27] This means for the author either (1) that Moses endured the same shame as Christ, or (2) that the shame of Christ was already laid on him, or (3) that Moses stood in relation to the pre-existent Christ.

[28] Here we find the artificial and rhetorical combination μισθὸν ἀντιμισθίας.

[29] Cf. H. Preisker, *Geist u. Leben. Das Telos-Ethos des Urchristentums* (1933), 179 ff.; 201 ff.

B. The Concept of Reward.

1. The Concept in the Graeco-Roman World.

(1) The Basic View of Greek Ethics. The basic view of Gk. ethics is that morality and happiness necessarily coincide.[30] Moral action contributes to a total state of felicity. Happiness is the supreme good. "Those live best, i.e., most happily, who are most concerned always to become better."[31] Socratic happiness consists in agreement with oneself, in health and harmony of soul. This is in keeping with Greek ethics, for which morality finds compensation and reward on this earth. The good are recompensed here and now for their uprightness and righteousness. In this respect Homer and the tragedians have in view only this world.

The just king enjoys happiness (Hom. Od., 19, 109-114) with the fruitfulness of the land and prosperity of the people. The faithful man has a fine progeny, Hes. Op., 219-227. The gods prosper a just cause, Xenoph. Hist. Graec., II, 4, 14; cf. Isoc., 15, 228; Soph. Oed. Tyr. 863-872. True knowledge leads by way of action to εὐδαιμονία — this is the genuine Gk. view of life. Similarly, wrong-doers are punished, Hom. Il., 2, 599 f. (blindness); Hdt., VI, 75-84 (madness); Eur. Phoen., 1172-1186 (lightning); Ael. Var. Hist., IV, 28 (severe illness), though this may often be later (Hom. Il., 4, 160; Soph. Oed. Col., 1536) and may affect only their descendants (Hdt., 1, 91; 6, 86; Plat. Resp., II, 363d; Isocr., 8, 120). Punishments are particularly depicted in Aristoph. Ra., 147, 282 f. (those who violate the laws of hospitality, perjurers and patricides lie in the mud); Plat. Resp., II, 363d (carrying water in vessels with holes). The certainty of the Greeks that there will be recompense on earth makes any belief in future rewards unnecessary. Plato finds the final moral goal and supreme good of men primarily in the ordering of the different spiritual powers, the higher above the lower. Happy is the man who possesses virtue on this way of righteousness.[32] Man's greatness lies in striving for the idea of the good and in the actualising of this idea in practical life. The man is not good who fulfils the moral demand merely for a good reputation or for a future reward[33] or to escape greater evils[34] or not to appear bad.[35] The good man is the one who in wisdom and perception of supreme truth practises the idea of the good, i.e., righteousness. Happiness lies in this practice of virtue.

(2) The Absence of the Biblical Concept of Reward from Greek Philosophy. It is thus apparent that the Greek world does not have the concept of reward found in the OT and NT.

This is amply seen in the debate between Socrates and the Sophists.[36] Here the way in which Hom. and Hes. speak of rewards is very definitely rejected. Plato deals ironically with a striving for righteousness which is less concerned about this than about respectability, offices etc., or even the approval of the gods. He rejects esp. the hopes of reward depicted by Musaeus: eternal intoxication, lasting progeny, or popular rewards and punishments. Plato thus rejects the Orphic doctrine of reward and punishment. He speaks of the reward of the righteous in Resp., X, 614a, but the metaphor of the contest in X, 612d, 613c, 614a shows that he uses the term μισθός more in the sense

---

30 ὅτι ... τὸν ἄριστόν τε καὶ δικαιότατον εὐδαιμονέστατον ἔκρινε (that the best and most righteous is also the happiest), Plat. Resp., IX, 580b; cf. Aristot. (Diehl, 116, 4). Cf. F. Jodl, *Geschichte der Ethik* (1882), 5.

31 Xenoph. Mem., IV, 8, 6; cf. III, 9, 4 f.

32 F. Wagner, *op. cit.*, 39 ff.

33 Resp., II, 362e f.

34 Phaed., 68d.

35 Theaet., 176b.

36 Resp., II, 363a b.

of recognition or distinction, X, 612d: δικαιοσύνης, ὥσπερ ἔχει δόξης καὶ παρὰ θεῶν καὶ παρ' ἀνθρώπων. The decisive pt. for him is that righteousness carries its own reward within itself, X, 614a. In the myth in Resp., X, 614b ff. he is obviously adopting the Orphic idea of the rewarding of the righteous and punishing of the wicked. In the total context of his thought, however, this is to be regarded as an occasional and formal acceptance of Orphism. It does not result in the development of a concept of reward.[37] Hence even when Plato speaks of a reward — usually without the term μισθός — it is quite evident that, like the Gk. world generally, he is thinking in terms of an immanent law of being.[38] Above all, it is to be noted that reward is not for Plato a motive for action. He deliberately separates what he has to say about the nature and value of moral action from the concept of reward.[39] Moral acts are to be done for their own sake, not for the sake of reward.[40] The purity of ethics is thus safeguarded by Plato. As in Socrates, knowledge of the good is the true motive force of morality. Turning to the idea of the good is not a command or compulsion of God; it is man's free act.

In Aristot. reason is that which leads the soul to the moral, supported by man's immanent desire for happiness. In contrast to Plato, he does not accept any idea whatever of a future reward. This is keeping with the unrestricted orientation of his ethics to this world, with no ref. to God at all. Happiness, man's supreme good and goal on earth, is to act with unbroken virtue, to live a full life to the end, adequately supplied with external benefits.[41]

For Stoicism morality is obedience[42] to deity equated with the cosmic law, world reason. Epictet. esp. emphasises the omnipresence of God, who sees and hears all that man does,[43] and whom one should not disgrace.[44] This upright life leads to happiness. Because happiness resides in virtue, the reward for good and punishment for sin are not beyond virtue and sin. Thus we read in Sen. Vit. Beat., 9, 4: (*virtus*) *ipsa pretium sui,* and Epictet. has the same emphasis in Diss., III, 24, 50. For M. Ant. (IX, 42, 13) it is enough to have done something acc. to nature, so that there can be no further talk of reward. Sen. does, of course, point to life above (Marc., 23, 2), to the better state (24, 5; Ep., 102, 26 ff.). Acc. to him the thought of the higher world of light can banish what is lower from the soul. But in general he no more needs this motive for morality than the other Stoics. Particularly when everything ends with death, as in M. Ant., VIII, 2, the thought of reward is ruled out. Epictet. thinks similarly; there is for him no life after death, Diss., II, 8, 28. When the rule is to follow nature, innermost being (M. Ant., VII, 55 and 59), reward simply consists in fulfilling the goal of life, in the happiness of a virtuous life, and punishment is that the sinner himself makes himself wretched (M. Ant., IX, 4). Hence for Cic. too (Fin., II, 14, 45) *honestum* (the morally good) is what can be praised for its own sake quite apart from reward.

(3) The Mysteries. Orientation to the life and reward hereafter is a particular feature of the Eleusinian mysteries.

Concerning these Soph. Fr., 753 (TGF, 308) writes: "How thrice blessed are they of men who, when they have seen these rites, go to Hades; for to these alone is it given

---

[37] Cf. also Gorg., 526c.
[38] [Kleinknecht].
[39] Resp., II, 367d; X, 612b.
[40] *Ibid.*, II, 366e; 367a.
[41] Eth. Nic., I, 10, p. 1099b, 9-1100a, 9. The word μισθός occurs 6 times in Aristot. (Bonitz, *Index Aristotelicus* [1870]), once as a fee for doctors, 5 times as a reward for participation in court sessions.
[42] Sen. Vit. Beat., 15, 4; Ep., 107, 9 and 11; Epict. Ench., 53; M. Ant., III, 16; VII, 31 and 67; IX, 1.
[43] Diss., I, 3, 1 ff.; 6, 40; 9, 22; II, 8, 11-14; III, 22 and 69 etc.
[44] Diss., II, 8, 21.

to live, and only misery to the rest."[45] This eternal future salvation is attained only by participation in the mysterious sacramental cult of the mother and daughter (Demeter and Kore), not by pure conduct.[46] In the earliest days we find something similar in Orphic circles. Word and spirit, body and soul, are in sharp dualism. In the ascetic life one meets the whole test demanded by Orphic teaching, and a final judgment decides whether a man will hereafter drink from the source of life or be handed over to the awful torments of hell.[47]

(4) The Hellenistic Cults. In contrast to Greek philosophy, the Hellenistic cults find a considerable place for the concept of reward.

Egypt was early renowned for its care for the dead. In the Egyptian Serapis-Isis cult[48] final expectation, with the notions of reward and punishment, is of decisive significance. Acc. to the ancient books of the dead the deceased comes before the judge Osiris and must make a confession of sins before 42 assessors, which is written down by the god Thoth. The heart of the dead is then weighed. So that it should not be weighed and found too light, the stone heart scarab is laid on the breast of the corpse. These ideas are later transferred to Serapis, and in an Egyptian story[49] of the Graeco-Roman period it is said of the judgment:[50] "The man whose evil deeds are more numerous than the good will be given to the devourer of the underworld; his body and soul will be destroyed, and he may live no longer. The man whose good deeds are more numerous than the bad will be set among the divine councillors of the Lord of the underworld, while his soul will go to heaven with the blest in glory." Similarly, in the Mithras cult the one who fights for the kingdom of light, whose merits, when placed on the scales of God, are heavier than his sins, will be given the reward of protection by Mithra against the servants of Ahriman and of being conducted to the heavenly spheres of light beyond the stars and to the throne of Jupiter-Ormuzd.[51]

(5) Roman Religion, Sacrificial Language. The principle of *do ut des* has a different signification in Roman religion.

At issue here is a commercial relation between men and gods. The Roman fulfils his contractual obligations to the gods. He makes his vows in times of distress. To the god on whom he calls he dedicates a sacrifice or temple or games should he be answered, or he promises that he will do so in return for assistance. In the prayer of the Arval brethren for the emperor and his house we read: "If thou performest this, then in the name of the college of the Arval brethren I will offer thee such and such sacrifices."[52] Here the deity does not give a reward, but man pays for divine help with corresponding offerings.

The language of sacrifice commonly leads to the concept of reward. The righteous man reminds the deity of the gifts and offerings which he has brought, and expects in return that his requests will be heard and answered, Hom. Il., 1, 37 ff.[53]

---

[45] Cf. also Plat. Men., 81a b.

[46] Hence the scorn of the Cynic Diogenes (Plut. Aud. Poet., 2, 21 f) that acc. to Eleusinian belief the thief Pataikion can expect a better fate than an Epaminondas.

[47] H. Haas, 9-11 (Leipoldt), No. 174.

[48] Cf. H. Preisker, *Nt.liche Zeitgeschichte* (1937), 134; bibl., 145.

[49] Cf. H. Gressmann, "Vom reichen Mann u. armen Lazarus," AAB (1918), 7.

[50] Acc. to A. Erman, *Die Religion d. Ägypter* (1934), 408.

[51] F. Cumont, *Die orientalischen Religionen im römischen Heidentum*³ (1931), 145; *Die Mysterien des Mithra* (1923), 103 ff.

[52] W. Kroll, "Die Kultur der ciceronischen Zeit," II = *Das Erbe der Alten*, 23 (1933), 15.

[53] Cf. Hom. Il., 1, 503; Od., 17, 240; Il., 15, 372; Hdt., 1, 87. Further examples in C. Ausfeld, "De Graecorum precationibus quaestiones," *Jbch. f. kl. Phil.*, 28, Suppl. (1903), 526 ff.

Granting prayers is a kind of reward for the good deeds of him who prays. In a different form one recognises something of the reciprocal operation of the *do ut des.*[54]

(6) Death as Reward. The religiously and philosophically controlled view of life in antiquity finally perceives the supreme recognition of man by deity in the fact that the deity takes man to itself.

This may be in an early death. A classical instance is Plut. Cons. ad Apoll., 14 (II, 108 f.), where early death is a reward (ἀμοιβή) for the piety of Cleobis and Biton; cf. Plut., *ibid.*, 14 (II, 109b) where Apollo grants Trophonios and Agamedes an early death as a μισθός for building him a temple. But man may also be deified. In the Hermet. writings deification is attained in ecstasy and fulfilled in a heavenly journey (Poimandres, 25) or a sacrament of baptism (Corp. Herm., IV, 5 and 7). By mystical vision man becomes ἀγαθὸς καὶ εὐσεβὴς καὶ ἤδη θεῖος (X, 9). The Hermet. writings show definite links with Orphic ideas, concerning which Hipp. Ref., I, 19, 11 says: οἱ δὲ (sc. Πλατωνικοί) ἀθάνατον αὐτὴν (sc. τὴν ψυχὴν) εἶναι λέγοντες μάλιστα ἐκείνοις ἰσχυρίζονται, (ἐν) ὅσοις καὶ κρίσεις φησὶν εἶναι μετὰ τελευτὴν καὶ ἐν Ἅιδου δικαστήρια, καὶ τὰς μὲν ἀγαθὰς ἀγαθοῦ μισθοῦ τυγχάνειν, τὰς δὲ πονηρὰς ἀκολούθων δικῶν (note the adding of ἀγαθός to μισθός). We find the same in the mysteries, e.g., the Isis mystery in Apul. Met., XI, 23 f. Here the process is combined with a sacramental dedication. In Plato, however, it is dissociated from such sacraments and thoroughly spiritualised.

Preisker

2. The Old Testament Belief in Recompense.

(1) The Origin. The origin of the OT belief in recompense escapes historical observation. It is so naturally presupposed in the very earliest OT testimonies, and it is so fruitful in historical and theological reflection, that it is obviously an ancient view current from the very outset in the thinking of Israel. Its roots are perhaps to be found in the primitive idea, independent of the concept of a personal God and fashioned by the profound optimism of peoples close to nature, that a good action will have, in accordance with its character, good and happy consequences,[55] whereas sin can bring neither peace nor good fortune.[56] In the OT the concept of a personal God plays a predominant role, so that only relics of the original form of this idea are to be found, especially in the use of the terms associated with the roots צדק and רשע.[57] For the rest, it is combined with the belief in a personal God and thus becomes a belief in recompense in the strict sense. The close connection which is assumed between action and destiny, and which on the primitive view is thought to lie in the very nature of things, is now attributed to God. Like all the gods of the Semites,[58] Yahweh in particular is a righteous God. Hence there is seen in Him a guarantee that a correct relation

[54] ARW, 20 (1920/21), 241 ff.; H. Kleinknecht, *Die Gebetsparodie in der Antike* (1937), 55; in criticism of this attitude, Plat. Resp., III, 394a.

[55] J. Pedersen, *Israel,* I-II (1926), 411; cf. G. Hölscher, ThStKr, 108 (1937/38), 234-262.

[56] Pedersen, *op. cit.*, 429.

[57] K. H. Fahlgren, *s^e^dāḳā, nahestehende u. entgegengesetzte Begriffe im AT,* Diss. Uppsala (1932).

[58] W. W. Graf Baudissin, *Festgabe Harnack* (1921), 1-23.

between conduct and destiny, a true harmony between deed and reward or punishment, which is so important for Israel, will in fact be maintained.

(2) The Meaning and Significance of the Belief. Since the belief is found throughout the OT, there is no need to document it in detail. Our present concern will be to take some typical examples and work out the function ascribed to it in the narratives, history, prophetic writings and wisdom literature. By means of the function we may then see the interests behind it, and finally apprehend its meaning and significance. In view of the varied character of the writings in which it occurs, we cannot always count in advance on a uniform answer.

Ju. 9:23 f. interprets the conflict between the Shechemites and Abimelech, which finally destroys both parties, as Yahweh's retribution for the sin of Abimelech towards his brethren, and for the help of Shechemites in this shameful act: "Then God sent an evil spirit between Abimelech and the men of Shechem, and the men of Shechem fell away from Abimelech, in order that the cruelty done to the sons of Jerubbaal might be avenged (לָבוֹא), and that he might lay their blood on their brother Abimelech, who had killed them, and on the men of Shechem, who had helped him to kill his brothers." Similarly 1 S. 15:2 f. regards the war of Saul against Amalek, though with very different means, as a divine visitation: "Thus saith Yahweh Zebaoth: I will visit (פָּקַד) that which Amalek has done to Israel, that he laid wait for him in the way when he came out of Egypt. Now go and smite Amalek, and fulfil the ban on him and[59] all his possessions, and do not spare, but kill both man and woman, infant and suckling, ox and sheep, camel and ass."

In both cases it is clear that the desire to exact recompense does not shape the historical action. In Ju. 9 it is obvious that the Shechemites did not undertake their machinations against Abimelech to avenge a crime in which they had a part. They did not truly realise what they were doing, but were instruments of God. The narrator from his higher vantage-point brings out the meaning immanent in their action and its consequences by introducing the motif of recompense. But the situation is not really different in 1 S. 15.[60] Saul is compelled to fight the Amalekites for other reasons than the consideration that the much earlier hampering of the Israelites by them is as yet unavenged. The sayings in v. 2 and v. 3 are subsequent explanations, first of the war, then of the terrible execution of the ban. In both cases, then, the belief in recompense is an instrument of reflection. It serves a consideration of history which does not merely take the facts but tries to understand them. It helps to understanding by trying to find the meaning of all historical events in terms of the God who according to the OT view is present in these events. Thus the belief in recompense has a rational function. It links the events of history, explaining them in terms of one another.[61] It does, of course, refer to God, and in so doing transcends the limit of the

---

[59] In v. 3 read וְהַחֲרַמְתּוֹ ו for וְהַחֲרַמְתֶּם with LXX Tg.

[60] On the reflective character of 1 S. 15:1-3 cf. A. Weiser, ZAW, NF, 13 (1936), 5 f.

[61] On this rational function of the belief in recompense and its connection with the definite rational aptitude of Israel, cf. J. Hempel, *AT u. Geschichte* (1930), 55 f. That the doctrine of recompense, with whose help the variety of life is reduced to a single formula, is accompanied by other motifs, should not be overlooked in connection with the limitation of this belief and its validity in the OT, cf. on this Hempel, *op. cit.*, 56 and W. Stärk, *Vorsehung und Vergeltung* (1931), 14 f.

rational. But this does not alter the fact that a need of *ratio* is here satisfied. For to OT man the belief in God is in no sense irrational in our sense.

Along with the rational element apparent in both cases, there is, of course, in the use of the concept of recompense a no less important religious motif which should not be overlooked. For when the events of history or everyday life are explained with the help of this belief, there is expressed a confidence that the divine action is radically outside the sphere of caprice, and even where events raise serious questions, as in the case of the dreadful fulfilment of the ban in 1 S. 15, the overthrow of the Shechemites in Ju. 9, the destruction of the city of Sodom in Gn. 18:20 ff.; 19, the tragic death of a king after a short rule in 2 K. 1:2 ff., an inner justification is found for this action.

The way in which the interests of *ratio* and faith can intertwine when the belief in recompense is used to interpret history may be finely seen when this takes place on the most grandiose scale in the earliest J narratives in Gn. 2:4-11:9. Here very naive questions are answered: why there is hostility between man and serpent, why the life of woman is so painful and so subject to man, why the work of man is so hard and stands always under the threat of disaster, why the flood destroyed the first race, why man is now divided into many nations. But as the reasons for the present suffering and distress of man are given, God is absolved from all charges of caprice or cruelty. Man's sin, not God, is to be regarded as responsible for the pitiable state of the world. This way of regarding history has, of course, a limitation plainly seen in lesser spirits, namely, that history constantly escapes from God. Man is active, and God only reacts. History cannot move to any firm goal because man's sin and error are continually thwarting the divine plan. For this reason, when J thinks in terms of a divine goal for history, he has to give up recompense as a guiding motif in his presentation. God Himself now takes history in hand, and in spite of human weakness leads it to the goal which He has set for it in the promise to Abraham (Gn. 12 ff.).

Thus far we have learned to know the belief in recompense only as belief in God's penal recompense. In fact, the idea that good conduct will find a reward plays little part in the earlier narratives and histories. If it is not altogether absent, its role is minor. This is no accident. It shows what is the ultimate and most profound concern, not equally strong at every point, but plainly apparent in the earliest J stories, namely, that God should be believed in and depicted as the unconditional enemy of sin who comes with strict judgment where the will of man resists His rule and goes its own ungodly ways. In these circumstances God's deity is demonstrated in the penal recompensing of sin, in strict judgment on it.

(3) The Belief in the Prophets. We are now ready to discuss the belief in the prophets. For them the holy God is in basic antithesis to every sinful creature. This means that the annihilating judgment of divine retribution must fall wherever sin reigns. Is., as a man of unclean lips dwelling among a people of unclean lips, is forced to regard himself as lost in the presence of the holiness of Yahweh the King (Is. 6:5). Similarly the prophets expect God's penal recompense on all sins. They thus proclaim approaching judgment to the people. The principle of recompense, present in all the prophets, is nowhere so strong as in Amos, who had cause to emphasise it particularly in answer to wrong conclusions from the belief in election. God does not forget the acts of sinful men (8:7; 5:11). Israel's sins do not receive from Him different treatment from that meted out to the sins of other nations (1:3-2:16). Indeed, just because God has elected Israel He visits all its sins upon it (3:2). The message of retribution is thus a testimony to the living

and personal nature of the relation between Yahweh and Israel. Obedience and disobedience have within this relation the character of decision. The belief in recompense has the significance of a safeguard against the — obviously widespread — frivolous view of election that this has taken place once for all in Israel's favour, that it is a decision which binds God Himself, and that there is thus good reason not to take sin so seriously.[62] In the other prophets as well as Amos the doctrine of divine recompense, in the specific form of the message of coming judgment, underlines the proclamation of the seriousness of the divine reality and the unconditional nature of God's religious and ethical claim even, and precisely, upon the chosen people. Whether this is accepted or not signifies decision for the future. At the same time the belief in recompense enables the prophets to understand history as the purposeful action of God. Faith understands the disaster which approaches, or which has already fallen, in relation to God and in close connection with His holy and moral will. The belief in recompense is the instrument best adapted for trying to understand God in the reality of history.

On the basis of the distinctive ancient Israelite idea that Israel is a unity in all its members and generations, recompense has first to be understood as collective retribution. The guilty must suffer punishment like the innocent. Children must expiate the sins of the fathers. This leaves no sense of injustice. That the concept has a measure of justification is obvious. But where it is carried through too logically it can lead to apathetic despair and damage the will for amendment, since the judgment which approaches, already incurred through the sins of the fathers, cannot be arrested. A sense of this perhaps led to the relaxation which we see for the first time in Jer. The principle of recompense is not affected. But the link with the past is not so indissoluble that a people cannot break free from the sinful past and its penalty by the resolute conversion of its way. If a people turns from its wickedness, Yahweh, too, will repent of the evil which He intended to bring (Jer. 18:1 ff.). Ezekiel suffers even more strongly from the difficulties of collective retribution which the people stated in the proverb that the fathers had eaten sour grapes and the children's teeth were set on edge. Ezekiel's generation had to see in itself the scapegoat for the misdoings of the fathers. Ezekiel, however, firmly releases the destiny of the individual Israelite from entanglement in the guilt of others, whether fathers or contemporaries. It is the sinful soul which will die in the catastrophe which is about to overwhelm the people. The son will not share the guilt of the father, nor the father that of the son. The righteousness of the righteous will rest on him, and the wickedness of the wicked will rest on him (Ez. 18:20). Indeed, the principle is carried further, for in the case of the individual only the present is decisive. Past sins will not be imputed against the converted sinner, nor will earlier good acts avail the righteous who stumbles (Ez. 18:21 ff.). The answer which Ez. gives to the urgent question of his age is stated in so general and theoretical a way that the dogma of individual recompense has been found in his exposition. This can hardly be right, as the constant reference to imminent judgment shows.[63] His word is specifically for his own generation, and he is telling it that God's retribution is absolutely just (18:25). But he also wants to show the possibility of deliverance from approaching destruction. In his view of recompense the holy God of the older prophets, who judges all

---

[62] On Am. 3:1 f. cf. esp. A. Weiser, "Die Profetie des Amos," BZAW, 53 (1929), 116 ff.
[63] Cf. A. Bertholet, "Hesekiel," HAT (1936), 67 f.

sinful beings, is also the merciful God who has no pleasure in the death of the wicked but rather that he should be converted and live (Ez. 18:23).

(4) The Idea of Twofold Recompense. In older narrative (especially J) and the prophets the belief in recompense is one-sided and primarily negative, and nowhere is the possible deduction that good conduct must be given a special reward of any particular significance.[64] In this respect, a clearly discernible change takes place with Dt. This promises rich blessing in earthly goods, numerous descendants, cattle and fruits of the field, for observance of the Law, and it prescribes the most terrible curses for disobedience to it, Dt. 28. This version of the doctrine of recompense serves the purpose of Dt., namely, to help towards deliverance from imminent judgment. "One should act according to the will of God laid down in it in order that one may escape judgment (i.e., live) and in order that it may go well with one. לְמַעַן (47 times in Dt.) is a characteristic term."[65] The prophetic message meant criticism, the proclamation of approaching judgment. This message was based on the fact that Yahweh cannot allow sin to go unpunished. Dt. calls for a fashioning of life with reference to the divine law of recompense which also recognises God's blessing upon obedience. One can hardly deny that here, as always when twofold retribution is taught, there lurks the danger that knowledge of reward will lead to calculating upon it — a danger which was to become acute in later developments in Judaism. This danger is the greater inasmuch as the OT does not know life after death and has to expect recompense in this world.

The concept of twofold recompense, once expounded so unequivocally, is in the so-called Deuteronomistic histories the core and centre of the view of history, as may be seen with particular clarity in Judges. The whole course of history is schematically understood in terms of national sin and divine punishment, national conversion and divine aid. Though this understanding seems rational to us, it is not primarily constructed out of a desire to fit history into a rational schema. Its true root is to be sought in the desire of a generation which had passed through the terrors of the last days of the monarchy, and possibly the exile, to explain its own history by that of the fathers, and to show to it what it should do, and what alone could help, in the existing situation.

Freed from this concern and adopted, it would almost seem, as a schema which is applied for its own sake, the interpretation of history from the standpoint of twofold recompense bears singular fruit in the Books of Chronicles. Since it is hard to find a place either for piety without happiness or sin without misfortune, many things are left out of the story. Thus, apart from the census, we find none of the unfavourable things which are said about David in Samuel and Kings. On the other hand, other things are put in. Thus the death of the pious Josiah in the battle of Megiddo, which constitutes a difficulty for a consistent belief in

---

[64] This thought is not present in Ex. 20:12b, which is simply showing that remaining in the land given by Yahweh depends upon obedience to the divine command. Ex. 20:5 f. could well be a Dt. gloss, cf. H. Holzinger, *Exodus KH* (1900), 72. Cf. also W. Eichrodt, *Theol. d. AT*, 3 (1939), 74: "Apart from the fact that in early days Israel did not know the precise reckoning with God's recompense in individual life which we see in Judaism, the occasional references to divine blessing associated with right conduct (Gn. 26:5; Ex. 15:25, 26b; 19:5, 8) have a non-reflective character and are simply a vital expression of certainty that in His personal action God shows Himself to be faithful and good to the individual."

[65] A. Bertholet, *Deuteronomium KH* (1899), XXVII.

recompense, is said to be due to the fact that he resists the demand of Pharaoh Necho to be allowed to pass through Judah even though Yahweh Himself was speaking in this demand (2 Ch. 35:21 f.). The wicked Manasseh, however, is allowed to reign so long because, deported to Babylon for his sins, he repented there, and after his return did works pleasing to God (2 Ch. 33). There is no reference to these matters in 2 K.

(5) The Wisdom Literature. The belief in recompense finds in the Wisdom literature its final and most conspicuous form in the OT. Here it is dinned into the pupil with wearying insistence that the righteous can expect a reward and the ungodly punishment. "My hand upon it, the wicked shall not be unpunished, but the seed of the righteous escapes" (Prv. 11:21). "If the righteous experiences recompense (יְשֻׁלָּם) on earth, how much more the wicked and the sinner" (11:31). "He that hath pity upon the poor lendeth unto Yahweh, and his righteous act will he recompense him (יְשַׁלֶּם)" (19:17).[66] We here have to understand the meaning and significance of the belief in the light of the living movement which impresses it into service. OT Wisdom is not a development of the specific mentality of Israel. It is closely connected with ancient oriental wisdom in general. The belief in recompense plays here the same role, though worked out more consistently in the OT. Its importance results from the basic concern of Wisdom as such. This seeks the greatest possible happiness for man (always earthly happiness in the OT),[67] and it tries to shows its students the way to this. The enterprise makes sense, however, only on the assumption that life can count upon the constant law that a good way will lead to a good end. Thus Wisdom stands or falls with the validity of the doctrine of recompense. The optimism with which the doctrine is affirmed in Wisdom links this with the primitive view of the correspondence between action and result to which we referred at the outset. Nevertheless, even where this is not clear from the wording, one must assume that Wisdom trusts, not in immanent law, but in God, though in the God who has so subjected Himself to the law of recompense that He is more its servant than its master, while the power of man is increased out of all measure, since it is in his own hands to shape his future.[68]

If this optimism which tends to do violence to the realities of life raises suspicion against Wisdom, even more so does the fact that it quite naturally commends the following of its counsels by emphasising the advantages to be expected therefrom. "The wise man does what is morally good, not because he perceives the absolute validity or high worth of the good, but primarily because he believes that there will be a reward for it, and punishment for wrong."[69] This type of piety,

---

[66] Outside Wisdom, though partly influenced by it, many post-exilic writings present the belief in the form of a sharp antithesis between the fortunes of the righteous and the ungodly (Ps. 1; 37:25 f.; 11:5-7; 34:15 ff.; 112 etc.). The predominant place of the belief in the Jewish community is to be traced back both to legal piety and to rationalistic Wisdom. With the reign of this belief there is a tendency for fear to determine the personal relation to God in the form of anxiety in face of the omnipresent and omniscient divine Judge, cf. W. Eichrodt, 42.

[67] Cf. J. Fichtner, "Die altorientalische Weisheit in ihrer isr.-jüd. Ausprägung," BZAW, 62 (1933), 61 ff.

[68] This is the diametrical opposite of the prophetic use of the belief. Instead of being a means to understand reality in terms of God, it has now become a means to shape reality by man.

[69] J. Fichtner, *op. cit.*, 75 f.

which can even make the commended fear of God a means to attain happiness, is finely characterised in Satan's question in the Book of Job: "Doth Job fear God for nought?" (1:9), and also in the question in which the poet has the friends pass judgment on themselves: "Has God any profit from man? No — the righteous is of profit only to himself" (22:2).

It was inevitable that the consistent optimism of the belief in recompense should be shown to be hollow when confronted with real life. Qoh. confesses with resignation: "What takes place on earth is vanity; there are just men to whom happens what is appropriate to the work of the wicked, wicked men to whom happens what is appropriate to the work of the righteous" (8:14). But deeper than this resignation is the contradiction of living faith. Job utters the sharpest protest against Wisdom's view of God as represented by the friends. By understanding all His dealings with man simply as a fulfilment of a human view of recompense, this makes of God no more than a petty judge. Thus in the dialogue and in God's speeches in Job the belief in recompense, which once served to set before men the unconditional seriousness of the holiness and greatness of God, is finally disputed in order to preserve this same holiness and greatness, in order that God should be known as the One whose action cannot be measured by the schema of recompense, but before whom it is proper that man should bow in silence. Ps. 73 transcends in a different way both the belief and the difficulties caused by measuring the whole of life by it. The poet here looks beyond the need which Wisdom with its understanding of existence necessarily felt to see and experience recompense. He is led to the certainty of faith that fellowship with God means more than all recompense in heaven or earth (73:25 f.).

Würthwein

3. The Concept of Reward in Later Judaism.

Later Judaism developed particularly the belief in recompense and combined eschatological expectation with it. Where the belief in strict recompense does not apply in this world, it is simply set in the next and closely connected with the concept of judgment and resurrection. The problem of theodicy is thus seen in the light of retribution. That this has to be so in Judaism is connected with another of its essential features, namely, that for Judaism salvation is predominantly future. There is no present reality of salvation which can be the force impelling to moral life, like the NT kingdom of God which is already incipiently present, or the possession of the Spirit. Future salvation has to be earned by human achievement. In spite of God's mercy it depends on man's attainment, and the main function of God is simply to recompense the work of man.[70] This Judaistic principle of human achievement leads logically to the dogma of merit and recompense. We see this everywhere in Judaism, with emphasis on the hereafter. The last judgment plays an increasingly decisive part, for rewards will then be given the righteous and punishment meted out to sinners.

On Wisdom lit. cf. what was said under → 2. (5). For Philo the reward of virtue is the blessedness of the virtuous on earth, Det. Pot. Ins., 120 ff.; Leg. All., III, 77, and then the immortality which finds its consummation in the vision of God, whereas evil souls sink into matter and sensuality, Gig., 6-18; Som., I, 133-156; Abr., 37 ff.; Leg. All., I, 107; Det. Pot. Ins., 163 ff.

---

[70] Cf. Braun, 41.

Apocalyptic promises eternal life to the righteous as a merited reward, Da. 12:1 f.; Ps. Sol. 3:12; 9:5; 13:11; Eth. En. 37:4; 40:9; 4 Esr. 14:35; S. Bar. 14:13, or, as we also read, light and life, Eth. En. 58:3, comparable with the angels and stars, Eth. En. 51:4; S. Bar. 51:10, 12. The alternative is full destruction, Eth. En. 94:1, 6 f., 10; 95:6 etc.; Ps. Sol. 3:12; 13:11; 14:6; Sib., IV, 43; 4 Esr. 7:125, or eternal damnation, Da. 12:2; Eth. En. 91:5-10; 103:8; S. Bar. 44:12; 78:6; 83:10 ff.; 4 Esr. 7:36 f.; 8:59, with terrible fiery torments, Eth. En. 10:6, 13; 90:24 ff.; 4 Esr. 7:36 f.; S. Bar. 44:15, or a sojourn in darkness, chains and blazing flames, Eth. En. 103:8; 63:10 f.

Rabb. tradition speaks of reward in this life, bShab., 127a; bQid., 39b; bTaan., 19b; Pea, I, 1 etc., and also of eternal reward, bEr., 22a; Dt. r., 7, 10 on 29:1 par.: God has said: "You reserve for me knowledge of the Torah and observance of the commandments in this life, and I reserve for you a good reward in the future world," cf. Str.-B., IV, 1,-490 ff. Some Talmudic passages refer only to the resurrection of the just, bTaan., 7a; bKet., 111b. [71] On this view punishment strikes sinners already on earth acc. to the principle of "measure for measure," bSot., 8b par. This is carried so far that — in acc. with the ancient *lex talionis* — it is believed that the eyes of those who sin with the eyes will be punished, bSot., 9b. Originally the Synagogue sees in the creation of man or the redemption out of Egypt divine acts which pledge every Israelite constantly to serve God by observance of His will, Ab., 2, 8 (Rabban Jochanan b. Zakkai, d. c. 80): "When you have studied the Torah a great deal, do not be proud of it; for you were created for this." But this standpoint of the so-called reward of grace was abandoned, and commandments were regarded as given only to produce achievements which could be evaluated as merits and carry a reward, Mak., 3, 16 (R. Chanania b. Aqashia, c. 150): "God willed to let Israel win merits, hence He gave them the Torah and many commandments." "The reward is acc. to the effort," Ab., 5, 23. The idea of merit is worked out in a commercial schema, Ab., 3, 17: By merits man amasses a capital on the interest of which he can live on earth, while the full payment will come in the future world. Not only is the righteous himself rewarded, but his presence is of benefit to his fellows, bTaan., 20b. For the righteous, death is a means to atone for sin, bBer., 60a, and thus to attain to a reward in the resurrection. For sinners, however, it is the completion of divine punishment, Weber, 321 ff. Since Judaism does not have a decisive incentive to moral action in the present possession of salvation (cf. πνεῦμα in the NT), and since man does not rely wholly and absolutely on God's grace but, for all the emphasis on the divine mercy, suspends salvation on his own work or meritorious achievement, the thought of judgment is a powerful incentive. Man's moral action must be controlled by the consideration of judgment with its merited reward or just punishment, cf. Ab., 3, 1. The Synagogue certainly tried to limit too wild a growth of the desire for reward. It pointed out that with a right disposition one should fulfil the Torah for its own sake, Ab., 1, 3: "Do not be like servants who serve the master with the prospect of receiving a reward but be like servants who serve the master without prospect of receiving a reward." These voices are present (Str.-B., IV, 496 f.) but they do not prevail. They cannot overcome the principle of achievement and the associated concept of reward. God is the Judge, and He allots to man what is in keeping with his good or evil deeds.

It should be noted that with this principle of achievement Judaism could not enjoy confidence of faith or assurance of salvation. Just because God is believed in as the Holy One, and the seriousness of His moral demands is perceived, a piety which soberly recognises human limitations and sins cannot but doubt whether its achievements will stand before the strict divine Judge. One has only to read 4 Esr. to see what uncertainty the thought of judgment arouses, → κρίνω (III, 935), and to understand the zeal of Jewish-Pharisaic casuistry to pile up with God good works which may counterbalance the number and weight of sins. We also find optimistic notes, e.g., in Ps. Sol. 2:35; 3:4; 10:3; 15:4-6; Wis. 3:9; 4:15 f.; 11:9 f.; bSanh., 97b; S. Dt., 252 on 23:8. But

---

71 But cf. Volz Esch., 241-249; Str.-B., IV, 1166 ff., esp. 1175 ff., 1180 ff.

the pessimistic and anxious are more common, 4 Esr. 3:22; 4:30, 38; 7:48, 68 f., 118 f.; S. Bar. 14:14; 48:42 f.; 84:10; M. Ex. on 17:14; Ab., 4, 22; 2, 4; Gn. r., 93, 11 on 45:9 par.; bSanh., 81a; bBer., 28b (cf. Str.-B., III, 219 f., esp. k; I, 581). Judaism, however, does not dare to rest man wholly on God's grace. It insists on man and his achievement. It seeks to merit a just reward and hence does not escape impotence and anxiety. It does not find confidence or joy because it does not take the idea of grace absolutely, and in relation to God relies on the human achievement which it is forced to recognise to be unattainable.

4. The Concept of Reward in the New Testament.

(1) The Synoptists.

a. In the Synoptic Gospels the concept of reward is presented just as freely as the threat of punishment. Mt. 6:19-21 = Lk. 12:33 f. speak in current Jewish imagery (cf. Str.-B., I, 429 ff.). To do God's will by not heaping up earthly treasures, or, as Lk. says, by giving them away, is to lay up treasure in heaven which will one day be paid out as a reward. There will be a particular reward for disciples who prove faithful in days of persecution and conflict, Mt. 5:12 = Lk. 6:23.[72] No less uninhibited is Mk. 10:21 = Mt. 19:21 = Lk. 18:22 where the rich young ruler is told that he will have a sure portion in the kingdom of God as a reward for giving all his possessions to the poor. The life of those who subject themselves to the will of God and the coming kingdom of God is presented in terms of the metaphor of work in the vineyard or house, at the plough or harvest, and there is prospect of a great reward for this service of God,[73] Mt. 20:2; 24:45-51 = Lk. 12:42-46; Mk. 9:41. To the very Jewish question of Mt. 19:27, cf. Mk. 10:28 = Lk. 18:28, what the disciples will get for giving up everything to follow Jesus, the reply is not given that the concept of reward is sub-moral. A rich recompense is promised both here and hereafter. The sayings treated on → 699 f. may also be cited here. In these the actual term μισθός is used. The reward is either recompense for achievement, Mt. 5:7; 6:14; 10:32, 39; 25:29, or compensation for what the disciples have given up or denied themselves, Mt. 10:39; Lk. 14:8-11. Varied though the achievements may be in detail (Mk. 9:41 ff.; Mt. 10:41 f.), the reward is always the same (cf. Mt. 20:9 f.), namely, the kingdom of God.

Corresponding to the reward there is also in the Synoptists a penal recompense for those who are disobedient to God, Mt. 11:20-24; 13:40 f.; 10:28 = Lk. 12:5; Mt. 18:8 f. = Mk. 9:43 ff.; Mt. 18:23-35; Mt. 23:37-39 = Lk. 13:34; Mk. 12:9 = Mt. 21:40 f. = Lk. 20:15; Lk. 13:1-5; 16:9. In this connection it should be noted that reward and punishment are almost always future. As in Judaism, a reward in this world is ruled out by the fact that the destiny of the disciples on earth is to be conflict and persecution. As the Ruler and Guarantor of the kingdom of God must die to fulfil the final revelation of God, to secure the victory of the

---

[72] Mt. 5:3 ff. should not be adduced in this connection, for what we have here is not the belief in recompense but the message of the grace of God who helps because man needs His gift, Schl. Mt., *ad loc.* The belief in recompense is present, however, in Mt. 5:7-10, found only in Mt.

[73] H. J. Holtzmann, *Lehrbuch d. nt.lichen Theologie*² (1911), 259.

kingdom, so suffering and battle are the natural destiny of His disciples,[74] Mk. 8:34 ff. = Mt. 16:24 ff. = Lk. 9:23 ff. Only once is a reward promised in this life, Mk. 10:29 f. = Lk. 18:29 f.[75] Those who have given up family and property for the sake of Jesus and the Gospel will receive them back a hundredfold, with future eternal life, now in this time, houses, brothers, sisters, mothers, children, and lands. The only possible meaning of these words is that the man who is persecuted will find a substitute and reward in the community, in which each is the other's brother.[76] This is connected with the evaluation of the community. As Jesus in His coming and work is the irruption of the divine lordship, as the risen Christ, invisible to the world, is now embodied in the community, so, in spite of persecution in the world, there is in the fellowship and love of the community a commencement of the reward which will find its consummation only in the final manifestation of the kingdom of God. If the community is the historical sign of the irruption of the divine rule, the sign of the power of the risen Christ in this world, then the reward which the righteous will receive in fulness in the kingdom of God begins in the fellowship of brethren.[77]

In the Synopt. the thought of reward is naturally connected very closely with the concept of judgment taken over from Jewish tradition. Every reward and punishment will be received at the judgment: "With what judgment you judge, you shall be judged, and with what measure you mete, it shall be measured to you again" (Mt. 7:2).

b. The question arises whether this concept of reward is to be ascribed to Jesus. It would seem indisputable that many Jewish sayings and later traditions of the Church are to be found in this view of reward and retribution.

In detail it is very difficult to come to any sure conclusions in this area where there are so many Jewish par., cf. Mt. 6:19 f. = Lk. 12:33 with T. Pea, 4, 18 par.: "My fathers have gathered treasures at a place over which the hand can gain control, and I have gathered treasures at a place over which no hand can gain control."[78] No light is shed by the common saying in Mt.: ἐκεῖ ἔσται ὁ κλαυθμὸς καὶ ὁ βρυγμὸς τῶν ὀδόντων, 8:12; 13:42, 50; 22:13; 24:51b; 25:30; cf. Lk. 13:28. There is debate as to the Woes pronounced on the privileged cities in Mt. 11:20-24 = Lk. 10:13-15, cf. Mt. 10:15 = Lk. 10:12. Weinel[79] thinks that the present form derives from Christian irritation at the home cities of Jesus, but he contends for a genuine core, whereas Wellhausen and Bultmann[80] believe the sayings were a later product of the community. When a sense of Messianic mission is found in Jesus, a historical core can be seen in the sayings, though the form may be later. Mt. 13:36 ff. might be a later tradition.[81] Mk. 11:25 could also be a product of later community needs.[82] Mk. 10:29 f. perhaps ended originally

[74] E. Lohmeyer, "Die Idee des Martyriums im Judt. u. Urchristentum," ZSTh, 5 (1928), 236 ff.

[75] Mt. alone omits the ref. to the present order, an obvious softening.

[76] Kl. Mk. and Loh. Mk., *ad loc.*

[77] Though Jesus rejects the rigid schema of retribution which finds a sin behind every misfortune (Lk. 13:1 ff.; cf. Jn. 9:1 ff.), He sees a connection between sin and evil, as is evident from the mere fact that the kingdom of God brings salvation from physical distress (Mk. 2:1-12 = Mt. 9:1-8 = Lk. 5:17-26), and also from the fact that for Him the rule of demons means evil for both body and soul (Mk. 3:23 ff. = Mt. 12:25 ff. = Lk. 11:17 ff.).

[78] Cf. Str.-B. on the individual passages.

[79] *Bibl. Theol. des NT*[4] (1928), 107.

[80] Trad., 118.

[81] *Ibid.*, 202 f.

[82] Loh. Mk., *ad loc.*

with ἑκατονταπλασίονα. Mt. 25:14-30 in its authentic form could have promised a reward in God's kingdom for faithful service.[83] No less debated is Mt. 25:31-46. Referring to Mandaean, Egyptian and Persian par., Klostermann, Bultmann etc. assume that the passage was taken from Jewish tradition by the community, the Son of Man being put in place of God. Schlatter, on the other hand, emphasises the full universality of the norm. It is "the measure by which Jesus judges all, whether they know Him or not, among whom He places the nations with their many religions and varied moral capabilities, as in the universal promise of 5:3-10."[84] But the same universalism leads Bultmann to think that the story comes from a time when the contrast between Christians and non-Christians no longer played any part.[85] Equally open to dispute is Lk. 16:9. The authenticity of Lk. 16:19-31 is also challenged. The first part is full of a sense of resentment which after the manner of the En. Apc. expects schematic counterbalancing in the future aeon (though cf. v. 28) for both poor and rich, here no less schematically equated with righteous and unrighteous. The second part champions the very Jewish view that men may expect no miracle from God in confirmation of His will.[86] These sayings provide no certain starting-point, and it is thus better to disregard them rather than burdening our presentation with disputed texts.

On the other hand, there is little doubt as to the authenticity of sayings like Mk. 9:43-48 = Mt. 18:8 f. concerning the battle against one's own sin and the final destiny connected therewith. The same is true of the saying about blaspheming the Son of Man and the Holy Spirit, Mk. 3:28 f. = Mt. 12:31 f., and of the parable of the wicked husbandmen, Mk. 12:1 ff. = Mt. 21:33 ff. = Lk. 20:9 ff. One must also regard as authentic the saying about cowardly fear of men and the true fear of God in Mt. 10:28 = Lk. 12:4 f., that about the narrow door to life in Mt. 7:13 f. = Lk. 13:23 f., the parable of the unmerciful servant in Mt. 18:23-35, and the warning against false (i.e., nationalistic and political) Messianic expectations in Lk. 13:1-5,[87] to mention only some.[88] But here we also move forward, since Jesus transcends in His own way the Jewish concept of reward.

c. It can hardly be contested that in Jesus the concept of reward has decisive significance in connection with the thought of the kingdom of God and the judgment. As Lord and King God demands obedience and promises a reward, Mt. 25:14 ff. Just because Jesus emphasises man's responsibility toward God in obedience, He everywhere underlines God's acceptance or rejection of man's conduct. What human arrogance regards as the result or return, the claim or merit, of one's own work, Jesus adjudges to be simply God's reward.[89] It is, of course, the joyful message of Jesus that God does not give His reward as a judge who judges justly, but as a father who gives generously, Mt. 6:1, 4, 6, 18; 25:34. Even in the parable in Mt. 25:14 ff. (cf. Lk. 19:12 ff.), which on the one side lays stress on the fact that God demands diligence and faithfulness from man, and on the other underlines the claim of God the King to man's obedience, the reward is great out of all proportion (Mt. 25:21, 23; cf. Mt. 24:47 = Lk. 12:44) in relation to man's conduct. It thus emerges already that the reward is God's generosity, not

[83] Kl. Mt., *ad loc.*
[84] Mt., *ad loc.*
[85] Trad., 130. Cf. G. Klein, *Der älteste christl. Katechismus u. die jüd. Propagandalit.* (1909), 49.
[86] Bultmann Trad., 220.
[87] J. Pickl, *Messiaskönig Jesus* (1935), 48.
[88] The other materials regarded as essential will be found in the ensuing discussion of the distinctive elements in Jesus' concept of reward.
[89] Wagner, 112.

man's deserving. Certainly the concept remains, but it is taken out of the sphere of law and calculation, and consequently purified.[90] The same is true in Mk. 10:29 f. = Mt. 19:29 = Lk. 18:29 f., where a hundredfold reward is promised, and in Lk. 6:38, where an overflowing measure is held out as reward. Special attention has rightly been devoted to the parable in Mt. 20:1 ff. in respect of this question. The parable starts with the concept of reward and works with it as with a self-evident reality. The owner promises and pays a legitimate reward. But if we are to understand the parable we cannot begin by assuming that the owner is primarily evaluating the will to work. This, it is argued, is the same in every case, though the opportunity comes much later for some; hence it is equally rewarded in all. According to the divine justice the reward can be the same for all, or so the argument runs, because the will to work, not the actual achievement, is estimated.[91] But this distinction between will and achievement has to be imported into the text. I believe rather that these are the essential points to be noted. i. The heart of the parable is in vv. 6, 7, 9, 14, 15. The labourers who worked the whole day and thus received a just recompense are in the parable only to bring out the more bluntly the singularity of the situation and the nature of the reward given to those who were last. It is not intended seriously to suggest that in fact there are those who merit the divine reward, just as Mk. 2:17; Lk. 5:32; 15:7; Mt. 5:45 do not deal with the question whether some are righteous or not. Their function is simply to bring out more vividly the fact of reward without merit or worth. ii. Those enlisted for work early in the morning, like the correct son in the parable of Lk. 15:11 ff., are put in merely to show that human righteousness simply cannot understand the divine generosity. In content, the parable is thus the Matthean parallel to the parable of the Prodigal Son in Lk. 15:11 ff. It declares the greatness of God's generous love. All individuals and individual traits serve this thought and constitute the dark background for the fact that the last to be called are so generously treated.[92] Naturally, this does not mean that there is no thought of divine reward. The one point that is made is that reward is not according to achievement. Achievement and reward stand in a mutual relation which is incomprehensible to those who think in terms of a correct schema of merit and reward, and who thus regard God's relation to man as that of a precisely calculating employer to his employees. The parable radically discards all thought of merit.[93] Its core is the message of the generous love of God for highly imperfect man: ὅτι ἐγὼ ἀγαθός εἰμι, v. 15. So great is this love of God that those who think in correct human terms, and for whom God is simply King and Judge, cannot understand it, and are confused by the mystery of the glad tidings of Jesus. The Jewish concept of merit is radically removed from the preaching of Jesus concerning the love of God, which rewards very differently. It is not that justice like that of a judge or employer pays a merited recompense. God's love lavishes itself prodigally, in a unique way which is possible only for God, upon children whose intentions, though imperfect, are good. If Jesus still retains the concept of reward (and punishment), this is to express the obligation of man to the holy will of God. In relation to God, man stands in responsibility and obedience, and God recognises his attitude and action to be either good or bad.

---

[90] Michel, 51.

[91] K. Weiss, 75 ff.; 87 ff.; Weinel, *Bibl. Theologie,* 119.

[92] The explanation suggested in Zn. Mt., *ad loc.* is thus impossible.

[93] Hence the argument of Michel, 52 that the concept of reward is not excluded, because the owner promises and pays a just reward, cannot be sustained.

But there is need to affirm all the more definitely that the calculating view of a merited reward is completely ruled out. Lk. 17:7-10 says clearly: λέγετε, ὅτι δοῦλοι ἀχρεῖοί ἐσμεν, ὃ ὠφείλομεν ποιῆσαι πεποιήκαμεν. The reference here is not to the overwhelming generosity of God, but on the basis of God's claim on man as Lord and King there is flat rejection of any right of man to reward. The concept of merit is completely repudiated. That of reward remains, but man is conceded no title to a divine reward. This saying in Lk. 17:7-10 can be appreciated only when one considers that the reference is to the reward which God gives, and only when the nature of this reward is remembered, namely, that it is the will of God's love to give the kingdom to men, Lk. 12:32; cf. Mt. 5:3. The kingdom of God is the miraculous act and gift of God, a gift incomparable and unique in value, such as only God can give.[94] This reward cannot be earned by any achievement. It cannot be merited. Before it all men are δοῦλοι ἀχρεῖοι. Because the reward is so incomparable, it allows no place for calculation of reward. For those who desire human recognition, who want their good deeds to be praised and extolled by men, God's reward is not enough. But the greatness of God's gift cannot be compared with any earthly gift or praise of men. Hence God alone has the prerogative of recompensing, and those who count on human rewards disqualify themselves from God's reward.[95] The claim to reward is thus rebuffed as radically as possible. Man can set before God no merit commensurate with this reward. No one may speculate on it, for in so doing he betrays himself into a hypocritical and self-seeking pettiness outside the sphere of the blessing of divine love.[96]

This is strengthened by Jesus when He promises the reward of the kingdom of heaven to children (Mk. 10:15 = Mt. 18:3 = Lk. 18:17), i.e., to those who act in a way which is natural and uncalculating, and who believe in the plenitude of divine possibilities, and also when He promises the kingdom to the πτωχοὶ τῷ πνεύματι, to those in inner need, to those who are poor even inwardly in the struggle for the necessities of life.[97] If God alone is good (Mk. 10:18 = Mt. 19:17 = Lk. 18:18), then no one can lay claim to a reward. Like a child who believes in a thousand possibilities, each must allow the unique possibility of God, the kingdom, to be granted to him.

From another angle, too, the meritorious character of the reward is ruled out. All that men do in actualisation of the will of God they do as the children of God, i.e., as those who have already been caught up in the living power of the kingdom of God. Their whole life stands under the sign of the breaking in of the kingdom. They live by possession of the living spiritual power of this onrushing kingdom. This kingdom is not just future, as in Judaism. With Jesus it has broken into time and is incipiently present, cf. Mt. 12:28; Lk. 11:20.[98] The reference, then, is not to a moral action on the part of autonomous man, but to volition and action in terms of the final reality of the coming kingdom of God. Thus moral action is not an achievement which deserves a reward. It is living power in all its fulness,

---

[94] → I, 583 ff.; H. D. Wendland, *Die Eschatologie des Reiches Gottes bei Jesus* (1931), 59 ff.

[95] ἀπέχω means to be satisfied, paid in full; cf. Deissmann LO, 88 f.; Schl. Mt., *ad loc.*

[96] → 699 f.

[97] Mt. 5:3; Lk. 6:20; Schl., *ad loc.*

[98] Wendland, *op. cit.*, 106; H. Preisker, *Geist u. Leben. Das Telos-Ethos des Urchristentums* (1933), 32 ff.; 37.

the power which is given by God. Hence it can raise no claim on God. It is simply the result of being placed in the insurgent power of the kingdom of heaven.

Jesus speaks, then, of reward, but all thought of merit is unconditionally excluded. His reference to reward implies i. that man stands under the eyes of the holy God; ii. that he owes obedience to God as Lord and King; iii. that man's salvation can be accomplished only by God Himself; iv. that only God's generosity grants a reward, and that it does so only to men with receptive hearts which are open to be blessed by the wonders of the kingdom of God; and v. that reward is not a claim or just recompense, but the incomprehensible rewarding which derives from God's love and which finds in the kingdom of God the beginning and completion of this overflowing generosity. The question naturally arises why, then, Jesus should speak of reward at all. There can be no doubt that He found the term in the world around Him, that He retained it, but that He did so only at the same time to transcend it. In fact, Jesus freed Himself radically from the Jewish concept of merit. He also rejected quite unconditionally any speculation concerning our reward with God or men. For Him the idea of reward arises with faith in the consummation of the kingdom of God. In His love the Father God gives His children the greatest gift there is, namely, the kingdom of God. He there perfects their moral will, their obedience to God, because human life is played out before God and is related to Him. [99] Thus the concept of reward is taken up into calling to the kingdom of God and the message of the coming and consummation of this kingdom. Because God is understood quite absolutely in the greatness of His being and the incomparability of His generous love, because He is in no way dependent on or conditioned by human action, the idea of merit is left behind and in no human action is there any place for counting on divine or human reward. There is a reward only in so far as God in sheer love, which is unintelligible to mere justice, draws human obedience, for all its limitations, into the power and glory of the kingdom of God. Thus the reward is simply the divine glory undeservedly received. This is the distinctive new revelation of Jesus as compared with Judaism and all other religions. [100]

(2) Paul.

a. In Paul the idea of twofold recompense, both punishment and reward, is undoubtedly present: τοὺς γὰρ πάντας ἡμᾶς φανερωθῆναι δεῖ ἔμπροσθεν τοῦ βήματος τοῦ Χριστοῦ, ἵνα κομίσηται ἕκαστος ... εἴτε ἀγαθὸν εἴτε φαῦλον, 2 C. 5:10. The harvest corresponds to the seed, Gl. 6:7 f.; R. 6:21. God repays each man according to his works, R. 2:1-11; 13:12; 14:10 ff.; 1 C. 15:32; → III, 938. In this respect Paul follows Jewish custom by ending his moral admonitions with threats and promises, Gl. 5:21; 1 C. 6:9 f. It is logical that Paul exerts himself to stand in the judgment. He runs like a contestant in a race seeking the prize, 1 C. 9:24-27. He wants to please his Lord, 2 C. 5:9. His churches must go forward sincere and without offence to the day of Christ, Phil. 1:10, and await heavenly glory, 2 C. 4:17; R. 8:17 f.; 1 Th. 1:10; 3:13; 1 C. 15:30-32, 58. The judgment is a matter of ἔργον, 1 Th. 5:23; Gl. 6:4; 1 C. 3:13 ff.; 9:1; R. 2:7; Phil. 1:22; 2:12. Hence Paul strives to have praise before God, 1 C. 9:14 f.; 2 C. 11:10, 12; Phil. 2:16;

---

[99] Cf. Karner, 97 f.
[100] → 704 f.; 712 f.

1 Th. 2:19; 2 C. 11:16 ff. In all these thoughts the apostle is obviously using, formally at least (→ 712 ff.), his ancient Pharisaic heritage.[101]

Nevertheless, it should not be overlooked that, Jewish though this sounds, there is a great difference. For Paul the day of judgment is a day in which he rejoices, the day in which the glory of Christ and His victory over all the powers of darkness will be manifested, the day on which the hope of the righteous will be actuality and they will be for ever with Christ in the kingdom of God. It is not, as for the Jews, a day of terror. It is a day of joy, of definitive redemption, to which he goes forward, not with trembling, but with παρρησία. This is possible only because the concept of achievement and reward, which always implies for man uncertainty before the holy God, has been overcome. Paul expresses his standpoint most succinctly in R.4:4 when he speaks of the μισθὸς ... κατὰ χάριν. The doctrine of justification vanquishes the concept of reward. If there is justification only for faith, and if the believer is one who gives place to the saving act of God, if he is thus a recipient, if faith itself is simply a gift of God, then any thought of merit is ruled out and reward is completely impossible.[102] Moreover, a new reality has broken in for Paul with the death and resurrection of Jesus, and to be a Christian is to live by this reality of redemption. This reality of the kingdom of God imparts itself to the individual as πνεῦμα,[103] and all the life and work of the Christian is no longer a matter of his own ability, but is simply a matter of being controlled, filled and impelled by this Spirit of God, R. 8:14; cf. 2 C. 1:22; 5:5. Thus the whole moral action of the Christian is for Paul the totality of capacity and volition on the one basis of life, the development of the spiritual power with which he has been endowed. It is all the fruit of the Spirit of God, and consequently the gift of grace, Gl. 5:22; Phil. 2:13; cf. 1 Th. 3:12; Col. 1:22; Eph. 5:9 𝔎. Again all merit and all thought of reward is ruled out, for the apostle is able to achieve all that he can, not of himself or by nature, but only in the strength of Him who is mighty in him, Phil. 4:13. If this means that all things are possible, if he has accomplished more than all the other apostles, it is not he, but ἡ χάρις τοῦ θεοῦ σὺν ἐμοί, 1 C. 15:10. For this reason, while he speaks of θάνατος as ὀψώνια τῆς ἁμαρτίας in R. 6:23, he expressly and basically describes ζωὴ αἰώνιος as χάρισμα τοῦ θεοῦ. For this reason, too, he draws the conclusion in R. 3:27: Ποῦ οὖν ἡ καύχησις; ἐξεκλείσθη ... διὰ νόμου πίστεως. Paul here gives masterly didactic form to the most profound content of the message of Jesus. The boasting of the apostle is not self-boasting. It is not insistence on his own power. It is boasting of what God has done for him in Christ. What God gives in His grace is naturally what He alone can give. It is the kingdom of God, 1 C. 15:50; Gl. 5:21; Col. 1:13, the δόξα Χριστοῦ, Col. 3:4; R. 8:18, and it is so unique and unheard of that this reward cannot be compared with anything on earth, 1 C. 15:42 f.

We may thus state that, purely externally, there are in Paul two apparently contradictory lines. The one is the idea of reward and judgment which comes from the Jewish religion of Law; the other is the early Christian circle of concepts which comes with the belief in justification and the certainty of endowment with

---

[101] How natural the concept of reward is for the apostle may also be seen from the fact that acc. to Phil. 2:4-11 exaltation was given to Christ as a reward for His humiliation (A. Schweizer, *Die Mystik des Apostels Pls.* [1930], 302).

[102] → II, 215 ff.; cf. Heidland, 112 ff.

[103] → πνεῦμα.

the Spirit. Both are consequences of the eschatological orientation. But while the first has the form of Jewish eschatology, the second draws on the primitive Christian belief that the righteous man lives already by the living and spiritual fulness of the kingdom of God, and will be perfected in it.

The tension between the lines of thought has first to be noted. In this respect it is immediately apparent that Paul speaks most unequivocally as a disciple of Jesus when he starts with the belief in justification and the endowment of the Spirit. It may also be said that the Jewish ideas and modes of expression often make it more difficult to perceive the distinctiveness of the Gospel. In Paul the concept of reward does not stand in the same direct and natural context of ethical acknowledgment of God as in the preaching of Jesus. It lies in the framework of theological deliberation and systematisation. For this very reason it can easily seem to have a disruptive and confusing influence on the doctrine of justification and spiritual endowment, which is elsewhere such a clear and fundamental mark of the Gospel.

b. While this is all true, however, it cannot be our final word. For a direct antithesis of this type would be quite intolerable to Paul the theologian. To him the concept of reward is more than a legacy carried over from Judaism. It has to have positive significance. On this three further points must be made.

i. Paul speaks of reward because God is the Holy One. As such He demands from man obedience, the recognition of His will, service with the whole of life, R. 12:1 f. As with Jesus, reward is God's acknowledgment of the moral will of man. Two further considerations force Paul to emphasise moral demands by means of the concept of reward and punishment, and thereby to establish in the churches a sense of responsibility before God.

ii. The early Christian doctrine of the Spirit stands in danger of being absorbed into the enthusiasm or ecstasy of the Hellenistic mysteries, and thereby transformed. Though the mysteries included moral demands,[104] it is evident that purity was made very largely dependent on cultic matters, and that the otherworldly orientation, i.e., the pledge of immortality particularly sought in the mysteries, did not always permit the ethical element to be of decisive significance.[105] The example of the Corinthian church, which is influenced by these cults, shows that the main emphasis was laid on ecstatic rapture rather than moral requirements. In answer, Paul stresses that the mark of the Christian is not γνῶσις and enthusiastic speaking in tongues, but brotherly love (ἀγάπη), 1 C. 13. The concept of recompense (reward) and judgment is designed to point out that God, who in Jesus reveals Himself in the moral will effected by the Spirit, not, like Dionysus, in enthusiastic rapture, decides in the judgment whether the pious have lived by the Spirit or allowed themselves to be impelled by the demonism of sin.[106]

The Spirit of God manifests Himself, not in ecstatic vision, but in moral activity. Hence judgment will be by works,[107] by deeds as the fruits of the Spirit, Gl. 5:22.

---

[104] H. Preisker, *Nt.liche Zeitgeschichte* (1937), 125 f.

[105] The greatest seriousness is shown by the Isis and Mithra cults, which are strongly eschatological and teach a judgment with reward and punishment.

[106] Cf. H. Lietzmann, *Geschichte der alten Kirche,* I (1932), 123.

[107] It is to be noted that for Paul judgment is by ἔργον (1 C. 3:13 ff.; Gl. 6:4; Phil. 1:6; Col. 1:10; 1 Th. 1:3), not ἔργα; on the other hand he often speaks of ἔργα νόμου.

iii. The apostle's doctrine of justification is to the same effect. The charge might obviously be brought against Paul that with his opposition to the Jewish righteousness of works and doctrine of merit he is destroying all ethical commitment and moral obligation, indeed, all responsibility before God, R. 3:8; 6:1; cf. Jm. 2:24. In face of this objection Paul explains that arbitrary assessment of one's moral attitude cannot give peace. Everything depends on God's judgment, and the divine kindness which gives is the acceptance which man must know in relation to his life, 1 C. 4:4 f.

Thus the preaching of reward and punishment is for the apostle the safeguard which he erects to prevent his message from being distorted into Hellenistic enthusiasm, libertinism, or moral passivity, Gl. 5:22. It is incontestable that with this form he adopts ancient ideas from his Jewish past which might disturb the purity of his proclamation. But this belief in rewards lays unlimited stress on the grace of God and is thus quite different from the concept of achievement. It is developed in the interests of moral will and effort and in opposition to threats against the doctrine of justification and the peril presented by pagan enthusiasm to the doctrine of the Spirit, with its orientation to moral activity. At these points one may see clearly the impress of primitive Christian belief. Paul certainly thinks in terms of the Jewish schema of reward. But with all the realities of faith associated with the terms χάρις, πίστις, παρρησία, εἰρήνη he transcends his Jewish heritage. Thus in 1 C. 3:5-15 he uninhibitedly applies the schema of rewards to his own work and that of his colleagues, and yet he speaks of it only in terms of the χάρις τοῦ θεοῦ ... δοθεῖσά μοι (v. 10). How radical this new impress is may be seen quite easily at a decisive point. The Jew seeks to be righteous before God on the basis of his own attainments, his good works. But he can never escape uncertainty whether his good works will be enough in the judgment, whether they will outweigh the bad, whether his sufferings and death are adequate to atone for his sins, so that on the basis of his good works he may be declared righteous and rewarded at the last day. One has only to read 4 Esr. or the account of the death of R. Jochanan ben Zakkai (→ II, 527) to be aware of this torturing uncertainty. Paul, too, speaks of the judgment. For him, too, the judgment means God's reward or punishment. But there is in him no trace of uncertainty or anxiety. He looks forward to this day with joy (→ κρίνω, III, 938). As a child of God who is already justified and blessed, the disciple of Jesus should be certain of salvation, R. 8:31-39; 5:9, 10. For Paul it is not a matter of counting the number of good works, as in Judaism. He knows that the Christian, even though endowed with the Spirit, is still a sinner (→ I, 308 ff.). There is for the apostle no need even to add up individual achievements before God and to seek a reward for them. The radical decision for him is whether a man lives by the Spirit or is controlled by ἁμαρτία: Πᾶν δὲ ὃ οὐκ ἐκ πίστεως ἁμαρτία ἐστίν, R. 14:23. The simple issue is whether the decisive factor in the Christian's life is God or sin. It is granted that during life on earth man's fate is never to be free from conflict with sin or to attain to complete victory over it, R. 8:10. The only important thing is that the life of faith and the power of the Spirit should have dominion over man. This is very different from the Jewish belief in recompense and achievement which looks to the individual work. This is the religion of joyous assurance which Jesus proclaimed and guaranteed in antithesis to the religion of fear. Because the Christian lives by grace and stands in the living power of the kingdom of God which broke into the world with Christ, he is certain of the love of God which will bring the work of God begun in him to glorious consummation, Phil. 1:6. The externalism and legalism of the concept of reward is transcended, and for all the remnants of legalism the concept is lifted up into the pure air of the religion of faith and grace, of the Spirit and joy.

c. The Pauline authorship of Eph. is much disputed, and for this reason we treat it separately. But the thinking is wholly Pauline. Apart from 6:8, where the thought of recompense occurs in the context of admonitions, the idea of achievement and merit is completely absent. The existence of the righteous is plainly grounded in God's saving work through Christ, 2:5. Only as children of light (5:9), as creatures of God, are Christians capable of the divine works which God expects of them: καὶ τοῦτο οὐκ ἐξ ὑμῶν, θεοῦ τὸ δῶρον· οὐκ ἐξ ἔργων, ἵνα μή τις καυχήσηται. αὐτοῦ γάρ ἐσμεν ποίημα, κτισθέντες ἐν Χριστῷ Ἰησοῦ ἐπὶ ἔργοις ἀγαθοῖς, 2:8 f. Only in virtue of the fulness of Christ is there power for a life of truth and love, 4:13, cf. 4:24. Only the wealth of the glory of light and power, only the incomparable living and spiritual fulness of divine empowering, of divine plenitude, makes possible the works of the children of God. One may see from 3:16-21 that the author goes out of his way to heap up extravagant expressions in order that this should be emphasised as impressively as possible. The slightest idea of a claim to reward is also ruled right out by the fact that Christians are regarded as children of God chosen before the foundation of the world, 1:4, 11. If they may hope for the glory of the inheritance, their joyful assurance does not rest on their own works. It rests on the fact that they are already seized by this new reality of the coming kingdom. It rests on the fact of the Spirit of God ruling within them. For this Spirit is the sign of the invading and victorious world of God, 1:13 f. All salvation, all confidence as to the future, is thus placed, not on human achievement, but on God's grace (2:8), on the power of God which works in Christians and which enables them even now to live in the strength of the heavenly world (2:6).

d. The Pastoral Epistles also see that God did not send the Saviour because of works, Tt. 3:5; 2 Tm. 1:9. But the antithesis to ἔργα is not now the faith which is brought into being by God. It is not the empty hand stretched out to God. Instead, it is God's own grace and pity, Tt. 3:5. Faith has lost its central position. The main concern is with practical moral conduct. Salvation is less a present possession and more one-sidedly future expectation. But where faith, i.e., the religious starting-point, yields before practical moral concerns, and a one-sidedly future eschatology arises, there is a tendency for the thought of reward to come to the fore.[108] This may be seen in the Past. The righteous Judge (2 Tm. 4:8) judges on the basis of works (1 Tm. 5:24 f.).[109] For women child-bearing is one such work (1 Tm. 2:15). The reward is both in this world (1 Tm. 4:8) and the world to come (1 Tm. 4:16; 6:19). This practical piety wins eternal life. The sober morality and calculating gaze on the future — apart from the centre of faith — cause a not inconsiderable shift in the whole outlook and allow the concept of reward a place alongside the divine mercy. This enables us to see that Paul's preaching of justification by faith is the central point which correctly integrates and subordinates all the other factors and in the light of which alone it is possible to make use of adopted Jewish ideas. It is true that in the Past. the concept of achievement is transcended. Salvation by good works is possible only on the ground of relation to

---

[108] Wetter, 194.
[109] The Past. do not use the sing. ἔργον but speak of ἔργα ἀγαθά.

Christ (1 Tm. 2:15; 4:8). Nevertheless, the righteous can hope for a reward corresponding to their works.

(3) The Johannine Writings.

a. The position is very different in the Gospel and Epistles of John. One may find an echo of the Jewish belief in recompense at Jn. 9:31, where on the lips of a Jew (οἴδαμεν) it is said that God does not hear the petitions of sinners, but of the righteous.[110] Otherwise all thought of reward is transcended by two radical considerations of faith. i. The resurrection simply corresponds to the life already present in the righteous, 6:39 f., 44, 47, 50. The judgment is merely the conclusion of the κρίσις which Jesus has already brought upon men, 3:18; 5:29 ff., 40.[111] He who already on earth has experienced in faith the revelation of the life of God in Jesus cannot be torn away from the nexus of life. Eternal life is not his desert or reward. It is the divinely ordained fulfilment of the miracle of birth from above (3:3, 6) which for faith has begun already on earth, 5:24; 6:39 f., 50; 8:51; 11:25; 12:46; 1 Jn. 4:16 ff.; 5:18 ff. ii. All that the disciple achieves is simply the gift of God, action in virtue of the divinely given ἐξουσία, 1:12; cf. 1 Jn. 2:6, 11. Jn. 1:16 has the sonorous formula: ὅτι ἐκ τοῦ πληρώματος αὐτοῦ ἡμεῖς πάντες ἐλάβομεν, καὶ χάριν ἀντὶ χάριτος. Only he who is born of God does what is right, 1 Jn. 2:29. For Jn. this gift of divine life received already on earth is so great and mighty that he sees both sin (1 Jn. 3:9 f.; 5:18) and death (Jn. 5:24 ff.; 11:25 ff.) overcome by it. The doctrine of the sinlessness of the Christian expresses the force which this revelation of new life had for Jn. He does not deny human sin, but when he speaks of life he cannot think also of sin and death. Because this life has appeared,[112] all moral volition and capacity are simply an outworking of its impartation by God, which all those have and demonstrate who believe in Him whom God has sent. This is consequently an ethos of the fulness of power which Jesus Himself had (Jn. 1:12). This clear and radical outlook leaves no place for the concept of reward or merit, and Jn. has eliminated all formulae even remotely reminiscent of this concept.

b. In Rev. the thoughts are more strongly clothed in Jewish terms and concepts. Thus the idea of judgment is the dominant eschatological form in which the greatness and majesty of God also find expression, Rev. 1:18; 14:7, 17 ff.; 15:1 ff.; 19:1 f.; 20:12; 22:12. The punishment of sinners takes place already on earth (2:22 f.), but ultimately only the last time will bring the full destruction of wrongdoers (11:18; 14:8, 10, 19; 15:1 ff.; 16:1 ff.; 17:1 ff.; 18:1 ff.; 21:8). For the righteous the last time will bring full blessing in all the fulness of the kingdom of God, 2:7, 10, 17, 26; 3:4 f., 10, 12, 20; 7:15 f.; 11:12, 18; 14:1 ff., 13; 19:9; 21:7; 22:3, 12, 17. Good works are strongly emphasised: οἶδά σου τὰ ἔργα, 2:19. The judgment will decide according to works, 20:12 f.; 22:12. Good works follow those who die in the Lord, 14:13. The reference is primarily to the special works of martyrs (7:9-17; 15:2-4) and ascetics (14:4), but love, faith, service and patience are also among the moral works (2:19) which will be rewarded (22:12). It thus seems as though Rev. is turning its back on the primitive Christian view and reverting to

110 Cf. Is. 1:15; ψ 65:18; 108:7; Prv. 15:29.
111 Bau. J., *ad loc.*
112 1 Jn. 1:2.

the Jewish schema of judgment, achievement and reward. In keeping is the fact that faith is not here the receptive attitude of man towards God but much more his perseverance or faithfulness (2:13; 13:10); indeed, it is even equated with patience.[113] Nevertheless, this would set Rev. at an unhistorical distance from John's Gospel and completely overlook the ultimate motifs of the book. In Rev. believers are written in the book of life from the foundation of the world, 17:8. Already on earth they are kings and priests, 1:6; 5:10. They are thus called to be witnesses even unto death.[114] This inner renewal is also expressed in the metaphor of the white clothes which the righteous wear, 3:4, 18, cf. 7:14. Works, therefore, are not their own meritorious achievement. They are the working out of an experienced encounter with Christ (3:20), of a known redemption (14:4). The reward is consequently not a rightly deserved recompense for one's own good works. For God's children in the great judgment, it is simply the public declaration before the world of that which, as those written in the book of life (17:8), as kings (vl.) and priests (1:6; 5:10), they already are, and have as God's gift of salvation, even here on earth, though hidden, of course, from the eyes of the world. They are sealed, and there is for them no judgment. They do not tremble before it; as God's children and witnesses, which God has ordained them to be through Christ, 5:9 f. — they await the manifestation of their secret kingship, of the glory of God which lives in them. Thus in spite of the Jewish form the concept of reward is here only the expression of a blessing which has been experienced already and which in the last time will be manifested to the eyes of the world.

(4) The Post-Pauline Writings.

a. Acts knows of a reward in this life for obedience to God. He who obeys God receives as a reward, not earthly goods, but the one and only gift of the last time by which early Christianity differentiates itself from Judaism (Ac. 1:5; 2:1 ff.; 8:15; 15:8; 19:1-6), namely, the Spirit of God (5:32; 10:4 ff., 44). Punishment for sin is also operative in this world, 5:4 f., 9 f.; 8:20 ff.; 12:22 f.; 13:11. This is not just the Jewish belief in recompense. It is linked with the dynamic view of the Spirit found in Lk. Endowment with the Spirit is endowment with power.[115] Sin breaks on the omnipotent power of the Spirit. There are thus judgments in the community, which is the manifestation of the κύριος. Because the community is the earthly embodiment of the Spirit of the κύριος, there arises this conflict between the kingdoms of Christ and the devil which agitates this world and destroys him who deceitfully and selfishly opposes the power of this Spirit. This dynamic of conflict, with its effects on those who oppose the κύριος, is rather different from the OT belief in recompense.[116] A primitive view of recompense is found in 15:29. This is perhaps taken from a directive common in Jewish communities of the *diaspora*. Adopted from Judaism, it gives evidence of the Jewish view of recompense. In Ac. the apostles speak of judgment on the whole world (10:42; 17:31) only in missionary addresses and in the hearing before Felix (24:15, 25). The life of the righteous is built wholly on the life, death and resurrection of Jesus and the activity of the Spirit in the community and the individual. All

---

113 πιστός in the sense of "faithful," 2:10.
114 Loh. Apk., 186.
115 → II, 300 ff.
116 → 706 ff.

meritorious claim is transcended by the Gospel of grace, 20:24, 32. The κληρονομία ἐν τοῖς ἡγιασμένοις is not an earned reward but is established with the fact of God's omnipotence.[117] In 26:18 the inheritance of the saints is bound up with the divine act of calling to light and liberating from the power of Satan. There is no question of merit.

b. Hebrews is seeking to warn its readers against growing weary and relapsing from Christianity. This purpose, and the contacts with the spirit of Alexandrian Judaism, as our examination of the terms has already shown (→ 701), cause the idea of recompense to come out more strongly than in other writings of the Pauline and post-Pauline period. Thus the author threatens Christians with judgment (10:27, 29) and also promises as a reward for faithfulness the rest of God (4:3), the salvation of God (9:28), and the kingdom of God (12:28; cf. 10:36). The clear distinction from Paul may be seen in the concept of faith found in Hb. Faith is strongly emphasised, but it is not, as in Pl., a protest against the righteousness of works, nor the presupposition of being in Christ with all that this means in terms of the *pneuma*. On the contrary, faith and recompense belong together. He who believes fulfils the condition of entry into the time of consummation, the prerequisite of recompense by God (11:6, 26, 33 f.). Faith is faithfulness which is rewarded, hope which becomes fulfilment. If in spite of all these clear echoes of Judaism Hb. still avoids the Jewish idea of merit, there may be seen in this the distinction of the basic Christian attitude from Judaism. No matter how strongly the faith of Hb. is orientated to the future, the attitude of men is that of those who have knowledge of, and are on the watch for, the final coming reality. Indeed, this faith has experienced the reality already in this world. Hence Hb. speaks of the anchor which reaches from this world into the world to come, 6:19. It also speaks of Christians as those who are enlightened, who have tasted the heavenly gift, who have received the Holy Spirit, 6:4, cf. 2:11. Christians are for Hb. men who live by the Spirit of grace (10:29) and bear in themselves the powers of the future aeon (6:5). As their whole life is built on God's grace, so the last judgment is for them simply God's grace, 4:16. Though Hb. uses Jewish images and concepts, it has fully transcended the idea of merit, as may be seen from the simple fact that it stands in awe of the greatness and majesty of God, and is fully aware of the weakness and guilt of man. Nevertheless, the righteous do not tremble at the judgment. They move forward towards the time of consummation with joyful confidence, 10:19 ff. This shows that they are not relying on the uncertain schema of human achievement and merit. They live already by their present experience of the power of the kingdom of God. They rest simply on the grace of God, 4:16. In virtue of this reality faith becomes confirmation in all the storms of persecution, and the salvation already experienced proves itself in emphatic righteousness of life, 12:10.

c. James, too, speaks of regeneration by the word of truth, 1:18. Works are a proof of faith, so that James affirms only the faith which unfolds itself in works, 2:14 ff. This faith alone leads to true prayer (1:6) and to confirmation in suffering (1:2 f.). This faith alone determines man for the truth even in what he says,

---

[117] This is the meaning if one links the participial addition τῷ δυναμένῳ ... with κυρίῳ. The more obvious link with λόγῳ would mean that the inheritance is given with the endowment of the community with the Word, and this, too, would exclude any thought of merit.

3:1 ff.[118] Whereas in Paul the point at issue is that man as a believer looks away from himself and his own achievement, and simply receives, the concern of James is that true faith produces works which will be acknowledged in the judgment and rewarded with the crown of life (1:12) and the inheritance of the kingdom (2:5, cf. 1:25), while just punishment falls on sinners (2:13; 4:12; 5:9). The idea of reward in this life is ruled out, since persecution and suffering are marks of the righteous, 1:2; 4:1 ff.; 5:7 ff. The thought of merit is also shattered, since the faith which leads to works is a gift of God (2:5), the reward of God's kingdom has its origin in God's gracious election (2:5), and all salvation rests on the ἔμφυτος λόγος (1:21) and the Spirit dwelling in believers (4:5). Thus Jm., for all that he borrows heavily from OT and Jewish wisdom and the hortatory tradition of Hellenism,[119] does not abandon the primitive Christian transcending of Jewish piety and its claim upon God for reward. It is true, of course, that the preaching of faith and redemption is in Jm. strongly secondary to the ethical admonition which is the main content and purpose of the work. For this reason Jm. always makes the impression of being an early Christian exhortation which uses the concept of achievement and reward, as though there had not been a complete and radical transcending of the concept.

d. The First Epistle of Peter seeks to strengthen Christians who are undergoing persecution so that they will make a faithful confession, display resolute endurance, and live a holy life. Faith here is close to hope. Its object is Christ, who has victoriously passed through death, and the future glory, 1:3, 7, 13; 3:22; 4:13. But it is the basis of the whole Christian life, liberating for moral action (1:15 f., 22; 5:10) and leading to salvation (1:5, 9). The author's aim to enable his readers to endure persecution naturally leads him to refer to future glory, the future inheritance, as the sure recompense for present distress, 5:6. Along the same lines, the righteous are reminded of the fear of God who judges each man, not according to his faith or general attitude to God, but according to his works. There is here a definite bias towards the Jewish view. Nevertheless, this is not the decisive note. This is heard when it is said that Christians are regenerate (2:2), that they are begotten anew by God (1:3), that they are lifted up into the world of the reality of the resurrection (1:3, 4), that they are called (3:9). The blessing which they win in 3:9, the glorification of 1:11; 4:12 ff.; 5:1, the salvation of their souls in 1:9, is not a reward based upon merits; it is the consummation which is already posited and guaranteed by God with their calling to salvation. Hence all idea of merit is fundamentally excluded, though it cannot be denied that the thought of reward and works is to be found here and there in the practical admonitions. Finally, the Pauline concept of all-creating grace which redeems, which places us even now in God's kingdom, and which is the presupposition of future glory, is more plainly upheld here than in any other of the Catholic Epistles.

Jude and 2 Peter are contending against false libertine and Gnostic teachers, and these are threatened with terrible punishments in the divine judgment, 2 Pt. 2:3, 9; 3:7; Jd. 4, 6 f., 9 ff., 13 ff. The righteous, on the other hand, have to attain to the kingdom of God, 2 Pt. 3:13. Nevertheless, both epistles cling to the fact that

---

[118] Instead of the older formula "faith and works" Jm. has "faith in works." Cf. H. Preisker, "Der Eigenwert des Jakobusbriefes in d. Geschichte des Urchristentums," ThBl, 8 (1934), 233.
[119] Dib. Jk., *passim.*

the righteous receive the promises only because, in the Hellenistic terminology of 2 Pt. 1:3 f., the θεῖα δύναμις is the basis of εὐσέβεια, and they have become θείας κοινωνοὶ φύσεως, so that ἄσπιλοι καὶ ἀμώμητοι they exhibit peace with God in the judgment, 2 Pt. 3:14. In Jd. 20 f. entry into eternal life accompanies faith, possession of the Spirit, and the love of God.

In post-Pauline writings faith is no longer so central as the giving to man of God's salvation. There is thus a marked orientation of believing faith to the future consummation as a spur to faithfulness and hope in time of persecution. There is also a strong emphasis on good works as the condition of deliverance before the righteous Judge. This means that the concept of reward has an essential place and there is considerable borrowing from the vocabulary of the OT and Judaism. Nevertheless, the idea of merit is ruled out, for the righteous know that the attitude which results in good works is possible for them only as they are called to the living power of Christ, i.e., only by God's action.

(5) The Meaning of Reward for Jesus and Early Christianity.

Jesus and early Christianity obviously spoke quite freely of reward. But for all the formal dependence, the Jewish idea of reward is completely transcended. The Christian cannot count on a reward either from man or God. Just recompense would mean for men absolute and definitive destruction, for God alone is good, Mk. 10:18, 26 f.; R. 3:22-24, and consequently He alone is life and the living One. If the NT still speaks of reward, this is simply a temporally conditioned term for the incomparably rich gift of God's love to man in spite of all his weakness and sin. One may thus speak of reward in the NT sense only i. as a reference to the fact that man is set before God, and that the most excellent fruit of faith which God demands and recognises is not enthusiasm or ecstasy, but moral volition and action; ii. with an awareness that God's gift, i.e., the kingdom, is so uniquely and incomparably great that it can only be given by God and no man can merit it, so that all reward is simply God's generous love; iii. in the faith that this final reward is God's gift, because there is at the beginning endowment with God's Spirit and adoption into the living power of the kingdom of God, so that man is conceivable as the child of God only in terms of his endowment by God; iv. with the clear perspective that the incomparable greatness of this gift frees man completely from calculating on rewards from men; v. in the experience that the power of faith, the omnipotence of God, the possession of the Spirit, is a simple and natural incentive to moral action, so that there neither can nor should be any thought or talk of reward; vi. in the attitude of the child of God, who goes forward to the final decision of God, not with fear and uncertainty, but with uniquely great confidence and cheerful and childlike trust in the love of God which will perfect the calling of God's children in the glory of His kingdom. Thus what is said about reward summons to moral seriousness before the holy God but it is also an expression of blessing already experienced and of the most joyous certainty of the love of God which overcomes all things, including all man's weakness and guilt. The old form can thus be used only with this completely different content and significance.

Preisker

μνεία, μνήμη, μνῆμα, μνημεῖον, μνημονεύω → 678 ff.

† μοιχεύω, † μοιχάω, † μοιχεία, † μοῖχος, † μοιχαλίς

Contents: A. The Use of the Word Group. B. Adultery in the Old Testament and Judaism. C. Adultery in the Greek and Roman World. D. The Word Group in the New Testament: 1. In the Literal Sense; 2. In the Figurative Sense.

A. The Use of the Word Group.

μοιχεύω. The Attic uses the act. of the man in the abs. "I act as an adulterer," and with the acc. "to commit adultery with a woman," Aristoph. Av., 558; Lys., 1, 4, then gen. "to seduce or violate a woman," Luc. Dial. Mar., 12, 1, fig. "to adulterate," Achill. Tat., IV, 8, p. 117 (Hercher). Pass. and med. "to be, or to allow oneself to be, seduced," of the woman "to commit adultery," fig. of the intermingling of animals and men or of different races, Aristot. Hist. An., 32, p. 619a, 10 f.: τὰ γὰρ ἄλλα γένη μέμικται καὶ μεμοίχευται ὑπ' ἀλλήλων. The LXX uses μοιχεύειν and derivates for the root נאף and derivates, abs. Ex. 20:14(13); Dt. 5:18(17); Ez. 23:43; Hos. 4:14; 7:4; cf. Test. Jos. 4:6; 5:1; with acc. Jer. 3:9 (fig. ἐμοίχευσεν [sc. Ἰσραήλ] τὸ ξύλον καὶ τὸν λίθον), also med. with acc. of the man, pass. of the woman, Lv. 20:10: ἄνθρωπος ὃς ἂν μοιχεύσηται γυναῖκα ἀνδρὸς ἢ ὃς ἂν μοιχεύσηται γυναῖκα τοῦ πλησίον, θανάτῳ θανατούσθωσαν, ὁ μοιχεύων καὶ ἡ μοιχευομένη, Sir. 23:23 of the woman: ἐν πορνείᾳ ἐμοιχεύθη.

Cf. also the NT quoting the 7th commandment, Mt. 5:27; 19:18; Mk. 10:19; Lk. 18:20; R. 13:9; Jm. 2:11; in Lk. 16:18 and R. 2:22 the man is evidently meant; with acc. of adultery against a woman, Mt. 5:28, and pass. of the woman with whom it is committed, Mt. 5:32. Jn. 8:4 (ἡ γυνὴ κατείληπται ἐπ' αὐτοφώρῳ μοιχευομένη); Rev. 2:22 (τοὺς μοιχεύοντας μετ' αὐτῆς).

μοιχεύω κτλ. RGG², II, 38 f.; ERE, I, 122 ff. (Adultery); RW, 299 f.; Jew. Enc., I, 216 ff. (Adultery); Pauly-W., V (1905), 1241 ff. (Leonhard); XV, 2 (1932), 2446-2449 (Latte); F. Lübker, *Reallexikon d. klass. Altertums*⁸ (1914), 318 f.; J. H. H. Schmidt, *Synonymik d. griech. Sprache*, II (1878), 412 ff.; L. Schmidt, *Ethik d. Griechen*, II (1882), 175 ff., 191 ff.; A. Lipsius, *Das attische Recht u. Rechtsverfahren*, I (1915), 429 ff.; P. F. Girard, *Gesch. u. System d. röm. Rechts* (1908), 175, 185 ff.; L. Wahrmund, *D. Institut d. Ehe im Altertum* (1933); L. Friedländer, *Darstellungen aus der Sittengeschichte Roms*, I⁹ (1919), 283 ff.; II, 114 ff.; H. Bennecke, *Die strafrechtliche Lehre vom Ehebruch in ihrer historisch-dogmatischen Entwicklung* (1884); O. Karlowa, *Römische Rechtsgeschichte*, II (1892), 186 ff.; J. Dölger, *Antike u. Christentum*, III (1932), 132 ff.; IV (1934), 149 ff., 284 ff. RE³, V, 738 ff., "Familie u. Ehe bei den Hebräern"; B. Stade-A. Bertholet, *Bibl. Theol. des AT*, I and II (1905/1911), Index *s.v.* "Ehebruch"; A. Eberharter, "Das Ehe- und Familienrecht der Hebräer," *At.liche Abh.*, 5, 1 and 2 (1914); J. L. Saalschütz, *Mosaisches Recht* (1853), 570 ff.; L. Lichtschein, *Das Ehe nach mos.-talm. Auffassung* (1879); S. Krauss, *Talmudische Archäologie*, II (1911), 51 f.; H. Nordin, *Die eheliche Ethik d. Juden z. Zt. Jesu* (1911); R. H. Charles, *The Teaching of the NT on Divorce* (1921); J. Leipoldt, *Jesus u. d. Frauen* (1921), 49 ff.; G. Delling, *Des Pls. Stellung z. Frau u. Ehe* (1931); H. Preisker, *Christentum u. Ehe in den ersten 3 Jhdten.* (1927). For further bibl. → γυνή, I, 776.

μοιχάω, a subsidiary Doric form,[1] "to commit adultery," fig. "to adulterate," Ael. Nat. An., 7, 39 (τὸ λεχθέν); Xenoph. Hist. Graec., I, 6, 15 τὴν θάλατταν (to bring cunningly and illegally into one's power). In the LXX (for נאף only Jer. and Ez.) and the NT only in the pres. stem of the med. and pass., "to commit adultery," "to be led into adultery," of the man in Jer. 5:7; 9:1; 23:14 (μοιχωμένους); Mt. 5:32; 19:9; Mk. 10:11, the woman in Jer. 3:8; 29:23 (Ἰερ. 36:23); Ez. 16:32; 23:37; Mk. 10:12 (ἐὰν αὐτὴ ἀπολύσασα τὸν ἄνδρα αὐτῆς γαμήσῃ ἄλλον μοιχᾶται).

μοιχεία, "adultery," "illicit intercourse," Lys., 1, 36; Plat. Resp., IV, 443a; Leg., VIII, 839a; astrologically. P, Tebt., II, 276, 16 (2nd/3rd. cent. A.D.): ἡ Ἀφροδίτ]η παρατυγχάνουσα τῷ τοῦ ["Αρεως πορ]νίας <καὶ> μοιχείας κατίσ[τ]ησιν, Venus in conjunction with Mars causes fornication and adultery. In the LXX for נאף (Hos. 4:2), נִאֻפִים (Jer. 13:27) and נַאֲפוּפִים (Hos. 2:4); also Wis. 14:26. In the NT Mt. 15:19: μοιχεῖαι (along with πορνεῖαι); Mk. 7:22; Jn. 8:3 (ἐπὶ μοιχείᾳ κατειλημμένην).

μοιχός, "adulterer," "lover," Aristoph. Pl., 168; Lys., 1, 30; Soph. Fr., 1026, 6 (Nock); Plat. Symp., 191d; P. Oxy., VIII, 1160, 26 f. (3rd/4th cent.). In the LXX for נֹאֵף, Job 24:15; Prv. 6:32; מְנָאֵף, ψ 49:18; Is. 57:3; Jer. 23:10; Sir. 25:2. In the NT Lk. 18:11; 1 C. 6:9; Hb. 13:4.

μοιχαλίς, first adj. "adulterous," Plut. Plac. Philos., I, 7 (II, 881d), then subst. "adulteress," "mistress," "harlot," P. Masp., 94, II, 42 (6th cent.). In the LXX and NT lit., Prv. 30:20; Hos. 3:1 (both times for מְנָאָפֶת); R. 7:3; 2 Pt. 2:14; also fig. for the unfaithfulness of Israel to its Husband, Yahweh: Ez. 16:38; 23:45 (נֹאֶפֶת); Mal. 3:5 (מְנָאֵף); Mt. 12:39; 16:4; Mk. 8:38; Jm. 4:4 (→ 734, 41 ff.).

B. Adultery in the Old Testament and Judaism.

1. The Decalogue numbers the inviolability of marriage among the fundamental commandments for the community life of the people of Israel, Ex. 20:14(13); Dt. 5:18(17).[2] But adultery is possible only if there is carnal intercourse between a married man and a married or betrothed Israelitess, Dt. 22:22 ff.; Lv. 20:10. Adultery is the violation of the marriage of another, Gn. 39:10 ff. Hence a man is not under obligation to avoid all non-marital intercourse (→ πορνεία). Unconditional fidelity is demanded only of the woman, who in marriage becomes the possession of her husband. The adulterer and the guilty woman, if caught in the act, are to be punished by death (Dt. 22:22), since the covenant with the holy God demands the rooting out of everything evil from within Israel. The punishment is usually stoning (Dt. 22:22; Ez. 16:40; cf. Jn. 8:5).[3] If there is suspicion against a wife, the husband can demand that she be purified from it by the ceremony of bitter water, Nu. 5:16 ff.[4] But the husband is not forced to take steps against her, cf. Mt. 1:19.

---

[1] Bl.-Debr. § 101, p. 59; J. Wackernagel, *Hellenistica* (1907), 7 ff.

[2] LXX B etc. put the 7th commandment before the 6th, cf. Εξ. 20:13; Δτ. 5:17; cf. also Philo Decal., 51, 121, 168-170; Spec. Leg., III, 8; also R. 13:9; Jm. 2:11 and many fathers, though Mt. 5:21, 27; 19:18 follow the Heb. Zn. Mt., 598, n. 65; Zn. R., 563, n. 82; Dib. Jk., 137.

[3] Cf. Lv. 20:10 ff., more lenient against a slave (Lv. 19:20 ff.), more severe against a priest's daughter (burning, Lv. 21:9; Jos. Ant., 4, 248, καιέσθω ζῶσα). In the Mishnah strangling is the penalty for adultery, Sanh., 11, 1 → n. 7; Saalschütz, 463 f., 570 ff.

[4] Stade-Bertholet, II, 49 f.; B. Stade, ZAW, 15 (1895), 166 ff.; Jos. Ant., 3, 270 ff.; Strabo, 16, 773.

2. Hosea, who depicts the relation of Yahweh to His people in terms of his own experience, views this relation as a marriage (2:21 f.) and thereby emphasises the exclusive loyalty which Israel owes its God, to whom it belongs as does the wife to her husband. By its apostasy to alien cults Israel is guilty of adultery against God. The religious unfaithfulness of Israel is thereby stigmatised as the most serious conceivable offence (3:1 f.; 2:4 ff.). The worship of high places is religious adultery (4:12 ff.).[5] Jeremiah, engaged in serious conflict with the admixture of worship of Yahweh with alien elements (Baal, star worship), makes further use of the metaphor of Hosea in 2:1; 5:7; 9:1. Israel breaks the marriage bond, by which it belongs to God alone, to flirt with wood and stone (3:8 f.). Faithless Jerusalem will bear the punishment of an adulteress (13:22, 26 f.). In exile Ez. applies Hosea's figure of speech to the religious history of Israel (c. 16; 23). By apostasy to alien cults Israel both past and present has soiled itself with whoring and adultery (16:32, 37; 23:37, 43, 45).[6]

3. The many warnings against fornication (→ πορνεία) and adultery in the Wisdom literature show that marital infidelity was common. The adulterer violates the law of God and also attacks the rights of God, before whom his marriage was concluded (Prv. 2:16 ff., cf. Mal. 2:14). He will undoubtedly suffer punishment (Prv. 6:26 ff.). He is a fool who brings ruin on himself (v. 32). He brings down on himself suffering and shame (v. 32 f.). The anger of the jealous husband will not spare him (v. 34 f.). One should be on guard against the smooth enticement of the strange woman (7:5 ff.), who after the act treats it with frivolity (30:20). One should also be on guard against wine, which kindles adulterous desire (23:31 ff.) and robs a man of prudence (v. 34 ff.). Sir. depicts the serious sin of the adulteress. She does threefold wrong by disobeying the command of God, sinning against her husband and bearing to another the children of adultery. She will be put out of the congregation and her children must expiate her sin. Particularly offensive is the adulterous old man (25:2). In Test. XII Joseph is a model of chastity who resists the temptation to adultery as something which is against God (Test. Jos. 4:6; 5:1) and who overcomes unlawful sexual desire by prayer and fasting (4:8).

Philo describes adultery as μέγιστον ἀδικημάτων (Decal., 121); it is στυγητὸν καὶ θεομίσητον πρᾶγμα (131). The adulterer fills three families with ὕβρις and ἀτιμία (126, 129). The source of adultery is φιληδονία (122). Not merely the body, but esp. the soul is corrupted by it (124). By his transgression the adulterer sows a blameworthy seed (129), though procreation as such is sacred to the Jew.

4. The Mishnah (esp. tractate Sota) and Talmud give more precise legal definitions of the act and the punishment. So far as possible they seek to evade the death penalty. Only adultery with an Israelitess is to be punished. There is no penalty for intercourse with the wife of a non-Israelite. Adultery can only be by adults. There is no penalty if there is no preceding warning and no witness.[7] Only the wife, who is set apart for

---

[5] Eichr. Theol. AT, I, 127 ff.; H. Schmidt, "Die Ehe d. Hosea," ZAW, 42 (1924), 245 ff.; A. Allwohn, "Die Ehe d. Propheten Hosea in psychoanalytischer Beleuchtung," ZAW *Beih.*, 44 (1926); F. Heiler, *Das Gebet* (1920), 331 ff.

[6] Some passages hover between a lit. and fig. sense, cf. Jer. 23:10, 14; 13:27; Is. 57:3; Hos. 4:14; 7:4.

[7] Cf. Str.-B., I, 295; S. Lv., 10 ("If a man commits adultery with the wife of a man, with the wife of his neighbour, both adulterer and adulteress are to be put to death"): " 'If a man' — this excludes a minor; 'with the wife of a man' — this excludes the wife of a minor (not yet 9 years and a day old); 'commits adultery with the wife of his neighbour' — this excludes the wife of another (a non-Israelite); 'are to be put to death,' namely, by strangling. You say: By strangling, and not by one of the death penalties to be found in the Torah? I say: Go and see! No penalty mentioned in the Torah without more precise

her husband alone by the ceremony of *qiddušin* (→ μνηστεύω), and not the husband, who has behind him the ancient right of polygamy, is exposed to the full threat of the penalties. In the Roman period the death penalty drops away.[8] The husband is simply forced to divorce an adulterous wife, who forfeits the money assigned her under the marriage contract (Sota, IV, 3), and is not permitted to marry her lover (Sota, 5, 1). Divorce is sufficient protection against an adulterous wife. In Rabb. exposition the ceremony of bitter water acquires an essentially moral sense. The wife must be forced to confess her fault. It is effective only if the husband is free from guilt (bSota, 47b). Hence the ceremony gradually disappears. The child of incest or adultery is called *mamzer,* and cannot be a member of the community (Dt. 23:3) or marry an Israelite (Qid., 3, 12).

Along with these legal definitions there are in the Haggadic parts of the Talmud and Midrash many warnings against adultery which oppose this as a serious sin from the moral standpoint, and which warn against any yielding to sensual desire. In contrast to the legal judgment, the sinful thought is repeatedly equated with the act, e.g., Pesikt. r., 24 (124b): "We find that even he who commits adultery with the eyes is called an adulterer, *v.* Job 24:15." "He who regards a woman with lustful intention is as one who cohabits with her ..." "He who touches the little finger of a woman is as one who touches a certain spot," Tract. Kalla, 1.[9] Cf. jChalla, 58c, 48 f. (Str.-B., I, 301). The adulterer is deeply despised. No virtues can save him from hell-fire (Sota, 4b).

C. Adultery in the Greek and Roman World.

A mark of the ancient view of marriage is that unconditional fidelity is demanded of the wife alone. The married man is not forbidden to have intercourse with an unmarried woman.[10] In Gk. law μοιχεία is simply "secret sexual intercourse with a free woman without the consent of her κύριος."[11] In face of such violation (ὕβρις) the husband or family (father, brother, son) has the right of private revenge (by killing,[12] maltreatment[13] or fine[14]). In practice the laws were extended to cover a girl of good repute or a widow.[15] The open harlot was not covered by the law of revenge.[16] Public law limited the right of revenge (seizure in the act).[17] Attic law allows a complaint to be lodged (γραφὴ μοιχείας) if private revenge is waived.[18] If the wounded husband is

---

definition is to be expounded so as to make it more severe, but rather so as to make it lighter." M. Ex. 20:14 (77b): "'Thou shalt not commit adultery.' Why does it say this? When it is said in Lv. 20:10 that both adulterer and adulteress are to be put to death, we have the penalty but not the warning. Hence the Scripture says instructively in Ex. 20:14: 'Thou shalt not commit adultery' (to pronounce the warning)." Cf. also Str.-B., I, 295 ff.

[8] Acc. to bSanh., 41a it was done away 40 yrs. before the destruction of Jerusalem. Later whipping is mentioned as a penalty, cf. Jew. Enc., I, 216 ff. Acc. to Sota, 9, 9, the water of cursing was also done away by R. Jochanan b. Zakkai when adultery flourished. Cf. Str.-B., III, 109 f., e.g., bJeb., 37b.

[9] Str.-B., I, 299; cf. Kittel Probleme, 99; Schl. Theol. d. Judt., 165 ff.

[10] Cf. Ps.-Demosth. Or., 59, 122 (Stob. Ecl., IV, 497, 15 ff.): τὰς μὲν γὰρ ἑταίρας ἡδονῆς ἕνεκα ἔχομεν, τὰς <δὲ> παλλακὰς τῆς καθ' ἡμέραν θεραπείας τοῦ σώματος, τὰς δὲ γυναῖκας τοῦ παιδοποιεῖσθαι γνησίως καὶ τῶν ἔνδον φύλακα πιστὴν ἔχειν.

[11] Latte, 2446.

[12] Aeschin. Or., 1, 91; Demosth. Or., 23, 53.

[13] Through the so-called ῥαφανίδωσις, Aristoph. Nu., 1083; Latte.

[14] Hom. Od., 8, 332: μοιχάγρια. Ps.-Demosth. Or., 59, 65. City law of Gortyna, Gt. Inscr., II, 20 ff. (J. Kohler-E. Ziebarth, *Das Stadtrecht von Gortyn* [1912], 5).

[15] Terentius (ed. A. Fleckeisen [1898]) Eunuchus, V, 4, 35 (957).

[16] Ps.-Demosth. Or., 59, 67.

[17] Luc. Eun., 10; Demosth. Or., 23, 53; Lys., 1, 30; Aristot. Ath. (ed. F. Blass-T. Thalheim), 57, 3.

[18] Poll. Onom., 8, 40 f.

not himself to fall victim to ἀτιμία he must put away the guilty wife. The adulteress is not allowed to visit the public temple.[19] The best men judged adultery sharply.[20] Plato warns against intercourse with the ἑταίρα, though his words show that this was more or less taken for granted on the common view.[21]

In Roman law up to the time of the Republic the husband has, in a case of *adulterium,*[22] the one-sided right of private revenge against the guilty wife even to putting to death, whereas the wife must accept the adultery of her husband.[23] The father can also put the adulterer to death if he at once strikes down his daughter too.[24] The punishment of adultery is thus a family affair (*iudicium domesticum*).[25] Only the increasing moral disintegration of the imperial period led to legal measures by the state. Augustus passed the Lex Julia de Adulteriis.[26] This declares adultery a penal offence, punishes offenders by banishment and forbids the husband to pardon or to quash the matter. He may be punished himself if he continues the marriage.[27] The law was not followed by an improvement of the situation. This was poor. Divorces were very common.[28] Plays,[29] banquets (→ ἀσέλγεια)[30] and slavery[31] contributed to moral deterioration. The infidelity of wives was almost an accepted fact.[32]

D. The Word Group in the New Testament.

1. In the Literal Sense. A mark of the NT is the sharp intensifying of the concept of adultery. The right of a man to sexual freedom is denied. Like the wife, the husband is under an obligation of fidelity. The wife is exalted to the same dignity as the husband. Marriage (→ γαμέω, I, 648 ff.) is a life-long fellowship of the partners. Only thus does it actualise the ideal intended in creation (Mt. 5:32; 19:8). On this ground Jesus rejects the provisions of the Law and the scribes concerning divorce of the wife under the legal form of a bill of divorcement (Dt. 24:1 → ἀπολύω, ἀποστάσιον). This is in conflict with the will of God (Mt. 19:6 ff.). For this reason the remarriage of a man after divorcing his wife, or the remarrying of the divorced woman, is tantamount to adultery (Mt. 5:32; 19:9; Mk. 10:11 f.; Lk. 16:18; cf. 1 C. 7:10 f.).[33] From the religious standpoint

---

19 Ps.-Demosth. Or., 59, 87; Aeschin. Or., 1, 183.

20 Isoc. Nikokl., 40 f.; Aristot. Pol., VIII, 16, p. 1335b, 38 ff.

21 Leg., VIII, 838e ff.

22 The older derivation of *adulterare* from *ad alteram* (*se conferre*) is not certain; more likely is derivation from **ad-alterare,* "to falsify," "to corrupt"; A. Walde-J. B. Hofmann, *Lat. etym. Wörterb.,* I³ (1938), 15 [Debrunner].

23 Cato in Gellius Noct. Att., 10, 23, 5: *in adulterio uxorem tuam si prehendisses, sine judicio impune necares; illa te, si adulterares ... digito non auderet contingere, neque jus est.*

24 C. G. Bruns, *Fontes Juris Romani Antiqui*⁷ (1909), 112: [*Lex permittit*] *ut is pater eum adulterum sine fraude occidat, ita ut in continenti filiam occidat.*

25 Girard, 185; Dion. Hal. Ant. Rom., II, 25; Suet. Caes. (Tib.), 35.

26 Girard, 175, 185; Bruns, 112; Suet. Caes. (Aug.), 34; Dio C., 54, 30, 4.

27 Girard, 185.

28 Sen. Ben., III, 16, 2: Women count the years, not by the consuls, but by their husbands; Friedländer, I, 283 ff.

29 Tert. Spect., 25; Cl. Al. Paed., III, 11, 76: ἀναμὶξ ἀνδρῶν καὶ γυναικῶν συνιόντων ἐπὶ τὴν ἀλλήλων θέαν.

30 Plut. Quaest. Conv., VII, 8, 4 (II, 712e f).

31 Plut. Praec. Coniug., 16 (II, 140b); Friedländer, I, 283 ff.

32 Mart., IV, 71.

33 The addition, in Mt. only, of παρεκτὸς λόγου πορνείας (5:32; μὴ ἐπὶ πορνείᾳ, 19:9), is not original acc. to the par., but is based on later Church law, Bultmann Trad., 140; M. Dibelius, *Formgeschichte d. Ev.*² (1933), 249; cf. *ad loc.* E. v. Dobschütz, ZNW, 29 (1928), 344; Kl. Mt., 46 and 154 f.; Kl. Mk., 112 f.; A. Merx, *Die 4 kanon. Ev.,* II, 1 (1902), 94; Schl. Mt., 179 f., 572; Zn. Mt., 241 f.; → πορνεία.

adultery does not consist merely in physical intercourse with a strange woman; it is present already in the desire which negates fidelity (Mt. 5:28). In distinction from the scribes, who as lawyers give definitions and relativise the divine commandment by assimilating it to the actualities of life, Jesus as a religious teacher tries to make men realise how absolute is the divine requirement. The great seriousness of Jesus in face of the sin of adultery goes hand in hand with His mercy for the sinner and His resolute rejection of hypocritical self-righteousness, as is shown by the story of the woman taken in adultery (Jn. 8:1 ff.) which, even if it does not belong originally to Jn., rests on an authentic tradition.[34] Against a purely legal view, on which a woman taken in the act (8:4) undoubtedly came under the death penalty, He maintains a moral and religious position. He disarms the human desire to punish — the witness had to cast the first stone — by appealing to the judgment of conscience. He grants the guilty woman a pardon which does not sap the moral demand because it presupposes repentance (cf. Mt. 21:31 f.). He preserves the unconditional validity of the sacred command of God by adding the warning to sin no more (Jn. 8:11).

The apostolic preaching presupposes the holy seriousness of Jesus in the assessment of adultery. Christian determination was the more significant at this point in view of the degeneration of sexual morality in the Hellenistic world, which regarded offences in this sphere as quite natural (1 C. 5:2) and accepted quasi-marital relations as no less ethically possible than marriage (→ 732). By contrast, it was most significant, both religiously and culturally, that the apostolic message from the very outset made it clear to the churches that the full marital fidelity of both spouses is an unconditional divine command (1 C. 5:1 ff.; 6:9). Adultery is not just a matter of civil law (R. 7:3). It is to be judged in accordance with the holy will of God (1 Th. 4:3; 1 C. 6:18 f.). Women are fellow-heirs of the kingdom of God and are thus worthy of the same honour as men (1 Pt. 3:7). According to the absolute judgment of Paul, adultery excludes from God's kingdom (1 C. 6:9). Marital fidelity is to be maintained intact (ἡ κοίτη ἀμίαντος, Hb. 13:4), even though there are no human witnesses. The omniscient God is the Judge of the adulterer (*loc. cit.*). The OT prohibition of adultery is not confined to the negative avoidance of the sinful act. It finds it true fulfilment only in the love of spouses who are joined together by God (R. 13:9).[35] Impulsive and uncontrolled desire is sinful even in the lustful glance (2 Pt. 2:14). It is a mark of the inwardly impious and licentious nature of bold heretics, who in doubting the *parousia* (3:3 f.) also undermine belief in the divine judgment (3:5 ff.).

2. In the Figurative Sense. The NT, too, uses μοιχεύειν fig. for religious unfaithfulness to God. Thus Jesus calls the evil generation of His time γενεὰ πονηρὰ καὶ μοιχαλίς (Mt. 12:39; 16:4; Mk. 8:38 alongside ἁμαρτωλός). Like the people in the days of the prophets, it shows itself to be unfaithful to God by its rejection of Jesus. In Jm. 4:4, too, the sharp term μοιχαλίδες refers to the religious unfaithfulness to God implied in φιλία τοῦ κόσμου. The feminine seems to be chosen because God is seen as the Husband (→ 731).[36] The adultery with

[34] Bau. J., 111 ff.; Zn. J., 723 ff.

[35] Warnings against adultery are rare in Paul because he usually issues sexual admonitions in terms of the broader term → πορνεία.

[36] There is an even smoother explanation of the fem. if one accepts the thesis of A. Meyer, *Das Rätsel des Jk.* (1930), 264 that behind the warning are the symbolical figures of the wives of Jacob, Rachel and Leah, whose ambitious and unscrupulous desire for children is an expression of the love of the world which despises God.

the prophetess mentioned in Rev. 2:2 is also a figure for acceptance of her false teaching and the implied infidelity to God. The τέκνα of this adulterous relation are the followers of the prophetess.

Hauck

† μόλις, † μόγις

"Hardly," "with difficulty." In literature μόλις and μόγις are interchangeable. Hom. uses only μόγις, but both occur in Aesch. and Eur. Soph. has only μόλις, Thuc., Aristoph. and Plat. prefer μόγις, Xenoph., Demosth. and Aristot. μόλις. In B.C. pap.,[1] with a few exceptions in the 3rd cent., we find only μόλις.[2] Then μόγις becomes more common again. The LXX usually has μόλις; μόγις occurs only twice at Wis. 9:16 AS; 3 Macc. 7:6. μόλις is also more common in the NT, 7 times, μόγις twice at Lk. 9:39 (B μόλις, hence Nestle) and Ac. 14:18 D. It is thus apparent that μόλις is more favoured than μόγις. μόλις is popular, μόγις is taken to be Attic.[3]

There is no Heb. equivalent. It is used in the LXX only in Prv., Wis., Sir. and 3 Macc. in the sense of "hardly." In Wis. 9:16 it corresponds to μετὰ πόνου. The word has the same meaning in the NT ("hardly" in Lk. 9:39; R. 5:7; 1 Pt. 4:18 quoting Prv. 11:31; "with difficulty" in Ac. 14:18; 27:7, 8, 16).

Only R. 5:7 and 1 Pt. 4:18 are of theological significance. R. 5:7 runs as follows: μόλις γὰρ ὑπὲρ δικαίου τις ἀποθανεῖται. V. 7 is a parenthetical note. Paul wants to emphasise the extraordinary nature of the death of Jesus. To set the unique sacrifice of Christ in its true light, he stresses the fact that in ordinary life it is unlikely that any would give himself for a righteous man.[4] But when he has said this, Paul feels compelled to make a reservation. It is not quite right that no one would sacrifice his life for another. Someone might die for the good.[5] But it is ruled out altogether than any would offer his life for the ungodly. This, however, is what Christ has done.

1 Pt. 4:18 is a quotation from Prv. 11:31 LXX: καὶ εἰ ὁ δίκαιος μόλις σῴζεται, ὁ ἀσεβὴς καὶ ἁμαρτωλὸς ποῦ φανεῖται; In the Hebrew[6] the saying applies to recompense in this life, but the author uses it of recompense in the last judgment.

μόλις κτλ. [1] The pap. refs. are listed in Mayser, I, 17, n. 1 and I², 3, 120, 6 ff.; cf. also I, 188 and Preisigke Wört., *s.v.*

[2] Cf. on this F. Solmsen, *Beiträge z. griech. Wortforschung* (1909), 169 f.

[3] Cf. Luc. Schol., 28, 21 (ed. H. Rabe [1906]); also Helladius in Phot. Bibliotheca (MPG, 103), 530a, 38 ff. Cf. G. Crönert, Memoria Graeca Herculanensis (1913), 98, n. 2; Bl.-Debr. § 33. The etym. of μόλις and μόγις is uncertain, *v.* Solmsen, 169 and 171 and H. Osthoff, *Zur Gesch. d. Perf. im Indogermanischen* (1884), 450, n. 1.

[4] Cf. on this Schl. R., 181: "But only rarely in special circumstances may it happen that a righteous man is so highly estimated that one will be prepared to die to save him."

[5] Ltzm. R., 59 takes a different view of the statements about the sacrifice of life for the righteous and good man; he detects two thoughts which are par. in so far as they set the act of Christ in v. 6 in a proper light, but in the strict sense cancel out one another.

[6] The LXX is an incorrect rendering of the Heb., which runs: "Behold, the righteous is recompensed in the land, much more the wicked and the sinner." Cf. on 1 Pt. 4:18 Sir. 26:29: μόλις ἐξελεῖται ἔμπορος ἀπὸ πλημμελείας.

The reference of the section in which v. 18 stands is to the sufferings of Christians, which are regarded as the fiery glow and beginning of judgment. They make great demands on Christians and above all represent a great temptation. Only with great difficulty will Christians pass through this hard time and stand in the divine judgment. The author wants to spur his readers on to faithfulness and to show them the seriousness of their responsibility.[7]

J. Schneider

† μολύνω, † μολυσμός

μολύνω.

a. "To soil," "to smear," with dirt, e.g., of pigs τῷ πηλῷ μολύνοντες ... ἑαυτούς, Aristot. Hist. An., VII, 18, p. 571b, 18; Epict. Diss., IV, 11, 10 (with πηλοῦσθαι of the feet), Plat. Resp., VII, 535e (ὥσπερ θηρίον ὕειον ἐν ἀμαθίᾳ μολύνηται). μολύνειν thus differs from the original sense of the synon. → μιαίνειν "to paint." It is used esp. of sexual defilement, Procl. Ad Hesiodi Opera et Dies, 733 (T. Gaisford, Poetae Graeci Minores, II [1823], 395, 34): μεμολυσμένον ἀπὸ γονῆς; Artemid., II, 26, p. 121, 6 f.: εἰ δὲ αὐτός τις ἑαυτὸν μολύνειν δόξειε κατὰ τῶν σκελῶν ἀφείς. Suid. (ed. Adler, II, p. 52), *s.v.* Διαγνώμων: τοὺς μολυσμοὺς τῆς φύσεως. b. Censoriously, in the religious and moral sphere, "to defile." Plut. Superst., 3 (II, 166b): τὴν ἑαυτῶν γλῶσσαν διαστρέφοντας καὶ μολύνοντας; Epict. Diss., II, 8, 13: μολύνων (sc. the God in us) ἀκαθάρτοις μὲν διανοήμασι, ῥυπαραῖς δὲ πράξεσι. The word is rare in the LXX.[1] It is used a. lit. of the feet in Cant. 5:3 (טָנַף), clothes in Gn. 37:31 (טבל); Is. 59:3 (ni גאל). b. Fig. of cultic defilement, Jer. 23:11 (חָנֵף) of a profaned priest, Is. 65:4 (פִּגּוּל) of a vessel defiled by unclean food, Zech. 14:2 (שׁגל) of the ravishing of women, Ez. 7:17; 21:12 (הָלַךְ).[2] In the apocr. of physical soiling in Sir. 13:1 (pitch) and cultic desecration in Tob 3:15 (the name of God), 1 Εσδρ. 8:80 (the land), Macc. 1:37; 2 Macc. 6:2 (the sanctuary of God); 14:3 (μεμολυσμένος ἐν τοῖς τῆς ἀμιξίας χρόνοις, of participating in what is pagan); of moral staining in Sir. 22:13; 21:28 (ὁ ψιθυρίζων); cf. Test. A. 4:4 (τὴν ψυχὴν μολυνεῖ).

μολύνω occurs three times in the NT in the sense of religious and cultic defilement. In 1 C. 8:7 contact with what is pagan (εἰδωλόθυτον) means defilement of conscience for the weak in faith. The two passages in Rev. (3:4: ἃ οὐκ ἐμόλυναν τὰ ἱμάτια αὐτῶν, and 14:4: οὗτοί εἰσιν οἳ μετὰ γυναικῶν οὐκ ἐμολύνθησαν· παρθένοι γάρ εἰσιν) are inter-related. 14:4 refers to all the members of the community (14:1). Hence it cannot imply just sexual continence in the ascetic

---

[7] Wbg. 1 Pt.[3] (1923), 141 translates μόλις "with great difficulty." J. H. Usteri, *Wissenschaftl. u. praktischer Komm. zu 1 Pt.* (1887), 203 has a similar rendering. Cf. also E. Kühl (Meyer's Komm., XII, 6[6] [1897], 273; v. Soden (H. J. Holtzmann, *Hand-Komm. z. NT*, III, 2[3] [1899]), 164: "with difficulty"; F. Hauck, *NT Deutsch*, 10, 72: "hardly"; also W. Michaelis, *Das NT*, II (1935), 423.

μ ο λ ύ ν ω. Trench, 104.

[1] 10 times in the canonical writings for 8 Heb. equivalents, and 8 times in the Apocr.

[2] Cf. A. B. Ehrlich, *Randglossen z. hbr. Bibel* (1912) on Ez. 7:17.

sense. On the other hand, μολύνω cannot mean only sexual transgression, for the subject παρθένοι would rule out those that are married in the community. In both places the οὐ μολύνειν is surely a symbolical expression for the faithfulness which has been maintained by the community, the bride (2 C. 11:2: παρθένον ἁγνὴν παραστῆσαι τῷ Χριστῷ), to its Bridegroom, Christ[3] (→ I, 486).

† μολυσμός.

"Defilement" (→ μολύνειν), physical, Plut. Maxime cum principibus Viris Philosopho esse disserendum, 4 (II, 779c) εὗρε Διονύσιον ὥσπερ βιβλίον παλίψηστον ἤδη μολυσμῶν ἀνάπλεων. Suid. (→ 736): τοὺς μολυσμοὺς τῆς φύσεως, cultic, Jos. Ap., I, 289; religious and moral, Ep. Ar., 106 (μιανθέντες ... τῷ τῆς ἀσεβείας μολυσμῷ); Test. S. 2:13 (with φθόνου). In the LXX only Jer. 23:15 (חֲנֻפָּה, unfaithfulness to God); 1 Εσδρ. 8:80 (τῶν ἀλλογενῶν); 2 Macc. 5:27, of defilement with what is pagan.

It occurs in the NT only at 2 C. 7:1: καθαρίσωμεν ἀπὸ παντὸς μολυσμοῦ σαρκὸς καὶ πνεύματος ἐπιτελοῦντες ἁγιωσύνην ἐν φόβῳ θεοῦ. As one would expect in the NT, the reference is to the moral defilement entailed by sharing a pagan way of life. The term is chosen in order to correspond to the earlier demand (6:14 ff.) for separation from everything pagan.

Hauck

μομφή → 572, 573.
μονή → 579 ff.

† μονογενής

A. The Usage outside the New Testament.

The word does not occur in Homer but is attested from the time of Hesiod.[1] In compounds like διο-γενής, γη-γενής, εὐ-γενής, συγ-γενής the -γενής suggests

[3] Cf. C. Rückert, Theol. Quart., 68 (1886), 391 ff.; 69 (1887), 105 ff.: "Die Begriffe παρθένος u. ἀπαρχή in Apk. 14:4, 5"; Zn. Apk., 515 f.; Had. Apk., 150. Bss. Apk., 381, on the other hand, favours Christian ascetics (cf. Mt. 19:12; Aug. Sct. Virg., 27), cf. also Loh. Apk., 120: οὐκ ἐμολύνθησαν need refer only to avoidance of licentiousness, but παρθένοι means full sexual abstinence, cf. 1 C. 7:1, 8.

μολυσμός. Trench, 104.

μονογενής. Pr.-Bauer[3], Liddell-Scott, Cr.-Kö., *s.v.* Bau. J.; Zn. J.; Bultmann J.; H. J. Holtzmann, *Theol. d. NT*, II (1897), 436-441.

[1] The absence from Hom. may be due to the fact that it does not fit the hexameter. Parm. and Hes. use the form μουνογενής in the hexameter, and in Hom. we find μοῦνος for μόνος. There is a fem. μο(υ)νογένεια in poetry, Apoll. Rhod., 3, 847; Orph. (Abel), 29, 2; also Procl. in Tim., 31 (ed. E. Diehl, I [1903], p. 457). Oppian Halieutica (ed. F. S. Lehrs, Poetae Bucolici et Didactici [1862], 3, 489 codd.; IG 9 (2), 305 (Tricca, 2nd cent. B.C.); Suppl. Epigr., 4, 634 (Sardes, 1st cent. B.C.) also have μο(υ)νόγονος in the sense of μονογενής. On the accent cf. Debr. Griech. Wortb. § 155.

derivation (γένος) rather than birth. Nouns as the first part of the compound give the source, e.g., from Zeus, the earth. Adverbs describe the nature of the derivation, e.g., noble or common. μονο-γενής is to be explained along the lines of εὐγενής rather than διο-γενής. The μονο- does not denote the source [2] but the nature of derivation. Hence μονογενής means "of sole descent," i.e., without brothers or sisters. This gives us the sense of only-begotten. [3] The ref. is to the only child of one's parents, primarily in relation to them. μονογενής is stronger than μόνος, for it denotes that they have never had more than this child. [4] But the word can also be used more generally without ref. to derivation in the sense of "unique," "unparalleled," "incomparable," though one should not confuse the refs. to class or species [5] and to manner. [6]

The LXX uses μονογενής for יָחִיד, e.g., Ju. 11:34, where it means the only child; cf. also Tob. 3:15; 6:11 (BA), 15 (S); 8:17; Bar. 4:16 vl. This rendering is also found in ψ 21:20; 34:17, where יְחִידָתִי is par. to נַפְשִׁי and the ref. is to the uniqueness of the

---

[2] "Deriving from one alone" would be meaningless.

[3] "Only-begotten" comes from the Lat. *unigenitus,* which is a rendering of μονογενής, cf. *uni-cornis* for μονοκέρως. Compounds with *soli-* (*soli-loquium* for μονολογία) are rare in Lat.; those with *uni* (*uni-vira*) are more common. In Gk. those with μονο- are very numerous and those with ἑνι- and ἑνο- are rare. With *unigenitus* we also find *unigena* (cf. *indigena, terrigena* = γηγενής). For Paulinus of Nola Christ is *unigena* (Carm., 5, 46), and for Cicero the world is *singularis hic mundus atque unigena* (Tim., 4 § 12) (in both cases for μονογενής).

[4] Aesch. Ag., 898 : μονογονὲς τέκνον πατρί, Plat. Critias, 113d; Hes. Op., 376; Theog., 426; Hdt., VII, 221; Antoninus Liberalis (ed. E. Martini, Mythographi Graeci, II [1896]), 32, 1. It is often a predicate of the gods in this sense, cf. the catena in Bau. J. on 1:14 and Bultmann J., 47, n. 2.

[5] Parm. in his description of being says : "because unbegotten, incorruptible, whole (not in parts), unique (μουνογενές), and without end." One cannot use "only-begotten" here, because it is unbegotten, and Parm. is certainly not thinking in terms of a γένος to which being belongs. Plat. Tim., 31b : διὰ ταῦτα οὔτε δύο οὔτε ἀπείρους ἐποίησεν ὁ ποιῶν κόσμους, ἀλλ' εἷς ὅδε μονογενὴς οὐρανὸς γεγονὼς ἔστιν καὶ ἔτ' ἔσται, uses μονογενής with εἷς ὅδε to strengthen the εἷς, so that the sense is "one and only." The meaning is not that this heaven is unique in kind. Procl. (→ n. 1) takes μονογενής in the sense of unique. For further instances of the use in cosmological speculations cf. Bultmann J., 48. In the magic pap. μονογενής often occurs in invocation of the deity, Preisigke Sammelbuch, 4324, 15 : ἐν τῷ οὐρανῷ θεός, ὁ μονογενής, R. Wünsch, *Antike Fluchtafeln*[2] (1912), 4, 34 : ὁρκίζω σε τὸν θεὸν ... τὸν μονογενῆ τὸν ἐξ αὐτοῦ ἀναφανέντα, Preis. Zaub., IV, 1585 : εἰσάκουσόν μου, ὁ εἷς μονογενής, here in the sense of incomparable or only-begotten, not alone in its kind. In 1 Cl., 25, 2 the fabulous bird, the Phoenix, is μονογονὲς ὑπάρχον, "unique." In Wis. 7:22 the πνεῦμα in wisdom is νοερὸν ἅγιον μονογονές, "intelligible," "holy," "incomparable." μονογενοῦς ἀφ' αἵματος in Eur. Hell., 1685 (doubtful reading, the other is ὁμογενοῦς) means "of one blood." The adv. μονογενῶς (in a way found only once) occurs in Periplus Maris Rubri (ed. H. Frisk [1927]) (1st cent. B.C.), 56, cf. 11: πέπερι μονογενῶς ἐν ἑνὶ τόπῳ (singly in one place) ... γεννώμενον πολύ.

[6] In the -γενής in μονο-γενής and related words the stem is γενεσ- (cf. γένος), Debr. Griech. Wortb. § 140. In accordance with the strict meaning of γένος, -γενής always denotes derivation, cf. the Lat. *unigenitus* from *gigno, genitum,* which takes μονογενής in this way. μονογενής is an exception in its use by grammarians for one gender, Apollon. Dyscol. De Adverbiis (in Grammatici Graeci, I, 1 [1878, ed. R. Schneider]), p. 145, 18 (cf. διγενής, Eustath. Thessal. Comm. in Il., 150, 27 and τριγενής). [This is a later ref. back to the most common type of compounds with adj. and noun, μονο-γενής "of one gender" (γένος = grammatical gender) like λευκώλενος etc. Debrunner.] The later philosophical use of γένος for kind, cf. Plat. Parm., 129c, does not arise in respect of γενής in μονογενής etc. There is no attestation for this sense later, though it has been fostered by the rendering "unique" when the refs. to class and manner are confused, and widespread misunderstanding has been caused (cf. the German *einzigartig*). It is true, of course, that μονογενής does not always carry a ref. to descent or birth, → n. 5.

soul. The transl. is possible on the basis of the general use of μονογενής for "unique," "unparalleled," "incomparable."[7]

The LXX also renders יָחִיד by ἀγαπητός, Gn. 22:2, 12, 16; Jer. 6:26; Am. 8:10; Zech. 12:10. Hence the question arises how far μονογενής has the sense of "beloved"? Undoubtedly an only child is particularly dear to his parents.[8] One might also say that the ὁ υἱός μου ὁ ἀγαπητός of Mk. 1:11; Mt. 3:17; Lk. 3:22 and Mk. 9:7; Mt. 17:5 is materially close to the ὁ μονογενὴς υἱός of Jn., esp. as the Messianic Son of God is unique and without par. as such. But there is a distinction between ἀγαπητός and μονογενής. It is a mistake to subsume the meaning of the latter under that of the former. μονογενής is not just a predicate of value. If the LXX has different terms for יָחִיד, this is perhaps because different translators were at work. Philo calls the λόγος, not μονογενής, but πρωτόγονος, Conf. Ling., 146 etc. μονογενής is not a significant word for him.[9] Joseph. has μονογενής in the usual sense of "only born."[10] There is a striking use of μονογενής in Ps. Sol. 18:4 : "Thy chastisement comes upon us (in love) as the first born and only begotten son." With this may be compared 4 Esr. 6:58 : "But we, thy people, whom thou hast called the first born, the only begotten, the dearest friend, are given up into their hands." After πρωτότοκος (Ex. 4:22) μονογενής denotes an intensifying. It is most unlikely that the sense here is simply that of ἀγαπητός.

B. The Use in the New Testament.

1. In the NT μονογενής occurs only in Lk., Jn. and Hb., not Mk., Mt. or Pl. It is thus found only in later writings. It means "only-begotten." Thus in Hb. Isaac is the μονογενής of Abraham (11:17), in Lk. the dead man raised up again at Nain is the only son of his mother (7:12), the daughter of Jairus is the only child (8:42), and the demoniac boy is the only son of his father (8:42).[11]

2. Only Jn. uses μονογενής to describe the relation of Jesus to God. Mk. and Mt. have ὁ υἱός μου ὁ ἀγαπητός; Pl. uses τὸν ἑαυτοῦ υἱόν at R. 8:3, τοῦ ἰδίου υἱοῦ at R. 8:32, and πρωτότοκος at R. 8:29; Col. 1:15, 18, but not μονογενής. The further step taken by Jn. to describe Jesus corresponds to the fact that believers who as children of God are called υἱοὶ θεοῦ — the same word as is applied to Jesus — in Mt., Pl. etc., are always called τέκνα θεοῦ in Jn., 1:12; 11:52; 1 Jn.

---

[7] At ψ 24:16 כִּי־יָחִיד וְעָנִי אָנִי is rendered ὅτι μονογενὴς καὶ πτωχός εἰμι ἐγώ. This is an unfortunate transl. based on the mistaken belief that here, too, יָחִיד should be rendered μονογενής. It is incorrect, however, to understand μονογενής in the sense of lonely, like a man without brothers or sisters, with emphasis on the misfortune of being an only child. In ψ 67:6 יָחִיד is transl. μονότροπος (living by oneself, alone, cf. Eur. Andr., 281). ['Α has μονογενής here, cf. Gn. 22:2 (Σ μόνος); Σ Gn. 22:12; 'ΑΣ Jer. 6:26; Prv. 4:3 'ΑΣΘ μονογενής but the LXX ἀγαπώμενος. Philo follows LXX in his quotation of the verse in Ebriet., 84. Bertram.]

[8] Cf. Mk. 12:6 : ἔτι ἕνα εἶχεν υἱὸν ἀγαπητόν.

[9] Following Plato in the Timaeus, Philo calls the world the son of God. He can speak of two sons, the younger and sensual, the older and intelligible, Deus Imm., 30-32. Cf. on this J. Leisegang, *Angelos*, 1 (1925), 27-31, also the notes in his translation, *Schriften d. hell.-jüd. Lit.*, IV (1923), 78 f. Leisegang does not have μονογενής in his Index, presumably because it does not occur. In Ebr., 30 Philo described this world as τὸν μόνον καὶ ἀγαπητὸν αἰσθητὸν υἱόν of God and ἐπιστήμη. Since this expression recurs in Deus Imm., 4 in the form τὸ ἀγαπητὸν καὶ μόνον ... ἔγγονον (the beloved and only progeny, used of Isaac as the son of Abraham), it was presumably Philo's way of stating the NT μονογενής. Jn.'s use of μονογενής thus shows the difference between him and Philo.

[10] Ant., 1, 222 = Gn. 22:2; Ant., 5, 264 = Ju. 11:34, cf. Schl. J., 26. These refs. make it unlikely that Jos. used μονογενής in the sense of unique.

[11] In their par. to Lk. 8:42; 9:38 Mk. and Mt. do not have this added touch of pathos.

3:1, 2, 10; 5:2, while υἱός is reserved for Jesus. Jn. emphasises more strongly the distinction between Jesus and believers and the uniqueness of Jesus in His divine sonship. It is not that Jesus is not unique in this sonship for Mt., Pl. etc. also. His Messiahship proves this. But Jn. puts it in an illuminating and easily remembered formula which was taken up into the baptismal confession and which ever since has formed an inalienable part of the creed of the Church. [12] To μονογενής as a designation of Jesus corresponds the fact that God is the πατὴρ ἴδιος of Jesus, Jn. 5:18; for ἴδιος means to be in a special relation to Jesus which excludes the same relation to others. [13]

μονογενής occurs in Jn. 1:14, 18; 3:16, 18; 1 Jn. 4:9. What is meant is plainest in Jn. 3:16 and 1 Jn. 4:9. Because Jesus is the only Son of God, His sending into the world is the supreme proof of God's love for the world. On the other side, it is only as the only-begotten Son of God that Jesus can mediate life and salvation from perdition. For life is given only in Him, Jn. 5:26. But the fact that He is the only-begotten Son means also that men are obligated to believe in Him, and that they come under judgment, indeed, have done so already, if they withhold faith from Him, 3:18. μονογενής is thus a predicate of majesty. This is true in Jn. 1:18. Here we are to read ὁ μονογενὴς υἱός. [14] As the only-begotten Son Jesus is in the closest intimacy with God. There is no other with whom God can have similar fellowship. He shares everything with this Son. For this reason Jesus can give what no man can give, namely, the fullest possible eye-witness account of God. He knows God, not just from hearsay, but from incomparably close intercourse with Him. In 3:16, 18; 1 Jn. 4:9; 1:18 the relation of Jesus is not just compared to that of an only child to its father. It *is* the relation of the only-begotten to the Father. Similarly in Jn. 1:14: δόξαν ὡς μονογενοῦς παρὰ πατρὸς, His glory is not just compared with that of an only child; it is described as that of the only-begotten Son. Grammatically both interpretations are justifiable. [15] But the total usage of

---

[12] No significance is to be attached to the fact that before Irenaeus μονογενής occurs only in Just. Dial., 105; Mart. Pol., 20, 2; Dg., 10, 2 (Bau. J.[3] on 1:14). Cf. the bibl. in Bultmann J., 47.

[13] Pl. speaks of ὁ ἴδιος υἱός, Jn. of πατὴρ ἴδιος.

[14] The only readings to call for consideration are (1) ὁ μονογενὴς υἱός and (2) μονογενὴς θεός. (1) is attested by the old Syriac, sy^c (no sy^s) sy^h and the Lat., Hipp. (Contra Noetum [MPG, 10], 5), the Lat. fathers from Tert., the Gk. from the 4th cent. The oldest attestation of (2) is in the Valentinians, Iren. Haer., I, 8, 5, Cl. Al., Exc. Theod., 6, 2, later Cl. Al., Orig. etc. Not very clear is the reading of Iren., who has *unigenitus filius* in III, 11, 6; IV, 20, 6, and *unigenitus deus* in IV, 20, 11. Very important is the fact that Hipp. read (1). For this proves that it does not come from the Lat. transl. (1) alone gives a non-artificial sense. υἱός fits best with εἰς τὸν κόλπον τοῦ πατρός. (2) can only mean "an only-begotten God"; to render "an only-begotten, one who is God," is an exegetical invention. It can hardly be credited of Jn., who is distinguished by monumental simplicity of expression. An only-begotten God corresponds to the weakening of monotheism in Gnosticism. It derives from this, and came into the Egyptian texts by way of its influence on the theology of Alexandria. The original was preserved in the Western text (cf. also 1:13). On this whole matter cf. the exhaustive discussion of the tradition in Zn. J., 703 ff. and Bultmann J., 55 f., who also supports (1). W. Bauer's preference for (2) corresponds to his attempt to relate John's Gospel as closely as possible to Gnosticism.

[15] Though ὡς can introduce a comparison, it can also introduce a solid fact, cf. Mt. 14:5: ὡς προφήτην, which does not mean "like a prophet" (which he is not), but "as one of the prophets" (because he is one), R. 1:21: οὐχ ὡς θεόν ἐδόξασαν, not: "They have not worshipped him as a god," but: "They have not worshipped him as the God he is," R. 3:7: ὡς ἁμαρτωλὸς κρίνομαι, "as a sinner," 1 C. 3:1; 4:1; 7:25; 8:7; Hb. 3:5, 6. It makes no difference that the ὡς μονογενοῦς in Jn. 1:14 has no article. In all the verses in which ὡς introduces a fact the noun is without article, cf. esp. Hb. 3:6: ὡς υἱός, "as the Son he is."

μονογενής is very emphatically against taking ὡς μονογενοῦς as a mere comparison.

In Jn. 1:14, 18; 3:16, 18; 1 Jn. 4:9 μονογενής denotes more than the uniqueness or incomparability of Jesus. In all these verses He is expressly called the Son, and He is regarded as such in 1:14. In Jn. μονογενής denotes the origin of Jesus. He is μονογενής as the only-begotten.

What Jn. means by ὁ μονογενὴς υἱός in detail can be known in its full import only in the light of the whole of John's proclamation. For ὁ μονογενὴς υἱός is simply a special form of ὁ υἱὸς τοῦ θεοῦ. When Jn. speaks of the Son of God, he has primarily in view the man Jesus Christ, though not exclusively the man, but also the risen and pre-existent Lord. The relation of the pre-existent Lord to God is that of Son to Father. This comes out indisputably in 17:5, 24. Jesus is aware that He was with God, and was loved by Him, and endued with glory, before the foundation of the world. This is personal fellowship with God, divine sonship. It is true that neither in the prologue, nor 8:58, nor c. 17 does Jn. use the term "son" for the pre-existent Lord. But He describes His relation to God as that of a son. [16] To maintain that in Jn. the pre-existent Lord is only the Word, and that the Son is only the historical and risen Lord, [17] is to draw too sharp a line between the pre-existence on the one side and the historical and post-historical life on the other. In Jn. the Lord is always the Son. Because He alone was God's Son before the foundation of the world, because the whole love of the Father is for Him alone, because He alone is one with God, because the title God may be ascribed to Him alone, He is the only-begotten Son of God.

It is not wholly clear whether μονογενής in Jn. denotes also the birth or begetting from God; it probably does, Jn. calls Jesus ὁ γεννηθεὶς ἐκ τοῦ θεοῦ, 1 Jn. 5:18. [18] Though many will not accept this, he here understands the concept of sonship in terms of begetting. For him to be the Son of God is not just to be the recipient of God's love. It is to be begotten of God. This is true both of believers and also of Jesus. [19] For this reason μονογενής probably includes also begetting by God. [20] To be sure, Jn. does not lift the veil of mystery which lies over the eternal begetting. But this does not entitle us to assume that he had no awareness of it. Johannine preaching and doctrine is designed to awaken faith, 20:30 f., not to give full and systematic knowledge. Hence it does not have to dispel all mysteries.

Büchsel

---

[16] One can hardly argue from expressions like "God sent his Son," 3:17; 1 Jn. 4:9, 10; cf. Jn. 3:16, since here the term "son" might be used proleptically, with ref. only to the man. But we see from 1 Jn. 4:14: "The Father sent the Son to be the Saviour of the world," that by His sending He who was already the Son became the Saviour, so that there is no room for doubt that the pre-existent Lord was already the Son. The fact that Jn. also uses ὁ λόγος for the pre-existent Lord gives us no right to assume that this λόγος was for him a power of God standing in an impersonal relation to Him.

[17] Zn. J., cf. also H. J. Holtzmann, *Theologie des NT*, II (1897), 436, n. 1.

[18] On the problems of this verse and the various attempts to avoid the only satisfactory solution cf. F. Büchsel on 1 Jn. 5:18.

[19] Jn. 1:13 (cf. Zn. J., *ad loc.*) probably reads, not οἳ ... ἐγεννήθησαν, but ὃς ... ἐγεννήθη.

[20] That the idea of begetting could be used of the relation of the Messiah to God in Judaism may be seen from ψ 2:7: σήμερον γεγέννηκά σε, and ψ 109:3: ἐκ γαστρὸς πρὸ ἑωσφόρου ἐξεγέννησά σε, cf. also Prv. 8:25: γεννᾷ με (wisdom). One should not refer the μονογενής to the virgin birth of Jesus (Zn. J., 82), for the pre-existent as well as the historical Jesus is the Son of God.

μορφή, μορφόω, μόρφωσις, μεταμορφόω → σύμμορφος, συμμορφίζω, συμμορφόω.

† μορφή.

Contents: A. Greek Usage: 1. The Meaning of the Word; 2. Synonyms; 3. Philosophical Use; 4. μορφή in the LXX. B. μορφὴ θεοῦ in the Greek World: 1. Manifestations of Deity; 2. Doubt as to the Physical Manifestation of Deity. C. The Form of God in the Old Testament and Judaism. D. The μορφή of Christ in the New Testament.

A. Greek Usage. [1]

1. The Meaning of the Word.

Rare in Hom., common later, μορφή means a. "form," "external appearance." Of men, e.g., Pind. Isthm., 4, 53: μορφὰν βραχύς, ψυχὰν δ' ἄκαμπτος, Aesch. Prom., 21 f.: ἵν' οὔτε φωνὴν οὔτε του μορφὴν βροτῶν ὄψηι, Suppl., 496: μορφῆς δ' οὐχ ὁμόστολος φύσις, Xenoph. Oec., 6, 16: ἐνίους ἐδόκουν καταμανθάνειν τῶν καλῶν τὰς μορφὰς πάνυ μοχθηροὺς ὄντας τὰς ψυχάς, Plut. Pericl., 31 (I, 169c): (Phidias) τὴν πρὸς 'Αμαζόνας μάχην ἐν τῇ ἀσπίδι ποιῶν αὑτοῦ τινα μορφὴν ἐνετύπωσε. Philo Leg. Gaj., 299: ἀσπίδας μήτε μορφὴν ἐχούσας, Cl. Al. Paed., III, 2, 11, 3 (I, 242, O. Stählin): τῆς ἐπιπλάστου μορφῆς τῆς ἑαυτῶν ... κάτοπτρα ἐπινενοήκασιν, and even "bearer of form, person," [2] e.g., Soph. El., 1159: The demon of misfortune sent the urn with his ashes ἀντὶ φιλτάτης μορφῆς (Orestes himself); also Aesch. Prom., 210, where it is said of the goddess Themis-Gaia: πολλῶν ὀνομάτων μορφὴ μία (one person), cf. Philo Vit. Mos., I, 66 (→ 749), Herm. v., 3, 10, 2: αὐτὴν ἠρώτων, ἵνα μοι ἀποκαλύψῃ περὶ τῶν τριῶν μορφῶν, ἐν αἷς μοι ἐνεφανίσθη, Cl. Al. Prot., X, 99, 2 (I, 72, O. Stählin): πολλὰς τῶν δαιμόνων ἐπινοήσασα μορφάς. Of animals, e.g., Aristot. Hist. An., II, 14, p. 505b, 8 f.: θαλάττιοι ὄφεις, παραπλήσιοι τὴν μορφὴν τοῖς χερσαίοις τἆλλα· πλὴν τὴν κεφαλὴν κτλ. Of plants or their leaves or buds as distinctive forms, e.g., Theophr. Hist. Plant., I, 14, 4: τοῖς καρποῖς τε καὶ φύλλοις

μορφή. On A: Pass., Liddell-Scott, Moult.-Mill., Preisigke Wört., Pr.-Bauer,[3] *s.v.*; on the syn. esp. J. H. H. Schmidt, *Synonymik d. gr. Sprache,* 4 (1886), 345 ff.; *Handbuch d. lat. u. gr. Synonymik* (1889), 550 ff.; J. B. Lightfoot, *Saint Paul's Epistle to the Philippians*[4] (1927 reprint), 127 ff.; Trench, 172 ff.; Cr.-Kö., 736 f., 389, 465 f. On D: Comm. on Phil. 2:6 f.; E. Gifford, *The Incarnation, Study on Phil. 2* (1897), 26 ff.; J. Kögel, "Christus der Herr. Erläuterungen z. Phil. 2:5-11," BFTh, 12, 2 (1908); H. Schumacher, *Christus in seiner Präexistenz u. Kenose,* I (1914), II (1921); E. Lohmeyer, "Kyrios Jesus," SAH 1927/1928, 4 (1928); "Die Verklärung Jesu nach dem Mk.-Ev.," ZNW, 21 (1922), 185 ff.; F. Loofs, "Das altkirchliche Zeugnis gegen d. herrschende Auffassung der Kenosisstelle (Phil. 2:5-11)," ThStKr, 100 (1927-28), 1 ff., esp. 80 ff.; F. Kattenbusch, "'Αρπαγμόν? Ἄπραγμον! Phil. 2:6. Ein Beitrag zur paul. Christologie," ThStKr, 104 (1932), 373 ff., esp. 398 ff.; K. Bornhäuser, "Zum Verständnis von Phil. 2:5-11," NkZ, 44 (1933), 428 ff., 453 ff.; A. Fridrichsen, "Epikureisches im NT," *Symbolae Osloenses,* 12 (1933), 52 ff.; P. Joüon, "Notes philologiques sur quelque versets de l'épître aux Philippiens," *Recherches de Science Religieuse,* 28 (1938), 223 ff.

[1] On the etym. → n. 16.

[2] Esp. for supernatural beings, as in other languages; cf. from the ancient East Eth. En. 64; Lidz. Ginza R., III, 94, 16 ff.; 96, 17 (p. 99, 18 ff.; 102, 16) etc.

καὶ ταῖς ἄλλαις μορφαῖς τε καὶ τοῖς μορίοις. But also of things and abstract ideas,[3] e.g., Soph. Trach., 699 f. μορφῇ μάλιστ' εἰκαστὸν ὥστε πρίονος ἐκβρώματ', El., 198 f.: δεινὰν δεινῶς προφυτεύσαντες μορφάν (of murder); Aesch. Prom., 448 f.: ὀνειράτων ἀλίγκιοι μορφαῖσι (figures in dreams); Plut. Ad Principem Ineruditum, 2 (II, 780a): (of statues) τὴν ἔξωθεν ἡρωικὴν καὶ θεοπρεπῆ μορφὴν ἔχοντες, esp. "beautiful figure," "beauty," "grace of form," e.g., Xenoph. Sym., 8, 16: θάλλουσα μορφῇ, Plat. Phaedr., 271a: κατὰ σώματος μορφὴν πολυειδές, also Hom. Od., 11, 367: σοὶ δ' ἔπι μὲν μορφὴ ἐπέων (cf. 8, 170), IG, IV, 1 (1929), 121, 119: νεανίσκον εὐπρεπῆ τὰμ μορφάν, Ditt. Or., 383, 40 f.: σῶμα μορφῆς ἐμῆς. b. Fig. "good-pleasure," Tob. 1:13: καὶ ἔδωκεν ὁ ὕψιστος χάριν καὶ μορφὴν ἐνώπιον Ενεμεσσαρου, Wilcken Ptol., 33, 8 ff.: δῷ σοι ὁ Σάραπις καὶ ἡ Εἶσις ἐπαφροδοσίαν χάρειν μορφὴν πρὸς τὸν βασιλέα καὶ τὴν βασίλισσαν etc. The term can also take on another sense in Dion. Hal. Ant. Rom., XIV, 15: κατά τε μορφὰς ("gestures," "miming") καὶ φωνάς. c. It can also be used generally for "kind," "manner," Eur. Ion, 381 f.: πολλαί γε πολλοῖς εἰσι συμφοραὶ βροτῶν, μορφαὶ δὲ διαφέρουσιν, *ibid.*, 1067: ἄλλας βιότου μορφάς, Plat. Resp., III, 397c: A specific mode of delivery has at its command παντοδαπὰς μορφὰς τῶν μεταβολῶν (kinds of alterations).

2. Synonyms.

μορφή in its fundamental meaning is synon. with εἶδος, ἰδέα (→ II, 373 ff.) and → σχῆμα,[4] cf. also the judgment of the older lexicographers, Hesych., Suid. (III, 413, Adler) etc. But in spite of much interchanging or piling up of related words, e.g., Aristot. Hist. An., II, 14, p. 505b, 13 f.: σκολόπενδραι θαλάττιαι, παραπλήσιαι τὸ εἶδος ταῖς χερσαίαις, τὸ δὲ μέγεθος μικρῷ ἐλάττους in comparison with *ibid.*, 8 f. (→ *supra*), Plut. Quaest. Conv., VIII, 9, 2 (II, 731c): φόβου ... σχήματα, τὰς δὲ λύπης καὶ ἡδονῆς μορφάς, Apoll. Rhod. Argonautica, 4, 1192 (→ 746); Eur. Iph. Taur., 291 ff.: παρῆν δ' ὁρᾶν οὐ ταὐτὰ μορφῆς σχήματ', ἀλλ' ἠλλάσσετο φθογγάς τε μόσχων καὶ κυνῶν ὑλάγματα, Ion, 992; Plat. Gorg., 465b, or Theaet., 163b (χρῶμα and σχῆμα) compared with Aristot. De Coloribus, 6, p. 799b, 16 ff.: τὰ λοιπὰ τῶν ζῴων ... παντοδαπὰς ἴσχει χρωμάτων μορφάς, Theophr. Physicorum Opiniones, Fr. De Sensibus, 64 ff. (H. Diels, Doxographi Graeci[2] [1929], 519 ff., cf. Index *s.v.*); Hipp. Philos., 12, 2: τὰ ὁμοιοσχήμονα καὶ παραπλήσια τὰς μορφάς, Cl. Al. Strom., IV, 23, 150, 3 (II, 315, Stählin): οὐδὲν ... τῶν χαρακτηριζόντων τὴν ἀνθρώπου ἰδέαν τε καὶ μορφὴν ἐνεδέησεν αὐτῷ (sc. Adam), there are still obvious differences of meaning, cf. Hom. Od., 8, 169 f.: ἄλλος μὲν γὰρ εἶδος ἀκιδνότερος πέλει ἀνήρ, ἀλλὰ θεὸς μορφὴν ἔπεσι στέφει, Philolaus Fr., 5 (I, 408, Diels[5]): ἑκατέρω δὲ τῶ εἴδεος πολλαὶ μορφαί, Plat. Resp., II, 380d: ἀλλάττοντα τὸ αὑτοῦ εἶδος εἰς πολλὰς μορφάς, Aristot. Part. An., I, 1, p. 640b, 34: ὁ τεθνεὼς ἔχει τὴν αὐτὴν τοῦ σχήματος μορφήν, ἀλλ' ὅμως οὐκ ἔστιν ἄνθρωπος, Plut. Comm. Not., 11 (II, 1064a): μεταβαλεῖν εἰς θηρίου μορφὴν τὸ εἶδος, Stob. Ecl., I, 30, 1 (I, 239, 26, Wachsmuth): (explanation of the rainbow): εἰσὶ δὲ αἱ ῥανίδες (drops of rain) οὐ σχήματος μορφαί, ἀλλὰ χρώματος, Act. Joh., 29 and 98; cf. the judgment of Theodoret (on R. 12:2, MPG, 82, 185d): ἡ μορφὴ ... ἀληθῶν πραγμάτων σημαντική, τὸ δὲ σχῆμα εὐδιάλυτον χρῆμα. μορφή, the form proper to a being, is not the same as εἶδος, his total visible appearance. εἶδος denotes the appearance of the kind, what is common to the individuals, while μορφή is the individual form of appearance. To εἶδος clings the idea of what may be perceived and known by others, but μορφή indicates what is objectively there. μορφή differs from σχῆμα inasmuch as it indicates the individual appearance as it is, while σχῆμα refers to its outward representation. μορφή is the whole (of the body etc.) in and for itself, while σχῆμα is what belongs or has

---

[3] Hence Thes. Steph., *s.v.* μορφή, *forma: generaliter de quavis re.*
[4] On εἰκών (→ II, 388 f.) as a synon. of μορφή *v.* H. Willms, ΕΙΚΩΝ, I (1935), 46 etc.

ref. to the whole (form, outward characteristics, manner of appearance etc.), cf. Bengel on Phil. 2:6 f.: μορφή, *forma dicit quiddam absolutum* ... σχῆμα, *habitus, cultus, vestitus, victus, gestus, sermones et actiones.* [5] But in view of the interchangeable use the nuances here indicated are not enough to establish firm boundaries between the terms.

3. Philosophical Use.

In the language of philosophy, too, μορφή has no unequivocal and definite sense. Parmenides, the first to use it, speaks of light and darkness as two forms of being (on the popular view), Fr., 8, 53 (I, 239, Diels[5]): μορφὰς γὰρ κατέθεντο δύο γνώμας ὀνομάζειν. Similarly, μορφή is a concept of pure form, equivalent to σχῆμα, in other pre-Socratics like Empedocles, who in Fr., 21, 2 (I, 319, Diels[5]) speaks of the form of the elements, [6] Philolaus Fr., 5 (I, 408, Diels[5]) (→ 743): the many forms of appearance of even or odd number, or Democrit., of whom Aristot. maintains in Part. An., I, 1, p. 640b, 31 ff.: φησὶ γοῦν παντὶ δῆλον εἶναι οἷόν τι τὴν μορφήν ἐστιν ὁ ἄνθρωπος, ὡς ὄντος αὐτοῦ τῷ τε σχήματι καὶ τῷ χρώματι γνωρίμου. Plato, [7] who does not use the word much, can treat it as an equivalent of εἶδος or ἰδέα for external appearance or form, Phaedr., 271a (→ 743); Resp., II, 380d (→ 748); Phileb., 12c : the many forms in which ἡδονή expresses itself, cf. 34d; Tim., 50c-51a, the characteristic or distinctiveness of a concept, Phaed., 103e, and finally also the concept itself, Phaed., 104d. But in the same context in Phaed. (103e : ἔστιν ἄρα ... περὶ ἔνια τῶν τοιούτων, ὥστε μὴ μόνον αὐτὸ τὸ εἶδος ἀξιοῦσθαι τοῦ αὐτοῦ ὀνόματος εἰς τὸν ἀεὶ χρόνον, ἀλλὰ καὶ ἄλλο τι, ὃ ἔστι μὲν οὐκ ἐκεῖνο, ἔχει δὲ τὴν ἐκείνου μορφὴν ἀεί, ὅτανπερ ᾖ, 104d : ἃ ἂν ἡ τῶν τριῶν ἰδέα κατάσχῃ, ἀνάγκη αὐτοῖς οὐ μόνον τρισὶν εἶναι ἀλλὰ καὶ περιττοῖς. ... ἐπὶ τὸ τοιοῦτον δή, φαμέν, ἡ ἐναντία ἰδέα ἐκείνη τῇ μορφῇ, ἣ ἂν τοῦτο ἀπεργάζηται, οὐδέποτ' ἂν ἔλθοι [sc. ἡ τοῦ ἀρτίου ἰδέα]), he distinguishes μορφή, the characteristic or distinctive form, from εἶδος, the concept. Thus the concept 3 has the μορφή of odd number. [8] He does not discuss whether μορφή in this sense is proper to every concept, nor does he deal with the relation of μορφή to οὐσία, → φύσις etc. (→ 748). In Aristot. [9] μορφή acquires a fixed meaning, and it occupies a central place in his structure. The four principles of all being (form or nature, matter, moving cause and end) may be reduced finally to two, form (μορφή, εἶδος) and matter (ὕλη, τὸ ὑποκείμενον, Phys., I, 7, p. 190b, 20 : γίγνεται πᾶν ἔκ τε τοῦ ὑποκειμένου καὶ τῆς μορφῆς. μορφή and εἶδος, which often occur together (e.g., An., II, 1, p. 412a, 8; II, 2, p. 414a, 9; Metaph., IV, 8, p. 1017b, 25 f.; IX, 1, p. 1052a, 22 f.), are interchangeable concepts for "form," i.e., that which may be perceived, but which is real only by ref. to that which in some way shapes it, [10] the fulfilment of the possibility of form which matter has within it. As being (τὸ τί ἐστι), cause (τὸ ὅθεν ἡ κίνησις) and end (τὸ οὗ ἕνεκα) find their unity in form (Phys., II, 7, p. 198a, 25 ff. etc.), so essence (τὸ τί ἦν εἶναι = οὐσία) and form are related, Gen. Corr., II, 9, p. 335b, 35; the point is to grasp through *eidos* that in a thing which it really was. [11] So, too, are nature (→ φύσις) and form (Phys., II, 1, p. 193a,

---

[5] For further examples and aspects cf. J. H. H. Schmidt, Trench, Cr.-Kö.

[6] For "form" cf. also Fr., 137, 1 (I, 367, Diels[5]): μορφὴν δ' ἀλλάξαντα ... φίλον υἱὸν κτλ.

[7] Cf. C. Ritter, *Neue Untersuchungen über Platon, 6* : εἶδος, ἰδέα *u. verwandte Wörter in den Schriften Platons* (1910), 228 ff.

[8] Ritter, 283 f.

[9] Cf. for material H. Bonitz, *Index Aristotelicus* (*Aristot. Opera, Akademie-Ausgabe,* V), 474; Schumacher, *op. cit.,* II, 182 ff.; for appraisal E. Zeller, *Die Philosophie d. Griechen*[3] (1879), II, 2, 313 ff.; W. Jaeger, *Aristoteles* (1923), 407 ff.; W. D. Ross, *Aristotle* (1923), 65 f., 71 ff., 167 ff.; J. Stenzel, *Zahl u. Gestalt bei Platon u. Aristoteles*[2] (1933), 132 f. etc.

[10] Stenzel, 132.

[11] Jaeger, 408. Cf. also Metaph., VI, 3, p. 1029a, 3 ff.: λέγω ... τὴν δὲ μορφὴν τὸ σχῆμα τῆς ἰδέας.

28 ff.; II, 8, p. 199a, 30 f.). Finally, there is unity between form and matter, Metaphys., VII, 6, p. 1045b, 17 ff.: ἔστι δ' ... ἡ ἐσχάτη ὕλη καὶ ἡ μορφὴ ταὐτὸ καὶ δυνάμει, τὸ δὲ ἐνεργείᾳ. Outside his true system of thought Aristot. can use μορφή qualitatively (→ 743), e.g., in Pol., VII, 1, p. 1323b, 33 ff., where he refers to the same kind of courage, righteousness and cleverness in national as in individual life (τὴν αὐτὴν ἔχει δύναμιν καὶ μορφήν), or Gen. An., II, 3, p. 737b, 4, the similarity of the matter from which skin and veins are made (τῆς δ' αὐτῆς μορφῆς ἐστι), or Part. An., I, 1, p. 640b, 34, the similarity of μορφὴ τοῦ σχήματος in a living person and a corpse.

In later philosophical terminology up to Neo-Platonism we catch reminiscences of Aristotle's understanding of μορφή, e.g., Theophr. Metaph. Fr., 17 (III, 156, F. Wimmer); Plut. De Animae Procreatione, 3 (II, 1013c): αὐτός τε γὰρ ὁ κόσμος οὗτος καὶ τῶν μερῶν ἕκαστον αὐτοῦ συνέστηκεν ἔκ τε σωματικῆς οὐσίας καὶ νοητῆς, ὧν ἡ μὲν ὕλην καὶ ὑποκείμενον, ἡ δὲ μορφὴν καὶ εἶδος τῷ γενομένῳ παρέσχε, cf. 21 (II, 1022e), Quaest. Conv., VIII, 2 (II, 719d); Stob. Ecl., I, 12 (I, 134 f., Wachsmuth); Plot. Enn., I, 6, 2; Damascius De Primis Principiis, 304 (ed. C. A. Ruelle [1889], II, 170) etc. But the nuances in the other usage are so great (cf. Ps.-Aristot. Physiognomica, 5, p. 809a, 28 ff.: διαιρετέον ... τὸ τῶν ζῴων γένος εἰς δύο μορφάς (mode of manifestation), εἰς ἄρσεν καὶ θῆλυ, προσάπτοντα τὸ πρέπον ἑκατέρᾳ μορφῇ, Epict. Diss., IV, 5, 19 f.: μορφή = ἡ ἐκτὸς περιγραφή) that there can be no question of a definite adoption of the term by philosophy which then influences everyday use. From Stoicism onwards μορφή is rare in philosophical writings (→ 748). Philo in his partly Platonic and partly Stoic cosmology contrasts matter and the world fashioned from it, ἄμορφος ὕλη and creation, in which everything has received its appropriate form, Spec. Leg., I, 329: from the unformed essence behind the elements, πάντ' ἐγέννησεν ὁ θεός, not by personal contact which must not take place between Him and ὕλη, ἀλλὰ ταῖς ἀσωμάτοις δυνάμεσιν, ὧν ἔτυμον ὄνομα αἱ ἰδέαι, κατεχρήσατο πρὸς τὸ γένος ἕκαστον τὴν ἁρμόττουσαν λαβεῖν μορφήν (cf. 47), e.g., the body of the first man, formed from the dust, ἀνθρωπεία μορφή (Migr. Abr., 3; Op. Mund., 135).[12] Here μορφή is in the strict sense the form proper to a being, cf. Op. Mund., 76 and Fr. (Philonis Iudaei Opera, ed. T. Mangey [1742], II, 654): καὶ ἄνθρωπος οὐδενὶ γνωρίζεται μᾶλλον ἢ προσώπῳ κατὰ τὴν ἰδίαν ποιότητα καὶ μορφήν. Elsewhere Philo vacillates between "form" (Op. Mund., 151; Abr., 147; Aet. Mund., 5 and 79; Leg. Gaj., 80: ἑνὸς σώματος οὐσίαν μετασχηματίζων καὶ μεταχαράττων εἰς πολυτρόπους μορφάς, *ibid.*, 211: ἐναργεῖς τύπους καὶ μορφὰς αὐτῶν [the divine λόγια in the laws] καθορῶντες, 55; 110; 290; 346), and appearance (Spec. Leg., I, 325: γυναικῶν μορφάς), personal appearance, Vit. Mos., I, 66 → 749). In Neo-Platonism,[13] too, μορφή is the individual material form which is no longer creative but is a νεκρὸς λόγος, cf. Plot. Enn., III, 8, 2 (p. 333, 24 ff., Volkmann): ὁ μὲν οὖν λόγος ὁ κατὰ τὴν μορφὴν τὴν ὁρωμένην ἔσχατος ἤδη καὶ νεκρὸς καὶ οὐκέτι ποιεῖν δύναται ἄλλον, ὁ δὲ ζωὴν ἔχων ὁ τοῦ ποιήσαντος τὴν μορφὴν[14] ἀδελφὸς ὤν ...

In sum, it may be seen from the majority of instances that in all its many nuances μορφή represents something which may be perceived by the senses,[15] and that it

---

[12] Acc. to Op. Mund., 140 the weaker μορφαί of his descendants resemble less and less the μορφή of the first man, cf. Plotinus and his later law of diminishing perfection, E. Zeller, *op. cit.*, III, 2^4 (1903), 558 f.

[13] This sentence, and n. 14, are by H. Kleinknecht.

[14] What are meant are, e.g., the hairs in the animal organism which cannot propagate themselves (this is μορφή). The species of animal or man can do this, but cannot be seen (→ opp. τὴν μορφὴν τὴν ὁρωμένην).

[15] Wettstein on Phil. 2:6: μορφή *denotat aliquid, quod in oculos incurrit.* Schumacher, II, 161 ff. has to strain hard to try to show from Gk. lit. that μορφή can mean both sensual and mental apprehension, both form and concept.

does so strictly, not even touching lightly the concept of being or appearance.[16]

4. μορφή in the LXX.

μορφή is rare in the LXX. It is used once each for תְּמוּנָה, "form" (Job 4:16),[17] תֹּאַר, "form" (Ju. 8:18 A:[18] ὡς εἶδος μορφὴ υἱῶν βασιλέων), תַּבְנִית, "likeness" (Is. 44:13) and Aram. צְלֵם, "image," "expression" (Da. 3:19: ἡ μορφὴ τοῦ προσώπου αὐτοῦ ἠλλοιώθη).[19] Peculiar to Θ is the use of μορφή for זִיו, "radiance," "healthy colour," in Da. 5:6: τότε τοῦ βασιλέως ἡ μορφὴ ἠλλοιώθη (cf. v. 9 f.; 7:28) and 4:36(33): ἡ μορφή μου ἐπέστρεψεν ἐπ' ἐμέ. The term always refers to the exterior, to that in man which may be seen. So also Wis. 18:1; 4 Macc. 15:4.[20]

B. μορφὴ θεοῦ in the Greek World.

1. The idea that the deity has form and appears in visible form to man, is found in Gk. religion (→ III, 71), esp. where there is a dominant belief in sensual divine revelation, in the epiphany of suprahuman beings (→ ἐπιφάνεια).[21]

In Hom.[22] the gods walk on earth in their own or other forms[23] and play a personal part in the affairs of men; so, too, in the Gk. epic generally, e.g., Apoll. Rhod. Argonautica, 4, 1192: θάμβευν δ' εἰσορόωσαι ἀριπρεπέων ἡρώων εἴδεα καὶ μορφάς. A feature of myth is that the gods continually take and change forms, cf. the myth of Aphrodite (e.g., Hom. Hymn. Ven., 81 ff.), and esp. of Demeter (Hom. Hymn. Cer., 275 ff. etc.) and Dionysus (Hom. Hymn. Bacch., 2 ff.; Eur. Ba., 4 f.: μορφὴν δ' ἀμείψας ἐκ θεοῦ βροτησίαν | πάρειμι, and 53 f.: ὧν οὕνεκ' εἶδος θνητὸν ἀλλάξας ἔχω | μορφήν τ' ἐμὴν μετέβαλον εἰς ἀνδρὸς φύσιν, Nonnus Dionys., 14 ff.) etc.[24] Fairy-stories and legends[25] tell of the presence, either for good or evil, of gods, spirits and heroes in bodily form, cf. Ovid Metamorphoseis, VIII, 626 ff. (visit of Jupiter and Mercury to Philemon and Baucis); Cic. Nat. Deor., II, 2, 6: *praesentes saepe di vim suam declarant ... saepe visae formae deorum quemvis non aut hebetem aut impium deos praesentes esse confiteri coegerunt*; Paus., VIII, 10, 8 f.; Xenoph. Mem., II, 1, 21 ff. (Just. Epit., 11, 3); Dion. Hal. Ant. Rom., V, 16, 3: τούτῳ γὰρ ἀνατιθέασι τῷ δαίμονι (Faunus = Pan) Ῥωμαῖοι τὰ πανικὰ καὶ ὅσα φάσματα μορφὰς ἄλλοτε ἀλλοίας

---

16 Even by its as yet obscure etym. (*v.* Walde-Pok., II, 274; A. Walde-J. B. Hofmann, *Lat. etym. Wörterbuch*, I³ [1938], 530; A. Ernout-A. Meillet, *Dict. étym.* [1932], 363), μορφή, like the Lat. *forma*, seems to belong originally to the visual sphere.

17 Cf. also Σ Dt. 4:12.

18 Cf. also Ἀ Is. 52:14.

19 Cf. the note by E. Nestle in ThStKr, 66 (1893), 173 f. opposing the view of Lohmeyer, *Kyrios Jesus*, 17, n. 1.

20 On Tob. 1:13 → 743. On LXX usage, cf. K. F. Euler, *Die Verkündigung vom leidenden Gottesknecht aus Js. 53 in d. gr. Bibel* (1934), 101 ff.

21 For excellent material and a comprehensive review cf. F. Pfister, Art. "Epiphanie," Pauly-W. Suppl., IV (1924), 277 ff. Cf. also L. Weniger, "Theophanien, altgriech. Götteradvente," ARW, 22 (1923/24), 16 ff. On the concept of the form of the gods in religious history cf. Chant. de la Saussaye, Index, *s.v.*; G. van der Leeuw, *Phänomenologie d. Religion* (1933), 156 ff., 427 ff. etc.

22 Cf. the fine account of Homer's religion as a religion of form in W. F. Otto, *Die Götter Griechenlands* (1929).

23 δέμας, εἶδος, φυή are the relevant terms in Hom., Il., 21, 285; 2, 58 etc.

24 Cf. Iambl. Vit. Pyth. § 30.

25 Cf. later Christian legends, e.g., Act. Pt. et Andr., 2 and 16; Act. Phil., 148; Act. Thom., 34 and 43 f. Cf., too, the changing form of the old lady in which the Church appears in Herm. v., 3, 10 ff., with its earlier models (Sibyl ?).

ἴσχοντα εἰς ὄψιν ἀνθρώπων ἔρχεται, Iambl. Vit. Pyth., § 151 etc.[26] Magical prayers invoke spiritual powers to appear in visible form and impart their strength to the petitioner, e.g., Preis. Zaub., XIII, 581 ff.: ἐπικαλοῦμαί σε, κύριε (here Αἰὼν Αἰῶνος) ἵνα μοι φανῇ ἡ ἀληθινή σου μορφή (which none of the gods can see, cf. 580 f.), IV, 3219 ff.: ἐπικαλοῦμαί σε, τὴν μητέρα καὶ δέσποιν[αν] νυμφῶν (i.e., Aphrodite) . . ., εἴσ<ελθε>, φῶς ἱερόν, καὶ δὸς ἀπόκρισιν δείξασα τὴν καλήν σου μορφήν, VII, 559 ff.: ἧκέ μοι, τὸ πνεῦμα τὸ ἀεροπετές . . . ἐπὶ τὴν λυχνομαντείαν ταύτην, ἣν ποιῶ, καὶ ἔμβηθι αὐτοῦ (sc. the boy) εἰς τὴν ψυχήν, ἵνα τυπώσηται τὴν ἀθάνατον μορφὴν ἐν φωτὶ κραταιῷ καὶ ἀφθάρτῳ,[27] VIII, 2 f., 8 ff.: ἐλθέ μοι, κύριε Ἑρμῆ, . . . οἶδά σου καὶ τὰς μορφάς αἵ εἰσι (in the East Ibis, in the West an ape with a dog's head, in the North a serpent, in the South a wolf) (cf. II, 106 ff.), V, 400, 415 ff.: Ἑρμῆ κοσμοκράτωρ, . . . σῇ μορφῇ ἱλαρός τε φάνηθι ἱλαρός τ' ἐπίτειλον ἀνθρώπῳ ὁσίῳ μορφὴν θ' ἱλαρὰν ἐπίτειλον ἐμοί, τῷ δεῖνα, ὄφρα σε μαντοσύναις, ταῖς σαῖς ἀρεταῖσι, λάβοιμι.[28] In IV, 1174 f. the spirit is addressed : μορφὴ καὶ πνεῦμα καὶ γῆ καὶ θάλασσα. Cf. also Test. Sol., II, 3; XIII, 1; XV, 4 f. and 44; XVI, 1; XVII, 1. If the god appears, the magician should thank him with an offering and prayer : συνεστάθην (I have been united) σου τῇ ἱερᾷ μορφῇ and return ἰσοθέου φύσεως κυριεύσας τῆς διὰ ταύτης τῆς συστάσεως ἐπιτελουμένης αὐθοπτικῆς λεκανομαντείας (oracle of the keys) ἅμα καὶ νεκυοαγωγῆς,[29] Preis. Zaub., IV, 215 ff. In the speculative Gnostic view the thought of the μορφὴ θεοῦ recurs in Hermes mysticism : The ἄνθρωπος (primal man), the son of the πατὴρ πάντων, is of the same form, οὗ ἠγάσθη ὡς ἰδίου τόκου· περικαλλὴς γὰρ ἦν, τὴν τοῦ πατρὸς εἰκόνα ἔχων· εἰκότως ἄρα ὁ θεὸς ἠγάσθη τῆς ἰδίας μορφῆς (Corp. Herm., I, 12, p. 120, 5 ff., Scott). The ἄνθρωπος shows in himself the καλὴ τοῦ θεοῦ μορφή to κατωφερὴς φύσις. φύσις appropriates the form, reflecting it on earth in water and in the shadow. The ἄνθρωπος, filled with love for the ὁμοία αὐτῷ μορφή on earth and in water, allows himself to become one with nature, I, 14, p. 120, 23 ff., Scott).[30]

2. Doubt as to the Physical Manifestation of Deity. But doubt quickly arises whether it is fitting to think of divine beings as ἀνθρωποφυεῖς (Hdt., I, 131, 1) or ἀνθρωποειδεῖς (II, 86, 7; 142, 3), or to imagine that they are manifested in physical form.

For Hom. experience of the physical proximity of the gods is early, and happens only rarely to the heroes of his epics (Od., 16, 161: οὐ γάρ πως πάντεσσι θεοὶ φαίνονται ἐναργεῖς) and not at all in the historical period of his own life.[31] Herodot. suggests (II, 53) that the Gks. before Homer and Hesiod had no knowledge of the gods or acquaintance with their form (ὁκοῖοί τέ τινες τὰ εἴδεα). These poets were the first to create a theogony, divine names etc. and to make known their figures (εἴδεα αὐτῶν σημήναντες). The popular belief that the gods have figures, once established

[26] It is only natural that the idea of the divine figure should recur in the ruler cult. Thus Demetrius Poliorketes is ἡλιόμορφος in the hymn in Athen., XII, 60 (p. 542e). Cf. also Philo Leg. Gaj., 110 on Jewish resistance to the emperor's claim to θεοῦ μορφή, also (75 ff.) the mocking of Gaius' methods of self-deification, which even goes so far that he changes one assumed form, like Proteus in Hom., into many others (80 → 745).

[27] The halo around the supraterrestrial figure is a typical feature like miraculous size and beauty, *v.* Pfister, 314 f.

[28] On μορφὴ θεοῦ in the magic pap. cf. G. Harder, *Pls. u. das Gebet* (1936), 56, n. 1.

[29] Cf. Reitzenstein Hell. Myst., 357 f.

[30] Cf. on the Corp. Herm. C. H. Dodd, *The Bible and the Greeks* (1935), Index, *s.v.* μορφή. On μορφή speculation in Gnosticism, cf. Cl. Al. Exc. Theod., 10, 1 f.; 11, 2; 31, 3 f.; an apocryphon of Jn. (*Philotesia, P. Kleinert zum 70. Geburtstag dargebracht* [1907], 327); Hipp. Ref., V, 10 (Naassene hymn); VI, 14, 4 etc.; Coptic Gnostic writings, ed. C. Schmidt, I (GCS, 13), Index, *s.v.* μορφή.

[31] Cf. K. F. Nägelsbach, *Homerische Theol.*[3] (1884), 144 ff.

by Hom., persisted, and was nourished by myth and the cultus.[32] But philosophical criticism also produced increasing scepticism. Xenophanes with passionate severity rejects the popular anthropomorphism as unworthy of the gods: ἀλλ' οἱ βροτοὶ δοκέουσι γεννᾶσθαι θεούς, | τὴν σφετέρην δ' ἐσθῆτα ἔχειν φωνήν τε δέμας τε (Fr., 14 [I, 132, 16 f., Diels⁵]); if oxen, horses and lions could paint, they would depict the gods in the form of their own bodies (Fr., 15 [I, 132, 19 ff., Diels⁵]); the one god is οὔτι δέμας θνητοῖσιν ὁμοίιος [sic!] οὔτε νόημα (Fr., 23 [I, 135, 5, Diels⁵]).[33] Socrates, instead of looking for theophanies, considers with awe the revelation of the nature of the deity in its works, Xenoph. Mem., IV, 3, 13: ὅτι δέ γε ἀληθῆ λέγω, καὶ σὺ γνώσῃ, ἂν μὴ ἀναμένῃς ἕως ἂν τὰς μορφὰς τῶν θεῶν ἴδῃς, ἀλλ' ἐξαρκῇ σοι τὰ ἔργα αὐτῶν ὁρῶντι σέβεσθαι καὶ τιμᾶν τοὺς θεούς. Plato fights against the false and misleading myths in Hom. and other poets with their bad reports and deceiving metamorphoses. In Resp., II, 380d he raises the question whether the deity is a magician appearing in many different guises (ἄλλοτε ἐν ἄλλαις ἰδέαις), sometimes really taking different forms and exchanging its own for them (ἀλλάττοντα τὸ αὑτοῦ εἶδος εἰς πολλὰς μορφάς), sometimes merely cheating us and causing us to think that this is so, or whether it is quite simple and does not ever leave its own form (τῆς ἑαυτοῦ ἰδέας ἐκβαίνειν). The answer is (381c) that "it is impossible for a god to seek to change himself, but each of them remains, as it seems, since he is as beautiful and good as possible, quite simply in his own form (μένει ἀεὶ ἁπλῶς ἐν τῇ αὑτοῦ μορφῇ)," also 382e: "Thus God is absolutely simple and true in word and work; he does not change nor deceive others whether in manifestations (κατὰ φαντασίας) or speeches or by sending signs in wakefulness or sleep." Here μορφή, like ἰδέα and εἶδος, is obviously the one unchanging form of manifestation proper to each god; the god does not reveal himself in changing and always inadequate forms, but in the form which reflects his nature.[34] Stoic monism tackles the problem of the μορφὴ θεοῦ, cf. Aetius Placita, I, 6, 1 (p. 292, 22 ff., H. Diels, Doxographi graeci² [1929]): ὁρίζονται δὲ τὴν τοῦ θεοῦ οὐσίαν οἱ Στωικοὶ οὕτως· πνεῦμα νοερὸν καὶ πυρῶδες οὐκ ἔχον μὲν μορφήν, μεταβάλλον δὲ εἰς ὃ βούλεται καὶ συνεξομοιούμενον πᾶσιν, Ps.-Gal. Hist. Philosopha, 16 (p. 608, 19, Diels, *op. cit.*): Zeno speaks of the σῶμα but not the μορφή of deity. The teaching of Epicurus, which allows the gods to lead a life of bliss in their own dwelling between the worlds, untroubled by the world or men, has crassly anthropomorphic notions of the gods.[35] It ascribes to them *tamquam corpus* and *tamquam sanguinem* (Cic. Nat. Deor., I, 25, 71), and imagines their form (Philodem. Philos. περὶ θεῶν, 3;[36] Cic. Nat. Deor., I, 18, 47 ff.) etc.[37] On the other hand euhemerism, with its deifying of kings and humanising of the gods, has no place for reflection on the divine form. There is a complete negation of a visible form for the idea of the good, representing deity, in Corp. Herm., IV, 9 (p. 154, 22 f., Scott): τὸ δὲ ἀγαθὸν ἀφανὲς τοῖς φανεροῖς· οὐ γὰρ μορφὴ οὔτε τύπος ἐστὶν αὐτῷ. Along with the concept of immortality, belief in the supraterrestrial form of the gods, which will be imparted to believers after death, may be found in the burial inscr. in Preisigke Sammelbuch, 4230 (2nd cent. A.D.): εὐψύχει Κύριλλα θεοῖς ἐναλίγκιε μορφήν· | νῦν γὰρ χῶρον ἔχεις ἥσυχον ἀθανάτων.

On the whole the divine form as a concrete phenomenon, though challenged or sublimated in philosophy, remains current in Hellenistic and Greek thought.

---

32 Of older lit., cf. K. F. Nägelsbach, *Die nachhomerische Theol. des gr. Volksglaubens bis auf Alexander* (1857), 1 ff., and of newer lit. esp. O. Kern, *Die Religion d. Griechen*, I (1926), 49 ff.; II (1935), 215 ff. etc.

33 Cf. on this J. Hempel, "Gott, Mensch u. Tier im AT," ZSTh, 9 (1931), 212 ff.

34 The problem whether God has one or many μορφαί is also discussed in Corp. Herm., XI, 16 (p. 218, 9 ff., Scott) along Platonic lines, cf. Hermetica, ed. W. Scott, II (1925), 321 ff.

35 Cf. Aetius Placita, I, 7, 34 (p. 306, 13 ff., H. Diels); Ps. Gal. Hist. Philos., 16 (p. 608, 19 f., Diels).

36 H. Diels, *Philodemus Über d. Götter*, III, 1: Gk. text (AAB [1916]), No. 4, Col. 9, line 10.

37 *Ibid.*, 2: Exposition (AAB [1916]), No. 6, Index of Subjects, *s.v.* "Gott," "Götter."

C. The Form of God in the Old Testament and Judaism.

1. In the OT it is a fundamentally alien and impossible thought that God should have a form open to human perception, or that He should reveal Himself in sensual form.[38] To be sure, there are many references to God as a being which, like man, has a face, eyes, ears, nose, mouth, lips, tongue, arms, fingers, back, clothes, shoes, staff etc.; but this is so obviously figurative that the LXX corrections (→ III, 109) were not necessary to maintain the purity of the concept of God. In none of the many OT theophanies or angelophanies (not even Gn. 18:1 ff. or 32:25 ff.) is there a manifestation in full human form of the supraterrestrial beings, and nowhere is there a depiction of the divine form which is seen (cf. Ez. 1:26 ff.; Job 4:12 ff.). In the OT the theomorphic understanding of man is more important than the anthropomorphic view of God (→ II, 390 ff.). The presentation in human form does not involve a humanisation.[39] The fire and smoke, storm and tempest, which indicate the personal presence of Yahweh (Gn. 15:17; Ex. 3:2 ff.; 19:16 ff.; 24:17; 1 K. 19:11 f.; Is. 6:4; Ps. 18:7 ff. etc.) also denote the limits which are drawn for the sensual apprehension of the divine. Man is not allowed to see face to face the God whose will is revealed in the Word. This applies even to those specially commissioned by Him (cf. Ex. 33:20, in spite of 24:9 ff.; 1 K. 19:11 ff.; Is. 6:1 ff. → πρόσωπον, → ὁράω). The fact that there is no image in the worship of Yahweh (→ II, 381 ff.) reflects the personal and ethical conception which resists any attempt at a sensual objectification of the divine form.

2. In Judaism, too, with its basic emphasis on the transcendence of God, there is no room for positive statements about the form of God.[40]

Jub. expunges features in the Gen. stories which seem to be too anthropomorphic (cf. 16:1 ff. with Gn. 18:1 ff.; 29:13 ff. with 32:25 ff.). The Sib. do not speak of the form of the Creator God, only of His giving form in creation: αὐτὸς δ᾽ ἐστήριξε τύπον μορφῆς μερόπων (3:27). Philo constantly maintains with emphasis: God is not ἀνθρωπόμορφος (Mut. Nom., 54; Congr., 115; Conf. Ling., 135 etc.). His account of the burning bush (Ex. 3) in Vit. Mos., I, 66: κατὰ δὲ μέσην τὴν φλόγα μορφή τις ἦν περικαλλεστάτη, τῶν ὁρατῶν ἐμφερὴς οὐδενί, θεοειδέστατον ἄγαλμα, φῶς αὐγοειδέστερον τοῦ πυρὸς ἀπαστράπτουσα, ἣν ἄν τις ὑπετόπησεν εἰκόνα τοῦ ὄντος εἶναι· καλείσθω δὲ ἄγγελος, has some Platonic features, but in the main its insistence on the imprecision of the miraculous manifestation conforms with Jewish belief. Josephus[41] in Ap., 2, 239 ff. accepts the philosophical criticism of the Gk. myths for unworthy anthropomorphism (248: τί γὰρ οὐχὶ τῶν κακίστων παθῶν εἰς θεοῦ φύσιν καὶ μορφὴν ἀνέπλασαν), and scoffs at the invented depictions of painters and sculptors (252: ἕκαστός τινα μορφὴν ἐπινοῶν). He says of the one true God in 2, 190: ὁ θεὸς ... ἔργοις μὲν καὶ χάρισιν ἐναργὴς καὶ παντὸς οὔτινος φανερώ-

[38] On anthropomorphism in the OT *v.* the OT theologies, e.g., W. Eichrodt, *Theol. d. AT*, I (1933), 104 ff.; II (1935), 1 ff.; L. Köhler, *Theol. d. AT* (1936), 4 ff.; E. Sellin, *Theol. d. AT*² (1936), 18 and 45 f.; also H. Duhm, *Der Verkehr Gottes mit dem Menschen im AT* (1926), 12 ff.; E. Fascher, "Deus invisibilis," *Marburger Theol. Studien*, I (1931), 43 ff.; H. Middendorf, *Gott sieht. Eine terminologische Studie über das Schauen Gottes im AT* (Diss. Theol., Freiburg, 1935), 102 ff.; J. Hempel, *Gott u. Mensch im AT*² (1936), 267 etc.; "Die Grenzen des Anthropomorphismus Jahwes im AT," ZAW, NF, 16 (1939), 75 f.

[39] L. Köhler, *op. cit.*, 6.

[40] → also I, 262 and n. 18.

[41] Cf. A. Schlatter, "Wie sprach Josephus von Gott?" BFTh, 14, 1 (1910), 22 f.; Schl. Theol. d. Judt., 22 f.

τερος, μορφὴν δὲ καὶ μέγεθος ἡμῖν ἄφατος. If in Ant., 6, 333 it is said of Saul, when he sees Samuel coming from the realm of the dead: βλέπειν εἶπεν ἀνελθόντα τῷ θεῷ τινα τὴν μορφὴν ὅμοιον, the "God-like figure" simply suggests the total otherness of a manifestation from the beyond.[42] As the Hellenists speak of the μορφή of God, so the Rabbis speaks of the דְּמוּת (→ II, 374),[43] but with a clear sense that this is figurative, just as the Torah, when it uses anthropomorphic expressions, "speaks in the language of the children of men" (S. Nu., 112 on 15:31 → III, 110).[44]

D. The μορφή of Christ in the New Testament.

1. The ἑτέρα μορφή in which, acc. to Mk. 16:12 (inauthentic ending, 𝔎 form), the risen Lord appears to two disciples by the way (Lk. 24:13 ff.) (→ II, 702), is a human form, but different from that which Jesus bore during his life on earth. The idea rests on reflection on Lk. 24:16, but is also reminiscent of popular Gk. beliefs concerning the epiphany of divine beings (→ 746).

2. On the change in the μορφή of Jesus at the transfiguration in Mk. 9:2 ff. and par. → 758 f.

3. The only important statement concerning Christ's μορφή is in Phil. 2:6 f.: ἐν μορφῇ θεοῦ ὑπάρχων οὐχ ἁρπαγμὸν ἡγήσατο τὸ εἶναι ἴσα θεῷ, ἀλλὰ ἑαυτὸν ἐκένωσεν μορφὴν δούλου λαβών, though this is not easy to grasp by reason of its liturgical and hymnic form. If the hymn (vv. 5-11), in the exhortatory context of 1:27-2:18 with its call for the unselfishness which does not seek its own (v. 3 f.), is laying a true foundation by glorifying Christ as the unique example of selfless renunciation of what is His, the assuming of the μορφὴ δούλου (→ II, 278) is to be regarded as an act of exemplary restraint on the part of Christ, as a concrete demonstration of this restraint.[45] As the One who became man (ἐν → ὁμοιώματι ἀνθρώπων γενόμενος),[46] Jesus was in the position of a slave, or, more concretely, He bore the figure or form of a slave, of a being which is wholly dependent on the will of another, which has to bow to and obey this other (cf. also v. 8). This does not merely describe the whole attitude reflected in the earthly work of Jesus[47] according to Mk. 10:45 (or Jn. 13:4 ff.). In the sequence of Phil. 2:5-11 it is also the opposite of the μορφὴ θεοῦ which He had before, and of the position of κύριος (→ III, 1088 ff.) which He will receive at His exaltation (vv. 9 ff.). The renunciation of the pre-existent Lord (→ III, 661)[48] finds ex-

[42] In Ant., 2, 232 the Egyptian princess calls the young Moses παῖδα μορφῇ τε θεῖον; Jos. himself simply refers to his εὐμορφία and χάρις (231).

[43] Jalkut Shimeoni, I § 20 on Gn. 2:8 says of the angels in Paradise that the ugliest among them is (as beautiful) in form as Joseph and Rabbi Jochanan (Weber, 346).

[44] On the alteration or reinterpretation of more violent OT anthropomorphisms cf. Str.-B., II, 320 ff., 326 ff. etc.

[45] Though cf. the Christian interpolation in Test. B. 10:7: τὸν ἐπὶ γῆς φανέντα ἐν μορφῇ ἀνθρώπου ἐν ταπεινώσει.

[46] This addition prevents us referring the μορφὴν δούλου λαβών to the incarnation, as has been constantly attempted from Cl. Al. Paed., III, 1, 2, 2 (I, 237, Stählin).

[47] The → σχήματι εὑρεθεὶς ὡς ἄνθρωπος of v. 7 points to this. On the difference between μορφή and σχῆμα in Pl. cf. also Schl. K., 243.

[48] That the pre-existent Christ is meant may be seen from the structure of the hymn, which traces the whole path of the Redeemer from its beginning in heaven by way of the *status exinanitionis* to the goal of exaltation and glorification. The ref. to the historical Jesus (Eus. Hist. Eccl., V, 2, 2 ff., Letter of the Churches of Vienne and Lyons; *v.* Loofs, 67 ff.; cf. also Loofs, 92 ff.; Kattenbusch, 404 f.; Bornhäuser, 461) is unable to explain the

pression in a μορφή which is the absolute antithesis to His prior μορφή. Thus the phrase μορφὴ θεοῦ, which Paul coins in obvious antithesis to μορφὴ δούλου, can be understood only in the light of the context. The appearance assumed by the incarnate Lord, the image of humiliation and obedient submission, stands in the sharpest conceivable contrast to His former appearance, the image of sovereign divine majesty,[49] whose restoration in a new and even more glorious form is depicted for the exalted κύριος at the conclusion of the hymn, v. 10 f. The specific outward sign of the humanity of Jesus is the μορφὴ δούλου, and of His essential divine likeness (τὸ εἶναι ἴσα θεῷ → III, 353 f.) the μορφὴ θεοῦ. The lofty terminology of the hymn can venture to speak of the form or visible appearance of God in this antithesis[50] on the theological basis of the δόξα concept of the Greek Bible, which is also that of Paul, and according to which the majesty of God is visibly expressed in the radiance of heavenly light (→ II, 237 ff.).[51] The μορφὴ θεοῦ in which the pre-existent Christ was[52] is simply the divine δόξα;[53] Paul's ἐν μορφῇ θεοῦ ὑπάρχων corresponds exactly to Jn. 17:5: τῇ δόξῃ ᾗ εἶχον πρὸ τοῦ τὸν κόσμον εἶναι παρὰ σοί.[54]

ἐν μορφῇ θεοῦ ὑπάρχων satisfactorily. Because of the pre-existent Christology there is no cause to reject the Pauline authorship of Phil. 2:6 f. (so E. Barnikol, "Phil. 2. Der marcionitische Ursprung des Mythos-Satzes Phil. 2:6-7," *Forschungen zur Entstehung des Urchristentums, des NT u. d. Kirche,* VII, 1932; cf. also his "Mensch u. Messias. Der nichtpaulinische Ursprung d. Präexistenz-Christologie," *ibid.,* VI, 1932).

[49] Calvin, *ad loc.: forma dei hic maiestatem significat.* Cf. Hofmann, *ad loc.*

[50] Only from the 2nd cent. on (under the influence of Phil. 2:6?) does it recur in Christian lit., cf. O. Sol. 7:4, where God says of Christ: "In form (דמותא) he appeared as I"; Just. Apol., 9, 3: God has ἄρρητον δόξαν καὶ μορφήν; Asc. Is. 3:13; 9:13; Sib., 8, 256 ff. and 264 ff.; Gnostic, Cl. Al. Exc. Theod., 31, 4 (III, 117, Stählin): ὅπερ ἐστὶν υἱός, μορφὴ τῶν αἰώνων. Much stronger, however, in the apologetic debate with paganism is the protest against the understanding of the form and epiphany of the gods which prevailed in pagan myth and worship, Dg., 2, 3; Just. Apol., 9, 1: The temple idols do not have θεοῦ μορφήν (οὐ γὰρ τοιαύτην ἡγούμεθα τὸν θεὸν ἔχειν τὴν μορφήν, ἥν φασί τινες εἰς τιμὴν μεμιμῆσθαι); 64, 5; Epit., 11, 3; Tat. Or. Graec., 21, 1: Christian preaching θεὸν ἐν ἀνθρώπου μορφῇ γεγονέναι is no foolish fable like the Gk. myths of the appearances of the gods in human or animal form (cf. 10, 2); Cl. Al. Prot., IV, e.g., 56, 6 (I, 44, O. Stählin): τὸ ἄγαλμά σου ... γῆ ἐστιν ... μορφὴν παρὰ τοῦ τεχνίτου προσλαβοῦσα, Strom., VII, 4, 22, 1 (III, 16, Stählin) etc.

[51] It has been rightly emphasised by H. Kittel, "Die Herrlichkeit Gottes," *Beih.* ZNW, 16 (1934) that the sensual (visual) element does not hold unlimited sway in the δόξα concept.

[52] ὑπάρχειν ἐν here in the sense of "to be wrapped or clothed in," cf. Lk. 7:25. For δόξα as the form of divine manifestation (garment) in similar phrases with ἐν cf. Mk. 8:38 and par.; Mt. 25:31, cf. Pr.-Bauer,[3] 428. How related are garment and form for the Gks. may be seen from Cl. Al. Prot., I, 4, 3 (I, 5, Stählin) on Mt. 7:15: "λύκους" δὲ ἄλλους ἀλληγορεῖ προβάτων κῳδίοις ἠμφιεσμένους, τοὺς ἐν ἀνθρώπων μορφαῖς ἁρπακτικοὺς αἰνιττόμενος.

[53] In LXX theophanies, too, we find μορφή (Job 4:16) and δόξα (Nu. 12:8; ψ 16:15) for תְּמוּנָה. Cf. also the two terms in Cl. Al. Exc. Theod., 11, 2; 10, 1 f. (III, 109 f., Stählin). Bertram pts. esp. to the christologically important Is. 52:14, where ʼA has ὅρασις αὐτοῦ καὶ μορφή for מַרְאֵהוּ וְתֹאֲרוֹ, the LXX τὸ εἶδός σου καὶ ἡ δόξα σου (μορφή and δόξα correspond). Perhaps μορφή in ʼA and Phil. 2:6 may even pt. to an earlier Gk. rendering of Is. 52. Cf. K. F. Euler, 47 f., 102 f. μορφὴ θεοῦ could also be צֶלֶם אֱלֹהִים (Gn. 1:27) in Heb. Delitzsch has דְּמוּת הָאֱלֹהִים at Phil. 2:6 (cf. Gn. 5:1). In both cases the LXX has εἰκὼν θεοῦ. Cf. 2 C. 4:4; Col. 1:15, where Delitzsch has צֶלֶם. In the LXX the Aram. is צְלֵם = μορφή, Da. 3:19 (→ 746). → καλός, III, 550 f. This has an important bearing on the idea of the ἔσχατος ʼΑδάμ in 1 C. 15:45.

[54] Cf. esp. Calvin, *ad loc.: maiestas, quae in deo relucet, ipsius est figura ... Christus ergo*

The wealth of the christological content of Phil. 2:6 f. rests on the fact that Paul does not regard the incomparable measure of the self-denial displayed by the pre-existent Christ in His incarnation merely as the opposite of the egotistic exploitation of what He possessed (→ I, 474) or as the surrender of His own will,[55] nor is he concerned merely to emphasise the contrast between His eternal and temporal existence, His deity and humanity, but he brings out in clear-cut contrast the absolute distinction between the modes of being. Christ came down from the height of power and splendour to the abyss of weakness and lowliness proper to a slave, and herein is revealed for the apostle the inner nature of the Redeemer who is both above history and yet also in history. He did not consider Himself; He set before the eyes of those who believe in Him the example of forgetfulness of His own ego.

It may thus be seen that there is no trace of a Hellenistic philosophical understanding of μορφή in this passage,[56] and certainly not of any supposed popular philosophical concept of μορφὴ θεοῦ = οὐσία or φύσις[57] (→ 745). Similarly, what Paul understands by μορφὴ θεοῦ and μορφὴ δούλου is remote from the epiphany ideas of myth or legend. Christ did not play the role of a god in human form.[58] Again, there can be no thought of a metamorphosis (→ 756) in the sense of Hellenistic belief or superstition. Paul does not speak of the exchanging of one's own form for another; in 1 C. 2:8 the man Jesus is the κύριος τῆς δόξης. Materially, if not linguistically, the apostle's paradoxical phrase μορφὴ θεοῦ is wholly in the sphere of the biblical view of God. εἰκὼν τοῦ θεοῦ cannot be equated with μορφὴ θεοῦ (2 C. 4:4; Col. 1:15; → II, 395 f.).[59] The image of God is Christ, while the μορφὴ θεοῦ is the garment by which His divine nature may be known.

† μορφόω.

"To form," "to fashion," of artists who shape their material into an image, esp. an idol, Poll. Onom., I, 13: τὸ μορφῶσαι ... κοιλᾶναι λίθον εἰς θεοῦ μορφήν, Is. 44:13 Ἀ (of making idols): ἐμόρφωσεν αὐτὸ ἐν παραγραφίδι, Philo Decal., 7: μυρίας γὰρ ὅσας διὰ γραφικῆς καὶ πλαστικῆς μορφώσαντες ἰδέας (cf. 66), Spec. Leg., I, 21: ἀργὴν ὕλην (namely, gold and silver) θνητῷ παραδείγματι προσχρησάμενοι, ... θεοὺς ὅσα τῷ δοκεῖν ἐμόρφωσαν, cf. Spec. Leg., II, 255; Decal., 72; Cl. Al. Prot., IV, 51, 6 (I, 40, Stählin); Strom., VI, 5, 40, 1 (II, 451) etc. Esp. of the creator of the world who gives specific form to matter, Alex. Aphr. (v. Arnim, II, p. 112, 29 ff.): μεμῖχθαι τῇ ὕλῃ λέγειν τὸν θεόν, διὰ πάσης αὐτῆς διήκοντα καὶ σχηματίζοντα καὶ μορφοῦντα καὶ κοσμοποιοῦντα τούτῳ τῷ τρόπῳ, Philo Plant., 3: τὴν οὐσίαν ... ὁ κοσμοπλάστης μορφοῦν ἤρξατο, Som., II, 45: ἀσχημάτιστον οὖσαν τὴν τῶν πάντων οὐσίαν ἐσχημάτισε καὶ ἀτύπωτον ἐτύπωσε καὶ ἄποιον ἐμόρφωσε, Aet. Mund., 41: ἐμπρεπὲς δὲ θεῷ τὰ ἄμορφα μορφοῦν.[1] Synon. with πλάσσω (Gn.

---

ante mundum conditum in forma dei erat, quia apud patrem gloriam suam obtinebat ab initio. Cf. Kögel, 26 ff.

[55] Cf. Schl. Theol. d. Ap., 342; Mich. Ph., 36 f. on ἑαυτὸν ἐκένωσεν.

[56] Lightfoot, 132 f. and Ew. Ph., *ad loc.* assume this. Lohmeyer *ad loc.* rightly says that it is "impossible to see in μορφή a philosophical term, however attenuated."

[57] So most of the fathers (Loofs, 10 ff.), also Schumacher. But cf. Cr.-Kö., 737; Schl. Theol. d. Ap., 343.

[58] G. Heinzelmann, *NT Deutsch*, 8, *ad loc.* It is artificial to see a contrast to the emperors Caligula and Nero, who were honoured as gods (so Bornhäuser, 453 ff.).

[59] So Novatian (?), Ambrosiaster, Pelagius, and more recently Loofs, 95 ff.

μορφόω. Cr.-Kö., Liddell-Scott, Moult.-Mill., Pr.-Bauer,[3] *s.v.*; J. H. H. Schmidt, *Handbuch d. lat. u. gr. Synonymik* (1889), 566; Comm. on Gl. 4:19.

[1] In Conf. Ling., 87 ἄμορφα μορφῶσαι is also ascribed to spirits inimical to God.

2:7 f.; Jer. 1:5 etc.), cf. Philo Fug., 69 (on Gn. 1:26): τὸ λογικὸν ἐν ἡμῖν ἐμόρφου (*v.* also Spec. Leg., I, 171), Conf. Ling., 63 (of the *logos*): ἐμόρφου τὰ εἴδη. Accordingly, the pass. is "to win, to assume form," Theophr. De Causis Plantarum, V, 6, 7: μεμορφωμένα ... εὐθὺς ἐκεῖνα ταῦτα δ' ἅμα τῇ γενέσει μορφοῦται (cf. also Fr., XII, 14 and 17 [III, 155 f., F. Wimmer]), Plut. De Animae Procreatione in Timaeo Platonis, 3 (II, 1013c): τῆς μὲν ὕλης τὸ μετοχῇ καὶ εἰκασίᾳ τοῦ νοητοῦ μορφωθέν, Diog. L., VII, 1, 68 (134): The Stoics teach καὶ ἀσωμάτους εἶναι τὰς ἀρχὰς καὶ ἀμόρφους, τὰ δὲ (sc. στοιχεῖα) μεμορφῶσθαι, Philo Fug., 12: τῶν ὄντων ἕκαστον μεμόρφωται, Abr., 118 (of the 3 men in Gn. 18): ἀσωμάτους ὄντας ... εἰς ἰδέαν ἀνθρώπων μεμορφῶσθαι, Just. Apol., 5, 4: τοῦ λόγου μορφωθέντος καὶ ἀνθρώπου γενομένου, Cl. Al. Paed., II, 8, 75, 1 (I, 203, Stählin): There showed itself to Moses (Ex. 3:2 ff.) ὄψις ... θεοειδὴς φωτὸς μεμοφωμένου. μορφοῦσθαι is also used of the fruit in the mother's womb, Aetius Placita, V, 21 (p. 433, 5 f., H. Diels, Doxographi Graeci² [1929]) has the heading: Ἐν πόσῳ χρόνῳ μορφοῦται τὰ ζῷα ἐν γαστρὶ ὄντα, *ibid.*, V, 12, 2 (p. 423, 17 ff.), which ascribes to Empedocles the saying: τῇ κατὰ τὴν σύλληψιν φαντασίᾳ τῆς γυναικὸς μορφοῦσθαι τὰ βρέφη, cf. also Philo Spec. Leg., III, 108: ἤδη μεμορφωμένον (sc. the embryo) ἁπάντων μελῶν τὰς οἰκείας τάξεις καὶ ποιότητας ἀπειληφότων, III, 117: τὰ μεμορφωμένα ἤδη (sc. βρέφη), Const. Ap., V, 7, 20: (of God) ὁ ... ἐν τῇ κοιλίᾳ τὸν ἄνθρωπον ἐκ μικροῦ σπέρματος μορφῶν.

The fig. use in Gnostic terminology derives partly from cosmogony and partly from growth in the womb.[2] Cf. Cl. Al. Exc. Theod., 34, 1 (III, 118, Stählin): <αἱ> εὐώνυμοι δυνάμεις ... ὑπὸ τῆς τοῦ φωτὸς παρουσίας οὐ μορφοῦται, κατελείφθησαν δὲ αἱ ἀριστεραὶ ὑπὸ τοῦ Τόπου μορφωθῆναι, 59, 1 (III, 126): σπέρμα ... ὃ κατὰ μικρὸν μορφοῦται διὰ γνώσεως, 79 (III, 131): ἕως οὖν ἀμόρφωτον, φασίν, ἔτι τὸ σπέρμα, θηλείας ἐστὶ τέκνον· μορφωθὲν δὲ μετετέθη εἰς ἄνδρα καὶ υἱὸς νυμφίου γίνεται, cf. 68 (III, 129): ἄχρι μὲν γὰρ ἦμεν τῆς θηλείας μόνης τέκνα, ὡς ἂν αἰσχρᾶς συζυγίας, ἀτελῆ καὶ νήπια καὶ ἄφρονα καὶ ἀσθενῆ καὶ ἄμορφα, οἷον ἐκτρώματα προ[σ]ενεχθέντα, τῆς γυναικὸς ἦμεν τέκνα, ὑπὸ δὲ τοῦ σωτῆρος μορφωθέντες ἀνδρὸς καὶ νυμφῶνος γεγόναμεν τέκνα, Cl. Al. Strom., VII, 14, 88, 3 (III, 62): The true Christian is μορφούμενος τῇ τοῦ κυρίου διδασκαλίᾳ, Hipp. Ref., VI, 31, 7 f.; 32, 2 f.; 42, 8; 46, 2; VII, 18, 1; VIII, 9, 4.

The only NT occurrence is at Gl. 4:19: τέκνα μου, οὓς πάλιν ὠδίνω μέχρις οὗ μορφωθῇ Χριστὸς ἐν ὑμῖν. Becoming a Christian is here depicted in terms of birth[3] (→ ὠδίνω; → I, 667 f.), and the goal is the fashioning of Christ in man. According to the apostle's view Christ lives in Christians (Gl. 2:20; R. 8:10; 2 C. 13:3, 5; Col. 1:27; 3:11). He dwells in their hearts (Eph. 3:17). They have → σπλάγχνα Χριστοῦ Ἰησοῦ (Phil. 1:8) etc. In order that this Christ-life may come into being in believers, Christ must take form in them. He must in some sense be incarnate afresh in each individual.[4] The nerve of this metaphor, which is based on the development of the child in the mother's womb (→ *supra*), is

---

[2] We may disregard the examples from Herm. mysticism. Corp. Herm., I, 31 (p. 130, 17, Scott) has the saying: ὃν ἡ φύσις οὐκ ἐμόρφωσεν, but ἠμαύρωσεν is here the better reading (cf. *Hermetica*, ed. W. Scott, II [1925], 70 f.). Stob. Ecl., I, 4, 8 (I, 73, Wachsmuth = *Hermetica*, I [1924], 422, 8): ἡ μεμορφωμένη μορφή, is unintelligible (cf. *Hermetica*, III [1926], 393 f.).

[3] In interpretation of the metaphor cf. E. D. Burton (ICC), *ad loc.* and G. S. Duncan, *The Epistle of Paul to the Galatians* (1934), *ad loc.*

[4] An idea current in later Christian mysticism, cf. Ltzm. Gl., *ad loc.* Calvin, *ad loc.* says: *nascitur in nobis, ut vivamus eius vitam.* The form of Christ is mentioned in this connection in, e.g., Cl. Al. Paed., III, 1, 1, 5 (I, 236, Stählin): ὁ δὲ ἄνθρωπος ἐκεῖνος, ᾧ σύνοικος ὁ λόγος, ... μορφὴν ἔχει τὴν τοῦ λόγου.

that Christ should come to full growth, to maturity, in the Christian.[5] That this is a process which is never completed in this aeon, that it is both open and secret, both gift and task (→ II, 542), corresponds to the distinctive nature of Paul's Christ mysticism and gives evidence of the distinction from formally similar ideas in Hellenistic mysticism, e.g., Preis. Zaub., VIII, 2 f., 49 f.: ἐλ[θ]έ μοι, κύριε Ἑρμῆ, ὡς τὰ βρέφη εἰς τὰ<ς> κοιλίας τῶν γυναικῶν ... οἶδά σε, Ἑρμῆ, καὶ σὺ ἐμέ. ἐγώ εἰμι σὺ καὶ σὺ ἐγώ, also VII, 561 ff.; → 747, 7 ff.

Gl. 4:19 is interpreted in Gnostic fashion in a Copt. Apocr., c. 14 (*Koptisch-gnostische Schriften*, 1 [GCS, 13], 355, 26 ff., cf. 21 ff.). In later Christian mysticism, cf. Symeon, the new theologian: μακάριος ὁ τὸ φῶς τοῦ κόσμου ἐν ἑαυτῷ μορφωθὲν θεασάμενος, ὅτι αὐτὸς ὡς ἔμβρυον ἔχων τὸν Χριστὸν μήτηρ αὐτοῦ λογισθήσεται (Cod. Coislinianus, 291 f., 296 verso).[6]

† μόρφωσις.

"Forming," "shaping." This verbal noun denotes a. the activity of shaping, e.g., trees, Theophr. De Causis Plantarum, III, 7, 4: μόρφωσις τῶν δένδρων ὕψει τε καὶ ταπεινότητι καὶ πλάτει καὶ τοῖς ἄλλοις, the embryo, Gal. De Semine (IV, 640, C. G. Kühn); Cl. Al. Paed., I, 6, 48, 1 (I, 118, O. Stählin), anal. Exc. Theod., 57 (III, 126): τοῦ μὲν μόρφωσις τοῦ πνευματικοῦ (sc. ἀνθρώπου, b. the result of this activity, abstr. Test. B. 10:1: ἐπεθύμουν ἰδεῖν ... τὴν μόρφωσιν τῆς ὄψεως αὐτοῦ, Hipp. Ref., VI, 51, 5 (p. 184, P. Wendland): τὸν Ἰησοῦν ... λέγει τεθεῖσθαι ... <εἰς> ἐξομοίωσιν καὶ μόρφωσιν τοῦ μέλλοντος εἰς αὐτὸν κατέρχεσθαι Ἀνθρώπου, cf. VI, 31, 2 (p. 158), concretely what is fashioned, "form," "external figure," more or less synon. → μορφή,[1] Catal. Cod. Astr. Graec., V, 1 (p. 188, 25): τὰς μορφώσεις τῶν δεκανῶν, VIII, 4 (p. 122, 34); Cl. Al. Exc. Theod., 60 (III, 127, Stählin): "δύναμις δὲ ὑψίστου ἐπισκιάσει σοι" (Lk. 1:35) τὴν μόρφωσιν δηλοῖ τοῦ θεοῦ, ἣν ἐνετύπωσεν τῷ σώμα<τι> ἐν τῇ παρθένῳ, 44, 2 (III, 121): εὐθὺς οὖν ὁ Σωτὴρ ἐπιφέρει αὐτῇ (sc. τῇ Σοφίᾳ) μόρφωσιν τὴν κατὰ γνῶσιν καὶ ἴασιν τῶν παθῶν (cf. Iren. Haer., I, 4, 5).[2]

In the list (Rom. 2:17 ff.) of titles of honour which were used by Jews proud of the Law, and which Paul took from the speech of Pharisaic rabbis, if not from a Pharisaic catechism for instructing proselytes,[3] the predicate ἔχοντα τὴν μόρφωσιν τῆς γνώσεως καὶ τῆς ἀληθείας ἐν τῷ νόμῳ (v. 20) refers to the high sense of pride with which a Jew who feels himself to be a teacher regards a book of the Law as a physical representation, indeed, the actual embodiment of absolute knowledge and truth, as the true depiction and representation of the idea of a divine norm.[4,5] This judgment, which is stated with obvious irony by Paul, is not

---

[5] There is no ref. to "the μορφή, the palpable and visible form of Christ" (Zn. Gl., *ad loc.*) or "the visible representation of the invisible Christ" (Ltzm. Gl., *ad loc.*), though cf. Cl. Al. Paed., III, 1, 1, 5 (→ n. 4).

[6] Acc. to K. Holl, *Enthusiasmus u. Bussgewalt beim gr. Mönchtum* (1898), 71. Cf. W. Bousset on Gl. 4:19 (*Schriften d. NT*, 2).

μόρφωσις. Cr.-Kö., Liddell-Scott, Pr.-Bauer[3], *s.v.* Comm. on R. 2:20 and 2 Tm. 3:5.

[1] The difference between μορφή and μόρφωσις for which J. B. Lightfoot contends, *op. cit.*, 131 (cf. *The Journal of Classical and Sacred Philology*, 3 [1857], 115) cannot be sustained.

[2] μόρφωσις is not found in the Gk. transl. of the OT. Ἀ has μόρφωμα for תְּרָפִים, apparently in the sense of "form" (Gn. 31:19; Ju. 17:5; 1 Βασ. 15:23; 19:13; Hos. 3:4).

[3] Cf. Ltzm. R., *ad loc.*

[4] H. J. Holtzmann, *Lehrbuch d. nt.lichen Theol.*[2] (1911), II, 259. This is to be accepted in spite of Schl. R., 103, n. 1, since Paul is not stating his own view but using a Jewish expression.

[5] Theod. Mops. on R. 2:20: μόρφωσιν λέγει οὐ τὴν προτύπωσιν, ἀλλ' αὐτὴν τὴν ὑπόστασιν καὶ τὴν γνῶσιν καὶ τὴν ἀλήθειαν, ὡς τό· "ὃς ἐν μορφῇ θεοῦ ὑπάρχων"

the same as his own estimate of the significance of the Law, in spite of R. 7:7 ff.; 2:13 ff.; 3:31; 9:4; 13:8 (→ νόμος).

In 2 Tm. 3:5 it is said of sinners of the last time: ἔχοντες μόρφωσιν → εὐσεβείας τὴν δὲ δύναμιν αὐτῆς ἠρνημένοι. What is meant is the external form of the Christian life with no inner power, the mere appearance[6] or mask of pious conduct[7] without the corresponding reality which derives from inner piety.

† μεταμορφόω.

Contents: A. Linguistic Data. B. Comparative Religion. C. μεταμορφοῦσθαι in the New Testament.

A. Linguistic Data.

"To remodel," "to change into another form," predominantly pass. or med. (though act., e.g., Σ ψ 33:1: μετεμόρφωσε τὸν τρόπον τὸν ἑαυτοῦ,[1] Appian Bell. Civ., 4, 41: ὁ πρεσβύτης μεταμορφῶν ἑαυτὸν ἐπεδήσατο διφθέραν ἐς τὸν ἕτερον ὀφθαλμόν, Ps.-Gal. Quod Qualitates Incorporeae, 6 [XIX, 479, C. G. Kühn]: ὁ μὲν γὰρ [sc. the mythological Proteus] εἰς ὀλίγας φύσεις ἑαυτὸν μετεποίει καὶ μετεμόρφου καὶ ταύτας οὐκ ἀπρεπεῖς, Corp. Herm., XVI, 8 f. [I, 268, Scott]: <τὰ> ζῷα [ἕλικος τρόπον] μεταποιῶν καὶ μεταμορφῶν εἰς ἄλληλα γένη γενῶν καὶ εἴδη εἰδῶν, Preis. Zaub., I, 117 ff.: [the god] μεταμορφοῖ δὲ εἰς ἣν ἐὰν βούλῃ μορφὴν θη[ρίου] πετηνοῦ, ἐνύδρου, τετραπόδου, ἑρπετοῦ) is a synonym of ἀλλοιόω, ἑτεροιόω, μεταβάλλω etc. which first became common in the *koine*. When Ps.-Ammon. Adfin. Vocab. Diff., 93 expounds μεταμορφοῦσθαι as μεταχαρακτηρισμὸς καὶ μετατύπωσις σώματος εἰς ἕτερον χαρακτῆρα,[2] the reference to an outward change of form perceptible to the senses determines the use of the word, Diod. S., IV, 81, 5: εἰς

(Phil. 2:6). Thdrt. on R. 2:20 (MPG, 82, 73a): τούτων γάρ σοι πάντων τοὺς χαρακτῆρας ὁ θεῖος προσέφερε νόμος. Calvin acutely notes the use of μόρφωσις here rather than → τύπος (*v.* 6:17), and adds: *puto* (sc. *Paulum*) *voluisse conspicuam doctrinae pompam indicare, quae Apparentia vulgo dicitur.* Schl. R., *ad loc.* suggests "shaping" (→ 754, 14 ff.), but this fits no better than the attempted equation with παίδευσις or διδασκαλία in A. Pallis, *To the Romans* (1920).

[6] Vg: *habentes speciem quidem pietatis.*

[7] Cf. Philo Plant., 70: καὶ νῦν εἰσί τινες τῶν ἐπιμορφαζόντων εὐσέβειαν.

μεταμορφόω. On A: Cr.-Kö., Liddell-Scott, Pr.-Bauer[3], *s.v.*; J. H. H. Schmidt, *Synonymik d. gr. Sprache,* 4 (1886), 567; Trench, 174 ff. On B: Reitzenstein Hell. Myst., 39 ff., 262 ff., 357; K. Deissner, *Auferstehungshoffnung u. Pneumagedanke bei Pls.* (1912), 104 ff.; *Pls. u. d. Mystik seiner Zeit*[2] (1921), 68 f., 103 f., 111 ff., 129; M. Dibelius, "Die Isisweihe bei Apulejus u. verwandte Initiationsriten," SHA (1917), 4, 26 f. etc.; Clemen, 333; E. Lohmeyer, "Die Verklärung Jesu nach dem Mk.-Ev.," ZNW, 21 (1922), 203 ff. On C: G. Wohlenberg, *Das Ev. d. Mk.*[3, 4] (1930) on 9:2; Zn. Mt. on 17:2; Kl. Mk.[3], Hck. Mk., Schl. Mk., Loh. Mk. on 9:2; J. Schniewind, *Das Ev. nach Mk.* (*NT Deutsch,* 1) on 9:2; J. Jeremias, "Jesus als Weltvollender," BFTh, 30, 4 (1930), 57; M. Dibelius, *Die Formgeschichte d. Ev.*[2] (1933), 275 f.; M. Goguel, *La Foi à la Résurrection de Jésus dans le Christianisme primitif* (1933), 317 ff.; A. Plummer (ICC), Ltzm. K., Bchm. 2 K., Wnd. 2 K., H. D. Wendland (*NT Deutsch,* 7[3], 1937) on 2 C. 3:18; Zn. R., Ltzm. R., W. Sanday-C. Headlam (ICC), T. Haering, *Der Römerbrief des Ap. Pls.* (1926), Schl. R., P. Althaus (*NT Deutsch,* 6) on R. 12:2; P. Feine, *Theologie des NT*[6] (1934), 243.

[1] The LXX, in which μεταμορφόω does not occur, has ἠλλοίωσεν τὸ πρόσωπον αὐτοῦ (Mas. בְּשַׁנּוֹתוֹ אֶת־טַעְמוֹ) at ψ 33:1.

[2] Cf. also Eustath. Thessal. Comm. in Od., p. 1799, 30 ff.

τὴν τῶν ἁλισκομένων θηρίων μεταμορφωθεὶς ἰδέαν ὑπὸ τῶν ... κυνῶν διεφθάρη, Plut. Adulat., 7 (II, 52d) → n. 3, Athen., VIII, 10 (p. 334c): τὴν Νέμεσιν ποιεῖ διωκομένην ὑπὸ Διὸς καὶ εἰς ἰχθὺν μεταμορφουμένην, Longus, 4, 3: ἐπῆσαν καὶ ... Τυρρηνοὶ μεταμορφούμενοι, Ps.-Luc. Asin., 11: ὦ φιλτάτη, δεῖξόν μοι μαγγανεύουσαν ἢ μεταμορφουμένην τὴν δέσποιναν ... πειράσομαι παρασχεῖν σοι τὸ ἰδεῖν μεταμορφουμένην τὴν κεκτημένην, Ps.-Demetr. De Elocutione, 189 (Rhet. Graec., III, 303, 23 f.), also Philo Leg. Gaj., 95 (of Hermes): ὁπότε δόξειεν αὐτῷ, τὰ μὲν ἀπετίθετο, εἰς δὲ Ἀπόλλωνα μετεμορφοῦτο καὶ μετεσκευάζετο, Vit. Mos., I, 57 (of transition into a state of ecstasy which arouses fear): λέγων ἅμα ἐνεθουσία μεταμορφούμενος εἰς προφήτην, Dg., 2, 3 (of images): οὐ πρὶν ἢ ταῖς τέχναις τούτων (sc. artisans) εἰς τὴν μορφὴν τούτων ἐκτυπωθῆναι ἦν ἕκαστον αὐτῶν ἑκάστῳ εἰκάζειν μεταμεμορφωμένον, Preis. Zaub., XIII, 581 f.: ὁ μεταμορφούμενος ἐν ταῖς ὁράσεσιν (sc. those who see), Αἰὼν Αἰῶνος. But in some cases the verb refers to an inner spiritual change, e.g., Philo Spec. Leg., IV, 147: τὸν αὐτὸν μὲν τρόπον κἂν τῇ βασιλίδι τῶν ἀρετῶν, εὐσεβείᾳ, προσθῇ τις ὁτιοῦν μικρὸν ἢ μέγα ἢ τοὐναντίον ἀφέλῃ, καθ' ἑκάτερον ἐπαλλάξει καὶ μεταμορφώσει τὸ εἶδος, 2 C. 3:18; R. 12:2; Cl. Al. Prot., I, 4, 3 (I, 5, Stählin), where Jesus is the allegorical counterpart of Orpheus, Arion etc.: καὶ πάντα ἄρα ταῦτα <τὰ> ἀγριώτατα θηρία (cf. Mt. 3:7) καὶ τοὺς τοιούτους λίθους (cf. Mt. 3:9) ἡ οὐράνιος ᾠδὴ αὐτὴ μετεμόρφωσεν εἰς ἀνθρώπους ἡμέρους. The relation of μεταμορφόω to → μετασχηματίζω corresponds to the relation between the two synon. root words μορφή and σχῆμα (→ 743, 19 ff.). In the one case the change concerns the appearance as such, in the other the external marks.[3] In the one the ref. is to the whole, in the other something within the whole. In the one it is a matter of the *quid*, in the other the *quale*. μεταμορφοῦσθαι can be "to change into something different," μετασχηματίζεσθαι "to become different."[4] But the basic distinction is as little observed in practice in the case of the verbs as in that of the nouns.[5]

B. Comparative Religion.

The belief that gods and spirits can transform themselves, and demonstrate this power on others, is widespread in religion.[6] An inexhaustible fund of myths and sagas of change bears witness to this, esp. in the Hellenistic Roman world,[7] in which metamorphoses produced a whole literary genre (Ovid, Apuleius, Ps.-Luc. Asin. etc.).[8] The dominant motif is that the gods, to draw near to men, change themselves into earthly and perceptible beings (→ 746, 14 ff.).[9] But in apocalyptic and mysticism the thought of change applies to the transition of man from earthly to supraterrestrial appearance. In

---

[3] E.g., Plut. Adulat., 7 (II, 52b): (The flatterer) ὥσπερ τὸ μετερώμενον ὕδωρ περιρρέων ἀεὶ καὶ μετασχηματιζόμενος τοῖς ὑποδεχομένοις, but also (II, 52d): ἅπαντας (who had indulged so long in philosophy) ὥσπερ ἐν Κίρκης μεταμορφωθέντας ἀμουσία καὶ λήθη καὶ συηνία κατέσχε.

[4] Cf. Cr.-Kö., 468; cf. also Dib. Ph.[3] on 3:21 and Zn. R. on 12:2.

[5] Cf. Trench, 174 ff.

[6] Cf. Chant. de la Saussaye[4], Index *s.v.* "Verwandlung," "Metamorphose."

[7] Cf. O. Gruppe, *Gr. Mythologie u. Religionsgeschichte*, II (1906), Index of Subjects, *s.v.* "Verwandlung."

[8] Cf. W. v. Christ-W. Schmid, *Gesch. d. gr. Lit.*, II, 1[6] (1920), 115, 168 etc.; M. Schanz-C. Hosius, *Gesch. d. röm. Lit.*, II[4] (1935), 235 f. etc.

[9] For early Christian criticism of these metamorphoses cf. Aristid. Apol., 8, 2; 9, 6 f.; Tat. Or. Graec., 10, 1. But already Asc. Is. 3:13 regards the incarnation as a metamorphosis (*v.* P. Amh., 1, p. 10: [ἡ] ἐξέλευσις [τοῦ ἀγα]πητοῦ ἐκ [τοῦ ἑβδ]όμου οὐρα[νοῦ καὶ ἡ] μεταμόρφωσις αὐτοῦ, καὶ ἡ κατάβασις αὐτοῦ, καὶ ἡ ἰδέα ἣν δεῖ αὐτὸν μεταμορφωθῆναι ἐν εἴδει ἀνθρώπου). And in later apocrypha the same motif occurs in Christophanies, e.g., Act. Andr. et Matth., 17 (p. 85, 6 f., Bonnet): μετεμόρφωσεν ... ἑαυτὸν ὥσπερ πρῳρεὺς ἐν τῷ πλοίῳ. On the transformation of the bearer of revelation in Herm. v., 5, 4 (ἠλλοιώθη ἡ ἰδέα αὐτοῦ), *v.* Dib. Herm., *ad loc.*

Jewish apocalyptic a miraculous change of form is one of the gifts of eschatological salvation which the blessed receive after the resurrection, S. Bar. 51:3 : "The appearance of their faces will be transformed into radiant beauty," 5 : "They will be changed into the splendour of angels," 10 : "They will resemble angels, and be like the stars, and will be changed into the form they desire, from beauty to splendour, and from light to the radiance of glory," 12 : "Then will the glory of the righteous be greater than that of the angels." [10] In the Hell. mystery religions transfiguration (μεταμόρφωσις, *transfigurari, reformari*) is a par. idea to regeneration [11] or deification. [12] To be changed into a god-like being is the great goal which the initiate, moving from one stage to another, strives to reach by vision of the deity. In Isis initiation in Apul. Met., XI, 23 f., where the way of vision leads the devotee through the realm of the dead and the world of the elements to the sphere of light of the gods of heaven, there takes place in the symbolical rites a twelve-fold change of form, and then the worship of the community is ascribed to the one who has been deified. The initiate experiences what happened to the god himself (30 : Osiris ... *reformatus*). The transformation involves the freeing of the body from the bonds of material nature ; it is physical transfiguration (Apul. Met., XI, 29 : *illustrari ;* Corp. Herm., 13, 3 [I, 240, Scott]: ὁρω[ν] τι<ν'> ἐν ἐμοὶ ἄπλαστον ἰδέαν γεγενημένην ἐξ ἐλέου θεοῦ, καὶ ἐμαυτὸν <δι>εξελήλυθα εἰς ἀθάνατον σῶμα· καί εἰμι νῦν οὐχ ὁ πρίν, ἀλλ' <ἀν>εγεννήθην ἐν νῷ, cf. 13, 14; [13] 10, 6 [I, 190]: πασῶν γὰρ τῶν σωματικῶν αἰσθήσεών τε καὶ κινήσεων ἐπιλαθόμενος ἀτρεμεῖ· περιλάμψαν δὲ [πάντα] τὸν νοῦν, [καὶ] τὴν ὅλην ψυχὴν ἀναλαμβ<άν>ει καὶ ἀνέλκει διὰ τοῦ σώματος, καὶ ὅλον αὐτὸν εἰς οὐσίαν μεταβάλλει, cf. 4, 11b etc., cf. Zosimus [Berthelot, 108, 17 f.]: ἕως ἂν ἔμαθον μετασωματούμενος πνεῦμα γενέσθαι). But it also carries with it a change in spiritual nature, *v.* Sen. Ep., 6, 1 f.: *Intelligo ... non emendari me tantum, sed transfigurari. nec hoc promitto iam aut spero, nihil in me superesse, quod mutandum sit ... et hoc ipsum argumentum est in melius translati animi, quod vitia sua, quae adhuc ignorabat, videt ... cuperem itaque tecum communicare tam subitam mutationem mei ;* 94, 48 : *qui didicit et facienda ac vitanda percepit, nondum sapiens est, nisi in ea quae didicit animus eius transfiguratus est.* In a passive form the same belief is also found in Hell. magic lit. The ability of the gods to transform themselves is highly lauded, and man can attain to the manner and power of deity by magical change into divine form, e.g., Preis. Zaub., XIII, 270 ff.: σὲ μόνον ἐπικαλοῦμαι. τὸν μόνον ἐν κόσμῳ διατάξαντα θεοῖς καὶ ἀνθρώποις, τὸν ἑαυτὸν ἀλλάξαντα μορφαῖς ἁγίαις καὶ ἐκ μὴ ὄντων εἶναι ποιήσαντα καὶ ἐξ ὄντων μὴ εἶναι, Θαῦθ ἅγιος ..., [14] *ibid.*, 70 f.: ὁ μεταμορφούμενος εἰς πάντας, ἀόρατος εἶ Αἰὼν Αἰῶνος, 581 f. → 747; VIII, 8 f. → 747; Test. Sol. 2:3 (words of a spirit) εἰμὶ δὲ καὶ ὑπνωτικὸν εἰς τρεῖς μορφὰς μεταβαλλόμενος, *ibid.*, 16:2, 4; Preis. Zaub., V, 416 ff. → 747; I, 117 f. → 756; IV, 215 ff. → 747: Through union with the sacred form of the deity the magician is in possession of a god-like nature ; VII, 560 ff. → 747: magic brings it about that the human soul reflects the immortal form of deity.

---

[10] For individual features, esp. the form of δόξα, cf. Da. 12:3; Eth. En. 38:4; 104:2; 4 Esr. 7:97; also Ex. 34:29 (Moses after the encounter on Sinai) LXX : δεδόξασται ἡ ὄψις τοῦ χρώματος τοῦ προσώπου αὐτοῦ. For the totality cf. the broad depiction in Jalkut Shimeoni, Bereshit, 20 (Weber, 345 f.). The reverse side of eschatological change is found in S. Bar. 51:1 f., 5 : "Both these and those shall be changed, the former into the glory of angels, the latter will vanish more and more into awful apparitions and ghostly images." Cf. also the idea of the change (ἀλλάσσω → I, 251) of heaven and the heavenly bodies at the last judgment, Ps. 102:26 (Hb. 1:12; Barn., 15, 5); Ass. Mos. 10:5 etc. "Change" is a word which characterises expectation of final salvation and judgment.

[11] ἀναγεννᾶσθαι (*renasci*) → I, 673, cf. 669. παλιγγενεσία → I, 687.

[12] Cf. Reitzenstein Hell. Myst., 262 ff.; also Bousset, *Kyrios Christos*² (1921), 165 ff.

[13] Cf. also Deissner, *Pls. u. d. Mystik seiner Zeit,* 68 f.

[14] Cf. Reitzenstein Poim., 22, n. 2 and 256 f.

C. μεταμορφοῦσθαι in the New Testament.

The story of the transfiguration of Jesus offers an example of perceptible change, Mk. 9:2 = Mt. 17:2: μετεμορφώθη ἔμπροσθεν αὐτῶν.[15] The miracle of transformation from an earthly form into a supraterrestrial, which is denoted by the radiance of the garments (also the countenance in Mt. and Lk.), has nothing whatever to do with metamorphosis in the Hellenistic sense (→ 757, 7 ff.) but suggests the context of apocalyptic ideas (→ 756, 34 ff., cf. also Rev. 1:14 f.; S. Bar. 30:4).[16] What is promised to the righteous in the new aeon (cf. also 1 C. 15:51 f.) happens already to Jesus in this world, not as one among many others, but as the bearer of a unique call. Before the eyes of His most intimate disciples the human appearance of Jesus was for a moment changed into that of a heavenly being in the transfigured world. This is the anticipation and guarantee of an eschatological reality.[17] Jesus is manifested to the disciples as the Son of Man of the hope of final salvation (ὁ → υἱὸς τοῦ ἀνθρώπου). They are to realise that the goal of His way through suffering and death (Mk. 8:31) is the glory of the Consummator (Mk. 8:38 f. and par.).[18]

In Paul the idea of transformation, in the two passages in which it occurs (2 C. 3:18; R. 12:2), refers to an invisible process in Christians which takes place, or begins to take place, already during their life in this aeon. In 2 C. 3:18 the apostle concludes his demonstration of the superiority of the new διαθήκη, whose gift and mark is the Spirit, by contrasting with the Jewish attitude (v. 13 ff.: κάλυμμα, which conceals the δόξα) that of Christians: ἡμεῖς δὲ πάντες ἀνακεκαλυμμένῳ προσώπῳ τὴν δόξαν κυρίου κατοπτριζόμενοι τὴν αὐτὴν εἰκόνα μεταμορφούμεθα ἀπὸ δόξης εἰς δόξαν, καθάπερ ἀπὸ κυρίου πνεύματος. To Christians the Spirit has granted free vision of the heavenly glory of the Lord, Christ. In this vision they undergo an unceasing and progressive change into the image[19] of the One whose glory they see. It is the Lord Himself, present and active by the Spirit, who brings about this change. Paul obviously shares formally the ideas of Hellenistic mysticism in respect of transformation by vision, transformation into the seen image of God, and transformation as a process which is progressively worked out in the righteous (→ 757, 7 ff.). Materially, however, he stands far removed from the piety of the mysteries. Man cannot bring about the change by his own activity; it is effected by Christ in Christians. There is no vision of God by oft-repeated ritual *opus operatum*; it is by the Spirit that Christians see the δόξα of Christ (→ II, 696). Mystical deification finds no place; the change into the likeness of Christ (cf. also R. 8:29) is a re-attainment of the divine likeness of man at creation (→ II, 396), and it maintains the characteristically biblical distance between God and man. The initiate has no aristocratic claim to a special

---

[15] Lk. 9:29: ἐγένετο ... τὸ εἶδος τοῦ προσώπου αὐτοῦ ἕτερον (𝔓[45] etc. + καὶ ἠλλοιώθη). Materially → II, 248. For the Evangelists this is not a "vision" (cf. R. Hartstock, "Die Visionsberichte in den synpt. Evv.," *Festgabe f. J. Kaftan* [1920], 133 f.).

[16] So Loh. Mk., *ad loc.* (as against ZNW, 21 [1922], 204 ff.).

[17] For an imitation cf. Act. Phil., 60, and on this *ibid.*, 144.

[18] To think of the δόξα of the pre-existent Messiah of apocalyptic (so J. B. Bernardin, "The Transfiguration," JBL, 52 [1933], 181 ff.), or to equate the other form of Jesus with the μορφὴ θεοῦ of the pre-existent Christ acc. to Phil. 2:6 (→ 750), as does Kl. Mk.[3], *ad loc.*, is to miss the eschatological character of the features which elucidate the event and the general eschatological orientation of the pericope Mk. 9:2-8 and par.

[19] On the acc. τὴν αὐτὴν εἰκόνα with μεταμορφούμεθα cf. Kühner-Blass-Gerth § 597, 2c; Bl.-Debr.[6] § 159, 4.

experience of God; all Christians participate in the miracle of transformation. Above all, what Paul means by transformation is not an autonomous, immanent, mystical event. It is a process by which the transcendent eschatological reality of salvation works determinatively in the earthly lives of Christians. After the manner of apocalyptic (→ 757, 1 ff.), Paul declares the hope of the physical transformation of believers at the end of the days (1 C. 15:44 ff., 51 f.; Phil. 3:21 → μετασχηματίζω). But he is also certain that the new aeon has already come with Christ (→ III, 449). The Spirit, the ἀπαρχή and ἀρραβών of eschatological salvation, is already the possession of Christians. In virtue of the presence of the → πνεῦμα, in whom the risen Lord is Himself present (v. 17 f.), the transformation begins already, and from within, though not only inwardly,[20] refashions after the likeness of the Lord, by giving them to share in the δόξα (→ II, 696 f.). There is still tension, however, between the "already" and the "not yet": ἀπὸ δόξης εἰς δόξαν (→ II, 251). In R. 12:2 the thought of transformation is changed from an indicative into an imperative and set in the sharp light of the doctrine of the two aeons (→ I, 204 ff.): μὴ → συσχηματίζεσθε τῷ αἰῶνι τούτῳ, ἀλλὰ μεταμορφοῦσθε[21] τῇ ἀνακαινώσει (→ III, 453) τοῦ → νοός, "Do not conform yourselves to this aeon, but be transformed by the renewing of the consciousness." Redeemed by Christ, Christians no longer stand in this aeon but in the coming aeon (Gl. 1:4). In conduct, then, they must not follow the forms of life in this aeon but the very different form of life in the coming aeon.[22] But they cannot give themselves this form. They are changed into it on the basis of the renewing of their thinking and willing by the πνεῦμα (→ 758; III, 453). The paradoxical μεταμορφοῦσθε[23] which echoes Jesus' call for repentance (→ μετανοέω, μετάνοια), has in view the responsibility of Christians for the change becoming and remaining effective. Its concern is the new moral life in the Spirit as an obligation:[24] "Become what you are."

Behm

---

[20] Cf. on this H. F. Weber, *"Eschatologie" u. "Mystik" im NT* (1930), 81 ff.

[21] 𝔓[46] Orig B lat syr guarantee the authenticity of the imperative.

[22] On the obviously deliberate contrasting of συσχηματίζεσθαι and μεταμορφοῦσθαι *v.* Chrys. Hom. in R., 20, *ad loc.* (MPG, 60, 597 f.). Cf. also J. B. Lightfoot, *St. Paul's Epistle to the Phil.*[4] (1927 reprint), 130 f.; Trench, 174 f.; Zn. R., *ad loc.*; A. Pallis, *To the Romans* (1920), 133; M. J. Lagrange, *St. Paul Épître aux Romains*[4] (1931), *ad loc.*

[23] On the pass. here cf. Bl.-Debr.[6] § 314.

[24] Cf. Ltzm. R.[4], Exc. on 6:4; P. Althaus (*NT Deutsch,* 6), Exc. "Das neue Leben als Wirklichkeit u. Aufgabe" on 6:1-14.

† μόσχος

A general and common word for "calf," "young cow or bull." We find it on class. and Hell. soil, also inscr. and pap. It is common in the LXX for various Heb. terms (note esp. בָּקָר, עֵגֶל, פַּר, שׁוֹר). As in Gk. literature (Hom.) there is in OT narrative a distinction between large and small cattle (LXX πρόβατα καὶ μόσχοι). Cattle figure among the possessions of the patriarchs (Gn. 12:16; 20:14; 21:27; 24:35), but esp. as sacrificial animals in the various expiatory rites (περὶ τῆς ἁμαρτίας) of the Law (Ex. 20:24; 29:10-14; Lv. 4:3 ff.; 8:2 ff.; 16:3 ff.). Worth noting are the explicit rules in preparation for the great festival of atonement. A bullock is to be killed for the reconciliation of the priest and his house to God (Lv. 16:3 ff.; Yoma, 3, 8; 4, 2; 5, 3-5; 6, 7). In the later tradition there are constant refs. to the account of the molten calf (μόσχος χωνευτός, Ex. 32:4; cf. Dt. 9:16, 21; Neh. 9:18), an early example of the sin of Israel and the mercy of God. In the vision of the heavenly throne chariot in Ez. 1:4 ff. four mysterious living creatures (חַיָּה, LXX: ζῷον), each with four faces and four wings, are mentioned; the four faces are those of a man, a lion, a bull and an eagle. The distinctive feature of the text of Ez. as compared with Assyrian and Babylonian par., as also of the NT account of the same scene in Rev. 4:7-8, is the fact that each watcher has four faces.[1] Along with μόσχος both the LXX and the NT use the similar ταῦρος (cf. the combination ταῦροι καὶ τράγοι in Dt. 32:14; Is. 1:11; Hb. 9:13; 10:4).[2] En. in his visions speaks of white, black and red bulls, though the white is the most prominent. 85:3: "Then came a bull from the earth, and this bull was white," 85:9: "I now saw in my sleep how this white bull grew and became a great bull. From it sprang many white bulls like unto it." 89:1: "Each of them went to the white bull and taught it a secret at which it trembled. It was born as a bull, but now became a man;

μόσχος. [1] A. Jeremias, *Das AT im Lichte des Alten Orients* (1930), 699 ff., thinks that the four heads of the text are a misunderstanding: Each of the four mixed creatures has a head, bull, lion, eagle, man. As he sees it, these are the divinely appointed watchers at the four corners of the earth. An astral-mythological origin is supposed, for the four figures correspond to certain signs of the zodiac, the bull April (spring), the lion July (summer), the scorpion October (autumn) and the aquarian January (winter). But on later Jewish and early Christian soil the four watchers are angelic powers, cf. Michael, Raphael, Gabriel and Phanuel, En. 40:1-10. Cf. Cant. r. on 3:10: R. Berechia and R. Bun said in the name of R. Abbahu: There are four majestic creatures, the eagle among birds, the bull among domestic animals, the lion among wild animals, but the highest of all is man; God has taken them all and engraved them in the throne of glory, as it is said in Ps. 103: "The Lord has established his throne in the heavens," i.e., above all heights, whereby thou mayest perceive that He rules over all (Str.-B., III, 799). Cf. also the par. Midr. Ps. 103:16 on 19; Tanch. בשלח, 14 (31a, Buber); Ex. r., 23 on 15:1. Cf. also PRE, 4 in Str.-B., III, 799 with its description (based on Ez.) of four living creatures identical with the cherubim (Ez. 10:20), who are here clearly differentiated from the seraphim. A. Jeremias' interpretation of Ez. and Rev. in terms of the zodiac is very doubtful.

[2] μόσχος also occurs with βοῦς and κριός: Prv. 14:4 LXX: βοῦς, Σ: μόσχος (שׁוֹר). Is. 27:10 LXX: different, Σ: μόσχος (עֵגֶל). 34:7 LXX: καὶ οἱ κριοὶ καὶ οἱ ταῦροι, Ἀ: καὶ δαμάλεις μετὰ δυναστῶν, Σ: καὶ μόσχοι μετὰ κραταιῶν, Θ: καὶ ταῦροι μετὰ ἰσχυρῶν (וּפָרִים עִם־אַבִּירִים). Jer. 50(27):11 LXX: βοΐδια, Ἀ: μόσχοι (עֶגְלָה). [Bertram.]

it built a ship and dwelt in it; three bulls also lived in the ship with it, and it was covered over them."[3]

The parable in Lk. 15:11-32 speaks of the fatted calf which was killed in honour of the prodigal son (μόσχος σιτευτός, 15:23, 27, 30; Ju. 6:25 [A]; Ιερ. 26:21 LXX). Hb. 9:12 in connection with the sacrifices of the great Day of Atonement mentions the blood of goats and calves (τράγων καὶ μόσχων), and the same animals are mentioned in reverse order (τῶν μόσχων καὶ τῶν τράγων) in 9:19 in connection with the covenant sacrifices at Sinai (Ex. 24:3 ff.). Hb. also refers to the blood of goats and bulls (τράγων καὶ ταύρων) in 9:13, and the same animals in reverse order are expiatory offerings of the old covenant according to 10:4. The external variations are a mark of the stylistic refinement of Hb., but exposition must take account of Is. 1:11 (αἷμα ταύρων καὶ τράγων οὐ βούλομαι).[4] ταῦρος is a more specific term than μόσχος, since only male animals were sacrificed. The great apocalyptic scene in Rev. 4 (v. 7: τὸ δεύτερον ζῷον ὅμοιον μόσχῳ) is obviously based on Ez. 1:4 ff.; 10:1 ff., though there are deviations from the OT presuppositions. The cherubim of Rev. do not belong directly to the throne or throne chariot, but are to some degree independent. Each is a living creature (ζῷον) of a specific kind, and the order is not the same as in Ez. (now lion, calf, man, eagle). The further description of their form and cry borrows features from the seraphim of Is. 6:1-3 (Rev. 4:8).[5] We are thus dealing with angelic powers who attest to God's presence in the visible world. They are in no sense representatives of creation and history before God. In the early Church the four watchers were largely understood as the four Evangelists, with some vacillation of order.[6] In their distinction and unity these cherubim represent the perfect holiness and glory of God. "The intelligence of man, the aggressive strength of the lion, the carrying and pulling power of the ox, the sharp glance and winged strength of the eagle, are distributed among them and yet are united in harmonious operation," Zn. Apk., I, 326. A feature of the total picture is that it goes beyond the individual OT depictions (Ez. 1:4 ff.; 10:12; Is. 6:1-3), and the subsidiary motifs are more simple and direct.

In the post-apost. period 1 Cl., 52 quotes various verses from the Ps. (7:16; 50:14 f.; 51:17; 69:31) to show that God needs nothing but accepts the confession of man (ἐξομολογεῖσθαι). This confession pleases God better than a bullock (ὑπὲρ μόσχον νέον) with horns and hoofs (69:31). The full content of the quotations (εὐφραίνεσθαι, ἐπικαλεῖσθαι, δοξάζειν = θυσία αἰνέσεως, εὐχαί, πνεῦμα συντετριμμένον) is to be deployed in this understanding of ἐξομολογεῖσθαι. The new sacrifice is more than

---

[3] The white bull (white is the colour of innocence and uprightness) is Adam in En. 85:3, Seth in 85:9, Noah in 89:1, cf. Kautzsch Apkr. u. Pseudepigr., II, 289 f.; R. H. Charles, *The Apocrypha and Pseudepigrapha of the OT*, II (1913), 250 f.

[4] F. Bleek, II, 2 (1840), 542.

[5] The four living creatures have six wings each (cf. Is. 6:1-3), as distinct from the four of Ez. Cf. the depiction of angels in apocalyptic, En. 39:12: "Those who never sleep praise thee; they stand before thy glory, praise, laud and magnify thee with words: Holy, holy, holy is the Lord of spirits; he fills the earth with spirits"; 71:7: "Round about were seraphim, cherubim and ophanim; these are they who never sleep, who watch over the throne of his glory."

[6] Acc. to Iren. Haer., III, 11, 8 the four cherubim are the Evangelists (John the lion, Lk. the calf, Mt. the man and Mk. the eagle), and the number four has mysterious ramifications in Christology and salvation history. Mk. and Jn. are now linked with the lion, now with the eagle, but the difference is connected with the fluctuating order of the Gospels in the Canon, cf. T. Zahn, *Forschungen z. Geschichte d. nt.lichen Kanons u. d. altkirchlichen Lit.*, II (1883), 257-275; Kan., II, 364-375.

the offering of a bull. Barn., 8, 1 ff. tries to interpret christologically and allegorically the killing of the red heifer in Nu. 19; the ref. to this expiatory statute seems also to have had particular significance in Hb. 9:13 (σποδὸς δαμάλεως).[7] Acc. to the "simple" exposition of Barn. each feature of the OT command (the men who sacrifice, the boys who sprinkle, the wool and hyssop) is reflected in the history of Jesus, in His cross, and in the preaching of the apostles. The heifer which is slain is Christ Himself (ὁ μόσχος ὁ Ἰησοῦς ἐστιν, 8, 2); as in Hb. 9:12 f. μόσχος = ταῦρος, so here μόσχος = δάμαλις, a sign that the term μόσχος can include the other two.

Michel

† μῦθος

(→ ἀλήθεια, I, 238 f.; → γενεαλογία, I, 663-665; → λόγος, IV, 69-136, esp. 73 f.; 77-91; 100 ff.; → παραμυθέομαι).

Contents: A. The Problems raised by the Term Myth. B. The Development of the Meaning: Etymology; Main Stages of Meaning: 1. "Thought" as the Root Meaning; 2. Thought μῦθοι; 3. Expressed μῦθοι: a. "Word," plur. "Sayings"; b. "Word," plur. "Words"; c. "Account," "Story": (a) "True Story," "Fact"; (b) "Untrue Story (Saga, Fairy-story, Fable, Myth, Poetry). C. Myth in the Greek World and Hellenism: 1. The Many Senses of Myth; 2. Counterparts of μῦθος: ἔργον, ἔπος, λόγος; 3. The Position of μῦθοι in the Intellectual World of Greece: a. In the Cultus and Religious Teaching; b. In Poetry; c. In Philosophy; d. In Spiritual Direction and Education; 4. The Allegorical Interpretation of Myth; 5. The Evaluation and Use of Myth: a. In Stoicism; b. in Posidonius; c. In the Mysteries; d. In Grave Symbolism; e. In Gnosticism; 6. Criticism and Repudiation of

[7] On the ashes of the red heifer in Rabb. Judaism cf. Nu. r., 19, 4 on 19:2, where we also find the saying of R. Acha in the name of R. Chanina: "In the hour when Moses went up on high, he heard the voice of the Holy One, blessed be He, who sat there and was occupied with the section on the red heifer, and pronounced the halacha in the name of the one who has said it (from whom it comes)." There were thus in Judaism many speculations on the chapter (not followed up in Hb.). W. Vischer, *Das Christuszeugnis des AT*, I² (1935) sees here a direct ref. to Jesus Christ: "This is the Gospel which is proclaimed in the section on the red heifer and confirmed by the sacraments of baptism and the Lord's Supper" (278).

μῦθος. In general: Cr.-Kö., 739-741; also 240 f. (*s.v.* γενεαλογία); B. Lindner, RE³, VII, 549, 4-47, *s.v.* "Heidentum"; W. Aly, Pauly-W., XVI (1935), 1374-1411, *s.v.* "Mythos"; E. A. Gardner, ERE, IX, 117-121, *s.v.* "Mythology"; P. Tillich, O. Rühle etc., RGG², IV, 363-394, Art. "Mythus u. Mythologie"; W. Baumgartner, H. Gunkel, G. Bertram, RGG², V, 41-64, Art. "Sagen u. Legenden"; L. Walk and P. Simon, LexThK², VII (1935), 412-418, *s.v.* "Mythologie"; K. Eisler, Wörterbuch d. philosophischen Begriffe⁴ (1927), *s.v.* "Mythus"; E. v. Schmidt, *Die Philosophie der Mythologie u. Max Müller* (1880); K. T. Preuss, *Der religiöse Gehalt d. Mythen* (1933); W. Wundt, *Völkerpsychologie. Eine Untersuchung d. Entwicklungsgesetze von Sprache, Mythus u. Sitte*, Vol. II: "Mythus u. Religion," IV⁴ (1926), V³ (1923), VI³ (1923), and on this R. Otto, "Mythus u. Religion in Wundts Völkerpsychologie," ThR, 13 (1910), 251 ff.; 293 ff. = "Sünde u. Urschuld," *Aufsätze das Numinose betreffend*⁴ (1929), 213 ff.; E. Kassirer, "Sprache u. Mythus," *Studien d. Bibliothek Warburg*, VI (1925); *Philosophie d. symbolischen Formen*, II: "Das mythische Denken" (1925); A. Jolles, *Einfache Formen, Legende/Sage/Mythe/Rätsel/Spruch/Kasus/Memorabile/Märchen/Witz* (1930), 91-125; J. and W. Grimm, *Deutsches Wörterbuch*, VI (1885), 2848, *s.v.* "Mythe." On A: F. W. v. Schelling, *Über Mythen, historische Sagen u. Philosopheme d. ältesten Welt* (1793); *Philosophie d. Mythologie* (1842); *Historisch-kritische Einleitung in d. Philosophie d. Mythologie* (1842); cf. A. Allwohn, *Der Mythos bei Schelling* (1927); G. Dekker, *Die Rückwendung zum Mythos. Schellings letzte Wandlung* (1930). J. v. Görres, *Mythengeschichte d. asiatischen Welt* (1810); F. Creuzer, *Symbolik u. Mythologie d. alten Völker* (1810 ff.; ³1836 ff.); cf. E. Howald, *Der Kampf um Creuzers Symbolik* (1926); C. F. Baur, *Die Symbolik u. Mythologie oder die Naturreligion des Altertums* (1824/25). J. J. Bachofen, *Versuch über die Gräbersymbolik d. Alten* (1859; ²1925);

Myth; 7. Conclusion. D. μῦθος and myths in the OT (LXX) and Judaism. E. μῦθος in the NT: I. Myth an Alien Body in the NT. II. The Problem of the NT μῦθοι: 1. Uniformity of the μῦθοι in the Past.; 2. Origin and Nature of the μῦθοι in the Past.: a. "Stories of the gods"? b. "Gnostic myths"? c. "Jewish Fables"? 3. The Nature of the μῦθοι in 2 Pt. III. Myth, Truth and History: 1. Myth and Truth for the Greeks; 2. Myth and History in Antiquity; 3. Myth, Truth and History in the NT; IV. Designations and Relations of the NT μῦθοι: 1. In 2 Tm. 4:4: a. μῦθος and λόγος; b. Teachers of μῦθοι; 2. In 1 Tm. 4:7: a. μῦθοι βέβηλοι; b. μῦθοι γραώδεις; 3. In 1 Tm. 1:4; 4. In Tt. 1:14; 5. In 2 Pt. 1:16: a. Invention of μῦθοι; b. μῦθος and Biblical History. V. Myths in the Gospel? F. The Evaluation of Myths in the Early Church. G. Conclusions: Is there any Place for Myth in the NT Message? 1. As a Form of Religious Communication? 2. As Parable? 3. As Symbol? 4. A New Use of the Term?

Der Mythus von Orient u. Occident (1926), with intro. by A. Baeumler: "Bachofen, der Mythologe d. Romantik" (pp. XXV-CCXCIV); cf. M. Schröter, "Mythus u. Metaphysik bei Bachofen u. Schelling," *Orient u. Occident*, 10 (1932), 18-22; N. Berdyaev, *Der Sinn d. Geschichte* (1925), 45 ff.; *Die Philosophie des freien Geistes* (1930), 88 ff.; A. Rosenberg, *Der Mythus d. 20. Jhdts.* (1930), cf. W. Schloz and W. Laiblin, "Vom Sinn d. Mythos," *Schriften d. Deutschen Glaubensbewegung*, 7 (1936), but also P. Simon, "Mythos oder Religion," *Der Christ in der Zeit*, 7[4] (1935); A. W. Macholz, "Die Sage u. das Wort, der Gesetzescharakter d. Mythos u. die chr. Verkündigung," ThBl, 13 (1934), 161 ff.; R. Frick, "Mythos u. Offenbarung," *Monatsschrift f. Pastoraltheologie*, 30 (1934), 224 ff.; P. Tillich, RGG[2], IV, 363-370, *s.v.* "Mythus, begrifflich u. religionsgeschichtlich." On B: Pass., Liddell-Scott, Pr.-Bauer[3], *s.v.*; E. Hofmann, *Qua ratione* ΕΠΟΣ, ΜΥΘΟΣ, ΑΙΝΟΣ, ΛΟΓΟΣ *et vocabula ab eisdem stirpibus derivata in antiquo Graecorum sermone ... adhibita sint* (Diss. Göttingen, 1923), esp. 28-48; bibl., 31, n. 1; J. H. H. Schmidt, *Synonymik d. gr. Sprache*, I (1876), 13 ff. Through my father O. Stählin I had access to much unpublished linguistic material prepared by Kopp of Erlangen for a lex. on Aristotle; I am also indebted to my father in other respects. On C: F. Lübker, *Reallexikon d. klass. Altertums*[8] (1914), Art. "Mythologie"; O. Gruppe, *Gr. Mythologie u. Religionsgeschichte* (1906), 14 f. with bibl.; "Gesch. d. klass. Mythologie u. Religionsgeschichte," Suppl. to Roscher (1921); M. P. Nilsson, *History of Gk. Religion* (1925); W. F. Otto, *Dionysos. Mythos u. Kultus* (1933), esp. 11-46; E. Bethe, *Mythus, Sage, Märchen* (1905); L. Radermacher, *Mythus u. Sage bei d. Griechen* (1938); E. Howald, *Mythus u. Tragödie* (1927); *Die gr. Tragödie* (1930), 2 ff.; P. Friedländer, *Platon*, I (1928), c. 9: Mythos (199-241); K. Reinhardt, *Platons Mythen* (1927); W. Willi, *Versuch einer Grundlegung d. platonischen Mythopoiie* (1925); H. W. Thomas, ΕΠΕΚΕΙΝΑ, *Untersuchungen über das Überlieferungsgut in den Jenseitsmythen Platons* (Diss. München, 1938); A. Nygren, *Eros u. Agape*, I (1930); E. Rohde, *Der gr. Roman u. seine Vorläufer*[3] (1914). On D: H. Gunkel, RGG[2], IV, 381-390, Art. "Mythus u. Mythologie im AT"; V, 49-60, Art. "Sagen u. Legenden in Israel"; *Genesis*[4] (1917), *passim*; M. Noth, "Die Historisierung d. Mythus im AT," *Christentum u. Wissenschaft*, 4 (1928), 265-272; 301-309; A. Weiser, *Glaube u. Geschichte im AT* (1931), 23-32; R. Kittel, *Die hell. Mysterienreligion u. das AT* (1924), esp. 67 ff.; J. Bergel, *Mythologie der alten Hebräer*, I and II (1882/83). On E: Wettstein, II, 701 on 2 Pt. 1:16; B. Weiss, *Die Briefe Pauli an Tm. u. Tt.*[7] (1902), 79 n., 171 n.; J. E. Belser, *Die Briefe d. Ap. Pls. an Tm. u. Tt.* (1907), 5 ff., 33; Wbg. Past., 24-49, and *ad loc.*; Dib. Past. on 1 Tm. 1:4 and Exc. on 1 Tm. 4:5: 1c; W. Lock, ICC (1924), XVII, 8 f. and *ad loc.*; Schl. Past., 33 f., 36, 123, 186 f.; F. Spitta, 2 Pt. (1885), *ad loc.*; J. B. Mayor (1907), on 2 Pt. 1:16 (103 and n.); C. Bigg, ICC[2] (1910), on 2 Pt. 1:16; Wbg. Pt., *ad loc.*; Wnd. Kath. Br. on 2 Pt. 1:16; Kn. Pt., *ad loc.*; H. Colson, "Myths and Genealogies," JThSt, 19 (1917/18), 265-271; G. Kittel, "Die γενεαλογίαι d. Past.," ZNW, 20 (1921), 49 ff.; R. Bultmann, RGG[2], IV, 390-394, Art. "Mythus u. Mythologie im NT"; J. M. Robertson, *Christianity and Mythology* (1900), esp. 181 ff. → n. 7; G. Bertram, RGG[2], V, 60-64, Art. "Sagen u. Legenden im NT"; *NT u. historische Methode* (1928). On F: Harnack Miss., 31 and 33 ff.; J. Geffcken, *Zwei gr. Apologeten* (1907); E. Hatch, *Griechentum u. Christentum* (1892), esp. 36 ff.; P. Heinisch, "Der Einfluss Philos auf die älteste chr. Exegese," *At.liche Abhandlungen*, ed. J. Nikel, I, 1/2 (1908); G. Bornkamm, *Mythos u. Legende in den apokr. Thomasakten* (1933). On G: A. Jeremias, "Die Bedeutung des Mythos f. d. Dogmatik," *Festschr. f. L. Ihmels* (1928), 236-257; "Die Bedeutung des Mythos f. das ap. Glaubensbekenntnis," *Religionswissenschaftliche Darstellungen f. d. Gegenwart, Heft* 5 (1930).

A. The Problems raised by the Term Myth.

The history of μῦθος = "word" both in Greek itself and as a loan word in other European languages is an instructive example of the way in which the same term can enjoy high estimation at one time and suffer severe devaluation at another. Particularly as a religious term [1] this word has moved from one extreme to the other, and sometimes, as in our own day, there have been great differences in its assessment.

Decisive points in its evaluation are first the way in which one relates it to the truth and reality of history, and second the degree to which one regards the truth and reality as religious values.

a. If myth is regarded as expressing a total view, [2] as partially in Plato, then in Schelling and the more modern myth idealism, [3] or if it is taken to be an account of reality (→ n. 37) in a supreme sense, as often in our own century, [4] it can have the dignity of supreme religious value. Basic here is the judgment that "life can only be expressed in terms of 'myth' when the natural and the supernatural meet as Plato knew." [5] Myth is exalted to the position of being the adequate expression of a revelation, and there is no place for interest in the historical character of revelation.

b. There is a similar high estimation of myth — both in antiquity and to-day — when myth, viewed as a unity of form and content and understood as a symbol, allows any philosophical system to be dated back to the earliest times with the help of allegorical interpretation (→ C. 4).

---

[1] Whether the term is originally religious is much discussed in academic enquiry. Howald thinks it was originally poetry, equally indifferent to religion, ethics and truth; cf. also F. Kauffmann, "Zur Theorie des Mythos," *Arch. f. die gesamte Psychologie*, 46 (1924), 61 ff.

[2] "The sensual expression, by way of personification, of the total inward and outward world view of the man of a given age" (→ Simon, LexThK[2], VII, 412), "the inner, unified, spiritual, moral and philosophical core of a race or people" (O. Gros, *850 Worte 'Mythus des XX. Jhdts.'* [1938], 57) — these are modern definitions embodying Nietzsche's idea of the correlation of myth and race. Cf. also Eisler, *op. cit.*

[3] Cf. Aly, Allwohn, Walk, 412, also Simon, *op. cit.*, 414 f. (myth to-day). To this level belong esp. the grandiose if varying conceptions of myth in Bachofen, Nietzsche, Stefan George and Rosenberg.

[4] Cf. F. A. Schmid Noerr, in "Luthertum" = NkZ, NF, 48 (1937), 82, and esp. Berdyaev, for whom myth is a reality incomparably greater than all perception, though not without ambivalence regarding reality, as in the statement in *Philosophie*, 96: "Myth always expresses a reality, but the reality of myth is symbolical" (with ref. to the story of the fall), → b. The tendency to regard myth as a term for transhistorical reality of supreme significance may also be seen in a philosophical theologian like P. Tillich with his symbolical-realistic theory of myth, cf. *op. cit.*, 364: "Myth is a symbol, constructed from elements of reality, for the unconditioned which is in view in the religious act." Very different is E. Brunner's attempt (*Der Mittler* [1927, [2]1930], 337-356) to introduce the concept of Christian mythology. On the relation of such attempts to the NT → G., esp. 4 (→ 794 f.).

[5] R. Niebuhr, *An Interpretation of Christian Ethics* (1937), 24, n. 1; cf. ExpT, 48 (1937), 212. Martin Buber describes the march of the Jewish myth through time; the Gospel is the greatest of all the triumphs of myth (*Die Chassidischen Bücher* [1928], 129). There is also an a-religious understanding of myth — in the ordinary sense — as a reality, cf. O. Goldberg, *Die Wirklichkeit d. Hebräer*, I (1925); and on this E. Unger, *Das Problem der mythischen Realität* (1926). On the basis of the idea of the authentic people and its collective life myths are here viewed as a scientifically recognisable reality; the events of the Bible constitute a specific form. But this is all said with the important reservation that with the actual people the gods are now dead. Cf. also Jolles, 122 f. on the story of the Maid of Orleans as a myth.

c. A decisive step is taken when it is argued that the unhistorical is the mark of myth, when the historical is no longer regarded as a religious value, and when religious significance can be claimed for myth even without allegorical interpretation, as in C. F. Nösgen's definition: [6] "Any unhistorical tale, however it may have arisen, in which a religious society finds a constituent part of its sacred foundations, because an absolute expression of its institutions, experiences and ideas, is a myth." In this sense D. F. Strauss, without denying the historical existence of Jesus, can call the NT a myth, a saga-like garment for early Christian ideas, and yet maintain its relative religious value.

d. But if the concept of myth is brought into antithesis to both historical reality and to truth as such, and if reality and truth are thought to be essential to genuine revelation and the only possible basis of faith, myth can have no religious value. The result is either that the NT stories are dismissed as myths, as errors and deceptions, [7] or that there is a sharp cleavage between the Gospel and myth. The latter is the judgment of the NT itself, which opposes myth to history on the one side (2 Pt. 1:16: ἐπόπται) and ἀλήθεια (2 Tm. 4:4; Tt. 1:14) on the other, and thus declares μῦθος to be incompatible with the οἰκονομία θεοῦ (1 Tm. 1:4) and true εὐσέβεια (4:7). → E. The Christian Church, in so far as it is true to itself, accepts this judgment that myth is untrue and consequently of no religious value.

B. The Development of the Meaning.

Etymology. This is debated. [8] Derivation from μύω "to close" (the eyes) is unacceptable on grounds of content, [9] and from μυέω "to instruct," "to initiate" (→ μυστήριον) on formal linguistic grounds. Nor is the connection with the cry μύ! very satisfactory (cf. Aristoph. Eq., 10); Prellwitz [10] tries to derive both the above verbs from this on the theory that the original ejaculation gave rise to terms both for silence (μύω) and for speech, e.g., μῦθος. A possible derivation is from a stem *mēudh-, mudh-* which is found in many Indo-European languages in many different but related meanings, esp. the Slav. *myslĭ,* "thought," "consideration." If this derivation is correct, [11] the original meaning of μῦθος is "thought," and it is in fact best to take this as the starting-point for the history of the meaning of the word.

Main Stages of Meaning. These are as follows.

---

6 *Geschichte Jesu Christi* = (*Gesch. d. nt.lichen Offenbarung,* I) (1891), 76; there is here (75-84) a — partially dated — rejection of all mythical theories of the NT. The definition describes the basic position of Hinduism with its basis in a rich and profound mythology and its lofty indifference to history (→ n. 182).

7 Cf. the mythical theories of J. M. Robertson, *Die Evangelienmythen* (1910); A. Drews, *Die Christusmythe*² (1924); W. B. Smith, *Der vorchristliche Jesus* (1906); S. Lublinski, *Der urchr. Erdkreis u. sein Mythos,* 2 Vols. (1910); bibl. in H. Windisch, "Das Problem d. Geschichtlichkeit Jesu: die Christusmythe," ThR, NF, 2 (1930), 207-252. Robertson's definition (*op. cit.,* 1) is typical: Myth is simply a term to classify a varied mass of traditional error. Against this cf. J. Weiss, *Jesus von Nazareth — Mythus oder Geschichte?* (1910); J. Leipoldt, *Hat Jesus gelebt?* (1920); *Vom Jesusbilde der Gegenwart*² (1925), 190 ff. Cf. the related view of the Gospel history as saga in G. Brandes, *Die Jesus-Sage* (1925); T. Kappstein, *Bibel u. Sage* (1913), 1-217 (saga, myth and legend in the Bible).

8 With the masc. μῦθος Hesych. (alone) also has a fem. μύθα (Cypriot dialect form) and a neut. μῦθαρ. The Germ. fem. "Mythe" is not Gk., but is formed by analogy with "Erzählung," "Fabel" etc. (→ Grimm). Modern distinctions between "Mythe" and "Mythos" (e.g., Jolles, 100) are quite arbitrary.

9 Hofmann, 31, n. 1 calls the derivation from μύω ridiculous.

10 Etym. Wört., 301; cf. Walde-Pok., II, 256; *ibid.,* 310 we also find the suggestion that the formation of μῦθος is par. to the guttural extension in the Sanskrit *múkha,* "mouth."

11 So Boisacq, 649; Hofmann, 47 f.; also → 74, n. 14.

1. "Thought" as the Root Meaning.[12] This is supported a. by the etym., b. by par. observations regarding the use of the verb μυθέομαι,[13] c. by the fact that, apart from two instances in Eur. (Med., 1082; Hipp., 197), who uses μῦθος far more often than Aesch. and Soph., only Hom. has this sense with any frequency, cf. esp. Il., 1, 545; 9, 309: τὸν μῦθον ἀπηλεγέως ἀποειπεῖν, Od., 11, 511: οὐχ ἡμάρτανε μύθων, "he did not go astray in his thoughts (or counsels)." The common question of Hera:[14] ποῖον τὸν μῦθον ἔειπες; also has the sense: "What do you really think?" as distinct from the expression ποῖόν σε ἔπος φύγεν ἕρκος ὀδόντων, where ἔπος means an empty word, which often contains only a false or foolish thought.

2. Thought μῦθοι. So long as a thought is unexpressed, it can have the form of an intention,[15] purpose,[16] opinion or idea,[17] reason,[18] rule,[19] or counsel,[20] with a natural tendency to communicate itself.

3. Expressed μῦθοι. Deliberation often implies inner dialogue, and every thought carries within it an urge for expression. For the Gks. thought and speech were originally identical.[21] As expressed thought μῦθος, "word," can take many forms,[22] like λόγος (→ 77) in all Gk. and → παράκλησις in the NT. Three main lines may be followed.

a. "Word" (plur. "Sayings"),[23] with the emphasis on content, in such varied forms and nuances as "saying," "proverb,"[24] "statement,"[25] "answer,"[26] "command,"[27]

---

[12] Hofmann, 30-36, with further instances, e.g., of μῦθος in connection with βουλή, νόημα etc. Schmidt, 13-19 is wrongly critical of this assumption and its implications.

[13] μυθέομαι (Schmidt, 19 f.), which is almost exclusive to poetry, but does not occur in Eur., Aristoph. or Attic prose (in the NT only → παραμυθέομαι) can mean not only "to speak," "to tell" (e.g., Hom. Il., 3, 235; 17, 200: "to speak to oneself") but also "to think," "to deliberate" (Democr. Fr., 30 [II, 151, Diels[5]]: πάντα Ζεὺς μυθέεται), and "to expound" (e.g., Il., 1, 74, "to interpret"). Par. to the development of μῦθος the later form μυθεύω usually means "to recount a fable" (whence μύθευμα, e.g., Plut. Mar., 11 [I, 411 f.]; Ign. Mg., 8, 1).

[14] The only exception is Il., 8, 209 (not v. 462, Hofmann, 34 f.).

[15] Il., 9, 625 f.: μύθοιο τελευτή, cf. 16, 83; Od., 4, 776 f.: σιγῇ τοῖον ἀναστάντες τελέωμεν μῦθον.

[16] Od., 4, 675 f.: ἄπυστος μύθων οὓς μνηστῆρες ἐνὶ φρεσὶ βυσσοδόμευον, "in ignorance of the resolves which the suitors secretly took in their minds."

[17] Emped. Fr., 24 (I, 322, Diels[5]) etc.; Plat. Symp., 177a: οὐ γὰρ ἐμὸς ὁ μῦθος ... ὃν μέλλω λέγειν, "the following idea does not come from me, in what follows I do not speak" (but Phaidros); this (or a similar phrase) was obviously a proverbial quotation from Eur. Melan. (Fr., 484, 1 [TGF, 511]; cf. Stallbaum on Plat. Ap., 20e), so also Plut. Symposiacon, 4 (II, 661a) and 8 (II, 718a); Philo Som., I, 172; Mut. Nom., 152: οὗτος δ' οὐκ ἐμὸς μῦθος, ἀλλὰ χρησμῶν τῶν ἱεροτάτων ἐστίν. Here there is already interwoven the thought of an assertion of my own, cf. Hor. Sat., II, 2, 2: *nec meus hic sermo est.*

[18] So in the fig. etym. μῦθον μυθεῖσθαι ("to declare the reason" for something, Od., 3, 140), which is a link between a. and b: "to express a thought."

[19] Plat. Leg., VI, 773b: κατὰ παντὸς εἷς ἔστω μῦθος γάμου.

[20] Hom. Il., 7, 358: οἶσθα καὶ ἄλλον μῦθον ἀμείνονα τοῦδε νοῆσαι.

[21] Stenzel in NJbch., 47 (1921), 152; → n. 18; though cf. also Schmidt, 17.

[22] Cf. already C. G. Heyne in his ed. of Homer, I (1802), 33 f. on Il., 1, 221.

[23] E.g., Od., 3, 124; 7, 157: μύθοισι κεκάσθαι, "to be armed with words, eloquent"; cf. also the play on words in Sir. 20:19: ἄνθρωπος ἄχαρις, μῦθος ἄκαιρος, "like a distasteful person is a word out of season" (which does not need to be foolish or evil in itself); cf. V. Ryssel in Kautzsch Apkr., *ad loc.*

[24] Aesch. Choeph., 314: τριγέρων μῦθος, "an ancient saying"; cf. Thes. Steph., *s.v.* (V, 1251 B); cf. λόγος in Jn. 4:37.

[25] Aristoph. Vesp., 725 f.: πρὶν ἂν ἀμφοῖν μῦθον ἀκούσῃς, οὐκ ἂν δικάσαις. Cf. Ps.-Hes. Fr., 271 (p. 412, Rzach, with further instances); Ps.-Phokylides, 87 (I, 200, Anthologia Lyrica, ed. E. Diehl).

[26] Hom. Od., 5, 97 f.: εἰρωτᾷς ... τὸν μῦθον ἐνισπήσω.

[27] *Ibid.*, 17, 348: ἐπεὶ τὸν μῦθον ἄκουσεν.

"commission,"[28] "proposal,"[29] "promise,"[30] but esp. "speech,"[31] "report,"[32] "discussion," "conference."[33]

b. "Word" in the formal sense (plur. "words"), a secondary sense on the analogy of ἔπος (→ 769 f.) and not very common in Hom.[34]

c. "Account," "Story." But the main emphasis is on content. There thus arise the meanings "report," "message,"[35] "account," "story,"[36] and this raises the question whether the story is true or not, and leads to a further distinction in meaning, the most important from the NT standpoint. (a) On the one side μῦθος can be an "account of facts,"[37] then the "fact"[38] itself, then in a weakened form a "circumstance," "matter."[39] (b) On the other side it means "rumour,"[40] or (unauthenticated) "story," in such varied form as primitive history, saga, legend,[41] the precursor of true history, → 785; then "fairy-story" such as women tell children, which is not true, but is valued for the kernel

---

[28] Il., 9, 625 f.: ἴομεν· οὐ γάρ μοι δοκέει μύθοιο τελευτὴ τῇδε γ' ὁδῷ κρανέεσθαι.

[29] Od., 21, 143: τοῖσιν δ' ἐπιήνδανε μῦθος.

[30] Il., 5, 715: ἅλιος μῦθος, "empty promise."

[31] E.g., Il., 2, 335 with ref. to vv. 284-332; Od., 17, 57 etc.: ἄπτερος ἔπλετο μῦθος, the sense of the speech did not fly away, i.e., she kept it in remembrance (so Hofmann, 3 f., 29 f., also Seiler-Capelle, Hom.-Wörterbuch[9] (1889), *s.v.* ἄπτερος etc., though many take the view that the word, or thought, was unfledged, i.e., unanswered, so Ameis-Hentze, *ad loc.* cf. esp. the express discussion in the *Anhang,* III, 111 f.; Liddell-Scott, *s.v.* ἄπτερος). Since a speech consists of many thoughts and words, the plur. is common, and sing. and plur. can be used *promiscue,* cf. Il., 2, 245 with Od., 2, 82 f.

[32] Sib., 3, 226: The inhabitants of Ur think nothing of μύθων μωρῶν ἀπάτας ἐγγαστεριμύθων, the misleading and foolish reports of professional orators. On ἐγγαστρίμυθος cf. 1 S. 28:7 ff. and Orig., *ad loc.* (GCS Orig., 3, 283 ff.).

[33] Since this also (→ n. 31) consists of many μῦθοι, the plur. is mostly used, e.g., Hom. Od., 4, 214.

[34] So Il., 9, 443; Eur. Iph. Taur., 900: μύθων πέρα (= ἀμύθητος), "inexpressible in words"; cf. also A. Nauck on IG, XII, 1, 40, 7 in *Rheinisches Museum,* 6 (1848), 443.

[35] Hom. Il., 9, 627: ἀπαγγεῖλαι μῦθον, Soph. Trach., 67.

[36] Od., 11, 368, cf. 376: μυθήσασθαι, "to recount," Aesch. Prom., 505: βραχεῖ δὲ μύθῳ πάντα συλλήβδην μάθε, "comprised in a short report," though cf. Pers., 713: πάντα ... ἀκούσῃ μῦθον ἐν βραχεῖ λόγῳ, "the whole matter (→ n. 38) in a short account." On the corresponding phrases μῦθος ἀπώλετο (Plat. Theaet., 164d) and μῦθος ἐσώθη (Resp., X, 621b; cf. Leg., I, 645b) cf. Liddell-Scott, *s.v.*

[37] Hom. Od., 11, 492 μῦθος παιδός, "tell me now the truth about the son"; IG, XII, 7, 449, 10 (2nd cent. B.C.): ἔχεις ἅπαντα μῦθον, "the whole (brief) story" (of a youth who died young); cf. Aesch. Pers., 713, → n. 36. Eur. Phoen., 469: ὁ μῦθος τῆς ἀληθείας, "the truthful account," cf. Plut. Adulat., II, 62.

[38] Hom. Od., 4, 744: μῦθον δέ τοι οὐκ ἐπικεύσω, "I will not conceal the matter from you." Eur. El., 346: τὸν ὄντα μῦθον, "the real facts," though cf. Plat. Tim., 29d: τὸν εἰκότα μῦθον, "poetry which is nevertheless probable" (→ 772, 7 f.).

[39] Hom. Od., 22, 289: θεοῖσι μῦθον ἐπιτρέψαι (cf. 19, 502). Schmidt, 18 sees here simply the usual sense of "word" ("leave the word to the gods"), but Jolles, 103 finds the deeper sense of "the word which is true."

[40] Soph. Ai., 226: ἀγγελίαν ... τὰν ὁ μέγας μῦθος ἀέξει.

[41] Eur. Ion, 994: ὁ μῦθος ὃν κλύω πάλαι, cf. Theocr., 15, 107 (on the saga of Berenice); Cl. Al. Protr., 1, 3: ὡς ὁ μῦθος βούλεται, though there is characteristic restriction in Paed., III, 11, 3: ὡς ὁ μῦθος Ἑλλήνων ἔχει: for Clement μῦθος is specifically "pagan myth" (→ n. 44), for, while the Greek thinks in myths, the Christian rejects mythical thinking, actual facts being decisive for him in religion. Ditt. Syll.[3], 382, 7 (290/280 B.C.): a poet Demoteles τοὺς μύθους τοὺς ἐπιχωρίους (local sagas) γέγραφεν (cf. Christ-Schmid-Stählin, *Gesch. d. gr. Lit.*[6] [1920], II, 1, 148, 231, n. 5). P. Herm., 6, 23 (3rd cent. A.D.): τὰ τῶν μύθων πάσχομεν, "we suffer that which is known otherwise only from ancient stories."

of truth in it; [42] the "fable" in the technical sense, esp. the animal fable, but also more broadly the "fabulous account," esp. from the sphere of nature, [43] hence "myth" in the narrower sense of a story dealing with gods and demi-gods, or a story in which deities are seen in action; [44] finally, the "plot" of a drama, i.e., the material and composition of tragedy or even comedy, [45] and hence more generally poetic creations (which claim the

---

[42] Plat. Resp., I, 350e: ὥσπερ ταῖς γραυσὶ ταῖς τοὺς μύθους λεγούσαις (→ 787, 8 ff.), *ibid.*, II, 377c (→ 775, 20 ff.). *Ibid.*, a: πρῶτον τοῖς παιδίοις μύθους λέγομεν· τοῦτο δέ που ὡς τὸ ὅλον εἰπεῖν ψεῦδος· ἔνι δὲ καὶ ἀληθῆ. Hence in the rhetorical schools it was required on pedagogic grounds that a μῦθος, esp. an animal fable, should have something πιθανόν in it even though essentially ψευδής (Joh. Sardicus Aphthonium, p. 4, 5 ff., Rabe; cf. Schmid-Stählin, *Gesch. d. gr. Lit.*, I, 1 [1929], 667, n. 5, 668, n. 4). Cf. also Plat. Tim., 23b: τὰ γενεαλογηθέντα ... παίδων βραχύ τι διαφέρει μύθων, and on this the typical remarks in Cl. Al. Strom., I, 180, 4 f. concerning τὸ παῖς μῦθος. Aristoph. Lys., 781: μῦθον βούλομαι λέξαι τιν' ὑμῖν, ὅν ποτ' ἤκουσ' αὐτὸς ἔτι παῖς ὤν. Synesius De Providentia, 1, 2 (MPG, 66, p. 1213 B): ὁ μῦθος φιλοσόφημα παίδων ἐστίν. In the phrase of Demosth. (Or., 50, 40): μύθους λέγειν, "to recount fables," the element of the false is dominant, so also in IG, XII, 7, 494, 2 (= Epigr. Graec., 277, 1 f.): καὶ οὐκέτι μοι μῦθον ἐρεῖτ' ἀρετήν, cf. also the formal antithesis in Plut. Def. Orac., 19 (II, 420b), → n. 102. In keeping is the fact that the μῦθος is for Christians an untrue story (e.g., Orig. Comm. in Joh., 13, 27 [162; GCS, p. 251, 17]), and μυθολογέω, esp. the part. μυθολογούμενος, means "invented," "fabricated," in the Apol. (Just. Apol., II, 12, 4; cf. I, 26, 7; cf. μυθοποιέω, I, 23, 3).

[43] a. Fables which are construed allegorically and give instruction under the mask of animals, Plat. Phaed., 60c; Aristot. Meteor., II, 3, p. 356b, 11: οἱ 'Αἰσώπου μῦθοι (but Plat., *loc. cit.* d: οἱ τοῦ Αἰσώπου λόγοι, Aristot. Rhet., II, 20, p. 1393a, 30: λόγοι Αἰσώπειοι). αἶνος is more common for animal fable, distinguished from μῦθος ("fairy-story") as in the following note of Julian (Or., VII, p. 268, 9 ff.): (ὁ αἶνος) τοῦ μύθου διαφέρει τῷ μὴ πρὸς παῖδας, ἀλλὰ πρὸς ἄνδρας πεποιῆσθαι καὶ μὴ ψυχαγωγίαν μόνον, ἀλλὰ καὶ παραίνεσιν ἔχειν τινά (→ C. 3d); cf. Ps.-Ammon., *s.v.* αἶνος, also Schmid-Stählin, *op. cit.*, 676 ff. Tat. Or. Graec., 34, 2 contemptuously uses μυθολόγημα for the fables of the "lying poet" Aesop. For ancient animal fables in Jewish lit. cf. Str.-B., IV, 409 f. and III, 655 on 1 Tm. 6:7. b. Stories about animals and other natural phenomena which are to be classified as fables, so probably μῦθοι Λιβυστικοί in Aesch. Fr., 139, 1 (TGF, 45), cf. Schmid-Stählin, 671, n. 3; Καρικοὶ μῦθοι in Theon. Progymnasmata, 3; also Aristot. Hist. An., VIII, 12, p. 597a, 7 of the pygmies: οὐ γάρ ἐστι τοῦτο μῦθος, ἀλλ' ἔστι κατὰ τὴν ἀλήθειαν γένος μικρόν, *ibid.*, VI, 31, p. 579b, 2 f., so also Ael. Nat. An., 4, 34 on fables concerning the birth of lions (ὁ λόγος, ὅστις λέγει ..., μῦθός ἐστιν), *ibid.*, 16, 5 (→ n. 151) on strange Athenian tales about the lark; Hdt., 2, 23 on those about fluctuations in the water of the Nile; Theophr. Hist. Plant., 4, 13, 2: φῆμαι παραδεδομέναι παρὰ τῶν μυθολόγων on the age of three trees. But cf. Aristot. Hist. An., VI, 35, p. 580a, 14 f.: λέγεται δέ τις περὶ τοῦ τόκου λόγος πρὸς μῦθον συνάπτων, here λόγος is a fable about the 12 nights for the conception of wolves, and μῦθος an aetiological myth.

[44] When the Gk. speaks of ἀρχαῖοι μῦθοι (Plat. Leg., IX, 865d) or μῦθοι παλαιοί (VII, 804e; Heracl. Hom. All., 42, p. 63, 12 f.) or ὁ τῶν παλαιῶν μῦθος (Philo Plant., 130), he is thinking primarily of stories of the gods and heroes, cf. Orig. Cels., 1, 67: οἱ παλαιοὶ μῦθοι Περσεῖ κτλ. θείαν σπορὰν νείμαντες. From Plato on this sense is to the fore, and it is almost the only one in Jewish and Chr. authors, always with an evaluation (but → 769); cf. in Cl. and Orig. μῦθοι 'Ελλήνων (Paed., III, 11, 3, → n. 41; Cels., 8, 68), μῦθοι 'Ελληνικοί (Protr., 1, 1; Cels., 1, 37), also ὁ ἔξω μῦθος (Comm. in Thr., XCVI [GCS, VI, p. 270, 11]), or more plainly οἱ 'Ελλήνων μῦθοι περὶ θεῶν (Cels., 1, 23). Philo (Aet. Mund., 131) speaks of τῶν ἐπιτραγῳδουμένων θεοῖς μύθων, "myths solemnly and tragically narrated of the gods," Cl. Al. once (Strom., V, 21, 1 → n. 142) of θεολογούμενοι μῦθοι. Cf. also esp. → C. 3-5.

[45] μῦθος here is close to ὑπόθεσις, "subject" (of a poem), cf. R. C. Kukula (*Bibliothek der Kirchenväter: Frühchr. Apologeten,* I [1913], 233) on Tat. Or. Graec., 24, 2. As an example cf. Luc. Philopatris, 1: μῦθος τοῖς ποιηταῖς γενήσομαι ὡς καὶ Νιόβη τὸ πρίν. Most examples, and the most important, are found in the Poet. of Aristot. (cf. the index in the ed. of I. Bywater [1909], *s.v.*), who here (6, p. 1450a, 4 f., 22 f., 38 f.) calls μῦθος the σύνθεσις τῶν πραγμάτων, "the heart and soul of tragedy," or its τέλος (cf. p. 1450b, 22 f.). For it serves to attain the main end of tragedy, the purging of the παθήματα by

liberty to alter real facts and invent new ones), the legends of the singer, the sagas of the epic poem, the stories of the novel. [46]

C. Myth in the Greek World and Hellenism.

1. The Many Senses of Myth.

The ancients felt the paradox that the term for "word," which can also be a "fact," means also "invented story." Thus Eustath. Thessal. Comm. in Il. (I, 26, 20 f., Stallbaum) comments: "The poet (sc. Homer) always has the simple μῦθος for 'word'; only later is this term used for an untrue word (an invented story)." [47] This inner tension in the concept naturally comes to light when the word is translated, and the possibility that words with several senses have been wrongly translated is one of the most common problems in antiquity. Thus it seems that Origen, who like the other fathers normally uses μῦθος for "myth" or "saga," can occasionally use it in the sense of "story," and yet *fabula* is still the rendering in Jer. This can hardly be a deliberate substitution of the scorned *fabula* because of a deviation from Orig. in attitude to the apocr.; [48] it is probably just the usual translation. [49] The tension in the semasiological picture of μῦθος hereby illustrated is later reflected in the many problems associated with "myth."

2. Counterparts of μῦθος: ἔργον, ἔπος, λόγος.

The paradoxical development of μῦθος may be seen esp. in the inter-relation to the terms associated with it in the course of its development.

Originally μῦθος means "thought," "content of a speech or conversation" (→ 766)

---

kindling pity and fear, 14, p. 1453b, 3 ff.: δεῖ γὰρ καὶ ἄνευ τοῦ ὁρᾶν οὕτω συνεστάναι τὸν μῦθον ὥστε τὸν ἀκούοντα τὰ πράγματα γινόμενα καὶ φρίττειν καὶ ἐλεεῖν ἐκ τῶν συμβαινόντων· ἅπερ ἂν πάθοι τις ἀκούων τὸν τοῦ Οἰδίποδος μῦθον (cf. 6, p. 1449b, 27 f. and Bywater, *ad loc.* [p. 152 ff.]). μῦθοι δραματικοί are not necessarily sagas or myths; they may be history (cf. Aesch. Pers.) and should resemble reality (Aristot. Poet., 9, p. 1451b, 33-1452a, 1).

[46] → C. 3b. Homer's songs are later called μῦθοι, e.g., Epict., III, 24, 18 → n. 151, in accordance with his own saying in Od., 11, 368: μῦθον δ' ὡς ὅτ' ἀοιδὸς ἐπισταμένως κατέλεξας. He is the μυθολόγος κατ' ἐξοχήν, cf. Plat. Resp., III, 398a. After him poets enjoy, along with μυθολόγος, honorary titles like μυθογράφος Ἀπόλλωνος καὶ Μουσῶν (IG, XII, 7, 273) and μύθων ταμίης (IG, III, 637, 2). For others, esp. Luc., (e.g., Hermot., 73) μυθοποιός etc. are far from honorary titles, since freedom in μυθολογεῖν (Vera Hist., I, 4) is simply freedom to lie, → n. 42. Christians esp. speak disparagingly of poets and their μῦθοι, cf. Athenag., 10, 1; 30, 3; Just. Apol., II, 5, 5 (ποιηταὶ καὶ μυθολόγοι), I, 54, 1 etc. But it was reserved for a later development to make of the μυθολόγος an itinerant singer (P. Masp., 97, II, 44). In the imperial period the stories of the novel are called μῦθοι. Achill. Tat. uses the title μῦθοι ἐρωτικοί, "stories of love" (cf. also Cl. Al. Paed., III, 27, 2). In fact the novel developed out of myth (cf. Rohde, → Bibl. C.). "The story of the Clementines is finally the 'humanised' form of an Egyptian myth" (cf. K. Kerényi, *Die gr.-orientalische Romanlit. in religionsgeschichtlicher Beleuchtung* [1927], 13 [esp. n. 67], 53, 89); in the Clementines myth is also seen to be important for the theory and practice of Gnosticism, in which the historical finally leaves the field wide open for myth (→ C. 5e).

[47] Μῦθον ἀεὶ ὁ ποιητὴς ἁπλῶς τὸν λόγον φησί· τὸ δὲ ἐπὶ ψευδοῦς λόγου τεθῆναι αὐτὸν τῶν ὑστέρων ἐστί. Later Etym. M., *s.v.* says: μῦθος σημαίνει δύο, τόν τε σκοτεινὸν λόγον ... καὶ τὸν ἁπλῶς λόγον.

[48] So Zn. Einl., I, 48 f.

[49] So A. v. Harnack, "Der kirchengeschichtliche Ertrag d. exegetischen Arbeiten des Orig., II," TU, 42, 4 (1919), 145, n. 3, though he adduces no examples of μῦθος = *historia* in Orig.

as distinct from ἔπος,[50] (mere) "word," "sound of speech."[51] But there is then a gradual rapprochement, and on the analogy of ἔπος (as "word," "words," → 767) it becomes the antonym of ἔργον (→ II, 650).[52]

The relation to λόγος (→ 74) is the reverse of that to ἔπος; an original relation becomes a sharp antithesis. The language of Hom., and the Ionic dialect from which, i.e., the speech of the educated, Eur. takes his common use of μῦθος, prefers this to λόγος, and uses it in very much the same sense as λόγος has in Attic.[53] Thus λόγος, with μῦθος (and ἔπος, → n. 52) is also contrasted with ἔργον, e.g., Thuc., 1, 22; Democr. Fr., 82 (II, 160, Diels[5]), and covers very much the same conceptual ground as μῦθος;[54] it, too, can mean "rumour" (Jn. 21:23), "saga," "fable" (→ n. 43a), "lying tale" (Mt. 28:15), and can be an antonym of ἀλήθεια[55] like μῦθος (→ E. III, 1). Yet in terms of Greek linguistic sense the distinction between true and false is as little developed in relation to λόγος as to μῦθος; it is a later, though dominant, development[56] when, esp. in Attic, λόγος comes to mean a true story as distinct from μῦθος, the false.[57] This makes λόγος and ἀλήθεια correlative on the one side, μῦθος and ψεῦδος on the other.[58] But in the Gk. world the distinction is never absolute. This may be seen from the late definition of Hesych. and Suid., who equate μῦθος and λόγος κενός or ψευδής, but then add: εἰκονίζων τὴν ἀλήθειαν. This does not simply mean what is said in Plut. Athen., 4 (II, 348a): ὁ δὲ μῦθος εἶναι βούλεται λόγος ψευδὴς ἐοικὼς ἀληθινῷ. Acc. to another saying of Plut. (Is. et Os., 20 [II, 359a]; → 776) μῦθος is a reflection of λόγος and indirectly mediates the truth which can be culled from it by means of rich allegorical exposition.

Thus μῦθος has a threefold relation to λόγος: 1. the fairy-tale or marvel as distinct from credible history; 2. the mythical form of an idea as distinct from its dialectical presentation (esp. Plato, → 774), and 3. popular myth as distinct

---

50 ἔπος occurs only once in the NT (Hb. 7:9) in the literary fig. etym. ὡς ἔπος εἰπεῖν, "if the word might be ventured, one might almost say."

51 Hofmann, 29 on Od., 11, 561 and 367: ἔπος *ad verborum ornatum,* μῦθος *ad narrationem* (the content of what is narrated) *spectat,* like the two similar, but in content different, expressions ποῖον τὸν μῦθον ἔειπες; and ποῖόν σε ἔπος φύγεν ἕρκος ὀδόντων (→ 766).

52 μῦθος and ἔργον may complement one another (cf. ἔπος and ἔργον in Plat. Leg., IX, 879c), as in Hom. Il., 19, 242: αὐτίκ' ἔπειθ' ἅμα μῦθος ἔην, τετέλεστο δὲ ἔργον ("said," "done"); 9, 442 f.: τοὔνεκά με προέηκε διδασκέμεναι τάδε πάντα: μύθων τε ῥητῆρ' ἔμεναι, πρηκτῆρά τε ἔργων, or they may be contrasted, e.g., Aesch. Prom., 1080: ἔργῳ κοὐκέτι μύθῳ, cf. also Il., 18, 252. The further development of μῦθος separates it more and more from ἔργον, cf. Plut. Athen., 4 (II, 348a): πολὺ τῶν ἔργων ἀφέστηκεν (sc. ὁ μῦθος), εἰ λόγος μὲν ἔργου, λόγου δὲ μῦθος εἰκὼν καὶ εἴδωλόν ἐστι.

53 Cf. Greg. Corinth. De Dialecto Ionica, 81: ὁ δὲ λόγος· μῦθος, and cf. Hesych. (→ *infra*) and Etym. M. (→ n. 47).

54 → 74. Cf. Pass., Liddell-Scott, *s.v.*

55 E.g., Aristot. Pol., III, 9, p. 1280b, 8: λόγου χάριν — ὡς ἀληθῶς (in word, ostensibly, but in reality), also the other instances in Liddell-Scott, *s.v.* λόγος (VI, 1c), also Col. 2:23. There are many instances of μῦθος and λόγος in exactly the same sense, e.g., at random Heracl. Hom. All., 73, p. 96, 15 ff. where Homer's μῦθοι πλόκιοι are explained by λόγος ἐκ λόγου; Luc. Halcyon, 1: παλαιὸς ἀνθρώποις μεμύθευται λόγος.

56 Cf. Pass., *s.v.* μῦθος. E. Howald, *Mythos,* 19: There is no love of historical truth; this is a concept discovered only by Herodot. (Hence myths) are not limited by any obligation of truth.

57 So Thuc., 1, 21; Plat. Tim., 26e. But λόγος keeps its many meanings, e.g., Aristid., 13, 7: εἰ μὲν γὰρ μυθικαὶ αἱ περὶ αὐτῶν (sc. θεῶν) ἱστορίαι, οὐδέν εἰσιν εἰ μὴ μόνον λόγοι ..., εἰ δὲ ἀλληγορικαί, μῦθοί εἰσι καὶ οὐκ ἄλλο τι. In the compounds μυθολογέω, μυθολόγος etc., which sound paradoxical in view of the later cleavage (cf. Jolles, 107), the stem λογ (= λεγ) is used in the same general sense as in other compounds.

58 E.g. Plat. Tim., 26e: ... μὴ πλασθέντα μῦθον, ἀλλ' ἀληθινὸν λόγον etc. (→ n. 60).

from the deeper meaning (the kernel of truth) which can be extracted from it.[59]

It is understandable that in general instruction, esp. philosophical and later religious, λόγος should be more highly esteemed than μῦθος (apart from the Platonic myth).[60]

3. The Position of μῦθοι in the Intellectual World of Greece.*

In spite of its deficiency in truth content, and the other objections that could be brought against it (→ C. 6), myth has a solid place in the intellectual world of Greece.

a. In the Cultus and Religious Teaching. The relations between the cultus and myth are very old in Greece, as in the ancient oriental world. The question which of them is older is often raised, but it is probably falsely put, and hence the answers, namely, that the cultus derives from myth, or that mythical narration is imaginatively evoked by cultic action, fall to the ground. Originally myth and the cultus are a unity in which neither has the priority.[61] The religious experience underlying both takes shape on the one side as cultic action in whose motions the nature and acts of deity are given form (W. F. Otto), and on the other side as mythical narrative, in which the same nature and acts are proclaimed to believers. Thus the cultus and myth constantly complement and fructify one another so long as they remain vital.

The guardians of the cultus and myth were priestly theologians — once called ἐξηγηταὶ τῶν μύθων by Luc. (Macrobii, 4) — and in some sense also the poets. For a third factor quickly to appear in this process of mutual fructifying was poetry, whose dramas were performed as cultic actions. In part this took place in the οἶκοι ἱεροί only before the eyes of devotees, as in the mysteries, whose cultic myths were kept a close secret (→ n. 64). But in part it took place on the open stage, which in Athens was the official cultic site of the state religion until it was emancipated from religious domination under the impulse of Euripides.

In the transition from religious drama — Euripides is on the border — there is reflected the ambivalent relation of the educated Greek to the national myths. Even in Homer it is doubtful how much vital religious belief stands behind the

---

59 Cf. Cr.-Kö., 740, and as example Orig. Cels., 1, 12 οἱ ἰδιῶται (the laity as distinct from Egyptian priests) μύθους τινὰς ἀκούοντες ὧν τοὺς λόγους οὐκ ἐπίστανται. Hence a narration of myths which have no λόγος, no hidden sense, is an ἀλόγως μυθεύειν, cf. Heracl. Hom. All., 26, p. 42, 2 (→ 791 and n. 164).

60 So Plat. Gorg., 523a: ἄκουε δή ... μάλα καλοῦ λόγου ὃν σὺ μὲν ἡγήσῃ μῦθον, ὡς ἐγὼ οἶμαι, ἐγὼ δὲ λόγον· ὡς ἀληθῆ γὰρ ὄντα σοι λέξω ἃ μέλλω λέγειν (cf. U. v. Wilamowitz-Moellendorff, *Platon*, I² [1920], 226, n. 1) and in dependence on this Cl. Al. Quis Div. Salv., 42, 1: ἄκουσον μῦθον, οὐ μῦθον, ἀλλὰ ὄντα λόγον, περὶ Ἰωάννου τοῦ ἀποστόλου παραδεδομένον καὶ μνήμῃ πεφυλαγμένον (with ref. to what is assumed by Herder to be the true history of John and the young man); cf. also Ael. Arist. Or., 46, 32: τὸν περὶ τοῖν θεοῖν ... εἴτε καὶ λόγον εἴτε καὶ μῦθον χρὴ φάναι, Orig. in Jer. 20:2 (GCS, VI, p. 178, 12): εἴτε μῦθον — εἴτε λόγον with ref. to a piece of Rabb. exposition. Nevertheless, we often find λόγοι καὶ μῦθοι (e.g., Dio Chrys., XII, 39 and 43 [I, 166, v. Arnim]; Strabo, 10, 3, 23).

* I owe many refs. in this section (esp. b and c) to H. Kleinknecht.

61 W. F. Otto, 20, 24, 44; Radermacher, 16, 299, n. 70; Aly, 1397 f. ("Der Mythos im Kultus"); Jeremias, *Ap. Glaubensbekenntnis*, 15; A. Bertholet, RGG², III, 1370 f., Art. "Kultus," 8; A. Lang, *Myth, Ritual and Religion*² (1899); *Custom and Myth*³ (1890); A. J. Wensinck, "The Semitic New Year and the Origin of Eschatology," *Acta Orientalia*, I (1923), 169 f.

songs — cf. especially his humorous scenes with the gods [62] — and Aeschylus and Sophocles, who "succeeded again in breathing into myth the life of their own mighty souls" (Rohde), were accompanied by Euripides, the destroyer of myths, under whose hands religious myth "disintegrated into a colourful game" (Thomas), and by Aristophanes, for whom nothing was sacred. There is a similar cleavage in philosophy. The Socrates of Plato confesses to personal conviction regarding myth [63] (πέπεισμαι, Phaed., 108e, 109a; cf. Gorg., 523a [n. 60]; 524a ταῦτ' ἔστιν ... ἃ ἐγὼ ἀκηκοὼς πιστεύω ἀληθῆ εἶναι), for final insights are expressed in myth, cf. Tim., 29d: περὶ τούτων τὸν εἰκότα μῦθον ("a poem which has a claim to verisimilitude") ἀποδεχομένους πρέπει τούτου μηδὲν ἔτι πέρα ζητεῖν. Aristotle, on the other hand, finds in myths only symbolical ways of expressing a pantheistic theology, Metaph., XI, 8, p. 1074b, 1 ff. → n. 130, "and indeed the mythical form (μυθικῶς) is chosen to make apprehension possible for the masses, for their religious and ethical instruction."

This saying betrays clearly the inner tension of the Greeks in relation to the ancient myths. This was caused especially by two insights, first that of destiny, which is greater than the figures of myth, and then that of δίκη, by whose criterion the authority of myth is dispelled. On the one side there are traces even into the Hellenistic period that belief in myth even in the realistic sense did not wholly disappear. [64] On the other side, the enlightened, following the example of Critias and Phaedros, regard the world of myths as a crafty invention and hence as a free object of criticism and wit (Friedländer, cf. Plat. Phaedr., 229c), or, after the example of the rationalist Euhemeros, they take myth to be an exaggeration of historical events in terms of marvels, or, like many at a later period, they see in it the sphere of children. [65] Nevertheless, the mythical heritage of antiquity lives on in changing forms and manifests its vitality in the soul of the people. The validity of a theologoumenon at any given time is, of course, very difficult to determine to-day. [66]

b. In Poetry. Myth and poetry are both found on the soil of the cultus. They belong together during the whole of the ancient period. Even when it lost its

[62] Cf. W. Nestle in N. Jbch. Kl. Alt., 8 (1905), 161 ff., esp. 176 ff.; E. Drerup, *Das fünfte Buch d. Ilias* (1913), 85 ff., 174 ff., 332 ff., 394 ff.; K. Bielohlawek, ARW, 28 (1930), 106 ff., 185 ff.; Nilsson, 175 f. On Eur. cf. Aly, 1397 f. Myth in its connection with the related cultus stands in distinctive analogy to the Gospel in relation to early Christian worship. In this cultic connection "myth" and "Gospel" can even be interchangeable terms in Aly, 1395 ("Der Mythos als 'Evangelium'"). This analogy plays some part in the theories of the so-called cultic-historical school, cf. G. Bertram, *Die Leidensgeschichte Jesu u. der Christuskult* (1922); K. L. Schmidt in *Eucharisterion f. H. Gunkel* (1923), II, 114 ff.; also W. Bousset, *Kyrios Christos*² (1921), 138 ff.

[63] Cf. Thomas ΕΠΕΚΕΙΝΑ, 84, n. 135; though cf. v. Wilamowitz, II, 170 f., who thinks that only belief is expressed, a lower stage as distinct from what can be proved and known logically.

[64] Very interesting in this connection is the peculiar awe which keeps Pausanias from narrating the cultic myths of many of the sanctuaries described by him; for, he says (IX, 25, 6), οὐκ ἐφαίνετο ὅσιόν μοι γράφειν. These are usually mysteries, of course, for he does tell many cultic myths, cf. G. Krueger, *Theologumena Pausaniae* (Diss. Bonn, 1860). On the shattering of belief in myth cf. also R. Bultmann, ThBl, 19 (1940), 3.

[65] Lib. Or., 31, 43: παίδων γὰρ ταῦτα μυθολογήματα (of the myth of Apollo and Daphne). μῦθος and παῖς are correlative terms for most people, cf. Cl. Al. Strom., I, 180, 4 f. on τὸ παῖς μῦθος as distinct from προγενεστάτη ἀλήθεια.

[66] Cf. the classical discussions of this in Harnack Miss., 32 f.; Rohde, 13 ff.; Radermacher, 20 ff.; cf. also Schmid-Stählin, *Geschichte d. gr. Lit.*, I, 2 (1934), 696 ff.

religious power over souls, myth maintained its heroic greatness. It still had power to evoke fear and pity (→ n. 45). Hence it remained so much the raw material of poetry that the products of poetry could simply be called μῦθοι (→ n. 46). Plat. Phaed., 61b establishes the canon ὅτι τὸν ποιητὴν δέοι ... ποιεῖν μύθους, ἀλλ' οὐ λόγους.[67] "We know sacrifices without the playing of flutes and dancing, but not poetry without myths and invented stories," says Plutarch,[68] and Philodem. Philos. calls him the best poet who is equally lofty in his μῦθοι, his presentation of character, and his language.[69] Nor is it merely in classical epic and drama that heroic myth holds the field. Even in the Hellenistic period, which follows the ancient laws of style and craft, it maintained its place, though more and more as a mere stylistic adornment. The point was reached, of course, when myth died because it lost not merely its credibility but also its force as an ideal and example.

c. In Philosophy. For the philosopher myths are not just the original sources of the religious ideas and yearnings of the Greek people, cf. Dio Chrys. in his address on the knowledge of God, XII, 39 (I, 166, v. Arnim). He himself can take refuge in myth to present his ideas. Aristot. Metaph., I, 2 (p. 982b, 18) says: φιλόμυθος ὁ φιλόσοφός πώς ἐστιν· ὁ γὰρ μῦθος σύγκειται ἐκ θαυμασίων.[70] These θαυμάσια can even counterbalance to some degree the incredibility of myth. The older Greek philosophers made use of myth.[71] But Plato is the example for this μύθῳ φιλοσοφεῖν, Plut. Quaest. Conv., 1, 1, 3 (II, 613d). While his teacher Socrates, who was neither an inventor of myths (Plat. Phaed., 61b: μυθολογικός) like Plato nor a destroyer of myths like the Sophists, was cool towards myth (e.g., Phaedr., 229c-e), in increasing measure it plays an extraordinary role in Plato's dialogues.

Plato was well acquainted with the myths of Homer, and all his life he had a great affection and reverence for them.[72] He resisted the contemptuous treatment of myths by the educated.[73] For him myths were the symbolical reality of the sphere of ἐπέκεινα which is accessible only to faith, "fragments of a great

---

[67] Cf. Resp., II, 379a, Procl. in Rem. Publ., I, p. 65, 26 f.: πάντως γὰρ τὸ μυθολογικὸν καὶ Πλάτων ἀποδίδωσιν τοῖς ποιηταῖς, Plut. Athen., 4 (II, 348a): ὅτι μὲν ἡ ποιητικὴ περὶ μυθοποιίαν ἐστί, καὶ Πλάτων εἴρηκεν, also the close connection between ποιητής and μυθολόγος in Plat. Resp., III, 392d (→ n. 177), 398a (→ 779, 4 ff.).

[68] Aud. Poet., 2 (II, 16c): θυσίας μὲν γὰρ ἀχόρους καὶ ἀναύλους ἴσμεν, οὐκ ἴσμεν δ' ἄμυθον οὐδ' ἀψευδῆ ποίησιν. Cf. Luc. Jup. Trag., 39: The poets hold their hearers μύθοις in tension (κατέχειν), and the common use of ποιητικὸς μῦθος in Cl. Al., e.g., Protr., 112, 2.

[69] Poem., V, 9, 12 ff., Jensen: οἱ μὲν οἰόμενοι τὸν ἐν τοῖς μύθοις καὶ ταῖς ἄλλαις ἠθοποιίαις κἂν τῇ λέξει παραπλησίως ὁμαλίζοντα ποιητὴν ἄριστον εἶναι.

[70] There is a different reading: ὁ φιλόμυθος φιλόσοφός πώς ἐστιν, which yields the reverse sense: "He who is occupied in mythical ideas is in some degree philosophically inclined" (Lasson), i.e., myth is a preliminary stage of philosophy (Friedländer, 207). This fits the context and is undoubtedly correct (cf. Eisler, *op. cit.*: Myth is a primitive view of things, protophilosophy; cf. Strabo, I, 2, 3). But the second half of the verse would then have to be explained artificially. Cf. also Fr., 618, p. 1582b, 14.

[71] Aly, 1402; cf. also Aly, *Philol. Suppl.*, XXI, 3 (1929), 70 ff.; on the style of these philosophical μῦθοι cf. E. Norden, *Agnostos Theos* (1913), 368 ff.

[72] Resp., X, 595b; cf. v. Wilamowitz, *op. cit.*, I, 335.

[73] Resp., I, 330d: οἵ τε γὰρ λεγόμενοι μῦθοι περὶ τῶν ἐν Ἅιδου, ὡς τὸν ἐνθάδε ἀδικήσαντα δεῖ ἐκεῖ διδόναι δίκην, καταγελώμενοι τέως, τότε (on the approach of death) δὴ στρέφουσιν αὐτοῦ τὴν ψυχὴν μὴ ἀληθεῖς ὦσιν. Cf. Plut. Ser. Num. Pun., 18 (II, 561b): ὕστερον δὲ τὸν μῦθον ... κινήσομεν (treat) εἴ γε δὴ μῦθός ἐστιν. Diod. S., I, 93, 3 (→ n. 145); Ael. Arist. Or., 46, 32 (→ n. 60).

myth half-extinguished and disintegrated by the movement of time, which must be purified, assembled and refashioned" [74] (esp. Polit., 268d ff.).

This means that Plato no longer believes in myths as they are, and especially in their colourful world of the gods. Only individual pieces fit into his new teaching, especially those which relate to the destiny of the soul. "From the great stream of the Greek world of belief and mythology, which in Plato's time had absorbed almost indistinguishably the most varied sources," Plato did in fact pick out various bits of myth and "make of them new myths which derived from his philosophical outlook" (Thomas). In particular he used epic myths, often in their later form in popular belief or poetry. There are also connections with the mystery religions, Eleusinian rather than Orphic, and particularly with the circles of the Pythagoreans, Empedocles and Pindar. [75] Plato's myths are thus the product of great imaginative and inventive power which both fuses traditional elements to create new philosophical and mythical statements, and also produces completely new mythical constructs as alone adequate to express the wealth of thought clothed by them. In distinction from the purely intellectual abstraction of Kant, Plato uses both *logos,* the dialectical presentation of thought, and *mythos,* the plastic illustration of the metaphysical. Myth carries the lines of *logos* organically beyond the frontiers of conceptual knowledge, and is itself discovered rather than experienced as inwardly necessary vision. This distinctive union of *logos* and *mythos* in Plato is linked with the fact that his philosophy is also a doctrine of salvation. For Plato's doctrine of salvation, which is concerned with the destiny of the human soul, the most valuable sources are undoubtedly the myths, at the heart of which this destiny stands, cf. the eros myth in Symp., the myth of the world to come in Gorg., Men., Phaed. and Resp., the myth of the world and the soul in Resp. and Phaedr., the myth of creation in Tim.; [76] for this is the method of Plato, as Orig. says (Cels., 4, 39): τὰ μεγάλα δόγματα κρύψαι ἐν τῷ τοῦ μύθου σχήματι. The Platonic myth both conceals and reveals. "It has a place in Plato's dialogues wherever the other world and the fulness of what belongs to the ideas projects into this life" (Friedländer). Hence it is not just protophilosophy, → n. 70. In Plato it stands at the end of the philosophical path as final wisdom.

d. In Spiritual Direction and Education. Apart from the inner necessities of philosophical knowledge myth also serves the psychagogic and pedagogic purpose of all ancient philosophy. This is true both of traditional myth and also of newly invented myth. [77]

---

[74] Thomas, 4; Friedländer, 201, cf. 203 ff. on the change in the significance and place of myth in Platonic dialogue; cf. also W. Windelband, *Platon*[7] (1923), c. 5 and Reinhardt; v. Wilamowitz, II, 175 f. shows less understanding of this, and it is only more recent work on Plato which has given such prominence to myth; cf. Nygren, 145 (Eng. ed. 124 f.).

[75] These connections are fruitfully explored by H. W. Thomas, whom we follow in part, cf. esp. 1-4. There has been much discussion of possible links with Orphism; on the basis of the witness of Olympiodor. and Neo-Platonic exegesis it has usually been thought that Plato used much Orphic material, and was even a prophet of Orphism, but following the lead of v. Wilamowitz, *Glaube d. Hellenen,* II (1932), 197 f. etc. Thomas hotly contests this (25 ff., esp. 45 f., 55 f.).

[76] Friedländer, 203-241; Reinhardt, *passim*; cf. also Nygren, 143 f. (Eng. ed., 123 f.). The link between *logos* and *mythos* in Plat. is confirmed in one case by Plut. (Quaest. Conv., 9, 5, 2 [II, 740b]): μῦθόν τινα τῷ περὶ ψυχῆς λόγῳ μείγνυσι.

[77] → E. IV, 5 (a). Cf. Jul. Or., I, p. 2, 7 ff.: οἱ μὲν ἐπειδὰν καινόν τινα μῦθον ... φέρωσιν αὐτοὶ ξυνθέντες τῷ ξένῳ (through the unusual) τοὺς ἀκούοντας ψυχαγωγήσαντες πλέον θαυμάζονται. *Ibid.,* VII, p. 268 9 (→ n. 43a).

This may be seen already in Hesiod (the Pandora myth), and then in more developed form in sophistry, e.g., Prodikos (Heracles at the cross-roads). Here μῦθος is a suitable illustration for the theoretical instruction of λόγος. The Sophist (Protagoras) has both λόγος and μῦθος at his command, and he chooses the more engaging, i.e., μῦθος.[78] In Plato there can be no question of an arbitrary choice of this kind; for him myth is much more than an illustration of *logos*. When he uses it, it corresponds to an inner necessity. It arises when there is need to express something which can be expressed in no other way. The concluding myth, too, serves the one great educational goal of the Platonic dialogue.[79] After Plato myth falls from its high place. Aristot. (Polit., VII, 17, p. 1336a, 30) re-assumes on the one side the Sophist position, arguing that λόγος alone has educational value and μῦθος merely has the task of pleasing. On the other side, he still expects something significant from the μῦθος of tragedy (→ n. 45).[80] A step further, and the only right of existence granted to μῦθος is in virtue of the element of τερπνόν,[81] or the second Aristotelian view is watered down to a threadbare moralism.[82] Finally, μῦθος maintains a place only as the first exercise in rhetorical instruction.[83]

A special form of myth, the fairy-story, the φιλοσόφημα παίδων (Synesius, → n. 42), ought, in Plato's view, to have a special place in the teaching of children. The pedagogic value of the fairy-story rests on its twofold character, which Plato describes thus (Resp., II, 377a, → n. 42), namely, that it is invented (ψεῦδος) and yet contains truth within it. The best of such stories are naturally good enough only for the training of the young (*loc. cit.*, e); a point worth noting (c) is that Plato associates μῦθοι as a force in the training of the soul with the physical training of the body: πλάττειν τὰς ψυχὰς αὐτῶν τοῖς μύθοις ... τὰ σώματα ταῖς χερσίν.

4. The Allegorical Interpretation of Myth.

No other people on earth, except the Indians, produced such a rich world of myth as the Greeks. Rosenberg claimed that in Greece and India "the myth-creating force of the Nordic race" found its most powerful embodiment.[84] Never-

---

78 Plat. Prot., 320c: πότερον ὑμῖν, ὡς πρεσβύτερος νεωτέροις, μῦθον λέγων ἐπιδείξω ἢ λόγῳ διεξελθών; ... δοκεῖ τοίνυν μοι, ἔφη, χαριέστερον εἶναι μῦθον ὑμῖν λέγειν (sc. the myth of Prometheus and Epimetheus). Of course, the sophist, obviously by rule, adds the λόγος (324d: οὐκέτι μῦθόν σοι ἐρῶ ἀλλὰ λόγον, cf. 328c). Cf. also Plut. Gen. Socr., 23 (II, 592 f.): ἀπέχεις μετὰ τοῦ λόγου τὸν μῦθον.

79 Friedländer, 204, 207, 219; cf. J. Stenzel, *Platon der Erzieher* (1928).

80 Poet., 6, p. 1450a, 33-35: τὰ μέγιστα οἷς ψυχαγωγεῖ ἡ τραγῳδία τοῦ μύθου μέρη ἐστίν, αἵ τε περιπέτειαι καὶ ἀναγνωρίσεις (the sudden turns of fate by which the knot is loosed, and the scenes of recognition).

81 Cf. Luc. Philops., 4; also Procl. in Rem Publ., I, p. 46, 14: φύσει γὰρ τὴν ψυχὴν ἡμῶν χαίρειν τοῖς μιμήμασιν, διὸ καὶ φιλόμυθοι (better φιλόμιμοι?) πάντες ἐσμέν.

82 Cf. Hermogenes, p. 1, 3 ff., Rabe: τὸν μῦθον πρῶτον ἀξιοῦσι προσάγειν τοῖς νέοις, ὅτι τὰς ψυχὰς αὐτῶν πρὸς τὸ βέλτιον ῥυθμίζειν δύναται. But cf. Orig. Cels., 4, 48: ὡς μηδὲ ... μῦθόν τινα παραδέξασθαι ἐπὶ βλάβῃ τῶν νέων, also Critias Fr., 4, 9 (Diehl, Anth. Lyr., I, p. 83): αἰσχροὶ μῦθοι, → E. IV, 2 (a).

83 Cf. Schmid-Stählin, 667, n. 6.

84 Rosenberg, 700. Hinduism has reached the critical stage only in our own time under western influences. It is true that the mystical exposition of some myths, esp. those of Krishna and Rama, is old. But to-day an exclusive figurative sense is often claimed for them, since there is a sharper sense of the abstruseness and immorality of many myths. Yet there are also protests against the unreality of such exposition, e.g., in Radhakrishna, as in the ancient world; cf. Reinhardt, 12; Wendland Hell. Kult., 100, 115 f.; → C. 6 and n. 92.

theless, in the Greek world, as shown already (→ 771 f.), myth quickly became a problem. From criticism and doubt of myth, i.e., of all traditional religion, there came the renewal of myth by Plato, who carried forward many ancient fragments to the higher level of Greek religion (→ 773 f.), and also the allegorical understanding of myths,[85] one of the most influential and crucial developments in intellectual history. Plato's myths, the final expression of the greatest pagan theology of antiquity, through the nature which their author designed for them summon us ἀπὸ μύθων εὑρίσκειν τὸ περὶ ἀληθείας τοῦ ταῦτα συντάξαντος βούλημα (Orig. Cels., 4, 39). For, according to the saying of a perspicacious Neo-Platonist (Sallust., 3: Περὶ μύθων), their nature is like that of the cosmos with its body and soul.[86] But this discovery of the soul of myths hidden under the visible corporeality is not yet true allegorising, for the content of the most important of Plato's myths, e.g., the migration of the soul in Phaedr. and Phaed., cannot be translated from the figurative into the conceptual (Windelband).

It was rather another matter when the same line of thought was applied to the ancient popular myths, for now something was read in which no συντάξας had ever put there. It was the express goal of all allegorising to find the core of truth in myths, the λόγος in the μῦθος (→ n. 59), the ὑπόνοια (or basic meaning), the underlying main thoughts (τὰ κεφάλαια),[87] in accordance with the fundamental view of myth expressed, e.g., in Plut. Is. et Os., 20 (II, 359a): ὁ μῦθος ... λόγου τινὸς ἔμφασίς ἐστιν ἀνακλῶντος ἐπ' ἄλλα τὴν διάνοιαν.[88] Behind this goal, however, the chief aim of allegorising was to ward off attacks on the irrationality and immorality of myths. It serves as an antidote to their alleged ungodliness. For if Homer had not meant many things to be taken allegorically, he would have been thoroughly ungodly,[89] → E. IV, 2 (a).

The first attempts at allegorising seem to have sprung from an unbelieving attitude which made even the finest stories of the gods into a tasteless garment for natural things and processes. Theagenes of Rhegion was the pioneer, followed by Anaxagoras and esp. Metrodor. of Lampsacos, whose main efforts were in the allegorical interpretation of Hom. But Stoicism produced the masters in the art of allegorical exegesis.[90]

---

[85] Apart from the bibl. on C, *v.* the older bibl. in Gruppe, *Geschichte,* 10 ff. and the newer in Radermacher, n. 10 (p. 293 f.); ERE, I, 327, Art. "Allegory, Allegorical Interpretation"; K. Müller in Pauly-W., Suppl. IV (1924), 16-22, Art. "Allegorische Dichtererklärung"; O. Seeck, *Geschichte des Untergangs der antiken Welt,* III (1909), 53 ff., 148, 238 ff.; Hatch, 42 ff. (bibl., 44, n. 2).

[86] ἔξεστι ... τὸν κόσμον μῦθον εἰπεῖν, σωμάτων μὲν καὶ χρημάτων ἐν αὐτῷ φαινομένων, ψυχῶν δὲ καὶ νοῶν κρυπτομένων.

[87] Plut. Is. et Os., 20 (II, 358e): ταῦτα σχεδόν ἐστι τοῦ μύθου τὰ κεφάλαια, cf. Pind. Pyth., 4, 116: κεφάλαια λόγων. Other terms used are ἀλληγορία, ψυσιολογία etc.

[88] "(As the rainbow is an ἔμφασις τοῦ ἡλίου ποικιλλομένη), so myth is the reflection of a *logos* which directs thought to something else." Another metaphor justifying allegorising is found in Philo Providentia, 41: "He who does not accept the rules of allegory proceeds like boys who in their ignorance show no interest in the original of Apelles but only in the copy on coins; they admire a pitiable imitation and despise the original which is truly worthy of admiration."

[89] Heracl. Hom. All., 22, p. 32, 18 f.: ταύτης τοίνυν τῆς ἀσεβείας ἕν ἐστιν ἀντιφάρμακον ἐὰν ἐπιδείξωμεν ἠλληγορημένον τὸν μῦθον, *ibid.,* 1, p. 1, 5: πάντα γὰρ ἠσέβησεν, εἰ μηδὲν ἠλληγόρησεν, cf. *ibid.,* 71, p. 93, 20-94, 1; 41, p. 62, 6 f.

[90] The allegorisers of antiquity (→ 790 with n. 160) have found zealous disciples in the Middle Ages and the modern period. Some, like the Stoics, have sought to derive profound

5. The Evaluation and Use of Myth.

a. In Stoicism. The Stoics no longer had any direct relation to the world of myth. But they tried to maintain it by finding support for it in their philosophy, and by basing their philosophy on allegorical interpretation. They made out that the stories of gods and heroes were primitive philosophy in historical dress,[91] *ut etiam veterrimi poetae, qui haec ne suspicati quidem sint, Stoici fuisse videantur* (Cic. Nat. Deor., I, 15). In part the Stoics found in the myths their ideas of natural philosophy, like Cornutus in his Greek theology. In part they found their ethical teachings, like Heraclitus in his Homeric allegories. A third main representative at a later time is Porphyrius with his Ὁμηρικὰ ζητήματα. The presupposition, partly believed and partly just asserted, was the same as that which guides modern metaphysicians like Bachofen in their interpretation of myths, namely, that the symbolical content of myth is inherent in it from the very first and is in no sense a product of later exposition.[92] The difference is that the Stoics were rationalists, whereas the moderns are mystics and Romantics.

b. For Stoicism myth is valid as symbol. Poseidonius goes a step further and regards it as "the matter in which the higher needs of the mind and religion find expression, because their true nature and manner remain closed to thinkers."[93] As in Plato, myth is thought to be of religious value by reason of its own inner vision.

c. Even before Poseidonius myth had been for the mystery religions a primary means whereby to represent religious presuppositions and experiences which either could not be expressed rationally or were better not stated in that way. οἱ τὰ μυστήρια θέμενοι ... τὰ αὐτῶν δόγματα τοῖς μύθοις κατέχωσαν, "the founders of the mysteries concealed their own teachings behind mythical stories."[94] For to present the content of mystery teaching in words would be a crime against the

philosophical wisdom from myths, e.g., Görres and Creuzer; some have thought that Christian doctrines were concealed therein (→ F. 2 and n. 176), e.g., Chateaubriand (cf. also H. Lüken in *Wetzer u. Welte, Kirchenlexikon,* VIII² [1893], 2105-2118, Art. "Mythologie," acc. to whom myth contains corrupted original revelation). The most exaggerated and fantastic allegorising of our own day is to be found in G. A. Gaskell, *A Dictionary of the Sacred Language of All Scriptures and Myths* (1923).

[91] Cr.-Kö., 240; cf. Wendland Hell. Kult., 112 ff.; Radermacher 17 and n. 32.

[92] Plut. Aud. Poet., 4 (II, 19e) represents the opp. conviction to that of Stoicism: οὓς (sc. τοὺς μύθους) ταῖς πάλαι μὲν ὑπονοίαις, ἀλληγορίαις δὲ νῦν λεγομέναις παραβιαζόμενοι καὶ διαστρέφοντες. Opposition to allegorising is old (cf. Wendland Hell. Kult., 108; Rohde, 291, n. 1); Plat. himself is reserved, cf. Phaedr., 229c ff.; Resp., II, 378d. The most determined opponents were the schools of the new academy and Epicurus. The main sources for ancient attacks on allegorising are Cic. Nat. Deor. and the work Περὶ εὐσεβείας by Philodem. Philos. (for the ridiculing of allegory cf. Radermacher, 295, n. 25). The arguments of pagan opponents recur in Christian polemic, esp. that of the Apologists e.g., Athenag., 22, → F. 1. Even Origen, though a master at allegorising the Bible, rejects the allegorical method whereby it is sought to make false and foolish myths respectable, Cels., 5, 38, → 792. Bar. 3:23 may also refer to those who expound myths philosophically when it mentions οἱ μυθολόγοι along with ἐκζητηταὶ τῆς συνέσεως, and says of both: ὁδὸν τῆς σοφίας οὐκ ἔγνωσαν — a par. to 1 C. 1:20 (cf. Ltzm., *ad loc.*), where we merely have συζητητής for ἐκζητητής.

[93] So Harnack Miss., 31, who regards this as a mistaken development. Bachofen (cf. *Gräbersymbolik,* 46 ff.), on the other hand, sees in it one of the highest stages in man's intellectual development.

[94] Cl. Al. Strom., V, 58, 4 (cf. O. Stählin, *Bibliothek d. Kirchenväter: Cl. v. Alex.,* IV [1937], 171). Cf. also Hatch, 42, n. 3 on the link between allegory and the mysteries.

supreme law; the only permissible way is to represent it in myths,"[95] e.g., the Dionysus myth, cf. Plut. Carn. Es., 1, 7 (II, 996c): τὰ γὰρ δὴ περὶ τὸν Διόνυσον μεμυθευμένα πάθη ... ᾐνιγμένος (vl. ἀνηγμένος) ἐστὶ μῦθος εἰς τὴν παλιγγενεσίαν, "a myth which relates like an enigmatic saying to regeneration." The same is true of the myths of the Pythagoreans (cf. Aristot. An., I, 3, p. 407b, 22: κατὰ τοὺς Πυθαγορικοὺς μύθους, Cl. Al. Strom., V, 58, 6: οἱ μῦθοι οἱ Πυθαγόρειοι) by which they supported their ascetic teachings.[96] Later, of course, the meaning of the myth was put in words even in the mystery religions. By means of allegorising, all their teachings were taken from the myth. "The myth becomes speculation" (Bousset).

d. Closely connected with these mystery myths are the many mythical depictions on ancient monuments and sarcophagi, where the symbol and its development represent speech and writing. "Though myth was no longer accepted as belief, it was held in the highest regard because of its connection with the mysteries and the grave ... Myths became images and shadows of higher thoughts," cf. the OT stories and personages in Hb. "The same mythical treasury in which the ancient world had deposited the earliest recollections of its history etc. ... now becomes the representation of religious truths, the illustration of the great laws of nature, the expression of ethical and moral truths, and the spur to comforting surmisings which leap the tragic frontier of the material data."[97] Myths which had been simply narrated were now taken as symbols,[98] and the later world becomes one with the earlier, for, with its power to interpret and experience, "it grasps the content of the symbol again in all its basic elements, and can thus apprehend the ancient myths with new vitality."[99]

e. Gnosticism, with its theologies of redemption, is an opponent of this mystical piety. It dethrones impartially both ancient myth and history, and a new myth completely takes the place of the historical, or rather this is completely swallowed up by the myth.[100] In the hands of the Gnostics allegory becomes a revolutionary instrument for the heretical transvaluation of all values, whether pagan or biblical. The distinction between these two worlds is broken down, and allegory, applied to both, mixes everything in a witches' cauldron of Gnostic speculation.

6. Criticism and Repudiation of Myth.

The same Plato who gives myth, in the form peculiar to him, so prominent a place in his system (→ C. 3, c and d) is openly critical of traditional myths, cf. esp. Resp., II, 377 ff., also Leg., XII, 941b, and ἐκβάλλει τῆς ἑαυτοῦ πολιτείας

---

95 Bachofen, 46; cf. also Schelling, and on Schelling Allwohn. On the various forms of the central mystery myth, i.e., that of the suffering, dying and rising god, cf. W. Bousset, *Kyrios Christos*[2] (1921), 134 ff.; there are examples of allegorising of the mystery myths, 136 f.

96 Cf. Orig. Cels., 5, 49: ἐκεῖνοι διὰ μὲν γὰρ τὸν περὶ ψυχῆς μετενσωματουμένης μῦθον ἐμψύχων ἀπέχονται. Cl. Al. Strom., VII, 33, 8: ἰχθύων οὐχ ἅπτονται καὶ δι' ἄλλους μέν τινας μύθους.

97 Bachofen, 47.

98 Cf. Rosenberg, 614.

99 Schröter, 20; cf. Aly, 1401 f.; Jolles, 125.

100 Cf. W. Bousset, *op. cit.*, 203 ff.; also *Hauptprobleme d. Gnosis* (1907), 238 ff.; cf. Bornkamm, 8-16 (cf. 121 f.) for examples of Gnostic redeemer myths. On Gnostic allegorising C. Barth, *Die Interpretation d. NT in der valentinianischen Gnosis* = TU, 37, 3 (1911); W. Völker, *Heracleons Stellung in seiner Zeit im Licht seiner Schriftauslegung* (Diss., 1922); Hatch, 51 and 54; W. v. Loewenich, *Das Johannesverständnis im 2. Jhdt.* (1932), e.g., 85 ff., 93, 141 ff.; H. Jonas, *Gnosis u. spätantiker Geist,* I (1934), 216 ff.; Bornkamm, 117 ff.

τοὺς τοιουσδὶ μύθους καὶ τὰ τοιαδὶ ποιήματα, Orig. Cels., 4, 50. For this reason he would not allow μυθολόγοι or poets (→ n. 46), including Homer, any place in his ideal state,[101] ἵνα δὴ μὴ τὴν ὀρθὴν δόξαν περὶ θεοῦ τοῖς μύθοις ἀφανίσειε, Jos. Ap., II, 256, though in the same context in Resp., III, 398a he confesses personally: αὐτοὶ δ' ἂν τῷ αὐστηροτέρῳ καὶ ἀηδεστέρῳ ποιητῇ χρῴμεθα καὶ μυθολόγῳ ὠφελίας ἕνεκα, ὃς ἡμῖν τὴν τοῦ ἐπιεικοῦς λέξιν μιμοῖτο, "who represents to us figuratively the idea of what is fitting," though → n. 89.

A critical attitude is also to be seen in Aristotle, Epicurus — in this, too, the direct opposite of the Stoa — and Plutarch etc. It applies not only to religious myth as such[102] but also to its allegorical exegesis, → n. 92. The main objections, with different emphases according to the differing standpoints of those concerned, are as follows: a. myths are of little moral value (→ E. IV, 2 [a]); b. they are childish or nonsensical (→ E. IV, 2 [b] and n. 149); c. they are deficient in truth (→ 770; E. III), being only fables, fairy-stories (→ n. 42) or λόγοι ψευδεῖς (Suid.).[103]

7. Conclusion.

Thus μῦθος, in so far as it denotes myth in the true sense, is variously evaluated in antiquity according to the outlook and standard of the person concerned. There is joyous acceptance in poetry and popular religion, profound interpretation in the mysteries and Plato, allegorical reinterpretation in nature philosophy and Stoicism, to the overthrow of any independent significance of myth,[104] frivolous mockery in many literary and educated circles, criticism and rejection on ethical and rational grounds in several writers, especially philosophers. There is, however, no fundamental repudiation on religious grounds until we come to the NT and the Christian writers of the first centuries (→ E.-G.).

---

101 Cf. H.-G. Gadamer, *Plato u. d. Dichter* (= *Wissenschaft u. Gegenwart*, 5 [1934]). A Christian counterpart is to be seen in the Egyptian Church Order and that of Hippolytus (TU, 6, 4 [1891], p. 81 f.), which have doubts as to admitting a teacher (γραμματικός) into the Church because myths are on the curriculum; in the Egyptian order the teacher is rather oddly linked with actors. Cf. Achelis, *op. cit.*, p. 79 n., also Harnack Miss., 365 ff., 999.

102 Epictures despises equally the belief in the ancient myths and the new belief in destiny; yet he writes in Ep., 3, p. 65, 12, Usener: ἐπεὶ κρεῖττον ἦν τῷ περὶ θεῶν μύθῳ κατακολουθεῖν ἢ τῇ τῶν φυσικῶν εἱμαρμένῃ δουλεύειν. This contempt for myths is the presupposition when the Epicurean school (cf. Wendland Hell. Kult., 107) calls the belief in providence a μῦθος, an empty illusion (Plut. Def. Orac., 19 [II, 420b]). The Neo-Platonic school also follows its master in criticising poetic myths, e.g., Jul. Gal., I, p. 167, ed. C. J. Neumann (1880) (→ 791, 15).

103 Cf. already Pind. Olymp., 1, 28b f.: φάτις ὑπὲρ τὸν ἀληθῆ λόγον δεδαιδαλμένοι ψεύδεσι ποικίλοις ἐξαπατῶντι μῦθοι, Eur. Cyc., 376: κοὐ πιστὰ μύθοις εἰκότ' οὐκ ἔργοις (history) βροτῶν, Plut. Artax., 1 (I, 1012): μύθων ἀπιθάνων καὶ παραφόρων ... παντοδαπὴν πυλαίαν, "a gay throng of incredible and nonsensical myths." Corp. Herm. Exc., XXIII, 50 (I, p. 460, Scott): ἄπιστος τοῖς μεταγενεστέροις μῦθος δὴ δοξάσθω <τὸ> χάος εἶναι. How strongly to the very latest period the linguistic sense of the Greeks attached the idea of the fabulous to μῦθος may be seen from the name of a garden in Syracuse which was called Μῦθος (Athen., XII, 59, p. 542a) διὰ τὸ μὴ ἂν πιστεύεσθαι τοῖς πολλοῖς οὕτω καλῶς εἶναι, ἀλλὰ μυθικὰ δοκεῖν τὰ ὑπὲρ αὐτοῦ λαλούμενα, as Eustath. Thessal. Comm. in Il., 23, 157 (p. 275, Stallbaum) conjectures.

104 Cf. Tillich in RGG², IV, 364.

D. μῦθος and Myths in the OT (LXX) and Judaism.

1. The word μῦθος and its derivates are almost completely alien to the OT. There is only one instance [105] at Sir. 20:19 → n. 23, and here the sense is the old one of "word." On the other hand, there is a remarkable use of the compound μυθολόγος in Bar. 3:23, if it really means here an "interpreter of myths" (→ n. 92).

2. Whether the thing itself, i.e., myth, is also alien to the OT is another question to which various answers are given. Representatives of the "history of religion" school like Gunkel [106] and Gressmann speak quite freely of myths, esp. in relation to Gn. 1-11 and many passages in the prophets. Other investigators believe that both the word and the thing itself are unthinkable in connection with the Bible. Gunkel himself allows that Israel was not partial to myths because they are essentially polytheistic, they represent deity in an unbiblical relation to nature, and they often allow things to be done or tolerated by deity which are quite unworthy of it. On the other hand, it is hard to deny that in spite of the protest of ethical and transcendental monotheism Israel did adopt mythical elements both in the earlier and again in the later period. In particular, its view of nature is related to that of myth. [107] Nevertheless, it transformed all mythical materials in a decisive way. It historicised them, [108] taking them out of the circular thinking which is typical of nature myths and placing them in the once-for-all history of God (even a mythical torso like that in Gn. 6:1-4).

Except in the primitive history most of the original mythical elements are found in the poetic parts of the OT, for the poets of all peoples are in some way φιλόμυθοι (→ n. 46; C. 3, b). This may be seen in the OT primarily in the prophets, who are the sternest opponents of all mythical falsification but who are also in many cases great poets, and who thus make use of many images of mythical derivation, especially in their prophecies of the future (cf. Is. 14; Ez. 29). [109]

Under the influence of the prophets apocalyptic made a much greater use of mythical materials and related many ancient myths to the last time. [110]

In Wisdom literature, too, there is perhaps concealed an original myth of Σοφία, the daughter of the gods. [111]

In the Ps.-Clem. Hom. (2, 25), which are at least under strong Jewish influence, the place of Sophia is taken by the Helena of Homer, the embodiment of all motherhood

---

[105] A has μῦθος in Wis. 17:4, but this is obviously a scribal error for μυχός.

[106] *Genesis*, XIV sqq., 33-40, 67-77, 124 ff.; cf. also his *Schriften d. AT*, I, 1² (1921), 13 ff., 17 f., 37 ff.; and RGG², IV, 381-390; V, 49-60. On the Jewish side, Bergel, I; Micha Josef bin Gorion (= M. J. Berditschewski), *Die Sagen d. Juden*, 7 Vols. (1913 ff.); *Der Born Judas* (1934).

[107] Sellin in RGG², V, 1832.

[108] Noth and Weiser [v. Rad].

[109] Cf. R. Kittel, *op. cit.* It is not true, however, that Israel took its eschatology, along with Messianic expectation and the mythical forms of presentation, from the Canaanites (so H. Schmidt, *Der Mythos vom wiederkehrenden König im AT²* [1933], 8 f.). The fusion of existing myth into visions of the future is a creation of the prophets which already has in itself the character of fulfilment.

[110] RGG², IV, 382 and 387; H. Gunkel, *Schöpfung u. Chaos in Urzeit u. Endzeit²* (1921); P. Volz, *Die Eschatologie d. jüdischen Gemeinde im nt.lichen Zeitalter* (1934); Bousset-Gressm., 469 ff.

[111] Cf. RGG², IV, 389; F. Büchsel, *Theologie d. NT* (1935), 164, n. 14; R. Bultmann in *Eucharisterion f. H. Gunkel*, II (1923), 10 ff. tries to trace this myth even in Jn. 1:1; cf. his *Joh.* (1937 ff.), 8 f., esp. 8, n. 10; 9, n. 1. Cf. also → n. 126; H. Schmidt, *op. cit.*, 21, n. 2.

and wisdom, "and," we read, "when he (sc. Simon Magus) expounds in an illuminating way many similar inventions of the Hellenic saga, he deceives many." [112]

Greek myths are later found alongside the earlier oriental myths. As parables they are used by the Rabbis for various purposes. Thus the stories of the Danaids (Lv. r., 19, 1 on 15:25) and Ariadne (Cant. r., 1, 8 on 1:1) are parables for the study and interpretation of the Torah. [113] Again, with the alteration of various features they can be applied to Jewish personages. [114] Even one of the great Platonic myths, the concluding myth in Resp., X, 614b-621d, made its way into Rabb. literature (Tanch. Pikkude, 3 [I. A. Eisenstein, *Ozar Midraschim*, 1928, 243 ff.]), presumably by way of Egypt where the Horus myth imposed some changes, and it here experienced rejuvenation as an almost purely Jewish myth. [115] But Judaism seems hardly to have been aware of the fact that the figures and materials (the primal man etc.) which played no insignificant a role in its thinking were in fact mythical. [116]

E. μῦθοι in the NT.

I. Myth an Alien Body in the NT.

The position of the NT regarding what it calls μῦθος is quite unequivocal. The only occurrences of the term are in negative statements (1 Tm. 1:4; 4:7; Tt. 1:14; 2 Pt. 1:16; and in sense 2 Tm. 4:4). There is obviously a complete repudiation of μῦθος. It is the means and mark of an alien proclamation, especially of the error combatted in the Past.

The Gospel is concerned with the μεγαλεῖα τοῦ θεοῦ (Ac. 2:11), the great acts of God in history and the last time. It is thus λόγος (→ *IV, 1 [a]*), the account of historical facts, or προφητικὸς λόγος (cf. 2 Pt. 1:19), the account of prophetic facts. The μῦθοι of the error, on the other hand, are invented stories or fables destitute of truth.

II. The Problem of the NT μῦθοι.

What we are to understand by the μῦθοι to which the NT refers, however, was already a subject of much discussion in the early Church, and is still debated to-day, for Paul, who did not have the same interest in μῦθοι as the 2nd century or we ourselves (Schlatter), does not give us any information on the point.

The first question must be whether the NT μῦθοι, which are mentioned only in the Past. and a single verse in 2 Pt., are a single magnitude, or whether there are two or many different kinds.

1. Uniformity of the μῦθοι in the Past. As regards the μῦθοι mentioned in the Past., there arises first the question whether one should differentiate between the μῦθοι of present (cf. 1 Tm. 4) and future (cf. 2 Tm. 4) heretics. But if one examines more closely the relevant sections in the epistles to Tm. it is at once apparent that a clear-cut distinction between present and future cannot be sustained. [117]

---

112 Hennecke, 217. Here there is also an example of the Gnostic interpretation of myth (→ C. 5, e ff.); cf. W. Bousset, *Hauptprobleme d. Gnosis* (1907), 78 ff.

113 Str.-B., IV, 408; I, 654; also 573 (bed of Procrustes) and IV, 408 f.

114 Cf. Bergel, II, 5 f., 68.

115 Cf. R. Meyer, *Hellenistisches in d. rabb. Anthropologie* (1937), 88-114.

116 Cf. Meyer, 1 and 74 ff.; on the ambivalent attitude of Philo, esp. in questions of allegory, → 790.

117 Wohlenberg (Past., 27 f.) makes this distinction, but the following considerations tell against him. First, Paul moves from depiction of the future in 2 Tm. 3:1-5 to that of

The question has also to be put whether the μῦθοι of the Ephesian error of 1 and 2 Tm. and those of the Cretan error of Tt. are basically different or whether they are one and the same. From the epistles themselves it is hardly possible to give a definite answer. It is significant, however, that in both cases the μῦθοι or their proponents are open to moral question (cf. Tt. 1:16; 1 Tm. 4:7: βέβηλος, → IV, 2[a]), and also that in both cases the truth of the Gospel (2 Tm. 4:4; Tt. 1:14) and the stability of the life of faith (Tt. 1:13; 1 Tm. 1:4) seem to be threatened by the μῦθοι. More important, however, is the fact that both groups seem to have a common derivation (→ II, 2). Thus it seems most likely that the μῦθοι of the Past. are to be regarded as manifestations of the same genus.

2. Origin and Nature of the μῦθοι in the Past. But if the μῦθοι of 1 and 2 Tm., to take these first, are to be regarded as a unity, are they a phenomenon of the Hellenistic or the Jewish world? In relation to this question expositors are divided into two groups, as in so many NT problems, and as in the days of the early Church.

a. "Stories of the Gods"? The history of the word and concept μῦθοι prior to the NT leaves us in no doubt that it derives from the Gk. world. In fact many expositors, like John Chrysostom of old, see here a ref. to the ancient stories of the gods, and to a Christian allegorising of these, such as is actually found in the ancient world (→ n. 160). Against this view it must be argued that faced by such an aberration Paul would surely have said something much plainer against the μῦθοι. But there are also other indications (→ 783) that the μῦθος of the Past. is not myth in the strict sense, but should be construed more generally as "untrue story," "fable."

b. "Gnostic Myths"? Most attempts at explaining the NT μῦθοι Hellenistically turn, however, to Gnosticism. Tert. (Praescr. Haer., 7, 33; Adv. Valentinianos, 3) and Iren. (Haer., 1, 1, cf. also Epiph. Haer., 31, 9) already refer 1 Tm. 1:4; 4:7 to the Valentinians, and the critical exegesis of the 19th cent. followed their example, sometimes referring (as they did) to a concrete form of Gnosticism, [118] sometimes leaving the question open what type it was, or even whether it was Hellen. or Jewish Gnosticism. [119] Particular support was found for this exposition in the γενεαλογίαι connected with the μῦθοι in 1 Tm. 1:4, for in these a ref. was seen to the series of aeons in Gnosticism. [120] But the history of the meaning of the word makes an explanation in terms of Gnosticism unlikely. As there is no doubt that μῦθος belongs originally and essentially to the world of polytheism, so γενεαλογία in the NT bears unmistakably the marks of an origin in Judaism. [121] But if μῦθοι and γενεαλογίαι are linked in a traditional formula, [122] and the μῦθοι of the Past. are to be regarded as a unity (→ II, 1), the ex-

---

the present in v. 6, but the opponents in view are obviously the same. Again, the link between the future sayings in 2 Tm. 4:3 f. and the present admonitions in the preceding and following vv. is so close that there is no doubt Paul finds the predictions fulfilled in the present, which has an eschatological character. Moreover, the fusion of present and future is indissoluble in 1 Tm. 4, where the predictions (vv. 1 ff.) which Timothy must set before the brethren (v. 6) have obvious significance for the present, and the warning against over-evaluation of σωματικὴ γυμνασία in v. 8 seems to refer back to v. 3, so that the μῦθοι of v. 7 belong to this series of statements which are both future and present (so also Schl., *ad loc.*).

118 Thus A. Neander suggested Cerinthus, J. Lightfoot the Naassenes, O. Pfleiderer (*Urchristentum*² [1902], II, 271) the Valentinians or an early Syrian Gnosticism.

119 Cf. Jülicher-Fascher, *Einleitung in das NT*⁷ (1931), 181 f.; H. J. Holtzmann, *Lehrbuch d. hist.-krit. Einl. in d. NT*³ (1892), 288.

120 So A. Klöpper in ZwTh (1902), 344 ;W. J. Mangold, *D. Irrlehrer d. Past.* (1856), 64 ff.; Dib. Past., *ad loc.* etc.; though cf. Feine-Behm, *Einl. in d. NT*⁸ (1936), 203 f.

121 → I, 664; Cr.-Kö., 240 f.; G. Kittel, *op. cit.*

122 → I, 664. Cf. Plat. Tim., 22a (→ I, 663); Polyb., 9, 2, 1: πολλῶν γὰρ καὶ πολλαχῶς ἐξηριθμένων τά τε περὶ τὰς γενεαλογίας καὶ μύθους ..., "after many in many ways have dealt with the portion of historical writing which is concerned with the saga of gods and heroes." Here γενεαλογία serves polytheistic notions.

pression Ἰουδαϊκοὶ μῦθοι in Tt. 1:14 is a significant pointer. The μῦθοι καὶ γενεαλογίαι ἀπέραντοι are of Jewish origin (cf. also νομοδιδάσκαλοι in 1 Tm. 1:7 etc.).

c. "Jewish Fables"? Many fathers of both East and West made this their starting-point. Theod. of Mopsuestia and Theodoret, like Augustine (c. adversarium legis et prophetarum, 2, 1 f.), found the μῦθοι in the Jewish δευτέρωσις (Mishnah), while the opponent of Aug. related them directly to the Law and the prophets. This interpretation in a modified form — not the OT stories themselves but their treatment after the manner of the common exposition of pagan stories of heroes and the gods is called μῦθος [123] — finds many champions to-day. [124]

Most deserving of notice, perhaps, are the interpretations (Schl., Lock etc.) which refer the μῦθοι to the Jewish haggada and which assume that the μῦθοι are proclaimed by a Jewish or Jewish-Christian Gnostic sect. Ambrosiaster obviously had the haggada in mind when in relation to 1 Tm. 1:4 he spoke of the *fabulae quas narrare consueti sunt Iudaei de generatione suarum originum* (cf. also on Tt. 1:14). The significant conception of a Jewish Gnosticism, which has found more general recognition only in our own time, [125] was also anticipated by Campegius Vitringa with his reference to *Iudaei aliqui Platonicae aut Pythagoricae philosophiae studiosi* and their *subtilissimae disputationes de divinitate eiusque variis emanationibus* (he has in view the Cabbala). [126] In fact it is highly probable that the Past. are concerned with the early form of a Gnosticism which flourished on the soil of Hellenistic Jewish Christianity, like the rather different Gnosticism to which Colossians refers. For certain references to dualistic ideas such as those contained in 1 Tm. 4:1-5 and 2 Tm. 2:18 clearly take us beyond the sphere of Judaism proper. In this Gnosis haggadic stories and their religious (allegorical) interpretation, along with the OT, were probably given a quite unfitting role, [127] and they were contemptuously described by opponents in terms of the pagan expression μῦθοι, with a primary reference to the method of exposition, which was fundamentally the same as that of the Hellenic myths. In this type of interpretation, which opened the door to Gnostic caprice (cf. ἀπέραντος in 1 Tm. 1:4), the Church saw a danger which caused it to hoist a warning signal even though it did not have to be totally opposed to the Jewish haggada in other respects (cf. Jd. 9). For this reason the terms in which the Past. refer to this secondary form

---

[123] Cf. already Ambrosiaster on Tt. 3:9: *Fabulosa non lex, sed haeresis est.*

[124] So Cr.-Kö., 241; F. H. Colson in JThSt, 19 (1917/18), 265-271, esp. 268. On this view it is tempting to think of Philo (→ *IV, 5[b]*), but in the Past. there can be no question of the Alexandrian Jewish religious philosophy represented by him, since the ref. is to a specific Christian group and teaching. The view that μῦθος and γενεαλογία denote only form and value, not content, is too artificial to commend itself, and it does not tally with the use of the terms elsewhere.

[125] → I, 664 and n. 3.

[126] Observationes Sacrae, V[2] (1717), 174; cf. Wbg. Past., 43-45. F. C. Baur linked the μῦθοι of the Past. with the Achamoth myth and A. Ritschl (*Die Entstehung d. altkatholischen Kirche*[2] [1857], 342, n. 2; more explicitly the essay "Über die Essener," Theol. Jbch. [1855], 354 ff.) with the Therapeutae. A. Knopf, *Das nachap. Zeitalter* (1905), 302 f. relates the μῦθοι and γενεαλογίαι to Jewish-Gnostic speculations on the sphere of angels, and thus brings them into the vicinity of the Colossian heresy.

[127] Cf. the extracts from Jub. in Wbg. Past., 32-37 and the instances in Lock on 1 Tm. 1:4 and Schl. Past., 33 f., cf. 123. Schl. thinks that the ref. is to myths of Jewish origin concerning God and nature, the origin and future of the soul etc., which served to support the dualistic-ascetic-docetic tendencies in the doctrine. A lively impression of the aberrations in Jewish myths may be gained from Bergel, I and esp. II.

of Gnosticism (βέβηλος, *IV, 2 [a]*, γραώδης → b, παραιτέομαι) are not so sharp as other expressions used of error.[128]

3. The Nature of the μῦθοι in 2 Pt.

What is the concept of μῦθος in the only passage in which the NT refers to μῦθοι outside the Past., namely, in 2 Pt. 1:16? The reference in 2 Pt. 1 (cf. esp. vv. 19-21) is to the eschatological proclamation of the apostles. This is grounded upon an anticipatory view of the glory of the returning Lord which was granted to them, i.e., on experience, autopsy (ἐπόπται γενηθέντες τῆς ἐκείνου μεγαλειότητος not merely on the Mount of Transfiguration, cf. Jn. 1:14, but there particularly, 2 Pt. 1:17 f.), not on fantastic speculations, as to some degree in apocalyptic, nor on empty fables, as obviously in Jewish Hellenistic Gnosticism. The eschatological context leads at once to the conclusion that the μῦθοι of 2 Pt. are also of Jewish origin like those of Tt. 1:14 and the Past. generally.[129] This is confirmed by Ignatius, for whom (Mg., 8, 1) πλανᾶσθαι μυθεύμασιν παλαιοῖς belongs with κατὰ Ἰουδαϊσμὸν ζῆν. It thus seems probable that we are dealing with the same type of μῦθοι throughout the NT. We shall now consider some further features and peculiarities of these μῦθοι.

III. Myth, Truth and History.

Of fundamental significance is the antithesis between μῦθος and ἀλήθεια of which the Greek world was already conscious (→ 770; 779), though it did not yet grasp how profound and radical it was. This was possible only on the basis of the NT understanding (→ I, 241-247). The basic NT verse in this respect is 1 Tm. 4:4 (→ *IV, 1*).

1. Myth and Truth for the Greeks.

Eur. could still speak of a μῦθος τῆς ἀληθείας (Phoen., 469 → n. 37), and further development of the concept μῦθος regarded it as expressing truth ἐν μύθου σχήματι, including, of course, the deepest religious truth.[130] For it is still possible to glean from myths the view of their creator (cf. Plato) concerning the truth (Orig. Cels., 4, 39 → 776). Nevertheless, the Platonic myth, even though it is for the philosopher a λόγος (Gorg., 523a, → n. 60), is characterised essentially by a final uncertainty, cf. Men., 86b, Phaed., 114d. It can never be more than probable speech, Tim., 29d. The essential thing in it is only ἡ τῶν εἰκότων μύθων ἰδέα, Tim., 59c d. Though it is a reflection of the truth (εἰκονίζων τὴν ἀλήθειαν, Suid.), or image of the λόγος,[131] as a μῦθος πλασθείς (→ n. 58 and 139) it is itself only a λόγος ψευδής.[132]

---

[128] Cf. Wbg., 159.

[129] On the question of the identity of the false teachers and μῦθοι in 2 Pt. and Past. cf. Mayor, CLXVII ff.

[130] Aristot. Metaph., XI, 8, p. 1074b, 1 ff.: παραδέδοται δὲ παρὰ τῶν ἀρχαίων καὶ παμπαλαίων ἐν μύθου σχήματι καταλελειμμένα τοῖς ὕστερον ὅτι θεοί τέ εἰσιν οὗτοι καὶ περιέχει τὸ θεῖον τὴν ὅλην φύσιν. This principle is particularly true of Socratic myth, which in Plato's works is clearly differentiated from other μῦθοι, e.g., Socrates' account of the birth of Eros in Symp., 203b ff. as compared with the five preceding Eros myths (Friedländer, 207 ff.). Cf. also Plat. Tim., 22c: τοῦτο μύθου μὲν σχῆμα ἔχον λέγεται, τὸ δ' ἀληθές ἐστι. Strabo, I, 2, 35; Orig. Cels., 4, 38 f. (→ 774).

[131] Plut. Is. et Os., 20 (II, 359a; → 776 and n. 88): λόγου τινὸς ἔμφασις, Athen., 4 (II, 348a; → n. 52): λόγου εἰκὼν καὶ εἴδωλον.

[132] *Loc. cit.* and Suid., *s.v.*, → 770.

Thus μῦθος eventually comes to be the complete opposite of ἀλήθεια, as is emphasised by Jewish and Christian and other later authors. Philo Exsecr., 162 sets ἄπλαστος ἀλήθεια and πεπλασμένοι μῦθοι in antithesis,[133] and Orig. Cels., 8, 66 says that a ζητῶν ἀλήθειαν is necessary as well as a φεύγων μύθους. Significant for the devaluation of μῦθος along these lines are finally the μυθιστορίαι and *mythistorica volumina* in later historical works,[134] which are probably lying tales.

2. Myth and History in Antiquity.

Antiquity makes no sharp distinction between myth and history. Up to the end of the classical period the so-called logographi, esp. Hecataios and his disciples, treated myth as a preliminary stage of true historical writing.[135] Polybius (9, 1, 4; 9, 2, 1 → n. 122) still regards μῦθος and ἱστορία as two genera of historical work.[136]

Even when there was a radical demand to separate the two,[137] and the myths of the so-called mythographi[138] were abandoned, Sext. Emp. (Math., I, 263) still associates ἱστορία, μῦθος and πλάσμα[139] as elements in historical writing.[140]

In practice history constantly turns into myth and *vice versa*. As there is a historicising of myth (→ 780), the reverse is also true. Alexander's exploits are projected into myth in accordance with the oriental way of thinking and speaking mythically; the battle of the god-king against his enemies is finally regarded as a conflict with hellish powers.[141] Pertinent here is Cl. Al. Strom., V, 21, 1: "In reliefs they (sc. the Egyptians) perpetuate the praise of kings in the vesture of myths of the gods."[142] The use of mythical pictures in grave symbolism is an analogous phenomenon in the history of individuals (→ C, 5, d).

3. Myth, Truth and History in the NT.

The antithesis between myth and truth, already present before, takes on a new

---

133 The antithesis μῦθος-ἀλήθεια is already a commonplace in early Gk. rationalism which was handed down to a late period, cf. Schmid-Stählin, 697 and n. 2. Examples: Dion. Hal. Ant. Rom., I, 39, 1 etc. For Luc. myths are definitely swindles, cf. Philop., *passim*, e.g., 4, the antithesis μυθώδη-ἀληθές. Longus, IV, 19, 3: ἀληθὴς λόγος-ψεύδεσθαι. Philodem. Philos. Rhetorica, II, p. 53, Sudhaus: ἀληθῶς-μυθικῶς etc. → n. 103.

134 Capitolinus Macrinus, 1, 5 (Script. Hist. Augustae, I, 201, ed. E. Hohl); Vopiscus Quadrigae Tyrannorum, 1, 2 (*ibid.*, II, 222).

135 Cf. Wendland Hell. Kult., 115 ff.

136 Cf. Ausonius (Commemoratio professorum, 22, 26 of two *grammatici latini et graeci*): *callentes mython plasmata et historiam.*

137 Luc. Quomodo Historia Conscribenda Sit, 42: μὴ τὸ μυθῶδες ἀσπάζεσθαι ἀλλὰ τὴν ἀλήθειαν τῶν γεγενημένων ἀπολείπειν τοῖς ὕστερον. Cf. Strabo, 10, 3, 20 (μυθολογεῖν μᾶλλον ἢ ἱστορεῖν); Aristot. Poet., 9, p. 1451b, 4 f.: Historians and poets are distinguished τῷ τὸν μὲν τὰ γενόμενα λέγειν, τὸν δὲ οἷα ἂν γένοιτο.

138 Christ-Schmid-Stählin, *Gesch. d. gr. Lit.*, II^6 (1920), 231 ff.

139 πλάσμα acc. to Sext. Emp. is fiction which resembles reality, μῦθος is πραγμάτων ἀγενήτων καὶ ψευδῶν ἔκθεσις, cf. his Pyrrh. Hyp., I, 147: μυθικὴ πίστις ἐστὶ πραγμάτων ἀγενήτων καὶ πεπλασμένων παραδοχή. But as this passage shows, μῦθος and πλάσμα (πλάττω) are mostly correlative terms; this is proved by the many expressions which combine the two, e.g., μῦθος πλασθείς (Plat. Tim., 26e; → n. 58); πλαστὸς μῦθος (Ps.-Callisth., p. 83, 21; cf. πλαστοὶ λόγοι, 2 Pt. 2:3 and Bigg, *ad loc.*); μῦθος καὶ πλάσμα, Plut. Def. Orac., 46 (II, 435d); Thes. 28, 1 (I, 13), Philo Congr., 61; μύθου πλάσμα, μύθων πλάσματα, and πλάσμα μυθικόν are very common in Philo, and sometimes also the compounds μυθοπλαστέω and μυθοπλάστης (*v.* Leisegang, *s.v.*); cf. P. Wendland, *Philos Schrift über die Vorsehung* (1892), 110.

140 Cf. Cr.-Kö., 740.

141 Jeremias, *Ap. Glaubensbekenntnis*, 47.

142 τοὺς γοῦν τῶν βασιλέων ἐπαίνους θεολογουμένοις μύθοις παραδιδόντες, ἀναγράφουσι διὰ τῶν ἀναγλύφων.

depth in the NT. For the term ἀλήθεια is given a new fulness by the actuality of salvation in history and the divine fulness of Christ in the incarnation. The opposite of myth here is not an abstract concept of truth, nor the sober fact of earthly events. It is a divine fact with all the weight of historical reality. The NT could not say that a word or history contains truth if it has nothing in common with reality, → *infra*; IV, 5. One is either on the side of myth or on that of NT truth. To this general thesis may be appended the following detailed observations.

IV. Designations and Relations of the NT μῦθοι.

1. In 2 Tm. 4:4. 2 Tm. 4:4 reads: ἀπὸ μὲν τῆς ἀληθείας τὴν ἀκοὴν ἀποστρέψουσιν, ἐπὶ δὲ τοὺς μύθους ἐκτραπήσονται. These myths, being obviously known to the Christians of the time, are not described more precisely. But the definite article is added, perhaps with an undertone of scorn as in 1 Tm. 4:7. The myths seem to be a heretical alternative to the truth of the Gospel, → *III, 3*. As the preceding verses show, they come within the framework of a teaching which is opposed to the ὑγιαίνουσα διδασκαλία (v. 3) [143] of the apostles. They stand in antithesis (a) to the λόγος of the Gospel, and they are spread (b) by teachers who in a suspicious way satisfy the ἐπιθυμίαι of men (→ 2, a), though signs of asceticism are also to be noted in them.

(a) μῦθος and λόγος. On the relation between λόγος and μῦθος in the Gk. world → 770 f. For Plato λόγος, in contrast to μῦθος, is that on which one can rely, cf. esp. Tim., 26e, → n. 58; Gorg., 523a, → n. 60. In the NT the deeper antithesis between ἀλήθεια and μῦθος implies a deeper antithesis between λόγος and μῦθος. John, who puts the NT Logos at the beginning of his message, never contrasts this with myth — perhaps because he is addressing Jews rather than Greeks. All the plainer, then, is the contrast in Paul (2 Tm. 4:2, 4; 1 Tm. 4:6, 7; cf. 2 Pt. 1:16, 19). λόγος is the absolutely valid and incarnate Word of God on which everything rests, the faith of the individual, the structure of the Church. If the Logos is replaced by myth, all is lost; the Word is betrayed. But even if an attempt is made to couple together God's Word and myth, as in earlier and later Gnosticism, the Logos is betrayed. Both errors are resisted by the fathers. On the second cf. Iren. (I, 8, 1), who, in plain allusion to 1 Tm. 4:7, says of the Valentinians: οὗτοι γραῶν μύθους συγκαττύσαντες ... ἐφαρμόζειν βούλονται τοῖς μύθοις αὐτῶν τὰ λόγια τοῦ θεοῦ.

(b) The primary teachers of myths in antiquity were the poets. They were the true μυθολόγοι (→ n. 46), cf. esp. Plat. Resp., III, 392d, 398a (→ 779), and their model and master was Hermes, cf. Manetho Apotelesmatica, 4, 444 f. [144] In a more definite sense, closer to that of the NT, the teachers of myths are philosophers like Pythagoras or Plato and the theologians of the mystery religions who concealed their doctrines behind mysterious myths (→ C. 3, c and d, 5, c), but also other philosophers who read their rationalistic teaching into ancient myths and thought that they could thereby commend both (→ C. 5, a).

2. In 1 Tm. 4:7. The antitheses relating to the future μῦθοι of 2 Tm. are also true of the present μῦθοι of 1 Tm. 4:6 f.: καλὸς ... διάκονος Χριστοῦ Ἰησοῦ, ἐντρεφόμενος τοῖς λόγοις τῆς πίστεως καὶ τῆς καλῆς διδασκαλίας ᾗ παρηκο-

[143] Plat. fears that myths can harm the correct doctrine of God, cf. Jos. Ap., II, 256 (→ 779); also Orig. Cels., 4, 48 (→ n. 82) and → F.

[144] Τούτοις δ' Ἑρμείας φαύλοις ἐν σχήμασιν ὀφθεὶς | μυθολόγους τεύχει τε καὶ αἰσχεορήμονας ἄνδρας. In Maximus of Tyre (18, 9, p. 232, 8) Ἔρως is described as μυθοπλόκος. This means much the same as when desire is called μυθολόγος in Philo Sacr. AC, 28.

λούθηκας· τοὺς δὲ βεβήλους καὶ γραώδεις μύθους παραιτοῦ. In 2 Tm. 4:4 (→ 1.) we have two antitheses to μῦθοι: λόγοι τῆς πίστεως[145] and ἡ καλὴ διδασκαλία. Here we have two epithets to describe μῦθοι: (a) βέβηλος and (b) γραώδης. There is also an express direction to reject the μῦθοι: παραιτοῦ (→ I, 195).

(a) μῦθοι βέβηλοι. The warning not to replace the simple food of the evangelical truths of pure teaching by μῦθοι, nor to mix it with μῦθοι (→ 1. (a)), is given emphasis by the addition of the epithet βέβηλος (→ I, 604 f.).[146] The μῦθοι with which the heretics offer supposed religious truths are profane. They have nothing to do with the true God and lead astray from Him. It can hardly be said more plainly that the μῦθοι and NT religion are mutually exclusive. But the line of demarcation drawn by βέβηλος is even sharper when one considers that the word includes the concept of what is unholy in the moral sense. That is to say, it can mean "impure," "immoral" (→ I, 604 f.), though this aspect is not stressed in this passage.

The connection between the myths and immorality was neither overlooked nor denied by the Gks. themselves from the time of the verses of Xenophanes on the bad example of the gods, Fr., 11 (I, 132, Diels[5]). This was, e.g., one of the reasons for the division in the assessment of myth on the part of Plato, → 779, who even suspected immoral motives in the creation of many myths, cf. Leg., I, 636c and d: The Cretans invented the myth of Ganymede κατὰ τοῦ Διός ἵνα ἑπόμενοι δὴ τῷ θεῷ καρπῶνται καὶ ταύτην τὴν ἡδονήν, cf. Philo Prov., 39; Ps.-Clem. Recg., 10, 28 etc. The Cynics, Stoics, and Epicureans, the Academicians and Peripatetics, were all agreed in their moral condemnation of the myths. It is said of Epicurus (Heracl. Hom. All., 4, p. 5, 4 f.) that he avoided all poetry as a dangerous bait of myths, ἅπασαν ὁμοῦ ποιητικὴν ὥσπερ ὀλέθριον μύθων δέλεαρ ἀφοσιούμενος.[147] But the moral failings of myth are really lashed for the first time only by Christian and Jewish writers, esp. Philo and the Ps.-Clem. In agreement with Plato's dictum (→ *supra*) Philo in Sacr. AC, 28 calls ἡδονή the author of myths (→ n. 144), and in Providentia, 38 Philo's nephew Alexander, after a sharp criticism of the myths of Hesiod and Homer, opines that the poets deserved to have their tongues cut out.[148] There were strong attacks on the allegorising which tried

[145] In the Gk. world one could speak of μῦθοι τῆς πίστεως, cf. Dion. Hal. De Thucydide, 5 (ed. H. Usener-L. Radermacher, p. 331, 9): μῦθοι ... ἀπὸ (vl. ὑπὸ) τοῦ πολλοῦ πεπιστευμένοι χρόνου, Diod. S., 1, 93, 3: οἱ μὲν γὰρ Ἕλληνες μύθοις πεπλασμένοις καὶ φήμαις διαβεβλημέναις (in incredible sagas) τὴν περὶ τούτων (sc. the dead) πίστιν παρέδωκαν, τήν τε τῶν εὐσεβῶν τιμὴν καὶ τὴν τῶν πονηρῶν τιμωρίαν. But already one may see here a sense of the discrepancy of the linking of μῦθοι and πίστις; cf. the note on the mingling of ἀρεταλογία (recitation of ἱεροὶ λόγοι) and μυθεύματα in Manetho, Apotelesmatica, 4, 447 and the related condemnation of Gnosis in Iren., I, 8, 1 (→ 786). It is surprising but significant that even the Christian philosopher Synesios (Prov., 1, 1; MPG, 66, 1212 B) makes a distinction between a μῦθος and a (pagan) ἱερὸς λόγος.

[146] The κενοφωνίαι of 1 Tm. 6:20; 2 Tm. 2:16 are also called βέβηλοι. Perhaps the meaning is the same as in the case of the μῦθοι. They are not only "profane" and "morally suspect," but also "empty," "devoid of truth"; cf. λόγος κενός or ψευδής for μῦθος in Hesych. and Suid., also Iren. (Epiph. Haer., 31, 9), Athenag., 30, 3 and the common use of κενοὶ μῦθοι, e.g., Cl. Al. Protr., 2, 1, also the correlative terms ματαιολογία (1 Tm. 1:6) and ψευδολόγος (4:2); → 770, 784, 791 and n. 164.

[147] Cf. Geffcken, XVIII sq.; P. Wendland, *Philos Schrift über d. Vorsehung* (1892), 58 ff.; examples, Luc. Sacrif., 5-7; Philop., 2; from a later period the scornful verse of Manetho (→ n. 144) concerning the μυθολόγοι, which he associates with αἰσχεορήμονες ἄνδρες, and which P. Masp., 97, II, 44 (6th cent. A.D.) calls ἀνάρμοστος, "unbecoming."

[148] Cf. also Jos. Ant., I, 22: οἱ μὲν γὰρ ἄλλοι νομοθέται τοῖς μύθοις ἐξακολουθήσαντες τῶν ἀνθρωπίνων ἁμαρτημάτων εἰς τοὺς θεοὺς τῷ λόγῳ τὴν αἰσχύνην μετέθεσαν (transferred in their presentation the shame of human sins to the gods) καὶ πολλὴν ὑποτίμησιν (a good excuse) τοῖς πονηροῖς ἔδωκαν, cf. also Orig. Cels., 1, 16; 4, 48 etc.

to draw profound and even religious wisdom from bad stories (→ n. 92). What a contradiction between the stories and the meaning is created by such expositors τὰ σεμνὰ ἀσέμνοις μύθοις καλύψαντες (Ps.-Clem. Hom., 6, 17; cf. Recg., 10, 30 ff., esp. 36)!

The myths of the false teachers can hardly have contained the same immoralities as the ancient myths, but they still found an echo in human sensuality, cf. 2 Tm. 4:3 f.

(b) μῦθοι γραώδεις. The concept of μῦθοι "as old women narrate them" is not originally contemptuous. On the contrary, a much lauded gift of old women was that of being excellent tellers of fairy-stories, Plat. Resp., I, 350e, → n. 42. As such they had a place in education acc. to Plato, → 775. But there is then combined with the concept of the γραώδης μῦθος, the *anilis fabula* (e.g., Orig. Princ., II, 4, 3; Apul. Apol., 25 [p. 29, Helm]) the idea of the "old-womanish," "the childish," "that which is unworthy of a man." [149] This judgment applies to the μῦθοι of the false teachers in 1 Tm. 4 (cf. also Iren., I, 8, 1: γραῶν μῦθοι, → 786). The Apologists judge the myths of the ancient gods similarly (Athenag., 21, 2), and opponents of Christianity use the same phrase to try to bring the stories of the Bible (Orig. Cels., 4, 36 and 39, → n. 163) and Christian doctrines (Lact. Inst., 5, 1 ff.) [150] into contempt.

3. In 1 Tm. 1:4. 1 Tm. 1:3 f. contains the apostle's warning to Timothy ἵνα παραγγείλῃς τισὶν μὴ ἑτεροδιδασκαλεῖν μηδὲ προσέχειν [151] μύθοις καὶ γενεαλογίαις ἀπεράντοις, αἵτινες ἐκζητήσεις παρέχουσιν μᾶλλον ἢ οἰκονομίαν θεοῦ τὴν ἐν πίστει. Here it is plain that in a group (τινές) within the congregations — they are under the pastoral authority (παραγγέλλειν) of Timothy — there has arisen an alien doctrine characterised by a lively interest in, and intensive concern with, a host of μῦθοι and γενεαλογίαι (→ 782). Paul warns against this by-product, possibly harmless enough in itself, because it does not serve — and this is his decisive criterion — the divine work of salvation which is built on faith and received in faith, but leads to (ἐκ)ζητήσεις (→ II, 894), perhaps about the allegorical exposition and speculative exploitation of these haggadic stories. [152]

4. In Tt. 1:14. The same point is at issue in Tt. 1:13 f.: ἔλεγχε αὐτοὺς (sc. the Cretan Christians) ἀποτόμως, ἵνα ὑγιαίνωσιν ἐν τῇ πίστει, μὴ προσέχοντες Ἰουδαϊκοῖς μύθοις καὶ ἐντολαῖς ἀνθρώπων ἀποστρεφομένων τὴν ἀλήθειαν. The first importance of this passage is that here the Jewish nature and origin (→ 783) of the μῦθοι is most evident (cf. not only the attribute Ἰουδαϊκός but also the link with ἐντολαί). But the passage is also important because the warning against the false teachers and their μῦθοι is particularly sharp. The development

---

[149] Cf. Strabo, I, 2, 3: τὴν ποιητικὴν γραώδη μυθολογίαν ἀποφαίνων, Luc. Philop., 9: ἔτι σοι γραῶν μῦθοι τὰ λεγόμενά ἐστιν. Worth noting in *ibid.*, 2 is the expression "very curious and marvellous stories" (μυθίδια) with which one can bewitch the souls of children so long as they still fear Mormo and Lamia (→ II, 2, n. 4); also Jul. Or., VII, p. 264, 7 ff.: κυνὸς ... ὥσπερ αἱ τίτθαι (nurses) μύθους ᾄδοντος. παιδαριώδης in Aristot. Metaph., I, 3, p. 995a, 4 and εὐήθης in Hdt., 2, 45 strike the same note as γραώδης in connection with μῦθος, cf. Friedländer, 199 f.

[150] Cf. Harnack Miss., 389; also Jul. Gal., I, p. 163, 4 f., Neumann.

[151] Cf. προσέχειν μύθοις in Tt. 1:14: μὴ προσέχοντες Ἰουδαϊκοῖς μύθοις. Epict., III, 24, 18: Ὁμήρῳ πάντα προσέχεις καὶ τοῖς μύθοις αὐτοῦ, Ael. Nat. An., 16, 5: τοιαῦτα ἄττα καὶ Ἀθηναῖοι ὑπὲρ τοῦ κορύδου τερατευόμενοι (telling such marvellous tales about the lark) προσεῖχον μύθῳ τινί, ᾧπερ οὖν ἀκολουθῆσαί μοι δοκεῖ καὶ Ἀριστοφάνης (Aristoph. Av.).

[152] Cf. Bigg, *ad loc.*, also the ζητήσεις in 1 Tm. 6:4; 2 Tm. 2:23; Tt. 3:9: μωρὰς ζητήσεις καὶ γενεαλογίας, and Bar. 3:23 (→ n. 92); also the Ὁμηρικὰ ζητήματα of Porphyrius.

of haggadic and halachic (ἐντολαί) pieces, probably by allegorical methods,[153] is branded as a wresting of the truth, and the speculations based on them are rejected as unsound because they turn aside from the simple faith.

5. In 2 Pt. 1:16. Finally, there is in 2 Pt. 1:16 the same antithesis between the apostolic testimony and μῦθοι as in the Past.: οὐ γὰρ σεσοφισμένοις μύθοις ἐξακολουθήσαντες (not resting on invented fables) ἐγνωρίσαμεν ὑμῖν τὴν τοῦ κυρίου ἡμῶν Ἰησοῦ Χριστοῦ δύναμιν καὶ παρουσίαν, ἀλλ᾽ ἐπόπται γενηθέντες τῆς ἐκείνου μεγαλειότητος. The author claims autopsy (→ 784)[154] as the basis of his apostolic proclamation, and especially his eschatological message. What the ἐπόπται were allowed to see at very solemn moments during the first παρουσία of the Lord, namely, the μεγαλειότης of Jesus, will be manifested to the whole world at His second παρουσία in power. If in contrast he refers to οὐ γὰρ σεσοφισμένοις μύθοις ἐξακολουθήσαντες,[155] he is presumably rejecting two things, first, proclamation in the form of (a) self-invented fantastic speculations (cf. πλαστοὶ λόγοι, 2:3), which, like his heretical opponents, were probably of Jewish origin, and secondly, the accusation that the apostolic message, (b) the underlying history, and the eschatological message based on OT prophecy and the Gospel history, contain μῦθοι.

(a) Invention of μῦθοι. Kögel[156] tries to distinguish between μῦθος as self-forming saga deriving from primitive times and πλάσμα as intentional artistic invention. But this distinction cannot be upheld, → n. 139. For, though there is some general truth in it, there are many refs. to the intentional invention of μῦθοι.

Nature fables in particular are often called deliberate constructs. Thus acc. to Aristot. Hist. An., VI, 31, p. 579b, 4 → n. 43b the rarity of the lion gave rise to the creation (συντίθημι) of a special μῦθος, and acc. to Ael. Nat. An., 16, 5; → n. 151, the Athenians composed (τερατεύομαι) one on the crested lark.

More important, however, is the fact that this is maintained of myths in the true sense. Acc. to Plat. Leg., I, 636c and d; → 787, the Ganymede myth was invented (λογοποιέω) by the Cretans and appended to the laws given by Zeus. If the goal here was apparently to cover moral laxity, the opp. purpose was served in Jul. Or., I, p. 2, 7 ff. (→ n. 77) by the self-invented myths of spiritual direction; cf. *ibid.*, VII, p. 264, 3 f.: εἰ πρέπει τῷ κυνὶ μύθους πλάττειν.

Above all others Plato himself is the great author of myths (→ C. 3, c). We might also mention the poets, whose occupation is μυθοποιία (→ n. 46; → C. 3, b). They compose on the basis of traditional λόγοι τε καὶ μῦθοι καὶ ἔθη, not arbitrarily, but guided by an inner voice (ἔμφυτος ἐπίνοια or ἔννοια, cf. Dio Chrys. Or., 12, 39; I, 165 f., v. Arnim). On the other hand the successors of the poets, the professional μυθογράφοι (e.g., Philo Decal., 55), often altered the myths with palpable caprice in their work of assembling and re-telling. They did so in acc. with their various purposes of making a living, glorifying their native place, or political ends.[157]

---

[153] Possibly ἀποστρέφομαι alludes directly to allegorical falsification.

[154] Already Hom. emphasises occasionally the distinction between direct perception and the μῦθος of others (in the sense of "word," "report"), so Od., 3, 93 ff.; 4, 323 ff.: εἴ που ὄπωπας ὀφθαλμοῖσι τεοῖσιν ἢ ἄλλου μῦθον ἄκουσας πλαζομένου, cf. also Eur. Med., 653 f.: εἴδομεν, οὐκ ἐξ ἑτέρων μῦθον ἔχω φράσασθαι. In the NT autopsy is a correlative of λόγος (cf. Lk. 1:2, also 1 Jn. 1:1), an example of the complete reorientation of a term deriving from the vocabulary of the mysteries (cf. Wnd., *ad loc.*).

[155] Cf. ἐξακολουθεῖν μύθοις in Jos. Ant., I, 22 (→ n. 148), ἀκολουθεῖν μύθῳ, Ael. Nat. An., 16, 5 (→ n. 151), κατακολουθεῖν μύθῳ, Epic. Ep., 3 (→ n. 102); the opp. is παρακολουθεῖν τῇ καλῇ διδασκαλίᾳ (1 Tm. 4:6).

[156] Cr.-Kö., 740.

[157] Radermacher, 298, n. 47.

In this respect the priests of the various sanctuaries play a particular part with particular problems (→ 771). They certainly added many new cultic myths to the old ones.[158] The Apologists, however, undertook to show that the heathen myths were invented under the influence of demons to confuse and seduce the human race, cf. Just. Apol., I, 54, 1.

That the reference in 2 Pt. 1:16 is to artistically composed[159] μῦθοι is supported by the θελήματι ἀνθρώπου of v. 21 (the opp. here is προφητεία, cf. the ὁ προφητικὸς λόγος of v. 19). If this contains an actual allusion to specific heretical phenomena, the σεσοφισμένος denotes a distinction from the μῦθοι of the Past., which were obviously taken from tradition, → 783.

(b) μῦθος and Biblical History. Philo already perceived that the essential distinction between the Bible and the religions of the ἔθνη lies in the fact that the latter rest largely on myths (Conf. Ling., 3 : αἱ ἱεραὶ λεγόμεναι βίβλοι παρ' ὑμῖν καὶ μύθους περιέχουσιν), whereas the Bible contains history. He also saw that everything depends on clearly maintaining this distinction. He thus objected to the fact that other Jewish apologists before him had devalued the biblical stories by explaining them as myths; cf. Ep. Ar., 168 : οὐδὲν εἰκῇ κατατέτακται διὰ τῆς γραφῆς οὐδὲ μυθωδῶς (in Scripture everything has its historical basis [opp. μυθωδῶς] and divine purpose [opp. εἰκῇ]). Philo Gig., 7: μηδεὶς ὑπολάβῃ μῦθον εἶναι τὸ εἰρημένον, Op. Mund., 2 : (Μωϋσῆς) μήτε ... μύθους πλασάμενος.

On the other hand, Philo himself basically treated biblical history like mythology by following the example of Aristobulus and applying to it the same methods of allegorical exegesis with which the eclectic philosophy of his time rediscovered its wisdom in the Gk. myths. The difficulty was the same, namely, the apparent foolishness and immorality of many parts of the Bible.[160] Philo found his most zealous disciples in the Alexandrian fathers.[161] Origen, like the Ep. of Barn. and its radical allegorising before him, makes the Bible a collection of myths with his exegetical procedures,[162] and yet he very firmly rejects the statements of his opponents that the accounts are in fact myths

---

158 Cf. O. Kern, "Griech. Kultlegenden," ARW, 26 (1928), 1-16. Critias Fr., 1 (TGF, 771 f.) even maintained that all myths rested on the invention and falsification of priests. This view was often adopted later, on the one side critically, as by the Encyclopedists, who charged the priests with inventing myths simply to hold down the masses, on the other side positively, e.g., by Creuzer, who dreamed of a priestly monarchy which composed myths to disseminate morality and religion.

159 Liddell-Scott: "craftily (Bigg, *ad loc.*: "cunningly") devised," Moffatt: "fabricated fables." For σεσοφισμένοι μῦθοι cf. Aristot. Metaph., II, 4, p. 1000a, 18 : οἱ μυθικῶς σοφιζόμενοι, "those who philosophise in mythical form, or about myths," also Ps.-Callisth., p. 60, 1, Kroll : σοφιστικούς μοι καὶ πεπλασμένους μύθους εἰπών. It is open to question whether the use of σεσοφισμένος in 2 Pt. 1:16 contains the thought of "a fiction which embodies a truth, an allegorism" (Bigg, *ad loc.*); cf. Mayor, 103 f., n.

160 Cf. C. Siegfried, *Philo v. Alexandrien als Ausleger d. AT* (1875). It is striking, of course, that Philo himself followed his Stoic masters in occasionally allegorising the Gk. myths (e.g., Providentia, 41), and even more so that the fathers found biblical theology in the sagas of Homer, e.g., Ps.-Just., Cohortatio ad Gentiles, 17 and 28; Cl. Al. Strom., V, 100, 5; 116 f.; 130, 2; cf. Hatch, 50 (though n. 6 is mistaken, cf. O. Stählin on Cl. Al. Strom., V, 116, 1 in *Bibliothek d. Kirchenväter : Clemens v. Alex.*, IV [1937], 215, n. 7); → n. 176.

161 Cf. P. Heinisch, *Der Einfluss Philos auf d. älteste chr. Exegese* (= *At.liche Abh.en*, ed. by J. Nikel, *Heft*, 1/2 [1908]); Hatch, 52 ff. How common and natural was the figurative understanding of religious and other stories may be seen from the fact that there are allegorical interpretations of biblical stories even in Iren.; cf. W. v. Loewenich, *D. Joh.-Verständnis im 2. Jhdt.* (1932), 135; P. Heinisch, 40 f. Later, Alexandrian allegorising was chiefly opposed in Antioch, Hatch, 58 f.

162 Orig. definitely rejects the literal understanding of many biblical stories (Princ., IV, 3, 1), but was sharply attacked for this (cf. Pamphylus, Apologia pro Orig., 5; MPG, 17, 585 ff.).

or fairy-stories, cf. Cels., 5, 57: οὐ χλεύη οὐδὲ γέλως (no subject for mocking laughter) τὰ λεγόμενα οὐδὲ πλάσματα καὶ μῦθοί εἰσιν.[163] Celsus had called the biblical stories inferior or empty myths from which nothing could be extracted even by allegory, 1, 20: μῦθοι κενοὶ νομίζονται μηδ' ἀλληγορίαν ἐπιδεχόμενοι οἱ λόγοι αὐτοῦ (sc. of Moses).[164] He thus says of allegorising — probably that of Philo — in 4, 51: αἱ περὶ αὐτῶν (sc. the OT stories) ἀλληγορίαι πολὺ τῶν μύθων (sc. the biblical stories themselves) αἰσχίους εἰσὶ καὶ ἀτοπώτεραι, and Porphyrius said critically of Origen (Eus. Hist. Eccl., VI, 19, 7) that he intruded Gk. ideas into alien myths (i.e., the biblical texts) (τὰ Ἑλλήνων τοῖς ὀθνείοις ὑποβαλλόμενος μύθοις) by applying to them the allegorical mode of exposition which he had learned from the Stoics Chaeremon and Cornutus.

This scornful assessment of the evangelical history by educated non-Christians was fashionable for a long time, cf. Arnobius, 1, 56 ff. Its most zealous champions were Porphyrius, who was at great pains to try to unmask and destroy the Christian myths,[165] and Julian — esp. at the beginning of his work against the Christians, Gal., p. 167 ff., Neumann — who compared the Gk. myths and biblical stories with a view to showing that both were meaningless and religiously suspect,[166] and esp. the latter, though with the highly remarkable reservation: "If it is not a myth with a secret teaching (μῦθος ἔχων θεωρίαν ἀπόρρητον), as I believe," p. 169, 4 f.

The 19th and 20th centuries produced the same method once again, and equally zealous proponents, → n. 7.

V. Myths in the Gospel?

This question has been raised by a historical comparison of the stories and concepts of the NT with the mythical legacy of contemporary antiquity, and even of such distant fields as that of India. We can touch on this only briefly in the present context. It might be argued against the testimony of the passages treated above, with their clear exclusion of myth from the NT, that there are in fact many mythical elements in the Gospels,[167] that there is a causal connection between Pauline and Johannine thinking in particular and the mythical ideas of the age, and that the world-view, the eschatology, and consequently also the chris-

---

[163] Cf. also 8, 47: ἐροῦσιν Ἕλληνες ταῦτα (the biblical stories) μύθους ... Τί δὲ οὐχὶ μᾶλλον τὰ Ἑλλήνων μῦθοι ἢ ταῦτα, 8, 45: (Celsus) τὰ παρ' ἡμῖν ἀναγεγραμμένα τεράστια ... μύθους εἶναι νενόμικε, 4, 36: μῦθον τινὰ παραπλήσιον τοῖς παραδεδομένοις ταῖς γραυσὶν ὑπολαβὼν (sc. Celsus) εἶναι τὸν λόγον (sc. in Gn. 2; cf. here the antithesis λόγος-μῦθος), 4, 39; 5, 54; 3, 27: περὶ πλασμάτων, ὥς οἴει, καὶ μύθων καὶ τερατειῶν τοσοῦτον ἀγωνίζονται (sc. Christians). Obviously the view that the NT miracle stories were myths was widespread at the time of Orig., cf. Comm. in Joh., 2, 34 (GCS, X, p. 92, 10); also Harnack Miss.

[164] In the same sense κενῶς μυθεύειν ("to tell myths with no fig. meaning") in Heracl. Hom. All., 21 (p. 31, 14 f. → n. 59). The same phrase as that of Celsus, but without the specific sense, is found in Just. Dial., 9, 1, which manifests an unmistakable similarity to 2 Pt. 1:16: οὐ κενοῖς ἐπιστεύσαμεν μύθοις οὐδὲ ἀναποδείκτοις λόγοις, ἀλλὰ μεστοῖς πνεύματος θείου καὶ δυνάμει βρύουσι καὶ τεθηλόσι χάριτι.

[165] Cf. Harnack Miss., 519 and n. 3; 521 f. On the other hand, the idea that Christian stories and teachings might appear as myths is sometimes used by the fathers themselves in theological and ethical discussions, e.g., Cl. Al. Strom., I, 52, 2: "If one rejects the doctrine of providence, μῦθος ἡ περὶ τὸν σωτῆρα οἰκονομία φαίνεται, or 2 Cl., 13, 3: "If the life and message of Christians do not tally, τὰ ἔθνη ... εἰς βλασφημίαν τρέπονται λέγοντες εἶναι μῦθόν τινα καὶ πλάνην, sc. τὰ λόγια τοῦ θεοῦ (→ II, 650 f.).

[166] Cf. p. 168, 4 f.: τί διαφέρει τῶν παρὰ τοῖς Ἕλλησι πεπλασμένων μύθων τὰ τοιαῦτα (sc. the story of Eve and the serpent), p. 167, 15 f.: ταῦτα γάρ ἐστι μυθώδη παντελῶς.

[167] Cf. the bibl. → n. 7, also P. Saintyves, *Essais de folklore biblique* (1923).

tology of the NT are very largely mythological.[168] To this we may reply that borrowings from the thinking and vocabulary of the age with which the messengers of the Gospel had to wrestle are to be expected in advance, and did in fact take place in many points of detail. On the other hand, many things are to be explained as analogy rather than borrowing. Furthermore, in the NT even more clearly than the OT what is borrowed is historicised, or better, baptised, i.e., integrated into the sphere of God's kingdom. Here, too, a μεταμορφοῦσθαι καθάπερ ἀπὸ κυρίου πνεύματος has taken place (2 C. 3:18). For one thing is firm and definite. For the apostles, as for the Gospels, everything was grounded in history. They preached the mighty reality of Christ, not as the followers of cunningly devised myths, but as ἐπόπται.

F. The Evaluation of Myths in the Early Church.

1. If pagan polemics eagerly sought to discredit the NT stories as empty myths, Christian authors were no less zealous to mock pagans for their own myths. Both sides rejected the right of the other to allegorise its own stories, and argued that it was motivated by shame or the immorality of the stories thus expounded.[169] Yet both sides engaged cheerfully in extensive allegorisation, and the result was "a genuine chaos of inconsistent polemics."[170]

The first to enter this unhappy polemical circle on the Christian side were the Apologists. Like their Jewish predecessors (cf. Jos. Ap., II, 236 ff.) they were only too ready to attack pagan myths (cf. Aristid., 13, 7),[171] and in particular they disputed the right of allegorical exegesis, e.g., Tat. Or. Graec., 21, 2: μηδὲ τοὺς μύθους μηδὲ τοὺς θεοὺς ὑμῶν ἀλληγορήσητε (→ C. 4). They disparagingly contrast myths with the Gospel accounts, *ibid.*, 21, 1: συγκρίνατε τοὺς μύθους ὑμῶν τοῖς ἡμετέροις διηγήμασιν, though they also allow themselves to compare, e.g., the divine sonship of Jesus with Gk. analogies (cf. Athenag., 10, 1: οὐ γὰρ ὡς ποιηταὶ μυθοποιοῦσιν ...) and can even make the exaggerated claim that many Gk. sophists perverted biblical truth into myths, Tat. Or. Graec., 40, 1: ... ὡς μυθολογίαν τὴν ἀλήθειαν παραβραβεύσωσι.

The great Alexandrians, Cl. and Orig., follow the Apologists. Cl. cannot abide μῦθοι (Prot., 2, 2: δυσανασχετῶ); they are ἄθεοι (13, 5). In answer to Cels. and his ridiculing of the biblical narratives as μῦθοι, Orig. argues that the ancient myths, being open to historical and religious question (cf. Cels., 1, 16 and 23), cannot be combined with the Bible. Above all, they are inseparable from the pagan view of God, cf. 8, 66. Even though one interprets them allegorically (κἂν τροπολογῶνται), they remain what they are, i.e., myths, 5, 38. The ancient Church took the same view, as may be seen from the church order of Hipp. with its ruling that schoolmasters, as teachers of myths, can be received into the Church only with great reserve (→ n. 101). The same outlook is reflected in the common description of Gnostic teaching and stories as μῦθοι, e.g., Orig. Comm. in Joh. 2:28; 13:27, → n. 42, or μυθολογία, *ibid.*, 2:24.

---

[168] → 765; cf. also W. Wrede, *Paulus* (1904), 103 f.; W. Bousset, *Kyrios Christos*² (1921), 139 ff., 26 ff. etc.; R. Reitzenstein Hell. Myst., also A. Jeremias, *Dogmatik*, 249 f., esp. R. Bultmann, RGG², IV, 390 ff.; *Joh.* (1940), 330 etc. on the Johannine Christ: Oriental myth has lost its mythical content and has been historicised; also J. Behm, *Geschichte u. Geheimnis d. NT* (1939), 23 on the mythical origin of the Son of Man concept.

[169] Cf. on the one side Arnobius Adv. Nationes, V, 43, on the other Celsus in Orig. Cels., 4, 48 (cf. A. Miura-Stange, *Cels. u. Origenes* [1926], 54-58).

[170] Geffcken, 82, cf. 61, 246, also 297 on the inconsistency of Cels., Orig. and Porphyrius; cf. Hatch, 57 f.

[171] εἰ μὲν γὰρ μυθικαὶ αἱ περὶ αὐτῶν ἱστορίαι, οὐδέν εἰσιν εἰ μὴ μόνον λόγοι· εἰ δὲ φυσικαί, οὐκέτι θεοί εἰσιν οἱ ταῦτα ποιήσαντες καὶ παθόντες· εἰ δὲ ἀλληγορικαί, μῦθοί εἰσι καὶ οὐκ ἄλλο τι (→ n. 57).

2. A distinctive exception was made for a brief period by early Christian (and contemporary Jewish, → II, 383) art, which borrowed mythical themes from antiquity [172] and portrayed Helios on the chariot of the sun, [173] the head of Medusa, Eros and Psyche, Nike and esp. Orpheus, the director of souls and tamer of wild nature, [174] or depicted the Good Shepherd in the form of Hermes. [175] Other later religions, e.g., Mithraism, did this far more freely. Yet one sees here, obviously on the basis of an allegorical interpretation of certain myths, a specific trend towards an early Christian mythology of which there are traces on and off later. [176]

In the main, however, there can be no doubt that the Church in every age has insisted that there can be no relation between the Logos of the NT and myth.

G. Conclusions.

The firm rejection of myth is one of the decisions characteristic of the NT. Myth is a pagan category. Though it may be seen in rudimentary form in many parts of the OT, and in metamorphic form in the NT (→ 780, 792), myth as such has no place on biblical soil either 1. as a direct impartation of religious truths, 2. as parable, or 3. as symbol.

1. As a Form of Religious Communication. As in the secular world the fairy-story is for childhood, and the novel, the fairy-story of adults, for the age of maturity, so in the religious development of the non-Christian world myth is for the age of childhood and then, after a period of disparagement, it arises afresh at a later stage as myth interpreted by philosophy and the mystery religions, → C. 5. In the Bible, however, we have from first to last the account and narration of facts. This may undergo certain changes in form and consciousness from the childlikeness of many of the ancient stories to the maturity of the Johannine view

---

172 Cf. F. Piper, *Mythologie u. Symbolik d. chr. Kunst,* I (1847); L. Walk, 416-418, who argues too strongly for the influence of lunar mythological motifs on Chr. art; J. Wilpert, *Die Malereien d. Katakomben Roms* (1903), 31 ff.; C. M. Kaufmann, *Handb. d. chr. Archäologie* (1905), 306 ff., 451; F. X. Kraus, *Gesch. d. chr. Kunst,* I (1895/96), 212 ff.; A. Mailly, "Abgötter an chr. Kirchen," *Chr. Kunst,* 25 (1928/29), 42-52; O. Wulff, *Altchr. u. byzantinische Kunst,* I (1914), 60 ff.

173 Cf. on a catacomb picture, Wilpert, 32, also "Passio S Semproniani etc.," ed. W. Wattenbach, SAB, 1896, 2, 1293, cf. 1282 f.

174 F. Piper, 121-128; J. Sauer in LexThK², VII (1935), 786 f., Art. "Orpheus," III; C. M. Kaufmann, 451; A. Heussner, *Die altchr. Orpheusdarstellungen* (Diss., 1893); V. Schultze, "Orpheus in d. frühchr. Kunst," ZNW, 23 (1924), 173-183; Wilpert, 38 f., 241 ff.; Wulff, 71 and 107; A. Boulanger, *Orphée, Rapports de l'orphisme et du christianisme* (1925); H. Leclercq, Cabrol-Leclercq, *Dict. d'archéologie chrétienne et de liturgie,* 12 (1936), 2735-2755, Art. "Orphée."

175 Cf. Kaufmann, 360; Wulff, 63, also art. "Hermulae" in Cabrol-Leclercq, 6 (1924), 2349 f.

176 Cf. Synesius, Prov., 1, 1 (MPG, 66, 1212 B): τάχ' ἂν οὖν ὅδε καὶ μῦθος ὢν μύθου τι πλέον αἰνίττοιτο διότι ἐστὶν Αἰγύπτιος, with a (non-theological) interpretation of the Osiris myth, also the allegorical expositions in *Ovide moralisé* (ed., Tarbé, 1850), e.g., the Daphne saga as a symbol of the incarnation of God in Mary (Gruppe, *Geschichte,* 17), the Aeneas saga as a parable of human life, and Juno as an image of the Church (God's bride) in the Ovid allegories of Berchorius (Gruppe, 19). But with this dogmatic allegorising there is also naturalistic, moral and euhemeristic interpretation of myths throughout the M. Ages; the writings of Fabius Planciades Fulgentius, esp. his Vergiliana Continentia, are a common model, cf. F. Piper, "Virgilius als Theolog u. Prophet des Heidenthums in d. Kirche," *Evang. Kalender, Jbch. f. 1862,* ed. F. Piper, 13 (1862), 17-82; N. Söderblom, "Natürliche Theologie u. allg. Religionsgeschichte," *Beiträge zur Religionswissenschaft,* I (1914), 24; also → n. 160 and 90.

of Christ. But the essential theme is the same throughout, namely, what God says and what God does.

2. As Parable. In the later stages of paganism myth is often no more than a parable for deeper and intrinsically inexpressible truths. No religious proclamation can dispense with these illustrations. In the Gospel they belong directly to the very essence of condescension. But the NT uses genuine parable rather than myth.

What μῦθος is in the Greek world, whether as the fairy-story or fable for children or the myth in the moral and religious education of adolescents and adults (→ C. 3, d), parable is in the Gospels. Parable is from the very first thought of as a transparency. It makes no odds whether it is historically true. Because it is like things which happen in this world, [177] and consequently has the stamp of truth as a simple story, it is adapted to reflect parabolically the events of God's world. [178] Jesus Himself, however, looks forward to a stage of proclamation when the parable can be dispensed with (Jn. 16:25).

3. As Symbol. The final stage in the understanding of myth is that it is a symbol, → C. 5, d. In both ancient and modern idealism, which is congenial to paganism in the sense of having a common "genius," myth is a symbol of eternal verities which are independent of all history and of all their individual proponents. "In an ever new and deeper sense the mythical symbol can bring an almost inexhaustible answer to those who ask concerning ultimate unity." [179] The central symbol of the Gospel, however, is the cross, and this embodies a hard and unromantic historical reality. No myth can be integrated into or imposed upon this symbol in any form, [180] for the λόγος τοῦ σταυροῦ would be made of none effect hereby (cf. 1 C. 1:17). Nor can this symbol be separated from its personal representative or historical setting, for without Christ at Golgotha the cross is indeed a κενὸς μῦθος, a meaningless symbol or pagan sign.

4. A New Use of the Term? Is there a fourth way to make myth at home in the biblical world? This question has to be faced in view of the present situation.

In spite of the facts adduced above there have been and are many attempts to introduce myth into Christian terminology as something of positive value. [181] But no matter how the term is understood, and no matter how it is extended, as, e.g., by Bultmann, there is within it an inherent antithesis to truth and reality which is quite intolerable on NT soil. [182]

---

[177] Cf. the related understanding of myth in Plato Resp., III, 392d: ἆρ' οὐ πάντα ὅσα ὑπὸ μυθολόγων ἢ ποιητῶν λέγεται διήγησις οὖσα τυγχάνει ἢ γεγονότων ἢ ὄντων ἢ μελλόντων;

[178] Allegorically interpreted myth and parable have much in common, cf. Aristot. Probl., XVIII, 3, p. 916b, 34 f.: τὸ παράδειγμα καὶ οἱ μῦθοι τὸ ὅμοιον δεικνύουσιν. Both are a concrete garment whereby to teach wisdom to the immature, Radermacher, 18, with a ref. to Mk. 4:33 f. But interpretation does not detract from the substance of the parable, which usually applies to man processes actually taken from nature or the world. Allegory, however, basically contests the independent validity of myth and underlines its unreality.

[179] Schröter, 22.

[180] Hence the use of expressions like the Christ myth, which is common in form criticism, is to be strictly avoided as a μετάβασις εἰς ἄλλο γένος.

[181] → A.; cf. esp. Bultmann in RGG², IV, 390 ff.

[182] For there applies absolutely to myth what Hinduism says of its mythical writings, that their validity "does not depend on any historical fact" (D. S. Sarma, *A Primer of Hinduism* [1929], 15); cf. for an example of the problem G. Stählin, "Avatar and Incarnation," *The Way of Christ*, I (1938), 11-22.

There are only two ways of construing myth if a worthwhile attempt is to be made to bring it into the context of the biblical data.

The one seeks by a *salto mortale* to change it into its opposite, to make it an account of facts in the supreme sense, namely, an account of events in the world beyond earthly history (→ n. 4). Now it would be a tempting prospect to have a special term for these events of true history as distinct from the ordinary world history made up of heroes and kings. But two doubts remain. For one thing, the very strong historical loading of the term, which is increasingly powerful in our own time, makes the chances of a successful reorientation very slim indeed, and a lasting uncertainty at the essential heart of the concept would be the greatest possible evil in these matters. Myth is a hotly contested term, as it was for Paul.[183] But where there is dispute conceptual clarity is of the greatest importance. Again, the application of the term "myth" to the transcendental divine history — especially if the character of reality is to be preserved for this — carries with it the danger that history will be devalued even on the part of Christian theologians. One can speak ever so eloquently of this reality of myth and still finally lose the σὰρξ ἐγένετο, the point at which the divine history intersects earthly history in the Gospel, and on which everything depends, unless it is expressly stated that this real myth of transcendent history has become sober earthly history in Christ.

The second way to introduce the term "myth" into the world of biblical facts is to regard the Gospel as fulfilled myth. "The original of all myths became history in Christ."[184] This involves, however, far-reaching presuppositions, and especially that myth is not just a product of our longing for and feeling after God, to refer to what is best in it, but also that it rests on a (perverted) revelation.[185] The Christ myth of the pre-Christian world is then understood as "creation" in the sphere of religion, a parallel to creation in the sphere of nature, along with which it is involved in the fall of man.[186] On this view the mythical theologians of paganism and the prophetic theologians of the old covenant, as those who in different ways proclaim the movement of world occurrence to redemption, are brought into what is at first an alien proximity. But this is to raise again the ancient and as yet unanswered question of the content of truth in the world religions, which is a burning point of controversy in the younger churches of the East.[187] All that we can say, with all due reserve in the light of Jn. 14:6, is that in μῦθος, too, are concealed σπέρματα τοῦ Λόγου.

Stählin

---

183 Cf. Schl. Past., 17.

184 A. v. Harnack, *Die Entstehung d. chr. Theologie u. des kirchlichen Dogmas* (1927), 16: "In its final core, i.e., its historical reality, the Gospel was not a new myth alongside others, but fulfilled myth." Orig., to whom Harnack refers, had the brilliant conception that the higher and lower forms of Christianity, which he differentiated as a Christian Gnostic, were the fulfilment of primitive belief in myth and the spiritual piety of the mysteries, cf. Harnack Dg., I, 656, n. 6. A. Jeremias in his two and in part par. essays (Bibl. under G.) has taken up and developed this idea; cf. esp. *Ap. Glaubensbekenntnis,* 17-26, where he writes (22): "The mythical style proffered by oriental Aram. and Hellen. was alone able to give linguistic shape to the unheard of transcendental factor which had become a reality in Christ, because myth, which conceals itself in this symbolical style, had represented this occurrence in idea." Cf. also his *Dogmatik,* 250; other voices, *ibid.,* 240 f.; P. Schütz, *Evangelium* (1940), 342 ff.

185 Cf. Lüken, *op. cit.*

186 Jeremias, *Ap. Glaubensbekenntnis,* 12 ff.

187 Cf. *Das Wunder d. Kirche unter den Völkern d. Erde,* ed. M. Schlunk (1939), esp. 74 ff.

μυκτηρίζω, ἐκμυκτηρίζω

† μυκτηρίζω.

μυκτηρίζω, derived from μυκτήρ, "nose," means "to suffer from nose bleeding" in Hippocr. Epid., 7, 123. Lys. in Poll. Onom., II, 78 equates it with μυσάττεσθαι ("to abhor") in the sense of "turn up one's nose," "treat contemptuously," cf. also Sext. Emp. Math., I, 217.

μυκτηρίζειν is more common in the LXX. It is used of Israel's mocking of its enemies, 4 Βασ. 19:21, of scorn for the intellectually slothful, Prv. 12:8, for heathen gods, 3 Βασ. 18:27. It becomes a sin when directed against God's messengers, 2 Ch. 36:16, or parents, Prv. 15:5, 20, or God's chastisements, Prv. 1:30.[1] The victim of this scorn suffers greatly from it, ψ 79:6; Jer. 20:7.

The only NT use is at Gl. 6:7. The apostle has given the admonition to walk in the Spirit, 5:25, and in contrast he portrays for the Galatians a walk in the flesh, i.e., an attitude of life which is disobedient to God and which will not place itself under the power of His Spirit. Both ways involve a stance in relation to the will of God. He who decides against this, says Paul, will learn in his whole being, both in time and also in the last judgment, that he has set himself against none other than God Himself. And God will not allow His will and grace to be treated with contempt through man's obeying and trusting his carnal and sinful nature and not God. Thus μυκτηρίζω is a term for despising God, His grace and His will, by an attitude to life which is sinful because it will not accept the lordship of the power of the Spirit. The reference is not to verbal scoffing but to the despising of God by a man's being, by his whole manner of life.[2]

Preisker

† ἐκμυκτηρίζω.

Like the simple form, ἐκμυκτηρίζω means "to turn up one's nose," hence "to despise," "to deride." The compound is hardly any stronger than the simple form. It owes its origin more to the love of Hellen. Gk. for compounds. It is attested only in biblical and post-biblical Gk. In the NT it occurs only in Lk. at 23:35 (quoting ψ 21:7) and at 16:14. In both instances it describes the conduct of the opponents of Jesus as they treat the bearer of revelation with scorn and contempt. The term is thus used in the context of suffering righteousness, as already in the OT, esp. the Gk. OT.

μυκτηρίζω. [1] It is thus wrong to say that the word is used in the LXX only for disdainful treatment of the defenceless, A. Oepke, *Der Brief d. Pls. an die Gl.* (1937), *ad loc.*

[2] Moult.-Mill., *s.v.* take μυκτηρίζειν in Gl. 6:7 in the sense "to let oneself be deceived." Pol. also seems to have construed it thus when one considers in what connection he quotes the verse in Phil., 4, 3; 5, 1: λέληθεν αὐτὸν οὐδὲν οὔτε λογισμῶν οὔτε ἐννοιῶν οὔτε τι τῶν κρυπτῶν τῆς καρδίας. εἰδότες οὖν ὅτι θεὸς οὐ μυκτηρίζεται [Bertram].

ἐκμυκτηρίζω. R. Helbing, *Die Kasussyntax der Verba bei den Septuaginta* (1928), 23.

A. ἐκμυκτηρίζω in the LXX.

While the compound alone is used in the NT in this sense, the simple form often has the same meaning in the OT. We also find the noun μυκτηρισμός. There is a comparatively large no. of underlying Heb. terms. Thus the group is used for the roots בוז, בזה, "to despise," התל pi, "to mock," which in the Mas. occurs only at 3 Βασ. 18:27, but also in Sir. 11:4 (καυχᾶσθαι); 13:7 (καταμωκᾶσθαι), for לעב hi, "to mock" (only 2 Ch. 36:16 = 1 Esr. 1:49), לעג, "to mock," and נאף, "to reject," cf. also כעס hi, "to insult," "irritate," Ez. 8:17 (Hatch-Redp. give אַף for it here, but the Gk. abbreviated the difficult sentence in acc. with its understanding, and found the decisive active word in כעס. Only the Hexapla LXX column tried to make אַף the original of μυκτηρίζω and to render כעס by παροργίζειν, which in the Gk. OT is the normal transl. of כעס. It was natural to link אַף, μυκτήρ, "nose," with μυκτηρίζειν; 'ΑΣΘ translated אַף lit. as μυκτήρ). In Prv. 2:15 Θ rendered לוז part. ni, the corrupt, the sinner, by μυκτηρίζειν act., and Σ once uses the verb for נגע, "to strike," part. ni (LXX μεμαστιγωμένος). This multiplicity of underlying words shows that the LXX here uses a stock term for various individual expressions. This stock term is used in three connections.

1. It is used to depict the ungodly in their personal attitude in which they are obstinately and arrogantly opposed to God Himself, to His messengers, to the pious and righteous, and to their doctrine and admonition. This may be seen in Prv. 1:30 in a saying which is quoted in 1 Cl., 57, 5 directed against those responsible for the disputes in Corinth. 1 Cl., 39, 1 uses the same line of thought: "Unwise, unreasonable, foolish and ignorant people are those who ridicule and despise us (χλευάζουσιν ἡμᾶς καὶ μυκτηρίζουσιν) because they are puffed up in their imaginations." [1] As wisdom and its censures are treated with scorn and contempt in Prv. 1:30, so are the representatives of wisdom, instruction and teaching. In Prv. 23:9 we read: "Speak not in the ears of a fool; for he will despise the wisdom of thy words." The same basic thought is present in 11:12: the fool despises his fellow-citizens; 15:5: he despises the instruction of his father; 15:20: he despises his mother. [2] That this is an essential mark of the fool, not a condemnation of his contempt as folly, may be seen in 2:15, where Θ uses the term for the concept of sinful perversion. The fool is a scoffer. Herein his true being is disclosed. Under this judgment fall not only enemies of the people of God like Nicanor in 1 Macc. 7:34, [3] but the people itself in its history leading to the overthrow of Jerusalem, namely, in its idolatry and apostasy (Ez. 8:17), in its contempt for the messengers of God (1 Esr. 1:49 = 2 Ch. 36:16).

2. If this scorn finally reveals the foolish arrogance of the ungodly, the ungodly, as a fool, will finally come under the scorn of the righteous and even of God. This is true of Sennacherib in Is. 37:22 = 4 Βασ. 19:21 and also of Antiochus Epiphanes IV, 2 Macc. 7:39, who is mocked by the martyred youth. It applies also to peoples and kings who resist God, ψ 2:4, [4] to fools who will not listen to wisdom and instruction, Prv. 1:26;

---

[1] Cf. R. Knopf, *Handbuch z. NT*, Suppl. Vol.

[2] Cf. 10:1: "But a foolish son is a grief to his mother." Perhaps the original Heb. had the noun בּוּזָה ("contempt") rather than the part. בּוֹזֶה in 15:20: "A fool of a man is a (cause of) contempt to his mother." This is in keeping with the view of collective family responsibility in ancient Israel. The ethical sense of "fool" in the sense of one who breaks the 5th commandment accords with the spiritual attitude of Hellen. Judaism. At this pt., then, the Mas. probably followed the LXX.

[3] "He (Nicanor) mocked and derided them (the priests), despised their ministry and spoke arrogantly."

[4] ὁ κύριος ἐκμυκτηριεῖ αὐτούς. Cf. Prv. 1:26: Wisdom makes mock of fools. 'ΑΣΘ have μυκτηρίζειν here, the LXX καταχαροῦμαι. In the par. ψ 58:8 LXX has ἐξουδενώσεις πάντα τὰ ἔθνη, and in 36:13 ὁ δὲ κύριος ἐκγελάσεται αὐτόν (the sinner).

12:8, to idolaters and their foolish trust in their gods, 3 Βασ. 18:27, and to the ungodly upon whom God's punishment falls, Job 22:19.[5] Finally, the prayer of the righteous in 2 Esr. 13:36 is to this effect: δὸς αὐτοὺς εἰς μυκτηρισμόν. The LXX itself introduces the stock term here. The Mas. has בִּזָּה, "prey," from בזז: "Give them for a prey," but the LXX substitutes a form of בזה.

3. The last passage shows, however, that it is now the specific historical situation of the righteous, of the people of God, to be exposed to the derision and contempt of their enemies, the ungodly. This is both punishment (→ *supra*) and grace. Thus we read in Ez. 23:32 (Θ and LXX Orig): τὸ ποτήριον τῆς ἀδελφῆς σου πίεσαι τὸ βαθὺ καὶ πλατύ (namely, the cup of Yahweh's anger which Samaria had already had to drink), *καὶ ἔσται εἰς γέλωτα καὶ εἰς μυκτηρισμόν, ⱶ καὶ τὸ πλεονάζον τοῦ συντελέσαι μέθην. In Job 34:7, too, there is a lit. rendering of the Mas. only in Θ and LXX Orig: *τὶς ἀνὴρ ὥσπερ Ιωβ πίνων μυκτηρισμὸν ὥσπερ ὕδωρ ⱶ· Nevertheless, the Mas. is the original. We find here the same image as that of Ez., namely, the cup of derision. The original meaning is that Job drinks blasphemy like water, and is thus full of it. Because this seems to be impossible in view of 42:8, the original LXX leaves out the verse and states the opposite in 34:8: οὐχ ἁμαρτὼν οὐδὲ ἀσεβήσας. Θ and LXX Orig give a lit. transl., but they probably read in a different sense: Job must drink his self-contempt like water. He is in a similar position to that of the prophet Jer. in 20:7: Ἠπάτησάς με, κύριε, καὶ ἠπατήθην, ἐκράτησας καὶ ἠδυνάσθης· ἐγενόμην εἰς γέλωτα, πᾶσαν ἡμέραν διετέλεσα μυκτηριζόμενος (Σ: πᾶς τις καταφλυαρεῖ μου. Ἀ: πᾶς ἐμπαίζει μοι). As the bearer of revelation a Job or Jeremiah is a target for the scoffing and contempt of the ungodly world around. Jewish Christian legend worked this out particularly plainly in the case of Noah, the type of the messenger of God, κῆρυξ τῆς δικαιοσύνης, 2 Pt. 2:5. It is said of him in Apc. Pauli, p. 68 (ed. Tischendorf): καὶ οὐδεὶς συνῆκεν, ἀλλὰ πάντες ἐξεμυκτήριζόν με. Orac. Sibyl., 1, 17 refers to the same scene of Noah's preaching of repentance to the godless generation before the flood: οἳ δέ μιν εἰσαΐοντες ἐμυκτήριζον ἕκαστος. This scoffing falls on all the righteous, 2 Esr. 13:36 (Neh. 4:4); ψ 34:16, where the thought is clear in the LXX as compared with the difficult Mas.; ψ 43:13; 72:14 Σ; 78:4; 79:6; and esp. 21:7.

B. ἐκμυκτηρίζω in the NT.

In the NT Lk. 23:35 quotes ψ 21:6 f. in the story of the passion. The LXX is used: ἐγὼ δέ εἰμι σκώληξ καὶ οὐκ ἄνθρωπος, ὄνειδος ἀνθρώπου καὶ ἐξουδένημα λαοῦ. πάντες οἱ θεωροῦντές με ἐξεμυκτήρισάν με, ἐλάλησαν ἐν χείλεσιν, ἐκίνησαν κεφαλήν. Just., who lists the verse in his OT proofs from prophecy in Dial., 98, 3 and 101, 3, paraphrases the ἐκμυκτηρίζειν in the second instance as follows: τοῖς μυξωτῆρσιν ἐν ἀλλήλοις διαρρινοῦντες ἔλεγον εἰρωνευόμενοι (there then follow the words of Lk. 23:35b). The OT prophecy is thus historicised. The words of the psalm are no longer a typical characterisation of the enemies of the righteous; they apply directly to the given situation. The θεωρεῖν refers to the people, the ἐκμυκτηρίζειν to the ἄρχοντες, who scornfully and ironically remind the one who is crucified of His own claim to power. Another LXX term: ἐμπαίζειν,[6] is used in Mt. 27:41 and Mk. 15:31, and in Lk. this occurs immediately after in v. 36: ἐνέπαιζον δὲ αὐτῷ καὶ οἱ στρατιῶται. It is used with ἐκμυκτηρίζειν in the LXX at 1 Esr. 1:49 = 2 Ch. 36:16.[7] In the NT it occurs constantly in

[5] He who violates good manners is exposed to derision in Cant. 8:1.

[6] Cf. ἐμπαίζειν → παίζειν.

[7] As compared with the par. in 2 Ch. and 2 Esr. the text of 1 Esr. is to be regarded as the more original transl., cf. S. S. Tedesche *A Critical Edition of 1 Esdras* (1928), *ad loc.*; Swete and Rahlfs, *ad loc.*: ἐκπαίζοντες.

prophecies of the passion and the various scoffing incidents in the passion narrative.[8] As compared with it, ἐκμυκτηρίζειν in the present verse denotes not so much the outward action but rather the inward attitude of the mockers and the emptiness of this apparent triumph of human wickedness over Christ.

The other instance in Lk. 16:14 is to be taken more schematically. The verb occurs here in a transitional marginal note[9] of the Evangelist attached to the parable of the unjust steward and the saying about serving two masters. Hence it is not easy to find the reason for the derision in the context. It can hardly be the Pharisees' love of money,[10] whether in the sense of laughing at the poor Jesus teaching His poor disciples about wealth, or in the sense that they do not, like Jesus, regard riches and piety as incompatible[11] (which is not really true of Jesus either). The real point emerges in the saying of Jesus in v. 15, which shows us that according to the Evangelist's intention the Pharisees are expressing an inward attitude of conceited superiority. In the context, then, ἐκμυκτηρίζειν is connected with a claim which can perhaps stand before men but whose inner emptiness as human *hubris* is manifest before God and is an abomination to Him. In the NT, then, the verb denotes an *a priori* rejection of the bearer of revelation on the basis of man's foolish sense of superiority. It is a sign of obduracy.

Neither here nor at the cross do we have intrinsically a psychological depiction of the opponents of Jesus. The point is rather that, as the bearer of revelation, He necessarily meets with derision in the same way as the righteous of the OT. The mockery of Jesus is an integral part of His Messianic suffering.

Bertram

---

[8] G. Bertram, *Die Leidensgeschichte Jesu u. d. Christuskult* (1922), 85.
[9] Bultmann Trad., 360.
[10] B. Weiss (1892), *ad loc.*
[11] Kl. Lk., *ad loc.*

† μύρον, † μυρίζω

The use of "ointment," not animal fat but vegetable oil to which sweet-smelling materials were added, is very ancient (as early as the 3rd millennium B.C. for Egypt). The custom of anointing the body, though often a luxury later, must have been regarded as a necessity by the people of the South. Ointments were also used in medicine, embalming, the cultus, magic etc. [1] In Gk. μύρον is the common word, along with rarer terms like ἄλειμμα, → χρῖσμα. [2] In the OT, too, we find mention of the use of ointments, both secular (esp. in Cant.; Am. 6:6; Prv. 27:9; Wis. 2:7) and cultic (e.g., Ex. 30:25). [3] In Philo Sacr. AC, 21, in the depiction of the female figure Ἡδονή decked out like a harlot: μύρων εὐωδεστάτων ἀποπνέουσα. Joseph. has μύρον at cultic functions, Ant., 3, 205, in feminine adornment, Bell., 4, 561, and in festal decoration (with crowning), Ant., 19, 358; Ap., 2, 256; cf. also Ant., 14, 54.

μύρον κτλ. [1] Cf. Hug, Art. "Salben" in Pauly-W., I, A (1920), 1851-1866; A. Schmidt, Art. "Drogen" in Pauly-W., Suppl. V (1931), 172-182, and esp. A. Schmidt, *Drogen u. Drogenhandel im Altertum*² (1927).

[2] Cf. Liddell-Scott, *s.v.*; Ditt. Or., 629, 35, 45, 149; Preisigke Wört., II, 122 f.; Moult.-Mill., 419; T. Reil, *Beiträge z. Kenntnis des Gewerbes im hell. Ägypten,* Diss. Leipzig (1913), 144 f., 149. On the etym. Athen., XV, p. 688c: μύρρα γὰρ ἡ σμύρνα παρ' Αἰολεῦσιν, ἐπειδὴ τὰ πολλὰ τῶν μύρων διὰ σμύρνης ἐσκευάζετο, already associates μύρον with σμύρνα, and the resultant confusion has left its mark even to-day (cf. the obscurities in Hug, Pass., *s.v.*, Mayser, I, 40 f., also H. Lewy, *Die semitischen Fremdwörter im Gr.* [1895], 42 f.; cf. also → n. 9, 15). Yet it would seem that originally we are to assume 2 different groups: 1. μυρ- "to anoint," in μύρον ("ointment") from the time of Archiloch.; also σμυρ- in σμυρίζω ("to anoint") (Archiloch.) = μυρίζω (from Hdt., Aristoph.), related to the Indo-European root *smer,* "to smear," and 2. σμύρνη, also σμύρνα and μύρρα, "myrrh," a loan word from the Semitic (whereas μύρον is a Gk. word); → σμύρνα; the initial letter was probably by analogy with the Gk. word for "ointment," with the initial σμ- and μ-. Cf. Walde-Pok., II, 690; Boisacq, 652, 886 [Debrunner]. R. Steier, Art. "Myrrha," 2, Pauly-W., XVI, 1 (1933), 1134-1146, also supports separation into two groups. There must be clear distinction from μύρτος, "myrtle." By interrelating myrrh and myrtle Pass. and Preisigke Wört. (II, 122: μύρον, "myrtle balsam," I, 647: ζμύρνα, "myrrh balsam," II, 473: μύρον, "myrtle balsam") unfortunately increase the confusion.

[3] Cf. Hug, 1852; K. Galling, Art. "Salbe," *Bibl. Reallexikon* (1937), 435-7; Str.-B., I, 426 ff., 986 ff.; I. Löw, *Die Flora d. Juden,* I, 1 (1926), 311. The LXX strictly differentiates μύρον and σμύρνα (→ n. 2). For מוֹר, מֹר it always has σμύρνα, and μύρον mostly for שֶׁמֶן, also rendered ἔλαιον. In the historical books μύρον occurs only 7 times for שֶׁמֶן. But it is used 9 other times for other words or with no definite original. It is not found in the Hellen. books. ἔλαιον is not found in some and is rare in others. Σ in Eccl. 7:1 and 'A in 10:1 have μύρον for שֶׁמֶן. LXX ἔλαιον. The LXX changes the Mas. at Is. 25:6, for, while the Mas. refers only to eating and drinking, the LXX puts μύρον for fatty foods (root שֶׁמֶן). χρίσονται μύρον is a sign of joy at the eschatological banquet. In the prophecy of disaster in Jer. 25:10 the LXX similarly has ὀσμὴ μύρου for the noise of the handmill, which is hardly festive. We thus have an arbitrary alteration on material grounds. The LXX did not have a different text (Kittel BHK² רֵיחַ מֹר), nor is there corruption in the Gk. (Rudolph in Kittel BHK³ from φωνὴ μύλου). The Hellenists used anointing oil at feasts and weddings. [Bertram.]

The main use of μύρον in the NT is in the stories of anointing. In the anointing at Bethany we find it in Mt. 26:7 par. Mk. 14:3 par. Jn. 12:3; Mk. 14:4 f. par. Jn. 12:5; Mt. 26:12 cf. Mk. 14:8 (the only use of the verb μυρίζω[4] in the NT); cf. also Jn. 11:2. The costly ointment used is called spikenard in Mk. 14:3 par. Jn. 12:3.[5] The head of Jesus is anointed in Mt. and Mk.,[6] while Mary anoints the feet of the Lord in Jn.[7] μύρον also occurs in the anointing story in Lk. 7:36 ff. (cf. 37, 38, 46), and here again the feet are anointed. This is regarded as a mark of particular attention,[8] as is also the use of μύρον rather than → ἔλαιον, II, 470 f.[9] In Mt. 26:7; Mk. 14:3; Lk. 7:37 it is emphasised that the ointment was contained in an alabaster box, as was customary in antiquity and also in Palestine.[10] When it is noted in Mk. 14:3 that the woman broke it (συντρίψασα), this is not to show that she intended to use all the contents,[11] but more likely indicates that she followed the custom of opening the container by breaking off the neck.[12]

In Mt. 26:12 par. Mk. 14:8 par. Jn. 12:7 Jesus explains that the anointing is an anticipation of the anointing of His body for burial.[13] In Lk. 23:56 the women prepared ἀρώματα καὶ μύρα for subsequent anointing of the body of Jesus, which was already buried, unless the point is that they wished to fill the sepulchre with the odour of sweet spices.[14]

In Rev. 18:13, in the list of the merchandise of the great merchant fleet, μύρον (ointment) is mentioned after odours and before frankincense, wine and oil (ἔλαιον).[15]

Michaelis

---

4 → n. 2. μυρίζω does not occur in the LXX, though cf. Jos. Ant., 19, 358.

5 On νάρδος cf. Pr.-Bauer³, *s.v.*, Zn. J.⁵,⁶, 501, n. 9, Wbg. Mk., 342, n. 59.

6 Cf. Hug, 1856; ψ 22:5; Schl. Mt. on 26:8 → I, 230.

7 Hug, 1856 describes this as rather extraordinary in antiquity, but cf. Str.-B., I, 427 f.

8 On the relation of Lk. 7:36 ff. to the anointing in Bethany cf. the comm.

9 Oil is a native product, ointments are imported or are made with imported materials. It is best (→ n. 2) not to equate μύρον and myrrh salve (so H. Schlier → II, 472; also Str.-B., II, 48 f. and Hck. Lk., 101 f.).

10 Cf. Hug, 1861; A. Mau, Art. "Alabastron," 2, Pauly-W., I (1894), 1272 f.; Galling, *op. cit.*, also Art. "Alabaster," *Bibl. Reallex.*, 7-13 (with illustr.).

11 So Kl. Lk.; Schl. Mk., *ad loc.*

12 Cf. Hck. Mk., *ad loc.* If the breaking was natural, Mt. and Jn. (Lk.) do not need to mention it. This was certainly the usual way of opening flasks of oil with a long neck (Galling, 13). Mk. 14:3; Mt. 26:7 (cf. κατέχεεν) clearly refer to fluid oil; μύρον can mean anointing oil as well as ointment, cf. Hug, 1852.

13 An ancient custom (Hug, 1857) also attested of the Jews, Hck. Mk. on 14:8 (cf. Shab., 23, 5). Ign. Eph., 17, 1 (the only instance of μύρον in the post-apost. fathers) suggests that the Lord allowed His hair to be anointed to waft the scent of incorruptibility to the Church. Cf. → I, 232. On the prayer over the μύρον in the Coptic fr. on Did., 10 ff. (cf. Const. Ap., VII, 27) cf. the bibl. → I, 231, n. 8.

14 Cf. Hck. Lk. on 24:1; Schmidt, *Drogen u. Drogenhandel* (→ n. 1), 46.

15 The weakly attested vl. σμύρναν (cf. Tisch. NT) is no reason for transl. "myrrh and frankincense" (Bss. Apk., 422; Had. Apk., 180, though not *Erklärung*, 181; Loh. Apk. etc.). Under the influence of the confusion mentioned in n. 2 there is in the vl. a reminiscence of Mt. 2:11: "Frankincense and myrrh." Cf. A. Deissmann, "Weihrauch u. Myrrhe," ThBl, 1 (1922), 13.

μυστήριον, μυέω

† μυστήριον.

Contents: Etymology. A. The Mysteries in the Greek World and Hellenism: 1. The Cultic Concept of Mysteries; 2. The Mysteries in Philosophy; 3. The Mysteries in Magic; 4. The Mysteries in Secular Usage; 5. The Mysteries in Gnosticism. B. μυστήριον in the LXX, Apocalyptic and Rabbinic Judaism. C. μυστήριον in the New Testament: 1. The Mystery of the Divine Lordship, Mk. 4:11 f. and Par.; 2. The Mystery of Christ; 3. The General Use of μυστήριον in Paul and the Rest of the NT. D. μυστήριον in the Early Church: 1. The Post-Apostolic Fathers; 2. Apologetic; 3. Alexandrian Theology; 4. μυστήρια as a Term for the Sacraments; 5. μυστήριον and *sacramentum*.

μυστήριον. There is no comprehensive monograph on μυστήριον. On the whole field cf. G. Anrich, *Das antike Mysterienwesen in seinem Einfluss auf d. Christentum* (1894); C. Clemen, "Der Einfluss der Mysterienreligionen auf das älteste Christentum" = RVV, 13, 1 (1913); A. Loisy, *Les mystères paiens et le mystère chrétien*² (1930); B. Heigl, *Antike Mysterienreligionen u. Urchristentum* (1932); K. Prümm, *Der chr. Glaube u. d. altheidn. Welt* (1935). On A. 1: C. A. Lobeck, *Aglaophamus* (1829); A. Tresp, "Die Fragmente d. griech. Kultschriftsteller," RVV, 15, 1 (1914); N. Turchi, *Fontes historiae mysteriorum aevi hellenistici* (1923); O. Casel, "De Philosophorum Graecorum silentio mystico," RVV, 16, 2 (1919); P. Foucart, *Les mystères d'Eleusis* (1914); R. Pettazzoni, *Misteri* (1924); O. Kern, *D. gr. Mysterien d. klass. Zeit* (1927); *D. Religion d. Griechen*, I (1926), II (1935), III (1938); Pauly-W., 16, 2 (1935), 1209 ff. (with bibl.); U. v. Wilamowitz-Moellendorff, *Der Glaube d. Hellenen* (1931); T. Hopfner, "Die orientalisch-hellenistischen Mysterien," Pauly-W., 16, 2 (1935), 1315 ff. (with bibl.); Mithr. Liturg.; R. Reitzenstein Hell. Myst.; Ir. Erl.; M. Dibelius, *Die Isisweihe bei Apulejus u. verwandte Initiationsriten* (*Sitzungsber. d. Heidelberg Akad., phil.-hist. Kl., Abh.*, 4 [1917]). On A. 2: J. Pascher, "Η ΒΑΣΙΛΙΚΗ ΟΔΟΣ, Der Königsweg zu Wiedergeburt u. Vergottung bei Philon v. Alex.," *Studien z. Gesch. u. Kultur d. Altertums*, 17, 3 and 4 (1931); W. Völker, "Fortschritt u. Vollendung bei Philo v. Alex.," TU, 49, 1 (1938). On A. 3: T. Hopfner, "Griech.-ägypt. Offenbarungszauber," *Stud. z. Paläograph. u. Papyruskunde*, 21 and 23 (1922/24). On A. 5: R. Liechtenhan, *D. Offenbarung im Gnostizismus* (1901); W. Bousset, *Hauptprobleme d. Gnosis* (1907); L. Fendt, *Gnostische Mysterien* (1922). On B: R. Kittel, "Die hell. Mysterienreligion u. d. AT," BWANT, 32 (1924). On C and D: H. v. Soden, "μυστήριον u. *sacramentum* in d. ersten zwei Jhdten. d. Kirche," ZNW, 12 (1911), 188 ff.; J. Schneider, "Mysterion im NT," ThStKr (1932), 255 ff.; F. Prat, *La théologie de St. Paul* (1913), 393 ff.; D. Deden, "Le 'mystère' Paulinien," *Ephem. Theol. Lovan*, 13 (1936), 405 f.; A. Robinson, *Ephesians* (1904), 234 ff.; H. Windisch, "Paulus u. Christus," UNT, 24 (1934), 215 ff.; K. Prümm, " 'Mysterion' von Paulus bis Origenes," *Zschr. f. kath. Theol.*, 61 (1937), 391 ff.; " 'Mysterion' u. Verwandtes bei Hippolyt.," *ibid.*, 63 (1939), 207 ff.; " 'Mysterion' u. Verwandtes bei Athanasius," *ibid.*, 350 ff. There are many studies on the link between the ancient mysteries and Christian worship (in the sense of a theological analogy) by O. Casel in the *Jbch. f. Liturgiewissenschaft*, cf. "Das Mysteriengedächtnis der Messliturgie im Lichte d. Tradition," 6 (1926), 113 ff.; "Mysteriengegenwart," 8 (1928), 145 ff.; cf. also in *Mysterium = Ges. Arbeiten Laacher Mönche* (1926), 9 ff., 29 ff.; *Die Liturgie als Mysterienfeier = Ecclesia orans*, IX (1923); *Das christliche Kult-Mysterium* (1932); "Zum Worte *sacramentum*," *Jbch. f. Liturgiewiss.*, 8 (1928), 225 ff.; "Das Wort *sacramentum*," *Theol. Rev.*, 24 (1925), 41 ff.; J. d. Ghellinek, E. de Baecker, J. Poukens, G. Lebacqz, *Pour l'histoire du mot* sacramentum (1924); Marsh, "The Use of ΜΥΣΤΗΡΙΟΝ in the Writings of Cl. Al. with Special Ref. to His Sacramental Doctrine," JThSt, 37 (1936), 64 ff.; H. v. Balthasar, "Le Mysterion d'Origène," *Recherches de science religieuse*, 26 (1936), 513 ff.; 27 (1937), 38 ff. In criticism of the work of Casel cf. esp. K. Soehngen, *Der Wesensaufbau des Mysteriums* (1938).

The etym. of the word is itself a mystery. Probable, though not certain, is derivation from μύειν "to close" (the mouth, lips), not to be confused with μυεῖν "to dedicate," Schol. Aristoph. Ra., 456: μυστήρια δὲ ἐκλήθη παρὰ τὸ τοὺς ἀκούοντας μύειν τὸ στόμα καὶ μηδενὶ ταῦτα ἐξηγεῖσθαι. μύειν δέ ἐστι τὸ κλείειν τὸ στόμα.[1] Other traditional derivations only demonstrate the uncertainty and are valueless, e.g., derivation from the evil done to Dionysus (μύσος), from a Μυοῦς τις 'Αττικός, appeal to the punning and late μυθήρια (all in Cl. Al. Prot., II, 13, 1 f.), or the pun which links it with "mouse-hole" (Athen., III, 98d: ὅτι τοὺς μῦς τηρεῖ), a bit of etym. nonsense which rests on the linking of homonymous words and which Aristot. explains already by a similar example (Rhet., II, 24, p. 1401a, 12 ff.). The suffix (-τήριον) is no help; it is common in terms which fix the place of an action (πωλητήριον, ὁρμητήριον, παιδευτήριον, δεσμωτήριον, φροντιστήριον etc.) or denote a means to an end (φυλακτήριον, διδακτήριον etc.), and it may be noted that in both cases there are many cultic examples (τελεστήριον, σφαγιστήριον, θυσιαστήριον, ἱλαστήριον, χαριστήριον, χρηστήριον).[2] Thus the etym. leads only to the fairly certain general conclusion that a μυστήριον is something on which silence must be kept. For the rest we are wholly dependent on usage, which quickly established the word as a precise term, especially in the religious field.

A. The Mysteries in the Greek World and Hellenism.

1. The Cultic Concept of Mysteries.

μυστήριον (predominantly plur.) is the term for the many ancient mystery cults whose intensive development can be studied from the 7th cent. B.C. to the 4th A.D.

In line with the command of silence typically imposed by them — a command strictly enjoined and in the main carefully observed — our knowledge of the mysteries is so fragmentary that we can only approximately delineate the main features. There can be no doubt that even at an early date the term was not restricted to Eleusis, the site of the most important mysteries.[3] It is thus a mistake to try to find a specific place where the concept originated. For all the multiplicity of cults, we can descry certain common features which are constitutive of the μυστήρια.

a. Mysteries are cultic rites[4] in which the destinies of a god are portrayed by sacred actions before a circle of devotees in such a way as to give them a part in the fate of the god.

The verbs used in this connection correspond to the cultic meaning: ὁ ἱερεὺς τῶν

---

[1] Walde-Pok., II, 310; but cf. W. Schulze, *Quaestiones epicae* (1892), 334, 3 (deriv. from the Sanskrit root *mush,* "to steal"); cf. also L. Malten, ARW, 12 (1909), 302, n. 4; U. v. Wilamowitz-Moellendorff, II, 45, n. 4; Kern, Pauly-W., 16, 2 (1935), 1209 f. The oldest instance of μυστήρια is Heracl. Fr., 14, I, 154, Diels[5] (also μύστης and μυεῖν); of μυστικός, Aesch. Fr., 387, Nauck; Hdt., 8, 65.

[2] Wilamowitz-Moellendorff illustrates the many meanings of the suffix by χρηστήριον, → n. 1. The nouns in -τηριον may be found in H. Hoogeveen, *Dictionarium analogicum linguae Graecae* (1810), 142 f. It cannot be shown that μυστήριον originally denoted the site of a sacred action. Equally unsuccessful is the attempt, on the analogy of other -ηριον words, to connect a noun in ηρ to a derived adj. in ηριος; neither is to be found. Cf. also P. Chantraine, *La formation des noms en grec ancien* (1933), 63 f.

[3] Hdt., 2, 51 refers to the Samothracian mysteries, 2, 171 to the Egyptian Osiris mysteries, Heracl. Fr., 14, I, 154, Diels[5] probably to the Dionysus mysteries.

[4] Ditt. Syll.[3], 83, 25; 717, 10; 820, 12.

θεῶν οἷς τὰ μυστήρια γίνεται,[5] τελεῖν (?),[6] more often ἐπιτελεῖν,[7] ἱεροποιεῖν,[8] λειτουργεῖν,[9] ποιεῖν, Andoc.., I, 11; Lys., 14, 42; Thuc., 6, 28; cf. also the related terms τέλη, Soph. Oed. Col., 1050; Eur. Med., 1382; Plat. Resp., VIII, 560e: τελετή (or τελεταί);[10] Hdt., 2, 171; Isoc., 4, 28; Paus., 10, 31, 11; τελετή and μυστήρια together: τά τε ἀπόρρητα τῆς κατὰ τὰ μυστήρια τελετῆς.[11] The oldest and most important source of the Eleusinian mysteries, the Hom. hymn to Demeter, has ὄργια instead of μυστήρια, Hom. Hymn. Cer., 273, 476;[12] cf. also Aristoph. Thes., 948; Hdt., 2, 51; 5, 61; Eur. Ba., 78 f. etc.

b. Integral to the concept of the mysteries is the fact that those who wish to take part in their celebration must undergo initiation; the uninitiated are denied both access to the sacred actions and knowledge of them.

The ceremony which makes the candidate a devotee of the deity embraces many different offerings and purifications. It is so firm a part of the whole mystery ritual that it is often hard to fix any precise distinction between the initiatory actions and the true mystery celebrations.

The linguistic usage shows this inasmuch as the word μυστήρια covers the whole celebration, including those parts of the cultus which have only initiatory significance. Thus in the Eleusinian cult, whose devotees experience the Eleusinian night of consecration only after long preparation,[13] the first cultic celebrations in Agrai are also called mysteries (the little mysteries).[14] To the same effect is the use of the same word in the two distinct expressions μυστήρια παραλαμβάνειν (to which there corresponds a μυστήρια παραδιδόναι)[15] and μυστήρια ἐπιτελεῖν. The first of these relates to the initial dedication which makes the adept a μυηθείς or μύστης, while the second is the fulfilment of the whole consecration whereby one becomes an ἐπόπτης.[16]

Receiving the mysteries is thus linked to certain conditions which are more or less difficult to attain in the individual mysteries.[17] By entrance qualification and dedication the candidate is separated from the host of the uninitiated and enters into the fellowship of initiates who know each other by confessional formulae or symbolical signs.[18] This society-forming element is of the very nature of the mysteries.

---

5 *Ibid.*, 736, 29.

6 *Ibid.*, 885, 5 (τελοῦντας supplied).

7 *Ibid.*, 735, 27; 820, 3 f., 14; Ditt. Or., 331, 54 f.

8 Ditt. Syll.³, 944 B, 39.

9 *Ibid.*, 736, 74.

10 τελετή does not contain the secret element like μυστήριον; hence it quickly comes to be used for acts of worship which have nothing to do with consecration, Kern, *Relig.*, II, 187 f. This difference in nuance explains why the two are often combined.

11 Ditt. Syll.³, 873, 9 f.

12 Cf. here the instructive par. δρησμοσύνη ἱερῶν.

13 Kern, II, 196 ff.

14 Cf. Schol. Aristoph. Pl., 1013 etc.; on the little mysteries of Agrai cf. A. Mommsen, *Feste d. Stadt Athen* (1898), 405 ff.; L. Deubner, *Attische Feste* (1932), 70.

15 On παραλαμβάνειν and παραδιδόναι as tt. in the mysteries cf. Lobeck, 39; Anrich, 54; Mithr. Liturg., 53 f. → II, 171, n. 18 and 19.

16 On these stages cf. Dibelius, 33 ff. μύησις is usually the introductory rite, though it can denote the whole. The same is true of the παράδοσις of the mysteries and the use of μυεῖσθαι; on the latter cf. Class. Rev., 14 (1900), 427a.

17 In Eleusis barbarians and murderers alone are at first excluded; the exclusion (πρόρρησις) is solemnly made at the beginning, Isoc., 4, 157. The lack of moral prerequisites to be met by candidates is derided by Diogenes in Plut. Aud. Poet., 4 (II, 21 f.): κρείττονα μοῖραν ἕξει Παταικίων ὁ κλέπτης ἀποθανὼν ἢ Ἐπαμεινώνδας ὅτι μεμύηται; cf. Philo Spec. Leg., I, 323. In other mysteries there are stricter moral and religious demands, Orig. Cels., III, 59; cf. F. J. Dölger, *Antike u. Christentum*, 3 (1932), 132 f.; Luc. Alex., 38 tells of the exclusion of atheists, Christians and Epicureans.

18 Dibelius, 14.

c. All mysteries promise their devotees salvation (σωτηρία) by the dispensing of cosmic life.

Their deities are chthonic gods[19] (Demeter and Kore, Dionysus, the great gods of Samothrace, Cybele and Attis, Adonis, Isis and Osiris).[20] Their myths and feasts are closely connected with the change of seasons, also with human life and death. Life and death are not just in their sphere of power, but are their own destiny. In the first instance in a general sense, these are suffering gods. Their πάθη, which are enacted in the cultic drama,[21] embrace sorrow and joy, seeking and finding, conception and birth, death and life, end and beginning.

These πάθη are not present equally in all the mysteries, but it is true of all mystery gods that in their mythical-personal destiny the living forces of periodically perishing and returning nature hold sway. The gods are involved in change. But they do not succumb to it. In their own destiny, which unites natural occurrence and human experience, they dispose of the powers of life which are not available to man, but which are necessary for protection here and eternal bliss hereafter.[22]

The holy mystery of the rites is this sanctifying union between the suffering deity and the devotees, who in the mysteries acquire a share in the destiny of the god and hence in the divine power of life.

The details of the cult are prefigured already in the cultic saga.[23] The deity plays first the role of the initiate. Then in the cultic drama hierophants, priests and devotees play the role of the deity. The παθεῖν of devotees is the true experience which corresponds to the πάθη of the deity.[24] The devotees weep and rejoice, seek and find, die and live with their gods.[25] The union with the gods is effected supremely by the sacramental actions[26] with divine symbols which differ in the individual mysteries. Thus we find sacred meals and weddings, fertility and birth rites, baptisms, investitures with sacred garments, rites of death and resurrection, or cultically symbolised journeys to Hades and heaven.

The traditions which speak of the decisive sacramental rites are so fragmentary and allusive than in many cases we can hardly make conjectures, let alone definite statements. But it may be seen more or less clearly in all the mysteries that they lead initiates to the border of death and cause them to undergo a change which has taken place typically in the destiny of the god, which is enacted in the rite, and which assures them of a life of salvation hereafter. Cultic participation in the birth of a divine child, the experience of one's own regeneration, the climax of vision of the living symbol of deity,

---

19 Mithr. Liturg., 145; Kern, I, 136 ff.

20 Mithras may be added as a cosmic deity.

21 Hdt., 2, 171: ἐν δὲ τῇ λίμνῃ ταύτῃ τὰ δείκηλα τῶν παθέων αὐτοῦ (Osiris) νυκτὸς ποιεῦσιν, τὰ καλέουσι μυστήρια Αἰγύπτιοι, Athenag., 32, 1: τὰ πάθη αὐτῶν (sc. θεῶν) δεικνύουσιν μυστήρια, Cl. Al. Protr., 2, 12, 2 (I, 11, 20 ff.): Δηὼ δὲ καὶ Κόρη δρᾶμα ἤδη ἐγενέσθην μυστικόν, καὶ τὴν πλάνην καὶ τὴν ἁρπαγὴν καὶ τὸ πένθος αὐταῖν Ἐλευσὶς δᾳδουχεῖ, Apul. Met., 11, 9 ff.; Luc. Salt., 37 ff.; Ps.-Luc. Syr. Dea, 6; Plut. Is. et Os., 27 (II, 361d f.).

22 Cf. G. v. d. Leeuw, *Phänomenologie d. Religion* (1933), 459 f.

23 H. Diels, *Sibyll. Blätter* (1890), 122 ff.; Kern, Pauly-W., 16 (1935), 1221.

24 Synesius de Dione, 10 (MPG, 66, 1133 f.): Ἀριστοτέλης ἀξιοῖ τοὺς τετελεσμένους οὐ μαθεῖν τι δεῖν, ἀλλὰ παθεῖν καὶ διατεθῆναι δηλονότι γινομένους ἐπιτηδείους. Cf. W. Jaeger, *Aristoteles* (1923), 164.

25 The formulae preserved (cf. Mithr. Liturg., 213 ff.) are mostly in the 1st or 2nd person. They are thus cultic promises, prayers or confessions which indicate the share of the devotee in the fate of the deity. Cf., e.g., the Attis (?) formulae: θαρρεῖτε μύσται τοῦ θεοῦ σεσωσμένου· ἔσται γὰρ ὑμῖν ἐκ πόνων σωτηρία, Firm. Mat. Err. Prof. Rel., 22, 1. ἐκ τυμπάνου βέβρωκα, ἐκ κυμβάλου πέπωκα, γέγονα μύστης Ἄττεως, 18, 1; also the Isis formula εὑρήκαμεν συγχαίρομεν, 2, 9.

26 But also with direct Bacchic ἐνθουσιασμός.

as at Eleusis,[27] all carry with them the same promise as the cultic dying with Osiris and Attis, which is followed by the deliverance of the god and the assurance of σωτηρία for the devotee, or the journey of the Isis initiate to the *dii inferi* and *superi*, in which the initiate summoned by the goddess accepts a voluntary death, is deified, and finds gracious salvation both in this world and the next (*precaria salus*, Apul. Met., XI, 21). The lively alternation of sorrow and jubilation, anxiety and hope, noise and silence, darkness and light, which is fostered by many psychological and technical means,[28] points to the fact that in the cultus the initiate is prepared for the life to come. He receives a share in the destiny of the god, becomes his, is made like him, and can now enter without terrible harm the sphere of divine rule under the earth, just as he can approach the earthly sanctuary of the gods. The mysteries are thus rituals of both death and life, and it makes little difference whether the predominant symbolism is that of life or death.

The connection between mystery celebrations and future hope may be seen in the following examples from Eleusis, Pind. Fr., 137 (ed. O. Schroeder): "Blessed is he who sees this and then goes under the earth. He knows the end of life, but he also knows the beginning given by God." Soph. Fr., 753, ed. Nauck: "Thrice blessed are those who after seeing these rites descend into Hades. To them alone is life given below; all others experience only evil there." The difference between initiates and the uninitiated may be seen in the final benediction of the hymn to Demeter, Hom. Hymn. Cer., 480 ff.[29] That the devotees of Dionysus hope in Hades to remain in the blessed following of their frenzied god may be seen from the depictions and symbols on their monuments.[30] For the Attis mysteries the most important example is in Firm. Mat. Err. Prof. Rel., 22, 1: θαρρεῖτε μύσται.[31] σωτηρία means salvation after death. It can even be represented as liberation from death.[32] In any case there is given the deified devotee the ability to go through Hades without being destroyed.[33] Cf. the corresponding rites in the Isis mystery[34] and the so-called Mithr. Lit.[35] It could be that the forms of the Attis and Isis mysteries which have come down to us serve as credentials for the devotee when he enters the realm of the dead, as is proved beyond doubt by the burial inscriptions of devotees of Dionysus.[36]

d. In all the mysteries the distinction between initiates and non-initiates finds expression not only in the ritual of the celebrations but also in the vow of silence laid on devotees. This is essential to all the mysteries, and is a feature implicit in the etymology.

---

[27] Hipp. Ref., V, 8, 39 ff.; cf. Kern, *Rel.*, II, 194 f.

[28] Aristoph. Ra., 341 ff.; cf. Anrich, 32 ff.

[29] Cf. Lobeck, 69 ff.; Kern, II, 194 ff.; Wilamowitz, II, 56 ff.; cf. also Casel, *De Philosoph. Graec. sil. myst.*, 12.

[30] Wilamowitz, II, 377 ff.; Kern, III, 201 ff.

[31] → n. 25. The ref. to Attis is contested. The traditional view is not accepted by R. P. Lagrange, *Rev. Bibl.*, NS, 16, 448 ff. or F. Cumont, *D. orient. Rel.*³, 228, n. 46, who refer the formula to Osiris; Wilamowitz suggests Dionysus, II, 381. In the present context the possibility of many refs. is more important than a correct decision.

[32] Cf. J. Kroll, "Gott u. Hölle," *Stud. d. Bibl. Warburg*, 20 (1932), 498.

[33] It is worth noting that one can nowhere see clearly the favourite motif of the overcoming of the realm of the dead by the deity and associated devotees. This must have played a not inconsiderable role in the mysteries; only the defectiveness of the sources prevents us from seeing it. Cf. J. Kroll, 505.

[34] Cf. Dibelius, 21 ff.

[35] Mithr. Liturg., 179 ff.; Hopfner, Pauly-W., 16, 2 (1935), 1346 ff.; J. Kroll, 506; cf. esp. Preis. Zaub., IV, 719 ff.: παλινγενόμενος ἀπογίγνομαι, αὐξόμενος καὶ αὐξηθεὶς τελευτῶ, ἀπὸ γενέσεως ζωογόνου γενόμενος, εἰς ἀπογενεσίαν ἀναλυθεὶς πορεύομαι, ὡς σὺ (sc. the god) ἔκτισας, ὡς σὺ ἐνομοθέτησας καὶ ἐποίησας μυστήριον.

[36] Cf. Dibelius, 14 f.

Examples of the injunction of silence are extraordinarily numerous and rich from the earliest time to that of the decline of the cults and primitive Christianity.[37] Herodot. already, in his many refs. to the cults and mysteries, breaks off his presentation because it is not proper to give a full exposition.[38] The fact that the silence formulae are a literary convention in his writings (cf. 2, 171, the repeated εὔστομα κείσθω) shows how old and fixed the injunctions are. Apul. Met., XI, 23 breaks off the account of the Isis mysteries in the same way. The oldest example for Eleusis is Hom. Hymn. Cer., 476 ff.: Δημήτηρ ... δεῖξε ... δρησμοσύνην θ' ἱερῶν καὶ ἐπέφραδεν ὄργια καλὰ ... σεμνά, τά τ' οὔ πως ἔστι παρεξίμεν οὔτε πυθέσθαι οὔτ' ἀχέειν· μέγα γάρ τι θεῶν σέβας ἰσχάνει αὐδήν. This command is obviously issued at the commencement of the rites, and is a sacred law.[39] The μυστήρια are ἄρρητα (or ἀπόρρητα), which means that they are not to be divulged.[40] On those who violate the duty of silence[41] the sternest punishments descend.[42] They are criminals, for the πόλις is angry εἴ τις εἰς τὰ μυστήρια φαίνοιτ' ἐξαμαρτάνων, Isoc., 16, 6.

More difficult are the questions how far the obligation extends and what is the reason for it. It obviously does not include the hopes for blessedness in the hereafter which devotees receive in the mysteries, for these are confidently extolled, → 806, and they form the main attraction to initiation. The cultic sagas of the mystery deities could also be the themes of poetry, cf. also the ecstatic elements in the Bacchants (Eur. Ba., 72 ff., 378 ff., 694 ff.) or the dances of the Eleusinian mystery procession on the day of Iakchos, Eur. Ion, 1074 ff., Aristoph. Ra., 324 ff., 340 ff.[43] Secrets to be strictly guarded are the details[44] of the cult, i.e., the sacramental rites which constitute the true event of the mystery, the cultic actualisation of the deity, which shows itself to be present in the sacred drama, in the exposition by the hierophants of the sacred symbols and the pronouncement of the accompanying formulae, and which enters into sanctifying sacramental fellowship with the devotees.[45] Because this encounter takes place in the mystery liturgy, the sacred actions and objects[46] must be protected from all profanation.

Such profanation might take the form of unauthorised and frivolous imitation of the sacred rites; Alcibiades and his friends give the best known example of this. It is instructive that in the texts which deal with violation of the mysteries we find the same terms used for sacrilege as are used to denote the right fulfilment of the mysteries.[47]

---

[37] Cf. the catena in Casel, 3 ff. (and older bibl.).

[38] This silence does not extend here to the cultic usages, but to the ἱερὸς λόγος underlying the actions and revealed in the mysteries (2, 51; cf. 2, 46 ff.).

[39] Sopater Rhet. Graec., VIII, 112, 7 f.; 118, 13 ff., ed. C. Walz (1835).

[40] Schol. Soph. Oed. Col., 1051 (ed. P. N. Papageorgios [1888]): ἐπεὶ ἄρρητα τὰ μυστήρια καὶ καθάπερ κλεισὶν ἡ γλῶσσα κατείληπται ὑπὲρ τοῦ μὴ ἐξενεγκεῖν. Cf. Casel, 5 ff.

[41] Andoc., I, 29 calls it ἁμαρτάνειν and ἀσεβεῖν περὶ τὼ θεώ (sc. Demeter and Kore).

[42] Sopater, *op. cit.*, 117, 13: ἐάν τις τὰ μυστήρια εἴπῃ τιμωρείσθω.

[43] Kern, II, 202 f., with illustrations.

[44] Cf. Diod. S., II, 62, 8: οὐ θέμις τοῖς ἀμυήτοις ἱστορεῖν τὰ κατὰ μέρος, V, 49, 5: καὶ τὰ μὲν κατὰ μέρος τῆς τελετῆς ἐν ἀπορρήτοις τελούμενα μόνοις παραδίδοται τοῖς μυηθεῖσι. Cf. Casel, 15 f.

[45] On the distinction of δρώμενα, δεικνύμενα, λεγόμενα, A. Persson, ARW, 21 (1922), 305.

[46] The ἱερά or sacred objects, with whose bringing to Athens from Eleusis the festival began, and which were brought back in solemn procession to Eleusis, can thus be called μυστήρια in Aristoph. Ra., 159.

[47] τὰ μυστήρια ποιεῖν, Andoc., I, 11, 12, 16; δεικνύειν τὰ ἱερά, Ps.-Lys., VI, 51, λέγειν τῇ φωνῇ τὰ ἀπόρρητα (i.e., the sacred formula to be pronounced by the hierophant in the rite), *loc. cit.*; ἐξορχεῖσθαι (lit. "to dance," namely, the δρᾶμα μυστικόν) is also a tt. for the profanation of the mysteries. Epict., III, 21, 13 ff. finely calls the pseudophilosopher a violator of the mysteries who disregards the sacred ordinances. To intrude into the rites without initiation is also profanation, Liv., 31, 14, 7; Anrich, 32; E. Rohde, *Psyche*[5, 6] (1910), 289; Casel, 16 f.

As regards the reason for the command of silence one might adduce the fact that the cults were originally linked with specific sanctuaries and districts, and that the deities were national deities who had to be protected against the attacks of strangers and enemies.[48] But this reason is shown to be inadequate by the fact that the injunction remained even when the original national boundaries were crossed, e.g., in Eleusis when the mystery had been elevated to be the state cult of Athens and recognised by the Roman Empire. The true reason for the command is to be sought in the special sanctity of the actions (μέγα γάρ τι θεῶν σέβας ἰσχάνει αὐδήν, Hom. Hymn. Cer., 479)[49] which establish a μετουσία with the deity.[50]

2. The Mysteries in Philosophy.

Already in Plato we find a conscious adoption of the ideas and terminology of the mysteries in philosophy. There is a considerable analogy between the mysteries and philosophy inasmuch as the vision of the divine is the goal of both, and a specific divinely appointed way leads in both to this end and fulfilment. Plato accordingly has described the toilsome yet certain ascent from changing being to the one constant being as the path of true consecration.[51]

In Symp., 210a-212c Diotima speaks as a hierophant when, significantly differentiating preparatory initiation from the τέλεα καὶ ἐποπτικά (sc. μυστήρια, 210a), she shows Socrates the way to knowledge of what is the beautiful (211c).[52] In Phaedr., 249a-250c there is a similar ascent of philosophical knowledge to the vision of true being (249c), or radiant beauty (250b); this is the way to the divine (249c) in the sense of mystery dedication.[53] Esp. instructive is Theaet., 156a, where Socrates undertakes to expound and explain to Theaet. a difficult theory of Protagoras and others and ironically[54] calls his task a declaration of mysteries of which the uninitiated may have no knowledge. Directly before Socrates has given the assurance that he will investigate the hidden wisdom of this theory (called μῦθος in 156c). The significance of the passage for the history of μυστήριον is that here the mysteries are not cultic actions but obscure and secret doctrines whose hidden wisdom may be understood only by those capable of knowledge. The gradual ascent of knowledge to full vision is here the true initiation.[55]

The transforming of the mysteries, discernible already in Plato, into mysterious teachings which elevate the soul to union with the divine[56] has had a long subsequent

[48] Lobeck, 270 ff.; Casel, 19 f.

[49] This is confirmed by the common use of σεμνός in connection with the mystery terms, Soph. Oed. Col., 1050 σεμνὰ τέλη; Eur. Hipp., 25; Athen., VI, 253d; there are further examples for ἅγιος in Casel, 21, for ἱερά, cf. Hdt., 8, 65; Hom. Hymn. Cer., 476.

[50] Procl. in Alc. (ed. V. Cousin [1864]), p. 293, lines 19 ff.: ὥσπερ οὖν ἐν ταῖς τελεταῖς καθάρσεις ἡγοῦνται καὶ περιῤῥαντήρια καὶ ἁγνισμοί, ἃ τῶν ἐν ἀπορρήτοις δρωμένων καὶ τῆς τοῦ θείου μετουσίας γυμνάσματά εἰσιν ...

[51] Cf. Rohde, *Psyche*, II, 279 ff.; G. Krüger, *Einsicht u. Leidenschaft* (1939), 16 f., 142 ff.

[52] *Ibid.*, 210 e (cf. 211 e), a description of the final stage. The passage is full of other mystery expressions, cf. W. Krantz, "Diotima von Mantineia," *Hermes*, 61 (1926), 445 f. Perhaps ἅτε οὐκ εἰδώλου and τοῦ ἀληθοῦς ἐφάπτεσθαι in 212a is to be understood in the light of the Eleusinian sacramental rite; on this Kern, II, 192 f.

[53] Here obviously alluding to the Dionysus mysteries; cf. ἐξιστάμενος, ὡς παρακινῶν ἐνθουσιάζων, 249d; also ἡ ψυχὴ συμπορευθεῖσα θεῷ, 249c.

[54] The unmistakable irony here lies in the mysterious solemnity with which the ideas of the Sophists are treated. The usage is thus wholly cultic, though figuratively. Cf. Men., 76e: ἀπιέναι πρὸ τῶν μυστηρίων ("to make off before one has grasped the main point"), and facetiously Gorg., 497c: εὐδαίμων εἶ ... ὅτι τὰ μεγάλα μεμύησαι πρὶν τὰ σμικρά.

[55] Phaedr., 249c: τελέους ἀεὶ τελετὰς τελούμενος, τέλεος ὄντως μόνος γίγνεται.

[56] Cf. in the Symp. the characteristic terms ἕπεσθαι, 210a, παιδαγωγεῖν, 210e, ὥσπερ ἐπαναβασμοῖς χρώμενον, 211c.

history by way of Alexandrian theology (→ 825) and Neo-Platonism to early medieval mysticism. Plato is still averse to mystery terminology, but in later philosophy [57] the relation to the mysteries is much closer; philosophy becomes mystagogy and the procedures of the cultic mysteries become its object of interpretation and source of terms. Philosophy leads its initiates through all the stages of μύησις; [58] its doctrines are hierophantically presented and kept secret from the uninitiated; [59] those who babble them out to the unworthy deprive them of force; [60] the worthy are by their truth initiated into the mysteries of being. [61] In Eleusinian fashion Philo can describe the individual stages of consecration as initiation into the little and great mysteries, Sacr. AC, 62; Cher., 49; Leg. All. III, 100. [62]

The aim of the knowledge of this mystagogic philosophy is to distinguish between real truth and its symbolical appearance or concealment. As concerns origin it often claims divine inspiration. [63] Its greatly varied theme is the allegorical interpretation of the mysteries, their divine names, rites, myths and symbols. [64] The mysteries are an adequate envelope for truth even in their incongruity, for they express the fact that the secrets of the divine cannot be declared openly but there can only be representation of certain reflections (symbols) τῶν μυστικῶν καὶ ἀποκεκρυμμένων καὶ ἀφανῶν νοήσεων. [65] The terms μυστικά and μυστήρια are now ontological rather than cultic terms. [66] They denote that which not only ought not to be declared but also that which by nature cannot be declared. Mystical speech, being inexact and symbolical, discloses hereby its knowledge of ineffable μυστήρια, and mediates this knowledge to initiates. [67]

---

57 On the relation of Aristot. to the mysteries cf. W. Jaeger, *op. cit.*, 164; Kern, III, 29. The terminology is also used in Stoicism, cf. the epigram ascribed to Cleanthes in K. Deichgräber, *Philologus*, 93 (1938), 28 ff. concerning the philosophy of Heraclit.: ὄρφνη καὶ σκότος ἐστὶν ἀλάμπετον· ἢν δέ σε μύστης || εἰσαγάγῃ, φανεροῦ λαμπρότερ' ἠελίου (Anth. Pal., IX, 540). [For later Stoicism cf. the fine passage in Dio Chrys. Or., XII, 33 f. Kleinknecht.]

58 Theo. Smyrnaeus Expositio rerum mathematicarum, ed. E. Hiller (1878), p. 14: τὴν φιλοσοφίαν μύησιν φαίη τις ἂν ἀληθοῦς τελετῆς καὶ τῶν ὄντων ὡς ἀληθῶς μυστηρίων παράδοσιν (there follow 5 stages of μύησις); the Proclus ref. in → n. 50 continues: οὕτω μοι δοκεῖ καὶ φιλόσοφος τελεσιουργία προκαθαίρειν καὶ προπαρασκευάζειν εἰς τὴν ἑαυτῶν γνῶσιν καὶ τὴν αὐτοφανῆ τῆς οὐσίας ἡμῶν θεωρίαν.

59 Examples in Anrich, 68 ff.; esp. Casel, 28 ff.

60 Philo Quaest. in Gn., IV, 8; Plut. Is. et Os., 2 (II, 351e ff.).

61 Philo Deus Imm., 61: παρ' ἧς (sc. ἀλήθεια) μυηθέντες τὰ περὶ τοῦ ὄντος ἀψευδῆ μυστήρια. For Philo Moses and Jeremiah are true hierophants, Cher., 49. The relation between teachers and pupils is understood in the same way in Neo-Pythagoreanism, Neo-Platonism, Hermetic Gnosticism, and, with ref. to Christ, Alexandrian theology.

62 There were long-standing connections between Alexandria and Eleusis; one need only recall the establishment of the Serapis cult after the pattern of Eleusis and with the addition of the Eumolp. Timotheos, Plut. Is. et Os., 28 (II, 362a). Cl. Al. Protr. shows exact knowledge of the Eleusinian mysteries (2). There is a close link also between Eleusis and the mystery of the birth of Aion celebrated in the Koreion at Alexandria, Epiph. Haer., 51, 22, 8 ff. Cf. K. Holl, *Ges. Aufs.*, II (1928), 144 ff.; R. Kittel, 37 ff.

63 Hermes is esp. the god of revelation in Corp. Herm.; cf. also the beginning and end of Iambl. Myst.: Isis, Plut. Is. et Os., 2 (II, 351 f.).

64 Cf. the allegorical interpretation of the Isis-Osiris myth in Plut. Is. et Os., 2, 3, 33, 38 f., 49, 53, 63 f.; the theology of Julian (cf. W. Nestle, *Griech. Religiosität von Alex. d. Gr. bis auf Proclus* [1934], 164 ff.). For Philo and the Christian Alexandrians the Bible is the book of mysteries; its figures and events conceal mysteries appointed only for initiates, cf. Cher., 42-49. Pascher reconstructs a single mystery of regeneration and deification in Philo. There is important material in Völker, *passim.*

65 Iambl. Myst., VII, 1.

66 On μυστικός cf. H. Leisegang, *Philol. Wochenschrift*, 44 (1924), 138 ff.

67 Greg. Naz. Or. Theol., 27, 5 (MPG, 36, 17): μυστικῶς τὰ μυστικὰ φθέγγεσθαι καὶ ἁγίως τὰ ἅγια. → ἀλληγορέω, I, 260.

The adoption of the vocabulary of the mysteries by philosophy led to a significant change in the understanding of μυστήρια. They were divested of their sacramental character and became secret teachings. In the theology of the philosophical mysteries the cults, strictly speaking, are no longer true mysteries; they conceal mysteries. The term implies, not the cultic event of encounter with deity, but the divine ground of being. Interest has shifted from the earthly contingency of the divine to the divine transcendence of the cosmos.

3. The Mysteries in Magic.

There is an intensive continuation of mystery terminology in the magic texts. Here there is a recognisable change as compared with the original meaning only in so far as magic involves individual practice without cultic connection. The vocabulary is richly represented. μυστήριον is used as follows: a. for a magical action; [68] b. for the formula which effects the magic: μηδενὶ [ἄλλῳ με]ταδῷς, ἀλλὰ κρύβε, πρὸς Ἡλίου ἀξιωθεὶς ὑπὸ τοῦ κυρί[ου θεοῦ], τὸ μέγα τοῦτο μυστήριον. [69] A precise direction [70] as to the way in which the magician, by means of a magic song, can command the god and stir him to give life to magic images, [71] closes with the demand: ὃ καὶ ἔχε ἐν ἀποκρύφῳ ὡς μεγαλομυστήριον. κρύβε, κρύβε. [72] It is also used c. for the magically potent mystery writing: ἵλαθί μοι, Πρόνοια καὶ Ψυχή, τάδε γράφοντι τὰ (ἄ)πρατα, παραδοτὰ μυστήρια, [73] and: ἄρξαι λέγειν τὴν στήλην (formula of prayer) καὶ τὸ μυστήριον τοῦ θεοῦ ὅ ἐστιν κάνθαρος (title of the writing), [74] and d. for other means employed in magic, a magic ointment, [75] a material from the scarab, [76] sacred animals, [77] an amulet (?) prepared by the magician. [78]

4. The Mysteries in Secular Usage.

Outside philosophy there was a transfer of the mystery terminology to non-cultic secular spheres. In the first instance, however, the influence of religious concepts may be seen. [79] Thus, when we read: ὕπνος τὰ μικρὰ τοῦ θανάτου μυστήρια, [80] the cultic

---

68 ὡς σύ (sc. the god) ... ἐποίησας μυστήριον, Preis. Zaub., IV, 722 ff. (so-called Mithr. Liturg.).

69 Preis. Zaub., I, 130 f. In I, 127 the one versed in magic is addressed μύστα τῆς ἱερᾶς μαγείας; the mysteries may be declared only to συμμύσται, XII, 94. Other derivates are μυσταγωγός, IV, 172; ἀμυστηρίαστος, XIII, 380, 428; μυστικῶς, III, 702; σύμβολα μυστικά (for magic words), IV, 945; μυστοδόκος (δόμος), XX, 8.

70 *Ibid.*, XII, 316 ff.

71 The whole action is called τελετὴ τοῦ μεγίστου καὶ θείου ἐνεργήματος.

72 On the formula cf. A. Dieterich, *Abraxas* (1891), 162 f.; there is mention of a violation in Preis. Zaub., IV, 2476 ff.: διέβαλεν γάρ σου τὰ ἱερὰ μυστήρια ἀνθρώποις εἰς γνῶσιν.

73 Preis. Zaub., IV, 475 f.; cf. Mithr. Liturg., 49 ff.

74 Preis. Zaub., XIII, 127 f.; cf. Reitzenstein Hell. Myst., 242; on mysteries, book mysteries and magic cf. J. Kroll, 495 f.

75 Preis. Zaub., IV, 746.

76 *Ibid.*, 794 f.

77 *Ibid.*, 2590 ff.

78 *Ibid.*, XII, 331: δότε οὖν πνεῦμα τῷ ὑπ' ἐμοῦ κατεσκευασμένῳ μυστηρίῳ.

79 For the sake of analogy one should note the fig. and secular use of other mystery terms: Hippocr. Nomos, 5 (ed. Heiberg, I, 1, p. 8): τὰ δὲ ἱερὰ ἐόντα πρήγματα ἱεροῖσιν ἀνθρώποισι δείκνυται, βεβήλοισι δὲ οὐ θέμις, πρὶν ἢ τελεσθῶσιν ὀργίοισιν ἐπιστήμης. Menand. Fr., 550 (FCA, III, 167 f.) refers to a μυσταγωγὸς (leader) τοῦ βίου ἀγαθός. Later μυσταγωγός can mean "guide," Kern, Pauly-W., 1209. → μυεῖν and μυσταγωγεῖν can also be used generally for instruction and μυστικός for secret.

80 Mnesimachus Fr., 11, CAF, II, 442; cf. also Lidz. Joh., 168: "The mystery of death is sleep."

concept is the basis, for the metaphor, which is obviously describing sleep as the preliminary stage and mysterious reflection of the eternal sleep, carries an allusion to Eleusinian ritual. [81] Figurative use [82] prepares the way for the secular use attested later, e.g., μυστήριον = a "private secret" not to be divulged even to a friend: [83] Ps.-Phocylides, Γνῶμαι, 229 (Poetae Lyrici Graeci[4], ed. T. Bergk, II [1915], 475): ταῦτα δικαιοσύνης μυστήρια, Soran (CMG, IV, ed. J. Ilberg, 1927, 5, 29): συνηθὲς μυστήριον, "a widespread superstition" (which a midwife must not accept lest she neglect her duty); esp. *ibid.*, 4, 25 and 5, 27: μυστήρια βίου, "intimacies of life," "family secrets." The term is also common in medical writings, Aret., VIII, 7, 3 (CMG, II [Hude, 1923], p. 166, 12): τοὐμὸν τὸ μυστήριον (with ref. to the prescription); cf. also Galen, ed. Kühn, XIII, 96; Alex. Trallianus, 5, 4. But the word can also be used generally, e.g., Cic. Att., 4, 17, 1 of letters: *tantum habent mysteriorum* (cf. also 6, 4: *illud praeterea* μυστικώτερον *ad te scribam,* i.e., in such a way that no one can understand; there follows the Gk. text). The LXX also has μυστήριον in the secular sense, → 814.

The secular use is obviously a later phase in the development of the term. Its history moves from the cultic and religious to the general and profane, not *vice versa.* The fact that examples of secular use are on the whole rare, and are repeatedly shown by the context to be figurative, demonstrates that the term was never wholly secularised. The religious use maintained its dominance.

5. The Mysteries in Gnosticism.

Like mystical philosophy, Gnosticism presupposes [84] and fosters [85] a process of intermingling and reinterpreting the ancient mystery cults.

The most important documentation of this reinterpretation of the ancient mysteries is to be found in the so-called preaching of the Naassenes, Hipp. Ref., V, 7 ff. [86] This is an example of the Gnostic reduction of all conceivable oriental and Gk. myths to the myth of the heavenly primal man who has fallen into the chaotic cosmos, and will be redeemed and brought to his original destiny. [87] Understanding of the mysteries is now controlled by this redemption myth. The ἀλάλως λαλοῦν μυστήριον ἄρρητον (Hipp. Ref., V, 8, 7) declares to the one ordained for redemption: ποδαπὸν αὐτὸν δεῖ γενέσθαι, τουτέστιν πνευματικόν. He becomes pneumatic when he hears the hidden mystery in silence. The mystery event, achieved in the giving and receiving of knowledge, means also, as shown by the images of the two gods in Samothrace, the union of the original man and the newly born pneumatic, who is fully like that man in nature, V, 8, 10. The resurrection of the τέλειος ἄνθρωπος, who is fashioned after the heavenly original, and his entry into heaven, are the ἄρρητα μυστήρια of the Spirit which only perfect

---

[81] From Plato to Christian theology the little and great mysteries are a common metaphor for the stages of a process of knowledge up to completion.

[82] The original religious sense and the generalising of usage may both be seen also in Μύστης as a proper name, Horat. Carm., II, 9; later we find Μύστις as a feminine name.

[83] Menand. Fr., 695, CAF, III, 200.

[84] It should be noted, of course, that the ideas of the later philosophy of antiquity are themselves largely dependent on Gnostic mythology.

[85] In Hipp. Ref., I prooem, 8 the syncretistic character of Gnosis is rightly indicated; it is a product ἐκ ... μυστηρίων ἐπικεχειρημένων, cf. also 2: πρόειμι δείξων αὐτῶν τὰ ἀπόρρητα μυστήρια (there follow allusions to the παράδοσις and the mystical oath of initiation).

[86] For a reconstruction of the text *v.* R. Reitzenstein-H. H. Schaeder, *Studien zum antiken Synkretismus* (1926), 161 ff.

[87] There is an excellent summary in H. Jonas, *Gnosis u. spätantiker Geist,* I (1934), 348 ff.

Gnostics perceive, V, 8, 24 ff.[88] It is their redemption, in the double sense of the term imparted, i.e., declared and made over, to them in the mysteries.[89] All the figures and symbols of the Eleusinian cult, the cut ears of corn, the hierophant, the new-born divine child, and also the individual features of other cults, are symbols of the regeneration[90] and deification of the Gnostics, V, 8, 39 ff., and this is the point of the whole mystery action.[91] The mysteries are both mystery and disclosure: mystery in so far as they can be perceived only by those who because of their more than earthly origin can hear the message which comes from the other world; and disclosure in so far as the redeeming message is imparted to these τέλειοι γνωστικοί through them.[92] They are thus secret divine-human revelations which assure the perfect of their origin and lead them to their destiny.

These definitions of the μυστήρια are simply theological formulations of the total Gnostic view that everything is μυστήριον which refers to the hidden heavenly world beyond, to the origin and redemption of man. The connection and difference between this Gnostic concept of the mysteries and the original cultic view are thus apparent. The framework in which mysteries are given and concealed, received and fulfilled, is now so broad that it embraces heaven, earth, and the spheres of the *archontes*. Within this sphere significance may be attached to the cultic action,[93] but the cultus is here a by-product of myth, whereas in the ancient mysteries myth is a by-product of the cultus.

The mysteries have their origin in the sphere of light, in "the universal mystery from or out of which all mysteries have come,"[94] in the first mystery, the father of light himself.[95] The sphere of the heavenly is the true sphere of the mysteries.[96] The secrets of the all are concealed in them, and disclosed to the perfect.[97] In accordance with the correspondence between Gnostic cosmology and soteriology, this means the secret of the primal man who comprehends the whole cosmos in himself.[98] The bringer of these mysteries of the other world, which reveal the origin of fallen and constantly erring man and bring him to redemption, is the redeemed redeemer, who promises in the Naassene hymn:

---

[88] Reitzenstein-Schaeder, 169 f.

[89] Hence the Gnostic redemption myth is derived, with an allegorical etym. (Hipp. Ref., V, 8, 41), from the designations Ἐλευσὶν καὶ ἀνακτόρειον: Ἐλευσίν, ὅτι ἤλθομεν, φησίν, οἱ πνευματικοὶ ἄνωθεν ἀπὸ τοῦ Ἀδάμαντος ῥυέντες κάτω — ἐλεύσεσθαι γάρ, φησίν, ἐστὶν ἐλθεῖν —, τὸ δὲ ἀνακτόρειον <διὰ> τὸ ἀνελθεῖν ἄνω.

[90] Hipp. Ref., V, 8, 40 relates the call of the Eleusinian hierophant ἱερὸν ἔτεκε πότνια κοῦρον Βριμὼ Βριμόν to the new birth of the devotee. Koerte, ARW, 18 (1915), 123 ff. thinks this is the right explanation, but cf. Kern, II, 194.

[91] V, 8, 42 (96, 24 f.): τοῦτο, φησίν, ἐστὶν ὃ λέγουσιν οἱ κατωργιασμένοι τῶν Ἐλευσινίων τὰ <μεγάλα> μυστήρια.

[92] This tension in the nature of the mysteries may be seen in paradoxical expressions like ἀλάλως λαλοῦν or κεκαλυμμένον καὶ ἀνακεκαλυμμένον, Hipp. Ref., V, 7, 27.

[93] Acc. to Epiph. Haer., 31, 7, 8 (I, 397, 11, Holl) the pneumatic is, of course, referred only to the knowledge and forms of the mysteries.

[94] Unknown Ancient Gnostic Work, 2 (*Koptisch-gnostische Schriften* [GCS], ed. C. Schmidt, I [1905], 336, 28 f.).

[95] So in innumerable passages in Pist. Soph., in which the unwearied and wearying repetition of the term mystery suggests a fixed formula, though the typically Gnostic view of the origin of the mysteries is plain to see. Cf. C. Schmidt, "Gnost. Schriften in kopt. Sprache," TU, VIII, 1-2 (1893), 475 ff.; cf. Anrich, 87.

[96] Lidz. Ginza, 381, 17 f.: "... the mighty mysteries of light which rest beneath the throne of the king of the earth of the aether."

[97] Hipp. Ref., V, 7, 27: τὸ μέγα καὶ κρύφιον τῶν ὅλων ἄγνωστον μυστήριον ... κεκαλυμμένον καὶ ἀνακεκαλυμμένον. Cf. also Pist. Soph., 91 (134 ff., Schmidt).

[98] Corp. Herm., I, 16: τοῦτό ἐστι τὸ [κεκρυμμένον] μυστήριον μέχρι τῆσδε τῆς ἡμέρας. ἡ γὰρ φύσις ἐπιμιγεῖσα τῷ ἀνθρώπῳ ἤνεγκέ τι θαῦμα θαυμασιώτατον. The primal man who comprises all mysteries in himself is depicted in the Unknown Anc. Gnostic Work, 21 (363 f., Schmidt).

μυστήρια πάντα δ' ἀνοίξω,
μορφὰς δὲ θεῶν ἐπιδείξω·
[καὶ] τὰ κεκρυμμένα τῆς ἁγίας ὁδοῦ,
γνῶσιν καλέσας, παραδώσω (Hipp. Ref., V, 10, 2).[99]

The disclosure of the mysteries, the conferring of knowledge, is itself enactment of redemption, not just the granting of its possibility. We simply have another way of stating the deifying effect of γνῶσις when in Pist. Soph., 91 (133, 33 ff.) it is said of him who has received the supreme mystery: "He has the power to go through all the orders of the inheritance of light."[100] In this fulfilment he has also come back to himself.[101]

In detail the concept of the mysteries finds in Gnosticism a varied use which also illustrates the connection with magic. The term may denote the secret means of redemption freighted with heavenly power, e.g., sacred books,[102] rites and sacraments,[103] and conjurations[104] which the redeemed practise to protect themselves on their heavenly journey against the evil forces which confront them by the way.[105] The common feature here is the understanding of the mysteries as powerfull secret instruments which must not be betrayed lest they lose their power. In the light of this uniform significance one can see why there can also be refs. to the mysteries of evil powers — mysteries which are disclosed by the heavenly redeemer and thereby wrested from these forces.[106]

B. μυστήριον in the LXX, Apocalyptic and Rabbinic Judaism.

1. LXX Usage.

In the LXX the term occurs for the first time only in the writings of the Hellen. period, Tob., Jdt., Wis., Sir., Da., 2 Macc. In some cases there is express ref. to the mystery cults, Wis. 14:15: μυστήρια καὶ τελετάς, 14:23: κρύφια μυστήρια (with τεκνοφόνους τελετάς), 3 Macc. 2:30: ἐν τοῖς κατὰ τὰς τελετὰς (sc. of Dionysus)

---

99 Jesus is sometimes called μυστήριον, Pist. Soph., 10; Act. Thom., 47.

100 γνῶσις is one of the heavenly powers from the unfathomable deep; we read of it: "Through it one has known the first father for whose sake one exists, and one has known the mystery of silence which speaks for all things and is hidden, the first unity for the sake of which the all became unreal," Unknown Ancient Gnostic Work, 10 (348 f., Schmidt). Stob. Herm. Exc., 25, 11 (Scott, I, 512, 15 ff.) ἀρρήτων γὰρ ἐπακούεις μυστηρίων γῆς τε καὶ οὐρανοῦ καὶ παντὸς τοῦ μέσου [ἱεροῦ] πνεύματος. Cf. also Scott, I, 456, 19 f.; 484, 35 f.; 494, 1 ff.

101 Unknown Anc. Gnost. Work, 7 (341, 33 ff.): "It is because man is a relative of the mysteries that he has received the mystery"; *ibid.*, 15 (356, 33 ff.): "I will give them the mystery of my hidden father because they have loved their own." Act. Andr., 15: μακαρίους οὖν ἐκείνους τίθεμαι τοὺς κατηκόους τῶν κεκηρυγμένων λόγων γεγονότας καὶ δι' αὐτῶν μυστήρια ὀπτριζομένους περὶ τὴν ἰδίαν φύσιν, ἧς ἕνεκεν τὰ πάντα ᾠκοδόμηται.

102 → n. 74; cf. Lidz. Ginza, 65, 27; 142, 15; 150, 30 etc. for an introductory "mystery."

103 Esp. Act. Joh., 96 (ed. Bonnet, p. 198) (after the preceding cultic dance): ἰδὼν ὃ πράσσω τὰ μυστήριά μου σίγα. The mystery of baptisms, Pist. Soph., 115 (193, 32); of oil, Lidz. Liturg., 121; the sacramental celebration of the Ophites, Epiph., 37, 5; in Mandaean texts a magical preparation, Lidz. Ginza, 228, 21; 232, 14 and 18, or the matter of the sacrament, 122.

104 Acc. to Corp. Herm., 16, 2 the power of the formulae depends on their not being translated. They must be protected against the empty rhetoric of Gk. philosophy.

105 Lidz. Ginza, 111, 27 f.: "I showed you (Rūhā) the great mystery through which the rebels were put down," *ibid.*, 144, 1: "The pass and the great mystery." When the redeemed come the *archontes* recognise the mysteries by name and prostrate themselves, Pist. Soph., 11 ff., 28; Ophite conjurations, in Orig. Cels., 6, 31 (Hennecke, 432 ff.). Such protective formulae are obviously also the ἐπιρρήματα which the pneumatic needs for redemption, Epiph. Haer., 31, 7, 8, → n. 93).

106 Lidz. Ginza, 131, 35 ff.; Liturg., 4, 10 ff.; 184, 5 ff.

μεμυημένοις ἀναστρέφεσθαι. Elsewhere the terms can denote idolatry: μύστης, Wis. 12:5; μυεῖσθαι, Σ Nu. 25:5 (LXX: τελεῖσθαι, also Nu. 25:3; ψ 105[106]:28); τελίσκεσθαι, Dt. 23:18 etc. [107] A few passages in Wis. show clearly the influence of mystery ideas; thus in 6:22 the teaching on the nature and origin of wisdom is introduced as the revelation of a mystery, [108] though with no distinction between initiates and the uninitiated; in 8:4 wisdom is μύστις ... τῆς τοῦ θεοῦ ἐπιστήμης, Solomon desires it as a bride, [109] and hopes for immortality through union with it (8:13). Cf. also 2:22: (the ungodly) οὐκ ἔγνωσαν μυστήρια θεοῦ. The righteous man knows them and keeps to them as the law, for he knows of man's eternal destiny in creation and hopes for it as a reward for holy conduct (2:22 f.). [110] These passages display no more than influence; the mysteries here are linked neither with sacramental rites not with the Gnostic redemption myth.

A few verses use the term in a secular sense [111] for secrets which must not be divulged, e.g., the secret plans of a king (Tob. 12:7, 11; Jdt. 2:2), secrets of war (2 Macc. 13:21), the secrets of a friend (Sir. 22:22; 27:16 f., 21; Σ Prv. 11:13; Θ Prv. 20:19). The one to whom they are imparted is worthy of special trust; he justifies this by keeping the secret, since only the other has the right to enlarge the circle of those in whom he confides. [112] In the Hexapla transl. the Heb. equivalent is סוֹד = "confidential speech or advice," "secret," then the "circle of confidants who are consulted." Only where the sense is "secret" or "secret plan" is μυστήριον a possible rendering. The Heb. word can be used for the intimate converse of men with men or of God with men. [113] The sparse use of μυστήριον may be explained by the alien religious significance which the term had in accordance with its origin. Only with reservations, then, can one speak of the transition of the religious word to general profane use or of an uninhibited new religious application.

The LXX and Θ are constant in their rendering of the Aram. רָז plur. רָזִין (which is of Persian derivation), cf. Da. 2:18 f., 27, 28, 29, 30, 47; in Θ Da. 4:9 Nebuchadnezzar's vision is a μυστήριον. The vision is a divine answer to the thoughts of the heart, to the king's concern for the future (ὅσα δεῖ γενέσθαι ἐπ' ἐσχάτων τῶν ἡμερῶν, 2:29; cf. 2:28, 30), but the revelation is veiled in images.

In Da. μυστήριον takes on for the first time a sense which is important for the further development of the word, namely, that of an eschatological mystery,

---

[107] Cf. also τελεταί in 3 Βασ. 15:12; Am. 7:9.

[108] τί δέ ἐστιν σοφία καὶ πῶς ἐγένετο, ἀπαγγελῶ καὶ οὐκ ἀποκρύψω ὑμῖν μυστήρια.

[109] Here one sees plainly the influence of the idea of the ἱερὸς γάμος. On wisdom teaching as a mystery cf. T. Arvedson, *Das Mysterium Christi* (1937), 80 ff., 162 ff.

[110] Cf. R. Kittel, 95.

[111] → 810.

[112] 2 Macc. 3:10: μυστικῶς, "secretly."

[113] סוֹד is never the Heb. original of μυστήριον in the LXX. We find it 3 times in Θ (ψ 24:14 [also E']; Prv. 20:19; Job 15:8), and once in Σ (Prv. 11:13). Σ usually has ὁμιλία (ὁμιλεῖν, συνόμιλος), 'A ἀπόρρητον (only Jer. 6:11 σύστρεμμα and ψ 110:1 ἱκετία?). LXX has no uniform rendering. סוֹד occurs 21 times in the Mas. LXX omits it in Prv. 20:19 and follows a different text in Prv. 25:9. In the other 19 instances it has no less than 12 different words, mostly intellectualistic. None is close to μυστήριον even where the context might suggest a corresponding idea. Cf. G. Bertram, "Der Begriff d. Erziehung in d. gr. Bibel," *Imago Dei, Festgabe f. G. Krüger* (1932), 48 f. On the other hand a mystical understanding is obviously presupposed in Sir. 3:19, which has been maintained in Gk. only by the Suppl. of S: πραέσιν ἀποκαλύπτει τὰ μυστήρια αὐτοῦ (סוֹד) → νήπιος, III B. Elsewhere in Sir. סוֹד is σύμβουλος (בַּעַל סוֹד, 6:6), λόγος (8:17), βουλή (37:10), διήγησις (9:15). The Aram. רָז is twice rendered μυστήριον in ΣΘ (Is. 24:16). The Heb. has רָזִי from רזה "to diminish." But perhaps the Mas. with its pointing had רָז ("secret") in view. At Sir. 8:18 רָז is κρυπτός, cf. Da. 2:47. [Bertram.]

a concealed intimation of divinely ordained future events whose disclosure and interpretation is reserved for God alone (ὁ ἀνακαλύπτων μυστήρια, 2:28, 29, cf. 2:47) and for those inspired by His Spirit (4:9 Θ). God's power to reveal mysteries raises him above heathen gods.

2. Apocalyptic.

The disclosure of divine secrets is the true theme of later Jewish apocalyptic. The fantastic fulness of statements does not conceal the underlying and explicit sense that God is infinitely remote, that heaven and earth, creation, history and its end, are full of puzzles, that the present is incapable of answering innumerable questions without a concrete prophetic word and human apprehension. Thus the concept of mystery has now a very significant role. The being and rule of God are unsearchable. "Deep and without number are thy mysteries, and there is no calculating thy righteousness," En. 63:3. Only the Son of Man "is mighty in all the secrets of righteousness," 49:2.

Apocalyptic speaks objectively of these mysteries. They have the character of hidden realities which are prepared (Eth. En. 9:6) and kept in heaven, and disclosed and shown to the enraptured seer as he wanders through the heavenly spheres under the guidance of an angel.[114] Nevertheless, while the sphere of mysteries constitutes in apoc. its own world of hidden things, the mysteries are the hidden other-worldly basis of reality. This is shown by the many combinations, e.g., mysteries of heaven, of creation, of the aeon, of lightning, thunder, the winds, the clouds etc., also the mystery of the Torah, sinners, the righteous. What is, what happens, what is to come, has its being in heaven rather than in itself, since it is there that it is prepared and may be seen or read on tables.

He who receives the revelation of the mysteries of the heavenly and the earthly knows "what inwardly holds the world together." He knows the power by which all things have come into being, "the mystery by which were created heaven and earth, sea and land, mountains and hills, rivers and springs, Gehenna, fire and hail, the Garden of Eden and the tree of life, and by which were formed Adam and Eve, cattle and wild beasts etc."[115] Mysteries as the hidden forces by which things find reality and fulfilment[116] comprehend their true being. Hence the disclosure of mysteries involves the revelation of the secret names, measurements,[117] times and numerical relationships which make up the whole.[118] The "total" character of mysteries is also plainly expressed in the common phrase "all mysteries."

The apocalyptist who sees mysteries and thus surveys the totality of heavenly and earthly realities and events is able to perceive the time of the world's course. He knows the mysteries of times and the approach of periods, S. Bar. 81:4.[119] He already sees what will then be manifest when the elect sits on the divine throne and "all the mysteries of wisdom proceed from the thoughts of his mouth," Eth. En. 51:3. "When the mysteries of the righteous are manifested, sinners will be judged," 38:3. These mysteries are the final destiny of sinners and righteous, punishment and salvation, 106:19; 103:2 ff. etc. They are the divine judgment (41:1) and the preceding and accompanying cosmic convulsions and disasters (Heb. En. 48 C 9 [cf. 7]; Eth. En. 83:7; 61:5). All that will then take place is already concealed in heaven. At the end it will simply be brought to light.

---

[114] In Heb. En. Metatron, instructed by God and appointed guardian of the heavenly treasures, knows and reveals mysteries; in Eth. En., Enoch in heaven is led to all mysteries by Michael (71:3 f.; cf. also 40:2; 46:2 etc.).

[115] Heb. En. 48 D 8. The Heb. equivalent is רז, as in Da., but also סתר and סוד, *v.* H. Odeberg's Index and notes on 11, p. 30.

[116] Cf. also Eth. En. 69:15 ff.

[117] Eth. En. 61.

[118] Eth. En. 10:7, acc. to the Eth., which diverges from the Gk. text, τῷ μυστηρίῳ ὅλου (G ὅλῳ).

[119] 4 Esr. 14:5: *temporum secreta et temporum finem*; Aram.: *mysteria horarum*.

The two points give the essence of the concept of the mysteries in apocalyptic. The mysteries are God's counsels destined finally to be disclosed. They are the final events and states which are already truly existent in heaven [120] and may be seen there, and which will in the last days emerge from their concealment and become manifest events. Thus Eth. En. 104:10 reads: "And now I know this mystery, that sinners will often alter and wrest the word of truth," and v. 12: "... and so I know another mystery, that the books (i.e., these revelations) will be given to the righteous and wise to their joy." Implied is that both these things will take place at the end of the days with a divine necessity which man cannot fathom.

These mysteries are revealed to apocalyptists either by rapture into heaven or by signs and visions. The connection between signs and mysteries is plain in, e.g., 4 Esr. 14:6, where the Lat. *signa, quae demonstravi,* is to be rendered in acc. with the Armenian, *mysterium hoc, quod antea significavi,* or Eth. En. 68:1: "And then my ancestor Enoch gave me in a book the signs of all mysteries and the metaphorical sayings"; [121] cf. also 4 Esr. 10:38, where the interpretation of the preceding vision of a woman bewailing her son, who changes suddenly into a city, is introduced as follows: ... *Altissimus revelavit tibi mysteria multa,* also 12:8 Armen., where *dicta* (often *oracula*) *et res* is a rendering of μυστήριον = רָז. [122] The mysteries are revealed to the apocalyptist in concealing signs and visions in which the coming destinies of Israel and the world are intimated. Their declaration is also enigmatic. It takes the form of concealing oracles which are themselves μυστήρια. [123] Full revelation will come only at the end. Hence apoc. insights must be carefully preserved by the seers and passed on only to the wise, 4 Esr. 12:36 ff.; 14:5 ff., 26, 45 f.; cf. also S. Bar. 20:3; 48:3 etc. [124]

There can also be an unseemly prying into heavenly mysteries of which the wicked angels were guilty. These have shown man what is hidden (Eth. En. 65:11), the mystery which is from God (16:3). [125] Thereby men have come into the possession of forbidden powers and have given themselves to magical arts, e.g., the winning of metals (65:6 ff.), the use of ink and paper (69:9 f.). The result is that judgment is passed on them (65). The mystery betrayed by angels brings them to destruction (10:7).

Apocalyptic usage discloses clear connections with that of the mystery cults and Gnosticism. We find the same demand for silence. The angel plays in apocalyptic the role of the mystagogue. [126] The journey to heaven and hell, liturgically depicted in the cults, takes visionary form in Gnosticism and apocalyptic. [127] Yet for all the common features there are decisive distinctions: 1. The apocalyptic mysteries do not relate to a destiny which the deity or the heavenly redeemer suffers, but to one which the deity decides and ordains; 2. reception of the mysteries is not deification in apocalyptic; 3. the mysteries are in apocalyptic orientated to an eschatological cosmic revelation.

---

[120] Cf. Anrich, 144.

[121] The two things are obviously one and the same; cf. the usage in Hermas, who acc. to Violet's illuminating conjecture ("Die Apk. d. Esra u. d. Baruch," GCS [1924], 191) has παραβολαί for the signs of 4 Esr. 14:8.

[122] Cf. Violet, *op. cit.,* 161.

[123] *Ibid.,* 167.

[124] Hence the literary form, cf. P. Volz, *Jüd. Eschatologie,* 5, 26, 46; G. Hölscher, *Kanonisch u. Apokryph* (1905), 47 ff.; *Gesch. d. isr. u. jüd. Rel.* (1922), 187 ff. → III, 971.

[125] Perhaps with Charles acc. to the Eth. we should read μυστήριον τὸ ἐξουθενημένον for μυστήριον τὸ ἐκ τοῦ θεοῦ γεγενημένον.

[126] Cf. G. Bornkamm, "Mythos u. Legende in d. apokr. Thomasakten," FRL, 49 (1933), 52 ff.

[127] On the Gnostic character of Heb. En. cf. the introduction and notes of H. Odeberg.

3. Rabbinic Judaism.

Rabb. Judaism increasingly expunged and came to have a strong contempt for the secret doctrines of apocalyptic.[128] Da. was the only apoc. book to find a place in the Canon. The objection was not a primitive one. It dated only from the destruction of Jerusalem. Earlier the Rabbinate itself had engaged in the cosmological and theosophical speculations of apocal. and had seen a value in them.[129] The concept of the mystery (סוד, רז, מסטירין = μυστήρια) is also found in Rabb. lit. Among secret doctrines are the exposition of the laws of incest and esp. theosophical speculations (e.g., on the vision of the chariot in Ez. 1:10) on cosmogonic and apocalyptic events. Discussion of these is allowed only with strict reservations. But a mystery, too, is the whole of the oral tradition by which the Israelites show themselves to be God's children, also circumcision and the calculation of the calendar.[130] Israel is under obligation to keep its secrets for itself and from the Gentiles (Ex. r., 19 on 12:50).[131] Cosmological and theosophical insights are promised to him who "occupies himself with the Torah for its own sake" (Aboth, 6, 2): "The mysteries of the Torah will be revealed to him." These mysteries are the grounds of the Torah from which God gave the detailed provisions. The Torah is thus an envelope for the mystery of the divine creation which underlies it and all being and to which one must seek to penetrate in mystical interpretation.[132]

C. μυστήριον in the New Testament.

1. The Mystery of the Divine Lordship, Mk. 4:11 f. and Par.

In the Gospels the term μυστήριον occurs only in the obscure saying of Jesus about the purpose of parables which the Synoptists interpose between the parable of the Sower and its interpretation. Mk. 4:11: ὑμῖν τὸ μυστήριον δέδοται τῆς βασιλείας τοῦ θεοῦ, Mt. 13:11; Lk. 8:10: ὑμῖν δέδοται γνῶναι τὰ μυστήρια τῆς βασιλείας τῶν οὐρανῶν (Lk. τοῦ θεοῦ). The saying differentiates between the disciples and those who are without (→ II, 575), i.e., the mass of the people not committed to discipleship. This differentiation is the basis of the rule of Jesus in His preaching to speak to the uncomprehending people only in parables (→ παραβολή), not in order to bring them by an appropriate method to understanding, but to withhold knowledge and complete their hardening, Mk. 4:12 par. The basic and comprehensive character of the saying (cf. the τὰ πάντα of Mk. 4:11) and the introductory question of the disciples in Mk. and Mt., with its reference to parables, show that there can be no limiting the principle to individual parables (only one has so far been told in all the Gospels) or to individual and special experiences of Jesus. There is in the saying a specific understanding of Jesus' general method of teaching in parables. This method serves to conceal the mystery of the divine rule — a mystery disclosed to the disciples but not to others.[133]

---

128 They re-emerge only in medieval mysticism and the Cabbala.

129 For details cf. G. Hölscher, *Kanonisch u. Apokryph* (1905), 54 ff.; J. Jeremias, *Jerusalem zur Zeit Jesu*, II B (1929), 106 ff.; *Die Abendmahlsworte Jesu* (1935), 49 ff. (with refs. to secret discipline among the Essenes and the community of the new covenant in Damascus).

130 Str.-B., I, 659 f.

131 *Loc. cit.*

132 In Heb. En. 11:1 "mysteries of the Torah" comprehends mysteries of wisdom, deep things of the perfect law and mysteries of creation, cf. H. Odeberg, *ad loc.* 31 and 177 f.

133 Mk. 4:11 f. does not fit smoothly into the context. V. 13 presupposes that the disciples have asked Jesus for an explanation of the preceding parable, cf. the question of v. 10: τίς αὕτη εἴη ἡ παραβολή (so Lk. 8:9). But v. 11 f. answers as though the question were: διὰ τί ἐν παραβολαῖς λαλεῖς αὐτοῖς (so Mt. 13:10). Moreover, it is not easy to

Mt. and Lk. vary slightly on Mk. and stress more heavily the enigmatic meaning of parables revealed to disciples: ὑμῖν δέδοται γνῶναι τὰ μυστήρια τῆς βασιλείας τῶν οὐρανῶν (Lk. τοῦ θεοῦ).[134] Mk. certainly does not mean that the parables have nothing to say to the disciples; this may be seen from the continuation in 4:13 ff., 34, where an explanation is given to them as distinct from the rest. Mk. 4:11 is very sharply formulated, since the antithesis is between the revelation of the mystery already given to the disciples and the parabolic instruction designed for others, not between parables which are elucidated and those which are left obscure. All the Evangelists agree that parables are a mode of speech which conceals, and that they are meant to withhold the mystery of God's lordship from the people.[135] The difference between Mk. (Lk.) and Mt., namely, that hardening is in one case the reason and in the other it is the result (ὅτι/ἵνα) of speaking in parables, is of little consequence, since all the Evangelists see fulfilled in Jesus' action a divine necessity established in Scripture (Mt. 13:14 f., 35; Is. 6:9 f. is also the basis of Mk. 4:12; Lk. 8:10, so that the ἵνα suggests the motif of Scripture fulfilment). The decision effected by the mode of instruction presupposes already in the people a state which makes it ripe for the judgment of hardening.[136]

The question what is the mystery (or mysteries) of the divine lordship finds no answer in the parable. But attention to the context leads to an answer. The antithesis at issue in the text implies first that the parables contain the mystery, but concealed in such sort that it may be found only by special revelation. This certainly does not mean that for those who do not understand the parables remain on the level of meaningless stories. That they are mysteries of the divine lordship is not added by the explanation but belongs essentially to the story itself.[137] The parables mediate a certain general understanding of the nature of the kingdom of God without disclosing its mystery. Obviously the interpretation, which is simply added with no artificial allegorising, does not carry any such disclosure either. The mystery of the divine rule, then, must obviously denote something which is not intimated, or intimated only very indirectly, in the parables. This can refer, not to some general content of the βασιλεία, but only to the fact of its coming. Hence the step from image to matter can be taken only by the faith which grasps the real event of this coming of the divine rule as this event is concealed in the parable but takes place with its proclamation. This view is confirmed by the fact that the phrase μυστήριον τῆς βασιλείας had long been current in apocalyptic usage to indicate the counsel of God which is concealed from human eyes, which is disclosed only by revelation, and which will be enacted at the end. If the disciples know the mysteries of the kingdom, this means that their eyes are opened to the dawn of the Messianic time (Mt. 13:16 f.). They are enabled to understand the parables of Jesus in a different way from the people, for the parables mediate

---

bring the total character of the parables of Jesus into accord with the view that the parabolic mode of instruction is a method of concealing the μυστήρια τῆς βασιλείας, i.e., with the theory of hardening. Objections have thus been raised against the authenticity of the verse, cf. Jülicher, I, 118 ff.; W. Wrede, *Das Messiasgeheimnis* (1901), 54 ff.; Bultmann Trad., 351, n. 1.

[134] Mt.: ἐκείνοις δὲ οὐ δέδοται, Lk.: τοῖς δὲ λοιποῖς ἐν παραβολαῖς (to be suppl. acc. to 10a δέδοται τὰ μυστήρια τῆς βασιλείας τοῦ θεοῦ). Cf. Jülicher, I, 127.

[135] Wrede, 56.

[136] The linking of the preaching of mysteries with the thought of judgment, i.e., the motif of election and hardening, is a distinction from typical Hell. mystagogies not noted in Windisch, 223 f.

[137] It is of little importance that the parable of the Sower does not begin: "The kingdom of God is like"; this is the exception which confirms the rule.

to them more than a general understanding of the nature of the βασιλεία; they point them to the incursion of the divine rule in the word and work of Jesus. This perception is not the result of their own perspicacity or a reward for their own achievement. It is the gift of God's free and sovereign grace. [138] The μυστήριον τῆς βασιλείας τοῦ θεοῦ which is revealed to the disciples is thus Jesus Himself as Messiah. [139] This mystery is in fact veiled by the parables, not because they are obscure or complicated, but precisely because of their simplicity — an interpretation which is demanded by the relation of the μυστήριον saying to the parable of the Sower and its explanation. For "a sower goes out to sow, no more; and this means the new world of God." [140]

2. The Mystery of Christ.

In the Pauline corpus the term μυστήριον is firmly connected with the *kerygma* of Christ. κηρύσσειν Χριστὸν ἐσταυρωμένον in 1 C. 1:23 means with reference to the community καταγγέλλειν τὸ μυστήριον τοῦ θεοῦ (2:1), [141] λαλεῖν θεοῦ σοφίαν ἐν μυστηρίῳ (2:7). Christ is the μυστήριον of God, Col. 2:2; cf. 1:27; 4:3. The section 1 C. 2:6-16, which receives its theme from the phrase quoted from 2:7, arouses at first the impression that Paul is presenting a mystery teaching which is designed only for the mature and which must be kept from the immature. This is how he actually begins in 2:6, in clear polemical dependence on the Corinthian Gnostics, whose terminology may be seen plainly throughout the section. In fact, however, Paul never abandons the λόγος τοῦ σταυροῦ which has been proclaimed to the whole community. Indeed, he is resisting the ecstatic demand of Corinthian mystery *gnosis* for a σοφία which will go beyond the message of the cross, and pointing to the wisdom of God which in this message is concealed from the world and its rulers, but revealed to those endowed with the Spirit of God. The addition ἐν μυστηρίῳ in 2:7 characterises, not the nature of the mysterious instruction of 2:6, but the σοφία of God, [142] which for its part is the divine will to save fulfilled in the crucifixion of Christ (1:24).

It is, of course, equally possible to combine ἐν μυστηρίῳ with λαλοῦμεν; [143] the phrase would then refer to the form of the instruction which is reserved for the τέλειοι and as yet inaccessible to the νήπιοι. But it should be noted that in this case 2:6 f. is a purely formal and polemical accommodation to Corinthian *gnosis*, and that for Paul the antithesis which arises with ref. to the wisdom of God is not that between mature and immature Christians, as it was for his Corinthian adversaries, but a radical and absolute antithesis between the rulers and ourselves, the spirit of the world and the Spirit of God, human wisdom and spiritual wisdom, the ψυχικοί and the πνευματικοί. Materially,

---

[138] On this sense of δέδοται cf. Mt. 13:12; 19:11 etc.

[139] Wrede, 58 f.

[140] Schn. on Mk. 4:11. On Mk. 4:11 f. cf. also J. Kögel, "Der Zweck d. Gleichnisse Jesu im Rahmen seiner Verkündigung," BFTh, 19, H. 6 (1915); C. A. Bugge, *Das Christus-mysterium* (1915); T. Arvedson, *Das Mysterium Christi, Eine Studie zu Mt. 11:25-30* (1937), 219 f.

[141] It is impossible to say for certain whether one should read μυστήριον with the Egypt. (א* AC bo syr^p etc.) or μαρτύριον with the Western (DEG vulg, but also B sa etc.). Since μαρτύριον τοῦ θεοῦ reflects 1:6, and the linking of μαρτύριον with καταγγέλλειν and τοῦ θεοῦ is unusual in the NT, μυστήριον is to be preferred.

[142] So with Lietzmann, Bachmann etc.

[143] Cf. J. Weiss, *ad loc.*

then, 2:6-16 remains within the sphere of the λόγος τοῦ σταυροῦ. It is thus misleading to seek in this section thoughts which are not included in the *kerygma* itself.[144]

Thus Paul could simply say μυστήριον for θεοῦ σοφίαν ἐν μυστηρίῳ, τὴν ἀποκεκρυμμένην. The μυστήριον is God's pre-temporal counsel which is hidden from the world but revealed to the spiritual. This has been eschatologically fulfilled in the cross of the κύριος τῆς δόξης, and it carries with it the glorification of believers. As thus used, the term displays evident dependence on the later Jewish apocalyptic concept, and distinction from that of the mystery cults and Gnosticism.

a. As μυστήριον τοῦ θεοῦ the history of the crucifixion and glorification of Jesus is removed from the grasp of worldly wisdom and characterised as a history which is prepared and fulfilled in the sphere of God. The μυστήριον, i.e., the mysterious wisdom of God, is (a) prepared before the world was (1 C. 2:7), (b) concealed from the aeons (1 C. 2:8; Eph. 3:9; Col. 1:26; R. 16:25, a later doxology), and (c) hidden in God, the Creator of all things (Eph. 3:9). The μυστήριον of the will of God (Eph. 1:9) is brought by God Himself to execution (οἰκονομία, Eph. 3:9) and manifestation. As the divine μυστήριον is fulfilled in Christ, the creation and consummation, the beginning and end of the world are comprised in Him and taken out of the sphere of their own control and apprehension. The times come to their end in the revelation of the divine mystery (Eph. 1:10).

b. The concept of μυστήριον, however, embraces not only a history which is outside the laws of cosmic occurrence and apprehension and which takes place according to God's secret counsel, but also the fact that this history is enacted in the world. In the mystery a heavenly reality breaks into the sphere of the old aeon. The κύριος τῆς δόξης dies on the cross which the rulers of the world set up. In the cross is manifested the radical antithesis between the hitherto hidden wisdom of God and the wisdom of the powers, or of the world which has fallen victim to them, to the destruction of the world and the salvation of those who believe the *kerygma* (1 C. 2:6-8). In Col. 1:27 the content of the μυστήριον is stated in the formula Χριστὸς ἐν ὑμῖν. That is to say, it consists in the indwelling of the exalted Christ in you, the Gentiles. In Eph. 3:4 ff. the mystery is the share of the Gentiles in the inheritance, in the body of the Church, in the promise in Christ. This joining of Jews and Gentiles in one body under the head Christ is a cosmic eschatological event. There takes place in it already the mystery of the comprehending of the whole created world in Christ, in whom the totality receives its head and sum (Eph. 1:9, 10).[145]

c. The mystery is not itself revelation; it is the object of revelation. This belongs constitutively to the term. It is not as though the mystery were a pre-

---

[144] As against J. Weiss, who takes the relative clause in 2:7 in this sense. Windisch, *op. cit.*, 215 distinguishes between the facts of the revelation of salvation and their interpretation, and the deeper insights connected therewith, which are reserved for the perfect.

[145] → III, 681 f. Cf. E. Käsemann, *Leib u. Leib Christi* (1933), 156 f. Since the Church composed of Jews and Gentiles is in Eph. too a cosmic eschatological entity, the fact that in Col. the μυστήριον is the eschatological Christ mystery, whereas in Eph. it is the reception of the Gentiles, is a distinction rather than a contradiction. For a different view cf. Dib. Gefbr., 64; W. Ochel, *Die Annahme einer Bearbeitung des Kol.-Briefes im Eph.-Brief* (Marb. Diss., 1934), 3.

supposition of revelation which is set aside when this takes place. Rather, revelation discloses the mystery as such. Hence the mystery of God does not disclose itself. At the appointed time it is in free grace[146] declared by God Himself to those who are selected and blessed by Him.

Hence μυστήριον is mostly used with terms for revelation: ἀποκάλυψις, R. 16:25; Eph. 3:3; ἀποκαλύπτειν, 1 C. 2:10; Eph. 3:5; γνωρίζειν, R. 16:26; Eph. 1:9; 3:3, 5; Col. 1:27; φανεροῦν, R. 16:26; Col. 1:26. The revelation of the μυστήριον takes place in the apostolic preaching (καταγγέλλειν, 1 C. 2:1; λαλεῖν, 1 C. 2:7; Col. 4:3; εὐαγγελίσασθαι, Eph. 3:8; φωτίσαι, Eph. 3:9; φανεροῦν, Col. 4:4; γνωρίζειν τὸ μυστήριον τοῦ εὐαγγελίου, Eph. 6:19; καταγγέλλειν includes both νουθετεῖν and διδάσκειν, Col. 1:28; the apostles are οἰκονόμοι μυστηρίων θεοῦ, 1 C. 4:1).

The terminological data themselves show that proclamation does not merely give information about the effected revelation of the μυστήριον of God (or Christ, Col. 2:2; 4:3) but itself belongs to the event of the μυστήριον and the occurrence of revelation. To the οἰκονομία τοῦ μυστηρίου (Eph. 3:9), to the divinely ordained execution of the hitherto concealed plan of salvation, belongs οἰκονομία as an (apostolic) office, Eph. 3:2; Col. 1:25. In the proclamation of God's Word, which is the task of the apostle as the διάκονος of the Church and the ὑπηρέτης of Christ (1 C. 4:1), the apostle fulfils the mystery of Christ which was concealed from aeons and generations but is now revealed to the saints (Col. 1:25 f.), as he also bears in his body the measure of the sufferings of Christ (Col. 1:24).

Mediation of revelation through the apostolic word leads in Eph. to a logical elevation of the grace of apostolic office which makes the apostle the bearer of ἀποκάλυψις and endows him with his own sanctity. The apostles and prophets possess a spiritual insight into the mystery of Christ which distinguishes them from the rest of the community, Eph. 3:2-6. At this point Eph., for all its dependence on Col., goes further. The statement in Col. 1:26: νῦν δὲ ἐφανερώθη τοῖς ἁγίοις αὐτοῦ, recurs in Eph. 3:5 in the more limited phrase: νῦν ἀπεκαλύφθη τοῖς ἁγίοις ἀποστόλοις αὐτοῦ καὶ προφήταις ἐν πνεύματι.[147]

In the reception of the revelation of the mystery there takes place the election of believers, whose origin is coincident with that of the divine mystery.[148] In Christ they are taken out of the old nature of distance from and hostility to God.[149] Saved by grace and awakened with Christ, as Jews and Gentiles[150] united in the Church under the head Christ, they are set in the sphere of heaven (Eph. 2:5 f.). Herewith the Church in its factual being becomes the revealer of the manifold wisdom of God for the ἀρχαί and ἐξουσίαι ἐν τοῖς ἐπουρανίοις, Eph. 3:10.[151] The fact that this takes place through the Church, and that it is said of Christ as the mystery of God ἐν ᾧ εἰσιν πάντες οἱ θησαυροὶ τῆς σοφίας

[146] Eph. 1:9: κατὰ τὴν εὐδοκίαν αὐτοῦ, cf. also R. 16:26: κατ' ἐπιταγὴν τοῦ αἰωνίου θεοῦ.

[147] Cf. Dib., *ad loc.* and esp. W. Ochel, 51 ff.; there is no reason to restrict the ἅγιοι of Col. 1:26 to the apostles. On the other side cf. E. Käsemann, 146.

[148] The πρὸ καταβολῆς κόσμου of election (Eph. 1:4) corresponds to the πρὸ τῶν αἰώνων of the mystery (1 C. 2:7; cf. Col. 1:26 f.).

[149] Eph. 2:11 ff.; 3:6.

[150] The common mention of the ἔθνη in connection with the μυστήριον (R. 16:26; Col. 1:27; Eph. 3:6, 8) shows that the pt. of their bringing into the sphere of the apostolic message is eschatological.

[151] Cf. H. Schlier, *Christus u. d. Kirche im Eph.* (1930), 6, n. 1; 56; 62.

καὶ γνώσεως ἀπόκρυφοι (Col. 2:3), is a further confirmation (cf. already 1 C. 1:18-25 and 2:6 ff.) that the original destiny of the world does not reside in itself and may not be known in and of itself.

Since the μυστήριον of God as such is disclosed in revelation, its concealment is always manifest with its proclamation. The antithesis implied in the μυστήριον is 1. the antithesis between the then and the now, R. 16:25; Eph. 3:5, 9 f.; Col. 1:26; 2. the constant antithesis between the rulers of the world and those who love God, 1 C. 2:6 ff.; and 3. the antithesis between the now and the one day. For the coming glorification of believers is only intimated in the μυστήριον. The riches of glory are already included in it, but they are still included in it, Christ being the "hope" of glory in whom the treasures of wisdom and knowledge are still concealed, Col. 2:3. Hence the revealed mystery still conceals the final consummation. The eschatological enactment is still only in word, the fulfilment of all things is as yet only through the Church, δόξα is only in the concealment of θλίψεις, Col. 1:24 f.; Eph. 3:13.

d. The transition from the hidden event to its proclamation in the term μυστήριον explains the formal use in 1 Tm. 3:9: τὸ μυστήριον τῆς πίστεως,[152] and 3:16: τὸ τῆς εὐσεβείας μυστήριον. In the first case it simply means πίστις and in the second εὐσέβεια, but the phrase derives its point from the reference to the eschatological[153] manifestation of Christ, as may be seen from the quasi-confessional hymn in 3:16.[154]

3. The General Use of μυστήριον in Paul and the Rest of the New Testament.

The term μυστήριον does not everywhere in the NT take its content from the Christ revelation, nor is it always part of the *kerygma*. But it always has an eschatological sense.

a. To penetrate the mysteries of God, the divine counsels concealed in Him, is the special spiritual gift of the prophet (1 C. 13:2). The contents of speaking in tongues are also μυστήρια (1 C. 14:2), though these are not hereby manifested, but remain ineffable divine mysteries.

In R. 11:25 Paul unfolds the final destiny of Israel as a specific mystery. In so doing Paul disclaims personal cleverness (ἵνα μὴ ἦτε ἐν ἑαυτοῖς φρόνιμοι). To his own intelligence the hardening of Israel would be either a pure enigma or a temptation to arbitrary rational conclusions. Putting the historical fact of the obduracy of Israel into the context of a μυστήριον, Paul discloses the eschatological significance of this event (ἄχρι οὗ ... σωθήσεται, 25 f.). In the present πώρωσις there is intimated in hidden form the entrance of the πλήρωμα τῶν ἐθνῶν into salvation history, and hence the final deliverance of Israel too. In respect of this proclamation Paul does not appeal to a revelation imparted to him. His interpretation is based on the fact that he sets the promise implied in the divine election of Israel in relation to what is on a human view the contradictory present

152 Cf. Dibelius, *ad loc.*

153 Cf. v. Soden, 194 f.

154 The two elements of meaning in μυστήριον, both mysterious event and declaration of this event, make possible the textual variation in 3:16, where for the ὅς of G Western witnesses have ὅ (vg: *magnum est pietatis sacramentum, quod* ...). In the first case the confessional hymn itself is the content of the μυστήριον, in the second the occurrence of revelation.

(κατὰ μὲν τὸ εὐαγγέλιον ἐχθροὶ δι' ὑμᾶς, κατὰ δὲ τὴν ἐκλογὴν ἀγαπητοὶ διὰ τοὺς πατέρας, 28 f.), and he is thus able to see the eschatological meaning of what takes place here and now. To this μυστήριον in its full inaccessibility to human investigation or perception applies the exclamation in 11:33 ff.: ὦ βάθος πλούτου κτλ.

Another specific mystery is what Paul tells the Corinthians about the change which will overtake Christians still alive at the *parousia*, 1 C. 15:51. He does not tell us whence he derived this apocalyptic insight. He simply calls it a μυστήριον, and says of the coming event that it is enclosed in God's counsel and will be fulfilled with divine necessity in a way which is beyond human calculation or comprehension.

b. In Eph. 5:32, after the quotation (5:31) of the saying about marriage in Gn. 2:24, there comes the statement: τὸ μυστήριον τοῦτο μέγα ἐστίν, ἐγὼ δὲ λέγω εἰς Χριστὸν καὶ εἰς τὴν ἐκκλησίαν. Since an exhortatory conclusion regarding marital life is drawn from the text and its exposition, μυστήριον refers to the text and not to the institution of marriage itself. The μυστήριον is thus the allegorical meaning of the OT saying, its mysteriously concealed prophecy of the relation of Christ to the ἐκκλησία. One should not overlook the link with the other μυστήριον verses in Eph. Eph. 5:32 is valid because the eschatological mystery of Christ and the Church is mysteriously pre-figured in Gn. 2:24. The interpretation introduced by ἐγὼ δὲ λέγω is in express opposition to other interpretations which also find a μυστήριον in the text but differ from Eph. in exposition. Opponents have been sought among champions of a Gnostic syzygy teaching.[155]

c. The passages still remaining all have apocalyptic significance. In 2 Th. 2:3 ff. the successive phases of the last events preceding the *parousia* are revealed: apostasy, and the manifestation of Antichrist (ὁ ἄνθρωπος τῆς ἀνομίας, ὁ υἱὸς τῆς ἀπωλείας), 2:3 f. The time of apostasy is mysteriously described in 2:7: τὸ γὰρ μυστήριον ἤδη ἐνεργεῖται τῆς ἀνομίας, "for the mystery of iniquity is already at work."[156] This is the eschatological mark of the present, that in it, in hidden yet no less effective fashion, the ἄνομος or Antichrist is manifested. As yet he is restrained only by the κατέχων but this will soon be set aside, and then he will be fully revealed until the Lord destroys him at His appearing. There is thus allusion to the mystery of iniquity in relation to the imminent revelation of the ἄνομος (2:6-8). In so far as the work of the Antichrist is already seen to be a μυστήριον, he is disclosed as a power which hastens not only towards its full manifestation but also towards its destruction by the κύριος.

Rev. 17:5, 7 speaks similarly of the μυστήριον of the harlot Babylon. The name on her forehead is Babylon the great, the mother of harlots and the abomination of the earth. This is her μυστήριον (17:5), i.e., the hidden significance of her appearing. Her name holds the mystery of her power. But the disclosure of her secret by the angel (17:7) makes it clear that the beast and the woman are delivered up to destruction, that they are already condemned to annihilation (17:8). Here then, with the disclosure of the hidden meaning of Satanic power, the

---

[155] Cf. v. Soden, 194; Dibelius, *ad loc.*; H. Schlier, ThBl (1927), 12 n.; *Christus u. d. Kirche im Eph.* (1930), 65 f.

[156] A historical interpretation is misleading and is not required by the text. Cf. Dibelius, 2 Th. Exc. on 2:10.

present manifestation is understood in terms of the future which destroys it. Since the power of Antichrist possesses a μυστήριον, it enjoys present power. But this μυστήριον also indicates that its doom is sealed.[157]

One can thus speak of the μυστήριον of anti-godly powers only because the μυστήριον of God, the hidden eschatological plan of God declared to His servants and prophets, moves to its fulfilment. This fulfilment of the divine μυστήριον is proleptically invoked already in 10:7; with it the time ends. In the light of this fulfilment the divine, who is summoned to write what he saw, what is, and what shall be hereafter (1:19; cf. Da. 2:28 f., 45), receives the interpretation of the seven stars which the one like unto the Son of Man holds in His right hand (1:16, 20). They contain a hidden sense; Christ, who is even now surrounded by His churches and who holds the symbol of dominion, will be the Lord of a new world.[158]

The use of μυστήριον in the NT never allows us to think in terms of a secret discipline.[159] Nowhere is there any accompanying warning against profanation of the mysteries.

In sum, μυστήριον is a rare expression in the NT which betrays no relation to the mystery cults. Where there seem to be connections (e.g., in sacramental passages), the term is not used; where it is used, there are no such connections. In spite of certain analogies, there are thus serious objections against bringing Jesus or Paul under the category of the mystagogue.[160]

D. μυστήριον in the Early Church.

1. The Post-Apostolic Fathers. Here μυστήριον is rare. It occurs 3 times in Ign., once in the Didache. There is allusion to 1 C. 2:6 ff. (→ 819) in Ign. Eph., 19, 1, where the virginity of Mary, her conceiving, and the death of the Lord are brought together as τρία μυστήρια κραυγῆς, ἅτινα ἐν ἡσυχίᾳ θεοῦ ἐπράχθη; they were concealed from the prince of this world. As the whole of c. 19 may be explained in terms of the Gnostic myth of the secret descent and victorious ascension of the Redeemer, to the terror and destruction of the powers,[161] so, too, may the phrase μυστήρια κραυγῆς. It denotes the arrangements for salvation which were secretly prepared in heaven and then openly revealed.[162] The death and resurrection of Christ are also a μυστήριον in Mg., 9, 1. In Ign. Tr., 2, 3 the deacons (a designation of office) are διάκονοι μυστηρίων Ἰησοῦ Χριστοῦ. There is here an echo of 1 C. 4:1, though with no ref. to the proclamation of the Word. Since Ign. has in view the table service of the διάκονοι, one might suspect in μυστήρια Ἰησοῦ Χριστοῦ an allusion to the Eucharist. But this would be an isolated ref. and it is not demanded by the context. The par. description of the deacons as ἐκκλησίας θεοῦ ὑπηρέται suggest that what Ign. really has in view are the mysteries of Christ to be set forth in the Church.[163] Even though sacramental action is important here, this does not mean that the rites are themselves called μυστήρια.

Did., 11, 11 is difficult. The approved prophet ποιῶν εἰς μυστήριον κοσμικὸν ἐκκλησίας ("who in his action has in view the earthly mystery of the Church"), μὴ διδάσκων δὲ ποιεῖν ὅσα αὐτὸς ποιεῖ, is not subject to the judgment of the com-

---

157 Cf. G. Bornkamm, ZNW, 36 (1937), 138 f.

158 Cf. Lohmeyer, Behm, *ad loc.*

159 Though cf. J. Jeremias, *D. Abendmahlsworte Jesu* (1935), 55 f.

160 So Windisch, 215 ff.

161 Cf. H. Schlier, *Religionsgesch. Unters. zu d. Ignatiusbriefen* (1929), 5 ff.

162 ἡσυχία is a Gnostic tt. for the pleroma, κραυγή the eschatological shout which announces the end of the world, cf. Schlier, 27 f.

163 Ign. Tr., 2, 3: οὐ γὰρ βρωμάτων καὶ ποτῶν εἰσὶν διάκονοι.

munity. What is probably meant is the spiritual marriage of a prophet who allegorically represents in an earthly copy the heavenly mystery of the marriage between Christ and the Church (Eph. 5:32).[164, 165]

2. Apologetic. From the time of early apologetic the term acquires increasing importance. At first used unreflectingly and occasionally, in the struggle with Gnosticism and the mystery religions it comes to be a central concept. The most important uses are as follows.[166]

a. It is naturally used quite often for the mystery cults, Just. Apol., I, 25, 27, 54, 66; II, 12; Tat. Or. Graec., 29; Athenag. Suppl., 28; Hipp. Ref., V, 7, 22 (84, 3); Tert. Praescr. Haer., 40 etc.; also for the secret teachings of the Gnostics, Iren.[167] Praef. (Harvey, 4); Hipp. Ref. Praef., 1 (1, 19 f.); Tert. De anima, 18 etc.

b. Fig. applied to Christianity, it is used in various ways: (a) for the basic facts of salvation, esp. the birth and crucifixion of Christ, Just. Apol., I, 13; Dial., 74, 91 etc.;[168] (b) for OT figures and events with typological significance. Acc. to Just. Dial., 44 the OT, when not a simple direction to true worship and right conduct, is appointed εἰς μυστήριον τοῦ Χριστοῦ, i.e., as a veiled prophecy of Christ.[169] μυστήριον in this sense is a synon. of παραβολή, σύμβολον, τύπος.[170] Thus the outstretched arms of Moses (Ex. 17:11 f.), the name Joshua (Just. Dial., 111), the 8th day of circumcision (*ibid.*, 24), the slaying of the Passover lamb (40), having allegorical significance, are μυστήρια[171] inasmuch as they reflect the mysteries of the Logos.[172]

3. Alexandrian Theology. Alexandrian theology adopts the Gk., or more precisely the Gnostic-Neo-Platonic mystery concept, and it thus regards the truths of the Christian religion as mysteries. Led by Christ the Mystagogue,[173] the Gnostic receives initiation and perfection[174] by going through the stages from the little mysteries (e.g., the doctrine of creation) to the great mysteries, in which the mystical initiation takes place.[175] The supreme mysteries, to be protected against profanation, must be passed on only in veiled form,[176] just as Scripture offers them only in parable and enigma.[177]

---

164 The Gnostics mentioned in Iren., 1, 6, 4, who zealously cultivate sexual intercourse, also think they are conforming to the μυστήριον of the heavenly syzygy.

165 This interpretation is to be preferred to that which suggests symbolical actions after the manner of the prophetic signs of the OT. The context suggests that what is done might be regarded as embarrassing and suspicious in the community. Cf. Harnack, TU, II, 1. 2 (1884), 44 ff.; also P. Drews in *Hndbch. z. d. nt.lichen Apokr.* (1904), 274 ff.; H. Weinel, *Die Wirkungen d. Geistes u. d. Geister* (1899), 131 ff.; R. Knopf, *Hndbch. z. d. NT*, Suppl. 2 (1920), *ad loc.*; H. Schlier, *Christus u. d. Kirche im Eph.* (1930), 68 f.

166 Since μυστήριον and *sacramentum* are equivalents (→ D. 5), some Lat. refs. are included.

167 Iren. mostly uses the word in anti-Gnostic polemic.

168 Cf. also Prot. Ev. Jc., 12, 3; Melito of Sardis Fr., 13 (Otto).

169 Cf. also Just. Dial., 78.

170 v. Soden, 202.

171 Cf. Tert. Marc., 2, 27: *totum denique dei mei penes vos dedecus sacramentum est humanae salutis.* For other instances cf. v. Soden, 208 f.

172 Hipp. De Antichristo, 2.

173 Cl. Al. Strom., IV, 162, 3 etc.

174 Cl. Al. Prot., XII, 120, 1: ὢ τῶν ἁγίων ὡς ἀληθῶς μυστηρίων ... ἅγιος γίνομαι μυούμενος, ἱεροφαντεῖ δὲ ὁ κύριος καὶ τὸν μύστην σφραγίζεται φωταγωγῶν, καὶ παρατίθεται τῷ πατρὶ τὸν πεπιστευκότα αἰῶσι τηρούμενον, ταῦτα τῶν ἐμῶν μυστηρίων βακχεύματα.

175 Cl. Al. Strom., IV, 3, 1. Cf. esp. c. 12 of the Protr.

176 Strom., V, 57, 2 reproduces literally a command of silence found in Iambl. Vit. Pyth., 17, 75 except that we have τὰ τοῦ λόγου μυστήρια for τὰ ταῖν Ἐλευσινίαιν θεαῖν μυστήρια. Cf. Anrich, 135, n. 1.

177 Cl. Al. Strom., VI, 124, 6; Orig. Cels., 7, 10.

Thus Origen, in a characteristic example, teaches that only he who undergoes preparatory purification in Proverbs and Ecclesiastes is led by the Spirit into the hidden truths of Canticles, namely, the mysteries of union with the heavenly Logos and knowledge of the Trinity.[178]

In the later Church dogma can sometimes be called μυστήριον, since it can never be fully disclosed to the understanding even of the believer, and it is profaned by discussion or heretical attack.[179] A dubious result of this conception of dogma is the separation of the mystery from the *kerygma*, with which it is always firmly connected by Paul.[180]

4. μυστήριον as a Term for the Sacraments. The original cultic concept of mystery found rejuvenation in the early Church when μυστήριον became a fixed term for the sacraments. Already Just.[181] and Tert.[182] can compare the pagan mysteries with the Christian sacraments, though the former does not call the Christian rites μυστήρια, and the latter does not call the pagan rites *sacramenta*.[183] The pagan mysteries are for them a devilish imitation of the Christian sacraments. For all the passionate polemicising, the same basic idea is seen in both, though the content differs. As the pagan mysteries actualise the destinies and acts of their gods in sacred actions, and thus give participants a share in them, so in the symbolical[184] ritual of the Christian sacraments there takes place a cultic repetition and re-presentation of the historically unrepeatable redeeming act of Christ.[185] In this sense Cyprian (Ep., 63, 14) calls the Eucharist *dominicae passionis et nostrae redemptionis sacramentum* (= μυστήριον). The action of Christ's self-sacrifice is cultically repeated, in symbolical concealment, in the eucharistic offering. Terminologically, this understanding comes to be fixed only in the 4th cent. μυστήριον now becomes a term for baptism and the Lord's Supper, and we also find a host of mystery terms: μυστικός, μύησις, μύστης, μυεῖν, τελετή, τελειοῦν, τελεῖν, ἐπιτελεῖν, παράδοσις, *repraesentare, ostendere, imitari,* ἅγια, ἱερά, ἀπόρρητα, φρικτά in connection with the μυστήρια.[186]

The nature of the relation between the saving acts and the cultic representation is brought out particularly well by the fact that both are called μυστήριον. "The Lord and Saviour Himself, and the priests who go out from Him ... present in veiled form in the bread and wine the mysteries of His body and saving blood (τοῦ τε σώματος αὐτοῦ καὶ τοῦ σωτηρίου αἵματος αἰνίττονται μυστήρια).[187] Remembrance of His sacrifice takes place κατὰ τὰ πρὸς αὐτοῦ παραδοθέντα μυστήρια.[188] Greg. Naz., 2, 95 calls the Eucharist τὴν τῶν μεγάλων μυστηρίων ἀντίτυπον. But these mysteries of Christ embrace, not merely His passion and resurrection, but also His epiphany in the flesh and His enthronement. Recollection of these is concentrated in the mass[189]

---

178 Hom. on Cant. = GCS, 33: Orig., 8 (1925), 76, 7 ff.; cf. A. Lieske, *Die Theologie d. Logosmystik bei Orig.* (1938), 24 ff., 45 ff.; W. Völker, *Das Vollkommenheitsideal des Origenes* (1931), 91 ff.

179 Chrys. on 1 C. 7:2 (MPG, 61, 56); cf. Anrich, 150 ff. for other examples.

180 Bas. Spir. Sct., 27, 66 (MPG, 32, 189): ... ἄλλο γὰρ δόγμα καὶ ἄλλο κήρυγμα. τὸ μὲν γὰρ σιωπᾶται, τὰ δὲ κηρύγματα δημοσιεύεται. Hom. Chrys. spur. in incarn. Dom. (MPG, 59, 687): πᾶν δὲ περὶ Χριστοῦ λεγόμενον οὐκ ἔστιν ἁπλοῦν κήρυγμα, ἀλλ' εὐσεβείας μυστήριον (quoted in Anrich, 153 n., 154 n. 4).

181 Apol., I, 66.

182 Praescr. Haer., 40; Bapt., 2.

183 → n. 199.

184 σύμβολον always having the sense of a *signum efficax*.

185 Cf. O. Casel on this significance of the cultic action, esp. *Jahrb. f. Liturgiewissenschaft*, 6 (1926), 113 ff.; *ibid.*, 13 (1935), 109 ff.

186 Cf. Anrich, 155 ff., and Casel, *passim*. The Church's *arcana disciplina* is now developed after the model of the mystery cults.

187 Eus. Dem. Ev., V, 3, 19.

188 *Ibid.*, I, 10, 38.

189 Cf. Casel, *Jahrb. f. Lit.*, 6, 116 ff.

and reflected in the calendar of feasts.[190] By cultic celebration of the mysteries believers are taken up into the event of redemption. Where the Church fulfils the sacramental action, Christ Himself is present.[191] Of many examples cf. Ambr. De Sacramento, 2, 2, 6: "Whence might baptism be if not from the cross of Christ, from the death of Christ? Herein is the whole mystery (*ibi est omne mysterium*) that He suffered for thee. In him thou art redeemed and saved"; Aug. Civ. D., 10, 20 on Christ as both Sacrificer and Sacrifice: *cuius rei sacramentum* (sacramental representation) *cottidianum esse voluit ecclesiae sacrificium.* Whereas His sacrifice was promised only fig. in the old covenant, the *sacramentum memoriae* (Faust., 20, 21) contains within it the reality of His sacrifice, not merely as the gift, but as the act of salvation symbolically represented in the sacramental action.[192]

5. μυστήριον and *sacramentum.* In the Lat. Bible *sacramentum* is at the outset the usual word for μυστήριον. With trifling exceptions this is so in the African text,[193] and there are many instances in the Itala[194] along with *mysterium,* which becomes predominant in the Vulg. Where the renderings are mixed, no material motivation can be discerned.[195] The meaning of *sacramentum* is wholly co-extensive with that of the Gk. word.

Since *sacramentum* is a tt. for the soldier's oath, the question arises how it could become a transl. of μυστήριον. The possibility is created by both the Lat. and the Gk. terms. Taking an oath has originally the character of an initiation, a *devotio* to beings under the earth. It is an *occultum sacrum,*[196] in which there is no place for the unworthy, like the state-persecuted followers of the Bacchus mysteries.[197] The mystery rites also help inasmuch as initiation often entailed an oath, and the view that the ministry of initiates was a *sancta militia* must have been fairly widespread.[198] Originally, then, *sacramentum* is an initiatory act and means much the same as μυστήριον. The terms first become full equivalents only in Christian texts, since the Romans conscripted *sacramentum* for military use. Tert. and some later writers applied the military use to the Christian concept of the *sacramentum.* The content in this case is the rule of faith to which the Christian is engaged at baptism. By this application of *sacramentum* to the contents of faith Tert. is able to differentiate once again between μυστήριον and *sacramentum,* and to ascribe to the pagan *mysteria idolorum* only the *res sacramentorum,* i.e., not in this case the true character of a sacrament.[199] This distinction on the basis of the military image is found again only in Cyprian, Arnobius and occasionally Ambr., and it fades out completely after the 4th cent.[200]

---

190 Greg. Naz. (MPG, 36, 136): πᾶσαί μοι πανηγύρεις καθ' ἕκαστον τῶν τοῦ Χριστοῦ μυστηρίων.

191 Ambr. De Mysteriis § 27: *ubi est ecclesia, ubi mysteria sua sunt, ibi dignatur suam impertire praesentiam.*

192 Aug. Ep., 55; cf. Casel, *op. cit.,* 162 ff.

193 Cf. v. Soden, 225 f.

194 For examples cf. Casel, *Jahrb. f. Liturgiewissenschaft,* 8 (1928), 230 f.

195 Cf. the promiscuous use in Eph. and Col. in the Vulg.

196 Cf. Liv., 10, 41; 38 f.; Herodian., 8, 7, 8: τὸν στρατιωτικὸν ὅρκον, ὅς ἐστιν τῆς Ῥωμαίων ἀρχῆς σεμνὸν μυστήριον.

197 Liv., 39, 15.

198 Cf. Apul. Met., 11, 15. On this cf. Reitzenstein Hell. Myst., 192 ff.

199 In Nat., 1, 16 he expressly calls them *non sacramenta.*

200 J. Huhn, *D. Bedeutung des Wortes* sacramentum *bei dem Kirchenvater Ambrosius* (1928), 9 f.; Casel, *Jahrb.,* 8 (1928), 226 ff.

† μυέω.

A cultic tt. "to initiate into the mysteries" (mostly pass. "to be initiated"), from Heracl. Fr., 14, I, 154, Diels[5]; Hdt., 2, 51; 8, 65; Aristoph. Ra., 158, 456 etc.; Ditt. Or., 530, 15; 764, 12 etc. In the LXX 3 Macc. 2:30: ἐν τοῖς κατὰ τὰς τελετὰς μεμυημένοις ἀναστρέφεσθαι (Σ Nu. 25:5); fig., esp. political, Plut., II, 795e. Also gen. "to be instructed in" followed by inf., e.g., Alciphr., III, 19, 4; Anth. Pal., 7, 385.

It occurs in the NT only at Phil. 4:12: ἐν παντὶ καὶ ἐν πᾶσιν μεμύημαι, καὶ χορτάζεσθαι καὶ πεινᾶν, καὶ περισσεύειν καὶ ὑστερεῖσθαι. It is hard to decide whether here there is an echo of the mysteries or a general use ("in each and everything I know," cf. v. 11).[1] If the former is more likely, since the term is predominantly cultic, then the expression is ironical. The concrete stresses and gifts of daily life are the place where Paul undergoes the mysteries, i.e., experiences the power of Christ.[2]

Bornkamm

μυέω. [1] Cf. the comm. One can hardly say that the term denotes more specifically the situation of the martyr (Loh., *ad loc.*).

[2] Cf. H. Windisch, "Paulus u. Christus," UNT, 24 (1934), 217 f.

† μώλωψ

There is an etym. connection with μολύνω and μέλας, and the word is esp. common among physicians for "weal" or "welt," Hyperides in Poll. Onom., III, 79; Aristot. Probl., IX, 1, p. 889b, 10; Daphitas in Strabo, XIV, 1, 39, p. 647; Macho in Athen., XIII, 43, 28 (580a); Dion. Hal. Ant. Rom., XVI, 5, 2; Plut. Ser. Num. Pun., 25 (II, 565b); Hesych., *s.v.*: ὁ ἐκ τῆς πληγῆς αἱματώδης τύπος. ἔναιμον ἄλγος θλασθέντος τοῦ σώματος ἐκ τῆς ἀντιτυπίας τοῦ πλήξαντος; also "swelling" from a sting, Aetius Amidenus, 5, 129 (ed. Venet, 1534, p. 96, verso line 6). The verb μωλωπίζω and adj. μωλωπικός do not occur in the NT.[1] It is used in the LXX for חַבּוּרָה at Gn. 4:23; Ex. 21:25 (*lex talionis*); Sir. 23:10 (beating of slaves); 28:17 (result of whipping); Is. 53:5 (of the Ebed Yahweh); 1:6; ψ 37:5 (fig. for human guilt); Jdt. 9:13 (fig. for the overthrow of enemies).

The only NT instance is at 1 Pt. 2:24 quoting Is. 53:5[2] in discussion of slavery (→ δοῦλος, II, 272 ff.). When a Christian slave is unjustly beaten he should remember that paradoxically the blows which the δοῦλος Christ suffered accomplished the world's salvation. This does not justify unjust beating, but leaves the judgment thereof to God alone (v. 23).[3] → μαστιγόω.

Carl Schneider

μῶμος, ἄμωμος, ἀμώμητος

† μῶμος.

μῶμος is the "censure" which derives from ill-will towards another, whether on the ground of his deficiency or of one's own censoriousness. In context it has the sense of

---

μ ώ λ ω ψ. Pr.-Bauer, 837, [3]879; Liddell-Scott, 1158; Wilke-Grimm, 292.

[1] Though cf. Cant. 5:7 (᾿Α).

[2] Is. 53:5 is also quoted in 1 Cl., 16, 5; Barn., 5, 2. Cf. K. F. Euler, *Die Verkündigung vom leidenden Gottesknecht aus Js. 53 in der gr. Bibel* (1934), 114. On Is. 53:5 cf. Prv. 20:30: Mas. "Bloody stripes cleanse away evil," ᾿Α: μώλωπες τραυμάτων, Σ: τραῦμα μώλωπος, LXX: ὑπώπια καὶ συντρίμματα συναντᾷ κακοῖς [Bertram].

[3] On the beating of slaves cf. the bibl. under → δοῦλος, also H. Wallon, *Histoire de l'esclavage*[2], II (1879), 277 ff.; E. Meyer, "Die Sklaverei im Altertum," *Kl. Schriften*, I (1910), 169 ff.; W. Soltau, "Humanität u. Christentum in ihren Beziehungen zur Sklaverei," *N. Jbch. Kl. Alt.* (1908), 335 ff. Even female slaves were whipped frequently, Herond. Mim., V; Juv., VI, 219 ff. etc., but it was also regarded as a sign of poor breeding and uneducated cruelty to beat slaves needlessly, Horat. Serm., II, 2, 66 ff.; Sen. Ep., V, 6, 1. For an illustr. cf. the Berlin terracotta from Priene, T. Wiegand-H. Schrader, *Priene* (1904), 358, Ill. 436 f.

μ ῶ μ ο ς. J. H. H. Schmidt, *Synonymik d. gr. Sprache*, III (1879), 458 f.; Trench (1906), 354 ff.

"reproach," "contempt," "scorn," "insult," or "ignominy,"[1] cf. Gorg. Hel., 1 (II, 288, Diels[5]): χρὴ τὸ μὲν ἄξιον ἐπαίνου ἐπαίνῳ τιμᾶν, τῷ δὲ ἀναξίῳ μῶμον ἐπιτιθέναι. Hom. Od., 2, 86; 6, 273 f.; Soph. Fr., 235, Nauck: μῶμον ἅπτεσθαι, "to cast a slur on someone"; Semonides of Amorgos, 7, 105 (I, 252, Diehl[2]): of a bad wife: εὑροῦσα μῶμον (sc. on the husband) ἐς μάχην κορύσσεται. Test. L. 9:10: λαβὲ οὖν σεαυτῷ γυναῖκα, ἔτι νέος ὤν, μὴ ἔχουσαν μῶμον μήτε βεβηλωμένην μήτε ἀπὸ γένους ἀλλοφύλων ἐθνῶν.

In the LXX it is used a. in the class. sense of "reproach," "ignominy," Sir. 11:33 (μήποτε μῶμον [מום] ... δῷ σοι, "to cast a reproach"); 18:15; 20:24 (μῶμος πονηρὸς ἐν ἀνθρώπῳ ψεῦδος); 47:20 (ἔδωκας μῶμον [מום] ἐν τῇ δόξῃ σου); often with ref. to physical blemishes, 2 Βασ. 14:25; Da. 1:4; Cant. 4:7. These verses border on the second use b., in which the LXX translators, because of the affinity of sound, choose μῶμος for the Heb. מְאוּם, מוּם, which first means concretely and objectively a "blemish" or "physical defect" (Lv. 24:19 f.) and only secondly a "moral flaw or fault." In the LXX, then, μῶμος takes on the first sense and becomes something which it is not in class. Gk., namely, an important cultic term. Freedom from physical blemish is a cultic demand in the priest (Lv. 21:16 ff.) and the offering (Lv. 22:20; Dt. 15:21 → ἄμωμος).

Philo uses the word accordingly when speaking both of the cultic perfection of sacrifices[2] and also of moral perfection.[3]

In the NT the word occurs only at 2 Pt. 2:13 where it is used in the objective and concrete LXX sense of false teachers who by reason of their moral libertinism are felt to be "defacing blemishes" (alongside σπίλοι) in the sacred table fellowship of believers.

† ἄμωμος.

"One who is without reproach," "blameless," either physically (κάλλει τ' ἀμώμω, Aesch. Pers., 185) or morally (νόμος, Hdt., II, 177); used thus on burial inscr.[1]

In the LXX it is almost always the rendering of תָּמִים and thus signifies "religious and moral blamelessness." It carries the greater weight inasmuch as it has to stand in God's judgment, though we find traces of the naïver view that this blamelessness is possible, 2 Βασ. 22:24; ψ 14:2; 36:18; Prv. 11:5; 20:7. The supreme use is for the absolute blamelessness of God Himself (2 Βασ. 22:31) and of the things of God (ψ 17:30: His way; 18:7: His law). In the LXX, however, ἄμωμος is most commonly used by far for physical perfection as a presupposition of cultic use, e.g., of the offering — a use alien to class. Gk. (→ μῶμος)[2] — in, e.g., Ex. 29:1; Lv. 1:3; 4:3; 5:15; Ez. 43:22 f., or the

---

[1] Μῶμος personified is the god of reproach and blame, cf. Suid., *s.v.*: Ἑρμείας: ἦν τὰ δὲ πρὸς ἀρετὴν εὖ ἠσκημένος. ὥστε μηδ' ἂν τὸν Μῶμον αὐτὸν ἐπιμωμήσασθαι μηδ' αὖ τὸν φθόνον μισῆσαι, τοσαύτη πρᾳότης ἐνῆν τῷ ἀνδρὶ καὶ τοιαύτη δικαιοσύνη. μῶμος is linguistically related to μῶκος (cf. Walde-Pok., II, 249).

[2] Spec. Leg., I, 166: [ζῷα] μώμων ἀμέτοχα; I, 259; acc. to Philo μωμοσκόποι were appointed among the priests for this purpose, Agric., 130; cf. Cl. Al. Strom., IV, 18, 117, 4.

[3] Leg. All., III, 141: ὅλην γὰρ τὴν ψυχὴν ἀξίαν οὖσαν θεῷ προσάγεσθαι διὰ τὸ μηδένα ἔχειν μήθ' ἑκούσιον μητ' ἀκούσιον μῶμον ὁ σοφὸς καθαγιάζει. Mut. Nom., 60.

ἄμωμος. Trench (1906), 355: "ἄμωμος is thus the 'unblemished,' ἄμεμπτος ... the 'unblamed.'"

[1] CIG, II, 1974: Λαΐδι ἀμώμῳ μνήμης χάριν. APF, 1, 220: δικνὺς σέλας αἰὲν ἄμωμον. Cf. Moult.-Mill., *s.v.*; Preisigke Sammelbuch, 625: Βεροττᾶτος ἀψόγου καὶ ἀμώμου.

[2] The usual terms are ὁλόκληρος, τέλειος etc., cf. Poll. Onom., I, 29; Aristot. in Athen., XV (p. 674 f.); Ditt. Syll.[3], 993, 12; 672, 49 f.; P. Stengel, "Gr. Kultusaltertümer," *Hndbch. Kl. AW*, V, 3 (1920), 121.

priest who is qualified to perform the most sacred actions by his most stringent fulfilment of the Law, 1 Macc. 4:42.

In Philo, too, it is used both of the cultic perfection of the offering [3] and of the blamelessness of the righteous before God. [4] In a further spiritualising of the cultic concept the virtues themselves are described by Philo as ἄμωμα καὶ πρεπωδέστατα ἱερεῖα. [5]

In the NT ἄμωμος is used of the perfect moral and religious piety of Christians to which believers are obligated by membership of the holy community of the last time, Eph. 1:4 (with ἅγιος); 5:27 (of the ἐκκλησία); Phil. 2:15 (opp. γενεὰ σκολιά, cf. Dt. 32:5); Col. 1:22 (with ἅγιος, ἀνέγκλητος); Jd. 24 (with ἄπταιστος); Rev. 14:5 (ἀπαρχὴ τῷ θεῷ). The point is always that Christians must manifest this blamelessness before the judgment of God and of Christ. The orientation is thus religious and eschatological.

The image of sacrifices without blemish is used in 1 Pt. 1:19 (ὡς ἀμνοῦ ἀμώμου καὶ ἀσπίλου) and Hb. 9:14 (ἑαυτὸν προσήνεγκεν ἄμωμον τῷ θεῷ). But in both cases, in accordance with the total character of NT religion, the statement is on the moral and religious plane rather than the ritual and cultic. The OT demand that sacrifices be without physical blemish finds its NT fulfilment in the perfect moral blamelessness (Hb. 4:15; 7:26) of the Redeemer who sacrifices Himself.

† ἀμώμητος.

"Blameless," "without reproach," Hom. Il., 12, 109 (of a hero), used on burial inscr. (CIG, III, 4642; Preisigke Sammelbuch, 332 of a three-year old child [ἀμ]ώμητε, εὐψύχ[ε]ι); Ep. Ar., 93 (of an offering); Philo Aet. Mund., 41 (of the work of God); in glorifying address to God, 8th Book of Moses in A. Dieterich, *Abraxas* (1891), 177, 8 f.: κύριε, ἀμώμητος, ὁ μηδένα τόπον μιαίνων, also Apocr. Moses, P. Leid., W 3a, 3 : ἧκε, κύριε ἀμώμητος καὶ ἀπήμαντος.

The only NT use is at 2 Pt. 3:14 for the blamelessness of believers (along with ἄσπιλοι) in the divine judgment. [1]

Hauck

---

[3] Leg. All., I, 50 : τὰ δὲ ἄμωμα τῷ θεῷ προσάγεται.
[4] Mut. Nom., 60.
[5] Sacr. AC, 51; H. Wenschkewitz, *D. Spiritualisierung d. Kultbegriffe* (1932), 81.

ἀ μ ώ μ η τ ο ς. [1] Phil. 2:15 vl. D𝔎G instead of ἄμωμα; along with ἄμεμπτοι and ἀκέραιοι.

† μωρός, † μωραίνω, † μωρία, † μωρολογία

Contents: A. μωρός κτλ. in Classical Greek. B. μωρός and Cognates in the Greek OT and the Corresponding Hebrew Originals. C. μωρός κτλ. in Philo. D. The Concept of Folly in the New Testament: 1. The Salt of Mt. 5:13; Lk. 14:34; 2. "Fool" as an Insult: 3. The "Fool" in Parables; 4. Foolish Words and Thoughts: Eph. 5:4; 2 Tm. 2:23; Tt. 3:9; 5. "Folly" in Paul: R. 1:22; 1 C. 1:18 ff.; 2:14; 3:18, 19; 4:10.

A. μωρός κτλ. in Classical Greek.

μωρός is related to the Sanskr. *mūras* ("dull-witted") and the Indo-European root mō[u]ro-, mūro-. We also find the Attic μῶρος.[1] The Lat. *morus,* "foolish," "absurd," derives from the Gk.[2] Etym. explanations in terms of the Gk. alone, such as we find in Eustathius and even up to the 19th cent., are scientifically untenable. μωρός has nothing to do with either μὴ ὁρᾶν or μὴ ὤρα (= φροντίς, ὁ μηδὲν φροντίζων). Nor is it a loan word from the Heb. מרה, as older lexicographers argued at least in the case of biblical Gk.[3] The Rabbis, indeed, took it over from the Gk.[4] μωρός and cognates denote a physical or intellectual deficiency in animals or men, in their conduct and actions, also in things. The word can refer to physical sloth or dullness, but its main ref. is to the intellectual life.

It takes on various meanings in different contexts. Thus it can mean "insipid" of insufficiently seasoned foods. The lexicographer Photius bears witness to this, and the use occurs in doctors and comedians. Thus Dioscurides Medicus, who was a contemporary of Paul and also from Cilicia, speaks of insipid roots (ῥίζαι γευσαμένῳ μωραί, Mat. Med., IV, 19). There is a similar use in an unknown comedian, Comica Adespota, 596.[5] Elsewhere in medicine it is used of the slackness, fatigue or dulling of the nerves, Hippocr. De Genitura, 2 (VII, 472, Littre). It is also used in respect of the sluggishness of animals in winter, Aristot. Hist. An., IX, 41, p. 628a, of wasps: χειμῶνος ἀρχομένου μωροὶ γίνονται οἱ ἐργάται [τῶν σφηκῶν]. A strong or unexpected impression on animals stupefies them; for this Aristot. Hist. An., IX, 3, p. 610b, 30 has the verb: [αἶγες] ἑστᾶσιν ὥσπερ μεμωραμέναι.[6] With ref. to men the use is predominantly psychological. The word implies censure on man himself; his acts, thoughts, counsels, and words are not as they should be. The weakness may be due to a specific failure in judgment or decision, but a general deficiency of intellectual and spiritual capacities may also be asserted.

The charge of folly does not have to be a definitive judgment. In many cases it is more in the nature of an admonition or warning, or it expresses the impossibility of understanding or following the thinking or acts of someone. Thus we read in Soph. Ai., 594: μῶρά μοι δοκεῖς φρονεῖν, εἰ τοὐμὸν ἦθος ἄρτι παιδεύειν νοεῖς (cf. also

---

μωρός κτλ. W. Caspari, "Über den biblischen Begriff d. Torheit," NkZ, 39 (1928), 668-695; K. H. J. Fahlgren, *Sᵉdaka, nahestehende u. entgegengesetzte Begriffe im AT* (1932), 28-32.

[1] Bl.-Debr.[6] § 13.

[2] Walde-Pok., II, 303.

[3] Cf. P. Mintert, *Lexicon Graeco-Latinum* (1728), *s.v.*: *ab* Hebr. מוֹרָה *cuius radix est* מָרָה *rebellis fuit.*

[4] → 840, 17 ff. on Mt. 5:22.

[5] CAF, III, 515.

[6] Though a vl. presupposes a form of μωρόομαι.

Oed. Tyr., 433). But the judgment can also imply condemnation of the whole personality. Hence Chrysothemis pleads for understanding before too hasty a judgment (Soph. El., 889 f.): πρὸς νῦν θεῶν ἄκουσον, ὡς μαθοῦσά μου τὸ λοιπὸν ἢ φρονοῦσαν ἢ μώραν λέγῃς. The man is above such a judgment who can say (Aristoph. Eccl., 474): ἀνόηθ᾽ ὅς᾽ ἂν καὶ μῶρα βουλευσώμεθα, ἅπαντ᾽ ἐπὶ τὸ βέλτιον ἡμῖν ξυμφέρειν. Eur. Med., 614: καὶ ταῦτα μὴ θέλουσα μωρανεῖς, obviously carries a warning. Demosthenes has in view the political conduct of his fellow-citizens when he says in the 3rd Philippic (Or., 9, 54): εἰς τοῦτ᾽ ἀφῖχθε μωρίας ἢ παρανοίας. Thucydides uses the expression with ref. to a proposal of peace from Argos to Lacedaemon in the sense that acceptance of the conditions would be folly because of the incalculable consequences for both parties. Soph. Oed. Tyr., 540 is also political: μῶρόν ἐστι τοὐγχείρημά σου ἄνευ τε πλήθους καὶ φίλων τυρρανίδα θηρᾶν, ὃ πλήθει χρήμασίν θ᾽ ἁλίσκεται,[7] and cf. Aesch. Pers., 719: πεζὸς ἢ ναύτης δὲ πεῖραν τήνδ᾽ ἐμώρανεν τάλας; which implies not merely a lack of rational consideration but the madness of the whole enterprise. In other cases, too, it is implied that there is not just a deficiency, a mere stupidity or irrationality, which would not occur if there were better mental equipment, but that man is controlled by a power which confuses his understanding, causes him to do mad things, and hides the right path from him. This is true of the impulsive action described in Eur. Hipp., 966: ἀλλ᾽ ὡς τὸ μῶρον ἀνδράσιν μὲν οὐκ ἔνι, γυναιξὶ δ᾽ ἐμπέφυκεν· οἶδ᾽ ἐγὼ νέους οὐδὲν γυναικῶν ὄντας ἀσφαλεστέρους, ὅταν ταράξῃ Κύπρις ἡβῶσαν φρένα, and it is also presupposed in Soph. Ant., 220: οὐκ ἔστιν οὕτω μῶρος ὃς θανεῖν ἐρᾷ, and 469 f.: σοὶ δ᾽ εἰ δοκῶ νῦν μῶρα δρῶσα τυγχάνειν, σχεδόν τι μώρῳ μωρίαν ὀφλισκάνω. This element of confusion is particularly present in Soph. Ai., 1150: ἐγὼ δέ γ᾽ ἄνδρ᾽ ὄπωπα μωρίας πλέων ὃς ἐν κακοῖς ὕβριζε τοῖσι τῶν πέλας. Here folly comes to expression as arrogance against the unfortunate. Cf. also Fr. Incert., 839, TGF: ἡ δὲ μωρία μάλιστ᾽ ἀδελφὴ τῆς πονηρίας ἔφυ. In Soph. El., 1326 μῶροι is used in address along with φρενῶν τητώμενοι. Folly is a fate; this view is found along with a more rationalistic understanding in classical Gk., and it is of fundamental importance in respect of the distinctive orientation of the concept in biblical Gk.

B. μωρός and Cognates in the Greek OT and the Corresponding Hebrew Originals.

μωρός and cognates are not common in the Gk. OT. In most of the Wisdom writings, Prv., Qoh., Wis., Ps., ἄφρων is used exclusively or almost exclusively for the fool.[8] Only in Sir. is the adj. fairly common. It here denotes an incidental failure sometimes caused by fate.[9] In so far as we have the Heb. originals, they are varied. In isolated instances the group is used for all the important Heb. words for fool.

Thus it is used for the old נָבָל, נְבָלָה in Dt. 32:6; Is. 32:5, 6, also Sir. 4:27; 21:22a; 50:26; Prv. 17:21 Σ. In Dt. 32:6 the people is addressed as עַם נָבָל וְלֹא חָכָם. The LXX has λαὸς μωρὸς καὶ οὐχὶ σοφός, and it uses the same word in Jer. 5:21: λαὸς μωρὸς καὶ ἀκάρδιος for עַם־סָכָל וְאֵין לֵב. The ref. is obviously to something other than a want of understanding. What is missing is true knowledge of God, acknowledgment of God and confession of God. The people is hardened. They have eyes and do not see,

[7] The term is used politically in a 6th cent. pap.: μωρία καὶ ἀκαταστασία, cf. Preisigke Wört., *s.v.*

[8] There are many related terms in the OT and NT: ἀνόητος, ἀπαίδευτος, ἀσύνετος, ἄφρων (→ φρονέω), → III, 659 f. κενός, → 519 ff. μάταιος, → νήπιος.

[9] Caspari, 684 tries to distinguish as follows between ἀφροσύνη and μωρία: "ἀφροσύνη is finally episodic failure, whereas μωρία, with the Attic μώρωσις, is degeneration which has become habitual." But shortly before he himself says: "μωρόν in (Sir.) 16:23 is the individual action of an ἄφρων" (ἀνὴρ ἄφρων καὶ πλανώμενος διανοεῖται μωρά). Sharp differentiation is thus impossible.

ears and do not hear, as we go on to read in Jer. 5:21. The folly condemned here is thus apostasy from God. In the same sense the judgment of Dt. 32:6 is applied in Sir. 50:26 to the Samaritans as dangerous schismatics.[10] נָבָל = μωρός is also used in Is. 32:5, 6 of one who has contemptuously broken off fellowship with God, i.e., of a practical atheist.[11] Acc. to the LXX a fool leads astray others who are seeking salvation.[12]

In Sir. 4:27 LXX, however, there is a softening along the lines of a purely intellectual understanding.[13] נבל is here par. to משלים. As in Is. 32:5 LXX, then, the ref. is to the ruler and his (Hellenistic) attitude of religious indifference or rejection.[14] The LXX has: καὶ μὴ ὑποστρώσῃς ἀνθρώπῳ μωρῷ σαυτόν. This is a warning against obsequiousness to the fool or the mighty, and is a clever rule of life[15] which even the following verses do not lift to a higher plane. In Sir. 21:22a μωρός = נבל is simply used of a man who disregards good manners.[16] The influence of Gk. moral thought is particularly clear in Prv. 17:21, where the LXX renders נָבָל[17] by ἀπαίδευτος (cf. Dt. 13:7 ff.).[18]

כְּסִיל, which replaces the older נָבָל in later Heb. works,[19] is transl. μωρός only once (ψ 93:8) in the LXX.[20] The folly of those addressed consists in what is quoted as their view in v. 7: "The Lord shall not see, and the God of Jacob has no understanding." This is again practical atheism (cf. Ps. 14:1). With *impietas* is combined *improbitas*.[21] Fools are arrogant (ὑπερήφανοι, גֵּאִים), sinners (ἁμαρτωλοί, רְשָׁעִים),[22] evil-doers (ἐργαζόμενοι τὴν ἀνομίαν, פֹּעֲלֵי־אָוֶן).[23] The ref. is again to political rulers. That we are to honour the truth against such is stated in Sir. 4:27 (Heb.) and also 42:8. For the παιδεία ἀνοήτου καὶ μωροῦ, על מוסר פותה וכסיל demanded here is more than the championing of education against those who are deficiently instructed. There is need for relentless opposition to fools who may very well be powerful. That the discipline of faith is here addressed to rulers corresponds to the admonition in ψ 2:10 LXX: καὶ νῦν, βασιλεῖς, σύνετε· παιδεύθητε, πάντες οἱ κρίνοντες τὴν γῆν. μωρός[24] in

[10] Caspari, 684.

[11] Fahlgren, 28 f. Caspari in his essay, which Fahlgren apparently did not know, understands נְבָלָה as sacrilege and נָבָל as one who exploits the connection with Yahweh for himself and thus forfeits salvation, 676.

[12] → II, 228. → διψάω.

[13] R. Smend, *D. Weisheit des Jesus Sirach hebräisch u. deutsch* (1906), *ad loc.* Cf. Ges.-Buhl, *s.v.* יצע derived from Sab. וצע "to bring low." The transl. of Ryssel in Kautzsch does not do justice to the parallelism.

[14] Sir. is after 132 B.C. The Is. transl. is in the first part of the 2nd cent. Thus the latter belongs to pre-Maccabean Hellenisation, the former to the Hasmonean recommencement of Hellenisation (John Hyrcanus, 135-105). This is the historical background against which the views represented by the LXX are best understood.

[15] This, at any rate, is how the Gk. reader would understand it.

[16] On the custom of knocking disregarded by the fool → κρούω and the refs. given there in → n. 3.

[17] 'A takes נבל here in the sense of physical fading and renders ἀπορρέων. Caspari, 670 hints at a possible connection between נבל ("to fade") and נבל ("fool"). Θ (ἀναίσθητος) takes a similar line to that of the LXX.

[18] Caspari, 674.

[19] *Ibid.*, 676.

[20] Hatch-Redp. here inadvertently equates μωρός with שכל, Caspari erroneously with בער (683).

[21] F. Baethgen, *Die Ps.*[2] (1897), on Ps. 14:1.

[22] On arrogance and folly as a sin in the LXX → ἁμαρτία, I, 286, 288, → ὕβρις.

[23] → ἔργον, II, 644.

[24] So only א: otherwise usually μοιχόν, which Rahlfs admits into the text. But μωρόν is perhaps the freer older transl.

Sir. 25:2 [25] is used censoriously for a blunder in the sense of a moral mistake on the part of an old "fool," [26] as in the euphemistic usage of class. Gk. [27]

For אֱוִיל, אִוֶּלֶת μωρός is used only at Sir. 41:15 and Is. 19:11. The ref. here is to rulers in Egypt who become fools. [28] Normal earthly relations are turned into their opposite as a sign of divine judgment, like the sign of eschatological catastrophe in S. Bar. 70: "The wise are silent and fools will speak," [29] and also like the signs of eschatological salvation in the NT, esp. in the preaching of Paul. [30] For סכל (in the LXX mostly ἄφρων and cognates) μωρός is used at Jer. 5:21 (→ 833) and μωρεύω at Is. 44:25, ABS, vl. μωραίνω. [31] ἀποστρέφων φρονίμους εἰς τὰ ὀπίσω καὶ τὴν βουλὴν αὐτῶν μωρεύων refers to God's intervention in the history of the nations when, contrary to all human (Jewish) expectation, he makes the Persian king Cyrus His anointed instrument for the deliverance of His people. The way in which God thus acts in defiance of human wisdom corresponds to His nature, glory and majesty, and to the fact that He is the Creator of the world. [32]

In 2 S. 24:10 סכל is used in David's prayer for the forgiveness of the guilt which he incurred by the census. Two renderings are offered. BA have ἐμωράνθην, and most of the others ἐματαιώθην (also 1 Ch. 21:8). The latter verb denotes foolish action in the psychological sense [33] (cf. Vg: *quia stulte egi nimis,* A.V.: "For I have done very foolishly"). ἐμωράνθην, however, denotes demonic confusion [34] ("for I was seriously deluded"). [35]

בַּעַר means "beast," "irrational man," and in its 4 or 5 occurrences the LXX has ἄφρων. For the verb בער we find ἄφρων once and ἀφρονεύεσθαι once. In Ez. 21:36 the rendering is βάρβαρος, but in the other 4 passages we find μωραίνω or μωρός: Is. 19:11 (μωραίνω for בער and μωρός for אֱוִיל)→ *supra*; Jer. 10:8 Σ [36] (בער and סכל alongside one another; Θ takes בער to mean "to burn"); Jer. 10:14; 51 (28):17. The context is the same in the last two verses, namely, that in face of God's power as Creator all human art, and esp. the erection of idols, is sheer folly: נִבְעַר כָּל־אָדָם מִדַּעַת: ἐμωράνθη (51 [28]:17, so only A; ἐματαιώθη, BS) πᾶς ἄνθρωπος ἀπὸ γνώσεως. ᾿Α, too, has ἐμωράνθη, but Σ ἠφρόνησε. The Mas. is translated: "Every man is

[25] Cf. the continuation in Sir. 42:8.

[26] At Sir. 42:8 the LXX with its ἐσχατογήρως κρινομένου πρὸς νέους is obviously alluding to the Daniel-Susanna story.

[27] So Eur. Ion, 545 speaks of the μωρία γε τοῦ νέου. Cf. also Andr., 674: ἀνὴρ γυναῖκα μωραίνουσαν ἐν δόμοις ἔχων, Hipp., 643 f.: ἡ δ' ἀμήχανος γυνὴ γνώμῃ βραχείᾳ μωρίαν ἀφῃρέθη.

[28] Historically the Mas. refers to the political confusion in Egypt at the beginning of the 7th cent. B.C., though Guthe in Kautzsch suggests the attacks of Artaxerxes III Ochus in the middle of the 4th cent. B.C. The LXX in v. 13, unlike the Mas., does not associate the officials of Memphis and Tanis as deluded fools, but contrasts the two cities: ἐξέλιπον οἱ ἄρχοντες Τάνεως καὶ ὑψώθησαν οἱ ἄρχοντες Μέμφεως. The historical situation which the LXX has in view cannot be established with any certainty.

[29] Cf. Ryssel in Kautzsch, *ad loc.*

[30] E. v. Dobschütz, "Religionsgeschichtliche Parallelen z. NT," ZNW, 21 (1922), 70 f. compares Bar. 70 and 1 C. 1:26-29.

[31] Μωρεύω in the LXX is a hapax legomenon, and hence it could easily be replaced in assimilation to NT passages.

[32] → ἔργον II, 641.

[33] Cf. Liddell-Scott, *s.v.*

[34] Cf. the flight and confusion of the disciples at the arrest of Jesus under the influence of Satan, and on this G. Bertram, *Die Leidensgeschichte Jesu u. der Christuskult* (1922), 45, with additional material.

[35] R. Kittel in Kautzsch, *ad loc.* At the par. 1 Ch. 21:8 Rothstein in Kautzsch translates: "I have acted very foolishly," but in Ch., where Satan, not God, is the instigator, there is even more reason than in 2 S. for a demonological understanding.

[36] Acc. to Field, *ad loc.* following Syro-hex.

confounded, there is no understanding," [37] or: "All men are fools in their craft." [38] The LXX and other Gk. translations seem to take this view, cf. the Vg: *stultus factus est omnis homo a scientia*.

In the passages cited becoming a fool is obviously a divine judgment on men in their fancied superior wisdom. Job 16:7 LXX is to be construed in the same way: God has made Job a fool. μωρόν is here used with σεσηπότα, "delivered up to decay," so that it might be taken in a purely physical sense as perhaps a rendering of the Mas. שׁמם, which in the hi means "subject to corruption." The verb also occurs in Job 38:36 Σ for שֶׂכְוִי, a term of uncertain meaning: ἢ τίς ἔδωκε μεμωραμένῳ ἔννοιαν; Σ has the noun in Job 24:12: ὁ θεὸς δὲ οὐκ ἐμπνέει μωρίαν. [39] The text is difficult and was taken in many different ways by the older translators. The Σ rendering could again be taken physically: God does not inspire debility. Otherwise we are to think in terms of sinful confusion of spirit which cannot be attributed to God. This would be the same judgment as that of Ch., which makes Satan the instigator of David rather than God. Finally μωρός occurs in Daniel's judgment on the inability of the Israelites to judge rightly in the case of Susanna, Sus. 48 LXX and Θ. In this judgment lies a religious reproach. The ability to judge rightly, which the Israelites do not have, is a gift of God to His people.

Elsewhere μωρός and cognates occur only in Sir. The verb is found only at 23:14 with no Heb. original, the noun at 20:31 and 41:15 (→ 835). The adj. is common. We have dealt already with the verses where the Heb. has been preserved apart from 8:17. Here, as elsewhere, the word is used in a purely intellectual sense: "Make no plan with a simpleton." This is a sober rule of practical wisdom. Warning against fools is a rule of life which runs through the whole wisdom of Sir. The concept of the fool is frequently expressed by our present word: 18:18; 19:11, 12; 20:13, 16, 20; 21:14 ff.; 22:9 ff.; 27:13; 33(36):5, 6. [40] μωρός here denotes a man acc. to his nature. He is always a fool. This is his unalterable destiny. He is excluded from the company of the wise, and, if this is civic society, he is an a-social man against whom society must be on guard and whom it must drive out. Thus the idea of the fool is a general moral and social matter. Nevertheless, there is also a religious connection in Gk. Sir. Thus in 16:23 (cf. v. 22) folly implies a practical denial of God as the Judge and Avenger of good and evil. In 22:12 the Gk. has "fool" and "ungodly" probably as a double translation.

Thus, in spite of considerable secularisation in detail, the religious basis has still to be remembered even here, the more so as the position of Sir. in Scripture caused this element to be brought out in the religious or ecclesiastical use of this collection by means of the corresponding religious explanation, interpretation and application.

---

[37] Rothstein in Kautzsch, also F. Giesebrecht, *Das Buch Jer.* (1894), *ad loc.*: "Then every man is silent in folly."

[38] Cf. Luther.

[39] The Mas. has תִּפְלָה from the root תפל, which perhaps in the Aram. underlies Mt. 5:13. Cf. also Job 6:6 תָּפֵל, Σ ἀνάρτυτον, and → n. 101.

[40] Caspari, 684. Verse 6: μωρός only in א[2]; AB א: μῶκος.

C. μωρός κτλ. in Philo.

There is in the OT a special religious concept of folly which became current in Judaism, including Hellenistic Judaism. This may be seen in Philo.

Philo uses the term in a way which implies criticism of all worldly wisdom. Man is ensnared in folly. He cannot escape by means of his own reason. There is almost an echo of Hellen. pessimism [41] when Philo states this as follows in Cher., 116: ὁ δὲ νοῦς ἐμόν ἐστιν διαίτημα; ὁ ψευδῶν εἰκαστικός, ὁ πλάνης, ὁ οἰητικός, ὁ παρανοῶν, ὁ μωραίνων, ὁ εὑρισκόμενος ἄνους ἐν ἐκστάσει καὶ μελαγχολίᾳ καὶ μακρῷ γήρᾳ. In Leg. All., II, 70 one finds the same link between arrogance and folly as in the OT: ἕως οὖν γυμνοί εἰσιν, ὁ μὲν νοῦς τοῦ νοεῖν, ἡ δὲ αἴσθησις τοῦ αἰσθάνεσθαι, οὐδὲν ἔχουσιν αἰσχρόν· ἐπειδὰν δὲ ἄρξωνται καταλαμβάνειν, ἐν αἰσχύνῃ καὶ ὕβρει γίνονται, εὑρεθήσονται γὰρ εὐηθείᾳ καὶ μωρίᾳ πολλάκις χρώμενοι, μᾶλλον ἢ ὑγιαινούσῃ ἐπιστήμῃ. In Sobr., 11, with ref. to Dt. 32:6, Philo maintains from God's standpoint that folly is inherent in man's nature. But the term is used here as Paul in the NT uses νήπιος in the sense of apology. God regards men as children in respect of their irrational conduct, which is childish in relation to truth: τὸ ... πρὸς ἀλήθειαν βρεφῶδες, cf. 1 C. 3:1 ff., also Hb. 5:11. This reinterpretation of Dt. 32:6 along the lines of a pessimistic view of man had apologetic significance for Judaism. Pagan anti-Semitism had already gone to the OT for weapons to fight Judaism. Christian polemics did the same, and Just. in Dial., 123, 4 quotes the verse from Dt. Just. gives it a historical sense. The OT people, which the Jews claim to be, has fallen victim to folly and ungodliness. Philo, however, integrates folly into his doctrine of man in Deus Imm., 164. Here stupidity and cunning are the two culpable extremes which stand in contrast to the correct mean of reflection: μέση δὲ πανουργίας τε αὖ καὶ μωρίας φρόνησις. This is wholly in the spirit of Hellen. anthropology. Philo feels that he is wise as a Jewish philosopher. From this standpoint, in the learned discussion in Cher., 75 he addresses as a fool the man who has no deeper understanding of the world and life with their paradoxes: λέληθέ σε, ὦ μωρέ, ὅτι πᾶς ὁ δοκῶν ἐν γενέσει διώκειν, διώκεται (on Ex. 15:9, the boast, in the Song of Moses, of the enemy who is swiftly humiliated).

D. The Concept of Folly in the New Testament.

In the OT the synonyms, specifically → ἄφρων and cognates, are far more numerous and important than μωρός. In the NT, however, the main weight of the concept of folly is borne by μωρός. This word has now acquired theological significance. Though used in much the same way, ἄφρων retreats into the background.

1. The Salt of Mt. 5:13; Lk. 14:34.

We turn first to Mt. 5:13: ἐὰν δὲ τὸ ἅλας μωρανθῇ, ἐν τίνι ἁλισθήσεται; Lk. 14:34 is to much the same effect: ἐὰν δὲ καὶ τὸ ἅλας μωρανθῇ, ἐν τίνι ἀρτυθήσεται; Mk. 9:50 has the saying in a different context and a divergent form: ἐὰν δὲ τὸ ἅλας ἄναλον γένηται, ἐν τίνι αὐτὸ ἀρτύσετε; [42]

---

[41] Cf. already Eur. Tro., 612 f.: ὁρῶ τὰ τῶν θεῶν, ὡς τὰ μὲν πυργοῦσ' ἄνω τὸ μηδὲν ὄντα, τὰ δὲ δοκοῦντ' ἀπώλεσαν.

[42] The Mk. text with αὐτό shows that the point of the saying lies in the indestructibility of salt. If salt were to lose its saltness, there could be no means of restoring it. In other words, there can be no substitute. The same text is to be found in the Rabb. saying quoted under → ἅλας, I, 229. Schl. Mt., *ad loc.* translates this into Gk. as follows: τὸ ἅλας, ἐὰν σαπρὸν γίνηται, ἐν τίνι ἁλίζουσι αὐτό;

The difficulty of the saying as thus attested in three different forms is that salt cannot lose its chemical qualities. It is usually assumed that this is not chemically pure salt, but an impure natural salt whose sediment might in certain circumstances lose all salt content.[43] Ref. has also been made to the use of salt by Arab bakers to help burning. The floor of the oven would be lined with blocks of salt, and under the effect of burning these would undergo a process of crystallisation and suffer a chemical change, so that after many years they would have to be thrown out as unserviceable. This is supposed by some to underlie the NT saying.[44] Finally the reading μαρανθῇ at Lk. 14:34, conjectured also for Mt. 5:13,[45] is regarded as an alleviation. μαραίνω in the pass. means gradually to fade out, to disappear, and would make possible an explanation of the saying in terms of impure salt whose salt content wastes away.

There is also, of course, the explanation that Jesus uses the image intentionally. He does not forget that salt does not become inactive[46] — attempts have been made to understand the saying in this way — but the *tertium comparationis*, the whole point of the parable, lies in this very fact. What He is saying is that, as salt cannot become inactive, so this or that cannot happen. We thus have a similar metaphor to that of the camel and the needle's eye. Jesus uses such images to characterise something as impossible. In Mk. 10:25 and par. the impossibility is that of a rich man entering the kingdom of God. Here the point is different. It is impossible that what Jesus brought, what He gave His disciples, what He made of them, should become insipid and perish. The Gospel is as incorruptible and indestructible as salt (Mk. 13:31). Jesus expresses this fact after the manner of popular *meshalim* in the distinctive metaphor preserved materially by all three Synoptists.[47] The image is almost a kind of parable of the kingdom, a parallel to the parables of the mustard seed and the leaven. As in these parables the greatness and might of God's kingdom are depicted in terms of its miraculous power, so here its indestructibility is illustrated. The permanence of God's gift in Christ is not dependent on men. By God's will this gift is the salvation of the world and hence it cannot perish. The interpretation in Mt.: "You are the salt of the earth," the application in Mk.: "Have salt among yourselves," and the admonition in Lk.: "Who has ears to hear, let him hear," weaken the unconditional element. As a demand or admonition to men, even to Christians, the saying is limited as to its fulfilment by human sin. Thus it cannot be correctly understood along these lines. The μωρανθῇ now suggests, not the physical impossibility of a change in the chemical constitution of salt, but the psychical possibility of a change in the faith of disciples. The warning concerns the earthly being of the disciple. He who through the powerful Word of Christ has become an apostle, a fisher of men, a shepherd, a rock, loses all value if his faith vacillates and he falls away (Lk.

---

[43] RE³, XVII, 405, *s.v.* "Salz"; Zn. Mt., *ad loc.*, 205, 55; → ἅλας, I, 229.

[44] L. Köhler, "Salz, das dumm wird," ZDPV, 59 (1936), 133 f.

[45] S. A. Naber, *Mnemosyne* (1881), 275, cf. Kl. Mt., *ad loc.*

[46] The ironical Rabb. saying quoted under → ἅλας, I, 229 shows how difficult it was truly to understand the message of Jesus as a message of grace. Even the Evangelists make of it an admonition and warning (→ *infra*).

[47] Cf. Bultmann Trad.,² for whom the popular image is one of the secular *meshalim* which the tradition later made into sayings of Jesus (107, cf. 102). The interpretation in the introduction in Mt. also comes from the community rather than Jesus acc. to Bultmann (95 f.). But the authenticity of the saying is perhaps supported by its radical saving character, even though the Rabbis scoffed and the Christian tradition did not properly understand it (→ n. 46).

14:34).[48] Thus the Lord's word of grace[49] becomes a word of judgment. This was how the Evangelists understood it, and this was how it was taken in patristic exegesis.

Cf. Cyril of Alex.: ἔστωσαν ἐν ὑμῖν οἱ ἅλες, τουτέστιν, οἱ θεῖοι καὶ σωτήριοι λόγοι, ὧν ἐὰν καταφρονήσωμεν, ἐσόμεθα μωροὶ καὶ ἀσύνετοι καὶ ἄχρειοι παντελῶς.[50] And in another place: ἔδειξε μωρανθεῖσαν πᾶσαν τὴν ἀνθρωπότητα καὶ κατασαπεῖσαν ὑπὸ τῶν ἁμαρτημάτων.[51] Cf. also the interpretation of Lk. 14:34 in the Coptic Gnostic work entitled *Pistis Sophia*:[52] "Blessed are all souls who will be received by the mysteries of the ineffable, but if they commit transgression they are not fit from this hour to return to the body or to anything else, but will be cast into outer darkness and consumed in that place." Protestant commentaries generally emphasise the moral and religious warning addressed to the disciples in the saying. It makes very little difference whether the lack (of salt) is then identified with *superbia*,[53] with a lack of readiness for suffering or service, with deficient love or self-sacrifice,[54] or with inadequate self-denial.[55] As the Evangelists, or at least Mt., present it, μωρανθῆναι causes us to think of the disciple rather than salt, and it is to be taken, not physiologically, but psychologically in terms of the biblical concept of folly. Apostasy from God, falling[56] from the state of grace, destroys the value of the Christian.

But in front of this admonition and warning of the early Christian community stands the saying of Jesus concerning the indestructibility of salvation. The Word of God is like salt. If man cannot give power to it, he also cannot deprive it of its efficacy.

2. "Fool" as an Insult.

Mt. 5:22[57] also raises a well-known problem of philological and theological interpretation. What is really meant by μωρέ? How is the condemnation of this term related both to the context and also to the general message of Jesus? We must try to answer both these questions.

---

[48] Cf. H. Grotius, *Annotationes in NT*, I² (1755), *ad loc.*: *Quo quaeque res bona sit, est melior, eo eadem mala est peior. Sal, dum salis naturam retinet, optimum est: idem si naturam suam exuat, peius gleba et fimo. Ita Christianismi professione nihil excellentius, si vita respondeat; nihil peius, nihil nocentius, si nomini vis absit, quod accidere necesse est aliud agentibus.*

[49] Cf. Cramer Cat. on Mk. 9:50: καὶ τάχα τοσοῦτον ἔχει τις ἁλῶν, ὅσον κεχώρηκε τῶν τοῦ θεοῦ χαρίτων. For the gracious character of the gift of salvation the exegete points to Col. 4:6: ὁ λόγος ὑμῶν πάντοτε ἐν χάριτι ἅλατι ἠρτυμένος. Cf. Ign. Eph., 17, 2, → n. 123.

[50] Cramer Cat. on Lk. 14:34.

[51] *Ibid.* on Mt. 5:13.

[52] Cf. C. Schmidt, *Pistis Sophia. Ein gnostisches Originalwerk des 3. Jhdts. aus dem Koptischen übers.* (1925), c. 120.

[53] Bengel on Mk. 9:50.

[54] Hck. Mk. on 9:50.

[55] Zn. Mk. on 9:50.

[56] ἐκβάλλειν is also a tt. for judgment in Mt. 8:12; 22:13; 25:30; Lk. 13:28; Jn. 12:31 → βάλλειν, I, 527. On καταπατεῖν cf. Lk. 8:5 and Cyril of Alex. in Cramer Cat. on Mt. 5:13: ἐὰν γὰρ φοβηθῆτε ὀνειδισμοὺς καὶ διωγμούς, καταφρονηθήσεσθε, ὅπερ ἐστὶν καταπατηθῆναι. Here, too, the thing is immediately suggested by the image. Treading underfoot in an OT symbol of contempt. Cf. καταπατεῖν in the Ps. (7:5) and the prophets (Am. 5:12).

[57] Zn. Mt. 5:22, cf. K. Köhler, ZNW, 19 (1920), 91 ff.; F. Schulthess, "Zur Sprache d. Evangelien," ZNW, 21 (1922), 241; A. Fridrichsen, "Exegetisches z. NT," I, *Symb. Osl.*, 13 (1934), 38-40.

The saying can be taken in many different ways.

a. It may be regarded as the rendering of a Heb.-Aram. term from the stem מרר (מוֹרָה) מרה or מרא, "to be bitter, recalcitrant." [58] There would then be allusion to Mas. Ps. 78:8: [59] דּוֹר סוֹרֵר וּמֹרֶה, LXX: γενεὰ σκολιὰ καὶ παραπικραίνουσα, Σ: γενεὰ ἀπειθὴς καὶ προσερίζουσα. 4 Esr. 7:22 links the ideas of stubbornness and folly: "But they (the living), rebellious and disobedient, conceived thoughts of folly" [60] (Vg: *cogitamen vanitatis*; foolish and sinful thoughts of revolt). In the Mishnah, in Tract. Sanh., 7, 4a; 8, 1-5, Rabb. tradition, on the basis of Dt. 21:18, speaks of the unruly and recalcitrant son: [61] בֵּן סוֹרֵר וּמוֹרֶה (υἱὸς ἀπειθὴς καὶ ἐρεθιστής, LXX). The conduct of such a son is stated to be worthy of death and is to be punished by stoning. To call someone a fool in this sense would be to deny him fellowship with God and man and to charge him with a capital offence. It is understandable that a heavy punishment should be prescribed for so doing. But it would be hard to see here an extension or intensification of the OT prohibition of killing along NT lines. The saying would perhaps be possible on the lips of Jesus if it bore this sense, but it is unlikely that He would give the full authority of His "But I say unto you," to such a saying.

b. It may also be regarded as a rendering of the Rabbinically adopted Gk. loan word מוֹרוֹס used by Jesus in the Aram. In this case, too, we should have to take into account similar Heb. or Aram. stems and words. Thus in Pesikt., 118b/119a on Nu. 20:10 הַמּוֹרִים becomes μωροί, "fools." The concept is thus related to the stems נבל and רשׁע, and is taken to have the sense of "ungodly." [62]

c. But it may be that we simply have a Gk. term unrelated to the loan word. In this case the Aram. equivalent would be שׁוֹטֶה, "fool" or "blockhead." The word occurs in Ed., 5, 6: "It would be better to be called a fool my whole life long than even for a single hour to act in an ungodly way towards him." [63] The ref. here is not to the insulting of another, which is obviously punishable only if without cause, [64] but to the experience of the righteous, who know that they are constantly exposed to the insults of the ungodly. To insult one's neighbour in this way is thus to rank oneself with the ungodly and to fall victim to death. Such an understanding of Mt. 5:22 would correspond to other Synoptic sayings and also to the Pauline tradition. Mt. 18:10 warns us against despising little ones, and this does not refer only to children, but to the "babes" whom Jesus describes as the recipients of revelation in Mt. 11:25. Those who give offence to little ones come under the full severity of Christ's judgment (Mt. 18:6-7). In Paul designation as a fool is the typical expression of the contempt of the Greeks [65] (and also of Jews) [66] for those who believe in Christ.

---

[58] Cf. Zn. Mt., *ad loc.*, who sees no essential distinction between the two insults, *racha* having no technical significance in the sense of atheist.

[59] Cf. B. Weiss, 10 (1910), *ad loc.*

[60] B. Violet, *Die Apk. d. Esr. u. d. Bar. in deutscher Gestalt* (1924), 71.

[61] Cf. S. Krauss, *Giessener Mischna*, IV, 4, Sanh. (1933), 216 f., 240 ff.

[62] Str.-B. on Mt. 5:22, 279 f.

[63] מוּטָב לִי לִקָּרוֹת שׁוֹטֶה כָּל־יָמַי וְלֹא לֵעָשׂוֹת שָׁעָה אַחַת רָשָׁע לִפְנֵי הַמָּקוֹם. Schl. Mt. on 5:22 translates as follows: κρεῖττόν μοι κληθῆναι μωρὸς πάσας τὰς ἡμέρας μου καὶ μὴ γενέσθαι ὥραν μίαν ἀσεβὴς ἐνώπιον τοῦ θεοῦ.

[64] There are only a few MSS in addition to B and S into which the explanatory εἰκῇ has not penetrated.

[65] The Apologists offer material on this, cf. Tat. Or. Graec., 21, 1: οὐ γὰρ μωραίνομεν, ἄνδρες Ἕλληνες, οὐδὲ ληροὺς ἀπαγγέλλομεν, θεὸν ἐν ἀνθρώπου μορφῇ γεγονέναι καταγγέλλοντες.

[66] In Just. Dial., 48, 1 the Jew says: θεὸν ὄντα ... τὸν Χριστὸν ἄνθρωπον γενόμενον ... οὐ μόνον παράδοξον δοκεῖ μοι εἶναι ἀλλὰ καὶ μωρόν. Cf. also 67, 2, where Christians as well as pagans are fools to the Jew.

d. The term may also be taken as a transl. of the preceding loan word ῥακά. ῥακά is probably רֵיק, which means empty head and which is best rendered κενός (cf. Jm. 2:20: ἄνθρωπε κενέ, or Ju. 11:3: ἄνδρες κενοί B, A: λιτοί, אֲנָשִׁים רֵיקִים). ἀνόητος in Lk. 24:25 and Gl. 3:1, 3, and μωροί in Mt. 23:17, might well be appropriate renderings of what was obviously a common term of opprobrium.[67] The material significance of this assumption is to be found in the historical fact that in this case the three NT statements concerning the commandment are reduced to two, and one of the main difficulties, the casuistic sequence, drops away.

This leads us to the second question as to the material understanding within the context of the preaching of Jesus. Only a few modern expositors try to relate the threefold warning in its traditional form to the intention of Jesus.

The saying about anger is usually related to the disposition. To call someone empty-headed is to charge him with frivolity and to wound his honour. Fool suggests that the one thus charged has no capacity for right thought or action, and he is thus denied all confidence and fellowship.[68] The passage does not express the true view of Jesus if the casuistic sequence is regarded as a mocking and challenging imitation of the casuistry of His opponents.[69] There are, in fact, par. in Jewish tradition, e.g., bQid., 28a, Bar.: "If a man calls his neighbour a slave, he is to be excommunicated; if he calls him a bastard, he is to receive forty stripes; if he calls him a malefactor, this is to cost him his life."[70] In a conversation between two Babylonian Amoreans in bBM, 58b ref. is made without differentiation to three who will never escape from Gehinnom, one of whom is the man "who calls his neighbour by an abusive name."[71]

It is hard to think that Jesus engaged in this kind of casuistry. For this reason these casuistical sayings in the Sermon on the Mount are often ascribed to the early Jewish Christian community and are regarded as a relapse into Jewish casuistry. Philologically the fact that ῥακά and μωρέ may be equivalents can serve as a starting-point.[72] It is in fact difficult to distinguish between these two, or to differentiate them from anger.[73] Hence these sayings may be regarded as an explanatory addition to the saying about anger, and this gives us a saying we might well expect from Jesus, in which all such things as anger and terms of abuse are characterised as equally reprehensible and culpable.[74]

The inner connection between anger and terms of abuse is already laid down in a saying of doubtful authorship: τὴν κακολογίαν ἡ ὀργὴ φαίνεται ἀπογεννῶσα ὥστε ἡ μήτηρ οὐκ ἀστεῖα.[75] This is confirmed not only in the Hellenistic world but also in Judaism and early Christianity, where sins of the tongue and anger are closely related, cf. especially Jm. 1:19: ἔστω δὲ πᾶς ἄνθρωπος ... βραδὺς εἰς τὸ λαλῆσαι, βραδὺς εἰς ὀργήν, and 3:5 ff. Patristic exegesis of Mt. 5:22 is to the same effect:[76] αἱ πλείους τῶν τιμωριῶν καὶ τῶν ἁμαρτιῶν ἀπὸ ῥημάτων ἔχουσι τὴν ἀρχήν. καὶ γὰρ βλασφημία ῥημάτων, καὶ ἄρνησις διὰ ῥημάτων καὶ λοιδορίαι καὶ ὕβρεις καὶ ἅπαξ ἁπλῶς πάντα τὰ διὰ τῆς γλώσσης κακά. This implies that there can hardly be a crescendo in the three sayings. Terms of abuse are not a heightened form of anger; they are its most

---

67 For examples cf. Wettstein, *ad loc.* Cf. also Grotius, *ad loc.*
68 Schl. Mt., *ad loc.* takes this view.
69 Zn. Mt., *ad loc.*
70 Cf. L. Goldschmidt, VI (1932), 597; also Wettstein, *ad loc.*
71 Goldschmidt, VII, 635; cf. Str.-B., I, 281.
72 Köhler, 92.
73 Though cf. Schlatter's exposition → *supra* and n. 68.
74 Fridrichsen (→ n. 57).
75 Quoted by Wettstein on the basis of an untraceable pseudo-Aristotelian tradition.
76 Cramer Cat., *ad loc.*

obvious and common expression. It is also hard to make any basic distinction between the two terms of abuse, namely, ῥακά and μωρέ. They both belong to the category of sins of the tongue, and are both subject to judgment. Again, the three statements do not distinguish between different courts. κρίσις is the general and comprehensive concept which in the following synonymous and parallel sentences [77] comprises the supreme human and ultimate divine judgment, so that the full content and scope of the term is brought out and it is given the strongest possible emphasis. All material arguments against the authenticity of Mt. 5:22 are thus dispelled at once. We have here a threefold statement underlined by the repetition in different forms.

Judaism, too, distinguishes between a wrong which affects property and injury done by words. [78] The latter is regarded as the more serious. [79] Sometimes public humiliation and the shedding of blood are equated, but the grounds are purely external and formal. The reason for the equation is that when a man is insulted the redness of shame is followed by paleness, just as the paleness of death follows the redness of blood when a man is murdered. [80] This is a clever interpretation of the sixth commandment rather than a moral intensification. Jesus refuses to mediate property disputes, and He sees the destructive kinship between anger and vilification. Where there neither is nor can be fellowship, He Himself can say: "Ye fools and blind" (Mt. 23:17), [81] thereby turning the honourable titles of the rabbis into their opposite. [82] Jesus is not merely thinking here of the μωρολογία, the hair-splitting, which can try to find reasons for distinguishing between swearing by the temple and the gold of the temple. [83] The saying is directed against the scribes and Pharisees as such. Thus the saying of Jesus is not a moral warning which seeks to banish anger and abuse from the world. It is designed to establish fellowship on the basis of the personal authority of Jesus. Those who follow Him stand in unconditional and indestructible fellowship with one another (cf. also 1 C. 6:6 f.).

3. The "Fool" in Parables.

In the parables of the wise and foolish builders (Mt. 7:24-27) and the wise and foolish virgins (Mt. 25:1-13) the concepts "wise" and "foolish" are contrasted from the standpoint of sound common sense. The first parable is also found in Lk. 6:47-49, but without the evaluation. Both parables are taken from life, [84] and are thus readily understandable. The action of the righteous corresponds finally to the demands of prudence, and that of the ungodly is ultimately shown to be foolish. Both parables presuppose that we cannot at once distinguish between what is wise and what is foolish; we have to learn this by testing. Hence both parables are orientated to the last judgment.

---

[77] Cf. Fridrichsen.

[78] Moore, II, 147 ff. (ref. to S. Lv., 25, 17 [Weiss, 107d]); Str.-B., I, 281.

[79] bBM, 58b.

[80] *Loc. cit.* The NT is presupposed, but the strange basis of an apparently lofty moral principle overthrows the principle. May it be that the author is caricaturing the saying of Jesus?

[81] The repetition in 23:19 is simply a secondary textual variant.

[82] Schl. Mt., *ad loc.*

[83] H. Olshausen (1830), *ad loc.*

[84] This is true even though one cannot discern clearly the wedding customs presupposed in the parable of the ten virgins. Cf. E. Hommel, "Ein uralter Hochzeitsbrauch im NT (zugleich ein Beitrag zur Lehre von den heiligen Zahlen)," ZNW, 23 (1924), 305-310.

The concepts "wise" and "foolish" are to be found in other NT parables, or may be brought into them, cf. the parable of building in Lk. as compared with Mt. Thus one may refer to the parable of the rich fool [85] in Lk. 12:13-21, or to that of the clever (or unjust) steward in Lk. 16:1-13, or to that of the foolish guests who did not hold themselves in readiness in Lk. 14:15-24. [86]

There is a similar parable to this in Jewish tradition, bShab., 153a. [87] The situation is the same as in Lk. The wise guests, who wait at the palace door, are contrasted with the foolish, who go about their business. This parable is linked with Is. 65:13, 14, [88] and thus carries an eschatological implication. The same is true of the preceding (152b) parable of the majestic robes lent by a king. [89] The wise preserve them, fools use them for working in. This parable is interpreted in terms of 1 S. 25:29, a metaphor which quite early became an almost confessional expression of Judaism's hope of the resurrection. [90]

Like all the others, the parable of the ten virgins has in view approaching judgment. The main admonition is to readiness. For the day and hour when the Lord comes are not known. If the foolish virgins are not ready, it is their own fault. The fault is one of lukewarmness rather than wickedness. [91] They love the Lord and want to meet Him. But the foolish virgins take their participation for granted. They make no preparations, and thus their hope does not influence their conduct. [92] The parable is thus a type of the judgment which is not executed by the Lord, but which men pass on themselves by their own conduct. The foolish virgins exclude themselves.

The parable secured a firm place for itself in the story of eschatologically orientated Christian piety. We find relatively early refs. to the wise virgins on the burial inscr. of dedicated virgins. [93] Both groups are sometimes found on depictions in the catacombs. [94] The foolish virgins, as the opposite of the wise who have attained to eternal bliss, are a warning and admonition to the living. The parable is used in the same way

[85] ἄφρων is used here. μωρός and esp. the antithesis μωρός/φρόνιμος are peculiar to Mt. apart from 1 C. 4:10, cf. Kl. Mt. (1927), Exc. p. 9. Cf. also Lk. 16:19-21, where it is pointed out that wisdom and folly are not just a matter of our own willing and running, but of divine gift and endowment.

[86] Cf. Mt. 22:1-10, where the ref. can only be to wicked rejection.

[87] Goldschmidt, I, 927 f.

[88] Cf. Guthe in Kautzsch, *ad loc.*

[89] Goldschmidt, I, 925 f.

[90] → ζάω, II, 853.

[91] Olshausen, *ad loc.* Ep. Apost. Aeth., 43 (c. 36) paraphrases the parable. The foolish virgins are not mortal sinners, but daughters of God like the wise. They are γνῶσις, σύνεσις (ἐπιστήμη), ὑπακοή, μακροθυμία (ὑπομονή), ἐλεημοσύνη. They have been overtaken by moral slumber, and hence they are thrown to the wolves and a painful death outside the Shepherd's fold. The urgent question whether they are finally saved through the intercession of their wise sisters is not answered. Cf. C. Schmidt, *Gespräche Jesu mit seinen Jüngern nach d. Auferstehung* (1919), 136 ff., 379 ff.

[92] Schl. Mt., *ad loc.*, cf. also Well. Mt.

[93] The inscr. in C. M. Kaufmann, *Hndbch. d. altchristl. Epigraphik* (1917), 285 and 358. On what follows cf. also H. Heyne, *Das Gleichnis von d. klugen u. törichten Jungfrauen, eine literarisch-ikonographische Studie zur altchr. Zeit* (1922), and W. Lehmann, *Die Parabel von den klugen u. törichten Jungfrauen* (1916).

[94] Cf. the catacomb of St. Cyriaca in Rome, from the 2nd half of the 4th cent. The pt. is the separation of the good and bad in the hereafter. The corresponding request for the dead girl (again a dedicated virgin) is that her soul should be saved like the wise virgins and not rejected like the foolish, cf. Heyne, also C. M. Kaufmann, *Hndbch. d. christl. Archäologie* (1922), 350 ff.

in the liturgical tradition.[95] *Pist. Soph.*, 125 gives evidence, too, of an understanding in terms of judgment:[96] "The foolish virgins are the souls who find the gates of light closed, and to whom the saying of the Lord applies: 'I know not who you are, you who thus far are workers of unrighteousness and iniquity.'" From the art of the catacombs a tradition leads on to the miniatures of Bible MSS[97] and depictions esp. in the entrances to Gothic cathedrals, where this parable has a fixed place.[98] Here the foolish virgins are always a type of the reprobate. Each represents a particular sin. In the well-known representation at Strassburg the tempter seduces them with an apple. They are thus an impressive depiction of the NT admonition to readiness and the associated warning against the folly which makes light of salvation and consequently falls victim to judgment.

4. Foolish Words and Thoughts: Eph. 5:4; 2 Tm. 2:23; Tt. 3:9.

Among the warnings in Eph. 5 there is found in v. 4 that against μωρολογία. The word occurs alongside εὐτραπελία, which means adroitness of speech both in the good sense[99] and the bad. The reference is thus to sins of the tongue, and words like κενοφωνία (1 Tm. 6:20), ματαιολογία (1 Tm. 1:16), αἰσχρολογία (Col. 3:8), πιθανολογία (Col. 2:4) etc. are closely related to μωρολογία. In Eph. 5:4 μωρολογία follows αἰσχρότης, and the three terms αἰσχρότης, μωρολογία and εὐτραπελία are then taken up again in the ensuing ἃ οὐκ ἀνῆκεν. Hence one is to think in terms of offensive, equivocal and foolish speech. But the terms are taken up yet again in the μηδεὶς ὑμᾶς ἀπατάτω κενοῖς λόγοις of v. 6, and this seems to carry a warning against heresy. The μωρολογία of Eph. 5:4 must also be compared with the μωραὶ ζητήσεις of 2 Tm. 2:23; Tt. 3:9 and the μωραὶ διδαχαί of Herm. s., 8, 6, 5, and Mt. 23:17 (→ 842) has also to be taken into account.[100] Jesus and early Christian exhortation are opposed to the empty verbal debates which are found in Jewish schools and also in Gnosticising Christianity (1 Tm. 6:4: νοσῶν περὶ ζητήσεις καὶ λογομαχίας). These are described as foolish, *non quod primo adspectu tales appareant (quin saepe inani sapientiae ostentatione fallunt), sed quia nihil ad pietatem conducunt.*[101] They are דִּבְרֵי בוּרוּת, foolish questions,[102] like the problem whether Lot's wife as a pillar of salt, or one who has risen from the dead, will make unclean according to the laws of uncleanness through contact with the dead.[103] The question of genealogies[104] (Tt. 3:9; 1 Tm. 1:4), whether these be generations of spirits or haggadic stories,[105] is relevant here. So, too, are speculations on the hereafter, which are

---

[95] Kaufmann, 350.

[96] Schmidt (→ n. 52), 212, 31 ff.

[97] In later editions of the Armen. Bible depictions of the foolish virgins are a type of persecutors falling down before Christ. W. Molsdorf, *Christl. Symbolik d. mittelalterlichen Kunst* (1926), 55, 320.

[98] Cf. Heyne and Lehmann, also F. X. Kraus, *Geschichte d. christl. Kunst,* I (1896), 134, also Molsdorf, 110, 793; 180, 1008; 221, 1081.

[99] In pagan writers, acc. to Calvin, *ad loc.*, εὐτραπελία means *acuta et salsa urbanitas.* In Aristot. Eth. Nic., II, 7, p. 1108a, 24 the term is the right mean between βωμολοχία and ἀγροικότης. In Rhet., II, 12, p. 1389b, 11 it is characterised as πεπαιδευμένη ὕβρις.

[100] Cf. also Mk. 7:13 D: ἀκυροῦντες τὸν λόγον τοῦ θεοῦ τῇ παραδόσει ὑμῶν τῇ μωρᾷ.

[101] Calvin on Tt. 3:9.

[102] Str.-B., III, 606. Cf. also דִּבְרֵי תַפְלוּת, foolish words in the sense of stupid resistance to God's decree.

[103] Cf. also the question of the Sadducees in Mk. 12:18-27 and par.

[104] B. Weiss (1902) on Tt. 3:9.

[105] Dib. Past. on Tt. 3:9; Wbg. Past., 263 on Tt. 3:9.

expressly stated to be dangerous to salvation in e.g., 4 Esr. 6:34: "And do not fall into foolish thoughts about the first times, that you be not felled by the last times."[106] Finally the subtleties which Jesus combatted in Mt. 23:16 ff., 23 ff. and elsewhere, and all questions which do not relate to the truth of salvation,[107] are dismissed as foolish. Nor is the concept of folly regarded as an excuse in this connection. Occupation with such questions is taken to be sinful and culpable.[108] The reference is to false teaching and false teachers, though what is at issue is the mode of thought rather than the content of the teaching. In this struggle similar means are used to those which philosophy adopted in its conflict with sophistry.[109] The Past. in particular champion sound doctrine against all foolish and morbid speculation.

5.. "Folly" in Paul: R. 1:22; 1 C. 1:18 ff.; 2:14; 3:18, 19; 4:10.

The transvaluation of values in the Gospel is the basis of the use of the word group by Paul. Sometimes a critical use is to be seen elsewhere as well, but the transvaluation of values in the sense of the NT revelation was accomplished by Jesus Himself, not by Paul. The only point is that νήπιος is more common than μωρός in the actual usage of Jesus. Paul does not raise the question of the power of the abusive term to destroy fellowship. Nor does he use it to draw boundaries which are already there. He sees that he himself and his churches stand under the burden and suffering of the term. He recognises in it the essential judgment of the world on believers. "The word of the cross is foolishness to those who are lost" (1 C. 1:18), to Gentiles or Greeks (1:23), to the natural man in general (2:14). Paul is obviously right in this. In his own work he constantly came up against this judgment. The philosophers at Athens mocked him (Ac. 17:18: σπερμολόγος,[110] 17:32: χλευάζειν).[111] The pro-consul Gallio, stepbrother of Seneca, regarded the dispute between Paul and the Jews as Jewish μωρολογία (Ac. 18:15: ζητήματα περὶ λόγου καὶ ὀνομάτων καὶ νόμου τοῦ καθ' ὑμᾶς). Festus declared him to be out of his mind (Ac. 26:24: μαίνῃ, Παῦλε, τὰ πολλά σε γράμματα εἰς μανίαν περιτρέπει). He thus knew from his own experience that those who are outside will always come to this unfavourable judgment of the man who is proud of his own reason. That Paul should speak of a crucified man must have seemed very tactless to many of his hearers,[112] and hence foolish in the superficial sense which the word can sometimes have in the Greek Bible, i.e., in the

---

[106] Vg: *cogitare vana.* Violet, 55.

[107] Cf. also Ps.-Pl. Ep. to the Laodiceans, ed. A. Harnack, Kl. T. (1905), 4: *neque destituant vos quorundam vaniloquia insinuantium, ut vos evertant a veritate evangelii.*

[108] Whereas OT usage generally equates fools with the ungodly and thus excludes them from salvation, primitive Christianity calls sinners in the congregation fools. The ref. is to venial sins, and folly is in some sense an excuse. This may be seen esp. in Herm. Thus s., 9, 22, 4 refers to those who are not wicked but foolish and stupid. Presumption caused their fall, but they had the possibility of repentance, 22, 2, 3; 8, 6, 5. In the sense of something which is wholly reprehensible Herm. refers to a πνεῦμα μωρόν (m., 11, 11) and to things which are improper for Christians (m., 5, 2, 2; 12, 2, 1; cf. also 5, 2, 4; s., 8, 7, 4). There is an even sharper warning against all manticism, and against μύθων μωρῶν ἀπάτας ἐγγαστεριμύθων in Orac. Sibyll., III, 226.

[109] Cf. Dib. Past. on 1 Tm. 4:6; 2 Tm. 2:23.

[110] A babbler with second-hand ideas.

[111] → παίζειν, ἐμπαίζειν.

[112] Cic. Pro Rabirio, 5: *Nomen ipsum crucis absit non modo a corpore civium Romanorum sed etiam a cogitatione, oculis, auribus.*

practical wisdom of the Greek Sir. When the Hellenist passes the judgment of folly, he is not thinking of the mystery of the cross which he does not know or understand, but of the violation of etiquette, which forbids any reference to the ugly execution of slaves in the company of worthy citizens. This rejection on grounds of taste rather than intellect is part of the hardening and blinding of the world, of the divinely willed corruption of its nature, which is both punishment and sin, R. 1:21, 22: ἐματαιώθησαν, ἐσκοτίσθη ἡ ἀσύνετος αὐτῶν καρδία, φάσκοντες (this expresses the fact that the assertion is objectively false) εἶναι σοφοὶ ἐμωράνθησαν.[113] This thought is further developed in 1 C. Paul finds the OT basis in Is. 29:14: ἀπολῶ τὴν σοφίαν τῶν σοφῶν καὶ τὴν σύνεσιν τῶν συνετῶν κρύψω. The LXX made a general judgment out of the Mas. judgment on the wise among the people of Israel.[114] Paul can use the verse only in this form. In so doing, he replaces the weak κρύψω by the stronger ἀθετήσω from ψ 32:10. In 1 C. 1:10 there is an echo of Is. 19:11, → 835. This saying from the prophecy against Egypt receives its radical significance from Paul's addition of τοῦ κόσμου. God has made the world's wisdom folly.[115] This is His miraculous and astonishing work in the world.[116] God fixes values without regard to human assessment and according to His own good-pleasure. Thus the wisdom of this world is folly before Him (1 C. 3:19). This is attested in the OT (Job 5:12 f.; Ps. 94:11). This means, of course, that the world's judgment on the foolishness of the cross is shown to be without substance. It simply serves to characterise those who have fallen victim to destruction.

Nevertheless, in two chains of thought Paul is prepared to accept the term "folly" as a correct assessment of the word of the cross. First, to do this is to gain a clear insight into human wisdom. God does not have to put forth His own wisdom to overcome the wisdom of man. Folly is the content of the preaching, a foolish act contrary to all human logic, to all human expectation of God's power, 1 C. 1:21.[117] For the act of God which is unintelligible to human reason, God's foolishness, is wiser than human wisdom, 1:25.[118] Behind these statements there undoubtedly stand Paul's own experiences and revelations (2 C. 12:9; cf. also 13:3, 4), though in a different sense the community can see something of the same in itself (1 C. 1:26 ff.).[119]

But secondly he uses "folly" in an unconditional sense. The act by which God reconciled the world really was foolish.[120] No doctrine of justification, atonement, or vicarious satisfaction, not even the reference to the revelation of the

---

[113] This verse often forms the starting-point for Christian apologetic and polemic against polytheism, cf. Aristid. Apol., 8, 2. Mistrust of philosophers was current in Hellenism from the time of Socrates. For material cf. Wettstein, for Jewish material Str.-B., III, 47. Cf. already Prv. 3:7.

[114] Cf. Philo's reinterpretation of Dt. 32:6, → 837.

[115] *Ita ut rationem divini consilii et beneplaciti non possit mundus exputare* (Bengel).

[116] → θαῦμα, III, 31 ff. Cf. also Is. 28:21, and on this → ἔργον, II, 640.

[117] Cf. Bengel: *Deus cum homine perverso agit per contraria, ut homo se abneget ac Deo gloriam reddat, per fidem crucis.*

[118] Calvin on 1 C. 1:21: *Concessio est, quod Evangelium stultitiam praedicationis vocat, quae in speciem talis censetur istis* μωροσόφοις, *qui falsa confidentia ebrii nihil verentur sacrosanctam Dei veritatem insipidae suae censurae subiicere.* Of the many compounds with μωρο-, that mentioned by Calvin, i.e., μωρόσοφος, is found in the satirist Luc. Alex., 40.

[119] Here exegetes from an early date have tended to soften; thus Orig. on Mt. 15:24 ascribes the folly to those who do not belong to Israel and have no clear insight (Comm. in Mt. § 17).

[120] Bchm. on 1 C. 1:22, 90 and 98.

mystery to Paul himself (1 C. 2:6, 7), can alter this. Wisdom as Paul uses the term here, and knowledge as he speaks of it in 1 C. 13:12, are not an earthly possession of Christians. They have them only in hope. Nor does this take away the foolishness of preaching. This consists in the humiliation of Christ, in the historical reality of His life and passion. Hence Christians, too, are always fools in the judgment of the world. They share in the folly of humiliation. They enter into fellowship with the suffering of Christ: "If any man among you would be wise, let him become a fool (that he may be wise)." For Paul's view is that as folly is part of the humiliation of Christ, so wisdom belongs to His glory.[121] Only ironically can Paul say that in their present earthly life Christians have already attained to wisdom. The present life is that of the fellowship of sufferings. Hence Paul can claim to be a fool for Christ's sake (1 C. 4:10).[122] Wisdom is a possession of hope, a gift of the Spirit.

The criticism of culture in Paul's preaching is perhaps most clearly displayed in his transvaluation of wisdom and folly. But it finds its most pertinent expression, on the basis of NT salvation history,[123] in the contrasting of strength and weakness. The comparison of wisdom and folly must always be related to this, as may be seen from the antithesis between folly and strength in 1 C. 1:18. Strength and wisdom are never man's own possession. They are the gift of God, which manifests itself precisely in weakness and folly (2 C. 12:9).

Bertram

---

121 H. St. J. Thackeray, *The LXX and Jewish Worship* (1923), 95 ff., emphasises the relation between Paul's discussion of the wisdom of the world and Jewish ideas, and refers to Bar. 3:9-4:4. In Bar. 3:28 we read: καὶ ἀπώλοντο παρὰ τὸ μὴ ἔχειν φρόνησιν, ἀπώλοντο διὰ τὴν ἀβουλίαν αὐτῶν. ἀβουλία is folly, being used for אִוֶּלֶת in Prv. 14:17. Acc. to Thackeray 1 C. 1:18-2:16 contains Paul's recollections of a Jewish sermon which he had heard on the day of mourning for the capture of Jerusalem by Nebuchadnezzar (9th Ab) on the text Jer. 8:13-9:24, the *haphtara* of the fast. But this is to misunderstand Paul. He is not deploring the human folly whose punishment the Israelites suffered so terribly with the overthrow of Jerusalem (cf. the Intr. Bar. 3:1-8). He is rather rejoicing in the power of the message which overcomes all the wisdom of the world.

122 That Pl. is serious is shown by the fact that he is not ashamed to be regarded as mad, cf. the verses already quoted from Ac. 17:18, 32 etc.

123 The transvaluation of values in the NT consists, not in the reversal of concepts, but in the overthrow of man's claim to independent validity, in the repulsing of arrogance. Wisdom still remains in force as God's gift, Eph. 5:15: "Walk ..., not as fools, but as wise." In Ign., too, it is stressed that Jesus Christ, and the knowledge given in Him, are a gift of God's grace, cf. Eph., 17, 2: "Why, then, have not all we who have received God's knowledge, i.e., Jesus Christ, become wise? Why do we perish in folly without insight into the gift of grace which the Lord has truly sent?" (Bau. Ign.).

Μωυσῆς [1]

Contents: A. Moses in Later Judaism: 1. The View of Moses in Later Judaism: a. Hellenistic Judaism; b. Palestinian Judaism; c. The Death and Ascension of Moses; d. The Distinction between the Hellenistic and the Palestinian View. 2. Moses in the Eschatological Expectation of Later Judaism: The Return of Moses. 3. Moses as a Type of the Messiah: a. The Coming "Prophet like Moses"; b. The Messiah as a Second Moses;

Μωυσῆς. On A. 1: J. A. Fabricius, *Codex pseudepigraphicus Veteris Testamenti* (1713), I, 825-868; II, 111-113; E. Carmoly, "La légende de Moïse," *Rev. Orientale*, 1 (1841), 373-382; B. Beer, "Leben Moses nach Auffassung d. jüdischen Sage," *Jahrbuch f. d. Geschichte der Juden u. d. Jdts.*, 3 (1863), 11-64; M. Grünbaum, *Neue Beiträge zur semitischen Sagenkunde* (1893), 152-185; J. H. Dorion, *Moïse dans les traditions biblique, grecque, latine et égyptienne* (1898-1899); J. Z. Lauterbach-K. Kohler, Art. "Moses" in *Jew. Enc.*, IX (1905), 44-57, 57 f.; N. Bonwetsch, "Die Mosessage in d. slavischen kirchlichen Lit.," *NGG phil.-hist. Kl.* (1908), 583-607 (with transl. of a Slavic life of Moses); Schürer, Index, *s.v.* "Moses"; L. Ginzberg, *The Legends of the Jews*, II, III (1910-11); E. Sellin, *Mose u. seine Bedeutung f. d. isr.-jüdische Religionsgeschichte* (1922); J. Morgenstern, "Moses with the Shining Face," *Hbr. Un. Coll. Ann.*, II (1925), 1-27; M. Abraham, *Légendes juives apocr. sur la vie de Moïse* (1925); M. J. bin Gorion (= M. J. Berdiczewski), *D. Sagen der Juden, Mose* (1926); Bousset-Gressm., 121 f.; M. A. Halévy, *Moïse dans l'histoire et dans la légende* (1927); M. Gaster, *The Asātīr, the Samaritan Book of the "Secrets of Moses"* (1927); Str.-B., Index, *s.v.* "Moses," IV, 1249; Schl. Mt., 528; A. Kristianpoller, Art. "Moses" (2: "In der rabb. Überlieferung"), Jüd. Lex., IV (1930), 310-313; S. Rappaport, *Agada u. Exegese bei Flavius Jos.* (1930), 25-39, 113-127; A. Rosmarin, *Moses im Lichte d. Agada* (1932); B. Heller, MGWJ, 77 (1933), 390-392; H. Windisch, "Paulus u. Christus," UNT, 24 (1934), 89 ff., 103 ff., 242 ff.; L. Bieler, ΘΕΙΟΣ ΑΝΗΡ, II (1936), 5-8, 30-36; I. Heinemann, Art. "Moses," Pauly-W., 16 (1935), 359-375. On A. 3: A. F. Gfrörer, *Das Jhdt. des Heils* (1838), II, 318 ff.; G. Dalman, *Der leidende u. d. sterbende Messias d. Synagoge* (1888), 28 f.; W. Baldensperger, *Das Selbstbewusstsein Jesu im Lichte der messianischen Hoffnungen seiner Zeit*² (1892), Exc. 138-142; K. Bornhäuser, *Das Wirken des Christus durch Taten u. Worte* (1921); B. Murmelstein, "Adam, ein Beitrag zur Messiaslehre," WZKM, 25 (1928), 242-275; 26 (1929), 51-86, esp. 51-64; J. Fischer, "Das Problem des neuen Exodus in Js. 40-55," Theol. Quart., 110 (1929), 111-130; J. Jeremias, "Erlöser u. Erlösung im Spätjudt. u. im Urchristentum," *Deutsche Theologie*, II. "Der Erlösungsgedanke" (1929), 112-115; W. Staerk, *Soter* (1933), 61 ff., 79 f.; Volz Esch., 191-197; W. Staerk, *Die Erlösererwartung in d. östlichen Religionen* (1938), esp. 50 ff. (and addendum, 487), 105 ff., 375, 408; L. Goppelt, *Typos. D. typologische Deutung d. AT im Neuen* (1940); W. Wiebe, *Die Wüstenzeit als Typus der messianischen Heilszeit* (Göttinger Diss.). On B. 1: There is no comprehensive study. On B. 3 cf. the bibl. listed under A. 3.

[1] On the orthography cf. Winer (Schmiedel) § 5, 21e; Tisch. NT, III, 119; E. Nestle, ZAW, 27 (1907), 111-113; Thackeray, 163, n. 3; Schürer, III, 478, n. 23; Bl.-Debr. § 38 and 53, 1; Preisigke Namenbuch; Schl. Gesch. Isr., 421 f.; Pr.-Bauer³, 880. We find both Μωυσης and Μωσης in the NT MSS; the only older maj. which is uniform is the Chester-Beatty pap. 𝔓⁴⁶ (early 3rd cent.), always Μωυσης (17 times). In all others there is vacillation. Μωυσης is predominant in א BDK, Μωσης in AEFG. Chester-Beatty pap. 𝔓⁴⁵ (early 3rd cent.) has Μωσης 6 times, Μωυσης at Ac. 7:20; pap. 𝔓⁴⁷ (3rd cent.) has Μωσεως at the one verse Rev. 15:3, but corr. Μωυσεως. C vacillates considerably. The same vacillation may be seen in the LXX, pap., Ep. Ar., Philo, Joseph., Sib., Test. Sol. The form Μωυσης (also Μουσης in the pap., so CIG, III, 4668g, Test. Sol. 25:4, and Μουσες, Preisigke Namenbuch, 221 ff.) is supported by the best NT MSS, and the same is true in the LXX, Joseph., and most sources. That it is pre-Christian is shown by the Egypt. etym. found in Philo (Vit. Mos., I, 17: τὸ γὰρ ὕδωρ μῶυ ὀνομάζουσιν Αἰγύπτιοι) and Joseph. (Ap., I, 286, and in more extended form Ant., 2, 228). The use of ωυ is perhaps an attempt to reproduce the Egypt pronunciation of מֹשֶׁה (Thackeray, 163, n. 3), for the diphthong ωυ is found in the early Ptolem. period (Mayser, 185), cf. the Gk. rendering of Egypt.

c. The Second Moses as a Figure of Suffering. B. Moses in the New Testament: 1. The Historical Moses: a. As the Mediator of the Law; b. As Prophet; c. As the Suffering Messenger of God and the Model of Faith for the Community; d. The Moses Legend in the NT. 2. Moses as a Figure of the Last Time. 3. The Moses/Christ Typology: a. The Baptist; b. Jesus; c. The Primitive Community; d. Paul; e. Matthew; f. Hebrews; g. The Johannine Writings; h. The Suffering Moses as a Type of Christ. C. The Post-Apostolic Age.

A. Moses in Later Judaism.

1. The View of Moses in Later Judaism.

For later Judaism the Torah is the one eternal main revelation of God to which the other books of the Canon are added only because of sin [2] and with limited validity in time. [3, 4] Similarly, Moses is for later Judaism the most important figure in salvation history thus far. As distinct from the basic OT approach to Moses, especially in the prophets, [5] his person is now panegyrically magnified, and his life and work are surrounded by an almost innumerable host of legends [6] which find ready points of contact in the biblical account, where numerous miraculous events accompany the life of Moses from his birth to his death. In this respect note should be taken of the difference between Hellenistic and Palestinian Judaism.

---

proper names and names of months (Θωυθ, Σαμῶυς, Mayser, 138). Acc. to Eus. Praep. Ev., 1, 9, 24 (Τάαυτος ..., ὃν Αἰγύπτιοι μὲν ἐκάλεσαν Θωύθ, Ἀλεξανδρεῖς δὲ Θώθ) we may assume that this pronounciation was native to Upper Egypt. It is thus highly likely that ωυ was pronounced as a diphthong (Thackeray, 163, n. 3; Heinemann, 360), and the modern custom of separating the vowels to give three syllables (Μωϋσῆς) can hardly be correct. The form Μωσης (Strabo, 16, 2, 35, mostly in metrical texts like Sib., 2, 245; 3, 253; 8, 251) is not to be regarded as an assimilation of Μωυσης to the Heb. form but as the usual Gk. rendering of מֹשֶׁה outside Egypt (Strabo) and probably in Lower Egypt (→ *supra*, hence 𝔓 [45, 47] *supra*). On the declension cf. Winer (Schmiedel) § 10, 5 and n. 4; Thackeray, 163 f.; Bl.-Debr. § 55, 1d; Pr.-Bauer[3], 880. The LXX declines with few exceptions Μωυσῆς, -ῆ (rarely -έως), -ῆ (more often -εῖ, but only as an orthographic variant), -ῆν, vocative -ῆ. In the 1st cent. A.D. we find in Philo and Joseph. the gen. and dat. of the 3rd declension (-έως [-έος], -εῖ), but -ῆν is still the acc. So also the NT, gen. always -έως, dat. -εῖ (also -ῆ in the MSS), acc. -ῆν (-έα only Lk. 16:29 and 𝔓 [46] 1 C. 10:2), vocative -ῆ (Barn., 4, 8; 1 Cl., 53, 2).

[2] bNed., 22b.

[3] jMeg., 70d, 60 f.

[4] Hellen. Judaism goes further than Palestinian in this exalting of the Torah over the other OT books, as the example of Philo shows. In fact Philo quotes little more than the Torah apart from a few verses from the Prophets and Writings (cf. J. Leisegang, Indices to Philo, ed. L. Cohn and P. Wendland, VII [1926], 29-43; I. Heinemann, *Philons gr. u. jüd. Bildung* [1932], 527).

[5] → 429, 431, 438 f. (Rengstorf), though it should be noted with ref. to 441 that there are a few impulses towards the glorifying of Moses in the OT, esp. the story of his radiant countenance (Ex. 34:29 ff., Morgenstern, Moses as "demi-god"), also the story of his exposure and deliverance (2:1 ff., cf. F. Dornseiff, "Antikes zum AT," ZAW, 53, NF, 12 [1935], 155 f.; →Bieler, II, 5 f.) and that of his death (Dt. 34; Windisch, 93; Bieler 8). But we must not forget the basic distinction between the OT ἄνθρωπος θεοῦ, who is always God-related, and the deified Hellenistic θεῖος ἀνήρ, Bieler, 24 f.

[6] Fabricius, Carmoly, Beer, Grünbaum, Dorion, Lauterbach, Kohler, Bonwetsch, Schürer (II, 405 f., III, 301 f., 402, 477 f.), Ginzberg, Abraham, bin Gorion, Halévy, Str.-B., Kristianpoller, Rappaport, Rosmarin, Heinemann.

a. Hellenistic Judaism.

The view which Hellenistic Judaism had of Moses may be seen first in Eupolemos (middle of the 2nd cent. B.C.). Unfortunately only a small fragment remains of the part of his historical work which relates to Moses. [7] We know a good deal more about Artapanus, who wrote a legendary romance about Moses in the 1st cent. B.C. [8] This is based on Eupolemos, [9] who also stands behind the glorification of Moses in Ps.-Aristobulus. [10] There are many points of contact between Artapanus and Joseph. (Ant., 2, 201-4, 331), [11] who follows a form of the Moses legend native to Egypt. [12] Philo is another source of our knowledge of the view of Moses in Hellenistic Judaism, Vit. Mos., I and II. Philo sticks closer to the biblical account that the others, though he gives it a typical Hellenistic form.

The Moses romance of Hellen. Judaism [13] displays all the features of the Hellen. βίος in glorification of heroes. [14] The biblical account is imaginatively expanded beyond all recognition. Moses' birth is prophesied by an Egyptian seer, Jos. Ant., 2, 205 → n. 238). As a child he tramples on the crown of Pharaoh. [15] As general and hero he leads the Egyptian army against the Ethiopians, [16] and marries the daughter of the Ethiopian king, Jos. Ant., 2, 252 f. He is the father of all wisdom and culture and the inventor of the alphabetic script. [17] As the father of Egyptian sailing, architecture, armaments, politics and even worship [18] he is the author of Egyptian civilisation. Gk. philosophy is based on Moses; [19] Pythagoras, [20] Anaxagoras, [21] Socrates, [20] Plato, [22] Heraclitus [23] and Zeno [24] took their doctrines from Moses, as deduced from similarities. Poets like Homer and Hesiod borrowed from his books. [25] He is identical with Musaios, the teacher of Orpheus. [26] In short, he is the true teacher of the race. [27]

The obvious apologetic motives behind this picture find expression also in the removal of all offensive features from the account. The Jewish historian Demetrius (3rd cent. B.C.) shows that Zipporah, his wife, descends from Abraham and Keturah. [28] Artapanus

[7] In Cl. Al. Strom., I, 23 § 153, 4 and Eus. Praep. Ev., 9, 26. Moses is exalted in the fragment as the first sage and the inventor of the alphabet.

[8] For this we are much indebted to Eus. Praep. Ev., 9, 27.

[9] Artapanus lauds Moses as the interpreter of the sacred letters of the Egyptians (cf. → n. 7), Eus. Praep. Ev., 9, 27, 6.

[10] On Ps.-Aristob. cf. Schürer, III, 514-519. On the dating Bousset-Gressm., 28 f., who put it in the Roman period (Schürer, middle of the 2nd cent. B.C.).

[11] The material in Joseph. which goes beyond the biblical account has been assembled by Rappaport, 25-39, 115-127. Windisch, 113 and Bieler, 30-34 relate it to Hellenistic depictions of the θεῖος ἀνήρ. On Joseph.'s contacts with Artapanus cf. J. Freudenthal, Alexander Polyhist. (1875), 169-171; Schl. Gesch. Isr., 190, 422, n. 179; Heinemann, 372-374; Bieler, 30, 32 f., where there is a comparison between the depiction of Moses in Artapanus and that in Joseph.

[12] For examples of local colour in the account in Joseph. cf. Schl. Gesch. Isr., 420, n. 170.

[13] Heinemann, 365 ff.

[14] On the freeing of Moses by the automatic opening of the prison doors (important as a par. to Ac. 5:19; 12:6-11; 16:26 f.) → III, 175, n. 34 (θύρα).

[15] Jos. Ant., 2, 233 (cf. Ex. r., 1 on 2:10 : Moses as a child puts the crown on his head).

[16] Artapanus in Eus. Praep. Ev., 9, 27; Jos. Ant., 2, 238-253.

[17] Eupolemos ; cf. Artapanus.

[18] Artapanus in Eus. Praep. Ev., 9, 27.

[19] Jos. Ap., II, 281.

[20] Ps.-Aristob. in Eus. Praep. Ev., 13, 12, 4.

[21] Jos. Ap., II, 168.

[22] Ps.-Aristob. → n. 20; Jos. Ap., II, 168, 257.

[23] Philo Leg. All., I, 108.

[24] Philo Omn. Prob. Lib., 57.

[25] Ps.-Aristob. in Eus. Praep. Ev., 13, 12, 13.

[26] Artapanus in Eus. Praep. Ev., 9, 27.

[27] On the rise of individual features cf. Heinemann, 367 ff.

[28] Eus. Praep. Ev., 9, 29, 1-3.

argues that Moses slew the Egyptian in self-defence,[29] and Joseph. omits this episode altogether.[30]

The strong apologetic thrust is understandable in view of the existence of an anti-Semitic Moses legend which Joseph. ascribes to the Egypt. priest Manetho (c. 270-250 B.C.)[31] and which was often repeated after the 1st cent. B.C.[32] This makes out that Moses was a leprous priest of Heliopolis originally called Osarsiph.[33] This man made himself the leader of 80,000 lepers expelled from the country.[34] Worship of the ass, which was ascribed to the Jews[35] and which even Tacitus believed of them,[36] was linked to Moses. Antiochus Epiphanes supposedly found in the Holy of Holies the stone statue of a long-bearded man with a book in his hand and riding on an ass; he conjectured that this represented Moses, and sprinkled it with swine's blood.[37]

Though Philo keeps closer to the OT, his depiction is no less Hellenistic.[38] Typical is the sentence with which he begins his Vita: "I will recount the life of Moses ..., in every respect the greatest and most perfect of men" (I, 1). Moses shows himself to be most perfect as the sage who fashions his life in harmony with nature[39] and the prophetic ecstatic who ascends to God (Ex. 24) and is deified.[40] He thus embodies Philo's religious ideal of the βίος θεωρητικὸς καὶ ὁρατικός.[41] Philo is not slack to enumerate the virtues of his hero.[42] He was the Law personified, the mediator (→ 617), the reconciler of his people.[43] He was king, law-giver, high-priest and prophet[44] in one.[45]

It is evident that Philo's view is at root just as remote from the biblical presentation as that of the fantastic romance. In both cases Moses is extolled as a unique personality. He is the genius, idealised man.

---

[29] *Ibid.*, 9, 27.
[30] For further apologetic features in Jos. → Rappaport, *passim*.
[31] Jos. Ap., I, 228-251. Jos. can hardly be right, since the decisive § 250 interrupts the context and does not originally belong here (I. Heinemann, Pauly-W., Art. "Antisemitismus," Suppl. V, 27).
[32] Schürer, III, 151, n. 7; I. Heinemann (→ n. 31), 27 f.
[33] Jos. Ap., I, 238, 250.
[34] Schürer, III, 151 f., 529 f.
[35] *Ibid.*, III, 152; I. Heinemann (→ n. 31), 28-30.
[36] Hist., V, 3-4.
[37] Diod. S., 34, 1 (Phot. Bibl., 244, p. 379a, 34), prob. based on Posidonius.
[38] There is a comprehensive historical survey of Philo's view of Moses in Bieler, 34-36. He follows Windisch, 103-113, who refers esp. to what is said about the deification of Moses (→ n. 40).
[39] Vit. Mos., I, 48. The goal of Moses is ὁ ὀρθὸς τῆς φύσεως λόγος (the Stoic ideal).
[40] R. Reitzenstein, *D. Vorgeschichte d. christl. Taufe* (1929), 103 ff.; J. Pascher, *Der Königsweg zu Wiedergeburt u. Vergottung bei Philon* (1931), 249 ff.; Windisch, 104 f. Cf. esp. Quaest. in Ex. 2:29: *transmutatur in divinum, ita ut fiat deo cognatus vereque divinus.*
[41] Heinemann, 371. Bieler, 36 rightly says: "This Moses is not the OT prophet, nor is he the usual θεῖος of Hellenism; he is the πνευματικός in whom centuries later both pagan and Christian Gnosis found the perfect man."
[42] Cf. esp. the long list in Vit. Mos., I, 153 f.
[43] Vit. Mos., I, 162: αὐτὸς ἐγένετο νόμος ἔμψυχός τε καὶ λογικός. II, 166.
[44] Vit. Mos., II, 292 (concluding sentence). The structure of the Vita corresponds to these four attributes. It depicts Moses as national leader (Book I), as law-giver (II, 8-65), high-priest (II, 66-186), prophet (II, 187-287).
[45] Cf. Test. L. 8: The Messiah is king-priest-prophet. On this threefold dignity which Moses also had acc. to the haggada (Murmelstein, 63 f.) as a mark of the primal man and redeemer, cf. Murmelstein, 268-275 (cf. 83 f.: the three dignities of antichrist as the devilish counterpart of the redeemer); Staerk, *Erlösererwartung*, 12 ff., 102 (Adam), 24 ff. (Christ), 52, 66, n. 2 (Moses), 60 f. (Elijah) and *passim*.

b. Palestinian Judaism.

Writings: 1. The Book of Jubilees is often called 'Ἀποκάλυψις Μωυσέως (so Syncellus, ed. Dindorf, 1, 5 and 49). It contains a free version of primitive history from creation to Ex. 14. According to Jub. 1:1 ff. it rests on a revelation given to Moses on Sinai and written down at God's behest (1:5, 7, 26; 23:32).[46] It was written soon after 110 B.C.[47] 2. The Assumption of Moses,[48] shortly after Herod's death[49] and preserved in at least the first part,[50] contains a disclosure made by Moses to Joshua on Mt. Nebo of coming events up to the end. 3. The Life of Adam and Eve in the Gk. MSS ABCD is entitled the Apocalypse of Moses,[51] though this is undoubtedly secondary.[52] Of mediaeval works, which use older materials, we might mention 4. גְּדֻלַּת מֹשֶׁה, The Greatness of Moses. This describes revelations to Moses on his heavenly ascent prior to the exodus.[53] The midrash is much older than the Moses Chronicle compiled in the 10th cent. (→ *infra*).[54] 5. פְּטִירַת מֹשֶׁה, The Midrash of the Decease of Moses, in two (not three)[55] recensions.[56] This contains legends about the death of Moses. It was compiled prior to 900.[57] 6. דִּבְרֵי הַיָּמִים שֶׁל מֹשֶׁה, The Chronicle of Moses.[58] This is an account of his life with legendary embellishment (war against the Cushites, → 850) of the biblical account. The midrash is dependent on סֵפֶר הַיָּשָׁר, which recounts world history from Abraham to the judges.[59] It was compiled by an unknown hand in the 10th cent.[60]

In its desire to magnify Moses with supreme attributes[61] Palestinian Judaism was not behind Hellenistic.[62] It was strongly influenced by the latter's depiction of Moses as a hero[63] and by its Moses legend.[64] Nevertheless, it saw Moses differently. He was not now the hero and ideal man, but primarily the mediator of revelation.

---

[46] Acc. to 1, 27 the angel of the countenance writes for Moses (→ n. 210).
[47] Cf. S. Klein, "Palästinisches im Jubiläenbuch," ZDPV, 57 (1934), 7-27, esp. 25.
[48] Schürer, III, 294-305.
[49] *Ibid.*, III, 298-300.
[50] The fragment, a palimpsest MS in Latin, was ed. by the man who found it, A. M. Ceriani, *Monumenta sacra et profana*, I, 1 (1861), 55-64.
[51] Ed. C. Tischendorff, *Apocalypses apocryphae* (1866), 1 ff.
[52] C. Fuchs in Kautzsch Pseudepigr., 506 f.; Schürer, III, 397 f.
[53] Bibl. Abraham, 26 f. (transl. 75-92).
[54] *Ibid.*, 23.
[55] Schürer, III, 301; Strack Einl., 218.
[56] First ed. Constantinople, 1516; cf. the ed. of A. Jellinek, *Bet ha-Midrasch*, 1 (1853), 115-129 (Rec. A) and 6 (1877), 73-78 (Rec. B); transl. into German, A. Wünsche, *Aus Israels Lehrhallen*, 1 (1907), 134-162; Abraham, 92-113, with full bibl. 41-45.
[57] Abraham, 31 f.
[58] First ed. Constantinople, 1516; cf. the ed. of A. Jellinek, *op. cit.*, 2 (1853), 1-11; transl. into German A. Wünsche, *op. cit.*, 61-80; Abraham, 46-74, with bibl. 16-22.
[59] Abraham, 13-15.
[60] Gfrörer, 354 f.; Abraham, 15.
[61] Rosmarin, 18-27 lists the attributes ascribed to Moses in Rabb. lit.
[62] The oldest instance is Sir. 44:22-45:5, esp. v. 2 (Heb.), where on the basis of Ex. 4:16 (cf. 7:1) we read: "And he (God) (magnified him [Moses] as) a god," (ויכבדהו כא)להים; LXX obviously softens this: ὡμοίωσεν αὐτὸν δόξῃ ἁγίων. The Ass. Mos. calls him "the divine prophet for the whole world, the most perfect teacher of this time" (11:16). In Rabb. lit. (though this is disputed) the supreme degree of piety and sinlessness is ascribed to Moses, bShab., 55b. There is no word of the Torah which he has not received, bChag., 4b. The world was created for him, R. Shemuel, b. 254, bSanh., 98b, etc. But for the Palestinian tradition Moses is primarily fallible man (→ 615). On the Samaritans, for whom Moses inherited the divine likeness which Adam lost, cf. Dalman, *Worte Jesu*², 385.
[63] E.g., Jos. Ant., 3, 180: Moses is θεῖος ἀνήρ. The OT offers only a few impulses towards glorification (→ n. 5). In its later Jewish form this comes from Gk. influences (→ 438 f.) and arises first in Hellen. Judaism.
[64] For examples of this influence → n. 15, n. 238.

Moses is the servant of God.[65] Because of his faithfulness and meekness he is selected from among all men.[66] Indeed, he is ordained mediator of the covenant from the beginning of the world.[67] God allowed him to see His glory,[68] to hear His voice,[69] and to mediate the chief revelation (→ 849), the pre-existent[70] Torah, to Israel. The oral Torah, the many statutes derived from the Torah, he also learned from God's lips on Sinai and passed on to his people by way of oral tradition.[71] His wisdom and dignity are by ordination transferred in unbroken succession to the scribes, and authorise them for their office.[72] He is Israel's absolute teacher.[73]

But he is more. He is the divine prophet for the whole world.[74] "All the secrets of the times and the end of the hours"[75] have been revealed to him by God.[76] He is the faithful shepherd (→ ποιμήν)[77] who rescues his people from Pharaoh. He is the man of patience who suffers many things in Egypt, at the Red Sea, for forty years in the desert,[78] where he finally dies and is buried, → 854. He is the great man of prayer, who as Israel's defender "hourly day and night bowed his knees to the earth in prayer,"[79] and who "poured out his soul unto death" (Is. 53:12) when he vicariously sought to take to himself the sin with the golden calf, Ex. 32:32.[80]

c. The Death and Ascension of Moses.

These deserve special treatment. The dominant tradition follows Scripture (Dt. 34:5-8) in teaching Moses' death.[81] But the miraculous events associated with this death in Dt. 34 provide the stimulus for various legends.

Moses vainly resists death with all his might. His request to be allowed to enter the promised land before death is not granted. Samael, the angel of death, does not manage to fetch his soul. Hence he dies עַל־פִּי יְהוָה (Dt. 34:5), i.e., according to the usual

---

65 Thus Moses is often called this in the OT, Ex. 14:31; Nu. 12:7, 8; Dt. 34:5 etc.; he is δοῦλος in Jos. Ant., 5, 39, παῖς in Bar. 1:20; 2:28 and עבד in T. Yoma, 2, 1.

66 Sir. 45:4. Cf. S. Bar. 17:4: "For he was subject to him who created him," but cf. Ass. Mos. 12:7: "Not on account of my virtue or firmness (Lat. *firmitatem*), but through the gentleness (Lat. *temperantia*) of his mercy."

67 Ass. Mos. 1:14; → 615.

68 Sir. 45:3; Str.-B., III, 513 ff.

69 Sir. 45:5; Jn. 9:29; Str.-B., IV, 439 ff.

70 Str.-B., IV, 435 ff.

71 jPea, 17a, 59 f.: "Scripture, Mishnah, Talmud, Haggada, whatever a sharp pupil learns from his teacher, it was all said (by God) to Moses on Sinai"; Ex. r., 46, 1 on 34:1 (Halakot, Midrash, Aggadot); 47, 1 on 34:27. Cf. the expression הֲלָכָה לְמשֶׁה מִסִּינַי, which is used some 50-60 times in Talmudic lit. for an ancient statute handed down by word of mouth.

72 Str.-B., II, 654 f.

73 For examples of the very common phrase "Moses our teacher" cf. Rosmarin, 27, n. 105, 106; also 19, n. 18 and 29; 26, n. 104. → n. 62 and → 437.

74 Ass. Mos. 11:16; Rabb. examples, Rosmarin, 19 f.

75 4 Esr. 14:5.

76 This is the theme of Ass. Mos., → 852; cf. also S. Bar. 4:5 and the long account of the secrets revealed to Moses in 59:4-11.

77 For this common designation cf. Rosmarin, 82, n. 293, e.g., Mek. Ex. on 14:31.

78 Ass. Mos. 3:11.

79 Ass. Mos. 11:17; also 11:11, 14; 12:6; Jub. 1:19-21.

80 bSota, 14a. Here Is. 53:12: "And he made intercession for the transgressors," is related to Moses's intercession: "For he begged for mercy for the transgressors of Israel" (R. Simlai, c. 250). M. Ex., 12, 1 and Dt. r., 3, 17 on 10:1 say of this intercession (Ex. 32:32) that "he gave his soul for Israel."

81 Eth. En. 89:38 (vision of the shepherd); Ass. Mos. → n. 95; Philo Vit. Mos., II, 288, 291 and Sacr. AC, 8 and 10; Jd. 9; Rabb. materials may be found fully (though uncritically) in Rosmarin, 133-149; cf. also Str.-B., I, 753-756; for the midr. on the decease of Moses → 852. Older bibl. (up to 1909) may be found in Schürer, III, 301 f.

interpretation, "through the kiss of Yahweh."[82] Michael contends with the devil for his body, Jd. 9 → n. 211. God buries him with the help of angels. His grave is subterraneously connected with the cave of Macpelah, S. Dt. § 357 on 34:5. Corruption has no power over his corpse.[83]

In particular, atoning power was ascribed to his death and burial in the wilderness.[84]

The midr. פְּטִירַת מֹשֶׁה (→ 852) concludes with the words: "The death of Moses is an expiatory altar מזבח כפרה for all Israel, as our teachers, their memory be blessed, have said, says R. Jiçchaq."[85] The fact that Moses died in the wilderness gave his death special atoning power for the wilderness generation. "Why did Moses die in the wilderness? In order that the wilderness generation should return and rise again through his merits."[86] In the reference of Is. 53:12 to Moses (by R. Simlai, *c.* 250) we read: " 'And he is numbered with the transgressors,' for he is numbered among those who died in the wilderness" (bSota, 14a; in this context his death in the wilderness is an atonement for the sin with the golden calf).[87]

His burial in the wilderness as well as his death has atoning power. "God spoke to Moses: If you will be buried here (in the wilderness) with them (the wilderness generation),[88] these by your merits will come with you (at the resurrection)."[89] Another passage widens the circle of those for whom the burial of Moses avails: "Why was Moses buried in a foreign land? In order that those who die abroad may rise to life again through his merits."[90] R. Chama bR. Chanina (*c.* 260) thinks in terms of a specific expiation: "Why was Moses buried at Beth Pe'or (Dt. 34:6)? In order to make expiation for the act with Pe'or (Nu. 25)."[91]

Along with the dominant view that Moses died we also find a few references to his bodily rapture.[92] That this idea should occur at all is surprising, for it is contrary to the plain statement of Dt. 34:5. Its native home was probably Hellenistic Judaism.[93]

---

[82] The ref. is to the view common to many peoples that the soul leaves the body with the last breath and can be intercepted with the mouth. Acc. to bBer., 8a "death by (God's) kiss" is the easiest of 903 ways of dying. Cf. K. M. Hofmann, *Philema hagion,* 1938, 72 f.

[83] For examples of the individual legends cf. Rosmarin, 133-149.

[84] The examples are from the 3rd cent. on, but the doctrine may be older.

[85] A. Jellinek, *Bet ha-Midrasch,* 6 (1877), 78; par. 1 (1853), 129. Cf. Murmelstein, 70, n. 1, who boldly combines this passage with Moses sacrificing in the heavenly sanctuary, → n. 98.

[86] Pesikt. r. Add. 3 (199a); par. Pesikt., 159b.

[87] This statement is not found in the par. in Midr. פְּטִירַת מֹשֶׁה (ed. A. Jellinek, 6, 75), probably rightly, because it does not fit the context.

[88] Read with Str.-B., I, 757, IV, 1187 אצלן (for אצלך).

[89] Dt. r., 2, 9 on 3:24. Cf. Tanch. חקת § 10 (Vienna, 1863, 227a) and par.: "Remain at their side and then come in fellowship with them" (Str.-B., I, 757 f.).

[90] Tanch. ואתחנן 5b (§ 6) (Str.-B., I, 757).

[91] bSota, 14a. Cf. Raschi on Dt. 34:6 (A. Berliner, *Raschi. Der Kommentar des Salomo b. Isak über den Pentateuch*² [1905], 423): "His grave was prepared there from the six days of creation to make expiation for the act with Pe'or. It is one of the (ten, Ab., 5, 6; bPes., 54a) things made in the twilight on the Friday evening (of creation week)."

[92] This is the point. If only an assumption of the soul is taught (Philo → n. 81) his death is probably accepted in Ass. Mos., → n. 95.

[93] The fact that the first attestation is in Joseph. and that there are few Rabb. refs. — those mentioned → *infra* are the only ones — suggests that the idea of bodily translation was native to Hellen. rather than Palestinian Judaism. Cf. on the rapture of the θεῖος ἀνήρ Philostr. Vit. Ap., VIII, 29; Philostr. is not sure whether Apollonius of Tyana died, Bieler, I (1935), 48, n. 64.

It is first attested in Joseph., who is intentionally ambiguous when he says in Ant., 4, 326: "A cloud suddenly stood over him, and he was taken from view into a valley. It is written in the sacred books that he died in order that on the ground of his outstanding virtues it should not be said that he went back up to deity." Joseph. is acquainted with the idea of the bodily rapture of Moses [94] even if he does not personally accept it. On the other hand the idea that the (lost) ending of the Ass. Mos. contained a rapture of Moses (→ II, 939, n. 92) cannot be sustained if we are thinking of a bodily process (→ n. 92). [95] This view, however, could very well be assumed in Mk. 9:4 f. and par., partly because Moses is mentioned along with Elijah, and partly because Enoch (who was also bodily translated) is elsewhere mentioned in place of Moses (→ II, 938, 931, n. 19). [96] Clear refs. to the rapture of Moses are found only in a few Rabb. passages, e.g., in the Bar. in S. Dt. § 357 on 34:5: [97] "Some say Moses did not die but stands and discharges above the (priestly) [98] ministry," and Midr. ha-gadol on Dt.: "Three went up alive into heaven: Enoch, Moses and Elijah." [99]

These different views on the end of Moses reflect again the distinction between Hellenistic and Palestinian Judaism. The former speaks of the apotheosis of Moses, [100] the latter asks concerning the cause and value of the death of this man of God.

d. The Distinction between the Hellenistic and the Palestinian View.

There thus develops in later Judaism a whole new view of Moses. This development occurs first in the *diaspora* under Greek influence. Moses is now magnified in a way for which there is little basis in the OT (→ n. 5). Nevertheless, there are basic differences between Hellenistic and Palestinian Judaism in the attempt to glorify Moses.

Hellenistic Judaism is under the influence of Hellenistic depictions of the θεῖος ἀνήρ. Moses becomes a superman, whether as a genius whose figure undergoes

---

[94] Schl. Mt., 528.

[95] In the portions extant the Ass. Mos. frequently speaks of the death of Moses (1:15; 10:12, 14; 11:7, 8). The fathers also state that the legend of Michael's conflict with the devil about the body of Moses comes from the Ass. Mos. (Jd. 9 → n. 211). The assumption of Moses which is described in the lost ending and which gives the book its name can have referred, then, only to the ascension of his soul. In keeping with this is a quotation which Origen (Hom. in Jos. 2:1) found *in libello quodam, ... licet in canone non habeatur,* if we can believe with Schürer, III, 303 that this *libellus* was the Ass. Mos.: *refertur quia duo Moyses videbantur, unus vivus in spiritu et alius mortuus in corpore.* Cf. also Euodii epistula ad Augustinum (Aug. Ep., 259): *tunc cum ascenderet in montem ut moreretur vi corporis, efficitur ut aliud esset quod terrae mandaretur, aliud quod angelo comitanti sociaretur.* Cf. also a statement handed down in Cl. Al. Strom., VI, 15, § 132, 2 (which perhaps comes from the Book of Initiates mentioned in Cl. Al. Strom., I, 23, § 153, 1; § 154, 1, Schl. Gesch. Isr., 321 and 444, n. 312) and which tells us that Joshua saw the soul of Moses parted from his body: τὸν Μωυσέα ἀναλαμβανόμενον διττὸν εἶδεν Ἰησοῦς ὁ τοῦ Ναυῆ, καὶ τὸν μὲν μετ' ἀγγέλων, τὸν δὲ ἐπὶ τὰ ὄρη περὶ τὰς φάραγγας κηδείας (burial) ἀξιούμενον. These three passages do not teach a bodily rapture of Moses but the ascension of his soul at the hour of death (cf. Philo Vita Mos., II, 288, 291; Sacr. AC, 8 and 10).

[96] In Rabb. lit. there is only one late ref. (Str.-B., I, 756; IV, 785) to a joint coming of Moses and Elijah in the last time, Dt. r., 3, 17 on 10:1: "One day when I cause the prophet Elijah to come you shall both come together."

[97] Par. bSota, 13b and Midr. Tannaim on Dt. 34:5 (ed. D. Hoffmann [1908/9], 224).

[98] Cf. Murmelstein, 70, n. 1, who refers to the Samaritan view of Moses as one who offers in the heavenly sanctuary (Marqa, Comm. on Pent., ed. M. Heidenheim, *Bibliotheca Samaritana,* III [1896], 71).

[99] Acc. to a Berlin MS (p. 123) quoted in M. J. bin Gorion, 373.

[100] Philo Vit. Mos., II, 288 ff.: Moses is transfigured εἰς νοῦν ἡλιοειδέστατον (288, cf. Windisch, 106); Sacr. AC, 8 and 10.

legendary embellishment (the Moses romance) or as the perfect man in whom may be seen the ideal of the righteous elevating themselves to God (Philo).

The Palestinian view develops differently. What Scripture says about Moses is here extended and embellished. In addition — and the later the sources the clearer this is — there are transferred to Moses, the deliverer from Egypt, the motifs of redeemer expectation as these are known to us from Palestinian speculation on Adam-primal man on the one side and Messianic expectation on the other.[101] On the whole Palestinian Judaism is closer to the OT, for here Moses, unaffected by the influences of the Hellenistic romance, is for the most part a fallible man (→ n. 62), and he is primarily magnified as the mediator of God's Word to Israel.

2. Moses in the Eschatological Expectation of Later Judaism: The Return of Moses.

There are few references to the return of Moses in the last time. The combination of Moses and Elijah in Mk. 9:4 f. and par. leads us to suspect that alongside the early Christian expectation that Enoch and Elijah would appear as forerunners of the Messiah[102] there was another tradition that Moses and Elijah would be the two precursors (→ II, 938).[103] Elsewhere there is reference to the return of Moses only in passages which speak of his death and burial in the wilderness. Moses had to suffer death and burial in order that the text Dt. 33:21 (referred by the Midr. to Moses): "He comes at the head of the people" (Midr.), might be fulfilled, i.e., in order that the wilderness generation might one day be raised again by virtue of his merits, and under his leadership enter into the promised land, → 855.

It was debated in the 1st cent. A. D. whether the wilderness generation would have a share in the resurrection and the world to come.[104] The referring of Dt. 33:21 (→ *supra*) to Moses expresses the more lenient and triumphant view. So Tanch. חקת § 10 (Vienna, 1863, 227a): (God demanded that Moses should remain in the wilderness) "Remain at their side (the side of those who died in the wilderness) and then come in fellowship with them, *v.* Dt. 33:21: He comes at the head of the people."[105] How this was envisaged may be seen from S. Dt. § 355 on 33:21; Tg. J. I II O Dt. 33:21, which show Moses coming into the land of Israel at the head of individual groups (those who are learned in Scripture, the Mishnah, the Talmud), there to receive a reward with each individual.[106] Also to be related to the leading of the wilderness generation into the promised land is the following passage from the Tg. fragment which sets Moses alongside the Messiah, Tg. J. II Ex. 15:18: "Moses will come out of the wilderness and

---

[101] For proof cf. Murmelstein, 51-64, to be supplemented by what was said under c., and Staerk, *Erlösererwartung*, 50-56. Cf. also → n. 45.

[102] The oldest instance is Eth. En. 90:31 → II, 931; then 4 Esr. 6:26 → II, 931, n. 19; Apc. Pt. 2; Copt. Apc. Elias (Steindorff, TU, NF, 2, *Heft* 3a, 1899), 163 f., 169 → II, 940. Abundant further materials may be found in W. Bousset, *Der Antichrist* (1895), 134-139.

[103] In Rabb. lit. this expectation is found only in the passage quoted in → n. 96.

[104] Sanh., 10, 3; T. Sanh., 13, 10, cf. Bacher Tannaiten, I, 135 f., esp. 136, n. 3.

[105] Cf. Dt. r., 2, 9 on 3:24, → 854; also Ex. r., 2, 5 on 3:1: "You will leave them in the wilderness and one day you will lead them out of the wilderness, *v.* Hos. 2:16."

[106] Though it does not expressly mention the wilderness generation Tanch. ויקרא (Vienna, 1863), 133b says that Moses "will come at the head of all in the future world when the righteous come to receive their reward," Tanch. Buber ויקרא 6, p. 3a; Dt. r., 9, 5 on 31:14.

the king Messiah will come out of Rome;[107] the one will lead (the wilderness generation) at the head of a cloud (read עננא for ענא), the other will lead (the *diaspora*)[108] at the head of a cloud (→ *supra*), and the *memra* of Yahweh[109] will lead between both, and they will come in together, and the children of Israel will say: To Yahweh belongs royal dominion in this world, and it is his in the world to come."

Nowhere,[110] however, in the older literature do we find the idea that the returning Moses will be the Messiah.[111]

3. Moses as a Type of the Messiah.

In the Haggada Moses is a type in two senses. On the one side he is a reflection of Adam, on the other a model of the Messiah. We have referred already to the parallel between Moses and Adam as ideal primal man (→ 856). We must now consider the strongly developing view that Moses is a prototype of the Messiah. An important question for NT studies is when Moses came to be regarded as such.

a. The Coming "Prophet like Moses."

How later Judaism understood the promise that God would send a prophet like Moses from among his brethren (Dt. 18:15, 18) is a very difficult problem. (1) It is not enough to say that the few[112] Rabb. refs. which quote the saying relate it to one of the past prophets,[113] esp. Jeremiah (Pesikt., 112a; cf. S. Dt. § 175 on 18:15), though it may be seen from Philo that this was an old view.[114] (2) For we have good reason to believe that a future interpretation also existed, though surprisingly not attested in Rabb. lit. On Dt. 18:15, 18 was based not only expectation of *the* prophet,[115] but probably also

107 Thus far also Tg. J. II Ex. 12:42 acc. to Elia Levita *s.v.* משיחא and משה (M. Ginsburger, *Das Fragmenten-Tg.* [1899], 105).

108 For examples of the leading in of the *diaspora* by the Messiah, cf. Str.-B., IV, 907 f.

109 I.e., God. For bibl. → 71, n. *s.v.* "Memra."

110 As against Bousset-Gressm., 233. The only possible older ref. is Sib., 5, 256-259: "(256) But one will come again from heaven, an outstanding man (257) whose hands he spread out on the fruitful wood (258), the best of the Hebrews who once caused the sun to stand still (ὃς ἠέλιόν ποτε στῆσεν)." If one strikes out v. 257 and perhaps also 258a as Christian interpolations or emendations, the passage expects as the son of man (v. 256: Da. 7:13) the one who caused the sun to stand still (→ υἱὸς τοῦ ἀνθρώπου), i.e., Joshua (Jos. 10:12). One might relate the passage to Moses on the ground that in Rabb. lit. and already in the Tannaitic period causing the sun to stand still was also ascribed to Moses (Str.-B., I, 13; II, 414). But it is doubtful whether Sib. knew this transference to Moses (also to Elijah, Aggadat Bereshit [Warsaw, 1876], 76, p. 52a, 5 ff.). The biblical text would suggest Joshua, unless we eliminate the problem by accepting στήσει in v. 258 with Buresch and Geffcken (→ III, 291).

111 This idea is first found only in Natan bSolomon Spira ספר מגלה עמוקות (91c), M. J. bin Gorion, 378: "Everyone knows that Moses is the Messiah of the stem of David. Until Shiloh comes, we read in the prophecy of the Messiah (Gn. 49:10). But Shiloh and Moses are one."

112 The list in Str.-B., II, 626 f. (only 3 refs.) seems to be complete.

113 S. Dt. § 176 on 18:16, cf. G. Dalman, *Ergänzungen u. Verbesserungen z. Jesus-Jeschua* (1929), 4.

114 Philo seems to refer to Dt. 18:15 in Spec. Leg., I, 65 and to relate the verse to past prophets (Str.-B., II, 479, though cf. Dalman, 28, n. 2). He did not take the verse Messianically (as against Gfrörer, 333 and Volz Esch., 194). That Ass. Mos. 10:15 (*te [Josua] elegit deus esse mihi [Moses] successorem eiusdem testamenti*) refers Dt. 18:15, 18 to Joshua is a widespread (e.g., H. J. Cadbury in Jackson-Lake, I, 5, p. 372, n. 2) but by no means certain assumption.

115 Jn. 1:21, 25; 7:40.

the hope of the coming of an acknowledged prophet [116] of the last days who would repeat the plagues of Egypt, [117] and finally [118] the popular reference to the arising of a prophet after the manner of the prophets [119] or the return of one of the (old) [120] prophets. [121]

All these passages agree in not equating the expected prophet with the Messiah. [122] It may be seen esp. from Jn. 1:21, 25 that *the* prophet was expected along with the Messiah and Elijah, obviously as a forerunner of the Messiah. [123] In notable distinction from apocalyptic (→ II, 931, 938, 940) the future expectation expressed here is thus restricted to three figures whose eschatological tasks were attested in Scripture, namely, the Messiah, Elijah (Mal. 3:23) and the prophet (Dt. 18:15, 18). [124]

(3) A lively issue for more than 100 years is whether there was in later Judaism a future interpretation of Dt. 18:15, 18 in Messianic as well as non-Messianic terms. [125]

The fact that the NT refers Dt. 18:15, 18 to Christ (Ac. 3:22 f. → 865, 873) may be left on one side, since this is a Christian proof from Scripture. More important is the Samaritan ref. of the verses to the Messiah, [126] though this does not for certain imply a corresponding understanding of the verses in later Judaism, since the Samaritan Canon was restricted to the Pentateuch and hence the Samaritans had to derive their Messianic expectation from the Law. Apart from this, only the following passages can be adduced in support of a Messianic interpretation of Dt. 18:15, 18. (a) In Jn. 6:14 f. (as distinct

---

[116] 1 Macc. 14:41: ἕως τοῦ ἀναστῆναι προφήτην πιστόν, cf. 4:46.

[117] Rev. 11:3 ff., cf. Dalman, 29, n. 2.

[118] Dalman, 29, n. 2.

[119] Mk. 6:15 : προφήτης ὡς (Aram. כְּגוֹן, כְּעֵין) εἷς (Aram. חַד indefinite pronoun = τὶς) τῶν προφητῶν, par. Lk. 9:8.

[120] + τῶν ἀρχαίων, Lk. 9:8, 19.

[121] Mk. 8:28 (εἷς [→ n. 119) τῶν προφητῶν); Mt. 16:14 (→ Ἰερεμίας); Lk. 9:19. On the connection of Mk. 6:15 and par. and 8:28 and par. with Dt. 18:15, 18 cf. Dalman, 29, n. 2, K. H. Rengstorf, *NT Deutsch* on Lk. 7:15 f. and O. Bauernfeind, *Die Ag.* (1939), 70.

[122] Note esp. that in Jn. 1:21, 25 and 7:40 f. *the* prophet is distinguished from the Messiah. Mk. 8:29 yields a non-Messianic understanding of 6:15; 8:28.

[123] P. Billerbeck, *Nathanael,* 19 (1903), 122, n. 62.

[124] Schl. J. on 1:21; "Die Sprache u. Heimat des 4. Evangelisten," BFTh, 6 (1902), 26; O. Bauernfeind, *op. cit.,* 70.

[125] Gfrörer, 318-413 gave a definite answer in the affirmative in 1838, but without critically reviewing the material adduced. He says on p. 324 : "There is no verse in the books of the old covenant which in the time of Christ was referred so definitely and by so many to the Messiah as Dt. 18:15." Bornhäuser, who takes into account the difficult data in Jn. → *infra,* says more cautiously (58) that "opinions vacillated whether the prophet and the Messiah would appear in one person or not." Str.-B., II, 480 answers with a qualified affirmative : "Expectation of a prophet Messiah, which is attested by Jn. 6:14 f. and indirectly by Joseph., is mostly, and correctly, traced back to Dt. 18:15, 18." Staerk, *Soter,* 61-72 is more confident, and cf. also Volz Esch., 194 and K. H. Rengstorf, *NT Deutsch* on Lk. 7:15 f. A negative answer is given by Baldensperger, 138 f., who omits pre-Christian refs., suggests that Jn. 6:14 might be a popular idea of the moment, and dismisses the Joseph. passages on the flimsy ground that they prove nothing as regards pre-Christian Judaism. A similar answer is given by R. Bultmann, *Das J. Ev.* (1937), 61, who calls the Messianic interpretation of Dt. 18:15, 18 a specifically Christian interpretation. One can hardly say this in view of the Samaritan tradition (→ n. 126).

[126] Eus. Theoph., 4, 35 (p. 216); Ps. Cl. Recg., I, 54, 5; 57, 1 and 5 (ed. W. Frankenberg, TU, 48, 3 [1937], 60, 62, 64); VII, 33 (ed. E. G. Gersdorf [1838], 168). Cf. also Orig. Cels., 1, 57: Dositheus ἠθέλησε ... πεῖσαι Σαμαρεῖς, ὅτι αὐτὸς εἴη ὁ προφητευόμενος ὑπὸ Μωυσέως Χριστός. In view of Dt. 18:15, 18 the Samaritan Messiah is called the "teacher" (*muri* or *mudi,* cf. H. Odeberg, *The Fourth Gospel* [1929], 183); Jn. 4:25 is in agreement with this. How important Dt. 18:15 was for the Samaritans may be seen from the fact that they added it to the 10th commandment.

from Jn. 1:21, 25; 7:40 f. → n. 122) *the* prophet is a Messianic figure in the judgment of the crowd.[127] (b) Joseph. says that the two revolutionary leaders Theudas and the Egyptian, who both presented themselves as redeemers and thus raised Messianic claims, described themselves as prophets.[128] This is the only clear point. (c) The Damascus document refers Dt. 18:15 to the "teacher of what is true"[129] who bears the characteristics of the second Moses and whose return as the Messiah is obviously expected (→ n. 169). (d) Test. L. 8:14 f., a passage which belongs to the Jewish original of Test. XII,[130] ascribes to the Messiah the three dignities of king, priest and prophet,[131] though it may be questioned whether the last of these is derived from Dt. 18:15 and not from the sphere of speculation on the first man and the redeemer (→ n. 45). (e) The same question whether the prophetic dignity is deduced from Dt. 18:15 arises in relation to the intrinsically possible conjecture[132] that the hymn in Lk. 1:68 ff., which calls the Baptist προφήτης ὑψίστου (Lk. 1:76), glorifies him as the prophetic Messiah, for here the prophetic dignity might well be an attribute of Elijah. (f) No weight can be attached to the statement in Ps. Cl. Recg., I, 43, 1 that through messengers the Jewish priests repeatedly initiated discussions whether Jesus was the prophet whom Moses had announced as the appointed Messiah from all eternity.[133]

When one reviews the material, the paucity of references makes any assured judgment impossible. On the other hand, as we shall see under b., it seems extremely likely that later Judaism, like the Samaritans, did know a Messianic interpretation of Dt. 18:15, 18. The sparse attestation might easily be explained by the fact that we have here a form of the Messianic hope native to popular expectation.[134, 135]

b. The Messiah as a Second Moses.[136]

It would be a fatal error to assume that investigation of later Jewish exegesis of Dt. 18:15, 18 settles definitively the question whether the figure of Moses influenced Messianic expectation. In many passages the Messiah is depicted as a second Moses even though there is no reference to Dt. 18. These are passages which have as their basis the doctrine that the redemption out of Egypt is a type of Messianic redemption.[137] Taught by the OT itself,[138] this doctrine "as no

---

127 An attempt will be made (→ 863 f.) to show that a Messianic interpretation of Dt. 18:15, 18 underlies the apocalyptic tradition in Rev. 11:3 ff.

128 Ant., 20, 97 of Theudas: προφήτης γὰρ ἔλεγεν εἶναι, 20, 169 of the Egyptian: προφήτης εἶναι λέγων, also Bell., 2, 261: προφήτου πίστιν ἐπιθεὶς ἑαυτῷ. Cf. on these passages as instances of the Messianic interpretation of Dt. 18:15, 18 Gfrörer, 331-333 and esp. Str.-B., II, 479 f.

129 Damasc. 1:11: ויקם; 20:28: וישמעו לקול מורה.

130 Murmelstein, 274 f. (with Bousset, Charles, Beer, Volz against Schnapp).

131 "A king will arise in Judah and set up a new priesthood (after the model of the Gentiles for all Gentiles [Christian interpolation]), his appearance is inexpressibly like that of a prophet of the Most High of the posterity of our father Abraham." On Test. B. 9:2 (perhaps a Christian interpolation) cf. Staerk, *Soter*, 68.

132 Staerk, *Soter*, 65.

133 Ed. Frankenberg (→ n. 126), 48.

134 Jn. 6:14 f.; Joseph. → *supra*; cf. Staerk, *Soter*, 64.

135 There is also anti-Christian polemic in the Rabb., → n. 154; Goppelt, 73, n. 4.

136 Gfrörer, 318-352; J. Jeremias; Murmelstein; Staerk, *Erlösererwartung*; esp. the work of Wiebe.

137 Str.-B., I, 68 ff., 85 ff.; II, 284 f., 293; IV, 55 f., 783 f. etc. → II, 658 (G. Kittel); Wiebe.

138 Mi. 7:15; Hos. 2:16; 12:10; Is. 11:11; 48:21 → Fischer, *op. cit.*; also *Jesajas cap. 40-55 und d. Perikopen vom leidenden Gottesknecht* (1916), 193 ff.; *Th. Revue*, 36 (1937), 269 f.; Sellin, *op. cit.*; also NKZ, 41 (1930), 152, n. 1; Wiebe.

other" "comprehensively determined at an early period the shape of the teaching concerning the final redemption." [139]

(1) Within the context of this typology of the first and final redemption there is found in Rabb. literature the much repeated principle, developed in all kinds of different ways: "As the first redeemer (Moses), so the final redeemer (the Messiah)." [140]

In this precise form the typology of Moses and the Messiah is first found in Qoh. r., 1, 28 on 1:9: "R. Berekia (*c.* 350) said in the name of R. Jiçchaq (II, *c.* 300): [141] As the first redeemer, so the last [142] redeemer. As it is said of the first redeemer: And Moses took his wife and his sons and had them ride on an ass (Ex. 4:20), so the last redeemer, for it is said: Lowly and riding on an ass (Zech. 9:9). [143] As the first redeemer caused manna to come down, for it is said: Lo, I cause bread to rain down upon you from heaven (Ex. 16:4), so the last redeemer will cause manna to come down, for it is said: White bread will lie on the earth (Ps. 72:16 Midr.). As the first redeemer caused the well to spring forth (Nu. 20:11), so the last redeemer will cause water to spring forth, for it is said: And a fountain will break forth out of the house of Yahweh (Joel 3:18)."

Apart from those mentioned the main parallels are as follows. Moses was brought up in Pharaoh's court (Ex. 2:10), and similarly the Messiah, before his public manifestation, will stay in the main enemy city of Rome. [144] Moses and Aaron called the people to freedom on the night of the passover, and it will be similarly called to freedom by the Messiah, [145] also on the night of the passover. [146] Moses revealed himself and then hid, and the Messiah will do the same. [147] Moses had Aaron at his side, and so, too, the Messiah is accompanied by Elijah. [148] Like Moses, the Messiah will lead the people into the wilderness. [149] etc. [150]

The oldest [151] Rabb. instance of this typology is in Tanch. עקב (Vienna, 1863), 7b: "How long will the days of the Messiah last? R. Aqiba (*c.* 90-135) said: Forty years. As the Israelites spent 40 years in the wilderness, so he (the Messiah) will lead them forth and take them into the wilderness and cause them to eat bitter herbs and roots (Job 30:4)." [152] Like Moses, the Messiah will lead the people into the wilderness to undergo a period of distress and suffering. Whether R. Eli'ezer (*c.* 90) already reckoned the Messianic

[139] Str.-B., I, 85.

[140] Qoh. r., 1, 28 on 1:9; Par. Midr. Samuel, 14 § 9 on 1 S. 12:3. Also Ruth r., 5, 6 on 2:14 and par.: Nu. r., 11 on 6:23; Pesikt., 49b; Pesikt. r., 15 (72b), cf. Cant. r., 2, 22 on 2:9 f.

[141] In the par. Midr. Samuel the author is R. Levi (*c.* 300).

[142] Midr. Samuel: the second redeemer.

[143] Midr. Samuel only up to this pt.

[144] Ex. r., 1, 31 on 2:10; Par. Tanch. שמות (Vienna, 1863, 61b).

[145] Tg. Lam., 2, 22.

[146] Hier. Comm. in Mt. 25:6 (MPL, 26, 184 f.): *traditio Judaeorum est Christum media nocte uenturum in similitudinem Aegyptii temporis, quando pascha celebratum est ... unde reor et traditionem apostolicam permansisse, ut in die uigiliarum paschae ante noctis dimidium populos dimittere non liceat exspectantes aduentum Christi.*

[147] Ruth r., 5 on 2:14 (par. → n. 140). Cf. Str.-B., I, 86 f.; II, 284 f.; also Bacher Pal. Am., 3, 482, n. 3.

[148] Midr. Ps. 43, § 1; in place of Elijah Tg. Cant., 4, 5; 7, 4 mentions the Messiah ben Ephraim.

[149] Pirqe Maschiach (A. Jellinek, *Bet ha-Midrasch,* III [1855], 72, 1 ff. Cf. Str.-B., IV, 798); Gfrörer, 336 ff.

[150] For further details cf. Gfrörer, 333 ff.; Murmelstein, 54-64; Staerk, *Erlösererwartung,* 50-56.

[151] But cf. → *infra.*

[152] Par. Midr. Ps. 90, § 17 and Pesikt. r., 1 (4a) on the biblical basis of Dt. 8:3 ("he oppressed thee and suffered thee to hunger").

period as 40 yrs. is not certain.[153] The silence of Rabb. lit. in the time between 135 (Aqiba) and 300 (Jiçchaq II, → 860) is connected with the attack on Christianity, which also used the Moses/Messiah typology.[154]

This typology does not arise first in Rabb. literature or in the time after Aqiba. There are references to show that it goes back to a period prior to the NT. If it is not mentioned in the OT apocrypha and pseudepigrapha,[155] it finds attestation in the Damascus document, Joseph. and the NT.

(2) The Damascus document may be assigned to the early first half of the 1st cent. A.D. on the grounds of vocabulary, language (pre-Mishnah Heb.), theology and halaka. It introduces us to a sect which went to Damascus in the Herodian period.[156] The whole teaching of this sect rests on the idea that the time in the wilderness is a prototype of the Messianic age of salvation. The community lives in tabernacles after the model of the wilderness period.[157] Its members are "numbered" (Ex. 30:13 f.)[158] and divided after the manner of Ex. 18:25.[159] They have entered into covenant,[160] the covenant of God,[161] the new covenant,[162] which as the last covenant is a counterpart to that made at Sinai. In the present context, however, the decisive pt. is a. that their leader, who is compared to Moses in many other things,[163] is, like Moses,[164] a teacher[165] and lawgiver,[166] and b. that he has called them to an exodus[167] which is compared to the journey of Israel into the promised land.[168] Since it is wholly probable that the "teacher of what is true" is a Messianic figure,[169] we have in him a second Moses[170] who led the exodus of the last time.

---

[153] The Babylonian tradition, known to us in 2 Bar. in bSanh., 99a, affirms this, but not the Palestinian tradition, where R. Eli'ezer reckons the period as three generations (60 yrs.) in M. Ex., 17, 16, 400 yrs. in Pesikt. r., 1, and 1000 in Tanch. עקב 7b; Midr. Ps. 90 § 17, cf. Str.-B., III, 824 f.; Bacher, *Tannaiten*², 139, n. 4. Bacher, 139 f. thinks the 60 yrs. the original view, but Str.-B., III, 826 disagrees and argues for the 1000.

[154] Wiebe. Cf. for arguments against the Christian Moses/Messiah typology Dt. r., 8, 6 on 30:11: "'It (the Torah) is not in heaven,' Dt. 30:12. Moses said to them: In order that you may not say that another Moses will arise and bring us another Torah, I have already told you: 'It is not in heaven,' i.e., nothing of it has remained in heaven." On later anti-Christian polemic in general cf. Jeremias, *op. cit.*, 116; also ZNW, 25 (1926), 128; *Die Abendmahlsworte Jesu,* 83 f.; → II, 940.

[155] Wiebe.

[156] 20:15. There can hardly be 40 yrs. between the death of the leader and the composition of the document.

[157] 7:6 ff.; 9:11; 12:23; 13:4 ff., 16, 20; 14:3, 9; 19:2; 20:26.

[158] 10:2; 14:3.

[159] 13:1.

[160] 2:2; 3:13; 8:1; 9:2; 15:5, 8; 16:1; 19:1, 13; 20:25, 30.

[161] 5:12; 7:5; 13:14; 14:2; 19:14; 20:17; covenant of repentance, 19:16.

[162] 6:19; 8:21; 19:33 f.; 20:12.

[163] Bes. 5:18 ff.

[164] 3:8: יוריהם. On Moses as *the* teacher of Israel → n. 73.

[165] יורה הצדק (based on Hos. 10:12 יורה צדק): 6:11, cf. 20:14; מורה צדק (on the basis of Joel 2:23: המורה לצדקה): 1:11; 20:32, cf. 20:1, 28. → II, 932.

[166] 6:4, 7, 9: מחוקק (Nu. 21:18) is understood in the sense of lawgiver (H. Odeberg, *The Fourth Gospel* [1929], 155).

[167] 4:3; 6:5: to Damascus on the basis of Am. 5:26 f. (Dam. 7:15). Wiebe perceived a par. to the Exodus.

[168] 1:7 f.; 8:14 ff. Cf. also 20:15: The time between the death of the teacher of what is true and the end is calculated to be 40 yrs., corresponding to the period of the sojourn in the wilderness.

[169] This can be affirmed more confidently than in → II, 932. Cf. S. Schechter, *Documents of Jewish Sectaries,* I (1910), 211, n. 11; H. Odeberg, 154; J. Brierre-Narbonne, *Exégèse apocryphe des prophéties messianiques* (1932); Wiebe.

[170] → n. 129.

(3) No less significant is the testimony of Joseph., whose accounts of the revolutionary movements of the 1st cent. A.D. display the almost stereotyped feature that the leaders were calling for a new exodus into the wilderness.[171]

Thus Theudas, who called himself a προφήτης (cf. Dt. 18:15, 18 → n. 128) led his followers to the Jordan and promised to part the waters, obviously for the journey into the desert.[172] There then follow anonymous popular leaders who lead the people εἰς τὴν ἐρημίαν.[173] The Egyptian, who arose shortly before Paul was imprisoned, also προφήτης εἶναι λέγων (→ n. 128), leads his followers εἰς τὴν ἔρημον.[174] Under Festus there arises a deceiver who promises the multitude good fortune and the end of all misery if they will follow him into the wilderness.[175] In 73 A.D. a weaver Jonathan in Cyrene, promising signs and wonders, again leads his followers εἰς τὴν ἔρημον.[176]

All these messiahs follow the example of Moses by calling for an exodus into the wilderness and promising signs and wonders, and also deliverance. The series is an impressive testimony to the strength with which the idea that the Messiah would be a second Moses was anchored in popular expectation.

(4) The witness of the NT is to the same effect. The NT gives evidence of widespread popular expectation that the Messiah would be a second Moses even when it tells of the Egyptian who led his followers εἰς τὴν ἔρημον (Ac. 21:38) and also when it reports the warning of Jesus against false Messianic rumours in the words: ἐὰν οὖν εἴπωσιν ὑμῖν· ἰδοὺ ἐν τῇ ἐρήμῳ ἐστίν, μὴ ἐξέλθητε (Mt. 24:26), for the Messiah who appears in the wilderness will be regarded as a second Moses. When the people debated whether the Baptist might be the Messiah (Lk. 3:15 etc.) it was probably because he was regarded as the second Moses both in virtue of his baptism (→ 867) and also in virtue of his appearing in the wilderness.

In Jn., too, there is reference to the later Jewish Moses/Messiah typology in 6:14 f., where after the feeding of the five thousand the crowd wants to make Him king, and also in 6:30 f., 34, where He is asked to repeat the miracle of the manna. In these passages not only is there ascribed to the crowd the popular expectation that the last time will bring a repetition of the miracle of the manna,[177] but it is presupposed that this miracle will be expected of the Messiah.[178]

(5) One may finally refer to the Messianic expectation of the Samaritans. The older Ta'eb expectation (→ I, 388 f.), which looked for a prophet like Moses, → n. 126,[179] ascribed to him a repetition of the acts of Moses.[180]

---

171 → II, 658 f. (G. Kittel); Wiebe.
172 Ant., 20, 97-99; Wiebe.
173 Bell., II, 259; par. Ant., 20, 167 f.
174 Ac. 21:38; Bell., 2, 261 f. Gfrörer, 332 f. conjectures that the emphasis on the man's coming from Egypt is linked with the Moses/Messiah typology.
175 Ant., 20, 188.
176 Bell., VII, 438, cf. also VI, 351 and → II, 659.
177 → 468; cf. in the NT Rev. 2:17; 1 C. 10:3 f.
178 E. Lohmeyer, ZSTh, 14 (1937), 628 f.; → 860.
179 The conjecture of D. Rettig, *Memar Marqa, ein samaritanischer Midr. z. Pent.* (Bonn Diss., 1934), 31 that Ta'eb expectation arises only after the time of Marqa (4th cent. A.D.) is shattered by Jn. 4:25, cf. Jos. Ant., 18, 85; Bell., 3, 207 f.; Just. Apol., I, 53, 6 and the refs. in → n. 126 (cf. also Odeberg, 183). The view that the Ta'eb is a second Joshua is later than that of a second Moses.
180 Examples in M. Gaster, *The Samaritan Oral Law and Ancient Traditions.* I. "The Samaritan Eschatology" (1932), 224-228. (This work, which is usually quoted uncritically, suffers from a tendency to give the Samaritan sources too much weight by ascribing to them very early dates which cannot be supported.)

The unanimous testimony of the Damascus document, Jos., the NT and the Samaritan tradition shows that Moses/Messiah typology was very much alive in the NT period and repeatedly exercised a decisive influence on the course of events. The nature of the sources and the silence of the OT apocrypha and pseudepigrapha suggest that this form of Messianic expectation was less at home in official theology [181] than in popular expectation. [182]

c. The Second Moses as a Figure of Suffering.

When one considers the statements about the second Moses, it is plain that in Rabb. writings elements of suffering are constantly linked with this figure. [183] This is not surprising when one recalls that Moses was regarded as the great example of patience [184] and that atoning efficacy was ascribed to his death and burial in the wilderness, → 854.

The following traits esp. call for notice. (1) The oldest Rabb. proponent of the Moses/Messiah typology, R. Aqiba, teaches that the Messiah will lead the people into the wilderness and there cause them to endure distress and hunger for forty yrs. [185] (2) Before his coming the Messiah (a leper acc. to bSanh., 98a, cf. Is. 53:3 f.) will stay for a while at the hated enemy city of Rome as Moses grew up at Pharaoh's court. [186] (3) The Messiah will come in lowliness and riding on an ass as Moses caused his wife and sons to ride on an ass (Ex. 4:20). [187] (4) After his appearing he will be concealed again as Moses was. [188]

Hence Rev. 11:3 ff., does not stand alone when the preacher of repentance whom it depicts as the second Moses (→ II, 939) [189] is a figure of suffering. In this passage, which undoubtedly comes from the pre-Christian apocalyptic tradition preserved in the El. Apc. (→ II, 940), there is reference to the martyrdom of the second Moses and the exposure of his corpse to public shame, but also to his resurrection after 3½ days and his assumption into heaven before the eyes of his enemies (11:11 f.).

In the present text of Rev. 11:3 ff., and its immediate model, this martyr figure of the second Moses is regarded as the forerunner of the Messiah. But (a) the surprising fact the Elijah comes first, which does not correspond to the historical sequence, (b) the fact that in Midr. Ps. 43 § 1 Elijah as the second Aaron is accompanied by the Messiah as the second Moses, [190] and esp. (c) the fact that the two olive-trees (Rev. 11:4 = Zech. 4:14)

---

181 Gfrörer felt this, though there are no grounds for his view that the Mosaic Messiah belongs to esoteric teaching or Essene dogma.

182 → 859, 862.

183 Jeremias, 112-115; Staerk, *Soter*, 63 f. (though not 63, n. 1; the supposed testimony of Orig. to the stoning of Moses does not exist; Comm. in Mt. X, 18 refers only to the repeated intention of stoning him), 79 f.; also Staerk, *Erlösererwartung*, 408.

184 On the aspects of suffering in the Moses of Dt. → 612 (Oepke); Ass. Mos. 3:11.

185 → 860. Cf. Str.-B., III, 824, esp. n. 1 and 4 (on R. Aqiba and Barcochba) and the general development of the thought in the passage mentioned in → n. 147.

186 → n. 144.

187 → 860. In bSanh., 98a riding on an ass as a sign of the lowliness of the Messiah is contrasted with coming on the clouds (Da. 7:13).

188 → n. 147, cf. n. 168. On concealment as a feature of suffering cf. Str.-B., II, 286 f.

189 Rev. 11:5 (cf. 2 C. 1:10) alludes to Nu. 16:35, Rev. 11:6b to Ex. 7:17, 19 f., Rev. 11:6, 10 to the plagues of Egypt. The two witnesses of Rev. 11:3 ff. are the prophet like Moses (Dt. 18:15, 18) and the returning Elijah (Mal. 3:23), cf. Dalman, 29, n. 2. To the bibl. → II, 939, n. 97 should be added Dalman, 29, n. 2; D. Haugg, "D. zwei Zeugen," *Nt.liche Abh.*, 17, 1 (1936), and → 327, n. 28 (Michaelis).

190 → 860.

are referred in Rabb. lit. to the Deliverer and the one who accompanies Him [191] make it very propable that originally the two witnesses of Rev. 11:3 ff. were the precursor (Elijah) and the Messiah (the second Moses). If so, we have here a proof that there existed in the later Judaism of the period a tradition which speaks of the martyrdom of both the Messiah [192] and His forerunner. The exact material agreement in Mk. 9:12 f. shows that this is by no means impossible: "Do you not know that it is written of the Son of man that he must suffer many things and be despised? But I tell you that Elias has come and they have done to him what they desired, as is written of him."

B. Moses in the New Testament.

Moses is mentioned more times in the NT (some 80 times) than any other OT figure.

1. The Historical Moses.

a. As Mediator of the Law. For the NT, as for the OT and Palestinian Judaism, Moses is primarily the messenger (Ac. 7:35) and servant (Rev. 15:3) of God who is validated by miracles (Ac. 7:36; Jn. 6:32; 3:14) and whose supreme dignity is that God spoke to him (Ac. 7:33 f.) [193] and that from the lips of an angel he received the living Word of the divine will to pass on to the people (Ac. 7:38). Hence Moses is predominantly mentioned in the NT as the lawgiver (→ νόμος). So strongly is this side of his activity felt to be decisive that Μωυσῆς is repeatedly an abbreviation for ὁ νόμος Μωυσέως. [194] Moses is read (2 C. 3:15). He has those who preach him (Ac. 15:21). Stephen speaks blasphemously against him (6:11; the Law in v. 13). Paul teaches apostasy from him (21:21). "Moses and the prophets" embraces the content of the OT (Lk. 16:29, 31; 24:27). More strictly, Moses is not the lawgiver; he is the mediator of the Law (which was given him by angels, → 865 f.).

But according to Jesus, and in contrast to the glorifying of Moses in later Judaism, Moses arbitrarily extended the Law in opposition to the true will of God (Mk. 10:5 and par.). Again, when the Rabbinate claims that by virtue of the wisdom of Moses [195] transmitted in unbroken succession through ordination it exercises teaching authority in the same sense as Moses himself did (ἐπὶ τῆς Μωυσέως καθέδρας [196] ἐκάθισαν οἱ γραμματεῖς, [197] Mt. 23:2), Jesus raised against this claim of the scribes to be the guardians and watchmen of the Mosaic legislation and tradition the objection that they did not practise what they taught (23:3-7). It is no accident, but a sign of profound religious distinction, that the

---

[191] The two olive-trees are Moses and Aaron; David representing the monarchy and Aaron the priesthood; Zerubbabel and Joshua; the Messiah and the high-priest of the Messianic age; the Messiah b. David and the Messiah b. Ephraim (Str.-B., III, 811 f.).

[192] Analogies: Str.-B., II, 282, n. 1; 292 ff.

[193] Cf. Jn. 9:29 and Unknown Gospel, lines 14-16: α[ὐ]τῶν δὲ λε[γόντω]ν ἔ[α˙] οἴδαμεν ὅτι Μω(υσεῖ) ἐλά[λησεν] ὁ θ(εό)ς ...

[194] This full form is found in Lk. 2:22; 24:44; Jn. 7:23; Ac. 13:38; 15:5; 28:23; 1 C. 9:9; Hb. 10:28.

[195] → 853.

[196] S. Krauss, *Talmudische Archäologie*, III (1912), 208, 340, n. 54; Str.-B., I, 909. Stone "seats of Moses" have been found in synagogues in Hamath (near Tiberias), Chorazin and Delos (K. Galling, *Bibl. Reallexikon* [1937], 510).

[197] The added καὶ οἱ Φαρισαῖοι does not fit materially, since it ascribes theological education to the Pharisees (→ I, 741) and is shown to be secondary by Lk. 11:45 f.

Ἰουδαῖοι of Jn. called themselves τοῦ Μωυσέως μαθηταί when they disputed the full authority of Jesus (Jn. 9:28).[198]

b. As Prophet. Moses is a prophet as well as the mediator of the Law,[199] and in the NT he is predominantly a prophet of Christ (Lk. 24:27, 44; Jn. 1:45; 5:46; Ac. 3:22; 7:37; 26:22; 28:23)[200] who intimated His coming and also His suffering (Lk. 24:27, 44 ff.; Ac. 26:22 f. He also prophesied the resurrection (Lk. 20:37; cf. 16:29, 31), the Gentile mission (R. 10:19) and the sovereignty of the divine election of grace (9:15). But the → Ἰουδαῖοι did not believe his words (Jn. 5:46 f.; cf. Mt. 22:29).

The statement in the two Lucan writings that Moses prophesied the sufferings of Christ (→ *supra*) is surprising, because there is no express prophecy to this effect in the Pentateuch. Perhaps the ref. is to Dt. 18:15, 18;[201] the prophet like Moses is understood as a figure of suffering, just as Moses was, → 873, 14 ff.[202]

c. As the Suffering Messenger of God and the Model of Faith for the Community. A more developed picture of the historical Moses, which goes beyond what has been said already, is to be found only in Ac. and Hb. Ac. paints a picture of the suffering messenger of God who was misunderstood and rejected, 7:17-44. The Moses of Hb. (11:23-29) is one of the heroic models of faith, and his faith finds fourfold attestation: as trust that God will recompense him because he renounced his dignity as the son of the king's daughter (24-26), as trust in God's help at leaving notwithstanding the anger of Pharaoh (27), as trust in God's promise in the sprinkling of the blood of the passover (28), and as trust in God's wonderful power at the passage of the Red Sea (29).[203]

d. The Moses Legend in the NT. At a few points of detail the depiction of Moses in the NT goes beyond the OT account and shows traces of the Moses legend. Thus we are told, without OT authority,[204] that Moses was learned in all the wisdom of the Egyptians,[205] that before he came to the fore he was already δυνατὸς ἐν λόγοις (cf. Ex. 4:10) καὶ ἔργοις αὐτοῦ (Ac. 7:22), that he was forty years old when he fled to Midian,[206] that he stayed in Midian forty years,[207] that two men called Jannes and Jambres withstood him,[208] that it was

---

198 → 443.

199 Moses is called a prophet in the OT at Dt. 18:15, 18; 34:10; in Hell. Judaism, Philo → n. 44 etc. (cf. H. Leisegang, *Index zu Philo,* II [1930], 692 f.); in Palestinian Judaism, → 853; in the early fathers, Barn., 6, 8; Ps. Cl. Recg., I, 34, 4 and 6.

200 Primarily Dt. 18:15, 18 is always in view.

201 This may be seen from the context of Ac. 7:37. → 868. Bornhäuser, 258 ff.

202 → 863. Bornhäuser, 282 conjectures that the word יָקִים (LXX ἀναστήσει) in Dt. 18:15 or אָקִים (LXX ἀναστήσω) in 18:18 is taken in the sense of "to raise again."

203 It is interesting to see how 4 Macc. views Moses as an example. He shows us how to tame passion by reason, for he does not take action against the conspiracy of Korah at the first attempt (Nu. 16).

204 On the echoes of the legendary account of Moses' birth in Mt. 2 → 870.

205 Ac. 7:22. There are par. for this only in the Hellen. legend. Philo in Vit. Mos., I, 21-24 mentions the spheres in which he was taught; cf. also the excerpt from the tragedian Ez. in Eus. Praep. Ev., 9, 28. On this as a feature of the θεῖος ἀνήρ, cf. Bieler, 34.

206 Ac. 7:23, cf. S. Dt. § 357 on 34:7 and Gn. r., 100, 8 on 50:14. We also find 20 in a few places, Ex. r., 1, 32 on 2:11 and 1, 35 on 2:14; Tanch. (Vienna, 1863) שמות, 61b (Str.-B., II, 679 f.).

207 Ac. 7:30; this is the common view, S. Dt., Gn. r., Tanch. (→ n. 206).

208 2 Tm. 3:8; → III, 192 f. (which should be supplemented by the oldest ref., Damasc. 5:18 f.).

an angel who spoke to him on Sinai,[209] that the Law was given him by angels to be passed on to Israel,[210] and that the archangel Michael strove with Satan for his body.[211] This review shows that the legendary features in the NT are of Palestinian origin. There is no trace of the wild flights of imagination found in the Egyptian-Jewish legend.

To summarise, it is plain that the Moses of the NT has nothing whatever to do with either the hero of the Moses romance or the ideal sage of Philo. This depiction is closer to that of the surrounding Palestinian world, though with the decisive distinction that it avoids any glorifying of Moses and can repeatedly offer relentless criticism.[212] The true basis is the OT.

2. Moses as a Figure of the Last Time.

As in later Palestinian Judaism, → 856 f., so in the NT Moses is given only a peripheral eschatological task.

He appears with Elijah on the Mount of Transfiguration (Mk. 9:4 f. and par.). Probably underlying this passage is the idea that these are the two precursors of the Messiah (→ II, 938),[213] but the idea is weakened, for Mk. 9:13 rules out the possibility

---

[209] Ac. 7:38: Οὗτός ἐστιν ὁ γενόμενος ἐν τῇ ἐκκλησίᾳ ἐν τῇ ἐρήμῳ μετὰ τοῦ ἀγγέλου τοῦ λαλοῦντος αὐτῷ ἐν τῷ ὄρει Σινᾶ. The usual explanation in the comm. that this angel handed Moses the Law is not supported by the text. This is only one angel, whereas the NT speaks of the handing of the Law to Moses by angels in the plur. (→ n. 210). Ac. 7:38 (cf. v. 35) is surely avoiding anthropomorphism. The OT says that God spoke to Moses on Mt. Sinai (Ex. 19:19 ff.), and Ac. 7:38 takes this to mean that He did so through an angel (cf. W. M. L. de Wette-F. Overbeck, Kurze Erklärung der Ag.[4] [1870], 106).

[210] Gl. 3:19. Though without mention of Moses, we also find in Hb. and Ac. the idea that the Law was spoken (Hb. 2:2) or ordained (Ac. 7:53) by angels (on Ac. 7:38 → n. 209). The co-operation of angels is to the magnifying of the Law in Ac. 7:53 but to its depreciation in Gl. 3:19 and Hb. 2:2 as compared with the promise to Abraham in Gl. and the Gospel in Hb. There are no exact par. in non-Christian writings; the idea is a different one in those usually adduced in the comm. Thus LXX Dt. 33:2 (ἐκ δεξιῶν αὐτοῦ [God's] ἄγγελοι μετ' αὐτοῦ) presupposes the presence of angels at the giving of the Law, but simply as God's entourage (Str.-B., III, 554). The closest to the NT seems to be Jos. Ant., 15, 136: The Jews have learned τὰ κάλλιστα τῶν δογμάτων καὶ τὰ ὁσιώτατα τῶν ἐν τοῖς νόμοις δι' ἀγγέλων παρὰ τοῦ θεοῦ, though the idea in Joseph. seems to be the rather different one, attested in Cant. r., 1, 13 on 1:2, that when the Law was given each law was presented and explained to each Israelite by an angel (Str.-B., III, 556). Acc. to Jub. 1:27 ff.; 6:22; 30:12, 21; 50:6, the angel of the presence wrote down the Law for Moses; acc. to 2:1 ff. this angel (Michael in Apc. Mos. 1) dictated the early history to him; acc. to Dt. r., 11, 6 on 31:14 (par. Midr. on the Decease of Moses, ed. A. Jellinek, *Bet ha-Midr.*, 6 [1877], 75) Michael says of Moses: "I was his teacher, he was my pupil." But the NT verses (Gl. 3:19; Ac. 7:53; Hb. 2:2) speak of many angels, and these had a part in the composition of the Law. Finally, Philo Som., I, 141, which says of angels that they teach children the commands of their father and the father the needs of their children, is hardly relevant here.

[211] Jd. 9. There are no Rabb. par. (Str.-B., III, 786). According to the fathers (first Cl. Al., ed. O. Stählin, III, 207; for others *v.* Schürer, III, 303) the legend comes from the Ass. Mos. Jd. 9 does not tell us how the conflict arose. We read in Cram. Cat., VIII, 163 and the Slav. Moses saga, 16 (N. Bonwetsch, NGG, 1908, 607) that Satan accused Moses of being a murderer because of the slaying of the Egyptian (Ex. 2:12), and that he would not permit his burial for this reason (Wnd. Kath. Br., *ad loc.*).

[212] For Jesus' criticism → 864. Paul (with no support in Ex. 34:29-35) says that Moses hid his radiant countenance so that the Israelites would not see how transitory the radiance was (2 C. 3:13).

[213] Mk. 9:4 f. seems to presuppose that Moses was translated like Elijah and Enoch (who appears elsewhere with Elijah, → II, 938), → 855.

that the community expected a personal return of Moses before the end. The significance of the appearance of the two divine messengers is limited to the fact that they proclaim the coming of the end, or Jesus' path of suffering acc. to Lk. 9:31, → II, 939.[214]

Only in one verse (Jn. 5:45) is Moses unequivocally allotted an eschatological function. The Jews set their hopes on him because they expect that he will intercede for them in the last judgment. But in fact he will be the accuser, i.e., the chief witness against them[215] (Jn. 5:45),[216] for lack of faith in Jesus is lack of faith in the writings of Moses which announce the coming of Jesus (5:46 f.). The Gospel Fr. of 1935 adds that this accusation is brought even now: νῦν κατηγορεῖται [ὑμῶν ἡ ἀ]πιστεί[α.[217]

3. The Moses/Christ Typology.

Theologically the most significant NT statements about Moses are those in which, like Adam (R. 5:12 ff.; 1 C. 15:15 ff.), Abel (Hb. 12:24), Melchisedec (Hb. 7:1 ff.), Jacob (Jn. 1:51), Solomon (Mt. 12:42),[218] David (Mt. 1:17;[219] Lk. 1:32; Mk. 2:25 and par.; 11:10; Rev. 3:7) and Jonah (Mt. 12:39 f. and par.), he is a type or antitype of Jesus. This Moses/Christ typology is not equally clear in all the books. It is plainly formulated only in Ac., Hb. and Jn., briefly indicated in Pl. and Rev., and presupposed in Mk. and Mt., but does not occur in any form in the Past. and the 7 Cath. Epistles.

a. The Baptist.

Expectation that the Messiah will be a second Moses is not unrelated to the appearing of the Baptist, for when John, on the basis of Is. 40:3, arose in the wilderness, according to the thinking of the age (→ 860 f.; → II, 658 f.) this was an indication that the Messiah, as the second Moses, would manifest Himself in the wilderness. That this was the thinking of the Baptist himself is very likely, since his baptism was a counterpart to the washing which according to contemporary tradition (cf. 1 C. 10:1-2, → 870) Moses made the wilderness generation undergo before receiving salvation.[220] Certainly the widespread popular opinion that the Baptist might be the Messiah (Lk. 3:15 etc.) rested on the fact that there was perceived in him the second Moses who would come in the wilderness.

b. Jesus.

As may be seen from Mt. 24:26, → 862, Jesus was acquainted with the Moses/

---

214 Rev. 11:3 ff. refers to the prophet like Moses, not Moses himself, → n. 189.

215 There is no state prosecutor in Palestinian law, but the chief witness undertakes the prosecution, cf. K. Bornhäuser, NkZ, 27 (1926), 353-363; H. v. Campenhausen, *D. Idee des Martyriums in d. alten Kirche* (1936), 33 ff.

216 Ἔστιν ὁ κατηγορῶν ὑμῶν Μωυσῆς, εἰς ὃν ὑμεῖς ἠλπίκατε (Jn. 5:45). As the immediately preceding κατηγορήσω shows, one should translate: "There is one here who will accuse you." As often in Jn. this is a present part. with a future sense — a usage which betrays the Semitic linguistic sense of the author. The part. is a-temporal in Aram.

217 Unknown Gospel, line 18 (the context refers to Moses as the accuser). The part. κατηγορῶν (for Jn. 5:45 → n. 216) is here obviously meant to be present.

218 Windisch, 96.

219 In Mt. 1:17 the number 14 carries an allusion to David: ד (= 4) + ו (= 6) + ד (= 4).

220 J. Jeremias, ZNW, 28 (1929), 320; also *Hat d. älteste Christenheit die Kindertaufe geübt?* (1938), 9-12.

Messiah typology. That He applied it to Himself may be seen from the fact that He repeatedly compared Himself to Moses as the Bringer of the true and definitive will of God (Mk. 10:1-12, and esp. the antitheses of the Sermon on the Mount, Mt. 5:21 ff.).[221] Indirectly, too, Jesus compares Himself with Moses as the Mediator of the new divine covenant, Mk. 14:24 and par.[222] If, as is likely, Jesus in Mt. 4:3 f. is refusing to repeat the miracle of the manna (cf. Jn. 6:30 ff.),[223] this teaches us that he regarded the popular expectation of a second Moses as a Satanic temptation.[224]

c. The Primitive Community.

Christian Moses/Messiah typology experienced its true development in the primitive community, which referred Dt. 18:15, 18 to Christ (Ac. 3:22 f., cf. 7:37)[225] and found affinities between the story of Moses and that of Jesus. These may be seen in Stephen's speech, which, with Jesus in view,[226] depicts Moses as the divinely sent Deliverer whom the people misunderstood and rejected, 7:17-44. Ac. 7 shows us that the prophet like Moses (Dt. 18:15, 18) was in the early Church identified with the suffering Messiah, of whom the suffering Moses is a type (cf. Hb. 11:26).

Ac. 3:22 f. and 7:17-44 cannot be regarded as a theologoumenon developed by Lk. Quite apart from 1 C. 10:1-2, this is shown by the fact that in one passage at least[227]

---

[221] Cf. esp. πληρῶσαι in Mt. 5:17. This is one of the few sayings of Jesus which we have in His native Aram., namely, in bShab., 116b, where the rendering of πληρῶσαι is לאוסופי ("to supplement"). As the Bringer of the supplementary and definitive divine will Jesus contrasts Himself with Moses, the bringer of the provisional divine will.

[222] Cf. also Jesus' self-designation as prophet (Lk. 13:33), perhaps in allusion to Dt. 18:15, 18 (so K. H. Rengstorf, *NT Deutsch* on Lk. 7:15 f.). K. Bornhäuser, in his *Das Wirken des Christus durch Taten u. Worte* (1921), advances the thesis that Jesus knew Himself to be both *the* prophet (the second Moses) and the Messiah, but distinguished between the two; He was to be *the* prophet on earth and to take on Messianic dignity only at the *parousia*. This is an exaggeration of a true point, for, while Jesus does sometimes apply the Moses/Messiah typology to Himself, it does not play in His consciousness the basic role allotted to it by Bornhäuser. The distinction between an earthly (prophetic) and a future (Messianic) dignity rests on an untenable exegesis of the phrase → υἱὸς τοῦ ἀνθρώπου, which Bornhäuser regards as a prophetic title in terms of Ez. (rather than Da. 7:13).

[223] Cf. J. Schniewind, *NT Deutsch* on Mt. 4:3 f.; J. Jeremias, ZDPV, 59 (1936), 207; E. Lohmeyer, ZSTh, 14 (1937), 628 f.

[224] In view of Mk. 3:27 (cf. also the first person in Ev. Hb. on Mt. 4:1, 8) it is highly probable that behind the temptation story, whose subject is the rejection of the political conception of the Messiah, there lies the account of a personal experience of Jesus. Attempts to attribute the whole story to the primitive community are decisively countered by the consideration that the political conception of the Messiah was no problem for the first community, which saw the life of Jesus in the light of the resurrection, but it was a very real problem for Jesus and His disciples in His own lifetime.

[225] Dt. 18:15 is referred to Jesus in Mk. 9:7 and par.; the passages adduced → 865, which speak of Messianic prophecies of Moses, also have Dt. 18:15, 18 primarily in view.

[226] The most important par. are Ac. 7:22b: Moses was δυνατὸς ἐν λόγοις καὶ ἔργοις αὐτοῦ (cf. Lk. 24:19); Ac. 7:25: ὁ θεὸς διὰ χειρὸς αὐτοῦ (Moses) δίδωσιν σωτηρίαν αὐτοῖς (the interruption of the narrative by this verse, the absence of an OT original, and the word σωτηρία betray an intentional par. with Jesus); v. 35: Moses is sent as ἄρχων and λυτρωτής (Moses is never called λυτρωτής in the LXX; the word has a Messianic ring, cf. λυτροῦσθαι in Lk. 24:21 and λύτρωσις in 1:68; 2:38, and generally, → 328 ff.): v. 36: τέρατα καὶ σημεῖα (cf. 2:22); v. 37: Dt. 18:15.

[227] Whether the ref. to the ἔρημος in Mk. 1:13 is connected with the typology is at least open to doubt is view of what was said → *supra* and 871.

the pre-Lucan Gospel tradition is shaped by the Moses/Messiah typology, namely, in the account of the transfiguration in Mk. 9:2-8 and par. The heavenly voice with its ἀκούετε αὐτοῦ (Mk. 9:7) contains an allusion to Dt. 18:15, and this leads us to conclude that in this story the many echoes of the account of Moses' ascent of the Mount of God and his transfiguration there (Ex. 24:9-18; 34:28-35)[228] are not accidental but are designed to characterise Jesus as the prophet like Moses.[229] The feeding of the five thousand in the desert (Mk. 6:32, 35 and par.) already in the Synoptic form (on Jn. 6 → 872) seeks to depict Jesus as the second Moses.

d. Paul.

Paul deals expressly with Moses as a type in 2 C. 3. But he develops the typology differently. (1) Moses with the veil on his face (→ III, 560 f.), which is designed to conceal the disappearance of the δόξα from the eyes of the people (v. 13), is for Paul a type of the office-bearer of the old covenant, who exercises a διακονία τοῦ θανάτου (v. 7) and τῆς κατακρίσεως (v. 9). With him is contrasted the NT office-bearer, who has no need of concealment but can speak with all openness (παρρησία, v. 12) because he exercises a διακονία τοῦ πνεύματος (v. 8) and τῆς δικαιοσύνης (v. 9) whose δόξα is imperishable (vv. 7-13). (2) Moses with his concealed δόξα is also for Paul a type of the concealment which lies over the OT for Judaism (v. 14), namely, over the hearts of those who hear the reading of the OT (v. 15). Contrasted with the community of the old covenant represented by Moses is the community of the new covenant which sees the δόξα of the Lord without concealment (→ II, 696 f.). In this respect, then, we may say that Paul applies the Moses typology in a way which differs from that of the primitive community. For him Moses represents the office-bearers and community of the old covenant, with whom he contrasts the office-bearers and community of the new.

Closely related, though without the contrast between the old and the new covenant, is 2 Tm. 3:8. As Moses met with futile opposition from Jannes and Jambres (v. 9), so the Christian community of the last time (v. 1) experiences opposition from licentious and blasphemous men (vv. 2-7) whose irrationality will, however, be made manifest (v. 9). Here Moses is a type of the Messianic community of salvation. It is a significant mark of the inner relation between the Past. and Pauline theology that here — as elsewhere in the NT only in Pl. — Moses is regarded as a type of the community rather than Christ.[230]

If in 2 C. Moses is not a type of Christ but a representative of the office-bearers and community of the old covenant in distinction from those of the new, this is related to the fact that Paul prefers → Adam as a type of Christ. The more significant, then, is the only passage in which the Moses/Messiah typology occurs

---

228 On Mk. 9:2a (6 days), cf. Ex. 24:16 (on this E. Lohmeyer, *Das Ev. des Mk.* [1937], 173, n. 3); on Mk. 9:2a (taking 3 disciples), cf. Ex. 24:1, 9 (Moses takes Aaron, Nadab, Abihu and the 70 elders); on Mk. 9:2b (ascent of the mount), cf. Ex. 24:9, 12 f., 15, 18; on Mk. 9:2b-3 (the transfiguration), cf. Ex. 34:29; on Mk. 9:7a (God reveals Himself in veiled form through the cloud, only here stated of God in the NT), cf. Ex. 24:15 f., 18; on Mk. 9:7b (the voice out of the cloud), cf. Ex. 24:16.

229 D. F. Strauss, *Das Leben Jesu*[3] (1874), 516 ff. emphasised these connections, but he went much too far, of course, when he argued that the transfiguration story was simply a mythical imitation of the story of Moses (518). Cf. A. Wünsche, *Neue Beiträge zur Erläuterung der Ev. aus Talmud u. Midr.* (1878), 201; Baldensperger, 141; Joh. Jeremias, *Der Gottesberg* (1919), 149 f.; E. Lohmeyer, ZNW, 28 (1929), 185-215; Wiebe.

230 The difference that in 2 C. 3:14 f. Moses represents the OT community whereas in 2 Tm. 3:8 he is a type of the NT community is not important, since it is not outside the limits of Paul's view of Moses. Thus, Pl. contrasts himself with Moses in 2 C. 3:12 f. (→ lines 11 ff.) but he also takes Moses as an example in R. 9:3 (Ex. 32:32; cf. Windisch, 242).

in Paul.[231] This is 1 C. 10:1-2, where it is said of the wilderness generation that when its members passed through the Red Sea. and were enveloped in the cloud and water,[232] εἰς τὸν Μωυσῆν ἐβαπτίσαντο.[233] The idea of a baptism of this generation was common in later Judaism from the 1st century A.D. on; it was prompted by the desire to find for proselyte baptism the biblical grounds which could not be found elsewhere.[234] Nevertheless, the description of this baptism as a baptism "into Moses" is unique. It is to be explained by the fact that the Moses/Christ typology led Paul to coin an analogous formula to εἰς Χριστὸν βαπτίζεσθαι (cf. 1 C. 1:13). The unprepared occurrence of the typology in 1 C. 10:2 suggests that it is pre-Pauline in origin.

Elsewhere Paul uses the typology only allusively, without expansion, and in such a way that the subordination of Moses to Christ is evident. Thus R. 10:4-5 opposes the righteousness of works which Moses proclaimed (Lv. 18:5) to the righteousness of faith. Gl. 3:19 ff. contrasts the Law given through the → μεσίτης Moses with the promise fulfilled in Jesus Christ. The same antithesis tacitly underlies Eph. 4:8. Ps. 68:18, which is here referred to Jesus, is always interpreted of Moses in Rabb. tradition. Moses went up into heaven, received the Torah (as prisoner) and gave it to men.[235] Paul in his exposition puts Christ in the place of Moses and divinely gifted χάρις in place of the Law (Eph. 4:7 ff.).

e. Matthew.

In Mt. the main influence of the typology is to be seen in the fact that the infancy story in Mt. 2 follows at many points the model of the Moses legend.[236] Thus according to a legend attested in Joseph. and Rabb. tradition the prophecy of the birth of the liberator of Israel by an Egyptian scribe[237] (cf. Mt. 2:4-6) provided the occasion for the startled Pharaoh (cf. 2:3) to order the slaying of the children of the Israelites (cf. 2:16).[238] But the father of Moses was told by God in a dream (cf. 2:13) that his child would be saved.[239] If one adds that in Joseph., quoting from the story of Moses (Ex. 4:19), the death of the persecutor is also foretold (2:20), and that mention of Egypt (2:13-15) necessarily suggests

[231] The statement that Pl. compares Moses only with himself and not with Jesus (Schl. K., 258) thus stands in need of qualification.

[232] In 1 C. 10:1-2 Pl. is not, of course, speaking of a twofold baptism of the wilderness generation, first in the cloud, then in the water, but he has in view the fact that the Israelites were enveloped by the cloud as they passed through the sea.

[233] The less frequent mid. form (**P**[46] **[ex corr] B 𝔎**) has a stronger claim to authenticity than the pass. (ἐβαπτίσθησαν, אACDG).

[234] Joach. Jeremias, ZNW, 28 (1929), 316-319.

[235] Str.-B., III, 596-598.

[236] Gfrörer, 354-364; Kl. Mt., 12; Schl. Mt., 32; Staerk, *Erlösererwartung*, 374; Wiebe.

[237] Jos. Ant., 2, 205. By astrologers acc. to Ex. r., 1, 22 on 1:22; by magicians acc. to PRE, 48; by Jannes and Jambres, the chief magicians, acc. to Tg. J. I Ex., 1, 15. The OT knows nothing of this. Acc. to Ex. 1:9 ff. the increased numbers of the Israelites were the reason for the order to kill.

[238] Jos. Ant., 2, 205: τῶν ἱερογραμματέων τις (cf. Mt. 2:4) ... ἀγγέλλει τῷ βασιλεῖ τεχθήσεσθαί τινα κατ' ἐκεῖνον τὸν καιρὸν τοῖς 'Ισραηλίταις ὃς ταπεινώσει μὲν τὴν Αἰγυπτίων ἡγεμονίαν, αὐξήσει δὲ τοὺς 'Ισραηλίτας (cf. Mt. 2:5 f.) ... (§ 206) Δείσας δ' ὁ βασιλεὺς (cf. Mt. 2:3) ... κελεύει πᾶν τὸ γεννηθὲν ἄρσεν ὑπὸ τῶν 'Ισραηλιτῶν ... διαφθείρειν (cf. Mt. 2:16). Ex. r., 1, 22 on 1:22: "The astrologers had said to him (Pharaoh): a mother is carrying the redeemer of Israel," whereupon Pharaoh had both Israelite and Egyptian children slain; PRE, 48; in much embellished form Tg. J. I Ex. 1, 15 (quoted in Str.-B., III, 661). For further par. and bibl. on the Arab Moses legend cf. Rappaport, 113, n. 126.

[239] Jos. Ant., 2, 212.

the story of Moses,[240] one is forced to the conclusion that the fact that the infancy story of Moses provides a model for that of Jesus implicitly characterises Jesus as the second Moses.[241]

The Moses/Christ typology is implicitly present in a few other passages in Mt. as well. Thus Mt. in his account of the temptation says that Jesus fasted forty days and forty nights (4:2). The addition of the nights, not mentioned in Mk. 1:13 or Lk. 4:2, is possibly based on Ex. 34:28; Dt. 9:9, 18, which tell us that Moses fasted for forty days and forty nights on the Mount of God.[242] Again, in the introduction to the Sermon on the Mount we read: ἀνέβη εἰς τὸ ὄρος. Here the art. is originally indefinite, as often in Aram. (= טוּרָא = a mountain), but this does not exclude the possibility that Mt. sees in "the" mountain of the Sermon on the Mount a counterpart to the Mount of God on which Moses received the Law,[243] for in Mt. 5:17, 21 f. Jesus is contrasted with Moses as the One who declares the true will of God (→ 868), and it is thus highly probable that Mt. had this comparison in view in the composition of the whole of the Sermon on the Mount.[244]

f. Hebrews.

If the Moses/Christ comparison is only implicit in Mt., it is plainly declared and repeatedly developed in Hb., which is also characterised by the fact that the model is transcended by the fulfilment. Moses is first compared with Christ in respect of the faithfulness which he displayed as a steward of God (Nu. 12:7). But this was the faithfulness of a servant, whereas Christ displayed that of a son, just as Christ's house, the saved community of the NT, is higher than that of Moses (3:1-6). Then Moses is a type of Christ as the mediator of a divine → διαθήκη. Like the Mosaic covenant, the νέα διαθήκη (12:24) demanded that atoning blood be shed first (9:15 ff.). But again, the fulfilment is incomparably greater than the prototype. God's new economy of salvation is better (7:22; 8:6) and eternal (13:20), for it was put in force by the blood of Christ which was offered in the heavenly sanctuary and which effected true purgation of sins (9:23 ff.). If it is finally said of Moses that he despised his dignity as the son of the king's daughter (11:24) and regarded τὸν ὀνειδισμὸν τοῦ Χριστοῦ as greater riches than the treasures of Egypt (v. 26), the *tertium comparationis*[245] is that, as Moses freely renounced his glory as the son of the king's daughter in order to suffer with his people (v. 25), so Christ in His incarnation freely surrendered the heavenly glory of the Son of God and accepted the shame of abasement (2:7, 9, 14).[246] In this respect, too, Moses is a type of the suffering Christ (→ 868).[247]

---

240 Gfrörer, 363 conjectures that the story of the flight to Egypt arose out of a desire that in this, too, Jesus should be like Moses, who grew up in Egypt.

241 Cf. J. Schniewind, *NT Deutsch, Das Ev. nach Mt.*, 19; Bieler, 7.

242 Bornhäuser, 30; Schl. Mt., 100; cf. also J. Schniewind, 28; Goppelt, 118. But acc. to Apc. Abr., 12, 1 Abraham also fasted for forty days and forty nights on the way to Horeb (cf. 1 K. 19:8). On the other hand, only the days are mentioned in the case of Adam (Vit. Ad., 6).

243 Kl. Mt., *ad loc.*; Wiebe. On the anonymous Mount of God cf. Joh. Jeremias, *Der Gottesberg* (1919), 143 f.

244 Bornhäuser, 62-67.

245 Though cf. the comm.

246 In Hb. 13:13, too, τὸν ὀνειδισμὸν αὐτοῦ (of Christ) means the same shame as Christ.

247 Christ's designation as ὁ ποιμὴν τῶν προβάτων (Hb. 13:20, based on LXX Is. 63:11) is hardly relevant here, since the way Hb. uses Scripture makes it doubtful whether the author was aware that the "shepherd of the sheep" of Is. 63:11 referred to Moses (Rgg. Hb., *ad loc.*).

g. The Johannine Writings.

In Rev. the Moses/Christ typology occurs only in 15:3.[248] Those who overcome, standing on the shore of the crystal sea, ᾄδουσιν τὴν ᾠδὴν Μωυσέως τοῦ δούλου τοῦ θεοῦ καὶ τὴν ᾠδὴν τοῦ ἀρνίου. The divine sees beginning and end, prototype and fulfilment, together. The exodus from Egypt is a type of the redemption from the aeon of sin, the passage through the Red Sea is a type of the passage of the redeemed through the crystal sea to their heavenly home, the triumph song of Moses (Ex. 15) is a type of the triumphant rejoicing of those who overcome,[249] and Moses as the divinely sent liberator is a type of the Lamb.[250]

In Jn. the lifting up of the serpent by Moses is a type of the lifting up of the Son of Man (3:14), and the giving of the manna by Moses is a type of the giving of the true bread of life which is to be found in the person of Jesus (6:32 ff.). In this case there is the strongest possible contrast between Moses and Christ: "Moses gave you not that bread from heaven; but my Father giveth you the true bread from heaven" (v. 32). The same contrast is to be seen in Jn. 10:11, 14: ἐγώ εἰμι ὁ ποιμὴν ὁ καλός ("The good shepherd am I"),[251] if — though this is not certain — the I-saying is aimed against the description of Moses (e.g., M. Ex. on 14:31) as the רוֹעֶה נֶאֱמָן ("faithful shepherd").[252, 253]

Jn. 1:17, an expansion of the original hymn to the Logos,[254] is to be assessed differently: ὁ νόμος διὰ Μωυσέως ἐδόθη. ἡ χάρις καὶ ἡ ἀλήθεια διὰ Ἰησοῦ Χριστοῦ

[248] With Wiebe we should see an indirect ref. in the mention of the wilderness in 12:6, 14. It is here that the Messiah manifests Himself as the second Moses, → 860 f., 867. On 11:3 ff. → 863.

[249] On the new song of the Messianic age cf. Str.-B., III, 801.

[250] To understand Rev. 15:2-4 within the whole of Rev., it is vital to note that Rev. 8:2-14:20 and 15:1-20:15 are 2 par. apocalypses, and that the same content is to be found more briefly in 6:1-8:1, G. Bornkamm, ZNW, 36 (1937), 134 ff. On p. 147 Bornkamm also argues plausibly that 6:1-2, the disputed opening of the first of the three, is to be interpreted in the light of 19:11. As the overture to the events of the end time the divine sees Christ, the Victor, on the white horse. 15:2-4 is to be taken analogously. As the overture to the third apocalypse (15:1-20:15), introducing here the vision of the seven last plagues (15:1-16:21), we have a depiction of the redeemed striking up a song of victory. In 15:2-4 we are thus given an anticipatory vision of the perfected community, with a par. in 7:9-17 (originally the conclusion of the second apocalypse). As concerns the origin of the material used in 15:2-4, Staerk, *Erlösererwartung*, 153 (on the basis of observations in Loh. Apk., *ad loc.*) makes the illuminating suggestion that behind the verses stands a myth of the soul's salvation which has been combined with an allegorical interpretation of the Exodus motif and eschatologically transmuted.

[251] Ἐγώ εἰμι is strictly the predicate, cf. R. Bultmann, *Das J. Ev.* (1939), 167, n. 2 ("formula of recognition").

[252] Ref. is made to this passage in connection with Jn. 10:11, 14 by A. Schlatter, "D. Sprache u. Heimat des 4. Evangelisten," BFTh, 6, 4 (1902), 124; P. Fiebig, *Angelos*, 1 (1925), 57 f.; H. Odeberg, *The Fourth Gospel* (1929), 138 f., 314 f. For other instances of the designation of Moses as the faithful shepherd cf. Rosmarin, 82, n. 293.

[253] It is possible that the contrast is present in other sayings in Jn., cf. the emphatic ἐγώ in Jn. 6:63: τὰ ῥήματα ἃ ἐγὼ λελάληκα ὑμῖν πνεῦμά ἐστιν καὶ ζωή ἐστιν. But this cannot be proved; a wider antithesis may be in view.

[254] Jn. 1:17 is shown to be an expansion by the fact (1) that it does not have the step parallelism typical of the hymn, and (2) that the name of Jesus, previously unmentioned, is now given directly. Jn. 1:17 and 17:3 are the only verses in Jn. where there is no art. before Χριστός, and we may suspect that the same hand is at work in both, cf. R. Bultmann, *op. cit.* (1937), 53, n. 3.

ἐγένετο. Most probably the parallelism here is not antithetical but synthetic. This is evident when one notes that the divine name stands behind the pass. ἐδόθη.[255] Moses, too, mediated divine revelation, even though this was only the preliminary revelation of the Law. As a mediator of revelation he is thus a type of Him who brought the full revelation of God.

In general it is a mark of the Moses/Christ typology in John's Gospel that it emphasises more strongly than other early Christian literature the contrast between Moses and Christ. This is probably due to the situation of the Church as the 1st century was drawing to its close. Judaism and Christianity now confronted one another as two different religions represented by Moses and Christ. Yet it should not be overlooked that the antithesis between Moses and Christ is emphasised already in the preaching of Jesus, → 867 f.[256]

h. The Suffering Moses as a Type of Christ.

When one considers the NT statements concerning Moses, it is striking how strongly Moses is depicted as a figure of suffering. This is most evident in the speech of Stephen (Ac. 7:17-44). But Hb., too, regards Moses as one who suffers (11:24-26), and cf. also → 870 on Mt. 2; Lk. 9:31; 2 Tm. 3:8. We should also add the verses in which the prophecy of a "prophet like Moses" (Dt. 18:15, 18) is construed as an intimation of the suffering Messiah (Lk. 24:27, 44 ff.; Ac. 26:22 f.). This emphasis on the elements of suffering is to be explained by the fact that biblical interpretation in the early Church was orientated to the cross. The prototype was seen in the light of the fulfilment. The reality of the second Moses determines the view of the first.

It may be asked whether it is purely accidental that later Judaism itself not only saw in the historical Moses a figure of suffering, esp. in connection with his death and burial in the wilderness (→ 853 ff.), but also linked elements of suffering with the figure of the second Moses (→ 863). If one answers in the negative, it may be concluded that this factor contributed to the early acceptance of the later Jewish Moses/Christ typology by the primitive Church.

In sum, it may be said that the Moses/Christ typology did not exercise a central or controlling influence on NT Christology. Nevertheless, whether explicit or implicit, whether with emphasis on points of comparison or on points of contrast, it is almost everywhere expressed in the NT, and it was one of the motifs which helped to shape NT Christology. Moses and Christ are the two divine messengers of the old covenant and the new. They are linked by the same fate of rejection and misunderstanding. They stand for the combination and yet also the contrast of Law and Gospel.

C. The Post-Apostolic Age.

The story of Moses is used in exhortation. Warning examples are taken from it in 1 Cl., 4, 10 and 12; 51, 3-5, and things to imitate in 17, 5; 43, 1-6; 53, 1-5. A varied allegorical interpretation of the story is also to be found in Barn., 4, 6-8; 6, 8 ff.; 10, 1-12; 12, 2-3 and 5-7, also 8 f.; 14, 2-4. Here for the first time (12, 2-3) the outstretched hands of Moses as he prays for victory over the Amalekites (Ex. 17:11 f.) are referred to the cross of Christ. This exposition enjoyed a great vogue in the time which followed.[257]

J. Jeremias

---

[255] On the passive for the name of God cf. Dalman WJ, I, 183-185.
[256] On Jn. 6:32 ff. cf. what is said on Mt. 4:3 f. → 868.
[257] Just. Dial., 90; Sib., 8, 251-255; cf. also the examples in Wnd. Barn., 370.

† Ναζαρηνός, † Ναζωραῖος

Jesus is always called Ναζαρηνός in Mk.: 1:24; 10:47 (vl. Ναζωραῖος); 14:67; 16:6, also in Lk. 4:34 (based on Mk. 1:24) and 24:19 (vl. Ναζωραίου). The more common form Ναζωραῖος is found in Mt. 2:23; 26:69 (vl. Γαλιλαῖος); 26:71; Lk. 18:37 (vl. Ναζαρηνός); Jn. 18:5 (vl. Ναζαρηνός); 18:7; 19:19; Ac. 2:22; 3:6; 4:10; 6:14; 22:8; 26:9. Christians are given the same name in Ac. 24:5; the accuser Tertullus calls Paul πρωτοστάτης τῆς τῶν Ναζωραίων αἱρέσεως. Lk. took Ναζαρηνός from an older tradition but prefers Ναζωραῖος, though the two forms mean the same for him. Their connection with Ναζαρέθ (Ναζαρέτ, also Ναζαρά, Mt. 4:13; Lk. 4:16), the home-town of Jesus in Galilee (πατρίς, Mk. 6:1; Lk. 4:23; Mt. 13:54), where His mother and brethren lived and where He grew up, is presupposed in Mk., Lk. and Jn. (cf. ὁ ἀπὸ Ναζαρέθ, Mt. 21:11; Ac. 10:38; Jn. 1:45) and is openly stated, in connection with a prophecy, in Mt. 2:23: τὸ ῥηθὲν διὰ τῶν προφητῶν ὅτι Ναζωραῖος κληθήσεται. A comparison of Mt. 26:69 and 26:71 shows that Ναζωραῖος and Γαλιλαῖος mean much the same. The disciples of Jesus are Γαλιλαῖοι in Ac. 1:11. The passages adduced show that the two terms are not self-designations on the part of Jesus and His disciples, but that they were called this by the world around. In Ac. 24:5 Ναζωραῖος is used by the Jews to denote members of the original community in Jerusalem. It indicates their place of origin and has a derogatory nuance, cf. Jn. 1:46.[1]

Paul uses neither of the two terms, nor does any later Christian author in Greek. The reason for this is that in Gentile Christian churches the name Χριστιανοί (Χρηστιανοί), first given to Christians in Antioch (Ac. 11:26), was generally accepted. Ναζαρηνός and Ναζωραῖος were restricted to the Jewish Christian tradition. Their influence on missions to the Syrians and Syriac versions of the

---

Ναζαρηνός, Ναζωραῖος. Comm. on Mt. 2:23: W. C. Allen, *A Critical and Exegetical Commentary on the Gospel according to St. Matthew*[3] (1912); Zn.; Kl.; Schl.; Str.-B., I, 92-96; Wellh. Mt.[2] on 26:71. Arts.: *s.v.* in Pr.-Bauer[3], 881 f.; "Nazoräer" in RGG[2], IV, 475; H. Guthe, "Nazareth," in PRE[3], 13, 676-678. Cf. also J. K. Zenner, "Philologisches zum Namen Nazareth," *Ztschr. f. kath. Theol.*, 18 (1894), 744-747; Dalman Gr., 152 and 178; P. Schwen, "Nazoräer u. Nasaräer bei Epiphanius," *Prot. Monatshefte*, 14 (1910), 208-13; "Nazareth u. d. Nazoräer," ZwTh, 54 (1912), 31-35; F. C. Burkitt, "The Syriac Forms of the New Testament Proper Names" (*Proceedings of the British Academy*, 1911/2, 374-408), 391-400, and on this R. H. Conolly, JThSt, 14 (1912/3), 475 f.; G. F. Moore, "Nazarene and Nazareth," in F. J. Foakes-Jackson and K. Lake, *The Beginnings of Christianity*, I, 1 (1920), 426-32; I, 5 (1933), 356 f.; Lidz. Liturg., XVI-XIX; Lidz., *Ztschr. f. Semitistik*, 1 (1922), 230-33; Lidz. Ginza, IX f.; H. Zimmern, "Nazoräer (Nazarener)," ZDMG, 74 (1920), 429-38; Meyer Ursprung, II, 408 f., 423-25; W. Caspari, "Ναζωραῖος Mt. 2:23 nach alttestamentlichen Voraussetzungen," ZNW, 21 (1922), 122-27; H. Smith, Ναζωραῖος, JThSt, 28 (1926/7), 60; G. Dalman, *Orte u. Wege Jesu*[3] (1924), 61-88.

[1] Cf. Tertullian Marc., IV, 8 (3, 437, Kroymann): *Nazaraeus vocari habebat secundum prophetiam Christus creatoris. unde et ipso nomine nos Judaei Nazarenos appellant per eum. nam et sumus de quibus scriptum est: Nazaraei exalbati sunt super nivem* [Lam. 4:7].

NT[2] explains why *nāṣrājā* (or more exactly *nāṣ^e^rājā*) is the consistent Syr. rendering of both Ναζαρηνός and Ναζωραῖος and is also the name of Syrian Christians, adopted also by the Persians, the Armenians, and later the Arabs. This single rendering of the two words in the whole of the Syr. Gospel tradition (cf. already Syr^sin^ and Syr^cur^) leads to the conclusion that *nāṣrājā* derives directly from the usage of the Aram. speaking disciples of Jesus and the primitive Jerusalem community. In secondary forms we find the Gk. Ναζαρηνός or Ναζωραῖος and the Hebrew *nōṣrī* (or *nōṣ^e^rī*), as Jesus and the disciples are sometimes called in the Talmud.[3]

But there are several difficulties. 1. In respect of the ending there are parallels elsewhere for the variation between Ναζαρηνός and Ναζωραῖος, cf. the Essene names Ἐσσηνοί and Ἐσσαῖοι, but in view of the difference in the second syllable (the vowels α and ω) they can hardly be treated as identical. 2. The ζ of both forms is in keeping with Ναζαρέθ-Ναζαρά, but does not seem to correspond to the *ṣ* in נצרת, *nāṣraṯ*, the Syr. rendering of the name, which is confirmed by the Arab name *an-Nāṣira* and also by *nāṣrājā* and *nōṣrī*. For the Semitic *ṣ* one would expect the Gk. σ rather than ζ. 3. It is hard to find an OT prophecy directly corresponding to Mt. 2:23.

a. The first difficulty explains the attempts to separate Ναζωραῖος materially from Ναζαρέθ. In this ref. is made to what Epiphanius (Haer., 29, 6) tells us about a pre-Christian Jewish sect of Νασαραῖοι. After earlier fantastic proposals[4] this attempt seemed to have reached its goal when Lidz. pointed to the Gnostic sect of the Mandaeans, which appeared in Southern Babylonia in the Christian era. In their sacred writings, composed in an East Aram. dialect, these call themselves without distinction מאנדאייא (*mandājē*) and נאצוראייא. The latter Lidz. transcribed as *nāṣōrājē*,[5] which he equated with Ναζωραῖος (though this leaves us with the second difficulty of the unrelated *ṣ* and ζ). He took both forms to be Aram. renderings of the Heb. *nōṣrī* attested in the Talmud. This he took to be an adjectival derivation (expressing membership) from *nōṣēr*, "observant" (i.e., of specific cultic usages). He thought he saw here the name of a pre-Christian sect from which Jesus came. As he saw it, this name was transmitted 1. in the Heb. form as a name for Jesus in the Talmud, 2. in the Aram. form *nāṣrājā* (derived from the part. *nāṣar*), the Syr. for Ναζαρηνός/Ναζωραῖος, 3. in the Aram. form *nāṣōrājā* (derived from a *nomen agentis* **nāṣōrā*), represented by the Gk. Ναζωραῖος and the Mand. *nāṣōrājā*. This explanation is one of the main props of his theory that the Mandaeans belonged to the Jordan area and were directly connected with sectarian movements in Palestinian Judaism at the time of the rise of Christianity. This hypothesis, esp. the assertion that Ναζωραῖος cannot be connected with Ναζαρέθ and

---

2 This is proved by the Syr. renderings of NT proper names, P. Schwen, ZAW, 31 (1911), 267-303, esp. 300.

3 bAZ, 17a; bTaan., 27b; bBer., 17b; bSota, 47a; bSanh., 103a, 107b (43a only נֵצֶר) etc. The passages not found in censored copies of the Talmud have been collected by G. Dalman in an app. to H. Laible, *Jesus Christus im Talmud* (1891), cf. H. L. Strack, *Jesus, die Häretiker und die Christen* (1910), also Str.-B., I, 94 f.

4 For attempts designed to dispute the historicity of Jesus or to prove a pre-historical Jesus cf. J. M. Robertson and W. B. Smith, and on these J. Weiss, *Jesus v. Nazareth, Mythus oder Geschichte?* (1910), 20-22; H. Weinel, *Ist das 'liberale' Jesusbild widerlegt?* (1910), 96-102; M. Brückner, "Nazareth als Heimat Jesu," *Palästinajahrbuch,* 1911, 74-84; A. Schweitzer, *Geschichte d. Leben-Jesu-Forschung*[5] (1933), 465, 475 f., 533 f.

5 → Bibl. Before him cf. already T. Nöldeke, *Mandäische Grammatik* (1875), XX and W. Brandt, *Die mandäische Religion* (1889), 140.

its equation with *nāṣōrājā*, has found a good deal of acceptance.[6] But it does not stand up to closer inspection, as we shall see.

The main arguments for a western origin of the Mandaeans were 1. the adoption of West Aram. elements in Mandaean usage, both generally and esp. in the religious sphere; 2. the Mandaean use of "Jordan" (*jardnā*) for the flowing water used in baptism; Lidz. takes this to imply that the Mandaeans, when they migrated from the Jordan area, took with them the name of their sacred river, in which they had held their lustrations, and 3. the Mandaean self-designation *nāṣōrājā*. Since then it has been shown 1. that the distinction between West and East Aram. arose only in the Christian era when there developed a distinction between the Jewish and Christian dialect of Palestine, which included the Nabatean and Samaritan, and the eastern dialects of the Christian Syrians, the Babylonian Talmud and the Mandaeans.[7] The phenomena which Lidz. asserted to be West Aram. may all be explained as archaisms inherited in Babylonian Aram.; none of them demands a derivation outside Babylon. 2. H. Lietzmann[8] has cogently shown that the Mandaeans borrowed not only their description of the baptismal water as "Jordan" but their whole baptismal ritual from the East Syrian church.

As regards 3. the explanation of נאצוראיא cannot be sustained even on purely linguistic grounds. Lidz. himself has shown that that the collective abstract noun in *-ūṯā* for *nāsōrajā* is not *nāṣōrūtā*, as his thesis would demand, but נאצארותא, נאצירותא, and once, in a later text, נאצרות.[9] All these forms, though Lidz. does not draw this inescapable conclusion, are relevant only if one assumes that the ו in נאצוראיא no more denotes a long ō than the א in נאצארותא a long ā and the י in נאצירותא a long ī. In all three cases the "full" form in Mandaean orthography has an indifferent *shwa* vowel between the *ṣ* and *r*, and this need not be denoted, as the form נאצרות shows. Thus on the one side we have *nāsᵒrājā* (not *nāsorājā-*), on the other *nāsᵃrūtā, nāsⁱrūtā*. It is in keeping with *nāṣᵒrājā* that earlier European travellers heard and listed the Southern Babylonian city Baṣra as Bassora.

This is confirmed by a statement[10] of the Syrian ecclesiastical author Theodore bar Kōnai (8th cent.) concerning the sect of the Dostaeans: "In Maišān (the Baṣra district)

[6] So T. Nöldeke, *Ztschr. f. Assyriologie*, 33 (1920), 73 f. (wanting to separate Ναζωραῖος and Ναζαρέθ); Zimmern; Reitzenstein Ir. Erl., VI etc.; R. Bultmann, ZNW, 24 (1925), 143 f.; also *Jesus* (1926), 26; A. v. Gall, "Βασιλεία τοῦ θεοῦ," *Religionswissenschaftliche Bibliothek*, 7 (1926), 411 f., 432; H. H. Schaeder, *Studien zum antiken Synkretismus* (1926), 308 f.; C. H. Kraeling, *Journal of the American Oriental Soc.*, 491 (1929), 214 ff. Lidz., *Ztschr. f. Sem.*, 1, 230 ff. met in part the criticisms of his linguistic data by E. Meyer, repeated by C. Clemen, *Religionsgesch. Erkl. des NT*[2] (1924), 202. The observations of H. Gressmann, ZKG, 41 (1922), 166 f. and M. J. Lagrange, *Revue biblique*, 36 (1927), 498 ff., do not seriously weaken his linguistic case.

[7] W. Baumgartner, "Das Aramäische im Buche Daniel," ZAW, 45 (1927), 81-133; C. Bergsträsser, *Einführung in d. semitischen Sprachen* (1928), 59; H. H. Schaeder, *Iranische Beiträge*, I (1930), 27-56; F. Rosenthal, *Die Sprache der palmyrenischen Inschriften* (1936), 99-105.

[8] "Ein Beitrag zur Mandäerfrage," SAB, 1930, XXVII, 596-608, and previously by way of conjecture E. Peterson, ZNW, 25 (1926), 243; 27 (1928), 89; ThBl, 7 (1928), 318. The objections to Lidz. in H. Schlier, ThR, NF, 5 (1933), 76 f. carry little weight.

[9] In Ginza MS A almost always has נאצארותא, while B and D prefer נאצירותא, with C in a middle position. The passages here are GR, 25, 21; 197, 22; 276, 23; 288, 10: נאצארותא קאשישא מן יאהדותא, "Nāsᵃraeanism is older than Judaism"; 301, 18; 317, 3; GL., 76, 7. Cf. Lidz., *Das Johannesbuch der Mandäer*, 2 (1915), 124, n. 2. נאצרות occurs in Liturg., 257, 4; cf. Nöldeke, *Mand. Gramm.*, 155, 11.

[10] H. Pognon, *Inscr. mandaïtes des coupes de Khouabir* (1898/9), 154, 15-17, cf. 224 f.; also K. Kessler, Art. "Mandaer" in PRE[3], 12, 159.

they are called Mandaeans (*mandājē*), *mašknājē* and followers of the benefactor, in Bet Aramājē (the Kūfā district) *nāṣrājē* and followers of Dōstai."

But in this case *nāṣ^{o}rājā* is simply a rendering of *nāṣrājā*, the common term for Christians in Syr. territory. That this is so is shown beyond doubt by a testimony in the Mandaean tradition itself which Lidz. ignored. In Ginza R., 184, 20-185, 4, in the context of a kind of parody of Mt. 25:31-46, departed souls who follow the false Mšīhā (Christ) rather than the God of the Mandaeans answer the question in whose name they have done good works during their lifetime as follows: "In the name of the upper being and in the name of the lower being, in the name of Jesus Christ (עשו משיהא) and in the name of the Holy Ghost (רוהא דקודשא), in the name of the God of the *Nāṣ^{o}rājē* (אלאהא דנאצוראייא) and in the name of the Virgin, the daughter of her father." [11] In rather a different expression the same term undoubtedly means Christians in 185, 23. Instead of testing his hypothesis by this usage, Lidz. here translates the decisive words as "the God of the Nazarenes," and adds the note: "Nasoraeans is the term used in the text."

Support is found here for the earlier view [12] that the Mandaean self-description as *Nāṣ^{o}rājē* may be traced back to the Syrian name for Christians. The Mandaeans, or one of the South Babylonian sects from which they sprang, adopted this at an unknown date; the more precise historical circumstances escape our knowledge. It is thus impossible to prove the direct connection between *nāṣ^{o}rājē* and Ναζωραῖος which Lidz. had in view.

b. But this explanation of the form of the Mandaean term raises the question how we are to understand the ω in Ναζωραῖος, i.e., whether the generally tacit presupposition that it is a long ō is right. For the early Christian tradition Ναζωραῖος and Ναζαρηνός, which appears only in Mk., the earliest witness, are equivalent, as shown by the usage of Lk. and the common Syr. rendering as *nāṣrājā*. The α of the second syllable of Ναζαρέθ and Ναζαρηνός is undoubtedly the "full" form of a shwa vowel between *ṣ* and *r*, as in the Mandaean נאצארותא *nāṣ^{a}rūṯā*. There is no reason why this should not also be true of the ω in Ναζωραῖος. The Gk. transcription of Heb. words gives us a list of assured examples of ω for the shwa simplex: [13] μωκωρ מְקוֹר in Ps. 36:10 Hexapla; δωδανιμ דְּדָנִים in Is. 21:13 ʼΑΣ; μωουλαθει מְחֹלָתִי in 2 S. 21:8 B; ρωμελιου (with ρομελιου) רְמַלְיָה in Is. 7:5 G^Luc; σωβενια שְׁבַנְיָהוּ in 1 Ch. 15:24 A; σωφηρα סְפָרָה in Gn. 10:30 BA; χωνενια כְּנַנְיָהוּ in 1 Ch. 15:22 A (κωνενια BS). Thus we may confidently say that Ναζωραῖος, like Ναζαρηνός, is the Gk. form of the Aram. *nāṣrājā*, derived from *nāṣraṯ*, [14] Ναζαρέθ.

---

11 The expression "daughter of her father," like the Arab "son of his father," denotes dubious origin.

12 Cf. esp. T. Nöldeke and W. Brandt; also Lietzmann, *op. cit.*, 607.

13 Cf. E. Nestle in Schwen, ZwTh, 48, n. 2. Schwen compares the Syr. *nāṣrājā* and the Mand. נאצוראיא but does not draw the right conclusion in relation to the latter term.

14 On the form *nāṣrāṯ* cf. צָרְפַת in 1 K. 17:9, 10; Ob. 20 and דָּבְרַת in Jos. 19:12; 21:28; 1 Ch. 6:57. The construction of the Aram. adj. *nāṣr-ājā* with elimination of the fem. ending *-at* is normal. If along with the correct forms Ναζαρέθ, Ναζαρέτ, Ναζαρά we find Ναζωρέθ in Mt. 2:23, this shows obvious assimilation to the nearby Ναζωραῖος. It does not give any more support than the imitated נזורת of the Evangeliarium Hierosolymitanum to the construction of a subsidiary form *nāṣōraṯ* proposed by Dalman Gr., 178, n. 2 and accepted by various scholars. Nor is there any evidence for the Heb. *nōṣereṯ* advanced by Dalman, 152, n. In the Arab period, probably in assimilation to city names in the form of a partic. fem. (e.g., *al-qāhira*, Cairo), *nāṣraṯ* became *an-Nāṣira*, the first example of which belongs to the time of the Umayyad caliph Hišām (724-43), cf. T. Nöldeke, *Ztschr. f. Assyriologie*, 33 (1920), 73 on the basis of Ibn al-Aṯīr, Chronicon, 5, 197. The Mandaean form ניצרת in GR, 56, 16 is a corruption of the Syr. *nāṣraṯ*.

Also untenable is the assumption of Lidz. that there are two Aram. forms of what he takes to be the initial *nōṣrī*:[15] 1. *nāṣrāјā*, derived from the part. *nāṣar*, and 2. *nāṣorāja*, assimilated to designations of calling in the form *ḟā'ōl* (like *amōrā'ē*, Amoraean, and *sāḇōrā'ē*, Saboraean). The objections to this are 1. that such twofold development is inconceivable, 2. that there are no names of religious societies in the form *ḟā'ōl*, 3. in such a thoroughgoing Aramaicising as construction in *ḟā'ōl* would presuppose the retention of the non-Aram. *ṣ* (instead of *ṭ*) is inexplicable, and 4. it has to be shown that the Mandaean form does not contain an o. Moreover Lidz., if not so firmly as others before him, is led to doubt not only whether Jesus was called after Nazareth but whether there was even a Galilean town of this name in His day. But the assumption which this necessitates, i.e., that the name of the city, or the city itself, belongs to the early Christian period, involves a *reductio ad absurdum*. One has only to think of the pains which Mt. and Lk. had to take to reconcile the fact that Jesus was a native of Nazareth with the birth in Bethlehem demanded by Micah 5:1. It is of little moment that there is no mention of Nazareth in Joseph. or Rabb. writings, and that the first ref. outside the NT is only in the 3rd cent. in Julius Africanus.

c. As concerns the prophecy in Mt. 2:23 the first point is that the words: ὅτι Ναζωραῖος κληθήσεται, contain the content of the prophecy; it is not necessary that they should be the exact wording.[16] It must be admitted that there is no exact equivalent in either the Heb. or Gk. OT. The usual ref. is to *nēṣer*, the shoot from the roots of Jesse, Is. 11:1, though it is hard to see the connection, since *nēṣer* was not a name borne by the Messiah. The equivalent "branch" of Is. 4:2; Jer. 23:5; 33:15 and esp. Zech. 3:8; 6:12 is certainly a name, but in this case the word is *ṣemaḥ* rather than *nēṣer*, and there is no link with Ναζαρέθ, Ναζωραῖος. Billerbeck[17] offers the following solution acc. to the Rabb. rule of interpretation Al-tiqri, which allows a word to be replaced by an equivalent: "Joseph settled in Nazareth in order that there should be fulfilled what was said by the prophet (in the words נצר and צמח): he shall be called נִצְרִי, a Nazarene." But apart from the substitution this does not carry with it any connection of signification, but is a pun which only experts in Rabbinic interpretation can unravel. Mt., however, was trying to make himself understood by Gk. readers. If, then, it is possible to find a serviceable explanation in Gk. or LXX terms, this deserves precedence. Such an explanation is offered by the similarity of Ναζωραῖος and ναζιραῖος (Nazirite), which was familiar to Mt.'s readers from the prophecy concerning Samson in Ju. 13:5, 7 (cf. 16:17): ὅτι ἡγιασμένον ναζιραῖον (ναζιρ B) ἔσται τῷ θεῷ τὸ παιδάριον ἐκ τῆς γαστρός A. That there was an old tradition which linked Ναζωραῖος with ναζιραῖος may be seen from Tertullian Marc., IV, 8.[18] The prophets of Mt. 2:23 embrace the former prophets of the Heb. Bible, which include the Book of Judges. Since, as we have shown, an explanation in Gk. is demanded, one

[15] G. F. Moore, 428 rejects the form *nōṣrī* and reads *noṣrī*, but the common נוֹצְרִי (→ n. 3) is against this.

[16] So Allen, who refers to Mt. 26:54, though he also considers elimination of the words as a scribal addition. Str.-B. refers pertinently to Ezr. 9:10 ff. and similar free quotations in the Talmud.

[17] Str.-B., I, 92 ff. Zn. Mt., following A. v. Harnack, *Mission u. Ausbreitung des Christentums*^{4} (1924), 414 n., wrests the words when he translates: "In order that the saying of the prophets should be fulfilled; for he was to be called a Nazarene." This would demand ἔμελλε κληθῆναι rather than κληθήσεται.

[18] → n. 1. Cf. the anonymous book of names in P. de Lagarde, *Onomastica sacra*^{2} (1887), 205, 23 f.: Ναζαρὲτ ἀκρεμόνος αὐτοῦ ἢ καθαρός. Ναζωραῖος καθαρός; 206, 60: Ναζαρὲθ καθαριότης; 220, 89 ff.: Ναζωραῖος ἅγιος ἢ καθαρός. Ναζηραῖος ἅγιος ἢ καθαρώτατος ἢ ἐκ κοιλίας μητρὸς ἀφωρισμένος θεῷ. Eus. Dem. Evang., VII, 2, p. 349 (MPG, 22, 548 f.) suggests *nēzer* in Lv. 21:12, where the LXX has ἅγιον, Aqu. ἀφόρισμα, Symm. ἄθικτον, Theod. ναζερ. Burkitt, believing it to be impossible to link Ναζωραῖος with Ναζαρέθ, tries to derive it directly from ναζιραῖος, as though this were easier.

cannot consider OT passages where we have *nāzīr* in the Heb. but not ναζιραῖος in the Gk., e.g., the blessing of Joseph in Gn. 49:26; Dt. 33:16 or Am. 2:11, 12.

But this also alleviates the second difficulty (→ 875) regarding the ζ for *s* in Ναζαρέθ etc. Similar examples are really adequate to explain this:[19] αδωνιζεδεκ אֲדֹנִי צֶדֶק in Ju. 1:5 ff. (corr. Jos. 10:1, 3) ᾿ΑΣΘ; βαζες בּוֹצֵץ 1 S. 14:4 B (βαζεθ G^Luc); εζρων חֶצְרוֹן Ruth 4:18 G^Luc (εσρων BA); ωζ עוּץ, Gn. 22:21 G^Luc (ωξ A), ους id. 1 Ch. 1:17 G^Luc (ως B); μαζαρ מִבְצָר Gn. 36:42; 1 Ch. 1:53 B; σωαζ יוֹעֵץ, 1 Ch. 26:14 B (ιωιας A); Ζεβὴν καὶ Ζαρμούνην, Jos. Ant., 5, 228 for זֶבַח וְצַלְמֻנָּע, Ju. 8:5 ff.; ζογορα צֹעַר Gn. 13:10; Jer. 31(48):4; ζογορ id. Jer. 31(48):34 (in 8 other OT passages σηγωρ); μᾶζα מַצָּה, Jos. Ant., 5, 219.[20] Thus there is ample support for the possibility of ζ for *s* in Ναζαρέθ. It is also possible, however, that when the name of Jesus' home town and His own surname were put in Gk. they were from the very first influenced by the ναζιραῖος of the Gk. Bible.[21]

d. Finally, in relation to the pre-Christian Jewish sect of the Nasarenes to which Epiphanius refers in Haer., 18; 29, 6, it may be emphasised that by the form Νασαραῖοι he distinguishes them plainly from the Jewish Christian Ναζωραῖοι. Hence they have no contribution to make in explanation of the NT Ναζωραῖος. Acc. to Epiphanius the characteristics of this sect are that they keep the Jewish commandments but reject the Torah as a falsification, reject bloody offerings and the eating of flesh, and contest εἱμαρμένη and astrology. Materially, then, they have nothing in common with either the Baptist, Jesus, or later Jewish Christianity. The only question is whether they ever existed at all. Epiphanius in the 4th century is the first and only writer to speak of them. In estimating the historical value of his reference the primary question is that of his sources. Following H. Hilgenfeld and A. Schmidtke, W. Bousset[22] has conjectured that the Νασαραῖοι of Epiphanius come from a list of sects which seems to have been used by Justin and Hegesipp. in the 2nd cent. and Ephraem the Syr. and the Apostolic Constitutions in the 4th. Bousset believes this list was of Jewish origin, and argues that the Νασαραῖοι were in fact Christians, the word being indeed an exact rendering of the Aram. *nāsrājē,* "Christians." In the Christian tradition this was no longer understood, and because of a second misunderstanding, namely, that the list dealt with pre-Christian Jewish heresies, the Νασαραῖοι of Epiphanius came into being. There is much to be said for this explanation.

In sum, it may be said that the understanding of Ναζωραῖος as a rendering of the Aram. *nāsrājā,* derived from the name of the city Nazareth (Aram. *nāsrat̲*), is linguistically and materially unassailable. Neither the self-designation of the Mandaeans as *nāsᵒrājē,* which derives from the Syr. name for Christians, nor the name of a supposed pre-Christian sect of Νασαραῖοι, can provide a different and more basic meaning for Ναζωραῖος.

Schaeder

19 Burkitt, *The Syriac Forms,* 404. Cf. also F. Wutz, *Die Transkriptionen der Septuaginta bis Hieronymus* (1937), 75.

20 Schl. Mt., 49.

21 So, apart from Burkitt, esp. E. Nestle, *Prot. Monatshefte,* 1910, 349.

22 H. Hilgenfeld, *Die Ketzergeschichte des Urchristentums* (1884), 84 f.; A. Schmidtke, "Neue Fragmente u. Untersuchungen zu den judenchristlichen Evangelien," TU, 37 (= III, 7) (1911); W. Bousset, "Noch einmal der 'vorchristliche Jesus,'" ThR, 14 (1911), 373-85.

† ναός

1. Non-Biblical Usage.

The noun ναός, Ion. νηός, Att. νεώς, denotes in Gk. the "abode of the gods," "temple," and it derives from ναίω, "to dwell," "inhabit." The noun has a cultic nuance, whereas the verb is used generally.[1] The word occurs in Hom. Il., 1, 39; Od., 6, 10; 12, 346, and is also common elsewhere in tragedy, historical writings, temple laws, inscr. and pap. Soph. El., 8; Eur. Hipp., 30 f., "She built there a temple to Cypris which looks over this coast, on Pallas rock, far-looking," also 620 ff.: ἀλλ' ἀντιθέντας σοῖσιν ἐν ναοῖς βροτοὺς ἢ χρυσὸν ἢ σίδηρον ἢ χαλκοῦ βάρος παίδων πρίασθαι σπέρμα, τοῦ τιμήματος τῆς ἀξίας ἕκαστον. ἐν δὲ δώμασιν ναίειν ἐλευθέροισι θηλειῶν ἄτερ (the cultic ναός and general ναίω are here closely related). Cf. Critias: "But, he said, the gods dwell in a place the naming of which would greatly terrify men" (Diels[5], II, 388). An interesting inscr. is that of Gortyn in Crete (GD, III, 2, 4991, 38 f.): "But when the slave on account of whom he was defeated in the trial makes use of the right of asylum (αἰ δέ κα ναεύηι ὁ δῶλος ..., ναεύειν derived from ναός in this sense), the loser should invite his opponent into the presence of two free and adult witnesses and try the case in the temple where the slave enjoys refuge, either in his own person or through a representative" (I, 38 ff.). ναός, νεώς and related forms (e.g., ναοποιία, ναοποιεῖν) are common on other inscr., cf. Ditt. Syll.[3], IV, 456 f. Hdt. uses νηός fairly often, e.g., I, 19; I, 21; II, 63 and 155; IV, 108; VI, 19 f., and associates the altar, the statue and the house as the three essential parts of a Hellenic temple, I, 131; II, 4; IV, 59 and 108. He tells us how in Egypt a statue (ἄγαλμα) in a small wooden but richly gilded temple (νηός) is taken out with solemn pomp (πομπαί, ἐξοδεῖαι) and on its return given a different dwelling: τὸ δὲ ἄγαλμα ἐὸν ἐν νηῷ μικρῷ ξυλίνῳ κατακεχρυσωμένῳ προεκκομίζουσι τῇ προτεραίῃ ἐς ἄλλο οἴκημα ἱρόν (II, 63). The νηός here seems to be a small temple which could be carried on a cart.[2] ναός (νηός) is, then, the dwelling of the deity, but can be more narrowly understood as ἱερόν, οἴκημα ἱερόν, τέμενος. In II, 155 Hdt. describes the sanctuaries in the Egyptian Buto and mentions the various terms alongside one another: ἱρὸν δὲ ἔστι ἐν τῇ Βουτοῖ ταύτῃ Ἀπόλλωνος καὶ Ἀρτέμιδος, καὶ ὅ γε νηὸς τῆς Λητοῦς, ἐν τῷ δὴ τὸ χρηστήριον ἔνι, αὐτός τε τυγχάνει ἐὼν μέγας καὶ τὰ προπύλαια ἔχει ἐς ὕψος δέκα ὀργυιέων ... ἔστι ἐν τῷ τεμένεϊ τούτῳ Λητοῦς νηὸς ἐξ ἑνὸς λίθου πεποιημένος ... (II, 155). οὗτος μὲν νῦν ὁ νηὸς τῶν φανερῶν μοι τῶν περὶ τοῦτο τὸ ἱρόν ἐστι θαυμαστότατον (156).[3] νηός is the sanctuary in the strict sense

---

ναός. [1] On ναός cf. Liddell-Scott, 1160.

[2] A. Wiedemann, *Hdt.'s zweites Buch* (1890), 265: "The *naos* with the image of the god was generally carried on the shoulders of the priests, though it was sometimes put on a cart." A cart drawn by men is depicted on an Ethiopian relief, W. Otto, *Priester u. Tempel im hellenistischen Ägypten,* I (1905), 94, n. 1: "When we read in Rosetta: ἐν ταῖς μεγάλαις πανηγύρεσιν, ἐν αἷς ἐξοδεῖαι τῶν ναῶν γίνονται, we must see in these ναοί, which were placed in the innermost sanctuaries of temples (line 42), the temple-like part of the boats of the gods, cf. also Hdt., II, 63 and Diod. S., I, 97, 9-10." Cf. also *ibid.,* 332: "The little ναοί in which the statues were put are always essential items in the lists of furnishings; in one inventory (unpubl. P. Rainer, 8) they are described as made of wood overlaid by gold."

[3] Wiedemann, *op. cit.,* 555: "The oracle at Buto, which Hdt. treats as the Egyptian oracle κατ' ἐξοχήν, is mentioned in II, 83, 111, 133 and 152, and it also plays a role in III, 64."

(*aedes*) as compared with the broader τέμενος or even ἱερόν. The Gnomon of the Idios Logos (ed. Schubart), 79 (BGU, 5, 1 [1919], 31) ordains: Ἐν παντὶ ἱερῷ, ὅπου ναός ἐστιν, δέον προφήτην εἶναι καὶ λαμβάνειν τῶν προσόδων (in every sanctuary where there is a ναός there must be a prophet who receives a fifth of the income). Plat. can also use ναός occasionally, Resp., III, 394a; Leg., V, 738c; VII, 814b. Leg., V, 738cd is interesting with its advice to legislators (νομοθέτης) not to disturb religious and cultic practices (οὐδεὶς ἐπιχειρήσει κινεῖν ... τούτων νομοθέτῃ τὸ σμικρότατον ἁπάντων οὐδὲν κινητέον, "neither when a man builds a new city nor when he re-establishes an old and decayed city should he, unless he is completely lacking in understanding, attempt, in respect of the gods and the temples which are to be built in the city, or the gods and demons whose names they are to bear, to disturb anything which has been commanded by Delphi or Dodona or Ammon, or ordained by certain ancient accounts of miraculous phenomena or proclamations of divine inspiration, in accordance with which they established dedication festivals, whether new and native, Tyrrhenian, Cypriot, or borrowed from any other place, and as a result of which instructions they dedicated traditions, statues, altars and temples, and allotted to each their consecrated precincts (καθιέρωσαν δὲ τοῖς τοιούτοις λόγοις φήμας τε καὶ ἀγάλματα καὶ βωμοὺς καὶ ναούς, τεμένη τε τούτων ἑκάστοις ἐτεμένισαν)." [4] The term must have an even more specialised meaning in the petition of Ptolemaios against the rapacious Amosis when it is said of him: οὐ μὴν [ἀ]λλὰ καὶ εἰς τὸ ἄδυτον τῆς θεᾶς εἰσελθὼν ἐσκύλη[σε]ν τὸν ναὸν ὥστε κινδυνεῦσαι καὶ συντρῖψαι αὐτόν, "indeed, he even forced his way into the innermost sanctuary of the goddess and plundered the holy shrine, so that he almost broke it in pieces"; Wilcken Ptol., I (1927), N, 6, 22 f. Perhaps here too, as in Hdt., the ref. is to the sacred shrine which houses the god. The word occurs several times in the inscr. from Dura Europos (Inscr. 867, 868, 817, 888, 917, 918). Here we find the verb ἀνήγειρεν (τὸν ναὸν τοῦτον) or οἰκοδομήσας (τὸν ναὸν τοῦτον). In Inscr., 916 there is a striking use of הֵיכָל, which corresponds to the word ναός. [5]

---

[4] The following understanding of Gk. temples is to be found in the essay of K. Lehmann-Hartleben, "Wesen u. Gestalt griechischer Heiligtümer," *Antike*, 7 (1931), 11-48, 161-180: "A mountain site and a boulder are from antiquity basic elements in Gk. sanctuaries. They are broadly dominated by the fundamental idea. What is strictly necessary is not a temple or cultic image. It is an open site under the free heavens in which these may be present. Such sites enclosed by walls, restricted sections of nature for divine power and ministry to the gods, have their prototypes already in pre-Greek religion" (16-18). In the 7th century, cultic enclosure begins along with political. The house of the king becomes a temple, his castle a sanctuary. Images come in at the same time. "At the very period when the ancient royal houses change into temples and temples are built elsewhere, images appear as well" (43).

[5] For Inscr. 916 cf. "The Excavations at Dura-Europos," ed. M. I. Rostovtzeff, F. E. Brown and C. B. Welles, 7th and 8th Seasons, 1933-34a/1934-5 (1939), 320: "The use of the term היכל *haikal* to designate this shrine is interesting and unexpected. The word ordinarily denotes a somewhat pretentious building, and is thus rendered 'temple,' 'palace' etc. It is used in Vog. 16 (= CIS, II, no. 3959) of a temple (ναός in the Greek text) which was built in Palmyra in the year 131. It also occurs once (for a temple) in the Palmyrene Tariff (= CIS, II, 3913, 1. 10)." On 867: Ἀνήγειρεν Ἐπίνικος κῆρυξ καὶ ἱερεὺς τοῦ θεοῦ τὸν ναὸν τοῦτον θεῶι ὑπὲρ τῆς ἑαυτοῦ τέκνων σωτηρίας καὶ ζωγραφήσας εἰκόνας. 877: Δημήτρι[ος or ου] ἀνήγειρεν τὸν ναόν, 888: Ἔτους βλυ'. Σέλευκος Θεομνήστου τοῦ Ἀντιόχου Εὐρωπαῖος καὶ τῶν πρώτων, ἀνήγειρεν Διὶ θεῶι τὸν ναὸν καὶ τὰ θυρώματα καὶ τὴν τῶν εἰκόνων γραφὴν πᾶσαν, 917-918: ... ἀνήγειρα ἐγὼ θεῶι περίβολον (?) καὶ ἄλλον ναὸν παρακείμενον, cf. also 868.

2. Biblical Usage.

ναός is relatively common in the LXX ; ναιώς and νεώς are rarer subsidiary forms. [6] ναός corresponds primarily to the Heb. אוּלָם, 1 Ch. 28:11; 2 Ch. 8:12 (cf. 15:8); 29:7, 17. We often find ναός for הֵיכָל, so 1 Βασ. 1:9; 3:3; 2 Βασ. 22:7. [7] ναὸς κυρίου, ναὸς ἅγιος, ναὸς τῆς ἁγίας δόξης σου (Δα. 3:53) and similar expressions relate to the temple in Jerusalem ; ψ 44:15 speaks of the ναὸς βασιλέως. Ez. uses ἱερόν (or τὰ ἱερά) for pagan cultic sites, 27:6; 28:18 LXX, but in 1 Εσδρ. and the Macc. the Jerusalem temple is τὸ ἱερόν. ναός is used by Joseph. for the temple building in Bell., 5, 207, 209 and 211; Ant., 15, 391, but also for the precincts in Ap., 2, 119; Bell., 6, 293. Originally ἱερόν, ναός and τέμενος are distinct, but a different usage seems to have effaced the original distinctions, Hdt., LXX, Macc. → III, 230-237.

In the NT, in addition to ἱερόν, ἅγιον (or τὰ ἅγια), not τέμενος, we also find ναός (ναὸς τοῦ θεοῦ), with no real distinction between the terms in either meaning or range. In the NT, too, ναός, ναὸς θεοῦ, ναὸς ἅγιος is used of the Jerusalem temple. Ac. 17:24 refers generally to χειροποίητοι ναοί, and Ac. 19:24 to ναοὶ ἀργυροῖ Ἀρτέμιδος, but in the NT the word occurs esp. in the in new Christian statements about the wonderful spiritual temple. In the NT, then, ναός takes precedence of the various other terms or concepts for a sanctuary. Perhaps this is because the LXX already shows special interest in it, or perhaps because the motif of building (οἰκοδομήσω) goes well with ναός (*aedes*). [8] Certainly ναός is more capable of development and richer in content that the par. terms already mentioned.

Gospels. In Mt. 23:16, 17, 21 we find the expression ὀμνύναι ἐν τῷ ναῷ or ὀμνύναι ἐν τῷ χρυσῷ τοῦ ναοῦ. This presupposes the custom of swearing by the temple or the gold adornment of the temple.

In the Rabb. cf. Qid., 71a, swearing by the temple, and Taan., 24a, by its ministry. "The distinction between the temple and the gold of the temple, the altar and the sacrifice laid on it, rests on the principle that the more binding oath is by that which is indubitably God's possession. The gold adornment of the temple, which was consecrated to God, is to a greater degree God's property than the walls, and the sacrifice on the altar belongs more to God than the stones of the altar. This casuistical distinction was not accepted by everyone." "The answer of Jesus to the casuists was that God is invoked with everything that belongs to Him. The gold and the house, the offering and the altar, the temple and God, heaven and God, are all related. The casuist seeks to put asunder that which cannot be parted. Hence there is no non-binding oath." [9]

---

[6] ναιώς 2 Macc. 4:14 A; 10:3 A. νεώς 2 Macc. 6:2 A; 9:16 A; 10:3 R; 10:5 (along with ναοῦ in the same verse); 13:23; 14:33 R. Bl.-Debr.[6] § 44, 1: For the Att. λεώς and νεώς always the Doric λαός (also Ἀρχέλαος and Λαοδίκεια) and ναός, but νεωκόρος in Ac. 19:35 as Hell. (Helbing, 39; for bibl. cf. Bl.-Debr., *loc. cit.*).

[7] Hatch-Redp., 939 on ναός (ναιώς, νεώς). In the Mas. ναός corresponds to 1. אוּלָם, 2. בַּיִת, 3. דְּבִיר, 4. הֵיכָל ,הֵיכַל ,חֵיכָל, cf. דְּבִיר in 1 K. 6:5, properly a "back room" (in the temple); LXX reproduces the Heb. (τῷ δαβίρ), Ἀ and Σ : χρηματστήριον, Vulg *oraculum* (with דִּבֵּר). הֵיכָל "palace of kings" (Hos. 8:14; 1 K. 21:1), "temple" (Am. 8:3; Is. 6:1), esp. the "great room of the temple," "sanctuary" (1 K. 6:5; 17; 7:50; Ez. 41:1 ff.). Cf. E. König, *Hebräisches u. Aram. Wörterbuch zum AT*[6, 7] (1936).

[8] G. Dalman, *Orte u. Wege Jesu*[3] (1924), 301 believes that there is a definite distinction in NT usage : "The Jerusalem sanctuary is always τὸ ἱερόν in the Gospels as distinct from the actual temple within it, which is ὁ ναός. Jesus teaches in the sanctuary (Mt. 26:55; Mk. 14:49; Lk. 21:37; Jn. 7:28) but he will destroy the temple (Mt. 27:40; Mk. 15:29; Jn. 2:19), whose curtain is torn at His death (Mt. 27:51; Mk. 15:33; Lk. 23:45). The Aram. equivalents would be *bet makdesha* and *hekhela*. But the Syr. version always uses *haikela*, the Pal. Evangeliarium *naosa*, Jerome, whom Luther follows, *templum*. It would be a good thing to restore the distinction. It is topographically indispensable."

[9] Schl. Mt., 677 f.

Mt. 23:35: μεταξὺ τοῦ ναοῦ καὶ τοῦ θυσιαστηρίου, between the temple and the altar, a place of refuge (Ex. 21:14; 1 K. 1:51; 2:28 ff.).[10]

Acc. to Mt. Zechariah, the son of Berachiah, was murdered between the temple and the altar. The ref. is probably to Zechariah, the son of Jehoiada, in 2 Ch. 24.[11]

In the trial of Jesus an important part is played by an alleged saying which is attested in different forms in Mk. 14:58; 15:29; Mt. 26:61; 27:40 and Jn. 2:19 (2:21). The saying seems to occur again in the Stephen tradition in Ac., where it initiates a new turn in the relations with Judaism (Ac. 6:14; cf. 6:13).[12]

Mk. makes the explanation of the historical data more difficult by calling the witness in the trial false (14:56 f.: ἐψευδομαρτύρουν). One possibility is that the primitive community could not accept the saying and therefore described it as false witness.[13] The antithesis χειροποίητον/ἀχειροποίητον occurs only in Mk. (not Mt., Jn.), so that one might ask whether it is original.[14] Mk. distinguishes between the temple made with hands and the wonderful new structure of the eschatological community which is not made with hands, whereas Mt. and Jn. draw attention to the power (Mt. δύναμαι) and person (Jn. ναὸς τοῦ σώματος) of Jesus.[15] We have here an enigmatic saying

---

[10] Wettstein, I, 491; Schl. Mt., 688.

[11] *NT Deutsch*, Schn. Mt., 229: "The Zechariah of 2 Ch. 24 is not, of course the son of Berechiah, but the name probably came in here because it was that of the prophet (Zech. 1:1). The killing of Zechariah was particularly serious because he was struck down in the holy place, which was also a refuge. Because of the difficulty of the name it has been assumed from the days of the early Church that this was another Zechariah, namely, the son of Bariscaeus (Baruch) mentioned by Jos. in Bell., 4, 334 ff. This Zechariah was put to death by the Zealots in 67-68 A.D. because he belonged to the Jewish aristocratic party. But it may well be asked whether this event would be recorded in the Gospels or the tradition behind them. We also know that Jewish tradition took a lively interest in the killing of the Zechariah of 2 Ch. 24, and Chronicles already came at the end of OT Canon in the days of Jesus.

[12] On Lk. 13:35 = Mt. 23:38: ἰδοὺ ἀφίεται ὑμῖν ὁ οἶκος ὑμῶν (ἔρημος), note the apocr. prayer: ὅθεν λέγει· γενηθήτω, ὁ πάτερ, ὁ ναὸς αὐτῶν ἠρημωμένος (Hippolyt., Demonstratio adv. Judaeos, VII). A. Resch, "Agrapha, Ausserkanonische Evangelienfragmente, gesammelt u. untersucht," TU, 5 (1889), 98 and 143; Logion, 6.

[13] R. A. Hoffmann, "Das Wort Jesu von d. Zerstörung u. dem Wiederaufbau des Tempels," *Nt.liche Studien f. G. Heinrici* (1914), 130-139 tries to do justice to the ἐψευδομαρτύρουν: "One cannot doubt, then, that Jesus prophesied the destruction of the Jerusalem temple. But He would hardly have described Himself as καταλύων. Only the misunderstanding or malice of His opponents ascribed this idea to Him. It is true, of course, that this confusion of the true content shows what a sense of sovereign power was ascribed to Him. To that degree the statement of the witnesses was not without interest to the Sanhedrin."

[14] Loh. Mk., 326: "It is surely an explanatory addition of the community, since it robs the accusation of all point and is not found in Mk. 15:29. Lk. leaves it out here, but brings it in Stephen's speech in Ac. 6:14: Ἰησοῦς ὁ Ναζωραῖος καταλύσει τὸν τόπον τοῦτον καὶ ἀλλάξει τὰ ἔθη ἃ παρέδωκεν ἡμῖν Μωϋσῆς. A comparison of the texts shows that the first part originally read: καταλύσω τὸν ναὸν τοῦτον, the second: καὶ διὰ τριῶν ἡμερῶν οἰκοδομήσω αὐτόν. One can only ask whether the second part belonged originally to the saying; Ac. 6:14 expands differently and in conscious correction, to formulate an accusation. To reject the second part as secondary because of the διὰ (ἐν) τριῶν (-σὶν) ἡμερῶν (-αις) is arbitrary."

[15] Bultmann Trad., 126 f.; Joh. Ev., 88 f.: "The source linked with the cleansing of the temple a saying which is a simple threat of destruction in Mk. 13:2 and Ac. 6:14, and which is associated with the building of the temple in three days in Mk. 14:58 (Mt. 26:61); 15:29. One can no longer say which is the original form of the saying and how far it goes back to Jesus. It is certainly old, and the earliest tradition found it difficult and suggested various interpretations. Mk. (14:58) calls the new temple an ἄλλον ἀχειροποίητον and obviously sees in it the Christian community. Mt. (26:61) maintains the original identity of the old

belonging to the oldest tradition, and it is hard to fix the exact form or meaning. One may assume that it belongs to the Son of Man sayings, that its context is the cleansing of the temple, that Jesus was conscious of being the builder and consummator of the Messianic temple, and that He thought of the *parousia* and the temple together, cf. the par. from the later Jewish hope (Ez. 40-44; Eth. En. 90:28 f.; Tob. 13:15 ff.; 14:5) and the Gospel tradition itself (Mt. 12:6; Mk. 12:10; the use of Ps. 118).[16] When the Gospels view the community as well as Jesus Himself as the Messianic temple — He is the head of the corner which completes the new building acc. to Ps. 118:22 — specific exegetical traditions find expression. The Johannine interpretation of the saying is highly individual and corresponds to a basic thrust of the Fourth Gospel.[17] The later Jewish parable (*mashal*) has become a mystery of Hellenistic revelation.[18]

Mt. 27:5 tells us that Judas cast the thirty shekels into the temple (εἰς τὸν ναόν) and went out and hanged himself.

If ναός is taken to mean the temple in the narrower sense, one may ask how Judas could bring the money into it, since only priests were allowed access. We may thus assume that it is used in a broader sense, as in Jn.[19]

---

temple and the new, but with his δύναμαι καταλῦσαι ... καὶ ... οἰκοδομῆσαι makes the prophecy a mere statement of possibility. The source of Jn. (2:19) also maintains the identity: τοῦτον τὸν ναὸν ... αὐτόν, but does not rob the saying of its character as an eschatological prophecy. Hence the form in Jn. could well be relatively original." Cf. F. Büchsel (*NT Deutsch*), 48, who also thinks that Jn. has a better form than the enigmatic saying of the Synoptists: "That Jesus uttered it as found in the Jewish accusation: 'I will destroy this temple made with hands and in three days set up another not made with hands,' is most unlikely. On the other hand, the Synoptic form of the saying is readily understandable as a Jewish perversion of the enigmatic saying handed down in Jn."

[16] Cf. Bousset-Gressm., 239; Str.-B., IV, 928 f. How enthronement and temple renewal are linked in antiquity is shown in J. Jeremias, "Jesus als Weltvollender," BFTh, 33, 4 (1930), 37 ff. by many examples from the OT and late Jewish, Hell. and Mohammedan legend. On Mk. 14:58 and par.: "The meaning of the *mashal* is plain. The temple will be destroyed, but the destruction of the temple will be followed by the *parousia* of Jesus and the building of the heavenly temple, the transformed community." 40. "He refers to the fact that He will set up a new temple not made with hands, and compares Himself with the builder of the new house of God. The same image of a new temple is used by Jesus rather differently when He refers to Himself the saying in Ps. 118: 'The stone which the builders rejected, God has made the chief corner-stone.' This image, too, speaks of the new temple," 79 f.

[17] Cf. Bultmann, *Joh. Ev.*, 89 f. Acc. to Bultmann the source ended with 2:19; 2:20 f. are added by the Evangelist. "That the interpretation derives from the Evangelist may be seen from the type of misunderstanding and also from the characteristic ἐκεῖνος, the formal (ἐκεῖνος) δὲ ἔλεγεν περί, cf. 7:39; 11:13; 12:33, and finally the fact that v. 22, which is to be taken with v. 20 f., is so plainly the work of the Evangelist," 89, n. 1. "The basis of the interpretation (cf. Mt. 12:40) is provided by the three days, which in early Christian tradition denote the period between the crucifixion and resurrection of Jesus (on the various formulations cf., e.g., Klostermann on Mk. 8:31); note should also be taken of the twofold ἐγερῶ (possibly understood by the Evangelist in the emphatic sense of Jn. 10:17 f.). The interpretation is probably strengthened by the fact that temple and house were common metaphors for the body, though such images (1 C. 6:19; 2 C. 6:16; Barn., 16, 8) are controlled by the idea of the body as a dwelling (for the immanent Spirit), which is not present in Jn. The Rabb. habit of speaking of the body as a little city (Str.-B., II, 412) is certainly no par. A better par. is the Mandaean use of 'building,' 'palace,' 'house' for the human body; *v.* H. Schlier, *Christus u. d. Kirche im Epheserbrief* (1930), 50."

[18] For this type of misunderstanding in Jn. cf. 2:20; 3:3 f.; 4:10 ff., 32 f.; 6:32 ff.; 7:34 ff.; 14:4 f., 7 ff., 22 f.; 16:17 f. The same technique may be seen in Herm. and the Hermetic lit., R. Bultmann, *Joh. Ev.*, 89-90, n. 2. The distinctive phrase ναὸς τοῦ σώματος (Jn. 2:21) is gen. appos. or explic.

[19] Zn. Mt.[2], 699, n. 73, though cf. Schl. Mt., 768 f.: "Perhaps the rendering 'to the temple' is adequate. 'Into the temple' would presuppose dealings with the priests in the innermost court. The fore-court was open." It may be seen here quite plainly that neither Jn. nor the

Mk. 15:38 (Mt. 27:51; Lk. 23:45) refers to miraculous signs on the death of Jesus. Among these is the ripping of the veil of the temple from top to bottom.

The miracle is narrated only briefly. Is the ref. to the inner or the outer curtain? What is the meaning of the sign? R. Bultmann[20] shows that there are many Jewish and Hell. par. to the τέρατα of the Synoptics, but the feature is to be interpreted against the background of the *kerygma* of Jesus (Mk. 13:1 ff.). God's judgment has fallen on the temple.[21]

Luke's Gospel and Acts. A distinctive feature here is that whereas τὸ ἱερόν is common in Lk. ὁ ναός is much less frequent. Apart from Lk. 23:45 it occurs only in the infancy stories in 1:9, 21, 22. Striking, too, is the usage in Ac. 17:24; 19:24. This fact is linked with the nature of the Synoptic sources, as the parallels in the other Gospels show, but one must also recognise that in the Gospels, as in Joseph., it is possible to distinguish to some degree between ἱερόν as the whole temple and ναός as the actual house, cf. G. Dalman, A. Schlatter, → n. 9, 19. The antithesis χειροποίητος/ἀχειροποίητος, which the Mk. tradition associates with Mk. 14:58, is not restricted to the apocalyptic view of the temple; it can also be found in a similar form in the Hellenistic polemic and missionary preaching of primitive Christianity, Ac. 7:48; 17:24. It is also possible, however, that the apocalyptic and Hellenistic traditions meet in the statement that God as Spirit does not dwell in a house made with hands, cf. later Barn., 4, 11; 6, 15 f.; 16. Both rest on the scriptural support of Is. 66:1 (Ac. 7:49; Barn., 16, 2).[22] According to Ac. 19:24 a silversmith, Demetrius, makes silver images of the temple of Artemis, and in so doing renders no small service to the craftsmen.

Miniature representations of the temple in silver or terracotta, with the statue of the goddess inside, were partly taken by foreign visitors to the temple (Amm. Marc., 22, 13; Dio C., 39, 20) and partly presented as offerings in the temple.[23]

NT takes ναός in the strict sense for the temple proper. Though it seems that we might often make a distinction between ναός and ἱερόν, this is not always possible. Cf. Zn., *Forsch.*, VI, 234: Jos., too, often uses ὁ ναός, τὸ ἱερόν, τὰ ἅγια, ὁ οἶκος τοῦ θεοῦ without distinction, e.g., Bell., 6, 2, 1 (all the words), cf. 6, 2, 4, though he can also distinguish between τὸ ἱερόν or τὸ ἔξωθεν ἱερόν and ὁ ναός or αὐτὸς ὁ ναός, 6, 2, 3; 4, 1."

[20] Bultmann Trad., 305.

[21] Zn. Mt.[2], 706: "The expression τὸ καταπέτασμα τοῦ ναοῦ does not favour the view of some recent scholars that the ref. is to the curtain which separates the Holy of Holies from the sanctuary (פָּרֹכֶת, Ex. 26:31-35; τὸ δεύτερον καταπέτασμα, Hb. 9:3), but it favours that of older authors, who saw in it the magnificent curtain which in Herod's temple hung before the entrance, opened during the day, from the fore-court to the sanctuary. This is supported by the fact that Jewish and Jewish Christian traditions, which are divergent but which obviously refer to the same event, speak of an astounding happening at this door of the temple, not at the partition between the sanctuary and the Holy of Holies." Cf. NkZ, 13 (1902), 729-756, and for contemporary refs. Str.-B., I, 1043-1046.

[22] Just. Dial., 22: καὶ γὰρ τὸν ναὸν τὸν ἐν Ἰερουσαλὴμ ἐπικληθέντα, οὐχ ὡς ἐνδεὴς ὢν ὡμολόγησεν οἶκον αὐτοῦ ἢ αὐλήν, ἀλλ' ὅπως κἂν κατὰ τοῦτο προσέχοντες αὐτῷ μὴ εἰδωλολατρῆτε. Καὶ ὅτι τοῦτό ἐστιν, Ἡσαίας λέγει· Ποῖον οἶκον ᾠκοδομήσατέ μοι; λέγει κύριος. Ὁ οὐρανός μοὶ θρόνος, καὶ ἡ γῆ ὑποπόδιον τῶν ποδῶν μου (MPG, 6, 526).

[23] Wdt. Ag., 277; E. Preuschen, *Apostelgesch.* (1912), 118. Hicks, Exp., 1890, II, 401 ff., suggests that Demetrius mades silver statues of Artemis, and that the statement of Ac. that he made silver temples is due to a misunderstanding of the title νεωποιός ("member of the civil board of temple assistants"). On the office of νεωποιός or νεωποίης cf. Ditt. Syll.[3], 353, 1; 354, 9; 364, 21.

Apostolic Epistles. Writing to the Corinthians, Paul appeals again and again to the principle that they are the temple of God and God's Spirit dwells in them (1 C. 3:16; 6:19; 2 C. 6:16 f.). He does not tell us the source of the statement, but assumes that the Corinthians are familiar with it (οὐκ οἴδατε ὅτι ..., 1 C. 3:16; 6:19). It may be conjectured that the apostle catechetically interprets the prophecy of Jesus in a form related to Mk. 14:58.[24]

On the other hand it should not be overlooked that there are some Hell. par. for the personal application of the idea in 1 C. 6:19: ἢ οὐκ οἴδατε ὅτι τὸ σῶμα ὑμῶν ναὸς τοῦ ἐν ὑμῖν ἁγίου πνεύματός ἐστιν. In Philo the metaphor of the soul as God's house is common, Som., I, 149; Sobr., 62 f.; Cher., 98 and 106. The Stoic concept of the δαίμων ἑκάστου which God has associated with each individual may also be cited, Epict. Diss., I, 14, 14 f.; II, 8, 11 f.; M. Ant., III, 6, 2. Yet one should also note the hesitation to call the body the dwelling-place of deity; the main emphasis of Paul is on the fact that the body is the temple of God.[25]

The primary allusion of 1 C. 6:19 f. is to the cultic legislation of the OT, for which the presence of an εἴδωλον in the temple is an abomination, 2 K. 21:7; 23:6; Da. 9:27.

---

[24] Cf. Schl. K., 137. Joh. W. K., 84: "Paul must be recalling a thought which belonged to the first preaching (cf. 6:9). It seems to have been an established part of Jewish eschatology that in the last time God will erect a new, glorious and perfect temple in which He can dwell (Is. 28:16 f.; En. 91:13; Jub. 1:17). Primitive Christianity regards this prophecy as already fulfilled. Since it is an evident idea of primitive Christianity from the very outset that a temple made with hands is impossible in the last time (cf. Ac. 7:48; Mk. 14:58; Rev. 21:22), the prophecy is spiritualised. The community itself, this οἶκος πνευματικός (1 Pt. 2:5), is the promised temple of the last time." H. Wenschkewitz, "Die Spiritualisierung der Kultusbegriffe Tempel, Priester und Opfer im NT," *Angelos*, 4 (1932), 70-230 concludes that the spiritualising of the temple concept is to be explained in terms of Hellen. presuppositions; for him the Jewish elements are only additional and auxiliary. "In primitive Palestinian Christianity and in Jesus we do not find the idea that the community is the temple of the last time," 178.

[25] There is a good collection of material in Joh. W. K., 166, n. 1: "The distinction is that the Stoic thinks in terms of innate divine reason, the invisible divine nobility which man only too easily forgets, whereas in Philo the divine indwelling is the result of conscious mystical surrender and union, in Paul the result of special blessing through the impartation of the Spirit." H. Wenschkewitz, *op. cit.*, 180 believes that the spiritualising of the concept of the temple in Paul is Stoic in origin. There has been added a Jewish and specifically Christian motif, and Wenschkewitz has to reckon with the fact that it is important for Paul that the body is the temple of God (175), and that neither in Stoicism nor Philo do we find the idea that the temple of God is the community. "Neither in Stoicism nor in Philo do we find this idea, for here the whole orientation is to the individual" (176). These differences from Hellenism warn us against seeking the source of Paul's thought here, though the Hellenistic aspect and the analogy to Hellenism should not be overlooked. On the question of spiritualising the temple concept, note Jos. in Bell., 5, 458 f.: πατρίδος δὲ οὐ μέλειν τῆς ὡς αὐτός φησιν ἀπολουμένης, καὶ ναοῦ (ἀπολομένου). ἀμείνω τούτου τῷ θεῷ τὸν κόσμον εἶναι. σωθήσεσθαί γε μὴν καὶ τοῦτον ὑπὸ τοῦ κατοικοῦντος, ὃν καὶ αὐτοὶ σύμμαχον ἔχοντες πᾶσαν χλευάσειν ἀπειλὴν ὑστεροῦσαν ἔργων· τὸ γὰρ τέλος εἶναι τοῦ θεοῦ. "The strongly Gk. formulation seems to be a literary redaction of Joseph., esp. as he is acquainted with an allegorical application of the temple to the world and the parts of the temple to the parts of the cosmos (Ant., 3, 123, 181 ff.; Bell., 5, 213 ff.)" (Wenschkewitz, 87). Philo in Som., I, 146 ff. describes how the soul, purified by God's λόγοι, becomes the temple of God, and he expounds Jacob's dream at Bethel allegorically ("Prepare, O soul, to become a house of God, a holy temple, a most beautiful dwelling" 149). "The introduction of the temple concept serves to strengthen the ethical admonition. By bringing in this idea Philo combines ethics and mysticism" (Wenschkewitz, 147).

Here, too, we have to think of the εἴδωλα of the pagan gods which unbelievers worship but with which Christians must have no fellowship.[26]

According to 2 Th. 2:3 f., in the ancient apocalyptic tradition, the man of lawlessness (ὁ ἄνθρωπος τῆς ἀνομίας), the son of perdition (ὁ υἱὸς τῆς ἀπωλείας), will be made manifest, the opponent who lifts up himself against everything called God or the sanctuary, so that he finally puts himself in the temple of God and makes himself God.

The idea that ungodly power will try to occupy God's throne is an old one and has mythological roots (cf. the traces in Is. 14:13 f.; Ez. 28:2). In the Jewish version the Jerusalem temple replaces the mythological seat. To occupy this is the decisive mark of ungodly power, mentioned here in the context of apocalyptic tradition rather than cosmological myth. Has 2 Th. 2:3 f. simply taken over this tradition? Is it referring to the real historical temple in Jerusalem? If so, this presumes composition prior to 70 A.D.[27] If older ecclesiastical tradition uniformly saw a ref. to the historical temple, from the 4th cent. the predominant view has been that the temple of God acc. to 1 C. 3:16; 2 C. 6:16 is the Christian community, into which heresy has penetrated[28] or in which the papacy has established itself.

The motif of the community as a temple (ναός) or as God's house (οἶκος πνευματικός) is still to be found in the later apostolic tradition. As in the older tradition, it combines with the motifs of the corner stone (λίθος ἀκρογωνιαῖος) and the building (οἰκοδομή): "Built on the foundation of the apostles and prophets, with Jesus Christ as the chief corner stone, in whom the whole building, being fitted together, grows into a holy temple in the Lord, in whom you also are to be built up together a habitation for God in the Spirit."[29] 1 Pt. 2:5; 4:17 speaks similarly of the οἶκος πνευματικός or οἶκος τοῦ θεοῦ. In this οἶκος Christ is the living stone, the corner stone, the stone which the builders rejected, the stone of stumbling and rock of offence. The members of the community are the living stones in this πνευματικὸς οἶκος. Is. 28:16; Ps. 118:22 (cf. already Mk. 12:10; R. 9:33) stand always behind this firm apostolic tradition.

Possibly related to the image is the motif of the στῦλος in Gl. 2:9; Rev. 3:12. Individual men play a special role as pillars in this spiritual house of God.

Revelation. The term ναός is used in different ways in Rev., since different traditions and strata are brought together here. In 11:1 the command to the divine is: ἔγειρε καὶ μέτρησον τὸν ναὸν τοῦ θεοῦ καὶ τὸ θυσιαστήριον καὶ τοὺς προσκυνοῦντας ἐν αὐτῷ. In this case we are fairly obviously to think in terms of the earthly temple in Jerusalem, for the distinction of the forecourt from the

[26] Cf. Wnd. 2 K., 215.

[27] *Quum autem devastaverit antichristus hic omnia in hoc mundo ... sedebit in templis Hierosolymis;* Ps. Ephraem in Caspari, *Briefe, Abhandlungen u. Predigten aus den letzten zwei Jahrhunderten des kirchlichen Altertums,* 217: *qui ingressus in eo (templo) sedebit ut deus et iubet se adorari ab omnibus gentibus.* Under the influence of the destruction of Jerusalem Hippolyt. writes in De Antichristo, 6, p. 8 (ed. Achelis): ἀναστήσει τὸν ἐν Ἱεροσολύμοις λίθινον ναόν; Ps. Ephraem, 7 (Caspari, 216 f.): *iubet sibi reaedificari templum dei quod est in Hierusalem.* Cf. Dib. Th., 39; Dob. Th., 276.

[28] Jerome, Thdrt., Oicum., Theophyl., Calvin. Cf. Dob. Th., 276.

[29] Cf. *NT Deutsch* Rff. Eph., *ad loc.*: "The terms used are house, erection, foundation, corner stone, building, fitting together, temple, built up together, habitation. Even a first glance shows that this is not a single metaphor but a group of images with many different relations and swift changes of meaning (cf. 1 C. 3:10; 1 Pt. 2:4 f.; Herm. v., 3; s., 9; Is. 28:16; Ps. 118:22)." Cf. J. Jeremias, "Der Eckstein," *Angelos,* 1 (1925), 65 ff.; "Golgotha u. der heilige Felsen," *ibid.,* 2 (1926), 74 ff.

temple proper corresponds not only to the position prior to 70 A.D. but also to the description in Ez. The temple and altar denote the sacred precincts, the altar the inner court.

It is thus understandable that J. Wellhausen should see in 11:1-2 the oracle of a Zealot prophet.[30] It is more likely, however, that a Palestinian trend in primitive Christianity wished to hold on to the existence of the temple and expressed this expectation in an apocalyptic prophecy.[31] After the catastrophe of 70 A.D. Christianity no longer thought in terms of the earthly temple or the historical origin of the saying but rather in terms of the spiritual temple and the community. This is the line taken by J. Behm: "The first task of the seer, equipped with a new prophetic witness (10:8 ff., 11), is to set before the Christianity of his day the fact that it is God's holy domain, protected against the storms of the final period of tribulation, kept for the salvation of fulfilment, separated from the pagan world, which desecrates the divine territory that falls into its hands."[32]

In a different apocalyptic tradition Rev. presupposes the existence of a heavenly temple, though apart from the primitive Christian metaphor that the temple is the community of the new covenant. According to 7:15 the great host of the purified stands before God's throne and serves Him day and night in His temple. That is to say, it is called to a priestly office. According to 11:19 the heavenly temple is opened, the ark of the covenant may be seen in it, and there are lightnings, voices, thunder, an earthquake, and a great hailstorm. We are often told that an angel comes out of the temple (14:15, 17; 15:5-6). The solemn phrase is used: καὶ ἠνοίγη ὁ ναὸς τῆς σκηνῆς τοῦ μαρτυρίου ἐν τῷ οὐρανῷ (15:5), which rests on a Hebrew original.[33] A particular climax is reached in the depiction of the inaccessibility of the God of wrath in 15:8: "And the temple was filled with smoke from the glory of God, and from his power; and no man was able to enter into the temple, till the seven plagues of the seven angels were fulfilled." One is reminded of the great OT models in Is. 6:4; 65:5; Ez. 10:4; 44:4; also Ex. 19:18; 1 K. 8:11; 2 Ch. 7:1-3. From this temple, too, comes the voice which commissions the angels of the plagues to execute judgment on the earth, 16:1. From the same temple comes the voice and confirmatory word of fulfilment: "It is done" (γέγονεν, 16:17). For the divine, then, the heavenly temple is the habitation of the majesty of God, the mysterious source of the divine commands. But Rev. also

---

[30] J. Wellhausen, "Analyse d. Offenbarung Johannis," *Abh. d. königl. Ges. der Wiss. zu Göttingen* (1907), 15: "An oracle of one of the Zealot prophets, who acc. to Joseph. were very numerous and had great influence, has been preserved here. Those who cling to the temple are the Messianic remnant." This hypothesis is also to be found in R. H. Charles, *Revelation of St. John* (1920), I, 274 ff. (ICC). Charles then argues that the age of the composition of Rev. spiritualised the oracle. Loh. Apk., 88 is also aware of the historical element and refers the saying to the Jerusalem temple. He argues for a Jewish origin, but thinks that here, as in Rev. as a whole, the ναὸς τοῦ θεοῦ is to be equated with the community.

[31] When Stephen renews the radical attitude of the dominical saying in Mk. 14:58 it is not impossible that he is introducing a new element into primitive Christianity, whose initial relation to the temple is much more positive. Hence the tension between Rev. 11:1-2 and Mk. 14:58 is not quite so unbearable as J. Wellhausen supposes (*op. cit.*, 15).

[32] J. Behm, *Die Off. d. Joh., NT Deutsch* (1935), 58. Behm also mentions the fact that 11:1 ff. is an established link in the chain of John's visions, though this does not decide the question of a traditional origin. Dib. Th., 39 and Loh. Apk., 106 f., 144, 189 f. point out that apocalyptic traditions do not have to be changed as a result of historical events.

[33] Loh. Apk., 129 suggests מִשְׁכַּן אֹהֶל מוֹעֵד as the Heb. original, but Charles says in II, 37: "The phrase in the text cannot be a rendering of מִשְׁכַּן אֹהֶל מוֹעֵד." Charles proposes הֵיכָל אֹהֶל מוֹעֵד בַּשָּׁמַיִם, and he has in view the original of 11:19.

shows acquaintance with the metaphor of the temple for the community as in primitive Christian tradition elsewhere. In the victorious saying in 3:12 it is promised: "Him that overcometh will I make a pillar in the temple of my God, and he will never leave it." The presence of the acknowledged metaphor στῦλος suggests that ναός is also to be taken metaphorically. [34] In a final great saying apocalyptic realism works out something previously intimated in mysterious symbolism: In the new Jerusalem there is no temple, 21:22. God the Lord, the sole Ruler, is its temple, and the Lamb. [35] In this respect primitive Christianity differs completely from later Judaism, for which the idea of the new Jerusalem was necessarily linked with the concept of a rich and famous temple. [36] "In the statement of Rev. lies one of the boldest transpositions of the whole concept of the temple. God Himself is the temple. What he means is that imperfect representations of the presence of God in the temple are replaced by God and the Lamb in person, so that unrestricted dealings with God are possible. At this point the influence of Christian ideas is seen to break down the firm structure of Jewish thought and to introduce new elements into it." [37]

3. The Usage of the Post-Apostolic Age.

The term played an important role in the post-apostolic age as a metaphor and an expression of theological truth. The proximity of Greek Stoic and Hellenistic mystical thought exerted an influence and pressed it in this direction. This is particularly clear in Barn., who begins his anti-Jewish polemic at this point. Barn., 4, 11 demands: "Let us become spiritual, let us become a perfect temple for God." Even to the formulation this Christian admonition reminds us of the similar basic motif in Philo: σπούδαζε οὖν, ὦ ψυχή, θεοῦ οἶκος γενέσθαι, ἱερὸν ἅγιον, ἐνδιαίτημα κάλλιστον, Som., I, 149. The words of Barn., of course, are addressed to Christian pneumatics, and terms like πνευματικός and ναὸς τοῦ θεοῦ are common in this circle; Barn. takes them

---

[34] The image of the "pillar" is common in antiquity, Eur. Iph. Taur., 57; Aesch. Ag., 897 f.; Hor. Carm., I, 35, 14. R. Jochanan b. Zakkai is the true (i.e., strong) pillar in Ber., 28b, and Abraham is the pillar of the world, in Levy Wört., III, 660. This metaphor is given a new significance, however, when it is combined with the primitive Christian idea of the ναὸς τοῦ θεοῦ.

[35] Charles, II, 170 conjectures that the original text of 21:22 is as follows: ὁ γὰρ κύριος, ὁ θεὸς, ὁ παντοκράτωρ ναὸς αὐτῆς ἐστιν, καὶ τὸ ἀρνίον ἡ κιβωτὸς τῆς διαθήκης αὐτῆς.

[36] Already in Da. 8:14 the new temple is the centre of eschatological expectation. Acc. to Tob. 14:5 those who return will build the temple: καὶ πάλιν ἐλεήσει αὐτοὺς ὁ θεὸς καὶ ἐπιστρέψει αὐτοὺς εἰς τὴν γῆν καὶ οἰκοδομήσουσιν τὸν οἶκον, οὐχ οἷος ὁ πρότερος, ἕως πληρωθῶσιν καιροὶ τοῦ αἰῶνος. καὶ μετὰ ταῦτα ἐπιστρέψουσιν ἐκ τῶν αἰχμαλωσιῶν καὶ οἰκοδομήσουσιν Ἰηρουσαλὴμ ἐντίμως, καὶ ὁ οἶκος τοῦ θεοῦ ἐν αὐτῇ οἰκοδομηθήσεται εἰς πάσας τὰς γενεὰς τοῦ αἰῶνος οἰκοδομῇ ἐνδόξῳ, καθὼς ἐλάλησαν περὶ αὐτῆς οἱ προφῆται. Or God Himself will build a temple in the midst of His people, that He may dwell among them on Mt. Zion (Jub. 1:17; 28). Acc. to Sib., 3, 290: 5, 422 the Son of Man builds the temple, and acc. to Tg. Is. 53:5 the Messiah. Acc. to Sib. 3:657 the temple of the great God will be magnificently adorned with gold and silver and purple. It will be more renowned than the first temple, Test. B. 9:2; Tob. 14:5. It is the temple of glory, Test. L. 18:6. It will be built for ever as the house of glory and dominion, En. 93:7. With the re-erection of the temple is expected the return of the holy vessels which acc. to 2 Macc. 7:4-8 Jeremiah, and acc. to 2 Bar. 6:5-11; 80:2 angels saved from destruction. The Samaritans give evidence of a similar expectation when on the Day of Atonement they pray for a remanifestation of the tabernacle (A. Merx, *Der Messias oder Taeb der Samaritaner* [1909], 28, 17 f.). Cf. also Jos. Ant., 18, 4, 1. Str.-B., III, 852: "The future Jerusalem without a temple is an impossible thought for the ancient Synagogue."

[37] **Wenschkewitz, 219.**

from it.[38] Developing the thought of 6, 14, Barn., 6:15 issues the reminder: "For a holy temple, my brother, is for the Lord the habitation of our heart." Christ would be manifest in the flesh and dwell in us (cf. Ez. 11:19; 36:26). Here again one is reminded of the similar phrase in Philo: οἶκος γάρ τις ἢ νεὼς ἱερὸς ἐτεκταίνετο ψυχῆς λογικῆς, ἣν ἔμελλεν ἀγαλματοφορήσειν ἀγαλμάτων τὸ θεοειδέστατον, Op. Mund., 137.[39] Barn., 16 shows theologically what is the true temple and what is the false. Part of the error of the Jews is to believe that their temple is the house of God (ὡς ὄντα οἶκον θεοῦ, 16, 1). This false idea is disproved by many verses of Scripture, among which we find Is. 66:1 (cf. Just. Dial., 22). But there is a true temple of God: "Before we believed in God, the habitation of our heart was dedicated to corruption and was decayed, like a temple made with hands," 16, 7. "But after we had receive forgiveness of sins ... we became new and were rebuilt from the foundation up, so that in our habitation God dwells in us (διὸ ἐν τῷ κατοικητηρίῳ ἡμῶν ἀληθῶς ὁ θεὸς κατοικεῖ ἐν ἡμῖν, 16, 8)." Prophecy is a specific proof that the Christian is a temple. "He Himself prophesying in us, He Himself dwelling in us, leads those enslaved to death, by opening to us the door of the temple, that is, the mouth, and granting us repentance, into the imperishable temple," 16, 9. Barn. thus plays on the image. Man is the temple, his mouth is the door, and yet God's heavenly dwelling is the temple to which God conducts man. Ign., too, is fond of the theme of the ναὸς τοῦ θεοῦ. The metaphor is worked out expressly in Eph., 9, 1: "Be, then, stones for the sanctuary of the Father, prepared for the building of God the Father, lifted up by the pulley of Jesus Christ, i.e., the cross, for which the Holy Spirit serves as the rope." A different metaphor in 9,2 reminds us of the pagan procession: "All of you, then, be companions on the way, bearers of God and bearers of the temple, bearers of Christ, and bearers of salvation, adorned at all points with the commandments of Jesus Christ." ναοφόρος reminds us that representations of the temple were carried in solemn procession along with the statue of the god, or were used for adornment by devotees to serve as a reminder and amulet, Hdt., II, 63; Diod. S., I, 97, 9.[40] Eph., 15, 3 contains the admonition: "So let us now do all things, He dwelling in us, that we may be His temple, and that He may be in us as our God." In Phld., 7, 2 the Spirit declares: "Do nothing without the bishop. Keep your flesh as the sanctuary of God (τὴν σάρκα ὑμῶν ὡς ναὸν θεοῦ τηρεῖτε)." The precise ref. to the flesh is important for Ign., and distinguishes him from the usual formulations of Gk. mysticism. There is a similar demand in 2 Cl., 9, 3: "We must keep the flesh as the temple of God" (δεῖ οὖν ἡμᾶς ὡς ναὸν θεοῦ φυλάσσειν τὴν σάρκα). Both commands are obviously anti-Gnostic. Magn., 7, 2 is close to the Pauline and primitive Christian view: "All of you come together as one temple of God" (πάντες ὡς εἰς ἕνα ναὸν συντρέχετε θεοῦ ὡς ἐπὶ ἓν θυσιαστήριον). The basic biblical and spiritual motif has approximated considerably to Hell. mysticism, but it still displays its distinctive origin.

Michel

[38] Wnd. Barn., 324 f.
[39] *Ibid.*, 337.
[40] W. Bauer Ign., 209.

† ναυαγέω

ναυαγέω (cf. ναυαγία from the time of Pindar and the tragedians; ναυαγός from that of Hdt.) means "to suffer shipwreck": Hdt., VII, 236 (νέες νεναυηγήκασι τετρακόσιαι); Xenoph. Cyrop., III, 1, 24; Demosth., 34, 10 (ὁ δὲ Λάμπις ἀναχθεὶς ἐναυάγησεν οὐ μακρὰν ἀπὸ τοῦ ἐμπορίου); Polyb., VI, 44, 7; P. Oxy., IV, 839, 6 ff. It is used fig. of other things, an earthen vessel in Aesch. Fr., 180, a broken vehicle in Ps.-Demosth., 61, 29 (ὡς ἐν τοῖς ἱππικοῖς ἀγῶσιν ἡδίστην θέαν παρέχεται τὰ ναυαγοῦντα).

Fig. it can also mean "to fail," "to be put to shame," Diog. L., V, 55: ἐν τοῖς ἰδίοις, "in one's own finances"; Plut., II, 622 B: ἐν οἷς τὰ πλεῖστα ναυαγεῖ συμπόσια. Ceb. Tab., 24, 2: ὡς κακῶς διατρίβουσι καὶ ἀθλίως ζῶσι καὶ ὡς ναυαγοῦσιν ἐν τῷ βίῳ. Philo Mut. Nom., 215; Som., II, 147: εἶτ' ἐν αὐταῖς τοῦ βίου ταῖς δυσμαῖς ἐξοκείλαντάς τε καὶ ναυαγήσαντας ... The word does not occur in the LXX.[1]

ναυαγεῖν is found twice in the NT. In 2 C. 11:25 Paul mentions among the many grievous sufferings and afflictions which he underwent in his work as an apostle the fact that he was shipwrecked three times (τρὶς ἐναυάγησα). Ac. 27:9 ff. refers to one such incident, though the apostle cannot have been thinking of this. We have no idea when Paul had these experiences; this shows how defective is our knowledge of the details of his life in spite of Ac. and his epistles, and it also shows how exciting the life and work of the apostle were.

1 Tm. 1:19 uses ναυαγεῖν figuratively. Timothy must fight the good fight of faith. Because opponents have not done this, their life of faith has suffered shipwreck. The apostle knows of no Christian life which does not involve serious and manly moral striving. Without this there is both theoretical and practical aberration. The life falls victim to both error and perversion of conduct, in other words: περὶ τὴν πίστιν ἐναυάγησαν.

Preisker

ναυαγέω. [1] The LXX has χειμάζεσθαι instead, fig. at Prv. 26:10 (cf. 1 Tm. 1:19).

νεκρός, νεκρόω, νέκρωσις

νεκρός.

In Gk. νεκρός is a common noun (from Homer) and adj. (from Pindar). The noun denotes the "dead person or body." The adj. means "dead" and is used of men and animals.[1] It can also be used of things without life, which are νεκρά as distinct from ἔμψυχα, Plot. Enn., III, 6, 6. Thus acc. to Plot. Enn., V, 1, 2 heaven was a σῶμα νεκρόν before the ψυχή came; λίθος and ξύλον are also νεκρά, IV, 7, 9. The fig. use, found from the classical period,[2] is much favoured by Stoicism (→ III, 12, n. 33). The false philosopher and his word are νεκρός, Epict. Diss., III, 23, 28. So, too, are the false παιδευτής and those taught by him, I, 9, 19. Things of the sensual world (τὰ αἰσθητά) are εὔφθαρτα καὶ νεκρά, M. Ant., II, 12, 1. νεκρὰ καὶ καπνός may be said of all that does not belong to the realm of the νοῦς, XII, 33, 2. Hence man's relationship with ζῷα as distinct from his relationship with God is an ἀτυχὴς καὶ νεκρὰ συγγένεια, Epict. Diss., I, 3, 3. Above all, the σῶμα or σωμάτιον of man is a νεκρόν, II, 19, 27; M. Ant., X, 33, 6. What is man? ψυχάριον εἶ, βαστάζον νεκρόν.[3] The same material and even formal view is to be found in Gnostic and Neo-platonic dualism (→ III, 12 f.). Acc. to Philostr. Vit. Soph., II, 1, 1 the πλοῦτος is νεκρός. In Corp. Herm., VII, 2 the σῶμα is characterised as ὁ αἰσθη<τι>κὸς νεκρός. Philo esp. bears witness to this usage, → III, 13. He combines description of the σῶμα as the σύνδετος νεκρός[4] with the old pun σῶμα/σῆμα, Leg. All., I, 108.[5] He characterises the state of man or the ψυχή, which must carry the body around with it, as a νεκροφορεῖν.[6]

In the LXX νεκρός is fairly common (mostly for מֵת) and it is used mainly as a noun, though also as an adj.[7] It means the deceased,[8] also the dead body,[9] and the dead in the underworld.[10] It can also be used for inanimate objects, Wis. 15:5, esp. images of false gods,[11] so that in ψ 105:28 idols themselves may be called νεκροί. Fig. the Rabbis call the ungodly dead.[12]

On belief in the resurrection of the dead → II, 856 f. It is God who will raise them; hence in the 2nd of the Eighteen Benedictions and elsewhere He is glorified as the One who makes the dead alive.[13]

νεκρός. [1] Cf. Liddell-Scott.

[2] Philoctetus complains in Soph. Phil., 1018: ἄφιλον, ἔρημον, ἄπολιν, ἐν ζῶσιν νεκρὸν (sc. προὐβάλου με). Cf. also Schol. on Aristoph. Ra., 420: διὰ τὴν κακοπραγίαν νεκροὺς τοὺς Ἀθηναίους λέγει.

[3] M. Ant., IV, 41; cf. IX, 24: πνευμάτια νεκροὺς βαστάζοντα.

[4] The expression derives from the Etruscan custom of tying prisoners to corpses (Aristot. Fr., 60, ed. V. Rose [1886]).

[5] For the σῶμα as νεκρόν cf. also Philo Leg. All., III, 69 ff.; Gig., 15 (the σῶμα as συμφυὴς νεκρός). The unrighteous or non-philosophical are νεκροί in Leg. All., III, 35; Conf. Ling., 55; Fug., 56. There is also fig. usage in Fug., 61; Mut. Nom., 173; Som., II, 213.

[6] Leg. All., III, 69 and 74; Agric., 25; Migr. Abr., 21; Som., II, 237.

[7] E.g., Ju. 4:22; 2 Βασ. 19:7; Is. 37:36.

[8] ψ 30:12; 87:10; Is. 22:2; 26:14 etc.

[9] Gn. 23:3 ff.; Dt. 28:26; Jer. 7:33; 9:21.

[10] Dt. 18:11; ψ 113:25; Qoh. 9:3, 5.

[11] Wis. 13:10, 18; 15:17. Idols are simply compared with the dead in Ep. Jer. 26. 31.

[12] Str.-B., I, 489 on Mt. 8:22; III, 652 on 1 Tm. 5:6.

[13] מְחַיֵּה הַמֵּתִים. Str.-B., III, 212 on R. 4:17; G. Harder, *Paulus u. das Gebet* (1936), 106, 1.

In the NT νεκρός is used as both noun and adj. As adj., in the sense "dead," it is used of men,[14] as of Jesus Christ.[15] Inanimate objects can also be described as νεκρός: τὸ σῶμα χωρὶς πνεύματος νεκρόν (Jm. 2:26; → 892). According to Barn., 12, 7 the brazen serpent was νεκρός; Did., 6, 3 and 2 Cl., 3, 1 refer to pagan gods as νεκροὶ θεοί. In this connection we might also mention R. 7:8: χωρὶς γὰρ νόμου ἁμαρτία νεκρά, i.e., "lifeless" (cf. v. 9: ἀνέζησεν).

As a subst. νεκρός means the dead as distinct from the living, Mk. 12:27 and par.: ζῶντες καὶ νεκροί are often associated as those over whom Christ's dominion extends (R. 14:9) and on whom His or God's judgment will be passed.[16] The NT tells of the dead whom Jesus raised up,[17] and the disciples were also given power to raise the dead (Mt. 10:8). The νεκροί are often the dead in the underworld of whom Christ is the πρωτότοκος.[18] The Jewish description of God as the One who raises the dead is repeated in different forms.[19] But belief in the resurrection of the dead receives a new basis and new strength from the resurrection of Jesus (→ II, 865, III, 18). As God raised Him from the dead,[20] or as He was raised[21] and has arisen from the dead,[22] so at the end of time the dead will be raised[23] and will arise[24] at the (general) ἀνάστασις (τῶν) νεκρῶν[25] or ἀνάστασις ἐκ (τῶν) νεκρῶν.[26] The sea, death and Hades will have to give up their dead for judgment according to Rev. 20:13.

νεκρός (mostly as adj.) is also used fig. The prodigal son was dead and then alive again (Lk. 15:24, 32), i.e., he was lost (better than sunk in sins) and then restored to the father. The church of Sardis is castigated for its imperfect ἔργα: ὄνομα ἔχεις ὅτι ζῇς, καὶ νεκρὸς εἶ, Rev. 3:1. According to Ign. Phld., 6, 1 heretics are στῆλαι καὶ τάφοι νεκρῶν. πίστις without ἔργα is νεκρά, Jm. 2:17, 26; v. 20 vl. Hb. 6:1; 9:14 speaks of the νεκρὰ ἔργα of the pre-Christian period, cf. also Herm. s., 9, 21, 2. In Col. 2:13 the whole pre-Christian existence is dead, because sinful: ὑμᾶς νεκροὺς ὄντας ἐν τοῖς παραπτώμασιν, cf. Eph. 2:1, 5. Men are νεκροί before baptism according to Herm. s., 9, 16, 3 f., and it is said of semi-Christians, who let themselves be entangled in the world: τὸ ἥμισυ αὐτῶν ζῇ, τὸ δὲ ἥμισυ νεκρόν ἐστιν, s., 8, 8, 1.

The noun is used figuratively as follows. There is a play on the word in the saying of Jesus in Mt. 8:22 and par.: ἄφες τοὺς νεκροὺς θάψαι τοὺς ἑαυτῶν νεκρούς, where those who resist the call of Jesus are put on the same level as the dead.[27] In Jn. 5:25 all are dead until the call of Jesus strikes them. They are also reckoned as dead in the cry to awake in Eph. 5:14: ἀνάστα ἐκ τῶν νεκρῶν.[28]

[14] Ac. 5:10; 28:6 etc.
[15] Rev. 1:18; 2:8.
[16] Ac. 10:42; 2 Tm. 4:1; 1 Pt. 4:5; Barn., 7, 2; Pol., 2, 1; 2 Cl., 1, 1.
[17] Jn. 12:1, 9, 17; cf. Mt. 11:5: νεκροὶ ἐγείρονται.
[18] Col. 1:18; Rev. 1:5.
[19] R. 4:17; 2 C. 1:9; Jn. 5:21; cf. Ac. 26:8.
[20] 1 Th. 1:10; Gl. 1:1; R. 4:24; 1 Pt. 1:21; Ac. 3:15; 4:10; 1 Cl., 24, 1 etc.
[21] R. 6:4, 9; Mt. 28:7; Jn. 2:22; 21:14 etc.
[22] Mk. 9:9; Lk. 24:46; Ac. 10:41; Jn. 20:9; Barn., 15, 9 etc.; cf. R. 4:24.
[23] 1 C. 15:35, 52; Mk. 12:26; Jn. 5:21 etc.
[24] Mk. 12:25.
[25] 1 C. 15:12 f., 21, 42; Mt. 22:31; Ac. 23:6; Hb. 6:2; Did., 16, 6 etc.
[26] Phil. 3:11; Lk. 20:35; Ac. 4:2; Barn., 5, 6. On the linguistic variants (ἐγείρειν or ἀναστῆναι) ἐκ (ἀπὸ) νεκρῶν or τῶν νεκρῶν *v.* Pr.-Bauer³.
[27] On the other hand the νεκροί of Mt. 11:5 are not dead in the fig. sense; the ref. is to miracles of resurrection.
[28] The basis here may be a baptismal song couched in Gnostic terminology, Reitzenstein Ir. Erl., 135 f.; F. J. Dölger, *Sol salutis*² (1925), 364 ff.

The dualistic terminology which describes the human σῶμα as νεκρόν (or a νεκρός) is not found, though Ign. uses it in Sm., 5, 2 when he says of the μὴ ὁμολογῶν αὐτὸν (Χριστὸν) σαρκοφόρον that any such is himself a νεκροφόρος. On this whole question → II, 863, n. 267; III, 17, n. 76.

There is a very different use of the adjective νεκρός in R. 6:11: λογίζεσθε ἑαυτοὺς εἶναι νεκροὺς μὲν τῇ ἁμαρτίᾳ, ζῶντας δὲ τῷ θεῷ ἐν Χριστῷ Ἰησοῦ. The usage in this case is sacramental rather than figurative. To be dead here is death with Christ (→ III, 19), i.e., appropriation of the real death of Christ already effected in the sacrament of baptism. R. 6:13 can thus give the admonition: παραστήσατε ἑαυτοὺς τῷ θεῷ ὡσεὶ ἐκ νεκρῶν ζῶντας, namely, as those who have already anticipated death and resurrection by virtue of their union with Christ. R. 8:10 is to be taken in the same way: εἰ δὲ Χριστὸς ἐν ὑμῖν, τὸ μὲν σῶμα νεκρὸν διὰ ἁμαρτίαν, τὸ δὲ πνεῦμα ζωὴ διὰ δικαιοσύνην, "Your body is dead because (by virtue of your fellowship with Christ) you are already dead to sin, i.e., because judgment has already been executed on sin (in your dying with Christ), your spirit is alive because you are (for this reason) pronounced righteous" (cf. 6:7).[29]

† νεκρόω.

νεκρόω means "to put to death," "kill." It is first attested in the Hell. period. Among physicians it denotes the atrophy of a part of the body through sickness.[1] Max. Tyr., 41, 3h says of the σῶμα in old age: κατὰ βραχὺ νεκρούμενον καὶ ἀποσβεννύμενον. In a burial insc.[2] the corpse is called the σῶμα τὸ νενεκρωμένον. The later Stoics use νεκροῦν and ἀπονεκροῦν fig., cf. Epict. Diss., I, 5, 4 f.: οἱ δὲ πολλοὶ τὴν μὲν σωματικὴν ἀπονέκρωσιν φοβούμεθα ..., τῆς ψυχῆς δ' ἀπονεκρουμένης οὐδὲν ἡμῖν μέλει ... ἂν δέ τινος τὸ ἐντρεπτικὸν καὶ αἰδῆμον ἀπονεκρωθῇ, τοῦτο ἔτι καὶ δύναμιν καλοῦμεν.[3] M. Ant., VII, 2 speaks of the νεκρωθῆναι of δόγματα which takes place when the corresponding φαντασίαι (representations of phenomena) are lost. The term does not occur in the LXX. It is found in Philo at Aet. Mund., 125: ... τὸ ὕδωρ, ἀκίνητον ἐαθὲν οὐχ ὑφ' ἡσυχίας νεκροῦται.

In the NT[4] the word is used literally in R. 4:19 when Paul says of Abraham: κατενόησεν τὸ ἑαυτοῦ σῶμα νενεκρωμένον (→ *supra*). Cf. also Hb. 11:12: ἀφ' ἑνὸς (Abraham) ἐγενήθησαν (innumerable descendants), καὶ ταῦτα νενεκρωμένου. The use in Col. 3:5 is figurative: νεκρώσατε οὖν τὰ μέλη τὰ ἐπὶ τῆς γῆς. In this case Paul's sacramental use of νεκρός (→ *supra*) is probably not without influence.

---

[29] Hence one must prefer to Ltzm. R. *propter peccatum commissum* and *propter iustitiam exercendam* Barth's "on account of judged sin" and "on account of established righteousness" (Barth R.).

νεκρόω. [1] E.g., Gal. Opera, Vol. 18, 1, p. 156, ed. G. Kühn (1829); also CMG, V, 9, 2, p. 45, 28. Also of the killing of a tree by frost, *ibid.*, V, 9, 1, p. 31, 5. The act. is used in V, 9, 1, p. 151, 11 of narcotics: νεκροῦν τὴν αἴσθησιν.

[2] IG, III, 2, 1355 (Deissmann LO, 75, 7); IG, XIV, 1976: νεκρωθείς, "the deceased."

[3] Cf. Epict. Diss., IV, 5, 21: τούτου τὸ αἰδῆμον ἀπονενέκρωται. Of the sceptic in I, 5, 7: νενέκρωται.

[4] 2 C. 10:12 in Chester Beatty Papyrus (𝔓[46]) erroneously has νεκροῦντες for μετροῦντες καὶ συνκρίνοντες [Debrunner].

† νέκρωσις.

This, too, is attested only from the Hell. period. It means among physicians the withering or mortification of the body or of a sick member.[1] ἀπονέκρωσις is used fig. in Epict. (→ 894). The term does not occur in the LXX or Philo.

It is used in the NT at R. 4:19 for the deadness of Sarah's womb (→ n. 1) and figuratively in Mk. 3:5 D it Syr^{sin} for the deadness of the heart (πώρωσις and πήρωσις are found in other witnesses). Paul uses the term in a sacramental sense at 2 C. 4:10 (→ 894): πάντοτε τὴν νέκρωσιν τοῦ Ἰησοῦ ἐν τῷ σώματι περιφέροντες, ἵνα καὶ ἡ ζωὴ τοῦ Ἰησοῦ ἐν τῷ σώματι ἡμῶν φανερωθῇ. The word is obviously chosen instead of θάνατος because the reference is to dying with Christ, not as basically fulfilled in the act of baptism, but as continually actualised in the concrete life of the apostle. Paul regards the suffering to which he is constantly exposed in his work as the process in which the death of Jesus is effected in him as a continual mortifying or mortification.[2]

There is a distinctive mingling of the fig. and sacramental use in Herm. s., 9, 16, 2 f., where baptism is interpreted, not as νέκρωσις, but as the ἀποτιθέναι of νέκρωσις, the earlier life.

Bultmann

νέκρωσις. [1] Galen., 18, 1, p. 156, Kühn; also CMG, V, 9, 2, p. 226, 17; 230, 2 (τῆς διοικούσης τὸ σῶμα δυνάμεως); 313, 16 (τοῦ σώματος ὅλου); Aret., II, 10, p. 32; 16; Phot. Lex., p. 513a, 36, Becker. On the unfruitfulness of the generative organs cf. Porphyr. Abst., IV, 20 (262, 20, Nauck).

[2] Cf. dualistic usage (→ 892) and C. H. Dodd, *The Bible and the Greeks* (1935), 182, 191 ff.

νέος, ἀνανεόω

νέος.

1. Linguistic and Historical Data.

νέος, an adj. to denote time, originally "belonging to the present moment," [1] combines the meanings a. "new," "fresh," "not previously there," or "not long there," and b. "young," "youthful."

In sense a., synon. with καινός (→ III, 447 f.) and → πρόσφατος, νέος is used predominantly of things, e.g., Gorg. Pal. Fr., 11a (II, 301, 3 f., Diels[5]): ἀντικατηγορῆσαι δέ σου πολλὰ καὶ μεγάλα καὶ παλαιὰ καὶ νέα πράσσοντος δυνάμενος οὐ βούλομαι, Philo Aet. Mund., 89: μετὰ τὴν ἐκπύρωσιν, ἐπειδὰν ὁ νέος κόσμος μέλλῃ δημιουργεῖσθαι (cf. 145), Cl. Al. Strom., I, 72, 3: αὗται (sc. holy women among the Teutons) γοῦν οὐκ εἴασαν αὐτοὺς τὴν μάχην θέσθαι πρὸς Καίσαρα πρὶν ἐπιλάμψαι σελήνην τὴν νέαν. In many cases (cf. → καινός, III, 447) it has the subsidiary sense of "unexpected," "strange," "odd," "contrary," e.g., Plat. Polit., 294c: ἄν τι νέον ἄρα τῳ συμβαίνῃ βέλτιον παρὰ τὸν λόγον, Thuc., V, 50, 4: πολλῷ δὴ μᾶλλον ἐπεφόβηντο πάντες καὶ ἐδόκει τι νέον ἔσεσθαι, and cf. esp. the comparative Hdt., V, 106, 4; V, 35, 4 ("evil," "misfortune"); V, 19, 2: νεώτερα πρήγματα ("revolution"); Xenoph. Hist. Graec., V, 2, 9; Demosth. Or., 11, 17 (of the Athenians): πυνθανόμενοι κατὰ τὴν ἀγορὰν εἴ τι λέγεται νεώτερον (cf. Ac. 17:21) [2] etc. In relation to people it can be used for a newly attained position or dignity, [3] e.g., Aesch. Prom., 96: ὁ νέος ταγὸς μακάρων, 149 f.: νέοι γὰρ οἰακονόμοι κρατοῦσ' Ὀλύμπου. With these predicates Aesch. ironically links the title οἱ νέοι θεοί or οἱ νεώτεροι θεοί for Zeus or the Olympian gods in general, who have overthrown the ancient divine race of the Titans, *v.* Prom., 955 and 960; Eum., 162, 721 f. and 778 (cf. Aristoph. Pl., 959 f.). In the Hell. and Roman ruler cult νέος is often combined with the name of a god (νέος Διόνυσος, νέος Ἀσκληπιός) to express the fact that the divinely venerated ruler represents the deity concerned in a present-day form. [4] In Act. Thom., 69 etc. the Christ preached to the Indians is ὁ νέος θεός, and in 123 He is worshipped by the newly converted: νέε θεέ, [5] cf. the invocations in Manichean hymns to Jesus: [6]

νέος. On 1: Cr.-Kö., Moult.-Mill., Liddell-Scott, Preisigke Wört., Pr.-Bauer[3], *s.v.*; also → III, 447, n. 1; cf. in addition J. A. H. Tittmann, *De Synonymis in Novo Testamento,* Lib. I (1829), 59 ff. On 2: A. v. Harnack, "Die Terminologie der Wiedergeburt u. verwandter Erlebnisse in d. ältesten Kirche," TU, 42, 3 (1918), 101 ff., 136.

[1] → III, 447, n. 1.

[2] → III, 448, and cf. E. Norden, *Agnostos Theos* (1913), 333 f.

[3] Cf. J. H. H. Schmidt, *Synonymik d. gr. Sprache,* II (1878), 97.

[4] Examples in G. Gerlach, *Griech. Ehreninschriften* (1908), 38; O. Weinreich, "De dis ignotis quaestiones selectae," ARW, 18 (1915), 23 ff. A. D. Nock, "Notes on Ruler-Cult," I-IV, JHS, 48 (1928), 21 ff., esp. 30 ff.: II. "Neos Dionysos."

[5] Though cf. Marcion's doctrine of the καινὸς θεός (Orig. Comm. in Joh., I, 82: τὴν καινὴν θεότητα, Tert. Marc., I, 8: *novus deus,* cf. 9; IV, 11 and 18), and on this A. v. Harnack, *Marcion*[2] (1924), 87 f., 126 f.; H. Jonas, "Gnosis u. spätantiker Geist," FRL, NF, 33 (1934), 247 ff.

[6] F. C. Andreas-W. Henning, "Mitteliranische Manichaica aus Chinesisch-Turkestan," II, SAB (1933), 314 and 317.

"To salvation, new ruler and new day! To salvation, new ruler and new physician! To salvation, new redeemer, new redeemed! To salvation, new God!" The new man, in contrast to the old, is found as a predicate or metaphor for the redeemed both in ancient Christian lit. (e.g., Hipp. Ref., X, 34, 5 of Christ: νέον τὸν παλαιὸν ἄνθρωπον ἀποτελῶν) and also in Manichean texts from N. Africa to China.[7] The source of the idea, as of that of Christ as the new man, which passed into Gnosticism (→ III, 449; acc. to Hipp. Ref., VI, 35, 4 Jesus was for the Valentinians ὁ καινὸς ἄνθρωπος), is not to be sought in Oriental-Hellenistic syncretism, but in primitive Christianity, cf. Paul[8] in Col. 3:10; Eph. 4:23 f. (→ 899; 900 f.).

In sense b. νέος denotes the age (up to 30 at most, cf. Xenoph. Mem., I, 2, 35) of a child or young man (proverb in Lib. Ep., 910, 3: ὁ νέος ἔσται νέος, cf. Phil. Poster. C., 109: πρεσβύτῃ γὰρ ἑτέρως ὁμιλητέον καὶ νέῳ). οἱ νέοι or οἱ νεώτεροι can be used for young men as compared with πρεσβύτεροι or γέροντες e.g., Xenoph. Cyrop., V, 1, 25; P. Par., 66, 24; Lib. Progymnasmata, 7, 3, 7 [VIII, p. 185, 4, R. Foerster]; 2 Παρ. 10:14; 2 Macc. 5:13, 24; 4 Macc. 9:6; Jos. Ant., 3, 47; 1 Cl., 3, 3). In the grouping of citizens in Hellenistic cities or in relation to societies it becomes a tt. for younger men over 20 as a group or body (distinct from γερουσία on the one side, ἔφηβοι or παῖδες on the other), cf. Ditt. Syll.³, 589, 38; 831, 8; 959, 5. Ditt. Or., 339, 31; 48, 15 etc.;[9] cf. the inscr. of Hypaepa:[10] Ἰουδαίων νεωτέρων. The idea of youthful temperament or immaturity can be linked with νέος or νεώτερος, which has little comparative significance,[11] Hesych.: νέος· ... ἀμαθής, προπετής, cf. Aristot. Pol., VIII, 6, p. 1340b, 29: οὐ γὰρ δύναται τὸ νέον ἡσυχάζειν, Lys., 24, 16: τοὺς ἔτι νέους καὶ νέαις ταῖς διανοίαις χρωμένους, Plat. Resp., II, 378a: ῥᾳδίως οὕτως λέγεσθαι πρὸς ἄφρονάς τε καὶ νέους, Plat. Gorg., 463e: πῶλος δὲ ὅδε νέος ἐστὶ καὶ ὀξύς, Demosth. Or., 18, 50: τοὺς νεωτέρους τῶν πεπραγμένων (too young to remember things). There is also an element of disparagement in Philo's description of the corporeal world in its relation to the spiritual: πρεσβυτέρου νεώτερον ἀπεικόνισμα, Op. Mund., 16.

In the LXX νέος is used for חָדָשׁ only at Lv. 23:16; 26:10; Nu. 18:26; Cant. 7:14 (cf. also Sir. 9:10; Wis. 19:11).[12] The usual term for new is καινός (→ III, 447). νέος is used for נַעַר in the sense of "young," subst. "boy" (Prv. 1:4: παῖς νέος).[13] The much more common comparative is found for נַעַר,[14] also צָעִיר "young,"[15] or קָטֹן[קָטָן], "younger," "youngest," and νεώτερος once for יֶלֶד, 2 Ch. 10:14.[16]

---

[7] Cf. Aug. Contra Faustum, 24, 1 (CSEL, 25, 717 ff.); É. Chavannes-P. Pelliot, "Traité Manichéen retrouvé en Chine," *Journal Asiatique*, 10, 18 (1911), 566 f.; E. Waldschmidt-W. Lentz, "Die Stellung Jesu im Manichäismus," AAB (1926), *Abh.* 4, 31 ff., 52 f.; also "Manichäische Dogmatik aus chinesischen u. iranischen Texten," SAB (1933), 487, 523, 547 f., 570 ff.; C. Schmidt-H. J. Polotsky, "Ein Mani-Fund aus Ägypten," SAB (1933), 23; *Kephalaia*, 33 (*Manichäische Handschriften der Staatlichen Museen Berlin*, I, 1935 ff., p. 96, 25—97, 21, etc.

[8] → I, 366, n. 12. Cf. also W. Lentz, "Mani u. Zarathustra," ZDMG, NF, 7 (1928), 192 f.; C. Schmidt, SAB (1933), 23, n. 1 and 33, n. 1.

[9] Cf. W. M. Ramsay, *Cities and Bishoprics of Phrygia*, I (1895), 110 f.; Schürer, III, 91; M. San Nicolò, *Ägyptisches Vereinswesen zur Zeit d. Ptolemäer u. d. Römer*, I (1913), 36 ff.; Moult.-Mill., *s.v.*; E. G. Turner, "The Gerousia of Oxyrhynchus," APF, 12 (1937), 181 ff.

[10] REJ, 10 (1885), 74 f.

[11] The non-comparative sense is the older, E. Schwyzer, *Gr. Grammatik*, I (1939), 533 f. [A. Debrunner]. Cf. also Bl.-Debr. § 244.

[12] Σ Job 32:19: οἶνος νέος has no Heb. original.

[13] So always in ΣΘ. Only in Σ Is. 60:22 do we have νέος for צָעִיר.

[14] Also Σ ψ 118:9; Θ Job 24:5 and Is. 65:20.

[15] Σ Ιερ. 48:4; Θ Job 30:1. οἱ νεώτεροι for הַצְּעָרִים in Θ Zech. 13:7.

[16] In the LXX, too, νέος can sometimes mean youthful immaturity as such or in the sense of susceptibility to evil and educability to good. Thus πᾶς νεώτερος ἄπειρος in

In the NT νέος is less common than καινός (→ III, 448 f.). It can mean "new" in time, with ref. to "now" as compared with "then" either past or future. νέον φύραμα in 1 C. 5:7 is fresh dough which is not yet leavened, οἶνος νέος in Mk. 2:22 and par. is new wine which is still fermenting. The νέος (sc. ἄνθρωπος) is contrasted with the παλαιός in Col. 3:9 f., the διαθήκη νέα (→ II, 132) in Hb. 12:24 with the outdated first διαθήκη (Hb. 8:13; 9:1, 15, 18; cf. 2 C. 3:14).[17] The ref. is to belonging to a new age, but in both cases the related καινός can suggest a difference in nature (→ III, 449).[18] The two will always have the quality of καινός, not always of νέος. νέος in the sense of "young" occurs only at Tt. 2:4 : αἱ νέαι, the age-group of young women. Elsewhere we find the comparative, which has comp. significance only in Lk. 15:12 f.,[19] e.g., in Ac. 5:6 (= νεανίσκος, v. 10); Tt. 2:6 : οἱ νεώτεροι, the young men as a class in the community; 1 Pt. 5:5; 1 Tm. 5:1, expressly contrasted with the πρεσβύτεροι (→ πρεσβύτερος); cf. 1 Tm. 5:2 : νεώτεραι.

2. Theological Implications.

In the NT νέος does not have, like καινός (→ III, 448 f.), an unequivocal eschatological content. It bears no specific reference to the consummation of salvation. What is envisaged is the reality of salvation in the present, the new thing which was not there before, which Jesus is and brings, the new being in which the Christian stands.

Though the dominical metaphor of the new wine in old wineskins (Mk. 2:22 and par.) is not originally linked with the question of fasting,[20] it is not a de-

---

Nu. 14:23 is to be taken in the sense of the preceding τὰ τέκνα ... ὅσοι οὐκ οἴδασιν ἀγαθὸν οὐδὲ κακόν (no Mas.; cf. Dt. 1:39 : πᾶν παιδίον νέον, ὅστις οὐκ οἶδεν ...). This usage is more common in the Wisdom lit. So Job 13:12 A : καί γε νεώτερος ὑμῶν οὔκ εἰμι ἀσυνετώτερος ὑμῶν, where the ἀσυνετώτερος is either a double translation or a clarification of νεώτερος. The Mas. merely has נפל מִן in the sense of "to stand back." The LXX translates very freely. In Prv. 22:15 ἄνοια is described as of the essence of the νέος without ῥάβδος and παιδεία. 7:10 LXX refers to the harlot "Folly" who seduces youth (Mas. different). Cf. 2:16 and on this G. Bertram, "Die religiöse Umdeutung der altorientalischen Lebensweisheit in d. gr. Übers. d. AT," ZAW, NF, 13 (1936), 162 f. In Sir. 51:13 the lack of a Heb. original for πρὶν ἢ πλανηθῆναί με seems to confirm the older view of Luther, Bretschneider, De Wette etc., which takes πλανηθῆναι in the moral sense, as compared with the modern rendering "to go journeying abroad" (Smend, Ryssel). For in the Gk. a psychological understanding is more likely than a materially unimportant amplification. πρὶν ἢ πλανηθῆναι denotes youth as yet untouched by sin and error (cf. Nu. 14:23), and therefore not led astray in the desire for wisdom. 2 Macc. 6:28, 31; 15:17 refer to good examples for youth, 4 Macc. 6:19 to an example of ungodliness (τύπος ἀσεβείας). That temptation is esp. linked with youth may be seen from the later transl. of Ps. 1:1 in E' and Σ : τέλειος ὁ νεώτερος, ὃς οὐκ ἀπῆλθεν ... in place of the μακάριος ἀνὴρ ... of the LXX. This rendering, and the whole pedagogic and psychological understanding of νέος in the Gk. OT, is undoubtedly linked with the penetration of the idea of education into the Gk. Bible. Cf. G. Bertram, "Der Begriff d. Erziehung in der gr. Bibel," Imago Dei. *Festschrift f. G. Krüger* (1932), 33-51. [Bertram.]

[17] The idea of the νέα διαθήκη is still to be found in the post-apostolic period, e.g., Cl. Al. Paed., I, 59, 2; Strom., I, 28, 2; III, 71, 3; V, 3, 3; 85, 1; Cramer Cat. on Mk. 2:2 f.; Apollinarius Laod., Antirrheticus contra Eunomium, p. 228, 20, J. Dräseke (1892); Test. Sol. D, I, 2 (p. 88*, 9 f., McCown), cf. also ἡ καινὴ διαθήκη, e.g., Cl. Al. Paed., I, 59, 1: πρεσβυτέρα διαθήκη ... καινὴ καὶ νέα διαθήκη.

[18] *V.* Trench, 137 f. In Hb. 12:24 Rgg. and Michel Hb. (cf. also J. Moffatt, ICC, *ad loc.*) see no difference between νέος and καινός. διαθήκης νέας might be used for διαθήκης καινῆς on grounds of rhythm.

[19] At Lk. 22:26 ὁ νεώτερος, like ὁ μείζων, has a superlative sense, cf. Bl.-Debr. § 244.

[20] Cf. A. Loisy, *Les Évangiles Synoptiques,* I (1907), 500 f.; Kl. and Loh. Mk. on 2:21 f.; Bultmann Trad., 102 f.; C. G. Montefiore, *The Synoptic Gospels,* I (1927), 59, though cf. J. Jeremias, "Jesus als Weltvollender," BFTh, 33, 4 (1930), 21.

tached and enigmatic saying.[21] As testimony to the new and unheard of element in the person and message of Jesus (→ III, 450) it is connected with the antitheses of the Sermon on the Mount or sayings like Mt. 12:6, 41, 42; Lk. 4:21; 16:16; Mk. 10:6 ff. and par., though it goes beyond them with its demand that the old and the new must not be confused.[22] The old age and the new (→ I, 204 ff.), i.e., that which has come with Jesus (→ I, 588 f.), are irreconcilable opposites. The attempt to bring them together has explosive consequences with mortal danger on both sides.[23]

In the allegorical exposition of the figure of the leaven in 1 C. 5:6 ff.[24] the words ἵνα ἦτε νέον φύραμα, καθώς ἐστε ἄζυμοι (v. 7) state the goal of the exhortation. The fresh dough, only just prepared and as yet unleavened, stands for the Christian community,[25] which must keep itself pure from its earlier sin (this is the point of the preceding imperative ἐκκαθάρατε [→ III, 430] τὴν → παλαιὰν ζύμην) in order to be in fact what it is by nature.[26] We have here the characteristically Pauline thought of the indissoluble unity of gift and task, of reality and the duty of actualisation laid on Christians by the Gospel. The new life is present in Christ (v. 7); it must now be actualised by Christians themselves.[27] The same thought occurs in another form in Col. 3:9 f.: ἀπεκδυσάμενοι τὸν → παλαιὸν ἄνθρωπον σὺν ταῖς πράξεσιν αὐτοῦ καὶ ἐνδυσάμενοι τὸν νέον τὸν ἀνακαινούμενον (→ III, 452, cf. 449). The new man is present (→ III, 453; I, 671) just as certainly as Christ, *the* new man, is present,[28] but it is also true that the new man continually arises afresh by religious and moral renewal.[29]

On διαθήκη νέα in Hb. 12:24 → 898; II, 130; III, 451.

† ἀνανεόω → ἀνακαινίζω, III, 451; → ἀνακαινόω, III, 452.

The rare basic word νεόω means in the act. and mid. trans. "to make new," "to

---

21 So *Schr. NT* (J. Weiss) on Mk. 2:22; R. Bultmann, *Jesus* (1926), 61 f., cf. Trad., 102 f.; Montefiore, *op. cit.*, 59 ff., though also Jülicher Gl. J., II, 199.

22 It thus follows that the old and the new are entities which differ not merely externally (e.g., the life and worship of the disciples of John and Jesus or Judaism and primitive Christianity), but essentially and absolutely.

23 Cf. J. Schniewind (*NT Deutsch*) on Mk. 2:22 and Mt. 9:17. Loh. Mk. on 2:22 is basically right when he says that the saying is negative.

24 → II, 903; W. Straub, *Die Bildersprache d. Ap. Pls.* (1937), 80 f. Cf. the same allegorical use in Ign. Mg., 10, 2; Just. Dial., 14, 2 f. → II, 904, n. 19.

25 Cramer Cat., *ad loc.* (V, 96) has on νέον φύραμα : νέον γὰρ ἄνθρωπον οἶδεν ἡ γραφὴ τὸν ἄρτιον, παλαιὸν δὲ τὸν ἀσεβῆ.

26 Cf. v. Hofmann, Joh. W. 1 K., Schl. K., H. D. Wendland (*NT Deutsch,* II), *ad loc.*

27 Cf. H. Windisch, "Das Problem d. paul. Imperativs," ZNW, 23 (1924), 265 ff.; P. Althaus on R. 6:1-14 : "The New Life as Reality and Task (Indicative and Imperative)" in *NT Deutsch,* II^4 (1938), 213 ff.; Oepke Gl. on 5:24 f.: "Indicative and Imperative in Pauline Exhortation."

28 → II, 320. It is probable that in Col. 2:11 (cf. Gl. 3:27) there is a ref. to baptism as the recent birth of the new man. For a par. with a Gnostic tinge cf. Cl. Al. Paed., I, 20, 2 : αἱ νέαι φρένες ..., ἐν παλαιᾷ τῇ ἀφροσύνῃ αἱ νεωστὶ συνεταί (just come to understanding), αἱ κατὰ τὴν διαθήκην τὴν καινὴν ἀνατείλασαι.

29 Cf. v. Hofmann, *ad loc.* (in spite of his failure to see the imperative significance of the two aor. part.); J. B. Lightfoot, *St. Paul's Epistles to the Colossians and Philemon* (1875, reprinted 1927), *ad loc.*; J. A. C. van Leeuwen, *Paulus' Zendbrieven aan Efeze, Colosse* ... (1926), 226; Dib. Gefbr., Loh. Kol., *ad loc.*

ἀνανεόω. Suid., 1973 f. (I, 177, 14 ff., Adler); Liddell-Scott, 113, cf. 1170; E. Fraenkel, *Gr. Denominativa* (1906), 144; Cr.-Kö., Moult.-Mill., Pr.-Bauer^3, *s.v.*; Trench, 138; v. Hofmann, T. K. Abbott (ICC), Haupt, Dib., Ew. Gefbr., H. Rendtorff (*NT Deutsch,* II) on Eph. 4:23; A. v. Harnack (→ νέος Bibl.).

renew," Aesch. Suppl., 534: νέωσον εὔφρον' αἶνον, IG, XIV, 1721, 7: ὅς <σ>φισι τούσδε τάφους ἐνεώσατο. The pass. in a true pass. sense occurs in Hesych. (*s.v.*): νεουμένη· δευτερουμένη. In Ιερ. 4:3, as elsewhere (*v.* Poll. Onom., I, 221), νεόω is used for νεάω, "to break or till new land."

ἀνανεόω, "to renew (again)," [1] is the same as the simple form even to the undifferentiated use of the act. and mid., the more common form. The act. occurs, e.g., in Job 33:24; 1 Macc. 12:1 vl.; Herm. s., 9, 14, 3: ἀνενέωσε τὴν ζωὴν ἡμῶν, M. Ant., VI, 15, 1: ῥύσεις καὶ ἀλλοιώσεις ἀνανεοῦσι τὸν κόσμον διηνεκῶς, Corp. Herm., IX, 6: (of the life-creating cosmos) διαλύων πάντα, ἀνανεοῖ [καὶ] <τὰ> δια-[τοῦτο]-λυθέντα, ὥσπερ ἀγαθὸς [ζωῆς] γεωργὸς τῇ καταβολῇ ἀνανέωσιν αὐτοὺς [φερόμενος] παρέχων. The mid. may be found in Thuc., V, 80, 2: τούς τε παλαιοὺς ὅρκους ἀνενεώσαντο καὶ ἄλλους ὤμοσαν, Dion. Hal. Ant. Rom., VI, 21, 2; Est. 3:13b; 1 Macc. 12:1, 3 etc.; 4 Macc. 18:4; Jos. Ant., 1, 290: τὴν προϋπάρχουσαν ἡμῖν συγγένειαν ἀνανεωσόμενος, Herm. v., 3, 12, 3: ἀνενεώσατο (sc. ὁ κύριος) τὰ πνεύματα ὑμῶν, [2] Cl. Al. Strom., I, 149, 3: (Ezra) πάσας τὰς παλαιὰς αὖθις ἀνανεούμενος ... γραφάς. From the meaning "to give new life to something by recollection" (cf. Thom. Mag., Ecloga Vocum Atticarum [p. 28, 17, F. Ritschl]: ἀνανεοῦμαι τῇ μνήμῃ τόδε) the mid. can take on the sense "to remember," Polyb., V, 36, 7: ἀεὶ τὸν λόγον ἀνενεοῦτο, Jos. Bell., I, 283: Καίσαρα μὲν οὖν εἶχεν ἑτοιμότερον αὐτοῦ τὰς Ἀντιπάτρου στρατείας ἀνανεούμενον, though this does not establish a reflexive use of the mid. ἀνανεοῦσθαι. The pass. "to be renewed" occurs in Jos. Ant., 12, 321 (of the temple): ἀνενεώθη δὲ κατὰ τὴν αὐτὴν ἡμέραν, cf. also Gal. Historia Philosopha, 17 (H. Diels, Doxographi Graeci² [1929], p. 609, 18 ff.): αὖθις δὲ τῶν ὄντων ἀνανεουμένων ἐκ πυρὸς καὶ μεταβαλλόντων κατ' ἀρχὰς εἰς τὴν τῶν ἄλλων στοιχείων φύσιν καὶ πάλιν συγκρινομένων καὶ σωματοποιουμένων ὑπὸ τοῦ θεοῦ καὶ τῶν πάντων ἐκ νέας κοσμοποιουμένων, M. Ant., X, 7, 5; also Test. B. 9:1: καὶ πάλιν ἀνανεωθήσεσθε, [3] Herm. v., 3, 12, 2 (cf. 13, 2); Corp. Herm., III, 4 (p. 148, 13, W. Scott; cf. p. 148, 10 ff.); also Eph. 4:23, where many attempts have been made to give ἀνανεοῦσθαι a reflexive meaning "to renew oneself," [4] but a pass. should be seen ("to be, or to let oneself be, renewed") in view of the usage, which has no reflexive mid. The relation to an earlier state which is now restored (cf. the ἀνα-) is seldom to be seen in ἀνανεόω (cf. Dion. Hal. Ant. Rom., VI, 21, 2 → *supra*; Herm. v., 3, 11, 3; Cl. Al. Strom., I, 149, 3 → *supra*). But as νέος can contain an antithesis to something earlier (→ 896 f.), so ἀνανεόω can denote a renewing activity which replaces an earlier state, i.e., "to renew what is old," "to refresh or reinvigorate a tired being." ἀνανεόω (cf. *recentare*) is to be distinguished from ἀνακαινόω (cf. *renovare*) as νέος is from καινός. It involves a new beginning in time as distinct from qualitative renewal.

Eph. 4:23, which occurs in the context of exhortation (vv. 17 ff.), is to be taken with v. 22: ἀποθέσθαι ὑμᾶς ... τὸν παλαιὸν ἄνθρωπον, and v. 24: ἐνδύσασθαι

---

[1] Intrans. "to become young again," "to receive strength again" only in Herm. v., 3, 11, 3: οἱ πρεσβύτεροι, μηκέτι ἔχοντες ἐλπίδα τοῦ ἀνανεῶσαι.

[2] Corresponding to the noun ἀνανέωσις (→ ἀνακαίνωσις, III, 453) Jos. Ant., 9, 161; 12, 324; Herm. v., 3, 13, 2; s., 6, 2, 4; Corp. Herm., III, 1a, 4 (→ *infra*); IX, 6 (→ *supra*); XI (2), 15b. On the word, which occurs in the Gk. Bible only at 1 Macc. 12:17, cf. Liddell-Scott and Pr.-Bauer³, *s.v.*, and on its legal use in the pap. Preisigke Wört., *s.v.*; Preisigke Fachwörter, 16 f.; APF, 12 (1937), 196 ff.

[3] Meaning, as in the Armen. version: "You will be betrayed again into sin with women"? R. H. Charles, who in his ed. of the Test. XII thinks it possible that the Gk. transl. of the Heb. original is wrong, prefers the vl. ἀνανεώσησθε ἐν γυναιξὶν στρίνους (= στρήνους, "excesses"), *The Apocrypha and Pseudepigrapha of the OT*, II (1913), 358. In any case, the verb is used here, contrary to the rule, in a bad sense.

[4] Cf. Luther, more recently H. v. Soden, *ad loc.* (*Hand-Commentar z. NT*², 3, 1 [1893], 141) and E. Preuschen, *Vollständiges Griechisch-Deutsches Handwörterbuch zu d. Schriften d. NT* ... (1910), 88, cf. also the transl. in Dib. Gefbr., Weizsäcker, Stage, Menge etc.

τὸν καινὸν ἄνθρωπον, as part of the doctrine of Christ (v. 21: ἐδιδάχθητε): ἀνανεοῦσθαι ... τῷ → πνεύματι τοῦ → νοὸς ὑμῶν. Since the point here is not to describe a fact but to assert obligations this infinitive, like the others, has an imperative sense.[5] The change which must be constantly brought about in the lives of Christians is finally accomplished on them rather than through them. It means that they are constantly set in the miraculous and mysterious magnetic field of this renewal which is effected in them. It is an inner "being renewed" or "letting themselves be renewed" which takes place in the centre of personal life. The effective subject of the renewal is obviously Christ Himself, cf. v. 20 f., also R. 7:6, → III, 451, though this does not contradict Paul's doctrine of the operation of the Spirit of God or of Christ in Christians, R. 8:9 ff.; 1 C. 12:13; Gl. 5:16 etc.[6] The thought expressed by ἀνακαινοῦσθαι in the par. passage Col. 3:10 (cf. ἀνακαίνωσις in R. 12:2) is given by the ἀνανεοῦσθαι of Eph. 4:23 a nuance which characterises the connection with v. 22 and v. 24, namely, that through the operation of Christ upon him the Christian is constantly rejuvenated and begins afresh,[7] free from the old being and free for the new.[8]

Behm

---

[5] This is correctly expressed by the easier ἀνανεοῦσθε 𝔓 46, 33 etc. The defenders of an indicative (v. Hofmann, Ew. Gefbr., *ad loc.*) are unable to give it any convincing sense.

[6] The linguistic argument for a pass. understanding of ἀνανεοῦσθαι (→ 900) is thus supported by a theological argument from the context of Eph., and from Paul's thinking generally.

[7] Ther is no ref. to a restoration of man's first estate, the *status paradisicus, v.* Haupt Gefbr., *ad loc.*, and cf. G. B. Winer, *De Verborum cum Praepositionibus compositorum in NT usu*, 3 (1838), 10 f.

[8] Cf. Chrys., *ad loc.* (Hom. in Eph., 13, MPG, 62, 95 f.): ἵνα μή τις νομίσῃ, ὅτι ἐπεισάγει ἄνθρωπον ἕτερον, εἰπὼν παλαιὸν καὶ καινόν, ὅρα τί φησιν· "ἀνανεοῦσθε." ἀνανεοῦσθαί ἐστιν ὅταν αὐτὸ τὸ γεγηρακὸς ἀνανεῶται ἄλλο ἐξ ἄλλου γενόμενον ... ὁ νέος ἰσχυρός ἐστιν ... ὁ νέος ῥυτίδα οὐκ ἔχει ... ὁ νέος οὐ περιφέρεται.

† νεφέλη, † νέφος

Contents : A. The Terms in General Religious and Moral Imagery : 1. In an Emphatically Low Sense ; 2. In an Emphatically Lofty Sense. B. The Cloud as an Embodiment and Attribute of Deity. 1. The Greek and Hellenistic World ; 2. The Old Testament : a. The Cloud in Theophany ; b. The Cloud in Rapture ; c. The Cloud in the Story of the Covenant ; d. The Cloud in Belief in the Creator ; 3. Judaism (including the Mandaeans); 4. The New Testament : a. The Cloud in Nature Theology ; b. The Cloud in the Wilderness ; c. The Cloud in Theophany (the Transfiguration); d. The Cloud in Apotheosis (the Ascension); e. The Cloud in Eschatology.

Both words are old. [1] At first they are predominantly poetic, rare in inscr. and pap. [2] There is no distinction of meaning, though both differ from ὁμίχλη "mist" (Aristot. Meteor., I, 9, p. 346b, 33) and ἀχλύς "haze." They mean "cloud," also "mass," "heap" (νέφος Τρώων, Hom. Il., 16, 66, ἀνθρώπων, Hdt., VIII, 109, [3] and as hapax legomenon in the NT at Hb. 12:1). Fig. usually νεφέλη, though also νέφος : of care in Il., 17, 591, war and murder, sickness and death. In the LXX for עָנָן (clouds), עָב (lit. thicket, Jer. 4:29, LXX ἄλσος), מַאֲפֵל (only Jos. 24:7), נָשִׂיא (Jer. 10:13 etc.), שַׁחַק (cloud, Is. 40:15, dust, elsewhere for atmospheric and astronomical terms); עָנָן also σκότος in Ex. 14:20 and γνόφος in Dt. 4:11; Is. 44:22; both in Δτ 5:22. [4]

A. The Terms in General Religious and Moral Imagery.

1. In an Emphatically Low Sense.

Figurative use is little developed on Gk. soil apart from what was said → *supra*. Aristoph. calls the utopian city of the birds, the building of whose walls began with the parody of a sacrifice, [5] Νεφελοκοκκυγία, Cloud-Cuckoo-Land, Av., 818 etc. What is meant, as earlier in the *Clouds* (→ 904), is the sophistry which introduces new gods.

νεφέλη, νέφος. Roscher, *s.v.* "Nephele"; H. Kleinknecht, "Die Gebetsparodie in d. Antike," *Tüb. Beitr. z. Altertumsw.*, 28 (1937); Str.-B., esp. I, 753, 956 f.; II, 154; III, 405, 407, 635; IV, 953; Kl. Mt., Mk., Lk.; Hck. Mk., Lk. on Mt. 17:5 and par.; 24:30 and par.; Ltzm. 1 K. on 10:1 ff.; Bss., ICC, Zn., Loh., Had., *NT Deutsch* on Rev. 1:7; 10:1; 11:12; 14:14 ff.; E. Lohmeyer, "D. Verklärung Jesu nach d. Mk.-Evangelium," ZNW, 21 (1922), 185 ff., esp. 196 ff.

[1] Walde-Pok., I, 131: νεφέλη Lat. *nebula*, Old High German *nebul*, νέφος Sansk. *nábhas* ("mist," "clouds," "heaven"), Old Slavic, *nebo* ("heaven").

[2] For νέφος (cf. Epigr. Graec., 375 for νεφέλη) Moult.-Mill. give only two instances from inscr.: Epigr. Graec., 1028, 68 (Isis hymn of Andros, 1st cent. B.C.) and 1068, 2 (6th cent. A.D.?). Neither word is in Preisigke Wört. The only instance from the pap. known so far is in an epiclesis of 'Esiês (→ I, 533) who was impelled three days and three nights, surrounded by the waves of the sea καὶ ὑπὸ τῆς τοῦ ἀέρος νεφέλης (Preis. Zaub., V, 277 f. = P. Lond., I, 46, 266 [p. 73]).

[3] For further examples cf. F. Bleek Hb., *ad loc.* By way of exception νεφέλη seems to come close to this meaning in Apc. Pt. 25 : ἐπέκειντο δὲ αὐτοῖς σκώληκες ὥσπερ νεφέλαι σκότους.

[4] This sentence is by Bertram.

[5] Kleinknecht, 27 ff.

The cloud is a figure of what is extravagant. Cf. Qoh. 11:4; Philo Som., I, 54: τί δὲ βαίνων ἐπὶ γῆς ὑπὲρ νεφέλας πηδᾷς; What is transitory is like a cloud, and so is man, Job 7:9; Wis. 2:4; cf. Jm. 4:14 ἀτμίς, esp. when God's wrath lies on him, Hos. 13:3; cf. ψ 89:7 ff. Salvation slips away from him like a cloud, Job 30:15, but Yahweh also blots out transgressions like a cloud, Is. 44:22. Israel's love for its God is as fleeting as a morning cloud, Hos. 6:4. Like cloud and wind with no rain is a man who boasts of gifts and does not give, Prv. 25:14. The Gnostic heretics are νεφέλαι ἄνυδροι ὑπὸ ἀνέμων παραφερόμεναι, Jd. 12.[6] For Jesus taking note of clouds and the weather, but not of God's time, is hypocrisy, Lk. 12:54.

2. In an Emphatically Lofty Sense.

The chariots of the destroyer of the people are as swift as clouds in Jer. 4:13, but so, too, are those who bring tribute to Israel in Is. 60:8 → 907. The benevolence of the king is as refreshing as spring clouds, Prv. 16:15 (LXX erroneous). Even more so is God's mercy, Sir. 35:24. In the time of salvation the clouds will rain down righteousness, Is. 45:8. Like the cloud at an inaccessible height, God is incomprehensible, Job 35:5; cf. Bar. 3:29. "Up to the clouds" is a common comparison, of titanic human well-being, Job 20:6 (LXX erroneous); Is. 14:14; Ez. 31:3, 10, 14; Δα. 4:11; Sir. 13:23. The arrogance which reaches to the clouds contests God's honour, but God's faithfulness also reaches to the clouds, ψ 35:5; 56:10; 107:5.

B. The Cloud as an Embodiment and Attribute of Deity.

In all times and places mythical[7] imagination has been occupied with the shapes of clouds. γίγνονται πάνθ' ὅ τι βούλονται (Aristoph. Nu., 348). The religious connection of the cloud is rooted in primitive animism,[8] but it is increased by human dependence. From the cloud comes rain, lightning, hail, and destructive flood. The sinister thunder cloud is particularly numinous in its effects.

1. The Greek and Hellenistic World.

The thunder cloud seems to be personified in the Gorgons or Old Women or ἠεροφοῖτις Ἐρινύς, the storm cloud in the Harpies. There is a goddess Nephele, mother of Centauros, the father of all the Centaurs (Pind. Pyth., II, 36 ff. etc.), or more generally of the Centaurs (Diod. S., IV, 69, 5), the *nubigenae* (Verg. Aen., 7, 674). Nephele, the spouse of Athamas, sends Phrixos and Helle, when they are to be sacrificed, the golden ram (of clouds) given her by the wind god, and on this they escape through the air (Ps.-Apollodorus Bibliotheca, I, 80 ff., ed. R. Wagner, Mythographi Graeci, I [1926], p. 28 f. etc.). Nephele as a nymph accompanies Artemis (Ovid Metam., III, 171).[9]

There is no cult of the clouds in Greece. Orphism, however, makes much of them. In Orphic cosmogony the νεφέλη has a role as the origin of the male-female Phanes (Orph. Fr., 60). In a hymn there is at the offering of incense an invocation of the clouds — immediately after Zeus Astrapios — with many epithets: ὑμᾶς νῦν λίτομαι,

---

[6] In the par. 2 Pt. 2:17 we should read with ℌ οὗτοί εἰσιν πηγαὶ ἄνυδροι καὶ ὁμίχλαι (ℜ syr^ph νεφέλαι) ὑπὸ λαίλαπος ἐλαυνόμεναι.

[7] L. Laistner, *Nebelsagen* (1879), *passim*; W. Mannhardt, *Germanische Mythen* (1858), *s.v.* "Wolke"; F. W. Schwartz, *Poetische Naturanschauungen*, I and II (1864/79), *s.v.* "Wolke." On the significance of the cloud in religious history, RGG³, V, 2011 f.; Chant. de la Saussaye, *s.v.* "Wolke."

[8] Cf. RGG³, I, 346 f.; N. Söderblom, *D. Werden d. Gottesglaubens* (1916), 11.

[9] For further examples cf. Roscher, 180 ff.

δροσοείμονες, εὔπνοιοι αὔραις, | πέμπειν καρποτρόφους ὄμβρους ἐπὶ μητέρα γαῖαν (Orph., 21).

Something of a parody of this Orphic worship is to be found in the *Clouds* of Aristoph. Here Socrates initiates Strepsiades into the mystery of sophistry, and he directs a prayer (Nu., 263 ff.),[10] a travesty of Homeric and liturgical formulae, to the σεμναὶ θεαὶ Νεφέλαι βροντησικέραυνοι. The latter fulfil the request for their appearance (266, 269 ff.) as a chorus of women (275 ff.). When Socrates lauds them as dispensers of sophistry and dialectic and enlightens Strepsiades on the manner of their appearance (317 f., 331 ff., 346 ff.), Strepsiades also greets them: χαίρετε τοίνυν, ὦ δέσποιναι (356 f.). They then complain that to them alone among the gods there is no sacrifice although they prevent wars by thunder and lightning (575 ff.), and they promise to those who venerate them the blessing of rain and protection against cloud-burst and hail, and to their detractors all kinds of hurt (1118 ff.). The aim of the poet is not, however, to establish a cult of the clouds. The clouds represent the new gods of sophistry. The latter is pilloried as the pace-maker of the demagogy of Cleon (581). Socrates, a well-known oddity, already (*c.* 424) suspected of ἀσέβεια, offers a useful target. In reality he was no true sophist, much less μετεωροσοφιστής or ἄθεος. The author was mistaken.

A cult of the clouds was impossible in Greece because the cloud was already at an early period an attribute of deity. Acc. to Paus., VIII, 38, 4 a primitive rain magic was associated with Zeus Lycaios. The νεφεληγερέτης (Hom. Il., 1, 511 etc.) is also the κελαινεφής (1, 397 etc.). Orphism itself often places the clouds at the service of the supreme deity which is personally invoked (Bromios, Orph. Fr., 248a, 6 and 12; the obscure refs. are perhaps to Zeus, 256 and 270, 1). The people says: ὗε Ζεύς (Il., 12, 25). The cloud is the tent in which the deity conceals itself. The guards are the Horae, τῇς ἐπιτέτραπται μέγας οὐρανὸς Οὔλυμπός τε, | ἠμὲν ἀνακλῖναι πυκινὸν νέφος ἠδ᾽ ἐπιθεῖναι Il., 5, 750 f.; 8, 394 f. Gods who wish to watch a battle or unite in love on mountain tops conceal themselves in clouds, Il., 20, 150; 14, 343 ff. ἠέρα ἑσσαμένω Hera and Hypnos hasten to Ida, 14, 282. Apollo and Iris find Zeus wrapped in a cloud on Gargaron, 15, 153. The idea is spiritualised in Orphism: αὐτὸν (Zeus) δ᾽ οὐχ ὁρόω· περὶ γὰρ νέφος ἐστήρικται. | πᾶσιν γὰρ θνητοῖς θνηταὶ κόραι εἰσὶν ἐν ὄσσοις, | ἀσθενέες δ᾽ ἰδέειν Δία τὸν πάντων μεδέοντα, Orph. Fr., 245, 14 ff.; cf. 247, 20 ff. The gods also conceal their assistants and favourites in clouds (often ἀήρ), e.g., Aphrodite and Paris, Il., 3, 380 f., or Hephaistos and Idaios, 5, 23, or Apollo and Hector, 20, 444, or Athene and Odysseus, Od., 7, 15 and 41; cf. also 23, 372. Mythology can envisage the concealment of whole districts or fleets by clouds, Od., 13, 189; 8, 561 f. The helmet of Cyclops, like the hat of Odin or the cloud-cap of German mythology,[11] can make the wearer invisible, Hes. Scutum Herculis, 227. Eustath. Thessal. Comm. in Il., p. 613, 24 f. calls it νέφος τι πυκνότατον. Finally the cloud is the chariot of the gods which leads the hero to them. It falls on Oeta and takes up Heracles in thunder and lightning to heaven, Apollodor. Bibliotheca, II, 160, ed. R. Wagner, Mythographi Graeci, I (1926), p. 99.

Numinous experiences are less prominent in Hellenism. In later writers the cloud has a stylised part in divine appearances or journeys, Ovid. Metam., V, 251; Horat. Carm., I, 2, 31. But it does not occur in the Mithr. Liturg.[12] or even in the cosmogony of Hermes mysticism.[13] The cloud is demythologised and partly despiritualised, partly spiritualised. Its place is taken by the → στοιχεῖα.

---

[10] Kleinknecht, 21 ff.

[11] J. Grimm, *Deutsche Mythologie*, I⁴ (1875), 383 f. has drawn attention to the analogy. The *helkappe* may carry a ref. to the underworld, though *helm* is also related to *helan* as *hut* is to *huoten*. Cf. the Old Norse *hialmr huliz* (a name for cloud in the Edda).

[12] Cf. index.

[13] Neither word is in the index to Corp. Herm.

2. The Old Testament.

The course taken in the OT is externally much the same, but here the very different understanding of God may be detected even in the "mythological" elements. This means that the "demythologisation" is also unique.

a. The Cloud in Theophany. In the Song of Deborah there is a depiction of the appearance of Yahweh in the thunderstorm, Ju. 5:4 f.; cf. Job 38:1. One might also refer to Ps. 18 with its use of ancient motifs. Dark clouds are Yahweh's tent (Ps. 18:11 = 2 S. 22:12), though He dispels them by His radiance (v. 12). Yahweh emerges from clouds in Ez. 1:4, cf. 1:28 and Zech. 2:17 LXX, with its distinctive theology. The cover of cloud is represented as so dense that the question is raised whether He sees what goes on on earth, Job 22:13 f., or whether man's prayer reaches Him, Sir. 35:16 f.; Lam., 3:44, cf. 56. The cloud fills the temple as the hem of His garment, 1 K. 8:10 f.; 2 Ch. 5:13 f.; Ez. 10:3 f.; cf. Is. 6:1. The splendour of the rainbow encircles His form, Ez. 1:28. The cloud is His chariot, Is. 19:1; Ps. 104:3, or the dust of His feet, Na. 1:3. This is also to be found in more or less eschatological statements or enthronement psalms, Zeph. 1:15; Jl. 2:2; Ez. 30:3; 34:12; 38:9; 2 Macc. 2:8; Ps. 97:2; Wis. 5:21: the clouds as God's bow. The majesty of the descriptions far surpasses what is found in paganism. Moreover the God hereby depicted is the one holy God in the absolute. The deceptions of pagan gods have no place. If heavenly beings share the glory of Yahweh in the clouds, it is only in subordination to Him. This is true of the one like unto the Son of Man in the vision in Da. 7:13. As a visionary embodiment of theocracy in distinction from worldly powers, he comes with the clouds of heaven (so also Θ, LXX with the more Hellen. ἐπὶ τῶν νεφελῶν). He receives all power [14] from the Ancient of days (God).

b. The Cloud in Rapture. In the two rapture stories of the OT (Enoch in Gn. 5:24, Elijah in 2 K. 2:1 ff.), there is no express mention of a cloud. But the first of the two has no details, and behind the heavenly chariot of the second (possibly plur. acc. to 6:17) there undoubtedly stands the storm cloud (רֶכֶב־אֵשׁ וְסוּסֵי אֵשׁ v. 11, סְעָרָה v. 1, 11). If the story makes a much deeper impression than that of the taking up of Heracles (→ 904), this is because of the incomparable depiction, not unlike that of the ascension of Jesus (→ 909), and the figure of Elijah himself.

c. The Cloud in the Story of the Covenant. It is the covenant God who conceals and manifests Himself in the cloud. P shows this already in the story of Noah, Gn. 9:13 ff. → III, 340. The manifestation of Yahweh in the cloud is in all the narratives a characteristic feature of the account of the wilderness wandering.

The pillar of cloud (עַמּוּד עָנָן, στῦλος [τῆς] νεφέλης) points the way on the march out of Egypt, Ex. 13:21 f. On the passage through the Red Sea it rests protectively and menacingly between Israel and its enemies, Ex. 14:19 ff. It accompanies the people throughout the journeyings, Nu. 14:14; 10:36 LXX (Mas. 34). At each special revelation it rests on the tent of meeting, Ex. 33:9 f.; 40:34; Lv. 16:2; Dt. 31:15 etc. It gives the sign for breaking camp, Ex. 40:36 f.; Nu. 9:15 ff. It serves each individual theophany which is significant in the history of the covenant, Ex. 16:10; 34:5; Nu. 11:25; 17:7; 14:10 LXX. Above all, at the making of the covenant the dark cloud, with lightning, on the top of the mountain conceals and displays the presence of Yahweh, Ex. 19:16; 24:15 ff.; Dt. 5:19(22); Ex. 19:13, LXX much abbreviated. In later writings there are constant refs. to these accounts, Ps. 77:18; 78:14; 99:7; 105:39; cf. Sir. 24:4; Ps. 78:23 f. A renewal is promised for the time of salvation, Is. 4:5; 2 Macc. 2:8.

---

14 There is no room here to discuss detailed exposition, esp. the question whether the Iranian myth of the primal man stands behind the description.

If there is here an obvious belief in miracle, there can be no doubt as to the movement from mythology, through legend, to history.

d. The Cloud in Belief in the Creator. The OT belief in creation is nourished and strengthened by the historical leading of the covenant people. Already at an early date dependence on cloud and rain takes on deeper religious significance than in the Greek world, 1 K. 18:44 f.; cf. 17:1; 18:1; Is. 5:6, → 904. There thus develops a view of nature which sees in the cloud, as an integral part of the course of nature, the power and glory of Yahweh, and in such a way that the God of the historical covenant relation is recalled.

In Jer. Yahweh is contrasted with idols as the One who gathers the clouds together, 10:13; 51:16. In various ways Job says that Yahweh stretches out and separates the clouds (LXX usually νέφος), 36:29; 37:16, LXX with its own distinctive theology. He gives them to the sea as clothing (38:9), binds the cosmic waters in them (26:8), and creates dew and rain therein (36:27 f.; 37:11; 38:37). Cf. also the Ps. (ψ 134:7; 146:8), Prv. (3:20; 8:28), Da. (Δα. 3:73), Ep. Jer. (61) and Sir. (43:14 f.). The norm of demythologisation is not rationalism, but the concrete personality of the historical covenant God. ψ 88:7 might be mentioned in this connection.

3. Judaism (including the Mandaeans).

If the mythological view of clouds is not prominent in Judaism, neither is that of nature theology. Interest is now entirely focused on the miraculous cloud of the wilderness and the last days.

Philo in Vit. Mos., I, 200 regards regular meteorological phenomena as par. to the raining down of manna and links the plagues of Egypt with the clouds, Vit. Mos., I, 118 : νεφῶν ῥήξεις, I, 123 : darkness because of the closing in of clouds. He also speaks of the pillar of cloud. A hyparch of the great king was invisibly present in this, Vit. Mos., I, 166. It formed the rearguard at the Red Sea, I, 178, cf. 176 and II, 254; it was a σκεπαστήριον καὶ σωτήριον τῶν φίλων, ἀμυντήριον καὶ κολαστήριον τῶν ἐχθρῶν ὅπλον, Rer. Div. Her., 203. In this way God differentiates the good from the bad. At Sinai the cloud stood with its foot on earth and its body reaching in fire and smoke to heaven as a sign that everything stands in Yahweh's service, Decal., 44. To the rationalist Joseph. the ref. to the miraculous cloud is a difficulty. At the passage of the Red Sea and the dedication of the tent of revelation he omits it (Ant., 2, 320 ff.; 3, 207: fire from the altar). At Sinai the cloud, with storm and rain, thunder and lightning, lies over the camp of the Israelites rather than the mountain. But the writer is not at ease here. He makes the excuse that each must form his own opinion, but he himself has to tell what is in the sacred books, 3, 79-81. In fact he does not do this. He weakens the account whenever possible, so that the final result is a bizarre exaggeration of the miracle. God revealed His presence in the tent of meeting. The whole sky was clear, but over the tent was a cloud, not as dense as a winter raincloud, but not so light that one could see through it. A sweet dew flowed from it, Ant., 3, 203. When Moses came to leave the earth, at the entrance to a ravine a cloud suddenly stood over him. He himself wrote in the Scriptures that he died, but he did so merely to prevent any question of his apotheosis, Ant., 4, 326.

Apocalyptic and Rabb. Judaism show little interest in the cloud, cf. Eth. En. 18:5; 41:3 f.; 60:20; bChag., 12b [15] for a cosmic-apocalyptic view, Eth. En. 2:3 for nature theology and 100:11 for the standpoint of practical religion. The visionary significance of the cloud is not forgotten, Eth. En. 14:8; 108:4. The vision of the clouds in S. Bar. 53-74 depicts salvation history from creation to the Messiah. The real interest is in the wonderful cloud of the wilderness and the last time. The former is multiplied to seven or

[15] Str.-B., III, 532.

thirteen, while other Rabb. reduce the number to four or two, and it is said of the cloud which goes before that it smites scorpions and serpents, levels out the ground and rushes and leaps on ahead of the people, M. Ex., 13, 21.[16] Even more imaginative is the description of the last time. On the basis of Da. 7:13 it is often maintained that the Messiah will come with the clouds of heaven, → 905. The oldest instance is 4 Esr. 13:1 ff. Cf. also many Rabb., R. Jehoshua b. Levi (*c.* 250) with the characteristic observation: If they have merits, he comes with the clouds of heaven; if they have none, he comes lowly and riding on an ass (bSanh., 98a).[17] The cloud is also the vehicle of Israel in the time of salvation, Is. 60:8. Jerusalem and the Israelites will mount up on a cloud to the 7th heaven, to the throne of glory, Tanch. B צו § 16 (10b/11a).[18] But the place of salvation is still earth. From Is. 66:23, along with 60:8, one may conclude that Israelites all the world over will be brought back on clouds to Jerusalem and their native cities for worship each new moon and Sabbath, and twice the same day if the new moon falls on the Sabbath, Pesikt. r., 1 (2a).[19]

The cloud has even more fantastic significance for the Mandaeans. The "great first cloud of light"[20] is the place of original life. The *škīnās* of radiance are set up in the clouds.[21] The clouds serve as seats for exalted beings.[22] These appear in a cloud of splendour.[23] He who has a share in the divine glory will be enveloped in a cloud of radiance, so Hibil,[24] also the perfected soul.[25] To the Nasoraean, who holds the *pandāmā*[26] as he effects baptism, there will one day come the cloud which comes to the *uthras.*[27] On the other hand, dark clouds conceal the guard-houses of the she-devil Rūhā.[28] If numinous experiences still lie behind this wild growth of fantasy, there is a profound difference from the OT. In the OT the dark cloud is a sign of the intrinsically inaccessible God who graciously offers Himself in fellowship. Here, however, the dark and light clouds are apportioned to evil and good powers. The cloud of radiance meets a need for display.

4. The New Testament.

What the NT says about the cloud in theologically significant passages seems at a first glance to be a mixture of OT, Jewish and Hellenistic motifs. But closer examination shows the distinctiveness of NT usage.

a. The Cloud in Nature Theology. This aspect is not found in the NT, though there is, of course, belief in the One who sets the clouds, the air and the winds their appointed courses and paths. Mt. 5:45 is a formal parallel to Ζεὺς ὕει, → 904. But the connection between the rain-cloud, the love of God for His enemies and man's love for his enemies is very different from the nature theology of Hellenism[29] and finds no parallel in relatively similar Rabbinic statements.[30] Again, in Ac. 14:17 we find neither a weakened mythology nor nature theology but

[16] *Ibid.*, 405; cf. 407; II, 154.
[17] *Ibid.*, I, 956 f.
[18] *Ibid.*, III, 635.
[19] *Ibid.*, 635 f.
[20] Lidz. Liturg., 73, 1.
[21] Lidz. Ginza R., II, 1, 11 (p. 32).
[22] *Ibid.*, XVII, 1, 374 (p. 401 f.).
[23] *Ibid.*, III, 116 (p. 130); XI, 266 (p. 264).
[24] *Ibid.*, XV, 2, 304 (p. 302).
[25] *Ibid.*, L., III, 21, 104 (p. 546) etc.
[26] The end of the turban hanging down to the left.
[27] Lidz. Liturg., 59, 11.
[28] Lidz. Ginza R., V, 3, 182 (p. 186).
[29] Ethical par. in Sen., e.g., Ben., I, 1, 9 and 11; I, 2, 5.
[30] Str.-B., I, 374.

the self-attestation of the God of revelation as a summons to conversion, v. 15.[31] The combining of concreteness and universalism is neither Hellenistic nor Jewish.[32]

b. The Cloud in the Wilderness (→ 905 f.). This is expressly mentioned in the NT only at 1 C. 10:1 ff., again in close connection with the passage through the Red Sea. Worth noting here is the typological and soteriological interpretation. The properties of the cloud to which Judaism refers (→ 906 f.) are not mentioned. Instead, the cloud is a type of baptism into Christ; it is thus recognised to involve a genuine encounter with God. But as Paul avoids gross materialising of baptism and the Lord's Supper, so materialising of the cloud is remote from his thinking. God had no pleasure in most of those who were baptised in the cloud because of their disobedience. They fell in the wilderness and did not reach the goal, vv. 5 ff. Sacramental grace is not a talisman for unconditional salvation; it sets us before the final decision.[33]

c. The Cloud in Theophany (→ 905). This is found in a different form in the NT, where there are no true theophanies, though → ἶρις, III, 341. The garment of the angel of revelation in Rev. 10:1 is a cloud.[34] One may perhaps assume that the vision had a basis in nature.[35] But the στῦλοι πυρός also remind us of Ex. 13:21. It might be that the divine, like Philo (→ 906), saw in the cloud in the wilderness a concealed angel. In the story of the transfiguration of Jesus we also read: καὶ ἐγένετο νεφέλη ἐπισκιάζουσα αὐτοῖς (Mk. 9:7 and par.).[36]

Cf. Ex. 24:15 ff.; 40:35. The idea is not that the cloud threw its shadow over those outside it[37] but that it enveloped God and what belonged to Him. In this case the reading αὐτῷ[38] (Jesus) is pertinent. But αὐτοῖς can be referred to Jesus with Elijah and Moses (v. 4). That the disciples were outside the cloud may be seen from the fact that acc. to all the Synoptists the heavenly voice ἐκ τῆς νεφέλης was addressed to them. Hence the meaning of Lk. 9:34b is that the disciples were afraid as the three other men were taken up to God.[39] Mt. describes the cloud as φωτεινή.[40] This expresses the kindly nature of the encounter with God in the NT, though against the background of the divine majesty (cf. also the ἐφοβήθησαν σφόδρα in Mt., v. 6). The appearance of the cloud is the divine answer to the saying of Peter in v. 5. The cloud is God's tabernacle (→ 904, 905). It is the manifestation of His presence promised for the last

---

31 M. Dibelius, "Pls. auf d. Areopag.," SAH, 1938/39, 2 (1939), cf. esp. 50 f., has justly called attention to the different emphasis in the speeches in Ac. 14:15-17 and 17:19-34 on the one side and the genuine Paul of the epistles on the other (→ III, 587). But Paul, in spite of his strong christological conception, could still adopt the concepts and formulae of Hellen. nature theology, though in the sense of accusation. Hence one cannot isolate the speeches to which we have referred from the contents of Paul's missionary preaching which have been interwoven into the narrative by the same hand, as Dibelius admits (50), and which give prominence to the christological rather than the rational element, cf. A. Oepke, *Die Missionspredigt des Ap. Pls.* (1920), 179 ff.; → III, 586.

32 Str.-B., II, 727; → 577.

33 Cf. H. v. Soden, "Sakrament u. Ethik bei Paulus," *Marburger Theol. Studien*, I (1931), esp. 23 ff., 31 ff.

34 That the cloud as a garment is unique (Loh. Apk., *ad loc.*) is an error (→ 904, 905). There is no need to think in terms of borrowing in relation to the Mandaeans.

35 So Had. and *NT Deutsch*, Apk., *ad loc.*

36 For attempts to isolate various parts of the pericope as redactional additions cf. Kl. Mk. on 9:2-13. → 25, n. 30.

37 Hck. Mk., *ad loc.*

38 Only sy^{s}, and accepted only by Wellhausen. The reading in the Athos min. 1604 Lk.: αὐτόν, pts. in the same direction, but finds no support.

39 So also Hck. Lk., *ad loc.*

40 The Ferrar group and sy^{c} read φωτός.

time (Rev. 21:3 → σκηνή). It is here a theophany. The one whom God hides in His pavilion belongs very closely to Him (Ps. 27:5). If Jesus is taken up into the cloud with the two divine messengers of the last time, this means that He brings final deliverance and that He brings it now.[41] The motif of theophany is thus deepened and broadened in the NT. Corresponding observations will be made in what follows.

d. The Cloud in Apotheosis (→ 905). What is perhaps the only NT account of the ascension of Jesus (Ac. 1:9)[42] reminds us of this. The story combines plasticity, especially for Hellenistic readers, with a chaste safeguarding of the mystery. Since the cloud simply covers the external form, the personal relation of Jesus to the disciples who watch Him go can still be maintained. This aspect is disrupted by the cruder Hellenistic reading: καὶ ταῦτα εἰπόντος αὐτοῦ νεφέλη ὑπέλαβεν αὐτὸν καὶ ἀπήρθη ἀπὸ τῶν ὀφθαλμῶν αὐτῶν. The cloud was not originally a vehicle of rapture.[43] Translated into apocalyptic, the motif recurs in Rev. 11:12.[44] The definite article shows that the use of the term is traditional here. It should be noted, however, that the cloud is more of a veil than a means of transport.

e. The Cloud in Eschatology. Familiar motifs are to be found in the eschatological use in the narrower sense. The new element is that they are now firmly linked with the person of Jesus. Along these lines Jesus warns His judges that they will see the Son of Man, i.e., Himself, coming with the clouds of heaven[45] (Mk. 14:62, corresponding to the original Da. 7:13 Θ: μετὰ τῶν νεφελῶν τοῦ οὐρανοῦ, Mt. 26:64 following LXX: ἐπὶ τῶν νεφελῶν τοῦ οὐρανοῦ, not in Lk.). The same note is to be heard in the Synoptic apocalypse (Mk. 13:26: ἐν νεφέλαις, Mt. 24:30 the same as 26:64, Lk. 21:27 more Hellenistically: ἐν νεφέλῃ). The linking of the Daniel motif with the saying in Zech. 12:10 ff., which is taken to be a threat, seems to be traditional (cf. Mt. 24:30 with Rev. 1:7: μετὰ τῶν

---

41 Lohmeyer, ZNW, *loc. cit.*

42 In Lk. 24:51 the words καὶ ἀνεφέρετο εἰς τὸν οὐρανόν do not occur in א* D it sy^s. If they are to be excised, this is not originally an account of the ascension. Mk. 16:19 is secondary. In neither verse is there any mention of the cloud.

43 Cf. A. Oepke, "Unser Glaube an d. Himmelfahrt Jesu," *Luthertum,* 49 (1938), 161 ff.

44 → μάρτυς. The suggestion that the two witnesses are James, the Lord's brother, and John, the son of Zebedee, who suffered martyrdom at the hands of the Jews contemporaneously in Jerusalem (B. W. Bacon, *The Gospel of the Hellenists* [1933], 28 f.), does not stand up to closer investigation. The ref. is again to the OT men of God who were expected as forerunners of the last day, namely, Moses (→ 869) and Elijah (v. 6), whose figures are apocalyptically magnified by the application of relevant OT stories (Ex. 7:17, 19; 1 K. 17:1) and the saying of Zech. concerning the two olive-trees (4:2 ff.), and whose end is assimilated to the perfecting of Jesus on the basis of OT accounts (Dt. 34:5 f.; 2 K. 2:1 ff.) and Jewish traditions like the Ass. Mos. (cf. Cl. Al., → III, 994; also the fragments in M. R. James, *Texts and Studies,* II, 3 [1893], 170 f., where it is said of the grave of Moses: φωτοειδὴς νεφέλη ἐπισκιάζει τὸν τόπον ἐκεῖνον, and: ἐγένετο δὲ νεφέλη καὶ σκότος κατὰ τὸν τόπον, → 906) and the Apc. Elias (ed. G. Steindorff [1899], 164). Cf. Bss., ICC, Zn., Loh., Had., *NT Deutsch, ad loc.*

45 H. Lietzmann, SAB, 1931, 313 ff. is too sceptical about the Gospel accounts of the trial of Jesus before the Sanhedrin. On questions of competence cf. F. Büchsel, ZNW, 30 (1931), 202 ff.; H. Lietzmann, *op. cit.,* 211 ff., 31 (1932), 78 ff.; M. Goguel, *op. cit.,* 289 ff.; A. Oepke, ThStKr, 105 (1933), 390 ff., and from the standpoint of form criticism M. Dibelius, ZNW, 30 (1931), 193 ff. (tending to agree with Lietzmann in rejection of the trial before the Sanhedrin, 200 f.). G. Bertram, "Die Leidensgeschichte Jesu u. der Christuskult," FRL, NF, 15 (1922), 57 accepts the historicity of the fact that "in the main Jesus ignored the accusation, but then in full prophetic power revealed Himself to His opponents with a powerful eschatological threat."

νεφελῶν). In Rev. 14:14-16 the Christ who comes again in power and glory is already described as the One who sits on the cloud. The white colour of the cloud corresponds to the fact that this coming is a heavenly triumph, → 27, 250.[46] Believers will also comes on the clouds at the *parousia,* 1 Th. 4:17 (→ ἀπάντησις, I, 380 f.).

The NT use of νεφέλη hardly differs from current usage from an external standpoint. But the consistent application to Christ gives a new significance to the ancient motifs. The cloud is a sign of the Father of Jesus Christ who in the concealment of revelation offers Himself for fellowship and victoriously establishes this fellowship. But with this new meaning the symbolical force of the word is exhausted. The known reality begins to transcend the figurative representation. Hence the term no longer has any history worth mentioning in the Church.

Oepke

[46] Acc. to Moult.-Mill., *s.v.* νεφέλη, who cites F. J. A. Hort, *The Apocalypse of St. John* (1908), p. 12, "Son of the cloud" was a Jewish term for the Messiah. A false impression is left by Loh. Apk., *ad loc.* when he quotes Lidz. Joh., 116, 15 and Apc. Pt. 6 as par. but ignores the most obvious parallels in Mt. 17:5 (→ 908) and Ass. Mos. → n. 44.

† νεφρός

An Indo-Eur. word, etym. related to the German *Niere,* cf. Lat. dial. *nefrones, nefrundines,* usually plur. "kidneys," Aristoph. Ra., 475, 1280; Lys., 962 (sing.); Plat. Tim., 91a; cf. νέφριον, P. Oxy., I, 108, I, 9. Very common in the LXX in the laws of sacrifice, where the kidneys as well as the liver and fat are to be sacrificed and to go up in smoke on the altar, Ex. 29:13; cf. 29:22; Lv. 3:4, 10, 15; 4:9 etc. In Dt. 32:14 the fat of the kidneys is lauded as most excellent and nourishing, along with other divine gifts, God's protection and care, fruits of the field and oil etc. [1] νεφρός is often used fig. for the inward part of man. The "reins" are the hidden parts, ψ 138:13 where a. grief is most bitter (Job 16:13), b. conscience sits (ψ 15:7), [2] and c. there is the deepest spiritual distress, cf. ψ 72:21, which speaks of the sorrow and inner confusion caused by the contradiction between the moral seriousness of the righteous and their external afflictions. Because only God can see the inward parts, it is said to His glory : ἐτάζων (ψ 7:9), δοκιμάζων (Jer. 11:20; 17:10), συνίων (Jer. 20:12) νεφροὺς καὶ καρδίας. God is far from the inward parts of the wicked (πόρρω ἀπὸ τῶν νεφρῶν αὐτῶν), Jer. 12:2. [3] In Philo the kidneys are mong the 7 inner parts of the body, Op. Mund., 118; cf. Leg. All., I, 12. In Spec. Leg., I, 212 ff. Philo considers the question why the liver, fat and kidneys are offered, not the heart and brain. His explanation is as follows. The heart and brain are the seat of the hegemonicon, which often grants access to all kinds of irrationality and unrighteousness. Since, then, the heart and brain are often an occasion for sin, they cannot be sacrificed on the altar, the place of forgiveness. The kidneys, on the other hand, help to sift out waste material, and "the seed created by nature finds its way unhindered," cf. esp. §§ 214-216. In Sacr. AC, 136; Spec. Leg., I, 232 and 239 Philo quotes Lv. 3:3 ff.; 4:9; 7:4 etc.

In the NT νεφρός occurs (in the plur.) only in Rev. 2:23 in quotation of Jer. 11:20 (17:10), though not accurately according to the LXX. In the suffering which God sends on false prophets and their adherents the community may see that God demands ultimate truth and purity and does not overlook the danger which threatens the faith of the community from a small circle. The total claim which God makes on the community finds expression in the OT saying that He tries the reins and the heart.

Preisker

νεφρός. [1] Kautzsch, I, *ad loc.*

[2] Cf. E. König, *Psalmen* (1927), *ad loc.*; R. Kittel, *Psalmen*[3,4] (1922), *ad loc.*

[3] The Gk. of Job 19:27 has πάντα δέ μοι instead of the Mas. כִּלְיֹתַי In Is. 34:6 νεφρός occurs only in ΑΣΘ. With no Mas. original the term also occurs in 1 Macc. 2:24; Wis. 1:6 for the innermost parts of man. Elsewhere νεφρός is used for כִּלְיָה [Bertram].

† νήπιος, † νηπιάζω

Contents: A. νήπιος in General Greek Usage. B. νήπιος in the OT. C. νήπιος in the NT: 1. Paul and Hb.; 2. Little Children in the Message of Jesus.

A. νήπιος in General Greek Usage.

For νήπιος, "immature," "foolish," no convincing derivation has yet been found. The old connection with ἔπος εἰπεῖν (with negation = Lat. *infans*),[1] and with ἤπιος, "gentle,"[2] has been given up, but interpretation as "without understanding," in terms of πινυτός, "understanding" and πινυτή, "the understanding," which is built on the apparently related Homeric νηπύτιος[3] (though this is not used of children), causes great difficulties. More likely is a link with the Ion. νηπελέω, "to be without power" etc.,[4] which gives the meaning "impotent," "weak." In fact the term comprises the concept of a child as well as that of the person who in various ways is without understanding.

In the first instance it is often used for the small child. In medical writers (Hippocrates, Galen. etc.)[5] it is used with different qualifications for the age of the foetus, the infant,[6] the small child up to 5 or 6,[7] or even the child up to the time of puberty. In general use, e.g., on burial inscr., it is used accordingly for small children from 1 to 10. Examples are to be found esp. in the Jewish catacombs of Monteverde and the Villa Torlonia in Rome.[8] (ἄωρος is used in the same way.) The death of a small child is keenly felt. It here denotes a child who has only just come to independent life. In contrast, there is the use for young orphans. Here the term signifies the weak and helpless and it arouses particular pity. In a pap. petition from c. 280 A.D.[9] etc.[10] there is a transition to legal use for minors in the sense of legal incompetence.[11]

The word is often used for the child as a member of the family, frequently with the wife or mother, cf. already Hom. Il., 5, 480. νήπιος as an attribute of υἱός can even correspond here to φίλος as an attribute of ἄλοχος. It expresses an inner personal

νήπιος κτλ.

1 Thes. Steph.

2 H. Ebeling, *Lexicon Homericum* (1880-85), *s.v.*

3 Walde-Pok., II (1927), 13.

4 F. Specht, *Zschr. f. vergl. Sprachforschung*, 56 (1928), 122 f.

5 For detailed examples cf. the lexicons.

6 E.g., Ps.-Plat., Ax., 366d: Τί μέρος τῆς ἡλικίας ἄμοιρον τῶν ἀνιαρῶν; οὐ κατὰ μὲν τὴν πρώτην γένεσιν τὸ νήπιον κλάει, τοῦ ζῆν ἀπὸ λύπης ἀρχόμενον; so also Plut. Quaest. Conv., III, 10 (p. 658 E): διὸ τὰ μὲν νήπια παντάπασιν αἱ τίτθαι δεικνύναι πρὸς τὴν σελήνην φυλάττονται, though obviously in Alex. Fort. Virt., II, 5 (II, 337d) Aridaeus, who as a child is put on the throne of Alexander, must be regarded as older.

7 Cf. also Luc. Halcyon, 5: τὰ νήπια παντελῶς βρέφη τὰ πεμπταῖα ἐκ γενετῆς ἢ δεκαταῖα.

8 H. Lietzmann-W. Beyer, *D. jüd. Katakombe d. Villa Torlonia zu Rom* (1930); N. Müller-N. Bees, *D. Inschriften d. jüd. Katakombe am Monteverde in Rom* (1919). Further instances are given esp. in relation to No. 12 and No. 42.

9 P. Ryl., II, 114, 3, cf. Moult.-Mill., *s.v.*

10 P. Tebt., II, 326, 6.

11 → 918 on Gl. 4:1 ff.

relation between father and son, e.g., 6, 366. The noun νηπιότης is also used for the age of childhood, e.g., Aristot. Probl., XI, 50, p. 896b, 6. Elsewhere in the same work (XI, 24, p. 901b, 24 ff.) the philosopher sets the nature of the young of men and animals alongside that of woman. The word can be used for the young of animals too, cf. Hom. Il., 2, 311; 11, 113; 17, 134 (cf. ינק in the OT), also of plants, e.g., Theophr. Hist. Plant., VIII, 1, 7, where the ref. is to sowing at the right time, ὅπως ἂν οἱ χειμῶνες μὴ νήπια καταλαμβάνωσιν.

But the sense of "foolish," "inexperienced," is more dominant in Gk. The ref. is often to the child who has little knowledge of the world. Or it may be to childlike or childish conduct, cf. Eur. Iph. Aul., 1243 f. Finally there is the man who, although adult, is a child in relation to the world. This is how the mocker Lucian in Halcyon, 3 explains the childlike inexperience of man (ἀπειρία and νηπιότης). Joseph. uses νηπιότης in the sense of childlike joy in Ant., 1, 287; he also uses the term in relation to the harmlessness of childlike play, 2, 233.

But from the very first the word can also be used with no obvious ref. to childhood. Hom. and Hes. use it thus. In both is found the saying ῥεχθὲν δέ τε νήπιος ἔγνω (Il., 17, 32, cf. 7, 401) or παθὼν δέ τε νήπιος ἔγνω (Hes. Op., 218). The statement is called a proverb in Plat. Symp., 222b. A man is νήπιος who in goals and conduct takes no account of reality because he lacks experience and insight. This is how we are to understand Hesiod's judgment on the men of the silver age who remained children for 100 years, Op., 130, and esp. the warning to his brother Perses, who with the majority is on the false path of apparently easy gain, and whom Hes. seeks to help back to the right path with his praise of all honest work and with this specific admonition, Op., 286 ff.: μέγα νήπιε Πέρση : τῆς δ' ἀρετῆς ἱδρῶτα θεοὶ προπάροιθεν ἔθηκαν. In Hom. it is the power of the gods, the force of destiny, which so often reveals the futility of men's thought and action. Agamemnon is νήπιος in Il., 2, 38, Patroclus in 16, 46 (cf. 833), Andromache in 22, 445, Achilles in 20, 264. For all these brave realists of the sunlit world of the heroic poet of Greece there is a dark and hidden destiny in face of which their joyous certainty in this life, the foundation of the Homeric world, is unable to stand. The man who trusts in fortune is a fool.

In the tragic poets, too, νήπιος is the antithesis of the attitude of the realist who takes account of facts in what he does and does not do, though it is often debatable on whose side the right of reality stands. Soph. El., 145 represents the standpoint of pious tradition : νήπιος, ὃς τῶν οἰκτρῶς οἰχομένων γονέων ἐπιλάθεται. The struggle is more bitter in Oed. Tyr., 652 f.: τὸν οὔτε πρὶν νήπιον νῦν τ' ἐν ὅρκῳ μέγαν καταίδεσαι. The Medea of Eur. judges herself when she says : ἐγὼ δ' ἄφρων ... οὔκουν χρῆν σ' ὁμοιοῦσθαι κακοῖς οὐδ' ἀντιτείνειν νήπι' ἀντὶ νηπίων (885, 890 f.). νήπιος and ἔννους are contrasted in Aesch. Prom., 443. In Aristoph. Pax, 1063 ff. it is obvious that man's unreason is deficient insight into the will of the gods. The limit set by destiny is transgressed herewith : σφῇσιν ἀτασθαλίῃσιν ὑπὲρ μόρον ἄλγε' ἔχουσιν, Hom. Od., 1, 34, cf. 7 f. Human hybris is guilty. The same is said in Hes. Op., 217 f.: δίκη δ' ὑπὲρ ὕβριος ἴσχει ἐς τέλος ἐξελθοῦσα. But man's bright faith in the right, which is also expressed in Hes., has to yield to a sinister belief in fate in Hom. This dark belief is the first and last word of antiquity. To trust in fortune is folly. Such foolish belief shows that man has remained a child, that he has no real experience of life no matter what his age. In a certain sense this is true of all men. Thus Epictet. (cf. Arrian), in the work περὶ τοῦ μὴ δεῖν προσπάσχειν τοῖς οὐκ ἐφ' ἡμῖν shows to man the way to freedom from bondage to fate in the admonition of the title, which follows the general outlook of the time as reflected, e.g., in the consolatory writings of Sen. In so doing he puts to the hearer or reader the question (III, 24, 53): οὕτως οὐδέποτε παύσει παιδίον ὢν νήπιον; οὐκ οἶσθ' ὅτι ὁ τὰ παιδίου ποιῶν ὅσῳ πρεσβύτερος τοσούτῳ γελοιότερος; For him obviously (III, 24, 9): οὐκ ἀπογαλακτίσομεν ἤδη ποθ' ἑαυτοὺς καὶ μεμνησόμεθα, ὧν ἠκούσαμεν παρὰ τῶν φιλοσόφων; (cf. also II, 16, 39). Philosophers lead to a true knowledge of the world. He who does not follow them is a νήπιος, a fool. Thus Empedocles in Περὶ φύσεως

(Fr., 11, 1 [I, 313, Diels[5]]) says of those who do not accept his doctrine of the mixing and separating of material which is always the same in amount: νήπιοι, ... οἳ δὴ γίγνεσθαι πάρος οὐκ ἐὸν ἐλπίζουσιν ἤ τι καταθνῄσκειν τε καὶ ἐξόλλυσθαι ἁπάντῃ, "They are fools who believe that something which did not exist can arise or that anything can die and completely perish." This hard judgment does not have its source merely in the pride of an opinion. It is passed on the ground of practical consequences. At any rate the most important place of such a judgment is in practical wisdom. The man who has not come to terms with life and who does not know how to meet death is a νήπιος. One is thus bound irrevocably to philosophical insight: παρεπιδημία τίς ἐστιν ὁ βίος, καὶ ὅτι δεῖ ἐπιεικῶς διαγαγόντας εὐθύμως μόνον οὐχὶ παιανίζοντας εἰς τὸ χρεὼν ἀπιέναι; τὸ δὲ οὕτω μαλακῶς καὶ δυσαποσπάστως ἔχειν νηπίου δίκην οὐ περὶ φρονοῦσαν ἡλικίαν ἔχειν, as Ps.-Plat. Ax. writes (365b) in a dialogue which is devoted to the problem of death. Already here we are on the way to Sen. and Epictet. But we are also confronted by the claim of this worldly wisdom to solve the final problems of life, a claim which each philosopher naturally advanced for himself. Thus Plut., 960d writes of Dio: οὕτω διελέχθη ... ὥστε τοὺς ἄλλους ἅπαντας τῇ μὲν φρονήσει παῖδας ἀποδεῖξαι. This is also how a Lucian deals with Christianity in Peregr. Mort., 11: σοφίαν τῶν Χριστιανῶν ἐξέμαθε ... ἐν βραχεῖ παῖδας αὐτοὺς (Christian priests and scholars) ἀπέφηνε προφήτης καὶ θιασάρχης καὶ ξυναγωγεὺς καὶ πάντα μόνος αὐτὸς ὤν. In the eyes of the Hell. philosopher Christians are really νήπιοι. That they wish to be so is what really evokes scorn and contempt. Not merely for apologetic reasons, but for its own sake and that of the Gospel, 1st century Christian theology had to struggle seriously for the true content and use of this concept.

B. νήπιος in the Old Testament.

What does νήπιος mean in the Bible? The LXX gives the first answer. νήπιος is used 31 times with a Mas. original, and once in Sir. and 16 times in Jdt., Wis., Macc. with no Heb. basis. It usually denotes children in age, weakness and helplessness, esp. in times of war and persecution (Wis. 11:7: νηπιοκτόνος of Pharaoh acc. to Ex. 1:16, 22; cf. Wis. 18:5). From this source ἀναμάρτητα νήπια came into the vocabulary of Christian martyrdom and secured a firm historical basis in connection with the slaughter of the innocents by Herod (cf. e.g., the νήπια παίζοντα μικρά in Paradise acc. to Act. Andr. et Matth.[12] and Mart. Mt., 1). In addition to the verse already mentioned (18:5), Wis. uses νήπιος 3 times with ref. to the nature of a child in the sense of lacking true understanding (12:24 with ἄφρων; 15:14;[13] 10:21; cf. ψ 8:2).

In the translation Gk. of the OT the presence of different senses is to be explained first in terms of different Heb. originals.

There are obviously two main groups. In the one the meaning is "child," in the other "simple." None of the Heb. terms corresponds wholly to the Gk. νήπιος. Among Heb. originals there are 4 words for "child," of which יוֹנֵק and עוּל denote infant. טַף denotes the pattering child, נַעַר perhaps the change of voice, i.e., the time of puberty. None of the words is definitely affixed to a specific age. Hence the translators proceed somewhat arbitrarily acc. to their own assessment of the context.

The verb עוּל is used in the OT only 4 times for suckling animals, but many derived nouns occur in the sense of child or boy. עֲוִיל is either misunderstood by the LXX (Job 19:18; 21:11 αἰώνιος, עולם for עוילים), or it is derived from the similar root עָוַל, "to act wickedly," and translated ἄδικος in Job 16:11.[14] At Job 19:18 Θ has ἄφρων,

[12] In Bonnet, II, 1, Praef. XXII.
[13] Cf. Is. 44:9 ff.
[14] One might argue for a development of meaning from child to (insolent) scamp, as in the case of מְעוֹלֵל (only Is. 3:12). *Ad loc.* the LXX has only the gen. sense. Cf. Ges.-Buhl, *s.v.*

and Σ acc. to the Syr. tradition has βρέφη at 21:11, ἐπίγονος being also attested for another transl. For עוּל, which occurs only in Is. 49:15 and 65:20, the LXX has παιδίον in the former case and ἄωρος in the latter, cf. the use of ἄωρος and νήπιος on Jewish Gk. burial inscr. (→ 912).[15] עוֹלֵל (מְעוֹלֵל) or עוֹלָל means a "little child," and it is usually rendered νήπιος in the LXX (16 times), though sometimes τέκνον or ὑποτίτθιον. Of the Hexapla translators Σ seems to have preferred νήπιος and 'Α βρέφος; ἔμβρυον is attested once for Θ. עֲלִילָה is obviously presupposed in Mi. 2:9 : πονηρὸν ἐπιτήδευμα.

The LXX uses νήπιος for עוֹלָל in various senses. The expression עוֹלָלִים וְיֹנְקִים is regularly transl. νήπιος (-οι) καὶ θηλάζων (-οντες). Cf. 1 Βασ. 15:3; 22:19; 4 Βασ. 8:12; Nah. 3:10; Hos. 14:1 Σ; ψ 136:9; Jer. 6:11 etc.; Jl. 2:16; ψ 16:14.

In Job 3:16 there is the idea of those not yet born, as in the Gk. physicians.[16] The ref. in Ps. 8:2 is to a miracle. It is debatable whether the LXX correctly renders the Mas. or whether the Mas. preserves the original Heb. Can עֹז mean praise, and how is מִפִּי to be construed? Attempts have been made to take it prepositionally like מִפְּנֵי (on account of children and infants).[17] Or the Mas. has been emended: "Out of the mouths of children thou dost rebuke the insolent"[18] (עָז for עֹז). The LXX and Heb. would then be in basic agreement except that the LXX read עֹז and took it subjectively in the sense of acknowledgement of power, i.e., glory or praise. With θηλάζων νήπιος can only mean a small child which cannot speak. God makes lisping infants His witnesses to put His enemies to shame (cf. Wis. 10:21). The opposite may be found in ψ 63:8, 9 where the ungodly are as weak as children.

In the OT ינק is more common than עול. It means in the qal "to suck" and in the hi caus. "to suckle." In the Gk. OT it is usually rendered θηλάζειν, which in the act. can mean both. Oddly enough the word is also used of plants. Thus in Is. 53:2[19] the LXX has παιδίον, 'Α τιθηνιζόμενον, Θ θηλάζον and Σ κλάδος.[20] νήπιος is used for יוֹנֵק only at Is. 11:8. The Heb. has גָּמוּל (weaned child) in parallelism, but the LXX has the comprehensive rendering: καὶ παιδίον νήπιον ἐπὶ τρώγλην ἀσπίδων καὶ ἐπὶ κοίτην ἐκγόνων ἀσπίδων τὴν χεῖρα ἐπιβαλεῖ.[21] A sign of the time of salvation is found in the fact that the harmlessness of a child, who is ignorant of the dangers of the wicked world, is not disappointed but in the new creation proves to be the right attitude.

טַף means collectively "(little) children" along with young men and girls or women, and it is a common term for the whole family or for camp-followers. The term derives from טפף, which seeks to represent the pattering of children. In the OT the verb is used only at Is. 3:16 of mincing women. παίζω seems to be the rendering in the LXX. In the stories of the wanderings of the patriarchs and people the LXX often has ἀποσκευή for טַף, and acc. to context we find σῶμα, οἰκία, συγγένεια, and more commonly παιδία, τέκνα or ἔκγονα. The others, specifically 'Α, usually have νήπια, which occurs in the LXX only at Ez. 9:6. Used for טַף, νήπιος means children generally and indefinitely; it includes all who do not bear arms. The LXX avoided this imprecise use.

---

15 This corresponds to the context: None will die an untimely death in the new Jerusalem.

16 Θ ἔμβρυον.

17 G. E. Paulus, *Commentar* (1812) on Mt. 21:16. So far as I have been able to see, he found no supporters. Gottfried Kittel, Chr. W., 52 (1938), 740 has the rendering: "Children who are as a breath."

18 Omit יונקים and put יִסַּרְתָּ for יסדת, so H. Gunkel, *Die Psalmen* (1913), cf. H. Grimme.

19 K. F. Euler, *Die Verkündigung vom leidenden Gottesknecht aus Js. 53 in d. gr. Bibel* (1934), 12 ff.

20 Ges.-Buhl lists 8 instances for יוֹנֵק.

21 Or should ἔκγονος correspond to גָּמוּל?

The context gives precision in Ez. 9:6, where the ref. is to innocent and helpless infants who fall under God's wrath along with all the ungodly inhabitants of the city. The pitiless severity of the divine judgment is expressed herein. In Est. 3:13; 8:11 and Ιερ. 50:6 νήπιος does not seem to be part of the original LXX.[22]

נַעַר, "boy," is usually rendered παιδάριον in Gk., also παῖς and παιδίον, νέος, νεανίας, and occasionally διάκονος. Twice in Prv. 23:13 and Hos. 11:1 it is the original of νήπιος. The ref. in Prv. 23:13 it to the young man in process of education who is subjected to discipline in order that he may not fall victim to sin and death (Dt. 21:18 ff.). This is a thought characteristic of OT wisdom, cf. Prv. 13:24; 29:15 etc.[23] Sir. 30:12, and 30:1-13 as a whole, may also be cited here. In the LXX the one word νήπιος represents the par. Heb. נערות and קטן. Severity does not rule out love; it presupposes it, 30:1. In Hos. 11:1 νήπιος is a simple term for youth. When Israel was young, Yahweh loved it. He treated it as a son. The LXX applies the term historically to the early days of the people and in what follows speaks of the sons of the people rather than of Israel as Yahweh's son. In OT tradition the early days, the wilderness period, are often regarded as the normative sinless age. Later the people came under the influence of the Canaanites and fell into sin and idolatry. νήπιος expresses rather more clearly than נַעַר the childlike innocence of the people in that early period.

The noun נְעוּרִים is usually rendered → νεότης (some 40 times). In Hos. 2:17; Ez. 16:22, 43, 60 we find νηπιότης, which elsewhere in the Gk. Bible occurs only in 'A. Here, as in Hos. 11:1, the ref. is to the youth of the people in its innocence and helplessness. Once νήπιος is also used for נֹעַר, which is present only 4 times in the Mas. Job 33:25 speaks of the deliverance of the man who is already a victim of death. His youth is restored to him. He becomes like a child again. This is manifested in his rejuvenated love.

All these verses are related even acc. to the Heb. original. They do not express any preconceived or derogatory view of the nature of the child.[25] Such a view is not naturally expressed by the word νήπιος. On the contrary, the OT use of this word with ref. to children rules out any such conception.

The position is different, however, when the term occurs in connection with the concept of simplicity expressed in the underlying root פתה. This root can be taken in both a good sense and a bad. Thus the adj. or noun פֶּתִי, which occurs three times in the Ps., once in Ez., elsewhere only in Prv., is eight times rendered ἄφρων (ἀφροσύνη), five times ἄκακος and five νήπιος, which is always used in the good sense in the LXX. How different the conception may be is apparent in Prv. 1:22. Here the LXX independently gives the saying a positive sense which does not correspond to the Mas. at all. This may be seen from the continuation, where פֶּתִי is set in parallelism to לֵץ and כְּסִיל, whereas the LXX puts the corresponding Gk. expressions in antithesis to the first part of the verse. Since the context as a whole speaks of instruction by wisdom, only an admonition to the simple seems to fit in smoothly. Hence the warning to mockers and fools has been regarded as an addition to the Heb.[26] 'A rightly reproduces the sense of the Mas. Here νήπιος is taken in a negative and censorious sense: ἕως πότε, νήπιοι, ἀγαπᾶτε νηπιότητα; Cf. also 1:32 Σ: ὅτι ἀποστροφὴ νηπίων ἀνελεῖ αὐ-

[22] Cf. the MSS.

[23] G. Bertram, "D. Begriff d. Erziehung in d. gr. Bibel," Imago Dei. *Festschrift f. G. Krüger* (1932), 36 f. → παιδεία.

[24] Job 24:12 and 31:10, where the LXX itself introduces νήπιος, are to be understood along the same lines.

[25] Cf. R. Renner, "D. Kind, ein Gleichnismittel bei Epiktet," *Festschrift des Hist.-philol. Vereins,* Munich (1905), 54 ff.

[26] So K. Steuernagel in E. Kautzsch. B. Gemser, *Sprüche Salomos* (1927), *ad loc.* omits 22c on metrical grounds.

τούς. Here, too, νήπιος has a negative sense, and 32b is par. in both form and content, as in the Mas.: καὶ εὐθηνία ἀφρόνων ἀπολεῖ αὐτούς. The LXX, however, takes 32a quite differently: ἀνθ' ὧν γὰρ ἠδίκουν νηπίους, φονευθήσονται, and it has to understand 32b accordingly: καὶ ἐξετασμὸς ἀσεβεῖς ὀλεῖ. In other places the Σ has νήπιος where the LXX uses ἄφρων. Thus 9:4 Mas. is a warning of wisdom to the simple to come to it and be instructed. Here the LXX uses ἄφρων, since νήπιος does not denote intellectual deficiency in its use of the term. Cf. also 9:16. In 14:15 the LXX has ἄκακος in a censorious sense, but Σ has νήπιος and 'Α θελγόμενος, which here as often is the most literal rendering of the root פתה ("to seduce"), LXX ἀπατᾶν, πλανᾶν. In 21:11 פֶּתִי is to be taken in the sense of one who can be instructed. Here, too, the LXX has ἄκακος and Σ νήπιος.

The distinctive LXX use of νήπιος is most clearly evident in the Ps. The righteous man who is under God's special protection is νήπιος. God is He who gives wisdom to the simple, ψ 18:7. He it is who protects and keeps the innocent, 114:6. He enlightens the simple by His revelation and gives them understanding, 118:130. Thus the thought of the original is sharpened. νήπιος has now become one of the dialectical terms for the righteous which are peculiar to the biblical revelation. The derogatory and critical description of the righteous as νήπιοι in a worldly sense is adopted and transmuted. Thus νήπιος is set alongside ἀσθενής, πτωχός, μικρός, also ἄπειρος and ἁπλοῦς. The closest par. to this usage, however, is to be found in the use of → μωρός in Paul.[27]

In the LXX, then, νήπιος bears a twofold sense. On the one hand it denotes the weak and innocent child who is helplessly implicated in the world's misfortune. On the other hand it denotes the righteous who are simple as the world sees it. The two meanings flow together in the emphatic use of the word in the Gospel of Jesus. In the Pauline sphere, however, other influences have obviously to be taken into account as well as the biblical presuppositions.

C. νήπιος in the New Testament.

1. Paul and Hb.

There is no uniform use of the term in the NT. One has to differentiate between the use in the Gospel tradition, which is based on the OT and is genuinely theological, and the use in Pl. and Hb., which is more ethical and pedagogic.

In detail Pl. fitted the word into his thinking in many different ways. In the first instance νήπιος is always connected with the idea of the child. But he has in view, not the child in the absolute, but the child in a specific connection. Cf. 1 C. 14:20.[28] It is childish of the Corinthians to stress unduly a spiritual gift which is outwardly so impressive, but inwardly of so little significance, as speaking in tongues.[29] Here at least the summons: "Become as little children" (Mt. 18:3), is not applicable, though it is sounded frequently in Christian preaching in Corinth too. The summons does apply, of course, when it is a question of the malice and wickedness in which children have no part. The νηπιάζειν (the only use of the verb in the Bible) is essentially negative like ἄκακος or ἄπειρος. The child does not yet have the instructive but in many cases corrupting experience of the

[27] The word can hardly be original in Ez. 45:20 A, where with ἀγνοῶν it has ref. to sins of ignorance. B here has ἀπόμοιρα, which denotes a share in the offering.
[28] Cf. R. 16:19.
[29] Cf. H. Grotius, *ad loc.*: *puerorum est se ostentare rebus inutilibus.*

wickedness of the world and the malice of man. Hence the child can serve as a model.

Childlikeness,[30] however, is not for Pl. the most obvious hallmark of Christianity. His view is better expressed by what is said in Eph. 4:13 f. The goal, delimited and defined according to the measure of the maturity which Christ gives, is the full-grown Christian. As the clarifying participles show, the concept of the νήπιος corresponds here to the OT פֶּתִי in the sense of the child which can easily be led astray, whereas the νηπιάζειν τῇ κακίᾳ is based on עוֹלְלִים וְיֹנְקִים (παιδία ἀναμάρτητα), and elsewhere Paul seems to use νήπιοι in the sense of נְעָרִים, i.e., children in the years of instruction. Only Σ uses νήπιος in this way, though it is common in the Hellenistic diatribe, whose view of the child is essentially negative.[31] Nevertheless, we are not perhaps to think in terms of analogies from the Hellenistic sphere, but rather in terms of the twofold concept of פֶּתִי in the OT.

Whether or not Pl. is to be regarded as the author of Eph., there is in Pl. a material tension between the ethical concept of childhood as something to be left behind and the theological view of childhood (sonship) as the supreme gift of the Spirit (R. 8:14 ff.). This tension finds particular expression in 1 C. in the wrestling with → μωρία, δύναμις, σοφία/γνῶσις.

If the state of νήπιος is something to be left behind in Eph. 4:14, it is something which has already been left behind in Gl. 4:1, 3. This runs as follows: ὅτε ἦμεν νήπιοι, "when we were children," then we were in a state of minority and dependence, like the son for whom the father in his will appoints a guardian who sees to his education and controls his income. Pl. seems to have these three elements in view in the three main terms in the comparison, προθεσμία, ἐπίτροποι, οἰκονόμοι, to which we should also add παιδαγωγοί. The plurals do not suggests a plurality of teachers and administrators in any given case, but the various possibilities which are open.[32] νήπιος[33] is to be regarded here as a tt. in the law of inheritance, though one cannot point to a specific law which fully corresponds to the situation described.

An example of the προθεσμία τοῦ πατρός is to be found in a pap. text of 126 A.D.[34] Materially it is of little moment whether the ref. is to a final testamentary disposition. The heir[35] — this is an eschatological concept, so that in the metaphor the heir is one who is still waiting for his inheritance, not one whose father is dead — so long as he is a minor, is in no better position than a slave. Plato had already discussed this problem of the minor and his pedagogues, who were usually slaves, cf. the commonly quoted Lys., 208c and also Leg., VII, 808d e.[36] The child has a harder time than the young animal; it is held in check by the pedagogues.

The *tertium comparationis* in Gl. 4 is the subjection which arises through minority and according to the father's will. As an earthly father sets a time of

---

[30] On the derogatory use of the comparison in the Rabb. cf. Str.-B., I, 427; III, 462. But there is another side, cf. R. Meyer, "Hellenistisches in d. rabb. Anthropologie," BWANT, IV, 22 (1937), 84 f.
[31] Cf. R. Renner, *loc. cit.*
[32] Cf. the comm., esp. Oepke, *ad loc.*; also Mitteis-Wilcken, II, 304; P. Oxy., III, 491, 9.
[33] K. Eger, *Rechtsgesch. z. NT* (1919), 35 f.
[34] Cf. Mitteis-Wilcken, *loc. cit.*
[35] → κληρονόμος.
[36] For additional material cf. the comm.

majority, so the heavenly Father has given us the full rights of sonship by sending the Son. The pedagogue who guided the νήπιος was the *nomos* in the sense of the *stoicheia* of the cosmos — an expression which is certainly to be understood astrologically, but which in practice refers to all kinds of regulations (cf. Luther), i.e., the selection of days by astrological calculation, asceticism, and apotropaic customs, which, in connection with the sanctifying of the Sabbath, often found entry into Hellenistic or syncretistic Judaism and its sphere of influence.

The metaphor in 1 C. 13:11 contrasts the child and the man. Paul is here adopting a favourite figure of Hellenistic rhetoric.[37] This may be found in Euripides (Fr., 606). The point is particularly clear in Xenoph. Cyrop., VIII, 7, 6. Every age has its own quality and value, which must be taken into account. The goal of human development is the τέλειος ἀνήρ. In 1 C. 13, however, the man and the child are mutually exclusive opposites. The meaning of the illustration is as follows. As the adult sets aside the nature of the child, so the Christian, ὅταν ἔλθῃ τὸ τέλειον, sets aside the *gnosis* which seems to be essential now, i.e., in the stage of the νήπιος.

Even Origen[38] recognises the disparagement of *gnosis*: νῦν νηπία ἡμῖν ἐστιν ἡ γνῶσις, ἐπεὶ καὶ ἡμεῖς νήπιοί ἐσμεν. ὅταν τοίνυν τέλειοι γενώμεθα, ἐσόμεθα δὲ ἐν τῷ μέλλοντι χρόνῳ, πάντα τὰ νηπιώδη ἀπορρίψομεν. Paul is reckoning himself among the νήπιοι, as may be seen in other refs. to himself, e.g., in 1 C. 4:9 f., where he accepts the designations μωροί, ἀσθενεῖς, ἄτιμοι. In its general pedagogical and ethical use in Paul, however, νήπιος does not have the same dialectical ring as these terms.

There is a simple non-dialectical self-designation in 1 Th. 2:7: ἐγενήθημεν νήπιοι ἐν μέσῳ ὑμῶν. But though this reading is well attested, the reading with ἤπιοι is to be preferred.[39] From the days of Origen much attention has been devoted to the material explanation of νήπιοι in this verse.[40]

The fact that in both biblical and Hellenistic Greek νήπιος can be used in such varied and even antithetical ways makes it understandable that Paul should apply it differently both figuratively and materially. To the fore is the ethical use of the image and the orientation to education. Paul, however, is not just νήπιος; he is also διδάσκαλος νηπίων, a title falsely claimed by the Jew (R. 2:20). One does not have to quote the well-known saying from the Judaised Sib. (3, 195) to recognise how justly Paul describes the attitude of the Judaism of his day when he describes the Jew as παιδαγωγὸς ἀφρόνων, διδάσκαλος νηπίων, or, in biblical terms, ὁδηγὸς τυφλῶν. This raises genuine and inalienable claims which arise directly from revelation. Against the related dangers for sinful man Christianity is fundamentally armed by Mt. 23:8, but it can hardly understand these claims except in the form of human pedagogy, and this is true of Paul too. He is always διδάσκαλος νηπίων, and he expressly says so when he calls the Corinthians νήπιοι (1 C. 3:1) whom he nourishes with milk, the word for basic doctrines in the diatribe. Paul's primary answer to the divisions in Corinth is theological. The μωρία θεοῦ is stated to be δύναμις in face of all human σοφία. But he refers also to a θεοῦ σοφία ἐν τοῖς τελείοις, and he speaks ἐν διδακτοῖς λόγοις πνεύματος. He could only regard the Corinthians as σάρκινοι, not

[37] E. Lehmann-A. Fridrichsen, "1 Kor. 13 eine christlich-stoische Diatribe," ThStKr (1922), 80 ff. Cf. also J. Weiss, *ad loc.*

[38] Cramer Cat., *ad loc.*, n. 44.

[39] Cf. esp. E. v. Dobschütz, *ad loc.*

[40] Cf. Wbg. Th., *ad loc.*; also 2 Tm. 2:24 and on this the comm.

πνευματικοί. To speak pedagogically rather than in terms of the sharp antithesis of spirit and flesh, they are νήπιοι, [41] i.e., children who are not yet ripe enough for the final and most profound instruction. The image used here is found frequently in Epictet. and Philo, [42] and the milk fed to neophytes in the mystery religions has symbolical significance. But a sharp distinction must be made. In the mystery religions the taking of milk by the initiate is connected with new birth. Milk is part of a sacrament of regeneration. This is how we are to take the image in, e.g., 1 Pt. 2:2. In Pl. and Hb. 5:12 f., however, the reference is to the nourishment of a child as distinct from that of an adult. The theme in 1 Cor. 3 is the gradual pedagogic mediation of the divine mystery to the young churches. In view of the immaturity of the Corinthians Paul could offer them only what he did. Apollos went further in the imparting of *gnosis* and hence he had enthusiastic hearers. But divisions were the result, and herein the Corinthians showed yet again that they were νήπιοι. The situation of the community is assessed similarly in Hb. 5 and 6. There has been no progress in doctrine. It here seems to be assumed of all those addressed that they should have been διδάσκαλοι νηπίων. But they themselves have remained νήπιοι, i.e., they have not gone beyond the basic doctrines, and they must be admonished to go on ἐπὶ τὴν τελειότητα. What are the initial doctrines for the immature is hard to say. The list in 6:1 f. certainly forms the basis of the Christian message, but it may be questioned whether it is the pedagogic basis. Those addressed in Hb. do not lack *gnosis* but σπουδή (6:11), παρρησία (10:35), ὑπομονή (10:36), i.e., the power to translate Christianity into action. Even greater material difficulties confront us if we try to separate in Paul the basic doctrines from the Christian teaching which should be given to the more advanced. For according to the statements of Paul in 1 C. 1:18; 2:2 the message of the cross is the one comprehensive theme of Christian teaching, and all *gnosis*, every attempt to pierce the divine mystery, involves the danger implicit in all theological speculation, namely, that of dissolving the historical reality of revelation in a docetic conception of Christ. The danger is overcome in Paul because for him the decisive thing is not the *gnosis* of man but the power of God, the power which is folly in human eyes and which is granted to the μωροί (νήπιοι).

2. Little Children in the Message of Jesus.

In this sense Paul stands on fundamentally the same ground as the revelation of Jesus, which is appointed for νήπιοι and makes them carriers of the Gospel. The Gospel tradition says this again and again in different ways. The message is directed to πτωχοί, πραεῖς; it is designed for the ἀσθενεῖς, μικροί. It sets up παιδία and δοῦλοι as examples. It makes of the proud διάκονοι and ταπεινοί.

The term νήπιοι occurs only twice in the Gospels, at Mt. 11:25 = Lk. 10:21 in the thanksgiving [43] of the cry of jubilation, and in Mt. 21:16 in the story of the entry into Jerusalem, where Jesus quotes Ps. 8:2 to explain and defend the rejoicing of the children at His coming. [44]

---

[41] Cf. the vl.: ὡς νηπίους ἐν Χριστῷ γάλα ὑμᾶς ἐπότισα.

[42] → γάλα.

[43] T. Arvedson, "Das Mysterium Christi. Eine Studie zu Mt. 11:25-30," *A. M. Upps.*, VII (1937), 10 ff., 155 ff.; W. Grundmann, *Jesus d. Galiläer u. d. Judentum* (1939), 209 ff.

[44] That we have here a *topos* based on Ps. 8:2 may be seen plainly from the par. Rabb. tradition about children who saw the *shekinah* when Israel passed through the Red Sea (also based on Ps. 8:2). Cf. on this R. Meyer, *op. cit.*, 84 f.; Str.-B., I, 854. → τέκνον.

In the latter passage the ref. is to children by age (cf. v. 15 παῖδες), though in view of the par. in Lk. 19:39 [45] we are perhaps to think in terms of the disciples generally (cf. Jn. 12:12, 17). From the story of Jesus at 12 yrs. of age it may be seen that parents used to take children up to the feasts before they attained the obligatory age of 13. There is, of course, no precise definition of minors who were not yet under obligation. The school of Shammai took as the test riding up the temple hill on the father's shoulder, that of Hillel taking the father's hand. [46] This could imply an earlier age (cf. the oriental custom of quietening toddling children), possibly even νήπιοι and θηλάζοντες. In Mt. the reality of Ps. 8:2 finds wonderful confirmation and elucidation, as early exegesis already pointed out: οὐ γὰρ τῆς διανοίας αὐτῶν ἦν τὸ λεγόμενον ἀλλὰ τῆς αὐτοῦ δυνάμεως τρανούσης τὴν γλῶτταν αὐτῶν. [47] Attempts have also been made to interpret Ps. 8:2 metaphorically. Thus ancient Jewish exegesis sees in the proverbial עוללים ויונקים a ref. to Israel as the weak and helpless people. Rashi even referred the saying to priests and Levites. [48] But it is going too far when Grotius says with ref. to the quotation: David περὶ νηπίων καὶ θηλαζόντων *dixerat figurate, innocentes et simplices intelligens,* with the historicising addition: *et pueros fuisse in clamantium turba.*

Fulfilment of the saying from the Ps. in the NT is not restricted to this one scene. The scene merely makes evident something which is recurrent in the Gospel. Those whom the world does not notice, children, the lowly, the disciples [49] and the masses bear witness to Jesus. They acknowledge Him to the praise and glory of God (Phil. 2:11). Flesh and blood did not reveal this to them any more than to Peter (Mt. 16:17), but God Himself. To them is given understanding of the μυστήρια (Mt. 13:11) (vl. μυστήριον) τῆς βασιλείας τῶν οὐρανῶν.

The NT, then, is a continuation of the story of OT revelation, which is also addressed to the elect rather than to the wise or rich or powerful of this world. In the OT the elect are undoubtedly the righteous. Thus we read in Ps. 24(25):14: סוֹד יְהוָֹה לִירֵאָיו וּבְרִיתוֹ לְהוֹדִיעָם, Θ μυστήριον κυρίου τοῖς φοβουμένοις αὐτὸν καὶ τὴν συνθήκην αὐτοῦ δηλώσει αὐτοῖς. Even more plainly wisdom addresses the κωφοί and νήπιοι in Wis. 10:21: ὅτι ἡ σοφία ἤνοιξεν στόμα κωφῶν καὶ γλώσσας νηπίων ἔθηκεν τρανάς. Sir. 3:19 is a direct precursor of Mt. 11:25. Though this verse in the Gk. is found only in the augmentation of S, it may be regarded as an original part of the transl. [50] The Heb. runs: ולענוים יגלה סודו. גלה סוד, "to reveal a secret," occurs also in Am. 3:7, where LXX has: ἐὰν μὴ ἀποκαλύψῃ παιδείαν αὐτοῦ πρὸς τοὺς δούλους αὐτοῦ τούς προφήτας, cf. also Prv. 20:19 (of men, no LXX). Sir 3:19 runs in the LXX vl.: πολλοί εἰσιν ὑψηλοὶ καὶ ἐπίδοξοι, ἀλλὰ πραέσιν ἀποκαλύπτει τὰ μυστήρια αὐτοῦ. Already, then, God's revelation in the OT is not tied to human criteria. Par. from religious history simply confirm the distinctiveness and uniqueness of the biblical revelation. [51] Typical is a report like that of Plato that the mysterious divine wisdom disclosed to Musaeus and his son is passed on only τοῖς δικαίοις. Cf. also the mystery religions. Judaism itself could not and did not make much of a saying like Sir. 3:19. The revelation was not denied by the Rabb., but they regarded it as a sign of judgment rather than salvation. Thus we read in BB, 12b: R. Jochanan (279) has said: "From the

---

45 The stones would perhaps cry out in accusation rather than acclaim, → λίθος.
46 Str.-B., II, 141 f.
47 Cram. Cat., *ad loc.*
48 Cf. Baethgen (1904), on Ps. 8:2.
49 Cf. also O. Michel, "'Diese Kleinen' — eine Jüngerbezeichnung Jesu," ThStKr, 1937/38.
50 Cf. Ryssel in Kautzsch, *ad loc.*
51 For material cf. E. Norden, *Agnostos Theos* (1913), 277 ff.

day when the sanctuary was destroyed prophecy has been taken from the prophets and given to fools and children." [52]

The saying of Jesus is thus to be set against the total background of the OT and NT revelation. The specific context in which it is pronounced is more difficult to determine. One cannot even say whether Mt. intentionally sets the Saviour's cry of jubilation in antithesis to the Woes which He pronounced just before. There can be no doubt, however, that the cry is not an attempt to overcome disappointment at rejection and failure in influential circles. Lk. puts the saying after the return of the 70, but one simply imports a historicising intention if one supposes that the 70 had told of their acceptance by the simple (פתאים) but not by rabbis, priests and politicians. [53] No, the saying of Jesus is not the result of experiences of Himself or His disciples. The insight into the nature of the Gospel expressed herein is fundamental to the Lord's preaching and conduct. Because God so wills it, because it corresponds to the nature of revelation, Jesus has not garbed Himself in power, wealth and wisdom. He is poor, mean and lowly, and He comes to those who are themselves νήπιοι. In His coming the whole greatness of God's grace is manifested to children and to the lowly. [54] The saying does not merely correspond to the nature of the Gospel. It discloses the nature of Jesus Himself. As πραΰς and ταπεινός (v. 29), He invites the νήπιοι to Himself. [55] The unrelated ταῦτα is determined in content by the content of the Gospel. It thus relates to acknowledgment of Jesus, e.g., with the fulfilment of the saying from the Psalms by the νήπιοι in Mt. 21:6 or with the revelation to Peter presupposed in Mt. 16:17. The ταῦτα is thus to be taken christologically. Recognition of the Son as the bearer of revelation is the presupposition of the acceptance of revelation. This is fulfilled in the νήπιοι; to them is given a share in knowledge of the Lord.

It has not been easy for the Christian Church in its history to keep to this fundamental presupposition of the evangelical message. Time and again from the days of Paul pedagogic modes of thought have attacked the radical character of the cry of jubilation. From the very first tradition and exposition have sought to weaken and change it. Thus Marcion [56] tried at least to soften the antithesis between ἀπόκρυψις for the σοφοί and συνετοί and ἀποκάλυψις for the νήπιοι by reading: εὐχαριστῶ (σοι) καὶ ἐξομολογοῦμαι, κύριε τοῦ οὐρανοῦ, ὅτι ἅτινα ἦν κρυπτὰ σοφοῖς καὶ συνετοῖς, ἀπεκάλυψας νηπίοις. But the emphasis falls, not merely on revelation to the νήπιοι, but also on concealement from the σοφοί who regard themselves as such. Paul shows awareness of this when, perhaps consciously echoing the saying of Jesus, he writes in 1 C. 1:19 f.: ἀπολῶ τὴν σοφίαν τῶν σοφῶν καὶ τὴν σύνεσιν τῶν συνετῶν ἀθετήσω ... οὐκ ἔγνω ὁ κόσμος τὸν θεόν ... εὐδόκησεν ὁ θεός ... [57]

In the battle to maintain the message for the simple the idea of Jesus Himself as a child became particularly significant for the Church. Witness is borne to this by many apocryphal traditions, not only the so-called gospels of the childhood of Jesus, but also

[52] Str.-B., I, 607, with examples of children's prophecies. On the charismatic type of the holy fool cf. E. Benz, "Heilige Narrheit," *Kyrios*, 3 (1938), 1 ff.
[53] G. E. Paulus (→ n. 17), II, 755, also J. Weiss-Bousset, *ad loc.*
[54] A. Schlatter, *ad loc.*
[55] J. Wellhausen, *ad loc.*
[56] A. Harnack, *Marcion* (1921), 187*; *Sprüche u. Reden Jesu* (1907), 206 ff.
[57] *Ibid.*, 210.

the apostolic stories in which the Saviour constantly appears as a child. [58] Revelation through a child perhaps belongs to a specific type which is at work on the margin of the NT. It is to be found on the contemporary scene. The figure of Harpocrates as a child, [59] or the divine child of the 4th Eclogue of Vergil, may be mentioned in this connection. Childhood stories are associated with many biblical characters, from Moses to Jesus. The motif is perhaps discernible also when teachers are young and little known, like Elihu in Job 32:4, 7. [60] Such ideas form a counterweight to an intellectualistic understanding of Christianity and consequently to its secularisation in the form of theological and philosophical speculation. But even where Christianity became a doctrine of wisdom, as in Cl. and Origen, revelation to the simple was never abandoned in principle. Origen argues against Celsus when the latter scorns as unworthy the self-description of Christians as νήπιοι. It is true that in this philosophical Christianity the μωροί [61] are ultimately mere believers. But the fact remains that even Clement Al. has to bear witness that the Gospel is for νήπιοι. [62] Jesus Himself is ὁ υἱὸς τοῦ θεοῦ, ὁ νήπιος τοῦ πατρός. [63] He is the Revealer of childhood, and through Him all Christians are νήπιοι in spite of all the distinctions and gradations which the wise of the world, and especially theologians, have sought from the time of the Alexandrians.

Bertram

[58] → III, 555 for examples.
[59] Arvedson, 48 : Har-pe-chrot meaning Horus, the child.
[60] *Ibid.*, 84.
[61] Orig. Cels., I, 16; V, 16. Cf. A. Miura-Stange, *Celsus u. Orig.* (1926), 31.
[62] Cf. the liturgically significant description of the baptised as νήπιοι, Cl. Al. Paed., I, 6, 23, 4 : νήπιοι ἄρα εἰκότως οἱ παῖδες τοῦ θεοῦ οἱ τὸν μὲν παλαιὸν ἀποθέμενοι ἄνθρωπον καὶ τῆς κακίας ἐκδυσάμενοι τὸν χιτῶνα, ἐπενδυσάμενοι δὲ τὴν ἀφθαρσίαν τοῦ Χριστοῦ, ἵνα καινοὶ γενόμενοι, λαὸς ἅγιος, ἀναγεννηθέντες ἀμίαντον φυλάξωμεν τὸν ἄνθρωπον καὶ νήπιοι ὡς βρέφος τοῦ θεοῦ κεκαθαρμένον πορνείας καὶ πονηρίας. Dölger, *Ichthys*, 1 (1928), 183 ff., who quotes this passage, seeks accordingly to understand the νήπιος of Christian burial inscr. with ref. to sinless youth.
[63] Cl. Al. Paed., I, 24, 4.

† νῆστις, † νηστεύω, † νηστεία

Contents: 1. Meaning of the Word. 2. Fasting in Antiquity. 3. Fasting in the Old Testament and Judaism. 4. Fasting in the New Testament. 5. Fasting in the Early Church.

1. Meaning of the Word.

The basic word νῆστις, from the Indo-Europ. *nĕ-ĕdtis*, [1] means generally "one who has not eaten, who is empty," Hom. Il., 19, 206 f.: ἀνώγοιμι πτολεμιζέμεν υἷας Ἀχαιῶν νήστιας ἀκμήνους ("unsatisfied"). Onosander, De Imperatoris Officio, 1, 12:

νῆστις κτλ. On 1: Thes. Steph., V, 1501 ff.; Liddell-Scott, *s.v.*; Pr.-Bauer³, *s.v.*; Moult.-Mill., 426. On 2: O. Zöckler, *Askese u. Mönchtum* (1897), I, 97 ff.; H. Strathmann, *Geschichte d. frühchristlichen Askese*, 1 (1914); R. Arbesmann, "Das Fasten bei d. Griechen u. Römern," RVV, 21, 1 (1929); L. Ziehen, Art. Νηστεία, Pauly-W., XVII, 1 (1936), 88 ff. On 3: G. B. Winer, *Biblisches Realwörterbuch*³ (1847), I, 364 ff.; H. J. Holtzmann, Art. "Fasten," Schenkel, II, 260 ff.; W. Nowack, *Lehrbuch d. hbr. Archäologie*, II (1894), 201 f., 270 ff.; F. Buhl, Art. "Fasten," RE³, V, 768 ff.; V. H. Stanton, Art. "Fasting," Hastings DB, I, 854 f.; I. Benzinger, Art. "Fastings, Fast," EB, II, 1505 ff.; also *Hbr. Archäologie*³ (1927), Index, *s.v.* "Fasten," "Fasttage"; A. W. Groenman, Het Vasten bij Israel (Diss. Leiden, 1906); K. Fruhstorfer, "Fastenvorschriften u. Fastenlehren der Heiligen Schrift d. Alten Bundes," *Theol.-Praktische Quartalschrift*, 69 (1916), 59 ff.; O. Kirn, Art. "Fasten," Calwer Bibellex.⁴ (1924), 182 f.; P. Volz, *D. biblischen Altertümer* (1925), 108, 112 f., 248 f.; T. Lewis, Art. "Fast, Fasting," ISBE, II (1925), 1099; M. Freiberger, *Das Fasten im alten Israel* (Diss. Würzburg, 1927); H. Gressmann-L. Baeck, Art. "Askese II: Im AT u. Judt.," RGG², I, 574 f.; E. Kalt, *Biblisches Reallex.*, Art. "Fasten," I (1931), 511 ff.; Weber, Index, *s.v.*; Schürer, II, 572 ff.; O. Holtzmann, *Nt.liche Zeitgeschichte*² (1906), 350 ff.; B. Stade-A. Bertholet, *Bibl. Theologie d. AT*, II (1911), 425 f. etc.; Bousset-Gressm., 179 f.; Schl. Theol. d. Judt., 120 ff.; A. Neuwirth, *Das Verhältnis d. jüdischen Fasten zu denen d. alten Heiden* (Diss. Bern, 1910); I. Abrahams, *Studies in Pharisaism and the Gospels*, I (1917), 121 ff.; Str.-B., IV, 77 ff. (Exc. "Vom altjüd. Fasten"), II, 241 ff.; I. Elbogen, *Der jüd. Gottesdienst*² (1924), 126 ff. etc.; Moore, II, 55 ff., 257 ff.; J. A. Montgomery, "Ascetic Strains in Early Judaism," JBL, 51 (1932), 183 ff.; Jüd. Lex., II (1928), 591 f.; EJ, VI, 940 ff. On 4 and 5: Comm.; H. Strathmann, Art. "Askese III: Im Urchristentum," RGG², I, 575 ff.; F. H. Dudden, Art. "Fasting," DCG, I, 579; D. Mackenzie, Art. "Abstinence," DAC, I, 6 ff.; Suic. Thes., 400 ff.; A. Linsenmayr, *Entwicklung d. kirchlichen Fastendisziplin bis zum Konzil v. Nicäa* (1877); F. Kattenbusch, *Lehrbuch d. vergleichenden Konfessionskunde*, I (1892), 475 ff.; H. Achelis, Art. "Fasten in der Kirche," RE³, V, 770 ff.; *Das Christentum in d. ersten 3 Jahrhunderten* (1912), Index, *s.v.* "Fasten," "Fastenverbote," "Fasttage"; O. Zöckler, I, 151 ff. etc.; E. v. Dobschütz, *D. urchristlichen Gemeinden* (1902), Index, *s.v.* "Fasten," "Fasttage"; C. Schmidt, "Gespräche mit seinen Jüngern nach der Auferstehung," TU, 43 (1919), Ind., *s.v.* "fasten"; F. Cabrol, Art. "Jeûnes," Dictionnaire d'Archéologie Chrétienne, VII, 2 (1927), 2481 ff.; K. Holl, *Ges. Aufsätze zur Kirchengeschichte*, II (1928), Ind., s.v. "Fasten," "Fastenzeit"; J. Svennung, "Statio = 'Fasten'" ZNW, 32 (1933), 294 ff.; H. J. Ebeling, "Die Fastenfrage (Mk. 2:18-22)," ThStKr, NF, 3 (1937/38), 387 ff.

[1] Cf. E. Risch, *Wortbildung d. homerischen Sprache* (1937), 35; A. Debrunner, *Gr. Wortbildungslehre* (1917), § 56 f. [Debrunner], and cf. already Suid., III, 463, 20 ff. (Adler): Νῆστις· ὁ ἄσιτος ... παρὰ τὸ νηστερητικὸν μόριον καὶ τὸ ἔδειν, ὁ ἐστερημένος τοῦ ἔδειν, ἢ παρὰ τὸ νηστερητικὸν καὶ τὸ σῖτος, also Etym. M. and Etym. Gud. etc. On the derivation of the verb νηστεύω from νῆστις, *v.* E. Fraenkel, *Gr. Denominativa* (1906), 184, 265.

(the general) μὴ ὀκνείτω καὶ ἀριστοποιεῖσθαι σημαίνειν, μὴ φθάσωσι νήστισιν ἐπιθέντες οἱ πολέμιοι τὴν ἀνάγκην τοῦ μάχεσθαι, Da. 6:19 LXX (Θ ἄδειπνος), Mk. 8:3 par. With specific ref. to intentional abstention from food on religious grounds, νῆστις becomes the tt. for one who fasts, cf. the hymn to Demeter in Orph. Fr., 47 (p. 118, 8 ff., Kern):

μητέρι Πῦρ μέν μ' ἄγ[ε], εἰ νῆστις οἰδ' <ὑπομεῖνα>
ἑπτά τε νῆστιν ἢ μεθ' ἡμέραν ἐλινύεν
ἑπτῆμαρ μὲν νῆστις ἔην.

νηστεύω can also mean generally "to be hungry, without food," Aristot. Probl., XII, 7 (→ *infra*). Part. An., 14, p. 675b, 36 f.: ἐν τοῖς μείζοσι καὶ νηστεύσασιν, ἀλλ' οὐκ ἐδηδοκόσιν. But it usually means "to fast" in a religious and ritual sense, Aristoph. Av., 1519: ὥσπερεὶ Θεσμοφορίοις νηστεύομεν, Aristoph. Thes., 983 f.: παίσωμεν, ὦ γυναῖκες, οἷά περ νόμος· νηστεύομεν δὲ πάντως, Chrysippus in Plut. Quaest. Conv., 1, 9, 1 (II, 626 f.): νηστεύσαντας ἀργότερον ἐσθίειν ἢ προφαγόντας, Ju. 20:26; 1 Παρ. 10:12; Zech. 7:5 etc.; Philo Spec. Leg., II, 197; Joseph. Ant., 20, 89: (Izates) ἐπὶ τὴν ἱκετείαν ἐτρέπετο τοῦ θεοῦ, χαμαί τε ῥίψας αὐτὸν καὶ σποδῷ τὴν κεφαλὴν καταισχύνας μετὰ γυναικὸς καὶ τέκνων ἐνήστευεν ἀνακαλῶν τὸν θεόν etc., Mt. 4:2; 6:16 ff.; Mk. 2:18 ff. par.; Lk. 18:12; Ac. 13:2 f.

The noun νηστεία can also have the general sense of "not having eaten," "being without nourishment," "suffering hunger," e.g., Aristot. Probl., XII, 7, p. 908b, 11 f.: τὰ στόματα μηδὲν ἐδηδοκότων, ἀλλὰ νηστευσάντων ὄζει μᾶλλον (ὃ καλεῖται νηστείας ὄζειν), Hippocr. Aphor., 2 [16] (23, 709, C. G. Kühn): γέροντες εὐφορώτατα νηστείην φέρουσι, 2 C. 6:5; 11:27 (in the list of the apostle's sufferings): νηστεῖαι is here "the resultant sum of λιμός and δίψος"[2] (cf. 1 C. 4:11; Phil. 4:12). But the word usually has the special religious sense of fasting, e.g., Hdt., 4, 186: νηστείας αὐτῇ (Isis) καὶ ὁρτὰς ἐπιτελέουσι, Plut. Is. et Os., 26 (II, 361a) → 926; 2 Βασ. 12:16; ψ 68:10; Jl. 1:14 etc.; Philo Migr. Abr., 98 (→ 930) etc.; Jos. Ant., 11, 134: (Ezra) νηστείαν αὐτοῖς (those who had returned from captivity) παρήγγειλεν, ὅπως εὐχὰς ποιήσονται τῷ θεῷ etc.; Lk. 2:37; Ac. 14:23. ἡ Νηστεία can also be a name for the fast-day, e.g., in the Athenian cult for a day in the festival of Thesmophoria, Alciphr., 2, 37, 2; Athen., VII, 80a,[3] and in Judaism for the great Day of Atonement on the 10th Tishri,[4] e.g., Philo Decal., 159: νηστείαν, ἐν ᾗ σιτίων καὶ ποτῶν ἀποχὴ διείρηται, Spec. Leg., I, 186, 168; II, 41, 197, 193 f. (νηστεία ἑορτή), 200 (ἡ ἡμέρα τῆς νηστείας); Vit. Mos., II, 23: τὴν λεγομένην νηστείαν, cf. Leg. Gaj., 306; Jos. Ant., 18, 94: κατὰ τὴν νηστείαν, cf. 17, 165 f.; 14, 487: τῇ ἑορτῇ τῆς νηστείας, 14, 66: τῇ τῆς νηστείας ἡμέρᾳ, cf. Damasc. 6:19: יוֹם הַתַּעֲנִית, Ac. 27:9; Plut. Quaest. Conv., 4, 6, 2 (II, 671d);[5] Just. Dial., 40, 4 f. etc.

The word νῆστις occurs in the LXX only at Da. 6:19 (→ *supra*) for the Aram. טְוָת. νηστεία is the fixed equivalent of צוֹם, νηστεύω of צוּם; only in 1 K. 21:9 (= 3 Βασ. 20:9) is קָרָא צוֹם rendered νηστεύειν νηστείαν. νηστεύω means the same as οὐ γεύομαι etc. in the LXX and Jewish Gk. lit. (→ I, 676; II, 690).

---

[2] A. Fridrichsen, "Zum Stil des paul. Peristasenkatalogs," *Symb. Osl.*, 7 (1928), 27. Cf. Wnd. 2 K. on 6:5 and 11:27.

[3] The νηστεία τῆς Δήμητρος, P. Zenon, 59350, 5 (III, 78, C. C. Edgar) is probably an imitation of the Athenian fast-day.

[4] The LXX does not yet use νηστεία for the ἡμέρα τοῦ ἱλασμοῦ or ἐξιλασμοῦ (יוֹם הַכִּפֻּרִים). In jJoma, 8, 44d, 42 the Day of Atonement is צוֹמָא רַבָּא.

[5] Here the Day of Atonement and the Feast of Tabernacles are confused, cf. Zn. Ag., II, 823, n. 64.

2. Fasting in Antiquity.

The practice of fasting,[6] found in all religions, and used here in the specific sense of temporary abstention from all nourishment on religious grounds,[7] is at first more common among the Greeks than the Romans, but then under foreign influences it spread across the whole of the ancient world. The original and most powerful motive for fasting in antiquity is to be found in fear of demons who gained power over men through eating. Fasting was also an effective means of preparing for intercourse with the deity and for the reception of ecstatic or magical powers.

The idea that fasting can ward off evil spirits is to be found already in Xenocrates acc. to Plutarch, Is. et Os., 26 (II, 361b): ὁ δὲ Ξενοκράτης ... τῶν ἑορτῶν, ὅσαι πληγάς τινας ἢ κοπετοὺς ἢ νηστείας ... ἔχουσιν, οὔτε θεῶν τιμαῖς οὔτε δαιμόνων οἴεται προσήκειν χρηστῶν, ἀλλ' εἶναι φύσεις ἐν τῷ περιέχοντι μεγάλας μὲν καὶ ἰσχυράς, δυστρόπους δὲ καὶ σκυθρωπάς, αἳ χαίρουσι τοῖς τοιούτοις καὶ τυγχάνουσαι πρὸς οὐδὲν ἄλλο χεῖρον τρέπονται.[8] Plut. himself in Def. Orac., 14 (II, 417c) believes that fasting takes place δαιμόνων φαύλων ἀποτροπῆς ἕνεκα.[9] The ancient view is still heard on Christian lips: πρὸς τὴν τῶν δαιμόνων φυγὴν ... ἡ νηστεία ... οἰκειότατόν ἐστιν βοήθημα, Ps.-Cl. Hom., 9, 10. It is probable also that the custom of the mourning fast had apotropaic significance. Luc. De Luctu, 24 makes fun of this (the parents of the deceased up to the burial, for 3 days, abstained from all food), and there is also allusion to it in Apul. Met., II, 24, where a man watching over the corpse is not allowed food and wine. So long as the soul of a dead person is near, there is danger of demonic infection through eating and drinking.[10] Herodot. speaks of fasts which priests had to observe in Egypt before entering the sanctuary, offering sacrifices or performing cultic actions (2, 40: προνηστεύσαντες δὲ θύουσιν), but there is no similar tradition in respect of Gk. and Roman cults.[11] The Themosphoria festival in Athens (→ 925), which was in honour of Demeter, imposed a one day fast on women, which they had to keep χαμαὶ καθήμεναι, Plut. Is. et Os., 69 (II, 738d).[12] In the mysteries[13] abstention from food and drink was an important obligation for those about to be initiated. Along with other prescribed rites fasting was supposed to make them fit for union with the deity. In the Eleusinian mysteries the neophyte fasted up to receiving the mixed sacramental drink (cf. Cl. Al. Prot., II, 21, 2: ἐνήστευσα, ἔπιον τὸν κυκεῶνα). Demeter's own fast in the myth (Hom. Hymn. Cer., 47 ff., 200 f. etc.) gives evidence of established cultic use. In the Phrygian mysteries of Cybele and Attis partial fasts culminated in total νηστεία during the 3 days of mourning for the death of Attis, Sallust. De Deis, 4 (p. 8, 19 ff., A. D. Nock). Initiation into the Isis mysteries seems not to have demanded a complete fast, though there was a 10 day abstention from flesh and wine before each of the 3 acts, *v.* Apul. Met., XI, 23, 28, 30. The Mithras mys-

[6] Cf. E. Westermarck, "The Principles of Fasting," *Folklore*, 18 (1907), 391 ff.; J. A. MacCulloch, Art. "Fasting (Introductory and nonChristian)," ERE, 5, 759 ff.; Chant. de la Saussaye, Index, *s.v.*; A. Bertholet, Art. "Fasten: I. Religionsgeschichtlich," RGG², II, 518 f.

[7] The temporary or permanent abstention from particular foods is a different phenomenon which is not considered here, though sometimes the motives and practice of this type of abstinence are much the same as those of true fasting.

[8] Cf. Strathmann, 255 f.

[9] Cf. F. J. Dölger, *Antike u. Christentum,* 3 (1932), 160 f.

[10] Strathmann, 195 ff.; Arbesmann, 25 ff., though cf. Ziehen, 95.

[11] On the forbidding of specific foods to priests, Strathmann, 166 ff. and 215 ff.; Arbesmann, 72 ff.; Ziehen, 97 ff.

[12] For the 7 day fast in the Demeter cult → 925. In the Roman par., the fast on the *sacrum anniversarium Cereris* and the festival *ieiunium Cereris,* there seems to have been abstention only from bread, Strathmann, 185; Arbesmann, 94 ff.; Ziehen, 92.

[13] Cf. Kn. Did. on 7, 4; Strathmann, 218 ff., 230 ff.; Arbesmann, 74 ff.; Ziehen, 90 ff.

teries imposed strict rules of asceticism,[14] but there is no evidence of true fasting. The Gks. and Romans knew that abstention makes receptive to ecstatic revelations. Thus fasting plays an important role in the history of ancient manticism,[15] cf. Cic. Divin., I, 51, 115: *animus ... omnia, quae in natura rerum sunt, videt, si modo temperatis escis modicisque potionibus ita est adfectus, ut sopito corpore ipse vigilet.* As the prophet of the oracle of Apollo at Clarus fasted a day and a night before receiving the revelation, and as the priestess of the oracle of the Branchidae at Didymoi fasted three days (Iambl. Myst., III, 11), so many others who dispensed oracles, e.g., the Pythian, mortified themselves prior to the discharge of their office. Preparation by strict fasting was made for the dream oracles through which gods revealed the future to those asleep in their temples, with promises of healing from sickness etc.,[16] Philostr. Vit. Ap., II, 37; Strabo, XIV, 649 etc. Tert. is hardly guilty of exaggeration in De Anima, 48 (CSEL, 20, 379): *apud oracula incubaturis ieiunium indicitur.* In magic fasting is often a pre-condition of success in the magical arts.[17] The texts always demand sobriety, if not extended fasting, to strengthen the magical force, e.g., Pap. (5025) d. Staatlichen Museen Berlin, 235 (Preis. Zaub., I, 14); Catal. Cod. Astr. Graec., III, 53, 13 f.

It is striking that the fasting of antiquity stands in no close connection with ethos and ethics. Conversely, the moral idea of ἐγκράτεια (→ II, 340 f.) which the philosophers proclaimed and sought to achieve in their schools never led to a demand for times of νηστεία, though we do find the utopian desire for a life without any nourishment at all, e.g., Porphyr. Abst., I, 27: λεπτὸν δὲ τὸ σιτίον καὶ ἐγγὺς τεῖνον ἀποσιτίας cf. 37 f. The fasting of the Graeco-Roman world is not asceticism (→ I, 494). It is a rite which is observed for the sake of relations to the spirits and the gods.

3. Fasting in the Old Testament and Judaism.

With צוֹם (→ 925), the OT also uses for fasting עִנָּה נֶפֶשׁ, "to humble the soul," "to mortify oneself,"[18] Lv. 16:29, 31; 23:27, 32; Nu. 29:7; Is. 58:3; pleonastically Ps. 35:13: עִנֵּיתִי בַצּוֹם נַפְשִׁי (originally Ps. 69:10 ?). In Ezr. 8:21 הִתְעַנָּה too means "to fast," and then in Rabb. writings, where צוֹם and הִתְעַנָּה are used synon. תַּעֲנִית, "self-mortification" in the sense of fasting, occurs in the Mas. only in Ezr. 9:5; it is a tt. in Rabb. Heb.[19]

Many aspects of OT fasting are the same as in other religions. Fasting in case of death (→ III, 838) has its roots here too in belief in demons (→ 926), though in the historical period it has the character of a mourning custom expressing sorrow for the deceased, 1 S. 31:13 (1 Ch. 10:12); 2 S. 1:12; 3:35; 12:21. Before receiving the Ten Commandments, Moses spent forty days and forty nights with Yahweh on Mt. Sinai neither eating nor drinking (Ex. 34:28; Dt. 9:9). Daniel fasted and mortified himself prior to his visions (Da. 9:3; 10:2 f., 12). In

---

[14] F. Cumont-G. Gehrich, *D. Mysterien d. Mithra*³ (1923), 126; Arbesmann, 87 ff.

[15] Arbesmann, 97 ff.; Ziehen, 93 f.

[16] Cf. L. Deubner, *De Incubatione* (1900), 14 ff.; W. Kroll, Art. "Incubatio," Pauly-W., IX, 1258 f.

[17] Arbesmann, 63 ff.; Ziehen, 94.

[18] Self-mortification generally in Nu. 30:14. For the Heb. the LXX always uses ταπεινοῦν τὴν ἑαυτοῦ ψυχήν (cf. Herm. m., 4, 2, 2) except for κακοῦν τὴν ἑαυτοῦ ψυχήν in Nu. 29:7 (and 30:14). ταπεινοῦσθαι has the same sense in 2 Εσδρ. 8:21 (for הִתְעַנָּה → *supra*); Sir. 34:26; Ditt. Syll.³, 1181, 11 (→ n. 27). The noun ταπείνωσις is used for fasting or mortification in 2 Εσδρ. 9:5 (= תַּעֲנִית → *supra*); 1 Cl., 53, 2; 55, 6 → ταπεινόω, → ταπείνωσις.

[19] On the Rabb. terms for "fast" cf. Levy Wört., IV, 178 f., IV, 657; Levy Chald. Wört., 318 f., 228, 548; Dalman Wört., *s.v.* צוֹם, עֲנָא and derivates.

these cases fasting would seem to be preparation for receiving revelation (→ 926). It makes Moses and Daniel capable of encounter with God and the hearing of His words. The most prominent feature, and one which is singular to the OT, is, however, the fact that fasting expresses submission to God, as the phrase עִנָּה נֶפֶשׁ shows. The fast is an act of self-renunciation and self-discipline which is designed to make an impression on God, to mollify His wrath and to move Him to grant what man desires.

Thus the individual fasts when he hopes that God will liberate him from tormenting care, 2 S. 12:16 ff.; 1 K. 21:27; Ps. 35:12; Ps. 69:10. In times of emergency the whole people fasts in order that God may turn aside calamity,[20] Ju. 20:26; 1 S. 7:6; 1 K. 21:9; Jer. 36:6, 9; 2 Ch. 20:3 f.; Jl. 1:14; 2:12 ff.; Jon. 3:5 ff. (where even the animals fast). Fasting and prayer go hand in hand to cause God to answer, Jer. 14:12; Neh. 1:4; Ezr. 8:21, 23; Est. 4:16, especially penitential prayer and confession, 1 S. 7:6; Jl. 1:14; 2:12 ff.; Neh. 9:1 ff.; Jon. 3:8 (→ II, 794), also fasting and vows, 1 S. 14:24; cf. Nu. 30:14. The one who fasts often takes up the attitude of a mourner, → III, 837 f.; cf. 1 K. 21:27; Jl. 2:13; also Is. 58:5; Est. 4:3; Neh. 9:1; Jon. 3:5 ff.; Da. 9:3. The rule is a fast of one day from morning to evening, Ju. 20:26; 1 S. 14:24; 2 S. 1:12. The only instance of a severer fast of 3 days, including the nights, is in Est. 4:16. The 7 day fast of 1 S. 31:13, cf. 2 S. 3:35, involves fasting only during the day, up to sunset. The 3 week self-mortification of Da. 10:2 f. is not a total fast. How severe fasting affects the body may be seen in Ps. 109:24.

The only fast prescribed by the Law and closely related to the cultus[21] was the fast of the Day of Atonement, the great day of national repentance, Lv. 16:29 ff.; 23:27 ff; Nu. 29:7. The fast, and complete rest from work, lasted the whole day. Death was the punishment for violation. After the destruction of Jerusalem 4 days, in the fourth, fifth, seventh and tenth months,[22] were set aside to remember this national disaster. These were days of fasting and prayer, Zech. 7:3, 5; 8:19.

Fasting, like sacrifice (→ III, 183), with which it is associated as a cultic action, tends to become a material achievement performed to one's own advantage. The prophets protest against this externalisation. In Jer. 14:12[23] Yahweh declares: "When they fast, I will not hear their cry." Is. 58:1 ff. inveighs with cutting sharpness against the current observance of fast days. Gainful commerce, strife, wrangling and violence are to be found in spite of the sham holiness of external observance. It is no wonder that Yahweh takes no pleasure in such rites. True fasting which leads to salvation is a real bowing of the soul (v. 5) in moral action, in loving service to the poor and unfortunate among the people. Cf. Zech. 7:5 ff. (also 8:16 f.); 8:19; Jl. 2:13. Yet the prophetic outcry against a hollow *opus operatum* is as good as disregarded. In exilic Judaism, with its legalistic trends, fasting is one of the most important of religious activities.

---

[20] Cf. the community in Aswan, P. Eleph., 1, 15.

[21] The injunction to fast at the feast of Purim in Est. 9:31 is unintelligible, *v.* Kautzsch, II, 445.

[22] Cf. Kautzsch on Zech. 8:19.

[23] It is an open question whether Is. 1:13 (Mas. אָוֶן, LXX νηστείαν) includes criticism of fasting within its criticism of the cultus.

Up to NT days fasting comes to occupy so high a place in the practice and estimation of Judaism [24] that for Gentiles it is one of the marks of the Jew, cf. Tacitus Hist., V, 4: *longam olim* (during the wilderness wanderings) *famem crebris adhuc ieiuniis fatentur*; Suet. Aug. Caes., 76, 3: *ne Judaeus quidem tam diligenter sabbatis ieiunium servat quam ego hodie servavi.* [25] Like Daniel, the later apocalyptists prepare themselves by fasting for ecstatic inspiration, 4 Esr. 5:13, 19 f.; 6:31, 35 (cf. 9:23; 12:51); S. Bar. 9:2; 12:5; 20:5; 21:1 ff.; 43:3; 47:2. A vow is confirmed by fasting, Tob. 7:12; Ac. 23:12, 14 (→ I, 676). So, too, in many cases is prayer, 1 Macc. 3:47; 2 Macc. 13:12; Bar. 1:5; Jdt. 4:9 ff.; Lk. 2:37; Test. Jos. 4:8; 10:1; Test. B. 1:4; Jos. Ant., 19, 349; 20, 89 (→ 925); cf. Tob. 12:8: ἀγαθὸν προσευχὴ μετὰ νηστείας. Remorse and penitence find expression in fasting, Ps. Sol. 3:8; 2 Εσδρ. 9:3 ff.; Test. R. 1:10; S. Bar. 5:7; 4 Esr. 10:4; Ass. Mos. 9:5 ff.; Vit. Ad. 6. Fasting is an exercise in virtue, as may be seen from the example of Jos. in Egypt, Test. Jos. 3:4 f.; 4:8; 10:1. God loves the virtuous man who fasts. 9:2; cf. 3:4: οἱ νηστεύοντες διὰ τὸν θεὸν τοῦ προσώπου τὴν χάριν λαμβάνουσιν. The meritoriousness of fasting is mentioned, e.g., Eth. En. 108:7 ff.; Philo Spec. Leg., II, 197, and Apc. Eliae 22 f. (here definitely Jewish), [26] which magnifies fasting as something which God created: "It forgives sins and heals diseases, it drives out spirits and has power even to the throne of God." Only rarely do we hear voices declaring that fasting is useless without true turning from sin, e.g., Sir. 34:26; Test. A. 2:8; Apc. Eliae 23: "Whoso fasts without being pure angers the Lord ... but I have created a pure fast with a pure heart and hands." Alongside the generally obligatory fast of the Day of Atonement, *the* νηστεία (→ 925; 928), [27] and other prescribed fast days (cf. S. Bar. 86:2; Jos. Ant., 11, 134; Vit., 290; Ap., 2, 282) the zealous among the righteous select two days in the week, the second and the fifth (Did., 8, 1 → 933) and voluntarily make them regular fast days which they keep strictly, Lk. 18:12 (Mk. 2:18 and par.). A fast may often last, not just one day (1 Macc. 3:47; S. Bar. 5:7), but three (2 Macc. 13:12, cf. also Ac. 9:9, 19), or seven (4 Esr. 5:13, 20 etc.; S. Bar. 9:2; 12:5 etc.) or even forty days (Vit. Ad. 6). Days which do not permit of fasting are the preparation of the Sabbath and the Sabbath, the preparation of the new moon and the new moon, and the various feasts and festivals (Jdt. 8:6; cf. Jub. 50:10, 12). Longer fasting, if possible for the whole of life, is a distinguishing mark of the ideal figures of Jewish piety, Jdt. 8:6; Eth. En. 108:9 f.; Test. S. 3:4; Test. Jud. 15:4; Test. Jos. 3:4; Lk. 2:37 (Ex. 38:26 LXX?). Much stress is laid on gestures of mourning in fasting (→ 928), cf. 1 Macc. 3:47; Jos. Ant., 19, 349; 20, 89 and esp. Mt. 6:16 f. As the representatives of the most zealous Jewish religion the Pharisees are particularly strict in their fasts, [28] Ps. Sol. 3:8. They observe voluntary fasts (Mk. 2:18 par.) [29] and value the practice

---

[24] In this connection one should also mention sobriety on the Sabbath morning, *v.* Jos. Vit., 279: ἕκτη ὥρα, καθ' ἣν τοῖς σάββασιν ἀριστοποιεῖσθαι νόμιμόν ἐστιν ἡμῖν, and on this Str.-B., II, 615.

[25] On the common Roman error that the Jews fasted on the Sabbath (→ *infra*) cf. O. Holtzmann, 350.

[26] TU, NF, 2, 3a (1899), 70 ff.

[27] Cf. also Jos. Bell., 5, 236: ἐν ᾗ νηστεύειν ἔθος ἡμέρᾳ πάντας τῷ θεῷ, Ant., 3, 240: δεκάτῃ δὲ τοῦ αὐτοῦ (i.e., the seventh) μηνὸς κατὰ σελήνην διανηστεύοντες ἕως ἑσπέρας. The Rheneia prayers for vengeance also allude to this day, Ditt. Syll.[3], 1181, cf. lines 10 ff.: ᾧ πᾶσα ψυχὴ ἐν τῇ σήμερον ἡμέρᾳ ταπεινοῦται μεθ' ἱκετείας, and on this cf. Deissmann LO, 357 f. Deissmann's view that penitential fasting and prayer for revenge are not mutually exclusive seems to be confirmed by a note in Midr. Ps. 41 § 8, where the prayer of Ps. 35:12, uttered in sackcloth as a garment of fasting, could have been a prayer for vengeance, as God Himself assumes acc. to the Midr. Cf. Str.-B., I, 371 [Bertram].

[28] One cannot say the same of the priests (because of their subjection to the laws of cleanness?) (Loh. Mk., 59).

[29] Lk. 5:33: νηστεύουσιν πυκνά, cf. Mt. 9:14 vl.

as highly meritorious, Lk. 18:12.[30] Characteristic of the piety of the disciples of John[31] was the fact that they observed voluntary fasts (Mk. 2:18 par.). In the severity of extraordinary pious exercises they were thus at one with the exemplary righteous of Judaism. Whether they followed a rule of their master similar to the rule of prayer which he gave (Lk. 11:1, cf. 5:33), or whether they followed his example, which illustrated the call for conversion (→ μετάνοια) by ascetic practice (Mk. 1:6 par.; Mt. 11:18 par.), we are not told. Among the Therapeutae a complete abstention from nourishment for 3 or even 6 days (Philo Vit. Cont., 35) represents a supreme ascetic achievement in the contemplative life of a host of pious hermits devoted to the study of Scripture.[32] We are not told that the Essenes included fasts among their pious exercises. Indeed, the sources do not tell us for certain that they would not eat flesh or wine in their striving for ἐγκράτεια (→ II, 341).[33] Philo's praise of νηστεία above all things in Spec. Leg., II, 193-203[34] applies not so much to ritual fasting as to the highest possible achievement of the ascetic ideal of restraint (→ II, 341) with ref. also to eating and drinking, *ibid.*, 197. In Migr. Abr., 98 the most fitting and perfect of all offerings is τὸ νηστείας καὶ καρτερίας ἀνάθημα, cf. *ibid.*, 204.[35]

Rabb. Judaism came to many decisions regarding fasting (יָשַׁב בְּתַעֲנִית, הִתְעַנָּה, צום),[36] both the public fast of the congregation obligatory for everyone (תַּעֲנִית צִבּוּר) and also the voluntary fasts of individuals (תַּעֲנִית יָחִיד). The main fast is still the Day of Atonement, the 10th Tishri (Yoma, 8, 1a). Judaism also observes as a day of national mourning the 9th Ab, the day of the first and second destruction of the temple (Taan., 4, 6 f.).[37] General fasts could also be ordered by the authorities in times of emergency (drought, pestilence, war etc.).[38] Monday and Thursday were the days preferred for these extraordinary national fasts (bTaan., 10a, cf. Taan., 1, 4 f.).[39] There are to be no fasts on the Sabbath and feasts.[40] After the cessation of the sacrificial cultus the Jew was more strongly impelled toward private fasting because of the power and meritoriousness of this work which is pleasing to God. Fasting replaces sacrifice, bBer., 17a: a pronouncement of R. Shesheth.[41] It is greater than alms, for it involves the body and not just money, bBer., 32b: a statement of R. Eleazar.[42] It brings about and guarantees a divine answer: "He who prays and is not answered must fast," jBer., 8a; "He who puts on sackcloth and fasts, let him not lay it off until what he prays for takes place," Midr.

---

[30] Fasting on Monday and Thursday (Lk. 18:12) is not to be regarded as a rule binding on all Pharisees.

[31] The presentation in E. Lohmeyer, *Das Urchristentum*, 1: "Johannes d. Täufer" (1932), 114 ff. is clearer than the sources permit.

[32] Strathmann, 148 ff.; Bousset-Gressm., 465 ff.

[33] Strathmann, 87 ff.; Bousset-Gressm., 465; W. Bauer, Art. "Essener," Pauly-W., Suppl. IV, 424.

[34] Cf. I. Heinemann, *Philons gr. u. jüd. Bildung* (1932), 132 ff.; W. Völker, "Fortschritt u. Vollendung bei Philo v. Alexandrien," TU, 49, 1 (1938), 132 f.

[35] When Philo in Ebr., 148 speaks of a ceaseless fasting and hungering (νηστείαν συνεχῆ καὶ λιμόν) for φρόνησις, he is following a fig. use found from time to time from Emped. Fr., 144 (I, 277, 23, Diels[5]): νηστεῦσαι κακότητος, and recurrent also in earlier Chr. lit., e.g., Cl. Al. Strom., VII, 75, 3; 76, 1, or Chrys. Ad. Populum Antiochenum Hom., 3 (MPG, 49, 53): νηστευέτω καὶ στόμα ἀπὸ ῥημάτων αἰσχρῶν καὶ λοιδορίας (cf. Lidz. Ginza, 18, 25 ff.; 39, 27 ff. etc.); cf. also the agraphon, → n. 66.

[36] First in the roll of fasts (Megillat Taan.) from the 1st cent. A.D. For the original Aram. form cf. G. Dalman, *Aram. Dialektproben*[2] (1927), 1 ff. The ed. of A. Neubauer in *Anecdota Oxoniensia, Semitic Ser.*, I, 6 (1895), 3 ff. contains also later Heb. additions.

[37] Str.-B., IV, 77 ff.

[38] *Ibid.*, 82 ff.

[39] For their choice on grounds of expediency, *ibid.*, 89; II, 243, n. 2.

[40] The roll of fasts (→ n. 36) forbids for the first time fasting not only on cultic feasts (cf. Jdt. 8:6 → 929) but also on national festivals.

[41] Str.-B., IV, 107, No. 9c.

[42] *Ibid.*, No. 9d.

Abba Gorjon, 6a (ed. Buber, 21a).[43] Fasting makes a saint, bTaan., 11a: pronouncement of R. Eleazar.[44] The pt. of fasting is not just to expiate sin, to avert calamity or to attain the fulfilment of a desire. Fasting is for its own sake. Its self-evident character can be understood only in terms of the conviction that God recognises the achievement as such.[45] There is lively recollection of Is.58:3 ff.,[46] bTaan., 16a (cf. Taan., 2, 1), where in a sermon on fasting we are told that the power lies, not in the sackcloth and fasting, but in penitence and good works.[47] But these are subsidiary notes which are drowned by the chorus of voices lauding fasting as an end in itself. How far fasting can sometimes be carried may be seen from the objections advanced against it on various rational grounds.[48] The student of Scripture should not engage in private fasts because he thereby reduces his work for heaven, bTaan., 11b; he weakens himself and cannot study.[49] R. Shesheth said: "If a young man keeps on fasting, a dog may eat up his meal," bTaan., 11b. A special form of private fasting, along with occasional fasts, is the voluntary, and later obligatory, setting aside of specific days for fasting.[50] The two days selected were those usually appointed for national fasts, i.e., Monday and Thursday, → 930. That this custom went back to the 1st cent. is not proved decisively by Rabb. sources,[51] but it is apparent from Did., 8, 1, → 933, cf. 929. The reason for such fasts may be quite old, cf. bGit., 56a: "R. Çadoq sat fasting 40 years that Jerusalem might not be destroyed."[52] The individual fasts representatively.[53] His exercise in piety is for the salvation of the whole body. In this light one can understand the concern of the Pharisee in Lk. 18:12: "He stands before God as one who in fasting and prayer bears on his heart the weal and woe of the people. He thus thinks that he should be seen before God."[54]

4. Fasting in the New Testament.

The position which Jesus adopts towards fasting is new and distinctive. At the beginning of the story of the temptation (Mt. 4:2; Lk. 4:2)[55] He spent 40 days (and 40 nights) fasting in the wilderness. This already does not accord with current practice. Behind the story there obviously stands reminiscence of Moses' fast on Sinai (Ex. 34:28; Dt. 9:9, → 927).[56] The way of the Messiah (Mt. 3:17; Lk. 3:22) corresponds to that of Moses. But whereas the mediator of the covenant of the

---

[43] *Ibid.*, 103, No. 8a.
[44] *Ibid.*, 108, No. 9 l.
[45] *Ibid.*, 94 and 105.
[46] *Ibid.*, 107, No. 9a.
[47] *Loc. cit.*
[48] *Ibid.*, II, 95.
[49] II, 100, No. 6w.
[50] II, 242 ff.
[51] In its original form the Megillat Taan. does not deal with voluntary fasting on the second and fifth days. The first ref. to this is in a much later Heb. comm. On c. 12 and in Megillat Taan., 13, which is a later addition, we have the explanation: "Our teachers have also ordained that one should fast on the second and fifth days for three reasons: because of the destruction of the temple; because of the Torah which has been burned; and because of the desecration of the divine name," cf. Str.-B., II, 243.
[52] Str.-B., II, 243 f. refers to the Monday-to-Thursday fast of the laity present at the *tamid* sacrifice in the temple (Taan., 4, 3), which had ref. to the special needs of the people, cf., e.g., bTaan., 27b Bar. (Str.-B., II, 65, No. 3h).
[53] Moore, II, 261 f.
[54] Str.-B., II, 244; cf. Schl. Lk., *ad loc.*
[55] Cf. Zn. Mt. and Lk., *ad loc.*; Schl. Mt., *ad loc.*; Hck. Lk., *ad loc.*; S. Eitrem, *D. Versuchung Christi* (1924), 19 ff., 37 (concluding remark by A. Fridrichsen); E. Lohmeyer, "D. Versuchung Jesu," ZSTh, 14 (1937), 626 ff.
[56] Tertullian Bapt., 20 arbitrarily suggests an antithetical relation between Israel's 40 yrs. of wandering with its sins of excess and the 40 days fast of Jesus.

OT fasted in preparation for the revelation of God, Jesus had already received it, and He fasted in order to be equipped to confirm the Messianic dignity and power with which He had been invested. His refusal of nourishment (Lk.: οὐκ ἔφαγεν οὐδὲν ἐν ταῖς ἡμέραις ἐκείναις) is no mere ascetic exercise.[57] As One who has been apprehended by the Spirit (Mt. 4:1; Lk. 4:1) He lives in a world where different conditions of life apply from those of earth (cf. also Mt. 4:11b).[58] The sources give us no reason to suppose that He fasted during the period of His public ministry,[59] though His external attitude to the dominant cultus leaves us in no doubt that He would observe the general days of fasting.[60] Nor does He forbid His hearers to fast.[61] In Mt. 6:16 ff.[62] He presupposes that they might engage in voluntary fasting as one of the common forms of religious discipline. But the significance which He ascribes to fasting is wholly different from that which Judaism in fateful misunderstanding tends to associate with the custom. Fasting is service of God. It is a sign and symbol of the conversion to God (→ μετάνοια) which takes place in concealment. Impressive display before men defeats the end of true fasting. Fasting before God, the Father of those who turn to Him, is joy. Hence there is no place for melancholy signs of mourning. Mk. 2:18 ff. par. goes further.[63] The immediate disciples of Jesus do not fast like the more pious of the people, the disciples of John and the Pharisees. When complaint is made about this, Jesus will not accept it. He defends the disciples on the ground that fasting in the presence of the Bridegroom is nonsensical. The presence of the Messiah (→ νυμφίος), the time of salvation which has dawned (→ I, 654), means joy. Joy and fasting, i.e., sorrow (Mt. 9:15), are mutually exclusive (→ III, 848). Sorrow and fasting belong to the time of waiting for salvation. This is true for the disciples too, who by His death will be rudely put back in the state of waiting, cf. Jn. 16:20.[64] Seen from the standpoint of the Messianic eschatological centre of the message of Jesus, fasting is transcended. But since Jesus is aware of an interval between Now and Then, between the dawn of salvation on earth and its consummation, He finds a place for fasting between the times.[65] It is not, of course, a pious work. It is a sign and symbol of the inner attitude which perhaps

---

57 Holtzmann NT on Mt. 4:2.

58 Cf. F. Büchsel, *Der Geist Gottes im NT* (1926), 172.

59 It is going too far to conclude from the practice of the disciples in Mk. 2:18 that non-fasting was for Jesus a form of life.

60 His opponents obviously could not charge Him with violating the laws of fasting. The adverse judgment of the Jews in Mt. 11:19 par. obviously has no more to do with despising fasts than the judgment on the Baptist in 11:18 par. has to do with zealously keeping them.

61 Cf. H. Preisker, *Geist u. Leben. Das Telos-Ethos des Urchristentums* (1933), 93.

62 Cf. Zn. Mt., Kl. Mt., Schl. Mt., J. Schniewind (*NT Deutsch,* I³ [1937]), *ad loc.*

63 Cf. Zn. Mt. and Lk., Schl. Mt., Kl. Mk., Hck. Mk., J. Schniewind, *Das Ev. nach Mk.* (*NT Deutsch,* I³ [1937]) and *Das Ev. nach Mt.* (*NT Deutsch,* I³ [1937]), Loh. Mk., K. H. Rengstorf, *Das Ev. nach Lk.* (*NT Deutsch,* I³ [1937]), *ad loc.*; M. Dibelius, *D. urchristl. Überlieferung von Johannes dem Täufer* (1911), 39 ff.; A. Blakiston, *John Baptist and his Relation to Jesus* (1912), 32 ff.; J. Jeremias, "Jesus als Weltvollender," BFTh, 33, 4 (1930), 21 ff.; Ebeling, 392 ff.

64 On the historicity of the prophecy of death here *v.* Schl. Gesch. d. Chr., 358; Hck. Mk. and Lk.; Schniewind, Mk. and Mt., *ad loc.*

65 ἐν ἐκείνῃ τῇ ἡμέρᾳ (only Mk. 2:20) may be a ref. of the Evangelist to the (Good) Friday fast, *v.* A. Loisy, *L'Évangile selon Marc* (1912), Wbg. Mk., Loh. Mk., *ad loc.*

hardly needs such a sign and symbol.[66] The attitude of Jesus to fasting is not unlike that of the prophets. But the reasons and concrete expression are His own, uniquely determined by His Messianic consciousness.

In the Gospel tradition primitive Christianity links the parables of the new patch on the old garment and the new wine in the old wineskins (Mk. 2:21 and par.) with the question of fasting (2:18 ff.).[67] In so doing it preserves a recollection of the fact that fasting does not belong to the new age introduced by Jesus. Nor does the 1st cent. tell us that Christians practised voluntary fasts.[68] But[69] the habit of strengthening prayer by fasting is adopted by Christians in Ac. 13:3 (on the sending out of the missionaries Barnabas and Paul from Antioch) and in Ac. 14:23 (when elders are appointed by Paul and Barnabas in the newly founded churches of South Asia Minor). In common worship (→ λειτουργέω) the prophets and teachers of Antioch prepare themselves by fasting for the revelation of the Spirit which will decide which missionaries are to be set apart, Ac. 13:2.[70] In the Pauline circle "the fast day" is familiar from the Jewish calendar (Ac. 27:9, → 925; 929), though this does not imply its observance. The NT epistles say nothing about fasting.[71] This applies especially to Hb. 13:16, which mentions prayer, thanksgiving and well-doing as sacrifices which are pleasing to God (→ III, 182, 186), but not fasting (unlike Mt. 6 and Did., 8, 1 f. and 15, 4). In R. 14 and Col. 2[72] Paul discusses ascetic and ritualistic leanings in the churches (→ I, 642 f., 675; II, 693), but he does not even mention the subject of fasting. This leaves us with the impression that the question did not even arise, at least for Hellenistic congregations.[73]

5: Fasting in the Early Church.

From the post-apostolic period onwards a different trend is evident. Voluntary fasting on specific days returns. The Christian practice of fasting on Wednesday and Friday is contrasted with the Jewish practice in Did., 8, 1: αἱ δὲ νηστεῖαι ὑμῶν μὴ ἔστωσαν μετὰ τῶν ὑποκριτῶν· νηστεύουσι γὰρ δευτέρᾳ σαββάτων καὶ πέμπτῃ· ὑμεῖς δὲ νηστεύσατε τετράδα καὶ παρασκευήν.[74] The Christian who fasts on these days is vigilantly expectant of the Lord's coming, cf. Herm. s., 5, 1, 1 f.: στατίωνα ἔχω = νηστεύω, Tertullian De Oratione, 19 (CSEL, 20, 192, 11).[75] There is no rule of fasting on these days prior to the 3rd cent. One fasts *ex arbitrio, non ex imperio novae disci-*

[66] This would follow from Mk. 2:21 f. if we could be sure of the original relation to the question of fasting or not, though → 898 f. Cf. also the agraphon in P. Oxy., I, 3 : ἐὰν μὴ νηστεύσητε τὸν κόσμον, οὐ μὴ εὕρητε τὴν βασιλείαν τοῦ θεοῦ (on νηστεύειν in the fig. sense → n. 35).

[67] → 898 f.

[68] But → n. 65 and II, 693, n. 29.

[69] That on the day of Pentecost the disciples went sober to the temple in fidelity to Jewish custom (→ n. 24) may well be the pt. of the ref. of Peter to the third hour in Ac. 2:15.

[70] Cf. Holtzmann NT, *ad loc.*

[71] On 2 C. 6:5 and 11:27 → 925, on 1 C. 7:5 vl. → n. 80.

[72] Whether → ταπεινοφροσύνη in Col. 2:18 includes fasting is uncertain, cf. Dib. Gefbr. and Loh. Col., *ad loc.*

[73] On νηστεία or νηστεύω in Mk. 9:29 vl. (Mt. 17:21); Ac. 10:30 vl. and 1 C. 7:5 vl. → n. 80.

[74] For later instances cf. A. Harnack, *Die Lehre d. 12 Apostel* (1884), *ad loc.* and T. Zahn, *Skizzen aus dem Leben d. alten Kirche*[3] (1908), 359, n. 27.

[75] On the expression cf. Svennung, on the matter Achelis, *Christentum,* I, 149; Holl, 213; H. Lietzmann, *Gesch. d. alten Kirche,* II (1936), 129.

plinae pro temporibus et causis uniuscuiusque, Tert. De Ieiunio, 2 (CSEL, 20, 275, 22 f.). Friday is chosen because it is the day of the crucifixion, Wednesday (from the very first?) because it is the day of the arrest of Jesus, Didasc., 21, p. 107, 25, J. Flemming.[76] During the course of the 2nd cent. there is laid on all Christians the duty of fasting during the time that the Lord was in the tomb[77] (the Easter fast), cf. Iren. in Eus. Hist. Eccl., V, 24, 12 ff.; Mk. 2:20 par. supplied the biblical basis for this, Tert. De Ieiunio, 2, 13 (CSEL, 20, 275, 17 ff.; 291, 16 f.); Const. Ap., V, 18, 2. To fast on Sunday is forbidden, Tert. De Corona, 3. In Act. Joh., 6 the apostle breaks his continuous fast on Sunday.[78] It soon becomes a practice for the candidate to fast before baptism, Did., 7, 4; Just. Apol., 61, 2; Ps. Clem. Recg., 6, 15; 7, 34; Ps. Clem. Hom., 13, 9; Tert. Bapt., 20. The baptiser and others who also take part in the baptism fast as well, Did., *loc. cit.*; Just., *loc. cit.*; Ps. Clem. Recg., 7, 37; Ps. Clem. Hom., 13, 11; Cl. Al. Exc. Theod., 84; Tert. Bapt., *loc. cit.* The fast of neophytes begins already during the catechumenate acc. to Ps. Clem. Recg., 3, 67; Ps. Clem. Hom., 11, 35. The custom of fasting communion is found already in Ac. Pl. Pap. Hamb., 6, 36 f.: τοῦ [δὲ Παύ]λου ... τὴν νηστίαν μετ' αὐτῶν ἀποθέ[ντος] προσφορᾶς γενομένης ὑπὸ τοῦ Παύλου ..., cf. Tert. De Oratione 19. Fasting is commonly practised along with and to strengthen prayer,[79] *v.* Pol., 7, 2; Act. Thom., 20 and 145,[80] and also to prepare for receiving God's revelation,[81] *v.* Herm. v., 2, 2, 1; 3, 1, 2; 3, 10, 6 f.;[82] Fr. Muratorianum, lines 10 ff. (Kl. T., 1^2, 5): (*Johannes*) *cohortantibus condiscipulis et episcopis suis dixit: conieiunate mihi hodie triduo, et quid cuique fuerit revelatum, alterutrum nobis enarremus;* Act. Pt. Verc., 17 (p. 63, 11 f., R. A. Lipsius), and esp. the Montanist fasts (Tert. De Ieiunio, 1; 2; 10; Hier. Ep., 41, 3; Hipp. Ref., 8, 19, 2).[83] Fasting to express sorrow is found in Act. Pl., Pap. Hamb., 5, 19. In the service of well-doing, to help the poor with the food saved, fasting is a good work, cf. the agraphon in Orig. Hom. in Lv., 10, 2: *beatus est, qui etiam ieiunat pro eo, ut alat pauperem;* Herm. s., 5, 3, 7 f.; Aristid. Apol., 15, 9: *si apud eos eget aut pauper est et copia victus eis non est, duo aut tres dies ieiunant, ut egentibus victum necessarium suppeditent,* cf. Sextus Pythagor., 267 (Gnomica, I, ed. A. Elter [1892]): ὑπὲρ τοῦ πτωχὸν τραφῆναι καὶ νηστεῦσαι καλόν. This fasting is meritorious, Herm. s., 5, 3, 8, cf. 2 Cl., 16, 4: κρείσσων νηστεία προσευχῆς. Even before he became a Montanist Tert. saw in fasting a sacrifice which reconciles God, De Patientia, 13; De Oratione, 18; De Carnis Resurrectione, 8. In all the fasting established by the Church from the 2nd cent. on[84] there is a continuation of OT and Jewish piety. The motives, which are related to a dualistic view, may be seen plainly in Marcion (Epiph. Haer., 42, 3, 3),[85] the Gnostics (e.g., Act. Phil., 142; the Manichees: Fihrist, 64 ff.;[86] Aug. Contra Epistulam Fundamenti, 8 [CSEL, 25, 202, 7 ff.] etc.) and the precursors of monasticism.[87]

---

[76] Cf. Holl, 210; Lietzmann, I (1932), 61.

[77] Cf. Achelis RE³, 5, 773 f.

[78] Cf. also T. Zahn, 360, n. 29.

[79] Thus in Did., 1, 3 (without par. in Mt. 5:44; Lk. 6:27 f.) νηστεύετε ...· ὑπὲρ τῶν διωκόντων ὑμᾶς is added to προσεύχεσθε ὑπὲρ τῶν ἐχθρῶν ὑμῶν. Cf. Kn. Did., *ad loc.*

[80] The addition of νηστείᾳ to προσευχῇ in Mk. 9:29 P⁴⁵ ACD etc. (cf. Mt. 17:21 CD Orig.) and 1 C. 7:5 𝔎 or of νηστεύων to προσευχόμενος in Ac. 10:30 D 𝔎 is to be explained by the sense that prayer and fasting belong inseparably together.

[81] Cf. the later interpretation in Chrys. Hom. in Cap. 1 Gn., X, 2 (MPG, 53, 83): ἡ ... νηστεία τὸ μὲν σῶμα κατατείνει καὶ χαλινοῖ τὰ ἄτακτα σκιρτήματα, τὴν δε ψυχὴν διαυγεστέραν ἐργάζεται καὶ πτεροῖ καὶ μετάρσιον (lifted up on high) καὶ κούφην ποιεῖ.

[82] Cf. on this H. Weinel, *Die Wirkungen des Geistes u. der Geister im nachapostolischen Zeitalter bis auf Irenaeus* (1899), 224 ff.

[83] Cf. F. J. Dölger, *Antike u. Christentum,* I (1929), 113 f. etc.

[84] Cf. in this connection fasting in penitential discipline, Cl. Al. Quis Div. Salv., 42, 15; Tert. De Poenitentia, 9.

[85] Cf. G. Flügel, *Mani* (1862), 160; A. v. Harnack, *Marcion²* (1924), 149 f.

[86] Flügel, *loc. cit.*; cf. also 95 ff.

[87] Achelis, *Christentum,* II, 334, n. 2.

Where there is criticism of fasting,[88] it is based on the OT prophets, cf. Barn., 3, 1 ff. (Is. 58:4 ff.); Just. Dial., 15, 1 ff. (Is. 58:1 ff.); Cl. Al. Paed., III, 90, 1 f. (Is. 58:4 ff.); Tert. De Ieiunio, 2 (Is. 58:4 f.) etc., and materially Herm. s., 5, 1; Ptolemaeus Ep. ad Floram (Epiph., 33, 5, 13 f.): οὐχὶ τὴν σωματικὴν βούλεται (sc. ὁ σωτήρ) νηστείαν ἡμᾶς νηστεύειν, ἀλλὰ τὴν πνευματικήν, ἐν ᾗ ἐστιν ἀποχὴ πάντων τῶν φαύλων. φυλάσσεται μέντοι γε καὶ παρὰ τοῖς ἡμετέροις ἡ κατὰ τὸ φαινόμενον νηστεία, ἐπεὶ καὶ ψυχῇ τι συμβάλλεσθαι δύναται αὕτη μετὰ λόγου γινομένη, ὁπότε μηδὲ διὰ τὴν πρός τινας μίμησιν γίνεται μήτε διὰ τὸ ἔθος μήτε διὰ τὴν ἡμέραν, ὡς ὡρισμένης <εἰς> τοῦτο ἡμέρας ἅμα δε καὶ εἰς ἀνάμνησιν τῆς ἀληθινῆς νηστείας, ἵνα οἱ μηδέπω ἐκείνην δυνάμενοι νηστεύειν ἀπὸ τῆς κατὰ τὸ φαινόμενον νηστείας ἔχωσι τὴν ἀνάμνησιν αὐτῆς. Along with sharp rejection (Barn., 3; Herm. s., 5, 1, 3 ff.) we find a trend toward inwardness and the subordination of the rite to the ethos, cf. Herm. s., 5, 3, 5 ff.; Ptolemaeus Ep. ad Floram (→ *supra*); Cl. Al. Strom., 6, 102, 3: νηστεῖαι δὲ ἀποχὰς κακῶν μηνύουσιν πάντων ἀπαξαπλῶς, τῶν τε κατ' ἐνέργειαν καὶ κατὰ λόγον καὶ κατὰ τὴν διάνοιαν αὐτήν, cf. Ecl. Proph., 14, 1 (III, 140, 23 ff., O. Stählin). There is no longer any clear awareness of the way in which Jesus viewed fasting.

Behm

---

[88] Dg., 4, 1 lashes Jewish fasting as εἰρωνεία.

νήφω, νηφάλιος, ἐκνήφω

† νήφω.

The concept which underlies the verb νήφω = "to be sober" and the whole word group, is formally negative. It is the opp. of "intoxication"[1] (→ μεθύω) both 1. in the lit. sense of intoxication with wine, and 2. in the fig. sense of states of spiritual intoxication attributable to other causes.

1. Sobriety in the Literal Sense.

a. The usage is originally radical. A man is νήφων[2] who is at the time completely unaffected by wine, Theogn., 478: οὔτ' ἔτι γὰρ νήφω οὔτε λίην μεθύω, Epict. Diss., IV, 27: οὐ δύνασαι δ' ἐν ἀμφοτέρῳ τῷ εἴδει διενεγκεῖν ... ἑλοῦ οὖν, πότερον μεθυστὴς εἶναι θέλεις ἢ νήφων, cf. also in Plut. De Garrulitate, 4 (II, 503) the proverb: τὸ γὰρ ἐν τῇ καρδίᾳ τοῦ νήφοντος ἐπὶ τῆς γλώττης ἐστὶ τοῦ μεθύοντος. b. But in the same context Pluto, like many others,[3] makes a distinction between mere οἴνωσις and strict → μέθη. This distinction must surely have had a relativising effect on the idea of sobriety.[4] This may be seen in Philo, where instead of the older middle way between the mutually exclusive opposites of drunkenness and sobriety there can even be ref. to a synthesis between the two. Thus in Quaest. in Gn., 2, 68 the abstemious person (*constans*) can be intoxicated,[5] cf. also Fug., 32: σὺ ... ἐὰν δέ που βιασθῇς εἰς πλειόνων ἀπόλαυσιν ἐλθεῖν, ... εἰ χρὴ τὸν τρόπον εἰπεῖν τοῦτον, → νηφάλια μεθυσθήσῃ.

The intermediate clause εἰ χρὴ ... shows, of course, that this is a concession on the part of the ascetic Philo, and does not represent his basic conviction. It is also likely that the circles whose view Philo is discussing were already using the word νήφω in a less stringent sense.[6] Cf. Leg. All., II, 29; Plant., 142 ff. In a similitude Plat. Leg., VI (773 ed) speaks of water as νήφων θεός. In the mixing vessel (κρατήρ) of national life (πόλις) the sober element (which is poor in wealth and influence) has a moderating effect on the equally necessary intoxicating (μαινόμενος οἶνος) element.[7] Here, however, the metaphor is simply speaking in terms of a profitable mixture, and the true synthesis applies to the reality rather than the figure. In other words, the use is predominantly figurative.

νήφω. Dob. Th., 209 ff. On the etym. cf. Walde-Pok., II, 317.

[1] Philo Plant., 172: τό γε νήφειν καὶ τὸ μεθύειν ἐναντία.

[2] In earlier times the pres. part. is the most common form of the verb; the aor. does not occur prior to Philo and Nicolas of Damascus.

[3] On the early history of this distinction cf. H. v. Arnim, *Philol. Untersuchungen*, II (1888), 103 and 139.

[4] Cf. Philostr. Vit. Ap., II, 35: πεπωκότα μὲν οἴνου, νήφοντα δὲ ...

[5] Cf. P. Wendland, *Neu entdeckte Fragmente Philos* (1891), 63.

[6] Cf. Lit. ZNW, Beih. 9 (1929), 26, n. 1.

[7] ... πόλιν εἶναι δεῖ δίκην κρατῆρος κεκραμένην, οὗ μαινόμενος μὲν οἶνος ἐγκεχυμένος ζεῖ, κολαζόμενος δὲ ὑπὸ νήφοντος ἑτέρου θεοῦ καλὴν κοινωνίαν λαβὼν ἀγαθὸν πῶμα καὶ μέτριον ἀπεργάζεται.

2. Sobriety in the Figurative Sense.

a. In general, when the word is used in a fig. sense, the subject of νήφειν is not a god or an element but the individual or his λογισμός (Epic. Ep., 3 § 132, p. 64; Philo Ebr., 166), and what is in view is the unequivocal and immediately self-evident antithesis to all kinds of mental fuzziness, Epicharmus Comicus, 250 (CGF, 1, 1, 137): νᾶφε καὶ μέμνασ' ἀπιστεῖν, ἄρθρα ταῦτα τῶν φρενῶν. Νήφων is a predicate of honour, positive rather than negative, along with such others as, e.g., ἀγρυπνῶν and πεφροντικώς, Plut. Praec. Ger. Reip., 4, 3 (II, 800b): Θεμιστοκλῆς ἅπτεσθαι τῆς πολιτείας διανοούμενος, ἀπέστησε τῶν πότων καὶ τῶν κώμων ἑαυτόν, ἀγρυπνῶν δὲ καὶ νήφων καὶ πεφροντικώς, λέγει ..., ὡς οὐκ ἐᾷ καθεύδειν αὐτὸν τὸ Μιλτιάδου τρόπαιον. [8] νήφειν is necessary not merely in terms of individual worth but also and esp. for public service. How highly a state should value sober judgment, esp. in financial and commercial affairs, may be seen quite plainly in Plat. Leg., XI (918d). [9] Acc. to Plato true νήφειν, which even in face of favourable opportunity is able to prefer μέτρου ἐχόμενον (moderate possessions) to πολύ, arises, of course, only in the rare cases in which nature and education co-operate most favourably. This shows us clearly what the fig. use of the term suggested in the Gk. world.

b. Each man is called to a form of service which demands νήφειν, though it must be recognised in practice that the demand is generally too high for the forces of empirical man. It would be surprising if at this pt. we did not catch an echo from the world of OT monotheism. In this world there is knowledge of a living God whose service constantly means obedience. Also known are the severe, and to the pagan world absurd, burdens of this obedience. Nevertheless, there is also an unperturbed and proud readiness to bear them. In Gk. terms this readiness is νήφειν or sobriety. The simple form does not occur in the LXX (→ ἐκνήφω) but Philo often uses it both in derivation of sobriety from the nature of God and in description of sobriety as an acknowledgment of God. When children or subjects approach their parents or lords, the first and obvious requirement is νήφειν, the conscious avoidance of all offence; how much more obvious is this requirement for him who would worship the Guide and Father of all things, Ebr., 131: δεσπόταις μὲν καὶ γονεῦσι καὶ ἄρχουσιν οἰκέται καὶ υἱοὶ καὶ ὑπήκοοι μέλλοντες προσέρχεσθαι πρόνοιαν ἕξουσι τοῦ νήφειν, ὡς μήτε ἐν τοῖς λεγομένοις καὶ πραττομένοις διαμάρτοιεν ... τὸν δὲ τοῦ παντὸς ἡγεμόνα καὶ πατέρα τις θεραπεύειν δικαιῶν οὐ καὶ σιτίων καὶ ποτῶν καὶ ὕπνου ... περιέσται; [10] The requirement is so obvious that the νόμιμον αἰώνιον (Lv. 10:8-10) in which Philo finds it stated is to be regarded, not strictly as a prohibition, but simply as a γνώμη which expresses a fact grounded in the nature of the universe; it is impossible (ἀμήχανον) to deny it recognition, Ebr., 138 ff. He who has to do with the living God cannot for the sake of God desire otherwise than that he should soberly regulate the powers which he has been given. He will choose παιδεία as his guide (Ebr., 153) and keep God's commandment (sobriety in respect of the 3rd commandment, Decal., 89). Philo can even say that to be sober is to recognise that God is God, Poster. C., 175: νήφοντος μὲν γὰρ ἔργον λογισμοῦ καὶ <σώφρονος> τὸν θεὸν ὁμολογεῖν ποιητὴν καὶ πατέρα τοῦ παντός. [11] This fundamental statement means that drunkenness, which is usually presupposed tacitly as the positive counterpart of the negative term, is a subject of theological reflection. The obscurity and fuzziness of the human mind rests ultimately on the fact that in some form it sets the creaturely, the human ego, in the place which

---

[8] νήφειν is meant fig. (Liddell-Scott), but the sentence shows that the lit. sense could be in view when the fig. was used (in contrast to the Germ. "nüchtern" or Eng. "sober").

[9] Σμικρὸν γένος ἀνθρώπων καὶ φύσει ὀλίγον καὶ ἄκρᾳ τροφῇ τεθραμμένον, ὅταν εἰς χρείας τε καὶ ἐπιθυμίας τινῶν ἐμπίπτῃ, καρτερεῖν πρὸς τὸ μέτριον δυνατόν ἐστιν, καὶ ὅταν ἐξῇ χρήματα λαβεῖν πολλά, νήφει καὶ πρότερον αἱρεῖται τοῦ πολλοῦ τὸ μέτρου ἐχόμενον.

[10] This is true of νήφειν both in the lit. (131) and the fig. (132-138) senses, → n. 8.

[11] νήφω is here used on the basis of Gn. 9:24 LXX, hence as a full synon. of → ἐκνήφω.

belongs to God alone (*loc. cit.*: πίπτοντος δ' ὑπὸ μέθης καὶ παροινίας (sc. ἔργον ὁμολογεῖν) ἑαυτὸν ἑκάστου τῶν ἀνθρωπείων πραγμάτων εἶναι δημιουργόν, Som., II, 291: ἡμεῖς οἱ ἡγεμόνες, ἡμεῖς οἱ δυναστεύοντες· ἐφ' ἡμῖν ὁρμεῖ τὰ πάντα. A further implication is the unequivocal saying on the state in which a way is found from intoxication to soberness, i.e., on becoming sober. The man who has become sober sees what κακία has wrought in him during intoxication, Sob., 30: Νήψας οὖν ὁ δίκαιος ... αἰσθάνεται, ὅσα ἡ νεωτεροποιὸς ἐν αὐτῷ κακία πρότερον εἰργάζετο. To become sober is to come to μετάνοια, which for him who has become sober is the advisor who cannot be suborned or won over by flattery. The final goal which can be pointed out to the one who has thus become sober is a full amnesty on the part of the gracious power of the supreme being, Som., II, 292: ἐὰν μὲν ὥσπερ ἐκ μέθης νήψαντες ἐν ἑαυτοῖς γένωνται ... ἀκολακεύτῳ καὶ ἀδεκάστῳ χρησάμενοι συμβούλῳ μετανοίᾳ τὴν ἵλεω τοῦ ὄντος δύναμιν ἐξευμενισάμενοι ... ἀμνηστίαν εὑρήσονται παντελῆ. In these statements Philo shows that in his own way he is a serious expositor of the OT message. This judgment is not prejudicially affected even by the fact that he might have taken his equation of drunkenness and rejection or ignorance of God (→ μεθύω) from the older Gnostic tradition, or by the fact that in these circles the term νήφω might have undergone already a religious conversion.[12]

c. But we find a very different use when Philo considers intoxication (and drunkenness) predominantly from the standpoint of religious psychology. Is there really a concept of sobriety which applies to all men without qualification? No, empirical men are often ἄφρονες to such a degree that there are no criteria of intoxication and sobriety and the two merge into one another, Ebr., 147: πολλοὶ τῶν ἀφρόνων ἀπατηθέντες τοὺς νήφοντας μεθύειν ὑπετόπασαν, cf. 5. Philo himself is forced to acknowledge that psychologically the two intersect, that τρόπον τινὰ the sober are intoxicated, 148. The synthesis of sobriety and intoxication consists in νηφάλιος μέθη (→ 940; Op. Mund., 71; Leg. All., III, 82; Vit. Mos., I, 187; Omn. Prob. Lib., 13) or νήφουσα μέθη (Fug., 166; Leg. All., I, 83) or καλὴ μέθη (Vit. Cont., 88). When Philo endorses this synthesis (→ 1. b) lit. it is always by way of concession; he uses his oxymoron only hesitantly. But when the sense is figurative, he uses it with the joy of discovery; it is the paradoxical solution to a problem for which there is no other solution. At this pt. we see adaptability, knowledge of human nature, and in the oxymoron originality.[13] But the powerful one-sidedness of the concept as originally developed is undoubtedly weakened and diluted. The fig. use undergoes a softening similar to that of the lit. (→ 1. b), and in this instance, too, the process began before Philo. It had often happened that states of Dionysiac inspiration, whether cultic or non-cultic, had been affirmed, that they had been described in terms of intoxication, and yet an attempt had been made to express their soberness, cf. Περὶ ὕψους, 16 (De Sublimitate Libellus, ed. J. Vahlen^3, 41): κἂν βακχεύμασι νήφειν, or Philostr. Vit. Ap., 2, 37: βάκχοι τοῦ νήφειν. These passages are neither dependent on Philo nor are they models for his oxymoron.[14] Indeed, they are independent of one another, and in their independence they give evidence of a relatively early use of the sense described under 2. b. The passage from Plat. Leg., VI (773c d) mentioned under 1. a points in this direction.

In the NT the word is used only in the figurative sense (2.), and even here it is noteworthy that sense 2. b does not occur. Equation of spiritual endowment with Dionysiac intoxication might seem natural to outsiders (Ac. 2:12 ff.; cf.

---

[12] Later attestation is found in the much quoted Corp. Herm., 1, 27: ὯΩ λαοί, ἄνδρες γηγενεῖς, οἱ μέθῃ καὶ ὕπνῳ ἑαυτοὺς ἐκδεδωκότες καὶ τῇ ἀγνωσίᾳ τοῦ θεοῦ, νήψατε, παύσασθε δὲ κραιπαλῶντες, θελγόμενοι ὕπνῳ ἀλόγῳ. *Ibid.*, 7, 1 f.: ποῖ φέρεσθε, ὦ ἄνθρωποι, μεθύοντες, τὸν τῆς ἀγνωσίας ἄκρατον [λόγον] ἐκπιόντες ... στῆτε νήψαντες, ἀναβλέψατε τοῖς ὀφθαλμοῖς τῆς καρδίας — ὅπου οὐδεὶς μεθύει, ἀλλὰ πάντες νήφουσιν ἀφορῶντες εἰς τὸν ὁραθῆναι θέλοντα —.

[13] ZNW, Beih. 9 (1929), 82 and 89.

[14] *Ibid.*, 62 and 70.

Eph. 5:18), but it is quite misleading. There is thus no reason for a relativising or paradoxical estimation of soberness. The five passages in which the word is used (1 Th. 5:6, 8; 2 Tm. 4:5; 1 Pt. 1:13; 4:7; 5:8) make it clear from the immediate context that νήφειν consists in acknowledgment of the reality given with God's revelation [15] and in discharge of the resultant ministry [16] by worship, [17] hope, [18] love [19] and warfare. [20] The basis of the obviously uniform use in the NT is the usage established by the spirit (not the letter) of the OT.

For the continuation of the NT use in the period which followed cf. Pol., 11, 4 (helping love) and Ign. Pol., 2, 3 : νῆφε ὡς θεοῦ ἀθλητής. [21]

† νηφάλιος.

1. a. "Holding no wine." This word is distinguished from the verb → νήφω mainly by the fact that in the first instance it is used only of materials (esp. cultic), Aesch. Eum., 107: χοάς τ' ἀοίνους, [1] νηφάλια μειλίγματα, Polemo Historicus, 42 (Fr. Historicorum Graecorum, ed. C. Müller³ [1849], 127): νηφάλιοι θυσίαι, IG, III, 77, 15 and 18 : πόπανον νηφάλιον; Apoll. Rhod., 4, 712 : ἡ δ' εἴσω πελάνους μείλικτρά τε νηφαλίῃσιν καῖεν ἐπ' εὐχωλῇσι [2] παρέστιος. In Plut. Quaest. Conv., 4, 6 (τίς ὁ παρ' Ἰουδαίοις θεός [II, 672b]) the neut. plur. νηφάλια is used without closer definition for the offerings without wine which are made alongside μελίσπονδα, cf. also De Cohibenda Ira, 16 (II, 464c), though here νηφάλια θύειν is a symbol for abstemious (ἄοινος) conduct : ἡμέρας ... ὀλίγας οἷον ἀμεθύστους καὶ ἀοίνους διαγαγεῖν, ὥσπερ νηφάλια καὶ μελίσπονδα θύοντα. This natural shift of emphasis from offerings without wine to the sober manner of life of those who make them must have been common before Plut., who is already acquainted with the expression τῷ Διονύσῳ ... νηφάλια θύειν as a proverbial description of a modest meal, De Tuenda Sanitate Praecepta, 19 (II, 132e).

b. The word then comes to be used not merely for the materials of sacrifice but also for the related altars [3] and fuel, which is not to come from the vine or fig tree. [4] The

---

[15] 1 Th. 5:5 : υἱοὶ φωτός. 2 Tm. 4:4 : ἀπὸ τῆς ἀληθείας ... ἀποστρέψουσιν, ἐπὶ δὲ τοὺς μύθους ἐκτραπήσονται. σὺ δὲ νῆφε ἐν πᾶσιν. 1 Pt. 1:13 f.: ... ἐπὶ τὴν ... χάριν ἐν ἀποκαλύψει Ἰησοῦ Χριστοῦ ... μὴ συσχηματιζόμενοι ταῖς πρότερον ἐν τῇ ἀγνοίᾳ ὑμῶν ἐπιθυμίαις. 1 Pt. 4:7 f.: πάντων τὸ τέλος ἤγγικεν. σωφρονήσατε οὖν καὶ νήψατε. 1 Pt. 5:7 ff.: αὐτῷ μέλει περὶ ὑμῶν ... ἀντίστητε στερεοὶ τῇ πίστει.

[16] 2 Tm. 4:5 : τὴν διακονίαν σου πληροφόρησον. 1 Pt. 1:14 : ὡς τέκνα ὑπακοῆς. 1 Pt. 4:10 : διακονοῦντες. 1 Th. 5:6; 1 Pt. 5:8 : γρηγορεῖν.

[17] 1 Pt. 4:7: νήψατε εἰς προσευχάς.

[18] 1 Th. 5:6 : The eschatological content of the whole section ; 1 Pt. 1:13 : τελείως ἐλπίσατε.

[19] 2 Tm. 4:2 : ἐν πάσῃ μακροθυμίᾳ. 1 Pt. 4:8 : τὴν ... ἀγάπην ἐκτενῆ ἔχοντες.

[20] 1 Th. 5:8 : The spiritual armour ; 2 Tm. 4:5 : κακοπάθησον. 1 Pt. 1:13 : ἀναζωσάμενοι τὰς ὀσφύας. 1 Pt. 5:8 f.: ὁ ἀντίδικος ... ἀντίστητε.

[21] On the later usage 2. c, cf. ZNW, Beih. 9, 108 ff.

νηφάλιος. B. Weiss, *Die Briefe Pauli an Tm. u. Tt.*⁷ (1902), 130 f., 353; Dib. Past., 33.

[1] Often synon. with νηφάλιος.

[2] Here at least an offering, cf. Preisigke Sammelbuch, 1719 and 2548 f.

[3] IG, II, 1651 (4th cent. B.C.): [νη]φάλιοι τρεῖς βωμοί, cf. U. v. Wilamowitz-Moellendorff, "Isyll. von Epidaurus" (*Philol. Untersuchungen*, 9 [1886]), 100; K. Elliger draws attention to an altar set up in Palmyra in 132 A.D. and bearing an Aram. inscr., which could well be a νηφάλιος βωμός (לא שתא חמר): Corpus Inscr. Semiticarum, 2, 3, 1, No. 3973 (line 4 f.), with bibl.

[4] Cf. the Scholion on Soph. Oed. Col., 100 : οὐ μόνον θυσίας νηφαλίους, ἀλλὰ καὶ ξύλα τινὰ ἐφ' ὧν ἔκαιον ... Philochoros, 31 (Fr. Historicorum Graecorum, ed. C. Müller, 1 [1841], 389).

term νηφάλιος applies not merely to use in sacrifice but also to a quality independent thereof. To the same sphere of cultic objects belongs the image of the κρατὴρ νηφάλιος without beaker or tankard which is proffered by the Muses. Plut. Sept. Sap. Conv., 13 (II, 156d): ὅταν δὲ τοιοῦτοι συνέλθωσιν ἄνδρες ... οὐδὲν ἔργον ἐστὶν οἶμαι κύλικος οὐδ' οἰνοχόης, ἀλλ' αἱ Μοῦσαι καθάπερ κρατῆρα νηφάλιον ἐν μέσῳ προθέμεναι τὸν λόγον, ᾧ πλεῖστον ἡδονῆς ἔνεστιν, ἐγείρουσι ... τὴν φιλοφροσύνην. But the essential thing about the λόγος illustrated by the κρατὴρ νηφάλιος is abstention from states of intoxication. Plut. leaves the sphere of cultic objects, if not the cultus, in a counterpart to the praise of musical speech, namely, the praise of silence, and indeed of silence in πότος, De garrulitate, 4 (II, 504 A): οὕτω τι βαθὺ καὶ μυστηριῶδες ἡ σιγὴ καὶ νηφάλιος, ἡ δὲ μέθη λάλον. Here human conduct is described, not just analogically, but directly as νηφάλιος in something of the sense of "reminding of sacred actions without wine." νηφάλιος is close to the part. of νήφω (→ νήφω n. 2).

2. a. The neut. sing. is often almost equivalent to the part. of νήφω in Philo in the sense of "what is sober," "soberness," Sobr., 2: ὅσων δημιουργὸς κακῶν ἡ μέθη, τοσούτων ἔμπαλιν ἀγαθῶν τὸ νηφάλιον. This statement differs from that quoted above (1. b) from Plut. II, 504 A mainly in the fact that we no longer catch a cultic echo. The same is true of Ebr., 123; Sobr., 4; Abr., 260. In Vit. Cont., 14 νηφάλιον is used synon. with μετὰ φρονήσεως ἠκριβωμένον περιττῆς. Yet one can hardly conclude from these refs. that there had been a widespread secularising approximation to νήφω. It is more probable that the monotheist Philo imperceptibly asserted his rejection of polytheistic sacrifice, and anticipated future development.

b. Philo's total attitude shows that he did not carry this through consistently. The inconsistency is twofold. (a) Proclaiming ecstasy, Philo must take a positive view of states of religious intoxication, in defining which the oxymoron νηφάλιος μέθη is of service, Op. Mund., 71; Leg. All., III, 82; Vit. Mos., I, 187; Omn. Prob. Lib., 13; cf. Leg. All., III, 210; Fug., 32.[5] In description of this drunkenness, to which the celebration of cultic actions without wine appertains, the word νηφάλιος is thus used in something of the pagan cultic sense. (b) The expression νηφάλια θύειν (cf. → νηφάλιος 1. a) is also referred by Philo to the cultic actions of the OT (Lv. 10:8-10). Abstemiousness, which is a duty of priests (and Therapeutae) during their period of office, is a demand of the ὀρθὸς λόγος, Vit. Cont., 74, cf. Ebr., 138 → νήφω 2. a. It distinguishes those who accept it from other men (Ebr., 126) and ensures them of immortality (Ebr., 140).[6] The requirement of Lv. 10:8-10 is twice (Spec. Leg., I, 100; IV, 191) rendered by προστέτακται ... νηφαλίους θύειν. Here, so far as is known, man himself is for the first time called νηφάλιος. In accordance with Philo's ascetic ideal the word in used in the sense of νήφω 1. a, but the context of Spec. Leg., IV, 191 shows that 1. b is in the offing. The priest must officiate as νηφάλιος because he has to carry out the directions which are contained in the picture of rulers given in Spec. Leg., IV, 183 ff. If he who is called to be judge is uncertain in his judgment, then the priest must be in a position to decide as the final earthly court. In Jos. Ant., 3, 12, 2 the priests are again called νηφάλιοι: ἄμωμοί τέ εἰσιν καὶ περὶ πάντα καθαροὶ καὶ νηφάλιοι, πίνειν οἶνον ἕως τὴν στολὴν ἔχουσι κεκωλυμένοι. The origin of the personal use is thus to be sought, not in the secular sphere, but in the sacral area to which the term belongs from the very outset. This origin can no longer be discerned in later usage, Max. Tyr., 3, 3 B.[7]

In the NT the term occurs only amongst the asyndetically listed requirements of the Past. The bishops of 1 Tm. 3:2, the women of 1 Tm. 3:11 and the elders

---

[5] Cf. on these passages ZNW, Beih. 9 (1929), 3 ff. → νήφω 2. b.

[6] λέγει δέ, ὡς οὐκ ἀποθανεῖται ὁ νηφάλια θύων (intentional?) misunderstanding of Lv. 10:9, cf. *Schriften d. jüdisch-hellenistischen Lit. in deutscher Übersetzung,* ed. Cohn-Heinemann, 5 (1929), 53, n. 4.

[7] Here the late subsidiary form νηφαλέος, cf. Pr.-Bauer[3].

of Tt. 2:2 are to be νηφάλιοι, "sober." The lists are not so systematic that one is justified in asking why νηφάλιος is left out in e.g., 1 Tm. 3:8 or Tt. 2:3. On the other hand, it may be asked whether they are so loose that one is to regard different members of the same series are wholly equivalent in meaning. If so, one may interpret νηφάλιος, the third member of the list 1 Tm. 3:2 f., in terms of the eighth member of the same series, μὴ πάροινον, and the synonymous μὴ οἴνῳ πολλῷ προσέχοντας of 1 Tm. 3:8 (δεδουλωμένας, Tt. 2:3). This would give the sense "temperate in the use of wine," and we should then have something not found elsewhere in the Past., namely, a personal application of the secularised use mentioned under 2. a. The weight of probability, however, favours the use referred to under 2. b. νηφάλιος is one of the many cultic words which are not used in the same way in the Past. as in the other Pauline epistles. The reference is to the clarity and self-control necessary for sacred ministry in God's work. The distinction from Philo and Jos. is that the use here is figurative, though with a hint of the literal sense which does not come through so well in translation (→ νήφω n. 8 and 10).

† ἐκνήφω.

"To become sober," Athen., IV, 130 from intoxication, Plut. Demosthenes, 20 (I, 855) from the intoxication of victory. From intoxication in the LXX at Gn. 9:24 (יקץ); 1 Βασ. 25:37 (היין יצא מן); Jl. 1:5 (קיץ). As a rendering of יקץ (Hab. 2:7) and קיץ hiph (2:19) it can also mean "to awake" out of sleep. In Sir. 34:2 (if original) we have the same meaning trans. "to waken" (Heb. פרע, "to cause to disappear"). In Gn. 45:26 'A it is used for the root פוג in the sense of "to cease."

1 C. 15:34 : ἐκνήψατε δικαίως καὶ μὴ ἁμαρτάνετε· ἀγνωσίαν γὰρ θεοῦ τινες ἔχουσιν ("become truly sober"), is directed against intoxication with one's own thoughts about life and death, which are not God's thoughts and which consequently mean in the last resort ἀγνωσία θεοῦ (→ νήφω 2. a, esp. n. 11 and 12).

Bauernfeind

† νικάω, † νίκη, † νῖκος, † ὑπερνικάω

A. The Usage outside the NT.

1. The word group denotes "victory" or "superiority," whether in the physical, legal or metaphorical sense, whether in mortal conflict or peaceful competition. The verb νικάω is used both intr. "to win" and trans. "to defeat," the former also impersonally. The noun τὸ νῖκος (also Itacistic νεῖκος) is a secondary form of νίκη attested from the 2nd cent. B.C. The very common use carries with it variation in meaning, and impersonally we find a weaker νικᾶν (Plat. Polit., I, 303b: ἐν δημοκρατίᾳ νικᾷ ζῆν, "it is to be preferred"). But the distinctions are of degree only; the basic sense of genuine superiority and overwhelming success generally remains. It is also generally assumed that a νικᾶν or νίκη is demonstrated by an action, by the overthrow of an opposing force, and that the success is palpable and manifest to all eyes.[1] Against this fundamental prerequisite, however, there are objections which are suggested by the realities of life and which are also reflected in the usage: a. Is the human eye sharp enough to discern between genuine and apparent victory? b. Can mortals ever finally achieve true victory?

a. There can be ref. to νικᾶν even where there is no direct or public manifestation and appeal has to be made exclusively to the judgment of those who see more deeply. The widespread pessimistic principle that it is better never to have been born (Stob. Ecl., 5, 1080) takes in Soph. Oed. Col., 1224 the form: μὴ φῦναι τὸν ἅπαντα νικᾷ λόγον. Not to have been born is beyond all computation, i.e., it is an incalculable benefit; but this νικᾶν will be recognised only by those who do not take natural pleasure in life, not by all. Epict. Diss., I, 18, 22 calls the fighter ἀνίκητος (unconquerable) whom neither δοξάριον nor λοιδορία, neither ἔπαινος nor θάνατος, can cause to deviate from the right path, δύναται ταῦτα πάντα νικῆσαι. His victoriousness is quite independent of public success. He can be victorious even though externally he marches from defeat to defeat. True victory can thus be a hidden victory.

b. We often read that victory cannot be an achievement of mortals; only divine power can bring it about. A god alone conquers, is unconquered and unconquerable. Gk. art was the first to proclaim the divine origin of victory in numerous depictions of the goddess Νίκη.[2] Nike is also crowned as victor on monuments. But the problems raised at this pt. are basically answered by religion rather than art.[3] The divine Nike is finally "an abstraction of the concept of victory fashioned by a developed and civilised people."[4] A separate field is that of confidence in the victorious gods of the mystery

νικάω κτλ. E. Peterson, ΕΙΣ ΘΕΟΣ, FRL, NF, 24 (1926), 152 ff., 314; O. Weinreich, *Neue Urkunden zur Serapisreligion* (1919), esp. 20 ff.; Pauly-W., 17, 285-307.

[1] Cf. such materially though not etym. related words as the German *Sieg* (Walde-Pok., II, 335, 481). The etym. of the group νικάω is uncertain. On the use of νίκη Bl.-Debr.[6] § 51, 1. Almost the only LXX use is in Macc.; νῖκος is thus more popular [Debrunner].

[2] Nike is not found in Hom.; the first ref. is in Hes. Theog., 383 ff.

[3] In Aesch. Ag., 163 ff. the victory of the new cosmic ruler Zeus is a proof of his divinity; on the dubious nature of the proof → μάταιος, IV, 520. On the meaning of victory in hymns and prayers cf. K. Keyssner, "Gottesvorstellung u. Lebensauffassung im gr. Hymnus," *Würzburger Studien zur Altertumswissenschaft*, ed. K. Hosius, No. 2 (1932).

[4] Pauly-W., 17, 285.

religions. To a believer in Serapis who is plunged into difficulties when he builds a shrine to Serapis the god promises: νικήσομεν, IG, XI, 4, 1299 (2nd cent. B.C.), and the word may well have more than the legal significance suggested by the context. But though there is here greater inwardness and warmth, on the whole it may still be asked whether the two qualifications of a simple and unreflecting view of victory stand in any relation or are brought into any kind of synthesis. Is the hidden victory which Epict.'s warrior strives to achieve by inner fortitude really a concern of the victorious god to whom one can pray and say Thou? "Many prayed for Νίκη. Eur. and Menand. did so at the conclusion of their dramas. But no one ever prayed seriously to her." [5]

2. The Gk. translations of the Bible yield no very striking data regarding the use of the word group. In the LXX νικάω κτλ. are not used for גבר and צלח, but for זכה (to stand innocent before the judgment, ψ 50:4), [6] חמד (to strive, Prv. 6:25), and esp. נצח. [7] In many instances there is considerable deviation from the original sense of the Heb. Detailed questions, and the interchangeability of νίκη and ν(ε)ῖκος, may be disregarded. Is. 25:8 Θ is quoted in 1 C. 15:55: κατεπόθη ὁ θάνατος εἰς νῖκος (for לָנֶצַח). Worth noting is the conclusion of Hab. in 3:19 LXX: ἐπὶ τὰ ὑψηλὰ ἐπιβιβᾷ με τοῦ νικῆσαι ἐν τῇ ᾠδῇ αὐτοῦ (for לַמְנַצֵּחַ). So, too, is the rendering of לַמְנַצֵּחַ in 55 Psalm titles by εἰς τὸ νῖκος in Θ and τῷ νικοποιῷ in 'Α. לַמְנַצֵּחַ has no intrinsic relation to any supposed victorious content of the psalm in question. It probably denotes the conductor. But for the translators, however wide of the mark they may be philologically, victory is the true word to suggest the power of these songs of prayer. [8] Success in the battle of weapons (2 S. 2:26; 1 Esr. 4:5; Wis. 16:10) or words (2 Macc. 3:5) can be described as victory, though statements like ὅτι οὐκ ἐν πλήθει δυνάμεως νίκη πολέμου ἐστίν (1 Macc. 3:19) characterise not merely Macc. but the whole of the Gk. OT. [9] The victory of Israel (2 Macc. 10:38) or the prophet (Ez. 3:8) is victory because it is God's victory. The watchword is: θεοῦ νίκην (2 Macc. 13:15; cf. 1 Ch. 29:11). God's victory is also the only answer one can give to the question of the meaning of evil (ψ 50:4: ὅπως νικήσῃς ἐν τῷ κρίνεσθαί σε, cf. R. 3:4).

A witness to the victory of the righteous against their own πάθη (13:7) and the assaults of men (6:10; 7:4 etc., cf. Hatch-Redp.) is to be found in 4 Macc. It must have sounded well to Gk. ears when 6:33 asserts that λογισμός overcomes the πάθη and when the conclusion is reached in 17:12: ἠθλοτέτει γὰρ τότε ἀρετὴ δι' ὑπομονῆς δοκιμάζουσα, τὸ νῖκος ἀφθαρσία ἐν ζωῇ πολυχρονίῳ. But it should not be forgotten that the victorious λογισμός, the total attitude of victory, which is described here is that of the martyr who has already reached the λιμήν of ἀθάνατος νίκη (7:3). The same can be said of his victory as is to be

[5] U. v. Wilamowitz-Moellendorf, *Der Glaube d. Hellenen*, II (1932), 180.

[6] Similarly זכא became a tt. in the Mandaean world. The noun means both purity of soul and victoriousness. The confession that life is victorious over all works is basic for the Mandaeans. The concept is also common elsewhere. Cf. R. Bultmann, "Die neuerschlossenen mandäischen u. manichäischen Quellen," ZNW, 24 (1925), 128 ff.; T. Arvedson, *Das Mysterium Christi* (1937), 39 f. [Bertram.]

[7] The verb נָצַח is rendered by νικάω in Hab. 3:19, the noun נֶצַח is on 8 occasions the original for νίκη (νῖκος), though more commonly translated τέλος.

[8] Cf. K. v. Pfeil (1712-1784): "O the unknown power of holy prayer ... Step by step it helps towards the victory of friends and the end of foes."

[9] Cf. 2 Macc. 15:8, 21; 1 S. 17:45 and Jos. Bell., 5, 390 in the speech of Jos. to the defenders of Jerusalem: μένοντες μέν γε κατὰ χώραν ἐνίκων ὡς ἐδόκει τῷ κριτῇ, μαχόμενοι δὲ ἔπταισαν ἀεί.

said of his → ἀρετή. In the last resort it is just as much divine gift as moral achievement.

B. The Usage in the NT.

νικάω. The only Synoptic saying of Jesus in which the group occurs is in the parable of the vanquished strong man in the Lucan version, Lk. 11:22: ἐπὰν δὲ ἰσχυρότερος αὐτοῦ ἐπελθὼν νικήσῃ αὐτόν, "but when a stronger than he shall come upon him, and overcome him." Νικάω is here used synonymously with δέω ("to bind"), as may be seen from Mt. 12:29; Mk. 3:27. The reference of the image is to a superiority obvious to all. But the truly decisive victory which the parable seeks to illustrate does not rest on the achievement of man, but on that of Christ. The reality of the victory should be recognised by all, but it is not recognised. The enemies of Jesus are more inclined to take refuge in the most fatal self-delusion, namely, the theory of discord in the kingdom of evil (Lk. 11:17 f.), than to acknowledge the victory of Jesus. The same decisive but unrecognised victory of Christ is in view in the only Johannine saying of Jesus in which the group occurs, Jn. 16:33: ἐγὼ νενίκηκα τὸν κόσμον.

The fact that there is temporal defeat and victory in earthly life is nowhere divested of its seriousness in the NT. Victory in the games is often used as a metaphor. The only point is that such successes are not the one decisive victory. They are only provisional victories. Except in the metaphors mentioned the powerful word group is used for such provisional earthly superiority only in Rev., and even here only in instances in which the victory is over the community on earth. Thus the beast in 11:7 overcomes (νικήσει) the two witnesses whom God sends in the time of supreme tribulation. The first horseman in 6:2 comes forth νικῶν καὶ ἵνα νικήσῃ, "conquering and to conquer." War and great terrors (6:3-8) await the afflicted children of men, and they have to expect that the bewitching magic of success, of constant, self-evident, irresistible and cumulative success, will accompany the afflicting powers and even precede them. Believers have the "heavenly music of the word" [10] "victory" against them. Of the victory of the rider on the white horse the same is finally true, of course, as is said of the victorious war of Antichrist against the saints in 13:7: Victory is given to him (ἐδόθη). It is limited by Him who gives it. The reader of Rev. should have no illusions as to the dreadfulness and reality of these provisional victories, but even before they are revealed to him, even before the book with the seven seals is opened, he already knows the message of the elder of 5:5: ἐνίκησεν ὁ λέων ἐκ τῆς φυλῆς Ἰούδα, and he knows that this is not a provisional victory but the final and unlimited victory which only the ἀρνίον, the κύριος κυρίων καὶ βασιλεὺς βασιλέων (17:14), can win.

With and through the Lord those whom He engages in His warfare become victors in a definitive rather than a provisional sense. The beast overcomes the saints in 13:7, and yet there stand on the crystal sea in 15:2 the νικῶντες ἐκ τοῦ θηρίου, those who overcome the beast. Even before the invincible rider on the white horse begins his journey, the believer knows that he himself, not the horseman, is called to be the true νικῶν in spite of all his defects before both God and man. In part the seven churches all suffer serious disabilities, but none of them,

---

[10] Schiller, *Die Jungfrau von Orleans*, 1, 8.

no congregation on earth and no believer, does not have the promise of the νικῶν: "He who overcomes ...," 2:7, 11, 17, 26; 3:5, 12, 21.

This νικῶν will be manifested as such and receive his inheritance, and the "heavenly music of the word" "victory" will find true realisation, when there is a new heaven and a new earth, 21:7: ὁ νικῶν κληρονομήσει ταῦτα. The word νικάω is in the NT a word of promise, an eschatological word. But the promised νικᾶν is materially no other than the νικᾶν of Christ, 3:21: ὡς κἀγὼ ἐνίκησα. It takes place through His blood, 12:11. It rests on the fact that God makes believers His children (→ γεννάω) and that through faith in His promise (→ πίστις) it makes men victors. Hence the promised victory is present already, 1 Jn. 5:4 f.: πᾶν τὸ γεγεννημένον ἐκ τοῦ θεοῦ νικᾷ τὸν κόσμον ... τίς ἐστιν ὁ νικῶν τὸν κόσμον εἰ μὴ ὁ πιστεύων ὅτι Ἰησοῦς ἐστιν ὁ υἱὸς τοῦ θεοῦ. Indeed, it is a past event, 1 Jn. 5:4: αὕτη ἐστὶν ἡ νίκη ἡ νικήσασα τὸν κόσμον, ἡ πίστις ἡμῶν. Though the horseman of the Apocalypse seems to win an obvious provisional victory, both yesterday and to-day the ultimate victory of believers is being worked out, not merely in hope, but also in faith and love. Nor is this victory less real than that of the horseman. The fresh power of the young men is successfully deployed against the ancient foe (1 Jn. 2:13 f.), evil is overcome by good (R. 12:21), those who through human ἀπιστία have been plunged into doubt and temptation are re-established by the biblical promise of divine victory (ψ 50:4, → νικάω 2.; cf. R. 3:4), and the severest onslaught of the enemy, the falsification of the Gospel, is beaten back (1 Jn. 4:4).

νίκη, νῖκος. The use of the noun corresponds to that of νικάω. Mt. 12:20, on the basis of Is. 42:1-4,[11] speaks of the victory of the Servant of God, Christ, over wrong: ἕως ἂν ἐκβάλῃ εἰς νῖκος τὴν κρίσιν, "until he leads right to victory." Paul in 1 C. 15:54 ff., as mentioned already, quotes Is. 25:8 Θ: The victory given to us is victory over death, or, in terms of the Apocalypse, over the fourth horseman (Rev. 6:8). Though apparently death and other hostile powers have still to be abolished, those who are called to ἀφθαρσία can already to-day put, without arrogance, the biblical question:[12] ποῦ σου, θάνατε, τὸ νῖκος; "Death, where is thy victory?" Finally, in 1 Jn. 5:4 faith is νίκη (→ *supra*).

ὑπερνικάω. This rare word[13] is used in R. 8:37 in a connection which reminds us of the saying in Epict. Diss., I, 18, 22 quoted earlier. For the warrior whom no earthly affliction or defeat perturbs νικάω is almost too weak a term. Paul does not have to restrict himself to δύναται ταῦτα πάντα νικῆσαι. He can say: ὑπερνικῶμεν διὰ τοῦ ἀγαπήσαντος ἡμᾶς, "we win the supreme victory through Him who loved us."

Bauernfeind

---

[11] In this verse, of course, none of the translations has εἰς νῖκος for the Heb. לֶאֱמֶת.

[12] Hos. 13:14 LXX: ποῦ ἡ δίκη σου, θάνατε; the replacement of δίκη by νῖκος is occasioned by the preceding Is. quotation.

[13] Cf. Pr.-Bauer[3].

νίπτω, ἄνιπτος

† νίπτω [1] → βαπτίζω, λούω, καθαρός.

"To wash," first for ordinary washing, then for cultic washing to establish or restore cultic cleanness. Preference was given to running water, esp. that from springs thought to be efficacious, or from salt sea-water. [2] For the Gk. πλύνειν applies to the washing of inanimate objects, [3] νίπτειν to the partial washing of living persons, [4] and λούειν or λούεσθαι to full washing or bathing. [5] The requirement of ritual washings is connected with the ancient religious idea that ritual defilement (→ μιαίνω, μολύνω) is material and can and must be removed by washing. [6] When the stage is reached at which the deity is thought to be holy, it becomes a principle that there can be approach only in a clean condition. Hence the requirement arises that one should draw near for prayer or sacrifice only when one has bathed or at least washed the hands. [7] Not until later does the thought that moral purity is decisive in relation to deity become predominant. [8]

In the OT, too, washings are important, esp. to establish cultic purity. The LXX follows the Gk. use of νίπτειν for the partial washing of persons (Gn. 18:4; 19:2 רחץ), then for cultic washings (Ex. 30:18 f.; Dt. 21:6; ψ 25:6; [9] 2 Ch. 4:6 etc.). [10]

Later Judaism, with its strong ritualistic character, extends the OT requirements. [11] Acc. to tradition (jShab., 3d) the custom, e.g., of washing the hands before meals (→ III, 421 f.) goes back to regulations imposed by Hillel and Shammai. The rule is an extension of the priestly ordinance to the more general sphere (Chag., 2, 5; bChull., 106a; Str.-B., I, 696d). This washing took place both before and after meals and was the

---

νίπτω. Str.-B., I, 695 ff.; IV, 620 ff.; Tract. Chul. and Jad.; W. Brandt, "D. jüd. Baptismen" (1910), ZAW Beih. 18; RE³ XVI, 564 ff., *s.v.* "Reinigungen"; S. Krauss, *Talm. Archäologie,* I (1910), 209 ff.; T. Wächter, "Reinheitsvorschriften im gr. Kult," RVV, 9, 1 (1910); RGG², V, 1768 f., *s.v.* "Waschungen"; Trench, 93 ff. → III, 413, Bibl. on καθαρός.

1 Attic form of the present: νίζειν, Bl.-Debr. § 73; *Indogerm. Forsch.,* 21 (1907), 211 f.

2 Stengel, *Gr. Kultusaltertümer,* 162.

3 Hom. Il., 22, 155 (εἵματα); cf. also LXX Lv. 13:6 etc.; also NT Lk. 5:2; Rev. 7:14; 22:14.

4 Plut. Thes., 10 (I, 4e); Hom. Od., 6, 224; Ep. Ar., 305 (χεῖρας before prayer); Jos. Ant., 8, 87 (χεῖρας καὶ πόδας of the priest before ministering).

5 Hdt., I, 126; Plat. Phaed., 115a; P. Oxy., III, 528, 10. On exceptions to this regular use cf. Trench, 94. For correct use of all three cf. Lv. 15:11.

6 Cf. Rohde, *Psyche,* II, 74 f.

7 Hom. Il., 6, 266 f.; 16, 228 ff.; Hes. Op., 724 f.; Poll. Onom., I, 25: νεοπλυνεῖ ἐσθῆτι on visiting the temple; cf. T. Wächter, *Reinheitsvorschriften.*

8 Anth. Pal., XIV n. 74 οὔποτε γὰρ σὴν ψυχὴν ἐκνίψει σῶμα διαινόμενον, on Jewish soil Philo Cher., 95 (τὰ τῆς ψυχῆς πάθη); Spec. Leg., I, 188 and 259; Deus Imm., 7.

9 Cf. R. Kittel, *Die Psalmen*⁵, 102 (1929).

10 The only exception is at Lv. 15:12 (σκεῦος); the LXX uses πλύνειν for כִּבֵּס at Lv. 6:20; 11:25, 28, 40 etc.; λούειν, esp. for רחץ act., at Lv. 8:6; Ez. 16:9; mid. "to bathe," Ex. 2:5; 2 Βασ. 11:2; 4 Βασ. 5:10, esp. also the cultic bath, Lv. 15:5 ff.; 16:4; Dt. 23:12; βάπτειν (טבל) for "to dip" in Ex. 12:22; Lv. 4:6, 17; 9:9.

11 Test. L. 9:11: πρὸ τοῦ εἰσελθεῖν σε εἰς τὰ ἅγια λούου καὶ ἐν τῷ θύειν σε νίπτου καὶ ἀπαρτίζων πάλιν τὴν θυσίαν νίπτου, Schürer, II, 478 and 567.

subject of detailed casuistical legislation. Further washings when new dishes were brought in during the meal were a matter of individual choice (bChull., 105a; Str.-B., I, 697). In accordance with his general mode of thought, Philo in particular sees in priestly washing a symbol of ethically pure conduct. [12]

The NT, too, uses νίπτειν in the Greek sense of partial washing. But here the ritual and cultic stage of religion has been transcended. Hence the term is of no great importance. It is used for mere washing in Jn. 9:7, 11, 15, and for ritual washing in the Jewish sense in Mt. 15:2; Mk. 7:3 (χεῖρας, → ἄνιπτος). Jesus expressly defends His disciples when they are the target of religious attacks for neglecting ritual handwashings. He also opposes the religious hypocrisy of the Pharisees, who make a display of their piety by not washing when they fast, Mt. 6:17.

In the foot-washing of Jn. 13 νίπτεσθαι becomes the symbol of an ethico-religious concept. Here, too, it means partial washing (τοὺς πόδας, 5 f., 8, 10, 12; 8 also νίψω σε), and is differentiated from λούεσθαι for bathing. As often in Jn., cf. 10:7-10, 11-15, the significance of the symbolical action may be worked out in various ways. The older interpretation is ethical (13:12 ff.). When Jesus washes the feet of His disciples He shows that He is prepared for the most menial service, and in this the disciples should follow their Master. The foot-washing is an act of humility (so in the community, 1 Tm. 5:10). [13] A later interpretation is religious. In going to His death Christ purifies His people from all sin. By the full washing of baptism (ὁ λελουμένος, v. 10) the believer participates in this cleansing (καθαρὸς ὅλος, v. 10), which does not need to be supplemented by partial washing (νίψασθαι). [14] Christian baptism is thus far superior to Judaism, which has to repeat its washings time and again. [15]

† ἄνιπτος.

"Unwashed," esp. in the cultic sense. The religious concept of God's purity and holiness means that man may approach God only in a pure condition (→ καθαρός, νίπτειν). In particular, the hands must be cultically purified for the sacred actions in which they are used, namely, prayer and sacrifice. Hence ἀνίπτοις χερσίν is an important cultic concept. [1]

The concept is known in the OT (Lv. 15:11; Ex. 30:19-21 etc.), though the word ἄνιπτος, which for reasons of language formation has no Heb. equivalent, is not found in the OT (LXX).

---

12 Vit. Mos., II, 138: οἱ μέλλοντες εἰς τὸν νεὼν εἰσιέναι ἱερεῖς ... πόδας μάλιστα καὶ χεῖρας ἀπονιπτόμενοι, σύμβολον ἀνυπαιτίου ζωῆς καὶ βίου καθαρεύοντος ἐν πράξεσιν ἐπαινεταῖς.

13 Cf. R. Knopf, *Das nachapostolische Zeitalter* (1905), 442.

14 Cf. Heitmüller, *Schr. NT*,[3] *ad loc.*

15 So acc. to the reading ℵ c Orig Tert vg^{codd}. If we read with (𝔎) 𝔖 lat + ει μη τους ποδας, the sense is the direct opposite: the full bath must be supplemented by partial washing. This would refer to cleansing from daily sins, so Zn. J., 538 f.; Bau. J., 164. Wellhausen Joh., 60 does not think the addition authentic, cf. also Merx, *D. 4 kanonischen Ev.*, II, 2b (1911), 349 ff., who thinks that there has been considerable and perhaps irremediable textual corruption.

ἄνιπτος. → νίπτω. J. Hamburger, *Realencycl.* (1883), 332 ff., *s.v.* "Händewaschen"; A. Wünsche, *Neue Beiträge z. Erläut. d. Ev.* (1878), 180 f.; Schürer, II, 481 ff.; Str.-B., I, 695 ff.

1 Hom. Il., 6, 266 f.: χερσὶ δ' ἀνίπτοισιν Διὶ λείβειν αἴθοπα οἶνον. Hes. Op., 725.

In later Judaism many requirements which originally applied only to the priests were transferred to the laity (Pharisaism). Thus washing the hands before meals became a religious rule, → νίπτω. At the time of Jesus this seems not yet to have achieved general recognition.[2] But the disciples of Jesus are attacked because they begin to eat with unwashed hands, Mk. 7:2; Mt. 15:20. In terms of ethical and spiritual religion Jesus shows that the requirement is of no religious significance.

Hauck

νοέω, νοῦς, νόημα, ἀνόητος, ἄνοια, δυσνόητος, διάνοια, διανόημα, ἔννοια, εὐνοέω, εὔνοια, κατανοέω, μετανοέω, μετάνοια, ἀμετανόητος, προνοέω, πρόνοια, ὑπονοέω, ὑπόνοια, νουθετέω, νουθεσία

† νοέω.

1. Linguistic Data.

The verb νοέω, lit. "to direct one's mind to a subject," had in older Gk. a broader meaning than the subst. νοῦς, namely, "to perceive," "to notice" in the sense of receiving both sensual and mental impressions. Cf. on the one side Hom. Il., 15, 422: ἐνόησεν ἀνεψιὸν ὀφθαλμοῖσιν,[1] Hes. Theog., 838: ὀξὺ νόησε πατὴρ ἀνδρῶν τε θεῶν τε, Aristot. An., III, 3, p. 427a, 26 f.: (the ancients) τὸ νοεῖν σωματικὸν ὥσπερ τὸ αἰσθάνεσθαι ὑπολαμβάνουσιν, and on the other side Hom. Il., 11, 599: τὸν δὲ ἰδὼν ἐνόησε, Od., 13, 318: οὐ ... ἴδον ... οὐδ' ἐνόησα etc., where ἰδεῖν denotes sensual perception and νοεῖν mental; Xenophanes Fr., 24 (Diels[5], I, 135): (God) οὖλος ὁρᾷ, οὖλος δὲ νοεῖ, οὖλος δέ τ' ἀκούει. Claimed by philosophical use for the sense "to know," "to grasp," "to think," cf. Parm. Fr., 3, Diels[5], I, 231: τὸ γὰρ τὸ αὐτὸ νοεῖν ἐστίν τε καὶ εἶναι, Fr., 8, 34 ff., Diels[5], I, 238: ταὐτὸν δ' ἐστὶ νοεῖν τε καὶ οὕνεκεν ἔστι νόημα. ‖ οὐ γὰρ ἄνευ τοῦ ἐόντος, ἐν ᾧι πεφατισμένον ἐστιν, ‖ εὑρήσεις τὸ νοεῖν ..., cf. *ibid.*, 7 f., the verb then comes to be understood only in the mental sense,[2] whether in terms of strict epistemology, Plat. Resp., VI, 507b: καὶ

---

[2] jShab., 1, 3d (40): Hillel (*c.* 20 B.C.) and Shammai (*c.* 30 B.C.) made rules about the cleanness of the hands, cf. Str.-B., I, 696; J. Jeremias, ZNW, 30 (1931), 294.

νοέω. On 1.: Pass., Liddell-Scott, Preisigke Wört., Moult.-Mill., Pr.-Bauer[3], *s.v.*; J. H. H. Schmidt, *Synonymik d. gr. Sprache*, III (1879), 634 ff.; also *Hndbch. d. lat. u. gr. Synonymik* (1889), 639; R. Schottlaender, "Nus als Terminus," *Herm.*, 64 (1929), 239 ff. On 2.: Wettstein on R. 1:20; Cr.-Kö., *s.v.*; E. Weber, "Die Beziehungen von R. 1-3 zur Missionspraxis des Pls.," BFTh, 9, 4 (1905), 86 ff.; H. Daxer, *R. 1:18-2:10 im Verhältnis zur spätjüd. Lehrauffassung*. (Diss. Rostock, 1914), 8-17, 37 ff.; A. Fridrichsen, "Zur Auslegung von R. 1:19 f.," ZNW, 17 (1916), 159 ff.; G. Bornkamm, "Die Offenbarung des Zornes Gottes (R. 1-3)," ZNW, 34 (1935), 243 ff.; P. Althaus, *Pls. u. Luther über den Menschen* (1938), 35 f., and the comm. on the relevant verses.

[1] Cf. on this Schottlaender, 240.

[2] To conclude from the use of → κατανοέω that νοέω too kept the sense "to perceive with the senses" up to the Hell. period (so Zn. on R. 1:20) is highly precarious, since there are no examples. The passage adduced in Fridrichsen, 164, Polyb., I, 49, 8: Ἀτάρβας ...

τὰ μὲν δὴ ὁρᾶσθαί φαμεν, νοεῖσθαι δ' οὔ, τὰς δ' αὖ ἰδέας νοεῖσθαι μέν, ὁρᾶσθαι δ' οὔ, cf. 508d; Aristot. An., I, 1, p. 403a, 7 f.: μάλιστα δ' ἔοικεν ἴδιον (sc. ψυχῆς, ἄνευ σώματος) τὸ νοεῖν, cf. III, 4, p. 429a, 13-430a, 9; Eth. Nic., IX, p. 1166a, 22 f., p. 1170a, 18 f.; Diog. L., VII, 52 (II, 29, 9 ff., v. Arnim), etc., or more broadly, like νοῦς (→ 952), for "to think," "to have understanding" (cf. the formula τάδε διέθετο νοῶν καὶ φρονῶν ... P. Petr., I, 16 (1), 12 etc. in the Test.), "to suppose," "to weigh," "to think out," "to intend," "to purpose," or, of words, "to have a definite sense," "to mean."[3] νοεῖν in the sense "to know" differs from the synon. γι[γ]νώσκειν (→ I, 689), αἰσθάνεσθαι (→ I, 187), συνιέναι and → φρονεῖν inasmuch as it is usually thought of as a function of the νοῦς, e.g., Aristot. An., I, 1, p. 402b, 12 : τὰ μόρια ... ἢ τὰ ἔργα αὐτῶν, οἷον τὸ νοεῖν ἢ τὸν νοῦν, Philo Cher., 73 : νοεῖν a child of νοῦς, whereas γινώσκειν denotes esp. the critical apprehension of a theme or object, αἰσθάνεσθαι is a general term for "to experience," "to perceive," in the sensual as well as the mental sense (→ I, 690), συνιέναι is the purely mental activity of combinative inference, and φρονεῖν has to do with the soul, esp. the emotional life and ethical disposition. But there is no strict differentiation in actual use, cf., e.g., Hippocr. De Arte, 2 (CMG, I, 10, 10); Morb. Sacr., 14; Cl. Al. Strom., IV, 130, 4.

In the LXX νοέω is mostly used for בִּין q, hi, hitp (with συνίημι and γινώσκω), e.g., 2 Βασ. 12:19; Prv. 20:24; 1:2, 6; Jer. 2:10; 23:20, or for שָׂכַל hi (with συνίημι), Prv. 1:3; Jer. 10:21; 20:11 etc.[4] That νοέω and συνίημι are felt to be synon. may be seen from their par. use in Prv. 28:5 (not 2 Βασ. 12:19) and the vl. Job 15:9; Prv. 28:5; 29:7 (cf. also Da. 12:10 Θ; ψ 49:22 Ἀλλ.). In the LXX the organ of νοεῖν is often the καρδία in acc. with OT thinking (→ III, 609 f.), cf. 1 Βασ. 4:20; Job 33:23; Prv. 16:23; Is. 32:6; 44:18; 47:7.[5] Hence the rendering of לֹא־שַׂמְתְּ אֵלֶּה עַל־לִבֵּךְ (Is. 47:7) by οὐκ ἐνόησας ταῦτα ἐν τῇ καρδίᾳ σου and of וְלֹא־שָׁתָה לִבָּהּ (1 S. 4:20) by καὶ οὐκ ἐνόησεν ἡ καρδία αὐτῆς. The senses in which the LXX uses the verb, "to note," "to recognise" (2 Βασ. 12:19; Wis. 13:4), "to understand" (Prv. 1:2, 6), "to take note" (Prv. 23:1), "to judge" (Sir. 31:15), "to ponder" (Is. 44:18; cf. νοήμων, Prv. 10:5, 19 etc.), are all in the mental sphere. There is no sign that νοέω might also denote sensual perceptions. The same is true of later Hell.-Jewish writings, cf. Ep. Ar., 224 : πρῶτον εἰ νοήσαι, ὅτι

νοήσας τὸν ἐπίπλουν τῶν ὑπεναντίων refers to strategic perception. To understand the "mental perception" implied by νοέω as the "perception of something brought near by sensual impression" (J. C. K. v. Hofmann, *D. heilige Schrift d. NT*, 3 [1868], 31; cf. Cr.-Kö., 766; Zn. R. on 1:20; Fridrichsen, *op. cit.*, 164 : νοεῖν = "to form a conception of something on the basis of what has been seen") is to limit the concept in a way not necessarily implied by the examples from Epict. Diss. Fr., 7, 5 and M. Ant., IV, 10, 2 (Fridrichsen, 164 f.).

[3] Cf. the lexicons, *s.v.*

[4] νοέω seems also to be used for חָשַׁב, for in 2 Βασ. 20:15 ἐνοοῦσαν corresponds to מְחַשְּׁבִים (BHK, *ad loc.*), and in Is. 32:6 καὶ ἡ καρδία αὐτοῦ μάταια νοήσει presupposes the Heb. וְלִבּוֹ יַחֲשָׁב־אָוֶן (*loc. cit.*). In Prv. 30:18 ἀδύνατά μοι νοῆσαι is a paraphrase of נִפְלְאוּ מִמֶּנִּי.

[5] Cf. Prv. 8:5 Σ : νοήσατε τῇ καρδίᾳ, Qoh. 2:3 Ἀ Σ : καὶ ἐνοήθην ἐν τῇ καρδίᾳ μου. Otherwise ἐννοεῖν is more common in the Hexapla translators, esp. Σ. In Sir. 11:7 νοεῖν is used for בקר, "to examine diligently," "consider" (elsewhere ἐκζητεῖν or ἐπισκέπτειν). At Sir. 34(31):15 we find a par. to the Golden Rule : רעה רעך כנפשך, "care for your neighbour as yourself." The marginal reading רעה is probably original. In the text we find דעה from ידע; the LXX has νόει τὰ τοῦ πλησίον ἐκ σεαυτοῦ, "assess your neighbour's interests in terms of yourself." This νόει does not have to presuppose דעה; it is a free but pertinent rendering of רעה, which is to be taken in the sense "to care for," "to tend." In 38:1 the LXX renders the same form by τίμα. Smend, *ad loc.* suggests "honour" in the former case and "befriend" in the latter [Bertram].

ὁ θεὸς πᾶσι μερίζει δόξαν τε καὶ πλούτου μέγεθος τοῖς βασιλεῦσι, 123 ("to perceive"), 153: τοῖς νοοῦσιν, "those who have insight," Test. Jos. 3:9; 7:4 ("to note"); Test. D. 4:4 ("to take note of"); Test. Iss. 3:5 vl. ("to ponder"), Jos. Vit., 298; Ant., 13, 97; Bell., 5, 257 ("to judge"); Ant., 16, 81; 1, 167; Philo Leg. All., II, 70: νοεῖν, "to think," opp. of αἰσθάνεσθαι, "to perceive with the senses" (cf. III, 198); Abr., 44: ὃ μήτε εἰπεῖν μήτε νοῆσαι θέμις.

In accordance with the usage of the *koine* νοέω means in the NT "to perceive," "to note," "to grasp," "to recognise," "to understand," Mk. 7:18 and par.; 8:17: οὔπω νοεῖτε οὐδὲ → συνίετε; (cf. Mt. 16:9); Mt. 16:11: πῶς οὐ νοεῖτε ...; (cf. Mk. 8:21: οὔπω → συνίετε; 6:52); Ac. 16:10 D; Eph. 3:4; 1 Tm. 1:7 etc.; "to consider," "to note," "to pay attention to," Mk. 13:14 and par.; 2 Tm. 2:7; "to conceive," "to imagine," Eph. 3:20. [6]

The usage of the post-apostol. fathers, Apologists and Gk. fathers is similar. Worth noting theologically is Dg., 11, 2: ὁ λόγος ... ὑπὸ ἀπίστων μὴ νοούμενος. In Just. Dial., 4, 3 man as distinct from the beast has something ᾧ νοεῖ τὸν θεόν (cf. 7).

2. Biblical Theology.

Jn. 12:40: ἵνα μὴ ἴδωσιν τοῖς ὀφθαλμοῖς καὶ νοήσωσιν τῇ καρδίᾳ (= Is. 6:10), [7] adopts the OT view that the activity of νοεῖν takes place in the heart (→ 949); this is wholly in keeping with the NT understanding of the term καρδία (→ III, 611 ff.). Knowledge has religious and moral significance as a function of the central organ of the life of the human spirit. [8]

In R. 1:20 Paul explains the fact of a revelation of God accessible to all men, through which τὸ γνωστὸν τοῦ θεοῦ φανερόν ἐστιν ἐν αὐτοῖς (v. 19a), in the statement: τὰ γὰρ ἀόρατα αὐτοῦ ἀπὸ κτίσεως κόσμου τοῖς ποιήμασιν νοούμενα καθορᾶται, ἥ τε ἀΐδιος αὐτοῦ δύναμις καὶ θειότης. [9] God's invisible being, His eternal power and divine majesty, may be apprehended from the beginning of the world in His works. The rule of the Creator God in nature and history reflects His eternal being, His almightiness and transcendence. The invisible God is seen — *finitum capax infiniti* — as contemplation of His works directs the mind to their author. From that which is before him, the meaningful order of the universe and its course, man can and should work back to Him who gives it meaning and recognise not only His existence but also His nature. [10] The paradox τὰ ἀόρατα ... καθορᾶται is removed by νοούμενα. Here, then, νοεῖν can denote only a purely intellectual process, [11] "attentive thought which takes note of what is seen and by means of which the observer apprehends what is before him." [12] Far from pointing to the activity of the νοῦς as the natural human instrument for knowledge of God — there is no such instrument for Paul (→ 958) — the apostle

---

[6] J. C. K. v. Hofmann, *Die heilige Schrift NT*, 4, 1 (1870), 140 f. and Haupt Gefbr., *ad loc.*

[7] Simply interchanging συνιέναι and νοεῖν, which is used in a similar context in Is. 44:18: ἀπημαυρώθησαν τοῦ βλέπειν τοῖς ὀφθαλμοῖς αὐτῶν καὶ τοῦ νοῆσαι τῇ καρδίᾳ αὐτῶν.

[8] Schl. J., *ad loc.* rightly concludes from the combination of νοεῖν and καρδία that there can have been no Gk. influence on the choice of the verb.

[9] → I, 719; II, 306; → ἀόρατος, → καθοράω, → ποίημα. Cf. also the comm. on R. 1:20, esp. Schl. R., *ad loc.*

[10] Cf. Fridrichsen, 159.

[11] In opposition to the expositors mentioned in → n.2, though cf. E. Weber, 86.

[12] Schl. R., *ad loc.*

makes it plain from the conclusion of v. 20 (εἰς τὸ εἶναι αὐτοὺς ἀναπολογήτους) that man himself must bear responsibility for the actualisation or non-actualisation by his νοεῖν of the possibility of knowledge of God which he is given (cf. v. 19a).

In the Stoic par. to Rom. 1:20 [13] there is no analogy to the characteristically Pauline expression τὰ ἀόρατα ... νοούμενα καθορᾶται. Closest to Paul in Hell. Judaism (→ II, 306), and perhaps known to him, is Wis. 13:4 (→ II, 297). Athenag. Suppl., 5, 2 platonises Paul when he expounds Eur. Fr., 951 as follows: "He saw God from the works (ἀπὸ τῶν ἔργων, in the next sentence τὰ ποιήματα) when he found in phenomena (the aether, the earth) a manifestation of the invisible" (ὄψιν τῶν ἀδήλων νοῶν τὰ φαινόμενα). In a particular way which deviates from Paul mysticism understands νοῆσαι τὸν θεόν as direct inner perception, as spiritual intuition which leads to ecstatic apprehension of God. [14] Cf. Corp. Herm., XI (2), 20b: ἐὰν οὖν μὴ σεαυτὸν ἐξισάσῃς τῷ θεῷ, τὸν θεὸν νοῆσαι οὐ δύνασαι· τὸ γὰρ ὅμοιον τῷ[ν] ὁμοίω[ν] νοητόν. "παντὸς σώματος ἐκπηδήσας" συναύξησον σεαυτὸν τῷ ἀμετρήτῳ μεγέθει ..., καὶ πάντα χρόνον ὑπεράρας αἰών<ιος> γενοῦ, καὶ νοήσεις τὸν θεόν etc. [15] (cf. X, 5 f.); Philo Leg. All., III, 100 ff.: Higher than the rational answer (of the Stoics) to the question πῶς ἐνοήσαμεν τὸ θεῖον (*ibid.*, 97) is the mystical; Plot. Enn., 3, 9, 1. 3 etc.: νοεῖν of the νοῦς as mental vision; cf. also the magical prayer in Pap. Mimaut. (Preis. Zaub., III), 595 f.: χαρισάμενος ἡμῖν νοῦν, λόγον, γνῶσιν· νοῦν μέ[ν], ἵνα σε νοήσωμεν ..., and the hymn of Jesus in Act. Joh., 95: νοηθῆναι θέλω νοῦς ὢν ὅλος ... ἔσοπτρον εἰμί σοι τῷ νοοῦντί με, p. 198, 1 f., 12, Bonnet.

Hb. 11:3 goes further than R. 1:20: → πίστει νοοῦμεν κατηρτίσθαι (→ I, 476) τοὺς αἰῶνας (→ I, 204) ῥήματι θεοῦ, "through faith we perceive that the universe is ordered by the Word of God." The reality of the invisible (v. 1b), exemplified here by the truth of the origin of the world in God's Word, is accessible neither to the senses nor the *ratio* of man, but only to the capacity for knowledge to be found in faith. To understand, perceive and acknowledge that God's will as Creator is the basis of all things is to think in terms of faith. It presupposes πίστις in the sense of v. 1b, namely, inner conviction that the invisible is the true reality which alone is worth seeking. For the author of Hb. this reality is, however, the reality of salvation. For him, then, knowledge of God the Creator is rooted in faith in the God revealed in salvation history.

† νοῦς.

Contents: A. Meaning of the Term. B. The Term νοῦς in Greek Philosophy and Religion. C. νοῦς in the New Testament. D. νοῦς in the Oldest Christian Literature after the New Testament.

---

[13] Cf. the list in Ltzm. R., *ad loc.*

[14] Synon. with γινώσκειν (→ I, 692 ff.) but also with the verbs of seeing (→ ὁρᾶν, θεᾶσθαι, θεωρεῖν), touching and tasting mystically understood.

[15] Cf. Hermetica, ed. W. Scott, II (1925), 328 ff. In other parts of the Corp. Herm. νοῆσαι τὸν θεόν has more a philosophical than a mystical sense, cf. VI, 5; XII (2), 20b; V, 2.

νοῦς. On A: Pape, Liddell-Scott, Moult.-Mill., Pr.-Bauer³, *s.v.*; J. H. H. Schmidt, *Synonymik d. gr. Sprache*, III (1879), 621 ff.; also *Hndbch. d. lat. u. gr. Synonymik* (1889), 637 f. On B: E. Zeller, *D. Philosophie d. Gr.*, Index (1882), *s.v.* "Nus"; G. Teichmüller, *Studien z. Gesch. d. Begriffe* (1874), Index, s.v. νοῦς; also *Neue Studien z. Gesch. d. Begriffe*, I (1876), 190 ff. etc.; II (1878), 31 f. etc.; III (1879), Index, *s.v.* νοῦς; H. Siebeck, *Geschichte d. Psychologie*, I, 2 (1884), 51 ff.; 331 ff. etc.; also "Neue Beiträge zur Entwicklungsgeschichte d. Geist-Begriffes," *Archiv f. Geschichte d. Philosophie*, 27 (1914), 1 ff.; J. B. Lightfoot, *Notes on Epistles of St. Paul*² (1904), 88 f.; J. Stenzel, "Zur Entwicklung des Geist-Begriffes in d. gr. Philosophie," *Antike*, 1 (1925), 244 ff.; R. Eisler, *Wörter-*

This art. deals only with the linguistic and historical presuppositions for an understanding of the word νοῦς. The theological significance of this as of other anthropological terms (καρδία, ψυχή, πνεῦμα etc.) as they are used in the NT is expounded in the art. ψυχή.

A. Meaning of the Term.

1. νοῦς, a contracted form of νόος, [1] probably belongs etym. [2] to a root *snū* or *snu* which is found in the German "schnau-fen," "schnu-ppern" (Eng. "snoop") etc.; cf. the Gothic *snutrs* ("scenting keenly"), "clever," "wise," and the history of the meaning of θυμός (→ III, 167, n. 1), → πνεῦμα, → ψυχή, also the Lat. *animus* = ἄνεμος. The original meaning of νοῦς, "(inner) sense directed on an object," embraces "sensation," "power of spiritual perception," "capacity for intellectual apprehension" (Hom. Od., 8, 78 : χαῖρε νόῳ, Il., 1, 363 : κεῦθε νόῳ ("hide it in the heart"), Hdt., VIII, 97: ὡς ἐκ παντὸς νόου ("from the heart," "very willingly") παρεσκεύασται μένων πολεμήσειν, Epicharmos Fr., 12 [I, 200, 16, Diels[5]]: νοῦς ὁρῆι καὶ νοῦς ἀκούει· τἄλλα κωφὰ καὶ τυφλά), also "mode of thought," "moral nature" (Hom. Od., 1, 3 : πολλῶν δ' ἀνθρώπων ... νόον ἔγνω, Il., 3, 63 : ἐνὶ στήθεσσιν ἀτάρβητος νόος ἐστί, Od., 6, 121: καί σφιν νόος ἐστὶ θεουδής). Of the wealth of possibilities of meaning contained in the term the following are the chief senses found in actual usage.

a. "Mind," "disposition," for the total inner or moral attitude, e.g., Epicharmos Fr., 26 (I, 202, 15, Diels[5]): καθαρὸν ἂν τὸν νοῦν ἔχῃς, ἅπαν τὸ σῶμα καθαρὸς εἶ, Hdt., VII, 150 : ἢν γὰρ ἐμοὶ γένηται κατὰ νόον ("mind," "inclination," "will") ..., Soph. Oed. Tyr., 600 : οὐκ ἂν γένοιτο νοῦς κακὸς καλῶς φρονῶν, Antiphon. Fr., 58 (II, 363, 16 f., Diels[5]): πολλάκις ὁ διὰ μέσου χρόνος ἀπέστρεψε τὸν νοῦν τῶν θελημάτων, Philo Congr., 118 : τὸν ἀντίθεον ... νοῦν, Plut. De Vitioso Pudore, 2 (II, 529d): ὡς φιλάνθρωπον καὶ πολιτικὸν καὶ κοινὸν ἔχοντα νοῦν, Porphyr. Abst., II, 61: θεοῖς δὲ ἀρίστη μὲν ἀπαρχὴ νοῦς καθαρὸς καὶ ψυχὴ ἀπαθής, P. Tebt., 334, 9 : μὴ ἔχουσα κατὰ νοῦν (in the heart) ἄλλον.

b. "Insight," "inventiveness," e.g., Euphron. in Athen., I, 13, p. 16 : οὐδὲν ὁ μάγειρος τοῦ ποιητοῦ διαφέρει· ὁ νοῦς γάρ ἐστιν ἑκατέρῳ τούτων τέχνη, generally "spirit," "reason," "consciousness," the mental side of man by which he shows himself to be a feeling, willing, thinking being, e.g., Parm. Fr., 16, 2 (I, 244, 9, Diels[5]): νόος ἀνθρώποισι παρίσταται, Plut. Lib. Educ., 8 (II, 5e): δύο τὰ πάντων ἐστὶ κυριώτατα ἐν ἀνθρωπίνῃ φύσει, νοῦς καὶ λόγος. καὶ ὁ μὲν νοῦς ἀρχικός ἐστι τοῦ λόγου, ὁ δὲ λόγος ὑπηρετικὸς τοῦ νοῦ ... μόνος γὰρ ὁ νοῦς παλαιούμενος ἀνηβᾷ, but also "divine spirit," so Xenophanes Fr., 25 (I, 135, 9, Diels[5]): ἀλλ' ἀπάνευθε

---

buch d. philos. Begriffe (1927 ff.), *s.v.* "Geist," "Intellekt," "Vernunft"; R. Schottländer, "Nus als Terminus," *Herm.*, 64 (1929), 228 ff.; A. Baeumler-M. Schröter, *Hndbch. d. Philosophie*, I (1934), and III (1931), Index, *s.v.* νοῦς; Reitzenstein Hell. Myst., 50, 328, 408; W. Bousset, *Kyrios Christos*[2] (1921), Ind., *s.v.* "Nus"; H. Hanse, " 'Gott haben' in d. Antike u. im frühen Christentum," RVV, 27 (1939), 45 ff. etc. On C : J. T. Beck, *Umriss d. bibl. Seelenlehre*[3] (1871), 54 ff.; F. Delitzsch, *Bibl. Psychologie*[2] (1861), 178 ff.; C. Holsten, *Zum Ev. d. Pls. u. des Pt.* (1868), 382 f. etc.; H. Lüdemann, *Die Anthropologie d. Pls.* (1872), 12 ff.; H. H. Wendt, *Die Begriffe Fleisch u. Geist im bibl. Sprachgebrauch* (1878), 134 ff.; T. Simon, *Die Psychologie d. Apostels Pls.* (1897), 38 ff.; E. Weber, "Die Beziehungen von R. 1-3 zur Missionspraxis d. Pls.," BFTh, 9, 4 (1905), 86 ff., 98 ff.; Cr.-Kö., *s.v.;* W. G. Kümmel, "R. 7 u. d. Bekehrung d. Pls.," UNT, 17 (1929), 27 ff., 62, 134 ff.; W. Gutbrod, *D. paulinische Anthropologie* (1934), 351 ff.; O. Moe, "Vernunft u. Geist im NT," ZSTh, 11 (1934), 351 ff.; H. Hanse, *op. cit.,* 61 ff.

[1] On the history of the form and cases of the word cf. Liddell-Scott, Moult.-Mill., Pr.-Bauer[3], *s.v.*

[2] Acc. to a communication from A. Debrunner, who refers to E. Schwyzer, "Beiträge zur gr. Wortforschung," *Festschrift f. P. Kretschmer* (1926), 247 ff. Prellwitz Etym. Wört., 215; Boisacq, 672; Walde-Pok., II, 324 do not attempt a derivation.

πόνοιο νόου φρενὶ πάντα κραδαίνει ("shakes all things with the intellectual power of the spirit"), Democr. Fr., 112 (II, 164, 13, Diels[5]): "It is θείου νοῦ ("of the divine spirit") always to conceive something beautiful."

c. "Understanding," "thinking ability," "capacity of intellectual perception," Democr. Fr., 105 (II, 163, 11 f., Diels[5]): σώματος κάλλος ζῳῶδες ("something animal"), ἢν μὴ νοῦς ὑπῇ ("is concealed behind"), Menand. (acc. to Stob. Florilegium, 37, 8): μέγιστον ἀγαθόν ἐστι μετὰ νοῦ χρηστότης, Plat. Gorg., 500c: σμικρὸν νοῦν ἔχων ἄνθρωπος, Plut. Stoic. Rep., 20 (II, 1043 f.), Philo Vit. Mos., I, 141 etc.: οἱ νοῦν ἔχοντες, "the understanding," "the wise"; the opp., Just. Dial., 30, 1: οἱ νοῦν μὴ ἔχοντες.

d. As the result of mental activity, sometimes with the participation of the will, "thought," "opinion," "judgment," "resolve," "purpose," "plan," Hom. Il., 9, 104 f.: οὐ γάρ τις νόον ἄλλος ἀμείνονα τοῦδε νοήσει, οἷον ἐγὼ νοέω, Hdt., I, 27: ἐπὶ σὲ ἐν νόῳ ἔχοντες ("have in mind," "intend," "purpose") στρατεύεσθαι etc., cf. also Plat. Resp., VI, 490a.

e. Fig. of words, statements etc., "meaning," "significance," e.g., Hdt., VII, 162: οὗτος δὲ ὁ νόος τοῦ ῥήματος, Polyb., V, 83, 4; Philo Sacr. AC, 114 etc.: τοιοῦτον ὑποβάλλει νοῦν, Just. Dial., 29, 2: ἀναγινώσκοντες οὐ νοεῖτε τὸν ἐν αὐτοῖς (sc. the OT Scriptures) νοῦν, Cl. Al. Quis Div. Salv., 5, 2: τὸν ἐν αὐτοῖς (sc. the words of the Saviour) κεκρυμμένον νοῦν ... ἐρευνᾶν καὶ καταμανθάνειν.

2. In the LXX νοῦς is surprisingly rare and indefinite.[3] It is used 6 times for לֵב or לֵבָב, though without affecting καρδία as the normal equivalent of לֵב (→ III, 609): Ex. 7:23; Jos. 14:7 (κατὰ τὸν νοῦν αὐτοῦ inaccurately for כַּאֲשֶׁר עִם־לְבָבִי); Job 7:17; Is. 10:7b (in 7a ψυχή is used for לְבָב); 10:12; 41:22. רוּחַ is once transl. νοῦς in Is. 40:13: מִי־תִכֵּן אֶת־רוּחַ יְהוָה = τίς ἔγνω νοῦν κυρίου. Here, too, there is no obvious relaxation of the rule that πνεῦμα corresponds to רוּחַ. The rendering of אֹזֶן by νοῦς at Job 33:16; 12:11 vl.; 34:3 vl. is either a scribal error (νοῦς for ους) or a very free transl. The organ of intellectual perception is used instead of the organ of sensual perception. Where the Heb. original is obscure or missing (Job 7:20: ὁ ἐπιστάμενος τὸν νοῦν ἀνθρώπων, 36:19: μή σε ἐκκλινάτω ἑκὼν ὁ νοῦς δεήσεως ἐν ἀνάγκῃ ὄντων ἀδυνάτων, Prv. 31:3: μὴ δῷς γυναιξὶ ... τὸν σὸν νοῦν, 29:7: πτωχῷ οὐχ ὑπάρχει νοῦς ἐπιγνώμων), the popular use of νοῦς predominates; cf. also the apocr.[4] where νοῦς usually means "mind," "disposition," e.g., 1 Εσδρ. 2:6 (πνεῦμα, v. 5); Sus. 9; Wis. 4:12: νοῦν ἄκακον, 3 Macc. 1:25: τὸν ἀγέρωχον αὐτοῦ νοῦν, Jdt. 8:14: God's νοῦς (cf. Is. 40:13). Everyday expressions are also found in 2 Macc. 15:8: ἔχειν κατὰ νοῦν, "to bear in mind," "to be mindful of," 1 Εσδρ. 9:41: ἐπιδιδόναι τὸν νοῦν εἰς, "to direct one's mind or attention to something." Even in the philosophical 4 Macc., which distinguishes sharply between the understanding (νοῦς) and reason (λογισμός) (1:15; 2:22; 5:11; ὁ σώφρων νοῦς, 1:35; 2:16, 18; 3:17), νοῦς can denote "character," 16:13: ἀδαμάντινον ἔχουσα τὸν νοῦν ("adamant mind"), cf. 14:11.

3. In the post-biblical Jewish writings, apart from Philo,[5] the term is again imprecise. It can mean the "mind" or "moral nature," e.g., Test. B. 8:3: ὁ καθαρὸς νοῦς, Test. Jud. 14:2 f.; the "mode of thought" or "understanding," Ep. Ar., 276: τὸ δὲ νοῦν ἔχειν ὀξὺν ... θεοῦ δώρημα καλόν ἐστιν, Test. R. 3:8; Test. S. 2:8 etc. In Joseph.[6] the basic sense is always that of "mind," "power of spiritual perception," "inner habit," cf. Ant., 8, 23: δός μοι ... νοῦν ὑγιῆ, Ap., II, 142: τυφλὸς ἦν τὸν νοῦν Ἀπίων,

---

[3] Cf. Cr.-Kö., 763 f. In Sir. and the Hexapla translators we do not find νοῦς (except for Sus. 9 Θ). There is in fact no clear Heb. equivalent for the Gk. term. Though νοῦς has many meanings, it is in the main too intellectualistic to be easily used by OT translators. Heb. cannot express intellect or reason, and this was the aspect of νοῦς which was obviously felt to be determinative, and which was avoided [G. Bertram].

[4] Apart from Wis. 9:15, → n. 18.

[5] → 955; cf. Sib., 3, 771, → n. 21.

[6] Cf. Schl. Lk., 462; Schl. Theol. d. Judt., 27.

sometimes more in the sense of understanding (Ant., 19, 321: ἐν τῷ λαμβάνων ὅσους ... πόνους ἐκεῖνος ἀνέτλη, 6, 287: ἃ ... εἰς νοῦν ἐβαλόμην), sometimes more in that of feeling (Ant., 16, 194: πρὸς δὲ τῇ δούλῃ τὸν νοῦν εἶχεν, 12, 55: τὸ πλῆθος εὐχὰς ἐποιήσατο γενέσθαι σοι τὰ κατὰ νοῦν.

B. The Term νοῦς in Greek Philosophy and Religion.

The transition of the word from popular usage to the vocabulary of philosophy gives it greater pregnancy and in so doing restricts its meaning. It comes to denote the organ of knowledge, and from the more general sense of "mind" it becomes equivalent to "reason" or "spirit" (→ πνεῦμα). The practical relation (of feeling, willing and acting) to an object retreats into the background, and the theoretical relation (of thinking and perceiving) comes to the fore.

Anaxagoras,[7] who finds in νοῦς, or cosmic reason, the principle which orders the universe, links perception and creative fashioning in Fr., 12 (II, 38, 9 ff., Diels[5]): πάντα ἔγνω νοῦς ... πάντα διεκόσμησε νοῦς. Knowledge and power over things (line 5: πάντων νοῦς κρατεῖ) are among the qualities which distinguish νοῦς, the finest and purest of all things, from bodily entities (p. 37, 17 ff.). But perhaps Archelaus, the pupil of Anaxagoras, was already limiting the sphere of the νοῦς which rules in the world to perception[8] when he taught: ἀέρα καὶ νοῦν τὸν θεόν, οὐ μέντοι κοσμοποιὸν τὸν νοῦν (Aetius Placita, I, 7, 15 [II, 47, 17 f., Diels[5]]).

Plato with his threefold division of the soul of man gives to reason (νοῦς = τὸ λογιστικόν), the most excellent part, an independent sphere, i.e., pure thought whose object is the idea,[9] Phaedr., 247c; Resp., VI, 508d; cf. Phaed., 83b etc. That reason, in virtue of its knowledge of virtue, also controls moral action, is made clear in the metaphor of the helmsman, Phaedr., 247c d; Leg., XII, 961e. As in the microcosm, man, so in the universe there rules as king of heaven and earth (Phileb., 28c), ἀληθινὸς καὶ θεῖος νοῦς (22c; Tim., 30a b, 46c ff.). In intercourse and marriage with pure being (τῷ ὄντι ὄντως) man brings forth νοῦς and ἀλήθεια, Resp., VI, 490b. With his insight that consciousness of God rests in reason, the supreme function of man's spiritual life,[10] Plato contributed to the religious philosophy of antiquity one of its most fruitful concepts.

Aristot.[11] goes beyond Plato's division of the soul when he sets νοῦς over the δυνάμεις of the soul as the ἐνέργεια which characterises man, An., II, 3, p. 414a, 29-414b, 19; III, 3, p. 429a, 6 ff.). He then gives a more precise definition. Theoretical reason, the power of logical thought (νοῦς θεωρητικός), is distinguished from practical reason (νοῦς πρακτικός) which sets goals for the will, An., III, 9, p. 432b, 27 ff.; III, 10, p. 433a, 14 ff.; Eth. Nic., VI, 2, p. 1139a, 17 ff. The sphere of the νοῦς is wholly limited to perception. Translation of this into practice is not effected by the νοῦς (An., III, 10, p. 433a). By nature the νοῦς is not intermingled with the body (III, 4, p. 429a, 24 f.). It

---

7 As regards Heraclit. H. Kleinknecht draws attention to the etym. theological pun in Fr., 114 (I, 176, 5 f., Diels[5]), which speaks of the ξυνόν (cosmic law) which must be grasped by the νοῦς (ξὺν νῷ). The pun is still found up to Stoic times, cf. Cleanthes, Hymn to Zeus, Fr., 537 (I, 122, 21, v. Arnim): ᾧ (the θεοῦ κοινὸς νόμος) κεν πειθόμενοι σὺν νῷ βίον ἐσθλὸν ἔχοιεν — the ξυνόν is the νοῦς. For the close connection between νοῦς, νόμος and θεός → νόμος [Kleinknecht]. On νοῦς in the Eleatic school cf. Stenzel, 248 ff. On νοῦς in relation to God and the cosmos cf. the valuable refs. in the index to Diels[5], III, 296 f. *s.v.* νοῦς.

8 Cf. on this Schottlaender, 235.

9 On νοῦς and ecstasy in Plato, → II, 453. But even enthusiastic knowledge is by way of the νοῦς, Tim., 90a-c.

10 Eur. already equated νοῦς and θεός: ὁ νοῦς γὰρ ἡμῶν ἐστιν ἐν ἑκάστῳ θεός (TGF Fr., 1018; cf. also *ibid.*, p. 685), cf. Eur. Tro., 886: Ζεύς = νοῦς βροτῶν.

11 Cf. G. Teichmüller, *Neue Studien,* III, esp. 110 ff.; F. Seifert, "Psychologie" in Baeumler-Schröter, III E, 8 ff.

is immortal and divine. It comes from without into the body (Gen. An., II, 3, p. 736b, 27 f.: λείπεται δὲ τὸν νοῦν μόνον θύραθεν ἐπεισιέναι καὶ θεῖον εἶναι μόνον, cf. *ibid.*, 6, p. 744b, 21 f.; Eth. Eud., IV, 14, p. 1248a, 24 ff.). But Aristot. then limits and obscures these statements by distinguishing between passive and active reason (νοῦς παθητικός and νοῦς ποιητικός, An., III, 5, p. 430a, 10 ff.),[12] between the principle of potential reason which receives form and the principle of the actualising power of thought which gives form. Only this ποιοῦν τοῦ πάσχοντος is immortal and eternal, lines 19 and 23. The significance of νοῦς in the theology of Aristot. may be seen from Fr., 49 (p. 55, 19 f., Rose): ὁ θεὸς ἢ νοῦς ἐστὶν ἢ ἐπέκεινά τι τοῦ νοῦ,[13] An., I, 4, p. 408b, 29 f.: ὁ δὲ νοῦς ἴσως θειότερόν τι καὶ ἀπαθές ἐστιν, Eth. Nic., X, 7, p. 1177a, 15 f.: εἴτε θεῖον ὂν καὶ αὐτὸ [sc. νοῦς] εἴτε τῶν ἐν ἡμῖν τὸ θειότατον, *ibid.*, 9, p. 1179a, 26: νοῦς is τὸ συγγενέστατον to the gods, the element of the logical, the finest part of man's spiritual life, the epitome of the divine. Though there is variation in their outworking, these insights of classical Gk. philosophy became the common legacy of ancient thought, cutting right across the antitheses of the schools.[14]

Thus they are found in the anthropology and theology of Stoicism at every stage.[15] For Zeno and his school reason is the first of the κριτήρια (Diog. L., VII, 54 [II, 33, 3 ff., v. Arnim]), and God is cosmic reason (Aetius Placita, I, 7, 23 [I, 42, 7 f., v. Arnim] etc.); cf. Poseidonius (cf. Diog. L., VII, 138 [I, 192, 1 ff., v. Arnim]), Epict.: God's οὐσία is νοῦς (Diss., II, 8, 1 f.), Marc. Aurel.: the νοῦς of man is the δαίμων in him, an ἀπόσπασμα of deity (M. Ant., V, 27, cf. Sen. Ep. ad Lucilium, IV, 2 (31), 11; Epict. Diss., II, 8, 11; I, 14, 6).

In Philo's[16] speculative and mystical fusion of Gk. philosophy and Jewish religion one may also detect clear signs of the legacy of Gk. psychology and cosmology in respect of the concept νοῦς = "reason," "spirit" → πνεῦμα. But the clarity of the term is often obscured by the fog of mysticism. Reason is the best in man (Mut. Nom., 246), ψυχῆς ἡγεμονικόν (Leg. All., I, 39, cf. Agric., 66 etc.), the ruler of soul and body (Leg. All., III, 80).[17] Essentially earthly and corruptible (Leg. All., I, 90; III, 29; cf. I, 49), enclosed in the narrow dimensions of the brain or heart (Det. Pot. Ins., 90), the νοῦς could not achieve what is correct were it not that a divine breath (θεῖον

---

[12] The term νοῦς ποιητικός occurs first in Alex. Aphr. An. (p. 88, 24, Bruns etc.; cf. Siebeck, *Gesch. d. Psychologie*, I, 2, 202 ff.). But it is a logical development of the statements of Aristot. On the problem of passive and active reason in Aristot. cf. G. Teichmüller, *Studien*, 344 ff., 378 ff., 428 ff.

[13] It is worth noting that this statement is found in the work περὶ εὐχῆς.

[14] Aristot.'s influence may be seen in Plut., for whom the νοῦς is higher than the ψυχή. Cf. De Procreatione Animae, 27 (II, 1026e): τὸ γὰρ παθητικὸν ἀναδίδωσιν ἐξ ἑαυτῆς ἡ ψυχή, τοῦ δὲ νοῦ μετέσχεν ἀπὸ τῆς κρείττονος ἀρχῆς ἐγγενομένου, also Fac. Lun., 28 (II, 943a); Gen. Socr., 22 (II, 591b); Lib. Educ., 8 (II, 5e) → 952. Of debated origin are the statements in Phot. Bibl. Cod., 249, which O. Immisch, "Agatharchidea," SAH, 1919, 7 ascribes to the Hell. peripatetic Agatharchides. On νοῦς, *ibid.*, 98 and 101.

[15] Cf. v. Arnim, Index, *s.v.*; cf. also L. Stein, "D. Psychologie d. Stoa," 1 (*Berliner Studien f. kl. Philologie* etc., 3, 1 [1886]), 125 ff.; 2 (*ibid.*, 7, 1 [1888]), 212 ff. etc.; A. Bonhöffer, *Epict. u. d. Stoa* (1898), 120 f.; P. Barth, *Die Stoa* ^{3,4} (1922), 59 ff.

[16] Cf. Leisegang, II, 557-564; C. Siegfried, *Philo v. Alexandria als Ausleger d. AT* (1875), 240 ff.; E. Hatch, *Essays in Biblical Greek* (1889), 125 ff.; H. Leisegang, *Der heilige Geist*, I, 1 (1919), 77 ff. etc.; J. S. Boughton, *The Idea of Progress in Philo Iudaeus* (Diss. New York, Columbia Univ., 1932), 249 ff.; W. Völker, "Fortschritt u. Vollendung bei Philo v. Alex.," TU, 49, 1 (1938), 159 ff., 212 f., 303 f. etc.; J. Pascher, "Η ΒΑΣΙΛΙΚΗ ΟΔΟΣ, Der Königsweg zu Wiedergeburt u. Vergottung bei Philon v. Alex.," *Studien zur Gesch. u. Kultur des Altertums*, 17, 3/4 (1931), 21 f., 61, 83, 127, 163; H. Schmidt, *D. Anthropologie Philons v. Alex.* (Diss. Leipzig, 1933), 3 ff., 49 ff., 59 ff., 70 ff. etc.; → II, 394.

[17] But sometimes, as here and there in the pre-Socratics (cf. Diog. L., IX, 22; Aetius Placita, IV, 5, 12 = Doxographi Graeci, ed. H. Diels^2 [1929], 392b, 4 ff.) or Stoicism (cf. Gal. Histor. Philos., 24 = Doxographi ...^{2}, 615, 5 f. etc.) νοῦς and ψυχή are equated, e.g., Gig., 15: τὸ κράτιστον ἐν ἡμῖν, ψυχὴν ἢ νοῦν, Rer. Div. Her., 108. Cf. Schmidt, 49.

πνεῦμα) shows it the way to truth (Vit. Mos., II, 265). The οὐσία of reason is not linked to anything created,[18] but ὑπὸ θεοῦ καταπνευσθεῖσα (Rer. Div. Her., 56). Hence reason can lift up man to heaven (Det. Pot. Ins., 85), lead to knowledge of God (Leg. All., I, 33 ff.; Det. Pot. Ins., 89; Praem. Poen., 122), and instruct in virtue (Leg. All., I, 47). The νοῦς is τὸ οὐράνιον τῶν ἐν ἡμῖν (Gig., 60), and hence immortal (Sacr. AC, 8). θεοειδὴς ὁ ἀνθρώπινος νοῦς πρὸς ἀρχέτυπον ἰδέαν, τὸν ἀνωτάτω λόγον, τυπωθείς (Spec. Leg., III, 207, cf. Decal., 134; Exsecr., 163 etc.). This is supremely true of the first man, whose νοῦς, directly reflecting the λόγος, was far superior to that of his descendants (cf. Op. Mund., 140). Reason is in the soul of man and in the whole cosmos (Abr., 272; Migr. Abr., 186; Fug., 46; Rer. Div. Her., 236). What the great Director is in the universe, that the human νοῦς is in man (Op. Mund., 69).[19] God has sent pure reason into the soul as an unmixed and unadulterated part (Rer. Div. Her., 184 and 274). It is God's gift that the νοῦς can embrace the νοητὸς κόσμος (Rer. Div. Her., 111), rise up aloft from earth (Sobr., 64), and penetrate to γνῶσις καὶ ἐπιστήμη θεοῦ (Deus Imm., 143). When reason serves God purely, it is divine rather than human (Rer. Div. Her., 84, cf. Ebr., 144). It then moves out of itself (ἐκβῇ ἑαυτοῦ), is initiated into the mysteries of God, and makes confession of Him who truly is (Leg. All., I, 82, cf. III, 71 and 100). In the ecstatic state, e.g., of the prophet, the human νοῦς departs with the coming of the divine πνεῦμα and then returns as this moves on (Rer. Div. Her., 265, cf. 257; Leg. All., II, 31), cf. the inspired psalmist who ὅλον τὸν νοῦν ὑπὸ θείας κατοχῆς συναρπασθεὶς οἴστρῳ finds his joy in God alone (Plant., 39), or the recipient of a vision, ἐν ᾧ ὁ ἡμέτερος νοῦς τῷ τῶν ὅλων συγκινούμενος ἐξ ἑαυτοῦ κατέχεσθαί τε καὶ θεοφορεῖσθαι δοκεῖ, ὡς ἱκανὸς εἶναι προλαμβάνειν καὶ προγινώσκειν τι τῶν μελλόντων (Som., I, 2), ἐξ ἔρωτος θείου κατασχεθεὶς ὁ νοῦς (II, 232).[20] The human νοῦς is limited as compared with the divine. It may grasp things but not itself, let alone the nature of God (Leg. All., I, 91). Because cosmic reason, ὁ καλὸς καὶ περιπόθητος καὶ μακάριος ὄντως νοῦς (Spec. Leg., III, 1), has created the universe, human reason has the promise that it will finally come to the Father of piety and know its own ego (Migr. Abr., 193 ff.).[21] Every heavenly thing is νοῦς (Gig., 60). Each star is pure νοῦς (Som., I, 135; Gig., 8; Op. Mund., 73 etc.). God Himself is νοῦς in the final and deepest sense, ὁ τῶν ὅλων νοῦς (Migr. Abr., 192; Leg. All., III, 29 etc.). He is the great and perfect cosmic reason (Spec. Leg., I, 18) creative and at work in all things (Op. Mund., 8; Migr. Abr., 193), the good of the soul and of all things (Gig., 40).

In the Neo-Platonism of Plotinus, the last great construction of Hell. philosophy, the doctrine of the νοῦς is a main part of the system, which is worked out with extreme logical consistency.[22] In the transcendental world the νοῦς, the thinking substance, is the highest entity next to ἕν, from which it proceeds. It is the supreme hypostasis in the realm of the intelligible, Plot. Enn., V, 6, 1 ff.; V, 1, 4 and 7; V, 9, 5. In the νοῦς the unity of original being divides into two, into the antithesis of thinking and what is thought, III, 8, 9; V, 1, 4. The νοῦς, δημιουργός (V, 1, 8 etc.) and κόσμος νοητός (V, 9, 9) in one, both thinks and is being, V, 5, 1 ff.; esp. V, 4, 2: ἔστι μὲν οὖν καὶ αὐτὸς (sc. ὁ νοῦς) νοητόν, ἀλλὰ καὶ νοῶν ... νοῦς δὴ καὶ ὂν ταὐτόν, οὐ γὰρ τῶν πραγμάτων ὁ νοῦς, ὥσπερ ἡ αἴσθησις τῶν αἰσθητῶν προόντων, ἀλλ' αὐτὸς [ὁ] νοῦς τὰ πράγματα [I owe this ref. to H. Kleinknecht]. The νοῦς works directly

[18] Cf. Wis. 9:15: φθαρτὸν γὰρ σῶμα βαρύνει ψυχήν, καὶ βρίθει τὸ γεῶδες σκῆνος νοῦν πολυφρόντιδα ("the earthly tent burdens the highly reflective spirit"), cf. Cr.-Kö., 764.

[19] Cf. Sen. Ep. ad Lucilium, VII, 3 (65), 24: *quem in hoc mundo locum deus obtinet, in homine animus.*

[20] The thought of the exclusion of the νοῦς in ecstasy separates Philo from Plato, for whom reason is at work in enthusiasm, → n. 9. Cf. Bousset-Gressm., 449.

[21] Sib., 3, 771 promises among the gifts of the Messianic age νοῦν ἀθάνατον αἰώνιον εὐφροσύνην τε.

[22] Cf. Seifert, 14 ff.

or indirectly even in the subordinate spheres of the suprasensual and sensual worlds right down to the individual soul, for which the νοῦς is the chief force alien to the world of sense:[23] πολὺς οὖν οὗτος ὁ θεὸς (sc. ὁ νοῦς) ἐπὶ τῇ ψυχῇ τῇδε ὑπάρχει (V, 1, 5).

In the Corp. Herm. the philosophical concept νοῦς is brought into close connection with mystical religious ideas, though with an ambiguity of content which defies analysis.[24] Deity is νοῦς, cf. σὺ ὁ νοῦς in XIII, 21. νοῦς or reason in supreme abstraction is the original divine principle (I, 6; V, 11), ὁ πάντων πατήρ (I, 12), ὁ τῶν ὅλων δημιουργός, σοφώτατος νοῦς καὶ ἀΐδιος (Stob. Ecl., I, 34, 5 f.). But we also read: ὁ οὖν θεὸς οὐ νοῦς ἐστιν, αἴτιος δὲ τοῦ <νοῦν> εἶναι (II, 13). From πρῶτος νοῦς, which is bi-sexual, there is begotten the distinct δημιουργὸς νοῦς, which out of fire and water creates the seven rulers of the world, the planets (I, 9 ff.; X, 18), and which is also called ἐνέργεια or ψυχὴ τοῦ θεοῦ (XI, 2; XII, 8) and depicted in the form of fire (X, 18). This second νοῦς, which derives from God's οὐσία in so far as we can speak of such (XII, 1), finds its reflection in the λόγος (XII, 14a), but also seems to be identical with it (II, 12). Though not in the original form of fire (X, 18), divine νοῦς is also a property of man (I, 17; XII, 1, cf. 19) acc. to the will of the Father. This is true of man alone among earthly creatures (VIII, 5). Only through νοῦς can man know God (V, 10a; cf. X, 4b etc. "the eye of reason"). The νοῦς is a benefactor of the soul; as an ἀγαθὸς δαίμων (X, 23) it works in its favour (XII, 2; I, 22). It brings knowledge and insight (X, 10a). But the texts diverge in answer to the question whether νοῦς is given to all men (XII, 9) or only to the righteous (IV, 3 ff.; XII, 3 f.; X, 19, 23 f.). In the latter case παλιγγενεσία takes place through νοῦς (XIII, 3 ff.): God sends a vessel full of νοῦς, the soul bathes (βαπτίζει ἑαυτόν) in it, and thus comes to partake of the divine element. Men blessed in this way are τέλειοι, ἀθάνατοι. They receive τῷ ἑαυτῶν νοΐ everything on earth, in heaven and beyond (IV, 4 f.), ἐν θεῷ γίνονται (I, 26a). In other words, νοῦς enters the pious soul and leads it to the light of γνῶσις (X, 21), the pious soul ὅλη νοῦς γίνεται (X, 19), it is deified (X, 6: ἀποθεωθῆναι).[25] But νοῦς can also be an avenging δαίμων for the soul (I, 23; X, 16). Alongside the idea that divine νοῦς is a possession of man we also find the different view that human reason may be fructified by God or a demon and bring forth good or bad thoughts accordingly (IX, 3). A haphazard fusion of the philosophical legacy and syncretistic soteriology characterises the discussions of νοῦς, which are in part little more than compilations.

As in Hermetic mysticism, so in Gnosticism and magic νοῦς is sometimes a divine hypostastis, the god Νοῦς. In the cosmology of the Leiden Pap. J 395,[26] there appears on the third laugh of the creator god Νοῦς [ἢ Φρένες] κατέχων καρδίαν· ἐκλήθη δὲ Ἑρμῆς.[27] In another place[28] we find among the gods to whom appeal is made

---

[23] Cf. Porphyr. Abst., I, 29: αὐτὸς δὲ ὄντως (the true self) ὁ νοῦς, ὥστε καὶ τὸ τέλος τὸ ζῆν κατὰ νοῦν, Ad Marc., 19: σοὶ δέ, ὥσπερ εἴρηται, νεὼς μὲν ἔστω τοῦ θεοῦ ὁ ἐν σοὶ νοῦς. Theodoret Graecorum Affectionum Curatio, 85 (p. 59, 5 ff., ed. J. Raeder [1904]) draws a par. between the Christian and a Neo-Platonic trinity: Τἀγαθόν, Νοῦς, Ψυχή.

[24] For material cf. Corp. Herm., Index *s.v.*; cf. also the comm. and J. Kroll, *Die Lehren des Hermes Trismegistos* (1914), Index, *s.v.* "Nus"; W. Kroll, Pauly-W., VIII (1913), 805 ff., Art. "Hermes Trismegistos"; F. Bräuninger *Untersuchungen zu den Schriften des Hermes Trismegistos* (Diss. Berlin, 1926); F. Büchsel, *Der Geist Gottes im NT* (1926), 114 ff. Reitzenstein Hell. Myst., 408 ff. etc. conjectures Persian influences on the understanding of the term.

[25] Cf. also the par. to the concluding prayer of Poimandres (Corp. Herm., I, 31) in Berlin Pap., 9794, col. 2, lines 43 ff. (*Berliner Klassikertexte,* 6 [1910], 112): ἅγιος [ὁ θεὸς ὁ ὑποδ]είξας μοι ἀπὸ τοῦ νιος ζωὴν καὶ φ[ῶς], where instead of the unintelligible νιος we should read νοός with Bousset, 175, n. 1.

[26] Preis. Zaub., XIII, 173 f.

[27] *Ibid.,* 487 f.

[28] *Ibid.,* V (London), 465.

ὁ μέγας Νοῦς. In the Gnostic systems of emanations Nous is among the masculine aeons in Valentinus (Iren., I, 1, 1; 2, 1 f. etc.), the Barbelo-Gnostics (I, 29),[29] the Sethians (Hipp. Ref., V, 19, 14 f., GCS, 26, 119, 1 ff.) etc. In the Naassene hymn Nous is the original principle: νόμος ἦν γενικὸς τοῦ παντὸς ὁ πρωτότοκος νόος (Hipp. Ref., V, 10, 2, GCS, 26, 102, 23). The aeon Nous still has an important role in the Manichean myth.[30] The origin of this syncretistic divine name is often forgotten; it is to be found in the ancient philosophical term.

C. νοῦς in the New Testament.

Except at Lk. 24:45; Rev. 13:18; 17:9, the term occurs in the NT only in Paul (21 times). There is no connection with the philosophical or mystico-religious use. νοῦς is not the divine or the divinely related element in man.[31] It is equated neither with the → πνεῦμα nor the → ψυχή. As in the popular usage of the Greeks the term has no precise meaning, and it is used in the various senses known to us from A. (→ 952 f.).[32]

a. "Mind," "disposition." In this sense it expresses the inner orientation or moral attitude, whether of the natural man or of the Christian, but only in formal terms. ἀδόκιμος νοῦς is used of the Gentiles under God's penal judgment in R. 1:28. They walk ἐν ματαιότητι τοῦ νοὸς αὐτῶν, Eph. 4:17. He who follows errors is vainly puffed up ὑπὸ τοῦ νοὸς τῆς → σαρκὸς αὐτοῦ, Col. 2:18, διεφθαρμένος τὸν νοῦν, 1 Tm. 6:5 (cf. 2 Tm. 3:8). His νοῦς and → συνείδησις are spotted, Tt. 1:15. In the νοῦς of Christians, i.e., in the inner direction of their thought and will and the orientation of their moral consciousness, there should be constant renewal, R. 12:2: μεταμορφοῦσθε (→ 758) τῇ ἀνακαινώσει τοῦ νοός, Eph. 4:23: ἀνανεοῦσθαι δὲ τῷ → πνεύματι τοῦ νοὸς ὑμῶν (→ III, 453; IV, 900 f.). The unity of a Christian congregation finds expression when the members are confirmed in the same mind, 1 C. 1:10 (νοῦς and γνώμη synon. → I, 717 f.).

b. "Practical reason." This is the moral consciousness as it concretely determines will and action. It is a purely human function, though its presence implies man's responsibility towards God.[33] The "I" of R. 7 realises that it is bound by the νόμος of God according to the ἔσω ἄνθρωπος (v. 22). The νοῦς affirms it to be His νόμος (v. 23), and in terms of its moral consciousness the "I" acts according to the norm of the νόμος of God: ἄρα οὖν αὐτὸς ἐγὼ τῷ μὲν νοΐ δουλεύω νόμῳ θεοῦ (v. 25)[34] → ἐγώ II, 358 ff., → νόμος, → ψυχή.

---

[29] Cf. C. Schmidt, "Iren. u. seine Quelle in Adv. Haer., I, 29," *Philotesia, P. Kleinert ... dargebracht* (1907), 324 f.

[30] Cf. H. J. Polotsky, Pauly-W. Suppl., VI (1935), 256 ff., Art. "Manichäismus."

[31] There is a typical misunderstanding in Simon, 44: "The νοῦς is the function of the divine likeness in man."

[32] To say that in Paul νοῦς is basically "thought" (so esp. R. Bultmann, cf. RGG², IV, 1033 f., Art. "Paulus" etc.; cf. F. C. Baur, *Vorlesungen über Nt.liche Theologie* [1864], 145: "νοῦς is a purely theoretical faculty," "νοῦς is the principle of thought and knowledge, of clear and intelligent thought") is to oversimplify a complicated semasiological situation. Nor is justice done to the facts by the development of the conceptual concept of νοῦς in terms of thought, cf. the skilful attempt of Gutbrod along these lines (*op. cit.*, 49 ff.) in the wake of Schlatter (cf. also F. Büchsel, *Der Geist Gottes im NT* [1926], 415).

[33] Gutbrod, 54; cf. P. Althaus, *Pls. und Luther über den Menschen* (1938) 35 ff.

[34] Though cf. R. 1:9: ὁ θεός, ᾧ λατρεύω ἐν τῷ → πνεύματί μου, or 2 Tm. 1:3: τῷ θεῷ, ᾧ λατρεύω ... ἐν καθαρᾷ → συνειδήσει.

c. "Understanding." In this sense it is an intellectual organ, the faculty of knowledge whether as state or act. [35] It is the understanding which understands the OT in Lk. 24:45, which penetrates apocalyptic secrets in Rev. 13:18; 17:9: ὧδε ὁ νοῦς ὁ ἔχων → σοφίαν, which is illuminated by divine wisdom. The peace which God gives to those who pray is a liberating power far beyond the human thought which is dominated by anxiety, Phil. 4:7: ἡ εἰρήνη τοῦ θεοῦ ἡ ὑπερέχουσα πάντα νοῦν. [36] νοῦς is especially understanding in contrast to the → πνεῦμα which lies behind the obscure ecstatic utterances of those who speak in tongues. As such, it is a function of the man who is in possession of his senses. It is the understanding which produces clear thoughts in intelligible words and whose activity is suspended during a state of spiritual rapture, 1 C. 14:14 f., 19. [37] The reference in 2 Th. 2:2: εἰς τὸ μὴ ταχέως σαλευθῆναι ὑμᾶς ἀπὸ τοῦ νοὸς μηδὲ θροεῖσθαι, is to the sure power of judgment which is always at the command of sober understanding. The sense here is that of discretion or circumspection in face of extravagant ideas of the *parousia*. [38]

d. "Thought," "judgment," "resolve." In the debate between the strong and the weak Paul advances in R. 14:5 the rule: ἕκαστος ἐν τῷ ἰδίῳ νοῒ πληροφορείσθω, "each should be established in his own judgment" (cf. Sir. 5:10). In the quotation from Is. (→ 953) in R. 11:34: τίς γὰρ ἔγνω νοῦν κυρίου; νοῦς is undoubtedly the saving purpose of God in which Paul finds the solution to the problem of R. 9-11. The same words are quoted from Is. 40:13 in 1 C. 2:16a, and here again the context (v. 7 ff.) points to the hidden plan of salvation which is now manifested. The sharp change of meaning which the word undergoes in v. 16b: ἡμεῖς δὲ νοῦν Χριστοῦ (= τὸ πνεῦμα τοῦ θεοῦ, v. 11, 14) ἔχομεν, represents a play on the word, which now bears sense a., i.e., "mind." There is no need to suppose that Paul is equating νοῦς and πνεῦμα after the manner of Hellenistic mysticism. [39]

D. νοῦς in the Oldest Christian Literature after the New Testament.

The rare use of the term in the post-apost. fathers is just as naïve and imprecise as that of the NT. Barn., 6, 10: εὐλογητὸς ὁ κύριος ἡμῶν ..., ὁ σοφίαν καὶ νοῦν θέμενος ἐν ἡμῖν τῶν κρυφίων αὐτοῦ, refers, like Lk. 24:45 (→ *supra*), to ability to understand the OT. Ign. Mg., 7, 1 and Herm. s., 9, 17, 4; 9, 18, 4 use εἷς νοῦς in the sense of the one mind of the Christian community or baptised Christians, who previously were men of different modes of thought and outlook (Herm. s., 9, 17, 2).

But the moment Christianity draws closer to the world around and begins discussion with it the Gk. concept of νοῦς, whether philosophical or syncretistic, reappears in

---

[35] Cf. also Mk. 12:34: νουνεχῶς ἀπεκρίθη.

[36] Even on the view that the peace is beyond all conceiving, that it is above what man can think, νοῦς still has reference to power of thought. But the present interpretation is demanded by the context, cf. Haupt Gefbr., Ew. Phil., *ad loc.*; Pr.-Bauer³, 901.

[37] Though some features remind us of Philo's depiction of ecstasy (→ 956) it should not be overlooked that the man who speaks with tongues retains his νοῦς even though it is seized by the πνεῦμα. The νοῦς is present, though inactive, cf. Joh. Weiss, 1 K., 328 f.; E. Sommerlath, *Der Ursprung d. neuen Lebens nach Pls.*² (1927), 47 n.; in the larger context of biblical theology G. Schrenk, "Geist u. Enthusiasmus," *Wort u. Geist, Festgabe f. K. Heim* (1934), 75 ff.

[38] Cf. Dob. Th., *ad loc.*

[39] In opposition to Reitzenstein Hell. Myst., 337 ff. cf. K. Deissner, *Pls. u. d. Mystik seiner Zeit*² (1921), 24 f.; Cr.-Kö., 765; Sommerlath, 46, n. 2; Kümmel, 28; Moe, 359; Hanse, 61 f.

Christian works, penetrates Christian thinking and affects Christian theology. [40] Uniting ancient theory (→ 957 f.) and new faith, Christian Gnosticism sees in Christ the *primogenitus Nus* which proceeded forth from the unbegotten and nameless Father (Basilides acc. to Iren., I, 24, 4). There are also echoes of mystery cults in the liturgical hymnic words of Act. Joh., 95: νοηθῆναι θέλω νοῦς ὢν ὅλος (sc. Christ), [41] Act. Thom., 27: ἐλθὲ ὁ πρεσβύτερος τῶν πέντε μελῶν, νοὸς ἐννοίας φρονήσεως ἐνθυμήσεως, λογισμοῦ, [42] or Act. Phil., 132 (p. 63, 17, M. Bonnet): ὁ νοῦς ὁ ὑπερύψωτος ἐν τῇ αὐτοῦ δόξῃ (sc. Christ). The Apologists take up Gk. ideas of the strict transcendence of God and the possibility of access to Him only through νοῦς, Just. Dial., 3, 7-4, 5; Athenag. Suppl., 4, 1; 10, 1; 23, 4. For them God and Christ are by nature νοῦς, Athenag. Suppl., 10, 2: ὁ θεός, νοῦς ἀίδιος ὤν, *loc. cit.*: νοῦς καὶ λόγος, τοῦ πατρὸς ὁ υἱὸς τοῦ θεοῦ, 24, 1: νοῦς, λόγος, σοφία ὁ υἱὸς τοῦ πατρός, Dg., 9, 6: Christ νοῦς, φῶς ... ζωή. [43] Cl. Al., [44] who is well acquainted with the philosophical doctrine of the νοῦς from Anaxag. to Philo, makes its essential content a theologoumenon of the Church. God the Father is νοῦς; the Logos is the Son of νοῦς (Strom., IV, 162, 5), εἰκὼν ... θεοῦ ..., εἰκὼν δ' εἰκόνος ἀνθρώπινος νοῦς (Strom., V, 94, 5; Prot., X, 98, 3). The Logos is the sun of the soul. By this alone, when it pierces to the inner depths of the νοῦς, is the eye of the soul illumined (Prot., VI, 68, 4). The human νοῦς, when free and pure from all evil, is in some sense able to receive the power of God as God's image is set up in it (Strom., III, 42, 6). He who penetrates things αὐτῷ καθαρῷ τῷ νῷ is the true philosopher (Strom., V, 67, 2) and also the truly righteous man who both hopes and believes τῷ νῷ ὁρᾷ τὰ νοητὰ καὶ τὰ μέλλοντα (Strom., V, 16, 1). Cf. also Hipp. Homilia contra Noëtianos (p. 49, 9 ff., ed. P. de Lagarde [1858]): εἷς ... νοῦς πατρός, ὁ παῖς. οἱ νοῦν πατρὸς ἔχοντες τούτῳ πιστεύομεν, οἱ δὲ τὸν νοῦν μὴ ἔχοντες τὸν υἱὸν ἤρνηνται.

The naïve view of νοῦς found in the NT can be understood only on the assumption that primitive Christianity stood quite apart from the philosophical reflection and religious mysticism of the surrounding world.

† νόημα.

Common in class. and Hell. Gk., νόημα is the result of the activity of the νοῦς (cf. Corp. Herm., IX, 3: ὁ γὰρ νοῦς κύει [to be pregnant, to bear] πάντα τὰ νοήματα). Hence acc. to the various senses of νοῦς (→ 952) it can mean "what is thought," "thought" (in the poets, everyday speech and philosophy, e.g., Hom. Od., 7, 36: νέες ὠκεῖαι ὡς εἰ πτερὸν ἠὲ νόημα, Parm. Fr., 8, 34 (I, 238, 3, Diels[5]) (→ 948), Aristot. Fr., 87 (89, 9 f., V. Rose): φύσει γὰρ εὐθὺς διῄρηται τά τε νοήματα καὶ τὰ αἰσθήματα, Philo Spec. Leg., IV, 108: ἡ τῶν νοημάτων βεβαία κατάληψις (cf. Det. Pot. Ins., 131), also "concept" (Aristot. An., III, 6, p. 430a, 27 f.: σύνθεσίς τις ἤδη νοημάτων, Cl. Al. Strom., VIII, 23, 1 ff.), the "point" of a matter (e.g., Epigr. Graec., 632: Τραιανοῦ τάφος οὗτος, ὃς εὐσεβὲς εἶχε νόημα), "what is willed," "resolve," "plan" (Plat. Polit., 260d: οὐκοῦν καὶ τὸ κηρυκικὸν φῦλον ἐπιταχθέντ'

[40] The popular understanding still persists, cf. Just. Apol., 60, 11; Dial., 2, 1; 68, 1: γνῶναι νοῦν καὶ θέλημα τοῦ θεοῦ. Just. Apol., 15, 16 gives to Mt. 6:21 and par. (→ III, 612, cf. 608) the more Hell. form: ὅπου γὰρ ὁ θησαυρός ἐστιν, ἐκεῖ καὶ ὁ νοῦς τοῦ ἀνθρώπου.

[41] *Ibid.*, 98 John as an initiate sees the cross of light which is now the Logos, now νοῦς, now Jesus, now Christ etc. On this passage of Act. Joh. cf. Hennecke, 172 f.

[42] For exposition of the obscure cultic text to which this petition belongs cf. the bibl. in Hennecke, 256 f.

[43] Cf. in this connection Sib., 8, 284 f., where Christ is πάντων ἀκοὴ καὶ νοῦς καὶ ὅρασις καὶ λόγος.

[44] Cf. the index in O. Stählin, *s.v.*

νόημα. Pass., Liddell-Scott, Cr.-Kö., Moult.-Mill., Pr.-Bauer[3] *s.v.*

ἀλλότρια νοήματα παραδεχόμενον αὐτὸ δεύτερον ἐπιτάττει πάλιν ἑτέροις) etc. The LXX uses νόημα only in the special sense of an "evil plan," "attack," Bar. 2:8: ἀποστρέψαι ἕκαστον ἀπὸ τῶν νοημάτων τῆς καρδίας αὐτῶν τῆς πονηρᾶς,[1] 3 Macc. 5:30.

In the NT the word occurs only in Paul (5 times in 2 C., once in Phil.). It is found only in the plur. or with a plural sense, and always (apart from Phil. 4:7) *sensu malo*. It means corrupt human thoughts in 2 C. 3:14: ἐπωρώθη τὰ νοήματα αὐτῶν, 4:4: ὁ θεὸς τοῦ αἰῶνος τούτου ἐτύφλωσεν τὰ νοήματα τῶν ἀπίστων,[2] 11:3. In Phil. 4:7, with no adverse judgment, it means the thoughts which proceed from the heart of Christians, ἡ εἰρήνη τοῦ θεοῦ ... φρουρήσει τὰς καρδίας ὑμῶν καὶ τὰ νοήματα[3] ὑμῶν ἐν Χριστῷ Ἰησοῦ (→ n. 1). In 2 C. 2:11 (cf. Eph. 6:11; 1 Pt. 5:8; Test. D. 6:3; Barn., 2, 10) the reference is to the devices of Satan, and in 10:5: αἰχμαλωτίζοντες πᾶν νόημα εἰς τὴν ὑπακοὴν Χριστοῦ,[4] to human devices against the Christian knowledge of God which the warrior Paul, as in the occupation of a captured fortress, takes captive and forces into obedient subjection to Christ.

νόημα is also rare in the Christian lit. of the 2nd cent. It usually has the stamp of what is bad, cf. Just. Dial., 23, 1; Athenag. Suppl., 27, 2; Cl. Al. Ecl. Proph., 30, 1; Strom., III, 94, 3; VII, 76, 4, though cf. also Just. Dial., 62, 1; Cl. Al. Strom., V, 65, 2; VII, 37, 3.

† ἀνόητος.

Rarely pass. "unthought of," "unsuspected" (Hom. Hymn. Merc., 80), "unintelligible," "inconceivable" (Plat. Parm., 132c: νοήματα ... ἀνόητα) this word is predominantly act. "unwise," "irrational," "foolish" (Hesych.: μωρός, ἠλίθιος, ἀσύνετος, ἄφρων), both intellectually and ethically, of persons lacking in understanding or judgment (→ 952) (Soph. Ai., 162 f.: οὐ δυνατὸν τοὺς ἀνοήτους τούτων γνώμας προδιδάσκειν, Plat. Gorg., 464d: ἐν ἀνδράσιν οὕτως ἀνοήτοις ὥσπερ οἱ παῖδες), whose folly is manifested in their acts (Anaxippus Fr., 4, CAF, III, 299: οἴμοι, φιλοσοφεῖς. ἀλλά τούς γε φιλοσόφους / ἐν τοῖς λόγοις φρονοῦντας εὑρίσκω μόνον, / ἐν τοῖσι δ' ἔργοις ὄντας ἀνοήτους ὁρῶ, Plut. Quomodo Adulescens Poetas audire debeat, 5 (II, 22b c): τοῖς ἄφροσι καὶ ἀνοήτοις, οὓς δειλαίους καὶ οἰκτροὺς διὰ μοχθηρίαν ὄντας εἴωθε "δειλοὺς" καὶ "διζυροὺς" προσαγορεύειν, Corp. Herm., I, 23: τοῖς δὲ ἀνοήτοις καὶ κακοῖς καὶ πονηροῖς ... πόρρωθέν εἰμι), but also of subjects, human thoughts, utterances etc. (Aristoph. Nu., 417: οἴνου τ' ἀπέχει καὶ γυμνασίων καὶ τῶν ἄλλων ἀνοήτων, Plat. Phileb., 12d: τὸν ... ἀνοήτων δοξῶν καὶ ἐλπίδων μεστόν, Xenoph. Oec., 11, 3: τὸ πάντων δὴ ἀνοητότατον δοκοῦν εἶναι ἔγκλημα). It is also used of men in the LXX, for אֱוִיל at Prv. 17:28 or אִוֶּלֶת (→ 962) at 15:21;

---

1 On καρδία as the seat of νοήματα → 949.

2 In these two passages there is a shift in usage inasmuch as statements which should be made of the organ νοῦς are transferred to the products of its activity. But the word νόημα does not thereby lose the sense of "thought," as against Wnd. 2 K., Ltzm. K., *ad loc.*

3 νοήματα P^{46} ℵ ABD as the more difficult reading is to be preferred to σώματα FG it (P. Oxy., VII, 1009, verso 36 f.: καὶ τὰ νοήματα καὶ τὰ σώματα). The fact that the νοήματα come from the καρδία (cf. Bar. 2:8) and the divergent use in 2 C. do not militate against Paul's use of νόημα for "thought" as in the *koine* (in spite of Loh. Phil., *ad loc.*).

4 A purely intellectual view of νόημα in 2 C. 2:11; 10:5 does not do justice to the context, which suggests the activity of the will (as against Bchm. K. and Schl. K., *ad loc.*).

ἀνόητος. Lexicons, *s.v.*; J. H. H. Schmidt, *Synonymik d. gr. Sprache*, 3 (1879), 652; C. H. Dodd, *The Bible and the Greeks* (1935), 174; Nägeli, 77 and 85.

Dt. 32:31;[1] cf. also Sir. 21:19; 42:8: ἀνοήτου καὶ μωροῦ (Heb. פוחה), 4 Macc. 8:17, and of animals in ψ 48:12, 20 (no Heb.), also neutrally in 4 Macc. 5:9: καὶ γὰρ ἀνόητον τοῦτο, τὸ μὴ ἀπολαύειν τῶν χωρὶς ὀνείδους ἡδέων. 'A and esp. Σ, but not so much Θ, often use ἀνόητος elsewhere, esp. for כְּסִיל, e.g., Prv. 10:23 'A; 13:19; 17:16 'AΣ; 19:29 Θ. For non-biblical Hell. Jewish usage cf. Ep. Ar., 136; Philo Fug., 14: βλαβεραὶ ... αἱ μετὰ ἀνοήτων συνουσίαι, Jos. Ant., 8, 264 and 243, perhaps also the apocryphon 1 Cl., 23, 4 = 2 Cl., 11, 3.

In R. 1:14 the ἀνόητοι as distinct from the σοφοί are the simple and uneducated whose power of thought is undeveloped.[2] Elsewhere in the NT ἀνόητος involves an adverse religious and moral judgment, Lk. 24:25: ὦ ἀνόητοι καὶ βραδεῖς τῇ καρδίᾳ (lack of understanding); Gl. 3:1: ὦ ἀνόητοι Γαλάται, 3:3: οὕτως ἀνόητοί ἐστε (deficient understanding of salvation); Tt. 2:3: ἦμεν γάρ ποτε καὶ ἡμεῖς ἀνόητοι, ἀπειθεῖς, πλανώμενοι, δουλεύοντες ἐπιθυμίαις καὶ ἡδοναῖς ποικίλαις ... (folly as a mark of the religious and ethical constitution of Christians prior to conversion, cf. Eph. 4:17 f.; R. 1:21 ff.). Similarly, in 1 Tm. 6:9 the many ἐπιθυμίαι which beset those who strive for wealth are called ἀνόητοι,[3] not merely because they are without substance[4] but because they are also morally suspect.

ἀνόητος suggests what is foolish and to be avoided from the Christian standpoint esp. in Just., cf. Apol., 12, 6; 63, 10; Dial., 39, 5; 134, 1; 68, 8; cf. also Cl. Al. Paed., II, 103, 4; Strom., IV, 168, 2 f.

† ἄνοια.

"Unreason," "folly," in the sense both of *insipientia* (vg) and also of *dementia* (Plat. Tim., 86b: δύο δ' ἀνοίας γένη, τὸ μὲν μανίαν, τὸ δὲ ἀμαθίαν (cf. ἄνοια and παράνοια, Cl. Al. Prot., X, 96, 4). Cf. on the one side Thuc., III, 48, 2: μετ' ἔργων ἰσχύος ἀνοίᾳ ἐπιών, Hdt., VI, 69, and on the other Plat. Leg., IV, 716a: νεότητι καὶ ἀνοίᾳ. In the mature man this ἄνοια denotes a moral defect, e.g., Ps.-Heracl. Ep., 2 (p. 8, 21 f., J. Bernays): ἀπληστίῃ (insatiability) δὲ καὶ δόξῃ κενῇ προσέχουσι κακῆς εἵνεκεν ἀνοίης, Philo Leg. All., III, 164: δυσελπιστίαν καὶ ἀπιστίαν μετὰ πολλῆς ἀνοίας, *ibid.*, 211 etc., Jos. Vit., 323; Ant., 8, 318: ἀνοίᾳ καὶ πονηρίᾳ πάντας ὑπερβεβληκὼς τοὺς πρὸ αὐτοῦ, Corp. Herm., XIV, 8: ὦ τῆς πολλῆς ἀνοίας καὶ ἀγνωσίας τῆς περὶ τὸν θεόν. In the LXX the usual sense is "folly" for אִוֶּלֶת, Prv. 14:8; 22:15, with no Heb. Eccl. 11:10; Job 33:23; ψ 21:2 (?). Cf. also in the apocr. Wis.

---

[1] Here, too, the LXX presupposes אֱוִיל (cf. BHK[3], *ad loc.*), but it is guessing. For the word פְּלִיל (meaning uncertain, cf. Ges.-Buhl) is unfamiliar to it. Except in this verse it occurs only twice in the OT, at Job 31:11, where the LXX gives a free rendering and at Ex. 21:22, where ἀξίωμα accidentally comes close to what is probably the true meaning. The verb פלל I also seems to be unfamiliar to the LXX translators. It is rendered arbitrarily at Gn. 48:11 and Ez. 16:52, and the sense is perhaps intentionally altered. At 1 Βασ. 2:25 and ψ 105:30 פלל II ("to pray," "to intercede for") is presupposed. At Dt. 32:31 Σ, following syr[hex], has the conjectured βίαιοι, and at Ez. 16:52 the arbitrary ὑπερέβαλεν is the rendering chosen for פלל [G. Bertram].

[2] The context hardly supports the sense of "unable and unwilling to grasp what is said" (Schl. R., *ad loc.*).

[3] The weakly attested vl. ἀνονήτους ("useless," cf. the play on words in Cl. Al. Prot., X, 92, 4: ἀνονήτους καὶ ἀνοήτους ἐκβόσκονται τρυφάς) is obviously not original.

[4] So Schl. Past., *ad loc.*

ἄνοια. Liddell-Scott, Cr.-Kö., Pr.-Bauer[3], *s.v.*; J. H. H. Schmidt, *Synonymik d. gr. Sprache*[3] (1879), 651 f.

19:3; 15:18 (animals); 2 Macc. 4:6, 40; 14:5; 15:33 (in these 4 instances "infamy"); 3 Macc. 3:16, 20. Σ has ἄνοια for כֶּסֶל at ψ 48:13. In Jos. Ap., I, 210 Agatharchides describes as ἄνοια the Jewish observance of the Sabbath even in war.

At Lk. 6:11: ἐπλήσθησαν ἀνοίας, the sense is pathological, "they were filled with madness" (at Jesus). 2 Tm. 3:9 refers to the dreadful folly of errors both new and old: ἡ γὰρ ἄνοια [1] αὐτῶν ἔκδηλος ἔσται πᾶσιν, ὡς καὶ ἡ ἐκείνων (sc. Jannes and Jambres, v. 8) ἐγένετο.

ἄνοια as sin, [2] with πονηρία, 2 Cl., 13, 1; cf. also Cl. Al. Prot., I, 4, 2: τοὺς ἐν ἀγνοίᾳ καὶ ἀνοίᾳ κατατετριμμένους. ἄνοια of the absurdity of the Gk. Kronos legend, Aristid. Apol., 9, 5.

† δυσνόητος.

"Something which is hard to understand," e.g., Aristot. De Plantis, I, 1, p. 816a, 3; Luc. Alex., 54: χρησμοὺς ..., ἀνοήτους δὲ καὶ δυσνοήτους ἅπαντας, Diog. L., IX, 13: λόγον ... δυσνόητόν τε καὶ δυσεξήγητον.

2 Pt. 3:16 tells us that in Paul's epistles we find δυσνόητά τινα, "things hard to understand" [1] which are wrested by the Gnostics. There can be no knowing whether the reference is to Paul's judgments on Christian freedom, on the πνευματικὸς ἄνθρωπος, on flesh and spirit, or to his eschatological statements, e.g., in 1 C. 15:50, 53 ff.; 2 Th. 2:2.

In the request for an interpretation of the vision of the building of the tower in Herm. s., 9, 14, 4 we read: τὰ γὰρ πάντα ... δυσνόητα τοῖς ἀνθρώποις.

† διάνοια.

1. The Use outside the NT.

This is a very common word throughout Gk. prose. The basic sense of "thought" or "reflection" (cf. the verb διανοέομαι, "to reflect on," "to ponder," not found in the NT) [1] opens up many possibilities of meaning as in the case of νοῦς (→ 952), so that διάνοια can be used as an alternative for νοῦς.

1. It means "thought" as a function, the activity of thinking, Plat. Soph., 263e: ὁ μὲν ἐντὸς τῆς ψυχῆς πρὸς αὑτὴν διάλογος ... ἐπωνομάσθη, διάνοια (cf. 264a), Resp., VI, 511d: ὡς μεταξύ τι δόξης τε καὶ νοῦ τὴν διάνοιαν οὖσαν, Aristot. Metaph., V, 1, p. 1025b, 25: πᾶσα διάνοια ἢ πρακτικὴ ἢ ποιητικὴ ἢ θεωρητική.

2. It also means the "power of thought," "understanding," "the ability to perceive," "the thinking consciousness" (including moral reflection), cf. the philosophers, [2] e.g., Democr. Fr., 11 (II, 140, 9 ff., Diels[5]), in whom two types of knowledge are distinguished,

---

[1] The vl. διάνοια A is a scribal error.

[2] So already LXX Job 33:23. Cf. BHK[3], which retranslates τὴν δὲ ἄνοιαν αὐτοῦ δείξῃ by וְחַטָּאתוֹ יוֹדִיעֶהוּ. In Eccl. 11:10 the arbitrary replacement of the hapax legomenon שַׁחֲרוּת, whose meaning is unknown, by ἄνοια is a negative characterisation of youth from the moral standpoint. In ψ 48:13 Σ has ἄνοια (Ἀ ἀνόησις, LXX σκάνδαλον) for כֶּסֶל, which means "false confidence," "folly" [G. Bertram].

δυσνόητος. Cr.-Kö., Pr.-Bauer, *s.v.*

[1] Cyril Al. (Cramer Cat., *ad loc.*): δυσχερῆ τινα.

διάνοια. Pass., Liddell-Scott, Moult.-Mill., Preisigke Wört., Cr.-Kö., Pr.-Bauer[3], *s.v.*

[1] In the LXX (Da., Sir.) διανοεῖσθαι is fairly common, esp. for בִּין [G. Bertram].

[2] Cf. H. Siebeck, *Gesch. d. Psychologie,* I, 2 (1884), Index, *s.v.*

τὴν μὲν διὰ τῶν αἰσθήσεων, τὴν δὲ διὰ τῆς διανοίας, the first obscure (σκοτίη), the second genuine (γνωσίη); Plat. Phaedr., 279a: φύσει ... ἔνεστί τις φιλοσοφία τῇ τοῦ ἀνδρὸς διανοίᾳ, 256c: ἅτε οὐ πάσῃ δεδογμένα τῇ διανοίᾳ πράττοντες ("moral consciousness"), [3] Aristot. Metaph., III, 7, p. 1012a, 2: πᾶν τὸ διανοητὸν καὶ νοητὸν ἡ διάνοια ἢ κατάφησιν ἢ ἀπόφησιν (confirms or rejects). The Stoics see in the διάνοια τὸ ἡγεμονικὸν μέρος αὐτῆς (scil. τῆς ψυχῆς [III, 75, 8 f., v. Arnim, cf. I, 50, 6]); [4] it is the proper subject of the philosopher's activity, cf. Epict. Diss., 3, 22, 20; M. Ant., 6, 16, 10; it can be fully identified with the ψυχή, 2, 2, 13: ἐξ ὅλης τῆς διανοίας = 2, 23, 42: ἐξ ὅλης ψυχῆς; its seat acc. to the Stoics is in the brain, I, 40, 30 f., v. Arnim, ἀλλ' ἐν τοῖς κατωτέρω τόποις, μάλιστά πως περὶ τὴν καρδίαν (III, 216, 9 f.). For Philo διάνοια [5] is what distinguishes man from the beasts and mediates to him the divine likeness (Plant., 40 and 42), τὸ θειότατον τῶν ἐν ἡμῖν (Det. Pot. Ins., 29, cf.Fug., 148; Jos., 71 etc. → 956), the organ of the knowledge of God, Virt., 57: θεόν, ᾧ μόνῳ διάνοιαν ἔξεστιν ἀκριβῶς θεωρεῖν (cf. Spec. Leg., I, 20; Gig., 53 etc., cf. Corp. Herm., V, 2). Like νοῦς, διάνοια can denote man's spiritual side as distinct from the body in the sense of "spirit" or "soul," e.g., Democr. acc. to Plut. Quaest. Conv., V, 7, 6 (II, 683a): κακοῦν αὐτῶν τό τε σῶμα καὶ τὴν διάνοιαν, Plat. Leg., XI, 916a: κατὰ τὸ σῶμα ἢ κατὰ τὴν διάνοιαν, cf. Resp., III, 395d, II, 371e; Theaet., 173e; Aristot. Pol., II, 9, p. 1270b, 40 f.: ἔστι γάρ, ὥσπερ καὶ σώματος, καὶ διανοίας γῆρας, *ibid.*, I, 2, p. 1252a, 32 f.: τῇ διανοίᾳ προορᾶν ... τῷ σώματι ταῦτα ποιεῖν. Philo Op. Mund., 135 (of man): θνητὸν μὲν κατὰ τὸ σῶμα, κατὰ δὲ τὴν διάνοιαν ἀθάνατον, [6] in typical deviation from the materialism of the Stoa: τὴν γὰρ διάνοιαν καὶ τὴν ψυχὴν σῶμα εἶναι (III, 75, 5, v. Arnim). διάνοια is one spiritual faculty among others in popular usage, e.g., R. Wünsch, *Antike Fluchtafeln,* Kl. T., 20^2 (1912), 1, 8 ff. ἀναθεμα[τί]ζομεν σῶμα πνεῦμα ψ[υ]χὴν [δι]άνοιαν φρόνησιν αἴσθησιν ζοὴν [καρδ]ίαν ..., *ibid.*, 4, 55 ff.: βασάνισον αὐτῶν τὴν διάνοιαν τὰς φρένας τὴν αἴσθησιν ἵνα μὴ νοῶσιν τί π[ο]ιῶσιν. Philosophically it is still one of the five faculties of the soul in Joh. Damascenus Fr. (MPG, 95, 232b): τῆς ψυχῆς εἰσι δυνάμεις πέντε· νοῦς, διάνοια, δόξα, φαντασία, αἴσθησις ... διάνοιά ἐστι δύναμις τῆς ψυχῆς, καθ' ἣν μετὰ συλλογισμοῦ δύναται γινώσκειν τὰ πράγματα· διὸ καὶ λέγεται διάνοια, παρὰ τὸ ὁδόν τινα διανοίγειν.

3. "Way of thought," "disposition," e.g., Plat. Tim., 71c: πρᾳότητός τις ἐκ διανοίας ἐπίπνοια, Phaedr., 234b: τοὺς ἐρῶντας ταύτην ἔχειν τὴν διάνοιαν, Leg., X, 888a: τοῖς οὕτω τὴν διάνοιαν διεφθαρμένοις, cf. Prot., 326b; Philo Spec. Leg., III, 121: τἀληθὲς ... διανοίας ἀφανεῖς εἰς τοὐμφανὲς ἄγον.

4. The result of the activity of thought, a "thought," "idea," "opinion," "judgment," Hdt., 2, 169, 2; Plat. Phaed., 63c: αὐτὸς ἔχων τὴν διάνοιαν ταύτην, cf. Theaet., 155d; Aristot. Meteor., II, 3, p. 356b, 31; Plut. De Animae Procreatione in Timaeo Platonis, 5 (II, 1014a) etc.

5. Fig. in the sphere of the will "purpose," "resolve," "intention," Hdt., 1, 90, 3; 8, 97, 3; Thuc., 5, 9, 6; Plat. Tim., 38c: ἐξ οὖν λόγου καὶ διανοίας θεοῦ τοιαύτης πρὸς χρόνου γένεσιν, ἵνα γεννηθῇ χρόνος, ἥλιος καὶ σελήνη καὶ πέντε ἄλλα ἄστρα ... εἰς διορισμὸν καὶ φυλακὴν ἀριθμῶν χρόνου γέγονεν, Plat. Apol., 41d; P. Masp., 2, II, 17: μετέβαλλεν τὰς διανοίας ὑμῶν.

---

[3] In Resp., VII, 533d, V, 476d etc. Plat. uses the term in a special sense and differentiates διάνοια as the power to understand mathematical relations from ἐπιστήμη as the knowledge of the ideas.

[4] For further material cf. A. Bonhöffer, *Epiktet u. die Stoa* (1890), 113 ff.

[5] On the philosophical equation of διάνοια, νοῦς etc. cf. H. Schmidt, *Die Anthropologie Philons v. Alex.* (Diss. phil. Leipzig, 1933), 50, 139 ff. (n. 13 and 14); W. Völker, "Fortschitt u. Vollendung bei Philo v. Alex.," TU, 49, 1 (1938), 160, 213, 303 f.

[6] In Rer. Div. Her., 257 διάνοια as an alternative for νοῦς means the spirit as distinct from the sensual nature (αἴσθησις), cf. Corp. Herm., I, 1: ἡ διάνοια — αἱ σωματικαὶ αἰσθήσεις.

6. Of words, statements, writings etc. the "meaning," "content," "significance," Plat. Critias, 113a: ἑκάστου τὴν διάνοιαν ὀνόματος ἀναλαμβάνων εἰς τὴν ἡμετέραν ἄγων φωνὴν ἀπεγράφετο, Crat., 418a, Phaedr., 228d, Ep. Ar., 171: τὴν ... φυσικὴν διάνοιαν τοῦ νόμου, Jos. Ant., 8, 143 etc.

The LXX mostly uses διάνοια for לֵב or לֵבָב. It is thus a — better Hell. — equivalent of καρδία (→ III, 609). Sometimes in his choice of the word the translator shows awareness of the connection of the Heb. with the activity or faculty of thought (→ III, 606), e.g., Job 1:5; Gn. 17:17; 45:26; Is. 57:11; Ex. 28:3 : οἱ σοφοὶ τῇ διανοίᾳ (cf. 35:25; 36:1; Job 9:4); Prv. 2:10; Ex. 35:35 : σύνεσις διανοίας; Dt. 28:28 : ἔκστασις διανοίας.[7] In Nu. 15:39 : οὐ διαστραφήσεσθε ὀπίσω τῶν διανοιῶν ὑμῶν καὶ ὀπίσω τῶν ὀφθαλμῶν ὑμῶν, the meaning of the plur. is thinking or considering (in the bad sense). But διάνοια is also used with ref. to emotions (Lv. 19:17; Is. 35:4) or acts of will (Ex. 35:22, 26; Dt. 29:17 etc.) or the totality of man's spiritual nature (Gn. 8:21; Dt. 4:39; Jos. 22:5 etc.). In sum, it is, like καρδία (→ III, 609), co-extensive with the לֵב and לֵבָב of the Mas.; this is shown by the textual vacillation between the two Gk. terms (e.g., Dt. 28:47; Jos. 14:8; Prv. 4:4; 27:19; cf. also the deviations from the LXX at ψ 12:2 Σ and Qoh. 7:3 Σ). At Ιερ. 38:33 the Gk. διάνοια and καρδία correspond to the Heb. synon. קֶרֶב and לֵב.[8] At Is. 55:9; Da. 11:25, where διάνοια occurs for מַחֲשָׁבוֹת, and 1 Ch. 29:18, where לְיֵצֶר מַחְשְׁבוֹת לְבַב עַמֶּךָ is rendered ἐν διανοίᾳ καρδίας λαοῦ σου, the meaning is "thought." Only at Da. 9:22 is διάνοια used for בִּינָה, "perception," "insight" (in the same sense Prv. 9:10a; 13:15, no Heb.).[9] In the OT apocr. and pseudepigr., too, the main sense is "understanding," "spirit," "mind," e.g., Sir. 29:16; Wis. 4:14; Bar. 4:28; 1 Εσδρ. 3:18 ff.; Jdt. 8:14; 1 Macc. 10:74; 2 Macc. 5:17; 4 Macc. 11:14. We also find the occasional meanings "thought" at Bar. 1:22 : καὶ ᾠχόμεθα ἕκαστος ἐν διανοίᾳ καρδίας αὐτοῦ τῆς πονηρᾶς, and Sir. 3:24 : ὑπόνοια πονηρὰ ὠλίσθησεν διανοίας αὐτῶν, and "insight" at Sir. 22:17: καρδία ἡδρασμένη ἐπὶ διανοίας συνέσεως.

The usage is much the same as that of the LXX in the two Jewish works where διάνοια is most common, Ep. Ar. and Test. XII, where it usually means "consciousness," "spirit," "mind" (e.g., Ep. Ar., 238 : θεὸς τῆς διανοίας ἡγεμών, cf. 227, 247, 122, 287; Test. B. 3:2; Test. Jos. 10:5 : οὐχὶ ὑψούμην ἐν τῇ διανοίᾳ μου, Test. Jud. 11:1: τὸ διαβούλιον τῆς νεότητος ἐτύφλωσε τὴν διάνοιάν μου, D. 2:4). In Test. XII it is an alternative for καρδία, which Ep. Ar. avoids. We also find the meanings "thought" (Test. Jos. 10:4 : ἢ ἐν ἔργῳ ἢ ἐν λόγῳ ἢ ἐν διανοίᾳ) and "disposition" (Ep. Ar., 292 : ἔχειν ἁγνὴν καὶ ἀμιγῆ παντὸς κακοῦ τὴν διάνοιαν, Test. B. 5:1; 6:5; 8:2 β : ὁ ἔχων διάνοιαν καθαρὰν ἐν ἀγάπῃ, Test. G. 6:1; Test. R. 6:2 etc.). Joseph. uses διάνοια in all the usual senses, esp. "consciousness," "spirit,"[10] e.g., Ant., 9, 57: τὰς ὄψεις ὑπὸ θεοῦ καὶ τὴν διάνοιαν ἐπεσκοτημένοι, 6, 21: ὅλαις ταῖς διανοίαις προστρέπεσθε τὸ θεῖον, 7, 269 etc.

2. The Usage in the New Testament.

Though not common, the word is used by almost all the NT writers. In general, the usage is popular, but closer inspection reveals LXX influence in most passages. There are no echoes of philosophical usage.

---

[7] The same applies to Qoh. 1:16 ᾿ΑΣ and 2 Βασ. 7:27 Σ.

[8] διάνοια for קֶרֶב also at ψ 63:6 Θ. Once διάνοια is used (Ez. 14:4) for גִּלּוּלִים "idols." The translator gives evidence here of the common LXX tendency to psychologise. For גִּלּוּלִים he also uses διανόημα 2 times, ἐνθύμημα 15 times, ἐπιθύμημα once, ἐπιτήδευμα 7 times. εἴδωλον is used 13 times [G. Bertram].

[9] At Ez. 14:4 the Heb. presupposed by the LXX (ἀποκριθήσομαι αὐτῷ ἐν οἷς ἐνέχεται ἡ διάνοια αὐτοῦ) is doubtful, in spite of → n. 8.

[10] Cf. Thackeray Lex Jos., 155 f.

In the Synoptic Gospels and Hb., where διάνοια occurs only in expressions influenced by the OT, the main sense is "understanding," "mind." The fulfilling of the first commandment, namely, to love God (Mk. 12:30 and par., Dt. 6:5;[11] cf. 4 Βασ. 23:25) claims the whole man, his whole heart (καρδία), his whole soul (ψυχή), his whole spiritual life (διάνοια), his whole strength (ἰσχύς). The requirements of the new divine order affect the moral consciousness, the point in man's being which determines his ethical attitude, Hb. 8:10; 10:16 (Ιερ. 38:33). The alternation of διάνοια and καρδία (8:10: διδοὺς νόμους μου εἰς τὴν διάνοιαν αὐτῶν, καὶ ἐπὶ καρδίας αὐτῶν ἐπιγράψω αὐτούς, 10:16: διδοὺς νόμους μου ἐπὶ καρδίας αὐτῶν, καὶ ἐπὶ τὴν διάνοιαν αὐτῶν ἐπιγράψω αὐτούς)[12] shows that both are synonymously related to the centre of man's inner life (→ III, 611, 612).[13] Lk. 1:51: ὑπερηφάνους διανοίᾳ καρδίας αὐτῶν refers to a proud disposition or mode of thought, cf. 1 Ch. 29:18, → 965; Bar. 1:22, → 965; Test. Jos. 10:5, → 965.

When Paul in Eph. 4:18[14] calls the Gentiles who live ἐν ματαιότητι τοῦ νοὸς αὐτῶν (v. 17 → 958) ἐσκοτωμένοι τῇ διανοίᾳ ὄντες,[15] he traces the defect of disposition (νοῦς) back to a defect of consciousness, of the faculty of spiritual and moral understanding (διάνοια) — a defect which is finally called → πώρωσις τῆς καρδίας, v. 18. In Col. 1:21: ὑμᾶς ποτε ὄντας ἀπηλλοτριωμένους (→ I, 265) καὶ ἐχθροὺς (→ II, 814) τῇ διανοίᾳ ἐν τοῖς ἔργοις τοῖς πονηροῖς, he has in view the pre-Christian disposition and mode of thought. The sense of "thought"[16] or "impulse of will" underlies the plur. διάνοιαι in Eph. 2:3: ποιοῦντες τὰ θελήματα (→ III, 61) τῆς → σαρκὸς καὶ τῶν διανοιῶν.[17] The context yields the special sense of "evil thoughts or inclinations" (cf. Nu. 15:39, → 965; Sir. 3:24, → 965; 1 Cl., 39, 1, → 967),[18] namely, the σάρξ, the whole sinful nature of man

---

[11] Here only B^r has διάνοια for καρδία. In the fourfold formula in Mk. and Lk., which strengthens the total claim of the commandment by the heaping up of synons., ἐξ ὅλης τῆς διανοίας σου or ἐν ὅλῃ τῇ διανοίᾳ σου is a second rendering of בְּכָל־לְבָבְךָ. The same applies to the threefold formula in Mt., in which ἐν ὅλῃ τῇ διανοίᾳ σου, for בְּכָל־מְאֹדֶךָ, establishes the harmony of related anthropological concepts, cf. Schl. Mt., Mk., Lk. and Zn. Lk., *ad loc.* Loh. Mk., 258, n. 3, in defiance of the usage of the Gk. Bible, takes διάνοια (like σύνεσις at 12:33) to mean "perception."

[12] The text of Ιερ. 38:33 also vacillates in the first clause, though Hb. 10:16 is a free rendering from memory, Rgg. Hb.$^{2, 3}$, 310, n. 62.

[13] Luther's fine exposition is not quite exact (Schol. on Hb. 8:10 in E. Hirsch-H. Rückert, *Luthers Vorlesung über den Hb.* [1929], 208): *igitur intelligendus scripturae modus <loquendi>, ubi dicit leges scribi "in mentes" et "in corda." nam per mentem et cor intellectum et affectum (ita enim nunc loquimur) accipit. esse enim in mente est intelligi, esse in corde est diligi.*

[14] The weakly attested vl. τῆς διανοίας for τῆς καρδίας in Eph. 1:18 attempts elucidation (in terms of 4:18 ?) by making the faculty of perception the central organ of the inner life. For the unusual expression ὀφθαλμοὶ τῆς διανοίας cf. Corp. Herm., X, 4b: ὁ τοῦ νοῦ ὀφθαλμός or Orig. Comm. in Joh. Fr., 46 (GCS, Orig., IV, 521, 23): οἱ προφῆται ... εἶδον διανοίᾳ καὶ ἤκουσαν τοῖς ὠσὶ τοῦ ἔσω ἀνθρώπου, also Act. Thom., 65 (p. 182, 6 ff., Bonnet): οὐ φαίνεται (sc. Jesus) τούτοις τοῖς ὀφθαλμοῖς τοῖς σωματικοῖς, ἀλλ' ἐν τοῖς ὀφθαλμοῖς τῆς ἐννοίας εὑρίσκεται.

[15] On the metaphor cf. Test. Jud. 11:1, → 965; D. 2:4, → 965; Jos. Ant., 9, 57, → 965; 1 Cl., 36, 2; 2 Cl., 19, 2; 1, 6.

[16] So also W. Gutbrod, *D. paul. Anthropologie* (1934), 51.

[17] To render διάνοιαι "hearts" (Ew. Gefbr., *ad loc.*; for the individualising plur. cf. Jos. 5:1; 1 Macc. 11:49) is impossible, since it would demand the co-ordination of the incompatible "flesh" and "heart."

[18] In 1 Εσδρ. 4:26 and 2 Macc. 2:2 also διάνοια has a derogatory sense.

(not just sexuality) which finds active expression sensually in his θελήματα and intellectually in his διάνοιαι.

The metaphor in 1 Pt. 1:13: ἀναζωσάμενοι τὰς ὀσφύας τῆς διανοίας ὑμῶν, is a summons to readiness of mind and soul. In their inner attitude Christians should be prepared for right conduct without hampering ἐπιθυμίαι (1:14; 2:11). In 2 Pt. 3:1 the εἰλικρινὴς διάνοια which the author seeks to maintain in his readers through the epistle is a "pure disposition," cf. Ep. Ar., 292, → 965; Test. B. 8:2 β, → 965.

In the Johannine writings διάνοια occurs only at 1 Jn. 5:20: οἴδαμεν δὲ ὅτι ὁ υἱὸς τοῦ θεοῦ ἥκει καὶ δέδωκεν ἡμῖν διάνοιαν ἵνα γινώσκομεν τὸν ἀληθινόν. To argue that the word has here the sense of γνῶσις, i.e., knowledge with a specific content, is to fly in the face of its history. Known usage allows only the meaning "faculty of perception" or "gift of apprehension." [19] The idea is that the Son of God has awakened in us the mind and given our thinking the orientation to know God, to receive His revelation, to share fellowship with Him. The reference is not to a natural disposition for knowledge of God and fellowship with Him. The NT, in distinction from Hellenistic mysticism (→ 964), never understands either διάνοια or νοῦς (→ 958) in this way. It is speaking of the ability which is given to Christians with experience of saving revelation. Here — with no contradiction of 2:20, 27; 3:24; 4:13 — this ability is a direct gift of the Son of God, Jesus Christ, whereas Paul traces it back to the operation of God through the Spirit, 1 C. 2:12; 2 C. 4:6; Eph. 4:17 f., cf. 1:17 f. [20]

The common use of διάνοια in the post-apost. fathers is along NT lines. The dominant meanings are "faculty of thought," "spirit" (e.g., Herm. m., 10, 1, 5; 1 Cl., 35, 2 and 5), or "mind," "disposition" (e.g., 1 Cl., 21, 8; 23, 1; Ign. Eph., 20, 2); plur. in a bad sense "evil thoughts," "imaginations," 1 Cl., 39, 1: ἑαυτοὺς βουλόμενοι ἐπαίρεσθαι ταῖς διανοίαις αὐτῶν. In the Apologists διάνοια is far less common than νοῦς or καρδία. Worth noting is the quotation from Jl. 2:13 in Just. Apol., 52, 11, which has διανοίας for καρδίας, and Just. Apol., 61, 12: Baptism is φωτισμός, ὡς φωτιζομένων τὴν διάνοιαν ("in the spirit") τῶν ταῦτα μανθανόντων. Cl. Al. uses διάνοια in all the current Gk. meanings, e.g., Strom., I, 50, 1 ("faculty of thought"); VI, 25, 1 (plur. "thoughts"); Paed., I, 14, 2; II, 14, 1; III, 20, 6: τὸ κάλλιστον ἐν ἀνθρώπῳ, τὴν διάνοιαν ("disposition"); I, 37, 3; Strom., VII, 84, 4, τὴν διάνοιαν τοῦ ῥητοῦ τοῦ ἀποστόλου ("meaning," "sense") etc. It is also a better Gk. alternative for καρδία, as in the LXX and NT, at Paed., III, 94, 1: κατεάγασιν αἱ πλάκες τῶν σκληροκαρδίων, ἵν' αἱ πίστεις τῶν νηπίων ἐν μαλθακαῖς τυπωθῶσιν διανοίαις (cf. 2 C. 3:3; Barn., 4, 8).

---

[19] Cf. the comm., esp. Bü. J., *ad loc.* A. Schlatter, "Herz u. Gehirn im ersten Jhdt.," *Studien zur systematischen Theologie, T. v. Haering ... dargebracht* (1918), 93, n. 20, correctly calls the expression δέδωκεν ἡμῖν διάνοιαν ἵνα ... a "slightly Hellenised form" of the Semitic expression in Rev. 17:17: ἔδωκεν εἰς τὰς καρδίας αὐτῶν with inf.

[20] διάνοια is not the Holy Spirit (so H. J. Holtzmann, *Lehrbuch d. nt.lichen Theologie*^{2} [1911], II, 518, and long before Cl. Al. Adumbrationes, *ad loc.* [III, 214, 31 ff., O. Stählin]: "*filius dei ... dedit nobis intellectum,*" *secundum fidem advenientem in nos, qui etiam spiritus sanctus appellatur,* and materially Luther, *Vorlesung über 1 J.* = *Werke, Weimarer Ausgabe,* 20, 800, 4 ff. [lines 23 f. expressly: *sensum, mentem, id est, Spiritum Sanctum*]). Nor can the διάνοια of 1 Jn. 5:20 be equated with the νοῦς Χριστοῦ of 1 C. 2:16 (→ 959), as against Cr.-Kö., 768, and earlier Didym., *ad loc.* (F. Zoepfl, Didymi Alexandrini in epistolas canonicas brevis enarratio = *Nt.liche Abhandlungen,* 4, 1 [1914], 81, 22 ff.).

† διανόημα.

This is the result of διανοεῖσθαι (→ 963), of the activity of thought, i.e., "thought," "opinion," "resolve," "plan," synon. διάνοια 4. and 5. (→ 964), e.g., Xenoph. Hist. Graec., 7, 5, 19; Isoc., 3, 9 : καὶ τῶν ἔργων καὶ τῶν διανοημάτων ἁπάντων ἡγεμόνα λόγον ὄντα, Plat. Symp., 210d : To know the beauty of academic disciplines the learner should bring forth πολλοὺς καὶ καλοὺς λόγους καὶ μεγαλοπρεπεῖς ... καὶ διανοήματα ἐν φιλοσοφίᾳ ἀφθόνῳ. It is often used in an adverse sense, Plut. Aud., 6 (II, 40c): διανοήματος εὐτέλεια καὶ ῥήματος κενότης, Epict. Diss., 2, 8, 13 : "Thou bearest God in thee and dost not observe how thou defilest him ἀκαθάρτοις μὲν διανοήμασι, ῥυπαραῖς δὲ πράξεσι, P. Lond., V, 1724, 13 and 15 : The partner in an agreement should act ἄνευ ... φαύλου διανοήματος ("mental reservations"). In medical speech διανοήματα are the "confused thoughts and imaginings" of fever, e.g., Hippocr. Epid., 1, 23 (I, 199, 16 f., Kühlewein); Gal. Comm., 3 in Hippocr. Epid., I (XVII, 1, 213, C. G. Kühn). In the LXX διανόημα is neutral at Prv. 14:14; 15:24 (HT ?). As a rendering of מַחֲשָׁבָה (Is. 55:9) and שֵׂכֶל (Da. 8:25) [1] or as a free paraphrase of גִּלּוּלִים [2] (Ez. 14:3 f.: idols as "constructs of human thought") the word means "arbitrary, foolish or evil thoughts" (Is. 55:9 : the thoughts of men in contrast to the διάνοια of God). [3] So also Sir. 23:2 : διανόημα (collective sing.) human thoughts in their moral ambivalence ; elsewhere in Sir. neutral "thought," "resolve" (e.g., 22:16, 18) or even *sensu bono*, "clever thought," "insight" (25:5; 32[35]:18; 42:20 [4] etc.). διανόημα does not occur in the other apocr. and pseudepigr., or in Philo or Joseph.

The only NT occurrence is at Lk. 11:17 in an unfavourable sense. τὰ διανοήματα are the hostile reservations of the Jews with regard to Jesus and His miraculous power over demons (= ἐνθυμήσεις, Mt. 12:25, → III, 172). [5]

In the early Chr. writings of the 2nd cent. διανόημα is rare. Apart from Just. Dial., 14, 5 (quoting Is. 55:9) it occurs only in Cl. Al.: εὐσυνειδησία keeps the soul pure διανοήμασι σεμνοῖς καὶ λόγοις ἁγνοῖς καὶ τοῖς δικαίοις ἔργοις (Strom., VI, 113, 2, cf. IV, 142, 4); to press on to Christian *gnosis* one must put off πρότερα διανοήματα (VI, 150, 4).

† ἔννοια.

1. Use outside the New Testament.

"What takes place in the → νοῦς," [1] "deliberation," "consideration" as an act, Plat. Leg., II, 657a : τοῦτο ... τὸ περὶ μουσικὴν ἀληθές τε καὶ ἄξιον ἐννοίας, Ps.-Plat.

διανόημα. Liddell-Scott, Preisigke Wört., Cr.-Kö., Pr.-Bauer, *s.v.* H. J. Cadbury, "The Style and Literary Method of Luke," *Harvard Theol. Studies*, 6 (1920), 14.

[1] Heb. וְעַל־קְדֹשִׁים שִׂכְלוֹ to be presupposed as the original of καὶ ἐπὶ τοὺς ἁγίους τὸ διανόημα αὐτοῦ.

[2] → Art. διάνοια, 965, n. 8.

[3] Cf. also the LXX rendering of Gn. 6:5 : וְכָל־יֵצֶר מַחְשְׁבֹת לִבּוֹ רַק רַע כָּל־הַיּוֹם, by καὶ πᾶς τις διανοεῖται ἐν τῇ καρδίᾳ αὐτοῦ ἐπιμελῶς ἐπὶ τὰ πονηρὰ πάσας τὰς ἡμέρας.

[4] Heb. in the last two passages שכל. Cf. R. Smend, *Die Weisheit d. Jesus Sirach erklärt* (1906), on 24:29.

[5] The attempt of W. K. Hobart, *The Medical Language of St. Luke* (1882), 72 f. to explain Lk.'s use of διανόημα along medical lines is refuted both by general Gk. usage (→ Cadbury) and also by the context of Lk. 11:17, where there can be no question of the illusions of sickness.

ἔννοια. Pass., Liddell-Scott, Preisigke Wört., Moult.-Mill., Cr.-Kö., Pr.-Bauer, *s.v.*; J. H. H. Schmidt, *Synonymik d. gr. Sprache*, 3 (1879), 642; Comm. on Hb. 4:12 and 1 Pt. 4:1.

[1] The corresponding verb ἐννοέω ("to bear in mind," "to ponder," "to consider"), which is very common in class. and Hell. Gk. (cf. the lexicons, *s.v.*) and which is also found in the LXX, does not occur in the NT. Its first appearance in Chr. lit. is in Dg., 8, 9 in the pregnant expression : ἐννοήσας δὲ μεγάλην καὶ ἄφραστον ἔννοιαν.

Def., 414a: ἔννοια συντονία διανοίας, Cl. Al. Strom., VI, 136, 1: τὰς πράξεις ... τὰς κατ' ἔννοιάν τε καὶ διάνοιαν, cf. 137, 1; then "what arises in the νοῦς," "thought," "insight," "perception," Xenoph. Cyrop., 1, 1, 1: ἔννοιά ποθ' ἡμῖν ἐγένετο, Polyb., 10, 27, 8: παρὰ τὴν κοινὴν ἔννοιαν, Diod. S., 14, 56, 3: οὐ τὰς αὐτὰς ἀλλήλοις ἐννοίας εἶχον περὶ τοῦ πολέμου, P. Reinach, 7, 15: τῶι μηδεμίαν ἔννοιαν (suspicion) [κ]ακίας ἔχειν, "purpose," Hesych.: ἔννοια· βουλή, "disposition," Eur. Hel., 1026; Isoc., 5, 150: ἑκάστοις τοιαύτην ἔννοιαν ἐμποιοῦσιν, Diod. S., 2, 30, 4: ἑρμηνεύοντες τοῖς ἀνθρώποις τὴν τῶν θεῶν ἔννοιαν, Just. Apol., 64, 5: Athena the πρώτη ἔννοια of Zeus, Act. Joh., 54 etc.

In the vocabulary of philosophy ἔννοια means "idea," "concept," as κριτήριον ζητήσεως, Democr., II, 110, 30, Diels[5], e.g., Plat. Tim., 47a: χρόνου ... ἔννοιαν, Phileb., 59d: ἐν ταῖς περὶ τὸ ὂν ὄντως ἐννοίαις, Aristot. Eth. Nic., X, 10, p. 1179b, 15: τοῦ δὲ καλοῦ ... οὐδ' ἔννοιαν ἔχουσιν, cf. IX, 11, p. 1171a, 32: ἡ ἔννοια τοῦ συναλγεῖν (sc. τοὺς φίλους) ἐλάττω τὴν λύπην ποιεῖ, also p. 1171b, 14 etc.; opp. αἴσθησις, Plat. Phaed., 73c; Aristot. Mot. An., 7, p. 701b, 17; Diog. L., III, 79 (of Plato): ἔννοιάν τε καλοῦ πρῶτος ἀπεφήνατο ..., Plut. Plac. Phil., I, 6 (II, 880a): ἔννοιαν θεοῦ, cf. Porphyr. Ad. Marc., 11: καθαίρεται ... ἄνθρωπος ἐννοίᾳ θεοῦ,[2] Cl. Al. Strom., II, 106, 3: ἔννοια of ἡδονή etc. The term took on and maintained a fixed meaning in Stoicism.[3] Acc. to Stoic teaching all philosophical thought rests on ἔννοιαι, empirical concepts. There is no true knowledge of things without conceptual thought: διὰ γὰρ τῶν ἐννοιῶν τὰ πράγματα λαμβάνεται, Diog. L., VII, 42; cf. Cic. Academici, II, 22; Aug. Civ. D., VIII, 7: *notiones, quas appellant* ἐννοίας. Acc. to a work of Chrysipp. which has not come down to us, and which bore the title περὶ τῶν ἐννοιῶν (cf. II, 9, 25, v. Arnim), concepts arise out of the understanding by way of experience, or they are formed on the ground of deliberate observation: τῶν δὲ ἐννοιῶν αἱ μὲν φυσικῶς γίνονται κατὰ τοὺς εἰρημένους τρόπους (namely, through experience) καὶ ἀνεπιτεχνήτως, αἱ δὲ ἤδη δι' ἡμετέρας διδασκαλίας καὶ ἐπιμελείας· αὗται μὲν οὖν ἔννοιαι καλοῦνται μόνον, ἐκεῖναι δὲ καὶ προλήψεις (II, 28, 19 ff., v. Arnim;[4] cf. Cic. Fin., III, 33; Epict. Diss., II, 17, 7 etc.). These προλήψεις, or, as the Stoics prefer to call them, κοιναὶ ἔννοιαι (*v.* Cic. Tusc., IV, 53): *notiones communes*; Sext. Emp. Math., XI, 22) are not the insights which come to individuals but the common intellectual legacy of all men. They are not innate, but they are originally reached by all and impressed on the consciousness, II, 28, 14 ff., v. Arnim. They thus guarantee their own authenticity: (τὰς κοινὰς ἐννοίας) ... κριτήρια τῆς ἀληθείας φησὶν (sc. Chrysipp.) ἡμᾶς παρὰ τῆς φύσεως λαβεῖν, II, 154, 29 f., v. Arnim. These elementary concepts common to all men are esp. the metaphysical and ethical concepts of God, providence, immortality, good and evil, etc., II, 299 ff., III, 51, 41 f., v. Arnim; Cic. Tusc., I, 30, 36; III, 2; Fin., V, 43 and 59; Epict. Diss., II, 11, 3; Just. Dial., 93, 1 etc.; cf. gen. Diog. L., VII, 54: ἔστι δ' ἡ πρόληψις ἔννοια φυσικὴ τῶν καθόλου.

In the LXX ἔννοια is a favourite word in Prv., where it occurs 12 times, always in the sense of "consideration," "insight," "perception," "cleverness." It is used for מְזִמָּה (1:4; 3:21; cf. 8:12), בִּינָה (4:1; 23:4),[5] תְּבוּנָה (2:11), שֶׂכֶל (16:22), or דַּעַת (18:15). The addition of ἀγαθή or ὁσία stresses the fact that it has a good sense (5:2; 19:7; 24:7; 2:11). In the plur. it denotes ethical thoughts, 23:19: ἄκουε, υἱέ, καὶ σοφὸς γίνου

[2] This is used in early Chr. lit. for the theological concept of God, e.g., Cl. Al. Strom., VII, 8, 2: At creation an ἔννοια θεοῦ came into man alone of all living creatures, cf. VI, 166, 3.

[3] Cf. L. Stein, "Die Erkenntnistheorie d. Stoa," *Berliner Studien f. klass. Philologie u. Archäologie*, 7, 1 (1888), 228 ff.; A. Bonhöffer, *Epict. u. d. Stoa* (1890), 187 ff.; P. Barth, *Die Stoa*[3,4] (1922), 81 ff.

[4] Cf. 14 f.: εἰς τοῦτο (sc. τὸ ἡγεμονικὸν μέρος τῆς ψυχῆς) μίαν ἑκάστην τῶν ἐννοιῶν ἐναπογράφεται (sc. ὁ ἄνθρωπος).

[5] So also Job 38:36 Σ.

καὶ κατεύθυνε ἐννοίας σῆς καρδίας.[6] For an adverse sense cf. Wis. 2:14: The righteous man ἐγένετο ἡμῖν εἰς ἔλεγχον ἐννοιῶν ἡμῶν.[7] Outside the Wis. lit. the word does not occur in the LXX, and even in Prv. and Sir. there is no echo of philosophical usage.

In other Hell. Jewish writings the word is rare (Jos. Ant., 6, 37: τὰς περὶ τῶν πραγμάτων ἐννοίας, "thoughts about the state of things"); it is more common only in Test. XII and Philo. The dominant meaning in Test. XII is "thought"[8] with a religious and moral nuance: οὐκ ἔστι πλάσμα καὶ πᾶσα ἔννοια ἣν οὐκ ἔγνω κύριος (Test. N. 2:5; B. 2:8 A). The righteous keep their thoughts pure (R. 4:8) and try to avoid sins of thought (G. 5:5: οὐ θέλει τὸ καθόλου οὐδὲ ἕως ἐννοίας ἀδικῆσαι ἄνθρωπον, Jos. 9:2; Zeb. 1:4). Philo can speak of ἔννοια in the everyday Gk. manner, e.g., Deus Imm., 7: ἔν τε λόγοις καὶ ἐννοίαις καὶ ἔργοις,[9] Poster. C., 115: μετεωρισθέντες ὑπὸ κούφης ἐννοίας ("puffed up with a vain mind"), Abr., 143: κατά γε τὴν ἐμὴν ἔννοιαν ("opinion"), cf. also the expressions εἰς ἔννοιαν ἐλθεῖν, "to come to knowledge or awareness" (Vit. Mos., I, 122 and 140; Praem. Poen., 42 etc.) and λαμβάνειν ἐννοίας, "to become or be aware" (Conf. Ling., 120). But usually the term has for Philo a philosophical nuance,[10] denoting the "thoughts" with which reason fructifies the νοῦς (Spec. Leg., II, 30; cf. Rer. Div. Her., 240 f.; Poster. C., 135; Conf. Ling., 127), the "ideas" or "concepts" of many varied subjects both corporal and spiritual (Leg. All., III, 234; Det. Pot. Ins., 68 and 87; Abr., 102 etc.), with a distinction between ἔννοια as ἐναποκειμένη οὖσα νόησις and διανόησις as νοήσεως διέξοδος (Deus Imm., 34); ἔννοια is used in def. (Op. Mund., 36: The ἔννοια of a solid body, its conceptual characteristic, is extension on various sides; Sacr. AC, 91: ὅρκου γὰρ ἔννοιά ἐστι μαρτυρία θεοῦ περὶ πράγματος ἀμφισβητουμένου [contested], Op. Mund., 59). Like the Stoa Philo refers constantly to the ἔννοια of God (Det. Pot. Ins., 86: πῶς ἔννοιαν ἔλαβεν ἄνθρωπος θεοῦ τοῦ ἀειδοῦς, cf. 91; Decal., 60; Leg. All., I, 37, III, 81 and 215; Spec. Leg., I, 34: ἔννοιαν ... τοῦ ποιητοῦ καὶ πατρὸς καὶ προσέτι ἡγεμόνος, cf. 65; Sacr. AC, 101 etc.), also to that of good and evil (Fug., 70: ἔμελλεν ἡ ἀνθρωπίνη ψυχὴ μόνη κακῶν καὶ ἀγαθῶν ἐννοίας λαμβάνειν, cf. Decal., 146; Leg. All., I, 35; II, 32; Rer. Div. Her., 299; Spec. Leg., IV, 138; Agric., 126 etc.). But the Stoic category of κοιναὶ ἔννοιαι is mentioned expressly only in Aet. Mund., 103.

Gnosticism, too, is influenced by the philosophical understanding. The Corp. Herm. uses the term in strict abstraction, e.g., I, 1: ἐννοίας μοί ποτε γενομένης περὶ τῶν ὄντων, VIII, 5 (of man): οὐ μόνον πρὸς τὸν δεύτερον θεὸν συμπάθειαν ἔχων, ἀλλὰ καὶ ἔννοιαν τοῦ πρώτου. Hypostatised and given concretion as the Gnostic aeon Ἔννοια appears in the Valentinian system acc. to Iren. Haer., I, 1, 1:[11] Ἔννοια,

---

[6] A free transl. of the Heb. וַאֲשֶׁר בַּדֶּרֶךְ לִבֶּךָ.

[7] Also for the Heb. מְזִמּוֹת ψ 9:25 ʼΑΣ (Ps. 10:4); ψ 20:11 Σ; Job 21:27 Σ, also as a free transl. of עֲלִילוֹת, ψ 140:4 Σ; Ez. 20:44 Σ. Cf. also Qoh. 7:26 (25) Σ: ἔννοιαν θορυβώδη for the Mas. הוֹלֵלוֹת; Prv. 16:22 Σ, where ἔννοια is hardly a rendering of מוּסָר but the transl. has reconstructed the half verse; Sus. 28 Θ: πλήρεις τῆς ἀνόμου ἐννοίας, Prv. 24:9 ʼΑΘ: ἔννοια ἀφροσύνης ἁμαρτία (for זִמָּה "plan"). ʼΑ takes the Heb. in the same sense at ψ 25:10 but at Prv. 21:27 misunderstands זִמָּה ("misdeed"), which comes from a different root.

[8] Even in the one exception in Test. R. 4:11: κατισχύσει ἡ πορνεία τὴν ἔννοιαν ὑμῶν ("mind," "disposition") it may be asked whether we should not take into account the τὰς ἐννοίας ("thoughts") of 4:8.

[9] Cf. similar expressions in Cl. Al., e.g., Strom., VI, 97, 2; VII, 54, 1; 88, 1.

[10] Cf. on this H. Schmidt, *D. Anthropologie Philons v. Alex.* (Diss. phil. Leipzig, 1933), 83, 159 (n. 301-309).

[11] Only passing ref. can be made to the modification of this account of Iren. in Epiph. Haer., 31, 5, 2 ff., to the special features in the Ἔννοια speculation of Theodotus acc. to Cl. Al. Exc. Theod., 22, 7; 41, 4 (also 32, 2; 33, 3 ?), to the related questions, and to Helena = Ἔννοια in the supposed system of Simon Magus (Iren. Haer., I, 23, 2).

also called Χάρις καὶ Σιγή, is united in syzygy with the original and eternal principle of all being, the Προπάτωρ or Βυθός, and from this first duality proceed Νοῦς and Ἀλήθεια. Thus at the beginning of this "metaphysical ontology of the spirit" [12] there stands not only the original spirit but also "conception" as the *locus* of its operation. [13] A degenerate form of this Ἔννοια speculation is to be found in the teaching of the Barbelo-Gnostics that the feminine aeon and maiden spirit Barbelo came forth as the first Ἔννοια from the original spirit, the unnamable father (Iren. Haer., I, 29, 1, cf. Apocryphon of John). [14] The obscure words in the Gnostic prayer of initiation in Act. Thom., 27: ἐλθὲ ὁ πρεσβύτερος τῶν πέντε μελῶν, νοὸς ἐννοίας φρονήσεως ἐνθυμήσεως λογισμοῦ, also refer to an aeon Ἔννοια, the personification of the concept ἔννοια. [15]

2. Use in the New Testament.

The term is infrequent in the NT and the use popular. There is no trace either of the technical philosophical sense or of Gnostic interpretations.

In Hb. 4:12 (ὁ λόγος τοῦ θεοῦ ... κριτικὸς ἐνθυμήσεων [16] καὶ ἐννοιῶν καρδίας) the ἔννοιαι which the Word of God unerringly discerns are the morally questionable thoughts [17] in the hidden innermost part of man (cf. Wis. 2:14, → 970; Test. N. 2:5, → 970; 1 Cl., 21, 3 and 9; Pol., 4, 3).

In 1 Pt. 4:1 the general truth expressed in Christ's passion, ὅτι ὁ παθὼν σαρκὶ πέπαυται ἁμαρτίας [18] (cf. R. 6:7), is an ἔννοια with which Christians must arm themselves, namely, a "thought" which, appropriated by them, will be insight and knowledge — the ethically binding recognition that those who have suffered death like Christ (cf. R. 6:2 ff.) can no longer have any truck with sin.

† εὐνοέω, † εὔνοια.

εὐνοέω, usually with the dat. of person, means "to be well-disposed," "friendly," "attached," "to meet half-way," in general dealings between men, Xenoph. Cyrop., 8, 2, 1: ἡγούμενος, ὥσπερ οὐ ῥᾴδιόν ἐστι φιλεῖν τοὺς μισεῖν δοκοῦντας οὐδ' εὐνοεῖν τοῖς κακόνοις, οὕτω καὶ τοὺς γνωσθέντας ὡς φιλοῦσι καὶ εὐνοοῦσιν, οὐκ ἂν δύνασθαι μισεῖσθαι ὑπὸ τῶν φιλεῖσθαι ἡγουμένων, Ditt. Syll.³ 1268, 15: φίλοις εὐνόει, P. Ryl., II, 153, 10 f. (of a relative): εὐνοήσας ἐμα[υτῷ κ]αὶ τῷ πατρί μου ... ἐν πολλοῖς, cf. P. Strassb., II, 122, 7: οὐκ εὐνοηκὼς αὐτῇ κατὰ τὸν

---

[12] R. Seeberg, *Lehrbuch d. Dogmengeschichte,* I³ (1922), 293.

[13] On Valentinian thinking concerning Ἔννοια cf. H. Jonas, "Gnosis u. spätantiker Geist," I FRL, NF, 33 (1934), 362 ff.

[14] Cf. the bibl. in C. Schmidt, Art. "Barbelo-Gnostiker," RGG², I, 760; also J. Pascher, Η ΒΑΣΙΛΙΚΗ ΟΔΟΣ, *Studien z. Geschichte u. Kultur d. Altertums,* 17, 3/4 (1931), 111 f.; H. Jonas, *op. cit.,* 361 f.

[15] Cf. on this the bibl. in Hennecke, 256 f.; also E. Hennecke, *Handbuch z. d. nt.lichen Apokryphen* (1904), 574; W. Bousset, "Hauptprobleme d. Gnosis," FRL, 10 (1907), 234 ff., who points to similar series of aeons in Hipp. Ref., VI, 12 ff.; Acta Archelai, 10 etc. and connects with them the 5 supreme hypostases of the Mandaean system.

[16] → III, 172. For ἐνθυμήσεις in synon. parallelism with ἔννοιαι cf. also Job 21:27 Σ; 1 Cl., 21, 9.

[17] Cf. the excellent distinction between "expressions of his thinking" and "expressions of his will" in Hofmann, *ad loc.*; cf. also T. Haering, *Der Brief an d. Hebräer* (1925), 25.

[18] On the constr. (ὅτι explicative) and the material understanding of this much wrested verse cf. Calvin, Bengel, Hofmann, H. v. Soden (*Hand-Kommentar z. NT,* III, 2³ [1899]), Wbg. Pt., W. Zoellner (*Der 1 Pt. für die Gemeinde ausgelegt* [1935]), *ad loc.*

εὐνοέω, εὔνοια. Pass., Liddell-Scott, Moult.-Mill., Preisigke Wört., Cr.-Kö., Pr.-Bauer, *s.v.*; Comm. on Mt. 5:25; Eph. 6:7 and 1 C. 7:3.

βίον, Cl. Al. Paed., I, 66, 1: The friend chides εὐνοῶν (with a benevolent purpose); esp. in law, in private relations like marriage (cf. the marriage contract, P. Greci e Latini, I, 64, 4 ff., in which the wife adds to the solemn declaration that she will live as γνησ[ία] γαμετή with the husband the statement: καὶ εὐνοεῖν [σο]ι, or the will, P. Oxy., III, 494, 9 which says of the wife of the testator: εὐνοούσῃ μοι καὶ πᾶσαν πίστιν μοι ἐκδεικνυμένῃ), or that of a steward to his master (Xenoph. Oec., 12, 5: τὸ εὐνοεῖν ἐμοὶ καὶ τοῖς ἐμοῖς) etc., also in public legal relations between persons or nations (e.g., Demosth. Or., 23, 181: μετὰ πάσης δ' ἀληθείας ἁπλῶς εὐνοεῖν ἡμῖν, Polyb., 3, 11, 7: ὀμνύναι μηδέποτε Ῥωμαίοις εὐνοήσειν, Ditt. Syll.³, 524, 17 [oath with a declaration of political fidelity]: εὐνοήσω Σταλίταις, Plut. Sull., 10, 6 [I, 458a]: ἀραῖς καὶ ὅρκοις καταλαβὼν εὐνοήσειν τοῖς ἑαυτοῦ πράγμασιν, Herodian. Hist., 8, 8, 5: ᾔδει γὰρ τοὺς Γερμανοὺς τῷ Μαξίμῳ εὐνοοῦντας, Gn. 35:15 'E [1]; Est. 8:12; Da. 2:43; [2] 3 Macc. 7:11; Jos. Bell., 4, 214: εὐνοήσειν τῷ δήμῳ, 1, 93: τὸ εὐνοοῦν Ἰουδαϊκόν [the portion of the Jews loyal to Alexander Jannaeus]; oaths of fidelity such as that in Ditt. Syll.³, 797, 30 f.: ὀμνύομεν Δία Σωτῆρα καὶ θεὸν Καίσαρα Σεβαστὸν ... εὐνοήσειν Γαίωι Καίσαρι Σεβαστῶι, cf. Ditt. Or., 532, 10 ff. etc.).

εὔνοια, which is common in the *koine,* means "goodwill," "affection," opp. "servility," Democr. Fr., 268 (II, 200, 14 f., Diels⁵): φόβος κολακείην μὲν ἐργάζεται, εὔνοιαν δὲ οὐκ ἔχει, differentiated from φιλία in Aristot. Eth. Nic., IX, 5, p. 1166b, 30 ff.: ἡ δὲ εὔνοια φιλίᾳ μὲν ἔοικεν, οὐ μὴν ἐστί γε φιλία· γίνεται γὰρ εὔνοια καὶ πρὸς ἀγνῶτας καὶ λανθάνουσα, φιλία δὲ οὔ, cf. VIII, 2, p. 1155b, 31 ff.; Eth. Eud., IV, 7, p. 1241a, 2 ff.; Plut. Quaest. Conv., IV Prooem (II, 660a b). Plat. Gorg., 487a lists εὔνοια, with ἐπιστήμη and παρρησία, among the qualities of the wise. Stoic def. of εὔνοια: βούλησις ἀγαθῶν (ἑτέρῳ) αὐτοῦ ἕνεκεν ἐκείνου (III, 105, 31, cf. 22, v. Arnim; cf. Philo Plant., 106; Cl. Al. Paed., I, 97, 3, Strom., II, 28, 3). Proverbially, ἄκαιρος εὔνοι' οὐδὲν ἔχθρας διαφέρει (Zenobius, 1, 50 [3]), cf. Ign. R., 4, 1. There is εὔνοια downward as well as upward, cf. Thom. Mag. (p. 162, 3 f., F. Ritschl): εὔνοια καὶ ἀπὸ τοῦ ἐλάττονος πρὸς μείζονα καὶ ἀπὸ τοῦ μείζονος πρὸς ἐλάττονα, cf. the goodwill of a ruler to his subjects or a superior to those under him, Ps.-Democr. Fr., 302 (II, 222, 19 f., Diels⁵): τὸν ἄρχοντα δεῖ ἔχειν ... πρὸς ... τοὺς ὑποτεταγμένους εὔνοιαν, Ditt. Syll.³, 390, 18 f.: King Ptolemy τὴν αὐτὴν εὔνοιαν καὶ ἐπιμέλειαν [π]αρεχόμενος διατελεῖ εἴς τε τοὺς Νησιώτας κα[ὶ] τοὺς ἄλλους Ἕλληνας (cf. 762, 27 f. etc. as an expression in the court style of diplomacy); it is also used, though more rarely, of the goodwill of the gods, Ditt. Syll.³, 560, 37: μετὰ τᾶς τῶν θε[ῶν εὐ]νοίας, Joseph.; [4] Preis. Zaub., III, 594 f. (magic prayer): πρ[ὸ]ς πάντας καὶ πρὸς πάντα πατρικὴν [εὔ]νοιαν κ[α]ὶ στοργὴν καὶ φιλίαν ... ἐνεδείξω, Cl. Al. Paed., I, 97, 3: ἀξιόπιστος ὁ θεῖος παιδαγωγὸς τρισὶ τοῖς καλλίστοις κεκοσμημένος, ἐπιστήμῃ, εὐνοίᾳ, παρρησίᾳ. [5] In the *koine,* esp. Jewish and Christian, it also means "affection," "love," between relatives, 4 Macc. 2:10; 13:25; Jos. Ant., 2, 161; Philo Spec. Leg., 1, 114, often described as φυσικὴ or ἐκ φύσεως εὔνοια, εὔνοια συγγενική etc., cf. Abr., 168; Virt., 192, 53; cf. also Cl. Al. Strom., I, 151, 3; Paed., I, 49, 2 etc.; love between husband and wide, cf. Philo Abr., 249; Jos. Ant., 1, 318, *v.* also 17, 49 and 58; P. Lond., V, 1711, 34 ff., sometimes for sexual union, Jos. Ant., 16, 201; Cl. Al. Paed., II, 97, 3. [6] Esp. "devotion," "fidelity," "goodwill," "loyalty" as a civic

---

[1] For אות "to accede to." Apart from this verse and Da. 2:43 (→ n. 2) there is no Heb. original for εὐνοέω and εὔνοια [G. Bertram].

[2] LXX: οὐκ ἔσονται δὲ ὁμονοοῦντες οὔτε εὐνοοῦντες ἀλλήλοις deviates more strongly from the Aram. original than Θ: οὐκ ἔσονται προσκολλώμενοι οὗτος μετὰ τούτου.

[3] Corpus Paroemiographorum Graecorum, ed. E. L. Leutsch-G. F. Schneidewin, I (1839), 20, 1.

[4] Schl. Theol. d. Judt., 27, cf. A. Schlatter, "Wie sprach Josephus von Gott?" BFTh, 14, 1 (1910), 62. No examples have been found thus far.

[5] Cl. Al. applies to God the qualities of the wise in Plat. Gorg., 487a (→ *supra*).

[6] The instances in Wettstein on 1 C. 7:3 are only partially relevant.

virtue, e.g., Ditt. Syll.³, 721, 13: τὰν εὔνοιαν ἂν ἔχει πορτὶ τὰν πόλιν, P. Herm., 53, 16 f.; Philo Virt., 75; cf. also Ditt. Syll.³, Index, *s.v.*, also in relation to fellow-citizens, compatriots or neighbours (2 Macc. 12:30; 14:37; 15:30), or of subject to ruler, subordinate to superior, provincial to the whole kingdom, Est. 3:13c; cf. 2:23; 6:4; 1 Macc. 11:33, 53 (plur. "proofs of allegiance"); 2 Macc. 9:21, 26; 3 Macc. 3:3; 6:26; 7:7; Ep. Ar., 270: τοῖς διὰ τὴν εὔνοιαν ... συνοῦσί σοι (those who serve thee out of affection), cf. 205, 230, 264 f.; Philo Spec. Leg., IV, 166; P. Oxy., IV, 705, 31 f.; of slave to master (Xenoph. Oec., 12, 5-7; P. Oxy., III, 494, 6; cf. Luc. Bis. Accusatus, 16).[7] "Willingness," "devotion," as seen in sacral gifts and endowments, Ditt. Syll.³, 330, 8: [μετὰ] πολλῆς εὐνοίας or a Jewish appendix:[8] διὰ ... τὴν π[ρ]ὸς τὴν συναγωγὴν εὔνοιάν τε καὶ σπουδήν.

The direction given to the debtor in the eschatological parable in Mt. 5:25 f.:[9] ἴσθι εὐνοῶν τῷ ἀντιδίκῳ σου ταχὺ ἕως ὅτου εἶ μετ' αὐτοῦ ἐν τῇ ὁδῷ (v. 25), "agree with thine adversary quickly, while thou art in the way with him" (i.e., come to quick agreement by a generous settlement), sets before the disciples of Jesus the urgency of removing the wrongs which men do one another. The reference is to evil which will be requited on the judgment day. Hence the man who does the wrong must repent quickly before it is too late, and show goodwill to the other (cf. v. 24: διαλλάγηθι τῷ ἀδελφῷ σου).

The demand addressed to slaves in the household table of Eph.: μετ' εὐνοίας δουλεύοντες, "render your service with goodwill" (6:7), corresponds to the ancient view that εὔνοια is fit and proper for the slave, → 972. But the service of the Christian slave is finally τῷ κυρίῳ καὶ οὐκ ἀνθρώποις. He discharges it as δοῦλος Χριστοῦ (cf. v. 6). His readiness has a religious basis. The slave virtue of εὔνοια is integrated into the Christian ethos controlled by the personal relation of the Christian to his κύριος, Christ.[10]

Mart. Pol., 17, 3: ἕνεκα εὐνοίας ἀνυπερβλήτου (sc. of martyrs) τῆς εἰς τὸν ἴδιον βασιλέα καὶ διδάσκαλον, transfers the loyalty or self-sacrifice of subjects directly to the relation of Christians to Christ. The view of Cl. Al. Strom., VII, 42, 3 that the piety of the Gnostic is an ἀντίστροφος (directed back, i.e., to God) εὔνοια τοῦ φίλου τοῦ θεοῦ rests on certainty of the experienced εὔνοια of God, e.g., in the revelation of salvation in Christ (Prot., X, 110, 1).

† κατανοέω.

κατανοέω, trans.[1] is closely related to the simple νοέω, → 948, whose lit. meaning is intensified, "to direct one's whole mind to an object," also from a higher standpoint to immerse oneself in it and hence to apprehend it in its whole compass.[2]

---

[7] For additional material cf. Wettstein on Eph. 6:7.
[8] Cf. W. M. Ramsay, *The Cities and Bishoprics of Phrygia*, II (1897), 650.
[9] Schl. Mt., 174 f.; Jülicher GlJ, II, 240 ff.
[10] The only other NT instance is at 1 C. 7:3 𝔎: τῇ γυναικὶ ὁ ἀνὴρ τὴν ὀφειλομένην εὔνοιαν ἀποδιδότω, ὁμοίως δὲ καὶ ἡ γυνὴ τῷ ἀνδρί, as a softened form of the undoubtedly original τὴν → ὀφειλήν of 𝔖. On this change (Chrys. Hom. in C., *ad loc.* [MPG, 61, 152]: τὴν ὀφειλομένην τιμήν) cf. the material → 972 and Cramer Cat., V, 122 on 1 C. 7:3; Oecumenius, *ad loc.* (MPG, 118, 724): ἔδειξε χρέος οὖσαν τὴν εὔνοιαν, ἤγουν τὴν πίστιν καὶ τὴν ἀγάπην, καὶ οὐ δωρεὰν παρεχομένην ... καὶ φαίνεται εὔνοια ἡ φιλία, εὐνούστατος ὁ πιστὸς φίλος, Euthymius Zigabenus (I, 246, N. Calogeras), *ad loc.*: εὐνοοῦντες δὲ ἀλλήλοις καὶ ὁμογνωμονοῦντες οὐ περὶ τὴν συνουσίαν διαστασιάσουσιν.

κατανοέω. Pass., Liddell-Scott, Moult.-Mill., Preisigke Wört., Cr.-Kö., Pr.-Bauer, *s.v.*; J. H. H. Schmidt, *Synonymik d. gr. Sprache*, 3 (1879), 645 ff.
[1] Only in Hippocr. do we find an intrans. use, "to be in one's right mind," cf. Epid., I, 26, 3 (I, 205, 4, H. Kühlewein).
[2] Cf. J. H. H. Schmidt, *op. cit.*, 645.

Since there is no clear distinction between apprehending with the senses and with the mind, this can involve 1. sensual perception, as in the case of νοέω, so that κατανοέω means "to perceive," "to note," e.g., Xenoph. Cyrop., 2, 2, 28 : (of Cyrus) κατανοήσας γάρ τινα τῶν λοχαγῶν σύνδειπνον καὶ παρακλίτην πεποιημένον ἄνδρα ὑπέρδασύν τε καὶ ὑπέραισχρον, cf. Hesych., *s.v.* : καταν[ο]οῦντι : καταβλέποντι, Thom. Mag. (p. 60, 9 f., F. Ritschl): ἔστι δὲ θεᾶσθαι καὶ τὸ κατανοεῖν.[3] While the simple form soon lost this sense because of its technical philosophical development, the compound still retains it in the *koine,* esp. Jewish and Christian. The LXX uses it for רָאָה in this sense at Is. 5:12.[4] As an equivalent of הִבִּיט at ψ 93:9 the Gk. verb can even have the meaning "to see," cf. also for רָאָה at Ex. 19:21; also in Is. 59:16 and ψ 9:34, where LXX deviates from the HT, κατανοέω is a synon. of βλέπω (as in Da. 7:21 for Aram. חזה pe, Θ θεωρέω). Cf. also Jdt. 10:14; Philo Vit. Mos., I, 158 (of Moses, cf. Ex. 20:21): τὰ ἀθέατα φύσει θνητῇ κατανοῶν, Jos., 182 : προσιόντας καὶ δεξιουμένους κατενόει, Jos. Ant., 3, 203 : so thin mist, ὥστε τὴν ὄψιν ἰσχῦσαι[5] τι δι᾽ αὐτοῦ κατανοῆσαι, Herm. s., 2, 1.

It can also denote 2. critical observation of an object: "to consider reflectively," "to study," "to examine," Athen., 5, 179a : κατανοῆσαι τὴν οἰκίαν, Hipp. Ref., I, 1, 4 (of Thales): ἀποβλέπων πρὸς τὸν οὐρανὸν καὶ τὰ ἄνω ἐπιμελῶς κατανοεῖν λέγων, Gn. 42:9; Ex. 2:11; Nu. 32:8 f. (for רָאָה);[6] Ex. 33:8; ψ 21:17; 90:8; 141:5 (for הִבִּיט); ψ 36:32 (for צָפָה, "to scout," "to watch"); 3 Βασ. 3:21; Job 30:20 (for הִתְבּוֹנֵן);[7] Hab. 3:2 (no Heb.); Sir. 23:19; Ep. Ar., 103 : κατανοῆσαι τὰ τῶν θυσιῶν (*v.* earlier : πρὸς θεωρίαν), cf. 155; Gk. En. 2:1; Philo Leg. Gaj., 358; Jos. Ant., 5, 5 : The spies ἅπασαν ἐπ᾽ ἀδείας αὐτῶν τὴν πόλιν κατενόησαν, cf. 3, 302; 8, 29 : ἀκριβῶς ... κατανοήσασα τοῦτο (sc. the child) ἐπέγνων, Herm. s., 8, 1, 5 etc.; Just. Dial., 3, 2; Apol., 55, 2; Corp. Herm., I, 13a (I, 120, 9 ff., W. Scott): "κατενόησε (sc. ὁ Ἄνθρωπος) τοῦ ἀδελφοῦ (sc. of Νοῦς) τὰ δημιουργήματα" .... κατανοήσας δὲ τὴν τοῦ δημιουργοῦ κτίσιν ἐν τῷ πυρί, ἠβουλήθη καὶ αὐτός δημιουργεῖν.

3. In literary Gk. κατανοέω, as distinct from αἰσθάνομαι (→ I, 187 f.), means esp. apprehension of a subject by intellectual absorption in it : "to consider," "to ponder," "to come to know," "to grasp," "to understand" (synon. συνίημι), e.g., Hdt., II, 93, 6, cf. 28, 5; Thuc., II, 3, 1 f.: οἱ δὲ Πλαταιῆς ὡς ᾔσθοντο ἔνδον ... ὄντας τοὺς Θηβαίους ... κατενόησαν οὐ πολλοὺς τοὺς Θηβαίους ὄντας, Plat. Soph., 233a : οὐ ... κατανοῶ τὸ νῦν ἐρωτώμενον, P. Par., 63, 190 ff.: ὅταν ... τὸ συμφέρον κατανοῶσι κοινὸν νομιζόμενον, Gn. 3:6 (for הַשְׂכִּיל); Job 23:15a;[8] Is. 57:1 (for הָבִין); ψ 118:15 (for הִבִּיט);[9] Jdt. 8:14 : πῶς ... τὸν λογισμὸν αὐτοῦ κατανοήσετε; Sir. 33:18; 2 Macc. 9:25; Ep. Ar., 3 : τὰ θεῖα κατανοεῖν, Philo Ebr., 137: κατανοῶν ... αὐτῆς (sc. τῆς ἰδέας) τὸ θεοειδέστατον κάλλος, Leg. All., III, 99 : διὰ σκιᾶς τὸν θεὸν καταλαμβάνουσι, διὰ τῶν ἔργων τὸν τεχνίτην κατανοοῦντες (→ 950 on R. 1:20), Jos. Ant., 7, 204 : τὰ ... ἀπόρρητα τῆς διανοίας αὐτοῦ κατανοεῖν, Vit., 72 : κατανοήσας δὲ ἐγὼ τὴν ἐπιχείρησιν αὐτοῦ καὶ τί διανοοῖτο πράσσειν, 1 Cl., 32, 1 etc.; Just. Dial., 87, 4; Tat. Or. Graec., 12, 3; 34, 1; Cl. Al. Prot., IV, 59, 3; cf. Paed.,

---

[3] Synon. ἐπινοέω (not in the NT, but cf. LXX, post-apost. fathers etc.), *v.* the lexicons, also E. C. E. Owen, "ἐπινοέω, ἐπίνοια and Allied Words," JThSt, 35 (1934), 368 ff.

[4] Cf. Hab. 3:7 Ἀλλ.

[5] As against Niese (ἰσγύσαι) [Debrunner].

[6] Cf. Hab. 3:16 Ἀλλ.

[7] Cf. Job 38:18 Ἀ. Here, then, the Mas. and the translation part company, the one referring to a pure process of consciousness, the other to a mixture of sensual apprehension and deliberation.

[8] Hexapla addition acc. to ἈΘ [G. Bertram]. Job 37:14 Ἀ; ψ 118:100 Ἀ Ἐ have κατανοέω for הִתְבּוֹנֵן.

[9] The distinction here is the reverse of that in → n. 7.

I, 44, 1; I, 90, 2; cf. Strom., V, 56, 5; Stob. Ecl., I, 386, 20 ff.: (Hermes) εἶδε τὰ σύμπαντα καὶ ἰδὼν κατενόησε καὶ κατανοήσας ἴσχυσε δηλῶσαί τε καὶ δεῖξαι.

The emphasis in NT usage lies in the visual sphere.[10] As a verb of seeing (→ ὁράω) alongside βλέπω, εἶδον, ἀτενίζω, παρακύπτω, κατανοέω, esp. in Lk., where it is most common, denotes perception by the eyes (Mt. 7:3 = Lk. 6:41, here paradoxically impossible; Ac. 27:39, opp. ἐπιγινώσκω), attentive scrutiny of an object (Jm. 1:23 f.),[11] the observation or consideration of a fact or process, whether natural or miraculous (Lk. 12:24, 27;[12] R. 4:19;[13] Ac. 7:31 f.; 11:6). This sensual perception or contemplation mediates impressions which can be points of contact for the attaining of important religious or ethical insights. Intellectual perception is at issue in Lk. 20:23: κατανοήσας δὲ αὐτῶν τὴν πανουργίαν.[14] In Hb.[15] κατανοέω is one of the verbal concepts which, used imperatively, impress upon the readers the duties involved in being a Christian: 3:1 f. (κατανοήσατε τὸν ἀπόστολον καὶ ἀρχιερέα τῆς ὁμολογίας ἡμῶν Ἰησοῦν, πιστὸν ὄντα ...) the duty of looking to the Mediator of salvation, of concentration upon His exemplary moral conduct; 10:24 (κατανοῶμεν ἀλλήλους εἰς παροξυσμὸν ἀγάπης καὶ καλῶν ἔργων) the duty of brotherly regard for one another with a view to the moral demonstration of Christianity. κατανοέω has the same sense "to take note of" in the free rendering of Lk. 11:42 in Just. Dial., 17, 4: ἀποδεκατοῦτε τὸ ἡδύοσμον καὶ τὸ πήγανον, τὴν δὲ ἀγάπην τοῦ θεοῦ καὶ τὴν κρίσιν οὐ κατανοεῖτε.

† μετανοέω, † μετάνοια.

Contents: A. Greek Usage: I. μετανοέω, II. μετάνοια, III. Historical Significance of the Data. B. Repentance and Conversion in the Old Testament: I. Cultic and Ritual Forms of Penitence: 1. The Occasion and Development of Penitential Observances; 2. External Forms; 3. Liturgies; 4. Days of Penitence; 5. Prophetic Criticism of Cultic and Ritual Penitence. II. The Prophetic Concept of Conversion: 1. The Personal View of Sin; 2. The Personal View of Repentance as Turning to Yahweh: a. Obedience to Yahweh's Will, b. Trust in Yahweh, c. Turning from Everything Ungodly; 3. The Possibility of Conversion and Its Historical Significance: a. Amos, b. Hosea, c. Isaiah, d. Jeremiah, e. Conclusion. III. The Exilic and Post-Exilic Period. C. μετανοέω/μετάνοια in Hellenistic Jewish Literature: I. The LXX: 1. μετανοέω; 2. μετάνοια. II. Other Writings: 1. Apocrypha and Pseudepigrapha; 2. Philo; 3. Josephus. D. Conversion in Rabbinic Literature. E. μετανοέω/μετάνοια in the New Testament: I. The Linguistic Understanding; II. The Concept of Conversion: 1. John the Baptist; 2. Jesus; 3. Primitive Christianity: a. In General, b. Paul, c. John, d. The Impossibility of a Second μετάνοια in Hb. F. μετανοέω/μετάνοια in the Ecclesiastical Writings of the Post-Apostolic and Early Catholic Period.

---

10 Artificial acc. to J. T. Beck, *Umriss d. biblischen Seelenlehre*² (1862), 57 f.

11 Cf. Hck. Jk., Schl. Jk., *ad loc.*

12 Mt. 6:26: ἐμβλέπειν, v. 28: καταμανθάνειν.

13 Cf. Hofmann, Zn. R. and Schl. R., *ad loc.*

14 Mt. 22:18: γνοὺς ... τὴν πονηρίαν αὐτῶν, cf. Xenoph. An., 7, 5, 11: ὁ δὲ γνοὺς ... τὴν πανουργίαν.

15 Cf. Rgg. Hb.²,³ and Michel Hb. on 3:1 and 10:24.

μετανοέω κτλ. On A.: Pass., Liddell-Scott, Moult.-Mill., Preisigke Wört., Cr.-Kö., Pr.-Bauer, *s.v.*; Trench, 167 ff.; E. F. Thompson, "Μετανοέω and Μεταμέλει in Gk. Literature until 100 A.D.," *Historical and Linguistic Studies in Literature Related to the NT*, 2nd. Ser., Vol. I (Chicago, 1909), 358-364; E. Norden, *Agnostos Theos* (1913), 134 ff.; Wnd. 2 K., 233; A. H. Dirksen, *The New Testament Concept of Metanoia*, Diss. Theol. Washington, The Catholic Univ. of America (1932), 165-197; A. D. Nock, *Conversion*

A. Greek Usage.

I. μετανοέω.

In compounds the preposition μετά can have many different meanings ("after," "with," "around" etc.) which can often be present at the same time, thus giving rise to a certain ambiguity.[1] Thus μετανοέω, which is comparatively rare in both class. and Hell. Gk., can have various senses.

1. It can first mean "to note after, later," often with the implication "too late," Epicharmus Fr., 41 (I, 204, Diels[5]): οὐ μετανοεῖν ἀλλὰ προνοεῖν χρὴ τὸν ἄνδρα τὸν σοφόν, Democr. Fr., 66 (II, 158, Diels[5]): προβουλεύεσθαι κρεῖσσον πρὸ τῶν πράξεων ἢ μετανοεῖν, "to agree subsequently," BGU, 747, I, 10 ff.: καὶ οἰό[μ]ενος με[τ]ανοή[σι]ν ἡμεῖν ἐπῖχό[ν] σοι τῷ κυρίῳ δηλῶσαι.

2. It can then mean "to change one's mind (νοῦς)," which, in view of the many senses of νοῦς → 952, might mean "to adopt another view," "to change one's feelings," Plut. Camillus, 12 (I, 135b): The exile prays the gods ταχὺ Ῥωμαίους μετανοῆσαι

(1933), 180, 296; Kl. Mk.[3], 6; E. K. Dietrich, *Die Umkehr* (*Bekehrung u. Busse*) *im AT u. im Judt.* (1936), 226 ff. On B.: W. Eichrodt, *Theol. d. AT,* III (1939), 171-176; J. Köberle, *Sünde u. Gnade im religiösen Leben des Volkes Israel* (1905), *passim*; H. Windisch, *Taufe u. Sünde im ältesten Christentum* (1908), 8-18; A. Eberharter, "Sünde u. Busse im AT," *Bibl. Zeitfragen,* 11 (1924); K. Paraskeuaides, Τὸ κήρυγμα περὶ μετανοίας τοῦ Προφήτου Ἱερεμίου, in Θεολογία, 6 (1928), 310 ff.; A. H. Dirksen, 109-128, 148-151; E. K. Dietrich, 8-217; O. Dilschneider, *Ev. Offenbarung* (1939), 75 ff. On C.: J. Köberle, 597-613; H. Windisch, 18-34, 54-60; E. F. Thompson, 367-370; Bousset-Gressm., 389 f.; A. H. Dirksen, 128 ff., 148-164; Schl. Theol. d. Judt., 146-148; Volz Esch., 103 f. etc.; E. K. Dietrich, 218-313. On D.: Weber, 316 ff. etc. (Index, *s.v.* "Busse"); Jew. Enc., 10, 376 ff.; C. G. Montefiore, "Rabbinic Conceptions of Repentance," *The Jewish Quarterly Review,* 16 (1904), 209 ff. (pp. 211 ff. reprinted with additions in C. G. Montefiore, *Rabbinic Lit. and Gospel Teachings* [1930], 390 ff.); Str.-B., I, 162-172, Index, *s.v.* "Busse"; Moore, I, 323-353, 507-534 etc.; A. Büchler, *Studies in Sin and Atonement in the Rabb. Lit. of the First Century* (1928), 270 ff.; A. H. Dirksen, 135-147; E. K. Dietrich, 314-457; E. Sjöberg, "Gott u. d. Sünder im palästinischen Judt.," BWANT, IV, 27 (1938), 125 ff. etc. On E.: Comm. on the relevant verses; NT Theol.; P. Müllensiefen, "Über den Begriff METANOIA im NT," I, *Programm Gymnasium Arnstadt* (1888); Cr.-Kö., *s.v.*; W. Wrede, *Miscellen,* 1 "μετάνοια — Sinnesänderung?" ZNW, 1 (1900), 66 ff.; H. Windisch, 74-97, 294 ff. etc.; E. F. Thompson, 372 ff.; Clemen, 213; E. De Witt Burton, *NT Word Studies,* ed. H. R. Willoughby (1927), 3 f.; A. Donini, "Escatologia e Penitenza nel Cristianesimo primitivo," *Ricerche Religiose,* 3 (1927), 489 ff.; H. D. Wendland, *Die Eschatologie d. Reiches Gottes bei Jesus* (1931), 93 ff.; A. H. Dirksen, 201-218; E. R. Smothers, "The NT Conception of Metanoia," *The Classical Bulletin* (Chicago), 10 (1933/34), 7 f.; F. P. Shipham, "Repentance — Metanoia," Exp. T., 46 (1934/35), 277 ff.; J. Schniewind, "Evangelische Metanoia," *Bekennende Kirche,* H. 25 (1935), 18-31 (Schniewind I); "Was verstand Jesus unter Umkehr?", *H. Asmussen, Rechtgläubigkeit u. Frömmigkeit* (1939), II, 70-84 (Schniewind II); O. Michel, "Die Umkehr nach d. Verkündigung Jesu," *Ev. Theol.,* 5 (1938), 403 ff.; O. Dilschneider, *op. cit.*; B. Poschmann, "*Paenitentia secunda,* Die kirchliche Busse im ältesten Christentum bis Cyprian u. Origenes," *Theophaneia, Beiträge zur Religions- und Kirchengeschichte d. Altertums,* ed. F. J. Dölger and T. Klauser (1940), 1-84; J. Behm, "Metanoia, Ein Grundbegriff d. nt.lichen Verkündigung," DTh 7 (1940), 75-86. On F.: Harnack DG, I, 231, 439 ff.; R. Seeberg, *Lehrbuch d. Dogmengeschichte,* I[3] (1922), 157 ff.; H. Windisch, 321 ff.; Dib. Herm., Exc. on m., 4, 3, 7 etc.; Wnd. Hb., Exc. on 6:8; A. Donini, 498 ff.; H. Weinel, *Bibl. Theol. d. NT*[4] (1928), 469 ff.; A. H. Dirksen, 8 ff.; Poschmann, 85 ff., and the writers listed by these authors in their bibl.

[1] H. Kleinknecht drew my attention to the recognised ambiguity of μετά in compounds like μεταβάλλω, μεταβαίνω, μετατίθημι, μεταλλάττω, etc. In the case of μετανοεῖν the μετα suggests "to think" both "later" and "otherwise." The fact that the different thinking is later is a mark of the term and gives it a strongly negative emphasis in Gk. This pt. is particularly important when μετανοεῖν primarily denotes an intellectual act, → 979, 980.

καὶ πᾶσιν ἀνθρώποις φανεροὺς γενέσθαι δεομένους αὐτοῦ καὶ ποθοῦντας Κάμιλλον, "to change one's resolve or purpose," Diod. S., 1, 67, 5 (of Psammetichus to the men bent on migration): προαγόντων δ' αὐτῶν παρὰ τὸν Νεῖλον καὶ τοὺς ὅρους ὑπερβαλλόντων τῆς Αἰγύπτου, ἐδεῖτο μετανοῆσαι καὶ τῶν τε ἱερῶν καὶ τῶν πατρίδων, ἔτι δὲ καὶ γυναικῶν καὶ τέκνων ὑπεμίμνησκεν, "to come to a different opinion," "to change one' view," Antiphon, Tetralogia, 1, 4, 12 (in a defence in court): ταῦτα οὖν σεβόμενοι ὁσίως καὶ δικαίως ἀπολύετέ με, καὶ μὴ μετανοήσαντες τὴν ἁμαρτίαν γνῶτε. ἀνίατος γὰρ ἡ μετάνοια τῶν τοιούτων ἐστίν, Xenoph. Cyrop., 1, 1, 3: ἠναγκαζόμεθα μετανοεῖν, Plat. Euthyd., 279c; Chrysippus (v. Arnim, III, 147, 21 ff.): οὐδὲ μετανοεῖν δ' ὑπολαμβάνουσι τὸν νοῦν ἔχοντα· καὶ γὰρ τὴν μετάνοιαν ἔχεσθαι ψευδοῦς συνκαταθέσεως, <ὡς> ἂν προδιαπεπτωκότος, Menand. Epit., 71 ff.: εἶ τοῦτ' ἀρεστόν ἐστί σοι, καὶ νῦν ἔχε. εἰ δ' οὐκ ἀρέσκει, μετανοεῖς δ', ἀπόδος πά[λιν] καὶ μηδὲν ἀδίκε[ι] μηδ' ἐλαττοῦ etc.

3. From sense 2., if the change of mind derives from recognition that the earlier view was foolish, improper or evil, there arises the sense "to regret," "to feel remorse," "to rue,"[2] e.g., Xenoph. Hist. Graec., 1, 7, 19: οὔκ, ἂν ὑμεῖς γέ μοι πείθησθε τὰ δίκαια καὶ ὅσια ποιοῦντες, καὶ ὅθεν μάλιστα τἀληθῆ πεύσεσθε καὶ οὐ μετανοήσαντες ὕστερον εὑρήσετε σφᾶς αὐτοὺς ἡμαρτηκότας τὰ μέγιστα εἰς θεούς τε καὶ ὑμᾶς αὐτούς, P. Greci e Latini, V, 495, 9 f.: νυνὶ δὲ μετανενόηκεν διὰ τὸ ἐπ[ι]τετιμῆσθαι ὑπό τε ἑκάσ[τ-] ..., Ditt. Syll.³, 1268, 8 (among the rules of the Praecepta Delphica): ἁμαρτὼν μετανόει, Plut. Adulat., 36 (II, 74c): βέλτιον δὲ τὰς ἁμαρτίας φυλάττεσθαι τοῖς συμβουλεύουσι πειθόμενον ἢ μετανοεῖν ἁμαρτάνοντα διὰ τοὺς κακῶς λέγοντας, Epict. Ench., 34: ἔπειτα μνήσθητι ἀμφοτέρων τῶν χρόνων, καθ' ὅν τε ἀπολαύσεις τῆς ἡδονῆς, καὶ καθ' ὃν ἀπολαύσας ὕστερον μετανοήσεις καὶ αὐτὸς σεαυτῷ λοιδορήσῃ, Diss., II, 22, 35: μὴ μετανοῶν as a characteristic of the wise man acc. to Epict. Along with the abs. use of the verb we find esp. the construction with ἐπί and dat., e.g., Ditt. Or., 751, 9: θεωρῶν οὖν ὑμᾶς μετανενοηκότας τε ἐπὶ τοῖς προημαρτημένοις, Luc. Salt., 84 (of Ajax): καὶ αὐτὸν μέντοι, φασίν, ἀνανήψαντα (become sober again) οὕτως μετανοῆσαι ἐφ' οἷς ἐποίησεν, ὥστε καὶ νοσῆσαι ὑπὸ λύπης, ὡς ἀληθῶς ἐπὶ μανίᾳ κατεγνωσμένον, M. Ant., 8, 2: καθ' ἑκάστην πρᾶξιν ἐρώτα σεαυτόν· πῶς μοι αὕτη ἔχει; μὴ μετανοήσω ἐπ' αὐτῇ; 8, 53: ἀρέσκει ἑαυτῷ ὁ μετανοῶν ἐφ' ἅπασι σχεδὸν οἷς πράσσει; or the construction with περί and gen., Plut. Galb., 6, 4 (I, 1055e): ἐν τῷ μετανοεῖν περὶ τῶν γεγονότων, or with the dat., Plut. Ages., 19, 7 (I, 803e): ἠρώτησεν, εἰ μετανοεῖ τοῖς πεπραγμένοις. μετανοεῖν is not restricted to rational self-criticism: "If I had known better I would have acted otherwise," cf. Plut. Lib. Educ., 14 (II, 10 f.), Sept. Sap. Conv., 12 (II, 155d). It is often accompanied by lively feelings, cf. Plut. Adulat., 12 (II, 56a); Luc. Salt., 84 (→ *supra*). Ethical self-dissatisfaction can often lead to μετανοῶν, cf. Epict. Ench., 34 (→ *supra*), also Plut. Tranq. An., 19 (II, 476 f.) (→ 978), etc. But a good act can be regretted, *v.* Plut. Sept. Sap. Conv., 21 (II, 163 f.): Murderers had spared a child καὶ πάλιν μετανοήσαντες ἐζήτουν καὶ οὐχ εὗρον, or Fr. of an unknown Hellen. romance (*Münchener Beiträge zur Papyrus-Forschung u. antiken Rechtsgeschichte*, 19 [1934], 23, line 16 f.): ἰδοῦσα ἡ Ἱππότις μετενόει ἐφ' οἷς εὔξατο, → 978.

---

[2] μεταμέλει (-ομαι) is synon. with μετανοέω in this sense, → 626 ff.

II. μετάνοια.[3]

The noun, too, is rare is classical Gk. and becomes more frequent only in the *koine.*[4] Sense 1., corresponding to the verb, is "later knowledge," "subsequent emendation." There is no literary attestation,[5] but the Lat. Rhetor Rutilius Lupus (prior to 50 A.D.) has a ref. to this meaning.[6] The usual senses correspond to μετανοέω 2. and 3.

The first of these is "change of mind."[7] This may affect a. the feelings, b. the will, or c. thought. It is seldom a function of the intellect alone. a. is found in Thuc., 3, 36, 4 (of the Athenians who had resolved to put the Mitylenians to death): καὶ τῇ ὑστεραίᾳ μετάνοιά τις εὐθὺς ἦν αὐτοῖς, Ps.-Hom. Batrachomyomachia, 69 f.: πολλὰ δακρύων ἄχρηστον μετάνοιαν ἐμέμφετο. b. occurs in Polyb., 4, 66, 7: Φίλιππος δὲ πυθόμενος τὴν τῶν Δαρδανέων μετάνοιαν, i.e., the decision to give up the fight. c. occurs in Bias, Fr., 4 (I, 65, 4 f., Diels[5]): μίσει τὸ ταχὺ λαλεῖν, μὴ ἁμάρτῃς· μετάνοια γὰρ ἀκολουθεῖ, Antiphon., 1, 4, 12, → 977; Chrysippus, → 977.

The second is "regret," "remorse." This expresses dissatisfaction with thoughts cherished, plans followed, acts performed etc.[8] In the dissatisfaction there may reside no more than the wish that these things had not been thought, willed, or done, even though good,[9] cf. Philemo Fr., 198 (CAF, II, 531): γαμεῖν ὃς ἐθέλει, εἰς μετάνοιαν ἔρχεται, Plut. Timoleon, 6 (I, 238d): αἰσχρὸν γὰρ ἡ μετάνοια ποιεῖ καὶ τὸ καλῶς πεπραγμένον. But μετάνοια is usually something other than ἡ ἐπὶ τὸ χεῖρον μεταβολή, Polyb., 18, 33 (16), 6 f., cf. Lycon in Diog. L., 5, 66: αὐτῶν κατηγορεῖν, ἀδυνάτῳ μηνύοντας εὐχῇ μετάνοιαν ἀργίας ἀδιορθώτου, M. Ant., 8, 10: ἡ μετάνοιά ἐστιν ἐπίληψίς τις ἑαυτοῦ ὡς χρήσιμόν τι παρεικότος. It bears witness to a sense of committed faults which must be corrected. It expresses pain or grief at what has happened (e.g., Plut. De Cohibenda Ira, 11 [II, 459d]: μετάνοιαν ... τοῦ κακουργεῖν) and in this way has an ethical character. Cf. Plut. De Sollertia Animalium 3 (II, 961d): αὐτοὶ δὲ καὶ κύνας ἁμαρτάνοντας καὶ ἵππους κολάζουσιν, οὐ διὰ κενῆς ἀλλ' ἐπὶ σωφρονισμῷ, λύπην δι' ἀλγηδόνος (painful sensation) ἐμποιοῦντες αὐτοῖς, ἣν μετάνοιαν ὀνομάζομεν, Tranq. An., 19 (II, 476 f.): τὰς μὲν γὰρ ἄλλας ἀναιρεῖ λύπας ὁ λόγος, τὴν δὲ μετάνοιαν αὐτὸς ἐνεργάζεται δακνομένης σὺν αἰσχύνῃ

---

[3] On the synon. μεταμέλεια, → 626 f.

[4] As Norden shows (137 ff.), there is no corresponding term in older Lat. lit. *Paenitentia* is not found prior to Liv., XXXI, 32, 2 : *celerem enim paenitentiam, sed eandem seram atque inutilem sequi.* "Cicero either did not know *paenitentia* or he avoided it. This is thought to be so remarkable by Ausonius that he says in an epigram (p. 332 f. [not 323 as in Norden], XXXIII, Peiper): *sum dea, cui nomen nec Cicero ipse dedit. Sum dea, quae factique et non facti exigo poenas, Nempe ut poeniteat ; sic Metanoea vocor*" (Norden, 138).

[5] But cf. the def. of μετάνοια as βραδεῖα ... γνῶσις ("knowledge which comes only later") in Cl. Al. Strom., II, 26, 5. In IV, 143, 1 Cl. explains μετάνοια etym. in terms of μετὰ ταῦτα νοήσαντες.

[6] I, 16 (Rhetores Latini Minores, ed. C. Halm [1863], 10): "Μετάνοια. *Hoc schema fieri solet, cum ipse se, qui loquitur, reprehendit, et id quod prius dixit, posteriori sententia commutat.*"

[7] Tert. is right in Marc., II, 24 (III, 369, 20 ff., CSEL): *in Graeco sono paenitentiae nomen non ex delicti confessione, sed ex animi demutatione compositum est.* Cf. also Lact. Inst., VI, 24, 6, who explains the Christian tt. *paenitentia* in terms of *resipiscentia,* which, like μετάνοια, suggests self-consideration : *quem ... facti sui paenitet, errorem suum pristinum intellegit, ideoque Graeci melius et significantius* μετάνοιαν *dicunt quam nos Latine possumus resipiscentiam dicere.* On μετανοέω and μετάνοια in the Lat. Bible, → n. 148.

[8] Tertullian De Paenitentia, 1 regards the *paenitentia* of pagans as *passio animi quaedam, quae veniat de offensa sententiae prioris.*

[9] *Ibid.,* 1: *illam* (sc. *paenitentiam*) *etiam in bonis factis suis adhibent* (sc. pagans). *paenitet fidei, amoris, simplicitatis, patientiae, misericordiae, prout quid in ingratiam cecidit.* On Tert. *v.* S. W. J. Teeuwen, "De voce 'paenitentia' apud Tertullianum," *Mnemosyne, Nova Series,* 55 (1927), 410 ff.

τῆς ψυχῆς καὶ κολαζομένης ὑφ' αὐτῆς, Adulat., 28 (II, 68 f.); Ser. Num. Pun., 6 (II, 551c d), Mar., 10, 5 (I, 410 f.): ἔσχε μέν τις τροπὴ γνώμης καὶ μετάνοια τὸν βάρβαρον, *ibid.*, 39, 5 (I, 428c): πάντας οὖν ἔκπληξις ἔσχεν, εἶτ' οἶκτος (sympathy) καὶ μετάνοια τῆς γνώμης καὶ κατάμεμψις ἑαυτῶν, cf. Pericl., 10, 3 (I, 157c): μετάνοια δεινὴ τοὺς Ἀθηναίους καὶ πόθος ἔσχε τοῦ Κίμωνος. Μετάνοια is allegorically personified in the pinax of Ceb., Ceb. Tab., 10 f.: It leads man out of the misery in which he must otherwise pass his life, ἂν μὴ ἡ Μετάνοια αὐτῷ ἐπιτύχῃ ... συναντήσασα (10, 4) by freeing him from false thoughts, passions and joys and showing him the way to true, rational and ethical development: ἐξαιρεῖ αὐτὸν ἐκ τῶν κακῶν καὶ συνίστησιν αὐτῷ ἑτέραν Δόξαν [καὶ Ἐπιθυμίαν] τῆς εἰς τὴν ἀληθινὴν Παιδείαν ἄγουσαν, ἅμα δὲ καὶ τὴν Ψευδοπαιδείαν καλουμένην (11, 1). Ἐὰν μὲν ... τὴν Δόξαν ταύτην προσδέξηται τὴν ἄξουσαν αὐτὸν εἰς τὴν ἀληθινὴν Παιδείαν, καθαρθεὶς ὑπ' αὐτῆς σῴζεται καὶ μακάριος καὶ εὐδαίμων γίνεται ἐν τῷ βίῳ· εἰ δὲ μή, πάλιν πλανᾶται ὑπὸ τῆς Ψευδοδοξίας (11, 2). The same figure appears again at the bitter end of the story of a poor simpleton in Luc. De Merc. Cond., 42: ἀπαντάτω δ' ἐξιόντι ἡ Μετάνοια δακρύουσα εἰς οὐδὲν ὄφελος καὶ τὸν ἄθλιον ἐπαπολλύουσα, and Ps.-Luc. Calumniatori non temere Credendum, 5 depicts Μετάνοια, who follows Διαβολή, as follows: κατόπιν δὲ ἠκολούθει πάνυ πενθικῶς τις ἐσκευασμένη, μελανείμων (clothed in black) καὶ κατεσπαραγμένη (dishevelled). Μετάνοια οἶμαι αὕτη ἐλέγετο· ἐπεστρέφετο γοῦν ἐς τοὐπίσω δακρύουσα καὶ μετ' αἰδοῦς πάνυ τὴν Ἀλήθειαν προσιοῦσαν ὑπέβλεπεν. Cf. also Hierocl. Carm. Aur., 14 [10] (Fragmenta Philosophorum Graecorum, ed. F. G. A. Mullach, I [1860], 451 f.): ἡ δὲ μετάνοια αὕτη φιλοσοφίας ἀρχὴ γίνεται, καὶ τῶν ἀνοήτων ἔργων τε καὶ λόγων φυγή, καὶ τῆς ἀμεταμελήτου ζωῆς ἡ πρώτη παρασκευή.

III. Historical Significance of the Data.

In pre-biblical and extra-biblical usage μετανοέω and μετάνοια are not firmly related to any specific concepts. At the first stage they bear the intellectual sense of "subsequent knowledge." With further development both verb and noun then come to mean "change of mind," "repentance," in an emotional and volitional sense as well. The change of opinion or decision, the alteration in mood or feeling, which finds expression in the terms, is not in any sense ethical. It may be for the bad as well as the good. [11] In the latter case, when μετάνοια denotes a change in moral judgment, regret for wrongs etc. which have been committed, the reference is always to an individual instance of change of judgment or remorse in respect of a specific act which is now no longer approved (→ συνείδησις). For the Greeks μετάνοια never suggests an alteration in the total moral attitude, a profound change in life's direction, a conversion which affects the whole of conduct. [12] Before himself and before the gods the Greek can μετανοεῖν a sin *in actu* (Xenoph. Hist. Graec., 1, 7, 19, → 977), but he has no knowledge of μετάνοια as repentance or conversion in the sense found in the OT and NT (→ B., C. I, E.).

---

[10] But here we have to take into account the possibility of Christian influence on the concept, far more so than does K. Praechter, "Christl.-neuplat. Beziehungen," *Byzantinische Zeitschrift,* 21 (1912), 24 f.

[11] Cf. Bengel on 2 C. 7:10.

[12] Rather less cautiously than W. W. Jaeger, GGA, 175 (1913), 589 ff., K. Latte, "Schuld u. Sühne in d. gr. Religion," *Archiv f. Religionswissenschaft,* 20 [1920/21], 281, n. 1, regards Ditt. Or., 751, 9 (→ 977) as the first example of the concept of a "lasting change of mind" in the Gk. world. Dirksen, 174 ff. concludes esp. from Ceb. Tab., 10 f. (→ *supra*) that in secular Gk. μετάνοια and μετανοέω have the technical sense of "conversion in an ethical sense." Nock is nearer the mark, *op. cit.*, 180 (→ n. 13).

The Hellenistic philosophers use μετάνοια predominantly in the intellectual sense, though the ethical element is also included. By a penitent alteration of judgment, by reconsideration, e.g., by the correction of a mistaken view, the fool becomes a wise man, Ceb. Tab., → 979; [13] Hierocl., → 979. On the Stoic view however (Chrysippus, → 977; Epict., → 977; M. Ant., → 977/8; 975) [14] the wise man is above a μετάνοια. This would not show him to be in harmony with himself. It would represent him as the victim of error, which as the opposite of the virtue of wisdom is beneath the dignity of the sage. [15] These ideas do not constitute a bridge to what the NT understands by μετάνοια.

Whether linguistically or materially, one searches the Greek world in vain for the origin of the NT understanding of μετανοέω and μετάνοια. [16]

Behm

B. Repentance and Conversion in the Old Testament.

There is in the OT no special tt. for "repentance" or "to repent." But the concept is by no means absent. It is found in two forms. On the one side is the cultic and ritual form, where the religion of Israel makes use of elements found elsewhere. On the other side is the prophetic form, namely, the concept of conversion. This developed out of the prophetic view of the relation between God and man, which is peculiar to the OT, and which is particularly significant inasmuch as it corresponds to and prepares the way for the μετανοεῖν of the NT.

I. Cultic and Ritual Forms of Penitence.

1. The Occasion and Development of Penitential Observances. When a special emergency arises, in Israel as elsewhere it is traced back to the wrath of God at transgressions of His will even though there is no particular sense of sin nor knowledge of the specific offence or the one who has committed it. Whether the offence is recognised or not, resort is had to penitential observance as a means to placate the divine wrath. Since the occasions which demand penitence are often general in scope, affecting the whole people or the major part of it, [17] the penitence designed to avert it is often a public matter.

Such a public event, which takes from its main component the name צוֹם or fast (→ νηστεία, 927 f.), is mentioned already in the story of Naboth. For a reason no longer known to us, a general fast is appointed. Obviously there must have been some misfortune whose cause was unknown, and it would seem that the occasion was seized to try to find out what had called down the wrath of God. [18] Through the false witness of two worthless men it is surprisingly discovered that Naboth, who had been given the

[13] Cf. Nock, 180: "The term implies an intellectual value judgement and commonly a momentary realization rather than the entry on a state."

[14] Cf. also Sen. Ben., IV, 34, 4: *non mutat sapiens consilium ...; ideo numquam illum paenitentia subit*; Sen. Ep., 115, 18: *hoc tibi philosophia praestabit, quo equidem nihil maius existimo: numquam te paenitebit tui*; also Cic. Tusc., V, 28 (81).

[15] Cf. P. Barth, *Die Stoa* [3, 4] (1922), 92 f.; → III, 52.

[16] Cf. on this Cr.-Kö., *s.v.*; Norden, 134 ff.; Thompson, 28 ff.; Clemen, 213; Wnd. 2 K., 233 f.; Dietrich, 226 ff. etc.

[17] 1 K. 8:33 ff. mentions defeat, drought, famine, pestilence, fire, mildew, locusts, enemy attacks.

[18] H. Gressmann, *Schriften d. AT*, II, 1[2] (1921), 272.

honour of presiding over the assembly, was the one who by blaspheming the king and God, and thus violating the commandment in Ex. 22:27, had incurred the guilt. The opportunity is thus provided for eradicating the guilty man from the community and thereby averting the curse brought down on it by his transgression. Usually common afflictions seem not to have been attributed to the sins of individuals. A sense of common guilt led to the appointment of penitential exercises whose course may be roughly determined from the fast described in Joel on the occasion of the plague of locusts. The summons to the fast is issued by the priests (1:13). At the sound of the ram's horn the whole community assembles, including old people and children, brides and bridegrooms. The priests are to weep between the porch and the altar and say: "Have mercy, Yahweh, on thy people, and give not thine heritage to reproach, that the heathen should mock them. Why should they say among the people, Where is their God?" (2:15-18).

2. External Forms. Along with fasting, which is the most important element and gave its name to the whole practice, other external forms characterise the day of penitence. The people clothed themselves in the garb of mourning, i.e., sackcloth,[19] and sat in ashes or strewed them on their heads.[20] Hos. 7:14[21] speaks not only of crying and wailing before Yahweh but also of the people scratching themselves "for corn and wine." Once in this connection there is a ref. to pouring out water before Yahweh — a rite whose meaning is not clear (1 S. 7:6). Later even greater significance was attached to the external signs of repentance. Thus the author of Jonah says that not only the people but also the cattle of Nineveh fasted and wore mourning (3:7 f.). In Est. 4:16 there is a fast of three days and nights. In Jdt. 4:10 ff. men, women, children, cattle, aliens, day labourers and slaves all wear sackcloth, and the altar of the burnt offering is also draped in it.

3. Liturgies. A chief feature of the fast, however, is calling on Yahweh for help, usually with an appropriate confession of sin.[22] It is likely that there developed quite soon a fixed penitential liturgy in which the congregation could present its petition and receive God's answer.[23] Prophetic reproductions of such liturgies may be found in Hos. 6:1 ff.; 14:2 ff.; Jer. 3:21-4:2 etc.[24] In view of the close similarity between Neh. 9; Da. 9:4-19; Bar. 1:15-3:8 there can be little doubt that the prayers were fixed, for these passages derive from a common source.[25] In the passages mentioned there is a strong sense of sinning against Yahweh (Da. 9:8-11), though in Neh. 9 the offences are those of the fathers rather than the present generation. In the moving penitential liturgy of Is. 63:7-64:12 this sense of guilt takes the bold form: "Yahweh, why hast thou made us to err from thy ways, and hardened our heart from thy fear?" (Is. 63:17). Cf. Ezr. 9:6 ff.; Neh. 1:5 ff., which also express a strong conviction of sin. Other prayers, which perhaps go back to special fasts on specific occasions,[26] in many cases do not contain the motif expressed in confession of sin. Especially in psalms probably dating from the Maccabean period, e.g., Ps. 44, there emerges a strong religious sense which calls on God for help in the boldest expressions. These national laments, as they have been called, were probably used at special fasts. If so, they show how often, esp. later, the motif of genuine penitence deriving from a sense of guilt had retreated into the background in favour of a protestation of innocence. One gains this impression from the prayer in 2 Ch. 20:3 ff., which was supposedly uttered at a fast summoned because of

---

[19] 1 K. 21:27; Is. 58:5; Jl. 1:8; Jon. 3:6, 8; Neh. 9:1; Da. 9:3 etc.
[20] Is. 58:5; Neh. 9:1; Da. 9:3; Est. 4:3; Jdt. 4:11 etc.
[21] Acc. to the LXX.
[22] 1 S. 7:6; Is. 63:7-64:11; Neh. 9:1 ff.; Da. 9:4 ff. etc.
[23] H. Schmidt, *Sellinfestschrift* (1927), 116 ff.; O. Eissfeldt, *Einl.* (1934), 126 f.
[24] H. Schmidt, *loc. cit.*; O. Eissfeldt, *loc. cit.*
[25] K. Marti, *Daniel* (1901), 65.
[26] Cf. Ps. 12; 44; 60; 74; 79; 80; 83; 85; 89; Lam. 5; Sir. 36:1-17; Ps. Sol. 7; cf. H. Schmidt, *op. cit.*, 116.

enemy threats, and which certainly shows acquaintance with the liturgical style customary on such occasions. Here, too, one misses the profound penitence expressed in confession of sin.

It is noteworthy that the texts in question never refer to the bringing of the offerings which one would expect in full measure on such occasions. Perhaps this is accidental and one may deduce from Mi. 6:6 f. and Is. 1:10-14 that large-scale sacrifices preceded such assemblies for prayer. Indeed, it has been conjectured that at this pt. in the cultus the offering of the firstborn son, esp. of the king, persisted to a late period (Mi. 6:7; 2 K. 16:3; 21:6).[27] But in view of the absence of direct evidence this is most uncertain, at least in the form suggested.[28]

4. Days of Penitence. General days of penitence must have been fairly common in the pre-exilic period. This is shown by the express reference to and naming of occasions in the great temple prayer of Solomon in 1 K. 8:33 ff. A fast day (יום צום) is mentioned from the time of Jeremiah.[29] The reason is to be sought either in the Babylonian invasion[30] or a drought.[31] The whole people from the various cities of Judah assembles in Jerusalem. In the exilic period the fateful days connected with the fall of Jerusalem (the beginning of Nebuchadnezzar's siege, the capture of Jerusalem, the burning of the temple and the murder of Gedaliah) were commemorated by fasting and lamentation in the 4th, 5th, 7th and 10th months.[32] In the post-exilic period the day of penance mentioned in Neh. 9 achieved particular significance and renown.

5. Prophetic Criticism of Cultic and Ritual Penitence. It has already become clear that in cultic and ritual penitence there are many different elements, and in our estimation of the meaning and significance of this penitence it matters a great deal which element is to the fore in a given case, whether external ceremonial and wild lamentation or prayer and the confession of sin. Prophetic statements enable us to see fairly clearly what form the appointed fasts took in practice, to what depths of the existence of those participating they reached, what significance was attached to them. A theological understanding of this kind of penitence is thus made possible.

From Amos to Joel the prophets express themselves critically.

Thus Amos maintains that in spite of famine, drought, poor harvests, sicknesses and earthquakes the people has not returned (ולא שבתם עדי).[33] Naturally one cannot take it that the prophet is referring to a failure on the part of the people to observe penitential practices like fasting, wearing sackcloth, and crying to Yahweh. "For Amos could hardly have denied that the people engaged in this form of penitence."[34] What the prophet is saying is that the people's penitence is not firmly anchored at the depth where it becomes genuine encounter with God. It does not lead, then, to a personal and existential relation between God and man. Hosea in his criticism starts with the fact that penitence is frivolous and confident of results. In 6:1-3 he lays on the lips of the people a song which it sings in pilgrimage to a service of prayer.[35] "Up and let us return to Yahweh ! For he has torn and he will heal us, he has smitten and he will bind us up . . .

---

27 H. Schmidt, 115.

28 Hos. 6:6 and Ps. 51:16 obviously presuppose sacrifices also, though we are not told to what extent.

29 Jer. 36:6, 9.

30 Rothstein in Kautzsch, *ad loc.*

31 Volz, Komm., *ad loc.*

32 Zech. 7:3, 5; 8:19.

33 Am. 4:6, 8, 9, 10, 11.

34 A. Weiser, *Prof. d. Am.* (1929), 176.

35 For this understanding of Hos. 6:1 ff. cf. H. Schmidt, 111 ff.

and let us know, let us follow on to know Yahweh: as we seek him, so shall we find him"[36] (Hos. 6:1, 3). The answer which Yahweh then gives the people is as follows "O Ephraim, what shall I do to thee? O Judah, what shall I do to thee? Your חֶסֶד is as a morning cloud and as the dew which quickly vanishes ... I have pleasure in חֶסֶד and not in sacrifice, in the knowledge of God and not in burnt offerings" (6:4, 6). Without final seriousness and readiness for the practical consequences of relationship with God, for חֶסֶד as the mode of conduct corresponding to the divine will,[37] the people expects that its penitential exercise will bring about a divine change in its favour. Yahweh thus directs it away from the path of its own choice to what corresponds to His will, חֶסֶד and דַּעַת אֱלֹהִים. Is. 58:5-7 demands instead of mortification and bowing the head, instead of sackcloth and ashes, a fast such as Yahweh loves, namely, liberation of the oppressed, feeding the hungry, sheltering the homeless, clothing the naked. The kind of fasting now practised is not adapted to find a hearing on high, 58:4b. Zech. destroys cultic practices from within when in his criticism of the fasts observed in the exilic period he ascribes to them only immanental significance: "When you fast and mourn, do you fast at all to me? When you eat and when you drink, are not you those who eat and those who drink?" (7:5b-6). Instead the old prophetic demand for social righteousness is raised again (7:7 ff.). Finally we might mention Joel again with his demand for inner turning rather than outward gestures: "Rend your heart, and not your garments" (2:13).

But the same Joel can also issue in Yahweh's name the command: "Turn to me with all your heart, and with fasting, and with weeping, and with mourning" (2:12; cf. Is. 22:12 f.).

One should not underestimate a verse like this. It forces us to conclude that prophetic criticism did not ask for a repudiation of all external forms in favour of the inner attitude. All prophetic criticism is agreed that the penitence of the people lacks the one thing that matters, namely, that in penitence one is before the God of unconditional requirement, that one has to take Him with full seriousness, that it is not enough to be sorry for past sins and to pray for their remission or for the aversion of calamity, that what counts is a turning from the sinful nature as such. If the external form is severed from what it is designed to express, if it becomes autonomous, it sinks to the level of magic and acquires a significance which the prophets could never accord it. The fact that specific emergencies are the occasion of penitence can easily give rise to the view that the main goal is dealing with the emergency rather than establishing a new relation to Yahweh. Thus David fasts and weeps so long in the hope that, who knows, Yahweh might have mercy and keep the child alive, but once the child is dead he stops, because he can no longer bring it back to life.[38] This shows that penitence was obviously thought of in this way in many circles. Finally the general or public character of penitence can easily mean that the individual, though he participates, is not fully and personally involved. "The very custom carries with it the danger that in distress the lips make confession ... but there is no forsaking of the old ungodly nature."[39] In the last resort, then, the prophets frequently perceive in this kind of penitence a veiling of the seriousness of the relationship between God and man, and so they are forced to protest against it.

---

[36] Read with Giesebrecht etc.: כְּשַׁחֲרֵנוּ כֵּן נִמְצָאֵנוּ.
[37] E. Sellin, *Zwölfprophetenbuch* $^{2, 3}$ (1929), I, 73.
[38] 2 S. 12:15 ff.
[39] J. Hempel, *Gott u. Mensch*^{2} (1936), 145.

II. The Prophetic Concept of Conversion.

The prophets did not, of course, invent a special term for their own view of penitence. They regarded a common secular term as quite adequate to express the process they had in view, and they thus preferred it in their own usage. This word is שׁוּב.

שׁוּב usually means "to go back again," "to return." But the statement of Hupfeld that "שׁוּב always includes an 'again,' and clings to it tenaciously,"[40] though true even in cases where first appearances might seem to refute it, cannot claim exclusive validity. Thus in Jer. 8:4: אִם יָשׁוּב וְלֹא יָשׁוּב, the sense "to go back again" does not fit the first יָשׁוּב. Here we must render: "Shall he turn aside and not turn back?"[41] Again in verses like Ez. 18:26; 33:18: בְּשׁוּב־צַדִּיק מִצִּדְקָתוֹ, where there is no suggestion of a relapse, one must assume "to turn aside," and translate: "If the righteous man turns from his righteousness." The element of return is certainly present in most instances, but not always. In the sense last mentioned the contrast to an earlier action or state[42] certainly plays a role. In the religious use, then, one has to decide in each case whether the element of return or that of contrast to what has gone before is more prominent. Conversion in the sense of turning about is perhaps the best general rendering.

There is a hint of the distinction mentioned in the prep. with which שׁוּב is combined. There are in all some 1056 instances[43] of שׁוּב. Of these about 118 bear a religious sense, 12 times in the hi, once the polel. The main occurrences are 5 times in Am., 7 in Hos., 7 in Is., 28 in Jer., 20 in Ez., 16 in Ezr.-Ch., 3 each in Dt., Dt. Is., Zech. and Mal., 5 in Ps. The element of return is prominent when we have the prep. אֶל, עַד, עַל, לְ (in all some 48 times). Contrast to what has preceded is emphasised by מִן (some 40 times, only from the time of Jer.) and once by the st. c. combination שָׁבֵי פֶשַׁע. שׁוּב abs. is found some 30 times.

The obj. of return in combination with אֶל, עַד, עַל, לְ is either expressly or contextually Yahweh, only once (Neh. 9:29) the Torah. The object of turning from is evil conduct (דרך הרעה or דרך הרע or דרך הרעים) in some 14 cases, previous conduct (דרך) in 6 cases, evil (רעה) in 3, wicked acts (מעללים רעים) in 2, violence (חמס) once, idols (גלולים) once, abomination (תועבות), once, sin in the various terms רשע 4 times, חטא 4, פשע 3, עון 2, and און once.[44]

If prophetic criticism of the cultic form of penitence common among the people is particularly directed against the lack of a sense of standing before God and of the implied need for seriousness, the concept of conversion emphasises positively the fact that penitence involves a new relation to God which embraces all spheres of human life, that it claims the will, and that man cannot make good this or that fault by this or that measure. Any magical element which ignores the highly

---

[40] H. Hupfeld, *Psalmen*², I (1868), 279.

[41] J. Barth, *Wurzeluntersuchungen* (1902), 48 f. traces back this meaning, which is present esp. in מְשׁוּבָה שׁוֹבָב, שׁוֹבֵב, to a radix which differs from the usual שׁוּב, which corresponds to the Arab. ساب (med. j), and whose basic sense is "free," "unbound." Whether or not Jer. 8:4 reflects awareness of the distinction of roots as Barth supposes is, of course, debatable.

[42] Hupfeld, 201.

[43] Brown-Driver-Briggs, *Hebrew and English Lexicon* (1906), 996.

[44] A noun "conversion" occurs only in Is. 30:15 (שׁוּבָה, a fem. inf., Procksch, *ad loc.*). תְּשׁוּבָה, the common Jewish word for "conversion," "penitence," has in the OT only the secular sense of "return," "the return of the year," "answer"; cf. Ges.-Buhl, *s.v.*

personal relation between God and man is thus carefully avoided by the prophets. The question of man's position before God is *the* question of existence. Everything else depends on it, the relation to fellow-men, the cultus, the state, politics etc. This has to be maintained in opposition to the misunderstanding that the prophetic message of conversion bases its claim to the various areas of life on immanent grounds — a misunderstanding which can easily arise in view of what are often the very concrete requirements of the prophets in ethical, political and other matters.

1. The Personal View of Sin. The strongly personal and total element in the prophetic understanding of the God-man relationship may be seen clearly in the prophetic view of sin, which it is important that we present here as a correlative to the concept of repentance. Sin does find visible manifestation, of course, in individual faults, idolatry, the cult of the high places, political coalitions, moral decay and social offences. But all these individual things form a great single entity when understood by the prophets as the result of a wrong attitude to God. Hence Hos. can depict the relation between Yahweh and Israel in terms of a marriage in which the wife is unfaithful to her husband.[45] Again, Is. can speak of sons who rebel,[46] and Jer. can describe sin as forsaking Yahweh.[47] All these expressions show that sin is simply turning away or apostasy from God. It is the more serious because Israel stands in a special relation to Yahweh. Yahweh has shown Israel favours for which it should be grateful. Again, He has constantly declared His will to it through the prophets and the Law, and summoned it to obedience. Thus sin is a corrupt attitude to Yahweh. It is backsliding from Him, esp. in the sense of ingratitude, unfaithfulness and disobedience.

2. The Personal View of Repentance as Turning to Yahweh. To the personal view of sin corresponds the personal view of repentance. As conversion to Yahweh this must be orientated to Yahweh and His will, for He is Israel's God.

With particular clarity in Hos., and also, if not so exclusively, in Is. and Jer., conversion is so strictly related to sin as apostasy that it is presented as a return to the earlier good relation between Israel and Yahweh.[48] In Am., Hos. and Is. שׁוּב is always used with the prep. אֶל and עַד (obj. always Yahweh) or in the abs., and this again shows how strongly they regard penitence as a converting or returning to Yahweh, with no special emphasis on the turning from sin, which is necessarily implied and obviously felt to be self-evident. In particular the great conversion verse in Am. (4:6 ff.): וְלֹא שַׁבְתֶּם עָדַי, whose עַד is stronger than אֶל because it also includes the goal, expresses the fact that the prophet wants true penitence to be regarded as a breaking through to the true God,[49] i.e., as a treatment of this God with unconditional seriousness.

Of the basic structure of prophetic repentance as proclaimed from Hos. to Jer. it may thus be maintained that the chief concern is a turning to Yahweh with all one's being, an absolutely serious reckoning with Him as Israel's God in all decisions. This basic structure is concretely exemplified at the following points.

a. Obedience to Yahweh's Will. As a turning of the whole existence to Yahweh conversion is actualised in obedience to His will.

Thus in Hos. 6:1-6, where the people's conversion (v. 1) is described as not deep or serious enough (v. 4), the lesson of v. 6 has the significance of a lesson on true con-

[45] Hos. 1-3.
[46] Is. 1:2.
[47] Jer. 1:16; 2:13, 17, 19; 5:7, 19 etc.
[48] Cf. esp. Hos. 2:9.
[49] A. Weiser, *op. cit.*, 176.

version, which is obedience to that wherein Yahweh takes pleasure, חסד and דעת אלהים, i.e., unconditional recognition of God in the form of conduct corresponding to God and His will. Similarly, Jer. can say with ref. to keeping the commandment to release slaves in the 7th year: "Turn now, and do what is right in my sight" (Jer. 34:15). Turning is hearing and following the Law of Yahweh and the words of the prophets sent by Him (26:3-5).

b. Trust in Yahweh. Turning to Yahweh, the orientation of one's being to Him (which also means from Him), demands unconditional trust in Him and the renunciation of all human help (coalitions), of false gods and idols. According to all that Israel had experienced of God's help in its history, refusal of confidence necessarily took the direction of sin.[50]

For this reason Hos. in the Spirit sees that the genuine conversion of his people after judgment is accompanied by words of trust: "Assur shall not save us; we will not ride upon horses; neither will we say any more to the work of our hands, Ye are our gods; for in thee the righteous[51] findeth mercy" (14:4). Even more fervently Jer. in inward experience hears the people which has been brought by the goodness of God to repentance[52] confess its trust: "We are here, we come unto thee, for thou, Yahweh, art our God. Valueless indeed are the hills,[53] the noise[54] of the mountains; truly in Yahweh, our God, is the help of Israel" (Jer. 3:22b, 23). Similarly in Is. 30:15 שׁוּבָה, which is correctly understood by Procksch as willing "conversion to God" in spite of Duhm and Marti,[55] is coupled with confident composure (נחת and השקט) and trust (בטחה). Of the remnant which, delivered from judgment, will return to Yahweh, it can also be said that it will no longer lean on him who smote it (Assur) but on Yahweh (Is. 10:20 f.). Hence even in the demand for conversion we can find the call not to go after other gods to serve them (Jer. 25:5 f.). For the worship of false gods is not just disobedience. It has its source in deficient trust in Yahweh.

c. Turning from Everything Ungodly. Conversion to Yahweh naturally carries with it a new attitude to everything else. This is displayed negatively in a turning away from all evil and ungodliness. This aspect is less prominent in the older prophets, to whom it seemed to be so inescapable a consequence of the new attitude to Yahweh that little stress had to be laid on it. Only with Jer. do we begin to find a more common שׁוב with מן, which then becomes exclusive in Ez. The demand to turn from is more concrete and urgent than the more abstract call for conversion to Yahweh, and in Jer. it takes on even greater force as an individual summons (איש מדרכו הרעה).[56] This is perhaps the reason for its use in the two prophets whose concern is more pastoral. The accompanying disadvantage is that this form cannot bring out so clearly the strongly personal orientation of all renewal to Yahweh or the comprehensive character of the concept of conversion on the positive side.

---

[50] A. Weiser, *Glaube u. Geschichte* (1931), 53.

[51] Read with Sellin, *ad loc.*: תָּמִים for יָתוֹם.

[52] Volz, *Komm. zu Jer.*[2] (1928), 39.

[53] Read הַגְּבָעוֹת.

[54] Read הֲמוֹן הֶהָרִים.

[55] Procksch, *ad loc.* Duhm and Marti, on the basis of Mi. 2:8, understand שׁוּבָה as a peaceful disposition, a conversion from all warlike plans etc.

[56] Jer. 26:3; 36:3 etc. Eichrodt, III, 132 traces the significance of conversion in the message of Jer. (as in that of Hos. before him) to the fact "that in them such prominence is given to the seeking love of God which woos a response of love."

3. The Possibility of Conversion and Its Historical Significance.

a. Amos. Amos realises that he is sent to prophesy against the people Israel (7:15). What he proclaims is supported by an awareness that Yahweh will no longer pardon (7:8; 8:2). His section on conversion (ולא שבתם עדי, 4:6 ff.) is not an admonition; it is a statement of fact. In view of 5:5 there is room for doubt whether even the "seek me" of 5:4 is a summons to repentance.[57] Certainly 5:14 f. falls under suspicion of not being part of the original text in view of the pure message of judgment which we find elsewhere in Amos.[58] At any rate, one may say with confidence that the summons to conversion has no historical significance here as compared with the proclamation of judgment. Yahweh comes, and this means judgment. Am. obviously does not think in terms of the human possibility of deliverance by conversion to Yahweh.

b. Hosea. Hosea, too, is aware of the ineluctable approach of judgment. He regards the people's sin as so serious that it is a hard and invincible reality between God and the people. The people no longer has the power to acknowledge God with final seriousness. "Their deeds will not allow them[59] to turn back to their God" (5:4). But whereas Am. preaches only judgment, Hos. discerns behind it a pedagogic purpose. Judgment will make the people ready for conversion (2:8 f.; 3:5; 14:2). Conversion does not imply human ability to escape judgment. It is the goal of the divine direction of history and as such it carries with it the promise of salvation (14:5 f.).

c. Isaiah. Is. has a different view again of the relation between history and conversion. In a few passages it seems that he counts on the possibility of finding salvation through conversion. Thus the mission to harden the people lest it should turn and be saved (6:10) presupposes that conversion is followed by salvation. In 30:15: "Through returning and rest you will be helped," it should be noted that the ref. is obviously to a past time when salvation by conversion was still possible. But because the people would not have it, judgment will come. A remnant, however, will still be saved and return, as may be seen from the symbolical name of the prophet's son, שְׁאָר יָשׁוּב. 10:20 f. makes it clear that deliverance is not merited by repentance. On the contrary, the remnant which escapes disaster will turn in trust to Yahweh. Conversion is the consequence, not the presupposition, of deliverance.

d. Jeremiah. It is at first surprising how often Jer., as compared with the Am., Hos. and Is., calls for conversion, affirms its possibility (4:1), and values its efficacy in averting judgment. He proclaims the evil which Yahweh purposes in order that each may turn from his wicked way (26:3; 36:3; cf. 36:7) and cause Yahweh to repent of the evil which He has purposed (26:3), and to forgive the guilt and sin (36:3). On the other hand, one cannot fail to detect a more sceptical note: "Can the Ethiopian change his skin, or the leopard his spots? then may ye also do good, that are accustomed to do evil" (13:23). This and similar passages show that Jer., for all the hopeful and winsome notes evoked by his profound love for the people, is well aware of the difficulty of conversion. And after the rich experiences of his life he no longer expects from men a comprehensive renewing of the people. He expects this only from God, who will write His Law on the people's hearts (31:33).

e. Conclusion. In sum it may be said that the older prophets had no great hopes of conversion. There are verses, especially in Jer., which might seem to suggest that the course of history and the coming of judgment could be arrested by conversion. But these should "not be pressed as a proof that judgment has only a casual and not a principial character; they are ... simply witnesses to the

[57] Cf. A. Weiser, *Prof. d. Am.* (1929), 190 ff.
[58] *Ibid.*, 185 ff.
[59] Read יְתְּנוּם.

fact that even ineluctable judgment is not for the prophets a blind fate, but leaves inviolate the living quality of the relation to God and the validity of the moral order." [60]

III. The Exilic and Post-Exilic Period.

The period after Jer. was hardly able to maintain the concept of conversion at the level of the classical prophets. Dt. Is. and Ps. 51 [61] are the only exceptions. The latter, with its view that all sin is directed against God alone (v. 4), believes that there can be true renewal only in a pure heart and new and strong spirit which God creates (v. 10). The former orientates conversion exclusively to Yahweh. [62] The basis is new: Return to me, for I redeem thee, [63] but there is a parallel for this in a statement which is common in the older prophets in the context of conversion, namely, that Yahweh is the God of Israel.

Distinctive in many ways is the position of Ez. For him conversion is primarily the conversion of the individual, or, more precisely, the רשע (18:21, 27; 33:9, 11, 12, 14 etc.). The רשע is defined more casuistically as the one who offends in cultic, ritual, or ethical matters (18:5 ff.). His offences are not expressly done out of opposition to Yahweh, nor do they find here their focus. For Ez., then, to convert is to change one's sinful way (3:19; 18:21, 23, 27; 33:12, 14, 19 etc.), to leave off the sins of the רשע, to become צדיק rather than רשע. [64] The point at issue here is a new attitude to sin, not explicitly a new attitude to God and His will. [65] The pastoral emphasising of responsibility may be seen clearly in this setting of action above the inner attitude. It may be seen also in the fact that Ez. fundamentally presupposes that man has the power to choose freely whether he will be a רשע or a צדיק. The profound insight into the enslaving power of sin, which is a mark of the older prophets, is necessarily less prominent on this view. Ez. counts far more on the possibility of conversion than did the earlier prophets. He also speaks in terms of individual retribution (c. 18). Hence conversion has for him enhanced significance in the life of man. For it is a means whereby he can attain to salvation, or, as Ez. puts it, to life (18:21-23; 33:11 etc.). Since man's action makes him a רשע or צדיק and change from the one to the other cancels all that has gone before, man can begin again with each conversion (18:21 ff.; 33:12 ff.). The being of man is not, then, a unity; it is fragmented. [66] On the other hand, it should not be overlooked that Ez., too, demands a new heart and a new spirit (18:31) which elsewhere — and here scepticism and profundity may be found in him too — he promises as a gift of Yahweh (11:19; 36:26).

---

[60] W. Eichrodt, *Theol. d. AT*, I (1933), 202, n. 1.

[61] A. Weiser, *Psalmen* (1935), 138: "... evidence of a struggle for faith which is not surpassed even by what the NT has to say about repentance."

[62] Is. 44:22. Cf. on Dt. Is. E. K. Dietrich, 152 ff. and W. Eichrodt, *Theol. d. AT*, III (1939), 133.

[63] Is. 44:22.

[64] On this basis Windisch, *Taufe u. Sünde im ält. Christentum* (1908), 9, rightly says: "Repentance is the conversion, represented in an act, by which one becomes a righteous man instead of a sinner." But he overlooks the distinctiveness of Ez. here as compared with the older prophets, and believes that his concept of conversion is a particularly radical development of the prophetic concept in general. For a different view cf. Dietrich, 216.

[65] J. Köberle, 222: "Here, then, conversion is naturally a moral turning, but, taking place in a moment, it is an act which no longer has any independent religious content."

[66] A. Bertholet, *Hesekiel* (1936), 15.

In general one may sum up the development of the concept of conversion in the exilic and post-exilic periods by saying that the legal thrust of the age left its mark also on the understanding of conversion. This means that the radical and total character of conversion was to a large extent lost. Thus in those parts of Dt. thought to be exilic conversion is equated with obedience to the Deuteronomic Law (Dt. 30:2, 10). The Deuteronomic revision of the history books says of Josiah that "according to the law of Moses" there was none before or after him "that turned to the Lord" (2 K. 23:25), and it finds the essence of conversion above all in turning away from cultic sins (1 S. 7:3; 1 K. 13:33; 2 K. 17:19 ff.). Mal. bases the need for conversion on the fact that attempts have been made to deceive Yahweh in respect of tithes and taxes (Mal. 3:7 f.). Orientation to the Law is especially pronounced in Neh. 9:29, where conversion is expressly understood as conversion to the Law. In 2 Ch. 30:6 ff. conversion involves keeping the Feast of the Passover as prescribed by the Law. On the other hand, attention may be drawn to the linking of the thought of conversion with the cultic and ritual forms of penitence in Joel and Jonah (Jl. 2:12-18; Jon. 3:8-10).

We are thus forced to the conclusion that in view of the weakness of a sense of guilt in the post-exilic community[67] the prophetic concept of conversion, which demanded a great power of religious thought and derived from a total and personal understanding of the relation between God and man, could not maintain its former grandeur and profundity. It had to accommodate itself to the possibilities and necessities of the time and to fall in with its dominant legal trends. If we are to know it in its full greatness and significance, we must always turn to the great prophets from Amos to Jeremiah.

Würthwein

C. μετανοέω/μετάνοια in Hellenistic Jewish Literature.

I. The LXX.

In the LXX, as in secular Gk., μετανοέω and μετάνοια are comparatively rare, and only in the case of the verb does one detect the beginnings of conceptual development.[68]

1. μετανοέω. This is used 14 times for נִחַם ni, "to regret something," for which μεταμέλομαι is also used (→ 626). The Heb. can also mean "to alter one's purpose out of pity" (of God, who gives up His intention of punishing, 1 S. 15:29; Jer. 18:8; cf. 4:28; Am. 7:3, 6; Jl. 2:13 f.; Jon. 3:9 f.; 4:2; Zech. 8:14) and "to repent" (of God, who repents of His promise of good, Jer. 18:10; of man, who repents of the sins he has committed, Jer. 8:6; 31:19). Hence in these passage the Gk. equivalent oscillates between "to change one's mind or intention" and "to repent." For שׁוּב, the verbal expression of the Mas. for religious and moral conversion, the LXX never uses μετανοέω but always → ἐπιστρέφω (-ομαι) or ἀποστρέφω (-ομαι). But נִחַם and שׁוּב, though they have different basic meanings, both denote movement away from a position previously adopted (whether lit. or fig.), and are thus often used as par. (Jer. 4:28; Ex. 32:12); religiously, they can be almost synon., cf. Jer. 8:6: נִחָם עַל־רָעָתוֹ... with

[67] J. Köberle, 282.

[68] In Prv. 20:25; 24:32 μετανοέω has the popular sense "to consider later."

31:18 ff.: הֲשִׁבֵנִי וְאָשׁוּבָה...כִּי־אַחֲרֵי שׁוּבִי נִחַמְתִּי... [69]. The result is that in the LXX μετανοέω and ἐπιστρέφω seem to be related in meaning, Jer. 8:6: ἄνθρωπος μετανοῶν ἀπὸ τῆς κακίας αὐτοῦ λέγων Τί ἐποίησα, Ιερ. 38:18 f.: ἐπίστρεψόν με, καὶ ἐπιστρέψω ... ὅτι ὕστερον αἰχμαλωσίας μου [70] μετενόησα, Is. 46:8 (deviating from the Heb.): μετανοήσατε, οἱ πεπλανημένοι, ἐπιστρέψατε τῇ καρδίᾳ. [71] μετανοέω thus approximates to ἐπιστρέφω = שׁוּב, the OT tt. for religious and ethical conversion. In the three prophetic passages it also refers not merely to the individual case of penitent change of mind but to an alteration in total attitude, to the relation to God which embraces the whole of life, to a change in nature which results from a reorientation brought about by God (Ιερ. 38:18 f.).

On the basis of the religious concepts of the OT it is thus easy for μετανοέω to take on in the LXX a religious and ethical sense which, with its connotation of a lasting change, is far removed from the secular understanding.

In the extant fragments of later Gk. transl. of the OT there are clear traces of a complete equation of μετανοέω and שׁוּב. [72] In 6 cases where שׁוּב means "to convert" in the religious sense Σ transl. it by μετανοέω, Is. 31:6; 55:7; Jer. 18:8; [73] Ez. 33:12; Hos. 11:5; Job 36:10 (LXX always ἐπιστρέφομαι or ἀποστρέφω). The same is true of 'Α (Σ?) at Ps. 7:12 and Ε' Hos. 7:10.

The linguistic material leads to the conclusion that for the Jewish Hellenistic world of the 2nd cent. A.D. μετανοέω was a common and even preferred equivalent of ἐπιστρέφομαι = שׁוּב, "to turn," "to convert."

---

69 Cf. Dietrich, 223 f.

70 The LXX presupposes שְׁבִיִי for שׁוּבִי.

71 [G. Bertram:] In Is. 46:8 הָשִׁיבוּ עַל־לֵב is rendered twice: μετανοήσατε ... ἐπιστρέψατε τῇ καρδίᾳ, so strongly did the translator feel the two terms to be related. The Hexapla translators apparently avoided rendering נחם by μετανοεῖν or ἐπιστρέφειν. 'Α regularly uses παρακαλεῖν in the sense "to let oneself be persuaded." This anthropopathic concept is esp. avoided where the ref. is to the נחם of God. παρακαλεῖν is common in the LXX too for נחם, which contains esp. the idea of consolation. Cf. on this G. B. Mitchell, "A Note on the Hebrew Root נחם," ExpT, 44 (1932/3), 428. In the LXX μετανοεῖν and ἐπιστρέφειν were gradually taking on the positive sense "to convert"; this is shown clearly by the opposite development of the synon. μεταβάλλειν in 4 Macc. As med. μεταβάλλειν means "to change one's mind," and it occurs in this sense in Est. 5:1e; Ac. 28:6; cf. also the noun μεταβολή in 3 Macc. 5:40, 42. In just the same way as μετανοεῖν, μεταβάλλειν is used of God in Job 10:8, 16. In the first case it represents a form of סבב (conjecture), in the second it occurs twice for שׁוּב. In Ign. Mg., 10, 2 the meaning is "to convert." The verb has the same sense as the μετανοεῖν of the Gospels in the preaching of Barn., Ps.-Cl. Hom., I, 7. In 3 and esp. 4 Macc., however, μεταβάλλειν is used *in malam partem*. Cf. 3 Macc. 1:3: ὕστερον δὲ μεταβαλὼν τὰ νόμιμα, or 4 Macc. 6:18, 24; 15:14. Here it means "to turn aside," "to become apostate." In 4 Macc. there may be some influence of the Stoic view which finds its ideal in the rejection of remorse or change of mind, → 980. For here μεταβάλλειν in the negative is used of the inflexible attitude of the Maccabean martyrs. In secular Gk. μεταβάλλειν and μεταδοξάζειν are used only intellectually. μετάθεσις is used in 2 Macc. 11:24 and μεταδιαιτᾶν in 4 Macc. 8:8 for the going over to a Hellenistic mode of life by the Jews. Materially the words are thus related to μεταβάλλειν in the negative, though apparently in the Hell. sense with no moral or religious implication. In 1 Εσδρ. 1:48 μετακαλεῖν is "to summon to repentance" (Mas. 2 Ch. 36:15 different). In 1:45 ἐντρέπειν ("to turn") is used for כנע ("to humble"). ἐντρέπειν often occurs alongside μετανοεῖν in the OT.

72 Cf. Field and the relevant refs.

73 On the other hand Σ at v. 8b and elsewhere does not have μετανοέω for נִחַם (like the LXX).

2. μετάνοια. The LXX does not use μετάνοια in transl. of the Heb. OT. At Prv. 14:15 : ἄκακος πιστεύει παντὶ λόγῳ, πανοῦργος δὲ ἔρχεται εἰς μετάνοιαν, the second clause does not correspond to the Heb. וְעָרוּם יָבִין לַאֲשֻׁרוֹ. If we are to read לְתִשׁוּבָה לַאֲשֻׁרוֹ,[74] the rendering εἰς μετάνοιαν would still be puzzling, for μετάνοια does not correspond to the Heb. term in this sense. Only an insight gained elsewhere, namely, that μετάνοια served as a rendering of תְּשׁוּבָה in the post-OT sense of conversion (→ 995 f.), enables us to conjecture that μετάνοια is here used mechanically and meaninglessly for תְּשׁוּבָה. But the basic text is uncertain and does not form a solid reason for concluding that the Gk. term changed its meaning.

In Σ Is. 30:15 μετάνοια corresponds to שׁוּבָה in the sense of religious and moral conversion. For this translator the noun shares the same shift of meaning as the verb, → 990.

II. Other Literature.

1. Apocrypha and Pseudepigrapha.

The OT apocr. and pseudepigr. give evidence of the break-through for which the way was prepared in the OT. The predominant sense of μετανοέω is now "to convert"[75] and of μετάνοια "conversion." Sir. 48:15 has μετανοέω for שׁוּב; Heb. לֹא שָׁב הָעָם וְלֹא חָדְלוּ מֵחַטֹּאתָם, Gk. οὐ μετενόησεν ὁ λαὸς καὶ οὐκ ἀπέστησαν ἀπὸ τῶν ἁμαρτιῶν αὐτῶν. In view of the fragmentary nature of Heb. Sir., this is the only instance ; at 5:7; 21:6; 48:10 ἐπιστρέφω occurs for שׁוּב. But the fact that the Gk. translator uses both terms for שׁוּב with no recognisable distinction shows clearly what meaning he attaches to μετανοέω. Test. XII is the work in which μετανοέω is most common, and here again, as in Sir. (cf. 17:24 f., 29), ἐπιστρέφω and μετανοέω stand in synon. parallelism in the religious and moral sense "to convert" (cf. Test. Zeb. 9:7 β[76] with N. 4:3, B. 5:1 with 5:4 etc.). How common μετανοέω was in this sense among Jewish Gk. writers between 200 B.C. and 100 A.D. may be seen also from Test. A. 1:6 : κἂν ἁμάρτῃ, εὐθὺς μετανοεῖ, G. 6:3 β : ἐὰν ὁμολογήσας μετανοήσῃ, ἄφες αὐτῷ, ibid., 6:6; 7:5; 5:6 : μετὰ τὸ μετανοῆσαί με περὶ Ἰωσήφ, R. 1:9; S. 2:13; Jos. 6:6; Jud. 15:4; Prayer of Man. 13 : σὺ εἶ, κύριε, ὁ θεὸς τῶν μετανοούντων. μετάνοια too, like the verb, has now the main sense of "conversion." Cf. Sir. 44:16 (of Enoch): ὑπόδειγμα μετανοίας[77] ταῖς γενεαῖς, Wis. 11:23 : παρορᾷς ἁμαρτήματα ἀνθρήπων εἰς μετάνοιαν, 12:10 : ἐδίδους τόπον μετανοίας,[78] cf. v. 19 : διδοῖς ἐπὶ ἁμαρτήμασιν μετάνοιαν, Test. G. 5:7 : ἡ γὰρ κατὰ Θεὸν ἀληθὴς μετάνοια ... φυγαδεύει τὸ σκότος, R. 2:1; Jud. 19:2; Prayer of Man. 8 : σὺ οὖν, κύριε, ὁ θεὸς τῶν δικαίων, οὐκ ἔθου μετάνοιαν δικαίοις ..., ἀλλ' ἔθου μετάνοιαν ἐμοὶ τῷ ἁμαρτωλῷ, Sib., 1, 128 f. (God's Word to Noah); ibid., 1, 167 ff. (Noah's preaching of conversion); 4, 162 f., 166-170; also Ep. Ar., 188 (where the king is counselled to imitate God): μακροθυμίᾳ γὰρ χρώμενος καὶ βλιμάζων τοὺς ἀξίους ἐπιεικέστερον, καθώς εἰσιν ἄξιοι, μετατιθεὶς ἐκ τῆς κακίας [καὶ] εἰς μετάνοιαν ἄξεις.[79]

Under the terms μετανοέω and μετάνοια the OT religious and moral concept of

---

[74] Cf. BHK, ad loc. → n. 44.
[75] With "to rue," Wis. 5:3; Prayer of Man. 7.
[76] Note the variant readings β and α : μετανοήσετε-ἐπιστρέψετε.
[77] Interpretation of אוֹת דַּעַת, cf. A. Schlatter, "Das neugefundene hbr. Stück des Sir." BFTh, I, 5/6 (1897), 127.
[78] Cf. S. Bar. 85:12 and the notes in B. Violet, "Die Apokalypsen d. Esr. u. Bar. in deutscher Gestalt" (GCS, 32 [1924]), 334.
[79] Also Ass. Mos. 1:18 : in diem paenitentiae suggests an original μετάνοια.

conversion (→ B.) returns.[80] Echoes from the prophetic call for conversion are heard again. The core is a total change in the relation to God as a gift and task from God. Cf. Pray. Man. esp. v. 7 (longer rec.):[81] σὺ εἶ κύριος ... μετανοῶν ἐπὶ ταῖς κακίαις τῶν ἀνθρώπων· ὅτι σύ, ὁ θεός, κατὰ τὴν χρηστότητα τῆς ἀγαθωσύνης σου ἐπηγγείλω μετανοίας ἄφεσιν τοῖς ἡμαρτηκόσιν, καὶ τῷ πλήθει τῶν οἰκτιρμῶν σου ὥρισας μετάνοιαν ἁμαρτωλοῖς εἰς σωτηρίαν. The God who judges with grace those who turn (Prayer of Man. 13) overlooks the sins of men in order that they may do so (Wis. 11:23). He leads to conversion (cf. Ep. Ar., 188). He grants μετάνοια (Wis. 12:19; Prayer of Man. 8; Sib., 4, 168). He makes space for it (Wis. 12:10). His rule in history (Sir. 48:14 f.) in goodness (Wis. 11:23; 12:18 ff.; cf. Ep. Ar., 188) and severity (Wis. 12:10) aims at μετάνοια. In heaven a special angel, Phanuel, is set over the conversion to hope of those who are to inherit eternal life (Eth. En. 40:9). The stronger emphasis on turning from sin (Sir. 48:15; Wis. 12:19; Test. S. 2:13 f.; Sib., 1, 168 ff.) as compared with turning to God (Sir. 17:24-26) is also in keeping with the prophetic demand for conversion (*v.* Ez.). God has instituted μετάνοια for sinners rather than the righteous (Prayer of Man. 8). As in the story of the Bible (Sir. 44:16; Test. G. 6:3 etc.; cf. Vit. Ad. 4 ff., 27), so now (Sir. 17:24; Prayer of Man. 8), it is for individuals. But it is for all (Wis. 11:23; Sib., 1, 128), for the people (Sir. 48:15; Wis. 12:19; Test. Zeb. 9:7 β; cf. Ass. Mos. 1:18). Doubts are still heard as to whether it will be effective, concern whether the mind of man will truly change (Wis. 12:10). But the genuine prophetic concept tends to yield to the moralising of Jewish piety, to the increasing development of legalism. The goal is still an alteration of the whole of moral conduct, a change of disposition, e.g., Test. G. 6:3, 6; A. 1:6; S. 2:13; 3:4). But according to the casuistic ethics commonly taught to turn is to cease from individual sins and to obey individual commandments, e.g., to leave off licentiousness (Test. R. 1:9; Jud. 15:4; Jos. 6:6), jealousy (Test. S. 2:13), avarice (Test. Jud. 19:2), hatred (Test. G. 5:6 ff.), contempt for the righteous (Test. B. 5:4), and to turn to the fulfilment of the corresponding positive commandments (e.g., Test. R. 4:1; S. 3:5; G. 5:2 ff.; B. 5:2 f.). Conversion is the presupposition of deliverance (Sir. 17:24; Vit. Ad. 4:6; cf. 4 Esr. 7:82).[82] It is an external achievement of man which is necessary to salvation and whose achievement can be promoted by customary or selected cultic and ritual forms, e.g., penance or penitential exercises to pay for offences committed or specific sins. Thus we find prayers of lamentation (Test. S. 2:13), confession of sin (Ps. Sol. 9:6 f.; Prayer of Man. 9 ff.; Test. G. 6:3; Apc. Mos. 32) accompanied by self-imposed punishments of varying severity, fasting (→ νῆστις), asceticism etc. (Test. S. 3:4; R. 1:9 f.; Jud. 15:4; 19:2; Apc. Mos. 32; cf. Vit. Ad. 4 ff., 17). A petty legalistic zeal for penance tends to crowd out the great concept of a conversion embracing man's whole being, cf. Test. A. 1:6 : When the soul sins, εὐθὺς μετανοεῖ, also Wis. 12:19. On true and godly μετάνοια — there may also be a false — is grounded assurance of salvation: φυγαδεύει τὸ σκότος, καὶ φωτίζει τοὺς ὀφθαλμοὺς καὶ γνῶσιν παρέχει τῇ ψυχῇ, καὶ ὁδηγεῖ τὸ διαβούλιον πρὸς σωτηρίαν (Test. G. 5:7, cf. 8). Jub. 1:23 gives the promise: "And then they will turn to me with all sincerity, with all their heart and soul" (cf. 1:15), and Ass. Mos. 1:18 contains the expectation of a *dies paenitentiae in respectu quo respiciet illos Dominus in consummatione exitus dierum.* Here in an eschatological connection conversion again seems to be regarded in the prophetic sense as a gift and work of God for Israel (cf. Ps. Sol. 18:4 f.; Jub. 23:26 ff.). Before the coming of the Messiah to establish the royal dominion of God there is a final period of grace to allow Israel to turn back to God. At any rate the concept of conversion in the Jewish lit. consulted in this section is also related to the final goal of faith and hope.

---

[80] Cf. Dietrich, 242-286 and Sjöberg, 212 ff., 250 ff. for a full discussion. Only a sketch of the thoughts expressed in μετανοέω and μετάνοια is given in this art.

[81] Preserved in Const. Ap., II, 22, 12.

[82] Perhaps also Slav. En. 42:10 : "Blessed is he who turns from the fickle (crooked?) way of this vain world and takes the straight way which leads to eternal life."

2. Philo.[83]

Even the linguistic understanding of μετανοέω and μετάνοια in Philo displays the synthesis of Gk. culture and Jewish religion which is a general mark of this Alexandrian Jew. Philo uses the terms in the same sense as the Gk. world around him for "change of mind" or "repentance" (→ 976 f.). Cf. on the one side Leg. All., II, 60 f., where the μετανοεῖν of the wise is "reconsideration," or Deus Imm., 33, where the alteration of God's judgment or purpose, μεταγινώσκειν in 21, is described as μετάνοια,[84] or Fr. (ed. P. Wendland [1891], 86): ἀποδεξάμενος δὲ αὐτῶν τὴν μετάνοιαν, and on the other side Vit. Mos., I, 167; Virt., 152 and 208; Spec. Leg., IV, 18 and 221; Leg. Gaj., 303: μετανοεῖ ἐπὶ τοῖς πεπραγμένοις, cf. 337 and 339, where μετανοέω and μετάνοια denote the feelings of remorse in man. Nor is Philo distinguished from other Hell. authors by his ethical evaluation of penitence, e.g., Leg. All., III, 211; Det. Pot. Ins., 95 f. But the religious flavour which he also gives to penitence (cf. Sacr. AC, 132 etc.: μετάνοια ἁμαρτημάτων) is an indication of the Jewish influence on his thinking. The predominant use of both noun and verb for "conversion" in the religious and moral sense also makes it plain that for all the lapses into popular usage Philo's understanding of the words is decisively determined by the specific emphasis which they had already been given in Judaism. The tractate περὶ μετανοίας in Virt., 175-186 discusses the conversion of the Gentiles to Judaism. In many other places, too, μετάνοια or μετανοέω denotes a full change in being and conduct, cf. Praem. Poen., 15: μετάνοια ... ζήλῳ δὲ καὶ ἔρωτι τοῦ βελτίονος ἐξαίφνης κατασχεθεῖσα καὶ σπεύδουσα καταλιπεῖν μὲν τὴν σύντροφον πλεονεξίαν καὶ ἀδικίαν, μεθορμίσασθαι δὲ πρὸς σωφροσύνην καὶ δικαιοσύνην καὶ τὰς ἄλλας ἀρετάς, Abr., 26: μετάνοια is the second stage next to perfection; as ἀπό τινος χρόνου βελτίωσις it is ἴδιον ἀγαθὸν εὐφυοῦς ψυχῆς ἀδροτέροις καὶ ἀνδρὸς ὄντως φρονήμασιν ἐπιζητούσης εὔδιον κατάστασιν [ψυχῆς] καὶ τῇ φαντασίᾳ τῶν καλῶν ἐπιτρεχούσης, Spec. Leg., I, 187: The gracious God values μετάνοια as highly as μηδὲ ἁμαρτάνειν, Poster. C., 178: ἡμεῖς ... ὥσπερ ἐκ κλύδωνος ἀνανηξάμενοι λαβώμεθα μετανοίας, ἐχυροῦ καὶ σωτηρίου πράγματος, καὶ μὴ πρότερον μεθώμεθα ἢ κατὰ τὸ παντελὲς τὸ κυμαῖνον πέλαγος, τὴν φορὰν τῆς τροπῆς διεκδῦναι, Deus Imm., 8: ὑπομενεῖ δέ τις τῷ θεῷ προσελθεῖν ἀκάθαρτος ὢν ψυχὴν τὴν ἑαυτοῦ τῷ καθαρωτάτῳ καὶ ταῦτα μὴ μέλλων μετανοήσειν, Spec. Leg., I, 236: The sinner has achieved μετάνοια, οὐχ ὑποσχέσει ἀλλ' ἔργοις, Som., I, 91. μετανοέω and μετάνοια are in Philo the proper terms for the concept of religious and moral conversion; the synon. → ἐπιστρέφω (Jos., 87) and ἐπιστροφή (cf. Jos. Ant., 2, 293), μεταβάλλω (Abr., 17 etc.) and μεταβολή (*loc. cit.*), βελτιοῦμαι (Jos., 88, cf. 87) and βελτίωσις (Abr., 17) etc. are less prominent. In no non-Christian author of antiquity are μετανοέω and μετάνοια so common as in Philo. The noun is used even more frequently than the verb, in keeping with the theoretical and abstract character of Philo's world of religious thought, which derives its vocabulary in this instance from the LXX and the modes of expression of Hell. Judaism.

What Philo denotes by μετάνοια or μετανοέω is the OT and Jewish concept of conversion, namely, radical turning to God (Virt., 179 f.; Spec. Leg., I, 309, 51), turning from sin (Virt., 177; Fug., 99 and 158; Leg. All., III, 106), change of nature (Praem. Poen., 15 → *supra*; Spec. Leg., I, 253). To turn from the many false gods to the one true God is the first and most essential part of μετάνοια (Virt., 179 f.; Spec. Leg., I, 51, cf. 58). To turn from sin is to draw a line under past sins (Virt., 176 f.; Fug., 157) and to sin no more (Fug., 160; Deus Imm., 8 f.). Part of μετάνοια is that the penitent

---

[83] On the usage cf. Leisegang, *s.v.*; Dietrich, 287 ff.; on content, cf. Windisch, *Taufe u. Sünde,* 54 ff.; also J. S. Boughton, *The Idea of Progress in Philo Judaeus* (Diss. Phil. New York, Columbia Univ. [1932], 154 ff.); esp. Dietrich 291 ff. and W. Völker, "Fortschritt u. Vollendung bei Philo v. Al.," TU, 49, 1 (1938), 105 ff., 339.

[84] Though cf. Vit. Mos., I, 283: οὐδ' ὡς υἱὸς ἀνθρώπου μετανοεῖ (sc. ὁ θεός), cf. Deus Imm., 72.

sinner (Leg. All., III, 211; Jos., 87) should publicly confess his sin in common worship (Exsecr., 163; Leg. All., II, 78; Som., I, 90 f.) and thus attain forgiveness (Exsecr., 163). Conversion is no longer turning from individual sins (Spec. Leg., I, 102 f., 238; Jos., 87; Leg. All., III, 106); it affects the whole man (Mut. Nom., 124; Sobr., 62). The reality of life must correspond at once to the reconstruction of mind. A sinless walk must replace the former sinning, cf. the fixed terms μηκέτι and ἀμεταστρεπτί (Abr., 19; Poster. C., 95; Ebr., 71; Migr. Abr., 25; Virt., 181 etc.). Without conversion there is no salvation, no rewarding with the prizes of victory (Virt., 175 and 184 f.; Det. Pot. Ins., 95; Spec. Leg., I, 239 and 253). μετάνοια is a task for man (Leg. All., III, 106; Spec. Leg., I, 236; Poster. C., 178; Leg. All., II, 78; Det. Pot. Ins., 96). But God helps by giving opportunity (Leg. All., III, 106 and 211 ff.; Praem. Poen., 117 and 119; Deus Imm., 116; Som., II, 25). What Philo finely says about conversion is much in line with Jewish thinking (→ 991 f.), but in his exposition he uses alien expressions which Hell. philosophy and mysticism introduce into meditations controlled by the OT. He depicts conversion as a fulfilment of the ideal of the Stoic sage; it is "becoming good in time." [85] As the shadow accompanies the body, so the garland of virtues necessarily follows the true knowledge of God with which μετάνοια begins (Virt., 181: πᾶσαν τὴν τῶν ἄλλων ἀρετῶν κοινωνίαν): the μετανοῶν turns from ignorance to knowledge, from lack of understanding to perception, from license to restraint, from unrighteousness to righteousness, from cowardice to bravery (*ibid.*, 180 ff.; Praem. Poen., 15, → 993). Conversion is a break with vice and a walk on the path of virtue (Cher., 2; cf. Leg. All., II, 60 f.), a radical change ἀπὸ χείρονος βίου πρὸς τὸν ἀμείνω (Abr., 17; cf. Som., II, 105 ff.). It brings harmony into the discord of thought and word; it brings resolution and action (Virt., 183 f.; cf. Praem. Poen., 81). It frees the soul from the shackles of sensuality (Praem. Poen., 15 ff.), purifies it, and opens for it access to God (Mut. Nom., 124; cf. Deus Imm., 8 f.; Rer. Div. Her., 6 f.; Spec. Leg., I, 201). Conversion is not a prolonged, gradual, progressive process; it is a sudden, once-for-all event (Praem. Poen., 15, → 993), an amendment which is there from a given moment onwards (Abr., 26, → 993). The perfect man reeds no amendment; over against him stands Enoch as the type of μετάνοια καὶ βελτίωσις: τοῦ βίου τὸν μὲν πρότερον χρόνον ἀναθεὶς κακίᾳ, τὸν δὲ ὕστερον ἀρετῇ, πρὸς ἣν μετανέστη καὶ μετῳκίσατο (Abr., 47; cf. 17; Praem. Poen., 17 f.). Enoch is also a type of the wise; in antithesis to the Stoic teaching that the sage does not need μετάνοια (→ 980) Philo takes the view: τὸ μὲν μηδὲν ἁμαρτεῖν ἴδιον θεοῦ, τὸ δὲ μετανοεῖν σοφοῦ (Fug., 157; cf. Virt., 177; Abr., 26, → 993; Leg. All., II, 60). μετάνοια is close to perfection, like convalescence to health (Virt., 176). But he who needs μετάνοια is below him who has not sinned at all (Som., I, 91). The μετανοήσας has become perfect and spotless, and must remain so to have and to hold the bliss of spiritual fellowship with God (Rer. Div. Her., 93). In Philo, then, the OT and Jewish concept of conversion takes from Hellenism elements not only of moral philosophy but also of religious syncretism. Nevertheless, it maintains its distinctive flavour as nowhere else either before or after. [86]

3. Josephus. [87]

The linguistic data are the same as in Philo. Both μετανοέω and μετάνοια are common in the traditional sense of "change of mind" (Ant., 5, 151; 12, 273; Vit., 17;

---

[85] Windisch, *Taufe u. Sünde*, 59, cf. 54.

[86] At best one might adduce Corp. Herm., I, 28: Τί ἑαυτούς, ὦ ἄνδρες [γηγενεῖς], εἰς θάνατον ἐκδεδώκατε, ἔχοντες ἐξουσίαν τῆς ἀθανασίας μεταλαβεῖν; μετανοήσατε, οἱ συνοδεύσαντες τῇ πλάνῃ καὶ συγκοινωνήσαντες τῇ ἀγνοίᾳ· ἀπαλλάγητε τοῦ σκότ[ειν]ου<ς, ἅψασθε τοῦ> φωτός· μεταλάβετε τῆς ἀθανασίας, καταλείψαντες τὴν φθοράν. On the Jewish syncretistic character of this preaching of conversion cf. Norden, 139; Meyer Ursprung, II, 371 ff.; Wnd. 2 K., 233; C. H. Dodd, *The Bible and the Greeks* (1935), 180 f., 183 ff.; also the profound observations of J. Kroll, *Die Lehren d. Hermes Trismegistos* (1914), 376, n. 3.

[87] Cf. the material and appraisal in Dietrich, 306 ff.

Bell., 1, 10; 3, 127 f.; 5, 360; Ap., 1, 274 etc.) and "repentance" (Ant., 10, 123; 2, 315; 4, 195; 6, 143; Vit., 113; Ant., 4, 191; Bell., 4, 367; 2, 203; 7, 378; Ant., 5, 166; 7, 54 : οὐ γὰρ ἔσεσθαι μετάνοιαν αὐτοῖς ἐκ τοῦ τοιούτου etc.). The "change of mind" is usually an alteration of will or purpose which is then translated into action, e.g., Vit., 110 and 370; so also the giving up of evil or ungodly plans, Ant., 2, 23 : ἀποστάντας ... τῆς πράξεως ἀγαπήσει (sc. ὁ θεός) μετανοίᾳ καὶ τῷ σωφρονεῖν εἴξαντας. As distinct from popular usage, but in line with Jewish Hellenistic, Jos. also likes to use μετανοέω and μετάνοια for the concept of religious and moral conversion, e.g., Bell., 5, 415 : καταλείπεται δὲ ὅμως ἔτι σωτηρίας ὁδός, ἐὰν θέλητε, καὶ τὸ θεῖον εὐδιάλλακτον ἐξομολογουμένοις καὶ μετανοοῦσιν, Ant., 4, 142 (of Moses): μὴ βουλόμενος εἰς ἀπόνοιαν περιστῆσαι τοὺς ἐκ τοῦ λανθάνειν μετανοῆσαι δυναμένους, explained as follows, *ibid.*, 144 : ἐπειρᾶτο τοὺς νέους ἐπανορθοῦν καὶ εἰς μετάνοιαν ἄγειν ὧν ἔπραττον (to turning from what impelled them, idolatry etc.); Ant., 9, 168; 10, 60 : No disaster or prophetic admonition could bring the people to conversion.

The statements of Jos. about conversion are not profound and echo common thoughts. His view is orientated to the OT, and lessons are drawn from OT examples (Ant., 7, 153 and 320; 10, 53; 2, 23, → *supra* ; 4, 142 and 144, → *supra*). Jos. does not proclaim the prophetic concept. He is a Jew of the Law and understands conversion legalistically, cf. Ant., 11, 156. Individual transgressions must cease and the Law must be scrupulously obeyed. Behind the avoidance of relapse into earlier sins (φυλακὴν τοῦ μηδὲν ὅμοιον συμπεσεῖν, Ant., 11, 156) is the positive turning to God (cf. Bell., 5, 377), behind the casuistry of prohibitions [88] the designation of the goal of the new life, e.g., Ant., 4, 191. Importance is attached to ritual penance in the ancient forms (Ant., 2, 107 f.; 4, 195; 8, 362; 11, 156) and to confession of sin (Ant., 7, 153; 8, 256 f., 362; Bell., 5, 415, → *supra*). Not to convert brings down the punishment of God (Ant., 10, 60). Conversion is the sure way to God's good-pleasure (Bell., 5, 415, → *supra*; Ant., 9, 176 : ὁ δὲ θεὸς καὶ τὴν μετάνοιαν ὡς ἀρετὴν ἀποδεχόμενος ...), which is expressed in His causing things to go well with us (Ant., 7, 153; 8, 257; 10, 60).

D. Conversion in Rabbinic Literature.

In essence, only the content of Jewish Hell. writings enables us to conclude that the OT concept of religious and moral conversion passed over into Judaism. When we turn to Rabb. writings, however, this fact also finds linguistic expression. [89] For in the new Heb. of these works the verb שׁוּב, though not very common and mostly in the abs., retains the OT sense "to turn," "to be converted." Cf. Ab., 2, 10b (R. Eliezer): שׁוּב יוֹם אֶחָד לִפְנֵי מִיתָתְךָ, "turn a day before thy death," or Shemone Esre, 5th petition (Palestinian recension) [90] (= Lam. 5:21): הֲשִׁיבֵנוּ יְיָ אֵלֶיךָ וְנָשׁוּבָה, "bring us back, Yahweh, to thyself, that we may convert." The real tt. for religious conversion in new Heb. is the noun תְּשׁוּבָה, which in the OT does not occur in this sense, [91] but which must have taken on this sense in Judaism quite early, i.e., certainly in the pre-Christian period. This is supported by its fixed use in this sense both in the Rabb. and also in the earliest texts e.g., Shemone Esre, 5th petition (Pal. recension): [92] בָּרוּךְ אַתָּה הָרוֹצֶה

[88] Cf. Schl. Theol. d. Judt., 131 ff.

[89] Cf. Levy Wört., 4, 516, 675, 678; Levy Chald. Wört., 2, 531 and 566; Dalman Wört.[2], 416 and 450 f.; Dietrich, 316 ff.

[90] Dalman WJ[1], I, 299.

[91] Though cf. at Is. 30:15 שׁוּבָה in the same sense (→ n. 44; 991). This verse is often adduced by the Rabb. in proof of what is said about תְּשׁוּבָה, cf. the quotation from Tanch., → 996.

[92] Dalman WJ[1], *loc. cit.*

בִּתְשׁוּבָה, "blessed be thou who takest pleasure in conversion," *ibid.* (Babylonian recension):[93] הַחֲזִירֵנוּ בִּתְשׁוּבָה שְׁלֵמָה לְפָנֶיךָ, "turn us to perfect conversion before thy countenance"; Tanch. (Buber) בחקתי § 5 (56a): R. Eliezer says: אם ישראל עושים תשובה נגאלים, "when Israel converts, it will be redeemed" (Is. 30:15 is then adduced in support). In Damasc., 9, 15 B (Kl. T., 167, p. 29, 16) the community of the new covenant in Damascus calls itself בְּרִית תְּשׁוּבָה, the covenant of conversion. In Jewish Gk. "conversion" is equally firmly embedded as the meaning of μετάνοια from the time of the LXX (→ 991, 993, 995). This in itself is an indication that at least some of the Jewish authors and translators were acquainted with a corresponding Heb. noun. The abstract noun תְּשׁוּבָה seems to have controlled Rabb. terminology for the concept of conversion to such a degree that the newly coined expression עָשָׂה תְּשׁוּבָה more or less replaced the simple verb שׁוּב. For עָשָׂה תְּשׁוּבָה means the same as שׁוּב, "to turn." The עָשָׂה does not indicate penitential achievement on man's part.[94] The new phrase expresses for the Rabb. exactly the same as the older שׁוּב. Rabb. exegetes discussing Jer. 3:22 (שׁוּבוּ) use עָשָׂה תְּשׁוּבָה (e.g., T. Yoma, 5, 6 ff., R. Jishmael;[95] bSanh., 97b, R. Eliezer).[96] In Yoma, 8, 9a we find the two: "If anyone says: I will sin and turn again (אָשׁוּב) . . ., the power will not be given him (by God) to turn (לַעֲשׂוֹת תְּשׁוּבָה) etc." The corresponding Aram. terms are תּוּב, תְּתוּבְתָּא,[97] עֲבַד תְּתוּבְתָּא. They, too, acquired their technical sense in the pre-Christian period. It is thus highly probable that the Heb. or Aram. equivalents for μετανοέω and μετάνοια in the Palestine of the NT period were (שׁוּב), תְּשׁוּבָה, עָשָׂה תְּשׁוּבָה or (תּוּב), תְּתוּבְתָּא, עֲבַד תְּתוּבְתָּא. And the concept which they express is unequivocally "conversion," "to convert," not "penance," "to do penance."[98]

The doctrine of conversion was much discussed in Rabb. theology. To more than one Rabbi it was an inner religious concern and not just a theme for pettifogging rational reflection. Nowhere was it developed systematically. Various intersecting lines of thought are to be found. But in the light of their origin they are seen to have the same motifs of faith and thought. In the following sketch the older Rabb. writings are, if possible, consulted first.[99]

גדולה תשובה ("great is conversion") — this is a statement which echoes through the Rabb. writings (bYoma, 86a b etc.).[100] Conversion is lavishly extolled: "Better is an hour in conversion and good works in this world than the whole life of the future world" (Ab., 4, 17, R. Jaaqob).[101] How highly the saving significance of תְּשׁוּבָה is esteemed may be seen from the fact that it is among the seven things created before the foundation of the world, and that it comes first next to the Torah (bNed., 39b, Bar.; bPes., 54a, Bar.). "The gates of conversion are always open" (Dt. r., 2 on 3:24). The ungodly and lukewarm can become converts (בעלי תשובה) (jRH, 57a, 49, R. Jochanan b. Nappacha); so, too, can the righteous who have committed a sin (bBer., 19a, school of R. Jishmael). This applies to Jews; Gentiles who are not proselytes are excluded

---

93 *Ibid.*, 302.

94 So Dirksen, 141 in spite of Moore, I, 508; III, 155, n. 220.

95 Cf. Str.-B., I, 169.

96 *Ibid.*, 163.

97 Cf. also S. Bar. 85:12.

98 So rightly Dietrich, 321 and 324 ff. on the basis of his comprehensive and careful examination of Rabb. usage; this is confirmed by Damasc. (→ *supra*; cf. also Sjöberg, 258 ff.).

99 For a full presentation and evaluation of the material cf. Moore, I, 323 ff., 507 ff. and Dietrich, 350-457.

100 Str.-B., I, 165 f.

101 Dietrich, 443.

(Pesikt., 156a/b).[102] The prevailing view of תְּשׁוּבָה is legal. To convert is to turn from wicked works (Pesikt., 153b; bBer., 10a, R. Meir), from violations of the Law. Part of it is a public act which shows that one has broken with the past (bSanh., 25b:[103] dicers should break their little stones and stop playing even without money; those who lend for usury should tear up their promissory notes and cease lending even to non-Israelites etc.). Restitution should be made, e.g., in cases of theft, robbery, usury (bBQ, 94b;[104] bTaan., 16a, R. Shemuel).[105] This is a perfect conversion (תְּשׁוּבָה שְׁלֵמָה, Shemone Esre, 5th petition, Bab. rec., → 995 f. etc.) as distinct from what was later called false conversion (תשובה של רמיות, *v.* Gn. r., 9, 6 on 1:31; jTaan., 65b, 27 ff.).[106] But conversion is also expressed in penitential prayer (bSanh., 103a, R. Jochanan in the name of R. Shimon b. Jochai). Genuine conversion is shown to be inner conversion (T. Yoma, 5, 6, R. Jishmael)[107] by confession of sin (Lv. r., 10, 5 on 8:2, R. Jehuda b. Chiyya;[108] Tanch. [Buber] חקת § 46 [63b];[109] cf. Midr. Ps. 92 § 7 [203b, 1]: "Everyone who confesses and forsakes sins" will be "delivered from the judgment of Gehinnom")[110] and in prayer for forgiveness of sins (bYoma, 86b, Bar., R. Meir;[111] Midr. Ps. 32 § 2 [121b], R. Jose b. Jehuda).[112] The OT idea that conversion is turning from evil and supremely turning to God finds pale echoes in Rabb. Judaism, e.g., in the Pal. rec. of the 5th petition of the Shemone Esre: "Bring us back, Yahweh, to thyself, that we may convert" (→ 995 f.), also in the Bab. rec.:[113] "Bring us back, our Father, to thy Torah (לְתוֹרָתֶךָ) ... and turn us to perfect conversion before thy countenance" (→ 995 f.). Only rarely do we find a statement like that of Abba bar Zabdai (jTaan., 65a, 57 f.): "Then we lift up our hearts to God in heaven." The positive side of conversion is obedience to the Law as an expression of the will of God. It is the doing of good works.[114] Hence there is ref. not only to the yoke of the Law but also to the yoke of conversion (עולה של תשובה, bAZ, 5a; bMQ, 16b). We find awareness that God must effect conversion, e.g., Shemone Esre, 5th petition, → 995 f.; T. Ber., 7, 4: "Convert the heart of those who worship (i.e., idolaters) that they may serve thee."[115] But even stronger is the conviction that man must achieve conversion, e.g., S. Nu., 27, 12 § 134: R. Jehuda bBaba puts on God's lips the saying: "Convert and I will receive you"; Tanch. (Buber) בחקתי § 5 (56a) → 995 f.; jBer., 8a, 49 (in R. Shemuel's short version of the Prayer of Eighteen Petitions): "Let our conversion please thee";[116] jTaan., 63d, 59 ff.;[117] Midr. Ps. 32 § 2 (121b): "When a man achieves perfect conversion, so that his heart is rooted in it, God forgives him."[118] תְּשׁוּבָה is a divinely given possibility which man realises; man acts first and then God. The synergism of human work and divine grace can change into the monergism of human achievement under the domination of a radical

---

102 Cf. Dietrich, 398 f. for individual Rabb. discussions of the possibility of Gentile conversion in the first and last times.

103 Str.-B., II, 250.

104 But here there is also clever evasion, Dietrich, 356 f.

105 Str.-B., I, 648.

106 *Loc. cit.*

107 *Ibid.*, 169; cf. jTaan., 65a, 57: Abba bar Zabdai (Dietrich, 452).

108 Dietrich, 449.

109 Str.-B., III, 776.

110 *Ibid.*, IV, 1069. Already in the days of Aqiba it was a disputed issue whether one should enumerate sins individually, *v.* jJoma, 45c, 34 (Str.-B., I, 113).

111 Str.-B., I, 166.

112 Dietrich, 444, cf. 353.

113 Dalman WJ[1], I, 302.

114 Cf. Dietrich, 360 f.

115 Str.-B., III, 150; Dietrich, 447.

116 Str.-B., IV, 222.

117 *Ibid.*, I, 162 f.

118 Dietrich, 444.

religion of Law. This achievement is sometimes thought of apart from penitential exercises. It is turning from sin rather than sackcloth and fasting, Taan., 2, 1; bTaan., 16a. Even where it takes the form of penitential sorrow the emphasis may be on prayer and amendment of life, Tanch. (Buber) בראשית § 23 (86 f.);[119] Midr. Ps. 14 § 5 (57a).[120] But there are also traces of a very different view which throws all the stress on the *opus operatum* of penitential exercises, Pirqe R. Eliezer, 43 : the example of the people of Nineveh ;[121] bAZ, 17a etc.: the meritorious penance of R. Eleazar bDurdaja ;[122] Gn. r., 65 on 27:23 : the self-torture of a fourfold capital punishment which a desecrator of the Sabbath imposes on himself. Different views may be seen in discussions of conversion and cultic expiation. Yoma, 8, 8, e.g., binds the expiatory power of the Day of Atonement to תְּשׁוּבָה, though this alone has less atoning power than the Day of Atonement. Later conversion is a condition for receiving atonement on the Day of Atonement, R. Jiṣhaq, Pesikt. r., 40 (169a);[123] Ex. r., 15 on 12:1 f.[124] Indeed, even without this relation to the cultus conversion is extolled as *the* means of salvation : "How far does an arrow usually fly when shot by a man ? The length of a field which brings one or two Kor. Great is the power of conversion ; for it extends to the throne of glory," Pesikt., 163b : R. Judan in the name of R. Shemuel b. Nachman.[125] Conversion is mostly regarded as something which will often be repeated in the life of a Jew, e.g., when the commandments are broken (T. Yoma, 5, 6),[126] on penitential days (jRH, 57a, 49),[127] etc. The necessity of daily conversion is emphatically recommended by R. Eliezer in his saying : "Turn a day before thy death" (Ab., 2, 10b), and also in his answer to the question of disciples whether a man may thus know the day of his death : "The more should he convert to-day, since he may die tomorrow, and so will be found in conversion his whole life long" (bShab., 153a).[128] This may bear a profound inward sense, but it can also be taken superficially and schematically ; hence the warning that "he who converts frequently" does not achieve forgiveness (Ab. R. Nat., 39).[129] By obstinate sinning man can forfeit the possibility of conversion and fall victim to the divine punishment of hardening, Yoma, 8, 9; Ex. r., 112 on 9:13, R. Pinchas bChama.[130] The blessing of conversion is the promise of future salvation for those who convert, Qoh. r. on 1:8, R. Shimon bChalaphta,[131] cf. bBer., 34b.[132] But it is also the promise of earthly fortune and the restoration of the Jewish state, jTaan., 65b, 5 ff., R. Eleazar : "When they turn, I will hear them from heaven . . . and heal their land."[133] Various answers were given to the question whether the conversion of Israel is a pre-condition of the coming of the Messiah. R. Eliezer b. Hyrcanos declared : "If Israel converts, it will be redeemed ; if it does not convert, it will not be redeemed," Tanch. (Buber) בחקתי § 5 (56a),[134] and he was followed by others like R. Eliezer (bSanh., 97b),[135] Shimon b. Laqish (Gn. r., 2 on 1:1 ff.: "In what merit does the Messiah come ? The answer is : In the merit of

---

[119] Cf. Weber, 321.
[120] Str.-B., IV, 1069.
[121] *Ibid.*, I, 647 f.
[122] Dietrich, 371.
[123] Str.-B., I, 169.
[124] *Ibid.*, IV, 474.
[125] *Ibid.*, I, 168.
[126] *Ibid.*, 169.
[127] *Ibid.*, 168.
[128] *Ibid.*, 165.
[129] *Ibid.*, 171, where the correct explanation is given : "Because he will not stop sinning."
[130] *Ibid.*, 172. Cf. the same statement in Midr. Ps. 1 § 22 (12b) (Str.-B., III, 690 on Midr. Ps. 1 § 22).
[131] Dietrich, 445.
[132] Str.-B., I, 167.
[133] *Ibid.*, 169.
[134] Dietrich, 430.
[135] Str.-B., I, 164.

conversion") [136] and the anon. jTaan., 64a, 19 ff., which expects from God morning for Israel and night for the nations of the world so soon as Israel sets aside the hindrance which holds up redemption, i.e., so soon as it converts. [137] But with Eliezer's partner in debate, R. Jehoshua b. Chananya (Tanch. → 998: "Whether they convert or not, as soon as the end has come, they will be redeemed"), many clung to the expectation that the coming of the Messiah stands under the norm, not of Israel's conversion, but of the times appointed in Da. 12:7. [138] Later the view is expressed that the Messiah will lead all the dwellers on earth to God through conversion (Cant. r., 7, 10 on 7:5). [139] Here finally the understanding of conversion as a human task and its understanding as a divine gift come together, though with no mutual adjustment.

The core of the concept of conversion is the same in the Rabbis as in the Jewish Hellenistic writings. Jewish theology and popular piety are at one in total outlook as the B.C. era closes and the A.D. period begins. We may thus conclude that, as sketched above, this leading doctrine, which a scholar like G. F. Moore calls "the Jewish doctrine of salvation," [140] enjoyed general validity in Palestine in the days of Jesus.

E. μετανοέω and μετάνοια in the New Testament.

I. The Linguistic Understanding.

Both words are most common in the Synoptic Gospels (μετανοέω 16 times, 9 in Lk.; μετάνοια 8 times, 5 in Lk.) and Ac. (verb 5 times, noun 6), cf. also μετανοέω 12 times in Rev. Paul uses the verb only once, the noun 4 times (once in Past.). Elsewhere μετάνοια is found 3 times in Hb. and once in 2 Pt.

The popular Gk. sense (→ A.) is most likely at Lk. 17:3 f., where μετανοεῖν denotes regret for a fault against one's brother, and 2 C. 7:9 f., where the combination with → μεταμέλομαι, → λύπη and → λυπέω suggests remorse (though → 1004 f.). Elsewhere the only possible meanings are "to change one's mind," "change of mind," or "to convert," "conversion." But the terms have religious and ethical significance along the lines of the OT and Jewish concept of conversion (→ B.-D.), for which there is no analogy in secular Greek. Again the NT use betrays certain peculiarities like the Jewish Hellenistic (μετανοέω synon. of → ἐπιστρέφω, Ac. 3:19; 26:20; [141] constr. with prep. ἀπό or ἐκ, Ac. 8:22; Rev. 2:21 f.; 9:20 f.; 16:11; Hb. 6:1; [142] constr. with εἰς, Ac. 20:21), [143] and rests on the underlying Aramaic, the speech of Jesus and primitive Palestinian Christianity. Hence the only apposite renderings are "to convert" and "conversion." What the religious language of the OT expressed by שׁוּב, and the theological terminology of the Rabbis by תְּשׁוּבָה, עָשָׂה תְשׁוּבָה or תְּתוּבְתָּא, עֲבַד תְּתוּבְתָּא, the NT, like the Jewish Hellenistic writings, expresses by μετανοέω and μετάνοια. This is no

136 *Loc. cit.*
137 *Loc. cit.*
138 Dietrich, 419 ff.
139 Str.-B., I, 165.
140 Moore, I, 500. Cf. *ibid.*, 515 for a comparison of the Rabb. doctrine with that of the Westminster Shorter Catechism.
141 → 989; 991; 993.
142 Cf. Jer. 8:6; Test. Jos. 3:10 (ἐπιστρέφω); Jos. Ant., 7, 54, → 995; 1 Cl., 8, 3 (quoting an apocryphon ?) etc.
143 Cf. Test. B. 5:1 (ἐπιστρέφω) etc.

idle philological finding. For as the call μετανοεῖτε which Jesus issued in the steps of the Baptist is construed as an emotional appeal: "Feel sorry,"[144] or as a stirring of the whole consciousness: "Change your mind,"[145] or as a demand for acts of expiation for wrongs committed: "Do penance,"[146] or as a summons to a radical change in the relation of God to man and man to God: "Convert," "be converted,"[147] so according to these various interpretations there will be radically different understandings of the message of Jesus. Investigation of the history of the term up to NT days has shown us, however, the only path which may be followed, and exposition of the theological usage of the NT will pursue this to its destination, namely, that μετανοέω and μετάνοια are the forms in which the NT gives new expression to the ancient concept of religious and moral conversion.[148]

II. The Concept of Conversion.

1. John the Baptist.

Conversion was the basic note in the message of the Baptist (Mk. 1:4 par.; Mt. 3:2,[149] 8 par., 11, cf. Ac. 13:24; 19:4; Lk. 1:16). The coming of God's lordship (→ I, 581 ff.) is imminent and His judgment is close at hand; in the last span of time there is thus only one task for man, μετάνοια. What John advances is the ancient prophetic summons for conversion, for a break with the ungodly and sinful past, for turning to God, because God, active in history, turns to man (→ 984 ff.). But the summons is more categorical than it was on the lips of any prophet, for it stands under the urgency of the eschatological revelation of God. The term

---

144 So H. Weinel, *Bibl. Theol. d. NT*⁴ (1928), 147, who describes the process of repentance psychologically (147 ff.).

145 So among many others B. Weiss, *Lehrbuch d. Bibl. Theol.*⁷ (1903), 72 ff.; Zn. Mt. on 3:2; though cf. in opposition T. Zahn, *Grundriss d. nt.lichen Theol.* (1928), 9.

146 There can be no doubt that Luther's transl. was not meant in this sense, cf. his defence of the first thesis (*Werke*, WA, I, 530): *poenitentiam agite, quod rigidissime transferri potest "transmentamini," id est "mentem et sensum alium induite, resipiscite, transitum mentis et phase spiritus facite"*; cf. also the accompanying letter to Staupitz (*ibid.*, 525 ff.), where Luther derives *"metanoea"* from *"trans"* and *"mentem"* rather than *"post"* and *"mentem," ut "metania" transmutationem mentis et affectus significet, quod non modo affectus mutationem, sed et modum mutandi, id est gratiam dei, videbatur spirare.* The feeling that "do penance" does not correspond to the demand of Jesus is expressed already in the dislike of Lact. for *paenitentia* as a rendering of μετάνοια (→ n. 7), cf. Norden, 137 ff.

147 So Cr.-Kö., 771; Dirksen, 207; Dietrich, 349, 425 ff.; J. Schniewind (*NT Deutsch*) on Mk. 1:4, 15; Schniewind, I, 18 ff.; Schniewind, II, 70 f.; F. Büchsel, *Theol. d. NT*² (1937), 19, 22; Pohlmann, 36 ff. P. de Lagarde has shown most impressively from the Aram. that "conversion" is the only sound transl. of μετάνοια in the preaching of Jesus (*Deutsche Schriften* [1886], 292, cf. *Mitteilungen*, 4 [1891], 308), and that "conversion" and "new birth" are related concepts (*Deutsche Schriften, loc. cit.*). On the other hand F. Field in his essay "Is 'Conversion' a Scriptural Term?" (*Notes on the Translation of the NT* [1899], 246 ff.) surprisingly does not discuss μετανοέω and μετάνοια along with ἐπιστρέφω, ἐπιστροφή etc. P. Feine, *Bekehrung im NT u. in d. Gegenwart* (1908), 6 f. concludes his somewhat inadequate discussion of NT usage with the dubious assertion: "The concept of conversion is not very precise in the NT, nor is it sharply differentiated from doing penance" (7).

148 On the rendering of the Gk. terms by *poenitere, poenitentia* in the Vetus Latina and Vg cf. W. Matzkow, *De vocabulis quibusdam Italae et Vulgatae Christianis quaestiones lexicographae*, Diss. Phil. Berlin (1933), 29 ff.

149 On the question of the authenticity of this saying cf. W. Michaelis, *Täufer, Jesus, Urgemeinde* (1928), 11; Schl. Mt. on 4:17; *NT Deutsch*, Schn. Mt., 23.

which John makes his slogan is familiar to his Jewish contemporaries. It is the epitome of their unwearied and manifold exertions to throw off sin and to fulfil the commandments. But the slogan gives the word a wholly new significance. Conversion is once and for all. It must be genuine and not in appearance only. It is demanded of all, not just of notorious sinners (Lk. 3:12 f.) or Gentiles (Lk. 3:14). Conversion is required of righteous Jews who do not think they need it (Mt. 3:7 ff.). It implies a change from within. This change must be demonstrated in the totality of a corresponding life (Mt. 3:8: ποιήσατε οὖν καρπὸν ἄξιον τῆς μετανοίας, cf. v. 10),[150] a life of love and righteousness in accordance with the will of God (Lk. 3:10-14). With the preaching of conversion John connects the baptism of conversion[151] (βάπτισμα μετανοίας, Mk. 1:4 par.; Ac. 13:24; 19:4), a sacramental act of purification which effects both remission of sins (εἰς ἄφεσιν ἁμαρτιῶν, Mk. 1:4 par.) and conversion (ἐγὼ μὲν ὑμᾶς βαπτίζω ἐν ὕδατι εἰς μετάνοιαν, Mt. 3:11).[152] The meaning is that the complete change of man's nature for the coming aeon is God's work in baptism. Through the eschatological sacrament of John's baptism God fashions for Himself a community of the converted who are given a place in the coming salvation. μετάνοια is both God's gift and man's task. God grants conversion through baptism, man is summoned by the call thereto to let it be given him, "to maintain and authenticate it as the divine basis of his own existence so long as this aeon lasts."[153] At the portal of the NT we thus find a concept of conversion which transcends Judaism and renews the ultimate insights of the prophetic piety of the OT (cf. Jer. 31:33; Ps. 51:10), but with a new eschatological certainty.

2. Jesus.

In the teaching of Jesus according to the Synoptists μετανοεῖτε is again the imperative which is indissolubly bound up with the indicative of the message of the βασιλεία (Mk. 1:15; Mt. 4:17).[154] But Jesus does not merely repeat the call of the Baptist. He modifies and transcends it by making conversion a fundamental requirement which necessarily follows from the present reality of the eschatological βασιλεία in His own person (→ I, 588 f.). To call to conversion is the purpose of His sending (Lk. 5:32).[155] His preaching of conversion far surpasses even the

150 Lk. 3:8: καρπούς does not affect this, esp. as the sing. occurs here too in v. 9. Cf. also J. Weiss, *Schriften d. NT* and Schl. Mt. on Mt. 3:8.

151 → I, 536, also F. Büchsel, *Theol. d. NT*^{2} (1937), 19 f. and esp. E. Lohmeyer, *Das Urchristentum*, I: "Joh. d. Täufer" (1932), 67-82, 141-145 etc.; "Vom urchr. Sakrament, I," DTh, 6 (1939), 118 ff.; Loh. Mk., 14 f. The basic ideas which Loh. develops in these works are important even though we cannot accept all his conclusions.

152 Cf. Loh. Mk., 15 and Schl. Mt., 77 f.

153 E. Lohmeyer, *Das Urchristentum*, I, 78.

154 The elimination of the μετανοεῖτε of Mt. 4:17 in syr^{sin} syr^{cur} Cl Al Orig Eus rests on false ideas of the difference between the preaching of Jesus and that of the Baptist, cf. *NT Deutsch*, Schn. Mt., *ad loc.* Neither M. E. Winkel, *Das Ev. nach Mk.* (1937), who describes the μετανοεῖτε of both Syn. passages as a "dogmatic intrusion of the views of the first Jewish Christians who could not outgrow their Jewish ideas (p. 7*, cf. 33* for the corresponding note on Mk. 6:12) nor R. Thiel, *Die 3 Markus-Evangelien* (1938), 119 (cf. 140) can find any place in the earliest tradition for the preaching of conversion by Jesus, Thiel on grounds of source criticism with no mention of the theological issue, Winkel on the basis of a mistaken preconception that Jesus demanded faith rather than Jewish penitence (→ 1002 f.).

155 εἰς μετάνοιαν does not occur in Mk. 2:17 or Mt. 9:13 (C 𝔎 etc. have it in Mk. and C𝔎Θ syr^{sin} sah have imported it into Mt. from Lk. 5:32). But it is fully in keeping

most powerful of such preaching before (Mt. 12:39 ff. par.: Jonah). The miracles which Jesus performs are also a summons to conversion (Mt. 11:20 ff. par.; cf. Lk. 5:8). μετάνοια, related to the will of God which He proclaims, is the way of salvation indicated by Jesus. It is a way which must be taken, not the theoretical description of a way. In characteristic distinction from the Jewish partiality for the abstract תְּשׁוּבָה the active aspect is to the fore in the Synoptic sayings of Jesus (μετανοέω 14 times, μετάνοια only 3). Jesus transcends the OT proclamation of conversion (cf. Lk. 16:30 f.) and especially the conversion piety of Judaism. In view of the coming of the βασιλεία the traditional Jewish forms of expressing תְּשׁוּבָה, e.g., feelings of remorse, gestures of sorrow, works of penance or self-mortification (cf. Mt. 11:21 par.), have no value. God's definitive revelation demands final and unconditional decision on man's part. It demands radical conversion, a transformation of nature, a definitive turning from evil, a resolute turning to God in total obedience (Mk. 1:15; Mt. 4:17; 18:3).[156] He who does not convert falls under divine judgment (Mt. 11:20 ff. par.; Lk. 13:3, 5; 19:40 ff.; 23:28 ff.). This conversion is once-for-all. There can be no going back, only advance in responsible movement along the way now taken. It affects the whole man, first and basically the centre of personal life, then logically his conduct at all times and in all situations, his thoughts, words and acts (Mt. 12:33 ff. par.; 23:26; Mk. 7:15 par.). The whole proclamation of Jesus, with its categorical demands for the sake of God's kingdom (the Sermon on the Mount, the sayings about discipleship), is a proclamation of μετάνοια even when the term is not used. It is a proclamation of unconditional turning to God, of unconditional turning from all that is against God, not merely that which is downright evil, but that which in a given case makes total turning to God impossible (Mt. 5:29 f., 44; 6:19 f.; 7:13 f. par.; 10:32-39 par.; Mk. 3:31 ff. par.; Lk. 14:33, cf. Mk. 10:21 par. etc., → I, 589). As distinct from all forms of eschatological enthusiasm, or moralism, or casuistry, the demand for conversion is the one and only imperative in Jesus' preaching of the kingdom of God. It is addressed to all without distinction and presented with unmitigated severity in order to indicate the only way of salvation there is. It calls for total surrender, total commitment to the will of God: God, be merciful to me, a sinner (Lk. 18:13).[157] It is a conversion to the God who seeks out sinners rather than the righteous (Lk. 15:7, 10, cf. 17 ff.; 5:32; 13:3, 5, → I, 303 f.). Jesus brought out the radicalism of His summons to conversion in His mortal conflict with the Pharisees.[158] In the preaching of Jesus faith grows out of conversion (Mk. 1:15; → πίστις, → πιστεύω), not as a

---

with the significance of the call of Jesus acc. to the Synoptists, → III, 488 (as against Kl. Mk.[3] on 2:17). Just. Apol., 15, 8 comments on Lk. 5:32: θέλει γὰρ ὁ πατὴρ ὁ οὐράνιος τὴν μετάνοιαν τοῦ ἁμαρτωλοῦ ἢ τὴν κόλασιν αὐτοῦ.

[156] H. D. Wendland, *Geschichtsanschauung u. Geschichtsbewusstsein im NT* (1938), 12 has an excellent comment on the demand for conversion in Mk. 1:15 from the standpoint of a theology of history: "Man must accept God's *kairos* in heart, will and life; he must place himself under the decision which God has taken and be obedient to it alone. To convert is to draw the conclusion from the act of God which takes place for men, to say Yes to the *kairos* of God, to set oneself on the way which God will take from the Now of the time of decision to the end."

[157] Wendland, *Die Eschatologie des Reiches Gottes*, 95.

[158] C. G. Montefiore, *Rabbinic Literature and Gospel Teachings* (1930), 260, fails to see the diametrical antithesis between Jesus and the Rabbis in the understanding of conversion when he concludes: "Nothing that Jesus says about it beats, or goes beyond, what the Rabbis say about it."

second thing which He requires, but as the development of the positive side of μετάνοια, the turning to God.[159] Conversion as Jesus understands it is not just negative. It is more than a break with the old nature in face of the threat of eschatological judgment. It embraces the whole walk of the man who is claimed by the divine lordship. It carries with it the founding of a new personal relation of man to God, i.e., of πίστις. "To convert," "to be converted," embraces all that the dawn of God's kingdom demands of man.

But this unconditional requirement is not met by man's own achievement. In Mt. 18:3[160] Jesus shows from the example of the child what "to convert," "to become another man," means for Him: ἐὰν μὴ → στραφῆτε καὶ γένησθε ὡς τὰ παιδία, οὐ μὴ εἰσέλθητε εἰς τὴν βασιλείαν τῶν οὐρανῶν. To be a child (→ παιδίον) is to be little, to need help, to be receptive to it. He who is converted becomes little before God (cf. v. 4 → ταπεινόω), ready to let God work in him. The children of the heavenly Father whom Jesus proclaims (→ πατήρ) are those who simply receive from Him. He gives them what they cannot give themselves (cf. Mk. 10:27 par.). This is true of μετάνοια.[161] It is God's gift, and yet it does not cease to be a binding requirement. It is both these at one and the same time; it is this so unconditionally as to rule out any calculated playing off of the one aspect against the other (→ 996 ff.). Behind the call for conversion which Jesus issues with His announcement of the rule of God there stands the promise of the transformation which He effects as the One who brings in this rule (cf. Mt. 11:28 ff.). If the water baptism of John, whose divine commission Jesus recognised (Mk. 11:30 par.), effected the conversion of those who awaited the fulfilment of salvation (Mt. 3:11, → 1001), the spiritual baptism which Jesus gives in the full might of the Consummator of the world is none other than the impartation of divine power which creates men who are subject to the divine rule, i.e., converted men. For all its pitiless severity the message of Jesus concerning μετάνοια does not drive us to the torture of penitential works or to despair. It awakens joyous obedience for a life according to God's will.[162] This is because μετάνοια here is no longer Law, as in Judaism, but Gospel.

3. Primitive Christianity.

a. General. In the apostolic *kerygma*, too, conversion is the basic requirement. Already in the lifetime of Jesus, and on His commission, the disciples took up His call for conversion (Mk. 6:12). They were then directed by the risen Lord to preach conversion in His name to all peoples (Lk. 24:47). According to Ac. the heart of the apostolic mission is the message of μετάνοια (2:38; 3:19: μετανοήσατε ... καὶ → ἐπιστρέψατε, 5:31; 8:22; 11:18; 17:30;[163] 20:21; 26:20).

---

[159] On conversion and faith cf. A. Schlatter, *Der Glaube im NT*⁴ (1927), 143 ff.; Schl. Mk., 39 ff.; Schniewind, I, 21 ff. and esp. Pohlmann, 50 f., cf. 22 ff.

[160] The only verse where we find the fully synon. → στρέφομαι instead of μετανοέω in the Synoptic tradition. O. Michel, "'Diese Kleinen' — eine Jüngerbezeichnung Jesu," ThStKr, NF, 3 (1937/38), 401 ff., believes that the parable of the child is just as much a part of the preaching of conversion as the use of the term "little ones" for the disciples.

[161] Cf. on this P. Gennrich, *Die Lehre von d. Wiedergeburt* (1907), 50 ff. and esp. W. Grundmann, *Die Gotteskindschaft in d. Geschichte Jesu* (1938), 78 ff., 86, n. 2, → 532 f. Cf. also P. de Lagarde (→ n. 147).

[162] On conversion and joy cf. Schl. Theol. d. Ap., 75; Schniewind, I, 23 f.; Schniewind, II, 78 ff.; Schniewind, *NT Deutsch*³, Mk. on 1:15.

[163] To take μετανοεῖν here in the secular sense (T. Birt, *Rheinisches Museum*, 69 [1914], 372, n. 1) is to misunderstand the language and thought of Lk. For a correct interpretation cf. Norden, 134 ff.

Hb. 6:1 numbers the teaching about μετάνοια among the basic articles of the primitive Christian catechism. Not to convert is a mark of culpable obduracy (Rev. 2:21 f.; 9:20 f.; 16:9, 11). In Jn. conversion and baptism are related, cf. also Ac. 13:24; 19:4. Similarly, Peter's sermon at Pentecost, which obviously accords with early practice, connects conversion and baptism (Ac. 2:38).[164] The nature of conversion may be described in traits familiar from the preaching of conversion in the OT prophets. It is a turning away from evil (Ac. 8:22, cf. 3:26; Hb. 6:1; Rev. 2:22; 9:20 f.; 16:11) and a turning towards God (Ac. 20:21; 26:20: μετανοεῖν καὶ → ἐπιστρέφειν ἐπὶ τὸν θεόν; Rev. 16:9, cf. 1 Pt. 2:25). It is man's task (Ac. 2:38; 3:19; 8:22; 17:30; 26:20, embracing the demonstration of a changed manner of life), and it is also God's gift (Ac. 5:31, cf. 3:26; 11:18; Rev. 2:21). The concept is given a distinctive NT impress, however, by its grounding in the saving historical revelation in Christ (Ac. 5:31). It is also understood with eschatological realism (Ac. 3:19 ff.; 17:30) and in universal terms (Ac. 11:18; 17:30;[165] 20:21; 26:20,[166] cf. Lk. 24:47; 2 Pt. 3:9). The fact that μετάνοια is a work of the Spirit (cf. Ac. 11:18 with 11:15 ff. and 10:45) is to be explained only on the assumption that Jesus fulfilled John's promise of a baptism of the Spirit. As in the evangelical message of Jesus, μετάνοια and πίστις are not only associated (Ac. 20:21: τὴν εἰς θεὸν μετάνοιαν καὶ πίστιν εἰς τὸν κύριον ἡμῶν Ἰησοῦν, Hb. 6:1, cf. also Ac. 26:18) but belong together.[167] The urgent call for conversion in the epistles of Rev. (2:5, 16; 3:3, 19) is based on the prospect of the imminent end. This summons carries a threat to the Christian churches, calling them back to reflection, to turning from sin and weakness, to the renewal of their former state of life. The emphasis here is an enduring to the end. To convert is not just to give one's life a new direction but in practice to reorientate oneself continually to the goal by the radical setting aside of evil. In Ac., too, the goal of conversion is the final salvation (11:18: ζωή, → II, 864), and especially the forgiveness and washing away of sins (Lk. 24:47; Ac. 3:19, cf. 8:22, → I, 511). Remission of sins is connected with baptism in Ac. 2:38 and with faith in 10:43. But as a blessing of eschatological salvation it is also found alongside μετάνοια in 5:31. There is no binding of forgiveness to conversion such as we find in Judaism, → 997.

b. Paul.[168] The concept of conversion occurs also in Paul's epistles. R. 2:4: man's μετάνοια with a view to the Last Judgment (cf. v. 3, 5 ff.) is the goal to which the goodness of God would lead him; cf. 2 Tm. 2:25, where μετάνοια εἰς ἐπίγνωσιν ἀληθείας is described as a gift of God. 2 C. 12:21: to convert implies a radical break with the sins of the past.[169] In 2 C. 7:9 f. the μετάνοια of the Corinthian Christians is the result of a concern awakened in them by Paul.

---

[164] Cf. on this pt. Schl. Theol. d. Ap., 36 ff.

[165] Cf. 14:15: ἀπὸ τούτων τῶν ματαίων → ἐπιστρέφειν ἐπὶ θεὸν ζῶντα, also 1 Th. 1:9.

[166] Cf. also 15:3: τὴν → ἐπιστροφὴν τῶν ἐθνῶν, 11:21.

[167] Ac. 20:21 gives strong linguistic expression to this by placing both nouns under the same article, cf. B. Weiss, *Das NT Handausgabe*, IIII[2] (1902), *ad loc.* On conversion and faith in primitive Christianity cf. A. Schlatter, *Der Glaube im NT*[4] (1927), 292 ff., 444.

[168] The brief observations of M. E. Andrews, "Paul and Repentance," JBL, 54 (1935), 125, do not deal with the present subject.

[169] Cf. on this W. Bousset, *Schriften d. NT, ad loc.*; Wnd. 2 K., 410 f.; Schl. K., 674 f.

Psychologically[170] — after the analogy of Plut. Tranq. An., 19 (II, 476 f.), → 978; Ceb. Tab., 11, → 979 — it is a revulsion of feeling, a sense of remorse. But Paul understands μετάνοια religiously as the result of divine action (v. 9 : ἐλυπήθητε ... κατὰ θεόν, v. 10 : ἡ ... κατὰ θεὸν λύπη) and as a means of salvation (v. 10 : μετάνοιαν εἰς σωτηρίαν). In Christian rather than Hellenistic terms, he regards μετάνοια as "the change of thought and will which releases from evil and renders obedient to the will of God."[171] Yet it is noteworthy how seldom Paul has the usual words for conversion. He expresses their meaning in his own distinctive theological terms.[172] If in Jesus conversion includes faith, in Paul μετάνοια is comprised in → πίστις, the central concept in his doctrine of salvation. He states the idea of conversion as a total refashioning of man's nature and conduct by the grace of God in his own characteristic vocabulary of dying and becoming, i.e., the death of the old man and the rising again of the new man (→ II, 336, III, 18 f.), καινὴ κτίσις (→ III, 1034), renewal (→ III, 449 f., cf. Tt. 3:5 : → παλιγγενεσία), etc. Different reasons may be advanced for Paul's restating in this way of a basic concept of primitive Christian piety. Along with antipathy to a term devalued by penitential practices we must certainly take into account the decisive motifs of his own Christian experience. But however that may be, the concept of a radical transformation effected by the revelation of God in Christ is still for Paul the foundation of his whole theology. And this is precisely the thought of conversion as understood by Jesus.

c. John. John avoids the loaded terms μετανοέω and μετάνοια, but he, too, has the matter itself no less definitely than Paul.[173] For him, too, faith (→ πιστεύω) includes conversion. The preaching of John the Baptist, Jesus' own preaching in this Gospel, and the exhortation of John himself in 1 Jn. all press for faith in Jesus and thus demand conversion to Him. The reverse side, turning from evil, is self-evident in view of the sharp line which the Johannine Jesus and the author of 1 Jn. draw between light and darkness, truth and falsehood, love and hate, life and death, God and the world. Again, the concept of birth from God (ἐκ τοῦ → πνεύματος) as the way into God's kingdom (Jn. 3:3-8, → I, 671) is another form of the thought of Mt. 18:3, and behind it stands the same conviction about the spiritual power which works miracles as is found in the Synoptic message of Jesus.[174] There is an inner continuity of the idea of conversion throughout the NT.

d. The Impossibility of a Second μετάνοια in Hb. Hb. emphasises the seriousness of the total change implied in conversion when this is considered in relation to the obvious danger that Christians will grow slack in their Christianity and sink into dull indifference. It shows that man cannot command μετάνοια at will (12:7: the example of Esau, who μετανοίας ... τόπον οὐχ εὗρεν καίπερ μετὰ

---

[170] Cf. Wnd. 2 K., *ad loc.*

[171] Schl. K., 586. Cf. for an understanding of the train of thought in 2 C. 7:9 f., *ibid.*, 586 ff.; C. F. G. Heinrici, *Das zweite Sendschreiben d. Ap. Pls. an d. Korinthier* (1887), 346 ff.; Bchm. K., *ad loc.*; W. Gutbrod, "D. paulinische Anthropologie," BWANT, IV, 15 (1934), 50. On 1 Th. 1:9; 2 C. 3:16; Gl. 4:9 → ἐπιστρέφω.

[172] Cf. on this Schl. Theol. d. Ap., 334, 374 ff.; P. Feine, *Theol. d. NT*[7] (1936), 242 ff.; Wnd. 2 K., 234; Pohlmann, 54 ff.

[173] Cf. Schl. Theol. d. Ap., 153, 170, 183, 210 f.

[174] Cf. also Gennrich, 52 ff.

δακρύων ἐκζητήσας αὐτήν),[175] indeed, that there is no renewal of μετάνοια for apostates (6:4-6: ἀδύνατον γὰρ τοὺς ἅπαξ φωτισθέντας ..., καὶ παραπεσόντας, πάλιν ἀνακαινίζειν εἰς μετάνοιαν ...).[176] The difficulty posed by this reference to the impossibility of a second repentance, which occurs in the context of exhortation, cannot be solved if we think in terms of casuistry or ritual penitence in the sense of Jewish or OT practice.[177] Against the background of the NT view of conversion, however, the thinking and concern of the author are quite understandable. The man who has once experienced this decisive change in his life and become a καινὴ κτίσις (→ 1005), entering the circle of the revelation of eschatological salvation, has been set thereby in an eternal movement. If he arrests this movement, he turns from the living God (3:12), sins with full awareness and will (10:26), and is thus exposed to eschatological judgment (6:8; 10:27 ff.). In this case no human possibility[178] exists of bringing him afresh to conversion. In the form of a sharp pastoral warning on a specific occasion Hb. expresses the conviction that μετάνοια is a totality and that its surrender is consequently a total surrender.

F. μετανοέω/μετάνοια in the Ecclesiastical Writings of the Post-Apostolic and Early Catholic Period.

The terms are much used by the post-apostolic fathers in the technical religious sense. Linguistically they have here the same sense as in the NT, namely, "to convert," "conversion."

μετανοεῖν is a synon. of ἐπιστρέφειν (-εσθαι), e.g., 1 Cl., 8, 3 (cf. 7, 5); 2 Cl., 16, 1; Cl. Al. Paed., I, 92, 3; Strom., II, 144, 4; Quis Div. Salv., 29, 2 f.; Iren. Haer., IV, 40, 1; Act. Andr., 5 (II, 1, 40, 13 ff., Bonnet), μετάνοια as a synon. of ἐπιστροφή, Just. Dial., 30, 1; Act. Joh., 56 (II, 1, 179, 19 f., Bonnet) etc. μετανοεῖν means "to turn away" ἀπὸ τῆς κακίας (Just. Dial., 109, 1, cf. 121, 3; Cl. Al. Quis Div. Salv., 39, 2), μηκέτι ἁμαρτάνειν (Herm. m., 4, 3, 2) and "to turn to" God (Ign. Sm., 9, 1; Herm. v., 4, 2, 5), to the passion of Christ (Ign. Sm., 5, 3), to the unity of God and the assembly of the bishop (Ign. Phld., 8, 1, cf. 3, 2), to change one's life from one full of discord to a better one (Cl. Al. Strom., II, 97, 3).

But popular Gk. ideas are fused with the NT understanding.[179]

---

[175] The attempt of Rgg. Hb., *ad loc.* (cf. also *NT Deutsch* [H. Strathmann] and O. Michel, *Der Brief an d. Hebräer* [1936], *ad loc.*) to take μετάνοια here in the secular sense of a change of opinion and conduct, and to relate it to a revocation of Esau's previous renunciation of the birthright, certainly accords with the Gn. narrative but hardly does justice to the context of Hb. Hb. is allegorising the OT story in order to establish the theological concept that there is no conversion of man without the work of God. Hb. is thus using the term μετάνοια in the religious and moral sense common to the NT. Cf. Wnd. Hb., *ad loc.*

[176] For details → I, 382, 676; II, 32, III, 451; → φωτίζω, → παραπίπτω, → ἀνασταυρόω. On the general understanding of the passage cf. Rgg. Hb., *ad loc.*; Wnd. Hb., 51 ff.; O. Michel, *op. cit.*, 66 ff., 72 f.; F. Büchsel, *Theol. d. NT*² (1937), 170 f.

[177] For Jewish practice → 992, 998; Str.-B., III, 689 f.; for the practice of the early Church, Rgg. Hb. and Wnd. Hb., *ad loc.*

[178] → III, 451, n. 1. Hb. 6 does not discuss the divine possibility, though 12:17 shows that the author, with his emphasis on the seriousness of divine judgment, considers the thought that God will not provide another τόπος μετανοίας.

[179] Cl. Al. defines μετάνοια in wholly Gk. terms, → n. 5.

We frequently find the meanings "to come to be of another mind," "change of mind" (Herm. v., 3, 7, 3; m., 11, 4; 4, 2, 2 : μετάνοια = σύνεσις; Cl. Al. Strom., I, 83, 2; VII, 85, 1 etc.) or "to bewail," "remorse" (Herm. m., 10, 2 and 3; 2 Cl., 15, 1; 16, 4 etc.; μετανοεῖν ἐπί [→ 977], Mart. Pol., 7, 3; Just. Apol., 61, 10; Dial., 17, 1; 26, 1; 106, 1; 141, 2; Cl. Al. Paed., I, 32, 1; Strom., IV, 37, 6 f.; Act. Phil., 138 [II, 2, 71, 10 f., Bonnet] etc.). In the martyrologies from Mart. Pol. onwards μετανοεῖν is often a legal tt. for "to recant," "to renounce Christianity."[180] The pro-consul demands of Polycarp : ὄμοσον τὴν Καίσαρος τύχην, μετανόησον (Mart. Pol., 9, 2). Polycarp rejects the threat : "I will throw you to the wild beasts, ἐὰν μὴ μετανοήσῃς, by confronting the legal tt. with Christian μετάνοια: ἀμετάθετος γὰρ ἡμῖν ἡ ἀπὸ τῶν κρειττόνων ἐπὶ τὰ χείρω μετάνοια·[181] καλὸν δὲ μετατίθεσθαι ἀπὸ τῶν χαλεπῶν ἐπὶ τὰ δίκαια, *ibid.*, 11, 1.

Ideas of conversion show primitive Christian influence.

The post-apost. fathers. To become a Christian is μετανοεῖν (Did., 10, 6; cf. Ign. Eph., 10, 1). God gives μετάνοια, creating new men who are His temple (Barn., 16, 9, cf. 8). The blood of Christ, shed for our deliverance, παντὶ τῷ κόσμῳ μετανοίας χάριν ἐπήνεγκεν (1 Cl., 7, 4). Conversion and baptism go together : μετάνοια ... ἐκείνη, ὅτε εἰς ὕδωρ κατέβημεν καὶ ἐλάβομεν ἄφεσιν ἁμαρτιῶν ἡμῶν τῶν προτέρων (Herm. m., 4, 3, 1). Faith is the fruit of conversion (Herm. s., 9, 22, 3; v., 3, 5, 5; m., 12, 6, 1). The call for conversion, which is sounded in 1 Cl., Ign., and esp. urgently in Herm. and 2 Cl., is addressed not merely to unbelievers and heretics but also and specifically to Christians. Just. expressly recalls the preaching of conversion by Jesus and John the Baptist (Apol., 15, 7 f.; Dial., 49, 3; 51, 2; 88, 7). Christ came in the power of the almighty Father to proclaim conversion (Dial., 139, 4). He sent a sceptre to Jerusalem τὸν λόγον τῆς κλήσεως καὶ τῆς μετανοίας πρὸς τὰ ἔθνη ἅπαντα (83, 4), and effects a full conversion ἀπὸ τῆς παλαιᾶς κακῆς ἑκάστου γένους πολιτείας (121, 3). Just. himself points emphatically to the saving way of μετάνοια which must be trodden before the Day of Judgment comes (Apol., 28, 2; 40, 7; Dial., 118, 1 etc.). Baptism is for him the λουτρὸν τῆς μετανοίας ..., τὸ βάπτισμα, τὸ μόνον καθαρίσαι τοὺς μετανοήσαντας δυνάμενον (Dial., 14, 1). Cl. Al., like the NT, sees in conversion both gift and task, the work of God (Paed., I, 70, 1; Quis Div. Salv., 42, 15 : μετάνοια par. παλιγγενεσία) and the responsibility of man (Prot., I, 4, 3 : εἴ τις ... μετανοήσαι ἑκών, ... "ἄνθρωπος" γίνεται "θεοῦ"). Cf. Act. Joh., 81 etc.

Characteristic of the understanding of μετάνοια in the post-apostolic period is the strong orientation to the OT.

The prophetic preaching of conversion is often adduced as Scripture proof for the saving significance of conversion in the present (1 Cl., 8; Just. Dial., 25, 4; 47, 5; Apol., 61, 6; Cl. Al. Paed., I, 58, 2; Strom., II, 35, 3; Paed., I, 69, 3 f. etc.). Through the prophets God has called the people of Israel εἰς ἐπιστροφὴν καὶ μετάνοιαν πνεύματος (Just. Dial., 30, 1). Noah (1 Cl., 7, 6, cf. 9, 4; Theophil. Ad Autol., III, 19) and Jonah among the Ninevites (1 Cl., 7, 7; Just. Dial., 107, 2; Cl. Al. Prot., X, 99, 4) are types of the effective preaching of μετάνοια to men. Judaism had already argued in this way.[182] Jewish tradition may also be discerned in the figure of the ἄγγελος τῆς μετανοίας (Herm. v., 5, 8; m., 12, 4, 7; 12, 6, 1; s., 9, 1, 1; 9, 14, 3; 9, 23, 5; 9, 24, 4; Cl. Al. Quis Div. Salv., 42, 18), cf. En. 40:9, → 992.

The primitive Christian view of conversion is greatly affected by Jewish ideas.

---

180 Cf. on this Rgg. Hb. [2, 3], 409, n. 5. At root is the idea of an alteration of religious standpoint expressed in a legally binding declaration.

181 Cf. on this expression Polyb., 18, 33 (16), 6 f., → 978.

182 → 992-998. For Noah cf. Sib., 1, 128 f., 167 ff., → 992, cf. Jos. Ant., 1, 74; for Jonah and the Ninevites (→ 998) cf. the Rabb. from Taan., 2, 1 on, *v.* Str.-B., I, 647 f.

μετάνοια is one mark of the pious life among others (1 Cl., 62, 2). Like almsgiving, it is a good work (2 Cl., 16, 4). Part of μετάνοια is keeping the commandments (Herm. v., 5, 6 f.; m., 2, 7; s., 6, 1, 3 f.; 7, 6). μετανοῆσαι ἐξ εἰλικρινοῦς καρδίας is the ἀντιμισθία one pays to God (2 Cl., 9, 8), the achievement by which one secures salvation and life (2 Cl., 19, 1, cf. Ign. Phld., 8, 1). Only penitence with weeping and wailing gives hope of God's forgiveness (Just. Dial., 141, 3). The μετάνοια one achieves must be genuine, pure and strong (Herm. m., 2, 7; 12, 3, 2; s., 7, 6 etc.).

The fateful relapse of post-apostolic and early Catholic Christianity into Jewish legalism finds striking expression in the changed understanding of μετάνοια. The primitive Christian view is moralised. Conversion becomes — for the second time — penance. Penance must be done and suffered (Did., 15, 3; 1 Cl., 57, 1 etc.). The development of a penitential discipline analogous to that of the Synagogue is the inevitable result, and there are distinct traces of this by the end of the 2nd century, Tert. Paen., 9 etc.

The great book of μετάνοια in early Christian literature is *The Shepherd of Hermas.*[183] Here one finds cheek by jowl conflicting elements from the NT preaching of conversion on the one side and the Judaised doctrine of penance on the other.

Hermas, an apocalyptic prophet, belongs to the NT line. For him Christianity in its original sense is an "eschatological religion of conversion."[184] As regards the present problem this means that μετάνοια is the basic change which, sealed by baptism, makes Christians into Christians. As such it is unique and cannot be repeated. There is no second conversion (cf. Hb., → 1005 f.). He who has received remission of sins should not sin any more; he must maintain his purity (m., 4, 3, 1 f.).[185] But the Christianity of Hermas' day is sunk in sins. Instead of resembling a virgin without spot or wrinkle, it is more like a wizened old woman. And Hermas can still promise a renewal of its original form with a view to the coming of the Bridegroom (v., 3, 11 ff.). That is to say, he can proclaim yet another extraordinary possibility of conversion, the theme of his book. How? He can do it only on the basis of a special revelation of the merciful God who has granted a last time of grace before the end (v., 2, 2, 3 ff.; m., 4, 3, 4 ff.; 4, 1, 8). But this eschatological τόπος μετανοίας is only for those who were converted long before and have now been tempted by the devil and fallen into fresh sin. It is not a license to sin for the newly converted (v., 2, 2, 5; m., 4, 3, 3 ff.).[186] μετάνοια is by nature σύνεσις: "The sinner sees that he has done evil before the Lord; the act which he has committed comes to his remembrance; he repents and does no more evil. He does good in rich measure, and humbles and vexes his soul because he has sinned" (m., 4, 2, 2). Herm. conceives of the fulfilment of μετάνοια in Jewish terms. It is man's task, a keeping of the commandments (s., 6, 1, 2 ff.; 9, 33, 3, cf. m., 4, 4, 4), moral achievement according to the many ethical injunctions given by the Shepherd (m., 1-12). Asceticism and penal suffering are the school of conversion (cf. esp. s., 7, 4: δεῖ τὸν μετανοοῦντα βασανίσαι τὴν ἑαυτοῦ ψυχὴν καὶ ταπεινοφρονῆσαι ἐν πάσῃ πράξει αὐτοῦ ἰσχυρῶς καὶ θλιβῆναι ἐν πάσαις θλίψεσι ποικίλαις, *ibid.*, 5; m., 4, 2, 2, → *supra*). Sure success can be expected only when God "sees that the heart of those who repent is pure from every wicked act" (s., 7, 5).

At the very beginning of the story of the NT concept in the early Church the Jewish misunderstanding is already present.

---

183 Cf. on what follows H. Windisch, *Taufe u. Sünde,* 356 ff.; Dib. Herm., 510 ff.; Poschmann, 134 ff.

184 Dib. Herm., 510.

185 On the problem of baptism and sin in early Christianity → I, 304 ff., 540 ff.

186 Cl. Al. Strom., II, 56 ff. took up the thought of Herm. Cf. esp. 58, 3; 59, 1: τὸ πολλάκις μετανοεῖν is an exercise in sinning, merely a δόκησις μετανοίας, οὐ μετάνοια.

† ἀμετανόητος → ἀμεταμέλητος, 626 ff.

Koine adj., firmly attested only from the imperial period, mostly in the pass. sense "exposed to no change of mind," "beyond repentance or recall," "unshakable," e.g., Luc. Abdicatus, 11: ἀμετανόητον ... τὴν ἀνάληψιν καὶ τὴν διαλλαγὴν βέβαιον εἶναι προσήκει, Plot. Enn., 6, 7 and 26; Vett. Val., 7 (p. 263, 16, Kroll); P. Grenf., II, 68, 3 f.: ὁμολογῶ χαρίζεσθαι σοὶ χάριτι ἀναφαιρέτῳ καὶ ἀμετανοήτῳ P. Strassb., 29, 30 f.: ὁμολογοῦμεν ... διῃρῆσθαι (that the inheritance will be divided) πρὸς ἀλλήλους ... αὐθαιρέ[τ]ως καὶ ἀμετανοήτως, and other legal pap.[1] Act. in the sense of "free from remorse" and to denote the Stoic ideal of never repenting (→ 980), Epict. Diss. Fr., 25: οὐδὲν ἄγριον δράσας ἀμετανόητος καὶ ἀνεύθυνος διαγενήσῃ. As here the philosophical understanding of μετανοέω and μετάνοια gives the adj. a new meaning, so the religious understanding in Judaism (→ 991-999) and primitive Christianity (→ 999-1006) conveys to it the sense of "one who does not convert," "impenitent." Cf. on the one hand Test. G. 7:5: ἀμετανόητος τηρεῖται εἰς αἰωνίαν κόλασιν, and on the other R. 2:5: κατὰ δὲ τὴν σκληρότητά σου καὶ ἀμετανόητον καρδίαν θησαυρίζεις σεαυτῷ ὀργήν ...[2] The antithesis between Stoicism and Judaism or primitive Christianity in the understanding of μετάνοια (→ 980; 991 ff.; 999 ff.) is also reflected in the positive assessment of ἀμετανόητος in the one case, and the negative in the other.

In R. 2:5 Paul sets the will of the self-righteous Jew, his hardened mind, his heart which resists conversion,[3] in effective contrast with the goodness of God which seeks to bring him to μετάνοια (v. 4, → 1004). Arbitrary man is incapable of decisive conversion to God, → 1005. "Because the heart is ἀμετανόητος, Paul is an evangelist, not a preacher of repentance."[4]

† προνοέω, πρόνοια.

Contents: A. The Usage. 1. προνοέω. 2. πρόνοια. B. The Concept of Divine Providence. 1. In Greek and Roman Antiquity. 2. In the Old Testament. 3. In Judaism. 4. In the New Testament. 5. In the Early Church.

A. The Usage.

1. προνοέω. The verb means "to perceive in advance," "to note beforehand," "to foresee," *praevidere*, though it can easily come to mean "to know or to think in

---

ἀμετανόητος. Liddell-Scott, Pass.-Cr., Cr.-Kö., Pr.-Bauer, Moult.-Mill., Preisigke Wört., *s.v.*; Deissmann NB, 84; Nägeli, 45, 52; A. Bonhöffer, "Epict. u. d. NT," RVV, 10 (1911), 106 f.; E. Norden, *Agnostos Theos* (1913), 135; A. H. Dirksen, *The New Testament Concept of Metanoia* (Diss. Theol. Washington, The Catholic Univ. of America [1932]), 186; Comm. on R. 2:5.

[1] Cf. also Philo Praem. Poen., 15 vl.: τῆς ἀμετανοήτου ... φύσεως (a mistake for ἀμεταβλήτου, "unalterable").

[2] Cr.-Kö., *s.v.* conjectures that Paul imparts his own sense in R. 2:5: "(a heart) which cannot be brought to repentance," but this is unnecessary in view of the attestation of the active use.

[3] τὴν σκληρότητά σου καὶ ἀμετανόητον καρδίαν is a kind of hendiadys suggested by the common linking of → σκληρότης etc. with καρδία in the Gk. Bible (→ III, 613 f.). ἀμετανόητος καρδία does not have to do duty for a missing abstract noun (ἀμετανοησία), as against Bengel, Zn. R., *ad loc.*

[4] Schl. R., 77, n. 1.

προνοέω κτλ. On A: Pass., Liddell-Scott, Moult.-Mill., Preisigke Wört., Cr.-Kö., Pr.-Bauer, *s.v.*; Bl.-Debr.[6] § 176, 2 (also p. 300); Nägeli, 64; A. P. M. Meuwese, *De rerum gestarum divi Augusti versione Graeca* (Diss. phil. Amsterdam [1920]), 82 ff.; S. Lösch,

advance," cf. Epicharmus Fr., 41 (I, 204, 9, Diels[5]): οὐ μετανοεῖν ἀλλὰ προνοεῖν χρὴ τὸν ἄνδρα τὸν σοφόν, Porphyr. Sententiae, 26 (p. 11, 8 ff., B. Mommert), another reminder of the sensual meaning of the simple form (→ 948), cf., e.g., Eur. Hipp., 685 : οὐ σῆς προὐνοησάμην φρενός, Thuc., 3, 38, 6 : προαισθέσθαι ... τὰ λεγόμενα καὶ προνοῆσαι βραδεῖς τὰ ἐξ αὐτῶν ἀποβησόμενα, Xenoph. Cyrop., 8, 1, 13 : προνοῶν ὅτι πολλὰ καὶ τελεῖν ἀνάγκη ἔσοιτο εἰς μεγάλην ἀρχήν, Aristot. Cael., II, 9, p. 291a, 24 f.: τὸ μέλλον ἔσεσθαι προνοούσης τῆς φύσεως, hence also Nu. 23:9 B[c]; Job 24:15 C; 17:15 Θ, where שׁוּר is rendered by προνοέω. The most common sense, for act. as well as mid. (with pass. aor.),[1] where the prep. can hardly have temporal significance, is in both class. and later Gk. (cf. Hesych.) *providere*, "to care for," "to be concerned about," "to make provision for," "to take thought for" (abs., with gen., more rarely acc., or clause); examples from secular Gk. may be found in the lexicons ; cf. also Da. 11:37 (for בִּין); Prv. 3:4 (deviating from HT); 1 Εσδρ. 2:24; Wis. 13:16; 2 Macc. 14:9; 3 Macc. 3:24; 4 Macc. 7:18; Philo Jos., 115 : δεῖν, καθάπερ ἐν εἰρήνῃ προνοεῖν τῶν ἐν τῷ πολέμῳ παρασκευῶν, καὶ ἐν εὐπορίαις τῶν κατ' ἔνδειαν (cf. Virt., 153), Jos. Ant., 1, 53 : Ἄβελος ... δικαιοσύνης ἐπεμελεῖτο καὶ ... ἀρετῆς προενόει, Did., 12, 4; Pol., 5, 3; 6, 1 (= Prv. 3:4); Athenag. Suppl., 1, 3 (with ref. to rulers): μὴ προνενόησθε καὶ ἡμῶν, Cl. Al. Fr., 44 (III, 222, 3 f., O. Stählin): φυλάττου δὲ ὅπως μηδέν ποτε λαλήσῃς ὃ μὴ προεσκέψω καὶ προενόησας etc. So of God, who provides for the world and men, Wis. 6:7: προνοεῖ περὶ πάντων, Philo Op. Mund., 171: προνοεῖ τοῦ κόσμου ὁ θεός, *ibid.*, 172 : ἀεὶ προνοεῖ τοῦ γεγονότος, Spec. Leg., III, 189 : ὁ γεννήσας (sc. τὸν κόσμον) πατὴρ νόμῳ φύσεως ἐπιμελεῖται τοῦ γενομένου προνοούμενος καὶ τοῦ ὅλου καὶ τῶν μερῶν, Leg. Gaj., 3 : ἄπιστοι γεγόνασί τινες τοῦ προνοεῖν τὸ θεῖον ἀνθρώπων, Just. Apol., 44, 11: μέλον ἐστὶν αὐτῷ καὶ προνοεῖται αὐτῶν (sc. τῶν ἀνθρώπων), Athenag. Suppl., 8, 4 : God creates and takes care of (προνοεῖ); 25, 2 etc.; τὸ προνοοῦν, "divine providence," Cl. Al. Strom., IV, 82, 2, cf. also Ael. Arist. In Sarapin, 17, 17 (II, 357, Keil) of Sarapis : ἐξ ἀρχῆς τε ἡμᾶς ἄγων εἰς φῶς καὶ τὴν ἑαυτοῦ καὶ γενομένοις ὅπως ἕκαστα ὑπάρξει προνοούμενος (soul, body etc.),[2] Procl. Inst. Theol., 134 (p. 118, 20, E. R. Dodds): πᾶς θεῖος νοῦς νοεῖ μὲν ὡς νοῦς, προνοεῖ δὲ ὡς θεός.

In the NT it is used only in the current sense, "to care for" dependents, esp. in one's own household,[3] 1 Tm. 5:8. In 2 C. 8:21: προνοοῦμεν ... καλά, and

---

"Die Dankesrede des Tertullus : Apg., 24, 1-4," *Theol. Quartalschrift*, 112 (1931), 310 ff.; M. P. Charlesworth, "*Providentia* and *Aeternitas*," HThR, 29 (1936), 107 ff. On B : Cr.-Kö., *s.v.* πρόνοια; P. Lobstein, Art. "Vorsehung," RE[3], 20, 740 ff.; P. Wendland, *Philos Schrift über d. Vorsehung* (1892), 9 ff.; P. Barth, *Die Stoa* [3, 4] (1922), 42 ff.; W. Capelle, "Zur antiken Theodicee," *Archiv f. Gesch. d. Philosophie*, 20 (1907), 176 ff.; R. Liechtenhan, "D. göttliche Vorherbestimmung bei Pls. u. in d. Posidonianischen Philosophie," FRL, NF, 18 (1922), 52 ff., 124 ff.; H. Koch, "*Pronoia u. Paideusis*," *Arbeiten z. Kirchengeschichte*, 22 (1932), 205 ff., etc.; H. Preisker, *Nt.-liche Zeitgeschichte* (1937), 58 ff., 86; W. Staerk, *Vorsehung u. Vergeltung* (1931); W. Eichrodt, "Vorsehungsglaube u. Theodizee im AT," *Procksch-Festschrift* (1934), 45 ff.; *Theologie d. AT*, II (1935), 77-79; E. Sellin, *Theol. d. AT*[2] (1936), 42 f.; L. Köhler, *Theol. d. AT* (1936), 68-82; Weber, 205 ff.; A. Schlatter, "Wie sprach Josephus von Gott?" BFTh, 14, 1 (1910), 49 f.; Schl. Theol. d. Judt., Index *s.v.* πρόνοια; A. Meyer, *Vorsehungsglaube u. Schicksalsidee in ihrem Verhältnis bei Philo v. Alex.* (Diss. Tübingen [1939]); H. J. Holtzmann, *Lehrbuch d. nt.-lichen Theol.*[2] (1911), I, 124, 212 ff.; II, 185; Schl. Theol. d. Ap., 13 f.; W. Grundmann, *D. Gotteskindschaft in d. Geschichte Jesu u. ihre religionsgeschichtliche Voraussetzungen* (1938), 14 ff.

[1] The dep. is found in the act. mostly with ἐπιμέλεσθαι etc., hence in the sense of *providere*, less frequently *praevidere* [A. Debrunner].

[2] Cf. on this A. Höfler, "Der Sarapishymnus d. Ailios Aristeides," *Tübinger Beiträge zur Altertumswissenschaft*, 27 (1935), 48.

[3] The ref. is to any kind of provision, not just testamentary provision for those left behind as in Xenoph. Cyrop., 8, 1, 1: οἵ τε γὰρ πατέρες προνοοῦσι τῶν παίδων, ὅπως μήποτε αὐτοὺς τἀγαθὰ ἐπιλείψει (so Hofmann and Wbg. Past., *ad loc.*).

R. 12:17: προνοούμενοι καλά (in both verses there is allusion to Prv. 3:4 LXX), the meaning is "to have regard for" what is noble and praiseworthy (→ III, 549).

2. πρόνοια. The use corresponds to that of the verb, cf. Hesych., *s.v.*: πρόνοια· προενθύμησις, ἐπιμέλεια, φροντίς. The meaning, "prior vision or knowledge," is found mainly in older poetry (Soph., Aesch.).[4] The word is more common in the sense of "provision" or "forethought" (Ps.-Plat. Def., 414a: πρόνοια παρασκευὴ πρός μέλλοντά τινα), "intention," "deliberation," e.g., Soph. Ai., 536; Oed. Tyr., 978; Plat. Tim., 44c: δι' ἅς τε αἰτίας καὶ προνοίας γέγονε θεῶν, cf. Phaedr., 254e; Aristot. Pol., IV, 16, p. 1300b, 25 f.: περί τε τῶν ἐκ προνοίας καὶ περὶ τῶν ἀκουσίων, Menand. Epit., 18 f.: ἔχειν πρόνοιαν κοινόν ἐστι τῷ βίῳ πάντων (cf. 126 ff.), Philo Jos., 161: ἤδη γὰρ ἡ πρόνοια τοῦ νεανίσκου πανταχόσε διηγγέλλετο ταμιευσαμένου τροφὰς ἀφθόνους εἰς καιρὸν ἐνδείας. Πρόνοια is a name for the Delphic Athene as the goddess of clever forethought, Demosth. Or., 25, 34 etc., cf. Suid., *s.v.* The word can mean "care," "provision," P. Flor., II, 131, 6 f.: τὴν τοῦ χό[ρ]του προνοίαν, Cl. Al. Strom., VII, 70, 7: τῇ τοῦ οἴκου προνοίᾳ, esp. in the phrase πρόνοιαν ποιεῖσθαί τινος, Demosth. Or., 21, 97; Dion. Hal. Ant. Rom., 10, 1, 1; P.Amh., II, 40, 12 f.: ὑμῶν μηδεμίαν πρόνοιαν ποιησαμένων, Da. 6:19; Ep. Ar., 80 and 190; Jos. Ant., 12, 153: πρόνοιαν δὲ ποιοῦ καὶ τοῦ ἔθνους κατὰ τὸ δυνατόν, Philo Spec. Leg., III, 205: τοσαύτην δὲ πρόνοιαν ἐποιήσατο τοῦ μηδένα παραίτιόν τινι γενέσθαι θανάτου, Papias Fr. (Eus. Hist. Eccl., III, 39, 15); Cl. Al. Strom., II, 114, 5; *ibid.*, VIII, 8, 2 etc. A common Hell. custom is to praise the πρόνοια of the ruler (Dio Chrys. Or., III, 43, a πρόνοια ἀνθρώπων κατὰ νόμον), the general or the statesman, cf. 2 Macc. 4:6: ἄνευ βασιλικῆς προνοίας ἀδύνατον εἶναι τυχεῖν εἰρήνης, Ep. Ar., 30: προνοίας γὰρ βασιλικῆς οὐ τέτευχε, Diod. S., XXIX, Fr. 19 (of Hannibal): οὐδέποτε στάσιν ἔσχεν ἐν τῷ στρατεύματι, ἀλλὰ ... διὰ τῆς ἰδίας προνοίας ἐν ὁμονοίᾳ καὶ συμφωνίᾳ διετήρησεν, P. Herm., 119 B, III, 3: προνο[ία]ς [τ]οῦ κυρίου μου λαμπρ[οτά]του ἡγεμόνος etc.[5] When the term is applied to the gods to produce the sense of divine foresight or providence the various meanings merge into one another, namely, foreknowledge, foreordination, foresight and provision. The emphasis is on the temporal aspect, and also on the rational element in the stem. But the constant providing for events which corresponds to the foreseeing of events may also become timeless provision for those affected by these events. The word is first used of divine providence in Hdt., 3, 108, 2: τοῦ θείου ἡ προνοίη, ὥσπερ καὶ οἰκός ἐστι, ἐοῦσα σοφή, ὅσα μὲν [γὰρ] ψυχήν τε δειλὰ καὶ ἐδώδιμα, ταῦτα μὲν πάντα πολύγονα πεποίηκε, ἵνα μὴ ἐπιλίπῃ κατεσθιόμενα, ὅσα δὲ σχέτλια καὶ ἀνιηρά ὀλιγόγονα. From the time of Xenoph. (Mem., 1, 4, 6: to the προνοίας ἔργα belongs the purposeful arrangement of the eyelids; cf. προνοητικόν, *ibid.*, 4, 3, 6) and Plat. (Tim., 30b: τόνδε τὸν κόσμον ζῷον ἔμψυχον ἔννουν τε τῇ ἀληθείᾳ διὰ τὴν τοῦ θεοῦ γενέσθαι πρόνοιαν) it is a philosophical tt.,[6] also used abs. as an abstr. designation for God, and esp. common in Stoicism (→ 1012), then Plut. Cons. Apoll., 34 (II, 119 f.): κατὰ τὴν τῶν ὅλων πρόνοιαν καὶ τὴν κοσμικὴν διάταξιν (→ 1013), cf. also Corp. Herm., I, 19; XII, 14b, 21; the formula μετὰ τῆς τῶν θεῶν προνοίας in Polyb., 23, 17, 10[7] corresponds to the "God willing" of Jm. 4:15, cf. also the Delphic precept, Ditt. Syll.³, 1268, I, 7: π]ρόνοιαν τ[ί]μ[α] and the oath in P. Lips., 40, III, 3: μὰ τὴν πρόνοιαν etc. In Jewish Hell. lit.[8] cf. Wis. 14:3; 17:2; Ep. Ar., 201: προνοίᾳ γὰρ τῶν ὅλων διοικουμένων, 3 Macc. 4:21; 5:30; 4 Macc. 9:24; 13:19; 17:22; Philo Ebr., 199: πρόνοιαν καὶ ἐπιμέλειαν ὅλου καὶ τῶν μερῶν θαυμαστήν τιν' εἶναι ἡνιοχοῦντος καὶ κυβερ-

---

4 Cf. the lexicons, *s.v.*

5 For further examples from Hell. lit., pap. and coins of the imperial period cf. Lösch, 311 ff.; Charlesworth, 107 ff.

6 For the pre-Socratics cf. Diels⁵, Index, *s.v.*

7 Cf. also P. Osl., III, 148, 4: τῆι τῶ[ν θε]ῶν προνοίαι etc.

8 Not in works originally written in Heb. or Aram., cf. Sir., Test. XII, apocalypses etc.

νῶντος ἀπταίστως καὶ σωτηρίως θεοῦ, Leg. Gaj., 336; Rer. Div. Her., 58 etc.; Jos. Ant., 4, 47 (prayer of Moses): ὅτι πάντα σῇ προνοίᾳ διοικεῖται καὶ μηδὲν αὐτομάτως ἀλλὰ κατὰ βούλησιν βραβευόμενον τὴν σὴν εἰς τέλος ἔρχεται, 18, 309; Bell., 3, 391: εἴτε ὑπὸ τύχης χρὴ λέγειν, εἴτε ὑπὸ θεοῦ προνοίας, cf. also Test. Sol. D 1:13 (p. 89*, 29 f., McCown): ἐπαιδεύθη (sc. Solomon) ταύτην τὴν σοφίαν ... παρὰ τῆς ἄνω προνοίας. In Chr. lit., 1 Cl., 24, 5: ἡ μεγαλειότης τῆς προνοίας τοῦ δεσπότου ἀνίστησιν αὐτά (sc. τὰ σπέρματα), Herm. v., 1, 3, 4: ὁ θεὸς τῶν δυνάμεων, ὁ ... τῇ ἰδίᾳ σοφίᾳ καὶ προνοίᾳ κτίσας τὴν ἁγίαν ἐκκλησίαν αὐτοῦ, Apologists, Cl. Al., etc., *passim*, cf. also Act. Joh. 20: σύ με τὴν πρόνοιαν ἐβιάσω ἐνυβρίσαι, P. Oxy., XIV, 1682, 6 ff.:[9] ἡ μὲν τοῦ θεοῦ πρόνοια παρέξει τὸ μετὰ ὁλοκληρίας σε τὰ οἰκεῖα ἀπολαβεῖν.

The NT never speaks of divine πρόνοια. In Ac. 24:2 πρόνοια is rhetorically ascribed to the procurator Felix in current style (→ 1011). In R. 13:14: τῆς → σαρκὸς πρόνοιαν μὴ ποιεῖσθε εἰς ἐπιθυμίας ("do not care for the flesh in such a way that desires arise"), Paul requires that care for the body (→ σάρξ) should be dominated by a moral attitude which by strict discipline prevents this care giving an entry to sinful lusts (→ III, 170 f.).[10]

B. The Concept of Divine Providence.[11]

1. In Greek and Roman Antiquity.

Beginning with recognition of the purposeful rule of cosmic reason in the macrocosm and microcosm (Anaxagoras, → 954 etc.), Gk. thought moves on to the concept of a divine πρόνοια which works in nature to man's benefit (Hdt., → 1011; Socrates acc. to Xenoph., → 1011). This wise and just care of the gods binds man to obedience and trust. It underlies faith in the absolute purposiveness of the ways of the gods with the righteous (Plat. Resp., X, 612e: τῷ δὲ θεοφιλεῖ οὐχ ὁμολογήσομεν, ὅσα γε ἀπὸ θεῶν γίγνεται, πάντα γίγνεσθαι ὡς οἷόν τε ἄριστα; cf. Leg., X, 899d ff.). Expressing the conviction that a salutary teleology obtains in the divine overruling of the world, the concept of providence becomes a dogma for the Stoics; indeed, it is the heart of their theology[12] (→ I, 121). There is no contingency. The original divine power immanent in the world inter-relates all things. A kindly providence which has the goal in view ordains for the best everything that takes place in history and human life.[13]

---

[9] Cf. APF, 12 (1937), 225.

[10] Cf. on this interpretation along the lines of Luther (already in the *Vorlesung über den Römerbrief* of 1515/16 = *Anfänge reformatorischer Bibelauslegung*, ed. J. Ficker, I³ [1925], 312) esp. Zn. and Schl. R., *ad loc.*; T. Haering, *Der Römerbr. d. Ap. Pls.* (1926), 128; W. Gutbrod, "Die paul. Anthropologie," BWANT, F. 4, *Heft* 15 (1934), 156. Chrys. and Theodoret took R. 13:14 in the same way, cf. Cramer Cat., *ad loc.* (IV, 469 f.), cf. also Euthymius Zigabenus, Commentarius in XIV epistolas S. Pauli ..., ed. N. Calogeras (1887), *ad loc.* The radical interpretation: "Care not for the flesh because this serves only to satisfy its lusts," which is advocated by A. Jülicher (*Schriften d. NT*), *ad loc.*; F. Kühl, *D. Brief d. Pls. an d. Römer* (1913), 443; Ltzm. R., *ad loc.*, is demanded neither by the order of words nor the context and is suspect from the standpoint of biblical theology, → σῶμα, → σάρξ.

[11] The problems of theodicy and predestination are not discussed here.

[12] Cf. for the older Stoicism, which already wrote περὶ προνοίας (Chrysipp.), II, 322 ff., v. Arnim (No. 1106-1186); I, 44, *ibid.* (No. 172, 174 and 176), for Posidonius, e.g., Cic. Nat. Deor., II, 73 ff., for the later Stoa, Sen. De Providentia; Epict. Diss., I, 6 and 16; III, 17 etc.; M. Ant., II, 3, 1; IV, 3 and 5; V, 32, 2; XII, 30 etc.; cf. the material in Wendland, 9 ff. The main opponents of the Stoic doctrine of providence were the Epicureans and, following Carneades, the newer Academy.

[13] For Zeno cf. Cic. Nat. Deor., II, 58 (I, 44, v. Arnim, No. 172), for Posidonius, cf. Plut. De Fato, 9 f. (II, 572 f-574b).

The true nature of Εἱμαρμένη, of ineluctable destiny, of the hard necessity which controls all events by the law of cause and effect, is to be seen only in providence, in the wise, purposeful and benevolent care of the gods, cf. Cleanthes, Hymn to Zeus, lines 14 ff. (I, 122, v. Arnim, No. 537, cf. also I, 124 f., v. Arnim, No. 549). ἔστι θεὸς καὶ προνοεῖ τῶν ὅλων (Epict. Diss., II, 14, 11, cf. III, 15, 14). God rules the great cosmic organism. He orders it like the head of a household. He controls it as does the artist his works. He sets tasks for the constellations and for living creatures, for animals and men (Epict. Diss., I, 6 and 16, 9 ff.; III, 22, 2 ff.). All events are in His hand, moral as well as temporal (M. Ant., IV, 10: κατὰ τὸ δίκαιον καὶ ὡς ἂν ὑπό τινος ἀπονέμοντος τὸ κατ' ἀξίαν). "The worse is there for the better, the better the one for the other. Better than lifeless things are living creatures, better than these rational creatures" (M. Ant., V, 16, 5, cf. VII, 55, 2; XI, 10). Rational man is the true goal of creation (Epict., I, 6, 19 ff., cf. Cic. Nat. Deor., II, 37). There thus arises the naïve view that even in detail providence serves the good of man[14] and also the insight that what is incomprehensible and apparently capricious serves a higher purpose concealed from men. Stoic speculation on πρόνοια finally nurtures a piety of joyous confidence. The deity is stronger than evil. The gods neither will nor can fail (Sen. Ep., 95, 50; M. Ant., V, 8). To be unhappy is a subjective thing, ὁ γὰρ θεὸς πάντας ἀνθρώπους ἐπὶ τὸ εὐδαιμονεῖν, ἐπὶ τὸ εὐσταθεῖν ἐποίησεν (Epict. Diss., IV, 24, 2 f.). God is the Father who makes provision for all (Sen. De Providentia, I, 2 and 6). He is well-disposed and friendly to all (Sen. Ben., IV, 5, 1 ff.; II, 29, 4 ff.), or at least to the good (Sen. De Providentia, I, 1, 5). Plut. separates the concept of πρόνοια from the Stoic belief in destiny (Stoic. Rep., 46 [II, 1055e f]). He believes that not only nature (Lib. Educ., 5 [II, 3c]; Def. Or., 30 [II, 426e] etc.) but also history is guided by it (Suav. Viv. Epic., 22 [II, 1103b]).[15] Through its organs, gods and demons, he thinks that providence enters into living relations with men to protect and discipline them, to show them love and righteousness (Praec. Coniug., 19 [II, 140d]; Adulat., 22 [II, 63 f]).[16] But here, too, the belief is intentionally related to man and to the human race.

2. In the Old Testament.

The concept of providence is found in the OT only at Job 10:12: the פְּקֻדָּה[17] or guardianship of God sustains the man whom He has created. But the implications of the concept are by no means alien to the OT. The belief that the God of creation continues to work powerfully and directly in the world, upholding it with fatherly care and guiding it acc. to His plans (Ps. 65:6 ff.; 104; 145:15 f.; 147:8 f.; Hos. 2:10; Job 9:5 ff.; Gn. 8:22; Is. 6:3 etc.) is just as firmly established as the conviction that nature is controlled by a purposeful order which sees to it that the divine ends are reached (Ps. 19:6; Job 38:33, 8 ff.; Prv. 8:29; Jer. 5:22, 24; 8:7; 31:35 f.; 33:25 etc.).[18] From the very outset the reference to a personal God, the almighty Lord of the world, distinguishes the OT concept of providence from the view of antiquity, which is linked to neutral and abstract ideas. By His

---

[14] For this reason the older Stoicism is derided even in Plut. Stoic. Rep., 21 (II, 1044c d). There was ref. to the good of rational beings, gods and men, from the time of Chrysipp., Cic. Fin., III, 67, cf. Nat. Deor., II, 133 etc.

[15] The historical sway of providence is extolled already in the Priene inscr. in Ditt. Or., II, 458, 32 f.: ἡ πάντα] διατάξασα τοῦ βίου ἡμῶν πρόνοια has "shown to us its solicitude and kindness and crowned the order of our life by sending Augustus to us."

[16] Related ideas may be seen in Apul. Met., XI, 5 f., 25, cf. Reitzenstein Hell. Myst., 255.

[17] LXX: ἐπισκοπή, → II, 606.

[18] → III, 1011; 1013. On the concept of time as an expression of the OT belief in providence cf. Köhler, *op. cit.*, 74 f., esp. the concluding sentences on 75: "Everything has its time and is foreseen, appointed and limited. It is God's time. Hence it is in God's will."

own proper nature the God of the OT is the God of history, whose will directs history.[19] According to predeterminate counsel He supervises the history of His people (the exodus from Egypt etc.; Dt. 32:39; 2 K. 19:25 ff.; Is. 5:12; 43:19 f.; 45:4; 46:9 ff. etc.) and shapes the destiny of all peoples (e.g., Am. 9:7; 2:1 ff.; Gn. 11:1 ff.; 49:10; Job 12:13 ff.; 1 K. 19:15 ff.; Is. 10:5 ff.; 2:2 ff.; Jer. 27:3 ff.; Is. 41:2 ff.; 45:1 ff.). He displays by miracles His proximity, His presence, and His power to save (1 S. 12:16 ff.; Is. 10:33). He foresees history (Is. 22:11; 44:7), and appoints instruments to achieve His purposes (Jer. 1:5; Is. 49:1 ff.; 54:16).[20] The individual is caught up in the purposive events directed by God. As a member of the people He experiences God's guidance. He realises that his life is in God's hands (Prv. 20:24; Job 5:18 ff.; 10:12; Ps. 16:5 ff.; 73:23 f.; 139:5, 16; Is. 4:3; Jl. 2:32 etc.). At all points, in great and little things alike, the care and providence of God may be seen at work (as regards human life cf. also Ps. 22:9 f.; 90:3; Job 10:8 ff.; Is. 41:4).[21] What seems to take place contingently, chance (מִקְרֶה, 1 S. 6:9; Rt. 2:3) or the decision of the lot (e.g., 1 S. 10:19 ff.; 14:41; Prv. 16:33), comes from God. Even evil is a means in the hand of the God of sovereign disposition (Am. 3:5 f.; Is. 45:7; Ex. 4:21 ff.; Is. 6:9 f.; Jer. 25:15 ff.; Is. 63:17). It serves His plan of salvation, which is beyond all human comprehension (e.g., Gn. 50:20; Is. 10:7 ff.; 47:1 ff.; Hab. 1:12 ff.; Is. 55:8 f.; Job 42:1 f.). Even at points in the OT where the Law is a normative expression of God's will in the world[22] there is still a conviction that God's providence holds sway, by judgment and punishment upholding against all opposition the inviolable orders which with wise foresight He has established (Ps. 75:3; the priestly interpretation of history in 1 and 2 S., 2 K. and 2 Ch.).[23] The OT concept of providence is theocentric and volitional. It is thus separated by a deep cleft from the anthropocentric and rational ideas which the world of Greek and Roman antiquity linked with πρόνοια.

3. In Judaism.

Through all the pressures and puzzles of its history Judaism maintained the core of the OT belief in providence, namely, belief in God's purposeful government of the world. The destiny of creation follows a plan (4 Esr. 6:1 ff.). God foresees the course of history (Eth. En. 39:11). The great theological view of history in the apocalypses from Da. to 4 Esr. and Baruch[24] is "a kind of world-conquering belief in providence,"[25] the original and striking expression of a tireless investigation of the mystery of God's overruling of universal history. God's sovereign will determines history's course (Da. 2:21; 4 Esr. 13:58). Historical figures, times and events are foreordained by Him from creation to the end of the world (Ass. Mos. 12:4 f.; 4 Esr. 4:36 f.; S. Bar. 48:2 ff. etc.). The fact that the predetermined course of history follows a regular plan may be seen in the schema of periods (4 kingdoms in Da. 2; 7; 4 Esr. 11:39; S. Bar. 39:3 ff.; 70 weeks of years in Da. 9; Eth. En. 89:59 ff.; 10 weeks of the world in Eth. En. 93; 91:12 ff.; cf. the 10 generations in Sib., 4, 47 ff.; 12 periods of world history in S. Bar. 53 ff.).

---

[19] Cf. on this H. D. Wendland, *Geschichtsanschauung u. Geschichtsbewusstsein im NT* (1938), 13 ff., with bibl.

[20] Eichrodt, II, 88: The one entrusted with a great historical mission stands under the special providence of Yahweh.

[21] On this cf. Köhler, 79 ff.

[22] Cf. Eichrodt, II, 90 f.

[23] *Ibid.*, 91.

[24] Cf. J. Behm, "Joh. Apk. u. Geschichtsphilosophie," ZSTh, 2 (1924), 333 ff.; E. Stauffer, "Das theol. Weltbild d. Apokalyptik," *ibid.*, 8 (1931), 203 ff.; Wendland, 16 ff.

[25] Volz Esch., 6.

The goal and end of history is the establishment of God's rule (Da. 2:44; 7:13, 27; Ass. Mos. 10:1; Sib., 3, 767 etc.). The Law, the embodiment of the eternal wisdom of God the Creator (Sir. 24:8, 10, 23 ff.) is for Judaism a providential guarantee of the effectual presence of God,[26] S. Bar. 85:3: "We now have no more than the Almighty and his law" (cf. 4 Esr. 9:37); Philo Vit. Mos., II, 51 calls it ἐμφερεστάτην εἰκόνα τῆς τοῦ κόσμου πολιτείας, R. Aqiba regards the individual commandments as educational tools of providence, Tanch. B תזריע § 7 (18a):[27] "God has given Israel the commandments simply in order to purify them thereby"; in bBer., 6a it is emphasised that even God Himself is bound to the ordinances of the Torah.[28] The Jewish belief in providence found its special sphere in the everyday life of the individual. God cares for His creatures (Ass. Mos. 12:9; S. Bar. 21:9; Ep. Ar., 157 and 190). In prayer, then, one may commit oneself in all situations to His almighty provision.[29] The Rabb. incessantly refine the doctrine of God's most special providence, e.g., jShebi, 9, 38d, 27 (saying of R. Shim'on b. Jochai) etc.: "A bird does not perish without heaven, how much less man"; bSanh., 29a: "Rab. Ashi has said: ... pestilence may last seven years and no one will die if his time has not yet come"; bChul., 7b: "R. Chanina has said: A man cannot hurt his finger here below if it has not been proclaimed concerning him above"; bBB, 91b: R. Chanan b. Raba has said in the name of Rab: "Even the overseer of the well is appointed by heaven."[30] And in relation to the further problem of predestination and the freedom of the will[31] we find statements like Ab., 3, 16: "All is foreseen (by God), but freedom is granted (to man)"; bBer., 33b: "Everything lies in the hand of heaven except for the fear of God," etc.

Into this terminologically imprecise circle of Jewish ideas Hell. Judaism imports the Stoic concept of πρόνοια. This serves to demonstrate the historical dispositions of God (Wis. 14:3 Noah; 17:2 Egyptian darkness; 3 Macc. 4:21: the lack of writing material for a record of the Jews of Egypt an ἐνέργεια τῆς τοῦ βοηθοῦντος τοῖς Ἰουδαίοις ἐξ οὐρανοῦ προνοίας ἀνικήτου, 4 Macc. 17:22; Sib., 5, 323; Jos. Bell., 7, 453: The dreadful end of a persecutor of the Jews a clear sign of God's πρόνοια, ὅτι τοῖς πονηροῖς δίκην ἐπιτίθησιν, Ant., 13, 80) and also to show His care for all,[32] esp. for Israel[33] (Wis. 6:7, → 1010; Jos. Ant., 11, 169 [words of Jeremiah to the people of Jerusalem]: "In virtue of the righteousness of the patriarchs God does not abandon τὴν ὑπὲρ ὑμῶν πρόνοιαν; 1, 225: Abraham knows that everything takes place ἐκ τῆς ἐκείνου προνοίας). But the predominantly eudaemonistic view of the rule of providence (3 Macc. 4:21; 5:30 [cf. 35]; 4 Macc. 13:19; Philo Jos., 99; Spec. Leg., I, 308 ff.; Praem. Poen., 104; Flacc., 125; Conf. Ling., 115 etc.; Jos. Ant., 2, 60 and 349; 18, 309, → 1012), the rational treatment of the theme (Philo Op. Mund., 9 f.: providence is τὸ ὠφελιμώτατον καὶ ἀναγκαιότατον τῶν εἰς εὐσέβειαν, for reason teaches that the Father and Creator is concerned about what He has created as a father is concerned for his children or an artist for his works; what is disadvantageous or hurtful He averts in every possible way, and what is advantageous and beneficial He seeks to bring about in every possible way;[34] Jos. Ant., 2, 24: αὐτοῦ [sc. τοῦ θεοῦ] τὴν πανταχοῦ

---

[26] → III, 1020.
[27] Str.-B., IV, 35.
[28] Cf. Weber, 159.
[29] Cf. the examples from Jewish prayer life in Bousset-Gressm., 366 ff.
[30] Str.-B., I, 582 f., with further material on 583 f.
[31] → προορίζω, → ἐκλέγω etc. On Joseph.'s account of the difference between the Pharisaic and Sadducean views cf. Schürer, II, 460 ff.; Str.-B., IV, 344.
[32] To the denial of providence, which abandons human life to chance there is a reply in Wis. 2:1 ff., cf. also Jos. Ant., 4, 47, → 1012, though Bell., 3, 391 (→ 1012); Ant., 2, 347 leave it open whether a thing happens by God's providence or contingently (cf. Schl. Theol. d. Judt., 32).
[33] On Jos. cf. Schl. Theol. d. Judt., 48.
[34] Philo arrives at the concept of providence through consideration of the starry heaven, Quaest. in Gn., II, 34 (J. B. Aucher, Philonis Judaei paralipomena Armena [1826], 114; Gk.

παροῦσαν πρόνοιαν καὶ μήτε τῶν ἐπ' ἐρημίᾳ πραττομένων ὑστεροῦσαν μήτε τῶν κατὰ τὰς πόλεις), and the habit of referring to providence instead of God (Wis. 17:2: ἡ αἰώνιος πρόνοια, Ep. Ar., 201 → 1011; 4 Macc. 9:24: ἡ δικαία καὶ πάτριος ἡμῶν πρόνοια, 13, 19: ἡ θεία καὶ πάνσοφος πρόνοια, 17:22; cf. also Jos. Ant., 2, 336: εἴ τι παρὰ τῆς σῆς ἔλθοι προνοίας ἐξαρπάσαι τῆς Αἰγυπτίων ὀργῆς ἡμᾶς δυνάμενον ἀφορῶμεν) show clearly how the Hell. concept affected Jewish thought. What Philo says about the providential purposiveness which holds sway in nature, and also how he says it, is purely Stoic (cf. esp. the work Περὶ προνοίας [35] but also Spec. Leg., III, 189, → 1010; Ebr., 199, → 1011; Virt., 216 [of God]: προνοεῖ τοῦ τε κόσμου καὶ τῶν ἐν αὐτῷ). [36]

4. In the New Testament.

That the concept of providence did not come to expression in the NT is one of the many pointers to the independence of the NT world of thought and its distinction from the world-views of philosophy. The belief in providence is implicitly present in the NT. But it is belief in the God whose will controls the world and achieves the goal of salvation. The same starting-point is adopted as in the OT. God the Creator is the Lord of heaven and earth (Mt. 11:25 and par.; Ac. 17:24 f.). As such He is actively and providentially at work in creation. He is the Lord of history who directs the course of events to the *telos* set by Him (R. 11:36: εἰς αὐτὸν τὰ πάντα, cf. 1 C. 15:28). But the new proclamation brought by Jesus and the reality of salvation present in His person give the concept a wholly new form. The fatherly goodness of God manifested in His care for His creatures, e.g., sunshine and rain on all without distinction (Mt. 5:45), care and protection for even the smallest animals and plants (Mt. 6:26 ff. and par.; 10:29 ff. and par.), is simply a reflection of the nature and work of the God of saving revelation (→ πατήρ). God's love enacted in Christ, His eternal redemptive counsel proclaimed in the golden chain of saving acts (R. 8:29 f.), [37] underlies the certainty of Paul that "all things work together for good to them that love God" (R. 8:28), and that no power in this world can separate them from the love of God in Christ (8:35-39). This is "the NT faith in providence in its most individual form (*providentia specialissima*)," [38] cf. also Phil. 2:13. This faith gives the individual his place in God's universal, teleological control of history (R. 9-11; Rev.; [39] also Ac. 17:26 f., 30 f.; 14:16 f.), whose goal is the establishment of His βασιλεία. The eternal plan of salvation which God has foreseen, and which has been revealed by Christ in history, reaches its definitive consummation beyond history.

---

text in J. R. Harris, *Fragments of Philo Judaeus* [1886], 22 f.): θεασάμενος ... ἡλίου κίνησιν καὶ σελήνης ... εὐθὺς εἰς ἔννοιαν ἦλθε θεοῦ καὶ γενέσεως καὶ προνοίας. On the difference between Stoicism and Philo at this pt. cf. W. Völker, "Fortschritt u. Vollendung bei Philo v. Alex.," TU, 49, 1 (1938), 178 (n. 5), 182 f.

[35] Fully extant only in Armenian (Lat. transl. in J. B. Aucher, Philonis Judaei sermones tres hactenus inediti ... [1822], 1 ff.); Gk. fr. in Eus. Praep. Ev., VII, 21 and VIII, 14, cf. also J. R. Harris, 75 f. and Wendland, 88 f.

[36] Cf. Wendland, 9 ff. 39, 86 etc. In Aet. Mund., 47 it is said of πρόνοια: ψυχὴ δ' ἐστὶ τοῦ κόσμου.

[37] Cf. *NT Deutsch* (P. Althaus) on R. 8:29.

[38] Holtzmann, II, 185.

[39] Cf. on this Behm, 327 ff.; Wendland, *passim*.

5. In the Early Church.

For the post-apost. fathers the concept of divine πρόνοια is naturally part of the Christian concept of God. That the Lord's noble concern causes seeds to rise up again from corruption (1 Cl., 24, 5, → 1012) is an intimation of the future resurrection of the dead. Herm. v., 1, 3, 4, → 1012, speaks of the founding of the Church by God's providence. The soteriological understanding of the concept points to dependence on the thinking of the NT. The Apologists, on the other hand, integrate the Gk. philosophical view of providence into Christian theology [40] and use it as one of their main arguments for belief in the one God who rules the world (Athenag. Suppl., 8, 4, → 1010; 25, 2; Theophil. Autol., III, 9: προνοίᾳ τὰ πάντα διοικεῖσθαι ἐπιστάμεθα, ἀλλ' ὑπ' αὐτοῦ μόνου) and cares for each man (Aristid. Apol., 1, 1: ἐγὼ ... προνοίᾳ θεοῦ ἦλθον εἰς <τόνδε> τὸν κόσμον, Just. Apol., 44, 11, → 1010 etc.) [41] as opposed to polytheism or a blind belief in fate (Aristid. Apol., 13, 2; Just. Dial., 1, 3 f.; Tat. Or. Graec., 2, 1 f.; Athenag. Suppl., 8, 1 ff.; 22, 8; 25, 2). But in so doing they relate the doctrine of God so strongly to cosmology that insufficient justice is done to the basic biblical concept of the God who works spiritually and personally and carries through His will to save (though cf. Just. Dial., 118, 3; 116, 2). In Iren. providence is ascribed to the God of saving revelation (Adv. Haer., IV, 36, 6; 38, 4), but providence is still an article of natural theology, cf. Fr., 5 (I, 828, A. Stieren): θέλησις καὶ ἐνέργεια θεοῦ ἐστιν ἡ παντὸς χρόνου ... καὶ πάσης φύσεως ποιητική τε καὶ προνοητικὴ αἰτία, Adv. Haer., I, 6, 1; II, 26, 2 f.; III, 25, 1. Cl., who wrote a work Περὶ προνοίας, [42] shows even more clearly what way the doctrine of providence was now to take in the Gk. church. God's πρόνοια is a fundamental truth of reason, to doubt which would be unchristian (Strom., I, 52, 1 ff.; V, 6, 1 f.). It is manifest ἔκ τε τῆς ὄψεως τῶν ὁρωμένων πάντων, τεχνικῶν καὶ σοφῶν ποιημάτων, καὶ τῶν μὲν τάξει γινομένων, τῶν δὲ τάξει φανερουμένων (V, 6, 2) and extends even to detailed events (I, 52, 3; VI, 153, 4). Philosophy is in some sense θείας ἔργον προνοίας (I, 18, 4), ordained to prepare the way for fulfilment in Christ (VI, 153, 1). Similarly prophecy and the plan of salvation fulfilled in Christ take place in accordance with providence (V, 6, 2, cf. VI, 128, 3). But even formulae like ἡ κατὰ τὴν πρόνοιαν οἰκονομία (VI, 123, 2, cf. I, 28, 1) cannot conceal the fact that providence and saving revelation are different branches of the divine operation which the Gk. church never succeeded in bringing into organic relation with one another. [43]

† ὑπονοέω, ὑπόνοια.

ὑπονοέω, class. and Hell., with acc. of person or object, acc. and inf., or clause following, means "to think in secret." Hence in a bad sense "to suspect," "to hold a (or in) suspicion," [1] Hdt., 9, 99; Plat. Leg., III, 679c: ψεῦδος ... ὑπονοεῖν οὐδεὶς ἠπίστατο, Plut. Adulat., 20 (II, 61 f.): ὑπονοεῖς; πίστευσον, P. Ryl., II, 139, 14 f.; Philo Decal., 84: ὁ γε ὀμνὺς εἰς ἀπιστίαν ὑπονοεῖται (stands in suspicion as though one could not fully trust him), Jos. Ant., 4, 41 and 220; mid. P. Oxy., XIV, 1680, 14 f.: ὑπονοοῦμαι ὅτι πάντως πάλιν τί ποτε ἔχει πρὸς σέ. Or generally "to conjecture,"

---

[40] Athenag. Suppl., 19, 2 refers expressly to the Stoic doctrine of providence.

[41] Angels are instruments of God's care and providence (Just. Epit., 5, 2; Athenag. Suppl., 24, 3). The Logos is not connected with the concept of providence.

[42] The few remaining fragments (in O. Stählin's ed. of Cl. Al., III, 219 ff.) give no adequate idea of the contents.

[43] Cf. Harnack Dg., II, 125. For the doctrine of providence in Orig., cf. Koch, 28 ff., 214 ff., 240 ff., etc., and for its development in the later Gk. church cf. H. Beck, "Vorsehung u. Vorherbestimmung in d. theol. Lit. d. Byzantiner," *Orientalia Christiana Analecta*, 114 (1937), 187 ff. etc.

ὑ π ο ν ο έ ω, ὑ π ό ν ο ι α. Pass., Preisigke Wört., Moult.-Mill., Cr.-Kö., Pr.-Bauer, Sophocles Lex., *s.v.*; Br.-Debr.[6] § 397, 2 and 298, 4 (cf. suppl., p. 307).

[1] Hesych., *s.v.*: ὑπονοεῖ· ὑποπτεύει.

"assume," "think," e.g., Plat. Gorg., 454c: ὑπονοοῦντες προαρπάζειν ἀλλήλων τὰ λεγόμενα, Aristot. Fr., 12, p. 1476a, 4: ὑπενόησαν οἱ ἄνθρωποι εἶναί τι θεόν, Plut. Sept. Sap. Conv., 2 (II, 146e): οὐδ' αὐτὸς ᾔδει, πλὴν ὑπενόει . . ., cf. De Garrulitate, 14 (II, 509e);[2] Sir. 23:21; Tob. 8:16; Jdt. 14:14; Da. Θ 7:25 ("to be intent on" for סְבַר; LXX: προσδέχομαι); Test. B. 9:1 β: ὑπονοῶ δὲ καὶ πράξεις οὐ καλὰς ἐν ὑμῖν ἔσεσθαι, Philo Op. Mund., 17: λέγειν ἢ ὑπονοεῖν οὐ θεμιτόν (cf. Aet. Mund., 73), Jos. Ant., 3, 98; 6, 328; 8, 136; 13, 315; Herm. v., 4, 1, 6: ὑπενόησα εἶναί τι θεῖον, Just. Dial., 44, 1; 103, 3; Cl. Al. Prot., V, 66, 5 (of Theophrastus): πῇ μὲν οὐρανόν, πῇ δὲ πνεῦμα τὸν θεὸν ὑπονοεῖ, "to guess," Thuc., 7, 73, 1: ὑπονοήσας αὐτῶν τὴν διάνοιαν, Stob. Ecl., II, 7 (II, 113, 3 ff., Wachsmuth) of the Stoics: οὐδ' ὑπονοεῖν δέ φασι τὸν σοφόν, καὶ γὰρ τὴν ὑπόνοιαν ἀκαταλήπτῳ εἶναι τῷ γένει συγκατάθεσιν.

In the NT only Ac. uses the verb, with no theological significance. The sense is "to suspect" at 25:18: αἰτίαν . . . ὧν ἐγὼ ὑπενόουν πονηρῶν. Elsewhere it means "to assume" on the basis of definite observations, 27:27; "to conjecture," with acc. and inf. "to regard as," 13:25 (saying of the Baptist): τί ἐμὲ[3] ὑπονοεῖτε εἶναι, οὐκ εἰμὶ ἐγώ.

ὑπόνοια, "secret opinion." 1. What one thinks inwardly, e.g., Athenag. Suppl., 1, 4: οὐδὲ μέχρις ὑπονοίας, "not even in thoughts." Esp. "conjecture," "unfounded opinion,"[4] "imagination," "illusion,"[5] e.g., Thuc. II, 41, 4: τῶν δ' ἔργων τὴν ὑπόνοιαν (arbitrary view) ἡ ἀλήθεια βλάψει, Demosth. Or., 48, 39; Chrysipp. Fr., 131 (II, 41, 16 f., v. Arnim): ἡ μὲν γὰρ ὑπόν[ο]ια καὶ ἡ ἄγ[ν]οι[α] . . . φαῦ[λ]ά ἐστι[ν (sc. for the wise), Stob. Ecl., II, 7 → *supra*; Plut. Solon, 28, 5 (I, 94e): μὴ θρασυνόμενον ἀβεβαίοις ὑπονοίαις ὑβρίζειν, Sir. 3:24: ὑπόνοια (Heb. דִּמְיוֹן) (synon. in the preceding part of the verse ὑπόληψις), Da. 5:6: φόβοι καὶ ὑπόνοιαι (imaginations, visions) αὐτὸν κατέσπευδον, cf. 4:19, 33b;[6] Ep. Ar., 316: λαβὼν ὑπόνοιαν (conjecture), Agatharchides in Jos. Ap., 1, 211: τὴν περὶ τοῦ νόμου παραδεδομένην ὑπόνοιαν (illusion, sc. of the Jews). Or "suspicion," Polyb., V, 15, 1: ἦσαν . . . ἐν ὑπονοίᾳ τῷ τε βασιλεῖ καὶ τοῖς ἄλλοις, P. Lond., 1912, 97: ἐξ οὗ μείζονας ὑπονοίας ἀναγκασθήσομαι λαμβάνειν, Philo Spec. Leg., IV, 36: φαύλης ὑπονοίας ῥυόμενος ἑαυτόν, Jos. Bell., 1, 227: καθ' ὑπόνοιαν τῆς φαρμακείας etc. 2. "The basic, hidden allegorical meaning of an expression, figure of speech, allegory, parable" etc., Xenoph. Sym., III, 6: τὰς ὑπονοίας οὐκ ἐπίστανται, Plat. Resp., II, 378d: Socrates has no interest in Homer's accounts of the conflicts of the gods οὔτ' ἐν ὑπονοίαις πεποιημένας οὔτε ἄνευ ὑπονοιῶν· ὁ γὰρ νέος οὐχ οἷός τε κρίνειν ὅ τι τε ὑπόνοια καὶ ὃ μή, Aristot. Eth. Nic., IV, 14, p. 1128a, 23 f.: τοῖς μὲν γὰρ ἦν γελοῖον ἡ αἰσχρολογία, τοῖς δὲ μᾶλλον ἡ ὑπόνοια (the concealed expression), Plut. Aud. Poet., 4 (II, 19e): ταῖς πάλαι μὲν ὑπονοίαις ἀλληγορίαις δὲ νῦν λεγομέναις, Philo Jos., 28: the story acc. to the OT wording καὶ τὰ ἐν ὑπονοίαις προσαποδοῦναι, Cl. Al. Strom., V, 24, 1: δι' ὑπονοίας (by a parable), Quis Div. Salv., 26, 1 etc.

In the list of vices in 1 Tm. 6:4 f., which depicts the terrible effects of the pathological penchant of false teachers for debate and wordy warfare, ὑπόνοιαι

---

[2] Cf. Etym. M., 783: ὑπονοεῖν οὖν, τὸ μὴ τελέως νοεῖν τὸ προκείμενον.

[3] C℞D(𝔓[45] ?): τίνα με, though this is not original (in spite of Zn. Ag., *ad loc.*).

[4] Cf. Etym. M., 783: ἡ ὑπὸ πρόθεσις (the prep. ὑπο-) ἐντελοῦς διανοίας ἔλλειψιν δηλοῖ.

[5] Cf. Hesych., *s.v.*: ὑπόνοια· ὑπερηφανία, θράσος.

[6] In LXX 4:19 (v. 16 in Aram. text) and 5:6 ὑπόνοια corresponds to the Aram. רַעְיוֹנָא "thought" (Θ: διαλογισμός), but only verbally, since the meaning of the stories is changed in the LXX text.

πονηραί, alongside βλασφημίαι,[7] are wicked intrigues and common insinuations which in the disputes, moving from the material aspect to the personal, they raise against their opponents in an attempt to discredit them in every possible way and to magnify themselves.[8]

† νουθετέω, νουθεσία.

νουθετέω (= νοῦν τίθημι, sc. in the heart, mind, etc., cf. Hom. Il., 13, 732; Od., 2, 124 f.), strictly νοῦς (→ 952), i.e., "to impart understanding (a mind for something)," with acc. of person (e.g., Test. Jos. 6:8), "to set right," "to have a corrective influence on someone," with double acc. "to lay on the heart of someone." νουθετεῖν can mean "to impart understanding," "to teach" (Democr. Fr., 52 [II, 156, 15 f., Diels[5]]: τὸν οἰόμενον νοῦν ἔχειν ὁ νουθετέων ματαιοπονεῖ) but it is not a direct synon. of διδάσκειν (→ II, 135 f.), though often linked with it, e.g., Plat. Ap., 26a, where Socrates takes aside someone who has unintentionally given a false account of something in order to instruct and warn him (ἰδίᾳ λαβόντα διδάσκειν καὶ νουθετεῖν), Leg., VIII, 845b (→ n. 4), Prot., 323d (→ n. 4), Plut. Aud., 3, 15 (II, 39a, 46b); Phil. Decal., 87 (of conscience): ὡς δικαστὴς διδάσκει, νουθετεῖ, παραινεῖ μεταβάλλεσθαι. In the case of διδάσκειν the primary effect is on the intellect, and someone qualified exercises the influence. νουθετεῖν, however, describes an effect on the will and disposition, and it presupposes an opposition which has to be overcome. It seeks to correct the mind, to put right what is wrong, to improve the spiritual attitude.[1] "The basic idea is that of the well-meaning earnestness with which one seeks to influence the mind and disposition by appropriate instruction, exhortation, warning and correction,"[2] cf. Plat. Euthyd., 284e : φιλῶ σε, ἀλλὰ νουθετῶ σε ὡς ἑταῖρον, Ep. Ar., 207: εἰ τοὺς καλοὺς καὶ ἀγαθοὺς τῶν ἀνθρώπων ἐπιεικέστερον νουθετεῖς, Dio Chrys. Or., 51, 5 : ὁ δὲ μετ' εὐνοίας νουθετῶν, *ibid.*, 7: νουθετεῖν ἠβούλετο τοὺς ἁμαρτάνοντας καὶ τὸ γοῦν καθ' αὐτὸν βελτίονας ποιεῖν. Hence the dominant meanings "to admonish, warn, soothe, remind, correct," Aesch. Prom., 264 f.: παραινεῖν νουθετεῖν τε τοὺς κακῶς πράσσοντας, Soph. Oed. Col., 1193 f.: νουθετούμενοι φίλων ἐπῳδαῖς, Aristot. Pol., I, 13, p. 1260b, 5 ff.: λέγουσιν οὐ καλῶς οἱ λόγου τοὺς δούλους ἀποστεροῦντες καὶ φάσκοντες ἐπιτάξει χρῆσθαι μόνον· νουθετητέον γὰρ μᾶλλον τοὺς δούλους ἢ τοὺς παῖδας, Ps.-Democr. Fr., 302, 168 (II, 222, 7 f., Diels[5]): νεκρὸν ἰατρεύειν καὶ γέροντα νουθετεῖν ταὐτόν ἐστι, Philo Virt., 94 : ἄκοντας νουθετεῖ καὶ σωφρονίζει νόμοις ἱεροῖς, Vit. Mos., I, 110 : τοὺς οἰκήτορας τῆς χώρας ὁ θεὸς νουθετῆσαι μᾶλλον ἐβούλετο ἢ διαφθεῖραι, Jos. Ant., 20, 162 etc. Aiming both to ward off and to impel, νουθετεῖν takes place through the word, *v.* Aristot. Rhet., II, 18, p. 1391b, 10 f.: ἄν τε πρὸς ἕνα τις τῷ λόγῳ χρώμενος προτρέπῃ ἢ ἀποτρέπῃ, οἷον οἱ νουθετοῦντες ποιοῦσιν. It is an elementary means of education (→ παιδεύω)[3] which the father uses, Plat. Resp., VIII, 560a. A divine pedagogue like the *logos* of

---

[7] → I, 622 f. On βλασφημία and ὑπόνοια together cf. Cl. Al. Paed., III, 81, 3 : καὶ τοῦτο ἐκπέπληκεν ὑπονοίας αἰσχρᾶς καὶ βλασφημίας τὸ ἀνέδην χρῆσθαι τῷ φιλήματι.

[8] Cf. Schl. Past., *ad loc.* The expression is not found even in the Cynic Stoic diatribe, of which the polemic of 1 Tm. reminds us (cf. Dib. Past., *ad loc.*). The similarity to Sir. 3:24 (→ 1018) is purely formal, not material. The idea of wicked allegories is wide of the mark here, in spite of 1 Tm. 1:4; Tt. 3:9; 2 Tm. 2:14.

νουθετέω, νουθεσία. Pass., Liddell-Scott, Moult.-Mill., Preisigke Wört., Cr.-Kö., Pr.-Bauer, *s.v.*; Trench, 68 f.; W. Crönert, "De critici arte in papyris exercenda," *Raccolta di scritti in onore di Giacomo Lumbroso* (1925), 500.

[1] διδάσκειν means "to show how," νουθετεῖν "to show what is wrong" [A. Debrunner].

[2] Cr.-Kö., 773.

[3] νουθετεῖν as a synon. of παιδεύειν, e.g., Plut. Aud. Poet., 4 (II, 20b): οἱ γοῦν φιλόσοφοι παραδείγμασι χρῶνται, νουθετοῦντες καὶ παιδεύοντες ἐξ ὑποκειμένων, Philo Spec. Leg., IV, 96.

Philo or the Christ of Cl. Al. is also depicted νουθετῶν; encouraging, warning, censuring, he instructs men, cf. Philo Poster. C., 68; Cl. Al. Paed., I, 75, 1; 76, 1; Prot., I, 6, 2 etc. There is, however, no technical use of νουθετεῖν for the educational work of the philosopher, not even in Plut. Aud. Poet., 4, → n. 3). νουθετεῖν in this sense is a means of pedagogical discipline. It does not mean "to punish," [4] but through the word (Xenoph. Mem., I, 2, 21: νουθετικοὶ λόγοι) to cause the appeal to the moral consciousness to gain a hold over men and bring them to repentance and shame, [5] so that punishment is superfluous. [6] In keeping with pedagogic experience, however, the word can have the secondary sense of actively affecting the mind, i.e., "to discipline," e.g., Aristoph. Vesp., 254 : κονδύλοις (blows) νουθετήσεθ' ἡμᾶς, Plat. Leg., IX, 879d : The youth must not presume πληγαῖς νουθετεῖν a stranger, Plut. Aetia Romana, 82 (II, 283e): αἱ μὲν ῥάβδοι (sc. of the praetors) νουθετοῦσι τὸ μεταθέσθαι δυνάμενον, οἱ δὲ πελέκεις ἀποκόπτουσι τὸ ἀνουθέτητον, Philo Congr., 118 : δέκα πληγαῖς καὶ τιμωρίαις ὁ τῶν ὅλων ἐπίτροπος καὶ κηδεμὼν νουθετεῖ, Jos. Ant., 8, 217: εἰ μάστιξιν αὐτοὺς ἐκεῖνος (Solomon) ἐνουθέτει, [7] σκορπίοις τοῦτο ποιήσειν αὐτὸν (Rehoboam) προσδοκᾶν.

The LXX, which hardly uses νουθετέω to render Heb. terms except in Job, shares for the most part the general Gk. understanding. In 1 Βασ. 3:13 it is used for כָּהָה pi, "to reproach, reprimand," Job 4:3 יָסַר pi, "urge, admonish." In Job 40:4 νουθετούμενος (no Heb.) means "him whom God has chastened," i.e., Job. In Job 30:1; 36:12 (no apparent relation to the HT) the verb means "to warn, correct," cf. also (of God) Wis. 11:10 : πατὴρ νουθετῶν, 12:2, 26; Ps. Sol. 13:9 : νουθετήσει δίκαιον ὡς υἱὸν ἀγαπήσεως. [8] The unusual νουθετεῖσθαι (for בִּין, hitp or q) occurs at Job 23:15; 37:14; 38:18; 34:16 in the sense "to let oneself be taught," "to understand," "to have understanding."

νουθεσία, [9] the corresponding noun, means "admonition," Aristoph. Ra., 1009 f.: νουθεσία is one of the most admirable qualities of poets, who make men better ; Plat. Resp., III, 399b: νουθέτησις ("exhortation") with διδαχή ("instruction"), Diod. S., XV, 7: φιλικὴν νουθεσίαν ἐπιφθεγξάμενοι, Dio Chrys. Or., 78, 42 : σφοδροτέραν τὴν

---

[4] In so far as punishment is educative on the Gk. view admonition or reprimand might be regarded as its mildest form, Plat. Gorg., 478e : ὁ νουθετούμενός τε καὶ ἐπιπληττόμενος καὶ δίκην διδούς, *loc. cit.:* μήτε νουθετεῖσθαι μήτε κολάζεσθαι μήτε δίκην διδόναι, Plat. Prot., 323d : οὐδεὶς θυμοῦται οὐδὲ νουθετεῖ οὐδὲ διδάσκει οὐδὲ κολάζει . . ., ἵνα μὴ τοιοῦτοι ὦσιν, Philo Spec. Leg., II, 232 : the father has authority to scold a child (κακηγορεῖν), to correct it firmly (ἐμβριθέστερον νουθετεῖν), and then if it ignores verbal warnings to beat it etc. But νουθετεῖν occupies a special position, cf. Plat. Leg., VIII, 845b: τὸν μὲν δοῦλον πληγαῖς κολάζειν, τὸν δὲ ἐλεύθερον ἀποπέμπειν νουθετήσαντα καὶ διδάξαντα, Themist. Or., 22 (p. 336, Dindorf): οἱ . . . ἀληθινοὶ καὶ μεστοὶ παρρησίας οὐκ ὀνειδίζουσι — πάμπολυ γὰρ διαφέρει νουθεσία μὲν λοιδορίας, ἐπίπληξις δὲ ὀνείδους, οὐ τῇ διανοίᾳ μόνῃ τοῦ λέγοντος, ἀλλὰ καὶ αὐτῷ τῷ λόγῳ εὐνοίας καὶ παρρησίας — νουθετοῦντες, οὐ λοιδορούμενοι, καὶ ἐπανορθοῦντες, οὐκ ὀνειδίζοντες.

[5] Cf. Plut. Adulat., 28 (II, 68 f.): ἔνεστι τὸ νουθετοῦν καὶ μετάνοιαν ἐμποιοῦν, De Virtute Morali, 12 (II, 452c): ἡ νουθεσία καὶ ὁ ψόγος ἐμποιεῖ μετάνοιαν καὶ αἰσχύνην.

[6] Pythagorean pedagogy emphasised esp. in νουθετεῖν = πεδαρτᾶν (παιδαρτᾶν *v.* Pass. and Liddell-Scott, *s.v.*) the silent and quietly expectant attitude, *v.* Iambl. Vit. Pyth., 31, 197 (I, 471, 11 f., Diels[5]).

[7] LXX at 3 Βασ. 12:11; 2 Ch. 10:11: ἐπαίδευσεν.

[8] Cf. also Test. B. 4:5 β (the good man) τὸν ἀθετοῦντα τὸν ὕψιστον νουθετῶν ἐπιστρέψει.

[9] Like νουθετ(ε)ία a rarer synon. of νουθέτησις; on the various words cf. Liddell-Scott, Moult.-Mill. and Pr.-Bauer. In def. cf. Cl. Al. Paed., I, 94, 2 : By derivation νουθέτησις means νοῦ ἐνθεματισμός (establishing of understanding); hence education by νουθέτησις is adapted to create understanding (νοῦ περιποιητικόν). Cf. I, 76, 1: νουθέτησις . . . ψόγος κηδεμονικός (concerned censure), νοῦ ἐμποιητικός (which brings amendment).

νουθεσίαν καὶ παρακέλευσιν ποιούμενος αὐτῷ τε κἀκείνοις, "correction," Plut. De Virtute Morali, 12 (II, 452c): αὐτούς γε μὴν τούτους ὁρᾶν ἔστι ... τοὺς νέους ... πολλάκις ... νουθεσίαις κολάζοντας, "chastisement," cf. Gellius, Noctes Atticae, VII, 14 (I, 298, C. Hosius): *poeniendis peccatis tres esse debere causas existimatum est. una est causa quae Graece* <*vel* κόλασις> *vel* νουθεσία *dicitur, cum poena adhibetur castigandi atque emendandi gratia, ut is, qui fortuito deliquit, attentior fiat correctiorque.* The word is common in Philo in the sense "admonition," "warning," "correction," e.g., Vit. Mos., II, 241, Leg. All., III, 193, Migr. Abr., 14 (with σωφρονισμός), Deus Imm., 54 (with παιδεία), Vit. Mos., I, 98 (with ἐπίπληξις), Spec. Leg., III, 141: πληγὰς ἕνεκα νουθεσίας ἐντεῖναι, cf. also Jos. Ant., 3, 311: τιμωρίαν ..., οἵαν δὲ οἱ πατέρες ἐπὶ νουθεσίᾳ τοῖς τέκνοις ἐπιφέρουσιν, Test. R. 3:8: μήτε ἀκούων νουθεσίας πατέρων αὐτοῦ. νουθεσίαι as a means of divine chastening, Philo Op. Mund., 128: God is not afraid to punish like a judge, now through more violent threats, now through milder warnings (νουθεσίαις) ..., through warnings when a man has sinned involuntarily and unthinkingly, so that he will not commit the same offence again."

The only LXX use is at Wis. 16:6 (of the warning of the wilderness generation by divinely sent plagues): εἰς νουθεσίαν δὲ πρὸς ὀλίγον ἐταράχθησαν. νουθέτημα is synon. at Job 5:17 (HT מוּסָר) of the chastening of man by God.[10] Cf. νουθέτησις, Jdt. 8:27: εἰς νουθέτησιν μαστιγοῖ κύριος τοὺς ἐγγίζοντας αὐτῷ, though at Prv. 2:2 the ref. is to the educative admonition of the son by the father.

The group occurs in the NT only in Paul and the sphere of his influence. The pedagogic sense may be discerned in the noun (→ 1019 f.). νουθεσία (κυρίου), with → παιδεία,[11] is a means of Christian upbringing in the household table of Eph. (6:4b). It denotes the word of admonition which is designed to correct while not provoking or embittering (cf. v. 4a: μὴ παροργίζετε).[12] Divine judgments in the OT have saving pedagogic significance as warning examples πρὸς νουθεσίαν ἡμῶν,[13] 1 C. 10:11 (→ 1019 f.). A peculiarity of the NT use of the verb is that νουθετεῖν, like → παρακαλεῖν, → παραμυθεῖσθαι, → στηρίζειν, is now a task and function of the pastor. The man who by admonition and correction seeks to turn others from what is wrong and to lay the good on their hearts is the apostle, the preacher of the Gospel, the one who bears responsibility for the faith and life of the primitive churches. Thus Paul's own preaching of Christ seeks to show the hearer what he is and what he should be, τέλειος ἐν Χριστῷ (Col. 1:28).[14]

---

[10] This verse is quoted in 1 Cl., 52, 6 acc. to the LXX. On discipline and education cf. G. Bertram, "Der Begriff d. Erziehung in d. griech. Bibel," *Imago Dei, Festschrift f. G. Krüger* (1932), 33 ff.

[11] παιδεία and νουθέτησις are interchangeable in 1 Cl., 56, 2.

[12] Cf. Calvin, In omnes Pauli apostoli epistolas ... comm., *ad loc.* (II, 67, A. Tholuck): *Sit igitur comitas temperata, ut contineantur in disciplina Domini et corrigantur etiam dum errant.*

[13] Conversely acc. to Philo Abr., 4 the moral conduct of the OT saints is providentially ordained ὑπὲρ τοῦ τοὺς ἐντυγχάνοντας προτρέψασθαι (encourage) καὶ ἐπὶ τὸν ὅμοιον ζῆλον ἀγαγεῖν.

[14] So J. C. K. v. Hofmann, *D. heilige Schrift NTs,* IV, 2 (1870), 46 f. Along with and prior to → διδάσκειν (→ also 1019), the influence on the intellect, νουθετεῖν here emphasises the influencing of the disposition and will, cf. Haupt Gefbr., *ad loc.* That νουθετεῖν aims at μετάνοια and διδάσκειν at πίστις (J. B. Lightfoot, *Epistles to the Colossians and Philemon* [1875] and Loh. Kol., *ad loc.*) would imply a Gk. rather than NT view, → n. 5; 978; 999. νουθετέω and μετάνοια are linked in Gk. fashion in Cl. Al. Strom., VII, 102, 3: παιδευθεῖεν (sc. the false teachers) γοῦν πρὸς τοῦ θεοῦ, τὰς πρὸ τῆς κρίσεως πατρῴας νουθεσίας ὑπομένοντες, ἔστ' ἂν καταισχυνθέντες μετανοήσωσιν. Herm. v., 1, 3, 2 (cf. 2 Cl., 17, 2) thinks in moral terms that the aim of pastoral νουθετεῖν is penitence (μετανοεῖν) (→ 1008), cf. also 2 Cl., 19, 1 f., where ἐπιστρέφειν and νουθετεῖν are closely connected.

His pastoral work in a congregation is retrospectively presented as a special, inwardly motivated cure of souls by means of indefatigable exhortation with a view to correction and amendment (Ac. 20:31). His sharp criticism in letters is simply the corrective word of a father to his children (1 C. 4:14 f.). Similarly a congregation admonishes or corrects whether by its pastors (1 Th. 5:12: τοὺς ... νουθετοῦντας ὑμᾶς) [15] or by the reciprocal brotherly ministry of the members exercising pastoral oversight with a sense of congregational obligation (1 Th. 5:14; R. 15:14; [16] Col. 3:16). [17] If the ref. in 2 Th. 3:15 is to the correction of the refractory, in Tt. 3:10: αἱρετικὸν ἄνθρωπον μετὰ μίαν καὶ δευτέραν νουθεσίαν παραιτοῦ, νουθεσία is the attempt to make the heretic aware of the falsity of his position, a pastoral attempt to reclaim rather than a disciplinary measure, [18] though there is place for this if the corrective word is of no avail.

The NT understanding of the terms lives on in the post-apost. fathers. Only in Herm. v., 1, 3, 1 f. is there ref. to the paternal duty of νουθετεῖν. In the vocabulary of the Christian community νουθετέω, νουθεσία and νουθέτησις are common terms for pastoral admonition, for mutual exhortation to amendment of life, repentance and conversion, [19] cf. 1 Cl., 7, 1; 56, 2; Ign. Eph., 3, 1; Herm. v., 2, 4, 3; m., 8, 10; 2 Cl., 17, 2; 19, 2. [20] The terms can also apply more specifically to the admonitory sermon preached at divine worship, cf. 2 Cl., 17:3: ἐν τῷ νουθετεῖσθαι ἡμᾶς ὑπὸ τῶν πρεσβυτέρων, Just. Apol., 67, 4: ὁ προεστὼς διὰ λόγου τὴν νουθεσίαν ... ποιεῖται.

Behm

νόμος, ἀνομία, ἄνομος, ἔννομος, νομικός, νόμιμος, νομοθέτης, νομοθεσία, νομοθετέω, παρανομία, παρανομέω

νομοδιδάσκαλος → II, 159

νόμος.

Contents: A. νόμος in the Greek and Hellenistic World: 1. The Meaning of νόμος; 2. The Nature and Development of the Concept in the Greek World; 3. νόμος in Hellenism; 4. The Greek Concept of νόμος and the New Testament. B. The Law in the Old

---

[15] Cf. on this Dob. Th., *ad loc.*

[16] Even if the preceding word in the original is not ἀλλήλους but ἄλλους 𝔎 33 etc., though cf. syr Orig; so Zn. R. as opposed to Ltzm. R., *ad loc.*), the ref. is to the education or pastoral admonition of Christians.

[17] On the construction, which is less complicated than Loh. Kol., *ad loc.* supposes, cf. Ew. and Dib. Gefbr.

[18] So Joachim Jeremias (*NT Deutsch*, 9^3, 1937), *ad loc.*

[19] → n. 14.

[20] There is a singular usage in Herm. v., 3, 5, 4 where the angel admonishes new converts to good works.

νόμος. On A.: In Plat. Leg. Gk. thinking on law and the historical concept find philosophically refined expression. From the rich and only partially preserved lit. περὶ νόμου one might mention Ps.-Plat. Min.; Ps.-Demosth. Or., 25, 15 ff.; Chrysipp. Fr., 314 ff. (III, 77 ff., v. Arnim); Cic. De legibus; Dio Chrys. Or., 58 (Budé); Stob. Ecl., IV, 115-183; Orph. Hymn., 64. Modern works: U. v. Wilamowitz, "Aus Kydathen, Exc. 1: Die Herrschaft des Gesetzes," PhU, 1 (1880), 47 ff.; R. Hirzel, *Themis, Dike u. Verwandtes* (1907), 133 ff.; ΑΓΡΑΦΟΣ ΝΟΜΟΣ in *Abhdl. Sächs. Akad. Wiss.*, 20 (1900), 65 ff.; V. Ehren-

Testament: 1. The Law in Ancient Israel; 2. The Understanding of the Law in the Older Historical Books; 3. The Attitude of the Prophets towards the Law; 4. The Deuteronomic Understanding of the Law; 5. The Understanding of the Law in the Priestly Writing and Related Works; 6. The Law in the Post-Exilic Period; 7. The Meaning of תּוֹרָה; 8. νόμος in the LXX. C. The Law in Judaism: 1. The Law in the Pseudepigrapha and Apocrypha; 2. Josephus; 3. Philo; 4. The Law in Rabbinic Judaism. D. The Law in the New Testament: I. Jesus and the Law in the Synoptic Gospels: 1. The Occurrence of the Word νόμος; 2. Jesus' Negation of the Law; 3. Jesus' Affirmation of the Law; 4. The Interrelation of Negation and Affirmation of the Law. II. The Conflict concerning the Law: 1. The Primitive Community; 2. The Usage of Paul; 3. The Material Understanding of the Law in Paul; III. The Period after the Conflict: 1. Hebrews; 2. James; 3. John's Gospel.

A. νόμος in the Greek and Hellenistic World.

1. The Meaning of νόμος.

a. νόμος belongs etym. to νέμω, "to allot," and thus has the sense of "what is proper," "what is assigned to someone."[1] In ancient times it has a comprehensive range

berg, *D. Rechtsidee im frühen Griechentum* (1921), 103 ff.; W. Jaeger, "D. griech. Staatsethik im Zeitalter d. Plato" (1924), in *Humanistische Reden u. Vortr.* (1937), 96 ff.; *Paideia* (1934), 152 ff.; H. E. Stier, ΝΟΜΟΣ ΒΑΣΙΛΕΥΣ in *Philol.*, 83 (1928), 225 ff.; H. Bogner, "D. griech. Nomos. Die Zersetzung d. griech. Nomos," *Deutsches Volkstum,* 13 (1931), 745 ff.; 854 ff.; M. Mühl, "Unters. z. altorient. u. althell. Gesetzgebung," *Klio Beih.*, 29 (1933), 85 ff.; U. Galli, *Platone e il Nomos* (1937); A. Bill, *La morale et la loi dans la philosophie antique* (1928), esp. 261 ff., where the most important ancient texts are assembled; K. Kerényi, *D. antike Religion* (1940), 77 ff. On B.: A. Alt, "Die Ursprünge d. isr. Rechts," SAW phil. hist. Kl. (1934); J. Begrich, "Die priesterliche Thora," *Werden u. Wesen d. AT,* ed. Volz, Stummer, Hempel (1936), 63 ff.; A. Jepsen, *Untersuchungen zum Bundesbuch* (1927); O. Procksch, *Die Elohimquelle* (1906), 225 ff., 263 ff.; L. Köhler, "Der Dekalog," ThR (1929), 161 ff.; G. v. Rad, *Das Gottesvolk im Deuteronomium* (1929); H. H. Schaeder, *Esra d. Schreiber* (1930). On C.: Bousset-Gressm.; L. Couard, *Die religiösen u. sittlichen Anschauungen d. at.lichen Apokryphen u. Pseudepigr.* (1907); S. Kaatz, *Die mündliche Lehre u. ihr Dogma* (1921/22); M. Löwy, "Die paul. Lehre vom Gesetz," *Monatsschrift f. Geschichte u. Wissenschaft des Judentums* (1903 f.); E. Stein, *Die allegorische Exegese d. Philo aus Alex.* (1929); *Philo u. d. Midrasch* (1931); J. Wohlgemuth, "Das jüdische Religionsgesetz in jüdischer Beleuchtung," *Jahresbericht 1918/19 des Rabbinerseminars Berlin* (1919). On D.: K. Benz, "Die Stellung Jesu zum at.lichen Gesetz," *Bibl. Studien,* XIX, 1 (1914); W. Brandt, *Das Gesetz Israels u. d. Gesetze d. Heiden bei Paulus und im Hebräerbrief* (1934); B. H. Branscomb, *Jesus and the Law of Moses* (New York, 1930); R. Bultmann, "Die Bedeutung des geschichtl. Jesus f. d. Theol. d. Paulus," *Glauben u. Verstehen* (1933); Cr.-Kö., *s.v.*; E. Grafe, *Die paul. Lehre vom Gesetz*[2] (1893); A. Harnack, "Hat Jesus das at.liche Gesetz abgeschafft?" *Aus Wissenschaft u. Leben,* II (1911), 225 ff.; J. Herkenrath, *Die Ethik Jesu in ihren Grundzügen* (1926); A. Juncker, *Die Ethik d. Apostels Paulus,* I (1904), II (1919); G. Kittel, "Die Stellung des Jakobus zu Judentum u. Heidenchristentum," ZNW, 30 (1931), 145 ff.; E. Lohmeyer, *Grundlagen paul. Theologie,* c. I (1929); O. Michel, *Paulus u. seine Bibel* (1929); A. W. Slaten, "The Qualitative Use of 'Nomos' in the Pauline Epistles," AThJ, XXIII (1919), 213 ff.; E. Brunner, *Der Mensch im Widerspruch* (1937), 150 ff., 532 ff.

[1] Walde-Pok., 2 (1927), 330. Gk. philosophy liked to appeal to this etym. derivation in its interpretation of the concept (Plat. Leg., IV, 714a; Ps.-Plat. Min., 317d; M. Ant., 10, 25; Plut. Quaest. Conv., 2, 10 [II, 644c]). The basic idea behind νέμειν explains why νόμος, in the course of development, is often connected and even equated with → δίκη, δίκαιον, ἴσον (→ II, 179, 13 ff., 182, 26 ff.; Pind. Fr., 215; Plat. Resp., II, 359a; Aristot. Eth. Nic., 5, 2, p. 1129a, 33 f.; Xenoph. Mem., IV, 4, 13; Eur. Phoen., 538), → τάξις (Plat. Resp., IX, 587a; Leg., VI, 780d; Phileb., 26b; Aristot. Pol., 7, 4, p. 1326a, 30), → λόγος (→ IV, 79; Plat. Resp., X, 604a; Leg., II, 659d; Chrysipp. Fr., 4 [III, 4, 2 f., v. Arnim]; Plut. Stoic. Rep., 1 [II, 1033b]; Plot. Enn., III, 2, 4), → νοῦς (Plat., Leg., XII, 957c; Aristot. Pol., 3, 16, p. 1287a, 32; Plot. Enn., V, 9, 5).

of meaning which embraces any kind of existing or accepted norm, order, custom, usage or tradition. Νόμος is what is valid and in use: τί οὖν ἄλλο νόμος εἴη ἂν ... ἢ τὰ νομιζόμενα (Ps.-Plat. Min., 313b; cf. Aristoph. Nu., 1185 f.; 1420 ff.; Xenoph. Mem., IV, 4, 19). The concept is religious in origin and plays a main role in the cultus. The connection between νόμος and veneration of the gods finds linguistic expression in the fixed phrase νομίζειν θεούς (Hdt., 1, 131; 4, 59; Aristoph. Nu., 329; 423), i.e., to honour the gods, according to the cultic usage of the *polis,* by participation in (national) worship:[2] ὥς κε πόλις ῥέζῃσι, νόμος δ' ἀρχαῖος ἄριστος (Hes. Fr., 221 [Rzach], cf. Plat. Crat., 400e: ἐν ταῖς εὐχαῖς νόμος ἐστίν). Marriage, procreation (Plat. Leg., IV, 720e ff.), the erotic life (Plat. Symp., 182a), common meals, gymnastic schools, the use of weapons (Plat. Leg., I, 625c) and esp. the honouring and burial of the dead (Thuc., 2, 35; Eur. Suppl., 563; Isoc. Or., 12, 169) all come under the concept. The establishment and regulation of the Nemean games (Pind. Nem., 10, 28; cf. Isthm., 2, 38) can be described as νόμος no less than a political order and constitution (Pind. Pyth., 2, 86; 10, 70). The gods, too, have νόμοι (Pind. Pyth., 2, 43; Nem., 1, 72; cf. Hes. Theog., 66). This extensive usage is always maintained.

b. As political order developed in Greece, however, the word came into specialised use in the juridical sphere. The legal norm or use becomes consciously stabilised and binding νόμος or law. No distinction is here made between political and absolute law (Heracl. Fr., 114 [I, 176, 5 ff., Diels[5]]; Aesch. Prom., 150 f.; Pind. Fr., 169; Soph. Oed. Tyr., 865). νόμος broadens out into the (divine) law of the world (Plat. Leg., IV, 716a; Callim. Hymn., 5, 100; M. Ant., 7, 9), the law of nature (Plat. Gorg., 483e; Dio Chrys. Or., 58, 5 [Budé]; Porphyr. Abst., 2, 61), the (philosophical) moral law (Epict. Diss., I, 26, 1; Muson., p. 87, 5 ff. [Hense]). c. Only in the 5th cent., as the νόμος came to be written down in individual νόμοι, does the word acquire, in the context of democratic development, the special sense of a "written law," "a fixed expression of legal order and the national constitution in a democratic *polis*" (Aristot. Resp. Ath., 7, 1; Andoc. Myst., 83). The legal definition may be seen in Xenoph. Mem., I, 2, 42 ff.: νόμοι εἰσίν, οὓς τὸ πλῆθος συνελθὸν καὶ δοκιμάσαν ἔγραψε. Νόμος is the compulsory command or order of a state, with punishment for violation (Antiphon. Or., 6, 4; Democr. Fr., 181 [II, 181, 11 ff., Diels[5]]; Ps.-Aristot. Rhet. Al., 2, p. 1422a, 2 ff.). d. When νόμος, as distinct from the divine → φύσις, came to be understood essentially as a human statute (Hippocr. Vict., 1, 11; Diod. S. Excerpta Vaticana, 7, 26 [p. 26, Dindorf]) it could finally become, in the Sophist writers at the end of the 5th cent., a "contract" or "convention" (Aristoph. Av., 755 ff.; esp. in the formula νόμῳ/φύσει, Democr. Fr., 9 [II, 139, 10 ff.]; Hippias in Plat. Prot., 337c) — a degenerate sense which has nothing to do with the original meaning of νόμος. e. The basic meaning νόμος = τάξις caused νόμος to become a tt. in music in the sense of "mode of singing," "melody" (Alcman. Fr., 93, Diehl; Hom. Hymn. Ap., 20; Aesch. Prom., 576). From the time of Plato it became a habit to play on the twofold political and musical sense (Plat. Leg., IV, 722d f; 800a; Archytas Pythagoraeus in Stob. Ecl., IV, 1, 138 [p. 88, 2 ff., Hense]; Max. Tyr., 6, 7).

In relation to Jn. 7:51 and R. 3:19 it is not unimportant that like so many other basic Gk. concepts Νόμος was personified and presented as a divine figure in poetry (Eur. Hec., 799 f.; Plat. Crito, 50a ff.) and later in theology (Procl. in Rem. Publ., II, 307, 20 ff. [Kroll]). In the same connection one might mention the expressions ὁ νόμος συντάσσει, ἀγορεύει, λέγει (Inscr. Magn., 92a, 11; b 16; Plat. Resp., V, 451b; Callim. Hymn., 5, 100),[3] the description of νόμος as δεσπότης (Hdt., 7, 104), τύραννος (Plat. Prot., 337c), βασιλεύς (Pind. Fr., 169 etc.), and finally even as θεός (Plat. Ep., VIII, 354e;

---

[2] So also in the charge against Socrates: ἀδικεῖ Σωκράτης οὓς μὲν ἡ πόλις νομίζει θεοὺς οὐ νομίζων, Xenoph. Mem., I, 1, 1 f. Only in Plat. Apol., 26c ff. does νομίζειν come to have the intellectual sense "to acknowledge," "to believe" (cf. Aristoph. Nu., 819; Eur. Suppl., 732). Cf. A. Menzel, *Hellenika* (1938), 17 f.; J. Tate, Class. Rev., 51 (1937), 3 ff.

[3] Cf. W. Schubart, "Das Gesetz u. der Kaiser in Gr. Urkunden," *Klio,* 30 (1937), 56 ff.

TGF Fr. adesp. 471). In mythical form Dio Chrys. Or., 58, 8 (Budé) extols νόμος as τοῦ Διὸς ὄντως υἱός. As πάρεδρος τοῦ Διός (Orph. Fr., 160, Kern), as the daughter of Δικαιοσύνη and Εὐσέβεια (Fr., 159), it appears alongside Δικαιοσύνη in Orphism, which addresses a special hymn to it as a cosmic power (Hymn. Orph., 64, ed. Quandt, 1941).

2. The Nature and Development of the Concept in the Greek World.

As the epitome of what is valid in social dealings νόμος in its unwritten form is first rooted in religion. In the phrases τὰ νομιζόμενα, νομίζειν θεούς (→ 1024) it constantly maintained its relation to the cultus and to worship of the gods (cf. the Pythagorean precept: ἀθανάτους μὲν πρῶτα θεούς, νόμῳ ὡς διάκεινται, τίμα Carmen Aureum, 1 f.; Iambl. Vit. Pyth., 144; Diog. L., 8, 33). Even the written law of the νόμος is still an expression of the will of the deity which holds sway in the city: ὁ μὲν οὖν τὸν νόμον κελεύων ἄρχειν δοκεῖ κελεύειν ἄρχειν τὸν θεὸν καὶ τὸν νοῦν μόνους, Aristot. Pol., 3, 16, p. 1287a, 28 ff., cf. Plat. Leg., IV, 712b. This rootage in the divine sphere, which always persists, gives to the Gk. νόμος concept its characteristic significance and true strength.

This applies particularly to the origin of νόμος. It is of the nature of νόμος to have an author. Either the gods give it: πᾶς ἐστιν νόμος εὕρημα μὲν καὶ δῶρον θεῶν, Ps.-Demosth. Or., 25, 16 (cf. Philo Decal., 15; Soph. Ant., 450 ff.; Xenoph. Mem., IV, 4, 19), or it is the work of a great personality, the law-giver: νόμους ..., ἀγαθῶν καὶ παλαιῶν νομοθετῶν εὑρήματα (Plat. Prot., 326d; cf. Hdt., 1, 29; Critias Fr., 25, 5 ff. [II, 386 f., Diels[5]]). This is the man who has special insight either by divine endowment or from within himself (πόλιν δὲ ἢ παρὰ θεῶν τινος ἢ παρὰ τούτου τοῦ γνόντος ταῦτα λόγον παραλαβοῦσαν, νόμον θεμένην, Plat. Leg., I, 645b, cf. Polit., 300c. The νόμος is thus a work of supreme skill (Plat. Leg., X, 890d; Polit., 297a) and wisdom (Hdt., 1, 196 f.; Eur. Ion, 1312 f.; Plat. Leg., IV, 712a; Max. Tyr., 6, 7). This does not prevent the mythico-historical legislation of the nation from being directly attributed in many cases to specific gods or to the religious authority of Delphi: τόν τε Μίνω παρὰ Διὸς δι' ἐνάτου ἔτους λαμβάνειν τοὺς νόμους ἱστοροῦσι φοιτῶντα εἰς τὸ τοῦ Διὸς ἄντρον, τόν τε αὖ Λυκοῦργον τὰ νομοθετικὰ εἰς Δελφοὺς πρὸς τὸν Ἀπόλλωνα συνεχὲς ἀπιόντα παιδεύεσθαι γράφουσι Πλάτων τε καὶ Ἀριστοτέλης καὶ Ἔφορος, ... Ζάλευκον τὸν Λοκρὸν παρὰ τῆς Ἀθηνᾶς τοὺς νόμους λαμβάνειν ἀπομνημονεύουσιν. οἳ δὲ τὸ ἀξιόπιστον τῆς παρ' Ἕλλησι νομοθεσίας, ὡς οἷόν τε αὐτοῖς, ἐπαίροντες εἰς τὸ θεῖον ... (Cl. Al. Strom., I, 170, 3 with Adnotatio).[4] When finally the νόμοι came into being in the *polis* by mutual agreement and decision (Xenoph. Mem., I, 2, 42 f.), this was the beginning of their downfall; they soon became mere ψηφίσματα rather than νόμοι (Demosth. Or., 20, 89 ff.).

a. In the earliest period νόμος is a creation and revelation of Zeus βασιλεύς. It is thus anchored in a divine sphere in which there is true belief.

Myth traces back the nomothesia of King Minos (βασιλεὺς καὶ νομοθέτης, Plut. Thes., 16 [I, 7]) to his dealings with Zeus (cf. Plat. Leg., I, 624a). The god is the original of the kingly power and wisdom reflected in νόμος. In Hes. Theog., 901 ff. the θεῶν βασιλεύς (886), after defeating the Titans, contracts a marriage with Themis,

[4] Cf. J. Mewaldt, *Wiener Studien*, 58 (1940), 8 f. In Stoicism God is the wisest and oldest law-giver of the whole world, Dio Chrys. Or., 19, 32 (Budé). This thought is particularly common in Philo: νομοθέτης γὰρ καὶ πηγὴ νόμων αὐτός (sc. θεός), Sacr. AC, 131; Op. Mund., 61; Spec. Leg., I, 279 etc. In the Isis aretalogy of Kyme the goddess extols herself as a law-giver (W. Peek, *Der Isishymnos von Andros* [1930], p. 122, 4): ἐγὼ νόμους ἀνθρώποις ἐθέμην καὶ ἐνομοθέτησα ἃ οὐθεὶς δύναται μεταθεῖναι.

from which spring Δίκη, Εἰρήνη and Εὐνομίη, i.e., true order or good νόμος.[5] Pindar Fr., 169 lauds νόμος as ὁ πάντων βασιλεὺς θνατῶν τε καὶ ἀθανάτων who ἄγει δικαιῶν τὸ βιαιότατον ὑπερτάτᾳ χειρί. Here the language and the train of thought both show that νόμος occupies the place of him who is πάντων βασιλεύς (Democr. Fr., 30 [II, 151, 14, Diels[5]]; Hes. Fr., 195 [Rzach], cf. Theog., 923) and who unites power and right in his hand, namely, Zeus.[6] Zeus it was who established the νόμος that animals should prey on one another in βία but that men should live in accordance with the δίκη which he gave them, Hes. Op., 276 ff. Κράτει νόμου, i.e., in virtue of the perfection of such a divine norm, of an order of will and a personal sense of right — for all these are inherent in νόμος — the law-giver Solon boasts that he has united βία and δίκη, Fr., 24, 15 f., Diehl.

Growing out of the struggle for right in the order of human life, νόμος is by its very nature righteousness (δίκη μὲν οὖν νόμου τέλος ἐστίν, Plut. Princ. Inerud., 3 [II, 780e]), → 1023, n. 1. But the δίκη or αἰδώς expressed in νόμος resides with Zeus, Plat. Prot., 322d; Ael. Arist. Or., 43, 20 (344, Keil). In terms of religious myth, the goddess Dike, obeying the supreme ruler (βασιλεύς, Plut. Exil., 5 [II, 601b]), watches over the θεῖος νόμος, Orph. Fr., 21 (Kern); Plat. Leg., IV, 716a. To late antiquity νόμος is thus connected in a special way with Zeus, → 1024.

In the *polis* established usage is given constitutional form and thus, as the epitome of all legal norms, it becomes law. Along these lines the concept can then come to specific development and mastery. For the state as a theoretical form is itself νόμος for the Greeks: πόλεως εἶναι ψυχὴν τοὺς νόμους (Aristot. of Demosth. in Stob. Ecl., IV, 1, 144 [p. 90, Hense]); ὅπου γὰρ μὴ νόμοι ἄρχουσιν, οὐκ ἔστι πολιτεία (Aristot. Pol., 4, 4, p. 1292a, 32). The people must contend for its νόμος as for its wall, Heracl. Fr., 44 (I, 160, 13 f., Diels[5]). It is the reigning power which commands as βασιλεύς or δεσπότης (→ 1030) in the *polis* and, e.g., bids the Spartans either triumph in battle or die, Hdt., 7, 104.

b. In the 6th century the new understanding of the divine world brought a corresponding change in the content of νόμος. It is still connected with deity but the Zeus of an earlier age is now reconstructed as a divine principle. The concept of the cosmos produces the view that νόμος is a reflection of the universe in which the same νόμος rules as in political life. Earthly law is simply a specific instance of divine law in the cosmos: ξὺν νόῳ λέγοντας ἰσχυρίζεσθαι χρὴ τῷ ξυνῷ πάντων, ὅκωσπερ νόμῳ πόλις, καὶ πολὺ ἰσχυροτέρως. τρέφονται γὰρ πάντες οἱ ἀνθρώπειοι νόμοι ὑπὸ ἑνὸς τοῦ θείου. κρατεῖ γὰρ τοσοῦτον ὁκόσον ἐθέλει καὶ ἐξαρκεῖ πᾶσι καὶ περιγίνεται, Heracl. Fr., 114 (I, 176, 5 ff., Diels[5]). Man cannot exist without the νόμος of his *polis*, even less so without the νόμος of the cosmos.

The Stoics who followed Heracl. regarded this later as the first mark of their cosmopolitanism, cf. Cleanthes Fr., 537 (I, 121, 34 f., v. Arnim); Dio Chrys. Or., 58, 2 (Budé). In contrast, Heracl. himself advocates rootage in the concrete νόμος πόλεως. Indeed, national law is so powerful a norm (cf. Fr., 44 [I, 160, 13 f., Diels[5]]) that Heracl. understands the universe in terms of it. The νόμος of a *polis* is common (ξυνόν

---

[5] In the early Gk. world kingship and the establishment of εὐνομίη are often connected, cf. Hdt., 1, 97 ff.; Plut. Num., 4. Plato takes up this idea when he derives the νόμοι as μιμήματα ... τῆς ἀληθείας from the βασιλικὴ τέχνη, Polit., 300c/e.

[6] So K. Kerényi, 78. On the history of this much quoted and expounded saying of Pind. (Hdt., 3, 38; Anonym. Iambl., 6, 1 [II, 402, 28 f., Diels[5]]; Plat. Gorg., 484b; Leg., III, 690b/c; IV, 714c; Chrysipp. Fr., 314 [III, 77, 34 ff., v. Arnim]), cf. H. E. Stier, 225 ff.

or κοινόν, Ps.-Demosth. Or., 25, 15 f.;[7] cf. Plat. Crito, 50a; Leg., I, 645a; Plut. Quaest. Conv., II, 10, 2 [II, 644c]). In life κατὰ νόμον the citizen lives as it were the κοινὸς βίος in contrast to private life. Similarly there is in the cosmos τὸ ξυνὸν πάντων which is explained in terms of the *polis* and its νόμος. It is the divine law of the world which one can grasp with the νοῦς (ξὺν νόῳ) and which must be followed like the λόγος and deity, Fr., 2 (I, 151, 1 ff., Diels[5]). Knowledge here is knowledge of a universal law and at the same time the keeping of this law. Both together are Gk. φρονεῖν, for ξυνόν ἐστι πᾶσι τὸ φρονέειν, Fr., 113 (I, 176, 4, Diels[5]) and ξυνόν is the universal law.

c. Greek tragedy tackles for the first time the problem of the νόμος which is against another νόμος (cf. Democr. Fr., 259 [II, 198, 2 ff., Diels[5]]), which is thus ambiguous[8] and which cannot be kept. In the midst of criticism of the νόμος in many different forms (→ 1028), Sophocles in Antigone causes the νόμος to triumph in both its aspects.[9] If the law of the state rests originally on divine law, then in the defence of Antigone (450 ff.) an unwritten divine law is set over against the law of the *polis*. Neither Zeus nor Dike, οἳ τούσδ' ἐν ἀνθρώποισιν ὥρισαν νόμους (as we should read, 452), commands Antigone to do what she does, but the ἄγραπτα κἀσφαλῆ θεῶν νόμιμα (454 f.).[10] Above the law of the state which derives from divine law is another divine law of ancient origin. But when the law which comes from God is no longer reconcilable with God, cleavage arises for the individual, cf. the tragic end of Antigone and Creon's destruction. Nothing is more distinctive of the Greek's understanding of existence than that at the point where he sees that the νόμος is equivocal and cannot be observed, since to keep one νόμος is necessarily to violate another, he never even imagines that it is he himself who absolutely and essentially is incapable of obedience to the law. The contradiction which results in the death of Antigone is for him the eternal, tragic contradiction of a law which comes from God but is no longer reconcilable with God. He traces back the contradiction to deity itself. In general inability to keep the law is no problem to the Greek. When such inability arises, it is given a tragic interpretation. It is not attributed to human sinfulness before the law.[11]

Out of the contradiction, and supplementing the written law of the *polis*, the ἄγραφος νόμος took on greater significance from the 5th century onwards (Thuc., II, 37, 3; Ps.-Aristot. Rhet. Al., 2, p. 1421b, 35 ff.).[12] In detail it is thought of in various ways,

---

[7] There is reflected here a tractate Περὶ Νόμων (cf. M. Pohlenz, NGG, 1924, 19 ff.) in which the various aspects of the traditional view of νόμος are summarised as follows: ἅπας ὁ τῶν ἀνθρώπων βίος ... φύσει καὶ νόμοις διοικεῖται. τούτων ἡ μὲν φύσις ἐστὶν ἄτακτον καὶ ἀνώμαλον (dissimilar, different) καὶ κατ' ἄνδρ' ἴδιον τοῦ ἔχοντος, οἱ δὲ νόμοι κοινὸν καὶ τεταγμένον καὶ ταὐτὸ πᾶσιν ... οἱ δὲ νόμοι τὸ δίκαιον καὶ τὸ καλὸν καὶ τὸ συμφέρον βούλονται, καὶ τοῦτο ζητοῦσιν, καὶ ἐπειδὰν εὑρεθῇ, κοινὸν τοῦτο πρόσταγμ' ἀπεδείχθη, πᾶσιν ἴσον καὶ ὅμοιον, καὶ τοῦτ' ἔστι νόμος. ᾧ πάντας πείθεσθαι προσήκει διὰ πολλά, καὶ μάλισθ' ὅτι πᾶς ἐστι νόμος εὕρημα μὲν καὶ δῶρον θεῶν, δόγμα δ' ἀνθρώπων φρονίμων, ἐπανόρθωμα δὲ τῶν ἑκουσίων καὶ ἀκουσίων ἁμαρτημάτων, πόλεως δὲ συνθήκη κοινή, καθ' ἣν πᾶσι προσήκει ζῆν τοῖς ἐν τῇ πόλει.

[8] R. Bultmann, "Polis u. Hades in d. Antigone des Sophokles," *Theol. Aufs. K. Barth zum 50. Geburtstag* (1936), 80.

[9] W. Schadewaldt, "Sophokles' Aias u. Antigone," *Neue Wege zur Antike*, 8 (1929), 114.

[10] These are the same laws as those whose divine origin is proclaimed in Soph. Oed. Tyr., 865 ff.: νόμοι πρόκεινται ὑψίποδες οὐρανίαν δι' αἰθέρα τεκνωθέντες, ὧν Ὄλυμπος πατὴρ μόνος, οὐδέ νιν θνατὰ φύσις ἀνέρων ἔτικτεν, οὐδὲ μήποτε λάθα κατακοιμάσῃ· μέγας ἐν τούτοις θεὸς οὐδὲ γηράσκει.

[11] Cf. G. Kittel, *Die Religionsgeschichte u. das Urchristentum* (1932), 118 ff.

[12] Cf. → R. Hirzel, ΑΓΡΑΦΟΣ ΝΟΜΟΣ, 29 ff.

as the ancient popular ἔθος of this or that *polis* (Diog. L., 3, 86), or more commonly as a natural or divine law valid for all men (Xenoph. Mem., IV, 4, 19 f.; Demosth. Or., 18, 275; 23, 61 and 85; Plat. Resp., VIII, 563d). Hence it is rather obscurely identified partly with the natural law of the Sophists and partly with the cosmic law of the Stoics (Maxim. Tyr., 6, 7). To the main ἄγραφοι or ἱεροὶ νόμοι which constantly recur in tradition belong not only ritual religious commandments but also ethical and social statutes which Xenoph. Mem., IV, 4, 20 already groups under the title θεοῦ νόμος. The most explicit list is to be found in Plut. Lib. Educ., 10 (II, 7e): δεῖ θεοὺς μὲν σέβεσθαι, γονέας δὲ τιμᾶν, πρεσβυτέρους αἰδεῖσθαι, νόμοις πειθαρχεῖν, ἄρχουσιν ὑπείκειν, φίλους ἀγαπᾶν, πρὸς γυναῖκας σωφρονεῖν, τέκνων στερκτικοὺς εἶναι, δούλους μὴ περιυβρίζειν, cf. Aesch. Eum., 545 ff.; Eur. Fr., 853; Ditt. Syll.², 1268. In keeping with the high regard which these ἄγραφοι νόμοι always enjoyed they are described by Plato as δεσμοὶ πάσης πολιτείας (Plat. Leg., VII, 973b) and later they can even be regarded as the source of all earthly laws (Archytas in Stob. Ecl., IV, 1, 132 [p. 79, Hense]).

d. In the 5th century the authority of νόμος was shaken. One factor was the learning of other νόμοι in the world. These had already been depicted by Herodot. with some respect and admiration (3, 38). He found in the νόμοι of the peoples their → σοφίη and also the breaking of an original σοφίη, 1, 196 f.; 7, 102; cf. Heracl. Fr., 114. In the relentless fight for existence, however, the subject soon began to make itself the norm of what is absolutely valid (ἔγωγε φημὶ καὶ νόμον γε μὴ σέβειν ἐν τοῖσι δεινοῖς τῶν ἀναγκαίων πλέον, Eur. Fr., 433; ἄνθρωποι τύραννοι νόμων, Plat. Ep., VIII, 354c).

"Human nature gained mastery over the laws and became stronger than right," affirms Thucydides in the Peloponnesian War (III, 84; cf. 45, 7). Among the Sophists νόμος was then put aside theoretically; man is rather set over against → φύσις (ἡ φύσις ἐβούλεθ', ᾗ νόμων οὐδὲν μέλει, Eur. Fr., 920). There thus arises a cleft between what is right by law (νόμῳ) and what is right by nature (φύσει), Plat. Gorg., 483a ff.; Leg., X, 889e. For the prescriptions of the law usually come into being arbitrarily, by human convention, Antiphon Fr., 44, Col. 1, 23 ff. (II, 346 f., Diels⁵). Nature, on the other hand, has its own law which even in the sphere of ethics and politics is recognised as a true norm, the νόμος τῆς φύσεως (Callicles in Plat. Gorg., 483e). νόμος is thus anchored in something higher. Instead of a divine sphere in which one believes, however, this is now φύσις, cf. Hippocr. Vict., 1, 11.

But this involves a dedivinised view of nature which is dominated by reciprocal conflict and in which the only rule is that of πλεονεξία, Plat. Gorg., 483c f, cf. Leg., IX, 875b. It thus carries with it the destruction not merely of the old political νόμος orientated to society but also necessarily of religion. For belief in the gods stands or falls with respect for νόμος.

Οἱ θεοὶ σθένουσι χὠ κείνων κρατῶν Νόμος· νόμῳ γὰρ τοὺς θεοὺς ἡγούμεθα, Eur. Hec., 799 f., cf. Antiphon Or., 6, 4. That is to say, if the gods evade the dominant rule (namely, that all wrong must be expiated, 791 f.), they thereby corrupt their divinity, cf. Eur. Ion, 442 f. They prove their own right to existence by accepting the validity of just νόμος. Hence belief in God and justice rests on the νόμος, cf. Plat. Menex., 237d: δίκην καὶ θεοὺς νομίζειν. For the Sophists, however, religion is not in tension with νόμος. In the last analysis it is unmasked as a fiction of the law-giver, Critias Fr., 25, 5 ff. (II, 386 f., Diels⁵). The νόμοι are the work of men and are not kept without witnesses. Hence a clever mind invented the gods of retribution as constant observers and guarantors of the laws, esp. against secret infringements. [13] On this view there

[13] As against λάθρῃ ἁμαρτέειν (Fr., 181 [II, 181, 11 ff., Diels⁵]) Democr. demands that νόμος should stand before the soul of man, i.e., that its inner contemplation should be normative for action (τοῦτον νόμον τῇ ψυχῇ καθεστάναι, Fr., 264 [II, 199, 6 ff., Diels⁵]).

are not really any gods; it is just that νόμος demands belief in them (Plat. Leg., X, 889e/890a: θεοὺς ... εἶναι πρῶτόν φασιν οὗτοι ... οὐ φύσει, ἀλλά τισι νόμοις, καὶ τούτους ἄλλους ἄλλῃ, ὅπῃ ἕκαστοι ἑαυτοῖσι συνωμολόγησαν νομοθετούμενοι ... ἀσέβειαί τε ἀνθρώποις ἐμπίπτουσι νέοις, ὡς οὐκ ὄντων θεῶν οἵους ὁ νόμος προστάττει διανοεῖσθαι δεῖν).

Two conclusions follow. The first is that νόμος can be overthrown only by an attack on religion, since the two are so essentially and fundamentally related. The second is that the crisis of νόμος originates and culminates in the dedivinisation of the world which is the final contribution of the 5th century: *quae religionis eversio 'naturae' nomen invenit* (Lact. Inst., III, 28, 3). This is how Plato saw it. For him rejection of the rule of the laws is equivalent to apostasy from God (Plat. Leg., IV, 701b/c; Ep., VII, 336b; in the myth of the inhabitants of Atlantis we read: μέχριπερ ἡ τοῦ θεοῦ φύσις αὐτοῖς ἐξήρκει, κατήκοοί τε ἦσαν τῶν νόμων καὶ πρὸς τὸ συγγενὲς θεῖον φιλοφρόνως εἶχον, Critias, 120e). For the mode of being and mode of operation of the gods are essentially known (cf. Plat. Leg., XII, 966c) in νόμος (θεοὺς ἡγούμενος εἶναι κατὰ νόμους οὐδεὶς πώποτε οὔτε ἔργον ἀσεβὲς ἠργάσατο ἑκὼν οὔτε λόγον ἀφῆκεν ἄνομον, *ibid.*, X, 885b, cf. Resp., II, 365e; Leg., X, 904a). νόμος lays down how they are to be worshipped and understood, Plat. Leg., X, 890a/b. The Platonic interrelating of theology and law is simply a philosophical expression of what the fact of νομίζειν θεούς (→ 1024) implied for the Greek world.

The rescuing of νόμος which Plato attempts rests first on proving the existence of the gods and secondly on the affirmation that νόμος, as a child of νοῦς, is related to the soul and is thus also φύσει[14] (Leg., X, 892a ff.): δεῖ ... τὸν ... νομοθέτην ... τῷ παλαιῷ νόμῳ ἐπίκουρον γίγνεσθαι λόγῳ ὡς εἰσὶ θεοί ..., καὶ δὴ καὶ νόμῳ αὐτῷ βοηθῆσαι[15] καὶ τέχνῃ, ὡς ἐστὸν φύσει ἢ φύσεως οὐχ ἧττον, εἴπερ νοῦ γέ ἐστι γεννήματα (Leg., X, 890d). By finally exalting νόμος (Ep., VIII, 354e) to divine rank[16] Plato overcame Sophist criticism of *nomos* at the decisive point.

e. In opposition to the Sophists Socrates' whole thinking on νόμος begins with the very positive content of the *polis*. The νόμος τῆς πόλεως is the norm of his life to such a degree that he not only does not act contrary to the laws but dies because they require it, even though they are unjustly manipulated by men: προείλετο μᾶλλον τοῖς νόμοις ἐμμένων ἀποθανεῖν ἢ παρανομῶν ζῆν (Xenoph. Mem., IV, 4, 4). To this conviction of Socrates Plato gave magnificent expression in the Crito when he caused the venerable Νόμοι καὶ τὸ κοινὸν τῆς πόλεως to appear to Socrates in prison in a kind of epiphany. There is a discussion of the

---

[14] In this connection Plato develops the anti-Sophist concept of an ἔμφρων φύσις (cf. the par. passage in Tim., 46d) which is almost the same as his concept of the ψυχή, Leg., X, 891c ff. On Plato's position regarding law cf. A. Capelle, *Platos Dialog Politikos* (Diss. Hamburg, 1939), 53 ff.

[15] Cf. Plat. Leg., X, 891b; Iambl. Vit. Pyth., 171; 223.

[16] Θεὸς δὲ ἀνθρώποις σώφροσι νόμος, ἄφροσι δὲ ἡδονή. νόυος and ἡδονή are here the two opposing powers on the divine level. Like Thucydides (II, 53; III, 82, 8), Plato continually advanced ἡδονή as the reason for the decline of νόμος (Leg., IV, 714a; Resp., VIII, 548b; IV, 429c). Life acc. to law is the very opposite of ἡδέως ζῆν (Leg., II, 662c/663a f). The general lawlessness of the Athenian state arose from the cultivation of art, which was too strongly dominated by ἡδονή (Leg., III, 700d/701a). The final result is the disintegration of the νόμος βασιλεύς through the rule of ἡδονή and λύπη (Resp., X, 607a).

right of the individual to renounce νόμος (Crito, 50a ff.). The νόμοι are here presented as parents to sustain and instruct man, 51c. Man is their ἔκγονος and → δοῦλος, 50e. His relation of dependence to them differs from that to his physical parents. These νόμοι have brothers in Hades (54c), i.e., they are still valid in face of death and beyond.

f. The relation of Socrates to the laws of the state illustrates the significance of νόμος for Greek ethics. Socrates does not distinguish between his pure conscience and degenerate political morality. For the classical Greek world does not speak of personal moral conscience (→ συνείδησις) but of objective knowledge of what is right and wrong.[17] This knowledge takes the form of law. Obedience to law is righteousness : ὁ δίκαιος ἔσται ὅ τε νόμιμος καὶ ὁ ἴσος. τὸ μὲν δίκαιον ἄρα τὸ νόμιμον καὶ τὸ ἴσον, τὸ δ' ἄδικον τὸ παράνομον καὶ ἄνισον (Aristot. Eth. Nic., 5, 1, p. 1129a, 33 ff., cf. Xenoph. Mem., IV, 4, 13 ff.). But all virtues are included in righteousness, → δίκη, II, 179. It is impossible to exhaust in detail the full content of νόμος, which embraces the whole of life (δοκοῦσιν ... τὸ καθόλου μόνον οἱ νόμοι λέγειν, Aristot. Pol., 3, 15, p. 1286a, 9 ff.), though for a more general account cf. Aristot. Eth. Nic., 5, 4, p. 1130a, 18 ff.

The goal of education is thus instruction in the spirit and ethos of the laws : παιδεία μέν ἐσθ' ἡ παίδων ... ἀγωγὴ πρὸς τὸν ὑπὸ τοῦ νόμου λόγον ὀρθὸν εἰρημένον, Plat. Leg., II, 659d; τεθράφθαι ἐν ἤθεσι νόμων εὖ πεπαιδευμένους, Plat. Leg., VI, 751c, cf. Prot., 326c/d. Indeed, law itself is an instructor, though in a very different sense from that of Paul in Gl. 3:24 : πῶς ἂν ἡμῖν ὁ νόμος αὐτὸς παιδεύσειεν ἱκανῶς (Plat. Leg., VII, 809a, cf. Aristot. Pol., 3, 16, p. 1287b, 25 f.; Archytas Pyth. in Stob. Ecl., IV, 1, 135 [p. 82, 16 f., Hense]).

Obedience to law is carried so far that there can even be ref. to → δουλεύειν τοῖς νόμοις without the disparagement elsewhere implied by the term (Plat. Leg., III, 698c; 700a; IV, 715d, cf. Pl. R. 7:25). This almost paradoxical usage makes it clear that νόμος exercises a dominion.[18] Law rules (νόμοι ἄρχουσιν, Aristot. Pol., 4, 4, p. 1292a, 32, cf. Plat. Leg., IV, 715d). It does so as δεσπότης, τύραννος (Plat. Prot., 337d) or βασιλεύς (οἱ τῶν πόλεων βασιλεῖς νόμοι, Alcidamas in Aristot. Rhet., 3, 3, p. 1406a, 23, cf. Anonym. Iambl., 6, 1 [II, 402, 29, Diels[5]]; Plat. Ep., VIII, 354c: νόμος ... κύριος ἐγένετο βασιλεὺς τῶν ἀνθρώπων). Acc. to Aristot. Eth. Nic., 10, 10, p. 1180a, 17 ff., he who lives acc. to νόμος lives κατά τινα νοῦν καὶ τάξιν ὀρθήν ἔχουσαν ἰσχύν, i.e., acc. to a spiritually determined order which also has power to enforce itself. νόμος has coercive power (ἀναγκαστικὴν ἔχει δύναμιν, a 21, cf. Antiph. Or., 6, 4). This power goes far beyond that of an individual, e.g., the father, or even the βασιλεύς etc. Bondage under law makes man a citizen in the *polis* (as later in the cosmos) and differentiates him from the slave, who by nature has no part or lot in the νόμοι (TGF, Fr. adesp., 326), by making him free : *legum ... idcirco omnes servi sumus, ut liberi esse possimus* (Cic. Pro Cluent., 53, 146, cf. Plat. Leg., III, 701b; Aristot. Pol., 5, 9, p. 1310a, 34 ff.).

δουλεία is used positively elsewhere only in respect of the gods (esp. Apollo at Delphi), cf. Soph. Oed. Tyr., 410; Eur. Orest., 418; Ion, 309; Plat. Phaed., 85b. To be at the service of the laws is to serve the gods : καλῶς δουλεῦσαι ... πρῶτον μὲν τοῖς νόμοις, ὡς ταύτην τοῖς θεοῖς οὖσαν δουλείαν (Plat. Leg., VI, 762e, cf. Plat.

---

17 "Conscience has no rights in the state, only what is legal. What true conscience will see to be right must be objective, ... not residing only within" (Hegel, *Werke* [Lasson], XIII, 2, 127 [*Vorlesungen über die Philosophie der Religion*]).

18 Pittacos is supposed to have answered the question of king Croesus concerning the ἀρχὴ κρατίστη with a ref. to the νόμοι (Diod. S. Excerpta Vaticana, 7, 27; Diog. L., 1, 77).

Ep., VIII, 354e). To be νόμιμος is to be, not merely δίκαιος, but also εὐσεβής (Xenoph. Mem., IV, 6, 2). This seems to be esp. the Delphic piety followed by Socrates (*ibid.*, I, 3, 1; par. IV, 3, 16). Among the many παραγγέλματα ascribed to the Delphic Apollo we find the saying:[19] ἕπου θεῷ· νόμῳ πείθου (Stob. Ecl., III, 1, 173 [p. 125, 5, Hense]). Following God and obeying law are not without inward relationship.[20]

For the dominion of law and the blessing of the gods guarantee the preservation of the state and the possibility of human life: ἐν ᾗ (sc. πόλει) μὲν γὰρ ἂν ἀρχόμενος ᾖ καὶ ἄκυρος νόμος, φθορὰν ὁρῶ τῇ τοιαύτῃ ἑτοίμην οὖσαν. ἐν ᾗ δ' ἂν δεσπότης τῶν ἀρχόντων, οἱ δὲ ἄρχοντες δοῦλοι τοῦ νόμου, σωτηρίαν καὶ πάντα ὅσα θεοὶ πόλεσιν ἔδοσαν ἀγαθὰ γιγνόμενα καθορῶ (Plat. Leg., IV, 715d). The soteriological function remained a constant mark of νόμος (cf. Ps.-Plat. Min., 314d; Aristot. Rhet., 1, 4, p. 1360a, 19 f.; Dio Chrys. Or., 58, 1 [Budé]; Porphyr. Marc., 25; Ep. Arist., 240; Just. Apol., 1, 65, 1): ὁ νόμος βούλεται μὲν εὐεργετεῖν βίον ἀνθρώπων. But only when one obeys law out of conviction τὴν ἰδίην ἀρετὴν ἐνδείκνυται (Democr. Fr., 248 [II, 194, 18 ff., Diels⁵]). Without νόμος men would inevitably lead a θηρίων βίος (Plut. Col., 30, 1 [II, 1124d] on the basis of Plat. Leg., IX, 874e).

g. The death of Socrates in obedience to the law Plato regarded as the transition of norm and law from state institutions to the ψυχή of Socrates, i.e., to the spirit.

Within the human → ψυχή as it manifested itself to the Greeks with Socrates Plato seeks and finds, after the model of medicine, a → κόσμος and a → τάξις. Medicine obviously had no single term for the physical norm; it spoke of health, force, beauty, etc. But Plato has a single term for the κόσμος and τάξις of the soul: νόμος. Plat. Gorg., 504c: ἐμοὶ γὰρ δοκεῖ ταῖς μὲν τοῦ σώματος τάξεσιν ὄνομα εἶναι ὑγιεινόν, ἐξ οὗ ἐν αὐτῷ ἡ ὑγίεια γίγνεται καὶ ἡ ἄλλη ἀρετὴ τοῦ σώματος ... ταῖς δὲ τῆς ψυχῆς τάξεσιν καὶ κοσμήσεσιν νόμιμόν τε καὶ νόμος (cf. Plat. Crit., 53c), ὅθεν καὶ νόμιμοι γίγνονται καὶ κόσμιοι· ταῦτα δ' ἔστιν δικαιοσύνη τε καὶ σωφροσύνη.[21]

Here is the basis of the Republic and the utopian legislation of the Νόμοι (cf. Leg., XII, 960d). Plato's new and inner νόμος is that whose τάξις is controlled by the norm of the ψυχή, i.e., δικαιοσύνη and σωφροσύνη.[22] This law is newly begotten[23] in Plato from a generally valid principle, i.e., knowledge: νοῦ γέ

---

19 Cf. W. H. Roscher, *Philol.*, 59 (1900), 37 f.

20 The Apollonian saying about following God by the way of law was taken up in M. Ant., 7, 31, though expounded in Stoic fashion: ἀκολούθησον θεῷ· ἐκεῖνος (Apollo) μέν φησιν, ὅτι 'πάντα νομιστί' ...

21 Cf. Plat. Phileb., 26b: καὶ ἄλλα δὴ μυρία ἐπιλείπω λέγων, οἷον μεθ' ὑγιείας κάλλος καὶ ἰσχύν, καὶ ἐν ψυχαῖς αὖ πάμπολλα ἕτερα καὶ πάγκαλα ... ἡ θεός ... πέρας οὔτε ἡδονῶν οὐδὲν οὔτε πλησμονῶν ἐνὸν ἐν αὐτοῖς, νόμον καὶ τάξιν πέρας ἐχόντων ἔθετο· καὶ σὺ μὲν ἀποκναῖσαι φῂς αὐτήν, ἐγὼ δὲ τοὐναντίον ἀποσῶσαι λέγω.

22 The converse may be seen in Plat. Leg., V, 728a/b: violation of the laws and contempt for them corrupt the soul.

23 Cf. Plat. Symp., 209d: τίμιος δὲ παρ' ὑμῖν καὶ Σόλων διὰ τὴν τῶν νόμων γέννησιν. In his use of this image Plato stands in a worthy tradition. Sophocles speaks of the generation of the eternal νόμοι (τεκνωθέντες, Oed. Tyr., 865 ff.) and also of their life (ζῇ, Ant., 457). Their πατήρ is the Olympian, and no θνατὰ φύσις ἀνέρων has borne them (ἔτικτεν, Oed. Tyr., 869 f.). Children (παῖδες) is the word used in Plat. Symp., 209d for the laws which Lycurgus left, and the Νόμοι which appear to Socrates in prison appeal to their brethren in Hades (Plat. Crito, 54c). The τρέφεσθαι of the νόμοι in Heracl. (Fr., 114 [I, 176, 7 f., Diels⁵]) belongs to the same sphere of biological and organic understanding. The influence of Plato's phraseology may be seen when Joseph. (Ant., 4, 319), who never speaks elsewhere of a γεννᾶν (→ I, 668) of God, says of the Jewish laws: νόμων οὓς αὐτὸς (sc. God) γεννήσας ἡμῖν ἔδωκεν.

ἐστι γεννήματα (sc. νόμος and τέχνη) (Plat. Leg., X, 890d; cf. I, 645a/b; IV, 712a). What speaks forth from law is the spirit. In an etymological play on words in which an essential relation may be discerned Plato calls νόμος the τοῦ νοῦ διανομή (Leg., IV, 714a; cf. XII, 967c; II, 674b). In the coercive force of νόμος Aristot. sees embodied the dominion of νοῦς (Eth. Nic., X, 10, p. 1180a, 21: ὁ δὲ νόμος ἀναγκαστικὴν ἔχει δύναμιν, λόγος ὢν ἀπό τινος φρονήσεως καὶ νοῦ). He who allows νοῦς to rule in the state constitutes as ruler τὸν θεὸν καὶ τὸν νοῦν μόνους (Aristot. Pol., 3, 16, p. 1287a, 28 ff.). With this anchoring in the νοῦς the Greek concept of law again finds absolute validity in philosophical form. For it is herewith linked afresh to the divine world (cf. Plat. Leg., IV, 713a/e).

On the other hand, it is a revolutionary thought, which points to future Hellenism, when the same Plato states for the first time that the ideal is not the dominion of law, which is constantly and necessarily left behind by developments, but the rule of a righteous and kingly figure who possesses true knowledge (τὸ δ' ἄριστον οὐ τοὺς νόμους ἐστὶν ἰσχύειν, ἀλλ' ἄνδρα τὸν μετὰ φρονήσεως βασιλικόν ... ὅτι νόμος οὐκ ἄν ποτε δύναιτο τό τε ἄριστον καὶ τὸ δικαιότατον ἀκριβῶς πᾶσιν ἅμα περιλαβὼν τὸ βέλτιστον ἐπιτάττειν, Pol., 294a/b; cf. Plat. Leg., IX, 875c/d). In Aristotle too (Pol., 3, 13, p. 1284a, 3 ff.) the man who towers over all others by reason of his ἀρετή seems to be no longer bound to any law. Not only is he over law; he himself, ὥσπερ θεὸς ἐν ἀνθρώποις (10 f.), is law both for himself and for others (κατὰ δὲ τῶν τοιούτων οὐκ ἔστι νόμος· αὐτοὶ γάρ εἰσι νόμος, 13 f.; cf. Eth. Nic., IV, 14, p. 1128a, 32; Plut. Alex., 52 [I, 694 f.]).

3. νόμος in Hellenism.

a. This philosophical theory became a historical reality in Hellenism. Here νόμος no longer rules as king in the *polis*. The will and person of the βασιλεύς has itself become νόμος (ὁ δὲ νόμος βασιλέως δόγμα, Dio Chrys. Or., 3, 43 [Budé]; cf. Anaxarch. in Plut. Alex., 52 [I, 694 f.] ὁ δὲ [sc. Alexander] ... ἀνθρώπων νόμον καὶ ψόγον δεδοικώς, οἷς αὐτὸν προσήκει νόμον εἶναι καὶ ὅρον τῶν δικαίων). The divine king is the new divine source of νόμος, which is linked to him in a special way (αὐτῷ ... τὸν νόμον δὲ συνόντα ἀεί, Themist. Or., 9, p. 123a [Dindorf]; cf. Isoc. Demonax., 36; Isis Hymn of Andros, 4 f. [p. 15, Peek]) and which can sometimes be called expressly → βασιλικὸς νόμος (Ps.-Plat. Min., 317a/c; Ditt. Or., II, 483, 1 [Pergamon]; cf. I, 329, 14; Jm. 2:8).[24] In keeping with his veneration as εἰκὼν ζῶσα (Ditt. Or., I, 90, 3) and ζηλωτὴς τοῦ Διός (Muson., p. 37, 3 f. [Hense]) the king, or even the philosopher himself, is the visible manifestation of eternal law in the cosmos, the νόμος ἔμψυχος (Muson., p. 37, 2 ff.; Archytas Pyth. in Stob. Ecl., IV, 1, 135 [p. 82, 20 f., Hense]; Diotogenes Pyth. in Stob. Ecl., IV, 7, 61 [p. 263, 19 Hense]; Philo Vit. Mos., 2, 4).[25]

b. In Stoicism, which regards law as a basic concept, the historically developed πολιτικὸς νόμος of the class. period is replaced by cosmic and universal law. The term νόμος no longer applies with any strictness to state laws.[26] These have sunk to the level of δόξαι ψευδεῖς: ὁ δὲ νοῦς τὸ τιμιώτατον ἐν ψυχῇ καὶ ἀρχικώτατον,

---

[24] Cf. Eus. De Laude Constantini, 3 (p. 201, 27) of Constantine: εἷς βασιλεὺς καὶ ὁ τούτου λόγος καὶ νόμος βασιλικὸς εἷς.

[25] Cf. E. R. Goodenough, "The Political Philosophy of Hellenistic Kingship," *Yale Class. Studies*, 1 (1928), 55 ff.

[26] The νόμος of the *polis* is now simply a comparison. What law is in the state God is for the world, cf. Ps.-Aristot. Mund., 6, p. 400b, 7 ff. (cf. Epict. Diss., I, 12, 7 etc.).

καθάπερ ἐν πόλει νόμος, οὐκ ἐπ' ἀξόνων (axle; then the wooden tablets of law in Athens which were turned on an axle) γεγραμμένος, ... οὐδ' ὑπὸ Σόλωνος ἢ Λυκούργου τεθείς· ἀλλὰ θεὸς μὲν ὁ νομοθέτης, ἄγραφος δὲ ὁ νόμος ... Καὶ μόνος ἂν εἴη οὗτος νόμος· οἱ δὲ ἄλλως, οἱ καλούμενοι, δόξαι ψευδεῖς ... κατ' ἐκείνους τοὺς νόμους καὶ 'Αριστείδης ἔφευγεν ... καὶ Σωκράτης ἀπέθνησκεν, κατὰ δὲ τὸν θεῖον τοῦτον νόμον καὶ 'Αριστείδης δίκαιος ἦν ... καὶ Σωκράτης φιλόσοφος. ἐκείνων τῶν νόμων ἔργον δημοκρατία καὶ δικαστήρια ... τούτου τοῦ νόμου ἔργον ἐλευθερία καὶ ἀρετή ... ὑπ' ἐκείνων τῶν νόμων ... ἐκπέμπονται ... οἱ στόλοι ... πολεμεῖται θάλαττα ... ὑπὸ τούτων τῶν νόμων ... εὐνομεῖται πόλις, εἰρήνην ἄγει γῆ καὶ θάλαττα ... ὦ νόμοι νόμων πρεσβύτεροι ... οἷς ὁ μὲν ἑκὼν ὑπορρίψας ἑαυτὸν, ἐλεύθερος ... καὶ ἀδεὴς ἐφημέρων νόμων (Max. Tyr., 6, 5 [Hobein]). The individual of the Hell. world can now seek and find the one true and divine νόμος only in the cosmos (cf. Plut. De Exilio, 5 [II, 601b]). For him the world is the state. Here there reigns a single law (ἡ μὲν γὰρ μεγαλόπολις ὅδε ὁ κόσμος ἐστὶ καὶ μιᾷ χρῆται πολιτείᾳ καὶ νόμῳ ἑνί, Chrysipp. Fr., 323 [III, 79, 38 f., v. Arnim]; Plut. Alex. Fort. Virt., 1, 6 [II, 329a]; Philo Op. Mund., 143) which, being the foundation of all society, binds even men and gods together (Chrysipp. Fr., 335 [III, 82, 18, v. Arnim]). As general and supreme reason (νόμος εἷς, λόγος κοινὸς πάντων τῶν νοερῶν ζῴων, M. Ant., 7, 9) this permeates all nature and determines the moral conduct of men (Chrysipp. Fr., 314 [III, 77, 34 ff., v. Arnim]). The spiritually determined order of the world is identical with the concept of law. Law again finds its ultimate basis in the religious sphere, whether νόμος be directly equated with θεός (II, 315, 23, v. Arnim) or deity equated with the unmoved[27] but all-moving law of the cosmos (νόμος μὲν γὰρ ἡμῖν ἰσοκλινὴς ὁ θεός, Ps.-Aristot. Mund., 6, p. 400b, 28 ff.). Adjustment is made to popular religion by giving the name of Zeus to this cosmic νόμος (ὁ νόμος ὁ κοινός, ὅσπερ ἐστὶν ὁ ὀρθὸς λόγος, διὰ πάντων ἐρχόμενος, ὁ αὐτὸς ὢν τῷ Διΐ καθηγεμόνι τούτῳ τῆς τῶν ὄντων διοικήσεως ὄντι, Zeno Fr., 162 [I, 43, v. Arnim = Diog. L., 7, 88]). In the Cleanthes hymn too (Fr., 537 [I, 121 ff., v. Arnim]) all-powerful Zeus controls the world by νόμος on the one side, but on the other, in the final verses, he is identified with the cosmic order whose magnifying is the supreme code for both men and gods (v. 38 f. [I, 123, 4 f., v. Arnim]). Only the κακοί ... οὔτ' ἐσορῶσι[28] θεοῦ κοινὸν νόμον, οὔτε κλύουσιν, ᾧ κεν πειθόμενοι σὺν νῷ (cf. Heracl. Fr., 114) βίον ἐσθλὸν ἔχοιεν (v. 24 f. [I, 122, 20 f., v. Arnim]).

In the strength of the indwelling νοῦς or λόγος man must decide for νόμος and a life commensurate with it (ὁ γὰρ λόγος τοῦ φιλοσόφου νόμος αὐθαίρετος καὶ ἴδιός ἐστιν, Plut. Stoic. Rep., 1 [II, 1033b]). But in so doing he does not obey an absolute demand which comes from without or from another world. He comes to himself and achieves his freedom (ὅσοι δὲ μετὰ νόμου ζῶσιν ἐλεύθεροι, Chrysipp. Fr., 360 [III, 87, 43 f., v. Arnim], cf. Max. Tyr., 33, 5; M. Ant., 10, 25). To fulfil the law, then, is no basic impossibility. It is that whereto the efforts and destiny of man are directed by nature. Thus the νόμος τῆς φύσεως καὶ τοῦ θεοῦ or the θεῖος νόμος which Epictet. proclaims (Diss., I, 29, 13/19) is in content simply the moral law of philosophy:[29] τίς δ' ὁ νόμος ὁ θεῖος; τὰ ἴδια τηρεῖν, τῶν ἀλλοτρίων μὴ ἀντιποιεῖσθαι, ἀλλὰ διδομένοις μὲν χρῆσθαι, μὴ διδόμενα δὲ μὴ ποθεῖν, ἀφαιρουμένου δέ τινος ἀποδιδόναι εὐλύτως καὶ αὐτόθεν (by easy and immediate release), χάριν εἰδότα οὗ ἐχρήσατο χρόνου (Diss., II, 16, 28, cf. I, 29, 4). These are for Epictetus οἱ ἐκεῖθεν ἀπεσταλμένοι νόμοι (Diss., IV, 3, 11/12) which alone can lead to a happy life. When

---

27 On the unalterability of law (ἀκίνητος νόμος) cf. Plat. Leg., XII, 960d; Ps.-Plat. Min., 321b; Max. Tyr., 11, 12; Plut. Vit. Lycurg., 29 (I, 57d); Philo Op. Mund., 61; → M. Mühl, 88 ff.

28 It is in keeping with the logical structure of this νόμος that one sees and perceives rather than hears it (cf. Dio Chrys. Or., 63, 5 [v. Arnim]): νόμον δὲ τὸν ἀληθῆ καὶ κύριον καὶ φανερὸν οὔτε ὁρῶσιν οὔτε ἡγεμόνα ποιοῦνται τοῦ βίου).

29 Cf. A. Bonhoeffer, "Epiktet u. d. NT," RVV, 10 (1911), 154 f.

the philosopher voluntarily follows them he is ἐλεύθερος ... καὶ φίλος θεοῦ (IV, 3, 9). For in so doing he follows God.[30] This happens, for instance, when to the saying in Plut. Aud., 1 (II, 37d): ταὐτόν ἐστιν τὸ ἕπεσθαι θεῷ καὶ τὸ πείθεσθαι λόγῳ, is added Plut. Ad Principem Ineruditum, 3, 1 (II, 780c): ὁ "νόμος ὁ πάντων βασιλεὺς θνατῶν τε καὶ ἀθανάτων" ὥς ἔφη Πίνδαρος, οὐκ ἐν βιβλίοις ἔξω γεγραμμένος οὐδέ τισι ξύλοις, ἀλλ' ἔμψυχος ὢν ἐν αὐτῷ λόγος, ἀεὶ συνοικῶν καὶ παραφυλάττων καὶ μηδέποτε τὴν ψυχὴν ἐῶν ἔρημον ἡγεμονίας.

Along with its cosmic extension νόμος thus undergoes on the other side very strong interiorisation. It is now written on the inward parts of man, on the soul (Max. Tyr., 27, 6).[31] Hence M. Ant., X, 13, 2 can list it with πίστις, αἰδώς, ἀλήθεια, ἀγαθὸς δαίμων as one of the most valuable constituents of man's being.

c. Neo-Platonism added no new features to the Gk. concept of law. In it different basic motifs replaced the constitutive Platonic and Stoic view of this matter. For Plotin. νόμος has only a subordinate role in ethics and the doctrine of the soul. A happy life cannot be allotted to those who have not done what makes them worthy of happiness, Plot. Enn., III, 2, 4. This is the aim of οἱ ἐν τῷ παντὶ νόμοι, III, 2, 8. Plot. sees here the operation of the divine world which keeps man in being by the νόμος of providence, III, 2, 9. Accusation is made against Gnostic teaching that with the divine πρόνοια it undervalues also the legal order of this world (πάντας νόμους τοὺς ἐνταῦθα) and makes a mockery of ἀρετή, II, 9, 15. For all wrong is punished, and nothing can evade what is laid down ἐν τῷ τοῦ παντὸς νόμῳ, III, 2, 4.[32] The same applies to all embodiments of the soul:[33] ἀναπόδραστος γὰρ ὁ θεῖος νόμος ὁμοῦ ἔχων ἐν ἑαυτῷ τὸ ποιῆσαι τὸ κριθὲν ἤδη, IV, 3, 24. The Neo-Platonic thinker Porphyrios (Ad Marc., 25/27) developed an express doctrine of νόμος in three stages: τρεῖς δὲ νόμοι διακεκρίσθωσαν οἵδε· εἷς μὲν ὁ τοῦ θεοῦ, ἕτερος δὲ ὁ τῆς θνητῆς φύσεως, τρίτος δὲ ὁ θετὸς κατ' ἔθνη καὶ πόλεις ... ὁ δ' αὖ θεῖος (sc. νόμος) ὑπὸ μὲν τοῦ νοῦ σωτηρίας ἕνεκα ταῖς λογικαῖς ψυχαῖς ... διετάχθη, δι' ἀληθείας δὲ τῶν ... πεπραγμένων εὑρίσκεται (25) ... ἀγνοεῖται μὲν ψυχῇ δι' ἀφροσύνην καὶ ἀκολασίαν ἀκαθάρτῳ, ἐκλάμπει δὲ δι' ἀπαθείας καὶ φρονήσεως (26).

d. Late antiquity follows for the most part Orphic Platonic views of νόμος, esp. Plat. Leg., IV, 716a = Orph. Fr., 21 (Kern); Gorg., 523a; Phaedr., 248c; Tim., 41e etc.; but it interprets these in terms of cosmic theology: τὸν δὲ δὴ Νόμον τοῦτον ὅτι θεὸν ἡγεῖσθαι δεῖ συνοχέα τῶν τε εἱμαρμένων νόμων, οὓς ὁ ἐν Τιμαίῳ δημιουργὸς ἐγγράφει ταῖς ψυχαῖς, καὶ τῶν εἰς πᾶσαν τὴν τοῦ κόσμου πολιτείαν διατεινόντων, ἠκούσαμεν πολλάκις τῶν τε θεολόγων αὐτὸν ἐξυμνούντων καὶ τοῦ Πλάτωνος ἔν τε Γοργίᾳ καὶ ἐν Νόμοις ... οἱ μὲν ἀληθεῖς νόμοι τῶν κοσμικῶν εἰσι νόμων εἰκόνες, οἱ δὲ ἡμαρτημένοι νόμοι μέν, ἀλλ' ἐσκιαγραφημένοι τινὲς ὄντες ἀποπτώσεις ἐκείνων ὑπάρχουσιν, Procl. in Rem Publ., II, 307, 20 ff. (Kroll), cf. in Tim., I, 203, 28 f. Along with a creative Νόμος, which is God and πάρεδρος τοῦ Διός (Orph. Fr., 160 [Kern]) — πρὸ γὰρ τῶν ἐγκοσμίων ἐστὶν ὁ δημιουργικὸς νόμος τῷ Διὶ παρεδρεύων καὶ συνδιακοσμῶν αὐτῷ πᾶσαν τὴν ἐν τῷ παντὶ προμηθίαν, Procl. in Tim., I, 156, 9 ff., cf. Orph. Fr., 159 (Kern) — there is a richly integrated system of cosmic νόμοι (Procl. in Tim., I, 136, 13 ff.; 397, 22 ff.) which find

---

[30] In Muson., p. 86, 19 ff., Hense, the ideal of the Stoic sage is the law of Zeus: ἀγαθὸν (i.e., φιλόσοφον) εἶναι κελεύει τὸν ἄνθρωπον ὁ νόμος ὁ τοῦ Διός.

[31] Cf. Jul. Or., 7, p. 209c: νόμοι ἐκ τῶν θεῶν ἡμῖν ὥσπερ ἐγγραφέντες ταῖς ψυχαῖς (cf. Pl. R. 2:15); cf. Plot. Enn., V, 3, 4; Procl. in Rem Publ., II, 307, 7 ff. (Kroll).

[32] Plotin. links with this the significant assertion: ἔστι δὲ οὐ διὰ τὴν ἀταξίαν τάξις οὐδὲ διὰ τὴν ἀνομίαν νόμος, ὥς τις οἴεται, ἵνα γένοιτο ἐκεῖνα διὰ τὰ χείρω καὶ ἵνα φαίνοιτο ... καὶ ὅτι τάξις ἀταξία καὶ διὰ τὸν νόμον καὶ τὸν λόγον, καὶ ὅτι λόγος παρανομία.

[33] Cf. Plat. Phaedr., 248c; Tim., 41e; in Herm. writings, cf. Stob. Ecl., I, 49, 49 (p. 418, 6, Hense); I, 49, 69 (p. 463, 23, Hense).

their comprehensive unity in Adrasteia: ἡ πάντων ὁμοῦ τῶν νόμων τῶν τε ἐγκοσμίων καὶ ὑπερκοσμίων, τῶν τε εἱμαρμένων καὶ Διΐων (εἰσὶ γὰρ καὶ Δίϊοι νόμοι καὶ Κρόνιοι, θεῖοί τε καὶ ὑπερκόσμιοι καὶ ἐγκόσμιοι) ἡ πάντων τούτων τὰ μέτρα ἑναίως ἐν ἑαυτῇ συλλαβοῦσα καὶ συνέχουσα. αὕτη ἐστὶν ἡ θεὸς Ἀδράστεια (Hermias in Plat. Phaedr., 248c [p. 161, 15 ff., Couvr.] = Orph. Fr., 105 [Kern]).

4. The Greek Concept of νόμος and the New Testament.

As distinct from the law which comes by revelation the νόμος of the Greeks proceeds from the spirit (νοῦς). Hence genuine law is no mere imperative. It is that wherein a being, or something of intrinsic validity, is discovered and apprehended: ὁ νόμος ἄρα βούλεται τοῦ ὄντος εἶναι ἐξεύρεσις (Ps.-Plat. Min., 315a, cf. Plat. Polit., 300c/e). It is "the ancient, valid and effective order which does not merely issue orders but creates order, which does not merely command, require or prohibit but rules, which evokes as it were its own fulfilment, and which upholds itself, or is upheld, in face of non-fulfilment," Cr.-Kö., 749.[34] In this its essential nature νόμος has something in common with the Greek gods.[35] Only thus can one explain the command: δεῖ δὲ καὶ τοὺς νόμους τῆς πατρίδος καθάπερ τινὰς θεοὺς δευτέρους συντηρεῖν (Hierocles Stoicus in Stob. Ecl., III, 39, 36 [p. 733, 10 f.]). Like the gods, νόμος has supreme and terrible power over all who seek to evade it. Like them, however, it is also encircled by supreme ideality, for it is the only ↦ σωτηρία (→ 1031) for those who are obedient to it (οὐ γὰρ κρεῖσσόν ποτε τῶν νόμων γιγνώσκειν χρὴ καὶ μελετᾶν. κούφα γὰρ δαπάνα (not much exertion is required) νομίζειν ἰσχὺν τόδ' ἔχειν, ὅ τι ποτ' ἄρα τὸ δαιμόνιον, τό τ' ἐν χρόνῳ μακρῷ νόμιμον ἀεὶ φύσει τε πεφυκός, Eur. Ba., 890 ff.). It is only natural that the νόμος both of the *polis* and the cosmos should thus be presented continually as God: ὁ γὰρ θεὸς μέγιστος ἀνθρώποις νόμος (TGF Fr. adesp., 471, cf. Plat. Ep., 8, 354e; Pind. Fr., 169; Aristot. Pol., 3, 16, p. 1287a, 28 ff.; Procl. in Rem Publ., II, 307, 20 [Kroll]; Philodem. Philos. Pietat., 11 [II, 315, 23, v. Arnim]) or mythico-theologically as Zeus: ὁ μὲν Ζεὺς ... αὐτὸς ... νόμων ὁ πρεσβύτατος καὶ τελειότατος (Plut. Ad Principem Ineruditum, 4, 2 [II, 781b], cf. Zeno Fr., 162 [I, 43, v. Arnim = Diog. L., 7, 88]; → 1024 f.).

With its understanding of the concept of law the Greek world missed the true meaning of law from the NT standpoint. For, to the Greek, law is never that which, rightly understood, crushes him and reduces him to despair by making him aware that he cannot keep it.[36] On the contrary, because it no longer has an objective historical νόμος, and philosophy can no longer supply this, later antiquity despairs of law.[37]

Kleinknecht

---

[34] Cf. Xenoph. Mem., IV, 4, 24: τὸ γὰρ τοὺς νόμους αὐτοὺς τοῖς παραβαίνουσι τὰς τιμωρίας ἔχειν βελτίονος ἢ κατ' ἄνθρωπον νομοθέτου δοκεῖ μοι εἶναι (cf. Plat. Leg., IV, 716a; Plot. Enn., IV, 3, 13/24).

[35] There is often explicit comparison, e.g., Aristot. Pol., 3, 13, p. 1284a, 10; Ps.-Aristot. Mund., 6, p. 400b, 7 ff.

[36] No Gk. could speak of the νόμος τῆς ἁμαρτίας as Pl. does in R. 7:23 (cf. 1 C. 15:56). For him the law could not be one of the causes of transgression (οὔτε νόμος τοῦ παρανομεῖν παραίτιος γένοιτο ἂν οὔτε οἱ θεοὶ τοῦ ἀσεβεῖν, Chrysipp. Fr., 1125 [II, 326, 35, v. Arnim]).

[37] Cf. the pious wish of Celsus in Orig. Cels., 8, 72: εἰ γὰρ δὴ οἷόν τε εἰς ἕνα συμφρονῆσαι νόμον τοὺς τὴν Ἀσίαν καὶ Εὐρώπην καὶ Λιβύην Ἕλληνάς τε καὶ βαρ-

B. The Law in the Old Testament.

1. The Law in Ancient Israel.

Within the total body of legal writing in the OT, literary and form criticism has enabled us to discern the oldest corpora at least to the point of making clear the essential and distinctive features of the Law of ancient Israel.[38] Such corpora are to be found esp. in the five-unit sayings (originally 12) concluding with מוֹת יוּמָת,[39] the four-unit sayings (originally 12) beginning with אָרוּר,[40] and the historically more solidly grounded Decalogue,[41] which has certainly surrendered formal symmetry for the sake of content, but for this very reason brings out the more sharply the essential features of this ancient legislation.

The historical *locus* of these laws was the act which regularly took place in the central sanctuary[42] in renewal and recollection of the covenant between Yahweh and Israel. As regards their origin we are referred to Sinai and what took place there, though it is hard to elucidate this in detail.[43]

What we have said about the probable *locus* of these laws in the period of the judges corresponds to, and is illuminated by, the theological setting of these laws in Israel's belief in God. The laws have their place in the doctrine of the covenant.[44] Yahweh has chosen Israel as His people, and Israel has acknowledged Yahweh as its God. This fundamental OT principle[45] is the direct basis of these laws. They express the claim of Yahweh to dominion over the whole life of this people which belongs to Him in virtue of His election. The first commandment of the Decalogue expresses this with full clarity.

The laws are not regarded, then, as a fair adjustment of human interests which is then divinely sanctioned. Nor is their observance the achievement which Israel presents to its God in gratitude for the covenant and election. In particular, it is not the achievement which establishes the divine relationship. The laws are in the strictest sense the requirements of the God to whom Israel belongs because He has revealed Himself in the exodus from Egypt and because in all future wars He will show Himself to be the God of this people. Thus the motive for keeping this Law is simply that of obedience in so far as there is any conscious reflection on the question of motivation.

βάρους ἄχρι περάτων νενεμημένους. The νόμος of Christ (Just. Dial., 11: αἰώνιός τε ἡμῖν νόμος καὶ τελευταῖος ὁ Χριστὸς ἐδόθη) has dissolved both the national νόμοι of antiquity and also the Stoic ideal of a single, all-embracing νόμος. Cf. E. Peterson, *Der Monotheismus also politisches Problem* (1935), 62 f.

[38] Cf. on what follows esp. Alt, *Die Ursprünge d. isr. Rechts,* 33 ff.

[39] Ex. 21:12, 15-17; 22:18 f.; 31:14 f.; Lv. 20:2, 9-16, 27; 24:16; 27:29. In part the original sayings can be reconstituted only by reconstruction, cf. Alt, 45 f.

[40] Dt. 27:15-26 with minor emendations.

[41] Ex. 20:2 ff.; Dt. 5:6 ff. On the question of the original form cf. L. Köhler, "Der Dekalog," ThR (1929), 161 ff.

[42] Cf. M. Noth, *Das System d. 12 Stämme Israels* (1930). Perhaps the focal object of the cult was the ark in which the laws of the covenant were kept. Cf. P. Volz, *Mose und sein Werk²* (1932), 100 ff.; Galling in RGG², III, 1449 f.

[43] Though those who pronounced these laws were presumably priests (Dt. 31:11; 33:10), tradition pts. to Moses, who was not a priest, as the author of the Ten Commandments. No cogent reason can be advanced against this. Cf. Volz, 20 ff.; Köhler, 178 ff., 184.

[44] W. Eichrodt, *Theol. d. AT,* I² (1939), 26 ff.; Volz, 73 f. It may be admitted that the thought of election was not present in the later theological form.

[45] As against L. Köhler, *Theol. d. AT* (1936), 12.

In detail, the nature of the law is in keeping with this.

a. Its demand is unconditional.

This may be seen in the style of the series of laws, in their harsh severity, in their uncompromising formulation, which weighs the act as such and not the background or special circumstances. It may be seen also in the threatened punishment, which can only be death, i.e., extirpation from the people of God, or the curse, which abandons the culprit to divine destruction when the act is one which cannot be brought to human judgment. It may be seen even more clearly in the fact that this law can be formulated with no mention of punishment for violation and it can take, not the common imperative or jussive form, but that of a simple indicative: "Thou shalt not kill." [46]

b. The form of the commands (or prohibitions) is negative.

Here is fresh confirmation that the theological setting of this Law is the covenant of election. There is not commanded what establishes the relation to Yahweh, but prohibited what destroys it.

c. This does not exclude the persuasive aspect of the commandments.

This may be seen in the way in which the proclamation of the Law seeks to make an impression on the will of the hearer and to make transgression inwardly impossible by recollection of Yahweh's acts. This aspect does not consist, however, in the promise of a reward, for, since the covenant precedes the prohibition, the only reward can be perseverance in this positive relation to Yahweh. [47] For this reason there is reference to punishment for violation but not to any special reward for fulfilment.

d. Moreover, for all its brevity this Law is comprehensive.

Not merely the cultus but the whole of life stands under this Law. The claim of this God to dominion leaves no neutral zone. Yet developed casuistry is not of the essence of these laws, though more precise catalogues became necessary in the course of time, to some degree as more detailed rulings on the basic prohibitions. [48]

e. Finally, it belongs to the very essence of these laws that they should be addressed to all Israel.

The individual is treated as a member of the people, and the neighbour to whom the Law refers is a compatriot. Similarly, punishment in cases of infringement is a matter for the whole body. Stoning as the prescribed mode of execution allows all to participate (Dt. 13:9 f.), and when a murder is not cleared up the nearest community is under obligation to make atonement (Dt. 21:1 ff.).

To say all this is to indicate already the aim of the Law. It is designed to bind the people and the individual to Yahweh. Hence the commandment: "Thou shalt have no other gods before me." Hence the separation from all magic and sorcery. [49] But linked with this is also the fashioning of the people as the people of God, and the exclusion of deeds which disrupt the relationship of the members one to another, and which threaten the life of the whole. It should be emphasised, however, that the validity of the commandment does not reside in its social utility, but in the underlying will of the covenant God. Hence the Law seeks to regulate the relation of the covenant people and the individual to the covenant God and to the member of the people belonging to this God, to regulate it on the basis of

---

[46] On this whole matter cf. Alt, 37 ff.; Volz, 26.
[47] E.g., the (perhaps secondary) promise along with the commandment to honour father and mother.
[48] For details cf. Alt, 49 ff.
[49] Cf. Volz, 27 ff., 40 ff.

the election of this people by this God, and by the avoidance of things which might destroy or disrupt the relation.[50]

2. The Understanding of the Law in the Older Historical Books.

To the understanding of the Law expressed in the ancient corpora corresponds the interpretation of Israel's history in the so-called J and E source, more particularly as regards the position here assigned to the Law. Though J and E end only with the fulfilment of the promise that Israel should possess the land of Palestine,[51] the climax in both is the giving of the Law. The way is prepared for this by viewing the preceding history from the standpoint of the totally unmerited election of Israel from among the nations. In this respect it is energetically maintained that there are no grounds of election in the people as such.[52] The history of the gracious dealings of God with a people which is often refractory reaches its climax in the fact that Yahweh reveals Himself to the whole people, constituting Himself its God and the people His people, Ex. 19. This gives the Law its significance as the divine gift which will show the people what conduct accords with its position as God's own people, or what conduct undermines it. The Law is thus a demonstration of grace inasmuch as it shows how the people lives before God because it lives by Him. Because "the redeeming God gives the Law," "obedience is made a proof of faith."[53]

In content the Law adopted in the history books is that of the ancient corpora and then esp. the Book of the Covenant.[54] This contains, along with the earliest Israelite material, the practical law of the pre-Israelite population of Palestine. Its main thrust is the seizure and impregnation of the adopted legislation by belief in Yahweh.[55] An essential pt. is that there is no conscious distinction between law and morality.[56] The validity of the laws is primarily based on the fact that they are divinely posited, not on their immanent goodness or utility. Naturally God demands what is good, but it is to be done because God demands it.

The Law also includes divine ordinances regulating the cultus. These are understood as statutes by which Yahweh orders the worship to be offered to Him (Ex. 20:24b).[57] Once again it is not man who decides what form the worship of God should take as though it were a free achievement of his own. The only legitimate worship is that which is based upon, and which consists in recognition of, the fact that God has revealed Himself to the people. The cultic law as these writers recount it may be fragmentary and primitive, but it is perfectly clear that the cultus is basically understood as the gracious divine ordinance by which the people is told how it can and should worship its holy God. But to say this is also to say that law and cultus cannot be differentiated in the understanding of the Law in J and E.

Of a piece with this is the ancient practice of priestly legislation in the narrower

---

[50] Cf. the rousing of a national conscience (Ju. 19 f.), Noth, 100 ff., Volz, 500.
[51] Cf. H. Holzinger, *Einleitung in d. Hexateuch* (1893), 71 ff.
[52] No natural grounds (cf. Ishmael and Esau) nor moral (Jacob, the wilderness journey).
[53] A. Schlatter, *Einleitung in d. Bibel*[4] (1923), 15.
[54] The Book of the Covenant (Ex. 21-23) derives from the pre-monarchy Palestinian period, but was for a long time the basis of law. Cf. Procksch, 231 f.; A. Jepsen, *Untersuchungen zum Bundesbuch* (1927), 96 ff.; Alt, 18, 25 ff.
[55] Eichrodt, I, 28 ff.; Jepsen, 100 ff.
[56] To view this as fatal (cf. Jepsen, 102 ff.) is to adopt a modern standpoint of dubious objectivity or relevance. The equation of law and morality derives from the whole concept of God in the OT.
[57] Cf. the transl. in Kautzsch[4]. The text is not wholly clear.

sense, and the understanding of the Law implicit therein. The essential content of specific priestly direction is the definition of clean and unclean. The main point, however, is that this instruction on what is clean and unclean is given on the commission and as the commandment of Yahweh. The question is, not what has the best effect on the deity, but what does Yahweh Himself declare to be the worship which may be appropriately offered by His people. Nor is the task of the priest confined to differentiating between clean and unclean. At national assemblies he must also declare the Law which has been handed down, and he must keep it safe in the sanctuary. He is also needed when in difficult cases the legal community approaches the sanctuary for the judgment of God, [58] though this does not mean that the priest discharges a true judicial function. It would be in keeping with this relation between priests and the Law to seek the development of the Book of the Covenant in priestly circles. [59]

All law is the will of Yahweh. It rests on the fact that in history God has given Himself to be the God of this people, and would see this people live as His possession. Since the relation of Yahweh to His people is historical, this understanding of the Law is in no way contradicted if the Law itself arises in the course of history. It is still the Law of God. This finds expression in the fact that all valid law is linked with the revelation of God at Sinai. Hence this is more of a theological than a historical judgment.

3. The Attitude of the Prophets towards the Law.

Prophetic preaching rests on a new encounter with God and on the breaking of this divine reality into the pious, yet ungodly activity of the people. Not a new idea of God, but a new encounter with God, is the essence and basis of prophetic preaching. [60] This enables us to understand the attitude of the prophets towards the Law. They do not think that they have to tell the people what God requires for the first time. Their preaching of repentance presupposes that man has been told already what is good, and what the Lord his God requires of him (Mi. 6:8). The prophets often formulate the divine will in a new way. They often bring out new features. But they neither have nor do they seek to arouse the sense of posing a hitherto unknown demand. Indeed, prophetic preaching recognises not merely the Law but also its basis. Israel is the divinely chosen people (Am. 2:9; 3:2; Is. 1:2; Hos. 8:13 f.). Violation of the Law is apostasy from Yahweh (Is. 1:27 f.). The prophets always condemn infringements of the commandments (Am. 5:7, 10 ff.; Hos. 5:10; 4:2; Jer. 7:9). Hos. 8:12 expressly presupposes a written law.

Nevertheless, direct ref. to formulated law, e.g., the Decalogue or Book of the Covenant, is comparatively rare (Hos. 4:2; Jer. 7:9). Even when it occurs, it carries no special emphasis. In view of what has been said, this cannot be explained in terms of either ignorance or rejection of the commandments. Hence the explanation may be sought only (1) in a specific prophetic insight into the nature of the Law and (2) in the different aim of prophetic preaching.

As regards the first pt. the prophets were confronted by the fact that appeal to the Law and its letter could be accompanied by the refusal of true obedience and a real lack of love for one's neighbours [61] (Am. 2:6; 8:4 ff.; Jer. 8:8). They thus radicalise the Law, as when Am. simply says: "Hate the evil, and love the good" (5:15). This does not mean that they abandon a narrower standpoint for one which is "purely moral." [62] It means that they resist attempts to introduce disobedience through gaps in the fence of

---

[58] L. Köhler, *D. hbr. Rechtsgemeinde* (Rectoral Address at Zürich, 1931), 13 ff.
[59] Procksch, 230; Jepsen, 99 f.
[60] On what follows cf. Eichrodt, I, 185 ff.; K. Marti, *Gesch. d. isr. Religion*[5] (1907), 184 ff.
[61] Eichrodt, 198 f.; Marti, 184 ff.
[62] Marti, 189: The good in a general human, international, purely moral sense, as that which is always and everywhere to be regarded as good.

the positive law which is outwardly respected (cf. Hos. 6:6; Mi. 6:8). This radicalising is thus at the same time an interiorising and unifying which coincides with the true purpose of the ancient Law, e.g., the Decalogue. Because the Law is not designed to hamper total obedience to the God who meets His people and the individual in living and directly menacing encounter, the Law is not quoted or used explicitly, though it is recognised to be an institution appointed by Yahweh.

This leads us to the second pt. In face of their direct encounter with God, and in face of the situation of the people as viewed from this standpoint, the prophets could no longer expect salvation from a legal order of life, esp. when Yahweh's will was now understood in this radical fashion. A new possibility arises for Israel only in the free, miraculous and creative act of God for which the prophets look, and it is "only where a new national existence is envisaged beyond the destruction of what has obtained thus far, (that) the divine imperatives, too, acquire a greater stringency."[63] After judgment and restoration Jerusalem will be called the city of right (Is. 1:26); the Gentiles will come to the new Zion to receive תּוֹרָה (Is. 2:3). The prophetic attitude towards the Law, with its simultaneous affirmation and (tacit) criticism and abolition, can be understood only in terms of direct apprehension by the holiness of God.

Only on this basis, too, can one understand the attitude of the prophets towards the worship of God in the narrower sense of the cultus.[64] As the prophets find it, the cultus serves to gloss over disobedience and to manipulate God. Because injustice and lovelessness are combined with this worship, and even justified thereby, the prophets engage in conflict with it (Jer. 7:11; Hos. 4:6; Zeph. 3:4b; Jer. 2:8). Many prophetic sayings seem to go even further and to involve a total rejection of the cultus[65] as something which God has not commanded (Am. 5:25; Is. 1:12; Jer. 7:22). They presumably concluded that the worship of the day was beyond remedy. In essence, however, prophetic criticism is not advocating non-cultic worship. The criticism can be properly understood only in terms of a recognition of the unbridgeable cleft between the God who calls His people to account and the supposed veneration of God in worship as the prophets knew it.

4. The Deuteronomic Understanding of the Law.

Dt. contains a definite view of the Law of Yahweh which in the original form of the book[66] is consistently worked out on the basis and in development of ancient legal material. The distinctive feature of this view is the urgency with which the requirement is grounded in the act by which God made Israel His people, עַם קָדוֹשׁ. No less strongly than J and E, D emphasises that the religious and national existence of the people of Israel rests solely and simply in the covenant sworn to the fathers (4:32 ff.; 7:8, 12 ff.; 9:5 etc.). Hence one of the main tasks of the Law is to safeguard the one link between Israel and this God. This explains the passionate battle against the אֱלֹהִים אֲחֵרִים and the fight for the one sanctuary of the one God, 13:7 ff. Another distinctive feature of the Dt. Law is the great earnestness with which it seeks to impart the blessing of the relation with God to the individual member of the people. In D, too, the destiny of the individual is closely linked with that of the whole people. But very strong emphasis is now laid on the just allotment of duties and especially rights to all members of God's people, so that none shall be deprived of God's blessing in this life.

---

[63] Eichrodt, 190.

[64] On what follows cf. esp. Eichrodt, 193 ff.; E. Kautzsch, *Bibl. Theol. d. AT* (1911), 233 ff.

[65] Cf. P. Volz, "Die radikale Ablehnung der Kultreligion durch d. at.lichen Propheten," ZSTh (1937), 63 ff.

[66] Cf. esp. the parts in which there is address in the sing. On this pt., and the whole section, cf. esp. G. v. Rad, *Das Gottesvolk im Dt.* (1929).

In the light of these general characteristics we may now understand the special features of the Dt. Law in detail.

a. In Dt., too, proclamation of the Law is preaching. It is not a neutral enumeration of legal norms. It is exhortation [67] which seeks to encourage cheerful fulfilment in gratitude for God's action. This is implied already in the whole concern of the book. The people is not confronted by a mere code of law. It is set before the living God Himself, who will not let Himself be concealed behind His Law. All instruction concerning the Law is in the first instance instruction concerning God's action. [68] The Law gives this history contemporary force. In keeping with this is the tendency towards inwardness manifested in the frequent expression בְּכָל־לְבָבְךָ וּבְכָל־נַפְשְׁךָ (6:5; 10:12; 26:16 etc.) or in the demand for a close relation to Yahweh (10:20; 30:20). What is to be attained is not just external legality. Inward love of God must be the root of all concrete action.

b. This Law seeks to encompass every field of life, though its main interest is ethical rather than ritual. [69] While comprehensive, however, it does not attempt a casuistic regulation of life. It simply indicates the general direction (cf. the relative lack of concern for absolute correctness in the cultic legislation).

c. Dt. has a central interest in the relation to the neighbour, esp. the compatriot. [70] The starting-point is the right ordering of God's people, not humanity. The neighbour is no mere object for my fulfilment of the Law; he is truly present as a brother. The word אָח plays a special role in Dt. (15:2 f., 7, 9, 11 f.; 19:18 f. etc.). This means, however, that the obligation to the neighbour is that of love, not of individual commandments. Hence the Law is repeatedly summed up in the law of love (6:5; 7:9; 10:12).

d. Nevertheless, Dt. also seeks to maintain the distance between God and man. Nor does it do this merely in the general sense that the one partner in this covenant is absolutely superior to the other. It also does it concretely by contesting, esp. in cultic regulation, a sub-moral nature worship. In this connection one might mention the rule in 14:24 ff. that cultic gifts can be turned into money, or the insistence in 21:7 f. that forgiveness is by the grace of God rather than expiatory action. Even the centralisation is not an upsurgence of magical ideas. It is a restriction of the cultus to the place which God has commanded, and which is holy only for this reason, not intrinsically.

The aim of the Law, then, is the fashioning of the people as God's people and its commitment to God alone — and both on the basis of the historical adoption of this people by this God. This being so, it is only natural that God's blessing should be promised for observance of the Law. For this blessing consists in the full and unhampered enjoyment of what the people is given by its God in its land, just as the curse for despising the Law consists in withdrawal of this gift.

This is perhaps the most profound attempt to understand the OT covenant and to shape life in accordance with it. Similarly, it is in criticism of this attempt that the OT attains to its deepest insight into the nature of the Law. Such criticism is most probably to be found in Jer. 31:31 ff. [71] This exposition presupposes that Jer. was in sympathy with the Dt. reform and its goals. [72] But Jer. finds the weak point of this attempt in the fact of sin, which breaks the undisrupted relation

---

[67] Cf. on this H. Breit, *Die Predigt des Deuteronomisten* (1933), 228 etc.

[68] Cf. O. Weber, *Bibelkunde d. AT,* I (1935), 49.

[69] Thus v. Rad, 36 draws attention to the fact that ethical interest in the situation of the Levites is stronger than interest in the machinery of the cultus in Jerusalem.

[70] Here esp. one may see the new conception as compared with the Book of the Covenant, cf. v. Rad, 14 ff.

[71] v. Rad, 98 ff.

[72] Marti, 182 f., 186 interprets many verses in Jer. in such a way as to make it appear that Dt. was rejected by Jer., but this is in most cases very arbitrary.

between God and His people and which does not allow of its restoration by any law. Only the act of God which creates the whole man anew by putting the Law in his heart, only a new covenant of God, can guarantee the time of salvation. Thus Jer. points to something which is outside OT revelation but is fulfilled in the NT.

5. The Understanding of the Law in the Priestly Writing and Related Works.

In typical distinction from D, P does not attempt to influence the reader pedagogically after the manner of the preacher. He presents his material austerely and sternly, "which a dignity which almost repels." [73] This is no mere stylistic difference. It is connected with a different view of God. In P to a far greater extent than D the transcendent holiness and absolute supraterrestriality of God are the basis of all theological thinking. Even the distinctive view of the people which is to be found in D does not have the same normativeness in P. P is not dealing merely with Israel. Though the special position of Israel is central, P takes much greater account of the world outside Israel. Yahweh's relation to Israel is viewed not so much from the standpoint of loving election as from that of the establishment of divine order with a view to salvation. It is precisely here that the Law finds in P its theological setting and purpose. The Law protects the purity of divine revelation by safeguarding God's supremacy and transcendence. The more significant is it, then, that P purports to be a historical presentation, not with edificatory or aesthetic intent, but with the aim of demonstrating the validity and binding character of the religious constitution of Israel, and indeed of the world, in God's action and therewith in God's revelation. In so doing P underscores the fact that the transcendent and holy God is not impersonal power, but personal will.

The divine order established by God's creative action tells both individuals and the people how they can and should live without forfeiting their existence by violation of the glory of God as Creator. The people of God's possession is constituted by God's new revelation to Abraham. The promise implicit in the making of the covenant is fulfilled at Sinai. Thus history acc. to P is a manifestation of the ordinances which establish and ensure the salvation of God's people. [74] There is expressed in the Law the sovereignty of the God of creation and election. The Law lays down how the life of the race, and esp. of Israel, can be consonant with this holy God. The positive Law of P is to be understood in the light of this understanding.

In the tent of revelation — for in P the tabernacle is characteristically the place of manifestation rather than the dwelling-place, Ex. 25:22; Nu. 14:10 — Moses receives ordinances and directions for the people (Ex. 25:22; Nu. 7:89). In the divine will which is revealed here the moral and cultic norms find their higher unity, [75] for both are witnesses to the lordship of God, the one as regulation of the relation to the neighbour, the other as a sign of the inner relation with God. This unity is expressed in the fact that Aaron acts only through Moses and at his direction, which is received from God and then passed on by him (Lv. 16; Nu. 17:11 ff.). To be sure, the cult is very important for P, [76] but it stands within the total revelation of the Law to Moses. Hence, with no

[73] Cf. G. v. Rad, *Die Priesterschrift im Hexateuch* (1934), 187; on what follows cf. also Eichrodt, *Theol.*, I, 209 ff.; W. Eichrodt, "Gottes ewiges Reich u. seine Wirklichkeit in d. Gesch. nach at.licher Offenbarung," ThStKr (1937), 1.

[74] v. Rad, *op. cit.*, 188.

[75] Eichrodt, *Theol.*, I, 228.

[76] And this seems to increase, as may be seen from a comparison of the two features of the P tradition to which v. Rad draws attention, *op. cit.*, 163.

difference in importance, there stand alongside the cultus the other legal and religious ordinances established and justified by history, and also the moral norms in the narrower sense.

This understanding of the Law, however, does not exclude profound joy, humble and reverent worship, or selfless self-giving. The whole presentation of P bears witness to this, e.g., the creation story in Gn. 1. In this respect it corresponds to the tenor of the Law psalms, e.g., Ps. 19; 119. P is thus very far from what is usually called legalism or nomism in relation to the NT conflict with Judaism.[77]

The so-called Holiness Code (H) of Lv. 17-26 displays an inner relation to the understanding of the Law in P. Here, too, man finds his supreme dignity in subjection to the will of God. The difference from P is to be found not so much in the emphasis on moral obligation to one's neighbour (Lv. 19:15 ff.; 25:35 ff.) as in the lesser importance attached to the historical validation of laws and institutions, though this is not completely absent (Lv. 18:1 ff.).

6. The Law in the Post-Exilic Period.

The Exile brought a major development in the attitude of Israel towards the Law, and consequently in the understanding of the Law. The threat of the prophets had been carried out. Israel had come under the judgment of Yahweh because of its disobedience to Him. After the return its decisive concern was to do His will. Israel had to obey God's Law to live. The Exile had made this plain.

This did not lead in the first instance to a change in theoretical attitude. In a new way the task of keeping the Law was still a result of election rather than its basis. This is true in the Chronicler's depiction of history and esp. in Ezra. Ezra's work stands or falls with the certainty that the transcendent God has chosen this particular people (Ezr. 9:5 ff.).[78]

Observing the Law does not create the relation to God; it keeps the people in this continuing relation, e.g., 2 Ch. 33:8. In fact, however, the emphasis and concern rest increasingly on the second aspect, so that everything depends on observance of the Law. The transition to the later view of the Law, whereby observance establishes the relation to God, is fluid. The Law takes on increasingly independent significance. It comes to have primary importance as regards the relation to God. Praise of God's deeds in relation to the fathers is increasingly accompanied by independent praise of the Law (cf. the two parts of Ps. 19) as the means which God has given the people to keep itself in His grace.

a. The historical presentation acc. to Dt. and Chronicles is an important stage in the progress of the Law towards a key position in the religious world of Judaism.[78a] This presentation presupposes a legal norm. Saul is rejected because he violates the commandment of God. All Israel's kings are judged acc. to the Law. The Davidic kingship is guaranteed by God's promise, but concretely it depends on observance of the Law (e.g., 2 Ch. 27 f.). The reconstruction of earlier historical materials in Ju. depicts the period acc. to the schema of sin, punishment calling upon God in distress, God's help through an appointed judge, and then new sin on the part of the people (Ju. 2:11 ff.). This depiction is informed by a zealous spirit of penitence which regards disaster as a righteous punishment for violation of God's will. On the other hand, this standpoint means that the idea of guilt is impossible in respect of periods or individuals who obviously stand under the grace of God. Thus the sin of David and the fall of Solomon

---

[77] Cf. v. Rad, *Priesterschrift*, 187, n. 34.
[78] Cf. Schaeder.
[78a] G. v. Rad, *Das Geschichtsbild des chronistischen Werks* (1930).

are not mentioned in Chronicles. Nevertheless, this presentation of history does bring home to the people the fact that its continued life is bound up with observance of the Law. The prophets themselves are commandeered for the Law and made its guardians and heralds (e.g., 2 K. 17:13).

b. The mounting significance of the Law is seen not only in this form of historical writing but also in the fact that the Law becomes increasingly the basis of the whole life of the community. [79] This is the point and purpose of the work of Ezra (Ezr. 9 f.). But this is also the starting-point for a logical development which will come only later. Bound to the Law, the people of Israel becomes a religious community centred in the Law. [80] Keeping the Law is the badge of membership of this people. This is naturally of decisive importance in the problem of proselytising, just as proselytising obviously contributes to this inner development.

c. There is a change in the cultus too. That worship should be acc. to the Law becomes so overwhelmingly important [81] that finally it is understood solely, or at least primarily, as a fulfilment of the Law, and it finds not merely its justification but its whole point and purpose as such. This is why Judaism could later survive the loss of the temple without any serious weakening of its religious structure.

d. Finally, the new position of the Law may be seen in the fact that a new class, i.e., that of the scribes, takes over the religious leadership of the people (Ezr. 7:10). If the priest had previously administered the Torah, the study of the Law now became an independent task separable from the priesthood. [82] In the high estimation of the scribes there is expressed the will of the community to recognise only the authority of the Law, to which all must bow, including the priest.

This does not have to mean [83] that casuistry predominates, or that the neighbour as a personal Thou is lost behind the neighbour as an object for my fulfilment of the Law. It does not have to mean that attachment to the Law is exploited as an evasion of obedience and a means of security before God. That it does not have to mean these things is shown by the genuine piety of many psalms which date from this period (Ps. 19; 37; 40; 119). On the other hand, it can mean these things. Indeed, it leads to them with a certain inner logic. This is enough to show how dangerous was this whole development, whose indubitable greatness lies in the fact that to a great extent it did in fact create a readiness for unconditional subjection to God's judgment and Law.

7. The Meaning of תּוֹרָה.

Of the many words which the OT uses with various nuances for "law," [84] תורה is the term which has the most comprehensive sense, which establishes itself most strongly, and which exerts the widest influence through its translation as νόμος in the LXX.

תורה occurs in the HT some 220 times, with sharp differences of meaning. The J

---

[79] Cf. E. Würthwein, *Der* 'am-ha'arez *im AT* (1936), 66 .

[80] Cf. G. Kittel, *Die Religionsgeschichte u. das Urchristentum* (1932), 69. One part of the wisdom of Prv. is clearly based on this standpoint (cf. Prv. 28:4 ff.), though elsewhere wisdom is a subsidiary movement with little relation to the Law.

[81] Cf. the exclusion of priests from the cultus if they cannot prove for certain their priestly descent (Ezr. 2:62).

[82] Cf. Eichrodt Theol., I, 214. Is there in 2 Ch. 15:3 a distinction between the Torah and priestly teaching along these lines ?

[83] Cf. Kautzsch, 352 f.; Schaeder, 3 f.

[84] Cf. the list in L. Köhler, *Theol. d. AT* (1936), 191 ff.

source does not have it. It occurs very rarely, if at all, in E.[85] The older prophets use it sparingly though sometimes emphatically. The Deuteronomic history and Dt. bring it into common use in its modern form. It also occurs frequently in the Priestly laws, in the Chronicler and in some psalms.

The etym., even if this were secure, could make no very solid contribution towards an understanding of the term.[86] The only possibility is to explain the content of תורה in terms of the oldest literary sources and then to work backwards and forwards from this pt. Such passages show that administration of the Torah was the special task of the priest (Hos. 4:6; Zeph. 3:4; Mi. 3:11; cf. also Jer. 18:18; Ez. 7:26; 22:26). On the other hand, Jer. 2:8 seems to imply that the Torah was already administered by others, not priests.

The older prophets also use תורה for the Word of God which comes to them[87] (Is. 8:16, cf. also v. 20; 30:9 f.; perhaps also 1:10). It should also be noted that some passages in the older prophets use the word תורה for the written commandment of Yahweh. Hos. 8:12 etc. plainly deal with ethical as well as purely ritual questions.

It thus follows that in this period at least תורה had the sense of a divine direction, whether this had come down from an earlier age as the Law preserved and proclaimed by the priest, whether it was now given by the priest (Lam. 2:9; Ez. 7:26; Mal. 2:4 ff.), or whether the divinely commissioned prophet gave it in a specific situation (cf. Is. 30:9).

The essential pt. in תורה is not the form but the divine authority. Normally the ref. will be to specific cases decided by Toroth,[88] though תורה can also embrace a greater whole (e.g., Is. 1:10 and later 2:3; Mi. 4:2; Is. 42:4; 51:4, 7). It is obvious, however, that the word Torah as used by the older prophets does not seem to admit of closer material definition, so that legal, cultic, political and other directions can all be described as Torah if they have divine authority. This is in keeping with the basic OT understanding of the Law as outlined above.

Nevertheless, account must also be taken of the fact that in some of the priestly corpora of Lv. and Nu. Torah is a term for the regulation of specific cultic or ritual practices and can sometimes be used as such at the head or the conclusion of a smaller related section.[89] In such cases the pt. may be that these regulations are part of the greater whole of the Law,[90] though this might also be a later reflection.

The meaning as thus far ascertained was worked out in two directions at a later period. On the one hand תורה occurs later as a term for the cultic direction of the priest (Hag. 2:11; Mal. 2:6 ff.). It can then take on in Prv. the general sense of instruction.[91] Other strata of this collection know תורה, of course, only in the sense which became customary later (Prv. 28:4, 7, 9; 29:18).

The change in the sense of תורה which was to be decisive for a later age takes place in the Deuteronomic writings. In the basic core of Dt. itself תורה still seems to be used in the older sense (Dt. 17:11; often it is hard to decide, cf. 32:46). The original Dt. would not yet have described itself as the Torah. But this occurs in the later strata

[85] Ex. 13:9; 16:4; 18:16, 20; 24:12 call for consideration, but they are disputable except perhaps for 18:16, 20. On 16:4 cf. Procksch, 203, n. 2.

[86] The customary derivation from ירה, "to throw," "to cast an oracle," is contested by Begrich, 68 f., 69, n. 1, though he has no explicit alternative to suggest.

[87] Jer. apparently not. Perhaps the Deuteronomic movement already inclines him to see the other aspect of תורה.

[88] Köhler, *Theol.*, 194.

[89] Lv. 6:2, 7, 18; 7:1, 11, 37; 11:46; Nu. 5:29 f. Cf. also Ez. 43:11 ff.

[90] There is, e.g., a חֻקַּת הַתּוֹרָה, Nu. 19:2; 31:21, cf. Köhler, 195.

[91] Instruction of the mother (Prv. 1:8; 6:20), or father (4:2), or teaching of the wise (3:1; 7:2). Perhaps Job 22:22 should be quoted in this connection.

and in the Deuteronomic history books (e.g., 2 K. 22:8, 11). There is now ref. to the דִּבְרֵי הַתּוֹרָה, the individual provisions of the Law, where previously the plur. תּוֹרוֹת had been used.[92] Dt. itself is סֵפֶר הַתּוֹרָה, and when the king has a copy made of this Law, this written Law is תורה (Dt. 17:18 f.; Jos. 8:32).

In content the תורה in the Deuteronomic writings is in the first instance Dt. itself, which is to be written on stones (Dt. 27:3, 8) and kept in the ark (31:26). In context the ref. could be specifically to the Decalogue (Dt. 4:44), but this is not customary. This תורה contains more than laws. Thus it includes also the covenant curse (29; 30). Yahweh can send sicknesses and plagues which are not mentioned in this book of the Law (28:61; Jos. 8:34). The book of the Law also contains the exposition or exhortatory application of the Law (1:5). In many cases, then, "law" is too narrow a rendering. תורה often has the general sense of teaching or instruction, cf. 2 Ch. 17:9; 19:10; Neh. 8; it can even mean divine revelation in general, esp. in the Psalms: 1:2; 19:8; 94:12. Nevertheless, the LXX rendering by νόμος is pertinent inasmuch as this Torah is still *a parte potiori* authoritative instruction. Confirmation may be found in the prior Aram. translation of תורה by דָּת, which points in the same direction.[93]

In the Chronicler and the later psalms this use of Torah does not undergo any fundamental change. But there is a change in content, since the Pentateuch as a whole is now called the Torah.[94] The chief titles for this Torah are תּוֹרַת יְהוָה (1 Ch. 16:40; 22:12 etc.), תּוֹרַת מֹשֶׁה (2 Ch. 23:18; 30:16 etc.), or a combination of both (2 Ch. 34:14; Ezr. 7:6 etc.), though תורה alone is no longer misleading.

8. νόμος in the LXX.

In the LXX תורה is in the vast majority of cases translated νόμος (some 200 times out of 220). νόμος, however, is even more common than תורה (some 240 times). There is an inner shift due to the fact that the LXX νόμος renders the תורה of a later stage of development, and the later meaning establishes itself in other cases too. Thus in Is. 8:16, what the prophet passes on to his disciples is in the LXX immediately identified with the Torah in the later sense; it is the epitome of divine teaching and the divine Law. In other passages, too, there is a fuller equation due to the suppression of the older senses of תורה. This may be seen particularly in the replacement of the old plur. of תורה by the sing. νόμος (e.g., Ex. 16:28; 18:16, 20; Is. 24:5).

The same trend emerges in those instances in which תורה is not rendered by νόμος. The change is usually to be explained by the fact that in the Heb. תורה bears a sense which does not accord with the main post-exilic meaning of νόμος and תורה. This applies to the use of תורה in the plur. (in Gn. 26:5; Prv. 3:1; Jer. 26:4 [Ιερ. 33:4]; Ez. 43:11; 44:5, 24; Hos. 8:12; Jer. 32:23 [Ιερ. 39:23]).[95] In such cases the LXX mostly has νόμιμα, once προστάγματα. Then there are the cases where תורה means a direction issued by men, Prv. 1:8; 6:20 (θεσμοί);[96] 31:26 (paraphrase). Finally, there are

---

[92] Gn. 26:5; Ex. 16:28; Lv. 26:46; Ez. 44:5; Ps. 105:45; also Dt. 33:10 (Begrich, 64, n. 9) and esp. Ex. 18:16, 20. Since many of these verses are later, it may be seen that there is no fixed rule.

[93] Schaeder, 44; Ezr. 7:12, 14, 25 f.; Est. 1:8 ff.; 8:13.

[94] For the Chronicler cf. v. Rad, *Geschichtsbild,* 38 ff. and "Die levitische Predigt in d. Büchern d. Chronik," *Festschrift f. O. Procksch* (1934), 113 ff. It should not be assumed that the present-day Pentateuch is always meant in these writings.

[95] In some of these verses the MT now has the sing., though this is secondary.

[96] In Gk. θεσμός is a more solemn term than νόμος. But since in Judaism νόμος is the equivalent of תורה, there can be no more solemn word than this.

passages in which the ref. is to an individual statute, 2 Ch. 19:10; Ez. 43:12.[97] It should be noted, however, that the changes in this direction are not in any way consistent. These instances simply indicate the general character of the shift.

The gains made by νόμος outside the sphere of תּוֹרָה do not affect the picture. They consist primarily in the assimilating of the Aram. terms דָּת (some 14 times) and פִּתְגָּם (once) and in the appropriation of many passages which use חֹק (3 times) or חֻקָּה (some 12 times). The same is true of many smaller variations which add nothing essential in detail (some 12 times) and in which we often find a vl. in the LXX.

The rendering of תּוֹרָה by νόμος means on the one side that the predominant later view of the Law triumphs and achieves domination. It also means on the other hand that the nuances of תּוֹרָה which supplement the understanding of the Law in terms of teaching, instruction and revelation also pass over to some degree into νόμος. Hence there is an expansion of meaning beyond the boundaries of traditional Gk. usage.[98]

C. The Law in Judaism.

1. The Law in the Pseudepigrapha and Apocrypha.

Though the apocryphal and pseudepigraphical writings do not form a material or linguistic unity, they are firmly connected in respect of the Law. In all of them the Law is the basis.[99] One part of these works is specifically devoted to the Law, seeking to apply, defend and commend it. Even in the works which have other concerns (esp. the apocalypses), the Law is of decisive significance.

a. Linguistically the abs. ὁ νόμος is largely dominant not merely in Pal. works like 1 Macc., where νόμος is almost always abs. and in the sing., but also in typically Hell. books like Ep. Ar. (39; 122; 309). But νόμος can also be used without the art. with no discernible distinction of meaning. ἐξέκλιναν ἐκ νόμου θεοῦ in Bar. 4:12 simply means that they have gone astray from the Torah of God.[100] Cf. also 1 Macc. 4:42 and esp. Sir., e.g., 19:20, 24; 21:11 etc.

Along with the predominant sense of God's commanding will, however, νόμος can often mean the Pentateuch, of which the Law was felt to be the main part. This may be seen from the twofold formula ὁ νόμος καὶ οἱ προφῆται, 2 Macc. 15:9; Sir. Prol. 1, 8 ff., 24 (cf. already in substance Zech. 7:12), and also from the more precise designation τὸ βιβλίον τοῦ νόμου (1 Εσδρ. 9:45). There can also be ref. to bringing the Law (1 Εσδρ. 9:39) or having the Law (Ep. Ar., 46) when the book is meant. νόμος also denotes the writing when it is not to be taken as law in the strict sense. Thus 2 Macc. 2:17 f. speaks of the inheritance, the monarchy, the priesthood, the sanctification of the people καθὼς ἐπηγγείλατο (sc. ὁ θεός) διὰ τοῦ νόμου. The deeds of the Shechemites are written in the Law acc. to Jub. 30:12.

Along with the abs. use, and in the same sense, we find fuller expressions like ὁ νόμος

---

[97] These can hardly be simple slips as, e.g., in Is. 42:21, where the LXX presupposes תודה for תורה; cf. also Job 22:22 (and the opp. in Am. 4:5). In other cases the deviation is hard to explain, e.g., Dt. 17:19; 2 K. 21:8 etc. In Dt. 17:18; Jos. 8:32 the LXX takes the Heb. משנה התורה in the technical sense and thus translates τὸ δευτερονόμιον τοῦτο.

[98] On the relation between νόμος and תּוֹרָה cf. C. H. Dodd, *The Bible and the Greeks* (1935), 25 ff.

[99] Cf. Bousset-Gressm., 119 ff.

[100] There can be no question here of a qualitative sense of the use without the art. (→ 1070, 15 f.).

κυρίου (1 Εσδρ. 1:31 etc.), ὁ νόμος τοῦ θεοῦ (3 Macc. 7:10, 12; Test. R. 3), ὁ νόμος Μωυσέως (1 Εσδρ. 8:3; Tob. 6:13 BA; 7:13 BA).

But there are other expressions which do not derive from a direct rendering of the Heb. תורה, esp. the plur. οἱ νόμοι. This is obviously an accommodation to Gk. readers or a Gk. form of expression current among the translators, 1 Macc. 10:37; 13:3; additions to Est. 3:13d e; 8:12p; Jdt. 11:12; esp. 2 Macc. 3:10; Jub. *passim*. That this term does in fact betray Gk. influence may be seen from other formulations which are not present in the OT but which remind us strongly of Gk. modes of thought, e.g., ὑπὲρ τῶν νόμων καὶ τῆς πατρίδος ἀποθνῄσκειν, 2 Macc. 8:21; 13:10, 14. Other phrases which are quite untypical of the OT are ὁ πατρῷος νόμος (3 Macc. 1:23 etc.), οἱ πάτριοι νόμοι (2 Macc. 6:1, identical here with οἱ τοῦ θεοῦ νόμοι), also νόμος ὑψίστου (Sir. 42:2; 44:20 etc.); ὁ θεῖος νόμος (Ep. Ar., 3). But these do not involve material change. In particular 2 Macc. with its strong Pharisaic orientation shows no weakening of the Jewish view of the Law in favour of Gk. influences. In the main the specifically OT mode of expression is still present even in writings which are open to the Hellenistic spirit. Thus Ep. Ar. usually has the sing. Only at 111 do we find the plur. for the Jewish Law. At 279 οἱ νόμοι is used in the more general sense.

b. In the material understanding of the Law one may see the same duality as in the usage. The position reached in the post-exilic period is maintained, with some sharpening of the contours, partly through inner development and partly through historical events. Yet new features also arise under intellectual influences from without.

(a) The first pt. to be noted in this whole lit. is the unconditional divine validity of the Law, which is fully accepted even in the Hell. Jewish works.[101] In the specifically Palestinian pieces no attempt is made to prove this validity or to engage in apologetic against apostates, though the material of, e.g., 1 Macc. might have suggested this. God's Law is eternally valid; this is part and parcel of its divine origin, Bar. 4:1; Jub. 2:33; 6:14 etc.

Again, the supremacy of the Law over all other religious functions is apparent. The prophets apply the Law (2 Macc. 2:1 ff.; 1 Εσδρ. 8:79 etc.). Temple worship is significant only if it is in strict accordance with the Law (Jub. 49:15; 50:11; Sir. 35:1 ff.; 1 Macc. 4:42 ff.). Indeed, the Law is more important than the temple, and scribal learning more important than priestly action.[102] In the time of the Macc. the different religious groups united in the battle for the Law. The revolt was kindled over a legal question (1 Macc. 1:41 ff.), and it is typical that a strong group very plainly withdrew from the conflict when the pt. at issue became political freedom rather than freedom to keep the Law.[103]

This was the Pharisaic group, composed of men who were determined in all circumstances and irrespective of the consequences to adhere to the Law and to the Law alone. The layman conversant with the Torah becomes increasingly the ideal of the righteous man, cf. the depiction in Sir. 38:24-39:11.[104] The fact of apostasy within and proselytising without led to the insight that the religious orientation of the individual depends, not on his membership of the people, but on his attitude to the Law.

---

[101] If more cautious formulae are sometimes found in Ep. Ar., this is due to the situation rather than the liberal view of the author, e.g., at 31: διὰ τὸ καὶ φιλοσοφωτέραν εἶναι καὶ ἀκέραιον τὴν νομοθεσίαν ταύτην, ὡς ἂν οὖσαν θείαν. For the author himself the Law has divine validity prior to any demonstration of its rationality, but not for the Gentile whom he causes to speak.

[102] Cf. L. Couard, *D. rel. u. sittl. Anschauungen d. at.lichen Apkr. u. Pseudepigr.* (1907), 141 f.

[103] Cf. W. Förster, "Der Ursprung d. Pharisäismus," ZNW, 34 (1935), 35 ff.

[104] Schaeder, 59, n. 1.

The historical situation of foreign domination and the *diaspora* leads to increased emphasis on those parts of the Law which differentiate the Jew externally from others, e.g., the Sabbath, circumcision, and the rules governing foods. These are at issue in the Maccabean revolt. Apologetic is mostly concerned with them. Historical writings lay particularly strong emphasis on these laws, esp. Jub. [105] The separation of the Jews from other peoples is often regarded, indeed, as the main purpose of the Law. [106]

Above all, there is increasing stress on the importance of the Law and its observance for the well-being of the individual and the people. God's acceptance or rejection depends on this observance. The whole history of the people is, so far as possible and more consistently than hitherto, viewed from the standpoint of reward or punishment for the keeping or transgressing of the Law, 1 Εσδρ. 8:81 ff.; Bar. 4:12; Prayer of Manasses. This can lead to external calculation, as in 2 Macc. 12:40, where it is said of all who fell in a particular battle that they carried charms ἀφ' ὧν ὁ νόμος ἀπείργει τοὺς Ἰουδαίους, and it became clear to all that they fell for this reason. That the reward for observance of the Law may be attained in the hereafter [107] is naturally a great help to this whole theory. The reward of resurrection is assigned for faithful observance, 2 Macc. 7:9. Hence the Law is the hope of the righteous, S. Bar. 51:7; Test. Jud. 26. The schema of reward for observance and judgment for violation dominates to a large extent the eschatological expectation of the future in Apocalyptic, even when, as in Jub. 1:23 ff., what is expected is a perfect keeping of the Law through the Spirit. For God, observance of the Law decides the verdict on individual and people. It thus fixes their temporal and eternal destiny.

(b) But there are also new features in the understanding of the Law in this lit. These arise esp. out of contacts with the intellectual and cultural world of Hellenism. The essential concern is to interpret the Law as true wisdom, and its observance as genuine reason. The fact that the debate with Hellenism is so strongly bound up with this question demonstrates yet again the predominant importance of the Law for the consciousness of the Jewish community. The Jewish part of Sib. (esp. 3-5), Ep. Ar., 3 and 4 Macc., Wis. of Sol., Sir., all seek either with a missionary or an apologetic thrust to make this synthesis between the Law and wisdom, observance of the Law and reason. [108] Bar. 4:1: αὕτη (sc. ἡ ἐπιστήμη, wisdom) ἡ βίβλος τῶν προσταγμάτων τοῦ θεοῦ καὶ ὁ νόμος ὁ ὑπάρχων εἰς τὸν αἰῶνα, Sir. 15:1: ὁ ἐγκρατὴς τοῦ νόμου κατακλήμψεται αὐτήν (sc. wisdom). The piety of wisdom had already found a home in Judaism, but it can now be upheld only if brought into relation with that of the Law. The way is prepared for this in Prv. by an equation of the wise and the righteous, the fool and the sinner. But now a mere assertion of this identity is not enough, for there are parts of the Law which are not obviously rational, esp. some on which particular stress has to be put for other reasons. [109] For the apologetic treatment of this question at the beginning of the 2nd cent. B.C. [110] Ep. Ar. is particularly instructive.

A rather different result of the equation of Law and wisdom is the idea that strictly all men equally are to keep the Law. This arises mainly in the form of an eschatological hope, and as such it is a favourite notion of Hell. Judaism. [111] God's Torah, like wisdom, becomes a universal law in Hell. Judaism. "It will be a common law on the whole

---

[105] In at least two of these matters we find a similar battle for the Law in primitive Christianity.

[106] Cf. Couard, 142.

[107] Volz, *Esch.*, § 37 f.

[108] Kautzsch Apokr. u. Pseudepigr., XVI f.; Couard, 143. On the whole question of Judaism and Hellenism cf. W. Knox, "Pharisaism and Hellenism," *Judaism and Christianity*, II (1937), also *St. Paul and the Church of the Gentiles* (1939).

[109] → *supra*.

[110] Cf. Schürer, III^4, 608 ff.

[111] Volz, 172. On this whole question cf. Knox.

earth," is the promise of Sib., III, 757, cf. 719 f. The Law is no longer an order of life within the election, as in the OT. It will no longer be kept only on the basis of the election. It is a timeless, intrinsically valid expression of the divine will. [112] The fact that the fathers of Israel before Moses are represented with increasing rigidity as men who kept the Law points in the same direction. No stain of lawlessness must be seen on them. This is esp. a concern of Jub. Abraham observed the Law of God, 24:11. [113]

It is only a step from this pt. to the idea of the pre-existence of the Law. The Law is now identical with the self-reposing and intrinsically valid divine wisdom. [114]

Thus the Law comes to have a full mediatorial position between God and man not merely in practice but also in theory. This is, however, the presupposition for the hopelessness and despair to which the Law gives rise in, e.g., 4 Esr. and S. Bar. No doubt is cast on the divine origin or eternal validity of the Law (4 Esr. 3:19; 5:27; 7:81; 9:36 f.). It is fully allowed that the Law confers life on him who does it (7:21; 14:30). But this is precisely what makes the position so hopeless when the fact of transgression is recognised and taken seriously. For sin prevents the bringing forth of the fruit of the Law. 4 Esr. 3:20 : *non abstulisti ab eis* (sc. the fathers) *cor malignum, ut faceret lex tua in eis fructum.* The very knowledge of the Law gives weight to sin ; 7:72 : *mandata accipientes non servaverunt ea et legem consecuti fraudaverunt eam, quam acceperunt.* Hence the complaint in 7:46 : *quis enim est de praesentibus, qui non peccavit, vel quis natorum, qui non praeterivit sponsionem tuam ?* 9:36 : *nos quidem, qui legem accepimus, peccantes peribimus.* This is where the Jewish understanding of the Law leads when taken seriously.

2. Josephus.

a. In Joseph. νόμος is normally used to denote the Jewish religious Law. οἱ νόμοι is more common in view of the concern of Joseph. to speak good Gk. and to make himself intelligible to Hellenistically educated readers. νόμος or οἱ νόμοι can often be used poetically as the subject of activities. The laws sigh, Bell., 3, 356. They command, Ant., 16, 3. There can, of course, be no question of personification. νόμος without art. is rare for the divine Law. [115] In other cases νόμος is the book of the OT or the Pentateuch, ἔνθα τῶν στρατιωτῶν τις εὑρὼν ἔν τινι κώμῃ τὸν ἱερὸν νόμον διέρρηξέν τε τὸ βιβλίον, Bell., 2, 229. λαβὼν εἰς χεῖρας τοὺς Μωυσέως νόμους, Vit., 134. Joseph. distinguishes between νόμος (the Pentateuch) and the other writings, Ap., 1, 39.

When Joseph. does not have the Jewish Law in view, he can often use νόμος for the laws of other nations, sometimes in comparison with the Jewish Law, Ap., 2, 172. There are also laws of war, Bell., 5, 123 f.: οἱ τῆς στρατείας νόμοι. νόμος can also mean custom not publicly elevated to the rank of law, e.g., Ant., 16, 277 of the νόμος of blood revenge. In this direction νόμος can also be usage, order or the law of nature. One should not fret at death ὡς κατὰ βούλησιν αὐτὸ πάσχοντας θεοῦ καὶ φύσεως νόμῳ, Ant., 4, 322 (cf. Bell., 3, 370, 374; also 5, 367; 4, 382). On the other hand, Joseph. does not identify this natural order with the Mosaic Law, though they do not stand in antithesis (Ant., 1, 24) and he can be impressed by the cosmic significance of certain cultic statutes (Ant., 3, 179 ff.).

Less Jewish is the use of νόμος for the norm of something, Bell., 5, 20 : καθεκτέον

---

112 Cf. the theory that the Gentiles knew and then rejected or forgot God's Law, though with no obvious reflection on the How of these events, 4 Esr. 3:33 ff.; S. Bar. 48:38 ff.

113 Sometimes Jub. can say that the Law was not perfectly revealed before Moses, but only after Moses became an eternal law for all races, Jub. 33:16. We can thus find occasional refs. to a first law, 2:24; 6:22. Relevant to R. 2:15 is the application of this thought in S. Bar. 57:2 : The works of the Law were done by the fathers, the Law was known to them in unwritten form.

114 Couard, 145 f.; Bousset-Gressm., 121.

115 Schl. Theol. d. Judt., 64.

καὶ τὰ πάθη τῷ νόμῳ τῆς συγγραφῆς, the manner corresponding to historical writing, the customary objective norm, demands ... (cf. πολέμου νόμῳ τὰς πληγὰς ἐθέλειν δέχεσθαι, Bell., 2, 90). But this use is rare in Joseph. and does not control his understanding of the Law.

b. The material understanding of Joseph. gives evidence of the same intermediary position as his usage. In all essentials his thought is Jewish, but he keeps firmly in view the needs of readers of non-Jewish culture. The Law has for Joseph. a dominant position in religion.[116] The Jews are people τὸ φυλάττειν τοὺς νόμους καὶ τὴν κατὰ τούτους παραδεδομένην εὐσέβειαν ἔργον ἀναγκαιότατον παντὸς τοῦ βίου πεποιημένοι, Ap., 1, 60. He admires those who set the Law above all else, Ant., 11, 152. The Law controls all life: οὐδὲν οὐδὲ τῶν βραχυτάτων αὐτεξούσιον ἐπὶ ταῖς βουλήσεσι τῶν χρησομένων κατέλιπεν (sc. Moses), but for all things he gave as ὅρον καὶ κανόνα τὸν νόμον, Ap., 2, 173 f., Ant., 3, 94. Customs are part of the Law, Ant., 12, 324; cf. 20, 218; 13, 297. This shows his orientation to Pharisaism.[117] The circumcision demanded by the Law, with acceptance of the Law, implies incorporation into the Jewish world, Ant., 13, 257 f. This means also that man's relationship with God is established by the Law. For this reason Joseph. is no mystic.

The basis of the significance and authority of the Law lies in its divine origin, which Joseph. firmly accepts. ταύτην Μωυσῆς τὴν διάταξιν τῶν νόμων ... ἐξέμαθε παρὰ τοῦ θεοῦ καὶ τοῖς Ἑβραίοις γεγραμμένην παραδίδωσιν, Ant., 3, 286. To be disobedient to the laws is to be disobedient to God, Ant., 20, 44. More cautiously formulated expressions are also found, Ap., 2, 184. Above all, there is strong emphasis on Moses' work as law-giver, Ant., 3, 266: οὐκ ἂν ἐπὶ τῇ αὐτοῦ ἀτιμίᾳ (sc. Moses — the laws of leprosy) ἐνομοθέτησεν. Moses sought a form of government in which God is the final authority, i.e., theocracy, Ap., 2, 165. This extolling of Moses as a wise and pious man obviously derives from accommodation to the Gk. world of thought, esp. when one adds thereto the proof of the superiority of the Law by its antiquity (Ap., 2, 154, 279) and immutability (Ap., 2, 184 and 221; Ant., 20, 218). The strongest pointer in this direction, however, is the attempt to give a rational interpretation and basis for the laws. Typical is Ant., 3, 274. The reason for the prohibition of adultery is that Moses believes that legitimate children are profitable civically and domestically. Hence Joseph. resolves upon a work in which he will expound the αἰτίαι of the laws, Ant., 4, 198 etc. Certainly the laws are not evidence of human wisdom, Ant., 3, 223. But Joseph. finds it meaningful to attempt to show which laws are the best by comparing the different laws and constitutions of the nations, Ap., 2, 163 ff. Hence recognition of the Law by men of all nations is important for him, Ap., 2, 284.

The two streams also meet in Joseph.'s reflection on the purpose and goal of the Law. The Law mediates a life well-pleasing to God, Ant., 3, 213; but in particular — and this shows again his Pharisaism — it is designed to prevent sin: μάθησις τῶν ἡμετέρων ἐθῶν καὶ νόμου ... δι' ὧν οὐχ ἁμαρτησόμεθα, Ant., 16, 43, cf. Ap., 2, 173 f. The Law blocks the attempt to excuse sin on the ground of ignorance, Ant., 4, 210. It is also valued as the order of public life. In giving laws God is βίον εὐδαίμονα καὶ πολιτείας κόσμον ὑπαγορεύσας, Ant., 3, 84. He who keeps the Law receives happiness. In even stronger dependence on Gk. thought Joseph. can interpret the Law as the commandment of virtues, esp. love: καὶ πρὸς εὐσέβειαν καὶ πρὸς κοινωνίαν τὴν μετ' ἀλλήλων καὶ πρὸς τὴν καθόλου φιλανθρωπίαν, ἔτι δὲ πρὸς δικαιοσύνην καὶ τὴν ἐν τοῖς πόνοις καρτερίαν καὶ θανάτου περιφρόνησιν ἄριστα κειμένους ἔχομεν τοὺς νόμους, Ap., 2, 146 (cf. 2, 291; Ant., 16, 42).[118]

---

[116] P. Krüger, *Philo u. Josephus als Apologeten des Judts.* (1906), 20.

[117] Schlatter, 63.

[118] Joseph. does, of course, lay emphasis on the fact that all these virtues have their root in piety: οὐ γὰρ μέρος τῆς ἀρετῆς ἐποίησε (sc. Moses) τὴν εὐσέβειαν, ἀλλὰ ταύτης μέρη τἆλλα, Ap., 2, 170 f.

In his deliberations on the motives for observing the Law Joseph. keeps for the most part to familiar paths. Fear of punishment and hope of reward play a part, Ant., 3, 321; 4, 210; 6, 93 etc. Joseph. emphasises above all the fact that the Law is impressed upon Jews from youth up, Ap., 2, 178, cf. Ant., 4, 211; Bell., 7, 343. In the stress laid on practical exercise in the Law Joseph. sees one of the main advantages of the Law of the Jews over that of other peoples, Ap., 2, 172; Ant., 20, 44. But it is added again, esp. from an apologetic standpoint, that in Judaism the following of the Law is voluntary and cheerful. There is manifest to all τὴν ἐθελούσιον ἡμῶν τοῖς νόμοις ἀκολουθίαν, Ap., 2, 220. Indeed, it is conscience which constrains the Jew to keep the Law, Ant., 3, 319.

On the one side Joseph.'s understanding of the Law gives evidence of an essential material basis in Jewish and even Pharisaic thought. But on the other there is a strong and primarily apologetic orientation to the rationalistic and moralistic world of Hellenistic culture.

3. Philo of Alexandria.

a. As regards usage there is no essential difference between Philo and Joseph. Ὁ νόμος or νόμος is usually the Torah of the Palestinians. The φιλανθρωπία νόμου (Spec. Leg., 2, 138) is the love of the OT Law. There are διὰ τῶν νόμων εἰς εὐσέβειαν παρακελεύσεις, Deus Imm., 69. But the laws of a state can also be οἱ νόμοι: ἰατροῖς μὲν οὖν ἐοίκασιν ἐν δήμῳ νόμοι (Jos., 63) is generally valid. Even among the Gentiles there is a κατὰ μοιχῶν νόμος, Vit. Mos., 1, 300. ὁ νόμος is also the Pentateuch. The Law says that the amount of grain collected by Joseph was beyond computation, Poster. C., 96. Acc. to Abr., 1 the sacred laws are written down in 5 books. Indeed, a single text of Scripture can be called νόμος even though it has no imperative character: τῶν ... νόμων, οἳ δὴ κυρίως εἰσὶ νόμοι ... ἓν μὲν ὅτι οὐχ ὡς ἄνθρωπος ὁ θεός (Nu. 23:19), ἕτερον δὲ ὡς ἄνθρωπος (Dt. 1:31), Deus Imm., 53.

More broadly than Joseph. Philo uses νόμος for the order and law of nature (ὁ τῆς φύσεως νόμος, Abr., 135). He does this in a twofold (though often barely distinguishable) sense: (1) for order: It is a νόμος φύσεως ἀνεπίληπτος that what has come into being should be of lower rank than its author, Plant., 132; and (2) for ordinance: Laban does not observe τοὺς ἀληθεῖς τῆς φύσεως νόμους, Ebr., 17. Something can indeed be written ἐν ταῖς τῆς φύσεως στήλαις (Spec. Leg., 1, 31) as other things are written ἐν ταῖς ἱερωτάταις τοῦ νόμου στήλαις (Op. Mund., 128).

The use of νόμος for the norm which is set for, or which corresponds to, a specific sphere or matter, is also found in Philo, κατὰ τοὺς μουσικῆς τελείας νόμους, Op. Mund., 70, 54; Omn. Prob. Lib., 51. κατὰ τοὺς ἐν ἀλληγορίᾳ νόμους, Abr., 68.

Finally, a man can be fig. νόμος as the embodiment of the Law. Vit. Mos., 1, 162: Before Moses became a law-giver αὐτὸς ἐγίνετο νόμος ἔμψυχός τε καὶ λογικὸς θείᾳ προνοίᾳ. The life of Abraham is not merely a νόμιμος βίος but νόμος αὐτὸς ὢν καὶ θεσμὸς ἄγραφος, Abr., 276, cf. 5.

b. It is hardly possible to give a uniform material exposition of Philo's statements about the Law or his understanding of it, for neither the Law nor legal religion is the true centre of his spiritual life. His basic theologico-philosophical position is that of a mystical ecstatic. For him the highest stage of religion is the vision which is also unity with the Godhead, the solitary sojourn in the supraterrestrial world of wisdom, Spec. Leg., 3, 1.[119] In relation to this central point the Law can have only a broken position; indeed, in the last resort it ought to be abandoned. But Philo cannot do this, and above all he will not. He prefers to cling to the unique authority of the divine Law, for he is and remains a Jew.[120]

---

119 Krüger, 57; Bousset-Gressm., 443 f., 449 ff.

120 Schürer, III, 700. Another reason why there is no uniformity in Philo is that he draws from different sources.

What he has to say about the Law is to be construed in terms of this tension between presuppositions which he will not surrender and the true centre of his theological and philosophical life.

The decisive concern of Philo in his discussion of the Law is to show the agreement between the OT Law and the cosmic order in reason and nature at large. This is for him a supremely personal question, nor is he controlled here merely by apologetic interests.

Moses gives the Law τοὺς νόμους ἐμφερεστάτην εἰκόνα τῆς τοῦ κόσμου πολιτείας ἡγησάμενος εἶναι, Vit. Mos., 2, 51. νόμοι τε καὶ θεσμοὶ τί ἕτερον ἢ φύσεως ἱεροὶ λόγοι; Spec. Leg., 2, 13.[121] He finds the strongest proof for this agreement between Law on the one side, reason, cosmic order and nature on the other, in the unity of God. In this unity creation and revelation are one. Vit. Mos., 2, 48: Moses shows τὸν αὐτὸν πατέρα καὶ ποιητὴν τοῦ κόσμου καὶ ἀληθείᾳ νομοθέτην. As he sees it, the order of the Pent. supports this, for the story of creation precedes the account of the giving of the Law.

Philo also finds this agreement in the patriarchs, for without knowing the revealed Law they live in full agreement with it.[122] Indeed, they are its embodiment, the unwritten Law (Abr., *passim*). They do the Law by nature and thus natural reason and revealed Law are in harmony.

Philo by no means denies the supernatural origin of the Law. In Decal., 15 he speaks περὶ τοῦ μὴ εὑρήματα ἀνθρώπου τοὺς νόμους ἀλλὰ θεοῦ χρησμοὺς σαφεστάτους εἶναι. God Himself has miraculously promulgated the Decalogue without human mediation (Decal., 18). This is in keeping with his other principle that man cannot elevate himself by his own power to the world of deity.[123]

To work out concretely this basic theological and philosophical concern, to show the agreement between nature and revelation, philosophy and Law, Philo has need of an allegorical interpretation of the Law.[124] He does, of course, allow a place for the literal sense, but from this one must move on ἐπὶ τὰς τροπικὰς ἀποδόσεις, Conf. Ling., 190. ἡμεῖς δὲ πειθόμενοι τῷ ὑποβάλλοντι ὀρθῷ λόγῳ τὴν ἐγκειμένην ἀπόδοσιν διερμηνεύσωμεν, Sobr., 33.

To be sure, Philo opposes those who relax the keeping of the commandments on the ground of allegorical exposition. He urges against them the fact that the commandments are obligatory in the literal sense too, Migr. Abr., 89. But this materially rather slender reasoning simply discloses that this position does not follow consistently from his starting-point. It is an illogicality which is to be charged to his Jewish heart.

Along with his allegorical treatment of the Law Philo has a rational discussion which is different in method though finally it meets the same need. The first point here is to unify and systematise the legal material, and then to show its rational basis, esp. as concerns the laws of separation.[125] The result in both cases is to minimise or evade whatever gives offence before the forum of speculative reason and cosmopolitan morality.[126] The apologetic intention is stronger here, and hence one can hardly miss the striking agreement between Philo and Ep. Ar. at this point. But Philo is still sufficiently distinctive. The whole Law can be reduced to a single requirement: ἔστι δ' ὡς ἔπος εἰπεῖν τῶν κατὰ μέρος ἀμυθήτων λόγων καὶ δογμάτων δύο τὰ ἀνωτάτω κεφά-

121 In contrast the laws of other nations are not a genuine expression of the natural order but additions to it, Jos., 31.

122 This is a self-evident axiom which needs no proof, → 1050.

123 Schürer, III, 714.

124 E. Stein, "Die allegorische Exegese d. Philo aus Alexandreia," *Beihefte*, ZAW, 51 (1929); "Philo und der Midr.," *Beihefte*, ZAW, 57 (1931).

125 → 1049.

126 This aspect is especially to the fore when Philo speaks of the Law admonishing and instructing in virtue, Virt., 119.

λαια τό τε πρὸς θεὸν δι' εὐσεβείας καὶ ὁσιότητος καὶ τὸ πρὸς ἀνθρώπους διὰ φιλανθρωπίας καὶ δικαιοσύνης· ὧν ἑκάτερον εἰς πολυσχιδεῖς ἰδέας καὶ πάσας ἐπαινετὰς τέμνεται (Spec. Leg., 2, 63, cf. 1, 300). In particular, the Decalogue is a sum of the whole Law, and the basis of all else. The goal of systematisation and unification is to show the rationality of the Law, a typically Hellenistic concern.[127] The rational explanation of the individual commandments is along the same lines. Thus circumcision in Spec. Leg., 1, 3 ff. is shown to be the only right thing by a whole series of hygienic considerations and theological allegorisings.

Finally, as concerns the way in which the Law works, Philo lays special stress on its voluntary character. It encourages rather than commands. Vit. Mos., 2, 51: ἔν τε γὰρ ταῖς προστάξεσι καὶ ἀπαγορεύσεσιν ὑποτίθεται (sc. Moses) καὶ παρηγορεῖ τὸ πλέον ἢ κελεύει, μετὰ προοιμιῶν καὶ ἐπιλόγων τὰ πλεῖστα καὶ ἀναγκαιότατα πειρώμενος ὑφηγεῖσθαι, τοῦ προτρέψασθαι χάριν μᾶλλον ἢ βιάσασθαι. To be sure, it is important that the Law should make its impress by daily reading and meditation, Spec. Leg., 4, 161. But in the last analysis the perfect man does not need its admonition, Leg. All., 1, 93 f. The Law is for him something external and alien. By nature he himself acts in accordance with the divine reason and wisdom expressed in the Law. Hence observance of the Law is not really a difficult matter.

Philo is thus the champion of allegorical exposition, rational explanation and moral unification. His continued practice of the Law may conceal the fact, but along these lines he carries through an obvious material dissolution of the Law in favour of Hellenistic speculation and moralism.[128]

4. The Law in Rabbinic Judaism.

The whole Rabb. understanding of the Law is denoted by the term תורה. The Rabb. תורה is also in most instances the equivalent of the NT νόμος.

a. The use of תורה in the Rabb. writings is basically the same as that of the end of the OT epoch, though there are some distinctive developments.

The Torah is primarily the Mosaic Law as Law (for examples cf. what follows, *passim*). This is the basis of all other meanings of תורה in the Rabb. writings. Thus תורה can be used specifically for the Decalogue, but the Decalogue is not in any exclusive sense the Torah. "Truly one should recite the Ten Commandments daily; and why does one not recite them? Because one does not wish to give a foothold to the assertion of heretics, that they may not be able to say that these alone were given on Sinai (and are divine)," jBer., 3c, 32 f.[129]

Along with the use of Torah for the Law of Moses we often find the word in the sense of that part of the OT Canon which contains the Law, i.e., the Pentateuch.[130] In most cases it is hard to distinguish between Torah as the Law and Torah as the Pentateuch. Nevertheless, the Pent. is called Torah even when the ref. is to contents which have no legal character (proofs from the Torah, i.e., the Pent., S. Dt., 1 on 1:1; 47 on 11:21; TBM, 11, 23; bTaan., 9a). In extension of this normal use of Torah all the writings of the OT can be called Torah, since the other writings agree with the Torah and are authoritative only in virtue of this agreement. S. Dt., 54 on 11, 26 introduces

---

127 Similar phenomena in the Rabb. and the NT have a different orientation.

128 Though there is a striking formal similarity between Philo's attitude to the Law and that of the NT, the two are separated by a deep material gulf, for the starting-points are quite different. It was natural, however, that in the early Church Christian criticism of the Law should soon be understood in Philonic fashion (Barn.).

129 J. Wohlgemuth, "Das jüd. Religionsgesetz in jüd. Beleuchtung," *Beilage z. Jahresbericht d. Rabbinerseminars in Berlin* (1921), 21.

130 On what follows → III, 978 ff.

Ps. 34:14 and Prv. 16:4 with the formula אמרה תורה. M. Ex., 15, 8 adduces passages from Is., Ez., Jer., Hos. etc. in support of the principle of the school of Ismael: "There is no earlier or later in the Torah." [131] The juxtaposition of the broader and narrower senses is particularly evident in Tanch. יתרו § 10 (ed. Horeb, 123b): תורה משלשת תורה נביאים וכתובים, "the Torah (the OT) contains Torah (Pentateuch), prophets and writings." [132]

But in a given context Torah can also have the sense of valid teaching generally. Tradition as distinct from Scripture is תורה שבעל פה. [133] In relation to this broadest sense the translation "law" is often not very apposite. Torah has here the more general meaning of "valid teaching," "revelation," though with particular ref. to man's action which this Torah regulates. Torah is thus necessarily singular. The plural תורות arises as it were only *per negationem,* e.g., when it is said that the difference between two schools is so sharp that one might think the Torah has been split into two Toroth, bSanh., 80b.

Finally Torah can have the special sense of study of the Torah, esp. in contrast to מצוה as the keeping of the commandment. Thus acc. to Ex. r., 31 on 22:26 the study of the Torah [134] is inseparable from keeping the commandment, and *vice versa.* bSota, 21a: עבירה מכבה מצוה ואין עבירה מכבה תורה. [135] Indeed, study of the Torah can sometimes be rated higher than fulfilment.

b. Materially, the Rabbinic understanding of the Torah may be summed up in two inwardly related principles: 1. God has revealed Himself once and for all and exclusively in the Torah; 2. man has his relationship with God only in his relationship with the Torah. Thus the basic starting-point of the OT, which can be summed up in the proposition that God has revealed Himself to Israel as its God, and hence Israel is bound to obey this God, is characteristically and decisively changed and annulled. Theoretically the two principles remain in force, but for all practical purposes the Torah comes fully to the forefront, primarily as the Law which claims the will of man.

(a) The central and dominant position of the Torah as the Law contained in the Pent. may be seen already in the relation of dependence in which all other authoritative writings stand to the Torah. This is indeed the inner presupposition of the extension of the concept Torah to which we have already referred. The other OT writings fundamentally contain nothing other than the Pent. There must be at least an indication of everything in it. Thus Qoh. is not withdrawn from use "because it begins with the words of the Torah and ends with the words of the Torah," bShab., 30b. [136] This view finds characteristic expression in the use of קבלה for the books of the OT apart from the Pent. [137] These works are valid because they are Sinaitic (→ 1056), though they

---

131 Bacher Term., I, 167 f.

132 Bacher Tannaiten, I², 476.

133 For refs. and discussion cf. W. Bacher, *Tradition u. Tradenten in den Schulen Palästinas u. Babyloniens* (1914), 22 ff.

134 Wohlgemuth, 77, n. 1.

135 A particularly interesting passage is Shab., 30a: "Once a man is dead, he is free from the Torah and the commandments." This statement seems at first sight to be a par. to R. 7:1. But just before we read: "Let a man continually occupy himself in the Torah and the commandments before he dies; for once he is dead the Torah and the commandments have ceased for him, and the Holy One, blessed be He, will no longer be praised through him." This makes it clear that here the Torah is study of the Law and the commandments are observance, so that there is no true par. to R. 7:1.

136 Moore, I, 246 f. For details → III, 985.

137 Bacher, *Tradition,* 2 f.

are formulated only later. This part of the OT is an explanation and application of the Law which in and of itself is not unconditionally necessary. "If Israel had not sinned, only the 5 parts of the Torah and the Book of Joshua would have been given to it," bNed., 22b. Basically the relation between written and oral Torah is the same. Agreement with the Torah is a presupposition of the latter. This was tacit at first, but from the time of Jochanan ben Zakkai [138] the traditional material was given a basis in the Torah acc. to specific exegetical methods. What could not be integrated in this way was accepted as הלכה למשה מסיני.[139] In reality the theory that traditional material has its origin in exegesis of the Torah is, of course, artificial. The validity of this material is dogmatic rather than historical. But the theory shows with what force the concept of the Law lays hold of all other parts of authoritative teaching. This can be authoritative only if it can be understood as exposition, development or even reconstruction [140] of the Torah.

(b) The authoritative character of the Law is supported by a strict view of the direct divine origin of the Pent. [141] bSanh., 99a: "Even if a man should say that the whole Torah is from heaven with the exception of this verse, which Moses spoke from his own lips rather than God, it is true of this man that he has despised the Word of Yahweh." This is the place for the distinctive affirmation that every valid doctrine, every recognised Rabbinic statement, every acknowledged exegetical conclusion, was revealed to Moses at Sinai. [142] This thesis plainly owes its origin to a concern for the comprehensive divinity, and hence also the uniqueness and unity, of the Sinai revelation. It is a judgment of faith rather than a historical theory; hence it is not uniformly followed. We read in bPes., 54a that the Torah is one of the 7 things created before the world, [143] and since it is of more value than all else, it was created first (Prv. 8:22), S. Dt., 37 on 11:10. [144] The Torah was already in existence when given to Moses. His role is purely passive. He is a middleman. The Torah is given to him in writing, or dictated to his pen, or taught him orally. [145] He is never regarded as its true author. [146] The sin for which he was punished is recorded "lest it should be said that it seems that Moses has falsified the Torah or said something which was not commanded" (which could then be regarded as the reason for his punishment), S. Dt., 26 on 3:23. Thus in copying the Torah it is like destroying a world to write a letter too much or too little, bSota, 20a. The sanctity of the Torah is further expressed in the principle that the Holy Scriptures "pollute the hands" (i.e., make washing essential before turning to secular activity), Jad., 3, 5 etc. Study of the Torah derives its outstanding dignity from this sanctity. God says to David: "Dearer to me is a day when you sit and study the Torah than the 1000 burnt offerings which thy son Solomon will one day offer me on the altar," bShab., 30a.

(c) Rooted in this divine authority of the Law is the reserve which the Rabbis — increasingly — display in respect of the question as to the טעמי התורה or reasons behind

[138] N. Glatzer, *Untersuchungen zur Geschichtslehre d. Tannaiten* (1933), 5. Cf. also R. Herford, "The Law and Pharisaism," *Judaism and Christianity*, Vol. III (ed. E. Rosenthal, London, 1938).

[139] Bacher, *Tradition*, 21 f.; 33 ff.; S. Kaatz, *D. mündliche Lehre und ihr Dogma* (I [1922], II [1923]), II, 11 ff.

[140] Kaatz, II, 5.

[141] Pesikt. r., 22; 111a; Str.-B., IV, 438. For the age of this view cf. Philo, → 1053.

[142] Kaatz, I, 30 ff.

[143] Not eternal pre-existence, as against F. Weber, *Jüdische Theol.*^{2} (1897), 15. The Torah is created, though first. It is the more important to keep to this when one recalls that the pre-existence of the Torah derives from the Hell. Jewish equation of Torah and cosmic principle, cf. p. 32, 35, also W. Knox.

[144] For refs. and details, Str.-B., II, 353 ff.

[145] *Ibid.*, IV, 439.

[146] The wisdom of the Law is not traced back to that of Moses, as in Philo and Joseph.

the Torah (the αἰτίαι of Joseph.). Jochanan ben Zakkai says: "By your life neither the dead pollutes nor does water purify, but it is a statute of the Most High the reasons for which one should not seek out," Pesikt., 40a. Thus one should not attribute to God's mercy the command not to offer a mother beast and offspring on the same day, jBer., 9c, 20 ff. To be sure this is again only the basic theoretical position designed to offset the danger of sublimation.[147] In practice it is one of the favourite proofs of perspicacity and a tool of edification to find reasons for the commandments.[148] But this does not rest on any essential concern, least of all an apologetic. There is no question of showing the profound significance of the Law by means of a norm which lies outside it. This is intentionally avoided in respect of laws for which reasons are commonly adduced in Hell. Jewish apologetic, or in debate with Gentiles.[149] Where reasons are alleged, they are mostly taken from the Torah itself.

(d) The strict and logical development of the authoritative character of the Torah is carried to such a degree that God Himself is bound to it, bAZ, 3b: "The first three hours of the day God sits and occupies Himself with the Torah." Naturally, this should not be pressed dogmatically. It is a more or less poetic mode of expression. But it is a typical sign of the all-dominant position of the Torah, in which God has wholly and utterly bound Himself.[150] The Torah is thus of eternal validity. R. Jochanan (c. 250) can say: "Prophets and writings will cease, but not the 5 books of the Torah" (jMeg., 70d, 60).

Even the Messiah will not bring a new Torah. He will Himself study and keep the Torah, teach the reasons for it,[151] bring defaulters back into subjection to it,[152] and give the Gentiles at least one part of the Law.[153] He receives the promises applicable to Him because He occupies Himself with the Torah, Midr. Ps. 2:9.

All this establishes the unique mediation of the Torah in respect of the relation between God and man, and even God and the world. "If two sit and occupy themselves with the words of the Torah, the Shekinah dwells among them," Ab., 3, 2. "When a man buys something valuable at the market, can he usually acquire the owner as well? But God has given Israel the Torah and says to them: In some sense you receive Me," Ex. r., 33, 7 on 25:2.

(e) All other relations between God on the one side, man, Israel and the world on the other, are subject to the Torah. The Torah is "the tool by which the world was made," Ab., 3, 14; S. Dt., 48 on 11:22. At creation God took counsel with the Torah; it is the master builder of every work.[154] Indeed, the world, man and Israel are created simply for the sake of the Torah, Gn. r., 1 on 1:1; Ab., 2, 8; cf. bBer., 6b; Midr. Ps. 78:1 (172b); Ab., 3, 14; M. Ex., 14, 29. History, too, is consistently brought under the schema of the Law, its transgression or observance. Thus the Law holds a key position in the whole religious life of Rabb. Judaism.

(f) For this reason the Torah has divisive power in the interrelations of men with one another. Israel and the Gentiles are essentially differentiated by possession or non-possession of the Torah. To be sure, it was given (bShab., 88b) or offered[155] to the nations in 70 languages. But they did not receive it, or at least do not keep it, S. Dt., 343 on 33:2. R. Meir (c. 150) has said, though without majority support, that even a

[147] Str.-B., III, 398.
[148] Wohlgemuth, 39 ff. adduces a host of examples, and cf. his discussion, 30 ff.
[149] Examples in Wohlgemuth, 71 f.
[150] *Ibid.*, 80 ff.; Weber, 17 f., 159 f.
[151] E.g., Tg. Cant., 8, 1 f., Str.-B., III, 570 f.
[152] E.g., Tg. Is. 53:11b, 12, Str.-B., I, 482 f.
[153] E.g., Midr. Ps. 21:8 (89a).
[154] In contrast to Philo, the indirectly stated Rabb. interrelating of creation and revelation is here wholly under the dominion of revelation.
[155] For details, and views of how this took place, cf. Str.-B., III, 38 ff.

Gentile, if he occupies himself with the Law, is to be as highly regarded as the high-priest, Lv. 18:5 being adduced as a basis, with emphasis on the fact that the *man* who does it will live, bSanh., 59a. But individuals within Israel are also differentiated by their knowledge of the Torah and their position towards it. This is why the scribe comes to occupy so important a position in community life. Even if a man learns Scripture and the Mishnah but does not serve with a wise man (as a pupil) he is regarded as *'am ha'arez*. He who has learned Scripture without the Mishnah is regarded as *bor*. But he who has learned neither Scripture nor Mishnah comes under, e.g., Prv. 24:20, bSota, 22a.

(g) The aim of the Torah is to show man what he should do and not do [156] in order that, obedient to the Torah, he may have God's approval, righteousness, life, and a share in the future world of God. "Why has God given us commandments? Is it not that we may do them and receive a reward?" S. Nu., 115 on 15:41. R. Chananiah ben Akashiah (*c.* 150) said: "God willed to allow Israel to earn merits, and therefore He gave them much Torah and commandments, as it is said: In order to give Israel merits, it pleased Yahweh to make the Torah big and strong" (so Is. 42:21 acc. to the Midr.). [157] Thus the Torah means life. As food sustains the life of the fleeting hour, so the future world is contained in the Torah, M. Ex., 13, 3; R. Simeon (*c.* 150) has said: "So says God to man: My Torah is in thy hand and thy soul is in my hand; keep what is mine, and I will keep what is thine, but destroy what is mine and I will destroy what is thine," Dt. r., 4, 4 on 11:26. The Torah is for one man a flavour of life, for another a flavour of death, bYoma, 72b. Transgression of the Torah does not destroy the Torah but the transgressor, Lv. r., 19 on 15:25.

This subjection to the Torah can also be seen from the angle that it implies for all the danger of death and condemnation. As the Torah turned to the hurt of the Gentiles because they did not learn it as they could and should have done (bSota, 35b), so in Israel there are Rabb. voices which express alarm at the difficulty of perfect observance. "When Gamaliel (II) read this verse (Ez. 18:9) he wept and said: He who observes all this is righteous, but not, alas! he who observes only one part of it." But Akiba then said to him, on the authority of Lv. 18:24a, that one part is enough, bSanh., 81a. [158] In the main it is asserted in principle that the Law can be fulfilled. This is an inner necessity, and complete sinlessness is claimed for at least a few: "We find that Abraham, our father, kept the whole Torah before it was given," Qid., 4, 14. [159]

(h) The fact that there is life only by keeping the Torah gives special interest to the development of the Law in the form of casuistry. The Law and its development and practice give the Jew his distinctive religious position. But this does not have to mean that true fulfilment of the Law is construed in terms of a casuistical observance of individual commandments and prohibitions, predominant though this may be. [160] Alongside this we find sayings which maintain that the piety of the heart and fear of God are the essential prerequisite of study, bYoma, 72b. "All that you do, do only out of

[156] The negative side, not infringing prohibitions, is more strongly emphasised by the Rabb. than the fulfilling of positive commandments. In discussion there is usually much more precise statement of what if forbidden than of what is commanded. Avoiding sin redounds more to the praise of the righteous than knowing the Law, bShab., 31b.

[157] Str.-B., IV, 6; Bacher Tannaiten, II, 376.

[158] Cf. on this whole question M. Löwy, "Die paulinische Lehre vom Gesetz," MGWJ, NF, 11 (1903), 322 ff., 417 ff., 534 ff.

[159] Cf. further Str.-B., III, 186, 204 f. This thought is old, → 1050. Philo's interest in this proposition is not evident among the Rabb.

[160] One occasionally finds among the Rabb. a sum of the Law in one or two central commandments, but this summarising, like the distinction between light and heavy commandments (cf. Wohlgemuth, 13 ff.), is of no fundamental importance. In bShab., 31a it is recounted that a Gentile asked Hillel whether he could tell him the Law while he stood on one foot, and Hillel answered: "What you would not have done to you, do not do to your neighbour. This is the whole Torah. All else is exposition. Go and learn it." "David

love," S. Dt., 41 on 11:3. Rabba b. R. Hona said: "A man who has knowledge of the Law without the fear of God is like a treasurer to whom are entrusted the inner keys but not the outer keys (of the house); how is he to enter?" Nevertheless, this does not alter the fact that a man achieves righteousness and life by study and observance of the Torah.

D. The Law in the New Testament.

I. Jesus and the Law in the Synoptic Gospels.

1. The Occurrence of the Word νόμος. In the Synoptic Gospels the occurrence of the term does not by a long way correspond to the importance of the matter either positively or negatively. To understand materially the attitude of Jesus to the Law one has thus to take into account stories in which the word νόμος does not occur.[161] In Mt. νόμος is found only 8 times, in Lk. 9 and in Mk. not at all.

In the few verses where it occurs the use of νόμος is simple. Except at Lk. 2:23 we always find ὁ νόμος. In Lk. 2:23 there is no art., but we have the combination νόμος κυρίου, which is to be defined in the light of תורת יהוה.[162] Normally νόμος means the Pent. For the whole of Scripture we find ὁ νόμος καὶ οἱ προφῆται (Mt. 5:17; 7:12; 11:13; 22:40; Lk. 16:16; 24:44 [also ψαλμοί]). The twofold meaning of νόμος and תורה which we noted in Judaism applies also to the Synoptic use of νόμος. It signifies both the Law and the Pentateuch or Scripture. Predominant is the sense of the Law as that which governs what we should do and not do. In Mt. 22:36, in the question about the ποία ἐντολὴ μεγάλη ἐν τῷ νόμῳ, the meaning is, not which is the great commandment in the Pent., but what kind of commandment is important within the total context of the Law.[163] But this very ref. shows how hard it is to make a clear-cut distinction, for the Pent. is essentially Law, and the Law is to be found only in the Pent. Mt. 5:18 f. is particularly instructive as regards the interrelation of Law and Pent. in νόμος. Here we find alongside one another ἰῶτα ἓν ἢ μία κεραία οὐ μὴ παρέλθῃ ἀπὸ τοῦ νόμου (where the idea of Scripture is basic) and μία τῶν ἐντολῶν τούτων τῶν ἐλαχίστων (where the ref. is rather to the content of the commandments).

Even in the expression ὁ νόμος καὶ οἱ προφῆται the ref. is usually to the imperative content of the OT (Mt. 5:17; 7:12; 22:40). But in context the promise of the OT may also be in view (Lk. 24:44; Mt. 11:13, here in the by no means accidental reverse form οἱ προφῆται καὶ ὁ νόμος). Elsewhere γραφή or a form of γράφω is normally used for the OT in this sense.

It may be an accident that νόμος is never used for the whole of the OT, though possibly οὐκ ἀνέγνωτε ἐν τῷ νόμῳ; (Nu. 28:9) in Mt. 12:5 alongside the simple οὐκ ἀνέγνωτε; (1 S. 21:7) in v. 3 could be intentional. In the light of verses like Mk. 7:1 ff. it is certainly no accident that νόμος is never used for the oral Torah or the teaching of tradition. The παράδοσις τῶν πρεσβυτέρων of Mk. 7:5 is a παράδοσις τῶν ἀνθρώπων (7:8); hence it is not granted the character of νόμος.

---

reduced it to 11 (commandments), Isaiah to 6 ... Micah to 3 ... Amos to 1 (Am. 5:4) ... Habakkuk to 1 (Hab. 2:4)," Mak., 23b/24a. But fundamentally each commandment is just as valid as any other, and such statements are more playful and edifying than of serious significance.

[161] Moreover it is doubtful in many instances whether the term is part of the original saying or statement, cf., e.g., Mt. 7:12 with Lk. 6:31. A. Harnack, *Beiträge zur Einleitung in das NT*, II: "Sprüche u. Reden Jesu" (1907), 11 f.

[162] In Lk. 2:39, however, we find κατὰ τὸν νόμον κυρίου.

[163] Cf. Zn. Mt., *ad loc.*

2. Jesus' Negation of the Law.

In the proclamation of Jesus according to the Synoptists affirmation and recognition of the Law are inextricably interwoven with negation and criticism. There are no data on which to attempt a chronological listing of the relevant sayings.[164] We must try, then, to understand the negation and affirmation of the Law in their mutual relationship.

The essential and basic negation of the Law in Jesus consists in the fact that He deposes it from its position of mediation. What determines man's relation to God is no longer the Law and man's relation to it. This decisive position is now occupied by the Word of Jesus, indeed, by Jesus Himself. Man finds his relation to God in the relation to Jesus, to the lordship of God which has invaded the world in Him.

What finally separates man from God is not transgression or negation of the Law (Mt. 21:28 ff.). Acc. to v. 31b the ref. here is not to the cleavage between word and act but to the difference between actual refusal of the Law and the new event of conversion and doing the will of God. It is not denied that infringement of the Law is sin which separates from God. But the point is that this hopeless situation can be remedied. This is the meaning of the statement: οἱ τελῶναι καὶ αἱ πόρναι προάγουσιν ὑμᾶς εἰς τὴν βασιλείαν τοῦ θεοῦ (21:31b). The pt. is even clearer in the parables of Lk. 15. These are to be understood in the light of 15:1 f. The publicans and sinners are with Jesus, and He extends them His fellowship even to the pt. of eating with them. This means that the lost sheep and the lost coin are found, that the prodigal son comes home again (vv. 3 ff.; 8 ff.; 11 ff.). In vv. 25 ff. it is then shown by way of contrast that the elder brother who stayed at home did not profit by staying at home. It is not in his relation to the Law, whether in a consistent fulfilment which is not disputed or in a flagrant transgression which is not condoned, that the righteous or the sinner finds his definitive relation to God. If the sinner is received into pardoning fellowship with Jesus, he is at home in the Father's house, and this fact puts to the man who is legally righteous the challenge whether he is building on his obedience to the commandment as hard-earned merit — this seems to be suggested by his grumbling at the reception of the prodigal — or whether he regards his perseverance in obedience as a joyous being at home in the Father's house. This means, however, that in both cases the Law is deposed from its position of mediation. The relation to the word and deed of Jesus now decides the relation to God.

In essence the same pt. is made in the sayings in Mt. 10:32 ff. Confession or denial of Jesus decides the eternal destiny of man. Similarly the parables collected in Mk. 2 are possible only if the Law no longer plays a decisive role between God and man, and conduct either in accordance with or in opposition to the Law no longer justifies or condemns a man definitively before God.[165]

The blessing of the children in Mk. 10:13 ff., the beatitudes in Mt. 5:3 ff., and the saying in Mt. 11:28 ff. all point in the same direction. Jesus pronounces these words precisely to those who are so burdened under the Law that they no longer have any ἀνάπαυσις. On the publican who falls down in repentance before God, and counts on God's grace alone, the sentence is passed: κατέβη οὗτος δεδικαιωμένος εἰς τὸν οἶκον αὐτοῦ παρ' ἐκεῖνον (Lk. 18:14) — rather than on the man who can boast of his observance of the Law (cf. also Lk. 17:7 ff.). The scribes and Pharisees close the

---

[164] Cf., e.g., Harnack, "Hat Jesus das at.liche Gesetz abgeschafft?", 227 ff. On the other hand, H. J. Holtzmann, *Lehrbuch d. nt.lichen Theologie*, I (1911), 202 f. tries to show that Jesus moved on to a radical transcending of nomism.

[165] Schl. Mk., *ad loc.*: "What Jesus did was grounded in the fact that He determined man's relation to God, not acc. to the Law, but in the power of His mission."

kingdom of God (Mt. 23:13) because they will allow men to enter only by fulfilment of the Law which they themselves administer.

This radically different position of the Law may be seen also in sayings and contexts in which the breaking in of the new aeon is regarded as the essence of the new order of things. This supplements what has been said already by giving it direction and protecting it against misunderstanding. For it shows that what is at issue is not just the disclosure of something which had been there all the time, or the clearing up of a pernicious error, but in very truth a new act of God which had thus far been present only in promise, not in fulfilment.[166] Ὁ νόμος καὶ οἱ προφῆται μέχρι Ἰωάννου· ἀπὸ τότε ἡ βασιλεία τοῦ θεοῦ εὐαγγελίζεται, Lk. 16:16 (cf. Mt. 11:13). Lk. is not reading anything impossible into the saying when on the one side he puts before it the saying about those who justify themselves before men, but God knows their hearts, ὅτι τὸ ἐν ἀνθρώποις ὑψηλὸν βδέλυγμα ἐνώπιον τοῦ θεοῦ (16:15), and on the other hand he affirms in the verses which follow that the Law maintains its significance and its validity is not overthrown by transgression (16:17 f.). Now that the coming of God's kingdom is proclaimed, then, the measure by which God measures is no longer the Law or the achievement of legal works (cf. the metaphors of the old coat and wineskins in Mk. 2:21 f.).[167]

But this changed situation and age is wholly bound up with the word and person of Him who brings it. Mk. 2:21 itself shows this, for the occasion of the sayings is the contrast between the disciples of Jesus and those of John. Inasmuch as the disciples belong to Jesus they belong to the new age. This means that in the Synoptists the freedom of Jesus *vis-à-vis* the Law is Messianically and Christologically grounded (cf. Lk. 2:41 ff.). In Mt. 17:24 ff. Jesus, as the Son, is free from the Law even though He keeps it.

Jesus, then, bases the relation of men to God on their relation to Himself and to the lordship of God which comes in Him. His specific invitation as the One who pardons is to sinners. This means that He firmly negates the Law in so far as it stands as a mediator between God and man. He firmly negates the righteousness of the Law. The Law is forced out of its key position by the person of Jesus Himself.

3. Jesus' Affirmation of the Law.

In terms of this new position and its implied negation of the Law, however, Jesus also affirms the Law rightly understood. For obviously this deposition of the Law from its position of mediation is not meant to be a general repudiation of the Law.

a. Jesus recognises the Law when He acts as the One who forgives sins, i.e., when He calls publicans and sinners to fellowship with Himself (Lk. 15). A plain judgment is pronounced; He is dealing with the sick (Mk. 2:17), the lost, the

---

166 B. Weiss, *Lehrbuch d. bibl. Theol. d. NT*[7] (1903), 82 has the same pt. in view when he distinguishes Jesus' new understanding of the Law from the older view by saying that there "the norm of the perfect will of God . . . had not yet attained everywhere to adequate expression corresponding to the perfect state of theocracy or the kingdom of God." Jesus understands the Law in the light of the full revelation of God which is given in Him, *ibid.*, 86.

167 *NT Deutsch*, Rengstorf Lk., *ad loc.*; Wellh. Mk., *ad loc.*

victims of death (Lk. 15:3 ff., 24, 32). Thus Jesus validates the Law by the judgment implied in His pardon.

The Law rightly demands obedience, and to withhold this means death. For this reason the new situation cannot be brought in by a doctrine which enlightens a merely alleged sinner. It can be brought in only by the eschatological act of forgiveness, i.e., the act which bears witness to God's lordship. The new relation to God is constituted, not by a new doctrine of God and His will, not by a new religion, but by the coming of the time of salvation and hence by the fact of forgiveness. This being so, the Law is on the one side deposed from its position of mediation. But on the other side the judgment of the Law and its demand are recognized to be valid. Indeed, they are a necessary presupposition.[168]

b. Moreover all the incidents adduced show that Jesus is not seeking to overturn the Law when He will not make it the basis of the relation to God (cf. Mt. 21:28 ff.).

The conversion of the prodigal son means that he is ready to come back in obedience (Lk. 15:19; cf. also Lk. 19:1 ff.). The call of Jesus lifts the burden of the Law, but imposes His own yoke (Mt. 11:29). The righteousness of the disciples is to exceed that of the scribes and Pharisees, not in the pedantry of legal casuistry, but in the fulness of surrender to God's will (Mt. 5:20). Bringing in the βασιλεία τοῦ θεοῦ, Jesus proclaims and creates true obedience and thereby recognises the Law in such a way as to fulfil it. The good tree produces good fruits (Mt. 7:16 ff.). The ref. of this metaphor is not to the relation between act and disposition, but to the relation between both these on the one side and standing in the position of divine sonship inaugurated by Jesus on the other. If the tree is good in this sense, there can be no repudiating the good fruits.

c. Hence it is not surprising that according to the Synoptic account Jesus Himself keeps the Law.

Thus He obviously wears the clothing prescribed by the Law (Mt. 9:20; 14:36).[169] That He was under the Law is of essential interest in the infancy stories in Lk. (2:22 ff., 27, 39). The prophetic witness applies to Him precisely as One who is set under the Law (2:24 f., 27 f.).[170] Indeed, the very goal of the Messianic work of Jesus is: ἕως ἂν πάντα γένηται (Mt. 5:18).[171] His own coming is fulfilment[172] of the Law, and the crucifixion is understood as the uniting of perfect obedience to God's will as this is stated in Scripture with love for the brethren in the act of self-sacrifice. The Synoptists, of course, do not say directly that they see here the fulfilment of the Law by Jesus, but this is in line with their depiction (cf. Mt. 3:15).[173]

d. Jesus recognises the Law to be God's good will not only for Himself but also for others. To the question of right conduct He gives the answer: τὰς ἐντολὰς οἶδας (Mk. 10:19). He does not accept as good any other will than the will of God revealed in the Law.[174] Apart from this He does not champion any other goodness (Mk. 10:18, cf. also Lk. 10:25 ff.).

---

[168] Schl. Gesch. d. Chr., 174 says that "the ethical sayings (of Jesus) were not meditations on ethical problems but parts of His summons to repentance."

[169] Branscomb, 115 f.

[170] Zn. Lk., *ad loc.*

[171] Schl. Mt., *ad loc.*

[172] Acc. to v. 19 πληροῦν does not mean "to make perfect" in content but "to bring into effect." The opposite view is taken by, e.g., A. Harnack, "Geschichte eines programmatischen Wortes Jesu (Mt. 5:17) in d. ältesten Kirche," SAB phil.-hist. Kl. (1912), 184 ff.

[173] Cf. Schl. Mt. on 5:18.

[174] P. Feine, *Theol. d. NT*⁴ (1922), 24 ff.

Jesus affirms the Law because it demands obedient action and is not content merely with a disposition subject to no controls. He rejects confession of Himself as Lord when it is combined with the doing of ἀνομία (Mt. 7:23). The goal of the Law is action; mere knowledge of the good will of God is not enough (Lk. 10:28).

Concretely, the Law demands self-denying love for God and neighbour[175] (Mk. 12:28 ff. and par.; the addition in Mt. 22:40 is to the point). The summing up of all the commandments in the law of love is found also in other places, e.g., Mt. 7:12 or 24:12: διὰ τὸ πληθυνθῆναι τὴν ἀνομίαν ψυγήσεται ἡ ἀγάπη τῶν πολλῶν. Lawlessness and lovelessness are reciprocal (cf. also Mt. 5:43 ff.).

There is thus a direct and positive relation between the Law on the one side and Jesus as the Christ on the other. True obedience to the law is rendered in discipleship. The rich young ruler will achieve perfect observance of the Law when he surrenders himself and follows Jesus (Mk. 10:17 ff.). The questioner of Mk. 12:34 is not far from the kingdom of God when he recognises the Law's radical requirement of love, though he is not yet in the kingdom, since he still expects the fulfilment of the commandment by his own achievement.[176]

e. Along with this direct affirmation of the Law there is criticism, though in reality this criticism serves only to confirm and establish the Law, not to destroy it. The first point in Jesus' criticism is that the Law can serve to protect man's disobedience against the claim of God. Keeping the individual commandments when there is no readiness for full self-giving is not accepted as perfect obedience by Jesus (Mk. 10:21 and par.). Even the fifth commandment is set aside by Jesus if it hampers response to His call to discipleship (Mt. 8:21 f.; cf. also Lk. 12:52 f.). Similarly, observance of the Law which is primarily calculating on recognition by men is not recognised by Jesus (Mt. 23:5 ff.; 6:1 ff.). Hence Jesus does not reject only an appeal to the sayings of "them of old time" when they conflict with the clear obligation of the Law (ἀφέντες τὴν ἐντολὴν τοῦ θεοῦ κρατεῖτε τὴν παράδοσιν τῶν ἀνθρώπων, Mk. 7:8 ff.). He also rejects an appeal to the letter of what is demanded by the Law when it conflicts with the unconditional claim of God and the claim of the neighbour.

This is the pt., e.g., of the story about the Sabbath in Mk. 3:1 ff. The question of good and evil, i.e., the question here of the will of God manifested at this moment in the neighbour's urgent need, solves the problem of what is permissible or impermissible acc. to the fourth commandment. God's will is indeed set forth in the Law, but it is not so bound to the Law that by appeal thereto one may evade the will of God regarding obligation to one's neighbour.

This is no reduction of the Law to morality. It is a radicalising of the Law by the question of concrete obedience in love for one's neighbour.

The concentration of the Law on love for God and neighbour serves to extend the duty of obedience. As distinct from similar summaries in Judaism this concentration is not based on interest in systematisation of the many commandments of the Law, nor does it owe its origin to playful or edifying tendencies, nor does it seek to escape the commandment and render the will of God innocuous. On the contrary, it serves to radicalise the Law,[177] to permit of no fulfilment of the Law

---

175 Cf. also Harnack, 229.
176 *NT Deutsch,* Schn. Mk., *ad loc.*
177 R. Bultmann, "Jesus und Pls.," *Jesus Chr. im Zeugnis der hl. Schrift u. d. Kirche* (1936), 74 ff.

which is not at its very core obedience to God and service to the neighbour. It serves supremely to prevent any refusal of this obedience and service which might appeal to the fulfilment of commandments. In so doing it also overthrows the Rabbinic distinction between legal duty and voluntary acts of love (cf. Mt. 3:15; Lk. 10:28 ff.; Mk. 10:17 ff.).[178]

The criticism of the Law implicit in this concentration is thus an affirmation of the Law in the radical sense. It is a restoration of the Law to its original OT sense of a claiming of man by God whereby man is also directed to his neighbour. After the manner of the prophetic understanding of the Law, the Law thus brings us up against God Himself, whose will is to be accepted both in the concrete Law and outside it. Jesus stands apart from the prophets, however, in the fact that they simply promise the divine act which will create obedience, whereas Jesus brings and is this act in His own person.

The rejection of casuistry by Jesus is not to be regarded, then, as a humanising, rationalising or moralising of the OT commandments.[179] Nor is it a mere extension of the national bond on a cosmopolitan scale.[180] Its primary point is that the holiness of God which demands the whole man is now taken seriously as compared with the protection which is sought in the Law precisely against the unconditional nature of this demand. This is particularly clear in Mt. 23:23, where Jesus is in no sense attacking the observance of lesser commandments of the Law but sharply condemning the view that to keep these is to secure dispensation from the βαρύτερα τοῦ νόμου.

The second point in Jesus's criticism is closely linked with the first. He criticises the Law in so far as it does not expose sin at the root by condemning only the act and not also the attitude of the heart which underlies the act.

Finally, the third point in his criticism of the Law is that the Law as it is presupposes the sin of man as a given factor which cannot be altered. Mk. 10:5: πρὸς τὴν σκληροκαρδίαν ὑμῶν ἔγραψεν (sc. Moses) ὑμῖν τὴν ἐντολὴν ταύτην. With relationship to Jesus and membership of the βασιλεία τοῦ θεοῦ, however, there is restored the order of creation which does not accept sin as a given factor.[181] This is implied even in the antitheses of Mt. 5:21 ff., and especially clearly in vv. 38 ff., where the Law limits unrestrained vengeance but Jesus frees His disciples from the whole spirit of revenge. Inasmuch as the Law presupposes the sin of man, it is set aside by Jesus, since He establishes the obedience of love which foregoes itself and its own rights and relies wholly and utterly on God.

Hereby the Law is for the first time genuinely established, though it is also clear that in its reconstruction by Jesus the Law is no longer understood as some-

---

[178] Bultmann, "Die Bedeutung ...," 193 f. (→ Bibl. D.).

[179] It is true that Jesus illustrates man's position before the Law primarily in terms of the ethical rather than the ritual commandments, but even if it is legitimate to speak of a fundamental priority of the former the essential point which He makes in respect of the Law is not to be sought in this priority. Even Mt. 7 is not primarily concerned with the alternative between and ethical and ritual understanding of the Law but with the alternative between genuine obedience and the concealment of disobedience by an appeal to the Law. Cf. also F. Büchsel, *Theol. d. NT* (1935), 22 f., and for a different view H. Weinel, *Bibl. Theol. d. NT*[4] (1928), 82 ff.

[180] This is emphasised by Weinel, 85 ff., cf. also Herkenrath, 132.

[181] The treatment of this question shows that a consistent relating of the commandment to God by no means excludes freedom. Marriage is a divine ordinance. As such, it binds wholly and utterly the man who is committed to God. But for this very reason there is freedom from the ordinance for the sake of the kingdom of God.

thing which man has to fulfil in the sense of earning thereby the justifying sentence of God. On the contrary, fulfilment of the requirement presupposes the prior divine sonship [182] which arises in fellowship with Jesus and which consists essentially in the forgiveness granted herewith.

4. The Interrelation of Negation and Affirmation of the Law.

It may thus be seen that this acknowledgment of the Law which consists of both affirmation and criticism is to be regarded primarily from two standpoints. First, it calls for full repentance, which acquires depth and concreteness from the Law's requirement. Secondly, it exhibits true obedience, the new righteousness. Both aspects are indissolubly bound up with the fact that Jesus bases the relation between God and man, not on fulfilment of the Law, but on the new creative act of God. Confrontation with God's unconditional claim through the Law, together with recognition of condemnation by the newly understood Law on the one side, and liberation from the mediation of the Law and its observance on the other, mutually promote and control one another. [183] Only when he renounces his own achievement and receives forgiveness is man truly able to set himself under the judgment of the Law and to offer the obedience of love. At the same time the question of God's new act on man and the world is contained in the radical establishment of the demand and its judgment.

II. The Conflict Concerning the Law.

1. The Primitive Community.

The sources give us no certain picture of the understanding of the Law in the primitive community. There is no doubt that the community did in fact keep the Law, but in what sense it did so is not clear from the account in Ac., since a tendency to efface distinctions may be discerned in this record. [184] Initial theological reflection was less concerned with the Law as its theme than with the understanding of Jesus as the Messiah promised by Scripture. [185] The question of the Law first became a subject when the community moved out to onetime Gentiles or more generally to the Gentile world. [186] The first basic position on the matter of which we can be certain is adopted at the so-called Apostolic Council recorded, with a substantial measure of agreement, in Gl. 2 and Ac. 15. [187] It is in the light of the decision taken at this council that we can best work out the fundamental understanding of the Law in the primitive community.

a. According to Gl. 2 the data relevant to the council are as follows. First, agreement between Paul's Gospel and that preached by the primitive community

---

182 Cf. Büchsel, 26.

183 Conversely, the clinging of Judaism to the mediatorial position of the Law, and the attempt to win God's justifying sentence by one's own achievements, are inseparable from a secret refusal of obedience with the help of the Law, and an unreadiness for full repentance.

184 C. Weizsäcker, *Das apostol. Zeitalter d. christl. Kirche* (1902), 169 ff.

185 Cf. P. Wernle, *Die Anfänge unserer Rel.*[2] (1904), 108.

186 The question of winning the Samaritans was similar in many ways, though not so difficult, Ac. 8.

187 The thesis of Weizsäcker, 175 f., that the author of Ac. 15 knew Gl. 2, gives rise to too many difficulties.

is confirmed, and not just established. Gl. 2:2: ἀνεθέμην αὐτοῖς τὸ εὐαγγέλιον ὃ κηρύσσω ἐν τοῖς ἔθνεσιν, v. 6: ἐμοὶ οἱ δοκοῦντες οὐδὲν προσανέθεντο.

Since the Law was the point at issue from the very first, it is impossible to assume that the agreement was unrelated to this fundamental question of the attitude to the Law. The arrangement on the separation of the εὐαγγέλιον τῆς ἀκροβυστίας and the εὐαγγέλιον τῆς περιτομῆς in Gl. 2:7 is not the recognition of a ἕτερον εὐαγγέλιον (Gl. 1:6) on the part of Paul. This is confirmed by Gl. 2:16: εἰδότες δὲ ὅτι οὐ δικαιοῦται ἄνθρωπος ἐξ ἔργων νόμου . . ., καὶ ἡμεῖς εἰς Χριστὸν Ἰησοῦν ἐπιστεύσαμεν, ἵνα δικαιωθῶμεν ἐκ πίστεως Χριστοῦ καὶ οὐκ ἐξ ἔργων νόμου.[188] Whether or not the verses Gl. 2:15 ff. were spoken to Peter does not alter the fact that Paul takes for granted Peter's assent to this principle and presupposes that it was already known. The dispute is about the practical consequences of this common fundamental understanding. Ac. 15 confirms the point at issue and the common answer. Those who come from Judaea to Antioch teach the brethren ὅτι ἐὰν μὴ περιτμηθῆτε τῷ ἔθει τῷ Μωυσέως, οὐ δύνασθε σωθῆναι (Ac. 15:1, cf. v. 5). And Ac. 15:11 gives the answer: ἀλλὰ διὰ τῆς χάριτος τοῦ κυρίου Ἰησοῦ πιστεύομεν σωθῆναι καθ' ὃν τρόπον κἀκεῖνοι. Though it is most unlikely that this account gives the actual words of Peter, the agreement of Ac. 15 with Gl. 2 certainly shows that there was unanimity in answering the question of the necessity of the Law to salvation in the negative, since both parties agreed that σωτηρία or δικαιοῦσθαι is given only by faith in the Kurios, Jesus.

The second point is equally certain, namely, that practical questions over and above the unanimity of principle were not so fully cleared up as to make impossible the dispute at Antioch as Paul describes it in Gl. 2.

To understand this passage it should be noted that neither directly nor indirectly does Paul have any word of censure for those who come from James, nor does he doubt their authorisation by James (though cf. Gl. 2:4: παρείσακτοι ψευδάδελφοι).[189] The concrete question is whether and how far those born Jews may live together in fellowship with Gentile Christians who do not keep the Law. In particular, can they have fellowship with them at table and in the Lord's Supper?[190] For if they do, they necessarily surrender essential parts of the strict observance of the Law. The measure of clarity reached thus far was simply that purely Gentile Christian churches were free from the Law with the consent of the primitive community, and purely Jewish Christian churches should keep the Law with the consent of Paul.[191]

The findings of the Apostolic Council, then, are that the Law is not to be kept as though one could be righteous by its observance, that faith in Jesus brings salvation to both Gentiles and Jews, and that the Law is still binding on Jews. On this basis it seems that the separation of Gentile and Jewish evangelisation (Gl. 2:7) had to be accepted by both Paul and the primitive community as necessary and appropriate.

b. But this raises the question why Jewish Christians were obliged to keep the Law, and we can take as a criterion in dealing with it the further question whether Paul could accept the reasons. That reasons had now to be considered was due to the situation of conflict; previously it had been self-evident without any need to consider specific reasons.

---

188 Cf. Weizsäcker, 160.

189 Cf. Kittel, 145 ff., 152.

190 Acc. to Kittel, 149, n. 1 we cannot be sure that fellowship at the Lord's table was at issue.

191 Schl. Gesch. d. erst. Chr., 70, 150 ff.; J. Weiss, *Das Urchristentum* (1917), 205; Weizsäcker, 164 ff.; for a different view cf. Meyer Ursprung, III, 424 ff.

The main reason is concern for the possibility of the Jewish mission. The preaching of Jesus as the Christ of Scripture could not be believed by Jews if His followers left the Law of God. Hereby the community and its Head would be condemned from the very outset in their eyes.[192] That Paul could agree with this view is shown beyond any question in 1 C. 9:20 f. Paul himself, τοῖς ὑπὸ νόμον, acts ὡς ὑπὸ νόμον, μὴ ὢν αὐτὸς ὑπὸ νόμον, that he may win those under the Law. He neither demands nor makes any demonstration of his freedom from the Law which might consist in transgression of the Law.

The practical consequences were naturally difficult in mixed congregations. A decisive role in understanding these matters is played by the so-called apostolic decree (Ac. 15:23 ff.; 21:25). This is certainly no invention of Ac.[193] The only question is whether it is issued by the Apostolic Council or whether it is the result of the difficult situation which later arose at Antioch. The decree should not be regarded as in any sense a minimal ethics, an abstract of the Law which in a kind of compromise tries to make at least the fundamentals of the Law obligatory in place of the whole Law.[194] This is ruled out by the choice of conditions as well as by the Jewish understanding of the Law in general; furthermore, it could not have gained the assent of Paul. Nor does defence against libertinistic Gnosticism seem to have been the main concern, for in this case the third and fourth points would remain obscure, and in addition an explanation along these lines would surely have had to be given. We have, in fact, no ground for distrusting the reasons given in Ac., which are plain enough: Ac. 15:21: Μωυσῆς γὰρ ἐκ γενεῶν ἀρχαίων κατὰ πόλιν τοὺς κηρύσσοντας αὐτὸν ἔχει ἐν ταῖς συναγωγαῖς κατὰ πᾶν σάββατον ἀναγινωσκόμενος. Now since in Jewish synagogues of the *diaspora* there was already fellowship in worship with the uncircumcised, similar fellowship in a mixed congregation of Jews and Gentiles could be defended before the Jewish world if the conditions of the decree were accepted by the Gentile Christians. The obligation of the Law was not restricted to these points for Jewish Christians, but they could engage in fellowship with Gentiles who accepted these points without giving offence to the Jews.[195]

c. From the basic and practical decision of the primitive community in these matters we may work out its understanding of the Law during the preceding period. Its actual commitment to the Law was not nomism in the sense that fulfilment of the Law was regarded as a presupposition of belonging to the Messianic kingdom. On the contrary, it regarded observance of the Law as the obedience concretely required of it as this people — an obedience which it had also to render for love's sake in the service of the Gospel. What constituted the community and separated it from others, however, was not a specific understanding of the Law but faith in Jesus as Lord and Christ.

What is the source of this distinctive attitude to the Law, of this simultaneous freedom from and commitment to it? The presentation in the Synoptic Gospels tells us that this attitude to the Law derived from Jesus.[196] The harmony of the attitude of Jesus towards the Law as depicted by the Synoptics with the attitude of the primitive community is in fact so striking that there must be a direct connection between them. The only remaining question is whether the picture of Jesus' attitude to the Law does not, conversely, owe its origin to the understanding of the Law in primitive Christianity.

If so, the only possible origin of this attitude would be either that it is a development of the confession of the Kurios which was demanded both by logic and also by historical

---

192 Cf. J. Weiss, 198; Schl. Gesch. d. erst. Chr., 14.
193 Weizsäcker, 175 ff.
194 Cf. Schl. Gesch. d. erst. Chr., 158 f.
195 Cf. J. Weiss, 237; Weizsäcker, 180.
196 Cf. Weizsäcker, 625 f.

events and which the primitive community must have understood, therefore, as the revelation and direction of its Lord present by the Holy Spirit, or that there was a strong influence of Hell. Judaism with its many softenings of the strict Jewish outlook on the Law. Support for the first possibility seems to be present in the story of Cornelius (Ac. 10 f., cf. 15:7 ff.), support for the second in the events relating to Stephen (Ac. 6 f.). The second explanation breaks down, however, on closer inspection, for, if it were true, Stephen with his view of the Law should not have met with opposition precisely in Hell. Jewish synagogues (Ac. 6:9 ff.), and in any case no Hell. Jewish views of the Law even approximate in essentials, in attitude and motivation, to that of primitive Christianity. Perhaps it is going too far even to say that in these quarters one would expect at least a greater readiness and openness in respect of that aspect of the message of Jesus which proclaimed freedom from the Law.[197] Stephen was condemned, not for his Hellenistic attitude to the Law, but for his Christian attitude.

As regards the first possibility, it should at least be noted that development from confession of the Kurios to the primitive Christian attitude to the Law would not be furthered by the Messianic theology of Judaism and its ideas concerning the relation between the Messiah and the Law. On the contrary, it would be hindered.[198] In view of the nature of the tradition one would also be betrayed into almost insuperable difficulties in any attempted derivation of the Synoptic presentation from the primitive Christian attitude on this question.

Historically speaking, it is far more probable that the Synoptic accounts of Jesus' attitude to the Law are correct and that fundamentally the primitive community took its attitude to the Law from Jesus Himself.[199]

d. Further development in the primitive community is also to be understood in the light of the conflicts, motives and decisions brought to light in the Apostolic Council and the events relating to it. The radical party, traditionally called the Judaisers, insisted in spite of the council that circumcision and the Law must be laid on Gentile Christians, since otherwise they could not enjoy salvation or belong to the community of Christ[200] They evidently propagated this view with zeal, especially in the Pauline churches, though it is open to question whether the situation presupposed in R. can be explained by Judaising propaganda.[201]

Acc. to Gl. the reasons for this campaign were fear of persecution on account of the cross and lust for personal power (Gl. 6:12 f.). Behind these there might well be a reversal of the missionary concern of the first community, a desire to avoid trouble in the Jewish world even at the cost of the Gospel of justification by faith in Jesus alone.[202] It may be assumed that there were some morally less disreputable motives, for the idea that one could or should give up the Law through faith in Jesus must have seemed quite impossible to many of those who had grown up in the Law.

The arguments which the Judaisers advanced to support their teaching were obviously a ref. to the command of Scripture (as the refutation in Gl. 3 f. shows), a ref. to the practice of the primitive community and even of Jesus Himself, and a contesting of Paul's apostleship, as may be seen from 2 C. 11; 1 C. 1:12; Gl. 1 f. To some degree,

---

[197] On this matter cf. J. Weiss, 121 ff., 198; Meyer Ursprung, III, 271 ff.; Weizsäcker, 52 ff.; M. Maurenbrecher, *Von Jerusalem nach Rom* (1910), 113, 114 f., 115.

[198] → 1057.

[199] This does not render the Cornelius story superfluous, for the community could not decide for itself whether freedom from the Law was necessary or right for it.

[200] Weizsäcker, 216 ff.; Schl. Gesch. d. erst. Chr., 152.

[201] Weizsäcker, 424 ff.

[202] Some part might also have been played by the consideration that only in this way could Christianity retain the advantages which the protection of the Roman Empire carried with it for the Jews.

esp. in more serious cases, some part might have been played, perhaps even a major role, by a ref. to the ethical consequences which it was thought would necessarily follow from Paul's doctrine of the Law.[203] In this respect it is not intrinsically likely that behind the activity there was a unified theological position which would everywhere be the same, for the primary interest of these people seems to have been in the Law itself rather than its theological defence.

A further development of this movement, which in essence had both time and history against it, may be found in the separated group of the Ebionites, who maintained that the Law is binding on all Christians.[204] To be distinguished, perhaps, from the Ebionites are the Nazarenes,[205] who simply clung to the Law themselves but excused Gentile Christians and recognised Paul.

e. Distinct from the position of the Judaisers is that of James, Peter, and the community controlled by them, who seem to have kept essentially to the lines laid down by the Apostolic Council. This certainly corresponds to the depiction of James in Ac. 21:18 ff., and it is confirmed by the account of his death in Joseph.[206] As regards Peter, it is best to assume that he returned to the position of the Apostolic Council and James after accepting the view of Paul for a period in Antioch. Certainly the attempt to make Peter a champion of the Judaisers[207] lacks adequate exegetical support in the available sources and it also suffers from intrinsic improbability.

As concerns the understanding of the Law in the normative circles of primitive Christianity, it may thus be said that they regarded the Law as the obedience to be rendered by Jewish Christians. They were also conscious of being under this obligation for the sake of winning the Jewish world for the Gospel. They did not believe that by achieving this obedience man could attain to righteousness before God. They were prepared to extend brotherly fellowship to Gentile Christians even though the latter did not keep the Law. In mixed congregations Gentile Christians were obliged to observe such points as would make the fellowship of Jewish Christians with them defensible in the eyes of the Jewish world.

2. The Usage of Paul.

The use of νόμος in Paul is not wholly uniform, for he can sometimes employ the term when he does not have the OT Law in view. Nevertheless, he does not start with a general sense which is then predominantly used for the Mosaic Law.[208] His starting-point is the traditional use of νόμος for the specific OT Law. Hence it is self-evident what νόμος means, and usually no more precise definition is given.[209]

As in Rabb. usage, the gist of the νόμος can be stated in the Decalogue, which is thus to some degree the Law in a specific sense (R. 13:8 ff.; 2:20 ff.; 7:7). In Paul, however, no basic distinction is made between the Decalogue and the rest of the legal material in the OT. With a corresponding gen. νόμος can also be used for an individual law, e.g., R. 7:2: νόμος τοῦ ἀνδρός, primarily in the sense of the law per-

---

[203] Weizsäcker, 428.
[204] J. Weiss, 572.
[205] *Ibid.*, 523.
[206] Jos. Ant., 20, 200, cf. Weiss, 552, n. 2; Kittel, 146.
[207] Esp. Meyer Ursprung, III, 434 ff. For R. cf. H. Lietzmann, SAB, 1930, and in criticism E. Hirsch, ZNW, 29 (1930), 63 ff.
[208] Cr.-Kö. seeks to distinguish between νόμος in general and the specific use for the divine Law of Israel, but he himself says that the use of the term in Paul is controlled by what he says about the Law of Israel.
[209] 1 C. 9:9: ὁ Μωυσέως νόμος, R. 7:22, 25; 8:7: ὁ νόμος τοῦ θεοῦ (the context requires the addition of τοῦ θεοῦ for emphasis).

taining to the husband,[210] in content the law which binds the wife to her husband, not, e.g., the law issued by the husband.

In Paul νόμος is supremely that which demands action from man, a specific will. Hence one "does" the Law (R. 2:25; cf. Gl. 5:3; 6:13). There are ἔργα νόμου demanded by the Law, i.e., works which are to be performed in acc. with it (R. 3:28 etc.). Only along these lines is there any point to the question of R. 7:7: ὁ νόμος ἁμαρτία; i.e., is the will present in the Law sinful? The positive equivalent of R. 7:12 is to the same effect: ὁ νόμος ἅγιος, the will of the Law, the Law in its demand, is holy.[211]

But even though the emphasis in νόμος is on its character as demanding will, this will of the Law may be seen esp. in the Mosaic Law of the OT.[212] There is a shift of emphasis in Paul. He attaches value to the Law as the living will of God in contrast to the Rabbinic stress on the fact that this will has been laid down once and for all. Nor is this change accidental, for all the wide measure of agreement. Nevertheless, this must not be taken as an occasion to revive the issue whether there is a distinction between the use of νόμος without the article and its use with the article.[213] It is certainly not true that νόμος is "a" law as distinct from ὁ νόμος, "the" Law.

This fact should be taken into account e.g., in exposition of R. 2:12 ff. Ὅσοι ἐν νόμῳ ἥμαρτον are not those who have sinned under some law of their own choosing. In contrast to those who ἀνόμως ἥμαρτον (v. 12a), they are people who knew the one divine Law and still sinned. The Gentiles in R. 2:14: νόμον μὴ ἔχοντες, do not know the specific Law of the OT. So far as Paul was aware, there was no people which did not have a law of some kind, even if this law did not have religious sanction. If these Gentiles do by nature, i.e., without knowing the revealed Law, the deeds which are commanded by this Law, they are herewith ἑαυτοῖς νόμος, i.e., "the" Law, not "a" law, to themselves.[214] If νόμος without article implied here a generalisation of the concept of law, the train of thought would be broken.

Not every national moral or politico-social order has for Paul the character of νόμος.[215] Hence he does not use νόμος in the plur., not even after the manner of Hell. Judaism which uses οἱ νόμοι for the OT Law, and certainly not in such a way as to group the OT Law with similar laws among other peoples.[216] The Law is one, the revealed will of the one God.

The central significance of God's demanding will is also expressed in the fact that the Law can be referred to as if it were personal. R. 3:19: The Law speaks, 4:15: it works, 7:1: it rules, 1 C. 9:8: it says. Sometimes, indeed, one might render νόμος by God in so far as He reveals Himself in the Law. Nevertheless, there is here not even the suggestion of a hypostatising of the Law, for along with these expressions we always find others which are quite impersonal, R. 3:20; 4:15; 7:2; 1 C. 9:9.

Along with this main use of νόμος there also occurs the other essential meaning of the Rabb. תורה, νόμος = Pentateuch, even when its nature as command is not at

---

210 Cf. Lv. 6:18: ὁ νόμος τῆς ἁμαρτίας for the Law in respect of the sin-offering.

211 Schl. R., on 7:7.

212 Cf. A. W. Slaten, "The Qualitative Use of νόμος in the Pauline Epistles," *American Journ. of Theol.*, 23 (1919), 213 ff. Even if Pl. often uses νόμος qualitatively, "that is, with especial emphasis upon the essential law-quality of law, its 'lawness,' so to speak" (214), this is not to deny its specific connection with the OT Law (217, n. 1). ὁ νόμος with the art. (e.g., R. 4:15) has this qualitative sense no less than νόμος without it (R. 4:14).

213 Cf. on this E. Grafe, *D. paul. Lehre vom Gesetz*² (1893), with older bibl. Cf. P. Feine, *D. Theol. d. NT*⁴ (1922), 218; Blass-Debrunner⁶ § 258, 2.

214 Schl. R., *ad loc.*

215 Typical is R. 5:14, where νόμος is not used of Adam, though in his case, since he transgressed a specific command of God, παράβασις occurs in the same way as later under the Law. Here too, then, there is no extension of νόμος in the direction of a general concept of law.

216 Cf. Brandt, 8 f.; Lohmeyer, 14.

issue.[217] In Gl. 4:21 νόμος is obviously used intentionally in a double sense: λέγετέ μοι οἱ ὑπὸ νόμον θέλοντες εἶναι, τὸν νόμον οὐκ ἀκούετε; the second time it simply means the Pentateuch narrative. The prophets are combined with this in R. 3:21 to give the whole Scripture. In proof from Scripture Pl. likes to associate a verse from the Torah and a passage from the prophets.[218] But this does not prevent him using νόμος for the whole of the OT. In 1 C. 14:21 a verse from the prophets is quoted with the words ἐν τῷ νόμῳ γέγραπται.[219] Similarly R. 3:19 combines verses from all parts of Scripture under the one ὅσα ὁ νόμος λέγει.

Finally, Pl. also uses νόμος in a fig. sense. In this case it is mostly found with a corresponding gen. or a word of explanation. In R. 3:27 there is ref. to the νόμος πίστεως as distinct from the νόμος ἔργων. Here, then, νόμος is meant in the broader sense of the divine ordinance which describes faith, not works, as the right conduct of man, to the exclusion of self-boasting before God. In R. 7:21 we do best to take νόμος fig.[220] The content of this νόμος is then the fact that evil is present with me when I seek to do the good. This rule is called a "law" because there is no evading its validity. Elsewhere νόμος can sometimes be the claim or will which comes from some source denoted by a *gen. auctoris* and which controls my conduct. ὁ νόμος τῆς ἁμαρτίας is the evil will forced on me by sin (R. 7:25; 8:2).[221] The use of ὁ νόμος τοῦ πνεύματος τῆς ζωῆς (R. 8:2) and ὁ νόμος τοῦ Χριστοῦ (Gl. 6:2), both in typical contrast to the OT Law, is similar. Also of interest is R. 13:8, where ὁ ἕτερος νόμος seems to refer back to the summary of the Law in the twofold commandment of love. This is why ἐντολή, elsewhere used for the individual commandment, is avoided here.

3. The Material Understanding of the Law in Paul.[222]

a. As concerns the material understanding of the Law in Paul, the cross of Jesus is decisive. In the statement that the crucified Jesus is the Christ the whole of Paul's thinking has its controlling centre, including what he says about the Law. Only in this light is there a meaningful, indeed, an inwardly necessary, connection between His affirmation and negation of the Law. Otherwise one could only conclude that there are two unrelated trains of thought, the one conservative and affirmative, the other negative and radical.[223]

In Paul the negation of the Law is a consequence of the cross, Gl. 2:21: εἰ γὰρ διὰ νόμου δικαιοσύνη, ἄρα Χριστὸς δωρεὰν ἀπέθανεν, cf. R. 7:1 ff.; 8:1 ff.[224] Freedom from the Law could be achieved in this way alone. This is grounded in the specific nature and operation of the Spirit.

b. The nature of the Law is summed up in the statement that the Law is the good will of God. Hence not to be subject to the Law is enmity against God, R. 8:7.

---

217 Sometimes a scripture which contains no command, and the lesson to be drawn from it, may be made fruitful for conduct, but in this case νόμος is not understood directly as commandment (e.g., 1 C. 14:21).

218 E.g., R. 9:12 f.; 10:6 ff., 13, 19 ff.; 11:8 f.; 15:10 ff.; 2 C. 6:16 ff.; Gl. 4:27, 30. Cf. the list in Michel, 12 f., 53. For the underlying Rabb. view cf. Lv. r., 16, 4 on Simeon b. Azai, "who sat and expounded and correlated the sayings of the Torah to the sayings of the prophets, and the sayings of the prophets to those of the writings: a fire flamed round about him and the sayings of the Torah rejoiced as on the day when they were given at Sinai"; cf. Glatzer, 38.

219 Dt. 28:49 is, however, appended.

220 Though cf. Schl. R., *ad loc.*

221 Cf. also R. 7:23.

222 Cf. P. Bläser, "Das Gesetz bei Pls." = *Nt.liche Abh.*, 19 (1941); C. Maurer, *Die Gesetzeslehre des Pls. nach ihrem Ursprung u. in ihrer Entfaltung dargelegt* (1941).

223 Michel, 190 f.; cf. also A. Schweitzer, *Die Mystik d. Ap. Pls.* (1930), 184 f.

224 Cf. O. Pfleiderer, *Der Paulinismus*² (1890), 6 f., 93.

In content Pl. does not make any fundamental distinction between cultic and ethical commandments, or between the Decalogue and the rest of the Law. Nevertheless, he works out his position primarily with ref. to the ethical commandments, esp. those of the Decalogue which apply to all men.[225] This is characteristic just because it is not done at the level of principle.

Since the Law is a declaration of God's will, it is orientated to what man does. When Paul quotes the statement in Lv. 18:5: ὁ ποιήσας αὐτὰ ζήσεται ἐν αὐτοῖς (Gl. 3:12; R. 10:5), the emphasis rests on the ποιεῖν.

The criticism of the Jew in R. 2:17 ff. makes the same assumption. The Jew certainly has knowledge of the Law. Indeed, he has the form and attitude of one who possesses truth and knowledge through the Law, 2:20.[226] But he does not do the Law, and the goal of the Law is the rendering of obedience by man. This is not achieved by knowledge and recognition of the Law. Hence Paul, when he describes man's existence under the Law, takes as his illustration, not the man who rejects the Law, but the man who wants to keep it, who assents to it, but who falls under its judgment because of his non-observance.

The Law has to do with ἔργα in contrast to the πίστις which is associated with ἀκοή, Gl. 3:2 ff. In life under the Law the act which conforms to the Law constitutes religious existence. To stand in the Law is to have a life which is based on doing it, Gl. 3:10: εἶναι ἐξ ἔργων νόμου, R. 3:23: ἐν νόμῳ καυχᾶσθαι. It is necessarily to seek one's boasting before God in the Law and by its fulfilment. This obligation to the Law is for Paul the true characteristic of the Jew.[227]

Nevertheless, Paul says of the Law that it cannot give life, Gl. 3:21. This is because no one keeps it, not because Paul regards the works of the Law as sin.[228] When Gentiles do by nature the works of the Law, these are acknowledged by Paul to be good works, R. 2:14.

Paul, then, does not primarily consider the Law as revelation, as God's giving of a share in Himself, though it is the central privilege of the Jew that the λόγια τοῦ θεοῦ are entrusted to him, R. 3:2; cf. 9:4 f. The fact that man knows the Law is the very thing which means that he has no share in God. Only if he performs the Law is he justified before God, R. 2:13.[229] Within the Law God links His own attitude towards man with that of man towards the Law.[230] It is precisely at this point that the new message begins, not with criticism of the Law according to its statutes.[231]

What the Law demands and "the good" are identical for Paul. This is true, not in the sense that the Law enjoys authority only as its goodness may be perceived, but in the sense that the doing of evil by any man is the same as transgression of the Law by the Jew. Similarly, awareness of the good is the same as knowledge of the Law.

---

[225] For Pl. the fulfilment of the Law through the Spirit in believers is the real intention of the Law. This view controls his understanding of the Law in judging the position of the sinner before it. That is to say, it demands obedience to God and love for neighbour. But Paul calls the Jews to repentance in face of the concrete Law, not of ideas concerning it.

[226] Cf. Schl. R., *ad loc.*

[227] Ἰουδαῖος is identical with ὑπὸ νόμον εἶναι, 1 C. 9:20 ff., cf. Lohmeyer, 22 f.; → III, 380 ff.

[228] Cf. Schl. Theol. d. Ap., 281.

[229] As against G. Kuhlmann, Theologia naturalis *bei Philon u. bei Pls.* (1930), 114 ff.; K. Barth, *Der Römerbrief*[6] (1929), on R. 2.

[230] Cf. H. Asmussen, *Theologisch-kirchliche Erwägungen zum Galaterbrief* (1935), No. 188 on 3:10 ff.; Schl. R. on 10:5; Lohmeyer, 31; 49.

[231] Cf. Schl. Theol. d. Ap., 289 ff.

This is particularly clear in the juxtaposition of R. 2:6 ff. and 2:12 ff. The ἔργον ἀγαθόν of v. 7 and the κατεργάζεσθαι τὸ κακόν of v. 9 are assessed in the same way as being a ποιητὴς νόμου or ἐν νόμῳ ἁμαρτάνειν in v. 12 f. This does not mean that the Jew may neglect the Law in favour of a good which is in his possession and which has to be done by him.[232] It means that the Gentile is without excuse even though he does not know the Law. Alternatively, a basis is provided for the statement in 2:11: οὐ γάρ ἐστιν προσωπολημψία παρὰ τῷ θεῷ. The judgment of God on the sin of Gentiles is also just. It is worth noting that Paul does not adduce in support of this the Rabb. theory that the Law was once given to all nations. He appeals instead to the assent of man to the verdict of καθῆκον (R. 1:28), to man's awareness that the μὴ καθήκοντα mentioned in R. 1:29 f. are worthy of death (1:32), and to his knowledge of what is good as displayed in the phenomenon of conscience,[233] which judges an act, and the phenomenon of ethical debate[234] (R. 2:15).

Nevertheless, those who stand outside faith in Christ are essentially distinguished by whether or not they possess the Law.[235] This is why a twofold proof is given in R. 2, first for those without the Law (vv. 12 ff.), then for those with the Law (vv. 17 ff., cf. also R. 3:1 ff.; 9:4 f.; Gl. 2:15). At what is for Paul the decisive point, however, Jews and Gentiles come together. Neither can be justified on the basis of observance of the Law or any other kind of goodness. For all have sinned, R. 3:23. Hence both alike are referred to faith in Christ alone, and in this they are linked together in unity, Gl. 3:28 etc. For one God stands over both parts of humanity, R. 3:29 f.

c. If this is the nature of the Law, one may understand its effect, which is produced when it comes into contact with sinful man.

(a) In the first instance the relation of the Law to sin is quite simply one of prohibition. That the Law forbids sin is a negative expression of the fact that the Law is the good will of God. Thus the Law says: οὐκ ἐπιθυμήσεις, R. 7:7. The question of R. 6:15 cannot be properly understood unless one presupposes that the Law protects against sin. The question, then, is whether sin is not unavoidable if the Law be done away.[236] On the whole, therefore, Paul kept to the strongly negative character of the Law, as also to the negative form of the Decalogue. The Law is God's Word directed against sin. It is, of course, summed up positively in the statement: ἀγαπήσεις τὸν πλησίον σου ὡς σεαυτόν (R. 13:9; Gl. 5:14), but this does not alter the fact that primarily the Law forbids sin as τῷ πλησίον κακὸν ἐργάζεσθαι, R. 13:10.

(b) Forbidding sin, the Law also unmasks it. Sin is shown up in its sinfulness. The Law brings out plainly its character as rebellion against God. To be sure, sin is already there before man comes into contact with the Law, R. 5:13; 7:9. But it comes to life through the Law: ἐλθούσης δὲ τῆς ἐντολῆς ἡ ἁμαρτία ἀνέζησεν, R. 7:9. Through the commandment sin kindles desire, R. 7:8. The point of R. 7:7, then, is that through the Law sin does not merely come to my knowledge, but for the first time it becomes a reality for me.[237] Perhaps the saying in R. 4:15:

---

232 Lohmeyer, 32; the demand of the Law is also equated with "the good" in R. 7:19, 22.

233 In R. 2:15 conscience is not considered as the source of ethical direction but as the court for judging actions. Cf. W. Gutbrod, *Die paul. Anthropologie* (1934), 55 f.; Schl. R. on 2:15.

234 This is at issue in the statement: μεταξὺ ἀλλήλων τῶν λογισμῶν κατηγορούντων ἢ καὶ ἀπολογουμένων.

235 Cf. Brandt, 23.

236 Cf. Schl. R., *ad loc.*; Schl. R. on 13:8 ff. is also relevant.

237 Cf. W. G. Kümmel, *Rö. 7 u. d. Bekehrung des Pls.* (1929), 44 ff.

οὗ δὲ οὐκ ἔστιν νόμος οὐδὲ παράβασις, should also be taken in the sense that it is the Law which first makes sin real rebellion.[238] Quite unmistakable is R. 5:20: νόμος δὲ παρεισῆλθεν ἵνα πλεονάσῃ τὸ παράπτωμα (cf. Gl. 3:19); also R. 7:13: ... ἵνα γένηται καθ' ὑπερβολὴν ἁμαρτωλὸς ἡ ἁμαρτία διὰ τῆς ἐντολῆς. Paul can even call this effect of the law its purpose (R. 5:20; Gl. 3:19), since no effect of the Law can arise outside the divine will. This means, of course, that the statement that the Law secures life for the doer takes on an air of unreality. For this reason, one must always add to it in thought an emphatic "only."[239]

(c) If the Law forbids sin, and also intensifies it to the level of actual rebellion against God, this means that the condemnation of sin is pronounced herewith. ἁμαρτία δὲ οὐκ ἐλλογεῖται μὴ ὄντος νόμου, R. 5:13. With the fact of transgression of the Law and rebellion against God, κατάκριμα rests on man, R. 8:1. Indeed, the Law does not simply entail the factual condemnation of sin. In its capacity as Scripture it also declares this condemnation and demands submission to the verdict. In R. 3:10 the Law speaks as indicated in 3:10 ff. ἵνα πᾶν στόμα φραγῇ καὶ ὑπόδικος γένηται πᾶς ὁ κόσμος τῷ θεῷ. R. 2:12: ὅσοι ἐν νόμῳ ἥμαρτον, διὰ νόμου κριθήσονται. Hence the Law makes sin into a deadly force, 1 C. 15:56; R. 7:9 f. For it works wrath, R. 4:15. Hereby the Law leads him who hears it aright to the knowledge of sin, R. 3:20[240] (perhaps R. 7:7 should also be construed in this sense). Paul is not really suggesting that this knowledge of sin gives man a subjective insight into his need of redemption. What he means is that a man cannot appeal to the Law before God, since the Law is the very thing which unmasks him as a sinner.

One may thus see why there is in Paul no place for the attempt to compensate for violations of the Law by works of fulfilment. Transgression implies rebellion against God and provokes God's judgment. Unity is thus given to the concept of sin; sin is no longer the sum of individual faults. Obedience, too, can only be total obedience, not just the sum of individual good acts. Any attempt to balance good deeds against bad deeds means that man is in some sense absolving himself from half God's requirement and by this very effort he is already turning the nature of obedience into its opposite.

(d) All this means that the true effect of the Law is to nail man to his sin. As a prison holds the prisoner, as a παιδαγωγός keeps the boy under his authority, so man is shut up by the Law under sin. This is according to the verdict of Scripture, which means according to the will of God, Gl. 3:22 ff. Rightly understood, then, the Law prevents any attempt on man's part to secure righteousness before God in any other way than by faith in Jesus Christ and by the pardoning grace of God, i.e., in any other way than that promised to Abraham. For the Law nails man to his sin. According to Paul this is the real connection between the Law and Christ. The Law is not in the first instance that which leads to Christ by giving insight into the need of redemption.

The Law has this effect only because it binds man with divine authority. Awareness of human imperfection can be created by any demand. But the situation of him who is justly condemned by God can be produced only by the good will of God, whether man rejects it or acknowledges it and seeks to fulfil it, R. 7:7 ff.

---

[238] Unless with Schl. R., *ad loc.* we take the sentence to mean that the Law is done away in Christ, and with it the guilt.

[239] This purpose of the Law, namely, to intensify and increase sin, is meaningful and bearable, of course, only in terms of the end of the Law.

[240] No attention is here given to the question whether the Law can or even must lead man to this knowledge apart from faith in Christ.

(e) To say this is to describe what Paul calls the weakness of the Law. This lies essentially in the fact that it can meet sin only with prohibition and condemnation. The Law is weak διὰ τῆς σαρκός, R. 8:3. It is weak because of the fact of sin which it cannot overcome. Thus the weakness of the Law can also be expressed by saying that it has no power to give life, Gl. 3:21. On the contrary, through sin it brings death, R. 7:9 f.; 1 C. 15:56. This is also meant when the Law as the letter which kills is contrasted with the life-giving Spirit, 2 C. 3:6 ff. Service of the Law which is written on tables of stone, though it is a glorious ministry because the Law is the revealed will of God, brings condemnation and death, since it comes to man only from without and does not move him from the centre of his being. In other words, it allows him to live on as the sinner he is. Indeed, it nails him to this sin, having no ability to take this sin from him. In essentials, then, the thought of 2 C. 3:6 is the same as that of R. 7 or Gl. 3. The reference is not to the distinction between a religion of the letter and a religion of disposition, though many have been only too pleased to find this in the verse.

Perhaps the strongest result of this insight into the effect of the Law is that Paul reckons the Law among the στοιχεῖα τοῦ κόσμου, Gl. 4:3, 9; Col. 2:8, 20. The meaning of this expression is most clearly brought out in Col. 2:20. He who has died with Christ to the στοιχεῖα τοῦ κόσμου should no longer take orders as though he were still ἐν κόσμῳ. In Gl. 4:3, 9, too, the emphasis is on κόσμος. The Law is something which belongs to the essential constitution of this world.[241] Hence it cannot lead beyond this state or break the tie with sin. This weakness of the Law, however, is not in spite of, but precisely because of, its holiness as the revelation of the will of God with which it confronts man, cf. R. 7:14.

d. Paul's radical understanding of the Law can be apprehended only in the light of his inner starting-point, namely, the act of forgiveness and justification accomplished in the cross of Christ, and therewith the reconstitution by God of man's relation to God apart from man's achievement, and hence apart from the Law. Paul's negation of the Law derives from his affirmation of what has taken place in Jesus Christ, not from rational criticism or missionary tactics. Because righteousness before God is attributed to man in the cross, not on the basis of what man has done, but on the basis of his assumption by grace into this death, this negation is necessary, R. 3:21 ff. The aim of Paul, then, is that he may be found in Christ : μὴ ἔχων ἐμὴν δικαιοσύνην τὴν ἐκ νόμου, ἀλλὰ τὴν διὰ πίστεως Χριστοῦ, τὴν ἐκ θεοῦ δικαιοσύνην, Phil. 3:9. οὐδὲν ἄρα νῦν κατάκριμα τοῖς ἐν Χριστῷ Ἰησοῦ, R. 8:1.

But outside the death of Christ and death with Christ man is still ἐν κόσμῳ and hence delivered up to the Law, Col. 2:20. Thus the statement in R. 10:4 : τέλος γὰρ νόμου Χριστὸς εἰς δικαιοσύνην παντὶ τῷ πιστεύοντι, does not simply mean that the age of the Law has ended with the coming of Jesus. The Law and Christ do not succeed one another in temporal history or even religious history. The transition takes place in salvation history. Only for him who in faith appropriates the righteousness of God in Christ is the Law abolished. Paul gives expression to this by saying that translation from the sphere of the Law takes place only by death, R. 7:1 ff.; Gl. 2:19; Col. 2:20. But this death is simply participation in the death of Christ : ἐθανατώθητε τῷ νόμῳ διὰ τοῦ σώματος τοῦ Χριστοῦ, R. 7:4; Χριστῷ συνεσταύρωμαι, Gl. 2:19; ἀπεθάνετε σὺν Χριστῷ, Col. 2:20. Beside this there stands baptism into Christ by which we are sons of God and no longer

---

[241] Cf. M. Dibelius, *Die Geisterwelt im Glauben des Pls.* (1909), 84.

servants, and hence no longer subject to the Law, Gl. 3. Baptism is again linked to death with Christ in R. 6.[242] All this simply means that the relation to God no longer rests on man himself. The Law is closed off as the way of salvation. Christ has taken its place. Man is thus forbidden even to try to become righteous by the Law now that God has revealed Himself in Jesus Christ as the pardoning God who justifies the sinner rather than him who is righteous by his own achievement, R. 4:5. The man who still expects righteousness by observing the Law causes Christ to have died in vain, Gl. 2:21.

e. The positive link between the Law and Christ is preserved, however, by understanding the cross as an affirmation of the Law. It is first an affirmation of its verdict. The death to the Law which takes place in crucifixion with Christ takes place διὰ νόμου, Gl. 2:19.[243] Gl. 3:13 makes this even clearer: Χριστὸς ἡμᾶς ἐξηγόρασεν ἐκ τῆς κατάρας τοῦ νόμου γενόμενος ὑπὲρ ἡμῶν κατάρα (cf. 2 C. 5:21: Christ was made sin for us). The Law's sentence of condemnation on sin is thus fulfilled in the cross of Christ, R. 5:6 ff. Moreover, even if Paul does not explicitly say so, it is logically implied in the matter itself that the cross of Christ is also a fulfilling of the Law in so far as the central purpose of the Law is fulfilled herein. The cross is the full achievement of obedience to God (Phil. 2:5 ff.), and at the same time it is perfect love for men (R. 8:34 ff.). This is, however, the true goal of the Law. Hence it is disobedience to the Law to desire it other than in this fulfilment. To emphasise expressly that the Law is fulfilled here is not in Paul's interest, since it would suggest the primacy of the Law. His concern is the very different one of showing how the Law comes to fulfilment in believers with faith in Christ.

Only with faith is there full recognition of the condemnation implicit in the Law. The attempt to be justified by works of the Law necessarily weakens this verdict or renders it innocuous. This is why R. 1-3 and R. 7 were written. But in dying with Christ, in which the relation to God has been established in God's act apart from the Law, the new obedience has its root (R. 6:11 ff.), and there also arises in faith the fruit of the Spirit (Gl. 5:22). The Law is thus fulfilled, at any rate primarily in the negative sense that the commandment of the Law is not infringed nor its condemnation challenged (Gl. 5:23). This is true because the requirements of the Law can be summed up in the commandment of love, Gl. 5:14; R. 13:10. Indeed, the twofold commandment of love (cf. Jesus in Mt. 22:36 ff.) can even be called the νόμος, so that the command to love one's neighbour is ὁ ἕτερος νόμος in R. 13:8. The same is meant by ὁ νόμος τοῦ Χριστοῦ in Gl. 6:2. Thus the true intention of the Law is fulfilled in the man who is set in love by Christ. R. 8:4: ἵνα τὸ δικαίωμα τοῦ νόμου πληρωθῇ ἐν ἡμῖν τοῖς μὴ κατὰ σάρκα περιπατοῦσιν ἀλλὰ κατὰ πνεῦμα. Hence Paul can say in R. 3:31 that the Law is not only not abolished but truly established for the first time by the Gospel of justification by faith, and the Law here is indeed used, not in the sense of the Law which promises (cf. R. 4) or the Law which condemns (cf. R. 3:10 ff.), but in its specific sense as the Law which commands.

If by the acceptance of Jesus' death in faith the Law is fulfilled according to its true intention, namely, the bond of obedience towards God and love of one's

---

242 Cf. Gutbrod, 190 ff.

243 Zn. Gl., *ad loc.* takes this διὰ νόμου to mean "by the fact that the Law showed me my need of redemption and referred me to faith."

neighbour, Paul can also speak of a fulfilment of the concrete Law of the OT out of love and obedience. It is true that in principle he withstands the idea that this fulfilment of the OT Law, or even the fulfilment of a Christian norm, is demanded in the sense of being necessary to justification before God.[244] But he himself is quite ready to keep the Mosaic Law in ministering the Gospel to the Jews, 1 C. 9:20 ff. He can even advise native Jews not to go back on their circumcision, 1 C. 7:18 ff. In so doing, Paul is not leaving his doctrine of justification for a legalistic view. On the contrary, he is simply working out the logical implications of his doctrine of justification and his proclamation of freedom in Christ, since a man may renounce the exercise of his freedom out of love for the weaker brother, or for the sake of building up the community, or because he stands in a particular order. As he is not justified by the works of the Law, no more is he justified by putting his knowledge into practice or exercising the freedom imparted to him thereby. He is justified solely by the fact that he is known by God, 1 C. 8:3.

Finally, the Law is also used by Paul as the place where he can find instructions for the concrete life of the community, i.e., in διδαχή. In 1 C. 9:8 f.; 14:21, 34 the Law is expounded allegorically to provide answers (or to support answers already given) to questions relating to the life of the community. It is worth noting in this connection that the proof from the Law is not adduced as the decisive argument, but as confirmation of what is already known to be right on other grounds.[245] The OT is not regarded here as a binding law. It does not have the weight which an appeal to the Law has in Judaism. Furthermore, this use of the Law does not, on the whole, play any significant role.[246] At any rate, even when the conduct of the community conforms to the Law's demands, the validity of this conduct is not established merely by appeal to the Law. It is authoritative, and must be respected, only if it follows from obedience to Christ in faith, according to the measure of faith granted to each individual, R. 14:1 ff.; 12:3. No longer whatsoever is not of the Law, but whatsoever is not of faith, is sin, R. 14:23.

f. The question of the origin of this understanding of the Law by Paul admits of no simple answer. There is not enough exegetical support for the thesis that Paul's own painful experience under the demands of the Law[247] or his sense of unworthiness before it led him to think of it in this way.[248] On the one hand this is not required by R. 7, and on the other it is as good as ruled out by Phil. 3:16: κατὰ δικαιοσύνην τὴν ἐν νόμῳ γενόμενος ἄμεμπτος.

In contrast, it is a plain fact that for Paul the decisive point in his attitude to the Law is faith in the divine revelation which took place in the cross of Christ. The narrower question thus arises how far a consistent application to the Law of this faith in the crucified Lord is really the source of Paul's view of the Law, or how far it is simply the criterion by which he accepts or rejects the solutions and answers to the problem of the Law which were already put forward by those before him and around him. This is not the place, however, to answer this question.

Certainly Paul from the very outset sees clearly the antithesis between the way of

---

[244] So esp. in Gl. 2:3 ff. in the conflict about the circumcision of Titus; cf. also the controversy with Peter in Gl. 2:11 ff.

[245] This is indicated by the καί in 1 C. 14:34 and 1 C. 9:8.

[246] Cf. the absence of νόμος in R. 12 ff. (except at 13:8 ff., though here the concrete Law is replaced by the commandment of love). Cf. also the absence in Th. and 2 C.

[247] So, e.g., Grafe, 13 ff. The εἰδότες in Gl. 2:16 does not reflect the rise of this knowledge from experience.

[248] The main basis of this view is the attributing of Luther's development to Paul. Cf. Ltzm. Gl., 7, and in criticism Lohmeyer, 5 ff.

Law and that of faith.[249] Indeed, even before his conversion he had already perceived that this was the decisive point of separation between Judaism and Christianity. A gradual development of his understanding of the Law, whether in the direction of sharpening[250] or softening[251] his negation of the Law, is most unlikely at least as regards the central points.[252]

III. The Period after the Conflict.

1. Hebrews.

Formally νόμος is used in Hb. as elsewhere in the NT. It is usually the OT Law. Only in 7:16 does the question arise whether it should not be rendered more generally as "norm" or "order."[253] But since this is the only instance in the epistle, it is better to take it here, too, in the sense of the OT Law. ἐντολῆς σαρκίνης would then be a gen. of content:[254] the Law consisting in the carnal commandment. The plur. occurs twice in Hb., but only in quotations (8:10; 10:16). Moreover, as in Pl. there is no basic distinction between ὁ νόμος and νόμος. Thus 7:12 does not refer to a generally valid rule but to the specific Law of the OT. In content νόμος may not always imply the whole of the OT Law, but in the first instance only the part which concerns the priestly ministry and the priesthood, cf. 9:22: σχεδὸν ἐν αἵματι πάντα καθαρίζεται κατὰ τὸν νόμον. But in no case is there any fundamental distinction. As compared with ἐντολή as the individual commandment, νόμος is mostly the OT Law as a whole, e.g., 7:5.

a. The fact that in content the orientation of νόμος is to the law which orders the priestly ministry is based on the main interest of the epistle. In Hb. the Law is viewed from a standpoint essentially different from that of, e.g., either Jesus or Paul. For them the Law is the will of God which requires and regulates human action. It aims at works and gives life to the man who does it. In Hb., however, the Law is seen from the standpoint that it gives the OT priesthood its basis, dignity and force. It has a share in the nature and efficacy of this priestly ministry, and similarly the nature and efficacy of the ministry depend on the fact that it rests on the Law.[255] This also means, of course, that the true theme of Hb. is not the relation of Law and Gospel, but the relation of the priestly ministry of the OT to the priestly ministry and priesthood of Jesus. The comparison is extended to the Law only in so far as the power of the priestly ministry of the OT is its basis in the Law.

How strongly the fact that it is anchored in the Law gives force to the OT priesthood[256] is shown not only by the common emphatic κατὰ τὸν νόμον or κατὰ νόμον (7:5; 8:4; 10:8),[257] but also by certain material arguments.

---

[249] Cf. Schl. Gesch. d. erst. Chr., 127. Certainly Gl. 5:11 is not to be understood as a ref. back to Christian works in which Paul required circumcision as necessary to salvation.

[250] So C. Clemen, *Die Chronologie d. paulinischen Briefe* (1893), esp. 256 ff.; though cf. ThLZ (1902), No. 8, 233.

[251] So Sieffert, *Theologische Studien ... B. Weiss ... dargebracht* (1897).

[252] Cf. Juncker, 171 ff.; Grafe, 27 ff.

[253] So F. Bleek, *Der Brief an d. Hb.,* II, 2 (1840), *ad loc.*

[254] Cf. Bl.-Debr.[6] § 167.

[255] νόμος is certainly used in the normal sense at 10:28: He who transgresses the Law must die; how much more so he who tramples the Son of God under foot! Cf. also 2:2. These passages make it plain, however, that there is no longer any obligation to the concrete Law. Materially cf. Brandt, 34 f.

[256] Cf. T. Haering, *Der Br. an d. Hb.* (1925), 62 ff.

[257] κατά moves on from the sense "according to," "after the manner of," by way of "in the strength of," almost to "through."

The majesty of Christ's priesthood rests precisely in the fact that He is a priest, not κατὰ νόμον ἐντολῆς σαρκίνης, but κατὰ δύναμιν ζωῆς ἀκαταλύτου (7:16). But this does not invalidate the fact that the sanctity of the Law is recognised in these statements.[258]

b. Though the OT priesthood finds its strength and authority in the Law, it cannot bring τελείωσις (7:11). Hence the same can be said even of the Law by which the priesthood lives: οὐδὲν γὰρ ἐτελείωσεν ὁ νόμος (7:19).

The aim of the priestly ministry is strictly to bring man near to God (7:19). It is τελείωσις and its presupposition, καθαρίζειν τὴν συνείδησιν ἀπὸ νεκρῶν ἔργων εἰς τὸ λατρεύειν θεῷ ζῶντι (9:14), in short, ἀφαιρεῖν ἁμαρτίας (10:4).[259] This goal is summed up in, e.g., 9:28 or 10:19 ff., for the decisive element in what is allotted to the believer by the High-priest Christ is the very thing which the Law, and the priesthood based upon it, could not attain, or could do so only inadequately.

The reason for this weakness and futility of the Law (ἀσθενὲς καὶ ἀνωφελές, 7:18), which do not allow it to attain its goal, is expounded in 7:18 ff., and this again is summed up in 7:28 in the antithesis: ὁ νόμος γὰρ ἀνθρώπους καθίστησιν ἀρχιερεῖς ἔχοντας ἀσθένειαν, ὁ λόγος δὲ τῆς ὁρκωμοσίας τῆς μετὰ τὸν νόμον υἱὸν εἰς τὸν αἰῶνα τετελειωμένον. The weakness of the Law, and therewith of the priesthood, lies essentially in the weakness of the men with whom the Law has to do.

This weakness may be seen in the mortal nature of the priests (7:24 ff.) and esp. in the fact that they must first bring offerings for themselves, i.e., in their own implication in sin (7:27; 5:3). Connected herewith is the further fact that the OT sacrifice purifies only externally, not internally; it sets aside neither the sense of guilt nor sin itself (9:9 f.). Seeing, then, that the Law and its priesthood have to do with sinful men, they cannot attain their goal; they cannot secure for men access to the Holy of Holies, to God.

To put it epigrammatically, the Law is weak for Paul because man does *not* do it, whereas it is weak for Hb. because *man* does it. The two propositions start from different points, but fundamentally they contain the same verdict. How closely they are related may be seen in Hb. in the use of Jer. 31:31 ff., where the weakness of the old covenant is exposed by Israel's transgression of it, and also in the fact that the priesthood of Jesus sanctifies better because it rests on a sacrifice of obedience which is well-pleasing to God, 10:5 ff.

c. At this point we find in Hb., too, the same distinctive turn of thought as in Paul. In the light of the fulfilment[260] the verdict is reached that the Law not only could not reach its goal but that it was not meant to do so, that its true purpose is to point to Christ by nailing man to his sin in order that he may find access

---

[258] In typical contrast to this is Barn., in which Christological allegorising of the OT is carried to the pt. of even arguing that the literal execution of the commandments of the OT, e.g., that of circumcision, is to be ascribed to the seduction of a wicked angel (9, 4), since the commandment from the very first was not meant to be fulfilled literally. Cf. also 10, 2: ἄρα οὖν οὐκ ἔστιν ἐντολὴ θεοῦ τὸ μὴ τρώγειν (i.e., the animals forbidden in the Law), Μωυσῆς δὲ ἐν πνεύματι ἐλάλησεν, cf. 10, 9. This is a further development of the Hell. Jewish dissolving of the OT Law after the manner of Ep. Ar. and Philo. There is nothing along these lines in Hb. in spite of many formal similarities.

[259] In fact, sacrifice is viewed in Hb. predominantly from the standpoint of expiation (5:1). Cf. Haering, 42 f.

[260] In Hb., too, the verdict on the inadequacy of the old divine ministry is not based on rational criticism, for all that statements like 9:12a sound very much like this, but on the fact of the high-priesthood of Jesus, 8:1 ff.; 10:5 ff.

to God by the only way proclaimed in Scripture, namely, through the high-priestly ministry of Jesus. In the sacrifice offered according to the Law there was in fact an ἀνάμνησις ἁμαρτιῶν κατ' ἐνιαυτόν (10:3), for the Law does not have the εἰκὼν τῶν πραγμάτων, but only the σκιὰ τῶν μελλόντων ἀγαθῶν (10:1).[261] Only with the new covenant whose Mediator is Christ did there take place the blotting out τῶν ἐπὶ τῇ πρώτῃ διαθήκῃ παραβάσεων and the receiving of the promise, 9:15. Thus the eternal high-priesthood of Christ, which was there already before the Law, which from the very first was above[262] the Law, which was intimated by the figure of Melchisedec and assigned with an oath to Christ in Ps. 110:4 (7:17, 21), means not only the μετάθεσις νόμου (7:12) but also the fulfilment, the εἰκὼν τῶν πραγμάτων instead of merely the provisional σκιὰ τῶν μελλόντων ἀγαθῶν (10:1).[263]

d. For all the differences, the affinity to the Pauline understanding of the Law is striking, especially in the way in which the old and the new covenants are interrelated, and the abrogation and fulfilment of the old by the new are integrated. This does not enable us to determine whether there are any direct Pauline influences. In comparison it should at least be noted that in Hb. there is no question, or, better, there is no longer any question of trying to find in the Law good acts which will justify man. This fact links the situation in Hb. regarding the question of the Law rather more strongly with Jn. and Jm. than with Paul.

2. James.

Decision as to the date and authorship of the letter and the interpretation of its understanding of the Law are mutually related.[264] Unfortunately the material is not sufficient to yield an assured interpretation. Nevertheless, two facts are obvious. First, the question of the relation between faith and works is posed and answered without any reference to the Law, 2:14 ff. The theme is specifically the relation of faith and works, not, as in Paul and his opponents, that of faith and the Law.

To a great extent the two questions overlap, but they are not wholly identical. It is true that 2:14 ff. attacks a misunderstood Paul,[265] yet not in the name of the Law nor even with reference to the Law, but in the name of the practical expression of faith in works, in acts of love, 2:16.

Secondly, where there is reference to νόμος, a qualifying phrase or word is often added: νόμος τέλειος τῆς ἐλευθερίας (1:25), νόμος ἐλευθερίας (2:12), νόμος βασιλικός (2:8). In each case (certainly in the first two) this is obviously intended to differentiate what is meant from what would be denoted by a simple νόμος. These two points together suggest a time when the primitive community was still discussing the question of the Law, but had already decided against legalism.[266] The real danger is no longer seen in the keeping or abolishing of the Law but in a false understanding of faith such as might arise out of Paul's answer to the question. This is quite independent of the question whether or not the

---

261 These good things are future ("to come") from the standpoint of the Law.

262 This is the point of the express proof that in Abraham Levi paid tithes to Melchisedec, 7:5 ff.

263 Cf. Brandt, 40.

264 Cf. Dib. Jk., 15.

265 It makes no difference whether the author himself misunderstands Paul in this way, or is simply combatting a misunderstanding based on Paul.

266 Cf. J. Marty, *L'Epître de Jacques* (1935), 248, 60; Dib. Jk. on 1:25 and 2:8.

author was a Jew. (The style almost forces us to conclude that he was.) [267]

The three passages in which there is reference to the Law must be interpreted in the light of this total situation. These are 1:25; 2:8 ff.; 4:11 ff.

a. In 1:25 the νόμος τέλειος τῆς ἐλευθερίας is essentially identical with, or at least closely related to, the λόγος ἔμφυτος δυνάμενος σῶσαι τὰς ψυχάς of v. 21 and the παρακύψαι εἰς νόμον is identical with the δοκεῖν θρησκὸν εἶναι and the θρησκεία of v. 26. Hence the Word of God which underlies the position of the Christian is here called νόμος, [268] and it is thus characterised in terms of that side of it which is orientated not merely to inactive acceptance but to the regulation of life, esp., as v. 27 shows, in acts of love. [269] The addition τέλειος τῆς ἐλευθερίας is thus designed to protect the term against the misunderstanding that the commandment of the OT Law is meant. In so far as the evangelical message claims a man's life for action, it can be called νόμος, [270] but in contrast to the old Law it is a perfect law of liberty. The more precise meaning of the terms, however, does not appear from the context. [271] But further light will be thrown by the two other passages.

b. In 2:8 ff. νόμος is obviously in the first instance not just another term for the word of truth but "commandment" in the strict sense. The only question is whether it is used for the whole of the OT Law with all its commandments, or for the summary of this Law in the law of love. [272] Taken alone, v. 10 might be taken to mean that here the whole of the OT Law with all its commandments is obligatory. But the general attitude of the epistle and the context of the verse are against this interpretation. 2:8 says that if you really fulfil the law of love you do well. The following verse adds that if nevertheless there is προσωπολημψία among you (as depicted in 2:1 ff.), this is sin, and it is sin against this law, for only — this is the point of v. 10 — when the law is kept in its entirety [273] does one escape its condemnation. The law of v. 9 f. is thus the law of love which in v. 8 is called the royal law, and βασιλικός describes the nature of this law as contrasted with any other understanding of law rather than denoting this specific law alongside others which are equated with it in principle. [274] If those addressed should appeal to the law of love on behalf of their conduct, this law includes the rich too, and hence the letter says: Very well, but it must be taken with full seriousness. προσωπολημψία, however, denies an essential part of the law of love, [275] and consequently such action is condemned by the commandment. [276] If the passage is taken in this way, a uniform picture is presented except, perhaps, for the use of νόμος in v. 11. But in v. 11 an example is given to strengthen v. 10; hence v. 11 does not belong to the real train of thought. It is just because νόμος is used in v. 11 in the

---

[267] The use of νόμος with or without art., with no difference of meaning, points in the same direction.

[268] As against A. Meyer, *Das Rätsel d. Jk.* (1930), 153 ff.

[269] Hence Windisch is not wholly right to speak of a "reduction" of the Torah to the "religious and moral commandments."

[270] The phrase "conception of Christianity itself as law" (Weizsäcker, 365) is at the very least misleading.

[271] Non-Christian pars. (cf. the comm., *ad loc.*) do not give such a clear picture that one can expound in the light of them alone. Hence other statements in the epistle are more normative for exegesis.

[272] Though two of the Ten Commandments are used in v. 11 to illustrate the principle of v. 10, one cannot assume at once that for James νόμος means the Decalogue.

[273] ἐν ἑνί does not have to mean "in one commandment of the OT" but has the more general sense "in one point or concrete instance."

[274] Both senses of βασιλικός are intrinsically possible in the light of usage outside the NT, cf. the comm., *ad loc.*

[275] Marty, *ad loc.*

[276] Excusing the wicked on the ground of good intentions, or by quoting the Law, is rejected here, as elsewhere in the NT, since man has to do, not with the commandments, but with God (v. 11).

different sense which is closer to common usage that there is the further addition τῆς ἐλευθερίας in v. 12. The νόμος ἐλευθερίας of v. 12 is thus identical with the νόμος βασιλικός of v. 8, i.e., with the law of love which is the Law in the true sense. By this speech and action must be judged.

Hence an inner connection can be made between the view of the Law expressed here and that of 1:25. In so far as the Word is orientated to man's acts it is the law of love, and for this very reason it is the perfect law, not just the sum of individual commandments.

c. What it means that this law is the law of freedom is perhaps made clear in 4:11 f. Comparison of this passage with R. 2:1 f. or Mt. 7:1 ff. breaks down precisely at the point which is peculiar to Jm., for here the condemnation of others does not involve condemnation of self, but of the Law and only then and therewith of self. Comparison with R. 14:4 is most likely.[277] In this case νόμος is the will of God valid only for the individual. Another cannot know this off-hand, for this will of God will not let itself be enclosed in specific, unequivocal forms and actions.[278] To judge another because his act deviates from what is right for me is to presume to judge concerning the command which is valid for him. But herein one is no longer a doer of the law.[279] Thus understood, the passage is an indication of the seriousness of the principle that from the Christian standpoint the law is a law of liberty which binds the individual, not to specific commandments, but to the obedience of love which is specifically laid on him. This freedom, then, is freedom through the obligation of obedience to God. Therefore, though it is freedom from the individual commandments of the Law, it is no more a hindrance to ethical guidance and direction than in Paul, and the epistle seeks to give these. But it nowhere forces the freedom of obedience into a schema after the manner of law.

Thus Jm. in its understanding of the Law is in full agreement with the Christian understanding in terms of the obedience of faith, though chronologically it comes after the actual debate as to the validity of the OT Law.

3. John's Gospel.

νόμος is rather more common in Jn. (14 times) than in Mt. (8); nevertheless, the actual question of the Law is far less central in this Gospel.

The meaning of the word is the usual one. νόμος is the Torah, esp. the Pent., e.g., 1:45: ἔγραψεν Μωυσῆς ἐν τῷ νόμῳ καὶ οἱ προφῆται. But it is also used more generally for the whole of the OT; 10:34: the γεγραμμένον ἐν τῷ νόμῳ ὑμῶν is a verse from the Ps., cf. 12:34; 15:25. Naturally νόμος can also be law in the narrower sense of a specific commandment, cf. in the discussion of Jesus' breaking of the Sabbath in 7:19, 23. As such νόμος is also a legal ordinance, e.g., 7:51: μὴ ὁ νόμος ἡμῶν κρίνει τὸν ἄνθρωπον ἐὰν μὴ ἀκούσῃ πρῶτον παρ' αὐτοῦ καὶ γνῷ τί ποιεῖ; or 18:31 on the lips of Pilate: κατὰ τὸν νόμον ὑμῶν κρίνατε αὐτόν, or on the lips of the Jews before Pilate in 19:7. Normally it is used with the art. The exception is 19:7a, where the indefinite form is required by the content.

The chief material point is that Jn. has no particular interest in the Law as a

---

[277] Weizsäcker, 368.

[278] Cf. also the self-designation of the author as θεοῦ καὶ κυρίου Ἰησοῦ Χριστοῦ δοῦλος, 1:1, Schl. Jk. on 1:25.

[279] Schl. Jk., *ad loc.* at least offers a similar exegesis for consideration. Another line of exposition assumes that καταλαλεῖν and κρίνειν νόμον is simply an expression for transgressing, so that νόμος is the law of love (cf. Wnd. Jk., *ad loc.*; also Hck. Jk., *ad loc.*). In view of v. 12 this is less probable, for the principle of the unity of law-giving and judgment in God surely implies that only He who gives the individual a law has the right to judge his action.

possibility for regulating human or even Christian action. Even in cases where it is expressly recounted that Jesus set aside the Law, e.g., c. 5 (with 7:19 ff.) and c. 9, the true theme which interests him is not the validity of the Law. These cases and questions simply provide the occasion and starting-point for the development of the true theme.

The Law interests Jn. in the first instance as revelation, and in this sense it is set in confrontation with Jesus.

a. Thus we read in 1:17: ὁ νόμος διὰ Μωυσέως ἐδόθη, ἡ χάρις καὶ ἡ ἀλήθεια διὰ Ἰησοῦ Χριστοῦ ἐγένετο. This must be construed in the light of v. 18. Only in Jesus is God truly revealed. Only here, in the incarnate Word, is there a real declaration of God, in the gift of grace and truth (v. 14, 17).[280] In keeping with this, a whole series of expressions with which Jesus designates Himself, or with which He is designated, is set over against similar statements about the Torah. Jesus is the Light (8:12; 9:5; 12:35) in contrast with the Torah as light.[281] Jesus gives the water of life (c. 4) in confrontation with the Torah, without which Israel can no more live than a fish without water.[282] Jesus is the bread of life (c. 6), or the way, the truth and the life (14:6); in both cases there are parallel statements about the Torah.[283] Finally, the description of Jesus as the incarnate Word stands over against statements about the pre-existence of this Logos and its mediatorial role in creation.

But even apart from the fact that these implicit confrontations are in no sense with the Torah alone,[284] it should also be noted that the parallels are not simply due to a mechanical, point by point transfer of features in teaching about the Torah to Christology. Both in Jn. and in Jewish theology the expressions are controlled by the central statements, namely, that the revelation of God is present in the Torah, and that it is present in Jesus. To the degree that in non-Rabbinic circles similar basic theses are advanced and lead to similar expressions, the statements about Jesus are a counter-thesis to these too. As concerns the Torah, it is contrasted, as a word of revelation, with the Son who is the perfect revelation.

b. This does not mean, however, that the relation between the two is simply that of an "either-or." Between the Law as the word of Scripture and the revelation of God in Jesus there is a positive inner connection.[285] In the Law, in Scripture,

---

[280] Hence this is not a criticism in the way stated by Bau. J. on 1:16: In face of the high estimation of Moses among Jews "Christian criticism shows that not even the whole of the Law goes back to Moses (7:22), much less that his acts should be rated as real acts of God (6:32). Hence all the confidence reposed on him is in vain." In fact, 7:22 is only conferring a higher dignity on circumcision because it goes back even to the patriarchs. Nor is the deduction drawn from 6:32 consonant with the text.

[281] Str.-B., I, 237d; K. H. Rengstorf, "Zu den Fresken in d. jüd. Katakombe der Villa Torlonia in Rom," ZNW, 31 (1932), 52 ff.

[282] Str.-B., II, 435 f.

[283] *Ibid.*, II, 482 ff.; on this whole question cf. K. Bornhäuser, *D. Joh. Ev. eine Missionsschrift für Israel* (1928), also → 135.

[284] Cf. Bau. Jn., *ad loc.*

[285] E. Hirsch, *Das vierte Ev. in seiner urspr. Gestalt verdeutscht u. erklärt* (1936), advances the thesis that the "basic and all-dominant concept of the Gospel is that between Christianity and Judaism, between liberating and life-giving faith in the Word and the enslaving service of Judaism, there is an irreconcilable conflict" (p. 78 f.). As regards this thesis it is debatable not merely whether this is the basic and all-dominating concept of the Gospel but also whether only an irreconcilable conflict is here disclosed. Cf. also R. Bultmann, "Hirschs Auslegung d. Joh. Ev.," *Evangelische Theol.* (1937), 115 ff., esp. 128 ff.

Jesus is attested and promised as the Christ. 1:45: ὃν ἔγραψεν Μωυσῆς ἐν τῷ νόμῳ καὶ οἱ προφῆται εὑρήκαμεν (sc. in Jesus). Cf. also 5:39 f. Though the word νόμος is not used here, it is materially apposite, as is shown by 7:19 ff., which fits the context of c. 5. The Scriptures bear witness to Jesus. Jn. often speaks of the Law in this sense. What the Law says or ordains is fulfilled in the life and work of Jesus, 8:17; 10:34; 12:34; 15:25.[286]

There is, of course, a strong emphasis here on the critical result of this relation. If a man rejects Jesus as the Christ, his appeal to the Law is shown to be revolt against Scripture, cf. esp. 5:39 ff. True belief in Moses and hence in the Law, true hearing of this revelation, will necessarily lead to acknowledgment of Jesus. Rejection of Jesus, then, is also rejection of the revelation of the Law. In this light the emphatic ὁ νόμος ὁ ὑμέτερος of 8:17 and ὁ νόμος ὑμῶν of 10:34 are to be taken in the sense that it is precisely the Law to which you appeal in opposition to me, it is precisely the statement of this Law, which refers to me; hence if you do not hear me you do not hear Scripture either.[287] The meaning is not: Your Law with which I have nothing to do.[288]

c. The very same relation between Jesus and the Law may be seen also in passages in which the Law is envisaged as the regulation of human action. In the first place there is again an antithesis. Jesus is bound only to the will of the Father, not to the commandment of the Law (5:19). Similarly, the disciples are bound to the commandment which is given in the Son, which for them takes the place of the Law, and which finds expression in the law of love: ἐντολὴν καινὴν δίδωμι ὑμῖν, ἵνα ἀγαπᾶτε ἀλλήλους ... ἀγάπην ἔχητε ἐν ἀλλήλοις (13:34 f.). V. 35 in particular shows how the relation of discipleship to Jesus takes the place of, e.g., obligation to the Torah, and this relation finds appropriate expression in the law of love. By it they are also released from the relationship of servants, 15:15. Only in Christ can they do a fruitful work, 15:5.

But again there stands beside this the close positive connection. Christ is imparted to him who really does the Law. Nathanael is called to Jesus as ἀληθῶς Ἰσραηλίτης, ἐν ᾧ δόλος οὐκ ἔστιν, 1:47 ff. 7:17 might also be cited here: ἐάν τις θέλῃ τὸ θέλημα αὐτοῦ (sc. of God) ποιεῖν, γνώσεται περὶ τῆς διδαχῆς, πότερον ἐκ τοῦ θεοῦ ἐστιν ἢ ἐγὼ ἀπ' ἐμαυτοῦ λαλῶ.

This again has the negative implication that with the rejection of Jesus there is also rejection of the will of the Law. In 7:19 the purpose to kill Jesus discloses the οὐ ποιεῖν τὸν νόμον. Hatred of Jesus evades the commandment of the Law, 7:50 f. If the Jews seek to serve God by persecuting Jesus, this is because they know neither the Father nor Jesus, 16:3.[289]

In so far as Jesus as the Son and Christ replaces in every respect all other mediators, including the Torah, the Torah is both destroyed and fulfilled. This may be seen from the fact that true hearing of the Law leads to faith in Jesus, and rejection of Jesus is at the same time revolt against the Law.

In John, however, the Law is never used as the rule of Christian conduct for the community. The Epistles confirm this, and so, too, does Rev. It is no accident that νόμος does not occur at all in these writings. Nowhere in John is there any attempt to prove that when the law of love is kept the true intention of the Law is fulfilled.

---

[286] Hence we do not have merely a kind of adding of the OT and the Word of Jesus, as Bornhäuser, 77 understands Jn. 2:22.

[287] Cf. Zn. J. on 8:17 and 10:34. Zahn rightly compares the ὑμῖν in Mt. 22:31. Mt. 15:25 is more difficult, though cf. 16:2.

[288] So 18:31 on the lips of Pilate.

[289] Cf. also 3:10: If Nicodemus were a true teacher in Israel, the saying of Jesus would not be so incomprehensible to him.

All this puts the Gospel[290] in the generation and period after the real battle as to the validity of the Law. In this respect, then, it places it in the same class as Jm. and Hb.

† ἀνομία.

The privative prefix and the content of the word νόμος give two shades of meaning to ἀνομία. The ref. is either a. to a fact, "there is or was no law," "without a (the) law," or b. the word means "against the (a) law," with an implied judgment, since it is assumed that there is in fact a binding law. This gives ἀνομία the sense of "wrongdoing," "sin." In fact, of course, the two meanings cannot be sharply differentiated from one another in the majority of cases. The difference is merely one of emphasis.

For a. cf. P. Oxy., 1121, 20: ἅπαντα ὡς ἐν ἀνομία[ι]ς ἀπεσύλησαν.[1] Philo Leg. All., III, 79: Melchisedec is a righteous king, not a tyrant ὅτι ὁ μὲν νόμων, ὁ δὲ ἀνομίας ἐστὶν εἰσηγητής. For b. cf. Philo Conf. Ling., 108, which speaks of ὀχλοκρατία ..., ἐν ᾗ ἀδικία καὶ ἀνομία καταδυναστεύουσιν. In Ebr., 143 ἀνομία and ἀπαιδευσία are associated. This occurs already in class. Gk., e.g., Demosth., 24, 152: If a decision by plebiscite dissolves the constitution of the city νόμῳ καινῷ, this should be called ἀνομία rather than νόμος. Thus even though the alteration is legally defensible, it may have to be called ἀνομία.

In this sense ἀνομία can denote a general state of lawlessness or wickedness, Philo Spec. Leg., 1, 188: εὐνομίᾳ καινῇ παλαιὰν ἀνομίαν ἐκνιψάμενοι. Yet ἀνομία, esp. in the plur., can be used just as well for the specific act, Ps. Sol. 15:10: αἱ ἀνομίαι αὐτῶν (sinners) διώξονται αὐτοὺς ἕως ᾅδου κάτω, P. Flor., 382, 49: ἡ ἀνυπέρβλητος αὐτοῦ τόλμα ... καὶ ἀνομία.

ἀνομία is common in the LXX, though there is no fixed Heb. equivalent. It corresponds most frequently to עון (some 60 times), און (some 25 times, esp. in Ps.), פשע (some 20 times), תועבה (some 25 times, esp. in Ez.).[2] In the LXX it has all the meanings mentioned above. It is common in the plur. for individual acts, Gn. 19:15: ἵνα μὴ συναπόλῃ ταῖς ἀνομίαις τῆς πόλεως. The state of ἀνομία is at issue in, e.g., ψ 31:5: τὴν ἀνομίαν μου οὐκ ἐκάλυψα, ψ 17:24 etc. In general there is no direct connection with the Law, at any rate not to any fundamentally greater degree than is true of the OT concept of sin generally, which is, of course, orientated to the commandment of God. It is characteristic, of course, that ἀνομία should become one of the chief terms for sin. Increasing unification and colourlessness here go hand in hand.

In the NT ἀνομία has the same range of use as elsewhere. In the plur. (found only in quotations) it is the "sinful act," though the connection with the Law, measured by which the act in question is shown to be sin, is not directly in view, R. 4:7; Hb. 10:17 (Hb. 8:12 vl.). In Tt. 2:14 (a quotation) ἀπὸ πάσης ἀνομίας is to be construed less along the lines of a general condition in view of the antithesis to ζηλωτὴς καλῶν ἔργων.

In R. 6:19 ἀνομία for the individual act is found along with ἀνομία for the general condition which is the result of such acts, namely, that of alienation from the Law, though this is understood as a judgment rather than a statement. Service of ἀνομία leads to a general state of ἀνομία. Similarly (in antithesis) in Hb. 1:9 (a quotation): ἠγάπησας δικαιοσύνην καὶ ἐμίσησας ἀνομίαν, and cf. 2 C. 6:14: δικαιοσύνη and ἀνομία are as mutually exclusive as faith and unbelief or Christ and Belial. Since Paul is here addressing a Christian community which is not

---

290 Though not necessarily the author too.

ἀνομία. On this and the following arts. cf. esp. the dict.

1 Preisigke Wört. translates: "As though there were no legal protection."

2 It also corresponds to about 20 other Heb. terms, but in most cases only once each.

under the norm of the OT Law, it is apparent that ἀνομία does not here derive its main force from the OT Law, but simply means sin or unrighteousness. The same is true of the ἄνθρωπος τῆς ἀνομίας of 2 Th. 2:3. The depiction in v. 4 shows how ἀνομία works itself out. Naturally such conduct is also contrary to the commandment of the OT, but the judgment pronounced here is at once both more direct and more general, and ἀνομία has in fact no meaning other than that of ἁμαρτία, which is found in many texts. The same is true of the μυστήριον τῆς ἀνομίας of v. 7. The ἀποστασία of v. 3 is central for the description given in the following verses.

ἀνομία may have a stronger connection with the Law and its transgression in Mt; this at least appears to be true in 23:28, where the words ἔσωθεν δέ ἐστε μεστοὶ ὑποκρίσεως καὶ ἀνομίας are addressed specifically to the pious who strictly observe the Law. The connection is less close, however, in 7:23; 13:41 (both quotations), and 24:12.

1 Jn. 3:4: πᾶς ὁ ποιῶν τὴν ἁμαρτίαν καὶ τὴν ἀνομίαν ποιεῖ, καὶ ἡ ἁμαρτία ἐστὶν ἡ ἀνομία, is not wholly clear. The most natural interpretation seems to be: If a man commits ἁμαρτία, his action also stands under the judgment of ἀνομία. In this case ἁμαρτία is more or less fixed and limited in content (hence the art. τήν); the saying is directed against those who argue more or less as follows: Even if ἁμαρτία is present, it is no great evil; it cannot be held against the man of true knowledge, the spiritual man. If ἀνομία thus carries with it for the readers and author a stigma which apparently ἁμαρτία does not of itself imply for all of them, in 1 Jn. this can hardly be based on an inherent relation to the OT Law.[3] The inner force of ἀνομία is probably supplied by a more general sense such as rebellion or revolt against God, or alienation from Him, as suggested by v. 6b, 9 f. Freely translated v. 4 would then be to the effect that "he who commits sin is thereby in revolt against God; indeed, sin is nothing but rebellion against God."

Nevertheless, it may be asked whether one might not assume a Christian understanding of νόμος which regards the commandment to love God and one's neighbour as the Law of Christ and therefore as the Law in the true sense. This view finds support in the ref. to the work of Jesus in v. 5, and esp. in v. 11.[4]

† ἄνομος.

To ἄνομος, "having no law," there applies in essentials all that we have said about ἀνομία, which derives from it. The emphasis may be a. on the objective fact that a or the law is not present (this is understandably rare, since in general there are laws everywhere, though cf. Plat. Polit., 302e), or b. (the regular use) on the subjective attitude, "not paying heed to the law (which exists)," "acting as if there were no law or laws." Since this attitude is usually wrong in the eyes of others a judgment is thus declared. In this case ἄνομος can easily take on the more general sense of "unrighteous," with no strict ref. to a specific law.

---

[3] If the passage is to be construed as a plain repudiation of antinomianism (Wnd. Kath. Br., *ad loc.*), the sentence has to be deliberately reversed and understood as "ἀνομία is ἁμαρτία." This is ruled out, however, by the first part of the verse.

[4] It is hardly possible to carry through a differentiation between ἁμαρτία and ἀνομία along the lines that ἀνομία, as sin against the Law, is at the same time sin against one's neighbour, while ἁμαρτία is sin against God (or even *vice versa* with a corresponding change of sense), so that the verse is directed against a separation of the two when it states that transgression of the commandment which refers me to my neighbour is also sin against God (cf. H. H. Wendt, *Die Johannesbriefe und das johanneische Christentum* [1925], 60 f.).

In Judaism ὁ ἄνομος or οἱ ἄνομοι is a common term for the Gentiles. Here it is hard to distinguish between a mere affirmation that they do not have the Law and a judgment that they are sinners. In general the latter view seems to predominate. Ps. Sol. 17:18: εἰς πᾶσαν τὴν γῆν ἐγενήθη ὁ σκορπισμὸς αὐτῶν ὑπὸ ἀνόμων. Of Pompey it is said in Ps. Sol. 17:11: ἠρήμωσεν ὁ ἄνομος τὴν γῆν ἡμῶν. Here ἄνομος certainly has the more general sense of "wrongdoer." In the LXX ἄνομος is used some 30 times for רשׁע, but elsewhere it occurs for about 25 other Heb. terms, in most cases only once each. There can hardly be a direct Heb. equivalent any more than in the case of ἀνομία, since Heb. has no privative prefix.

In the NT we occasionally find the purely affirmative use of ἄνομος. When the ἀνόμως ἁμαρτάνειν of R. 2:12 is accompanied by an ἐν νόμῳ ἁμαρτάνειν, the first phrase simply means that the sin was committed without knowledge of the Law. The ἄνομοι to whom Paul adjusts himself in 1 C. 9:21 are distinguished as such from those who are ὑπὸ νόμον by the fact that they do not actually know the Law and are not aware that they are bound by it. οἱ ἄνομοι is also used in a weaker sense in Lk. 22:37 (a quotation, also as vl. in Mk. 15:28) and Ac. 2:23 (here for the Gentiles).

Even 1 C. 9:21, however, shows how strongly ἄνομος implies a judgment, for Paul immediately protects himself against an obvious misunderstanding by saying that though he is ὡς ἄνομος to these ἄνομοι, he is not for this reason ἄνομος θεοῦ (→ ἔννομος).

If ἄνομος is meant to imply a judgment, the ref. in the NT, too, it not always specifically to the Law, but may be more general. This is plain in 1 Tm. 1:9: δικαίῳ νόμος οὐ κεῖται, ἀνόμοις δὲ καὶ ἀνυποτάκτοις. Ἄνομοι are simply those who do evil. That this is judged by the Law is implied, not in this particular expression, but in the whole sentence.[1] The sense is also general in 2 Pt. 2:8: The men of Sodom vex Lot ἀνόμοις ἔργοις, by their wicked deeds. In 2 Th. 2:8, too, ἄνομος should be rendered, not "transgressor of the Law," but simply "evildoer" (→ ἀνομία, 1085).

† ἔννομος.

ἔννομος is the opp. of ἄνομος, but is not so common. In the first instance it simply means "according to law," "he who (or that which) remains within the law," P. Oxy., 1204, 24: ἵνα ἐννομώτερον ἀκουσθείη, of a hearing which should be conducted acc. to law. Aeschin. Tim., 3, 230 speaks of a ψήφισμα ἔννομον in contrast to a ψήφισμα παράνομον. Cf. *ibid.*, 1, 5; Philo Abr., 242; Poster. C., 176. When used of persons ἔννομος means "righteous," "upright." Plat. Resp., IV, 424e: ἐννόμους τε καὶ σπουδαίους ... ἄνδρας.

In Judaism ἔννομος mostly refers to the OT Law. Sir. Prol., 14: The grandfather wrote his work in order that πολλῷ μᾶλλον ἐπιπροσθῶσιν (the readers) διὰ τῆς ἐννόμου βιώσεως, the grandson translates the work for people προκατασκευαζομένους τὰ ἤθη ἐννόμως βιοτεύειν (35 f.). More generally at Prv. 31:25: στόμα αὐτῆς (the virtuous woman) διήνοιξεν προσεχόντως καὶ ἐννόμως.

In the NT ἔννομος is used at Ac. 19:39: The ἔννομος ἐκκλησία is the lawfully summoned assembly, against which no legal objection can be lodged, in contrast to the riotous gathering of the people depicted just before. In 1 C. 9:21 Paul says of himself that even though he sets aside the Law in his dealings with Gentiles he is not ἄνομος θεοῦ, but ἔννομος Χριστοῦ. The latter underlies the former.

ἄνομος. [1] Debrunner, however, thinks the statement is sharper if, as the ἀνυπότακτοι are those who will not subordinate themselves, so the ἄνομοι are those who have no concern for laws (the law) [Debrunner in a communication during proof-reading].

Because he is ἔννομος Χριστοῦ he is not ἄνομος θεοῦ. Both genitives refer to the νόμος implicit in ἄνομος and ἔννομος.[1]

† νομικός.

In class. Gk. νομικός is found only as an adj., Plat. Leg., I, 625a: ἐν τοιούτοις ἤθεσι τέθραφθε νομικοῖς. The meaning is "according to, corresponding to, law."[1] Later νομικός is extensively used as a tt. for a lawyer, esp. a notary. Epict. Diss., II, 13, 6: If one is not acquainted with the laws of a city, one consults a νομικός. In the pap. νομικός is often used as a title after a name. P. Oxy., 237, VIII, 2 ff.: ἀντίγραφον προσφων[ήσεως νομι]κοῦ ... Οὔλπιος ... νομικὸς Σαλουστίῳ ...[2] But it is also used as an adj. (and as an adv., e.g., Ep. Ar., 142). In Judaism the designation νομικός acquires a ref. to the OT Law. 4 Macc. 5:4: Ἐλεάζαρος, τὸ γένος ἱερεύς, τὴν ἐπιστήμην νομικός.

In the NT νομικός is once used as an adj. at Tt. 3:9: καὶ μάχας νομικὰς περιΐστασο, "contentions," "strivings" about the Law (or the OT as a whole). The expression leaves it an open question whether the issue is the validity of the Law as a norm of life for Christians or theories which are to be proved from Scripture. Since Tt. 1:10 speaks of those "of the circumcision," the former view calls for consideration, but the total picture of the errors combatted in the Past. favours the latter.

In Mt. and Lk. νομικός is often used for the leaders of the Jewish people, though they are given this name only in contexts which deal with the administration or understanding of the Law. In Mt. 22:35 (par. Lk. 10:25) it is a νομικός who puts the question as to the most important commandment. Mk.'s γραμματεύς (12:28) means the same, but in the context νομικός is more typical.[3]

In Lk. 7:30, too, νομικός is intentionally chosen, esp. if βουλὴ τοῦ θεοῦ refers to John the Baptist, not the Law. Those who particularly seek to concern themselves about the Law are not concerned about the will of God as it is now declared. In Lk. 11:45 f., 52 νομικός obviously underscores what a burden is imposed, and how the locking up is done. The understanding of the Law is also at issue in Lk. 14:3.

It is hard to decide for certain the meaning of νομικός in Tt. 3:13. But since Zenas is not among the opponents, and the addition of νομικός is common elsewhere as a title after a name, the more likely interpretation is "lawyer" or "notary."[4]

† νόμιμος.

νόμιμος usually has the sense of "according to rule or order or right."[1] P. Oxy., 1201, 18: οἱ νόμιμοι κληρονόμοι, Chr., II, 372, 13 (Preisigke Wört., *s.v.*): γάμος νόμιμος, "valid marriage"; Epict. Diss., III, 10, 8: ὁ θεός σοι λέγει "δός μοι ἀπόδειξιν, εἰ νομίμως ἤθλησας." As a noun τὸ νόμιμον is "what is right and fair"; P. Iandanae (1912/14), 16, 8 (Preisigke Wört., *s.v.*); BGU, IV, 1074, 2: νόμιμα καὶ φιλάνθρωπα = rights and favours;[2] Philo Decal., 37; Abr., 276.

In the LXX νόμιμος is used only once as an adj. (2 Macc. 4:11) in the sense of

---

ἔννομος. [1] Cf. Schl. K., *ad loc.*

νομικός. Preisigke Wört., III, 135; Moult.-Mill., *s.v.*

[1] Cf. Kühner-Blass-Gerth, I, 2, § 334, 5.

[2] For further instances cf. Preisigke Wört., III, 135.

[3] Since Mk. wrote for Romans, νομικός is open to misunderstanding in view of the technical aspect of the term mentioned above. Hence it is not used at all in Mk.

[4] Cf. Dib. Past., *ad loc.*

νόμιμος. C. Arbenz, *Die Adj. auf* -ιμος (Diss. Zürich, 1933), 72 ff.

[1] The word was formed at a time when νόμος did not yet mean "law" [Debrunner].

[2] Cf. the transl. in Preisigke Wört., *s.v.*

"according to law." Elsewhere τὸ νόμιμον or τὰ νόμιμα is the rendering of חק, חקה, תורה. This usage presupposes that there are specific regulations or commandments only in relation to the Law. Hence τὸ νόμιμον means "commandment of the Law."

In the NT νόμιμος is found only as an adverb, 1 Tm. 1:8; 2 Tm. 2:5. In the latter case it obviously does not mean according to the OT Law. Within the context of the image from the games it means either "according to the rules of the contest,"[3] "appropriately," or more generally "well," "skilfully."

In 1 Tm. 1:8, too, νομίμως does not mean "in correspondence with the OT Law,"[4] but simply "as is appropriate,"[5] though in the context the two mean exactly the same. At any rate the proper use of the Law is different from that made of it by those who seek to be teachers of the Law.

† νομοθέτης.

νομοθέτης means "lawgiver." Aristot. Pol., II, 12, p. 1274a, 31 f.: ἐγένετο δὲ καὶ Φιλόλαος ὁ Κορίνθιος νομοθέτης Θηβαίοις (cf. *ibid.*, II, 6, p. 1265a, 18 ff.). Diod. S., 12, 11, 3: εἵλοντο δὲ καὶ νομοθέτην τὸν ἄριστον τῶν ἐν παιδείᾳ θαυμαζομένων πολιτῶν ... Philo Spec. Leg., IV, 120: οἱ πολλοὶ τῶν παρ' Ἕλλησι καὶ βαρβάροις νομοθετῶν. In Judaism Moses is in a special sense νομοθέτης (Ep. Ar., 131, 148, 312). So is God (Philo Sacr. AC, 131: God is νομοθέτης καὶ πηγὴ νόμων αὐτός). The only LXX passage with νομοθέτης (Ps. 9:20) rests on the ketib (מורה) instead of the qere of the Mas. (מורא).

The only NT occurrence is at Jm. 4:12. The meaning of the title νομοθέτης for God in this passage must be controlled by the exposition of the preceding sentence and not *vice versa*[1] (→ 1082).

† νομοθεσία.

νομοθεσία (from → νομοθέτης) usually connotes, not the act of legislation, but the result of this act, i.e., the law, constitution or order as the case might be; in the Jewish world it is thus used, like νόμος, for the Pentateuch. Diod. S., 12, 11, 4: ἐπισκεψάμενος τὰς ἁπάντων νομοθεσίας ἐξελέξατο τὰ κράτιστα, P. Oxy., 1119, 18: εἴς τε τὰς θείας νομοθεσίας (imperial regulations). The only instance in the LXX is at 2 Macc. 6:23: Eleazar is fixed in his steadfastness by the ἁγία καὶ θεόκτιστος νομοθεσία. In Ep. Ar., 15 the νομοθεσία of the Jews is to be translated. In Philo even the unwritten law can be called ἄγραφος νομοθεσία, Abr., 5, though elsewhere he often uses the term for the Pent., Cher., 87: πολλαχοῦ τῆς νομοθεσίας, "in many passages of the Pentateuch."

Occasionally, of course, the sense of legislation is nearer the mark, e.g., Philo Vit. Mos., II, 2: One of the δυνάμεις of Moses πραγματεύεται περὶ νομοθεσίαν. Ditt. Or., 326, 26: καθὼς αὐτὸς ἐν τῆι νομοθεσίαι περὶ ἑκάστων δια[τέ]ταχεν. Here the act of legislation may at any rate be in view, cf. also Plat. Leg., III, 684e.

The only instance in the NT is at R. 9:4. Here the most natural sense is "Law," not the more specific giving of the Law. What is listed as one of the privileges of Israel is not the giving of the Law but its possession, cf. R. 3:1 f.

---

[3] Cf. Wbg. Past., *ad loc.*
[4] Cf. Wbg. Past., *ad loc.*
[5] Cf. Wbg. and Dib. Past., *ad loc.*

νομοθέτης. [1] Also relevant is Barn., 21, 4: ἑαυτῶν γίνεσθε νομοθέται ἀγαθοί. V. 5 shows that this is not meant in the sense of radical autonomy, but the usage shows how wide a range the term can have.

† νομοθετέω.

νομοθετεῖν (from νομοθέτης) means a. "to be active as a legislator," "to give laws," e.g., Plat. Polit., 294c : διὰ τί ἀναγκαῖον νομοθετεῖν, Ep. Ar., 240 : τὰς ἐπινοίας ὁ θεὸς δέδωκε τοῖς νομοθετήσασιν. The recipient of the law is in the dat. or the acc. Philo Poster. C., 143 : θεοῦ νομοθετοῦντος ἐκκλησίαν. But it also means b. "to order a matter by law," "to settle legally," Ep. Ar., 144 : ἐνομοθέτει ταῦτα Μωυσῆς. Both senses can occur in the pass. This is more common of "things which are settled by law," e.g., Philo Vit. Mos., II, 218 : ὅσα περὶ τοῦ σεβασμοῦ τῆς ἑβδόμης νενομοθέτηται. P. Oxy., 1119, 24 : πράσσειν παρὰ τὰ νενομοθετημένα.

In contrast there is no distinctive LXX use. It should merely be noted that the word does not always have to carry with it a strict ref. to the Mosaic Law. Cf. ψ 26:11: νομοθέτησόν με, κύριε, τῇ ὁδῷ σου, where νομοθετεῖν almost has the sense "to instruct" (Heb. ירה hi).

The two NT passages reflect the two main senses. In Hb. 7:11 νομοθετεῖν is used in the pass. of those to whom the Law is given. The precise connotation (whether one should translate "the Law" or "law") is decided, not by the word νομοθετεῖν, but by the context and the interpretation of ἐπ' αὐτῆς. ἐπί with the gen. to denote the object in respect of which law is given does not occur elsewhere with νομοθετεῖν (though cf. περί in 3 Macc. 3:15; Philo Vit. Mos., II, 218). In view of the further fact that the meaning of the parenthetical statement would otherwise be rather weak, the reference is surely to the whole Law, not to the specific law by which the cultus is regulated. In Hb. 8:6 the relative clause may refer either to λειτουργία or to διαθήκη. It makes no material difference, but the expression seems to fit λειτουργία better. In any case the new thing in question is established and settled. Here, then, the νόμος implicit in νομοθετεῖν is to be taken in a more general sense, with no specific reference to the OT.

† παρανομία.

a. παρανομία means in class. and later Gk. a total condition (expressed, of course, in individual acts). Ps. Sol. 17:20 : ὁ βασιλεὺς ἐν παρανομίᾳ καὶ ὁ κριτὴς ἐν ἀπειθείᾳ καὶ ὁ λαὸς ἐν ἁμαρτίᾳ. The word is not common in the LXX (9 times) and there is no fixed Heb. equivalent. παράνομος is more common. As in the case of ἀνομία the many distinctions of the original are generalised. In παρανομία, too, the ref. to a legal norm underlying the word is in many cases not clearly maintained. In the verse quoted from Ps. Sol. παρανομία no more refers to law than does ἀπείθεια or ἁμαρτία, though in Judaism the Law is, of course, the norm and standard of all such judgments. παρανομία can also mean b. an "individual wrong act," e.g., Philo Vit. Mos., I, 295 : Balaam advises Balak ... εἰδὼς Ἑβραίοις μίαν ὁδὸν ἁλώσεως παρανομίαν, P. Oxy., 1119, 18 : παρανομία against imperial orders must be punished.

The only use of παρανομία in the NT is at 2 Pt. 2:16 : Balaam ἔλεγξιν ἔσχεν ἰδίας παρανομίας. V. 16 is either concessive : "although ... had restrained him," in which case ἔλεγξις has the sense of punishment and the παρανομία is the promise to curse Israel for reward, or it is a development of the content of ἔλεγξιν ἔσχεν, in which case ἔλεγξις is a warning conviction prior to the act, and the παρανομία is the purpose to curse Israel. The distinction makes no difference as far as παρανομία is concerned. But the question strongly affects the meaning of the whole passage. Either the false teachers refuse to accept any warning or, if they will not pay heed to the warning, they will be punished as Balaam was when he ignored the warning. In any case παρανομία is a wrong act with no direct reference to the Law.

† παρανομέω.

παρανομέω means "to transgress a law or established ordinance." Ditt. Syll.[3], 218, 21 f.: οἱ παρανομοῦντες are people who infringe a specific regulation. Plat. Resp., I, 338e : Let what is useful to the ruling class be everywhere the law whose transgressors will be punished ὡς παρανομοῦντά τε καὶ ἀδικοῦντα. But παρανομεῖν also has the more general sense "to offend," Ps. Sol. 16:8 : μὴ ἀπατησάτω με κάλλος γυναικὸς παρανομούσης. In the LXX it occurs only 5 times, with different Heb. originals in each case. In Ps. 74:4 it is par. to ἁμαρτάνειν. In the pass. it can also be construed personally : ἀδίκως μετὰ βίας παρανομηθείς. [1]

The only NT occurrence is at Ac. 23:3 : σὺ κάθῃ κρίνων με κατὰ τὸν νόμον, καὶ παρανομῶν κελεύεις με τύπτεσθαι; Here the antithesis κατὰ τὸν νόμον shows that παρανομεῖν has the specific sense of "transgression of the Law" and is not just a general term for wrongdoing.

Gutbrod

† νόσος, † νοσέω, † νόσημα (μαλακία, μάστιξ, κακῶς ἔχω)

→ ἀσθενής κτλ., ἰάομαι.

Contents : A. Sickness and Sin : 1. Primitive Oriental and Greek Thinking ; 2. The Equation of Defect and Sickness in Greek Philosophy ; 3. Sickness and Sin in the Old Testament ; 4. In Judaism ; 5. In the New Testament. B. Sin as Vicarious Suffering. 1. The Suffering Hero in the Greek World. 2. The Suffering Servant of God in the Old Testament and Judaism. 3. The Suffering Man of God in the New Testament. C. The Church and Sickness : 1. Visiting and Caring for the Sick in the Primitive Church ; 2. The Influence of Isaiah 53 on the Concept of Christ.

νόσος. The etym. is uncertain. From the time of Hom. the most common meaning is "sickness," with a subsidiary (earlier ?) sense of "plague," "calamity" (e.g., whirlwind in Soph. Ant., 421; the suffering of Prometheus, Hes. Theog., 527; patricide, Soph. Oed. Col., 544; riches, Qoh. 5:12, 15 Σ, LXX : πονηρὰ ἀρρωστία, Heb. רָעָה חוֹלָה). Also inscr., pap., LXX [1] (Ex. 15:26; Dt. 7:15; Job 24:23 with distinctive theology etc.), Philo (Migr. Abr., 217: νόσος σώματος no hindrance to merchantmen). Other special senses are "epidemic" (Plat. Theaet., 169b), "licentiousness" (Sus. 57, Θ : ἀνομία, cf. Eur. Hipp., 765 f.: Ἀφροδίτας νόσος, Herm. s., 6, 5, 5 : ὁ μοιχὸς καὶ ὁ μέθυσος ... τῇ ἰδίᾳ νόσῳ [synon. πάθος] τὸ ἱκανὸν ποιεῖ), of persons, "plague" (Plat. Prot., 322d : τὸν μὴ δυνάμενον αἰδοῦς ... μετέχειν κτείνειν ὡς νόσον πόλεως), of society (wealth and poverty bring infirmity to the state, Plat. Leg., XI, 919c); νόσος καρπῶν (Ps.-Xenoph. Resp. Ath., 2, 6, cf. Dt. 29:21: νόσοι τῆς γῆς, Hebr. תַּחֲלֻאִים). In the NT exclusively in the Synoptic Gospels and Ac., always lit.: Mt. 4:23 f.; 8:17; 9:35; 10:1; Mk. 1:34; Lk. 4:40; 6:18; 7:21; 9:1; Ac. 19:12 synon. μαλακία, μάστιξ.

παρανομέω. [1] P. Greci e Latini (= P. Soc.), 330, 8, *v.* Preisigke Wört., *s.v.*

νόσος κτλ. RGG[2], III, 1274 ff.; Roscher, III, 457 ff., *s.v.* "Nosos"; J. Köberle, *Sünde u. Gnade im religiösen Leben d. Volkes Israel bis auf Christum* (1905), esp. 9 ff.; H. Zimmern, "Babylonische Hymnen u. Gebete in Auswahl," AO, 7, 3 (1905); A. van Selms, *De babylonische Termini voor Zonde* (Diss. Utrecht, 1933 [I owe this to A. Alt]); S. Mowinckel, *Psalmenstudien,* I : "Awän u. d. individuellen Klagepsalmen," *Skrifter utgit av Videnskapsselskapet i Kristiania* (1921), *Hist.-Filos. Kl.,* I (1922); K. F. Euler, *Die Verkündigung vom leidenden Gottesknecht aus Js. 53 in d. griech. Bibel* (1934); J. Preuss, *Biblisch-talmudische Medizin* (1911); F. Fenner, *Die Krankheit im NT* (1930); G. Uhlhorn, *Die christliche Liebesthätigkeit in d. alten Kirche* (1882). — III, 194 Bibl.

[1] νόσος corresponds to derivates of √חלה: חֳלִי, מַחֲלָה, מַחֲלֶה, תַּחֲלוּא, or √דוה: מַדְוֶה (not מַכָּה in Dt. 28:59, in spite of Hatch-Redp.) [Bertram].

νοσέω (from the time of Aesch.) "to be sick," in body or soul (νοσεῖν τὰς φρένας, Crat. Fr., 329, CAF, I, 110), fig. νοσεῖν περὶ δόξαν "to be full of (unhealthy) ambition," Plut. Laud. s. Inv., 20 (II, 546 f.), ἀπαιδίᾳ (Eur. Ion, 620), πονηρίᾳ (Xenoph. Mem., III, 5, 18). Also of national calamities, → 1091. The fig. use is more developed than in the case of the noun. The word is used in the OT both lit., Gn. 48:1 Σ; 1 Βασ. 30:13 Σ, and fig., Wis. 17:8. In the NT it is only fig., 1 Tm. 6:4 (of the false teacher).

νόσημα is used both lit. and fig. (Plat. Gorg., 480b: τὸ νόσημα τῆς ἀδικίας). It is synon. with νόσος, and like this very common in Philo. It does not occur in the LXX and in the NT only lit. at Jn. 5:4.[2]

A. Sickness and Sin.

1. Primitive Oriental and Greek Thinking.

Sickness and impurity are closely connected under the master concept miasma. Analogically both are thought of as substances, and the one always causes the other. Contact with miasma should be avoided or purged as quickly as possible (→ 296). Relics of this view are still to be found quite often even in higher religions. The boundary with more personal ideas is fluid. Now it is a taboo which reacts against violation, now demons which convey the material of sickness or are stirred up by it (→ III, 195), now personal gods who by means of sickness avenge offences, mostly ritual or cultic in character. If sin and sickness here begin to part company as guilt and punishment, the concepts are still so closely connected that they are often used interchangeably.

This is plain, e.g., in Babylonian texts. Many things are obscure in detail,[3] but it may be stated that many Babylonian words for sin also have the sense of "disease" or "infirmity" (*asakku*)[4] or are mentioned in the same breath as sickness and trouble (*ikkibu* = *mysterium*, taboo, ban).[5] The noun *killatu*, which derives from *kullulu* (to demean oneself before the cultus), corresponds in bilingual texts to the Sumerian PA-GA, to be read *sigga* = *miḫsu*, "stroke," "sickness," and more than the other words is linked with *mešû*, "to forgive."[6] In this light one may understand why there is such frequent complaint at sickness in the Babylonian penitential psalms,[7] and why this is often related to confession of sins or assurance that no sin is known, 20, 45 ff.; 21, 69 f. 79 f.: "There came upon me sickness, disease, wasting and destruction; there came upon me distress, turning aside of face and the fulness of wrath (cf. 23, 30 ff.). Mine ears take note of thee, my Lady (Ishtar), they are directed to thee, I pray to thee, yea, to thee; take the curse from me." 23, 11. 26 f.: "I know not the sin which I have done, I know not the offence which I have committed." In between, 23, 21: "O Lord, my sins are many, my transgressions are great" (cf. 26:25 ff.). 27, 39 f. (request of the priest): "Take his hand, take away his guilt, let fever (?) and oppression depart from him ... Let thy servant live that he may glorify thy power." Sin and sickness, though distinct, are interchangeable. 30: "My sins he caused to be borne away by the wind (there follows a description of recovery). I may lay aside my wickedness, the bird will carry it up to heaven" (30 A 4).

One may compare the sacral practice of the Near East. "With expiations and sacrifices I prayed to the Lord (Phrygian deity) that he might save my body, and he restored my body. For this reason I dissuaded any from eating the sacred unsacrificed

[2] The verse is not found in 𝔖 D sy^c etc. as compared with 𝔎 A it sy^p etc., but it is materially indispensable.
[3] In spite of the very creditable researches of van Selms.
[4] Van Selms, 24 f.
[5] *Ibid.*, 15 ff., esp. 19.
[6] *Ibid.*, 44 ff., 110.
[7] Quoted from Zimmern.

flesh of goats, since otherwise you will detect my chastisements."[8] The Greek, too, attributes sickness to the wrath of the deity. Thus Apollo, the god of pestilence (→ I, 397), avenges the wrong done to his priests, Hom. Il., 1, 9 ff.; cf. 43 ff. Epimenides is supposed to have fought a plague in Athens by letting loose black and white sheep on the Areopagus and sacrificing them τῷ προσήκοντι θεῷ where they lay, Diog. L., I, 110, 3. The miasma is still visible when one drives περικαθάρματα (→ III, 430 f.) and → περιψήματα out of the land. There are also examples from Egypt. Sarapis smites Zoilos with sickness because he does not pursue energetically enough the order to build the temple, P. Greci e Latini (Firenze, 1917), No. 435,[9] and Imhotep-Asklepios smites an unknown person because he is dilatory in translating a cultic inscr., P. Oxy., XI, 1381, 64 ff.

2. The Equation of Defect and Sickness in Greek Philosophy.

There is a rather different equation of defect and sickness from the time of Plato. Here the distinctive nature of morality is recognised. The derivation of immoral acts from physical degeneration, which is in close accord with modern thought, is only intimated: νόσοι ... ἐμποδίζουσιν ἡμῶν τὴν τοῦ ὄντος θήραν (Plat. Phaed., 66c). But by means of the genuinely Gk. category of analogy (→ III, 198) there is an equation of defect and sickness which is more than a mere figure of speech. The real suffering of the inward man is ignorance. Hence it is equally necessary to heal both outward and inward sickness, Plat. Resp., X, 609c ff. etc. Plat. Soph., 228a ff.: There are two kinds of κακία in relation to the soul, distinguished like νόσος and αἶσχος (mutilation), namely, cowardice, licentiousness and unrighteousness on the one side and ignorance (τὸ τῆς πολλῆς καὶ παντοδαπῆς ἀγνοίας πάθος) on the other. To medicine and gymnastics there correspond in the mental sphere discipline (ἡ κολαστικὴ τέχνη) and instruction (ἡ διδασκαλικὴ τέχνη). This way of looking at things is extended to the state and society. The reciprocal censoriousness of the prudent and the brave is νόσος ... ταῖς πόλεσιν, Polit., 307d.

3. Sickness and Sin in the Old Testament.

The idea that sin is a spiritual sickness is never found in the Heb. OT (on Sus. 57 → 1091). The Psalter in particular bears an obvious resemblance to the penitential psalms of Babylon. By way of the concepts of guilt and sin an approximation of sin and sickness is achieved here. The distinction, however, is that in face of the one holy and living God there is a different sense of moral guilt as compared with cultic and ritual. Whereas the nature deity demands the savour of sacrifice and the fulness of wheat, Yahweh seeks a contrite heart (Ps. 51:16 f.).[10]

Ps. 103:3: הַסֹּלֵחַ לְכָל־עֲוֺנֵכִי הָרֹפֵא לְכָל־תַּחֲלוּאָיְכִי, LXX: τὸν εὐιλατεύοντα πάσαις ταῖς ἀνομίαις σου, τὸν ἰώμενον πάσας τὰς νόσους σου (cf. v. 4), has in view a genuine and almost mortal sickness which is taken from the psalmist after his forgiveness.[11] Nevertheless, the parallelism should be noted. Sin and sickness are closely related, for both are hopeless states.[12] In Hos. 5:12 ff. and Is. 1:5 f. this thought is worked out

---

[8] Steinleitner, 32. Steinleitner has made it very probable that the κολάσεις are usually sicknesses, 96 ff.

[9] 258/57 B.C. Deissmann LO, 121 ff.

[10] R. Kittel, *Die at.liche Wissenschaft*[4] (1921), 272 ff.

[11] Cf. the comm. of R. Kittel, B. Duhm, *ad loc.* Other (penitential) psalms may be quoted in this connection even though the word "sickness" does not occur, cf. esp. Ps. 32.

[12] This may be illustrated particularly well from Is. 53. An allegorical exposition of חֳלִי in v. 3 f. (Wellhausen, etc.) has rightly been abandoned by most scholars. B. Duhm suggests leprosy, P. Volz no particular ailment but real physical suffering. Near equivalents are sorrows (מַכְאֹבוֹת, v. 3 f.), chastisement (מוּסָר, v. 5), stripes (חַבֻּרָה, v. 5), guilt (עָוֺן, v. 6), sin

with ref. to the whole people. But the distinction from Plato (→ 1093) is obvious. For Plato sickness is an analogy or figure of the inner corruption which causes failings, and of the mischief to which this leads by immanent causality. But here the starting-point is the transcendent connection between guilt and judgment. By the dogma of retribution the sick man is stamped as a sinner (Is. 53:4). A conscience which is aware of no sin rebels against this. The resultant problem, which is particularly evident in Job, is solved in Is. 53 with the help of the concept of vicariousness, → 1097.

4. Sickness and Sin in Judaism.

Judaism worked out the doctrine of retribution with great virtuosity in relation to sickness. Indeed, it became the central dogma. [13] In Rabb. Judaism a distinction is usually made between sickness and sin. In Hell. Judaism Gk. presuppositions (→ 1093) probably help to relate them. Thus at Is. 53:4 the LXX has τὰς ἁμαρτίας ἡμῶν for חֳלָיֵנוּ; [14] it construes it fig., as does Σ, cf. also Dt. 30:3, where שָׁב שְׁבוּתְךָ is freely transl. by the LXX: καὶ ἰάσεται κύριος τὰς ἁμαρτίας σου (→ I, 287). Philo adopts the Platonic usage except that one can hardly detect the basis in analogy and the application to the state yields to an individualistic view. Virt., 162: ἀλαζονεία γὰρ φύεται, ὡς καὶ τῶν ἄλλων ἕκαστον ψυχῆς παθῶν τε καὶ νοσημάτων. The man who is dedicated to God is concerned to purify the soul ὅπως αὐτὴν καθαρὰν ἴδῃ τὴν τῆς ψυχῆς (gen. epexeg.) οἰκίαν καί, εἴ τινες ἐν αὐτῇ νόσοι γεγόνασιν, ἰάσηται (Deus Imm., 135). Dialectic heals μεγάλην νόσον ψυχῆς, ἀπάτην (Congr., 18). Only later and in restricted circles did these immanentist ideas influence Palestinian Judaism. [15] The transcendental doctrine of retribution does not necessarily have all the consequences one would expect from the standpoint of rigid logic. If the sick have to make confession of sin, this is not because they are special sinners but because of the possible imminence of death. [16] There are also chastisements of love (→ III, 201). God is esp. near the sick. [17] They are not to be regarded as outlaws, but are to be visited. Prayer is to be offered for them and any possible help extended. [18] If Judaism had to overcome religious scruples in respect of medicine, it recognised it from an early date (Sir. 38:12) and in increasing measure, and developed it to a notable degree. [19]

5. Sickness and Sin in the New Testament (→ III, 204).

Christianity, though it did not exclude natural causes, adopted the view that

(חֵטְא, v. 12). Though distinguished on the one side from the standpoint of causal relation (v. 5), "bearing sicknesses" (v. 4) and "bearing sins" (v. 12) are closely related on the other. It is also plain to what degree the sick man is described as a sinner, v. 3, 4b.

[13] On the doctrine of retribution in general, Bousset-Gressm., 411 f.; examples of sickness as retribution, Weber, 245 f., 322 f.; → III, 201. Gad is visited for 11 months with a liver complaint because his liver had no pity for Joseph, for "wherewith a man sins, therewith shall he be punished," Test. G. 5:11; cf. Test. Zeb. 5:2; Test. S. 2:12.

[14] → I, 286. Euler's attempt to prove (59 ff.) that the original LXX text is preserved in Mt. 8:17 and that the present LXX text is of Christian origin rests on a series of acute but not very secure conclusions. If he is right, what is said above would have to apply to the Christianity of the post-apostolic period, but with restrictions, since the presuppositions are different here. Euler rightly contests Christian influence on the Σ text (62).

[15] At Is. 53:4 the Targum renders חֳלָיֵנוּ by חוֹבָנָא ("our guilt"), but this does not have to be taken Hellenistically. In Lv. r., 5 on 4:3 (Str.-B., II, 156) we read: "The anointed priest sins? R. Levi (c. 300) has said: Miserable the city whose doctor has the gout." Here Hell. influence is possible. But the expression is so concretely Jewish that it is more natural to think in terms of a spontaneous comparison.

[16] Str.-B., I, 114; IV, 576.

[17] *Ibid.*, IV, 573 f. One should not sit on a sick-bed because of the proximity of the Shechinah.

[18] *Loc. cit.*

[19] → III, 201. Cf. the vast amount of material in Preuss, also over 150 medical refs. (in the broadest sense) in Str.-B., *s.v.* Cf. also Schl. Mt. on 9:12. Jos. mentions Jewish

sickness is contrary to God's creative intention, that it is due to the influence of demonic powers, that it is grounded in a cosmic catastrophe, that there is a general penal connection between sin and sickness, and that this may also apply in particular cases (Mt. 12:22 ff. and par.; Lk. 13:16; Jn. 5:14; R. 8:20; 1 C. 11:30; Rev. *passim*). But Jesus bursts through the mechanical dogma of retribution (Jn. 9:3 f.; 11:4, cf. Lk. 13:1 f.). He grants the sick healing and forgiveness (Mk. 2:5 ff. and par.). For believers sickness in this aeon is a salutary discipline used by God's fatherly love against sin, esp. presumption (1 C. 11:32; 2 C. 4:17; 12:7 ff.). Yet counteraction is taken against it by prayer, miraculous healing and natural means (2 C. 12:8; Jm. 5:13 ff.; Mt. 10:8; 1 C. 12:28; Lk. 10:34; Col. 4:14; 1 Tm. 5:23) so long as reverence, submission to God's will and patience are maintained.

The equation of sickness and sin may be seen in the expression κακῶς ἔχειν, Mk. 2:17 and par. Since the reference is not to men who are physically sick, the use is metaphorical. Accepting the standpoint of His Pharisaical opponents, with a full realisation of the religious and moral distinctions present, and not perhaps without gentle irony, Jesus concedes that they are δίκαιοι, or metaphorically οἱ ἰσχύοντες (Lk. οἱ ὑγιαίνοντες), whereas the publicans are ἁμαρτωλοί, or metaphorically οἱ κακῶς ἔχοντες. But He then concludes that He Himself belongs to the sinners. The image would be Greek if Jesus were seeking herewith to describe it as His calling to help by means of instruction and dialectic. Cynic philosophers used the same figure of speech for their mission, → III, 205. But Jesus speaks as the One who, divinely sent, leads from ruin to salvation by restoring the fellowship with God which was disrupted by sin and penally abrogated.[20] This does not rule out the possibility that Greek influences helped to shape the expression.[21] But a spontaneous origin of the metaphor has also to be considered, → n. 15. One may best refer to the ancient oriental and OT view that sickness is a state of loss, → 1092.

On the other hand, the figurative use of νοσέω in 1 Tm. 6:4 is Hellenistic in context. This is supported by the construction (→ 1092), the popular philosophical character of the list of vices which follows in v. 4 f.,[22] and the strong emphasis on ignorance as the source of aberration. Here, as in Plato and Philo (→ 1093 f.), being sick is a metaphor to indicate the abnormal state of the inward man. In keeping is the fact that in 2 Tm. 2:17 the growth of error is compared with that of a cancer. Though the guilt of error is not disputed, neither this nor the penal consequences are emphasised. The accent in the comparison is on the abnormality and common threat.

B. Sickness as Vicarious Suffering.

1. The Suffering Hero in the Greek World.

In Gk. mythology the sick hero is a well-known phenomenon. Orestes, Alcmaion, Ajax, Bellerophontes, also women like Ino, Io, Antiope, and whole groups like the Pandarides, Proetides and esp. the Maenades are afflicted by madness. Above all others Heracles is the divine man who is tested by suffering. Apart from the "sacred malady"

---

doctors, Vit., 404; Bell., 1, 272; Ant., 14, 368. The assertion of H. Pohlmann, *Der Gottesgedanke Jesu als Gegensatz gg. d. israel.-jüd. Gottesgedanken* (1939), 60, that to all appearance the art of healing could not develop on Jewish soil, is based on false presuppositions.

[20] Rightly understood the addition in Lk. (εἰς μετάνοιαν) supports this.

[21] A Hell. influence on Jesus Himself is esp. argued, though with inadequate resources, by E. Wechssler, *Hellas im Evangelium* (1936), esp. 267 ff.

[22] Dib. Past., *ad loc.*, Exc. on 1 Tm. 4:5.

he is afflicted by an irritation of the skin (Ἡρακλέους ψώρα) connected with melancholy, and also by nightmares caused by the demon Ephialtes. Through the poison of the Hydra working in the blood of Nessus he finally contracts a leprous complaint which also brings seizures. Only his death and apotheosis put an end to his sufferings. If these mythological illnesses are often attributed in the first instance to the wrath of specific deities or demons, e.g., the jealousy of Hera in the cases of Heracles or the vengefulness of the Erinyes in that of Orestes, the religio-psychological problem lies deeper in the Gk. sense of tragedy. Behind the contrariness of the course of things and the envy of the gods there is a final demonism of destiny to which the gods are also subject (cf. esp. Dionysus, → II, 451 f.) and which alone can bring human life to its full richness. The hardly won confirmation is surely exemplary. But the tragedy of the sick hero also has saving significance. The vicariousness, however, is not that of historical expiation, and the approach is individualistic.

2. The Suffering Servant of God in the Old Testament and Judaism. In biblical thought there is a clash of unparalleled intensity between a realistic and an idealistic view of the world. The tension can finally be resolved only in the eschaton. In this light it hardly seems possible to find an inner reason for sickness in terms of the vocational burden laid on a man who has a special commission. Yet a distinctive understanding develops out of the experience of prophetic figures. It is possible that something of this is reflected in the account of wrestling Jacob (Gn. 32:25 ff.). But the matter is quite plain in Ez. and Dt. Is.

For Ez. a cataleptic type of sickness is both the occasion and the indispensable expression of his commission (Ez. 3:22-27; 4:4-8). The thought of substitution is present in the words: "Thou shalt bear the iniquity of the house of Israel and of the house of Judah," though the sense is symbolical and epideictic rather than expiatory. The true depths of the thought are plumbed in the interpretation which Tr. Is. probably found for the solemn fate of Dt. Is. (Is. 53:3-5). According to the doctrine of retribution the servant of God was marked off by God as a sinner beyond all others. But the sin was that of his people laid on him. He bore this in substitutionary expiation, → 612 f.

Only in part,[23] and in the main in the post-Christian era,[24] did Judaism relate Is. 53 to the Messiah, and out of this interpretation there arose the thesis that the Messiah would be a leper.[25] In the translation 'A is closest to the Mas. at the crucial verse (v. 4).[26] The LXX[27] and Σ[28] — like 'A with no clear ref. to the Messiah — take "sicknesses" fig., though they stress the thought of vicarious suffering (there is no Θ rendering). The prophetic Targum[29] relates the text to the Messiah, but reinterprets the

---

[23] Other refs. are to the righteous and to the people of Israel; the latter finally prevailed, Str.-B., I, 481 ff.

[24] The designation "the righteous one" for the Messiah in Eth. En. 38:2; 47:1, 4; 53:6 seems to come from Is. 53:11, and the attitude of the kings of the earth to the Messiah in Eth. En. 46:4; 62:5 f. seems to follow the depiction in Is. 52:13 ff. Whether this interpretation was widespread, and esp. whether Is. 53:4 was included, and in what sense, cannot be decided. The Messianic interpretation is first found in Rabb. Judaism in the 3rd cent. A.D. Its main proponent is the prophetic Targum. Cf. P. Seidelin, "Der Ebed Jahwe und d. Messiasgestalt im Jstargum," ZNW, 35 (1936), 194 ff., esp. 206 ff.

[25] Str.-B., I, 481; H. Gressmann, "Der aussätzige Messias," Chr. W., 34 (1920), 663 ff.

[26] ὄντως αὐτὸς τὰς νόσους ἡμῶν ἔλαβεν καὶ τοὺς πόνους ἡμῶν ὑπέμεινεν. The different transl. may be found in Euler, 12 ff. It is by no means certain that 'A is telling the story of what was at first an anonymous priest.

[27] οὗτος τὰς ἁμαρτίας ἡμῶν φέρει καὶ περὶ ἡμῶν ὀδυνᾶται. On the authenticity → n. 14.

[28] ὄντως τὰς ἁμαρτίας ἡμῶν ἀνέλαβε καὶ τοὺς πόνους ὑπέμεινεν.

[29] Hence he will pray for our sin and our iniquity will be forgiven for his sake (בכן על חובנא הוא יבעי ועויתנא בדיליה ישתבקון).

sicknesses and makes of the substitution vicarious intercession. Throughout the chapter it also refers the sufferings consistently to the enemies of Israel, → 616.

The suffering servant vicariously bearing sickness forms no constituent part of Judaism in the NT period.

3. The Suffering Man of God in the New Testament.

The most primitive Christian *kerygma*, and in all probability Jesus Himself, referred Is. 53 to Christ (Ac. 8:32 f.). The fact that Jesus was never ill [30] raises no difficulty, because the divinely smitten servant of God was found in the Crucified, the more so in view of the reference to violent death in the original. The dominant LXX text, or at least that which had established itself prior to 1 Cl., 16, 3 ff. (→ n. 27), arouses no misgivings. Quite apart from the Hellenistic equation of sickness and sin, those who know Hebrew could relate חֳלָיֵנוּ to the state caused by sin, including its penal consequences, or with a slight twist they could even refer it directly to the passion. It is easier, however, to relate Is. 53:7 f. or 53:5, 9, 12 to the Crucified, and for this reason these are the only references explicitly found in the NT (Ac. 8:32 f.; 1 Pt. 2:22, 24 f.).

Mt. 8:17 applies Is. 53:4 to the healing Christ in a version of its own. Since Mt. is bilingual, [31] we must reckon with the possibility that this understanding, which is not far from the original, is taken independently from it. [32] λαμβάνειν and βαστάζειν are understood in the sense "to bear away," "to remove." [33] But elsewhere Mt., like all the Evangelists, shows a good grasp of the fact that the healings of Jesus could not take place without His taking to His own heart the needs of those seeking help (Mt. 15:30 ff.: σπλαγχνίζομαι ἐπὶ τὸν ὄχλον, cf. 20:34 [only Mt.]; 17:17). It sounds like concrete recollection when Jesus, coming from the mount of transfiguration, plunges into the battle. Here already is the first impulse which leads to His death and passion. There is no reason to rule out such considerations in the case of 8:17. [34]

In a literal sense sickness is a vocational burden for Paul. How closely his sickness (→ III, 204) is bound up with his apostolic calling may be seen from 2 C. 12:7 ff. Though there is no hint of vicariousness here, cf. 2 C. 4:10 ff. The νέκρωσις depicted here does not exclude impairment of health, though persecution is to the fore, cf. 2 C. 11:27 ff. The same point is made by the expression παθήματα [35] or θλίψεις τοῦ Χριστοῦ in 2 C. 1:5 ff.; Col. 1:24. [36] By these sufferings in his own flesh the apostle fills up what is still lacking of the sufferings of Christ (ἀνταναπληρῶ τὰ ὑστερήματα τῶν θλίψεων τοῦ Χριστοῦ ἐν τῇ σαρκί μου ὑπὲρ

[30] This is particularly emphasised by O. Borchert, *Der Goldgrund des Lebensbildes Jesu*, II⁴ (1921), 21 ff. On Christ's physical health → II, 456 f., n. 39, 41, also A. Schweitzer, *Geschichte d. Leben-Jesu-Forschung*⁴ (1926), 362 ff.

[31] In spite of Euler, → n. 14.

[32] So Schl. Mt., *ad loc.* There is no need to speak of Mt. using a translation independent of the LXX (Kl. Mt., *ad loc.*).

[33] On λαμβάνειν cf. Mt. 5:40; 15:26; on βαστάζειν, 3:11, also Gal. De Compositione Medicamentorum per Genera, II, 14 (ed. Kühn, XIII, 527) (of an ointment): ψώρας τε θεραπεύει καὶ ὑπώπια βαστάζει, "it heals scratches and removes boils."

[34] Schl. Mt., *ad loc.*, though cf. Kl. Mt., *ad loc.* (unless this is just meant linguistically): "hardly co-bearing in sympathy and exhausting exertion."

[35] As against the view of older exegetes that Paul has in mind a severe illness from which he had just recovered in Ephesus, cf. Wnd. 2 K., *ad loc.*

[36] Cf. G. Kittel, "Kol. 1:24," ZSTh, 18 (1941), 186-191 (sufferings in the sense of Mt. 5:11).

τοῦ σώματος αὐτοῦ, ὅ ἐστιν ἡ ἐκκλησία). The basic idea is that of Christ as the universal man. As the One who appeared in history, Christ has done enough for sin. He died once and for all to its power and all its consequences, R. 6:10. He has now been placed as Head in another aeon, in heavenly being. Believers are there with Him, but for the time being only in concealment. In so far as Christ with His "body" still belongs to this aeon, He must still undergo a certain divinely appointed measure of suffering. Since Paul is a member of Christ's body, his sufferings are the sufferings of Christ and help to hasten the final redemption. There is no reference to a supplementing of the satisfaction made once and for all at the cross, but this is still the effective bearing of a burden which in the case of the apostle is particularly comprehensive and significant.

C. The Church and Sickness.

1. Visiting and Caring for the Sick in the Primitive Church.

A community which handed down the saying of the Lord in Mt. 25:36 and which knew the directions in Jm. 5:13 ff. was bound to regard visiting, caring and praying for the sick as important tasks. At the end of the 1st cent. the Roman church prayed: τοὺς ἀσθενεῖς ἴασαι, 1 Cl., 59, 4. In Pol., 1, 3, with a clear echo of Mt. 8:17 and therefore with ref. to the Lord's example, Ign. gives the admonition: πάντων τὰς νόσους βάσταζε.[37] The Canons of Hipp.[38] and the "Book of Clement"[39] refer explicitly to the fact that the bishop and deacons are to visit the sick, to pray over them, and to do all that is necessary in care for them. In times of pestilence, when pagans often left their sick relatives to lie helpless, and threw their dead bodies on the streets to avoid infection, many Christians devoted themselves to ministering to the sick and dying even among pagans, and to the point of self-sacrifice, Vita Cypriani, 9 and 10, CSEL, III, 3, XCIX f.; Cyprian, Ad Demetrianum, 10, CSEL, III, 1, 358; Eus. Hist. Eccl., 7, 22, 7-10; 9, 8, 4-15.[40]

2. The Influence of Is. 53 on the Concept of Christ.

It would have been natural if alongside the ugly Christ (Is. 52:14; 53:2 f. → III, 550 f.)[41] there had also been a sick Christ (Is. 53:4), → 1096 f. But apparently this did not happen. The obvious reason is that the dominant LXX text (→ n. 7) provided no basis for it. A deeper reason, however, is that in the main v. 4 was referred exclusively to the Crucified, while the teaching and healing Christ was thought of as the mighty Helper. This does not mean that Christ and sickness were incompatible for the Church. It is a sign of the increasing Hellenisation of Christianity, however, that when ἀσθένεια and νόσος are related to Mt. 8:17, they are more and more understood figuratively.[42]

Oepke

---

[37] On the influence of Mt. 8:17 in ecclesiastical literature cf. Euler, 59 ff., 137 f.

[38] Canon 24 (ed. H. Achelis, TU, VI, 4 [1891], 117).

[39] Ed. P. de Lagarde, Reliquiae Juris ecclesiastici antiquissimae (1856) 84, 19-24.

[40] The material has been assembled by Uhlhorn, 181 ff., 303.

[41] Euler, 55, 134 ff.; W. Bauer, *Das Leben Jesu im Zeitalter d. nt.lichen Apokryphen* (1909), 312 ff.; N. Müller in RE³, IV, 64. The best collection of material is in R. Eisler, Ἰησοῦς Βασιλεὺς οὐ βασιλεύσας, II (1930), 321 ff. (though this is often inaccurate in detail and is to be used with caution). When later fathers in their description of Jesus appealed to Jos. as a source, this simply shows that the apocryphal accounts were traced back to him, not that there had been such a description in the original Aram. version of the Bellum, and even less that the description has any historical value. These hypotheses stand or fall with the evaluation of Slav. Jos. by Eisler and others.

[42] For examples cf. Euler, 137 f.

† νύμφη, † νυμφίος (→ γαμέω, γάμος).

Contents: A. Background Material: 1. The Designation of the Bride as γυνή; 2. The Escort for the Bridegroom; 3. Λαμπάδες in the Bridal Procession; 4. The Best Man. B. Christ as Bridegroom in the Parables of Jesus? 1. The Allegory Bridegroom/Messiah Unknown to the OT and Later Judaism; 2. The Two νυμφίος Parables of Jesus: a. "Can Wedding-Guests Mourn?" (Mt. 9:15 and par.); b. "The Bridegroom Cometh" (Mt. 25:1-13). C. The Development of the Allegory Christ/Bridegroom, Christ-Community/Bride, Apostle/Best Man.

Νύμφη (from the time of Hom.) means "bride," "marriageable young woman," "young wife," νυμφίος (also from Hom.) "bridegroom," "young husband." In Jewish Gk. both words also acquire a meaning (from the time of the LXX) not found in Gk. elsewhere, namely, "daughter-in-law" (LXX Gn. 11:31; 38:11, 13, 16, 24; 1 Βασ. 4:19 etc.) or "son-in-law" (LXX Ju. 15:6 B; 2 Εσδρ. 23:28 etc.). This extension of meaning is brought about by Semitic usage, for the Heb. כַּלָּה (Aram. כַּלְּתָא) means both the bride and also (predominantly) the daughter-in-law, and the Heb. חָתָן (Aram. חַתְנָא) both the bridegroom and son-in-law.

In the NT the meaning is always bride/bridegroom except at Mt. 10:35 (par. Lk. 12:53). Here, on the basis of Mi. 7:6, we have a description of the moral collapse in the time of the curse preceding the coming of salvation. [1] In the disruption of the closest family ties the νύμφη and the mother-in-law will also be at variance. Νύμφη here is the daughter-in-law living in the house of her husband's parents. [2]

Though the words νύμφη and νυμφίος are comparatively rare [3] in the NT, the few instances raise a whole series of questions. These relate partly to the background material but esp. to the use of the metaphor of the bridegroom and bride for Christ and the community.

A. Background Material.

1. The Designation of the Bride as γυνή. In the NT the bride is repeatedly called γυνή (Mt. 1:20, 24; Rev. 19:7; 21:9; Jn. 8:1 ff., → n. 8). This usage is particularly striking in the apparently contradictory expression δείξω σοι τὴν νύμφην τὴν γυναῖκα τοῦ ἀρνίου (Rev. 21:9). The many artifices occasioned by the expression [4] are unnecessary when it is realised that the designation of the bride as γυνή is in keeping with current Palestinian usage. [5] According to later Jewish law the betrothal effects the "acquisition" (קִנְיָן) of the bride by the bridegroom and is thus a valid marriage. Though the bride still stands under the *patria potestas* until the marriage, [6] she is legally a married woman from the time of the betrothal. She is called אִשָּׁה (γυνή) and can become a widow, receive a bill of divorcement,

---

ν ύ μ φ η κ τ λ. [1] For similar descriptions cf. Jub. 23:19; Eth. En. 100:2; 4 Esr. 6:24; Mk. 13:12; Mt. 10:21; Lk. 21:16. Another motif of the time of the curse and judgment is that the voice of the bride and bridegroom is no longer heard (i.e., bridal jubilation, Jer. 7:34; 16:9; 25:10; Joel 1:8; Bar. 2:23; and in the NT, on the basis of Jer., Rev. 18:23); it is stilled because lamentation dominates and the city lies waste. On the other hand, the voice of the bride and bridegroom is heard in the time of salvation, Jer. 33:11; bKet., 7b.

[2] Cf. LXX Lv. 18:15 etc.

[3] Νύμφη Mt. 10:35 (par. Lk. 12:53 twice); Mt. 25:1 vl.; Jn. 3:29; Rev. 18:23; 21:2, 9; 22:17. νυμφίος: Mt. 9:15 twice (par. Mk. 2:19-20; Lk. 5:34 f.); Mt. 25:1, 5, 6, 10; Jn. 2:9; 3:29 three times; Rev. 18:23.

[4] Cf. Zn. Apk., *ad loc.*: The married woman who still wears her bridal attire.

[5] Gn. 29:21; Dt. 22:24; Str.-B., II, 393 f.

[6] J. Jeremias, *Jerusalem zur Zeit Jesu,* II B (1937), 241.

or be punished for infidelity etc.[7] Jn. 8:1 ff. illustrates the fact that a bride who has proved unfaithful can be punished as an adulteress.[8]

2. The Escort for the Bridegroom. There is much debate as to the situation presupposed in the parable of the ten virgins. The answer depends essentially on which reading of Mt. 25:1 is preferred.

Acc. to ℵ BCW ℜ pm the virgins go out εἰς ὑπάντησιν τοῦ νυμφίου, acc. to DΘλit vg sy εἰς ὑπ- (D ἀπ-) άντησιν τοῦ νυμφίου καὶ τῆς νύμφης. Before deciding the textual problem one must remember that the established custom was to hold the wedding in the house of the bridegroom or his parents.[9] The bridegroom fetches the bride and brings her to his house, where the bridal table and chamber are ready. If, as often happens, the second reading is preferred (εἰς ὑπάντησιν τοῦ νυμφίου καὶ τῆς νύμφης), then the virgins accompany the bridal couple from the house of the bride to the house of the bridegroom. The development of the first and shorter reading may then be explained as follows. The words καὶ τῆς νύμφης were later cut out because they seemed to contradict the allegorical interpretation of the bride as the community. The returning Christ does not make entry with His bride, the community, but hastens towards it.[10] Against selection of this second and longer reading may be argued not only the attestation but also the fact that only the bridegroom is mentioned in v. 5 and v. 6. In consequence one should read εἰς ὑπάντησιν τοῦ νυμφίου (with ℵBC etc.) in v. 1 as well. But why, then, is there no mention of the bride in v. 1, 5, 6? The answer is that the ten virgins are the friends of the bride who go out from her house to meet the bridegroom when he comes to fetch her.[11]

3. Λαμπάδες in the Bridal Procession. Mt. 25:1 ff. presupposes that the wedding took place late in the evening and that virgins with → λαμπάδες brought in the bridegroom and then accompanied the bridal couple to the house. Though probably by accident, there is not witness to any such Palestinian custom[12] except in Mt. 25:1 ff.

Whether the λαμπάδες are torches[13] or lamps[14] one cannot say for certain, since λαμπάς may mean either.[15] In the former case we are to think of staves with vessels

---

[7] Str.-B., II, 393 ff.

[8] Since an unfaithful wife was to be strangled acc. to Rabb. exegesis of Lv. 20:10; Dt. 22:22 (Str.-B., II, 519 f.), the ref. in Jn. 8:1 ff. is to an unfaithful bride, who was to be stoned acc. to Dt. 22:24. She would still be very young, since the normal age of betrothal was 12-12½.

[9] A wedding could presumably take place in the house of the bride's parents only if the daughter married abroad (Tob. 7:12 ff.; Midr. Est. on 1:4), and even then the ref. is to a prior festival followed by a seven day wedding in the bridegroom's house (Tob. 11:19).

[10] Cf. A. Merx, *D. vier kanonischen Evangelien*, II, 1 (1902), 363; A. H. McNeile, *The Gospel acc. to Matthew* (1915), 361; W. O. E. Oesterley, *The Gospel Parables* (1936), 134 ff.; *NT Deutsch*, Schn. Mt., *ad loc.*

[11] The words καὶ τῆς νύμφης were added by a glossator who thought the ten virgins were relatives of the bridegroom who went out to meet the bridal procession from his house.

[12] The use of bridal torches in Arabia is attested by R. Simson Abraham of Sens (*c.* 1200) on Kelim, 2, 8, cf. the passage → 17, n. 2. One can hardly compare Pesikt. r., 43 (180b) in Rabb. lit., → 17, n. 2. The word קירקנות which P. Billerbeck translates torches (Str.-B., I, 510; cf. ed. M. Friedmann [1909], 180b, 8 קורקנות) is a hapax legomenon of doubtful meaning. It certainly has nothing to do with κηρίων (wax light).

[13] So F. Zorell, Verbum Domini, 10 (1930), 176 ff. Schl. Mt., 719 pts. out that λαμπάς always means "torch" in Joseph.

[14] So Oepke, → 17, n. 2; Pr.-Bauer³, 772; G. Dalman, *Arbeit u. Sitte in Palästina*, IV (1935), 271.

[15] → 17; Pr.-Bauer³, 772. In the NT cf. Jn. 18:3 (torch) and Ac. 20:8 (lamp).

of oil, [16] in the latter of lamps on sticks [17] or storm lanterns [18] (which is very likely).

4. The Best Man. Jn. 3:29 refers to ὁ φίλος τοῦ νυμφίου (שׁוֹשְׁבִין) and his joy at the voice of the bridegroom.

The two best men [19] sometimes played a role in the wooing and betrothal too (cf. 2 C. 11:2). [20] At the wedding they conducted the bridegroom to the bride, [21] though their main task was to superintend the sexual intercourse of the young couple. [22] Hence the φωνὴ τοῦ νυμφίου of Jn. 3:29 is probably the call of the bridegroom from the bridal chamber for the friend who customarily fetches the *signum virginitatis.* [23] The vigour of the image, which would not be offensive to the sensibilities of antiquity, suggests that it is no allegory, but a true metaphor. [24] We may thus conjecture — there can be no question of certainty — that the ref. is not to the heavenly Bridegroom and His bride, the community, but that a common incident from life is used to express unselfish joy.

When in John's Gospel the Baptist describes himself figuratively as the best man, this indicates the ungrudging relation of the precursor to the consummator and his unselfish delight in the successes of the latter. There is probable allusion to the company of John's disciples, who are summoned to attain to a similar attitude.

B. Christ as Bridegroom in the Parables of Jesus?

It is generally accepted as self-evident that in the two νυμφίος parables of Jesus (that of the wedding-guests [Mk. 2:19 f.; Mt. 9:15; Lk. 5:34 f.] and that of the ten virgins [Mt. 25:1-13]) the bridegroom stands allegorically for the Messiah. This allegorical interpretation is very old, as may be seen from Mk. 2:20. Nevertheless, it is not so easily related to the original point of the two parables. Both the data of religious history and the exegetical findings are against it.

1. The Allegory Bridegroom/Messiah Unknown to the OT and Later Judaism.

From the time of Hosea the OT is, of course, acquainted with the metaphor of the marriage of Yahweh and Israel, which it uses to depict the covenant relation of God to His people, His covenant faithfulness and His forgiving patience. [25] Occasionally the metaphor is further developed and there is reference to the espousals. In Jer. 2:2 these are equated with the exodus from Egypt, i.e., the time before the conclusion of the covenant at Sinai, while Tr. Is. uses the image of the joy of the bridegroom to depict the age of salvation: "As the bridegroom rejoiceth over the bride, so shall thy God rejoice over thee" (62:5). [26] But nowhere in the OT is the Messiah presented as a bridegroom.

---

16 Acc. to Arabian custom, → 17, n. 2.
17 After the Gk. pattern, so K. Galling, ZDPV, 46 (1923), 32.
18 G. Dalman, → n. 14.
19 Str.-B., I, 500-504, cf. 45 f., has a collection of the most important Rabb. material concerning the best man.
20 This may be seen, e.g., from the fact that in Ex. r., 46, 1 on 34:1 the marriage agreement (drawn up at the betrothal, Str.-B., II, 387 ff.) was committed into the trusty hands of the best man.
21 Ex. r., 20, 6 on 13:7; bEr., 18b; Ab RN, 4 (Str.-B., I, 502 and 504).
22 Str.-B., I, 46 and 500 f.
23 So also Schl. J., 108.
24 So also R. Bultmann, *Das Ev. d. J.* (1941), 126.
25 Hos. 1-3, esp. 2:18, 21; Ex. 16:7 ff.; 23:4; Is. 50:1; 54:4 ff. → I, 654; Eichr. Theol. AT, I, 127 ff.
26 Cf. also Is. 61:10.

Later Judaism uses the image of bridegroom and bride for Yahweh and Israel more often than does the OT.[27] Thus in the 1st cent. A.D. there is no doubt but that the Song of Songs was allegorically understood of Israel as the bride of God.[28] This made possible the acceptance of the Song of Songs into the Canon,[29] which in turn naturalised the allegory. The days before the making of the covenant at Sinai[30] were now the bridal period for some, though it was usually identified with the present age:[31] "This world is the betrothal ..., the wedding will be in the days of the Messiah."[32] But in all later Jewish literature there is no instance of an application of the allegory of the bridegroom to the Messiah.

The Lat. transl. of 4 Esr. 7:26 reads: *apparebit sponsa apparescens civitas,* cf. the Syr. But the Armen. (*manifestabitur urbs quae nunc non apparet*) and the Arab. (ed. H. Ewald, 1863: "The city will appear which thus far has not appeared") offer another text which is shown by the parallelism to be original:

"Then will the as yet invisible city appear,
And the hidden land will show itself."

All more recent editors[33] rightly conclude that the word *sponsa* is due to textual corruption. Possibly an original ἡ νῦν μὴ φαινομένη πόλις was misread as ἡ νύμφη φαινομένη πόλις.[34] Hence 4 Esr. 7:26 is not an example to prove that later Judaism was acquainted with the idea that Jerusalem is the bride of the Messiah. In the fourth vision of 4 Esr. (9:26-10:59) there appears to the seer a woman lamenting for her son, who died on his wedding night. The woman is transformed into a glorious city — the seer is now looking on the Zion of the last time. If the son is the Messiah — which is much contested[35] — the vision refers to His wedding. But the metaphor is not worked out; the word bridegroom is not used; the bride is neither depicted nor mentioned; the whole emphasis is on the fact that Zion is the mother and that the son is torn from his mother. Finally ref. might be made to the Christian-Gnostic[36] novel Joseph and Asenath,[37] which tells the story of the conversion of Asenath, daughter of an Egyptian priest, and Joseph's marriage with her. Joseph here has supernatural traits which make it likely that he is a prototype of the Messiah (→ I, 657). But these traits are hardly a part of the probably Jewish basis of the story, for pre-Christian Judaism was undecided in its evaluation of Joseph, esp. in respect of his Egyptian marriage (Gn. 41:45, 50; 46:20),[38] and it nowhere found in him a prototype of the Messiah.

---

[27] → I, 654.

[28] R. Aqiba (d. 135 A.D.) championed the allegorical interpretation of the Song of Songs with particular vigour (Str.-B., I, 516 and 898, cf. IV, 432 f., also M. Ex. on 15:2 etc.). But the usual view that he was the first to do so is incorrect. This interpretation is found already in the 1st cent. A.D.: M. Ex. on 19:1 and par. (R. Jochanan b. Zakkai, *c.* 40-80); also 4 Esr. 5:24, 26 (cf. H. Gunkel in Kautzsch Pseudepigr., 361 n. e; J. Bonsirven, "Exégèse allégorique chez les Rabbins Tannaïtes," *Recherches de science religieuse,* 23 [1933], 513-541; 24 [1934], 35-46, esp. 35 f.).

[29] Str.-B., IV, 432 f.

[30] *Ibid.,* I, 501 f., 969, 970; II, 393; → 1101.

[31] *Ibid.,* I, 517 f.; IV, 827, 863, 926.

[32] Ex. r., 15, 30 on 15:2. The verse can also be translated: "In this world they (the Israelites) were betrothed ..., in the days of the Messiah they will be married," but the meaning is the same.

[33] After G. Volkmar, *Handbuch d. Einl. in d. Apkr.,* II (1863).

[34] H. Gunkel in Kautzsch Pseudepigr., 370. L. Gry, *Les dires prophétiques d'Esdras,* I (1938), 147 traces back the corruption to what he assumes to be the Aram. original. כרכתא (enclosure) became the twofold כרכא (city) and כלתא (bride).

[35] J. Wellhausen, *Skizzen u. Vorarbeiten,* VI (1899), 219, n. 1.

[36] H. Priebatsch, *D. Josephsgeschichte in d. Weltlit.* (1937), 132 tries to locate the author more precisely among the Valentinians.

[37] Ed. E. Batiffol, *Studia Patristica,* I (1889-1890).

[38] H. Priebatsch, 3 ff., 188 ff.

This is all the material there is, and none of the passages cited contains a clear instance of the Messiah/bridegroom allegory.

2. The Two νυμφίος Parables of Jesus.

a. "Can wedding-guests mourn?" (Mt. 9:15 and par.). To the accusing question why His disciples do not fast, Jesus replies[39] with the counter-question: "Can wedding-guests[40] mourn[41] so long as[42] the bridegroom is with them?" (Mt. 9:15a par. Mk. 2:19a; Lk. 5:34).

The secondary clause "so long as the bridegroom is with them" seems to demand that in the ref. to the bridegroom Jesus means Himself as the Messiah, and that He is referring to a time when He will no longer be among His people. But this poses the question of authenticity, for some scholars think it unlikely that He publicly confessed His Messiahship prior to the hearing on the night before Good Friday (Mk. 14:62). It should also be noted that this is not the only possible interpretation.

It is not improbable that the subsidiary clause ἐφ' ὅσον (Mk. Lk. ἐν ᾧ) μετ' αὐτῶν ἐστιν ὁ νυμφίος was originally simply a paraphrase for "during the wedding festival."[43] If so, the counter-question is a genuine metaphor, perhaps even a secular proverb:[44] "Can one weep at a wedding?" "Do the joy of a wedding and the sorrow of a funeral mix?"[45] Not at all! Similarly it would be nonsensical for the disciples of Jesus to fast when they have the joy of the coming age of salvation and they already possess the gifts of salvation. It could be that the saying has originally nothing whatever to do with the bridegroom/Messiah allegory; the choice of metaphor is simply due to the common comparison of the age of salvation with a wedding, → 1102.

Mt. 9:15b (par. Mk. 2:20; Lk. 5:35) adds a surprising qualification: "But days will come when the bridegroom will be taken from them; then shall they fast." According to this statement the rejection of fasting applies only to the earthly life of Jesus. In apparent contradiction of 9:15a, it not only proclaims that the disciples will fast but contains an open prophecy of the Messianic passion. To many this seems to suggest that the saying derives from the community. The bridegroom of Mt. 9:15a is allegorically interpreted as the Messiah, and the subsidiary clause ἐφ' ὅσον μετ' αὐτῶν ἐστιν ὁ νυμφίος is construed as a chronological limitation. This statement in 9:15b is one of the oldest instances of the Messiah/bridegroom allegory.

---

39 On the authenticity of Mt. 9:15a (much contested in the wake of Wellhausen Mk., 18) cf. the acute examination of H. J. Ebeling, ThStKr, 108 (1937), 387-396: Since the community fasts acc. to Mt. 9:15b, the attack on non-fasting (9:14) and the saying which meets the attack (9:15a) must surely be part of the story of Jesus. The fasting community gave no offence. Also significant as regards authenticity is the fact that a basic Aram. text of Mt. 9:15a can be discerned, → n. 40-42.

40 οἱ υἱοὶ τοῦ νυμφῶνος ("the sons of the bridechamber") is a Semitism; it is a slavishly lit. transl. of בְּנֵי הַחוּפָּה, the wedding-guests (Tos. Ber., 2, 10; jSukka, 53a, line 18; bSukka, 25b). The art. (οἱ [!] υἱοὶ τοῦ νυμφῶνος) has generic significance (Aramaism) and should be left out in transl.

41 So Mt. 9:15: πενθεῖν, Mk. 2:19 and Lk. 5:34: νηστεύειν. These are different renderings of the Aram. אִתְעַנֵּי, which means 1. "to be troubled, sad" (e.g., Tg. 1 K. 2:26) and 2. "to fast" (e.g., Tg. Zech. 7:5).

42 Ἐφ' ὅσον scil. χρόνον (Mt.) and ἐν ᾧ (Mk. Lk.) are different translations.

43 Kl. Mk., *ad loc.*; C. H. Dodd, *The Parables of the Kingdom*[4] (1938), 116, n. 2.

44 Bultmann Trad., 107, n. 1; Kl. Mk., *ad loc.*

45 If one translates with Mk. and Lk.: "Can wedding-guests fast at the wedding?" (→ n. 41), Jesus had in view the rule that wedding guests were absolved from certain religious duties (bSukka, 25b), which might well have included fasting.

b. "The bridegroom cometh" (Mt. 25:1-13). The parable of the ten virgins [46] is one of the group which deals with the sudden coming of the end. It belongs to the same series as the reference to the flood (Mt. 24:37-39; Lk. 17:26 f.), the parable of the thief by night (Mt. 24:42-44; Lk. 12:39 f.), that of the watchful servants (Mk. 13:33-37) and that of the faithful and evil servants (Mt. 24:45-51; Lk. 12:42-46). All these are parables of judgment. They warn the hearers to be ready for the unexpected coming of the end, which will bring judgment and separation. Just as the flood was a surprise, or the thief by night, or the return of the master of the house, or the call which wakened the sleeping virgins at midnight: "The bridegroom cometh" (Mt. 25:6), so the final catastrophe will be a surprise when it comes on a race unprepared.

In the parable of the ten virgins the feature of the awaited bridegroom (χρονίζοντος δὲ τοῦ νυμφίου, Mt. 25:5) understandably provided the primitive Church with an occasion to relate the parable to the delay of the *parousia,* and to see in the bridegroom an allegory of the Messiah. [47] But this can hardly be the original point. [48] This interpretation tacitly presupposes that the parable was addressed exclusively to the disciples of Jesus. There is, however, no ground for this assumption. If the crowd are the hearers, then the only possible point of the parable is to stir men to reflection in face of the crisis which hastens ineluctably towards the final catastrophe. [49] No emphasis is originally placed on the delay of the bridegroom. This is simply designed to explain why the foolish virgins are caught in the predicament of not having enough oil for their lamps (Mt. 25:8).

Mt. 25:1-13 is thus a comparison, not an allegory. It refers, not to the heavenly Bridegroom and the delay of the *parousia,* but to the suddenness with which the final catastrophe will break over men, and of the judgment which will overtake those who are not ready.

The conclusion that the Messiah/bridegroom allegory is no less alien to the preaching of Jesus than to the narrower world about Him is supported by the fact that the comparing of the community with the bride is also unknown in His preaching. Jesus compares His disciples, not with the bride, but with the wedding-guests (Mt. 9:15; 22:1 ff., 10 ff.).

C. The Development of the Allegory Christ/Bridegroom, Christ-Community/Bride, Apostle/Best Man.

The allegorical use of bridegroom/bride imagery occurs first in Paul at 2 C. 11:2: ἡρμοσάμην γὰρ ὑμᾶς ἑνὶ ἀνδρὶ παρθένον ἁγνὴν παραστῆσαι τῷ Χριστῷ. Describing his apostolic office, Paul compares the community with a bride, Christ with the bridegroom, and himself with the best man who has won the bride, who watches over her virginity, and who will lead her to the bridegroom at the wedding. The image is further developed in Eph. 5:22-33. The saying in Gn. 2:24 concerning

---

46 The main pt. in defence of the authenticity of the parable (except perhaps for v. 13, → n. 54) is the fact that the bride is not equated with the community. This equation is not found in the preaching of Jesus but is common in the primitive Church from the time of Paul.

47 Hence Bultmann's verdict that the parable is a creation of the community in which allegory has run riot, Bultmann Trad., 125.

48 C. H. Dodd, *op. cit.,* 171-174.

49 This is no less true of the other parables mentioned above, as the cogent expositions of Dodd (154-171) have shown.

the union of man and wife is referred in v. 31 f. to the union (at the *parousia*) [50] of Christ the Bridegroom, who leaves heaven and comes for His bride, and the community. In Eph. 5:22 ff. the point of the allegory is particularly clear. It serves to depict the love of Christ for His community, which is selfless even to the point of self-sacrifice, and the obligation of obedience and bridal purity which lies on the community.

The description of the community as a bride is found already in the OT (Is. 62:5; 49:18). Allegorical exposition of the Song of Songs made it familiar to later Judaism. [51] The new feature in Paul is that Christ now replaces God as the Bridegroom, and the apostle replaces Moses as the best man. [52]

The allegorical reference of the bride/bridegroom image to Christ and His community is found in the NT not only in Paul but also in the Synoptists and Rev. [53] As Mk. 2:20 and par. show, the Synoptists, possibly in extension of the original sense, → 1103, applied the saying about the wedding-guests in Mk. 2:19a to Christ the Bridegroom. The new feature here as compared with Paul or any other NT reference is that the metaphor of the wedding is applied to the historical Jesus. The days of His earthly ministry were already wedding days for the disciples. This is harmonised with the eschatological application of the image by the saying about the violent wresting away of the Bridegroom. Mt. 25:1 ff. (as shown by the τότε of 25:1, the addition of v. 13 by the Evangelist, [54] and comparison with Lk. 13:25 ff.) is also applied by the Evangelist to the νυμφίος Christ, again in possible extension of the original sense, → 1104. The parable is now interpreted as a warning to the community not to allow the delay in the *parousia* to betray it into spiritual sloth and slumber (v. 13). [55]

In Rev. the image of the Messianic bridal community is found in the final chapters which depict the ultimate consummation: 19:7, 9; 21:2, 9; 22:17. But the image of the bride is not now, as formerly, referred to the earthly community. It applies to the heavenly Jerusalem which comes down to the transfigured earth when the millennial kingdom ends (21:10). The equation of the bride of the Lamb (21:9) with the Jerusalem which comes down from heaven (21:10) is based on 21:2, which, borrowing from Is. 61:10, says of the heavenly city of God that it is "prepared as a bride adorned for her husband." Final fulfilment, certainty of salvation, joy, hope and longing are all expressed in what is said here about the Lamb's wife.

It may be conjectured, though it cannot be proved, that the mythologically derived and widespread Hellenistic (esp. Gnostic) reference of the νυμφίος image to the Soter [56] exerted some influence on the NT Christ/νυμφίος allegory as it is

---

[50] Eph. 5:31 f. is to be taken eschatologically, cf. the fut. in v. 31, and cf. παριστάναι in v. 27 with 2 C. 11:2.

[51] Str.-B., I, 517, 844, 969, 970; III, 501, 822.

[52] PREl, 41 (Str.-B., I, 970); Ex. r., 46, 1 on 34, 1.

[53] On Jn. 3:29, → 1101.

[54] The exhortation γρηγορεῖτε is hardly in keeping with the parable, which censures the virgins, not for sleeping, but for having no oil.

[55] Mt. probably has the νυμφίος Christ in view in 22:2 also.

[56] The Gnostic texts have been assembled by J. C. Thilo, Acta S. Thomae Apostoli (1823), 121 ff., cf. also H. Gunkel, *Zum religionsgeschichtlichen Verständnis des NT* (1903), 59; W. Bousset, *Hauptprobleme d. Gnosis* (1907), 267 ff.; *Kyrios Christos*² (1921), 204 f., 207 f.; E. Norden, *Die Geburt des Kindes* (1924), 67 ff.; Reitzenstein Hell. Myst., 34 ff.; 245 ff.; H. Schlier, "Religionsgeschichtliche Untersuchungen zu den Ign.-Briefen," Beih. ZNW, 8 (1929), 88 ff.; "Christus u. d. Kirche im Eph.," *Beiträge zur historischen Theologie,*

first found in Paul.[57] What is certain is that only in the post-NT period did mysticism seize on the allegory, divest it of its eschatological content, and fatally link with it instead the sensual content of Hellenistic ἱερὸς γάμος ideas, → I, 656.

J. Jeremias

νῦν (ἄρτι)

(→ αἰών, I, 197, esp. 204; ἡμέρα, II, 943, esp. 951; καιρός, III, 455; σήμερον, ὥρα).

Contents: A. The Presuppositions of the NT Concept of νῦν: I. The Forms of the Word (νῦν, νυνί, ἄρτι). II. The Forms of Use (Adv., Noun, Adj.). III. The Non-Temporal νῦν: 1. νῦν as a Connecting Particle; 2. νῦν as a Particle of Logical Antithesis; 3. καὶ νῦν = Nevertheless. IV. The Temporal νῦν: 1. νῦν as a Limit of Time; 2. νῦν as a Period of Time; 3. νῦν with Reference to Past and Future. B. The NT Now: I. νῦν as the Divine Hour. II. νῦν as a Divinely Delineated Period: 1. The History of Christ as Present; 2. The NT νῦν between the Comings; a. Intimations; b. The Uniqueness of the NT νῦν; 3. The NT Still: a. In the Old Aeon; b. In the Time of Christ between the Comings; 4. The NT Already: a. νῦν in Parallelism with the Past; b. νῦν in Antithesis to the Past; c. νῦν as an Anticipation of the Last Things; d. νῦν as a Proleptic First Stage of the Last Things; 5. Stages of the NT Now; 6. Once and Now in the Life of the Individual Christian. III. νῦν with the Imperative: 1. νῦν in NT Exhortation. 2. νῦν in NT Prayer. IV. The Significance of the NT View of the Now.

A. The Presuppositions of the NT Concept of νῦν.

I. The Forms of the Word (νῦν, νυνί, ἄρτι).

For the concept "now" the Greek language, like many other Indo-European tongues which have related forms,[1] uses νῦν and νυνί (with a strengthening or epideictic -ί).[2]

Whereas νυνί is in the *koine* pap. at least as common as νῦν,[3] it is much less frequent in the bibl. *koine*. In the LXX it is more common in the much more literary Gk. of some books like Job, 2 and 4 Macc.,[4] in the NT it occurs almost exclusively[5] in the Pauline Epistles (not the Past.)[6] and Hb.

---

6 (1930), 57-59, 60-74; G. Bornkamm, "Mythos u. Legende in den apokryphen Thomas-Akten," FRL, NF, 31 (1933), 68-89.

[57] Bau. J. on 3:29; Wnd. 2 K. on 11:2; Dib. Gefbr. on Eph. 5:22-24; H. Schlier, *Christus u. d. Kirche im Eph.* (→ n. 56); Loh. Apk. on 19:7.

νῦν. A. Weiser, *Glaube u. Geschichte im AT* (1931); E. v. Dobschütz, "Zeit u. Raum im Denken d. Urchristentums," JBL, 41 (1922), 212-223; K. Bornhäuser, *Tage u. Stunden im NT* (1937); G. Delling, *Das Zeitverständnis d. NT* (1940); H. D. Wendland, *Geschichtsanschauung u. Geschichtsbewusstsein im NT* (1938); G. Schrenk, "Die Geschichtsanschauung d. Pls. auf dem Hintergrund seines Zeitalters," *Jbch. d. Theol. Schule Bethel*, 3 (1932), 59-86. On antiquity cf. the bibl. in n. 35.

[1] E.g., Lat. *nunc*, German *nun*, English "now" etc.; cf. Boisacq, *s.v.*

[2] Cf. K. Meisterhans, *Grammatik d. attischen Inschriften* (1900), 147 with n. 1267; in the NT the strengthening -ί is found only here, Bl.-Debr. § 64, 2. It is now hardly possible, however, to find any distinction between νῦν and νυνί, for νῦν δέ is often used in emphatic antitheses. Hence the readings often vacillate between νῦν δέ and νυνὶ δέ, as already in the LXX, e.g., Jos. 22:4; Job 4:5; for the NT cf. R. 11:30; 1 C. 12:18, 20; Phlm. 9; Hb. 8:6. Nevertheless, it is true that in logical antithesis Paul prefers νυνὶ δέ (→ 1109); cf. J. Weiss 1 K., 305, n. 2.

[3] Mayser, I², 3, 119, 44.

[4] Thackeray, 191, cf. p. 13, 15 f.

[5] Elsewhere only Ac. 22:1; 24:13, the only places in the NT where νυνί is not in an adversative relation; in Pl. and Hb. it is regularly followed by δέ (→ n. 2).

[6] Nägeli, 83, 86, 88.

Yet νῦν is not equally distributed over the whole of the NT. It is common only in Pl. (52 times), Lk. (39) and Jn. (28).[7]

In NT Gk. ἄρτι is almost synon.[8] with νῦν in its temporal senses. But it is much less common, and is not found at all in Mk., Lk., Ac., Past. or Hb.

II. The Forms of Use (Adverb, Noun, Adjective).

νῦν is strictly an adv., but in the NT, mostly in fixed phrases, it is also used as a noun and adj. (cf. in part also νυνί and ἄρτι, → n. 10).

1. A transitional form to use as a noun is the occasional use of νῦν and ἄρτι in dependence on prepositions: ἀπ' ἄρτι (Mt. 23:39; 26:29, 64), "from now on," in Jn. (13:19; 14:7) just "now";[9] ἕως ἄρτι (e.g., 1 Jn. 2:9, cf. ἕως νῦν, 1 Βασ. 1:16; 3 Βασ. 3:2) and ἄχρι νῦν (Ac. 13:31 vl., cf. μέχρι νῦν ψ 70:17; Ign. Mg., 8, 1), "until now."

2. But more commonly in such cases νῦν[10] is a noun: ἀπὸ τοῦ νῦν (= ἀπ' ἄρτι), frequent in the LXX (e.g., Is. 48:6; Tob. 7:12),[11] for the most part only in Lk. in the NT (1:48; 5:10 etc.; Ac. 18:6, though cf. 2 C. 5:16);[12] ἄχρι τοῦ νῦν, only in Pl. (Phil. 1:5; R. 8:22; cf. μέχρι τοῦ νῦν, 3 Macc. 6:28; 1 Esr. 6:19), = ἕως τοῦ νῦν,[13] only in the Synoptists (Mk. 13:19 = Mt. 24:21) and common in the LXX, e.g., Gn. 15:16; 1 Macc. 2:33. The phrase[14] emphasises either the great distance in time[15] (up to the present day, e.g., Dt. 12:9), or the uninterrupted nature of the process[16] (Mk. 13:19; cf. R. 8:22).

---

[7] Cf. J. C. Hawkins, *Horae Synopticae* (1899), 17, though he leaves the erroneous impression that νῦν is found only in the Gospels, Ac. and Pl.

[8] Cf. Poll. Onom., I, 72: ἄρτι, ὅ ἐστι πρὸ μικροῦ, καὶ νῦν δή, ὅ ἐστι ταὐτόν. How closely ἄρτι and νῦν approximate may be seen from a whole series of expressions which have their roots in either the one or the other. Like the class. ἄρτι, νῦν too can denote what has just happened, the immediate past (ἄρτι, e.g., Mt. 9:18; Rev. 12:10; in the LXX Da. 9:22; νῦν, Jn. 11:8 "just now"; 21:10 "now"). On the other hand, in the *koine* ἄρτι may, with νῦν, denote the present strictly as a pt. of time, e.g., Gl. 1:9 f., or as a period of time, e.g., 1 C. 13:12. Thus the two are almost completely interchangeable in the NT, cf. esp. Jn. 13:36 f.; cf. also Jos. Ant., 1, 125 etc., but cf. → n. 46.

[9] But not the vl. in Jn. 1:51 (in the sense of Mt. 26:64); may one conclude from this that the reading is not Johannine? As a counterpart to ἀπ' ἄρτι cf. ἀπὸ τότε in Lk. 16:16.

[10] Not so νυνί and ἄρτι, which are used only as adv. and occasionally as adj. (νυνί, Ac. 22:1; ἄρτι 1 C. 4:11, → 1108).

[11] For instances from secular Gk. *v.* Pr.-Bauer, *s.v.* νῦν and Deissmann NB, 81. Like ἀπ' ἄρτι in Jn. (→ *supra*), ἀπὸ τοῦ νῦν in the LXX often has the simple sense of "now" (e.g., Gn. 46:30; 3 Βασ. 18:29, also in the common phrase ἀπὸ τοῦ νῦν καὶ ἕως τοῦ αἰῶνος, e.g., ψ 113:26 [Ps. 115:18]; 130:3 etc.); it can also be taken this way in some Pauline passages, e.g., 2 C. 5:16.

[12] Hck. Lk. calls it a rare term peculiar to Lk. (in the Synoptists); Mt. has instead ἀπ' ἄρτι (cf. Mt. 26:29 with Lk. 22:18; Mt. 26:64 with Lk. 22:69). Deissmann NB, 80 f. thinks it was common formal speech, as shown by many stereotyped additions of the LXX: καὶ ἕως τοῦ αἰῶνος (e.g., ψ 120:8; 124:2, → n. 11), καὶ εἰς τὸν αἰῶνα (χρόνον) (Is. 9:6; 59:21; cf. 18:7; Mi. 4:7), εἰς τὸν ἅπαντα χρόνον (1 Macc. 11:36; cf. 15:8), etc.

[13] Schleusner, *NT Lex.*, *s.v.* supplies ὄντος καιροῦ or μέρους τοῦ χρόνου. This might be justified on the basis of 1 Esr. 6:19 (ἀπ' ἐκείνου μέχρι τοῦ νῦν), where χρόνου has to be added to ἐκείνου, but cf. on the use of τὸ νῦν (τὰ νῦν) Bl.-Debr. § 266, 1 and 2 (→ n. 17).

[14] ἕως τοῦ νῦν is a formal expression like ἀπὸ τοῦ νῦν (→ n. 12), chiefly in manifestly stereotyped combinations with ἀπ' ἀρχῆς κόσμου (κτίσεως) Mt. 24:21 (Mk. 13:19) or ἐκ παιδός (παιδιόθεν, νεότητος), Gn. 46:34 (47:3 cod. A; 2 Βασ. 19:8; cf. Ez. 4:14: ἀπὸ γενέσεώς μου) etc. (Ex. 10:6 is esp. rich). Counterparts are ἀπ' ἀρχῆς κόσμου ἕως τοῦ νῦν and ἀπὸ τοῦ νῦν (καὶ) εἰς τὸν αἰῶνα.

[15] Cf. the similar expressions ἄχρι τῆς ἡμέρας ταύτης, Ac. 2:29, μέχρι τῆς σήμερον, Mt. 11:23; cf. 28:15, ἕως (τῆς) σήμερον, Sir. 47:7 (8); 2 C. 3:15 (Mt. 27:8). In the LXX we almost always find the stereotyped ἕως τῆς σήμερον ἡμέρας (e.g., Gn. 19:37 f.; Ez. 2:3; R. 11:8 = Dt. 29:3) or ἕως τῆς ἡμέρας ταύτης (e.g., Dt. 29:3; Is. 39:6).

[16] Cf. the related expressions ἄχρι τῆς ἄρτι ὥρας (1 C. 4:11), ἄχρι τῆς σήμερον

3. Without prep., as an acc. of time, the noun νῦν is rarer in the sing.[17] than the plur.: τὰ νῦν (often written τανῦν)[18] has either a purely temporal sense (= νῦν,[19] Ac. 17:30) or a very weak meaning (καὶ τὰ νῦν, "and now" corresponding to the common introductory formula of the LXX, καὶ νῦν → n. 24, so Ac. 4:29 etc.).

4. Like all Gk. adverbs of time νῦν, νυνί and ἄρτι can also be used as attributive adj. between the art. and noun; this does not have to imply that an original παρών has been dropped (cf. ὁ νῦν παρὼν χρόνος, Soph. Trach., 174). In the NT we find the following expressions: ὁ νῦν αἰών (1 Tm. 6:17 etc. → 1114), ὁ νῦν καιρός (R. 3:26 etc., → 1114), ἡ νῦν Ἰερουσαλήμ (Gl. 4:25, → 1114), οἱ νῦν οὐρανοί (2 Pt. 3:7, → 1114), ζωὴ ἡ νῦν (1 Tm. 4:8, → 1120), ἡ πρὸς ὑμᾶς νυνὶ ἀπολογία (Ac. 22:1),[20] ἄχρι τῆς ἄρτι ὥρας (1 C. 4:11).[21]

III. The Non-Temporal νῦν.

The chief meaning of νῦν (νυνί) is in the sphere of time (→ *IV*). But its use is not restricted to this sphere. There is extension of meaning 1. by a weakening of the original temporal sense, 2. by a changing of the temporal antithesis to past or future into a logical antithesis.

1. νῦν as a Connecting Particle. The weakened meaning, which has lost temporal significance (cf. the German *nun*, where the weak meaning is the main sense of the root and other words have to be used for "now" as the temporal present) and is simply a particle, is connected outside the NT esp. with the enclitic form νύν (νύ),[22] which is found in the NT only in the expression ἄγε νῦν[23] (Jm. 4:13; 5:1). In the NT νῦν has this weak non-temporal sense in some expressions which are specifically Lucan: καὶ νῦν (Ac. 20:22, 25; 22:16 [differing from Jn. 11:22, → 1110], very common in the LXX, → n. 24); καὶ τὰ νῦν (Ac. 4:29; 5:38; 20:32 [? → 1113]; 27:22),[24] νῦν οὖν (Ac. 10:33; 15:10; 16:36; 23:15; often in the LXX, e.g., 4 Βασ. 18:20), also in the ex-

---

ἡμέρας (2 C. 3:14), ἄχρι ταύτης τῆς ἡμέρας (Ac. 23:1; 26:22); cf. also ἄχρι νῦν (Ac. 13:31 D etc.), ἄχρι τοῦ δεῦρο (R. 1:13). The same thought often occurs in the LXX expressions mentioned in → n. 15 ἕως τῆς σήμερον ἡμέρας (e.g., Nu. 22:30; Dt. 11:4) and ἕως τῆς ἡμέρας ταύτης (e.g., Ex. 10:6, esp. often Jer., e.g., 3:25; 11:7 [Θ]), which with this ambiguity are true equivalents of ἕως τοῦ νῦν.

[17] τὸ νῦν can be a true noun in the sense of "the present," e.g., Aristot. Phys., IV, 10, p. 218a, 6. It is also used adv. for "now," e.g., Ex. 9:27; Jos. Bell., 7, 240; Ps. Clem. Hom., 12, 2; Plat. Theaet., 187b, but not in the NT, only once (Ac. 24:25) τὸ νῦν ἔχον, "as concerns the present," "for now" (cf. Bl.-Debr. § 160), cf. also Tob. 7:11 A B (א has καὶ νῦν), also Luc. Tyr., 13 etc. τὸ νῦν εἶναι is related to the pleonastic εἶναι (e.g., Plat. Resp., VI, 506e), cf. τὸ πρίν = τότε, e.g., (Luc.) Philopatris, 1.

[18] Cf. Tisch. NT Prolegomena, 111.

[19] Like τὸ νῦν, τὰ νῦν can be a true noun for "present events," e.g., 1 Esr. 1:31 (33); Jdt. 9:5, but it is also an adv. = νῦν, cf. already in Attic (Gregorius Corinthius, De Dialecto Attica, 56: Ἀττικὸν καὶ τὸ λέγειν ἀντὶ τοῦ νῦν "τανῦν," ed. Schaefer [1811], p. 120, n. 71), e.g., Eur. Med., 494. But it does not occur in this sense in the LXX; for the NT cf. Ac. 17:30 and perhaps also 20:32 (though → n. 24). The temporal element is particularly strong in phrases like τὰ νῦν τάδε (e.g., Hdt., 7, 104) and τὰ νῦν ταῦτα (e.g., Alciphr. Ep., III, 22 and 71).

[20] Cf. Plat. Theaet., 153e: ὁ ἄρτι λόγος, "the assertion just made."

[21] Cf. P. Lond., 121, 373: ἐν τῇ ἄρτι ὥρᾳ.

[22] Cf. Liddell-Scott, *s.v.* II; Pass., *s.v.*, 2a.

[23] In use elsewhere (Aristoph. Pax, 1056; Vesp., 381) this is the accent, as with similar imperatives (ἴθι, φέρε, σπεῦδε). On the question whether we are to read νῦν in R. 11:31 and 8:1 → n. 43 and n. 71. On νῦν and imp. → 1121.

[24] καὶ τὰ νῦν (also, e.g., Test. L. 10:1) seems to be a form of direct speech in Ac., but not the Gospels. The corresponding LXX formula (also Test. XII) καὶ νῦν (which falls under the strongly Semitic use of καί) is mostly in direct speech (e.g., Mi. 4:9, 11; Am. 7:16 etc.; Test. L. 14:1; 16:1 etc.), esp. in prayers (cf. Ac. 4:29 → 1122, esp. Da., e.g., 9:17, also Jon. 4:3; Is. 64:8) and admonitions (→ 1121, e.g., Ἱερ. 49[42]:19; Is. 2:10; Test. S. 3:1; L. 13:1 etc.), though also to introduce direct speech (e.g., Jl. 2:12; Hag. 1:5) and in other ways (e.g., Da. 8:26; Ez. 19:13).

pression νῦν (νυνὶ) δέ (cf. 1 C. 14:6 [25] and R. 7:17), [26] also the simple νῦν (Lk. 11:39, perhaps also 1 Th. 3:8). Like their Heb. equivalent וְעַתָּה, these expressions hardly have any greater weight than the connecting particles δέ, γέ, οὖν (cf. esp. Jos. 14:10 ff.).

2. νῦν as a Particle of Logical Antithesis. The same νῦν, however, can also have a very heavy stress when used to oppose something factually valid to a hypothetical but erroneous assumption or an incorrect idea. There is here a shift of meaning from "in the present" to "in actuality." Usually this logical νυνὶ (or νῦν) δέ [27] is preceded, then, by a hypothetical conditional statement. [28] An analogy may be found in the Aram. אִלּוּ ... וְכַדוּן, e.g., Tg. J. I on Gn. 3:22, [29] but it is not found in the LXX, and since it is common in class. Gk. (e.g., Thuc., 4, 126; Aristot. An., II, 1, 8, p. 412b, 15) [30] the NT use conforms to accepted Hell. style.

The NT statements with νυνὶ δέ show particularly impressively what the NT reckons, and would have reckoned, as decisive realities in the world. Almost always we find that facts are set in opposition to a supposition when νῦν (νυνὶ) δέ is used, e.g., the ungodly attitude of men, or the Jews (esp. in Jn., 8:40; 9:41; 15:22, 24; also Lk. 19:42; [31] Jm. 4:16, → n. 28), or divine facts, whether in opposition to earthly human reality (Jn. 18:36; 1 C. 7:14; Hb. 8:6; 11:16) or to erroneous thoughts (1 C. 12:18, 20; also 5:11 [32] and esp. 15:20; [33] Hb. 9:26).

---

[25] νῦν δέ = *quae cum ita sint*, cf. H. Heinrici, Bachmann and J. Weiss, *ad loc.*

[26] Ltzm. R., Althaus *NT Deutsch, ad loc.*: "but then"; Winer[5] (1844), § 67, 7: "but now," "now that I have made this observation"; "thus" is also a correct rendering (Albrecht). The exertions of Zahn, *ad loc.*, to construct an antithesis here are artificial, and the basic distinction ([3], 355) of three successive states in Paul is quite unconvincing.

[27] Cf. Buttmann § 151, 26; Jn. prefers νῦν δέ, Pl. νυνὶ δέ (→ n. 2).

[28] The places where this is not so are only apparent exceptions. In 1 C. 7:14 the saying with ἐπεί, and in Lk. 19:42 the desire with εἰ, are unreal. In Jm. 4:15, where the logical train of thought is far from smooth, we should supplement as follows: If you were true Christians you would say "If God wills," but instead of doing so (v. 16) you boast in your ungodliness etc. Where there is no hypothetical statement one may conclude that the use of νυνὶ δέ is not the logically adversative, e.g., R. 7:17 (→ n. 26) and 1 C. 13:13. Here the temporal sense is ruled out, since the καταργεῖσθαι which is the opp. of μένειν (vv. 8 ff.) applies only to the fut., i.e., the other *charismata* remain for the present. But a logical antithesis would have to be constructed (cf. J. Weiss, *ad loc.*). Hence νυνὶ δέ is here very close to a simple ἀλλά, which for its part can also be used after hypotheses when elsewhere one finds νυνὶ δέ, e.g., M. Ant., II, 11, cf. J. Weiss, 1 K., 355, n. 4: "But there remain," in contrast to the things of earth which are transitory and imperfect, "(now and to eternity) faith, hope, love." To the objection of J. Weiss that πίστις and ἐλπίς will be superfluous and will be discarded at the *parousia* it may be answered that their function will indeed cease, but in the NT their meaning includes the content of faith (e.g., Gl. 3:23 ff.) or hope (cf. esp. Col. 1:5, where the three again stand together), and this will remain to all eternity. Like νυνὶ δέ here, the Lat. *nunc* is also used in the sense of *sed*, e.g., Cic. Divin., I, 29; Tac. Ann., 2, 71. But the context would also permit of "hence," cf. Herwerden, *s.v.*

[29] Cf. J. Weiss on 1 C. 5:11.

[30] Cf. on this the ed. of F. A. Trendelenburg[3] (1877), 272, also the refs. in Pape, *s.v.* νῦν. Related to this construction is the use of εἰ statements and νῦν δέ in the comparisons of the philosophical diatribe, except that here the figure and the matter are related, not the hypothetical and the real; cf. R. Bultmann, *Der Stil d. paul. Predigt u. d. kynisch-stoische Diatribe* (1910), 42 with n. 7.

[31] Here the preceding ἐν τῇ ἡμέρᾳ ταύτῃ itself makes it clear that νῦν cannot be understood in the sense of a temporal antithesis.

[32] Paul is here championing God's claim that His community should be pure in opposition to the probably malicious misunderstanding of the Corinthians.

[33] It is in some sense true that R. 3:21 is a striking par. to 1 C. 15:20, so J. Weiss, *ad loc.*: "'But now,' God be praised, all this is purely academic dialectic, and in reality 'Christ is risen.'" But the temporal factor predominates in the νυνὶ δέ of R. 3:21, cf. esp. v. 26,

3. καὶ νῦν, "nevertheless." The use of καὶ νῦν in Jn. 11:22 is related. Here, too, a hypothetical conditional clause is assumed. With νυνὶ δέ the condition would run: But now he has died. Mary, however, says: καὶ νῦν οἶδα, "even so, I know."[34] To the conviction of faith there thus corresponds, not the earthly reality, but the even greater certainty of a divine reality.

IV. The Temporal νῦν.

1. νῦν as a Limit of Time. By nature νῦν is a limiting concept. It is the limit between past and future which is sharp, but which cannot be grasped because it is always fleeting.[35] It is thus the boundary a. at the end and b. at the beginning of specific periods.

a. At the End. In detail νῦν, often in stereotyped formulae like ἕως τοῦ νῦν (→ n. 14) etc., denotes the provisional boundary of the world (Mt. 24:21 and par.; R. 8:22),[36] of individual human life (e.g., Gn. 46:34; Ez. 4:14), of the age of grace (Nu. 14:19), but also of the time of the hardening of Israel (cf. 2 C. 3:14) etc. (cf. also Phil. 1:5; 1 C. 4:11, 13). Only once in the NT, so far as I can see, does ἄρτι seem to have this sense of a definitive limit, at Jn. 16:24: ἕως ἄρτι οὐκ ᾐτήσατε οὐδὲν τῷ ὀνόματί μου, in the future it will be different — the continuation might be introduced by (ἀπὸ τοῦ) νῦν δέ — in the future pray in my

---

→ n. 70; → 1114 f.; this may also be perceived elsewhere, e.g., Hb. 8:6; cf. also Aristid. Apol., 13, 7: ... νυνὶ δὲ οἱ νόμοι καλοί εἰσι καὶ δίκαιοι, obviously an allusion to R. 7:12. The preceding conditional clause contains a feigned assumption which is reduced *ad absurdum*. Cf. also Chrys. Hom. in Jo. 20:2, MPG, 59, 126.

[34] Formally similar is Xenoph. An., 7, 4, 24; 7, 7, 17; perhaps also Is. 40:28. Essentially different is the νῦν οἴδαμεν in Jn. 16:30 (→ 1119).

[35] This is the concept of the Now which Gk. philosophy developed and worked at until exhausted. In part., Aristot. and the Stoic and Sceptical school influenced by him undertook to examine the Now and its relation to time in general. But they contributed little to the NT understanding, for the Gks., for all their reflection, were entangled in formal and fruitless theorising. Aristot. deals with the problem of time in his Physics, esp. Bk. IV. His treatment "abounds in difficulties, puzzles and contradictions" (A. Torstrik, "Über d. Abhandlung d. Aristot. von d. Zeit. Phys. Δ, 10 ff.," Philol., 26 [1867], 523). τὸ νῦν is for him the indivisible boundary between two stretches of time. It relates to infinitely divisible time as does a mathematical pt. to a line (τὸ νῦν τὸ ἄτομον οἷον στιγμὴ γραμμῆς ἐστιν, VI, 3, p. 233b, 33). Hence it is no part of time (οὐδὲ μόριον τὸ νῦν τοῦ χρόνου, IV, 11, p. 220a, 19), though there are other statements to the contrary (cf., VI, 6, p. 237a, 5 f.: τοῦτο γάρ ἐστιν τὸ ὁρίζον καὶ τὸ μεταξὺ τῶν νῦν χρόνος). The limiting aspect of time is most impressively worked out by him: τὸ νῦν τελευτὴ καὶ ἀρχὴ χρόνου, ... τοῦ μὲν παρήκοντος τελευτή, ἀρχὴ δὲ τοῦ μέλλοντος (IV, 13, p. 222a, 33). In relation to the NT use it should be emphasised that νῦν is always taken in the strict sense of the present moment; νῦν in relation to a longer period finds no place in the sharp definition of Aristot. Stoicism used the same categories as Aristot. With the infinite divisibility of time it establishes the principle that in the strict sense no time is present (Chrysipp. Fr., 509; II, 164, v. Arnim: οὐδεὶς ὅλως ἐνίσταται χρόνος), and that τὸ νῦν is not strict time, i.e., a space of time, but a boundary (πέρας χρόνου, cf. Archedemus Tarsensis Fr., 14; III, 263, v. Arnim) which on the one side is still the past and on the other already the future (Fr., 517; II, 165, v. Arnim: ... τοῦ ἐνεστηκότος χρόνου τὸ μὲν μέλλον εἶναι, τὸ δὲ παρεληλυθός). On the other hand Stoicism also affirms that only the present truly "is" (ὑπάρχει) because the past no longer "is" and the future "is" not yet (cf. Fr., 509, 518; II, 164 f., v. Arnim; and on this Plut. Comm. Not., 41; II, 1081c-f). This thesis, then, rests on the equation of the terms "to be" and "to be present" — which is in fact a confusion of concepts. The resultant sophisms determine the Sceptics' view of time, e.g., in Sext. Emp. εἰ ἔστι χρόνος (Math., X, 169-247), where the present is said to be beyond our grasp because it is already the past and still future (cf. esp. 200 ff.). This leads to complete scepticism in relation to time generally.

name. In most cases, however, ἕως ἄρτι has lost most of its character as a boundary, e.g., 1 C. 8:7; 1 Jn. 2:9: ἕως ἄρτι, "until now"; it has lost it altogether at Jn. 5:17, for there is no temporal limit to God's work: ἕως ἄρτι = ἀεί.[37]

b. At the Beginning. Whereas the terminal boundary denoted by νῦν (and ἄρτι) is mostly fluid, since it moves back each moment as the Now advances, the character of the term as a limit is much more strong and fundamental when it marks the beginning of periods. In the Bible these are usually in some sense divinely appointed periods (→ B. II), whether the age of salvation for the world, the new aeon (e.g., Mi. 4:7; Is. 9:6; 59:21; cf. 18:7, → n. 12), or the time of salvation for the Gentiles, which also means the rejection of the Jews (Ac. 18:6), or the time of personal blessing, e.g., in the case of Mary (Lk. 1:48) or Peter (Lk. 5:10). In many ways the end of Jesus is a starting-point, namely, the beginning of the time between the comings, which is a time of separation and distress for the disciples and the world (Lk. 22:18 and par.; Mt. 23:39), the time of the Messianic woes (Lk. 12:52), but which is already for Christ a period of lordship (Lk. 22:69 and par.), for this νῦν is both the point of His deepest abasement and also the starting-point of His exaltation.

2. νῦν as a Period of Time. In the case of νῦν, however, the concept of a temporal limit may be extended until it is a concept of temporal duration. The point becomes a line. That is, νῦν in the NT may denote not merely a decisive point of time but also the present second of eternity, e.g., in formal expressions like Phil. 1:20: ὡς πάντοτε καὶ νῦν (cf. Plat. Conv., 212b: νῦν καὶ ἀεί), 2 Pt. 3:18: καὶ νῦν καὶ εἰς ἡμέραν αἰῶνος, Jd. 25: πρὸ παντὸς τοῦ αἰῶνος καὶ νῦν καὶ εἰς πάντας τοὺς αἰῶνας.[38] This may stretch over a longer period, as in the adjectival use of νῦν (→ 1108): ὁ νῦν αἰών, ὁ νῦν καιρός. The most important and frequent use of νῦν in this way is for the period between the comings. If on the one side, as indicated above, νῦν is in some Synoptic verses the starting-point of this time, on the other it embraces in its fulness the whole of the period, → 1114.

3. νῦν with Reference to Past and Future. In the light of this NT extension of νῦν to longer periods of time, one may easily see why here too, as in classical Greek, it can sometimes be used for past and future events.[39]

The formalism of these views of time stands out most strongly against the background of the reality of time, and esp. the Now, in the NT. Recognition of the limiting aspect of the Now is the only feature of significance in relation to the NT. But in the NT νῦν as a limit belongs to the relevant period, for in the strict sense it is not the boundary but the given present, cf. Zn. R., 405, n. 14. On this whole question cf. H. Eibl, "Das Problem d. Zeit bei den alten Denkern," *Archiv f. syst. Philosophie*, 27 (1922), 67-87, 153-170; J. Steffens, *Die Entwicklung des Zeitbegriffs in d. griech. Philosophie bis Plato* (Diss. Bonn, 1911); A. Torstrik, *op. cit.*, 446-523; Delling, 12 ff. For grammatical aspects cf. Debrunner, *Indogerm. Forschungen*, 48 (1930), 13 ff.

[36] Cf. Cl. Al. Prot., I, 7, 4: The serpent καταδουλοῦται καὶ αἰκίζεται εἰσέτι νῦν τοὺς ἀνθρώπους.

[37] Cf. Bultmann J., 183, n. 7 on Jn. 5:17; cf. μέχρι νῦν in Ign. Mg., 8, 1, also Qoh. 4:2: ὅσοι αὐτοὶ ζῶσιν ἕως τοῦ νῦν.

[38] Wnd. Kath. Br., *ad loc.*: For God the Now has an eternity both before it (Prv. 8:23; 1 C. 2:7) and behind it (Da. 2:20 etc.; Lk. 1:33; R. 1:25 etc.). Here αἰών means world period, as Delling rightly pts. out (43) in relation to the similar expression in Sib., 8, 67, though this is Christian and is influenced by NT expressions, even if some of the later parts of the LXX might also have served as models (→ I, 200, n. 10).

[39] Eustath. Thessal. Comm. in Il., II, p. 164: τὸ νῦν κατὰ τοὺς παλαιοὺς τοὺς τρεῖς χρόνους δηλοῖ, τὸν ἐνεστῶτα, τὸν παρῳχημένον καὶ τὸν μέλλοντα, cf. Hesych., *s.v.*

a. νῦν and ἄρτι with the preterite [40] mostly refer to what has just happened, esp. ἄρτι (Mt. 9:18; Rev. 12:10) but also νῦν (Mt. 26:65; Jn. 21:10; cf. LXX, e.g., Jos. 5:14), or to what is not too distant (Jn. 11:8; Ac. 7:52). But in many cases (cf. R. 11:30 f.; Jn. 8:52 as well as Ac. 7:52) νῦν refers not merely to the once-for-all event in the preterite, but rather to the process or state initiated by it. [41]

b. Analogically [42] νῦν, in virtue of its strong relation to the present, can also refer to the near [43] future. [44] The LXX makes considerable use of this future νῦν, e.g., to announce divine chastisements (e.g., Ex. 9:14 f. [ἐν τῷ νῦν καιρῷ = νῦν]; Jer. 7:13) and blessings (e.g., Is. 29:22). In the NT Jn. 12:31; R. 11:31 (→ n. 43), and perhaps also Phil. 1:20 (→ 1111) are the only examples, [45] though cf. ἄρτι in Mt. 26:53. These all express the certainty of faith of Jesus and His apostle.

B. The NT Now.

I. νῦν as the Divine Hour.

νῦν (and even more precisely ἄρτι) [46] denotes in the strict sense only a στιγμὴ χρόνου (Lk. 4:5), but since such moments can become a καιρός, each of them is intrinsically significant. From the apparently endless chain of hours, however,

---

[40] Cf. Hom. Il., 3, 439 : νῦν Μενέλαος ἐνίκησεν, Luc. Soloec., 2 : οὐδὲ νῦν ἔγνως, 3 : τὸ γὰρ νῦν ῥηθέν, often also in Plat., e.g., Prot., 329c : ἃ νῦν δὴ ἐγὼ ἔλεγον. Acc. to Timaeus, Λέξεις Πλατωνικαί, *s.v.*, νῦν δή is chiefly used with the preterite (though also the fut., → n. 44), but νῦν indicates the present. For further instances from secular Gk. cf. Liddell-Scott, *s.v.*; Pr.-Bauer, *s.v.*; cf. also Bultmann J., 303, n. 8.

[41] Cf. Pr.-Bauer, *s.v.* on the aor. with νῦν.

[42] On this analogy cf. the two renderings of Da. 11:2 : LXX καὶ νῦν ἦλθον ὑποδεῖξαί σοι, Θ καὶ νῦν ... ἀναγγελῶ σοι (but → 1108 with n. 24), also Is. 51:3.

[43] The difficult passage R. 11:31, already adduced as an example of νῦν with the preterite, seems to be an exception : οὗτοι (sc. the Jews) νῦν ἠπείθησαν ... ἵνα καὶ αὐτοὶ νῦν ἐλεηθῶσιν. There are four possible solutions to the riddle of the second νῦν : 1. with much of the tradition (also P[46]) to excise it on material grounds (Zn. R., 527 f., n. 76); but the attestation by א, B and D* is too strong ; 2. to take it as an enclitic νύν; but this is unusual in Paul (→ 1108); 3. to understand it as the eternal Now, the day of Christ, within which the conversion of the Jews will come (cf. Barth R., *ad loc.*); but the NT knows no *nunc aeternum,* no dialectical Now, which would finally negate biblical eschatology ; 4. rightly understood, this νῦν is the typical NT stage of transition (→ 1115), and since Paul in R. is still expecting an imminent *parousia* (cf. 13:11) the blessing of the Jews is expected any moment now in the νῦν of transition between the comings (cf. Ltzm. R., *ad loc.*).

[44] Cf. Xenoph. Cyrop. 4, 1, 23 : νῦν δὴ σὺ δηλώσεις, Plat. Leg., XII, 962d : νῦν δὴ μαθησόμεθα ὅτι θαυμαστὸν οὐδέν, cf. also Resp., I, p. 353a, Soph., 221c; Luc. Soloec., 8 : ἴσως μὲν οὐδὲ νῦν δυνήσομαι. Although there innumerable examples of νῦν with the fut. in class. lit., the Atticist Lucian, if the dial. Pseudosophista is authentic, regards it as a solecism ; cf. Soloec., 9 : ὑβριστὴς ἐγὼ νῦν δὴ γενήσομαί σοι διαλεγόμενος; ἔοικε δὲ σολοικίσαι τὸ "νῦν δὴ γενήσομαι," σὺ δ' οὐκ ἔγνως, cf. *ibid.*, 1: ἐπεὶ ὄφελον καὶ νῦν ἀκολουθῆσαι δυνήσῃ : on the supposed twofold solecism here cf. on the one side Jn. 13:36 f. (νῦν and ἄρτι in the fut. sense) and on the other Gl. 5:12 (ὄφελον with fut.). The case is rather different with ἄρτι and fut. This is a later and inferior use, cf. Phryn. Ecl., 12 and Rutherford, *ad loc.*, but also Appian De Bello Mithridatico, 69; Aesop Fabulae, 326, 7 Chambry [142 Schaefer, 81 de Furia ; this reading is not found in Halm, 386]: τεθνήξῃ ἄρτι. For further details cf. Pass., *s.v.* ἄρτι); Plat. would in such cases say αὐτίκα, μάλα, αὖθις or the like instead of ἄρτι. But in Hell. Gk. ἄρτι approximates so closely in meaning to νῦν (→ n. 8) that ἄρτι with the fut. becomes linguistically tolerable. Cf. also Luc., Editio Bipontina, IX, 445 ff., 494 ff.; Timaeus Sophista, Plat. Lexicon ed. D. Ruhnken (1789), 186, n. 4.

[45] The other texts adduced (Jn. 16:5; 17:13; Lk. 2:29) are not relevant here, → 1119; 1118.

[46] Cf. Mt. 26:53 (ἄρτι, "in a moment," "at once"); 2 Cl., 17, 3 (ἄρτι, "now," "for the moment," "so long as you are in the service of God"); here νῦν would not be suitable, since it does not have sufficient temporal pregnancy.

some stand out because on them the accent of eternity especially falls with its demand and gift. As God's οἰκονομία chooses men and nations, so it chooses specific hours for its purposes. In the OT, e.g., such an hour is that of Jos. 5:14, where God intervenes in history through the leader of His host. In the NT we might refer to Lk. 5:10, the call of the disciples, or Ac. 18:6, the commitment to Gentile missions, or Ac. 20:32, the beginning of the post-apostolic period. In particular, mention should be made of the νῦν of the exodus of Jesus, which is given distinctive form in Jn. (12:27;[47] 13:31;[48] 16:5; 17:13) and which Lk. shows to be a significant turning-point with his peculiar formula (→ n. 12) ἀπὸ τοῦ νῦν: 12:52; 22:18 and par. (cf. Mt. 23:39: [ἀπ' ἄρτι]); 22:69 and par. In the last of these passages Jesus anticipates His glorification and even His coming again in a paradoxical ἀπὸ τοῦ νῦν, cf. the "transfiguration" in Jn. 12:27 ff.: Now even in this state of humiliation, the exaltation begins.[49]

II. νῦν as the Divinely Delineated Period.

1. The History of Christ as Present.

But there is something special about this hour of all hours, as about the whole history of Christ. The distinctive emphasis of the Gospel is certainly on the fact that God once (→ ἅπαξ, I, 381 ff.) gave a completely new turn to the history of mankind. But in NT proclamation this new turn is not just past. It has present power; it has for Christians the full weight of the νῦν, cf. R. 5:9; Col. 1:22; 2 Tm. 1:10; R. 16:26 (with the addition found in Orig.),[50] perhaps also Hb. 9:26 (→ 1109, cf. v. 24), and Cl. Al. Prot., I, 7, 4. Analogous to this cosmic turn is that which takes place in the life of the individual, the decision for or against Christ. This, too, has contemporary weight, cf. R. 11:30; 1 Pt. 2:25; R. 11:31.

The "remarkable overleaping of historical distance" which is to be seen here finds an important OT parallel in the making contemporary of the initial election of Israel in Dt.[51] and esp. the prophets.[52] God's ancient people had the sense of being in this state of election and salvation, and this sense is a prototype of NT awareness of living in the νῦν of the history of Christ, → 1114.

Two important features of the NT νῦν are thus brought to light: 1. history is experienced as the present; 2. νῦν is in the NT predominantly a period with eternal significance. It is distinctive of this NT νῦν, however, that in it the future is also experienced as the present. This leads us to the next point.

---

47 Cf. Bultmann J., *ad loc.* (327, n. 7).

48 Cf. Jn. 17:5. Acc. to Bultmann's reconstruction this is the request which Jesus declares to be fulfilled in the νῦν of 13:31.

49 This is a shortening of perspective, as often in the Bible (cf. *NT Deutsch,* Schn. on Mt. 26:64). It is not a conception which differs from expectation and proclamation elsewhere, as though Jesus would go straight to His heavenly glory without resurrection, cf. J. Weiss, *Urchristentum* (1917), 19 f.; on Lk. 16:25 → 1119, on 22:69 → *supra*; on Jn. 16:5 and 17:13 → 1119; only Lk. 23:43 causes difficulty, but cf. E. Stauffer, *Die Theologie d. NT* (1941), 190.

50 μυστηρίου ... φανερωθέντος ... νῦν διὰ ... τῆς ἐπιφανείας τοῦ κυρίου ἡμῶν (accepted by Zahn). The work as well as the person of Christ is always present. We have a different conception, however, when Mithras is thought to be the living present, as compared with his attendants, *cantes* and *cantopates,* the beginning and the end, cf. A. Schütze, *Mithras-Mysterien u. Urchristentum* [1937], 31; this is a personification or even an apotheosis of the Now.

51 Weiser, 70 ff.; G. v. Rad, *Das Gottesvolk im Dt.* (1929), 60 ff.

52 Weiser, 85 ff.; K. Galling, "Die Geschichte als Wort Gottes bei d. Propheten," ThBl, 1929, 171; J. Hempel, *AT u. Geschichte* (1930), 29 ff.

2. The NT νῦν between the Comings.

a. Intimations. As in the case of the past seen from the standpoint of the present, so the viewing of the future from this perspective finds parallels in the OT. The prophets did not merely threaten judgment (e.g., Jer. 4:12) and promise salvation (Is. 33:10 f.). They also declared judgment (Is. 3:8) and salvation (Is. 48:7) to be taking place already as νῦν. Nevertheless, it is a general rule in the OT that every Now looks forward again to a new Then. The νῦν of the OT is always awaiting the expected turning-point; that of the NT coincides with it.[53]

Further intimations of the specific νῦν of the NT are to be seen in expressions relating to the doctrine of the two aeons which borrow from Jewish usage and which extend the period denoted by the νῦν to the whole length of this aeon: ὁ νῦν αἰών, "the present state of the world" in the Past. (2 Tm. 4:10; 1 Tm. 6:17; Tt. 2:12),[54] ἡ νῦν Ἰερουσαλήμ (Gl. 4:25), i.e., the community of the old covenant which is correlative to the present aeon, and οἱ νῦν οὐρανοὶ καὶ ἡ γῆ (2 Pt. 3:7), the form of the world between the disasters of the flood and the destruction of the world by fire (v. 6 f., 10, 12).

b. The Uniqueness of the NT νῦν. The expressions just quoted, especially that from 2 Pt. 3, already give to νῦν the value of an interim period. This value, which is peculiar to the NT, may be illustrated by a spatial image. The NT Now is like a range of mountains between two countries. It belongs to both and looks out on both. In literal terms, it is a transitional time between two times, namely, between the two comings, the first of which marks the beginning of the new aeon and the second the (definitive) end of the old. Hence this distinctive νῦν in which we still live belongs to both aeons.[55]

For those who live in this period the present is both a "still" (still in the old aeon) and an "already" (already in the new), and each is characterised by antithesis, whether to the new or to the old. This sense, which is typical of the NT Now, shows, of course, that the twilight nature of the time to which the NT νῦν refers is not related to the word as such but is experienced unequivocally either in the sense of the "still" or in that of the "already."

Paul is characterised by an expression which he almost always uses with reference to the time between the comings:[56] ὁ νῦν καιρός.[57] This is for Israel the time of the remnant of grace between its period as God's people and its reacceptance at the end (R. 11:5). For Christians it is on the one hand the time of suffering between joy at the presence of the Bridegoom and His reappearance

---

[53] Delling, 134 f.; cf. K. Galling, *loc. cit.*

[54] Cf. also the vl. in Mt. 12:32: οὔτε ἐν τῷ νῦν αἰῶνι οὔτε ἐν τῷ μέλλοντι. The temporal sense is also weakened in the Vulgate, which in all three passages from the Past. has *hoc saeculum* (elsewhere ὁ αἰὼν οὗτος or οὗτος ὁ αἰών Bl.-Debr.[6], 306), i.e., "this world," for *saeculum* follows αἰών in eliminating the temporal aspect.

[55] Though cf., e.g., Rgg. (Hb.[2, 3], 250), who maintains that acc. to all NT teaching the αἰὼν μέλλων begins only at the *parousia*. Delling, 101 rightly **pts.** out in answer that the Now of the NT is an eschatological present, which is to be understood, not as a dialectical paradox, but quite soberly as the time both of fulfilment and also of promise. On the Now which lasts until the consummation of all things cf. also Cl. Al. Prot., 84, 6.

[56] Only once (2 C. 8:14) is ἐν τῷ νῦν καιρῷ ("now," "for now") used by Paul without ref. to the time of Christ.

[57] In a few LXX passages ὁ νῦν καιρός is a time of either blessing (Gn. 29:34; 30:20) or punishment (Ex. 9:14). In the main the expression is not related in the OT to Messianic conceptions or eschatology.

(R. 8:18), and on the other the time of the unique revelation of God's righteousness between the period of the ἀνοχή τοῦ θεοῦ and the final judgment (R. 3:26).[58]

Similarly, ὁ καιρὸς οὗτος[59] in two Synoptic texts denotes this distinctive interim period. It is the Messianic period which the Jews have failed to see (Lk. 12:56). "This time," the unique significance of the νῦν, is seen only by him to whom the Messianic secret of Jesus has been disclosed in faith. For the specific aspect of this νῦν is itself part of the Messianic secret. For Christians, however, "this time" (Mk. 10:30) is a period of suffering εἵνεκεν τῆς βασιλείας τοῦ θεοῦ (Lk. 18:29 f.), as it is also already a time of divine retribution.

The present (ὁ καιρὸς ὁ ἐνεστηκώς) of Hb. (9:9) is also the time of Christ between His first coming and the *parousia* (v. 28). Here already the whole stress is on the contrast with the past, the time of παραβολαί and the δικαιώματα σαρκός. This present is already καιρὸς διορθώσεως, the time of the fulfilment of that which they prefigured.

3. The NT Still.

The unique present of the NT takes on different colours according to the angle of vision.

a. In the first instance it is part of the old aeon, the time of God's work as Creator (Jn. 5:17 ὁ πατήρ μου ἕως ἄρτι ἐργάζεται), but also of the fallen creation, which συστενάζει καὶ συνωδίνει ἄχρι τοῦ νῦν in the δουλεία τῆς φθορᾶς (R. 8:21 f.), and in which it is possible that one ἐν τῇ σκοτίᾳ ἐστὶν ἕως ἄρτι (1 Jn. 2:9).

b. But the darkness of this aeon is not due merely to the nature of this aeon. It belongs to the basic structure of the time of Christ between the comings. This is in view in Lk. 6 with its νῦν of unequal distribution (v. 21, 25) or in Jn. 16 with its corresponding νῦν of the suffering of disciples and the rejoicing of the world (v. 22, 20).[60] For this νῦν began with Christ (Lk. 12:52: ἀπὸ τοῦ νῦν there commences the tragic division of families, 22:36: νῦν is the time in which one must be ready for hardship and conflict), and it will also end with Christ[61]

---

[58] On the other hand ὁ νῦν καιρός in Barn., 4, 1 and 18, 2 obviously refers to this wicked aeon in contrast to the new divine aeon (ὁ μέλλων sc. καιρός, 4, 1). It is still used, or used again, in the sense of the pre-Christian, apocalyptic border between the aeons. The sense that after Christ the present, though still a time of distress, is already a time of salvation, may be seen to dwindle after the NT.

[59] It may thus be said that neither ὁ καιρὸς οὗτος nor ὁ νῦν καιρός is used for "this aeon" in the NT any more than is καιρὸς ἐρχόμενος (or μέλλων, cf. Barn., 4, 1) or ἐκεῖνος for "that aeon." For these only expressions with αἰών are used (→ 1114, → I, 204 ff.; it seems to me that Sasse → I, 205 f. is wrong not to distinguish between ὁ αἰὼν οὗτος and ὁ καιρὸς οὗτος). The one exception at Lk. 18:30; Mk. 10:30 is only an apparent exception. Here the time remaining before the end is contrasted with the new aeon — hence the change from καιρός to αἰών — not the one aeon with the other as in Mt. 12:32. Only outside the NT does the phrase ἐκεῖνος ὁ καιρός denote the new aeon (cf. S. Bar. 74:2). In the NT, except at Eph. 2:12 where it denotes the pre-Christian period, it serves as a connecting formula (Mt. 11:25; Ac. 12:1), the original sense of contemporaneity (cf. ἐν αὐτῷ τῷ καιρῷ, e.g., Lk. 13:1) being thereby weakened as in the case of the εὐθύς or εὐθέως of Mk. and Mt. Apart from Mk. 10:30 and Lk. 12:56 ὁ καιρὸς οὗτος occurs only in R. 9:9 (in a quotation) with reference to an individual promise.

[60] Acc. to the eschatological schema of Jn. (cf. v. 32) the fut. χαρήσεται is already present like the fut. λυπηθήσεσθε (cf. v. 20 with v. 22).

[61] This period is thus bounded by the two most striking points in world history, the beginning and end of the coming of the kingdom of God, Delling, 126.

(R. 8:18; 1 Pt. 1:6 f.: ὀλίγον ἄρτι ... λυπηθέντες before the ἀποκάλυψις Ἰησοῦ Χριστοῦ, cf. also 2 C. 4:17 W. text: τὸ παραυτίκα πρόσκαιρον καὶ ἐλαφρὸν τῆς θλίψεως).

In this time of Christ the world is still the world. It is not yet under Christ's dominion (Hb. 2:8) but in the power of the devil (Eph. 2:2). Nevertheless, the tension of the νῦν of the world presses towards a τότε of the victory of Christ (cf. the interplay of νῦν, ἤδη, ἄρτι, τότε in 2 Th. 2:6-8). To this world, i.e., to the υἱοὶ τῆς ἀπειθείας of Eph. 2:2, the Jews also belong according to the NT (the Fourth Gospel), in development of the prophetic νῦν, R. 11:31: νῦν ἠπείθησαν. This is why they understand neither their own Scriptures (2 C. 3:14) nor Christ Himself (cf. the νῦν of the error of Jn. 8:52, cf. also Mt. 26:65). But Christians also share in this "still" of the world. The apostle himself still lives in the flesh (Gl. 2:20), the sinful flesh. Christians, too, are ἄρτι μὴ ὁρῶντες (1 Pt. 1:8). They know what others do not, but ἄρτι δι' ἐσόπτρου ἐν αἰνίγματι ... ἄρτι ἐκ μέρους (1 C. 13:12), and more than all others they are still in suffering (Lk. 6:21; Jn. 16:22; 1 Pt. 1:6; 2 C. 4:17, → 1115), especially among them the apostles (1 C. 4:11, 13).

In all the distress of this "still" of the NT there is a special gift of grace. So long as this time of Christ endures, there will always be the νῦν of the possibility of conversion (Ac. 17:30), of awakening from sleep (R. 13:11). Thus in the νῦν of Ac. 17:30, as in the ἤδη of R. 13:11, there is an urgent "now at last" as well as a warning "still."

4. The NT Already.

The same νῦν which is covered by darkness as "still" is even now shining brightly into the future as "already." σκοτία still has power in the world ἕως ἄρτι, so that many fall victim to it. But τὸ φῶς τὸ ἀληθινὸν ἤδη φαίνει (1 Jn. 2:8 f.); now is the time of salvation.

Thus the NT Now stands in unique tension with this aeon even though is still belongs to it (→ 1115). There is a. a certain correspondence, and yet b. a sharp contrast between what was and what is. Similarly in relation to the future the Already of the NT is c. an anticipated ἔσχατον and yet also d. merely an indication of the greater thing which is to be.

a. νῦν in Parallelism with the Past.

An essential feature of the NT understanding of the OT is Messianic typology. In this connection the OT Now comes under the law of the correspondence of τύπος and ἀντίτυπος, e.g., in Gl. 4:29 (οὕτως καὶ νῦν),[62] Hb. 12:26 (τότε ... νῦν) and 1 Pt. 3:21 (baptism νῦν σῴζει as the ἀντίτυπον of the flood).

But already in this typological correspondence there is an element of antithesis, cf. the two redemptions in 1 Pt. 3:20 f. and especially Hb. 12:26: τὴν γῆν ἐσάλευσεν τότε, νῦν δὲ ... οὐ μόνον τὴν γῆν ἀλλὰ καὶ τὸν οὐρανόν.

b. νῦν in Antithesis to the Past.

In general, the Now stands exclusively in antithesis to what has been. Thus Paul is marked by fondness for the antithesis τότε/νῦν. This is not just imitation

[62] Cf. Oepke, *ad loc.* (89). In v. 25, however, the ref. is to the νῦν of the old aeon, → 1114.

of a direct model,[63] but an application of the category of antithesis which he has in common with the diatribe. The NT Now itself is undoubtedly completely new as compared with anything in the preceding or contemporary world. There the Now, if distinguished from another time, was usually the evil present as compared with the good old days.[64] In the NT, however, the νῦν shines out with radiant splendour as compared with the τότε.

For in this Now, in contrast to all previous ages, the whole salvation of the Gospel is present.

(a) It is the Now of a new relation to God. The antitheses of 1 Pt. 2:10 are carefully constructed: Once you were οἱ οὐκ ἠλεημένοι, νῦν δὲ ἐλεηθέντες,[65] once οὐ λαός,[66] νῦν δὲ λαὸς θεοῦ, cf. also the figure of the sheep and Shepherd in v. 25.[67] Paul describes the contrast along similar lines, but he draws an even finer distinction by attributing earlier ruin to men and present salvation to God, cf. R. 5:10 f.: We, who were once God's enemies, νῦν τὴν καταλλαγὴν ἐλάβομεν,[68] cf. also Col. 1:21 f. and especially R. 11:30 f.: ποτὲ ἠπειθήσατε, νῦν δὲ ἠλεήθητε (→ n. 65). This contrast may be seen most clearly, of course, in the lives of Gentile Christians, Eph. 2:12,[69] also Gl. 4:8 f.

(b) The Now of the new life. The Now of the new relation to God implies a radical and factual transformation of Christian life. This is no longer lived in bondage to sin (R. 6:20, also 5:8) or under the yoke of the Law (R. 7:1, 6) but in righteousness (R. 3:21;[70] 5:9) and freedom (R. 6:22) under the renewing power of the Spirit (R. 7:6). Hence acting, thinking and knowing κατὰ σάρκα are excluded (cf. 2 C. 5:16). As a direct result of the new relation to God (cf. Col. 1:21 f.), this means in practice, no longer ἔργα πονηρά, but νῦν ἅγιοι. The wonder of this change, which is very impressively described in Eph. 2:1 ff., may be seen most vividly in Gentile Christians whose past included so many vices (cf.,

---

[63] Cf. on the one side *NT Deutsch,* Rendtorff on Col. 3:5 f., on the other R. Bultmann in RGG², III, 1681 f.

[64] Cf. the OT intimations and analogies (Is. 1:21; Hos. 2:7 [9]), also those outside the Bible (Epict., III, 22, 69; Cl. Al. Prot., II, 22, 6; 37, 1 and 3).

[65] Cf. with this Ez. 39:25: νῦν ἀποστρέψω τὴν αἰχμαλωσίαν Ἰακὼβ καὶ ἐλεήσω τὸν οἶκον Ἰσραήλ. The two passages represent typically the prophetic νῦν of the near future on the one side and the NT νῦν of eschatological fulfilment on the other. The aor. emphasises the historical fact which is already in the past (→ n. 67) but which still controls the whole νῦν, → 1113.

[66] The οὐ λαός denotes esp. the Gentiles, cf. the paraphrase in Eph. 2:12 (ἀπηλλοτριωμένοι τῆς πολιτείας τοῦ Ἰσραὴλ καὶ ξένοι τῶν διαθηκῶν τῆς ἐπαγγελίας) and the expansion in 2 Cl., 2, 3 on the basis of a later situation: our people, which was once οὐ λαός (R. 9:25) or οὐκ ἔθνος (R. 10:19), which was once abandoned by God, is now believing and more numerous than the older people.

[67] This νῦν, in spite of the ἀρτιγέννητος of v. 2, can hardly be taken in the sense of "recently" (→ 1112), as though to emphasise that the recipients of the letter were novices (cf. Wnd. Pt., *ad loc.*). The ref. is rather to the contrast between the once and the now in the lives of Gentile Christians (ἐπεστράφητε is thus to be taken as med. like πλανώμενοι; cf. Bl.-Debr. § 308).

[68] Cf. Hos. 8:10: νῦν εἰσδέξομαι αὐτούς, to which what was said in → n. 65 applies; cf. also Bultmann Trad., 133; *Glauben u. Verstehen* (1933), 265.

[69] Cf. as an OT counterpart the promise of fellowship with God on the basis of the people's conversion with the prophetic νῦν (→ 1114), e.g., Ez. 43:9; Hos. 4:16.

[70] It has already been pointed out in n. 33 that νυνὶ δέ can be understood as a logical adversative after the analogy of 1 C. 15:20 (cf. J. Weiss on 1 C. 15:20, but also Zn. R., 173 f., *ad loc.*), but that in view of the par. in v. 26 and the general context of salvation history in R. one should not overlook the temporal aspect of νυνί. One might say that in this νυνί we have both the logical and the temporal aspects together (so also Kühl, *ad loc.*).

e.g., Col. 3:5 with v. 7). But fundamentally it is just as great a miracle in Jewish Christians (cf. R. 6:21 f.; 8:1;[71] Eph. 5:8). At this point in Paul the νῦν of proclamation often becomes the νῦν of exhortation. That is to say, the new ethos is frequently expressed by him in the form of νῦν with the imperative (→ *III, 1*).

(c) The Now of new knowledge. In the Gospel, and hence also in the Now which it proclaims, new spiritual knowledge is inseparably related to the renewal of life. The disclosure of the great transformation and its understanding are just as much a gift of the Holy Spirit as the renewal of man himself.

Thus Paul's antithesis between the past of ungodliness and the present of sanctification finds an exact and closely related parallel in the antithesis of the past of concealment and the present of disclosure.[72] The mystery of God which was hidden from eternity but is now revealed to the saints is a theme in Col. (1:26) and Eph. (3:5, 10) but also in the final doxology of Romans (16:26). The content of this secret which is now revealed can be described in just as many ways as the gift of Christ Himself, e.g., as the miracle of Christ in us (Col. 1:27; cf. 2:2) or the miracle of the one Church (Eph.).

But the Once which is contrasted with the NT Now is not just that of concealment. It is also the Once of incomplete revelation, as in the prophetic writings. Thus in later NT writings a τότε of prophetic intimation can be contrasted with the νῦν of apostolic proclamation, as in the οὐκ ... ὡς νῦν of Eph. 3:5, or especially 1 Pt. 1:12, also Lk. 2:29: Now when the time of prophecy has passed and salvation is present,[73] ἀπολύεις τὸν δοῦλόν σου, δέσποτα.

To God's revelation there corresponds in this Now of Christ man's knowledge. This comes from the Revealer Himself, specifically as the One who went to death (Jn. 16:30; 17:7),[74] though in such a way that there may also be terrible misunderstanding and blindness (cf. Jn. 8:52; Mt. 26:65, → 1116). The decisive thing about true knowledge is that it is no longer κατὰ σάρκα but κατὰ πνεῦμα (as we may legitimately add to the thought of 2 C. 5:16).[75] In other words, God Himself first comes to him who knows with the radically transforming knowledge of love (Gl. 4:8 f., also Hos. 12:1). NT knowledge is sustained by the mystery of this always present reciprocity, → I, 709, 700).

c. νῦν as an Anticipation of the Last Things.

In the light of these gifts of the NT Now it is understandable that the apostle should believe that the long-expected day of the Lord had come in this νῦν:

---

[71] In itself the νῦν here might suggest the time of earthly life as distinct from the last judgment (Hofmann, *ad loc.*; cf. Zn. R., 374, n. 37); but numerous analogies show that this νῦν also means "now in the time since Christ was manifested." Here as elsewhere one may see the value of systematic comparison. For this reason esp. (though also on other grounds, → 1108) one cannot take this as an enclitic νύν (cf. Zn. R., 375 with n. 39; *ibid.*, 373 with n. 34 on the question of the authenticity of νῦν here). Certainly it does not seem to me that to turn the sentence into a question makes it any clearer.

[72] Cf. R. Bultmann in RGG², III, 1682; IV, 995 f.

[73] Cf. Hck., *ad loc.*: here, then, νῦν is not used of the imminent fut., as Pr.-Bauer thinks. Cf. also Cl. Al. Prot., I, 7, 6: ... ὁ κύριος, προμηνύων ἀρχῆθεν προφητικῶς, νῦν δὲ ἤδη καὶ ἐναργῶς εἰς σωτηρίαν παρακαλῶν. The relation between now and once naturally seems different from the standpoint of prophecy and apocalyptic, cf. with 1 Pt. 1:12 En. 1:2: οὐκ εἰς τὴν νῦν γενεὰν διενοούμην, ἀλλ' ἐπὶ πόρρω οὖσαν ἐγὼ λαλῶ.

[74] Cf. Bultmann on Jn. 17:7 (p. 381).

[75] Cf. R. Bultmann, *Der Stil d. paul. Predigt u. die kynisch-stoische Diatribe* (1910), 84, n. 2.

ἰδοὺ νῦν καιρὸς εὐπρόσδεκτος, ἰδοὺ νῦν ἡμέρα σωτηρίας (2 C. 6:2). In so doing he simply took up the proclamation of Jesus Himself, who had declared His → σήμερον to be the ἐνιαυτὸς κυρίου δεκτός (Lk. 4:19, 21).[76] In the NT νῦν there is in fact expressed the certainty of eschatology already realised. The final tribulation has come (cf. Jn. 16:32; 1 Jn. 4:3), the judgment (Jn. 12:31; cf. 3:19), but also the fulness of eschatological salvation, life and immortality (2 Tm. 1:10),[77] even the vision of God (Jn. 14:7).[78]

The distinctive form of this νῦν which anticipates the ἔσχατα is the νῦν of Jn. This relates more broadly to the whole life of Jesus on earth (Jn. 4:23; 5:25), and more narrowly to the final crisis in which the terms νῦν and ὥρα for the first time take on their full significance. This is the hour of supreme affliction (12:27), but also herein it is already that of glorification (17:5), of victory over the devil (12:31), and of going up to the Father (16:5; 17:13).[79] Already in this νῦν of the Fourth Gospel, and then especially in the vision of Rev. (12:10 f.), there is awareness of being in transition, of being almost completely absorbed into the realisation that in the Now of Christ the end, the consummation, is present.[80] But the Johannine νῦν, as this art. makes clear, is not unique. It is simply an enhanced form of the general view of primitive Christianity.

A kind of anticipation, though in the form of a non-eschatological changing of the contrast between Once and Now into the antithesis between life in heaven and hell, may be seen in the singular νῦν of Lk. 16:25. Here the temporal and spatial antithesis is for all practical purposes one and the same, cf. the πρίν and νῦν of Hom. Od., 11, 484 f.[81] But related in this way to the provisional state in *sheol*, where the definitive decision has still to be made between glory and Gehenna, even this νῦν of a parable which borrows pre-Christian imagery still denotes a transitional period (→ 1111, 1114), though this is not specifically NT in character. Closely related is the thought of Rev. 14:13: "From now on (or now, → 1107), saith the Spirit, they (will) rest from their labours"; this is how we are to take the ἀπ' ἄρτι without the ναί (with P^{47} ℵ*), (ἀπ') ἄρτι being the Now inaugurated by Christ, which is also a time of affliction, → 1115 f.[82]

---

[76] It is no accident that Jesus selected this verse which spoke of the year of salvation rather than one dealing with the day of the Lord, for it is an essential mark of the NT νῦν that here eschatological events are no longer points of time. The day of salvation lasts as long as Christ is there, and so, too, does judgment (Jn. 3:19). Thus eschatological expectation of a series of "punctual" events is distinctively fulfilled by the occurrence of all these events in the period of Christ, cf. Delling, 121 f., 127.

[77] Cf. Dib. Past., *ad loc.*

[78] On ἀπ' ἄρτι → 1107.

[79] Cf. R. Bultmann J., 139, n. 7; 327, n. 7; 516 f.; 328; 377; 401 f.; esp. 324 ff.: "Everywhere the same Now is meant" (324, n. 5), probably also in the case of the symbolical ἕως ἄρτι of 2:10, for only now in Christ is the good or true wine of God present (*ibid.*, 85, n. 1; also W. Oehler, *Zum Missionscharakter des J. Ev.* [1941], 52).

[80] Cf. R. Bultmann, *Glauben u. Verstehen* (1933), 134 ff.; G. Stählin, ZNW, 33 (1934), 225 ff., esp. 234 f.

[81] This use of νῦν, not current elsewhere in the NT, seems to support the conjecture that Lk. 16:19 ff. is from some other source, cf. the comm. and H. Gressmann, "Vom reichen Mann u. armen Lazarus," AAB, 1918, No. 7, esp. 46 ff.; Bultmann Trad., 212 f. But in the light of the world of apocalyptic it is quite conceivable even on the lips of Jesus, cf. E. Stauffer, *Die Theologie d. NT* (1941), 190.

[82] Cf. Behm Apk. (*NT Deutsch*), 85: The Now denotes the beginning of the bloody conflict between Rome and Christianity, though cf. A. Fridrichsen [in a letter to A. Debrunner]: "Assuredly (ἀπαρτί), saith the Spirit."

d. νῦν as a Proleptic First Stage of the Last Things.

Though there seems to be in Jn. a full anticipation of the last things, the NT still speaks of eschatology beyond this Now, of the end which will consummate all things, so that in the Now there is both possession and hope, R. 5:8 f.: δικαιωθέντες νῦν ... σωθησόμεθα in the last judgment; 1 Jn. 3:2: νῦν τέκνα θεοῦ ἐσμεν ... (then) ὅμοιοι αὐτῷ ἐσόμεθα, 1 Tm. 4:8: ζωὴ ἡ νῦν καὶ ἡ μέλλουσα, i.e., (divine) life in which we already participate in the period of Christ, and to which we look forward in fulness then.[83] This thought of twofold fulfilment runs through the whole of the NT (cf., e.g., Eph. 1:13 f.).

Intimations of this eschatological νῦν of the NT may again be found in the LXX. Thus in Mi. 4:11 the future last judgment on Jerusalem is portrayed as present, as is also eschatological salvation in Is. 48:7, → 1114. But the present tense here is simply a more intensive form of prophecy.

5. Stages of the NT Now.

In the course of the day of salvation embraced by the NT νῦν one hour follows another, and each can bear the full weight of the νῦν in comparison with that which precedes or follows. Thus the Jesus of Jn. has a constant sense of the fleeting hours. He is aware of the νῦν of work, especially of preparing the disciples for the great tribulation (cf. Jn. 13:19, → 1107; 14:29; also 16:1, 4; this tribulation is at the doors in the νῦν of the hour of Lk. 22:36). For the disciples this νῦν is still a period of incompleteness in discipleship (Jn. 13:36 f.), in prayer (16:24) in understanding (16:12, cf. v. 25). This defective understanding may be seen in their ἴδε νῦν (v. 29), in which they already believe they have advanced a stage further in the progress of the hours.

Paul, too, is conscious of a moving on of the eschatological clock from νῦν to νῦν (R. 13:11 f.; 2 Th. 2:5 ff.; also 1 C. 3:2: Now when you have moved a stage further in the time of the πνεῦμα you are still σαρκικοί). Nor is this any less true of Jn., who sees the coming of the last hour in the appearance of antichrist (1 Jn. 2:18; 4:3).

6. Once and Now in the Life of the Individual Christian.

If Paul's own experience has basic significance in the fashioning of his theology in general, the fact of Gl. 1:23 (νῦν-ποτέ) particularly affects his conception of the Once and Now of salvation history. Many such antitheses are just as much personal confessions as they are theological statements on the historical economy of God, e.g., 2 C. 5:16;[84] R. 5:9;[85] 7:6 etc. But the objective validity is more important to a man like Paul than the personal aspect even in what seem to be the very personal τότε-νῦν passages in R. 6:21 f.; 11:30 f. (cf. also 1 Pt. 2:25). The fundamental significance of the τότε-νῦν relation is finely brought out in what we must assume to be the pun of Phlm. 11: εὔχρηστος-Χριστός,[86] cf. also Lk. 2:29

[83] So Hofman, Dib. Past., though cf. Wbg. Past., *ad loc.*

[84] Cf. Ltzm. R., *ad loc.*, who takes the νῦν to be the moment of Paul's conversion. This νῦν, however, includes the present tense of the great change effected in Christ (→ 1118) as well as the beginning of spiritual life in Paul.

[85] Cf. Zn. R., 258, n. 22, who seeks to relate the section only to personal experience.

[86] Cf. Loh. Phlm., *ad loc.* (p. 186, n. 3) *et. al.*

(→ 1118); Ac. 13:31 vl.[87] (also Epict., IV, 4, 7:[88] τότε καὶ ἐγὼ ἡμάρτανον· νῦν δ' οὐκέτι, χάρις τῷ θεῷ, Tat. Or. Graec., 42). Lk. 1:48 may also be mentioned in this connection, for the whole community speaks in the ancient canticle of Mary: ἀπὸ τοῦ νῦν μακαριοῦσίν με πᾶσαι αἱ γενεαί.

III. νῦν with the Imperative.

1. νῦν in NT Exhortation.

The great Already of the NT includes renewal of life, → 1117. But since Pauline ethics is constructed on the principle: "Be what you are," in this sphere of the NT Now a νῦν with the imperative corresponds to that with the indicative.

There are many instances of this use, too, prior to the NT.

In class. and Hell. Gk. νῦν or νύν with the imp. often serves to show how urgent a command or requirement is, → 1108 with n. 23. In such cases it should be rendered "but," "for," "so" etc.[89] In the NT only ἄγε νῦν is used in this way (Jm. 4:13; 5:1), though cf. ἄφες ἄρτι (Mt. 3:15). Equally unemphatic, as shown earlier (→ 1108 with n. 24), is νῦν or τὰ νῦν when used with καὶ or οὖν before an imp. or related expression (cf. Ac. 10:5; 2 Jn. 5 — Ac. 5:38; 27:22 — Ac. 16:36; 23:15). In other cases in the NT, however, νῦν has some temporal significance when used after an imp. (Mt. 27:42 f.; Jn. 2:8 etc.) or even before it (e.g., Col. 3:8). There is precedent for this, e.g., in the LXX: "Yet now hear when God speaks, O Israel" (Is. 44:1; cf. Am. 7:16). "Now when God commands the prophet he should be obeyed at once" (Jer. 18:11). "Now, in the judgment of God, hide yourselves" (Is. 2:10). "Now, when God gives opportunity therefor, repent" (Ιερ. 33[26]:13; Ez. 43:9 with the promise of grace; cf. Jos. 22:4 etc.).

In the NT we find the νῦν of exhortation (a) in basic missionary proclamation. But precedence is here given, not to the imperative of admonition, but to the indicative of the word of forgiveness on which it rests; cf. Jn. 8:11 and Ac. 17:30 f.: in the one case οὐ κατακρίνω, in the other ὑπεριδεῖν, is the presupposition of the exhortation. In Ac. 17 the νῦν stands significantly between the past of χρόνοι τῆς ἀγνοίας and the future of the day of judgment. It is the decisive interim of grace between the two.[90]

We also find this νῦν (b) in exhortation addressed to the community. From the Now of liberation from the Law and sin follows (ὥστε) the necessity of δουλεύειν ἐν καινότητι πνεύματος (R. 7:6) and the admonition: Now is the time to put an end to the pagan manner of life (Col. 3:8); now serve righteousness (R. 6:19).[91] The admonition which Jn. develops with particular seriousness for the νῦν of the Christian community is that now, in the hour of special danger, just before the *parousia*, we should abide in Him (1 Jn. 2:28).[92]

[87] Ac. 12:11, however, refers to individual direction in the life of Peter. Conversely the νῦν of 1 C. 16:12 is a point of time on which there is no divine stress and for which there is no θέλημα, → III, 59, n. 24. Contrasted with it is the expected time of εὐκαιρεῖν.

[88] Cf. on this A. Bonhöffer, *Epiktet u. das NT* (1911), 369 ff.; R. Bultmann, ZNW, 13 (1912), 184; T. Zahn, *Der Stoiker Epiktet u. sein Verhältnis zum Christentum*[2] (1895); O. Kuss, *Röm. 5:12-21* (Diss. Breslau, 1930), 28 ff.; also → I, 301.

[89] Pass., *s.v.*; cf. Bl.-Debr. § 474, 3; passages in Pass. and Liddell-Scott, *s.v.* In the NT νῦν does not occur with the exhortative (e.g., Luc. Soloec., 10, 12).

[90] M. Dibelius, "Pls. auf dem Areopag," SAH (1938/39), 34: In these two verses past, present and future seem to be compressed together; cf. 40 f.

[91] In this saying Pl. constructs a distinctive rhetorical form. Past and present are antithetically contrasted and associated.

[92] This can hardly be the common, colourless καὶ νῦν, → 1108. There is in the νῦν a new thought as compared with the μένετε ἐν αὐτῷ which immediately precedes in v. 27.

2. νῦν in NT Prayer.

In many an hour of eternal seriousness there rings out in the prayer of the community an urgent Now to God. This is true already under the old covenant (cf. LXX Jon. 4:3; Is. 37:20 B; 64:8), and we find it again under the new (Ac. 4:29; 20:32). It occurs in the greatest prayer in the NT, that of Jesus in Jn. 17 (v. 5). As in every hour of His Now, so in the last hour Jesus knows what must come, and in faith (13:31) and prayer He accepts this most difficult hour for what it is in the sight of God, the ὥρα of δοξασθῆναι.[93]

IV. The Significance of the NT View of the Now.

The NT understanding of the Now, like the whole world of NT history and thought, presents a unique picture. The man of pagan antiquity suffers under the ineluctable and ultimately meaningless transitoriness of time. Hence the motto *carpe diem* (Hor. Od., I, 11, 8). The Jew has a sense of the teleological movement of time, but within it each period has only the significance of what becomes at once an indifferent preparation for what is to come. In the NT, however, the whole emphasis falls precisely on the present which the Greeks, especially Aristotle, regarded as beyond our grasp and the Jews as merely an irrelevant point of transition.[94] For all the essentials which the NT has to proclaim are basically brought together in the present. The νῦν of the NT is wholly determined and filled by the Christ event. From a purely historical standpoint this embraces the life, work, death and resurrection of Jesus. That is to say, it is a past event which is narrated in the aorist. But as God's act, as the breaking of eternity into time, this event is also present. For "all time after Christ is the time of Christ."[95] In the NT as nowhere else in the world of religion everything depends on history. But in the Gospel history is made contemporaneous in a unique way. It belongs to the Now not merely as concept but as fact, though only faith, of course, can grasp this. This is the reason why the present as well as the aorist carries special emphasis in NT proclamation, cf., e.g., the participles σῳζόμενοι/ἀπολλύμενοι (1 C. 1:18; 2 C. 2:15). These participles show that Christian hope, the true mark of men of God as compared with pagans, ἄθεοι ἐν τῷ κόσμῳ, ἐλπίδα μὴ ἔχοντες (Eph. 2:12), is fulfilled in the νῦν of the NT as well as directed as a living hope to the future. In this νῦν the past of Christ and the future of Christ are both comprehended as the present of Christ.

The NT νῦν is the whole period between the comings, but for individual disciples it is continually compressed into hours of decision. They have to grasp this νῦν in faith, to set themselves in it in prayer, and to work it out in action. In the NT νῦν proclamation does not relate only to certain places. All life rests upon it. The

---

[93] Cf. R. Bultmann J., 374 ff. The same νῦν of prayer (concretely to the demons of the curse), which seeks an answer at the very moment of utterance, may be found in Soph. Oed. Col., 1376.

[94] Even T. Chag., 2, 7 does not go beyond this when it says that man should look neither to what was nor to what will be, but, as we may conclude, only to what is. The point here is that common sense will keep to the present without bewailing the past or worrying about the future. This does not confer on the present, however, the special significance which it is given in the NT.

[95] So Delling, 141, who presents many similar ideas to those found in this article, but who diverges from the present interpretation in his general view that time is fulfilled and overcome, so that the NT νῦν is de-eschatologised; I hope to expound and demonstrate this more fully in an essay on the present in NT thinking.

aim of all NT proclamation is both to evoke this νῦν as a fact (cf. 2 C. 6:2) and to help men to live in terms of this νῦν as the divinely given → καιρός (R. 6:19).

The NT thus binds faith with equal strength to past, present and future. The uniqueness of the Gospel story is significantly expressed in the fact that what has been accomplished once and for all (→ ἅπαξ, I, 381 ff.) continues to work to-day in the νῦν of the time of Christ. But as the τότε of the past stands always behind the NT νῦν, so the τότε of the future stands always before it. "He who has no hope does not stand in the Christian faith — but he who does not stand in the present of Christ has no ground for hope."[96] Only when the reality in which we now believe becomes sight and is thus consummated will the τότε of 1 C. 13:12 become a new νῦν, a true[97] *nunc aeternum*.

Stählin

νύξ

νύξ — an old Indo-European word, cf. Lat. *nox*, German *Nacht*, English "night" — means "night," the "time when there is no sunlight" (→ ἡμέρα), then "darkness" generally (sometimes among the Orphics primal being, Orph. Fr. [Kern], 28 and 86), the "dark" (cf. Gn. 1:5 : τὸ σκότος ἐκάλεσεν νύκτα; ψ 103:20 : ἔθου σκότος, καὶ ἐγένετο νύξ), fig. "blindness," "dereliction,"[1] "harm" (it is a bad omen to dream that it is night, Artemid. Oneirocr., IV, 42), "death."[2] That in the first instance νύξ suggests for the Gk. the dreadful character of the night may be seen in the etymology of Plato. After dark the light is longingly awaited by men (ἱμείρουσι, part.), and so they coined the word ἱμέρα (for ἡμέρα, Crat., 418c d). But night is also depicted sometimes as the giver of liberating sleep, e.g., Orph., 3, 5 ff.; Epigr. Graec., 312; Sib., 8, 354; Aesch. Ag., 355, where Νύξ is invoked as φιλία.

In mythology the deified figure of Νύξ still has this dreadful character.[3] Νύξ appears anthropomorphically (Hes. Theog., 748 and 755 f.) but it plays little role in the cultus (though cf. Aesch. Ag., 355, and for magic, Preis. Zaub., I, No. IV, 2858). It is the mother of a series of evil and influential figures in Hesiod (Theog., 211 ff.; cf. also 123 f.), esp. the avenging deities in Aesch. (Eum., 322 ff., 844 f.).

Night is the main time for magic, which has particular potency in the hours of darkness, (Preis. Zaub., I, No. IV, 1662). Each night is the time for a particular demon (*ibid.*, 1328 f.; II, 8 : [ὁ] τὴν νύκτα ταύτην κατέχων καὶ ταύτης δεσποτεύων, cf. II, 79) who is set over it. The fact that night is preferred for magic, because the demons can develop their activity then, influenced the development of the moon goddess into a magical deity (→ μήν, cf. also ψ 135:9 : τὴν σελήνην ... εἰς ἐξουσίαν τῆς νυκτός, even if the OT verse is meant to be taken purely cosmographically). On the other hand, faith in the miraculous power of the moon (→ μήν) also favoured the preferring of the night for magic.

Finally, the night is the special time of divine revelations. If the deity uses for its manifestations the time of the release of the human consciousness from the purely empirical world of the senses, then directions will obviously be found in the dreams

---

[96] Delling, 141.
[97] Cf. → n. 43 (*A, IV, 3*).

νύξ. [1] Cf. the instance in *Rev. Bibl.*, NS, 36 (1927), 561, line 6 (inscr.).
[2] Examples in H. Ebeling, Lexicon Homericum. Cf. B. Weiss on Jn. 9:4.
[3] Examples in C. F. H. Buchmann, Epitheta deorum graec. (1893), 182 f.

associated with this state.[4] Books of dreams are based on this idea.[5] The high estimation of dreams may be seen most clearly in accounts of healings in dreams and the practice of incubation.[6] The god often appears to the dreamer and heals him by manipulating the sick part of the body (Ditt. Syll.³, III, No. 1168-1173, esp. in the famous sanctuary of Epidauros where Aesculapius was at work). At a later date instructions as to the manner of healing were expected in incubation, e.g., Ael. Arist. Or. Sacr., 2, 30 ff.; double dreams finally decide whether the directions are right (*loc. cit.*). In 32 f. there is a fine depiction of the state of religious excitement when this nightly instruction is given.

1. In the NT νύξ occurs first in the literal sense for "night," which the Jews divided into three watches (bBer., 3a), the Greeks and Romans into four[7] (fourth Mt. 14:25, par. Mk. 6:48, cf. ψ 89:4; 129:6) or which was divided into hours (twelve of different length, → ὥρα; the third, Ac. 23:23). It is often used in the gen. temp. (or with διά, Ac.), with emphasis, "under cover of night." Nicodemus in Jn. 3:2 seeks not so much the cover of night as the blessing of its stillness.[8] Sometimes in longer notes of time the number of nights is given as well as that of the days. In some cases this is Jewish pleonasm, as usually in the LXX, where we read e.g., of forty days and forty nights. If not, the point is to emphasise the length of the time, e.g., Jesus' fast in Mt. 4:2, or Jonah's stay in the belly of the fish, and that of Jesus in the tomb, in Mt. 12:40 (→ gen. II, 948 ff.). Mt. 12:40 is a prophecy of the resurrection which is simply related to Jon. 2:1 by the addition "and three nights"; hence the phrase does not contain any theological or exegetical mysteries.[9]

For the Rabbis night is threatened by evil spirits which exercise power during it (e.g., Lilith, bShab., 151b). But the man who knows that the night also belongs to God (ψ 73:16) enjoys the Father's protection in the night too. Hence the righteous of the NT no longer fear the demons and other rulers of the night. Jesus spends whole nights in converse with God (Lk. 6:12). Mt. 26:36 ff. gives us the deepest insight into His nightly wrestling in prayer.

The Rabbis think that direction is given in most dreams, bBer., 55a. Dreams come from either angels or demons, 55b. Prayers are prescribed for preventing the fulfilment of contrary dreams; these are not far from magic (*loc. cit.*). The Rabbi is not afraid of consulting a professional interpreter of dreams (*loc. cit.*) and undertakes to interpret the dreams of others, 56b. The Rabbis had a whole list of rules for doing this, 56b-57b.[10]

In contrast, one should note the care with which the NT assigns significance to dreams only when they mediate divine commands. They are not given for the

---

[4] Cf. Weinreich, AH, 76.

[5] Artemid. Oneirocr.; Achmets (from the mediaeval period) rec. Drexl; lost writings are mentioned in Artemid. Oneirocr., V, 18 f.

[6] Cf. Weinreich, 77 ff.; R. Herzog, *Die Wunderheilungen v. Epidauros* (1931).

[7] F. K. Ginzel, *Handbuch der mathemat. u. techn. Chronologie*, II (1911), 4 f., 165, 304; S. Krauss, *Talmudische Archäologie*, II (1911), 420; D. Völter, *Schweizerische Theol. Zeitschr.*, 32 (1915), 189.

[8] Cf. K. Bornhäuser, *Das Joh.-Ev., eine Missionsschrift f. Israel* (1928), 26 f.; Schl. J., *ad loc.*, 85.

[9] It is not consonant with the self-understanding of the NT to construct a material contradiction between Mt. 12:40 and the fulfilment (K. Bornhäuser, *Tage u. Stunden im NT* [1937], 66 ff.): "Only if Jesus were a *goët* would his prophecy agree to the hour." The formal contradiction "is simply a proof of the authenticity of Mt. 12:40" (my review in ThLBl, 58 [1937], 198). Cf. G. Kittel, *Rabbinica* (1920), 37; DTh³ (1936), 171 f.

[10] Acc. to R. Meyer [in a written communication] we may see in bBer., 56b-57b a book of dreams, or part of such a book, which arises out of its environment.

satisfying of curiosity (cf. Mt. 1). Even in the mediation of divine commands their role is limited.

It is in keeping with the specific character of Ac. that only here are visions which either instruct or encourage expressly stated to occur at night, cf. 16:9; 18:9; 23:11; 27:23.

One might compare Gn. 26:24: ὤφθη αὐτῷ κύριος ἐν τῇ νυκτὶ ἐκείνῃ, 31:24: ἦλθεν ὁ θεὸς ... καθ' ὕπνον τὴν νύκτα, 40:5 and 41:11: ἐνύπνιον, that two have the same dream is particularly significant; 46:2: εἶπεν ... ἐν ὁράματι τῆς νυκτός, also 1 Βασ. 15:16; 3 Βασ. 3:5; 2 Ch. 7:12: ὤφθη κύριος τῷ Σαλωμὼν τὴν νύκτα, 3 Βασ. 3:5 with the addition ἐν ὕπνῳ.

The degree of actuality is obviously the same in the various formulations, from the realistic depiction in Ac. 23:11 (cf. Gn. 31:24) to the more suggestive method of Ac. 16:9 (cf. 2 Ch. 7:12). The ὅραμα, whether it be the Κύριος Himself who appears (Ac. 23:11), or a messenger of God (27:23), or a mortal man (16:9), is a revelation from the suprahuman world, which is in essentials to be evaluated from a positive religious standpoint. This uses night for its manifestations to man because this best guarantees openness to the revelation (other processes are obviously at issue in the announcements ἐν ὁράματι in Ac. 9:10 and ἐν ἐκστάσει in 22:17). The emphasis on the fact that directions are given at night shows that the author ascribes to them a different character than to revelations given directly by day, though religious awareness recognises that they are no less divine. The degree of actuality may best be seen in the formulation in Ac. 18:9 (cf. Gn. 46:2). That it is a relatively lower degree may be seen especially from the context of Ac. 16:9 (→ συμβιβάζω).

The darkness of night is, for very primitive reasons (cf. 1 Th. 5:2; Job 24:14; Ιερ. 30:3 [49:9]), sinister to the man of antiquity. Hence Rev. declares that in the time of judgment even the night stars will be darkened (8:12; cf. Job 3:9; → II, 948), and it promises that in the new Jerusalem there will be a cessation of the regular periods of darkness by night (21:25; 22:5; → II, 948). This corresponds to Slav. En. 65:9, which says that in the one great aeon of the righteous "there will be among them no work, ... nor night nor darkness, but a great light."

2. Metaphorically νύξ is used only by Jn. and Paul. On the lips of Jesus it means the time when there is no possibility of work. This time comes with death, Jn. 9:4. In Jn. 11:10 the idea of physical death suggested by νύξ (→ n. 2: Homer) is changed into that of defective spiritual understanding in virtue of which one cannot find the right path, προσκόπτει.

Paul uses νύξ in different connections. In R. 13:12 it is the time before the consummation of the rule of God. This has yielded in large part with the conversion of Paul and his readers, and it will soon be ended altogether. The day (→ II, 953) will soon dawn. Hence the Christian stands between the times. 1 Th. 5:5-7 develops even more strongly the thought that the members (→ υἱοί) of the kingdom of light already stand in its brightness, in sharp contrast to members of the kingdom of darkness which is destined to perish (οὐκ ἐσμὲν νυκτός, v. 5). Already in this aeon they are taken out of darkness, → II, 953.

The situation of man by night, which is one of uncertainty because of the darkness (cf. Jn. 11:10), of indecision by reason of vacillation between dreaming and unconscious sleep, and finally of confusion of intellectual and moral judgment in virtue of the drunkenness which is common by night (1 Th. 5:7), differs markedly from the normal state, and can thus be used as a figure for the man of corresponding moral and spiritual condition. It is used in this way in Alexandrian theology (Hos. 4:5 f.: νυκτὶ ... ὡμοιώθη ὁ λαός μου ὡς οὐκ ἔχων γνῶσιν, a complete wresting of the Mas.); in Palestinian it is used in a nationalistic sense for the oppression of Israel by the Gentiles.[11]

Philo in his dualistic philosophy uses νύξ for captivity to the senses, Ebr., 209. Hence, in spite of what is at times verbal similarity (cf. also Corp. Herm., I, 27: οἱ μέθῃ καὶ ὕπνῳ ἑαυτοὺς ἐκδεδωκότες ... νήψατε), his meaning is different from that of Paul in 1 Th. 5:5-7. The resemblance is that both speak of the man who is characterised by drunkenness (μέθη, Som., II, 104) and sleep (106), whereas the pure and religious man (106) is sober (νήφοντες, 101) and awake (ἐγρηγορώς, 106).

For Paul this whole condition is not the sphere of Christian life (1 Th. 5:5), nor can it be. Hence the apostle calls for a walk in the light (→ II, 953). The same thought may be found in R. 13:11 ff. (→ 1125).

Delling

† νωθρός

νωθρός means "sluggish," "obtuse," Polyb., XXXI, 23, 11 (along with ἡσύχιος); Luc. Demosth., 43; Aristot. Part. An., 696b, 6; Hist. An., 622b, 32; (Hom. has νωθής, Il., 11, 559 [of the ass]); fig. νωθροί πως ἀπαντῶσι πρὸς τὰς μαθήσεις, Plat. Theaet., 144b; Heliodor. Aeth., 5, 1: νωθρότερος ὢν τὴν ἀκοήν; of mental obtuseness, Polyb., III, 90, 6: ἀγεννῶς καὶ νωθρῶς, IV, 60, 2: ἀτόλμως ... καὶ νωθρῶς, cf. IV, 8, 5: ἐν ταῖς ἐπινοίαις, "making sluggish," Hippocr. Aphorism., 3, 5; νωθρεύω and νωθρ(ε)ία in pap. (though both are older). νωθρός is rare in the LXX. Prv. 22:29 tells us that a man who is diligent in his affairs (ὀξὺς ἐν τοῖς ἔργοις αὐτοῦ) can be of use to kings, but not ἀνδράσι νωθροῖς. Sir. 4:29 warns against indolence in work (μὴ γίνου ... νωθρὸς καὶ παρειμένος ἐν τοῖς ἔργοις σου).

In the NT νωθρός occurs only in Hb. In 5:11 the author tells the readers that he cannot lead them, as he would like, into the profundities of Christian theological knowledge. This is because their inward capacity to receive is blunted and dulled. They have become νωθροὶ ταῖς ἀκοαῖς (*v.* Heliodor. → *supra*), sluggish in hearing and receptivity. This is connected with the fact that the recipients of the epistle do not have the vitality of assured and persevering faith. This spiritual exhaustion, which is due to deficient confidence of hope in the future time of consummation, makes them νωθροί, 6:12. Thus the word expresses a twofold deficiency which is no true part of the Christian life: a lack of receptivity for Christian *gnosis*, and a stale, exhausted spirit instead of the glowing joy of hope. When Christian life shows exhaustion both in breathing in (hearing and receiving) and in breathing out (believing confidence in the future), the author of Hb. calls his readers νωθροί.

Preisker

11 Str.-B., IV, 853-855.